P9-CCW-031

Merriam-Webster's Spanish-English Dictionary

Merriam-Webster's Spanish-English Dictionary

MERRIAM-WEBSTER, INCORPORATED
Springfield, Massachusetts, U.S.A.

A GENUINE MERRIAM-WEBSTER

The name *Webster* alone is no guarantee of excellence. It is used by a number of publishers and may serve mainly to mislead an unwary buyer.

Merriam-Webster™ is the name you should look for when you consider the purchase of dictionaries or other fine reference books. It carries the reputation of a company that has been publishing since 1831 and is your assurance of quality and authority.

ISBN 0-87779-916-4

MADE IN THE UNITED STATES OF AMERICA

16QWB04

Contents

Preface

MERRIAM-WEBSTER'S SPANISH-ENGLISH DICTIONARY is a completely new dictionary designed to meet the needs of English and Spanish speakers in a time of ever-expanding communication among the countries of the Western Hemisphere. It is intended for language learners, teachers, office workers, tourists, business travelers—anyone who needs to communicate effectively in the Spanish and English languages as they are spoken and written in the Americas. This new dictionary provides accurate and up-to-date coverage of current vocabulary in both languages, as well as abundant examples of words used in context to illustrate idiomatic usage. The selection of Spanish words and idioms was based on evidence drawn from a wide variety of modern Latin-American sources and interpreted by trained Merriam-Webster bilingual lexicographers. The English entries were chosen by Merriam-Webster editors from the most recent Merriam-Webster dictionaries, and they represent the current basic vocabulary of American English.

All of this material is presented in a format which is based firmly upon and, in many important ways, is similar to the traditional styling found in the Merriam-Webster monolingual dictionaries. The reader who is familiar with Merriam-Webster dictionaries will immediately recognize this style, with its emphasis on convenience and ease of use, clarity and conciseness of the information presented, precise discrimination of senses, and frequent inclusion of example phrases showing words in actual use. Other features include pronunciations (in the International Phonetic Alphabet) for all English words, full coverage of irregular verbs in both languages, a section on basic Spanish grammar, tables of the most common Spanish and English abbreviations, and a detailed Explanatory Notes section which answers any questions the reader might have concerning the use of this book.

Merriam-Webster's Spanish-English Dictionary represents the combined efforts of many members of the Merriam-Webster Editorial Department, along with advice and assistance from consultants outside the company. The primary defining work was done by Charlene M. Chateauneuf, Seán O'Mannion-Espejo, Karen L. Wilkinson, and Jocelyn Woods; early contributions to the text were also submitted by Cèsar Alegre, Hilton Alers, Marién Díaz, Anne Gatschet, and María D. Guijarro, with Victoria E. Neufeldt, Ph.D., and James L. Rader providing helpful suggestions regarding style. Proofreading was done by Susan L. Brady, Daniel B. Brandon, Charlene M. Chateauneuf, Deanna Stathis Chiasson, Seán O'Mannion-Espejo, James L. Rader, Donna L. Rickerby, Adrienne M. Scholz, Amy West, Karen L. Wilkinson, and Linda Picard Wood. Brian M. Sietsema, Ph.D., provided the pronunciations. Cross-reference services were provided by Donna L. Rickerby. Karen L. Levister assisted in inputting revisions. Carol Fugiel contributed many hours of clerical assistance and other valuable support. The editorial work relating to typesetting and production was begun by Jennifer S. Goss and continued by Susan L. Brady, who also offered helpful suggestions regarding format. Madeline L. Novak provided guidance on typographic matters. John M. Morse was responsible for the conception of this book as well as for numerous ideas and continued support along the way.

Eileen M. Haraty
Editor

Explanatory Notes

Entries

1. Main Entries

A boldface letter, word, or phrase appearing flush with the left-hand margin of each column of type is a main entry or entry word. The main entry may consist of letters set solid, of letters joined by a hyphen, or of letters separated by a space:

> **cafetalero¹, -ra** *adj* . . .
>
> **eye–opener** . . . *n* . . .
>
> **walk out** *vi* . . .

The main entry, together with the material that follows it on the same line and succeeding indented lines, constitutes a dictionary entry.

2. Order of Main Entries

Alphabetical order throughout the book follows the order of the English alphabet, with one exception: words beginning with the Spanish letter *ñ* follow all entries for the letter *n*. The main entries follow one another alphabetically letter by letter without regard to intervening spaces or hyphens; for example, *shake-up* follows *shaker*.

Homographs (words with the same spelling) having different parts of speech are usually given separate dictionary entries. These entries are distinguished by superscript numerals following the entry word:

> **hail¹** . . . *vt* . . .
>
> **hail²** *n* . . .
>
> **hail³** *interj* . . .
>
> **madrileño¹, -ña** *adj* . . .
>
> **madrileño², -ña** *n* . . .

Numbered homograph entries are listed in the following order: verb, adverb, adjective, noun, conjunction, preposition, pronoun, interjection, article.

Homographs having the same part of speech are normally included at the same dictionary entry, without regard to their different semantic origins. On the English-to-Spanish side, however, separate entries are made if the homographs have distinct inflected forms or if they have distinct pronunciations.

3. Guide Words

A pair of guide words is printed at the top of each page, indicating the first and last main entries that appear on that page:

factura · faringe

4. Variants

When a main entry is followed by the word *or* and another spelling, the two spellings are variants. Both are standard, and either one may be used according to personal inclination:

jailer *or* **jailor** . . . *n* . . .

quizá *or* **quizás** *adv* . . .

Occasionally, a variant spelling is used only for a particular sense of a word. In these cases, the variant spelling is listed after the sense number of the sense to which it pertains:

electric . . . *adj* **1** *or* **electrical** . . .

Sometimes the entry word is used interchangeably with a longer phrase containing the entry word. For the purposes of this dictionary, such phrases are considered variants of the headword:

bunk[2] *n* **1** *or* **bunk bed** . . .

angina *nf* **1** *or* **angina de pecho** : angina . . .

Variant wordings of boldface phrases may also be shown:

> **madera** *nf* . . . **3 madera dura** *or* **madera noble** . . .

> **atención**[1] *nf* . . . **2 poner atención** *or* **prestar atención** . . .

5. Run-On Entries

A main entry may be followed by one or more derivatives or by a homograph with a different functional label. These are run-on entries. Each is introduced by a boldface dash and each has a functional label. They are not defined, however, since their equivalents can be readily derived by adding the corresponding foreign-language suffix to the terms used to define the entry word or, in the case of homographs, simply substituting the appropriate part of speech:

> **illegal** . . . *adj* : ilegal — **illegally** *adv* (the Spanish adverb is *ilegalmente*)

> **transferir** . . . *vt* trasladar : to transfer — **transferible** *adj* (the English adjective is **transferable**)

> **Bosnian** *n* : bosnio *m*, -nia *f* — **Bosnian** *adj* (the Spanish adjective is *bosnio, -nia*)

On the Spanish side of the book, reflexive verbs are sometimes run on undefined:

> **enrollar** *vt* : to roll up, to coil — **enrollarse** *vr*

The absence of a definition means that *enrollarse* has the simple reflexive meaning "to become rolled up or coiled," "to roll itself up."

6. Bold Notes

A main entry may be followed by one or more phrases containing the entry word or an inflected form of the entry word. These are bold notes. Each bold note is defined at its own numbered sense:

> **álamo** *nm* **1** : poplar **2 álamo temblón**
> : aspen

> **hold**¹ ... *vi* ... **4 to hold to** : ... **5 to
> hold with** : ...

If the bold note consists only of the entry word and a single preposition, the entry word is represented by a boldface swung dash ~.

> **pegar** ... *vi* ... **3** ~ **con** : to match, to
> go with ...

The same bold note phrase may appear at two or more senses if it has more than one distinct meaning:

> **wear**¹ ... *vt* ... **3 to wear out** : gastar
> ⟨he wore out his shoes ... ⟩ **4 to wear
> out** EXHAUST : agotar, fatigar ⟨to wear
> oneself out ... ⟩ ...

> **estar** ... *vi* ... **15** ~ **por** : to be in favor
> of **16** ~ **por** : to be about to ⟨está por
> cerrar ... ⟩ ...

If the use of the entry word is commonly restricted to one particular phrase, then a bold note may be given as the entry word's only sense:

> **ward**¹ ... *vt* to ward off : ...

Pronunciation

1. Pronunciation of English Entry Words

The matter between a pair of brackets [ ] following the entry word of an English-to-Spanish entry indicates the pronunciation. The symbols used are explained in the International Phonetic Alphabet chart on page 58a.

The presence of variant pronunciations indicates that not all educated speakers pronounce words the same way. A second-place variant is not to be regarded as less acceptable than the pronunciation that is given first. It may, in fact, be used by as many educated speakers as the first variant, but the requirements of the printed page are such that one must precede the other:

> **tomato** [tə'meɪ̞o, -'mɑ-] . . .

When a compound word has less than a full pronunciation, the missing part is to be supplied from the pronunciation at the entry for the unpronounced element of the compound:

> **gamma ray** ['gæmə] . . .
>
> **ray** ['reɪ] . . .
>
> **smoke¹** ['smoːk] . . .
>
> **smoke detector** [dɪ'tɛktər] . . .

In general, no pronunciation is given for open compounds consisting of two or more English words that are main entries at their own alphabetical place:

> **water lily** *n* : nenúfar *m*

Only the first entry in a series of numbered homographs is given a pronunciation if their pronunciations are the same:

> **dab¹** ['dæb] *vt* . . .
>
> **dab²** *n* . . .

No pronunciation is shown for principal parts of verbs that are formed by regular suffixation, nor for other derivative words formed by common suffixes.

2. Pronunciation of Spanish Entry Words

Spanish pronunciation is highly regular, so no pronunciations are given for most Spanish-to-English entries. Exceptions have been made for certain words (such as foreign borrowings) whose Spanish pronunciations are not evident from their spellings:

> **pizza** ['pitsa, 'pisa] . . .
>
> **footing** ['fu,tɪŋ] . . .

Functional Labels

An italic label indicating a part of speech or some other functional classification follows the pronunciation or, if no pronunciation is given, the main entry. The eight traditional parts of speech, adjective, adverb, conjunction, interjection, noun, preposition, pronoun, and verb, are indicated as follows:

> **daily**² *adj* . . .
>
> **vagamente** *adv* . . .
>
> **and** . . . *conj* . . .
>
> **huy** *interj* . . .
>
> **jackal** . . . *n* . . .
>
> **para** *prep* . . .
>
> **neither**³ *pron* . . .
>
> **leer** . . . *v* . . .

Verbs that are intransitive are labeled *vi*, and verbs that are transitive are labeled *vt*. Entries for verbs that are both transitive and intransitive are labeled *v;* if such an entry includes irregular verb inflections, it is labeled *v* immediately after the main entry, with the labels *vi* and *vt* serving to introduce transitive and intransitive subdivisions when both are present:

> **deliberar** *vi* : to deliberate
>
> **necessitate** . . . *vt* **-tated; -tating** : necesitar, requerir
>
> **satisfy** . . . *v* **-fied; -fying** *vt* . . . — *vi* . . .

Two other labels are used to indicate functional classifications of verbs: *v aux* (auxiliary verb) and *v impers* (impersonal verb).

> **may** . . . *v aux, past* **might** . . .
>
> **haber**¹ . . . *v aux* **1** : have . . . — *v impers* **1 hay** : there is, there are . . .

Gender Labels

In Spanish-to-English noun entries, the gender of the entry word is indicated by an italic *m* (masculine), *f* (feminine), or *mf* (masculine or feminine), immediately following the functional label:

> **magnesio** *nm* . . .
>
> **galaxia** *nf* . . .
>
> **turista** *nmf* . . .

If both the masculine and feminine forms are shown for a noun referring to a person, the label is simply *n:*

> **director, -tora** *n* . . .

Spanish noun equivalents of English entry words are also labeled for gender:

> **amnesia** . . . *n* : amnesia *f*
>
> **earache** . . . *n* : dolor *m* de oído
>
> **gamekeeper** . . . *n* : guardabosque *mf*

Inflected Forms

1. Nouns

The plurals of nouns are shown in this dictionary when they are irregular, when plural suffixation brings about a change in accentuation or in the spelling of the root word, when an English noun ends in a consonant plus *-o* or in *-ey*, when an English noun ends in *-oo*, when an English noun is a compound that pluralizes any element but the last, when a noun has variant plurals, or whenever the dictionary user might have reasonable doubts regarding the spelling of a plural:

> **tooth** . . . *n, pl* **teeth** . . .
>
> **garrafón** *nm, pl* **-fones** . . .
>
> **potato** . . . *n, pl* **-toes** . . .

> **abbey** . . . *n, pl* **-beys** . . .
>
> **cuckoo**[2] *n, pl* **-oos** . . .
>
> **brother–in–law** . . . *n, pl*
>   **brothers–in–law** . . .
>
> **quail**[2] *n, pl* **quail** *or* **quails** . . .
>
> **hábitat** *nm, pl* **-tats** . . .
>
> **tahúr** *nm, pl* **tahúres** . . .

Cutback inflected forms are used for most nouns on the English-to-Spanish side, regardless of the number of syllables. On the Spanish-to-English side, cutback inflections are given for nouns that have three or more syllables; plurals for shorter words are written out in full:

> **shampoo**[2] *n, pl* **-poos** . . .
>
> **calamity** . . . *n, pl* **-ties** . . .
>
> **mouse** . . . *n, pl* **mice** . . .
>
> **sartén** *nmf, pl* **sartenes** . . .
>
> **hámster** *nm, pl* **hámsters** . . .
>
> **federación** *nf, pl* **-ciones** . . .

If only one gender form has a plural which is irregular, that plural form will be given with the appropriate label:

> **campeón, -ona** *n, mpl* **-ones** : champi-
> on

The plurals of nouns are usually not shown when the base word is unchanged by the addition of the regular plural suffix or when the noun is unlikely to occur in the plural:

> **apple** . . . *n* : manzana *f*
>
> **inglés**[3] *nm* : English (language)

Nouns that are plural in form and that regularly occur in plural constructions are labeled as *npl* (for English nouns), *nmpl* (for Spanish masculine nouns), or *nfpl* (for Spanish feminine nouns):

> **knickers** . . . *npl* . . .
>
> **enseres** *nmpl* . . .
>
> **mancuernas** *nfpl* . . .

Entry words that are unchanged in the plural are labeled *ns &
pl* (for English nouns), *nms & pl* (for Spanish masculine nouns),
nfs & pl (for Spanish feminine nouns), and *nmfs & pl* (for Spanish
gender-variable nouns):

> **deer** . . . *ns & pl* . . .
>
> **lavaplatos** *nms & pl* . . .
>
> **tesis** *nfs & pl* . . .
>
> **rompehuelgas** *nmfs & pl* . . .

2. Verbs

ENGLISH VERBS

The principal parts of verbs are shown in English-to-Spanish
entries when they are irregular, when suffixation brings about a
change in spelling of the root word, when the verb ends in *-ey,*
when there are variant inflected forms, or whenever it is believed
that the dictionary user might have reasonable doubts about the
spelling of an inflected form:

> **break**[1] . . . *v* broke . . . ; broken . . . ;
> breaking . . .
>
> **drag**[1] . . . *v* dragged; dragging . . .
>
> **monkey**[1] . . . *vi* -keyed; -keying . . .
>
> **label**[1] . . . *vt* -beled *or* -belled; -beling
> *or* -belling . . .
>
> **imagine** . . . *vt* -ined; -ining . . .

Cutback inflected forms are usually used when the verb has
two or more syllables:

> **multiply** . . . *v* -plied; -plying . . .
>
> **bevel**[1] . . . *v* -eled *or* -elled; -eling *or*
> -elling . . .
>
> **forgo** *or* **forego** . . . *vt* -went; -gone;
> -going . . .
>
> **commit** . . . *vt* -mitted; -mitting . . .

The principal parts of an English verb are not shown when the
base word is unchanged by suffixation:

> **delay**[1] ... *vt*
>
> **pitch**[1] ... *vt*

SPANISH VERBS

Entries for irregular Spanish verbs are cross-referenced by number to the model conjugations appearing in the Conjugation of Spanish Verbs section:

> **abnegarse** {49} *vr* ...
>
> **volver** {89} *vi* ...

Entries for Spanish verbs with regular conjugations are not cross-referenced; however, model conjugations for regular Spanish verbs are included in the Conjugation of Spanish Verbs section beginning on page 38a.

Adverbs and Adjectives

The comparative and superlative forms of English adjective and adverb main entries are shown when suffixation brings about a change in spelling of the root word, when the inflection is irregular, and when there are variant inflected forms:

> **wet**[2] *adj* **wetter; wettest** ...
>
> **good**[2] *adj* **better** ... ; **best** ...
>
> **evil**[1] ... *adj* **eviler** *or* **eviller; evilest** *or* **evillest** ...

The superlative forms of adjectives and adverbs of two or more syllables are usually cut back; the superlative is shown in full, however, when it is desirable to indicate the pronunciation of the inflected form:

> **early**[1] ... *adv* **earlier; -est** ...
>
> **gaudy** ... *adj* **gaudier; -est** ...
>
> **secure**[2] *adj* **-curer; -est** ...
>
> *but*
>
> **young**[1] ... *adj* **younger** [ˈjʌŋgər]; **youngest** [-gəst] ...

At a few entries only the superlative form is shown:

mere *adj, superlative* **merest** . . .

The absence of the comparative form indicates that there is no evidence of its use.

The comparative and superlative forms of adjectives and adverbs are usually not shown when the base word is unchanged by suffixation:

quiet[3] *adj* **1** . . .

Usage

1. Usage Labels

Two types of usage labels are used in this dictionary—regional and stylistic. Spanish words that are limited in use to a specific area or areas of Latin America, or to Spain, are given labels indicating the countries in which they are most commonly used:

guarachear *vi Cuba, PRi fam* . . .

bucket . . . *n* : . . . cubeta *f Mex*

The following regional labels are used in this book: *Arg* (Argentina), *Bol* (Bolivia), *CA* (Central America), *Car* (Caribbean), *Chile* (Chile), *Col* (Colombia), *CoRi* (Costa Rica), *Cuba* (Cuba), *DomRep* (Dominican Republic), *Ecua* (Ecuador), *Sal* (El Salvador), *Guat* (Guatemala), *Hond* (Honduras), *Mex* (Mexico), *Nic* (Nicaragua), *Pan* (Panama), *Par* (Paraguay), *Peru* (Peru), *PRi* (Puerto Rico), *Spain* (Spain), *Uru* (Uruguay), *Ven* (Venezuela).

Since this book focuses on the Spanish spoken in Latin America, only the most common regionalisms from Spain have been included in order to allow for more thorough coverage of Latin-American forms.

A number of Spanish words are given a *fam* (familiar) label as well, indicating that these words are suitable for informal contexts but would not normally be used in formal writing or speaking. The stylistic label *usu considered vulgar* is added for a word which is usually considered vulgar or offensive but whose widespread use justifies its inclusion in this book. The label is intended to warn the reader that the word in question may be inappropriate in polite conversation.

2. Usage Notes

Definitions are sometimes preceded by parenthetical usage notes that give supplementary semantic information:

> **not** . . . *adv* **1** (*used to form a negative*) : no . . .
>
> **within²** *prep* . . . **2** (*in expressions of distance*) : . . . **3** (*in expressions of time*) : . . .
>
> **e²** *conj* (*used instead of* y *before words beginning with* i *or* hi) : . . .
>
> **poder¹** . . . *v aux* . . . **2** (*expressing possibility*) : . . . **3** (*expressing permission*) : . . .

Additional semantic orientation is also sometimes given in the form of parenthetical notes appearing within the definition:

> **calibrate** . . . *vt* . . . : calibrar (armas), graduar (termómetros)
>
> **palco** *nm* : box (in a theater or stadium)

Occasionally a usage note is used in place of a definition. This is usually done when the entry word has no single foreign-language equivalent. This type of usage note will be accompanied by examples of common use:

> **shall** . . . *v aux* . . . **1** (*used to express a command*) ⟨you shall do as I say : harás lo que te digo⟩ . . .

3. Illustrations of Usage

Definitions are sometimes followed by verbal illustrations that show a typical use of the word in context or a common idiomatic usage. These verbal illustrations include a translation and are enclosed in angle brackets:

> **lejos** *adv* **1** : far away, distant ⟨a lo lejos
> : in the distance, far off⟩ . . .

> **make**[1] . . . **9** . . . : ganar ⟨to make a liv-
> ing : ganarse la vida⟩ . . .

Sense Division

A boldface colon is used to introduce a definition:

> **fable** . . . *n* : fábula *f*

Boldface Arabic numerals separate the senses of a word that has more than one sense:

> **laguna** *nf* **1** : lagoon **2** : lacuna, gap

Whenever some information (such as a synonym, a boldface word or phrase, a usage note, a cross-reference, or a label) follows a sense number, it applies only to that specific numbered sense and not to any other boldface numbered senses:

> **abanico** *nm* . . . **2** GAMA : . . .
>
> **tonic**[2] *n* . . . **2** *or* **tonic water** : . . .
>
> **grillo** *nm* . . . **2 grillos** *nmpl* : . . .
>
> **fairy** . . . *n, pl* **fairies** . . . **2 fairy tale** : . . .
>
> **myself** . . . *pron* **1** (*used reflexively*) : . . .
>
> **pike** . . . *n* . . . **3** → **turnpike**
>
> **atado**[2] *nm* . . . **2** *Arg* : . . .

Cross-References

Three different kinds of cross-references are used in this dictionary: synonymous, cognate, and inflectional. In each instance the cross-reference is readily recognized by the boldface arrow following the entry word.

Synonymous and cognate cross-references indicate that a definition at the entry cross-referred to can be substituted for the entry word:

> scapula . . . → shoulder blade
>
> amuck . . . → amok

An inflectional cross-reference is used to identify the entry word as an inflected form of another word (as a noun or verb):

> fue, etc. → ir, ser
>
> mice → mouse

Synonyms

At many entries or senses in this book, a synonym in small capital letters is provided before the boldface colon and the following defining text. These synonyms are all main entries or bold notes elsewhere in the book. They serve as a helpful guide to the meaning of the entry or sense and also give the reader an additional term that might be substituted in a similar context. On the English-to-Spanish side synonyms are particularly abundant, since special care has been taken to guide the English speaker—by means of synonyms, verbal illustrations, or usage notes—to the meaning of the Spanish terms at each sense of a multisense entry.

Spanish Grammar

Accentuation

Spanish word stress is generally determined according to the following rules:

- Words ending in a vowel, or in *-n* or *-s,* are stressed on the penultimate syllable (*zapato*, *llaman*).

- Words ending in a consonant other than *-n* or *-s* are stressed on the last syllable (*perdiz, curiosidad*).

Exceptions to these rules have a written accent mark over the stressed vowel (*fácil, hablará, último*). There are also a few words which take accent marks in order to distinguish them from homonyms (*si, sí; que, qué; el, él; etc.*).

Adverbs ending in *-mente* have two stressed syllables since they retain both the stress of the root word and of the *-mente* suffix (*lentamente, difícilmente*). Many compounds also have two stressed syllables (*limpiaparabrisas*).

Punctuation and Capitalization

Questions and exclamations in Spanish are preceded by an inverted question mark ¿ and an inverted exclamation mark ¡, respectively:

> ¿Cuándo llamó Ana?
> Y tú, ¿qué piensas?
>
> ¡No hagas eso!
> Pero, ¡qué lástima!

In Spanish, unlike English, the following words are not capitalized:

- Names of days, months, and languages (*jueves, octubre, español*).

- Spanish adjectives or nouns derived from proper nouns (*los nicaragüenses, una teoría marxista*).

Articles

1. Definite Article

Spanish has five forms of the definite article: *el* (masculine singular), *la* (feminine singular), *los* (masculine plural), *las* (feminine plural), and *lo* (neuter). The first four agree in gender and number with the nouns they limit (*el carro*, the car; *las tijeras*, the scissors), although the form *el* is used with feminine singular nouns beginning with a stressed *a-* or *ha-* (*el águila, el hambre*).

The neuter article *lo* is used with the masculine singular form of an adjective to express an abstract concept (*lo mejor de este método*, the best thing about this method; *lo meticuloso de su trabajo*, the meticulousness of her work; *lo mismo para mí*, the same for me).

Whenever the masculine article *el* immediately follows the words *de* or *a*, it combines with them to form the contractions *del* and *al*, respectively (*viene del campo, vi al hermano de Roberto*).

The use of *el, la, los,* and *las* in Spanish corresponds largely to the use of *the* in English; some exceptions are noted below.

The definite article is used:

- When referring to something as a class (*los gatos son ágiles*, cats are agile; *me gusta el café*, I like coffee).

- In references to meals and in most expressions of time (*¿comiste el almuerzo?*, did you eat lunch?; *vino el año pasado*, he came last year; *son las dos*, it's two o'clock; *prefiero el verano*, I prefer summer; *la reunión es el lunes*, the meeting is on Monday; but: *hoy es lunes*, today is Monday).

- Before titles (except *don, doña, san, santo, santa, fray,* and *sor*) in third-person references to people (*la señora Rivera llamó*, Mrs. Rivera called; but: *hola, señora Rivera*, hello, Mrs. Rivera).

- In references to body parts and personal possessions (*me duele la cabeza,* my head hurts; *dejó el sombrero,* he left his hat).

- To mean "the one" or "the ones" when the subject is already understood (*la de madera,* the wooden one; *los que vi ayer,* the ones I saw yesterday).

The definite article is omitted:

- Before a noun in apposition, if the noun is not modified (*Caracas, capital de Venezuela;* but: *Pico Bolívar, la montaña más alta de Venezuela*).

- Before a number in a royal title (*Carlos Quinto,* Charles the Fifth).

2. Indefinite Article

The forms of the indefinite article in Spanish are *un* (masculine singular), *una* (feminine singular), *unos* (masculine plural), and *unas* (feminine plural). They agree in number and gender with the nouns they limit (*una mesa,* a table; *unos platos,* some plates), although the form *un* is used with feminine singular nouns beginning with a stressed *a-* or *ha-* (*un ala, un hacha*).

The use of *un, una, unos,* and *unas* in Spanish corresponds largely to the use of *a, an,* and *some* in English, with some exceptions:

- Indefinite articles are generally omitted before nouns identifying someone or something as a member of a class or category (*Paco es profesor/católico,* Paco is a professor/Catholic; *se llama páncreas,* it's called a pancreas).

- They are also often omitted in instances where quantity is understood from context (*vine sin chaqueta,* I came without a jacket; *no tengo carro,* I don't have a car).

Nouns

1. Gender

Nouns in Spanish are either masculine or feminine. A noun's gender can often be determined according to the following guidelines:

- Nouns ending in *-aje*, *-o*, or *-or* are usually masculine (*el traje, el libro, el sabor*), with some exceptions (*la mano, la foto, la labor,* etc.).

- Nouns ending in *-a*, *-dad*, *-ión*, *-tud*, or *-umbre* are usually feminine (*la alfombra, la capacidad, la excepción, la juventud, la certidumbre*). Exceptions include: *el día, el mapa,* and many learned borrowings ending in *-ma* (*el idioma, el tema*).

Most nouns referring to people or animals agree in gender with the subject (*el hombre, la mujer; el hermano, la hermana; el perro, la perra*). However, some nouns referring to people, including those ending in *-ista*, use the same form for both sexes (*el artista, la artista; el modelo, la modelo;* etc.).

A few names of animals exist in only one gender form (*la jirafa, el sapo,* etc.). In these instances, the adjectives *macho* and *hembra* are sometimes used to distinguish males and females (*una jirafa macho,* a male giraffe).

2. Pluralization

Plurals of Spanish nouns are formed as follows:

- Nouns ending in an unstressed vowel or an accented *-é* are pluralized by adding *-s* (*la vaca, las vacas; el café, los cafés*).

- Nouns ending in a consonant other than *-s*, or in a stressed vowel other than *-é*, are generally pluralized by adding *-es* (*el papel, los papeles; el rubí, los rubíes*). Exceptions include *papá* (*papás*) and *mamá* (*mamás*).

- Nouns with an unstressed final syllable ending in *-s* usually have a zero plural (*la crisis, las crisis; el jueves, los jueves*). Other nouns ending in *-s* add *-es* to form the plural (*el mes, los meses; el país, los países*).

- Nouns ending in *-z* are pluralized by changing the *-z* to *-c* and adding *-es* (*el lápiz, los lápices; la vez, las veces*).

- Many compound nouns have a zero plural (*el paraguas, los paraguas; el aguafiestas, los aguafiestas*).

- The plurals of *cualquiera* and *quienquiera* are *cualesquiera* and *quienesquiera*, respectively.

Adjectives

1. Gender and Number

Most adjectives agree in gender and number with the nouns they modify (un chico *alto,* una chica *alta,* unos chicos *altos,* unas chicas *altas*). Some adjectives, including those ending in *-e* and *-ista* (*fuerte, altruista*) and comparative adjectives ending in *-or* (*mayor, mejor*), vary only for number.

Adjectives whose masculine singular forms end in *-o* generally change the *-o* to *-a* to form the feminine (*pequeño → pequeña*). Masculine adjectives ending in *-án, -ón,* or *-dor,* and masculine adjectives of nationality which end in a consonant, usually add *-a* to form the feminine (*holgazán → holgazana; llorón → llorona; trabajador → trabajadora; irlandés → irlandesa*).

Adjectives are pluralized in much the same manner as nouns:

- The plurals of adjectives ending in an unstressed vowel or an accented *-é* are formed by adding an *-s* (un postre *rico,* unos postres *ricos;* una camisa *café,* unas camisas *cafés*).

- Adjectives ending in a consonant, or in a stressed vowel other than *-é,* are generally pluralized by adding *-es* (un niño *cortés,* unos niños *corteses;* una persona *iraní,* unas personas *iraníes*).

- Adjectives ending in *-z* are pluralized by changing the *-z* to *-c* and adding *-es* (una respuesta *sagaz,* unas respuestas *sagaces*).

2. Shortening

- The following masculine singular adjectives drop their final *-o* when they occur before a masculine singular noun: *bueno* (*buen*), *malo* (*mal*), *uno* (*un*), *alguno* (*algún*), *ninguno* (*ningún*), *primero* (*primer*), *tercero* (*tercer*).

- *Grande* shortens to *gran* before any singular noun.

- *Ciento* shortens to *cien* before any noun.

- The title *Santo* shortens to *San* before all masculine names except those beginning with *To-* or *Do-* (*San Juan, Santo Tomás*).

3. Position

Descriptive adjectives generally follow the nouns they modify (*una cosa útil, un actor famoso*). However, adjectives that express an inherent quality often precede the noun (*la blanca nieve*).

Some adjectives change meaning depending on whether they occur before or after the noun: *un pobre niño,* a poor (pitiable) child; *un niño pobre,* a poor (not rich) child; *un gran hombre,* a great man; *un hombre grande,* a big man; *el único libro,* the only book; *el libro único,* the unique book, etc.

4. Comparative and Superlative Forms

The comparative of Spanish adjectives is generally rendered as *más . . . que* (more . . . than) or *menos . . . que* (less . . . than): *soy más alta que él,* I'm taller than he; *son menos inteligentes que tú,* they're less intelligent than you.

The superlative of Spanish adjectives usually follows the formula *definite article + (noun +) más/menos + adjective: ella es la estudiante más trabajadora,* she is the hardest-working student; *él es el menos conocido,* he's the least known.

A few Spanish adjectives have irregular comparative and superlative forms:

Adjective	Comparative/Superlative
bueno (good)	**mejor** (better, best)
malo (bad)	**peor** (worse, worst)
grande[1] (big, great), **viejo** (old)	**mayor** (greater, older; greatest, oldest)
pequeño[1] (little), **joven** (young)	**menor** (lesser, younger; least, youngest)
mucho (much), **muchos** (many)	**más** (more, most)
poco (little), **pocos** (few)	**menos** (less, least)

[1] These words have regular comparative and superlative forms when used in reference to physical size: *él es más grande que yo; nuestra casa es la más pequeña.*

ABSOLUTE SUPERLATIVE

The absolute superlative is formed by placing *muy* before the adjective, or by adding the suffix *-ísimo* (*ella es muy simpática* or *ella es simpatiquísima*, she is very nice). The absolute superlative using *-ísimo* is formed according to the following rules:

- Adjectives ending in a consonant other than *-z* simply add the *-ísimo* ending (*fácil → facilísimo*).

- Adjectives ending in *-z* change this consonant to *-c* and add *-ísimo* (*feliz → felicísimo*).

- Adjectives ending in a vowel or diphthong drop the vowel or diphthong and add *-ísimo* (*claro → clarísimo; amplio → amplísimo*).

- Adjectives ending in *-co* or *-go* change these endings to *qu* and *gu*, respectively, and add *-ísimo* (*rico → riquísimo; largo → larguísimo*).

- Adjectives ending in *-ble* change this ending to *-bil* and add *-ísimo* (*notable → notabilísimo*).

- Adjectives containing the stressed diphthong *ie* or *ue* will sometimes change these to *e* and *o,* respectively (*ferviente → fervientísimo* or *ferventísimo; bueno → buenísimo* or *bonísimo*).

Adverbs

Adverbs can be formed by adding the adverbial suffix *-mente* to virtually any adjective (*fácil → fácilmente*). If the adjective varies for gender, the feminine form is used as the basis for forming the adverb (*rápido → rápidamente*).

Pronouns

1. Personal Pronouns

The personal pronouns in Spanish are:

Person		Singular	Plural	
FIRST	**yo**	I	**nosotros, nosotras**	we
SECOND	**tú**	you (familiar)	**vosotros[2], vosotras[2]**	you, all of you
	vos[1]	you		
	usted	you (formal)	**ustedes[3]**	you, all of you
THIRD	**él**	he	**ellos, ellas**	they
	ella	she		
	ello	it (neuter)		

[1] Familiar form used in addition to *tú* in South and Central America.

[2] Familiar form used in Spain.

[3] Formal form used in Spain; familiar and formal form used in Latin America.

FAMILIAR VS. FORMAL

The second person personal pronouns exist in both familiar and formal forms. The familiar forms are generally used when addressing relatives, friends, and children, although usage varies considerably from region to region; the formal forms are used in other contexts to show courtesy, respect, or emotional distance.

In Spain and in the Caribbean, *tú* is used exclusively as the familiar singular "you." In South and Central America, however, *vos* either competes with *tú* to varying degrees or replaces it entirely. (For a more detailed explanation of *vos* and its corresponding verb forms, refer to the Conjugation of Spanish Verbs section.)

The plural familiar form *vosotros, -as* is used only in Spain, where *ustedes* is reserved for formal contexts. In Latin America, *vosotros, -as* is not used, and *ustedes* serves as the all-purpose plural "you."

It should be noted that while *usted* and *ustedes* are regarded as second person pronouns, they take the third person form of the verb.

USAGE

In Spanish, personal pronouns are generally omitted (*voy al cine*, I'm going to the movies; *¿llamaron?*, did they call?), although they are sometimes used for purposes of emphasis or clarity (*se* *lo diré yo,* I will tell them; *vino ella, pero él se quedó,* she came, but he stayed behind). The forms *usted* and *ustedes* are usually included out of courtesy (*¿cómo está usted?,* how are you?).

Personal pronouns are not generally used in reference to inanimate objects or living creatures other than humans; in these instances, the pronoun is most often omitted (*¿es nuevo? no, es viejo,* is it new? no, it's old).

The neuter third person pronoun *ello* is reserved for indefinite subjects (as abstract concepts): *todo ello implica . . . ,* all of this implies . . . ; *por si ello fuera poco . . . ,* as if that weren't enough . . . . It most commonly appears in formal writing and speech. In less formal contexts, *ello* is often either omitted or replaced with *esto, eso,* or *aquello.*

2. Prepositional Pronouns

Prepositional pronouns are used as the objects of prepositions (*¿es para mí?,* is it for me?; *se lo dio a ellos,* he gave it to them).

The prepositional pronouns in Spanish are:

Singular		**Plural**	
mí	me	**nosotros, nosotras**	us
ti	you	**vosotros[1], vosotras[1]**	you
usted	you (formal)	**ustedes**	you
él	him	**ellos, ellas**	them
ella	her		
ello	it (neuter)		
sí	yourself, himself, herself, itself, oneself	**sí**	yourselves, themselves

[1] Used primarily in Spain.

When the preposition *con* is followed by *mí, ti,* or *sí,* both words are replaced by *conmigo, contigo,* and *consigo,* respectively (*¿vienes conmigo?,* are you coming with me?; *habló contigo,* he spoke with you; *no lo trajo consigo,* she didn't bring it with her).

3. Object Pronouns

DIRECT OBJECT PRONOUNS

Direct object pronouns represent the primary goal or result of the action of a verb. The direct object pronouns in Spanish are:

Singular		Plural	
me	me	**nos**	us
te	you	**os**[1]	you
le[2]	you, him	**les**[2]	you, them
lo	you, him, it	**los**	you, them
la	you, her, it	**las**	you, them

[1] Used only in Spain.

[2] Used mainly in Spain.

Agreement

The third person forms agree in both gender and number with the nouns they replace or the people they refer to (*pintó las paredes,* she painted the walls → *las pintó,* she painted them; *visitaron al señor Juárez,* they visited Mr. Juárez → *lo visitaron,* they visited him). The remaining forms vary only for number.

Position

Direct object pronouns are normally affixed to the end of an affirmative command, a simple infinitive, or a present participle (*¡hazlo!,* do it!; *es difícil hacerlo,* it's difficult to do it; *haciéndolo, aprenderás,* you'll learn by doing it). With constructions involving an auxiliary verb and an infinitive or present participle, the pronoun may occur either immediately before the construction or suffixed to it (*lo voy a hacer* or *voy a hacerlo,* I'm going to do it; *estoy haciéndolo* or *lo estoy haciendo,* I'm doing it). In all other cases, the pronoun immediately precedes the conjugated verb (*no lo haré,* I won't do it).

Regional Variation

In Spain and in a few areas of Latin America, *le* and *les* are used in place of *lo* and *los* when referring to or addressing people (*le vieron,* they saw him; *les vistió,* she dressed them). In most parts of Latin America, however, *los* and *las* are used for the second person plural in both formal and familiar contexts.

The second person plural familiar form *os* is restricted to Spain.

INDIRECT OBJECT PRONOUNS

Indirect object pronouns represent the secondary goal of the action of a verb (*me dio el regalo,* he gave me the gift; *les dije que no,* I told them no). The indirect object pronouns in Spanish are:

Singular		**Plural**	
me	(to, for, from) me	**nos**	(to, for, from) us
te	(to, for, from) you	**os**[1]	(to, for, from) you
le	(to, for, from) you, him, her, it	**les**	(to, for, from) you, them
se[2]		**se**[2]	

[1]Used only in Spain.
[2]See explanation below.

Position

Indirect object pronouns follow the same rules as direct object pronouns with regard to their position in relation to verbs. When they occur with direct object pronouns, the indirect object pronoun always precedes (*nos lo dio,* she gave it to us; *estoy trayéndotela,* I'm bringing it to you).

Use of *Se*

When the indirect object pronouns *le* or *les* occur before any direct object pronoun beginning with an *l-*, the indirect object pronouns *le* and *les* convert to *se* (*les mandé la carta,* I sent them the letter → *se la mandé,* I sent it to them; *vamos a comprarle los aretes,* let's buy her the earrings → *vamos a comprárselos,* let's buy them for her).

4. Reflexive Pronouns

Reflexive pronouns are used to refer back to the subject of the verb (*me hice daño,* I hurt myself; *se vistieron,* they got dressed, they dressed themselves; *nos lo compramos,* we bought it for ourselves).

The reflexive pronouns in Spanish are:

	Singular		**Plural**
me	myself	**nos**	ourselves
te	yourself	**os**[1]	yourselves
se	yourself, himself, herself, itself	**se**	yourselves, themselves

[1]Used only in Spain.

Reflexive pronouns are also used:

- When the verb describes an action performed to one's own body, clothing, etc. (*me quité los zapatos,* I took off my shoes; *se arregló el pelo,* he fixed his hair).

- In the plural, to indicate reciprocal action (*se hablan con frecuencia,* they speak with each other frequently).

- In the third person singular and plural, as an indefinite subject reference (*se dice que es verdad,* they say it's true; *nunca se sabe,* one never knows; *se escribieron miles de páginas,* thousands of pages were written).

It should be noted that many verbs which take reflexive pronouns in Spanish have intransitive equivalents in English (*ducharse,* to shower; *quejarse,* to complain; etc.).

5. Relative Pronouns

Relative pronouns introduce subordinate clauses acting as nouns or modifiers (*el libro que escribió* . . . , the book that he wrote . . . ; *las chicas a quienes conociste* . . . , the girls whom you met . . .). In Spanish, the relative pronouns are:

que (that, which, who, whom)

quien, quienes (who, whom, that, whoever, whomever)

el cual, la cual, los cuales, las cuales (which, who)

el que, la que, los que, las que (which, who, whoever)

lo cual (which)

lo que (what, which, whatever)

cuanto, cuanta, cuantos, cuantas (all those that, all that, whatever, whoever, as much as, as many as)

Relative pronouns are not omitted in Spanish as they often are in English: *el carro que vi ayer,* the car (that) I saw yesterday. When relative pronouns are used with prepositions, the preposition precedes the clause (*la película sobre la cual le hablé,* the film I spoke to you about).

The relative pronoun *que* can be used in reference to both people and things. Unlike other relative pronouns, *que* does not take the personal *a* when used as a direct object referring to a person (*el hombre que llamé,* the man that I called; but: *el hombre a quien llamé,* the man whom I called).

Quien is used only in reference to people. It varies in number with the explicit or implied antecedent (*las mujeres con quienes charlamos . . . ,* the women we chatted with; *quien lo hizo pagará,* whoever did it will pay).

El cual and *el que* vary for both number and gender, and are therefore often used in situations where *que* or *quien(es)* might create ambiguity: *nos contó algunas cosas sobre los libros, las cuales eran interesantes,* he told us some things about the books which (the things) were interesting.

Lo cual and *lo que* are used to refer back to a whole clause, or to something indefinite (*dijo que iría, lo cual me alegró,* he said he would go, which made me happy; *pide lo que quieras,* ask for whatever you want).

Cuanto varies for both number and gender with the implied antecedent: *conté a cuantas (personas) pude,* I counted as many (people) as I could. If an indefinite mass quantity is referred to, the masculine singular form is used (*anoté cuanto decía,* I jotted down whatever he said).

Possessives

1. Possessive Adjectives

UNSTRESSED FORMS

Singular		**Plural**	
mi(s)	my	nuestro(s), nuestra(s)	our
tu(s)	your	vuestro(s)[1], vuestra(s)[1]	your
su(s)	your, his, her, its	su(s)	your, their

[1] Used only in Spain.

STRESSED FORMS

Singular		Plural	
mío(s), **mía(s)**	my, mine, of mine	**nuestro(s),** **nuestra(s)**	our, ours, of ours
tuyo(s), **tuya(s)**	your, yours, of yours	**vuestro(s)[1],** **vuestra(s)[1]**	your, yours, of yours
suyo(s), **suya(s)**	your, yours, of yours; his, of his; her, hers, of hers; its, of its	**suyo(s),** **suya(s)**	your, yours, of yours; their, theirs, of theirs

[1]Used only in Spain.

The unstressed forms of possessive adjectives precede the nouns they modify (*mis zapatos,* my shoes; *nuestra escuela,* our school).

The stressed forms occur after the noun and are often used for purposes of emphasis (*el carro tuyo,* your car; *la pluma es mía,* the pen is mine; *unos amigos nuestros,* some friends of ours).

All possessive adjectives agree with the noun in number. The stressed forms, as well as the unstressed forms *nuestro* and *vuestro,* also vary for gender.

2. Possessive Pronouns

The possessive pronouns have the same forms as the stressed possessive adjectives (see table above). They are always preceded by the definite article, and they agree in number and gender with the nouns they replace (*las llaves mías,* my keys → *las mías,* mine; *los guantes nuestros,* our gloves → *los nuestros,* ours).

Demonstratives

1. Demonstrative Adjectives

The demonstrative adjectives in Spanish are:

Singular		Plural	
este, esta	this	estos, estas	these
ese, esa	that	esos, esas	those
aquel, aquella	that	aquellos, aquellas	those

Demonstrative adjectives agree with the nouns they modify in gender and number (*esta chica, aquellos árboles*). They normally precede the noun, but may occasionally occur after for purposes of emphasis or to express contempt: *en la época aquella de cambio,* in that era of change; *el perro ese ha ladrado toda la noche,* that (awful, annoying, etc.) dog barked all night long.

The forms *aquel, aquella, aquellos,* and *aquellas* are generally used in reference to people and things that are relatively distant from the speaker in space or time: *ese libro,* that book (a few feet away); *aquel libro,* that book (way over there).

2. Demonstrative Pronouns

The demonstrative pronouns in Spanish are orthographically identical to the demonstrative adjectives except that they take an accent mark over the stressed vowel (*éste, ése, aquél,* etc.). In addition, there are three neuter forms—*esto, eso,* and *aquello*—which are used when referring to abstract ideas or unidentified things (*¿te dijo eso?,* he said that to you?; *¿qué es esto?,* what is this?; *tráeme todo aquello,* bring me all that stuff).

Except for the neuter forms, demonstrative pronouns agree in gender and number with the nouns they replace (*esta silla,* this chair → *ésta,* this one; *aquellos vasos,* those glasses → *aquéllos,* those ones).

Abbreviations in This Work

adj	adjective	*nm*	masculine noun
adv	adverb	*nmf*	masculine or feminine noun
Arg	Argentina		
Bol	Bolivia	*nmfpl*	plural noun invariable for gender
Brit	British		
CA	Central America	*nmfs & pl*	noun invariable for both gender and number
Car	Caribbean region		
Col	Colombia		
conj	conjunction	*nmpl*	masculine plural noun
CoRi	Costa Rica		
DomRep	Dominican Republic	*nms & pl*	invariable singular or plural masculine noun
Ecua	Ecuador	*npl*	plural noun
esp	especially	*ns & pl*	noun invariable for plural
f	feminine		
fam	familiar or colloquial	*Pan*	Panama
		Par	Paraguay
fpl	feminine plural	*pl*	plural
Guat	Guatemala	*pp*	past participle
Hond	Honduras	*prep*	preposition
interj	interjection	*PRi*	Puerto Rico
m	masculine	*pron*	pronoun
Mex	Mexico	*s*	singular
mf	masculine or feminine	*Sal*	El Salvador
		Uru	Uruguay
mfpl	masculine or feminine plural	*usu*	usually
mpl	masculine plural	*v*	verb (transitive and intransitive)
n	noun		
nf	feminine noun	*v aux*	auxiliary verb
nfpl	feminine plural noun	*Ven*	Venezuela
		vi	intransitive verb
nfs & pl	invariable singular or plural feminine noun	*v impers*	impersonal verb
		vr	reflexive verb
Nic	Nicaragua	*vt*	transitive verb

Conjugation of Spanish Verbs

Simple Tenses

Tense	Regular Verbs Ending in -AR hablar	
PRESENT INDICATIVE	hablo	hablamos
	hablas	habláis
	habla	hablan
PRESENT SUBJUNCTIVE	hable	hablemos
	hables	habléis
	hable	hablen
PRETERIT INDICATIVE	hablé	hablamos
	hablaste	hablasteis
	habló	hablaron
IMPERFECT INDICATIVE	hablaba	hablábamos
	hablabas	hablabais
	hablaba	hablaban
IMPERFECT SUBJUNCTIVE	hablara	habláramos
	hablaras	hablarais
	hablara	hablaran
	or	
	hablase	hablásemos
	hablases	hablaseis
	hablase	hablasen
FUTURE INDICATIVE	hablaré	hablaremos
	hablarás	hablaréis
	hablará	hablarán
FUTURE SUBJUNCTIVE	hablare	habláremos
	hablares	hablareis
	hablare	hablaren
CONDITIONAL	hablaría	hablaríamos
	hablarías	hablaríais
	hablaría	hablarían
IMPERATIVE		hablemos
	habla	hablad
	hable	hablen
PRESENT PARTICIPLE (GERUND)	hablando	
PAST PARTICIPLE	hablado	

| Regular Verbs Ending in -ER | | Regular Verbs Ending in -IR | |
comer		vivir	
como	comemos	vivo	vivimos
comes	coméis	vives	vivís
come	comen	vive	viven
coma	comamos	viva	vivamos
comas	comáis	vivas	viváis
coma	coman	viva	vivan
comí	comimos	viví	vivimos
comiste	comisteis	viviste	vivisteis
comió	comieron	vivió	vivieron
comía	comíamos	vivía	vivíamos
comías	comíais	vivías	vivíais
comía	comían	vivía	vivían
comiera	comiéramos	viviera	viviéramos
comieras	comierais	vivieras	vivierais
comiera	comieran	viviera	vivieran
or		*or*	
comiese	comiésemos	viviese	viviésemos
comieses	comieseis	vivieses	vivieseis
comiese	comiesen	viviese	viviesen
comeré	comeremos	viviré	viviremos
comerás	comeréis	vivirás	viviréis
comerá	comerán	vivirá	vivirán
comiere	comiéremos	viviere	viviéremos
comieres	comiereis	vivieres	viviereis
comiere	comieren	viviere	vivieren
comería	comeríamos	viviría	viviríamos
comerías	comeríais	vivirías	viviríais
comería	comerían	viviría	vivirían
	comamos		vivamos
come	comed	vive	vivid
coma	coman	viva	vivan
comiendo		viviendo	
comido		vivido	

Compound Tenses

1. Perfect Tenses

The perfect tenses are formed with *haber* and the past participle:

PRESENT PERFECT

he hablado, etc. (*indicative*);
haya hablado, etc. (*subjunctive*)

PAST PERFECT

había hablado, etc. (*indicative*);
hubiera hablado, etc. (*subjunctive*)
or
hubiese hablado, etc. (*subjunctive*)

PRETERIT PERFECT

hube hablado, etc. (*indicative*)

FUTURE PERFECT

habré hablado, etc. (*indicative*)

CONDITIONAL PERFECT

habría hablado, etc. (*indicative*)

2. Progressive Tenses

The progressive tenses are formed with *estar* and the present participle:

PRESENT PROGRESSIVE

estoy llamando, etc. (*indicative*);
esté llamando, etc. (*subjunctive*)

IMPERFECT PROGRESSIVE

estaba llamando, etc. (*indicative*);
estuviera llamando, etc. (*subjunctive*)
or
estuviese llamando, etc. (*subjunctive*)

PRETERIT PROGRESSIVE

estuve llamando, etc. (*indicative*)

FUTURE PROGRESSIVE

estaré llamando, etc. (*indicative*)

CONDITIONAL PROGRESSIVE

estaría llamando, etc. (*indicative*)

PRESENT PERFECT PROGRESSIVE

he estado llamando, etc. (*indicative*);
haya estado llamando, etc. (*subjunctive*)

PAST PERFECT PROGRESSIVE

había estado llamando, etc. (*indicative*);
hubiera estado llamando, etc. (*subjunctive*)
or
hubiese estado llamando, etc. (*subjunctive*)

Use of *Vos*

In parts of South and Central America, *vos* often replaces or competes with *tú* as the second person familiar personal pronoun. It is particularly well established in the Río de la Plata region and much of Central America.

The pronoun *vos* often takes a distinct set of verb forms, usually in the present tense and the imperative. These vary widely from region to region; examples of the most common forms are shown below.

INFINITIVE FORM	hablar	comer	vivir
PRESENT INDICATIVE	vos hablás	vos comés	vos vivís
PRESENT SUBJUNCTIVE	vos hablés	vos comás	vos vivás
IMPERATIVE	hablá	comé	viví

In some areas, *vos* may take the *tú* or *vosotros* forms of the verb, while in others (as Uruguay), *tú* is combined with the *vos* verb forms.

Irregular Verbs

The *imperfect subjunctive,* the *future subjunctive,* the *conditional*, and most forms of the *imperative* are not included in the model conjugations list, but can be derived as follows:

The *imperfect subjunctive* and the *future subjunctive* are formed from the third person plural form of the preterit tense by removing the last syllable (*-ron*) and adding the appropriate suffix:

PRETERIT INDICATIVE, THIRD PERSON PLURAL (querer)	quisieron
IMPERFECT SUBJUNCTIVE (querer)	quisiera, quisieras, etc. *or* quisiese, quisieses, etc.
FUTURE SUBJUNCTIVE (querer)	quisiere, quisieres, etc.

The conditional uses the same stem as the future indicative:

FUTURE INDICATIVE (poner)	pondré, pondrás, etc.
CONDITIONAL (poner)	pondría, pondrías, etc.

The third person singular, first person plural, and third person plural forms of the *imperative* are the same as the corresponding forms of the present subjunctive.

The second person plural *(vosotros)* form of the *imperative* is formed by removing the final *-r* of the infinitive form and adding a *-d* (ex.: *oír → oíd*).

Model Conjugations of Irregular Verbs

The model conjugations below include the following simple tenses: the *present indicative* (IND), the *present subjunctive* (SUBJ), the *preterit indicative* (PRET), the *imperfect indicative* (IMPF), the *future indicative* (FUT), the second person singular form of the *imperative* (IMPER), the *present participle* or *gerund* (PRP), and the *past participle* (PP). Each set of conjugations is preceded by the corresponding infinitive form of the verb, shown in bold type. Only tenses containing irregularities are listed, and the irregular verb forms within each tense are displayed in bold type.

Each irregular verb entry in the Spanish-English section of this dictionary is cross-referred by number to one of the following model conjugations. These cross-reference numbers are shown in curly braces { } immediately following the entry's functional label.

1 **abolir** *(defective verb)* : IND abolimos, abolís *(other forms not used)*; SUBJ *(not used)*; IMPER *(only second person plural is used)*

2 **abrir** : PP abierto

3 **actuar** : IND **actúo**, **actúas**, **actúa**, actuamos, actuáis, **actúan**; SUBJ **actúe**, **actúes**, **actúe**, actuemos, actuéis, **actúen**; IMPER **actúa**

4 **adquirir** : IND **adquiero**, **adquieres**, **adquiere**, adquirimos, adquirís, **adquieren**; SUBJ **adquiera**, **adquieras**, **adquiera**, adquiramos, adquiráis, **adquieran**; IMPER **adquiere**

5 **airar** : IND **aíro**, **aíras**, **aíra**, airamos, airáis, **aíran**; SUBJ **aíre**, **aíres**, **aíre**, airemos, airéis, **aíren**; IMPER **aíra**

6 **andar** : PRET **anduve**, **anduviste**, **anduvo**, **anduvimos**, **anduvisteis**, **anduvieron**

7 **asir** : IND **asgo**, ases, ase, asimos, asís, asen; SUBJ **asga**, **asgas**, **asga**, **asgamos**, **asgáis**, **asgan**

8 **aunar** : IND **aúno**, **aúnas**, **aúna**, aunamos, aunáis, **aúnan**; SUBJ **aúne**, **aúnes**, **aúne**, aunemos, aunéis, **aúnen**; IMPER **aúna**

9 **avergonzar** : IND **avergüenzo**, **avergüenzas**, **avergüenza**, avergonzamos, avergonzáis, **avergüenzan**; SUBJ **avergüence**, **avergüences**, **avergüence**, avergoncemos, avergoncéis, **avergüencen**; PRET **avergoncé**; IMPER **avergüenza**

10 **averiguar** : SUBJ **averigüe**, **averigües**, **averigüe**, **averigüemos**, **averigüéis**, **averigüen**; PRET **averigüé**, averiguaste, averiguó, averiguamos, averiguasteis, averiguaron

11 **bendecir** : *IND* **bendigo, bendices, bendice,** bendecimos, ben-
   decís, **bendicen;** *SUBJ* **bendiga, bendigas, bendiga, bendig-
   amos, bendigáis, bendigan;** *PRET* **bendije, bendijiste,
   bendijo, bendijimos, bendijisteis, bendijeron;** *IMPER* **bendice**

12 **caber** : *IND* **quepo,** cabes, cabe, cabemos, cabéis, caben; *SUBJ*
   quepa, quepas, quepa, quepamos, quepáis, quepan; *PRET*
   cupe, cupiste, cupo, cupimos, cupisteis, cupieron; *FUT* **cabré,
   cabrás, cabrá, cabremos, cabréis, cabrán**

13 **caer** : *IND* **caigo,** caes, cae, caemos, caéis, caen; *SUBJ* **caiga,
   caigas, caiga, caigamos, caigáis, caigan;** *PRET* caí, **caíste,
   cayó, caímos, caísteis, cayeron;** *PRP* **cayendo;** *PP* **caído**

14 **cocer** : *IND* **cuezo, cueces, cuece,** cocemos, cocéis, **cuecen;**
   SUBJ **cueza, cuezas, cueza, cozamos, cozáis, cuezan;** *IMPER*
   cuece

15 **coger** : *IND* **cojo,** coges, coge, cogemos, cogéis, cogen; *SUBJ*
   coja, cojas, coja, cojamos, cojáis, cojan

16 **colgar** : *IND* **cuelgo, cuelgas, cuelga,** colgamos, colgáis, **cuel-
   gan;** *SUBJ* **cuelgue, cuelgues, cuelgue, colguemos, colguéis,
   cuelguen;** *PRET* **colgué,** colgaste, colgó, colgamos, colgasteis,
   colgaron; *IMPER* **cuelga**

17 **concernir** (*defective verb; used only in the third person singular
   and plural of the present indicative, present subjunctive, and
   imperfect subjunctive*) see 25 **discernir**

18 **conocer** : *IND* **conozco,** conoces, conoce, conocemos, cono-
   céis, conocen; *SUBJ* **conozca, conozcas, conozca, conoz-
   camos, conozcáis, conozcan**

19 **contar** : *IND* **cuento, cuentas, cuenta,** contamos, contáis, **cuen-
   tan;** *SUBJ* **cuente, cuentes, cuente,** contemos, contéis,
   cuenten; *IMPER* **cuenta**

20 **creer** : *PRET* creí, **creíste, creyó, creímos, creísteis, creyeron;**
   PRP **creyendo;** *PP* **creído**

21 **cruzar** : *SUBJ* **cruce, cruces, cruce, crucemos, crucéis, crucen;**
   PRET **crucé,** cruzaste, cruzó, cruzamos, cruzasteis, cruzaron

22 **dar** : *IND* **doy,** das, da, damos, **dais,** dan; *SUBJ* **dé,** des, **dé,**
   demos, **deis,** den; *PRET* **di, diste, dio, dimos, disteis, dieron**

23 **decir** : *IND* **digo, dices, dice**, decimos, decís, **dicen**; *SUBJ* **diga, digas, diga, digamos, digáis, digan**; *PRET* **dije, dijiste, dijo, dijimos, dijisteis, dijeron**; *FUT* **diré, dirás, dirá, diremos, diréis, dirán**; *IMPER* **di**; *PRP* **diciendo**; *PP* **dicho**

24 **delinquir** : *IND* **delinco**, delinques, delinque, delinquimos, delinquís, delinquen; *SUBJ* **delinca, delincas, delinca, delincamos, delincáis, delincan**

25 **discernir** : *IND* **discierno, disciernes, discierne**, discernimos, discernís, **disciernen**; *SUBJ* **discierna, disciernas, discierna**, discernamos, discernáis, **disciernan**; *IMPER* **discierne**

26 **distinguir** : *IND* **distingo**, distingues, distingue, distinguimos, distinguís, distinguen; *SUBJ* **distinga, distingas, distinga, distingamos, distingáis, distingan**

27 **dormir** : *IND* **duermo, duermes, duerme**, dormimos, dormís, **duermen**; *SUBJ* **duerma, duermas, duerma, durmamos, durmáis, duerman**; *PRET* dormí, dormiste, **durmió**, dormimos, dormisteis, **durmieron**; *IMPER* **duerme**; *PRP* **durmiendo**

28 **elegir** : *IND* **elijo, eliges, elige**, elegimos, elegís, **eligen**; *SUBJ* **elija, elijas, elija, elijamos, elijáis, elijan**; *PRET* elegí, elegiste, **eligió**, elegimos, elegisteis, **eligieron**; *IMPER* **elige**; *PRP* **eligiendo**

29 **empezar** : *IND* **empiezo, empiezas, empieza**, empezamos, empezáis, **empiezan**; *SUBJ* **empiece, empieces, empiece, empecemos, empecéis, empiecen**; *PRET* **empecé**, empezaste, empezó, empezamos, empezasteis, empezaron; *IMPER* **empieza**

30 **enraizar** : *IND* **enraízo, enraízas, enraíza**, enraizamos, enraizáis, **enraízan**; *SUBJ* **enraíce, enraíces, enraíce, enraicemos, enraicéis, enraícen**; *PRET* **enraicé**, enraizaste, enraizó, enraizamos, enraizasteis, enraizaron; *IMPER* **enraíza**

31 **erguir** : *IND* **irgo** *or* **yergo**, **irgues** *or* **yergues**, **irgue** *or* **yergue**, erguimos, erguís, **irguen** *or* **yerguen**; *SUBJ* **irga** *or* **yerga**, **irgas** *or* **yergas**, **irga** *or* **yerga**, **irgamos**, **irgáis**, **irgan** *or* **yergan**; *PRET* erguí, erguiste, **irguió**, erguimos, erguisteis, **irguieron**; *IMPER* **irgue** *or* **yergue**; *PRP* **irguiendo**

32 **errar** : *IND* **yerro, yerras, yerra,** erramos, erráis, **yerran;** *SUBJ*
    yerre, yerres, yerre, erremos, erréis, **yerren;** *IMPER* **yerra**

33 **escribir** : *PP* **escrito**

34 **estar** : *IND* **estoy, estás, está,** estamos, estáis, **están;** *SUBJ* **esté,**
    estés, esté, estemos, estéis, **estén;** *PRET* **estuve, estuviste,**
    estuvo, estuvimos, estuvisteis, estuvieron; *IMPER* **está**

35 **exigir** : *IND* **exijo,** exiges, exige, exigimos, exigís, exigen; *SUBJ*
    exija, exijas, exija, exijamos, exijáis, exijan

36 **forzar** : *IND* **fuerzo, fuerzas, fuerza,** forzamos, forzáis,
    fuerzan; *SUBJ* **fuerce, fuerces, fuerce, forcemos, forcéis,**
    fuercen; *PRET* **forcé,** forzaste, forzó, forzamos, forzasteis,
    forzaron; *IMPER* **fuerza**

37 **freír** : *IND* **frío, fríes, fríe,** freímos, freís, **fríen;** *SUBJ* **fría, frías,**
    fría, friamos, friáis, fríen; *PRET* **freí, freíste, frió, freímos,**
    freísteis, frieron; *IMPER* **fríe;** *PRP* **friendo;** *PP* **frito**

38 **gruñir** : *PRET* **gruñí,** gruñiste, **gruñó,** gruñimos, gruñisteis,
    gruñeron; *PRP* **gruñendo**

39 **haber** : *IND* **he, has, ha, hemos,** habéis, **han;** *SUBJ* **haya, hayas,**
    haya, hayamos, hayáis, hayan; *PRET* **hube, hubiste, hubo,**
    hubimos, hubisteis, hubieron; *FUT* **habré, habrás, habrá,**
    habremos, habréis, habrán; *IMPER* **he**

40 **hacer** : *IND* **hago,** haces, hace, hacemos, hacéis, hacen; *SUBJ*
    haga, hagas, haga, hagamos, hagáis, hagan; *PRET* **hice,**
    hiciste, hizo, hicimos, hicisteis, hicieron; *FUT* **haré, harás,**
    hará, haremos, haréis, harán; *IMPER* **haz;** *PP* **hecho**

41 **huir** : *IND* **huyo, huyes, huye,** huimos, huís, **huyen;** *SUBJ* **huya,**
    huyas, huya, huyamos, huyáis, huyan; *PRET* **huí,** huiste,
    huyó, huimos, huisteis, **huyeron;** *IMPER* **huye;** *PRP* **huyendo**

42 **imprimir** : *PP* **impreso**

43 **ir** : *IND* **voy, vas, va, vamos, vais, van;** *SUBJ* **vaya, vayas, vaya,**
    vayamos, vayáis, vayan; *PRET* **fui, fuiste, fue, fuimos, fuis-**
    teis, fueron; *IMPF* **iba, ibas, iba, íbamos, ibais, iban;** *IMPER*
    ve; *PRP* **yendo;** *PP* **ido**

44 **jugar** : *IND* **juego, juegas, juega,** jugamos, jugáis, **juegan;** *SUBJ*
    juegue, juegues, juegue, juguemos, juguéis, jueguen; *PRET*

jugué, jugaste, jugó, jugamos, jugasteis, jugaron; *IMPER* **juega**

45 **lucir** : *IND* **luzco**, luces, luce, lucimos, lucís, lucen; *SUBJ* **luzca, luzcas, luzca, luzcamos, luzcáis, luzcan**

46 **morir** : *IND* **muero, mueres, muere**, morimos, morís, **mueren**; *SUBJ* **muera, mueras, muera**, muramos, **muráis, mueran**; *PRET* morí, moriste, **murió**, morimos, moristeis, **murieron**; *IMPER* **muere**; *PRP* **muriendo**; *PP* **muerto**

47 **mover** : *IND* **muevo, mueves, mueve**, movemos, movéis, **mueven**; *SUBJ* **mueva, muevas, mueva**, movamos, mováis, **muevan**; *IMPER* **mueve**

48 **nacer** : *IND* **nazco**, naces, nace, nacemos, nacéis, nacen; *SUBJ* **nazca, nazcas, nazca, nazcamos, nazcáis, nazcan**

49 **negar** : *IND* **niego, niegas, niega**, negamos, negáis, **niegan**; *SUBJ* **niegue, niegues, niegue, neguemos, neguéis, nieguen**; *PRET* **negué**, negaste, negó, negamos, negasteis, negaron; *IMPER* **niega**

50 **oír** : *IND* **oigo, oyes, oye**, oímos, oís, **oyen**; *SUBJ* **oiga, oigas, oiga, oigamos, oigáis, oigan**; *PRET* oí, **oíste, oyó**, oímos, oísteis, **oyeron**; *IMPER* **oye**; *PRP* **oyendo**; *PP* **oído**

51 **oler** : *IND* **huelo, hueles, huele**, olemos, oléis, **huelen**; *SUBJ* **huela, huelas, huela**, olamos, oláis, **huelan**; *IMPER* **huele**

52 **pagar** : *SUBJ* **pague, pagues, pague, paguemos, paguéis, paguen**; *PRET* **pagué**, pagaste, pagó, pagamos, pagasteis, pagaron

53 **parecer** : *IND* **parezco**, pareces, parece, parecemos, parecéis, parecen; *SUBJ* **parezca, parezcas, parezca, parezcamos, parezcáis, parezcan**

54 **pedir** : *IND* **pido, pides, pide**, pedimos, pedís, **piden**; *SUBJ* **pida, pidas, pida, pidamos, pidáis, pidan**; *PRET* pedí, pediste, **pidió**, pedimos, pedisteis, **pidieron**; *IMPER* **pide**; *PRP* **pidiendo**

55 **pensar** : *IND* **pienso, piensas, piensa**, pensamos, pensáis, **piensan**; *SUBJ* **piense, pienses, piense**, pensemos, penséis, **piensen**; *IMPER* **piensa**

56 **perder** : *IND* **pierdo, pierdes, pierde**, perdemos, perdéis, **pierden**; *SUBJ* **pierda, pierdas, pierda**, perdamos, perdáis, **pierdan**; *IMPER* **pierde**

57 **placer** : *IND* **plazco**, places, place, placemos, placéis, placen; *SUBJ* **plazca, plazcas, plazca, plazcamos, plazcáis, plazcan**; *PRET* plací, placiste, plació *or* **plugo**, placimos, placisteis, placieron *or* **pluguieron**

58 **poder** : *IND* **puedo, puedes, puede**, podemos, podéis, **pueden**; *SUBJ* **pueda, puedas, pueda**, podamos, podáis, **puedan**; *PRET* **pude, pudiste, pudo, pudimos, pudisteis, pudieron**; *FUT* **podré, podrás, podrá, podremos, podréis, podrán**; *IMPER* **puede**; *PRP* **pudiendo**

59 **podrir** *or* **pudrir** : *PP* **podrido** (*all other forms based on* pudrir)

60 **poner** : *IND* **pongo**, pones, pone, ponemos, ponéis, ponen; *SUBJ* **ponga, pongas, ponga, pongamos, pongáis, pongan**; *PRET* **puse, pusiste, puso, pusimos, pusisteis, pusieron**; *FUT* **pondré, pondrás, pondrá, pondremos, pondréis, pondrán**; *IMPER* **pon**; *PP* **puesto**

61 **producir** : *IND* **produzco**, produces, produce, producimos, producís, producen; *SUBJ* **produzca, produzcas, produzca, produzcamos, produzcáis, produzcan**; *PRET* **produje, produjiste, produjo, produjimos, produjisteis, produjeron**

62 **prohibir** : *IND* **prohíbo, prohíbes, prohíbe**, prohibimos, prohibís, **prohíben**; *SUBJ* **prohíba, prohíbas, prohíba**, prohibamos, prohibáis, **prohíban**; *IMPER* **prohíbe**

63 **proveer** : *PRET* proveí, **proveíste, proveyó, proveímos, proveísteis, proveyeron**; *PRP* **proveyendo**; *PP* **provisto**

64 **querer** : *IND* **quiero, quieres, quiere**, queremos, queréis, **quieren**; *SUBJ* **quiera, quieras, quiera**, queramos, queráis, **quieran**; *PRET* **quise, quisiste, quiso, quisimos, quisisteis, quisieron**; *FUT* **querré, querrás, querrá, querremos, querréis, querrán**; *IMPER* **quiere**

65 **raer** : *IND* rao *or* **raigo** *or* **rayo**, raes, rae, raemos, raéis, raen; *SUBJ* **raiga** *or* **raya**, **raigas** *or* **rayas**, **raiga** *or* **raya**, **raigamos** *or* **rayamos**, **raigáis** *or* **rayáis**, **raigan** *or* **rayan**; *PRET* **raí, raíste, rayó, raímos, raísteis, rayeron**; *PRP* **rayendo**; *PP* **raído**

66 **reír** : *IND* **río, ríes, ríe, reímos**, reís, **ríen;** *SUBJ* **ría, rías, ría, riamos, riáis, rían;** *PRET* reí, **reíste, rió, reímos, reísteis, rieron;** *IMPER* **ríe;** *PRP* **riendo;** *PP* **reído**

67 **reñir** : *IND* **riño, riñes, riñe**, reñimos, reñís, **riñen;** *SUBJ* **riña, riñas, riña, riñamos, riñáis, riñan;** *PRET* reñí, reñiste, **riñó,** reñimos, reñisteis, **riñeron;** *IMPER* riñe; *PRP* riñendo

68 **reunir** : *IND* **reúno, reúnes, reúne**, reunimos, reunís, **reúnen;** *SUBJ* **reúna, reúnas, reúna,** reunamos, reunáis, **reúnan;** *IMPER* **reúne**

69 **roer** : *IND* **roo** *or* **roigo** *or* **royo**, roes, roe, roemos, roéis, roen; *SUBJ* roa *or* **roiga** *or* **roya,** roas *or* **roigas** *or* **royas,** roa *or* **roiga** *or* **roya,** roamos *or* **roigamos** *or* **royamos,** roáis *or* **roigáis** *or* **royáis,** roan *or* **roigan** *or* **royan;** *PRET* roí, **roíste, royó, roímos, roísteis, royeron;** *PRP* **royendo;** *PP* **roído**

70 **romper** : *PP* **roto**

71 **saber** : *IND* **sé**, sabes, sabe, sabemos, sabéis, saben; *SUBJ* **sepa, sepas, sepa, sepamos, sepáis, sepan;** *PRET* **supe, supiste, supo, supimos, supisteis, supieron;** *FUT* **sabré, sabrás, sabrá, sabremos, sabréis, sabrán**

72 **sacar** : *SUBJ* **saque, saques, saque, saquemos, saquéis, saquen;** *PRET* **saqué**, sacaste, sacó, sacamos, sacasteis, sacaron

73 **salir** : *IND* **salgo**, sales, sale, salimos, salís, salen; *SUBJ* **salga, salgas, salga, salgamos, salgáis, salgan;** *FUT* **saldré, saldrás, saldrá, saldremos, saldréis, saldrán;** *IMPER* **sal**

74 **satisfacer** : *IND* **satisfago**, satisfaces, satisface, satisfacemos, satisfacéis, satisfacen; *SUBJ* **satisfaga, satisfagas, satisfaga, satisfagamos, satisfagáis, satisfagan;** *PRET* **satisfice, satisficiste, satisfizo, satisficimos, satisficisteis, satisficieron;** *FUT* **satisfaré, satisfarás, satisfará, satisfaremos, satisfaréis, satisfarán;** *IMPER* **satisfaz** *or* satisface; *PP* **satisfecho**

75 **seguir** : *IND* **sigo, sigues, sigue**, seguimos, seguís, **siguen;** *SUBJ* **siga, sigas, siga, sigamos, sigáis, sigan;** *PRET* seguí, seguiste, **siguió,** seguimos, seguisteis, **siguieron;** *IMPER* **sigue;** *PRP* **siguiendo**

76 **sentir** : *IND* **siento, sientes, siente**, sentimos, sentís, **sienten;** *SUBJ* **sienta, sientas, sienta, sintamos, sintáis, sientan;** *PRET*

sentí, sentiste, **sintió**, sentimos, sentisteis, **sintieron**; *IMPER* **siente**; *PRP* **sintiendo**

77 **ser** : *IND* **soy, eres, es, somos, sois, son**; *SUBJ* **sea, seas, sea, seamos, seáis, sean**; *PRET* **fui, fuiste, fue, fuimos, fuisteis, fueron**; *IMPF* **era, eras, era, éramos, erais, eran**; *IMPER* **sé**; *PRP* **siendo**; *PP* **sido**

78 **soler** *(defective verb; used only in the present, preterit, and imperfect indicative, and the present and imperfect subjunctive)* see 47 **mover**

79 **tañer** : *PRET* **tañí**, tañiste, **tañó**, tañimos, tañisteis, **tañeron**; *PRP* **tañendo**

80 **tener** : *IND* **tengo, tienes, tiene**, tenemos, tenéis, **tienen**; *SUBJ* **tenga, tengas, tenga, tengamos, tengáis, tengan**; *PRET* **tuve, tuviste, tuvo, tuvimos, tuvisteis, tuvieron**; *FUT* **tendré, tendrás, tendrá, tendremos, tendréis, tendrán**; *IMPER* **ten**

81 **traer** : *IND* **traigo**, traes, trae, ·traemos, traéis, traen; *SUBJ* **traiga, traigas, traiga, traigamos, traigáis, traigan**; *PRET* **traje, trajiste, trajo, trajimos, trajisteis, trajeron**; *PRP* **trayendo**; *PP* **traído**

82 **trocar** : *IND* **trueco, truecas, trueca**, trocamos, trocáis, **truecan**; *SUBJ* **trueque, trueques, trueque, troquemos, troquéis, truequen**; *PRET* **troqué**, trocaste, trocó, trocamos, trocasteis, trocaron; *IMPER* **trueca**

83 **uncir** : *IND* **unzo**, unces, unce, uncimos, uncís, uncen; *SUBJ* **unza, unzas, unza, unzamos, unzáis, unzan**

84 **valer** : *IND* **valgo**, vales, vale, valemos, valéis, valen; *SUBJ* **valga, valgas, valga, valgamos, valgáis, valgan**; *FUT* **valdré, valdrás, valdrá, valdremos, valdréis, valdrán**

85 **variar** : *IND* **varío, varías, varía**, variamos, variáis, **varían**; *SUBJ* **varíe, varíes, varíe**, variemos, variéis, **varíen**; *IMPER* **varía**

86 **vencer** : *IND* **venzo**, vences, vence, vencemos, vencéis, vencen; *SUBJ* **venza, venzas, venza, venzamos, venzáis, venzan**

87 **venir** : *IND* **vengo, vienes, viene**, venimos, venís, **vienen**; *SUBJ* **venga, vengas, venga, vengamos, vengáis, vengan**; *PRET* **vine, viniste, vino, vinimos, vinisteis, vinieron**; *FUT* **vendré**,

vendrás, vendrá, vendremos, vendréis, vendrán; *IMPER* ven; *PRP* viniendo

88 **ver** : *IND* veo, ves, ve, vemos, veis, ven; *PRET* vi, viste, vio, vimos, visteis, vieron; *IMPER* ve; *PRP* viendo; *PP* visto

89 **volver** : *IND* vuelvo, vuelves, vuelve, volvemos, volvéis, vuelven; *SUBJ* vuelva, vuelvas, vuelva, volvamos, volváis, vuelvan; *IMPER* vuelve; *PP* vuelto

90 **yacer** : *IND* yazco *or* yazgo *or* yago, yaces, yace, yacemos, yacéis, yacen; *SUBJ* yazca *or* yazga *or* yaga, yazcas *or* yazgas *or* yagas, yazca *or* yazga *or* yaga, yazcamos *or* yazgamos *or* yagamos, yazcáis *or* yazgáis *or* yagáis, yazcan *or* yazgan *or* yagan; *IMPER* yace *or* yaz

Irregular English Verbs

INFINITIVE	PAST	PAST PARTICIPLE
arise	arose	arisen
awake	awoke	awoken *or* awaked
be	was, were	been
bear	bore	borne
beat	beat	beaten *or* beat
become	became	become
befall	befell	befallen
begin	began	begun
behold	beheld	beheld
bend	bent	bent
beseech	beseeched *or* besought	beseeched *or* besought
beset	beset	beset
bet	bet	bet
bid	bade *or* bid	bidden *or* bid
bind	bound	bound
bite	bit	bitten
bleed	bled	bled
blow	blew	blown
break	broke	broken
breed	bred	bred
bring	brought	brought
build	built	built
burn	burned *or* burnt	burned *or* burnt
burst	burst	burst
buy	bought	bought
can	could	—
cast	cast	cast
catch	caught	caught
choose	chose	chosen
cling	clung	clung
come	came	come
cost	cost	cost
creep	crept	crept
cut	cut	cut
deal	dealt	dealt
dig	dug	dug
do	did	done
draw	drew	drawn
dream	dreamed *or* dreamt	dreamed *or* dreamt
drink	drank	drunk *or* drank
drive	drove	driven
dwell	dwelled *or* dwelt	dwelled *or* dwelt

INFINITIVE	PAST	PAST PARTICIPLE
eat	ate	eaten
fall	fell	fallen
feed	fed	fed
feel	felt	felt
fight	fought	fought
find	found	found
flee	fled	fled
fling	flung	flung
fly	flew	flown
forbid	forbade	forbidden
forecast	forecast	forecast
forego	forewent	foregone
foresee	foresaw	foreseen
foretell	foretold	foretold
forget	forgot	forgotten *or* forgot
forgive	forgave	forgiven
forsake	forsook	forsaken
freeze	froze	frozen
get	got	got *or* gotten
give	gave	given
go	went	gone
grind	ground	ground
grow	grew	grown
hang	hung	hung
have	had	had
hear	heard	heard
hide	hid	hidden *or* hid
hit	hit	hit
hold	held	held
hurt	hurt	hurt
keep	kept	kept
kneel	knelt *or* kneeled	knelt *or* kneeled
know	knew	known
lay	laid	laid
lead	led	led
lean	leaned	leaned
leap	leaped *or* leapt	leaped *or* leapt
learn	learned	learned
leave	left	left
lend	lent	lent
let	let	let
lie	lay	lain
light	lit *or* lighted	lit *or* lighted
lose	lost	lost
make	made	made
may	might	—

INFINITIVE	PAST	PAST PARTICIPLE
mean	meant	meant
meet	met	met
mow	mowed	mowed *or* mown
pay	paid	paid
put	put	put
quit	quit	quit
read	read	read
rend	rent	rent
rid	rid	rid
ride	rode	ridden
ring	rang	rung
rise	rose	risen
run	ran	run
saw	sawed	sawed *or* sawn
say	said	said
see	saw	seen
seek	sought	sought
sell	sold	sold
send	sent	sent
set	set	set
shake	shook	shaken
shall	should	—
shear	sheared	sheared *or* shorn
shed	shed	shed
shine	shone *or* shined	shone *or* shined
shoot	shot	shot
show	showed	shown *or* showed
shrink	shrank *or* shrunk	shrunk *or* shrunken
shut	shut	shut
sing	sang *or* sung	sung
sink	sank *or* sunk	sunk
sit	sat	sat
slay	slew	slain
sleep	slept	slept
slide	slid	slid
sling	slung	slung
smell	smelled *or* smelt	smelled *or* smelt
sow	sowed	sown *or* sowed
speak	spoke	spoken
speed	sped *or* speeded	sped *or* speeded
spell	spelled	spelled
spend	spent	spent
spill	spilled	spilled
spin	spun	spun
spit	spit *or* spat	spit *or* spat
split	split	split

INFINITIVE	PAST	PAST PARTICIPLE
spoil	spoiled	spoiled
spread	spread	spread
spring	sprang *or* sprung	sprung
stand	stood	stood
steal	stole	stolen
stick	stuck	stuck
sting	stung	stung
stink	stank *or* stunk	stunk
stride	strode	stridden
strike	struck	struck
swear	swore	sworn
sweep	swept	swept
swell	swelled	swelled *or* swollen
swim	swam	swum
swing	swung	swung
take	took	taken
teach	taught	taught
tear	tore	torn
tell	told	told
think	thought	thought
throw	threw	thrown
thrust	thrust	thrust
tread	trod	trodden *or* trod
wake	woke	woken *or* waked
waylay	waylaid	waylaid
wear	wore	worn
weave	wove *or* weaved	woven *or* weaved
wed	wedded	wedded
weep	wept	wept
will	would	—
win	won	won
wind	wound	wound
withdraw	withdrew	withdrawn
withhold	withheld	withheld
withstand	withstood	withstood
wring	wrung	wrung
write	wrote	written

Spelling-to-Sound Correspondences in Spanish

For example words for the phonetic symbols below, see Pronunciation Symbols on page 58a.

VOWELS

a [a]

e [e] in open syllables (syllables ending with a vowel); [ɛ] in closed syllables (syllables ending with a consonant)

i [i]; before another vowel in the same syllable pronounced as [j] ([ʒ] or [ʃ] in Argentina and Uruguay; [ʤ] when at the beginning of a word in the Caribbean)

o [o] in open syllables (syllables ending with a vowel); [ɔ] in closed syllables (syllables ending with a consonant)

u [u]; before another vowel in the same syllable pronounced as [w]

y [i]; before another vowel in the same syllable pronounced as [j] ([ʒ] or [ʃ] in Argentina and Uruguay; [ʤ] when at the beginning of a word in the Caribbean)

CONSONANTS

b [b] at the beginning of a word or after *m* or *n*; [β] elsewhere

c [s] before *i* or *e* in Latin America and parts of southern Spain, [θ] in northern Spain; [k] elsewhere

ch [ʧ]; frequently [ʃ] in Chile and Panama; sometimes [ts] in Chile

d [d] at the beginning of a word or after *n* or *l*; [ð] elsewhere, frequently silent between vowels

f [f]; [Φ] in Honduras (no English equivalent for this sound; like [f] but made with both lips)

g [x] before *i* or *e* ([h] in the Caribbean and Central America); [g] at the beginning of a word or after *n* and not before *i* or *e*; [ɣ] elsewhere, frequently silent between vowels

gu [gw] at the beginning of a word before *a, o;* [ɣw] elsewhere before *a, o*; frequently just [w] between vowels; [g] at the beginning of a word before *i, e*; [ɣ] elsewhere before *i, e*; frequently silent between vowels

gü [gw] at the beginning of a word, [ɣw] elsewhere; frequently just [w] between vowels

h silent

j [x] ([h] in the Caribbean and Central America)

k [k]

l [l]

ll [j]; [ʒ] or [ʃ] in Argentina and Uruguay; [ʤ] when at the beginning of a word in the Caribbean;

[lʲ] in Bolivia, Paraguay, Peru, and parts of northern Spain (no English equivalent; like "lli" in *million*)

m [m]

n [n]; frequently [ŋ] at the end of a word when next word begins with a vowel

ñ [ɲ]

p [p]

qu [k]

r [r] (no English equivalent; a trilled sound) at the beginning of words; [t]/[ɾ] elsewhere

rr [r] (no English equivalent; a trilled sound)

s [s]; frequently [z] before

b, d, g, m, n, l, r; at the end of a word [h] or silent in many parts of Latin America and some parts of Spain

t [t]

v [b] at the beginning of a word or after *m* or *n*; [β] elsewhere

x [ks] or [gz] between vowels; [s] before consonants

z [s] in Latin America and parts of southern Spain, [θ] in northern Spain; at the end of a word [h] or silent in many parts of Latin America and some parts of Spain

Pronunciation Symbols

VOWELS

æ	ask, bat, glad
ɑ	cot, bomb
a	*New England* aunt, *British* ask, glass, *Spanish* casa
e	*Spanish* peso, jefe
ɛ	egg, bet, fed
ə	about, javelin, Alabama
ə	when italicized as in əl, əm, ən, indicates a syllabic pronunciation of the consonant as in bottle, prism, button
i	very, any, thirty, *Spanish* piña
i:	eat, bead, bee
ɪ	id, bid, pit
o	Ohio, yellower, potato, *Spanish* óvalo
o:	oats, own, zone, blow
ɔ	awl, maul, caught, paw
ʊ	sure, should, could
u	*Spanish* uva, culpa
u:	boot, few, coo
ʌ	under, putt, bud
eɪ	eight, wade, bay
aɪ	ice, bite, tie
aʊ	out, gown, plow
ɔɪ	oyster, coil, boy
ər	further, stir
ɒ	*British* bond, god
:	indicates that the preceding vowel is long. Long vowels are almost always diphthongs in English, but not in Spanish.

CONSONANTS

b	baby, labor, cab
β	*Spanish* cabo, óvalo
d	day, ready, kid
ʤ	just, badger, fudge
ð	then, either, bathe
f	foe, tough, buff
g	go, bigger, bag
ɣ	*Spanish* tragar, daga
h	hot, aha
j	yes, vineyard
k	cat, keep, lacquer, flock
l	law, hollow, boil
m	mat, hemp, hammer, rim
n	new, tent, tenor, run
ŋ	rung, hang, swinger
ɲ	*Spanish* cabaña, piña
p	pay, lapse, top
r	rope, burn, tar
s	sad, mist, kiss
ʃ	shoe, mission, slush
t	toe, button, mat
t̜	indicates that some speakers of English pronounce this as a voiced alveolar flap [ɾ], as in later, catty, battle
ʧ	choose, batch
θ	thin, ether, bath
v	vat, never, cave
w	wet, software
x	*German* Bach, *Scots* loch, *Spanish* gente, jefe
z	zoo, easy, buzz
ʒ	jaborandi, azure, beige
h, k,	when italicized indicate
p, t	sounds which are present in the pronunciation of some speakers of English but absent in that of others, so that *whence* ['hwɛnts] can be pronounced as ['wɛns], ['hwɛns], ['wɛnts], or ['hwɛnts]

STRESS MARKS

' high stress	**pen**manship
ˌ low stress	penman**ship**

Spanish–English Dictionary

A

a¹ *nf* : first letter of the Spanish alphabet

a² *prep* **1** : to ⟨nos vamos a México : we're going to Mexico⟩ **2** (*used before direct or indirect objects referring to persons*) ⟨¿llamaste a tu papá? : did you call your dad?⟩ ⟨como a usted le guste : as you wish⟩ **3** : in the manner of ⟨papas a la francesa : french fries⟩ **4** : on, by means of ⟨a pie : on foot⟩ **5** : per, each ⟨tres pastillas al día : three pills per day⟩ **6** : at ⟨a las dos : at two o'clock⟩ ⟨al principio : at first⟩ **7** (*with infinitive*) ⟨enséñales a leer : teach them to read⟩ ⟨problemas a resolver : problems to be solved⟩

ábaco *nm* : abacus

abad *nm* : abbot

abadesa *nf* : abbess

abadía *nf* : abbey

abajo *adv* **1** : down ⟨póngalo más abajo : put it further down⟩ ⟨arriba y abajo : up and down⟩ **2** : downstairs **3** : under, beneath ⟨el abajo firmante : the undersigned⟩ **4** : down with ⟨¡abajo la inflación! : down with inflation!⟩ **5 ~ de** : under, beneath **6 de ~** : bottom ⟨el cajón de abajo : the bottom drawer⟩ **7 hacia ~** *or* **para ~** : downwards **8 cuesta abajo** : downhill **9 río abajo** : downstream

abalanzarse {21} *vr* : to hurl oneself, to rush

abanderado, -da *n* : standard-bearer

abandonado, -da *adj* **1** : abandoned, deserted **2** : neglected **3** : slovenly, unkempt

abandonar *vt* **1** DEJAR : to abandon, to leave **2** : to give up, to quit ⟨abandonaron la búsqueda : they gave up the search⟩ — **abandonarse** *vr* **1** : to neglect oneself **2 ~ a** : to succumb to, to give oneself over to

abandono *nm* **1** : abandonment **2** : neglect **3** : withdrawal ⟨ganar por abandono : to win by default⟩

abanicar {72} *vt* : to fan — **abanicarse** *vr*

abanico *nm* **1** : fan **2** GAMA : range, gamut

abaratamiento *nm* : price reduction

abaratar *vt* : to lower the price of — **abaratarse** *vr* : to go down in price

abarcar {72} *vt* **1** : to cover, to include, to embrace **2** : to undertake **3** : to monopolize

abaritonado, -da *adj* : baritone

abarrotado, -da *adj* : packed, crammed

abarrotar *vt* : to fill up, to pack

abarrotería *nf CA, Mex* : grocery store

abarrotero, -ra *n Col, Mex* : grocer

abarrotes *nmpl* **1** : groceries, supplies **2 tienda de abarrotes** : general store, grocery store

abastecedor, -dora *n* : supplier

abastecer {53} *vt* : to supply, to stock — **abastecerse** *vr* : to stock up

abastecimiento → abasto

abasto *nm* : supply, supplying ⟨no da abasto : there isn't enough for all⟩

abatido, -da *adj* : dejected, depressed

abatimiento *nm* **1** : drop, reduction **2** : dejection, depression

abatir *vt* **1** DERRIBAR : to demolish, to knock down **2** : to shoot down **3** DEPRIMIR : to depress, to bring low — **abatirse** *vr* **1** DEPRIMIRSE : to get depressed **2 ~ sobre** : to swoop down on

abdicación *nf, pl* **-ciones** : abdication

abdicar {72} *vt* : to relinquish, to abdicate

abdomen *nm, pl* **-dómenes** : abdomen

abdominal *adj* : abdominal

abecé *nm* : ABC's *pl*

abecedario *nm* ALFABETO : alphabet

abedul *nm* : birch (tree)

abeja *nf* : bee

abejorro *nm* : bumblebee

aberración *nf, pl* **-ciones** : aberration

aberrante *adj* : aberrant, perverse

abertura *nf* **1** : aperture, opening **2** AGUJERO : hole **3** : slit (in a skirt, etc.) **4** GRIETA : crack

abeto *nm* : fir (tree)

abierto¹ *pp* → **abrir**

abierto², -ta *adj* **1** : open **2** : candid, frank **3** : generous — **abiertamente** *adv*

abigarrado, -da *adj* : multicolored, variegated

abigeato *nm* : rustling (of livestock)

abismal *adj* : abysmal, vast

abismo *nm* : abyss, chasm ⟨al borde del abismo : on the brink of ruin⟩

abjurar *vi* **~ de** : to abjure — **abjuración** *nf*

ablandamiento *nm* : softening, moderation

ablandar *vt* **1** SUAVIZAR : to soften **2** CALMAR : to soothe, to appease — *vi* : to moderate, to get milder — **ablandarse** *vr* **1** : to become soft, to soften **2** CEDER : to yield, to relent

ablución *nf, pl* **-ciones** : ablution

abnegación *nf, pl* **-ciones** : abnegation, self-denial

abnegado, -da *adj* : self-sacrificing, selfless

abnegarse {49} *vr* : to deny oneself

abobado, -da *adj* **1** : silly, stupid **2** : bewildered

abocarse {72} *vr* **1** DIRIGIRSE : to head, to direct oneself **2** DEDICARSE : to dedicate oneself

abochornar *vt* AVERGONZAR : to embarrass, to shame — **abochornarse** *vr*

abofetear *vt* : to slap

abogacía *nf* : law, legal profession

abogado, -da *n* : lawyer, attorney

abogar {52} *vi* **~ por** : to plead for, to defend, to advocate

abolengo *nm* LINAJE : lineage, ancestry
abolición *nf, pl* **-ciones** : abolition
abolir {1} *vt* DEROGAR : to abolish, to repeal
abolladura *nf* : dent
abollar *vt* : to dent
abombar *vt* : to warp, to cause to bulge — **abombarse** *vr* : to decompose, to go bad
abominable *adj* ABORRECIBLE : abominable
abominación *nf, pl* **-ciones** : abomination
abominar *vt* ABORRECER : to abominate, to abhor
abonado, -da *n* : subscriber
abonar *vt* **1** : to pay **2** FERTILIZAR : to fertilize — **abonarse** *vr* : to subscribe
abono *nm* **1** : payment, installment **2** FERTILIZANTE : fertilizer **3** : season ticket
abordaje *nm* : boarding
abordar *vt* **1** : to address, to broach **2** : to accost, to waylay **3** : to come on board
aborigen[1] *adj, pl* **-rígenes** : aboriginal, native
aborigen[2] *nmf, pl* **-rígenes** : aborigine, indigenous inhabitant
aborrecer {53} *vt* ABOMINAR, ODIAR : to abhor, to detest, to hate
aborrecible *adj* ABOMINABLE, ODIOSO : abominable, detestable
aborrecimiento *nm* : abhorrence, loathing
abortar *vi* : to have an abortion — *vt* **1** : to abort **2** : to quash, to suppress
abortista *nmf* : abortionist
abortivo, -va *adj* : abortive
aborto *nm* **1** : abortion **2** : miscarriage
abotonar *vt* : to button — **abotonarse** *vr* : to button up
abovedado, -da *adj* : vaulted
abrasador, -dora *adj* : burning, scorching
abrasar *vt* QUEMAR : to burn, to sear, to scorch
abrasivo[1], -va *adj* : abrasive
abrasivo[2] *nm* : abrasive
abrazadera *nf* : clamp, brace
abrazar {21} *vt* : to hug, to embrace — **abrazarse** *vr*
abrazo *nm* : hug, embrace
abrebotellas *nms & pl* : bottle opener
abrelatas *nms & pl* : can opener
abrevadero *nm* BEBEDERO : watering trough
abreviación *nf, pl* **-ciones** : abbreviation
abreviar *vt* **1** : to abbreviate **2** : to shorten, to cut short
abreviatura → **abreviación**
abridor *nm* : bottle opener, can opener
abrigadero *nm* : shelter, windbreak
abrigado, -da *adj* **1** : sheltered **2** : warm, wrapped up (with clothing)
abrigar {52} *vt* **1** : to shelter, to protect **2** : to keep warm, to dress warmly **3** : to cherish, to harbor ⟨abrigar esperanzas : to cherish hopes⟩ — **abrigarse** *vr* : to dress warmly
abrigo *nm* **1** : coat, overcoat **2** : shelter, refuge
abril *nm* : April
abrillantador *nm* : polish
abrillantar *vt* : to polish, to shine
abrir {2} *vt* **1** : to open **2** : to unlock, to undo **3** : to turn on (a tap or faucet) — *vi* : to open, to open up — **abrirse** *vr* **1** : to open up **2** : to clear (of the skies)
abrochar *vt* : to button, to fasten — **abrocharse** *vr* : to fasten, to hook up
abrogación *nf, pl* **-ciones** : abrogation, annulment, repeal
abrogar {52} *vt* : to abrogate, to annul, to repeal
abrojo *nm* : bur (of a plant)
abrumador, -dora *adj* : crushing, overwhelming
abrumar *vt* **1** AGOBIAR : to overwhelm **2** OPRIMIR : to oppress, to burden
abrupto, -ta *adj* **1** : abrupt **2** ESCARPADO : steep — **abruptamente** *adv*
absceso *nm* : abscess
absolución *nf, pl* **-ciones** **1** : absolution **2** : acquittal
absolutismo *nm* : absolutism
absoluto, -ta *adj* **1** : absolute, unconditional **2** **en ~** : not at all ⟨no me gustó en absoluto : I did not like it at all⟩ — **absolutamente** *adv*
absolver {89} *vt* **1** : to absolve **2** : to acquit
absorbente *adj* **1** : absorbent **2** : absorbing, engrossing
absorber *vt* **1** : to absorb, to soak up **2** : to occupy, to take up, to engross
absorción *nf, pl* **-ciones** : absorption
absorto, -ta *adj* : absorbed, engrossed
abstemio[1], -mia *adj* : abstemious, teetotal
abstemio[2], -mia *n* : teetotaler
abstención *nf, pl* **-ciones** : abstention
abstenerse {80} *vr* : to abstain, to refrain
abstinencia *nf* : abstinence
abstracción *nf, pl* **-ciones** : abstraction
abstracto, -ta *adj* : abstract
abstraer {81} *vt* : to abstract — **abstraerse** *vr* : to lose oneself in thought
abstraído, -da *adj* : preoccupied, withdrawn
abstruso, -sa *adj* : abstruse
abstuvo, etc. → **abstenerse**
absuelto *pp* → **absolver**
absurdo[1], -da *adj* DISPARATADO, RIDÍCULO : absurd, ridiculous — **absurdamente** *adv*
absurdo[2] *nm* : absurdity
abuchear *vt* : to boo, to jeer
abucheo *nm* : booing, jeering
abuela *nf* **1** : grandmother **2** : old woman **3** **¡tu abuela!** *fam* : no way!, forget about it!
abuelo *nm* **1** : grandfather **2** : old man **3** **abuelos** *nmpl* : grandparents, ancestors

abulia *nf* : apathy, lethargy

abúlico, -ca *adj* : lethargic, apathetic

abultado, -da *adj* : bulging, bulky

abultar *vi* : to bulge — *vt* : to enlarge, to expand

abundancia *nf* : abundance

abundante *adj* : abundant, plentiful — **abundantemente** *adv*

abundar *vi* 1 : to abound, to be plentiful 2 ~ **en** : to be in agreement with

aburrido, -da *adj* 1 : bored, tired, fed up 2 TEDIOSO : boring, tedious

aburrimiento *nm* : boredom, weariness

aburrir *vt* : to bore, to tire — **aburrirse** *vr* : to get bored

abusado, -da *adj Mex fam* : sharp, on the ball

abusador, -dora *n* : abuser

abusar *vi* 1 : to go too far, to do something to excess 2 ~ **de** : to abuse (as drugs) 3 ~ **de** : to take unfair advantage of

abusivo, -va *adj* 1 : abusive 2 : outrageous, excessive

abuso *nm* 1 : abuse 2 : injustice, outrage

abyecto, -ta *adj* : despicable, contemptible

acá *adv* AQUÍ : here, over here ⟨¡ven acá! : come here!⟩

acabado¹, -da *adj* 1 : finished, done, completed 2 : old, worn-out

acabado² *nm* : finish ⟨un acabado brillante : a glossy finish⟩

acabar *vi* 1 TERMINAR : to finish, to end 2 ~ **de** : to have just (done something) ⟨acabo de ver a tu hermano : I just saw your brother⟩ 3 ~ **con** : to put an end to, to stamp out — *vt* TERMINAR : to finish — **acabarse** *vr* TERMINARSE : to come to an end, to run out ⟨se me acabó el dinero : I ran out of money⟩

acacia *nf* : acacia

academia *nf* : academy

académico¹, -ca *adj* : academic, scholastic — **académicamente** *adv*

académico², -ca *n* : academic, academician

acaecer {53} *vt (3rd person only)* : to happen, to take place

acalambrarse *vr* : to cramp up, to get a cramp

acallar *vt* : to quiet, to silence

acalorado, -da *adj* : emotional, heated

acaloramiento *nm* 1 : heat 2 : ardor, passion

acalorar *vt* : to heat up, to inflame — **acalorarse** *vr* : to get upset, to get worked up

acampada *nf* : camp, camping ⟨ir de acampada : to go camping⟩

acampar *vi* : to camp

acanalar *vt* 1 : to groove, to furrow 2 : to corrugate

acantilado *nm* : cliff

acanto *nm* : acanthus

acantonar *vt* : to station, to quarter

acaparador, -dora *adj* : greedy, selfish

acaparar *vt* 1 : to stockpile, to hoard 2 : to monopolize

acápite *nm* : paragraph

acariciar *vt* : to caress, to stroke, to pet

ácaro *nm* : mite

acarrear *vt* 1 : to haul, to carry 2 : to bring, to give rise to ⟨los problemas que acarrea : the problems that come along with it⟩

acarreo *nm* : transport, haulage

acartonarse *vr* 1 : to stiffen 2 : to become wizened

acaso *adv* 1 : perhaps, by any chance 2 **por si acaso** : just in case

acatamiento *nm* : compliance, observance

acatar *vt* : to comply with, to respect

acaudalado, -da *adj* RICO : wealthy, rich

acaudillar *vt* : to lead, to command

acceder *vi* 1 ~ **a** : to accede to, to agree to 2 : to assume (a position) 3 : to gain access to

accesar *vt* : to access (on a computer)

accesibilidad *nf* : accessibility

accesible *adj* ASEQUIBLE : accessible, attainable

acceso *nm* 1 : access 2 : admittance, entrance

accesorio¹, -ria *adj* 1 : accessory 2 : incidental

accesorio² *nm* 1 : accessory 2 : prop (in the theater)

accidentado¹, -da *adj* 1 : eventful, turbulent 2 : rough, uneven 3 : injured

accidentado², -da *n* : accident victim

accidental *adj* : accidental, unintentional — **accidentalmente** *adv*

accidentarse *vr* : to have an accident

accidente *nm* 1 : accident 2 : unevenness 3 **accidente geográfico** : geographical feature

acción *nf, pl* **acciones** 1 : action 2 ACTO : act, deed 3 : share, stock

accionamiento *nm* : activation

accionar *vt* : to put into motion, to activate — *vi* : to gesticulate

accionario, -ria *adj* : stock ⟨mercado accionario : stock market⟩

accionista *nmf* : stockholder, shareholder

acebo *nm* : holly

acechar *vt* 1 : to watch, to spy on 2 : to stalk, to lie in wait for

acecho *nm* **al acecho** : lying in wait

acedera *nf* : sorrel (herb)

acéfalo, -la *adj* : leaderless

aceitar *vt* : to oil

aceite *nm* 1 : oil 2 **aceite de ricino** : castor oil 3 **aceite de oliva** : olive oil

aceitera *nf* 1 : cruet (for oil) 2 : oilcan 3 *Mex* : oil refinery

aceitoso, -sa *adj* : oily

aceituna *nf* OLIVA : olive

aceituno *nm* OLIVO : olive tree

aceleración *nf, pl* **-ciones** : acceleration, speeding up

acelerado, -da *adj* : accelerated, speedy

acelerador *nm* : accelerator

aceleramiento *nm* → **aceleración**

acelerar *vt* 1 : to accelerate, to speed up 2 AGILIZAR : to expedite — *vi* : to accelerate (of an automobile) — **acelerarse** *vr* : to hasten, to hurry up

acelga *nf* : chard, Swiss chard

acendrado, -da *adj* : pure, unblemished

acendrar *vt* : to purify, to refine

acento *nm* 1 : accent 2 : stress, emphasis

acentuación *nf*, *pl* **-ciones** : accentuation

acentuado, -da *adj* : marked, pronounced

acentuar {3} *vt* 1 : to accent 2 : to emphasize, to stress — **acentuarse** *vr* : to become more pronounced

acepción *nf*, *pl* **-ciones** SIGNIFICADO : sense, meaning

aceptabilidad *nf* : acceptability

aceptable *adj* : acceptable

aceptación *nf*, *pl* **-ciones** 1 : acceptance 2 APROBACIÓN : approval

aceptar *vt* 1 : to accept 2 : to approve

acequia *nf* 1 : irrigation ditch 2 *Mex* : sewer

acera *nf* : sidewalk

acerado, -da *adj* 1 : made of steel 2 : steely, tough

acerbo, -ba *adj* 1 : harsh, cutting ⟨comentarios acerbos : cutting remarks⟩ 2 : bitter — **acerbamente** *adv*

acerca *prep* ∼ **de** : about, concerning

acercamiento *nm* : rapprochement, reconciliation

acercar {72} *vt* APROXIMAR, ARRIMAR : to bring near, to bring closer — **acercarse** *vr* APROXIMARSE, ARRIMARSE : to approach, to draw near

acería *nf* : steel mill

acerico *nm* : pincushion

acero *nm* : steel ⟨acero inoxidable : stainless steel⟩

acérrimo, -ma *adj* 1 : staunch, steadfast 2 : bitter ⟨un acérrimo enemigo : a bitter enemy⟩

acertado, -da *adj* CORRECTO : accurate, correct, on target — **acertadamente** *adv*

acertante[1] *adj* : winning

acertante[2] *nmf* : winner

acertar {55} *vt* : to guess correctly — *vi* 1 ATINAR : to be correct, to be on target 2 ∼ **a** : to manage to

acertijo *nm* ADIVINANZA : riddle

acervo *nm* 1 : pile, heap 2 : wealth, heritage ⟨el acervo artístico del instituto : the artistic treasures of the institute⟩

acetato *nm* : acetate

acético, -ca *adj* : acetic ⟨ácido acético : acetic acid⟩

acetileno *nm* : acetylene

acetona *nf* 1 : acetone 2 : nail-polish remover

achacar {72} *vt* : to attribute, to impute ⟨te achaca todos sus problemas : he blames all his problems on you⟩

achacoso, -sa *adj* : frail, sickly

achaparrado, -da *adj* : stunted, scrubby ⟨árboles achaparrados : scrubby trees⟩

achaques *nmpl* : aches and pains

achatar *vt* : to flatten

achicar {72} *vt* 1 REDUCIR : to make smaller, to reduce 2 : to intimidate 3 : to bail out (water) — **achicarse** *vr* : to become intimidated

achicharrar *vt* : to scorch, to burn to a crisp

achicoria *nf* : chicory

achispado, -da *adj fam* : tipsy

achote *or* **achiote** *nm* : annatto seed

achuchón *nm*, *pl* **-chones** 1 : push, shove 2 *fam* : squeeze, hug 3 *fam* : mild illness

aciago, -ga *adj* : fateful, unlucky

acicalar *vt* 1 PULIR : to polish 2 : to dress up, to adorn — **acicalarse** *vr* : to get dressed up

acicate *nm* 1 : spur 2 INCENTIVO : incentive, stimulus

acidez *nf*, *pl* **-deces** 1 : acidity 2 : sourness 3 **acidez estomacal** : heartburn

acidificar {72} *vt* : to acidify

ácido[1], **-da** *adj* AGRIO : acid, sour

ácido[2] *nm* : acid

acierto *nm* 1 : correct answer, right choice 2 : accuracy, skill, deftness

acimut *nm* : azimuth

acitronar *vt Mex* : to fry until crisp

aclamación *nf*, *pl* **-ciones** : acclaim, acclamation

aclamar *vt* : to acclaim, to cheer, to applaud

aclaración *nf*, *pl* **-ciones** CLARIFICACIÓN : clarification, explanation

aclarar *vt* 1 CLARIFICAR : to clarify, to explain, to resolve 2 : to lighten 3 **aclarar la voz** : to clear one's throat — *vi* 1 : to get light, to dawn 2 : to clear up — **aclararse** *vr* : to become clear

aclaratorio, -ria *adj* : explanatory

aclimatar *vt* : to acclimatize — **aclimatarse** *vr* ∼ **a** : to get used to — **aclimatación** *nf*

acné *nm* : acne

acobardar *vt* INTIMIDAR : to frighten, to intimidate — **acobardarse** *vr* : to be frightened, to cower

acodarse *vr* ∼ **en** : to lean (one's elbows) on

acogedor, -dora *adj* : cozy, warm, friendly

acoger {15} *vt* 1 REFUGIAR : to take in, to shelter 2 : to receive, to welcome — **acogerse** *vr* 1 REFUGIARSE : to take refuge 2 ∼ **a** : to resort to, to avail oneself of

acogida *nf* 1 AMPARO, REFUGIO : refuge, protection 2 RECIBIMIENTO : reception, welcome

acolchar *vt* 1 : to pad (a wall, etc.) 2 : to quilt

acólito *nm* 1 MONAGUILLO : altar boy 2 : follower, helper, acolyte

acomedido, -da *adj* : helpful, obliging

acometer *vt* **1** ATACAR : to attack, to assail **2** EMPRENDER : to undertake, to begin — *vi* ~ **contra** : to rush against

acometida *nf* ATAQUE : attack, assault

acomodado, -da *adj* **1** : suitable, appropriate **2** : well-to-do, prosperous

acomodador, -dora *n* : usher, usherette

acomodar *vt* **1** : to accommodate, to make room for **2** : to adjust, to adapt — **acomodarse** *vr* **1** : to settle in **2** ~ **a** : to adapt to

acomodaticio, -cia *adj* : accommodating, obliging

acomodo *nm* **1** : job, position **2** : arrangement, placement **3** : accommodation, lodging

acompañamiento *nm* : accompaniment

acompañante *nmf* **1** COMPAÑERO : companion **2** : accompanist

acompañar *vt* : to accompany, to go with

acompasado, -da *adj* : rhythmic, regular, measured

acomplejado, -da *adj* : full of complexes, neurotic

acondicionado, -da *adj* **1** : equipped, fitted-out **2 bien acondicionado** : in good shape, in a fit state

acondicionador *nm* **1** : conditioner **2 acondicionador de aire** : air conditioner

acondicionar *vt* **1** : to condition **2** : to fit out, to furnish

acongojado, -da *adj* : distressed, upset

acongojarse *vr* : to grieve, to become distressed

aconsejable *adj* : advisable

aconsejar *vt* : to advise, to counsel

acontecer {53} *vt* (*3rd person only*) : to occur, to happen

acontecimiento *nm* SUCESO : event

acopiar *vt* : to gather, to collect, to stockpile

acopio *nm* : collection, stock

acoplamiento *nm* : connection, coupling

acoplar *vt* : to couple, to connect — **acoplarse** *vr* : to fit together

acoquinar *vt* : to intimidate

acorazado[1], -da *adj* BLINDADO : armored

acorazado[2] *nm* : battleship

acordado, -da *adj* : agreed upon

acordar {19} *vt* **1** : to agree on **2** OTORGAR : to award, to bestow — **acordarse** *vr* RECORDAR : to remember, to recall

acorde[1] *adj* **1** : in agreement, in accordance **2** ~ **con** : in keeping with

acorde[2] *nm* : chord

acordeón *nm, pl* **-deones** : accordion — **acordeonista** *nmf*

acordonar *vt* **1** : to cordon off **2** : to lace up **3** : to mill (coins)

acorralar *vt* ARRINCONAR : to corner, to hem in, to corral

acortar *vt* : to shorten, to cut short — **acortarse** *vr* **1** : to become shorter **2** : to end early

acosar *vt* PERSEGUIR : to pursue, to hound, to harass

acoso *nm* ASEDIO : harassment ⟨acoso sexual : sexual harassment⟩

acostar {19} *vt* **1** : to lay (something) down **2** : to put to bed — **acostarse** *vr* **1** : to lie down **2** : to go to bed

acostumbrado, -da *adj* **1** HABITUADO : accustomed **2** HABITUAL : usual, customary

acostumbrar *vt* : to accustom — *vi* : to be accustomed, to be in the habit — **acostumbrarse** *vr*

acotación *nf, pl* **-ciones** **1** : marginal note **2** : stage direction

acotado, -da *adj* : enclosed

acotamiento *nm Mex* : shoulder (of a road)

acotar *vt* **1** ANOTAR : to note, to annotate **2** DELIMITAR : to mark off (land), to demarcate

acre[1] *adj* **1** : acrid, pungent **2** MORDAZ : caustic, biting

acre[2] *nm* : acre

acrecentamiento *nm* : growth, increase

acrecentar {55} *vt* AUMENTAR : to increase, to augment

acreditación *nf, pl* **-ciones** : accreditation

acreditado, -da *adj* **1** : accredited, authorized **2** : reputable

acreditar *vt* **1** : to accredit, to authorize **2** : to credit **3** : to prove, to verify — **acreditarse** *vr* : to gain a reputation

acreedor[1], -dora *adj* : deserving, worthy

acreedor[2], -dora *n* : creditor

acribillar *vt* **1** : to riddle, to pepper (with bullets, etc.) **2** : to hound, to harass

acrílico *nm* : acrylic

acrimonia *nf* **1** : pungency **2** : acrimony

acrimonioso, -sa *adj* : acrimonious

acriollarse *vr* : to adopt local customs, to go native

acritud *nf* **1** : pungency, bitterness **2** : intensity, sharpness **3** : harshness, asperity

acrobacia *nf* : acrobatics

acróbata *nmf* : acrobat

acrobático, -ca *adj* : acrobatic

acrónimo *nm* : acronym

acta *nf* **1** : document, certificate ⟨acta de nacimiento : birth certificate⟩ **2 actas** *nfpl* : minutes (of a meeting)

actitud *nf* **1** : attitude **2** : posture, position

activación *nf, pl* **-ciones** **1** : activation, stimulation **2** ACELERACIÓN : acceleration, speeding up

activar *vt* **1** : to activate **2** : to stimulate, to energize **3** : to speed up

actividad *nf* : activity

activista *nmf* : activist

activo[1], -va *adj* : active — **activamente** *adv*

activo[2] *nm* : assets *pl* ⟨activo y pasivo : assets and liabilities⟩

acto nm **1** ACCIÓN : act, deed **2** : act (in a play) **3 el acto sexual** : sexual intercourse **4 en el acto** : right away, on the spot **5 acto seguido** : immediately after

actor nm ARTISTA : actor

actriz nf, pl **actrices** ARTISTA : actress

actuación nf, pl **-ciones 1** : performance **2 actuaciones** nfpl DILIGENCIAS : proceedings

actual adj PRESENTE : present, current

actualidad nf **1** : present time ⟨en la actualidad : at present⟩ **2 actualidades** nfpl : current affairs

actualización nf, pl **-ciones** : updating, modernization

actualizar {21} vt : to modernize, to bring up to date

actualmente adv : at present, nowadays

actuar {3} vi : to act, to perform

actuarial adj : actuarial

actuario, -ria n : actuary

acuarela nf : watercolor

acuario nm : aquarium

Acuario nmf : Aquarius, Aquarian

acuartelar vt : to quarter (troops)

acuático, -ca adj : aquatic, water

acuchillar vt APUÑALAR : to knife, to stab

acuciante adj : pressing, urgent

acucioso, -sa → **acuciante**

acudir vi **1** : to go, to come (someplace for a specific purpose) ⟨acudió a la puerta : he went to the door⟩ ⟨acudimos en su ayuda : we came to her aid⟩ **2** : to be present, to show up ⟨acudí a la cita : I showed up for the appointment⟩ **3 ~ a** : to turn to, to have recourse to ⟨hay que acudir al médico : you must consult the doctor⟩

acueducto nm : aqueduct

acuerdo nm **1** : agreement **2 estar de acuerdo** : to agree **3 de acuerdo con** : in accordance with **4 de ~** : OK, all right

acuicultura nf : aquaculture

acullá adv : yonder, over there

acumulación nf, pl **-ciones** : accumulation

acumulador nm : storage battery

acumular vt : to accumulate, to amass — **acumularse** vr : to build up, to pile up

acumulativo, -va adj : cumulative — **acumulativamente** adv

acunar vt : to rock, to cradle

acuñar vt : to coin, to mint

acuoso, -sa adj : aqueous, watery

acupuntura nf : acupuncture

acurrucarse {72} vr : to cuddle, to nestle, to curl up

acusación nf, pl **-ciones 1** : accusation, charge **2 la acusación** : the prosecution

acusado¹, -da adj : prominent, marked

acusado², -da n : defendant

acusador, -dora n **1** : accuser **2** FISCAL : prosecutor

acusar vt **1** : to accuse, to charge **2** : to reveal, to betray ⟨sus ojos acusaban la desconfianza : his eyes revealed distrust⟩ — **acusarse** vr : to confess

acusativo nm : objective (in grammar)

acusatorio, -ria adj : accusatory

acuse nm **acuse de recibo** : acknowledgment of receipt

acústica nf : acoustics

acústico, -ca adj : acoustic

adagio nm **1** REFRÁN : adage, proverb **2** : adagio

adalid nm : leader, champion

adaptable adj : adaptable — **adaptabilidad** nf

adaptación nf, pl **-ciones** : adaptation, adjustment

adaptado, -da adj : suited, adapted

adaptador nm : adapter (in electricity)

adaptar vt **1** MODIFICAR : to adapt **2** : to adjust, to fit — **adaptarse** vr : to adapt oneself, to conform

adecentar vt : to tidy up

adecuación nf, pl **-ciones** ADAPTACIÓN : adaptation

adecuadamente adv : adequately

adecuado, -da adj **1** IDÓNEO : suitable, appropriate **2** : adequate

adecuar {8} vt : to adapt, to make suitable — **adecuarse** vr **~ a** : to be appropriate for, to fit in with

adefesio nm : eyesore, monstrosity

adelantado, -da adj **1** : advanced, ahead **2** : fast (of a clock or watch) **3 por ~** : in advance

adelantamiento nm **1** : advancement **2** : speeding up

adelantar vt **1** : to advance, to move forward **2** : to overtake, to pass **3** : to reveal (information) in advance **4** : to advance, to lend (money) — **adelantarse** vr **1** : to advance, to get in front **2 ~ a** : to forestall, to preempt

adelante adv **1** : ahead, in front, forward **2 más adelante** : further on, later on **3 ¡adelante!** : come in!

adelanto nm **1** : advance, progress **2** : advance payment **3** : earliness ⟨llevamos una hora de adelanto : we're running an hour ahead of time⟩

adelfa nf : oleander

adelgazar {21} vt : to thin, to reduce — vi : to lose weight

ademán nm, pl **-manes 1** GESTO : gesture **2 ademanes** nmpl : manners

además adv **1** : besides, furthermore **2 ~ de** : in addition to, as well as

adenoides nfpl : adenoids

adentrarse vr **~ en** : to go into, to penetrate

adentro adv : inside, within

adentros nmpl **decirse para sus adentros** : to say to oneself ⟨me dije para mis adentros que nunca regresaría : I told myself that I'd never go back⟩

adepto¹, -ta adj : supportive ⟨ser adepto a : to be a follower of⟩

adepto², -ta n PARTIDARIO : follower, supporter

aderezar {21} *vt* **1** SAZONAR : to season, to dress (salad) **2** : to embellish, to adorn

aderezo *nm* **1** : dressing, seasoning **2** : adornment, embellishment

adeudar *vt* **1** : to debit **2** DEBER : to owe

adeudo *nm* **1** DÉBITO : debit **2** *Mex* : debt, indebtedness

adherencia *nf* **1** : adherence, adhesiveness **2** : appendage, accretion

adherente *adj* : adhesive, sticky

adherirse {76} *vr* : to adhere, to stick

adhesión *nf, pl* **-siones 1** : adhesion **2** : attachment, commitment (to a cause, etc.)

adhesivo[1], **-va** *adj* : adhesive

adhesivo[2] *nm* : adhesive

adicción *nf, pl* **-ciones** : addiction

adición *nf, pl* **-ciones** : addition

adicional *adj* : additional — **adicionalmente** *adv*

adicionar *vt* : to add

adictivo, -va *adj* : addictive

adicto[1], **-ta** *adj* **1** : addicted **2** : devoted, dedicated

adicto[2], **-ta** *n* **1** : addict **2** PARTIDARIO : supporter, advocate

adiestrador, -dora *n* : trainer

adiestramiento *nm* : training

adiestrar *vt* : to train

adinerado, -da *adj* : moneyed, wealthy

adiós *nm, pl* **adioses 1** DESPEDIDA : farewell, good-bye **2** ¡adiós! : good-bye!

aditamento *nm* : attachment, accessory

aditivo *nm* : additive

adivinación *nf, pl* **-ciones 1** : guess **2** : divination, prediction

adivinanza *nf* ACERTIJO : riddle

adivinar *vt* **1** : to guess **2** : to foretell, to predict

adivino, -na *n* : fortune-teller

adjetivo[1], **-va** *adj* : adjectival

adjetivo[2] *nm* : adjective

adjudicación *nf, pl* **-ciones 1** : adjudication **2** : allocation, awarding, granting

adjudicar {72} *vt* **1** : to adjudge, to adjudicate **2** : to assign, to allocate ⟨adjudicar la culpa : to assign the blame⟩ **3** : to award, to grant

adjuntar *vt* : to enclose, to attach

adjunto[1], **-ta** *adj* : enclosed, attached

adjunto[2], **-ta** *n* : deputy, assistant

adjunto[3] *nm* : adjunct

administración *nf, pl* **-ciones 1** : administration, management **2 administración de empresas** : business administration

administrador, -dora *n* : administrator, manager

administrar *vt* : to administer, to manage, to run

administrativo, -va *adj* : administrative

admirable *adj* : admirable, impressive — **admirablemente** *adv*

admiración *nf, pl* **-ciones** : admiration

admirador, -dora *n* : admirer

admirar *vt* **1** : to admire **2** : to amaze, to astonish — **admirarse** *vr* : to be amazed

admirativo, -va *adj* : admiring

admisibilidad *nf* : admissibility

admisible *adj* : admissible, allowable

admisión *nf, pl* **-siones** : admission, admittance

admitir *vt* **1** : to admit, to let in **2** : to acknowledge, to concede **3** : to allow, to make room for ⟨la ley no admite cambios : the law doesn't allow for changes⟩

admonición *nf, pl* **-ciones** : admonition, warning

admonitorio, -ria *adj* : admonitory

ADN *nm* (ácido desoxirribonucleico) : DNA

adobar *vt* : to marinate

adobe *nm* : adobe

adobo *nm* **1** : marinade, seasoning **2** *Mex* : spicy marinade used for cooking pork

adoctrinamiento *nm* : indoctrination

adoctrinar *vt* : to indoctrinate

adolecer {53} *vi* PADECER : to suffer ⟨adolece de timidez : he suffers from shyness⟩

adolescencia *nf* : adolescence

adolescente[1] *adj* : adolescent, teenage

adolescente[2] *nmf* : adolescent, teenager

adonde *conj* : where ⟨el lugar adonde vamos es bello : the place where we're going is beautiful⟩

adónde *adv* : where ⟨¿adónde vamos? : where are we going?⟩

adondequiera *adv* : wherever, anywhere ⟨adondequiera que vayas : anywhere you go⟩

adopción *nf, pl* **-ciones** : adoption

adoptar *vt* **1** : to adopt (a measure), to take (a decision) **2** : to adopt (children)

adoptivo, -va *adj* **1** : adopted (children, country) **2** : adoptive (parents)

adoquín *nm, pl* **-quines** : paving stone, cobblestone

adorable *adj* : adorable, lovable

adoración *nf, pl* **-ciones** : adoration, worship

adorador[1], **-dora** *adj* : adoring, worshipping

adorador[2], **-dora** *n* : worshipper

adorar *vt* : to adore, to worship

adormecer {53} *vt* **1** : to make sleepy, to lull to sleep **2** : to numb — **adormecerse** *vr* **1** : to doze off **2** : to go numb

adormecimiento *nm* **1** SUEÑO : drowsiness, sleepiness **2** INSENSIBILIDAD : numbness

adormilarse *vr* : to doze, to drowse

adornar *vt* DECORAR : to decorate, to adorn

adorno *nm* : ornament, decoration

adquirido, -da *adj* **1** : acquired **2 mal adquirido** : ill-gotten

adquirir {4} *vt* **1** : to acquire, to gain **2** COMPRAR : to purchase

adquisición *nf, pl* **-ciones 1** : acquisition **2** COMPRA : purchase
adquisitivo, -va *adj* **poder adquisitivo** : purchasing power
adrede *adv* : intentionally, on purpose
adrenalina *nf* : adrenaline
adscribir {33} *vt* : to assign, to appoint — **adscribirse** *vr* ~ **a** : to become a member of
adscripción *nf, pl* **-ciones** : assignment, appointment
adscrito *pp* → **adscribir**
aduana *nf* : customs, customs office
aduanero¹, -ra *adj* : customs
aduanero², -ra *n* : customs officer
aducir {61} *vt* : to adduce, to offer as proof
adueñarse *vr* ~ **de** : to take possession of, to take over
adulación *nf, pl* **-ciones** : adulation, flattery
adulador¹, -dora *adj* : flattering
adulador², -dora *n* : flatterer, toady
adular *vt* LISONJEAR : to flatter
adulteración *nf, pl* **-ciones** : adulteration
adulterar *vt* : to adulterate
adulterio *nm* : adultery
adúltero¹, -ra *adj* : adulterous
adúltero², -ra *n* : adulterer
adultez *nf* : adulthood
adulto, -ta *adj & n* : adult
adusto, -ta *adj* : harsh, severe
advenedizo, -za *n* **1** : upstart, parvenu **2** : newcomer
advenimiento *nm* : advent
adverbio *nm* : adverb — **adverbial** *adj*
adversario¹, -ria *adj* : opposing, contrary
adversario², -ria *n* OPOSITOR : adversary, opponent
adversidad *nf* : adversity
adverso, -sa *adj* DESFAVORABLE : adverse, unfavorable — **adversamente** *adv*
advertencia *nf* AVISO : warning
advertir {76} *vt* **1** AVISAR : to warn **2** : to notice, to tell ⟨no advertí que estuviera enojada : I couldn't tell she was angry⟩
Adviento *nm* : Advent
adyacente *adj* : adjacent
aéreo, -rea *adj* **1** : aerial, air **2 correo aéreo** : airmail
aeróbic *nm* : aerobics
aeróbico, -ca *adj* : aerobic
aerobio, -bia *adj* : aerobic
aerodinámica *nf* : aerodynamics
aerodinámico, -ca *adj* : aerodynamic, streamlined
aeródromo *nm* : airfield
aeroespacial *adj* : aerospace
aerolínea *nf* : airline
aeromozo, -za *n* : flight attendant, steward *m*, stewardess *f*
aeronáutica *nf* : aeronautics
aeronáutico, -ca *adj* : aeronautical
aeronave *nf* : aircraft

aeropostal *adj* : airmail
aeropuerto *nm* : airport
aerosol *nm* : aerosol, aerosol spray
aeróstata *nmf* : balloonist
aerotransportado, -da *adj* : airborne
aerotransportar *vt* : to airlift
afabilidad *nf* : affability
afable *adj* : affable — **afablemente** *adv*
afamado, -da *adj* : well-known, famous
afán *nm, pl* **afanes 1** ANHELO : eagerness, desire **2** EMPEÑO : effort, determination
afanador, -dora *n Mex* : cleaning person, cleaner
afanarse *vr* : to toil, to strive
afanosamente *adv* : zealously, industriously, busily
afanoso, -sa *adj* **1** : eager, industrious **2** : arduous, hard
afear *vt* : to make ugly, to disfigure
afección *nf, pl* **-ciones 1** : fondness, affection **2** : illness, complaint
afectación *nf, pl* **-ciones** : affectation
afectado, -da *adj* **1** : affected, mannered **2** : influenced **3** : afflicted **4** : feigned
afectar *vt* **1** : to affect **2** : to upset **3** : to feign, to pretend
afectísimo, -ma *adj* **suyo afectísimo** : yours truly
afectivo, -va *adj* : emotional
afecto¹, -ta *adj* **1** : affected, afflicted **2** : fond, affectionate
afecto² *nm* CARIÑO : affection
afectuoso, -sa *adj* CARIÑOSO : affectionate, caring
afeitadora *nf* : shaver, electric razor
afeitar *vt* RASURAR : to shave — **afeitarse** *vr*
afelpado, -da *adj* : plush
afeminado, -da *adj* : effeminate
aferrado, -da *adj* : obstinate, stubborn
aferrarse {55} *vr* : to cling, to hold on
affidávit *nm, pl* **-dávits** : affidavit
afgano, -na *adj & n* : Afghan
AFI *nm* (Alfabeto Fonético Internacional) : IPA
afianzar {21} *vt* **1** : to secure, to strengthen **2** : to guarantee, to vouch for — **afianzarse** *vr* ESTABLECERSE : to establish oneself
afiche *nm* : poster
afición *nf, pl* **-ciones 1** : enthusiasm, penchant, fondness ⟨afición al deporte : love of sports⟩ **2** PASATIEMPO : hobby
aficionado¹, -da *adj* ENTUSIASTA : enthusiastic, keen
aficionado², -da *n* **1** ENTUSIASTA : enthusiast, fan **2** : amateur
áfido *nm* : aphid
afiebrado, -da *adj* : feverish
afilado, -da *adj* **1** : sharp **2** : long, pointed ⟨una nariz afilada : a sharp nose⟩
afilador *nm* : sharpener
afilalápices *nms & pl* : pencil sharpener
afilar *vt* : to sharpen
afiliación *nf, pl* **-ciones** : affiliation

afiliado¹, -da *adj* : affiliated

afiliado², -da *n* : member

afiliarse *vr* : to become a member, to join, to affiliate

afín *adj, pl* **afines 1** PARECIDO : related, similar ⟨la biología y disciplinas afines : biology and related disciplines⟩ **2** PRÓXIMO : adjacent, nearby

afinación *nf, pl* **-ciones 1** : tune-up **2** : tuning (of an instrument)

afinador, -dora *n* : tuner (of musical instruments)

afinar *vt* **1** : to perfect, to refine **2** : to tune (an instrument) — *vi* : to sing or play in tune

afincarse {72} *vr* : to establish oneself, to settle in

afinidad *nf* : affinity, similarity

afirmación *nf, pl* **-ciones 1** : statement **2** : affirmation

afirmar *vt* **1** : to state, to affirm **2** REFORZAR : to make firm, to strengthen

afirmativo, -va *adj* : affirmative — **afirmativamente** *adv*

aflicción *nf, pl* **-ciones** DESCONSUELO, PESAR : grief, sorrow

afligido, -da *adj* : grief-stricken, sorrowful

afligir {35} *vt* **1** : to distress, to upset **2** : to afflict — **afligirse** *vr* : to grieve

aflojar *vt* **1** : to loosen, to slacken **2** *fam* : to pay up, to fork over — *vi* : to slacken, to ease up — **aflojarse** *vr* : to become loose, to slacken

afloramiento *nm* : outcropping, emergence

aflorar *vi* : to come to the surface, to emerge

afluencia *nf* **1** : flow, influx **2** : abundance, plenty

afluente *nm* : tributary

afluir {41} *vi* **1** : to flock ⟨la gente afluía a la frontera : people were flocking to the border⟩ **2** : to flow

aforismo *nm* : aphorism

aforo *nm* **1** : appraisal, assessment **2** : maximum capacity (of a theater, highway, etc.)

afortunado, -da *adj* : fortunate, lucky — **afortunadamente** *adv*

afrecho *nm* : bran, mash

afrenta *nf* : affront, insult

afrentar *vt* : to affront, to dishonor, to insult

africano, -na *adj & n* : African

afroamericano, -na *adj & n* : Afro-American

afrodisiaco *or* **afrodisíaco** *nm* : aphrodisiac

afrontamiento *nm* : confrontation

afrontar *vt* : to confront, to face up to

afrutado, -da *adj* : fruity

afuera *adv* **1** : out ⟨¡afuera! : get out!⟩ **2** : outside, outdoors

afueras *nfpl* ALEDAÑOS : outskirts

agachadiza *nf* : snipe (bird)

agachar *vt* : to lower (a part of the body) ⟨agachar la cabeza : to bow one's head⟩

— agacharse *vr* : to crouch, to stoop, to bend down

agalla *nf* **1** BRANQUIA : gill **2 tener agallas** *fam* : to have guts, to have courage

agarradera *nf* ASA, ASIDERO : handle, grip

agarrado, -da *adj fam* : cheap, stingy

agarrar *vt* **1** : to grab, to grasp **2** : to catch, to take — *vi* **agarrar y** *fam* : to do (something) abruptly ⟨el día siguiente agarró y se fue : the next day he up and left⟩ — **agarrarse** *vr* **1** : to hold on, to cling **2** *fam* : to get into a fight ⟨se agarraron a golpes : they came to blows⟩

agarre *nm* : grip, grasp

agarrotarse *vr* **1** : to stiffen up **2** : to seize up

agasajar *vt* : to fête, to wine and dine

agasajo *nm* : lavish attention

ágata *nf* : agate

agave *nm* : agave

agazaparse *vr* **1** AGACHARSE : to crouch **2** : to hide

agencia *nf* : agency, office

agenciar *vt* **1** : to obtain, to procure — **agenciarse** *vr* : to manage, to get by

agenda *nf* **1** : agenda **2** : appointment book

agente *nmf* **1** : agent **2 agente de viajes** : travel agent **3 agente de bolsa** : stockbroker **4 agente de tráfico** : traffic officer

agigantado, -da *adj* GIGANTESCO : gigantic

agigantar *vt* **1** : to increase greatly, to enlarge **2** : to exaggerate

ágil *adj* **1** : agile, nimble **2** : sharp, lively (of a response, etc.) — **ágilmente** *adv*

agilidad *nf* : agility, nimbleness

agilizar {21} *vt* ACELERAR : to expedite, to speed up

agitación *nf, pl* **-ciones 1** : agitation **2** NERVIOSISMO : nervousness

agitado, -da *adj* **1** : agitated, excited **2** : choppy, rough, turbulent

agitador, -dora *n* PROVOCADOR : agitator

agitar *vt* **1** : to agitate, to shake **2** : to wave, to flap **3** : to stir up — **agitarse** *vr* **1** : to toss about, to flap around **2** : to get upset

aglomeración *nf, pl* **-ciones 1** : conglomeration, mass **2** GENTÍO : crowd

aglomerar *vt* **1** : to cluster, to amass — **aglomerarse** *vr* : to crowd together

aglutinar *vt* : to bring together, to bind

agnóstico, -ca *adj & n* : agnostic

agobiado, -da *adj* : weary, worn-out, weighted-down

agobiante *adj* **1** : exhausting, overwhelming **2** : stifling, oppressive

agobiar *vt* **1** OPRIMIR : to oppress, to burden **2** ABRUMAR : to overwhelm **3** : to wear out, to exhaust

agonía *nf* : agony, death throes

agonizante *adj* : dying

agonizar {21} *vi* **1** : to be dying **2** : to be in agony **3** : to dim, to fade

agorero, -ra *adj* : ominous

agostar *vt* **1** : to parch **2** : to wither — **agostarse** *vr*

agosto *nm* **1** : August **2 hacer uno su agosto** : to make a fortune, to make a killing

agotado, -da *adj* **1** : exhausted, used up **2** : sold out **3** FATIGADO : worn-out, tired

agotador, -dora *adj* : exhausting

agotamiento *nm* FATIGA : exhaustion

agotar *vt* **1** : to exhaust, to use up **2** : to weary, to wear out — **agotarse** *vr*

agraciado[1], -da *adj* **1** : attractive **2** : fortunate

agraciado[2], -da *n* : winner

agradable *adj* GRATO, PLACENTERO : pleasant, agreeable — **agradablemente** *adv*

agradar *vi* : to be pleasing ⟨nos agradó mucho el resultado : we were very pleased with the result⟩

agradecer {53} *vt* **1** : to be grateful for **2** : to thank

agradecido, -da *adj* : grateful, thankful

agradecimiento *nm* : gratitude, thankfulness

agrado *nm* **1** GUSTO : taste, liking ⟨no es de su agrado : it's not to his liking⟩ **2** : graciousness, agreeableness **3 con ~** : with pleasure, willingly ⟨lo haré con agrado : I will be happy to do it⟩

agrandar *vt* **1** : to exaggerate **2** : to enlarge — **agrandarse** *vr*

agrario, -ria *adj* : agrarian, agricultural

agravación *nf, pl* **-ciones** : aggravation, worsening

agravante *adj* : aggravating

agravar *vt* **1** : to increase (weight), to make heavier **2** EMPEORAR : to aggravate, to worsen — **agravarse** *vr*

agraviar *vt* INJURIAR, OFENDER : to offend, to insult

agravio *nm* INJURIA : affront, offense, insult

agredir {1} *vt* : to assail, to attack

agregado[1], -da *n* **1** : attaché **2** : assistant professor

agregado[2] *nm* **1** : aggregate **2** AÑADIDURA : addition, something added

agregar {52} *vt* **1** AÑADIR : to add, to attach **2** : to appoint — **agregarse** *vr* : to join

agresión *nf, pl* **-siones** **1** : aggression **2** ATAQUE : attack

agresividad *nf* : aggressiveness, aggression

agresivo, -va *adj* : aggressive — **agresivamente** *adv*

agresor[1], -sora *adj* : hostile, attacking

agresor[2], -sora *n* **1** : aggressor **2** : assailant, attacker

agreste *adj* **1** CAMPESTRE : rural **2** : wild, untamed

agriar *vt* **1** : to sour, to make sour **2** : to embitter — **agriarse** *vr* : to turn sour

agrícola *adj* : agricultural

agricultor, -tora *n* : farmer, grower

agricultura *nf* : agriculture, farming

agridulce *adj* **1** : bittersweet **2** : sweet-and-sour

agrietar *vt* : to crack — **agrietarse** *vr* **1** : to crack **2** : to chap

agrimensor, -sora *n* : surveyor

agrimensura *nf* : surveying

agrio, agria *adj* **1** ÁCIDO : sour **2** : caustic, acrimonious

agriparse *vr* : to catch the flu

agroindustria *nf* : agribusiness

agronomía *nf* : agronomy

agropecuario, -ria *adj* : pertaining to livestock and agriculture

agrupación *nf, pl* **-ciones** GRUPO : group, association

agrupamiento *nm* : grouping, concentration

agrupar *vt* : to group together

agua *nf* **1** : water **2 agua oxigenada** : hydrogen peroxide **3 aguas negras** *or* **aguas residuales** : sewage **4 como agua para chocolate** *Mex fam* : furious **5 echar aguas** *Mex fam* : to keep an eye out, to be on the lookout

aguacate *nm* : avocado

aguacero *nm* : shower, downpour

aguado, -da *adj* **1** DILUIDO : watered-down, diluted **2** CA, Col, Mex fam : soft, flabby **3** Mex, Peru fam : dull, boring

aguafiestas *nmfs & pl* : killjoy, stick-in-the-mud, spoilsport

aguafuerte *nm* : etching

aguamanil *nm* : ewer, pitcher

aguanieve *nf* : sleet ⟨caer aguanieve : to be sleeting⟩

aguantar *vt* **1** SOPORTAR : to bear, to tolerate, to withstand **2** : to hold **3 aguantar las ganas** : to resist an urge ⟨no pude aguantar las ganas de reír : I couldn't keep myself from laughing⟩ — *vi* : to hold out, to last — **aguantarse** *vr* **1** : to resign oneself **2** : to restrain oneself

aguante *nm* **1** TOLERANCIA : tolerance, patience **2** RESISTENCIA : endurance, strength

aguar {10} *vt* **1** : to water down, to dilute **2 aguar la fiesta** *fam* : to spoil the party

aguardar *vt* ESPERAR : to wait for, to await — *vi* : to be in store

aguardiente *nm* : clear brandy

aguarrás *nm* : turpentine

agudeza *nf* **1** : keenness, sharpness **2** : shrillness **3** : witticism

agudizar {21} *vt* : to intensify, to heighten

agudo, -da *adj* **1** : acute, sharp **2** : shrill, high-pitched **3** PERSPICAZ : clever, shrewd

agüero *nm* AUGURIO, PRESAGIO : augury, omen

aguijón *nm, pl* **-jones** **1** : stinger (of a bee, etc.) **2** : goad

aguijonear *vt* : to goad
águila *nf* **1** : eagle **2 águila o sol** *Mex* : heads or tails
aguileño, -ña *adj* : aquiline
aguilera *nf* : aerie, eagle's nest
aguilón *nm, pl* **-lones** : gable
aguinaldo *nm* **1** : Christmas bonus, year-end bonus **2** *PRi, Ven* : Christmas carol
agüitarse *vr Mex fam* : to have the blues, to feel discouraged
aguja *nf* **1** : needle **2** : steeple, spire
agujerear *vt* : to make a hole in, to pierce
agujero *nm* **1** : hole **2 agujero negro** : black hole (in astronomy)
agujeta *nf* **1** *Mex* : shoelace **2 agujetas** *nfpl* : muscular soreness or stiffness
agusanado, -da *adj* : worm-eaten
aguzar {21} *vt* **1** : to sharpen ⟨aguzar el ingenio : to sharpen one's wits⟩ **2 aguzar el oído** : to prick up one's ears
ah *interj* : oh!
ahí *adv* **1** : there ⟨ahí está : there it is⟩ **2 por ~** : somewhere, thereabouts **3 de ahí que** : with the result that, so that
ahijado, -da *n* : godchild, godson *m*, goddaughter *f*
ahijar {5} *vt* : to adopt (a child)
ahínco *nm* : eagerness, zeal
ahogar {52} *vt* **1** : to drown **2** : to smother **3** : to choke back, to stifle — **ahogarse** *vr*
ahogo *nm* : breathlessness, suffocation
ahondar *vt* : to deepen — *vi* : to elaborate, to go into detail
ahora *adv* **1** : now **2 ahora mismo** : right now **3 hasta ~** : so far **4 por ~** : for the time being
ahorcar {72} *vt* : to hang, to kill by hanging — **ahorcarse** *vr*
ahorita *adv fam* : right now, right away
ahorquillado, -da *adj* : forked
ahorrador, -dora *adj* : thrifty
ahorrar *vt* **1** : to save (money) **2** : to spare, to conserve — *vi* : to save up — **ahorrarse** *vr* : to spare oneself
ahorrativo, -va *adj* : thrifty, frugal
ahorro *nm* : saving ⟨cuenta de ahorros : savings account⟩
ahuecar {72} *vt* **1** : to hollow out **2** : to cup (one's hands) **3** : to plump up, to fluff up
ahuizote *nm Mex fam* : annoying person, pain in the neck
ahumar {8} *vt* : to smoke, to cure
ahuyentar *vt* **1** : to scare away, to chase away **2** : to banish, to dispel ⟨ahuyentar las dudas : to dispel doubts⟩
airado, -da *adj FURIOSO* : angry, irate
airar {5} *vt* : to make angry, to anger
aire *nm* **1** : air **2 aire acondicionado** : air-conditioning **3 darse aires** : to give oneself airs
airear *vt* **1** : to air, to air out — **airearse** *vr* : to get some fresh air
airoso, -sa *adj* **1** : elegant, graceful **2 salir airoso** : to come out winning
aislacionismo *nm* : isolationism

aislacionista *adj & nmf* : isolationist
aislado, -da *adj* : isolated, alone
aislador *nm* : insulator (part)
aislamiento *nm* **1** : isolation **2** : insulation
aislante *nm* : insulator, nonconductor
aislar {5} *vt* **1** : to isolate **2** : to insulate
ajado, -da *adj* **1** : worn, shabby **2** : wrinkled, crumpled
ajar *vt* : to wear out, to spoil
ajardinado, -da *adj* : landscaped
ajedrecista *nmf* : chess player
ajedrez *nm, pl* **-dreces** **1** : chess **2** : chess set
ajeno, -na *adj* **1** : alien **2** : of another, of others ⟨propiedad ajena : somebody else's property⟩ **3 ~ a** : foreign to **4 ~ de** : devoid of, free from
ajetreado, -da *adj* : hectic, busy
ajetrearse *vr* : to bustle about, to rush around
ajetreo *nm* : hustle and bustle, fuss
ají *nm, pl* **ajíes** : chili pepper
ajo *nm* : garlic
ajonjolí *nm, pl* **-líes** : sesame
ajuar *nm* : trousseau
ajustable *adj* : adjustable
ajustado, -da *adj* **1** CEÑIDO : tight, tight-fitting **2** : close, tight ⟨una ajustada victoria : a close victory⟩
ajustar *vt* **1** : to adjust, to adapt **2** : to take in (clothing) **3** : to settle, to resolve — **ajustarse** *vr* : to fit, to conform
ajuste *nm* **1** : adjustment **2** : tightening
ajusticiar *vt EJECUTAR* : to execute, to put to death
al *prep* (contraction of *a* and *el*) → *a²*
ala *nf* **1** : wing **2** : brim (of a hat)
Alá *nm* : Allah
alabanza *nf ELOGIO* : praise
alabar *vt* : to praise — **alabarse** *vr* : to boast
alabastro *nm* : alabaster
alabear *vt* : to warp — **alabearse** *vr*
alabeo *nm* : warp, warping
alacena *nf* : cupboard, larder
alacrán *nm, pl* **-cranes** ESCORPIÓN : scorpion
alado, -da *adj* : winged
alambique *nm* : still (to distill alcohol)
alambre *nm* **1** : wire **2 alambre de púas** : barbed wire
alameda *nf* **1** : poplar grove **2** : tree-lined avenue
álamo *nm* **1** : poplar **2 álamo temblón** : aspen
alar *nm* : eaves *pl*
alarde *nm* **1** : show, display **2 hacer alarde de** : to make show of, to boast about
alardear *vi PRESUMIR* : to boast, to brag
alargado, -da *adj* : elongated, slender
alargamiento *nm* : lengthening, extension, elongation
alargar {52} *vt* **1** : to extend, to lengthen **2** PROLONGAR : to prolong — **alargarse** *vr*

alarido *nm* : howl, shriek

alarma *nf* : alarm

alarmante *adj* : alarming — **alarmantemente** *adv*

alarmar *vt* : to alarm

alazán *nm, pl* **-zanes** : sorrel (color or animal)

alba *nf* AMANECER : dawn, daybreak

albacea *nmf* TESTAMENTARIO : executor, executrix *f*

albahaca *nf* : basil

albanés, -nesa *adj & n, mpl* **-neses** : Albanian

albañil *nmf* : bricklayer, mason

albañilería *nf* : bricklaying, masonry

albaricoque *nm* : apricot

albatros *nm* : albatross

albedrío *nm* : will ⟨libre albedrío : free will⟩

alberca *nf* **1** : reservoir, tank **2** *Mex* : swimming pool

albergar {52} *vt* ALOJAR : to house, to lodge, to shelter

albergue *nm* **1** : shelter, refuge **2** : hostel

albino, -na *adj & n* : albino — **albinismo** *nm*

albóndiga *nf* : meatball

albor *nm* **1** : dawning, beginning **2** BLANCURA : whiteness

alborada *nf* : dawn

alborear *v impers* : to dawn

alborotado, -da *adj* **1** : excited, agitated **2** : rowdy, unruly

alborotador¹, -dora *adj* **1** : noisy, boisterous **2** : rowdy, unruly

alborotador², -dora *n* : agitator, troublemaker, rioter

alborotar *vt* **1** : to excite, to agitate **2** : to incite, to stir up — **alborotarse** *vr* **1** : to get excited **2** : to riot

alboroto *nm* **1** : disturbance, ruckus **2** MOTÍN : riot

alborozado, -da *adj* : jubilant

alborozar {21} *vt* : to gladden, to cheer

alborozo *nm* : joy, elation

álbum *nm* : album ⟨álbum de recortes : scrapbook⟩

albúmina *nf* : albumin

albur *nm* **1** : chance, risk **2** *Mex* : pun

alca *nf* : auk

alcachofa *nf* : artichoke

alcahuete, -ta *n* CHISMOSO : gossip

alcaide *nm* : warden (in a prison)

alcalde, -desa *n* : mayor

alcaldía *nf* **1** : mayoralty **2** AYUNTAMIENTO : city hall

álcali *nm* : alkali

alcalino, -na *adj* : alkaline — **alcalinidad** *nf*

alcance *nm* **1** : reach **2** : range, scope

alcancía *nf* **1** : piggy bank, money box **2** : collection box (for alms, etc.)

alcanfor *nm* : camphor

alcantarilla *nf* CLOACA : sewer, drain

alcanzar {21} *vt* **1** : to reach **2** : to catch up with **3** LOGRAR : to achieve, to attain — *vi* **1** DAR : to suffice, to be enough **2** ~ **a** : to manage to

alcaparra *nf* : caper

alcapurria *nf* PRi : stuffed fritter made with taro and green banana

alcaravea *nf* : caraway

alcatraz *nm, pl* **-traces** : gannet

alcázar *nm* : fortress, castle

alce¹, etc. → **alzar**

alce² *nm* : moose, European elk

alcoba *nf* : bedroom

alcohol *nm* : alcohol

alcohólico, -ca *adj & n* : alcoholic

alcoholismo *nm* : alcoholism

alcoholizarse {21} *vr* : to become an alcoholic

alcornoque *nm* **1** : cork oak **2** *fam* : idiot, fool

alcurnia *nf* : ancestry, lineage

aldaba *nf* : door knocker

aldea *nf* : village

aldeano¹, -na *adj* : village, rustic

aldeano², -na *n* : villager

aleación *nf, pl* **-ciones** : alloy

alear *vt* : to alloy

aleatorio, -ria *adj* : random, fortuitous — **aleatoriamente** *adv*

alebrestar *vt* : to excite, to make nervous — **alebrestarse** *vr*

aledaño, -ña *adj* : bordering, neighboring

aledaños *nmpl* AFUERAS : outskirts, surrounding area

alegar {52} *vt* : to assert, to allege — *vi* DISCUTIR : to argue

alegato *nm* **1** : allegation, claim **2** *Mex* : argument, summation (in law) **3** : argument, dispute

alegoría *nf* : allegory

alegórico, -ca *adj* : allegorical

alegrar *vt* : to make happy, to cheer up — **alegrarse** *vr* : to be glad, to rejoice

alegre *adj* **1** : glad, cheerful **2** : colorful, bright **3** *fam* : tipsy

alegremente *adv* : happily, cheerfully

alegría *nf* : joy, cheer, happiness

alejado, -da *adj* : remote

alejamiento *nm* **1** : removal, separation **2** : estrangement

alejar *vt* **1** : to remove, to move away **2** : to estrange, to alienate — **alejarse** *vr* **1** : to move away, to stray **2** : to drift apart

alelado, -da *adj* **1** : bewildered, stupefied **2** : foolish, stupid

aleluya *interj* : hallelujah!, alleluia!

alemán¹, -mana *adj & n, mpl* **-manes** : German

alemán² *nm* : German (language)

alentador, -dora *adj* : encouraging

alentar {55} *vt* : to encourage, to inspire — *vi* : to breathe

alerce *nm* : larch

alérgeno *nm* : allergen

alergia *nf* : allergy

alérgico, -ca *adj* : allergic

alero *nm* **1** : eaves *pl* **2** : forward (in basketball)

alerón *nm, pl* **-rones** : aileron
alerta[1] *adv* : on the alert
alerta[2] *adj & nf* : alert
alertar *vt* : to alert
aleta *nf* 1 : fin 2 : flipper 3 : small wing
aletargado, -da *adj* : lethargic, sluggish, torpid
aletargarse {52} *vr* : to feel drowsy, to become lethargic
aletear *vi* : to flutter, to flap one's wings
aleteo *nm* : flapping, flutter
alevín *nm, pl* **-vines** 1 : fry, young fish 2 PRINCIPIANTE : beginner
alevosía *nf* 1 : treachery 2 : premeditation
alevoso, -sa *adj* : treacherous
alfabético, -ca *adj* : alphabetical — **alfabéticamente** *adv*
alfabetismo *nm* : literacy
alfabetizado, -da *adj* : literate
alfabetizar {21} *vt* : to alphabetize
alfabeto *nm* : alphabet
alfalfa *nf* : alfalfa
alfanje *nm* : cutlass, scimitar
alfarería *nf* : pottery
alfarero, -ra *n* : potter
alféizar *nm* : sill, windowsill
alfeñique *nm fam* : wimp, weakling
alférez *nmf, pl* **-reces** 1 : second lieutenant 2 : ensign
alfil *nm* : bishop (in chess)
alfiler *nm* 1 : pin 2 BROCHE : brooch
alfiletero *nm* : pincushion
alfombra *nf* : carpet, rug
alfombrado *nm* : carpeting
alfombrar *vt* : to carpet
alfombrilla *nf* : small rug, mat
alforfón *nm, pl* **-fones** : buckwheat
alforja *nf* : saddlebag
alforza *nf* : pleat, tuck
alga *nf* 1 : aquatic plant, alga 2 : seaweed
algarabía *nf* 1 : gibberish, babble 2 : hubbub, uproar
álgebra *nf* : algebra
algebraico, -ca *adj* : algebraic
álgido, -da *adj* 1 : critical, decisive 2 : icy cold
algo[1] *adv* : somewhat, rather ⟨es simpático, pero algo tacaño : he's nice but rather stingy⟩
algo[2] *pron* 1 : something 2 **~ de** : some, a little ⟨tengo algo de dinero : I've got some money⟩
algodón *nm, pl* **-dones** : cotton
algoritmo *nm* : algorithm
alguacil *nm* : constable
alguien *pron* : somebody, someone
alguno[1]**, -na** *adj* (**algún** *before masculine singular nouns*) 1 : some, any ⟨algún día : someday, one day⟩ 2 (*in negative constructions*) : not any, not at all ⟨no tengo noticia alguna : I have no news at all⟩ 3 **algunas veces** : sometimes
alguno[2]**, -na** *pron* 1 : one, someone, somebody ⟨alguno de ellos : one of them⟩ 2 **algunos, -nas** *pron pl* : some,

a few ⟨algunos quieren trabajar : some want to work⟩
alhaja *nf* : jewel, gem
alhajar *vt* : to adorn with jewels
alharaca *nf* : fuss
alhelí *nm* : wallflower
aliado[1]**, -da** *adj* : allied
aliado[2]**, -da** *n* : ally
alianza *nf* : alliance
aliarse {85} *vr* : to form an alliance, to ally oneself
alias *adv & nm* : alias
alicaído, -da *adj* : depressed, discouraged
alicates *nmpl* PINZAS : pliers
aliciente *nm* 1 INCENTIVO : incentive 2 ATRACCIÓN : attraction
alienación *nf, pl* **-ciones** : alienation, derangement
alienar *vt* ENAJENAR : to alienate
aliento *nm* 1 : breath 2 : courage, strength 3 **dar aliento a** : to encourage
aligerar *vt* 1 : to lighten 2 ACELERAR : to hasten, to quicken
alijo *nm* : cache, consignment (of contraband)
alimaña *nf* : pest, vermin
alimentación *nf, pl* **-ciones** NUTRICIÓN : nutrition, nourishment
alimentar *vt* 1 NUTRIR : to feed, to nourish 2 MANTENER : to support (a family) 3 FOMENTAR : to nurture, to foster — **alimentarse** *vr* **~ con** : to live on
alimentario, -ria → **alimenticio**
alimenticio, -cia *adj* 1 : nutritional, food, dietary 2 : nutritious, nourishing
alimento *nm* : food, nourishment
aliñar *vt* 1 : to dress (salad) 2 CONDIMENTAR : to season
alineación *nf, pl* **-ciones** 1 : alignment 2 : lineup (in sports)
alineamiento *nm* : alignment
alinear *vt* 1 : to align 2 : to line up — **alinearse** *vr* 1 : to fall in, to line up 2 **~ con** : to align oneself with
aliño *nm* : seasoning, dressing
alipús *nm, pl* **-puses** *Mex fam* : booze, drink
alisar *vt* : to smooth
aliso *nm* : alder
alistamiento *nm* : enlistment, recruitment
alistar *vt* 1 : to recruit 2 : to make ready — **alistarse** *vr* : to join up, to enlist
aliteración *nf, pl* **-ciones** : alliteration
aliviar *vt* MITIGAR : to relieve, to alleviate, to soothe — **aliviarse** *vr* : to recover, to get better
alivio *nm* : relief
aljaba *nf* : quiver (for arrows)
aljibe *nm* : cistern, well
allá *adv* 1 : there, over there 2 **más allá** : farther away 3 **más allá de** : beyond 4 **allá tú** : that's up to you

allanamiento *nm* 1 : (police) raid 2 allanamiento de morada : breaking and entering

allanar *vt* 1 : to raid, to search 2 : to resolve, to solve 3 : to smooth, to level out

allegado¹, -da *adj* : close, intimate

allegado², -da *n* : close friend, relation ⟨parientes y allegados : friends and relations⟩

allegar {52} *vt* : to gather, to collect

allende¹ *adv* : beyond, on the other side

allende² *prep* : beyond ⟨allende las montañas : beyond the mountains⟩

allí *adv* : there, over there ⟨allí mismo : right there⟩ ⟨hasta allí : up to that point⟩

alma *nf* 1 : soul 2 : person, human being 3 no tener alma : to be pitiless 4 tener el alma en un hilo : to have one's heart in one's mouth

almacén *nm, pl* -cenes 1 BODEGA : warehouse, storehouse 2 TIENDA : shop, store 3 gran almacén *Spain* : department store

almacenaje → almacenamiento

almacenamiento *nm* : storage ⟨almacenamiento de datos : data storage⟩

almacenar *vt* : to store, to put in storage

almacenero, -ra *n* : shopkeeper

almacenista *nm* MAYORISTA : wholesaler

almádena *nf* : sledgehammer

almanaque *nm* : almanac

almeja *nf* : clam

almendra *nf* 1 : almond 2 : kernel

almendro *nm* : almond tree

almiar *nm* : haystack

almíbar *nm* : syrup

almidón *nm, pl* -dones : starch

almidonar *vt* : to starch

alminar *nm* MINARETE : minaret

almirante *nm* : admiral

almizcle *nm* : musk

almohada *nf* : pillow

almohadilla *nf* 1 : small pillow, cushion 2 : bag, base (in baseball)

almohadón *nm, pl* -dones : bolster, cushion

almohazar {21} *vt* : to curry (a horse)

almoneda *nf* SUBASTA : auction

almorranas *nfpl* HEMORROIDES : hemorrhoids, piles

almorzar {36} *vi* : to have lunch — *vt* : to have for lunch

almuerzo *nm* : lunch

alocado, -da *adj* 1 : crazy 2 : wild, reckless 3 : silly, scatterbrained

alocución *nf, pl* -ciones : speech, address

áloe *or* aloe *nm* : aloe

alojamiento *nm* : lodging, accommodations *pl*

alojar *vt* ALBERGAR : to house, to lodge — alojarse *vr* : to lodge, to room

alondra *nf* : lark, skylark

alpaca *nf* : alpaca

alpinismo *nm* : mountain climbing, mountaineering

alpinista *nmf* : mountain climber

alpino, -na *adj* : Alpine, alpine

alpiste *nm* : birdseed

alquilar *vt* ARRENDAR : to rent, to lease

alquiler *nm* ARRENDAMIENTO : rent, rental

alquimia *nf* : alchemy

alquimista *nmf* : alchemist

alquitrán *nm, pl* -tranes BREA : tar

alquitranar *vt* : to tar, to cover with tar

alrededor¹ *adv* 1 : around, about ⟨todo temblaba alrededor : all around things were shaking⟩ 2 ~ de : around, approximately ⟨alrededor de quince personas : around fifteen people⟩

alrededor² *prep* ~ de : around, about ⟨corrió alrededor de la casa : she ran around the house⟩ ⟨llegaré alrededor de diciembre : I will get there around December⟩

alrededores *nmpl* ALEDAÑOS : surroundings, outskirts

alta *nf* 1 : admission, entry, enrollment 2 dar de alta : to release, to discharge (a patient)

altanería *nf* ALTIVEZ, ARROGANCIA : arrogance, haughtiness

altanero, -ra *adj* ALTIVO, ARROGANTE : arrogant, haughty — altaneramente *adv*

altar *nm* : altar

altavoz *nm, pl* -voces ALTOPARLANTE : loudspeaker

alteración *nf, pl* -ciones 1 MODIFICACIÓN : alteration, modification 2 PERTURBACIÓN : disturbance, disruption

alterado, -da *adj* : upset

alterar *vt* 1 MODIFICAR : to alter, to modify 2 PERTURBAR : to disturb, to disrupt — alterarse *vr* : to get upset, to get worked up

altercado *nm* DISCUSIÓN, DISPUTA : altercation, argument, dispute

alternador *nm* : alternator

alternancia *nf* : alternation, rotation

alternar *vi* 1 : to alternate 2 : to mix, to socialize — *vt* : to alternate — alternarse *vr* : to take turns

alternativa *nf* OPCIÓN : alternative, option

alternativo, -va *adj* 1 : alternating 2 : alternative — alternativamente *adv*

alterno, -na *adj* : alternate ⟨corriente alterna : alternating current⟩

alteza *nf* 1 : loftiness, lofty height 2 Alteza : Highness

altibajos *nmpl* 1 : unevenness (of terrain) 2 : ups and downs

altímetro *nm* : altimeter

altiplanicie *nf* → altiplano

altiplano *nm* : high plateau, upland

altisonante *adj* 1 : pompous, affected (of language) 2 *Mex* : rude, obscene (of language)

altitud *nf* : altitude

altivez *nf, pl* **-veces** ALTANERÍA, ARRO-GANCIA : arrogance, haughtiness
altivo, -va *adj* ALTANERO, ARROGANTE : arrogant, haughty
alto¹ *adv* **1** : high **2** : loud, loudly
alto², -ta *adj* **1** : tall, high **2** : loud ⟨en voz alta : aloud, out loud⟩
alto³ *nm* **1** ALTURA : height, elevation **2** : stop, halt **3 altos** *nmpl* : upper floors
alto⁴ *interj* : halt!, stop!
altoparlante *nm* ALTAVOZ : loudspeaker
altozano *nm* : hillock
altruismo *nm* : altruism
altruista¹ *adj* : altruistic
altruista² *nmf* : altruist
altura *nf* **1** : height **2** : altitude **3** : lofti-ness, nobleness **4 a la altura de** : near, up by ⟨en la avenida San Antonio a la altura de la Calle Tres : on San Anto-nio Avenue up near Third Street⟩ **5 a estas alturas** : at this point, at this stage of the game
alubia *nf* : kidney bean
alucinación *nf, pl* **-ciones** : hallucina-tion
alucinante *adj* : hallucinatory
alucinar *vi* : to hallucinate
alucinógeno¹, -na *adj* : hallucinogenic
alucinógeno² *nm* : hallucinogen
alud *nm* AVALANCHA : avalanche, land-slide
aludido, -da *n* **1** : person in question ⟨el aludido : the aforesaid⟩ **2 darse por aludido** : to take it personally
aludir *vi* : to allude, to refer
alumbrado *nm* ILUMINACIÓN : lighting
alumbramiento *nm* **1** : lighting **2** : childbirth
alumbrar *vt* **1** ILUMINAR : to light, to il-luminate **2** : to give birth to
alumbre *nm* : alum
aluminio *nm* : aluminum
alumnado *nm* : student body
alumno, -na *n, pl* **-nos 1** : pupil, student **2 ex–alumno, -na** : alumnus, alumna *f* **3 ex–alumnos, -nas** *npl* : alumni, alum-nae *f*
alusión *nf, pl* **-siones** : allusion, refer-ence
alusivo, -va *adj* **1** : allusive **2 ∼ a** : in reference to, regarding
aluvión *nm, pl* **-viones** : flood, barrage
alza *nf* SUBIDA : rise ⟨precios en alza : rising prices⟩
alzamiento *nm* LEVANTAMIENTO : up-rising, insurrection
alzar {21} *vt* **1** ELEVAR, LEVANTAR : to lift, to raise **2** : to erect — **alzarse** *vr* LEVANTARSE : to rise up
ama *nf* → **amo**
amabilidad *nf* : kindness
amable *adj* : kind, nice — **amablemente** *adv*
amado¹, -da *adj* : beloved, darling
amado², -da *n* : sweetheart, loved one
amaestrar *vt* : to train (animals)
amafiarse *vr Mex fam* : to conspire, to be in cahoots

amagar {52} *vt* **1** : to show signs of (an illness, etc.) **2** : to be imminent, to threaten — *vi* **1** : to feint, to dissemble
amago *nm* **1** AMENAZA : threat **2** : sign, hint
amainar *vi* : to abate, to ease up, to die down
amalgama *nf* : amalgam
amalgamar *vt* : to amalgamate, to unite
amamantar *v* : to breast-feed, to nurse, to suckle
amanecer¹ {53} *v impers* **1** : to dawn **2** : to begin to show, to appear **3** : to wake up (in the morning)
amanecer² *nm* ALBA : dawn, daybreak
amanerado, -da *adj* : affected, man-nered
amansar *vt* **1** : to tame **2** : to soothe, to calm down — **amansarse** *vr*
amante¹ *adj* : loving, fond
amante² *nmf* : lover
amañar *vt* : to rig, to fix, to tamper with — **amañarse** *vr* **amañárselas** : to man-age
amaño *nm* **1** : skill, dexterity **2** : trick, ruse
amapola *nf* : poppy
amar *vt* : to love — **amarse** *vr*
amargado, -da *adj* : embittered, bitter
amargar {52} *vt* : to make bitter, to em-bitter — *vi* : to taste bitter
amargo¹, -ga *adj* : bitter — **amarga-mente** *adv*
amargo² *nm* : bitterness, tartness
amargura *nf* **1** : bitterness **2** : grief, sor-row
amarilis *nf* : amaryllis
amarillear *vi* : to yellow, to turn yellow
amarillento, -ta *adj* : yellowish
amarillismo *nm* : yellow journalism, sensationalism
amarillo¹, -lla *adj* : yellow
amarillo² *nm* : yellow
amarra *nf* **1** : mooring, mooring line **2 soltar las amarras de** : to loosen one's grip on
amarrar *vt* **1** : to moor (a boat) **2** ATAR : to fasten, to tie up, to tie down
amartillar *vt* : to cock (a gun)
amasar *vt* **1** : to amass **2** : to knead **3** : to mix, to prepare
amasijo *nm* : jumble, hodgepodge
amasio, -sia *n* : lover, paramour
amateur *adj & nmf* : amateur — **ama-teurismo** *nm*
amatista *nf* : amethyst
amatorio, -ria *adj* : amatory, sexual ⟨poesía amatoria : love poems⟩
amazona *nf* **1** : Amazon (in mythology) **2** : horsewoman
amazónico, -ca *adj* : amazonian
ambages *nmpl* **sin ∼** : without hesita-tion, straight to the point
ámbar *nm* **1** : amber **2 ámbar gris** : am-bergris
ambición *nf, pl* **-ciones** : ambition
ambicionar *vt* : to aspire to, to seek

ambicioso, -sa *adj* : ambitious — **ambiciosamente** *adv*

ambidextro, -tra *adj* : ambidextrous

ambientación *nf, pl* **-ciones** : setting, atmosphere

ambiental *adj* : environmental — **ambientalmente** *adv*

ambientalista *nmf* : environmentalist

ambientar *vt* : to give atmosphere to, to set (in literature and drama) — **ambientarse** *vr* : to adjust, to get one's bearings

ambiente *nm* **1** : atmosphere **2** : environment **3** : surroundings *pl*

ambigüedad *nf* : ambiguity

ambiguo, -gua *adj* : ambiguous

ámbito *nm* : domain, field, area

ambivalencia *nf* : ambivalence

ambivalente *adj* : ambivalent

ambos, -bas *adj & pron* : both

ambulancia *nf* : ambulance

ambulante *adj* **1** : traveling, itinerant **2** **vendedor ambulante** : street vendor

ameba *nf* : amoeba

amedrentar *vt* : to frighten, to intimidate — **amedrentarse** *vr*

amén *nm* **1** : amen **2** ~ **de** : in addition to, besides **3** **en un decir amén** : in an instant

amenaza *nf* : threat, menace

amenazador, -dora *adj* : threatening, menacing

amenazante → **amenazador**

amenazar {21} *v* : to threaten

amenguar {10} *vt* **1** : to diminish **2** : to belittle, to dishonor

amenidad *nf* : pleasantness, amenity

amenizar {21} *vt* **1** : to make pleasant : to brighten up, to add life to

ameno, -na *adj* : agreeable, pleasant

amento *nm* : catkin

americano, -na *adj & n* : American

amerindio, -dia *adj & n* : Amerindian

ameritar *vt* MERECER : to deserve

ametralladora *nf* : machine gun

amianto *nm* : asbestos

amiba → **ameba**

amigable *adj* : friendly, amicable — **amigablemente** *adv*

amígdala *nf* : tonsil

amigdalitis *nf* : tonsilitis

amigo¹, -ga *adj* : friendly, close

amigo², -ga *n* : friend

amigote *nm* : crony, pal

amilanar *vt* **1** : to frighten **2** : to daunt, to discourage — **amilanarse** *vr* : to lose heart

aminoácido *nm* : amino acid

aminorar *vt* : to reduce, to lessen — *vi* : to diminish

amistad *nf* : friendship

amistoso, -sa *adj* : friendly — **amistosamente** *adv*

amnesia *nf* : amnesia

amnésico, -ca *adj & n* : amnesiac, amnesic

amnistía *nf* : amnesty

amnistiar {85} *vt* : to grant amnesty to

amo, ama *n* **1** : master *m*, mistress *f* **2** : owner, keeper (of an animal) **3** **ama de casa** : housewife **4** **ama de llaves** : housekeeper

amodorrado, -da *adj* : drowsy

amolar {19} *vt* **1** : to grind, to sharpen **2** : to pester, to annoy

amoldable *adj* : adaptable

amoldar *vt* **1** : to mold **2** : to adapt, to adjust — **amoldarse** *vr*

amonestación *nf, pl* **-ciones** **1** APERCIBIMIENTO : admonition, warning **2** **amonestaciones** *nfpl* : banns

amonestar *vt* APERCIBIR : to admonish, to warn

amoníaco *or* **amoniaco** *nm* : ammonia

amontonamiento *nm* : accumulation, piling up

amontonar *vt* APILAR : to pile up, to heap up **2** : to collect, to gather **3** : to hoard — **amontonarse** *vr*

amor *nm* **1** : love **2** : loved one, beloved **3** **amor propio** : self-esteem **4** **hacer el amor** : to make love

amoral *adj* : amoral

amoratado, -da *adj* : black-and-blue, bruised, livid

amordazar {21} *vt* **1** : to gag, to muzzle **2** : to silence

amorfo, -fa *adj* : shapeless, amorphous

amorío *nm* : love affair, fling

amoroso, -sa *adj* **1** : loving, affectionate **2** : amorous ⟨una mirada amorosa : an amorous glance⟩ **3** : charming, cute — **amorosamente** *adv*

amortiguación *nf* : cushioning, absorption

amortiguador *nm* : shock absorber

amortiguar {10} *vt* : to soften (an impact)

amortizar {21} *vt* : to amortize, to pay off — **amortización** *nf*

amotinado¹, -da *adj* : rebellious, insurgent, mutinous

amotinado², -da *n* : rebel, insurgent, mutineer

amotinamiento *nm* : uprising, rebellion

amotinar *vt* : to incite (to riot), to agitate — **amotinarse** *vr* **1** : to riot, to rebel **2** : to mutiny

amparar *vt* : to safeguard, to protect — **ampararse** *vr* **1** ~ **de** : to take shelter from **2** ~ **en** : to have recourse to

amparo *nmi* ACOGIDA, REFUGIO : protection, refuge

amperímetro *nm* : ammeter

amperio *nm* : ampere

ampliable *adj* : expandable, enlargeable, extendible

ampliación *nf, pl* **-ciones** : expansion, extension

ampliar {85} *vt* **1** : to expand, to extend **2** : to widen **3** : to enlarge (photographs) **4** : to elaborate on, to develop (ideas)

amplificador *nm* : amplifier

amplificar {72} *vt* : to amplify — **amplificación** *nf*

amplio, -plia *adj* : broad, wide, ample — **ampliamente** *adj*

amplitud *nf* **1** : breadth, extent **2** : spaciousness

ampolla *nf* **1** : blister **2** : vial, ampoule

ampollar *vt* : to blister — **ampollarse** *vr*

ampolleta *nf* **1** : small vial **2** : hourglass **3** *Chile* : light bulb

ampulosidad *nf* : pompousness, bombast

ampuloso, -sa *adj* GRANDILOCUENTE : pompous, bombastic — **ampulosamente** *adv*

amputar *vt* : to amputate — **amputación** *nf*

amueblar *vt* : to furnish

amuleto *nm* TALISMÁN : amulet, charm

amurallar *vt* : to wall in, to fortify

anacardo *nm* : cashew nut

anaconda *nf* : anaconda

anacrónico, -ca *adj* : anachronistic

anacronismo *nm* : anachronism

ánade *nmf* **1** : duck **2 ánade real** : mallard

anagrama *nm* : anagram

anal *adj* : anal

anales *nmpl* : annals

analfabetismo *nm* : illiteracy

analfabeto, -ta *adj & n* : illiterate

analgésico[1]**, -ca** *adj* : analgesic, painkilling

analgésico[2] *nm* : painkiller, analgesic

análisis *nm* : analysis

analista *nmf* **1** : analyst **2** : annalist

analítico, -ca *adj* : analytical, analytic — **analíticamente** *adv*

analizar {21} *vt* : to analyze

analogía *nf* : analogy

analógico, -ca *adj* **1** : analogical **2** : analog ⟨computadora analógica : analog computer⟩

análogo, -ga *adj* : analogous, similar

ananá *or* **ananás** *nm, pl* **-nás** : pineapple

anaquel *nm* REPISA : shelf

anaranjado[1]**, -da** *adj* NARANJA : orange-colored

anaranjado[2] *nm* NARANJA : orange (color)

anarquía *nf* : anarchy

anárquico, -ca *adj* : anarchic

anarquismo *nm* : anarchism

anarquista *adj & nmf* : anarchist

anatema *nm* : anathema

anatomía *nf* : anatomy — **anatomista** *nmf*

anatómico, -ca *adj* : anatomical — **anatómicamente** *adv*

anca *nf* **1** : haunch, hindquarter **2 ancas de rana** : frogs' legs

ancestral *adj* **1** : ancient, traditional **2** : ancestral

ancestro *nm* ASCENDIENTE : ancestor, forefather *m*

ancho[1]**, -cha** *adj* **1** : wide, broad **2** : ample, loose-fitting

ancho[2] *nm* : width, breadth

anchoa *nf* : anchovy

anchura *nf* : width, breadth

ancianidad *nf* SENECTUD : old age

anciano[1]**, -na** *adj* : aged, old, elderly

anciano[2]**, -na** *n* : elderly person

ancla *nf* : anchor

ancladero → **anclaje**

anclaje *nm* : anchorage

anclar *v* FONDEAR : to anchor

andadas *nfpl* **1** : tracks **2 volver a las andadas** : to go back to one's old ways, to backslide

andador[1] *nm* **1** : walker, baby walker **2** *Mex* : walkway

andador[2]**, -dora** *n* : walker, one who walks

andadura *nf* : course, journey ⟨su agotadora andadura al campeonato : his exhausting journey to the championship⟩

andaluz, -luza *adj & n, mpl* **-luces** : Andalusian

andamiaje *nm* **1** : scaffolding **2** ESTRUCTURA : structure, framework

andamio *nm* : scaffold

andanada *nf* **1** : volley, broadside **2 soltar una andanada a** : to reprimand

andanzas *nfpl* : adventures

andar[1] {6} *vi* **1** CAMINAR : to walk **2** IR : to go, to travel **3** FUNCIONAR : to run, to function ⟨el auto anda bien : the car runs well⟩ **4** : to ride ⟨andar a caballo : to ride on horseback⟩ **5** : to be ⟨anda sin dinero : he's broke⟩ — *vt* : to walk, to travel

andar[2] *nm* : walk, gait

andas *nfpl* : stand (for a coffin), bier

andén *nm, pl* **andenes 1** : (train) platform **2** *CA, Col* : sidewalk

andino, -na *adj* : Andean

andorrano, -na *adj & n* : Andorran

andrajos *nmpl* : rags, tatters

andrajoso, -sa *adj* : ragged, tattered

andrógino, -na *adj* : androgynous

andurriales *nmpl* : remote place

anea *nf* : cattail

anduvo, etc. → **andar**

anécdota *nf* : anecdote

anecdótico, -ca *adj* : anecdotal

anegar {52} *vt* **1** INUNDAR : to flood **2** AHOGAR : to drown **3** : to overwhelm — **anegarse** *vr* : to be flooded

anejo *nm* → **anexo**[2]

anemia *nf* : anemia

anémico, -ca *adj* : anemic

anémona *nf* : anemone

anestesia *nf* : anesthesia

anestesiar *vt* : to anesthetize

anestésico[1]**, -ca** *adj* : anesthetic

anestésico[2] *nm* : anesthetic

anestesista *nmf* : anesthetist

aneurisma *nm* : aneurysm

anexar *vt* : to annex, to attach

anexión *nf, pl* **-xiones** : annexation

anexo[1]**, -xa** *adj* : attached, joined, annexed

anexo[2] *nm* **1** : annex **2** : supplement (to a book), appendix

anfetamina *nf* : amphetamine

anfibio¹, -bia *adj* : amphibious
**anfibio² ** *nm* : amphibian
anfiteatro *nm* **1** : amphitheater **2** : lecture hall
anfitrión, -triona *n, mpl* **-triones** : host, hostess *f*
ánfora *nf* **1** : amphora **2** *Mex, Peru* : ballot box
ángel *nm* : angel
angelical *adj* : angelic, angelical
angélico, -ca *adj* → **angelical**
angina *nf* **1** *or* **angina de pecho** : angina **2** *Mex* : tonsil
anglicano, -na *adj & n* : Anglican
angloparlante¹ *adj* : English-speaking
**angloparlante² ** *nmf* : English speaker
anglosajón, -jona *adj & n, mpl* **-jones** : Anglo-Saxon
angoleño, -ña *adj & n* : Angolan
angora *nf* : angora
angostar *vt* : to narrow — **angostarse** *vr*
angosto, -ta *adj* : narrow
angostura *nf* : narrowness
anguila *nf* : eel
angular *adj* : angular — **angularidad** *nf*
ángulo *nm* **1** : angle **2** : corner **3** **ángulo muerto** : blind spot
anguloso, -sa *adj* : angular, sharp ⟨una cara angulosa : an angular face⟩ — **angulosidad** *nf*
angustia *nf* **1** CONGOJA : anguish, distress **2** : anxiety, worry
angustiar *vt* **1** : to anguish, to distress **2** : to worry — **angustiarse** *vr*
angustioso, -sa *adj* **1** : anguished, distressed **2** : distressing, worrisome
anhelante *adj* : yearning, longing
anhelar *vt* : to yearn for, to crave
anhelo *nm* : longing, yearning
anidar *vi* **1** : to nest **2** : to make one's home, to dwell — *vt* : to shelter
anillo *nm* SORTIJA : ring
ánima *n* ALMA : soul
animación *nf, pl* **-ciones** **1** : animation **2** VIVEZA : liveliness
animado, -da *adj* **1** : animated, lively **2** : cheerful — **animadamente** *adv*
animador, -dora *n* **1** : (television) host **2** : cheerleader
animadversión *nf, pl* **-siones** ANIMOSIDAD : animosity, antagonism
animal¹ *adj* **1** : animal **2** ESTÚPIDO : stupid, idiotic **3** : rough, brutish
**animal² ** *nm* : animal
animal³ ** *nmf* **1 IDIOTA : idiot, fool **2** : brute, beastly person
animar *vt* **1** ALENTAR : to encourage, to inspire **2** : to animate, to enliven **3** : to brighten up, to cheer up — **animarse** *vr*
anímico, -ca *adj* : mental ⟨estado anímico : state of mind⟩
ánimo *nm* **1** ALMA : spirit, soul **2** : mood, spirits *pl* **3** : encouragement **4** PROPÓSITO : intention, purpose ⟨sociedad sin ánimo de lucro : nonprofit organization⟩ **5** : energy, vitality

animosidad *nf* ANIMADVERSIÓN : animosity, ill will
animoso, -sa *adj* : brave, spirited
aniñado, -da *adj* : childlike
aniquilación *nf* → **aniquilamiento**
aniquilamiento *nm* : annihilation, extermination
aniquilar *vt* **1** : to annihilate, to wipe out **2** : to overwhelm, to bring to one's knees — **aniquilarse** *vr*
anís *nm* **1** : anise **2 semilla de anís** : aniseed
aniversario *nm* : anniversary
ano *nm* : anus
anoche *adv* : last night
anochecer¹ {53} *v impers* : to get dark
**anochecer² ** *nm* : dusk, nightfall
anodino, -na *adj* : insipid, dull
ánodo *nm* : anode
anomalía *nf* : anomaly
anómalo, -la *adj* : anomalous
anonadado, -da *adj* : dumbfounded, speechless
anonadar *vt* : to dumbfound, to stun
anonimato *nm* : anonymity
anónimo, -ma *adj* : anonymous — **anónimamente** *adv*
anorexia *nf* : anorexia
anoréxico, -ca *adj* : anorexic
anormal *adj* : abnormal — **anormalmente** *adv*
anormalidad *nf* : abnormality
anotación *nf, pl* **-ciones** **1** : annotation, note **2** : scoring (in sports) ⟨lograron una anotación : they managed to score a goal⟩
anotar *vt* **1** : to annotate **2** APUNTAR, ESCRIBIR : to write down, to jot down **3** : to score (in sports) — *vi* : to score
anquilosado, -da *adj* **1** : stiff-jointed **2** : stagnated, stale
anquilosamiento *nm* **1** : stiffness (of joints) **2** : stagnation, paralysis
anquilosarse *vr* **1** : to stagnate **2** : to become stiff or paralyzed
anquilostoma *nm* : hookworm
ánsar *nm* : goose
ansarino *nm* : gosling
ansia *nf* **1** INQUIETUD : apprehensiveness, uneasiness **2** ANGUSTIA : anguish, distress **3** ANHELO : longing, yearning
ansiar {85} *vt* : to long for, to yearn for
ansiedad *nf* : anxiety
ansioso, -sa *adj* **1** : anxious, worried **2** : eager — **ansiosamente** *adv*
antagónico, -ca *adj* : conflicting, opposing
antagonismo *nm* : antagonism
antagonista¹ *adj* : antagonistic
**antagonista² ** *nmf* : antagonist, opponent
antagonizar {21} *vt* : to antagonize
antaño *adv* : yesteryear, long ago
antártico, -ca *adj* **1** : antarctic **2 círculo antártico** : antarctic circle
ante¹ *nm* **1** : elk, moose **2** : suede
ante² ** *prep* **1 : before, in front of **2** : considering, in view of **3 ante todo** : first and foremost, above all

anteanoche *adv* : the night before last

anteayer *adv* : the day before yesterday

antebrazo *nm* : forearm

antecedente[1] *adj* : previous, prior

antecedente[2] *nm* **1** : precedent **2 antecedentes** *nmpl* : record, background

anteceder *v* : to precede

antecesor, -sora *n* **1** ANTEPASADO : ancestor **2** PREDECESOR : predecessor

antedicho, -cha *adj* : aforesaid, above

antelación *nf, pl* **-ciones 1** : advance notice **2 con ∼** : in advance, beforehand

antemano *adv* **de ∼** : in advance ⟨se lo agradezco de antemano : I thank you in advance⟩

antena *nf* : antenna

antenoche → **anteanoche**

anteojera *nf* **1** : eyeglass case **2 anteojeras** *nfpl* : blinders

anteojos *nmpl* GAFAS : glasses, eyeglasses

antepasado[1], **-da** *adj* : before last ⟨el domingo antepasado : the Sunday before last⟩

antepasado[2], **-da** *n* ANTECESOR : ancestor

antepecho *nm* **1** : guardrail **2** : ledge, sill

antepenúltimo, -ma *adj* : third from last

anteponer {60} *vt* **1** : to place before ⟨anteponer al interés de la nación el interés de la comunidad : to place the interests of the community before national interest⟩ **2** : to prefer

anteproyecto *nm* **1** : draft, proposal **2 anteproyecto de ley** : bill

antera *nf* : anther

anterior *adj* **1** : previous **2** : earlier ⟨tiempos anteriores : earlier times⟩ **3** : anterior, forward, front

anterioridad *nf* **1** : priority **2 con ∼** : beforehand, in advance

anteriormente *adv* : previously, beforehand

antes *adv* **1** : before, earlier **2** : formerly, previously **3** : rather, sooner ⟨antes prefiero morir : I'd rather die⟩ **4 ∼ de** : before, previous to ⟨antes de hoy : before today⟩ **5 antes que** : before ⟨antes que llegue Luis : before Luis arrives⟩ **6 cuanto antes** : as soon as possible **7 antes bien** : on the contrary

antesala *nf* **1** : anteroom, waiting room, lobby **2** : prelude, prologue

antiaborto, -ta *adj* : antiabortion

antiácido *nm* : antacid

antiadherente *adj* : nonstick

antiaéreo, -rea *adj* : antiaircraft

antiamericano, -na *adj* : anti-American

antibalas *adj* : bulletproof

antibiótico[1], **-ca** *adj* : antibiotic

antibiótico[2] *nm* : antibiotic

antichoque *adj* : shockproof

anticipación *nf, pl* **-ciones 1** : expectation, anticipation **2 con ∼** : in advance

anticipado, -da *adj* **1** : advance, early **2 por ∼** : in advance

anticipar *vt* **1** : to anticipate, to forestall, to deal with in advance **2** : to pay in advance — **anticiparse** *vr* **1** : to be early **2** ADELANTARSE : to get ahead

anticipo *nm* **1** : advance (payment) **2** : foretaste, preview

anticlerical *adj* : anticlerical

anticlimático, -ca *adj* : anticlimactic

anticlímax *nm* : anticlimax

anticomunismo *nm* : anticommunism

anticomunista *adj & nmf* : anticommunist

anticoncepción *nf, pl* **-ciones** : birth control, contraception

anticonceptivo *nm* : contraceptive

anticongelante *nm* : antifreeze

anticuado, -da *adj* : antiquated, outdated

anticuario[1], **-ria** *adj* : antique, antiquarian

anticuario[2], **-ria** *n* : antiquarian, antiquary

anticuario[3] *nm* : antique shop

anticuerpo *nm* : antibody

antidemocrático, -ca *adj* : antidemocratic

antideportivo, -va *adj* : unsportsmanlike

antidepresivo *nm* : antidepressant

antídoto *nm* : antidote

antidrogas *adj* : antidrug

antier → **anteayer**

antiestético, -ca *adj* : unsightly, unattractive

antifascista *adj & nmf* : antifascist

antifaz *nm, pl* **-faces** : mask

antifeminista *adj & nmf* : antifeminist

antífona *nf* : anthem

antígeno *nm* : antigen

antigualla *nf* **1** : antique **2** : relic, old thing

antiguamente *adv* **1** : formerly, once **2** : long ago

antigüedad *nf* **1** : antiquity **2** : seniority **3** : age ⟨con siglos de antigüedad : centuries-old⟩ **4 antigüedades** *nfpl* : antiques

antiguo, -gua *adj* **1** : ancient, old **2** : former **3** : old-fashioned ⟨a la antigua : in the old-fashioned way⟩ **4 Antiguo Testamento** : Old Testament

antihigiénico, -ca *adj* INSALUBRE : unhygienic, unsanitary

antihistamínico *nm* : antihistamine

antiimperialismo *nm* : anti-imperialism

antiimperialista *adj & nmf* : anti-imperialist

antiinflacionario, -ria *adj* : anti-inflationary

antiinflamatorio, -ria *adj* : anti-inflammatory

antillano[1], **-na** *adj* CARIBEÑO : Caribbean, West Indian

antillano[2], **-na** *n* : West Indian

antílope *nm* : antelope

antimilitarismo *nm* : antimilitarism

antimilitarista adj & nmf : antimilitarist
antimonio nm : antimony
antimonopolista adj : antimonopoly, antitrust
antinatural adj : unnatural, perverse
antipatía nf : aversion, dislike
antipático, -ca adj : obnoxious, unpleasant
antipatriótico, -ca adj : unpatriotic
antirrábico, -ca : antirabies ⟨vacuna antirrábica : rabies vaccine⟩
antirreglamentario, -ria adj 1 : unlawful, illegal 2 : foul (in sports)
antirrevolucionario, -ria adj & n : antirevolutionary
antirrobo, -ba adj : antitheft
antisemita adj : anti-Semitic
antisemitismo nm : anti-Semitism
antiséptico¹, -ca adj : antiseptic
antiséptico² nm : antiseptic
antisocial adj : antisocial
antitabaco adj : antismoking
antiterrorista adj : antiterrorist
antítesis nf : antithesis
antitoxina nf : antitoxin
antitranspirante nm : antiperspirant
antojadizo, -za adj CAPRICHOSO : capricious
antojarse vr 1 APETECER : to be appealing, to be desirable ⟨se me antoja un helado : I feel like having ice cream⟩ 2 : to seem, to appear ⟨los árboles se antojan fantasmas : the trees seemed like ghosts⟩
antojitos nmpl Mex : traditional Mexican snack foods
antojo nm 1 CAPRICHO : whim 2 : craving
antología nf 1 : anthology 2 de ~ fam : fantastic, incredible
antónimo nm : antonym
antonomasia nf por ~ : par excellence
antorcha nf : torch
antracita nf : anthracite
antro nm 1 : cave, den 2 : dive, seedy nightclub
antropofagia nf CANIBALISMO : cannibalism
antropófago¹, -ga adj : cannibalistic
antropófago², -ga n CANÍBAL : cannibal
antropoide adj & nmf : anthropoid
antropología nf : anthropology
antropológico, -ca adj : anthropological
antropólogo, -ga n : anthropologist
anual adj : annual, yearly — **anualmente** adv
anualidad nf : annuity
anuario nm : yearbook, annual
anudar vt : to knot, to tie in a knot — **anudarse** vr
anuencia nf : consent
anulación nf, pl **-ciones** : annulment, nullification
anular vt : to annul, to cancel
anunciador, -dora n → **anunciante**
anunciante nmf : advertiser
anunciar vt 1 : to announce 2 : to advertise

anuncio nm 1 : announcement 2 : advertisement, commercial
anzuelo nm 1 : fishhook 2 **morder el anzuelo** : to take the bait
añadido nm : addition
añadidura nf 1 : additive, addition 2 **por ~** : in addition, furthermore
añadir vt 1 AGREGAR : to add 2 AUMENTAR : to increase
añejar vt : to age, to ripen
añejo, -ja adj 1 : aged, vintage 2 : age-old, musty, stale
añicos nmpl : smithereens, bits ⟨hacer(se) añicos : to shatter⟩
añil nm 1 : indigo 2 : bluing
año nm 1 : year ⟨en el año 1990 : in (the year) 1990⟩ ⟨tiene diez años : she is ten years old⟩ 2 : grade ⟨cuarto año : fourth grade⟩ 3 **año bisiesto** : leap year 4 **año luz** : light-year 5 **Año Nuevo** : New Year
añoranza nf : longing, yearning
añorar vt DESEAR : to long for 2 : to grieve for, to miss — vi : to mourn, to grieve
añoso, -sa adj : aged, old
aorta nf : aorta
apabullante adj : overwhelming, crushing
apabullar vt : to overwhelm
apacentar {55} vt : to pasture, to put to pasture
apache adj & nmf : Apache
apachurrado, -da adj fam : depressed, down
apachurrar vt : to crush, to squash
apacible adj : gentle, mild, calm — **apaciblemente** adv
apaciguador, -dora adj : calming
apaciguamiento nm : appeasement
apaciguar {10} vt APLACAR : to appease, to pacify — **apaciguarse** vr : to calm down
apadrinar vt 1 : to be a godparent to 2 : to sponsor, to support
apagado, -da adj 1 : off, out ⟨la luz está apagada : the light is off⟩ 2 : dull, subdued
apagador nm Mex : switch
apagar {52} vt 1 : to turn off, to shut off 2 : to extinguish, to put out — **apagarse** vr 1 : to go out, to fade 2 : to wane, to die down
apagón nm, pl **-gones** : blackout (of power)
apalancamiento nm : leverage
apalancar {72} vt 1 : to jack up 2 : to pry open
apalear vt : to beat up, to thrash
apantallar vt Mex : to dazzle, to impress
apañar vt 1 : to seize, to grasp 2 : to repair, to mend — **apañarse** vr : to manage, to get along
apaño nm fam 1 : patch 2 HABILIDAD : skill, knack
apapachar vt Mex fam : to cuddle, to caress — **apapacharse** vr

aparador *nm* **1** : sideboard, cupboard **2** ESCAPARATE, VITRINA : shop window

aparato *nm* **1** : machine, appliance, apparatus ⟨aparato auditivo : hearing aid⟩ ⟨aparato de televisión : television set⟩ **2** : system ⟨aparato digestivo : digestive system⟩ **3** : display, ostentation ⟨sin aparato : without ceremony⟩ **4 aparatos** *nmpl* : braces (for the teeth)

aparatoso, -sa *adj* **1** : ostentatious **2** : spectacular

aparcamiento *nm Spain* **1** : parking **2** : parking lot

aparcar {72} *v Spain* : to park

aparcero, -ra *n* : sharecropper

aparear *vt* **1** : to mate (animals) **2** : to match up — **aparearse** *vr* : to mate

aparecer {53} *vi* **1** : to appear **2** PRESENTARSE : to show up **3** : to turn up, to be found — **aparecerse** *vr* : to appear

aparejado, -da *adj* **1 ir aparejado con** : to go hand in hand with **2 llevar aparejado** : to entail

aparejar *vt* **1** PREPARAR : to prepare, to make ready **2** : to harness (a horse) **3** : to fit out (a ship)

aparejo *nm* **1** : equipment, gear **2** : harness, saddle **3** : rig, rigging (of a ship)

aparentar *vt* **1** : to seem, to appear ⟨no aparentas tu edad : you don't look your age⟩ **2** FINGIR : to feign, to pretend

aparente *adj* **1** : apparent **2** : showy, striking — **aparentemente** *adv*

aparición *nf, pl* **-ciones 1** : appearance **2** PUBLICACIÓN : publication, release **3** FANTASMA : apparition, vision

apariencia *nf* **1** ASPECTO : appearance, look **2 en ~** : seemingly, apparently

apartado *nm* **1** : section, paragraph **2 apartado postal** : post office box

apartamento *nm* DEPARTAMENTO : apartment

apartar *vt* **1** ALEJAR : to move away, to put at a distance **2** : to put aside, to set aside, to separate — **apartarse** *vr* **1** : to step aside, to move away **2** DESVIARSE : to stray

aparte[1] *adv* **1** : apart, aside ⟨modestia aparte : if I say so myself⟩ **2** : separately **3 ~ de** : apart from, besides

aparte[2] *adj* : separate, special

aparte[3] *nm* : aside (in theater)

apartheid *nm* : apartheid

apasionado, -da *adj* : passionate, enthusiastic — **apasionadamente** *adv*

apasionante *adj* : fascinating, exciting

apasionar *vt* : to enthuse, to excite — **apasionarse** *vr*

apatía *nf* : apathy

apático, -ca *adj* : apathetic

apearse *vr* **1** DESMONTAR : to dismount **2** : to get out of or off (a vehicle)

apedrear *vt* : to stone, to throw stones at

apegado, -da *adj* : attached, close, devoted ⟨es muy apegado a su familia : he is very devoted to his family⟩

apegarse {52} *vr* **~ a** : to become attached to, to grow fond of

apego *nm* AFICIÓN : attachment, fondness, inclination

apelación *nf, pl* **-ciones** : appeal (in court)

apelar *vi* **1** : to appeal **2 ~ a** : to resort to

apelativo *nm* APELLIDO : last name, surname

apellidarse *vr* : to have for a last name ⟨¿cómo se apellida? : what is your last name?⟩

apellido *nm* : last name, surname

apelotonar *vt* : to roll into a ball, to bundle up

apenar *vt* : to aggrieve, to sadden — **apenarse** *vr* **1** : to be saddened **2** : to become embarrassed

apenas[1] *adv* : hardly, scarcely

apenas[2] *conj* : as soon as

apéndice *nm* **1** : appendix **2** : appendage

apendicectomía *nf* : appendectomy

apendicitis *nf* : appendicitis

apercibimiento *nm* **1** : preparation **2** AMONESTACIÓN : warning

apercibir *vt* **1** DISPONER : to prepare, to make ready **2** AMONESTAR : to warn **3** OBSERVAR : to observe, to perceive — **apercibirse** *vr* **1** : to get ready **2 ~ de** : to notice

aperitivo *nm* **1** : appetizer **2** : aperitif

apero *nm* : tool, implement

apertura *nf* **1** : opening, aperture **2** : commencement, beginning **3** : openness

apesadumbrar *vt* : to distress, to sadden — **apesadumbrarse** *vr* : to be weighed down

apestar *vt* **1** : to infect with the plague **2** : to corrupt — *vi* : to stink

apestoso, -sa *adj* : stinking, foul

apetecer {53} *vt* **1** : to crave, to long for ⟨apeteció la fama : he longed for fame⟩ **2** : to appeal to ⟨me apetece un bistec : I feel like having a steak⟩ ⟨¿cuándo te apetece ir? : when do you want to go?⟩ — *vi* : to be appealing

apetecible *adj* : appetizing, appealing

apetito *nm* : appetite

apetitoso, -sa *adj* : appetizing

apiario *nm* : apiary

ápice *nm* **1** : apex, summit **2** PIZCA : bit, smidgen

apicultor, -tora *n* : beekeeper

apicultura *nf* : beekeeping

apilar *vt* : to heap up, to pile up — **apilarse** *vr*

apiñado, -da *adj* : jammed, crowded

apiñar *vt* : to pack, to cram — **apiñarse** *vr* : to crowd together, to huddle

apio *nm* : celery

apisonadora *nf* : steamroller

apisonar *vt* : to pack down, to tamp

aplacamiento *nm* : appeasement

aplacar {72} *vt* APACIGUAR : to appease, to placate — **aplacarse** *vr* : to calm down

aplanadora *nf* : steamroller
aplanar *vt* : to flatten, to level
aplastante *adj* : crushing, overwhelming
aplastar *vt* : to crush, to squash
aplaudir *v* : to applaud
aplauso *nm* **1** : applause, clapping **2** : praise, acclaim
aplazamiento *nm* : postponement
aplazar {21} *vt* : to postpone, to defer
aplicable *adj* : applicable — **aplicabilidad** *nf*
aplicación *nf, pl* **-ciones 1** : application **2** : diligence, dedication
aplicado, -da *adj* : diligent, industrious
aplicador *nm* : applicator
aplicar {72} *vt* : to apply — **aplicarse** *vr* : to apply oneself
aplique *or* **apliqué** *nm* : appliqué
aplomar *vt* : to plumb, to make vertical
aplomo *nm* : aplomb, composure
apocado, -da *adj* : timid
apocalipsis *nms & pl* : apocalypse ⟨el Libro del Apocalipsis : the Book of Revelation⟩
apocalíptico, -ca *adj* : apocalyptic
apocamiento *nm* : timidity
apocarse {72} *vr* **1** : to shy away, to be intimidated **2** : to humble oneself, to sell oneself short
apócrifo, -fa *adj* : apocryphal
apodar *vt* : to nickname, to call — **apodarse** *vr*
apoderado, -da *n* : proxy, agent
apoderar *vt* : to authorize, to empower — **apoderarse** *vr* ~ **de** : to seize, to take over
apodo *nm* SOBRENOMBRE : nickname
apogeo *nm* : acme, peak, zenith
apología *nf* : defense, apology
apoplejía *nf* : apoplexy, stroke
apopléctico, -ca *adj* : apoplectic
aporrear *vt* : to bang on, to beat, to bludgeon
aportación *nf, pl* **-ciones** : contribution
aportar *vt* CONTRIBUIR : to contribute, to provide
aporte *nm* → **aportación**
apostador, -dora *n* : bettor, better
apostar {19} *v* : to bet, to wager ⟨apuesto que no viene : I bet he's not coming⟩
apostasía *nf* : apostasy
apóstata *nmf* : apostate
apostilla *nf* : note
apostillar *vt* : to annotate
apóstol *nm* : apostle
apostólico, -ca *adj* : apostolic
apóstrofe *nmf* : apostrophe
apostura *nf* : elegance, gracefulness
apoyacabezas *nms & pl* : headrest
apoyapiés *nms & pl* : footrest
apoyar *vt* **1** : to support, to back **2** : to lean, to rest — **apoyarse** *vr* **1** ~ **en** : to lean on **2** ~ **en** : to be based on, to rest on
apoyo *nm* : support, backing
apreciable *adj* : appreciable, substantial, considerable

apreciación *nf, pl* **-ciones 1** : appreciation **2** : appraisal, evaluation
apreciar *vt* **1** ESTIMAR : to appreciate, to value **2** EVALUAR : to appraise, to assess — **apreciarse** *vr* : to appreciate, to increase in value
aprecio *nm* **1** ESTIMO : esteem, appreciation **2** EVALUACIÓN : appraisal, assessment
aprehender *vt* **1** : to apprehend, to capture **2** : to conceive of, to grasp
aprehensión *nf, pl* **-siones** : apprehension, capture, arrest
apremiante *adj* : pressing, urgent
apremiar *vt* INSTAR : to pressure, to urge — *vi* URGIR : to be urgent ⟨el tiempo apremia : time is of the essence⟩
apremio *nm* : pressure, urgency
aprender *v* : to learn — **aprenderse** *vr*
aprendiz, -diza *n, mpl* **-dices** : apprentice, trainee
aprendizaje *nm* : apprenticeship
aprensión *nf, pl* **-siones** : apprehension, dread
aprensivo, -va *adj* : apprehensive, worried
apresamiento *nm* : seizure, capture
apresar *vt* : to capture, to seize
aprestar *vt* : to make ready, to prepare — **aprestarse** *vr* : to get ready
apresuradamente *adv* **1** : hurriedly **2** : hastily, too fast
apresurado, -da *adj* : hurried, in a rush
apresuramiento *nm* : hurry, haste
apresurar *vt* : to quicken, to speed up — **apresurarse** *vr* : to hurry up, to make haste
apretado, -da *adj* **1** : tight **2** *fam* : cheap, tightfisted — **apretadamente** *adv*
apretar {55} *vt* **1** : to press, to push (a button) **2** : to tighten **3** : to squeeze — *vi* **1** : to press, to push **2** : to fit tightly, to be too tight ⟨los zapatos me aprietan : my shoes are tight⟩
apretón *nm, pl* **-tones 1** : squeeze **2**
apretón de manos : handshake
apretujar *vt* : to squash, to squeeze — **apretujarse** *vr*
aprieto *nm* APURO : predicament, difficulty ⟨estar en un aprieto : to be in a fix⟩
aprisa *adv* : quickly, hurriedly
aprisionar *vt* **1** : to imprison **2** : to trap, to box in
aprobación *nf, pl* **-ciones** : approval, endorsement
aprobar {19} *vt* **1** : to approve of **2** : to pass (a law, an exam) — *vi* : to pass (in school)
aprobatorio, -ria *adj* : approving
apropiación *nf, pl* **-ciones** : appropriation
apropiado, -da *adj* : appropriate, proper, suitable — **apropiadamente** *adv*
apropiarse *vr* ~ **de** : to take possession of, to appropriate
aprovechable *adj* : usable

aprovechado¹, -da *adj* **1** : diligent, hardworking **2** : pushy, opportunistic

aprovechado², -da *n* : pushy person, opportunist

aprovechamiento *nm* : use, exploitation

aprovechar *vt* : to take advantage of, to make good use of.of — *vi* **1** : to be of use **2** : to progress, to improve — **aprovecharse** *vr* ~ **de** : to take advantage of, to exploit

aprovisionamiento *nm* : provisions *pl*, supplies *pl*

aprovisionar *vt* : to provide, to supply (with provisions)

aproximación *nf, pl* **-ciones 1** : approximation, estimate **2** : rapprochement

aproximado, -da *adj* : approximate, estimated — **aproximadamente** *adv*

aproximar *vt* ACERCAR, ARRIMAR : to approximate, to bring closer — **aproximarse** *vr* ACERCARSE, ARRIMARSE : to approach, to move closer

aptitud *nf* : aptitude, capability

apto, -ta *adj* **1** : suitable, suited, fit **2** HÁBIL : capable, competent

apuesta *nf* : bet, wager

apuesto, -ta *adj* : elegant, good-looking

apuntador, -dora *n* : prompter

apuntalar *vt* : to prop up, to shore up

apuntar *vt* **1** : to aim, to point **2** ANOTAR : to write down, to jot down **3** INDICAR, SEÑALAR : to point to, to point out **4** : to prompt (in the theater) — *vi* **1** : to take aim **2** : to become evident — **apuntarse** *vr* **1** : to sign up, to enroll **2** : to score

apunte *nm* : note

apuñalar *vt* : to stab

apuradamente *adv* **1** : with difficulty **2** : hurriedly, hastily

apurado, -da *adj* **1** APRESURADO : rushed, pressured **2** : poor, needy **3** : difficult, awkward **4** embarrassed

apurar *vt* **1** APRESURAR : to hurry, to rush **2** : to use up, to exhaust **3** : to trouble — **apurarse** *vr* **1** APRESURARSE : to hurry up **2** PREOCUPARSE : to worry

apuro *nm* **1** APRIETO : predicament, jam **2** : rush, hurry **3** : embarrassment

aquejar *vt* : to afflict

aquel, aquella *adj, mpl* **aquellos** : that, those

aquél, aquélla *pron, mpl* **aquéllos 1** : that (one), those (ones) **2** : the former

aquello *pron (neuter)* : that, that matter, that business ⟨aquello fue algo serio : that was something serious⟩

aquí *adv* **1** : here **2** : now ⟨de aquí en adelante : from now on⟩ **3** por ~ : around here, hereabouts

aquiescencia *nf* : acquiescence, approval

aquietar *vt* : to allay, to calm — **aquietarse** *vr* : to calm down

aquilatar *vt* **1** : to assay **2** : to assess, to size up

ara *nf* **1** : altar **2 en aras de** : in the interests of, for the sake of

árabe¹ *adj & nmf* : Arab, Arabian

árabe² *nm* : Arabic (language)

arabesco *nm* : arabesque — **arabesco, -ca** *adj*

arábigo, -ga *adj* **1** : Arabic, Arabian **2 número arábigo** : Arabic numeral

arable *adj* : arable

arado *nm* : plow

aragonés, -nesa *adj & n, mpl* **-neses** : Aragonese

arancel *nm* : tariff, duty

arándano *nm* : blueberry

arandela *nf* : washer (for a faucet, etc.)

araña *nf* **1** : spider **2** : chandelier

arañar *v* : to scratch, to claw

arañazo *nm* : scratch

arar *v* : to plow

arbitraje *nm* **1** : arbitration **2** : refereeing (in sports)

arbitrar *v* **1** : to arbitrate **2** : to referee, to umpire

arbitrariedad *nf* **1** : arbitrariness **2** INJUSTICIA : injustice, wrong

arbitrario, -ria *adj* **1** : arbitrary **2** : unfair, unjust — **arbitrariamente** *adv*

arbitrio *nm* **1** ALBEDRÍO : will **2** JUICIO : judgment

árbitro, -tra *n* **1** : arbitrator, arbiter **2** : referee, umpire

árbol *nm* **1** : tree **2 árbol genealógico** : family tree

arbolado¹, -da *adj* : wooded

arbolado² *nm* : woodland

arboleda *nf* : grove, wood

arbóreo, -rea *adj* : arboreal

arbusto *nm* : shrub, bush, hedge

arca *nf* **1** : ark **2** : coffer, chest

arcada *nf* **1** : arcade, series of arches **2 arcadas** *nfpl* : retching ⟨hacer arcadas : to retch⟩

arcaico, -ca *adj* : archaic

arcángel *nm* : archangel

arcano, -na *adj* : arcane

arce *nm* : maple tree

arcén *nm, pl* **arcenes** : hard shoulder, berm

archidiócesis *nfs & pl* : archdiocese

archipiélago *nm* : archipelago

archivador *nm* : filing cabinet

archivar *vt* **1** : to file **2** : to archive

archivero, -ra *n* : archivist

archivista *nmf* : archivist

archivo *nm* **1** : file **2** : archive, archives *pl*

arcilla *nf* : clay

arco *nm* **1** : arch, archway **2** : bow (in archery) **3** : arc **4** : wicket (in croquet) **5** PORTERÍA : goal, goalposts *pl* **6 arco iris** : rainbow

arder *vi* **1** : to burn ⟨el bosque está ardiendo : the forest is in flames⟩ ⟨arder de ira : to burn with anger, to be seething⟩ **2** : to smart, to sting, to burn ⟨le ardía el estómago : he had heartburn⟩

ardid *nm* : scheme, ruse

ardiente *adj* 1 : burning 2 : ardent, passionate — **ardientemente** *adv*

ardilla *nf* 1 : squirrel 2 *or* **ardilla listada** : chipmunk

ardor *nm* 1 : heat 2 : passion, ardor

ardoroso, -sa *adj* : heated, impassioned

arduo, -dua *adj* : arduous, grueling — **arduamente** *adv*

área *nf* : area

arena *nf* 1 : sand ⟨arena movediza : quicksand⟩ 2 : arena

arenga *nf* : harangue, lecture

arengar {52} *vt* : to harangue, to lecture

arenilla *nf* 1 : fine sand 2 **arenillas** *nfpl* : kidney stones

arenisca *nf* : sandstone

arenoso, -sa *adj* : sandy, gritty

arenque *nm* : herring

arepa *nf* : cornmeal bread

arete *nm* : earring

argamasa *nf* : mortar (cement)

argelino, -na *adj & n* : Algerian

argentino, -na *adj & n* : Argentinian, Argentine

argolla *nf* : hoop, ring

argón *nm* : argon

argot *nm* : slang

argucia *nf* : sophistry, subtlety

argüir {41} *vi* : to argue — *vt* 1 ARGUMENTAR : to contend, to argue 2 INFERIR : to deduce 3 PROBAR : to prove

argumentación *nf, pl* **-ciones** : line of reasoning, argument

argumentar *vt* : to argue, to contend

argumento *nm* 1 : argument, reasoning 2 : plot, story line

aria *nf* : aria

aridez *nf, pl* **-deces** : aridity, dryness

árido, -da *adj* : arid, dry

Aries *nmf* : Aries

ariete *nm* : battering ram

arisco, -ca *adj* : surly, sullen, unsociable

arista *nf* 1 : ridge, edge 2 : beard (of a plant) 3 **aristas** *nfpl* : rough edges, complications, problems

aristocracia *nf* : aristocracy

aristócrata *nmf* : aristocrat

aristocrático, -ca *adj* : aristocratic

aritmética *nf* : arithmetic

aritmético, -ca *adj* : arithmetic, arithmetical — **aritméticamente** *adv*

arlequín *nm, pl* **-quines** : harlequin

arma *nf* 1 : weapon 2 **armas** *nfpl* : armed forces 3 **arma de fuego** : firearm

armada *nf* : navy, fleet

armadillo *nm* : armadillo

armado, -da *adj* 1 : armed 2 : assembled, put together 3 *PRi* : obstinate, stubborn

armador, -dora *n* : shipowner

armadura *nf* 1 : armor 2 ARMAZÓN : skeleton, framework

armamento *nm* : armament, arms *pl*, weaponry

armar *vt* 1 : to assemble, to put together 2 : to create, to cause ⟨armar un escándalo : to cause a scene⟩ 3 : to arm — **armarse** *vr* **armarse de valor** : to steel oneself

armario *nm* 1 CLÓSET, ROPERO : closet 2 ALACENA : cupboard

armatoste *nm fam* : monstrosity, contraption

armazón *nmf, pl* **-zones** 1 ESQUELETO : framework, skeleton ⟨armazón de acero : steel framework⟩ 2 : frames *pl* (of eyeglasses)

armenio, -nia *adj & n* : Armenian

armería *nf* 1 : armory 2 : arms museum 3 : gunsmith's shop 4 : gunsmith's craft

armiño *nm* : ermine

armisticio *nm* : armistice

armonía *nf* : harmony

armónica *nf* : harmonica

armónico, -ca *adj* 1 : harmonic 2 : harmonious — **armónicamente** *adv*

armonioso, -sa *adj* : harmonious — **armoniosamente** *adv*

armonizar {21} *vt* 1 : to harmonize 2 : to reconcile — *vi* : to harmonize, to blend together

arnés *nm, pl* **arneses** : harness

aro *nm* 1 : hoop 2 : napkin ring 3 *Arg, Chile, Uru* : earring

aroma *nm* : aroma, scent

aromático, -ca *adj* : aromatic

arpa *nf* : harp

arpegio *nm* : arpeggio

arpía *nf* : shrew, harpy

arpillera *nf* : burlap

arpista *nmf* : harpist

arpón *nm, pl* **arpones** : harpoon — **arponear** *vt*

arquear *vt* : to arch, to bend — **arquearse** *vr* : to bend, to bow

arqueología *nf* : archaeology

arqueológico, -ca *adj* : archaeological

arqueólogo, -ga *n* : archaeologist

arquero, -ra *n* 1 : archer 2 PORTERO : goalkeeper, goalie

arquetípico, -ca *adj* : archetypal

arquetipo *nm* : archetype

arquitecto, -ta *n* : architect

arquitectónico, -ca *adj* : architectural — **aquitectónicamente** *adv*

arquitectura *nf* : architecture

arrabal *nm* 1 : slum 2 **arrabales** *nmpl* : outskirts, outlying area

arracada *nf* : hoop earring

arracimarse *vr* : to cluster together

arraigado, -da *adj* : deep-seated, ingrained

arraigar {52} *vi* : to take root, to become established — **arraigarse** *vr*

arraigo *nm* : roots *pl* ⟨con mucho arraigo : deep-rooted⟩

arrancar {72} *vt* 1 : to pull out, to tear out 2 : to pick, to pluck (a flower) 3 : to start (an engine) 4 : to boot (a computer) — *vi* 1 : to start an engine 2 : to get going — **arrancarse** *vr* : to pull out, to pull off

arrancón *nm, pl* **-cones** *Mex* **1** : sudden loud start (of a car) **2 carrera de arrancones** : drag race

arranque *nm* **1** : starter (of a car) **2 ARREBATO** : outburst, fit **3 punto de arranque** : beginning, starting point

arrasar *vt* **1** : to level, to smooth **2** : to devastate, to destroy **3** : to fill to the brim

arrastrar *vt* **1** : to drag, to tow **2** : to draw, to attract — *vi* : to hang down, to trail — **arrastrarse** *vr* **1** : to crawl **2** : to grovel

arrastre *nm* **1** : dragging **2** : pull, attraction **3 red de arrastre** : dragnet, trawling net

arrayán *nm, pl* **-yanes 1** MIRTO : myrtle **2 arrayán brabántico** : bayberry, wax myrtle

arrear *vt* : to urge on, to drive — *vi* : to hurry along

arrebatado, -da *adj* **1** PRECIPITADO : impetuous, hotheaded, rash **2** : flushed, blushing

arrebatar *vt* **1** : to snatch, to seize **2** CAUTIVAR : to captivate — **arrebatarse** *vr* : to get carried away (with anger, etc.)

arrebato *nm* ARRANQUE : fit, outburst

arreciar *vi* : to intensify, to worsen

arrecife *nm* : reef

arreglado, -da *adj* **1** : fixed, repaired **2** : settled, sorted out **3** : neat, tidy **4** : smart, dressed-up

arreglar *vt* **1** COMPONER : to repair, to fix **2** : to tidy up ⟨arregla tu cuarto : pick up your room⟩ **3** : to solve, to work out ⟨quiero arreglar este asunto : I want to settle this matter⟩ — **arreglarse** *vr* **1** : to get dressed (up) ⟨arreglarse el pelo : to get one's hair done⟩ **2 arreglárselas** *fam* : to get by, to manage

arreglo *nm* **1** : repair **2** : arrangement **3** : agreement, understanding

arrellanarse *vr* : to settle (in a chair)

arremangarse {52} *vr* : to roll up one's sleeves

arremeter *vi* EMBESTIR : to attack, to charge

arremetida *nf* EMBESTIDA : attack, onslaught

arremolinarse *vr* **1** : to crowd around, to mill about **2** : to swirl (about)

arrendador, -dora *n* **1** : landlord, landlady *f* **2** : tenant, lessee

arrendajo *nm* : jay

arrendamiento *nm* **1** ALQUILER : rental, leasing **2 contrato de arrendamiento** : lease

arrendar {55} *vt* ALQUILAR : to rent, to lease

arrendatario, -ria *n* : tenant, lessee, renter

arreos *nmpl* GUARNICIONES : tack, harness, trappings

arrepentido, -da *adj* : repentant, remorseful

arrepentimiento *nm* : regret, remorse, repentance

arrepentirse {76} *vr* **1** : to regret, to be sorry **2** : to repent

arrestar *vt* DETENER : to arrest, to detain

arresto *nm* **1** DETENCIÓN : arrest **2 arrestos** *nmpl* : boldness, daring

arriar {85} *vt* **1** : to lower (a flag, etc.) **2** : to slacken (a rope, etc.)

arriate *nm Mex, Spain* : bed (for plants), border

arriba *adv* **1** : up, upwards **2** : above, overhead **3** : upstairs **4** ~ **de** : more than **5 de arriba abajo** : from top to bottom, from head to foot

arribar *vi* **1** : to arrive **2** : to dock, to put into port

arribista *nmf* : parvenu, upstart

arribo *nm* : arrival

arriendo *nm* ARRENDAMIENTO : rent, rental

arriero, -ra *n* : mule driver, muleteer

arriesgado, -da *adj* **1** : risky **2** : bold, daring

arriesgar {52} *vt* : to risk, to venture — **arriesgarse** *vr* : to take a chance

arrimado, -da *n Mex fam* : sponger, freeloader

arrimar *vt* ACERCAR, APROXIMAR : to bring closer, to draw near — **arrimarse** *vr* ACERCARSE, APROXIMARSE : to approach, to get close

arrinconar *vt* **1** ACORRALAR : to corner, to box in **2** : to push aside, to abandon

arroba *nf* : arroba (Spanish unit of measurement)

arrobamiento *nm* : rapture, ecstasy

arrobar *vt* : to enrapture, to enchant — **arrobarse** *vr*

arrocero¹, -ra *adj* : rice

arrocero², -ra *n* : rice grower

arrodillarse *vr* : to kneel (down)

arrogancia *nf* ALTANERÍA, ALTIVEZ : arrogance, haughtiness

arrogante *adj* ALTANERO, ALTIVO : arrogant, haughty

arrogarse {52} *vr* : to usurp, to arrogate

arrojado, -da *adj* : daring, fearless

arrojar *vt* **1** : to hurl, to cast, to throw **2** : to give off, to spew out **3** : to yield, to produce **4** *fam* : to vomit — **arrojarse** *vr* PRECIPITARSE : to throw oneself, to leap

arrojo *nm* : boldness, fearlessness

arrollador, -dora *adj* : sweeping, overwhelming

arrollar *vt* **1** : to sweep away, to carry away **2** : to crush, to overwhelm **3** : to run over (with a vehicle)

arropar *vt* : to clothe, to cover (up) — **arroparse** *vr*

arrostrar *vt* : to confront, to face (up to)

arroyo *nm* **1** RIACHUELO : brook, creek, stream **2** : gutter

arroz *nm, pl* **arroces** : rice

arrozal *nm* : rice field, rice paddy

arruga *nf* : wrinkle, fold, crease

arrugado, -da *adj* : wrinkled, creased, lined

arrugar {52} *vt* : to wrinkle, to crease, to pucker — **arrugarse** *vr*

arruinar *vt* : to ruin, to wreck — **arruinarse** *vr* **1** : to be ruined **2** : to fall into ruin, to go bankrupt

arrullar *vt* : to lull to sleep — *vi* : to coo

arrullo *nm* **1** : lullaby **2** : coo (of a dove)

arrumaco *nm fam* : kissing, cuddling

arrumbar *vt* **1** : to lay aside, to put away **2** : to floor, to leave speechless

arsenal *nm* : arsenal

arsénico *nm* : arsenic

arte *nmf (usually m in singular, f in plural)* **1** : art ⟨artes y oficios : arts and crafts⟩ ⟨bellas artes : fine arts⟩ **2** HABILIDAD : skill **3** : cunning, cleverness

artefacto *nm* **1** : artifact **2** DISPOSITIVO : device

artemisa *nf* : sagebrush

arteria *nf* : artery — **arterial** *adj*

arteriosclerosis *nf* : arteriosclerosis, hardening of the arteries

artero, -ra *adj* : wily, crafty

artesanal *adj* : pertaining to crafts or craftsmanship, handmade

artesanía *nf* **1** : craftsmanship **2** : handicrafts *pl*

artesano, -na *n* : artisan, craftsman *m*, craftsperson

artesiano, -na *adj* : artesian ⟨pozo artesiano : artesian well⟩

ártico, -ca *adj* : arctic

articulación *nf, pl* **-ciones** **1** : articulation, pronunciation **2** COYUNTURA : joint

articular *vt* **1** : to articulate, to utter **2** : to connect with a joint **3** : to coordinate, to orchestrate

articulista *nmf* : columnist

artículo *nm* **1** : article, thing **2** : item, feature, report **3** artículo de comercio : commodity **4** artículos de primera necesidad : essentials **5** artículos de tocador : toiletries

artífice *nmf* **1** ARTESANO : artisan **2** : mastermind, architect

artificial *adj* **1** : artificial, man-made **2** : feigned, false — **artificialmente** *adv*

artificio *nm* **1** HABILIDAD : skill **2** APARATO : device, appliance **3** ARDID : artifice, ruse

artificioso, -sa *adj* **1** : skillful **2** : cunning, deceptive

artillería *nf* : artillery

artillero, -ra *n* : artilleryman *m*, gunner

artilugio *nm* : gadget, contraption

artimaña *nf* : ruse, trick

artista *nmf* **1** : artist **2** ACTOR, ACTRIZ : actor, actress *f*

artístico, -ca *adj* : artistic — **artísticamente** *adv*

artrítico, -ca *adj* : arthritic

artritis *nfs & pl* : arthritis

artrópodo *nm* : arthropod

arveja *nf* GUISANTE : pea

arzobispado *nm* : archbishopric

arzobispo *nm* : archbishop

as *nm* : ace

asa *nf* AGARRADERA, ASIDERO : handle, grip

asado¹, -da *adj* : roasted, grilled, broiled

asado² *nm* **1** : roast **2** : barbecued meat **3** : barbecue, cookout

asador *nm* : spit, rotisserie

asaduras *nfpl* : entrails, offal

asalariado¹, -da *adj* : wage-earning, salaried

asalariado², -da *n* : wage earner

asaltante *nmf* **1** : mugger, robber **2** : assailant

asaltar *vt* **1** : to assault **2** : to mug, to rob **3** asaltar al poder : to seize power

asalto *nm* **1** : assault **2** : mugging, robbery **3** : round (in boxing) **4** asalto al poder : coup d'etat

asamblea *nf* : assembly, meeting

asambleísta *nmf* : assemblyman *m*, assemblywoman *f*

asar *vt* : to roast, to grill — **asarse** *vr fam* : to roast, to be dying from heat

asbesto *nm* : asbestos

ascendencia *nf* **1** : ancestry, descent **2** ~ **sobre** : influence over

ascendente *adj* : ascending, upward ⟨un curso ascendente : an upward trend⟩

ascender {56} *vt* **1** : to ascend, to rise up **2** : to be promoted ⟨ascendió a gerente : she was promoted to manager⟩ **3** ~ **a** : to amount to, to reach ⟨las deudas ascienden a 20 millones de pesos : the debt amounts to 20 million pesos⟩ — *vt* : to promote

ascendiente¹ *nmf* ANCESTRO : ancestor

ascendiente² *nm* INFLUENCIA : influence, ascendancy

ascensión *nf, pl* **-siones** **1** : ascent, rise **2** Fiesta de la Ascensión : Ascension Day

ascenso *nm* **1** : ascent, rise **2** : promotion

ascensor *nm* ELEVADOR : elevator

asceta *nmf* : ascetic

ascético, -ca *adj* : ascetic

ascetismo *nm* : asceticism

asco *nm* **1** : disgust ⟨¡qué asco! : that's disgusting!, how revolting!⟩ **2** darle asco (a alguien) : to sicken, to revolt **3** estar hecho un asco : to be filthy **4** hacerle ascos a : to turn up one's nose at

ascua *nf* **1** BRASA : ember **2** estar en ascuas *fam* : to be on edge

asear *vt* **1** : to wash, to clean **2** : to tidy up — **asearse** *vr*

asechanza *nf* : snare, trap

asechar *vt* : to set a trap for

asediar *vt* **1** SITIAR : to besiege **2** ACOSAR : to harass

asedio *nm* **1** : siege **2** ACOSO : harassment

asegurador¹, -dora *adj* **1** : insuring, assuring **2** : pertaining to insurance

asegurador², -dora *n* : insurer, underwriter

aseguradora *nf* : insurance company

asegurar *vt* **1** : to assure **2** : to secure **3** : to insure — **asegurarse** *vr* **1** CERCIORARSE : to make sure **2** : to take out insurance, to insure oneself

asemejar *vt* **1** : to make similar ⟨ese bigote te asemeja a tu abuelo : that mustache makes you look like your grandfather⟩ **2** *Mex* : to be similar to, to resemble — **asemejarse** *vr* ~ **a** : to look like, to resemble

asentaderas *nfpl fam* : bottom, buttocks *pl*

asentado, -da *adj* : settled, established

asentamiento *nm* : settlement

asentar {55} *vt* **1** : to lay down, to set down, to place **2** : to settle, to establish **3** *Mex* : to state, to affirm — **asentarse** *vr* **1** : to settle **2** ESTABLECERSE : to settle down, to establish oneself

asentimiento *nm* : assent, consent

asentir {76} *vt* : to consent, to agree

aseo *nm* : cleanliness

aséptico, -ca *adj* : aseptic, germ-free

asequible *adj* ACCESIBLE : accessible, attainable

aserción *nf* → aserto

aserradero *nm* : sawmill

aserrar {55} *vt* : to saw

aserrín *nm, pl* **-rrines** : sawdust

aserto *nm* : assertion, affirmation

asesinar *vt* **1** : to murder **2** : to assassinate

asesinato *nm* **1** : murder **2** : assassination

asesino¹, -na *adj* : murderous, homicidal

asesino², -na *n* **1** : murderer, killer **2** : assassin

asesor, -sora *n* : advisor, consultant

asesoramiento *nm* : advice, counsel

asesorar *vt* : to advise, to counsel — **asesorarse** *vr* ~ **de** : to consult

asesoría *nf* **1** : consulting, advising **2** : consultant's office

asestar {55} *vt* **1** : to aim, to point (a weapon) **2** : to deliver, to deal (a blow)

aseveración *nf, pl* **-ciones** : assertion, statement

aseverar *vt* : to assert, to state

asexual *adj* : asexual — **asexualmente** *adv*

asfaltado¹, -da *adj* : asphalted, paved

asfaltado² *nm* PAVIMENTO : pavement, asphalt

asfaltar *vt* : to pave, to blacktop

asfalto *nm* : asphalt

asfixia *nf* : asphyxia, asphyxiation, suffocation

asfixiar *vt* : to asphyxiate, to suffocate, to smother — **asfixiarse** *vr*

asga, etc. → asir

así¹ *adv* **1** : like this, like that **2** : so, thus ⟨así sea : so be it⟩ **3** ~ **de** : so, about so ⟨una caja así de grande : a box about so big⟩ **así que** : so, therefore

5 ~ **como** : as well as **6 así así** : so-so, fair

así² *adj* : such, such a ⟨un talento así es inestimable : a talent like this is priceless⟩

así³ *conj* AUNQUE : even if, even though ⟨no irá, así le paguen : he won't go, even if they pay him⟩

asiático¹, -ca *adj* : Asian, Asiatic

asiático², -ca *n* : Asian

asidero *nm* **1** AGARRADERA, ASA : grip, handle **2** AGARRE : grip, hold

asiduamente *adv* : regularly, frequently

asiduidad *nf* **1** : assiduousness **2** : regularity, frequency

asiduo, -dua *adj* **1** : assiduous **2** : frequent, regular

asiento *nm* **1** : seat, chair ⟨asiento trasero : back seat⟩ **2** : location, site

asignación *nf, pl* **-ciones 1** : allocation **2** : appointment, designation **3** : allowance, pay **4** *PRi* : homework, assignment

asignar *vt* **1** : to assign, to allocate **2** : to appoint

asignatura *nf* MATERIA : subject, course

asilado, -da *n* : exile, refugee

asilo *nm* : asylum, refuge, shelter

asimetría *nf* : asymmetry

asimétrico, -ca *adj* : asymmetrical, asymmetric

asimilación *nf, pl* **-ciones** : assimilation

asimilar *vt* : to assimilate — **asimilarse** *vr* ~ **a** : to be similar to, to resemble

asimismo *adv* **1** IGUALMENTE : similarly, likewise **2** TAMBIÉN : as well, also

asir {7} *vt* : to seize, to grasp — **asirse** *vr* ~ **a** : to cling to

asistencia *nf* **1** : attendance **2** : assistance **3** : assist (in sports)

asistente¹ *adj* : attending, in attendance

asistente² *nmf* **1** : assistant **2 los asistentes** : those present, those in attendance

asistir *vi* : to attend, to be present ⟨asistir a clase : to attend class⟩ — *vt* : to aid, to assist

asma *nf* : asthma

asmático, -ca *adj* : asthmatic

asno *nm* BURRO : ass, donkey

asociación *nf, pl* **-ciones 1** : association, relationship **2** : society, group, association

asociado¹, -da *adj* : associate, associated

asociado², -da *n* : associate, partner

asociar *vt* **1** : to associate, to connect **2** : to pool (resources) **3** : to take into partnership — **asociarse** *vr* **1** : to become partners **2** ~ **a** : to join, to become a member of

asolar {19} *vt* : to devastate, to destroy

asoleado, -da *adj* : sunny

asolear *vt* : to put in the sun — **asolearse** *vr* : to sunbathe

asomar *vt* : to show, to stick out — *vi* : to appear, to become visible — **aso-**

marse *vr* 1 : to show, to appear 2 : to lean out, to look out ⟨se asomó por la ventana : he leaned out the window⟩

asombrar *vt* MARAVILLAR : to amaze, to astonish — **asombrarse** *vr* : to marvel, to be amazed

asombro *nm* : amazement, astonishment

asombroso, -sa *adj* : amazing, astonishing — **asombrosamente** *adv*

asomo *nm* 1 : hint, trace 2 **ni por asomo** : by no means

aspa *nf* : blade (of a fan or propeller)

aspaviento *nm* : exaggerated movement, fuss, flounce

aspecto *nm* 1 : aspect 2 APARIENCIA : appearance, look

aspereza *nf* RUDEZA : roughness, coarseness

áspero, -ra *adj* : rough, coarse, abrasive — **ásperamente** *adv*

aspersión *nf, pl* **-siones** : sprinkling

aspersor *nm* : sprinkler

aspiración *nf, pl* **-ciones** 1 : inhalation, breathing in 2 ANHELO : aspiration, desire

aspiradora *nf* : vacuum cleaner

aspirante *nmf* : applicant, candidate

aspirar *vi* ~ **a** : to aspire to — *vt* : to inhale, to breathe in

aspirina *nf* : aspirin

asquear *vt* : to sicken, to disgust

asquerosidad *nf* : filth, foulness

asqueroso, -sa *adj* : disgusting, sickening, repulsive — **asquerosamente** *adv*

asta *nf* 1 : flagpole ⟨a media asta : at half-mast⟩ 2 : horn, antler 3 : shaft (of a weapon)

ástaco *nm* : crayfish

astado, -da *adj* : horned

aster *nm* : aster

asterisco *nm* : asterisk

asteroide *nm* : asteroid

astigmatismo *nm* : astigmatism

astil *nm* : shaft (of an arrow or feather)

astilla *nf* 1 : splinter, chip 2 **de tal palo, tal astilla** : like father, like son

astillar *vt* : to splinter — **astillarse** *vr*

astillero *nm* : dry dock, shipyard

astral *adj* : astral

astringente *adj & nm* : astringent — **astringencia** *nf*

astro *nm* 1 : heavenly body 2 : star

astrología *nf* : astrology

astrológico, -ca *adj* : astrological

astrólogo, -ga *n* : astrologer

astronauta *nmf* : astronaut

astronáutica *nf* : astronautics

astronáutico, -ca *adj* : astronautic, astronautical

astronave *nf* : spaceship

astronomía *nf* : astronomy

astronómico, -ca *adj* : astronomical — **astronómicamente** *adv*

astrónomo, -ma *n* : astronomer

astroso, -sa *adj* DESALIÑADO : slovenly, untidy

astucia *nf* 1 : astuteness, shrewdness 2 : cunning, guile

astuto, -ta *adj* 1 : astute, shrewd 2 : crafty, tricky — **astutamente** *adv*

asueto *nm* : time off, break

asumir *vt* 1 : to assume, to take on ⟨asumir el cargo : to take office⟩ 2 SUPONER : to assume, to suppose

asunción *nf, pl* **-ciones** : assumption

asunto *nm* 1 CUESTIÓN, TEMA : affair, matter, subject 2 **asuntos** *nmpl* : affairs, business

asustadizo, -za *adj* : nervous, jumpy, skittish

asustado, -da *adj* : frightened, afraid

asustar *vt* ESPANTAR : to scare, to frighten — **asustarse** *vr*

atacante *nmf* : assailant, attacker

atacar {72} *v* : to attack

atado¹, -da *adj* : shy, inhibited

atado² *nm* 1 : bundle, bunch 2 *Arg* : pack (of cigarettes)

atadura *nf* LIGADURA : tie, bond

atajar *vt* 1 IMPEDIR : to block, to stop 2 INTERRUMPIR : to interrupt, to cut off 3 CONTENER : to hold back, to restrain — *vi* ~ **por** : to take a shortcut through

atajo *nm* : shortcut

atalaya *nf* 1 : watchtower 2 : vantage point

atañer {79} *vt* ~ **a** (*3rd person only*) : to concern, to have to do with ⟨eso no me atañe : that does not concern me⟩

ataque *nm* 1 : attack, assault 2 : fit ⟨ataque de risa : fit of laughter⟩ 3 **ataque de nervios** : nervous breakdown 4 **ataque cardíaco** *or* **ataque al corazón** : heart attack

atar *vt* AMARRAR : to tie, to tie up, to tie down — **atarse** *vr*

atarantado, -da *adj fam* 1 : restless 2 : dazed, stunned

atarantar *vt fam* : to daze, to stun

atarazana *nf* : shipyard

atardecer¹ {53} *v impers* : to get dark

atardecer² *nm* : late afternoon, dusk

atareado, -da *adj* : busy, overworked

atascar {72} *vt* 1 ATORAR : to block, to clog, to stop up 2 : to hinder — **atascarse** *vr* 1 : to become obstructed 2 : to get bogged down 3 PARARSE : to stall

atasco *nm* 1 : blockage 2 EMBOTELLAMIENTO : traffic jam

ataúd *nm* : coffin, casket

ataviar {85} *vt* : to dress, to clothe — **ataviarse** *vr* : to dress up

atavío *nm* ATUENDO : dress, attire

ateísmo *nm* : atheism

atemorizar {21} *vt* : to frighten, to intimidate — **atemorizarse** *vr*

atemperar *vt* : to temper, to moderate

atención¹ *nf, pl* **-ciones** 1 : attention 2 **poner atención** *or* **prestar atención** : to pay attention 3 **llamar la atención** : to attract attention 4 **en atención a** : in view of

atención² *interj* 1 : attention! 2 : watch out!

atender {56} *vt* **1** : to help, to wait on **2** : to look after, to take care of **3** : to heed, to listen to — *vi* : to pay attention

atenerse {80} *vr* : to abide ⟨tendrás que atenerte a las reglas : you will have to abide by the rules⟩

atentado *nm* : attack, assault

atentamente *adv* **1** : attentively, carefully **2** (*used in correspondence*) : sincerely, sincerely yours

atentar {55} *vi* ~ **contra** : to make an attempt on, to threaten ⟨atentaron contra su vida : they made an attempt on his life⟩

atento, -ta *adj* **1** : attentive, mindful **2** CORTÉS : courteous

atenuación *nf, pl* **-ciones** **1** : lessening **2** : understatement

atenuante¹ *adj* : extenuating, mitigating

atenuante² *nmf* : extenuating circumstance, excuse

atenuar {3} *vt* **1** MITIGAR : to extenuate, to mitigate **2** : to dim (light), to tone down (colors) **3** : to minimize, to lessen

ateo¹, atea *adj* : atheistic

ateo², atea *n* : atheist

aterciopelado, -da *adj* : velvety, downy

aterido, -da *adj* : freezing, frozen

aterrador, -dora *adj* : terrifying

aterrar {55} *vt* : to terrify, to frighten

aterrizaje *nm* : landing (of a plane)

aterrizar {21} *vt* : to land, to touch down

aterrorizar {21} *vt* **1** : to terrify **2** : to terrorize — **aterrorizarse** *vr* : to be terrified

atesorar *vt* : to hoard, to amass

atestado, -da *adj* : crowded, packed

atestar {55} *vt* **1** ATIBORRAR : to crowd, to pack **2** : to witness, to testify to — *vi* : to testify

atestiguar {10} *vt* : to testify to, to bear witness to — *vi* DECLARAR : to testify

atiborrar *vt* : to pack, to crowd — **atiborrarse** *vr* : to stuff oneself

ático *nm* **1** : penthouse **2** BUHARDILLA, DESVÁN : attic

atigrado, -da *adj* : tabby (of cats), striped (of fur)

atildado, -da *adj* : smart, neat, dapper

atildar *vt* **1** : to put a tilde over **2** : to clean up, to smarten up — **atildarse** *vr* : to get spruced up

atinar *vi* ACERTAR : to be accurate, to be on target

atingencia *nf* : bearing, relevance

atípico, -ca *adj* : atypical

atiplado, -da *adj* : shrill, high-pitched

atirantar *vt* : to make taut, to tighten

atisbar *vt* **1** : to spy on, to watch **2** : to catch a glimpse of, to make out

atisbo *nm* : glimpse, sign, hint

atizador *nm* : poker (for a fire)

atizar {21} *vt* **1** : to poke, to stir, to stoke (a fire) **2** : to stir up, to rouse **3** *fam* : to give, to land (a blow)

atlántico, -ca *adj* : Atlantic

atlas *nm* : atlas

atleta *nmf* : athlete

atlético, -ca *adj* : athletic

atletismo *nm* : athletics

atmósfera *nf* : atmosphere

atmosférico, -ca *adj* : atmospheric

atole *nm Mex* **1** : thick hot beverage prepared with corn flour **2 darle atole con el dedo (a alguien)** : to string (someone) along

atollarse *vr* : to get stuck, to get bogged down

atolón *nm, pl* **-lones** : atoll

atolondrado, -da *adj* **1** ATURDIDO : bewildered, dazed **2** DESPISTADO : scatterbrained, absentminded

atómico, -ca *adj* : atomic

atomizador *nm* : atomizer

atomizar {21} *vt* FRAGMENTAR : to fragment, to break into bits

átomo *nm* : atom

atónito, -ta *adj* : astonished, amazed

atontar *vt* **1** : to stupefy **2** : to bewilder, to confuse

atorar *vt* ATASCAR : to block, to clog — **atorarse** *vr* **1** ATASCARSE : to get stuck **2** ATRAGANTARSE : to choke

atormentador, -dora *n* : tormenter

atormentar *vt* : to torment, to torture — **atormentarse** *vr* : to torment oneself, to agonize

atornillar *vt* : to screw (in, on, down)

atorrante *nmf Arg* : bum, loafer

atosigar {52} *vt* : to harass, to annoy

atracadero *nm* : dock, pier

atracador, -dora *n* : robber, mugger

atracar {72} *vt* : to dock, to land — *vt* : to hold up, to rob, to mug — **atracarse** *vr fam* ~ **de** : to gorge oneself with

atracción *nf, pl* **-ciones** : attraction

atraco *nm* : holdup, robbery

atractivo¹, -va *adj* : attractive

atractivo² *nm* : attraction, appeal, charm

atraer {81} *vt* : to attract — **atraerse** *vr* **1** : to attract (each other) **2** GANARSE : to gain, to win

atragantarse *vr* : to choke (on food)

atrancar {72} *vt* : to block, to bar — **atrancarse** *vr*

atrapada *nf* : catch

atrapar *vt* : to trap, to capture

atrás *adv* **1** DETRÁS : back, behind ⟨se quedó atrás : he stayed behind⟩ **2** ANTES : ago ⟨mucho tiempo atrás : long ago⟩ **3 para** ~ *or* **hacia** ~ : backwards, toward the rear **4** ~ **de** : in back of, behind

atrasado, -da *adj* **1** : late, overdue **2** : backward **3** : old-fashioned **4** : slow (of a clock or watch)

atrasar *vt* : to delay, to put off — *vi* : to lose time — **atrasarse** *vr* : to fall behind

atraso *nm* **1** RETRASO : lateness, delay ⟨llegó con 20 minutos de atraso : he was 20 minutes late⟩ **2** : backwardness **3 atrasos** *nmpl* : arrears

atravesar {55} *vt* **1** CRUZAR : to cross, to go across **2** : to pierce **3** : to lay across **4** : to go through (a situation or crisis) — **atravesarse** *vr* **1** : to be in the way ⟨se me atravesó : it blocked my path⟩ **2** : to interfere, to meddle

atrayente *adj* : attractive

atreverse *vr* **1** : to dare **2** : to be insolent

atrevido, -da *adj* **1** : bold, daring **2** : insolent

atrevimiento *nm* **1** : daring, boldness **2** : insolence

atribución *nf, pl* **-ciones** : attribution

atribuible *adj* IMPUTABLE : attributable, ascribable

atribuir {41} *vt* **1** : to attribute, to ascribe **2** : to grant, to confer — **atribuirse** *vr* : to take credit for

atribular *vt* : to afflict, to trouble — **atribularse** *vr*

atributo *nm* : attribute

atril *nm* : lectern, stand

atrincherar *vt* : to entrench — **atrincherarse** *vr* **1** : to dig in, to entrench oneself **2** ~ **en** : to hide behind

atrio *nm* **1** : atrium **2** : portico

atrocidad *nf* : atrocity

atrofia *nf* : atrophy

atrofiar *v* : to atrophy

atronador, -dora *adj* : thunderous, deafening

atropellado, -da *adj* **1** : rash, hasty **2** : brusque, abrupt

atropellamiento → **atropello**

atropellar *vt* **1** : to knock down, to run over **2** : to violate, to abuse — **atropellarse** *vr* : to rush through (a task), to trip over one's words

atropello *nm* : abuse, violation, outrage

atroz *adj, pl* **atroces** : atrocious, appalling — **atrozmente** *adv*

atuendo *nm* ATAVÍO : attire, costume

atufar *vt* : to vex, to irritate — **atufarse** *vr* **1** : to get angry **2** : to smell bad, to stink

atún *nm, pl* **atunes** : tuna fish, tuna

aturdimiento *nm* : bewilderment, confusion

aturdir *vt* **1** : to stun, to shock **2** : to bewilder, to confuse, to stupefy

atuvo, etc. → **atenerse**

audacia *nf* OSADÍA : boldness, audacity

audaz *adj, pl* **audaces** : bold, audacious, daring — **audazmente** *adv*

audible *adj* : audible

audición *nf, pl* **-ciones** **1** : hearing **2** : audition

audiencia *nf* : audience

audífono *nm* **1** : hearing aid **2** **audífonos** *nmpl* : headphones, earphones

audio *nm* : audio

audiovisual *adj* : audiovisual

auditar *vt* : to audit

auditivo, -va *adj* : auditory, hearing, aural ⟨aparato auditivo : hearing aid⟩

auditor, -tora *n* : auditor

auditoría *nf* : audit

auditorio *nm* **1** : auditorium **2** : audience

auge *nm* **1** : peak, height **2** : boom, upturn

augur *nm* : augur

augurar *vt* : to predict, to foretell

augurio *nm* AGÜERO, PRESAGIO : augury, omen

augusto, -ta *adj* : august

aula *nf* : classroom

aullar {8} *vi* : to howl, to wail

aullido *nm* : howl, wail

aumentar *vt* ACRECENTAR : to increase, to raise — *vi* : to rise, to increase, to grow

aumento *nm* INCREMENTO : increase, rise

aun *adv* **1** : even ⟨ni aun en coche llegaría a tiempo : I wouldn't arrive on time even if I drove⟩ **2 aun así** : even so **3 aun más** : even more

aún *adv* **1** TODAVÍA : still, yet ⟨¿aún no ha llegado el correo? : the mail still hasn't come?⟩ **2 más aún** : furthermore

aunar {8} *vt* : to join, to combine — **aunarse** *vr* : to unite

aunque *conj* **1** : though, although, even if, even though **2 aunque sea** : at least

aura *nf* **1** : aura **2** : turkey buzzard

áureo, -rea *adj* : golden

aureola *nf* **1** : halo **2** : aura (of power, fame, etc.)

aurícula *nf* : auricle

auricular *nm* : telephone receiver

aurora *nf* **1** : dawn **2 aurora boreal** : aurora borealis

ausencia *nf* : absence

ausentarse *vr* **1** : to leave, to go away **2** ~ **de** : to stay away from

ausente[1] *adj* : absent, missing

ausente[2] *nmf* **1** : absentee **2** : missing person

auspiciar *vt* **1** PATROCINAR : to sponsor **2** FOMENTAR : to foster, to promote

auspicios *nmpl* : sponsorship, auspices

austeridad *nf* : austerity

austero, -ra *adj* : austere

austral[1] *adj* : southern

austral[2] *nm* : former monetary unit of Argentina

australiano, -na *adj & n* : Australian

austriaco *or* **austríaco, -ca** *adj & n* : Austrian

autenticar {72} *vt* : to authenticate — **autenticación** *nf*

autenticidad *nf* : authenticity

auténtico, -ca *adj* : authentic — **auténticamente** *adv*

autentificar {72} *vt* : to authenticate — **autentificación** *nf*

autismo *nm* : autism

autista *adj* : autistic

auto *nm* : auto, car

autoayuda *nf* : self-help

autobiografía *nf* : autobiography

autobiográfico, -ca *adj* : autobiographical

autobús *nm, pl* **-buses** : bus

autocompasión *nf* : self-pity
autocontrol *nm* : self-control
autocracia *nf* : autocracy
autócrata *nmf* : autocrat
autocrático, -ca *adj* : autocratic
autóctono, -na *adj* : indigenous, native ⟨arte autóctono : indigenous art⟩
autodefensa *nf* : self-defense
autodestrucción *nf* : self-destruction — **autodestructivo, -va** *adj*
autodeterminación *nf* : self-determination
autodidacta[1] *adj* : self-taught
autodidacta[2] *nmf* : self-taught person, autodidact
autodidacto[1], **-ta** *adj* → **autodidacta**[1]
autodidacto[2], **-ta** *n* → **autodidacta**[2]
autodisciplina *nf* : self-discipline
autoestima *nf* : self-esteem
autogobierno *nm* : self-government
autografiar *vt* : to autograph
autógrafo *nm* : autograph
autoinfligido, -da *adj* : self-inflicted
automación → **automatización**
autómata *nm* : automaton
automático, -ca *adj* : automatic — **automáticamente** *adv*
automatización *nf* : automation
automatizar {21} *vt* : to automate
automotor, -tora *adj* **1** : self-propelled **2** : automotive, car
automotriz[1] *adj, pl* **-trices** : automotive, car
automotriz[2] *nf, pl* **-trices** : automaker
automóvil *nm* : automobile
automovilista *nmf* : motorist
automovilístico, -ca *adj* : automobile, car ⟨accidente automovilístico : automobile accident⟩
autonombrado, -da *adj* : self-appointed
autonomía *nf* : autonomy
autónomo, -ma *adj* : autonomous — **autónomamente** *adv*
autopista *nf* : expressway, highway
autoproclamado, -da *adj* : self-proclaimed, self-appointed
autopropulsado, -da *adj* : self-propelled
autopsia *nf* : autopsy
autor, -tora *n* **1** : author **2** : perpetrator
autoría *nf* : authorship
autoridad *nf* : authority
autoritario, -ria *adj* : authoritarian
autorización *nf, pl* **-ciones** : authorization
autorizado, -da *adj* **1** : authorized **2** : authoritative
autorizar {21} *vt* : to authorize, to approve
autorretrato *nm* : self-portrait
autoservicio *nm* **1** : self-service restaurant **2** SUPERMERCADO : supermarket
autostop *nm* **1** : hitchhiking **2 hacer autostop** : to hitchhike
autostopista *nmf* : hitchhiker
autosuficiencia *nf* : self-sufficiency — **autosuficiente** *adj*
auxiliar[1] *vt* : to aid, to assist

auxiliar[2] *adj* : assistant, auxiliary
auxiliar[3] *nmf* **1** : assistant, helper **2 auxiliar de vuelo** : flight attendant
auxilio *nm* **1** : aid, assistance **2 primeros auxilios** : first aid
aval *nm* : guarantee, endorsement
avalancha *nf* ALUD : avalanche
avalar *vt* : to guarantee, to endorse
avaluar {3} *vt* : to evaluate, to appraise
avalúo *nm* : appraisal, evaluation
avance *nm* ADELANTO : advance
avanzado, -da *adj* **1** : advanced **2** : progressive
avanzar {21} *v* : to advance, to move forward
avaricia *nf* CODICIA : greed, avarice
avaricioso, -sa *adj* : avaricious, greedy
avaro[1], **-ra** *adj* : miserly, greedy
avaro[2], **-ra** *n* : miser
avasallador, -dora *adj* : overwhelming
avasallamiento *nm* : subjugation, domination
avasallar *vt* : to overpower, to subjugate
ave *nf* **1** : bird **2 aves de corral** : poultry **3 ave rapaz** *or* **ave de presa** : bird of prey
avecinarse *vr* : to approach, to come near
avecindarse *vr* : to settle, to take up residence
avellana *nf* : hazelnut, filbert
avellano *nm* : hazel
avena *nf* **1** : oat, oats *pl* **2** : oatmeal
avenencia *nf* : agreement, pact
avenida *nf* : avenue
avenir {87} *vt* : to reconcile, to harmonize — **avenirse** *vr* **1** : to agree, to come to terms **2** : to get along
aventajado, -da *adj* : outstanding
aventajar *vt* **1** : to be ahead of, to lead **2** : to surpass, to outdo
aventar {55} *vt* **1** : to fan **2** : to winnow **3** *Col, Mex* : to throw, to toss — **aventarse** *vr* **1** *Col, Mex* : to hurl oneself **2** *Mex fam* : to dare, to take a chance
aventón *nm, pl* **-tones** *Col, Mex fam* : ride, lift
aventura *nf* **1** : adventure **2** RIESGO : venture, risk **3** : love affair
aventurado, -da *adj* : hazardous, risky
aventurar *vt* : to venture, to risk — **aventurarse** *vr* : to take a risk
aventurero[1], **-ra** *adj* : adventurous
aventurero[2], **-ra** *n* : adventurer
avergonzado, -da *adj* **1** : ashamed **2** : embarrassed
avergonzar {9} *vt* APENAR : to shame, to embarrass — **avergonzarse** *vr* APENARSE : to be ashamed, to be embarrassed
avería *nf* **1** : damage **2** : breakdown, malfunction
averiado, -da *adj* **1** : damaged, faulty **2** : broken down
averiar {85} *vt* : to damage — **averiarse** *vr* : to break down
averiguación *nf, pl* **-ciones** : investigation, inquiry

averiguar {10} vt 1 : to find out, to ascertain 2 : to investigate

aversión nf, pl -siones : aversion, dislike

avestruz nm, pl -truces : ostrich

avezado, -da adj : seasoned, experienced

aviación nf, pl -ciones : aviation

aviador, -dora n : aviator, flyer

aviar {85} vt 1 : to prepare, to make ready 2 : to tidy up 3 : to equip, to supply

avicultor, -tora n : poultry farmer

avicultura nf : poultry farming

avidez nf, pl -deces : eagerness

ávido, -da adj : eager, avid — ávidamente adv

avieso, -sa adj 1 : twisted, distorted 2 : wicked, depraved

avinagrado, -da adj : vinegary, sour

avio nm 1 : preparation, provision 2 : loan (for agriculture or mining) 3 avíos nmpl : gear, equipment

avión nm, pl aviones : airplane

avioneta nf : light airplane

avisar vt 1 : to notify, to inform 2 : to advise, to warn

aviso nm 1 : notice 2 : advertisement, ad 3 ADVERTENCIA : warning 4 estar sobre aviso : to be on the alert

avispa nf : wasp

avispado, -da adj fam : clever, sharp

avispero nm : wasps' nest

avispón nm, pl -pones : hornet

avistar vt : to sight, to catch sight of

avituallar vt : to suppy with food, to provision

avivar vt 1 : to enliven, to brighten 2 : to strengthen, to intensify

avizorar vt 1 ACECHAR : to spy on, to watch 2 : to observe, to perceive ⟨se avizoran dificultades : difficulties are expected⟩

axila nf : underarm, armpit

axioma nm : axiom

axiomático, -ca adj : axiomatic

ay interj 1 : oh! 2 : ouch!, ow!

ayer¹ adv : yesterday

ayer² nm ANTAÑO : yesteryear, days gone by

ayote nm CA, Mex : squash, pumpkin

ayuda nf 1 : help, assistance 2 ayuda de cámara : valet

ayudante nmf : helper, assistant

ayudar vt : to help, to assist — ayudarse vr ~ de : to make use of

ayunar vi : to fast

ayunas nfpl en ~ : fasting ⟨este medicamento ha de tomarse en ayunas : this medication should be taken on an empty stomach⟩

ayuno nm : fast

ayuntamiento nm 1 : town hall, city hall 2 : town or city council

azabache nm : jet ⟨negro azabache : jet black⟩

azada nf : hoe

azafata nf 1 : stewardess f 2 : hostess f (on a TV show)

azafrán nm, pl -franes 1 : saffron 2 : crocus

azahar nm : orange blossom

azalea nf : azalea

azar nm 1 : chance ⟨juegos de azar : games of chance⟩ 2 : accident, misfortune 3 al azar : at random, randomly

azaroso, -sa adj 1 : perilous, hazardous 2 : turbulent, eventful

azimut nm : azimuth

azogue nm : mercury, quicksilver

azorar vt 1 : to alarm, to startle 2 : to fluster, to embarrass — azorarse vr : to get embarrassed

azotar vt 1 : to whip, to flog 2 : to lash, to batter 3 : to devastate, to afflict

azote nm 1 LÁTIGO : whip, lash 2 fam : spanking, licking 3 : calamity, scourge

azotea nf : flat roof, terraced roof

azteca adj & nmf : Aztec

azúcar nmf : sugar — azucarar vt

azucarado, -da adj : sweetened, sugary

azucarera nf : sugar bowl

azucarero, -ra adj : sugar ⟨industria azucarera : sugar industry⟩

azucena nf : white lily

azuela nf : adze

azufre nm : sulphur — azufroso, -sa adj

azul adj & nm : blue

azulado, -da adj : bluish

azulejo nm : ceramic tile, floor tile

azuloso, -sa adj : bluish

azulete nm : bluing

azur¹ adj CELESTE : azure

azur² n CELESTE : azure, sky blue

azuzar {21} vt : to incite, to egg on

B

b nf : second letter of the Spanish alphabet

baba nf 1 : spittle, saliva 2 : dribble, drool (of a baby) 3 : slime, ooze

babear vi 1 : to drool, to slobber 2 : to ooze

babel nmf : babel, chaos, bedlam

babero nm : bib

babor nm : port, port side

babosa nf : slug (mollusk)

babosada nf CA, Mex : silly act or remark

baboso, -sa adj 1 : drooling, slobbering 2 : slimy 3 CA, Mex fam : silly, dumb

babucha nf : slipper

babuino nm : baboon

bacalao nm : cod (fish)

bache *nm* **1** : pothole **2** *PRi* : deep puddle **3** : bad period, rough time ⟨bache económico : economic slump⟩

bachiller *nmf* : high school graduate

bachillerato *nm* : high school diploma

bacilo *nm* : bacillus

bacon *nm Spain* : bacon

bacteria *nf* : bacterium

bacteriano, -na *adj* : bacterial

bacteriología *nf* : bacteriology

bacteriológico, -ca *adj* : bacteriologic, bacteriological

bacteriólogo, -ga *n* : bacteriologist

báculo *nm* **1** : staff, stick **2** : comfort, support

badajo *nm* : clapper (of a bell)

badén *nm, pl* **badenes** **1** : (paved) ford, channel **2** : dip, ditch (in a road) **3** : speed bump

bádminton *nm* : badminton

bafle *or* **baffle** *nm* **1** : baffle **2** : speaker, loudspeaker

bagaje *nm* **1** EQUIPAJE : baggage, luggage **2** : background ⟨bagaje cultural : cultural baggage⟩

bagatela *nf* : trifle, trinket

bagre *nm* : catfish

bahía *nf* : bay

bailar *vt* : to dance — *vi* **1** : to dance **2** : to spin **3** : to be loose, to be too big

bailarín[1], -rina *adj, mpl* **-rines** **1** : dancing **2** : fond of dancing

bailarín[2], -rina *n, mpl* **-rines** **1** : dancer **2** : ballet dancer, ballerina *f*

baile *nm* **1** : dance **2** : dance party, ball **3 llevarse al baile a** *Mex fam* : to take for a ride, to take advantage of

baja *nf* **1** DESCENSO : fall, drop **2** : slump, recession **3** : loss, casualty **4** : discharge, dismissal ⟨dar de baja **5** : to discharge, to dismiss **5 darse de baja** : to withdraw, to drop out

bajada *nf* **1** : descent **2** : dip, slope **3** : decrease, drop

bajar *vt* **1** DESCENDER : to lower, to let down, to take down **2** REDUCIR : to reduce (prices) **3** INCLINAR : to lower, to bow (the head) **4** : to go down, to descend **5 bajar de categoría** : to downgrade — *vi* **1** : to drop, to fall **2** : to come down, to go down **3** : to ebb (of tides) — **bajarse** *vr* ∼ **de** : to get off, to get out of (a vehicle)

bajeza *nf* **1** : low or despicable act **2** : baseness

bajío *nm* **1** : lowland **2** : shoal, sandbank, shallows

bajista *nmf* : bass player, bassist

bajo[1] *adv* **1** : down, low **2** : softly, quietly ⟨habla más bajo : speak more softly⟩

bajo[2], -ja *adj* **1** : low **2** : short (of stature) **3** : soft, faint, deep (of sounds) **4** : lower ⟨el bajo Amazonas : the lower Amazon⟩ **5** : lowered ⟨con la mirada baja : with lowered eyes⟩ **6** : base, vile **7 los bajos fondos** : the underworld

bajo[3] *nm* **1** : bass (musical instrument) **2** : first floor, ground floor **3** : hemline

bajo[4] *prep* : under, beneath, below

bajón *nm, pl* **bajones** : sharp drop, slump

bajorrelieve *nm* : bas-relief

bala *nf* **1** : bullet **2** : bale

balacera *nf* TIROTEO : shoot-out, gunfight

balada *nf* : ballad

balance *nm* **1** : balance **2** : balance sheet

balancear *vt* **1** : to balance **2** : to swing (one's arms, etc.) **3** : to rock (a boat) — **balancearse** *vr* **1** OSCILAR : to swing, to sway, to rock **2** VACILAR : to hesitate, to vacillate

balanceo *nm* **1** : swaying, rocking **2** : vacillation

balancín *nm, pl* **-cines** **1** : rocking chair **2** SUBIBAJA : seesaw

balandra *nf* : sloop

balanza *nf* BÁSCULA : scales *pl*, balance

balaustrada *nf* : balustrade

balaustre *nm* : baluster

balazo *nm* **1** TIRO : shot, gunshot **2** : bullet wound

balboa *nf* : balboa (monetary unit of Panama)

balbucear *vi* **1** : to mutter, to stammer **2** : to prattle, to babble ⟨los niños están balbuceando : the children are prattling away⟩

balbuceo *nm* : mumbling, stammering

balbucir → **balbucear**

balcánico, -ca *adj* : Balkan

balcón *nm, pl* **balcones** : balcony

balde *nm* **1** CUBO : bucket, pail **2 en** ∼ : in vain, to no avail

baldío[1], -día *adj* **1** : fallow, uncultivated **2** : useless, vain

baldío[2] *nm* **1** : wasteland **2** *Mex* : vacant lot

baldosa *nf* LOSETA : floor tile

balear *vt* : to shoot, to shoot at

balero *nm* **1** *Mex* : ball bearing **2** *Mex, PRi* : cup-and-ball toy

balido *nm* : bleat

balín *nm, pl* **balines** : pellet

balística *nf* : ballistics

balístico, -ca *adj* : ballistic

baliza *nf* **1** : buoy **2** : beacon (for aircraft)

ballena *nf* : whale

ballenero[1], -ra *adj* : whaling

ballenero[2], -ra *n* : whaler

ballenero[3] *nm* : whaleboat, whaler

ballesta *nf* **1** : crossbow **2** : spring (of an automobile)

ballet *nm* : ballet

balneario *nm* : spa, bathing resort

balompié *nm* FUTBOL : soccer

balón *nm, pl* **balones** : ball

baloncesto *nm* BASQUETBOL : basketball

balsa *nf* **1** : raft **2** : balsa **3** : pond, pool

balsámico, -ca *adj* : soothing

bálsamo *nm* : balsam, balm
báltico, -ca *adj* : Baltic
baluarte *nm* BASTIÓN : bulwark, bastion
bambolear *vi* **1** : to sway, to swing **2** : to wobble — **bambolearse** *vr*
bamboleo *nm* **1** : swaying, swinging **2** : wobbling
bambú *nm, pl* **bambúes** *or* **bambús** : bamboo
banal *adj* : banal, trivial
banalidad *nf* : banality
banana *nf* : banana
bananero¹, -ra *adj* : banana
bananero² *nm* : banana tree
banano *nm* **1** : banana tree **2** *CA, Col* : banana
banca *nf* **1** : banking **2** BANCO : bench
bancada *nf* **1** : group, faction **2** : workbench
bancal *nm* **1** : terrace (in agriculture) **2** : plot (of land)
bancario, -ria *adj* : bank, banking
bancarrota *nf* QUIEBRA : bankruptcy
banco *nm* **1** : bank ⟨banco central : central bank⟩ ⟨banco de datos : data bank⟩ ⟨banco de arena : sandbank⟩ ⟨banco de sangre : blood bank⟩ **2** BANCA : stool, bench **3** : pew **4** : school (of fish)
banda *nf* **1** : band, strip **2** *Mex* : belt ⟨banda transportadora : conveyor belt⟩ **3** : band (of musicians) **4** : gang (of persons), flock (of birds) **5 banda de rodadura** : tread (of a tire, etc.) **6 banda sonora** *or* **banda de sonido** : sound track
bandada *nf* : flock (of birds), school (of fish)
bandazo *nm* : swerving, lurch
bandearse *vr* : to look after oneself, to cope
bandeja *nf* : tray, platter
bandera *nf* : flag, banner
banderazo *nm* : starting signal (in sports)
banderilla *nf* : banderilla, dart (in bullfighting)
banderín *nm, pl* **-rines** : pennant, small flag
bandidaje *nm* : banditry
bandido, -da *n* BANDOLERO : bandit, outlaw
bando *nm* **1** FACCIÓN : faction, side **2** EDICTO : proclamation
bandolerismo *nm* : banditry
bandolero, -ra *n* BANDIDO : bandit, outlaw
bangladesí *adj & nmf* : Bangladeshi
banjo *nm* : banjo
banquero, -ra *n* : banker
banqueta *nf* **1** : footstool, stool, bench **2** *Mex* : sidewalk
banquete *nm* : banquet
banquetear *v* : to feast
banquillo *nm* **1** : bench (in sports) **2** : dock, defendant's seat
bañadera *nf* → **bañera**

bañar *vt* **1** : to bathe, to wash **2** : to immerse, to dip **3** : to coat, to cover ⟨bañado en lágrimas : bathed in tears⟩ — **bañarse** *vr* **1** : to take a bath, to bathe **2** : to go for a swim
bañera *nf* TINA : bathtub
bañista *nmf* : bather
baño *nm* **1** : bath **2** : swim, dip **3** : bathroom **4 baño María** : double boiler
baqueta *nf* **1** : ramrod **2 baquetas** *nfpl* : drumsticks
bar *nm* : bar, tavern
baraja *nf* : deck of cards
barajar *vt* **1** : to shuffle (cards) **2** : to consider, to toy with
baranda *nf* : rail, railing
barandal *nm* **1** : rail, railing **2** : banister, handrail
barandilla *nf Spain* : bannister, handrail, railing
barata *nf* **1** *Mex* : sale, bargain **2** *Chile* : cockroach
baratija *nf* : bauble, trinket
baratillo *nm* : rummage sale, flea market
barato¹ *adv* : cheap, cheaply ⟨te lo vendo barato : I'll sell it to you cheap⟩
barato², -ta *adj* : cheap, inexpensive
baratura *nf* **1** : cheapness **2** : cheap thing
barba *nf* **1** : beard, stubble **2** : chin
barbacoa *nf* : barbecue
bárbaramente *adv* : barbarously
barbaridad *nf* **1** : barbarity, atrocity **2** ¡qué barbaridad! : that's outrageous!
barbarie *nf* : barbarism, savagery
bárbaro¹ *adv fam* : wildly ⟨anoche lo pasamos bárbaro : we had a wild time last night⟩
bárbaro², -ra *adj* **1** : barbarous, wild, uncivilized **2** *fam* : great, fantastic
bárbaro³, -ra *n* : barbarian
barbecho *nm* : fallow land ⟨dejar en barbecho : to leave fallow⟩
barbero, -ra *n* : barber
barbilla *nf* MENTÓN : chin
barbitúrico *nm* : barbiturate
barbudo¹, -da *adj* : bearded
barbudo² *nm* : bearded man
barca *nf* **1** : boat **2 barca de pasaje** : ferryboat
barcaza *nf* : barge
barcia *nf* : chaff
barco *nm* **1** BARCA : boat **2** BUQUE, NAVE : ship
bardo *nm* : bard
bario *nm* : barium
barítono *nm* : baritone
barlovento *nm* : windward
barman *nm* : bartender
barniz *nm, pl* **barnices** **1** LACA : varnish, lacquer **2** : glaze (on ceramics, etc.)
barnizar {21} *vt* **1** : to varnish **2** : to glaze
barométrico, -ca *adj* : barometric
barómetro *nm* : barometer
barón *nm, pl* **barones** : baron

baronesa *nf* : baroness
baronet *nm* : baronet
barquero, -ra : boatman *m*, boatwoman *f*
barquillo *nm* : wafer, thin cookie or cracker
barra *nf* : bar
barraca *nf* 1 CABAÑA, CHOZA : hut, cabin 2 : booth, stall
barracuda *nf* : barracuda
barranca *nf* 1 : hillside, slope 2 → **barranco**
barranco *nm* : ravine, gorge
barredora *nf* : street sweeper (machine)
barrena *nf* 1 TALADRO : drill, auger, gimlet 2 : tailspin
barrenar *vt* 1 : to drill 2 : to undermine
barrendero, -ra *n* : sweeper, street cleaner
barrer *v* : to sweep — **barrerse** *vr* : to slide (in sports)
barrera *nf* OBSTÁCULO : barrier, obstacle ⟨barrera de sonido : sound barrier⟩
barreta *nf* : crowbar
barriada *nf* 1 : district, quarter 2 : slums *pl*
barrica *nf* BARRIL, TONEL : barrel, cask, keg
barricada *nf* : barricade
barrida *nf* 1 : sweep 2 : slide (in sports)
barrido *nm* : sweeping
barriga *nf* PANZA : belly, paunch
barrigón, -gona *adj, mpl* **-gones** *fam* : potbellied, paunchy
barril *nm* 1 BARRICA : barrel, keg 2 **cerveza de barril** : draft beer
barrio *nm* 1 : neighborhood, district 2 **barrios bajos** : slums *pl*
barro *nm* 1 LODO : mud 2 ARCILLA : clay 3 ESPINILLA, GRANO : pimple, blackhead
barroco, -ca *adj* : baroque
barroso, -sa *adj* ENLODADO : muddy
barrote *nm* : bar (on a window)
barrunto *nm* 1 SOSPECHA : suspicion 2 INDICIO : sign, indication, hint
bártulos *nmpl* : things, belongings ⟨liar los bártulos : to pack one's things⟩
barullo *nm* BULLA : racket, ruckus
basa *nf* : base, pedestal
basalto *nm* : basalt
basar *vt* FUNDAR : to base — **basarse** *vr* FUNDARSE ∼ **en** : to be based on
báscula *nf* BALANZA : balance, scales *pl*
base *nf* 1 : base, bottom 2 : base (in baseball) 3 FUNDAMENTO : basis, foundation 4 **base de datos** : database 5 **a base de** : based on, by means of 6 **en base a** : based on, on the basis of
básico, -ca *adj* FUNDAMENTAL : basic — **básicamente** *adv*
basílica *nf* : basilica
basquetbol *or* **básquetbol** *nm* BALONCESTO : basketball
basset *nm* : basset hound
bastante[1] *adv* 1 : enough, sufficiently ⟨he trabajado bastante : I have worked enough⟩ 2 : fairly, rather, quite ⟨llegaron bastante temprano : they arrived quite early⟩
bastante[2] *adj* : enough, sufficient
bastante[3] *pron* : enough ⟨hemos visto bastante : we have seen enough⟩
bastar *vi* : to be enough, to suffice
bastardilla *nf* CURSIVA : italic type, italics *pl*
bastardo, -da *adj & n* : bastard
bastidor *nm* 1 : framework, frame 2 : wing (in theater) ⟨entre bastidores : backstage, behind the scenes⟩
bastilla *nf* : hem
bastión *nf, pl* **bastiones** BALUARTE : bastion, bulwark
basto, -ta *adj* : coarse, rough
bastón *nm, pl* **bastones** 1 : cane, walking stick 2 : baton 3 **bastón de mando** : staff (of authority)
basura *nf* DESECHOS : garbage, waste, refuse
basurero[1], **-ra** *n* : garbage collector
basurero[2] *nm Mex* : garbage can
bata *nf* 1 : bathrobe, housecoat 2 : smock, coverall, lab coat
batalla *nf* 1 : battle 2 : fight, struggle 3 **de** ∼ : ordinary, everyday ⟨mis zapatos de batalla : my everyday shoes⟩
batallar *vi* LIDIAR, LUCHAR : to battle, to fight
batallón *nm, pl* **-llones** : battalion
batata *nf* : yam, sweet potato
batazo *nm* HIT : hit (in baseball)
bate *nm* : baseball bat
batea *nf* 1 : tray, pan 2 : flat-bottomed boat, punt
bateador, -dora *n* : batter, hitter
batear *vi* : to bat — *vt* : to hit
bateo *nm* : batting (in baseball)
batería *nf* 1 PILA : battery 2 : drum kit, drums *pl* 3 **batería de cocina** : kitchen utensils *pl*
baterista *nmf* : drummer
batido *nm* LICUADO : milk shake
batidor *nm* : eggbeater, whisk, mixer
batidora *nf* : (electric) mixer
batir *vt* 1 GOLPEAR : to beat, to hit 2 VENCER : to defeat 3 REVOLVER : to mix, to beat 4 : to break (a record) — **batirse** *vr* : to fight
batista *nf* : batiste, cambric
batuta *nf* 1 : baton 2 **llevar la batuta** : to be the leader, to call the tune
baúl *nm* : trunk, chest
bautismal *adj* : baptismal
bautismo *nm* : baptism, christening
bautista *adj & nmf* : Baptist
bautizar {21} *vt* : to baptize, to christen
bautizo → **bautismo**
bávaro, -ra *adj & n* : Bavarian
baya *nf* 1 : berry 2 **baya de saúco** : elderberry
bayeta *nf* : cleaning cloth
bayoneta *nf* : bayonet
baza *nf* 1 : trick (in card games) 2 **meter baza en** : to butt in on
bazar *nm* : bazaar
bazo *nm* : spleen

bazofia *nf* **1** : table scraps *pl* **2** : slop, swill **3** : hogwash, rubbish

bazuca *nf* : bazooka

beagle *nm* : beagle

beatificar {72} *vt* : to beatify — **beatificación** *nf*

beatífico, -ca *adj* : beatific

beatitud *nf* : beatitude

beato, -ta *adj* **1** : blessed **2** : pious, devout **3** : sanctimonious, overly devout

bebé *nm* : baby

bebedero *nm* **1** ABREVADERO : watering trough **2** *Mex* : drinking fountain

bebedor, -dora *n* : drinker

beber *v* TOMAR : to drink

bebida *nf* : drink, beverage

beca *nf* : grant, scholarship

becado, -da *n* : scholar, scholarship holder

becerro, -rra *n* : calf

begonia *nf* : begonia

beige *adj* & *nm* : beige

beisbol *or* **béisbol** *nm* : baseball

beisbolista *nmf* : baseball player

beldad *nf* BELLEZA, HERMOSURA : beauty

belén *nf*, *pl* **belenes** NACIMIENTO : Nativity scene

belga *adj* & *nmf* : Belgian

beliceño, -ña *adj* & *n* : Belizean

belicista[1] *adj* : militaristic

belicista[2] *nmf* : warmonger

bélico, -ca *adj* GUERRERO : war, fighting ⟨esfuerzos bélicos : war efforts⟩

belicosidad *nf* : bellicosity

belicoso, -sa *adj* **1** : warlike, martial **2** : aggressive, belligerent

beligerancia *nf* : belligerence

beligerante *adj* & *nmf* : belligerent

bellaco[1], **-ca** *adj* : sly, cunning

bellaco[2], **-ca** *n* : rogue, scoundrel

belleza *nf* BELDAD, HERMOSURA : beauty

bello, -lla *adj* **1** HERMOSO : beautiful **2** **bellas artes** : fine arts

bellota *nf* : acorn

bemol *nm* : flat (in music) — **bemol** *adj*

benceno *nm* : benzene

bendecir {11} *vt* **1** CONSAGRAR : to bless, to consecrate **2** ALABAR : to praise, to extol **3 bendecir la mesa** : to say grace

bendición *nf*, *pl* **-ciones** : benediction, blessing

bendiga, bendijo etc. → **bendecir**

bendito, -ta *adj* **1** : blessed, holy **2** : fortunate **3** : silly, simple-minded

benedictino, -na *adj* & *n* : Benedictine

benefactor[1], **-tora** *adj* : beneficent

benefactor[2], **-tora** *n* : benefactor, benefactress *f*

beneficencia *nf* : beneficence, charity

beneficiar *vt* : to benefit, to be of assistance to — **beneficiarse** *vr* : to benefit, to profit

beneficiario, -ria *n* : beneficiary

beneficio *nm* **1** GANANCIA, PROVECHO : gain, profit **2** : benefit

beneficioso, -sa *adj* PROVECHOSO : beneficial

benéfico, -ca *adj* : charitable, beneficent

benemérito, -ta *adj* : meritorious, worthy

beneplácito *nm* : approval, consent

benevolencia *nf* BONDAD : benevolence, kindness

benévolo, -la *adj* BONDADOSO : benevolent, kind, good

bengala *nf* **luz de bengala 1** : flare (signal) **2** : sparkler

bengalí[1] *adj* & *nmf* : Bengali

bengalí[2] *nm* : Bengali (language)

benignidad *nf* : mildness, kindness

benigno, -na *adj* : benign, mild

beninés, -nesa *adj* & *n* : Beninese

benjamín, -mina *n*, *mpl* **-mines** : youngest child

beodo[1], **-da** *adj* : drunk, inebriated

beodo[2], **-da** *n* : drunkard

berberecho *nm* : cockle

berbiquí *nm* : brace (in carpentry)

berenjena *nf* : eggplant

bergantín *nm*, *pl* **-tines** : brig (ship)

berilo *nm* : beryl

bermudas *nfpl* : Bermuda shorts

berrear *vi* **1** : to bellow, to low **2** : to bawl, to howl

berrido *nm* **1** : bellowing **2** : howl, scream

berrinche *nm fam* : tantrum, conniption

berro *nm* : watercress

berza *nf* : cabbage

besar *vt* : to kiss

beso *nm* : kiss

bestia[1] *adj* **1** : ignorant, stupid **2** : boorish, rude

bestia[2] *nf* : beast, animal

bestia[3] *nmf* **1** IGNORANTE : ignoramus **2** : brute

bestial *adj* **1** : bestial, beastly **2** *fam* : huge, enormous ⟨hace un frío bestial : it's terribly cold⟩ **3** *fam* : great, fantastic

besuquear *vt fam* : to cover with kisses — **besuquearse** *vr fam* : to neck, to smooch

betabel *nm Mex* : beet

betún *nm*, *pl* **betunes 1** : shoe polish **2** *Mex* : icing

bianual *adj* : biannual

biatlón *nm*, *pl* **-lones** : biathlon

biberón *nm*, *pl* **-rones** : baby's bottle

biblia *nf* **1** : bible **2 la Biblia** : the Bible

bíblico, -ca *adj* : biblical

bibliografía *nf* : bibliography

bibliográfico, -ca *adj* : bibliographic, bibliographical

bibliógrafo, -fa *n* : bibliographer

biblioteca *nf* : library

bibliotecario, -ria *n* : librarian

bicameral *adj* : bicameral

bicarbonato *nm* **1** : bicarbonate **2 bicarbonato de soda** : sodium bicarbonate, baking soda

bicentenario *nm* : bicentennial

bíceps *nms & pl* : biceps
bicho *nm* : small animal, bug, insect
bici *nf fam* : bike
bicicleta *nf* : bicycle
bicolor *adj* : two-tone
bicúspide *adj* : bicuspid
bidón *nm, pl* **bidones** 2 : large can, (oil) drum
bien¹ *adv* 1 : well ⟨¿dormiste bien? : did you sleep well?⟩ 2 CORRECTAMENTE : correctly, properly, right ⟨hay que hacerlo bien : it must be done correctly⟩ 3 : very, quite ⟨el libro era bien divertido : the book was very amusing⟩ 4 : easily ⟨bien puede acabarlo en un día : he can easily finish it in a day⟩ 5 : willingly, readily ⟨bien lo aceptaré : I'll gladly accept it⟩ 6 **bien que** : although 7 **más bien** : rather
bien² *adj* 1 : well, OK, all right ⟨¿te sientes bien? : are you feeling all right?⟩ 2 : pleasant, agreeable ⟨las flores huelen bien : the flowers smell very nice⟩ 3 : satisfactory 4 : correct, right
bien³ *nm* 1 : good ⟨el bien y el mal : good and evil⟩ 2 **bienes** *nmpl* : property, goods, possessions
bienal *adj & nf* : biennial — **bienalmente** *adv*
bienaventurado, -da *adj* 1 : blessed 2 : fortunate, happy
bienaventuranzas *nfpl* : Beatitudes
bienestar *nm* 1 : welfare, well-being 2 CONFORT : comfort
bienhechor¹, -chora *adj* : beneficent, benevolent
bienhechor², -chora *n* : benefactor, benefactress *f*
bienintencionado, -da *adj* : well-meaning
bienvenida *nf* 1 : welcome 2 **dar la bienvenida a** : to welcome
bienvenido, -da *adj* : welcome
bies *nm* : bias (in sewing)
bife *nm Arg, Chile, Uru* : steak
bífido, -da *adj* : forked
bifocal *adj* : bifocal
bifocales *nmpl* : bifocals
bifurcación *nf, pl* **-ciones** : fork (in a river or road)
bifurcarse {72} *vr* : to fork
bigamia *nf* : bigamy
bígamo, -ma *n* : bigamist
bigote *nm* 1 : mustache 2 : whisker (of an animal)
bigotudo, -da *adj* : mustached, having a big mustache
bikini *nm* : bikini
bilateral *adj* : bilateral — **bilateralmente** *adv*
bilingüe *adj* : bilingual
bilioso, -sa *adj* 1 : bilious 2 : irritable
bilis *nf* : bile
billar *nm* : pool, billiards
billete *nm* 1 : bill ⟨un billete de cinco dólares : a five-dollar bill⟩ 2 BOLETO : ticket ⟨billete de ida y vuelta : round-trip ticket⟩

billetera *nf* : billfold, wallet
billón *nm, pl* **billones** 1 : billion (Great Britain) 2 : trillion (U.S.A.)
bimestral *adj* : bimonthly — **bimestralmente** *adv*
bimotor *adj* : twin-engined
binacional *adj* : binational
binario, -ria *adj* : binary
bingo *nm* : bingo
binocular *adj* : binocular
binoculares *nmpl* : binoculars
binomio *nm* 1 : binomial 2 PAREJA : pair, duo
biodegradable *adj* : biodegradable
biodegradarse *vr* : to biodegrade
biodiversidad *nf* : biodiversity
biofísica *nf* : biophysics
biofísico¹, -ca *adj* : biophysical
biofísico², -ca *n* : biophysicist
biografía *nf* : biography
biográfico, -ca *adj* : biographical
biógrafo, -fa *n* : biographer
biología *nf* : biology
biológico, -ca *adj* : biological, biologic — **biológicamente** *adv*
biólogo, -ga *n* : biologist
biombo *nm* MAMPARA : folding screen, room divider
biomecánica *nf* : biomechanics
biopsia *nf* : biopsy
bioquímica *nf* : biochemistry
bioquímico¹, -ca *adj* : biochemical
bioquímico², -ca *n* : biochemist
biosfera *or* **biósfera** *nf* : biosphere
biotecnología *nf* : biotechnology
biótico, -ca *adj* : biotic
bipartidismo *nm* : two-party system
bipartidista *adj* : bipartisan
bípedo *nm* : biped
birlar *vt fam* : to swipe, to pinch
birmano, -na *adj & n* : Burmese
bis¹ *adv* 1 : twice, again (in music) 2 : a, A ⟨artículo 47 bis : Article 47A⟩ ⟨calle Bolívar, número 70 bis : Bolívar Street, number 70A⟩
bis² *nm* : encore
bisabuelo, -la *n* : great-grandfather *m*, great-grandmother *f*, great-grandparent
bisagra *nf* : hinge
bisecar {72} *vt* : bisect — **bisección** *nf*
bisel *nm* : bevel
biselar *vt* : to bevel
bisexual *adj* : bisexual
bisiesto *adj* **año bisiesto** : leap year
bismuto *nm* : bismuth
bisnieto, -ta *n* : great-grandson *m*, great-granddaughter *f*, great-grandchild
bisonte *nm* : bison, buffalo
bisoñé *nm* : hairpiece, toupee
bisoño¹, -ña *adj* : inexperienced, green
bisoño², -ña *n* : rookie, greenhorn
bistec *nm* : steak, beefsteak
bisturí *nm* ESCALPELO : scalpel
bisutería *nf* : costume jewelry
bit *nm* : bit (unit of information)
bivalvo *nm* : bivalve
bizarría *nf* 1 : courage, gallantry 2 : generosity

bizarro, -rra *adj* **1** VALIENTE : courageous, valiant **2** GENEROSO : generous

bizco, -ca *adj* : cross-eyed

bizcocho *nm* **1** : sponge cake **2** : biscuit **3** *Mex* : breadstick

bizquera *nf* : crossed eyes, squint

blanco¹, -ca *adj* : white

blanco², -ca *n* : white person

blanco³ *nm* **1** : white **2** : target, bull's-eye ⟨dar en el blanco : to hit the target, to hit the nail on the head⟩ **3** : blank space, blank ⟨un cheque en blanco : a blank check⟩

blancura *nf* : whiteness

blancuzco, -ca *adj* **1** : whitish, off-white **2** PÁLIDO : pale

blandir {1} *vt* : to wave, to brandish

blando, -da *adj* **1** SUAVE : soft, tender **2** : weak (in character) **3** : lenient

blandura *nf* **1** : softness, tenderness **2** : leniency

blanqueador *nm* : bleach, whitener

blanquear *vt* **1** : to whiten, to bleach **2** : to shut out (in sports) **3** : to launder (money) — *vi* **1** : to turn white

blanquillo *nm* *CA, Mex* : egg

blasfemar *vi* : to blaspheme

blasfemia *nf* : blasphemy

blasfemo, -ma *adj* : blasphemous

blazer *nm* : blazer

bledo *nm* **no me importa un bledo** *fam* : I couldn't care less, I don't give a damn

blindado, -da *adj* ACORAZADO : armored

blindaje *nm* **1** : armor, armor plating **2** : shield (for cables, machinery, etc.)

bloc *nm, pl* **blocs** : writing pad, pad of paper

blof *nm* *Col, Mex* : bluff

blofear *vi* *Col, Mex* : to bluff

blondo, -da *adj* : blond, flaxen

bloque *nm* **1** : block **2** GRUPO : bloc ⟨el bloque comunista : the Communist bloc⟩

bloquear *vt* **1** OBSTRUIR : to block, to obstruct **2** : to blockade

bloqueo *nm* **1** OBSTRUCCIÓN : blockage, obstruction **2** : blockade

blusa *nf* : blouse

blusón *nm, pl* **blusones** : loose shirt, smock

boa *nf* : boa

boato *nm* : ostentation, show

bobada *nf* **1** : stupid remark or action **2 decir bobadas** : to talk nonsense

bobalicón, -cona *adj, mpl* **-cones** *fam* : silly, stupid

bobina *nf* CARRETE : bobbin, reel

bobo¹, -ba *adj* : silly, stupid

bobo², -ba *n* : fool, simpleton

boca *nf* **1** : mouth **2 boca arriba** : face up, on one's back **3 boca abajo** : face down, prone **4 boca de riego** : hydrant **5 en boca de** : according to

bocacalle *nf* : entrance to a street ⟨gire a la última bocacalle : take the last turning⟩

bocadillo *nm* *Spain* : sandwich

bocado *nm* **1** : bite, mouthful **2** FRENO : bit (of a bridle)

bocajarro *nm* **a ~** : point-blank, directly

bocallave *nf* : keyhole

bocanada *nf* **1** : swig, swallow **2** : puff, mouthful (of smoke) **3** : gust (of air) **4** : stream (of people)

boceto *nm* : sketch, outline

bochinche *nm* *fam* : ruckus, uproar

bochorno *nm* **1** VERGÜENZA : embarrassment **2** : hot and humid weather **3** : hot flash

bochornoso, -sa *adj* EMBARAZOSO : embarrassing **2** : hot and muggy

bocina *nf* **1** : horn, trumpet **2** : automobile horn **3** : mouthpiece (of a telephone) **4** *Mex* : loudspeaker

bocinazo *nm* : honk (of a horn)

bocio *nm* : goiter

bocón, -cona *n, mpl* **bocones** *fam* : blabbermouth, loudmouth

boda *nf* : wedding

bodega *nf* **1** : wine cellar **2** *Chile, Col, Mex* : storeroom, warehouse **3** (*in various countries*) : grocery store

bofetada *nf* CACHETADA : slap on the face

bofetear *vt* CACHETEAR : to slap

bofetón *nm* → bofetada

bofo, -fa *adj* : flabby

boga *nf* : fashion, vogue ⟨estar en boga : to be in style⟩

bogotano¹, -na *adj* : of or from Bogotá

bogotano², -na *n* : person from Bogotá

bohemio, -mia *adj & n* : bohemian, Bohemian

boicot *nm, pl* **boicots** : boycott

boicotear *vt* : to boycott

boina *nf* : beret

boiserie *nf* : wood paneling, wainscoting

boj *nm, pl* **bojes** : box (plant), boxwood

bola *nf* **1** : ball ⟨bola de nieve : snowball⟩ **2** *fam* : lie, fib **3** *Mex fam* : bunch, group ⟨una bola de rateros : a bunch of thieves⟩ **4** *Mex* : uproar, tumult

bolear *vt* *Mex* : to polish (shoes)

bolera *nf* : bowling alley

bolero *nm* : bolero

boleta *nf* **1** : ballot **2** : ticket **3** : receipt

boletería *nf* TAQUILLA : box office, ticket office

boletín *nm, pl* **-tines** **1** : bulletin **2** : journal, review **3 boletín de prensa** : press release

boleto *nm* BILLETE : ticket

boliche *nm* **1** BOLOS : bowling **2** *Arg* : bar, tavern

bólido *nm* **1** : race car **2** METEORO : meteor

bolígrafo *nm* : ballpoint pen

bolillo *nm* **1** : bobbin **2** *Mex* : roll, bun

bolívar *nm* : bolivar (monetary unit of Venezuela)

boliviano¹, -na *adj & n* : Bolivian

boliviano² *nm* : boliviano (monetary unit of Bolivia)

bollo *nm* : bun, sweet roll

bolo *nm* : bowling pin, tenpin

bolos *nmpl* BOLICHE : bowling

bolsa *nf* **1** : bag, sack **2** *Mex* : pocketbook, purse **3** *Mex* : pocket **4 la Bolsa** : the stock market, the stock exchange **5 bolsa de trabajo** : employment agency

bolsear *vi Mex* : to pick pockets

bolsillo *nm* **1** : pocket **2 dinero de bolsillo** : pocket change, loose change

bolso *nm* : pocketbook, handbag

bomba *nf* **1** : bomb **2** : bubble **3** : pump ⟨bomba de gasolina : gas pump⟩

bombachos *nmpl* : baggy pants, bloomers

bombardear *vt* **1** : to bomb **2** : to bombard

bombardeo *nm* **1** : bombing, shelling **2** : bombardment

bombardero *nm* : bomber (airplane)

bombástico, -ca *adj* : bombastic

bombear *vt* : to pump

bombero, -ra *n* : firefighter, fireman *m*

bombilla *nf* : lightbulb

bombillo *nm CA, Col, Ven* : lightbulb

bombo *nm* **1** : bass drum **2** *fam* : exaggerated praise, hype ⟨con bombos y platillos : with great fanfare⟩

bombón *nm, pl* **bombones 1** : bonbon, chocolate **2** *Mex* : marshmallow

bonachón¹, -chona *adj, mpl* **-chones** *fam* : good-natured, kindhearted

bonachón², -chona *n, mpl* **-chones** *fam* BUENAZO : kindhearted person

bonaerense¹ *adj* : of or from Buenos Aires

bonaerense² *nmf* : person from Buenos Aires

bonanza *nf* **1** PROSPERIDAD : prosperity ⟨bonanza económica : economic boom⟩ **2** : calm weather **3** : rich ore deposit, bonanza

bondad *nf* BENEVOLENCIA : goodness, kindness ⟨tener la bondad de hacer algo : to be kind enough to do something⟩

bondadoso, -sa *adj* BENÉVOLO : kind, kindly, good — **bondadosamente** *adv*

bonete *nm* : cap, mortarboard

boniato *nm* : sweet potato

bonificación *nf, pl* **-ciones 1** : discount **2** : bonus, extra

bonito¹ *adv* : nicely, well ⟨¡qué bonito canta tu hermana! : your sister sings wonderfully!⟩

bonito², -ta *adj* LINDO : pretty, lovely ⟨tiene un apartamento bonito : she has a nice apartment⟩

bonito³ *nm* : bonito (tuna)

bono *nm* **1** : bond ⟨bono bancario : bank bond⟩ **2** : voucher

boqueada *nf* : gasp ⟨dar la última boqueada : to give one's last gasp⟩

boquear *vi* **1** : to gasp **2** : to be dying

boquete *nm* : gap, opening, breach

boquiabierto, -ta *adj* : open-mouthed, speechless, agape

boquilla *nf* : mouthpiece (of a musical instrument)

borbollar *vi* : to bubble

borbotar *or* **borbotear** *vi* : to boil, to bubble, to gurgle

borboteo *nm* : bubbling, gurgling

borda *nf* : gunwale

bordado *nm* : embroidery, needlework

bordar *v* : to embroider

borde *nm* **1** : border, edge **2 al borde de** : on the verge of ⟨estoy al borde de la locura : I'm about to go crazy⟩

bordear *vt* **1** : to border, to skirt ⟨el Río Este bordea Manhattan : the East River borders Manhattan⟩ **2** : to border on ⟨bordea la irrealidad : it borders on unreality⟩ **3** : to line ⟨una calle bordeada de árboles : a street lined with trees⟩

bordillo *nm* : curb

bordo *nm* **a** ~ : aboard, on board

boreal *adj* : northern

borgoña *nf* : burgundy

bórico, -ca *adj* : boric ⟨ácido bórico : boric acid⟩

boricua *adj & nmf fam* : Puerto Rican

borinqueño, -ña → **boricua**

borla *nf* **1** : pom-pom, tassel **2** : powder puff

boro *nm* : boron

borrachera *nf* : drunkenness ⟨agarró una borrachera : he got drunk⟩

borrachín, -china *n, mpl* **-chines** *fam* : lush, drunk

borracho¹, -cha *adj* EBRIO : drunk, intoxicated

borracho², -cha *n* : drunk, drunkard

borrador *nm* **1** : rough copy, first draft ⟨en borrador : in the rough⟩ **2** : eraser

borrar *vt* : to erase, to blot out — **borrarse** *vr* **1** : to fade, to fade away **2** : to resign, to drop out **3** *Mex fam* : to split, to leave ⟨me borro : I'm out of here⟩

borrascoso, -sa *adj* : gusty, blustery

borrego, -ga *n* **1** : lamb, sheep **2** : simpleton, fool

borrico → **burro**

borrón *nm, pl* **borrones** : smudge, blot ⟨borrón y cuenta nueva : let's start on a clean slate, let's start over again⟩

borronear *vt* : to smudge, to blot

borroso, -sa *adj* **1** : blurry, smudgy **2** CONFUSO : unclear, confused

boscoso, -sa *adj* : wooded

bosnio, -nia *adj & n* : Bosnian

bosque *nm* : woods, forest

bosquecillo *nm* : grove, copse, thicket

bosquejar *vt* ESBOZAR : to outline, to sketch

bosquejo *nm* **1** TRAZADO : outline, sketch **2** : draft

bostezar {21} *vi* : to yawn

bostezo *nm* : yawn

bota *nf* **1** : boot **2** : wineskin

botana *nf Mex* : snack, appetizer

botanear *vi Mex* : to have a snack

botánica *nf* : botany

botánico[1], **-ca** *adj* : botanical
botánico[2], **-ca** *n* : botanist
botar *vt* **1** ARROJAR : to throw, to fling, to hurl **2** TIRAR : to throw out, to throw away **3** : to launch (a ship)
bote *nm* **1** : small boat ⟨bote de remos : rowboat⟩ **2** : can, jar **3** : jump, bounce **4** *Mex fam* : jail
botella *nf* : bottle
botica *nf* FARMACIA : drugstore, pharmacy
boticario, -ria *n* FARMACÉUTICO : pharmacist, druggist
botín *nm, pl* **botines** **1** : baby's bootee **2** : ankle boot **3** : booty, plunder
botiquín *nm, pl* **-quines** **1** : medicine cabinet **2** : first-aid kit
botón *nm, pl* **botones** **1** : button **2** : bud **3** INSIGNIA : badge
botones *nmfs & pl* : bellhop
botulismo *nm* : botulism
boulevard [ˌbuleˈvar] → **bulevar**
bouquet *nm* **1** : fragrance, bouquet (of wine) **2** RAMILLETE : bouquet (of flowers)
boutique *nf* : boutique
bóveda *nf* **1** : vault, dome **2** CRIPTA : crypt
bovino, -na *adj* : bovine
box *nm, pl* **boxes** **1** : pit (in auto racing) **2** *Mex* : boxing
boxeador, -dora *n* : boxer
boxear *vi* : to box
boxeo *nm* : boxing
boya *nf* : buoy
boyante *adj* **1** : buoyant **2** : prosperous, thriving
bozal *nm* **1** : muzzle **2** : halter (for a horse)
bracear *vi* **1** : to wave one's arms **2** : to make strokes (in swimming)
bracero, -ra *n* : migrant worker, day laborer
braguero *nm* : truss (in medicine)
bragueta *nf* : fly, pants zipper
braille *adj & nm* : braille
bramante *nm* : twine, string
bramar *vi* **1** RUGIR : to roar, to bellow **2** : to howl (of the wind)
bramido *nm* : bellowing, roar
brandy *nm* : brandy
branquia *nf* AGALLA : gill
brasa *nf* ASCUA : ember, live coal
brasero *nm* : brazier
brasier *nm Col, Mex* : brassiere, bra
brasileño, -ña *adj & n* : Brazilian
bravata *nf* **1** JACTANCIA : boast, bravado **2** AMENAZA : threat
bravo, -va *adj* **1** FEROZ : ferocious, fierce ⟨un perro bravo : a ferocious dog⟩ **2** EXCELENTE : excellent, great ⟨¡bravo! : bravo!, well done!⟩ **3** : rough, rugged, wild **4** : annoyed, angry
bravucón, -cona *n, mpl* **-cones** : bully
bravuconadas *nfpl* : bravado
bravura *nf* **1** FEROCIDAD : fierceness, ferocity **2** VALENTÍA : bravery

braza *nf* **1** : breaststroke **2** : fathom (unit of length)
brazada *nf* : stroke (in swimming)
brazalete *nm* PULSERA : bracelet, bangle
brazo *nm* **1** : arm **2 brazo derecho** : right-hand man **3 brazos** *nmpl* : hands, laborers
brea *nf* ALQUITRÁN : tar, pitch
brebaje *nm* : potion, brew
brecha *nf* **1** : gap, breach ⟨estar siempre en la brecha : to be always there when needed, to stay in the thick of things⟩ **2** : gash
brécol *nm* : broccoli
brega *nf* **1** LUCHA : struggle, fight **2** : hard work
bregar {52} *vi* **1** LUCHAR : to struggle **2** : to toil, to work hard **3** ~ **con** : to deal with
brete *nm* : jam, tight spot
breve *adj* **1** CORTO : brief, short **2 en** ~ : shortly, in short — **brevemente** *adv*
brevedad *nf* : brevity, shortness
breviario *nm* : breviary
brezal *nm* : heath, moor
brezo *nm* : heather
bribón, -bona *n, mpl* **bribones** : rascal, scamp
bricolaje *or* **bricolage** *nm* : do-it-yourself
brida *nf* : bridle
brigada *nf* **1** : brigade **2** : gang, team, squad
brigadier *nm* : brigadier
brillante[1] *adj* : brilliant, bright — **brillantemente** *adv*
brillante[2] *nm* DIAMANTE : diamond
brillantez *nf* : brilliance, brightness
brillar *vi* : to shine, to sparkle
brillo *nm* **1** LUSTRE : luster, shine **2** : brilliance
brilloso, -sa *adj* LUSTROSO : lustrous, shiny
brincar {72} *vi* **1** SALTAR : to jump around, to leap about **2** : to frolic, to gambol
brinco *nm* **1** SALTO : jump, leap, skip **2 pegar un brinco** : to give a start, to jump
brindar *vi* : to drink a toast ⟨brindó por los vencedores : he toasted the victors⟩ — *vt* OFRECER, PROPORCIONAR : to offer, to provide — **brindarse** *vr* : to offer one's assistance, to volunteer
brindis *nm* : toast, drink ⟨hacer un brindis : to drink a toast⟩
brinque, etc. → **brincar**
brío *nm* **1** : force, determination **2** : spirit, verve
brioso, -sa *adj* : spirited, lively
briqueta *nf* : briquette
brisa *nf* : breeze
británico[1], **-ca** *adj* : British
británico[2], **-ca** *n* **1** : British person **2 los británicos** : the British
brizna *nf* **1** : strand, thread **2** : blade (of grass)

broca *nf* : drill bit
brocado *nm* : brocade
brocha *nf* : paintbrush
broche *nm* **1** ALFILER : brooch **2** : fastener, clasp **3 broche de oro** : finishing touch
brocheta *nf* : skewer
brócoli *nm* : broccoli
broma *nf* **1** CHISTE : joke, prank **2** : fun, merriment **3 en ~** : in jest, jokingly
bromear *vi* : to joke, to fool around ⟨sólo estaba bromeando : I was only kidding⟩
bromista[1] *adj* : fun-loving, joking
bromista[2] *nmf* : joker, prankster
bromo *nm* : bromine
bronca *nf fam* : fight, quarrel, fuss
bronce *nm* : bronze
bronceado[1], **-da** *adj* **1** : tanned, suntanned **2** : bronzing
bronceado[2] *nm* **1** : suntan, tan **2** : bronzing
broncearse *vr* : to get a suntan
bronco, -ca *adj* **1** : harsh, rough **2** : untamed, wild
bronquial *adj* : bronchial
bronquio *nm* : bronchial tube, bronchus
bronquitis *nf* : bronchitis
broqueta *nf* : skewer
brotar *vi* **1** : to bud, to sprout **2** : to spring up, to stream, to gush forth **3** : to break out, to appear
brote *nm* **1** : outbreak **2** : sprout, bud, shoot
broza *nf* **1** : brushwood **2** MALEZA : scrub, undergrowth
brujería *nf* HECHICERÍA : witchcraft, sorcery
brujo[1], **-ja** *adj* : bewitching
brujo[2], **-ja** *n* : warlock *m*, witch *f*, sorcerer
brújula *nf* : compass
bruma *nf* : haze, mist
brumoso, -sa *adj* : hazy, misty
bruñir {38} *vt* : to burnish, to polish (metals)
brusco, -ca *adj* **1** SÚBITO : sudden, abrupt **2** : curt, brusque — **bruscamente** *adv*
brusquedad *nf* **1** : abruptness, suddenness **2** : brusqueness
brutal *adj* **1** : brutal **2** *fam* : incredible, terrific — **brutalmente** *adv*
brutalidad *nf* CRUELDAD : brutality
brutalizar {21} *vt* : to brutalize, to maltreat
bruto[1], **-ta** *adj* **1** : gross ⟨peso bruto : gross weight⟩ ⟨ingresos brutos : gross income⟩ **2** : unrefined ⟨petróleo bruto : crude oil⟩ **3** : brutish, stupid
bruto[2], **-ta** *n* **1** : brute **2** : dunce, blockhead
bubónico, -ca *adj* : bubonic
bucal *adj* : oral
bucanero *nm* : buccaneer, pirate
buccino *nm* : whelk
buceador, -dora *n* : diver, scuba diver

bucear *vi* **1** : to dive, to swim underwater **2** : to explore, to delve
buceo *nm* **1** : diving, scuba diving **2** : exploration, searching
buche *nm* **1** : crop (of a bird) **2** *fam* : belly, gut **3** : mouthful ⟨hacer buches : to rinse one's mouth⟩
bucle *nm* **1** : curl, ringlet **2** : loop
bucólico, -ca *adj* : bucolic
budín *nm, pl* **budines** : pudding
budismo *nm* : Buddhism
budista *adj & nmf* : Buddhist
buen *adj* → **bueno**[1]
buenamente *adv* **1** : easily **2** : willingly
buenaventura *nf* **1** : good luck **2** : fortune, future ⟨le dijo la buenaventura : she told his fortune⟩
buenazo, -za *n fam* BONACHÓN : kindhearted person
bueno[1], **-na** *adj* (**buen** *before masculine singular nouns*) **1** : good ⟨una buena idea : a good idea⟩ **2** BONDADOSO : nice, kind **3** APROPIADO : proper, appropriate **4** SANO : well, healthy **5** : considerable, goodly ⟨una buena cantidad : a lot⟩ **6 buenos días** : hello, good day **7 buenas tardes** : good afternoon **8 buenas noches** : good evening, good night
bueno[2] *interj* **1** : OK!, all right! **2** *Mex* : hello! (on the telephone)
buey *nm* : ox, steer
búfalo *nm* **1** : buffalo **2 búfalo de agua** : water buffalo
bufanda *nf* : scarf, muffler
bufar *vi* : to snort
bufet *or* **bufé** *nm* : buffet-style meal
bufete *nm* **1** : law firm, law office **2** : writing desk
bufido *nm* : snort
bufo, -fa *adj* : comic
bufón, -fona *n, mpl* **bufones** : clown, buffoon, jester
bufonada *nf* **1** : jest, buffoonery **2** : sarcasm
buhardilla *nf* **1** ÁTICO, DESVÁN : attic **2** : dormer window
búho *nm* **1** : owl **2** *fam* : hermit, recluse
buhonero, -ra *n* MERCACHIFLE : peddler
buitre *nm* : vulture
bujía *nf* : spark plug
bula *nf* : papal bull
bulbo *nm* : bulb
bulboso, -sa *adj* : bulbous
bulevar *nm* : boulevard
búlgaro, -ra *adj & n* : Bulgarian
bulla *nf* BARULLO : racket, rowdiness
bullicio *nm* **1** : ruckus, uproar **2** : hustle and bustle
bullicioso, -sa *adj* : noisy, busy, turbulent
bullir {38} *vi* **1** HERVIR : to boil **2** MOVERSE : to stir, to bustle about
bulto *nm* **1** : package, bundle **2** : piece of luggage, bag **3** : size, bulk, volume **4** : form, shape **5** : lump (on the body), swelling, bulge

bumerán *nm, pl* **-ranes** : boomerang
búnker *nm, pl* **búnkers** : bunker
búnquer → **búnker**
buñuelo *nm* : fried pastry
buque *nm* BARCO : ship, vessel
burbuja *nf* : bubble, blister (on a surface)
burbujear *vi* **1** : to bubble **2** : to fizz
burbujeo *nm* : bubbling
burdel *nm* : brothel, whorehouse
burdo, -da *adj* **1** : coarse, rough **2** : crude, clumsy ⟨una burda mentira : a clumsy lie⟩ — **burdamente** *adj*
burgués, -guesa *adj & n, mpl* **burgueses** : bourgeois
burguesía *nf* : bourgeoisie, middle class
burla *nf* **1** : mockery, ridicule **2** : joke, trick **3 hacer burla de** : to make fun of, to mock
burlar *vt* ENGAÑAR : to trick, to deceive — **burlarse** *vr* ~ **de** : to make fun of, to ridicule
burlesco, -ca *adj* : burlesque, comic
burlón[1], -lona *adj, mpl* **burlones** : joking, mocking
burlón[2], -lona *n, mpl* **burlones** : joker
burocracia *nf* : bureaucracy
burócrata *nmf* : bureaucrat
burocrático, -ca *adj* : bureaucratic
burrada *nf fam* : stupid act, nonsense
burrito *nm* : burrito
burro[1], -rra *adj fam* : dumb, stupid

burro[2], -rra *n* ASNO : donkey, ass **2** *fam* : dunce, poor student
burro[3] *nm* **1** : sawhorse **2** *Mex* : ironing board **3** *Mex* : stepladder
bursátil *adj* : stock-market
bursitis *nf* : bursitis
burundés, -desa *adj & n* : Burundian
bus *nm* : bus
busca *nf* : search
buscador, -dora *n* : hunter (for treasure, etc.), prospector
buscapersonas *nms & pl* : beeper, pager
buscapleitos *nmfs & pl* : troublemaker
buscar {72} *vt* **1** : to look for, to seek **2** : to pick up, to collect **3** : to provoke — *vi* : to look, to search ⟨buscó en los bolsillos : he searched through his pockets⟩
buscavidas *nmf & pl* **1** : busybody **2** : go-getter
busque, etc. → **buscar**
búsqueda *nf* : search
busto *nm* : bust
butaca {72} *nf* **1** SILLÓN : armchair **2** : seat (in a theatre) **3** *Mex* : pupil's desk
butano *nm* : butane
buzo[1], -za *adj Mex fam* : smart, astute ⟨¡ponte buzo! : get with it!, get on the ball!⟩
buzo[2] *nm* : diver, scuba diver
buzón *nm, pl* **buzones** : mailbox
byte *nm* : byte

C

c *nf* : third letter of the Spanish alphabet
cabal *adj* **1** : exact, correct **2** : complete **3** : upright, honest
cabales *nmpl* **no estar en sus cabales** : not to be in one's right mind
cabalgar {52} *vi* : to ride (on horseback)
cabalgata *nf* : cavalcade, procession
cabalidad *nf a* ~ : thoroughly, conscientiously
caballa *nf* : mackerel
caballada *nf* **1** : herd of horses **2** *fam* : nonsense, stupidity, outrageousness
caballar *adj* EQUINO : horse, equine
caballeresco, -ca *adj* : gallant, chivalrous
caballería *nf* **1** : cavalry **2** : horse, mount **3** : knighthood, chivalry
caballeriza *nf* : stable
caballero[1] → **caballeroso**
caballero[2] *nm* **1** : gentleman **2** : knight
caballerosidad *nf* : chivalry, gallantry
caballeroso, -sa *adj* : gentlemanly, chivalrous
caballete *nm* **1** : ridge **2** : easel **3** : trestle (for a table, etc.) **4** : bridge (of the nose) **5** : sawhorse
caballista *nmf* : horseman *m*, horsewoman *f*
caballito *nm* **1** : rocking horse **2 caballito de mar** : seahorse **3 caballitos** *nmpl* : merry-go-round

caballo *nm* **1** : horse **2** : knight (in chess) **3 caballo de fuerza** *or* **caballo de vapor** : horsepower
cabalmente *adv* : fully, exactly
cabaña *nf* CHOZA : cabin, hut
cabaret *nm, pl* **-rets** : nightclub, cabaret
cabecear *vt* : to head (in soccer) — *vi* **1** : to nod one's head **2** : to lurch, to pitch
cabecera *nf* **1** : headboard **2** : head ⟨cabecera de la mesa : head of the table⟩ **3** : heading, headline **4** : headwaters *pl* **5 médico de cabecera** : family doctor **6 cabecera municipal** *CA, Mex* : downtown area
cabecilla *nmf* : ringleader, kingpin
cabellera *nf* : head of hair, mane
cabello *nm* : hair
cabelludo, -da *adj* **1** : hairy **2 cuero cabelludo** : scalp
caber {12} *vi* **1** : to fit, to go ⟨no sé si cabremos todos en el coche : I don't know if we'll all fit in the car⟩ **2** : to be possible ⟨no cabe duda alguna : there's no doubt about it⟩ ⟨cabe que llegue mañana : he may come tomorrow⟩
cabestrillo *nm* : sling ⟨llevo el brazo en cabestrillo : my arm is in a sling⟩
cabestro *nm* : halter (for an animal)
cabeza *nf* **1** : head **2 cabeza hueca** : scatterbrain **3 de** ~ : head first **4 dolor de cabeza** : headache

cabezada *nf* **1** : butt, blow with the head **2** : nod ⟨echar una cabezada : to take a nap, to doze off⟩

cabezal *nm* : bolster

cabezazo *nm* : butt, blow with the head

cabezón, -zona *adj, mpl* **-zones** *fam* **1** : having a big head **2** : pigheaded, stubborn

cabida *nf* **1** : room, space, capacity **2** dar cabida a : to accommodate, to hold

cabildear *vi* : to lobby

cabildeo *nm* : lobbying

cabildero, -ra *n* : lobbyist

cabildo *nm* AYUNTAMIENTO **1** : town or city hall **2** : town or city council

cabina *nf* **1** : cabin **2** : booth **3** : cab (of a truck), cockpit (of an airplane)

cabizbajo, -ja *adj* : dejected, downcast

cable *nm* : cable

cableado *nm* : wiring

cabo *nm* **1** : end ⟨al cabo de dos semanas : at the end of two weeks⟩ **2** : stub, end piece **3** : corporal **4** : cape, headland ⟨el Cabo Cañaveral : Cape Canaveral⟩ **5** al fin y al cabo : after all, in the end **6** llevar a cabo : to carry out, to do

caboverdiano, -na *adj & n* : Cape Verdean

cabrá, etc. → caber

cabra *nf* : goat

cabrestante *nm* : windlass

cabrío, -ría *adj* : goat, caprine

cabriola *nf* **1** : skip, jump **2** hacer cabriolas : to prance

cabriolar *vi* : to prance

cabrito *nm* : kid, baby goat

cabús *nm, pl* **cabuses** *Mex* : caboose

cacahuate *or* **cacahuete** *nm* : peanut

cacalote *nm Mex* : crow

cacao *nm* : cacao, cocoa bean

cacarear *vi* : to crow, to cackle, to cluck — *vt fam* : to boast about, to crow about ⟨cacarear un huevo : to brag about an accomplishment⟩

cacareo *nm* **1** : clucking (of a hen), crowing (of a rooster) **2** : boasting

cacatúa *nf* : cockatoo

cace, etc. → cazar

cacería *nf* **1** CAZA : hunt, hunting **2** : hunting party

cacerola *nf* : pan, saucepan

cacha *nf* : butt (of a gun)

cachar *vt fam* : to catch

cacharro *nm* **1** *fam* : thing, piece of junk **2** *fam* : jalopy **3** cacharros *nmpl* : pots and pans

cache *nm* : cache, cache memory

caché *nm* : cachet

cachear *vt* : to search, to frisk

cachemir *nm* : cashmere

cachetada *nf* BOFETADA : slap on the face

cachete *nm* : cheek

cachetear *vt* BOFETEAR : to slap

cachiporra *nf* : bludgeon, club, blackjack

cachirul *nm Mex fam* : cheating ⟨hacer cachirul : to cheat⟩

cachivache *nm fam* : thing ⟨mete tus cachivaches en el maletero : put your stuff in the trunk⟩

cacho *nm fam* : piece, bit

cachorro, -rra *n* **1** : cub **2** PERRITO : puppy

cachucha *nf Mex* : cap, baseball cap

cacique *nm* **1** : chief (of a tribe) **2** : boss (in politics)

cacofonía *nf* : cacophony

cacofónico, -ca *adj* : cacophonous

cacto *nm* : cactus

cactus → cacto

cada *adj* **1** : each ⟨cuestan diez pesos cada una : they cost ten pesos each⟩ **2** : every ⟨cada vez : every time⟩ **3** : such, some ⟨sales con cada historia : you come up with such crazy stories⟩ **4** cada vez más : more and more, increasingly **5** cada vez menos : less and less

cadalso *nm* : scaffold, gallows

cadáver *nm* : corpse, cadaver

cadavérico, -ca *adj* **1** : cadaverous **2** PÁLIDO : deathly pale

caddie *or* **caddy** *nmf, pl* **caddies** : caddy

cadena *nf* **1** : chain **2** : network, channel **3** cadena de montaje : assembly line **4** cadena perpetua : life sentence

cadencia *nf* : cadence, rhythm

cadencioso, -sa *adj* : rhythmic, rhythmical

cadera *nf* : hip

cadete *nmf* : cadet

cadmio *nm* : cadmium

caducar {72} *vi* : to expire

caducidad *nf* : expiration

caduco, -ca *adj* **1** : outdated, obsolete **2** : deciduous

caer {13} *vi* **1** : to fall, to drop **2** : to collapse **3** : to hang (down) **4** caer bien *fam* : to be pleasant, to be likeable ⟨me caes bien : I like you⟩ **5** caer mal *or* caer gordo *fam* : to be unpleasant, to be unlikeable — **caerse** *vr* : to fall down

café[1] *adj* : brown ⟨ojos cafés : brown eyes⟩

café[2] *nm* **1** : coffee **2** : café

cafeína *nf* : caffeine

cafetal *nm* : coffee plantation

cafetalero[1]**, -ra** *adj* : coffee ⟨cosecha cafetalera : coffee harvest⟩

cafetalero[2]**, -ra** *n* : coffee grower

cafetera *nf* : coffeepot, coffeemaker

cafetería *nf* **1** : coffee shop, café **2** : lunchroom, cafeteria

cafetero[1]**, -ra** *adj* : coffee-producing

cafetero[2]**, -ra** *n* : coffee grower

caficultura *nf Mex* : coffee industry

caguama *nf* **1** : large Caribbean turtle **2** *Mex* : large bottle of beer

caída *nf* **1** BAJA, DESCENSO : fall, drop **2** : collapse, downfall

caiga, etc. → caer

caimán *nm, pl* **caimanes** : alligator, caiman

caimito *nm* : star apple

caja *nf* **1** : box, case **2** : cash register, checkout counter **3** : bed (of a truck) **4** *fam* : coffin **5 caja fuerte** *or* **caja de caudales** : safe **6 caja de seguridad** : safe-deposit box **7 caja torácica** : rib cage

cajero, -ra *n* **1** : cashier **2** : teller **3 cajero automático** : automated teller machine, ATM

cajeta *nf Mex* : a sweet caramel-flavored spread

cajetilla *nf* : pack (of cigarettes)

cajón *nm, pl* **cajones 1** : drawer, till **2** : crate, case **3 cajón de estacionamiento** *Mex* : parking space

cajuela *nf Mex* : trunk (of a car)

cal *nf* : lime, quicklime

cala *nf* : cove, inlet

calabacín *nm, pl* **-cines** : zucchini

calabacita *nf Mex* : zucchini

calabaza *nf* **1** : pumpkin, squash **2** : gourd **3 dar calabazas a** : to give the brush-off to, to jilt

calabozo *nm* **1** : prison **2** : jail cell

calado¹, -da *adj* **1** : drenched **2** : open-worked

calado² *nm* **1** : draft (of a ship) **2** : open-work

calafatear *vt* : to caulk

calamar *nm* **1** : squid **2 calamares** *nmpl* : calamari

calambre *nm* **1** ESPASMO : cramp **2** : electric shock, jolt

calamidad *nf* DESASTRE : calamity, disaster

calamina *nf* : calamine

calamitoso, -sa *adj* : calamitous, disastrous

calaña *nf* : ilk, kind, sort ⟨una persona de mala calaña : a bad sort⟩

calar *vt* **1** : to soak through **2** : to pierce, to penetrate — *vi* : to catch on — **calarse** *vr* : to get drenched

calavera¹ *nf* **1** : skull **2** *Mex* : taillight

calavera² *nm* : rake, rogue

calcar {72} *vt* **1** : to trace **2** : to copy, to imitate

calce, etc. → **calzar**

calceta *nf* : knee-high stocking

calcetería *nf* : hosiery

calcetín *nm, pl* **-tines** : sock

calcificar {72} *v* : to calcify — **calcificarse** *vr*

calcinar *vt* : to char, to burn

calcio *nm* : calcium

calco *nm* **1** : transfer, tracing **2** : copy, image

calcomanía *nf* : decal, transfer

calculador, -dora *adj* : calculating

calculadora *nf* : calculator

calcular *vt* **1** : to calculate, to estimate **2** : to plan, to scheme

cálculo *nm* **1** : calculation, estimation **2** : calculus **3** : plan, scheme **4 cálculo biliar** : gallstone **5 hoja de cálculo** : spreadsheet

caldas *nfpl* : hot springs

caldear *vt* : to heat, to warm — **caldearse** *vr* **1** : to heat up **2** : to become heated, to get tense

caldera *nf* **1** : cauldron **2** : boiler

caldo *nm* **1** CONSOMÉ : broth, stock **2** **caldo de cultivo** : culture medium, breeding ground

caldoso, -sa *adj* : watery

calefacción *nf, pl* **-ciones** : heating, heat

calefactor *nm* : heater

caleidoscopio → **calidoscopio**

calendario *nm* **1** : calendar **2** : timetable, schedule

caléndula *nf* : marigold

calentador *nm* : heater

calentamiento *nm* **1** : heating, warming **2** : warm-up (in sports)

calentar {55} *vt* **1** : to heat, to warm **2** *fam* : to annoy, to anger **3** *fam* : to excite, to turn on — **calentarse** *vr* **1** : to get warm, to heat up **2** : to warm up (in sports) **3** *fam* : to become sexually aroused **4** *fam* : to get mad

calentura *nf* **1** FIEBRE : temperature, fever **2** : cold sore

calibrador *nm* : gauge, calipers *pl*

calibrar *vt* : to calibrate — **calibración** *nf*

calibre *nm* **1** : caliber, gauge **2** : importance, excellence **3** : kind, sort ⟨un problema de grueso calibre : a serious problem⟩

calidad *nf* **1** : quality, grade **2** : position, status **3 en calidad de** : as, in the capacity of

cálido, -da *adj* **1** : hot ⟨un clima cálido : a hot climate⟩ **2** : warm ⟨una cálida bienvenida : a warm welcome⟩

calidoscopio *nm* : kaleidoscope

caliente *adj* **1** : hot, warm ⟨mantenerse caliente : to stay warm⟩ **2** : heated, fiery ⟨una disputa caliente : a heated argument⟩ **3** *fam* : sexually excited, horny

califa *nm* : caliph

calificación *nf, pl* **-ciones 1** NOTA : grade (for a course) **2** : rating, score **3** CLASIFICACIÓN : qualification, qualifying ⟨ronda de calificación : qualifying round⟩

calificar {72} *vt* **1** : to grade **2** : to describe, to rate ⟨la calificaron de buena alumna : they described her as a good student⟩ **3** : to qualify, to modify (in grammar)

calificativo¹, -va *adj* : qualifying

calificativo² *nm* : qualifier, epithet

caligrafía *nf* **1** ESCRITURA : handwriting **2** : calligraphy

calipso *nm* : calypso

calistenia *nf* : calisthenics

cáliz *nm, pl* **cálices 1** : chalice, goblet **2** : calyx

caliza *nf* : limestone

callado, -da *adj* : quiet, silent — **calladamente** *adv*

callar *vi* : to keep quiet, to be silent — *vt* **1** : to silence, to hush ⟨¡calla a los niños! : keep the children quiet!〉 **2** : to keep secret — **callarse** *vr* : to remain silent 〈¡cállate! : be quiet!, shut up!〉

calle *nf* : street, road

callejear *vi* : to wander about the streets, to hang out

callejero, -ra *adj* : street 〈perro callejero : stray dog〉

callejón *nm, pl* **-jones 1** : alley **2 callejón sin salida** : dead-end street

callo *nm* **1** : callus, corn **2 callos** *nmpl* : tripe

calloso, -sa *adj* : callous

calma *nf* : calm, quiet

calmante[1] *adj* : calming, soothing

calmante[2] *nm* : tranquilizer, sedative

calmar *vt* TRANQUILIZAR : to calm, to soothe — **calmarse** *vr* : to calm down

calmo, -ma *adj* TRANQUILO : calm, tranquil

calmoso, -sa *adj* **1** TRANQUILO : calm, quiet **2** LENTO : slow, sluggish

calor *nm* **1** : heat 〈hace calor : it's hot outside〉 〈tener calor : to feel hot〉 **2** : warmth, affection **3** : ardor, passion

caloría *nf* : calorie

calórico, -ca *adj* : caloric

calorífico, -ca *adj* : caloric

calque, etc. → **calcar**

calumnia *nf* : slander, libel — **calumnioso, -sa** *adj*

calumniar *vt* : to slander, to libel

caluroso, -sa *adj* **1** : hot **2** : warm, enthusiastic

calva *nf* : bald spot, bald head

calvario *nm* **1** : Calvary **2** : Stations of the Cross *pl* **3 vivir un calvario** : to suffer great adversity

calvicie *nf* : baldness

calvo[1], **-va** *adj* : bald

calvo[2], **-va** *n* : bald person

calza *nf* : block, wedge

calzada *nf* : roadway, avenue

calzado *nm* : footwear

calzador *nm* : shoehorn

calzar {21} *vt* **1** : to wear (shoes) 〈¿de cuál calza? : what is your shoe size?〉 〈siempre calzaban tenis : they always wore sneakers〉 **2** : to provide with shoes

calzo *nm* : chock, wedge

calzoncillos *nmpl* : underpants, briefs

calzones *nmpl* : underpants, panties

cama *nf* **1** : bed **2 cama elástica** : trampoline

camada *nf* : litter, brood

camafeo *nm* : cameo

camaleón *nm, pl* **-leones** : chameleon

cámara *nf* **1** : camera **2** : chamber, room **3** : house (in government) **4** : inner tube

camarada *nmf* **1** : comrade, companion **2** : colleague

camaradería *nf* : camaraderie

camarero, -ra *n* **1** MESERO : waiter, waitress *f* **2** : bellhop *m*, chambermaid *f* (in a hotel) **3** : steward *m*, stewardess *f* (on a ship, etc.)

camarilla *nf* : political clique

camarógrafo, -fa *n* : cameraman *m*, camerawoman *f*

camarón *nm, pl* **-rones 1** : shrimp **2** : prawn

camarote *nm* : cabin, stateroom

camastro *nm* : small hard bed, pallet

cambalache *nm fam* : swap

cambiante *adj* **1** : changing **2** VARIABLE : changeable, variable

cambiar *vt* **1** ALTERAR, MODIFICAR : to change **2** : to exchange, to trade — *vi* **1** : to change **2 cambiar de velocidad** : to shift gears — **cambiarse** *vr* **1** : to change (clothing) **2** MUDARSE : to move (to a new address)

cambio *nm* **1** : change, alteration **2** : exchange **3** : change (money) **4 en cambio** : instead **5 en cambio** : however, on the other hand

cambista *nmf* : exchange broker

camboyano, -na *adj & n* : Cambodian

cambur *nm Ven* : banana

camelia *nf* : camellia

camello *nm* : camel

camellón *nm, pl* **-llones** *Mex* : traffic island

camerino *nm* : dressing room

camerunés, -nesa *adj, mpl* **-neses** : Cameroonian

camilla *nf* : stretcher

camillero, -ra *n* : orderly (in a hospital)

caminante *nmf* : wayfarer, walker

caminar *vi* ANDAR : to walk, to move — *vt* : to walk, to cover (a distance)

caminata *nf* : hike, long walk

camino *nm* **1** : path, road **2** : journey 〈ponerse en camino : to set off〉 **3** : way 〈a medio camino : halfway there〉

camión *nm, pl* **camiones 1** : truck **2** *Mex* : bus

camionero, -ra *n* **1** : truck driver **2** *Mex* : bus driver

camioneta *nf* : light truck, van

camisa *nf* **1** : shirt **2 camisa de fuerza** : straitjacket

camiseta *nf* **1** : T-shirt **2** : undershirt

camisón *nm, pl* **-sones** : nightshirt, nightgown

camorra *nf fam* : fight, trouble 〈buscar camorra : to pick a fight〉

camote *nm* **1** : root vegetable similar to the sweet potato **2 hacerse camote** *Mex fam* : to get mixed up

campal *adj* : pitched, fierce 〈batalla campal : pitched battle〉

campamento *nm* : camp

campana *nf* : bell

campanada *nf* TAÑIDO : stroke (of a bell), peal

campanario *nm* : bell tower, belfry

campanilla *nf* **1** : small bell, handbell **2** : uvula

campante *adj* : nonchalant, smug 〈seguir tan campante : to go on as if nothing had happened〉

campaña *nf* **1** CAMPO : countryside, country **2** : campaign **3 tienda de campaña** : tent
campañol *nm* : vole
campechana *nf Mex* : puff pastry
campechanía *nf* : geniality
campechano, -na *adj* : open, cordial, friendly
campeón, -peona *n, mpl* **-peones** : champion
campeonato *nm* : championship
cámper *nm* : camper (vehicle)
campero, -ra *adj* : country, rural
campesino, -na *n* : peasant, farm laborer
campestre *adj* : rural, rustic
camping *nm* **1** : camping **2** : campsite
campiña *nf* CAMPO : countryside, country
campista *nmf* : camper
campo *nm* **1** CAMPAÑA : countryside, country **2** : field ⟨campo de aviación : airfield⟩ ⟨su campo de responsabilidad : her field of responsibility⟩
camposanto *nm* : graveyard, cemetery
campus *nms & pl* : campus
camuflaje *nm* : camouflage
camuflajear *vt* : to camouflage
camuflar → **camuflajear**
can *nm* : hound, dog
cana *nf* **1** : gray hair **2 salirle canas** : to go gray, to get gray hair **3 echar una cana al aire** : to let one's hair down
canadiense *adj & nmf* : Canadian
canal[1] *nm* **1** : canal **2** : channel
canal[2] *nmf* : gutter, groove
canalé *nm* : rib, ribbing (in fabric)
canaleta *nf* : gutter
canalete *nm* : paddle
canalizar {21} *vt* : to channel
canalla[1] *adj fam* : low, rotten
canalla[2] *nmf fam* : bastard, swine
canapé *nm* **1** : hors d'oeuvre, canapé **2** SOFÁ : couch, sofa
canario[1], **-ria** *adj* : of or from the Canary Islands
canario[2], **-ria** *n* : Canarian, Canary Islander
canario[3] *nm* : canary
canasta *nf* **1** : basket **2** : canasta (card game)
cancel *nm* **1** : sliding door **2** : partition
cancelación *nf, pl* **-ciones 1** : cancellation **2** : payment in full
cancelar *vt* **1** : to cancel **2** : to pay off, to settle
cáncer *nm* : cancer
Cáncer *nmf* : Cancer
cancerígeno[1], **-na** *adj* : carcinogenic
cancerígeno[2] *nm* : carcinogen
canceroso, -sa *adj* : cancerous
cancha *nf* : court, field (for sports)
canciller *nm* : chancellor
cancillería *nf* : chancellery, ministry
canción *nf, pl* **canciones 1** : song **2 canción de cuna** : lullaby
cancionero[1] *nm* : songbook
cancionero[2], **-ra** *n Mex* : songster, songstress *f*

candado *nm* : padlock
candela *nf* **1** : flame, fire **2** : candle
candelabro *nm* : candelabra
candelero *nm* **1** : candlestick **2 estar en el candelero** : to be the center of attention
candente *adj* : red-hot
candidato, -ta *n* : candidate, applicant
candidatura *nf* : candidacy
candidez *nf* **1** : simplicity **2** INGENUIDAD : naïveté, ingenuousness
cándido, -da *adj* **1** : simple, unassuming **2** INGENUO : naive, ingenuous
candil *nm* : oil lamp
candilejas *nfpl* : footlights
candor *nm* : naïveté, innocence
candoroso, -sa *adj* : naive, innocent
canela *nf* : cinnamon
canesú *nm* : yoke (of clothing)
cangrejo *nm* JAIBA : crab
canguro *nm* **1** : kangaroo **2 hacer de canguro** *Spain* : to baby-sit
caníbal[1] *adj* : cannibalistic
caníbal[2] *nmf* ANTROPÓFAGO : cannibal
canibalismo *nm* ANTROPOFAGIA : cannibalism
canibalizar {21} *vt* : to cannibalize
canica *nf* : marble ⟨jugar a las canicas : to play marbles⟩
caniche *nm* : poodle
canijo, -ja *adj* **1** *fam* : puny, weak **2** *Mex fam* : tough, hard ⟨un examen muy canijo : a very tough exam⟩
canilla *nf* **1** : shin, shinbone **2** *Arg, Uru* : faucet
canino[1], **-na** *adj* : canine
canino[2] *nm* **1** COLMILLO : canine (tooth) **2** : dog, canine
canje *nm* INTERCAMBIO : exchange, trade
canjear *vt* INTERCAMBIAR : to exchange, to trade
cannabis *nm* : cannabis
cano, -na *adj* : gray ⟨un hombre de pelo cano : a gray-haired man⟩
canoa *nf* : canoe
canon *nm, pl* **cánones** : canon
canónico, -ca *adj* **1** : canonical **2 derecho canónico** : canon law
canónigo *nm* : canon (of a church)
canonizar {21} *vt* : to canonize — **canonización** *nf*
canoso, -sa → **cano**
cansado, -da *adj* **1** : tired ⟨estar cansado : to be tired⟩ **2** : tiresome, wearying ⟨ser cansado : to be tiring⟩
cansancio *nm* FATIGA : fatigue, weariness
cansar *vt* FATIGAR : to wear out, to tire — *vi* : to be tiresome — **cansarse** *vr* **1** : to wear oneself out **2** : to get bored
cansino, -na *adj* : slow, weary, lethargic
cantaleta *nf fam* : nagging ⟨la misma cantaleta : the same old story⟩
cantalupo *nm* : cantaloupe
cantante *nmf* : singer
cantar[1] *v* : to sing

cantar[2] *nm* : song, ballad
cántaro *nm* **1** : pitcher, jug **2 llover a cántaros** *fam* : to rain cats and dogs
cantata *nf* : cantata
cantera *nf* : quarry ⟨cantera de piedra : stone quarry⟩
cántico *nm* : canticle, chant
cantidad[1] *adv fam* : really ⟨ese carro me costó cantidad : that car cost me plenty⟩
cantidad[2] *nf* **1** : quantity **2** : sum, amount (of money) **3** : a lot, a great many ⟨había cantidad de niños en el parque : there were tons of kids in the park⟩
cantimplora *nf* : canteen, water bottle
cantina *nf* **1** : tavern, bar **2** : canteen, mess, dining quarters *pl*
cantinero, -ra *n* : bartender
canto *nm* **1** : singing **2** : chant ⟨canto gregoriano : Gregorian chant⟩ **3** : song (of a bird) **4** : edge, end ⟨de canto : on end, sideways⟩ **5 canto rodado** : boulder
cantón *nm, pl* **cantones 1** : canton **2** *Mex* : place, home
cantonés[1], **-nesa** *adj & n, mpl* **-neses** : Cantonese
cantonés[2] *nm, pl* **-neses** : Cantonese (language)
cantor[1], **-tora** *adj* **1** : singing **2 pájaro cantor** : songbird
cantor[2], **-tora** *n* **1** : singer **2** : cantor
caña *nf* **1** : cane ⟨caña de azúcar : sugarcane⟩ **2** : reed **3 caña de pescar** : fishing rod **4 caña del timón** : tiller (of a boat)
cañada *nf* : ravine, gully
cáñamo *nm* : hemp
cañaveral *nm* : sugarcane field
cañería *nf* TUBERÍA : pipes *pl*, piping
caño *nm* **1** : pipe **2** : spout **3** : channel (for navigation)
cañón *nm, pl* **cañones 1** : cannon **2** : barrel (of a gun) **3** : canyon
cañonear *vt* : to shell, to bombard
cañoneo *nm* : shelling, bombardment
cañonero *nm* : gunboat
caoba *nf* : mahogany
caolín *nm* : kaolin
caos *nm* : chaos
caótico, -ca *adj* : chaotic
capa *nf* **1** : cape, cloak **2** : coating **3** : layer, stratum **4** : (social) class, stratum
capacidad *nf* **1** : capacity **2** : capability, ability
capacitación *nf, pl* **-ciones** : training
capacitar *vt* : to train, to qualify
caparazón *nm, pl* **-zones** : shell, carapace
capataz *nmf, pl* **-taces** : foreman *m*, forewoman *f*
capaz *adj, pl* **capaces 1** APTO : capable, able **2** COMPETENTE : competent **3** : spacious ⟨capaz para : with room for⟩
capcioso, -sa *adj* : cunning, deceptive ⟨pregunta capciosa : trick question⟩

capea *nf* : amateur bullfight
capear *vt* **1** : to make a pass with the cape (in bullfighting) **2** : to dodge, to weather ⟨capear el temporal : to ride out the storm⟩
capellán *nm, pl* **-llanes** : chaplain
capilar *nm* : capillary — **capilar** *adj*
capilla *nf* : chapel
capirotada *nf Mex* : traditional bread pudding
capirotazo *nm* : flip, flick
capital[1] *adj* **1** : capital **2** : chief, principal
capital[2] *nm* : capital ⟨capital de riesgo : venture capital⟩
capital[3] *nf* : capital, capital city
capitalino[1], **-na** *adj* : of or from a capital city
capitalino[2], **-na** *n* : inhabitant of a capital city
capitalismo *nm* : capitalism
capitalista *adj & nmf* : capitalist
capitalizar {21} *vt* : to capitalize — **capitalización** *nf*
capitán, -tana *n, mpl* **-tanes** : captain
capitanear *vt* : to captain, to command
capitanía *nf* : captaincy
capitel *nm* : capital (of a column)
capitolio *nm* : capitol
capitulación *nf, pl* **-ciones** : capitulation
capitular *vi* : to capitulate, to surrender
capítulo *nm* **1** : chapter, section **2** : matter, subject
capó *nm* : hood (of a car)
capón *nm, pl* **capones** : capon
caporal *nm* **1** : chief, leader **2** : foreman (on a ranch)
capota *nf* : top (of a convertible)
capote *nm* **1** : cloak, overcoat **2** : bullfighter's cape **3** *Mex* COFRE : hood (of a car)
capricho *nm* ANTOJO : whim, caprice
caprichoso, -sa *adj* ANTOJADIZO : capricious, fickle
Capricornio *nmf* : Capricorn
cápsula *nf* : capsule
captar *vt* **1** : to catch, to grasp **2** : to gain, to attract **3** : to harness, to collect (waters)
captor, -tora *n* : captor
captura *nf* : capture, seizure
capturar *vt* : to capture, to seize
capucha *nf* : hood, cowl
capuchina *nf* : nasturtium
capuchino *nm* **1** : Capuchin (monk) **2** : capuchin (monkey) **3** : cappuccino
capullo *nm* **1** : cocoon **2** : bud (of a flower)
caqui *adj & nm* : khaki
cara *nf* **1** : face **2** ASPECTO : look, appearance ⟨¡qué buena cara tiene ese pastel! : that cake looks delicious!⟩ **3** *fam* : nerve, gall **4** ~ **a** *or* **de cara a** : facing **5 de cara a** : in view of, in the light of
carabina *nf* : carbine
caracol *nm* **1** : snail **2** CONCHA : conch, seashell **3** : cochlea **4** : ringlet

caracola *nf* : conch

carácter *nm, pl* caracteres 1 ÍNDOLE : character, kind, nature 2 TEMPERAMENTO : disposition, temperament 3 : letter, symbol ⟨caracteres chinos : Chinese characters⟩

característica *nf* RASGO : trait, feature, characteristic

característico, -ca *adj* : characteristic — característicamente *adv*

caracterizar {21} *vt* : to characterize — caracterización *nf*

caramba *interj* 1 *(expressing annoyance)* : darn!, heck! 2 *(expressing disgust or surprise)* : jeez!

carámbano *nm* : icicle

carambola *nf* 1 : carom 2 : ruse, trick ⟨por carambola : by a lucky chance⟩

caramelo *nm* 1 : caramel 2 DULCE : candy

caramillo *nm* 1 : pipe, small flute 2 : heap, pile

caraqueño[1], -ña *adj* : of or from Caracas

caraqueño[2], -ña *n* : person from Caracas

carátula *nf* 1 : title page 2 : cover, dust jacket 3 CARETA : mask 4 *Mex* : face, dial (of a clock or watch)

caravana *nf* 1 : caravan 2 : convoy, motorcade 3 REMOLQUE : trailer

caray → caramba

carbohidrato *nm* : carbohydrate

carbón *nm, pl* carbones 1 : coal 2 : charcoal

carbonatado, -da *adj* : carbonated

carbonato *nm* : carbonate

carboncillo *nm* : charcoal

carbonera *nf* : coal cellar, coal bunker (on a ship)

carbonero, -ra *adj* : coal

carbonizar {21} *vt* : to carbonize, to char

carbono *nm* : carbon

carbunco *or* carbunclo *nm* : carbuncle

carburador *nm* : carburetor

carburante *nm* : fuel

carca *nmf fam* : old fogy

carcacha *nf fam* : jalopy, wreck

carcaj *nm* : quiver (for arrows)

carcajada *nf* : loud laugh, guffaw ⟨reírse a carcajadas : to roar with laughter⟩

carcajearse *vr* : to roar with laughter, to be in stitches

cárcel *nf* PRISIÓN : jail, prison

carcelero, -ra *n* : jailer

carcinogénico, -ca *adj* : carcinogenic

carcinógeno *nm* CANCERÍGENO : carcinogen

carcinoma *nm* : carcinoma

carcomer *vt* : to eat away at, to consume

carcomido, -da *adj* 1 : worm-eaten 2 : decayed, rotten

cardán *nm, pl* cardanes : universal joint

cardar *vt* : to card, to comb

cardenal *nm* 1 : cardinal (in religion) 2 : bruise

cardíaco *or* cardiaco, -ca *adj* : cardiac, heart

cárdigan *nm, pl* -gans : cardigan

cardinal *adj* : cardinal

cardiología *nf* : cardiology

cardiólogo, -ga *n* : cardiologist

cardiovascular *adj* : cardiovascular

cardo *nm* : thistle

cardumen *nm* : school of fish

carear *vt* : to bring face-to-face

carecer {53} *vi* ~ de : to lack ⟨el cheque carecía de fondos : the check lacked funds⟩

carencia *nf* 1 FALTA : lack 2 ESCASEZ : shortage 3 DEFICIENCIA : deficiency

carente *adj* ~ de : lacking (in)

carero, -ra *adj fam* : pricey

carestía *nf* 1 : rise in cost ⟨la carestía de la vida : the high cost of living⟩ 2 : dearth, scarcity

careta *nf* MÁSCARA : mask

carey *nm* 1 : hawksbill turtle, sea turtle 2 : tortoiseshell

carga *nf* 1 : loading 2 : freight, load, cargo 3 : burden, responsibility 4 : charge ⟨carga eléctrica : electrical charge⟩ 5 : attack, charge

cargado, -da *adj* 1 : loaded 2 : bogged down, weighted down 3 : close, stuffy 4 : charged ⟨cargado de tensión : charged with tension⟩ 5 FUERTE : strong ⟨café cargado : strong coffee⟩ 6 cargado de hombros : stoop-shouldered

cargador[1], -dora *n* : longshoreman *m*, longshorewoman *f*

cargador[2] *nm* 1 : magazine (for a firearm) 2 : charger (for batteries)

cargamento *nm* : cargo, load

cargar {52} *vt* 1 : to carry 2 : to load, to fill 3 : to charge — *vi* 1 : to load 2 : to rest (in architecture) 3 ~ sobre : to fall upon

cargo *nm* 1 : burden, load 2 : charge ⟨a cargo de : in charge of⟩ 3 : position, office

cargue, etc. → cargar

carguero[1], -ra *adj* : freight, cargo ⟨tren carguero : freight train⟩

carguero[2] *nm* : freighter, cargo ship

cariarse *vr* : to decay (of teeth)

caribe *adj* : Caribbean ⟨el mar Caribe : the Caribbean Sea⟩

caribeño, -ña *adj* : Caribbean

caribú *nm* : caribou

caricatura *nf* 1 : caricature 2 : cartoon

caricaturista *nmf* : caricaturist, cartoonist

caricaturizar {21} *vt* : to caricature

caricia *nf* 1 : caress 2 hacer caricias : to pet, to stroke

caridad *nf* 1 : charity 2 LIMOSNA : alms *pl*

caries *nfs & pl* : cavity (in a tooth)

carillón *nm, pl* -llones 1 : carillon 2 : glockenspiel

cariño *nm* AFECTO : affection, love

cariñoso, -sa *adj* AFECTUOSO : affectionate, loving — cariñosamente *adv*

carioca[1] *adj* : of or from Rio de Janeiro

carioca[2] *nmf* : person from Rio de Janeiro

carisma *nf* : charisma

carismático, -ca *adj* : charismatic

carita *adj Mex fam* : cute (said of a man) ⟨tu primo se cree muy carita : your cousin thinks he's gorgeous⟩

caritativo, -va *adj* : charitable

cariz *nm, pl* **carices** : appearance, aspect

carmesí *adj & nm* : crimson

carmín *nm, pl* **carmines 1** : carmine **2 carmín de labios** : lipstick

carnada *nf* CEBO : bait

carnal *adj* **1** : carnal **2 primo carnal** : first cousin

carnaval *nm* : carnival

carnaza *nf* : bait

carne *nf* **1** : meat ⟨carne molida : ground beef⟩ **2** : flesh ⟨carne de gallina : goose bumps⟩

carné → carnet

carnero *nm* **1** : ram, sheep **2** : mutton

carnet *nm* **1** : identification card, ID **2** : membership card **3 carnet de conducir** *Spain* : driver's license

carnicería *nf* **1** : butcher shop **2** MATANZA : slaughter, carnage

carnicero, -ra *n* : butcher

carnívoro[1]**, -ra** *adj* : carnivorous

carnívoro[2] *nm* : carnivore

carnoso, -sa *adj* : fleshy, meaty

caro[1] *adv* : dearly, a lot ⟨pagué caro : I paid a high price⟩

caro[2]**, -ra** *adj* **1** : expensive, dear **2** QUERIDO : dear, beloved

carpa *nf* **1** : carp **2** : big top (of a circus) **3** : tent

carpelo *nm* : carpel

carpeta *nf* : folder, binder, portfolio (of drawings, etc.)

carpetazo *nm* **dar carpetazo a** : to shelve, to defer

carpintería *nf* **1** : carpentry **2** : carpenter's workshop

carpintero, -ra *n* : carpenter

carraspear *vi* : to clear one's throat

carraspera *nf* : hoarseness ⟨tener carraspera : to have a frog in one's throat⟩

carrera *nf* **1** : run, running ⟨a la carrera : at full speed⟩ ⟨de carrera : hastily⟩ **2** : race **3** : course of study **4** : career, profession **5** : run (in baseball)

carreta *nf* : cart, wagon

carrete *nm* **1** BOBINA : reel, spool **2** : roll of film

carretel → carrete

carretera *nf* : highway, road ⟨carretera de peaje : turnpike⟩

carretero, -ra *adj* : highway ⟨el sistema carretero nacional : the national highway system⟩

carretilla *nf* **1** : wheelbarrow **2 carretilla elevadora** : forklift

carril *nm* **1** : lane ⟨carretera de doble carril : two-lane highway⟩ **2** : rail (on a railroad track)

carrillo *nm* : cheek, jowl

carrito *nm* : cart ⟨carrito de compras : shopping cart⟩

carrizo *nm* JUNCO : reed

carro *nm* **1** COCHE : car **2** : cart **3** *Chile, Mex* : coach (of a train) **4 carro alegórico** : float (in a parade)

carrocería *nf* : bodywork, body (of a vehicle)

carroña *nf* : carrion

carroñero, -ra *n* : scavenger (animal)

carroza *nf* **1** : carriage **2** : float (in a parade)

carruaje *nm* : carriage

carrusel *nm* **1** : merry-go-round **2** : carousel ⟨carrusel de equipaje : luggage carousel⟩

carta *nf* **1** : letter **2** NAIPE : playing card **3** : charter, constitution **4** MENÚ : menu **5** : map, chart **6 tomar cartas en** : to intervene in

cártamo *nm* : safflower

cartearse *vr* ESCRIBIRSE : to write to one another, to correspond

cartel *nm* **1** : sign, poster

cártel *or* **cartel** *nm* : cartel

cartelera *nf* **1** : billboard **2** : marquee

cartera *nf* **1** BILLETERA : wallet, billfold **2** BOLSO : pocketbook, purse **3** : portfolio ⟨cartera de acciones : stock portfolio⟩

carterista *nmf* : pickpocket

cartero, -ra *n* : letter carrier, mailman *m*

cartilaginoso, -sa *adj* : cartilaginous, gristly

cartílago *nm* : cartilage

cartilla *nf* **1** : primer, reader **2** : booklet ⟨cartilla de ahorros : bankbook⟩

cartografía *nf* : cartography

cartógrafo, -fa *n* : cartographer

cartón *nm, pl* **cartones 1** : cardboard ⟨cartón madera : fiberboard⟩ **2** : carton

cartucho *nm* : cartridge

cartulina *nf* : poster board, cardboard

carúncula *nf* : wattle (of a bird)

casa *nf* **1** : house, building **2** HOGAR : home **3** : household, family **4** : company, firm **5 echar la casa por la ventana** : to spare no expense

casaca *nf* : jacket

casado[1]**, -da** *adj* : married

casado[2]**, -da** *n* : married person

casamentero, -ra *n* : matchmaker

casamiento *nm* **1** : marriage **2** BODA : wedding

casar *vt* : to marry — *vi* : to go together, to match up — **casarse** *vr* **1** : to get married **2 ~ con** : to marry

casateniente *nmf Mex* : landlord, landlady *f*

cascabel[1] *nm* : small bell

cascabel[2] *nf* : rattlesnake

cascada *nf* CATARATA, SALTO : waterfall, cascade

cascajo *nm* **1** : pebble, rock fragment **2** *fam* : piece of junk

cascanueces *nms & pl* : nutcracker

cascar {72} *vt* : to crack (a shell) — **cascarse** *vr* : to crack, to chip

cáscara *nf* 1 : skin, peel, rind, husk 2 : shell (of a nut or egg)

cascarón *nm, pl* **-rones** 1 : eggshell 2 *Mex* : shell filled with confetti

cascarrabias *nmfs & pl fam* : grouch, crab

casco *nm* 1 : helmet 2 : hull 3 : hoof 4 : fragment, shard 5 : center (of a town) 6 *Mex* : empty bottle 7 **cascos** *nmpl* : headphones

caserío *nm* 1 : country house 2 : hamlet

casero[1], **-ra** *adj* 1 : domestic, household 2 : homemade

casero[2], **-ra** *n* DUEÑO : landlord *m*, landlady *f*

caseta *nf* : booth, stand, stall ⟨caseta telefónica : telephone booth⟩

casete → **cassette**

casi *adv* 1 : almost, nearly, virtually 2 (*in negative phrases*) : hardly ⟨casi nunca : hardly ever⟩

casilla *nf* 1 : booth 2 : pigeonhole 3 : box (on a form)

casino *nm* 1 : casino 2 : (social) club

caso *nm* 1 : case 2 **en caso de** : in case of, in the event of 3 **hacer caso de** : to pay attention to, to notice 4 **hacer caso omiso de** : to ignore, to take no notice of 5 **no venir al caso** : to be beside the point

caspa *nf* : dandruff

casque, etc. → **cascar**

casquete *nm* 1 : skullcap 2 **casquete glaciar** : ice cap 3 **casquete corto** *Mex* : crew cut

casquillo *nm* : case, casing (of a bullet)

cassette *nmf* : cassette

casta *nf* 1 : caste 2 : lineage, stock ⟨de casta : thoroughbred, purebred⟩ 3 **sacar la casta** *Mex* : to come out ahead

castaña *nf* : chestnut

castañetear *vi* : to chatter (of teeth)

castaño[1], **-ña** *adj* : chestnut, brown

castaño[2] *nm* 1 : chestnut tree 2 : chestnut, brown

castañuela *nf* : castanet

castellano[1], **-na** *adj & n* : Castilian

castellano[2] *nm* ESPAÑOL : Spanish, Castilian (language)

castidad *nf* : chastity

castigar {52} *vt* : to punish

castigo *nm* : punishment

castillo *nm* 1 : castle 2 **castillo de proa** : forecastle

casto, -ta *adj* : chaste, pure — **castamente** *adv*

castor *nm* : beaver

castración *nf, pl* **-ciones** : castration

castrar *vt* 1 : to castrate, to spay, to neuter, to geld 2 DEBILITAR : to weaken, to debilitate

castrense *adj* : military

casual *adj* 1 FORTUITO : fortuitous, accidental 2 *Mex* : casual (of clothing)

casualidad *nf* 1 : chance 2 **por ~** or **de ~** : by chance, by any chance

casualmente *adv* : accidentally, by chance

casucha *or* **casuca** *nf* : shanty, hovel

cataclismo *nm* : cataclysm

catacumbas *nfpl* : catacombs

catador, -dora *n* : wine taster

catalán[1], **-lana** *adj & n, mpl* **-lanes** : Catalan

catalán[2] *nm* : Catalan (language)

catálisis *nf* : catalysis

catalítico, -ca *adj* : catalytic

catalizador *nm* 1 : catalyst 2 : catalytic converter

catalogar {52} *vt* : to catalog, to classify

catálogo *nm* : catalog

catamarán *nm, pl* **-ranes** : catamaran

cataplasma *nf* : poultice

catapulta *nf* : catapult

catapultar *vt* : to catapult

catar *vt* 1 : to taste, to sample 2 : to look at, to examine

catarata *nf* 1 CASCADA, SALTO : waterfall 2 : cataract

catarro *nm* RESFRIADO : cold, catarrh

catarsis *nf* : catharsis

catártico, -ca *adj* : cathartic

catástrofe *nf* DESASTRE : catastrophe, disaster

catastrófico, -ca *adj* DESASTROSO : catastrophic, disastrous

catcher *nmf* : catcher (in baseball)

catecismo *nm* : catechism

cátedra *nf* 1 : chair, professorship 2 : subject, class 3 **libertad de cátedra** : academic freedom

catedral *nf* : cathedral

catedrático, -ca *n* PROFESOR : professor

categoría *nf* 1 CLASE : category 2 RANGO : rank, standing 3 **categoría gramatical** : part of speech 4 **de ~** : first-rate, outstanding

categórico, -ca *adj* : categorical, unequivocal — **categóricamente** *adv*

catéter *nm* : catheter

cátodo *nm* : cathode

catolicismo *nm* : Catholicism

católico, -ca *adj & n* : Catholic

catorce *adj & nm* : fourteen

catorceavo *nm* : fourteenth

catre *nm* : cot

catsup *nm* : ketchup

caucásico, -ca *adj & n* : Caucasian

cauce *nm* 1 LECHO : riverbed 2 : means *pl*, channel

caucho *nm* 1 GOMA : rubber 2 : rubber tree 3 *Ven* : tire

caución *nf, pl* **cauciones** FIANZA : bail, security

caudal *nm* 1 : volume of water 2 RIQUEZA : capital, wealth 3 ABUNDANCIA : abundance

caudillaje *nm* : leadership

caudillo *nm* : leader, commander

causa *nf* **1** MOTIVO : cause, reason, motive ⟨a causa de : because of⟩ **2** IDEAL : cause ⟨morir por una causa : to die for a cause⟩ **3** : lawsuit

causal[1] *adj* : causal

causal[2] *nm* : cause, grounds *pl*

causalidad *nf* : causality

causante[1] *adj* ~ **de** : causing, responsible for

causante[2] *nmf Mex* : taxpayer

causar *vt* **1** : to cause **2** : to provoke, to arouse ⟨eso me causa gracia : that strikes me as being funny⟩

cáustico, -ca *adj* : caustic

cautela *nf* : caution, prudence

cautelar *adj* : precautionary, preventive

cauteloso, -sa *adj* : cautious, prudent — **cautelosamente** *adv*

cauterizar {21} *vt* : to cauterize

cautivador, -dora *adj* : captivating

cautivar *vt* HECHIZAR : to captivate, to charm

cautiverio *nm* : captivity

cautivo, -va *adj & n* : captive

cauto, -ta *adj* : cautious, careful

cavar *vt* : to dig — *vi* ~ **en** : to delve into, to probe

caverna *nf* : cavern, cave

cavernoso, -sa *adj* **1** : cavernous **2** : deep, resounding

caviar *nm* : caviar

cavidad *nf* : cavity

cavilar *vi* : to ponder, to deliberate

cayado *nm* : crook, staff, crosier

cayena *nf* : cayenne pepper

cayó, etc. → **caer**

caza[1] *nf* **1** CACERÍA : hunt, hunting **2** : game

caza[2] *nm* : fighter plane

cazador, -dora *n* **1** : hunter **2 cazador furtivo** : poacher

cazar {21} *vt* **1** : to hunt **2** : to catch, to bag **3** *fam* : to land (a job, a spouse) — *vi* : to go hunting

cazatalentos *nmfs & pl* : talent scout

cazo *nm* **1** : saucepan, pot **2** CUCHARÓN : ladle

cazuela *nf* **1** : pan, saucepan **2** : casserole

cazurro, -ra *adj* : sullen, surly

CD *nm* : CD, compact disk

cebada *nf* : barley

cebar *vt* **1** : to bait **2** : to feed, to fatten **3** : to prime (a pump, etc.) — **cebarse** *vr* ~ **en** : to take it out on

cebo *nm* **1** CARNADA : bait **2** : feed **3** : primer (for firearms)

cebolla *nf* : onion

cebolleta *nf* : scallion, green onion

cebollino *nm* **1** : chive **2** : scallion

cebra *nf* : zebra

cebú *nm, pl* **cebús** *or* **cebúes** : zebu (cattle)

cecear *vi* : to lisp

ceceo *nm* : lisp

cecina *nf* : dried beef, beef jerky

cedazo *nm* : sieve

ceder *vi* **1** : to yield, to give way **2** : to diminish, to abate **3** : to give in, to relent — *vt* : to cede, to hand over

cedro *nm* : cedar

cédula *nf* : document, certificate

céfiro *nm* : zephyr

cegador, -dora *adj* : blinding

cegar {49} *vt* **1** : to blind **2** : to block, to stop up — *vi* : to be blinded, to go blind

cegatón, -tona *adj, mpl* **-tones** *fam* : blind as a bat

ceguera *nf* : blindness

ceiba *nf* : ceiba, silk-cotton tree

ceja *nf* **1** : eyebrow ⟨fruncir las cejas : to knit one's brows⟩ **2** : flange, rim

cejar *vi* : to give in, to back down

celada *nf* : trap, ambush

celador, -dora *n* GUARDIA : guard, warden

celda *nf* : cell (of a jail)

celebración *nf, pl* **-ciones** : celebration

celebrado, -da *adj* CÉLEBRE, FAMOSO : famous, celebrated

celebrante *nmf* OFICIANTE : celebrant

celebrar *vt* **1** FESTEJAR : to celebrate **2** : to hold (a meeting) **3** : to say (Mass) **4** : to welcome, to be happy about — *vi* : to be glad — **celebrarse** *vr* **1** : to be celebrated, to fall **2** : to be held, to take place

célebre *adj* CELEBRADO, FAMOSO : celebrated, famous

celebridad *nf* **1** : celebrity **2** FAMA : fame, renown

celeridad *nf* : celerity, swiftness

celeste[1] *adj* **1** : celestial **2** : sky blue, azure

celeste[2] *nm* : sky blue

celestial *adj* : heavenly, celestial

celibato *nm* : celibacy

célibe *adj & nmf* : celibate

cello *nm* : cello

celo *nm* **1** : zeal, fervor **2** : heat (of females), rut (of males) **3 celos** *nmpl* : jealousy ⟨tenerle celos a alguien : to be jealous of someone⟩

celofán *nm, pl* **-fanes** : cellophane

celosía *nf* **1** : lattice window **2** : latticework, trellis

celoso, -sa *adj* **1** : jealous **2** : zealous — **celosamente** *adv*

celta[1] *adj* : Celtic

celta[2] *nmf* : Celt

célula *nf* : cell

celular *adj* : cellular

celuloide *nm* **1** : celluloid **2** : film, cinema

celulosa *nf* : cellulose

cementar *vt* : to cement

cementerio *nm* : cemetery

cemento *nm* : cement

cena *nf* : supper, dinner

cenador *nm* : arbor

cenagal *nm* : bog, quagmire

cenagoso, -sa *adj* : swampy

cenar *vi* : to have dinner, to have supper — *vt* : to have for dinner or supper

⟨anoche cenamos tamales : we had tamales for supper last night⟩

cencerro *nm* : cowbell

cenicero *nm* : ashtray

ceniciento, -ta *adj* : ashen

cenit *nm* : zenith, peak

ceniza *nf* 1 : ash 2 **cenizas** *nfpl* : ashes (of a deceased person)

cenizo, -za *n* : jinx

cenote *nm Mex* : natural deposit of spring water

censar *vt* : to take a census of

censo *nm* : census

censor, -sora *n* : censor, critic

censura *nf* 1 : censorship 2 : censure, criticism

censurable *adj* : reprehensible, blameworthy

censurar *vt* 1 : to censor 2 : to censure, to criticize

centauro *nm* : centaur

centavo *nm* 1 : cent (in English-speaking countries) 2 : unit of currency in various Latin-American countries

centella *nf* 1 : lightning flash 2 : spark

centellear *vi* 1 : to twinkle 2 : to gleam, to sparkle

centelleo *nm* : twinkling, sparkle

centenar *nm* 1 : hundred 2 **a centenares** : by the hundreds

centenario¹, -ria *adj & n* : centenarian

centenario² *nm* : centennial

centeno *nm* : rye

centésimo¹, -ma *adj* : hundredth

centésimo² *nm* : hundredth

centígrado *adj* : centigrade, Celsius

centigramo *nm* : centigram

centímetro *nm* : centimeter

centinela *nmf* : sentinel, sentry

central¹ *adj* 1 : central 2 PRINCIPAL : main, principal

central² *nf* 1 : main office, headquarters 2 **central camionera** *Mex* : bus terminal

centralita *nf* : switchboard

centralizar {21} *vt* : to centralize — **centralización** *nf*

centrar *vt* 1 : to center 2 : to focus — **centrarse** *vr* ~ **en** : to focus on, to concentrate on

céntrico, -ca *adj* : central

centrífugo, -ga *adj* : centrifugal

centrípeto, -ta *adj* : centripetal

centro¹ *nm* : center (in sports)

centro² *nm* 1 MEDIO : center ⟨centro de atención : center of attention⟩ ⟨centro de gravedad : center of gravity⟩ 2 : downtown 3 **centro de mesa** : centerpiece

centroamericano, -na *adj & n* : Central American

ceñido, -da *adj* AJUSTADO : tight, tight-fitting

ceñir {67} *vt* 1 : to encircle, to surround 2 : to hug, to cling to ⟨me ciñe demasiado : it's too tight on me⟩ — **ceñirse** *vr* ~ **a** : to restrict oneself to, to stick to

ceño *nm* 1 : frown, scowl 2 **fruncir el ceño** : to frown, to knit one's brows

cepa *nf* 1 : stump (of a tree) 2 : stock (of a vine) 3 LINAJE : ancestry, stock

cepillar *vt* 1 : to brush 2 : to plane (wood) — **cepillarse** *vr*

cepillo *nm* 1 : brush ⟨cepillo de dientes : toothbrush⟩ 2 : plane (for woodworking)

cepo *nm* : trap (for animals)

cera *nf* 1 : wax ⟨cera de abejas : beeswax⟩ 2 : polish

cerámica *nf* 1 : ceramics *pl* 2 : pottery

cerámico, -ca *adj* : ceramic

ceramista *nmf* ALFARERO : potter

cerca¹ *adv* 1 : close, near, nearby 2 ~ **de** : nearly, almost

cerca² *nf* 1 : fence 2 : (stone) wall

cercado *nm* : enclosure

cercanía *nf* 1 PROXIMIDAD : proximity, closeness 2 **cercanías** *nfpl* : outskirts, suburbs

cercano, -na *adj* : near, close

cercar {72} *vt* 1 : to fence in, to enclose 2 : to surround

cercenar *vt* 1 : to cut off, to amputate 2 : to diminish, to curtail

cerceta *nf* : teal (duck)

cerciorarse *vr* ASEGURARSE ~ **de** : to make sure of, to verify

cerco *nm* 1 : siege 2 : cordon, circle 3 : fence

cerda *nf* 1 : bristle 2 : sow

cerdo *nm* 1 : pig, hog 2 **carne de cerdo** : pork

cereal *nm* : cereal — **cereal** *adj*

cerebelo *nm* : cerebellum

cerebral *adj* : cerebral

cerebro *nm* : brain

ceremonia *nf* : ceremony — **ceremonial** *adj*

ceremonioso, -sa *adj* : ceremonious

cereza *nf* : cherry

cerezo *nm* : cherry tree

cerilla *nf* 1 : match 2 : earwax

cerillo *nm* (*in various countries*) : match

cerner {56} *vt* : to sift — **cernerse** *vr* 1 : to hover 2 ~ **sobre** : to loom over, to threaten

cernidor *nm* : sieve

cernir → **cerner**

cero *nm* : zero

ceroso, -sa *adj* : waxy

cerque, etc. → **cercar**

cerquita *adv fam* : very close, very near

cerrado, -da *adj* 1 : closed, shut 2 : thick, broad ⟨tiene un acento cerrado : she has a thick accent⟩ 3 : cloudy, overcast 4 : quiet, reserved 5 : dense, stupid

cerradura *nf* : lock

cerrajería *nf* : locksmith's shop

cerrajero, -ra *n* : locksmith

cerrar {55} *vt* 1 : to close, to shut 2 : to turn off 3 : to bring to an end — *vi* 1 : to close up, to lock up 2 : to close down — **cerrarse** *vr* 1 : to close 2 : to fasten, to button up 3 : to conclude, to end

cerrazón *nf, pl* **-zones** : obstinacy, stubbornness
cerro *nm* COLINA, LOMA : hill
cerrojo *nm* PESTILLO : bolt, latch
certamen *nm, pl* **-támenes** : competition, contest
certero, -ra *adj* : accurate, precise — **certeramente** *adv*
certeza *nf* : certainty
certidumbre *nf* : certainty
certificable *adj* : certifiable
certificación *nf, pl* **-ciones** : certification
certificado¹, -da *adj* **1** : certified **2** : registered (of mail)
certificado² *nm* **1** : certificate **2** : registered letter
certificar {72} *vt* **1** : to certify **2** : to register (mail)
cervato *nm* : fawn
cervecera *nf* : brewery
cervecería *nf* **1** : brewery **2** : beer hall, bar
cerveza *nf* : beer ⟨cerveza de barril : draft beer⟩
cervical *adj* : cervical
cerviz *nf, pl* **cervices** : nape of the neck, cervix
cesación *nf, pl* **-ciones** : cessation, suspension
cesante *adj* : laid off, unemployed
cesantía *nf* : unemployment
cesar *vi* : to cease, to stop — *vt* : to dismiss, to lay off
cesárea *nf* : cesarean, C-section
cese *nm* **1** : cessation, stop ⟨cese del fuego : cease-fire⟩ **2** : dismissal
cesio *nm* : cesium
cesión *nf, pl* **cesiones** : transfer, assignment ⟨cesión de bienes : transfer of property⟩
césped *nm* : lawn, grass
cesta *nf* **1** : basket **2** : jai alai racket
cesto *nm* **1** : hamper **2** : basket (in basketball) **3 cesto de (la) basura** : wastebasket
cetrería *nf* : falconry
cetrino, -na *adj* : sallow
cetro *nm* : scepter
chabacano¹, -na *adj* : tacky, tasteless
chabacano² *nm* *Mex* : apricot
chacal *nm* : jackal
cháchara *nf* *fam* **1** : small talk, chatter **2 chácharas** *nfpl* : trinkets, junk
chacharear *vi fam* : to chatter, to gab
chacra *nf* *Arg, Chile, Peru* : small farm
chadiano, -na *adj & n* : Chadian
chal *nm* MANTÓN : shawl
chalado¹, -da *adj fam* : crazy, nuts
chalado², -da *n* : nut, crazy person
chalán *nm, pl* **chalanes** *Mex* : barge
chalé → chalet
chaleco *nm* : vest
chalet *nm* *Spain* : house
chalupa *nf* **1** : small boat **2** *Mex* : small stuffed tortilla
chamaco, -ca *n Mex fam* : kid, boy *m*, girl *f*

chamarra *nf* **1** : sheepskin jacket **2** : poncho, blanket
chamba *nf Mex, Peru fam* : job, work
chambear *vi Mex, Peru fam* : to work
chamo, -ma *n Ven fam* **1** : kid, boy *m*, girl *f* **2** : buddy, pal
champaña *or* **champán** *nm* : champagne
champiñón *nm, pl* **-ñones** : mushroom
champú *nm, pl* **-pus** *or* **-púes** : shampoo
champurrado *nm Mex* : hot chocolate thickened with cornstarch
chamuco *nm Mex fam* : devil
chamuscar {72} *vt* : to singe, to scorch — **chamuscarse** *vr*
chamusquina *nf* : scorch
chance *nm* OPORTUNIDAD : chance, opportunity
chancho¹, -cha *adj fam* : dirty, filthy, gross
chancho², -cha *n* **1** : pig, hog **2** *fam* : slob
chanchullero, -ra *adj fam* : shady, crooked
chanchullo *nm fam* : shady deal, scam
chancla *nf* **1** : thong sandal, slipper **2** : old shoe
chancleta → chancla
chanclo *nm* **1** : clog **2 chanclos** *nmpl* : overshoes, galoshes, rubbers
chancro *nm* : chancre
changarro *nm Mex* : small shop, stall
chango, -ga *n Mex* : monkey
chantaje *nm* : blackmail
chantajear *vt* : to blackmail
chantajista *nmf* : blackmailer
chanza *nf* **1** : joke, jest **2** *Mex fam* : chance, opportunity
chapa *nf* **1** : sheet, panel, veneer **2** : lock **3** : badge
chapado, -da *adj* **1** : plated **2 chapado a la antigua** : old-fashioned
chapar *vt* **1** : to veneer **2** : to plate (metals)
chaparrón *nm, pl* **-rrones** **1** : downpour **2** : great quantity, torrent
chapeado, -da *adj Col, Mex* : flushed
chapopote *nm Mex* : tar, blacktop
chapotear *vi* : to splash about
chapucero¹, -ra *adj* **1** : crude, shoddy **2** *Mex fam* : dishonest
chapucero², -ra *n* **1** : sloppy worker, bungler **2** *Mex fam* : cheat, swindler
chapulín *nm, pl* **-lines** *CA, Mex* : grasshopper, locust
chapuza *nf* **1** : botched job **2** *Mex fam* : fraud, trick ⟨hacer chapuzas : to cheat⟩
chapuzón *nm, pl* **-zones** : dip, swim ⟨darse un chapuzón : to go for a quick dip⟩
chaqueta *nf* : jacket
charada *nf* : charades (game)
charango *nm* : traditional Andean stringed instrument
charca *nf* : pond, pool
charco *nm* : puddle, pool

charcutería *nf* : delicatessen
charla *nf* : chat, talk
charlar *vi* : to chat, to talk
charlatán[1], **-tana** *adj* : talkative, chatty
charlatán[2], **-tana** *n, mpl* **-tanes** 1 : chatterbox 2 FARSANTE : charlatan, phony
charlatanear *vi* : to chatter away
charol *nm* 1 : lacquer, varnish 2 : patent leather 3 : tray
charola *nf Bol, Mex, Peru* : tray
charreada *nf Mex* : charro show, rodeo
charretera *nf* : epaulet
charro[1], **-rra** *adj* 1 : gaudy, tacky 2 *Mex* : pertaining to charros
charro[2], **-rra** *n Mex* : charro (Mexican cowboy or cowgirl)
chascarrillo *nm fam* : joke, funny story
chasco *nm* 1 BROMA : trick, joke 2 DECEPCIÓN, DESILUSIÓN : disillusionment, disappointment
chasis *or* **chasís** *nm* : chassis
chasquear *vt* 1 : to click (the tongue, fingers, etc.) 2 : to snap (a whip)
chasquido *nm* 1 : click (of the tongue or fingers) 2 : snap, crack
chatarra *nf* : scrap metal
chato, -ta *adj* 1 : pug-nosed 2 : flat
chauvinismo *nm* : chauvinism
chauvinista[1] *adj* : chauvinistic
chauvinista[2] *nmf* : chauvinist
chaval, -vala *n fam* : kid, boy *m*, girl *f*
chavo[1], **-va** *adj Mex fam* : young
chavo[2], **-va** *n Mex fam* : kid, boy *m*, girl *f*
chavo[3] *nm fam* : cent, buck ⟨no tengo un chavo : I'm broke⟩
chayote *nm* : chayote (plant, fruit)
checar {72} *vt Mex* 1 : to check, to verify
checo[1], **-ca** *adj & n* : Czech
checo[2] *nm* : Czech (language)
checoslovaco, -ca *adj & n* : Czechoslovakian
chef *nm* : chef
chelín *nm, pl* **chelines** : shilling
cheque[1], **etc.** → **checar**
cheque[2] *nm* 1 : check 2 **cheque de viajero** : traveler's check
chequear *vt* 1 : to check, to verify 2 : to check in (baggage)
chequeo *nm* 1 INSPECCIÓN : check, inspection 2 : checkup, examination
chequera *nf* : checkbook
chévere *adj fam* : great, fantastic
chic *adj & nm* : chic
chica → **chico**
chicano, -na *adj & n* : Chicano *m*, Chicana *f*
chicha *nf* : fermented alcoholic beverage made from corn
chícharo *nm* : pea
chicharra *nf* 1 CIGARRA : cicada 2 : buzzer
chicharrón *nm, pl* **-rrones** 1 : pork rind 2 **darle chicharrón a** *Mex fam* : to get rid of
chichón *nm, pl* **chichones** : bump, swelling

chicle *nm* : chewing gum
chicloso *nm Mex* : taffy
chico[1], **-ca** *adj* 1 : little, small 2 : young
chico[2], **-ca** *n* 1 : child, boy *m*, girl *f* 2 : young man *m*, young woman *f*
chicote *nm* LÁTIGO : whip, lash
chiffon → **chifón**
chiflado[1], **-da** *adj fam* : nuts, crazy
chiflado[2], **-da** *n fam* : crazy person, lunatic
chiflar *vi* : to whistle — *vt* : to whistle at, to boo — **chiflarse** *vr fam* ~ **por** : to be crazy about
chiflido *nm* : whistle, whistling
chiflón *nm, pl* **chiflones** : draft (of air)
chifón *nm, pl* **chifones** : chiffon
chilango[1], **-ga** *adj Mex fam* : of or from Mexico City
chilango[2], **-ga** *n Mex fam* : person from Mexico City
chilaquiles *nmpl Mex* : shredded tortillas in sauce
chile *nm* : chili pepper
chileno, -na *adj & n* : Chilean
chillar *vi* 1 : to squeal, to screech 2 : to scream, to yell 3 : to be gaudy, to clash
chillido *nm* 1 : scream, shout 2 : squeal, screech, cry (of an animal)
chillo *nm PRi* : red snapper
chillón, -llona *adj, mpl* **chillones** 1 : piercing, shrill 2 : loud, gaudy
chilpayate *nmf Mex fam* : child, little kid
chimenea *nf* 1 : chimney 2 : fireplace
chimichurri *nm Arg* : traditional hot sauce
chimpancé *nm* : chimpanzee
china *nf* 1 : pebble, small stone 2 *PRi* : orange
chinchar *vt fam* : to annoy, to pester — **chincharse** *vr fam* : to put up with something, to grin and bear it
chinchayote *nm Mex* : chayote root
chinche[1] *nf* 1 : bedbug 2 *Ven* : ladybug 3 : thumbtack
chinche[2] *nmf fam* : nuisance, pain in the neck
chinchilla *nf* : chinchilla
chino[1], **-na** *adj* 1 : Chinese 2 *Mex* : curly, kinky
chino[2], **-na** *n* : Chinese person
chino[3] *nm* : Chinese (language)
chip *nm, pl* **chips** : chip ⟨chip de memoria : memory chip⟩
chipote *nm Mex fam* : bump (on the head)
chipotle *nm Mex* : type of chili pepper
chipriota *adj & nmf* : Cypriot
chiquear *vt Mex* : to spoil, to indulge
chiquero *nm* POCILGA : pigpen, pigsty
chiquillada *nf* : childish prank
chiquillo[1], **-lla** *adj* : very young, little
chiquillo[2], **-lla** *n* : kid, youngster
chiquito[1], **-ta** *adj* : tiny
chiquito[2], **-ta** *n* : little one, baby
chiribita *nf* 1 : spark 2 **chiribitas** *nfpl* : spots before the eyes
chiribitil *nm* 1 DESVÁN : attic, garret 2 : cubbyhole

chirigota *nf fam* : joke

chirimía *nf* : traditional reed pipe

chirimoya *nf* : cherimoya, custard apple

chiripa *nf* **1** : fluke **2 de ~** : by sheer luck

chirivía *nf* : parsnip

chirona *nf fam* : slammer, jail

chirriar {85} *vi* **1** : to squeak, to creak **2** : to screech — **chirriante** *adj*

chirrido *nm* **1** : squeak, squeaking **2** : screech, screeching

chirrión *nm, pl* **chirriones** *Mex* : whip, lash

chisme *nm* **1** : gossip, tale **2** *Spain fam* : gadget, thingamajig

chismear *vi* : to gossip

chismoso¹, -sa *adj* : gossipy, gossiping

chismoso², -sa *n* **1** : gossiper, gossip **2** *Mex fam* : tattletale

chispa¹ *adj* **1** *Mex fam* : lively, vivacious ⟨un perrito chispa : a frisky puppy⟩ **2** *Spain fam* : tipsy

chispa² *nf* **1** : spark **2 echar chispas** : to be furious

chispeante *adj* : sparkling, scintillating

chispear *vi* **1** : to give off sparks **2** : to sparkle

chisporrotear *vi* **1** : to crackle, to sizzle

chiste *nm* **1** : joke, funny story **2 tener chiste** : to be funny **3 tener su chiste** *Mex* : to be tricky

chistoso¹, -sa *adj* **1** : funny, humorous **2** : witty

chistoso², -sa *n* : wit, joker

chivas *nfpl Mex fam* : stuff, odds and ends

chivo¹, -va *n* **1** : kid, young goat **2 chivo expiatorio** : scapegoat

chivo² *nm* **1** : billy goat **2** : fit of anger

chocante *adj* **1** : shocking **2** : unpleasant, rude

chocar {72} *vi* **1** : to crash, to collide **2** : to clash, to conflict **3** : to be shocking ⟨le chocó : he was shocked⟩ **4** *Mex, Ven fam* : to be unpleasant or obnoxious ⟨me choca tu jefe : I can't stand your boss⟩ — *vt* **1** : to shake (hands) **2** : to clink glasses

chochear *vi* **1** : to be senile **2 ~ por** : to dote on, to be soft on

chochín *nm, pl* **-chines** : wren

chocho, -cha *adj* **1** : senile **2** : doting

choclo *nm* **1** : ear of corn, corncob **2** : corn **3 meter el choclo** *Mex fam* : to make a mistake

chocolate *nm* **1** : chocolate **2** : hot chocolate, cocoa

chofer *or* **chófer** *nm* **1** : chauffeur **2** : driver

choke *nm* : choke (of an automobile)

chole *interj Mex fam* ¡ya chole! : enough!, cut it out!

cholo, -la *adj & n* : mestizo

cholla *nf fam* : head

chollo *nm Spain fam* : bargain

chongo *nm* **1** *Mex* : bun (chignon) **2 chongos** *nmpl Mex* : dessert made with fried bread

choque¹, etc. → **chocar**

choque² *nm* **1** : crash, collision **2** : clash, conflict **3** : shock

chorizo *nm* : chorizo, sausage

chorrear *vi* **1** : to drip **2** : to pour out, to gush out

chorrito *nm* : squirt, splash

chorro *nm* **1** : flow, stream, jet **2** *Mex fam* : heap, ton

choteado, -da *adj Mex fam* : worn-out, stale ⟨esa canción está bien choteada : that song's been played to death⟩

chotear *vt* : to make fun of

choteo *nm* : joking around, kidding

chovinismo, chovinista → **chauvinismo, chauvinista**

choza *nf* BARRACA, CABAÑA : hut, shack

chubasco *nm* : downpour, storm

chuchería *nf* : knickknack, trinket

chueco, -ca *adj* **1** : crooked, bent **2** *Chile, Mex fam* : dishonest, shady

chulada *nf Mex, Spain fam* : cute or pretty thing ⟨¡qué chulada de vestido! : what a lovely dress!⟩

chulear *vt Mex fam* : to compliment

chuleta *nf* : cutlet, chop

chulo¹, -la *adj* **1** *fam* : cute, pretty **2** *Spain fam* : cocky, arrogant

chulo² *nm Spain* : pimp

chupada *nf* **1** : suck, sucking **2** : puff, drag (on a cigarette)

chupado, -da *adj fam* **1** : gaunt, skinny **2** : plastered, drunk

chupaflor *nm* COLIBRÍ : hummingbird

chupamirto *nm Mex* : hummingbird

chupar *vt* **1** : to suck **2** : to absorb **3** : to puff on **4** *fam* : to drink, to guzzle — *vi* : to suckle — **chuparse** *vr* **1** : to waste away **2** *fam* : to put up with **3** ¡chúpate esa! *fam* : take that!

chupete *nm* **1** : pacifier **2** *Chile, Peru* : lollipop

chupetear *vt* : to suck (at)

chupón *nm, pl* **chupones** **1** : sucker (of a plant) **2** : baby bottle, pacifier

churrasco *nm* **1** : steak **2** : barbecued meat

churro *nm* **1** : fried dough **2** *fam* : botch, mess **3** *fam* : attractive person, looker

chusco, -ca *adj* : funny, amusing

chusma *nf* GENTUZA : riffraff, rabble

chutar *vi* : to shoot (in soccer)

chute *nm* : shot (in soccer)

cianuro *nm* : cyanide

cibernética *nf* : cybernetics

cicatriz *nf, pl* **-trices** : scar

cicatrizarse {21} *vr* : to form a scar, to heal

cíclico, -ca *adj* : cyclical

ciclismo *nm* : bicycling

ciclista *nmf* : bicyclist

ciclo *nm* : cycle

ciclomotor *nm* : moped

ciclón *nm, pl* **ciclones** : cyclone

cicuta *nf* : hemlock

cidra *nf* : citron (fruit)

ciega, ciegue etc. → **cegar**

ciego¹, -ga *adj* **1** INVIDENTE : blind **2 a ciegas** : blindly **3 quedarse ciego** : to go blind — **ciegamente** *adv*

ciego², -ga *n* INVIDENTE : blind person

cielo *nm* **1** : sky **2** : heaven **3** : ceiling

ciempiés *nms & pl* : centipede

cien¹ *adj* **1** : a hundred, hundred ⟨las primeras cien páginas : the first hundred pages⟩ **2 cien por cien** *or* **cien por ciento** : a hundred percent, through and through, wholeheartedly

cien² *nm* : one hundred

ciénaga *nf* : swamp, bog

ciencia *nf* **1** : science **2** : learning, knowledge **3 a ciencia cierta** : for a fact, for certain

cieno *nm* : mire, mud, silt

científico¹, -ca *adj* : scientific — **científicamente** *adv*

científico², -ca *n* : scientist

ciento¹ *adj* (*used in compound numbers*) : one hundred ⟨ciento uno : one hundred and one⟩

ciento² *nm* **1** : hundred, group of a hundred **2 por ~** : percent

cierne, etc. → **cerner**

cierra, etc. → **cerrar**

cierre *nm* **1** : closing, closure **2** : fastener, clasp, zipper

cierto, -ta *adj* **1** : true, certain, definite ⟨lo cierto es que ... : the fact is that ... ⟩ **2** : certain, one ⟨cierto día de verano : one summer day⟩ ⟨bajo ciertas circunstancias : under certain circumstances⟩ **3 por ~** : in fact, as a matter of fact — **ciertamente** *adv*

ciervo, -va *n* : deer, stag *m*, hind *f*

cifra *nf* **1** : figure, number **2** : quantity, amount **3** CLAVE : code, cipher

cifrar *vt* **1** : to write in code **2** : to place, to pin ⟨cifró su esperanza en la lotería : he pinned his hopes on the lottery⟩ — **cifrarse** *vr* : to amount ⟨la multa se cifra en millares : the fine amounts to thousands⟩

cigarra *nf* CHICHARRA : cicada

cigarrera *nf* : cigarette case

cigarrillo *nm* : cigarette

cigarro *nm* **1** : cigarette **2** PURO : cigar

cigoto *nm* : zygote

cigüeña *nf* : stork

cilantro *nm* : cilantro, coriander

cilíndrico, -ca *adj* : cylindrical

cilindro *nm* : cylinder

cima *nf* CUMBRE : peak, summit, top

cimarrón, -rrona *adj, mpl* **-rrones** : untamed, wild

címbalo *nm* : cymbal

cimbel *nm* : decoy

cimbrar *vt* : to shake, to rock — **cimbrarse** *vr* : to sway, to swing

cimentar {55} *vt* **1** : to lay the foundation of, to establish **2** : to strengthen, to cement

cimientos *nmpl* : base, foundation(s)

cinc *nm* : zinc

cincel *nm* : chisel

cincelar *vt* **1** : to chisel **2** : to engrave

cincha *nf* : cinch, girth

cinchar *vt* : to cinch (a horse)

cinco *adj & nm* : five

cincuenta *adj & nm* : fifty

cincuentavo¹, -va *adj* : fiftieth

cincuentavo² *nm* : fiftieth (fraction)

cine *nm* **1** : cinema, movies *pl* **2** : movie theater

cineasta *nmf* : filmmaker

cinematográfico, -ca *adj* : movie, film, cinematic ⟨la industria cinematográfica : the film industry⟩

cingalés¹, -lesa *adj & n* : Sinhalese

cingalés² *nm* : Sinhalese (language)

cínico¹, -ca *adj* **1** : cynical **2** : shameless, brazen — **cínicamente** *adv*

cínico², -ca *n* : cynic

cinismo *nm* : cynicism

cinta *nf* **1** : ribbon **2** : tape ⟨cinta métrica : tape measure⟩ **3** : strap, belt ⟨cinta transportadora : conveyor belt⟩

cinto *nm* : strap, belt

cintura *nf* **1** : waist, waistline **2 meter en cintura** *fam* : to bring into line, to discipline

cinturón *nm, pl* **-rones 1** : belt **2 cinturón de seguridad** : seat belt

ciñe, etc. → **ceñir**

ciprés *nm, pl* **cipreses** : cypress

circo *nm* : circus

circón *nm, pl* **circones** : zircon

circonio *nm* : zirconium

circuitería *nf* : circuitry

circuito *nm* : circuit

circulación *nf, pl* **-ciones 1** : circulation **2** : movement **3** : traffic

circular¹ *vi* **1** : to circulate **2** : to move along **3** : to drive

circular² *adj* : circular

circular³ *nf* : circular, flier

circulatorio, -ria *adj* : circulatory

círculo *nm* **1** : circle **2** : club, group

circuncidar *vt* : to circumcise

circuncisión *nf, pl* **-siones** : circumcision

circundar *vt* : to surround — **circundante** *adj*

circunferencia *nf* : circumference

circunflejo, -ja *adj* **acento circunflejo** : circumflex

circunlocución *nf, pl* **-ciones** : circumlocution

circunloquio *nm* → **circunlocución**

circunnavegar {52} *vt* : to circumnavigate — **circunnavegación** *nf*

circunscribir {33} *vt* : to circumscribe, to constrict, to limit — **circunscribirse** *vr*

circunscripción *nf, pl* **-ciones 1** : limitation, restriction **2** : constituency

circunscrito *pp* → **circunscribir**

circunspección *nf, pl* **-ciones** : circumspection, prudence

circunspecto, -ta *adj* : circumspect, prudent

circunstancia *nf* : circumstance

circunstancial *adj* : circumstantial, incidental

circunstante *nmf* **1** : onlooker, bystander **2 los circunstantes** : those present

circunvalación *nf, pl* **-ciones** : surrounding, encircling ⟨carretera de circunvalación : bypass, beltway⟩

circunvecino, -na *adj* : surrounding, neighboring

cirio *nm* : large candle

cirro *nm* : cirrus (cloud)

cirrosis *nf* : cirrhosis

ciruela *nf* **1** : plum **2 ciruela pasa** : prune

cirugía *nf* : surgery

cirujano, -na *n* : surgeon

cisma *nm* : schism, rift

cisne *nm* : swan

cisterna *nf* : cistern, tank

cita *nf* **1** : quote, quotation **2** : appointment, date

citable *adj* : quotable

citación *nf, pl* **-ciones** EMPLAZAMIENTO : summons, subpoena

citadino¹, -na *adj* : of the city, urban

citadino², -na *n* : city dweller

citado, -da *adj* : said, aforementioned

citar *vt* **1** : to quote, to cite **2** : to make an appointment with **3** : to summon (to court), to subpoena — **citarse** *vr* ~ **con** : to arrange to meet (someone)

cítara *nf* : zither

citatorio *nm* : subpoena

citoplasma *nm* : cytoplasm

cítrico¹, -ca *adj* : citric

cítrico² *nm* : citrus fruit

ciudad *nf* **1** : city, town **2 ciudad universitaria** : college or university campus **3 ciudad perdida** *Mex* : shantytown

ciudadanía *nf* **1** : citizenship **2** : citizenry, citizens *pl*

ciudadano¹, -na *adj* : civic, city

ciudadano², -na *n* **1** NACIONAL : citizen **2** HABITANTE : resident, city dweller

ciudadela *nf* : citadel, fortress

cívico, -ca *adj* **1** : civic **2** : public-spirited

civil¹ *adj* **1** : civil **2** : civilian

civil² *nmf* : civilian

civilidad *nf* : civility, courtesy

civilización *nf, pl* **-ciones** : civilization

civilizar {21} *vt* : to civilize

civismo *nm* : community spirit, civic-mindedness, civics

cizaña *nf* : discord, rift

clamar *vi* : to clamor, to raise a protest — *vt* : to cry out for

clamor *nm* : clamor, outcry

clamoroso, -sa *adj* : clamorous, resounding, thunderous

clan *nm* : clan

clandestinidad *nf* : secrecy ⟨en la clandestinidad : underground⟩

clandestino, -na *adj* : clandestine, secret

clara *nf* : egg white

claraboya *nf* : skylight

claramente *adv* : clearly

clarear *v impers* **1** : to clear, to clear up **2** : to get light, to dawn — *vi* : to go gray, to turn white

claridad *nf* **1** NITIDEZ : clarity, clearness **2** : brightness, light

clarificación *nf, pl* **-ciones** ACLARACIÓN : clarification, explanation

clarificar {72} *vt* ACLARAR : to clarify, to explain

clarín *nm, pl* **clarines** : bugle

clarinete *nm* : clarinet

clarividencia *nf* **1** : clairvoyance **2** : perspicacity, discernment

clarividente¹ *adj* **1** : clairvoyant **2** : perspicacious, discerning

clarividente² *nmf* : clairvoyant

claro¹ *adv* **1** : clearly ⟨habla más claro : speak more clearly⟩ **2** : of course, surely ⟨¡claro!, ¡claro que sí! : absolutely!, of course!⟩ ⟨claro que entendió : of course she understood⟩

claro², -ra *adj* **1** : bright, clear **2** : pale, fair, light **3** : clear, evident

claro³ *nm* **1** : clearing **2 claro de luna** : moonlight

clase *nf* **1** : class **2** ÍNDOLE, TIPO : sort, kind, type

clasicismo *nm* : classicism

clásico¹, -ca *adj* **1** : classic **2** : classical

clásico² *nm* : classic

clasificación *nf, pl* **-ciones** **1** : classification, sorting out **2** : rating **3** CALIFICACIÓN : qualification (in competitions)

clasificado, -da *adj* : classified ⟨aviso clasificado : classified ad⟩

clasificar {72} *vt* **1** : to classify, to sort out **2** : to rate, to rank — *vi* CALIFICAR : to qualify (in competitions) — **clasificarse** *vr*

claudicación *nf, pl* **-ciones** : surrender, abandonment of one's principles

claudicar {72} *vi* : to back down, to abandon one's principles

claustro *nm* : cloister

claustrofobia *nf* : claustrophobia

claustrofóbico, -ca *adj* : claustrophobic

cláusula *nf* : clause

clausura *nf* **1** : closure, closing **2** : closing ceremony **3** : cloister

clausurar *vt* **1** : to close, to bring to a close **2** : to close down

clavadista *nmf* : diver

clavado¹, -da *adj* **1** : nailed, fixed, stuck **2** *fam* : punctual, on the dot **3** *fam* : identical ⟨es clavado a su padre : he's the image of his father⟩

clavado² *nm* : dive

clavar *vt* **1** : to nail, to hammer **2** HINCAR : to plunge, to stick **3** : to fix (one's eyes) on — **clavarse** *vr* : to stick oneself (with a sharp object)

clave¹ *adj* : key, essential

clave² *nf* **1** CIFRA : code **2** : key ⟨la clave del misterio : the key to the mystery⟩ **3** : clef **4** : keystone

clavel *nm* : carnation

clavelito *nm* : pink (flower)

clavicémbalo *nm* : harpsichord
clavícula *nf* : collarbone
clavija *nf* **1** : plug **2** : peg, pin
clavo *nm* **1** : nail ⟨clavo grande : spike⟩ **2** : clove **3 dar en el clavo** : to hit the nail on the head
claxon *nm, pl* **cláxones** : horn (of an automobile)
clemencia *nf* : clemency, mercy
clemente *adj* : merciful
cleptomanía *nf* : kleptomania
cleptómano, -na *n* : kleptomaniac
clerecía *nf* : ministry, ministers *pl*
clerical *adj* : clerical
clérigo, -ga *n* : cleric, member of the clergy
clero *nm* : clergy
cliché *nm* **1** : cliché **2** : stencil **3** : negative (of a photograph)
cliente, -ta *n* : customer, client
clientela *nf* : clientele, customers *pl*
clima *nm* **1** : climate **2** AMBIENTE : atmosphere, ambience
climático, -ca *adj* : climatic
climatización *nf, pl* **-ciones** : air-conditioning
climatizar {21} *vt* : to air-condition — **climatizado, -da** *adj*
clímax *nm* : climax
clínica *nf* : clinic
clínico, -ca *adj* : clinical — **clínicamente** *adv*
clip *nm, pl* **clips 1** : clip **2** : paper clip
clítoris *nms & pl* : clitoris
cloaca *nf* ALCANTARILLA : sewer
clocar {82} *vi* : to cluck
cloche *nm* CA, Car, Col, Ven : clutch (of an automobile)
clon *nm* : clone
cloqué, etc. → clocar
cloquear *vi* : to cluck
clorar *vt* : to chlorinate — **cloración** *nf*
cloro *nm* : chlorine
clorofila *nf* : chlorophyll
cloroformo *nm* : chloroform
cloruro *nm* : chloride
clóset *nm, pl* **clósets 1** : closet **2** : cupboard
club *nm* : club
clueca, clueque etc. → clocar
coa *nf Mex* : hoe
coacción *nf, pl* **-ciones** : coercion, duress
coaccionar *vt* : to coerce
coactivo, -va *adj* : coercive
coagular *v* : to clot, to coagulate — **coagulación** *nf*
coágulo *nm* : clot
coalición *nf, pl* **-ciones** : coalition
coartada *nf* : alibi
coartar *vt* : to restrict, to limit
cobalto *nm* : cobalt
cobarde[1] *adj* : cowardly
cobarde[2] *nmf* : coward
cobardía *nf* : cowardice
cobaya *nf* : guinea pig
cobertizo *nm* : shed, shelter
cobertor *nm* COLCHA : bedspread, quilt

cobertura *nf* **1** : coverage **2** : cover, collateral
cobija *nf* FRAZADA, MANTA : blanket
cobijar *vt* : to shelter — **cobijarse** *vr* : to take shelter
cobra *nf* : cobra
cobrador, -dora *n* **1** : collector **2** : conductor (of a bus or train)
cobrar *vt* **1** : to charge **2** : to collect, to draw, to earn **3** : to acquire, to gain **4** : to recover, to retrieve **5** : to cash (a check) **6** : to claim, to take (a life) **7** : to shoot (game), to bag — *vi* **1** : to be paid **2 llamar por cobrar** *Mex* : to call collect
cobre *nm* : copper
cobrizo, -za *adj* : coppery
cobro *nm* : collection (of money), cashing (of a check)
coca *nf* **1** : coca **2** *fam* : coke, cocaine
cocaína *nf* : cocaine
cocal *nm* : coca plantation
cocción *nf, pl* **cocciones** : cooking
cocear *vi* : to kick (of an animal)
cocer {14} *vt* **1** COCINAR : to cook **2** HERVIR : to boil
cochambre *nmf fam* : filth, grime
cochambroso, -sa *adj* : filthy, grimy
coche *nm* **1** : car, automobile **2** : coach, carriage **3 coche cama** : sleeping car **4 coche fúnebre** : hearse
cochecito *nm* : baby carriage, stroller
cochera *nf* : garage, carport
cochinada *nf fam* **1** : filthy language **2** : disgusting behavior **3** : dirty trick
cochinillo *nm* : suckling pig, piglet
cochino[1], **-na** *adj* **1** : dirty, filthy, disgusting **2** *fam* : rotten, lousy
cochino[2], **-na** *n* : pig, hog
cocido[1], **-da** *adj* **1** : boiled, cooked **2 bien cocido** : well-done
cocido[2] *nm* ESTOFADO, GUISADO : stew
cociente *nm* : quotient
cocimiento *nm* : cooking, baking
cocina *nf* **1** : kitchen **2** : stove **3** : cuisine, cooking
cocinar *v* : to cook
cocinero, -ra *n* : cook, chef
cocineta *nf Mex* : kitchenette
coco *nm* **1** : coconut **2** *fam* : head **3** *fam* : bogeyman
cocoa *nf* : cocoa, hot chocolate
cocodrilo *nm* : crocodile
cocotero *nm* : coconut palm
coctel *or* **cóctel** *nm* **1** : cocktail **2** : cocktail party
coctelera *nf* : cocktail shaker
codazo *nm* **1 darle un codazo a** : to elbow, to nudge **2 abrirse paso a codazos** : to elbow one's way through
codearse *vr* : to rub elbows, to hobnob
códice *nm* : codex, manuscript
codicia *nf* AVARICIA : avarice, covetousness
codiciar *vt* : to covet
codicilo *nm* : codicil
codicioso, -sa *adj* : avaricious, covetous

codificación *nf, pl* **-ciones 1** : codification **2** : coding, encoding

codificar {72} *vt* **1** : to codify **2** : to code, to encode

código *nm* **1** : code **2 código postal** : zip code **3 código morse** : Morse code

codo[1], **-da** *adj Mex* : cheap, stingy

codo[2], **-da** *n Mex* : tightwad, cheapskate

codo[3] *nm* : elbow

codorniz *nf, pl* **-nices** : quail

coeficiente *nm* **1** : coefficient **2 coeficiente intelectual** : IQ, intelligence quotient

coexistir *vi* : to coexist — **coexistencia** *nf*

cofa *nf* : crow's nest

cofre *nm* **1** BAÚL : trunk, chest **2** *Mex* CAPOTE : hood (of a car)

coger {15} *vt* **1** : to seize, to take hold of **2** : to catch **3** : to pick up **4** : to gather, to pick **5** : to gore — **cogerse** *vr* AGARRARSE : to hold on

cogida *nf* **1** : gathering, harvest **2** : goring

cognición *nf, pl* **-ciones** : cognition

cognitivo, -va *adj* : cognitive

cogollo *nm* **1** : heart (of a vegetable) **2** : bud, bulb **3** : core, crux ⟨el cogollo de la cuestión : the heart of the matter⟩

cogote *nm* : scruff, nape

cohabitar *vi* : to cohabit — **cohabitación** *nf*

cohechar *vt* SOBORNAR : to bribe

cohecho *nm* SOBORNO : bribe, bribery

coherencia *nf* : coherence — **coherente** *adj*

cohesión *nf, pl* **-siones** : cohesion

cohesivo, -va *adj* : cohesive

cohete *nm* : rocket

cohibición *nf, pl* **-ciones 1** : (legal) restraint **2** INHIBICIÓN : inhibition

cohibido, -da *adj* : inhibited, shy

cohibir {62} *vt* : to inhibit, to make self-conscious — **cohibirse** *vr* : to feel shy or embarrassed

cohorte *nf* : cohort

coima *nf Arg, Chile, Peru* : bribe

coimear *vt Arg, Chile, Peru* : to bribe

coincidencia *nf* : coincidence

coincidente *adj* **1** : coincident **2** ACORDE : coinciding

coincidir *vi* **1** : to coincide **2** : to agree

coito *nm* : sexual intercourse, coitus

coja, etc. → **coger**

cojear *vi* **1** : to limp **2** : to wobble, to rock **3 cojear del mismo pie** : to be two of a kind

cojera *nf* : limp

cojín *nm, pl* **cojines** : cushion, throw pillow

cojinete *nm* **1** : bearing, bushing **2 cojinete de bola** : ball bearing

cojo[1], **-ja** *adj* **1** : limping, lame **2** : wobbly **3** : weak, ineffectual

cojo[2], **-ja** *n* : lame person

cojones *nmpl usu considered vulgar* **1** : testicles *pl* **2** : guts *pl*, courage

col *nf* **1** REPOLLO : cabbage **2 col de Bruselas** : Brussels sprout **3 col rizada** : kale

cola *nf* **1** RABO : tail ⟨cola de caballo : ponytail⟩ **2** FILA : line (of people) ⟨hacer cola : to wait in line⟩ **3** : cola, drink **4** : train (of a dress) **5** : tails *pl* (of a tuxedo) **6** PEGAMENTO : glue **7** *fam* : buttocks *pl*, rear end

colaboracionista *nmf* : collaborator, traitor

colaborador, -dora *n* **1** : contributor (to a periodical) **2** : collaborator

colaborar *vi* : to collaborate — **colaboración** *nf*

colación *nf, pl* **-ciones 1** : light meal **2** : comparison, collation ⟨sacar a colación : to bring up, to broach⟩ **3** : conferral (of a degree)

colador *nm* **1** : colander, strainer **2** *PRi* : small coffeepot

colapso *nm* **1** : collapse **2** : standstill

colar {19} *vt* **1** : to strain, to filter — **colarse** *vr* **1** : to sneak in, to cut in line, to gate-crash **2** : to slip up, to make a mistake

colateral[1] *adj* : collateral — **colateralmente** *adv*

colateral[2] *nm* : collateral

colcha *nf* COBERTOR : bedspread, quilt

colchón *nm, pl* **colchones 1** : mattress **2** : cushion, padding, buffer

colchoneta *nf* : mat (for gymnastic sports)

colear *vi* **1** : to wag its tail **2 vivito y coleando** *fam* : alive and kicking

colección *nf, pl* **-ciones** : collection

coleccionar *vt* : to collect, to keep a collection of

coleccionista *nmf* : collector

colecta *nf* : collection (of donations)

colectar *vt* : to collect

colectividad *nf* : community, group

colectivo[1], **-va** *adj* : collective — **colectivamente** *adv*

colectivo[2] *nm* **1** : collective **2** *Arg, Bol, Peru* : city bus

colector[1], **-tora** *n* : collector ⟨colector de impuestos : tax collector⟩

colector[2] *nm* **1** : sewer **2** : manifold (of an engine)

colega *nmf* **1** : colleague **2** HOMÓLOGO : counterpart **3** *fam* : buddy

colegiado[1], **-da** *adj* : collegiate

colegiado[2], **-da** *n* **1** ÁRBITRO : referee **2** : member (of a professional association)

colegial[1], **-giala** *adj* **1** : school, collegiate **2** *Mex fam* : green, inexperienced

colegial[2], **-giala** *n* : schoolboy *m*, schoolgirl *f*

colegiatura *nf Mex* : tuition

colegio *nm* **1** : school **2** : college ⟨colegio electoral : electoral college⟩ **3** : professional association

colegir {28} *vt* **1** JUNTAR : to collect, to gather **2** INFERIR : to infer, to deduce

cólera¹ *nm* : cholera

cólera² *nf* FURIA, IRA : anger, rage

colérico, -ca *adj* **1** FURIOSO : angry **2** IRRITABLE : irritable

colesterol *nm* : cholesterol

coleta *nf* **1** : ponytail **2** : pigtail

coletazo *nm* : lash, flick (of a tail)

colgado, -da *adj* **1** : hanging, hanged **2** : pending **3 dejar colgado a** : to disappoint, to let down

colgante¹ *adj* : hanging, dangling

colgante² *nm* : pendant, charm (on a bracelet)

colgar {16} *vt* **1** : to hang (up), to put up **2** AHORCAR : to hang (someone) **3** : to hang up (a telephone) **4** *fam* : to fail (an exam) — **colgarse** *vr* **1** : to hang, to be suspended **2** AHORCARSE : to hang oneself **3** : to hang up a telephone

colibrí *nm* CHUPAFLOR : hummingbird

cólico *nm* : colic

coliflor *nf* : cauliflower

colilla *nf* : butt (of a cigarette)

colina *nf* CERRO, LOMA : hill

colindante *adj* CONTIGUO : adjacent, neighboring

colindar *vi* : to adjoin, to be adjacent

coliseo *nm* : coliseum

colisión *nf*, *pl* **-siones** : collision

colisionar *vi* : to collide

collage *nm* : collage

collar *nm* **1** : collar (for an animal) **2** : necklace ⟨collar de perlas : string of pearls⟩

colmado, -da *adj* : heaping

colmar *vt* **1** : to fill to the brim **2** : to fulfill, to satisfy **3** : to heap, to shower ⟨me colmaron de regalos : they showered me with gifts⟩

colmena *nf* : beehive

colmenar *nm* APIARIO : apiary

colmillo *nm* **1** CANINO : canine (tooth), fang **2** : tusk

colmilludo, -da *adj Mex, PRi* : astute, shrewd, crafty

colmo *nm* : height, extreme, limit ⟨el colmo de la locura : the height of folly⟩ ⟨¡eso es el colmo! : that's the last straw!⟩

colocación *nf*, *pl* **-ciones** **1** : placement, placing **2** : position, job **3** : investment

colocar {72} *vt* **1** PONER : to place, to put **2** : to find a job for **3** : to invest — **colocarse** *vr* **1** SITUARSE : to position oneself **2** : to get a job

colofón *nm*, *pl* **-fones** **1** : ending, finale **2** : colophon

colofonia *nf* : rosin

colombiano, -na *adj & n* : Colombian

colon *nm* : (intestinal) colon

colón *nm*, *pl* **colones** : Costa Rican and Salvadoran unit of currency

colonia *nf* **1** : colony **2** : cologne **3** *Mex* : residential area, neighborhood

colonial *adj* : colonial

colonización *nf*, *pl* **-ciones** : colonization

colonizador¹, -dora *adj* : colonizing

colonizador², -dora *n* : colonizer, colonist

colonizar {21} *vt* : to colonize, to settle

colono, -na *n* **1** : settler, colonist **2** : tenant farmer

coloquial *adj* : colloquial

coloquio *nm* **1** : discussion, talk **2** : conference, symposium

color *nm* **1** : color **2** : paint, dye **3 colores** *nmpl* : colored pencils

coloración *nf*, *pl* **-ciones** : coloring, coloration

colorado¹, -da *adj* **1** ROJO : red **2** **ponerse colorado** : to blush **3 chiste colorado** *Mex* : off-color joke

colorado² *nm* ROJO : red

colorante *nm* : coloring ⟨colorante de alimentos : food coloring⟩

colorear *vt* : to color — *vi* **1** : to redden **2** : to ripen

colorete *nm* : rouge, blusher

colorido *nm* : color, coloring

colorín *nm*, *pl* **-rines** **1** : bright color **2** : goldfinch

colosal *adj* : colossal

coloso *nm* : colossus

coludir *vi* : to be in collusion, to conspire

columna *nf* **1** : column **2 columna vertebral** : spine, backbone

columnata *nf* : colonnade

columnista *nmf* : columnist

columpiar *vt* : to push (on a swing) — **columpiarse** *vr* : to swing

columpio *nm* : swing

colusión *nf*, *pl* **-siones** : collusion

colza *nf* : rape (plant)

coma¹ *nm* : coma

coma² *nf* : comma

comadre *nf* **1** : godmother of one's child **2** : mother of one's godchild **3** *fam* : neighbor, female friend **4** *fam* : gossip

comadrear *vi fam* : to gossip

comadreja *nf* : weasel

comadrona *nf* : midwife

comanche *nmf* : Comanche

comandancia *nf* **1** : command headquarters **2** : command

comandante *nmf* **1** : commander, commanding officer **2** : major

comandar *vt* : to command, to lead

comando *nm* **1** : commando **2** : command (for computers)

comarca *nf* REGIÓN : region

comarcal *adj* REGIONAL : regional, local

comatoso, -sa *adj* : comatose

combar *vt* : to bend, to curve — **combarse** *vr* **1** : to bend, to buckle **2** : to warp, to bulge, to sag

combate *nm* **1** : combat **2** : fight, boxing match

combatiente *nmf* : combatant, fighter

combatir *vt* : to combat, to fight against — *vi* : to fight

combatividad *nf* : fighting spirit
combativo, -va *adj* : combative, spirited
combinación *nf, pl* **-ciones 1** : combination **2** : connection (in travel)
combinar *vt* **1** UNIR : to combine, to mix together **2** : to match, to put together — **combinarse** *vr* : to get together, to conspire
combo *nm* **1** : (musical) band **2** *Chile, Peru* : sledgehammer **3** *Chile, Peru* : punch
combustible¹ *adj* : combustible
combustible² *nm* : fuel
combustión *nf, pl* **-tiones** : combustion
comedero *nm* : trough, feeder
comedia *nf* : comedy
comediante *nmf* : actor, actress *f*
comedido, -da *adj* MESURADO : moderate, restrained
comediógrafo, -fa *n* : playwright
comedor *nm* : dining room
comején *nm, pl* **-jenes** : termite
comelón¹, -lona *adj, mpl* **-lones** *fam* : gluttonous
comelón², -lona *n, pl* **-lones** *fam* : big eater, glutton
comensal *nmf* : dinner guest
comentador, -dora *n* → **comentarista**
comentar *vt* **1** : to comment on, to discuss **2** : to mention, to remark
comentario *nm* **1** : comment, remark ⟨sin comentarios : no comment⟩ **2** : commentary
comentarista *nmf* : commentator
comenzar {29} *v* EMPEZAR : to begin, to start
comer¹ *vt* **1** : to eat **2** : to consume, to eat up, to eat into — *vi* **1** : to eat **2** CENAR : to have a meal **3 dar de comer** : to feed — **comerse** *vr* : to eat up
comer² *nm* : eating, dining
comercial *adj & nm* : commercial — **comercialmente** *adv*
comercializar {21} *vt* **1** : to commercialize **2** : to market
comerciante *nmf* : merchant, dealer
comerciar *vi* : to do business, to trade
comercio *nm* **1** : commerce, trade **2** NEGOCIO : business, place of business
comestible *adj* : edible
comestibles *nmpl* VÍVERES : groceries, food
cometa¹ *nm* : comet
cometa² *nf* : kite
cometer *vt* **1** : to commit **2 cometer un error** : to make a mistake
cometido *nm* : assignment, task
comezón *nf, pl* **-zones** PICAZÓN : itchiness, itching
comible *adj fam* : eatable, edible
comic *or* **cómic** *nm* : comic strip, comic book
comicastro, -tra *n* : second-rate actor, ham
comicidad *nf* HUMOR : humor, wit
comicios *nmpl* : elections, voting
cómico¹, -ca *adj* : comic, comical

cómico², -ca *n* HUMORISTA : comic, comedian, comedienne *f*
comida *nf* **1** : food **2** : meal **3** : dinner **4 comida basura** : junk food **5 comida rápida** : fast food
comidilla *nf* : talk, gossip
comienzo *nm* **1** : start, beginning **2 al comienzo** : at first **3 dar comienzo** : to begin
comillas *nfpl* : quotation marks ⟨entre comillas : in quotes⟩
comilón, -lona → **comelón, -lona**
comilona *nf fam* : feast
comino *nm* **1** : cumin **2 me vale un comino** *fam* : not to matter to someone ⟨no me importa un comino : I couldn't care less⟩
comisaría *nf* : police station
comisario, -ria *n* : commissioner
comisión *nf, pl* **-siones 1** : commission, committing **2** : committee **3** : percentage, commission ⟨comisión sobre las ventas : sales commission⟩
comisionado¹, -da *adj* : commissioned, entrusted
comisionado², -da *n* → **comisario**
comisionar *vt* : to commission
comité *nm* : committee
comitiva *nf* : retinue, entourage
como¹ *adv* **1** : around, about ⟨cuesta como 500 pesos : it costs around 500 pesos⟩ **2** : kind of, like ⟨tengo como mareos : I'm kind of dizzy⟩
como² *conj* **1** : how, as ⟨hazlo como dijiste que lo harías : do it the way you said you would⟩ **2** : since, given that ⟨como estaba lloviendo, no salí : since it was raining, I didn't go out⟩ **3** : if ⟨como lo vuelva a hacer lo arrestarán : if he does that again he'll be arrested⟩ **4 como quiera** : in any way
como³ *prep* **1** : like, as ⟨ligero como una pluma : light as a feather⟩ **2 así como** : as well as
cómo *adv* : how ⟨¿cómo estás? : how are you?⟩ ⟨¿a cómo están las manzanas? : how much are the apples?⟩ ⟨¿cómo? : excuse me?, what was that?⟩ ⟨¿se puede? ¡cómo no! : may I? please do!⟩
cómoda *nf* : bureau, chest of drawers
comodidad *nf* **1** : comfort **2** : convenience
comodín *nm, pl* **-dines 1** : joker, wild card **2** : all-purpose word or thing **3** : pretext, excuse
cómodo, -da *adj* **1** CONFORTABLE : comfortable **2** : convenient — **cómodamente** *adv*
comodoro *nm* : commodore
comoquiera *adv* **1** : in any way **2 comoquiera que** : in whatever way, however ⟨comoquiera que sea eso : however that may be⟩
compa *nm fam* : buddy, pal
compactar *vt* : to compact, to compress
compacto, -ta *adj* : compact

compadecer {53} *vt* : to sympathize with, to feel sorry for — **compadecerse** *vr* **1** ∼ **de** : to take pity on, to commiserate with **2** ∼ **con** : to fit, to accord (with)

compadre *nm* **1** : godfather of one's child **2** : father of one's godchild **3** *fam* : buddy, pal

compaginar *vt* **1** COORDINAR : to combine, to coordinate **2** : to collate

compañerismo *nm* : comradeship, camaraderie

compañero, -ra *n* : companion, mate, partner

compañía *nf* **1** : company ⟨llegó en compañía de su madre : he arrived with his mother⟩ **2** EMPRESA, FIRMA : firm, company

comparable *adj* : comparable

comparación *nf, pl* **-ciones** : comparison

comparado, -da *adj* : comparative ⟨literatura comparada : comparative literature⟩

comparar *vt* : to compare

comparativo¹, -va *adj* : comparative, relative — **comparativamente** *adv*

comparativo² *nm* : comparative degree or form

comparecencia *nf* **1** : appearance (in court) **2 orden de comparecencia** : subpoena, summons

comparecer {53} *vi* : to appear (in court)

compartimiento *or* **compartimento** *nm* : compartment

compartir *vt* : to share

compás *nm, pl* **-pases 1** : beat, rhythm, time **2** : compass

compasión *nf, pl* **-siones** : compassion, pity

compasivo, -va *adj* : compassionate, sympathetic

compatibilidad *nf* : compatibility

compatible *adj* : compatible

compatriota *nmf* PAISANO : compatriot, fellow countryman

compeler *vt* : to compel

compendiar *vt* : to summarize, to condense

compendio *nm* : summary

compenetración *nf, pl* **-ciones** : rapport, mutual understanding

compenetrarse *vr* **1** : to understand each other **2** ∼ **con** : to identify oneself with

compensación *nf, pl* **-ciones** : compensation

compensar *vt* : to compensate for, to make up for — *vi* : to be worth one's while

compensatorio, -ria *adj* : compensatory

competencia *nf* **1** : competition, rivalry **2** : competence

competente *adj* : competent, able — **competentemente** *adv*

competición *nf, pl* **-ciones** : competition

competidor¹, -dora *adj* RIVAL : competing, rival

competidor², -dora *n* RIVAL : competitor, rival

competir {54} *vi* : to compete

competitividad *nf* : competitiveness

competitivo, -va *adj* : competitive — **competitivamente** *adv*

compilar *vt* : to compile — **compilación** *nf*

compinche *nmf fam* **1** : buddy, pal **2** : partner in crime, accomplice

complacencia *nf* : pleasure, satisfaction

complacer {57} *vt* : to please — **complacerse** *vr* ∼ **en** : to take pleasure in

complaciente *adj* : obliging, eager to please

complejidad *nf* : complexity

complejo¹, -ja *adj* : complex

complejo² *nm* : complex

complementar *vt* : to complement, to supplement — **complementarse** *vr*

complementario, -ria *adj* : complementary

complemento *nm* **1** : complement, supplement **2** : supplementary pay, allowance

completamente *adv* : completely, totally

completar *vt* TERMINAR : to complete, to finish

completo, -ta *adj* **1** : complete **2** : perfect, absolute **3** : full, detailed

complexión *nf, pl* **-xiones** : (physical) constitution

complicación *nf, pl* **-ciones** : complication

complicado, -da *adj* : complicated

complicar {72} *vt* **1** : to complicate **2** : to involve — **complicarse** *vr*

cómplice *nmf* : accomplice

complicidad *nf* : complicity

complot *nm, pl* **complots** CONFABULACIÓN, CONSPIRACIÓN : conspiracy, plot

componenda *nf* : shady deal, scam

componente *adj & nm* : component, constituent

componer {60} *vt* **1** ARREGLAR : to fix, to repair **2** CONSTITUIR : to make up, to compose **3** : to compose, to write **4** : to set (a bone) — **componerse** *vr* **1** : to improve, to get better **2** ∼ **de** : to consist of

comportamiento *nm* CONDUCTA : behavior, conduct

comportarse *vr* : to behave, to conduct oneself

composición *nf, pl* **-ciones 1** OBRA : composition, work **2** : makeup, arrangement

compositor, -tora *n* : composer, songwriter

compostura *nf* **1** : composure **2** : mending, repair

compra *nf* **1** : purchase **2 ir de compras** : to go shopping **3 orden de compra** : purchase order

comprador, -dora n : buyer, shopper

comprar vt : to buy, to purchase

compraventa nf : buying and selling

comprender vt **1** ENTENDER : to comprehend, to understand **2** ABARCAR : to cover, to include — vi : to understand ⟨¡ya comprendo! : now I understand!⟩

comprensible adj : understandable — **comprensiblemente** adv

comprensión nf, pl **-siones 1** : comprehension, understanding, grasp **2** : understanding, sympathy

comprensivo, -va adj : understanding

compresa nf **1** : compress **2** or **compresa higiénica** : sanitary napkin

compresión nf, pl **-siones** : compression

compresor nm : compressor

comprimido nm PÍLDORA, TABLETA : pill, tablet

comprimir vt : to compress

comprobable adj : verifiable, provable

comprobación nf, pl **-ciones** : verification, confirmation

comprobante nm **1** : proof ⟨comprobante de identidad : proof of identity⟩ **2** : voucher, receipt ⟨comprobante de ventas : sales slip⟩

comprobar {19} vt **1** : to verify, to check **2** : to prove

comprometedor, -dora adj : compromising

comprometer vt **1** : to compromise **2** : to jeopardize **3** : to commit, to put under obligation — **comprometerse** vr **1** : to commit oneself **2** ~ **con** : to get engaged to

comprometido, -da adj **1** : compromising, awkward **2** : committed, obliged **3** : engaged (to be married)

compromiso nm **1** : obligation, commitment **2** : engagement ⟨anillo de compromiso : engagement ring⟩ **3** : agreement **4** : awkward situation, fix

compuerta nf : floodgate

compuesto¹ pp → **componer**

compuesto², -ta adj **1** : fixed, repaired **2** : compound, composite **3** : decked out, spruced up **4** ~ **de** : made up of, consisting of

compuesto³ nm : compound

compulsión nf, pl **-siones** : compulsion

compulsivo, -va adj **1** : compelling, urgent **2** : compulsive — **compulsivamente** adv

compungido, -da adj : contrite, remorseful

compungirse {35} vr : to feel remorse

compuso, etc. → **componer**

computable adj : countable ⟨años computables : years accrued⟩ ⟨ingresos computables : qualifying income⟩

computación nf, pl **-ciones** : computing, computers pl

computador nm → **computadora**

computadora nf **1** : computer **2 computadora portátil** : laptop computer

computar vt : to compute, to calculate

computarizar {21} vt : to computerize

cómputo nm : computation, calculation

comulgar {52} vi : to receive Communion

común adj, pl **comunes 1** : common **2 común y corriente** : ordinary, regular **3 por lo común** : generally, as a rule

comuna nf : commune

comunal adj : communal

comunicación nf, pl **-ciones 1** : communication **2** : access, link **3** : message, report

comunicado nm **1** : communiqué **2 comunicado de prensa** : press release

comunicar {72} vt **1** : to communicate, to convey **2** : to notify — **comunicarse** vr ~ **con 1** : to contact, to get in touch with **2** : to be connected to

comunicativo, -va adj : communicative, talkative

comunidad nf : community

comunión nf, pl **-niones 1** : communion, sharing **2** : Communion

comunismo nm : communism, Communism

comunista adj & nmf : communist

comúnmente adv : commonly

con prep **1** : with ⟨vengo con mi padre : I'm going with my father⟩ ⟨¿con quién hablas? : who are you speaking to?⟩ **2** : in spite of ⟨con todo : in spite of it all⟩ **3** : to, towards ⟨ella es amable con los niños : she is kind to the children⟩ **4** : by ⟨con llegar temprano : by arriving early⟩ **5 con (tal) que** : as long as, so long as

conato nm : attempt, effort ⟨conato de robo : attempted robbery⟩

cóncavo, -va adj : concave

concebible adj : conceivable

concebir {54} vt **1** : to conceive **2** : to conceive of, to imagine — vi : to conceive, to become pregnant

conceder vt **1** : to grant, to bestow **2** : to concede, to admit

concejal, -jala n : councilman m, councilwoman f, alderman m, alderwoman f

concejo nm : council ⟨concejo municipal : town council⟩

concentración nf, pl **-ciones** : concentration

concentrado nm : concentrate

concentrar vt : to concentrate — **concentrarse** vr

concéntrico, -ca adj : concentric

concepción nf, pl **-ciones** : conception

concepto nm NOCIÓN : concept, idea, opinion

conceptuar {3} vt : to regard, to judge

concernir {17} vi : to be of concern

concertar {55} vt **1** : to arrange, to set up **2** : to agree on, to settle **3** : to harmonize — vi : to be in harmony

concesión nf, pl **-siones 1** : concession **2** : awarding, granting

concha nf : conch, seashell

conciencia *nf* 1 : conscience 2 : consciousness, awareness

concientizar {21} *vt* : to make aware — **concientizarse** *vr* ~ **de** : to realize, to become aware of

concienzudo, -da *adj* : conscientious

concierto *nm* 1 : concert 2 : agreement 3 : concerto

conciliador¹, -dora *adj* : conciliatory

conciliador², -dora *n* : arbitrator, peacemaker

conciliar *vt* : to conciliate, to reconcile — **conciliación** *nf*

conciliatorio, -ria *adj* → **conciliador¹**

concilio *nm* : (church) council

conciso, -sa *adj* : concise — **concisión** *nf*

conciudadano, -na *n* : fellow citizen

cónclave *nm* : conclave, private meeting

concluir {41} *vt* 1 TERMINAR : to conclude, to finish 2 DEDUCIR : to deduce, to infer — *vi* : to end, to conclude

conclusión *nf, pl* **-siones** : conclusion

concluyente *adj* : conclusive

concomitante *adj* : concomitant

concordancia *nf* : agreement, accordance

concordar {19} *vi* : to agree, to coincide — *vt* : to reconcile

concordia *nf* : concord, harmony

concretar *vt* 1 : to pinpoint, to specify 2 : to fulfill, to realize — **concretarse** *vr* : to become real, to take shape

concretizar → **concretar**

concreto¹, -ta *adj* 1 : concrete, actual 2 : definite, specific ⟨en concreto : specifically⟩ — **concretamente** *adv*

concreto² *nm* HORMIGÓN : concrete

concubina *nf* : concubine

concurrencia *nf* 1 : audience, turnout 2 : concurrence

concurrente *adj* : concurrent — **concurrentemente** *adv*

concurrido, -da *adj* : busy, crowded

concurrir *vi* 1 : to converge, to come together 2 : to concur, to agree 3 : to take part, to participate 4 : to attend, to be present ⟨concurrir a una reunión : to attend a meeting⟩ 5 ~ **a** : to contribute to

concursante *nmf* : contestant, competitor

concursar *vt* : to compete in — *vi* : to compete, to participate

concurso *nm* 1 : contest, competition 2 : concurrence, coincidence 3 : crowd, gathering 4 : cooperation, assistance

condado *nm* 1 : county 2 : earldom

conde, -desa *n* : count *m*, earl *m*, countess *f*

condecoración *nf, pl* **-ciones** : decoration, medal

condecorar *vt* : to decorate, to award (a medal)

condena *nf* 1 REPROBACIÓN : disapproval, condemnation 2 SENTENCIA : sentence, conviction

condenable *adj* : reprehensible

condenación *nf, pl* **-ciones** 1 : condemnation 2 : damnation

condenado¹, -da *adj* 1 : fated, doomed 2 : convicted, sentenced 3 *fam* : darn, damned

condenado², -da *n* : convict

condenar *vt* 1 : to condemn 2 : to sentence 3 : to board up, to wall up — **condenarse** *vr* : to be damned

condensación *nf, pl* **-ciones** : condensation

condensar *vt* : to condense

condesa *nf* → **conde**

condescendencia *nf* : condescension

condescender {56} *vi* 1 : to condescend 2 : to agree, to acquiesce

condición *nf, pl* **-ciones** 1 : condition, state 2 : capacity, position 3 **condiciones** *nfpl* : conditions, circumstances ⟨condiciones de vida : living conditions⟩

condicional *adj* : conditional — **condicionalmente** *adv*

condicionamiento *nm* : conditioning

condicionar *vt* 1 : to condition, to determine 2 ~ **a** : to be contingent on, to depend on

condimentar *vt* SAZONAR : to season, to spice

condimento *nm* : condiment, seasoning, spice

condiscípulo, -la *n* : classmate

condolencia *nf* : condolence, sympathy

condolerse {47} *vr* : to sympathize

condominio *nm* : condominium, condo

condón *nm, pl* **condones** : condom

cóndor *nm* : condor

conducción *nf, pl* **-ciones** 1 : conduction (of electricity, etc.) 2 DIRECCIÓN : management, direction

conducir {61} *vt* 1 DIRIGIR, GUIAR : to direct, to lead 2 MANEJAR : to drive (a vehicle) — *vi* 1 : to drive a vehicle 2 ~ **a** : to lead to — **conducirse** *vr* PORTARSE : to behave, to conduct oneself

conducta *nf* COMPORTAMIENTO : conduct, behavior

conducto *nm* : conduit, channel, duct

conductor¹, -tora *adj* : conducting, leading

conductor², -tora *n* : driver

conductor³ *nm* : conductor (of electricity, etc.)

conectar *vt* : to connect — *vi* ~ **con** : to link up with, to communicate with

conector *nm* : connector

conejera *nf* : rabbit hutch

conejillo *nm* **conejillo de Indias** : guinea pig

conejo, -ja *n* : rabbit

conexión *nf, pl* **-xiones** : connection

confabulación *nf, pl* **-ciones** COMPLOT, CONSPIRACIÓN : plot, conspiracy

confabularse *vr* : to plot, to conspire

confección *nf, pl* **-ciones** 1 : preparation 2 : tailoring, dressmaking

confeccionar *vt* : to make, to produce, to prepare

confederación *nf, pl* **-ciones** : confederation

confederarse *vr* : to confederate, to form a confederation

conferencia *nf* **1** REUNIÓN : conference, meeting **2** : lecture

conferenciante *nmf* : lecturer

conferencista → **conferenciante**

conferir {76} *vt* : to confer, to bestow

confesar {55} *v* : to confess — **confesarse** *vr* : to go to confession

confesión *nf, pl* **-siones 1** : confession **2** : creed, denomination

confesionario *nm* : confessional

confesor *nm* : confessor

confeti *nm* : confetti

confiable *adj* : trustworthy, reliable

confiado, -da *adj* **1** : confident, self-confident **2** : trusting — **confiadamente** *adv*

confianza *nf* **1** : trust ⟨de poca confianza : untrustworthy⟩ **2** : confidence, self-confidence

confianzudo, -da *adj* : forward, presumptuous

confiar {85} *vi* : to have trust, to be trusting — *vt* **1** : to confide **2** : to entrust — **confiarse** *vr* **1** : to be overconfident **2 ~ a** : to confide in

confidencia *nf* : confidence, secret

confidencial *adj* : confidential — **confidencialmente** *adv*

confidencialidad *nf* : confidentiality

confidente *nmf* **1** : confidant, confidante *f* **2** : informer

configuración *nf, pl* **-ciones** : configuration, shape

configurar *vt* : to shape, to form

confín *nm, pl* **confines** : boundary, limit

confinamiento *nm* : confinement

confinar *vt* **1** : to confine, to limit **2** : to exile — *vi* **~ con** : to border on

confirmación *nf, pl* **-ciones** : confirmation

confirmar *vt* : to confirm, to substantiate

confiscación *nf, pl* **-ciones** : confiscation

confiscar {72} *vt* DECOMISAR : to confiscate, to seize

confitado, -da *adj* : candied

confite *nm* : comfit, candy

confitería *nf* **1** DULCERÍA : candy store, confectionery **2** : tearoom, café

confitero, -ra *n* : confectioner

confitura *nf* : preserves, jam

conflagración *nf, pl* **-ciones 1** : conflagration, fire **2** : war

conflictivo, -va *adj* **1** : troubled **2** : controversial

conflicto *nm* : conflict

confluencia *nf* : junction, confluence

confluir {41} *vi* **1** : to converge, to join **2** : to gather, to assemble

conformar *vt* **1** : to form, to create **2** : to constitute, to make up — **conformarse** *vr* **1** RESIGNARSE : to resign oneself **2** : to comply, to conform **3 ~ con** : to content oneself with, to be satisfied with

conforme[1] *adj* **1** : content, satisfied **2 ~ a** : in accordance with

conforme[2] *conj* : as ⟨entreguen sus tareas conforme vayan saliendo : hand in your homework as you leave⟩

conformidad *nf* **1** : agreement, consent **2** : resignation

confort *nm* : comfort

confortable *adj* CÓMODO : comfortable

confortar *vt* CONSOLAR : to comfort, to console

confraternidad *nf* : brotherhood, fraternity

confraternización *nf, pl* **-ciones** : fraternization

confraternizar *vi* : to fraternize

confrontación *nf, pl* **-ciones** : confrontation

confrontar *vt* **1** ENCARAR : to confront **2** : to compare **3** : to bring face-to-face — *vi* : to border — **confrontarse** *vr* **~ con** : to face up to

confundir *vt* : to confuse, to mix up — **confundirse** *vr* : to make a mistake, to be confused ⟨confundirse de número : to get the wrong number⟩

confusión *nf, pl* **-siones** : confusion

confuso, -sa *adj* **1** : confused, mixed-up **2** : obscure, indistinct

congelación *nf, pl* **-ciones 1** : freezing **2** : frostbite

congelado, -da *adj* HELADO : frozen

congelador *nm* HELADORA : freezer

congelamiento *nm* → **congelación**

congelar *vt* : to freeze — **congelarse** *vr*

congeniar *vi* : to get along (with someone)

congénito, -ta *adj* : congenital

congestión *nf, pl* **-tiones** : congestion

congestionado, -da *adj* : congested

congestionamiento *nm* → **congestión**

congestionarse *vr* **1** : to become flushed **2** : to become congested

conglomerado[1]**, -da** *adj* : conglomerate, mixed

conglomerado[2] *nm* : conglomerate, conglomeration

congoja *nf* ANGUSTIA : anguish, grief

congoleño, -ña *adj & n* : Congolese

congraciarse *vr* : to ingratiate oneself

congratular *vt* FELICITAR : to congratulate

congregación *nf, pl* **-ciones** : congregation, gathering

congregar {52} *vt* : to bring together — **congregarse** *vr* : to congregate, to assemble

congresista *nmf* : congressman *m*, congresswoman *f*

congreso *nm* : congress, conference

congruencia *nf* **1** : congruence **2** COHERENCIA : coherence — **congruente** *adj*

cónico, -ca *adj* : conical, conic

conífera *nf* : conifer

conífero, -ra *adj* : coniferous
conjetura *nf* : conjecture, guess
conjeturar *vt* : to guess, to conjecture
conjugación *nf, pl* **-ciones** : conjugation
conjugar {52} *vt* **1** : to conjugate **2** : to combine
conjunción *nf, pl* **-ciones** : conjunction
conjuntivo, -va *adj* : connective ⟨tejido conjuntivo : connective tissue⟩
conjunto[1], -ta *adj* : joint
conjunto[2] *nm* **1** : collection, group **2** : ensemble, outfit ⟨conjunto musical : musical ensemble⟩ **3** : whole, entirety ⟨en conjunto : as a whole, altogether⟩
conjurar *vt* **1** : to exorcise **2** : to avert, to ward off — *vi* CONSPIRAR : to conspire, to plot
conjuro *nm* **1** : exorcism **2** : spell
conllevar *vt* **1** : to bear, to suffer **2** IMPLICAR : to entail, to involve
conmemorar *vt* : to commemorate — **conmemoración** *nf*
conmemorativo, -va *adj* : commemorative, memorial
conmigo *pron* : with me ⟨habló conmigo : he talked with me⟩
conminar *vt* AMENAZAR : to threaten, to warn
conmiseración *nf, pl* **-ciones** : pity, commiseration
conmoción *nf, pl* **-ciones** **1** : shock, upheaval **2** *or* **conmoción cerebral** : concussion
conmocionar *vt* : to shake, to shock
conmovedor, -dora *adj* EMOCIONANTE : moving, touching
conmover {47} *vt* **1** EMOCIONAR : to move, to touch **2** : to shake up — **conmoverse** *vr*
conmutador *nm* **1** : switch **2** : switchboard
conmutar *vt* **1** : to commute (a sentence) **2** : to switch, to exchange
connivencia *nf* : connivance
connotación *nf, pl* **-ciones** : connotation
connotar *vt* : to connote, to imply
cono *nm* : cone
conocedor[1], -dora *adj* : knowledgeable
conocedor[2], -dora *n* : connoisseur, expert
conocer {18} *vt* **1** : to know, to be acquainted with ⟨ya lo conocí : I've already met him⟩ **2** : to meet **3** RECONOCER : to recognize — **conocerse** *vr* **1** : to know each other **2** : to meet **3** : to know oneself
conocido[1], -da *adj* **1** : familiar **2** : well-known, famous
conocido[2], -da *n* : acquaintance
conocimiento *nm* **1** : knowledge **2** SENTIDO : consciousness
conque *conj* : so, so then, and so ⟨ah, conque esas tenemos! : oh, so that's what's going on!⟩
conquista *nf* : conquest
conquistador[1], -dora *adj* : conquering

conquistador[2], -dora *n* : conqueror
conquistar *vt* : to conquer
consabido, -da *adj* : usual, typical
consagración *nf, pl* **-ciones** : consecration
consagrar *vt* **1** : to consecrate **2** DEDICAR : to dedicate, to devote
consciencia → **conciencia**
consciente *adj* : conscious, aware — **conscientemente** *adv*
conscripción *nf, pl* **-ciones** : conscription, draft
conscripto, -ta *n* : conscript, inductee
consecución *nf, pl* **-ciones** : attainment
consecuencia *nf* **1** : consequence, result ⟨a consecuencia de : as a result of⟩ **2 en ~** : accordingly
consecuente *adj* : consistent — **consecuentemente** *adv*
consecutivo, -va *adj* : consecutive, successive — **consecutivamente** *adv*
conseguir {75} *vt* **1** : to get, to obtain **2** : to achieve, to attain **3** : to manage to ⟨consiguió acabar el trabajo : she managed to finish the job⟩
consejero, -ra *n* : adviser, counselor
consejo *nm* **1** : advice, counsel **2** : council ⟨consejo de guerra : court-martial⟩
consenso *nm* : consensus
consentido, -da *adj* : spoiled, pampered
consentimiento *nm* : consent, permission
consentir {76} *vt* **1** PERMITIR : to consent to, to allow **2** MIMAR : to pamper, to spoil — *vi* **~ en** : to agree to, to approve of
conserje *nmf* : custodian, janitor, caretaker
conserva *nf* **1** : preserve(s), jam **2 conservas** *nfpl* : canned goods
conservación *nf, pl* **-ciones** : conservation, preservation
conservacionista *nmf* : conservationist
conservador[1], -dora *adj & n* : conservative
conservador[2] *nm* : preservative
conservadurismo *nf* : conservatism
conservante *nm* : preservative
conservar *vt* **1** : to preserve **2** GUARDAR : to keep, to conserve
conservatorio *nm* : conservatory
considerable *adj* : considerable — **considerablemente** *adv*
consideración *nf, pl* **-ciones** **1** : consideration **2** : respect **3 de ~** : considerable, important
considerado, -da *adj* **1** : considerate, thoughtful **2** : respected
considerar *vt* **1** : to consider, to think over **2** : to judge, to deem **3** : to treat with respect
consigna *nf* ESLOGAN : slogan **2** : assignment, orders *pl* **3** : checkroom
consignación *nf, pl* **-ciones** **1** : consignment **2** ASIGNACIÓN : allocation
consignar *vt* **1** : to consign **2** : to record, to write down **3** : to assign, to allocate

consigo *pron* : with her, with him, with you, with oneself ⟨se llevó las llaves consigo : she took the keys with her⟩
consiguiente *adj* **1** : resulting, consequent **2 por ~** : consequently, as a result
consistencia *nf* : consistency
consistente *adj* **1** : firm, strong, sound **2** : consistent — **consistentemente** *adv*
consistir *vi* **1 ~ en** : to consist of **2 ~ en** : to lie in, to consist in
consola *nf* : console
consolación *nf, pl* **-ciones** : consolation ⟨premio de consolación : consolation prize⟩
consolar {19} *vt* CONFORTAR : to console, to comfort
consolidar *vt* : to consolidate — **consolidación** *nf*
consomé *nm* CALDO : consommé, clear soup
consonancia *nf* **1** : consonance, harmony **2 en consonancia con** : in accordance with
consonante¹ *adj* : consonant, harmonious
consonante² *nf* : consonant
consorcio *nm* : consortium
consorte *nmf* : consort, spouse
conspicuo, -cua *adj* : eminent, famous
conspiración *nf, pl* **-ciones** COMPLOT, CONFABULACIÓN : conspiracy, plot
conspirador, -dora *n* : conspirator
conspirar *vi* CONJURAR : to conspire, to plot
constancia *nf* **1** PRUEBA : proof, certainty **2** : record, evidence ⟨que quede constancia : for the record⟩ **3** : perseverance, constancy
constante¹ *adj* : constant — **constantemente** *adv*
constante² *nf* : constant
constar *vi* **1** : to be evident, to be on record ⟨que conste : believe me, have no doubt⟩ **2 ~ de** : to consist of
constatación *nf, pl* **-ciones** : confirmation, proof
constatar *vt* **1** : to verify **2** : to state
constelación *nf, pl* **-ciones** : constellation
consternación *nf, pl* **-ciones** : consternation, dismay
consternar *vt* : to dismay, to appall
constipación *nf, pl* **-ciones** : constipation
constipado¹, -da *adj* **estar constipado** : to have a cold
constipado² *nm* RESFRIADO : cold
constiparse *vr* : to catch a cold
constitución *nf, pl* **-ciones** : constitution — **constitucional** *adj* — **constitucionalmente** *adv*
constitucionalidad *nf* : constitutionality
constituir {41} *vt* **1** FORMAR : to constitute, to make up, to form **2** FUNDAR : to establish, to set up — **constituirse**

vr **~ en** : to set oneself up as, to become
constitutivo, -va *adj* : constituent, component
constituyente *adj & nmf* : constituent
constreñir {67} *vt* **1** FORZAR, OBLIGAR : to constrain, to oblige **2** LIMITAR : to restrict, to limit
construcción *nf, pl* **-ciones** : construction, building
constructivo, -va *adj* : constructive — **constructivamente** *adv*
constructor, -tora *n* : builder
constructora *nf* : construction company
construir {41} *vt* : to build, to construct
consuelo *nm* : consolation, comfort
consuetudinario, -ria *adj* **1** : customary, habitual **2 derecho consuetudinario** : common law
cónsul *nmf* : consul — **consular** *adj*
consulado *nm* : consulate
consulta *nf* **1** : consultation **2** : inquiry
consultar *vt* : to consult
consultor¹, -tora *adj* : consulting ⟨firma consultora : consulting firm⟩
consultor², -tora *n* : consultant
consultorio *nm* : office (of a doctor or dentist)
consumación *nf, pl* **-ciones** : consummation
consumado, -da *adj* : consummate, perfect
consumar *vt* **1** : to consummate, to complete **2** : to commit, to carry out
consumible *adj* : consumable
consumición *nf, pl* **-ciones** **1** : consumption **2** : drink (in a restaurant)
consumido, -da *adj* : thin, emaciated
consumidor, -dora *n* : consumer
consumir *vt* : to consume — **consumirse** *vr* : to waste away
consumo *nm* : consumption
contabilidad *nf* **1** : accounting, bookkeeping **2** : accountancy
contabilizar {21} *vt* : to enter, to record (in accounting)
contable¹ *adj* : countable
contable² *nmf* *Spain* : accountant, bookkeeper
contactar *vt* : to contact — *vi* **~ con** : to get in touch with, to contact
contacto *nm* : contact
contado¹, -da *adj* **1** : counted ⟨tenía los días contados : his days were numbered⟩ **2** : rare, scarce ⟨en contadas ocasiones : on rare occasions⟩
contado² *nm* **al contado** : cash ⟨pagar al contado : to pay in cash⟩
contador¹, -dora *n* : accountant
contador² *nm* : meter ⟨contador de agua : water meter⟩
contaduría *nf* **1** : accounting office **2** CONTABILIDAD : accountancy
contagiar *vt* **1** : to infect **2** : to transmit (a disease) — **contagiarse** *vr* **1** : to be contagious **2** : to become infected
contagio *nm* : contagion, infection

contagioso, -sa *adj* : contagious, catching

contaminación *nf, pl* **-ciones** : contamination, pollution

contaminante *nm* : pollutant, contaminant

contaminar *vt* : to contaminate, to pollute

contar {19} *vt* **1** : to count **2** : to tell **3** : to include — *vi* **1** : to count (up) **2** : to matter, to be of concern ⟨eso no cuenta : that doesn't matter⟩ **3 ~ con** : to rely on, to count on — **contarse** *vr* **~ entre** : to be numbered among

contemplación *nf, pl* **-ciones** : contemplation — **contemplativo, -va** *adj*

contemplar *vt* **1** : to contemplate, to ponder **2** : to gaze at, to look at

contemporáneo, -nea *adj & n* : contemporary

contención *nf, pl* **-ciones** : containment, holding

contencioso, -sa *adj* : contentious

contender {56} *vi* **1** : to contend, to compete **2** : to fight

contendiente *nmf* : contender

contenedor *nm* **1** : container, receptacle **2** : Dumpster™

contener {80} *vt* **1** : to contain, to hold **2** ATAJAR : to restrain, to hold back — **contenerse** *vr* : to restrain oneself

contenido¹, -da *adj* : restrained, reserved

contenido² *nm* : contents *pl*, content

contentar *vt* : to please, to make happy — **contentarse** *vr* : to be satisfied, to be pleased

contento¹, -ta *adj* : contented, glad, happy

contento² *nm* : joy, happiness

contestación *nf, pl* **-ciones** **1** : answer, reply **2** : protest

contestar *vt* RESPONDER : to answer — *vi* **1** RESPONDER : to answer, to reply **2** REPLICAR : to answer back

contexto *nm* : context

contienda *nf* **1** : dispute, conflict **2** : contest, competition

contigo *pron* : with you ⟨voy contigo : I'm going with you⟩

contiguo, -gua *adj* COLINDANTE : contiguous, adjacent

continencia *nf* : continence

continente *nm* : continent — **continental** *adj*

contingencia *nf* : contingency, eventuality

contingente *adj & nm* : contingent

continuación *nf, pl* **-ciones** **1** : continuation **2 a ~** : next ⟨lo demás sigue a continuación : the rest follows⟩ **3 a continuación de** : after, following

continuar {3} *v* : to continue

continuidad *nf* : continuity

continuo, -nua *adj* : continuous, steady, constant — **continuamente** *adv*

contonearse *vr* : to sway one's hips

contoneo *nm* : swaying, wiggling (of the hips)

contorno *nm* **1** : outline **2 contornos** *nmpl* : outskirts

contorsión *nf, pl* **-siones** : contortion

contra¹ *nf* **1** : difficulty, snag **2 llevar la contra a** : to oppose, to contradict

contra² *prep* : con ⟨los pros y los contras : the pros and cons⟩

contra³ *prep* : against

contraalmirante *nm* : rear admiral

contraatacar {72} *v* : to counterattack — **contraataque** *nm*

contrabajo *nm* : double bass

contrabalancear *vt* : to counterbalance — **contrabalanza** *nf*

contrabandear *v* : to smuggle

contrabandista *nmf* : smuggler, black marketeer

contrabando *nm* **1** : smuggling **2** : contraband

contracción *nf, pl* **-ciones** : contraction

contracepción *nf, pl* **-ciones** : contraception

contraceptivo *nm* ANTICONCEPTIVO : contraceptive

contrachapado *nm* : plywood

contracorriente *nf* **1** : crosscurrent **2 ir a contracorriente** : to go against the tide

contractual *adj* : contractual

contradecir {11} *vt* DESMENTIR : to contradict — **contradecirse** *vr* DESDECIRSE : to contradict oneself

contradicción *nf, pl* **-ciones** : contradiction

contradictorio, -ria *adj* : contradictory

contraer {81} *vt* **1** : to contract (a disease) **2** : to establish by contract ⟨contraer matrimonio : to get married⟩ **3** : to tighten, to contract — **contraerse** *vr* : to contract, to tighten up

contrafuerte *nm* : buttress

contragolpe *nm* **1** : counterblow **2** : backlash

contrahecho, -cha *adj* : deformed, hunchbacked

contraindicado, -da *adj* : contraindicated — **contraindicación** *nf*

contralor, -lora *n* : comptroller

contralto *nm¹* : contralto

contramaestre *nm* **1** : boatswain **2** : foreman

contramandar *vt* : to countermand

contramano *nm* **a ~** : the wrong way (on a street)

contramedida *nf* : countermeasure

contraorden *nf* : countermand

contraparte *nf* **1** : counterpart **2 en ~** : on the other hand

contrapartida *nf* : compensation

contrapelo *nm* **a ~** : in the wrong direction, against the grain

contrapeso *nm* : counterbalance

contraponer {60} *vt* **1** : to counter, to oppose **2** : to contrast, to compare

contraposición *nf, pl* **-ciones** : comparison

contraproducente *adj* : counterproductive

contrapunto *nm* : counterpoint

contrariar {85} *vt* **1** : to contradict, to oppose **2** : to vex, to annoy

contrariedad *nf* **1** : setback, obstacle **2** : vexation, annoyance

contrario, -ria *adj* **1** : contrary, opposite ⟨al contrario : on the contrary⟩ **2** : conflicting, opposed

contrarrestar *vt* : to counteract

contrarrevolución *nf*, *pl* **-ciones** : counterrevolution — **contrarrevolucionario, -ria** *adj & n*

contrasentido *nm* : contradiction

contraseña *nf* : password

contrastante *adj* : contrasting

contrastar *vt* **1** : to resist **2** : to check, to confirm — *vi* : to contrast

contraste *nm* : contrast

contratar *vt* **1** : to contract for **2** : to hire, to engage

contratiempo *nm* **1** PERCANCE : mishap, accident **2** DIFICULTAD : setback, difficulty

contratista *nmf* : contractor

contrato *nm* : contract

contravenir {87} *vt* : to contravene, to infringe

contraventana *nf* : shutter

contribución *nf*, *pl* **-ciones** : contribution

contribuidor, -dora *n* : contributor

contribuir {41} *vt* **1** APORTAR : to contribute **2** : to pay (in taxes) — *vi* **1** : contribute, to help out **2** : to pay taxes

contribuyente[1] *adj* : contributing

contribuyente[2] *nmf* : taxpayer

contrición *nf*, *pl* **-ciones** : contrition

contrincante *nmf* : rival, opponent

contrito, -ta *adj* : contrite, repentant

control *nm* **1** : control **2** : inspection, check **3** : checkpoint, roadblock

controlador, -dora *n* : controller ⟨controlador aéreo : air traffic controller⟩

controlar *vt* : to control **2** : to monitor, to check

controversia *nf* : controversy

controversial → **controvertido**

controvertido, -da *adj* : controversial

controvertir {76} *vt* : to dispute, to argue about — *vi* : to argue, to debate

contubernio *nm* : conspiracy

contumacia *nf* : obstinacy, stubbornness

contumaz *adj*, *pl* **-maces** : obstinate, stubbornly disobedient

contundencia *nf* **1** : forcefulness, weight **2** : severity

contundente *adj* **1** : blunt ⟨un objeto contundente : a blunt instrument⟩ **2** : forceful, convincing — **contundentemente** *adv*

contusión *nf*, *pl* **-siones** : bruise, contusion

contuvo, etc. → **contener**

convalecencia *nf* : convalescence

convalecer {53} *vi* : to convalesce, to recover

convaleciente *adj & nmf* : convalescent

convección *nf*, *pl* **-ciones** : convection

convencer {86} *vt* : to convince, to persuade — **convencerse** *vr*

convencimiento *nm* : belief, conviction

convención *nf*, *pl* **-ciones** **1** : convention, conference **2** : pact, agreement **3** : convention, custom

convencional *adj* : conventional — **convencionalmente** *adv*

convencionalismo *nm* : conventionality

conveniencia *nf* **1** : convenience **2** : fitness, suitability, advisability

conveniente *adj* **1** : convenient **2** : suitable, advisable

convenio *nm* PACTO : agreement, pact

convenir {87} *vi* **1** : to be suitable, to be advisable **2** : to agree

convento *nm* **1** : convent **2** : monastery

convergencia *nf* : convergence

convergente *adj* : convergent, converging

converger {15} *vi* **1** : to converge **2** ~ **en** : to concur on

conversación *nf*, *pl* **-ciones** : conversation

conversador, -dora *n* : conversationalist, talker

conversar *vi* : to converse, to talk

conversión *nf*, *pl* **-siones** : conversion

converso, -sa *n* : convert

convertible *adj & nm* : convertible

convertidor *nm* : converter

convertir {76} *vt* **1** : to convert **2** : to transform, to change **3** : to exchange (money) — **convertirse** *vr* ~ **en** : to turn into

convexo, -xa *adj* : convex

convicción *nf*, *pl* **-ciones** : conviction

convicto[1], **-ta** *adj* : convicted

convicto[2], **-ta** *n* : convict, prisoner

convidado, -da *n* : guest

convidar *vt* **1** INVITAR : to invite **2** : to offer

convincente *adj* : convincing — **convincentemente** *adv*

convivencia *nf* **1** : coexistence **2** : cohabitation

convivir *vi* **1** : to coexist **2** : to live together

convocación *nf*, *pl* **-ciones** : convocation

convocar {72} *vt* : to convoke, to call together

convocatoria *nf* : summons, call

convoy *nm* : convoy

convulsión *nf*, *pl* **-siones** **1** : convulsion **2** : agitation, upheaval

convulsionar *vt* : to shake, to convulse — **convulsionarse** *vr*

convulsivo, -va *adj* : convulsive

conyugal *adj* : conjugal

cónyuge *nmf* : spouse, partner

coñac *nm* : cognac, brandy

cooperación *nf*, *pl* **-ciones** : cooperation

cooperador, -dora *adj* : cooperative

cooperar *vi* : to cooperate
cooperativa *nf* : cooperative, co-op
cooperativo, -va *adj* : cooperative
cooptar *vt* : to co-opt
coordenada *nf* : coordinate
coordinación *nf, pl* **-ciones** : coordination
coordinador, -dora *n* : coordinator
coordinar *vt* COMPAGINAR : to coordinate, to combine
copa *nf* 1 : wineglass, goblet 2 : drink ⟨irse de copas : to go out drinking⟩ 3 : cup, trophy
copar *vt* 1 : to take ⟨ya está copado el puesto : the job is already taken⟩ 2 : to fill, to crowd
copartícipe *nmf* : joint partner
copete *nm* 1 : tuft (of hair) 2 **estar hasta el copete** : to be completely fed up
copia *nf* 1 : copy 2 : imitation, replica
copiadora *nf* : photocopier
copiar *vt* : to copy
copiloto *nmf* : copilot
copioso, -sa *adj* : copious, abundant
copla *nf* 1 : popular song or ballad 2 : couplet, stanza
copo *nm* 1 : snowflake 2 **copos de avena** : rolled oats 3 **copos de maíz** : cornflakes
copra *nf* : copra
cópula *nf* : copulation
copular *vi* : to copulate
coque *nm* : coke (fuel)
coqueta *nf* : dressing table
coquetear *vi* : to flirt
coqueteo *nm* : flirting, coquetry
coqueto¹, -ta *adj* : flirtatious, coquettish
coqueto², -ta *n* : flirt
coraje *nm* 1 VALOR : valor, courage 2 IRA : anger ⟨darle coraje a alguien : to make someone angry⟩
corajudo, -da *adj* : brave
coral¹ *nm* 1 : coral 2 : chorale
coral² *nf* : choir
Corán *nm* **el Corán** : the Koran
coraza *nf* 1 : armor, armor plating 2 : shell (of an animal)
corazón *nm, pl* **-zones** 1 : heart ⟨de todo corazón : wholeheartedly⟩ ⟨de buen corazón : kindhearted⟩ 2 : core 3 : darling, sweetheart
corazonada *nf* : hunch, impulse
corbata *nf* : tie, necktie
corcel *nm* : steed, charger
corchete *nm* 1 : hook and eye, clasp 2 : square bracket
corcho *nm* : cork
corcholata *nf Mex* : cap, bottle top
corcovear *vi* : to buck
cordel *nm* : cord, string
cordero *nm* : lamb
cordial¹ *adj* : cordial, affable — **cordialmente** *adv*
cordial² *nm* : cordial (liqueur)
cordialidad *nf* : cordiality, warmth
cordillera *nf* : mountain range
córdoba *nf* : Nicaraguan unit of currency

cordón *nm, pl* **cordones** 1 : cord ⟨cordón umbilical : umbilical cord⟩ 2 : cordon
cordura *nf* 1 : sanity 2 : prudence, good judgment
coreano¹, -na *adj & n* : Korean
coreano² *nm* : Korean (language)
corear *vt* : to chant, to chorus
coreografía *nf* : choreography
coreografiar {85} *vt* : to choreograph
coreográfico, -ca *adj* : choreographic
coreógrafo, -fa *n* : choreographer
corista *nmf* 1 : chorister 2 : chorus girl *f*
cormorán *nm, pl* **-ranes** : cormorant
cornada *nf* : goring, butt (with the horns)
córnea *nf* : cornea
cornear *vt* : to gore
cornejo *nm* : dogwood (tree)
corneta *nf* : bugle, horn, cornet
cornisa *nf* : cornice
cornudo, -da *adj* : horned
coro *nm* 1 : choir 2 : chorus
corola *nf* : corolla
corolario *nm* : corollary
corona *nf* 1 : crown 2 : wreath, garland 3 : corona (in astronomy)
coronación *nf, pl* **-ciones** : coronation
coronar *vt* 1 : to crown 2 : to reach the top of, to culminate
coronario, -ria *adj* : coronary
coronel, -nela *n* : colonel
coronilla *nf* 1 : crown (of the head) 2 **estar hasta la coronilla** : to be completely fed up
corpiño *nm* 1 : bodice 2 *Arg* : brassiere, bra
corporación *nf, pl* **-ciones** : corporation
corporal *adj* : corporal, bodily
corporativo, -va *adj* : corporate
corpóreo, -rea *adj* : corporeal, physical
corpulencia *nf* : corpulence, stoutness, sturdiness
corpulento, -ta *adj* ROBUSTO : robust, stout, sturdy
corpúsculo *nm* : corpuscle
corral *nm* 1 : farmyard 2 : corral, pen, stockyard 3 *or* **corralito** : playpen
correa *nf* : strap, belt
correcaminos *nms & pl* : roadrunner
corrección *nf, pl* **-ciones** 1 : correction 2 : correctness, propriety 3 : rebuke, reprimand 4 **corrección de pruebas** : proofreading
correccional *nm* REFORMATORIO : reformatory
correctivo, -va *adj* : corrective ⟨lentes correctivos : corrective lenses⟩
correcto, -ta *adj* 1 : correct, right 2 : courteous, polite — **correctamente** *adv*
corrector, -tora *n* : proofreader
corredizo, -za *adj* : sliding ⟨puerta corrediza : sliding door⟩
corredor¹, -dora *n* 1 : runner, racer 2 : agent, broker ⟨corredor de bolsa : stockbroker⟩
corredor² *nm* PASILLO : corridor, hallway

correduría *nf* → **corretaje**
corregir {28} *vt* **1** ENMENDAR : to correct, to emend **2** : to reprimand **3 corregir pruebas** : to proofread — **corregirse** *vr* : to reform, to mend one's ways
correlación *nf, pl* **-ciones** : correlation
correo *nm* **1** : mail ⟨correo aéreo : airmail⟩ **2** : post office
correoso, -sa *adj* : leathery, rough
correr *vi* **1** : to run, to race **2** : to rush **3** : to flow — *vt* **1** : to travel over, to cover **2** : to move, to slide, to roll, to draw (curtains) **3 correr un riesgo** : to run a risk — **correrse** *vr* **1** : to move along **2** : to run, to spill over
correspondencia *nf* **1** : correspondence, mail **2** : equivalence **3** : connection, interchange
corresponder *vi* **1** : to correspond **2** : to pertain, to belong **3** : to be appropriate, to fit **4** : to reciprocate — **corresponderse** *vr* : to write to each other
correspondiente *adj* : corresponding, respective
corresponsal *nmf* : correspondent
corretaje *nm* : brokerage
corretear *vi* **1** VAGAR : to loiter, to wander about **2** : to run around, to scamper about — *vt* : to pursue, to chase
corrida *nf* **1** : run, dash **2** : bullfight
corrido¹, -da *adj* **1** : straight, continuous **2** : worldly, experienced
corrido² *nm* : Mexican narrative folk song
corriente¹ *adj* **1** : common, everyday **2** : current, present **3** *Mex* : cheap, trashy **4 perro corriente** *Mex* : mutt
corriente² *nf* **1** : current ⟨corriente alterna : alternating current⟩ ⟨direct current : corriente continua⟩ **2** : draft **3** TENDENCIA : tendency, trend
corrillo *nm* : small group, clique
corro *nm* : ring, circle (of people)
corroboración *nf, pl* **-ciones** : corroboration
corroborar *vt* : to corroborate
corroer {69} *vt* **1** : to corrode **2** : to erode, to wear away
corromper *vt* **1** : to corrupt **2** : to rot — **corromperse** *vr*
corrompido, -da *adj* CORRUPTO : corrupt, rotten
corrosión *nf, pl* **-siones** : corrosion
corrosivo, -va *adj* : corrosive
corrugar {52} *vt* : to corrugate — **corrugación** *nf*
corrupción *nf, pl* **-ciones** **1** : decay **2** : corruption
corruptela *nf* : corruption, abuse of power
corrupto, -ta *adj* CORROMPIDO : corrupt
corsario *nm* : privateer
corsé *nm* : corset
cortada *nf* : cut, gash
cortador, -dora *n* : cutter
cortadora *nf* : cutter, slicer
cortadura *nf* : cut, slash
cortafuegos *nms & pl* **1** : firebreak **2** : firewall (program)

cortante *adj* : cutting, sharp
cortar *vt* **1** : to cut, to slice, to trim **2** : to cut out, to omit **3** : to cut off, to interrupt **4** : to block, to close off **5** : to curdle (milk) — *vi* **1** : to cut **2** : to break up **3** : to hang up (the telephone) — **cortarse** *vr* **1** : to cut oneself ⟨cortarse el pelo : to cut one's hair⟩ **2** : to be cut off **3** : to sour (of milk)
cortaúñas *nms & pl* : nail clippers
corte¹ *nm* **1** : cut, cutting ⟨corte de pelo : haircut⟩ **2** : style, fit
corte² *nf* **1** : court ⟨corte suprema : supreme court⟩ **2 hacer la corte a** : to court, to woo
cortejar *vt* GALANTEAR : to court, to woo
cortejo *nm* **1** GALANTEO : courtship **2** : retinue, entourage
cortés *adj* : courteous, polite — **cortésmente** *adv*
cortesano¹, -na *adj* : courtly
cortesano², -na *n* : courtier
cortesía *nf* **1** : courtesy, politeness **2 de ∼** : complimentary, free
corteza *nf* **1** : bark **2** : crust **3** : peel, rind **4** : cortex ⟨corteza cerebral : cerebral cortex⟩
cortijo *nm* : farmhouse
cortina *nf* : curtain
cortisona *nf* : cortisone
corto, -ta *adj* **1** : short (in length or duration) **2** : scarce **3** : timid, shy **4 corto de vista** : nearsighted
cortocircuito *nm* : short circuit
corvejón *nm, pl* **-jones** JARRETE : hock
corvo, -va *adj* : curved, bent
cosa *nf* **1** : thing, object **2** : matter, affair **3 otra cosa** : anything else, something else
cosecha *nf* : harvest, crop
cosechador, -dora *n* : harvester, reaper
cosechadora *nf* : harvester (machine)
cosechar *vt* **1** : to harvest, to reap **2** : to win, to earn, to garner — *vi* : to harvest
coser *vt* **1** : to sew **2** : to stitch up — *vi* : to sew
cosmético¹, -ca *adj* : cosmetic
cosmético² *nm* : cosmetic
cósmico, -ca *adj* : cosmic
cosmonauta *nmf* : cosmonaut
cosmopolita *adj & nmf* : cosmopolitan
cosmos *nm* : cosmos
cosquillas *nfpl* **1** : tickling **2 hacer cosquillas** : to tickle
cosquilleo *nm* : tickling sensation, tingle
cosquilloso, -sa *adj* : ticklish
costa *nf* **1** : coast, shore **2** : cost ⟨a toda costa : at all costs⟩
costado *nm* **1** : side **2 al costado** : alongside
costar {19} *v* : to cost ⟨¿cuánto cuesta? : how much does it cost?⟩
costarricense *adj & nmf* : Costa Rican
costarriqueño, -ña → **costarricense**
coste → **costo**
costear *vt* : to pay for, to finance

costero, -ra *adj* : coastal, coast
costilla *nf* 1 : rib 2 : chop, cutlet 3 *fam* : better half, wife
costo *nm* 1 : cost, price 2 **costo de vida** : cost of living
costoso, -sa *adj* : costly, expensive
costra *nf* 1 : crust 2 POSTILLA : scab
costumbre *nf* 1 : custom 2 HÁBITO : habit
costura *nf* 1 : seam 2 : sewing, dressmaking 3 **alta costura** : haute couture
costurera *nf* : seamstress *f*
cotejar *vt* : to compare, to collate
cotejo *nm* : comparison, collation
cotidiano, -na *adj* : daily, everyday ⟨la vida cotidiana : daily life⟩
cotización *nf*, *pl* **-ciones** 1 : market price 2 : quote, estimate
cotizado, -da *adj* : in demand, sought after
cotizar {21} *vt* : to quote, to value — **cotizarse** *vr* : to be worth
coto *nm* 1 : enclosure, reserve 2 **poner coto a** : to put a stop to
cotorra *nf* 1 : small parrot 2 *fam* : chatterbox, windbag
cotorrear *vi fam* : to chatter, to gab, to blab
cotorreo *nm fam* : chatter, prattle
coyote *nm* 1 : coyote 2 *Mex fam* : smuggler (of illegal immigrants)
coyuntura *nf* 1 ARTICULACIÓN : joint 2 : occasion, moment
coz *nf*, *pl* **coces** : kick (of an animal)
crac *nm*, *pl* **cracs** : crash (of the stock market)
cozamos, etc. → **cocer**
craneal *adj* : cranial
cráneo *nm* : cranium, skull — **craneano, -na** *adj*
cráter *nm* : crater
crayón *nm*, *pl* **-yones** : crayon
creación *nf*, *pl* **-ciones** : creation
creador¹, -dora *adj* : creative, creating
creador², -dora *n* : creator
crear *vt* 1 : to create, to cause 2 : to originate
creatividad *nf* : creativity
creativo, -va *adj* : creative
crecer {53} *vi* 1 : to grow 2 : to increase
crecida *nf* : flooding, floodwater
crecido, -da *adj* 1 : grown, grown-up 2 : large (of numbers)
creciente *adj* 1 : growing, increasing 2 **luna creciente** : waxing moon
crecientemente *adv* : increasingly
crecimiento *nm* 1 : growth 2 : increase
credencial *adj* **cartas credenciales** : credentials
credenciales *nfpl* : documents, documentation, credentials
credibilidad *nf* : credibility
crédito *nm* : credit
credo *nm* : creed, credo
credulidad *nf* : credulity
crédulo, -la *adj* : credulous, gullible
creencia *nf* : belief
creer {20} *v* 1 : to believe 2 : to suppose, to think ⟨creo que sí : I think so⟩

— **creerse** *vr* 1 : to believe, to think 2 : to regard oneself as ⟨se cree guapísimo : he thinks he's so handsome⟩
creíble *adj* : believable, credible
creído, -da *adj* 1 *fam* : conceited 2 : confident, sure
crema *nf* 1 : cream 2 **la crema y nata** : the pick of the crop
cremación *nf*, *pl* **-ciones** : cremation
cremallera *nf* : zipper
cremar *vt* : to cremate
cremoso, -sa *adj* : creamy
crepa *nf Mex* : crepe (pancake)
crepe *or* **crep** *nmf* : crepe (pancake)
crepé *nm* 1 → **crespón** 2 **papel crepé** : crepe paper
crepitar *vi* : to crackle
crepúsculo *nm* : twilight
crescendo *nm* : crescendo
crespo, -pa *adj* : curly, frizzy
crespón *nm*, *pl* **crespones** : crepe (fabric)
cresta *nf* 1 : crest 2 : comb (of a rooster)
creta *nf* : chalk (mineral)
cretino, -na *n* : cretin
creyente *nmf* : believer
creyó, etc. → **creer**
crezca, etc. → **crecer**
cría *nf* 1 : breeding, rearing 2 : young 3 : litter
criadero *nm* : hatchery
criado¹, -da *adj* : raised, brought up 2 **bien criado** : well-bred
criado², -da *n* : servant, maid *f*
criador, -dora *n* : breeder
crianza *nf* : upbringing, rearing
criar {85} *vt* 1 : to breed 2 : to bring up, to raise
criatura *nf* 1 : baby, child 2 : creature
criba *nf* : sieve, screen
cribar *vt* : to sift
cric *nm*, *pl* **crics** : jack
crimen *nm*, *pl* **crímenes** : crime
criminal *adj* & *nmf* : criminal
crin *nf* 1 : mane 2 : horsehair
criollo¹, -lla *adj* 1 : Creole 2 : native, national ⟨comida criolla : native cuisine⟩
criollo², -lla *n* : Creole
criollo³ *nm* : Creole (language)
cripta *nf* : crypt
críptico, -ca *adj* 1 : cryptic, coded 2 : enigmatic, cryptic
criptón *nm* : krypton
criquet *nm* : cricket (game)
crisálida *nf* : chrysalis, pupa
crisantemo *nm* : chrysanthemum
crisis *nf* 1 : crisis 2 **crisis nerviosa** : nervous breakdown
crisma *nf fam* : head ⟨romperle la crisma a alguien : to knock someone's block off⟩
crisol *nm* 1 : crucible 2 : melting pot
crispar *vt* 1 : to cause to contract 2 : to irritate, to set on edge ⟨eso me crispa : that gets on my nerves⟩ — **crisparse** *vr* : to tense up

cristal nm **1** VIDRIO : glass, piece of glass **2** : crystal

cristalería nf **1** : glassware shop ⟨como chivo en cristalería : like a bull in a china shop⟩ **2** : glassware, crystal

cristalino¹, -na adj : crystalline, clear

cristalino² nm : lens (of the eye)

cristalizar {21} vi : to crystallize — **cristalización** nf

cristiandad nf : Christendom

cristianismo nm : Christianity

cristiano, -na adj & n : Christian

Cristo nm : Christ

criterio nm **1** : criterion **2** : judgment, sense

crítica nf **1** : criticism **2** : review, critique

criticar {72} vt : to criticize

crítico¹, -ca adj : critical — **críticamente** adv

crítico², -ca n : critic

criticón¹, -cona adj, mpl **-cones** fam : hypercritical, captious

criticón², -cona n, mpl **-cones** fam : faultfinder, critic

croar vi : to croak

croata adj & nmf : Croatian

crocante adj : crunchy

croché or **crochet** nm : crochet

cromático, -ca adj : chromatic

cromo nm **1** : chromium, chrome **2** : picture card, sports card

cromosoma nm : chromosome

crónica nf **1** : news report **2** : chronicle, history

crónico, -ca adj : chronic

cronista nmf **1** : reporter, newscaster **2** HISTORIADOR : chronicler, historian

cronología nf : chronology

cronológico, -ca adj : chronological — **cronológicamente** adv

cronometrador, -dora n : timekeeper

cronometrar vt : to time, to clock

cronómetro nm : chronometer

croquet nm : croquet

croqueta nf : croquette

croquis nm : rough sketch

cruce¹, etc. → **cruzar**

cruce² nm **1** : crossing, cross **2** : crossroads, intersection ⟨cruce peatonal : crosswalk⟩

crucero nm **1** : cruise **2** : cruiser, warship **3** Mex : intersection

crucial adj : crucial — **crucialmente** adv

crucificar {72} vt : to crucify

crucifijo nm : crucifix

crucifixión nf, pl **-fixiones** : crucifixion

crucigrama nm : crossword puzzle

crudo¹, -da adj **1** : raw **2** : crude, harsh

crudo² nm : crude oil

cruel adj : cruel — **cruelmente** adv

crueldad nf : cruelty

cruento, -ta adj : bloody

crujido nm **1** : rustling **2** : creaking **3** : crackling (of a fire) **4** : crunching

crujiente adj : crunchy, crisp

crujir vi **1** : to rustle **2** : to creak, to crack **3** : to crunch

crup nm : croup

crustáceo nm : crustacean

crutón nm, pl **crutones** : crouton

cruz nf, pl **cruces** : cross

cruza nf : cross (hybrid)

cruzada nf : crusade

cruzado¹, -da adj : crossed ⟨espadas cruzadas : crossed swords⟩

cruzado² nm **1** : crusader **2** : Brazilian unit of currency

cruzar {21} vt **1** : to cross **2** : to exchange (words, greetings) **3** : to cross, to interbreed — **cruzarse** vr **1** : to intersect **2** : to meet, to pass each other

cuaderno nm LIBRETA : notebook

cuadra nf **1** : city block **2** : stable

cuadrado¹, -da adj : square

cuadrado² nm : square ⟨elevar al cuadrado : to square (a number)⟩

cuadragésimo¹ adj : fortieth, forty-

cuadragésimo², -ma n : fortieth, forty- (in a series)

cuadrante nm **1** : quadrant **2** : dial

cuadrar vi : to conform, to agree — vt : to square — **cuadrarse** vr : to stand at attention

cuadriculado nm : grid (on a map, etc.)

cuadrilátero nm **1** : quadrilateral **2** : ring (in sports)

cuadrilla nf : gang, team, group

cuadro nm **1** : square ⟨una blusa a cuadros : a checkered blouse⟩ **2** : painting, picture **3** : baseball diamond, infield **4** : panel, board, cadre

cuadrúpedo nm : quadruped

cuádruple adj : quadruple

cuadruplicar {72} vt : to quadruple — **cuadruplicarse** vr

cuajada nf : curd

cuajar vi **1** : to curdle **2** COAGULAR : to clot, to coagulate **3** : to set, to jell **4** : to be accepted ⟨su idea no cuajó : his idea didn't catch on⟩ — vt **1** : to curdle **2** ~ **de** : to fill with

cual¹ prep : like, as

cual² pron **1** el cual, la cual, los cuales, las cuales : who, whom, which ⟨la razón por la cual lo dije : the reason I said it⟩ **2** lo cual : which ⟨se rió, lo cual me dio rabia : he laughed, which made me mad⟩ **3** cada cual : everyone, everybody

cuál¹ adj : which, what ⟨¿cuáles libros? : which books?⟩

cuál² pron **1** (in questions) : which (one), what (one) ⟨¿cuál es el mejor? : which one is the best?⟩ ⟨¿cuál es tu apellido? : what is your last name?⟩ **2** cuál más, cuál menos : some more, some less

cualidad nf : quality, trait

cualitativo, -va adj : qualitative — **cualitativamente** adv

cualquier adj → **cualquiera¹**

cualquiera¹ (**cualquier** before nouns) adj, pl **cualesquiera 1** : any, whichever ⟨cualquier persona : any person⟩ **2** : everyday, ordinary ⟨un hombre cualquiera : an ordinary man⟩

cualquiera[2] *pron, pl* **cualesquiera 1** : anyone, anybody, whoever **2** : whatever, whichever

cuán *adv* : how ⟨cuán risible fue todo eso! : how funny it all was!⟩

cuando[1] *conj* **1** : when ⟨cuando llegó : when he arrived⟩ **2** : since, if ⟨cuando lo dices : if you say so⟩ **3 cuando más** : at the most **4 de vez en cuando** : from time to time

cuando[2] *prep* : during, at the time of ⟨cuando la guerra : during the war⟩

cuándo *adv & conj* **1** : when ⟨¿cuándo llegará? : when will she arrive?⟩ ⟨no sabemos cuándo será : we don't know when it will be⟩ **2 ¿de cuándo acá?** : since when?, how come?

cuantía *nf* **1** : quantity, extent **2** : significance, import

cuántico, -ca *adj* : quantum ⟨teoría cuántica : quantum theory⟩

cuantioso, -sa *adj* **1** : abundant, considerable **2** : heavy, grave ⟨cuantiosos daños : heavy damage⟩

cuantitativo, -va *adj* : quantitative — **cuantitativamente** *adv*

cuanto[1] *adv* **1** : as much as ⟨come cuanto puedas : eat as much as you can⟩ **2 cuanto antes** : as soon as possible **3 en ~** : as soon as **4 en cuanto a** : as for, as regards

cuanto[2] *adj* : as many, whatever ⟨llévate cuantas flores quieras : take as many flowers as you wish⟩

cuanto[3], **-ta** *pron* **1** : as much as, all that, everything ⟨tengo cuanto deseo : I have all that I want⟩ **2 unos cuantos, unas cuantas** : a few

cuánto[1] *adv* : how much, how many ⟨¿a cuánto están las manzanas? : how much are the apples?⟩ ⟨no sé cuánto desean : I don't know how much they want⟩

cuánto[2], **-ta** *adj* : how much, how many ⟨¿cuántos niños tiene? : how many children do you have?⟩

cuánto[3] *pron* : how much, how many ⟨¿cuántos quieren participar? : how many want to take part?⟩ ⟨¿cuánto cuesta? : how much does it cost?⟩

cuarenta *adj & nm* : forty

cuarentavo[1], **-va** *adj* : fortieth

cuarentavo[2] *nm* : fortieth (fraction)

cuarentena *nf* **1** : group of forty **2** : quarantine

Cuaresma *nf* : Lent

cuartear *vt* **1** : to quarter **2** : to divide up — **cuartearse** *vr* AGRIETARSE : to crack, to split

cuartel *nm* **1** : barracks, headquarters **2** : mercy ⟨una guerra sin cuartel : a merciless war⟩

cuartelazo *nm* : coup d'état

cuarteto *nm* : quartet

cuartilla *nf* : sheet (of paper)

cuarto[1], **-ta** *adj* : fourth

cuarto[2], **-ta** *n* : fourth (in a series)

cuarto[3] *nm* **1** : quarter, fourth ⟨cuarto de galón : quart⟩ **2** HABITACIÓN : room

cuarzo *nm* : quartz

cuate, -ta *n Mex* **1** : twin **2** *fam* : buddy, pal

cuatrero, -ra *n* : rustler

cuatrillizo, -za *n* : quadruplet

cuatro *adj & nm* : four

cuatrocientos[1], **-tas** *adj* : four hundred

cuatrocientos[2] *nms & pl* : four hundred

cuba *nf* BARRIL : cask, barrel

cubano, -na *adj & n* : Cuban

cubertería *nf* : flatware, silverware

cubeta *nf* **1** : keg, cask **2** : bulb (of a thermometer) **3** *Mex* : bucket, pail

cúbico, -ca *adj* : cubic, cubed

cubículo *nm* : cubicle

cubierta *nf* **1** : covering **2** FORRO : cover, jacket (of a book) **3** : deck

cubierto[1] *pp* → **cubrir**

cubierto[2] *nm* **1** : cover, shelter ⟨bajo cubierto : under cover⟩ **2** : table setting **3** : utensil, piece of silverware

cubil *nm* : den, lair

cúbito *nm* : ulna

cubo *nm* **1** : cube **2** BALDE : pail, bucket, can ⟨cubo de basura : garbage can⟩ **3** : hub (of a wheel)

cubrecama *nm* COLCHA : bedspread

cubrir {2} *vt* : to cover — **cubrirse** *vr*

cucaracha *nf* : cockroach, roach

cuchara *nf* : spoon

cucharada *nf* : spoonful

cucharilla *or* **cucharita** *nf* : teaspoon

cucharón *nm, pl* **-rones** : ladle

cuchichear *vi* : to whisper

cuchicheo *nm* : whisper

cuchilla *nf* **1** : kitchen knife, cleaver **2** : blade ⟨cuchilla de afeitar : razor blade⟩ **3** : crest, ridge

cuchillada *nf* : stab, knife wound

cuchillo *nm* : knife

cuclillas *nfpl* **en ~** : squatting, crouching

cuco[1], **-ca** *adj fam* : pretty, cute

cuco[2] *nm* : cuckoo

cucurucho *nm* : ice-cream cone

cuece, cueza etc. → **cocer**

cuela, etc. → **colar**

cuelga, cuelgue etc. → **colgar**

cuello *nm* **1** : neck **2** : collar (of a shirt) **3 cuello del útero** : cervix

cuenca *nf* **1** : river basin **2** : eye socket

cuenco *nm* : bowl, basin

cuenta[1], etc. → **contar**

cuenta[2] *nf* **1** : calculation, count **2** : account **3** : check, bill **4 darse cuenta** : to realize **5 tener en cuenta** : to bear in mind

cuentagotas *nfs & pl* **1** : dropper **2 con ~** : little by little

cuentista *nmf* **1** : short story writer **2** *fam* : liar, fibber

cuentó *nm* **1** : story, tale **2 cuento de hadas** : fairy tale **3 sin ~** : countless

cuerda *nf* **1** : cord, rope, string **2 cuerdas vocales** : vocal cords **3 darle cuerda a** : to wind up (a clock, a toy, etc.)

cuerdo, -da adj : sane, sensible
cuerno nm **1** : horn, antler **2** : cusp (of the moon) **3** : horn (musical instrument)
cuero nm **1** : leather, hide **2 cuero cabelludo** : scalp
cuerpo nm **1** : body **2** : corps
cuervo nm : crow, raven
cuesta[1], etc. → costar
cuesta[2] nf **1** : slope ⟨cuesta arriba : uphill⟩ **2 a cuestas** : on one's back
cuestión nf, pl **-tiones** ASUNTO, TEMA : matter, affair
cuestionable adj : questionable, dubious
cuestionar vt : to question
cuestionario nm **1** : questionnaire **2** : quiz
cueva nf : cave
cuidado nm **1** : care **2** : worry, concern **3 tener cuidado** : to be careful **4 ¡cuidado!** nf : watch out!, be careful!
cuidador, -dora n : caretaker
cuidadoso, -sa adj : careful, attentive — **cuidadosamente** adv
cuidar vt **1** : to take care of, to look after **2** : to pay attention to — vi **1 ~ de** : to look after **2 cuidar de que** : to make sure that — **cuidarse** vr : to take care of oneself
culata nf : butt (of a gun)
culatazo nm : kick, recoil
culebra nf SERPIENTE : snake
culí nm : coolie
culinario, -ria adj : culinary
culminante adj **punto culminante** : peak, high point, climax
culminar vi : to culminate — **culminación** nf
culo nm **1** fam : backside, behind **2** : bottom (of a glass)
culpa nf **1** : fault, blame ⟨echarle la culpa a alguien : to blame someone⟩ **2** : sin
culpabilidad nf : guilt
culpable[1] adj : guilty
culpable[2] nmf : culprit, guilty party
culpar vt : to blame
cultivado, -da adj **1** : cultivated, farmed **2** : cultured
cultivador, -dora n : cultivator
cultivar vt **1** : to cultivate **2** : to foster
cultivo nm **1** : cultivation, farming **2** : crop
culto[1], -ta adj : cultured, educated
culto[2] nm **1** : worship **2** : cult
cultura nf : culture
cultural adj : cultural — **culturalmente** adv
cumbre nf CIMA : top, peak, summit
cumpleaños nms & pl : birthday
cumplido[1], -da adj **1** : complete, full **2** : courteous, correct
cumplido[2] nm : compliment, courtesy ⟨por cumplido : out of courtesy⟩ ⟨andarse con cumplidos : to stand on ceremony, to be formal⟩
cumplimentar vt **1** : to congratulate **2** : to carry out, to perform

cumplimiento nm **1** : completion, fulfillment **2** : performance
cumplir vt **1** : to accomplish, to carry out **2** : to comply with, to fulfill **3** : to attain, to reach ⟨su hermana cumple los 21 el viernes : her sister will be 21 on Friday⟩ — vi **1** : to expire, to fall due **2** : to fulfill one's obligations ⟨cumplir con el deber : to do one's duty⟩ ⟨cumplir con la palabra : to keep one's word⟩ — **cumplirse** vr **1** : to come true, to be fulfilled ⟨se cumplieron sus sueños : her dreams came true⟩ **2** : to run out, to expire
cúmulo nm **1** MONTÓN : heap, pile **2** : cumulus
cuna nf **1** : cradle **2** : birthplace ⟨Puerto Rico es la cuna de la música salsa : Puerto Rico is the birthplace of salsa music⟩
cundir vi **1** : to propagate, to spread ⟨cundió el pánico en el vecindario : panic spread throughout the neighborhood⟩ **2** : to progress, to make headway
cuneta nf : ditch (in a road), gutter
cuña nf : wedge
cuñado, -da n : brother-in-law m, sister-in-law f
cuño nm : die (for stamping)
cuota nf **1** : fee, dues **2** : quota, share **3** : installment, payment
cupé nm : coupe
cupo[1], etc. → caber
cupo[2] nm **1** : quota, share **2** : capacity, room
cupón nm, pl **cupones 1** : coupon, voucher **2 cupón federal** : food stamp
cúpula nf **1** : dome, cupola
cura[1] nm : priest
cura[2] nf **1** CURACIÓN, TRATAMIENTO : cure, treatment **2** : dressing, bandage
curación nf, pl **-ciones** CURA, TRATAMIENTO : cure, treatment
curandero, -ra nm **1** : witch doctor **2** : quack, charlatan
curar vt **1** : to cure, to heal **2** : to treat, to dress **3** CURTIR : to tan **4** : to cure (meat) — vi : to get well, to recover — **curarse** vr
curativo, -va adj : curative, healing
curiosear vi **1** : to snoop, to pry **2** : to browse — vt : to look over, to check
curiosidad nf **1** : curiosity **2** : curio
curioso, -sa adj **1** : curious, inquisitive **2** : strange, unusual, odd — **curiosamente** adv
currículo → currículum
currículum nm, pl **-lums 1** : résumé, curriculum vitae **2** : curriculum, course of study
curry ['kurri] nm, pl **-rries 1** : curry powder **2** : curry (dish)
cursar vt **1** : to attend (school), to take (a course) **2** : to dispatch, to pass on
cursi adj fam : affected, pretentious
cursilería nf **1** : vulgarity, poor taste **2** : pretentiousness

cursiva *nf* BASTARDILLA : italic type, italics *pl*
curso *nm* 1 : course, direction 2 : school year 3 : course, subject (in school)
cursor *nm* : cursor
curtido, -da *adj* : weather-beaten, leathery (of skin)
curtidor, -dora *n* : tanner
curtiduría *nf* : tannery
curtir *vt* 1 : to tan 2 : to harden, to weather — **curtirse** *vr*
curva *nf* : curve, bend
curvar *vt* : to bend

curvatura *nf* : curvature
curvilíneo, -nea *adj* : curvaceous, shapely
curvo, -va *adj* : curved, bent
cúspide *nf* : zenith, apex, peak
custodia *nf* : custody
custodiar *vt* : to guard, to look after
custodio, -dia *n* : keeper, guardian
cúter *nm* : cutter (boat)
cutícula *nf* : cuticle
cutis *nms & pl* : skin, cómplexion
cuyo, -ya *adj* 1 : whose, of whom, of which 2 **en cuyo caso** : in which case

D

d *nf* : fourth letter of the Spanish alphabet
dable *adj* : feasible, possible
dactilar *adj* **huellas dactilares** : fingerprints
dádiva *nf* : gift, handout
dadivoso, -sa *adj* : generous
dado, -da *adj* 1 : given 2 **dado que** : given that, since
dador, -dora *n* : giver, donor
dados *nmpl* : dice
daga *nf* : dagger
dalia *nf* : dahlia
dálmata *nm* : dalmatian
daltónico, -ca *adj* : color-blind
daltonismo *nm* : color blindness
dama *nf* 1 : lady 2 **damas** *nfpl* : checkers
damasco *nm* : damask
damisela *nf* : damsel
damnificado, -da *n* : victim (of a disaster)
damnificar {72} *vt* : to damage, to injure
dance, etc. → **danzar**
dandi *nm* : dandy, fop
danés¹, -nesa *adj* : Danish
danés², -nesa *n, mpl* **daneses** : Dane, Danish person
danza *nf* : dance, dancing ⟨danza folklórica : folk dance⟩
danzante, -ta *n* BAILARÍN : dancer
danzar {21} *v* BAILAR : to dance
dañar *vt* 1 : to damage, to spoil 2 : to harm, to hurt — **dañarse** *vr*
dañino, -na *adj* : harmful
daño *nm* 1 : damage 2 : harm, injury 3 **hacer daño a** : to harm, to damage 4 **daños y perjuicios** : damages
dar {22} *vt* 1 : to give 2 ENTREGAR : to deliver, to hand over 3 : to hit, to strike 4 : to yield, to produce 5 : to perform 6 : to give off, to emit 7 ~ **como** *or* ~ **por** : to regard as, to consider — *vi* 1 ALCANZAR : to suffice, to be enough ⟨no me da para dos pasajes : I don't have enough for two fares⟩ 2 ~ **a** *or* ~ **sobre** : to overlook, to look out on 3 ~ **con** : to run into 4 ~ **con** : to hit upon (an idea) 5 **dar de sí** : to give, to stretch — **darse** *vr* 1 : to give in, to

surrender 2 : to occur, to arise 3 : to grow, to come up 4 ~ **con** *or* ~ **contra** : to hit oneself against 5 **dárselas de** : to boast about ⟨se las da de muy listo : he thinks he's very smart⟩
dardo *nm* : dart
datar *vt* : to date — *vi* ~ **de** : to date from, to date back to
dátil *nm* : date (fruit)
dato *nm* 1 : fact, piece of information 2 **datos** *nmpl* : data, information
dé → **dar**
de *prep* 1 : of ⟨la casa de Pepe : Pepe's house⟩ ⟨un niño de tres años : a three-year-old boy⟩ 2 : from ⟨es de Managua : she's from Managua⟩ ⟨salió del edificio : he left the building⟩ 3 : in, at ⟨a las tres de la mañana : at three in the morning⟩ ⟨salen de noche : they go out at night⟩ 4 : than ⟨más de tres : more than three⟩
deambular *vi* : to wander, to roam
debacle *nf* : debacle
debajo *adv* 1 : underneath, below, on the bottom 2 ~ **de** : under, underneath 3 **por** ~ : below, beneath
debate *nm* : debate
debatir *vt* : to debate, to discuss — **debatirse** *vr* : to struggle
debe *nm* : debit column, debit
deber¹ *v* — *v aux* 1 : must, have to ⟨debo ir a la oficina : I must go to the office⟩ 2 : should, ought to ⟨deberías buscar trabajo : you ought to look for work⟩ 3 (*expressing probability*) : must ⟨debe ser mexicano : he must be Mexican⟩ — **deberse** *vr* ~ **a** : to be due to
deber² *nm* 1 OBLIGACIÓN : duty, obligation 2 **deberes** *nmpl, Spain* : homework
debidamente *adv* : properly, duly
debido, -da *adj* 1 : right, proper, due 2 ~ **a** : due to, owing to
débil *adj* : weak, feeble — **débilmente** *adv*
debilidad *nf* : weakness, debility, feebleness
debilitamiento *nm* : debilitation, weakening

debilitar *vt* : to debilitate, to weaken — **debilitarse** *vr*
debilucho¹, -cha *adj* : weak, frail
debilucho², -cha *n* : weakling
debitar *vt* : to debit
débito *nm* **1** DEUDA : debt **2** : debit
debut [de'but] *nm, pl* **debuts** : debut
debutante¹ *nmf* : beginner, newcomer
debutante² *nf* : debutante *f*
debutar *vi* : to debut, to make a debut
década *nf* DECENIO : decade
decadencia *nf* **1** : decadence **2** : decline
decadente *adj* **1** : decadent **2** : declining
decaer {13} *vi* **1** : to decline, to decay, to deteriorate **2** FLAQUEAR : to weaken, to flag
decaiga, etc. → **decaer**
decano, -na *n* **1** : dean **2** : senior member
decantar *vt* : to decant
decapitar *vt* : to decapitate, to behead
decayó, etc. → **decaer**
decena *nf* : group of ten
decencia *nf* : decency
decenio *nm* DÉCADA : decade
decente *adj* : decent — **decentemente** *adv*
decepción *nf, pl* **-ciones** : disappointment, letdown
decepcionante *adj* : disappointing
decepcionar *vt* : to disappoint, to let down — **decepcionarse** *vr*
deceso *nm* DEFUNCIÓN : death, passing
dechado *nm* **1** : sampler (of embroidery) **2** : model, paragon
decibelio *or* **decibel** *nm* : decibel
decidido, -da *adj* : decisive, determined, resolute — **decididamente** *adv*
decidir *vt* **1** : to decide, to determine ⟨no he decidido nada : I haven't made a decision⟩ **2** : to persuade, to decide ⟨su padre lo decidió a estudiar : his father persuaded him to study⟩ — *vi* : to decide — **decidirse** *vr* : to make up one's mind
decimal *adj* : decimal
décimo, -ma *adj* : tenth — **décimo, -ma** *n*
decimoctavo¹, -va *adj* : eighteenth
decimoctavo², -va *n* : eighteenth (in a series)
decimocuarto¹, -ta *adj* : fourteenth
decimocuarto², -ta *n* : fourteenth (in a series)
decimonoveno¹, -na *or* **decimonono, -na** *adj* : nineteenth
decimonoveno², -na *or* **decimonono, -na** *n* : nineteenth (in a series)
decimoquinto¹, -ta *adj* : fifteenth
decimoquinto², -ta *n* : fifteenth (in a series)
decimoséptimo¹, -ma *adj* : seventeenth
decimoséptimo², -ma *n* : seventeenth (in a series)
decimosexto¹, -ta *adj* : sixteenth
decimosexto², -ta *n* : sixteenth (in a series)

decimotercero¹, -ra *adj* : thirteenth
decimotercero², -ra *n* : thirteenth (in a series)
decir¹ {23} *vt* **1** : to say ⟨dice que no quiere ir : she says she doesn't want to go⟩ **2** : to tell ⟨dime lo que estás pensando : tell me what you're thinking⟩ **3** : to speak, to talk ⟨no digas tonterías : don't talk nonsense⟩ **4** : to call ⟨me dicen Rosy : they call me Rosy⟩ **5 es decir** : that is to say **6 querer decir** : to mean — **decirse** *vr* **1** : to say to oneself **2** : to be said ⟨¿cómo se dice "lápiz" en francés? : how do you say "pencil" in French?⟩
decir² *nm* DICHO : saying, expression
decisión *nf, pl* **-siones** : decision, choice
decisivo, -va *adj* : decisive, conclusive — **decisivamente** *adv*
declamar *vi* : to declaim — *vt* : to recite
declaración *nf, pl* **-ciones** **1** : declaration, statement **2** TESTIMONIO : deposition, testimony **3 declaración de derechos** : bill of rights **4 declaración jurada** : affidavit
declarado, -da *adj* : professed, open — **declaradamente** *adv*
declarar *vt* : to declare, to state — *vi* ATESTIGUAR : to testify — **declararse** *vr* **1** : to declare oneself, to make a statement **2** : to confess one's love **3** : to plead (in court) ⟨declararse inocente : to plead not guilty⟩
declinación *nf, pl* **-ciones** **1** : drop, downward trend **2** : declination **3** : declension (in grammar)
declinar *vt* : to decline, to turn down — *vi* **1** : to draw to a close **2** : to diminish, to decline
declive *nm* **1** DECADENCIA : decline **2** : slope, incline
decodificador *nm* : decoder
decolar *vi* Chile, Col, Ecua : to take off (of an airplane)
decolorar *vt* : to bleach — **decolorarse** *vr* : to fade
decomisar *vt* CONFISCAR : to seize, to confiscate
decomiso *nm* : seizure, confiscation
decoración *nf, pl* **-ciones** **1** : decoration **2** : decor **3** : stage set, scenery
decorado *nm* : stage set, scenery
decorador, -dora *n* : decorator
decorar *vt* ADORNAR : to decorate, to adorn
decorativo, -va *adj* : decorative, ornamental
decoro *nm* : decorum, propriety
decoroso, -sa *adj* : decent, proper, respectable
decrecer {53} *vi* : to decrease, to wane, to diminish — **decreciente** *adj*
decrecimiento *nm* : decrease, decline
decrépito, -ta *adj* : decrepit
decretar *vt* : to decree, to order
decreto *nm* : decree
decúbito *nm* : horizontal position ⟨en decúbito prono : prone⟩ ⟨en decúbito supino : supine⟩

dedal *nm* : thimble
dedalera *nf* DIGITAL : foxglove
dedicación *nf, pl* **-ciones** : dedication, devotion
dedicar {72} *vt* CONSAGRAR : to dedicate, to devote — **dedicarse** *vr* ~ **a** : to devote oneself to, to engage in
dedicatoria *nf* : dedication (of a book, song, etc.)
dedo *nm* 1 : finger ⟨dedo meñique : little finger⟩ 2 **dedo del pie** : toe
deducción *nf, pl* **-ciones** : deduction
deducible *adj* 1 : deducible, inferable 2 : deductible
deducir {61} *vt* 1 INFERIR : to deduce 2 DESCONTAR : to deduct
defecar {72} *vi* : to defecate — **defecación** *nf*
defecto *nm* 1 : defect, flaw, shortcoming 2 **en su defecto** : lacking that, in the absence of that
defectuoso, -sa *adj* : defective, faulty
defender {56} *vt* : to defend, to protect — **defenderse** *vr* 1 : to defend oneself 2 : to get by, to know the basics ⟨su inglés no es perfecto pero se defiende : his English isn't perfect but he gets by⟩
defendible *adj* : defensible, tenable
defensa[1] *nf* : defense
defensa[2] *nmf* : defender, back (in sports)
defensiva *nf* : defensive, defense
defensivo, -va *adj* : defensive — **defensivamente** *adv*
defensor[1], **-sora** *adj* : defending, defense
defensor[2], **-sora** *n* 1 : defender, advocate 2 : defense counsel
defeño, -ña *n* : person from the Federal District (Mexico City)
deferencia *nf* : deference
deficiencia *nf* : deficiency, flaw
deficiente *adj* : deficient
déficit *nm, pl* **-cits** 1 : deficit 2 : shortage, lack
definición *nf, pl* **-ciones** : definition
definido, -da *adj* : definite, well-defined
definir *vt* 1 : to define 2 : to determine
definitivamente *adv* 1 : finally 2 : permanently, for good 3 : definitely, absolutely
definitivo, -va *adj* 1 : definitive, conclusive 2 **en definitiva** : all in all, on the whole 3 **en definitiva** *Mex* : permanently, for good
deflación *nf, pl* **-ciones** : deflation
deforestación *nf, pl* **-ciones** : deforestation
deformación *nf, pl* **-ciones** 1 : deformation 2 : distortion
deformar *vt* 1 : to deform, to disfigure 2 : to distort — **deformarse** *vr*
deforme *adj* : deformed, misshapen
deformidad *nf* : deformity
defraudación *nf, pl* **-ciones** : fraud
defraudar *vt* 1 ESTAFAR : to defraud, to cheat 2 : to disappoint
defunción *nf, pl* **-ciones** DECESO : death, passing

degeneración *nf, pl* **-ciones** 1 : degeneration 2 : degeneracy, depravity
degenerado, -da *adj* DEPRAVADO : degenerate
degenerar *vi* : to degenerate
degenerativo, -va *adj* : degenerative
degollar {19} *vt* 1 : to slit the throat of, to slaughter 2 DECAPITAR : to behead 3 : to ruin, to destroy
degradación *nf, pl* **-ciones** 1 : degradation 2 : demotion
degradar *vt* 1 : to degrade, to debase 2 : to demote
degustación *nf, pl* **-ciones** : tasting, sampling
degustar *vt* : to taste
deidad *nf* : deity
deificar {72} *vt* : to idolize, to deify
dejado, -da *adj* 1 : slovenly 2 : careless, lazy
dejar *vt* 1 : to leave 2 ABANDONAR : to abandon, to forsake 3 : to let be, to let go 4 PERMITIR : to allow, to permit — *vi* ~ **de** : to stop, to quit ⟨dejar de fumar : to quit smoking⟩ — **dejarse** *vr* 1 : to let oneself be ⟨se deja insultar : he lets himself be insulted⟩ 2 : to forget, to leave ⟨me dejé las llaves en el carro : I left the keys in the car⟩ 3 : to neglect oneself, to let oneself go 4 : to grow ⟨nos estamos dejando el pelo largo : we're growing our hair long⟩
dejo *nm* 1 : aftertaste 2 : touch, hint 3 : (regional) accent
del (*contraction of* **de** *and* **el**) → **de**
delación *nf, pl* **-ciones** : denunciation, betrayal
delantal *nm* 1 : apron 2 : pinafore
delante *adv* 1 ENFRENTE : ahead, in front 2 ~ **de** : before, in front of
delantera *nf* 1 : front, front part, front row ⟨tomar la delantera : to take the lead⟩ 2 : forward line (in sports)
delantero[1], **-ra** *adj* 1 : front, forward 2 **tracción delantera** : front-wheel drive
delantero[2], **-ra** *n* : forward (in sports)
delatar *vt* 1 : to betray, to reveal 2 : to denounce, to inform against
delegación *nf, pl* **-ciones** : delegation
delegado, -da *n* : delegate, representative
delegar {52} *vt* : to delegate
deleitar *vt* : to delight, to please — **deleitarse** *vr*
deleite *nm* : delight, pleasure
deletrear *vi* : to spell ⟨¿como se deletrea? : how do you spell it?⟩
deleznable *adj* 1 : brittle, crumbly 2 : slippery 3 : weak, fragile ⟨una excusa deleznable : a weak excuse⟩
delfín *nm, pl* **delfines** 1 : dolphin 2 : dauphin, heir apparent
delgadez *nf* : thinness, skinniness
delgado, -da *adj* 1 FLACO : thin, skinny 2 ESBELTO : slender, slim 3 DELICADO : delicate, fine 4 AGUDO : sharp, clever
deliberación *nf, pl* **-ciones** : deliberation

deliberado, -da *adj* : deliberate, intentional — **deliberadamente** *adv*

deliberar *vi* : to deliberate

deliberativo, -va *adj* : deliberative

delicadeza *nf* 1 : delicacy, fineness 2 : gentleness, softness 3 : tact, discretion, consideration

delicado, -da *adj* 1 : delicate, fine 2 : sensitive, frail 3 : difficult, tricky 4 : fussy, hard to please 5 : tactful, considerate

delicia *nf* : delight

delicioso, -sa *adj* 1 RICO : delicious 2 : delightful

delictivo, -va *adj* : criminal

delictuoso, -sa → **delictivo**

delimitación *nf*, *pl* **-ciones** 1 : demarcation 2 : defining, specifying

delimitar *vt* 1 : to demarcate 2 : to define, to specify

delincuencia *nf* : delinquency, crime

delincuente[1] *adj* : delinquent

delincuente[2] *nmf* CRIMINAL : delinquent, criminal

delinear *vt* 1 : to delineate, to outline 2 : to draft, to draw up

delinquir {24} *vi* : to break the law

delirante *adj* : delirious

delirar *vi* 1 DESVARIAR : to be delirious 2 : to rave, to talk nonsense

delirio *nm* 1 DESVARÍO : delirium 2 DISPARATE : nonsense, ravings *pl* ⟨delirios de grandeza : delusions of grandeur⟩ 3 FRENESÍ : mania, frenzy ⟨¡fue el delirio! : it was wild!⟩

delito *nm* : crime, offense

delta *nm* : delta

demacrado, -da *adj* : emaciated, gaunt

demagogia *nf* : demagogy

demagógico, -ca *adj* : demagogic, demagogical

demagogo, -ga *n* : demagogue

demanda *nf* 1 : demand ⟨la oferta y la demanda : supply and demand⟩ 2 : petition, request 3 : lawsuit

demandado, -da *n* : defendant

demandante *nmf* : plaintiff

demandar *vt* 1 : to demand 2 REQUERIR : to call for, to require 3 : to sue, to file a lawsuit against

demarcar {72} *vt* : to demarcate — **demarcación** *nf*

demás[1] *adj* : remaining ⟨acabó las demás tareas : she finished the rest of the chores⟩

demás[2] *pron* 1 lo (la, los, las) demás : the rest, everyone else, everything else ⟨Pepe, Rosa, y los demás : Pepe, Rosa, and everybody else⟩ 2 estar por demás : to be of no use, to be pointless ⟨no estaría por demás : it couldn't hurt, it's worth a try⟩ 3 por demás : extremely 4 por lo demás : otherwise 5 y demás : and so on, et cetera

demasía *nf* en ∼ : excessively, in excess

demasiado[1] *adv* 1 : too ⟨vas demasiado aprisa : you're going too fast⟩ 2 : too

much ⟨estoy comiendo demasiado : I'm eating too much⟩

demasiado[2], **-da** *adj* : too much, too many, excessive

demencia *nf* 1 : dementia 2 LOCURA : madness, insanity

demente[1] *adj* : insane, mad

demente[2] *nmf* : insane person

demeritar *vt* 1 : to detract from 2 : to discredit

demérito *nm* 1 : fault 2 : discredit, disrepute

democracia *nf* : democracy

demócrata[1] *adj* : democratic

demócrata[2] *nmf* : democrat

democrático, -ca *adj* : democratic — **democráticamente** *adv*

democratizar {21} *vt* : to democratize, to make democratic

demografía *nf* : demography

demográfico, -ca *adj* : demographic

demoledor, -dora *adj* : devastating

demoler {47} *vt* DERRIBAR, DERRUMBAR : to demolish, to destroy

demolición *nf*, *pl* **-ciones** : demolition

demonio *nm* DIABLO : devil, demon

demora *nf* : delay

demorar *vt* 1 RETRASAR : to delay 2 TARDAR : to take, to last ⟨la reparación demorará varios días : the repair will take several days⟩ — *vi* : to delay, to linger — **demorarse** *vr* 1 : to be slow, to take a long time 2 : to take too long

demostración *nf*, *pl* **-ciones** : demonstration

demostrar {19} *vt* : to demonstrate, to show

demostrativo, -va *adj* : demonstrative

demudar *vt* : to change, to alter — **demudarse** *vr* : to change one's expression

denegación *nf*, *pl* **-ciones** : denial, refusal

denegar {49} *vt* : to deny, to turn down

denigrante *adj* : degrading, humiliating

denigrar *vt* 1 DIFAMAR : to denigrate, to disparage 2 : to degrade, to humiliate

denodado, -da *adj* : bold, dauntless

denominación *nf*, *pl* **-ciones** 1 : name, designation 2 : denomination (of money)

denominador *nm* : denominator

denominar *vt* : to designate, to name

denostar {19} *vt* : to revile

denotar *vt* : to denote, to show

densidad *nf* : density, thickness

denso, -sa *adj* : dense, thick — **densamente** *adv*

dentado, -da *adj* SERRADO : serrated, jagged

dentadura *nf* 1 : teeth *pl* 2 dentadura postiza : dentures *pl*

dental *adj* : dental

dentellada *nf* 1 : bite 2 : tooth mark

dentera *nf* 1 : envy, jealousy 2 dar dentera : to set one's teeth on edge

dentición *nf*, *pl* **-ciones** 1 : teething 2 : dentition, set of teeth

dentífrico *nm* : toothpaste

dentista *nmf* : dentist

dentro *adv* 1 : in, inside 2 : indoors 3 ~ **de** : within, inside, in 4 **dentro de poco** : soon, shortly 5 **dentro de todo** : all in all, all things considered 6 **por** ~ : inwardly, inside

denuedo *nm* : valor, courage

denuesto *nm* : insult

denuncia *nf* 1 : denunciation, condemnation 2 : police report

denunciante *nmf* : accuser (of a crime)

denunciar *vt* 1 : to denounce, to condemn 2 : to report (to the authorities)

deparar *vt* 1 : to have in store for, to provide with ⟨no sabemos lo que nos depara el destino : we don't know what fate has in store for us⟩

departamental *adj* 1 : departmental 2 **tienda departamental** *Mex* : department store

departamento *nm* 1 : department 2 APARTAMENTO : apartment

departir *vi* : to converse

dependencia *nf* 1 : dependence, dependency ⟨dependencia emocional : emotional dependence⟩ ⟨dependencia del alcohol : dependence on alcohol⟩ 2 : agency, branch office

depender *vi* 1 : to depend 2 ~ **de** : to depend on 3 ~ **de** : to be subordinate to

dependiente[1] *adj* : dependent

dependiente[2], -ta *n* : clerk, salesperson

deplorable *adj* : deplorable

deplorar *vt* 1 : to deplore 2 LAMENTAR : to regret

deponer {60} *vt* 1 : to depose, to overthrow 2 : to abandon (an attitude or stance) 3 **deponer las armas** : to lay down one's arms — *vi* 1 TESTIFICAR : to testify, to make a statement 2 EVACUAR : to defecate

deportación *nf, pl* **-ciones** : deportation

deportar *vt* : to deport

deporte *nm* : sport, sports *pl* ⟨hacer deporte : to engage in sports⟩

deportista[1] *adj* 1 : fond of sports 2 : sporty

deportista[2] *nmf* 1 : sports fan 2 : athlete, sportsman *m*, sportswoman *f*

deportividad *nf Spain* : sportsmanship

deportivo, -va *adj* 1 : sports, sporting ⟨artículos deportivos : sporting goods⟩ 2 : sporty

deposición *nf, pl* **-ciones** 1 : statement, testimony 2 : removal from office

depositante *nmf* : depositor

depositar *vt* 1 : to deposit, to place 2 : to store — **depositarse** *vr* : to settle

depósito *nm* 1 : deposit 2 : warehouse, storehouse

depravación *nf, pl* **-ciones** : depravity

depravado, -da *adj* DEGENERADO : depraved, degenerate

depravar *vt* : to deprave, to corrupt

depreciación *nf, pl* **-ciones** : depreciation

depreciar *vt* : to depreciate, to reduce the value of — **depreciarse** *vr* : to lose value

depredación *nf* SAQUEO : depredation, plunder

depredador[1], -dora *adj* : predatory

depredador[2] *nm* 1 : predator 2 SAQUEADOR : plunderer

depresión *nf, pl* **-siones** 1 : depression 2 : hollow, recess 3 : drop, fall 4 : slump, recession

depresivo[1], -va *adj* 1 : depressive 2 : depressant

depresivo[2] *nm* : depressant

deprimente *adj* : depressing

deprimir *vt* 1 : to depress 2 : to lower — **deprimirse** *vr* ABATIRSE : to get depressed

depuesto *pp* → **deponer**

depuración *nf, pl* **-ciones** 1 PURIFICACIÓN : purification 2 PURGA : purge 3 : refinement, polish

depurar *vt* 1 PURIFICAR : to purify 2 PURGAR : to purge

depuso, etc. → **deponer**

derecha *nf* 1 : right 2 : right hand, right side 3 : right wing, right (in politics)

derechazo *nm* 1 : pass with the cape on the right hand (in bullfighting) 2 : right (in boxing) 3 : forehand (in tennis)

derechista[1] *adj* : rightist, right-wing

derechista[2] *nmf* : right-winger

derecho[1] *adv* 1 : straight 2 : upright 3 : directly

derecho[2], -cha *adj* 1 : right 2 : right-hand 3 RECTO : straight, upright, erect

derecho[3] *nm* 1 : right ⟨derechos humanos : human rights⟩ 2 : law ⟨derecho civil : civil law⟩ 3 : right side (of cloth or clothing)

deriva *nf* 1 : drift 2 **a la deriva** : adrift

derivación *nf, pl* **-ciones** 1 : derivation 2 RAMIFICACIÓN : ramification, consequence

derivar *vi* 1 : to drift 2 ~ **de** : to come from, to derive from 3 ~ **en** : to result in — *vt* : to steer, to direct ⟨derivó la discusión hacia la política : he steered the discussion over to politics⟩ — **derivarse** *vr* : to be derived from, to arise from

dermatología *nf* : dermatology

dermatológico, -ca *adj* : dermatological

dermatólogo, -ga *n* : dermatologist

derogación *nf, pl* **-ciones** : abolition, repeal

derogar {52} *vt* ABOLIR : to abolish, to repeal

derramamiento *nm* 1 : spilling, overflowing 2 **derramamiento de sangre** : bloodshed

derramar *vt* 1 : to spill 2 : to shed (tears, blood) — **derramarse** *vr* 1 : to spill over 2 : to scatter

derrame *nm* 1 : spilling, shedding 2 : leakage, overflow 3 : discharge, hemorrhage

derrapar *vi* : to skid

derrape *nm* : skid
derredor *nm* **al derredor** *or* **en derredor** : around, round about
derrengado, -da *adj* 1 : bent, twisted 2 : exhausted
derretir {54} *vt* : to melt, to thaw — **derretirse** *vr* 1 : to melt, to thaw 2 ~ **por** *fam* : to be crazy about
derribar *vt* 1 DEMOLER, DERRUMBAR : to demolish, to knock down 2 : to shoot down, to bring down (an airplane) 3 DERROCAR : to overthrow
derribo *nm* 1 : demolition, razing 2 : shooting down 3 : overthrow
derrocamiento *nm* : overthrow
derrocar {72} *vt* DERRIBAR : to overthrow, to topple
derrochador¹, -dora *adj* : extravagant, wasteful
derrochador², -dora *n* : spendthrift
derrochar *vt* : to waste, to squander
derroche *nm* : extravagance, waste
derrota *nf* 1 : defeat, rout 2 : course (at sea)
derrotar *vt* : to defeat
derrotero *nm* RUTA : course
derrotista *adj & nmf* : defeatist
derruir {41} *vt* : to demolish, to tear down
derrumbamiento *nm* : collapse
derrumbar *vt* 1 DEMOLER, DERRIBAR : to demolish, to knock down 2 DESPEÑAR : to cast down, to topple — **derrumbarse** *vr* DESPLOMARSE : to collapse, to break down
derrumbe *nm* 1 DESPLOME : collapse, fall ⟨el derrumbe del comunismo : the fall of Communism⟩ 2 : landslide
desabastecimiento *nm* : shortage, scarcity
desabasto *nm Mex* : shortage, scarcity
desabrido, -da *adj* : tasteless, bland
desabrigar {52} *vt* 1 : to undress 2 : to uncover 3 : to deprive of shelter
desabrochar *vt* : to unbutton, to undo — **desabrocharse** *vr* : to come undone
desacatar *vt* 1 DESAFIAR : to defy 2 DESOBEDECER : to disobey
desacato *nm* 1 : disrespect 2 : contempt (of court)
desacelerar *vi* : to decelerate, to slow down
desacertado, -da *adj* 1 : mistaken 2 : unwise
desacertar {55} *vi* ERRAR : to err, to be mistaken
desacierto *nm* ERROR : error, mistake
desaconsejable *adj* : inadvisable
desaconsejado, -da *adj* : ill-advised, unwise
desacorde *adj* 1 : conflicting 2 : discordant
desacostumbrado, -da *adj* : unaccustomed, unusual
desacreditar *vt* DESPRESTIGIAR : to discredit, to disgrace
desactivar *vt* : to deactivate, to defuse
desacuerdo *nm* : disagreement
desafiante *adj* : defiant

desafiar {85} *vt* RETAR : to defy, to challenge
desafilado, -da *adj* : blunt
desafinado, -da *adj* : out-of-tune, off-key
desafinarse *vr* : to go out of tune
desafío *nm* 1 RETO : challenge 2 RESISTENCIA : defiance
desafortunado, -da *adj* : unfortunate, unlucky — **desafortunadamente** *adv*
desafuero *nm* ABUSO : injustice, outrage
desagradable *adj* : unpleasant, disagreeable — **desagradablemente** *adv*
desagradar *vi* : to be unpleasant, to be disagreeable
desagradecido, -da *adj* : ungrateful
desagrado *nm* 1 : displeasure 2 con ~ : reluctantly
desagravio *nm* 1 : apology 2 : amends, reparation
desagregarse {52} *vr* : to break up, to disintegrate
desaguar {10} *vi* : to drain, to empty
desagüe *nm* 1 : drain 2 : drainage
desahogado, -da *adj* 1 : well-off, comfortable 2 : spacious, roomy
desahogar {52} *vt* 1 : to relieve, to ease 2 : to give vent to — **desahogarse** *vr* 1 : to recover, to feel better 2 : to unburden oneself, to let off steam
desahogo *nm* 1 : relief, outlet 2 con ~ : comfortably
desahuciar *vt* 1 : to deprive of hope 2 : to evict — **desahuciarse** *vr* : to lose all hope
desahucio *nm* : eviction
desairar {5} *vt* : to snub, to rebuff
desaire *nm* : rebuff, snub, slight
desajustar *vt* 1 : to disarrange, to put out of order 2 : to upset (plans)
desajuste *nm* 1 : maladjustment 2 : imbalance 3 : upset, disruption
desalentador, -dora *adj* : discouraging, disheartening
desalentar {55} *vt* DESANIMAR : to discourage, to dishearten — **desalentarse** *vr*
desaliento *nm* : discouragement
desaliñado, -da *adj* : slovenly, untidy
desalmado, -da *adj* : heartless, callous
desalojar *vt* 1 : to remove, to clear 2 EVACUAR : to evacuate, to vacate 3 : to evict
desalojo *nm* 1 : removal, expulsion 2 : evacuation 3 : eviction
desamor *nm* 1 FRIALDAD : indifference 2 ENEMISTAD : dislike, enmity
desamparado, -da *adj* DESVALIDO : helpless, destitute
desamparar *vt* : to abandon, to forsake
desamparo *nm* 1 : abandonment, neglect 2 : helplessness
desamueblado, -da *adj* : unfurnished
desandar {6} *vt* : to go back, to return to the starting point
desangelado, -da *adj* : dull, lifeless
desangrar *vt* : to bleed, to bleed dry — **desangrarse** *vr* 1 : to be bleeding 2 : to bleed to death

desanimar vt DESALENTAR : to discourage, to dishearten — **desanimarse** vr

desánimo nm DESALIENTO : discouragement, dejection

desanudar vt : to untie, to disentangle

desapacible adj : unpleasant, disagreeable

desaparecer {53} vt : to cause to disappear — vi : to disappear, to vanish

desaparecido¹, -da adj 1 : late, deceased 2 : missing

desaparecido², -da n : missing person

desaparición nf, pl -ciones : disappearance

desapasionado, -da adj : dispassionate, impartial — **desapasionadamente** adv

desapego nm : coolness, indifference

desapercibido, -da adj 1 : unnoticed 2 DESPREVENIDO : unprepared, off guard

desaprobación nf, pl -ciones : disapproval

desaprobar {19} vt REPROBAR : to disapprove of

desaprovechar vt MALGASTAR : to waste, to misuse — vi : to lose ground, to slip back

desarmador nm Mex : screwdriver

desarmar vt 1 : to disarm 2 DESMONTAR : to disassemble, to take apart

desarme nm : disarmament

desarraigado, -da adj : rootless

desarraigar {52} vt : to uproot, to root out

desarreglado, -da adj : untidy, disorganized

desarreglar vt 1 : to mess up 2 : to upset, to disrupt

desarreglo nm 1 : untidiness 2 : disorder, confusion

desarrollar vt : to develop — **desarrollarse** vr : to take place

desarrollo nm : development

desarticulación nf, pl -ciones 1 : dislocation 2 : breaking up, dismantling

desarticular vt 1 DISLOCAR : to dislocate 2 : to break up, to dismantle

desaseado, -da adj 1 : dirty 2 : messy, untidy

desastre nm CATÁSTROFE : disaster

desastroso, -sa adj : disastrous, catastrophic

desatar vt 1 : to undo, to untie 2 : to unleash 3 : to trigger, to precipitate — **desatarse** vr 1 : to break out, to erupt

desatascar {72} vt : to unblock, to clear

desatención nf, pl -ciones 1 : absentmindedness, distraction 2 : discourtesy

desatender {56} vt 1 : to disregard 2 : to neglect

desatento, -ta adj 1 DISTRAÍDO : absentminded 2 GROSERO : discourteous, rude

desatinado, -da adj : foolish, silly

desatino nm : folly, mistake

desautorizar {21} vt : to deprive of authority, to discredit

desavenencia nf DISCORDANCIA : disagreement, dispute

desayunar vi : to have breakfast — vt : to have for breakfast

desayuno nm : breakfast

desazón nf, pl -zones INQUIETUD : uneasiness, anxiety

desbalance nm : imbalance

desbancar {72} vt : to displace, to oust

desbandada nf : scattering, dispersal

desbarajuste nm DESORDEN : disarray, disorder, mess

desbaratar vt 1 ARRUINAR : to destroy, to ruin 2 DESCOMPONER : to break, to break down — **desbaratarse** vr : to fall apart

desbloquear vt 1 : to open up, to clear, to break through 2 : to free, to release

desbocado, -da adj : unbridled, rampant

desbocarse {72} vr : to run away, to bolt

desbordamiento nm : overflowing

desbordante adj : overflowing, bursting ⟨desbordante de energía : bursting with energy⟩

desbordar vt 1 : to overflow, to spill over 2 : to surpass, to exceed — **desbordarse** vr

descabellado, -da adj : outlandish, ridiculous

descafeinado, -da adj : decaffeinated

descalabrar vt : to hit on the head — **descalabrarse** vr

descalabro nm : setback, misfortune, loss

descalificación nf, pl -ciones 1 : disqualification 2 : disparaging remark

descalificar {72} vt 1 : to disqualify 2 DESACREDITAR : to discredit — **descalificarse** vr

descalzarse {21} vr : take off one's shoes

descalzo, -za adj : barefoot

descansado, -da adj 1 : rested, refreshed 2 : restful, peaceful

descansar vi : to rest, to relax — vt : to rest ⟨descansar la vista : to rest one's eyes⟩

descansillo nm : landing (of a staircase)

descanso nm 1 : rest, relaxation 2 : break 3 : landing (of a staircase) 4 : intermission

descapotable adj & nm : convertible

descarado, -da adj : brazen, impudent — **descaradamente** adv

descarga nf 1 : discharge 2 : unloading

descargar {52} vt 1 : to discharge 2 : to unload 3 : to release, to free 4 : to take out, to vent (anger, etc.) — **descargarse** vr 1 : to unburden oneself 2 : to quit 3 : to lose power

descargo nm 1 : unloading 2 : defense ⟨testigo de descargo : witness for the defense⟩

descarnado, -da adj : scrawny, gaunt

descaro nm : audacity, nerve

descarriado, -da *adj* : lost, gone astray
descarrilar *vi* : to derail — **descarrilarse** *vr*
descartar *vt* : to rule out, to reject — **descartarse** *vr* : to discard
descascarar *vt* : to peel, to shell, to husk — **descascararse** *vr* : to peel off, to chip
descendencia *nf* **1** : descendants *pl* **2** LINAJE : descent, lineage
descendente *adj* : downward, descending
descender {56} *vt* **1** : to descend, to go down **2** BAJAR : to lower, to take down, to let down — *vi* **1** : to descend, to come down **2** : to drop, to fall **3** ~ **de** : to be a descendant of
descendiente *adj & nm* : descendant
descenso *nm* **1** : descent **2** BAJA, CAÍDA : drop, fall
descentralizar {21} *vt* : to decentralize — **descentralizarse** *vr* — **descentralización** *nf*
descifrable *adj* : decipherable
descifrar *vt* : to decipher, to decode
descodificar {72} *vt* : to decode
descolgar {16} *vt* **1** : to take down, to let down **2** : to pick up, to answer (the telephone)
descollar {19} *vi* SOBRESALIR : to stand out, to be outstanding, to excel
descolorarse *vr* : to fade
descolorido, -da *adj* : discolored, faded
descomponer {60} *vt* **1** : to rot, to decompose **2** DESBARATAR : to break, to break down — **descomponerse** *vr* **1** : to break down **2** : to decompose
descomposición *nf, pl* **-ciones 1** : breakdown, decomposition **2** : decay
descompresión *nf* : decompression
descompuesto[1] *pp* → **descomponer**
descompuesto[2], **-ta** *adj* **1** : broken down, out of order **2** : rotten, decomposed
descomunal *adj* **1** ENORME : enormous, huge **2** EXTRAORDINARIO : extraordinary
desconcertante *adj* : disconcerting
desconcertar {55} *vt* : to disconcert — **desconcertarse** *vr*
desconchar *vt* : to chip — **desconcharse** *vr* : to chip off, to peel
desconcierto *nm* : uncertainty, confusion
desconectar *vt* **1** : to disconnect, to switch off **2** : to unplug
desconfiado, -da *adj* : distrustful, suspicious
desconfianza *nf* RECELO : distrust, suspicion
desconfiar {85} *vi* ~ **de** : to distrust, to be suspicious of
descongelar *vt* **1** : to thaw **2** : to defrost **3** : to unfreeze (assets — **descongelarse** *vr*
descongestionante *adj & nm* : decongestant

desconocer {18} *vt* **1** IGNORAR : to be unaware of **2** : to fail to recognize
desconocido[1], **-da** *adj* : unknown, unfamiliar
desconocido[2], **-da** *n* EXTRAÑO : stranger
desconocimiento *nm* : ignorance
desconsiderado, -da *adj* : inconsiderate, thoughtless — **desconsideradamente** *adj*
desconsolado, -da *adj* : disconsolate, heartbroken
desconsuelo *nm* AFLICCIÓN : grief, distress, despair
descontaminar *vt* : to decontaminate — **descontaminación** *nf*
descontar {19} *vt* **1** : to discount, to deduct **2** EXCEPTUAR : to except, to exclude
descontento[1], **-ta** *adj* : discontented, dissatisfied
descontento[2] *nm* : discontent, dissatisfaction
descontrol *nm* : lack of control, disorder, chaos
descontrolarse *vr* : to get out of control, to be out of hand
descorazonado, -da *adj* : disheartened, discouraged
descorazonador, -dora *adj* : disheartening, discouraging
descorrer *vt* : to draw back
descortés *adj, pl* **-teses** : discourteous, rude
descortesía *nf* : discourtesy, rudeness
descrédito *nm* DESPRESTIGIO : discredit
descremado, -da *adj* : nonfat, skim
describir {33} *vt* : to describe
descripción *nf, pl* **-ciones** : description
descriptivo, -va *adj* : descriptive
descrito *pp* → **describir**
descuartizar {21} *vt* **1** : to cut up, to quarter **2** : to tear to pieces
descubierto[1] *pp* → **descubrir**
descubierto[2], **-ta** *adj* **1** : exposed, revealed **2 al descubierto** : out in the open
descubridor, -dora *n* : discoverer, explorer
descubrimiento *nm* : discovery
descubrir {2} *vt* **1** HALLAR : to discover, to find out **2** REVELAR : to uncover, to reveal — **descubrirse** *vr*
descuento *nm* REBAJA : discount
descuidado, -da *adj* **1** : neglectful, careless **2** : neglected, unkempt
descuidar *vt* : to neglect, to overlook — *vi* : to be careless — **descuidarse** *vr* **1** : to be careless, to drop one's guard **2** : to let oneself go
descuido *nm* **1** : carelessness, negligence **2** : slip, oversight
desde *prep* **1** : from **2** : since **3 desde ahora** : from now on **4 desde entonces** : since then **5 desde hace** : for, since (a time) ⟨ha estado nevando desde hace dos días : it's been snowing for

two days⟩ **6 desde luego** : of course
7 desde que : since, ever since **8 desde ya** : right now, immediately

desdecir {11} *vi* **1 ~ de** : to be unworthy of **2 ~ de** : to clash with — **desdecirse** *vr* **1** CONTRADECIRSE : to contradict oneself **2** RETRACTARSE : to go back on one's word

desdén *nm, pl* **desdenes** DESPRECIO : disdain, scorn

desdentado, -da *adj* : toothless

desdeñar *vt* DESPRECIAR : to disdain, to scorn, to despise

desdeñoso, -sa *adj* : disdainful, scornful — **desdeñosamente** *adv*

desdibujar *vt* : to blur — **desdibujarse** *vr*

desdicha *nf* **1** : misery **2** : misfortune

desdichado[1], -da *adj* **1** : unfortunate **2** : miserable, unhappy

desdichado[2], -da *n* : wretch

desdicho *pp* → **desdecir**

desdiga, desdijo etc. → **desdecir**

desdoblar *vt* DESPLEGAR : to unfold

deseable *adj* : desirable

desear *vt* **1** : to wish ⟨te deseo buena suerte : I wish you good luck⟩ **2** QUERER : to want, to desire

desecar {72} *vt* : to dry (flowers, etc.)

desechable *adj* : disposable

desechar *vt* **1** : to discard, to throw away **2** RECHAZAR : to reject

desecho *nm* **1** : reject **2 desechos** *nmpl* RESIDUOS : rubbish, waste

desembarazarse {21} *vr* **~ de** : to get rid of

desembarcadero *nm* : jetty, landing pier

desembarcar {72} *vi* : to disembark — *vt* : to unload

desembarco *nm* **1** : landing, arrival **2** : unloading

desembarque → **desembarco**

desembocadura *nf* **1** : mouth (of a river) **2** : opening, end (of a street)

desembocar {72} *vi* **~ en** *or* **~ a 1** : to flow into, to join **2** : to lead to, to result in

desembolsar *vt* PAGAR : to disburse, to pay out

desembolso *nm* PAGO : disbursement, payment

desempacar {72} *v* : to unpack

desempate *nm* : tiebreaker, play-off

desempeñar *vt* **1** : to play (a role) **2** : to fulfill, to carry out **3** : to redeem (from a pawnshop) — **desempeñarse** *vr* : to function, to act

desempeño *nm* **1** : fulfillment, carrying out **2** : performance

desempleado[1], -da *adj* : unemployed

desempleado[2], -da *n* : unemployed person

desempleo *nm* : unemployment

desempolvar *vt* **1** : to dust off **2** : to resurrect, to revive

desencadenar *vt* **1** : to unchain **2** : to trigger, to unleash — **desencadenarse** *vr*

desencajar *vt* **1** : to dislocate **2** : to disconnect, to disengage

desencantar *vt* : to disenchant, to disillusion — **desencantarse** *vr*

desencanto *nm* : disenchantment, disillusionment

desenchufar *vt* : to disconnect, to unplug

desenfadado, -da *adj* **1** : uninhibited, carefree **2** : confident, self-assured

desenfado *nm* **1** DESENVOLTURA : self-assurance, confidence **2** : naturalness, ease

desenfrenadamente *adv* : wildly, with abandon

desenfrenado, -da *adj* : unbridled, unrestrained

desenfreno *nm* : abandon, unrestraint

desenganchar *vt* : to unhitch, to uncouple

desengañar *vt* : to disillusion, to disenchant — **desengañarse** *vr*

desengaño *nm* : disenchantment, disillusionment

desenlace *nm* : ending, outcome

desenlazar {21} *vt* **1** : to untie **2** : to clear up, to resolve

desenmarañar *vt* : to disentangle, to unravel

desenmascarar *vt* : to unmask, to expose

desenredar *vt* : to untangle, to disentangle

desenrollar *vt* : to unroll, to unwind

desentenderse {56} *vr* **1 ~ de** : to want nothing to do with, to be uninterested in **2 ~ de** : to pretend ignorance of

desenterrar {55} *vt* **1** EXHUMAR : to exhume **2** : to unearth, to dig up

desentonar *vi* **1** : to clash, to conflict **2** : to be out of tune, to sing off-key

desentrañar *vt* : to get to the bottom of, to unravel

desenvainar *vt* : to draw, to unsheathe (a sword)

desenvoltura *nf* **1** DESENFADO : confidence, self-assurance **2** ELOCUENCIA : eloquence, fluency

desenvolver {89} *vt* : to unwrap, to open — **desenvolverse** *vr* **1** : to unfold, to develop **2** : to manage, to cope

desenvuelto[1] *pp* → **desenvolver**

desenvuelto[2], -ta *adj* : confident, relaxed, self-assured

deseo *nm* : wish, desire

deseoso, -sa *adj* : eager, anxious

desequilibrar *vt* : to unbalance, to throw off balance — **desequilibrarse** *vr*

desequilibrio *nm* : imbalance

deserción *nf, pl* **-ciones** : desertion, defection

desertar *vi* **1** : to desert, to defect **2 ~ de** : to abandon, to neglect

desertor, -tora *n* : deserter, defector

desesperación *nf, pl* **-ciones** : desperation, despair

desesperado, -da *adj* : desperate, despairing, hopeless — **desesperadamente** *adv*

desesperanza *nf* : despair, hopelessness

desesperar *vt* : to exasperate — *vi* : to despair, to lose hope — **desesperarse** *vr* : to become exasperated

desestimar *vt* **1** : to reject, to disallow **2** : to have a low opinion of

desfachatez *nf, pl* **-teces** : audacity, nerve, cheek

desfalcador, -dora *n* : embezzler

desfalcar {72} *vt* : to embezzle

desfalco *nm* : embezzlement

desfallecer {53} *vi* **1** : to weaken **2** : to faint

desfallecimiento *nm* **1** : weakness **2** : fainting

desfasado, -da *adj* **1** : out of sync **2** : out of step, behind the times

desfase *nm* : gap, lag ⟨desfase horario : jet lag⟩

desfavorable *adj* : unfavorable, adverse — **desfavorablemente** *adv*

desfavorecido, -da *adj* : underprivileged

desfigurar *vt* **1** : to disfigure, to mar **2** : to distort, to misrepresent

desfiladero *nm* : narrow gorge, defile

desfilar *vi* : to parade, to march

desfile *nm* : parade, procession

desfogar {52} *vt* **1** : to vent **2** *Mex* : to unclog, to unblock — **desfogarse** *vr* : to vent one's feelings, to let off steam

desforestación *nf, pl* **-ciones** : deforestation

desgajar *vt* **1** : to tear off **2** : to break apart — **desgajarse** *vr* : to come apart

desgana *nf* **1** INAPETENCIA : lack of appetite **2** APATÍA : apathy, unwillingness, reluctance

desgano *nm* → **desgana**

desgarbado, -da *adj* : ungainly

desgarrador, -dora *adj* : heartrending, heartbreaking

desgarradura *nf* : tear, rip

desgarrar *vt* **1** : to tear, to rip **2** : to break (one's heart) — **desgarrarse** *vr*

desgarre → **desgarro**

desgarro *nm* : tear

desgarrón *nm, pl* **-rrones** : rip, tear

desgastar *vt* **1** : to use up **2** : to wear away, to wear down

desgaste *nm* : deterioration, wear and tear

desglosar *vt* : to break down, to itemize

desglose *nm* : breakdown, itemization

desgobierno *nm* : anarchy, disorder

desgracia *nf* **1** : misfortune **2** : disgrace **3** **por ~** : unfortunately

desgraciadamente *adv* : unfortunately

desgraciado¹, -da *adj* **1** : unfortunate, unlucky **2** : vile, wretched

desgraciado², -da *n* : unfortunate person, wretch

desgranar *vt* : to shuck, to shell

deshabitado, -da *adj* : unoccupied, uninhabited

deshacer {40} *vt* **1** : to destroy, to ruin **2** DESATAR : to undo, to untie **3** : to break apart, to crumble **4** : to dissolve, to melt **5** : to break, to cancel — **deshacerse** *vr* **1** : to fall apart, to come undone **2** **~ de** : to get rid of

deshecho¹ *pp* → **deshacer**

deshecho², -cha *adj* **1** : destroyed, ruined **2** : devastated, shattered **3** : undone, untied

desheredado, -da *adj* MARGINADO : dispossessed, destitute

desheredar *vt* : to disinherit

deshicieron, etc. → **deshacer**

deshidratar *vt* : to dehydrate — **deshidratación** *nf*

deshielo *nm* : thaw, thawing

deshilachar *vt* : to fray — **deshilacharse** *vr*

deshizo → **deshacer**

deshonestidad *nf* : dishonesty

deshonesto, -ta *adj* : dishonest

deshonra *nf* : dishonor, disgrace

deshonrar *vt* : to dishonor, to disgrace

deshonroso, -sa *adj* : dishonorable, disgraceful

deshuesar *vt* **1** : to pit (a fruit, etc.) **2** : to bone, to debone

deshumanizar {21} *vt* : to dehumanize — **deshumanización** *nf*

desidia *nf* **1** APATÍA : apathy, indolence **2** NEGLIGENCIA : negligence, sloppiness

desierto¹, -ta *adj* : deserted, uninhabited

desierto² *nm* : desert

designación *nf, pl* **-ciones** NOMBRAMIENTO : appointment, naming (to an office, etc.)

designar *vt* NOMBRAR : to designate, to appoint, to name

designio *nm* : plan

desigual *adj* **1** : unequal **2** DISPAREJO : uneven

desigualdad *nf* **1** : inequality **2** : unevenness

desilusión *nf, pl* **-siones** DESENCANTO, DESENGAÑO : disillusionment, disenchantment

desilusionar *vt* DESENCANTAR, DESENGAÑAR : to disillusion, to disenchant — **desilusionarse** *vr*

desinfectante *adj & nm* : disinfectant

desinfectar *vt* : to disinfect — **desinfección** *nf*

desinflar *vt* : to deflate — **desinflarse** *vr*

desinhibido, -da *adj* : uninhibited, unrestrained

desintegración *nf, pl* **-ciones** : disintegration

desintegrar *vt* : to disintegrate, to break up — **desintegrarse** *vr*

desinterés *nm* **1** : lack of interest, indifference **2** : unselfishness

desinteresado, -da *adj* GENEROSO : unselfish

desintoxicar {72} *vt* : to detoxify, to detox

desistir *vi* 1 : to desist, to stop 2 ~ **de** : to give up, to relinquish

deslave *nm Mex* : landslide

desleal *adj* INFIEL : disloyal — **deslealmente** *adv*

deslealtad *nf* : disloyalty

desleír {66} *vt* : to dilute, to dissolve

desligar {52} *vt* 1 : to separate, to undo 2 : to free (from an obligation) — **desligarse** *vr* ~ **de** : to extricate oneself from

deslindar *vt* 1 : to mark the limits of, to demarcate 2 : to define, to clarify

deslinde *nm* : demarcation

desliz *nm*, *pl* **deslices** : error, mistake, slip ⟨desliz de la lengua : slip of the tongue⟩

deslizar {21} *vt* 1 : to slide, to slip 2 : to slip in — **deslizarse** *vr* 1 : to slide, to glide 2 : to slip away

deslucido, -da *adj* 1 : unimpressive, dull 2 : faded, dingy, tarnished

deslucir {45} *vt* 1 : to spoil 2 : to fade, to dull, to tarnish 3 : to discredit

deslumbrar *vt* : to dazzle — **deslumbrante** *adj*

deslustrado, -da *adj* : dull, lusterless

deslustrar *vt* : to tarnish, to dull

deslustre *nm* : tarnish

desmán *nm*, *pl* **desmanes** 1 : outrage, abuse 2 : misfortune

desmandarse *vr* : to behave badly, to get out of hand

desmantelar *vt* DESMONTAR : to dismantle

desmañado, -da *adj* : clumsy, awkward

desmayado, -da *adj* 1 : fainting, weak 2 : dull, pale

desmayar *vi* : to lose heart, to falter — **desmayarse** *vr* DESVANECERSE : to faint, to swoon

desmayo *nm* 1 : faint, fainting 2 **sufrir un desmayo** : to faint

desmedido, -da *adj* DESMESURADO : excessive, undue

desmejorar *vt* : to weaken, to make worse — *vi* : to decline (in health), to get worse

desmembramiento *nm* : dismemberment

desmembrar {55} *vt* 1 : to dismember 2 : to break up

desmemoriado, -da *adj* : absentminded, forgetful

desmentido *nm* : denial

desmentir {76} *vt* 1 NEGAR : to deny, to refute 2 CONTRADECIR : to contradict

desmenuzar {21} *vt* 1 : to break down, to scrutinize 2 : to crumble, to shred — **desmenuzarse** *vr*

desmerecer {53} *vt* : to be unworthy of — *vi* 1 : to decline in value 2 ~ **de** : to compare unfavorably with

desmesurado, -da *adj* DESMEDIDO : excessive, inordinate — **desmesuradamente** *adv*

desmigajar *vt* : to crumble — **desmigajarse** *vr*

desmilitarizado, -da *adj* : demilitarized

desmontar *vt* 1 : to clear, to level off 2 DESMANTELAR : to dismantle, to take apart — *vi* : to dismount

desmonte *nm* : clearing, leveling

desmoralizador, -dora *adj* : demoralizing

desmoralizar {21} *vt* DESALENTAR : to demoralize, to discourage

desmoronamiento *nm* : crumbling, falling apart

desmoronar *vt* : to wear away, to erode — **desmoronarse** *vr* : to crumble, to deteriorate, to fall apart

desmotadora *nf* : gin, cotton gin

desmovilizar {21} *vt* : to demobilize — **desmovilización** *nf*

desnaturalizar {21} *vt* 1 : to denature 2 : to distort, to alter

desnivel *nm* 1 : disparity, difference 2 : unevenness (of a surface)

desnivelado, -da *adj* 1 : uneven 2 : unbalanced

desnudar *vt* 1 : to undress 2 : to strip, to lay bare — **desnudarse** *vr* : to undress, to strip off one's clothing

desnudez *nf*, *pl* **-deces** : nudity, nakedness

desnudismo → **nudismo**

desnudista → **nudista**

desnudo[1], -da *adj* : nude, naked, bare

desnudo[2] *nm* : nude

desnutrición *nf*, *pl* **-ciones** MALNUTRICIÓN : malnutrition, undernourishment

desnutrido, -da *adj* MALNUTRIDO : malnourished, undernourished

desobedecer {53} *v* : to disobey

desobediencia *nf* : disobedience — **desobediente** *adj*

desocupación *nf*, *pl* **-ciones** : unemployment

desocupado, -da *adj* 1 : vacant, empty 2 : free, unoccupied 3 : unemployed

desocupar *vt* 1 : to empty 2 : to vacate, to move out of — **desocuparse** *vr* : to leave, to quit (a job)

desodorante *adj & nm* : deodorant

desolación *nf*, *pl* **-ciones** : desolation

desolado, -da *adj* 1 : desolate 2 : devastated, distressed

desolador, -dora *adj* 1 : devastating 2 : bleak, desolate

desollar *vt* : to skin, to flay

desorbitado, -da *adj* 1 : excessive, exorbitant 2 **con los ojos desorbitados** : with eyes popping out of one's head

desorden *nm*, *pl* **desórdenes** 1 DESBARAJUSTE : disorder, mess 2 : disorder, disturbance, upset

desordenado, -da *adj* 1 : untidy, messy 2 : disorderly, unruly

desordenar *vt* : to mess up — **desordenarse** *vr* : to get messed up

desorganización *nf*, *pl* **-ciones** : disorganization

desorganizar {21} *vt* : to disrupt, to disorganize

desorientación *nf, pl* **-ciones** : disorientation, confusion

desorientar *vt* : to disorient, to mislead, to confuse — **desorientarse** *vr* : to become disoriented, to lose one's way

desovar *vi* : to spawn

despachar *vt* **1** : to complete, to conclude **2** : to deal with, to take care of, to handle **3** : to dispatch, to send off **4** *fam* : to finish off, to kill — **despacharse** *vr fam* : to gulp down, to polish off

despacho *nm* **1** : dispatch, shipment **2** OFICINA : office, study

despacio *adv* LENTAMENTE, LENTO : slowly, slow ⟨despacio! : take it easy!, easy does it!⟩

desparasitar *vt* : to worm (an animal), to delouse

desparpajo *nm fam* **1** : self-confidence, nerve **2** *CA* : confusion, muddle

desparramar *vt* **1** : to spill, to splatter **2** : to spread, to scatter

despatarrarse *vr* : to sprawl (out)

despavorido, -da *adj* : terrified, horrified

despecho *nm* **1** : spite **2 a despecho de** : despite, in spite of

despectivo, -va *adj* **1** : contemptuous, disparaging **2** : derogatory, pejorative

despedazar {21} *vt* : to cut to pieces, to tear apart

despedida *nf* **1** : farewell, good-bye **2 despedida de soltera** : bridal shower

despedir {54} *vt* **1** : to see off, to show out **2** : to dismiss, to fire **3** EMITIR : to give off, to emit ⟨despedir un olor : to give off an odor⟩ — **despedirse** *vr* : to take one's leave, to say good-bye

despegado, -da *adj* **1** : separated, detached **2** : cold, distant

despegar {52} *vt* : to remove, to detach — *vi* : to take off, to lift off, to blast off

despegue *nm* : takeoff, liftoff

despeinado, -da *adj* : disheveled, tousled ⟨estoy despeinada : my hair's a mess⟩

despeinarse *vr* **1** : to mess up one's hair **2** : to become disheveled ⟨me despeiné : my hair got messed up⟩

despejado, -da *adj* **1** : clear, fair **2** : alert, clear-headed **3** : uncluttered, unobstructed

despejar *vt* **1** : to clear, to free **2** : to clarify — *vi* **1** : to clear up **2** : to punt (in sports)

despeje *nm* **1** : clearing **2** : punt (in sports)

despellejar *vt* : to skin (an animal)

despenalizar {21} *vt* : to legalize — **despenalización** *nf*

despensa *nf* **1** : pantry, larder **2** PROVISIONES : provisions *pl*, supplies *pl*

despeñar *vt* : to hurl down

despepitar *vt* : to seed, to remove the seeds from

desperdiciar *vt* **1** DESAPROVECHAR, MALGASTAR : to waste **2** : to miss, to miss out on

desperdicio *nm* **1** : waste **2 desperdicios** *nmpl* RESIDUOS : refuse, scraps, rubbish

desperdigar {52} *vt* DISPERSAR : to disperse, to scatter

desperfecto *nm* **1** DEFECTO : flaw, defect **2** : damage

despertador *nm* : alarm clock

despertar {55} *vi* **1** : to awaken, to wake up — *vt* **1** : to arouse, to wake **2** EVOCAR : to elicit, to evoke — **despertarse** *vr* : to wake (oneself) up

despiadado, -da *adj* CRUEL : cruel, merciless, pitiless — **despiadadamente** *adv*

despido *nm* : dismissal, layoff

despierto, -ta *adj* **1** : awake, alert **2** LISTO : clever, sharp ⟨con la mente despierta : with a sharp mind⟩

despilfarrador[1], **-dora** *adj* : extravagant, wasteful

despilfarrador[2], **-dora** *n* : spendthrift, prodigal

despilfarrar *vt* MALGASTAR : to squander, to waste

despilfarro *nm* : extravagance, wastefulness

despintar *vt* : to strip the paint from — **despintarse** *vr* : to fade, to wash off, to peel off

despistado[1], **-da** *adj* **1** DISTRAÍDO : absentminded, forgetful **2** CONFUSO : confused, bewildered

despistado[2], **-da** *n* : scatterbrain, absentminded person

despistar *vt* : to throw off the track, to confuse — **despistarse** *vr*

despiste *nm* **1** : absentmindedness **2** : mistake, slip

desplantador *nm* : garden trowel

desplante *nm* : insolence, rudeness

desplazamiento *nm* **1** : movement, displacement **2** : journey

desplazar {21} *vt* **1** : to replace, to displace **2** TRASLADAR : to move, to shift

desplegar {49} *vt* **1** : to display, to show, to manifest **2** DESDOBLAR : to unfold, to unfurl **3** : to spread (out) **4** : to deploy

despliegue *nm* **1** : display **2** : deployment

desplomarse *vr* **1** : to plummet, to fall **2** DERRUMBARSE : to collapse, to break down

desplome *nm* **1** : fall, drop **2** : collapse

desplumar *vt* : to pluck (a chicken, etc.)

despoblado[1], **-da** *adj* : uninhabited, deserted

despoblado[2] *nm* : open country, deserted area

despoblar {19} *vt* : to depopulate

despojar *vt* **1** : to strip, to clear **2** : to divest, to deprive — **despojarse** *vr* **1** ∼ **de** : to remove (clothing) **2** ∼ **de** : to relinquish, to renounce

despojos *nmpl* **1** : remains, scraps **2** : plunder, spoils

desportilladura *nf* : chip, nick

desportillar *vt* : to chip — **desportillarse** *vr*

desposeer {20} *vt* : to dispossess

déspota *nmf* : despot, tyrant

despotismo *nm* : despotism — **despótico, -ca** *adj*

despotricar {72} *vi* : to rant and rave, to complain excessively

despreciable *adj* **1** : despicable, contemptible **2** : negligible ⟨nada despreciable : not inconsiderable, significant⟩

despreciar *vt* DESDEÑAR, MENOSPRECIAR : to despise, to scorn, to disdain

despreciativo, -va *adj* : scornful, disdainful

desprecio *nm* DESDÉN, MENOSPRECIO : disdain, contempt, scorn

desprender *vt* **1** SOLTAR : to detach, to loosen, to unfasten **2** EMITIR : to emit, to give off — **desprenderse** *vr* **1** : to come off, to come undone **2** : to be inferred, to follow **3** ~ **de** : to part with, to get rid of

desprendido, -da *adj* : generous, unselfish, disinterested

desprendimiento *nm* **1** : detachment **2** GENEROSIDAD : generosity **3 desprendimiento de tierras** : landslide

despreocupación *nf, pl* **-ciones** : indifference, lack of concern

despreocupado, -da *adj* : carefree, easygoing, unconcerned

desprestigiar *vt* DESACREDITAR : to discredit, to disgrace — **desprestigiarse** *vr* : to lose prestige

desprestigio *nm* DESCRÉDITO : discredit, disrepute

desprevenido, -da *adj* DESAPERCIBIDO : unprepared, off guard, unsuspecting

desproporción *nf, pl* **-ciones** : disproportion, disparity

desproporcionado, -da : out of proportion

despropósito *nm* : piece of nonsense, absurdity

desprotegido, -da *adj* : unprotected, vulnerable

desprovisto, -ta *adj* ~ **de** : devoid of, lacking in

después *adv* **1** : afterward, later **2** : then, next **3** ~ **de** : after, next after ⟨después de comer : after eating⟩

después (de) que : after ⟨después que lo acabé : after I finished it⟩ **5 después de todo** : after all **6 poco después** : shortly after, soon thereafter

despuntado, -da *adj* : blunt, dull

despuntar *vt* : to blunt — *vi* **1** : to dawn **2** : to sprout **3** : to excel, to stand out

desquiciar *vt* **1** : to unhinge (a door) **2** : to drive crazy — **desquiciarse** *vr* : to go crazy

desquitar *vr* **1** : to get even, to retaliate **2** ~ **con** : to take it out on

desquite *nm* : revenge

desregulación *nf, pl* **-ciones** : deregulation

desregular *vt* : to deregulate

desregularización *nf* → **desregulación**

destacadamente *adv* : outstandingly, prominently

destacado, -da *adj* **1** : outstanding, prominent **2** : stationed, posted

destacamento *nm* : detachment (of troops)

destacar {72} *vt* **1** ENFATIZAR, SUBRAYAR : to emphasize, to highlight, to stress **2** : to station, to post — *vi* : to stand out

destajo *nm* **1** : piecework **2 a** ~ : by the item, by the job

destapador *nm* : bottle opener

destapar *vt* **1** : to open, to take the top off **2** DESCUBRIR : to reveal, to uncover **3** : to unblock, to unclog

destape *nm* : uncovering, revealing

destartalado, -da *adj* : dilapidated, tumbledown

destellar *vi* **1** : to sparkle, to flash, to glint **2** : to twinkle

destello *nm* **1** : flash, sparkle, twinkle **2** : glimmer, hint

destemplado, -da *adj* **1** : out of tune **2** : irritable, out of sorts **3** : unpleasant (of weather)

desteñir {67} *vi* : to run, to fade — **desteñirse** *vr* DESCOLORARSE : to fade

desterrado[1], **-da** *adj* : banished, exiled

desterrado[2], **-da** *n* : exile

desterrar {55} *vt* **1** EXILIAR : to banish, to exile **2** ERRADICAR : to eradicate, to do away with

destetar *vt* : to wean

destiempo *adv* **a** ~ : at the wrong time

destierro *nm* EXILIO : exile

destilación *nf, pl* **-ciones** : distillation

destilador, -dora *n* : distiller

destilar *vt* **1** : to exude **2** : to distill

destilería *nf* : distillery

destinación *nf, pl* **-ciones** DESTINO : destination

destinado, -da *adj* : destined, bound

destinar *vt* **1** : to appoint, to assign **2** ASIGNAR : to earmark, to allot

destinatario, -ria *n* **1** : addressee **2** : payee

destino *nm* **1** : destiny, fate **2** DESTINACIÓN : destination **3** : use **4** : assignment, post

destitución *nf, pl* **-ciones** : dismissal, removal from office

destituir {41} *vt* : to dismiss, to remove from office

destorcer {14} *vt* : to untwist

destornillador *nm* : screwdriver

destornillar *vt* : to unscrew

destrabar *vt* **1** : to untie, to undo, to ease up **2** : to separate

destreza *nf* HABILIDAD : dexterity, skill

destronar *vt* : to depose, to dethrone

destrozado, -da *adj* **1** : ruined, destroyed **2** : devastated, brokenhearted

destrozar {21} *vt* **1** : to smash, to shatter **2** : to destroy, to wreck — **destrozarse** *vr*

destrozo *nm* **1** DAÑO : damage **2** : havoc, destruction

destrucción *nf, pl* **-ciones** : destruction

destructivo, -va *adj* : destructive

destructor[1], **-tora** *adj* : destructive

destructor[2] *nm* : destroyer (ship)

destruir {41} *vt* : to destroy — **destruirse** *vr*

desubicado, -da *adj* **1** : out of place **2** : confused, disoriented

desunión *nf, pl* **-niones** : disunity

desunir *vt* : to split, to divide

desusado, -da *adj* **1** INSÓLITO : unusual **2** OBSOLETO : obsolete, disused, antiquated

desuso *nm* : disuse, obsolescence ⟨caer en desuso : to fall into disuse⟩

desvaído, -da *adj* **1** : pale, washed-out **2** : vague, blurred

desvainar *vt* : to shell

desvalido, -da *adj* DESAMPARADO : destitute, helpless

desvalijar *vt* **1** : to ransack **2** : to rob

desvalorización *nf, pl* **-ciones 1** DEVALUACIÓN : devaluation **2** : depreciation

desvalorizar {21} *vt* : to devalue

desván *nm, pl* **desvanes** ÁTICO, BUHARDILLA : attic

desvanecer {53} *vt* **1** DISIPAR : to make disappear, to dispel **2** : to fade, to blur — **desvanecerse** *vr* **1** : to vanish, to disappear **2** : to fade **3** DESMAYARSE : to faint, to swoon

desvanecimiento *nm* **1** : disappearance **2** DESMAYO : faint **3** : fading

desvariar {85} *vi* **1** DELIRAR : to be delirious **2** : to rave, to talk nonsense

desvarío *nm* DELIRIO : delirium

desvelado, -da *adj* : sleepless

desvelar *vt* **1** : to keep awake **2** REVELAR : to reveal, to disclose — **desvelarse** *vr* **1** : to stay awake **2** : to do one's utmost

desvelo *nm* **1** : sleeplessness **2** **desvelos** *nmpl* : efforts, pains

desvencijado, -da *adj* : dilapidated, rickety

desventaja *nf* : disadvantage, drawback

desventajoso, -sa *adj* : disadvantageous, unfavorable

desventura *nf* INFORTUNIO : misfortune

desventurado, -da *adj* : unfortunate, ill-fated

desvergonzado, -da *adj* : shameless, impudent

desvergüenza *nf* : shamelessness, impudence

desvestir {54} *vt* : to undress — **desvestirse** *vr* : to get undressed

desviación *nf, pl* **-ciones 1** : deviation, departure **2** : detour, diversion

desviar {85} *vt* **1** : to change the course of, to divert **2** : to turn away, to deflect — **desviarse** *vr* **1** : to branch off **2** APARTARSE : to stray

desvinculación *nf, pl* **-ciones** : dissociation

desvincular *vt* ~ **de** : to separate from, to dissociate from — **desvincularse** *vr*

desvío *nm* **1** : diversion, detour **2** : deviation

desvirtuar {3} *vt* **1** : to impair, to spoil **2** : to detract from **3** : to distort, to misrepresent

detalladamente *adv* : in detail, at great length

detallar *vt* : to detail

detalle *nm* **1** : detail **2 al detalle** : retail

detallista[1] *adj* **1** : meticulous **2** : retail

detallista[2] *nmf* **1** : perfectionist **2** : retailer

detección *nf, pl* **-ciones** : detection

detectar *vt* : to detect — **detectable** *adj*

detective *nmf* : detective

detector *nm* : detector ⟨detector de mentiras : lie detector⟩

detención *nf, pl* **-ciones 1** ARRESTO : detention, arrest **2** : stop, halt **3** : delay, holdup

detener {80} *vt* **1** ARRESTAR : to arrest, to detain **2** PARAR : to stop, to hold **3** : to keep, to hold back — **detenerse** *vr* **1** : to stop **2** : to delay, to linger

detenidamente *adv* : thoroughly, at length

detenimiento *nm* **con** ~ : carefully, in detail

detentar *vt* : to hold, to retain

detergente *nm* : detergent

deteriorado, -da *adj* : damaged, worn

deteriorar *vt* ESTROPEAR : to damage, to spoil — **deteriorarse** *vr* **1** : to get damaged, to wear out **2** : to deteriorate, to worsen

deterioro *nm* **1** : deterioration, wear **2** : worsening, decline

determinación *nf, pl* **-ciones 1** : determination, resolve **2 tomar una determinación** : to make a decision

determinado, -da *adj* **1** : certain, particular **2** : determined, resolute

determinante[1] *adj* : determining, deciding

determinante[2] *nm* : determinant

determinar *vt* **1** : to determine **2** : to cause, to bring about — **determinarse** *vr* : to make up one's mind, to decide

detestar *vt* : to detest — **detestable** *adj*

detonación *nf, pl* **-ciones** : detonation

detonador *nm* : detonator

detonante[1] *adj* : detonating, explosive

detonante[2] *nm* **1** → **detonador 2** : catalyst, cause

detonar *vi* : to detonate, to explode

detractor, -tora *n* : detractor, critic

detrás *adv* **1** : behind **2** ~ **de** : in back of **3 por** ~ : from behind

detrimento *nm* : detriment ⟨en detrimento de : to the detriment of⟩

detuvo, etc. → **detener**

deuda *nf* **1** DÉBITO : debt **2 en deuda con** : indebted to
deudo, -da *n* : relative
deudor¹, -dora *adj* : indebted
deudor², -dora *n* : debtor
devaluación *nf, pl* **-ciones** DESVAL-ORIZACIÓN : devaluation
devaluar {3} *vt* : to devalue — **devaluarse** *vr* : to depreciate
devanarse *vr* **devanarse los sesos** : to rack one's brains
devaneo *nm* **1** : flirtation, fling **2** : idle pursuit
devastador, -dora *adj* : devastating
devastar *vt* : to devastate — **devastación** *nf*
devenir {87} *vi* **1** : to come about **2 ~ en** : to become, to turn into
devoción *nf, pl* **-ciones** : devotion
devolución *nf, pl* **-ciones** REEMBOLSO : return, refund
devolver {89} *vt* **1** : to return, to give back **2** REEMBOLSAR : to refund, to pay back **3** : to vomit, to bring up — *vi* : to vomit, to throw up — **devolverse** *vr* : to return, to come back, to go back
devorar *vt* **1** : to devour **2** : to consume
devoto¹, -ta *adj* : devout — **devotamente** *adv*
devoto², -ta *n* : devotee, admirer
di → dar, decir
día *nm* **1** : day ⟨todos los días : every day⟩ **2** : daytime, daylight ⟨de día : by day, in the daytime⟩ ⟨en pleno día : in broad daylight⟩ **3 al día** : up-to-date **4 en su día** : in due time
diabetes *nf* : diabetes
diabético, -ca *adj & n* : diabetic
diablillo *nm* : little devil, imp
diablo *nm* DEMONIO : devil
diablura *nf* **1** : prank **2 diabluras** *nfpl* : mischief
diabólico, -ca *adj* : diabolical, diabolic, devilish
diaconisa *nf* : deaconess
diácono *nm* : deacon
diacrítico, -ca *adj* : diacritic, diacritical
diadema *nf* : diadem, crown
diáfano, -na *adj* : diaphanous
diafragma *nm* : diaphragm
diagnosticar {72} *vt* : to diagnose
diagnóstico¹, -ca *adj* : diagnostic
diagnóstico² *nm* : diagnosis
diagonal *adj & nf* : diagonal — **diagonalmente** *adv*
diagrama *nm* **1** : diagram **2 diagrama de flujo** ORGANIGRAMA : flowchart
dial *nm* : dial (on a radio, etc.)
dialecto *nm* : dialect
dialogar {52} *vi* : to have a talk, to converse
diálogo *nm* : dialogue
diamante *nm* : diamond
diametral *adj* : diametric, diametrical — **diametralmente** *adv*
diámetro *nm* : diameter
diana *nf* **1** : target, bull's-eye **2 or toque de diana** : reveille

diapositiva *nf* : slide, transparency
diario¹ *adv Mex* : every day, daily
diario², -ria *adj* : daily, everyday — **diariamente** *adv*
diario³ *nm* **1** : diary **2** PERIÓDICO : newspaper
diarrea *nf* : diarrhea
diatriba *nf* : diatribe, tirade
dibujante *nmf* **1** : draftsman *m*, draftswoman *f* **2** CARICATURISTA : cartoonist
dibujar *vt* **1** : to draw, to sketch **2** : to portray, to depict
dibujo *nm* **1** : drawing **2** : design, pattern **3 dibujos animados** : (animated) cartoons
dicción *nf, pl* **-ciones** : diction
diccionario *nm* : dictionary
dícese → decir
dicha *nf* **1** SUERTE : good luck **2** FELICIDAD : happiness, joy
dicho¹ *pp* **→ decir**
dicho², -cha *adj* : said, aforementioned
dicho³ *nm* DECIR : saying, proverb
dichoso, -sa *adj* **1** : blessed **2** FELIZ : happy **3** AFORTUNADO : fortunate, lucky
diciembre *nm* : December
diciendo → decir
dictado *nm* : dictation
dictador, -dora *n* : dictator
dictadura *nf* : dictatorship
dictamen *nm, pl* **dictámenes 1** : report **2** : judgment, opinion
dictaminar *vt* : to report — *vi* : to give an opinion, to pass judgment
dictar *vt* **1** : to dictate **2** : to pronounce (a judgment) **3** : to give, to deliver ⟨dictar una conferencia : to give a lecture⟩
dictatorial *adj* : dictatorial
didáctico, -ca *adj* : didactic
diecinueve *adj & nm* : nineteen
diecinueveavo¹, -va *adj* : nineteenth
diecinueveavo² *nm* : nineteenth (fraction)
dieciocho *adj & nm* : eighteen
dieciochoavo¹, -va *or* **dieciochavo, -va** *adj* : eighteenth
dieciochoavo² *or* **dieciochavo** *nm* : eighteenth (fraction)
dieciséis *adj & nm* : sixteen
dieciseisavo¹, -va *adj* : sixteenth
dieciseisavo² *nm* : sixteenth (fraction)
diecisiete *adj & nm* : seventeen
diecisieteavo¹, -va *adj* : seventeenth
diecisieteavo² *nm* : seventeenth
diente *nm* **1** : tooth ⟨diente canino : eyetooth, canine tooth⟩ **2** : tusk, fang **3** : prong, tine **4 diente de león** : dandelion
dieron, etc. → dar
diesel [ˈdisɛl] *nm* : diesel
diestra *nf* : right hand
diestramente *adv* : skillfully, adroitly
diestro¹, -tra *adj* **1** : right **2** : skillful, accomplished
diestro² *nm* : bullfighter, matador
dieta *nf* : diet

dietética *nf* : dietetics
dietético, -ca *adj* : dietetic
dietista *nmf* : dietitian
diez *adj & nm, pl* **dieces** : ten
difamación *nf, pl* **-ciones** : defamation, slander
difamar *vt* : to defame, to slander
difamatorio, -ria *adj* : slanderous, defamatory, libelous
diferencia *nf* 1 : difference 2 **a diferencia de** : unlike, in contrast to
diferenciación *nf, pl* **-ciones** : differentiation
diferenciar *vt* : to differentiate between, to distinguish — **diferenciarse** *vr* : to differ
diferendo *nm* : dispute, conflict
diferente *adj* DISTINTO : different — **diferentemente** *adv*
diferir {76} *vt* DILATAR, POSPONER : to postpone, to put off — *vi* : to differ
difícil *adj* : difficult, hard
difícilmente *adv* 1 : with difficulty 2 : hardly
dificultad *nf* : difficulty
dificultar *vt* : to make difficult, to obstruct
dificultoso, -sa *adj* : difficult, hard
difteria *nf* : diphtheria
difundir *vt* 1 : to diffuse, to spread out 2 : to broadcast, to spread
difunto, -ta *adj & n* FALLECIDO : deceased
difusión *nf, pl* **-siones** 1 : spreading 2 : diffusion (of heat, etc.) 3 : broadcast, broadcasting ⟨los medios de difusión : the media⟩
difuso, -sa *adj* : diffuse, widespread
diga, etc. → **decir**
digerir {76} *vt* : to digest — **digerible** *adj*
digestión *nf, pl* **-tiones** : digestion
digestivo, -va *adj* : digestive
digital[1] *adj* : digital — **digitalmente** *adv*
digital[2] *nf* 1 DEDALERA : foxglove 2 : digitalis
dígito *nm* : digit
dignarse *vr* : to deign, to condescend ⟨no se dignó contestar : he didn't deign to answer⟩
dignatario, -ria *n* : dignitary
dignidad *nf* 1 : dignity 2 : dignitary
dignificar {72} *vt* : to dignify
digno, -na *adj* 1 HONORABLE : honorable 2 : worthy — **dignamente** *adv*
digresión *nf, pl* **-ciones** : digression
dije *nm* : charm (on a bracelet)
dijo, etc. → **decir**
dilación *nf, pl* **-ciones** : delay
dilapidar *vt* : to waste, to squander
dilatar *vt* 1 : to dilate, to widen, to expand 2 DIFERIR, POSPONER : to put off, to postpone — **dilatarse** *vr* 1 : to expand (of gases, metals, etc.) 2 *Mex* : to take long, to be long
dilatorio, -ria *adj* : dilatory, delaying
dilema *nm* : dilemma
diletante *nmf* : dilettante

diligencia *nf* 1 : diligence, care 2 : promptness, speed 3 : action, step 4 : task, errand 5 : stagecoach 6 **diligencias** *nfpl* : judicial procedures, formalities
diligente *adj* : diligent — **diligentemente** *adv*
dilucidar *vt* : to elucidate, to clarify
dilución *nf, pl* **-ciones** : dilution
diluir {41} *vt* : to dilute
diluviar *v impers* : to pour (with rain), to pour down
diluvio *nm* 1 : flood 2 : downpour
dimensión *nf, pl* **-siones** : dimension — **dimensional** *adj*
dimensionar *vt* : to measure, to gauge
diminutivo[1], **-va** *adj* : diminutive
diminutivo[2] *nm* : diminutive
diminuto, -ta *adj* : minute, tiny
dimisión *nf, pl* **-siones** : resignation
dimitir *vi* : to resign, to step down
dimos → **dar**
dinámica *nf* : dynamics
dinámico, -ca *adj* : dynamic — **dinámicamente** *adv*
dinamismo *nm* : energy, vigor
dinamita *nf* : dynamite
dinamitar *vt* : to dynamite
dínamo *or* **dinamo** *nm* : dynamo
dinastía *nf* : dynasty
dineral *nm* : fortune, large sum of money
dinero *nm* : money
dinosaurio *nm* : dinosaur
dintel *nm* : lintel
dio, etc. → **dar**
diocesano, -na *adj* : diocesan
diócesis *nfs & pl* : diocese
dios, diosa *n* : god, goddess *f*
Dios *nm* : God
diploma *nm* : diploma
diplomacia *nf* : diplomacy
diplomado[1], **-da** *adj* : qualified, trained
diplomado[2] *nm Mex* : seminar
diplomático[1], **-ca** *adj* : diplomatic — **diplomáticamente** *adv*
diplomático[2], **-ca** *n* : diplomat
diptongo *nm* : diphthong
diputación *nf, pl* **-ciones** : deputation, delegation
diputado, -da *n* : delegate, representative
dique *nm* : dike
dirá, etc. → **decir**
dirección *nf, pl* **-ciones** 1 : address 2 : direction 3 : management, leadership 4 : steering (of an automobile)
direccional[1] *adj* : directional
direccional[2] *nf* : directional, turn signal
directa *nf* : high gear
directamente *adv* : straight, directly
directiva *nf* 1 ORDEN : directive 2 DIRECTORIO, JUNTA : board of directors
directivo[1], **-va** *adj* : executive, managerial
directivo[2], **-va** *n* : executive, director
directo, -ta *adj* 1 : direct, straight, immediate 2 **en ∼** : live (in broadcasting)

director, -tora n **1** : director, manager, head **2** : conductor (of an orchestra)
directorial adj : managing, executive
directorio nm **1** : directory **2** DIRECTIVA, JUNTA : board of directors
directriz nf, pl **-trices** : guideline
dirigencia nf : leaders pl, leadership
dirigente¹ adj : directing, leading
dirigente² nmf : director, leader
dirigible nm : dirigible, blimp
dirigir {35} vt **1** : to direct, to lead **2** : to address **3** : to aim, to point **4** : to conduct (music) — **dirigirse** vr ~ **a 1** : to go towards **2** : to speak to, to address
dirimir vt **1** : to resolve, to settle **2** : to annul, to dissolve (a marriage)
discapacidad nf MINUSVALÍA : disability, handicap
discapacitado¹, -da adj : disabled, handicapped
discapacitado², -da n : disabled person, handicapped person
discar {72} v : to dial
discernimiento nm : discernment
discernir {25} v : to discern, to distinguish
disciplina nf : discipline
disciplinar vt : to discipline — **disciplinario, -ria** adj
discípulo, -la n : disciple, follower
disc jockey [ˌdiskˈjoke, -ˈʤo-] nmf : disc jockey
disco nm **1** : phonograph record **2** : disc, disk ⟨disco compacto : compact disc⟩ **3** : discus
díscolo, -la adj : unruly, disobedient
disconforme adj : in disagreement
discontinuidad nf : discontinuity
discontinuo, -nua adj : discontinuous
discordancia nf DESAVENENCIA : conflict, disagreement
discordante adj **1** : discordant **2** : conflicting
discordia nf : discord
discoteca nf **1** : disco, discotheque **2** CA, Mex : record store
discreción nf, pl **-ciones** : discretion
discrecional adj : discretionary
discrepancia nf : discrepancy
discrepar vi **1** : to disagree **2** : to differ
discreto, -ta adj : discreet — **discretamente** adv
discriminación nf, pl **-ciones** : discrimination
discriminar vt **1** : to discriminate against **2** : to distinguish, to differentiate
discriminatorio, -ria adj : discriminatory
disculpa nf **1** : apology **2** : excuse
disculpable adj : excusable
disculpar vt : to excuse, to pardon — **disculparse** vr **1** : to apologize
discurrir vi **1** : to flow **2** : to pass, to go by **3** : to ponder, to reflect
discurso nm **1** ORACIÓN : speech, address **2** : discourse, treatise

discusión nf, pl **-siones 1** : discussion **2** ALTERCADO, DISPUTA : argument
discutible adj : arguable, debatable
discutidor, -dora adj : argumentative
discutir vt **1** : to discuss **2** : to dispute — vi ALTERCAR : to argue, to quarrel
disecar {72} vt **1** : to dissect **2** : to stuff (for preservation)
disección nf, pl **-ciones** : dissection
diseminación nf, pl **-ciones** : dissemination, spreading
diseminar vt : to disseminate, to spread
disensión nf, pl **-siones** : dissension, disagreement
disentería nf : dysentery
disentir {76} vi : to dissent, to disagree
diseñador, -dora n : designer
diseñar vt **1** : to design, to plan **2** : to lay out, to outline
diseño nm : design
disentimiento nm : dissent
disertación nf, pl **-ciones 1** : lecture, talk **2** : dissertation
disertar vi : to lecture, to give a talk
disfraz nm, pl **disfraces 1** : disguise **2** : costume **3** : front, pretense
disfrazar {21} vt **1** : to disguise **2** : to mask, to conceal — **disfrazarse** vr : to wear a costume, to be in disguise
disfrutar vt : to enjoy — vi : to enjoy oneself, to have a good time
disfrute nm : enjoyment
disfunción nf, pl **-ciones** : dysfunction — **disfuncional** adj
disgresión → **digresión**
disgustar vt : to upset, to displease, to make angry — **disgustarse** vr
disgusto nm **1** : annoyance, displeasure **2** : argument, quarrel **3** : trouble, misfortune
disidencia nf : dissidence, dissent
disidente adj & nmf : dissident
disímbolo, -la adj Mex : dissimilar
disímil adj : dissimilar
disimulado, -da adj **1** : concealed, disguised **2** : furtive, sly
disimular vi : to dissemble, to pretend — vt : to conceal, to hide
disimulo nm **1** : dissembling, pretense **2** : slyness, furtiveness **3** : tolerance
disipar vt **1** : to dissipate, to dispel **2** : to squander — **disiparse** vr
diskette [diˈsket] nm : floppy disk, diskette
dislocar {72} vt : to dislocate — **dislocación** nf
disminución nf, pl **-ciones** : decrease, drop, fall
disminuir {41} vt REDUCIR : to reduce, to decrease, to lower — vi **1** : to lower **2** : to drop, to fall
disociación nf, pl **-ciones** : dissociation
disociar vt : to dissociate, to separate
disolución nf, pl **-ciones 1** : dissolution, dissolving **2** : breaking up **3** : dissipation
disoluto, -ta adj : dissolute, dissipated

disolver {89} *vt* **1** : to dissolve **2** : to break up — **disolverse** *vr*

disonancia *nf* : dissonance — **disonante** *adj*

dispar *adj* **1** : different, disparate **2** DIVERSO : diverse **3** DESIGUAL : inconsistent

disparado, -da *adj* **salir disparado** *fam* : to take off in a hurry, to rush away

disparar *vi* **1** : to shoot, to fire **2** *Mex fam* : to pay — *vt* **1** : to shoot **2** *Mex fam* : to treat to, to buy — **dispararse** *vr* : to shoot up, to skyrocket

disparatado, -da *adj* ABSURDO, RIDÍCULO : absurd, ridiculous, crazy

disparate *nm* : silliness, stupidity ⟨decir disparates : to talk nonsense⟩

disparejo, -ja *adj* DESIGUAL : uneven

disparidad *nf* : disparity

disparo *nm* TIRO : shot

dispendio *nm* : wastefulness, extravagance

dispendioso, -sa *adj* : wasteful, extravagant

dispensa *nf* : dispensation

dispensable *adj* **1** : dispensable **2** : excusable

dispensar *vt* **1** : to dispense, to give, to grant **2** EXCUSAR : to excuse, to forgive **3** EXIMIR : to exempt

dispensario *nm* **1** : dispensary, clinic **2** *Mex* : dispenser

dispersar *vt* DESPERDIGAR : to disperse, to scatter

dispersión *nf, pl* **-siones** : dispersion

disperso, -sa *adj* : dispersed, scattered

displicencia *nf* : indifference, coldness, disdain

displicente *adj* : indifferent, cold, disdainful

disponer {60} *vt* **1** : to arrange, to lay out **2** : to stipulate, to order **3** : to prepare — *vi* ~ **de** : to have at one's disposal — **disponerse** *vr* ~ **a** : to prepare to, to be about to

disponibilidad *nf* : availability

disponible *adj* : available

disposición *nf, pl* **-ciones 1** : disposition **2** : aptitude, talent **3** : order, arrangement **4** : willingness, readiness **5 última disposición** : last will and testament

dispositivo *nm* **1** APARATO, MECANISMO : device, mechanism **2** : force, detachment

dispuesto[1] *pp* → **disponer**

dispuesto[2]**, -ta** *adj* PREPARADO : ready, prepared, disposed

dispuso, etc. → **disponer**

disputa *nf* ALTERCADO, DISCUSIÓN : dispute, argument

disputar *vi* : to argue, to contend, to vie — *vt* : to dispute, to question — **disputarse** *vr* : to be in competition for ⟨se disputan la corona : they're fighting for the crown⟩

disquera *nf* : record label, recording company

disquete → **diskette**

disquisición *nf, pl* **-ciones 1** : formal discourse **2 disquisiciones** *nfpl* : digressions

distancia *nf* : distance

distanciamiento *nm* **1** : distancing **2** : rift, estrangement

distanciar *vt* **1** : to space out **2** : to draw apart — **distanciarse** *vr* : to grow apart, to become estranged

distante *adj* **1** : distant, far-off **2** : aloof

distar *vi* ~ **de** : to be far from ⟨dista de ser perfecto : he is far from perfect⟩

diste → **dar**

distender {56} *vt* : to distend, to stretch

distensión *nf, pl* **-siones** : distension

distinción *nf, pl* **-ciones** : distinction

distinguible *adj* : distinguishable

distinguido, -da *adj* : distinguished, refined

distinguir {26} *vt* **1** : to distinguish **2** : to honor — **distinguirse** *vr*

distintivo, -va *adj* : distinctive, distinguishing

distinto, -ta *adj* **1** DIFERENTE : different **2** CLARO : distinct, clear, evident

distorsión *nf, pl* **-siones** : distortion

distorsionar *vt* : to distort

distracción *nf, pl* **-ciones 1** : distraction, amusement **2** : forgetfulness **3** : oversight

distraer {81} *vt* **1** : to distract **2** ENTRETENER : to entertain, to amuse — **distraerse** *vr* **1** : to get distracted **2** : to amuse oneself

distraídamente *adv* : absentmindedly

distraído[1] *pp* → **distraer**

distraído[2]**, -da** *adj* **1** : distracted, preoccupied **2** DESPISTADO : absentminded

distribución *nf, pl* **-ciones** : distribution

distribuidor, -dora *n* : distributor

distribuir {41} *vt* : to distribute

distributivo, -va *adj* : distributive

distrital *adj* : district, of the district

distrito *nm* : district

distrofia *nf* : dystrophy ⟨distrofia muscular : muscular dystrophy⟩

disturbio *nm* : disturbance

disuadir *vt* : to dissuade, to discourage

disuasión *nf, pl* **-siones** : dissuasion

disuasivo, -va *adj* : deterrent, discouraging

disuasorio, -ria *adj* : discouraging

disuelto *pp* → **disolver**

disyuntiva *nf* : dilemma

DIU ['diu] *nm* (*dispositivo intrauterino*) : IUD, intrauterine device

diurético[1]**, -ca** *adj* : diuretic

diurético[2] *nm* : diuretic

diurno, -na *adj* : day, daytime

diva *nf* → **divo**

divagar {52} *vi* : to digress

diván *nm, pl* **divanes** : divan

divergencia *nf* : divergence, difference

divergente *adj* : divergent, differing

divergir {35} *vi* **1** : to diverge **2** : to differ, to disagree

diversidad *nf* : diversity, variety
diversificación *nf, pl* **-ciones** : diversification
diversificar {72} *vt* : to diversify
diversión *nf, pl* **-siones** ENTRETENIMIENTO : fun, amusement, diversion
diverso, -sa *adj* : diverse, various
divertido, -da *adj* **1** : amusing, funny **2** : entertaining, enjoyable
divertir {76} *vt* ENTRETENER : to amuse, to entertain — **divertirse** *vr* : to have fun, to have a good time
dividendo *nm* : dividend
dividir *vt* **1** : to divide, to split **2** : to distribute, to share out — **dividirse** *vr*
divieso *nm* : boil
divinidad *nf* : divinity
divino, -na *adj* : divine
divisa *nf* **1** : currency **2** LEMA : motto **3** : emblem, insignia
divisar *vt* : to discern, to make out
divisible *adj* : divisible
división *nf, pl* **-siones** : division
divisionismo *nm* : factionalism
divisivo, -va *adj* : divisive
divisor *nm* : denominator
divisorio, -ria *adj* : dividing
divo, -va *n* **1** : prima donna **2** : celebrity, star
divorciado¹, -da *adj* **1** : divorced **2** : split, divided
divorciado², -da *n* : divorcé *m,*divorcée *f*
divorciar *vt* : to divorce — **divorciarse** *vr* : to get a divorce
divorcio *nm* : divorce
divulgación *nf, pl* **-ciones** **1** : spreading, dissemination **2** : popularization
divulgar {52} *vt* **1** : to spread, to circulate **2** REVELAR : to divulge, to reveal **3** : to popularize — **divulgarse** *vr*
dizque *adv* : supposedly, apparently
dobladillar *vt* : to hem
dobladillo *nm* : hem
doblar *vt* **1** : to double **2** PLEGAR : to fold, to bend **3** : to turn ⟨doblar la esquina : to turn the corner⟩ **4** : to dub — *vi* **1** : to turn **2** : to toll, to ring — **doblarse** *vr* **1** : to fold up, to double over **2** : to give in, to yield
doble¹ *adj* : double — **doblemente** *adv*
doble² *nm* **1** : double **2** : toll (of a bell), knell
doble³ *nmf* : stand-in, double
doblegar {52} *vt* **1** : to fold, to crease **2** : to force to yield — **doblegarse** *vr* : to yield, to bow
doblez¹ *nm, pl* **dobleces** : fold, crease
doblez² *nmf* : duplicity, deceitfulness
doce *adj & nm* : twelve
doceavo¹, -va *adj* : twelfth
doceavo² *nm* : twelfth (fraction)
docena *nf* **1** : dozen **2 docena de fraile** : baker's dozen
docencia *nf* : teaching
docente¹ *adj* : educational, teaching
docente² *n* : teacher, lecturer
dócil *adj* : docile — **dócilmente** *adv*

docilidad *nf* : docility
docto, -ta *adj* : learned, erudite
doctor, -tora *n* : doctor
doctorado *nm* : doctorate
doctrina *nf* : doctrine — **doctrinal** *adj*
documentación *nf, pl* **-ciones** : documentation
documental *adj & nm* : documentary
documentar *vt* : to document
documento *nm* : document
dogma *nm* : dogma
dogmático, -ca *adj* : dogmatic
dogmatismo *nm* : dogmatism
dólar *nm* : dollar
dolencia *nf* : ailment, malaise
doler {47} *vi* **1** : to hurt, to ache **2** : to grieve — **dolerse** *vr* **1** : to be distressed **2** : to complain
doliente *nmf* : mourner, bereaved
dolor *nm* **1** : pain, ache ⟨dolor de cabeza : headache⟩ **2** PENA, TRISTEZA : grief, sorrow
dolorido, -da *adj* **1** : sore, aching **2** : hurt, upset
doloroso, -sa *adj* **1** : painful **2** : distressing — **dolorosamente** *adv*
doloso, -sa *adj* : fraudulent — **dolosamente** *adv*
domador, -dora *n* : tamer
domar *vt* : to tame, to break in
domesticado, -da *adj* : domesticated, tame
domesticar {72} *vt* : to domesticate, to tame
doméstico, -ca *adj* : domestic, household
domiciliado, -da *adj* : residing
domiciliario, -ria *adj* **1** : home **2 arresto domiciliario** : house arrest
domiciliarse *vr* RESIDIR : to reside
domicilio *nm* : home, residence ⟨cambio de domicilio : change of address⟩
dominación *nf, pl* **-ciones** : domination
dominancia *nf* : dominance
dominante *adj* **1** : dominant **2** : domineering
dominar *vt* **1** : to dominate **2** : to master, to be proficient at — *vi* : to predominate, to prevail — **dominarse** *vr* : to control oneself
domingo *nm* : Sunday
dominical *adj* : Sunday ⟨periódico dominical : Sunday newspaper⟩
dominicano, -na *adj & n* : Dominican
dominio *nm* **1** : dominion, power **2** : mastery **3** : domain, field
dominó *nm, pl* **-nós** **1** : domino (tile) **2** : dominoes *pl* (game)
domo *nm* : dome
don¹ *nm* **1** : gift, present **2** : talent
don² *nm* **1** : title of courtesy preceding a man's first name **2 don nadie** : nobody, insignificant person
dona *nf Mex* : doughnut, donut
donación *nf, pl* **-ciones** : donation
donador, -dora *n* : donor
donaire *nm* **1** GARBO : grace, poise **2** : witticism

donante *nf* → **donador**
donar *vt* : to donate
donativo *nm* : donation
doncella *nf* : maiden, damsel
doncellez *nf* : maidenhood
donde[1] *conj* : where, in which ⟨el pueblo donde vivo : the town where I live⟩
donde[2] *prep* : over by ⟨lo encontré donde la silla : I found it over by the chair⟩
dónde *adv* : where ⟨¿dónde está su casa? : where is your house?⟩
dondequiera *adv* **1** : anywhere, no matter where **2 dondequiera que** : wherever, everywhere
doña *nf* : title of courtesy preceding a woman's first name
doquier *adv* **por ~** : everywhere, all over
dorado[1], **-da** *adj* : gold, golden
dorado[2], **-da** *nm* : gilt
dorar *vt* **1** : to gild **2** : to brown (food)
dormido, -da *adj* **1** : asleep **2** : numb ⟨tiene el pie dormido : her foot's numb, her foot's gone to sleep⟩
dormilón, -lona *n* : sleepyhead, late riser
dormir {27} *vt* : to put to sleep — *vi* : to sleep — **dormirse** *vr* : to fall asleep
dormitar *vi* : to snooze, to doze
dormitorio *nm* **1** : bedroom **2** : dormitory
dorsal[1] *adj* : dorsal
dorsal[2] *nm* : number (worn in sports)
dorso *nm* **1** : back ⟨el dorso de la mano : the back of the hand⟩ **2** *Mex* : backstroke
dos *adj & nm* : two
doscientos[1], **-tas** *adj* : two hundred
doscientos[2] *nms & pl* : two hundred
dosel *nm* : canopy
dosificación *nf, pl* **-ciones** : dosage
dosis *nfs & pl* **1** : dose **2** : amount, quantity
dossier *nm* : dossier
dotación *nf, pl* **-ciones** **1** : endowment, funding **2** : staff, personnel
dotado, -da *adj* **1** : gifted **2 ~ de** : endowed with, equipped with
dotar *vt* **1** : to provide, to equip **2** : to endow
dote *nf* **1** : dowry **2 dotes** *nfpl* : talent, gift
doy → **dar**
draga *nf* : dredge
dragado *nm* : dredging
dragar {52} *vt* : to dredge
dragón *nm, pl* **dragones** **1** : dragon **2** : snapdragon
drague, etc. → **dragar**
drama *nm* : drama
dramático, -ca *adj* : dramatic — **dramáticamente** *adv*
dramatizar {21} *vt* : to dramatize — **dramatización** *nf*
dramaturgo, -ga *n* : dramatist, playwright

drástico, -ca *adj* : drastic — **drásticamente** *adv*
drenaje *nm* : drainage
drenar *vt* : to drain
drene *nm Mex* : drain
driblar *vi* : to dribble (in basketball)
drible *nm* : dribble (in basketball)
droga *nf* : drug
drogadicción *nf, pl* **-ciones** : drug addiction
drogadicto, -ta *n* : drug addict
drogar {52} *vt* : to drug — **drogarse** *vr* : to take drugs
drogue, etc. → **drogar**
droguería *nf* FARMACIA : drugstore
dromedario *nm* : dromedary
dual *adj* : dual
dualidad *nf* : duality
dualismo *nm* : dualism
ducha *nf* : shower ⟨darse una ducha : to take a shower⟩
ducharse *vr* : to take a shower
ducho, -cha *adj* : experienced, skilled, expert
dúctil *adj* : ductile
ducto *nm* **1** : duct, shaft **2** : pipeline
duda *nf* : doubt ⟨no cabe duda : there's no doubt about it⟩
dudar *vt* : to doubt — *vi* **~ en** : to hesitate to ⟨no dudes en pedirme ayuda : don't hesitate to ask me for help⟩
dudoso, -sa *adj* **1** : doubtful **2** : dubious, questionable — **dudosamente** *adv*
duele, etc. → **doler**
duelo *nm* **1** : duel **2** LUTO : mourning
duende *nm* **1** : elf, goblin **2** ENCANTO : magic, charm ⟨una bailarina que tiene duende : a dancer with a certain magic⟩
dueño, -ña *n* **1** : owner, proprietor, proprietress *f* **2** : landlord, landlady *f*
duerme, etc. → **dormir**
dueto *nm* : duet
dulce[1] *adv* : sweetly, softly
dulce[2] *adj* **1** : sweet **2** : mild, gentle, mellow — **dulcemente** *adv*
dulce[3] *nm* : candy, sweet
dulcería *nf* : candy store
dulcificante *nm* : sweetener
dulzura *nf* **1** : sweetness **2** : gentleness, mellowness
duna *nf* : dune
dúo *nm* : duo, duet
duodécimo[1], **-ma** *adj* : twelfth
duodécimo[2], **-ma** *nm* : twelfth (in a series)
dúplex *nms & pl* : duplex apartment
duplicación *nf, pl* **-ciones** : duplication, copying
duplicado *nm* : duplicate, copy
duplicar {72} *vt* **1** : to double **2** : to duplicate, to copy
duplicidad *nf* : duplicity
duque *nm* : duke
duquesa *nf* : duchess
durabilidad *nf* : durability
durable → **duradero**

duración *nf, pl* **-ciones** : duration, length
duradero, -ra *adj* : durable, lasting
duramente *adv* 1 : harshly, severely 2 : hard
durante *prep* : during ⟨durante todo el día : all day long⟩ ⟨trabajó durante tres horas : he worked for three hours⟩
durar *vi* : to last, to endure
durazno *nm* 1 : peach 2 : peach tree

dureza *nf* 1 : hardness, toughness 2 : severity, harshness
durmiente[1] *adj* : sleeping
durmiente[2] *nmf* : sleeper
durmió, etc. → **dormir**
duro[1] *adv* : hard ⟨trabajé tan duro : I worked so hard⟩
duro[2] **, -ra** *adj* 1 : hard, tough 2 : harsh, severe

E

e[1] *nf* : fifth letter of the Spanish alphabet
e[2] *conj* (*used instead of* **y** *before words beginning with* i- *or* hi-) : and
ebanista *nmf* : cabinetmaker
ebanistería *nf* : cabinetmaking
ébano *nm* : ebony
ebriedad *nf* EMBRIAGUEZ : inebriation, drunkenness
ebrio, -bria *adj* EMBRIAGADO : inebriated, drunk
ebullición *nf, pl* **-ciones** : boiling
eccéntrico → **excéntrico**
echar *vt* 1 LANZAR : to throw, to cast, to hurl 2 EXPULSAR : to throw out, to expel 3 EMITIR : to emit, give off 4 BROTAR : to sprout, to put forth 5 DESPEDIR : to fire, to dismiss 6 : to put in, to add 7 **echar a perder** : to spoil, to ruin 8 **echar de menos** : to miss ⟨echan de menos a su madre : they miss their mother⟩ — *vi* 1 : to start off 2 ~ **a** : to begin to — **echarse** *vr* 1 : to throw oneself 2 : to lie down 3 : to put on 4 ~ **a** : to start to 5 **echarse a perder** : to go bad, to spoil 6 **echárselas de** : to pose as
ecléctico, -ca *adj* : eclectic
eclesiástico[1]**, -ca** *adj* : ecclesiastical, ecclesiastic
eclesiástico[2] *nm* CLÉRIGO : cleric, clergyman
eclipsar *vt* 1 : to eclipse 2 : to outshine, to surpass
eclipse *nm* : eclipse
eco *nm* : echo
ecografía *nf* : ultrasound scanning
ecología *nf* : ecology
ecológico, -ca *adj* : ecological — **ecológicamente** *adv*
ecologista *nmf* : ecologist, environmentalist
ecólogo, -ga *n* : ecologist
economía *nf* 1 : economy 2 : economics
económicamente *adv* : financially
económico, -ca *adj* : economic, economical
economista *nmf* : economist
economizar {21} *vt* : to save, to economize on — *vi* : to save up, to be frugal
ecosistema *nm* : ecosystem
ecuación *nf, pl* **-ciones** : equation
ecuador *nm* : equator

ecuánime *adj* 1 : even-tempered 2 : impartial
ecuanimidad *nf* 1 : equanimity 2 : impartiality
ecuatorial *adj* : equatorial
ecuatoriano, -na *adj & n* : Ecuadorian
ecuestre *adj* : equestrian
ecuménico, -ca *adj* : ecumenical
eczema *nm* : eczema
edad *nf* 1 : age ⟨¿qué edad tiene? : how old is she?⟩ 2 ÉPOCA, ERA : epoch, era
edema *nm* : edema
Edén *nm, pl* **Edenes** : Eden, paradise
edición *nf, pl* **-ciones** 1 : edition 2 : publication, publishing
edicto *nm* : edict, proclamation
edificación *nf, pl* **-ciones** 1 : edification 2 : construction, building
edificante *adj* : edifying
edificar {72} *vt* 1 : to edify 2 CONSTRUIR : to build, to construct
edificio *nm* : building, edifice
editar *vt* 1 : to edit 2 PUBLICAR : to publish
editor[1]**, -tora** *adj* : publishing ⟨casa editora : publishing house⟩
editor[2]**, -tora** *n* 1 : editor 2 : publisher
editora *nf* : publisher, publishing company
editorial[1] *adj* 1 : publishing 2 : editorial
editorial[2] *nm* : editorial
editorial[3] *nf* : publishing house
editorializar {21} *vi* : to editorialize
edredón *nm, pl* **-dones** COBERTOR, COLCHA : comforter, eiderdown, quilt
educable *adj* : educable, teachable
educación *nf, pl* **-ciones** 1 ENSEÑANZA : education 2 : manners *pl* — **educacional** *adj*
educado, -da *adj* : polite, well-mannered
educador, -dora *n* : educator
educando, -da *n* ALUMNO, PUPILO : pupil, student
educar {72} *vt* 1 : to educate 2 CRIAR : to bring up, to raise 3 : to train — **educarse** *vr* : to be educated
educativo, -va *adj* : educational
efectista *adj* : dramatic, sensational
efectivamente *adv* : really, actually
efectividad *nf* : effectiveness

efectivo¹, -va *adj* **1** : effective **2** : real, actual **3** : permanent, regular (of employment)

efectivo² *nm* : cash

efecto *nm* **1** : effect **2 en ~** : actually, in fact **3 efectos** *nmpl* : goods, property ⟨efectos personales : personal effects⟩

efectuar {3} *vt* : to carry out, to bring about

efervescencia *nf* **1** : effervescence **2** : vivacity, high spirits *pl*

efervescente *adj* **1** : effervescent **2** : vivacious

eficacia *nf* **1** : effectiveness, efficacy **2** : efficiency

eficaz *adj, pl* **-caces 1** : effective **2** EFICIENTE : efficient — **eficazmente** *adv*

eficiencia *nf* : efficiency

eficiente *adj* EFICAZ : efficient — **eficientemente** *adv*

eficientizar {21} *vt Mex* : to streamline, to make more efficient

efigie *nf* : effigy

efímera *nf* : mayfly

efímero, -ra *adj* : ephemeral

efusión *nf, pl* **-siones 1** : effusion **2** : warmth, effusiveness **3 con ~** : effusively

efusivo, -va *adj* : effusive — **efusivamente** *adv*

egipcio, -cia *adj & n* : Egyptian

eglefino *nm* : haddock

ego *nm* : ego

egocéntrico, -ca *adj* : egocentric, self-centered

egoísmo *nm* : selfishness, egoism

egoísta¹ *adj* : selfish, egoistic

egoísta² *nmf* : egoist, selfish person

egotismo *nm* : egotism, conceit

egotista¹ *adj* : egotistic, egotistical, conceited

egotista² *nmf* : egotist, conceited person

egresado, -da *n* : graduate

egresar *vi* : to graduate

egreso *nm* **1** : graduation **2 ingresos y egresos** : income and expenditure

eh *interj* **1** : hey! **2** : eh?, huh?

eje *nm* **1** : axle **2** : axis

ejecución *nf, pl* **-ciones** : execution

ejecutante *nmf* : performer

ejecutar *vt* **1** : to execute, to put to death **2** : to carry out, to perform

ejecutivo, -va *adj & n* : executive

ejecutor, -tora *n* : executor

ejemplar¹ *adj* : exemplary, model

ejemplar² *nm* **1** : copy (of a book, magazine, etc.) **2** : specimen, example

ejemplificar {72} *vt* : to exemplify, to illustrate

ejemplo *nm* **1** : example **2 por ~** : for example **3 dar ejemplo** : to set an example

ejercer {86} *vi* **~ de** : to practice as, to work as — *vt* **1** : to practice **2** : exercise (a right) **3** : to exert

ejercicio *nm* **1** : exercise **2** : practice

ejercitar *vt* **1** : to exercise **2** ADIESTRAR : to drill, to train

ejército *nm* : army

ejidal *adj Mex* : cooperative

ejido *nm* **1** : common land **2** *Mex* : cooperative

ejote *nm Mex* : green bean

el¹ *pron* (*referring to masculine nouns*) **1** : the one ⟨tengo mi libro y el tuyo : I have my book and yours⟩ ⟨de los cantantes me gusta el de México : I prefer the singer from México⟩ **2 el que** : he who, whoever, the one that ⟨el que vino ayer : the one who came yesterday⟩ ⟨el que trabaja duro estará contento : he who works hard will be happy⟩

el², la *art, pl* **los, las** : the ⟨los niños están en la casa : the boys are in the house⟩ ⟨me duele el pie : my foot hurts⟩

él *pron* : he, him ⟨él es mi amigo : he's my friend⟩ ⟨hablaremos con él : we will speak with him⟩

elaboración *nf, pl* **-ciones 1** PRODUCCIÓN : production, making **2** : preparation, devising

elaborado, -da *adj* : elaborate

elaborar *vt* **1** : to make, to produce **2** : to devise, to draw up

elasticidad *nf* : elasticity

elástico¹, -ca *adj* **1** FLEXIBLE : flexible **2** : elastic

elástico² *nm* **1** : elastic (material) **2** : rubber band

elección *nf, pl* **-ciones 1** SELECCIÓN : choice, selection **2** : election

electivo, -va *adj* : elective

electo, -ta *adj* : elect ⟨el presidente electo : the president-elect⟩

elector, -tora *n* : elector, voter

electorado *nm* : electorate

electoral *adj* : electoral, election

electricidad *nf* : electricity

electricista *nmf* : electrician

eléctrico, -ca *adj* : electric, electrical

electrificar {72} *vt* : to electrify — **electrificación** *nf*

electrizar {21} *vt* : to electrify, to thrill — **electrizante** *adj*

electrocardiógrafo *nm* : electrocardiograph

electrocardiograma *nm* : electrocardiogram

electrocutar *vt* : to electrocute — **electrocución** *nf*

electrodo *nm* : electrode

electrodoméstico *nm* : electric appliance

electroimán *nm, pl* **-manes** : electromagnet

electrólisis *nfs & pl* : electrolysis

electrolito *nm* : electrolyte

electromagnético, -ca *adj* : electromagnetic

electromagnetismo *nm* : electromagnetism

electrón *nm, pl* **-trones** : electron

electrónica *nf* : electronics

electrónico, -ca *adj* : electronic — **electrónicamente** *adv*

elefante, -ta *n* : elephant
elegancia *nf* : elegance
elegante *adj* : elegant, smart — **elegantemente** *adv*
elegía *nf* : elegy
elegíaco, -ca *adj* : elegiac
elegibilidad *nf* : eligibility
elegible *adj* : eligible
elegido, -da *adj* **1** : chosen, selected **2** : elected
elegir {28} *vt* **1** ESCOGER, SELECCIONAR : to choose, to select **2** : to elect
elemental *adj* **1** : elementary, basic **2** : fundamental, essential
elemento *nm* : element
elenco *nm* : cast (of actors)
elepé *nm* : long-playing record
elevación *nf, pl* **-ciones** : elevation, height
elevado, -da *adj* **1** : elevated, lofty **2** : high
elevador *nm* ASCENSOR : elevator
elevar *vt* **1** ALZAR : to raise, to lift **2** AUMENTAR : to raise, to increase **3** : to elevate (in a hierarchy), to promote **4** : to present, to submit — **elevarse** *vr* : to rise
elfo *nm* : elf
eliminación *nf, pl* **-ciones** : elimination, removal
eliminar *vt* **1** : to eliminate, to remove **2** : to do in, to kill
elipse *nf* : ellipse
elipsis *nf* : ellipsis
elíptico, -ca *adj* : elliptical, elliptic
elite *or* **élite** *nf* : elite
elixir *or* **elíxir** *nm* : elixir
ella *pron* : she, her ⟨ella es mi amiga : she is my friend⟩ ⟨nos fuimos con ella : we left with her⟩
ello *pron* : it ⟨es por ello que me voy : that's why I'm going⟩
ellos, ellas *pron pl* **1** : they, them **2 de ellos, de ellas** : theirs
elocución *nf, pl* **-ciones** : elocution
elocuencia *nf* : eloquence
elocuente *adj* : eloquent — **elocuentemente** *adv*
elogiar *vt* ENCOMIAR : to praise
elogio *nm* : praise
elote *nm* **1** *Mex* : corn, maize **2** *CA, Mex* : corncob
elucidación *nf, pl* **-ciones** ESCLARECIMIENTO : elucidation
elucidar *vt* ESCLARECER : to elucidate
eludir *vt* EVADIR : to evade, to avoid, to elude
emanación *nf, pl* **-ciones** : emanation
emanar *vi* ~ **de** : to emanate from — *vt* : to exude
emancipar *vt* : to emancipate — **emancipación** *nf*
embadurnar *vt* EMBARRAR : to smear, to daub
embajada *nf* : embassy
embajador, -dora *n* : ambassador
embalaje *nm* : packing, packaging
embalar *vt* EMPAQUETAR : to pack

embaldosar *vt* : to tile, to pave with tiles
embalsamar *vt* : to embalm
embalsar *vt* : to dam, to dam up
embalse *nm* : dam, reservoir
embarazada *adj* ENCINTA, PREÑADA : pregnant, expecting
embarazar {21} *vt* **1** : to obstruct, to hamper **2** PREÑAR : to make pregnant
embarazo *nm* : pregnancy
embarazoso, -sa *adj* : embarrassing, awkward
embarcación *nf, pl* **-ciones** : boat, craft
embarcadero *nm* : wharf, pier, jetty
embarcar {72} *vi* : to embark, to board — *vt* : to load
embarco *nm* : embarkation
embargar {52} *vt* **1** : to seize, to impound **2** : to overwhelm
embargo *nm* **1** : seizure **2** : embargo **3 sin ~** : however, nevertheless
embarque *nm* **1** : embarkation **2** : shipment
embarrancar {72} *vi* **1** : to run aground **2** : to get bogged down
embarrar *vt* **1** : to cover with mud **2** EMBADURNAR : to smear
embarullar *vt fam* : to muddle, to confuse — **embarullarse** *vr fam* : to get mixed up
embate *nm* **1** : onslaught **2** : battering (of waves or wind)
embaucador, -dora *n* : swindler, deceiver
embaucar {72} *vt* : to trick, to swindle
embeber *vt* : to absorb, to soak up — *vi* : to shrink
embelesado, -da *adj* : spellbound
embelesar *vt* : to enchant, to captivate
embellecer {53} *vt* : to embellish, to beautify
embellecimiento *nm* : beautification, embellishment
embestida *nf* **1** : charge (of a bull) **2** ARREMETIDA : attack, onslaught
embestir {54} *vt* : to hit, to run into, to charge at — *vi* ARREMETER : to charge, to attack
emblanquecer {53} *vt* BLANQUEAR : to bleach, to whiten — **emblanquecerse** *vr* : to turn white
emblema *nm* : emblem
emblemático, -ca *adj* : emblematic
embolia *nf* : embolism
émbolo *nm* : piston
embolsarse *vr* **1** : to pocket (money) **2** : to collect (payment)
emborracharse *vr* EMBRIAGARSE : to get drunk
emborronar *vt* **1** : to blot, to smudge **2** GARABATEAR : to scribble
emboscada *nf* : ambush
emboscar {72} *vt* : to ambush — **emboscarse** *vr* : to lie in ambush
embotadura *nf* : bluntness, dullness
embotar *vt* **1** : to dull, to blunt **2** : to weaken, to enervate
embotellamiento *nm* ATASCO : traffic jam

embotellar vt ENVASAR : to bottle

embragar {52} vi : to engage the clutch

embrague nm : clutch

embravecerse {53} vr **1** : to get furious **2** : to get rough ⟨el mar se embraveció : the sea became tempestuous⟩

embriagado, -da adj : inebriated, drunk

embriagador, -dora adj : intoxicating

embriagarse {52} vr EMBORRACHARSE : to get drunk

embriaguez nf EBRIEDAD : drunkenness, inebriation

embrión nm, pl **embriones** : embryo

embrionario, -ria adj : embryonic

embrollo nm ENREDO : imbroglio, confusion

embrujar vt HECHIZAR : to bewitch

embrujo nm : spell, curse

embudo nm : funnel

embuste nm **1** MENTIRA : lie, fib **2** ENGAÑO : trick, hoax

embustero¹, -ra adj : lying, deceitful

embustero², -ra n : liar, cheat

embutido nm **1** : sausage **2** : inlaid work

embutir vt **1** : to cram, to stuff, to jam **2** : to inlay

emergencia nf **1** : emergency **2** : emergence

emergente adj **1** : emergent **2** : consequent, resultant

emerger {15} vi : to emerge, to surface

emético¹, -ca adj : emetic

emético² nm : emetic

emigración nf, pl **-ciones 1** : emigration **2** : migration

emigrante adj & nmf : emigrant

emigrar vi **1** : to emigrate **2** : to migrate

eminencia nf : eminence

eminente adj : eminent, distinguished

eminentemente adv : basically, essentially

emisario¹, -ria n : emissary

emisario² nm : outlet (of a body of water)

emisión nf, pl **-siones 1** : emission **2** : broadcast **3** : issue ⟨emisión de acciones : stock issue⟩

emisor nm TRANSMISOR : television or radio transmitter

emisora nf : radio station

emitir vt **1** : to emit, to give off **2** : to broadcast **3** : to issue **4** : to cast (a vote)

emoción nf, pl **-ciones** : emotion — **emocional** adj — **emocionalmente** adv

emocionado, -da adj **1** : moved, affected by emotion **2** ENTUSIASMADO : excited

emocionante adj **1** CONMOVEDOR : moving, touching **2** EXCITANTE : exciting, thrilling

emocionar vt **1** CONMOVER : to move, to touch **2** : to excite, to thrill — **emocionarse** vr

emotivo, -va adj : emotional, moving

empacador, -dora n : packer

empacar {72} vt **1** EMPAQUETAR : to pack **2** : to bale — vi : to pack — **empacarse** vr **1** : to balk, to refuse to budge **2** Col, Mex fam : to eat ravenously, to devour

empachar vt **1** ESTORBAR : to obstruct **2** : to give indigestion to **3** DISFRAZAR : to disguise, to mask — **empacharse** vr **1** INDIGESTARSE : to get indigestion **2** AVERGONZARSE : to be embarrassed

empacho nm **1** INDIGESTIÓN : indigestion **2** VERGÜENZA : embarrassment **3** **no tener empacho en** : to have no qualms about

empadronarse vr : to register to vote

empalagar {52} vt **1** : to cloy, to surfeit **2** FASTIDIAR : to annoy, to bother

empalagoso, -sa adj MELOSO : cloying, excessively sweet

empalar vt : to impale

empalizada nf : palisade (fence)

empalmar vt **1** : to splice, to link **2** : to combine — vi : to meet, to converge

empalme nm **1** CONEXIÓN : connection, link **2** : junction

empanada nf : pie, turnover

empanadilla nf : meat or seafood pie

empanar vt : to bread

empantanado, -da adj : bogged down, delayed

empañar vt **1** : to steam up **2** : to tarnish, to sully

empapado, -da adj : soggy, sodden

empapar vt MOJAR : to soak, to drench — **empaparse** vr **1** : to get soaking wet **2 ~ de** : to absorb, to be imbued with

empapelar vt : to wallpaper

empaque nm fam **1** : presence, bearing **2** : pomposity **3** DESCARO : impudence, nerve

empaquetar vt EMBALAR : to pack, to package — **empaquetarse** vr fam : to dress up

emparedado nm : sandwich

emparedar vt : to wall in, to confine

emparejar vt **1** : to pair, to match up **2** : to make even — vi : to catch up — **emparejarse** vr : to pair up

emparentado, -da adj : related

emparentar {55} vi : to become related by marriage

emparrillado nm Mex : gridiron (in football)

empastar vt **1** : to fill (a tooth) **2** : to bind (a book)

empaste nm : filling (of a tooth)

empatar vt : to tie, to connect — vi : to result in a draw, to be tied — **empatarse** vr Ven : to hook up, to link together

empate nm : draw, tie

empatía nf : empathy

empecinado, -da adj TERCO : stubborn

empecinarse vr OBSTINARSE : to be stubborn, to persist

empedernido, -da adj INCORREGIBLE : hardened, inveterate

empedrado nm : paving, pavement

empedrar {55} *vt* : to pave (with stones)

empeine *nm* : instep

empellón *nm, pl* **-llones** : shove, push

empelotado, -da *adj* 1 *Mex fam* : madly in love 2 *fam* : stark naked

empeñado, -da *adj* : determined, committed

empeñar *vt* 1 : to pawn 2 : to pledge, to give (one's word) — **empeñarse** *vr* 1 : to insist stubbornly 2 : to make an effort

empeño *nm* 1 : pledge, commitment 2 : insistence 3 ESFUERZO : effort, determination 2 : pawning ⟨casa de empeños : pawnshop⟩

empeoramiento *nm* : worsening, deterioration

empeorar *vi* : to deteriorate, to get worse — *vt* : to make worse

empequeñecer {53} *vi* : to diminish, to become smaller — *vt* : to minimize, to make smaller

emperador *nm* : emperor

emperatriz *nf, pl* **-trices** : empress

empero *conj* : however, nevertheless

empezar {29} *v* COMENZAR : to start, to begin

empinado, -da *adj* : steep

empinar *vt* ELEVAR : to lift, to raise — **empinarse** *vr* : to stand on tiptoe

empírico, -ca *adj* : empirical — **empíricamente** *adv*

emplasto *nm* : poultice, dressing

emplazamiento *nm* 1 : location, site 2 CITACIÓN : summons, subpoena

emplazar {21} *vt* 1 CONVOCAR : to convene, to summon 2 : to subpoena 3 UBICAR : to place, to position

empleado, -da *n* : employee

empleador, -dora *n* PATRÓN : employer

emplear *vt* 1 : to employ 2 USAR : to use — **emplearse** *vr* 1 : to get a job 2 : to occupy oneself

empleo *nm* 1 OCUPACIÓN : employment, occupation, job 2 : use, usage

empobrecer {53} *vt* : to impoverish — *vi* : to become poor — **empobrecerse** *vr*

empobrecimiento *nm* : impoverishment

empollar *vi* : to brood eggs — *vt* : to incubate

empolvado, -da *adj* 1 : dusty 2 : powdered, powdery

empolvar *vt* 1 : to cover with dust 2 : to powder — **empolvarse** *vr* 1 : to gather dust 2 : to powder one's face

emporio *nm* 1 : center, capital, empire ⟨un emporio cultural : a cultural center⟩ ⟨un emporio financiero : a financial empire⟩ 2 : department store

empotrado, -da *adj* : built-in ⟨armarios empotrados : built-in cabinets⟩

empotrar *vt* : to build into, to embed

emprendedor, -dora *adj* : enterprising

emprender *vt* : to undertake, to begin

empresa *nf* 1 COMPAÑÍA, FIRMA : company, corporation, firm 2 : undertaking, venture

empresariado *nm* 1 : business world 2 : management, managers *pl*

empresarial *adj* : business, managerial, corporate

empresario, -ria *n* 1 : manager 2 : businessman *m*, businesswoman *f* 3 : impresario

empréstito *nm* : loan

empujar *vi* : to push, to shove — *vt* 1 : to push 2 PRESIONAR : to spur on, to press

empuje *nm* : impetus, drive

empujón *nm, pl* **-jones** : push, shove

empuñadura *nf* MANGO : hilt, handle

empuñar *vt* 1 ASIR : to grasp 2 **empuñar las armas** : to take up arms

emú *nm* : emu

emular *vt* IMITAR : to emulate — **emulación** *nf*

emulsión *nf, pl* **-siones** : emulsion

emulsionante *nm* : emulsifier

emulsionar *vt* : to emulsify

en *prep* 1 : in ⟨en el bolsillo : in one's pocket⟩ ⟨en una semana : in a week⟩ 2 : on ⟨en la mesa : on the table⟩ 3 : at ⟨en casa : at home⟩ ⟨en el trabajo : at work⟩ ⟨en ese momento : at that moment⟩

enagua *nf* : petticoat, slip

enajenación *nf, pl* **-ciones** 1 : transfer (of property) 2 : alienation 3 : absentmindedness

enajenado, -da *adj* : out of one's mind

enajenar *vt* 1 : to transfer (property) 2 : to alienate 3 : to enrapture — **enajenarse** *vr* 1 : to become estranged 2 : to go mad

enaltecer {53} *vt* : to praise, to extol

enamorado¹, -da *adj* : in love

enamorado², -da *n* : lover, sweetheart

enamoramiento *nm* : infatuation, crush

enamorar *vt* : to enamor, to win the love of — **enamorarse** *vr* : to fall in love

enamoriscarse {72} *vr fam* : to have a crush, to be infatuated

enamorizado, -da *adj* : amorous, passionate

enano¹, -na *adj* : tiny, minute

enano², -na *n* : dwarf, midget

enarbolar *vt* 1 : to hoist, to raise 2 : to brandish

enarcar {72} *vt* : to arch, to raise

enardecer {53} *vt* 1 : to arouse (anger, passions) 2 : to stir up, to excite — **enardecerse** *vr*

encabezado *nm Mex* : headline

encabezamiento *nm* 1 : heading 2 : salutation, opening

encabezar {21} *vt* 1 : to head, to lead 2 : to put a heading on

encabritarse *vr* 1 : to rear up 2 *fam* : to get angry

encadenar *vt* 1 : to chain 2 : to connect, to link 3 INMOVILIZAR : to immobilize

encajar vi : to fit, to fit together, to fit in — vt 1 : to insert, to stick 2 : to take, to cope with ⟨encajó el golpe : he withstood the blow⟩
encaje nm 1 : lace 2 : financial reserve
encajonar vt 1 : to box, to crate 2 : to cram in
encalar vt : to whitewash
encallar vi 1 : to run aground 2 : to get stuck
encallecido, -da adj : callused
encamar vt : to confine to a bed
encaminado, -da adj 1 : on the right track 2 ~ a : aimed at, designed to
encaminar vt 1 : to direct, to channel 2 : to head in the right direction — **encaminarse** vr ~ a : to head for, to aim at
encandilar vt : to dazzle
encanecer {53} vi : to gray, to go gray
encantado, -da adj 1 : charmed, bewitched 2 : delighted
encantador[1], **-dora** adj : charming, delightful
encantador[2], **-dora** n : magician
encantamiento nm : enchantment, spell
encantar vt 1 : to enchant, to bewitch 2 : to charm, to delight ⟨me encanta esta canción : I love this song⟩
encanto nm 1 : charm, fascination 2 HECHIZO : spell 3 : delightful person or thing
encañonar vt : to point (a gun) at, to hold up
encapotado, -da adj : cloudy, overcast
encapotarse vr : to cloud over, to become overcast
encaprichado, -da adj : infatuated
encaprichamiento nm : infatuation
encapuchado, -da adj : hooded
encarado, -da adj estar mal encarado fam : to be ugly-looking, to look mean
encaramar vt : to raise, to lift up — **encaramarse** vr : to perch
encarar vt CONFRONTAR : to face, to confront
encarcelación nf → encarcelamiento
encarcelamiento nm : incarceration, imprisonment
encarcelar vt : to incarcerate, to imprison
encarecer {53} vt 1 : to increase, to raise (price, value) 2 : to beseech, to entreat — **encarecerse** vr : to become more expensive
encarecidamente adv : insistently, urgently
encarecimiento nm : increase, rise (in price)
encargado[1], **-da** adj : in charge
encargado[2], **-da** n : manager, person in charge
encargar {52} vt 1 : to put in charge of 2 : to recommend, to advise 3 : to order, to request — **encargarse** vr ~ de : to take charge of
encargo nm 1 : errand 2 : job assignment 3 : order ⟨hecho de encargo : custom-made, made to order⟩

encariñarse vr ~ con : to become fond of, to grow attached to
encarnación nf, pl -ciones : incarnation, embodiment
encarnado[1], **-da** adj 1 : incarnate 2 : flesh-colored 3 : red 4 : ingrown
encarnado[2] nm : red
encarnar vt : to incarnate, to embody — **encarnarse** vr encarnarse una uña : to have an ingrown nail
encarnizado, -da adj 1 : bloodshot, inflamed 2 : fierce, bloody
encarnizar {21} vt : to enrage, to infuriate — **encarnizarse** vr : to be brutal, to attack viciously
encarrilar vt : to guide, to put on the right track
encasillar vt CLASIFICAR : to classify, to pigeonhole, to categorize
encausar vt : to prosecute, to charge
encauzar {21} vt : to channel, to guide — **encauzarse** vr
encebollado, -da adj : cooked with onions
encefalitis nms & pl : encephalitis
enceguecedor, -dora n : blinding
encendedor nm : lighter
encender {56} vi : to light — vt 1 : to light, to set fire to 2 PRENDER : to switch on 3 : to start (a motor) 4 : to arouse, to kindle — **encenderse** vr 1 : to get excited 2 : to blush
encendido[1], **-da** adj 1 : burning 2 : flushed 3 : fiery, passionate
encendido[2] nm : ignition
encerado nm 1 : waxing, polishing 2 : blackboard
encerar vt : to wax, to polish
encerrar {55} vt 1 : to lock up, to shut away 2 : to contain, to include 3 : to involve, to entail
encerrona nf 1 TRAMPA : trap, setup 2 prepararle una encerrona a alguien : to set a trap for someone, to set someone up
encestar vi : to make a basket (in basketball)
enchapado nm : plating, coating (of metal)
encharcamiento nm : flood, flooding
encharcar {72} vt : to flood, to swamp — **encharcarse** vr
enchilada nf : enchilada
enchilar vt Mex : to season with chili
enchuecar {72} vt Chile, Mex fam : to make crooked, to twist
enchufar vt 1 : to plug in 2 : to connect, to fit together
enchufe nm 1 : connection 2 : plug, socket
encía nf : gum (tissue)
encíclica nf : encyclical
enciclopedia nf : encyclopedia
enciclopédico, -ca adj : encyclopedic
encierro nm 1 : confinement 2 : enclosure
encima adv 1 : on top, above 2 ADEMÁS : as well, besides 3 ~ de : on, on top

of, over **4 por encima de** : above, beyond ⟨**por encima de la ley** : above the law⟩ **5 echarse encima** : to take upon oneself **6 estar encima de** *fam* : to nag, to criticize **7 quitarse de encima** : to get rid of

encina *nf* : evergreen oak

encinta *adj* EMBARAZADA, PREÑADA : pregnant, expecting

enclaustrado, -da *adj* : cloistered, shut away

enclavado, -da *adj* : buried

enclenque *adj* : weak, sickly

encoger {15} *vt* 1 : to shrink, to make smaller 2 : to intimidate — *vi* : to shrink, to contract — **encogerse** *vr* 1 : to shrink 2 : to be intimidated, to cower, to cringe **3 encogerse de hombros** : to shrug (one's shoulders)

encogido, -da *adj* 1 : shriveled, shrunken 2 TÍMIDO : shy, inhibited

encogimiento *nm* 1 : shrinking, shrinkage 2 : shrug 3 TIMIDEZ : shyness

encolar *vt* : to paste, to glue

encolerizar {21} *vt* ENFURECER : to enrage, to infuriate — **encolerizarse** *vr*

encomendar {55} *vt* CONFIAR : to entrust, to commend — **encomendarse** *vr*

encomiable *adj* : commendable, praiseworthy

encomiar *vt* ELOGIAR : to praise, to pay tribute to

encomienda *nf* 1 : charge, mission 2 : royal land grant 3 : parcel

encomio *nm* : praise, eulogy

encomioso, -sa *adj* : eulogistic, laudatory

enconar *vt* 1 : to irritate, to anger 2 : to inflame — **enconarse** *vr* 1 : to become heated 2 : to fester

encono *nm* 1 RENCOR : animosity, rancor 2 : inflammation, infection

encontrado, -da *adj* : contrary, opposing

encontrar {19} *vt* 1 HALLAR : to find 2 : to encounter, to meet — **encontrarse** *vr* 1 REUNIRSE : to meet 2 : to clash, to conflict 3 : to be ⟨su abuelo se encuentra mejor : her grandfather is doing better⟩

encorvar *vt* : to bend, to curve — **encorvarse** *vr* : to hunch over, to stoop

encrespar *vt* 1 : to curl, to ruffle, to ripple 2 : to annoy, to irritate — **encresparse** *vr* 1 : to curl one's hair 2 : to become choppy 3 : to get annoyed

encrucijada *nf* : crossroads

encuadernación *nf, pl* **-ciones** : bookbinding

encuadernar *vt* EMPASTAR : to bind (a book)

encuadrar *vt* 1 ENMARCAR : to frame 2 ENCAJAR : to fit, to insert 3 COMPRENDER : to contain, to include

encubierto *pp* → **encubrir**

encubrimiento *nm* : cover-up

encubrir {2} *vt* : to cover up, to conceal

encuentro *nm* 1 : meeting, encounter 2 : conference, congress

encuerado, -da *adj fam* : naked

encuerar *vt fam* : to undress

encuesta *nf* 1 INVESTIGACIÓN, PESQUISA : inquiry, investigation 2 SONDEO : survey

encuestador, -dora *n* : pollster

encuestar *vt* : to poll, to take a survey of

encumbrado, -da *adj* 1 : lofty, high 2 : eminent, distinguished

encumbrar *vt* 1 : to exalt, to elevate 2 : to extol — **encumbrarse** *vr* : to reach the top

encurtir *vt* ESCABECHAR : to pickle

ende *adv* **por ~** : therefore, consequently

endeble *adj* : feeble, weak

endeblez *nf* : weakness, frailty

endémico, -ca *adj* : endemic

endemoniado, -da *adj* : fiendish, diabolical

endentecer {53} *vi* : to teethe

enderezar {21} *vt* 1 : to straighten (out) 2 : to stand on end, to put upright

endeudado, -da *adj* : in debt, indebted

endeudamiento *nm* : indebtedness

endeudarse *vr* 1 : to go into debt 2 : to feel obliged

endiabladamente *adv* : extremely, diabolically

endiablado, -da *adj* 1 : devilish, diabolical 2 : complicated, difficult

endibia *or* **endivia** *nf* : endive

endilgar {52} *vt fam* : to spring, to foist ⟨me endilgó la responsabilidad : he saddled me with the responsibility⟩

endocrino, -na *adj* : endocrine

endogamia *nf* : inbreeding

endosar *vt* : to endorse

endoso *nm* : endorsement

endulzante *nm* : sweetener

endulzar {21} *vt* 1 : to sweeten 2 : to soften, to mellow — **endulzarse** *vr*

endurecer {53} *vt* : to harden, to toughen — **endurecerse** *vr*

enebro *nm* : juniper

eneldo *nm* : dill

enema *nm* : enema

enemigo, -ga *adj & n* : enemy

enemistad *nf* : enmity, hostility

enemistar *vt* : to make enemies of — **enemistarse** *vr* **con** : to fall out with

energía *nf* : energy

enérgico, -ca *adj* 1 : energetic, vigorous 2 : forceful, emphatic — **enérgicamente** *adv*

energúmeno, -na *n fam* : lunatic, crazy person

enero *nm* : January

enervar *vt* 1 : to enervate 2 *fam* : to annoy, to get on one's nerves — **enervante** *adj*

enésimo, -ma *adj* : umpteenth, nth

enfadar *vt* 1 : to annoy, to make angry 2 *Mex fam* : to bore — **enfadarse** *vr* : to get angry, to get annoyed

enfado *nm* : anger, annoyance
enfadoso, -sa *adj* : irritating, annoying
enfardar *vt* : to bale
énfasis *nms & pl* : emphasis
enfático, -ca *adj* : emphatic — **enfáticamente** *adv*
enfatizar {21} *vt* DESTACAR, SUBRAYAR : to emphasize
enfermar *vt* : to make sick — *vi* : to fall ill, to get sick — **enfermarse** *vr*
enfermedad *nf* 1 INDISPOSICIÓN : sickness, illness 2 : disease
enfermería *nf* : infirmary
enfermero, -ra *n* : nurse
enfermizo, -za *adj* : sickly
enfermo¹, -ma *adj* : sick, ill
enfermo², -ma *n* 1 : sick person, invalid 2 PACIENTE : patient
enfilar *vt* 1 : to take, to go along ⟨enfiló la carretera de Montevideo : she went up the road to Montevideo⟩ 2 : to line up, to put in a row 3 : to string, to thread 4 : to aim, to direct — *vi* : to make one's way
enflaquecer {53} *vi* : to lose weight, to become thin — *vt* : to emaciate
enfocar {72} *vt* 1 : to focus (on) 2 : to consider, to look at
enfoque *nm* : focus
enfrascamiento *nm* : immersion, absorption
enfrascarse {72} *vr* ~ **en** : to immerse oneself in, to get caught up in
enfrentamiento *nm* : clash, confrontation
enfrentar *vt* : to confront, to face — **enfrentarse** *vr* 1 ~ **con** : to clash with 2 ~ **a** : to face up to
enfrente *adv* 1 DELANTE : in front 2 : opposite
enfriamiento *nm* 1 CATARRO : chill, cold 2 : cooling off, damper
enfriar {85} *vt* 1 : to chill, to cool 2 : to cool down, to dampen — *vi* : to get cold — **enfriarse** *vr* : to get chilled, to catch a cold
enfundar *vt* : to sheathe, to encase
enfurecer {53} *vt* ENCOLERIZAR : to infuriate — **enfurecerse** *vr* : to fly into a rage
enfurecido, -da *adj* : furious, raging
enfurruñarse *vr fam* : to sulk
engalanar *vt* : to decorate, to deck out — **engalanarse** *vr* : to dress up
enganchar *vt* 1 : to hook, to snag 2 : to attach, to hitch up — **engancharse** *vr* 1 : to get snagged, to get hooked 2 : to enlist
enganche *nm* 1 : hook 2 : coupling, hitch 3 *Mex* : down payment
engañar *vt* 1 EMBAUCAR : to trick, to deceive, to mislead 2 : to cheat on, to be unfaithful to — **engañarse** *vr* 1 : to be mistaken 2 : to deceive oneself
engaño *nm* 1 : deception, trick 2 : fake, feint (in sports)
engañoso, -sa *adj* 1 : deceitful 2 : misleading, deceptive

engarrotarse *vr* : to stiffen up, to go numb
engatusamiento *nm* : cajolery
engatusar *vt* : to coax, to cajole
engendrar *vt* 1 : to beget, to father 2 : to give rise to, to engender
engentarse *vr Mex* : to be in a daze
englobar *vt* : to include, to embrace
engomar *vt* : to glue
engordar *vt* : to fatten, to fatten up — *vi* : to gain weight
engorro *nm* : nuisance, bother
engorroso, -sa *adj* : bothersome
engranaje *nm* : gears *pl*, cogs *pl*
engranar *vt* : to mesh, to engage — *vi* : to mesh gears
engrandecer {53} *vt* 1 : to enlarge 2 : to exaggerate 3 : to exalt
engrandecimiento *nm* 1 : enlargement 2 : exaggeration 3 : exaltation
engrane *nm Mex* : cogwheel
engrapadora *nf* : stapler
engrapar *vt* : to staple
engrasar *vt* : to grease, to lubricate
engrase *nm* : greasing, lubrication
engreído, -da *adj* PRESUMIDO, VANIDOSO : vain, conceited, stuck-up
engreimiento *nm* ARROGANCIA : arrogance, conceit
engreír {66} *vt* ENVANECER : to make vain — **engreírse** *vr* : to become conceited
engrosar {19} *vt* : to enlarge, to increase, to swell — *vi* ENGORDAR : to gain weight
engrudo *nm* : paste
engullir {38} *vt* : to gulp down, to gobble up — **engullirse** *vr*
enharinar *vt* : to flour
enhebrar *vt* ENSARTAR : to string, to thread
enhiesto, -ta *adj* 1 : erect, upright 2 : lofty, towering
enhilar *vt* : to thread (a needle, etc.)
enhorabuena *nf* FELICIDADES : congratulations *pl*
enigma *nm* : enigma, mystery
enigmático, -ca *adj* : enigmatic — **enigmáticamente** *adv*
enjabonar *vt* : to soap up, to lather — **enjabonarse** *vr*
enjaezar {21} *vt* : to harness
enjalbegar {52} *vt* : to whitewash
enjambrar *vi* : to swarm
enjambre *nm* 1 : swarm 2 MUCHEDUMBRE : crowd, mob
enjaular *vt* 1 : to cage 2 *fam* : to jail, to lock up
enjuagar {52} *vt* : to rinse — **enjuagarse** *vr* : to rinse out
enjuague *nm* 1 : rinse 2 **enjuague bucal** : mouthwash
enjugar {52} *vt* : to wipe away (tears)
enjuiciar *vt* 1 : to indict, to prosecute 2 JUZGAR : to try
enjundioso, -sa *adj* : substantial, weighty
enjuto, -ta *adj* : lean, gaunt

enlace *nm* 1 : bond, link, connection 2 : liaison
enladrillado *nm* : brick paving
enladrillar *vt* : to pave with bricks
enlatar *vt* ENVASAR : to can
enlazar {21} *v* : to join, to link, to fit together
enlistar *vt* : to list — **enlistarse** *vr* : to enlist
enlodado, -da *adj* BARROSO : muddy
enlodar *vt* 1 : to cover with mud 2 : to stain, to sully — **enlodarse** *vr*
enlodazar → **enlodar**
enloquecedor, -dora *adj* : maddening
enloquecer {53} *vt* ALOCAR : to drive crazy — **enloquecerse** *vr* : to go crazy
enlosado *nm* : flagstone pavement
enlosar *vt* : to pave with flagstone
enlutarse *vr* : to go into mourning
enmaderado *nm* 1 : wood paneling 2 : hardwood floor
enmarañar *vt* 1 : to tangle 2 : to complicate 3 : to confuse, to mix up — **enmarañarse** *vr*
enmarcar {72} *vt* ENCUADRAR : to frame 2 : to provide the setting for
enmascarar *vt* : to mask, to disguise
enmasillar *vt* : to putty, to caulk
enmendar {55} *vt* 1 : to amend 2 CORREGIR : to emend, to correct 3 COMPENSAR : to compensate for — **enmendarse** *vr* : to mend one's ways
enmienda *nf* 1 : amendment 2 : correction, emendation
enmohecerse {53} *vr* 1 : to become moldy 2 OXIDARSE : to rust, to become rusty
enmudecer {53} *vt* : to mute, to silence — *vi* : to fall silent
enmugrar *vt* : to soil, to make dirty — **enmugrarse** *vr* : to get dirty
ennegrecer {53} *vt* : to blacken, to darken — **ennegrecerse** *vr*
ennoblecer {53} *vt* 1 : to ennoble 2 : to embellish
enojadizo, -za *adj* IRRITABLE : irritable, cranky
enojado, -da *adj* 1 : annoyed 2 : angry, mad
enojar *vt* 1 : to anger 2 : to annoy, to upset — **enojarse** *vr*
enojo *nm* 1 CÓLERA : anger 2 : annoyance
enojón, -jona *adj, pl* **-jones** *Chile, Mex fam* : irritable, cranky
enojoso, -sa *adj* FASTIDIOSO, MOLESTOSO : annoying, irritating
enorgullecer {53} *vt* : to make proud — **enorgullecerse** *vr* : to pride oneself
enorme *adj* INMENSO : enormous, huge — **enormemente** *adv*
enormidad *nf* 1 : enormity, seriousness 2 : immensity, hugeness
enraizado, -da *adj* : deep-seated, deeply rooted
enraizar {30} *vi* : to take root
enramada *nf* : arbor, bower
enramar *vt* : to cover with branches

enrarecer {53} *vt* : to rarefy — **enrarecerse** *vr*
enredadera *nf* : climbing plant, vine
enredar *vt* 1 : to tangle up, to entangle 2 : to confuse, to complicate 3 : to involve, to implicate — **enredarse** *vr*
enredo *nm* 1 EMBROLLO : muddle, confusion 2 MARAÑA : tangle
enredoso, -sa *adj* : complicated, tricky
enrejado *nm* 1 : railing 2 : grating, grille 3 : trellis, lattice
enrevesado, -da *adj* : complicated, involved
enriquecer {53} *vt* : to enrich — **enriquecerse** *vr* : to get rich
enriquecido, -da *adj* : enriched
enriquecimiento *nm* : enrichment
enrojecer {53} *vt* : to make red, to redden — **enrojecerse** *vr* : to blush
enrolar *vt* RECLUTAR : to recruit — **enrolarse** *vr* INSCRIBIRSE : to enlist, to sign up
enrollar *vt* : to roll up, to coil — **enrollarse** *vr*
enronquecerse {53} *vr* : to become hoarse
enroscar {72} *vt* TORCER : to twist — **enroscarse** *vr* : to coil, to twine
ensacar {72} *vt* : to bag (up)
ensalada *nf* : salad
ensaladera *nf* : salad bowl
ensalmo *nm* : incantation, spell
ensalzar {21} *vt* 1 : to praise, to extol 2 EXALTAR : to exalt
ensamblaje *nm* : assembly
ensamblar *vt* 1 : to assemble 2 : to join, to fit together
ensanchar *vt* 1 : to widen 2 : to expand, to extend — **ensancharse** *vr*
ensanche *nm* 1 : widening 2 : expansion, development
ensangrentado, -da *adj* : bloody, bloodstained
ensañarse *vr* : to act cruelly, to be merciless
ensartar *vt* 1 ENHEBRAR : to string, to thread 2 : to skewer, to pierce
ensayar *vi* : to rehearse — *vt* 1 : to try out, to test 2 : to assay
ensayista *nmf* : essayist
ensayo *nm* 1 : essay 2 : trial, test 3 : rehearsal 4 : assay (of metals)
enseguida *adv* INMEDIATAMENTE : right away, immediately, at once
ensenada *nf* : cove, inlet
enseña *nf* 1 INSIGNIA : emblem, insignia 2 : standard, banner
enseñanza *nf* 1 EDUCACIÓN : education 2 : teaching
enseñar *vt* 1 : to teach 2 MOSTRAR : to show, to display — **enseñarse** *vr* ~ **a** : to learn to, to get used to
enseres *nmpl* : equipment, furnishings *pl* ⟨enseres domésticos : household goods⟩
ensillar *vt* : to saddle (up)
ensimismado, -da *adj* : absorbed, engrossed

ensimismarse *vr* : to lose oneself in thought

ensoberbecerse {53} *vr* : to become haughty

ensombrecer {53} *vt* : to cast a shadow over, to darken — **ensombrecerse** *vr*

ensoñación *nf, pl* **-ciones** : fantasy

ensopar *vt* **1** : to drench **2** : to dunk, to dip

ensordecedor, -dora *adj* : deafening, thunderous

ensordecer {53} *vt* : to deafen — *vi* : to go deaf

ensuciar *vt* : to soil, to dirty — **ensuciarse** *vr*

ensueño *nm* **1** : daydream, revery **2** FANTASÍA : illusion, fantasy

entablar *vt* **1** : to cover with boards **2** : to initiate, to enter into, to start

entallar *vt* AJUSTAR : to tailor, to fit, to take in — *vi* QUEDAR : to fit

ente *nm* **1** : being, entity **2** : body, organization ⟨ente rector : ruling body⟩ **3** *fam* : eccentric, crackpot

enteco, -ca *adj* : gaunt, frail

entenado, -da *n Mex* : stepchild, stepson *m*, stepdaughter *f*

entender[1] {56} *vt* **1** COMPRENDER : to understand **2** OPINAR : to think, to believe **3** : to mean, to intend **4** DEDUCIR : to infer, to deduce — *vi* **1** : to understand ⟨¡ya entiendo! : now I understand!⟩ **2** ~ **de** : to know about, to be good at **3** ~ **en** : to be in charge of — **entenderse** *vr* **1** : to be understood **2** : to get along well, to understand each other **3** ~ **con** : to deal with

entender[2] *nm* **a mi entender** : in my opinion

entendible *adj* : understandable

entendido[1], **-da** *adj* **1** : skilled, expert **2 tener entendido** : to understand, to be under the impression ⟨teníamos entendido que vendrías : we were under the impression you would come⟩ **3 darse por entendido** : to go without saying

entendido[2] *nm* : expert, authority, connoisseur

entendimiento *nm* **1** : intellect, mind **2** : understanding, agreement

enterado, -da *adj* : aware, well-informed ⟨estar enterado de : to be privy to⟩

enteramente *adv* : entirely, completely

enterar *vt* INFORMAR : to inform — **enterarse** *vr* INFORMARSE : to find out, to learn

entereza *nf* **1** INTEGRIDAD : integrity **2** FORTALEZA : fortitude **3** FIRMEZA : resolve

enternecedor, -dora *adj* CONMOVEDOR : touching, moving

enternecer {53} *vt* CONMOVER : to move, to touch

entero[1], **-ra** *adj* **1** : entire, whole **2** : complete, absolute **3** : intact — **enteramente** *adv*

entero[2] *nm* **1** : integer, whole number **2** : point (in finance)

enterramiento *nm* : burial

enterrar {55} *vt* : to bury

entibiar *vt* : to cool (down) — **entibiarse** *vr* : to become lukewarm

entidad *nf* **1** ENTE : entity **2** : body, organization **3** : firm, company **4** : importance, significance

entierro *nm* **1** : burial **2** : funeral

entintar *vt* : to ink

entoldado *nm* : awning

entomología *nf* : entomology

entomólogo, -ga *n* : entomologist

entonación *nf, pl* **-ciones** : intonation

entonar *vi* : to be in tune — *vt* **1** : to intone **2** : to tone up

entonces *adv* **1** : then **2 desde ~** : since then **3 en aquel entonces** : in those days

entornado, -da *adj* ENTREABIERTO : half-closed, ajar

entornar *vt* ENTREABRIR : to leave ajar

entorno *nm* : surroundings *pl*, environment

entorpecer {53} *vt* **1** : to hinder, to obstruct **2** : to dull — **entorpecerse** *vr* : to dull the senses

entrada *nf* **1** : entrance, entry **2** : ticket, admission **3** : beginning, onset **4** : entrée **5** : cue (in music) **6 entradas** *nfpl* : income ⟨entradas y salidas : income and expenditures⟩ **7 tener entradas** : to have a receding hairline

entrado, -da *adj* **entrado en años** : elderly

entramado *nm* : framework

entrampar *vt* **1** ATRAPAR : to entrap, to ensnare **2** ENGAÑAR : to deceive, to trick

entrante *adj* **1** : next, upcoming ⟨el año entrante : next year⟩ **2** : incoming, new ⟨el presidente entrante : the president elect⟩

entraña *nf* **1** MEOLLO : core, heart, crux **2 entrañas** *nfpl* VÍSCERAS : entrails

entrañable *adj* : close, intimate

entrañar *vt* : to entail, to involve

entrar *vi* **1** : to enter, to go in, to come in **2** : to begin — *vt* **1** : to bring in, to introduce **2** : to access

entre *prep* **1** : between **2** : among

entreabierto[1] *pp* → **entreabrir**

entreabierto[2], **-ta** *adj* ENTORNADO : half-open, ajar

entreabrir {2} *vt* ENTORNAR : to leave ajar

entreacto *nm* : intermission, interval

entrecano, -na *adj* : grayish, graying

entrecejo *nm* **fruncir el entrecejo** : to knit one's brows

entrecomillar *vt* : to place in quotation marks

entrecortado, -da *adj* **1** : labored, difficult ⟨respiración entrecortada : shortness of breath⟩ **2** : faltering, hesitant ⟨con la voz entrecortada : with a catch in his voice⟩

entrecruzar {21} *vt* ENTRELAZAR : to interweave, to intertwine — **entrecruzarse** *vr*
entredicho *nm* 1 DUDA : doubt, question 2 : prohibition
entrega *nf* 1 : delivery 2 : handing over, surrender 3 : installment ⟨entrega inicial : down payment⟩
entregar {52} *vt* 1 : to deliver 2 DAR : to give, to present 3 : to hand in, to hand over — **entregarse** *vr* 1 : to surrender, to give in 2 : to devote oneself
entrelazar {21} *vt* ENTRECRUZAR : to interweave, to intertwine
entremedias *adv* 1 : in between, halfway 2 : in the meantime
entremés *nm, pl* **-meses** 1 APERITIVO : appetizer, hors d'oeuvre 2 : interlude, short play
entremeterse → entrometerse
entremetido *nm* → entrometido
entremezclar *vt* : to intermingle
entrenador, -dora *n* : trainer, coach
entrenamiento *nm* : training, drill, practice
entrenar *vt* : to train, to drill, to practice — **entrenarse** *vr* : to train, to spar (in boxing)
entreoír {50} *vt* : to hear indistinctly
entrepierna *nf* 1 : inner thigh 2 : crotch 3 : inseam
entrepiso *nm* ENTRESUELO : mezzanine
entresacar {72} *vt* 1 SELECCIONAR : to pick out, to select 2 : to thin out
entresuelo *nm* ENTREPISO : mezzanine
entretanto[1] *adv* : meanwhile
entretanto[2] *nm* en el entretanto : in the meantime
entretejer *vt* : to interweave
entretela *nf* : facing (of a garment)
entretener {80} *vt* 1 DIVERTIR : to entertain, to amuse 2 DISTRAER : to distract 3 DEMORAR : to delay, to hold up — **entretenerse** *vr* 1 : to amuse oneself 2 : to dally
entretenido, -da *adj* DIVERTIDO : entertaining, amusing
entretenimiento *nm* 1 : entertainment, pastime 2 DIVERSIÓN : fun, amusement
entrever {88} *vt* 1 : to catch a glimpse of 2 : to make out, to see indistinctly
entreverar *vt* : to mix, to intermingle
entrevero *nm* : confusion, disorder
entrevista *nf* : interview
entrevistador, -dora *n* : interviewer
entrevistar *vt* : to interview — **entrevistarse** *vr* REUNIRSE ∼ con : to meet with
entristecer {53} *vt* : to sadden
entrometerse *vr* : to interfere, to meddle
entrometido, -da *n* : meddler, busybody
entroncar {72} *vt* RELACIONAR : to establish a relationship between, to connect — *vi* 1 : to be related 2 : to link up, to be connected
entronque *nm* 1 : kinship 2 VÍNCULO : link, connection

entuerto *nm* : wrong, injustice
entumecer {53} *vt* : to make numb, to be numb — **entumecerse** *vr* : to go numb, to fall asleep
entumecido, -da *adj* 1 : numb 2 : stiff (of muscles, joints, etc.)
entumecimiento *nm* : numbness
enturbiar *vt* 1 : to cloud 2 : to confuse — **enturbiarse** *vr*
entusiasmar *vt* : to excite, to fill with enthusiasm — **entusiasmarse** *vr* : to get excited
entusiasmo *nm* : enthusiasm
entusiasta[1] *adj* : enthusiastic
entusiasta[2] *nmf* AFICIONADO : enthusiast
enumerar *vt* : to enumerate — **enumeración** *nf*
enunciación *nf, pl* **-ciones** : enunciation, statement
enunciar *vt* : to enunciate, to state
envainar *vt* : to sheathe
envalentonar *vt* : to make bold, to encourage — **envalentonarse** *vr*
envanecer {53} *vt* ENGREÍR : to make vain — **envanecerse** *vr*
envasar *vt* 1 EMBOTELLAR : to bottle 2 ENLATAR : to can 3 : to pack in a container
envase *nm* 1 : packaging, packing 2 : container 3 LATA : can 4 : empty bottle
envejecer {53} *vt* : to age, to make look old — *vi* : to age, to grow old
envejecido, -da *adj* : aged, old-looking
envejecimiento *nm* : aging
envenenamiento *nm* : poisoning
envenenar *vt* 1 : to poison 2 : to embitter
envergadura *nf* 1 : span, breadth, spread 2 : importance, scope
envés *nm, pl* **enveses** : reverse, opposite side
enviado, -da *n* : envoy, correspondent
enviar {85} *vt* 1 : to send 2 : to ship
envidia *nf* : envy, jealousy
envidiar *vt* : to envy — **envidiable** *adj*
envidioso, -sa *adj* : envious, jealous
envilecer {53} *vt* : to degrade, to debase
envilecimiento *nm* : degradation, debasement
envío *nm* 1 : shipment 2 : remittance
enviudar *vi* : to be widowed, to become a widower
envoltorio *nm* 1 : bundle, package 2 : wrapping, wrap
envoltura *nf* : wrapper, wrapping
envolver {89} *vt* 1 : to wrap 2 : to envelop, to surround 3 : to entangle, to involve — **envolverse** *vr* 1 : to become involved 2 : to wrap oneself (up)
envuelto *pp* → envolver
enyerbar *vt Mex* : to bewitch
enyesar *vt* 1 : to plaster 2 ESCAYOLAR : to put in a plaster cast
enzima *nf* : enzyme
éon *nm, pl* **eones** : aeon
eperlano *nm* : smelt (fish)

épico, -ca *adj* : epic
epicúreo[1], -rea *adj* : epicurean
epicúreo[2], -rea *n* : epicure
epidemia *nf* : epidemic
epidémico, -ca *adj* : epidemic
epidermis *nf* : epidermis
epifanía *nf* : feast of the Epiphany (January 6th)
epigrama *nm* : epigram
epilepsia *nf* : epilepsy
epiléptico, -ca *adj & n* : epileptic
epílogo *nm* : epilogue
episcopal *adj* : episcopal
episcopaliano, -na *adj & n* : Episcopalian
episódico, -ca *adj* : episodic
episodio *nm* : episode
epístola *nf* : epistle
epitafio *nm* : epitaph
epíteto *nm* : epithet, name
epítome *nm* : summary, abstract
época *nf* **1** EDAD, ERA, PERÍODO : epoch, age, period **2** : time of year, season **3 de ~** : vintage, antique
epopeya *nf* : epic poem
equidad *nf* JUSTICIA : equity, justice, fairness
equilátero, -ra *adj* : equilateral
equilibrado, -da *adj* : well-balanced
equilibrar *vt* : to balance — **equilibrarse** *vr*
equilibrio *nm* **1** : balance, equilibrium ⟨perder el equilibrio : to lose one's balance⟩ ⟨equilibrio político : balance of power⟩ **2** : poise, aplomb
equilibrista *nmf* ACRÓBATA, FUNÁMBULO : acrobat, tightrope walker
equino, -na *adj* : equine
equinoccio *nm* : equinox
equipaje *nm* BAGAJE : baggage, luggage
equipamiento *nm* : equipping, equipment
equipar *vt* : to equip — **equiparse** *vr*
equiparable *adj* : comparable
equiparar *vt* **1** IGUALAR : to put on a same level, to make equal **2** COMPARAR : to compare
equipo *nm* **1** : team, crew **2** : gear, equipment
equitación *nf, pl* **-ciones** : horseback riding, horsemanship
equitativo, -va *adj* JUSTO : equitable, fair, just — **equitativamente** *adv*
equivalencia *nf* : equivalence
equivalente *adj & nm* : equivalent
equivaler {84} *vi* : to be equivalent
equivocación *nf, pl* **-ciones** ERROR : error, mistake
equivocado, -da *adj* : mistaken, wrong — **equivocadamente** *adv*
equivocar {72} *vt* : to mistake, to confuse — **equivocarse** *vr* : to make a mistake, to be wrong
equívoco[1], -ca *adj* AMBIGUO : ambiguous, equivocal
equívoco[2] *nm* : misunderstanding
era[1], etc. → **ser**
era[2] *nf* EDAD, ÉPOCA : era, age

erario *nm* : public treasury
erección *nf, pl* **-ciones** : erection, raising
eremita *nmf* ERMITAÑO : hermit
ergonomía *nf* : ergonomics
erguido, -da *adj* : erect, upright
erguir {31} *vt* : to raise, to lift up — **erguirse** *vr* : to straighten up
erial *nm* : uncultivated land
erigir {35} *vt* : to build, to erect — **erigirse** *vr* **~ en** : to set oneself up as
erizado, -da *adj* : bristly
erizarse {21} *vr* : to bristle, to stand on end
erizo *nm* **1** : hedgehog **2 erizo de mar** : sea urchin
ermitaño[1], -ña *n* ERMITA : hermit, recluse
ermitaño[2] *nm* : hermit crab
erogación *nf, pl* **-ciones** : expenditure
erogar {52} *vt* **1** : to pay out **2** : to distribute
erosión *nf, pl* **-siones** : erosion
erosionar *vt* : to erode
erótico, -ca *adj* : erotic
erotismo *nm* : eroticism
errabundo, -da *adj* ERRANTE, VAGABUNDO : wandering
erradicar {72} *vt* : to eradicate — **erradicación** *nf*
errado, -da *adj* : wrong, mistaken
errante *adj* ERRABUNDO, VAGABUNDO : errant, wandering
errar {32} *vt* FALLAR : to miss — *vi* **1** DESACERTAR : to be wrong, to be mistaken **2** VAGAR : to wander
errata *nf* : misprint, error
errático, -ca *adj* : erratic — **erráticamente** *adv*
erróneo, -nea *adj* EQUIVOCADO : erroneous, wrong — **erróneamente** *adv*
error *nm* EQUIVOCACIÓN : error, mistake
eructar *vi* : to belch, to burp
eructo *nm* : belch, burp
erudición *nf, pl* **-ciones** : erudition, learning
erudito[1], -ta *adj* LETRADO : erudite, learned
erudito[2], -ta *n* : scholar
erupción *nf, pl* **-ciones** : eruption **2** SARPULLIDO : rash
eruptivo, -va *adj* : eruptive
es → ser
esbelto, -ta *adj* DELGADO : slender, slim
esbirro *nm* : henchman
esbozar {21} *vt* BOSQUEJAR : to sketch, to outline
esbozo *nm* **1** : sketch **2** : rough draft
escabechar *vt* **1** ENCURTIR : to pickle **2** *fam* : to kill, to rub out
escabeche *nm* : brine (for pickling)
escabechina *nf* MASACRE : massacre, bloodbath
escabel *nm* : footstool
escabroso, -sa *adj* **1** : rugged, rough **2** : difficult, tough **3** : risqué
escabullirse {38} *vr* : to slip away, to escape

escala *nf* **1** : scale **2** ESCALERA : ladder **3** : stopover
escalada *nf* : ascent, climb
escalador, -dora *n* ALPINISTA : mountain climber
escalafón *nm, pl* **-fones 1** : list of personnel **2** : salary scale, rank
escalar *vt* : to climb, to scale — *vi* **1** : to go climbing **2** : to escalate
escaldar *vt* : to scald
escalera *nf* **1** : ladder ⟨escalera de tijera : stepladder⟩ **2** : stairs *pl*, staircase **3 escalera mecánica** : escalator
escalfador *nm* : chafing dish
escalfar *vt* : to poach (eggs)
escalinata *nf* : flight of stairs
escalofriante *adj* : horrifying, blood-curdling
escalofrío *nm* : shiver, chill, shudder
escalón *nm, pl* **-lones 1** : echelon **2** : step, rung
escalonado, -da *adj* GRADUAL : gradual, staggered
escalonar *vt* **1** : to terrace **2** : to stagger, to alternate
escalpelo *nm* BISTURÍ : scalpel
escama *nf* **1** : scale (of fish or reptiles) **2** : flake (of skin)
escamar *vt* **1** : to scale (fish) **2** : to make suspicious
escamocha *nf Mex* : fruit salad
escamoso, -sa *adj* : scaly
escamotear *vt* **1** : to palm, to conceal **2** *fam* : to lift, to swipe **3** : to hide, to cover up
escandalizar {21} *vt* : to shock, to scandalize — *vi* : to make a fuss — **escandalizarse** *vr* : to be shocked
escándalo *nm* **1** : scandal **2** : scene, commotion
escandaloso, -sa *adj* **1** : shocking, scandalous **2** RUIDOSO : noisy, rowdy **3** : flagrant, outrageous — **escandalosamente** *adv*
escandinavo, -va *adj & n* : Scandinavian
escandir *vt* : to scan (poetry)
escanear *vt* : to scan
escáner *nm* : scanner, scan
escaño *nm* **1** : seat (in a legislative body) **2** BANCO : bench
escapada *nf* HUIDA : flight, escape
escapar *vi* HUIR : to escape, to flee, to run away — **escaparse** *vr* : to escape notice, to leak out
escaparate *nm* **1** : shop window **2** : showcase
escapatoria *nf* **1** : loophole, excuse, pretext ⟨no tener escapatoria : to have no way out⟩ **2** ESCAPADA : escape, flight
escape *nm* **1** FUGA : escape **2** : exhaust (from a vehicle)
escapismo *nm* : escapism
escápula *nf* OMÓPLATO : scapula, shoulder blade
escapulario *nm* : scapular
escarabajo *nm* : beetle
escaramuza *nf* **1** : skirmish **2** : scrimmage

escaramuzar {21} *vi* : to skirmish
escarapela *nf* : rosette (ornament)
escarbar *vt* **1** : to dig, to scratch up **2** : to poke, to pick **3 ~ en** : to investigate, to pry into
escarcha *nf* **1** : frost **2** *Mex, PRi* : glitter
escarchar *vt* **1** : to frost (a cake) **2** : to candy (fruit)
escardar *vt* **1** : to weed, to hoe **2** : to weed out
escariar *vt* : to ream
escarlata *adj & nf* : scarlet
escarlatina *nf* : scarlet fever
escarmentar {55} *vt* : to punish, to teach a lesson to — *vi* : to learn one's lesson
escarmiento *nm* **1** : lesson, warning **2** CASTIGO : punishment
escarnecer {53} *vt* RIDICULIZAR : to ridicule, to mock
escarnio *nm* : ridicule, mockery
escarola *nf* : escarole
escarpa *nf* : escarpment, steep slope
escarpado, -da *adj* : steep, sheer
escarpia *nf* : hook, spike
escasamente *adv* : scarcely, barely
escasear *vi* : to be scarce, to run short
escasez *nf, pl* **-seces** : shortage, scarcity
escaso, -sa *adj* **1** : scarce, scant **2 ~ de** : short of
escatimar *vt* : to skimp on, to be sparing with ⟨no escatimar esfuerzos : to spare no effort⟩
escayola *nf* **1** : plaster (for casts) **2** : plaster cast
escayolar *vt* : to put in a plaster cast
escena *nf* **1** : scene **2** : stage
escenario *nm* **1** ESCENA : stage **2** : setting, scene ⟨el escenario del crimen : the scene of the crime⟩
escénico, -ca *adj* **1** : scenic **2** : stage
escenificar {72} *vt* : to stage, to dramatize
escepticismo *nm* : skepticism
escéptico[1], -ca *adj* : skeptical
escéptico[2], -ca *n* : skeptic
escindirse *vr* **1** : to split **2** : to break away
escisión *nf, pl* **-siones 1** : split, division **2** : excision
esclarecer {53} *vt* **1** ELUCIDAR : to elucidate, to clarify **2** ILUMINAR : to illuminate, to light up
esclarecimiento *nm* ELUCIDACIÓN : elucidation, clarification
esclavitud *nf* : slavery
esclavización *nf, pl* **-ciones** : enslavement
esclavizar {21} *vt* : to enslave
esclavo, -va *n* : slave
esclerosis *nf* **esclerosis múltiple** : multiple sclerosis
esclusa *nf* : floodgate, lock (of a canal)
escoba *nf* : broom
escobilla *nf* : small broom, brush, whisk broom
escobillón *nm, pl* **-llones** : swab

escocer {14} *vi* ARDER : to smart, to sting — **escocerse** *vr* : to be sore

escocés[1], **-cesa** *adj, mpl* **-ceses** 1 : Scottish 2 : tartan, plaid

escocés[2], **-cesa** *n, mpl* **-ceses** : Scottish person, Scot

escocés[3] *nm* 1 : Scots (language) 2 *pl* **-ceses** : Scotch (whiskey)

escofina *nf* : file, rasp

escoger {15} *vt* ELEGIR, SELECCIONAR : to choose, to select

escogido, -da *adj* : choice, select

escolar[1] *adj* : school

escolar[2] *nmf* : student, pupil

escolaridad *nf* : schooling ⟨escolaridad obligatoria : compulsory education⟩

escolarización *nf, pl* **-ciones** : education, schooling

escollo *nm* 1 : reef 2 OBSTÁCULO : obstacle

escolta *nmf* : escort

escoltar *vt* : to escort, to accompany

escombro *nm* 1 : debris, rubbish 2 **escombros** *nmpl* : ruins, rubble

esconder *vt* OCULTAR : to hide, to conceal

escondidas *nfpl* 1 : hide-and-seek 2 a ~ : secretly, in secret

escondimiento *nm* : concealment

escondite *nm* 1 ENCONDRIJO : hiding place 2 ESCONDIDAS : hide-and-seek

escondrijo *nm* ESCONDITE : hiding place

escopeta *nf* : shotgun

escoplear *vt* : to chisel (out)

escoplo *nm* : chisel

escora *nf* : list, heeling

escorar *vi* : to list, to heel (of a boat)

escorbuto *nm* : scurvy

escoria *nf* 1 : slag, dross 2 HEZ : dregs *pl*, scum ⟨la escoria de la sociedad : the dregs of society⟩

Escorpio *or* **Escorpión** *nmf* : Scorpio

escorpión *nm, pl* **-piones** ALACRÁN : scorpion

escote *nm* 1 : low neckline 2 **pagar a escote** : to go dutch

escotilla *nf* : hatch, hatchway

escotillón *nf, pl* **-llones** : trapdoor

escozor *nm* : smarting, stinging

escriba *nm* : scribe

escribano, -na *n* 1 : court clerk 2 NOTARIO : notary public

escribir {33} *v* 1 : to write 2 : to spell — **escribirse** *vr* CARTEARSE : to write to one another, to correspond

escrito[1] *pp* → **escribir**

escrito[2], **-ta** *adj* : written

escrito[3] *nm* 1 : written document 2 **escritos** *nmpl* : writings, works

escritor, -tora *n* : writer

escritorio *nm* : desk

escritorzuelo, -la *n* : hack (writer)

escritura *nf* 1 : writing, handwriting 2 : deed 3 **las Escrituras** : the Scriptures

escroto *nm* : scrotum

escrúpulo *nm* : scruple

escrupuloso, -sa *adj* 1 : scrupulous 2 METICULOSO : exact, meticulous — **escrupulosamente** *adv*

escrutador, -dora *adj* : penetrating, searching

escrutar *vt* ESCUDRIÑAR : to scrutinize, to examine closely

escrutinio *nm* : scrutiny

escuadra *nf* 1 : square (instrument) 2 : fleet, squadron

escuadrilla *nf* : squadron, formation, flight

escuadrón *nm, pl* **-drones** : squadron

escuálido, -da *adj* 1 : skinny, scrawny 2 INMUNDO : filthy, squalid

escuchar *vt* 1 : to listen to 2 : to hear — *vi* : to listen — **escucharse** *vr*

escudar *vt* : to shield — **escudarse** *vr* ~ **en** : to hide behind

escudero *nm* : squire

escudo *nm* 1 : shield 2 **escudo de armas** : coat of arms

escudriñar *vt* 1 ESCRUTAR : to scrutinize 2 : to inquire into, to investigate

escuela *nf* : school

escueto, -ta *adj* 1 : plain, simple 2 : succinct, concise — **escuetamente** *adv*

escuincle, -cla *n* Mex fam : child, kid

esculcar {72} *vt* : to search

esculpir *vt* 1 : to sculpt 2 : to carve, to engrave — *vi* : to sculpt

escultor, -tora *n* : sculptor

escultórico, -ca *adj* : sculptural

escultura *nf* : sculpture

escultural *adj* : statuesque

escupidera *nf* : spittoon, cuspidor

escupir *v* : to spit

escupitajo *nm* : spit

escurridizo, -za *adj* : slippery, elusive

escurridor *nm* 1 : dish rack 2 : colander

escurrir *vt* 1 : to wring out 2 : to drain — *vi* 1 : to drain 2 : to drip, to dripdry — **escurrirse** *vr* : to slip away

ese, esa *adj, mpl* **esos** : that, those

ése, ésa *pron, mpl* **ésos** : that one, those ones *pl*

esencia *nf* : essence

esencial *adj* : essential — **esencialmente** *adv*

esfera *nf* 1 : sphere 2 : face, dial (of a watch)

esférico[1], **-ca** *adj* : spherical

esférico[2] *nm* : ball (in sports)

esfinge *nf* : sphinx

esforzado, -da *adj* 1 : energetic, vigorous 2 VALIENTE : courageous, brave

esforzar {36} *vt* : to strain — **esforzarse** *vr* : to make an effort

esfuerzo *nm* 1 : effort 2 ÁNIMO, VIGOR : spirit, vigor 3 **sin** ~ : effortlessly

esfumar *vt* : to tone down, to soften — **esfumarse** *vr* 1 : to fade away, to vanish 2 *fam* : to take off, to leave

esgrima *nf* : fencing (sport)

esgrimidor, -dora *n* : fencer

esgrimir *vt* 1 : to brandish, to wield 2 : to use, to resort to — *vi* : to fence

esguince *nm* : sprain, strain (of a muscle)

eslabón *nm, pl* **-bones** : link

eslabonar *vt* : to link, to connect, to join

eslavo¹, -va *adj* : Slavic

eslavo², -va *n* : Slav

eslogan *nm, pl* **-lóganes** : slogan

eslovaco, -ca *adj & n* : Slovakian, Slovak

esloveno, -na *adj & nm* : Slovene, Slovenian

esmaltar *vt* : to enamel

esmalte *nm* 1 : enamel 2 **esmalte de uñas** : nail polish

esmerado, -da *adj* : careful, painstaking

esmeralda *nf* : emerald

esmerarse *vr* : to take great pains, to do one's utmost

esmeril *nm* : emery

esmero *nm* : meticulousness, great care

esmoquin *nm, pl* **-quins** : tuxedo

esnob¹ *adj, pl* **esnobs** : snobbish

esnob² *nmf, pl* **esnobs** : snob

esnobismo *nm* : snobbery, snobbishness

eso *pron (neuter)* 1 : that ⟨eso no me gusta : I don't like that⟩ 2 ¡eso es! : that's it!, that's right! 3 a eso de : around ⟨a eso de las tres : around three o'clock⟩ 4 en ~ : at that point, just then

esófago *nm* : esophagus

esos → ese

ésos → ése

esotérico, -ca *adj* : esoteric — **esotéricamente** *adv*

espabilado, -da *adj* : bright, smart

espabilarse *vr* 1 : to awaken 2 : to get a move on 3 : to get smart, to wise up

espacial *adj* 1 : space 2 : spatial

espaciar *vt* DISTANCIAR : to space out, to spread out

espacio *nm* 1 : space, room 2 : period, length (of time) 3 **espacio exterior** : outer space

espacioso, -sa *adj* : spacious, roomy

espada¹ *nf* 1 : sword 2 **espadas** *nfpl* : spades (in playing cards)

espada² *nm* MATADOR, TORERO : bullfighter, matador

espadaña *nf* 1 : belfry 2 : cattail

espadilla *nf* : scull, oar

espagueti *nm or* **espaguetis** *nmpl* : spaghetti

espalda *nf* 1 : back 2 **espaldas** *nfpl* : shoulders, back 3 **por la espalda** : from behind

espaldarazo *nm* 1 : recognition, support 2 : slap on the back

espaldera *nf* : trellis

espantajo *nm* : scarecrow

espantapájaros *nms & pl* : scarecrow

espantar *vt* ASUSTAR : to scare, to frighten — **espantarse** *vr*

espanto *nm* : fright, fear, horror

espantoso, -sa *adj* 1 : frightening, terrifying 2 : frightful, dreadful

español¹, -ñola *adj* : Spanish

español², -ñola *n* : Spaniard

español³ *nm* CASTELLANO : Spanish (language)

esparadrapo *nm* : adhesive bandage, Band-Aid™

esparcimiento *nm* 1 DIVERSIÓN, RECREO : entertainment, recreation 2 DESCANSO : relaxation 3 DISEMINACIÓN : dissemination, spreading

esparcir {83} *vt* DISPERSAR : to scatter, to spread — **esparcirse** *vr* 1 : to spread out 2 DESCANSARSE : to take it easy 3 DIVERTIRSE : to amuse oneself

espárrago *nm* : asparagus

espartano, -na *adj* : severe, austere

espasmo *nm* : spasm

espasmódico, -ca *adj* : spasmodic

espástico, -ca *adj* : spastic

espátula *nf* : spatula

especia *nf* : spice

especial *adj & nm* : special

especialidad *nf* : specialty

especialista *nmf* : specialist, expert

especialización *nf, pl* **-ciones** : specialization

especializarse {21} *vr* : to specialize

especialmente *adv* : especially, particularly

especie *nf* 1 : species 2 CLASE, TIPO : type, kind, sort

especificación *nf, pl* **-ciones** : specification

especificar {72} *vt* : to specify

específico, -ca *adj* : specific — **específicamente** *adv*

espécimen *nm, pl* **especímenes** : specimen

especioso, -sa *adj* : specious

espectacular *adj* : spectacular — **espectacularmente** *adv*

espectáculo *nm* 1 : spectacle, sight 2 : show, performance

espectador, -dora *n* : spectator, onlooker

espectro *nm* 1 : ghost, specter 2 : spectrum

especulación *nf, pl* **-ciones** : speculation

especulador, -dora *n* : speculator

especular *vi* : to speculate

especulativo, -va *adj* : speculative

espejismo *nm* 1 : mirage 2 : illusion

espejo *nm* : mirror

espejuelos *nmpl* ANTEOJOS : spectacles, glasses

espeluznante *adj* : hair-raising, terrifying

espera *nf* : wait

esperado, -da *adj* : anticipated

esperanza *nf* : hope, expectation

esperanzado, -da *adj* : hopeful

esperanzador, -dora *adj* : encouraging, promising

esperanzar {21} *vt* : to give hope to

esperar *vt* 1 AGUARDAR : to wait for, to await 2 : to expect 3 : to hope ⟨espero poder trabajar : I hope to be able to work⟩ ⟨espero que sí : I hope so⟩ — *vi*

: to wait — **esperarse** *vr* 1 : to expect, to be hoped ⟨como podría esperarse : as would be expected⟩ 2 : to hold on, to hang on ⟨espérate un momento : hold on a minute⟩

esperma *nmf* : sperm

esperpéntico, -ca *adj* GROTESCO : grotesque

esperpento *nm fam* MAMARRACHO : sight, fright ⟨voy hecha un esperpento : I really look a sight⟩

espesante *nm* : thickener

espesar *vt* : to thicken — **espesarse** *vr*

espeso, -sa *adj* : thick, heavy, dense

espesor *nm* : thickness, density

espesura *nf* 1 : thickness 2 : thicket

espetar *vt* 1 : to blurt out 2 : to skewer

espía *nmf* : spy

espiar {85} *vt* : to spy on, to observe — *vi* : to spy

espiga *nf* 1 : ear (of wheat) 2 : spike (of flowers)

espigado, -da *adj* : willowy, slender

espigar {52} *vt* : to glean, to gather — **espigarse** *vr* : to grow quickly, to shoot up

espigón *nm, pl* **-gones** : breakwater

espina *nf* 1 : thorn 2 : spine ⟨espina dorsal : spinal column⟩ 3 : fish bone

espinaca *nf* 1 : spinach (plant) 2 **espinacas** *nfpl* : spinach (food)

espinal *adj* : spinal

espinazo *nm* : backbone

espineta *nf* : spinet

espinilla *nf* 1 BARRO, GRANO : pimple 2 : shin

espino *nm* : hawthorn

espinoso, -sa *adj* 1 : thorny, prickly 2 : bony (of fish) 3 : knotty, difficult

espionaje *nm* : espionage

espiración *nf, pl* **-ciones** : exhalation

espiral *adj & nf* : spiral

espirar *vt* EXHALAR : to breathe out, to give off — *vi* : to exhale

espiritismo *nm* : spiritualism

espiritista *nmf* : spiritualist

espíritu *nm* 1 : spirit 2 ÁNIMO : state of mind, spirits *pl* 3 **el Espíritu Santo** : the Holy Ghost

espiritual *adj* : spiritual — **espiritualmente** *adv*

espiritualidad *nf* : spirituality

espita *nf* : spigot, tap

esplendidez *nf, pl* **-deces** ESPLENDOR : magnificence, splendor

espléndido, -da *adj* 1 : splendid, magnificent 2 : generous, lavish — **espléndidamente** *adv*

esplendor *nm* ESPLENDIDEZ : splendor

esplendoroso, -sa *adj* MAGNÍFICO : magnificent, grand

espliego *nm* LAVANDA : lavender

espolear *vt* : to spur on

espoleta *nf* 1 DETONADOR : detonator, fuse 2 : wishbone

espolón *nm, pl* **-lones** : spur (of poultry), fetlock (of a horse)

espolvorear *vt* : to sprinkle, to dust

esponja *nf* 1 : sponge 2 **tirar la esponja** : to throw in the towel

esponjado, -da *adj* : spongy

esponjoso, -sa *adj* 1 : spongy 2 : soft, fluffy

esponsales *nmpl* : betrothal, engagement

espontaneidad *nf* : spontaneity

espontáneo, -nea *adj* : spontaneous — **espontáneamente** *adv*

espora *nf* : spore

esporádico, -ca *adj* : sporadic — **esporádicamente** *adv*

esposar *vt* : to handcuff

esposas *nfpl* : handcuffs

esposo, -sa *n* : spouse, wife *f*, husband *m*

esprint *nm* : sprint

esprintar *vi* : to sprint

esprínter *nmf* : sprinter

espuela *nf* : spur

espuerta *nf* : two-handled basket

espulgar {52} *vt* 1 : to delouse 2 : to scrutinize

espuma *nf* 1 : foam 2 : lather 3 : froth, head (on beer)

espumar *vi* : to foam, to froth — *vt* : to skim off

espumoso, -sa *adj* : foamy, frothy

espurio, -ria *adj* : spurious

esputar *v* : to expectorate, to spit

esputo *nm* : spit, sputum

esqueje *nm* : cutting (from a plant)

esquela *nf* 1 : note 2 : notice, announcement

esquelético, -ca *adj* : emaciated, skeletal

esqueleto *nm* 1 : skeleton 2 ARMAZÓN : framework

esquema *nf* BOSQUEJO : outline, sketch, plan

esquemático, -ca *adj* : schematic

esquí *nm* 1 : ski 2 **esquí acuático** : water ski, waterskiing

esquiador, -dora *n* : skier

esquiar {85} *vi* : to ski

esquife *nm* : skiff

esquila *nf* 1 CENCERRO : cowbell 2 : shearing

esquilar *vt* TRASQUILAR : to shear

esquimal *adj & nmf* : Eskimo

esquina *nf* : corner

esquinazo *nm* 1 : corner 2 **dar esquinazo a** *fam* : to stand up, to give the slip to

esquirla *nf* : splinter (of bone, glass, etc.)

esquirol *nm* ROMPEHUELGAS : strikebreaker, scab

esquisto *nm* : shale

esquivar *vt* 1 EVADIR : to dodge, to evade 2 EVITAR : to avoid

esquivez *nf, pl* **-veces** 1 : aloofness 2 TIMIDEZ : shyness

esquivo, -va *adj* 1 HURAÑO : aloof, unsociable 2 : shy 3 : elusive, evasive

esquizofrenia *nf* : schizophrenia

esquizofrénico, -ca *adj & n* : schizophrenic

esta *adj* → **este**[1]
ésta → **éste**
estabilidad *nf* : stability
estabilización *nf, pl* **-ciones** : stabilization
estabilizador *nm* : stabilizer
estabilizar {21} *vt* : to stabilize — **estabilizarse** *vr*
estable *adj* : stable, steady
establecer {53} *vt* FUNDAR, INSTITUIR : to establish, to found, to set up — **establecerse** *vr* INSTALARSE : to settle, to establish oneself
establecimiento *nm* 1 : establishing 2 : establishment, institution, office
establo *nm* : stable
estaca *nf* : stake, picket, post
estacada *nf* 1 : picket fence 2 : stockade
estacar {72} *vt* 1 : to stake out 2 : to fasten down with stakes — **estacarse** *vr* : to remain rigid
estación *nf, pl* **-ciones** 1 : station ⟨estación de servicio : service station, gas station⟩ 2 : season
estacional *adj* : seasonal
estacionamiento *nm* 1 : parking 2 : parking lot
estacionar *vt* 1 : to place, to station 2 : to park — **estacionarse** *vr* 1 : to park 2 : to remain stationary
estacionario, -ria *adj* 1 : stationary 2 : stable
estada *nf* : stay
estadía *nf* ESTANCIA : stay, sojourn
estadio *nm* 1 : stadium 2 : phase, stage
estadista *nmf* : statesman
estadística *nf* 1 : statistic, figure 2 : statistics
estadístico[1], -ca *adj* : statistical — **estadísticamente** *adv*
estadístico[2], -ca *n* : statistician
estado *nm* 1 : state 2 : status ⟨estado civil : marital status⟩ 3 CONDICIÓN : condition
estadounidense *adj & nmf* AMERICANO, NORTEAMERICANO : American
estafa *nf* : swindle, fraud
estafador, -dora *n* : cheat, swindler
estafar *vt* DEFRAUDAR : to swindle, to defraud
estalactita *nf* : stalactite
estalagmita *nf* : stalagmite
estallar *vi* 1 REVENTAR : to burst, to explode, to erupt 2 : to break out
estallido *nm* 1 EXPLOSIÓN : explosion 2 : report (of a gun) 3 : outbreak, outburst
estambre *nm* 1 : worsted (fabric) 2 : stamen
estampa *nf* 1 ILUSTRACIÓN, IMAGEN : printed image, illustration 2 ASPECTO : appearance, demeanor
estampado[1], -da *adj* : patterned, printed
estampado[2] *nm* : print, pattern
estampar *vt* : to stamp, to print, to engrave

estampida *nf* : stampede
estampilla *nf* 1 : rubber stamp 2 SELLO, TIMBRE : postage stamp
estancado, -da *adj* : stagnant
estancamiento *nm* : stagnation
estancar {72} *vt* 1 : to dam up, to hold back 2 : to bring to a halt, to deadlock — **estancarse** *vr* 1 : to stagnate 2 : to be brought to a standstill, to be deadlocked
estancia *nf* 1 ESTADÍA : stay, sojourn 2 : ranch, farm
estanciero, -ra *n* : rancher, farmer
estanco, -ca *adj* : watertight
estándar *adj & nm* : standard
estandarización *nf, pl* **-ciones** : standardization
estandarizar {21} *vt* : to standardize
estandarte *nm* : standard, banner
estanque *nm* 1 : pool, pond 2 : tank, reservoir
estante *nm* REPISA : shelf
estantería *nf* : shelves *pl*, bookcase
estaño *nm* : tin
estaquilla *nf* 1 : peg 2 ESPIGA : spike
estar {34} *v aux* : to be ⟨estoy aprendiendo inglés : I'm learning English⟩ ⟨está terminado : it's finished⟩ — *vi* 1 (*indicating a state or condition*) : to be ⟨está muy alto : he's so tall, he's gotten very tall⟩ ⟨¿ya estás mejor? : are you feeling better now?⟩ ⟨estoy casado : I'm married⟩ 2 (*indicating location*) : to be ⟨están en la mesa : they're on the table⟩ ⟨estamos en la página 2 : we're on page 2⟩ 3 : to be at home ⟨¿está María? : is María in?⟩ 4 : to remain ⟨estaré aquí 5 días : I'll be here for 5 days⟩ 5 : to be ready, to be done ⟨estará para las diez : it will be ready by ten o'clock⟩ 6 : to agree ⟨¿estamos? : are we in agreement?⟩ ⟨estoy contigo : I'm with you⟩ 7 ¿**cómo estás?** : how are you? 8 **¡está bien!** : all right!, that's fine! 9 **~ a** : to cost 10 **~ a** : to be ⟨¿a qué día estamos? : what's today's date?⟩ 11 **~ con** : to have ⟨está con fiebre : she has a fever⟩ 12 **~ de** : to be ⟨estoy de vacaciones : I'm on vacation⟩ ⟨está de director hoy : he's acting as director today⟩ 13 **estar bien (mal)** : to be well (sick) 14 **~ para** : to be in the mood for 15 **~ por** : to be in favor of 16 **~ por** : to be about to ⟨está por cerrar : it's on the verge of closing⟩ 17 **estar de más** : to be unnecessary 18 **estar que** : to be (in a state or condition) ⟨está que echa chispas : he's hopping mad⟩ — **estarse** *vr* QUEDARSE : to stay, to remain ⟨¡estáte quieto! : be still!⟩
estarcir {83} *vt* : to stencil
estatal *adj* : state, national
estática *nf* : static
estático, -ca *adj* : static
estatizar {21} *vt* : to nationalize — **estatización** *nf*
estatua *nf* : statue

estatuilla *nf* : statuette, figurine
estatura *nf* : height, stature ⟨de mediana estatura : of medium height⟩
estatus *nm* : status, prestige
estatutario, -ria *adj* : statutory
estatuto *nm* : statute
este[1], esta *adj, mpl* **estos** : this, these
este[2] *adj* : eastern, east
este[3] *nm* **1** ORIENTE : east **2** : east wind **3 el Este** : the East, the Orient
éste, ésta *pron, mpl* **éstos 1** : this one, these ones *pl* **2** : the latter
estela *nf* **1** : wake (of a ship) **2** RASTRO : trail (of dust, smoke, etc.)
estelar *adj* : stellar
estelarizar {21} *vt Mex* : to star in, to be the star of
esténcil *nm* : stencil
estentóreo, -rea *adj* : loud, thundering
estepa *nf* : steppe
éster *nf* : ester
estera *nf* : mat
estercolero *nm* : dunghill
estéreo *adj & nm* : stereo
estereofónico, -ca *adj* : stereophonic
estereotipado, -da *adj* : stereotyped
estereotipar *vt* : to stereotype
estereotipo *nm* : stereotype
estéril *adj* **1** : sterile, germ-free **2** : infertile, barren **3** : futile, vain
esterilidad *nf* **1** : sterility **2** : infertility
esterilizar {21} *vt* **1** : to sterilize, to disinfect **2** : to sterilize (a person), to spay (an animal) — **esterilización** *nf*
esterlina *adj* : sterling
esternón *nm, pl* **-nones** : sternum
estero *nm* : estuary
estertor *nm* : death rattle
estética *nf* : aesthetics
estético, -ca *adj* : aesthetic — **estéticamente** *adv*
estetoscopio *nm* : stethoscope
estibador, -dora *n* : longshoreman, stevedore
estibar *vt* : to load (freight)
estiércol *nm* : dung, manure
estigma *nm* : stigma
estigmatizar {21} *vt* : to stigmatize, to brand
estilarse *vr* : to be in fashion
estilete *nm* : stiletto
estilista *nmf* : stylist
estilizar {21} *vt* : to stylize
estilo *nm* **1** : style **2** : fashion, manner **3** : stylus
estima *nf* ESTIMACIÓN : esteem, regard
estimable *adj* **1** : considerable **2** : estimable, esteemed
estimación *nf, pl* **-ciones 1** ESTIMA : esteem, regard **2** : estimate
estimado, -da *adj* : esteemed, dear ⟨Estimado señor Ortiz : Dear Mr. Ortiz⟩
estimar *vt* **1** APRECIAR : to esteem, to respect **2** EVALUAR : to estimate, to appraise **3** OPINAR : to consider, to deem
estimulación *nf, pl* **-ciones** : stimulation
estimulante[1] *adj* : stimulating
estimulante[2] *nm* : stimulant

estimular *vt* **1** : to stimulate **2** : to encourage
estímulo *nm* **1** : stimulus **2** INCENTIVO : incentive, encouragement
estío *nm* : summertime
estipendio *nm* **1** : salary **2** : stipend, remuneration
estipular *vt* : to stipulate — **estipulación** *nf*
estirado, -da *adj* **1** : stretched, extended **2** PRESUMIDO : stuck-up, conceited
estiramiento *nm* **1** : stretching **2 estiramiento facial** : face-lift
estirar *vt* : to stretch (out), to extend — **estirarse** *vr*
estirón *nm, pl* **-rones 1** : pull, tug **2 dar un estirón** : to grow quickly, to shoot up
estirpe *nf* LINAJE : lineage, stock
estival *adj* VERANIEGO : summer
esto *pron* (*neuter*) **1** : this ⟨¿qué es esto? : what is this?⟩ **2 en ~** : at this point **3 por ~** : for this reason
estocada *nf* **1** : final thrust (in bullfighting) **2** : thrust, lunge (in fencing)
estofa *nf* CLASE : class, quality ⟨de baja estofa : low-class, poor-quality⟩
estofado *nm* COCIDO, GUISADO : stew
estofar *vt* GUISAR : to stew
estoicismo *nm* : stoicism
estoico[1], -ca *adj* : stoic, stoical
estoico[2], -ca *n* : stoic
estola *nf* : stole
estomacal *adj* GÁSTRICO : stomach, gastric
estómago *nm* : stomach
estoniano, -na *adj & n* : Estonian
estonio, -nia *adj & n* : Estonian
estopa *nf* **1** : tow (yarn or cloth) **2** : burlap
estopilla *nf* : cheesecloth
estoque *nm* : rapier, sword
estorbar *vt* OBSTRUIR : to obstruct, to hinder — *vi* : to get in the way
estorbo *nm* **1** : obstacle, hindrance **2** : nuisance
estornino *nm* : starling
estornudar *vi* : to sneeze
estornudo *nm* : sneeze
estos *adj* → **este[1]**
éstos → **éste**
estoy → **estar**
estrabismo *nm* : squint
estrado *nm* **1** : dais, platform, bench (of a judge) **2 estrados** *nmpl* : courts of law
estrafalario, -ria *adj* ESTRAMBÓTICO, EXCÉNTRICO : eccentric, bizarre
estragar {52} *vt* DEVASTAR : to ruin, to devastate
estragón *nm* : tarragon
estragos *nmpl* **1** : ravages, destruction, devastation ⟨los estragos de la guerra : the ravages of war⟩ **2 hacer estragos en** *or* **causar estragos entre** : to play havoc with
estrambótico, -ca *adj* ESTRAFALARIO, EXCÉNTRICO : eccentric, bizarre

estrangulamiento *nm* : strangling, strangulation

estrangular *vt* AHOGAR : to strangle — **estrangulación** *nf*

estratagema *nf* ARTIMAÑA : stratagem, ruse

estratega *nmf* : strategist

estrategia *nf* : strategy

estratégico, -ca *adj* : strategic, tactical — **estratégicamente** *adv*

estratificación *nf, pl* **-ciones** : stratification

estratificado, -da *adj* : stratified

estrato *nm* : stratum, layer

estratosfera *nf* : stratosphere

estratosférico, -ca *adj* 1 : stratospheric 2 : astronomical, exorbitant

estrechamiento *nm* 1 : narrowing 2 : narrow point 3 : tightening, strengthening (of relations)

estrechar *vt* 1 : to narrow 2 : to tighten, to strengthen (a bond) 3 : to hug, to embrace 4 **estrechar la mano de** : to shake hands with — **estrecharse** *vr*

estrechez *nf, pl* **-checes** 1 : tightness, narrowness 2 **estrecheces** *nfpl* : financial problems

estrecho¹, -cha *adj* 1 : tight, narrow 2 ÍNTIMO : close — **estrechamente** *adv*

estrecho² *nm* : strait, narrows

estrella *nf* 1 ASTRO : star ⟨estrella fugaz : shooting star⟩ 2 : destiny ⟨tener buena estrella : to be born lucky⟩ 3 : movie star 4 **estrella de mar** : starfish

estrellado, -da *adj* 1 : starry 2 : star-shaped 3 **huevos estrellados** : fried eggs

estrellamiento *nm* : crash, collision

estrellar *vt* : to smash, to crash — **estrellarse** *vr* : to crash, to collide

estrellato *nm* : stardom

estremecedor, -dora *adj* : horrifying

estremecer {53} *vt* : to cause to shake — *vi* : to tremble, to shake — **estremecerse** *vr* : to shudder, to shiver (with emotion)

estremecimiento *nm* : trembling, shaking, shivering

estrenar *vt* 1 : to use for the first time 2 : to premiere, to open — **estrenarse** *vr* : to make one's debut

estreno *nm* DEBUT : debut, premiere

estreñimiento *nm* : constipation

estreñirse {67} *vr* : to be constipated

estrépito *nm* ESTRUENDO : clamor, din

estrepitoso, -sa *adj* : clamorous, noisy — **estrepitosamente** *adv*

estrés *nm, pl* **estreses** : stress

estresante *adj* : stressful

estresar *vt* : to stress, to stress out

estría *nf* : fluting, groove

estribación *nf, pl* **-ciones** 1 : spur, ridge 2 **estribaciones** *nfpl* : foothills

estribar *vi* FUNDARSE ∼ **en** : to be due to, to stem from

estribillo *nm* : refrain, chorus

estribo *nm* 1 : stirrup 2 : abutment, buttress 3 **perder los estribos** : to lose one's temper

estribor *nm* : starboard

estricnina *nf* : strychnine

estricto, -ta *adj* SEVERO : strict, severe — **estrictamente** *adv*

estridente *adj* : strident, shrill, loud — **estridentemente** *adv*

estrofa *nf* : stanza, verse

estrógeno *nm* : estrogen

estropajo *nm* : scouring pad

estropear *vt* 1 ARRUINAR : to ruin, to spoil 2 : to break, to damage — **estropearse** *vr* 1 : to spoil, to go bad 2 : to break down

estropicio *nm* DAÑO : damage, breakage

estructura *nf* : structure, framework

estructuración *nf, pl* **-ciones** : structuring, structure

estructural *adj* : structural — **estructuralmente** *adv*

estructurar *vt* : to structure, to organize

estruendo *nm* ESTRÉPITO : racket, din, roar

estruendoso, -sa *adj* : resounding, thunderous

estrujar *vt* APRETAR : to press, to squeeze

estuario *nm* : estuary

estuche *nm* : kit, case

estuco *nm* : stucco

estudiado, -da *adj* : affected, mannered

estudiantado *nm* : student body, students *pl*

estudiante *nmf* : student

estudiantil *adj* : student ⟨la vida estudiantil : student life⟩

estudiar *v* : to study

estudio *nm* 1 : study 2 : studio 3 **estudios** *nmpl* : studies, education

estudioso, -sa *adj* : studious

estufa *nf* 1 : stove, heater 2 *Col, Mex* : cooking stove, range

estupefacción *nf, pl* **-ciones** : stupefaction, astonishment

estupefaciente¹ *adj* : narcotic

estupefaciente² *nm* DROGA, NARCÓTICO : drug, narcotic

estupefacto, -ta *adj* : astonished, stunned

estupendo, -da *adj* MARAVILLOSO : stupendous, marvelous — **estupendamente** *adv*

estupidez *nf, pl* **-deces** 1 : stupidity 2 : nonsense

estúpido¹, -da *adj* : stupid — **estúpidamente** *adj*

estúpido², -da *n* IDIOTA : idiot, fool

estupor *nm* 1 : stupor 2 : amazement

esturión *nm, pl* **-riones** : sturgeon

estuvo, etc. → **estar**

etano *nm* : ethane

etanol *nm* : ethanol

etapa *nf* FASE : stage, phase

etcétera¹ : et cetera, and so on

etcétera² *nmf* : et cetera

éter *nm* : ether

etéreo, -rea *adj* : ethereal, heavenly
eternidad *nf* : eternity
eternizar {21} *vt* PERPETUAR : to make eternal, to perpetuate — **eternizarse** *vr fam* : to take forever
eterno, -na *adj* : eternal, endless — **eternamente** *adv*
ética *nf* : ethics
ético, -ca *adj* : ethical — **éticamente** *adv*
etimología *nf* : etymology
etimológico, -ca *adj* : etymological
etimólogo, -ga *n* : etymologist
etíope *adj & nmf* : Ethiopian
etiqueta *nf* 1 : etiquette 2 : tag, label 3 **de ~** : formal, dressy
etiquetar *vt* : to label
étnico, -ca *adj* : ethnic
etnología *nf* : ethnology
etnólogo, -ga *n* : ethnologist
eucalipto *nm* : eucalyptus
Eucaristía *nf* : Eucharist, communion
eucarístico, -ca *adj* : eucharistic
eufemismo *nm* : euphemism
eufemístico, -ca *adj* : euphemistic
eufonía *nf* : euphony
eufónico, -ca *adj* : euphonious
euforia *nf* : euphoria, joyousness
eufórico, -ca *adj* : euphoric, exuberant, joyous — **eufóricamente** *adv*
eunuco *nm* : eunuch
europeo, -pea *adj & n* : European
euskera *nm* : Basque (language)
eutanasia *nf* : euthanasia
evacuación *nf, pl* **-ciones** : evacuation
evacuar *vt* 1 : to evacuate, to vacate 2 : to carry out — *vi* : to have a bowel movement
evadir *vt* ELUDIR : to evade, to avoid — **evadirse** *vr* : to escape, to slip away
evaluación *nf, pl* **-ciones** : assessment, evaluation
evaluador, -dora *n* : assessor
evaluar {3} *vt* : to evaluate, to assess, to appraise
evangélico, -ca *adj* : evangelical — **evangélicamente** *adv*
evangelio *nm* : gospel
evangelismo *nm* : evangelism
evangelista *nm* : evangelist
evangelizador, -dora *n* : evangelist, missionary
evaporación *nf, pl* **-ciones** : evaporation
evaporar *vt* : to evaporate — **evaporarse** *vr* ESFUMARSE : to disappear, to vanish
evasión *nf, pl* **-siones** 1 : escape, flight 2 : evasion, dodge
evasiva *nf* : excuse, pretext
evasivo, -va *adj* : evasive
evento *nm* : event
eventual *adj* 1 : possible 2 : temporary ⟨trabajadores eventuales : temporary workers⟩ — **eventualmente** *adv*
eventualidad *nf* : possibility, eventuality
evidencia *nf* 1 : evidence, proof 2 **poner en evidencia** : to demonstrate, to make clear

evidenciar *vt* : to demonstrate, to show — **evidenciarse** *vr* : to be evident
evidente *adj* : evident, obvious, clear — **evidentemente** *adv*
eviscerar *vt* : to eviscerate
evitable *adj* : avoidable, preventable
evitar *vt* 1 : to avoid 2 PREVENIR : to prevent 3 ELUDIR : to escape, to elude
evocación *nf, pl* **-ciones** : evocation
evocador, -dora *adj* : evocative
evocar {72} *vt* 1 : to evoke 2 RECORDAR : to recall
evolución *nf, pl* **-ciones** 1 : evolution 2 : development, progress
evolucionar *vi* 1 : to evolve 2 : to change, to develop
evolutivo, -va *adj* : evolutionary
exabrupto *nm* : pointed remark
exacción *nf, pl* **-ciones** : levying, exaction
exacerbar *vt* 1 : to exacerbate, to aggravate 2 : to irritate, to exasperate
exactamente *adv* : exactly
exactitud *nf* PRECISIÓN : accuracy, precision, exactitude
exacto, -ta *adj* PRECISO : accurate, precise, exact
exageración *nf, pl* **-ciones** : exaggeration
exagerado, -da *adj* 1 : exaggerated 2 : excessive — **exageradamente** *adv*
exagerar *v* : to exaggerate
exaltación *nf, pl* **-ciones** 1 : exaltation 2 : excitement, agitation
exaltado[1], -da *adj* : excitable, hotheaded
exaltado[2], -da *n* : hothead
exaltar *vt* 1 ENSALZAR : to exalt, to extol 2 : to excite, to agitate — **exaltarse** *vr* ACALORARSE : to get overexcited
ex-alumno → *alumno*
examen *nm, pl* **exámenes** 1 : examination, test 2 : consideration, investigation
examinar *vt* 1 : to examine 2 INSPECCIONAR : to inspect — **examinarse** *vr* : to take an exam
exánime *adj* 1 : lifeless 2 : exhausted
exasperante *adj* : exasperating
exasperar *vt* IRRITAR : to exasperate, to irritate — **exasperación** *nf*
excavación *nf, pl* **-ciones** : excavation
excavadora *nf* : excavator
excavar *v* : to excavate, to dig
excedente[1] *adj* 1 : excessive 2 : excess, surplus
excedente[2] *nm* : surplus, excess
exceder *vt* : to exceed, to surpass — **excederse** *vr* : to go too far
excelencia *nf* 1 : excellence 2 : excellency ⟨Su Excelencia : His Excellency⟩
excelente *adj* : excellent — **excelentemente** *adv*
excelso, -sa *adj* : lofty, sublime
excentricidad *nf* : eccentricity
excéntrico, -ca *adj & n* : eccentric
excepción *nf, pl* **-ciones** : exception
excepcional *adj* EXTRAORDINARIO : exceptional, extraordinary, rare

excepto *prep* SALVO : except
exceptuar {3} *vt* EXCLUIR : to except, to exclude
excesivo, -va *adj* : excessive — **excesivamente** *adv*
exceso *nm* 1 : excess 2 **excesos** *nmpl* : excesses, abuses 3 **exceso de velocidad** : speeding
excitabilidad *nf* : excitability
excitación *nf, pl* **-ciones** : excitement
excitante *adj* : exciting
excitar *vt* : to excite, to arouse — **excitarse** *vr*
exclamación *nf, pl* **-ciones** : exclamation
exclamar *v* : to exclaim
excluir {41} *vt* EXCEPTUAR : to exclude, to leave out
exclusión *nf, pl* **-siones** : exclusion
exclusividad *nf* 1 : exclusiveness 2 : exclusive rights *pl*
exclusivista *adj & nmf* : exclusivist
exclusivo, -va *adj* : exclusive — **exclusivamente** *adv*
excomulgar {52} *vt* : to excommunicate
excomunión *nf, pl* **-niones** : excommunication
excreción *nf, pl* **-ciones** : excretion
excremento *nm* : excrement
excretar *vt* : to excrete
exculpar *vt* : to exonerate, to exculpate — **exculpación** *nf*
excursión *nf, pl* **-siones** : excursion, outing
excursionista *nmf* 1 : sightseer, tourist 2 : hiker
excusa *nf* 1 PRETEXTO : excuse 2 DISCULPA : apology
excusado *nm Mex* : toilet
excusar *vt* 1 : to excuse 2 : to exempt — **excusarse** *vr* : to apologize, to send one's regrets
execrable *adj* : detestable, abominable
exención *nf, pl* **-ciones** : exemption
exento, -ta *adj* 1 : exempt, free 2 **exento de impuestos** : tax-exempt
exequias *nfpl* FUNERALES : funeral rites
exhalación *nf, pl* **-ciones** 1 : exhalation 2 : shooting star ⟨salió como una exhalación : he took off like a shot⟩
exhalar *vt* ESPIRAR : to exhale, to give off
exhaustivo, -va *adj* : exhaustive — **exhaustivamente** *adv*
exhausto, -ta *adj* AGOTADO : exhausted, worn-out
exhibición *nf, pl* **-ciones** 1 : exhibition, show 2 : showing
exhibir *vt* : to exhibit, to show, to display — **exhibirse** *vr*
exhortación *nf, pl* **-ciones** : exhortation
exhortar *vt* : to exhort
exhumar *vt* DESENTERRAR : to exhume — **exhumación** *nf*
exigencia *nf* : demand, requirement
exigente *adj* : demanding, exacting
exigir {35} *vt* 1 : to demand, to require 2 : to exact, to levy

exiguo, -gua *adj* : meager
exiliado¹, -da *adj* : exiled, in exile
exiliado², -da *n* : exile
exiliar *vt* DESTERRAR : to exile, to banish — **exiliarse** *vr* : to go into exile
exilio *nm* DESTIERRO : exile
eximio, -mia *adj* : distinguished, eminent
eximir *vt* EXONERAR : to exempt
existencia *nf* 1 : existence 2 **existencias** *nfpl* MERCANCÍA : goods, stock
existente *adj* 1 : existing, in existence 2 : in stock
existir *vi* : to exist
éxito *nm* 1 TRIUNFO : success, hit 2 **tener éxito** : to be successful
exitoso, -sa *adj* : successful — **exitosamente** *adv*
éxodo *nm* : exodus
exoneración *nf, pl* **-ciones** EXENCIÓN : exoneration, exemption
exonerar *vt* 1 EXIMIR : to exempt, to exonerate 2 DESPEDIR : to dismiss
exorbitante *adj* : exorbitant
exorcismo *nm* : exorcism — **exorcista** *nmf*
exorcizar {21} *vt* : to exorcise
exótico, -ca *adj* : exotic
expandir *vt* EXPANSIONAR : to expand — **expandirse** *vr* : to spread
expansión *nf, pl* **-siones** 1 : expansion, spread 2 DIVERSIÓN : recreation, relaxation
expansionar *vt* EXPANDIR : to expand — **expansionarse** *vr* 1 : to expand 2 DIVERTIRSE : to amuse oneself, to relax
expansivo, -va *adj* : expansive
expatriado, -da *adj & n* : expatriate
expatriarse {85} *vr* 1 EMIGRAR : to emigrate 2 : to go into exile
expectación *nf, pl* **-ciones** : expectation, anticipation
expectante *adj* : expectant
expectativa *nf* 1 : expectation, hope 2 **expectativas** *nfpl* : prospects
expedición *nf, pl* **-ciones** : expedition
expediente *nm* 1 : expedient, means 2 ARCHIVO : file, dossier, record
expedir {54} *vt* 1 EMITIR : to issue 2 DESPACHAR : to dispatch, to send
expedito, -ta *adj* 1 : free, clear 2 : quick, easy
expeler *vt* : to expel, to eject
expendedor, -dora *n* : dealer, seller
expendio *nm* TIENDA : store, shop
expensas *nfpl* 1 : expenses, costs 2 **a expensas de** : at the expense of
experiencia *nf* 1 : experience 2 EXPERIMENTO : experiment
experimentación *nf, pl* **-ciones** : experimentation
experimental *adj* : experimental
experimentar *vi* : to experiment — *vt* 1 : to experiment with, to test out 2 : to experience
experimento *nm* EXPERIENCIA : experiment

experto, -ta *adj & n* : expert
expiación *nf, pl* **-ciones** : expiation, atonement
expiar {85} *vt* : to expiate, to atone for
expiración *nf, pl* **-ciones** VENCIMIENTO : expiration
expirar *vi* 1 FALLECER, MORIR : to pass away, to die 2 : to expire
explanada *nf* : esplanade, promenade
explayar *vt* : to extend — **explayarse** *vr* : to expound, to speak at length
explicable *adj* : explicable, explainable
explicación *nf, pl* **-ciones** : explanation
explicar {72} *vt* : to explain — **explicarse** *vr* : to understand
explicativo, -va *adj* : explanatory
explicitar *vt* : to state explicitly, to specify
explícito, -ta *adj* : explicit — **explícitamente** *adv*
exploración *nf, pl* **-ciones** : exploration
explorador, -dora *n* : explorer, scout
explorar *vt* : to explore — **exploratorio, -ria** *adj*
explosión *nf, pl* **-siones** 1 ESTALLIDO : explosion 2 : outburst ⟨una explosión de ira : an outburst of anger⟩
explosionar *vi* : to explode
explosivo, -va *adj* : explosive
explotación *nf, pl* **-ciones** 1 : exploitation 2 : operation, running
explotar *vt* 1 : to exploit 2 : to operate, to run — *vi* ESTALLAR, REVENTAR : to explode — **explotable** *adj*
exponencial *adj* : exponential — **exponencialmente** *adv*
exponente *nm* : exponent
exponer {60} *vt* 1 : to exhibit, to show, to display 2 : to explain, to present, to set forth 3 : to expose, to risk — *vi* : to exhibit
exportación *nf, pl* **-ciones** 1 : exportation 2 **exportaciones** *nfpl* : exports
exportador, -dora *n* : exporter
exportar *vt* : to export — **exportable** *adj*
exposición *nf, pl* **-ciones** 1 EXHIBICIÓN : exposition, exhibition 2 : exposure 3 : presentation, statement
expositor, -tora *n* 1 : exhibitor 2 : exponent
exprés *nms & pl* 1 : express, express train 2 : espresso
expresamente *adv* : expressly, on purpose
expresar *vt* : to express — **expresarse** *vr*
expresión *nf, pl* **-siones** : expression
expresivo, -va *adj* 1 : expressive 2 CARIÑOSO : affectionate — **expresivamente** *adv*
expreso¹, -sa *adj* : express, specific
**expreso² *nm* : express train, express
exprimidor *nm* : squeezer, juicer
exprimir *vt* 1 : to squeeze 2 : to exploit
expropiar *vt* 1 : to expropriate, to commandeer — **expropiación** *nf*
expuesto¹ *pp* → **exponer**
expuesto², -ta *adj* 1 : exposed 2 : hazardous, risky

expulsar *vt* : to expel, to eject
expulsión *nf, pl* **-siones** : expulsion
expurgar *vt* : to expurgate
expuso, etc. → **exponer**
exquisitez *nf, pl* **-teces** 1 : exquisiteness, refinement 2 : delicacy, special dish
exquisito, -ta *adj* 1 : exquisite 2 : delicious
extasiarse {85} *vr* : to be in ecstasy, to be enraptured
éxtasis *nms & pl* : ecstasy, rapture
extático, -ca *adj* : ecstatic
extemporáneo, -nea *adj* 1 : unseasonable 2 : untimely
extender {56} *vt* 1 : to spread out, to stretch out 2 : to broaden, to expand ⟨extender la influencia : to broaden one's influence⟩ 3 : to draw up (a document), to write out (a check) — **extenderse** *vr* 1 : to spread 2 : to last
extendido, -da *adj* 1 : outstretched 2 : widespread
extensamente *adv* : extensively, at length
extensible *adj* : extensible, extendable
extensión *nf, pl* **-siones** 1 : extension, stretching 2 : expanse, spread 3 : extent, range 4 : length, duration
extensivo, -va *adj* 1 : extensive 2 **hacer extensivo** : to extend
extenso, -sa *adj* 1 : extensive, detailed 2 : spacious, vast
extenuar {3} *vt* : to exhaust, to tire out — **extenuarse** *vr* — **extenuante** *adj*
exterior¹ *adj* 1 : exterior, external 2 : foreign ⟨asuntos exteriores : foreign affairs⟩
**exterior² *nm* 1 : outside 2 : abroad
exteriorizar {21} *vt* : to express, to reveal
exteriormente *adv* : outwardly
exterminar *vt* : to exterminate — **exterminación** *nf*
exterminio *nm* : extermination
externar *vt* *Mex* : to express, to display
externo, -na *adj* : external, outward
extinción *nf, pl* **-ciones** : extinction
extinguidor *nm* : fire extinguisher
extinguir {26} *vt* 1 APAGAR : to extinguish, to put out 2 : to wipe out — **extinguirse** *vr* 1 APAGARSE : to go out, to fade out 2 : to die out, to become extinct
extinto, -ta *adj* : extinct
extintor *nm* : extinguisher
extirpación *n, pl* **-ciones** : removal, excision
extirpar *vt* : to eradicate, to remove, to excise — **extirparse** *vr*
extorsión *nf, pl* **-siones** 1 : extortion 2 : harm, trouble
extorsionar *vt* : to extort
extra¹ *adv* : extra
**extra² *adj* 1 : additional, extra 2 : superior, top-quality
**extra³ *nmf* : extra (in movies)

extra[4] *nm* : extra expense ⟨paga extra : bonus⟩
extracción *nf, pl* **-ciones** : extraction
extracto *nm* **1** : extract ⟨extracto de vainilla : vanilla extract⟩ **2** : abstract, summary
extractor *nm* : extractor
extracurricular *adj* : extracurricular
extradición *nf, pl* **-ciones** : extradition
extraditar *vt* : to extradite
extraer {81} *vt* : to extract
extraído *pp* → **extraer**
extrajudicial *adj* : out-of-court
extramatrimonial *adj* : extramarital
extranjerizante *adj* : foreign-sounding, foreign-looking
extranjero[1], **-ra** *adj* : foreign
extranjero[2], **-ra** *n* : foreigner
extranjero[3] *nm* : foreign countries *pl* ⟨viajó al extranjero : he traveled abroad⟩ ⟨trabajan en el extranjero : they work overseas⟩
extrañamente *adv* : strangely, oddly
extrañamiento *nm* ASOMBRO : amazement, surprise, wonder
extrañar *vt* : to miss (someone) — **extrañarse** *vr* : to be surprised
extrañeza *nf* **1** : strangeness, oddness **2** : surprise
extraño[1], **-ña** *adj* **1** RARO : strange, odd **2** EXTRANJERO : foreign
extraño[2], **-ña** *n* DESCONOCIDO : stranger
extraoficial *adj* OFICIOSO : unofficial — **extraoficialmente** *adv*
extraordinario, -ria *adj* EXCEPCIONAL : extraordinary — **extraordinariamente** *adv*
extrasensorial *adj* : extrasensory ⟨percepción extrasensorial : extrasensory perception⟩
extraterrestre *adj & nmf* : extraterrestrial, alien

extravagancia *nf* : extravagance, outlandishness, flamboyance
extravagante *adj* : extravagant, outrageous, flamboyant
extraviar {85} *vt* **1** : to mislead, to lead astray **2** : to misplace, to lose — **extraviarse** *vr* : to get lost, to go astray
extravío *nm* **1** PÉRDIDA : loss, misplacement **2** : misconduct
extremado, -da *adj* : extreme — **extremadamente** *adv*
extremar *vt* : to carry to extremes — **extremarse** *vr* : to do one's utmost
extremidad *nf* **1** : extremity, tip, edge **2 extremidades** *nfpl* : extremities
extremista *adj & nmf* : extremist
extremo[1], **-ma** *adj* **1** : extreme, utmost **2** EXCESIVO : excessive **3 en caso extremo** : as a last resort
extremo[2] *nm* **1** : extreme, end **2 al extremo de** : to the point of **3 en ~** : in the extreme
extrovertido[1], **-da** *adj* : extroverted, outgoing
extrovertido[2], **-da** *n* : extrovert
extrudir *vt* : to extrude
exuberancia *nf* **1** : exuberance **2** : luxuriance, lushness
exuberante *adj* : exuberant, luxuriant — **exuberantemente** *adv*
exudar *vt* : to exude
exultación *nf, pl* **-ciones** : exultation, elation
exultante *adj* : exultant, elated — **exultantemente** *adv*
exultar *vi* : to exult, to rejoice
eyacular *vi* : to ejaculate — **eyaculación** *nf*
eyección *nf, pl* **-ciones** : ejection, expulsion
eyectar *vt* : to eject, to expel — **eyectarse** *vr*

F

f *nf* : sixth letter of the Spanish alphabet
fábrica *nf* FACTORÍA : factory
fabricación *nf, pl* **-ciones** : manufacture
fabricante *nmf* : manufacturer
fabricar {72} *vt* MANUFACTURAR : to manufacture, to make
fabril *adj* INDUSTRIAL : industrial, manufacturing
fábula *nf* **1** : fable **2** : fabrication, fib
fabuloso, -sa *adj* **1** : fabulous, fantastic **2** : mythical, fabled
facción *nf, pl* **-ciones 1** : faction **2 facciones** *nfpl* RASGOS : features
faccioso, -sa *adj* : factious
faceta *nf* : facet
facha *nf* : appearance, look ⟨estar hecho una facha : to look a sight⟩
fachada *nf* : facade
facial *adj* : facial

fácil *adj* **1** : easy **2** : likely, probable ⟨es fácil que no pase : it probably won't happen⟩
facilidad *nf* **1** : facility, ease **2 facilidades** *nfpl* : facilities, services **3 facilidades** *nfpl* : opportunities
facilitar *vt* **1** : to facilitate **2** : to provide, to supply
fácilmente *adv* : easily, readily
facsímil *or* **facsímile** *nm* **1** : facsimile, copy **2** : fax
facsimilar *adj* : facsimile
factibilidad *nf* : feasibility
factible *adj* : feasible, practicable
facticio, -cia *adj* : artificial, factitious
factor[1], **-tora** *n* **1** : agent, factor **2** : baggage clerk
factor[2] *nm* ELEMENTO : factor, element
factoría *nf* FÁBRICA : factory
factótum *nm* : factotum

factura nf 1 : making, manufacturing 2 : bill, invoice

facturación nf, pl **-ciones** 1 : invoicing, billing 2 : check-in

facturar vt 1 : to bill, to invoice 2 : to register, to check in

facultad nf 1 : faculty, ability ⟨facultades mentales : mental faculties⟩ 2 : authority, power 3 : school (of a university) ⟨facultad de derecho : law school⟩

facultar vt 1 : to authorize, to empower

facultativo, -va adj 1 OPTATIVO : voluntary, optional 2 : medical ⟨informe facultativo : medical report⟩

faena nf : task, job, work ⟨faenas domésticas : housework⟩

faenar vi 1 : to work, to labor 2 PESCAR : to fish

fagot nm : bassoon

faisán nm, pl **faisanes** : pheasant

faja nf 1 : sash, belt 2 : girdle 3 : strip (of land)

fajar vt 1 : to wrap (a sash or girdle) around 2 : to hit, to thrash — **fajarse** vr 1 : to put on a sash or girdle 2 : to come to blows

fajín nm, pl **-jines** : sash, belt

fajo nm : bundle, sheaf ⟨un fajo de billetes : a wad of cash⟩

falacia nf : fallacy

falaz, -laza adj, mpl **falaces** FALSO : fallacious, false

falda nf 1 : skirt ⟨falda escocesa : kilt⟩ 2 REGAZO : lap (of the body) 3 VERTIENTE : side, slope

faldón nm, pl **-dones** 1 : tail (of a shirt, etc.) 2 : full skirt 3 **faldón bautismal** : christening gown

falible adj : fallible

fálico, -ca adj : phallic

falla nf 1 : flaw, defect 2 : (geological) fault 3 : fault, failing

fallar vi 1 FRACASAR : to fail, to go wrong 2 : to rule (in a court of law) — vt 1 ERRAR : to miss (a target) 2 : to pronounce judgment on

fallecer {53} vi MORIR : to pass away, to die

fallecido, -da adj & n DIFUNTO : deceased

fallecimiento nm : demise, death

fallido, -da adj : failed, unsuccessful

fallo nm 1 SENTENCIA : sentence, judgment, verdict 2 : error, fault

falo nm : phallus, penis

falsamente adv : falsely

falsear vt 1 : to falsify, to fake 2 : to distort — vi 1 CEDER : to give way 2 : to be out of tune

falsedad nf 1 : falseness, hypocrisy 2 MENTIRA : falsehood, lie

falsete nm : falsetto

falsificación nf, pl **-ciones** 1 : counterfeit, forgery 2 : falsification

falsificador, -dora n : counterfeiter, forger

falsificar {72} vt 1 : to counterfeit, to forge 2 : to falsify

falso, -sa adj 1 FALAZ : false, untrue 2 : counterfeit, forged

falta nf 1 CARENCIA : lack ⟨hacer falta : to be lacking, to be needed⟩ 2 DEFECTO : defect, fault, error 3 : offense, misdemeanor 4 : foul (in basketball), fault (in tennis)

faltar vi 1 : to be lacking, to be needed ⟨me falta tiempo : I don't have enough time⟩ 2 : to be absent, to be missing 3 QUEDAR : to remain, to be left ⟨faltan pocos días para la fiesta : the party is just a few days away⟩ 4 **¡no faltaba más!** : don't mention it!, you're welcome!

falto, -ta adj ~ **de** : lacking (in), short of

fama nf 1 : fame 2 REPUTACIÓN : reputation 3 **de mala fama** : disreputable

famélico, -ca adj HAMBRIENTO : starving, famished

familia nf 1 : family 2 **familia política** : in-laws

familiar[1] adj 1 CONOCIDO : familiar 2 : familial, family 3 INFORMAL : informal

familiar[2] nmf PARIENTE : relation, relative

familiaridad nf 1 : familiarity 2 : informality

familiarizarse {21} vr ~ **con** : to familiarize oneself with

famoso[1], **-sa** adj CÉLEBRE : famous

famoso[2], **-sa** n : celebrity

fanal nm 1 : beacon, signal light 2 Mex : headlight

fanático, -ca adj & n : fanatic

fanatismo nm : fanaticism

fandango nm : fandango

fanfarria nf 1 : (musical) fanfare 2 : pomp, ceremony

fanfarrón[1], **-rrona** adj, mpl **-rrones** fam : bragging, boastful

fanfarrón[2], **-rrona** n, mpl **-rrones** fam : braggart

fanfarronada nf : boast, bluster

fanfarronear vi : to brag, to boast

fango nm LODO : mud, mire

fangosidad nf : muddiness

fangoso, -sa adj LODOSO : muddy

fantasear vi : to fantasize, to daydream

fantasía nf 1 : fantasy 2 : imagination

fantasioso, -sa adj : fanciful

fantasma nm : ghost, phantom

fantasmagórico, -ca adj : phantasmagoric

fantasmal adj : ghostly

fantástico, -ca adj 1 : fantastic, imaginary, unreal 2 fam : great, fantastic

faquir nm : fakir

farándula nf : show business, theater

faraón nm, pl **faraones** : pharaoh

fardo nm 1 : bale 2 : bundle

farfulla nf : jabbering

farfullar v : to jabber, to gabble

faringe nf : pharynx

faríngeo, -gea *adj* : pharyngeal
fariña *nf* : coarse manioc flour
farmacéutico[1]**, -ca** *adj* : pharmaceutical
farmacéutico[2]**, -ca** *n* : pharmacist
farmacia *nf* : drugstore, pharmacy
fármaco *nm* : medicine, drug
farmacodependencia *nf* : drug addiction
farmacología *nf* : pharmacology
faro *nm* **1** : lighthouse **2** : headlight
farol *nm* **1** : streetlight **2** : lantern, lamp **3** *fam* : bluff **4** *Mex* : headlight
farola *nf* **1** : lamppost **2** : streetlight
farolero, -ra *n fam* : bluffer
farra *nf* : spree, revelry
fárrago *nm* REVOLTIJO : hodgepodge, jumble
farsa *nf* **1** : farce **2** : fake, sham
farsante *nmf* CHARLATÁN : charlatan, fraud, phony
fascículo *nm* : fascicle, part (of a publication)
fascinación *nf, pl* **-ciones** : fascination
fascinante *adj* : fascinating
fascinar *vt* **1** : to fascinate **2** : to charm, to captivate
fascismo *nm* : fascism
fascista *adj & nmf* : fascist
fase *nf* : phase, stage
fastidiar *vt* **1** MOLESTAR : to annoy, to bother, to hassle **2** ABURRIR : to bore — *vi* : to be annoying or bothersome
fastidio *nm* **1** MOLESTIA : annoyance, nuisance, hassle **2** ABURRIMIENTO : boredom
fastidioso, -sa *adj* **1** MOLESTO : annoying, bothersome **2** ABURRIDO : boring
fatal *adj* **1** MORTAL : fatal **2** *fam* : awful, terrible **3** : fateful, unavoidable
fatalidad *nf* **1** : fatality **2** DESGRACIA : misfortune, bad luck
fatalismo *nm* : fatalism
fatalista[1] *adj* : fatalistic
fatalista[2] *nmf* : fatalist
fatalmente *adv* **1** : unavoidably **2** : unfortunately
fatídico, -ca *adj* : fateful, momentous
fatiga *nf* CANSANCIO : fatigue
fatigado, -da *adj* AGOTADO : weary, tired
fatigar {52} *vt* CANSAR : to fatigue, to tire — **fatigarse** *vr* : to wear oneself out
fatigoso, -sa *adj* : fatiguing, tiring
fatuidad *nf* **1** : fatuousness **2** VANIDAD : vanity, conceit
fatuo, -tua *adj* **1** : fatuous **2** PRESUMIDO : vain
fauces *nfpl* : jaws *pl*, maw
faul *nm, pl* **fauls** : foul, foul ball
fauna *nf* : fauna
fausto *nm* : splendor, magnificence
favor *nm* **1** : favor **2 a favor de** : in favor of **3 por ~** : please
favorable *adj* : favorable — **favorablemente** *adv*
favorecedor, -dora *adj* : becoming, flattering
favorecer {53} *vt* **1** : to favor **2** : to look well on, to suit

favorecido, -da *adj* **1** : flattering **2** : fortunate
favoritismo *nm* : favoritism
favorito, -ta *adj & n* : favorite
fax *nm* : fax, facsimile
fayuca *nf Mex* **1** : contraband **2** : black market
fayuquero *nm Mex* : smuggler, black marketeer
faz *nf* **1** : face, countenance ⟨la faz de la tierra : the face of the earth⟩ **2** : side (of coins, fabric, etc.)
fe *nf* **1** : faith **2** : assurance, testimony ⟨dar fe de : to bear witness to⟩ **3** : intention, will ⟨de buena fe : bona fide, in good faith⟩
fealdad *nf* : ugliness
febrero *nm* : February
febril *adj* : feverish — **febrilmente** *adv*
fecal *adj* : fecal
fecha *nf* **1** : date **2 fecha de caducidad** *or* **fecha de vencimiento** : expiration date **3 fecha límite** : deadline
fechar *vt* : to date, to put a date on
fechoría *nf* : misdeed
fécula *nf* : starch
fecundar *vt* : to fertilize (an egg) — **fecundación** *nf*
fecundidad *nf* **1** : fecundity, fertility **2** : productiveness
fecundo, -da *adj* FÉRTIL : fertile, fecund
federación *nf, pl* **-ciones** : federation
federal *adj* : federal
federalismo *nm* : federalism
federalista *adj & nmf* : federalist
federar *vt* : to federate
fehaciente *adj* : reliable, irrefutable — **fehacientemente** *adv*
feldespato *nm* : feldspar
felicidad *nf* **1** : happiness **2 ¡felicidades!** : best wishes!, congratulations!, happy birthday!
felicitación *nf, pl* **-ciones** **1** : congratulation ⟨¡felicitaciones! : congratulations!⟩ **2** : greeting card
felicitar *vt* CONGRATULAR : to congratulate — **felicitarse** *vr* **~ de** : to be glad about
feligrés, -gresa *n, mpl* **-greses** : parishioner
feligresía *nf* : parish
felino, -na *adj & n* : feline
feliz *adj, pl* **felices** **1** : happy **2 Feliz Navidad** : Merry Christmas
felizmente *adv* **1** : happily **2** : fortunately, luckily
felonía *nf* **1** : felony
felpa *nf* **1** : terry cloth **2** : plush
felpudo *nm* : doormat
femenil *adj* : women's, girls' ⟨futbol femenil : women's soccer⟩
femenino, -na *adj* **1** : feminine **2** : women's ⟨derechos femeninos : women's rights⟩ **3** : female
femineidad *nf* : femininity
feminidad *nf* : femininity
feminismo *nm* : feminism
feminista *adj & nmf* : feminist

femoral *adj* : femoral

fémur *nm* : femur, thighbone

fenecer {53} *vi* **1** : to die, to pass away **2** : to come to an end, to cease

fénix *nm* : phoenix

fenomenal *adj* **1** : phenomenal **2** *fam* : fantastic, terrific — **fenomenalmente** *adv*

fenómeno *nm* **1** : phenomenon **2** : prodigy, genius

feo¹ *adv* : badly, bad

feo², fea *adj* **1** : ugly **2** : unpleasant, nasty

féretro *nm* ATAÚD : coffin, casket

feria *nf* **1** : fair, market **2** : festival, holiday **3** *Mex* : change (money)

feriado, -da *adj* día feriado : public holiday

ferial *nm* : fairground

fermentar *v* : to ferment — **fermentación** *nf*

fermento *nm* : ferment

ferocidad *nf* : ferocity, fierceness

feroz *adj, pl* feroces FIERO : ferocious, fierce — **ferozmente** *adv*

férreo, -rrea *adj* **1** : iron **2** : strong, steely ⟨una voluntad férrea : an iron will⟩ **3** : strict, severe **4** vía férrea : railroad track

ferretería *nf* **1** : hardware store **2** : hardware **3** : foundry, ironworks

férrico, -ca *adj* : ferric

ferrocarril *nm* : railroad, railway

ferrocarrilero → **ferroviario**

ferroso, -sa *adj* : ferrous

ferroviario, -ria *adj* : rail, railroad

ferry *nm, pl* ferrys : ferry

fértil *adj* FECUNDO : fertile, fruitful

fertilidad *nf* : fertility

fertilizante¹ *adj* : fertilizing ⟨droga fertilizante : fertility drug⟩

fertilizante², nm ABONO : fertilizer

fertilizar *vt* ABONAR : to fertilize — **fertilización** *nf*

ferviente *adj* FERVOROSO : fervent

fervor *nm* : fervor, zeal

fervoroso, -sa *adj* FERVIENTE : fervent, zealous

festejar *vt* **1** CELEBRAR : to celebrate **2** AGASAJAR : to entertain, to wine and dine **3** *Mex fam* : to thrash, to beat

festejo *nm* : celebration, festivity

festín *nm, pl* festines : banquet, feast

festinar *vt* : to hasten, to hurry up

festival *nm* : festival

festividad *nf* **1** : festivity **2** : (religious) feast, holiday

festivo, -va *adj* **1** : festive **2** día festivo : holiday — **festivamente** *adv*

fetal *adj* : fetal

fetiche *nm* : fetish

fétido, -da *adj* : fetid, foul

feto *nm* : fetus

feudal *adj* : feudal — **feudalismo** *nm*

feudo *nm* **1** : fief **2** : domain, territory

fiabilidad *nf* : reliability, trustworthiness

fiable *adj* : trustworthy, reliable

fiado, -da *adj* : on credit

fiador, -dora *n* : bondsman, guarantor

fiambrería *nf* : delicatessen

fiambres *nfpl* : cold cuts

fianza *nf* **1** CAUCIÓN : bail, bond **2** : surety, deposit

fiar {85} *vt* **1** : to sell on credit **2** : to guarantee — **fiarse** *vr* ~ **de** : to place trust in

fiasco *nm* FRACASO : fiasco, failure

fibra *nf* **1** : fiber **2** fibra de vidrio : fiberglass

fibrilar *vi* : to fibrillate — **fibrilación** *nf*

fibroso, -sa *adj* : fibrous

ficción *nf, pl* ficciones **1** : fiction **2** : fabrication, lie

ficha *nf* **1** : index card **2** : file, record **3** : token **4** : domino, checker, counter, poker chip

fichar *vt* **1** : to open a file on **2** : to sign up — *vi* : to punch in, to punch out

fichero *nm* **1** : card file **2** : filing cabinet

ficticio, -cia *adj* : fictitious

fidedigno, -na *adj* FIABLE : reliable, trustworthy

fideicomisario, -ria *n* : trustee

fideicomiso *nm* : trusteeship, trust ⟨guardar en fideicomiso : to hold in trust⟩

fidelidad *nf* : fidelity, faithfulness

fideo *nm* : noodle

fiduciario¹, -ria *adj* : fiduciary

fiduciario², -ria *n* : trustee

fiebre *nf* **1** CALENTURA : fever, temperature ⟨fiebre amarilla : yellow fever⟩ ⟨fiebre palúdica : malaria⟩ **2** : fever, excitement

fiel¹ *adj* **1** : faithful, loyal **2** : accurate — **fielmente** *adv*

fiel², nm **1** : pointer (of a scale) **2** los fieles : the faithful

fieltro *nm* : felt

fiera *nf* **1** : wild animal, beast **2** : fiend, demon ⟨una fiera para el trabajo : a demon for work⟩

fiereza *nf* : fierceness, ferocity

fiero, -ra *adj* FEROZ : fierce, ferocious

fierro *nm* HIERRO : iron

fiesta *nf* **1** : party, fiesta **2** : holiday, feast day

figura *nf* **1** : figure **2** : shape, form **3** figura retórica : figure of speech

figurado, -da *adj* : figurative — **figuradamente** *adv*

figurar *vi* **1** : to figure, to be included ⟨Rivera figura entre los más grandes pintores de México : Rivera is among Mexico's greatest painters⟩ **2** : to be prominent, to stand out — *vt* : to represent ⟨esta línea figura el horizonte : this line represents the horizon⟩ — **figurarse** *vr* : to imagine, to think ⟨¡figúrate el lío en que se metió! : imagine the mess she got into!⟩

fijación *nf, pl* -ciones **1** : fixation, obsession **2** : fixing, establishing **3** : fastening, securing

fijador *nm* **1** : fixative **2** : hair spray

fijamente *adv* : fixedly

fijar *vt* **1** : to fasten, to affix **2** ES-TABLECER : to establish, to set up **3** CONCRETAR : to set, to fix ⟨fijar la fecha : to set the date⟩ — **fijarse** *vr* **1** : to settle, to become fixed **2** ~ **en** : to notice, to pay attention to

fijeza *nf* **1** : firmness (of convictions) **2** : persistence, constancy ⟨mirar con fijeza a : to stare at⟩

fijiano, -na *adj & n* : Fijian

fijo, -ja *adj* **1** : fixed, firm, steady **2** PER-MANENTE : permanent

fila *nf* **1** HILERA : line, file ⟨ponerse en fila : to get in line⟩ **2** : rank, row **3 filas** *nfpl* : ranks ⟨cerrar filas : to close ranks⟩

filamento *nm* : filament

filantropía *nf* : philanthropy

filantrópico, -ca *adj* : philanthropic

filántropo, -pa *n* : philanthropist

filatelia *nf* : philately, stamp collecting

filatelista *nmf* : stamp collector, philatelist

fildeador, -dora *n* : fielder

filete *nm* **1** : fillet **2** SOLOMILLO : sirloin **3** : thread (of a screw)

filiación *nf, pl* -**ciones 1** : affiliation, connection **2** : particulars *pl,* (police) description

filial¹ *adj* : filial

filial² *nf* : affiliate, subsidiary

filibustero *nm* : freebooter, pirate

filigrana *nf* **1** : filigree **2** : watermark (on paper)

filipino, -na *adj & n* : Filipino

filmación *nf, pl* -**ciones** : filming, shooting

filmar *vt* : to film, to shoot

filme *or* **film** *nm* PELÍCULA : film, movie

filmina *nf* : slide, transparency

filo *nm* **1** : cutting edge, blade **2** : edge ⟨al filo del escritorio : at the edge of the desk⟩ ⟨al filo de la medianoche : at the stroke of midnight⟩

filología *nf* : philology

filólogo, -ga *n* : philologist

filón *nm, pl* **filones 1** : seam, vein (of minerals) **2** *fam* : successful business, gold mine

filoso, -sa *adj* : sharp

filosofar *vi* : to philosophize

filosofía *nf* : philosophy

filosófico, -ca *adj* : philosophic, philosophical — **filosóficamente** *adv*

filósofo, -fa *n* : philosopher

filtración *nf* : seepage, leaking

filtrar *v* : to filter — **filtrarse** *vr* : to seep through, to leak

filtro *nm* : filter

filudo, -da *adj* : sharp

fin *nm* **1** : end **2** : purpose, aim, objective **3 en** ~ : in short **4 fin de semana** : weekend **5 por** ~ : finally, at last

finado, -da *adj & n* DIFUNTO : deceased

final¹ *adj* : final, ultimate — **finalmente** *adv*

final² *nm* : end, conclusion, finale

final³ *nf* : final, play-off

finalidad *nf* **1** : purpose, aim **2** : finality

finalista *nmf* : finalist

finalización *nf* : completion, end

finalizar {21} *v* : to finish, to end

financiación *nf, pl* -**ciones** : financing, funding

financiamiento *nm* → **financiación**

financiar *vt* : to finance, to fund

financiero¹, -ra *adj* : financial

financiero², -ra *n* : financier

financista *nmf* : financier

finanzas *nfpl* : finances, finance ⟨altas finanzas : high finance⟩

finca *nf* **1** : farm, ranch **2** : country house

fineza *nf* FINURA, REFINAMIENTO : refinement

fingido, -da *adj* : false, feigned

fingimiento *nm* : pretense

fingir {35} *v* : to feign, to pretend

finiquitar *vt* **1** : to settle (an account) **2** : to conclude, to bring to an end

finiquito *nm* : settlement (of an account)

finito, -ta *adj* : finite

finja, etc. → **fingir**

finlandés, -desa *adj & n* : Finnish

fino, -na *adj* **1** : fine, excellent **2** : delicate, slender **3** REFINADO : refined **4** : sharp, acute ⟨olfato fino : keen sense of smell⟩ **5** : subtle

finta *nf* : feint

fintar *or* **fintear** *vi* : to feint

finura *nf* **1** : fineness, high quality **2** FINEZA, REFINAMIENTO : refinement

fiordo *nm* : fjord

fique *nm* : sisal

firma *nf* **1** : signature **2** : signing **3** EM-PRESA : firm, company

firmamento *nm* : firmament, sky

firmante *nmf* : signer, signatory

firmar *v* : to sign

firme *adj* **1** : firm, resolute **2** : steady, stable

firmemente *adv* : firmly

firmeza *nf* **1** : firmness, stability **2** : strength, resolve

firuletes *nmpl* : frills, adornments

fiscal¹ *adj* : fiscal — **fiscalmente** *adv*

fiscal² *nmf* : district attorney, prosecutor

fiscalizar {21} *vt* **1** : to audit, to inspect **2** : to oversee **3** : to criticize

fisco *nm* : national treasury, exchequer

fisgar {52} *vt* HUSMEAR : to pry into, to snoop on

fisgón, -gona *n, mpl* **fisgones** : snoop, busybody

fisgonear *vi* : to snoop, to pry

fisgue, etc. → **fisgar**

física *nf* : physics

físico¹, -ca *adj* : physical — **físicamente** *adv*

físico², -ca *n* : physicist

físico³ *nm* : physique, figure

fisiología *nf* : physiology

fisiológico, -ca *adj* : physiological, physiologic

fisiólogo, -ga *n* : physiologist

fisión *nf*, *pl* **fisiones** : fission — **fisionable** *adj*

fisionomía → **fisonomía**

fisioterapeuta *nmf* : physical therapist

fisioterapia *nf* : physical therapy

fisonomía *nf* : physiognomy, features *pl*

fistol *nm Mex* : tie clip

fisura *nf* : fissure, crevasse

fláccido, -da *or* **flácido, -da** *adj* : flaccid, flabby

flaco, -ca *adj* **1** DELGADO : thin, skinny **2** : feeble, weak ⟨una flaca excusa : a feeble excuse⟩

flagelar *vt* : to flagellate — **flagelación** *nf*

flagelo *nm* **1** : scourge, whip **2** : calamity

flagrante *adj* : flagrant, glaring, blatant — **flagrantemente** *adv*

flama *nf* LLAMA : flame

flamante *adj* **1** : bright, brilliant **2** : brand-new

flamear *vi* **1** LLAMEAR : to flame, to blaze **2** : to flap, to flutter

flamenco¹, -ca *adj* **1** : flamenco **2** : Flemish

flamenco², -ca *n* : Fleming, Flemish person

flamenco³ *nm* **1** : Flemish (language) **2** : flamingo **3** : flamenco (music or dance)

flanco *nm* : flank, side

flanquear *vt* : to flank

flaquear *vi* DECAER : to flag, to weaken

flaqueza *nf* **1** DEBILIDAD : frailty, feebleness **2** : thinness **3** : weakness, failing

flato *nm* : gloom, melancholy

flatulento, -ta *adj* : flatulent — **flatulencia** *nf*

flauta *nf* **1** : flute **2** **flauta dulce** : recorder

flautín *nm*, *pl* **flautines** : piccolo

flautista *nmf* : flute player, flutist

flebitis *nf* : phlebitis

flecha *nf* : arrow

fleco *nm* **1** : bangs *pl* **2** : fringe

flema *nf* : phlegm

flemático, -ca *adj* : phlegmatic, stolid, impassive

flequillo *nm* : bangs *pl*

fletar *vt* **1** : to charter, to hire **2** : to load (freight)

flete *nm* **1** : charter fee **2** : shipping cost **3** : freight, cargo

fletero *nm* : shipper, carrier

flexibilidad *nf* : flexibility

flexibilizar {21} *vt* : to make more flexible

flexible¹ *adj* : flexible

flexible² *nm* **1** : flexible electrical cord **2** : soft hat

flirtear *vi* : to flirt

flojear *vi* **1** DEBILITARSE : to weaken, to flag **2** : to idle, to loaf around

flojedad *nf* : weakness

flojera *nf fam* **1** : lethargy, feeling of weakness **2** : laziness

flojo, -ja *adj* **1** SUELTO : loose, slack **2** : weak, poor ⟨está flojo en las ciencias : he's weak in science⟩ **3** PEREZOSO : lazy

flor *nf* **1** : flower **2** **flor de Pascua** : poinsettia

flora *nf* : flora

floración *nf* : flowering ⟨en plena floración : in full bloom⟩

floral *adj* : floral

floreado, -da *adj* : flowered, flowery

florear *vi* FLORECER : to flower, to bloom — *vt* **1** : to adorn with flowers **2** *Mex* : to flatter, to compliment

florecer {53} *vi* **1** : to bloom, to blossom **2** : to flourish, to thrive

floreciente *adj* **1** : flowering **2** PRÓSPERO : flourishing, thriving

florecimiento *nm* : flowering

floreo *nm* : flourish

florería *nf* : flower shop, florist's

florero¹, -ra *n* : florist

florero² *nm* JARRÓN : vase

floresta *nf* **1** : glade, grove **2** BOSQUE : woods

florido, -da *adj* **1** : full of flowers **2** : florid, flowery ⟨escritos floridos : flowery prose⟩

florista *nmf* : florist

floritura *nf* : frill, embellishment

flota *nf* : fleet

flotabilidad *nf* : buoyancy

flotación *nf*, *pl* **-ciones** : flotation

flotador *nm* **1** : float **2** : life preserver

flotante *adj* : floating, buoyant

flotar *vi* : to float

flote *nm* **a ~** : afloat

flotilla *nf* : flotilla, fleet

fluctuar {3} *vi* **1** : to fluctuate **2** VACILAR : to vacillate — **fluctuación** *nf* — **fluctuante** *adj*

fluidez *nf* **1** : fluency **2** : fluidity

fluido¹, -da *adj* **1** : flowing **2** : fluent **3** : fluid

fluido² *nm* : fluid

fluir {41} *vi* : to flow

flujo *nm* **1** : flow **2** : discharge

flúor *nm* : fluorine

fluoración *nf*, *pl* **-ciones** : fluoridation

fluorescencia *nf* : fluorescence — **fluorescente** *adj*

fluorizar {21} *vt* : to fluoridate

fluoruro *nm* : fluoride

fluvial *adj* : fluvial, river

fluye, etc. → **fluir**

fobia *nf* : phobia

foca *nf* : seal (animal)

focal *adj* : focal

focha *nf* : coot

foco *nm* **1** : focus **2** : center, pocket **3** : lightbulb **4** : spotlight **5** : headlight

fofo, -fa *adj* ESPONJOSO : soft, spongy **2** : flabby

fogaje *nm* **1** FUEGO : skin eruption, cold sore **2** BOCHORNO : hot and humid weather

fogata *nf* : bonfire
fogón *nm, pl* **fogones** : bonfire
fogonazo *nm* : flash, explosion
fogonero, -ra *n* : stoker (of a furnace), fireman
fogoso, -sa *adj* ARDIENTE : ardent
foguear *vt* : to inure, to accustom
foja *nf* : sheet (of paper)
folículo *nm* : follicle
folio *nm* : folio, leaf
folklore *nm* : folklore
folklórico, -ca *adj* : folk, traditional
follaje *nm* : foliage
folleto *nm* : pamphlet, leaflet, circular
fomentar *vt* **1** : to foment, to stir up **2** PROMOVER : to promote, to foster
fomento *nm* : promotion, encouragement
fonda *nf* **1** POSADA : inn **2** : small restaurant
fondeado, -da *adj fam* : rich, in the money
fondear *vt* **1** : to sound **2** : to sound out, to examine **3** *Mex* : to fund, to finance — *vi* ANCLAR : to anchor — **fondearse** *vr fam* : to get rich
fondeo *nm* **1** : anchoring **2** *Mex* : funding, financing
fondillos *mpl* : seat, bottom (of clothing)
fondo *nm* **1** : bottom **2** : rear, back, end **3** : depth **4** : background **5** : sea bed **6** : fund ⟨fondo de inversiones : investment fund⟩ **7** *Mex* : slip, petticoat **8 fondos** *nmpl* : funds, resources ⟨cheque sin fondos : bounced check⟩ **9** a ∼ : thoroughly, in depth **10 en** ∼ : abreast
fonema *nm* : phoneme
fonética *nf* : phonetics
fonético, -ca *adj* : phonetic
fontanería *nf* PLOMERÍA : plumbing
fontanero, -ra *n* PLOMERO : plumber
footing ['fu̞tɪŋ] *nm* : jogging ⟨hacer footing : to jog⟩
foque *nm* : jib
forajido, -da *n* : bandit, fugitive, outlaw
foráneo, -nea *adj* : foreign, strange
forastero, -ra *n* : stranger, outsider
forcejear *vi* : to struggle
forcejeo *nm* : struggle
fórceps *nms & pl* : forceps *pl*
forense *adj* : forensic, legal
forestal *adj* : forest
forja *nf* FRAGUA : forge
forjar *vt* **1** : to forge **2** : to shape, to create ⟨forjar un compromiso : to hammer out a compromise⟩ **3** : to invent, to concoct
forma *nf* **1** : form, shape **2** MANERA, MODO : manner, way **3** : fitness ⟨estar en forma : to be fit, to be in shape⟩ **4 formas** *nfpl* : appearances, conventions
formación *nf, pl* **-ciones 1** : formation **2** : training ⟨formación profesional : vocational training⟩

formal *adj* **1** : formal **2** : serious, dignified **3** : dependable, reliable
formaldehído *nm* : formaldehyde
formalidad *nf* **1** : formality **2** : seriousness, dignity **3** : dependability, reliability
formalizar {21} *vt* : to formalize, to make official
formalmente *adv* : formally
formar *vt* **1** : to form, to make **2** CONSTITUIR : to constitute, to make up **3** : to train, to educate — **formarse** *vr* **1** DESARROLLARSE : to develop, to take shape **2** EDUCARSE : to be educated
formatear *vt* : to format
formativo, -va *adj* : formative
formato *nm* : format
formidable *adj* **1** : formidable, tremendous **2** *fam* : fantastic, terrific
formón *nm, pl* **formones** : chisel
fórmula *nf* : formula
formulación *nf, pl* **-ciones** : formulation
formular *vt* **1** : to formulate, to draw up **2** : to make, to lodge (a protest or complaint)
formulario *nm* : form ⟨rellenar un formulario : to fill out a form⟩
fornicar {72} *vi* : to fornicate — **fornicación** *nf*
fornido, -da *adj* : well-built, burly, hefty
foro *nm* **1** : forum **2** : public assembly, open discussion
forraje *nm* **1** : forage, fodder **2** : foraging **3** *fam* : hodgepodge
forrajear *vi* : to forage
forrar *vt* **1** : to line (a garment) **2** : to cover (a book)
forro *nm* **1** : lining **2** CUBIERTA : book cover
forsitia *nf* : forsythia
fortachón, -chona *adj, pl* **-chones** *fam* : brawny, strong, tough
fortalecer {53} *vt* : to strengthen, to fortify — **fortalecerse** *vr*
fortalecimiento *nm* **1** : strengthening, fortifying **2** : fortifications
fortaleza *nf* **1** : fortress **2** FUERZA : strength **3** : resolution, fortitude
fortificación *nf, pl* **-ciones** : fortification
fortificar {72} *vt* **1** : to fortify **2** : to strengthen
fortín *nm, pl* **fortines** : small fort
fortuito, -ta *adj* : fortuitous
fortuna *nf* **1** SUERTE : fortune, luck **2** RIQUEZA : wealth, fortune
forzar {36} *vt* **1** OBLIGAR : to force, to compel **2** : to force open **3** : to strain ⟨forzar los ojos : to strain one's eyes⟩
forzosamente *adv* **1** : forcibly, by force **2** : necessarily, inevitably ⟨forzosamente tendrán que pagar : they'll have no choice but to pay⟩
forzoso, -sa *adj* **1** : forced, compulsory **2** : necessary, inevitable
fosa *nf* **1** : ditch, pit ⟨fosa séptica : septic tank⟩ **2** TUMBA : grave **3** : cavity ⟨fosas nasales : nasal cavities, nostrils⟩
fosfato *nm* : phosphate

fosforescencia *nf* : phosphorescence — **fosforescente** *adj*

fósforo *nm* **1** CERILLA : match **2** : phosphorus

fósil[1] *adj* : fossilized, fossil

fósil[2] *nm* : fossil

fosilizarse {21} *vr* : to fossilize, to become fossilized

foso *nm* **1** FOSA, ZANJA : ditch **2** : pit (of a theater) **3** : moat

foto *nf* : photo, picture

fotocopia *nf* : photocopy — **fotocopiar** *vt*

fotocopiadora *nf* COPIADORA : photocopier

fotoeléctrico, -ca *adj* : photoelectric

fotogénico, -ca *adj* : photogenic

fotografía *nf* **1** : photograph **2** : photography

fotografiar {85} *vt* : to photograph

fotográfico, -ca *adj* : photographic — **fotográficamente** *adv*

fotógrafo, -fa *n* : photographer

fotosíntesis *nf* : photosynthesis

fotosintético, -ca *adj* : photosynthetic

fracasado[1], **-da** *adj* : unsuccessful, failed

fracasado[2], **-da** *n* : failure

fracasar *vi* **1** FALLAR : to fail **2** : to fall through

fracaso *nm* FIASCO : failure

fracción *nf, pl* **fracciones 1** : fraction **2** : part, fragment **3** : faction, splinter group

fraccionamiento *nm* **1** : division, breaking up **2** *Mex* : residential area, housing development

fraccionar *vt* : to divide, to break up

fraccionario, -ria *adj* : fractional

fractura *nf* **1** : fracture **2 fractura complicada** : compound fracture

fracturarse *vr* QUEBRARSE, ROMPERSE : to fracture, to break ⟨fracturarse el brazo : to break one's arm⟩

fragancia *nf* : fragrance, scent

fragante *adj* : fragrant

fragata *nf* : frigate

frágil *adj* **1** : fragile **2** : frail, delicate

fragilidad *nf* **1** : fragility **2** : frailty, delicacy

fragmentar *vt* : to fragment — **fragmentación** *nf*

fragmentario, -ria *adj* : fragmentary, sketchy

fragmento *nm* **1** : fragment, shard **2** : bit, snippet **3** : excerpt, passage

fragor *nm* : clamor, din, roar

fragoroso, -sa *adj* : thunderous, deafening

fragoso, -sa *adj* **1** : rough, uneven **2** : thick, dense

fragua *nf* FORJA : forge

fraguar {10} *vt* **1** : to forge **2** : to conceive, to concoct, to hatch — *vi* : to set, to solidify

fraile *nm* : friar, monk

frambuesa *nf* : raspberry

francamente *adv* **1** : frankly, candidly **2** REALMENTE : really ⟨es francamente admirable : it's really impressive⟩

francés[1], **-cesa** *adj, mpl* **franceses** : French

francés[2], **-cesa** *n, mpl* **franceses** : French person, Frenchman *m*, Frenchwoman *f*

francés[3] *nm* : French (language)

franciscano, -na *adj & n* : Franciscan

francmasón, -sona *nm, mpl* **-sones** : Freemason — **francmasonería** *nf*

franco[1], **-ca** *adj* **1** CÁNDIDO : frank, candid **2** PATENTE : clear, obvious **3** : free ⟨franco a bordo : free on board⟩

franco[2] *nm* : franc

francotirador, -dora *n* : sniper

franela *nf* : flannel

franja *nf* **1** : stripe, band **2** : border, fringe

franquear *vt* **1** : to clear **2** ATRAVESAR : to cross, to go through **3** : to pay the postage on

franqueo *nm* : postage

franqueza *nf* : frankness

franquicia *nf* **1** EXENCIÓN : exemption **2** : franchise

frasco *nm* : small bottle, flask, vial

frase *nf* **1** : phrase **2** ORACIÓN : sentence

frasear *vt* : to phrase

fraternal *adj* : fraternal, brotherly

fraternidad *nf* **1** : brotherhood **2** : fraternity

fraternizar {21} *vi* : to fraternize — **fraternización** *nf*

fraterno, -na *adj* : fraternal, brotherly

fratricida *adj* : fratricidal

fratricidio *nm* : fratricide

fraude *nm* : fraud

fraudulento, -ta *adj* : fraudulent — **fraudulentamente** *adv*

fray *nm* : brother (title of a friar) ⟨Fray Bartolomé : Brother Bartholomew⟩

frazada *nf* COBIJA, MANTA : blanket

frecuencia *nf* : frequency

frecuentar *vt* : to frequent, to haunt

frecuente *adj* : frequent — **frecuentemente** *adv*

fregadera *nf fam* : hassle, pain in the neck

fregadero *nm* : kitchen sink

fregado[1], **-da** *adj fam* : annoying, bothersome

fregado[2] *nm* **1** : scrubbing, scouring **2** *fam* : mess, muddle

fregar {49} *vt* **1** : to scrub, to scour, to wash ⟨fregar los trastes : to do the dishes⟩ ⟨fregar el suelo : to scrub the floor⟩ **2** *fam* : to annoy — *vi* **1** : to wash the dishes **2** : to clean, to scrub **3** *fam* : to be annoying

freidera *nf Mex* : frying pan

freír {37} *vt* : to fry — **freírse** *vr*

frenar *vt* **1** : to brake **2** DETENER : to curb, to check — *vi* : to apply the brakes — **frenarse** *vr* : to restrain oneself

frenesí *nm* : frenzy

frenético, -ca *adj* : frantic, frenzied — **frenéticamente** *adv*

freno *nm* **1** : brake **2** : bit (of a bridle) **3** : check, restraint **4 frenos** *nmpl Mex* : braces (for teeth)

frente[1] *nm* **1** : front ⟨al frente de : at the head of⟩ ⟨en frente : in front, opposite⟩ **2** : facade **3** : front line, sphere of activity **4** : front (in meteorology) ⟨frente frío : cold front⟩ **5 hacer frente a** : to face up to, to brave

frente[2] *nf* **1** : forehead, brow **2 frente a frente** : face to face

fresa *nf* **1** : strawberry **2** : drill (in dentistry)

fresco[1], **-ca** *adj* **1** : fresh **2** : cool **3** *fam* : insolent, nervy

fresco[2] *nm* **1** : coolness **2** : fresh air ⟨al fresco : in the open air, outdoors⟩ **3** : fresco

frescor *nm* : cool air ⟨el frescor de la noche : the cool of the evening⟩

frescura *nf* **1** : freshness **2** : coolness **3** : calmness **4** DESCARO : nerve, audacity

fresno *nm* : ash (tree)

freza *nf* : spawn, roe

frezar {21} *vi* DESOVAR : to spawn

friable *adj* : friable

frialdad *nf* **1** : coldness **2** INDIFERENCIA : indifference, unconcern

fríamente *adv* : coldly, indifferently

fricasé *nm* : fricassee

fricción *nf, pl* **fricciones 1** : friction **2** : rubbing, massage **3** : discord, disagreement ⟨fricción entre los hermanos : friction between the brothers⟩

friccionar *vt* **1** FROTAR : to rub **2** : to massage

friega[1], **friegue, etc. → fregar**

friega[2] *nf* **1** FRICCIÓN : rubdown, massage **2** : annoyance, bother

frigidez *nf* : (sexual) frigidity

frigorífico *nm Spain* : refrigerator

frijol *nm* : bean ⟨frijoles refritos : refried beans⟩

frío[1], **fría** *adj* **1** : cold **2** INDIFERENTE : cool, indifferent

frío[2] *nm* **1** : cold ⟨hace mucho frío esta noche : it's very cold tonight⟩ **2** INDIFERENCIA : coldness, indifference **3 tener frío** : to feel cold ⟨tengo frío : I'm cold⟩ **4 tomar frío** RESFRIARSE : to catch a cold

friolento, -ta *adj* : sensitive to cold

friolera *nf* (*used ironically or humorously*) : trifling amount ⟨una friolera de mil dólares : a mere thousand dollars⟩

friso *nm* : frieze

fritar *vt* : to fry

frito[1] *pp* → **freír**

frito[2], **-ta** *adj* **1** : fried **2** *fam* : worn-out, fed up ⟨tener frito a alguien : to get on someone's nerves⟩ **3** *fam* : fast asleep ⟨se quedó frito en el sofá : she fell asleep on the couch⟩

fritura *nf* **1** : frying **2** : fried food

frivolidad *nf* : frivolity

frívolo, -la *adj* : frivolous — **frívolamente** *adv*

fronda *nf* **1** : frond **2 frondas** *nfpl* : foliage

frondoso, -sa *adj* : leafy, luxuriant

frontal *adj* : frontal, head-on ⟨un choque frontal : a head-on collision⟩

frontalmente *adv* : head-on

frontera *nf* : border, frontier

fronterizo, -za *adj* : border, on the border ⟨estados fronterizos : neighboring states⟩

frontispicio *nm* : frontispiece

frotar *vt* **1** : to rub **2** : to strike (a match) — **frotarse** *vr* : to rub (together)

frote *nm* : rubbing, rub

fructífero, -ra *adj* : fruitful, productive

fructificar {72} *vi* **1** : to bear or produce fruit **2** : to be productive

fructuoso, -sa *adj* : fruitful

frugal *adj* : frugal, thrifty — **frugalmente** *adv*

frugalidad *adj* : frugality

frunce *nm* : gather (in cloth), pucker

fruncido *nm* : gathering, shirring

fruncir {83} *vt* **1** : to gather, to shirr **2 fruncir el ceño** : to knit one's brow, to frown **3 fruncir la boca** : to pucker up, to purse one's lips

frunza, etc. → fruncir

frustración *nf, pl* **-ciones** : frustration

frustrado, -da *adj* **1** : frustrated **2** : failed, unsuccessful

frustrante *adj* : frustrating

frustrar *vt* : to frustrate, to thwart — **frustrarse** *vr* FRACASAR : to fail, to come to nothing ⟨se frustraron sus esperanzas : his hopes were dashed⟩

fruta *nf* : fruit

frutal[1] *adj* : fruit, fruit-bearing

frutal[2] *nm* : fruit tree

frutilla *nf* : South American strawberry

fruto *nm* **1** : fruit, agricultural product ⟨los frutos de la tierra : the fruits of the earth⟩ **2** : result, consequence ⟨los frutos de su trabajo : the fruits of his labor⟩

fucsia *adj & nm* : fuchsia

fue, etc. → ir, ser

fuego *nm* **1** : fire **2** : light ⟨¿tienes fuego? : have you got a light?⟩ **3** : flame, burner (on a stove) **4** : ardor, passion **5** FOGAJE : skin eruption, cold sore **6 fuegos artificiales** *nmpl* : fireworks

fuelle *nm* : bellows

fuente *nf* **1** MANANTIAL : spring **2** : fountain **3** ORIGEN : source ⟨fuentes informativas : sources of information⟩ **4** : platter, serving dish

fuera *adv* **1** : outside, out **2** : abroad, away **3 ~ de** : outside of, out of, beyond **4 ~ de** : besides, in addition to ⟨fuera de eso : aside from that⟩ **5 fuera de lugar** : out of place, amiss

fuerce, fuerza etc. → forzar

fuero *nm* **1** JURISDICCIÓN : jurisdiction **2** : privilege, exemption **3 fuero interno** : conscience, heart of hearts

fuerte[1] *adv* **1** : strongly, tightly, hard **2** : loudly **3** : abundantly

fuerte[2] *adj* **1** : strong **2** : intense ⟨un fuerte dolor : an intense pain⟩ **3** : loud **4** : extreme, excessive

fuerte[3] *nm* **1** : fort, stronghold **2** : forte, strong point

fuerza *nf* **1** : strength, vigor ⟨fuerza de voluntad : willpower⟩ **2** : force ⟨fuerza bruta : brute force⟩ **3** : power, might ⟨fuerza de brazos : manpower⟩ **4 fuerzas** *nfpl* : forces ⟨fuerzas armadas : armed forces⟩ **5 a fuerza de** : by, by dint of

fuetazo *nm* : lash

fuga *nf* **1** HUIDA : flight, escape **2** : fugue **3** : leak ⟨fuga de gas : gas leak⟩

fugarse {52} *vr* **1** : to escape **2** HUIR : to flee, to run away **3** : to elope

fugaz *adj, pl* **fugaces** : brief, fleeting

fugitivo, -va *adj & n* : fugitive

fulana *nf* : hooker, slut

fulano, -na *n* **1** : so-and-so, what's-his-name, what's-her-name ⟨fulano, mengano, y zutano : Tom, Dick, and Harry⟩ ⟨señora fulana de tal : Mrs. so-and-so⟩

fulcro *nm* : fulcrum

fulgor *nm* : brilliance, splendor

fulgurar *vi* : to shine brightly, to gleam, to glow

fulminante *adj* **1** : fulminating, explosive **2** : devastating, terrible ⟨una mirada fulminante : a withering look⟩

fulminar *vt* **1** : to strike with lightning **2** : to strike down ⟨fulminar a alguien con la mirada : to look daggers at someone⟩

fumador, -dora *n* : smoker

fumar *v* : to smoke

fumble *nm* : fumble (in football)

fumblear *vt* : to fumble (in football)

fumigante *nm* : fumigant

fumigar {52} *vt* : to fumigate — **fumigación** *nf*

funámbulo, -la *n* EQUILIBRISTA : tightrope walker

función *nf, pl* **funciones 1** : function **2** : duty **3** : performance, show

funcional *adj* : functional — **funcionalmente** *adv*

funcionamiento *nm* **1** : functioning **2 en ~** : in operation

funcionar *vi* **1** : to function **2** : to run, to work

funcionario, -ria *n* : civil servant, official

funda *nf* **1** : case, cover, sheath **2** : pillowcase

fundación *nf, pl* **-ciones** : foundation, establishment

fundado, -da *adj* : well-founded, justified

fundador, -dora *n* : founder

fundamental *adj* BÁSICO : fundamental, basic — **fundamentalmente** *adv*

fundamentalismo *nm* : fundamentalism

fundamentalista *nmf* : fundamentalist

fundamentar *vt* **1** : to lay the foundations for **2** : to support, to back up **3** : to base, to found

fundamento *nm* : basis, foundation, groundwork

fundar *vt* **1** ESTABLECER, INSTITUIR : to found, to establish **2** BASAR : to base — **fundarse** *vr* ~ **en** : to be based on, to stem from

fundición *nf, pl* **-ciones 1** : founding, smelting **2** : foundry

fundir *vt* **1** : to melt down, to smelt **2** : to fuse, to merge **3** : to burn out (a lightbulb) — **fundirse** *vr* **1** : to fuse together, to blend, to merge **2** : to melt, to thaw **3** : to fade (in television or movies)

fúnebre *adj* **1** : funeral, funereal **2** LÚGUBRE : gloomy, mournful

funeral[1] *adj* : funeral, funerary

funeral[2] *nm* **1** : funeral **2 funerales** *nmpl* EXEQUIAS : funeral rites

funeraria *nf* **1** : funeral home, funeral parlor **2 director de funeraria** : funeral director, undertaker

funerario, -ria *adj* : funeral

funesto, -ta *adj* : terrible, disastrous ⟨consecuencias funestas : disastrous consequences⟩

fungicida[1] *adj* : fungicidal

fungicida[2] *nm* : fungicide

fungir {35} *vi* : to act, to function ⟨fungir de asesor : to act as a consultant⟩

fungoso, -sa *adj* : fungous

funja, etc. → fungir

furgón *nm, pl* **furgones 1** : van, truck **2** : freight car, boxcar **3 furgón de cola** : caboose

furgoneta *nf* : van

furia *nf* **1** CÓLERA, IRA : fury, rage **2** : violence, fury ⟨la furia de la tormenta : the fury of the storm⟩

furibundo, -da *adj* : furious

furiosamente *adv* : furiously, frantically

furioso, -sa *adj* **1** AIRADO : furious, irate **2** : intense, violent

furor *nm* **1** : fury, rage **2** : violence (of the elements) **3** : passion, frenzy **4** : enthusiasm ⟨hacer furor : to be all the rage⟩

furtivo, -va *adj* : furtive — **furtivamente** *adv*

furúnculo *nm* DIVIESO : boil

fuselaje *nm* : fuselage

fusible *nm* : (electrical) fuse

fusil *nm* : rifle

fusilar *vt* **1** : to shoot, to execute (by firing squad) **2** *fam* : to plagiarize, to pirate

fusilería *nf* **1** : rifles *pl*, rifle fire **2 descarga de fusilería** : fusillade

fusión *nf, pl* **fusiones 1** : fusion **2** : union, merger

fusionar *vt* **1** : to fuse **2** : to merge, to amalgamate — **fusionarse** *vr*
fusta *nf* : riding crop
fustigar {52} *vt* **1** AZOTAR : to whip, to lash **2** : to upbraid, to berate
futbol *or* **fútbol** *nm* **1** : soccer **2 futbol americano** : football
futbolista *nmf* : soccer player
futesa *nf* **1** : small thing, trifle **2 futesas** *nfpl* : small talk
fútil *adj* : trifling, trivial
futurista *adj* : futuristic
futuro¹, -ra *adj* : future
futuro² *nm* PORVENIR : future

G

g *nf* : seventh letter of the Spanish alphabet
gabán *nm, pl* **gabanes** : topcoat, overcoat
gabardina *nf* **1** : gabardine **2** : trench coat, raincoat
gabarra *nf* : barge
gabinete *nm* **1** : cabinet (in government) **2** : study, office (in the home) **3** : (professional) office
gablete *nm* : gable
gabonés, -nesa *adj & n, mpl* **-neses** : Gabonese
gacela *nf* : gazelle
gaceta *nf* : gazette, newspaper
gachas *nfpl* : porridge
gacho, -cha *adj* **1** : drooping, turned downward **2** *Mex fam* : nasty, awful **3 ir a gachas** *fam* : to go on all fours
gaélico¹, -ca *adj* : Gaelic
gaélico² *nm* : Gaelic (language)
gafas *nfpl* ANTEOJOS : eyeglasses, glasses
gaita *nf* : bagpipes *pl*
gajes *nmpl* **gajes del oficio** : occupational hazards
gajo *nm* **1** : broken branch (of a tree) **2** : cluster, bunch (of fruit) **3** : segment (of citrus fruit)
gala *nf* **1** : gala ⟨vestido de gala : formal dress⟩ ⟨tener algo a gala : to be proud of something⟩ **2 galas** *nfpl* : finery, attire
galáctico, -ca *adj* : galactic
galán *nm, pl* **galanes 1** : ladies' man, gallant **2** : leading man, hero **3** : boyfriend, suitor
galano, -na *adj* **1** : elegant **2** *Mex* : mottled
galante *adj* : gallant, attentive — **galantemente** *adv*
galantear *vt* **1** CORTEJAR : to court, to woo **2** : to flirt with
galanteo *nm* **1** CORTEJO : courtship **2** : flirtation, flirting
galantería *nf* **1** : gallantry, attentiveness **2** : compliment
galápago *nm* : aquatic turtle
galardón *nm, pl* **-dones** : award, prize
galardonado, -da *adj* : prize-winning
galardonar *vt* : to give an award to
galaxia *nf* : galaxy
galeno *nm fam* : physician, doctor
galeón *nm, pl* **galeones** : galleon
galera *nf* : galley

galería *nf* **1** : gallery, balcony (in a theater) ⟨galería comercial : shopping mall⟩ **2** : corridor, passage
galerón *n, mpl* **-rones** *Mex* : large hall
galés¹, -lesa *adj* : Welsh
galés², -lesa *n, mpl* **galeses 1** : Welshman *m*, Welshwoman *f* **2 los galeses** : the Welsh
galés³ *nm* : Welsh (language)
galgo *nm* : greyhound
galimatías *nms & pl* : gibberish, nonsense
galio *nm* : gallium
gallardete *nm* : pennant, streamer
gallardía *nf* **1** VALENTÍA : bravery **2** APOSTURA : elegance, gracefulness
gallardo, -da *adj* **1** VALIENTE : brave **2** APUESTO : elegant, graceful
gallear *vi* : to show off, to strut around
gallego¹, -ga *adj* **1** : Galician **2** *fam* : Spanish
gallego², -ga *n* **1** : Galician **2** *fam* : Spaniard
galleta *nf* **1** : cookie **2** : cracker
gallina *nf* **1** : hen **2 gallina de Guinea** : guinea fowl
gallinazo *nm* : vulture, buzzard
gallinero *nm* : chicken coop, henhouse
gallito, -ta *adj fam* : cocky, belligerent
gallo *nm* **1** : rooster, cock **2** *fam* : squeak or crack in the voice **3** *Mex* : serenade **4 gallo de pelea** : gamecock
galo¹, -la *adj* **1** : Gaulish **2** : French
galo², -la *n* : Frenchman *m*, Frenchwoman *f*
galocha *nf* : galosh
galón *nm, pl* **galones 1** : gallon **2** : stripe (military insignia)
galopada *nf* : gallop
galopante *adj* : galloping ⟨inflación galopante : galloping inflation⟩
galopar *vi* : to gallop
galope *nm* : gallop
galpón *nm, pl* **galpones** : shed, storehouse
galvanizar {21} *vt* : to galvanize — **galvanización** *nf*
gama *nf* **1** : range, spectrum, gamut **2** → **gamo**
gamba *nf* : large shrimp, prawn
gamberro, -rra *n Spain* : hooligan, troublemaker
gambiano, -na *adj & n* : Gambian
gambito *nm* : gambit (in chess)
gameto *nm* : gamete

gamo, -ma n : fallow-deer

gamuza nf **1** : suede **2** : chamois

gana nf **1** : desire, inclination **2 de buena gana** : willingly, readily, gladly **3 de mala gana** : reluctantly, halfheartedly **4 tener ganas de** : to feel like, to be in the mood for ⟨tengo ganas de bailar : I feel like dancing⟩ **5 ponerle ganas a algo** : to put effort into something

ganadería nf **1** : cattle raising, stock-breeding **2** : cattle ranch **3** GANADO : cattle pl, livestock

ganadero¹, -ra adj : cattle, ranching

ganadero², -ra n : rancher, stockbreeder

ganado nm **1** : cattle pl, livestock **2 ganado ovino** : sheep pl **3 ganado porcino** : swine pl

ganador¹, -dora adj : winning

ganador², -dora n : winner

ganancia nf **1** : profit **2 ganancias** nfpl : winnings, gains

ganancioso, -sa adj : profitable

ganar vt **1** : to win **2** : to gain ⟨ganar tiempo : to buy time⟩ **3** : to earn ⟨ganar dinero : to make money⟩ **4** : to acquire, to obtain — vi **1** : to win **2** : to profit ⟨salir ganando : to come out ahead⟩ — **ganarse** vr **1** : to gain, to win ⟨ganarse a alguien : to win someone over⟩ **2** : to earn ⟨ganarse la vida : to make a living⟩ **3** : to deserve

gancho nm **1** : hook **2** : clothes hanger **3** : hairpin, bobby pin **4** Col : safety pin

gandul¹ nm CA, Car, Col : pigeon pea

gandul², -dula n fam : idler, lazybones

gandulear vi : to idle, to loaf, to lounge about

ganga nf : bargain

ganglio nm **1** : ganglion **2** : gland

gangrena nf : gangrene — **gangrenoso, -sa** adj

gángster nmf, pl **gángsters** : gangster

gansada nf : silly thing, nonsense

ganso, -sa n **1** : goose, gander m **2** : idiot, fool

gañido nm : yelp (of a dog)

gañir {38} vi : to yelp

garabatear v : to scribble, to scrawl, to doodle

garabato nm **1** : doodle **2 garabatos** nmpl : scribble, scrawl

garaje nm : garage

garante nmf : guarantor

garantía nf **1** : guarantee, warranty **2** : security ⟨garantía de trabajo : job security⟩

garantizar {21} vt : to guarantee

garapiña nf : pineapple drink

garapiñar vt : to candy

garbanzo nm : chickpea, garbanzo

garbo nm **1** DONAIRE : grace, poise **2** : jauntiness

garboso, -sa adj **1** : graceful **2** : elegant, stylish

garceta nf : egret

gardenia nf : gardenia

garfio nm : hook, gaff, grapnel

gargajo nm fam : phlegm

garganta nf **1** : throat **2** : neck (of a person or a bottle) **3** : ravine, narrow pass

gargantilla nf : choker, necklace

gárgara nf **1** : gargle, gargling **2 hacer gárgaras** : to gargle

gargarizar vi : to gargle

gárgola nf : gargoyle

garita nf **1** : cabin, hut **2** : sentry box, lookout post

garoso, -sa adj Col, Ven : gluttonous, greedy

garra nf **1** : claw **2** : hand, paw **3 garras** nfpl : claws, clutches ⟨caer en las garras de alguien : to fall into someone's clutches⟩

garrafa nf : decanter, carafe

garrafal adj : terrible, monstrous

garrafón nm, pl **-fones** : large decanter, large bottle

garrapata nf : tick

garrobo nm CA : large lizard, iguana

garrocha nf **1** PICA : lance, pike **2** : pole ⟨salto con garrocha : pole vault⟩

garrotazo nm : blow (with a club)

garrote nm **1** : club, stick **2** Mex : brake

garúa nf : drizzle

garuar {3} v impers LLOVIZNAR : to drizzle

garza nf : heron

gas nm : gas, vapor, fumes pl ⟨gas lagrimógeno : tear gas⟩

gasa nf : gauze

gasear vt **1** : to gas **2** : to aerate (a liquid)

gaseosa nf REFRESCO : soda, soft drink

gaseoso, -sa adj **1** : gaseous **2** : carbonated, fizzy

gasoducto nm : gas pipeline

gasolina nf : gasoline, gas

gasolinera nf : gas station, service station

gastado, -da adj **1** : spent **2** : worn, worn-out

gastador¹, -dora adj : extravagant, spendthrift

gastador², -dora n : spendthrift

gastar vt **1** : to spend **2** CONSUMIR : to consume, to use up **3** : to squander, to waste **4** : to wear ⟨gasta un bigote : he sports a mustache⟩ — **gastarse** vr **1** : to spend, to expend **2** : to run down, to wear out

gasto nm **1** : expense, expenditure **2** DETERIORO : wear **3 gastos generales** or **gastos indirectos** : overhead

gástrico, -ca adj : gastric

gastritis nf : gastritis

gastronomía nf : gastronomy

gastronómico, -ca adj : gastronomic

gastrónomo, -ma n : gourmet

gatas adv **andar a gatas** : to crawl, to go on all fours

gatear vi **1** : to crawl **2** : to climb, to clamber (up)

gatillero *nm Mex* : gunman
gatillo *nm* : trigger
gatito, -ta *n* : kitten
gato¹, -ta *n* : cat
gato² *nm* : jack (for an automobile)
gauchada *nf Arg, Uru* : favor, kindness
gaucho *nm* : gaucho
gaveta *nf* 1 CAJÓN : drawer 2 : till
gavilla *nf* 1 : gang, band 2 : sheaf
gaviota *nf* : gull, seagull
gay [ˈge, ˈgai] *adj* : gay (homosexual)
gaza *nf* : loop
gazapo *nm* 1 : young rabbit 2 : misprint, error
gazmoñería *nf* MOJIGATERÍA : prudery, primness
gazmoño¹, -ña *adj* : prudish, prim
gazmoño², -ña *n* MOJIGATO : prude, prig
gaznate *nm* : throat, gullet
gazpacho *nm* : gazpacho
géiser *or* **géyser** *nm* : geyser
gel *nm* : gel
gelatina *nf* : gelatin
gélido, -da *adj* : icy, freezing cold
gelificarse *vr* : to jell
gema *nf* : gem
gemelo¹, -la *adj & n* MELLIZO : twin
gemelo² *nm* 1 : cuff link 2 **gemelos** *nmpl* BINOCULARES : binoculars
gemido *nm* : moan, groan, wail
Géminis *nmf* : Gemini
gemir {54} *vi* : to moan, to groan, to wail
gen *or* **gene** *nm* : gene
gendarme *nmf* POLICÍA : police officer, policeman *m*, policewoman *f*
gendarmería *nf* : police
genealogía *nf* : genealogy
genealógico, -ca *adj* : genealogical
generación *nf, pl* **-ciones** 1 : generation ⟨tercera generación : third generation⟩ 2 : generating, creating 3 : class ⟨la generación del '97 : the class of '97⟩
generacional *adj* : generation, generational
generador *nm* : generator
general¹ *adj* 1 : general 2 **en ~** *or* **por lo general** : in general, generally
general² *nmf* 1 : general 2 **general de división** : major general
generalidad *nf* 1 : generality, generalization 2 : majority
generalización *nf, pl* **-ciones** 1 : generalization 2 : escalation, spread
generalizado, -da *adj* : generalized, widespread
generalizar {21} *vi* : to generalize — *vt* : to spread, to spread out — **generalizarse** *vr* : to become widespread
generalmente *adv* : usually, generally
generar *vt* : to generate — **generarse** *vr*
genérico, -ca *adj* : generic
género *nm* 1 : genre, class, kind ⟨el género humano : the human race, mankind⟩ 2 : gender (in grammar) 3 **géneros** *nmpl* : goods, commodities
generosidad *nf* : generosity
generoso, -sa *adj* 1 : generous, unselfish 2 : ample — **generosamente** *adv*

genética *nf* : genetics
genético, -ca *adj* : genetic — **genéticamente** *adv*
genetista *nmf* : geneticist
genial *adj* 1 AGRADABLE : genial, pleasant 2 : brilliant ⟨una obra genial : a work of genius⟩ 3 *fam* FORMIDABLE : fantastic, terrific
genialidad *nf* 1 : genius 2 : stroke of genius 3 : eccentricity
genio *nm* 1 : genius 2 : temper, disposition ⟨de mal genio : bad-tempered⟩ 3 : genie
genital *adj* : genital
genitales *nmpl* : genitals, genitalia
genocidio *nm* : genocide
genotipo *nm* : genotype
gente *nf* 1 : people 2 : relatives *pl*, folks *pl* 3 **gente menuda** *fam* : children, kids *pl* 4 **ser buena gente** : to be nice, to be kind
gentil¹ *adj* 1 AMABLE : kind 2 : gentile
gentil² *nmf* : gentile
gentileza *nf* 1 AMABILIDAD : kindness 2 CORTESÍA : courtesy
gentilicio, -cia *adj* 1 : national, tribal 2 : family
gentío *nm* MUCHEDUMBRE, MULTITUD : crowd, mob
gentuza *nf* CHUSMA : riffraff, rabble
genuflexión *nf, pl* **-xiones** 1 : genuflection 2 **hacer una genuflexión** : to genuflect
genuino, -na *adj* : genuine — **genuinamente** *adv*
geofísica *nf* : geophysics
geofísico, -ca *adj* : geophysical
geografía *nf* : geography
geográfico, -ca *adj* : geographic, geographical — **geográficamente** *adv*
geógrafo, -fa *n* : geographer
geología *nf* : geology
geológico, -ca *adj* : geologic, geological — **geológicamente** *adv*
geólogo, -ga *n* : geologist
geometría *nf* : geometry
geométrico, -ca *adj* : geometric, geometrical — **geométricamente** *adv*
geopolítica *nf* : geopolitics
geopolítico, -ca *adj* : geopolitical
georgiano, -na *adj & n* : Georgian
geranio *nm* : geranium
gerbo *nm* : gerbil
gerencia *nf* : management, administration
gerencial *adj* : managerial
gerente *nmf* : manager, director
geriatría *nf* : geriatrics
geriátrico, -ca *adj* : geriatric
germanio *nm* : germanium
germano, -na *adj* : Germanic, German
germen *nm, pl* **gérmenes** : germ
germicida *nf* : germicide
germinación *nf, pl* **-ciones** : germination
germinar *vi* : to germinate, to sprout
gerontología *nf* : gerontology
gerundio *nm* : gerund

gesta *nf* : deed, exploit
gestación *nf, pl* **-ciones** : gestation
gesticulación *nf, pl* **-ciones** : gesturing, gesticulation
gesticular *vi* : to gesticulate, to gesture
gestión *nf, pl* **gestiones 1** TRÁMITE : procedure, step **2** ADMINISTRACIÓN : management **3 gestiones** *nfpl* : negotiations
gestionar *vt* **1** : to negotiate, to work towards **2** ADMINISTRAR : to manage, to handle
gesto *nm* **1** ADEMÁN : gesture **2** : facial expression **3** MUECA : grimace
gestor¹, -tora *adj* : facilitating, negotiating, managing
gestor², -tora *n* : facilitator, manager
géyser → géiser
ghanés, -nesa *adj & n, mpl* **ghaneses** : Ghanaian
ghetto → gueto
giba *nf* **1** : hump (of an animal) **2** : hunchback (of a person)
gibón *nm, pl* **gibones** : gibbon
giboso¹, -sa *adj* : hunchbacked, humpbacked
giboso², -sa *n* : hunchback, humpback
gigabyte *nm* : gigabyte
gigante¹ *adj* : giant, gigantic
gigante², -ta *n* : giant
gigantesco, -ca *adj* : gigantic, huge
gime, etc. → gemir
gimnasia *nf* : gymnastics
gimnasio *nm* : gymnasium, gym
gimnasta *nmf* : gymnast
gimnástico, -ca *adj* : gymnastic
gimotear *vi* LLORIQUEAR : to whine, to whimper
gimoteo *nm* : whimpering
ginebra *nf* : gin
ginecología *nf* : gynecology
ginecológico, -ca *adj* : gynecologic, gynecological
ginecólogo, -ga *n* : gynecologist
ginseng *nm* : ginseng
gira *nf* : tour
giralda *nf* : weather vane
girar *vi* **1** : to turn around, to revolve **2** : to swing around, to swivel — *vt* **1** : to turn, to twist, to rotate **2** : to draft (checks) **3** : to transfer (funds)
girasol *nm* MIRASOL : sunflower
giratorio, -ria *adj* : revolving
giro *nm* **1** VUELTA : turn, rotation **2** : change of direction ⟨giro de 180 grados : U-turn, about-face⟩ **3 giro bancario** : bank draft **4 giro postal** : money order
giroscopio *or* **giróscopo** *nm* : gyroscope
gis *nm Mex* : chalk
gitano, -na *adj & n* : Gypsy
glacial *adj* : glacial, icy — **glacialmente** *adv*
glaciar *nm* : glacier
gladiador *nm* : gladiator
gladiolo *or* **gladíolo** *nm* : gladiolus
glándula *nf* : gland — **glandular** *adj*

glaseado *nm* : glaze, icing
glasear *vt* : to glaze
glaucoma *nm* : glaucoma
glicerina *nf* : glycerin, glycerol
glicinia *nf* : wisteria
global *adj* **1** : global, worldwide **2** : full, comprehensive **3** : total, overall
globalizar {21} *vt* **1** ABARCAR : to include, to encompass **2** : to extend worldwide
globalmente *adv* : globally, as a whole
globo *nm* **1** : globe, sphere **2** : balloon **3 globo ocular** : eyeball
glóbulo *nm* **1** : globule **2** : blood cell, corpuscle
gloria *nf* **1** : glory **2** : fame, renown **3** : delight, enjoyment **4** : star, legend ⟨las glorias del cine : the great names in motion pictures⟩
glorieta *nf* **1** : rotary, traffic circle **2** : bower, arbor
glorificar {72} *vt* ALABAR : to glorify — **glorificación** *nf*
glorioso, -sa *adj* : glorious — **gloriosamente** *adv*
glosa *nf* **1** : gloss **2** : annotation, commentary
glosar *vt* **1** : to gloss **2** : to annotate, to comment on (a text)
glosario *nm* : glossary
glotis *nf* : glottis
glotón¹, -tona *adj, mpl* **glotones** : gluttonous
glotón², -tona *n, mpl* **glotones** : glutton
glotón³ *nm, pl* **glotones** : wolverine
glotonería *nf* GULA : gluttony
glucosa *nf* : glucose
glutinoso, -sa *adj* : glutinous
gnomo [ˈnomo] *nm* : gnome
gobernación *nf, pl* **-ciones** : governing, government
gobernador, -dora *n* : governor
gobernante¹ *adj* : ruling, governing
gobernante² *nmf* : ruler, leader, governor
gobernar {55} *vt* **1** : to govern, to rule **2** : to steer, to sail (a ship) — *vi* **1** : to govern **2** : to steer
gobierno *nm* : government
goce¹, etc. → gozar
goce² *nm* **1** PLACER : enjoyment, pleasure **2** : use, possession
gol *nm* : goal (in soccer)
golear *vt* : to rout, to score many goals against (in soccer)
goleta *nf* : schooner
golf *nm* : golf
golfista *nmf* : golfer
golfo *nm* : gulf, bay
golondrina *nf* **1** : swallow (bird) **2 golondrina de mar** : tern
golosina *nf* : sweet, snack
goloso, -sa *adj* : fond of sweets ⟨ser goloso : to have a sweet tooth⟩
golpazo *nm* : heavy blow, bang, thump
golpe *nm* **1** : blow ⟨caerle a golpes a alguien : to give someone a beating⟩ **2** : knock **3 de ~** : suddenly **4 de un**

golpe : all at once, in one fell swoop 5
golpe de estado : coup, coup d'etat 6
golpe de suerte : stroke of luck
golpeado, -da adj 1 : beaten, hit 2 : bruised (of fruit) 3 : dented
golpear vt 1 : to beat (up), to hit 2 : to slam, to bang, to strike — vi 1 : to knock (at a door) 2 : to beat ⟨la lluvia golpeaba contra el tejado : the rain beat against the roof⟩ — **golpearse** vr
golpetear v : to knock, to rattle, to tap
golpeteo nm : banging, knocking, tapping
goma nf 1 : gum ⟨goma de mascar : chewing gum⟩ 2 CAUCHO : rubber ⟨goma espuma : foam rubber⟩ 3 PEGAMENTO : glue 4 : rubber band 5 Arg : tire 6 or **goma de borrar** : eraser
gomita nf : rubber band
gomoso, -sa adj : gummy, sticky
góndola nf : gondola
gong nm : gong
gonorrea nf : gonorrhea
gorda nf Mex : thick corn tortilla
gordinflón[1], -flona adj, mpl **-flones** fam : chubby, pudgy
gordinflón[2], -flona n, mpl **-flones** fam : chubby person
gordo[1], -da adj 1 : fat 2 : thick 3 : fatty, greasy, oily 4 : unpleasant ⟨me cae gorda tu tía : I can't stand your aunt⟩
gordo[2], -da n : fat person
gordo[3] nm 1 GRASA : fat 2 : jackpot
gordura nf : fatness, flab
gorgojo nm : weevil
gorgotear vi : to gurgle, to bubble
gorgoteo nm : gurgle
gorila nm : gorilla
gorjear vi : to chirp, to tweet, to warble 2 : to gurgle
gorjeo nm 1 : chirping, warbling 2 : gurgling
gorra nf 1 : bonnet 2 : cap 3 **de ~** fam : for free, at someone else's expense ⟨vivir de gorra : to sponge, to freeload⟩
gorrear vt fam : to bum, to scrounge — vi fam : to freeload
gorrero, -ra n fam : freeloader, sponger
gorrión nm, pl **gorriones** : sparrow
gorro nm 1 : cap 2 **estar hasta el gorro** : to be fed up
gorrón, -rrona n, mpl **gorrones** fam : freeloader, scrounger
gorronear vt fam : to bum, to scrounge — vi fam : to freeload
gota nf 1 : drop ⟨una gota de sudor : a bead of sweat⟩ ⟨como dos gotas de agua : like two peas in a pod⟩ ⟨sudar la gota gorda : to sweat buckets, to work very hard⟩ 2 : gout
gotear v 1 : to drip 2 : to leak — v impers LLOVIZNAR : to drizzle
goteo nm : drip, dripping
gotera nf 1 : leak 2 : stain (from dripping water)
gotero nm : (medicine) dropper
gótico, -ca adj : Gothic
gourmet nmf : gourmet

gozar {21} vi 1 : to enjoy oneself, to have a good time 2 **~ de** : to enjoy, to have, to possess ⟨gozar de buena salud : to enjoy good health⟩ 3 **~ con** : to take delight in
gozne nm BISAGRA : hinge
gozo nm 1 : joy 2 PLACER : enjoyment, pleasure
gozoso, -sa adj : joyful
grabación nf, pl **-ciones** : recording
grabado nm 1 : engraving 2 **grabado al aguafuerte** : etching
grabador, -dora n : engraver
grabadora nf : tape recorder
grabar vt 1 : to engrave 2 : to record, to tape — vi **grabar al aguafuerte** : to etch — **grabarse** vr **grabársele a alguien en la memoria** : to become engraved on someone's mind
gracia nf 1 : grace 2 : favor, kindness 3 : humor, wit ⟨su comentario no me hizo gracia : I wasn't amused by his remark⟩ 4 **gracias** nfpl : thanks ⟨gracias! : thank you!⟩ ⟨dar gracias : to give thanks⟩
grácil adj 1 : graceful 2 : delicate, slender, fine
gracilidad nm : gracefulness
gracioso, -sa adj 1 CHISTOSO : funny, amusing 2 : cute, attractive
grada nf 1 : harrow 2 PELDAÑO : step, stair 3 **gradas** nfpl : bleachers, grandstand
gradación nf, pl **-ciones** : gradation, scale
gradar vt : to harrow, to hoe
gradería nf : tiers pl, stands pl, rows pl (in a theater)
gradiente nf : gradient, slope
grado nm 1 : degree (in meteorology and mathematics) ⟨grado centígrado : degree centigrade⟩ 2 : extent, level, degree ⟨en grado sumo : greatly, to the highest degree⟩ 3 RANGO : rank 4 : year, class (in education) 5 **de buen grado** : willingly, readily
graduable adj : adjustable
graduación nf, pl **-ciones** 1 : graduation (from a school) 2 GRADO : rank 3 : alcohol content, proof
graduado[1], -da adj 1 : graduated 2 **lentes graduados** : prescription lenses
graduado[2], -da n : graduate
gradual adj : gradual — **gradualmente** adv
graduar {3} v 1 : to regulate, to adjust 2 CALIBRAR : to calibrate, to gauge — **graduarse** vr : to graduate (from a school)
graffiti or **grafiti** nmpl : graffiti pl
gráfica nf → **gráfico[2]**
gráfico[1], -ca adj : graphic — **gráficamente** adv
gráfico[2] nm 1 : graph, chart 2 : graphic (for a computer, etc.) 3 **gráfico de barras** : bar graph
grafismo nm : graphics pl

grafito *nm* : graphite
gragea *nf* 1 : coated pill or tablet 2 **grageas** *nfpl* : sprinkles, jimmies
grajo *nm* : rook (bird)
grama *nf* : grass
gramática *nf* : grammar
gramatical *adj* : grammatical — **gramaticalmente** *adv*
gramo *nm* : gram
gran → **grande**
grana *nf* : scarlet, deep red
granada *nf* 1 : pomegranate 2 : grenade ⟨granada de mano : hand grenade⟩
granadero *nm* 1 : grenadier 2 **granaderos** *nmpl Mex* : riot squad
granadino, -na *adj & n* : Grenadian
granado, -da *adj* 1 DISTINGUIDO : distinguished 2 : choice, select
granate *nm* 1 : garnet 2 : deep red, maroon
grande *adj* (**gran** *before singular nouns*) 1 : large, big ⟨un libro grande : a big book⟩ 2 ALTO : tall 3 NOTABLE : great ⟨un gran autor : a great writer⟩ 4 (*indicating intensity*) : great ⟨con gran placer : with great pleasure⟩ 5 : old, grown-up ⟨hijos grandes : grown children⟩
grandeza *nf* 1 MAGNITUD : greatness, size 2 : nobility 3 : generosity, graciousness 4 : grandeur, magnificence
grandilocuencia *nf* : grandiloquence — **grandilocuente** *adj*
grandiosidad *nf* : grandeur
grandioso, -sa *adj* 1 MAGNÍFICO : grand, magnificent 2 : grandiose
granel *adv* 1 a ~ : galore, in great quantities 2 a ~ : in bulk ⟨vender a granel : to sell in bulk⟩
granero *nm* : barn, granary
granito *nm* : granite
granizada *nf* : hailstorm
granizar {21} *v impers* : to hail
granizo *nm* : hail
granja *nf* : farm
granjear *vt* : to earn, to win — **granjearse** *vr* : to gain, to earn
granjero, -ra *n* : farmer
grano *nm* 1 PARTÍCULA : grain, particle ⟨un grano de arena : a grain of sand⟩ 2 : grain (of rice, etc.), bean (of coffee), seed 3 : grain (of wood or rock) 4 BARRO, ESPINILLA : pimple 5 **ir al grano** : to get to the point
granuja *nmf* PILLUELO : rascal, urchin
granular[1] *vt* : to granulate — **granularse** *vr* : to break out in spots
granular[2] *adj* : granular, grainy
granza *nf* : chaff
grapa *nf* 1 : staple 2 : clamp
grapadora *nf* ENGRAPADORA : stapler
grapar *vt* ENGRAPAR : to staple
grasa *nf* 1 : grease 2 : fat 3 *Mex* : shoe polish
grasiento, -ta *adj* : greasy, oily
graso, -sa *adj* 1 : fatty 2 : greasy, oily
grasoso, -sa *adj* GRASIENTO : greasy, oily

gratificación *nf, pl* **-ciones** 1 SATISFACCIÓN : gratification 2 : bonus 3 RECOMPENSA : recompense, reward
gratificar {72} *vt* 1 SATISFACER : to satisfy, to gratify 2 RECOMPENSAR : to reward 3 : to give a bonus to
gratinado, -da *adj* : au gratin
gratis[1] *adv* GRATUITAMENTE : free, for free, gratis
gratis[2] *adj* GRATUITO : free, gratis
gratitud *nf* : gratitude
grato, -ta *adj* AGRADABLE, PLACENTERO : pleasant, agreeable — **gratamente** *adv*
gratuitamente *adv* 1 : gratuitously 2 GRATIS : free, for free, gratis
gratuito, -ta *adj* 1 : gratuitous, unwarranted 2 GRATIS : free, gratis
grava *nf* : gravel
gravamen *nm, pl* **-vámenes** 1 : burden, obligation 2 : (property) tax
gravar *vt* 1 : to burden, to encumber 2 : to levy (a tax)
grave *adj* 1 : grave, important 2 : serious, somber 3 : serious (of an illness)
gravedad *nf* 1 : gravity ⟨centro de gravedad : center of gravity⟩ 2 : seriousness, severity
gravemente *adv* : gravely, seriously
gravilla *nf* : (fine) gravel
gravitación *nf, pl* **-ciones** : gravitation
gravitacional *adj* : gravitational
gravitar *vi* 1 : to gravitate 2 ~ **sobre** : to rest on 3 ~ **sobre** : to loom over
gravoso, -sa *adj* 1 ONEROSO : burdensome, onerous 2 : costly
graznar *vi* : to caw, to honk, to quack, to squawk
graznido *nm* : cawing, honking, quacking, squawking
gregario, -ria *adj* : gregarious
gregoriano, -na *adj* : Gregorian
gremial *adj* SINDICAL : union, labor
gremio *nm* SINDICATO : union, guild
greña *nf* 1 : mat, tangle 2 **greñas** *nfpl* MELENAS : shaggy hair, mop
greñudo, -da *n* HIPPIE, MELENUDO : longhair, hippie
grey *nf* : congregation, flock
griego[1], **-ga** *adj & n* : Greek
griego[2] *nm* : Greek (language)
grieta *nf* : crack, crevice
grifo *nm* 1 : faucet ⟨agua del grifo : tap water⟩ 2 : griffin
grillete *nm* : shackle
grillo *nm* 1 : cricket 2 **grillos** *nmpl* : fetters, shackles
grima *nf* 1 : disgust, uneasiness 2 **darle grima a alguien** : to get on someone's nerves
gringo, -ga *adj & n* YANQUI : Yankee, gringo
gripa *nf Col, Mex* : flu
gripe *nf* : flu
gris *adj* 1 : gray 2 : overcast, cloudy
grisáceo, -cea *adj* : grayish
gritar *v* : to shout, to scream, to cry
gritería *nf* : shouting, clamor

grito *nm* : shout, scream, cry ⟨a grito pelado : at the top of one's voice⟩

groenlandés, -desa *adj & n* : Greenlander

grogui *adj fam* : dazed, groggy

grosella *nf* **1** : currant **2 grosella espinosa** : gooseberry

grosería *nf* **1** : insult, coarse language **2** : rudeness, discourtesy

grosero¹, -ra *adj* **1** : rude, fresh **2** : coarse, vulgar

grosero², -ra *n* : rude person

grosor *nm* : thickness

grosso *adj* **a grosso modo** : roughly, broadly, approximately

grotesco, -ca *adj* : grotesque, hideous

grúa *nf* **1** : crane (machine) **2** : tow truck

gruesa *nf* : gross

grueso¹, -sa *adj* **1** : thick, bulky **2** : heavy, big **3** : heavyset, stout

grueso² *nm* **1** : thickness **2** : main body, mass **3 en ∼** : in bulk

grulla *nf* : crane (bird)

grumo *nm* : lump, glob

gruñido *nm* : growl, grunt

gruñir {38} *vi* **1** : to growl, to grunt **2** : to grumble

gruñón¹, -ñona *adj, mpl* **gruñones** *fam* : grumpy, crabby

gruñón², -ñona *n, mpl* **gruñones** *fam* : grumpy person, nag

grupa *nf* : rump, hindquarters *pl*

grupo *nm* : group

gruta *nf* : grotto, cave

guacal *nm Col, Mex, Ven* : crate

guacamayo *nm* : macaw

guacamole *or* **guacamol** *nm* : guacamole

guacamote *nm Mex* : yuca, cassava

guachinango → huachinango

guacho, -cha *adj* **1** *Arg, Col, Chile, Peru* : orphaned **2** *Chile, Peru* : odd, unmatched

guadaña *nf* : scythe

guagua *nf* **1** *Arg, Col, Chile, Peru* : baby **2** *Cuba, PRi* : bus

guaira *nf* **1** *CA* : traditional flute **2** *Peru* : smelting furnace

guajiro, -ra *n Cuba* : peasant

guajolote *nm Mex* : turkey

guanábana *nf* : guanabana, soursop (fruit)

guanaco *nm* : guanaco

guandú *nm CA, Car, Col* : pigeon pea

guango, -ga *adj Mex* **1** : loose-fitting, baggy **2** : slack, loose

guano *nm* : guano

guante *nm* **1** : glove ⟨guante de boxeo : boxing glove⟩ **2 arrojarle el guante (a alguien)** : to throw down the gauntlet (to someone)

guantelete *nm* : gauntlet

guapo, -pa *adj* **1** : handsome, good-looking, attractive **2** : elegant, smart **3** *fam* : bold, dashing

guapura *nf fam* : handsomeness, attractiveness, good looks *pl* ⟨¡qué guapura! : what a vision!⟩

guarache → huarache

guarachear *vi Cuba, PRi fam* : to go on a spree, to go out on the town

guaraní¹ *adj & nmf* : Guarani

guaraní² *nm* : Guarani (language of Paraguay)

guarda *nmf* **1** GUARDIÁN : security guard **2** : keeper, custodian

guardabarros *nms & pl* : fender, mudguard

guardabosque *nmf* : forest ranger, gamekeeper

guardacostas¹ *nmfs & pl* : coastguardsman

guardacostas² *nms & pl* : coast guard vessel

guardaespaldas *nmfs & pl* : bodyguard

guardafangos *nms & pl* : fender, mudguard

guardameta *nmf* ARQUERO, PORTERO : goalkeeper, goalie

guardapelo *nm* : locket

guardapolvo *nm* **1** : dustcover **2** : duster, housecoat

guardar *vt* **1** : to guard **2** : to maintain, to preserve **3** CONSERVAR : to put away **4** RESERVAR : to save **5** : to keep (a secret or promise) — **guardarse** *vr* **1** — **de** : to refrain from **2** ∼ **de** : to guard against, to be careful not to

guardarropa *nm* **1** : cloakroom, checkroom **2** ARMARIO : closet, wardrobe

guardería *nf* : nursery, day-care center

guardia¹ *nf* **1** : guard, defense **2** : guard duty, watch **3 en ∼** : on guard

guardia² *nmf* **1** : sentry, guardsman, guard **2** : police officer, policeman *m*, policewoman *f*

guardiamarina *nmf* : midshipman

guardián, -diana *n, mpl* **guardianes 1** GUARDA : security guard, watchman **2** : guardian, keeper **3 perro guardián** : watchdog

guarecer {53} *vt* : to shelter, to protect — **guarecerse** *vr* : to take shelter

guarida *nf* **1** : den, lair **2** : hideout

guarismo *nm* : figure, numeral

guarnecer {53} *vt* **1** : to adorn **2** : to garnish **3** : to garrison

guarnición *nf, pl* **-ciones 1** : garnish **2** : garrison **3** : decoration, trimming, setting (of a jewel)

guaro *nm CA* : liquor distilled from sugarcane

guasa *nf fam* **1** : joking, fooling around **2 de ∼** : in jest, as a joke

guasón¹, -sona *adj, mpl* **guasones** *fam* : funny, witty

guasón², -sona *n, mpl* **guasones** *fam* : joker, clown

guatemalteco, -ca *adj & n* : Guatemalan

guau *interj* : wow!

guayaba *nf* : guava (fruit)

gubernamental *adj* : governmental

gubernativo, -va → gubernamental

gubernatura *nf Mex* : governing body

guepardo *nm* : cheetah

güero, -ra *adj Mex* : blond, fair

guerra *nf* **1** : war ⟨declarar la guerra : to declare war⟩ ⟨guerra sin cuartel : all-out war⟩ **2** : warfare **3** LUCHA : conflict, struggle

guerrear *vi* : to wage war

guerrero[1], **-ra** *adj* **1** : war, fighting **2** : warlike

guerrero[2], **-ra** *n* : warrior

guerrilla *nf* : guerrilla warfare

guerrillero, -ra *adj & n* : guerrilla

gueto *nm* : ghetto

guía[1] *nf* **1** : directory, guidebook **2** ORIENTACIÓN : guidance, direction ⟨la conciencia me sirve como guía : conscience is my guide⟩

guía[2] *nmf* : guide, leader ⟨guía de turismo : tour guide⟩

guiar {85} *vt* **1** : to guide, to lead **2** CONDUCIR : to manage — **guiarse** *vr* : to be guided by, to go by

guija *nf* : pebble

guijarro *nm* : pebble

guillotina *nf* : guillotine — **guillotinar** *vt*

guinda[1] *adj & nm Mex* : burgundy (color)

guinda[2] *nf* : morello (cherry)

guineo *nm Car* : banana

guinga *nf* : gingham

guiñada → **guiño**

guiñar *vi* : to wink

guiño *nm* : wink

guión *nm, pl* **guiones 1** : script, screenplay **2** : hyphen, dash **3** ESTANDARTE : standard, banner

guirnalda *nf* : garland

guisa *nf* **1** : manner, fashion **2 a guisa de** : like, by way of **3 de tal guisa** : in such a way

guisado ESTOFADO *nm* : stew

guisante *nm* : pea

guisar *vt* **1** ESTOFAR : to stew **2** *Spain* : to cook

guiso *nm* **1** : stew **2** : casserole

güisqui → **whisky**

guita *nf* : string, twine

guitarra *nf* : guitar

guitarrista *nmf* : guitarist

gula *nf* GLOTONERÍA : gluttony, greed

gusano *nm* **1** LOMBRIZ : worm, earthworm ⟨gusano de seda : silkworm⟩ **2** : caterpillar, maggot, grub

gustar *vt* **1** : to taste **2** : to like ⟨¿gustan pasar? : would you like to come in?⟩ — *vi* **1** : to be pleasing ⟨me gustan los dulces : I like sweets⟩ ⟨a María le gusta Carlos : Maria is attracted to Carlos⟩ ⟨no me gusta que me griten : I don't like to be yelled at⟩ **2 ~ de** : to like, to enjoy ⟨no le gusta de chismes : she doesn't like gossip⟩ **3 como guste** : as you wish, as you like

gustativo, -va *adj* : taste ⟨papilas gustativas : taste buds⟩

gusto *nm* **1** : flavor, taste **2** : taste, style **3** : pleasure, liking **4** : whim, fancy ⟨a gusto : at will⟩ **5 a ~** : comfortable, at ease **6 al gusto** : to taste, as one likes **7 mucho gusto** : pleased to meet you

gustosamente *adv* : gladly

gustoso, -sa *adj* **1** : willing, glad ⟨nuestra empresa participará gustosa : our company will be pleased to participate⟩ **2** : zesty, tasty

gutural *adj* : guttural

H

h *nf* : eighth letter of the Spanish alphabet

ha → **haber**

haba *nf* : broad bean

habanero[1], **-ra** *adj* : of or from Havana

habanero[2], **-ra** *n* : native or resident of Havana

haber[1] {39} *v aux* **1** : have, has ⟨no ha llegado el envío : the shipment hasn't arrived⟩ **2 ~ de** : must ⟨ha de ser tarde : it must be late⟩ — *v impers* **1 hay** : there is, there are ⟨hay dos mensajes : there are two messages⟩ ⟨¿qué hay de nuevo? : what's new?⟩ **2 hay que** : it is necessary ⟨hay que trabajar más rápido : you have to work faster⟩

haber[2] *nm* **1** : assets *pl* **2** : credit, credit side **3 haberes** *nmpl* : salary, income, remuneration

habichuela *nf* **1** : bean, kidney bean **2** : green bean

hábil *adj* **1** : able, skillful **2** : working ⟨días hábiles : working days⟩

habilidad *nf* CAPACIDAD : ability, skill

habilidoso, -sa *adj* : skillful, clever

habilitación *nf, pl* **-ciones 1** : authorization **2** : furnishing, equipping

habilitar *vt* **1** : to enable, to authorize, to empower **2** : to equip, to furnish

hábilmente *adv* : skillfully, expertly

habitable *adj* : habitable, inhabitable

habitación *nf, pl* **-ciones 1** CUARTO : room **2** DORMITORIO : bedroom **3** : habitation, occupancy

habitante *nmf* : inhabitant, resident

habitar *vt* : to inhabit — *vi* : to reside, to dwell

hábitat *nm, pl* **-tats** : habitat

hábito *nm* **1** : habit, custom **2** : habit (of a monk or nun)

habitual *adj* : habitual, customary — **habitualmente** *adv*

habituar {3} *vt* **1** : to accustom, to habituate — **habituarse** *vr* **~ a** : to get used to, to grow accustomed to

habla *nf* **1** : speech **2** : language, dialect **3 de ~** : speaking ⟨de habla inglesa : English-speaking⟩

hablado, -da *adj* **1** : spoken **2 mal hablado** : foulmouthed

hablador¹, -dora adj : talkative
hablador², -dora n : chatterbox
habladuría nf 1 : rumor 2 **habladurías** nfpl : gossip, scandal
hablante nmf : speaker
hablar vi 1 : to speak, to talk ⟨hablar en broma : to be joking⟩ 2 ~ **de** : to mention, to talk about 3 **dar que hablar** : to make people talk — vt 1 : to speak (a language) 2 : to talk about, to discuss ⟨háblalo con tu jefe : discuss it with your boss⟩ — **hablarse** vr 1 : to speak to each other, to be on speaking terms 2 **se habla inglés** (etc.) : English (etc.) spoken
habrá, etc. → **haber**
hacedor, -dora n : creator, maker, doer
hacendado, -da n : landowner
hacer {40} vt 1 : to make 2 : to do, to perform 3 : to force, to oblige ⟨los hice esperar : I made them wait⟩ — vi 1 : to act ⟨haces bien : you're doing the right thing⟩ — v impers 1 (referring to weather) ⟨hacer frío : to be cold⟩ ⟨hace viento : it's windy⟩ 2 **hace** : ago ⟨hace mucho tiempo : a long time ago, for a long time⟩ 3 **no le hace** : it doesn't matter, it makes no difference 4 **hacer falta** : to be necessary, to be needed — **hacerse** vr 1 : to become 2 : to pretend, to act, to play ⟨hacerse el tonto : to play dumb⟩ 3 : to seem ⟨el examen se me hizo difícil : the exam seemed difficult to me⟩ 4 : to get, to grow ⟨se hace tarde : it's growing late⟩
hacha nf : hatchet, ax
hachazo nm : blow, chop (with an ax)
hachís nm : hashish
hacia prep 1 : toward, towards ⟨hacia abajo : downward⟩ ⟨hacia adelante : forward⟩ 2 : near, around, about ⟨hacia las seis : about six o'clock⟩
hacienda nf 1 : estate, ranch, farm 2 : property 3 : livestock 4 **la Hacienda** : department of revenue, tax office
hacinar vt 1 : to pile up, to stack 2 : to overcrowd — **hacinarse** vr : to crowd together
hada nf : fairy
hado nm : destiny, fate
haga, etc. → **hacer**
haitiano, -na adj & n : Haitian
hala interj Spain 1 (expressing encouragement or disbelief) : come on! 2 (expressing surprise) : wow! 3 (expressing protest) : hey!
halagador¹, -dora adj : flattering
halagador², -dora n : flatterer
halagar {52} vt : to flatter, to compliment
halago nm : flattery, praise
halagüeño, -ña adj 1 : flattering 2 : encouraging, promising
halar vt CA, Car → **jalar**
halcón nm, pl **halcones** : hawk, falcon
halibut nm, pl **-buts** : halibut
hálito nm 1 : breath 2 : gentle breeze

hallar vt 1 ENCONTRAR : to find 2 DESCUBRIR : to discover, to find out — **hallarse** vr 1 : to be situated, to find oneself 2 : to feel ⟨no se halla bien : he doesn't feel comfortable, he feels out of place⟩
hallazgo nm 1 : discovery 2 : find ⟨¡es un verdadero hallazgo! : it's a real find!⟩
halo nm 1 : halo 2 : aura
halógeno nm : halogen
hamaca nf : hammock
hambre nf 1 : hunger 2 : starvation 3 **tener hambre** : to be hungry 4 **dar hambre** : to make hungry
hambriento, -ta adj : hungry, starving
hambruna nf : famine
hamburguesa nf : hamburger
hampa nf : criminal underworld
hampón, -pona n, mpl **hampones** : criminal, thug
hámster [ˈxamster] nm, pl **hámsters** : hamster
han → **haber**
handicap or **hándicap** [ˈhandiˌkap] nm, pl **-caps** : handicap (in sports)
hangar nm : hangar
hará, etc. → **hacer**
haragán¹, -gana adj, mpl **-ganes** : lazy, idle
haragán², -gana n, mpl **-ganes** HOLGAZÁN : slacker, good-for-nothing
haraganear vi : to be lazy, to waste one's time
haraganería nf : laziness
harapiento, -ta adj : ragged, tattered
harapos nmpl ANDRAJOS : rags, tatters
hardware [ˈhardˌwer] nm : computer hardware
harén nm, pl **harenes** : harem
harina nf 1 : flour 2 **harina de maíz** : cornmeal
hartar vt 1 : to glut, to satiate 2 FASTIDIAR : to tire, to irritate, to annoy — **hartarse** vr : to be weary, to get fed up
harto¹ adv : most, extremely, very
harto², -ta adj 1 : full, satiated 2 : fed up
hartura nf 1 : surfeit 2 : abundance, plenty
has → **haber**
hasta¹ adv : even
hasta² prep 1 : until, up until ⟨hasta entonces : until then⟩ ⟨¡hasta luego! : see you later!⟩ 2 : as far as ⟨nos fuimos hasta Managua : we went all the way to Managua⟩ 3 : up to ⟨hasta cierto punto : up to a certain point⟩ 4 **hasta que** : until
hastiar {85} vt 1 : to make weary, to bore 2 : to disgust, to sicken — **hastiarse** vr ~ **de** : to get tired of
hastío nm 1 TEDIO : tedium 2 REPUGNANCIA : disgust
hato nm 1 : flock, herd 2 : bundle (of possessions)
hawaiano, -na adj & n : Hawaiian
hay → **haber¹**

haya¹, etc. → haber
haya² *nf* : beech (tree and wood)
hayuco *nm* : beechnut
haz¹ → hacer
haz² *nm, pl* **haces 1** FARDO : bundle **2** : beam (of light)
haz³ *nf, pl* **haces 1** : face **2 haz de la tierra** : surface of the earth
hazaña *nf* PROEZA : feat, exploit
hazmerreír *nm fam* : laughingstock
he¹ {39} → haber
he² *v impers* **he aquí** : here is, here are, behold
hebilla *nf* : buckle, clasp
hebra *nf* : strand, thread
hebreo¹, **-brea** *adj & n* : Hebrew
hebreo² *nm* : Hebrew (language)
hecatombe *nf* **1** MATANZA : massacre **2** : disaster
heces → hez
hechicería *nf* **1** BRUJERÍA : sorcery, witchcraft **2** : curse, spell
hechicero¹, **-ra** *adj* : bewitching, enchanting
hechicero², **-ra** *n* : sorcerer, sorceress *f*
hechizar {21} *vt* **1** EMBRUJAR : to bewitch **2** CAUTIVAR : to charm
hechizo *nm* **1** SORTILEGIO : spell, enchantment **2** ENCANTO : charm, fascination
hecho¹ *pp* → hacer
hecho², **-cha** *adj* **1** : made, done **2** : ready-to-wear **3** : complete, finished ⟨hecho y derecho : full-fledged⟩
hecho³ *nm* **1** : fact **2** : event ⟨hechos históricos : historic events⟩ **3** : act, action **4 de ~** : in fact, in reality
hechura *nf* **1** : style **2** : craftsmanship, workmanship **3** : product, creation
hectárea *nf* : hectare
heder {56} *vi* : to stink, to reek
hediondez *nf, pl* **-deces** : stink, stench
hediondo, **-da** *adj* MALOLIENTE : foulsmelling, stinking
hedor *nm* : stench, stink
hegemonía *nf* **1** : dominance **2** : hegemony (in politics)
helada *nf* : frost (in meteorology)
heladería *nf* : ice-cream parlor, icecream stand
helado¹, **-da** *adj* **1** GÉLIDO : icy, freezing cold **2** CONGELADO : frozen
helado² *nm* : ice cream
heladora *nf* CONGELADOR : freezer
helar {55} *v* CONGELAR : to freeze — *v impers* : to produce frost ⟨anoche heló : there was frost last night⟩ — **helarse** *vr*
helecho *nm* : fern, bracken
hélice *nf* **1** : spiral, helix **2** : propeller
helicóptero *nm* : helicopter
helio *nm* : helium
helipuerto *nm* : heliport
hembra *adj & nf* : female
hemisférico, **-ca** *adj* : hemispheric, hemispherical
hemisferio *nm* : hemisphere
hemofilia *nf* : hemophilia

hemofílico, **-ca** *adj & n* : hemophiliac
hemoglobina *nf* : hemoglobin
hemorragia *nf* **1** : hemorrhage **2 hemorragia nasal** : nosebleed
hemorroides *nfpl* ALMORRANAS : hemorrhoids, piles
hemos → haber
henchido, **-da** *adj* : swollen, bloated
henchir {54} *vt* **1** : to stuff, to fill **2** : to swell, to swell up — **henchirse** *vr* **1** : to stuff oneself **2** LLENARSE : to fill up, to be full
hender {56} *vt* : to cleave, to split
hendidura *nf* : crack, crevice, fissure
henequén *nm, pl* **-quenes** : sisal hemp
heno *nm* : hay
hepatitis *nf* : hepatitis
heráldica *nf* : heraldry
heráldico, **-ca** *adj* : heraldic
heraldo *nm* : herald
herbario, **-ria** *adj* : herbal
herbicida *nm* : herbicide, weed killer
herbívoro¹, **-ra** *adj* : herbivorous
herbívoro² *nm* : herbivore
herbolario, **-ria** *n* : herbalist
hercio *nm* : hertz
hercúleo, **-lea** *adj* : herculean
heredar *vt* : to inherit
heredero, **-ra** *n* : heir, heiress *f*
hereditario, **-ria** *adj* : hereditary
hereje *nmf* : heretic
herejía *nf* : heresy
herencia *nf* **1** : inheritance **2** : heritage **3** : heredity
herético, **-ca** *adj* : heretical
herida *nf* : injury, wound
herido¹, **-da** *adj* **1** : injured, wounded **2** : hurt, offended
herido², **-da** *n* : injured person, casualty
herir {76} *vt* **1** : to injure, to wound **2** : to hurt, to offend
hermafrodita *nmf* : hermaphrodite
hermanar *vt* **1** : to unite, to bring together **2** : to match up, to twin (cities)
hermanastro, **-tra** *n* : half brother *m*, half sister *f*
hermandad *nf* **1** FRATERNIDAD : brotherhood ⟨hermandad de mujeres : sisterhood, sorority⟩ **2** : association
hermano, **-na** *n* : sibling, brother *m*, sister *f*
hermético, **-ca** *adj* : hermetic, watertight — **herméticamente** *adv*
hermoso, **-sa** *adj* BELLO : beautiful, lovely — **hermosamente** *adv*
hermosura *nf* BELLEZA : beauty, loveliness
hernia *nf* : hernia
héroe *nm* : hero
heroicidad *nf* : heroism, heroic deed
heroico, **-ca** *adj* : heroic — **heroicamente** *adv*
heroína *nf* **1** : heroine **2** : heroin
heroísmo *nm* : heroism
herpes *nms & pl* **1** : herpes **2** : shingles
herradura *nf* : horseshoe
herraje *nm* : ironwork

herramienta *nf* : tool
herrar {55} *vt* : to shoe (a horse)
herrería *nf* : blacksmith's shop
herrero, -ra *n* : blacksmith
herrumbre *nf* ORÍN : rust
herrumbroso, -sa *adj* OXIDADO : rusty
hertzio *nm* : hertz
hervidero *nm* **1** : mass, swarm **2** : hotbed (of crime, etc.)
hervidor *nm* : kettle
hervir {76} *vi* **1** BULLIR : to boil, to bubble **2 ~ de** : to teem with, to be swarming with — *vt* : to boil
hervor *nm* **1** : boiling **2** : fervor, ardor
heterogeneidad *nf* : heterogeneity
heterogéneo, -nea *adj* : heterogeneous
heterosexual *adj & nmf* : heterosexual
heterosexualidad *nf* : heterosexuality
hexágono *nm* : hexagon — **hexagonal** *adj*
hez *nf*, *pl* **heces 1** ESCORIA : scum, dregs *pl* **2** : sediment, lees *pl* **3 heces** *nfpl* : feces, excrement
hiato *nm* : hiatus
hibernar *vi* : to hibernate — **hibernación** *nf*
híbrido[1]**, -da** *adj* : hybrid
híbrido[2] *nm* : hybrid
hicieron, etc. → **hacer**
hidalgo, -ga *n* : nobleman *m*, noblewoman *f*
hidrante *nm* CA, Col : hydrant
hidratar *vt* : to moisturize — **hidratante** *adj*
hidrato *nm* **1** : hydrate **2 hidrato de carbono** : carbohydrate
hidráulico, -ca *adj* : hydraulic
hidroavión *nm*, *pl* **-viones** : seaplane
hidrocarburo *nm* : hydrocarbon
hidroeléctrico, -ca *adj* : hydroelectric
hidrofobia *nf* RABIA : hydrophobia, rabies
hidrófugo, -ga *adj* : water-repellent
hidrógeno *nm* : hydrogen
hidroplano *nm* : hydroplane
hiede, etc. → **heder**
hiedra *nf* **1** : ivy **2 hiedra venenosa** : poison ivy
hiel *nf* **1** BILIS : bile **2** : bitterness
hiela, etc. → **helar**
hielo *nm* **1** : ice **2** : coldness, reserve ⟨romper el hielo : to break the ice⟩
hiena *nf* : hyena
hiende, etc. → **hender**
hierba *nf* **1** : herb **2** : grass **3 mala hierba** : weed
hierbabuena *nf* : mint, spearmint
hiere, etc. → **herir**
hierra, etc. → **herrar**
hierro *nm* **1** : iron ⟨hierro fundido : cast iron⟩ **2** : branding iron
hierve, etc. → **hervir**
hígado *nm* : liver
higiene *nf* : hygiene
higiénico, -ca *adj* : hygienic — **higiénicamente** *adv*
higienista *nmf* : hygienist
higo *nm* **1** : fig **2 higo chumbo** : prickly pear (fruit)

higrómetro *nm* : hygrometer
higuera *nf* : fig tree
hijastro, -tra *n* : stepson *m*, stepdaughter *f*
hijo, -ja *n* **1** : son *m*, daughter *f* **2 hijos** *nmpl* : children, offspring
híjole *interj Mex* : wow!, good grief!
hilacha *nf* **1** : ravel, loose thread **2 mostrar la hilacha** : to show one's true colors
hilado *nm* **1** : spinning **2** HILO : yarn, thread
hilar *vt* **1** : to spin (thread) **2** : to consider, to string together (ideas) — *vi* **1** : to spin **2 hilar delgado** : to split hairs
hilarante *adj* **1** : humorous, hilarious **2 gas hilarante** : laughing gas
hilaridad *nf* : hilarity
hilera *nf* FILA : file, row, line
hilo *nm* **1** : thread ⟨colgar de un hilo : to hang by a thread⟩ ⟨hilo dental : dental floss⟩ **2** LINO : linen **3** : (electric) wire **4** : theme, thread (of a discourse) **5** : trickle (of water, etc.)
hilvanar *vt* **1** : to baste, to tack **2** : to piece together
himnario *nm* : hymnal
himno *nm* **1** : hymn **2 himno nacional** : national anthem
hincapié *nm* **hacer hincapié en** : to emphasize, to stress
hincar {72} *vt* CLAVAR : to stick, to plunge — **hincarse** *vr* **hincarse de rodillas** : to kneel down, to fall to one's knees
hinchado, -da *adj* **1** : swollen, inflated **2** : pompous, overblown
hinchar *vt* **1** INFLAR : to inflate **2** : to exaggerate — **hincharse** *vr* **1** : to swell up **2** : to become conceited, to swell with pride
hinchazón *nf*, *pl* **-zones** : swelling
hinche, etc. → **henchir**
hindi *nm* : Hindi
hindú *adj & nmf* : Hindu
hinduismo *nm* : Hinduism
hiniesta *nf* : broom (plant)
hinojo *nm* **1** : fennel **2 de hinojos** : on bended knee
hinque, etc. → **hincar**
hipar *vi* : to hiccup
hiperactividad *nf* : hyperactivity
hiperactivo, -va *adj* : hyperactive, overactive
hipérbole *nf* : hyperbole
hiperbólico, -ca *adj* : hyperbolic, exaggerated
hipercrítico, -ca *adj* : hypercritical
hipermetropía *nf* : farsightedness
hipersensibilidad *nf* : hypersensitivity
hipersensible *adj* : hypersensitive
hipertensión *nf*, *pl* **-siones** : hypertension, high blood pressure
hip–hop [ˌxipˈxop] *nm* : hip-hop (music)
hípico, -ca *adj* : equestrian ⟨concurso hípico : horse show⟩
hipil → **huipil**
hipnosis *nfs & pl* : hypnosis

hipnótico, -ca *adj* : hypnotic
hipnotismo *nm* : hypnotism
hipnotizador[1], -dora *adj* **1** : hypnotic **2** : spellbinding, mesmerizing
hipnotizador[2], -dora *n* : hypnotist
hipnotizar {21} *vt* : to hypnotize
hipo *nm* : hiccup, hiccups *pl*
hipocampo *nm* : sea horse
hipocondría *nf* : hypochondria
hipocondríaco, -ca *adj & n* : hypochondriac
hipocresía *nf* : hypocrisy
hipócrita[1] *adj* : hypocritical — **hipócritamente** *adv*
hipócrita[2] *nmf* : hypocrite
hipodérmico, -ca *adj* **aguja hipodérmica** : hypodermic needle
hipódromo *nm* : racetrack
hipopótamo *nm* : hippopotamus
hipoteca *nf* : mortgage
hipotecar {72} *vt* **1** : to mortgage **2** : to compromise, to jeopardize
hipotecario, -ca *adj & n* : mortgage
hipotensión *nf* : low blood pressure
hipotenusa *nf* : hypotenuse
hipótesis *nfs & pl* : hypothesis
hipotético, -ca *adj* : hypothetical — **hipotéticamente** *adv*
hippie *or* **hippy** [ˈhipi] *nmf, pl* **hippies** [-pis] : hippie
hiriente *adj* : hurtful, offensive
hirió, etc. → **herir**
hirsuto, -ta *adj* **1** : hirsute, hairy **2** : bristly, wiry
hirviente *adj* : boiling
hirvió, etc. → **hervir**
hisopo *nm* **1** : hyssop **2** : cotton swab
hispánico, -ca *adj & n* **1** : Hispanic
hispano[1], -na *adj* : Hispanic ⟨de habla hispana : Spanish-speaking⟩
hispano[2], -na *n* : Hispanic (person)
hispanoamericano[1], -na *adj* LATINOAMERICANO : Latin-American
hispanoamericano[2], -na *n* LATINOAMERICANO : Latin American
hispanohablante[1] *adj* : Spanish-speaking
hispanohablante[2] *nmf* : Spanish speaker
histerectomía *nf* : hysterectomy
histeria *nf* **1** : hysteria **2** : hysterics
histérico, -ca *adj* : hysterical — **histéricamente** *adv*
histerismo *nm* **1** : hysteria **2** : hysterics
historia *nf* **1** : history **2** NARRACIÓN, RELATO : story
historiador, -dora *n* : historian
historial *nm* **1** : record, document **2** CURRÍCULUM : résumé, curriculum vitae
histórico, -ca *adj* **1** : historical **2** : historic, important — **históricamente** *adv*
historieta *nf* : comic strip
histrionismo *nm* : histrionics, acting
hit [ˈhit] *nm, pl* **hits** **1** ÉXITO : hit, popular song **2** : hit (in baseball)
hito *nm* : milestone, landmark

hizo → **hacer**
hobby [ˈhɔbi] *nm, pl* **hobbies** [-bis] : hobby
hocico *nm* : snout, muzzle
hockey [ˈhɔke, -ki] *nm* : hockey
hogar *nm* **1** : home **2** : hearth, fireplace
hogareño, -ña *adj* **1** : home-loving **2** : domestic, homelike
hogaza *nf* : large loaf (of bread)
hoguera *nf* **1** FOGATA : bonfire **2 morir en la hoguera** : to burn at the stake
hoja *nf* **1** : leaf, petal, blade (of grass) **2** : sheet (of paper), page (of a book) ⟨hoja de cálculo : spreadsheet⟩ **3** FORMULARIO : form ⟨hoja de pedido : order form⟩ **4** : blade (of a knife) ⟨hoja de afeitar : razor blade⟩
hojalata *nf* : tinplate
hojaldre *nm* : puff pastry
hojarasca *nf* : fallen leaves *pl*
hojear *vt* : to leaf through (a book or magazine)
hojuela *nf* **1** : leaflet, young leaf **2** : flake
hola *interj* : hello!, hi!
holandés[1], -desa *adj, mpl* **-deses** : Dutch
holandés[2], -desa *n, mpl* **-deses** : Dutch person, Dutchman *m*, Dutchwoman *f* ⟨los holandeses : the Dutch⟩
holandés[3] *nm* : Dutch (language)
holgadamente *adv* : comfortably, easily ⟨vivir holgadamente : to be well-off⟩
holgado, -da *adj* **1** : loose, baggy **2** : at ease, comfortable
holganza *nf* : leisure, idleness
holgazán[1], -zana *adj, mpl* **-zanes** : lazy
holgazán[2], -zana *n, mpl* **-zanes** HARAGÁN : slacker, idler
holgazanear *vi* HARAGANEAR : to laze around, to loaf
holgazanería *nf* PEREZA : idleness, laziness
holgura *nf* **1** : looseness **2** COMODIDAD : comfort, ease
holístico, -ca *adj* : holistic
hollar {19} *vt* : to tread on, to trample
hollín *nm, pl* **hollines** TIZNE : soot
holocausto *nm* : holocaust
holograma *nm* : hologram
hombre *nm* **1** : man ⟨el hombre : man, mankind⟩ **2 hombre de estado** : statesman **3 hombre de negocios** : businessman **4 hombre lobo** : werewolf
hombrera *nf* **1** : shoulder pad **2** : epaulet
hombría *nf* : manliness
hombro *nm* : shoulder ⟨encogerse de hombros : to shrug one's shoulders⟩
hombruno, -na *adj* : mannish
homenaje *nm* : homage, tribute ⟨rendir homenaje a : to pay tribute to⟩
homenajear *vt* : to pay homage to, to honor
homeopatía *nf* : homeopathy
homicida[1] *adj* : homicidal, murderous
homicida[2] *nmf* ASESINO : murderer
homicidio *nm* ASESINATO : homicide, murder

homilía *nf* : homily, sermon
homófono *nm* : homophone
homogeneidad *nf* : homogeneity
homogeneización *nf* : homogenization
homogeneizar {21} *vt* : to homogenize
homogéneo, -nea *adj* : homogeneous
homógrafo *nm* : homograph
homologación *nf, pl* **-ciones** 1 : sanctioning, approval 2 : parity
homologar {52} *vt* 1 : to sanction 2 : to bring into line
homólogo¹, -ga *adj* : homologous, equivalent
homólogo², -ga *n* : counterpart
homónimo¹, -ma *n* TOCAYO : namesake
homónimo² *nm* : homonym
homosexual *adj & nmf* : homosexual
homosexualidad *nf* : homosexuality
honda *nf* : sling
hondo¹ *adv* : deeply
hondo², -da *adj* PROFUNDO : deep ⟨en lo más hondo de : in the depths of⟩ — **hondamente** *adv*
hondonada *nf* 1 : hollow, depression 2 : ravine, gorge
hondura *nf* : depth
hondureño, -ña *adj & n* : Honduran
honestidad *nf* 1 : decency, modesty 2 : honesty, uprightness
honesto, -ta *adj* 1 : decent, virtuous 2 : honest, honorable — **honestamente** *adv*
hongo *nm* 1 : fungus 2 : mushroom
honor *nm* 1 : honor ⟨en honor a la verdad : to be quite honest⟩ 2 **honores** *nmpl* : honors ⟨hacer los honores : to do the honors⟩
honorable *adj* HONROSO : honorable — **honorablemente** *adv*
honorario, -ria *adj* : honorary
honorarios *nmpl* : payment, fees (for professional services)
honorífico, -ca *adj* : honorary ⟨mención honorífica : honorable mention⟩
honra *nf* 1 : dignity, self-respect ⟨tener a mucha honra : to take great pride in⟩ 2 : good name, reputation
honradamente *adv* : honestly, decently
honradez *nf, pl* **-deces** : honesty, integrity, probity
honrado, -da *adj* HONESTO : honest, upright 2 : honored
honrar *vt* 1 : to honor 2 : to be a credit to ⟨su generosidad lo honra : his generosity does him credit⟩
honroso, -sa *adj* HONORABLE : honorable — **honrosamente** *adv*
hora *nf* 1 : hour ⟨media hora : half an hour⟩ ⟨a la última hora : at the last minute⟩ ⟨a la hora en punto : on the dot⟩ ⟨horas de oficina : office hours⟩ 2 : time ⟨¿qué hora es? : what time is it?⟩ 3 CITA : appointment
horario *nm* 1 : schedule, timetable, hours *pl* ⟨horario de visita : visiting hours⟩
horca *nf* 1 : gallows *pl* 2 : pitchfork
horcajadas *nfpl* a ～ : astride, astraddle
horcón *nm, pl* **horcones** : wooden post, prop

horda *nf* : horde
horizontal *adj* : horizontal — **horizontalmente** *adv*
horizonte *nm* : horizon, skyline
horma *nf* 1 : shoe tree 2 : shoemaker's last
hormiga *nf* : ant
hormigón *nm, pl* **-gones** CONCRETO : concrete
hormigonera *nf* : cement mixer
hormigueo *nm* 1 : tingling, pins and needles *pl* 2 : uneasiness
hormiguero *nm* 1 : anthill 2 : swarm (of people)
hormona *nf* : hormone — **hormonal** *adj*
hornacina *nf* : niche, recess
hornada *nf* : batch
hornear *vt* : to bake
hornilla *nf* : burner (of a stove)
horno *nm* 1 : oven ⟨horno crematorio : crematorium⟩ ⟨horno de microondas : microwave oven⟩ 2 : kiln
horóscopo *nm* : horoscope
horqueta *nf* 1 : fork (in a river or road) 2 : crotch (in a tree) 3 : small pitchfork
horquilla *nf* 1 : hairpin, bobby pin 2 : pitchfork
horrendo, -da *adj* : horrendous, horrible
horrible *adj* : horrible, dreadful — **horriblemente** *adv*
horripilante *adj* : horrifying, hair-raising
horripilar *vt* : to horrify, to terrify
horror *nm* : horror, dread
horrorizado, -da *adj* : terrified
horrorizar {21} *vt* : to horrify, to terrify — **horrorizarse** *vr*
horroroso, -sa *adj* 1 : horrifying, terrifying 2 : dreadful, bad
hortaliza *nf* 1 : vegetable 2 **hortalizas** *nfpl* : garden produce
hortera *adj* Spain fam : tacky, gaudy
hortícola *adj* : horticultural
horticultor, -ra *n* : horticulturist
horticultura *nf* : horticulture
hosco, -ca *adj* : sullen, gloomy
hospedaje *nm* : lodging, accommodations *pl*
hospedar *vt* : to provide with lodging, to put up — **hospedarse** *vr* : to stay, to lodge
hospicio *nm* : orphanage
hospital *nm* : hospital
hospitalario, -ria *adj* : hospitable
hospitalidad *nf* : hospitality
hospitalización *nf, pl* **-ciones** : hospitalization
hospitalizar {21} *vt* : to hospitalize — **hospitalizarse** *vr*
hostería *nf* POSADA : inn
hostia *nf* : host, Eucharist
hostigamiento *nm* : harassment
hostigar {52} *vt* ACOSAR, ASEDIAR : to harass, to pester
hostil *adj* : hostile

hostilidad *nf* **1** : hostility, antagonism **2 hostilidades** *nfpl* : (military) hostilities

hostilizar {21} *vt* : to harass

hotel *nm* : hotel

hotelero[1], **-ra** *adj* : hotel ⟨la industria hotelera : the hotel business⟩

hotelero[2], **-ra** *n* : hotel manager, hotelier

hoy *adv* **1** : today ⟨hoy mismo : right now, this very day⟩ **2** : now, nowadays ⟨de hoy en adelante : from now on⟩

hoyo *nm* AGUJERO : hole

hoyuelo *nm* : dimple

hoz *nf, pl* **hoces** : sickle

hozar {21} *vi* : to root (of a pig)

huachinango *nm Mex* : red snapper

huarache *nm* : huarache sandal

hubo, etc. → **haber**

hueco[1], **-ca** *adj* **1** : hollow, empty **2** : soft, spongy **3** : hollow-sounding, resonant **4** : proud, conceited **5** : superficial

hueco[2] *nm* **1** : hole, hollow, cavity **2** : gap, space **3** : recess, alcove

huele, etc. → **oler**

huelga *nf* **1** PARO : strike **2 hacer huelga** : to strike, to go on strike

huelguista *nmf* : striker

huella[1], **etc.** → **hollar**

huella[2] *nf* **1** : footprint ⟨seguir las huellas de alguien : to follow in someone's footsteps⟩ **2** : mark, impact ⟨dejar huella : to leave one's mark⟩ ⟨sin dejar huella : without a trace⟩ **3 huella digital** *or* **huella dactilar** : fingerprint

huérfano[1], **-na** *adj* **1** : orphan, orphaned **2** : defenseless **3** ~ **de** : lacking, devoid of

huérfano[2], **-na** *n* : orphan

huerta *nf* **1** : large vegetable garden, truck farm **2** : orchard **3** : irrigated land

huerto *nm* **1** : vegetable garden **2** : orchard

hueso *nm* **1** : bone **2** : pit, stone (of a fruit)

huésped[1], **-peda** *n* INVITADO : guest

huésped[2] *nm* : host ⟨organismo huésped : host organism⟩

huestes *nfpl* **1** : followers **2** : troops, army

huesudo, -da *adj* : bony

hueva *nf* : roe, spawn

huevo *nm* : egg ⟨huevos revueltos : scrambled eggs⟩

huida *nf* : flight, escape

huidizo, -za *adj* **1** ESCURRIDIZO : elusive, slippery **2** : shy, evasive

huipil *nm CA, Mex* : traditional sleeveless blouse or dress

huir {41} *vi* **1** ESCAPAR : to escape, to flee **2** ~ **de** : to avoid

huiro *nm Chile, Peru* : seaweed

huizache *nm* : huisache, acacia

hule *nm* **1** : oilcloth, oilskin **2** *Mex* : rubber **3 hule espuma** *Mex* : foam rubber

humanidad *nf* **1** : humanity, mankind **2** : humaneness **3 humanidades** *nfpl* : humanities *pl*

humanismo *nm* : humanism

humanista *nmf* : humanist

humanístico, -ca *adj* : humanistic

humanitario, -ria *adj & n* : humanitarian

humano[1], **-na** *adj* **1** : human **2** BENÉVOLO : humane, benevolent — **humanamente** *adv*

humano[2] *nm* : human being, human

humareda *nf* : cloud of smoke

humeante *adj* **1** : smoky **2** : smoking, steaming

humear *vi* **1** : to smoke **2** : to steam

humectante[1] *adj* : moisturizing

humectante[2] *nm* : moisturizer

humedad *nf* **1** : humidity **2** : dampness, moistness

humedecer {53} *vt* **1** : to humidify **2** : to moisten, to dampen

húmedo, -da *adj* **1** : humid **2** : moist, damp

humidificador *nm* : humidifier

humidificar {72} *vt* : to humidify

humildad *nf* **1** : humility **2** : lowliness

humilde *adj* **1** : humble **2** : lowly ⟨gente humilde : poor people⟩

humildemente *adv* : meekly, humbly

humillación *nf, pl* **-ciones** : humiliation

humillante *adj* : humiliating

humillar *vt* : to humiliate — **humillarse** *vr* : to humble oneself ⟨humillarse a hacer algo : to stoop to doing something⟩

humo *nm* **1** : smoke, steam, fumes **2 humos** *nmpl* : airs *pl*, conceit

humor *nm* **1** : humor **2** : mood, temper ⟨está de buen humor : she's in a good mood⟩

humorada *nf* **1** BROMA : joke, witticism **2** : whim, caprice

humorismo *nm* : humor, wit

humorista *nmf* : humorist, comedian, comedienne *f*

humorístico, -ca *adj* : humorous — **humorísticamente** *adv*

humoso, -sa *adj* : smoky, steamy

humus *nm* : humus

hundido, -da *adj* **1** : sunken **2** : depressed

hundimiento *nm* **1** : sinking **2** : collapse, ruin

hundir *vt* **1** : to sink **2** : to destroy, to ruin — **hundirse** *vr* **1** : to sink down **2** : to cave in **3** : to break down, to go to pieces

húngaro[1], **-ra** *adj & n* : Hungarian

húngaro[2] *nm* : Hungarian (language)

huracán *nm, pl* **-canes** : hurricane

huraño, -ña *adj* **1** : unsociable, aloof **2** : timid, skittish (of an animal)

hurgar {52} *vt* : to poke, to jab, to rake (a fire) — *vi* ~ **en** : to rummage in, to poke through

hurgue, etc. → **hurgar**

hurón *nm, pl* **hurones** : ferret

huronear *vi* : to pry, to snoop

hurra *interj* : hurrah!, hooray!
hurtadillas *nfpl* a ~ : stealthily, on the sly
hurtar *vt* ROBAR : to steal
hurto *nm* 1 : theft, robbery 2 : stolen property, loot
husmear *vt* 1 : to follow the scent of, to track 2 : to sniff out, to pry into — *vi* 1 : to pry, to snoop 2 : to sniff around (of an animal)
huso *nm* 1 : spindle 2 **huso horario** : time zone
huy *interj* : ow!, ouch!
huye, etc. → **huir**

I

i *nf* : ninth letter of the Spanish alphabet
iba, etc. → **ir**
ibérico, -ca *adj* : Iberian
ibero, -ra *or* **íbero, -ra** *adj & n* : Iberian
iberoamericano, -na *adj* HISPANO-AMERICANO, LATINOAMERICANO : Latin-American
ibis *nfs & pl* : ibis
ice, etc. → **izar**
iceberg *nm, pl* **icebergs** : iceberg
icono *nm* : icon
iconoclasia *nf* : iconoclasm
iconoclasta *nmf* : iconoclast
ictericia *nf* : jaundice
ida *nf* 1 : going, departure 2 **ida y vuelta** : round-trip 3 **idas y venidas** : comings and goings
idea *nf* 1 : idea, notion 2 : opinion, belief 3 PROPÓSITO : intention
ideal *adj & nm* : ideal — **idealmente** *adv*
idealismo *nm* : idealism
idealista[1] *adj* : idealistic
idealista[2] *nmf* : idealist
idealizar {21} *vt* : to idealize — **idealización** *nf*
idear *vt* : to devise, to think up
ideario *nm* : ideology
ídem *nm* : idem, the same, ditto
idéntico, -ca *adj* : identical, alike — **idénticamente** *adv*
identidad *nf* : identity
identificable *adj* : identifiable
identificación *nf, pl* **-ciones** 1 : identification, identifying 2 : identification document, ID
identificar {72} *vt* : to identify — **identificarse** *vr* 1 : to identify oneself 2 ~ **con** : to identify with
ideología *nf* : ideology — **ideológicamente** *adv*
ideológico, -ca *adj* : ideological
idílico, -ca *adj* : idyllic
idilio *nm* : idyll
idioma *nm* : language ⟨el idioma inglés : the English language⟩
idiomático, -ca *adj* : idiomatic — **idiomáticamente** *adv*
idiosincrasia *nf* : idiosyncrasy
idiosincrásico, -ca *adj* : idiosyncratic
idiota[1] *adj* : idiotic, stupid, foolish
idiota[2] *nmf* : idiot, foolish person
idiotez *nf, pl* **-teces** 1 : idiocy 2 : idiotic act or remark ⟨no digas idioteces! : don't talk nonsense!⟩
ido *pp* → **ir**

idólatra[1] *adj* : idolatrous
idólatra[2] *nmf* : idolater
idolatrar *vt* : to idolize
idolatría *nf* : idolatry
ídolo *nm* : idol
idoneidad *nf* : suitability
idóneo, -nea *adj* ADECUADO : suitable, fitting
iglesia *nf* : church
iglú *nm* : igloo
ignición *nf, pl* **-ciones** : ignition
ignífugo, -ga *adj* : fire-resistant, fireproof
ignominia *nf* : ignominy, disgrace
ignominioso, -sa *adj* : ignominious, shameful
ignorancia *nf* : ignorance
ignorante[1] *adj* : ignorant
ignorante[2] *nmf* : ignorant person, ignoramus
ignorar *vt* 1 : to ignore 2 DESCONOCER : to be unaware of ⟨lo ignoramos por absoluto : we have no idea⟩
ignoto, -ta *adj* : unknown
igual[1] *adv* 1 : in the same way 2 **por** ~ : equally
igual[2] *adj* 1 : equal 2 IDÉNTICO : the same, alike 3 : even, smooth 4 SEMEJANTE : similar 5 CONSTANTE : constant
igual[3] *nmf* : equal, peer
igualación *nf* 1 : equalization 2 : leveling, smoothing 3 : equating (in mathematics)
igualado, -da *adj* 1 : even (of a score) 2 : level 3 *Mex* : disrespectful
igualar *vt* 1 : to equalize 2 : to tie ⟨igualar el marcador : to even the score⟩
igualdad *nf* 1 : equality 2 UNIFORMIDAD : evenness, uniformity
igualmente *adv* 1 : equally 2 ASIMISMO : likewise
iguana *nf* : iguana
ijada *nf* : flank, loin, side
ijar *nm* → **ijada**
ilegal[1] *adj* : illegal, unlawful — **ilegalmente** *adv*
ilegal[2] *nmf CA, Mex* : illegal alien
ilegalidad *nf* : illegality, unlawfulness
ilegibilidad *nf* : illegibility
ilegible *adj* : illegible — **ilegiblemente** *adv*
ilegitimidad *nf* : illegitimacy
ilegítimo, -ma *adj* : illegitimate, unlawful

ileso, -sa *adj* : uninjured, unharmed

ilícito, -ta *adj* : illicit — **ilícitamente** *adv*

ilimitado, -da *adj* : unlimited

ilógico, -ca *adj* : illogical — **ilógicamente** *adv*

iluminación *nf, pl* **-ciones 1** : illumination **2** ALUMBRADO : lighting

iluminado, -da *adj* : illuminated, lighted

iluminar *vt* **1** : to illuminate, to light (up) **2** : to enlighten

ilusión *nf, pl* **-siones 1** : illusion, delusion **2** ESPERANZA : hope ⟨hacerse ilusiones : to get one's hopes up⟩

ilusionado, -da *adj* ESPERANZADO : hopeful, eager

ilusionar *vt* : to build up hope, to excite — **ilusionarse** *vr* : to get one's hopes up

iluso¹, -sa *adj* : naive, gullible

iluso², -sa *n* SOÑADOR : dreamer, visionary

ilusorio, -ria *adj* ENGAÑOSO : illusory, misleading

ilustración *nf, pl* **-ciones 1** : illustration **2** : erudition, learning ⟨la Ilustración : the Enlightenment⟩

ilustrado, -da *adj* **1** : illustrated **2** DOCTO : learned, erudite

ilustrador, -dora *n* : illustrator

ilustrar *vt* **1** : to illustrate **2** ACLARAR, CLARIFICAR : to explain

ilustrativo, -va *adj* : illustrative

ilustre *adj* : illustrious, eminent

imagen *nf, pl* **imágenes** : image, picture

imaginable *adj* : imaginable, conceivable

imaginación *nf, pl* **-ciones** : imagination

imaginar *vt* : to imagine — **imaginarse** *vr* **1** : to suppose, to imagine **2** : to picture

imaginario, -ria *adj* : imaginary

imaginativo, -va *adj* : imaginative — **imaginativamente** *adv*

imaginería *nf* **1** : imagery **2** : image making (in religion)

imán *nm, pl* **imanes** : magnet

imantar *vt* : to magnetize

imbatible *adj* : unbeatable

imbécil¹ *adj* : stupid, idiotic

imbécil² *nmf* **1** : imbecile **2** *fam* : idiot, dope

imborrable *adj* : indelible

imbuir {41} *vt* : to imbue — **imbuirse** *vr*

imitación *nf, pl* **-ciones 1** : imitation **2** : mimicry, impersonation

imitador¹, -dora *adj* : imitative

imitador², -dora *n* **1** : imitator **2** : mimic

imitar *vt* **1** : to imitate, to copy **2** : to mimic, to impersonate

imitativo, -va *adj* → **imitador¹**

impaciencia *nf* : impatience

impacientar *vt* : to make impatient, to exasperate — **impacientarse** *vr*

impaciente *adj* : impatient — **impacientemente** *adv*

impactado, -da *adj* : shocked, stunned

impactante *adj* **1** : shocking **2** : impressive, powerful

impactar *vt* **1** GOLPEAR : to hit **2** IMPRESIONAR : to impact, to affect — **impactarse** *vr*

impacto *nm* **1** : impact, effect **2** : shock, collision

impagable *adj* **1** : unpayable **2** : priceless

impago *nm* : nonpayment

impalpable *adj* INTANGIBLE : impalpable, intangible

impar¹ *adj* : odd ⟨números impares : odd numbers⟩

impar² *nm* : odd number

imparable *adj* : unstoppable

imparcial *adj* : impartial — **imparcialmente** *adv*

imparcialidad *nf* : impartiality

impartir *vt* : to impart, to give

impasible *adj* : impassive, unmoved — **impasiblemente** *adv*

impasse *nm* : impasse

impávido, -da *adj* : undaunted, unperturbed

impecable *adj* INTACHABLE : impeccable, faultless — **impecablemente** *adv*

impedido, -da *adj* : disabled, crippled

impedimento *nm* **1** : impediment, obstacle **2** : disability

impedir {54} *vt* **1** : to prevent, to block **2** : to impede, to hinder

impeler *vt* **1** : to drive, to propel **2** : to impel

impenetrable *adj* : impenetrable — **impenetrabilidad** *nf*

impenitente *adj* : unrepentant, impenitent

impensable *adj* : unthinkable

impensado, -da *adj* : unforeseen, unexpected

imperante *adj* : prevailing

imperar *vi* **1** : to reign, to rule **2** PREDOMINAR : to prevail

imperativo¹, -va *adj* : imperative

imperativo² *nm* : imperative

imperceptible *adj* : imperceptible — **imperceptiblemente** *adv*

imperdible *nm Spain* : safety pin

imperdonable *adj* : unpardonable, unforgivable

imperecedero, -ra *adj* **1** : imperishable **2** INMORTAL : immortal, everlasting

imperfección *nf, pl* **-ciones 1** : imperfection **2** DEFECTO : defect, flaw

imperfecto¹, -ta *adj* : imperfect, flawed

imperfecto² *nm* : imperfect tense

imperial *adj* : imperial

imperialismo *nm* : imperialism

imperialista *adj & nmf* : imperialist

impericia *nf* : lack of skill, incompetence

imperio *nm* : empire

imperioso, -sa *adj* **1** : imperious **2** : pressing, urgent — **imperiosamente** *adv*

impermeabilizante *adj* : water-repellent

impermeabilizar {21} *vt* : to waterproof

impermeable¹ *adj* **1** : impervious **2** : impermeable, waterproof

impermeable² *nm* : raincoat

impersonal *adj* : impersonal — **impersonalmente** *adv*
impertinencia *nf* INSOLENCIA : impertinence, insolence
impertinente *adj* **1** INSOLENTE : impertinent, insolent **2** INOPORTUNO : inappropriate, uncalled-for **3** IRRELEVANTE : irrelevant
imperturbable *adj* : imperturbable, impassive, stolid
ímpetu *nm* **1** : impetus, momentum **2** : vigor, energy **3** : force, violence
impetuoso, -sa *adj* : impetuous, impulsive — **impetuosamente** *adv*
impiedad *nf* : impiety
impío, -pía *adj* : impious, ungodly
implacable *adj* : implacable, relentless — **implacablemente** *adv*
implantación *nf, pl* **-ciones 1** : implantation **2** ESTABLECIMIENTO : establishment, introduction
implantado, -da *adj* : well-established
implantar *vt* **1** : to implant **2** ESTABLECER : to establish, to introduce — **implantarse** *vr*
implante *nm* : implant
implementar *vt* : to implement — **implementarse** *vr* — **implementación** *nf*
implemento *nm* : implement, tool
implicación *nf, pl* **-ciones** : implication
implicar {72} *vt* **1** ENREDAR, ENVOLVER : to involve, to implicate **2** : to imply
implícito, -ta *adj* : implied, implicit — **implícitamente** *adv*
implorar *vt* : to implore
implosión *nf, pl* **-siones** : implosion — **implosivo, -va** *adj*
implosionar *vi* : to implode
imponderable *adj & nm* : imponderable
imponente *adj* : imposing, impressive
imponer {60} *vt* **1** : to impose **2** : to confer — *vi* : to be impressive, to command respect — **imponerse** *vr* **1** : to take on (a duty) **2** : to assert oneself **3** : to prevail
imponible *adj* : taxable
impopular *adj* : unpopular — **impopularidad** *nf*
importación *nf, pl* **-ciones 1** : importation **2 importaciones** *nfpl* : imports
importado, -da *adj* : imported
importador¹, -dora *adj* : importing
importador², -dora *n* : importer
importancia *nf* : importance
importante *adj* : important — **importantemente** *adv*
importar *vi* : to matter, to be important ⟨no le importa lo que piensen : she doesn't care what they think⟩ — *vt* : to import
importe *nm* **1** : price, cost **2** : sum, amount
importunar *vt* : to bother, to inconvenience — *vi* : to be inconvenient
importuno, -na *adj* **1** : inopportune, inconvenient **2** : bothersome, annoying
imposibilidad *nf* : impossibility

imposibilitado, -da *adj* **1** : disabled, crippled **2 verse imposibilitado** : to be unable (to do something)
imposibilitar *vt* **1** : to make impossible **2** : to disable, to incapacitate — **imposibilitarse** *vr* : to become disabled
imposible *adj* : impossible
imposición *nf, pl* **-ciones 1** : imposition **2** EXIGENCIA : demand, requirement **3** : tax **4** : deposit
impositivo, -va *adj* : tax ⟨tasa impositiva : tax rate⟩
impostor, -tora *n* : impostor
impostura *nf* **1** : fraud, imposture **2** CALUMNIA : slander
impotencia *nf* **1** : impotence, powerlessness **2** : impotence (in medicine)
impotente *adj* **1** : powerless **2** : impotent
impracticable *adj* : impracticable
imprecisión *nf, pl* **-siones 1** : imprecision, vagueness **2** : inaccuracy
impreciso, -sa *adj* **1** : imprecise, vague **2** : inaccurate
impredecible *adj* : unpredictable
impregnar *vt* : to impregnate
imprenta *nf* **1** : printing **2** : printing shop, press
imprescindible *adj* : essential, indispensable
impresentable *adj* : unpresentable, unfit
impresión *nf, pl* **-siones 1** : print, printing **2** : impression, feeling
impresionable *adj* : impressionable
impresionante *adj* : impressive, incredible, amazing — **impresionantemente** *adv*
impresionar *vt* **1** : to impress, to strike **2** : to affect, to move — *vi* : to make an impression — **impresionarse** *vr* : to be affected, to be removed
impresionismo *nm* : impressionism
impresionista¹ *adj* : impressionist, impressionistic
impresionista² *nmf* : impressionist
impreso¹ *pp* → **imprimir**
impreso², -sa *adj* : printed
impreso³ *nm* PUBLICACIÓN : printed matter, publication
impresor, -sora *n* : printer
impresora *nf* : (computer) printer
imprevisible *adj* : unforeseeable
imprevisión *nf, pl* **-siones** : lack of foresight, thoughtlessness
imprevisto¹, -ta *adj* : unexpected, unforeseen
imprevisto² *nm* : unexpected occurrence, contingency
imprimir {42} *vt* **1** : to print **2** : to imprint, to stamp, to impress
improbabilidad *nf* : improbability
improbable *adj* : improbable, unlikely
improcedente *adj* **1** : inadmissible **2** : inappropriate, improper
improductivo, -va *adj* : unproductive
improperio *nm* : affront, insult
impropiedad *nf* : impropriety

impropio, -pia *adj* **1** : improper, incorrect **2** INADECUADO : unsuitable, inappropriate
improvisación *nf, pl* **-ciones** : improvisation, ad-lib
improvisado, -da *adj* : improvised, ad-lib
improvisar *v* : to improvise, to ad-lib
improviso *adj* de ~ : all of a sudden, unexpectedly
imprudencia *nf* INDISCRECIÓN : imprudence, indiscretion
imprudente *adj* INDISCRETO : imprudent, indiscreet — **imprudentemente** *adv*
impúdico, -ca *adj* : shameless, indecent
impuesto[1] *pp* → **imponer**
impuesto[2] *nm* : tax
impugnar *vt* : to challenge, to contest
impulsar *vt* : to propel, to drive
impulsividad *nf* : impulsiveness
impulsivo, -va *adj* : impulsive — **impulsivamente** *adv*
impulso *nm* **1** : drive, thrust **2** : impulse, urge
impune *adj* : unpunished
impunemente *adv* : with impunity
impunidad *nf* : impunity
impureza *nf* : impurity
impuro, -ra *adj* : impure
impuso, etc. → **imponer**
imputable *adj* ATRIBUIBLE : attributable
imputación *nf, pl* **-ciones** **1** : attribution, imputation **2** : accusation
imputar *vt* ATRIBUIR : to impute, to attribute
inacabable *adj* : endless
inacabado, -da *adj* INCONCLUSO : unfinished
inaccesibilidad *nf* : inaccessibility
inaccesible *adj* **1** : inaccessible **2** : unattainable
inacción *nf, pl* **-ciones** : inactivity, inaction
inaceptable *adj* : unacceptable
inactividad *nf* : inactivity, idleness
inactivo, -va *adj* : inactive, idle
inadaptado[1]**, -da** *adj* : maladjusted
inadaptado[2]**, -da** *n* : misfit
inadecuación *nf, pl* **-ciones** : inadequacy
inadecuado, -da *adj* **1** : inadequate **2** IMPROPIO : inappropriate — **inadecuadamente** *adv*
inadmisible *adj* **1** : inadmissible **2** : unacceptable
inadvertencia *nf* : oversight
inadvertidamente *adv* : inadvertently
inadvertido, -da *adj* **1** : unnoticed ⟨pasar inadvertido : to go unnoticed⟩ **2** DESPISTADO, DISTRAÍDO : inattentive, distracted
inagotable *adj* : inexhaustible
inaguantable *adj* INSOPORTABLE : insufferable, unbearable
inalámbrico, -ca *adj* : wireless, cordless
inalcanzable *adj* : unreachable, unattainable

inalienable *adj* : inalienable
inalterable *adj* **1** : unalterable, unchangeable **2** : impassive **3** : colorfast
inamovible *adj* : immovable, fixed
inanición *nf, pl* **-ciones** : starvation
inanimado, -da *adj* : inanimate
inapelable *adj* : indisputable
inapetencia *nf* : lack of appetite
inaplicable *adj* : inapplicable
inapreciable *adj* **1** : imperceptible, negligible **2** : invaluable
inapropiado, -da *adj* : inappropriate, unsuitable
inarticulado, -da *adj* : inarticulate, unintelligible — **inarticuladamente** *adv*
inasequible *adj* : unattainable, inaccessible
inasistencia *nf* AUSENCIA : absence
inatacable *adj* : unassailable, indisputable
inaudible *adj* : inaudible
inaudito, -ta *adj* : unheard-of, unprecedented
inauguración *nf, pl* **-ciones** : inauguration
inaugural *adj* : inaugural, opening
inaugurar *vt* **1** : to inaugurate **2** : to open
inca *adj & nmf* : Inca
incalculable *adj* : incalculable
incalificable *adj* : indescribable
incandescencia *nf* : incandescence — **incandescente**
incansable *adj* INFATIGABLE : tireless — **incansablemente** *adv*
incapacidad *nf* **1** : inability, incapacity **2** : disability, handicap
incapacitado, -da *adj* **1** : disqualified **2** : disabled, handicapped
incapacitar *vt* **1** : to incapacitate, to disable **2** : to disqualify
incapaz *adj, pl* **-paces** **1** : incapable, unable **2** : incompetent, inept
incautación *nf, pl* **-ciones** : seizure, confiscation
incautar *vt* CONFISCAR : to confiscate, to seize — **incautarse** *vr*
incauto, -ta *adj* : unwary, unsuspecting
incendiar *vt* : to set fire to, to burn (down) — **incendiarse** *vr* : to catch fire
incendiario[1]**, -ria** *adj* : incendiary, inflammatory
incendiario[2]**, -ria** *n* : arsonist
incendio *nm* **1** : fire **2 incendio premeditado** : arson
incensario *nm* : censer
incentivar *vt* : to encourage, to stimulate
incentivo *nm* : incentive
incertidumbre *nf* : uncertainty, suspense
incesante *adj* : incessant — **incesantemente** *adv*
incesto *nm* : incest
incestuoso, -sa *adj* : incestuous
incidencia *nf* **1** : incident **2** : effect, impact **3** por ~ : by chance, accidentally

incidental *adj* : incidental
incidentalmente *adv* : by chance
incidente *nm* : incident, occurrence
incidir *vi* 1 ~ **en** : to fall into, to enter into ⟨incidimos en el mismo error : we fell into the same mistake⟩ 2 ~ **en** : to affect, to influence, to have a bearing on
incienso *nm* : incense
incierto, -ta *adj* 1 : uncertain 2 : untrue 3 : unsteady, insecure
incineración *nf, pl* **-ciones** 1 : incineration 2 : cremation
incinerador *nm* : incinerator
incinerar *vt* 1 : to incinerate 2 : to cremate
incipiente *adj* : incipient
incisión *nf, pl* **-siones** : incision
incisivo¹, -va *adj* : incisive
incisivo² *nm* : incisor
inciso *nm* : digression, aside
incitación *nf, pl* **-ciones** : incitement
incitador¹, -dora *n* : instigator, agitator
incitador², -dora *adj* : provocative
incitante *adj* : provocative
incitar *vt* : to incite, to rouse
incivilizado, -da *adj* : uncivilized
inclemencia *nf* : inclemency, severity
inclemente *adj* : inclement
inclinación *nf, pl* **-ciones** 1 PROPENSIÓN : inclination, tendency 2 : incline, slope
inclinado, -da *adj* 1 : sloping 2 : inclined, apt
inclinar *vt* : to tilt, to lean, to incline ⟨inclinar la cabeza : to bow one's head⟩ — **inclinarse** *vr* 1 : to lean, to lean over 2 ~ **a** : to be inclined to
incluir {41} *vt* : to include
inclusión *nf, pl* **-siones** : inclusion
inclusive *adv* : inclusively, up to and including
inclusivo, -va *adj* : inclusive
incluso *adv* 1 AUN : even, in fact ⟨es importante e incluso crucial : it is important and even crucial⟩ 2 : inclusively
incógnita *nf* 1 : unknown quantity (in mathematics) 2 : mystery
incógnito, -ta *adj* 1 : unknown 2 **de incógnito** : incognito
incoherencia *nf* : incoherence
incoherente *adj* : incoherent — **incoherentemente** *adv*
incoloro, -ra *adj* : colorless
incombustible *adj* : fireproof
incomible *adj* : inedible
incomodar *vt* 1 : to make uncomfortable 2 : to inconvenience — **incomodarse** *vr* : to put oneself out, to take the trouble
incomodidad *nf* 1 : discomfort, awkwardness 2 MOLESTIA : inconvenience, bother
incómodo, -da *adj* 1 : uncomfortable, awkward 2 INCONVENIENTE : inconvenient
incomparable *adj* : incomparable

incompatibilidad *nf* : incompatibility
incompatible *adj* : incompatible, uncongenial
incompetencia *nf* : incompetence
incompetente *adj & nmf* : incompetent
incompleto, -ta *adj* : incomplete
incomprendido, -da *adj* : misunderstood
incomprensible *adj* : incomprehensible
incomprensión *nf, pl* **-siones** : lack of understanding, incomprehension
incomunicación *nf, pl* **-ciones** : lack of communication
incomunicado, -da *adj* 1 : cut off, isolated 2 : in solitary confinement
inconcebible *adj* : inconceivable, unthinkable — **inconcebiblemente** *adv*
inconcluso, -sa *adj* INACABADO : unfinished
incondicional *adj* : unconditional — **incondicionalmente** *adv*
inconexo, -xa *adj* : unconnected, disconnected
inconfesable *adj* : unspeakable, shameful
inconforme *adj & nmf* : nonconformist
inconformidad *nf* : nonconformity
inconformista *adj & nmf* : nonconformist
inconfundible *adj* : unmistakable, obvious — **inconfundiblemente** *adv*
incongruencia *nf* : incongruity
incongruente *adj* : incongruous
inconmensurable *adj* : vast, immeasurable
inconquistable *adj* : unyielding
inconsciencia *nf* 1 : unconsciousness, unawareness 2 : irresponsibility
inconsciente¹ *adj* 1 : unconscious, unaware 2 : reckless, needless — **inconscientemente** *adv*
inconsciente² *nm* **el inconsciente** : the unconscious
inconsecuente *adj* : inconsistent — **inconsecuencia** *nf*
inconsiderado, -da *adj* : inconsiderate, thoughtless
inconsistencia *nf* : inconsistency
inconsistente *adj* 1 : weak, flimsy 2 : inconsistent, weak (of an argument)
inconsolable *adj* : inconsolable — **inconsolablemente** *adv*
inconstancia *nf* : inconstancy
inconstante *adj* : inconstant, fickle, changeable
inconstitucional *adj* : unconstitutional
inconstitucionalidad *nf* : unconstitutionality
incontable *adj* INNUMERABLE : countless, innumerable
incontenible *adj* : uncontrollable, unstoppable
incontestable *adj* INCUESTIONABLE, INDISCUTIBLE : irrefutable, indisputable
incontinencia *nf* : incontinence — **incontinente** *adj*
incontrolable *adj* : uncontrollable
incontrolado, -da *adj* : uncontrolled, out of control

incontrovertible *adj* : indisputable
inconveniencia *nf* 1 : inconvenience, trouble 2 : unsuitability, inappropriateness 3 : tactless remark
inconveniente[1] *adj* 1 INCÓMODO : inconvenient 2 INAPROPIADO : improper, unsuitable
inconveniente[2] *nm* : obstacle, problem, snag ⟨no tengo inconveniente en hacerlo : I don't mind doing it⟩
incorporación *nf, pl* **-ciones** : incorporation
incorporar *vt* 1 : to incorporate 2 : to add, to include — **incorporarse** *vr* 1 : to sit up 2 ~ **a** : to join
incorpóreo, -rea *adj* : incorporeal, bodiless
incorrección *n, pl* **-ciones** : impropriety, improper word or action
incorrecto, -ta *adj* : incorrect — **incorrectamente** *adv*
incorregible *adj* : incorrigible — **incorregibilidad** *nf*
incorruptible *adj* : incorruptible
incredulidad *nf* : incredulity, skepticism
incrédulo[1], **-la** *adj* : incredulous, skeptical
incrédulo[2], **-la** *n* : skeptic
increíble *adj* : incredible, unbelievable — **increíblemente** *adv*
incrementar *vt* : to increase — **incrementarse** *vr*
incremento *nm* AUMENTO : increase
incriminar *vt* : to incriminate — **incriminación** *nf*
incriminatorio, -ria *adj* : incriminating, incriminatory
incruento, -ta *adj* : bloodless
incrustación *nf, pl* **-ciones** : inlay
incrustar *vt* 1 : to embed 2 : to inlay — **incrustarse** *vr* : to become embedded
incubación *nf, pl* **-ciones** : incubation
incubadora *nf* : incubator
incubar *v* : to incubate
incuestionable *adj* INCONTESTABLE, INDISCUTIBLE : unquestionable, indisputable — **incuestionablemente** *adv*
inculcar {72} *vt* : to inculcate, to instill
inculpar *vt* ACUSAR : to accuse, to charge
inculto, -ta *adj* 1 : uncultured, ignorant 2 : uncultivated, fallow
incumbencia *nf* : obligation, responsibility
incumbir *vi (3rd person only)* ~ **a** : to be incumbent upon, to be of concern to ⟨a mí no me incumbe : it's not my concern⟩
incumplido, -da *adj* : irresponsible, unreliable
incumplimiento *nm* 1 : nonfulfillment, neglect 2 **incumplimiento de contrato** : breach of contract
incumplir *vt* : to fail to carry out, to break (a promise, a contract)
incurable *adj* : incurable
incurrir *vi* 1 ~ **en** : to incur ⟨incurrir en gastos : to incur expenses⟩ 2 ~ **en** : to fall into, to commit ⟨incurrió en un error : he made a mistake⟩

incursión *nf, pl* **-siones** : incursion, raid
incursionar *vi* 1 : to raid 2 ~ **en** : to go into, to enter ⟨el actor incursionó en el baile : the actor worked in dance for awhile⟩
indagación *nf, pl* **-ciones** : investigation, inquiry
indagar {52} *vt* : to inquire into, to investigate
indebido, -da *adj* : improper, undue — **indebidamente** *adv*
indecencia *nf* : indecency, obscenity
indecente *adj* : indecent, obscene
indecible *adj* : indescribable, inexpressible
indecisión *nf, pl* **-siones** : indecision
indeciso, -sa *adj* 1 IRRESOLUTO : indecisive 2 : undecided
indeclinable *adj* : unavoidable
indecoro *nm* : impropriety, indecorousness
indecoroso, -sa *adj* : indecorous, unseemly
indefectible *adj* : unfailing, sure
indefendible *adj* : indefensible
indefenso, -sa *adj* : defenseless, helpless
indefinible *adj* : indefinable
indefinido, -da *adj* 1 : undefined, vague 2 INDETERMINADO : indefinite — **indefinidamente** *adv*
indeleble *adj* : indelible — **indeleblemente** *adv*
indelicado, -da *adj* : indelicate, tactless
indemnización *nf, pl* **-ciones** 1 : indemnity 2 **indemnización por despido** : severance pay
indemnizar {21} *vt* : to indemnify, to compensate
independencia *nf* : independence
independiente *adj* : independent — **independientemente** *adv*
independizarse {21} *vr* : to become independent, to gain independence
indescifrable *adj* : indecipherable
indescriptible *adj* : indescribable — **indescriptiblemente** *adv*
indeseable *adj & nmf* : undesirable
indestructible *adj* : indestructible
indeterminación *nf, pl* **-ciones** : indeterminacy
indeterminado, -da *adj* 1 INDEFINIDO : indefinite 2 : indeterminate
indexar *vt* INDICIAR : to index (wages, prices, etc.)
indicación *nf, pl* **-ciones** 1 : sign, signal 2 : direction, instruction 3 : suggestion, hint
indicado, -da *adj* 1 APROPIADO : appropriate, suitable 2 : specified, indicated ⟨al día indicado : on the specified day⟩
indicador *nm* 1 : gauge, dial, meter 2 : indicator ⟨indicadores económicos : economic indicators⟩
indicar {72} *vt* 1 SEÑALAR : to indicate 2 ENSEÑAR, MOSTRAR : to show
indicativo[1], **-va** *adj* : indicative
indicativo[2] *nm* : indicative (mood)

índice *nm* **1** : index **2** : index finger, forefinger **3** INDICIO : indication
indiciar *vt* : to index (prices, wages, etc.)
indicio *nm* : indication, sign
indiferencia *nf* : indifference
indiferente *adj* **1** : indifferent, unconcerned **2** ser indiferente : to be of no concern ⟨me es indiferente : it doesn't matter to me⟩
indígena¹ *adj* : indigenous, native
indígena² *nmf* : native
indigencia *nf* MISERIA : poverty, destitution
indigente *adj & nmf* : indigent
indigestarse *vr* **1** EMPACHARSE : to have indigestion **2** *fam* : to nauseate, to disgust ⟨ese tipo se me indigesta : that guy makes me sick⟩
indigestión *nf, pl* **-tiones** EMPACHO : indigestion
indigesto, -ta *adj* : indigestible, difficult to digest
indignación *nf, pl* **-ciones** : indignation
indignado, -da *adj* : indignant
indignante *adj* : outrageous, infuriating
indignar *vt* : to outrage, to infuriate — **indignarse** *vr*
indignidad *nf* : indignity
indigno, -na *adj* : unworthy
índigo *nm* : indigo
indio¹, -dia *adj* **1** : American Indian, Indian, Amerindian **2** : Indian (from India)
indio², -dia *n* **1** : American Indian **2** : Indian (from India)
indirecta *nf* **1** : hint, innuendo **2** echar indirectas *or* lanzar indirectas : to drop a hint, to insinuate
indirecto, -ta *adj* : indirect — **indirectamente** *adv*
indisciplina *nf* : indiscipline, unruliness
indisciplinado, -da *adj* : undisciplined, unruly
indiscreción *nf, pl* **-ciones** **1** IMPRUDENCIA : indiscretion **2** : tactless remark
indiscreto, -ta *adj* IMPRUDENTE : indiscreet, imprudent — **indiscretamente** *adv*
indiscriminado, -da *adj* : indiscriminate — **indiscriminadamente** *adv*
indiscutible *adj* INCONTESTABLE, INCUESTIONABLE : indisputable, unquestionable — **indiscutiblemente** *adv*
indispensable *adj* : indispensable — **indispensablemente** *adv*
indisponer {60} *vt* **1** : to spoil, to upset **2** : to make ill — **indisponerse** *vr* **1** : to become ill **2** ~ con : to fall out with
indisposición *nf, pl* **-ciones** : indisposition, illness
indispuesto, -ta *adj* : unwell, indisposed
indistinguible *adj* : indistinguishable
indistintamente *adv* **1** : indistinctly **2** : indiscriminately
indistinto, -ta *adj* : indistinct, vague, faint

individual *adj* : individual — **individualmente** *adv*
individualidad *nf* : individuality
individualismo *nm* : individualism
individualista¹ *adj* : individualistic
individualista² *nmf* : individualist
individualizar {21} *vt* : to individualize
individuo *nm* : individual, person
indivisible *adj* : indivisible — **indivisibilidad** *nf*
indocumentado, -da *n* : illegal immigrant
índole *nf* **1** : nature, character **2** CLASE, TIPO : sort, kind
indolencia *nf* : indolence, laziness
indolente *adj* : indolent, lazy
indoloro, -ra *adj* : painless
indomable *adj* **1** : indomitable **2** : unruly, unmanageable
indómito, -ta *adj* : indomitable
indonesio, -sia *adj & n* : Indonesian
inducción *nf, pl* **-ciones** : induction
inducir {61} *vt* **1** : to induce, to cause **2** : to infer, to deduce
inductivo, -va *adj* : inductive
indudable *adj* : unquestionable, beyond doubt
indudablemente *adv* : undoubtedly, unquestionably
indulgencia *nf* **1** : indulgence, leniency **2** : indulgence (in religion)
indulgente *adj* : indulgent, lenient
indultar *vt* : to pardon, to reprieve
indulto *nm* : pardon, reprieve
indumentaria *nf* : clothing, attire
industria *nf* : industry
industrial¹ *adj* : industrial
industrial² *nmf* : industrialist, manufacturer
industrialización *nf, pl* **-ciones** : industrialization
industrializar {21} *vt* : to industrialize
industrioso, -sa *adj* : industrious
inédito, -ta *adj* **1** : unpublished **2** : unprecedented
inefable *adj* : ineffable
ineficacia *nf* **1** : inefficiency **2** : ineffectiveness
ineficaz *adj, pl* **-caces** **1** : inefficient **2** : ineffective — **ineficazmente** *adv*
ineficiencia *nf* : inefficiency
ineficiente *adj* : inefficient — **ineficientemente** *adv*
inelegancia *nf* : inelegance — **inelegante** *adj*
inelegible *adj* : ineligible — **inelegibilidad** *nf*
ineludible *adj* : inescapable, unavoidable — **ineludiblemente** *adv*
ineptitud *nf* : ineptitude, incompetence
inepto, -ta *adj* : inept, incompetent
inequidad *nf* : inequity
inequitativo, -va *adj* : inequitable
inequívoco, -ca *adj* : unequivocal, unmistakable — **inequívocamente** *adv*
inercia *nf* **1** : inertia **2** : apathy, passivity **3** por ~ : out of habit
inerme *adj* : unarmed, defenseless

inerte *adj* : inert
inescrupuloso, -sa *adj* : unscrupulous
inescrutable *adj* : inscrutable
inesperado, -da *adj* : unexpected — **inesperadamente** *adv*
inestabilidad *nf* : instability, unsteadiness
inestable *adj* : unstable, unsteady
inestimable *adj* : inestimable, invaluable
inevitabilidad *nf* : inevitability
inevitable *adj* : inevitable, unavoidable — **inevitablemente** *adv*
inexactitud *nf* : inaccuracy
inexacto, -ta *adj* : inexact, inaccurate
inexcusable *adj* : inexcusable, unforgivable
inexistencia *nf* : lack, nonexistence
inexistente *adj* : nonexistent
inexorable *adj* : inexorable — **inexorablemente** *adv*
inexperiencia *nf* : inexperience
inexperto, -ta *adj* : inexperienced, unskilled
inexplicable *adj* : inexplicable — **inexplicablemente** *adv*
inexplorado, -da *adj* : unexplored
inexpresable *adj* : inexpressible
inexpresivo, -va *adj* : inexpressive, expressionless
inexpugnable *adj* : impregnable
inextinguible *adj* **1** : inextinguishable **2** : unquenchable
inextricable *adj* : inextricable — **inextricablemente** *adv*
infalibilidad *nf* : infallibility
infalible *adj* : infallible — **infaliblemente** *adv*
infame *adj* **1** : infamous **2** : loathsome, vile ⟨tiempo infame : terrible weather⟩
infamia *nf* : infamy, disgrace
infancia *nf* **1** NIÑEZ : infancy, childhood **2** : children *pl* **3** : beginnings *pl*
infante *nm* **1** : infante, prince **2** : infantryman
infantería *nf* : infantry
infantil *adj* **1** : childish, infantile **2** : child's, children's
infantilismo *nm* **1** : infantilism **2** INMADUREZ : childishness
infarto *nm* : heart attack
infatigable *adj* : indefatigable, tireless — **infatigablemente** *adv*
infección *nf, pl* **-ciones** : infection
infeccioso, -sa *adj* : infectious
infectar *vt* : to infect — **infectarse** *vr*
infecto, -ta *adj* **1** : infected **2** : repulsive, sickening
infecundidad *nf* : infertility
infecundo, -da *adj* : infertile, barren
infelicidad *nf* : unhappiness
infeliz¹ *adj, pl* **-lices 1** : unhappy **2** : hapless, unfortunate, wretched
infeliz² *nmf, pl* **-lices** : wretch
inferencia *nf* : inference
inferior¹ *adj* : inferior, lower
inferior² *nmf* : inferior, underling
inferioridad *nf* : inferiority

inferir {76} *vt* **1** DEDUCIR : to infer, to deduce **2** : to cause (harm or injury), to inflict
infernal *adj* : infernal, hellish
infestación *n, pl* **-ciones** : infestation
infestar *vt* **1** : to infest **2** : to overrun, to invade
infición *nf, pl* **-ciones** *Mex* : pollution
infidelidad *nf* : unfaithfulness, infidelity
infiel¹ *adj* : unfaithful, disloyal
infiel² *nmf* : infidel, heathen
infierno *nm* **1** : hell **2 el quinto infierno** : the middle of nowhere
infiltrar *vt* : to infiltrate — **infiltrarse** *vr* — **infiltración** *nf*
infinidad *nf* **1** : infinity **2** SINFÍN : great number, huge quantity ⟨una infinidad de veces : countless times⟩
infinitesimal *adj* : infinitesimal
infinitivo *nm* : infinitive
infinito¹ *adv* : infinitely, vastly
infinito², -ta *adj* **1** : infinite **2** : limitless, endless **3 hasta lo infinito** : ad infinitum — **infinitamente** *adv*
infinito³ *nm* : infinity
inflable *adj* : inflatable
inflación *nf, pl* **-ciones** : inflation
inflacionario, -ria *adj* : inflationary
inflacionista → **inflacionario**
inflamable *adj* : flammable
inflamación *nf, pl* **-ciones** : inflammation
inflamar *vt* : to inflame
inflamatorio, -ria *adj* : inflammatory
inflar *vt* HINCHAR : to inflate — **inflarse** *vr* **1** : to swell **2** : to become conceited
inflexibilidad *nf* : inflexibility
inflexible *adj* : inflexible, unyielding
inflexión *nf, pl* **-xiones** : inflection
infligir {35} *vt* : to inflict
influencia *nf* INFLUJO : influence
influenciable *adj* : easily influenced, suggestible
influenciar *vt* : to influence
influenza *nf* : influenza
influir {41} *vt* : to influence — *vi* ~ **en** *or* ~ **sobre** : to have an influence on, to affect
influjo *nm* INFLUENCIA : influence
influyente *adj* : influential
información *nf, pl* **-ciones 1** : information **2** INFORME : report, inquiry **3** NOTICIAS : news
informado, -da *adj* : informed ⟨bien informado : well-informed⟩
informador, -dora *n* : informer, informant
informal *adj* **1** : unreliable (of persons) **2** : informal, casual — **informalmente** *adv*
informalidad *nf* : informality
informante *nmf* : informant
informar *vt* ENTERAR : to inform — *vi* : to report — **informarse** *vr* ENTERARSE : to get information, to find out
informática *nf* : computer science, computing

informativo[1], **-va** adj : informative
informativo[2] nm : news program, news
informatización nf, pl **-ciones** : computerization
informatizar {21} vt : to computerize
informe[1] adj AMORFO : shapeless, formless
informe[2] nm 1 : report 2 : reference (for employment) 3 **informes** nmpl : information, data
infortunado, -da adj : unfortunate, unlucky
infortunio nm 1 DESGRACIA : misfortune 2 CONTRATIEMPO : mishap
infracción nf, pl **-ciones** : violation, offense, infraction
infractor, -tora n : offender
infraestructura nf : infrastructure
infrahumano, -na adj : subhuman
infranqueable adj 1 : impassable 2 : insurmountable
infrarrojo, -ja adj : infrared
infrecuente adj : infrequent
infringir {35} vt : to infringe, to breach
infructuoso, -sa adj : fruitless — **infructuosamente** adv
ínfulas nfpl 1 : conceit 2 **darse ínfulas** : to put on airs
infundado, -da adj : unfounded, baseless
infundio nm : false story, lie, tall tale ⟨todo eso son infundios : that's a pack of lies⟩
infundir vt 1 : to instill 2 **infundir ánimo a** : to encourage 3 **infundir miedo a** : to intimidate
infusión nf, pl **-siones** : infusion
ingeniar vt : to devise, to think up — **ingeniarse** vr : to manage, to find a way
ingeniería nf : engineering
ingeniero, -ra n : engineer
ingenio nm 1 : ingenuity 2 CHISPA : wit, wits 3 : device, apparatus 4 **ingenio azucarero** : sugar refinery
ingenioso, -sa adj 1 : ingenious 2 : clever, witty — **ingeniosamente** adv
ingente adj : huge, enormous
ingenuidad nf : naïveté, ingenuousness
ingenuo[1], **-nua** adj CÁNDIDO : naive — **ingenuamente** adv
ingenuo[2], **-nua** n : naive person
ingerencia → **injerencia**
ingerir {76} vt : to ingest, to consume
ingestión nf, pl **-tiones** : ingestion
ingle nf : groin
inglés[1], **-glesa** adj, mpl **ingleses** : English
inglés[2], **-glesa** n, mpl **ingleses** : Englishman m, Englishwoman f
inglés[3] nm : English (language)
inglete nm : miter joint
ingobernable adj : ungovernable, lawless
ingratitud nf : ingratitude
ingrato[1], **-ta** adj 1 : ungrateful 2 : thankless
ingrato[2], **-ta** n : ingrate
ingrediente nm : ingredient

ingresar vt 1 : to admit ⟨ingresaron a Luis al hospital : Luis was admitted into the hospital⟩ 2 : to deposit — vi 1 : to enter, to go in 2 **~ en** : to join, to enroll in
ingreso nm 1 : entrance, entry 2 : admission 3 **ingresos** nmpl : income, earnings pl
íngrimo, -ma adj : all alone, all by oneself
inhábil adj : unskillful, clumsy
inhabilidad nf 1 : unskillfulness 2 : unfitness
inhabilitar vt 1 : to disqualify, to bar 2 : to disable
inhabitable adj : uninhabitable
inhabituado, -da adj **~ a** : unaccustomed to
inhalador nm : inhaler
inhalante nm : inhalant
inhalar vt : to inhale — **inhalación** nf
inherente adj : inherent
inhibición nf, pl **-ciones** COHIBICIÓN : inhibition
inhibir vt : to inhibit — **inhibirse** vr
inhóspito, -ta adj : inhospitable
inhumación nf, pl **-ciones** : interment, burial
inhumanidad nf : inhumanity
inhumano, -na adj : inhuman, cruel, inhumane
inhumar vt : to inter, to bury
iniciación nf, pl **-ciones** 1 : initiation 2 : introduction
iniciado, -da n : initiate
iniciador[1], **-dora** adj : initiatory
iniciador[2], **-dora** n : initiator, originator
inicial[1] adj : initial, original — **inicialmente** adv
inicial[2] nf : initial (letter)
iniciar vt COMENZAR : to initiate, to begin — **iniciarse** vr
iniciativa nf : initiative
inicio nm COMIENZO : beginning
inicuo, -cua adj : iniquitous, wicked
inigualado, -da adj : unequaled
inimaginable adj : unimaginable
inimitable adj : inimitable
inteligible adj : unintelligible
ininterrumpido, -da adj : uninterrupted, continuous — **ininterrumpidamente** adv
iniquidad nf : iniquity, wickedness
injerencia nf : interference
injerirse {76} vr ENTROMETERSE, INMISCUIRSE : to meddle, to interfere
injertar vt : to graft
injerto nm : graft ⟨injerto de piel : skin graft⟩
injuria nf AGRAVIO : affront, insult
injuriar vt INSULTAR : to insult, to revile
injurioso, -sa adj : insulting, abusive
injusticia nf : injustice, unfairness
injustificable adj : unjustifiable
injustificadamente adv : unjustifiably, unfairly
injustificado, -da adj : unjustified, unwarranted

injusto, -ta *adj* : unfair, unjust — **injustamente** *adv*

inmaculado, -da *adj* : immaculate, spotless

inmadurez *nf, pl* **-reces** : immaturity

inmaduro, -ra *adj* **1** : immature **2** : unripe

inmediaciones *nfpl* : environs, surrounding area

inmediatamente *adv* ENSEGUIDA : immediately

inmediatez *nf, pl* **-teces** : immediacy

inmediato, -ta *adj* **1** : immediate **2** CONTIGUO : adjoining **3 de ~** : immediately, right away **4 ~ a** : next to, close to

inmejorable *adj* : excellent, unbeatable

inmemorial *adj* : immemorial ⟨tiempos inmemoriales : time immemorial⟩

inmensidad *nf* : immensity, vastness

inmenso, -sa *adj* ENORME : immense, huge, vast — **inmensamente** *adv*

inmensurable *adj* : boundless, immeasurable

inmerecido, -da *adj* : undeserved — **inmerecidamente** *adv*

inmersión *nf, pl* **-siones** : immersion

inmerso, -sa *adj* **1** : immersed **2** : involved, absorbed

inmigración *nf, pl* **-ciones** : immigration

inmigrado, -da *adj & n* : immigrant

inmigrante *adj & nmf* : immigrant

inmigrar *vi* : to immigrate

inminencia *nf* : imminence

inminente *adj* : imminent — **inminentemente** *adv*

inmiscuirse {41} *vr* ENTROMETERSE, INJERIRSE : to meddle, to interfere

inmobiliario, -ria *adj* : real estate, property

inmoderación *n, pl* **-ciones** : immoderation, intemperance

inmoderado, -da *adj* : immoderate, excessive — **inmoderadamente** *adv*

inmodestia *nf* : immodesty — **inmodesto, -ta** *adj*

inmolar *vt* : to immolate — **inmolación** *nf*

inmoral *adj* : immoral

inmoralidad *nf* : immorality

inmortal *adj & nmf* : immortal

inmortalidad *nf* : immortality

inmortalizar {21} *vt* : to immortalize

inmotivado, -da *adj* **1** : unmotivated **2** : groundless

inmovible *adj* : immovable, fixed

inmóvil *adj* **1** : still, motionless **2** : steadfast

inmovilidad *nf* : immobility

inmovilizar {21} *vt* : to immobilize

inmueble *nm* : building, property

inmundicia *nf* : dirt, filth, trash

inmundo, -da *adj* : dirty, filthy, nasty

inmune *adj* : immune

inmunidad *nf* : immunity

inmunizar {21} *vt* : to immunize — **inmunización** *nf*

inmunología *nf* : immunology

inmunológico, -ca *adj* : immune ⟨sistema inmunológico : immune system⟩

inmutabilidad *nf* : immutability

inmutable *adj* : immutable, unchangeable

innato, -ta *adj* : innate, inborn

innecesario, -ria *adj* : unnecessary — **innecesariamente** *adv*

innegable *adj* : undeniable

innoble *adj* : ignoble — **innoblemente** *adv*

innovación *nf, pl* **-ciones** : innovation

innovador, -dora *adj* : innovative

innovar *vt* : to introduce — *vi* : to innovate

innumerable *adj* INCONTABLE : innumerable, countless

inobjetable *adj* : indisputable, unobjectionable

inocencia *nf* : innocence

inocente[1] *adj* **1** : innocent **2** INGENUO : naive — **inocentemente** *adv*

inocente[2] *nmf* : innocent person

inocentón[1], -tona *adj, mpl* **-tones** : naive, gullible

inocentón[2], -tona *n, mpl* **-tones** : simpleton, dupe

inocuidad *nf* : harmlessness

inocular *vt* : to inoculate, to vaccinate — **inoculación** *nf*

inocuo, -cua *adj* : innocuous, harmless

inodoro[1], -ra *adj* : odorless

inodoro[2] *nm* : toilet

inofensivo, -va *adj* : inoffensive, harmless

inolvidable *adj* : unforgettable

inoperable *adj* : inoperable

inoperante *adj* : ineffective, inoperative

inopinado, -da *adj* : unexpected — **inopinadamente** *adv*

inoportuno, -na *adj* : untimely, inopportune, inappropriate

inorgánico, -ca *adj* : inorganic

inoxidable *adj* **1** : rustproof **2 acero inoxidable** : stainless steel

inquebrantable *adj* : unshakable, unwavering

inquietante *adj* : disturbing, worrisome

inquietar *vt* PREOCUPAR : to disturb, to upset, to worry — **inquietarse** *vr*

inquieto, -ta *adj* **1** : anxious, uneasy, worried **2** : restless

inquietud *nf* **1** : anxiety, uneasiness, worry **2** AGITACIÓN : restlessness

inquilinato *nm* : tenancy

inquilino, -na *n* : tenant, occupant

inquina *nf* **1** : aversion, dislike **2** : ill will ⟨tener inquina a alguien : to have a grudge against someone⟩

inquirir {4} *vi* : to make inquiries — *vt* : to investigate

inquisición *nf, pl* **-ciones** : investigation, inquiry

inquisidor, -dora *adj* : inquisitive

inquisitivo, -va *adj* : inquisitive, curious — **inquisitivamente** *adv*

insaciable *adj* : insatiable

insalubre *adj* **1** : unhealthy **2** ANTIHIGIÉNICO : unsanitary

insalubridad *nf* : unhealthiness
insalvable *adj* : insuperable, insurmountable
insano, -na *adj* **1** LOCO : insane, mad **2** INSALUBRE : unhealthy
insatisfacción *nf, pl* **-ciones** : dissatisfaction
insatisfactorio *nm* : unsatisfactory
insatisfecho, -cha *adj* **1** : dissatisfied **2** : unsatisfied
inscribir {33} *vt* **1** MATRICULAR : to enroll, to register **2** GRABAR : to engrave — **inscribirse** *vr* : to register, to sign up
inscripción *nf, pl* **-ciones 1** MATRÍCULA : enrollment, registration **2** : inscription
inscrito *pp* → **inscribir**
insecticida[1] *adj* : insecticidal
insecticida[2] *nm* : insecticide
insecto *nm* : insect
inseguridad *nf* **1** : insecurity **2** : lack of safety **3** : uncertainty
inseguro, -ra *adj* **1** : insecure **2** : unsafe **3** : uncertain
inseminar *vt* : to inseminate — **inseminación** *nf*
insensatez *nf, pl* **-teces** : foolishness, stupidity
insensato[1], -ta *adj* : foolish, senseless
insensato[2], -ta *n* : fool
insensibilidad *nf* : insensitivity
insensible *adj* : insensitive, unfeeling
inseparable *adj* : inseparable — **inseparablemente** *adv*
inserción *nf, pl* **-ciones** : insertion
insertar *vt* : to insert
inservible *adj* INÚTIL : useless, unusable
insidia *nf* **1** : snare, trap **2** : malice
insidioso, -sa *adj* : insidious
insigne *adj* : noted, famous
insignia *nf* ENSEÑA : insignia, emblem, badge
insignificancia *nf* **1** : insignificance **2** NIMIEDAD : trifle, triviality
insignificante *adj* : insignificant
insincero, -ra *adj* : insincere — **insinceridad** *nf*
insinuación *nf, pl* **-ciones** : insinuation, hint
insinuante *adj* : suggestive
insinuar {3} *vt* : to insinuate, to hint at — **insinuarse** *vr* **1** ～ **a** : to make advances to **2** ～ **en** : to worm one's way into
insipidez *nf, pl* **-deces** : insipidness, blandness
insípido, -da *adj* : insipid, bland
insistencia *nf* : insistence
insistente *adj* : insistent — **insistentemente** *adv*
insistir *v* : to insist
insociable *adj* : unsociable
insolación *nf, pl* **-ciones** : sunstroke
insolencia *nf* IMPERTINENCIA : insolence
insolente *adj* IMPERTINENTE : insolent
insólito, -ta *adj* : rare, unusual

insoluble *adj* : insoluble — **insolubilidad** *nf*
insolvencia *nf* : insolvency, bankruptcy
insolvente *adj* : insolvent, bankrupt
insomne *adj & nmf* : insomniac
insomnio *nm* : insomnia
insondable *adj* : fathomless, deep
insonorizado, -da *adj* : soundproof
insoportable *adj* INAGUANTABLE : unbearable, intolerable
insoslayable *adj* : unavoidable, inescapable
insospechado, -da *adj* : unexpected, unforeseen
insostenible *adj* : untenable
inspección *nf, pl* **-ciones** : inspection
inspeccionar *vt* : to inspect
inspector, -tora *n* : inspector
inspiración *nf, pl* **-ciones 1** : inspiration **2** INHALACIÓN : inhalation
inspirador, -dora *adj* : inspiring
inspirar *vt* : to inspire — *vi* INHALAR : to inhale
instalación *nf, pl* **-ciones** : installation
instalar *vt* **1** : to install **2** : to instate — **instalarse** *vr* ESTABLECERSE : to settle, to establish oneself
instancia *nf* **1** : petition, request **2 en última instancia** : as a last resort
instantánea *nf* : snapshot
instantáneo, -nea *adj* : instantaneous — **instantáneamente** *adv*
instante *nm* **1** : instant, moment **2 al instante** : immediately **3 a cada instante** : frequently, all the time **4 por instantes** : constantly, incessantly
instar *vt* APREMIAR : to urge, to press — *vi* URGIR : to be urgent or pressing ⟨insta que vayamos pronto : it is imperative that we leave soon⟩
instauración *nf, pl* **-ciones** : establishment
instaurar *vt* : to establish
instigador, -dora *n* : instigator
instigar {52} *vt* : to instigate, to incite
instintivo, -va *adj* : instinctive — **instintivamente** *adv*
instinto *nm* : instinct
institución *nf, pl* **-ciones** : institution
institucional *adj* : institutional — **institucionalmente** *adv*
institucionalización *nf, pl* **-ciones** : institutionalization
institucionalizar {21} *vt* : to institutionalize
instituir {41} *vt* ESTABLECER, FUNDAR : to institute, to establish, to found
instituto *nm* : institute
institutriz *nf, pl* **-trices** : governess *f*
instrucción *nf, pl* **-ciones 1** EDUCACIÓN : education **2 instrucciones** *nfpl* : instructions, directions
instructivo, -va *adj* : instructive, educational
instructor, -tora *n* : instructor
instruir {41} *vt* **1** ADIESTRAR : to instruct, to train **2** ENSEÑAR : to educate, to teach

instrumentación *nf, pl* **-ciones** : orchestration
instrumental *adj* : instrumental
instrumentar *vt* : to orchestrate
instrumentista *nmf* : instrumentalist
instrumento *nm* : instrument
insubordinado, -da *adj* : insubordinate — **insubordinación** *nf*
insubordinarse *vr* : to rebel
insuficiencia *nf* **1** : insufficiency, inadequacy **2 insuficiencia cardíaca** : heart failure
insuficiente *adj* : insufficient, inadequate — **insuficientemente** *adv*
insufrible *adj* : insufferable
insular *adj* : insular
insularidad *nf* : insularity
insulina *nf* : insulin
insulso, -sa *adj* **1** INSÍPIDO : insipid, bland **2** : dull
insultante *adj* : insulting
insultar *vt* : to insult
insulto *nm* : insult
insumos *nmpl* : supplies ⟨insumos agrícolas : agricultural supplies⟩
insuperable *adj* : insuperable, insurmountable
insurgente *adj & nmf* : insurgent — **insurgencia** *nf*
insurrección *nf, pl* **-ciones** : insurrection, uprising
insustancial *adj* : insubstantial, flimsy
insustituible *adj* : irreplaceable
intachable *adj* : irreproachable, faultless
intacto, -ta *adj* : intact
intangible *adj* IMPALPABLE : intangible, impalpable
integración *nf, pl* **-ciones** : integration
integral *adj* **1** : integral, essential **2 pan integral** : whole grain bread
integrante[1] *adj* : integrating, integral
integrante[2] *nmf* : member
integrar *vt* : to make up, to compose — **integrarse** *vr* : to integrate, to fit in
integridad *nf* **1** RECTITUD : integrity, honesty **2** : wholeness, completeness
integrismo *nm* : fundamentalism
integrista *adj & nmf* : fundamentalist
íntegro, -gra *adj* **1** : honest, upright **2** ENTERO : whole, complete **3** : unabridged
intelecto *nm* : intellect
intelectual *adj & nmf* : intellectual — **intelectualmente** *adv*
intelectualidad *nf* : intelligentsia
inteligencia *nf* : intelligence
inteligente *adj* : intelligent — **inteligentemente** *adv*
inteligible *adj* : intelligible — **inteligibilidad** *nf*
intemperancia *adj* : intemperance, excess
intemperie *nf* **1** : bad weather, elements *pl* **2 a la intemperie** : in the open air, outside
intempestivo, -va *adj* : inopportune, untimely — **intempestivamente** *adv*

intención *nf, pl* **-ciones** : intention, plan
intencionado, -da → **intencional**
intencional *adj* : intentional — **intencionalmente** *adv*
intendencia *nf* : management, administration
intendente *nmf* : quartermaster
intensidad *nf* : intensity
intensificación *nf, pl* **-ciones** : intensification
intensificar {72} *vt* : to intensify — **intensificarse** *vr*
intensivo, -va *adj* : intensive — **intensivamente** *adv*
intenso, -sa *adj* : intense — **intensamente** *adv*
intentar *vt* : to attempt, to try
intento *nm* **1** PROPÓSITO : intent, intention **2** TENTATIVA : attempt, try
interacción *nf, pl* **-ciones** : interaction
interactivo, -va *adj* : interactive
interactuar {3} *vi* : to interact
intercalar *vt* : to intersperse, to insert
intercambiable *adj* : interchangeable
intercambiar *vt* CANJEAR : to exchange, to trade
intercambio *nm* CANJE : exchange, trade
interceder *vi* : to intercede
intercepción *nf, pl* **-ciones** : interception
interceptar *vt* **1** : to intercept, to block **2 interceptar las líneas** : to wiretap
intercesión *nf, pl* **-siones** : intercession
intercomunicación *nf, pl* **-ciones** : intercommunication
interconexión *nf, pl* **-xiones** : interconnection
interconfesional *adj* : interdenominational
interdepartamental *adj* : interdepartmental
interdependencia *nf* : interdependence — **interdependiente** *adj*
interdicción *nf, pl* **-ciones** : interdiction, prohibition
interés *nm, pl* **-reses** : interest
interesado, -da *adj* **1** : interested **2** : selfish, self-seeking
interesante *adj* : interesting
interesar *vt* : to interest — *vi* : to be of interest, to be interesting — **interesarse** *vr*
interestatal *adj* : interstate ⟨autopista interestatal : interstate highway⟩
interestelar *adj* : interstellar
interfase → **interfaz**
interfaz *nf, pl* **-faces** : interface
interferencia *nf* : interference, static
interferir {76} *vi* : to interfere, to meddle — *vt* : to interfere with, to obstruct
intergaláctico, -ca *adj* : intergalactic
intergubernamental *adj* : intergovernmental
interín[1] *or* **ínterin** *adv* : meanwhile
interín[2] *or* **ínterin** *nm, pl* **-rines** : meantime, interim ⟨en el interín : in the meantime⟩

interinamente *adv* : temporarily
interino, -na *adj* : acting, temporary, interim
interior[1] *adj* : interior, inner
interior[2] *nm* **1** : interior, inside **2** : inland region
interiormente *adv* : inwardly
interjección *nf, pl* **-ciones** : interjection
interlocutor, -tora *n* : interlocutor, speaker
interludio *nm* : interlude
intermediario, -ria *adj & n* : intermediary, go-between
intermedio[1] *adj* : intermediate
intermedio[2] *nm* **1** : intermission **2 por intermedio de** : by means of
interminable *adj* : interminable, endless — **interminablemente** *adv*
intermisión *nf, pl* **-siones** : intermission, pause
intermitente[1] *adj* **1** : intermittent **2** : flashing, blinking (of a light) — **intermitentemente** *adv*
intermitente[2] *nm* : blinker, turn signal
internacional *adj* : international — **internacionalmente** *adv*
internacionalismo *nm* : internationalism
internacionalizar {21} *vt* : to internationalize
internado *nm* : boarding school
internar *vt* : to commit, to confine — **internarse** *vr* **1** : to penetrate, to advance into **2 ~ en** : to go into, to enter
internista *nmf* : internist
interno[1], **-na** *adj* : internal — **internamente** *adv*
interno[2], **-na** *n* **1** : intern **2** : inmate, internee
interpelación *nf, pl* **-ciones** : appeal, plea
interpelar *vt* : to question (formally)
interpersonal *adj* : interpersonal
interpolar *vt* : to insert, to interpolate
interponer {60} *vt* : to interpose — **interponerse** *vr* : to intervene
interpretación *nf, pl* **-ciones** : interpretation
interpretar *vt* **1** : to interpret **2** : to play, to perform
interpretativo, -va *adj* : interpretive
intérprete *nmf* **1** TRADUCTOR : interpreter **2** : performer
interpuesto *pp* → **interponer**
interracial *adj* : interracial
interrelación *nf, pl* **-ciones** : interrelationship
interrelacionar *vi* : to interrelate
interrogación *nf, pl* **-ciones** **1** : interrogation, questioning **2 signo de interrogación** : question mark
interrogador, -dora *n* : interrogator, questioner
interrogante[1] *adj* : questioning
interrogante[2] *nm* **1** : question mark **2** : query
interrogar {52} *vt* : to interrogate, to question

interrogativo, -va *adj* : interrogative
interrogatorio *nm* : interrogation, questioning
interrumpir *v* : to interrupt
interrupción *nf, pl* **-ciones** : interruption
interruptor *nm* **1** : (electrical) switch **2** : circuit breaker
intersección *nf, pl* **-ciones** : intersection
intersticio *nm* : interstice — **intersticial** *adj*
interuniversitario, -ria *adj* : intercollegiate
interurbano, -na *adj* **1** : intercity **2** : long-distance ⟨llamadas interurbanas : long-distance calls⟩
intervalo *nm* : interval
intervención *nf, pl* **-ciones** **1** : intervention **2** : audit **3 intervención quirúrgica** : operation
intervencionista *adj & nmf* : interventionist
intervenir {87} *vi* **1** : to take part **2** INTERCEDER : to intervene, to intercede — *vt* **1** : to control, to supervise **2** : to audit **3** : to operate on **4** : to tap (a telephone)
interventor, -tora *n* **1** : inspector **2** : auditor, comptroller
intestado, -da *adj* : intestate
intestinal *adj* : intestinal
intestino *nm* : intestine
intimar *vi* **~ con** : to become friendly with — *vt* : to require, to call on
intimidación *nf, pl* **-ciones** : intimidation
intimidad *nf* **1** : intimacy **2** : privacy, private life
intimidar *vt* ACOBARDAR : to intimidate
íntimo, -ma *adj* **1** : intimate, close **2** PRIVADO : private — **íntimamente** *adv*
intitular *vt* : to entitle, to title
intocable *adj* : untouchable
intolerable *adj* : intolerable, unbearable
intolerancia *nf* : intolerance
intolerante[1] *adj* : intolerant
intolerante[2] *nmf* : intolerant person, bigot
intoxicación *nf, pl* **-ciones** : poisoning
intoxicante *nm* : poison
intoxicar {72} *vt* : to poison
intranquilidad *nf* PREOCUPACIÓN : worry, anxiety
intranquilizar {21} *vt* : to upset, to make uneasy — **intranquilizarse** *vr* : to get worried, to be anxious
intranquilo, -la *adj* PREOCUPADO : uneasy, worried
intransigencia *nf* : intransigence
intransigente *adj* : intransigent, unyielding
intransitable *adj* : impassable
intransitivo, -va *adj* : intransitive
intrascendente *adj* : unimportant, insignificant
intratable *adj* **1** : intractable **2** : awkward **3** : unsociable
intravenoso, -sa *adj* : intravenous

intrepidez *nf* : fearlessness
intrépido, -da *adj* : intrepid, fearless
intriga *nf* : intrigue
intrigante *nmf* : schemer
intrigar {52} *v* : to intrigue — **intrigante**
adj
intrincado, -da *adj* : intricate, involved
intrínseco, -ca *adj* : intrinsic — **intrínsecamente** *adv*
introducción *nf, pl* **-ciones** : introduction
introducir {61} *vt* **1** : to introduce **2** : to bring in **3** : to insert **4** : to input, to enter — **introducirse** *vr* : to penetrate, to get into
introductorio, -ria *adj* : introductory
intromisión *nf, pl* **-siones** : interference, meddling
introspección *nf, pl* **-ciones** : introspection
introspectivo, -va *adj* : introspective
introvertido[1], -da *adj* : introverted
introvertido[2], -da *n* : introvert
intrusión *nf, pl* **-siones** : intrusion
intruso[1], -sa *adj* : intrusive
intruso[2], -sa *n* : intruder
intuición *nf, pl* **-ciones** : intuition
intuir {41} *vt* : to intuit, to sense
intuitivo, -va *adj* : intuitive — **intuitivamente** *adv*
inundación *nf, pl* **-ciones** : flood, inundation
inundar *vt* : to flood, to inundate
inusitado, -da *adj* : unusual, uncommon — **inusitadamente** *adv*
inusual *adj* : unusual, uncommon — **inusualmente** *adv*
inútil[1] *adj* INSERVIBLE : useless — **inútilmente** *adv*
inútil[2] *nmf* : good-for-nothing
inutilidad *nf* : uselessness
inutilizar {21} *vt* **1** : to make useless **2** INCAPACITAR : to disable, to put out of commission
invadir *vt* : to invade
invalidar *vt* : to nullify, to invalidate
invalidez *nf, pl* **-deces 1** : invalidity **2** : disablement
inválido, -da *adj & n* : invalid
invalorable *adj* : invaluable
invariable *adj* : invariable — **invariablemente** *adv*
invasión *nf, pl* **-siones** : invasion
invasivo, -va *adj* : invasive
invasor[1], -sora *adj* : invading
invasor[2], -sora *n* : invader
invectiva *nf* : invective, abuse
invencibilidad *nf* : invincibility
invencible *adj* **1** : invincible **2** : insurmountable
invención *nf, pl* **-ciones 1** INVENTO : invention **2** MENTIRA : fabrication, lie
inventar *vt* **1** : to invent **2** : to fabricate, to make up
inventariar {85} *vt* : to inventory
inventario *nm* : inventory
inventiva *nf* : ingenuity, inventiveness
inventivo, -va *adj* : inventive

invento *nm* INVENCIÓN : invention
inventor, -tora *n* : inventor
invernadero *nm* : greenhouse, hothouse
invernal *adj* : winter, wintry
invernar {55} *vi* **1** : to spend the winter **2** HIBERNAR : to hibernate
inverosímil *adj* : unlikely, far-fetched
inversión *nf, pl* **-siones 1** : inversion **2** : investment
inversionista *nmf* : investor
inverso[1], -sa *adj* **1** : inverse, inverted **2** CONTRARIO : opposite **3 a la inversa** : on the contrary, vice versa **4 en orden inverso** : in reverse order — **inversamente** *adv*
inverso[2] *n* : inverse
inversor, -sora *n* : investor
invertebrado[1], -da *adj* : invertebrate
invertebrado[2] *nm* : invertebrate
invertir {76} *vt* **1** : to invert, to reverse **2** : to invest — *vi* : to make an investment — **invertirse** *vr* : to be reversed
investidura *nf* : investiture, inauguration
investigación *nf, pl* **-ciones 1** ENCUESTA, INDAGACIÓN : investigation, inquiry **2** : research
investigador[1], -dora *adj* : investigative
investigador[2], -dora *n* **1** : investigator **2** : researcher
investigar {52} *vt* **1** INDAGAR : to investigate **2** : to research — *vi* ~ **sobre** : to do research into
investir {54} *vt* **1** : to empower **2** : to swear in, to inaugurate
inveterado, -da *adj* : inveterate, deep-seated
invicto, -ta *adj* : undefeated
invidente[1] *adj* CIEGO : blind, sightless
invidente[2] *nmf* CIEGO : blind person
invierno *nm* : winter, wintertime
inviolable *adj* : inviolable — **inviolabilidad** *nf*
inviolado, -da *adj* : inviolate, pure
invisibilidad *nf* : invisibility
invisible *adj* : invisible — **invisiblemente** *adv*
invitación *nf, pl* **-ciones** : invitation
invitado, -da *n* : guest
invitar *vt* : to invite
invocación *nf, pl* **-ciones** : invocation
invocar {72} *vt* : to invoke, to call on
involucramiento *nm* : involvement
involucrar *vt* : to implicate, to involve — **involucrarse** *vr* : to get involved
involuntario, -ria *adj* : involuntary — **involuntariamente** *adv*
invulnerable *adj* : invulnerable
inyección *nf, pl* **-ciones** : injection, shot
inyectado, -da *adj* **ojos inyectados** : bloodshot eyes
inyectar *vt* : to inject
ion *nm* : ion
iónico, -ca *adj* : ionic
ionizar {21} *vt* : to ionize — **ionización** *nf*
ionosfera *nf* : ionosphere
ir {43} *vi* **1** : to go ⟨ir a pie : to go on foot, to walk⟩ ⟨ir a caballo : to ride

horseback⟩ ⟨ir a casa : to go home⟩ **2** : to lead, to extend, to stretch ⟨el camino va de Cali a Bogotá : the road goes from Cali to Bogotá⟩ **3** FUN-CIONAR : to work, to function ⟨esta computadora ya no va : this computer doesn't work anymore⟩ **4** : to get on, to get along ⟨¿cómo te va? : how are you?, how's it going?⟩ ⟨el negocio no va bien : the business isn't doing well⟩ **5** : to suit ⟨ese vestido te va bien : that dress really suits you⟩ **6 ~ con** : to go ⟨ir con prisa : to be in a hurry⟩ **7 ~ por** : to follow, to go along ⟨fueron por la costa : they followed the shoreline⟩ **8 dejarse ir** : to let oneself go **9 ir a parar** : to end up **10 vamos a ver** : let's see — *v aux* **1** (*with present participle*) ⟨ir caminando : to walk⟩ ⟨¡voy corriendo! : I'll be right there!⟩ **2 ~ a** : to be going to ⟨voy a hacerlo : I'm going to do it⟩ ⟨el avión va a despegar : the plane is about to take off⟩ — **irse** *vr* **1** : to leave, to go ⟨¡vámonos! : let's go!⟩ ⟨todo el mundo se fue : everyone left⟩ **2** ESCAPARSE : to leak **3** GASTARSE : to be used up, to be gone

ira *nf* CÓLERA, FURIA : wrath, anger

iracundo, -da *adj* : irate, angry

iraní *adj & nmf* : Iranian

iraquí *adj & nmf* : Iraqi

irascible *adj* : irascible, irritable — **irascibilidad** *nf*

irga, irgue etc. → **erguir**

iridio *nm* : iridium

iridiscencia *nf* : iridescence — **iridiscente** *adj*

iris *nms & pl* **1** : iris **2 arco iris** : rainbow

irlandés¹, -desa *adj, mpl* **-deses** : Irish

irlandés², -desa *n, pl* **-deses** : Irish person, Irishman *m*, Irishwoman *f*

irlandés³ *nm* : Irish (language)

ironía *nf* : irony

irónico, -ca *adj* : ironic, ironical — **irónicamente** *adv*

irracional *adj* : irrational — **irracionalmente** *adv*

irracionalidad *nf* : irrationality

irradiación *nf, pl* **-ciones** : irradiation

irradiar *vt* : to radiate, to irradiate

irrazonable *adj* : unreasonable

irreal *adj* : unreal

irrebatible *adj* : unanswerable, irrefutable

irreconciliable *adj* : irreconcilable

irreconocible *adj* : unrecognizable

irrecuperable *adj* : irrecoverable, irretrievable

irredimible *adj* : irredeemable

irreductible *adj* : unyielding

irreemplazable *adj* : irreplaceable

irreflexión *nf, pl* **-xiones** : thoughtlessness, impetuosity

irreflexivo, -va *adj* : rash, unthinking — **irreflexivamente** *adv*

irrefrenable *adj* : uncontrollable, unstoppable ⟨un impulso irrefrenable : an irresistable urge⟩

irrefutable *adj* : irrefutable

irregular *adj* : irregular — **irregularmente** *adv*

irregularidad *nf* : irregularity

irrelevante *adj* : irrelevant — **irrelevancia** *nf*

irreligioso, -sa *adj* : irreligious

irremediable *adj* : incurable — **irremediablemente** *adv*

irreparable *adj* : irreparable

irreprimible *adj* : irrepressible

irreprochable *adj* : irreproachable

irresistible *adj* : irresistible — **irresistiblemente** *adv*

irresolución *nf, pl* **-ciones** : indecision, hesitation

irresoluto, -ta *adj* INDECISO : undecided

irrespeto *nm* : disrespect

irrespetuoso, -sa *adj* : disrespectful — **irrespetuosamente** *adv*

irresponsabilidad *nf* : irresponsibility

irresponsable *adj* : irresponsible — **irresponsablemente** *adv*

irrestricto, -ta *adj* : unrestricted, unconditional

irreverencia *nf* : disrespect

irreverente *adj* : disrespectful

irreversible *adj* : irreversible

irrevocable *adj* : irrevocable — **irrevocablemente** *adv*

irrigar {52} *vt* : to irrigate — **irrigación** *nf*

irrisible *adj* : laughable

irrisión *nf, pl* **-siones** : derision, ridicule

irrisorio, -ria *adj* RISIBLE : ridiculous, ludicrous

irritabilidad *nf* : irritability

irritable *adj* : irritable

irritación *nf, pl* **-ciones** : irritation

irritante *adj* : irritating

irritar *vt* : to irritate — **irritación** *nf*

irrompible *adj* : unbreakable

irrumpir *vi* **~ en** : to burst into

irrupción *nf, pl* **-ciones** **1** : irruption **2** : invasion

isla *nf* : island

islámico, -ca *adj* : Islamic, Muslim

islandés¹, -desa *adj, mpl* **-deses** : Icelandic

islandés², -desa *n, mpl* **-deses** : Icelander

islandés³ *nm* : Icelandic (language)

isleño, -ña *n* : islander

islote *nm* : islet

isometría *nfs & pl* : isometrics

isométrico, -ca *adj* : isometric

isósceles *adj* : isosceles ⟨triángulo isósceles : isosceles triangle⟩

isótopo *nm* : isotope

israelí *adj & nmf* : Israeli

istmo *nm* : isthmus

itacate *nm Mex* : pack, provisions *pl*

italiano¹, -na *adj & n* : Italian

italiano² *nm* : Italian (language)

iterbio *nm* : ytterbium

itinerante *adj* AMBULANTE : traveling, itinerant

itinerario *nm* : itinerary, route

itrio *nm* : yttrium
izar {21} *vt* : to hoist, to raise ⟨izar la bandera : to raise the flag⟩

izquierda *nf* : left
izquierdista *adj & nmf* : leftist
izquierdo, -da *adj* : left

J

j *nf* : tenth letter of the Spanish alphabet
ja *interj* **1** : ha! **2 ja, ja, ja** : ha-ha!
jabalí *nm* : wild boar
jabalina *nf* : javelin
jabón *nm, pl* **jabones** : soap
jabonar *vt* ENJABONAR : to soap up, to lather — **jabonarse** *vr*
jabonera *nf* : soap dish
jabonoso, -sa *adj* : soapy
jaca *nf* **1** : pony **2** YEGUA : mare
jacal *nm Mex* : shack, hut
jacinto *nm* : hyacinth
jactancia *nf* **1** : boastfulness **2** : boasting, bragging
jactancioso¹, -sa *adj* : boastful
jactancioso², -sa *n* : boaster, braggart
jactarse *vr* : to boast, to brag
jade *nm* : jade
jadear *vi* : to pant, to gasp, to puff — **jadeante** *adj*
jadeo *nm* : panting, gasping, puffing
jaez *nm, pl* **jaeces 1** : harness **2** : kind, sort, ilk **3 jaeces** *nmpl* : trappings
jaguar *nm* : jaguar
jai alai *nm* : jai alai
jaiba *nf* CANGREJO : crab
jalapeño *nm Mex* : jalapeño pepper
jalar *vt* **1** : to pull, to tug **2** *fam* : to attract, to draw in ⟨las ideas nuevas lo jalan : new ideas appeal to him⟩ — *vi* **1** : to pull, to pull together **2** *fam* : to hurry up, to get going **3** *Mex fam* : to be in working order ⟨esta máquina no jala : this machine doesn't work⟩
jalbegue *nm* : whitewash
jalea *nf* : jelly
jalear *vt* : to encourage, to urge on
jaleo *nm* **1** *fam* : uproar, ruckus, racket **2** *fam* : confusion, hassle **3** : cheering and clapping (for a dance)
jalón *nm, pl* **jalones 1** : milestone, landmark **2** TIRÓN : pull, tug
jalonar *vt* : to mark, to stake out
jalonear *vt Mex, Peru fam* : to tug at — *vi* **1** *fam* : to pull, to tug **2** *CA fam* : to haggle
jamaica *nf* : hibiscus
jamaicano, -na → **jamaiquino**
jamaiquino, -na *adj & n* : Jamaican
jamás *adv* **1** NUNCA : never **2 nunca jamás** *or* **jamás de los jamases** : never ever **3 para siempre jamás** : for ever and ever
jamba *nf* : jamb
jamelgo *nm* : nag (horse)
jamón *nm, pl* **jamones** : ham
Januká *nmf* : Hanukkah
japonés¹, -nesa *adj & n, mpl* **-neses** : Japanese

japonés² *nm, pl* **-neses** : Japanese (language)
jaque *nm* **1** : check (in chess) ⟨jaque mate : checkmate⟩ **2 tener en jaque** : to intimidate, to bully
jaqueca *nf* : headache, migraine
jarabe *nm* **1** : syrup **2** : Mexican folk dance
jarana *nf* **1** *fam* : revelry, partying, spree **2** *fam* : joking, fooling around **3** : small guitar
jaranear *vi fam* : to go on a spree, to party
jarcia *nf* **1** : rigging **2** : fishing tackle
jardín *nm, pl* **jardines 1** : garden **2 jardín de niños** : kindergarten **3 los jardines** *nmpl* : the outfield
jardinería *nf* : gardening
jardinero, -ra *n* **1** : gardener **2** : outfielder (in baseball)
jarra *nf* **1** : pitcher, jug **2** : stein, mug **3 de jarras** *or* **en jarras** : akimbo
jarrete *nm* **1** : back of the knee **2** CORVEJÓN : hock
jarro *nm* **1** : pitcher, jug **2** : mug
jarrón *nm, pl* **jarrones** FLORERO : vase
jaspe *nm* : jasper
jaspeado, -da *adj* **1** VETEADO : streaked, veined **2** : speckled, mottled
jaula *nf* : cage
jauría *nf* : pack of hounds
javanés, -nesa *adj & n* : Javanese
jazmín *nm, pl* **jazmines** : jasmine
jazz ['jas, 'd͡ʒas] *nm* : jazz
jeans ['jins, 'd͡ʒins] *nmpl* : jeans
jeep ['jip, 'd͡ʒip] *nm, pl* **jeeps** : jeep
jefatura *nf* **1** : leadership **2** : headquarters ⟨jefatura de policía : police headquarters⟩
jefe, -fa *n* **1** : chief, head, leader ⟨jefe de bomberos : fire chief⟩ **2** : boss
Jehová *nm* : Jehovah
jején *nm, pl* **jejenes** : gnat, small mosquito
jengibre *nm* : ginger
jeque *nm* : sheikh, sheik
jerarca *nmf* : leader, chief
jerarquía *nf* **1** : hierarchy **2** RANGO : rank
jerárquico, -ca *adj* : hierarchical
jerbo *nm* : gerbil
jerez *nm, pl* **jereces** : sherry
jerga *nf* **1** : jargon, slang **2** : coarse cloth
jerigonza *nf* GALIMATÍAS : mumbo jumbo, gibberish
jeringa *nf* : syringe
jeringar {52} *vt* **1** : to inject **2** *fam* JOROBAR : to annoy, to pester — *vi fam*

JOROBAR : to be annoying, to be a nuisance

jeringuear → **jeringar**

jeringuilla → **jeringa**

jeroglífico nm : hieroglyphic

jersey nm, pl **jerseys 1** : jersey (fabric) **2** Spain : sweater

Jesucristo nm : Jesus Christ

jesuita adj & nm : Jesuit

Jesús nm **1** : Jesus **2 ¡Jesús!** : goodness!, good heavens!

jeta nf **1** : snout **2** fam : face, mug

jíbaro, -ra adj **1** : Jivaro **2** : rustic, rural

jibia nf : cuttlefish

jícama nf : jicama

jícara nf Mex : calabash

jilguero nm : European goldfinch

jinete nmf : horseman, horsewoman f, rider

jinetear vt **1** : to ride, to perform (on horseback) **2** DOMAR : to break in (a horse) — vi CABALGAR : to ride horseback

jingoísmo [ʤɪŋɡoˈizmo, ˌʤɪŋ-] nm : jingoism

jingoísta adj : jingoist, jingoistic

jiote nm Mex : rash

jira nf : outing, picnic

jirafa nf **1** : giraffe **2** : boom microphone

jirón nm, pl **jirones** : shred, rag ⟨hecho jirones : in tatters⟩

jitomate nm Mex : tomato

jockey [ˈjoki, ˈʤɔ-] nmf, pl **jockeys** [-kis] : jockey

jocosidad nf : humor, jocularity

jocoso, -sa adj : playful, jocular — **jocosamente** adv

jofaina nf : washbowl

jogging [ˈjogɪŋ, ˈʤɔ-] nm : jogging

jolgorio nm : merrymaking, fun

jonrón nm, pl **jonrones** : home run

jordano, -na adj & n : Jordanian

jornada nf **1** : expedition, day's journey **2 jornada de trabajo** : working day **3 jornadas** nfpl : conference, congress

jornal nm **1** : day's pay **2 a ~** : by the day

jornalero, -ra n : day laborer

joroba nf **1** GIBA : hump **2** fam : nuisance, pain in the neck

jorobado¹, -da adj GIBOSO : hunchbacked, humpbacked

jorobado², -da n GIBOSO : hunchback, humpback

jorobar vt fam JERINGAR : to bother, to annoy — vi fam JERINGAR : to be annoying, to be a nuisance

jorongo nm Mex : full-length poncho

jota nf **1** : jot, bit ⟨no entiendo ni jota : I don't understand a word of it⟩ ⟨no se ve ni jota : you can't see a thing⟩ **2** : jack (in playing cards)

joven¹ adj, pl **jóvenes 1** : young **2** : youthful

joven² nmf, pl **jóvenes** : young man m, young woman f, young person

jovial adj : jovial, cheerful — **jovialmente** adv

jovialidad nf : joviality, cheerfulness

joya nf **1** : jewel, piece of jewelry **2** : treasure, gem ⟨la nueva empleada es una joya : the new employee is a real gem⟩

joyería nf **1** : jewelry store **2** : jewelry **3 joyería de fantasía** : costume jewelry

joyero, -ra n : jeweler

juanete nm : bunion

jubilación nf, pl **-ciones 1** : retirement **2** PENSIÓN : pension

jubilado¹, -da adj : retired, in retirement

jubilado², -da nmf : retired person, retiree

jubilar vt **1** : to retire, to pension off **2** fam : to get rid of, to discard — **jubilarse** vr : to retire

jubileo nm : jubilee

júbilo nm : jubilation, joy

jubiloso, -sa adj : jubilant, joyous

judaico, -ca adj : Judaic, Jewish

judaísmo nm : Judaism

judía nf **1** : bean **2** or **judía verde** : green bean, string bean

judicatura nf **1** : judiciary, judges pl **2** : office of judge

judicial adj : judicial — **judicialmente** adv

judío¹, -día adj : Jewish

judío², -día n : Jewish person, Jew

judo [ˈjuðo, ˈʤu-] nm : judo

uega, juegue, etc. → **jugar**

juego nm **1** : play, playing ⟨poner en juego : to bring into play⟩ **2** : game, sport ⟨juego de cartas : card game⟩ ⟨Juegos Olímpicos : Olympic Games⟩ **3** : gaming, gambling ⟨estar en juego : to be at stake⟩ **4** : set ⟨un juego de llaves : a set of keys⟩ **5 hacer juego** : to go together, to match **6 juego de manos** : conjuring trick, sleight of hand

juerga nf : partying, binge ⟨irse de juerga : to go on a spree⟩

juerguista nmf : reveler, carouser

jueves nms & pl : Thursday

juez¹ nmf, pl **jueces 1** : judge **2** ÁRBITRO : umpire, referee

juez², jueza n → **juez¹**

jugada nf **1** : play, move **2** : trick ⟨hacer una mala jugada : to play a dirty trick⟩

jugador, -dora n **1** : player **2** : gambler

jugar {44} vi **1** : to play ⟨jugar a la pelota : to play ball⟩ **2** APOSTAR : to gamble, to bet **3** : to joke, to kid — vt **1** : to play ⟨jugar un papel : to play a role⟩ ⟨jugar una carta : to play a card⟩ **2** : to bet — **jugarse** vr **1** : to risk, to gamble away ⟨jugarse la vida : to risk one's life⟩ **2 jugarse el todo por el todo** : to risk everything

jugarreta nf fam : prank, dirty trick

juglar nm : minstrel

jugo *nm* **1** : juice **2** : substance, essence ⟨sacarle el jugo a algo : to get the most out of something⟩

jugosidad *nf* : juiciness, succulence

jugoso, -sa *adj* : juicy

juguete *nm* : toy

juguetear *vi* **1** : to play, to cavort, to frolic **2** : to toy, to fiddle

juguetería *nf* : toy store

juguetón, -tona *adj, mpl* **-tones** : playful — **juguetonamente** *adv*

juicio *nm* **1** : good judgment, reason, sense **2** : opinion ⟨a mi juicio : in my opinion⟩ **3** : trial ⟨llevar a juicio : to take to court⟩

juicioso, -sa *adj* : judicious, wise — **juiciosamente** *adv*

julio *nm* : July

juncia *nf* : sedge

junco *nm* **1** : reed, rush **2** : junk (boat)

jungla *nf* : jungle

junio *nm* : June

junquillo *nm* : jonquil

junta *nf* **1** : board, committee ⟨junta directiva : board of directors⟩ **2** REUNIÓN : meeting, session **3** : junta **4** : joint, gasket

juntamente *adv* **1** : jointly, together ⟨juntamente con : together with⟩ **2** : at the same time

juntar *vt* **1** UNIR : to unite, to combine, to put together **2** REUNIR : to collect, to gather together, to assemble **3** : to close partway ⟨juntar la puerta : to leave the door ajar⟩ — **juntarse** *vr* **1** : to join together **2** : to socialize, to get together

junto, -ta *adj* **1** UNIDO : joined, united **2** : close, adjacent ⟨colgaron los dos retratos juntos : they hung the two paintings side by side⟩ **3** (*used adverbially*) : together ⟨llegamos juntos : we arrived together⟩ **4** ~ **a** : next to, alongside of **5** ~ **con** : together with, along with

juntura *nf* : joint, coupling

Júpiter *nm* : Jupiter

jura *nf* : oath, pledge ⟨jura de bandera : pledge of allegiance⟩

jurado¹ *nm* : jury

jurado², -da *n* : juror

juramento *nm* **1** : oath ⟨juramento hipocrático : Hippocratic oath⟩ **2** : swearword, oath

jurar *vt* **1** : to swear ⟨jurar lealtad : to swear loyalty⟩ **2** : to take an oath ⟨el alcalde juró su cargo : the mayor took the oath of office⟩ — *vi* : to curse, to swear

jurídico, -ca *adj* : legal

jurisdicción *nf, pl* **-ciones** : jurisdiction

jurisdiccional *adj* : jurisdictional, territorial

jurisprudencia *nf* : jurisprudence, law

jurista *nmf* : jurist

justa *nf* **1** : joust **2** TORNEO : tournament, competition

justamente *adv* **1** PRECISAMENTE : precisely, exactly **2** : justly, fairly

justar *vi* : to joust

justicia *nf* **1** : justice, fairness ⟨hacerle justicia a : to do justice to⟩ ⟨ser de justicia : to be only fair⟩ **2 la justicia** : the law ⟨tomarse la justicia por su mano : to take the law into one's own hands⟩

justiciero, -ra *adj* : righteous, avenging

justificable *adj* : justifiable

justificación *nf, pl* **-ciones** : justification

justificante *nm* **1** : justification **2** : proof, voucher

justificar {72} *vt* **1** : to justify **2** : to excuse, to vindicate

justo¹ *adv* **1** : justly **2** : right, exactly ⟨justo a tiempo : just in time⟩ **3** : tightly

justo², -ta *adj* **1** : just, fair **2** : right, exact **3** : tight ⟨estos zapatos me quedan muy justos : these shoes are too tight⟩

justo³, -ta *n* : just person ⟨los justos : the just⟩

juvenil *adj* **1** : juvenile, young, youthful **2** ADOLESCENTE : teenage

juventud *nf* **1** : youth **2** : young people

juzgado *nm* TRIBUNAL : court, tribunal

juzgar {52} *vt* **1** : to try, to judge (a case in court) **2** : to pass judgment on **3** CONSIDERAR : to consider, to deem

juzgue, etc. → **juzgar**

K

k *nf* : eleventh letter of the Spanish alphabet

káiser *nm* : kaiser

kaki → **caqui**

kaleidoscopio → **caleidoscopio**

kamikaze *adj* & *nm* : kamikaze

kampucheano, -na *adj* & *n* : Kampuchean

kan *nm* : khan

karaoke *nm* : karaoke

karate *or* **karaté** *nm* : karate

kayac *or* **kayak** *nm, pl* **kayacs** *or* **kayaks** : kayak

keniano, -na *adj* & *n* : Kenyan

kepí *nm* : kepi

kermesse *or* **kermés** [kerˈmɛs] *nf, pl* **kermesses** *or* **kermeses** [-ˈmɛsɛs] : charity fair, bazaar

kerosene *or* **kerosén** *or* **keroseno** *nm* : kerosene, paraffin

kibutz *or* **kibbutz** *nms* & *pl* : kibbutz

kilo *nm* **1** : kilo, kilogram **2** *fam* : large amount

kilobyte [ˌkiloˈbait] *nm* : kilobyte

kilociclo *nm* : kilocycle

kilogramo *nm* : kilogram

kilohertzio *nm* : kilohertz
kilometraje *nm* : distance in kilometers, mileage
kilométrico, -ca *adj fam* : endless, very long
kilómetro *nm* : kilometer
kilovatio *nm* : kilowatt
kimono *nm* : kimono
kinder [ˈkɪndɛr] → **kindergarten**
kindergarten [ˌkɪndɛrˈgarten] *nm, pl* **kindergartens** [-tɛns] : kindergarten, nursery school
kinesiología *nf* : physical therapy
kinesiólogo, -ga *n* : physical therapist
kiosco → **quiosco**
kit *nm, pl* **kits** : kit
kiwi [ˈkiwi] *nm* **1** : kiwi (bird) **2** : kiwifruit
klaxon → **claxon**
knockout [nɔˈkaut] → **nocaut**
koala *nm* : koala bear
kriptón *nm* : krypton
kurdo¹, -da *adj* : Kurdish
kurdo², -da *n* : Kurd
kuwaití [kuˌwaiˈti] *adj & nmf* : Kuwaiti

L

l *nf* : twelfth letter of the Spanish alphabet
la¹ *pron* **1** : her, it ⟨llámala hoy : call her today⟩ ⟨sacó la botella y la abrió : he took out the bottle and opened it⟩ **2** (*formal*) : you ⟨no la vi a usted, Señora Díaz : I didn't see you, Mrs. Díaz⟩ **3** : the one ⟨mi casa y la de la puerta roja : my house and the one with the red door⟩ **4 la que** : the one who
la² *art* → **el²**
laberíntico, -ca *adj* : labyrinthine
laberinto *nm* : labyrinth, maze
labia *nf fam* : gift of gab ⟨tu amigo tiene labia : your friend has a way with words⟩
labial *adj* : labial, lip ⟨lápiz labial : lipstick⟩
labio *nm* **1** : lip **2 labio leporino** : harelip
labor *nf* : work, labor
laborable *adj* **1** : arable **2 día laborable** : workday, business day
laboral *adj* : work, labor ⟨costos laborales : labor costs⟩
laborar *vi* : to work
laboratorio *nm* : laboratory, lab
laboriosidad *nf* : industriousness, diligence
laborioso, -sa *adj* **1** : laborious, hard **2** : industrious, hardworking
labrado¹, -da *adj* **1** : cultivated, tilled **2** : carved, wrought
labrado² *nm* : cultivated field
labrador, -dora *n* : farmer
labranza *nf* : farming
labrar *vt* **1** : to carve, to work (metal) **2** : to cultivate, to till **3** : to cause, to bring about
laca *nf* **1** : lacquer, shellac **2** : hair spray **3 laca de uñas** : nail polish
lacayo *nm* : lackey
lace, etc. → **lazar**
lacear *vt* : to lasso
laceración *nf, pl* **-ciones** : laceration
lacerante *adj* : hurtful, wounding
lacerar *vt* **1** : to lacerate, to cut **2** : to hurt, to wound (one's feelings)
lacio, -cia *adj* **1** : limp, lank **2 pelo lacio** : straight hair
lacónico, -ca *adj* : laconic — **lacónicamente** *adv*
lacra *nf* **1** : scar, mark (on the skin) **2** : stigma, blemish
lacrar *vt* : to seal (with wax)
lacrimógeno, -na *adj* **gas lacrimógeno** : tear gas
lacrimoso, -sa *adj* : tearful, moving
lactancia *nf* **1** : lactation **2** : breast-feeding
lactante *nmf* : nursing infant, suckling
lactar *v* : to breast-feed
lácteo, -tea *adj* **1** : dairy **2 Vía Láctea** : Milky Way
láctico, -ca *adj* : lactic
lactosa *nf* : lactose
ladeado, -da *adj* : crooked, tilted, lopsided
ladear *vt* : to tilt, to tip — **ladearse** *vr* : to bend (over)
ladera *nf* : slope, hillside
ladino¹, -na *adj* **1** : cunning, shrewd **2** *CA, Mex* : mestizo
ladino², -na *n* **1** : trickster **2** *CA, Mex* : Spanish-speaking Indian **3** *CA, Mex* : mestizo
lado *nm* **1** : side **2 PARTE** : place ⟨miró por todos lados : he looked everywhere⟩ **3 al lado de** : next to, beside **4 de ~** : tilted, sideways ⟨está de lado : it's lying on its side⟩ **5 hacerse a un lado** : to step aside **6 lado a lado** : side by side **7 por otro lado** : on the other hand
ladrar *vi* : to bark
ladrido *nm* : bark (of a dog), barking
ladrillo *nm* **1** : brick **2 AZULEJO** : tile
ladrón, -drona *n, mpl* **ladrones** : robber, thief, burglar
lagartija *nf* : small lizard
lagarto *nm* **1** : lizard **2 lagarto de Indias** : alligator
lago *nm* : lake
lágrima *nf* : tear, teardrop
lagrimear *vi* **1** : to water (of eyes) **2** : to weep easily
laguna *nf* **1** : lagoon **2** : lacuna, gap
laicado *nm* : laity
laico¹, -ca *adj* : lay, secular
laico², -ca *n* : layman *m*, laywoman *f*

laja *nf* : slab
lama[1] *nf* : slime, ooze
lama[2] *nm* : lama
lamber *vt* : to lick
lamé *nm* : lamé
lamentable *adj* 1 : unfortunate, lamentable 2 : pitiful, sad
lamentablemente *adv* : unfortunately, regrettably
lamentación *nf, pl* **-ciones** : lamentation, groaning, moaning
lamentar *vt* 1 : to lament 2 : to regret ⟨lo lamento : I'm sorry⟩ — **lamentarse** *vr* : to grumble, to complain
lamento *nm* : lament, groan, cry
lamer *vt* 1 : to lick 2 : to lap against
lamida *nf* : lick
lámina *nf* 1 PLANCHA : sheet, plate 2 : plate, illustration
laminado[1], **-da** *adj* : laminated
laminado[2] *nm* : laminate
laminar *vt* : to laminate — **laminación** *nf*
lámpara *nf* : lamp
lampiño, -ña *adj* : hairless
lamprea *nf* : lamprey
lana *nf* 1 : wool ⟨lana de acero : steel wool⟩ 2 *Mex fam* : money, dough
lance[1], *etc.* → **lanzar**
lance[2] *nm* 1 INCIDENTE : event, incident 2 RIÑA : quarrel 3 : throw, cast (of a net, etc.) 4 : move, play (in a game), throw (of dice)
lancear *vt* : to spear
lanceta *nf* : lancet
lancha *nf* 1 : small boat, launch 2 **lancha motora** : motorboat, speedboat
langosta *nf* 1 : lobster 2 : locust
langostino *nm* : prawn, crayfish
languidecer {53} *vi* : to languish
languidez *nf, pl* **-deces** : languor, listlessness
lánguido, -da *adj* : languid, listless — **lánguidamente** *adv*
lanolina *nf* : lanolin
lanudo, -da *adj* : woolly
lanza *nf* : spear, lance
lanzadera *nf* 1 : shuttle (for weaving) 2 **lanzadera espacial** : space shuttle
lanzado, -da *adj* 1 : impulsive, brazen 2 : forward, determined ⟨ir lanzado : to hurtle along⟩
lanzador, -dora *n* : thrower, pitcher
lanzallamas *nms & pl* : flamethrower
lanzamiento *nm* 1 : throw 2 : pitch (in baseball) 3 : launching, launch
lanzar {21} *vt* 1 : to throw, to hurl 2 : to pitch 3 : to launch — **lanzarse** *vr* 1 : to throw oneself (at, into) 2 ~ **a** : to embark upon, to undertake
laosiano, -na *adj & n* : Laotian
lapicero *nm* 1 : mechanical pencil 2 *CA, Peru* : ballpoint pen
lápida *nf* : marker, tombstone
lapidar *vt* APEDREAR : to stone
lapidario, -ria *adj & n* : lapidary
lápiz *nm, pl* **lápices** 1 : pencil 2 **lápiz de labios** *or* **lápiz labial** : lipstick

lapón, -pona *adj & n, mpl* **lapones** : Lapp
lapso *nm* : lapse, space (of time)
lapsus *nms & pl* : error, slip
laptop *nm, pl* **laptops** : laptop
laquear *vt* : to lacquer, to varnish, to shellac
largamente *adv* 1 : at length, extensively 2 : easily, comfortably 3 : generously
largar {52} *vt* 1 SOLTAR : to let loose, to release 2 AFLOJAR : to loosen, to slacken 3 *fam* : to give, to hand over 4 *fam* : to hurl, to let fly (insults, etc.) — **largarse** *vr fam* : to scram, to beat it
largo[1], **-ga** *adj* 1 : long 2 **a lo largo** : lengthwise 3 **a lo largo de** : along 4 **a la larga** : in the long run
largo[2] *nm* : length ⟨tres metros de largo : three meters long⟩
largometraje *nm* : feature film
largue, *etc.* → **largar**
larguero *nm* : crossbeam
largueza *nf* : generosity, largesse
larguirucho, -cha *adj fam* : lanky
largura *nf* : length
laringe *nf* : larynx
laringitis *nfs & pl* : laryngitis
larva *nf* : larva — **larval** *adj*
las → el[2], **los**[1]
lasaña *nf* : lasagna
lasca *nf* : chip, chipping
lascivia *nf* : lasciviousness, lewdness
lascivo, -va *adj* : lascivious, lewd — **lascivamente** *adv*
láser *nm* : laser
lasitud *nf* : lassitude, weariness
laso, -sa *adj* : languid, weary
lástima *nf* 1 : compassion, pity 2 PENA : shame, pity ⟨qué lástima! : what a shame!⟩
lastimadura *nf* : injury, wound
lastimar *vt* 1 DAÑAR, HERIR : to hurt, to injure 2 AGRAVIAR : to offend — **lastimarse** *vr* : to hurt oneself
lastimero, -ra *adj* : pitiful, wretched
lastimoso, -sa *adj* 1 : shameful 2 : pitiful, terrible
lastrar *vt* 1 : to ballast 2 : to burden, to encumber
lastre *nm* 1 : burden 2 : ballast
lata *nf* 1 : tinplate 2 : tin can 3 *fam* : pest, bother, nuisance 4 **dar lata** *fam* : to bother, to annoy
latencia *nf* : latency
latente *adj* : latent
lateral[1] *adj* 1 : lateral, side 2 : indirect — **lateralmente** *adv*
lateral[2] *nm* : end piece, side
látex *nms & pl* : latex
latido *nm* : beat, throb ⟨latido del corazón : heartbeat⟩
latifundio *nm* : large estate
latigazo *nm* : lash (with a whip)
látigo *nm* AZOTE : whip
latín *nm* : Latin (language)
latino[1], **-na** *adj* 1 : Latin 2 *fam* : Latin-American

latino², **-na** *n fam* : Latin American

latinoamericano¹, **-na** *adj* HISPANO-AMERICANO : Latin American

latinoamericano, **-na** *n* : Latin American

latir *vi* **1** : to beat, to throb **2 latirle a uno** *Mex fam* : to have a hunch ⟨me late que no va a venir : I have a feeling he's not going to come⟩

latitud *nf* **1** : latitude **2** : breadth

lato, **-ta** *adj* **1** : extended, lengthy **2** : broad (in meaning)

latón *nm, pl* **latones** : brass

latoso¹, **-sa** *adj fam* : annoying, bothersome

latoso², **-sa** *n fam* : pest, nuisance

latrocinio *nm* : larceny

laúd *nm* : lute

laudable *adj* : laudable, praiseworthy

laudo *nm* : findings, decision

laureado, **-da** *adj & n* : laureate

laurear *vt* : to award, to honor

laurel *nm* **1** : laurel **2** : bay leaf **3 dormirse en sus laureles** : to rest on one's laurels

lava *nf* : lava

lavable *adj* : washable

lavabo *nm* **1** LAVAMANOS : sink, washbowl **2** : lavatory, toilet

lavadero *nm* : laundry room

lavado *nm* **1** : laundry, wash **2** : laundering ⟨lavado de dinero : money laundering⟩

lavadora *nf* : washing machine

lavamanos *nms & pl* LAVABO : sink, washbowl

lavanda *nf* ESPLIEGO : lavender

lavandería *nf* : laundry (service)

lavandero, **-ra** *n* : launderer, laundress *f*

lavaplatos *nms & pl* **1** : dishwasher **2** *Chile, Col, Mex* : kitchen sink

lavar *vt* **1** : to wash, to clean **2** : to launder (money) **3 lavar en seco** : to dry-clean — **lavarse** *vr* **1** : to wash oneself **2 lavarse las manos de** : to wash one's hands of

lavativa *nf* : enema

lavatorio *nm* : lavatory, washroom

lavavajillas *nms & pl* : dishwasher

laxante *adj & nm* : laxative

laxitud *nf* : laxity, slackness

laxo, **-xa** *adj* : lax, slack

lazada *nf* : bow, loop

lazar {21} *vt* : to rope, to lasso

lazo *nm* **1** VÍNCULO : link, bond **2** : bow, ribbon **3** : lasso, lariat

le *pron* **1** : to her, to him, to it ⟨¿qué le dijiste? : what did you tell him?⟩ **2** : from her, from him, from it ⟨el ladrón le robó la cartera : the thief stole his wallet⟩ **3** : for her, for him, for it ⟨cómprale flores a tu mamá : buy your mom some flowers⟩ **4** (*formal*) : to you, for you ⟨le traje un regalo : I brought you a gift⟩

leal *adj* : loyal, faithful — **lealmente** *adv*

lealtad *nf* : loyalty, allegiance

lebrel *nm* : hound

lección *nf, pl* **lecciones** : lesson

lechada *nf* **1** : whitewash **2** : grout

lechal *adj* : suckling, unweaned ⟨cordero lechal : suckling lamb⟩

leche *nf* **1** : milk ⟨leche en polvo : powdered milk⟩ ⟨leche de magnesia : milk of magnesia⟩ **2** : milky sap

lechera *nf* **1** : milk jug **2** : dairymaid *f*

lechería *nf* : dairy store

lechero¹, **-ra** *adj* : dairy

lechero², **-ra** *n* : milkman *m*, milk dealer

lecho *nm* **1** : bed ⟨un lecho de rosas : a bed of roses⟩ ⟨lecho de muerte : deathbed⟩ **2** : riverbed **3** : layer, stratum (in geology)

lechón, **-chona** *n, mpl* **lechones** : suckling pig

lechoso, **-sa** *adj* : milky

lechuga *nf* : lettuce

lechuza *nf* BÚHO : owl, barn owl

lectivo, **-va** *adj* : school ⟨año lectivo : school year⟩

lector¹, **-tora** *adj* : reading ⟨nivel lector : reading level⟩

lector², **-tora** *n* : reader

lector³ *nm* : scanner, reader ⟨lector óptico : optical scanner⟩

lectura *nf* **1** : reading **2** : reading matter

leer {20} *v* : to read

legación *nf, pl* **-ciones** : legation

legado *nm* **1** : legacy, bequest **2** : legate, emissary

legajo *nm* : dossier, file

legal *adj* : legal, lawful — **legalmente** *adv*

legalidad *nf* : legality, lawfulness

legalista *adj* : legalistic

legalizar {21} *vt* : to legalize — **legalización** *nf*

legar {52} *vt* **1** : to bequeath, to hand down **2** DELEGAR : to delegate

legendario, **-ria** *adj* : legendary

legible *adj* : legible

legión *nf, pl* **legiones** : legion

legionario, **-ria** *n* : legionnaire

legislación *nf* **1** : legislation, lawmaking **2** : laws *pl*, legislation

legislador¹, **-dora** *adj* : legislative

legislador², **-dora** *n* : legislator

legislar *vi* : to legislate

legislativo, **-va** *adj* : legislative

legislatura *nf* **1** : legislature **2** : term of office

legitimar *vt* **1** : to legitimize **2** : to authenticate — **legitimación** *nf*

legitimidad *nf* : legitimacy

legítimo, **-ma** *adj* **1** : legitimate **2** : genuine, authentic — **legítimamente** *adv*

lego¹, **-ga** *adj* **1** : secular, lay **2** : uninformed, ignorant

lego², **-ga** *n* : layperson, layman *m*, laywoman *f*

legua *nf* **1** : league **2 notarse a leguas** : to be very obvious ⟨se notaba a leguas : you could tell from a mile away⟩

legue, etc. → **legar**
legumbre nf 1 HORTALIZA : vegetable 2 : legume
leíble adj : readable
leída nf : reading, read ⟨de una leída : in one reading, at one go⟩
leído[1] pp → **leer**
leído[2], **-da** adj : well-read
lejanía nf : remoteness, distance
lejano, -na adj : remote, distant, far away
lejía nf 1 : lye 2 : bleach
lejos adv 1 : far away, distant ⟨a lo lejos : in the distance, far off⟩ ⟨desde lejos : from a distance⟩ 2 : long ago, a long way off ⟨está lejos de los 50 años : he's a long way from 50 years old⟩ 3 **de ~** : by far ⟨esta decisión fue de lejos la más fácil : this decision was by far the easiest⟩ 4 **~ de** : far from ⟨lejos de ser reprobado, recibió una nota de B : far from failing, he got a B⟩
lelo, -la adj : silly, stupid
lema nm : motto, slogan
lencería nf : lingerie
lengua nf 1 : tongue ⟨morderse la lengua : to bite one's tongue⟩ 2 IDIOMA : language ⟨lengua materna : mother tongue, native language⟩ ⟨lengua muerta : dead language⟩
lenguado nm : sole, flounder
lenguaje nm 1 : language, speech 2 **lenguaje gestual** or **lenguaje de gestos** : sign language 3 **lenguaje de programación** : programming language
lengüeta nf 1 : tongue (of a shoe), tab, flap 2 : reed (of a musical instrument) 3 : barb, point
lengüetada nf **beber a lengüetadas** : to lap (up)
lenidad nf : leniency
lenitivo, -va adj : soothing
lente nmf 1 : lens ⟨lentes de contacto : contact lenses⟩ 2 **lentes** nmpl ANTEOJOS : eyeglasses ⟨lentes de sol : sunglasses⟩
lenteja nf : lentil
lentejuela nf : sequin, spangle
lentitud nf : slowness
lento[1] adv DESPACIO : slowly
lento[2], **-ta** adj 1 : slow 2 : slow-witted, dull — **lentamente** adv
leña nf : wood, firewood
leñador, -dora n : lumberjack, woodcutter
leñera nf : woodshed
leño nm : log
leñoso, -sa adj : woody
Leo nmf : Leo
león, -ona n, mpl **leones** 1 : lion, lioness f 2 (in various countries) : puma, cougar
leonado, -da adj : tawny
leonino, -na adj 1 : leonine 2 : one-sided, unfair
leopardo nm : leopard
leotardo nm MALLA : leotard, tights pl
leperada nf Mex : obscenity

lépero, -ra adj Mex : vulgar, coarse
lepra nf : leprosy
leproso[1], **-sa** adj : leprous
leproso[2], **-sa** n : leper
lerdo, -da adj 1 : clumsy 2 : dull, oafish, slow-witted
les pron 1 : to them ⟨dales una propina : give them a tip⟩ 2 : from them ⟨se les privó de su herencia : they were deprived of their inheritance⟩ 3 : for them ⟨les hice sus tareas : I did their homework for them⟩ 4 : to you pl, for you pl ⟨les compré un regalo : I bought you all a present⟩
lesbiana nf : lesbian — **lesbiano, -na** adj
lesbianismo nm : lesbianism
lesión nf, pl **lesiones** HERIDA : lesion, wound, injury ⟨una lesión grave : a serious injury⟩
lesionado, -da adj HERIDO : injured, wounded
lesionar vt : to injure, to wound — **lesionarse** vr : to hurt oneself
lesivo, -va adj : harmful, damaging
letal adj MORTÍFERO : deadly, lethal — **letalmente** adv
letanía nf 1 : litany 2 fam : spiel, song and dance
letárgico, -ca adj : lethargic
letargo nm : lethargy, torpor
letón[1], **-tona** adj & n, mpl **letones** : Latvian
letón[2] nm : Latvian (language)
letra nf 1 : letter 2 CALIGRAFÍA : handwriting, lettering 3 : lyrics pl 4 **al pie de la letra** : word for word, by the book 5 **letras** nfpl : arts (in education)
letrado[1], **-da** adj ERUDITO : learned, erudite
letrado[2], **-da** n : attorney-at-law, lawyer
letrero nm RÓTULO : sign, notice
letrina nf : latrine
letrista nmf : lyricist, songwriter
leucemia nf : leukemia
leva nf : cam
levadizo, -za adj 1 : liftable 2 **puente levadizo** : drawbridge
levadura nf 1 : yeast, leavening 2 **levadura en polvo** : baking powder
levantamiento nm 1 ALZAMIENTO : uprising 2 : raising, lifting ⟨levantamiento de pesas : weight lifting⟩
levantar vt 1 ALZAR : to lift, to raise 2 : to put up, to erect 3 : to call off, to adjourn 4 : to give rise to, to arouse ⟨levantar sospechas : to arouse suspicion⟩ — **levantarse** vr 1 : to rise, to stand up 2 : to get out of bed
levar vt **levar anclas** : to weigh anchor
leve adj 1 : light, slight 2 : trivial, unimportant — **levemente** adv
levedad nf : lightness
levemente adv LIGERAMENTE : lightly, softly
leviatán nm, pl **-tanes** : leviathan
léxico[1], **-ca** adj : lexical
léxico[2] nm : lexicon, glossary
lexicografía nf : lexicography

lexicográfico, -ca *adj* : lexicographical, lexicographic

lexicógrafo, -fa *n* : lexicographer

ley *nf* **1** : law ⟨fuera de la ley : outside the law⟩ ⟨la ley de gravedad : the law of gravity⟩ **2** : purity (of metals) ⟨oro de ley : pure gold⟩

leyenda *nf* **1** : legend **2** : caption, inscription

leyó, etc. → **leer**

liar {85} *vt* **1** ATAR : to bind, to tie (up) **2** : to roll (a cigarette) **3** : to confuse — **liarse** *vr* : to get mixed up

libanés, -nesa *adj & n, mpl* **-neses** : Lebanese

libar *vt* **1** : to suck (nectar) **2** : to sip, to swig (liquor, etc.)

libelo *nm* **1** : libel, lampoon **2** : petition (in court)

libélula *nf* : dragonfly

liberación *nf, pl* **-ciones** : liberation, deliverance ⟨liberación de la mujer : women's liberation⟩

liberado, -da *adj* **1** : liberated ⟨una mujer liberada : a liberated woman⟩ **2** : freed, delivered

liberal *adj & nmf* : liberal

liberalidad *nf* : generosity, liberality

liberalismo *nm* : liberalism

liberalizar {21} *vt* : to liberalize — **liberalización** *nf*

liberar *vt* : to liberate, to free — **liberarse** *vr* : to get free of

liberiano, -na *adj & n* : Liberian

libertad *nf* **1** : freedom, liberty ⟨tomarse la libertad de : to take the liberty of⟩ **2 libertad bajo fianza** : bail **3 libertad condicional** : parole

libertador¹, -dora *adj* : liberating

libertador², -dora *n* : liberator

libertar *vt* LIBRAR : to set free

libertario, -ria *adj & n* : libertarian

libertinaje *nm* : licentiousness, dissipation

libertino¹, -na *adj* : licentious, dissolute

libertino², -na *n* : libertine

libidinoso, -sa *adj* : lustful, lewd

libido *nf* : libido

libio, -bia *adj & n* : Libyan

libra *nf* **1** : pound **2 libra esterlina** : pound sterling

Libra *nmf* : Libra

libramiento *nm* **1** : liberating, freeing **2** LIBRANZA : order of payment **3** *Mex* : beltway

libranza *nf* : order of payment

librar *vt* **1** LIBERTAR : to deliver, to set free **2** : to wage ⟨librar batalla : to do battle⟩ **3** : to issue ⟨librar una orden : to issue an order⟩ — **librarse** *vr* ~ **de** : to free oneself from, to get out of

libre¹ *adj* **1** : free ⟨un país libre : a free country⟩ ⟨libre de : free from, exempt from⟩ ⟨libre albedrío : free will⟩ **2** DESOCUPADO : vacant **3 día libre** : day off

libre² *nm Mex* : taxi

librea *nf* : livery

librecambio *nm* : free trade

libremente *adv* : freely

librería *nf* : bookstore

librero¹, -ra *n* : bookseller

librero² *nm Mex* : bookcase

libresco, -ca *adj* : bookish

libreta *nf* CUADERNO : notebook

libretista *nmf* **1** : librettist **2** : scriptwriter

libreto *nm* : libretto, script

libro *nm* **1** : book ⟨libro de texto : textbook⟩ **2 libros** *nmpl* : books (in bookkeeping), accounts ⟨llevar los libros : to keep the books⟩

licencia *nf* **1** : permission **2** : leave, leave of absence **3** : permit, license ⟨licencia de conducir : driver's license⟩

licenciado, -da *n* **1** : university graduate **2** ABOGADO : lawyer

licenciar *vt* **1** : to license, to permit, to allow **2** : to discharge **3** : to grant a university degree to — **licenciarse** *vr* : to graduate

licenciatura *nf* **1** : college degree **2** : course of study (at a college or university)

licencioso, -sa *adj* : licentious, lewd

liceo *nm* : secondary school, high school

licitación *nf, pl* **-ciones** : bid, bidding

licitar *vt* : to bid on

lícito, -ta *adj* **1** : lawful, licit **2** JUSTO : just, fair

licor *nm* **1** : liquor **2** : liqueur

licorera *nf* : decanter

licuado *nm* BATIDO : milk shake

licuadora *nf* : blender

licuar {3} *vt* : to liquefy — **licuarse** *vr*

lid *nf* **1** : fight, combat **2** : argument, dispute **3 lides** *nfpl* : matters, affairs **4 en buena lid** : fair and square

líder¹ *adj* : leading, foremost

líder² *nmf* : leader

liderar *vt* DIRIGIR : to lead, to head

liderato *nm* : leadership, leading

liderazgo → **liderato**

lidiar *vt* : to fight — *vi* BATALLAR, LUCHAR : to struggle, to battle, to wrestle

liebre *nf* : hare

liendre *nf* : nit

lienzo *nm* **1** : linen **2** : canvas, painting **3** : stretch of wall or fencing

liga *nf* **1** ASOCIACIÓN : league **2** GOMITA : rubber band **3** : garter

ligado, -da *adj* : linked, connected

ligadura *nf* **1** ATADURA : tie, bond **2** : ligature

ligamento *nm* : ligament

ligar {52} *vt* : to bind, to tie (up)

ligeramente *adv* **1** : slightly **2** LEVEMENTE : lightly, gently **3** : casually, flippantly

ligereza *nf* **1** : lightness **2** : flippancy **3** : agility

ligero, -ra *adj* **1** : light, lightweight **2** : slight, minor **3** : agile, quick **4** : light-hearted, superficial

lignito *nm* : lignite

ligue, etc. → ligar
lija nf or **papel de lija** : sandpaper
lijar vt : to sand
lila[1] adj : lilac, light purple
lila[2] nf : lilac
lima nf 1 : lime (fruit) 2 : file ⟨lima de uñas : nail file⟩
limadora nf : polisher
limar vt 1 : to file 2 : to polish, to put the final touch on 3 : to smooth over ⟨limar las diferencias : to iron out differences⟩
limbo nm 1 : limbo 2 : limb (in botany and astronomy)
limeño[1], **-ña** adj : of or from Lima, Peru
limeño[2], **-ña** n : person from Lima, Peru
limero nm : lime tree
limitación nf, pl **-ciones** 1 : limitation 2 : limit, restriction ⟨sin limitación : unlimited⟩
limitado, -da adj 1 RESTRINGIDO : limited 2 : dull, slow-witted
limitar vt RESTRINGIR : to limit, to restrict — vi ~ con : to border on — **limitarse** vr ~ a : to limit oneself to
límite nm 1 : boundary, border 2 : limit ⟨el límite de mi paciencia : the limit of my patience⟩ ⟨límite de velocidad : speed limit⟩ 3 **fecha límite** : deadline
limítrofe adj LINDANTE, LINDERO : bordering, adjoining
limo nm : slime, mud
limón nm, pl **limones** 1 : lemon 2 : lemon tree 3 **limón verde** Mex : lime
limonada nf : lemonade
limonar nm : lemon tree
limosna nf : alms, charity
limosnear vi : to beg (for alms)
limosnero, -ra n MENDIGO : beggar
limoso, -sa adj : slimy
limpiabotas nmfs & pl : bootblack
limpiador[1], **-dora** adj : cleaning
limpiador[2], **-dora** n : cleaning person, cleaner
limpiamente adv : cleanly, honestly, fairly
limpiaparabrisas nms & pl : windshield wiper
limpiar vt 1 : to clean, to cleanse 2 : to clean up, to remove defects 3 fam : to clean out (in a game) 4 fam : to swipe, to pinch — vi : to clean — **limpiarse** vr
limpiavidrios nmfs & pl Mex : windshield wiper
límpido, -da adj : limpid
limpieza nf 1 : cleanliness, tidiness 2 : cleaning 3 HONRADEZ : integrity, honesty 4 DESTREZA : skill, dexterity
limpio[1] adv : fairly
limpio[2], **-pia** adj 1 : clean, neat 2 : honest ⟨un juego limpio : a fair game⟩ 3 : free ⟨limpio de impurezas : pure, free from impurities⟩ 4 : clear, net ⟨ganancia limpia : clear profit⟩
limusina nf : limousine
linaje nm ABOLENGO : lineage, ancestry
linaza nf : linseed
lince nm : lynx

linchamiento nm : lynching
linchar vt : to lynch
lindante adj LIMÍTROFE, LINDERO : bordering, adjoining
lindar vi 1 ~ con : to border, to skirt 2 ~ con BORDEAR : to border on, to verge on
linde nmf : boundary, limit
lindero[1], **-ra** adj LIMÍTROFE, LINDANTE : bordering, adjoining
lindero[2] nm : boundary, limit
lindeza nf 1 : prettiness 2 : clever mark 3 **lindezas** nfpl, (used ironically) : insults
lindo[1] adv 1 : beautifully, wonderfully ⟨canta lindo tu mujer : your wife sings beautifully⟩ 2 **de lo lindo** : a lot, a great deal ⟨los zancudos nos picaban de lo lindo : the mosquitoes were biting away at us⟩
lindo[2], **-da** adj 1 BONITO : pretty, lovely 2 MONO : cute
línea nf 1 : line ⟨línea divisoria : dividing line⟩ ⟨línea de banda : sideline⟩ 2 : line, course, position ⟨línea de conducta : course of action⟩ ⟨en líneas generales : in general terms, along general lines⟩ 3 : line, service ⟨línea aérea : airline⟩ ⟨línea telefónica : telephone line⟩
lineal adj : linear
linfa nf : lymph
linfático, -ca adj : lymphatic
lingote nm : ingot
lingüista nmf : linguist
lingüística nf : linguistics
lingüístico, -ca adj : linguistic
linimento nm : liniment
lino nm 1 : linen 2 : flax
linóleo nm : linoleum
linterna nf 1 : lantern 2 : flashlight
lío nm fam 1 : confusion, mess 2 : hassle, trouble, jam ⟨meterse en un lío : to get into a jam⟩ 3 : affair, liaison
liofilizar {21} vt : to freeze-dry
lioso, -sa adj fam 1 : confusing, muddled 2 : troublemaking
liquen nm : lichen
liquidación nf, pl **-ciones** 1 : liquidation 2 : clearance sale 3 : settlement, payment
liquidar vt 1 : to liquefy 2 : to liquidate 3 : to settle, to pay off 4 fam : to rub out, to kill
liquidez nf, pl **-deces** : liquidity
líquido[1], **-da** adj 1 : liquid, fluid 2 : net ⟨ingresos líquidos : net income⟩
líquido[2] nm 1 : liquid, fluid ⟨líquido de frenos : brake fluid⟩ 2 : ready cash, liquid assets
lira nf : lyre
lírica nf : lyric poetry
lírico, -ca adj : lyric, lyrical
lirio nm 1 : iris 2 **lirio de los valles** MUGUETE : lily of the valley
lirismo nm : lyricism
lirón nm, pl **lirones** : dormouse
lisiado[1], **-da** adj : disabled, crippled

lisiado², -da n : disabled person, cripple

lisiar vt : to cripple, to disable — **lisiarse** vr

liso, -sa adj **1** : smooth **2** : flat **3** : straight ⟨pelo liso : straight hair⟩ **4** : plain, unadorned ⟨liso y llano : plain and simple⟩

lisonja nf : flattery

lisonjear vt ADULAR : to flatter

lista nf **1** : list **2** : roster, roll ⟨pasar lista : to take attendance⟩ **3** : stripe, strip **4** : menu

listado¹, -da adj : striped

listado² nm : listing

listar vt : to list

listeza nf : smartness, alertness

listo, -ta adj **1** DISPUESTO, PREPARADO : ready ⟨¿estás listo? : are you ready?⟩ **2** : clever, smart

listón nm, pl **listones 1** : ribbon **2** : strip (of wood), lath **3** : high bar (in sports)

lisura nf : smoothness

litera nf : bunk bed, berth

literal adj : literal — **literalmente** adv

literario, -ria adj : literary

literato, -ta n : writer, author

literatura nf : literature

litigante adj & nmf : litigant

litigar {52} vi : to litigate, to be in litigation

litigio nm **1** : litigation, lawsuit **2 en ~** : in dispute

litigioso, -sa adj : litigious

litio nm : lithium

litografía nf **1** : lithography **2** : lithograph

litógrafo, -fa n : lithographer

litoral¹ adj : coastal

litoral² nm : shore, seaboard

litosfera nf : lithosphere

litro nm : liter

lituano¹, -na adj & n : Lithuanian

lituano² nm : Lithuanian (language)

liturgia nf : liturgy

litúrgico, -ca adj : liturgical — **litúrgicamente** adv

liviandad nf LIGEREZA : lightness

liviano, -na adj **1** : light, slight **2** INCONSTANTE : fickle

lividez nf PALIDEZ : pallor

lívido, -da adj **1** AMORATADO : livid **2** PÁLIDO : pallid, extremely pale

living nm : living room

llaga nf : sore, wound

llama nf **1** : flame **2** : llama

llamada nf : call ⟨llamada a larga distancia : long-distance call⟩ ⟨llamada al orden : call to order⟩

llamado, -da adj : named, called ⟨una mujer llamada Rosa : a woman called Rosa⟩

llamado² → llamamiento

llamador nm : door knocker

llamamiento nm : call, appeal

llamar vt **1** : to name, to call **2** : to call, to summon **3** : to phone, to call up — **llamarse** vr : to be called, to be named ⟨¿cómo te llamas? : what's your name?⟩

llamarada nf **1** : flare-up, sudden blaze **2** : flushing (of the face)

llamativo, -va adj : flashy, showy, striking

llameante adj : flaming, blazing

llamear vi : to flame, to blaze

llana nf **1** : trowel **2 → llano²**

llanamente adv : simply, plainly, straightforwardly

llaneza nf : simplicity, naturalness

llano¹, -na adj **1** : even, flat **2** : frank, open **3** LISO : plain, simple

llano² nm : plain

llanta nf **1** NEUMÁTICO : tire **2** : rim

llantén nm, pl **llantenes** : plantain (weed)

llanto nm : crying, weeping

llanura nf : plain, prairie

llave nf **1** : key **2** : faucet **3** INTERRUPTOR : switch **4** : brace (punctuation mark) **5 llave inglesa** : monkey wrench

llavero nm : key chain, key ring

llegada nf : arrival

llegar {52} vi **1** : to arrive, to come **2 ~ a** : to arrive at, to reach, to amount to **3 ~ a** : to manage to ⟨llegó a terminar la novela : she managed to finish the novel⟩ **4 llegar a ser** : to become ⟨llegó a ser un miembro permanente : he became a permanent member⟩

llegue, etc. → llegar

llenar vt **1** : to fill, to fill up, to fill in **2** : to meet, to fulfill ⟨los regalos no llenaron sus expectativas : the gifts did not meet her expectations⟩ — **llenarse** vr : to fill up, to become full

llenito, -ta adj fam REGORDETE : chubby, plump

lleno¹, -na adj **1** : full, filled **2 de ~** : completely, fully **3 estar lleno de sí mismo** : to be full of oneself

lleno² nm **1** fam : plenty, abundance **2** : full house, sellout

llevadero, -ra adj : bearable

llevar vt **1** : to take away, to carry ⟨me gusta, me lo llevo : I like it, I'll take it⟩ **2** : to wear **3** : to take, to lead ⟨llevamos a Pedro al cine : we took Pedro to the movies⟩ **4 llevar a cabo** : to carry out **5 llevar adelante** : to carry on, to keep going — vi : to lead ⟨un problema lleva al otro : one problem leads to another⟩ — v aux : to have ⟨llevo mucho tiempo buscándolo : I've been looking for it for a long time⟩ ⟨lleva leído medio libro : he's halfway through the book⟩ — **llevarse** vr **1** : to take away, to carry off **2** : to get along ⟨siempre nos llevábamos bien : we always got along well⟩

llorar vi : to cry, to weep — vt : to mourn, to bewail

lloriquear vi : to whimper, to whine

lloriqueo nm : whimpering, whining

llorón, -rona n, mpl **llorones** : crybaby, whiner

lloroso, -sa adj : tearful, sad

llovedizo, -za *adj* : rain ⟨agua llovediza : rainwater⟩

llover {47} *v impers* : to rain ⟨está lloviendo : it's raining⟩ ⟨llover a cántaros : to rain cats and dogs⟩ — *vi* : to rain down, to shower ⟨le llovieron regalos : he was showered with gifts⟩

llovizna *nf* : drizzle, sprinkle

lloviznar *v impers* : to drizzle, to sprinkle

llueve, etc. → **llover**

lluvia *nf* **1** : rain, rainfall **2** : barrage, shower

lluvioso, -sa *adj* : rainy

lo[1] *pron* **1** : him, it ⟨lo vi ayer : I saw him yesterday⟩ ⟨lo entiendo : I understand it⟩ ⟨no lo creo : I don't believe so⟩ **2** (*formal, masculine*) : you ⟨disculpe, señor, no lo oí : excuse me sir, I didn't hear you⟩ **3 lo que** : what, that which ⟨eso es lo que más le gusta : that's what he likes the most⟩

lo[2] *art* **1** : the ⟨lo mejor : the best, the best thing⟩ **2** : how ⟨sé lo bueno que eres : I know how good you are⟩

loa *nf* : praise

loable *adj* : laudable, praiseworthy — **loablemente** *adv*

loar *vt* : to praise, to laud

lobato, -ta *n* : wolf cub

lobby *nm* : lobby, pressure group

lobo, -ba *n* : wolf

lóbrego, -ga *adj* SOMBRÍO : gloomy, dark

lobulado, -da *adj* : lobed

lóbulo *nm* : lobe ⟨lóbulo de la oreja : earlobe⟩

locación *nf, pl* **-ciones 1** : location (in moviemaking) **2** *Mex* : place

local[1] *adj* : local — **localmente** *adv*

local[2] *nm* : premises *pl*

localidad *nf* : town, locality

localización *nf, pl* **-ciones 1** : locating, localization **2** : location

localizar {21} *vt* **1** UBICAR : to locate, to find **2** : to localize — **localizarse** *vr* UBICARSE : to be located ⟨se localiza en el séptimo piso : it is located on the seventh floor⟩

locatario, -ria *n* : tenant

loción *nf, pl* **lociones** : lotion

lócker *nm, pl* **lóckers** : locker

loco, -ca *adj* **1** DEMENTE : crazy, insane, mad **2 a lo loco** : wildly, recklessly **3 volverse loco** : to go mad

loco[2]**, -ca** *n* **1** : crazy person, lunatic **2 hacerse el loco** : to act the fool

locomoción *nf, pl* **-ciones** : locomotion

locomotor, -tora *adj* : locomotive

locomotora *nf* **1** : locomotive **2** : driving force

locuacidad *nf* : loquacity, talkativeness

locuaz *adj, pl* **locuaces** : loquacious, talkative

locución *nf, pl* **-ciones** : locution, phrase ⟨locución adverbial : adverbial phrase⟩

locura *nf* **1** : insanity, madness **2** : crazy thing, folly

locutor, -tora *n* : announcer

lodazal *nm* : bog, quagmire

lodo *nm* BARRO : mud, mire

lodoso, -sa *adj* : muddy

logaritmo *nm* : logarithm

logia *nf* : lodge ⟨logia masónica : Masonic lodge⟩

lógica *nf* : logic

lógico, -ca *adj* : logical — **lógicamente** *adv*

logística *nf* : logistics *pl*

logístico, -ca *adj* : logistic, logistical

logo → **logotipo**

logotipo *nm* : logo

logrado, -da *adj* : successful, well done

lograr *vt* **1** : to get, to obtain **2** : to achieve, to attain — **lograrse** *vr* : to be successful

logro *nm* : achievement, attainment

loma *nf* : hill, hillock

lombriz *nf, pl* **lombrices** : worm ⟨lombriz de tierra : earthworm, night crawler⟩ ⟨lombriz solitaria : tapeworm⟩ ⟨tener lombrices : to have worms⟩

lomo *nm* **1** : back (of an animal) **2** : loin ⟨lomo de cerdo : pork loin⟩ **3** : spine (of a book) **4** : blunt edge (of a knife)

lona *nf* : canvas

loncha *nf* LONJA, REBANADA : slice

lonche *nm* **1** ALMUERZO : lunch **2** *Mex* : submarine sandwich

lonchería *nf Mex* : luncheonette

londinense[1] *adj* : of or from London

londinense[2] *nmf* : Londoner

longaniza *nf* : spicy pork sausage

longevidad *nf* : longevity

longevo, -va *adj* : long-lived

longitud *nf* **1** LARGO : length ⟨longitud de onda : wavelength⟩ **2** : longitude

longitudinal *adj* : longitudinal

lonja *nf* LONCHA, REBANADA : slice

lontananza *nf* : background ⟨en lontananza : in the distance, far away⟩

lord *nm, pl* **lores** (*title in England*) : lord

loro *nm* : parrot

los[1]**, las** *pron* **1** : them ⟨hice galletas y se las di a los nuevos vecinos : I made cookies and gave them to the new neighbors⟩ **2** : you ⟨voy a llevarlos a los dos : I am going to take both of you⟩ **3 los que, las que** : those, who, the ones ⟨los que van a cantar deben venir temprano : those who are singing must come early⟩ **4** (*used with* **haber**) ⟨los hay en varios colores : they come in various colors⟩

los[2] *art* → **el**[2]

losa *nf* : flagstone, paving stone

loseta *nf* BALDOSA : floor tile

lote *nm* **1** : part, share **2** : batch, lot **3** : plot of land, lot

lotería *nf* : lottery

loto *nm* : lotus

loza *nf* **1** : crockery, earthenware **2** : china

lozanía *nf* **1** : healthiness, robustness **2** : luxuriance, lushness

lozano, -na adj 1 : robust, healthy-looking ⟨un rostro lozano : a smooth, fresh face⟩ 2 : lush, luxuriant
LSD nm : LSD
lubricante[1] adj : lubricating
lubricante[2] nm : lubricant
lubricar {72} vt : to lubricate, to oil — **lubricación** nf
lucero nm : bright star ⟨lucero del alba : morning star⟩
lucha nf 1 : struggle, fight 2 : wrestling
luchador, -dora n 1 : fighter 2 : wrestler
luchar vi 1 : to fight, to struggle 2 : to wrestle
luchón, -chona adj, mpl **luchones** Mex : industrious, hardworking
lucidez nf, pl **-deces** : lucidity, clarity
lucido, -da adj MAGNÍFICO : magnificent, splendid
lúcido, -da adj : lucid
luciérnaga nf : firefly, glowworm
lucimiento nm 1 : brilliance, splendor, sparkle 2 : triumph, success ⟨salir con lucimiento : to succeed with flying colors⟩
lucio nm : pike (fish)
lucir {45} vi 1 : to shine 2 : to look good, to stand out 3 : to seem, to appear ⟨ahora luce contento : he looks happy now⟩ — vt 1 : to wear, to sport 2 : to flaunt, to show off — **lucirse** vr 1 : to distinguish oneself, to excel 2 : to show off
lucrarse vr : to make a profit
lucrativo, -va adj : lucrative, profitable — **lucrativamente** adv
lucro GANANCIA : profit, gain
luctuoso, -sa adj : mournful, tragic
luego[1] adv 1 DESPUÉS : then, afterwards 2 : later (on) 3 desde ~ : of course 4 ¡hasta luego! : see you later! 5 **luego que** : as soon as 6 **luego luego** Mex fam : right away, immediately
luego[2] conj : therefore ⟨pienso, luego existo : I think, therefore I am⟩
lugar nm 1 : place, position ⟨se llevó el primer lugar en su división : she took first place in her division⟩ 2 ESPACIO : space, room 3 **dar lugar a** : to give rise to, to lead to 4 **en lugar de** : instead of 5 **lugar común** : cliché, platitude 6 **tener lugar** : to take place
lugareño[1], **-ña** adj : village, rural
lugareño[2], **-ña** n : villager
lugarteniente nmf : lieutenant, deputy
lúgubre adj : gloomy, lugubrious
lujo nm 1 : luxury 2 **de** ~ : deluxe
lujoso, -sa adj : luxurious
lujuria nf : lust, lechery
lujurioso, -sa adj : lustful, lecherous
lumbago nm : lumbago
lumbar adj : lumbar
lumbre nf 1 FUEGO : fire 2 : brilliance, splendor 3 **poner en la lumbre** : to put on the stove, to warm up
lumbrera nf 1 : skylight 2 : vent, port 3 : brilliant person, luminary
luminaria nf 1 : altar lamp 2 LUMBRERA : luminary, celebrity
luminiscencia nf : luminescence — **luminiscente** adj
luminosidad nf : luminosity, brightness
luminoso, -sa adj : shining, luminous
luna nf 1 : moon 2 **luna de miel** : honeymoon
lunar[1] adj : lunar
lunar[2] nm 1 : mole, beauty spot 2 : defect, blemish 3 : polka dot
lunático, -ca adj & n : lunatic
lunes nms & pl : Monday
luneta nf 1 : lens (of eyeglasses) 2 : windshield (of an automobile) 3 : crescent
lupa nf : magnifying glass
lúpulo nm : hops (plant)
lustrar vt : to shine, to polish
lustre nm 1 BRILLO : luster, shine 2 : glory, distinction
lustroso, -sa adj BRILLOSO : lustrous, shiny
luto nm : mourning ⟨estar de luto : to be in mourning⟩
luz nf, pl **luces** 1 : light 2 : lighting 3 fam : electricity 4 : window, opening 5 : light, lamp 6 : span, spread (between supports) 7 **a la luz de** : in light of 8 **dar a luz** : to give birth 9 **traje de luces** : matador's costume
luzca, etc. → lucir

M

m nf : thirteenth letter of the Spanish alphabet
macabro, -bra adj : macabre
macaco[1], **-ca** adj : ugly, misshapen
macaco[2], **-ca** n : macaque
macadán nm, pl **-danes** : macadam
macana nf 1 : club, cudgel 2 fam : nonsense, silliness 3 fam : lie, fib
macanudo, -da adj fam : great, fantastic
macarrón nm, pl **-rrones** 1 : macaroon 2 **macarrones** nmpl : macaroni
maceta nf 1 : flowerpot 2 : mallet 3 Mex fam : head
macetero nm 1 : plant stand 2 TIESTO : flowerpot, planter
machacar {72} vt 1 : to crush, to grind 2 : to beat, to pound — vi : to insist, to go on (about)
machacón, -cona adj, mpl **-cones** : insistent, tiresome
machete nm : machete
machetear vt : to hack with a machete — vi Mex fam : to plod, to work tirelessly
machismo nm 1 : machismo 2 : male chauvinism
machista nm : male chauvinist

macho[1] *adj* **1** : male **2** : macho, virile, tough

macho[2] *nm* **1** : male **2** : he-man

machote *nm* **1** *fam* : tough guy, he-man **2** *CA*, *Mex* : rough draft, model **3** *Mex* : blank form

machucar {72} *vt* **1** : to pound, to beat, to crush **2** : to bruise

machucón *nm*, *pl* **-cones 1** MORETÓN : bruise **2** : smashing, pounding

macilento, -ta *adj* : gaunt, wan

macis *nm* : mace (spice)

macizo, -za *adj* **1** : solid ⟨oro macizo : solid gold⟩ **2** : strong, strapping **3** : massive

macrocosmo *nm* : macrocosm

mácula *nf* : blemish, stain

madeja *nf* **1** : skein, hank **2** : tangle (of hair)

madera *nf* **1** : wood **2** : lumber, timber **3 madera dura** *or* **madera noble** : hardwood

maderero, -ra *adj* : timber, lumber

madero *nm* : piece of lumber, plank

madrastra *nf* : stepmother

madrazo *nm Mex fam* : punch, blow ⟨se agarraron a madrazos : they beat each other up⟩

madre *nf* **1** : mother **2 madre política** : mother-in-law **3 la Madre Patria** : the mother country (said of Spain)

madrear *vt Mex fam* : to beat up

madreperla *nf* NÁCAR : mother-of-pearl

madreselva *nf* : honeysuckle

madriguera *nf* : burrow, den, lair

madrileño[1], **-ña** *adj* : of or from Madrid

madrileño[2], **-ña** *n* : person from Madrid

madrina *nf* **1** : godmother **2** : bridesmaid **3** : sponsor

madrugada *nf* **1** : early morning, wee hours **2** ALBA : dawn, daybreak

madrugador, -dora *n* : early riser

madrugar {52} *vi* **1** : to get up early **2** : to get a head start

madurar *v* **1** : to ripen **2** : to mature

madurez *nf*, *pl* **-reces 1** : maturity **2** : ripeness

maduro, -ra *adj* **1** : mature **2** : ripe

maestría *nf* **1** : mastery, skill **2** : master's degree

maestro[1], **-tra** *adj* **1** : masterly, skilled **2** : chief, main **3** : trained ⟨un elefante maestro : a trained elephant⟩

maestro[2], **-tra** *n* **1** : teacher (in grammar school) **2** : expert, master **3** : maestro

Mafia *nf* : Mafia

mafioso, -sa *n* : mafioso, gangster

magdalena *nf* : bun, muffin

magenta *adj & n* : magenta

magia *nf* : magic

mágico, -ca *adj* : magic, magical — **mágicamente** *adv*

magisterio *nm* **1** : teaching **2** : teachers *pl*, teaching profession

magistrado, -da *n* : magistrate, judge

magistral *adj* **1** : masterful, skillful **2** : magisterial

magistralmente *adv* : masterfully, brilliantly

magistratura *nf* : judgeship, magistracy

magma *nm* : magma

magnanimidad *nf* : magnanimity

magnánimo, -ma *adj* GENEROSO : magnanimous — **magnánimamente** *adv*

magnate *nmf* : magnate, tycoon

magnesia *nf* : magnesia

magnesio *nm* : magnesium

magnético, -ca *adj* : magnetic

magnetismo *nm* : magnetism

magnetizar {21} *vt* : to magnetize

magnetófono *nm* : tape recorder

magnetofónico, -ca *adj* **cinta magnetofónica** : magnetic tape

magnificar {72} *vt* **1** : to magnify **2** EXAGERAR : to exaggerate **3** ENSALZAR : to exalt, to extol, to praise highly

magnificencia *nf* : magnificence, splendor

magnífico, -ca *adj* ESPLENDOROSO : magnificent, splendid — **magníficamente** *adv*

magnitud *nf* : magnitude

magnolia *nf* : magnolia (flower)

magnolio *nm* : magnolia (tree)

mago, -ga *n* **1** : magician **2** : wizard (in folk tales, etc.) **3 los Reyes Magos** : the Magi

magro, -gra *adj* **1** : lean (of meat) **2** : meager

maguey *nm* : maguey

magulladura *nf* MORETÓN : bruise

magullar *vt* : to bruise — **magullarse** *vr*

mahometano[1], **-na** *adj* ISLÁMICO : Islamic, Muslim

mahometano[2], **-na** *n* : Muslim

mahonesa → **mayonesa**

maicena *nf* : cornstarch

mainframe ['mein,freim] *nm* : mainframe

maíz *nm* : corn, maize

maizal *nm* : cornfield

maja *nf* : pestle

majadería *nf* **1** TONTERÍA : stupidity, foolishness **2** *Mex* LEPERADA : insult, obscenity

majadero[1], **-ra** *adj* **1** : foolish, silly **2** *Mex* LÉPERO : crude, vulgar

majadero[2], **-ra** *n* **1** TONTO : fool **2** *Mex* : rude person, boor

majar *vt* : to crush, to mash

majestad *nf* : majesty ⟨Su Majestad : Your Majesty⟩

majestuosamente *adv* : majestically

majestuosidad *nf* : majesty, grandeur

majestuoso, -sa *adj* : majestic, stately

majo, -ja *adj Spain* **1** : nice, likeable **2** GUAPO : attractive, good-looking

mal[1] *adv* **1** : badly, poorly ⟨baila muy mal : he dances very badly⟩ **2** : wrong, incorrectly ⟨me entendió mal : she misunderstood me⟩ **3** : with difficulty, hardly ⟨mal puedo oírte : I can hardly hear you⟩ **4 de mal en peor** : from bad to worse **5 menos mal** : it could have been worse

mal² adj → malo

mal³ nm 1 : evil, wrong 2 DAÑO : harm, damage 3 DESGRACIA : misfortune 4 ENFERMEDAD : illness, sickness

malabar adj **juegos malabares** : juggling

malabarista nmf : juggler

malaconsejado, -da adj : ill-advised

malacostumbrado, -da adj CONSENTIDO : spoiled, pampered

malacostumbrar vt : to spoil

malagradecido, -da adj INGRATO : ungrateful

malaisio → **malasio**

malaquita nf : malachite

malaria nf PALUDISMO : malaria

malasio, -sia adj & n : Malaysian

malauiano, -na adj & n : Malawian

malaventura nf : misadventure, misfortune

malaventurado, -da adj MALHADADO : ill-fated, unfortunate

malayo, -ya adj & n : Malay, Malayan

malbaratar vt 1 MALGASTAR : to squander 2 : to undersell

malcriado¹, -da adj 1 : ill-bred, ill-mannered 2 : spoiled, pampered

malcriado², -da n : spoiled brat

maldad nf 1 : evil, wickedness 2 : evil deed

maldecir {11} vt 1 : to curse, to damn — vi 1 : to curse, to swear 2 ~ **de** : to speak ill of, to slander, to defame

maldición nf, pl **-ciones** : curse

maldiga, maldijo etc. → **maldecir**

maldito, -ta adj 1 : cursed, damned ⟨¡maldita sea! : damn it all!⟩ 2 : wicked

maldoso, -sa adj Mex : mischievous

maleable adj : malleable

maleante nmf : crook, thug

malecón nm, pl **-cones** : jetty, breakwater

maleducado, -da adj : ill-mannered, rude

maleficio nm : curse, hex

maléfico, -ca adj : evil, harmful

malentender {56} vt : to misunderstand

malentendido nm : misunderstanding

malestar nm 1 : discomfort 2 IRRITACIÓN : annoyance 3 INQUIETUD : uneasiness, unrest

maleta nf : suitcase, bag ⟨haz tus maletas : pack your bags⟩

maletero¹, -ra n : porter

maletero² nm : trunk (of an automobile)

maletín nm, pl **-tines** 1 PORTAFOLIO : briefcase 2 : overnight bag, satchel

malevolencia nf : malevolence, wickedness

malévolo, -la adj : malevolent, wicked

maleza nf 1 : thicket, underbrush 2 : weeds pl

malformación nf, pl **-ciones** : malformation

malgache adj & nmf : Madagascan

malgastar vt : to squander (resources), to waste (time, effort)

malhablado, -da adj : foul-mouthed

malhadado, -da adj MALAVENTURADO : ill-fated

malhechor, -chora n : criminal, delinquent, wrongdoer

malherir {76} vt : to injure seriously

malhumor nm : bad mood, sullenness

malhumorado, -da adj : bad-tempered, cross

malicia nf 1 : wickedness, malice 2 : mischief, naughtiness 3 : cunning, craftiness

malicioso, -sa adj 1 : malicious 2 PÍCARO : mischievous

malignidad nf 1 : malignancy 2 MALDAD : evil

maligno, -na adj 1 : malignant ⟨un tumor maligno : a malignant tumor⟩ 2 : evil, harmful, malign

malinchismo nm Mex : preference for foreign goods or people — **malinchista** adj

malintencionado, -da adj : malicious, spiteful

malinterpretar vt : to misinterpret

malla nf 1 : mesh 2 LEOTARDO : leotard, tights pl 3 **malla de baño** : bathing suit

mallorquín, -quina adj & n : Majorcan

malnutrición nf, pl **-ciones** DESNUTRICIÓN : malnutrition

malnutrido, -da adj DESNUTRIDO : malnourished, undernourished

malo¹, -la adj (**mal** before masculine singular nouns) 1 : bad ⟨mala suerte : bad luck⟩ 2 : wicked, naughty 3 : cheap, poor (quality) 4 : harmful ⟨malo para la salud : bad for one's health⟩ 5 (using the form **mal**) : unwell ⟨estar mal del corazón : to have heart trouble⟩ 6 **estar de malas** : to be in a bad mood

malo², -la n : villain, bad guy (in novels, movies, etc.)

malogrado, -da adj : failed, unsuccessful

malograr vt 1 : to spoil, to ruin 2 : to waste (an opportunity, time) — **malograrse** vr 1 FRACASAR : to fail 2 : to die young

malogro nm 1 : untimely death 2 FRACASO : failure

maloliente adj HEDIONDO : foul-smelling, smelly

malparado, -da adj **salir malparado** or **quedar malparado** : to come out of (something) badly, to end up in a bad state

malpensado, -da adj : distrustful, suspicious, nasty-minded

malquerencia nf AVERSIÓN : ill will, dislike

malquerer {64} vt : to dislike

malquiso, etc. → **malquerer**

malsano, -na adj : unhealthy

malsonante adj : rude, offensive ⟨palabras malsonantes : foul language⟩

malta nf : malt

malteada nf : malted milk ⟨malteada de chocolate : chocolate malt⟩

maltés, -tesa *adj & n, mpl* **malteses** : Maltese

maltratar *vt* **1** : to mistreat, to abuse **2** : to damage, to spoil

maltrato *nm* : mistreatment, abuse

maltrecho, -cha *adj* : battered, damaged

malucho, -cha *adj fam* : sick, under the weather

malva *adj & nm* : mauve

malvado¹, -da *adj* : evil, wicked

malvado², -da *n* : evildoer, wicked person

malvavisco *nm* : marshmallow

malvender *vt* : to sell at a loss

malversación *nf, pl* **-ciones** : misappropriation (of funds), embezzlement

malversador, -dora *n* : embezzler

malversar *vt* : to embezzle

malvivir *vi* : to live badly, to just scrape by

mamá *nf fam* : mom, mama

mamar *vi* **1** : to suckle **2 darle de mamar a** : to breast-feed — *vt* **1** : to suckle, to nurse **2** : to learn from childhood, to grow up with — **mamarse** *vr fam* : to get drunk

mamario, -ria *adj* : mammary

mamarracho *nm fam* **1** ESPERPENTO : mess, sight **2** : laughingstock, fool **3** : rubbish, junk

mambo *nm* : mambo

mami *nf fam* : mommy

mamífero¹, -ra *adj* : mammalian

mamífero² *nm* : mammal

mamila *nf* **1** : nipple **2** *Mex* : baby bottle, pacifier

mamografía *nf* : mammogram

mamola *nf* : pat, chuck under the chin

mamotreto *nm fam* **1** : huge book, tome **2** ARMATOSTE : hulk, monstrosity

mampara *nf* BIOMBO : screen, room divider

mamparo *nm* : bulkhead

mampostería *nf* : masonry, stonemasonry

mampostero *nm* : mason, stonemason

mamut *nm, pl* **mamuts** : mammoth

maná *nm* : manna

manada *nf* **1** : flock, herd, pack **2** *fam* : horde, mob ⟨llegaron en manada : they came in droves⟩

manantial *nm* **1** FUENTE : spring **2** : source

manar *vi* **1** : to flow **2** : to abound

manatí *nm* : manatee

mancha *nf* **1** : stain, spot, mark ⟨mancha de sangre : bloodstain⟩ **2** : blemish, blot ⟨una mancha en su reputación : a blemish on his reputation⟩ **3** : patch

manchado, -da *adj* : stained

manchar *vt* **1** ENSUCIAR : to stain, to soil **2** DESHONRAR : to sully, to tarnish — **mancharse** *vr* : to get dirty

mancillar *vt* : to sully, to besmirch

manco, -ca *adj* : one-armed, one-handed

mancomunar *vt* : to combine, to pool — **mancomunarse** *vr* : to unite, to join together

mancomunidad *nf* **1** : commonwealth **2** : association, confederation

mancuernas *nfpl* : cuff links

mancuernillas *nf Mex* : cuff links

mandadero, -ra *n* : errand boy *m*, errand girl *f*, messenger

mandado *nm* **1** : order, command **2** : errand ⟨hacer los mandados : to run errands, to go shopping⟩

mandamás *nmf, pl* **-mases** *fam* : boss, bigwig, honcho

mandamiento *nm* **1** : commandment **2** : command, order, warrant ⟨mandamiento judicial : warrant, court order⟩

mandar *vt* **1** ORDENAR : to command, to order **2** ENVIAR : to send ⟨te manda saludos : he sends you his regards⟩ **3** ECHAR : to hurl, to throw **4 ¿mande?** *Mex* : yes?, pardon? — *vi* : to be the boss, to be in charge — **mandarse** *vr* *Mex* : to take liberties, to take advantage

mandarín *nm* : Mandarin

mandarina *nf* : mandarin orange, tangerine

mandatario, -ria *n* **1** : leader (in politics) ⟨primer mandatario : head of state⟩ **2** : agent (in law)

mandato *nm* **1** : term of office **2** : mandate

mandíbula *nf* **1** : jaw **2** : mandible

mandil *nm* **1** DELANTAL : apron **2** : horse blanket

mandilón *nm, pl* **-lones** *fam* : wimp, coward

mandioca *nf* **1** : manioc, cassava **2** : tapioca

mando *nm* **1** : command, leadership **2** : control (for a device) ⟨mando a distancia : remote control⟩ **3 al mando de** : in charge of **4 al mando de** : under the command of

mandolina *nf* : mandolin

mandón, -dona *adj, mpl* **mandones** : bossy, domineering

mandonear *vt fam* MANGONEAR : to boss around

mandrágora *nf* : mandrake

manecilla *nf* : hand (of a clock), pointer

manejable *adj* **1** : manageable **2** : docile, easily led

manejar *vt* **1** CONDUCIR : to drive (a car) **2** OPERAR : to handle, to operate **3** : to manage **4** : to manipulate (a person) — *vi* : to drive — **manejarse** *vr* **1** COMPORTARSE : to behave **2** : to get along, to manage

manejo *nm* **1** : handling, operation **2** : management

manera *nf* **1** MODO : way, manner, fashion **2 de cualquier manera** *or* **de todas maneras** : anyway, anyhow **3 de manera que** : so, in order that **4 de ninguna manera** : by no means, absolutely not **5 manera de ser** : personality, demeanor

manga *nf* **1** : sleeve **2** MANGUERA : hose
manganeso *nm* : manganese
mangle *nm* : mangrove
mango *nm* **1** : hilt, handle **2** : mango
mangonear *vt fam* **1** : to boss around, to bully — *vi* **1** : to be bossy **2** : to loaf, to fool around
mangosta *nf* : mongoose
manguera *nf* : hose
manguito *nm* **1** : muff **2** : sleeve (of a pipe, etc.), hose (of a car)
maní *nm, pl* **maníes** : peanut
manía *nf* **1** OBSESIÓN : mania, obsession **2** : craze, fad **3** : odd habit, peculiarity **4** : dislike, aversion
maníaco[1], **-ca** *adj* : maniacal
maníaco[2], **-ca** *n* : maniac
maniatar *vt* : to tie the hands of, to manacle
maniático[1], **-ca** *adj* **1** MANÍACO : maniacal **2** : obsessive **3** : fussy, finicky
maniático[2], **-ca** *n* **1** MANÍACO : maniac, lunatic **2** : obsessive person, fanatic **3** : eccentric, crank
manicomio *nm* : insane asylum, madhouse
manicura *nf* : manicure
manicuro, -ra *n* : manicurist
manido, -da *adj* : hackneyed, stale, trite
manifestación *nf, pl* **-ciones 1** : manifestation, sign **2** : demonstration, rally
manifestante *nmf* : demonstrator
manifestar {55} *vt* **1** : to demonstrate, to show **2** : to declare — **manifestarse** *vr* **1** : to be or become evident **2** : to state one's position ⟨se han manifestado a favor del acuerdo : they have declared their support for the agreement⟩ **3** : to demonstrate, to rally
manifiesto[1], **-ta** *adj* : manifest, evident, clear — **manifiestamente** *adv*
manifiesto[2] *nm* : manifesto
manija *nf* MANGO : handle
manilla → **manecilla**
manillar *nm* : handlebars *pl*
maniobra *nf* : maneuver, stratagem
maniobrar *v* : to maneuver
manipulación *nf, pl* **-ciones** : manipulation
manipulador[1], **-dora** *adj* : manipulating, manipulative
manipulador[2], **-dora** *n* : manipulator
manipular *vt* **1** : to manipulate **2** MANEJAR : to handle
maniquí[1] *nmf, pl* **-quíes** : mannequin, model
maniquí[2] *nm, pl* **-quíes** : mannequin, dummy
manirroto[1], **-ta** *adj* : extravagant
manirroto[2], **-ta** *n* : spendthrift
manivela *nf* : crank
manjar *nm* : delicacy, special dish
mano[1] *nf* **1** : hand **2** : coat (of paint or varnish) **3 a ~** : by hand **4 a ~ or a la mano** : handy, at hand, nearby **5 darse la mano** : to shake hands **6 de la mano** : hand in hand ⟨la política y la economía van de la mano : politics

and economics go hand in hand⟩ **7 de primera mano** : firsthand, at firsthand **8 de segunda mano** : secondhand ⟨ropa de segunda mano : secondhand clothing⟩ **9 mano a mano** : one-on-one **10 mano de obra** : labor, manpower **11 mano de mortero** : pestle **12 echar una mano** : to lend a hand **13 mano negra** *Mex fam* : shady dealings *pl*
mano[2], **-na** *n Mex fam* : buddy, pal ⟨¡oye, mano! : hey man!⟩
manojo *nm* PUÑADO : handful, bunch
manopla *nf* **1** : mitten, mitt **2** : brass knuckles *pl*
manosear *vt* **1** : to handle or touch excessively **2** ACARICIAR : to fondle, to caress
manotazo *nm* : slap, smack, swipe
manotear *vi* : to wave one's hands, to gesticulate
mansalva *adv* **a ~** : at close range
mansarda *nf* BUHARDILLA : attic
mansedumbre *nf* **1** : gentleness, meekness **2** : tameness
mansión *nf, pl* **-siones** : mansion
manso, -sa *adj* **1** : gentle, meek **2** : tame — **mansamente** *adv*
manta *nf* **1** COBIJA, FRAZADA : blanket **2** : poncho **3** *Mex* : coarse cotton fabric
manteca *nf* **1** GRASA : lard, fat **2** : butter
mantecoso, -sa *adj* : buttery
mantel *nm* **1** : tablecloth **2** : altar cloth
mantelería *nf* : table linen
mantener {80} *vt* **1** SUSTENTAR : to support, to feed ⟨mantener uno su familia : to support one's family⟩ **2** CONSERVAR : to keep, to preserve **3** CONTINUAR : to keep up, to sustain ⟨mantener una correspondencia : to keep up a correspondence⟩ **4** AFIRMAR : to maintain, to affirm — **mantenerse** *vr* **1** : to support oneself, to subsist **2 mantenerse firme** : to hold one's ground
mantenimiento *nm* **1** : maintenance, upkeep **2** : sustenance, food **3** : preservation
mantequera *nf* **1** : churn **2** : butter dish
mantequería *nf* **1** : creamery, dairy **2** : grocery store
mantequilla *nf* : butter
mantilla *nf* : mantilla
mantis *nf* **mantis religiosa** : praying mantis
manto *nm* **1** : cloak **2** : mantle (in geology)
mantón *nm, pl* **-tones** CHAL : shawl
mantuvo, etc. → **mantener**
manual[1] *adj* **1** : manual ⟨trabajo manual : manual labor⟩ **2** : handy, manageable — **manualmente** *adv*
manual[2] *nm* : manual, handbook
manualidades *nfpl* : handicrafts (in schools)
manubrio *nm* **1** : handle, crank **2** : handlebars *pl*

manufactura *nf* **1** FABRICACIÓN : manufacture **2** : manufactured item, product **3** FÁBRICA : factory

manufacturar *vt* FABRICAR : to manufacture

manufacturero¹, -ra *adj* : manufacturing

manufacturero², -ra *n* FABRICANTE : manufacturer

manuscrito¹, -ta *adj* : handwritten

manuscrito² *nm* : manuscript

manutención *nf, pl* **-ciones** : maintenance, support

manzana *nf* **1** : apple **2** CUADRA : block (enclosed by streets or buildings) **3** *or* **manzana de Adán** : Adam's apple

manzanal *nm* **1** : apple orchard **2** MANZANO : apple tree

manzanar *nm* : apple orchard

manzanilla *nf* **1** : chamomile **2** : chamomile tea

manzano *nm* : apple tree

maña *nf* **1** : dexterity, skill **2** : cunning, guile **3 mañas** *or* **malas mañas** *nfpl* : bad habits, vices

mañana *nf* **1** : morning **2** : tomorrow

mañanero, -ra *adj* MATUTINO : morning ⟨rocío mañanero : morning dew⟩

mañanitas *nfpl Mex* : birthday serenade

mañoso, -sa *adj* **1** HÁBIL : skillful **2** ASTUTO : cunning, crafty **3** : fussy, finicky

mapa *nm* CARTA : map

mapache *nm* : raccoon

mapamundi *nm* : map of the world

maqueta *nf* : model, mock-up

maquillador, -dora *n* : makeup artist

maquillaje *nm* : makeup

maquillarse *vr* : to put on makeup, to make oneself up

máquina *nf* **1** : machine ⟨máquina de coser : sewing machine⟩ ⟨máquina de escribir : typewriter⟩ **2** LOCOMOTORA : engine, locomotive **3** : machine (in politics) **4 a toda máquina** : at full speed

maquinación *nf, pl* **-ciones** : machination, scheme, plot

maquinal *adj* : mechanical, automatic — **maquinalmente** *adv*

maquinar *vt* : to plot, to scheme

maquinaria *nf* **1** : machinery **2** : mechanism, works *pl*

maquinilla *nf* **1** : small machine or device **2** *CA, Car* : typewriter

maquinista *nmf* **1** : machinist **2** : railroad engineer

mar *nmf* **1** : sea ⟨un mar agitado : a rough sea⟩ ⟨hacerse a la mar : to set sail⟩ **2 alta mar** : high seas

maraca *nf* : maraca

maraña *nf* **1** : thicket **2** ENREDO : tangle, mess

marasmo *nm* : paralysis, stagnation

maratón *nm, pl* **-tones** : marathon

maravilla *nf* **1** : wonder, marvel ⟨a las mil maravillas : wonderfully, marvelously⟩ ⟨hacer maravillas : to work wonders⟩ **2** : marigold

maravillar *vt* ASOMBRAR : to astonish, to amaze — **maravillarse** *vr* : to be amazed, to marvel

maravilloso, -sa *adj* ESTUPENDO : wonderful, marvelous — **maravillosamente** *adv*

marbete *nm* **1** ETIQUETA : label, tag **2** *PRi* : registration sticker (of a car)

marca *nf* **1** : mark **2** : brand, make **3** : trademark ⟨marca registrada : registered trademark⟩ **4** : record (in sports) ⟨batir la marca : to beat the record⟩

marcado, -da *adj* : marked ⟨un marcado contraste : a marked contrast⟩

marcador *nm* **1** TANTEADOR : scoreboard **2** : marker, felt-tipped pen **3 marcador de libros** : bookmark

marcaje *nm* **1** : scoring (in sports) **2** : guarding (in sports)

marcapasos *nms & pl* : pacemaker

marcar {72} *vt* **1** : to mark **2** : to brand (livestock) **3** : to indicate, to show **4** RESALTAR : to emphasize **5** : to dial (a telephone) **6** : to guard (an opponent) **7** ANOTAR : to score (a goal, a point) — *vi* **1** ANOTAR : to score **2** : to dial

marcha *nf* **1** : march **2** : hike, walk ⟨ir de marcha : to go hiking⟩ **3** : pace, speed ⟨a toda marcha : at top speed⟩ **4** : gear (of an automobile) ⟨marcha atrás : reverse, reverse gear⟩ **5 en ~** : in motion, in gear, under way

marchar *vi* **1** IR : to go, to travel **2** ANDAR : to walk **3** FUNCIONAR : to work, to go **4** : to march — **marcharse** *vr* : to leave

marchitar *vt* : to make wither, to wilt — **marchitarse** *vr* **1** : to wither, to shrivel up, to wilt **2** : to languish, to fade away

marchito, -ta *adj* : withered, faded

marcial *adj* : martial, military

marco *nm* **1** : frame, framework **2** : goalposts *pl* **3** AMBIENTE : setting, atmosphere **4** : mark (unit of currency)

marea *nf* : tide

mareado, -da *adj* **1** : dizzy, lightheaded **2** : queasy, nauseous **3** : seasick

marear *vt* **1** : to make sick ⟨los gases me marearon : the fumes made me sick⟩ **2** : to bother, to annoy — **marearse** *vr* **1** : to get sick, to become nauseated **2** : to feel dizzy **3** : to get tipsy

marejada *nf* **1** : surge, swell (of the sea) **2** : undercurrent, ferment, unrest

maremoto *nm* : tidal wave

mareo *nm* **1** : dizzy spell **2** : nausea **3** : seasickness, motion sickness **4** : annoyance, vexation

marfil *nm* : ivory

margarina *nf* : margarine

margarita *nf* **1** : daisy **2** : margarita (cocktail)

margen¹ *nf, pl* **márgenes** : bank (of a river), side (of a street)

margen[2] *nm, pl* **márgenes** 1 : edge, border 2 : margin ⟨margen de ganancia : profit margin⟩

marginación *nf, pl* **-ciones** : marginalization, exclusion

marginado[1], **-da** *adj* 1 DESHEREDADO : outcast, alienated, dispossessed 2 clases marginadas : underclass

marginado[2], **-da** *n* : outcast, misfit

marginal *adj* : marginal, fringe

marginalidad *nf* : marginality

marginar *vt* : to ostracize, to exclude

mariachi *nm* : mariachi musician or band

maridaje *nm* : marriage, union

maridar *vt* UNIR : to marry, to unite

marido *nm* ESPOSO : husband

marihuana *or* **mariguana** *or* **marijuana** *nf* : marihuana

marimacho *nmf fam* 1 : mannish woman · 2 : tomboy

marimba *nf* : marimba

marina *nf* 1 : coast, coastal area 2 : navy, fleet ⟨marina mercante : merchant marine⟩

marinada *nf* : marinade

marinar *vt* : to marinate

marinero[1], **-ra** *adj* 1 : seaworthy 2 : sea, marine

marinero[2] *nm* : sailor

marino[1], **-na** *adj* : marine, sea

marino[2] *nm* : sailor, seaman

marioneta *nf* TÍTERE : puppet, marionette

mariposa *nf* 1 : butterfly 2 mariposa nocturna : moth

mariquita[1] *nf* : ladybug

mariquita[2] *nm fam* : sissy, wimp

mariscal *nm* 1 : marshal 2 mariscal de campo : field marshal (in the military), quarterback (in football)

marisco *nm* 1 : shellfish 2 mariscos *nmpl* : seafood

marisma *nf* : marsh, salt marsh

marital *adj* : marital, married ⟨la vida marital : married life⟩

marítimo, **-ma** *adj* : maritime, shipping ⟨la industria marítima : the shipping industry⟩

marmita *nf* : (cooking) pot

mármol *nm* : marble

marmóreo, **-rea** *adj* : marble, marmoreal

marmota *nf* 1 : marmot 2 marmota de América : woodchuck, groundhog

maroma *nf* 1 : rope 2 : acrobatic stunt 3 *Mex* : somersault

marque, *etc.* → marcar

marqués, **-quesa** *n, mpl* **marqueses** : marquis *m*, marquess *m*, marquise *f*, marchioness *f*

marquesina *nf* : marquee, canopy

marqueta *nf Mex* : block (of chocolate), lump (of sugar or salt)

marranada *nf* 1 : disgusting thing 2 : dirty trick

marrano, **-na** *adj* : filthy, disgusting

marrano[2], **-na** *n* CERDO : pig, hog 2 : dirty pig, slob

marrar *vt* : to miss (a target) — *vi* : to fail, to go wrong

marras *adv* 1 : long ago 2 de ∼ : said, aforementioned ⟨el individuo de marras : the individual in question⟩

marrasquino *nm* : maraschino

marrón *adj & nm, pl* **marrones** CASTAÑO : brown

marroquí *adj & nmf, pl* **-quíes** : Moroccan

marsopa *nf* : porpoise

marsupial *nm* : marsupial

marta *nf* 1 : marten 2 marta cebellina : sable (animal)

Marte *nm* : Mars

martes *nms & pl* : Tuesday

martillar *v* : to hammer

martillazo *nm* : blow with a hammer

martillo *nm* 1 : hammer 2 martillo neumático : jackhammer

martinete *nm* 1 : heron 2 : pile driver

mártir *nmf* : martyr

martirio *nm* 1 : martyrdom 2 : ordeal, torment

martirizar {21} *vt* 1 : to martyr 2 ATORMENTAR : to torment

marxismo *nm* : Marxism

marxista *adj & nmf* : Marxist

marzo *nm* : March

mas *conj* PERO : but

más[1] *adv* 1 : more ⟨¿hay algo más grande? : is there anything bigger?⟩ 2 : most ⟨Luis es el más alto : Luis is the tallest⟩ 3 : longer ⟨el sabor dura más : the flavor lasts longer⟩ 4 : rather ⟨más querría andar : I would rather walk⟩ 5 a ∼ : besides, in addition 6 más allá : further 7 qué ... más ... : what ..., what a ... ⟨qué día más bonito! : what a beautiful day!⟩

más[2] *adj* 1 : more ⟨dáme dos kilos más : give me two more kilos⟩ 2 : most ⟨la que ganó más dinero : the one who earned the most money⟩ 3 : else ⟨¿quién más quiere vino? : who else wants wine?⟩

más[3] *n* : plus sign

más[4] *prep* : plus ⟨tres más dos es igual a cinco : three plus two equals five⟩

más[5] *pron* 1 : more ⟨¿tienes más? : do you have more?⟩ 2 a lo más : at most 3 de ∼ : extra, excess 4 más o menos : more or less, approximately 5 por más que : no matter how much ⟨por más que corras no llegarás a tiempo : no matter how fast you run you won't arrive on time⟩

masa *nf* 1 : mass, volume ⟨masa atómica : atomic mass⟩ ⟨producción en masa : mass production⟩ 2 : dough, batter 3 masas *nfpl* : people, masses ⟨las masas populares : the common people⟩ 4 masa harina *Mex* : corn flour (for tortillas, etc.)

masacrar *vt* : to massacre

masacre *nf* : massacre

masaje *nm* : massage

masajear *vt* : to massage

masajista *nmf* : masseur *m*, masseuse *f*
mascar {72} *v* MASCAR : to chew
máscara *nf* **1** CARETA : mask **2** : appearance, pretense **3 máscara antigás** : gas mask
mascarada *nf* : masquerade
mascarilla *nf* **1** : mask (in medicine) ⟨mascarilla de oxígeno : oxygen mask⟩ **2** : facial mask (in cosmetology)
mascota *nf* : mascot
masculinidad *nf* : masculinity
masculino, -na *adj* **1** : masculine, male **2** : manly **3** : masculine (in grammar)
mascullar *v* : to mumble, to mutter
masificado, -da *adj* : overcrowded
masilla *nf* : putty
masivamente *adv* : en masse
masivo, -va *adj* : mass ⟨comunicación masiva : mass communication⟩
masón *nm*, *pl* **masones** FRANCMASÓN : Mason, Freemason
masonería *nf* FRANCMASONERÍA : Masonry, Freemasonry
masónico, -ca *adj* : Masonic
masoquismo *nm* : masochism
masoquista[1] *adj* : masochistic
masoquista[2] *nmf* : masochist
masque, etc. → **mascar**
masticar {72} *v* MASCAR : to chew, to masticate
mástil *nm* **1** : mast **2** ASTA : flagpole **3** : neck (of a stringed instrument)
mastín *nm*, *pl* **mastines** : mastiff
mástique *nm* : putty, filler
mastodonte *nm* : mastodon
masturbación *nf*, *pl* **-ciones** : masturbation
masturbarse *vr* : to masturbate
mata *nf* **1** ARBUSTO : bush, shrub **2** : plant ⟨mata de tomate : tomato plant⟩ **3** : sprig, tuft **4 mata de pelo** : mop of hair
matadero *nm* : slaughterhouse, abattoir
matado, -da *adj Mex* : strenuous, exhausting
matador *nm* TORERO : matador, bullfighter
matamoscas *nms & pl* : flyswatter
matanza *nf* MASACRE : slaughter, butchering
matar *vt* **1** : to kill **2** : to slaughter, to butcher **3** APAGAR : to extinguish, to put out (fire, light) **4** : to tone down (colors) **5** : to pass, to waste (time) **6** : to trump (in card games) — *vi* : to kill — **matarse** *vr* **1** : to be killed **2** SUICIDARSE : to commit suicide **3** *fam* : to exhaust oneself ⟨se mató tratando de terminarlo : he knocked himself out trying to finish it⟩
matasanos *nms & pl fam* : quack
matasellar *vt* : to cancel (a stamp), to postmark
matasellos *nms & pl* : postmark
matatena *nf Mex* : jacks
mate[1] *adj* : matte, dull
mate[2] *nm* **1** : maté **2 jaque mate** : checkmate ⟨darle mate a *or* darle jaque mate a : to checkmate⟩

matemática → **matemáticas**
matemáticas *nfpl* : mathematics, math
matemático[1]**, -ca** *adj* : mathematical — **matemáticamente** *adv*
matemático[2]**, -ca** *n* : mathematician
materia *nf* **1** : matter ⟨materia gris : gray matter⟩ **2** : material ⟨materia prima : raw material⟩ **3** : (academic) subject **4 en materia de** : on the subject of, concerning
material[1] *adj* **1** : material, physical, real **2 daños materiales** : property damage
material[2] *nm* **1** : material ⟨material de construcción : building material⟩ **2** EQUIPO : equipment, gear
materialismo *nm* : materialism
materialista[1] *adj* : materialistic
materialista[2] *nmf* **1** : materialist **2** *Mex* : truck driver
materializar {21} *vt* : to bring to fruition, to realize — **materializarse** *vr* : to materialize, to come into being
materialmente *adv* **1** : materially, physically ⟨materialmente imposible : physically impossible⟩ **2** : really, absolutely
maternal *adj* : maternal, motherly
maternidad *nf* **1** : maternity, motherhood **2** : maternity hospital, maternity ward
materno, -na *adj* : maternal
matinal *adj* MATUTINO : morning ⟨la pálida luz matinal : the pale morning light⟩
matinée *or* **matiné** *nf* : matinee
matiz *nm*, *pl* **matices** **1** : hue, shade **2** : nuance
matización *nf*, *pl* **-ciones** **1** : tinting, toning, shading **2** : clarification (of a statement)
matizar {21} *vt* **1** : to tinge, to tint (colors) **2** : to vary, to modulate (sounds) **3** : to qualify (statements)
matón *nm*, *pl* **matones** : thug, bully
matorral *nm* **1** : thicket **2** : scrub, scrubland
matraca *nf* **1** : rattle, noisemaker **2 dar la matraca a** : to pester, to nag
matriarca *nf* : matriarch
matriarcado *nm* : matriarchy
matrícula *nf* **1** : list, roll, register **2** INSCRIPCIÓN : registration, enrollment **3** : license plate, registration number
matriculación *nf*, *pl* **-ciones** : matriculation, registration
matricular *vt* **1** INSCRIBIR : to enroll, to register (a person) **2** : to register (a vehicle) — **matricularse** *vr* : to matriculate
matrimonial *adj* : marital, matrimonial ⟨la vida matrimonial : married life⟩
matrimonio *nm* **1** : marriage, matrimony **2** : married couple
matriz *nf*, *pl* **matrices** **1** : uterus, womb **2** : original, master copy **3** : main office, headquarters **4** : stub (of a check) **5** : matrix ⟨matriz de puntos : dot matrix⟩

matrona *nf* : matron
matronal *adj* : matronly
matutino¹, -na *adj* : morning ⟨la edición matutina : the morning edition⟩
matutino² *nm* : morning paper
maullar {8} *vi* : to meow
maullido *nm* : meow
mauritano, -na *adj & n* : Mauritanian
mausoleo *nm* : mausoleum
maxilar *nm* : jaw, jawbone
máxima *nf* : maxim
máxime *adv* ESPECIALMENTE : especially, principally
maximizar {21} *vt* : to maximize
máximo¹, -ma *adj* : maximum, greatest, highest
máximo² *nm* **1** : maximum **2 al máximo** : to the utmost **3 como ~ : at the** most, at the latest
maya¹ *adj & nmf* : Mayan
maya² *nmf* : Maya, Mayan
mayo *nm* : May
mayonesa *nf* : mayonnaise
mayor¹ *adj* **1** (*comparative of* **grande**) : bigger, larger, greater, elder, older **2** (*superlative of* **grande**) : biggest, largest, greatest, eldest, oldest **3** : grown-up, mature **4** : main, major **5 mayor de edad** : of (legal) age **6 al por mayor** *or* **por ~** : wholesale
mayor² *nmf* **1** : major (in the military) **2** : adult
mayoral *nm* CAPATAZ : foreman, overseer
mayordomo *nm* : butler, majordomo
mayoreo *nm* : wholesale
mayores *nmpl* : grown-ups, elders
mayoría *nf* **1** : majority **2 en su mayoría** : on the whole
mayorista¹ *adj* ALMACENISTA : wholesale
mayorista² *nmf* : wholesaler
mayoritariamente *adv* : primarily, chiefly
mayoritario, -ria *adj & n* : majority ⟨un consenso mayoritario : a majority consensus⟩
mayormente *adv* : primarily, chiefly
mayúscula *nf* : capital letter
mayúsculo, -la *adj* **1** : capital, uppercase **2** : huge, terrible ⟨un problema mayúsculo : a huge problem⟩
maza *nf* **1** : mace (weapon) **2** : drumstick **3** *fam* : bore, pest
mazacote *nm* **1** : concrete **2** : lumpy mess (of food) **3** : eyesore, crude work of art
mazapán *nm, pl* **-panes** : marzipan
mazmorra *nf* CALABOZO : dungeon
mazo *nm* **1** : mallet **2** : pestle **3** MANOJO : handful, bunch
mazorca *nf* **1** CHOCLO : cob, ear of corn **2 pelar la mazorca** *Mex fam* : to smile from ear to ear
me *pron* **1** : me ⟨me vieron : they saw me⟩ **2** : to me, for me, from me ⟨dame el libro : give me the book⟩ ⟨me lo compró : he bought it for me⟩ ⟨me robaron la cartera : they stole my pocketbook⟩

3 : myself, to myself, for myself, from myself ⟨me preparé una buena comida : I cooked myself a good dinner⟩ ⟨me equivoqué : I made a mistake⟩
mecánica *nf* : mechanics
mecánico¹, -ca *adj* : mechanical — **mecánicamente** *adv*
mecánico², -ca *n* **1** : mechanic **2** : technician ⟨mecánico dental : dental technician⟩
mecanismo *nm* : mechanism
mecanización *nf, pl* **-ciones** : mechanization
mecanizar {21} *vt* : to mechanize
mecanografía *nf* : typing
mecanografiar {85} *vt* : to type
mecanógrafo, -fa *n* : typist
mecate *nm* CA, Mex, Ven : rope, twine, cord
mecedor *nm* : glider (seat)
mecedora *nf* : rocking chair
mecenas *nmfs & pl* : patron (of the arts), sponsor
mecenazgo *nm* PATROCINIO : sponsorship, patronage
mecer {86} *vt* **1** : to rock **2** COLUMPIAR : to push (on a swing) — **mecerse** *vr* : to rock, to swing, to sway
mecha *nf* **1** : fuse **2** : wick **3 mechas** *nfpl* : highlights (in hair)
mechero *nm* **1** : burner **2** *Spain* : lighter
mechón *nm, pl* **mechones** : lock (of hair)
medalla *nf* : medal, medallion
medallista *nmf* : medalist
medallón *nm, pl* **-llones** **1** : medallion **2** : locket
media *nf* **1** CALCETÍN : sock **2** : average, mean **3 medias** *nfpl* : stockings, hose, tights **4 a medias** : by halves, half and half, halfway ⟨ir a medias : to go halves⟩ ⟨verdad a medias : half-truth⟩
mediación *nf, pl* **-ciones** : mediation
mediado, -da *adj* **1** : half full, half empty, half over **2** : halfway through ⟨mediada la tarea : halfway through the job⟩
mediador, -dora *n* : mediator
mediados *nmpl* **a mediados de** : halfway through, in the middle of ⟨a mediados del mes : towards the middle of the month, mid-month⟩
medialuna *nf* **1** : crescent **2** : croissant, crescent roll
medianamente *adv* : fairly, moderately
medianero, -ra *adj* **1** : dividing **2** : mediating
medianía *nf* **1** : middle position **2** : mediocre person, mediocrity
mediano, -na *adj* **1** : medium, average ⟨la mediana edad : middle age⟩ **2** : mediocre
medianoche *nf* : midnight
mediante *prep* : through, by means of ⟨Dios mediante : God willing⟩
mediar *vi* **1** : to mediate **2** : to be in the middle, to be halfway through **3** : to elapse, to pass ⟨mediaron cinco años entre el inicio de la guerra y el armisti-

cio : five years passed between the start of the war and the armistice〉 **4** : to be a consideration 〈media el hecho de que cuesta mucho : one must take into account that it is costly〉 **5** : to come up, to happen 〈medió algo urgente : something pressing came up〉

mediatizar {21} *vt* : to influence, to interfere with

medicación *nf, pl* **-ciones** : medication, treatment

medicamento *nm* : medication, medicine, drug

medicar {72} *vt* : to medicate — **medicarse** *vr* : to take medicine

medicina *nf* : medicine

medicinal *adj* **1** : medicinal **2** : medicated

medicinar *vt* : to give medication to, to dose

medición *nf, pl* **-ciones** : measuring, measurement

médico[1], **-ca** *adj* : medical 〈una receta médica : a doctor's prescription〉

médico[2], **-ca** *n* DOCTOR : doctor, physician

medida *nf* **1** : measurement, measure 〈hecho a medida : custom-made〉 **2** : measure, step 〈tomar medidas : to take steps〉 **3** : moderation, prudence 〈sin medida : immoderately〉 **4** : extent, degree 〈en gran medida : to a great extent〉

medidor *nm* : meter, gauge

medieval *adj* : medieval — **medievalista** *nmf*

medievo → **medioevo**

medio[1] *adv* **1** : half 〈está medio dormida : she's half asleep〉 **2** : rather, kind of 〈está medio aburrida esta fiesta : this party is rather boring〉

medio[2], **-dia** *adj* **1** : half 〈una media hora : half an hour〉 〈medio hermano : half brother〉 〈a media luz : in the half-light〉 〈son las tres y media : it's half past three, it's three-thirty〉 **2** : midway, halfway 〈a medio camino : halfway there〉 **3** : middle 〈la clase media : the middle class〉 **4** : average 〈la temperatura media : the average temperature〉

medio[3] *nm* **1** CENTRO : middle, center 〈en medio de : in the middle of, amid〉 **2** AMBIENTE : milieu, environment **3** : medium, spiritualist **4** : means *pl*, way 〈por medio de : by means of〉 〈los medios de comunicación : the media〉 **5 medios** *nmpl* : means, resources

mediocampista *nmf* : midfielder

mediocre *adj* : mediocre, average

mediocridad *nf* : mediocrity

mediodía *nm* : noon, midday

medioevo *nm* : Middle Ages

medir {54} *vt* **1** : to measure **2** : to weigh, to consider 〈medir los riesgos : to weigh the risks〉 — *vi* : to measure — **medirse** *vr* : to be moderate, to exercise restraint

meditabundo, -da *adj* PENSATIVO : pensive, thoughtful

meditación *nf, pl* **-ciones** : meditation, thought

meditar *vi* : to meditate, to think 〈meditar sobre la vida : to contemplate life〉 — *vt* **1** : to think over, to consider **2** : to plan, to work out

meditativo, -va *adj* : pensive

mediterráneo, -nea *adj* : Mediterranean

medrar *vi* **1** PROSPERAR : to prosper, to thrive **2** AUMENTAR : to increase, to grow

medro *nm* PROSPERIDAD : prosperity, growth

medroso, -sa *adj* : fainthearted, fearful

médula *nf* **1** : marrow, pith **2 médula espinal** : spinal cord

medular *adj* : fundamental, core 〈el punto medular : the crux of the matter〉

medusa *nf* : jellyfish, medusa

megabyte *nm* : megabyte

megáfono *nm* : megaphone

megahercio *nm* : megahertz

megahertzio *nm* : megahertz

megatón *nm, pl* **-tones** : megaton

megavatio *nm* : megawatt

mejicano → **mexicano**

mejilla *nf* : cheek

mejillón *nm, pl* **-llones** : mussel

mejor[1] *adv* **1** : better 〈Carla cocina mejor que Ana : Carla cooks better than Ann〉 **2** : best 〈ella es la que lo hace mejor : she's the one who does it best〉 **3** : rather 〈mejor morir que rendirme : I'd rather die than give up〉 **4** : it's better that . . . 〈mejor te vas : you'd better go〉 **5 a lo mejor** : maybe, perhaps

mejor[2] *adj* **1** (*comparative of* **bueno**) : better 〈a falta de algo mejor : for lack of something better〉 **2** (*comparative of* **bien**) : better 〈está mucho mejor : he's much better〉 **3** (*superlative of* **bueno**) : best, the better 〈mi mejor amigo : my best friend〉 **4** (*superlative of* **bien**) : best, the better 〈duermo mejor en un clima seco : I sleep best in a dry climate〉 **5** PREFERIBLE : preferable, better **6 lo mejor** : the best thing, the best part

mejor[3] *nmf* (*with definite article*) : the better (one), the best (one)

mejora *nf* : improvement

mejoramiento *nm* : improvement

mejorana *nf* : marjoram

mejorar *vt* : to improve, to make better — *vi* : to improve, to get better — **mejorarse** *vr*

mejoría *nf* : improvement, betterment

mejunje *nm* : concoction, brew

melancolía *nf* : melancholy, sadness

melancólico, -ca *adj* : melancholy, sad

melanoma *nm* : melanoma

melaza *nf* : molasses

melena *nf* **1** : mane **2** : long hair **3 melenas** *nfpl* GREÑAS : shaggy hair, mop

melenudo[1], **-da** *adj fam* : longhaired
melenudo[2], **-da** *n* GREÑUDO : longhair, hippie
melindres *nmpl* **1** : affectation, airs *pl* **2** : finickiness
melindroso[1], **-sa** *adj* **1** : affected **2** : fussy, finicky
melindroso[2], **-sa** *n* : finicky person, fussbudget
melisa *nf* : lemon balm
mella *nf* **1** : dent, nick **2 hacer mella en** : to have an effect on, to make an impression on
mellado, -da *adj* **1** : chipped, dented **2** : gap-toothed
mellar *vt* : to dent, to nick
mellizo, -za *adj & n* GEMELO : twin
melocotón *nm, pl* **-tones** : peach
melodía *nf* : melody, tune
melódico, -ca *adj* : melodic
melodioso, -sa *adj* : melodious
melodrama *nm* : melodrama
melodramático, -ca *adj* : melodramatic
melón *nm, pl* **melones** : melon, cantaloupe
meloso, -sa *adj* **1** : honeyed, sweet **2** EMPALAGOSO : cloying, saccharine
membrana *nf* **1** : membrane **2 membrana interdigital** : web, webbing (of a bird's foot) — **membranoso, -sa** *adj*
membresía *nf* : membership, members *pl*
membrete *nm* : letterhead, heading
membrillo *nm* : quince
membrudo, -da *adj* FORNIDO : muscular, well-built
memez *nf, pl* **memeces** : stupid thing
memo, -ma *adj* : silly, stupid
memorabilia *nf* : memorabilia
memorable *adj* : memorable
memorándum *or* **memorando** *nm, pl* **-dums** *or* **-dos** **1** : memorandum, memo **2** : memo book, appointment book
memoria *nf* **1** : memory ⟨de memoria : by heart⟩ ⟨hacer memoria : to try to remember⟩ ⟨traer a la memoria : to call to mind⟩ **2** RECUERDO : remembrance, memory ⟨su memoria perdurará para siempre : his memory will live forever⟩ **3** : report ⟨memoria annual : annual report⟩ **4 memorias** *nfpl* : memoirs
memorizar {21} *vt* : to memorize — **memorización** *nf*
mena *nf* : ore
menaje *nm* : household goods *pl*, furnishings *pl*
mención *nf, pl* **-ciones** : mention
mencionar *vt* : to mention, to refer to
mendaz *adj, pl* **mendaces** : mendacious, lying
mendicidad *nf* : begging
mendigar {52} *vi* : to beg — *vt* : to beg for
mendigo, -ga *n* LIMOSNERO : beggar
mendrugo *nm* : crust (of bread)

menear *vt* **1** : to shake (one's head) **2** : to sway, to wiggle (one's hips) **3** : to wag (a tail) **4** : to stir (a liquid) — **menearse** *vr* **1** : to wiggle one's hips **2** : to fidget
meneo *nm* **1** : movement **2** : shake, toss **3** : swaying, wagging, wiggling **4** : stir, stirring
menester *nm* **1** : activity, occupation, duties *pl* **2 ser menester** : to be necessary ⟨es menester que vengas : you must come⟩
mengano, -na → **fulano**
mengua *nf* **1** : decrease, decline **2** : lack, want **3** : discredit, dishonor
menguar *vt* : to diminish, to lessen — *vi* **1** : to decline, to decrease **2** : to wane — **menguante** *adj*
meningitis *nf* : meningitis
menisco *nm* : meniscus, cartilage
menjurje → **mejunje**
menopausia *nf* : menopause
menor[1] *adj* **1** (*comparative of* **pequeño**) : smaller, lesser, younger **2** (*superlative of* **pequeño**) : smallest, least, youngest **3** : minor **4 al por menor** : retail **5 ser menor de edad** : to be a minor, to be underage
menor[2] *nmf* : minor, juvenile
menos[1] *adv* **1** : less ⟨llueve menos en agosto : it rains less in August⟩ **2** : least ⟨el coche menos caro : the least expensive car⟩ **3 ~ de** : less than, fewer than
menos[2] *adj* **1** : less, fewer ⟨tengo más trabajo y menos tiempo : I have more work and less time⟩ **2** : least, fewest ⟨la clase que tiene menos estudiantes : the class that has the fewest students⟩
menos[3] *prep* **1** SALVO, EXCEPTO : except **2** : minus ⟨quince menos cuatro son once : fifteen minus four is eleven⟩
menos[4] *pron* **1** : less, fewer ⟨no deberías aceptar menos : you shouldn't accept less⟩ **2 al menos** *or* **por lo menos** : at least **3 a menos que** : unless
menoscabar *vt* **1** : to lessen, to diminish **2** : to disgrace, to discredit **3** PERJUDICAR : to harm, to damage
menoscabo *nm* **1** : lessening, diminishing **2** : disgrace, discredit **3** : harm, damage
menospreciar *vt* **1** DESPRECIAR : to scorn, to look down on **2** : to underestimate, to undervalue
menosprecio *nm* DESPRECIO : contempt, scorn
mensaje *nm* : message
mensajero, -ra *n* : messenger
menso, -sa *adj Mex fam* : foolish, stupid
menstrual *adj* : menstrual
menstruar {3} *vi* : to menstruate — **menstruación** *nf*
mensual *adj* : monthly
mensualidad *nf* **1** : monthly payment, installment **2** : monthly salary
mensualmente *adv* : every month, monthly

mensurable *adj* : measurable
menta *nf* **1** : mint, peppermint **2 menta verde** : spearmint
mentado, -da *adj* **1** : aforementioned **2** FAMOSO : renowned, famous
mental *adj* : mental, intellectual — **mentalmente** *adv*
mentalidad *nf* : mentality
mentar {55} *vt* **1** : to mention, to name **2 mentar la madre a** *fam* : to insult, to swear at
mente *nf* : mind ⟨tener en mente : to have in mind⟩
mentecato¹, -ta *adj* : foolish, simple
mentecato², -ta *n* : fool, idiot
mentir {76} *vi* : to lie
mentira *nf* : lie
mentiroso¹, -sa *adj* EMBUSTERO : lying, untruthful
mentiroso², -sa *n* EMBUSTERO : liar
mentís *nm, pl* **mentises** : denial, repudiation ⟨dar el mentís a : to deny, to refute⟩
mentol *nm* : menthol
mentón *nm, pl* **mentones** BARBILLA : chin
mentor *nm* : mentor, counselor
menú *nm, pl* **menús** : menu
menudear *vi* : to occur frequently — *vt* : to do repeatedly
menudencia *nf* **1** : trifle **2 menudencias** *nfpl* : giblets
menudeo *nm* : retail, retailing
menudillos *nmpl* : giblets
menudo¹, -da *adj* **1** : minute, small **2 a ~** FRECUENTEMENTE : often, frequently
menudo² *nm* **1** *Mex* : tripe stew **2 menudos** *nmpl* : giblets
meñique *nf or* **dedo meñique** : little finger, pinkie
meollo *nm* **1** MÉDULA : marrow **2** SESO : brains *pl* **3** ENTRAÑA : essence, core ⟨el meollo del asunto : the heart of the matter⟩
mequetrefe *nm fam* : good-for-nothing
mercachifle *nm* : peddler, hawker
mercadeo *nm* : marketing
mercadería *nf* : merchandise, goods *pl*
mercado *nm* : market ⟨mercado de trabajo *or* mercado laboral : labor market⟩ ⟨mercado de valores *or* mercado bursátil : stock market⟩
mercadotecnia *nf* : marketing
mercancía *nf* : merchandise, goods *pl*
mercante *nmf* : merchant, dealer
mercantil *adj* COMERCIAL : commercial, mercantile
merced *nf* **1** : favor **2 ~ a** : thanks to, due to **3 a merced de** : at the mercy of
mercenario, -ria *adj & n* : mercenary
mercería *nf* : notions store
Mercosur *nm* : economic community consisting of Argentina, Brazil, Paraguay, and Uruguay
mercurio *nm* : mercury
Mercurio *nm* : Mercury (planet)

merecedor, -dora *adj* : deserving, worthy
merecer {53} *vt* : to deserve, to merit — *vi* : to be worthy
merecidamente *adv* : rightfully, deservedly
merecido *nm* : something merited, due ⟨recibieron su merecido : they got their just deserts⟩
merecimiento *nm* : merit, worth
merendar {55} *vi* : to have an afternoon snack — *vt* : to have as an afternoon snack
merendero *nm* **1** : lunchroom, snack bar **2** : picnic area
merengue *nm* **1** : meringue **2** : merengue (dance)
meridiano¹, -na *adj* **1** : midday **2** : crystal clear
meridiano² *nm* : meridian
meridional *adj* SUREÑO : southern
merienda *nf* : afternoon snack, tea
mérito *nm* : merit
meritorio¹, -ria *adj* : deserving, meritorious
meritorio², -ria *n* : intern, trainee
merluza *nf* : hake
merma *nf* **1** : decrease, cut **2** : waste, loss
mermar *vi* : to decrease, to diminish — *vt* : to reduce, to cut down
mermelada *nf* : marmalade, jam
mero¹, -ra *adv Mex fam* **1** : nearly, almost ⟨ya mero me caí : I almost fell⟩ **2** : just, exactly ⟨aquí mero : right here⟩
mero², -ra *adj* **1** : mere, simple **2** *Mex fam* (used as an intensifier) : very ⟨en el mero centro : in the very center of town⟩
mero³ *nm* : grouper
merodeador, -dora *n* **1** : marauder **2** : prowler
merodear *vi* **1** : to maraud, to pillage **2** : to prowl around, to skulk
mes *nm* : month
mesa *nf* **1** : table **2** : committee, board
mesada *nf* : allowance, pocket money
mesarse *vr* : to pull at ⟨mesarse los cabellos : to tear one's hair⟩
mesero, -ra *n* CAMARERO : waiter, waitress *f*
meseta *nf* : plateau, tableland
Mesías *nm* : Messiah
mesón *nm, pl* **mesones** : inn
mesonero, -ra *nm* : innkeeper
mestizo¹, -za *adj* **1** : of mixed ancestry **2** HÍBRIDO : hybrid
mestizo², -za *n* : person of mixed ancestry
mesura *nf* **1** MODERACIÓN : moderation, discretion **2** CORTESÍA : courtesy **3** GRAVEDAD : seriousness, dignity
mesurado, -da *adj* COMEDIDO : moderate, restrained
mesurar *vt* : to moderate, to restrain, to temper — **mesurarse** *vr* : to restrain oneself
meta *nf* : goal, objective

metabólico, -ca *adj* : metabolic
metabolismo *nm* : metabolism
metabolizar {21} *vt* : to metabolize
metafísica *nf* : metaphysics
metafísico, -ca *adj* : metaphysical
metáfora *nf* : metaphor
metafórico, -ca *adj* : metaphoric, metaphorical
metal *nm* **1** : metal **2** : brass section (in an orchestra)
metálico, -ca *adj* : metallic, metal
metalistería *nf* : metalworking
metalurgia *nf* : metallurgy
metalúrgico¹, -ca *adj* : metallurgical
metalúrgico², -ca *n* : metallurgist
metamorfosis *nfs & pl* : metamorphosis
metano *nm* : methane
metedura *nf* **metedura de pata** : blunder, faux pas
meteórico, -ca *adj* : meteoric
meteorito *nm* : meteorite
meteoro *nm* : meteor
meteorología *nf* : meteorology
meteorológico, -ca *adj* : meteorologic, meteorological
meteorólogo, -ga *n* : meteorologist
meter *vt* **1** : to put (in) ⟨metieron su dinero en el banco : they put their money in the bank⟩ **2** : to fit, to squeeze ⟨puedes meter dos líneas más en esa página : you can fit two more lines on that page⟩ **3** : to place (in a job) ⟨lo metieron de barrendero : they got him a job as a street sweeper⟩ **4** : to involve ⟨lo metió en un buen lío : she got him in an awful mess⟩ **5** : to make, to cause ⟨meten demasiado ruido : they make too much noise⟩ **6** : to spread (a rumor) **7** : to strike (a blow) **8** : to take up, to take in (clothing) **9 a todo meter** : at top speed — **meterse** *vr* **1** : to get into, to enter **2** *fam* : to meddle ⟨no te metas en lo que no te importa : mind your own business⟩ **3 ~ con** *fam* : to pick a fight with, to provoke ⟨no te metas conmigo : don't mess with me⟩
metiche¹ *adj Mex fam* : nosy
metiche² *nmf Mex fam* : busybody
meticulosidad *nf* : thoroughness, meticulousness
meticuloso, -sa *adj* : meticulous, thorough — **meticulosamente** *adv*
metida *nf* **metida de pata** *fam* : blunder, gaffe, blooper
metódico, -ca *adj* : methodical — **metódicamente** *adv*
metodista *adj & nmf* : Methodist
método *nm* : method
metodología *nf* : methodology
metomentodo *nmf fam* : busybody
metraje *nm* : length (of a film) ⟨de largo metraje : feature-length⟩
metralla *nf* : shrapnel
metralleta *nf* : submachine gun
métrico, -ca *adj* **1** : metric **2 cinta métrica** : tape measure
metro *nm* **1** : meter **2** : subway
metrónomo *nm* : metronome

metrópoli *nf or* **metrópolis** *nfs & pl* : metropolis
metropolitano, -na *adj* : metropolitan
mexicanismo *nm* : Mexican word or expression
mexicano, -na *adj & n* : Mexican
mexicoamericano, -na *adj & n* : Mexican-American
meza, etc. → **mecer**
mezcla *nf* **1** : mixing **2** : mixture, blend **3** : mortar (masonry material)
mezclar *vt* **1** : to mix, to blend **2** : to mix up, to muddle **3** INVOLUCRAR : to involve — **mezclarse** *vr* **1** : to get mixed up (in) **2** : to mix, to mingle (socially)
mezclilla *nf* *Chile, Mex* : denim ⟨pantalones de mezclilla : jeans⟩
mezcolanza *nf* : jumble, hodgepodge
mezquindad *nf* **1** : meanness, stinginess **2** : petty deed, mean action
mezquino¹, -na *adj* **1** : mean, petty **2** : stingy **3** : paltry
mezquino² *nm Mex* : wart
mezquita *nf* : mosque
mezquite *nm* : mesquite
mi *adj* : my
mi *pron* **1** : me ⟨es para mí : it's for me⟩ ⟨a mí no me importa : it doesn't matter to me⟩ **2 mí mismo, mí misma** : myself
miasma *nm* : miasma
miau *nm* : meow
mica *nf* : mica
mico *nm* : monkey, long-tailed monkey
micra *nf* : micron
microbio *nm* : microbe, germ
microbiología *nf* : microbiology
microbiológico, -ca *adj* : microbiological
microbús *nm, pl* **-buses** : minibus
microcomputadora *nf* : microcomputer
microcosmos *nms & pl* : microcosm
microficha *nf* : microfiche
microfilm *nm, pl* **-films** : microfilm
micrófono *nm* : microphone
micrómetro *nm* : micrometer
microonda *nf* : microwave
microondas *nms & pl* : microwave, microwave oven
microordenador *nm Spain* : microcomputer
microorganismo *nm* : microorganism
microprocesador *nm* : microprocessor
microscópico, -ca *adj* : microscopic
microscopio *nm* : microscope
mide, etc. → **medir**
miedo *nm* **1** TEMOR : fear ⟨le tiene miedo al perro : he's scared of the dog⟩ ⟨tenían miedo de hablar : they were afraid to speak⟩ **2 dar miedo** : to frighten
miedoso, -sa *adj* TEMEROSO : fearful
miel *nf* : honey
miembro *nm* **1** : member **2** EXTREMIDAD : limb, extremity
mienta, etc. → **mentar**
miente, etc. → **mentir**

mientras[1] *adv* **1** *or* **mientras tanto** : meanwhile, in the meantime **2 mientras más** : the more ⟨mientras más como, más quiero : the more I eat, the more I want⟩

mientras[2] *conj* **1** : while, as ⟨roncaba mientras dormía : he snored while he was sleeping⟩ **2** : as long as ⟨luchará mientras pueda : he will fight as long as he is able⟩ **3 mientras que** : while, whereas ⟨él es alto mientras que ella es muy baja : he is tall, whereas she is very short⟩

miércoles *nms & pl* : Wednesday

miga *nf* **1** : crumb **2 hacer buenas (malas) migas con** : to get along well (poorly) with

migaja *nf* **1** : crumb **2 migajas** *nfpl* SOBRAS : leftovers, scraps

migración *nf, pl* **-ciones** : migration

migrante *nmf* : migrant

migraña *nf* : migraine

migratorio, -ria *adj* : migratory

mijo *nm* : millet

mil[1] *adj* : thousand

mil[2] *nm* : one thousand, a thousand

milagro *nm* : miracle ⟨de milagro : miraculously⟩

milagroso, -sa *adj* : miraculous, marvelous — **milagrosamente** *adv*

milenio *nm* : millennium

milésimo, -ma *adj* : thousandth — **milésimo** *nm*

milicia *nf* **1** : militia **2** : military service

miligramo *nm* : milligram

mililitro *nm* : milliliter

milímetro *nm* : millimeter

militancia *nf* : militancy

militante[1] *adj* : militant

militante[2] *nmf* : militant, activist

militar[1] *vi* **1** : to serve (in the military) **2** : to be active (in politics)

militar[2] *adj* : military

militar[3] *nmf* SOLDADO : soldier

militarismo *nm* : militarism

militarista *adj & nmf* : militarist

militarizar {21} *vt* : to militarize

milla *nf* : mile

millar *nm* : thousand

millón *nm, pl* **millones** : million

millonario, -ria *n* : millionaire

millonésimo[1], **-ma** *adj* : millionth

millonésimo[2] *nm* : millionth

mil millones *nms & pl* : billion

milpa *nf CA, Mex* : cornfield

milpiés *nms & pl* : millipede

mimar *vt* CONSENTIR : to pamper, to spoil

mimbre *nm* : wicker

mimeógrafo *nm* : mimeograph

mímica *nf* **1** : mime, sign language **2** IMITACIÓN : mimicry

mimo *nm* **1** : pampering, indulgence ⟨hacerle mimos a alguien : to pamper someone⟩ **2** : mime

mimoso, -sa *adj* **1** : fussy, finicky **2** : affectionate, clinging

mina *nf* **1** : mine **2** : lead (for pencils)

minar *vt* **1** : to mine **2** DEBILITAR : to undermine

minarete *nm* ALMINAR : minaret

mineral *adj & nm* : mineral

minería *nf* : mining

minero[1], **-ra** *adj* : mining

minero[2], **-ra** *n* : miner, mine worker

miniatura *nf* : miniature

minicomputadora *nf* : minicomputer

minifalda *nf* : miniskirt

minifundio *nm* : small farm

minimizar {21} *vt* : to minimize

mínimo[1], **-ma** *adj* **1** : minimum ⟨salario mínimo : minimum wage⟩ **2** : least, smallest **3** : very small, minute

mínimo[2] *nm* **1** : minimum, least amount **2** : modicum, small amount **3 como ~** : at least

minino, -na *n fam* : pussy, pussycat

miniserie *nf* : miniseries

ministerial *adj* : ministerial

ministerio *nm* : ministry, department

ministro, -tra *n* : minister, secretary ⟨primer ministro : prime minister⟩ ⟨Ministro de Defensa : Secretary of Defense⟩

minivan [ˌminiˈban, -ˈvan] *nf, pl* **-vanes** : minivan

minoría *nf* : minority

minorista[1] *adj* : retail

minorista[2] *nmf* : retailer

minoritario, -ria *adj* : minority

mintió, etc. → **mentir**

minuciosamente *adv* **1** : minutely **2** : in great detail **3** : thoroughly, meticulously

minucioso, -sa *adj* **1** : minute **2** DETALLADO : detailed **3** : thorough, meticulous

minué *nm* : minuet

minúsculo, -la *adj* DIMINUTO : tiny, miniscule

minusvalía *nf* : disability, handicap

minusválido[1], **-da** *adj* : handicapped, disabled

minusválido[2], **-da** *n* : handicapped person

minuta *nf* **1** BORRADOR : rough draft **2** : bill, fee

minutero *nm* : minute hand

minuto *nm* : minute

mío[1], **mía** *adj* **1** : my, of mine ⟨¡Dios mío! : my God!, good heavens!⟩ ⟨una amiga mía : a friend of mine⟩ **2** : mine ⟨es mío : it's mine⟩

mío[2], **mía** *pron (with definite article)* : mine, my own ⟨tus zapatos son iguales a los míos : your shoes are just like mine⟩

miope *adj* : nearsighted, myopic

miopía *nf* : myopia, nearsightedness

mira *nf* **1** : sight (of a firearm or instrument) **2** : aim, objective ⟨con miras a : with the intention of, with a view to⟩ ⟨de amplias miras : broad-minded⟩ ⟨poner la mira en : to aim at, to aspire to⟩

mirada *nf* **1** : look, glance, gaze **2** EXPRESIÓN : look, expression ⟨una mirada de sorpresa : a look of surprise⟩

mirado, -da *adj* **1** : cautious, careful **2** : considerate **3 bien mirado** : well thought of **4 mal mirado** : disliked, disapproved of

mirador *nm* : balcony, lookout, vantage point

miramiento *nm* **1** CONSIDERACIÓN : consideration, respect **2 sin miramientos** : without due consideration, carelessly

mirar *vt* **1** : to look at **2** OBSERVAR : to watch **3** REFLEXIONAR : to consider, to think over — *vi* **1** : to look **2** : to face, to overlook **3 ∼ por** : to look after, to look out for — **mirarse** *vr* **1** : to look at oneself **2** : to look at each other

mirasol *nm* GIRASOL : sunflower

miríada *nf* : myriad

mirlo *nm* : blackbird

mirra *nf* : myrrh

mirto *nm* ARRAYÁN : myrtle

misa *nf* : Mass

misantropía *nf* : misanthropy

misantrópico, -ca *adj* : misanthropic

misántropo, -pa *n* : misanthrope

miscelánea *nf* : miscellany

misceláneo, -nea *adj* : miscellaneous

miserable *adj* **1** LASTIMOSO : miserable, wretched **2** : paltry, meager **3** MEZQUINO : stingy, miserly **4** : despicable, vile

miseria *nf* **1** POBREZA : poverty **2** : misery, suffering **3** : pittance, meager amount

misericordia *nf* COMPASIÓN : mercy, compassion

misericordioso, -sa *adj* : merciful

mísero, -ra *adj* **1** : wretched, miserable **2** : stingy **3** : paltry, meager

misil *nm* : missile

misión *nf, pl* **misiones** : mission

misionero, -ra *adj & n* : missionary

misiva *nf* : missive, letter

mismísimo, -ma *adj* (*used as an intensifier*) : very, selfsame ⟨el mismísimo día : that very same day⟩

mismo[1] *adv* (*used as an intensifier*) : right, exactly ⟨hazlo ahora mismo : do it right now⟩ ⟨te llamará hoy mismo : he'll definitely call you today⟩

mismo[2]**, -ma** *adj* **1** : same **2** (*used as an intensifier*) : very ⟨en ese mismo momento : at that very moment⟩ **3** : oneself ⟨lo hizo ella misma : she made it herself⟩ **4 por lo mismo** : for that reason

misoginia *nf* : misogyny

misógino *nm* : misogynist

misterio *nm* : mystery

misterioso, -sa *adj* : mysterious — **misteriosamente** *adv*

misticismo *nm* : mysticism

místico[1]**, -ca** *adj* : mystic, mystical

místico[2]**, -ca** *n* : mystic

mitad *nf* **1** : half ⟨mitad y mitad : half and half⟩ **2** MEDIO : middle ⟨a mitad de : halfway through⟩ ⟨por la mitad : in half⟩

mítico, -ca *adj* : mythical, mythic

mitigar {52} *vt* ALIVIAR : to mitigate, to alleviate — **mitigación** *nf*

mitin *nm, pl* **mítines** : (political) meeting, rally

mito *nm* LEYENDA : myth, legend

mitología *nf* : mythology

mitológico, -ca *adj* : mythological

mitosis *nfs & pl* : mitosis

mitra *nf* : miter (bishop's hat)

mixto, -ta *adj* **1** : mixed, joint **2** : coeducational

mixtura *nf* : mixture, blend

mnemónico, -ca *adj* : mnemonic

mobiliario *nm* : furniture

mocasín *nm, pl* **-sines** : moccasin

mocedad *nf* **1** JUVENTUD : youth **2** : youthful prank

mochila *nf* MORRAL : backpack, knapsack

moción *nf, pl* **-ciones** **1** MOVIMIENTO : motion, movement **2** : motion (to a court or assembly)

moco *nm* **1** : mucus **2** *fam* : snot ⟨limpiarse los mocos : to wipe one's (runny) nose⟩

mocoso, -sa *n* : kid, brat

moda *nf* **1** : fashion, style **2 a la moda** *or* **de ∼** : in style, fashionable **3 moda pasajera** : fad

modales *nmpl* : manners

modalidad *nf* **1** CLASE : kind, type **2** MANERA : way, manner

modelar *vt* : to model, to mold — **modelarse** *vr* : to model oneself after, to emulate

modelo[1] *adj* : model ⟨una casa modelo : a model home⟩

modelo[2] *nm* : model, example, pattern

modelo[3] *nmf* : model, mannequin

módem *or* **modem** ['mo̞ðɛm] *nm* : modem

moderación *nf, pl* **-ciones** MESURA : moderation

moderado, -da *adj & n* : moderate — **moderadamente** *adv*

moderador, -dora *n* : moderator, chair

moderar *vt* **1** TEMPERAR : to temper, to moderate **2** : to curb, to reduce ⟨moderar gastos : to curb spending⟩ **3** PRESIDIR : to chair (a meeting) — **moderarse** *vr* **1** : to restrain oneself **2** : to diminish, to calm down

modernidad *nf* **1** : modernity, modernness **2** : modern age

modernismo *nm* : modernism

modernista[1] *adj* : modernist, modernistic

modernista[2] *nmf* : modernist

modernizar {21} *vt* : to modernize — **modernización** *nf*

moderno, -na *adj* : modern, up-to-date

modestia *nf* : modesty

modesto, -ta *adj* : modest — **modestamente** *adv*
modificación *nf, pl* **-ciones** : alteration
modificador¹, -dora *adj* : modifying, moderating
modificador² → **modificante**
modificante *nm* : modifier
modificar {72} *vt* ALTERAR : to modify, to alter, to adapt
modismo *nm* : idiom
modista *nmf* **1** : dressmaker **2** : fashion designer
modo *nm* **1** MANERA : way, manner, mode ⟨de un modo u otro : one way or another⟩ ⟨a mi modo de ver : to my way of thinking⟩ **2** : mood (in grammar) **3** : mode (in music) **4 a modo de** : by way of, in the manner of, like ⟨a modo de ejemplo : by way of example⟩ **5 de cualquier modo** : in any case, anyway **6 de modo que** : so, in such a way that **7 de todos modos** : in any case, anyway **8 en cierto modo** : in a way, to a certain extent
modorra *nf* : drowsiness, lethargy
modular¹ *v* : to modulate — **modulación** *nf*
modular² *adj* : modular
módulo *nm* : module, unit
mofa *nf* **1** : mockery, ridicule **2 hacer mofa de** : to make fun of, to ridicule
mofarse *vr* ~ **de** : to scoff at, to make fun of
mofeta *nf* ZORRILLO : skunk
mofle *nm* CA, Mex : muffler (of a car)
moflete *nm fam* : fat cheek
mofletudo, -da *adj fam* : fat-cheeked, chubby
mohín *nm, pl* **mohines** : grimace, face
mohíno, -na *adj* : gloomy, melancholy
moho *nm* **1** : mold, mildew **2** : rust
mohoso, -sa *adj* **1** : moldy **2** : rusty
moisés *nm, pl* **moiseses** : bassinet, cradle
mojado¹, -da *adj* : wet
mojado², -da *n Mex fam* : illegal immigrant
mojar *vt* **1** : to wet, to moisten **2** : to dunk — **mojarse** *vr* : to get wet
mojigatería *nf* **1** : hypocrisy **2** GAZMOÑERÍA : primness, prudery
mojigato¹, -ta *adj* : prudish, prim — **mojigatamente** *adv*
mojigato², -ta *n* : prude, prig
mojón *nm, pl* **mojones** : boundary stone, marker
molar *nm* MUELA : molar
molcajete *nm Mex* : mortar
molde *nm* **1** : mold, form **2 letras de molde** : printing, block lettering
moldear *vt* **1** FORMAR : to mold, to shape **2** : to cast
moldura *nf* : molding
mole¹ *nm Mex* : spicy sauce made with chilies and usually chocolate **2** : meat served with mole sauce
mole² *nf* : mass, bulk
molécula *nf* : molecule — **molecular** *adj*

moler {47} *vt* **1** : to grind, to crush **2** CANSAR : to exhaust, to wear out
molestar *vt* **1** FASTIDIAR : to annoy, to bother **2** : to disturb, to disrupt — *vi* : to be a nuisance — **molestarse** *vr* ~ **en** : to take the trouble to
molestia *nf* **1** FASTIDIO : annoyance, bother, nuisance **2** : trouble ⟨se tomó la molestia de investigar : she took the trouble to investigate⟩ **3** MALESTAR : discomfort
molesto, -ta *adj* **1** ENOJADO : bothered, annoyed **2** FASTIDIOSO : bothersome, annoying
molestoso, -sa *adj* : bothersome, annoying
molido, -da *adj* **1** MACHACADO : ground, crushed **2 estar molido** : to be exhausted
molienda *nf* : milling, grinding
molinero, -ra *n* : miller
molinillo *nm* : grinder, mill ⟨molinillo de café : coffee grinder⟩
molino *nm* **1** : mill **2 molino de viento** : windmill
molla *nf* : soft fleshy part, flesh (of fruit), lean part (of meat)
molleja *nf* : gizzard
molusco *nm* : mollusk
momentáneamente *adv* : momentarily
momentáneo, -nea *adj* **1** : momentary **2** TEMPORARIO : temporary
momento *nm* **1** : moment, instant ⟨espera un momentito : wait just a moment⟩ **2** : time, period of time ⟨momentos difíciles : hard times⟩ **3** : present, moment ⟨los atletas del momento : the athletes of the moment, today's popular athletes⟩ **4** : momentum **5 al momento** : right away, at once **6 de** ~ : at the moment, for the moment **7 de un momento a otro** : any time now **8 por momentos** : at times
momia *nf* : mummy
monaguillo *nm* ACÓLITO : altar boy
monarca *nmf* : monarch
monarquía *nf* : monarchy
monárquico, -ca *n* : monarchist
monasterio *nm* : monastery
monástico, -ca *adj* : monastic
mondadientes *nms & pl* PALILLO : toothpick
mondar *vt* : to peel
mondongo *nm* ENTRAÑAS : innards *pl*, insides *pl*, guts *pl*
moneda *nf* **1** : coin **2** : money, currency
monedero *nm* : change purse
monetario, -ria *adj* : monetary, financial
mongol, -gola *adj & n* : Mongol, Mongolian
monitor¹, -tora *n* : instructor (in sports)
monitor² *nm* : monitor ⟨monitor de televisión : television monitor⟩
monitorear *vt* : to monitor
monja *nf* : nun
monje *nm* : monk
mono¹, -na *adj fam* : lovely, pretty, cute, darling

mono², **-na** *n* : monkey

monóculo *nm* : monocle

monogamia *nf* : monogamy

monógamo, **-ma** *adj* : monogamous

monografía *nf* : monograph

monograma *nm* : monogram

monolingüe *adj* : monolingual

monolítico, **-ca** *adj* : monolithic

monolito *nm* : monolith

monólogo *nm* : monologue

monomanía *nf* : obsession

monopatín *nm*, *pl* **-tines** 1 : scooter 2 : skateboard

monopolio *nm* : monopoly

monopolizar {21} *vt* : to monopolize — **monopolización** *nf*

monosilábico, **-ca** *adj* : monosyllabic

monosílabo *nm* : monosyllable

monoteísmo *nm* : monotheism

monoteísta¹ *adj* : monotheistic

monoteísta² *nmf* : monotheist

monotonía *nf* 1 : monotony 2 : monotone

monótono, **-na** *adj* : monotonous — **monótonamente** *adv*

monóxido *nm* : monoxide ⟨monóxido de carbono : carbon monoxide⟩

monserga *nf* : gibberish, drivel

monstruo *nm* : monster

monstruosidad *nf* : monstrosity

monstruoso, **-sa** *adj* : monstrous — **monstruosamente** *adv*

monta *nf* 1 : sum, total 2 : importance, value ⟨de poca monta : unimportant, insignificant⟩

montaje *nm* 1 : assembling, assembly 2 : montage

montante *nm* : transom, fanlight

montaña *nf* 1 MONTE : mountain 2 **montaña rusa** : roller coaster

montañero, **-ra** *n* : mountaineer, mountain climber

montañoso, **-sa** *adj* : mountainous

montar *vt* 1 : to mount 2 ESTABLECER : to set up, to establish 3 ARMAR : to assemble, to put together 4 : to edit (a film) 5 : to stage, to put on (a show) 6 : to cock (a gun) 7 **montar en bicicleta** : to get on a bicycle 8 **montar a caballo** CABALGAR : to ride horseback

monte *nm* 1 MONTAÑA : mountain, mount 2 : woodland, scrubland ⟨monte bajo : underbrush⟩ 3 : outskirts (of a town), surrounding country 4 **monte de piedad** : pawnshop

montés *adj*, *pl* **monteses** : wild (of animals or plants)

montículo *nm* 1 : mound, heap 2 : hillock, knoll

monto *nm* : amount, total

montón *nm*, *pl* **-tones** 1 : heap, pile 2 *fam* : ton, load ⟨un montón de preguntas : a ton of questions⟩ ⟨montones de gente : loads of people⟩

montura *nf* 1 : mount (horse) 2 : saddle, tack 3 : setting, mounting (of jewelry) 4 : frame (of glasses)

monumental *adj fam* 1 : tremendous, terrific 2 : massive, huge

monumento *nm* : monument

monzón *nm*, *pl* **monzones** : monsoon

moño *nm* 1 : bun (chignon) 2 LAZO : bow, knot ⟨corbata de moño : bow tie⟩

moquear *vi* : to snivel

moquillo *nm* : distemper

mora *nf* 1 : blackberry 2 : mulberry

morada *nf* RESIDENCIA : dwelling, abode

morado¹, **-da** *adj* : purple

morado² *nm* : purple

morador, **-dora** *n* : dweller, inhabitant

moral¹ *adj* : moral — **moralmente** *adv*

moral² *nf* 1 MORALIDAD : ethics, morality, morals *pl* 2 ÁNIMO : morale, spirits *pl*

moraleja *nf* : moral (of a story)

moralidad *nf* : morality

moralista¹ *adj* : moralistic

moralista² *nmf* : moralist

morar *vi* : to dwell, to reside

moratoria *nf* : moratorium

mórbido, **-da** *adj* : morbid

morboso, **-sa** *adj* : morbid — **morbosidad** *nf*

morcilla *nf* : blood sausage, blood pudding

mordacidad *nf* : bite, sharpness

mordaz *adj* : caustic, scathing

mordaza *nf* 1 : gag 2 : clamp

mordedura *nf* : bite (of an animal)

morder {47} *v* : to bite

mordida *nf* 1 : bite 2 *CA, Mex* : bribe, payoff

mordisco *nm* : bite, nibble

mordisquear *vt* : to nibble (on), to bite

morena *nf* 1 : moraine 2 : moray (eel)

moreno¹, **-na** *adj* 1 : brunette 2 : dark, dark-skinned

moreno², **-na** *n* 1 : brunette 2 : dark-skinned person

moretón *nm*, *pl* **-tones** : bruise

morfina *nf* : morphine

morfología *nf* : morphology

morgue *nf* : morgue

moribundo¹, **-da** *adj* : dying, moribund

moribundo², **-da** *n* : dying person

morillo *nm* : andiron

morir {46} *vi* 1 FALLECER : to die 2 APAGARSE : to die out, to go out

mormón, **-mona** *adj & n*, *pl* **mormones** : Mormon

moro¹, **-ra** *adj* : Moorish

moro², **-ra** *n* 1 : Moor 2 : Muslim

morosidad *nf* 1 : delinquency (in payment) 2 : slowness

moroso, **-sa** *adj* 1 : delinquent, in arrears ⟨cuentas morosas : delinquent accounts⟩ 2 : slow, sluggish

morral *nm* MOCHILA : backpack, knapsack

morralla *nf* 1 : small fish 2 : trash, riffraff 3 *Mex* : small change

morriña *nf* : homesickness

morro *nm* HOCICO : snout

morsa *nf* : walrus
morse *nm* : Morse code
mortaja *nf* SUDARIO : shroud
mortal[1] *adj* **1** : mortal **2** FATAL : fatal, deadly — **mortalmente** *adv*
mortal[2] *nmf* : mortal
mortalidad *nf* : mortality
mortandad *nf* **1** : loss of life, death toll **2** : carnage, slaughter
mortero *nm* : mortar (bowl, cannon, or building material)
mortífero, -ra *adj* LETAL : deadly, fatal
mortificación *nf, pl* **-ciones 1** : mortification **2** TORMENTO : anguish, torment
mortificar {72} *vt* **1** : to mortify **2** TORTURAR : to trouble, to torment — **mortificarse** *vr* : to be mortified, to feel embarrassed
mosaico *nm* : mosaic
mosca *nf* **1** : fly **2 mosca común** : housefly
moscada *adj* **nuez moscada** : nutmeg
moscovita *adj* & *nmf* : Muscovite
mosquearse *vr* **1** : to become suspicious **2** : to take offense
mosquete *nm* : musket
mosquetero *nm* : musketeer
mosquitero *nm* : mosquito net
mosquito *nm* ZANCUDO : mosquito
mostachón *nm, pl* **-chones** : macaroon
mostaza *nf* : mustard
mostrador *nm* : counter (in a store)
mostrar {19} *vt* **1** : to show **2** EXHIBIR : to exhibit, to display — **mostrarse** *vr* : to show oneself, to appear
mota *nf* **1** : fleck, speck **2** : defect, blemish
mote *nm* SOBRENOMBRE : nickname
moteado, -da *adj* : dotted, spotted, dappled
motel *nm* : motel
motín *nm, pl* **motines 1** : riot **2** : rebellion, mutiny
motivación *nf, pl* **-ciones** : motivation — **motivacional** *adj*
motivar *vt* **1** CAUSAR : to cause **2** IMPULSAR : to motivate
motivo *nm* **1** MÓVIL : motive **2** CAUSA : cause, reason **3** TEMA : theme, motif
moto *nf* : motorcycle, motorbike
motocicleta *nf* : motorcycle
motociclismo *nm* : motorcycling
motociclista *nmf* : motorcyclist
motor[1], **-ra** *adj* MOTRIZ : motor
motor[2] *nm* **1** : motor, engine **2** : driving force, cause
motorista *nmf* : motorist
motriz *adj, pl* **motrices** : driving
motu proprio *adv* **de motu proprio** [de ˈmotu ˈproprio] : voluntarily, of one's own accord
mousse [ˈmus] *nmf* : mousse
mover {47} *vt* **1** TRASLADAR : to move, to shift **2** AGITAR : to shake, to nod (the head) **3** ACCIONAR : to power, to drive **4** INDUCIR : to provoke, to cause **5** : to excite, to stir — **moverse** *vr* **1**

: to move, to move over **2** : to hurry, to get a move on **3** : to get moving, to make an effort
movible *adj* : movable
movida *nf* : move (in a game)
móvil[1] *adj* : mobile
móvil[2] *nm* **1** MOTIVO : motive **2** : mobile
movilidad *nf* : mobility
movilizar {21} *vt* : to mobilize — **movilización** *nf*
movimiento *nm* : movement, motion ⟨movimiento del cuerpo : bodily movement⟩ ⟨movimiento sindicalista : labor movement⟩
mozo[1], **-za** *adj* : young, youthful
mozo[2], **-za** *n* **1** JOVEN : young man *m*, young woman *f*, youth **2** : helper, servant **3** *Arg, Chile, Col, Peru* : waiter *m*, waitress *f*
mucamo, -ma *n* : servant, maid *f*
muchacha *nf* : maid
muchacho, -cha *n* **1** : kid, boy *m*, girl *f* **2** JOVEN : young man *m*, young woman *f*
muchedumbre *nf* MULTITUD : crowd, multitude
mucho[1] *adv* **1** : much, a lot ⟨mucho más : much more⟩ ⟨le gusta mucho : he likes it a lot⟩ **2** : long, a long time ⟨tardó mucho en venir : he was a long time getting here⟩ **3 por mucho que** : no matter how much
mucho[2], **-cha** *adj* **1** : a lot of, many, much ⟨mucha gente : a lot of people⟩ ⟨hace mucho tiempo que no lo veo : I haven't seen him in ages⟩ **2 muchas veces** : often
mucho[3], **-cha** *pron* **1** : a lot, many, much ⟨hay mucho que hacer : there is a lot to do⟩ ⟨muchas no vinieron : many didn't come⟩ **2 cuando ~ or como ~** : at most **3 con ~** : by far **4 ni mucho menos** : not at all, far from it
mucílago *nm* : mucilage
mucosidad *nf* : mucus
mucoso, -sa *adj* : mucous, slimy
muda *nf* **1** : change ⟨muda de ropa : change of clothes⟩ **2** : molt, molting
mudanza *nf* **1** CAMBIO : change **2** TRASLADO : move, moving
mudar *v* **1** CAMBIAR : to change **2** : to molt, to shed — **mudarse** *vr* **1** TRASLADARSE : to move (one's residence) **2** : to change (clothes)
mudo[1], **-da** *adj* **1** SILENCIOSO : silent ⟨cine mudo : silent films⟩ **2** : mute, dumb
mudo[2], **-da** *n* : mute
mueble *nm* **1** : piece of furniture **2 muebles** *nmpl* : furniture, furnishings
mueblería *nf* : furniture store
mueca *nf* : grimace, face
muela *nf* **1** : tooth, molar ⟨dolor de muelas : toothache⟩ ⟨muela de juicio : wisdom tooth⟩ **2** : millstone **3** : whetstone
muele, etc. → **moler**

muelle¹ *adj* : soft, comfortable, easy
muelle² *nm* **1** : wharf, dock **2** RESORTE : spring
muérdago *nm* : mistletoe
muerde, etc. → **morder**
muere, etc. → **morir**
muerte *nf* : death
muerto¹ *pp* → **morir**
muerto², -ta *adj* **1** : dead **2** : lifeless, flat, dull **3** ~ **de** : dying of ⟨estoy muerto de hambre : I'm dying of hunger⟩
muerto³, -ta *nm* DIFUNTO : dead person, deceased
muesca *nf* : nick, notch
muestra¹, etc. → **mostrar**
muestra² *nf* **1** : sample **2** SEÑAL : sign, show ⟨una muestra de respeto : a show of respect⟩ **3** EXPOSICIÓN : exhibition, exposition **4** : pattern, model
mueve, etc. → **mover**
mugido *nm* : moo, lowing, bellow
mugir {35} *vi* : to moo, to low, to bellow
mugre *nf* SUCIEDAD : grime, filth
mugriento, -ta *adj* : filthy
muguete *nm* : lily of the valley
muja, etc. → **mugir**
mujer *nf* **1** : woman **2** ESPOSA : wife
mulato, -ta *adj* & *n* : mulatto
muleta *nf* : crutch
mullido, -da *adj* **1** : soft, fluffy **2** : spongy, springy
mulo, -la *n* : mule
multa *nf* : fine
multar *vt* : to fine
multicolor *adj* : multicolored
multicultural *adj* : multicultural
multidisciplinario, -ria *adj* : multidisciplinary
multifacético, -ca *adj* : multifaceted
multifamiliar *adj* : multifamily
multilateral *adj* : multilateral
multimedia *nf* : multimedia
multimillonario, -ria *n* : multimillionaire
multinacional *adj* : multinational
múltiple *adj* : multiple
multiplicación *nf*, *pl* **-ciones** : multiplication
multiplicar {72} *v* **1** : to multiply **2** : to increase — **multiplicarse** *vr* : to multiply, to reproduce
multiplicidad *nf* : multiplicity
múltiplo *nm* : multiple
multitud *nf* MUCHEDUMBRE : crowd, multitude
multiuso, -sa *adj* : multipurpose
multivitamínico, -ca *adj* : multivitamin
mundano, -na *adj* : worldly, earthly
mundial *adj* : world, worldwide
mundialmente *adv* : worldwide, all over the world

mundo *nm* **1** : world **2 todo el mundo** : everyone, everybody
municiones *nfpl* : ammunition, munitions
municipal *adj* : municipal
municipio *nm* **1** : municipality **2** AYUNTAMIENTO : town council
muñeca *nf* **1** : doll **2** MANIQUÍ : mannequin **3** : wrist
muñeco *nm* **1** : doll, boy doll **2** MARIONETA : puppet
muñón *nm*, *pl* **muñones** : stump (of an arm or leg)
mural *adj* & *nm* : mural
muralista *nmf* : muralist
muralla *nf* : rampart, wall
murciélago *nm* : bat (animal)
murga *nf* : band of street musicians
murió, etc. → **morir**
murmullo *nm* **1** : murmur, murmuring **2** : rustling, rustle ⟨el murmullo de las hojas : the rustling of the leaves⟩
murmurar *vt* **1** : to murmur, to mutter **2** : to whisper (gossip) — *vi* **1** : to murmur **2** CHISMEAR : to gossip
muro *nm* : wall
musa *nf* : muse
musaraña *nf* : shrew
muscular *adj* : muscular
musculatura *nf* : muscles *pl*, musculature
músculo *nm* : muscle
musculoso, -sa *adj* : muscular, brawny
muselina *nf* : muslin
museo *nm* : museum
musgo *nm* : moss
musgoso, -sa *adj* : mossy
música *nf* : music
musical *adj* : musical — **musicalmente** *adv*
músico¹, -ca *adj* : musical
músico², -ca *n* : musician
musitar *vt* : to mumble, to murmur
muslo *nm* : thigh
musulmán, -mana *adj* & *n*, *mpl* **-manes** : Muslim
mutación *nf*, *pl* **-ciones** : mutation
mutante *adj* & *nm* : mutant
mutar *v* : to mutate
mutilar *vt* : to mutilate — **mutilación** *nf*
mutis *nm* **1** : exit (in theater) **2** : silence
mutual *adj* : mutual
mutuo, -tua *adj* : mutual, reciprocal — **mutuamente** *adv*
muy *adv* **1** : very, quite ⟨es muy inteligente : she's very intelligent⟩ ⟨muy bien : very well, fine⟩ ⟨eso es muy americano : that's typically American⟩ **2** : too ⟨es muy grande para él : it's too big for him⟩

N

n *nf* : fourteenth letter of the Spanish alphabet

nabo *nm* : turnip

nácar *nm* MADREPERLA : nacre, mother-of-pearl

nacarado, -da *adj* : pearly

nacer {48} *vi* **1** : to be born ⟨nací en Guatemala : I was born in Guatemala⟩ ⟨no nació ayer : he wasn't born yesterday⟩ **2** : to hatch **3** : to bud, to sprout **4** : to rise, to originate **5 nacer para algo** : to be born to be something **6 volver a nacer** : to have a lucky escape

nacido¹, -da *adj* **1** : born **2 recién nacido** : newborn

nacido², -da *n* **1 los nacidos** : those born (at a particular time) **2 recién nacido** : newborn baby

naciente *adj* **1** : newfound, growing **2** : rising ⟨el sol naciente : the rising sun⟩

nacimiento *nm* **1** : birth **2** : source (of a river) **3** : beginning, origin **4** BELÉN : Nativity scene, crèche

nación *nf, pl* **-ciones** : nation, country, people (of a country)

nacional¹ *adj* : national

nacional² *nmf* CIUDADANO : national, citizen

nacionalidad *nf* : nationality

nacionalismo *nm* : nationalism

nacionalista¹ *adj* : nationalist, nationalistic

nacionalista² *nmf* : nationalist

nacionalización *nf, pl* **-ciones 1** : nationalization **2** : naturalization

nacionalizar {21} *vt* **1** : to nationalize **2** : to naturalize (as a citizen) — **nacionalizarse** *vr*

naco, -ca *adj Mex* : trashy, vulgar, common

nada¹ *adv* : not at all, not in the least ⟨no estamos nada cansados : we are not at all tired⟩

nada² *nf* **1** : nothingness **2** : smidgen, bit ⟨una nada le disgusta : the slightest thing upsets him⟩

nada³ *pron* **1** : nothing ⟨no estoy haciendo nada : I'm not doing anything⟩ **2 casi nada** : next to nothing **3 de —** : you're welcome **4 dentro de nada** : very soon, in no time **5 nada más** : nothing else, nothing more

nadador, -dora *n* : swimmer

nadar *vi* **1** : to swim **2 ~ en** : to be swimming in, to be rolling in — *vt* : to swim

nadería *nf* : small thing, trifle

nadie *pron* : nobody, no one ⟨no vi a nadie : I didn't see anyone⟩

nadir *nm* : nadir

nado *nm* **1** *Mex* : swimming **2 a ~** : swimming ⟨cruzó el río a nado : he swam across the river⟩

nafta *nf* **1** : naphtha **2** (*in various countries*) : gasoline

naftalina *nf* : naphthalene, mothballs *pl*

náhuatl¹ *adj & nmf, pl* **nahuas** : Nahuatl

náhuatl² *nm* : Nahuatl (language)

nailon → **nilón**

naipe *nm* : playing card

nalga *nf* **1** : buttock **2 nalgas** *nfpl* : buttocks, bottom

nalgada *nf* : smack on the bottom, spanking

namibio, -bia *adj & n* : Namibian

nana *nf* **1** : lullaby **2** *fam* : grandma **3** *CA, Col, Mex, Ven* : nanny

nanay *interj fam* : no way!, not likely!

naranja¹ *adj & nm* : orange (color)

naranja² *nf* : orange (fruit)

naranjal *nm* : orange grove

naranjo *nm* : orange tree

narcisismo *nm* : narcissism

narcisista¹ *adj* : narcissistic

narcisista² *nmf* : narcissist

narciso *nm* : narcissus, daffodil

narcótico¹, -ca *adj* : narcotic

narcótico² *nm* : narcotic

narcotizar {21} *vt* : to drug, to dope

narcotraficante *nmf* : drug trafficker

narcotráfico *nm* : drug trafficking

narigón, -gona *adj, mpl* **-gones** : big-nosed

narigudo → **narigón**

nariz *nf, pl* **narices 1** : nose ⟨sonar(se) la nariz : to blow one's nose⟩ **2** : sense of smell

narración *nf, pl* **-ciones** : narration, account

narrador, -dora *n* : narrator

narrar *vt* : to narrate, to tell

narrativa *nf* : narrative, story

narrativo, -va *adj* : narrative

narval *nm* : narwhal

nasa *nf* : creel

nasal *adj* : nasal

nata *nf* **1** : cream ⟨nata batida : whipped cream⟩ **2** : skin (on boiled milk)

natación *nf, pl* **-ciones** : swimming

natal *adj* : native, natal

natalicio *nm* : birthday ⟨el natalicio de George Washington : George Washington's birthday⟩

natalidad *nf* : birthrate

natillas *nfpl* : custard

natividad *nf* : birth, nativity

nativo, -va *adj & n* : native

nato, -ta *adj* : born, natural

natural¹ *adj* **1** : natural **2** : normal ⟨como es natural : naturally, as expected⟩ **3 ~ de** : native of, from **4 de tamaño natural** : life-size

natural² *nm* **1** CARÁCTER : disposition, temperament **2** : native ⟨un natural de Venezuela : a native of Venezuela⟩

naturaleza *nf* **1** : nature ⟨la madre naturaleza : mother nature⟩ **2** ÍNDOLE : nature, disposition, constitution ⟨la naturaleza humana : human nature⟩ **3 naturaleza muerta** : still life

naturalidad *nf* : simplicity, naturalness
naturalismo *nm* : naturalism
naturalista¹ *adj* : naturalistic
naturalista² *nmf* : naturalist
naturalización *nf, pl* **-ciones** : naturalization
naturalizar {21} *vt* : to naturalize — **naturalizarse** *vr* NACIONALIZARSE : to become naturalized
naturalmente *adv* 1 : naturally, inherently 2 : of course
naufragar {52} *vi* 1 : to be shipwrecked 2 FRACASAR : to fail, to collapse
naufragio *nm* 1 : shipwreck 2 FRACASO : failure, collapse
náufrago¹, -ga *adj* : shipwrecked, castaway
náufrago², -ga *n* : shipwrecked person, castaway
náusea *nf* 1 : nausea 2 **dar náuseas** : to nauseate, to disgust 3 **náuseas matutinas** : morning sickness
nauseabundo, -da *adj* : nauseating, sickening
náutica *nf* : navigation
náutico, -ca *adj* : nautical
nautilo *nm* : nautilus
navaja *nf* 1 : pocketknife, penknife ⟨navaja de muelle : switchblade⟩ 2 **navaja de afeitar** : straight razor, razor blade
navajo, -ja *adj & n* : Navajo
naval *adj* : naval
nave *nf* 1 : ship ⟨nave capitana : flagship⟩ ⟨nave espacial : spaceship⟩ 2 : nave ⟨nave lateral : aisle⟩ 3 **quemar uno sus naves** : to burn one's bridges
navegabilidad *nf* : navigability
navegable *adj* : navigable
navegación *nf, pl* **-ciones** : navigation
navegante¹ *adj* : sailing, seafaring
navegante² *nmf* : navigator
navegar {52} *v* : to navigate, to sail
Navidad *nf* : Christmas, Christmastime ⟨Feliz Navidad : Merry Christmas⟩
navideño, -ña *adj* : Christmas
naviero, -ra *adj* : shipping
náyade *nf* : naiad
nazca, etc. → **nacer**
nazi *adj & nmf* : Nazi
nazismo *nm* : Nazism
nébeda *nf* : catnip
neblina *nf* : light fog, mist
neblinoso, -sa *adj* : misty, foggy
nebulosa *nf* : nebula
nebulosidad *nf* : mistiness, haziness
nebuloso, -sa *adj* 1 : hazy, misty 2 : nebulous, vague
necedad *nf* : stupidity, foolishness ⟨decir necedades : to talk nonsense⟩
necesariamente *adv* : necessarily
necesario, -ria *adj* 1 : necessary 2 **si es necesario** : if need be 3 **hacerse necesario** : to be required
neceser *nm* : toilet kit, vanity case
necesidad *nf* 1 : need, necessity 2 : poverty, want 3 **necesidades** *nfpl* : hardships 4 **hacer sus necesidades** : to relieve oneself

necesitado, -da *adj* : needy
necesitar *vt* 1 : to need 2 : to necessitate, to require — *vi* ~ **de** : to have need of
necio¹, -cia *adj* 1 : foolish, silly, dumb 2 *fam* : naughty
necio², -cia *n* ESTÚPIDO : fool, idiot
necrología *nf* : obituary
necrópolis *nfs & pl* : cemetery
néctar *nm* : nectar
nectarina *nf* : nectarine
neerlandés¹, -desa *adj, mpl* **-deses** HOLANDÉS : Dutch
neerlandés², -desa *n, mpl* **-deses** HOLANDÉS : Dutch person, Dutchman *m*
nefando, -da *adj* : unspeakable, heinous
nefario, -ria *adj* : nefarious
nefasto, -ta *adj* 1 : ill-fated, unlucky 2 : disastrous, terrible
negación *nf, pl* **-ciones** 1 : negation, denial 2 : negative (in grammar)
negar {49} *vt* 1 : to deny 2 REHUSAR : to refuse 3 : to disown — **negarse** *vr* 1 : to refuse 2 : to deny oneself
negativa *nf* 1 : denial 2 : refusal
negativo¹, -va *adj* : negative
negativo² *nm* : negative (of a photograph)
negligé *nm* : negligee
negligencia *nf* : negligence
negligente *adj* : neglectful, negligent — **negligentemente** *adv*
negociable *adj* : negotiable
negociación *nf, pl* **-ciones** 1 : negotiation 2 **negociación colectiva** : collective bargaining
negociador, -dora *n* : negotiator
negociante *nmf* : businessman *m*, businesswoman *f*
negociar *vt* : to negotiate — *vi* : to deal, to do business
negocio *nm* 1 : business, place of business 2 : deal, transaction 3 **negocios** *nmpl* : commerce, trade, business
negrero, -ra *n* 1 : slave trader 2 *fam* : slave driver, brutal boss
negrita *nf* : boldface (type)
negro¹, -gra *adj* 1 : black, dark 2 BRONCEADO : suntanned 3 : gloomy, awful, desperate ⟨la cosa se está poniendo negra : things are looking bad⟩ 4 **mercado negro** : black market
negro², -gra *n* : dark-skinned person, black person 2 *fam* : darling, dear
negro³ *nm* : black (color)
negrura *nf* : blackness
negruzco, -ca *adj* : blackish
nene, -na *n* : baby, small child
nenúfar *nm* : water lily
neocelandés → **neozelandés**
neoclasicismo *nm* : neoclassicism
neoclásico, -ca *adj* : neoclassical
neófito, -ta *n* : neophyte, novice
neologismo *nm* : neologism
neón *nm, pl* **neones** : neon
neoyorquino¹, -na *adj* : of or from New York

neoyorquino², **-na** *n* : New Yorker
neozelandés¹, **-desa** *adj, mpl* **-deses**
: of or from New Zealand
neozelandés², **-desa** *n, mpl* **-deses**
: New Zealander
nepalés, **-lesa** *adj & n, mpl* **-leses**
: Nepali
nepotismo *nm* : nepotism
neptunio *nm* : neptunium
Neptuno *nm* : Neptune
nervio *nm* **1** : nerve **2** : tendon, sinew,
gristle (in meat) **3** : energy, drive **4**
: rib (of a vault) **5 nervios** *nmpl*
: nerves ⟨estar mal de los nervios : to
be a bundle of nerves⟩ ⟨ataque de
nervios : nervous breakdown⟩
nerviosamente *adv* : nervously
nerviosidad → **nerviosismo**
nerviosismo *nm* : nervousness, anxiety
nervioso, **-sa** *adj* **1** : nervous, nerve ⟨sis-
tema nervioso : nervous system⟩ **2**
: high-strung, restless, anxious ⟨pon-
erse nervioso : to get nervous⟩ **3** : vigorous, energetic
nervudo, **-da** *adj* : sinewy, wiry
neta *nf Mex fam* : truth ⟨la neta es que
me cae mal : the truth is, I don't like
her⟩
netamente *adv* : clearly, obviously
neto, **-ta** *adj* **1** : net ⟨peso neto : net
weight⟩ **2** : clear, distinct
neumático¹, **-ca** *adj* : pneumatic
neumático² *nm* LLANTA : tire
neumonía *nf* PULMONÍA : pneumonia
neural *adj* : neural
neuralgia *nf* : neuralgia
neuritis *nf* : neuritis
neurología *nf* : neurology
neurológico, **-ca** *adj* : neurological,
neurologic
neurólogo, **-ga** *n* : neurologist
neurosis *nfs & pl* : neurosis
neurótico, **-ca** *adj & n* : neurotic
neutral *adj* : neutral
neutralidad *nf* : neutrality
neutralizar {21} *vt* : to neutralize — **neutralización** *nf*
neutro, **-tra** *adj* **1** : neutral **2** : neuter
neutrón *nm, pl* **neutrones** : neutron
nevada *nf* : snowfall
nevado, **-da** *adj* **1** : snowcapped **2**
: snow-white
nevar {55} *v impers* : to snow
nevasca *nf* : snowstorm, blizzard
nevera *nf* REFRIGERADOR : refrigerator
nevería *nf Mex* : ice cream parlor
nevisca *nf* : light snowfall, flurry
nevoso, **-sa** *adj* : snowy
nexo *nm* VÍNCULO : link, connection,
nexus
ni *conj* **1** : neither, nor ⟨afuera no hace
ni frío ni calor : it's neither cold nor
hot outside⟩ **2 ni que** : not even if, not
as if ⟨ni que me pagaran : not even if
they paid me⟩ ⟨ni que fuera (yo) su
madre : it's not as if I were his moth-
er⟩ **3 ni siquiera** : not even ⟨ni siquiera
nos llamaron : they didn't even call us⟩

nicaragüense *adj & nmf* : Nicaraguan
nicho *nm* : niche
nicotina *nf* : nicotine
nido *nm* **1** : nest **2** : hiding place, den
niebla *nf* : fog, mist
niega, **niegue** etc. → **negar**
nieto, **-ta** *n* **1** : grandson *m*, granddaughter *f* **2 nietos** *nmpl* : grandchil-
dren
nieva, etc. → **nevar**
nieve *nf* **1** : snow **2** *Cuba, Mex, PRi*
: sherbet
nigeriano, **-na** *adj & n* : Nigerian
nigua *nf* : sand flea, chigger
nihilismo *nm* : nihilism
nilón *or* **nilon** *nm, pl* **nilones** : nylon
nimbo *nm* **1** : halo **2** : nimbus
nimiedad *nf* INSIGNIFICANCIA : trifle,
triviality
nimio, **-mia** *adj* INSIGNIFICANTE : insignificant, trivial
ninfa *nf* : nymph
ningunear *vt Mex fam* : to disrespect
ninguno¹, **-na** (**ningún** *before masculine
singular nouns*) *adj, mpl* **ningunos** : no,
none ⟨no es ninguna tonta : she's no
fool⟩ ⟨no debe hacerse en ningún momento : that should never be done⟩
ninguno², **-na** *pron* **1** : neither, none
⟨ninguno de los dos ha vuelto aún : neither one has returned yet⟩ **2** : no one,
no other ⟨te quiero más que a ninguna : I love you more than any other⟩
niña *nf* **1** PUPILA : pupil (of the eye) **2**
la niña de los ojos : the apple of one's
eye
niñada *nf* **1** : childishness **2** : trifle, silly thing
niñería → **niñada**
niñero, **-ra** *n* : baby-sitter, nanny
niñez *nf, pl* **niñeces** INFANCIA : childhood
niño, **-ña** *n* : child, boy *m*, girl *f*
niobio *nm* : niobium
nipón, **-pona** *adj & n, mpl* **nipones**
JAPONÉS : Japanese
níquel *nm* : nickel
nitidez *nf, pl* **-deces** CLARIDAD : clarity, vividness, sharpness
nítido, **-da** *adj* CLARO : clear, vivid, sharp
nitrato *nm* : nitrate
nítrico, **-ca** *adj* **ácido nítrico** : nitric acid
nitrito *nm* : nitrite
nitrógeno *nm* : nitrogen
nitroglicerina *nf* : nitroglycerin
nivel *nm* **1** : level, height ⟨nivel del mar
: sea level⟩ **2** : level, standard ⟨nivel
de vida : standard of living⟩
nivelar *vt* : to level (out)
nixtamal *nm Mex* : limed corn used for
tortillas
no *adv* **1** : no ⟨¿quieres ir al mercado?
no, voy más tarde : do you want to go
shopping? no, I'm going later⟩ **2** : not
⟨¡no hagas eso! : don't do that!⟩ ⟨creo
que no : I don't think so⟩ **3** : non- ⟨no
fumador : non-smoker⟩ **4 ¡como no!**
: of course! **5 no bien** : as soon as, no
sooner

nobelio *nm* : nobelium
noble[1] *adj* : noble — **noblemente** *adv*
noble[2] *nmf* : nobleman *m*, noblewoman *f*
nobleza *nf* 1 : nobility 2 HONRADEZ : honesty, integrity
nocaut *nm* : knockout, KO
noche *nf* 1 : night, nighttime, evening 2 **buenas noches** : good evening, good night 3 **de noche** *or* **por la noche** : at night 4 **hacerse de noche** : to get dark
Nochebuena *nf* : Christmas Eve
nochecita *nf* : dusk
Nochevieja *nf* : New Year's Eve
noción *nf, pl* **nociones** 1 CONCEPTO : notion, concept 2 **nociones** *nfpl* : smattering, rudiments *pl*
nocivo, -va *adj* DAÑINO : harmful, noxious
noctámbulo, -la *n* 1 : sleepwalker 2 : night owl
nocturno[1], **-na** *adj* : night, nocturnal
nocturno[2] *nm* : nocturne
nodriza *nf* : wet nurse
nódulo *nm* : nodule
nogal *nm* 1 : walnut tree 2 *Mex* : pecan tree 3 **nogal americano** : hickory
nómada[1] *adj* : nomadic
nómada[2] *nmf* : nomad
nomás *adv* : only, just ⟨lo hice nomás porque sí : I did it just because⟩ ⟨nomás de recordarlo me enojo : I get angry just remembering it⟩ ⟨nomás faltan dos semanas para Navidad : there are only two weeks left till Christmas⟩
nombradía *nf* RENOMBRE : fame, renown
nombrado, -da *adj* : famous, well-known
nombramiento *nm* : appointment, nomination
nombrar *vt* 1 : to appoint 2 : to mention, to name
nombre *nm* 1 : name ⟨nombre de pluma : pseudonym, pen name⟩ ⟨en nombre : on behalf of⟩ ⟨sin nombre : nameless⟩ 2 : noun ⟨nombre propio : proper noun⟩ 3 : fame, renown
nomenclatura *nf* : nomenclature
nomeolvides *nmfs & pl* : forget-me-not
nómina *nf* : payroll
nominación *nf, pl* **-ciones** : nomination
nominal *adj* : nominal — **nominalmente** *adv*
nominar *vt* : to nominate
nominativo[1], **-va** *adj* : nominative
nominativo[2] *nm* : nominative (case)
nomo *nm* : gnome
non[1] *adj* IMPAR : odd, not even
non[2] *nm* : odd number
nonagésimo[1], **-ma** *adj* : ninetieth, ninety-
nonagésimo[2], **-ma** *n* : ninetieth, ninety- (in a series)
nono, -na *adj* : ninth — **nono** *nm*
nopal *nm* : nopal, cactus
nopalitos *nmpl Mex* : pickled cactus leaves
noquear *vt* : to knock out, to KO

norcoreano, -na *adj & n* : North Korean
nordeste[1] *or* **noreste** *adj* 1 : northeastern 2 : northeasterly
nordeste[2] *or* **noreste** *nm* : northeast
nórdico, -ca *adj & n* 1 ESCANDINAVO : Scandinavian 2 : Norse
noreste → **nordeste**
noria *nf* 1 : waterwheel 2 : Ferris wheel
norirlandés[1], **-desa** *adj, mpl* **-deses** : Northern Irish
norirlandés[2], **-desa** *n, mpl* **-deses** : person from Northern Ireland
norma *nf* 1 : rule, regulation 2 : norm, standard
normal *adj* 1 : normal, usual 2 : standard 3 **escuela normal** : teacher-training college
normalidad *nf* : normality, normalcy
normalización *nf, pl* **-ciones** *nf* 1 REGULARIZACIÓN : normalization 2 ESTANDARIZACIÓN : standardization
normalizar {21} *vt* 1 REGULARIZAR : to normalize 2 ESTANDARIZAR : to standardize — **normalizarse** *vr* : to return to normal
normalmente *adv* GENERALMENTE : ordinarily, generally
noroeste[1] *adj* 1 : northwestern 2 : northwesterly
noroeste[2] *nm* : northwest
norte[1] *adj* : north, northern
norte[2] *nm* 1 : north 2 : north wind 3 META : aim, objective
norteamericano, -na *adj & n* 1 : North American 2 AMERICANO, ESTADOUNIDENSE : American, native or inhabitant of the United States
norteño[1], **-ña** *adj* : northern
norteño[2], **-ña** *n* : Northerner
noruego[1], **-ga** *adj & n* : Norwegian
noruego[2] *nm* : Norwegian (language)
nos *pron* 1 : us ⟨nos enviaron a la frontera : they sent us to the border⟩ 2 : ourselves ⟨nos divertimos muchísimo : we enjoyed ourselves a great deal⟩ 3 : each other, one another ⟨nos vimos desde lejos : we saw each other from far away⟩ 4 : to us, for us, from us ⟨nos lo dio : he gave it to us⟩ ⟨nos lo compraron : they bought it from us⟩
nosotros, -tras *pron* 1 : we ⟨nosotros llegamos ayer : we arrived yesterday⟩ 2 : us ⟨ven con nosotros : come with us⟩ 3 **nosotros mismos** : ourselves ⟨lo arreglamos nosotros mismos : we fixed it ourselves⟩
nostalgia *nf* 1 : nostalgia, longing 2 : homesickness
nostálgico, -ca *adj* 1 : nostalgic 2 : homesick
nota *nf* 1 : note, message 2 : announcement ⟨nota de prensa : press release⟩ 3 : grade, mark (in school) 4 : characteristic, feature, touch 5 : note (in music) 6 : bill, check (in a restaurant)

notable *adj* **1** : notable, noteworthy **2** : outstanding

notación *nf, pl* **-ciones** : notation

notar *vt* **1** : to notice ⟨hacer notar algo : to point out something⟩ **2** : to tell ⟨la diferencia se nota inmediatamente : you can tell the difference right away⟩ — **notarse** *vr* **1** : to be evident, to show **2** : to feel, to seem

notario, -ria *n* : notary, notary public

noticia *nf* **1** : news item, piece of news **2 noticias** *nfpl* : news

noticiero *nm* : news program, newscast

noticioso, -sa *adj* : news ⟨agencia noticiosa : news agency⟩

notificación *nf, pl* **-ciones** : notification

notificar {72} *vt* : to notify, to inform

notoriedad *nf* **1** : knowledge, obviousness **2** : fame, notoriety

notorio, -ria *adj* **1** OBVIO : obvious, evident **2** CONOCIDO : well-known

novato¹, -ta *adj* : inexperienced, new

novato², -ta *n* : beginner, novice

novecientos¹, -tas *adj* : nine hundred

novecientos² *nms & pl* : nine hundred

novedad *nf* **1** : newness, novelty **2** : innovation

novedoso, -sa *adj* : original, novel

novel *adj* NOVATO : inexperienced, new

novela *nf* **1** : novel **2** : soap opera

novelar *vt* : to fictionalize, to make a novel out of

novelesco, -ca *adj* **1** : fictional **2** : fantastic, fabulous

novelista *nmf* : novelist

novena *nf* : novena

noveno, -na *adj* : ninth — **noveno, -na** *n*

noventa *adj & nm* : ninety

noventavo¹, -va *adj* : ninetieth

noventavo², -va *nm* : ninetieth (fraction)

noviazgo *nm* **1** : courtship, relationship **2** : engagement, betrothal

novicio, -cia *n* **1** : novice (in religion) **2** PRINCIPIANTE : novice, beginner

noviembre *nm* : November

novilla *nf* : heifer

novillada *nf* : bullfight featuring young bulls

novillero, -ra *n* : apprentice bullfighter

novillo *nm* : young bull

novio, -via *n* **1** : boyfriend *m*, girlfriend *f* **2** PROMETIDO : fiancé *m*, fiancée *f* **3** : bridegroom *m*, bride *f*

novocaína *nf* : novocaine

nubarrón *nm, pl* **-rrones** : storm cloud

nube *nf* **1** : cloud ⟨andar en las nubes : to have one's head in the clouds⟩ ⟨por las nubes : sky-high⟩ **2** : cloud (of dust), swarm (of insects, etc.)

nublado¹, -da *adj* **1** NUBOSO : cloudy, overcast **2** : clouded, dim

nublado² *nm* **1** : storm cloud **2** AMENAZA : menace, threat

nublar *vt* **1** : to cloud **2** OSCURECER : to obscure — **nublarse** *vr* : to get cloudy

nubosidad *nf* : cloudiness

nuboso, -sa *adj* NUBLADO : cloudy

nuca *nf* : nape, back of the neck

nuclear *adj* : nuclear

núcleo *nm* **1** : nucleus **2** : center, heart, core

nudillo *nm* : knuckle

nudismo *nm* : nudism

nudista *adj & nmf* : nudist

nudo *nm* **1** : knot ⟨nudo de rizo : square knot⟩ ⟨un nudo en la garganta : a lump in one's throat⟩ **2** : node **3** : junction, hub ⟨nudo de comunicaciones : communication center⟩ **4** : crux, heart (of a problem, etc.)

nudoso, -sa *adj* : knotty, gnarled

nuera *nf* : daughter-in-law

nuestro¹, -tra *adj* : our

nuestro², -tra *pron* (*with definite article*) : ours, our own ⟨el nuestro es más grande : ours is bigger⟩ ⟨es de los nuestros : it's one of ours⟩

nuevamente *adv* : again, anew

nuevas *nfpl* : tidings *pl*

nueve *adj & nm* : nine

nuevecito, -ta *adj* : brand-new

nuevo, -va *adj* **1** : new ⟨una casa nueva : a new house⟩ ⟨¿qué hay de nuevo? : what's new?⟩ **2 de ~** : again, once more **3 Nuevo Testamento** : New Testament

nuez *nf, pl* **nueces 1** : nut **2** : walnut **3** *Mex* : pecan **4 nuez de Adán** : Adam's apple **5 nuez moscada** : nutmeg

nulidad *nf* **1** : nullity **2** : incompetent person ⟨es una nulidad! : he's hopeless!⟩

nulo, -la *adj* **1** : null, null and void **2** INEPTO : useless, inept ⟨es nula para la cocina : she's hopeless at cooking⟩

numen *nm* : poetic muse, inspiration

numerable *adj* : countable

numeración *nf, pl* **-ciones 1** : numbering **2** : numbers *pl*, numerals *pl* ⟨numeración romana : Roman numerals⟩

numerador *nm* : numerator

numeral *adj* : numeral

numerar *vt* : to number

numerario, -ria *adj* : long-standing, permanent ⟨profesor numerario : tenured professor⟩

numérico, -ca *adj* : numerical — **numéricamente** *adv*

número *nm* **1** : number ⟨número impar : odd number⟩ ⟨número ordinal : ordinal number⟩ ⟨número arábico : Arabic numeral⟩ ⟨número quebrado : fraction⟩ **2** : issue (of a publication) **3 sin ~** : countless

numeroso, -sa *adj* : numerous

numismática *nf* : numismatics

nunca *adv* **1** : never, ever ⟨nunca es tarde : it's never too late⟩ ⟨no trabaja casi nunca : he hardly ever works⟩ **2 nunca más** : never again **3 nunca jamás** : never ever

nuncio *nm* : harbinger, herald

nupcial *adj* : nuptial, wedding

nupcias *nfpl* : nuptials *pl*, wedding

nutria *nf* **1** : otter **2** : nutria
nutrición *nf, pl* **-ciones** : nutrition, nourishment
nutrido, -da *adj* **1** : nourished ⟨mal nutrido : undernourished, malnourished⟩ **2** : considerable, abundant ⟨de nutrido : full of, abounding in⟩
nutriente *nm* : nutrient
nutrimento *nm* : nutriment
nutrir *vt* **1** ALIMENTAR : to feed, to nourish **2** : to foster, to provide
nutritivo, -va *adj* : nourishing, nutritious

nylon → nilón
ñ *nf* : fifteenth letter of the Spanish alphabet
ñame *nm* : yam
ñandú *nm* : rhea
ñapa *nf* : extra amount ⟨de ñapa : for good measure⟩
ñoñear *vi fam* : to whine
ñoño, -ña *adj fam* : whiny, fussy ⟨no seas tan ñoño : don't be such a wimp⟩
ñoquis *nmpl* : gnocchi *pl*
ñu *nm* : gnu, wildebeest

O

o¹ *nf* : sixteenth letter of the Spanish alphabet
o² *conj* (**u** *before words beginning with o-or ho-*) **1** : or ⟨¿vienes con nosotros o te quedas? : are you coming with us or staying?⟩ **2** : either ⟨o vienes con nosotros o te quedas : either you come with us or you stay⟩ **3 o sea** : that is to say, in other words
oasis *ms & pl* : oasis
obcecado, -da *adj* **1** : blinded ⟨obcecado por la ira : blinded by rage⟩ **2** : stubborn, obstinate
obcecar {72} *vt* : to blind (by emotions) — **obcecarse** *vr* : to become stubborn
obedecer {53} *vt* : to obey ⟨obedecer órdenes : to obey orders⟩ ⟨obedece a tus padres : obey your parents⟩ — *vi* **1** : to obey **2** ~ **a** : to respond to **3** ~ **a** : to be due to, to result from
obediencia *nf* : obedience
obediente *adj* : obedient — **obedientemente** *adv*
obelisco *nm* : obelisk
obertura *nf* : overture
obesidad *nf* : obesity
obeso, -sa *adj* : obese
óbice *nm* : obstacle, impediment
obispado *nm* DIÓCESIS : bishopric, diocese
obispo *nm* : bishop
obituario *nm* : obituary
objeción *nf, pl* **-ciones** : objection ⟨ponerle objeciones a algo : to object to something⟩
objetar *v* : to object ⟨no tengo nada que objetar : I have no objections⟩
objetividad *nf* : objectivity
objetivo¹, -va *adj* : objective — **objetivamente** *adv*
objetivo² *nm* **1** META : objective, goal, target **2** : lens
objeto *nm* **1** COSA : object, thing **2** OBJETIVO : objective, purpose ⟨con objeto de : in order to, with the aim of⟩ **3 objeto volador no identificado** : unidentified flying object
objetor, -tora *n* : objector ⟨objetor de conciencia : conscientious objector⟩
oblea *nf* **1** : wafer **2 hecho una oblea** *fam* : skinny as a rail

oblicuo, -cua *adj* : oblique — **oblicuamente** *adv*
obligación *nf, pl* **-ciones** **1** DEBER : obligation, duty **2** : bond, debenture
obligado, -da *adj* **1** : obliged **2** : obligatory, compulsory **3** : customary
obligar {52} *vt* : to force, to require, to oblige — **obligarse** *vr* : to commit oneself, to undertake (to do something)
obligatorio, -ria *adj* : mandatory, required, compulsory
obliterar *vt* : to obliterate, to destroy — **obliteración** *nf*
oblongo, -ga *adj* : oblong
obnubilación *nf, pl* **-ciones** : bewilderment, confusion
obnubilar *vt* : to daze, to bewilder
oboe¹ *nm* : oboe
oboe² *nmf* : oboist
obra *nf* **1** : work ⟨obra de arte : work of art⟩ ⟨obra de teatro : play⟩ ⟨obra de consulta : reference work⟩ **2** : deed ⟨una buena obra : a good deed⟩ **3** : construction work **4 obra maestra** : masterpiece **5 obras públicas** : public works **6 por obra de** : thanks to, because of
obrar *vt* : to work, to produce ⟨obrar milagros : to work miracles⟩ — *vi* **1** : to act, to behave ⟨obrar con cautela : to act with caution⟩ **2 obrar en poder de** : to be in possession of
obrero¹, -ra *adj* : working ⟨la clase obrera : the working class⟩
obrero², -ra *n* : worker, laborer
obscenidad *nf* : obscenity
obsceno, -na *adj* : obscene
obscurecer, obscuridad, obscuro → oscurecer, oscuridad, oscuro
obsequiar *vt* REGALAR : to give, to present ⟨lo obsequiaron con una placa : they presented him with a plaque⟩
obsequio *nm* REGALO : gift, present
obsequiosidad *nf* : attentiveness, deference
obsequioso, -sa *adj* : obliging, attentive
observable *adj* : observable
observación *nf, pl* **-ciones** **1** : observation, watching **2** : remark, comment
observador¹, -dora *adj* : observant

observador², **-dora** *n* : observer, watcher

observancia *nf* : observance

observante *adj* : observant ⟨los judíos observantes : observant Jews⟩

observar *vt* 1 : to observe, to watch ⟨estábamos observando a los niños : we were watching the children⟩ 2 NOTAR : to notice 3 ACATAR : to obey, to abide by 4 COMENTAR : to remark, to comment

observatorio *nm* : observatory

obsesión *nf, pl* **-siones** : obsession

obsesionar *vt* : to obsess, to preoccupy excessively — **obsesionarse** *vr*

obsesivo, -va *adj* : obsessive

obseso, -sa *adj* : obsessed

obsolescencia *nf* DESUSO : obsolescence — **obsolescente** *adj*

obsoleto, -ta *adj* DESUSADO : obsolete

obstaculizar {21} *vt* IMPEDIR : to obstruct, to hinder

obstáculo *nm* IMPEDIMENTO : obstacle

obstante¹ *conj* **no obstante** : nevertheless, however

obstante² *prep* **no obstante** : in spite of, despite ⟨mantuvo su inocencia no obstante la evidencia : he maintained his innocence in spite of the evidence⟩

obstar *v impers* **~ a** *or* **~ para** : to hinder, to prevent ⟨eso no obsta para que me vaya : that doesn't prevent me from leaving⟩

obstetra *nmf* TOCÓLOGO : obstetrician

obstetricia *nf* : obstetrics

obstétrico, -ca *adj* : obstetric, obstetrical

obstinación *nf, pl* **-ciones** 1 TERQUEDAD : obstinacy, stubbornness 2 : perseverance, tenacity

obstinado, -da *adj* 1 TERCO : obstinate, stubborn 2 : persistent — **obstinadamente** *adv*

obstinarse *vr* EMPECINARSE : to be obstinate, to be stubborn

obstrucción *nf, pl* **-ciones** : obstruction, blockage

obstruccionismo *nm* : obstructionism, filibustering

obstruccionista *adj* : obstructionist, filibustering

obstructor, -tora *adj* : obstructive

obstruir {41} *vt* BLOQUEAR : to obstruct, to block, to clog — **obstruirse** *vr*

obtención *nf* : obtaining, procurement

obtener {80} *vt* : to obtain, to secure, to get — **obtenible** *adj*

obturador *nm* : shutter (of a camera)

obtuso, -sa *adj* : obtuse

obtuvo, etc. → **obtener**

obús *nm, pl* **obuses** 1 : mortar (weapon) 2 : mortar shell

obviar *vt* : to get around (a difficulty), to avoid

obvio, -via *adj* : obvious — **obviamente** *adv*

oca *nf* : goose

ocasión *nf, pl* **-siones** 1 : occasion, time 2 : opportunity, chance 3 : bargain 4 **de ~** : secondhand 5 **aviso de ocasión** *Mex* : classified ad

ocasional *adj* 1 : occasional 2 : chance, fortuitous

ocasionalmente *adv* 1 : occasionally 2 : by chance

ocasionar *vt* CAUSAR : to cause, to occasion

ocaso *nm* 1 ANOCHECER : sunset, sundown 2 DECADENCIA : decline, fall

occidental *adj* : western, occidental

occidente *nm* 1 OESTE, PONIENTE : west 2 **el Occidente** : the West

oceánico, -ca *adj* : oceanic

océano *nm* : ocean

oceanografía *nf* : oceanography

oceanográfico, -ca *adj* : oceanographic

ocelote *nm* : ocelot

ochenta *adj & nm* : eighty

ochentavo¹, -va *adj* : eightieth

ochentavo² *nm* : eightieth (fraction)

ocho *adj & nm* : eight

ochocientos¹, -tas *adj* : eight hundred

ochocientos² *ms & pl* : eight hundred

ocio *nm* 1 : free time, leisure 2 : idleness

ociosidad *nf* : idleness, inactivity

ocioso, -sa *adj* 1 INACTIVO : idle, inactive 2 INÚTIL : pointless, useless

ocre *nm* : ocher

octágono *nm* : octagon — **octagonal** *adj*

octava *nf* : octave

octavo, -va *adj* : eighth — **octavo, -va** *n*

octeto *nm* 1 : octet 2 : byte

octogésimo¹, -ma *adj* : eightieth, eighty-

octogésimo², -ma *n* : eightieth, eighty-(in a series)

octubre *nm* : October

ocular *adj* 1 : ocular, eye ⟨músculos oculares : eye muscles⟩ 2 **testigo ocular** : eyewitness

oculista *nmf* : oculist, ophthalmologist

ocultación *nf, pl* **-ciones** : concealment

ocultar *vt* ESCONDER : to conceal, to hide — **ocultarse** *vr*

oculto, -ta *adj* 1 ESCONDIDO : hidden, concealed 2 : occult

ocupación *nf, pl* **-ciones** 1 : occupation, activity 2 : occupancy 3 EMPLEO : employment, job

ocupacional *adj* : occupational, job-related

ocupado, -da *adj* 1 : busy 2 : taken ⟨este asiento está ocupado : this seat is taken⟩ 3 : occupied ⟨territorios ocupados : occupied territories⟩ 4 **señal de ocupado** : busy signal

ocupante *nmf* : occupant

ocupar *vt* 1 : to occupy, to take possession of 2 : to hold (a position) 3 : to employ, to keep busy 4 : to fill (space, time) 5 : to inhabit (a dwelling) 6 : to bother, to concern — **ocuparse** *vr* **~ de** 1 : to be concerned with 2 : to take care of

ocurrencia *nf* **1** : occurrence, event **2** : witticism **3** : bright idea

ocurrente *adj* **1** : witty **2** : clever, sharp

ocurrir *vi* : to occur, to happen — **ocurrirse** *vr* ~ **a** : to occur to, to strike ⟨se me ocurrió una mejor idea : a better idea occurred to me⟩

oda *nf* : ode

odiar *vt* ABOMINAR, ABORRECER : to hate

odio *nm* : hate, hatred

odioso, -sa *adj* ABOMINABLE, ABORRECIBLE : hateful, detestable

odisea *nf* : odyssey

odontología *nf* : dentistry, dental surgery

odontólogo, -ga *n* : dentist, dental surgeon

oeste[1] *adj* **1** : west, western ⟨la región oeste : the western region⟩ **2** : westerly

oeste[2] *nm* **1** : west, West **2** : west wind

ofender *vt* AGRAVIAR : to offend, to insult — *vi* : to offend, to be insulting — **ofenderse** *vr* : to take offense

ofensa *nf* : offense, insult

ofensiva *nf* : offensive ⟨pasar a la ofensiva : to go on the offensive⟩

ofensivo, -va *adj* : offensive, insulting

ofensor, -sora *n* : offender

oferente *nmf* **1** : supplier **2** FUENTE : source ⟨un oferente no identificado : an unidentified source⟩

oferta *nf* **1** : offer **2** : sale, bargain ⟨las camisas están en oferta : the shirts are on sale⟩ **3 oferta y demanda** : supply and demand

ofertar *vt* OFRECER : to offer

oficial[1] *adj* : official — **oficialmente** *adv*

oficial[2] *nmf* **1** : officer, police officer, commissioned officer (in the military) **2** : skilled worker

oficializar {21} *vt* : to make official

oficiante *nmf* : celebrant

oficiar *vt* **1** : to inform officially **2** : to officiate at, to celebrate (Mass) — *vi* ~ **de** : to act as

oficina *nf* : office

oficinista *nmf* : office worker

oficio *nm* **1** : trade, profession ⟨es electricista de oficio : he's an electrician by trade⟩ **2** : function, role **3** : official communication **4** : experience ⟨tener oficio : to be experienced⟩ **5** : religious ceremony

oficioso, -sa *adj* **1** EXTRAOFICIAL : unofficial **2** : officious — **oficiosamente** *adv*

ofrecer {53} *vt* **1** : to offer **2** : to provide, to give **3** : to present (an appearance, etc.) — **ofrecerse** *vr* **1** : to offer oneself, to volunteer **2** : to open up, to present itself

ofrecimiento *nm* : offer, offering

ofrenda *nf* : offering

oftalmología *nf* : ophthalmology

oftalmólogo, -ga *n* : ophthalmologist

ofuscación *nf*, *pl* **-ciones** : blindness, confusion

ofuscar {72} *vt* **1** : to blind, to dazzle **2** CONFUNDIR : to bewilder, to confuse — **ofuscarse** *vr* ~ **con** : to be blinded by

ogro *nm* : ogre

ohm *nm*, *pl* **ohms** : ohm

ohmio → **ohm**

oídas *nfpl* **de** ~ : by hearsay

oído *nm* **1** : ear ⟨oído interno : inner ear⟩ **2** : hearing ⟨duro de oído : hard of hearing⟩ **3 tocar de oído** : to play by ear

oiga, etc. → **oír**

oír {50} *vi* : to hear — *vt* **1** : to hear **2** ESCUCHAR : to listen to **3** : to pay attention to, to heed **4** ¡oye! *or* ¡oiga! : listen!, excuse me!, look here!

ojal *nm* : buttonhole

ojalá *interj* **1** : I hope so!, if only!, God willing! **2** : I hope, I wish, hopefully ⟨ojalá que le vaya bien! : I hope things go well for her!⟩ ⟨ojalá no llueva! : hopefully it won't rain!⟩

ojeada *nf* : glimpse, glance ⟨echar una ojeada : to have a quick look⟩

ojear *vt* : to eye, to have a look at

ojete *nm* : eyelet

ojiva *nf* : warhead

ojo *nm* **1** : eye **2** : judgment, sharpness ⟨tener buen ojo para : to be a good judge of, to have a good eye for⟩ **3** : hole (in cheese), eye (in a needle), center (of a storm) **4** : span (of a bridge) **5 a ojos vistas** : openly, publicly **6 andar con ojo** : to be careful **7 ojo de agua** *Mex* : spring, source **8 ¡ojo!** : look out!, pay attention!

ola *nf* **1** : wave **2 ola de calor** : heat wave

oleada *nf* : swell, wave ⟨una oleada de protestas : a wave of protests⟩

oleaje *nm* : waves *pl*, surf

óleo *nm* **1** : oil **2** : oil painting

oleoducto *nm* : oil pipeline

oleoso, -sa *adj* : oily

oler {51} *vt* **1** : to smell **2** INQUIRIR : to pry into, to investigate **3** AVERIGUAR : to smell out, to uncover — *vi* **1** : to smell ⟨huele mal : it smells bad⟩ **2** ~ **a** : to smell like, to smell of ⟨huele a pino : it smells like pine⟩ — **olerse** *vr* : to have a hunch, to suspect

olfatear *vt* **1** : to sniff **2** : to sense, to sniff out

olfativo, -va *adj* : olfactory

olfato *nm* **1** : sense of smell **2** : nose, instinct

oligarquía *nf* : oligarchy

olimpiada *or* **olimpíada** *nf* **1** : Olympiad **2** *or* **olimpiadas** *nfpl* : Olympics *pl*

olímpico, -ca *adj* : Olympic

olisquear *vt* : to sniff at

oliva *nf* ACEITUNA : olive ⟨aceite de oliva : olive oil⟩

olivo *nm* : olive tree

olla *nf* **1** : pot ⟨olla de presión : pressure cooker⟩ **2 olla podrida** : Spanish stew

olmeca *adj & nmf* : Olmec
olmo *nm* : elm
olor *nm* : smell, odor
oloroso, -sa *adj* : scented, fragrant
olote *nm Mex* : cob, corncob
olvidadizo, -za *adj* : forgetful, absent-minded
olvidar *vt* **1** : to forget, to forget about ⟨olvida lo que pasó : forget about what happened⟩ **2** : to leave behind ⟨olvidé mi chequera en la casa : I left my checkbook at home⟩ — **olvidarse** *vr* : to forget ⟨se me olvidó mi cuaderno : I forgot my notebook⟩ ⟨se le olvidó llamarme : he forgot to call me⟩
olvido *nm* **1** : forgetfulness **2** : oblivion **3** DESCUIDO : oversight
omaní *adj & nmf* : Omani
ombligo *nm* : navel, belly button
ombudsman *nmfs & pl* : ombudsman
omelette *nmf* : omelet
ominoso, -sa *adj* : ominous — **ominosamente** *adv*
omisión *nf, pl* **-siones** : omission, neglect
omiso, -sa *adj* **1** NEGLIGENTE : neglectful **2 hacer caso omiso de** : to ignore
omitir *vt* **1** : to omit, to leave out **2** : to fail to ⟨omitió dar su nombre : he failed to give his name⟩
ómnibus *n, pl* **-bus** *or* **-buses** : bus, coach
omnipotencia *nf* : omnipotence
omnipotente *adj* TODOPODEROSO : omnipotent, almighty
omnipresencia *nf* : ubiquity, omnipresence
omnipresente *adj* : ubiquitous, omnipresent
omnisciente *adj* : omniscient — **omnisciencia** *nf*
omnívoro, -ra *adj* : omnivorous
omóplato *or* **omoplato** *nm* : shoulder blade
once *adj & nm* : eleven
onceavo¹, -va *adj* : eleventh
onceavo² *nm* : eleventh (fraction)
onda *nf* **1** : wave, ripple, undulation ⟨onda sonora : sound wave⟩ **2** : wave (in hair) **3** : scallop (on clothing) **4** *fam* : wavelength, understanding ⟨agarrar la onda : to get the point⟩ ⟨en la onda : on the ball, with it⟩ **5 ¿qué onda?** *fam* : what's happening?, what's up?
ondear *vi* : to ripple, to undulate, to flutter
ondulación *nf, pl* **-ciones** : undulation
ondulado, -da *adj* **1** : wavy ⟨pelo ondulado : wavy hair⟩ **2** : undulating
ondulante *adj* : undulating
ondular *vt* : to wave (hair) — *vi* : to undulate, to ripple
oneroso, -sa *adj* GRAVOSO : onerous, burdensome
ónix *nm* : onyx
onza *nf* : ounce

opacar {72} *vt* **1** : to make opaque or dull **2** : to outshine, to overshadow
opacidad *nf* **1** : opacity **2** : dullness
opaco, -ca *adj* **1** : opaque **2** : dull
ópalo *nm* : opal
opción *nf, pl* **opciones 1** ALTERNATIVA : option, choice **2** : right, chance ⟨tener opción a : to be eligible for⟩
opcional *adj* : optional — **opcionalmente** *adv*
ópera *nf* : opera
operación *nf, pl* **-ciones 1** : operation **2** : transaction, deal
operacional *adj* : operational
operador, -dora *n* **1** : operator **2** : cameraman, projectionist
operante *adj* : operating, working
operar *vt* **1** : to produce, to bring about **2** INTERVENIR : to operate on **3** *Mex* : to operate, to run (a machine) — *vi* **1** : to operate, to function **2** : to deal, to do business — **operarse** *vr* **1** : to come about, to take place **2** : to have an operation
operario, -ria *n* : laborer, worker
operático, -ca → operístico
operativo¹, -va *adj* **1** : operating ⟨capacidad operativa : operating capacity⟩ **2** : operative
operativo² *nm* : operation ⟨operativo militar : military operation⟩
opereta *nf* : operetta
operístico, -ca *adj* : operatic
opiable *adj* : opiate
opinable *adj* : arguable
opinar *vi* **1** : to think, to have an opinion **2** : to express an opinion **3 opinar bien de** : to think highly of — *vt* : to think ⟨opinamos lo mismo : we're of the same opinion, we're in agreement⟩
opinión *nf, pl* **-niones** : opinion, belief
opio *nm* : opium
oponente *nmf* : opponent
oponer {60} *vt* **1** CONTRAPONER : to oppose, to place against **2 oponer resistencia** : to resist, to put up a fight — **oponerse** *vr* ~ **a** : to object to, to be against
oporto *nm* : port (wine)
oportunamente *adv* **1** : at the right time, opportunely **2** : appropriately
oportunidad *nf* : opportunity, chance
oportunismo *nm* : opportunism
oportunista¹ *adj* : opportunistic
oportunista² *nmf* : opportunist
oportuno, -na *adj* **1** : opportune, timely **2** : suitable, appropriate
oposición *nf, pl* **-ciones** : opposition
opositor, -tora *n* ADVERSARIO : opponent
oposum *nm* ZARIGÜEYA : opossum
opresión *nf, pl* **-siones 1** : oppression **2 opresión de pecho** : tightness in the chest
opresivo, -va *adj* : oppressive
opresor¹, -sora *adj* : oppressive
opresor², -sora *n* : oppressor

oprimir *vt* **1** : to oppress **2** : to press, to squeeze ⟨oprima el botón : push the button⟩

oprobio *nm* : opprobrium, shame

optar *vi* **1** ~ **por** : to opt for, to choose **2** ~ **a** : to aspire to, to apply for ⟨dos candidatos optan a la presidencia : two candidates are running for president⟩

optativo, -va *adj* FACULTATIVO : optional

óptica *nf* **1** : optics **2** : optician's shop **3** : viewpoint

óptico¹, -ca *adj* : optical, optic

óptico², -ca *n* : optician

optimismo *nm* : optimism

optimista¹ *adj* : optimistic

optimista² *nmf* : optimist

óptimo, -ma *adj* : optimum, optimal

optometría *nf* : optometry — **optometrista** *nmf*

opuesto¹ *pp* → **oponer**

opuesto² *adj* **1** : opposite, contrary **2** : opposed

opulencia *nf* : opulence — **opulento, -ta** *adj*

opus *nm* : opus

opuso, etc. → **oponer**

ora *conj* : now ⟨los matices eran variados, ora verdes, ora ocres : the hues were varied, now green, now ocher⟩

oración *nf, pl* **-ciones 1** DISCURSO : oration, speech **2** PLEGARIA : prayer **3** FRASE : sentence, clause

oráculo *nm* : oracle

orador, -dora *n* : speaker, orator

oral *adj* : oral — **oralmente** *adv*

órale *interj Mex fam* **1** : sure!, OK! ⟨¿los dos por cinco pesos? ¡órale! : for five pesos? you've got a deal!⟩ **2** : come on! ⟨¡órale, vámonos! : come on, let's go!⟩

orangután *nm, pl* **-tanes** : orangutan

orar *vi* REZAR : to pray

oratoria *nf* : oratory

oratorio *nm* **1** CAPILLA : oratory, chapel **2** : oratorio

orbe *nm* **1** : orb, sphere **2** GLOBO : globe, world

órbita *nf* **1** : orbit **2** : eye socket **3** ÁMBITO : sphere, field

orbitador *nm* : space shuttle, orbiter

orbital *adj* : orbital

orbitar *v* : to orbit

orden¹ *nm, pl* **órdenes 1** : order ⟨todo está en orden : everything's in order⟩ ⟨por orden cronológico : in chronological order⟩ **2 orden del día** : agenda (at a meeting) **3 orden público** : law and order

orden² *nf, pl* **órdenes 1** : order ⟨una orden religiosa : a religious order⟩ ⟨una orden de tacos : an order of tacos⟩ **2 orden de compra** : purchase order **3 estar a la orden del día** : to be the order of the day, to be prevalent

ordenación *nf, pl* **-ciones 1** : ordination **2** : ordering, organizing

ordenadamente *adv* : in an orderly fashion, neatly

ordenado, -da *adj* : orderly, neat

ordenador *nm Spain* : computer

ordenamiento *nm* **1** : ordering, organizing **2** : code (of laws)

ordenanza¹ *nf* REGLAMENTO : ordinance, regulation

ordenanza² *nm* : orderly (in the armed forces)

ordenar *vt* **1** MANDAR : to order, to command **2** ARREGLAR : to put in order, to arrange **3** : to ordain (a priest)

ordeñar *vt* : to milk

ordeño *nm* : milking

ordinal *nm* : ordinal (number)

ordinariamente *adv* **1** : usually **2** : coarsely

ordinariez *nf* : coarseness, vulgarity

ordinario, -ria *adj* **1** : ordinary **2** : coarse, common, vulgar **3 de** ~ : usually

orear *vt* : to air

orégano *nm* : oregano

oreja *nf* : ear

orfanato *nm* : orphanage

orfanatorio *nm Mex* : orphanage

orfebre *nmf* : goldsmith, silversmith

orfebrería *nf* : articles of gold or silver

orfelinato *nm* : orphanage

orgánico, -ca *adj* : organic — **orgánicamente** *adv*

organigrama *nm* : organization chart, flowchart

organismo *nm* **1** : organism **2** : agency, organization

organista *nmf* : organist

organización *nf, pl* **-ciones** : organization

organizador¹, -dora *adj* : organizing

organizador², -dora *n* : organizer

organizar {21} *vt* : to organize, to arrange — **organizarse** *vr* : to get organized

organizativo, -va *adj* : organizational

órgano *nm* : organ

orgasmo *nm* : orgasm

orgía *nf* : orgy

orgullo *nm* : pride

orgulloso, -sa *adj* : proud — **orgullosamente** *adv*

orientación *nf, pl* **-ciones 1** : orientation **2** DIRECCIÓN : direction, course **3** GUÍA : guidance, direction

oriental¹ *adj* **1** : eastern **2** : oriental **3** *Arg, Uru* : Uruguayan

oriental² *nmf* **1** : Easterner **2** : Oriental **3** *Arg, Uru* : Uruguayan

orientar *vt* **1** : to orient, to position **2** : to guide, to direct — **orientarse** *vr* **1** : to orient oneself, to get one's bearings **2** ~ **hacia** : to turn towards, to lean towards

oriente *nm* **1** : east, East **2 el Oriente** : the Orient

orífice *nmf* : goldsmith

orificio *nm* : orifice, opening

origen *nm, pl* **orígenes 1** : origin **2** : lineage, birth **3 dar origen a** : to give rise to **4 en su origen** : originally

original *adj & nm* : original — **originalmente** *adv*
originalidad *nf* : originality
originar *vt* : to originate, to give rise to — **originarse** *vr* : to originate, to begin
originario, -ria *adj* ~ **de** : native of
originariamente *adv* : originally
orilla *nf* **1** BORDE : border, edge **2** : bank (of a river) **3** : shore
orillar *vt* **1** : to skirt, to go around **2** : to trim, to edge (cloth) **3** : to settle, to wind up **4** *Mex* : to pull over (a vehicle)
orín *nm* **1** HERRUMBRE : rust **2 orines** *nmpl* : urine
orina *nf* : urine
orinación *nf* : urination
orinal *nm* : urinal (vessel)
orinar *vi* : to urinate — **orinarse** *vr* : to wet oneself
oriol *nm* OROPÉNDOLA : oriole
oriundo, -da *adj* ~ **de** : native of
orla *nf* : border, edging
orlar *vt* : to edge, to trim
ornamentación *nf, pl* **-ciones** : ornamentation
ornamental *adj* : ornamental
ornamentar *vt* ADORNAR : to ornament, to adorn
ornamento *nm* : ornament, adornment
ornar *vt* : to adorn, to decorate
ornitología *nf* : ornithology
ornitólogo, -ga *n* : ornithologist
ornitorrinco *nm* : platypus
oro *nm* : gold
orondo, -da *adj* **1** : rounded, potbellied (of a container) **2** *fam* : smug, self-satisfied
oropel *nm* : glitz, glitter, tinsel
oropéndola *nf* : oriole
orquesta *nf* : orchestra — **orquestal** *adj*
orquestar *vt* : to orchestrate — **orquestación** *nf*
orquídea *nf* : orchid
ortiga *nf* : nettle
ortodoncia *nf* : orthodontics
ortodoncista *nmf* : orthodontist
ortodoxia *nf* : orthodoxy
ortodoxo, -xa *adj* : orthodox
ortografía *nf* : orthography, spelling
ortográfico, -ca *adj* : orthographic, spelling
ortopedia *nf* : orthopedics
ortopédico, -ca *adj* : orthopedic
ortopedista *nmf* : orthopedist
oruga *nf* **1** : caterpillar **2** : track (of a tank, etc.)
orzuelo *nm* : sty, stye (in the eye)
os *pron pl (objective form of* **vosotros** *Spain)* **1** : you, to you **2** : yourselves, to yourselves **3** : each other, to each other
osa *nf* → **oso**
osadía *nf* VALOR : boldness, daring **2** AUDACIA : audacity, nerve
osado, -da *adj* **1** : bold, daring **2** : audacious, impudent — **osadamente** *adv*

osamenta *nf* : skeletal remains *pl*, bones *pl*
osar *vi* : to dare
oscilación *nf, pl* **-ciones** **1** : oscillation **2** : fluctuation **3** : vacillation, wavering
oscilar *vi* **1** BALANCEARSE : to swing, to sway, to oscillate **2** FLUCTUAR : to fluctuate **3** : to vacillate, to waver
oscuramente *adv* : obscurely
oscurecer {53} *vt* **1** : to darken **2** : to obscure, to confuse, to cloud **3 al oscurecer** : at dusk, at nightfall — *v impers* : to grow dark, to get dark — **oscurecerse** *vr* : to darken, to dim
oscuridad *nf* **1** : darkness **2** : obscurity
oscuro, -ra *adj* **1** : dark **2** : obscure **3 a oscuras** : in the dark, in darkness
óseo, ósea *adj* : skeletal, bony
ósmosis *or* **osmosis** *nf* : osmosis
oso, osa *n* **1** : bear **2 Osa Mayor** : Big Dipper **3 Osa Menor** : Little Dipper **4 oso blanco** : polar bear **5 oso hormiguero** : anteater **6 oso de peluche** : teddy bear
ostensible *adj* : ostensible, apparent — **ostensiblemente** *adv*
ostentación *nf, pl* **-ciones** : ostentation, display
ostentar *vt* **1** : to display, to flaunt **2** POSEER : to have, to hold ⟨ostenta el récord mundial : he holds the world record⟩
ostentoso, -sa *adj* : ostentatious, showy — **ostentosamente** *adv*
osteópata *nmf* : osteopath
osteopatía *n* : osteopathy
osteoporosis *nf* : osteoporosis
ostión *nm, pl* **ostiones** **1** *Mex* : oyster **2** *Chile* : scallop
ostra *nf* : oyster
ostracismo *nm* : ostracism
otear *vt* : to scan, to survey, to look over
otero *nm* : knoll, hillock
otomana *nf* : ottoman (mueble)
otomano, -na *adj & n* : Ottoman
otoñal *adj* : autumn, autumnal
otoño *nm* : autumn, fall
otorgamiento *nm* : granting, awarding
otorgar {52} *vt* **1** : to grant, to award **2** : to draw up, to frame (a legal document)
otro¹, otra *adj* **1** : other **2** : another ⟨en otro juego, ellos ganaron : in another game, they won⟩ **3 otra vez** : again **4 de otra manera** : otherwise **5 otra parte** : elsewhere **6 en otro tiempo** : once, formerly
otro², otra *pron* **1** : another one ⟨dame otro : give me another⟩ **2** : other one ⟨el uno o el otro : one or the other⟩ **3 los otros, las otras** : the others, the rest ⟨me dio una y se quedó con las otras : he gave me one and kept the rest⟩
ovación *nf, pl* **-ciones** : ovation
ovacionar *vt* : to cheer, to applaud

oval → ovalado
ovalado, -da *adj* : oval
óvalo *nm* : oval
ovárico, -ca *adj* : ovarian
ovario *nm* : ovary
oveja *nf* 1 : sheep, ewe 2 oveja negra : black sheep
overol *nm* : overalls *pl*
ovillar *vt* : to roll into a ball
ovillo *nm* 1 : ball (of yarn) 2 : tangle
ovni *or* OVNI *nm* (objeto volador no identificado) : UFO
ovoide *adj* : ovoid, ovoidal
ovulación *nf, pl* -ciones : ovulation
ovular *vi* : to ovulate
óvulo *nm* : ovum

oxidación *nf, pl* -ciones 1 : oxidation 2 : rusting
oxidado, -da *adj* : rusty
oxidar *vt* 1 : to cause to rust 2 : to oxidize — **oxidarse** *vr* : to rust, to become rusty
óxido *nm* 1 HERRUMBRE, ORÍN : rust 2 : oxide
oxigenar *vt* 1 : to oxygenate 2 : to bleach (hair)
oxígeno *nm* : oxygen
oxiuro *nm* : pinworm
oye, etc. → oír
oyente *nmf* 1 : listener 2 : auditor, auditing student
ozono *nm* : ozone

P

p *nf* : seventeenth letter of the Spanish alphabet
pabellón *nm, pl* -llones 1 : pavilion 2 : summerhouse, lodge 3 : flag (of a vessel)
pabilo *nm* MECHA : wick
paca *nf* FARDO : bale
pacana *nf* : pecan
pacer {48} *v* : to graze, to pasture
paces → paz
pachanga *nf fam* : party, bash
paciencia *nf* : patience
paciente *adj & nmf* : patient — **pacientemente** *adv*
pacificación *nf, pl* -ciones : pacification
pacíficamente *adv* : peacefully, peaceably
pacificar {72} *vt* : to pacify, to calm — **pacificarse** *vr* : to calm down, to abate
pacífico, -ca *adj* : peaceful, pacific
pacifismo *nm* : pacifism
pacifista *adj & nmf* : pacifist
pacotilla *nf* de ~ : shoddy, trashy
pactar *vt* : to agree on — *vi* : to come to an agreement
pacto *nm* CONVENIO : pact, agreement
padecer {53} *vt* : to suffer, to endure — *vi* ADOLECER ~ de : to suffer from
padecimiento *nm* 1 : suffering 2 : ailment, condition
padrastro *nm* 1 : stepfather 2 : hangnail
padre[1] *adj Mex fam* : fantastic, great
padre[2] *nm* 1 : father 2 padres *nmpl* : parents
padrenuestro *nm* : Lord's Prayer, paternoster
padrino *nm* 1 : godfather 2 : best man 3 : sponsor, patron
padrón *nm, pl* padrones : register, roll ⟨padrón municipal : city register⟩
paella *nf* : paella
paga *nf* 1 : payment 2 : pay, wages *pl*
pagadero, -ra *adj* : payable
pagado, -da *adj* 1 : paid 2 pagado de sí mismo : self-satisfied, smug
pagador, -dora *n* : payer

paganismo *nm* : paganism
pagano, -na *adj & n* : pagan
pagar {52} *vt* : to pay, to pay for, to repay — *vi* : to pay
pagaré *nm* VALE : promissory note, IOU
página *nf* : page
pago *nm* 1 : payment 2 en pago de : in return for
pagoda *nf* : pagoda
pague, etc. → pagar
país *nm* 1 NACIÓN : country, nation 2 REGIÓN : region, territory
paisaje *nm* : scenery, landscape
paisano, -na *n* COMPATRIOTA : compatriot, fellow countryman
paja *nf* 1 : straw 2 *fam* : trash, tripe
pajar *nm* : hayloft, haystack
pajarera *nf* : aviary
pájaro *nm* : bird ⟨pájaro cantor : songbird⟩ ⟨pájaro bobo : penguin⟩ ⟨pájaro carpintero : woodpecker⟩
pajita *nf* : (drinking) straw
pajote *nm* : straw, mulch
pala *nf* 1 : shovel, spade 2 : blade (of an oar or a rotor) 3 : paddle, racket
palabra *nf* 1 VOCABLO : word 2 PROMESA : word, promise ⟨un hombre de palabra : a man of his word⟩ 3 HABLA : speech 4 : right to speak ⟨tener la palabra : to have the floor⟩
palabrería *nf* : empty talk
palabrota *nf* : swearword
palacio *nm* 1 : palace, mansion 2 palacio de justicia : courthouse
paladar *nm* 1 : palate 2 GUSTO : taste
paladear *vt* SABOREAR : to savor
paladín *nm, pl* -dines : champion, defender
palanca *nf* 1 : lever, crowbar 2 *fam* : leverage, influence 3 palanca de cambio *or* palanca de velocidad : gearshift
palangana *nf* : washbowl
palanqueta *nf* : jimmy, small crowbar
palco *nm* : box (in a theater or stadium)
palear *vt* 1 : to shovel 2 : to paddle
palenque *nm* 1 ESTACADA : stockade, palisade 2 : arena, ring

paleontología *nf* : paleontology
paleontólogo, -ga *n* : paleontologist
palestino, -na *adj & n* : Palestinian
palestra *nf* : arena ⟨salir a la palestra : to join the fray⟩
paleta *nf* **1** : palette **2** : trowel **3** : spatula **4** : blade, vane **5** : paddle **6** *CA, Mex* : lollipop, Popsicle
paletilla *nf* : shoulder blade
paliar *vt* MITIGAR : to alleviate, to palliate
paliativo¹, -va *adj* : palliative
paliativo² *nm* : palliative
palidecer {53} *vi* : to turn pale
palidez *nf, pl* **-deces** : paleness, pallor
pálido, -da *adj* : pale
palillo *nm* **1** MONDADIENTES : toothpick **2 palillos** *nmpl* : chopsticks **3 palillo de tambor** : drumstick
paliza *nf* : beating, pummeling ⟨darle una paliza a : to beat, to thrash⟩
palma *nf* **1** : palm (of the hand) **2** : palm (tree or leaf) **3 batir palmas** : to clap, to applaud **4 llevarse la palma** *fam* : to take the cake
palmada *nf* **1** : pat **2** : slap **3** : clap
palmarés *nm* : record (of achievements)
palmario, -ria *adj* MANIFIESTO : clear, manifest
palmeado, -da *adj* : webbed
palmear *vt* : to slap on the back — *vi* : to clap, to applaud
palmera *nf* : palm tree
palmo *nm* **1** : span, small amount **2 palmo a palmo** : bit by bit, inch by inch **3 dejar con un palmo de narices** : to disappoint
palmotear *vi* : to applaud
palmoteo *nm* : clapping, applause
palo *nm* **1** : stick, pole, post **2** : shaft, handle ⟨palo de escoba : broomstick⟩ **3** : mast, spar **4** : wood **5** : blow (with a stick) **6** : suit (of cards)
paloma *nf* **1** : pigeon, dove **2 paloma mensajera** : carrier pigeon
palomilla *nf* : moth
palomitas *nfpl* : popcorn
palpable *adj* : palpable, tangible
palpar *vt* : to feel, to touch
palpitación *nf, pl* **-ciones** : palpitation
palpitar *vi* : to palpitate, to throb — **palpitante** *adj*
palta *nf* : avocado
paludismo *nm* MALARIA : malaria
palurdo, -da *n* : boor, yokel, bumpkin
pampa *nf* : pampa
pampeano, -na *adj* : pampean, pampas
pampero → pampeano
pan *nm* **1** : bread **2** : loaf of bread **3** : cake, bar ⟨pan de jabón : bar of soap⟩ **4 pan dulce** *CA, Mex* : traditional pastry **5 pan tostado** : toast **6 ser pan comido** *fam* : to be a piece of cake, to be a cinch
pana *nf* : corduroy
panacea *nf* : panacea
panadería *nf* : bakery, bread shop
panadero, -ra *n* : baker

panal *nm* : honeycomb
panameño, -ña *adj & n* : Panamanian
pancarta *nf* : placard, sign
pancita *nf* *Mex* : tripe
páncreas *nms & pl* : pancreas
panda *nmf* : panda
pandeado, -da *adj* : warped
pandearse *vr* **1** : to warp **2** : to bulge, to sag
pandemonio *or* **pandemónium** *nm* : pandemonium
pandereta *nf* : tambourine
pandero *nm* : tambourine
pandilla *nf* **1** : group, clique **2** : gang
panecito *nm* : roll, bread roll
panegírico¹, -ca *adj* : eulogistic, panegyrical
panegírico² *nm* : eulogy, panegyric
panel *nm* : panel — **panelista** *nmf*
panera *nf* : bread box
panfleto *nm* : pamphlet
pánico *nm* : panic
panorama *nm* **1** VISTA : panorama, view **2** : scene, situation ⟨el panorama nacional : the national scene⟩ **3** PERSPECTIVA : outlook
panorámico, -ca *adj* : panoramic
panqueque *nm* : pancake
pantaletas *nfpl* : panties
pantalla *nf* **1** : screen, monitor **2** : lampshade **3** : fan
pantalón *nm, pl* **-lones** **1** : pants *pl,* trousers *pl* **2 pantalones vaqueros** : jeans **3 pantalones de mezclilla** *Chile, Mex* : jeans **4 pantalones de montar** : jodhpurs
pantano *nm* **1** : swamp, marsh, bayou **2** : reservoir **3** : obstacle, difficulty
pantanoso, -sa *adj* **1** : marshy, swampy **2** : difficult, thorny
panteón *nm, pl* **-teones** **1** CEMENTERIO : cemetery **2** : pantheon, mausoleum
pantera *nf* : panther
pantimedias *nfpl* *Mex* : panty hose
pantomima *nf* : pantomime
pantorrilla *nf* : calf (of the leg)
pantufla *nf* ZAPATILLA : slipper
panza *nf* BARRIGA : belly, paunch
panzón, -zona *adj, mpl* **panzones** : pot-bellied, paunchy
pañal *nm* : diaper
pañería *nf* **1** : cloth, material **2** : fabric store
pañito *nm* : doily
paño *nm* **1** : cloth **2** : rag, dust cloth **3 paño de cocina** : dishcloth **4 paño higiénico** : sanitary napkin
pañuelo *nm* **1** : handkerchief **2** : scarf
papa¹ *nm* : pope
papa² *nf* **1** : potato **2 papa dulce** : sweet potato **3 papas fritas** : potato chips, french fries **4 papas a la francesa** *Mex* : french fries
papá *nm* *fam* **1** : dad, pop **2 papás** *nmpl* : parents, folks
papada *nf* **1** : double chin, jowl **2** : dewlap
papagayo *nm* LORO : parrot

papal *adj* : papal
papalote *nm Mex* : kite
papaya *nf* : papaya
papel *nm* **1** : paper, piece of paper **2** : role, part **3 papel de estaño** : tinfoil **4 papel de empapelar** *or* **papel pintado** : wallpaper **5 papel higiénico** : toilet paper **6 papel de lija** : sandpaper
papeleo *nm* : paperwork, red tape
papelera *nf* : wastebasket
papelería *nf* : stationery store
papelero, -ra *adj* : paper
papeleta *nf* **1** : ballot **2** : ticket, slip
paperas *nfpl* : mumps
papi *nm fam* : daddy, papa
papilla *nf* **1** : pap, mash **2 hacer papilla** : to beat to a pulp
papiro *nm* : papyrus
paquete *nm* BULTO : package, parcel
paquistaní *adj & nmf* : Pakistani
par¹ *adj* : even (in number)
par² *nm* **1** : pair, couple **2** : equal, peer ⟨sin par : matchless, peerless⟩ **3** : par (in golf) **4** : rafter **5 de par en par** : wide open
par³ *nf* **1** : par ⟨por encima de la par : above par⟩ **2 a la par que** : at the same time as, as well as ⟨interesante a la par que instructivo : both interesting and informative⟩
para *prep* **1** : for ⟨para ti : for you⟩ ⟨alta para su edad : tall for her age⟩ ⟨una cita para el lunes : an appointment for Monday⟩ **2** : to, towards ⟨para la derecha : to the right⟩ ⟨van para el río : they're heading towards the river⟩ **3** : to, in order to ⟨lo hace para molestarte : he does it to annoy me⟩ **4** : around, by (a time) ⟨para mañana estarán listos : they'll be ready for tomorrow⟩ **5 para adelante** : forwards **6 para atrás** : backwards **7 para que** : so, so that, in order that ⟨te lo digo para que sepas : I'm telling you so you'll know⟩
parabién *nm, pl* **-bienes** : congratulations *pl*
parábola *nf* **1** : parable **2** : parabola
parabrisas *nms & pl* : windshield
paracaídas *nms & pl* : parachute
paracaidista *nmf* **1** : parachutist **2** : paratrooper
parachoques *nms & pl* : bumper
parada *nf* **1** : stop ⟨parada de autobús : bus stop⟩ **2** : catch, save, parry (in sports) **3** DESFILE : parade
paradero *nm* : whereabouts
paradigma *nm* : paradigm
paradisíaco, -ca *or* **paradisiaco, -ca** *adj* : heavenly
parado, -da *adj* **1** : motionless, idle, stopped **2** : standing (up) **3** : confused, bewildered **4 bien (mal) parado** : in good (bad) shape ⟨salió bien parado : it turned out well for him⟩
paradoja *nf* : paradox
paradójico, -ca *adj* : paradoxical
parafernalia *nf* : paraphernalia

parafina *nf* : paraffin
parafrasear *vt* : to paraphrase
paráfrasis *nfs & pl* : paraphrase
paraguas *nms & pl* : umbrella
paraguayo, -ya *adj & n* : Paraguayan
paraíso *nm* **1** : paradise, heaven **2 paraíso fiscal** : tax shelter
paraje *nm* : spot, place
paralelismo *nm* : parallelism, similarity
paralelo¹, -la *adj* : parallel
paralelo² *nm* : parallel
paralelogramo *nm* : parallelogram
parálisis *nfs & pl* **1** : paralysis **2** : standstill **3 parálisis cerebral** : cerebral palsy
paralítico, -ca *adj & n* : paralytic
paralizar {21} *vt* **1** : to paralyze **2** : to bring to a standstill — **paralizarse** *vr*
parámetro *nm* : parameter
páramo *nm* : barren plateau, moor
parangón *nm, pl* **-gones** **1** : comparison **2 sin** ~ : incomparable
paraninfo *nm* : auditorium, assembly hall
paranoia *nf* : paranoia
paranoico, -ca *adj & n* : paranoid
parapeto *nm* : parapet, rampart
parapléjico, -ca *adj & n* : paraplegic
parar *vt* **1** DETENER : to stop **2** : to stand, to prop — *vi* **1** CESAR : to stop **2** : to stay, to put up **3 ir a parar** : to end up, to wind up — **pararse** *vr* **1** : to stop **2** ATASCARSE : to stall (out) **3** : to stand up, to get up
pararrayos *nms & pl* : lightning rod
parasitario, -ria *adj* : parasitic
parasitismo *nm* : parasitism
parásito *nm* : parasite
parasol *nm* SOMBRILLA : parasol
parcela *nf* : parcel, tract of land
parcelar *vt* : to parcel (land)
parchar *vt* : to patch, to patch up
parche *nm* : patch
parcial *adj* : partial — **parcialmente** *adv*
parcialidad *nf* : partiality, bias
parco, -ca *adj* **1** : sparing, frugal **2** : moderate, temperate
pardo, -da *adj* : brownish grey
pardusco → pardo
parecer¹ {53} *vi* **1** : to seem, to look, to appear to be ⟨parece bien fácil : it looks very easy⟩ ⟨así parece : so it seems⟩ ⟨pareces una princesa : you look like a princess⟩ **2** : to think, to have an opinion ⟨me parece que sí : I think so⟩ **3** : to like, to be in agreement ⟨si te parece : if you like, if it's all right with you⟩ — **parecerse** *vr* ~ **a** : to resemble
parecer² *nm* **1** OPINIÓN : opinion **2** ASPECTO : appearance ⟨al parecer : apparently⟩
parecido¹, -da *adj* **1** : similar, alike **2 bien parecido** : good-looking
parecido² *nm* : resemblance, similarity
pared *nf* : wall
pareja *nf* **1** : couple, pair **2** : partner, mate

parejo, -ja *adj* **1** : even, smooth, level **2** : equal, similar

parentela *nf* : relations *pl*, kinfolk

parentesco *nm* : relationship, kinship

paréntesis *nms & pl* **1** : parenthesis **2** : digression

parentético, -ca *adj* : parenthetic, parenthetical

paria *nmf* : pariah, outcast

paridad *nf* : parity, equality

pariente *nmf* : relative, relation

parir *vi* : to give birth — *vt* : to give birth to, to bear

parking *nm* : parking lot

parlamentar *vi* : to talk, to parley

parlamentario¹, -ria *adj* : parliamentary

parlamentario², -ria *n* : member of parliament

parlamento *nm* **1** : parliament **2** : negotiations *pl*, talks *pl*

parlanchín¹, -china *adj, mpl* **-chines** : chatty, talkative

parlanchín², -china *n, mpl* **-chines** : chatterbox

parlante *nm* ALTOPARLANTE : loudspeaker

parlotear *vi fam* : to gab, to chat, to prattle

parloteo *nm fam* : prattle, chatter

paro *nm* **1** HUELGA : strike **2** : stoppage, stopping **3 paro forzoso** : layoff

parodia *nf* : parody

parodiar *vt* : to parody

paroxismo *nm* **1** : fit, paroxysm **2** : peak, height ⟨llevar al paroxismo : to carry to the extreme⟩

parpadear *vi* **1** : to blink **2** : to flicker

parpadeo *nm* **1** : blink, blinking **2** : flickering

párpado *nm* : eyelid

parque *nm* **1** : park **2 parque de atracciones** : amusement park

parquear *vt* : to park — **parquearse** *vr*

parqueo *nm* : parking

parquet *or* **parqué** *nm* : parquet

parquímetro *nm* : parking meter

parra *nf* : vine, grapevine

párrafo *nm* : paragraph

parranda *nf fam* : party, spree

parrilla *nf* **1** : broiler, grill **2** : grate

parrillada *nf* BARBACOA : barbecue

párroco *nm* : parish priest

parroquia *nf* **1** : parish **2** : parish church **3** : customers *pl*, clientele

parroquial *adj* : parochial

parroquiano, -na *nm* **1** : parishioner **2** : customer, patron

parsimonia *nf* **1** : calm **2** : parsimony, thrift

parsimonioso, -sa *adj* **1** : calm, unhurried **2** : parsimonious, thrifty

parte¹ *nm* : report, dispatch

parte² *nf* **1** : part, share **2** : part, place ⟨en alguna parte : somewhere⟩ ⟨por todas partes : everywhere⟩ **3** : party (in negotiations, etc.) **4 de parte de** : on behalf of **5 ¿de parte de quién?** : may I ask who's calling? **6 tomar parte** : to take part

partero, -ra *n* : midwife

partición *nf, pl* **-ciones** : division, sharing

participación *nf, pl* **-ciones** **1** : participation **2** : share, interest **3** : announcement, notice

participante *nmf* **1** : participant **2** : competitor, entrant

participar *vi* **1** : to participate, to take part **2 — en** : to have a share in — *vt* : to announce, to notify

partícipe *nmf* : participant

participio *nm* : participle

partícula *nf* : particle

particular¹ *adj* **1** : particular, specific **2** : private, personal **3** : special, unique

particular² *nm* **1** : matter, detail **2** : individual

particularidad *nf* : characteristic, peculiarity

particularizar {21} *vt* **1** : to distinguish, to characterize **2** : to specify

partida *nf* **1** : departure **2** : item, entry **3** : certificate ⟨partida de nacimiento : birth certificate⟩ **4** : game, match, hand **5** : party, group

partidario, -ria *n* : follower, supporter

partido *nm* **1** : (political) party **2** : game, match ⟨partido de futbol : soccer game⟩ **3** APOYO : support, following **4** PROVECHO : profit, advantage ⟨sacar partido de : to profit from⟩

partir *vt* **1** : to cut, to split **2** : to break, to crack **3** : to share (out), to divide — *vi* **1** : to leave, to depart **2 — de** : to start from **3 a partir de** : as of, from ⟨a partir de hoy : as of today⟩ — **partirse** *vr* **1** : to smash, to split open **2** : to chap

partisano, -na *adj & n* : partisan

partitura *nf* : (musical) score

parto *nm* **1** : childbirth, delivery, labor ⟨estar de parto : to be in labor⟩ **2** : product, creation, brainchild

parvulario *nm* : nursery school

párvulo, -la *n* : toddler, preschooler

pasa *nf* **1** : raisin **2 pasa de Corinto** : currant

pasable *adj* : passable, tolerable — **pasablemente** *adv*

pasada *nf* **1** : passage, passing **2** : pass, wipe, coat (of paint) **3 de ~** : in passing **4 mala pasada** : dirty trick

pasadizo *nm* : passageway, corridor

pasado¹, -da *adj* **1** : past ⟨el año pasado : last year⟩ ⟨pasado mañana : the day after tomorrow⟩ ⟨pasadas las siete : after seven o'clock⟩ **2** : stale, bad, overripe **3** : old-fashioned, out-of-date **4** : overripe, slightly spoiled

pasado² *nm* : past

pasador *nm* **1** : bolt, latch **2** : barrette **3** *Mex* : bobby pin

pasaje *nm* **1** : ticket (for travel) **2** TARIFA : fare **3** : passageway **4** : passengers *pl*

pasajero¹, -ra *adj* : passing, fleeting

pasajero², -ra *n* : passenger

pasamanos *nms & pl* 1 : handrail 2 : bannister

pasante *nmf* : assistant

pasaporte *nm* : passport

pasar *vi* 1 : to pass, to go by, to come by 2 : to come in, to enter ⟨¿se puede pasar? : may we come in?⟩ 3 : to happen ⟨¿qué pasa? : what's happening?, what's going on?⟩ 4 : to manage, to get by 5 : to be over, to end 6 ~ **de** : to exceed, to go beyond 7 ~ **por** : to pretend to be — *vt* 1 : to pass, to give ⟨¿me pasas la sal? : would you pass me the salt?⟩ 2 : to pass (a test) 3 : to go over, to cross 4 : to spend (time) 5 : to tolerate 6 : to go through, to suffer 7 : to show (a movie, etc.) 8 : to overtake, to pass, to surpass 9 : to pass over, to wipe up 10 **pasarlo bien** *or* **pasarla bien** : to have a good time 11 **pasarlo mal** *or* **pasarla mal** : to have a bad time, to have a hard time 12 **pasar por alto** : to overlook, to omit — **pasarse** *vr* 1 : to move, to pass, to go away 2 : to slip one's mind, to forget 3 : to go too far

pasarela *nf* 1 : gangplank 2 : footbridge 3 : runway, catwalk

pasatiempo *nm* : pastime, hobby

Pascua *nf* 1 : Easter 2 : Passover 3 : Christmas 4 **Pascuas** *nfpl* : Christmas season

pase *nm* 1 **PERMISO** : pass, permit 2 **pase de abordar** *Mex* : boarding pass

pasear *vi* : to take a walk, to go for a ride — *vt* 1 : to take for a walk 2 : to parade around, to show off — **pasearse** *vr* : to walk around

paseo *nm* 1 : walk, stroll 2 : ride 3 **EXCURSIÓN** : outing, trip 4 : avenue, walk 5 *or* **paseo marítimo** : boardwalk

pasiflora *nf* : passionflower

pasillo *nm* **CORREDOR** : hallway, corridor, aisle

pasión *nf, pl* **pasiones** : passion

pasional *adj* : passionate ⟨crimen pasional : crime of passion⟩

pasionaria → **pasiflora**

pasivo¹, -va *adj* : passive — **pasivamente** *adv*

pasivo² *nm* 1 : liability ⟨activos y pasivos : assets and liabilities⟩ 2 : debit side (of an account)

pasmado, -da *adj* : stunned, flabbergasted

pasmar *vt* : to amaze, to stun — **pasmarse** *vr*

pasmo *nm* 1 : shock, astonishment 2 : wonder, marvel

pasmoso, -sa *adj* : incredible, amazing — **pasmosamente** *adv*

paso¹, -sa *adj* : dried ⟨ciruela pasa : prune⟩

paso² *nm* 1 : passage, passing ⟨de paso : in passing, on the way⟩ 2 : way, path ⟨abrirse paso : to make one's way⟩ 3 : crossing ⟨paso de peatones : crosswalk⟩ ⟨paso a desnivel : underpass⟩ ⟨paso elevado : overpass⟩ 4 : step

⟨paso a paso : step by step⟩ 5 : pace, gait ⟨a buen paso : quickly, at a good rate⟩

pasta *nf* 1 : paste ⟨pasta de dientes *or* pasta dental : toothpaste⟩ 2 : pasta 3 : pastry dough 4 **libro en pasta dura** : hardcover book 5 **tener pasta de** : to have the makings of

pastar *vi* : to graze — *vt* : to put to pasture

pastel¹ *adj* : pastel

pastel² *nm* 1 : cake ⟨pastel de cumpleaños : birthday cake⟩ 2 : pie; turnover 3 : pastel

pastelería *nf* : pastry shop

pasteurización *nf, pl* **-ciones** : pasteurization

pasteurizar {21} *vt* : to pasteurize

pastilla *nf* 1 **COMPRIMIDO, PÍLDORA** : pill, tablet 2 : lozenge ⟨pastilla para la tos : cough drop⟩ 3 : cake (of soap), bar (of chocolate)

pastizal *nm* : pasture, grazing land

pasto *nm* 1 : pasture 2 **HIERBA** : grass, lawn

pastor, -tora *n* 1 : shepherd, shepherdess *f* 2 : minister, pastor

pastoral *adj & nf* : pastoral

pastorear *vt* : to shepherd, to tend

pastorela *nf* 1 : pastoral, pastourelle 2 *Mex* : a traditional Christmas play

pastoso, -sa *adj* 1 : pasty, doughy 2 : smooth, mellow (of sounds)

pata *nf* 1 : paw, leg (of an animal) 2 : foot, leg (of furniture) 3 **patas de gallo** : crow's-feet 4 **meter la pata** *fam* : to put one's foot in it, to make a blunder

patada *nf* 1 **PUNTAPIÉ** : kick 2 : stamp (of the foot)

patalear *vi* 1 : to kick 2 : to stamp one's feet

pataleta *nf fam* : tantrum

patán¹ *adj, pl* **patanes** : boorish, crude

patán² *nm, pl* **patanes** : boor, lout

patata *nf Spain* : potato

pateador, -dora *n* : kicker (in sports)

patear *vt* : to kick — *vi* : to stamp one's foot

patentar *vt* : to patent

patente¹ *adj* **EVIDENTE** : obvious, patent — **patentemente** *adv*

patente² *nf* : patent

paternal *adj* : fatherly, paternal

paternidad *nf* 1 : fatherhood, paternity 2 : parenthood 3 : authorship

paterno, -na *adj* : paternal ⟨abuela paterna : paternal grandmother⟩

patético, -ca *adj* : pathetic, moving

patetismo *nm* : pathos

patíbulo *nm* : gallows, scaffold

patillas *nfpl* : sideburns

patín *nm, pl* **patines** : skate ⟨patín de ruedas : roller skate⟩

patinador, -dora *n* : skater

patinaje *nm* : skating

patinar *vi* 1 : to skate 2 : to skid, to slip 3 *fam* : to slip up, to blunder

patinazo *nm* 1 : skid 2 *fam* : blunder, slipup

patineta *nf* **1** : scooter **2** : skateboard
patinete *nm* : scooter
patio *nm* **1** : courtyard, patio **2 patio de recreo** : playground
patito, -ta *n* : duckling
pato, -ta *n* **1** : duck **2 pato real** : mallard **3 pagar el pato** *fam* : to take the blame
patología *nf* : pathology
patológico, -ca *adj* : pathological
patólogo, -ga *n* : pathologist
patraña *nf* : tall tale, humbug, nonsense
patria *nf* : native land
patriarca *nm* : patriarch — **patriarcal** *adj*
patriarcado *nm* : patriarchy
patrimonio *nm* : patrimony, legacy
patrio, -tria *adj* **1** : native, home ⟨suelo patrio : native soil⟩ **2** : paternal
patriota[1] *adj* : patriotic
patriota[2] *nmf* : patriot
patriotería *nf* : jingoism, chauvinism
patriotero[1]**, -ra** *adj* : jingoistic, chauvinistic
patriotero[2]**, -ra** *n* : jingoist, chauvinist
patriótico, -ca *adj* : patriotic
patriotismo *nm* : patriotism
patrocinador, -dora *n* : sponsor, patron
patrocinar *vt* : to sponsor
patrocinio *nm* : sponsorship, patronage
patrón[1]**, -trona** *n, mpl* **patrones 1 JEFE** : boss **2** : patron saint
patrón[2] *nm, pl* **patrones 1** : standard **2** : pattern (in sewing)
patronal *adj* **1** : management, employers' ⟨sindicato patronal : employers' association⟩ **2** : pertaining to a patron saint ⟨fiesta patronal : patron saint's day⟩
patronato *nm* **1** : board, council **2** : foundation, trust
patrono, -na *n* **1** : employer **2** : patron saint
patrulla *nf* **1** : patrol **2** : police car, cruiser
patrullar *v* : to patrol
patrullero *nm* **1** : police car **2** : patrol boat
paulatino, -na *adj* : gradual
paupérrimo, -ma *adj* : destitute, poverty-stricken
pausa *nf* : pause, break
pausado[1] *adv* : slowly, deliberately ⟨habla más pausado : speak more slowly⟩
pausado[2]**, -da** *adj* : slow, deliberate — **pausadamente** *adv*
pauta *nf* **1** : rule, guideline **2** : lines *pl* (on paper)
pava *nf Arg, Bol, Chile* : kettle
pavimentar *vt* : pave
pavimento *nm* : pavement
pavo, -va *n* **1** : turkey **2 pavo real** : peacock **3 comer pavo** : to be a wallflower
pavón *nm, pl* **pavones** : peacock
pavonearse *vr* : to strut, to swagger
pavoneo *nm* : strut, swagger
pavor *nm* **TERROR** : dread, terror

pavoroso, -sa *adj* **ATERRADOR** : dreadful, terrifying
payasada *nf* **BUFONADA** : antic, buffoonery
payasear *vi* : to clown around
payaso, -sa *n* : clown
paz *nf, pl* **paces 1** : peace **2 dejar en paz** : to leave alone **3 hacer las paces** : to make up, to reconcile
pazca, etc. → **pacer**
PC *nmf* : PC, personal computer
peaje *nm* : toll
peatón *nm, pl* **-tones** : pedestrian
peatonal *adj* : pedestrian
peca *nf* : freckle
pecado *nm* : sin
pecador[1]**, -dora** *adj* : sinful, sinning
pecador[2]**, -dora** *n* : sinner
pecaminoso, -sa *adj* : sinful
pecar {72} *vi* **1** : to sin **2 ∼ de** : to be too much (something) ⟨no pecan de amabilidad : they're not overly friendly⟩
pécari *or* **pecarí** *nm* : peccary
pececillo *nm* : small fish
pecera *nf* : fishbowl, fish tank
pecho *nm* **1** : chest **2 SENO** : breast, bosom **3** : heart, courage **4 dar el pecho** : to breast-feed **5 tomar a pecho** : to take to heart
pechuga *nf* : breast (of fowl)
pecoso, -sa *adj* : freckled
pectoral *adj* : pectoral
peculado *nm* : embezzlement
peculiar *adj* **1 CARACTERÍSTICO** : particular, characteristic **2 RARO** : peculiar, uncommon
peculiaridad *nf* : peculiarity
pecuniario, -ria *adj* : pecuniary
pedagogía *nf* : pedagogy
pedagógico, -ca *adj* : pedagogic, pedagogical
pedagogo, -ga *n* : educator, pedagogue
pedal *nm* : pedal
pedalear *vi* : to pedal
pedante[1] *adj* : pedantic
pedante[2] *nmf* : pedant
pedantería *nf* : pedantry
pedazo *nm* **TROZO** : piece, bit, chunk ⟨caerse a pedazos : to fall to pieces⟩ ⟨hacer pedazos : to tear into shreds, to smash to pieces⟩
pedernal *nm* : flint
pedestal *nm* : pedestal
pedestre *adj* : commonplace, pedestrian
pediatra *nmf* : pediatrician
pediatría *nf* : pediatrics
pediátrico, -ca *adj* : pediatric
pedido *nm* **1** : order (of merchandise) **2** : request
pedigrí *nm* : pedigree
pedir {54} *vt* **1** : to ask for, to request ⟨le pedí un préstamo a Claudia : I asked Claudia for a loan⟩ **2** : to order (food, merchandise) **3 pedir disculpas** *or* **pedir perdón** : to apologize — *vi* **1** : to order **2** : to beg

pedrada *nf* 1 : blow (with a rock or stone) ⟨la ventana se quebró de una pedrada : the window was broken by a rock⟩ 2 *fam* : cutting remark, dig
pedregal *nm* : rocky ground
pedregoso, -sa *adj* : rocky, stony
pedrera *nf* CANTERA : quarry
pedrería *nf* : precious stones *pl*, gems *pl*
pegado, -da *adj* 1 : glued, stuck, stuck together 2 ~ a : right next to
pegajoso, -sa *adj* 1 : sticky, gluey 2 : catchy ⟨una tonada pegajosa : a catchy tune⟩
pegamento *nm* : adhesive, glue
pegar {52} *vt* 1 : to glue, to stick, to paste 2 : to attach, to sew on 3 : to infect with, to give ⟨me pegó el resfriado : he gave me his cold⟩ 4 GOLPEAR : to hit, to deal, to strike ⟨me pegaron un puntapié : they gave me a kick⟩ 5 : to give (out with) ⟨pegó un grito : she let out a yell⟩ — *vi* 1 : to adhere, to stick 2 ~ en : to hit, to strike (against) 3 ~ con : to match, to go with — **pegarse** *vr* 1 GOLPEARSE : to hit oneself, to hit each other 2 : to stick, to take hold 3 : to be contagious 4 *fam* : to tag along, to stick around
pegote *nm* 1 : sticky mess 2 *Mex* : sticker, adhesive label
pegue, etc. → pegar
peinado *nm* : hairstyle, hairdo
peinador, -dora *n* : hairdresser
peinar *vt* : to comb — **peinarse** *vr*
peine *nm* : comb
peineta *nf* : ornamental comb
peladez *nf, pl* **-deces** *Mex fam* : obscenity, bad language
pelado, -da *adj* 1 : bald, hairless 2 : peeled 3 : bare, barren 4 : broke, penniless 5 *Mex fam* : coarse, crude
pelador *nm* : peeler
pelagra *nf* : pellagra
pelaje *nm* : coat (of an animal), fur
pelar *vt* 1 : to peel, to shell 2 : to skin 3 : to pluck 4 : to remove hair from 5 *fam* : to clean out (of money) — **pelarse** *vr* 1 : to peel 2 *fam* : to get a haircut 3 *Mex fam* : to split, to leave
peldaño *nm* 1 : step, stair 2 : rung
pelea *nf* 1 LUCHA : fight 2 : quarrel
pelear *vi* 1 LUCHA : to fight 2 DISPUTAR : to quarrel — **pelearse** *vr*
peleón, -leona *adj, mpl* **-ones** *Spain* : quarrelsome, argumentative
peleonero, -ra *adj Mex* : quarrelsome
peletería *nf* 1 : fur shop 2 : fur trade
peletero, -ra *n* : furrier
peliagudo, -da *adj* : tricky, difficult, ticklish
pelícano *nm* : pelican
película *nf* 1 : movie, film 2 : (photographic) film 3 : thin covering, layer
peligrar *vi* : to be in danger
peligro *nm* 1 : danger, peril 2 : risk ⟨correr peligro de : to run the risk of⟩
peligroso, -sa *adj* : dangerous, hazardous

pelirrojo[1], -ja *adj* : red-haired, redheaded
pelirrojo[2], -ja *n* : redhead
pellejo *nm* 1 : hide, skin 2 salvar el pellejo : to save one's neck
pellizcar {72} *vt* 1 : to pinch 2 : to nibble on
pellizco *nm* : pinch
pelo *nm* 1 : hair 2 : fur 3 : pile, nap 4 a pelo : bareback 5 con pelos y señales : in great detail 6 no tener pelos en la lengua : to not mince words, to be blunt 7 tomarle el pelo a alguien : to tease someone, to pull someone's leg
pelón, -lona *adj, mpl* **pelones** 1 : bald 2 *fam* : broke 3 *Mex fam* : tough, difficult
pelota *nf* 1 : ball 2 *fam* : head 3 en pelotas *fam* : naked 4 pelota vasca : jai alai 5 pasar la pelota *fam* : to pass the buck
pelotón *nm, pl* **-tones** : squad, detachment
peltre *nm* : pewter
peluca *nf* : wig
peluche *nm* : plush (fabric)
peludo, -da *adj* : hairy, shaggy, bushy
peluquería *nf* 1 : hairdresser's, barber shop 2 : hairdressing
peluquero, -ra *n* : barber, hairdresser
peluquín *nm, pl* **-quines** TUPÉ : hairpiece, toupee
pelusa *nf* : lint, fuzz
pélvico, -ca *adj* : pelvic
pelvis *nfs & pl* : pelvis
pena *nf* 1 CASTIGO : punishment, penalty ⟨pena de muerte : death penalty⟩ 2 AFLICCIÓN : sorrow, grief ⟨morir de pena : to die of a broken heart⟩ ⟨qué pena! : what a shame!, how sad!⟩ 3 DOLOR : pain, suffering 4 DIFICULTAD : difficulty, trouble ⟨a duras penas : with great difficulty⟩ 5 VERGÜENZA : shame, embarrassment 6 valer la pena : to be worthwhile
penacho *nm* 1 : crest, tuft 2 : plume (of feathers)
penal[1] *adj* : penal
penal[2] *nm* CÁRCEL : prison, penitentiary
penalidad *nf* 1 : hardship 2 : penalty, punishment
penalizar {21} *vt* : to penalize
penalty *nm* : penalty (in sports)
penar *vt* : to punish, to penalize — *vi* : to suffer, to grieve
pendenciero, -ra *adj* : argumentative, quarrelsome
pender *vi* 1 : to hang 2 : to be pending
pendiente[1] *adj* 1 : pending 2 estar pendiente de : to be watchful of, to be on the lookout for
pendiente[2] *nm Spain* : earring
pendiente[3] *nf* : slope, incline
pendón *nm, pl* **pendones** : banner
péndulo *nm* : pendulum
pene *nm* : penis

penetración *nf, pl* **-ciones 1** : penetration **2** : insight

penetrante *adj* **1** : penetrating, piercing **2** : sharp, acute **3** : deep (of a wound)

penetrar *vi* **1** : to penetrate, to sink in **2** ~ **por** *or* ~ **en** : to pierce, to go in, to enter into ⟨el frío penetra por la ventana : the cold comes right in through the window⟩ — *vt* **1** : to penetrate, to permeate **2** : to pierce ⟨el dolor penetró su corazón : sorrow pierced her heart⟩ **3** : to fathom, to understand

penicilina *nf* : penicillin

península *nf* : peninsula — **peninsular** *adj*

penitencia *nf* : penance, penitence

penitenciaría *nf* : penitentiary

penitente *adj & nmf* : penitent

penol *nm* : yardarm

penoso, -sa *adj* **1** : painful, distressing **2** : difficult, arduous **3** : shy, bashful

pensado, -da *adj* **1 bien pensado** : well thought-out **2 en el momento menos pensado** : when least expected **3 poco pensado** : badly thought-out **4 mal pensado** : evil-minded

pensador, -dora *n* : thinker

pensamiento *nm* **1** : thought **2** : thinking **3** : pansy

pensar {55} *vi* **1** : to think **2** ~ **en** : to think about — *vt* **1** : to think **2** : to think about **3** : to intend, to plan on — **pensarse** *vr* : to think over

pensativo, -va *adj* : pensive, thoughtful

pensión *nf, pl* **pensiones 1** JUBILACIÓN : pension **2** : boarding house **3 pensión alimenticia** : alimony

pensionado, -da *n* → **pensionista**

pensionista *nmf* **1** JUBILADO : pensioner, retiree **2** : boarder, lodger

pentágono *nm* : pentagon — **pentagonal** *adj*

pentagrama *nm* : staff (in music)

penúltimo, -ma *adj* : next to last, penultimate

penumbra *nf* : semidarkness

penuria *nf* **1** ESCASEZ : shortage, scarcity **2** : poverty

peña *nf* : rock, crag

peñasco *nm* : crag, large rock

peñón → **peñasco**

peón *nm, pl* **peones 1** : laborer, peon **2** : pawn (in chess)

peonía *nf* : peony

peor[1] *adv* **1** (*comparative of* **mal**) : worse ⟨se llevan peor que antes : they get along worse than before⟩ **2** (*superlative of* **mal**) : worst ⟨me fue peor que a nadie : I did the worst of all⟩

peor[2] *adj* **1** (*comparative of* **malo**) : worse ⟨es peor que el original : it's worse than the original⟩ **2** (*superlative of* **malo**) : worst ⟨el peor de todos : the worst of all⟩

pepa *nf* : seed, pit (of a fruit)

pepenador, -dora *n CA, Mex* : scavenger

pepenar *vt CA, Mex* : to scavenge, to scrounge

pepinillo *nm* : pickle, gherkin

pepino *nm* : cucumber

pepita *nf* **1** : seed, pip **2** : nugget **3** *Mex* : dried pumpkin seed

peque, etc. → **pecar**

pequeñez *nf, pl* **-ñeces 1** : smallness **2** : trifle, triviality **3 pequeñez de espíritu** : pettiness

pequeño[1], **-ña** *adj* **1** : small, little ⟨un libro pequeño : a small book⟩ **2** : young **3** BAJO : short

pequeño[2], **-ña** *n* : child, little one

pera *nf* : pear

peraltar *vt* : to bank (a road)

perca *nf* : perch (fish)

percal *nm* : percale

percance *nm* : mishap, misfortune

percatarse *vr* ~ **de** : to notice, to become aware of

percebe *nm* : barnacle

percepción *nf, pl* **-ciones 1** : perception **2** : idea, notion **3** COBRO : receipt (of payment), collection

perceptible *adj* : perceptible, noticeable — **perceptiblemente** *adv*

percha *nf* **1** : perch **2** : coat hanger **3** : coatrack, coat hook

perchero *nm* : coatrack

percibir *vt* **1** : to perceive, to notice, to sense **2** : to earn, to draw (a salary)

percudido, -da *adj* : grimy

percudir *vt* : to make grimy — **percudirse** *vr*

percusión *nf, pl* **-siones** : percussion

percusor *or* **percutor** *nm* : hammer (of a firearm)

perdedor[1], **-dora** *adj* : losing

perdedor[2], **-dora** *n* : loser

perder {56} *vt* **1** : to lose **2** : to miss ⟨perdimos la oportunidad : we missed the opportunity⟩ **3** : to waste (time) — *vi* : to lose — **perderse** *vr* EXTRAVIARSE : to get lost, to stray

perdición *nf, pl* **-ciones** : perdition, damnation

pérdida *nf* **1** : loss **2 pérdida de tiempo** : waste of time

perdidamente *adv* : hopelessly

perdido, -da *adj* **1** : lost **2** : inveterate, incorrigible ⟨es un caso perdido : he's a hopeless case⟩ **3** : in trouble, done for **4 de** ~ *Mex fam* : at least

perdigón *nm, pl* **-gones** : shot, pellet

perdiz *nf, pl* **perdices** : partridge

perdón[1] *nm, pl* **perdones** : forgiveness, pardon

perdón[2] *interj* : excuse me!, sorry!

perdonable *adj* : forgivable

perdonar *vt* **1** DISCULPAR : to forgive, to pardon **2** : to exempt, to excuse

perdurable *adj* : lasting

perdurar *vi* : to last, to endure, to survive

perecedero, -ra *adj* : perishable

perecer {53} *vi* : to perish, to die

peregrinación *nf, pl* **-ciones** : pilgrimage

peregrinaje *nm* → **peregrinación**

peregrino¹, -na *adj* 1 : unusual, odd 2 MIGRATORIO : migratory
peregrino², -na *n* : pilgrim
perejil *nm* : parsley
perenne *adj* : perennial
perentorio, -ria *adj* 1 : peremptory 2 URGENTE : urgent 3 FIJO : fixed, set
pereza *nf* FLOJERA, HOLGAZANERÍA : laziness, idleness
perezoso¹, -sa *adj* FLOJO, HOLGAZÁN : lazy
perezoso² *nm* : sloth (animal)
perfección *nf, pl* **-ciones** : perfection
perfeccionamiento *nm* : perfecting, refinement
perfeccionar *vt* : to perfect, to refine
perfeccionismo *nm* : perfectionism
perfeccionista *nmf* : perfectionist
perfecto, -ta *adj* : perfect — **perfectamente** *adv*
perfidia *nf* : perfidy, treachery
pérfido, -da *adj* : perfidious
perfil *nm* 1 : profile 2 **de ~** : sideways, from the side 3 **perfiles** *nmpl* RASGOS : features, characteristics
perfilar *vt* : to outline, to define — **perfilarse** *vr* 1 : to be outlined, to be silhouetted 2 : to take shape
perforación *nf, pl* **-ciones** 1 : perforation 2 : drilling
perforadora *nf* 1 : hole punch (for paper) 2 : drill (in mining, etc.)
perforar *vt* 1 : to perforate, to pierce 2 : to drill, to bore
perfumar *vt* : to perfume, to scent — **perfumarse** *vr*
perfume *nm* : perfume, scent
pergamino *nm* : parchment
pérgola *nf* : pergola, arbor
pericia *nf* : skill, expertise
pericial *adj* : expert ⟨testigo pericial : expert witness⟩
perico *nm* COTORRA : small parrot
periferia *nf* : periphery
periférico¹, -ca *adj* : peripheral
periférico² *nm* 1 CA, Mex : beltway 2 : peripheral
perilla *nf* 1 : goatee 2 : pommel (on a saddle) 3 Col, Mex : knob, handle 4 **perilla de la oreja** : earlobe 5 **de perillas** *fam* : handy, just right
perímetro *nm* : perimeter
periódico¹, -ca *adj* : periodic — **periódicamente** *adv*
periódico² *nm* DIARIO : newspaper
periodismo *nm* : journalism
periodista *nmf* : journalist
periodístico, -ca *adj* : journalistic, news
período *or* **periodo** *nm* : period
peripecia *nf* VICISITUD : vicissitude, reversal ⟨las peripecias de su carrera : the ups and downs of her career⟩
periquito *nm* 1 : parakeet 2 **periquito australiano** : budgerigar
periscopio *nm* : periscope
perito, -ta *adj & n* : expert
perjudicar {72} *vt* : to harm, to be detrimental to

perjudicial *adj* : harmful, detrimental
perjuicio *nm* 1 : harm, damage 2 **en perjuicio de** : to the detriment of
perjurar *vi* : to perjure oneself
perjurio *nm* : perjury
perjuro, -ra *n* : perjurer
perla *nf* 1 : pearl 2 **de perlas** *fam* : wonderfully ⟨me viene de perlas : it suits me just fine⟩
permanecer {53} *vi* 1 QUEDARSE : to remain, to stay 2 SEGUIR : to remain, to continue to be
permanencia *nf* 1 : permanence, continuance 2 ESTANCIA : stay
permanente¹ *adj* 1 : permanent 2 : constant — **permanentemente** *adv*
permanente² *nf* : permanent (wave)
permeabilidad *nf* : permeability
permeable *adj* : permeable
permisible *adj* : permissible, allowable
permisividad *nf* : permissiveness
permisivo, -va *adj* : permissive
permiso *nm* 1 : permission 2 : permit, license 3 : leave, furlough 4 **con ~** : excuse me, pardon me
permitir *vt* : to permit, to allow — **permitirse** *vr*
permuta *nf* : exchange
permutar *vt* INTERCAMBIAR : to exchange
pernicioso, -sa *adj* : pernicious, destructive
pernil *nm* 1 : haunch (of an animal) 2 : leg (of meat), ham 3 : trouser leg
perno *nm* : bolt, pin
pernoctar *vi* : to stay overnight, to spend the night
pero¹ *nm* 1 : fault, defect ⟨ponerle peros a : to find fault with⟩ 2 : objection
pero² *conj* : but
perogrullada *nf* : truism, platitude, cliché
peroné *nm* : fibula
perorar *vi* : to deliver a speech
perorata *nf* : oration, long-winded speech
peróxido *nm* : peroxide
perpendicular *adj & nf* : perpendicular
perpetrar *vt* : to perpetrate
perpetuar {3} *vt* ETERNIZAR : to perpetuate
perpetuidad *nf* : perpetuity
perpetuo, -tua *adj* : perpetual — **perpetuamente** *adv*
perplejidad *nf* : perplexity
perplejo, -ja *adj* : perplexed, puzzled
perrada *nf fam* : dirty trick
perrera *nf* : kennel, dog pound
perrero, -ra *n* : dogcatcher
perrito, -ta *n* CACHORRO : puppy, small dog
perro, -rra *n* 1 : dog, bitch *f* 2 **perro caliente** : hot dog 3 **perro salchicha** : dachshund 4 **perro faldero** : lapdog 5 **perro cobrador** : retriever
persa¹ *adj & nmf* : Persian
persa² *nm* : Persian (language)

persecución *nf, pl* **-ciones** 1 : pursuit, chase 2 : persecution
perseguidor, -dora *n* 1 : pursuer 2 : persecutor
perseguir {75} *vt* 1 : to pursue, to chase 2 : to persecute 3 : to pester, to annoy
perseverancia *nf* : perseverance
perseverar *vi* : to persevere
persiana *nf* : blind, venetian blind
persignarse *vr* SANTIGUARSE : to cross oneself, to make the sign of the cross
persistir *vi* : to persist — **persistencia** *nf* — **persistente** *adj*
persona *nf* : person
personaje *nm* 1 : character (in drama or literature) 2 : personage, celebrity
personal[1] *adj* : personal — **personalmente** *adv*
personal[2] *nm* : personnel, staff
personalidad *nf* : personality
personalizar {21} *vt* : to personalize
personificar {72} *vi* : to personify — **personificación** *nf*
perspectiva *nf* 1 : perspective, view 2 : prospect, outlook
perspicacia *nf* : shrewdness, perspicacity, insight
perspicaz *adj, pl* **-caces** : shrewd, perspicacious
persuadir *vt* : to persuade — **persuadirse** *vr* : to become convinced
persuasión *nf, pl* **-siones** : persuasion
persuasivo, -va *adj* : persuasive
pertenecer {53} *vi* : to belong
perteneciente *adj* ~ **a** : belonging to
pertenencia *nf* 1 : membership 2 : ownership 3 **pertenencias** *nfpl* : belongings, possessions
pértiga *nf* GARROCHA : pole ⟨salto de pértiga : pole vault⟩
pertinaz *adj, pl* **-naces** 1 OBSTINADO : obstinate 2 PERSISTENTE : persistent
pertinencia *nf* : pertinence, relevance — **pertinente** *adj*
pertrechos *nmpl* : equipment, gear
perturbación *nf, pl* **-ciones** : disturbance, disruption
perturbador, -dora *adj* 1 INQUIETANTE : disturbing, troubling 2 : disruptive
perturbar *vt* 1 : to disturb, to trouble 2 : to disrupt
peruano, -na *adj & n* : Peruvian
perversidad *nf* : perversity, depravity
perversión *nf, pl* **-siones** : perversion
perverso, -sa *adj* : wicked, depraved
pervertido[1], **-da** *adj* DEPRAVADO : perverted, depraved
pervertido[2], **-da** *n* : pervert
pervertir {76} *vt* : to pervert, to corrupt
pesa *nf* 1 : weight 2 **levantamiento de pesas** : weightlifting
pesadamente *adv* 1 : heavily 2 : slowly, clumsily
pesadez *nf, pl* **-deces** 1 : heaviness 2 : slowness 3 : tediousness
pesadilla *nf* : nightmare

pesado[1], **-da** *adj* 1 : heavy 2 : slow 3 : irritating, annoying 4 : tedious, boring 5 : tough, difficult
pesado[2], **-da** *n fam* : bore, pest
pesadumbre *nf* AFLICCIÓN : grief, sorrow, sadness
pésame *nm* : condolences *pl* ⟨mi más sentido pésame : my heartfelt condolences⟩
pesar[1] *vt* 1 : to weigh 2 EXAMINAR : to consider, to think over — *vi* 1 : to weigh ⟨¿cuánto pesa? : how much does it weigh?⟩ 2 : to be heavy 3 : to weigh heavily, to be a burden ⟨no le pesa : it's not a burden on him⟩ ⟨pesa sobre mi corazón : it weighs upon my heart⟩ 4 INFLUIR : to carry weight, to have bearing 5 (*with personal pronouns*) : to grieve, to sadden ⟨me pesa mucho : I'm very sorry⟩ 6 **pese a** : in spite of, despite
pesar[2] *nm* 1 AFLICCIÓN, PENA : sorrow, grief 2 REMORDIMIENTO : remorse 3 **a pesar de** : in spite of, despite
pesaroso, -sa *adj* 1 : sad, mournful 2 ARREPENTIDO : sorry, regretful
pesca *nf* : fishing
pescadería *nf* : fish market
pescado *nm* : fish (as food)
pescador, -dora *n* : fisherman *m*, fisherwoman *f*
pescar {72} *vt* 1 : to fish for 2 : to catch 3 *fam* : to get a hold of, to land — *vi* : to fish, to go fishing
pescuezo *nm* : neck
pesebre *nm* : manger
pesero *nm Mex* : minibus
peseta *nf* : peseta (Spanish unit of currency)
pesimismo *nm* : pessimism
pesimista[1] *adj* : pessimistic
pesimista[2] *nmf* : pessimist
pésimo, -ma *adj* : dreadful, abominable
peso *nm* 1 : weight, heaviness 2 : burden, responsibility 3 : weight (in sports) 4 BÁSCULA : scales *pl* 5 : peso
pesque, etc. → **pescar**
pesquería *nf* : fishery
pesquero[1], **-ra** *adj* : fishing ⟨pueblo pesquero : fishing village⟩
pesquero[2] *nm* : fishing boat
pesquisa *nf* INVESTIGACIÓN : inquiry, investigation
pestaña *nf* 1 : eyelash 2 : flange, rim
pestañear *vi* : to blink
pestañeo *nm* : blink
peste *nf* 1 : plague, pestilence 2 : stench, stink 3 : nuisance, pest
pesticida *nm* : pesticide
pestilencia *nf* 1 : stench, foul odor 2 : pestilence
pestilente *adj* 1 : foul, smelly 2 : pestilent
pestillo *nm* CERROJO : bolt, latch
petaca *nf* 1 *Mex* : suitcase 2 **petacas** *nfpl Mex fam* : bottom, behind
pétalo *nm* : petal
petardear *vi* : to backfire

petardeo nm : backfiring
petardo nm : firecracker
petate nm Mex : mat
petición nf, pl **-ciones** : petition, request
peticionar vt : to petition
peticionario, -ria n : petitioner
petirrojo nm : robin
peto nm : bib (of clothing)
pétreo, -trea adj : stone, stony
petrificar {72} vt : to petrify
petróleo nm : oil, petroleum
petrolero¹, -ra adj : oil ⟨industria petrolera : oil industry⟩
petrolero² nm : oil tanker
petrolífero, -ra adj → petrolero¹
petulancia nf INSOLENCIA : insolence, petulance
petulante adj INSOLENTE : insolent, petulant — **petulantemente** adv
petunia nf : petunia
peyorativo, -va adj : pejorative
pez¹ nm, pl **peces** : fish **2 pez de colores** : goldfish **3 pez espada** : swordfish **4 pez gordo** : big shot
pez² nf, pl **peces** : pitch, tar
pezón nm, pl **pezones** : nipple
pezuña nf : hoof ⟨pezuña hendida : cloven hoof⟩
pi nf : pi
piadoso, -sa adj **1** : compassionate, merciful **2** DEVOTO : pious, devout
pianista nmf : pianist, piano player
piano nm : piano
piar {85} vi : to chirp, to cheep, to tweet
pibe, -ba n Arg, Uru fam : kid, child
pica nf **1** : pike, lance **2** : goad (in bullfighting) **3** : spade (in playing cards)
picada nf **1** : bite, sting (of an insect) **2** : sharp descent
picadillo nm **1** : minced meat, hash **2 hacer picadillo a** : to beat to a pulp
picado, -da adj **1** : perforated **2** : minced, chopped **3** : decayed (of teeth) **4** : choppy, rough **5** fam : annoyed, miffed
picador nm : picador
picadura nf **1** : sting, bite **2** : prick, puncture **3** : decay, cavity
picaflor nm COLIBRÍ : hummingbird
picana nf : goad, prod
picante¹ adj **1** : hot, spicy **2** : sharp, cutting **3** : racy, risqué
picante² nm **1** : spiciness **2** : hot spices pl, hot sauce
picaporte nm **1** : latch **2** : door handle **3** ALDABA : door knocker
picar {72} vt **1** : to sting, to bite **2** : to peck at **3** : to nibble on **4** : to prick, to puncture, to punch (a ticket) **5** : to grind, to chop **6** : to goad, to incite **7** : to pique, to provoke — vi **1** : to itch **2** : to sting **3** : to be spicy **4** : to nibble **5** : to take the bait **6 ~ en** : to dabble in **7 picar muy alto** : to aim too high — **picarse** vr **1** : to get a cavity, to decay **2** : to get annoyed, to take offense
picardía nf **1** : cunning, craftiness **2** : prank, dirty trick

picaresco, -ca adj **1** : picaresque **2** : rascally, roguish
pícaro¹, -ra adj **1** : mischievous **2** : cunning, sly **3** : off-color, risqué
pícaro², -ra n **1** : rogue, scoundrel **2** : rascal
picazón nf, pl **-zones** COMEZÓN : itch
picea nf : spruce (tree)
pichel nm : pitcher, jug
pichón, -chona n, mpl **pichones 1** : young pigeon, squab **2** Mex fam : novice, greenhorn
picnic nm : picnic
pico nm **1** : peak **2** : point, spike **3** : beak, bill **4** : pick, pickax **5 y pico** : and a little, and a bit ⟨las siete y pico : a little after seven⟩ ⟨dos metros y pico : a bit over two meters⟩
picor nm : itch, irritation
picoso, -sa adj Mex : very hot, spicy
picota nf **1** : pillory, stock **2 poner a alguien en la picota** : to put someone on the spot
picotada nf → picotazo
picotazo nm : peck (of a bird)
picotear vt : to peck — vi : to nibble, to pick
pictórico, -ca adj : pictorial
picudo, -da adj **1** : pointy, sharp **2 ~ para** Mex fam : clever at, good at
pide, etc. → pedir
pie nm **1** : foot ⟨a pie : on foot⟩ ⟨de pie : on one's feet, standing⟩ **2** : base, bottom, stem, foot ⟨pie de la cama : foot of the bed⟩ ⟨pie de una lámpara : base of a lamp⟩ ⟨pie de la escalera : bottom of the stairs⟩ ⟨pie de una copa : stem of a glass⟩ **3** : foot (in measurement) ⟨pie cuadrado : square foot⟩ **4** : cue (in theater) **5 dar pie a** : to give cause for, to give rise to **6 en pie de igualdad** : on equal footing
piedad nf **1** COMPASIÓN : mercy, pity **2** DEVOCIÓN : piety, devotion
piedra nf **1** : stone **2** : flint (of a lighter) **3** : hailstone **4 piedra de afilar** : whetstone, grindstone **5 piedra angular** : cornerstone **6 piedra arenisca** : sandstone **7 piedra caliza** : limestone **8 piedra imán** : lodestone **9 piedra de molino** : millstone **10 piedra de toque** : touchstone
piel nf **1** : skin **2** CUERO : leather, hide ⟨piel de venado : deerskin⟩ **3** : fur, pelt **4** CÁSCARA : peel, skin **5 piel de gallina** : goose bumps pl ⟨me pone la piel de gallina : it gives me goose bumps⟩
piélago nm **el piélago** : the deep, the ocean
piensa, etc. → pensar
pienso nm : feed, fodder
pierde, etc. → perder
pierna nf : leg
pieza nf **1** ELEMENTO : piece, part, component ⟨vestido de dos piezas : two-piece dress⟩ ⟨pieza de recambio : spare part⟩ ⟨pieza clave : key element⟩ **2** : piece (in chess) **3** OBRA : piece, work

⟨pieza de teatro : play⟩ **4** : room, bed-room

pifia *nf fam* : goof, blunder
pigargo *nm* : osprey
pigmentación *nf, pl* **-ciones** : pigmentation
pigmento *nm* : pigment
pigmeo, -mea *adj & n* : pygmy, Pygmy
pijama *nm* : pajamas *pl*
pila *nf* **1** BATERÍA : battery ⟨pila de linterna : flashlight battery⟩ **2** MONTÓN : pile, heap **3** : sink, basin, font ⟨pila bautismal : baptismal font⟩ ⟨pila para pájaros : birdbath⟩
pilar *nm* **1** : pillar, column **2** : support, mainstay
píldora *nf* PASTILLA : pill
pillaje *nm* : pillage, plunder
pillar *vt* **1** *fam* : to catch ⟨¡cuidado! ¡nos pillarán! : watch out! they'll catch us!⟩ **2** *fam* : to grasp, to catch on ⟨¿no lo pillas? : don't you get it?⟩
pillo¹, -lla *adj* : cunning, crafty
pillo², -lla *n* **1** : rascal, brat **2** : rogue, scoundrel
pilluelo, -la *n* : urchin
pilón *nm, pl* **pilones 1** PILA : basin **2** : pillar, tower (for cables), pylon (of a bridge) **3** *Mex* : extra, lagniappe
pilotar *vt* : to pilot, to drive
pilote *nm* : pile (stake)
pilotear → **pilotar**
piloto *nm* **1** : pilot, driver **2** : pilot light
piltrafa *nf* **1** : poor quality meat **2** : wretch **3 piltrafas** *nfpl* : food scraps
pimentero *nm* : pepper shaker
pimentón *nm, pl* **-tones 1** : paprika **2** : cayenne pepper
pimienta *nf* **1** : pepper (condiment) **2 pimienta de Jamaica** : allspice
pimiento *nm* : pepper (fruit) ⟨pimiento verde : green pepper⟩
pináculo *nm* **1** : pinnacle (of a building) **2** : peak, acme
pincel *nm* : paintbrush
pincelada *nf* **1** : brushstroke **2 últimas pinceladas** : final touches
pinchar *vt* **1** PICAR : to puncture (a tire) **2** : to prick, to stick **3** : to goad, to tease, to needle — *vi* **1** : to be prickly **2** : to get a flat tire **3** *fam* : to get beaten, to lose out — **pincharse** *vr* : to give oneself an injection
pinchazo *nm* **1** : prick, jab **2** : puncture, flat tire
pingüe *adj* **1** : rich, huge (of profits) **2** : lucrative
pingüino *nm* : penguin
pininos *or* **pinitos** *nmpl* : first steps ⟨hacer pininos : to take one's first steps, to toddle⟩
pino *nm* : pine, pine tree
pinta *nf* **1** : dot, spot **2** : pint **3** *fam* : aspect, appearance ⟨las peras tienen buena pinta : the pears look good⟩ **4 pintas** *nfpl Mex* : graffiti
pintadas *nfpl* : graffiti

pintar *vt* **1** : to paint **2** : to draw, to mark **3** : to describe, to depict — *vi* **1** : to paint, to draw **2** : to look ⟨no pinta bien : it doesn't look good⟩ **3** *fam* : to count ⟨aquí no pinta nada : he has no say here⟩ — **pintarse** *vr* **1** MAQUILLARSE : to put on makeup **2 pintárselas solo** *fam* : to manage by oneself, to know it all
pintarrajear *vt* : to daub (with paint)
pinto, -ta *adj* : speckled, spotted
pintor, -tora *n* **1** : painter **2 pintor de brocha gorda** : housepainter, dauber
pintoresco, -ca *adj* : picturesque, quaint
pintura *nf* **1** : paint **2** : painting (art, work of art)
pinza *nf* **1** : clothespin **2** : claw, pincer **3** : pleat, dart **4 pinzas** *nfpl* : tweezers **5 pinzas** *nfpl* ALICATES : pliers, pincers
pinzón *nm, pl* **pinzones** : finch
piña *nf* **1** : pineapple **2** : pine cone
piñata *nf* : piñata
piñón *nm, pl* **piñones 1** : pine nut **2** : pinion
pío¹, pía *adj* **1** DEVOTO : pious, devout **2** : piebald, pied, dappled
pío² *nm* : peep, tweet, cheep
piocha *nf* **1** : pickax **2** *Mex* : goatee
piojo *nm* : louse
piojoso, -sa *adj* **1** : lousy **2** : filthy
pionero¹, -ra *adj* : pioneering
pionero², -ra *n* : pioneer
pipa *nf* : pipe (for smoking)
pipián *nm, pl* **pipianes** *Mex* : a spicy sauce or stew
pipiolo, -la *n fam* **1** : greenhorn, novice **2** : kid, youngster
pique¹, etc. → **picar**
pique² *nm* **1** : pique, resentment **2** : rivalry, competition **3 a pique de** : about to, on the verge of **4 irse a pique** : to sink, to founder
piqueta *nf* : pickax
piquete *nm* **1** : picketers *pl*, picket line **2** : squad, detachment **3** *Mex* : prick, jab
piquetear *vt* **1** : to picket **2** *Mex* : to prick, to jab
pira *nf* : pyre
piragua *nf* : canoe — **piragüista** *nmf*
pirámide *nf* : pyramid
piraña *nf* : piranha
pirata¹ *adj* : bootleg, pirated
pirata² *nmf* **1** : pirate **2** : bootlegger **3 pirata aéreo** : hijacker
piratear *vt* **1** : to hijack, to commandeer **2** : to bootleg, to pirate
piratería *nf* : piracy, bootlegging
piromanía *nf* : pyromania
pirómano, -na *n* : pyromaniac
piropo *nm* : flirtatious compliment
pirotecnia *nf* : fireworks *pl*, pyrotechnics *pl*
pirotécnico, -ca *adj* : fireworks, pyrotechnic
pírrico, -ca *adj* : Pyrrhic
pirueta *nf* : pirouette
pirulí *nm* : cone-shaped lollipop

pisada *nf* **1** : footstep **2** HUELLA : footprint

pisapapeles *nms & pl* : paperweight

pisar *vt* **1** : to step on, to set foot in **2** : to walk all over, to mistreat — *vi* : to step, to walk, to tread

piscina *nf* **1** : swimming pool **2** : fish pond

Piscis *nmf* : Pisces

piso *nm* **1** PLANTA : floor, story **2** SUELO : floor **3** *Spain* : apartment

pisotear *vt* **1** : to stamp on, to trample **2** PISAR : to walk all over **3** : to flout, to disregard

pisotón *nm*, *pl* **-tones** : stamp, step ⟨sufrieron empujones y pisotones : they were pushed and stepped on⟩

pista *nf* **1** RASTRO : trail, track ⟨siguen la pista de los sospechosos : they're on the trail of the suspects⟩ **2** : clue **3** CAMINO : road, trail **4** : track, racetrack **5** : ring, arena, rink **6 pista de aterrizaje** : runway, airstrip **7 pista de baile** : dance floor

pistacho *nm* : pistachio

pistilo *nm* : pistil

pistola *nf* **1** : pistol, handgun **2** : spray gun

pistolera *nf* : holster

pistolero *nm* : gunman

pistón *nm*, *pl* **pistones** : piston

pita *nf* **1** : agave **2** : pita fiber **3** : twine

pitar *vi* **1** : to blow a whistle **2** : to whistle, to boo **3** : to beep, to honk, to toot — *vi* : to whistle at, to boo

pitido *nm* **1** : whistle, whistling **2** : beep, honk, toot

pito *nm* **1** SILBATO : whistle **2 no me importa un pito** *fam* : I don't give a damn

pitón *nm*, *pl* **pitones** **1** : python **2** : point of a bull's horn

pituitario, -ria *adj* : pituitary

pívot *nmf*, *pl* **pívots** : center (in basketball)

pivote *nm* : pivot

piyama *nmf* : pajamas *pl*

pizarra *nf* **1** : slate **2** : blackboard **3** : scoreboard

pizarrón *nm*, *pl* **-rrones** : blackboard, chalkboard

pizca *nf* **1** : pinch ⟨una pizca de canela : a pinch of cinnamon⟩ **2** : speck, trace ⟨ni pizca : not a bit⟩ **3** *Mex* : harvest

pizcar {72} *vt Mex* : to harvest

pizque, etc. → **pizcar**

pizza [ˈpitsa, ˈpisa] *nf* : pizza

pizzería *nf* : pizzeria, pizza parlor

placa *nf* **1** : sheet, plate **2** : plaque, nameplate **3** : plate (in photography) **4** : badge, insignia **5 placa de matrícula** : license plate, tag **6 placa dental** : plaque, tartar

placebo *nm* : placebo

placenta *nf* : placenta, afterbirth

placentero, -ra *adj* AGRADABLE, GRATO : pleasant, agreeable

placer[1] {57} *vi* GUSTAR : to be pleasing ⟨hazlo como te plazca : do it however you please⟩

placer[2] *nm* **1** : pleasure, enjoyment **2 a ~** : as much as one wants

plácido, -da *adj* TRANQUILO : placid, calm

plaga *nf* **1** : plague, infestation, blight **2** CALAMIDAD : disaster, scourge

plagado, -da *adj* **~ de** : filled with, covered with

plagar {52} *vt* : to plague

plagiar *vt* **1** : to plagiarize **2** SECUESTRAR : to kidnap, to abduct

plagiario, -ria *n* **1** : plagiarist **2** SECUESTRADOR : kidnapper, abductor

plagio *nm* **1** : plagiarism **2** SECUESTRO : kidnapping, abduction

plague, etc. → **plagar**

plan *nm* **1** : plan, strategy, program ⟨plan de inversiones : investment plan⟩ ⟨plan de estudios : curriculum⟩ **2** PLANO : plan, diagram **3** : attitude, intent, purpose ⟨ponte en plan serio : be serious⟩ ⟨estamos en plan de divertirnos : we're looking to have some fun⟩

plana *nf* **1** : page ⟨noticias en primera plana : front-page news⟩ **2 plana mayor** : staff (in the military)

plancha *nf* **1** : iron, ironing **2** : grill, griddle ⟨a la plancha : grilled⟩ **3** : sheet, plate ⟨plancha para hornear : baking sheet⟩ **4** *fam* : blunder, blooper

planchada *nf* : ironing, pressing

planchado *nm* → **planchada**

planchar *v* : to iron

planchazo *nm fam* : goof, blunder

plancton *nm* : plankton

planeación *nf* → **planeamiento**

planeador *nm* : glider (aircraft)

planeamiento *nm* : plan, planning

planear *vt* : to plan — *vi* : to glide (in the air)

planeo *nm* : gliding, soaring

planeta *nm* : planet

planetario[1]**, -ria** *adj* **1** : planetary **2** : global, worldwide

planetario[2] *nm* : planetarium

planicie *nf* : plain

planificación *nf* : planning ⟨planificación familiar : family planning⟩

planificar {72} *vt* : to plan

planilla *nf* **1** LISTA : list **2** NÓMINA : payroll **3** TABLA : chart, table **4** *Mex* : slate, ticket (of candidates) **5 planilla de cálculo** *Arg, Chile* : spreadsheet

plano[1]**, -na** *adj* : flat, level, plane

plano[2] *nm* **1** PLAN : map, plan **2** : plane (surface) **3** NIVEL : level ⟨en un plano personal : on a personal level⟩ **4** : shot (in photography) **5 de ~** : flatly, outright, directly ⟨se negó de plano : he flatly refused⟩

planta *nf* **1** : plant ⟨planta de interior : houseplant⟩ **2** FÁBRICA : plant, factory **3** PISO : floor, story **4** : staff, employees *pl* **5** : sole (of the foot)

plantación *nf, pl* **-ciones 1** : plantation **2** : planting

plantado, -da *adj* **1** : planted **2 dejar plantado** : to stand up (a date), to dump (a lover)

plantar *vt* **1** : to plant, to sow ⟨plantar de flores : to plant with flowers⟩ **2** : to put in, to place **3** *fam* : to plant, to land ⟨plantar un beso : to plant a kiss⟩ **4** *fam* : to leave, to jilt — **plantarse** *vr* **1** : to stand firm **2** *fam* : to arrive, to show up **3** *fam* : to balk

planteamiento *nm* **1** : approach, position ⟨el planteamiento feminista : the feminist viewpoint⟩ **2** : explanation, exposition **3** : proposal, suggestion, plan

plantear *vt* **1** : to set forth, to bring up, to suggest **2** : to establish, to set up **3** : to create, to pose (a problem) — **plantearse** *vr* **1** : to think about **2** : to arise

plantel *nm* **1** : educational institution **2** : staff, team

planteo → **planteamiento**

plantilla *nf* **1** : insole **2** : pattern, template, stencil **3** *Mex, Spain* : staff, roster of employees

plantío *nm* : field (planted with a crop)

plantón *nm, pl* **plantones 1** : seedling **2** : long wait ⟨darle a alguien un plantón : to stand someone up⟩

plañidero[1], -ra *adj* : mournful

plañidero[2], -ra *nf* : hired mourner

plañir {38} *v* : to mourn, to lament

plasma *nm* : plasma

plasmar *vt* : to express, to give form to — **plasmarse** *vr*

plasta *nf* : soft mass, lump

plástica *nf* : modeling, sculpture

plasticidad *nf* : plasticity

plástico[1], -ca *adj* : plastic

plástico[2] *nm* : plastic

plastificar {72} *vt* : to laminate

plata *nf* **1** : silver **2** : money

plataforma *nf* **1** ESTRADO, TARIMA : platform, dais **2** : platform (in politics) **3** : springboard, stepping stone **4 plataforma continental** : continental shelf **5 plataforma de lanzamiento** : launchpad **6 plataforma petrolífera** : oil rig (at sea)

platal *nm* : large sum of money, fortune

platanal *nm* : banana plantation

platanero[1], -ra *adj* : banana, banana-producing

platanero[2], -ra *n* : banana grower

plátano *nm* **1** : banana **2** : plantain **3 plátano macho** *Mex* : plantain

platea *nf* : orchestra, pit (in a theater)

plateado, -da *adj* **1** : silver, silvery **2** : silver-plated

plática *nf* **1** : talk, lecture **2** : chat, conversation

platicar {72} *vi* : to talk, to chat — *vt Mex* : to tell, to say

platija *nf* : flatfish, flounder

platillo *nm* **1** : saucer ⟨platillo volador : flying saucer⟩ **2** : cymbal **3** *Mex* : dish ⟨platillos típicos : local dishes⟩

platino *nm* : platinum

plato *nm* **1** : plate, dish ⟨lavar los platos : to do the dishes⟩ **2** : serving, helping **3** : course (of a meal) **4** : dish ⟨plato típico : typical dish⟩ **5** : home plate (in baseball) **6 plato hondo** : soup bowl

plató *nm* : set (in the movies)

platónico, -ca *adj* : platonic

playa *nf* : beach, seashore

playera *nf* **1** : canvas sneaker **2** *CA, Mex* : T-shirt

plaza *nf* **1** : square, plaza **2** : marketplace **3** : room, space, seat (in a vehicle) **4** : post, position **5 plaza fuerte** : stronghold, fortified city **6 plaza de toros** : bullring

plazca, etc. → **placer**

plazo *nm* **1** : period, term ⟨un plazo de cinco días : a period of five days⟩ ⟨a largo plazo : long-term⟩ **2** ABONO : installment ⟨pagar a plazos : to pay in installments⟩

pleamar *nf* : high tide

plebe *nf* : common people, masses *pl*

plebeyo[1], -ya *adj* : plebeian

plebeyo[2], -ya *n* : plebeian, commoner

plegable *adj* : folding, collapsible

plegadizo → **plegable**

plegar {49} *vt* DOBLAR : to fold, to bend — **plegarse** *vr* : to give in, to yield

plegaria *nf* ORACIÓN : prayer

pleito *nm* **1** : lawsuit **2** : fight, argument, dispute

plenamente *adv* COMPLETAMENTE : fully, completely

plenario, -ria *adj* : plenary, full

plenilunio *nm* : full moon

plenipotenciario, -ria *n* : plenipotentiary

plenitud *nf* : fullness, abundance

pleno, -na *adj* COMPLETO ⟨⟨*often used as an intensifier*⟩⟩ : full, complete ⟨en pleno uso de sus facultades : in full command of his faculties⟩ ⟨en plena noche : in the middle of the night⟩ ⟨en pleno corazón de la ciudad : right in the heart of the city⟩

plétora *nf* : plethora

pleuresía *nf* : pleurisy

pliega, pliegue etc. → **plegar**

pliego *nm* **1** HOJA : sheet of paper **2** : sealed document

pliegue *nm* **1** DOBLEZ : crease, fold **2** : pleat

plisar *vt* : to pleat

plomada *nf* **1** : plumb line **2** : sinker

plomería *nf* FONTANERÍA : plumbing

plomero, -ra *n* FONTANERO : plumber

plomizo, -za *adj* : leaden

plomo *nm* **1** : lead **2** : plumb line **3** : fuse **4** *fam* : bore, drag **5 a ~** : plumb, straight

plugo, etc. → **placer**

pluma *nf* **1** : feather **2** : pen **3 pluma fuente** : fountain pen

plumaje *nm* : plumage
plumero *nm* : feather duster
plumilla *nf* : nib
plumón *nm, pl* **plumones** : down
plumoso, -sa *adj* : feathery, downy
plural *adj & nm* : plural
pluralidad *nf* : plurality
pluralizar {21} *vt* : to pluralize
pluriempleado, -da *adj* : holding more than one job
pluriempleo *nm* : moonlighting
plus *nm* : bonus
plusvalía *nf* : appreciation, capital gain
Plutón *nm* : Pluto
plutocracia *nf* : plutocracy
plutonio *nm* : plutonium
población *nf, pl* **-ciones 1** : population **2** : city, town, village
poblado¹, -da *adj* **1** : inhabited, populated **2** : full, thick ⟨cejas pobladas : bushy eyebrows⟩
poblado² *nm* : village, settlement
poblador, -dora *n* : settler
poblar {19} *vt* **1** : to populate, to inhabit **2** : to settle, to colonize **3** ~ **de** : to stock with, to plant with — **poblarse** *vr* : to fill up, to become crowded
pobre¹ *adj* **1** : poor, impoverished **2** : unfortunate ⟨pobre de mí! : poor me!⟩ **3** : weak, deficient ⟨una dieta pobre : a poor diet⟩
pobre² *nmf* : poor person ⟨los pobres : the poor⟩ ⟨¡pobre! : poor thing!⟩
pobremente *adv* : poorly
pobreza *nf* : poverty
pocilga *nf* CHIQUERO : pigsty, pigpen
pocillo *nm* : small coffee cup, demitasse
poción *nf, pl* **pociones** : potion
poco¹ *adv* **1** : little, not much ⟨poco probable : not very likely⟩ ⟨come poco : he doesn't eat much⟩ **2** : a short time, a while ⟨tardaremos poco : we won't be very long⟩ **3 poco antes** : shortly before **4 poco después** : shortly after
poco², -ca *adj* **1** : little, not much, (a) few ⟨tengo poco dinero : I don't have much money⟩ ⟨en no pocas ocasiones : on more than a few occasions⟩ ⟨poca gente : few people⟩ **2 pocas veces** : rarely
poco³, -ca *pron* **1** : little, few ⟨le falta poco para terminar : he's almost finished⟩ ⟨uno de los pocos que quedan : one of the remaining few⟩ **2 un poco** : a little, a bit ⟨un poco de vino : a little wine⟩ ⟨un poco extraño : a bit strange⟩ **3 a** ~ *Mex* (*used to express disbelief*) ⟨¿a poco no se te hizo difícil? : you mean you didn't find it difficult?⟩ **4 de a poco** : little by little **5 hace poco** : not long ago **6 poco a poco** : little by little **7 dentro de poco** : shortly, in a little while **8 por** ~ : nearly, almost
podar *vt* : to prune, to trim
poder¹ {58} *v aux* **1** : to be able to, can ⟨no puede hablar : he can't speak⟩ **2** (*expressing possibility*) : might, may ⟨puede llover : it may rain at any moment⟩ ⟨¿cómo puede ser? : how can that be?⟩ **3** (*expressing permission*) : can, may ⟨¿puedo ir a la fiesta? : can I go to the party?⟩ ⟨¿se puede? : may I come in?⟩ — *vi* **1** : to beat, to defeat ⟨cree que le puede a cualquiera : he thinks he can beat anyone⟩ **2** : to be possible ⟨¿crees que vendrán? — puede (que sí) : do you think they'll come? — maybe⟩ **3** ~ **con** : to cope with, to manage ⟨¡no puedo con estos niños! : I can't handle these children!⟩ **4 no poder más** : to have had enough ⟨no puede más : she can't take anymore⟩ **5 no poder menos que** : to not be able to help ⟨no pudo menos que asombrarse : she couldn't help but be amazed⟩
poder² *nm* **1** : control, power ⟨poder adquisitivo : purchasing power⟩ **2** : authority ⟨el poder legislativo : the legislature⟩ **3** : possession ⟨está en mi poder : it's in my hands⟩ **4** : strength, force ⟨poder militar : military might⟩
poderío *nm* **1** : power **2** : wealth, influence
poderoso, -sa *adj* **1** : powerful **2** : wealthy, influential **3** : effective
podiatría *nf* : podiatry
podio *nm* : podium
pódium → **podio**
podología *nf* : podiatry, chiropody
podólogo, -ga *n* : podiatrist, chiropodist
podrá, etc. → **poder**
podredumbre *nf* **1** : decay, rottenness **2** : corruption
podrido, -da *adj* **1** : rotten, decayed **2** : corrupt
podrir → **pudrir**
poema *nm* : poem
poesía *nf* **1** : poetry **2** POEMA : poem
poeta *nmf* : poet
poético, -ca *adj* : poetic, poetical
pogrom *nm* : pogrom
póker *or* **poker** *nm* : poker (card game)
polaco¹, -ca *adj* : Polish
polaco², -ca *n* : Pole, Polish person
polaco³ *nm* : Polish (language)
polar *adj* : polar
polarizar {21} *vt* : to polarize — **polarizarse** *vr* — **polarización** *nf*
polea *nf* : pulley
polémica *nf* CONTROVERSIA : controversy, polemics
polémico, -ca *adj* CONTROVERTIDO : controversial, polemical
polen *nm, pl* **pólenes** : pollen
policía¹ *nf* : police
policía² *nmf* : police officer, policeman *m*, policewoman *f*
policíaco, -ca *or* **policiaco, -ca** *adj* : police ⟨novela policíaca : detective story⟩
policial *adj* : police
poliéster *nm* : polyester
poligamia *nf* : polygamy
polígamo¹, -ma *adj* : polygamous
polígamo², -ma *n* : polygamist
polígono *nm* : polygon — **poligonal** *adj*

poliinsaturado, -da *adj* : polyunsaturated

polilla *nf* : moth

polimerizar {21} *vt* : to polymerize

polímero *nm* : polymer

polinesio, -sia *adj & n* : Polynesian

polinizar {21} *vt* : to pollinate — **polinización** *nf*

polio *nf* : polio

poliomielitis *nf* : poliomyelitis, polio

polisón *nm, pl* **-sones** : bustle (on clothing)

politécnico, -ca *adj* : polytechnic

politeísmo *nm* : polytheism — **politeísta** *adj & nmf*

política *nf* **1** : politics **2** : policy

políticamente *adv* : politically

político¹, -ca *adj* **1** : political **2** : tactful, politic **3** : by marriage ⟨padre político : father-in-law⟩

político², -ca *n* : politician

póliza *nf* : policy ⟨póliza de seguros : insurance policy⟩

polizón *nm, pl* **-zones** : stowaway ⟨viajar de polizón : to stow away⟩

polka *nf* : polka

polla *nf* APUESTA : bet

pollera *nf* **1** : chicken coop **2** : skirt

pollero, -ra *n* **1** : poulterer **2** : poultry farm **3** *Mex fam* COYOTE : smuggler of illegal immigrants

pollito, -ta *n* : chick, young bird, fledgling

pollo, -lla *n* **1** : chicken **2** POLLITO : chick **3** JOVEN : young man *m*, young lady *f*

polluelo *nm* → **pollito**

polo *nm* **1** : pole ⟨el Polo Norte : the North Pole⟩ ⟨polo negativo : negative pole⟩ **2** : polo (sport) **3** : polo shirt **4** : focal point, center **5 polo opuesto** : exact opposite

polución *nf, pl* **-ciones** CONTAMINACIÓN : pollution

polvareda *nf* **1** : cloud of dust **2** : uproar, fuss

polvera *nf* : compact (for face powder)

polvo *nm* **1** : dust **2** : powder **3 polvos** *nmpl* : face powder **4 polvos de hornear** : baking powder **5 hacer polvo** *fam* : to crush, to shatter ⟨vas a hacer polvo el reloj : you're going to destroy your watch⟩

pólvora *nf* **1** : gunpowder **2** : fireworks *pl*

polvoriento, -ta *adj* : dusty, powdery

polvorín *nm, pl* **-rines** : magazine, storehouse (for explosives)

pomada *nf* : ointment, cream

pomelo *nm* : grapefruit

pómez *nf or* **piedra pómez** : pumice

pomo *nm* **1** : pommel (on a sword) **2** : knob, handle **3** : perfume bottle

pompa *nf* **1** : bubble **2** : pomp, splendor **3 pompas fúnebres** : funeral

pompón *nm, pl* **pompones** BORLA : pom-pom

pomposidad *nf* **1** : pomp, splendor **2** : pomposity, ostentation

pomposo, -sa *adj* : pompous — **pomposamente** *adv*

pómulo *nm* : cheekbone

pon → **poner**

ponchadura *nf Mex* : puncture, flat (tire)

ponchar *vt* **1** : to strike out (in baseball) **2** *Mex* : to puncture — **poncharse** *vr* **1** *Col, Ven* : to strike out (in baseball) **2** *Mex* : to blow out (of a tire)

ponche *nm* **1** : punch (drink) **2 ponche de huevo** : eggnog

poncho *nm* : poncho

ponderación *nf, pl* **-ciones** **1** : consideration, deliberation **2** : high praise

ponderar *vt* **1** : to weigh, to consider **2** : to speak highly of

pondrá, etc. → **poner**

ponencia *nf* **1** DISCURSO : paper, presentation, address **2** INFORME : report

ponente *nmf* : speaker, presenter

poner {60} *vt* **1** COLOCAR : to put, to place ⟨pon el libro en la mesa : put the book on the table⟩ **2** AGREGAR, AÑADIR : to put in, to add **3** : to put on (clothes) **4** CONTRIBUIR : to contribute **5** ESCRIBIR : to put in writing ⟨no le puso su nombre : he didn't put his name on it⟩ **6** IMPONER : to set, to impose **7** EXPONER : to put, to expose ⟨lo puso en peligro : she put him in danger⟩ **8** : to prepare, to arrange ⟨poner la mesa : to set the table⟩ **9** : to name ⟨le pusimos Ana : we called her Ana⟩ **10** ESTABLECER : to set up, to establish ⟨puso un restaurante : he opened up a restaurant⟩ **11** INSTALAR : to install, to put in **12** (*with an adjective or adverb*) : to make ⟨siempre lo pones de mal humor : you always put him in a bad mood⟩ **13** : to turn on, to switch on **14** SUPONER : to suppose ⟨pongamos que no viene : supposing he doesn't come⟩ **15** : to lay (eggs) **16 ~ a** : to start (someone doing something) ⟨lo puse a trabajar : I put him to work⟩ **17 ~ de** : to place as ⟨la pusieron de directora : they made her director⟩ **18 ~ en** : to put in (a state or condition) ⟨poner en duda : to call into question⟩ — *vi* **1** : to contribute **2** : to lay eggs — **ponerse** *vr* **1** : to move (into a position) ⟨ponerse de pie : to stand up⟩ **2** : to put on, to wear **3** : to become, to turn ⟨se puso colorado : he turned red⟩ **4** : to set (of the sun or moon)

poni *or* **poney** *nm* : pony

ponga, etc. → **poner**

poniente *nm* **1** OCCIDENTE : west **2** : west wind

ponqué *nm Col, Ven* : cake

pontifical *adj* : pontifical

pontificar {72} *vi* : to pontificate

pontífice *nm* : pontiff, pope

pontón *nm, pl* **pontones** : pontoon

ponzoña *nf* VENENO : poison — **ponzoñoso, -sa** *adj*

popa *nf* **1** : stern **2 a ～** : astern, abaft, aft

popelín *nm, pl* **-lines** : poplin

popelina *nf* : poplin

popote *nm Mex* : (drinking) straw

populachero, -ra *adj* : common, popular, vulgar

populacho *nm* : rabble, masses *pl*

popular *adj* **1** : popular **2** : traditional **3** : colloquial

popularidad *nf* : popularity

popularizar {21} *vt* : to popularize — **popularizarse** *vr*

populista *adj & nmf* : populist — **populismo** *nm*

populoso, -sa *adj* : populous

popurrí *nm* : potpourri

por *prep* **1** : for, during ⟨se quedaron allí por la semana : they stayed there during the week⟩ ⟨por el momento : for now, at the moment⟩ **2** : around, during ⟨por noviembre empieza a nevar : around November it starts to snow⟩ ⟨por la mañana : in the morning⟩ **3** : around (a place) ⟨debe estar por allí : it must be over there⟩ ⟨por todas partes : everywhere⟩ **4** : by, through, along ⟨por la puerta : through the door⟩ ⟨pasé por tu casa : I stopped by your house⟩ ⟨por la costa : along the coast⟩ **5** : for, for the sake of ⟨lo hizo por su madre : he did it for his mother⟩ ⟨¡por Dios! : for heaven's sake!⟩ **6** : because of, on account of ⟨llegué tarde por el tráfico : I arrived late because of the traffic⟩ ⟨dejar por imposible : to give up as impossible⟩ **7** : per ⟨60 millas por hora : 60 miles per hour⟩ ⟨por docena : by the dozen⟩ **8** : for, in exchange for, instead of ⟨su hermana habló por él : his sister spoke on his behalf⟩ **9** : by means of ⟨hablar por teléfono : to talk on the phone⟩ ⟨por escrito : in writing⟩ **10** : as for ⟨por mí : as far as I'm concerned⟩ **11** : times ⟨tres por dos son seis : three times two is six⟩ **12** SEGÚN : from, according to ⟨por lo que dices : judging from what you're telling me⟩ **13** : as, for ⟨por ejemplo : for example⟩ **14** : by ⟨hecho por mi abuela : made by my grandmother⟩ ⟨por correo : by mail⟩ **15** : for, in order to ⟨lucha por ganar su respeto : he struggles to win her respect⟩ **16 estar ～** : to be about to **17 por ciento** : percent **18 por favor** : please **19 por lo tanto** : therefore, consequently **20 ¿por qué?** : why? **21 por que** o **porque 22 por . . . que** : no matter how ⟨por mucho que intente : no matter how hard I try⟩ **23 por si** o **por si acaso** : just in case

porcelana *nf* : china, porcelain

porcentaje *nm* : percentage

porche *nm* : porch

porción *nf, pl* **porciones 1** : portion **2** PARTE : part, share **3** RACIÓN : serving, helping

pordiosear *vi* MENDIGAR : beg

pordiosero, -ra *n* MENDIGO : beggar

porfiado, -da *adj* OBSTINADO, TERCO : obstinate, stubborn — **porfiadamente** *adv*

porfiar {85} *vi* : to insist, to persist

pormenor *nm* DETALLE : detail

pormenorizar {21} *vi* : to go into detail — *vt* : to tell in detail

pornografía *nf* : pornography

pornográfico, -ca *adj* : pornographic

poro *nm* : pore

poroso, -sa *adj* : porous — **porosidad** *nf*

poroto *nm Arg, Chile, Uru* : bean

porque *conj* **1** : because **2** o **por que** : in order that

porqué *nm* : reason, cause

porquería *nf* **1** SUCIEDAD : dirt, filth **2** : nastiness, vulgarity **3** : worthless thing, trifle **4** : junk food

porra *nf* **1** : nightstick, club **2** *Mex* : cheer, yell ⟨los aficionados le echaban porras : the fans cheered him on⟩

porrazo *nm* **1** : blow, whack **2 de golpe y porrazo** : suddenly

porrista *nmf* **1** : cheerleader **2** : fan, supporter

portaaviones *nms & pl* : aircraft carrier

portada *nf* **1** : title page **2** : cover **3** : facade, front

portador, -dora *n* : carrier, bearer

portafolio o **portafolios** *nm, pl* **-lios 1** MALETÍN : briefcase **2** : portfolio (of investments)

portal *nm* **1** : portal, doorway **2** VESTÍBULO : vestibule, hall

portar *vt* **1** : to carry, to bear **2** : to wear — **portarse** *vr* CONDUCIRSE : to behave ⟨pórtate bien : behave yourself⟩

portátil *adj* : portable

portaviandas *nms & pl* : lunch box

portaviones *nm* → **portaaviones**

portavoz *nmf, pl* **-voces** : spokesperson, spokesman *m*, spokeswoman *f*

portazo *nm* : slam (of a door)

porte *nm* **1** ASPECTO : bearing, demeanor **2** TRANSPORTE : transport, carrying ⟨porte pagado : postage paid⟩

portento *nm* MARAVILLA : marvel, wonder

portentoso, -sa *adj* MARAVILLOSO : marvelous, wonderful

porteño, -ña *adj* : of or from Buenos Aires

portería *nf* **1** ARCO : goal, goalposts *pl* **2** : superintendent's office

portero, -ra *n* **1** ARQUERO : goalkeeper, goalie **2** : doorman *m* : janitor, superintendent

pórtico *nm* : portico

portilla *nf* : porthole

portón *nm, pl* **portones 1** : main door **2** : gate

portugués¹, -guesa *adj & n, mpl* **-gueses** : Portuguese

portugués² *nm* : Portuguese (language)

porvenir nm FUTURO : future
pos adv en pos de : in pursuit of
posada nf 1 : inn 2 Mex : Advent celebration
posadero, -ra n : innkeeper
posar vi : to pose — vt : to place, to lay — **posarse** vr 1 : to land, to light, to perch 2 : to settle, to rest
posavasos nms & pl : coaster (for drinks)
posdata → postdata
pose nf : pose
poseedor, -dora n : possessor, holder
poseer {20} vt : to possess, to hold, to have
poseído, -da adj : possessed
posesión nf, pl -siones : possession
posesionarse vr ~ de : to take possession of, to take over
posesivo[1]**, -va** adj : possessive
posesivo[2] nm : possessive case
posguerra nf : postwar period
posibilidad nf 1 : possibility 2 **posibilidades** nfpl : means, income
posibilitar vt : to make possible, to permit
posible adj : possible — **posiblemente** adv
posición nf, pl -ciones 1 : position, place 2 : status, standing 3 : attitude, stance
posicionar vt 1 : to position, to place 2 : to establish — **posicionarse** vr
positivo[1]**, -va** adj : positive
positivo[2] nm : print (in photography)
poso nm 1 : sediment, dregs pl 2 : grounds pl (of coffee)
posoperatorio, -ria adj : postoperative
posponer {60} vt 1 : to postpone 2 : to put behind, to subordinate
pospuso, etc. → posponer
posta nf : relay race
postal[1] adj : postal
postal[2] nf : postcard
postdata nf : postscript
poste nm : post, pole ⟨poste de teléfonos : telephone pole⟩
póster or **poster** nm, pl **pósters** or **posters** : poster, placard
postergación nf, pl -ciones : postponement, deferring
postergar {52} vt 1 : to delay, to postpone 2 : to pass over (an employee)
posteridad nf : posterity
posterior adj 1 ULTERIOR : later, subsequent 2 TRASERO : back, rear
postgrado nm : graduate course
postgraduado, -da n : graduate student, postgraduate
postigo nm 1 CONTRAVENTANA : shutter 2 : small door, wicket gate
postilla nf : scab
postizo, -za adj : artificial, false ⟨dentadura postiza : dentures⟩
postnatal adj : postnatal
postor, -tora n : bidder ⟨mejor postor : highest bidder⟩

postración nf, pl -ciones 1 : prostration 2 ABATIMIENTO : depression
postrado, -da adj 1 : prostrate 2 **postrado en cama** : bedridden
potranco, -ca n → potro[1]
postrar vt DEBILITAR : to debilitate, to weaken — **postrarse** vr : to prostrate oneself
postre nm : dessert
postrero, -ra adj (**postrer** before masculine singular nouns) ÚLTIMO : last
postulación nf, pl -ciones 1 : collection 2 : nomination (of a candidate)
postulado nm : postulate, assumption
postulante, -ta n 1 : postulant 2 : candidate, applicant
postular vt 1 : to postulate 2 : to nominate 3 : to propose — **postularse** vr : to run, to be a candidate
póstumo, -ma adj : posthumous — **póstumamente** adv
postura nf 1 : posture, position (of the body) 2 ACTITUD, POSICIÓN : position, stance
potable adj : drinkable, potable
potaje nm : thick vegetable soup, pottage
potasa nf : potash
potasio nm : potassium
pote nm 1 OLLA : pot 2 : jar, container
potencia nf 1 : power ⟨potencias extranjeras : foreign powers⟩ ⟨elevado a la tercera potencia : raised to the third power⟩ 2 : capacity, potency
potencial adj & nm : potential
potenciar vt : to promote, to foster
potenciómetro nm : dimmer, dimmer switch
potentado, -da n 1 SOBERANO : potentate, sovereign 2 MAGNATE : tycoon, magnate
potente adj 1 : powerful, strong 2 : potent, virile
potestad nf 1 AUTORIDAD : authority, jurisdiction 2 **patria potestad** : custody, guardianship
potrero nm 1 : field, pasture 2 : cattle ranch
potro[1]**, -tra** n : colt m, filly f
potro[2] nm 1 : rack (for torture) 2 : horse (in gymnastics)
pozo nm 1 : well ⟨pozo de petróleo : oil well⟩ 2 : deep pool (in a river) 3 : mine shaft 4 Arg, Par, Uru : pothole 5 **pozo séptico** : cesspool
pozole nm Mex : spicy stew made with pork and hominy
práctica nf 1 : practice, experience 2 EJERCICIO : exercising ⟨la práctica de la medicina : the practice of medicine⟩ 3 APLICACIÓN : application, practice ⟨poner en práctica : to put into practice⟩ 4 **prácticas** nfpl : training
practicable adj : practicable, feasible
prácticamente adv : practically
practicante[1] adj : practicing ⟨católicos practicantes : practicing Catholics⟩

practicante[2] *nmf* : practicer, practitioner

practicar {72} *vt* **1** : to practice **2** : to perform, to carry out **3** : to exercise (a profession) — *vi* : to practice

práctico, -ca *adj* : practical, useful

pradera *nf* : grassland, prairie

prado *nm* **1** CAMPO : field, meadow **2** : park

pragmático, -ca *adj* : pragmatic — **pragmáticamente** *adv*

pragmatismo *nm* : pragmatism

preámbulo *nm* **1** INTRODUCCIÓN : preamble, introduction **2** RODEO : evasion ⟨gastar preámbulos : to beat around the bush⟩

prebélico, -ca *adj* : antebellum

prebenda *nf* : privilege, perquisite

precalentar {55} *vt* : to preheat

precariedad *nf* : precariousness

precario, -ria *adj* : precarious — **precariamente** *adv*

precaución *nf, pl* **-ciones** **1** : precaution ⟨medidas de precaución : precautionary measures⟩ **2** PRUDENCIA : caution, care ⟨con precaución : cautiously⟩

precautorio, -ria *adj* : precautionary

precaver *vt* PREVENIR : to prevent, to guard against — **precaverse** *vr* PREVENIRSE : to take precautions, to be on guard

precavido, -da *adj* CAUTELOSO : cautious, prudent

precedencia *nf* : precedence, priority

precedente[1] *adj* : preceding, previous

precedente[2] *nm* : precedent

preceder *v* : to precede

precepto *nm* : rule, precept

preciado, -da *adj* : esteemed, prized, valuable

preciarse *vr* **1** JACTARSE : to boast, to brag **2** ~ **de** : to pride oneself on

precinto *nm* : seal

precio *nm* **1** : price **2** : cost, sacrifice ⟨a cualquier precio : whatever the cost⟩

preciosidad *nf* : beautiful thing ⟨este vestido es una preciosidad : this dress is lovely⟩

precioso, -sa *adj* **1** HERMOSO : beautiful, exquisite **2** VALIOSO : precious, valuable

precipicio *nm* **1** : precipice **2** RUINA : ruin

precipitación *nf, pl* **-ciones** **1** PRISA : haste, hurry, rush **2** : precipitation, rain, snow

precipitado, -da *adj* **1** : hasty, sudden **2** : rash — **precipitadamente** *adv*

precipitar *vt* **1** APRESURAR : to hasten, to speed up **2** ARROJAR : to hurl, to throw — **precipitarse** *vr* **1** APRESURARSE : to rush **2** : to act rashly **3** ARROJARSE : to throw oneself

precisamente *adv* JUSTAMENTE : precisely, exactly

precisar *vt* **1** : to specify, to determine exactly **2** NECESITAR : to need, to require — *vi* : to be necessary

precisión *nf, pl* **-siones** **1** EXACTITUD : precision, accuracy **2** CLARIDAD : clarity (of style, etc.) **3** NECESIDAD : necessity ⟨tener precisión de : to have need of⟩

preciso, -sa *adj* **1** EXACTO : precise **2** : very, exact ⟨en ese preciso instante : at that very instant⟩ **3** NECESARIO : necessary

precocidad *nf* : precocity

precocinar *vt* : to precook

preconcebir {54} *vt* : to preconceive

precondición *nf, pl* **-ciones** : precondition

preconizar {21} *vt* **1** : to recommend, to advocate **2** : to extol

precoz *adj, pl* **precoces** **1** : precocious **2** : early, premature — **precozmente** *adv*

precursor, -sora *n* : forerunner, precursor

predecesor, -sora *n* ANTECESOR : predecessor

predecir {11} *vt* : to foretell, to predict

predestinado, -da *adj* : predestined, fated

predestinar *vt* : to predestine — **predestinación** *nf*

predeterminar *vt* : to predetermine

prédica *nf* SERMÓN : sermon

predicado *nm* : predicate

predicador, -dora *n* : preacher

predicar {72} *v* : to preach

predicción *nf, pl* **-ciones** **1** : prediction **2** PRONÓSTICO : forecast ⟨predicción del tiempo : weather forecast⟩

prediga, predijo etc. → **predecir**

predilección *nf, pl* **-ciones** : predilection, preference

predilecto, -ta *adj* : favorite

predio *nm* : property, piece of land

predisponer {60} *vt* **1** : to predispose, to incline **2** : to prejudice, to bias

predisposición *nf, pl* **-ciones** **1** : predisposition, tendency **2** : prejudice, bias

predominante *adj* : predominant — **predominantemente** *adv*

predominar *vi* PREVALECER : to predominate, to prevail

predominio *nm* : predominance, prevalence

preeminente *adj* : preeminent — **preeminencia** *nf*

preescolar *adj & nm* : preschool

preestreno *nm* : preview

prefabricado, -da *adj* : prefabricated

prefacio *nm* : preface

prefecto *nm* : prefect

preferencia *nf* **1** : preference **2** PRIORIDAD : priority **3 de** ~ : preferably

preferencial *adj* : preferential

preferente *adj* : preferential, special ⟨trato preferente : special treatment⟩

preferentemente *adv* : preferably

preferible *adj* : preferable
preferido, -da *adj & n* : favorite
preferir {76} *vt* : to prefer
prefigurar *vt* : foreshadow, prefigure
prefijo *nm* : prefix
pregonar *vt* **1** : to proclaim, to announce **2** : to hawk (merchandise) **3** : to extol **4** : to reveal, to disclose
pregunta *nf* **1** : question **2 hacer una pregunta** : to ask a question
preguntar *vt* : to ask, to question — *vi* : to ask, to inquire — **preguntarse** *vr* : to wonder
preguntón, -tona *adj, mpl* **-tones** : inquisitive
prehistórico, -ca *adj* : prehistoric
prejuiciado, -da *adj* : prejudiced
prejuicio *nm* : prejudice
prejuzgar {52} *vt* : to prejudge
prelado *nm* : prelate
preliminar *adj & nm* : preliminary
preludio *nm* : prelude
prematrimonial *adj* : premarital
prematuro, -ra *adj* : premature
premeditación *nf, pl* **-ciones** : premeditation
premeditar *vt* : to premeditate, to plan
premenstrual *adj* : premenstrual
premiado, -da *adj* : winning, prizewinning
premiar *vt* **1** : to award a prize to **2** : to reward
premier *nmf* : premier, prime minister
premio *nm* **1** : prize ⟨premio gordo : grand prize, jackpot⟩ **2** : reward **3** : premium
premisa *nf* : premise, basis
premolar *nm* : bicuspid (tooth)
premonición *nf, pl* **-ciones** : premonition
premura *nf* : haste, urgency
prenatal *adj* : prenatal
prenda *nf* **1** : piece of clothing **2** : security, pledge
prendar *vt* : to charm, to captivate **2** : to pawn, to pledge — **prendarse** *vr* ∼ **de** : to fall in love with
prendedor *nm* : brooch, pin
prender *vt* **1** SUJETAR : to pin, to fasten **2** APRESAR : to catch, to apprehend **3** : to light (a cigarette, a match) **4** : to turn on ⟨prende la luz : turn on the light⟩ **5 prender fuego a** : to set fire to — *vi* **1** : to take root **2** : to catch fire **3** : to catch on
prensa *nf* **1** : printing press **2** : press ⟨conferencia de prensa : press conference⟩
prensar *vt* : to press
prensil *adj* : prehensile
preñado, -da *adj* **1** : pregnant **2** ∼ **de** : filled with
preñar *vt* EMBARAZAR : to make pregnant
preñez *nf, pl* **preñeces** : pregnancy
preocupación *nf, pl* **-ciones** INQUIETUD : worry, concern
preocupante *adj* : worrisome

preocupar *vt* INQUIETAR : to worry, to concern — **preocuparse** *vr* APURARSE : to worry, to be concerned
preparación *nf, pl* **-ciones** **1** : preparation, readiness **2** : education, training **3** : (medicinal) preparation
preparado[1], -da *adj* **1** : ready, prepared **2** : trained
preparado[2] *nm* : preparation, mixture
preparar *vt* **1** : to prepare, to make ready **2** : to teach, to train, to coach — **prepararse** *vr*
preparativos *nmpl* : preparations
preparatoria *nf* *Mex* : high school
preparatorio, -ria *adj* : preparatory
preponderante *adj* : preponderant, predominant — **preponderancia** *nf* — **preponderantemente** *adv*
preposición *nf, pl* **-ciones** : preposition — **preposicional** *adj*
prepotente *adj* : arrogant, domineering, overbearing — **prepotencia** *nf*
prerrogativa *nf* : prerogative, privilege
presa *nf* **1** : capture, seizure ⟨hacer presa de : to seize⟩ **2** : catch, prey ⟨presa de : prey to, seized with⟩ **3** : claw, fang **4** DIQUE : dam **5** : morsel, piece (of food)
presagiar *vt* : to presage, to portend
presagio *nm* : omen, portent
presbiterio *nm* : presbytery, sanctuary (of a church)
presbítero *nm* : presbyter
presciencia *nf* : prescience
prescindible *adj* : expendable, dispensable
prescindir *vi* **1** ∼ **de** : to do without, to dispense with **2** DESATENDER : to ignore, to disregard **3** OMITIR : to omit, to skip
prescribir {33} *vt* : to prescribe
prescripción *nf, pl* **-ciones** : prescription
prescrito *pp* → **prescribir**
presencia *nf* **1** : presence **2** ASPECTO : appearance
presenciar *vt* : to be present at, to witness
presentable *adj* : presentable
presentación *nf, pl* **-ciones** **1** : presentation **2** : introduction **3** : appearance
presentador, -dora *n* : newscaster, anchorman *m*, anchorwoman *f*
presentar *vt* **1** : to present, to show **2** : to offer, to give **3** : to submit (a document), to launch (a product) **4** : to introduce (a person) — **presentarse** *vr* **1** : to show up, to appear **2** : to arise, to come up **3** : to introduce oneself
presente[1] *adj* **1** : present, in attendance **2** : present, current **3 tener presente** : to keep in mind
presente[2] *nm* **1** : present (time, tense) **2** : one present ⟨entre los presentes se encontraban . . . : those present included . . . ⟩
presentimiento *nm* : premonition, hunch, feeling

presentir {76} vt : to sense, to intuit ⟨presentía lo que iba a pasar : he sensed what was going to happen⟩
preservación nf, pl -ciones : preservation
preservar vt 1 : to preserve 2 : to protect
preservativo nm CONDÓN : condom
presidencia nf 1 : presidency 2 : chairmanship
presidencial adj : presidential
presidente, -ta n 1 : president 2 : chair, chairperson 3 : presiding judge
presidiario, -ria n : convict, prisoner
presidio nm : prison, penitentiary
presidir vt 1 MODERAR : to preside over, to chair 2 : to dominate, to rule over
presilla nf : eye, loop, fastener
presión nf, pl **presiones** 1 : pressure 2 **presión arterial** : blood pressure
presionar vt 1 : to pressure 2 : to press, to push — vi : to put on the pressure
preso¹, -sa adj : imprisoned
preso², -sa n : prisoner
prestado, -da adj 1 : borrowed, on loan 2 **pedir prestado** : to borrow
prestamista nmf : moneylender, pawnbroker
préstamo nm : loan
prestar vt 1 : to lend, to loan 2 : to render (a service), to give (aid) 3 **prestar atención** : to pay attention 4 **prestar juramento** : to take an oath — **prestarse** vr : to lend oneself ⟨se presta a confusiones : it lends itself to confusion⟩
prestatario, -ria n : borrower
presteza nf : promptness, speed
prestidigitación nf, pl -ciones : sleight of hand, prestidigitation
prestidigitador, -dora n : conjurer, magician
prestigio nm : prestige — **prestigioso, -sa** adj
presto¹ adv : promptly, at once
presto², -ta adj 1 : quick, prompt 2 DISPUESTO, PREPARADO : ready
presumido, -da adj VANIDOSO : conceited, vain
presumir vt SUPONER : to presume, to suppose — vi 1 ALARDEAR : to boast, to show off 2 ~ **de** : to consider oneself ⟨presume de inteligente : he thinks he's intelligent⟩
presunción nf, pl -ciones 1 SUPOSICIÓN : presumption, supposition 2 VANIDAD : conceit, vanity
presunto, -ta adj : presumed, supposed, alleged — **presuntamente** adv
presuntuoso, -sa adj : conceited
presuponer {60} vt : to presuppose
presupuestal adj : budget, budgetary
presupuestar vi : to budget — vt : to budget for
presupuestario, -ria adj : budget, budgetary
presupuesto nm 1 : budget, estimate 2 : assumption, supposition

presurizar {21} vt : to pressurize
presuroso, -sa adj : hasty, quick
pretencioso, -sa adj : pretentious
pretender vt 1 INTENTAR : to attempt, to try ⟨pretendo estudiar : I'm trying to study⟩ 2 AFIRMAR : to claim ⟨pretende ser pobre : he claims he's poor⟩ 3 : to seek, to aspire to ⟨¿qué pretendes tú? : what are you after?⟩ 4 CORTEJAR : to court 5 **pretender que** : to expect ⟨¿pretendes que lo crea? : do you expect me to believe you?⟩
pretendiente¹ nmf 1 : candidate, applicant 2 : pretender, claimant (to a throne, etc.)
pretendiente² nm : suitor
pretensión nf, pl -siones 1 : intention, hope, plan 2 : pretension ⟨sin pretensiones : unpretentious⟩
pretexto nm EXCUSA : pretext, excuse
pretil nm : parapet, railing
prevalecer {53} vi : to prevail, to triumph
prevaleciente adj : prevailing, prevalent
prevalerse {84} vr ~ **de** : to avail oneself of, to take advantage of
prevención nf, pl -ciones 1 : prevention 2 : preparation, readiness 3 : precautionary measure 4 : prejudice, bias
prevenido, -da adj 1 PREPARADO : prepared, ready 2 ADVERTIDO : forewarned 3 CAUTELOSO : cautious
prevenir {87} vt 1 : to prevent 2 : to warn — **prevenirse** vr ~ **contra** or ~ **de** : to take precautions
preventivo, -va adj : preventive, precautionary
prever {88} vt ANTICIPAR : to foresee, to anticipate
previo, -via adj 1 : previous, prior 2 : after, upon ⟨previo pago : after paying, upon payment⟩
previsible adj : foreseeable
previsión nf, pl -siones 1 : foresight 2 : prediction, forecast 3 : precaution
previsor, -sora adj : farsighted, prudent
prieto, -ta adj 1 : blackish, dark 2 : dark-skinned, swarthy 3 : tight, compressed
prima nf 1 : premium 2 : bonus 3 → primo
primacía nf 1 : precedence, priority 2 : superiority, supremacy
primado nm : primate (bishop)
primario, -ria adj : primary
primate nm : primate
primavera nf 1 : spring (season) 2 PRÍMULA : primrose
primaveral adj : spring, springlike
primero¹ adv 1 : first 2 : rather, sooner
primero², -ra adj (**primer** before masculine singular nouns) 1 : first 2 : top, leading 3 : fundamental, basic 4 **de primera** : first-rate
primero³, -ra n : first
primicia nf 1 : first fruits 2 : scoop, exclusive

primigenio, -nia *adj* : original, primary
primitivo, -va *adj* **1** : primitive **2** ORIG-
  INAL : original
primo, -ma *n* : cousin
primogénito, -ta *adj & n* : firstborn
primor *nm* **1** : skill, care **2** : beauty, elegance
primordial *adj* **1** : primordial **2** : basic,
  fundamental
primoroso, -sa *adj* **1** : exquisite, fine,
  delicate **2** : skillful
prímula *nf* : primrose
princesa *nf* : princess
principado *nm* : principality
principal¹ *adj* **1** : main, principal **2**
  : foremost, leading
principal² *nm* : capital, principal
príncipe *nm* : prince
principesco, -ca *adj* : princely
principiante¹ *adj* : beginning
principiante² *nmf* : beginner, novice
principiar *vt* EMPEZAR : to begin
principio *nm* **1** COMIENZO : beginning
  2 : principle **3 al principio** : at first **4**
  a principios de : at the beginning of ⟨a
  principios de agosto : at the beginning
  of August⟩ **5 en ~** : in principle
pringar {52} *vt* **1** : to dip (in grease) **2**
  : to soil, to spatter (with grease) —
  pringarse *vr*
pringoso, -sa *adj* : greasy
pringue¹, etc. → pringar
pringue² *nm* : grease, drippings *pl*
prior, priora *n* : prior *m*, prioress *f*
priorato *nm* : priory
prioridad *nf* : priority, precedence
prisa *nf* **1** : hurry, rush **2 a ~ or de ~**
  : quickly, fast **3 a toda prisa** : as fast
  as possible **4 darse prisa** : to hurry **5**
  tener prisa : to be in a hurry
prisión *nf, pl* **prisiones 1** CÁRCEL
  : prison, jail **2** ENCARCELAMIENTO
  : imprisonment
prisionero, -ra *n* : prisoner
prisma *nm* : prism
prismáticos *nmpl* : binoculars
prístino, -na *adj* : pristine
privacidad *nf* : privacy
privación *nf, pl* **-ciones 1** : deprivation
  2 : privation, want
privado, -da *adj* : private — **privada-**
  mente *adv*
privar *vt* **1** DESPOJAR : to deprive **2** : to
  stun, to knock out — **privarse** *vr* : to
  deprive oneself
privativo, -va *adj* : exclusive, particular
privilegiado, -da *adj* : privileged
privilegiar *vt* : to grant a privilege to, to
  favor
privilegio *nm* : privilege
pro¹ *nm* **1** : pro, advantage ⟨los pros y
  contras : the pros and cons⟩ **2 en pro**
  de : for, in favor of
pro² *prep* : for, in favor of ⟨grupos pro
  derechos humanos : groups supporting
  human rights⟩
proa *nf* : bow, prow
probabilidad *nf* : probability

probable *adj* : probable, likely
probablemente *adv* : probably
probar {19} *vt* **1** : to demonstrate, to
  prove **2** : to test, to try out **3** : to try
  on (clothing) **4** : to taste, to sample —
  vi : to try — **probarse** *vr* : to try on
  (clothing)
probeta *nf* : test tube
probidad *nf* : probity
problema *nm* : problem
problemática *nf* : set of problems ⟨la
  problemática que debemos enfrentar
  : the problems we must face⟩
proboscide *nf* : proboscis
problemático, -ca *adj* : problematic
procaz *adj, pl* **procaces 1** : insolent, impudent **2** : indecent
procedencia *nf* : origin, source
procedente *adj* **1** : proper, fitting **2 ~**
  de : coming from
proceder *vi* **1** AVANZAR : to proceed **2**
  : to act, to behave **3** : to be appropriate, to be fitting **4 ~ de** : to originate
  from, to come from
procedimiento *nm* : procedure, process
prócer *nmf* : eminent person, leader
procesado, -da *n* : accused, defendant
procesador *nm* : processor ⟨procesador
  de textos : word processor⟩
procesamiento *nm* : processing ⟨proce-
  samiento de datos : data processing⟩
procesar *vt* **1** : to prosecute, to try **2**
  : to process
procesión *nf, pl* **-siones** : procession
proceso *nm* **1** : process **2** : trial, proceedings *pl*
proclama *nf* : proclamation
proclamación *nf, pl* **-ciones** : proclamation
proclamar *vt* : to proclaim — **procla-**
  marse *vr*
proclive *adj* **~ a** : inclined to, prone to
proclividad *nf* : proclivity, inclination
procrear *vi* : to procreate — **pro-**
  creación *nf*
procurador, -dora *n* ABOGADO : attorney
procurar *vt* **1** INTENTAR : to try, to endeavor **2** CONSEGUIR : to obtain, to
  procure **3 procurar hacer** : to manage
  to do
prodigar {52} *vt* : to lavish, to be generous with
prodigio *nm* : wonder, marvel
prodigioso, -sa *adj* : prodigious, marvelous
pródigo¹, -ga *adj* **1** : generous, lavish **2**
  : wasteful, prodigal
pródigo², -ga *n* : spendthrift, prodigal
producción *nf, pl* **-ciones 1** : production **2 producción en serie** : mass production
producir {61} *vt* **1** : to produce, to make,
  to manufacture **2** : to cause, to bring
  about **3** : to bear (interest) — **pro-**
  ducirse *vr* : to take place, to occur
productividad *nf* : productivity
productivo, -va *adj* **1** : productive **2** LU-
  CRATIVO : profitable

producto *nm* 1 : product 2 : proceeds *pl*, yield

productor, -tora *n* : producer

proeza *nf* HAZAÑA : feat, exploit

profanar *vt* : to profane, to desecrate — **profanación** *nf*

profano¹, -na *adj* 1 : profane 2 : worldly, secular

profano², -na *n* : nonspecialist

profecía *nf* : prophecy

proferir {76} *vt* 1 : to utter 2 : to hurl (insults)

profesar *vt* 1 : to profess, to declare 2 : to practice, to exercise

profesión *nf, pl* **-siones** : profession

profesional *adj & nmf* : professional — **profesionalmente** *adv*

profesionalismo *nm* : professionalism

profesionalizar {21} *vt* : to professionalize

profesionista *nmf Mex* : professional

profesor, -sora *n* 1 MAESTRO : teacher 2 : professor

profesorado *nm* 1 : faculty 2 : teaching profession

profeta *nm* : prophet

profético, -ca *adj* : prophetic

profetisa *nf* : prophetess, prophet

profetizar {21} *vt* : to prophesy

prófugo, -ga *adj & n* : fugitive

profundidad *nf* : depth, profundity

profundizar {21} *vt* 1 : to deepen 2 : to study in depth — *vi* **en** : to go deeply into, to study in depth

profundo, -da *adj* 1 HONDO : deep 2 : profound — **profundamente** *adv*

profusión *nf, pl* **-siones** : abundance, profusion

profuso, -sa *adj* : profuse, abundant, extensive

progenie *nf* : progeny, offspring

progenitor, -tora *n* ANTEPASADO : ancestor, progenitor

progesterona *nf* : progesterone

prognóstico *nm* : prognosis

programa *nm* 1 : program 2 : plan 3 **programa de estudios** : curriculum

programable *adj* : programmable

programación *nf, pl* **-ciones** 1 : programming 2 : planning

programador, -dora *n* : programmer

programar *vt* 1 : to schedule, to plan 2 : to program (a computer, etc.)

progresar *vi* : to progress, to make progress

progresista *adj & nmf* : progressive

progresivo, -va *adj* : progressive, gradual

progreso *nm* : progress

prohibición *nf, pl* **-ciones** : ban, prohibition

prohibir {62} *vt* : to prohibit, to ban, to forbid

prohibitivo, -va *adj* : prohibitive

prohijar {5} *vt* ADOPTAR : to adopt

prójimo *nm* : neighbor, fellow man

prole *nf* : offspring, progeny

proletariado *nm* : proletariat, working class

proletario, -ria *adj & n* : proletarian

proliferar *vi* : to proliferate — **proliferación** *nf*

prolífico, -ca *adj* : prolific

prolijo, -ja *adj* : wordy, long-winded

prólogo *nm* : prologue, preface, foreword

prolongación *nf, pl* **-ciones** : extension, lengthening

prolongar {52} *vt* 1 : to prolong 2 : to extend, to lengthen — **prolongarse** *vr* CONTINUAR : to last, to continue

promediar *vt* 1 : to average 2 : to divide in half — *vi* : to be half over

promedio *nm* 1 : average 2 : middle, midpoint

promesa *nf* : promise

prometedor, -dora *adj* : promising, hopeful

prometer *vt* : to promise — *vi* : to show promise — **prometerse** *vr* COMPROMETERSE : to get engaged

prometido¹, -da *adj* : engaged

prometido², -da *n* NOVIO : fiancé *m*, fiancée *f*

prominente *adj* : prominent — **prominencia** *nf*

promiscuo, -cua *adj* : promiscuous — **promiscuidad** *nf*

promisorio, -ria *adj* 1 : promising 2 : promissory

promoción *nf, pl* **-ciones** 1 : promotion 2 : class, year 3 : play-off (in soccer)

promocionar *vt* : to promote — **promocional** *adj*

promontorio *nm* : promontory, headland

promotor, -tora *n* : promoter

promover {47} *vt* 1 : to promote, to advance 2 FOMENTAR : to foster, to encourage 3 PROVOCAR : to provoke, to cause

promulgación *nf, pl* **-ciones** 1 : enactment 2 : proclamation, enactment

promulgar {52} *vt* 1 : to promulgate, to proclaim 2 : to enact (a law or decree)

prono, -na *adj* : prone

pronombre *nm* : pronoun

pronosticar {72} *vt* : to predict, to forecast

pronóstico *nm* 1 PREDICCIÓN : forecast, prediction 2 : prognosis

prontitud *nf* 1 PRESTEZA : promptness, speed 2 **con ~** : promptly, quickly

pronto¹ *adv* 1 : quickly, promptly 2 : soon 3 **de ~** : suddenly 4 **lo más pronto posible** : as soon as possible 5 **tan pronto como** : as soon as

pronto², -ta *adj* 1 RÁPIDO : quick, speedy, prompt 2 PREPARADO : ready

pronunciación *nf, pl* **-ciones** : pronunciation

pronunciado, -da *adj* 1 : pronounced, sharp, steep 2 : marked, noticeable

pronunciamiento *nm* 1 : pronouncement 2 : military uprising

pronunciar *vt* 1 : to pronounce, to say 2 : to give, to deliver (a speech) 3 pro-

nunciar un fallo : to pronounce sentence — **pronunciarse** *vr* : to declare oneself

propagación *nf, pl* **-ciones** : propagation, spreading

propaganda *nf* **1** : propaganda **2** PUBLICIDAD : advertising

propagar {52} *vt* **1** : to propagate **2** : to spread, to disseminate — **propagarse** *vr*

propalar *vt* **1** : to divulge **2** : to spread

propano *nm* : propane

proparse *vr* : to go too far, to overstep one's bounds

propensión *nf, pl* **-siones** INCLINACIÓN : inclination, propensity

propenso, -sa *adj* : prone, susceptible

propiamente *adv* **1** : properly, correctly **2** : exactly, precisely ⟨propiamente dicho : strictly speaking⟩

propiciar *vt* **1** : to propitiate **2** : to favor, to foster

propicio, -cia *adj* : favorable, propitious

propiedad *nf* **1** : property ⟨propiedad privada : private property⟩ **2** : ownership **3** CUALIDAD : property, quality **4** : suitability, appropriateness

propietario¹, -ria *adj* : proprietary

propietario², -ria *n* DUEÑO : owner, proprietor

propina *nf* : tip, gratuity

propinar *vt* : to give, to strike ⟨propinar una paliza : to give a beating⟩

propio, -pia *adj* **1** : own ⟨su propia casa : his own house⟩ ⟨sus recursos propios : their own resources⟩ **2** APROPIADO : appropriate, suitable **3** CARACTERÍSTICO : characteristic, typical **4** MISMO : oneself ⟨el propio director : the director himself⟩

proponer {60} *vt* **1** : to propose, to suggest **2** : to nominate — **proponerse** *vr* : to intend, to plan, to set out ⟨lo que se propone lo cumple : he does what he sets out to do⟩

proporción *nf, pl* **-ciones** **1** : proportion **2** : ratio (in mathematics) **3** **proporciones** *nfpl* : proportions, size ⟨de grandes proporciones : very large⟩

proporcionado, -da *adj* **1** : proportionate **2** : proportioned ⟨bien proporcionado : well-proportioned⟩ — **proporcionadamente** *adv*

proporcional *adj* : proportional — **proporcionalmente** *adv*

proporcionar *vt* **1** : to provide, to give **2** : to proportion, to adapt

proposición *nf, pl* **-ciones** : proposal, proposition

propósito *nm* **1** INTENCIÓN : purpose, intention **2 a** ⟨~ : by the way **3 a** ⟨~ : on purpose, intentionally

propuesta *nf* PROPOSICIÓN : proposal

propulsar *vt* **1** IMPULSAR : to propel, to drive **2** PROMOVER : to promote, to encourage

propulsión *nf, pl* **-siones** : propulsion

propulsor *nm* : propellant

propuso, etc. → **proponer**

prorrata *nf* **1** : share, quota **2 a** ⟨~ : pro rata, proportionately

prórroga *nf* **1** : extension, deferment **2** : overtime (in sports)

prorrogar {52} *vt* **1** : to extend (a deadline) **2** : to postpone

prorrumpir *vi* : to burst forth, to break out ⟨prorrumpí en lágrimas : I burst into tears⟩

prosa *nf* : prose

prosaico, -ca *adj* : prosaic, mundane

proscribir {33} *v* **1** PROHIBIR : to prohibit, to ban, to proscribe **2** DESTERRAR : to banish, to exile

proscripción *nf, pl* **-ciones** **1** PROHIBICIÓN : ban, proscription **2** DESTIERRO : banishment

proscrito¹ *pp* → **proscribir**

proscrito², -ta *n* **1** DESTERRADO : exile **2** : outlaw

prosecución *nf, pl* **-ciones** **1** : continuation **2** : pursuit

proseguir {75} *vt* **1** CONTINUAR : to continue **2** : to pursue (studies, goals) — *vi* : to continue, to go on

prosélito, -ta *n* : proselyte

prospección *nf, pl* **-ciones** : prospecting, exploration

prospectar *vi* : to prospect

prospecto *nm* : prospectus, leaflet, brochure

prosperar *vi* : to prosper, to thrive

prosperidad *nf* : prosperity

próspero, -ra *adj* : prosperous, flourishing

próstata *nf* : prostate

prostitución *nf, pl* **-ciones** : prostitution

prostituir {41} *vt* : to prostitute — **prostituirse** *vr* : to prostitute oneself

prostituto, -ta *n* : prostitute

protagonista *nmf* **1** : protagonist, main character **2** : leader

protagonizar {21} *vt* : to star in

protección *nf, pl* **-ciones** : protection

protector¹, -tora *adj* : protective

protector², -tora *n* **1** : protector, guardian **2** : patron

protector³ *nm* : protector, guard ⟨chaleco protector : chest protector⟩

protectorado *nm* : protectorate

proteger {15} *vt* **1** : to protect, to defend — **protegerse** *vr*

protegido, -da *n* : protégé

proteína *nf* : protein

prótesis *nfs & pl* : prosthesis

protesta *nf* **1** : protest **2** *Mex* : promise, oath

protestante *adj & nmf* : Protestant

protestantismo *nm* : Protestantism

protestar *vi* : to protest, to object — *vt* **1** : to protest, to object to **2** : to declare, to profess

protocolo *nm* : protocol

protón *nm, pl* **protones** : proton

protoplasma *nm* : protoplasm

prototipo *nm* : prototype

protozoario *or* **protozoo** *nm* : protozoan

protuberancia *nf* : protuberance — **protuberante** *adj*

provecho *nm* : benefit, advantage

provechoso, -sa *adj* BENEFICIOSO : beneficial, profitable, useful — **provechosamente** *adv*

proveedor, -dora *n* : provider, supplier

proveer {63} *vt* : to provide, to supply — **proveerse** *vr* ~ **de** : to obtain, to supply oneself with

provenir {87} *vi* ~ **de** : to come from

provenzal[1] *adj* : Provençal

provenzal[2] *nmf* : Provençal

provenzal[3] *nm* : Provençal (language)

proverbio *nm* REFRÁN : proverb — **proverbial** *adj*

providencia *nf* 1 : providence, foresight 2 : Providence, God 3 **providencias** *nfpl* : steps, measures

providencial *adj* : providential

provincia *nf* : province — **provincial** *adj*

provinciano, -na *adj* : provincial, unsophisticated

provisión *nf, pl* -**siones** : provision

provisional *adj* : provisional, temporary

provisionalmente *adv* : provisionally, tentatively

provisorio, -ria *adj* : provisional, temporary

provisto *pp* → **proveer**

provocación *nf, pl* -**ciones** : provocation

provocador[1], **-dora** *adj* : provocative, provoking

provocador[2], **-dora** *n* AGITADOR : agitator

provocar {72} *vt* 1 CAUSAR : to provoke, to cause 2 IRRITAR : to provoke, to pique

provocativo, -va *adj* : provocative

proxeneta *nmf* : pimp *m*

próximamente *adv* : shortly, soon

proximidad *nf* 1 : nearness, proximity 2 **proximidades** *nfpl* : vicinity

próximo, -ma *adj* : near, close ⟨la Navidad está próxima : Christmas is almost here⟩ 2 SIGUIENTE : next, following ⟨la próxima semana : the following week⟩

proyección *nf, pl* -**ciones** 1 : projection 2 : showing, screening (of a film) 3 : range, influence, diffusion

proyectar *vt* 1 : to plan 2 LANZAR : to throw, to hurl 3 : to project, to cast (light or shadow) 4 : to show, to screen (a film)

proyectil *nm* : projectile, missile

proyecto *nm* 1 : plan, project 2 **proyecto de ley** : bill

proyector *nm* 1 : projector 2 : spotlight

prudencia *nf* : prudence, care, discretion

prudente *adj* : prudent, sensible, reasonable

prueba[1], etc. → **probar**

prueba[2] *nf* 1 : proof, evidence 2 : trial, test 3 : proof (in printing or photography) 4 : event, qualifying round (in sports) 5 **a prueba de agua** : waterproof 6 **prueba de fuego** : acid test 7 **poner a prueba** : to put to the test

prurito *nm* 1 : itching 2 : desire, urge

psicoanálisis *nm* : psychoanalysis — **psicoanalista** *nmf*

psicoanalítico, -ca *adj* : psychoanalytic

psicoanalizar {21} *vt* : to psychoanalyze

psicología *nf* : psychology

psicológico, -ca *adj* : psychological — **psicológicamente** *adv*

psicólogo, -ga *n* : psychologist

psicópata *nmf* : psychopath

psicopático, -ca *adj* : psycopathic

psicosis *nfs & pl* : psychosis

psicosomático, -ca *adj* : psychosomatic

psicoterapeuta *nmf* : psychotherapist

psicoterapia *nf* : psychotherapy

psicótico, -ca *adj & n* : psychotic

psique *nf* : psyche

psiquiatra *nmf* : psychiatrist

psiquiatría *nf* : psychiatry

psiquiátrico[1], **-ca** *adj* : psychiatric

psiquiátrico[2] *nm* : mental hospital

psíquico, -ca *adj* : psychic

psiquis *nfs & pl* : psyche

psoriasis *nf* : psoriasis

ptomaína *nf* : ptomaine

púa *nf* 1 : barb ⟨alambre de púas : barbed wire⟩ 2 : tooth (of a comb) 3 : quill, spine

pubertad *nf* : puberty

pubiano → **púbiano**

púbico, -ca *adj* : pubic

publicación *nf, pl* -**ciones** : publication

publicar {72} *vt* 1 : to publish 2 DIVULGAR : to divulge, to disclose

publicidad *nf* 1 : publicity 2 : advertising

publicista *nmf* : publicist

publicitar *vt* 1 : to publicize 2 : to advertise

publicitario, -ria *adj* : advertising, publicity ⟨agencia publicitaria : advertising agency⟩

público[1], **-ca** *adj* : public — **públicamente** *adv*

público[2] *nm* 1 : public 2 : audience, spectators *pl*

puchero *nm* 1 : pot 2 : stew 3 : pout ⟨hacer pucheros : to pout⟩

pucho *nm* 1 : waste, residue 2 : cigarette butt 3 **a puchos** : little by little, bit by bit

púdico, -ca *adj* : chaste, modest

pudiente *adj* 1 : powerful 2 : rich, wealthy

pudín *nm, pl* **pudines** BUDÍN : pudding

pudo, etc. → **poder**

pudor *nm* : modesty, reserve

pudoroso, -sa *adj* : modest, reserved, shy

pudrir {59} *vt* 1 : to rot 2 *fam* : to annoy, to upset — **pudrirse** *vr* 1 : to rot 2 : to languish

pueblerino, -na *adj* : provincial, countrified

puebla, etc. → **poblar**

pueblo nm **1** NACIÓN : people **2** : common people **3** ALDEA, POBLADO : town, village

puede, etc. → **poder**

puente nm **1** : bridge ⟨puente levadizo : drawbridge⟩ **2** : denture, bridge **3** **puente aéreo** : airlift

puerco[1], **-ca** adj : dirty, filthy

puerco[2], **-ca** n **1** CERDO, MARRANO : pig, hog **2** : pig, dirty or greedy person **3** **puerco espín** : porcupine

pueril adj : childish, puerile

puerro nm : leek

puerta nf **1** : door, entrance, gate **2** **a puerta cerrada** : behind closed doors

puerto nm **1** : port, harbor **2** : mountain pass **3** **puerto marítimo** : seaport

puertorriqueño, -ña adj & n : Puerto Rican

pues conj **1** : since, because, for ⟨no puedo ir, pues no tengo plata : I can't go, since I don't have any money⟩ ⟨lo hace, pues a él le gusta : he does it because he likes to⟩ **2** (used interjectionally) : well, then ⟨¡pues claro que sí! : well, of course!⟩ ⟨¡pues no voy! : well then, I'm not going!⟩

puesta nf **1** : setting ⟨puesta del sol : sunset⟩ **2** : laying (of eggs) **3** **puesta a punto** : tune-up **4** **puesta en marcha** : start, starting up

puestero, -ra n : seller, vendor

puesto[1] pp → **poner**

puesto[2], **-ta** adj : dressed ⟨bien puesto : well-dressed⟩

puesto[3] nm **1** LUGAR, SITIO : place, position **2** : position, job **3** : kiosk, stand, stall **4** **puesto que** : since, given that

pugilato nm BOXEO : boxing, pugilism

pugilista nm BOXEADOR : boxer, pugilist

pugna nf **1** CONFLICTO, LUCHA : conflict, struggle **2** **en ∼** : at odds, in conflict

pugnar vi LUCHAR : to fight, to strive, to struggle

pugnaz adj : pugnacious

pujante adj : mighty, powerful

pujanza nf : strength, vigor ⟨pujanza económica : economic strength⟩

pulcritud nf **1** : neatness, tidiness **2** ESMERO : meticulousness

pulcro, -cra adj **1** : clean, neat **2** : exquisite, delicate, refined

pulga nf **1** : flea **2** **tener malas pulgas** : to be bad-tempered

pulgada nf : inch

pulgar nm **1** : thumb **2** : big toe

pulir vt **1** : to polish, to shine **2** REFINAR : to refine, to perfect

pulla nf **1** : cutting remark, dig, gibe **2** : obscenity

pulmón nm, pl **pulmones** : lung

pulmonar adj : pulmonary

pulmonía nf NEUMONÍA : pneumonia

pulpa nf : pulp, flesh

pulpería nf : small grocery store

púlpito nm : pulpit

pulpo nm : octopus

pulsación nf, pl **-ciones 1** : beat, pulsation, throb **2** : keystroke

pulsar vt **1** APRETAR : to press, to push **2** : to strike (a key) **3** : to assess — vi : to beat, to throb

pulsera nf : bracelet

pulso nm **1** : pulse ⟨tomarle el pulso a alguien : to take someone's pulse⟩ ⟨tomarle el pulso a la opinión : to sound out opinion⟩ **2** : steadiness (of hand) ⟨dibujo a pulso : freehand sketch⟩

pulular vi ABUNDAR : to abound, to swarm ⟨en el río pululan los peces : the river is teeming with fish⟩

pulverizador nm **1** : atomizer, spray **2** : spray gun

pulverizar {21} vt **1** : to pulverize, to crush **2** : to spray

puma nf : cougar, puma

puna nf : bleak Andean tableland

punción nf, pl **punciones** : puncture

punible adj : punishable

punitivo, -va adj : punitive

punce, etc. → **punzar**

punta nf **1** : tip, end ⟨punta del dedo : fingertip⟩ ⟨en la punta de la lengua : at the tip of one's tongue⟩ **2** : point (of a weapon or pencil) ⟨punta de lanza : spearhead⟩ **3** : point, headland **4** : bunch, lot ⟨una punta de ladrones : a bunch of thieves⟩ **5** **a punta de** : by, by dint of

puntada nf **1** : stitch (in sewing) **2** PUNZADA : sharp pain, stitch, twinge **3** Mex : witticism, quip

puntal nm **1** : prop, support **2** : stanchion

puntapié nm PATADA : kick

puntazo nm CORNADA : wound (from a goring)

puntear vt **1** : to pluck (a guitar) **2** : to lead (in sports)

puntería nf : aim, marksmanship

puntero nm **1** : pointer **2** : leader

puntiagudo, -da adj : sharp, pointed

puntilla nf **1** : lace edging **2** : dagger (in bullfighting) **3** **de puntillas** : on tiptoe

puntilloso, -sa adj : punctilious

punto nm **1** : dot, point **2** : period (in punctuation) **3** : item, question **4** : spot, place **5** : moment, stage, degree **6** : point (in a score) **7** : stitch **8** **en ∼** : on the dot, sharp ⟨a las dos en punto : at two o'clock sharp⟩ **9** **al punto** : at once **10** **a punto fijo** : exactly, certainly **11** **dos puntos** : colon **12** **hasta cierto punto** : up to a point **13** **punto decimal** : decimal point **14** **punto de vista** : point of view **15** **punto y coma** : semicolon **16** **y punto** : period ⟨es el mejor que hay y punto : it's the best there is, period⟩ **17** **puntos cardinales** : points of the compass

puntuación *nf, pl* **-ciones 1** : punctuation **2** : scoring, score, grade
puntual *adj* **1** : prompt, punctual **2** : exact, accurate — **puntualmente** *adv*
puntualidad *nf* **1** : promptness, punctuality **2** : exactness, accuracy
puntualizar {21} *vt* **1** : to specify, to state **2** : to point out
puntuar {3} *vt* : to punctuate — *vi* : to score points
punzada *nf* : sharp pain, twinge, stitch
punzante *adj* **1** : sharp **2** CÁUSTICO : biting, caustic
punzar {21} *vt* **1** : to pierce, to puncture
punzón *nm, pl* **punzones 1** : awl **2** : hole punch
puñado *nm* **1** : handful **2 a puñados** : lots of, by the handful
puñal *nm* DAGA : dagger
puñalada *nf* : stab, stab wound
puñetazo *nm* : punch (with the fist)
puño *nm* **1** : fist **2** : handful, fistful **3** : cuff (of a shirt) **4** : handle, hilt
pupila *nf* : pupil (of the eye)
pupilo, -la *n* **1** : pupil, student **2** : ward, charge
pupitre *nm* : writing desk
puré *nm* : purée ⟨puré de papas : mashed potatoes⟩
pureza *nf* : purity
purga *nf* **1** : laxative **2** : purge
purgante *adj & nm* : laxative, purgative
purgar {52} *vt* **1** : to purge, to cleanse **2** : to liquidate (in politics) **3** : to give a

laxative to — **purgarse** *vr* **1** : to take a laxative **2 ~ de** : to purge oneself of
purgatorio *nm* : purgatory
purgue, etc. → **purgar**
purificador *nm* : purifier
purificar {72} *vt* : to purify — **purificación** *nf*
puritano¹, -na *adj* : puritanical, puritan
puritano², -na *n* **1** : Puritan **2** : puritan
puro¹ *adv* : sheer, much ⟨de puro terco : out of sheer stubbornness⟩
puro², -ra *adj* **1** : pure ⟨aire puro : fresh air⟩ **2** : plain, simple, sheer ⟨por pura curiosidad : from sheer curiosity⟩ **3** : only, just ⟨emplean puras mujeres : they only employ women⟩ **4 pura sangre** : Thoroughbred horse
puro³ *nm* : cigar
púrpura *nf* : purple
purpúreo, -rea *adj* : purple
purpurina *nf* : glitter (for decoration)
pus *nm* : pus
pusilánime *adj* COBARDE : pusillanimous, cowardly
puso, etc. → **poner**
pústula *nf* : pustule, pimple
puta *nf* : whore, slut
putrefacción *nf, pl* **-ciones** : putrefaction
putrefacto, -ta *adj* **1** PODRIDO : putrid, rotten **2** : decayed
pútrido, -da *adj* : putrid, rotten
puya *nf* **1** : point (of a lance) **2 lanzar una puya** : to gibe, to taunt

Q

q *nf* : eighteenth letter of the Spanish alphabet
que¹ *conj* **1** : that ⟨dice que está listo : he says that he's ready⟩ ⟨espero que lo haga : I hope that he does it⟩ **2** : than ⟨más que nada : more than anything⟩ **3** (*implying permission or desire*) ⟨¡que entre! : send him in!⟩ ⟨¡que te vaya bien! : I wish you well!⟩ **4** (*indicating a reason or cause*) ⟨¡cuidado, que te caes! : be careful, you're about to fall!⟩ ⟨no provoques al perro, que te va a morder : don't provoke the dog or (else) he'll bite⟩ **5 es que** : the thing is that, I'm afraid that **6 yo que tú** : if I were you
que² *pron* **1** : who, that ⟨la niña que viene : the girl who is coming⟩ **2** : whom, that ⟨los alumnos que enseñé : the students that I taught⟩ **3** : that, which ⟨el carro que me gusta : the car that I like⟩ **4 el (la, lo, las, los) que** → **el¹, la¹, lo¹, los¹**
qué¹ *adv* : how, what ⟨¡qué bonito! : how pretty!⟩
qué² *adj* : what, which ⟨¿qué hora es? : what time is it?⟩
qué³ *pron* : what ⟨¿qué quieres? : what do you want?⟩

quebracho *nm* : quebracho (tree)
quebrada *nf* DESFILADERO : ravine, gorge
quebradizo, -za *adj* FRÁGIL : breakable, delicate, fragile
quebrado¹, -da *adj* **1** : bankrupt **2** : rough, uneven **3** ROTO : broken
quebrado² *nm* : fraction
quebrantamiento *nm* **1** : breaking **2** : deterioration, weakening
quebrantar *vt* **1** : to break, to split, to crack **2** : to weaken **3** : to violate (a law or contract)
quebranto *nm* **1** : break, breaking **2** AFLICCIÓN : affliction, grief **3** PÉRDIDA : loss
quebrar {55} *vt* **1** ROMPER : to break **2** DOBLAR : to bend, to twist — *vi* **1** : to go bankrupt **2** : to fall out, to break up — **quebrarse** *vr*
queda *nf* : curfew
quedar *vi* **1** PERMANECER : to remain, to stay **2** : to be ⟨quedamos contentos con las mejoras : we were pleased with the improvements⟩ **3** : to be situated ⟨queda muy lejos : it's very far, it's too far away⟩ **4** : to be left ⟨quedan sólo dos alternativas : there are only two options left⟩ **5** : to fit, to suit ⟨estos zap-

atos no me quedan : these shoes don't fit⟩ **6 quedar bien (mal)** : to turn out well (badly) **7 ~ en** : to agree, to arrange ⟨¿en qué quedamos? : what's the arrangement, then?⟩ — **quedarse** vr **1** : to stay ⟨se quedó en casa : she stayed at home⟩ **2** : to keep on ⟨se quedó esperando : he kept on waiting⟩ **3 quedarse atrás** : to stay behind ⟨no quedarse atrás : to be no slouch⟩ **4 ~ con** : to remain ⟨me quedé con hambre después de comer : I was still hungry after I ate⟩

quedo¹ adv : softly, quietly

quedo², -da adj : quiet, still

quehacer nm **1** : work **2 quehaceres** nmpl : chores

queja nf : complaint

quejarse vr **1** : to complain **2** : to groan, to moan

quejido nm **1** : groan, moan **2** : whine, whimper

quejoso, -sa adj : complaining, whining

quejumbroso, -sa adj : querulous, whining

quema nf **1** FUEGO : fire **2** : burning

quemado, -da adj **1** : burned, burnt **2** : annoyed : burned-out

quemador nm : burner

quemadura nf : burn

quemar vt : to burn, to set fire to — vi : to be burning hot — **quemarse** vr

quemarropa nf a ~ : point-blank

quemazón nf, pl **-zones 1** : burning **2** : intense heat **3** : itch **4** : cutting remark

quena nf : Peruvian reed flute

quepa, etc. → caber

querella nf **1** : complaint **2** : lawsuit

querellante nmf : plaintiff

querellarse vr ~ **contra** : to bring suit against, to sue

querer¹ {64} vt **1** DESEAR : to want, to desire ⟨quiere ser profesor : he wants to be a teacher⟩ ⟨¿cuánto quieres por esta computadora? : how much do you want for this computer?⟩ **2** : to love, to like, to be fond of ⟨te quiero : I love you⟩ **3** (indicating a request) ⟨¿quieres pasarme la leche? : please pass the milk⟩ **4 querer decir** : to mean **5 sin ~** : unintentionally — vi : like, want ⟨si quieras : if you like⟩

querer² nm : love, affection

querido¹, -da adj : dear, beloved

querido², -da n : dear, sweetheart

queroseno nm : kerosene

querrá, etc. → querer

querúbico, -ca adj : cherubic

querubín nm, pl **-bines** : cherub

quesadilla nf : quesadilla

quesería nf : cheese shop

queso nm : cheese

quetzal nm **1** : quetzal (bird) **2** : monetary unit of Guatemala

quicio nm **1 estar fuera de quicio** : to be beside oneself **2 sacar de quicio** : to exasperate, to drive crazy

quid nm : crux, gist ⟨el quid de la cuestión : the crux of the matter⟩

quiebra¹, etc. → quebrar

quiebra² nf **1** : break, crack **2** BANCARROTA : failure, bankruptcy

quien pron, pl **quienes 1** : who, whom ⟨no sé quien ganará : I don't know who will win⟩ ⟨las personas con quienes trabajo : the people with whom I work⟩ **2** : whoever, whomever ⟨quien quiere salir que salga : whoever wants to can leave⟩ **3** : anyone, some people ⟨hay quienes no están de acuerdo : some people don't agree⟩

quién pron, pl **quiénes 1** : who, whom ⟨¿quién sabe? : who knows?⟩ ⟨¿con quién hablo? : with whom am I speaking?⟩ **2 de ~** : whose ⟨¿de quién es este libro? : whose book is this?⟩

quienquiera pron, pl **quienesquiera** : whoever, whomever

quiere, etc. → querer

quieto, -ta adj **1** : calm, quiet **2** INMÓVIL : still

quietud nf **1** : calm, tranquility **2** INMOVILIDAD : stillness

quijada nf : jaw, jawbone

quijotesco, -ca adj : quixotic

quilate nm : karat

quilla nf : keel

quimera nf : chimera, illusion

quimérico, -ca adj : chimeric, fanciful

química nf : chemistry

químico¹, -ca adj : chemical

químico², -ca n : chemist

quimioterapia nf : chemotherapy

quimono nm : kimono

quince adj & nm : fifteen

quinceañero, -ra n : fifteen-year-old, teenager

quinceavo¹, -va adj : fifteenth

quinceavo² nm : fifteenth (fraction)

quincena nf : two week period, fortnight

quincenal adj : bimonthly, twice a month

quincuagésimo¹, -ma adj : fiftieth, fifty-

quincuagésimo², -ma n : fiftieth, fifty-(in a series)

quingombó nm : okra

quiniela nf : sports lottery

quinientos¹, -tas adj : five hundred

quinientos² nms & pl : five hundred

quinina nf : quinine

quino nm : cinchona

quinqué nm : oil lamp

quinquenal adj : five-year ⟨un plan quinquenal : a five-year plan⟩

quinta nf : country house, villa

quintaesencia nf : quintessence — **quintaesencial** adj

quintal nm : hundredweight

quinteto nm : quintet

quintillizo, -za n : quintuplet

quinto, -ta adj : fifth — **quinto, -ta** n

quíntuplo, -la adj : quintuple, five-fold

quiosco nm **1** : kiosk **2** : newsstand **3 quiosco de música** : bandstand

quirófano nm : operating room

quiromancia *nf* : palmistry
quiropráctica *nf* : chiropractic
quiropráctico, -ca *n* : chiropractor
quirúrgico, -ca *adj* : surgical — **quirúrgicamente** *adv*
quiso, etc. → querer
quisquilloso[1], -sa *adj* : fastidious, fussy
quisquilloso[2], -sa *n* : fussy person, fussbudget
quiste *nm* : cyst
quitaesmalte *nm* : nail polish remover
quitamanchas *nms & pl* : stain remover

quitanieves *nms & pl* : snowplow
quitar *vt* **1** : to remove, to take away **2** : to take off (clothes) **3** : to get rid of, to relieve — **quitarse** *vr* **1** : to withdraw, to leave **2** : to take off (one's clothes) **3** ~ **de** : to give up (a habit) **4 quitar de encima** : to get rid of
quitasol *nm* : parasol
quiteño[1], -ña *adj* : of or from Quito
quiteño[2], -ña *n* : person from Quito
quizá *or* **quizás** *adv* : maybe, perhaps
quórum *nm, pl* **quórums** : quorum

R

r *nf* : nineteenth letter of the Spanish alphabet
rábano *nm* **1** : radish **2 rábano picante** : horseradish
rabí *nmf, pl* **rabíes** : rabbi
rabia *nf* **1** HIDROFOBIA : rabies, hydrophobia **2** : rage, anger
rabiar *vi* **1** : to rage, to be furious **2** : to be in great pain **3 a** ~ *fam* : like crazy, like mad
rabieta *nf* BERRINCHE : tantrum
rabino, -na *n* : rabbi
rabioso, -sa *adj* **1** : enraged, furious **2** : rabid
rabo *nm* **1** COLA : tail **2 el rabo del ojo** : the corner of one's eye
racha *nf* **1** : gust of wind **2** : run, series, string ⟨racha perdedora : losing streak⟩
racheado, -da *adj* : gusty, windy
racial *adj* : racial
racimo *nm* : bunch, cluster ⟨un racimo de uvas : a bunch of grapes⟩
raciocinio *nm* : reason, reasoning
ración *nf, pl* **raciones 1** : share, ration **2** PORCIÓN : portion, helping
racional *adj* : rational, reasonable — **racionalmente** *adv*
racionalidad *nf* : rationality
racionalización *nf, pl* **-ciones** : rationalization
racionalizar {21} *vt* **1** : to rationalize **2** : to streamline
racionamiento *nm* : rationing
racionar *vt* : to ration
racismo *nm* : racism
racista *adj & nmf* : racist
radar *nm* : radar
radiación *nf, pl* **-ciones** : radiation, irradiation
radiactividad *nf* : radioactivity
radiactivo, -va *adj* : radioactive
radiador *nm* : radiator
radial *adj* **1** : radial **2** : radio, broadcasting ⟨emisora radial : radio transmitter⟩
radiante *adj* : radiant
radiar *vt* **1** : to radiate **2** : to irradiate **3** : to broadcast (on the radio)
radical[1] *adj* : radical, extreme — **radicalmente** *adv*

radical[2] *nmf* : radical
radicalismo *nm* : radicalism
radicar {72} *vi* **1** : to be found, to lie **2** ARRAIGAR : to take root — **radicarse** *vr* : to settle, to establish oneself
radio[1] *nm* **1** : radius **2** : radium
radio[2] *nmf* : radio
radioactividad *nf* : radioactivity
radioactivo, -va *adj* : radioactive
radioaficionado, -da *n* : ham radio operator
radiodifusión *nf, pl* **-siones** : radio broadcasting
radiodifusora *nf* : radio station
radioemisora *nf* : radio station
radiofaro *nm* : radio beacon
radiofónico, -ca *adj* : radio ⟨estación radiofónica pública : public radio station⟩
radiofrecuencia *nf* : radio frequency
radiografía *nf* : X ray (photograph)
radiografiar {85} *vt* : to x-ray
radiología *nf* : radiology
radiólogo, -ga *n* : radiologist
radón *nm* : radon
raer {65} *vt* RASPAR : to scrape, to scrape off
ráfaga *nf* **1** : gust (of wind) **2** : flash, burst ⟨una ráfaga de luz : a flash of light⟩
raid *nm CA, Mex fam* : lift, ride
raído, -da *adj* : worn, shabby
raiga, etc. → raer
raíz *nf, pl* **raíces 1** : of root **2** : origin, source **3 a raíz de** : following, as a result of **4 echar raíces** : to take root
raja *nf* **1** : crack, slit **2** : slice, wedge
rajá *nm* : raja
rajadura *nf* : crack, split
rajar *vt* HENDER : to crack, to split — *vi* **1** *fam* : to chatter **2** *fam* : to boast, to brag — **rajarse** *vr* **1** : to crack, to split open **2** *fam* : to back out
rajatabla *adv* **a** ~ : strictly, to the letter
ralea *nf* : kind, sort, ilk ⟨son de la misma valea : they're two of a kind⟩
ralentí *nm* **dejar al ralentí** : to leave (a motor) idling
rallado, -da *adj* **1** : grated **2 pan rallado** : bread crumbs *pl*
rallador *nm* : grater

rallar *vt* : to grate

ralo, -la *adj* : sparse, thin

RAM *nf* : RAM, random-access memory

rama *nf* : branch

ramaje *nm* : branches *pl*

ramal *nm* 1 : branchline 2 : halter, strap

ramera *nf* : harlot, prostitute

ramificación *nf, pl* **-ciones** : ramification

ramificarse {72} *vr* : to branch out, to divide into branches

ramillete *nm* 1 RAMO : bouquet 2 : select group, cluster

ramo *nm* 1 : branch 2 RAMILLETE : bouquet 3 : division (of science or industry) 4 **Domingo de Ramos** : Palm Sunday

rampa *nf* : ramp, incline

rana *nf* 1 : frog 2 **rana toro** : bullfrog

ranchera *nf Mex* : traditional folk song

ranchería *nf* : settlement

ranchero, -ra *n* : rancher, farmer

rancho *nm* 1 : ranch, farm 2 : hut 3 : settlement, camp 4 : food, mess (for soldiers, etc.)

rancio, -cia *adj* 1 : aged, mellow (of wine) 2 : ancient, old 3 : rancid

rango *nm* 1 : rank, status 2 : high social standing 3 : pomp, splendor

ranúnculo *nm* : buttercup

ranura *nf* : groove, slot

rap *nm* : rap (music)

rapacidad *nf* : rapacity

rapar *vt* 1 : to crop 2 : to shave

rapaz¹ *adj, pl* **rapaces** : rapacious, predatory

rapaz², -paza *n, mpl* **rapaces** : youngster, child

rape *nm* : close haircut

rapé *nm* : snuff

rapero, -ra *n* : rapper, rap artist

rapidez *nf* : rapidity, speed

rápido¹ *adv* : quickly, fast ⟨manejas tan rápido! : you drive so fast!⟩

rápido², -da *adj* : rapid, quick — **rápidamente** *adv*

rápido³ *nm* 1 : express train 2 **rápidos** *nmpl* : rapids

rapiña *nf* 1 : plunder, pillage 2 **ave de rapiña** : bird of prey

raposa *nf* : vixen (fox)

rapsodia *nf* : rhapsody

raptar *vt* SECUESTRAR : to abduct, to kidnap

rapto *nm* 1 SECUESTRO : kidnapping, abduction 2 ARREBATO : fit, outburst

raptor, -tora *n* SECUESTRADOR : kidnapper

raque *nm* : beachcombing

raquero, -ra *n* : beachcomber

raqueta *nf* 1 : racket (in sports) 2 : snowshoe

raquítico, -ca *adj* 1 : scrawny, weak 2 : measly, skimpy

raquitismo *nm* : rickets

raramente *adv* : seldom, rarely

rareza *nf* 1 : rarity 2 : peculiarity, oddity

raro, -ra *adj* 1 EXTRAÑO : odd, strange, peculiar 2 : unusual, rare 3 : exceptional 4 **rara vez** : seldom, rarely

ras *nm* **a ras de** : level with

rasar *vt* 1 : to skim, to graze 2 : to level

rascacielos *nms & pl* : skyscraper

rascar {72} *vt* 1 : to scratch 2 : to scrape — **rascarse** *vr* : to scratch an itch

rasgadura *nf* : tear, rip

rasgar {52} *vt* : to rip, to tear — **rasgarse** *vr*

rasgo *nm* 1 : stroke (of a pen) ⟨a grandes rasgos : in broad outlines⟩ 2 CARACTERÍSTICA : trait, characteristic 3 : gesture, deed 4 **rasgos** *nmpl* FACCIONES : features

rasgón *nm, pl* **rasgones** : rip, tear

rasgue, etc. → **rasgar**

rasguear *vt* : to strum

rasguñar *vt* 1 : to scratch 2 : to sketch, to outline

rasguño *nm* 1 : scratch 2 : sketch

raso¹, -sa *adj* 1 : level, flat 2 **soldado raso** : private (in the army) ⟨los soldados rasos : the ranks⟩

raso² *nm* : satin

raspadura *nf* 1 : scratching, scraping 2 **raspaduras** *nfpl* : scrapings

raspar *vt* 1 : to scrape 2 : to file down, to smooth — *vi* : to be rough

rasque, etc. → **rascar**

rastra *nf* 1 : harrow 2 **a rastras** : by dragging, unwillingly

rastrear *vt* 1 : to track, to trace 2 : to comb, to search 3 : to trawl

rastrero, -ra *adj* 1 : creeping, crawling 2 : vile, despicable

rastrillar *vt* : to rake, to harrow

rastrillo *nm* 1 : rake 2 *Mex* : razor

rastro *nm* 1 PISTA : trail, track 2 VESTIGIO : trace, sign

rastrojo *nm* : stubble (of plants)

rasuradora *nf Mex, CA* : electric razor, shaver

rasurar *vt* AFEITAR : to shave — **rasurarse** *vr*

rata¹ *nm fam* : pickpocket, thief

rata² *nf* 1 : rat 2 *Col, Pan, Peru* : rate, percentage

ratear *vt* : to pilfer, to steal

ratero, -ra *n* : petty thief

ratificación *nf, pl* **-ciones** : ratification

ratificar {72} *vt* 1 : to ratify 2 : to confirm

rato *nm* 1 : while 2 **pasar el rato** : to pass the time 3 **a cada rato** : all the time, constantly ⟨les sacaba dinero a cada rato : he was always taking money from them⟩ 4 **al poco rato** : later, shortly after

ratón¹, -tona *n, mpl* **ratones** 1 : mouse 2 **ratón de biblioteca** *fam* : bookworm

ratón² *nm, pl* **ratones** 1 : (computer) mouse 2 *CoRi* : biceps

ratonera *nf* : mousetrap

raudal *nm* 1 : torrent 2 **a raudales** : in abundance

raya¹, etc. → raer
raya² *nf* **1** : line **2** : stripe **3** : skate, ray **4** : part (in the hair) **5** : crease (in clothing)
rayar *vt* **1** ARAÑAR : to scratch **2** : to scrawl on, to mark up ⟨rayaron las paredes : they covered the walls with graffiti⟩ — *vi* **1** : to scratch **2** AMANECER : to dawn, to break ⟨al rayar el alba : at break of day⟩ **3** ～ con : to be adjacent to, to be next to **4** ～ en : to border on, to verge on ⟨su respuesta raya en lo ridículo : his answer borders on the ridiculous⟩ — **rayarse** *vr*
rayo *nm* **1** : ray, beam ⟨rayo láser : laser beam⟩ ⟨rayo de gamma : gamma ray⟩ ⟨rayo de sol : sunbeam⟩ **2** RELÁMPAGO : lightning bolt **3 rayo X** : X-ray
rayón *nm, pl* **rayones** : rayon
raza *nf* **1** : race ⟨raza humana : human race⟩ **2** : breed, strain **3 de ～** : thoroughbred, pedigreed
razón *nf, pl* **razones 1** MOTIVO : reason, motive ⟨en razón de : by reason of, because of⟩ **2** JUSTICIA : rightness, justice ⟨tener razón : to be right⟩ **3** : reasoning, sense ⟨perder la razón : to lose one's mind⟩ **4** : ratio, proportion
razonable *adj* : reasonable — **razonablemente** *adv*
razonado, -da *adj* : itemized, detailed
razonamiento *nm* : reasoning
razonar *v* : to reason, to think
reabastecimiento *nm* : replenishment
reabierto *pp* → reabrir
reabrir {2} *vt* : to reopen — **reabrirse** *vr*
reacción *nf, pl* **-ciones 1** : reaction **2 motor a reacción** : jet engine
reaccionar *vi* : to react, to respond
reaccionario, -ria *adj & n* : reactionary
reacio, -cia *adj* : resistant, opposed
reacondicionar *vt* : to recondition
reactivación *nf, pl* **-ciones** : reactivation, revival
reactivar *vt* : to reactivate, revive
reactor *nm* **1** : reactor ⟨reactor nuclear : nuclear reactor⟩ **2** : jet engine **3** : jet airplane, jet
reafirmar *vt* : to reaffirm, to assert, to strengthen
reajustar *vt* : to readjust, to adjust
reajuste *nm* : readjustment ⟨reajuste de precios : price increase⟩
real *adj* **1** : real, true **2** : royal
realce *nm* **1** : embossing, relief **2 dar realce** : to highlight, to bring out
realeza *nf* : royalty
realidad *nf* **1** : reality **2 en ～** : in truth, actually
realinear *vt* : to realign
realismo *nm* **1** : realism **2** : royalism
realista¹ *adj* **1** : realistic **2** : realist **3** : royalist
realista² *nmf* **1** : realist **2** : royalist
realización *nf, pl* **-ciones** : execution, realization

realizar {21} *vt* **1** : to carry out, to execute **2** : to produce, to direct (a film or play) **3** : to fulfill, to achieve **4** : to realize (a profit) — **realizarse** *vr* **1** : to come true **2** : to fulfill oneself
realmente *adv* : really, in reality
realzar {21} *vt* **1** : to heighten, to raise **2** : to highlight, to enhance
reanimación *nf, pl* **-ciones** : revival, resuscitation
reanimar *vt* **1** : to revive, to restore **2** : to resuscitate — **reanimarse** *vr* : to come around, to recover
reanudación *nf, pl* **-ciones** : resumption, renewal
reanudar *vt* : to resume, to renew — **reanudarse** *vr* : to resume, to continue
reaparecer {53} *vi* **1** : to reappear **2** : to make a comeback
reaparición *nf, pl* **-ciones** : reappearance
reapertura *nf* : reopening
reata *nf* **1** : rope **2** *Mex* : lasso, lariat **3 de ～** : single file
reavivar *vt* : to revive, to reawaken
rebaja *nf* **1** : reduction **2** DESCUENTO : discount **3 rebajas** *nfpl* : sale
rebajar *vt* **1** : to reduce, to lower ⟨a precios rebajados : at reduced prices, on sale⟩ **2** : to lessen, to diminish **3** : to humiliate — **rebajarse** *vr* **1** : to humble oneself **2 rebajarse a** : to stoop to
rebanada *nf* : slice
rebañar *vt* : to mop up, to sop up
rebaño *nm* **1** : flock **2** : herd
rebasar *vt* **1** : to surpass, to exceed **2** *Mex* : to pass, to overtake
rebatiña *nf* : scramble, fight (over something)
rebatir *vt* REFUTAR : to refute
rebato *nm* **1** : surprise attack **2 tocar a rebato** : to sound the alarm
rebelarse *vr* : to rebel
rebelde¹ *adj* : rebellious, unruly
rebelde² *nmf* **1** : rebel **2** : defaulter
rebeldía *nf* **1** : rebelliousness **2 en ～** : in default
rebelión *nf, pl* **-liones** : rebellion
rebobinar *vt* : to rewind
reborde *nm* : border, flange, rim
rebosante *adj* : brimming, overflowing ⟨rebosante de salud : brimming with health⟩
rebosar *vi* **1** : to overflow **2** ～ **de** : to abound in, to be bursting with — *vt* : to radiate
rebotar *vi* **1** : to bounce **2** : to ricochet, to rebound
rebote *nm* **1** : bounce **2** : rebound, ricochet
rebozar {21} *vt* : to coat in batter
rebozo *nm* **1** : shawl, wrap **2 sin ～** : frankly, openly
rebullir {38} *v* : to move, to stir — **rebullirse** *vr*
rebuscado, -da *adj* : affected, pretentious
rebuscar {72} *vi* : to search thoroughly

rebuznar *vi* : to bray
rebuzno *nm* : bray, braying
recabar *vt* **1** : to gather, to obtain, to collect **2 recabar fondos** : to raise money
recado *nm* **1** : message ⟨mandar recado : to send word⟩ **2** *Spain* : errand
recaer {13} *vi* **1** : to relapse **2 ~ en** or **~ sobre** : to fall on, to fall to
recaída *nf* : relapse
recaiga, etc. → **recaer**
recalar *vi* : to arrive
recalcar {72} *vt* : to emphasize, to stress
recalcitrante *adj* : recalcitrant
recalentar {55} *vt* **1** : to reheat, to warm up **2** : to overheat
recámara *nf* **1** *Col, Mex, Pan* : bedroom **2** : chamber (of a firearm)
recamarera *nf Mex* : chambermaid
recambio *nm* **1** : spare part **2** : refill (for a pen, etc.)
recapacitar *vi* **1** : to reconsider **2 ~ en** : to reflect on, to weigh
recapitular *v* : to recapitulate — **recapitulación** *nf*
recargable *adj* : rechargeable
recargado, -da *adj* : overly elaborate or ornate
recargar {52} *vt* **1** : to recharge **2** : to overload
recargo *nm* : surcharge
recatado, -da *adj* MODESTO : modest, demure
recato *nm* PUDOR : modesty
recaudación *nf, pl* **-ciones** **1** : collection **2** : earnings *pl*, takings *pl*
recaudador, -dora *n* **recaudador de impuestos** : tax collector
recaudar *vt* : to collect
recaudo *nm* : safe place ⟨a (buen) recaudo : in safe keeping⟩
recayó, etc. → **recaer**
rece, etc. → **rezar**
recelo *nm* : distrust, suspicion
receloso, -sa *adj* : distrustful, suspicious
recepción *nf, pl* **-ciones** : reception
recepcionista *nmf* : receptionist
receptáculo *nm* : receptacle
receptividad *nf* : receptivity, receptiveness
receptivo, -va *adj* : receptive
receptor[1], -tora *adj* : receiving
receptor[2], -tora *n* **1** : recipient **2** : catcher (in baseball), receiver (in football)
receptor[3] *nm* : receiver ⟨receptor de televisión : television set⟩
recesión *nf, pl* **-siones** : recession
recesivo, -va *adj* : recessive
receso *nm* : recess, adjournment
receta *nf* **1** : recipe **2** : prescription
recetar *vt* : to prescribe (medications)
rechazar {21} *vt* **1** : to reject **2** : to turn down, to refuse
rechazo *nm* : rejection, refusal
rechifla *nf* : booing, jeering
rechinar *vi* **1** : to squeak **2** : to grind, to gnash ⟨hacer rechinar los dientes : to grind one's teeth⟩

rechoncho, -cha *adj fam* : chubby, squat
recibidor *nm* : vestibule, entrance hall
recibimiento *nm* : reception, welcome
recibir *vt* **1** : to receive, to get **2** : to welcome — *vi* : to receive visitors — **recibirse** *vr* **~ de** : to qualify as
recibo *nm* : receipt
reciclable *adj* : recyclable
reciclado → **reciclaje**
reciclaje *nm* **1** : recycling **2** : retraining
reciclar *vt* **1** : to recycle **2** : to retrain
recién *adv* **1** : newly, recently ⟨recién nacido : newborn⟩ ⟨recién casados : newlyweds⟩ ⟨recién llegado : newcomer⟩ **2** : just, only just ⟨recién ahora me acordé : I just now remembered⟩
reciente *adj* : recent — **recientemente** *adv*
recinto *nm* **1** : enclosure **2** : site, premises *pl*
recio[1] *adv* **1** : strongly, hard **2** : loudly, loud
recio[2], -cia *adj* **1** : severe, harsh **2** : tough, strong
recipiente[1] *nm* : container, receptacle
recipiente[2] *nmf* : recipient
reciprocar {72} *vi* : to reciprocate
reciprocidad *nf* : reciprocity
recíproco, -ca *adj* : reciprocal, mutual
recitación *nf, pl* **-ciones** : recitation, recital
recital *nm* : recital
recitar *vt* : to recite
reclamación *nf, pl* **-ciones** **1** : claim, demand **2** QUEJA : complaint
reclamar *vt* **1** EXIGIR : to demand, to require **2** : to claim — *vi* : to complain
reclamo *nm* **1** : bird call, lure **2** : lure, decoy **3** : inducement, attraction **4** : advertisement **5** : complaint
reclinar *vt* : to rest, to lean — **reclinarse** *vr* : to recline, to lean back
recluir {41} *vt* : to confine, to lock up — **recluirse** *vr* : to shut oneself up, to withdraw
reclusión *nf, pl* **-siones** : imprisonment
recluso, -sa *n* **1** : inmate, prisoner **2** SOLITARIO : recluse
recluta *nmf* : recruit, draftee
reclutamiento *nm* : recruitment, recruiting
reclutar *vt* ENROLAR : to recruit, to enlist
recobrar *vt* : to recover, to regain — **recobrarse** *vr* : to recover, to recuperate
recocer {14} *vt* : to overcook, to cook again
recodo *nm* : bend
recogedor *nm* : dustpan
recoger {15} *vt* **1** : to collect, to gather **2** : to get, to retrieve, to pick up **3** : to clean up, to tidy (up)
recogido, -da *adj* : quiet, secluded
recogimiento *nm* **1** : collecting, gathering **2** : withdrawal **3** : absorption, concentration

recolección *nf, pl* **-ciones 1** : collection ⟨recolección de basura : trash pickup⟩ **2** : harvest

recolectar *vt* **1** : to gather, to collect **2** : to harvest, to pick

recomendable *adj* : advisable, recommended

recomendación *nf, pl* **-ciones** : recommendation

recomendar {55} *vt* **1** : to recommend **2** ACONSEJAR : to advise

recompensa *nf* : reward, recompense

recompensar *vt* **1** PREMIAR : to reward **2** : to compensate

reconciliación *nf, pl* **-ciones** : reconciliation

reconciliar *vt* : to reconcile — **reconciliarse** *vr*

recóndito, -ta *adj* **1** : remote, isolated **2** : hidden, recondite **3 en lo más recóndito de** : in the depths of

reconfortar *vt* : to comfort — **reconfortante** *adj*

reconocer {18} *vt* **1** : to recognize **2** : to admit **3** : to examine

reconocible *adj* : recognizable

reconocido, -da *adj* **1** : recognized, accepted **2** : grateful

reconocimiento *nm* **1** : acknowledgment, recognition, avowal **2** : (medical) examination **3** : reconnaissance

reconquista *nf* : reconquest

reconquistar *vt* **1** : to reconquer, to recapture **2** RECUPERAR : to regain, to recover

reconsiderar *vt* : to reconsider — **reconsideración** *nf*

reconstrucción *nf, pl* **-ciones** : reconstruction

reconstruir {41} *vt* **1** : to rebuild, to reconstruct

reconversión *nf, pl* **-siones** : restructuring

reconvertir {76} *vt* **1** : to restructure **2** : to retrain

recopilación *nf, pl* **-ciones 1** : summary **2** : collection, compilation

recopilar *vt* : to compile, to collect

récord *or* **record** [ˈrɛkər] *nm, pl* **récords** *or* **records** [-kərs] : record ⟨record mundial : world record⟩ — **récord** *or* **record** *adj*

recordar {19} *vt* **1** : to recall, to remember **2** : to remind — *vi* **1** ACORDARSE : to remember **2** DESPERTAR : to wake up

recordatorio¹, -ria *adj* : commemorative

recordatorio² *nm* : reminder

recorrer *vt* **1** : to travel through, to tour **2** : to cover (a distance) **3** : to go over, to look over

recorrido *nm* **1** : journey, trip **2** : path, route, course **3** : round (in golf)

recortar *vt* **1** : to cut, to reduce **2** : to cut out **3** : to trim, to cut off **4** : to outline — **recortarse** *vr* : to stand out ⟨los árboles se recortaban en el horizonte : the trees were silhouetted against the horizon⟩

recorte *nm* **1** : cut, reduction **2** : clipping ⟨recortes de periódicos : newspaper clippings⟩

recostar {19} *vt* **1** : to lean, to rest — **recostarse** *vr* : to lie down, recline

recoveco *nm* **1** VUELTA : bend, turn **2** : nook, corner **3 recovecos** *nmpl* : intricacies, ins and outs

recreación *nf, pl* **-ciones 1** : re-creation **2** DIVERSIÓN : recreation, entertainment

recrear *vt* **1** : to re-create **2** : to entertain, to amuse — **recrearse** *vr* : to enjoy oneself

recreativo, -va *adj* : recreational

recreo *nm* **1** DIVERSIÓN : entertainment, amusement **2** : recess, break

recriminación *nf, pl* **-ciones** : reproach, recrimination

recriminar *vt* : to reproach — *vi* : to recriminate — **recriminarse** *vr*

recrudecer {53} *v* : to intensify, to worsen — **recrudecerse** *vr*

rectal *adj* : rectal

rectangular *adj* : rectangular

rectángulo *nm* : rectangle

rectificación *nf, pl* **-ciones** : rectification, correction

rectificar {72} *vt* **1** : to rectify, to correct **2** : to straighten (out)

rectitud *nf* **1** : straightness **2** : honesty, rectitude

recto¹ *adv* : straight

recto², -ta *adj* **1** : straight **2** : upright, honorable **3** : sound

recto³ *nm* : rectum

rector¹, -tora *adj* : governing, managing

rector², -tora *n* : rector

rectoría *nf* : rectory

recubierto *pp* → **recubrir**

recubrir {2} *vt* : to cover, to coat

recuento *nm* : recount, count ⟨un recuento de los votos : a recount of the votes⟩

recuerdo *nm* **1** : memory **2** : souvenir, memento **3 recuerdos** *nmpl* : regards

recular *vi* **1** : to back up **2** REPLEGARSE : to retreat, to fall back **3** RETRACTARSE : to back down

recuperación *nf, pl* **-ciones 1** : recovery, recuperation **2 recuperación de datos** : data retrieval

recuperar *vt* **1** : to recover, to get back, to retrieve **2** : to recuperate **3** : to make up for ⟨recuperar el tiempo perdido : to make up for lost time⟩ — **recuperarse** *vr* ~ **de** : to recover from, to get over

recurrente *adj* : recurrent, recurring

recurrir *vi* **1** ~ **a** : to turn to, to appeal to **2** ~ **a** : to resort to **3** : to appeal (in law)

recurso *nm* **1** : recourse ⟨el último recurso : the last resort⟩ **2** : appeal (in law) **3 recursos** *nmpl* : resources, means ⟨recursos naturales : natural resources⟩

red *nf* **1** : net, mesh **2** : network, system, chain **3** : trap, snare
redacción *nf, pl* **-ciones 1** : writing, composition **2** : editing
redactar *vt* **1** : to write, to draft **2** : to edit
redactor, -tora *n* : editor
redada *nf* **1** : raid **2** : catch, haul
redefinir *vt* : to redefine — **redefinición** *nf*
redención *nf, pl* **-ciones** : redemption
redentor¹, -tora *adj* : redeeming
redentor², -tora *n* : redeemer
redescubierto *pp* → **redescubrir**
redescubrir {2} *vt* : to rediscover
redicho, -cha *adj fam* : affected, pretentious
redil *nm* **1** : sheepfold **2 volver al redil** : to return to the fold
redimir *vt* : to redeem, to deliver (from sin)
rediseñar *vt* : to redesign
redistribuir {41} *vt* : to redistribute — **redistribución** *nf*
rédito *nm* : return, yield
redituar {3} *vt* : to produce, to yield
redoblar *vt* : to redouble, to strengthen — **redoblado, -da** *adj*
redoble *nm* : drum roll
redomado, -da *adj* **1** : sly, crafty **2** : utter, out-and-out
redonda *nf* **1** : region, surrounding area **2 a la redonda** ALREDEDOR : around ⟨de diez millas a la redonda : for ten miles around⟩
redondear *vt* : to round off, to round out
redondel *nm* **1** : ring, circle **2** : bullring, arena
redondez *nf* : roundness
redondo, -da *adj* **1** : round ⟨mesa redonda : round table⟩ **2** : great, perfect ⟨un negocio redondo : an excellent deal⟩ **3** : straightforward, flat ⟨un rechazo redondo : a flat refusal⟩ **4** *Mex* : round-trip **5 en ~** : around
reducción *nf, pl* **-ciones** : reduction, decrease
reducido, -da *adj* **1** : reduced, limited **2** : small
reducir {61} *vt* **1** DISMINUIR : to reduce, to decrease, to cut **2** : to subdue **3** : to boil down — **reducirse** *vr* **~ a** : to come down to, to be nothing more than
redundancia *nf* : redundancy
redundante *adj* : redundant
reedición *nf, pl* **-ciones** : reprint
reelegir {28} *vt* : to reelect — **reelección** *nf*
reembolsable *adj* : refundable
reembolsar *vt* **1** : to refund, to reimburse **2** : to repay
reembolso *nm* : refund, reimbursement
reemplazable *adj* : replaceable
reemplazar {21} *vt* : to replace, to substitute
reemplazo *nm* : replacement, substitution
reencarnación *nf, pl* **-ciones** : reincarnation

reencuentro *nm* : reunion
reestablecer {53} *vt* : to reestablish
reestructurar *vt* : to restructure
reexaminar *vt* : to reexamine
refaccionar *vt* : to repair, to renovate
refacciones *nfpl* : repairs, renovations
referencia *nf* **1** : reference **2 hacer referencia a** : to refer to
referendo → **referéndum**
referéndum *nm, pl* **-dums** : referendum
referente *adj* **~ a** : concerning
réferi *or* **referi** [ˈreferi] *nmf* : referee
referir {76} *vt* **1** : to relate, to tell **2** : to refer ⟨nos refirió al diccionario : she referred us to the dictionary⟩ — **referirse** *vr* **~ a 1** : to refer to **2** **~** : to be concerned, to be in reference to ⟨en lo que se refiere a la educación : as far as education is concerned⟩
refinado¹, -da *adj* : refined
refinado² *nm* : refining
refinamiento *nm* **1** : refining **2** FINURA : refinement
refinanciar *vt* : to refinance
refinar *vt* : to refine
refinería *nf* : refinery
reflectante *adj* : reflective, reflecting
reflector¹, -tora *adj* : reflecting
reflector² *nm* **1** : spotlight, searchlight **2** : reflector
reflejar *vt* : to reflect — **reflejarse** *vr* : to be reflected ⟨la decepción se refleja en su rostro : the disappointment shows on her face⟩
reflejo *nm* **1** : reflection **2** : reflex **3 reflejos** *nmpl* : highlights, streaks (in hair)
reflexión *nf, pl* **-xiones** : reflection, thought
reflexionar *vi* : to reflect, to think
reflexivo, -va *adj* **1** : reflective, thoughtful **2** : reflexive
reflujo *nm* : ebb, ebb tide
reforma *nf* **1** : reform **2** : alteration, renovation
reformador, -dora *n* : reformer
reformar *vt* **1** : to reform **2** : to change, to alter **3** : to renovate, to repair — **reformarse** *vr* : to mend one's ways
reformatorio *nm* : reformatory
reformular *vt* : to reformulate — **reformulación** *nf*
reforzar {36} *vt* **1** : to reinforce, to strengthen **2** : to encourage, to support
refracción *nf, pl* **-ciones** : refraction
refractar *vt* : to refract — **refractarse** *vr*
refractario, -ria *adj* : refractory, obstinate
refrán *nm, pl* **refranes** ADAGIO : proverb, saying
refregar {49} *vt* : to scrub
refrenar *vt* **1** : to rein in (a horse) **2** : to restrain, to check — **refrenarse** *vr* : to restrain oneself
refrendar *vt* **1** : to countersign, to endorse **2** : to stamp (a passport)
refrescante *adj* : refreshing

refrescar {72} vt 1 : to refresh, to cool 2 : to brush up (on) 3 **refrescar la memoria** : to refresh one's memory — vi : to turn cooler

refresco nm : refreshment, soft drink

refriega nf : skirmish, scuffle

refrigeración nf, pl **-ciones** 1 : refrigeration 2 : air-conditioning

refrigerador nmf NEVERA : refrigerator

refrigeradora nf Col, Peru : refrigerator

refrigerante nm : coolant

refrigerar vt 1 : to refrigerate 2 : to air-condition

refrigerio nm : snack, refreshments pl

refrito¹, -ta adj : refried

refrito² nm : rehash

refuerzo nm : reinforcement, support

refugiado, -da n : refugee

refugiar vt : to shelter — **refugiarse** vr ACOGERSE : to take refuge

refugio nm : refuge, shelter

refulgencia nf : brilliance, splendor

refulgir {35} vi : to shine brightly

refundir vt 1 : to recast (metals) 2 : to revise, to rewrite

refunfuñar vi : to grumble, to groan

refutar vt : to refute — **refutación** nf

regadera nf 1 : watering can 2 : shower head, shower 3 : sprinkler

regaderazo nm Mex : shower

regalar vt 1 OBSEQUIAR : to present (as a gift), to give away 2 : to regale, to entertain 3 : to flatter, to make a fuss over — **regalarse** vr : to pamper oneself

regalía nf : royalty, payment

regaliz nm, pl **-lices** : licorice

regalo nm 1 OBSEQUIO : gift, present 2 : pleasure, comfort 3 : treat

regañadientes mpl **a ~** : reluctantly, unwillingly

regañar vt : to scold, to give a talking to — vi 1 QUEJARSE : to grumble, to complain 2 REÑIR : to quarrel, to argue

regaño nm fam : scolding

regañon, -ñona adj, mpl **-ñones** fam : grumpy, irritable

regar {49} vt 1 : to irrigate 2 : to water 3 : to wash, to hose down 4 : to spill, to scatter

regata nf : regatta, yacht race

regate nm : dodge, feint

regatear vt 1 : to haggle over 2 ESCATIMAR : to skimp on, to be sparing with — vi : to bargain, to haggle

regateo nm : bargaining, haggling

regatón nm, pl **-tones** : ferrule, tip

regazo nm : lap (of a person)

regencia nf : regency

regenerar vt : to regenerate — **regenerarse** vr — **regeneración** nf

regentar vt : to run, to manage

regente nmf : regent

regidor, -dora n : town councillor

régimen nm, pl **regímenes** 1 : regime 2 : diet 3 : regimen, rules pl ⟨régimen de vida : lifestyle⟩

regimiento nm : regiment

regio, -gia adj 1 : great, magnificent 2 : regal, royal

región nf, pl **regiones** : region, area

regional adj : regional — **regionalmente** adv

regir {28} vt 1 : to rule 2 : to manage, to run 3 : to control, to govern ⟨las costumbres que rigen la conducta : the customs which govern behavior⟩ — vi : to apply, to be in force ⟨las leyes rigen en los tres países : the laws apply in all three countries⟩ — **regirse** vr ~ **por** : to go by, to be guided by

registrador¹, -dora adj **caja registradora** : cash register

registrador², -dora n : registrar, recorder

registrar vt 1 : to register, to record 2 GRABAR : to record, to tape 3 : to search, to examine — **registrarse** vr 1 INSCRIBIRSE : to register 2 OCURRIR : to happen, to occur

registro nm 1 : register 2 : registration 3 : registry, record office 4 : range (of a voice or musical instrument) 5 : search

regla nf 1 NORMA : rule, regulation 2 : ruler ⟨regla de cálculo : slide rule⟩ 3 MENSTRUACIÓN : period, menstruation

reglamentación nf, pl **-ciones** 1 : regulation 2 : rules pl

reglamentar vt : to regulate, to set rules for

reglamentario, -ria adj : regulation, official ⟨equipo reglamentario : standard equipment⟩

reglamento nm : regulations pl, rules pl ⟨reglamento de tráfico : traffic regulations⟩

regocijar vt : to gladden, to delight — **regocijarse** vr : to rejoice

regocijo nm : delight, rejoicing

regordete, -ta adj fam LLENITO : chubby

regresar vt DEVOLVER : to give back — vi : to return, to come back, to go back

regresión nf, pl **-siones** : regression, return

regresivo, -va adj : regressive

regreso nm 1 : return 2 **estar de regreso** : to be back, to be home

reguero nm 1 : irrigation ditch 2 : trail, trace 3 **propagarse como reguero de pólvora** : to spread like wildfire

regulable adj : adjustable

regulación nf, pl **-ciones** : regulation, control

regulador¹, -dora adj : regulating, regulatory

regulador² nm 1 : regulator, governor 2 **regulador de tiro** : damper (in a chimney)

regular¹ vt : to regulate, to control

regular² adj 1 : regular 2 : fair, OK, so-so 3 : medium, average 4 **por lo regular** : in general, generally

regularidad nf : regularity

regularización *nf, pl* **-ciones** NORMAL-IZACIÓN : normalization
regularizar {21} *vt* NORMALIZAR : to normalize, to make regular
regularmente *adv* : regularly
regusto *nm* : aftertaste
rehabilitar *vt* 1 : to rehabilitate 2 : to reinstate 3 : renovate, to restore — **rehabilitación** *nf*
rehacer {40} *vt* 1 : to redo 2 : to remake, to repair, to renew — **rehacerse** *vr* 1 : to recover 2 ~ **de** : to get over
rehecho *pp* → **rehacer**
rehén *nm, pl* **rehenes** : hostage
rehicieron, etc. → **rehacer**
rehizo → **rehacer**
rehuir {41} *vt* 1 : to avoid, to shun
rehusar {8} *v* : to refuse
reimprimir *vt* : to reprint
reina *nf* : queen
reinado *nm* : reign
reinante *adj* 1 : reigning 2 : prevailing, current
reinar *vi* 1 : to reign 2 : to prevail
reincidencia *nf* : recidivism, relapse
reincidente *nmf* : backslider, recidivist
reincidir *vi* 1 : to backslide, to retrogress 2 : to relapse
reincorporar *vt* : to reinstate — **reincorporarse** *vr* ~ **a** : to return to, to rejoin
reiniciar *vt* 1 : to resume, to restart 2 : to reboot (a computer)
reino *nm* : kingdom, realm ⟨reino animal : animal kingdom⟩
reinstalar *vt* 1 : to reinstall 2 : to reinstate
reintegración *nf, pl* **-ciones** 1 : reinstatement, reintegration 2 : refund, reimbursement
reintegrar *vt* 1 : to reintegrate, reinstate 2 : to refund, to reimburse — **reintegrarse** *vr* ~ **a** : to return to, to rejoin
reír {66} *vi* : to laugh — *vt* : to laugh at — **reírse** *vr*
reiteración *nf, pl* **-ciones** : reiteration, repetition
reiterado, -da *adj* : repeated ⟨lo explicó en reiteradas ocasiones : he explained it repeatedly⟩ — **reiteradamente** *adv*
reiterar *vt* : to reiterate, to repeat
reiterativo, -va *adj* : repetitive, repetitious
reivindicación *nf, pl* **-ciones** 1 : demand, claim 2 : vindication
reivindicar {72} *vt* 1 : to vindicate 2 : to demand, to claim 3 : to restore
reja *nf* 1 : grille, grating ⟨entre rejas : behind bars⟩ 2 : plowshare
rejilla *nf* : grille, grate, screen
rejuvenecer {53} *vt* : to rejuvenate — *vi* : to be rejuvenated — **rejuvenecerse** *vr*
rejuvenecimiento *nm* : rejuvenation
relación *nf, pl* **-ciones** 1 : relation, connection, relevance 2 : relationship 3 RELATO : account 4 LISTA : list 5 **con relación a** *or* **en relación con** : in re-

lation to, concerning 6 **relaciones públicas** : public relations
relacionar *vt* : to relate, to connect — **relacionarse** *vr* ~ **con** : to be connected to, to be linked with
relajación *nf, pl* **-ciones** : relaxation
relajado, -da *adj* 1 : relaxed, loose 2 : dissolute, depraved
relajante *adj* : relaxing
relajar *vt* : to relax, to slacken — *vi* : to be relaxing — **relajarse** *vr*
relajo *nm* 1 : commotion, ruckus 2 : joke, laugh ⟨lo hizo de relajo : he did it for a laugh⟩
relamerse *vr* : to smack one's lips, to lick one's chops
relámpago *nm* : flash of lightning
relampaguear *vi* : to flash
relanzar {21} *vt* : to relaunch
relatar *vt* : to relate, to tell
relatividad *nf* : relativity
relativo, -va *adj* 1 : relative 2 **en lo relativo a** : with regard to, concerning — **relativamente** *adv*
relato *nm* 1 : story, tale 2 : account
releer {20} *vt* : to reread
relegar {52} *vt* 1 : to relegate 2 **relegar al olvido** : to consign to oblivion
relevante *adj* : outstanding, important
relevar *vt* 1 : to relieve, to take over from 2 ~ **de** : to exempt from — **relevarse** *vr* : to take turns
relevo *nm* 1 : relief, replacement 2 : relay ⟨carrera de relevos : relay race⟩
relicario *nm* 1 : reliquary 2 : locket
relieve *nm* 1 : relief, projection ⟨mapa en relieve : relief map⟩ ⟨letras en relieve : embossed letters⟩ 2 : prominence, importance 3 **poner en relieve** : to highlight, to emphasize
religión *nf, pl* **-giones** : religion
religiosamente *adv* : religiously, faithfully
religioso[1], -sa *adj* : religious
religioso[2], -sa *n* : monk *m*, nun *f*
relinchar *vi* : to neigh, to whinny
relincho *nm* : neigh, whinny
reliquia *nf* 1 : relic 2 **reliquia de familia** : family heirloom
rellenar *vt* 1 : to refill 2 : to stuff, to fill 3 : to fill out
relleno[1], -na *adj* : stuffed, filled
relleno[2] *nm* : stuffing, filling
reloj *nm* 1 : clock 2 : watch 3 **reloj de arena** : hourglass 4 **reloj de pulsera** : wristwatch 5 **como un reloj** : like clockwork
relojería *nf* 1 : watchmaker's shop 2 : watchmaking, clockmaking
reluciente *adj* : brilliant, shining
relucir {45} *vi* 1 : to glitter, to shine 2 **salir a relucir** : to come to the surface 3 **sacar a relucir** : to bring up, to mention
relumbrante *adj* : dazzling
relumbrar *vi* : to shine brightly
relumbrón *nm, pl* **-brones** 1 : flash, glare 2 **de** ~ : flashy, showy

remachar *vt* **1** : to rivet **2** : to clinch (a nail) **3** : to stress, to drive home — *vi* : to smash, to spike (a ball)

remache *nm* **1** : rivet **2** : smash, spike (in sports)

remanente *nm* **1** : remainder, balance **2** : surplus

remanso *nm* : pool

remar *vi* **1** : to row, to paddle **2** : to struggle, to toil

remarcar {72} *vt* : to emphasize, to stress

rematado, -da *adj* : utter, complete

rematador, -dora *n* : auctioneer

rematar *vt* **1** : to finish off **2** : to auction — *vi* **1** : to shoot **2** : to end

remate *nm* **1** : shot (in sports) **2** : auction **3** : end, conclusion **4 como ~** : to top it off **5 de ~** : completely, utterly

remecer {86} *vt* : to sway, to swing

remedar *vt* **1** IMITAR : to imitate, to copy **2** : to mimic, to ape

remediar *vt* **1** : to remedy, to repair **2** : to help out, to assist **3** EVITAR : to prevent, to avoid

remedio *nm* **1** : remedy, cure **2** : solution **3** : option ⟨no me quedó más remedio : I had no other choice⟩ ⟨no hay remedio : it can't be helped⟩ **4 poner remedio a** : to put a stop to **5 sin ~** : unavoidable, inevitable

remedo *nm* : imitation

rememorar *vi* : to recall ⟨rememorar los viejos tiempos : to reminisce⟩

remendar {55} *vt* **1** : to mend, to patch, to darn **2** : to correct

remero, -ra *n* : rower

remesa *nf* **1** : remittance **2** : shipment

remezón *nm, pl* **-zones** : mild earthquake, tremor

remiendo *nm* **1** : patch **2** : correction

remilgado, -da *adj* **1** : prim, prudish **2** : affected

remilgo *nm* : primness, affectation

reminiscencia *nf* : reminiscence

remisión *nf, pl* **-siones** **1** ENVÍO : sending, delivery **2** : remission **3** : reference, cross-reference

remiso, -sa *adj* **1** : lax, remiss **2** : reluctant

remitente[1] *nm* : return address

remitente[2] *nmf* : sender (of a letter, etc.)

remitir *vt* **1** : to send, to remit **2** : to refer to, to direct to ⟨nos remitió al diccionario : he referred us to the dictionary⟩ — *vi* : to subside, to let up

remo *nm* **1** : paddle, oar **2** : rowing (sport)

remoción *nf, pl* **-ciones** **1** : removal **2** : dismissal

remodelación *nf, pl* **-ciones** **1** : remodeling **2** : reorganization, restructuring

remodelar *vt* **1** : to remodel **2** : to restructure

remojar *vt* **1** : to soak, to steep **2** : to dip, to dunk **3** : to celebrate with a drink

remojo *nm* **1** : soaking, steeping **2 poner en remojo** : to soak, to leave soaking

remolacha *nf* : beet

remolcador *nm* : tugboat

remolcar {72} *vt* : to tow, to haul

remolino *nm* **1** : whirlwind **2** : eddy, whirlpool **3** : crowd, throng **4** : cowlick

remolque *nm* **1** : towing, tow **2** : trailer **3 a ~** : in tow

remontar *vt* **1** : to overcome **2** SUBIR : to go up — **remontarse** *vr* **1** : to soar **2 ~ a** : to date from, to go back to

rémora *nf* : obstacle, hindrance

remorder {47} *vt* INQUIETAR : to trouble, to distress

remordimiento *nm* : remorse

remotamente *adv* : remotely, vaguely

remoto, -ta *adj* **1** : remote, unlikely ⟨hay una posibilidad remota : there is a slim possibility⟩ **2** : distant, far-off

remover {47} *vt* **1** : to stir **2** : to move around, to turn over **3** : to stir up **4** : to remove **5** : to dismiss

remozamiento *nm* : renovation

remozar {21} *vt* **1** : to renew, to brighten up **2** : to redo, to renovate

remuneración *nf, pl* **-ciones** : remuneration, pay

remunerar *vt* : to pay, to remunerate

remunerativo, -va *adj* : remunerative

renacer {48} *vi* : to be reborn, to revive

renacimiento *nm* **1** : rebirth, revival **2 el Renacimiento** : the Renaissance

renacuajo *nm* : tadpole, pollywog

renal *adj* : renal, kidney

rencilla *nf* : quarrel

renco, -ca *adj* : lame

rencor *nm* **1** : rancor, enmity, hostility **2 guardar rencor** : to hold a grudge

rencoroso, -sa *adj* : resentful, rancorous

rendición *nf, pl* **-ciones** **1** : surrender, submission **2** : yield, return

rendido, -da *adj* **1** : submissive **2** : worn-out, exhausted **3** : devoted

rendija *nf* GRIETA : crack, split

rendimiento *nm* **1** : performance **2** : yield

rendir {54} *vt* **1** : to render, to give ⟨rendir las gracias : to give thanks⟩ ⟨rendir homenaje a : to pay homage to⟩ **2** : to yield **3** CANSAR : to exhaust — *vi* **1** CUNDIR : to progress, to make headway **2** : to last, to go a long way — **rendirse** *vr* : to surrender, to give up

renegado, -da *n* : renegade

renegar {49} *vi* **1 ~ de** : to renounce, to disown, to give up **2 ~ de** : to complain about — *vt* **1** : to deny vigorously **2** : to abhor, to hate

renegociar *vt* : to renegotiate — **renegociación** *nf*

renglón *nm, pl* **renglones** **1** : line (of writing) **2** : merchandise, line (of products)

rengo, -ga *adj* : lame

renguear *vi* : to limp

reno *nm* : reindeer

renombrado, -da *adj* : renowned, famous

renombre *nm* NOMBRADÍA : renown, fame

renovable *adj* : renewable

renovación *nf, pl* **-ciones 1** : renewal ⟨renovación de un contrato : renewal of a contract⟩ **2** : change, renovation

renovar {19} *vt* **1** : to renew, to restore **2** : to renovate

renquear *vi* : to limp, to hobble

renquera *nf* COJERA : limp, lameness

renta *nf* **1** : income **2** : rent **3 impuesto sobre la renta** : income tax

rentable *adj* : profitable

rentar *vt* **1** : to produce, to yield **2** ALQUILAR : to rent

renuencia *nf* : reluctance, unwillingness

renuente *adj* : reluctant, unwilling

renuncia *nf* **1** : resignation **2** : renunciation **3** : waiver

renunciar *vi* **1** : to resign **2 ~ a** : to renounce, to relinquish ⟨renunció al título : he relinquished the title⟩

reñido, -da *adj* **1** : tough, hard-fought **2** : at odds, on bad terms

reñir {67} *vi* **1** : to argue **2 ~ con** : to fall out with, to go up against — *vt* : to scold, to reprimand

reo, rea *n* **1** : accused, defendant **2** : offender, culprit

reojo *nm* **de ~** : out of the corner of one's eye ⟨una mirada de reojo : a sidelong glance⟩

reorganizar {21} *vt* : to reorganize — **reorganización** *nf*

repantigarse {52} *vr* : to slouch, to loll about

reparación *nf, pl* **-ciones 1** : reparation, amends **2** : repair

reparar *vt* **1** : to repair, to fix, to mend **2** : to make amends for **3** : to correct **4** : to restore, to refresh — *vi* **1 ~ en** : to observe, to take notice of **2 ~ en** : to consider, to think about

reparo *nm* **1** : repair, restoration **2** : reservation, qualm ⟨no tuvieron reparos en decírmelo : they didn't hesitate to tell me⟩ **3 poner reparos a** : to find fault with, to object to

repartición *nf, pl* **-ciones 1** : distribution **2** : department, division

repartidor¹, -dora *adj* : delivery ⟨camión repartidor : delivery truck⟩

repartidor², -dora *n* : delivery person, distributor

repartimiento *nm* → **repartición**

repartir *vt* **1** : to allocate **2** DISTRIBUIR : to distribute, to hand out **3** : to spread

reparto *nm* **1** : allocation **2** : distribution **3** : cast (of characters)

repasar *vt* **1** : to pass by again **2** : to review, to go over **3** : to mend

repaso *nm* **1** : review **2** : mending **3** : checkup, overhaul

repatriar {85} *vt* : to repatriate — **repatriación** *nf*

repavimentar *vt* : to resurface

repelente¹ *adj* : repellent, repulsive

repelente² *nm* : repellent ⟨repelente de insectos : insect repellent⟩

repeler *vt* **1** : to repel, to resist, to repulse **2** : to reject **3** : to disgust ⟨el sabor me repele : I find the taste repulsive⟩

repensar {55} *v* : to rethink, to reconsider

repente *nm* **1** : sudden movement, start ⟨de repente : suddenly⟩ **2** : fit, outburst ⟨un repente de ira : a fit of anger⟩

repentino, -na *adj* : sudden — **repentinamente** *adv*

repercusión *nf, pl* **-siones** : repercussion

repercutir *vi* **1** : to reverberate, to echo **2 ~ en** : to have effects on, to have repercussions on

repertorio *nm* : repertoire

repetición *nf, pl* **-ciones 1** : repetition **2** : rerun, repeat

repetidamente *adv* : repeatedly

repetido, -da *adj* **1** : repeated, numerous **2 repetidas veces** : repeatedly, time and again

repetir {54} *vt* **1** : to repeat **2** : to have a second helping of — **repetirse** *vr* **1** : to repeat oneself **2** : to recur

repetitivo, -va *adj* : repetitive, repetitious

repicar {72} *vt* : to ring — *vi* : to ring out, to peal

repique *nm* : ringing, pealing

repisa *nf* : shelf, ledge ⟨repisa de chimenea : mantelpiece⟩ ⟨repisa de ventana : windowsill⟩

replantear *vt* : to redefine, to restate — **replantearse** *vr* : to reconsider

replegar {49} *vt* : to fold — **replegarse** *vr* RETIRARSE : to retreat, to withdraw

repleto, -ta *adj* **1** : replete, full **2 ~ de** : packed with, crammed with

réplica *nf* **1** : reply **2** : replica, reproduction **3** *Chile, Mex* : aftershock

replicación *nf, pl* **-ciones** : replication

replicar {72} *vi* **1** : to reply, to retort **2** : to argue, to answer back

repliegue *nm* **1** : fold **2** : retreat, withdrawal

repollo *nm* COL : cabbage

reponer {60} *vt* **1** : to replace, to put back **2** : to reinstate **3** : to reply — **reponerse** *vr* : to recover

reportaje *nm* : article, story, report

reportar *vt* **1** : to check, to restrain **2** : to bring, to carry, to yield ⟨me reportó numerosos beneficios : it brought me many benefits⟩ **3** : to report — **reportarse** *vr* **1** CONTENERSE : to control oneself **2** PRESENTARSE : to report, to show up

reporte *nm* : report

reportear *vt* : to report on, to cover

reportero, -ra n 1 : reporter 2 **reportero gráfico** : photojournalist
reposado, -da adj : calm
reposar vi 1 : to rest, to repose 2 : to stand, to settle ⟨deje reposar la masa media hora : let the dough stand for half an hour⟩ 3 : to lie, to be buried — **reposarse** vr : to settle
reposición nf, pl **-ciones** 1 : replacement 2 : reinstatement 3 : revival
repositorio nm : repository
reposo nm : repose, rest
repostar vi 1 : to stock up 2 : to refuel
repostería nf 1 : confectioner's shop 2 : pastry-making
repostero, -ra n : confectioner
repreguntar vt : to cross-examine
repreguntas nfpl : cross-examination
reprender vt : to reprimand, to scold
reprensible adj : reprehensible
represa nf : dam
represalia nf 1 : reprisal, retaliation 2 **tomar represalias** : to retaliate
represar vt : to dam
representación nf, pl **-ciones** 1 : representation 2 : performance 3 **en representación de** : on behalf of
representante nmf 1 : representative 2 : performer
representar vt 1 : to represent, to act for 2 : to perform 3 : to look, to appear as 4 : to symbolize, to stand for 5 : to signify, to mean — **representarse** vr : to imagine, to picture
representativo, -va adj : representative
represión nf, pl **-siones** : repression
represivo, -va adj : repressive
reprimenda nf : reprimand
reprimir vt 1 : to repress 2 : to suppress, to stifle
reprobable adj : reprehensible, culpable
reprobación nf : disapproval
reprobar {19} vt 1 DESAPROBAR : to condemn, to disapprove of 2 : to fail (a course)
reprobatorio, -ria adj : disapproving, admonitory
reprochable adj : reprehensible, reproachable
reprochar vt : to reproach — **reprocharse** vr
reproche nm : reproach
reproducción nf, pl **-ciones** : reproduction
reproducir {61} vt : to reproduce — **reproducirse** vr 1 : to breed, to reproduce 2 : to recur
reproductor, -tora adj : reproductive
reptar vi : to crawl, to slither
reptil[1] adj : reptilian
reptil[2] nm : reptile
república nf : republic
republicanismo nm : republicanism
republicano, -na adj & n : republican
repudiar vt : to repudiate — **repudiación** nf
repudio nm : repudiation
repuesto[1] pp → **reponer**

repuesto[2] nm 1 : spare part 2 **de** ~ : spare ⟨rueda de repuesto : spare wheel⟩
repugnancia nf : repugnance
repugnante adj : repulsive, repugnant, revolting
repugnar vt : to cause repugnance, to disgust — **repugnarse** vr
repujar vt : to emboss
repulsivo, -va adj : repulsive
repuntar vt Arg, Chile : to round up (cattle) — vi : to begin to appear — **repuntarse** vr : to fall out, to quarrel
repuso, etc. → **reponer**
reputación nf, pl **-ciones** : reputation
reputar vt : to consider, to deem
requerir {76} vt 1 : to require, to call for 2 : to summon, to send for
requesón nm, pl **-sones** : curd cheese, cottage cheese
réquiem nm : requiem
requisa nf 1 : requisition 2 : seizure 3 : inspection
requisar vt 1 : to requisition 2 : to seize 3 INSPECCIONAR : to inspect
requisito nm 1 : requirement 2 **requisito previo** : prerequisite
res nf 1 : beast, animal 2 CA, Mex : beef 3 **reses** nfpl : cattle ⟨60 reses : 60 head of cattle⟩
resabio nm 1 VICIO : bad habit, vice 2 DEJO : aftertaste
resaca nf 1 : undertow 2 : hangover
resaltar vi 1 SOBRESALIR : to stand out 2 **hacer resaltar** : to bring out, to highlight — vt : to stress, to emphasize
resarcimiento nm 1 : compensation 2 : reimbursement
resarcir {83} vt : to compensate, to indemnify — **resarcirse** vr ~ **de** : to make up for
resbaladizo, -za adj 1 RESBALOSO : slippery 2 : tricky, ticklish, delicate
resbalar vi 1 : to slip, to slide 2 : to slip up, to make a mistake 3 : to skid — **resbalarse** vr
resbalón nm, pl **-lones** : slip
resbaloso, -sa adj : slippery
rescatar vt 1 : to rescue, to save 2 : to recover, to get back
rescate nm 1 : rescue 2 : recovery 3 : ransom
rescindir vt : to rescind, to annul, to cancel
rescisión nf, pl **-siones** : annulment, cancellation
rescoldo nm : embers pl
resecar {72} vt : to make dry, to dry up — **resecarse** vr : to dry up
reseco, -ca adj : dry, dried-up
resentido, -da adj : resentful
resentimiento nm : resentment
resentirse {76} vr 1 : to suffer, to be weakened 2 OFENDERSE : to be upset ⟨se resintió porque la insultaron : she got upset when they insulted her, she resented being insulted⟩ 3 ~ **de** : to feel the effects of

reseña *nf* **1** : report, summary, review **2** : description

reseñar *vt* **1** : to review **2** DESCRIBIR : to describe

reserva *nf* **1** : reservation **2** : reserve **3** : confidence, privacy ⟨con la mayor reserva : in strictest confidence⟩ **4 de ~** : spare, in reserve **5 reservas** *nfpl* : reservations, doubts

reservación *nf, pl* **-ciones** : reservation

reservado, -da *adj* **1** : reserved, reticent **2** : confidential

reservar *vt* : to reserve — **reservarse** *vr* **1** : to save oneself **2** : to conceal, to keep to oneself

reservorio *nm* : reservoir, reserve

resfriado *nm* CATARRO : cold

resfriar {85} *vt* : to cool — **resfriarse** *vr* **1** : to cool off **2** : to catch a cold

resfrío *nm* : cold

resguardar *vt* : to safeguard, to protect — **resguardarse** *vr*

resguardo *nm* **1** : safeguard, protection **2** : receipt, voucher **3** : border guard, coast guard

residencia *nf* **1** : residence **2** : boarding house

residencial *adj* : residential

residente *adj & nmf* : resident

residir *vi* **1** VIVIR : to reside, to dwell **2 ~ en** : to lie in, to consist of

residual *adj* : residual

residuo *nm* **1** : residue **2** : remainder **3 residuos** *nmpl* : waste ⟨residuos nucleares : nuclear waste⟩

resignación *nf, pl* **-ciones** : resignation

resignar *vt* : to resign — **resignarse** *vr* **~ a** : to resign oneself to

resina *nf* **1** : resin **2 resina epoxídica** : epoxy

resistencia *nf* **1** : resistance **2** AGUANTE : endurance, strength, stamina

resistente *adj* : resistant **2** : strong, tough

resistir *vt* **1** : to stand, to bear, to tolerate **2** : to withstand — *vi* : to resist ⟨resistió hasta el último minuto : he held out until the last minute⟩ — **resistirse** *vr* **~ a** : to be resistant to, to be reluctant

resollar {19} *vi* : to breathe heavily, to wheeze

resolución *nf, pl* **-ciones** **1** : resolution, settlement **2** : decision **3** : determination, resolve

resolver {89} *vt* **1** : to resolve, to settle **2** : to decide — **resolverse** *vr* : to make up one's mind

resonancia *nf* **1** : resonance **2** : impact, repercussions *pl*

resonante *adj* **1** : resonant **2** : tremendous, resounding ⟨un éxito resonante : a resounding success⟩

resonar {19} *vi* : to resound, to ring

resoplar *vi* **1** : to puff, to pant **2** : to snort

resoplo *nm* **1** : puffing, panting **2** : snort

resorte *nm* **1** MUELLE : spring **2** : elasticity **3** : influence, means *pl* ⟨tocar resortes : to pull strings⟩

resortera *nf Mex* : slingshot

respaldar *vt* **1** : to back, to support, to endorse — **respaldarse** *vr* : to lean back

respaldo *nm* **1** : back (of an object) **2** : support, backing

respectar *vt* : to concern, to relate to ⟨por lo que a mí respecta : as far as I'm concerned⟩

respectivo, -va *adj* : respective — **respectivamente** *adv*

respecto *nm* **1 ~ a** : in regard to, concerning **2 al respecto** : on this matter, in this respect

respetable *adj* : respectable — **respetabilidad** *nf*

respetar *vt* : to respect

respeto *nm* **1** : respect, consideration **2 respetos** *nmpl* : respects ⟨presentar sus respetos : to pay one's respects⟩

respetuosidad *nf* : respectfulness

respetuoso, -sa *adj* : respectful — **respetuosamente** *adv*

respingo *nm* : start, jump

respiración *nf, pl* **-ciones** : respiration, breathing

respiradero *nm* : vent, ventilation shaft

respirador *nm* : respirator

respirar *v* : to breathe

respiratorio, -ria *adj* : respiratory

respiro *nm* **1** : breath **2** : respite, break

resplandecer {53} *vi* **1** : to shine **2** : to stand out

resplandeciente *adj* **1** : resplendent, shining **2** : radiant

resplandor *nm* **1** : brightness, brilliance **2** : radiance **3** : flash

responder *vt* : to answer — *vi* **1** : to answer, to reply, to respond **2 ~ a** : to respond to ⟨responder al tratamiento : to respond to treatment⟩ **3 ~ de** : to answer for, to vouch for (something) **4 ~ por** : to vouch for (someone)

responsabilidad *nf* : responsibility

responsable *adj* : responsible — **responsablemente** *adv*

respuesta *nf* : answer, response

resquebrajar *vt* : to split, to crack — **resquebrajarse** *vr*

resquemor *nm* : resentment, bitterness

resquicio *nm* **1** : crack **2** : opportunity, chance **3** : trace ⟨sin un resquicio de remordimiento : without a trace of remorse⟩ **4 resquicio legal** : loophole

resta *nf* SUSTRACCIÓN : subtraction

restablecer {53} *vt* : to reestablish, to restore — **restablecerse** *vr* : to recover

restablecimiento *nm* **1** : reestablishment, restoration **2** : recovery

restallar *vi* : to crack, to crackle, to click

restallido *nm* : crack, crackle

restante *adj* **1** : remaining **2 lo restante, los restantes** : the rest

restañar *vt* : to stanch

restar *vt* **1** : to deduct, to subtract ⟨restar un punto : to deduct a point⟩

2 : to minimize, to play down — vi : to remain, to be left

restauración nf, pl **-ciones 1** : restoration **2** : catering, food service

restaurante nm : restaurant

restaurar vt : to restore

restitución nf, pl **-ciones** : restitution, return

restituir {41} vt : to return, to restore, to reinstate

resto nm **1** : rest, remainder **2 restos** nmpl : remains ⟨restos de comida : leftovers⟩ ⟨restos arqueológicos : archeological ruins⟩ **3 restos mortales** : mortal remains

restorán nm, pl **-ranes** : restaurant

restregadura nf : scrub, scrubbing

restregar {49} vt **1** : to rub **2** : to scrub — **restregarse** vr

restricción nf, pl **-ciones** : restriction, limitation

restrictivo, -va adj : restrictive

restringido, -da adj LIMITADO : limited, restricted

restringir {35} vt LIMITAR : to restrict, to limit

restructuración nf : restructuring

restructurar vt : to restructure

resucitación nf : resuscitation ⟨resucitación cardiopulmonar : CPR, cardiopulmonary resuscitation⟩

resucitar vt **1** : to resuscitate, to revive, to resurrect **2** : to revitalize

resuello nm **1** : puffing, heavy breathing, wheezing **2** : break, breather

resuelto[1] pp → **resolver**

resuelto[2]**, -ta** adj : determined, resolved, resolute

resulta nf **1** : consequence, result **2 a resultas de** or **de resultas de** : as a result of

resultado nm : result, outcome

resultante adj & nf : resultant

resultar vi **1** : to work, to work out ⟨mi idea no resultó : my idea didn't work out⟩ **2** : to prove, to turn out to be ⟨resultó bien simpático : he turned out to be very nice⟩ **3** ~ **en** : to lead to, to result in **4** ~ **de** : to be the result of

resumen nm, pl **-súmenes 1** : summary, summation **2 en** ~ : in summary, in short

resumidero nm : drain

resumir v : to summarize, to sum up

resurgimiento nm : resurgence

resurgir {35} vi : to reappear, to revive

resurrección nf, pl **-ciones** : resurrection

retablo nm **1** : tableau **2** : altarpiece

retador, -dora n : challenger (in sports)

retaguardia nf : rear guard

retahíla nf : string, series ⟨una retahíla de insultos : a volley of insults⟩

retaliación nf, pl **-ciones** : retaliation

retama nf : broom (plant)

retar vt DESAFIAR : to challenge, to defy

retardante adj : retardant

retardar vt **1** RETRASAR : to delay, to retard **2** : to postpone

retazo nm **1** : remnant, scrap **2** : fragment, piece ⟨retazos de su obra : bits and pieces from his writings⟩

retención nf, pl **-ciones 1** : retention **2** : deduction, withholding

retener {80} vt **1** : to retain, to keep **2** : to withhold **3** : to detain

retentivo, -va adj : retentive

reticencia nf **1** : reluctance, reticence **2** : insinuation

reticente adj **1** : reluctant, reticent **2** : insinuating, misleading

retina nf : retina

retintín nm, pl **-tines 1** : jingle, jangle **2 con** ~ : sarcastically

retirada nf **1** : retreat ⟨batirse en retirada : to withdraw, to beat a retreat⟩ **2** : withdrawal (of funds) **3** : retirement **4** : refuge, haven

retirado, -da adj **1** : remote, distant, far off **2** : secluded, quiet

retirar vt **1** : to remove, to take away, to recall **2** : to withdraw, to take out — **retirarse** vr **1** REPLEGARSE : to retreat, to withdraw **2** JUBILARSE : to retire

retiro nm **1** JUBILACIÓN : retirement **2** : withdrawal, retreat **3** : seclusion

reto nm DESAFÍO : challenge, dare

retocar {72} vt : to touch up

retoñar vi : to sprout

retoño nm : sprout, shoot

retoque nm : retouching

retorcer {14} vt **1** : to twist **2** : to wring — **retorcerse** vr **1** : to get twisted, to get tangled up **2** : to squirm, to writhe, to wiggle about

retorcijón nm, pl **-jones** : cramp, sharp pain

retorcimiento nm **1** : twisting, wringing **2** : deviousness

retórica nf : rhetoric

retórico, -ca adj : rhetorical — **retóricamente** adv

retornar v : to return

retorno nm : return

retozar {21} vi : to frolic, to romp

retozo nm : frolicking

retozón, -zona adj, mpl **-zones** : playful

retracción nf, pl **-ciones** : retraction, withdrawal

retractable adj : retractable

retractación nf, pl **-ciones** : retraction (of a statement, etc.)

retractarse vr **1** : to withdraw, to back down **2** ~ **de** : to take back, to retract

retraer {81} vt **1** : to bring back **2** : to dissuade — **retraerse** vr **1** RETIRARSE : to withdraw, to retire **2** REFUGIARSE : to take refuge

retraído, -da adj : withdrawn, retiring, shy

retraimiento nm **1** : shyness, timidity **2** : withdrawal

retrasado, -da adj **1** : retarded, mentally slow **2** : behind, in arrears **3**

: backward (of a country) **4** : slow (of a watch)

retrasar *vt* **1** DEMORAR, RETARDAR : to delay, to hold up **2** : to put off, to postpone — **retrasarse** *vr* **1** : to be late **2** : to fall behind

retraso *nm* **1** ATRASO : delay, lateness **2 retraso mental** : mental retardation

retratar *vt* **1** : to portray, to depict **2** : to photograph **3** : to paint a portrait of

retrato *nm* **1** : depiction, portrayal **2** : portrait, photograph

retrete *nm* : restroom, toilet

retribución *nf, pl* **-ciones 1** : pay, payment **2** : reward

retribuir {41} *vt* **1** : to pay **2** : to reward

retroactivo, -va *adj* : retroactive — **retroactivamente** *adv*

retroalimentación *nf, pl* **-ciones** : feedback

retroceder *vi* **1** : to move back, to turn back **2** : to back off, to back down **3** : to recoil (of a firearm)

retroceso *nm* **1** : backward movement **2** : backing down **3** : setback, relapse **4** : recoil

retrógrado, -da *adj* **1** : reactionary **2** : retrograde

retropropulsión *nf* : jet propulsion

retrospectiva *nf* : retrospective, hindsight

retrospectivo, -va *adj* **1** : retrospective **2 mirada retrospectiva** : backward glance

retrovisor *nm* : rearview mirror

retruécano *nm* : pun, play on words

retumbar *vi* **1** : to boom, to thunder **2** : to resound, to reverberate

retumbo *nm* : booming, thundering, roll

retuvo, etc. → retener

reubicar {72} *vt* : to relocate — **reubicación** *nf*

reuma or **reúma** *nmf* → **reumatismo**

reumático, -ca *adj* : rheumatic

reumatismo *nm* : rheumatism

reunión *nf, pl* **-niones 1** : meeting **2** : gathering, reunion

reunir {68} *vt* **1** : to unite, to join, to bring together **2** : to have, to possess ⟨reunieron los requisitos necesarios : they fulfilled the necessary requirements⟩ **3** : to gather, to collect, to raise (funds) — **reunirse** *vr* : to meet

reutilizable *adj* : reusable

reutilizar {21} *vt* : to recycle, to reuse

revalidar *vt* **1** : to confirm, to ratify **2** : to defend (a title)

revaluar {3} *vt* : to reevaluate — **revaluación** *n*

revancha *nf* **1** DESQUITE : revenge, requital **2** : rematch

revelación *nf, pl* **-ciones** : revelation

revelado *nm* : developing (of film)

revelador¹, -dora *adj* : revealing

revelador² *nm* : developer

revelar *vt* **1** : to reveal, to disclose **2** : to develop (film)

revendedor, -dora *n* **1** : scalper **2** DETALLISTA : retailer

revender *vt* **1** : to resell **2** : to scalp

reventa *nf* **1** : resale **2** : scalping

reventar {55} *vi* **1** ESTALLAR, EXPLOTAR : to burst, to blow up **2 ~ de** : to be bursting with — *vt* **1** : to burst **2** *fam* : to annoy, to rile

reventón *nm, pl* **-tones 1** : burst, bursting **2** : blowout, flat tire **3** *Mex fam* : bash, party

reverberar *vi* : to reverberate — **reverberación** *nf*

reverdecer {53} *vi* **1** : to grow green again **2** : to revive

reverencia *nf* **1** : reverence **2** : bow, curtsy

reverenciar *vt* : to revere, to venerate

reverendo¹, -da *adj* **1** : reverend **2** *fam* : total, absolute ⟨es un reverendo imbécil : he is a complete idiot⟩

reverendo², -da *n* : reverend

reverente *adj* : reverent

reversa *nf* *Col, Mex* : reverse (gear)

reversible *adj* : reversible

reversión *nf, pl* **-siones** : reversion

reverso *nm* **1** : back, other side **2 el reverso de la medalla** : the complete opposite

revertir {76} *vi* **1** : to revert, to go back **2 ~ en** : to result in, to end up as

revés *nm, pl* **reveses 1** : back, wrong side **2** : setback, reversal **3** : backhand (in sports) **4 al revés** : the other way around, upside down, inside out **5 al revés de** : contrary to

revestimiento *nm* : covering, facing (of a building)

revestir {54} *vt* **1** : to coat, to cover, to surface **2** : to conceal, to disguise **3** : to take on, to assume ⟨la reunión revistió gravedad : the meeting took on a serious note⟩

revisar *vt* **1** : to examine, to inspect, to check **2** : to check over, to overhaul (machinery) **3** : to revise

revisión *nf, pl* **-siones 1** : revision **2** : inspection, check

revisor, -sora *n* **1** : inspector **2** : conductor (on a train)

revista *nf* **1** : magazine, journal **2** : revue **3 pasar revista** : to review, to inspect

revistar *vt* : to review, to inspect

revitalizar {21} *vt* : to revitalize — **revitalización** *nf*

revivir *vi* : to revive, to come alive again — *vt* : to relive

revocación *nf, pl* **-ciones** : revocation, repeal

revocar {72} *vt* **1** : to revoke, to repeal **2** : to plaster (a wall)

revolcar {82} *vt* : to knock over, to knock down — **revolcarse** *vr* : to roll around, to wallow

revolcón *nm, pl* **-cones** *fam* : tumble, fall

revolotear *vi* : to flutter around, to flit

revoloteo *nm* : fluttering, flitting

revoltijo *nm* **1** FÁRRAGO : mess, jumble **2** *Mex* : traditional seafood dish

revoltoso, -sa *adj* : unruly, rebellious

revolución *nf*, *pl* **-ciones** : revolution

revolucionar *vt* : to revolutionize

revolucionario, -ria *adj & n* : revolutionary

revolver {89} *vt* **1** : to move about, to mix, to shake, to stir **2** : to upset (one's stomach) **3** : to mess up, to rummage through ⟨revolver la casa : to turn the house upside down⟩ — **revolverse** *vr* **1** : to toss and turn **2** VOLVERSE : to turn around

revólver *nm* : revolver

revoque *nm* : plaster

revuelo *nm* **1** : fluttering **2** : commotion, stir

revuelta *nf* : uprising, revolt

revuelto[1] *pp* → revolver

revuelto[2]**, -ta** *adj* **1** : choppy, rough ⟨mar revuelto : rough sea⟩ **2** : untidy **3 huevos revueltos** : scrambled eggs

rey *nm* : king

reyerta *nf* : brawl, fight

rezagado, -da *n* : straggler, latecomer

rezagar {52} *vt* **1** : to leave behind **2** : to postpone — **rezagarse** *vr* : to fall behind, to lag

rezar {21} *vi* **1** : to pray **2** : to say ⟨como reza el refrán : as the saying goes⟩ **3** ~ **con** : to concern, to have to do with — *vt* : to say, to recite ⟨rezar un Ave María : to say a Hail Mary⟩

rezo *nm* : prayer, praying

rezongar {52} *vi* : to gripe, to grumble

rezumar *v* : to ooze, to leak

ría[1]**, etc.** → reír

ría[2] *nf* : estuary

riachuelo *nm* ARROYO : brook, stream

riada *nf* : flood

ribera *nf* : bank, shore

ribete *nm* **1** : border, trim **2** : frill, adornment **3 ribetes** *nmpl* : hint, touch ⟨tiene sus ribetes de genio : there's a touch of genius in him⟩

ribetear *vt* : to border, to edge, to trim

ricamente *adv* : richly, splendidly

rice, etc. → rizar

rico[1]**, -ca** *adj* **1** : rich, wealthy **2** : fertile **3** : luxurious, valuable **4** : delicious **5** : adorable, lovely **6** : great, wonderful

rico[2]**, -ca** *n* : rich person

ridiculez *nf*, *pl* **-leces** : ridiculousness, absurdity

ridiculizar {21} *vt* : to ridicule

ridículo[1]**, -la** *adj* ABSURDO, DISPARATADO : ridiculous, ludicrous — **ridículamente** *adv*

ridículo[2]**, -la** *n* **1 hacer el ridículo** : to make a fool of oneself **2 poner en ridículo** : to ridicule

ríe, etc. → reír

riega, riegue etc. → regar

riego *nm* : irrigation

riel *nm* : rail, track

rienda *nf* **1** : rein **2 dar rienda suelta a** : to give free rein to **3 llevar las riendas** : to be in charge **4 tomar las riendas** : to take control

riesgo *nm* : risk

riesgoso, -sa *adj* : risky

rifa *nf* : raffle

rifar *vt* : to raffle — *vi* : to quarrel, to fight

rifle *nm* : rifle

rige, rija etc. → regir

rigidez *nf*, *pl* **-deces 1** : rigidity, stiffness ⟨rigidez cadavérica : rigor mortis⟩ **2** : inflexibility

rígido, -da *adj* **1** : rigid, stiff **2** : strict — **rígidamente** *adv*

rigor *nm* **1** : rigor, harshness **2** : precision, meticulousness **3 de** ~ : usual ⟨la respuesta de rigor : the standard reply⟩ **4 de** ~ : essential, obligatory **5 en** ~ : strictly speaking, in reality

riguroso, -sa *adj* : rigorous — **rigurosamente** *adv*

rima *nf* **1** : rhyme **2 rimas** *nfpl* : verse, poetry

rimar *vi* : to rhyme

rimbombante *adj* **1** : grandiose, showy **2** : bombastic, pompous

rímel *or* **rimel** *nm* : mascara

rin *nm Col, Mex* : wheel, rim (of a tire)

rincón *nm*, *pl* **rincones** : corner, nook

rinde, etc. → rendir

rinoceronte *nm* : rhinoceros

riña *nf* **1** : fight, brawl **2** : dispute, quarrel

riñe, etc. → reñir

riñón *nm*, *pl* **riñones** : kidney

río[1] → reír

río[2] *nm* **1** : river **2** : torrent, stream ⟨un río de lágrimas : a flood of tears⟩

ripio *nm* **1** : debris, rubble **2** : gravel

riqueza *nf* **1** : wealth, riches *pl* **2** : richness **3 riquezas naturales** : natural resources

risa *nf* **1** : laughter, laugh **2 dar risa** : to make laugh ⟨me dio mucha risa : I found it very funny⟩ **3** *fam* **morirse de la risa** : to die laughing, to crack up

risco *nm* : crag, cliff

risible *adj* IRRISORIO : ludicrous, laughable

risita *nf* : giggle, titter, snicker

risotada *nf* : guffaw

ristra *nf* : string, series *pl*

risueño, -ña *adj* **1** : cheerful, pleasant **2** : promising

rítmico, -ca *adj* : rhythmical, rhythmic — **rítmicamente** *adv*

ritmo *nm* **1** : rhythm **2** : pace, tempo ⟨trabajó a ritmo lento : she worked at a slow pace⟩

rito *nm* : rite, ritual

ritual *adj & nm* : ritual — **ritualmente** *adv*

rival *adj & nmf* COMPETIDOR : rival

rivalidad *nf* : rivalry, competition

rivalizar {21} *vi* ~ **con** : to rival, to compete with

rizado, -da *adj* **1** : curly **2** : ridged **3** : ripply, undulating
rizar {21} *vt* **1** : to curl **2** : to ripple, to ruffle (a surface) **3** : to crumple, to fold — **rizarse** *vr* **1** : to frizz **2** : to ripple
rizo *nm* **1** : curl **2** : loop (in aviation)
robalo *or* **róbalo** *nm* : sea bass
robar *vt* **1** : to steal **2** : to rob, to burglarize **3** SECUESTRAR : to abduct, to kidnap **4** : to captivate — *vi* ~ **en** : to break into
roble *nm* : oak
robo *nm* : robbery, theft
robot *nm*, *pl* **robots** : robot
robótica *nf* : robotics
robustecer {53} *vt* : to grow stronger, to strengthen
robustez *nf* : sturdiness, robustness
robusto, -ta *adj* : robust, sturdy
roca *nf* : rock, boulder
roce[1], *etc.* → **rozar**
roce[2] *nm* **1** : rubbing, chafing **2** : brush, graze, touch **3** : close contact, familiarity **4** : friction, disagreement
rociador *nm* : sprinkler
rociar {85} *vt* : to spray, to sprinkle
rocío *nm* **1** : dew **2** : shower, light rain
rock *or* **rock and roll** *nm* : rock, rock and roll
rocola *nf* : jukebox
rocoso, -sa *adj* : rocky
rodada *nf* : track (of a tire), rut
rodado, -da *adj* **1** : wheeled **2** : dappled (of a horse)
rodadura *nf* : rolling, taxiing
rodaja *nf* : round, slice
rodaje *nm* **1** : filming, shooting **2** : breaking in (of a vehicle)
rodamiento *nm* **1** : bearing ⟨rodamiento de bolas : ball bearings⟩ **2** : rolling
rodante *adj* : rolling
rodar {19} *vi* **1** : to roll, to roll down, to roll along ⟨rodé por la escalera : I tumbled down the stairs⟩ ⟨todo rodaba bien : everthing was going along well⟩ **2** GIRAR : to turn, to go around **3** : to move about, to travel ⟨andábamos rodando por todas partes : we drifted along from place to place⟩ — *vt* **1** : to film, to shoot **2** : to break in (a new vehicle)
rodear *vt* **1** : to surround **2** : to round up (cattle) — *vi* **1** : to go around **2** : to beat around the bush — **rodearse** *vr* ~ **de** : to surround oneself with
rodeo *nm* **1** : rodeo, roundup **2** DESVÍO : detour **3** : evasion ⟨andar con rodeos : to beat around the bush⟩ ⟨sin rodeos : without reservations⟩
rodilla *nf* : knee
rodillo *nm* **1** : roller **2** : rolling pin
rododendro *nm* : rhododendron
roedor[1], **-dora** *adj* : gnawing
roedor[2] *nm* : rodent
roer {69} *vt* **1** : to gnaw **2** : to eat away at, to torment
rogar {16} *vt* : to beg, to request — *vi* **1** : to beg, to plead **2** : to pray

roiga, *etc.* → **roer**
rojez *nf* : redness
rojizo, -za *adj* : reddish
rojo[1], **-ja** *adj* **1** : red **2 ponerse rojo** : to blush
rojo[2] *nm* : red
rol *nm* **1** : role **2** : list, roll
rollo *nm* **1** : roll, coil ⟨un rollo de cinta : a roll of tape⟩ ⟨en rollo : rolled up⟩ **2** *fam* : roll of fat **3** *fam* : boring speech, lecture
romance *nm* **1** : Romance language **2** : ballad **3** : romance **4 en buen romance** : simply stated, simply put
romano, -na *adj* & *n* : Roman
romanticismo *nm* : romanticism
romántico, -ca *adj* : romantic — **románticamente** *adv*
rombo *nm* : rhombus
romería *nf* **1** : pilgrimage, procession **2** : crowd, gathering
romero[1], **-ra** *n* PEREGRINO : pilgrim
romero[2] *nm* : rosemary
romo, -ma *adj* : blunt, dull
rompecabezas *nms* & *pl* : puzzle, riddle
rompehielos *nms* & *pl* : icebreaker (ship)
rompehuelgas *nmfs* & *pl* ESQUIROL : strikebreaker, scab
rompenueces *nms* & *pl* : nutcracker
rompeolas *ns* & *pl* : breakwater, jetty
romper {70} *vt* **1** : to break, to smash **2** : to rip, to tear **3** : to break off (relations), to break (a contract) **4** : to break through, to break down **5** GASTAR : to wear out — *vi* **1** : to break ⟨al romper del día : at the break of day⟩ **2** ~ **a** : to begin to, to burst out with ⟨romper a llorar : to burst into tears⟩ **3** ~ **con** : to break off with
rompope *nm* CA, Mex : drink similar to eggnog
ron *nm* : rum
roncar {72} *vi* **1** : to snore **2** : to roar
ronco, -ca *adj* **1** : hoarse **2** : husky (of the voice) — **roncamente** *adv*
ronda *nf* **1** : beat, patrol **2** : round (of drinks, of negotiations, of a game)
rondar *vt* **1** : to patrol **2** : to hang around ⟨siempre está rondando la calle : he's always hanging around the street⟩ **3** : to be approximately ⟨debe rondar los cincuenta : he must be about 50⟩ — *vi* **1** : to be on patrol **2** : to prowl around, to roam about
ronque, *etc.* → **roncar**
ronquera *nf* : hoarseness
ronquido *nm* **1** : snore **2** : roar
ronronear *vi* : to purr
ronroneo *nm* : purr, purring
ronzal *nm* : halter (for an animal)
ronzar {21} *v* : to munch, to crunch
roña *nf* **1** : mange **2** : dirt, filth **3** *fam* : stinginess
roñoso, -sa *adj* **1** : mangy **2** : dirty **3** *fam* : stingy
ropa *nf* **1** : clothes *pl*, clothing **2 ropa interior** : underwear

ropaje *nm* : apparel, garments *pl*, regalia
ropero *nm* ARMARIO, CLÓSET : wardrobe, closet
rosa[1] *adj* : rose-colored, pink
rosa[2] *nm* : rose, pink (color)
rosa[3] *nf* : rose (flower)
rosáceo, -cea *adj* : pinkish
rosado[1], **-da** *adj* 1 : pink 2 **vino rosado** : rosé
rosado[2] *nm* : pink (color)
rosal *nm* : rosebush
rosario *nm* 1 : rosary 2 : series ⟨un rosario de islas : a string of islands⟩
rosbif *nm* : roast beef
rosca *nf* 1 : thread (of a screw) ⟨una tapa a rosca : a screw top⟩ 2 : ring, coil
roseta *nf* : rosette
rosquilla *nf* : ring-shaped pastry, doughnut
rostro *nm* : face, countenance
rotación *nf, pl* **-ciones** : rotation
rotar *vt* : to rotate, to turn — *vi* : to turn, to spin
rotativo[1], **-va** *adj* : rotary
rotativo[2] *nm* : newspaper
rotatorio, -ria *adj* → **rotativo**[1]
roto[1] *pp* → **romper**
roto[2], **-ta** *adj* 1 : broken 2 : ripped, torn
rotonda *nf* 1 : traffic circle, rotary 2 : rotunda
rotor *nm* : rotor
rótula *nf* : kneecap
rotular *vt* 1 : to head, to entitle 2 : to label
rótulo *nm* 1 : heading, title 2 : label, sign
rotundo, -da *adj* 1 REDONDO : round 2 : categorical, absolute ⟨un éxito rotundo : a resounding success⟩ — **rotundamente** *adv*
rotura *nf* : break, tear, fracture
roya *nf* : plant rust
roya, etc. → **roer**
rozado, -da *adj* GASTADO : worn
rozadura *nf* 1 : scratch, abrasion 2 : rubbed spot, sore
rozar {21} *vt* 1 : to chafe, to rub against 2 : to border on, to touch on 3 : to graze, to touch lightly — **rozarse** *vr* ∼ **con** *fam* : to rub shoulders with
ruandés, -desa *adj & n* : Rwandan
ruano, -na *adj* : roan
rubí *nm, pl* **rubíes** : ruby
rubio, -bia *adj & n* : blond
rublo *nm* : ruble
rubor *nm* 1 : flush, blush 2 : rouge, blusher
ruborizarse {21} *vr* : to blush
rúbrica *nf* : title, heading
rubricar {72} *vt* 1 : sign with a flourish ⟨firmado y rubricado : signed and sealed⟩ 2 : to endorse, to sanction
rubro *nm* 1 : heading, title 2 : line, area (in business)
rudeza *nf* ASPEREZA : roughness, coarseness

rudimentario, -ria *adj* : rudimentary — **rudimentariamente** *adv*
rudimento *nm* : rudiment, basics *pl*
rudo, -da *adj* 1 : rough, harsh 2 : coarse, unpolished — **rudamente** *adv*
rueda[1], **etc.** → **rodar**
rueda[2] *nf* 1 : wheel 2 RODAJA : round slice 3 : circle, ring 4 **rueda de andar** : treadmill 5 **rueda de prensa** : press conference 6 **ir sobre ruedas** : to go smoothly
ruedita *nf* : caster (on furniture)
ruedo *nm* 1 : bullring, arena 2 : rotation, turn 3 : hem
ruega, ruegue etc. → **rogar**
ruego *nm* : request, appeal, plea
rugido *nm* : roar
rugir {35} *vi* : to roar
ruibarbo *nm* : rhubarb
ruido *nm* : noise, sound
ruidoso, -sa *adj* : loud, noisy — **ruidosamente** *adv*
ruin *adj* 1 : base, despicable 2 : mean, stingy
ruina *nf* 1 : ruin, destruction 2 : downfall, collapse 3 **ruinas** *nfpl* : ruins, remains
ruinoso, -sa *adj* 1 : run-down, dilapidated 2 : ruinous, disastrous
ruiseñor *nm* : nightingale
ruja, etc. → **rugir**
ruleta *nf* : roulette
rulo *nm* : curler, roller
rumano, -na *n* : Romanian, Rumanian
rumbo *nm* 1 : direction, course ⟨con rumbo a : bound for, heading for⟩ ⟨perder el rumbo : to go off course, to lose one's bearings⟩ ⟨sin rumbo : aimless, aimlessly⟩ 2 : ostentation, pomp 3 : lavishness, generosity
rumiante *adj & n* : ruminant
rumiar *vt* : to ponder, to mull over — *vi* 1 : to chew the cud 2 : to ruminate, to ponder
rumor *nm* 1 : rumor 2 : murmur
rumorearse *or* **rumorarse** *vr* : to be rumored ⟨se rumorea que se va : rumor has it that she's leaving⟩
rumoroso, -sa *adj* : murmuring, babbling ⟨un arroyo rumoroso : a babbling brook⟩
rupia *nf* : rupee
ruptura *nf* 1 : break 2 : breaking, breach (of a contract) 3 : breaking off, breakup
rural *adj* : rural
ruso[1], **-sa** *adj & n* : Russian
ruso[2] *nm* : Russian (language)
rústico[1], **-ca** *adj* : rural, rustic
rústico[2], **-ca** *n* : rustic, country dweller
ruta *nf* : route
rutina *nf* : routine, habit
rutinario, -ria *adj* : routine, ordinary ⟨visita rutinaria : routine visit⟩ — **rutinariamente** *adv*

S

s *nf* : twentieth letter of the Spanish alphabet

sábado *nm* **1** : Saturday **2** : Sabbath

sábalo *nm* : shad

sabana *nf* : savanna

sábana *nf* : sheet, bedsheet

sabandija *nf* BICHO : bug, small reptile, pesky creature

sabático, -ca *adj* : sabbatical

sabedor, -dora *adj* : aware, informed

sabelotodo *nmf fam* : know-it-all

saber¹ {71} *vt* **1** : to know **2** : to know how to, to be able to ⟨sabe tocar el violín : she can play the violin⟩ **3** : to learn, to find out **4 a** ~ : to wit, namely — *vi* **1** : to know, to suppose **2** : to be informed ⟨supimos del desastre : we heard about the disaster⟩ **3** : to taste ⟨esto no sabe bien : this doesn't taste right⟩ **4** ~ **a** : to taste like ⟨sabe a naranja : it tastes like orange⟩ — **saberse** *vr* : to know ⟨ese chiste no me lo sé : I don't know that joke⟩

saber² *nm* : knowledge, learning

sabiamente *adv* : wisely

sabido, -da *adj* : well-known

sabiduría *nf* **1** : wisdom **2** : learning, knowledge

sabiendas *adv* **1 a** ~ : knowingly **2 a sabiendas de que** : knowing full well that

sabio¹, -bia *adj* **1** PRUDENTE : wise, sensible **2** DOCTO : learned

sabio², -bia *n* **1** : wise person **2** : savant, learned person

sable *nm* : saber, cutlass

sabor *nm* **1** : flavor, taste **2 sin** ~ : flavorless

saborear *vt* **1** : to taste, to savor **2** : to enjoy, to relish

sabotaje *nm* : sabotage

saboteador, -dora *n* : saboteur

sabotear *vt* : to sabotage

sabrá, etc. → **saber**

sabroso, -sa *adj* **1** RICO : delicious, tasty **2** AGRADABLE : pleasant, nice, lovely

sabueso *nm* **1** : bloodhound **2** *fam* : detective, sleuth

sacacorchos *nms & pl* : corkscrew

sacapuntas *nms & pl* : pencil sharpener

sacar {72} *vt* **1** : to pull out, to take out ⟨saca el pollo del congelador : take the chicken out of the freezer⟩ **2** : to get, to obtain ⟨saqué un 100 en el examen : I got 100 on the exam⟩ **3** : to get out, to extract ⟨le saqué la información : I got the information from him⟩ **4** : to stick out ⟨sacar la lengua : to stick out one's tongue⟩ **5** : to bring out, to introduce ⟨sacar un libro : to publish a book⟩ ⟨sacaron una moda nueva : they introduced a new style⟩ **6** : to take (photos) **7** : to make (copies) — *vi* **1**

: to kick off (in soccer or football) **2** : to serve (in sports)

sacarina *nf* : saccharin

sacarosa *nf* : sucrose

sacerdocio *nm* : priesthood

sacerdotal *adj* : priestly

sacerdote, -tisa *n* : priest *m*, priestess *f*

saciar *vt* **1** HARTAR : to sate, to satiate **2** SATISFACER : to satisfy

saciedad *nf* : satiety

saco *nm* **1** : bag, sack **2** : sac **3** : jacket, sport coat

sacramento *nm* : sacrament — **sacramental** *adj*

sacrificar {72} *vt* : to sacrifice — **sacrificarse** *vr* : to sacrifice oneself, to make sacrifices

sacrificio *nm* : sacrifice

sacrilegio *nm* : sacrilege

sacrílego, -ga *adj* : sacrilegious

sacristán *nm, pl* **-tanes** : sexton, sacristan

sacristía *nf* : sacristy, vestry

sacro, -cra *adj* SAGRADO : sacred ⟨arte sacro : sacred art⟩

sacrosanto, -ta *adj* : sacrosanct

sacudida *nf* **1** : shaking **2** : jerk, jolt, shock **3** : shake-up, upheaval

sacudir *vt* **1** : to shake, to beat **2** : to jerk, to jolt **3** : to dust off **4** CONMOVER : to shake up, to shock — **sacudirse** *vr* : to shake off

sacudón *nm, pl* **-dones** : intense jolt or shake-up

sádico¹, -ca *adj* : sadistic

sádico², -ca *n* : sadist

sadismo *nm* : sadism

safari *nm* : safari

saga *nf* : saga

sagacidad *nf* : sagacity, shrewdness

sagaz *adj, pl* **sagaces** PERSPICAZ : shrewd, discerning, sagacious

Sagitario *nmf* : Sagittarius, Sagittarian

sagrado, -da *adj* : sacred, holy

sainete *nm* : comedy sketch, one-act farce ⟨este proceso es un sainete : these proceedings are a farce⟩

sajar *vt* : to lance, to cut open

sal¹ → **salir**

sal² *nf* **1** : salt **2** *CA, Mex* : misfortune, bad luck

sala *nf* **1** : living room **2** : room, hall ⟨sala de conferencias : lecture hall⟩ ⟨sala de urgencias : emergency room⟩ ⟨sala de baile : ballroom⟩

salado, -da *adj* **1** : salty **2 agua salada** : salt water

salamandra *nf* : salamander

salami *nm* : salami

salar *vt* **1** : to salt **2** : to spoil, to ruin **3** *CoRi, Mex* : to jinx, to bring bad luck

salarial *adj* : salary, salary-related

salario *nm* **1** : salary **2 salario mínimo** : minimum wage

salaz *adj, pl* **salaces** : salacious, lecherous

salchicha *nf* 1 : sausage 2 : frankfurter, wiener

salchichón *nf, pl* **-chones** : a type of deli meat

salchichonería *nf Mex* 1 : delicatessen 2 : cold cuts *pl*

saldar *vt* : to settle, to pay off ⟨saldar una cuenta : to settle an account⟩

saldo *nm* 1 : settlement, payment 2 : balance ⟨saldo de cuenta : account balance⟩ 3 : remainder, leftover merchandise

saldrá, etc. → salir

salero *nm* 1 : saltshaker 2 : wit, charm

salga, etc. → salir

salida *nf* 1 : exit ⟨salida de emergencia : emergency exit⟩ 2 : leaving, departure 3 SOLUCIÓN : way out, solution 4 : start (of a race) 5 OCURRENCIA : wisecrack, joke 6 **salida del sol** : sunrise

saliente¹ *adj* 1 : departing, outgoing 2 : projecting 3 DESTACADO : salient, prominent

saliente² *nm* 1 : projection, protrusion 2 **ventana en saliente** : bay window

salinidad *nf* : salinity, saltiness

salino, -na *adj* : saline ⟨solución salina : saline solution⟩

salir {73} *vi* 1 : to go out, to come out, to get out ⟨salimos todas las noches : we go out every night⟩ ⟨su libro acaba de salir : her book just came out⟩ 2 PARTIR : to leave, to depart 3 APARECER : to appear ⟨salió en todos los diarios : it came out in all the papers⟩ 4 : to project, to stick out 5 : to cost, to come to 6 RESULTAR : to turn out, to prove 7 : to come up, to occur ⟨salga lo que salga : whatever happens⟩ ⟨salió una oportunidad : an opportunity came up⟩ 8 **~ a** : to take after, to look like, to resemble 9 **~ con** : to go out with, to date — **salirse** *vr* 1 : to escape, to get out, to leak out 2 : to come loose, to come off 3 **salirse con la suya** : to get one's own way

saliva *nf* : saliva

salivar *vi* : to salivate

salmo *nm* : psalm

salmón¹ *adj* : salmon-colored

salmón² *nm, pl* **salmones** : salmon

salmuera *nf* : brine

salobre *adj* : brackish, briny

salón *nm, pl* **salones** : hall, large room ⟨salón de clase : classroom⟩ ⟨salón de baile : ballroom⟩ 2 : salon ⟨salón de belleza : beauty salon⟩ 3 : parlor, sitting room

salpicadera *nf Mex* : fender

salpicadura *nf* : spatter, splash

salpicar {72} *vt* 1 : to spatter, to splash 2 : to sprinkle, to scatter about

salpimentar {55} *vt* 1 : to season (with salt and pepper) 2 : to spice up

salsa *nf* 1 : sauce ⟨salsa picante : hot sauce⟩ ⟨salsa inglesa : Worcestershire sauce⟩ ⟨salsa tártara : tartar sauce⟩ 2 : gravy 3 : salsa (music) 4 **salsa mexicana** : salsa (sauce)

salsero, -ra *n* : salsa musician

saltador, -dora *n* : jumper

saltamontes *nms & pl* ; grasshopper

saltar *vi* 1 BRINCAR : to jump, to leap 2 : to bounce 3 : to come off, to pop out 4 : to shatter, to break 5 : to explode, to blow up — *vt* 1 : to jump, to jump over 2 : to skip, to miss — **saltarse** *vr* OMITIR : to skip, to omit ⟨me salté ese capítulo : I skipped that chapter⟩

saltarín, -rina *adj, mpl* **-rines** : leaping, hopping ⟨frijol saltarín : jumping bean⟩

salteado, -da *adj* 1 : sautéed 2 : jumbled up ⟨los episodios se transmitieron salteados : the episodes were broadcast in random order⟩

salteador *nm* : highwayman

saltear *vt* 1 SOFREÍR : to sauté 2 : to skip around, to skip over

saltimbanqui *nmf* : acrobat

salto *nm* 1 BRINCO : jump, leap, skip 2 : jump, dive (in sports) 3 : gap, omission 4 **dar saltos** : to jump up and down 4 *or* **salto de agua** CATARATA : waterfall

saltón, -tona *adj, mpl* **saltones** : bulging, protruding

salubre *adj* : healthful, salubrious

salubridad *nf* : healthfulness, health

salud *nf* 1 : health ⟨buena salud : good health⟩ 2 **¡salud!** : bless you! (when someone sneezes) 3 **¡salud!** : cheers!, to your health!

saludable *adj* 1 SALUBRE : healthful 2 SANO : healthy, well

saludar *vt* 1 : to greet, to say hello to 2 : to salute — **saludarse** *vr*

saludo *nm* 1 : greeting, regards *pl* 2 : salute

salutación *nf, pl* **-ciones** : salutation

salva *nf* 1 : salvo, volley 2 **salva de aplausos** : round of applause

salvación *nf, pl* **-ciones** 1 : salvation 2 RESCATE : rescue

salvado *nm* : bran

salvador, -dora *n* 1 : savior, rescuer 2 **el Salvador** : the Savior

salvadoreño, -ña *adj & n* : Salvadoran, El Salvadoran

salvaguardar *vt* : to safeguard

salvaguardia *or* **salvaguarda** *nf* : safeguard, defense

salvajada *nf* ATROCIDAD : atrocity, act of savagery

salvaje¹ *adj* 1 : wild ⟨animales salvajes : wild animals⟩ 2 : savage, cruel 3 : primitive, uncivilized

salvaje² *nmf* : savage

salvajismo *nm* : savagery

salvamento *nm* 1 : rescuing, lifesaving 2 : salvation 3 : refuge

salvar *vt* 1 : to save, to rescue 2 : to cover (a distance) 3 : to get around (an obstacle), to overcome (a difficulty) 4

: to cross, to jump across **5 salvando**
: except for, excluding — **salvarse** vr
1 : to survive, to escape **2** : to save one's
soul

salvavidas[1] nms & pl **1** : life preserver
2 bote salvavidas : lifeboat

salvavidas[2] nmf : lifeguard

salvedad nf **1** EXCEPCIÓN : exception
2 : proviso, stipulation

salvia nf : sage (plant)

salvo[1], **-va** adj **1** : unharmed, sound
⟨sano y salvo : safe and sound⟩ **2 a ~**
: safe from danger

salvo[2] prep **1** EXCEPTO : except (for),
save ⟨todos asistirán salvo Jaime : all
will attend except for Jaime⟩ **2 salvo
que** : unless ⟨salvo que llueva : unless
it rains⟩

salvoconducto nm : safe-conduct

samba nf : samba

San adj → **santo**[1]

sanar vt : to heal, to cure — vi : to get
well, to recover

sanatorio nm **1** : sanatorium **2** : clinic, private hospital

sanción nf, pl **sanciones** : sanction

sancionar vt **1** : to penalize, to impose
a sanction on **2** : to sanction, to approve

sancochar vt : to parboil

sandalia nf : sandal

sándalo nm : sandalwood

sandez nf, pl **sandeces** ESTUPIDEZ
: nonsense, silly thing to say

sandía nf : watermelon

sandwich [ˈsandwitʃ, ˈsangwitʃ] nm, pl
sandwiches [-ˈditʃes, -ˈgwi-] EMPARE-
DADO : sandwich

saneamiento nm **1** : cleaning up, sanitation **2** : reorganizing, streamlining

sanear vt **1** : to clean up, to sanitize **2**
: to reorganize, to streamline

sangrante adj **1** : bleeding **2** : flagrant,
blatant

sangrar vi : to bleed — vt : to indent (a
paragraph, etc.)

sangre nf **1** : blood **2 a sangre fría** : in
cold blood **3 a sangre y fuego** : by violent force **4 pura sangre** : thoroughbred

sangría nf **1** : bloodletting **2** : sangria
(wine punch) **3** : drain, draining ⟨una
sangría fiscal : a financial drain⟩ **4** : indentation, indenting

sangriento, -ta adj **1** : bloody **2** : cruel

sanguijuela nf **1** : leech, bloodsucker **2**
: sponger, leech

sanguinario, -ria adj : bloodthirsty

sanguíneo, -nea adj : blood ⟨vaso
sanguíneo : blood vessel⟩ **2** : sanguine,
ruddy

sanidad nf **1** : health **2** : public health,
sanitation

sanitario[1], **-ria** adj **1** : sanitary **2** : health
⟨centro sanitario : health center⟩

sanitario[2], **-ria** n : sanitation worker

sanitario[3] nm Col, Mex, Ven : toilet ⟨los
sanitarios : the toilets, the restroom⟩

sano, -na adj **1** SALUDABLE : healthy **2**
: wholesome **3** : whole, intact

santiaguino, -na adj : of or from Santi-
ago, Chile

santiamén nm **en un santiamén** : in no
time at all

santidad nf : holiness, sanctity

santificar {72} vt : to sanctify, to consecrate, to hallow

santiguarse {10} vr PERSIGNARSE : to
cross oneself

santo[1], **-ta** adj **1** : holy, saintly ⟨el San-
to Padre : the Holy Father⟩ ⟨una vida
santa : a saintly life⟩ **2 Santo, Santa**
(**San** before names of masculine saints
except those beginning with D or T)
: Saint ⟨Santa Clara : Saint Claire⟩
⟨Santo Tomás : Saint Thomas⟩ ⟨San
Francisco : Saint Francis⟩

santo[2], **-ta** n : saint

santo[3] nm **1** : saint's day **2** CUMPLE-
AÑOS : birthday

santuario nm : sanctuary

santurrón, -rrona adj, mpl **-rrones**
: overly pious, sanctimonious — **santurronamente** adv

saña nf **1** : fury, rage **2** : viciousness
⟨con saña : viciously⟩

sapo nm : toad

saque[1], etc. → **sacar**

saque[2] nm **1** : kickoff (in soccer or football) **2** : serve, service (in sports)

saqueador, -dora n DEPREDADOR
: plunderer, looter

saquear vt : to sack, to plunder, to loot

saqueo nm DEPREDACIÓN : sacking,
plunder, looting

sarampión nm : measles pl

sarape nm CA, Mex : serape, blanket

sarcasmo nm : sarcasm

sarcástico, -ca adj : sarcastic

sarcófago nm : sarcophagus

sardina nf : sardine

sardónico, -ca adj : sardonic

sarga nf : serge

sargento nmf : sergeant

sarna nf : mange

sarnoso, -sa adj : mangy

sarpullido nm ERUPCIÓN : rash

sarro nm **1** : deposit, coating **2** : tartar,
plaque

sarta nf **1** : string, series (of insults, etc.)
2 : string (of pearls, etc.)

sartén nmf, pl **sartenes** **1** : frying pan
2 tener la sartén por el mango : to call
the shots, to be in control

sasafrás nm : sassafras

sastre, -tra n : tailor

sastrería nf **1** : tailoring **2** : tailor's shop

Satanás or **Satán** nm : Satan, the devil

satánico, -ca adj : satanic

satélite nm : satellite

satín or **satén** nm, pl **satines** or **satenes**
: satin

satinado, -da adj : satiny, glossy

sátira nf : satire

satírico, -ca adj : satirical, satiric

satirizar {21} vt : to satirize

sátiro *nm* : satyr

satisfacción *nf, pl* **-ciones** : satisfaction

satisfacer {74} *vt* **1** : to satisfy **2** : to fulfill, to meet **3** : to pay, to settle — **satisfacerse** *vr* **1** : to be satisfied **2** : to take revenge

satisfactorio, -ria *adj* : satisfactory — **satisfactoriamente** *adv*

satisfecho, -cha *adj* : satisfied, content, pleased

saturación *nf, pl* **-ciones** : saturation

saturar *vt* **1** : to saturate, to fill up **2** : to satiate, to surfeit

saturnismo *nm* : lead poisoning

Saturno *nm* : Saturn

sauce *nm* : willow

saúco *nm* : elder (tree)

saudí *or* **saudita** *adj & nmf* : Saudi, Saudi Arabian

sauna *nmf* : sauna

savia *nf* : sap

saxofón *nm, pl* **-fones** : saxophone

sazón[1] *nf, pl* **sazones** **1** : flavor, seasoning **2** : ripeness, maturity ⟨en sazón : in season, ripe⟩ **3 a la sazón** : at that time, then

sazón[2] *nmf, pl* **sazones** *Mex* : flavor, seasoning

sazonar *vt* CONDIMENTAR : to season, to spice

scanner *nm* → **escáner**

sé → **saber, ser**

se *pron* **1** : to him, to her, to you, to them ⟨se los daré a ella : I'll give them to her⟩ **2** : each other, one another ⟨se abrazaron : they hugged each other⟩ **3** : himself, herself, itself, yourself, yourselves, themselves ⟨se afeitó antes de salir : he shaved before leaving⟩ **4** (*used in passive constructions*) ⟨se dice que es hermosa : they say she's beautiful⟩ ⟨se habla inglés : English spoken⟩

sea, etc. → **ser**

sebo *nm* **1** : grease, fat **2** : tallow **3** : suet

secado *nm* : drying

secador *nm* : hair dryer

secadora *nf* **1** : dryer, clothes dryer **2** *Mex* : hair dryer

secante *nm* : blotting paper, blotter

secar {72} *v* **1** : to dry — **secarse** *vr* **1** : to get dry **2** : to dry up

sección *nf, pl* **secciones** **1** : section ⟨sección transversal : cross section⟩ **2** : department, division

seco, -ca *adj* **1** : dry **2** DISECADO : dried ⟨fruta seca : dried fruit⟩ **3** : thin, lean **4** : curt, brusque **5** : sharp ⟨un golpe seco : a sharp blow⟩ **6 a secas** : simply, just ⟨se llama Chico, a secas : he's just called Chico⟩ **7 en ~** : abruptly, suddenly ⟨frenar en seco : to make a sudden stop⟩

secoya *nf* : sequoia, redwood

secreción *nf, pl* **-ciones** : secretion

secretar *vt* : to secrete

secretaría *nf* **1** : secretariat, administrative department **2** *Mex* : ministry, cabinet office

secretariado *nm* **1** : secretariat **2** : secretarial profession

secretario, -ria *n* : secretary — **secretarial** *adj*

secreto[1], **-ta** *adj* **1** : secret **2** : secretive — **secretamente** *adv*

secreto[2] *nm* **1** : secret **2** : secrecy

secta *nf* : sect

sectario, -ria *adj & n* : sectarian

sector *nm* : sector

secuaz *nmf, pl* **secuaces** : follower, henchman, underling

secuela *nf* : consequence, sequel ⟨las secuelas de la guerra : the aftermath of the war⟩

secuencia *nf* : sequence

secuestrador, -dora *n* **1** : kidnapper, abductor **2** : hijacker

secuestrar *vt* **1** RAPTAR : to kidnap, to abduct **2** : to hijack, to commandeer **3** CONFISCAR : to confiscate, to seize

secuestro *nm* **1** RAPTO : kidnapping, abduction **2** : hijacking **3** : seizure, confiscation

secular *adj* : secular — **secularismo** *nm* — **secularización** *nf*

secundar *vt* : to support, to second

secundaria *nf* **1** : secondary education, high school **2** *Mex* : junior high school, middle school

secundario, -ria *adj* : secondary

secuoya *nf* : sequoia

sed *nf* **1** : thirst ⟨tener sed : to be thirsty⟩ **2 tener sed de** : to hunger for, to thirst for

seda *nf* : silk

sedación *nf, pl* **-ciones** : sedation

sedal *nm* : fishing line

sedán *nm, pl* **sedanes** : sedan

sedante *adj & nm* CALMANTE : sedative

sedar *vt* : to sedate

sede *nf* **1** : seat, headquarters **2** : venue, site **3 la Santa Sede** : the Holy See

sedentario, -ria *adj* : sedentary

sedición *nf, pl* **-ciones** : sedition — **sedicioso, -sa** *adj*

sediento, -ta *adj* : thirsty, thirsting

sedimentación *nf, pl* **-ciones** : sedimentation

sedimentario, -ria *adj* : sedimentary

sedimento *nm* : sediment

sedoso, -sa *adj* : silky, silken

seducción *nf, pl* **-ciones** : seduction

seducir {61} *vt* **1** : to seduce **2** : to captivate, to charm

seductivo, -va *adj* : seductive

seductor[1], **-tora** *adj* **1** SEDUCTIVO : seductive **2** ENCANTADOR : charming, alluring

seductor[2], **-tora** *n* : seducer

segador, -dora *n* : harvester

segar {49} *vt* **1** : to reap, to harvest, to cut **2** : to sever abruptly ⟨una vida segada por la enfermedad : a life cut short by illness⟩

seglar[1] *adj* LAICO : lay, secular

seglar[2] *nm* LAICO : layperson, layman *m*, laywoman *f*

segmentación *nf, pl* **-ciones** : segmentation

segmentado, -da *adj* : segmented

segmento *nm* : segment

segregar {52} *vt* **1** : to segregate **2** SECRETAR : to secrete

seguida *nf* en ~ : right away, immediately ⟨vuelvo en seguida : I'll be right back⟩

seguidamente *adv* **1** : next, immediately after **2** : without a break, continuously

seguido¹ *adv* **1** RECTO : straight, straight ahead **2** : often, frequently

seguido², -da *adj* **1** CONSECUTIVO : consecutive, successive ⟨tres días seguidos : three days in a row⟩ **2** : straight, unbroken **3** ~ por *or* ~ de : followed by

seguidor, -dora *n* : follower, supporter

seguimiento *nm* **1** : following, pursuit **2** : continuation **3** : tracking, monitoring

seguir {75} *vt* **1** : to follow ⟨el sol sigue la lluvia : sunshine follows the rain⟩ ⟨seguiré tu consejo : I'll follow your advice⟩ ⟨me siguieron con la mirada : they followed me with their eyes⟩ **2** : to go along, to keep on ⟨seguimos toda la carretera panamericana : we continued up the PanAmerican Highway⟩ ⟨siguió hablando : he kept on talking⟩ ⟨seguir el curso : to stay on course⟩ **3** : to take (a course, a treatment) — *vi* **1** : to go on, to keep going ⟨sigue adelante : keep going, carry on⟩ **2** : to remain, to continue to be ⟨¿todavía sigues aquí? : you're still here?⟩ ⟨sigue con vida : she's still alive⟩ **3** : to follow, to come after ⟨la frase que sigue : the following sentence⟩

según¹ *adv* : it depends ⟨según y como : it all depends on⟩

según² *conj* **1** COMO, CONFORME : as, just as ⟨según lo dejé : just as I left it⟩ **2** : depending on how ⟨según se vea : depending on how one sees it⟩

según³ *prep* **1** : according to ⟨según los rumores : according to the rumors⟩ **2** : depending on ⟨según los resultados : depending on the results⟩

segundo¹, -da *adj* : second ⟨el segundo lugar : second place⟩

segundo², -da *n* **1** : second (in a series) **2** : second (person), second-in-command

segundo³ *nm* : second ⟨sesenta segundos : sixty seconds⟩

seguramente *adv* **1** : for sure, surely **2** : probably

seguridad *nf* **1** : safety, security **2** : (financial) security ⟨seguridad social : Social Security⟩ **3** CERTEZA : certainty, assurance ⟨con toda seguridad : with complete certainty⟩ **4** : confidence, self-confidence

seguro¹ *adv* : certainly, definitely ⟨va a llover, seguro : it's going to rain for sure⟩ ⟨¡seguro que sí! : of course!⟩

seguro², -ra *adj* **1** : safe, secure **2** : sure, certain ⟨estoy segura que es él : I'm sure that's him⟩ **3** : reliable, trustworthy **4** : self-assured

seguro³ *nm* **1** : insurance ⟨seguro de vida : life insurance⟩ **2** : fastener, clasp **3** *Mex* : safety pin

seis *adj & nm* : six

seiscientos¹, -tas *adj* : six hundred

seiscientos² *nms & pl* : six hundred

selección *nf, pl* **-ciones 1** ELECCIÓN : selection, choice **2 selección natural** : natural selection

seleccionar *vt* ELEGIR : to select, to choose

selectivo, -va *adj* : selective — **selectivamente** *adv*

selecto, -ta *adj* **1** : choice, select **2** EXCLUSIVO : exclusive

selenio *nm* : selenium

sellar *vt* **1** : to seal **2** : to stamp

sello *nm* **1** : seal **2** ESTAMPILLA, TIMBRE : postage stamp **3** : hallmark, characteristic

selva *nf* **1** BOSQUE : woods *pl*, forest ⟨selva húmeda : rain forest⟩ **2** JUNGLA : jungle

selvático, -ca *adj* **1** : forest, jungle ⟨sendero selvático : jungle path⟩ **2** : wild

semáforo *nm* **1** : traffic light **2** : stop signal

semana *nf* : week

semanal *adj* : weekly — **semanalmente** *adv*

semanario *nm* : weekly (publication)

semántica *nf* : semantics

semántico, -ca *adj* : semantic

semblante *nm* **1** : countenance, face **2** : appearance, look

semblanza *nf* : biographical sketch, profile

sembrado *nm* : cultivated field

sembrador, -dora *n* : planter, sower

sembradora *nf* : seeder (machine)

sembrar {55} *vt* **1** : to plant, to sow **2** : to scatter, to strew ⟨sembrar el pánico : to spread panic⟩

semejante¹ *adj* **1** PARECIDO : similar, alike **2** TAL : such ⟨nunca he visto cosa semejante : I have never seen such a thing⟩

semejante² *nm* PRÓJIMO : fellowman

semejanza *nf* PARECIDO : similarity, resemblance

semejar *vi* : to resemble, to look like — **semejarse** *vr* : to be similar, to look alike

semen *nm* : semen

semental *nm* : stud (animal) ⟨caballo semental : stallion⟩

semestre *nm* : semester

semicírculo *nm* : semicircle, half circle

semiconductor *nm* : semiconductor

semidiós *nm, pl* **-dioses** : demigod *m*

semifinal *nf* : semifinal

semifinalista¹ *adj* : semifinal

semifinalista² *nmf* : semifinalist

semiformal *adj* : semiformal
semilla *nf* : seed
semillero *nm* **1** : seedbed **2** : hotbed, breeding ground
seminario *nm* **1** : seminary **2** : seminar, graduate course
seminarista *nm* : seminarian
semiprecioso, -sa *adj* : semiprecious
semita¹ *adj* : Semitic
semita² *nmf* : Semite
sémola *nf* : semolina
sempiterno, -na *adj* ETERNO : eternal, everlasting
senado *nm* : senate
senador, -dora *n* : senator
sencillamente *adv* : simply, plainly
sencillez *nf* : simplicity
sencillo¹, -lla *adj* **1** : simple, easy **2** : plain, unaffected **3** : single
sencillo² *nm* **1** : single (recording) **2** : small change (coins) **3** : one-way ticket
senda *nf* CAMINO, SENDERO : path, way
sendero *nm* CAMINO, SENDA : path, way
sendos, -das *adj pl* : each, both ⟨llevaban sendos vestidos nuevos : they were each wearing a new dress⟩
senectud *nf* ANCIANIDAD : old age
senegalés, -lesa *adj & n, mpl* **-leses** : Senegalese
senil *adj* : senile — **senilidad** *nf*
seno *nm* **1** : breast, bosom ⟨los senos : the breasts⟩ ⟨el seno de la familia : the bosom of the family⟩ **2** : sinus **3 seno materno** : womb
sensación *nf, pl* **-ciones 1** IMPRESIÓN : feeling ⟨tener la sensación : to have a feeling⟩ **2** : sensation ⟨causar sensación : to cause a sensation⟩
sensacional *adj* : sensational
sensacionalista *adj* : sensationalistic, lurid
sensatez *nf* **1** : good sense **2 con ∼** : sensibly
sensato, -ta *adj* : sensible, sound — **sensatamente** *adv*
sensibilidad *nf* **1** : sensitivity, sensibility **2** SENSACIÓN : feeling
sensibilizar {21} *vt* : to sensitize
sensible *adj* **1** : sensitive **2** APRECIABLE : considerable, significant
sensiblemente *adv* : considerably, significantly
sensiblería *nf* : sentimentality, mush
sensiblero, -ra *adj* : mawkish, sentimental, mushy
sensitivo, -va *adj* **1** : sense ⟨órganos sensitivos : sense organs⟩ **2** : sentient, capable of feeling
sensor *nm* : sensor
sensorial *adj* : sensory
sensual *adj* : sensual, sensuous — **sensualmente** *adv*
sensualidad *nf* : sensuality
sentado, -da *adj* **1** : sitting, seated **2** : established, settled ⟨dar por sentado : to take for granted⟩ ⟨dejar sentado : to make clear⟩ **3** : sensible, steady, judicious

sentar {55} *vt* **1** : to seat, to sit **2** : to establish, to set — *vi* **1** : to suit ⟨ese color te sienta : that color suits you⟩ **2** : to agree with (of food or drink) ⟨las cebollas no me sientan : onions don't agree with me⟩ **3** : to please ⟨le sentó mal el paseo : she didn't enjoy the trip⟩ — **sentarse** *vr* : to sit, to sit down ⟨siéntese, por favor : please have a seat⟩
sentencia *nf* **1** : sentence, judgment **2** : maxim, saying
sentenciar *vt* : to sentence
sentido¹, -da *adj* **1** : heartfelt, sincere ⟨mi más sentido pésame : my sincerest condolences⟩ **2** : touchy, sensitive **3** : offended, hurt
sentido² *nm* **1** : sense ⟨sentido común : common sense⟩ ⟨los cinco sentidos : the five senses⟩ ⟨sin sentido : senseless⟩ **2** CONOCIMIENTO : consciousness **3** SIGNIFICADO : meaning, sense ⟨doble sentido : double entendre⟩ **4** : direction ⟨calle de sentido único : one-way street⟩
sentimental¹ *adj* **1** : sentimental **2** : love, romantic ⟨vida sentimental : love life⟩
sentimental² *nmf* : sentimentalist
sentimentalismo *nm* : sentimentality, sentimentalism
sentimiento *nm* **1** : feeling, emotion **2** PESAR : regret, sorrow
sentir {76} *vt* **1** : to feel, to experience ⟨no siento nada de dolor : I don't feel any pain⟩ ⟨sentía sed : he was feeling thirsty⟩ ⟨sentir amor : to feel love⟩ **2** PERCIBIR : to perceive, to sense ⟨sentir un ruido : to hear a noise⟩ **3** LAMENTAR : to regret, to feel sorry for ⟨lo siento mucho : I'm very sorry⟩ — *vi* **1** : to have feeling, to feel **2 sin ∼** : without noticing, inadvertently — **sentirse** *vr* **1** : to feel ⟨¿te sientes mejor? : are you feeling better?⟩ **2** *Chile, Mex* : to take offense
seña *nf* **1** : sign, signal **2 dar señas de** : to show signs of
señal *nf* **1** : signal **2** : sign ⟨señal de tráfico : traffic sign⟩ **3** INDICIO : indication ⟨en señal de : as a token of⟩ **4** VESTIGIO : trace, vestige **5** : scar, mark **6** : deposit, down payment
señalado, -da *adj* : distinguished, notable
señalador *nm* : marker ⟨señalador de libros : bookmark⟩
señalar *vt* **1** INDICAR : to indicate, to show **2** : to mark **3** : to point out, to stress **4** : to fix, to set — **señalarse** *vr* : to distinguish oneself
señor, -ñora *n* **1** : gentleman *m*, man *m*, lady *f*, woman *f*, wife *f* **2** : Sir *m*, Madam *f* ⟨estimados señores : Dear Sirs⟩ **3** : Mr. *m*, Mrs. *f* **4** : lord *m*, lady *f* ⟨el Señor : the Lord⟩
señoría *nf* **1** : lordship **2 Su Señoría** : Your Honor
señorial *adj* : stately, regal

señorío *nm* **1** : manor, estate **2** : do-minion, power **3** : elegance, class
señorita *nf* **1** : young lady, young woman **2** : Miss
señuelo *nm* **1** : decoy **2** : bait
sépalo *nm* : sepal
sepa, etc. → **saber**
separación *nf, pl* **-ciones 1** : separation, division **2** : gap, space
separadamente *adv* : separately, apart
separado, -da *adj* **1** : separated **2** : sep-arate ⟨vidas separadas : separate lives⟩ **3 por ∼** : separately
separar *vt* **1** : to separate, to divide **2** : to split up, to pull apart — **separarse** *vr*
sepelio *nm* : interment, burial
sepia[1] *adj & nm* : sepia
sepia[2] *nf* : cuttlefish
septentrional *adj* : northern
séptico, -ca *adj* : septic
septiembre *nm* : September
séptimo[1], **-ma** *adj* : seventh
séptimo[2] *nm* : seventh
septuagésimo[1], **-ma** *adj* : seventieth
septuagésimo[2] *nm* : seventieth
sepulcral *adj* : sepulchral **2** : dismal, gloomy
sepulcro *nm* TUMBA : tomb, sepulchre
sepultar *vt* ENTERRAR : to bury
sepultura *nf* **1** : burial **2** TUMBA : grave, tomb
seque, etc. → **secar**
sequedad *nf* **1** : dryness **2** : brusque-ness, curtness
sequía *nf* : drought
séquito *nm* : retinue, entourage
ser[1] {77} *vi* **1** : to be ⟨él es mi hermano : he is my brother⟩ ⟨Camila es linda : Camila is pretty⟩ **2** : to exist, to live ⟨ser, o no ser : to be or not to be⟩ **3** : to take place, to occur ⟨el concierto es el domingo : the concert is on Sun-day⟩ **4** (*used with expressions of time, date, season*) ⟨son las diez : it's ten o'-clock⟩ ⟨hoy es el 9 : today's the 9th⟩ **5** : to cost, to come to ⟨¿cuánto es? : how much is it?⟩ **6** (*with the future tense*) : to be able to be ⟨¿será posible? : can it be possible?⟩ **7 ∼ de** : to come from ⟨somos de Managua : we're from Managua⟩ **8 ∼ de** : to belong to ⟨ese lápiz es de Juan : that's Juan's pencil⟩ **9 es que** : the thing is that ⟨es que no lo conozco : it's just that I don't know him⟩ **10 ¡sea!** : agreed!, all right! **11 sea...sea** : either...or — *v aux* (*used in passive constructions*) : to be ⟨la cuenta ha sido pagada : the bill has been paid⟩ ⟨él fue asesinado : he was murdered⟩
ser[2] *nm* : being ⟨ser humano : human being⟩
seráfico, -ca *adj* : angelic, seraphic
serbio[1], **-bia** *adj & n* : Serb, Serbian
serbio[2] *nm* : Serbian (language)
serbocroata[1] *adj* : Serbo-Croatian
serbocroata[2] *nm* : Serbo-Croatian (lan-guage)

serenar *vt* : to calm, to soothe — **sere-narse** *vr* CALMARSE : to calm down
serenata *nf* : serenade
serendipia *nf* : serendipity
serenidad *nf* : serenity, calmness
sereno[1], **-na** *adj* **1** SOSEGADO : serene, calm, composed **2** : fair, clear (of weather) **3** : calm, still (of the sea) — **serenamente** *adv*
sereno[2] *nm* : night watchman
seriado, -da *adj* : serial
serial *nm* : serial (on radio or television)
seriamente *adv* : seriously
serie *nf* **1** : series **2** SERIAL : serial **3 fabricación en serie** : mass production **4 fuera de serie** : extraordinary, amaz-ing
seriedad *nf* **1** : seriousness, earnestness **2** : gravity, importance
serio, -ria *adj* **1** : serious, earnest **2** : re-liable, responsible **3** : important **4 en ∼** : seriously, in earnest — **seriamente** *adv*
sermón *nm, pl* **sermones 1** : sermon **2** *fam* : harangue, lecture
sermonear *vt fam* : to harangue, to lec-ture
serpentear *vi* : to twist, to wind — **ser-penteante** *adj*
serpentina *nf* : paper streamer
serpiente *nf* : serpent, snake
serrado, -da *adj* DENTADO : serrated
serranía *nf* : mountainous area
serrano, -na *adj* : from the mountains
serrar {55} *vt* : to saw
serrín *nm, pl* **serrines** : sawdust
serruchar *vt* : to saw up
serrucho *nm* : saw, handsaw
servicentro *nm Peru* : gas station
servicial *adj* : obliging, helpful
servicio *nm* **1** : service **2** SAQUE : serve (in sports) **3** SERVICIOS *nmpl* : restroom
servidor, -dora *n* **1** : servant **2 su se-guro servidor** : yours truly (in corre-spondence)
servidumbre *nf* **1** : servitude **2** : help, servants *pl*
servil *adj* **1** : servile, subservient **2** : me-nial
servilismo *nm* : servility, subservience
servilleta *nf* : napkin
servir {54} *vt* **1** : to serve, to be of use to **2** : to serve, to wait **3** SURTIR : to fill (an order) — *vi* **1** : to work ⟨mi ra-dio no sirve : my radio isn't working⟩ **2** : to be of use, to be helpful ⟨esa com-putadora no sirve para nada : that com-puter's perfectly useless⟩ — **servirse** *vr* **1** : to help oneself to **2** : to be kind enough ⟨sírvase enviarnos un catálogo : please send us a catalog⟩
sésamo *nm* AJONJOLÍ : sesame, sesame seeds *pl*
sesenta *adj & nm* : sixty
sesentavo[1], **-va** *adj* : sixtieth
sesentavo[2] *n* : sixtieth (fraction)
sesgado, -da *adj* **1** : inclined, tilted **2** : slanted, biased

sesgar {52} *vt* **1** : to cut on the bias **2** : to tilt **3** : to bias, to slant

sesgo *nm* : bias

segue, etc. → **sesgar**

sesión *nf*, *pl* **sesiones 1** : session **2** : showing, performance

sesionar *vi* REUNIRSE : to meet, to be in session

seso *nm* **1** : brains, intelligence **2 sesos** *nmpl* : brains (as food)

sesudo, -da *adj* **1** : prudent, sensible **2** : brainy

set *nm*, *pl* **sets** : set (in tennis)

seta *nf* : mushroom

setecientos[1], **-tas** *adj* : seven hundred

setecientos[2] *nms & pl* : seven hundred

setenta *adj & nm* : seventy

setentavo[1], **-va** *adj* : seventieth

setentavo[2] *nm* : seventieth

setiembre → **septiembre**

seto *nm* **1** : fence, enclosure **2 seto vivo** : hedge

seudónimo *nm* : pseudonym

severidad *nf* **1** : harshness, severity **2** : strictness

severo, -ra *adj* **1** : harsh, severe **2** ESTRICTO : strict — **severamente** *adv*

sexagésimo[1], **-ma** *adj* : sixtieth, sixty-

sexagésimo[2], **-ma** *n* : sixtieth, sixty- (in a series)

sexismo *nm* : sexism — **sexista** *adj & nmf*

sexo *nm* : sex

sextante *nm* : sextant

sexteto *nm* : sextet

sexto, -ta *adj* : sixth — **sexto, -ta** *n*

sexual *adj* : sexual, sex (educación sexual : sex education) — **sexualmente** *adv*

sexualidad *nf* : sexuality

sexy *adj*, *pl* **sexy** *or* **sexys** : sexy

shock [ˈʃɔk, ˈtʃɔk] *nm* : shock (estado de shock : state of shock)

short *nm*, *pl* **shorts** : shorts *pl*

show *nm*, *pl* **shows** : show

si *conj* **1** : if (lo haré si me pagan : I'll do it if they pay me) (si lo supiera te lo diría : if I knew it I would tell you) **2** : whether, if (no importa si funciona o no : it doesn't matter whether it works (or not)) **3** (expressing desire, protest, or surprise) (si supiera la verdad : if only I knew the truth) (¡si no quiero! : but I don't want to!) **4 si bien** : although (si bien se ha progresado : although progress has been made) **5 si no** : otherwise, or else (si no, no voy : otherwise I won't go)

sí[1] *adv* **1** : yes (sí, gracias : yes, please) (creo que sí : I think so) **2 sí que** : indeed, absolutely (esta vez sí que ganaré : this time I'm sure to win) **3 porque sí** *fam* : because, just because (lo hizo porque sí : she did it just because)

sí[2] *nm* : yes (dar el sí : to say yes, to express consent)

sí[3] *pron* **1 de por sí** *or* **en sí** : by itself, in itself, per se **2 fuera de sí** : beside oneself **3 para sí (mismo)** : to himself, to herself, for himself, for herself **4 entre ~** : among themselves

siamés, -mesa *adj & n*, *mpl* **siameses** : Siamese

sibilante *adj & nf* : sibilant

siciliano, -na *adj & n* : Sicilian

sico- → **psico-**

sicomoro *or* **sicómoro** *nm* : sycamore

SIDA *or* **sida** *nm* (síndrome de inmunodeficiencia adquirida) : AIDS

siderurgia *nf* : iron and steel industry

siderúrgico, -ca *adj* : steel, iron (la industria siderúrgica : the steel industry)

sidra *nf* : hard cider

siega[1], **siegue**, etc. → **segar**

siega[2] *nf* **1** : harvesting **2** : harvest time **3** : harvested crop

siembra[1], etc. → **sembrar**

siembra[2] *nf* **1** : sowing **2** : sowing season **3** SEMBRADO : cultivated field

siempre *adv* **1** : always (siempre tienes hambre : you're always hungry) **2** : still (¿siempre te vas? : are you still going?) **3** *Mex* : after all (siempre no fui : I didn't go after all) **4 siempre que** : whenever, every time (siempre que pasa : every time he walks by) **5 para ~** : forever, for good **6 siempre y cuando** : provided that

sien *nf* : temple (on the forehead)

sienta, etc. → **sentar**

siente, etc. → **sentir**

sierpe *nf* : serpent, snake

sierra[1], etc. → **serrar**

sierra[2] *nf* **1** : saw (sierra de vaivén : jigsaw) **2** CORDILLERA : mountain range **3** : mountains *pl* (viven en la sierra : they live in the mountains)

siervo, -va *n* **1** : slave **2** : serf

siesta *nf* : nap, siesta

siete *adj & nm* : seven

sífilis *nf* : syphilis

sifón *nm*, *pl* **sifones** : siphon

siga, sigue etc. → **seguir**

sigilo *nm* : secrecy, stealth

sigiloso, -sa *adj* FURTIVO : furtive, stealthy — **sigilosamente** *adv*

sigla *nf* : acronym, abbreviation

siglo *nm* **1** : century **2** : age (el Siglo de Oro : the Golden Age) (hace siglos que no te veo : I haven't seen you in ages) **3** : world, secular life

signar *vt* : to sign (a treaty or agreement)

signatario, -ria *n* : signatory

significación *nf*, *pl* **-ciones 1** : significance, importance **2** : signification, meaning

significado *nm* **1** : sense, meaning **2** : significance

significante *adj* : significant

significar {72} *vt* **1** : to mean, to signify **2** : to express, to make known — **significarse** *vr* **1** : to draw attention, to become known **2** : to take a stance

significativo, -va *adj* **1** : significant, important **2** : meaningful — **significativamente** *adv*

signo *nm* **1** : sign ⟨signo de igual : equal sign⟩ ⟨un signo de alegría : a sign of happiness⟩ **2** : (punctuation) mark ⟨signo de interrogación : question mark⟩ ⟨signo de admiración : exclamation point⟩ ⟨signo de intercalación : caret⟩
siguiente *adj* : next, following
sílaba *nf* : syllable
silábico, -ca *adj* : syllabic
silbar *v* : to whistle
silbato *nm* PITO : whistle
silbido *nm* : whistle, whistling
silenciador *nm* **1** : muffler (of an automobile) **2** : silencer
silenciar *vt* **1** : to silence **2** : to muffle
silencio *nm* **1** : silence, quiet ⟨¡silencio! : be quiet!⟩ **2** : rest (in music)
silencioso, -sa *adj* : silent, quiet — **silenciosamente** *adv*
sílice *nf* : silica
silicio *nm* : silicon
silla *nf* **1** : chair **2 silla de ruedas** : wheelchair
sillón *nm, pl* **sillones** : armchair, easy chair
silo *nm* : silo
silueta *nf* **1** : silhouette **2** : figure, shape
silvestre *adj* : wild ⟨flor silvestre : wildflower⟩
silvicultor, -tora *n* : forester
silvicultura *nf* : forestry
sima *nf* ABISMO : chasm, abyss
simbólico, -ca *adj* : symbolic — **simbólicamente** *adj*
simbolismo *nm* : symbolism
simbolizar {21} *vt* : to symbolize
símbolo *nm* : symbol
simetría *nf* : symmetry
simétrico, -ca *adj* : symmetrical, symmetric
simiente *nf* : seed
símil *nm* **1** : simile **2** : analogy, comparison
similar *adj* SEMEJANTE : similar, alike
similitud *nf* : similarity, resemblance
simio *nm* : ape
simpatía *nf* **1** : liking, affection ⟨tomarle simpatía a : to take a liking to⟩ **2** : warmth, friendliness **3** : support, solidarity
simpático, -ca *adj* : nice, friendly, likeable
simpatizante *nf* : sympathizer, supporter
simpatizar {21} *vi* **1** : to get along, to hit it off ⟨simpaticé mucho con él : I really liked him⟩ **2 ~ con** : to sympathize with, to support
simple¹ *adj* **1** SENCILLO : plain, simple, easy **2** : pure, mere ⟨por simple vanidad : out of pure vanity⟩ **3** : simpleminded, foolish
simple² *n* : fool, simpleton
simplemente *adv* : simply, merely, just
simpleza *nf* **1** : foolishness, simpleness **2** NECEDAD : nonsense
simplicidad *nf* : simplicity

simplificar {72} *vt* : to simplify — **simplificación** *nf*
simplista *adj* : simplistic
simposio *or* **simposium** *nm* : symposium
simulación *nf, pl* **-ciones** : simulation
simulacro *nm* : imitation, sham ⟨simulacro de juicio : mock trial⟩
simular *vt* **1** : to simulate **2** : to feign, to pretend
simultáneo, -nea *adj* : simultaneous — **simultáneamente** *adv*
sin *prep* **1** : without ⟨sin querer : unintentionally⟩ ⟨sin refinar : unrefined⟩ **2**
sin que : without ⟨lo hicimos sin que él se diera cuenta : we did it without him noticing⟩
sinagoga *nf* : synagogue
sinceridad *nf* : sincerity
sincero, -ra *adj* : sincere, honest, true — **sinceramente** *adv*
síncopa *nf* : syncopation
sincopar *vt* : to syncopate
sincronizar {21} *vt* : to synchronize — **sincronización** *nf*
sindical *adj* GREMIAL : union, labor ⟨representante sindical : union representative⟩
sindicalización *nf, pl* **-ciones** : unionizing, unionization
sindicalizar {21} *vt* : to unionize — **sindicalizarse** *vr* **1** : to form a union **2** : to join a union
sindicar → **sindicalizar**
sindicato *nm* GREMIO : union, guild
síndrome *nm* : syndrome
sinecura *nf* : sinecure
sinfín *nm* : endless number ⟨un sinfín de problemas : no end of problems⟩
sinfonía *nf* : symphony
sinfónica *nf* : symphony orchestra
sinfónico, -ca *adj* : symphonic, symphony
singular¹ *adj* **1** : singular, unique **2** PARTICULAR : peculiar, odd **3** : singular (in grammar) — **singularmente** *adv*
singular² *nm* : singular
singularidad *nf* : uniqueness, singularity
singularizar {21} *vt* : to make unique or distinct — **singularizarse** *vr* : to stand out, to distinguish oneself
siniestrado, -da *adj* : damaged, wrecked ⟨zona siniestrada : disaster zone⟩
siniestro¹, -tra *adj* **1** IZQUIERDO : left, left-hand **2** MALVADO : sinister, evil
siniestro² *nm* : accident, disaster
sinnúmero → **sinfín**
sino *conj* **1** : but, rather ⟨no será hoy, sino mañana : it won't be today, but tomorrow⟩ **2** EXCEPTO : but, except ⟨no hace sino despertar suspicacias : it does nothing but arouse suspicion⟩
sinónimo¹, -ma *adj* : synonymous
sinónimo² *nm* : synonym
sinopsis *nfs & pl* RESUMEN : synopsis, summary
sinrazón *nf, pl* **-zones** : wrong, injustice

sinsabores *nmpl* : woes, troubles

sinsonte *nm* : mockingbird

sintáctico, -ca *adj* : syntactic, syntactical

sintaxis *nfs & pl* : syntax

síntesis *nfs & pl* 1 : synthesis, fusion 2 SINOPSIS : synopsis, summary

sintético, -ca *adj* : synthetic — **sintéticamente** *adv*

sintetizar {21} *vt* 1 : to synthesize 2 RESUMIR : to summarize

sintió, etc. → sentir

síntoma *nm* : symptom

sintomático, -ca *adj* : symptomatic

sintonía *nf* 1 : tuning in (of a radio) 2 **en sintonía con** : in tune with, attuned to

sintonizador *nm* : tuner, knob for tuning (of a radio, etc.)

sintonizar {21} *vt* : to tune (in) to — *vi* 1 : to tune in 2 **~ con** : to be in tune with, to empathize with

sinuosidad *nf* : sinuosity

sinuoso, -sa *adj* 1 : winding, sinuous 2 : devious

sinvergüenza¹ *adj* 1 DESCARADO : shameless, brazen, impudent 2 TRAVIESO : naughty

sinvergüenza² *nmf* 1 : rogue, scoundrel 2 : brat, rascal

sionista *adj & nmf* : Zionist — **sionismo** *nm*

siqui- → psiqui-

siquiera *adv* 1 : at least ⟨dame siquiera un poquito : at least give me a little bit⟩ 2 (*in negative constructions*) : not even ⟨ni siquiera nos saludaron : they didn't even say hello to us⟩

sirena *nf* 1 : mermaid 2 : siren ⟨sirena de niebla : foghorn⟩

sirio, -ria *adj & n* : Syrian

sirope *nm* : syrup

sirve, etc. → servir

sirviente, -ta *n* : servant, maid *f*

sisal *nm* : sisal

sisear *vi* : to hiss

siseo *nm* : hiss

sísmico, -ca *adj* : seismic

sismo *nm* 1 TERREMOTO : earthquake 2 TEMBLOR : tremor

sismógrafo *nm* : seismograph

sistema *nm* : system

sistemático, -ca *adj* : systematic — **sistemáticamente** *adv*

sistematizar {21} *vt* : to systematize

sistémico, -ca *adj* : systemic

sitiar *vt* ASEDIAR : to besiege

sitio *nm* 1 LUGAR : place, site ⟨vámonos a otro sitio : let's go somewhere else⟩ 2 ESPACIO : room, space ⟨hacer sitio a : to make room for⟩ 3 : siege ⟨estado de sitio : state of siege⟩ 4 *Mex* : taxi stand

situación *nf, pl* **-ciones** : situation

situado, -da *adj* : situated, placed

situar {3} *vt* UBICAR : to situate, to place, to locate — **situarse** *vr* 1 : to be placed, to be located 2 : to make a place for oneself, to do well

sketch *nm* : sketch, skit

slip *nm* : briefs *pl*, underpants *pl*

smog *nm* : smog

smoking *nm* ESMOQUIN : tuxedo

snob → esnob

so *prep* : under ⟨so pena de : under penalty of⟩

sobaco *nm* : armpit

sobado, -da *adj* 1 : worn, shabby 2 : well-worn, hackneyed

sobar *vt* 1 : to finger, to handle 2 : to knead 3 : to rub, to massage 4 *fam* : to beat, to pummel

soberanía *nf* : sovereignty

soberano, -na *adj & n* : sovereign

soberbia *nf* 1 ORGULLO : pride, arrogance 2 MAGNIFICENCIA : magnificence

soberbio, -bia *adj* 1 : proud, arrogant 2 : grand, magnificent

sobornable *adv* : venal, bribable

sobornar *vt* : to bribe

soborno *nm* 1 : bribery 2 : bribe

sobra *nf* 1 : excess, surplus 2 **de ~** : extra, to spare 3 **sobras** *nfpl* : leftovers, scraps

sobrado, -da *adj* : abundant, excessive, more than enough

sobrante¹ *adj* : remaining, superfluous

sobrante² *nm* : remainder, surplus

sobrar *vi* : to be in excess, to be superfluous ⟨más vale que sobre a que falte : it's better to have too much than not enough⟩

sobre¹ *nm* 1 : envelope 2 : packet ⟨un sobre de sazón : a packet of seasoning⟩

sobre² *prep* 1 : on, on top of ⟨sobre la mesa : on the table⟩ 2 : over, above 3 : about ⟨¿tiene libros sobre Bolivia? : do you have books on Bolivia?⟩ 4 **sobre todo** : especially, above all

sobrealimentar *vt* : to overfeed

sobrecalentar {55} *vt* : to overheat — **sobrecalentarse** *vr*

sobrecama *nmf* : bedspread

sobrecargar {52} *vt* : to overload, to overburden, to weigh down

sobrecoger {15} *vt* 1 : to surprise, to startle 2 : to scare — **sobrecogerse** *vr*

sobrecubierta *nf* : dust jacket

sobredosis *nfs & pl* : overdose

sobreentender {56} *vt* : to infer, to understand

sobreestimar *vt* : to overestimate, to overrate

sobreexcitado, -da *adj* : overexcited

sobreexponer {60} *vt* : to overexpose

sobregirar *vt* : to overdraw

sobregiro *nm* : overdraft

sobrehumano, -na *adj* : superhuman

sobrellevar *vt* : to endure, to bear

sobremanera *adv* : exceedingly

sobremesa *nf* : after-dinner conversation

sobrenatural *adj* : supernatural

sobrenombre *nm* APODO : nickname

sobrentender → sobreentender

sobrepasar *vt* : to exceed, to surpass — **sobrepasarse** *vr* PASARSE : to go too far

sobrepelliz *nf*, *pl* **-pellices** : surplice

sobrepeso *nm* **1** : excess weight **2** : overweight, obesity

sobrepoblación, sobrepoblado → **superpoblación, superpoblado**

sobreponer {60} *vt* **1** SUPERPONER : to superimpose **2** ANTEPONER : to put first, to give priority to — **sobreponerse** *vr* **1** : to pull oneself together **2** ∼ **a** : to overcome

sobreprecio *nm* : surcharge

sobreproducción *nf*, *pl* **-ciones** : overproduction

sobreproducir {61} *vt* : to overproduce

sobreprotector, -tora *adj* : overprotective

sobreproteger {15} *vt* : to overprotect

sobresaliente¹ *adj* **1** : protruding, projecting **2** : outstanding, noteworthy **3** : significant, salient

sobresaliente² *nmf* : understudy

sobresalir {73} *vi* **1** : to protrude, to jut out, to project **2** : to stand out, to excel

sobresaltar *vt* : to startle, to frighten — **sobresaltarse** *vr*

sobresalto *nm* : start, fright

sobresueldo *nm* : bonus, additional pay

sobretasa *nf* : surcharge ⟨sobretasa a la gasolina : gas tax⟩

sobretodo *nm* : overcoat

sobrevalorar *or* **sobrevaluar** {3} *vt* : to overvalue, to overrate

sobrevender *vt* : to oversell

sobrevenir {87} *vi* ACAECER : to take place, to come about ⟨podrían sobrevenir complicaciones : complications could occur⟩

sobrevivencia → **supervivencia**

sobreviviente → **superviviente**

sobrevivir *vi* : to survive — *vt* : to outlive, to outlast

sobrevolar {19} *vt* : to fly over, to overfly

sobriedad *nf* : sobriety, moderation

sobrino, -na *n* : nephew *m*, niece *f*

sobrio, -bria *adj* : sober — **sobriamente** *adv*

socarrón, -rrona *adj*, *mpl* **-rrones** **1** : sly, cunning **2** : sarcastic

socavar *vt* : to undermine

sociabilidad *nf* : sociability

sociable *adj* : sociable

social *adj* : social — **socialmente** *adv*

socialista *adj & nmf* : socialist — **socialismo** *nm*

sociedad *nf* **1** : society **2** : company, enterprise **3 sociedad anónima** : incorporated company

socio, -cia *n* **1** : member **2** : partner

socioeconómico, -ca *adj* : socioeconomic

sociología *nf* : sociology

sociológico, -ca *adj* : sociological — **sociológicamente** *adv*

sociólogo, -ga *n* : sociologist

socorrer *vt* : to assist, to come to the aid of

socorrido, -da *adj* ÚTIL : handy, practical

socorrista *nmf* **1** : rescue worker **2** : lifeguard

socorro *nm* AUXILIO **1** : aid, help ⟨equipo de socorro : rescue team⟩ **2** ¡**socorro**! : help!

soda *nf* : soda, soda water

sodio *nm* : sodium

soez *adj*, *pl* **soeces** GROSERO : rude, vulgar — **soezmente** *adv*

sofá *nm* : couch, sofa

sofistería *nf* : sophistry — **sofista** *nmf*

sofisticación *nf*, *pl* **-ciones** : sophistication

sofisticado, -da *adj* : sophisticated

sofocante *adj* : suffocating, stifling

sofocar {72} *vt* **1** AHOGAR : to suffocate, to smother **2** EXTINGUIR : to extinguish, to put out (a fire) **3** APLASTAR : to crush, to put down ⟨sofocar una rebelión : crush a rebellion⟩ — **sofocarse** *vr* **1** : to suffocate **2** *fam* : to get upset, to get mad

sofreír {66} *vt* : to sauté

sofrito¹, -ta *adj* : sautéed

sofrito² *nm* : seasoning sauce

softbol *nm* : softball

software *nm* : software

soga *nf* : rope

soja → **soya**

sojuzgar *vt* : to subdue, to conquer, to subjugate

sol *nm* **1** : sun **2** : Peruvian unit of currency

solamente *adv* SÓLO : only, just

solapa *nf* **1** : lapel (of a jacket) **2** : flap (of an envelope)

solapado, -da *adj* : secret, underhanded

solapar *vt* : to cover up, to keep secret — **solaparse** *vr* : to overlap

solar¹ {19} *vt* : to floor, to tile

solar² *adj* : solar, sun

solar³ *nm* **1** TERRENO : lot, piece of land, site **2** *Cuba, Peru* : tenement building

solariego, -ga *adj* : ancestral

solaz *nm*, *pl* **solaces** **1** CONSUELO : solace, comfort **2** DESCANSO : relaxation, recreation

solazarse {21} *vr* : to relax, to enjoy oneself

soldado *nm* **1** : soldier **2 soldado raso** : private, enlisted man

soldador¹, -dora *n* : welder

soldador² *nm* : soldering iron

soldadura *nf* **1** : welding **2** : soldering, solder

soldar {19} *vt* **1** : to weld **2** : to solder

soleado, -da *adj* : sunny

soledad *nf* : loneliness, solitude

solemne *adj* : solemn — **solemnemente** *adv*

solemnidad *nf* : solemnity

soler {78} *vi* : to be in the habit of, to tend to ⟨solía tomar café por la tarde : she usually drank coffee in the afternoon⟩ ⟨eso suele ocurrir : that frequently happens⟩

solera *nf* 1 : prop, support 2 : tradition

solicitante *nmf* : applicant

solicitar *vt* 1 : to request, to solicit 2 : to apply for ⟨solicitar empleo : to apply for employment⟩

solícito, -ta *adj* : solicitous, attentive, obliging

solicitud *nf* 1 : solicitude, concern 2 : request 3 : application

solidaridad *nf* : solidarity

solidario, -ria *adj* : supportive, united in support ⟨se declararon solidarios con la nueva ley : they declared their support for the new law⟩ ⟨espíritu solidario : spirit of solidarity⟩

solidarizar {21} *vi* : to be in solidarity ⟨solidarizamos con la huelga : we support the strike⟩

solidez *nf* 1 : solidity, firmness 2 : soundness (of an argument, etc.)

solidificar {72} *vt* : to solidify, to make solid — **solidificarse** *vr* — **solidificación** *nf*

sólido¹, -da *adj* 1 : solid, firm 2 : sturdy, well-made 3 : sound, well-founded — **sólidamente** *adv*

sólido² *nm* : solid

soliloquio *nm* : soliloquy

solista *nmf* : soloist

solitaria *nf* TENIA : tapeworm

solitario¹, -ria *adj* 1 : lonely 2 : lone, solitary 3 DESIERTO : deserted, lonely ⟨una calle solitaria : a deserted street⟩

solitario², -ria *n* : recluse, loner

solitario³ *nm* : solitaire

sollozar {21} *vi* : to sob

sollozo *nm* : sob

solo¹, -la *adj* 1 : alone, by oneself 2 : lonely 3 ÚNICO : only, sole, unique ⟨hay un solo problema : there's only one problem⟩ 4 **a solas** : alone

solo² *nm* : solo

sólo *adv* SOLAMENTE : just, only ⟨sólo quieren comer : they just want to eat⟩

solomillo *nm* : sirloin, loin

solsticio *nm* : solstice

soltar {19} *vt* 1 : to let go of, to drop 2 : to release, to set free 3 AFLOJAR : to loosen, to slacken

soltería *nf* : bachelorhood, spinsterhood

soltero¹, -ra *adj* : single, unmarried

soltero², -ra *n* : bachelor *m*, single man *m*, single woman *f* 2 **apellido de soltera** : maiden name

soltura *nf* 1 : looseness, slackness 2 : fluency (of language) 3 : agility, ease of movement

soluble *adj* : soluble — **solubilidad** *nf*

solución *nf, pl* **-ciones** 1 : solution (in a liquid) 2 : answer, solution

solucionar *vt* RESOLVER : to solve, to resolve — **solucionarse** *vr*

solvencia *nf* 1 : solvency 2 : settling, payment (of debts) 3 : reliability ⟨solvencia moral : trustworthiness⟩

solvente¹ *adj* 1 : solvent 2 : reliable, trustworthy

solvente² *nm* : solvent

somalí *adj & nmf* : Somalian

sombra *nf* 1 : shadow 2 : shade 3 **sombras** *nfpl* : darkness, shadows *pl* 4 **sin sombra de duda** : without a shadow of a doubt

sombreado, -da *adj* 1 : shady 2 : shaded, darkened

sombrear *vt* : to shade

sombrerero, -ra *n* : milliner, hatter

sombrero *nm* 1 : hat 2 **sin ∼** : bareheaded 3 **sombrero hongo** : derby

sombrilla *nf* : parasol, umbrella

sombrío, -bría *adj* LÓBREGO : dark, somber, gloomy — **sombríamente** *adv*

someramente *adv* : cursorily, summarily

somero, -ra *adj* : superficial, cursory, shallow

someter *vt* 1 : to subjugate, to conquer 2 : to subordinate 3 : to subject (to treatment or testing) 4 : to submit, to present — **someterse** *vr* 1 : to submit, to yield 2 : to undergo

sometimiento *nm* 1 : submission, subjection 2 : presentation

somnífero¹, -ra *adj* : soporific

somnífero² *nm* : sleeping pill

somnolencia *nf* : drowsiness, sleepiness

somnoliento, -ta *adj* : drowsy, sleepy

somorgujo *or* **somormujo** *nm* : loon, grebe

somos → **ser¹**

son¹ → **ser**

son² *nm* 1 : sound ⟨al son de la trompeta : at the sound of the trumpet⟩ 2 : news, rumor 3 **en son de** : as, in the manner of, by way of ⟨en son de broma : as a joke⟩ ⟨en son de paz : in peace⟩

sonado, -da *adj* : celebrated, famous, much-discussed

sonaja *nf* : rattle

sonajero *nm* : rattle (toy)

sonámbulo, -la *n* : sleepwalker

sonar¹ {19} *vi* 1 : to sound ⟨suena bien : it sounds good⟩ 2 : to ring (bells) 3 : to look or sound familiar ⟨me suena ese nombre : that name rings a bell⟩ 4 **∼ a** : to sound like — *vt* 1 : to ring 2 : to blow (a trumpet, a nose) — **sonarse** *vr* : to blow one's nose

sonar² *nm* : sonar

sonata *nf* : sonata

sonda *nf* 1 : sounding line 2 : probe 3 CATÉTER : catheter

sondar *vt* 1 : to sound, to probe (in medicine, drilling, etc.) 2 : to probe, to explore (outer space)

sondear *vt* 1 : to sound 2 : to probe 3 : to sound out, to test (opinions, markets)

sondeo *nm* **1** : sounding, probing **2** : drilling **3** ENCUESTA : survey, poll
soneto *nm* : sonnet
sónico, -ca *adj* : sonic
sonido *nm* : sound
sonoridad *nf* : sonority, resonance
sonoro, -ra *adj* **1** : resonant, sonorous, voiced (in linguistics) **2** : resounding, loud **3 banda sonora** : soundtrack
sonreír {66} *vi* : to smile
sonriente *adj* : smiling
sonrisa *nf* : smile
sonrojar *vt* : to cause to blush — **sonrojarse** *vr* : to blush
sonrojo *nm* RUBOR : blush
sonrosado, -da *adj* : rosy, pink
sonsacar {72} *vt* : to wheedle, to extract
sonsonete *nm* **1** : tapping **2** : drone **3** : mocking tone
soñador[1], **-dora** *adj* : dreamy
soñador[2], **-dora** *n* : dreamer
soñar {19} *v* **1** : to dream **2 ~ con** : to dream about **3 soñar despierto** : to daydream
soñoliento, -ta *adj* : sleepy, drowsy
sopa *nf* **1** : soup **2 estar hecho una sopa** : to be soaked to the bone
sopera *nf* : soup tureen
sopesar *vt* : to weigh, to evaluate
soplar *vi* : to blow — *vt* : to blow on, to blow out, to blow off
soplete *nm* : blowtorch
soplido *nm* : puff
soplo *nm* : puff, gust
soplón, -plona *n, mpl* **soplones** *fam* : tattletale, sneak
sopor *nm* SOMNOLENCIA : drowsiness, sleepiness
soporífero, -ra *adj* : soporific
soportable *adj* : bearable, tolerable
soportar *vt* **1** SOSTENER : to support, to hold up **2** RESISTIR : to withstand, to resist **3** AGUANTAR : to bear, to tolerate
soporte *nm* : base, stand, support
soprano *nmf* : soprano
sor *nf* : Sister (religious title)
sorber *vt* **1** : to sip, to suck in **2** : to absorb, to soak up
sorbete *nm* : sherbet
sorbo *nm* **1** : sip, gulp, swallow **2 beber a sorbos** : to sip
sordera *nf* : deafness
sordidez *nf, pl* **-deces** : sordidness, squalor
sórdido, -da *adj* : sordid, dirty, squalid
sordina *nf* : mute (for a musical instrument)
sordo, -da *adj* **1** : deaf **2** : muted, muffled
sordomudo, -da *n* : deaf-mute
sorgo *nm* : sorghum
soriasis *nfs & pl* : psoriasis
sorna *nf* : sarcasm, mocking tone
sorprendente *adj* : surprising — **sorprendentemente** *adv*
sorprender *vt* : to surprise — **sorprenderse** *vr*

sorpresa *nf* : surprise
sorpresivo, -va *adj* **1** : surprising, surprise **2** IMPREVISTO : sudden, unexpected
sortear *vt* **1** RIFAR : to raffle, to draw lots for **2** : to dodge, to avoid
sorteo *nm* : drawing, raffle
sortija *nf* **1** ANILLO : ring **2** : curl, ringlet
sortilegio *nm* **1** HECHIZO : spell, charm **2** HECHICERÍA : sorcery
SOS *nm* : SOS
sosegado, -da *adj* SERENO : calm, tranquil, serene
sosegar {49} *vt* : to calm, to pacify — **sosegarse** *vr*
sosiego *nm* : tranquillity, serenity, calm
soslayar *vt* ESQUIVAR : to dodge, to evade
soslayo *nm* **de ~** : obliquely, sideways ⟨mirar de soslayo : to look askance⟩
soso, -sa *adj* **1** INSÍPIDO : bland, flavorless **2** ABURRIDO : dull, boring
sospecha *nf* : suspicion
sospechar *vt* : to suspect — *vi* : to be suspicious
sospechosamente *adv* : suspiciously
sospechoso[1], **-sa** *adj* : suspicious, suspect
sospechoso[2], **-sa** *n* : suspect
sostén *nm, pl* **sostenes 1** APOYO : support **2** : sustenance **3** : brassiere, bra
sostener {80} *vt* **1** : to support, to hold up **2** : to hold ⟨sostenme la puerta : hold the door for me⟩ ⟨sostener una conversación : to hold a conversation⟩ **3** : to sustain, to maintain — **sostenerse** *vr* **1** : to stand, to hold oneself up **2** : to continue, to remain
sostenible *adj* : sustainable, tenable
sostenido[1], **-da** *adj* **1** : sustained, prolonged **2** : sharp (in music)
sostenido[2] *nm* : sharp (in music)
sostuvo, etc. → **sostener**
sotana *nf* : cassock
sótano *nm* : basement
sotavento *nm* : lee ⟨a sotavento : leeward⟩
soterrar {55} *vt* **1** : to bury **2** : to conceal, to hide away
soto *nm* : grove, copse
souvenir *nm, pl* **-nirs** RECUERDO : souvenir, memento
soviético, -ca *adj* : Soviet
soy → **ser**
soya *nf* : soy, soybean
spaghetti → **espagueti**
sport [ɛ'spor] *adj* : sport, casual
sprint [ɛ'sprin, -'sprint] *nm* : sprint — **sprinter** *nmf*
squash [ɛ'skwaʃ, -'skwatʃ] *nm* : squash (sport)
Sr. *nm* : Mr.
Sra. *nf* : Mrs., Ms.
Srta. or Srita. *nf* : Miss, Ms.
standard → **estándar**
stress → **estrés**
su *adj* **1** : his, her, its, their, one's ⟨su libro : her book⟩ ⟨sus consecuencias

: its consequences⟩ **2** (*formal*) : your ⟨tómese su medicina, señor : take your medicine, sir⟩

suave *adj* **1** BLANDO : soft **2** LISO : smooth **3** : gentle, mild **4** *Mex fam* : great, fantastic

suavemente *adv* : smoothly, gently, softly

suavidad *nf* : softness, smoothness, mellowness

suavizante *nm* : softener, fabric softener

suavizar {21} *vt* **1** : to soften, to smooth out **2** : to tone down — **suavizarse** *vr*

subacuático, -ca *adj* : underwater

subalterno¹, -na *adj* **1** SUBORDINADO : subordinate **2** SECUNDARIO : secondary

subalterno², -na *n* SUBORDINADO : subordinate

subarrendar {55} *vt* : to sublet

subasta *nf* : auction

subastador, -dora *n* : auctioneer

subastar *vt* : to auction, to auction off

subcampeón, -peona *n*, *mpl* **-peones** : runner-up

subcomité *nm* : subcommittee

subconsciente *adj & nm* : subconscious — **subconscientemente** *adv*

subcontratar *vt* : to subcontract

subcontratista *nmf* : subcontractor

subcultura *nf* : subculture

subdesarrollado, -da *adj* : underdeveloped

subdirector, -tora *n* : assistant manager

súbdito, -ta *n* : subject (of a monarch)

subdividir *vt* : to subdivide

subdivisión *nf*, *pl* **-siones** : subdivision

subestimar *vt* : to underestimate, to undervalue

subexponer {60} *vt* : to underexpose

subexposición *nf*, *pl* **-ciones** : underexposure

subgrupo *nm* : subgroup

subibaja *nm* : seesaw

subida *nf* **1** : ascent, climb **2** : rise, increase **3** : slope, hill ⟨ir de subida : to go uphill⟩

subido, -da *adj* **1** : intense, strong ⟨amarillo subido : bright yellow⟩ **2** **subido de tono** : risqué

subir *vt* **1** : to bring up, to take up **2** : to climb, to go up **3** : to raise — *vi* **1** : to go up, to come up **2** : to rise, to increase **3** : to be promoted **4** ~ **a** : to get on, to mount ⟨subir a un tren : to get on a train⟩ — **subirse** *vr* **1** : to climb (up) **2** : to pull up (clothing) **3** **subirse a la cabeza** : to go to one's head

súbito, -ta *adj* **1** REPENTINO : sudden **2 de** ~ : all of a sudden, suddenly — **súbitamente** *adv*

subjetivo, -va *adj* : subjective — **subjetivamente** *adv* — **subjetividad** *nf*

subjuntivo¹, -va *adj* : subjunctive

subjuntivo² *nm* : subjunctive

sublevación *nf*, *pl* **-ciones** ALZAMIENTO : uprising, rebellion

sublevar *vt* : to incite to rebellion — **sublevarse** *vr* : to rebel, to rise up

sublimar *vt* : to sublimate — **sublimación** *nf*

sublime *adj* : sublime

submarinismo *nm* : scuba diving

submarinista *nmf* : scuba diver

submarino¹, -na *adj* : submarine, undersea

submarino² *nm* : submarine

suboficial *nmf* : noncommissioned officer, petty officer

subordinado, -da *adj & n* : subordinate

subordinar *vt* : to subordinate — **subordinarse** *vr* — **subordinación** *nf*

subproducto *nm* : by-product

subrayar *vt* **1** : to underline, to underscore **2** ENFATIZAR : to highlight, to emphasize

subrepticio, -cia *adj* : surreptitious — **subrepticiamente** *adv*

subsahariano, -na *adj* : sub-Saharan

subsanar *vt* **1** RECTIFICAR : to rectify, to correct **2** : to overlook, to excuse **3** : to make up for

subscribir → suscribir

subsecretario, -ria *n* : undersecretary

subsecuente *adj* : subsequent — **subsecuentemente** *adv*

subsidiar *vt* : to subsidize

subsidiaria *nf* : subsidiary

subsidio *nm* : subsidy

subsiguiente *adj* : subsequent

subsistencia *nf* **1** : subsistence **2** : sustenance

subsistir *vi* **1** : to subsist, to live **2** : to endure, to survive

substancia → sustancia

subteniente *nmf* : second lieutenant

subterfugio *nm* : subterfuge

subterráneo¹, -nea *adj* : underground, subterranean

subterráneo² *nm* **1** : underground passage, tunnel **2** *Arg, Uru* : subway

subtítulo *nm* : subtitle, subheading

subtotal *nm* : subtotal

suburbano, -na *adj* : suburban

suburbio *nm* **1** : suburb **2** : slum (outside a city)

subvención *nf*, *pl* **-ciones** : subsidy, grant

subvencionar *vt* : to subsidize

subversivo, -va *adj & n* : subversive — **subversión** *nf*

subvertir {76} *vt* : to subvert

subyacente *adj* : underlying

subyugar {52} *vt* : to subjugate — **subyugación** *nf*

succión *nf*, *pl* **succiones** : suction

succionar *vt* : to suck up, to draw in

sucedáneo *nm* : substitute ⟨sucedáneo de azucar : sugar substitute⟩

suceder *vi* **1** OCURRIR : to happen, to occur ⟨¿qué sucede? : what's going on?⟩ ⟨suceda lo que suceda : come what may⟩ **2** ~ **a** : to follow, to succeed ⟨suceder al trono : to succeed to the throne⟩ ⟨a la primavera sucede el verano : summer follows spring⟩

sucesión *nf, pl* **-siones 1** : succession
2 : sequence, series **3** : issue, heirs *pl*
sucesivamente *adv* : successively, consecutively ⟨y así sucesivamente : and
so on⟩
sucesivo, -va *adj* : successive ⟨en los
días sucesivos : in the days that fol-
lowed⟩
suceso *nm* **1** : event, happening, occurrence **2** : incident, crime
sucesor, -sora *n* : successor
suciedad *nf* **1** : dirtiness, filthiness **2**
MUGRE : dirt, filth
sucinto, -ta *adj* CONCISO : succinct, concise — **sucintamente** *adv*
sucio, -cia *adj* : dirty, filthy
sucre *nm* : Ecuadoran unit of currency
suculento, -ta *adj* : succulent
sucumbir *vi* : to succumb
sucursal *nf* : branch (of a business)
sudadera *nf* : sweatshirt
sudado, -da *adj* → **sudoroso**
sudafricano, -na *adj & n* : South African
sudamericano, -na *adj & n* : South
American
sudanés, -nesa *adj & n, mpl* **-neses**
: Sudanese
sudar *vi* TRANSPIRAR : to sweat, to perspire
sudario *nm* : shroud
sudeste → **sureste**
sudoeste → **suroeste**
sudor *nm* TRANSPIRACIÓN : sweat, perspiration
sudoroso, -sa *adj* : sweaty
sueco¹, -ca *adj* : Swedish
sueco², -ca *n* : Swede
sueco³ *nm* : Swedish (language)
suegro, -gra *n* **1** : father-in-law *m*,
mother-in-law *f* **2 suegros** *nmpl* : in-
laws
suela *nf* : sole (of a shoe)
suelda, etc. → **soldar**
sueldo *nm* : salary, wage
suele, etc. → **soler**
suelo *nm* **1** : ground ⟨caerse al suelo
: to fall down, to hit the ground⟩ **2**
: floor, flooring **3** TIERRA : soil, land
suelta, etc. → **soltar**
suelto¹, -ta *adj* : loose, free, unattached
suelto² *nm* : loose change
suena, etc. → **sonar**
sueña, etc. → **soñar**
sueño *nm* **1** : dream **2** : sleep ⟨perder
el sueño : to lose sleep⟩ **3** : sleepiness
⟨tener sueño : to be sleepy⟩
suero *nm* **1** : serum **2** : whey
suerte *nf* **1** FORTUNA : luck, fortune
⟨tener suerte : to be lucky⟩ ⟨por suerte
: luckily⟩ **2** DESTINO : fate, destiny, lot
3 CLASE, GÉNERO : sort, kind ⟨toda
suerte de cosas : all kinds of things⟩
suertudo, -da *adj fam* : lucky
suéter *nm* : sweater
suficiencia *nf* **1** : adequacy, sufficiency **2** : competence, fitness **3** : smug-
ness, self-satisfaction
suficiente *adj* BASTANTE : enough,
sufficient ⟨tener suficiente : to have

enough⟩ **2** : suitable, fit **3** : smug, complacent
suficientemente *adv* : sufficiently,
enough
sufijo *nm* : suffix
suflé *nm* : soufflé
sufragar {52} *vt* **1** AYUDAR : to help out,
to support **2** : to defray (costs) — *vi*
: to vote
sufragio *nm* : suffrage, vote
sufrido, -da *adj* **1** : long-suffering, patient **2** : sturdy, serviceable (of clothing)
sufrimiento *nm* : suffering
sufrir *vt* **1** : to suffer ⟨sufrir una pérdida : to suffer a loss⟩ **2** : to tolerate, to
put up with ⟨ella no lo puede sufrir : she
can't stand him⟩ — *vi* : to suffer
sugerencia *nf* : suggestion
sugerir {76} *vt* **1** PROPONER, RE-
COMENDAR : to suggest, to recommend, to propose **2** : to suggest, to
bring to mind
sugestión *nf, pl* **-tiones** : suggestion,
prompting ⟨poder de sugestión : pow-
er of suggestion⟩
sugestionable *adj* : suggestible, impressionable
sugestionar *vt* : to influence, to sway —
sugestionarse *vr* ~ **con** : to talk oneself into, to become convinced of
sugestivo, -va *adj* **1** : suggestive **2** : interesting, stimulating
suicida¹ *adj* : suicidal
suicida² *nmf* : suicide victim, suicide
suicidarse *vr* : to commit suicide
suicidio *nm* : suicide
suite *nf* : suite
suizo, -za *adj & n* : Swiss
sujeción *nf, pl* **-ciones 1** : holding, fastening **2** : subjection
sujetador *nm* **1** : fastener **2** : holder
⟨sujetador de tazas : cup holder⟩
sujetalibros *nms & pl* : bookend
sujetapapeles *nms & pl* CLIP : paper clip
sujetar *vt* **1** : to hold on to, to steady, to
hold down **2** FIJAR : to fasten, to attach **3** DOMINAR : to subdue, to conquer — **sujetarse** *vr* **1** : to hold on, to
hang on **2** ~ **a** : to abide by
sujeto¹, -ta *adj* **1** : secure, fastened **2**
~ **a** : subject to
sujeto² *nm* **1** INDIVIDUO : individual,
character **2** : subject (in grammar)
sulfúrico, -ca *adj* : sulfuric
sulfuro *nm* : sulfur
sultán *nm, pl* **sultanes** : sultan
suma *nf* **1** CANTIDAD : sum, quantity **2**
: addition
sumamente *adv* : extremely, exceedingly
sumar *vt* **1** : to add, to add up **2** : to add
up to, to total — *vi* : to add up —
sumarse *vr* ~ **a** : to join
sumario¹, -ria *adj* SUCINTO : succinct,
summary — **sumariamente** *adv*
sumario² *nm* : summary

sumergir {35} *vt* : to submerge, to immerse, to plunge — **sumergirse** *vr*

sumersión *nf, pl* **-siones** : submersion, immersion

sumidero *nm* : drain, sewer

suministrar *vt* : to supply, to provide

suministro *nm* : supply, provision

sumir *vt* SUMERGIR : to plunge, to immerse, to sink — **sumirse** *vr*

sumisión *nf, pl* **-siones** 1 : submission 2 : submissiveness

sumiso, -sa *adj* : submissive, acquiescent, docile

sumo, -ma *adj* 1 : extreme, great, high ⟨la suma autoridad : the highest authority⟩ 2 **a lo sumo** : at the most — **sumamente** *adv*

suntuoso, -sa *adj* : sumptuous, lavish — **suntuosamente** *adv*

supeditar *vt* SUBORDINAR : to subordinate — **supeditación** *nf*

super¹ *or* **súper** *adj fam* : super, great

super² *nm* SUPERMERCADO : market, supermarket

superable *adj* : surmountable

superabundancia *nf* : overabundance, superabundance — **superabundante** *adj*

superar *vt* 1 : to surpass, to exceed 2 : to overcome, to surmount — **superarse** *vr* : to improve oneself

superávit *nm, pl* **-vit** *or* **-vits** : surplus

superchería *nf* : trickery, fraud

supercomputadora *nf* : supercomputer

superestructura *nf* : superstructure

superficial *adj* : superficial — **superficialmente** *adv*

superficialidad *nf* : superficiality

superficie *nf* 1 : surface 2 : area ⟨la superficie de un triángulo : the area of a triangle⟩

superfluidad *nf* : superfluity

superfluo, -flua *adj* : superfluous

superintendente *nmf* : supervisor, superintendent

superior¹ *adj* 1 : superior 2 : upper ⟨nivel superior : upper level⟩ 3 : higher ⟨educación superior : higher education⟩ 4 **~ a** : above, higher than, in excess of

superior² *nm* : superior

superioridad *nf* : superiority

superlativo¹, -va *adj* : superlative

superlativo² *nm* : superlative

supermercado *nm* : supermarket

superpoblación *nf, pl* **-ciones** : overpopulation

superpoblado, -da *adj* : overpopulated

superponer {60} *vt* : to superimpose

superpotencia *nf* : superpower

superproducción → **sobreproducción**

supersónico, -ca *adj* : supersonic

superstición *nf, pl* **-ciones** : superstition

supersticioso, -sa *adj* : superstitious

supervisar *vt* : to supervise, to oversee

supervisión *nf, pl* **-siones** : supervision

supervisor, -sora *n* : supervisor, overseer

supervivencia *nf* : survival

superviviente *nmf* : survivor

supino, -na *adj* : supine

suplantar *vt* : to supplant, to replace

suplemental → **suplementario**

suplementario, -ria *adj* : supplementary, additional, extra

suplemento *nm* : supplement

suplencia *nf* : substitution, replacement

suplente *adj & nmf* : substitute ⟨equipo suplente : replacement team⟩

supletorio, -ria *adj* : extra, additional ⟨teléfono supletorio : extension phone⟩ ⟨cama supletoria : spare bed⟩

súplica *nf* : plea, entreaty

suplicar {72} *vt* IMPLORAR, ROGAR : to entreat, to implore, to supplicate

suplicio *nm* TORMENTO : ordeal, torture

suplir *vt* 1 COMPENSAR : to make up for, to compensate for 2 REEMPLAZAR : to replace, to substitute

supo, etc. → **saber**

suponer {60} *vt* 1 PRESUMIR : to suppose, to assume ⟨supongo que sí : I guess so, I suppose so⟩ ⟨se supone que van a llegar mañana : they're supposed to arrive tomorrow⟩ 2 : to imply, to suggest 3 : to involve, to entail ⟨el éxito supone mucho trabajo : success involves a lot of work⟩

suposición *nf, pl* **-ciones** PRESUNCIÓN : supposition, assumption

supositorio *nm* : suppository

supremacía *nf* : supremacy

supremo, -ma *adj* : supreme

supresión *nf, pl* **-siones** 1 : suppression, elimination 2 : deletion

suprimir *vt* 1 : to suppress, to eliminate 2 : to delete

supuestamente *adv* : supposedly, allegedly

supuesto, -ta *adj* 1 : supposed, alleged 2 **por ~** : of course, absolutely

supurar *vi* : to ooze, to discharge

supuso, etc. → **suponer**

sur¹ *adj* : southern, southerly, south

sur² *nm* 1 : south, South 2 : south wind

surafricano, -na → **sudafricano**

suramericano, -na → **sudamericano**

surcar {72} *vt* 1 : to plow (through) 2 : to groove, to score, to furrow

surco *nm* : groove, furrow, rut

sureño, -ña *adj* : southern, Southern

sureño², -ña *n* : Southerner

sureste¹ *adj* 1 : southeast, southeastern 2 : southeasterly

sureste² *nm* : southeast, Southeast

surf *nm* : surfing

surfear *vi* : to surf

surfing → **surf**

surfista *nmf* : surfer

surgimiento *nm* : rise, emergence

surgir {35} *vi* : to rise, to arise, to emerge

suroeste¹ *adj* 1 : southwest, southwestern 2 : southwesterly

suroeste² *nm* : southwest, Southwest

surtido¹, -da *adj* 1 : assorted, varied 2 : stocked, provisioned

surtido² *nm* : assortment, selection
surtidor *nm* **1** : jet, spout **2** *Arg, Chile, Spain* : gas pump
surtir *vt* **1** : to supply, to provide ⟨surtir un pedido : to fill an order⟩ **2 surtir efecto** : to have an effect — *vi* : to spout, to spurt up — **surtirse** *vr* : to stock up
susceptible *adj* : susceptible, sensitive — **susceptibilidad** *nf*
suscitar *vt* : to provoke, to give rise to
suscribir {33} *vt* **1** : to sign (a formal document) **2** : to endorse, to sanction — **suscribirse** *vr* ~ **a** : to subscribe to
suscripción *nf, pl* **-ciones 1** : subscription **2** : endorsement, sanction **3** : signing
suscriptor, -tora *n* : subscriber
susodicho, -cha *adj* : aforementioned, aforesaid
suspender *vt* **1** COLGAR : to suspend, to hang **2** : to suspend, to discontinue **3** : to suspend, to dismiss
suspensión *nf, pl* **-siones** : suspension
suspenso *nm* : suspense
suspicacia *nf* : suspicion, mistrust
suspicaz *adj, pl* **-caces** DESCONFIADO : suspicious, wary
suspirar *vi* : to sigh
suspiro *nm* : sigh
surque, etc. → **surcar**
suscrito *pp* → **suscribir**
sustancia *nf* **1** : substance **2 sin** ~ : shallow, lacking substance
sustancial *adj* **1** : substantial **2** ESENCIAL, FUNDAMENTAL : essential, fundamental — **sustancialmente** *adv*
sustancioso, -sa *adj* **1** NUTRITIVO : hearty, nutritious **2** : substantial, solid
sustantivo *nm* : noun

sustentación *nf, pl* **-ciones** SOSTÉN : support
sustentar *vt* **1** : to support, to hold up **2** : to sustain, to nourish **3** : to maintain, to hold (an opinion) — **sustentarse** *vr* : to support oneself
sustento *nm* **1** : means of support, livelihood **2** : sustenance, food
sustitución *nf, pl* **-ciones** : replacement, substitution
sustituir {41} *vt* **1** : to replace, to substitute for **2** : to stand in for
sustituto, -ta *n* : substitute, stand-in
susto *nm* : fright, scare
sustracción *nf, pl* **-ciones 1** RESTA : subtraction **2** : theft
sustraer {81} *vt* **1** : to remove, to take away **2** RESTAR : to subtract **3** : to steal — **sustraerse** *vr* ~ **a** : to avoid, to evade
susurrar *vi* **1** : to whisper **2** : to murmur **3** : to rustle (leaves, etc.) — *vt* : to whisper
susurro *nm* **1** : whisper **2** : murmur **3** : rustle, rustling
sutil *adj* **1** : delicate, thin, fine **2** : subtle
sutileza *nf* **1** : delicacy **2** : subtlety
sutura *nf* : suture
suturar *vt* : to suture
suyo¹, -ya *adj* : his, her, its, theirs ⟨los libros suyos : his books⟩ ⟨un amigo suyo : a friend of hers⟩ ⟨esta casa es suya : this house is theirs⟩ **2** (*formal*) : yours ⟨¿este abrigo es suyo, señor? : is this your coat, sir?⟩
suyo², -ya *pron* **1** : his, hers, theirs ⟨mi guitarra y la suya : my guitar and hers⟩ ⟨ellos trajeron las suyas : they brought theirs, they brought their own⟩ **2** (*formal*) : yours ⟨usted olvidó la suya : you forgot yours⟩
switch *nm* : switch

T

t *nf* : twenty-first letter of the Spanish alphabet
taba *nf* : anklebone
tabacalero¹, -ra *adj* : tobacco ⟨industria tabacalera : tobacco industry⟩
tabacalero², -ra *n* : tobacco grower
tabaco *nm* : tobacco
tábano *nm* : horsefly
taberna *nf* : tavern, bar
tabernáculo *nm* : tabernacle
tabicar {72} *vt* : to wall up
tabique *nm* : thin wall, partition
tabla *nf* **1** : table, list ⟨tabla de multiplicar : multiplication table⟩ **2** : board, plank, slab ⟨tabla de planchar : ironing board⟩ **3** : plot, strip (of land) **4 tablas** *nfpl* : stage, boards *pl*
tablado *nm* **1** : floor **2** : platform, scaffold **3** : stage
tablero *nm* **1** : bulletin board **2** : board (in games) ⟨tablero de ajedrez : chess-

board⟩ ⟨tablero de damas : checkerboard⟩ **3** PIZARRA : blackboard **4** : switchboard **5. tablero de instrumentos** : dashboard, instrument panel
tableta *nf* **1** COMPRIMIDO, PÍLDORA : tablet, pill **2** : bar (of chocolate)
tabletear *vi* : to rattle, to clack
tableteo *nm* : clack, rattling
tablilla *nf* **1** : small board or tablet **2** : bulletin board **3** : splint
tabloide *nm* : tabloid
tablón *nm, pl* **tablones 1** : plank, beam **2 tablón de anuncios** : bulletin board
tabú¹ *adj* : taboo
tabú² *nm, pl* **tabúes** *or* **tabús** : taboo
tabulador *nm* : tabulator
tabular¹ *vt* : to tabulate
tabular² *adj* : tabular
taburete *nm* : footstool, stool
tacañería *nf* : miserliness, stinginess

tacaño¹, -ña *adj* MEZQUINO : stingy, miserly
tacaño², -ña *n* : miser, tightwad
tacha *nf* 1 : flaw, blemish, defect 2 **poner tacha a** : to find fault with 3 **sin ~** : flawless
tachadura *nf* : erasure, correction
tachar *vt* 1 : to cross out, to delete 2 **~ de** : to accuse of, to label as ⟨lo tacharon de mentiroso : they accused him of being a liar⟩
tachón *nm, pl* **tachones** : stud, hobnail
tachonar *vt* : to stud
tachuela *nf* : tack, hobnail, stud
tácito, -ta *adj* : tacit, implicit — **tácitamente** *adv*
taciturno, -na *adj* 1 : taciturn 2 : sullen, gloomy
tacle *nm* : tackle
taclear *vt* : to tackle (in football)
taco *nm* 1 : wad, stopper, plug 2 : pad (of paper) 3 : cleat 4 : heel (of a shoe) 5 : cue (in billiards) 6 : light snack, bite 7 : taco
tacón *nm, pl* **tacones** : heel (of a shoe) ⟨de tacón alto : high-heeled⟩
táctica *nf* : tactic, tactics *pl*
táctico¹, -ca *adj* : tactical
táctico², -ca *n* : tactician
táctil *adj* : tactile
tacto *nm* 1 : touch, touching, feel 2 DELICADEZA : tact
tafetán *nm, pl* **-tanes** : taffeta
tahúr *nm, pl* **tahúres** : gambler
tailandés¹, -desa *adj & n, pl* **-deses** : Thai
tailandés² *nm* : Thai (language)
taimado, -da *adj* 1 : crafty, sly 2 *Chile* : sullen, sulky
tajada *nf* 1 : slice 2 **sacar tajada** *fam* : to get one's share
tajante *adj* 1 : cutting, sharp 2 : decisive, categorical
tajantemente *adv* : emphatically, categorically
tajar *vt* : to cut, to slice
tajo *nm* 1 : cut, slash, gash 2 ESCARPA : steep cliff
tal¹ *adv* 1 : so, in such a way 2 **tal como** : just as ⟨tal como lo hice : just the way I did it⟩ 3 **con tal que** : provided that, as long as 4 **¿qué tal?** : how are you?, how's it going?
tal² *adj* 1 : such, such a 2 **tal vez** : maybe, perhaps
tal³ *pron* 1 : such a one, someone 2 : such a thing, something 3 **tal para cual** : two of a kind
tala *nf* : felling (of trees)
taladrar *vt* : to drill
taladro *nm* : drill, auger ⟨taladro eléctrico : power drill⟩
talante *nm* 1 HUMOR : mood, disposition 2 VOLUNTAD : will, willingness
talar *vt* 1 : to cut down, to fell 2 DEVASTAR : to devastate, to destroy
talco *nm* 1 : talc 2 : talcum powder
talego *nm* : sack

talento *nm* : talent, ability
talentoso, -sa *adj* : talented, gifted
talismán *nm, pl* **-manes** AMULETO : talisman, charm
talla *nf* 1 ESTATURA : height 2 : size (in clothing) 3 : stature, status 4 : sculpture, carving
tallar *vt* 1 : to sculpt, to carve 2 : to measure (someone's height) 3 : to deal (cards)
tallarín *nf, pl* **-rines** : noodle
talle *nm* 1 : size 2 : waist, waistline 3 : figure, shape
taller *nm* 1 : shop, workshop 2 : studio (of an artist)
tallo *nm* : stalk, stem ⟨tallo de maíz : cornstalk⟩
talón *nm, pl* **talones** 1 : heel (of the foot) 2 : stub (of a check) 3 **talón de Aquiles** : Achilles' heel
talud *nm* : slope, incline
tamal *nm* : tamale
tamaño¹, -ña *adj* : such a big ⟨¿crees tamaña mentira? : do you believe such a lie?⟩
tamaño² *nm* 1 : size 2 **de tamaño natural** : life-size
tamarindo *nm* : tamarind
tambalearse *vr* 1 : to teeter 2 : to totter, to stagger, to sway — **tambaleante** *adj*
tambaleo *nm* : staggering, lurching, swaying
también *adv* : too, as well, also
tambor *nm* : drum
tamborilear *vi* : to drum, to tap
tamborileo *nm* : tapping, drumming
tamiz *nm* : sieve
tamizar {21} *vt* : to sift
tampoco *adv* : neither, not either ⟨ni yo tampoco : me neither⟩
tampón *nm, pl* **tampones** 1 : ink pad 2 : tampon
tam–tam *nm* : tom-tom
tan *adv* 1 : so, so very ⟨no es tan difícil : it is not that difficult⟩ 2 : as ⟨tan pronto como : as soon as⟩ 3 **tan siquiera** : at least, at the least 4 **tan sólo** : only, merely
tanda *nf* 1 : turn, shift 2 : batch, lot, series
tándem *nm* 1 : tandem (bicycle) 2 : duo, pair
tangente *adj & nf* : tangent — **tangencial** *adj*
tangible *adj* : tangible
tango *nm* : tango
tanino *nm* : tannin
tanque *nm* 1 : tank, reservoir 2 : tanker, tank (vehicle)
tanteador *nm* MARCADOR : scoreboard
tantear *vt* 1 : to feel, to grope 2 : to size up, to weigh — *vi* 1 : to keep score 2 : to feel one's way
tanteo *nm* 1 : estimate, rough calculation 2 : testing, sizing up 3 : scoring
tanto¹ *adv* 1 : so much ⟨tanto mejor : so much the better⟩ 2 : so long ⟨¿por qué

te tardaste tanto? : why did you take so long?⟩

tanto², -ta *adj* **1** : so much, so many, such ⟨no hagas tantas preguntas : don't ask so many questions⟩ ⟨tiene tanto encanto : he has such charm, he's so charming⟩ **2** : as much, as many ⟨come tantos dulces como yo : she eats as many sweets as I do⟩ **3** : odd, however many ⟨cuarenta y tantos años : forty-odd years⟩

tanto³ *nm* **1** : certain amount **2** : goal, point (in sports) **3 al tanto** : abreast, in the picture **4 un tanto** : somewhat, rather ⟨un tanto cansado : rather tired⟩

tanto⁴, -ta *pron* **1** : so much, so many ⟨tiene tanto que hacer : she has so much to do⟩ ⟨¡no me des tantos! : don't give me so many!⟩ **2 entre ~** : meanwhile **3 por lo tanto** : therefore

tañer {79} *vt* **1** : to ring (a bell) **2** : to play (a musical instrument)

tañido *nm* **1** CAMPANADA : ring, peal, toll **2** : sound (of an instrument)

tapa *nf* **1** : cover, top, lid **2** *Spain* : bar snack

tapacubos *nms & pl* : hubcap

tapadera *nf* **1** : cover, lid **2** : front, cover (for an organization or person)

tapar *vt* **1** CUBRIR : to cover, to cover up **2** OBSTRUIR : to block, to obstruct — **taparse** *vr*

tapete *nm* **1** : small rug, mat **2** : table cover **3 poner sobre el tapete** : to bring up for discussion

tapia *nf* : (adobe) wall, garden wall

tapiar *vt* **1** : to wall in **2** : to enclose, to block off

tapicería *nf* **1** : upholstery **2** TAPIZ : tapestry

tapicero, -ra *n* : upholsterer

tapioca *nf* : tapioca

tapir *nm* : tapir

tapiz *nm, pl* **tapices** : tapestry

tapizar {21} *vt* **1** : to upholster **2** : to cover, to carpet

tapón *nm, pl* **tapones 1** : cork **2** : bottle cap **3** : plug, stopper

tapujo *nm* **1** : deceit, pretension **2 sin tapujos** : openly, frankly

taquigrafía *nf* : stenography, shorthand

taquigráfico, -ca *adj* : stenographic

taquígrafo, -fa *n* : stenographer

taquilla *nf* **1** : box office, ticket office **2** : earnings *pl*, take

taquillero, -ra *adj* : box-office, popular ⟨un éxito taquillero : a box-office success⟩

tarántula *nf* : tarantula

tararear *vt* : to hum

tardanza *nf* : lateness, delay

tardar *vi* **1** : to delay, to take a long time **2** : to be late **3 a más tardar** : at the latest — *vt* DEMORAR : to take (time) ⟨tarda una hora : it takes an hour⟩

tarde¹ *adv* **1** : late **2 tarde o temprano** : sooner or later

tarde² *nf* **1** : afternoon, evening **2 ¡buenas tardes!** : good afternoon!, good evening! **3 en la tarde** *or* **por la tarde** : in the afternoon, in the evening

tardío, -día *adj* : late, tardy

tardo, -da *adj* : slow

tarea *nf* **1** : task, job **2** : homework

tarifa *nf* **1** : rate ⟨tarifas postales : postal rates⟩ **2** : fare (for transportation) **3** : price list **4** ARANCEL : duty

tarima *nf* PLATAFORMA : dais, platform, stage

tarjeta *nf* : card ⟨tarjeta de crédito : credit card⟩ ⟨tarjeta postal : postcard⟩

tarro *nm* **1** : jar, pot **2** *Arg, Chile* : can, tin

tarta *nf* **1** : tart **2** : cake

tartaleta *nf* : tart

tartamudear *vi* : to stammer, to stutter

tartamudeo *nm* : stutter, stammer

tartán *nm, pl* **tartanes** : tartan, plaid

tártaro *nm* : tartar

tasa *nf* **1** : rate ⟨tasa de desempleo : unemployment rate⟩ **2** : tax, fee **3** : appraisal, valuation

tasación *nf, pl* **-ciones** : appraisal, assessment

tasador, -dora *n* : assessor, appraiser

tasar *vt* **1** VALORAR : to appraise, to value **2** : to set the price of **3** : to ration, to limit

tasca *nf* : cheap bar, dive

tatuaje *nm* : tattoo, tattooing

tatuar {3} *vt* : to tattoo

taurino, -na *adj* : bull, bullfighting

Tauro *nmf* : Taurus

tauromaquia *nf* : (art of) bullfighting

taxi *nm, pl* **taxis** : taxi, taxicab

taxidermia *nf* : taxidermy

taxidermista *nmf* : taxidermist

taxímetro *nm* : taximeter

taxista *nmf* : taxi driver

taza *nf* **1** : cup **2** : cupful **3** : (toilet) bowl **4** : basin (of a fountain)

tazón *nm, pl* **tazones 1** : bowl **2** : large cup, mug

te *pron* **1** : you ⟨te quiero : I love you⟩ **2** : for you, to you, from you ⟨me gustaría dártelo : I would like to give it to you⟩ **3** : yourself, for yourself, to yourself, from yourself ⟨¡cálmate! : calm yourself!⟩ ⟨¿te guardaste uno? : did you keep one for yourself?⟩ **4** : thee

té *nm* **1** : tea **2** : tea party

tea *nf* : torch

teatral *adj* : theatrical — **teatralmente** *adv*

teatro *nm* **1** : theater **2 hacer teatro** : to put on an act, to exaggerate

teca *nf* : teak

techado *nm* **1** : roof **2 bajo techado** : under cover, indoors

techar *vt* : to roof, to shingle

techo *nm* **1** TEJADO : roof **2** : ceiling **3** : upper limit, ceiling

techumbre *nf* : roofing

tecla *nf* **1** : key (of a musical instrument or a machine) **2 dar en la tecla** : to hit the nail on the head

teclado *nm* : keyboard
teclear *vt* : to type in, to enter
técnica *nf* **1** : technique, skill **2** : technology
técnico[1], **-ca** *adj* : technical — **técnicamente** *adv*
técnico[2], **-ca** *n* : technician, expert, engineer
tecnología *nf* : technology
tecnológico, -ca *adj* : technological — **tecnológicamente** *adv*
tecolote *nm Mex* : owl
tedio *nm* : tedium, boredom
tedioso, -sa *adj* : tedious, boring — **tediosamente** *adv*
teja *nf* : tile
tejado *nm* TECHO : roof
tejedor, -dora *n* : weaver
tejer *vt* **1** : to knit, to crochet **2** : to weave **3** FABRICAR : to concoct, to make up, to fabricate
tejido *nm* **1** TELA : fabric, cloth **2** : weave, texture **3** : tissue ⟨tejido muscular : muscle tissue⟩
tejo *nm* **1** : yew **2** : hopscotch (children's game)
tejón *nm, pl* **tejones** : badger
tela *nf* **1** : fabric, cloth, material **2 tela de araña** : spiderweb **3 poner en tela de juicio** : to call into question, to doubt
telar *nm* : loom
telaraña *nf* : spiderweb, cobweb
tele *nf fam* : TV, television
telecomunicación *nf, pl* **-ciones** : telecommunication
teleconferencia *nf* : teleconference
teledifusión *nf, pl* **-siones** : television broadcasting
teledirigido, -da *adj* : remote-controlled
telefonear *v* : to telephone, to call
telefónico, -ca *adj* : phone, telephone ⟨llamada telefónica : phone call⟩
telefonista *nmf* : telephone operator
teléfono *nm* **1** : telephone **2 llamar por teléfono** : to telephone, to make a phone call
telegrafiar {85} *v* : to telegraph
telegráfico, -ca *adj* : telegraphic
telégrafo *nm* : telegraph
telegrama *nm* : telegram
telenovela *nf* : soap opera
telepatía *nf* : telepathy
telepático, -ca *adj* : telepathic — **telepáticamente** *adv*
telescópico, -ca *adj* : telescopic
telescopio *nm* : telescope
telespectador, -dora *n* : television viewer
telesquí *nm, pl* **-squís** : ski lift
televidente *nmf* : television viewer
televisar *vt* : to televise
televisión *nf, pl* **-siones** : television, TV
televisivo, -va *adj* : television ⟨serie televisiva : television series⟩
televisor *nm* : television set
telón *nm, pl* **telones** **1** : curtain (in theater) **2 telón de fondo** : backdrop, background

tema *nm* **1** ASUNTO : theme, topic, subject **2** MOTIVO : motif, central theme
temario *nm* **1** : set of topics (for study) **2** : agenda
temática *nf* : subject matter
temático, -ca *adj* : thematic
temblar {55} *vi* **1** : to tremble, to shake, to shiver ⟨le temblaban las rodillas : his knees were shaking⟩ **2** : to shudder, to be afraid ⟨tiemblo con sólo pensarlo : I shudder to think of it⟩
temblor *nm* **1** : shaking, trembling **2** : tremor, earthquake
tembloroso, -sa *adj* : tremulous, trembling, shaking ⟨con la voz temblorosa : with a shaky voice⟩
temer *vt* : to fear, to dread — *vi* : to be afraid
temerario, -ria *adj* : reckless, rash — **temerariamente** *adv*
temeridad *nf* **1** : temerity, recklessness, rashness **2** : rash act
temeroso, -sa *adj* MIEDOSO : fearful, frightened
temible *adj* : fearsome, dreadful
temor *nm* MIEDO : fear, dread
témpano *nm* : ice floe
temperamento *nm* : temperament — **temperamental** *adj*
temperancia *nf* : temperance
temperar *vt* MODERAR : to temper, to moderate — *vi* : to have a change of air
temperatura *nf* : temperature
tempestad *nf* **1** : storm, tempest **2 tempestad de arena** : sandstorm
tempestuoso, -sa *adj* : tempestuous, stormy
templado, -da *adj* **1** : temperate, mild **2** : moderate, restrained **3** : warm, lukewarm **4** VALIENTE : courageous, bold
templanza *nf* **1** : temperance, moderation **2** : mildness (of weather)
templar *vt* **1** : to temper (steel) **2** : to restrain, to moderate **3** : to tune (a musical instrument) **4** : to warm up, to cool down — **templarse** *vr* **1** : to be moderate **2** : to warm up, to cool down
temple *nm* **1** : temper (of steel, etc.) **2** HUMOR : mood ⟨de buen temple : in a good mood⟩ **3** : tuning **4** VALOR : courage
templo *nm* **1** : temple **2** : church, chapel
tempo *nm* : tempo (in music)
temporada *nf* **1** : season, time ⟨temporada de béisbol : baseball season⟩ **2** : period, spell ⟨por temporadas : on and off⟩
temporal[1] *adj* **1** : temporal **2** : temporary
temporal[2] *nm* **1** : storm **2 capear el temporal** : to weather the storm
temporalmente *adv* : temporarily
temporario, -ria *adj* : temporary — **temporariamente** *adv*
temporero[1], **-ra** *adj* : temporary, seasonal

temporero², -ra *n* : temporary or seasonal worker
temporizador *nm* : timer
tempranero, -ra *adj* **1** : early **2** : early-rising
temprano¹ *adv* : early ⟨lo más temprano posible : as soon as possible⟩
temprano², -na *adj* : early ⟨la parte temprana del siglo : the early part of the century⟩
ten → **tener**
tenacidad *nf* : tenacity, perseverance
tenaz *adj, pl* **tenaces 1** : tenacious, persistent **2** : strong, tough
tenaza *nf, or* **tenazas** *nfpl* **1** : pliers, pincers **2** : tongs **3** : claw (of a crustacean)
tenazmente *adv* : tenaciously
tendedero *nm* : clothesline
tendencia *nf* **1** PROPENSIÓN : tendency, inclination **2** : trend
tendencioso, -sa *adj* : tendentious, biased
tendente → **tendiente**
tender {56} *vt* **1** EXTENDER : to spread out, to lay out **2** : to hang out (clothes) **3** : to lay (cables, etc.) **4** : to set (a trap) — *vi* ~ **a** : to tend to, to have a tendency towards — **tenderse** *vr* : to stretch out, to lie down
tendero, -ra *n* : shopkeeper, storekeeper
tendido *nm* **1** : laying (of cables, etc.) **2** : seats *pl*, section (at a bullfight)
tendiente *adj* ~ **a** : aimed at, designed to
tendón *nm, pl* **tendones** : tendon
tendrá, etc. → **tener**
tenebrosidad *nf* : darkness, gloom
tenebroso, -sa *adj* **1** OSCURO : gloomy, dark **2** SINIESTRO : sinister
tenedor¹, -dora *n* **1** : holder **2 tenedor de libros, tenedora de libros** : bookkeeper
tenedor² *nm* : table fork
tenencia *nf* **1** : possession, holding **2** : tenancy **3** : tenure
tener {80} *vt* **1** : to have ⟨tiene ojos verdes : she has green eyes⟩ ⟨tengo mucho que hacer : I have a lot to do⟩ ⟨tiene veinte años : he's twenty years old⟩ ⟨tiene un metro de largo : it's one meter long⟩ **2** : to hold ⟨ten esto un momento : hold this for a moment⟩ **3** : to feel, to make ⟨tengo frío : I'm cold⟩ ⟨eso nos tiene contentos : that makes us happy⟩ **4** ~ **por** : to think, to consider ⟨me tienes por loco : you think I'm crazy⟩ — *v aux* **1 tener que** : to have to ⟨tengo que salir : I have to leave⟩ ⟨tiene que estar aquí : it has to be here, it must be here⟩ **2** (*with past participle*) ⟨tenía pensado escribirte : I've been thinking of writing to you⟩ — **tenerse** *vr* **1** : to stand up **2** ~ **por** : to consider oneself ⟨me tengo por afortunado : I consider myself lucky⟩
tenería *nf* CURTIDURÍA : tannery
tenga, etc. → **tener**
tenia *nf* SOLITARIA : tapeworm

teniente *nmf* **1** : lieutenant **2 teniente coronel** : lieutenant colonel
tenis *nms & pl* **1** : tennis **2 tenis** *nmpl* : sneakers *pl*
tenista *nmf* : tennis player
tenor *nm* **1** : tenor **2** : tone, sense
tensar *vt* **1** : to tense, to make taut **2** : to draw (a bow) — **tensarse** *vr* : to become tense
tensión *nf, pl* **tensiones 1** : tension, tautness **2** : stress, strain **3 tensión arterial** : blood pressure
tenso, -sa *adj* : tense
tentación *nf, pl* **-ciones** : temptation
tentáculo *nm* : tentacle, feeler
tentador¹, -dora *adj* : tempting
tentador², -dora *n* : tempter, temptress *f*
tentar {55} *vt* **1** TOCAR : to feel, to touch **2** PROBAR : to test, to try **3** ATRAER : to tempt, to entice
tentativa *nf* : attempt, try
tentempié *nm fam* : snack, bite
tenue *adj* **1** : tenuous **2** : faint, weak, dim **3** : light, fine **4** : thin, slender
teñir {67} *vt* **1** : to dye **2** : to stain
teodolito *nm* : theodolite, transit (for surveying)
teología *nf* : theology
teológico, -ca *adj* : theological
teólogo, -ga *n* : theologian
teorema *nm* : theorem
teoría *nf* : theory
teórico¹, -ca *adj* : theoretical — **teóricamente** *adv*
teórico², -ca *n* : theorist
teorizar {21} *vi* : to theorize
tepe *nm* : sod, turf
teponaztle *nm Mex* : traditional drum
tequila *nm* : tequila
terapeuta *nmf* : therapist
terapéutica *nf* : therapeutics
terapéutico, -ca *adj* : therapeutic
terapia *nf* **1** : therapy **2 terapia intensiva** : intensive care
tercer → **tercero**
tercermundista *adj* : third-world
tercero¹, -ra *adj* (**tercer** *before masculine singular nouns*) **1** : third **2 el Tercer Mundo** : the Third World
tercero², -ra *n* : third (in a series)
terceto *nm* **1** : tercet, triplet (in literature) **2** : trio (in music)
terciar *vt* **1** : to place diagonally **2** : to divide into three parts — *vi* **1** : to mediate **2** ~ **en** : to take part in
terciario, -ria *adj* : tertiary
tercio¹, -cia → **tercero**
tercio² *nm* : third ⟨dos tercios : two thirds⟩
terciopelo *nm* : velvet
terco, -ca *adj* OBSTINADO : obstinate, stubborn
tergiversación *nf, pl* **-ciones** : distortion
tergiversar *vt* : to distort, to twist
termal *adj* : thermal, hot
termas *nfpl* : hot springs
térmico, -ca *adj* : thermal, heat ⟨energía térmica : thermal energy⟩

terminación *nf, pl* **-ciones** : termination, conclusion

terminal[1] *adj* : terminal — **terminalmente** *adv*

terminal[2] *nm* (*in some regions f*) : (electric or electronic) terminal

terminal[3] *nf* (*in some regions m*) : terminal, station

terminante *adj* : final, definitive, categorical — **terminantemente** *adv*

terminar *vt* **1** CONCLUIR : to end, to conclude **2** ACABAR : to complete, to finish off — *vi* **1** : to finish **2** : to stop, to end — **terminarse** *vr* **1** : to run out **2** : to come to an end

término *nm* **1** CONCLUSIÓN : end, conclusion **2** : term, expression **3** : period, term of office **4 término medio** : happy medium **5 términos** *nmpl* : terms, specifications ⟨los términos del acuerdo : the terms of the agreement⟩

terminología *nf* : terminology

termita *nf* : termite

termo *nm* : thermos

termodinámica *nf* : thermodynamics

termómetro *nm* : thermometer

termostato *nm* : thermostat

ternera *nf* : veal

ternero, -ra *n* : calf

terno *nm* **1** : set of three **2** : three-piece suit

ternura *nf* : tenderness

terquedad *nf* OBSTINACIÓN : obstinacy, stubbornness

terracota *nf* : terra-cotta

terraplén *nm, pl* **-plenes** : terrace, embankment

terráqueo, -quea *adj* **1** : earth **2 globo terráqueo** : the earth, globe (of the earth)

terrateniente *nmf* : landowner

terraza *nf* **1** : terrace, veranda **2** : balcony (in a theater) **3** : terrace (in agriculture)

terremoto *nm* : earthquake

terrenal *adj* : worldly, earthly

terreno *nm* **1** : terrain **2** SUELO : earth, ground **3** : plot, tract of land **4 perder terreno** : to lose ground **5 preparar el terreno** : to pave the way

terrestre *adj* : terrestrial

terrible *adj* : terrible, horrible — **terriblemente** *adv*

terrier *nmf* : terrier

territorial *adj* : territorial

territorio *nm* : territory

terrón *nm, pl* **terrones 1** : clod (of earth) **2 terrón de azúcar** : lump of sugar

terror *nm* : terror

terrorífico, -ca *adj* : horrific, terrifying

terrorismo *nm* : terrorism

terrorista *adj & nmf* : terrorist

terroso, -sa *adj* : earthy ⟨colores terrosos : earthy colors⟩

terruño *nm* : native land, homeland

terso, -sa *adj* **1** : smooth **2** : glossy, shiny **3** : polished, flowing (of a style)

tersura *nf* **1** : smoothness **2** : shine

tertulia *nf* : gathering, group ⟨tertulia literaria : literary circle⟩

tesauro *nm* : thesaurus

tesis *nfs & pl* : thesis

tesón *nm* : persistence, tenacity

tesonero, -ra *adj* : persistent, tenacious

tesorería *nf* : treasurer's office

tesorero, -ra *n* : treasurer

tesoro *nm* **1** : treasure **2** : thesaurus

test *nm* : test

testaferro *nm* : figurehead

testamentario[1], **-ria** *adj* : testamentary

testamentario[2], **-ria** *n* ALBACEA : executor, executrix *f*

testamento *nm* : testament, will

testar *vi* : to draw up a will

testarudo, -da *adj* : stubborn, pigheaded

testículo *nm* : testicle

testificar {72} *v* : to testify

testigo *nmf* : witness

testimonial *adj* **1** : testimonial **2** : token

testimoniar *vi* : to testify

testimonio *nm* : testimony, statement

teta *nf* : teat

tétano *or* **tétanos** *nm* : tetanus, lockjaw

tetera *nf* **1** : teapot **2** : teakettle

tetilla *nf* **1** : teat **2** : nipple

tetina *nf* : nipple (on a bottle)

tétrico, -ca *adj* : somber, gloomy

textil *adj & nm* : textile

texto *nm* : text

textual *adj* : literal, exact — **textualmente** *adv*

textura *nf* : texture

tez *nf, pl* **teces** : complexion, coloring

ti *pron* **1** : you ⟨es para ti : it's for you⟩ **2 ti mismo, ti misma** : yourself **3** : thee

tía → **tío**

tiamina *nf* : thiamine

tianguis *nm Mex* : open-air market

tibetano[1], **-na** *adj & n* : Tibetan

tibetano[2] *nm* : Tibetan (language)

tibia *nf* : tibia

tibieza *nf* **1** : tepidness **2** : halfheartedness

tibio, -bia *adj* **1** : lukewarm, tepid **2** : cool, unenthusiastic

tiburón *nm, pl* **-rones 1** : shark **2** : raider (in finance)

tic *nm* **1** : click, tick **2 tic nervioso** : tic

tico, -ca *adj & n fam* : Costa Rican

tictac *nm* **1** : ticking, tick-tock **2 hacer tictac** : to tick

tiembla, etc. → **temblar**

tiempo *nm* **1** : time ⟨justo a tiempo : just in time⟩ ⟨perder tiempo : to waste time⟩ ⟨tiempo libre : spare time⟩ **2** : period, age ⟨en los tiempos que corren : nowadays⟩ **3** : season, moment ⟨antes de tiempo : prematurely⟩ **4** : weather ⟨hace buen tiempo : the weather is fine, it's nice outside⟩ **5** : tempo (in music) **6** : half (in sports) **7** : tense (in grammar)

tienda *nf* **1** : store, shop **2** *or* **tienda de campaña** : tent

tiende, etc. → **tender**

tiene, etc. → **tener**
tienta[1], etc. → **tentar**
tienta[2] *nf* **andar a tientas** : to feel one's way, to grope around
tiernamente *adv* : tenderly
tierno, -na *adj* **1** : affectionate, tender **2** : tender, young
tierra *nf* **1** : land **2** SUELO : ground, earth **3** : country, homeland, soil **4 tierra natal** : native land **5 tierras altas** : highlands **6 la Tierra** : the Earth
tieso, -sa *adj* **1** : stiff, rigid **2** : upright, erect
tiesto *nm* **1** : potsherd **2** MACETA : flowerpot
tiesura *nf* : stiffness, rigidity
tifoidea *nf* : typhoid
tifoideo, -dea *adj* : typhoid ⟨**fiebre tifoidea** : typhoid fever⟩
tifón *nm*, *pl* **tifones** : typhoon
tifus *nm* : typhus
tigre, -gresa *n* **1** : tiger, tigress *f* **2** : jaguar
tijera *nf* **1** *or* **tijeras** *nfpl* : scissors **2 de** ~ : folding ⟨**escalera de tijera** : stepladder⟩
tijereta *nf* : earwig
tijeretada *nf or* **tijeretazo** *nm* : cut, snip
tildar *vt* ~ **de** : to brand as, to call ⟨**lo tildaron de traidor** : they branded him as a traitor⟩
tilde *nf* **1** : accent mark **2** : tilde (accent over *ñ*)
tilo *nm* : linden (tree)
timador, -dora *n* : swindler
timar *vt* : to swindle, to cheat
timbal *nm* **1** : kettledrum **2 timbales** *nmpl* : timpani
timbre *nm* **1** : bell ⟨**tocar el timbre** : to ring the doorbell⟩ **2** : tone, timbre **3** SELLO : seal, stamp **4** *CA, Mex* : postage stamp
timidez *nf* : timidity, shyness
tímido, -da *adj* : timid, shy — **tímidamente** *adv*
timo *nm fam* : swindle, trick, hoax
timón *nm*, *pl* **timones** : rudder ⟨**estar al timón** : to be at the helm⟩
timonel *nm* : helmsman, coxswain
timorato, -ta *adj* **1** : timorous **2** : sanctimonious
tímpano *nm* **1** : eardrum **2 tímpanos** *nmpl* : timpani, kettledrums
tina *nf* **1** BAÑERA : tub, bathtub **2** : vat
tinaco *nm Mex* : water tank
tinieblas *nfpl* **1** OSCURIDAD : darkness **2** : ignorance
tino *nm* **1** : good judgment, sense **2** : tact, sensitivity, insight
tinta *nf* : ink
tinte *nm* **1** : dye, coloring **2** : overtone ⟨**tintes raciales** : racial overtones⟩
tintero *nm* **1** : inkwell **2 quedarse en el tintero** : to remain unsaid
tintinear *vt* : to jingle, to clink, to tinkle
tintineo *nm* : clink, jingle, tinkle
tinto, -ta *adj* **1** : dyed, stained ⟨**tinto en sangre** : bloodstained⟩ **2** : red (of wine)

tintorería *nf* : dry cleaner (service)
tintura *nf* **1** : dye, tint **2** : tincture ⟨**tintura de yodo** : tincture of iodine⟩
tiña *nf* : ringworm
tiñe, etc. → **teñir**
tío, tía *n* : uncle *m*, aunt *f*
tiovivo *nm* : merry-go-round
tipi *nm* : tepee
típico, -ca *adj* : typical — **típicamente** *adv*
tipificar {72} *vt* **1** : to classify, to categorize **2** : to typify
tiple *nm* : soprano
tipo[1] *nm* **1** CLASE : type, kind, sort **2** : figure, build, appearance **3** : rate ⟨**tipo de interés** : interest rate⟩ **4** : (printing) type, typeface **5** : style, model ⟨**un vestido tipo 60's** : a 60's-style dress⟩
tipo[2], **-pa** *n fam* : guy *m*, gal *f*, character
tipografía *nf* : typography, printing
tipográfico, -ca *adj* : typographic, typographical
tipógrafo, -fa *n* : printer, typographer
tique *or* **tiquet** *nm* **1** : ticket **2** : receipt
tira *nf* **1** : strip, strap **2 tira cómica** : comic, comic strip
tirabuzón *nf*, *pl* **-zones** : corkscrew
tirada *nf* **1** : throw **2** : distance, stretch **3** IMPRESIÓN : printing, issue
tiradero *nm Mex* **1** : dump **2** : mess, clutter
tirador[1] *nm* : handle, knob
tirador[2], **-dora** *n* : marksman *m*, markswoman *f*
tiragomas *nms & pl* : slingshot
tiranía *nf* : tyranny
tiránico, -ca *adj* : tyrannical
tiranizar {21} *vt* : to tyrannize
tirano[1], **-na** *adj* : tyrannical, despotic
tirano[2], **-na** *n* : tyrant
tirante[1] *adj* **1** : tense, strained **2** : taut
tirante[2] *nm* **1** : shoulder strap **2 tirantes** *nmpl* : suspenders
tirantez *nf* **1** : tautness **2** : tension, friction, strain
tirar *vt* **1** : to throw, to hurl, to toss **2** BOTAR : to throw away, to throw out, to waste **3** DERRIBAR : to knock down **4** : to shoot, to fire, to launch **5** : to take (a photo) **6** : to print, to run off — *vi* **1** : to pull, to draw **2** : to shoot **3** : to attract **4** : to get by, to manage ⟨**va tirando** : he's getting along, he's managing⟩ **5** ~ **a** : to tend towards, to be rather ⟨**tira a picante** : it's a bit spicy⟩ — **tirarse** *vr* **1** : to throw oneself **2** *fam* : to spend (time)
tiritar *vi* : to shiver, to tremble
tiro *nm* **1** BALAZO, DISPARO : shot, gunshot **2** : shot, kick (in sports) **3** : flue **4** : team (of horses, etc.) **5 a** ~ : within range **6 al tiro** : right away **7 tiro de gracia** : coup de grace, death blow
tiroideo, -dea *adj* : thyroid
tiroides *nmf & pl* : thyroid, thyroid gland — **tiroides** *adj*

tirolés, -lesa *adj* : Tyrolean
tirón *nm, pl* **tirones 1** : pull, tug, yank **2 de un tirón** : all at once, in one go
tiroteo *nm* **1** : shooting **2** : gunfight, shoot-out
tirria *nf* **tener tirria a** *fam* : to have a grudge against
titánico, -ca *adj* : titanic, huge
titanio *nm* : titanium
títere *nm* : puppet
tití *nm* : marmoset
titilar *vi* : to twinkle, to flicker
titileo *nm* : twinkle, flickering
titiritero, -ra *n* **1** : puppeteer **2** : acrobat
titubéar *vi* **1** : to hesitate **2** : to stutter, to stammer — **titubeante** *adj*
titubeo *nm* **1** : hesitation **2** : stammering
titulado, -da *adj* **1** : titled, entitled **2** : qualified
titular¹ *vt* : to title, to entitle — **titularse** *vr* **1** : to be called, to be entitled **2** : to receive a degree
titular² *adj* : titular, official
titular³ *nm* : headline
titular⁴ *nmf* **1** : owner, holder **2** : officeholder, incumbent
titularidad *nf* **1** : ownership, title **2** : position, office (with a title) **3** : starting position (in sports)
título *nm* **1** : title **2** : degree, qualification **3** : security, bond **4 a título de** : by way of, in the capacity of
tiza *nf* : chalk
tiznar *vt* : to blacken (with soot, etc.)
tizne *nm* HOLLÍN : soot
tiznón *nm, pl* **tiznones** : stain, smudge
tlapalería *nf Mex* : hardware store
TNT *nm* (*trinitrotolueno*) : TNT
toalla *nf* : towel
toallita *nf* : washcloth
tobillo *nm* : ankle
tobogán *nm, pl* **-ganes 1** : toboggan, sled **2** : slide, chute
tocadiscos *nms & pl* : record player, phonograph
tocado, -da *adj* **1** : bad, bruised (of fruit) **2** *fam* : touched, not all there
tocado² *nm* : headdress
tocador¹ *nm* **1** : dressing table, vanity table **2 artículos de tocador** : toiletries
tocador², -dora *n* : player (of music)
tocante *adj* ~ **a** : with regard to, regarding
tocar {72} *vt* **1** : to touch, to feel, to handle **2** : to touch on, to refer to **3** : to concern, to affect **4** : to play (a musical instrument) — *vi* **1** : to knock, to ring ⟨tocar a la puerta : to rap on the door⟩ **2** ~ **en** : to touch on, to border on ⟨eso toca en lo ridículo : that's almost ludicrous⟩ **3 tocarle a** : to fall to, to be up to, to be one's turn ⟨¿a quién le toca manejar? : whose turn is it to drive?⟩
tocayo, -ya *n* : namesake
tocineta *nf Col, Ven* : bacon
tocino *nm* **1** : bacon **2** : salt pork

tocología *nf* OBSTETRICIA : obstetrics
tocólogo, -ga *n* OBSTETRA : obstetrician
tocón *nm, pl* **tocones** CEPA : stump (of a tree)
todavía *adv* **1** AÚN : still, yet ⟨todavía puedes verlo : you can still see it⟩ **2** : even ⟨todavía más rápido : even faster⟩ **3 todavía no** : not yet
todo¹, -da *adj* **1** : all, whole, entire ⟨con toda sinceridad : with all sincerity⟩ ⟨toda la comunidad : the whole community⟩ **2** : every, each ⟨a todo nivel : at every level⟩ **3** : maximum ⟨a toda velocidad : at top speed⟩ **4 todo el mundo** : everyone, everybody
todo² *nm* : whole
todo³, -da *pron* **1** : everything, all, every bit ⟨lo sabe todo : he knows it all⟩ ⟨es todo un soldado : he's every inch a soldier⟩ **2 todos, -das** *pl* : everybody, everyone, all
todopoderoso, -sa *adj* OMNIPOTENTE : almighty, all-powerful
toga *nf* **1** : toga **2** : gown, robe (for magistrates, etc.)
toldo *nm* : awning, canopy
tolerable *adj* : tolerable — **tolerablemente** *adv*
tolerancia *nf* : tolerance, toleration
tolerante *adj* : tolerant — **tolerantemente** *adv*
tolerar *vt* : to tolerate
tolete *nm* : oarlock
tolva *nf* : hopper (container)
toma *nf* **1** : taking, seizure, capture **2** DOSIS : dose **3** : take, shot **4 toma de corriente** : wall socket, outlet **5 toma y daca** : give-and-take
tomar *vt* **1** : to take ⟨tomé el libro : I took the book⟩ ⟨tomar un taxi : to take a taxi⟩ ⟨tomar una foto : to take a photo⟩ ⟨toma dos años : it takes two years⟩ ⟨tomaron medidas drásticas : they took drastic measures⟩ **2** BEBER : to drink **3** CAPTURAR : to capture, to seize **4 tomar el sol** : to sunbathe **5 tomar tierra** : to land — *vi* : to drink (alcohol) — **tomarse** *vr* **1** : to take ⟨tomarse la molestia de : to take the trouble to⟩ **2** : to drink, to eat, to have
tomate *nm* : tomato
tomillo *nm* : thyme
tomo *nm* : volume, tome
ton *nm* **sin ton ni son** : without rhyme or reason
tonada *nf* **1** : tune, song **2** : accent
tonalidad *nf* : tonality
tonel *nm* BARRICA : barrel, cask
tonelada *nf* : ton
tonelaje *nm* : tonnage
tónica *nf* **1** : tonic (water) **2** : tonic (in music) **3** : trend, tone ⟨dar la tónica : to set the tone⟩
tónico¹, -ca *adj* : tonic
tónico² *nm* : tonic ⟨tónico capilar : hair tonic⟩
tono *nm* **1** : tone ⟨tono muscular : muscle tone⟩ **2** : shade (of colors) **3** : key (in music)

tontamente *adv* : foolishly, stupidly

tontear *vi* **1** : to fool around, to play the fool **2** : to flirt

tontería *nf* **1** : foolishness **2** : stupid remark or action **3 decir tonterías** : to talk nonsense

tonto¹, -ta *adj* **1** : dumb, stupid **2** : silly **3 a tontas y a locas** : without thinking, haphazardly

tonto², -ta *n* : fool, idiot

topacio *nm* : topaz

toparse *vr* ~ **con** : to bump into, to run into, to come across ⟨me topé con algunas dificultades : I ran into some problems⟩

tope *nm* **1** : limit, end ⟨hasta el tope : to the limit, to the brim⟩ **2** : stop, check, buffer ⟨tope de puerta : doorstop⟩ **3** : bump, collision **4** *Mex* : speed bump

tópico¹, -ca *adj* **1** : topical, external **2** : trite, commonplace

tópico² *nm* **1** : topic, subject **2** : cliché, trite expression

topo *nm* **1** : mole (animal) **2** *fam* : clumsy person, blunderer

topografía *nf* : topography

topográfico, -ca *adj* : topographic, topographical

topógrafo, -fa *n* : topographer

toque¹, etc. → tocar

toque² *nm* **1** : touch ⟨el último toque : the finishing touch⟩ ⟨un toque de color : a touch of color⟩ **2** : ringing, peal, chime **3** *Mex* : shock, jolt **4 toque de queda** : curfew **5 toque de diana** : reveille

toquetear *vt* : to touch, to handle, to finger

tórax *nm* : thorax

torbellino *nm* : whirlwind

torcedura *nf* **1** : twisting, buckling **2** : sprain

torcer {14} *vt* **1** : to bend, to twist **2** : to sprain **3** : to wring, to wring out **4** : to turn (a corner) **5** : to distort — *vi* : to turn — **torcerse** *vr*

torcido, -da *adj* **1** : twisted, crooked **2** : devious

tordo *nm* ZORZAL : thrush

torear *vt* **1** : to fight (bulls) **2** : to dodge, to sidestep

toreo *nm* : bullfighting

torero, -ra *n* MATADOR : bullfighter, matador

tormenta *nf* **1** : storm ⟨tormenta de nieve : snowstorm⟩ **2** : turmoil, frenzy

tormento *nm* **1** : torment, anguish **2** : torture

tormentoso, -sa *adj* : stormy, turbulent

tornado *nm* : tornado

tornamesa *nmf* : turntable

tornar *vt* **1** : to return, to give back **2** : to make, to render — *vi* : to go back **3** : to become, to turn into

tornasol *nm* **1** : reflected light **2** : sunflower **3** : litmus

tornear *vt* : to turn (in carpentry)

torneo *nm* : tournament

tornillo *nm* **1** : screw **2 tornillo de banco** : vise

torniquete *nm* **1** : tourniquet **2** : turnstile

torno *nm* **1** : lathe **2** : winch **3 torno de banco** : vise **4 en torno a** : around, about ⟨en torno a este asunto : about this issue⟩ ⟨en torno suyo : around him⟩

toro *nm* : bull

toronja *nf* : grapefruit

toronjil *nm* : balm, lemon balm

torpe *adj* **1** DESMAÑADO : clumsy, awkward **2** : stupid, dull — **torpemente** *adv*

torpedear *vt* : to torpedo

torpedo *nm* : torpedo

torpeza *nf* **1** : clumsiness, awkwardness **2** : stupidity **3** : blunder

torre *nf* **1** : tower ⟨torre de perforación : oil rig⟩ **2** : turret **3** : rook, castle (in chess)

torrencial *adj* : torrential — **torrencialmente** *adv*

torrente *nm* **1** : torrent **2 torrente sanguíneo** : bloodstream

torreón *nm*, *pl* **-rreones** : tower (of a castle)

torreta *nf* : turret (of a tank, ship, etc.)

tórrido, -da *adj* : torrid

torsión *nf*, *pl* **torsiones** : torsion — **torsional** *adj*

torso *nm* : torso, trunk

torta *nf* **1** : torte, cake **2** *Mex* : sandwich

tortazo *nm fam* : blow, wallop

tortilla *nf* **1** : tortilla **2** *or* **tortilla de huevo** : omelet

tórtola *nf* : turtledove

tortuga *nf* **1** : turtle, tortoise **2 tortuga de agua dulce** : terrapin **3 tortuga boba** : loggerhead

tortuoso, -sa *adj* : tortuous, winding

tortura *nf* : torture

torturador, -dora *n* : torturer

torturar *vt* : to torture, to torment

torvo, -va *adj* : grim, stern, baleful

torzamos, etc. → torcer

tos *nf* **1** : cough **2 tos ferina** : whooping cough

tosco, -ca *adj* : rough, coarse

toser *vi* : to cough

tosquedad *nf* : crudeness, coarseness, roughness

tostada *nf* **1** : piece of toast **2** : tostada

tostador *nm* **1** : toaster **2** : roaster (for coffee)

tostar {19} *vt* **1** : to toast **2** : to roast (coffee) **3** : to tan — **tostarse** *vr* : to get a tan

tostón *nm*, *pl* **tostones** *Car* : fried plantain chip

total¹ *adv* : in the end, so ⟨total, que no fui : in short, I didn't go⟩

total² *adj* & *nm* : total — **totalmente** *adv*

totalidad *nf* : totality, whole

totalitario, -ria *adj* & *n* : totalitarian

totalitarismo *nm* : totalitarianism

totalizar {21} *vt* : total, to add up to

tótem *nm, pl* **tótems** : totem

totopo *nm CA, Mex* : tortilla chip

totuma *nf* : calabash

tour ['tur] *nm, pl* **tours** : tour, excursion

toxicidad *nf* : toxicity

tóxico[1], **-ca** *adj* : toxic, poisonous

tóxico[2] *nm* : poison

toxicomanía *nf* : drug addiction

toxicómano, -na *n* : drug addict

toxina *nf* : toxin

tozudez *nf* : stubbornness, obstinacy

tozudo, -da *adj* : stubborn, obstinate — **tozudamente** *adv*

traba *nf* **1** : tie, bond **2** : obstacle, hindrance

trabajador[1], **-dora** *adj* : hardworking

trabajador[2], **-dora** *n* : worker

trabajar *vi* **1** : to work ⟨trabaja mucho : he works hard⟩ ⟨trabajo de secretaria : I work as a secretary⟩ **2** : to strive ⟨trabajan por mejores oportunidades : they're striving for better opportunities⟩ **3** : to act, to perform ⟨trabajar en una película : to be in a movie⟩ — *vt* **1** : to work (metal) **2** : to knead **3** : to till **4** : to work on ⟨tienes que trabajar el español : you need to work on your Spanish⟩

trabajo *nm* **1** : work, job **2** LABOR : labor, work ⟨tengo mucho trabajo : I have a lot of work to do⟩ **3** TAREA : task **4** ESFUERZA : effort **5 costar trabajo** : to be difficult **6 tomarse el trabajo** : to take the trouble **7 trabajo en equipo** : teamwork **8 trabajos** *nmpl* : hardships, difficulties

trabajoso, -sa *adj* LABORIOSO : laborious — **trabajosamente** *adv*

trabalenguas *nms & pl* : tongue twister

trabar *vt* **1** : to join, to connect **2** : to impede, to hold back **3** : to strike up (a conversation), to form (a friendship) **4** : to thicken (sauces) — **trabarse** *vr* **1** : to jam **2** : to become entangled **3** : to be tongue-tied, to stammer

trabucar {72} *vt* : to confuse, to mix up

trabuco *nm* : blunderbuss

tracalero, -ra *adj Mex* : dishonest, tricky

tracción *nf* : traction

trace, etc. → **trazar**

tracto *nm* : tract

tractor *nm* : tractor

tradición *nf, pl* **-ciones** : tradition

tradicional *adj* : traditional — **tradicionalmente** *adv*

traducción *nf, pl* **-ciones** : translation

traducible *adj* : translatable

traducir {61} *vt* **1** : to translate **2** : to convey, to express — **traducirse** *vr* ~ **en** : to result in

traductor, -tora *n* : translator

traer {81} *vt* **1** : to bring ⟨trae una ensalada : bring a salad⟩ **2** CAUSAR : to cause, to bring about ⟨el problema puede traer graves consecuencias : the problem could have serious consequences⟩ **3** : to carry, to have ⟨todos los periódicos traían las mismas noti-

cias : all of the newspapers carried the same news⟩ **4** LLEVAR : to wear — **traerse** *vr* **1** : to bring along **2 traérselas** : to be difficult

traficante *nmf* : dealer, trafficker

traficar {72} *vi* **1** : to trade, to deal **2** ~ **con** : to traffic in

tráfico *nm* **1** : trade **2** : traffic

tragaluz *nf, pl* **-luces** : skylight, fanlight

tragar {52} *v* : to swallow — **tragarse** *vr*

tragedia *nf* : tragedy

trágico, -ca *adj* : tragic — **trágicamente** *adv*

trago *nm* **1** : swallow, swig **2** : drink, liquor **3 trago amargo** : hard time

trague, etc. → **tragar**

traición *nf, pl* **traiciones** **1** : treason **2** : betrayal, treachery

traicionar *vt* : to betray

traicionero, -ra → **traidor**

traidor[1], **-dora** *adj* : traitorous, treasonous

traidor[2], **-dora** *n* : traitor

traiga, etc. → **traer**

tráiler *or* **trailer** *nm* : trailer

trailla *nf* **1** : leash **2** : harrow

traje *nm* **1** : suit **2** : dress **3** : costume **4 traje de baño** : bathing suit

trajín *nm, pl* **trajines** **1** : transport **2** *fam* : hustle and bustle

trajinar *vt* : to transport, to carry — *vi* : to rush around

trajo, etc. → **traer**

trama *nf* **1** : plot **2** : weave, weft (fabric)

tramar *vt* **1** : to plot, to plan **2** : to weave

tramitar *vt* : to transact, to negotiate, to handle

trámite *nm* : procedure, step

tramo *nm* **1** : stretch, section **2** : flight (of stairs)

trampa *nf* **1** : trap **2 hacer trampas** : to cheat

trampear *vt* : to cheat

trampero, -ra *n* : trapper

trampilla *nf* : trapdoor

trampolín *nm, pl* **-lines** **1** : diving board **2** : trampoline **3** : springboard ⟨un trampolín al éxito : a springboard to success⟩

tramposo[1], **-sa** *adj* : crooked, cheating

tramposo[2], **-sa** *n* : cheat, swindler

tranca *nf* **1** : stick, club **2** : bar, crossbar

trancar {72} *vt* : to bar (a door or window)

trancazo *nm* GOLPE : blow, hit

trance *nm* **1** : critical juncture, tough time **2** : trance **3 en trance de** : in the process of ⟨en trance de extinción : on the verge of extinction⟩

tranco *nm* **1** : stride **2** UMBRAL : threshold

tranque, etc. → **trancar**

tranquilidad *nf* : tranquility, peace

tranquilizador, -dora *adj* **1** : soothing **2** : reassuring

tranquilizante[1] *adj* **1** : reassuring **2** : tranquilizing

tranquilizante² *nm* : tranquilizer
tranquilizar {21} *vt* CALMAR : to calm down, to soothe ⟨tranquilizar la conciencia : to ease the conscience⟩ — **tranquilizarse** *vr*
tranquilo, -la *adj* CALMO : calm, tranquil ⟨una vida tranquila : a quiet life⟩ — **tranquilamente** *adv*
transacción *nf, pl* **-ciones** : transaction
transar *vi* TRANSIGIR : to give way, to compromise — *vt* : to buy and sell
transatlántico¹, -ca *adj* : transatlantic
transatlántico² *nm* : ocean liner
transbordador *nm* **1** : ferry **2 transbordador espacial** : space shuttle
transbordar *v* : to transfer
transbordo *nm* : transfer
transcendencia → trascendencia
transcender → trascender
transcribir {33} *vt* : to transcribe
transcrito *pp* → **transcribir**
transcripción *nf, pl* **-ciones** : transcription
transcurrir *vi* : to elapse, to pass
transcurso *nm* : course, progression ⟨en el transcurso de cien años : over the course of a hundred years⟩
transeúnte *nmf* **1** : passerby **2** : transient
transferencia *nf* : transfer, transference
transferir {76} *vt* TRASLADAR : to transfer — **transferible** *adj*
transfigurar *vt* : to transfigure, to transform — **transfiguración** *nf*
transformación *nf, pl* **-ciones** : transformation, conversion
transformador *nm* : transformer
transformar *vt* **1** CONVERTIR : to convert **2** : to transform, to change, to alter — **transformarse** *vr*
transfusión *nf, pl* **-siones** : transfusion
transgredir {1} *vt* : to transgress — **transgresión** *nf*
transgresor, -sora *n* : transgressor
transición *nf, pl* **-ciones** : transition ⟨período de transición : transition period⟩
transido, -da *adj* : overcome, beset ⟨transido de dolor : racked with pain⟩
transigir {35} *vi* **1** : to give in, to compromise **2 ~ con** : to tolerate, to put up with
transistor *nm* : transistor
transitable *adj* : passable
transitar *vi* : to go, to pass, to travel ⟨transitar por la ciudad : to travel through the city⟩
transitivo, -va *adj* : transitive
tránsito *nm* **1** TRÁFICO : traffic ⟨hora de máximo tránsito : rush hour⟩ **2** : transit, passage, movement **3** : death, passing
transitorio, -ria *adj* **1** : transitory **2** : provisional, temporary — **transitoriamente** *adv*
translúcido, -da *adj* : translucent
translucir → traslucir
transmisible *adj* : transmissible

transmisión *nf, pl* **-siones 1** : transmission, broadcast **2** : transfer **3** : transmission (of an automobile)
transmisor *nm* : transmitter
transmitir *vt* **1** : to transmit, to broadcast **2** : to pass on, to transfer — *vi* : to transmit, to broadcast
transparencia *nf* : transparency
transparentar *vt* : to reveal, to betray — **transparentarse** *vr* **1** : to be transparent **2** : to show through
transparente¹ *adj* : transparent — **transparentemente** *adv*
transparente² *nm* : shade, blind
transpiración *nf, pl* **-ciones** SUDOR : perspiration, sweat
transpirado, -da *adj* : sweaty
transpirar *vi* **1** SUDAR : to perspire, to sweat **2** : to transpire
transplantar, transplante → trasplantar, trasplante
transponer {60} *vt* **1** : to transpose, to move about **2** TRASPLANTAR : to transplant — **transponerse** *vr* **1** OCULTARSE : to hide **2** PONERSE : to set, to go down (of the sun or moon) **3** DORMITAR : to doze off
transportación *nf, pl* **-ciones** : transportation
transportador *nm* **1** : protractor **2** : conveyor
transportar *vt* **1** : to transport, to carry **2** : to transmit **3** : to transpose (music) — **transportarse** *vr* : to get carried away
transporte *nm* : transport, transportation
transportista *nmf* : hauler, carrier, trucker
transpuso, etc. → transponer
transversal *adj* : transverse, cross ⟨corte transversal : cross section⟩
transversalmente *adv* : obliquely
transverso, -sa *adj* : transverse
tranvía *nm* : streetcar, trolley
trapeador *nm* : mop
trapear *vt* : to mop
trapecio *nm* `1 : trapezoid **2** : trapeze
trapezoide *nm* : trapezoid
trapo *nm* **1** : cloth, rag ⟨trapo de polvo : dust cloth⟩ **2 soltar el trapo** : to burst into tears **3 trapos** *nmpl fam* : clothes
tráquea *nf* : trachea, windpipe
traquetear *vi* : to clatter, to jolt
traqueteo *nm* **1** : jolting **2** : clattering, clatter
tras *prep* **1** : after ⟨día tras día : day after day⟩ ⟨uno tras otro : one after another⟩ **2** : behind ⟨tras la puerta : behind the door⟩
trasbordar, trasbordo → transbordar, transbordo
trascendencia *nf* **1** : importance, significance **2** : transcendence
trascendental *adj* **1** : transcendental **2** : important, momentous
trascendente *adj* **1** : important, significant **2** : transcendent

trascender {56} *vi* 1 : to leak out, to become known 2 : to spread, to have a wide effect 3 ~ **a** : to smell of ⟨la casa trascendía a flores : the house smelled of flowers⟩ 4 ~ **de** : to transcend, to go beyond — *vt* : to transcend

trasero¹, -ra *adj* POSTERIOR : rear, back

trasero² *nm* : buttocks

trasfondo *nm* 1 : background, backdrop 2 : undertone, undercurrent

trasformación → **transformación**

trasgo *nm* : goblin, imp

trasgredir → **transgredir**

trasladar *vt* 1 TRANSFERIR : to transfer, to move 2 POSPONER : to postpone 3 TRADUCIR : to translate 4 COPIAR : to copy, to transcribe — **trasladarse** *vr* MUDARSE : to move, to relocate

traslado *nm* 1 : transfer, move 2 : copy

traslapar *vt* : to overlap — **traslaparse** *vr*

traslapo *nm* : overlap

traslúcido, -da → **translúcido**

traslucir {45} *vi* : to reveal, to show — **traslucirse** *vr* : to show through

trasmano a ~ : out of the way, out of reach

trasmisión, trasmitir → **transmisión, transmitir**

trasnochar *vi* : to stay up all night

trasparencia *nf* **trasparente** → **transparencia, transparente**

traspasar *vt* 1 PERFORAR : to pierce, to go through 2 : to go beyond ⟨traspasar los límites : to overstep the limits⟩ 3 ATRAVESAR : to cross, to go across 4 : to sell, to transfer

traspaso *nm* : transfer, sale

traspié *nm* 1 : stumble 2 : blunder

traspiración → **transpiración**

trasplantar *vt* : to transplant

trasplante *nm* : transplant

trasponer → **transponer**

trasportar → **transportar**

trasquilar *vt* ESQUILAR : to shear

traste *nm* 1 : fret (on a guitar) 2 *CA, Mex, PRi* : kitchen utensil ⟨lavar los trastes : to do the dishes⟩ 3 **dar al traste con** : to ruin, to destroy 4 **irse al traste** : to fall through

trastornar *vt* : to disturb, to upset, to disrupt — **trastornarse** *vr*

trastorno *nm* 1 : disorder ⟨trastorno mental : mental disorder⟩ 2 : disturbance, upset

trastos *nmpl* 1 : implements, utensils 2 *fam* : pieces of junk, stuff

trasunto *nm* : image, likeness

tratable *adj* 1 : friendly, sociable 2 : treatable

tratado *nm* 1 : treatise 2 : treaty

tratamiento *nm* : treatment

tratante *nmf* : dealer, trader

tratar *vi* 1 ~ **con** : to deal with, to have contact with ⟨no trato mucho con los clientes : I don't have much contact with customers⟩ 2 ~ **de** : to try to ⟨estoy tratando de comer : I am trying to

eat⟩ 3 ~ **de** *or* ~ **sobre** : to be about, to concern ⟨el libro trata de las plantas : the book is about plants⟩ 4 ~ **en** : to deal in ⟨trata en herramientas : he deals in tools⟩ — *vt* 1 : to treat ⟨tratan bien a sus empleados : they treat their employees well⟩ 2 : to handle ⟨trató el tema con delicadeza : he handled the subject tactfully⟩ — **tratarse** *vr* ~ **de** : to be about, to concern

trato *nm* 1 : deal, agreement 2 : relationship, dealings *pl* 3 : treatment ⟨malos tratos : ill-treatment⟩

trauma *nm* : trauma

traumático, -ca *adj* : traumatic — **traumáticamente** *adv*

traumatismo *nm* : injury ⟨traumatismo cervical : whiplash⟩

través *nm* 1 **a través de** : across, through 2 **al través** : crosswise, across 3 **de través** : sideways

travesaño *nm* 1 : crossbar 2 : crossbeam, crosspiece, transom (of a window)

travesía *nf* : voyage, crossing (of the sea)

travesura *nf* 1 : prank, mischievous act 2 **travesuras** *nfpl* : mischief

travieso, -sa *adj* : mischievous, naughty — **traviesamente** *adv*

trayecto *nm* 1 : journey 2 : route 3 : trajectory, path

trayectoria *nf* : course, path, trajectory

trayendo → **traer**

traza *nf* 1 DISEÑO : design, plan 2 : appearance

trazado *nm* 1 BOSQUEJO : outline, sketch 2 PLAN : plan, layout

trazar {21} *vt* 1 : to trace 2 : to draw up, to devise 3 : to outline, to sketch

trazo *nm* 1 : stroke, line 2 : sketch, outline

trébol *nm* 1 : clover, shamrock 2 : club (playing card)

trece *adj & nm* : thirteen

treceavo¹, -va *adj* : thirteenth

treceavo² *nm* : thirteenth (fraction)

trecho *nm* 1 : stretch, period ⟨de trecho en trecho : at intervals⟩ 2 : distance, space

tregua *nf* 1 : truce 2 : lull, respite 3 **sin ~** : relentless, unrelenting

treinta *adj & nm* : thirty

treintavo¹, -va *adj* : thirtieth

treintavo² *nm* : thirtieth (fraction)

tremendo, -da *adj* 1 : tremendous, enormous 2 : terrible, dreadful 3 *fam* : great, super

trementina *nf* AGUARRÁS : turpentine

trémulo, -la *adj* 1 : trembling, shaky 2 : flickering

tren *nm* 1 : train 2 : set, assembly ⟨tren de aterrizaje : landing gear⟩ 3 : speed, pace ⟨a todo tren : at top speed⟩

trence, etc. → **trenzar**

trenza *nf* : braid, pigtail

trenzar {21} *vt* : to braid — **trenzarse** *vr* : to get involved

trepador, -dora *adj* : climbing ⟨rosal trepador : rambling rose⟩

trepadora *nf* **1** : climbing plant, climber **2** : nuthatch

trepar *vi* **1** : to climb ⟨trepar a un árbol : to climb up a tree⟩ **2** : to creep, to spread (of a plant)

trepidación *nf, pl* **-ciones** : vibration

trepidante *adj* **1** : vibrating **2** : fast, frantic

trepidar *vi* **1** : to shake, to vibrate **2** : to hesitate, to waver

tres *adj & nm* : three

trescientos¹, -tas *adj* : three hundred

trescientos² *nms & pl* : three hundred

treta *nf* : trick, ruse

tríada *nf* : triad

triángulo *nm* : triangle — **triangular** *adj*

tribal *adj* : tribal

tribu *nf* : tribe

tribulación *nf, pl* **-ciones** : tribulation

tribuna *nf* **1** : dais, platform **2** : stands *pl*, bleachers *pl*, grandstand

tribunal *nm* : court, tribunal

tributar *vt* : to pay, to render — *vi* : to pay taxes

tributario¹, -ria *adj* : tax ⟨evasión tributaria : tax evasion⟩

tributario² *nm* : tributary

tributo *nm* **1** : tax **2** : tribute

triciclo *nm* : tricycle

tricolor *adj* : tricolor, tricolored

tridente *nm* : trident

tridimensional *adj* : three-dimensional, 3-D

trienal *adj* : triennial

trifulca *nf fam* : row, ruckus

trigésimo¹, -ma *adj* : thirtieth, thirty-

trigésimo², -ma *n* : thirtieth, thirty- (in a series)

trigo *nm* **1** : wheat **2 trigo rubión** : buckwheat

trigonometría *nf* : trigonometry

trigueño, -ña *adj* **1** : light brown (of hair) **2** MORENO : dark, olive-skinned

trillado, -da *adj* : trite, hackneyed

trilladora *nf* : thresher, threshing machine

trillar *vt* : to thresh

trillizo, -za *n* : triplet

trilogía *nf* : trilogy

trimestral *adj* : quarterly — **trimestralmente** *adv*

trinar *vi* **1** : to thrill **2** : to warble

trinchar *vt* : to carve, to cut up

trinchera *nf* **1** : trench, ditch **2** : trench coat

trineo *nm* : sled, sleigh

trinidad *nf* **la Trinidad** : the Trinity

trino *nm* : trill, warble

trinquete *nm* : ratchet

trío *nm* : trio

tripa *nf* **1** INTESTINO : gut, intestine **2 tripas** *nfpl fam* : belly, tummy, insides *pl* ⟨dolerle a uno las tripas : to have a stomach ache⟩

tripartito, -ta *adj* : tripartite

triple *adj & nm* : triple

triplicado *nm* : triplicate

triplicar {72} *vt* : to triple, to treble

trípode *nm* : tripod

tripulación *nf, pl* **-ciones** : crew

tripulante *nmf* : crew member

tripular *vt* : to man

tris *nm* **estar en un tris de** : to be within an inch of, to be very close to

triste *adj* **1** : sad, gloomy ⟨ponerse triste : to become sad⟩ **2** : desolate, dismal ⟨una perspectiva triste : a dismal outlook⟩ **3** : sorry, sorry-looking ⟨la triste verdad : the sorry truth⟩

tristeza *nf* DOLOR : sadness, grief

tristón, -tona *adj, mpl* **-tones** : melancholy, downhearted

tritón *nm, pl* **tritones** : newt

triturar *vt* : to crush, to grind

triunfal *adj* : triumphal, triumphant — **triunfalmente** *adv*

triunfante *adj* : triumphant, victorious

triunfar *vi* : to triumph, to win

triunfo *nm* **1** : triumph, victory **2** ÉXITO : success **3** : trump (in card games)

triunvirato *nm* : triumvirate

trivial *adj* **1** : trivial **2** : trite, commonplace

trivialidad *nf* : triviality

triza *nf* **1** : shred, bit **2 hacer trizas** : to tear into shreds, to smash to pieces

trocar {82} *vt* **1** CAMBIAR : to exchange, to trade **2** CAMBIAR : to change, to alter, to transform **3** CONFUNDIR : to confuse, to mix up

trocha *nf* : path, trail

troce, etc. → **trozar**

trofeo *nm* : trophy

tromba *nf* **1** : whirlwind **2 tromba de agua** : downpour, cloudburst

trombón *nm, pl* **trombones** **1** : trombone **2** : trombonist — **trombonista** *nmf*

trombosis *nf* : thrombosis

trompa *nf* **1** : trunk (of an elephant), proboscis (of an insect) **2** : horn ⟨trompa de caza : hunting horn⟩ **3** : tube, duct (in the body)

trompada *nf fam* **1** : punch, blow **2** : bump, collision (of persons)

trompeta *nf* : trumpet

trompetista *nmf* : trumpet player, trumpeter

trompo *nm* : spinning top

tronada *nf* : thunderstorm

tronar {19} *vi* **1** : to thunder, to roar **2** : to be furious, to rage **3** *CA, Mex fam* : to shoot — *v impers* : to thunder ⟨está tronando : it's thundering⟩

tronchar *vt* **1** : to snap, to break off **2** : to cut off (relations)

tronco *nm* **1** : trunk (of a tree) **2** : log **3** : torso

trono *nm* **1** : throne **2** *fam* : toilet

tropa *nf* **1** : troop, soldiers *pl* **2** : crowd, mob **3** : herd (of livestock)

tropel *nm* : mob, swarm

tropezar {29} *vi* **1** : to trip, to stumble **2** : to slip up, to blunder **3 ~ con** : to run into, to bump into **4 ~ con** : to come up against (a problem)

tropezón *nm, pl* **-zones 1** : stumble **2** : mistake, slip

tropical *adj* : tropical

trópico *nm* **1** : tropic ⟨trópico de Cáncer : tropic of Cancer⟩ **2 el trópico** : the tropics

tropiezo *nm* **1** CONTRATIEMPO : snag, setback **2** EQUIVOCACIÓN : mistake, slip

troqué, etc. → **trocar**

troquel *nm* : die (for stamping)

trotamundos *nmf* : globe-trotter

trotar *vi* **1** : to trot **2** : to jog **3** *fam* : to rush about

trote *nm* **1** : trot **2** *fam* : rush, bustle **3 de ~** : durable, for everyday use

trovador, -dora *n* : troubadour

trozar {21} *vt* : to cut up, to dice

trozo *nm* **1** PEDAZO : piece, bit, chunk **2** : passage, extract

trucha *nf* : trout

truco *nm* **1** : trick **2** : knack

truculento, -ta *adj* : horrifying, gruesome

trueca, trueque etc. → **trocar**

truena, etc. → **tronar**

trueno *nm* : thunder

trueque *nm* : barter, exchange

trufa *nf* : truffle

truncar {72} *vt* **1** : to truncate, to cut short **2** : to thwart, to frustrate ⟨truncó sus esperanzas : she shattered their hopes⟩

trunco, -ca *adj* **1** : truncated **2** : unfinished, incomplete

trunque, etc. → **truncar**

tu *adj* **1** : your ⟨tu vestido : your dress⟩ ⟨toma tus vitaminas : take your vitamins⟩ **2** : thy

tú *pron* **1** : you ⟨tú eres mi hijo : you are my son⟩ **2** : thou

tuba *nf* : tuba

tubérculo *nm* : tuber

tuberculosis *nf* : tuberculosis

tuberculoso, -sa *adj* : tuberculous, tubercular

tubería *nf* : pipes *pl*, tubing

tuberoso, -sa *adj* : tuberous

tubo *nm* **1** : tube ⟨tubo de ensayo : test tube⟩ **2** : pipe ⟨tubo de desagüe : drainpipe⟩ **3 tubo digestivo** : alimentary canal

tubular *adj* : tubular

tuerca *nf* : nut ⟨tuercas y tornillos : nuts and bolts⟩

tuerce, etc. → **torcer**

tuerto, -ta *adj* : one-eyed, blind in one eye

tuerza, etc. → **torcer**

tuesta, etc. → **tostar**

tuétano *nm* : marrow

tufo *nm* **1** : fume, vapor **2** *fam* : stench, stink

tugurio *nm* : hovel

tulipán *nm, pl* **-panes** : tulip

tumba *nf* **1** SEPULCRO : tomb **2** FOSA : grave **3** : felling of trees

tumbar *vt* **1** : to knock down **2** : to fell, to cut down — *vi* : to fall down — **tumbarse** *vr* ACOSTARSE : to lie down

tumbo *nm* **1** : tumble, fall **2 dar tumbos** : to jolt, to bump around

tumor *nm* : tumor

túmulo *nm* : burial mound

tumulto *nm* **1** ALBOROTO : commotion, tumult **2** MOTÍN : riot **3** MULTITUD : crowd

tumultuoso, -sa *adj* : tumultuous

tuna *nf* : prickly pear (fruit)

tundra *nf* : tundra

tunecino, -na *adj & n* : Tunisian

túnel *nm* : tunnel

tungsteno *nm* : tungsten

túnica *nf* : tunic

tupé *nm* PELUQUÍN : toupee

tupido, -da *adj* **1** DENSO : dense, thick **2** OBSTRUIDO : obstructed, blocked up

turba *nf* **1** : peat **2** : mob, throng

turbación *nf, pl* **-ciones 1** : disturbance **2** : alarm, concern **3** : confusion

turbante *nm* : turban

turbar *vt* **1** : to disturb, to disrupt **2** : to worry, to upset **3** : to confuse

turbina *nf* : turbine

turbio, -bia *adj* **1** : cloudy, murky, turbid **2** : dim, blurred **3** : shady, crooked

turbopropulsor *nm* : turboprop

turborreactor *nm* : turbojet

turbulencia *nf* : turbulence

turbulento, -ta *adj* : turbulent

turco¹, -ca *adj* : Turkish

turco², -ca *n* : Turk

turco³ *nm* : Turkish (language)

turgente *adj* : turgid, swollen

turismo *nm* : tourism, tourist industry

turista *nmf* : tourist, vacationer

turístico, -ca *adj* : tourist, travel

turnar *vi* : to take turns, to alternate

turno *nm* **1** : turn ⟨ya te tocará tu turno : you'll get your turn⟩ **2** : shift, duty ⟨turno de noche : night shift⟩ **3 por turno** : alternately

turón *nm, pl* **turones** : polecat

turquesa *nf* : turquoise

turrón *nm, pl* **turrones** : nougat

tusa *nf* : corn husk

tutear *vt* : to address as *tú*

tutela *nf* **1** : guardianship **2** : tutelage, protection

tuteo *nm* : addressing as *tú*

tutor, -tora *n* **1** : tutor **2** : guardian

tuvo, etc. → **tener**

tuyo¹, -ya *adj* : yours, of yours ⟨un amigo tuyo : a friend of yours⟩ ⟨¿es tuya esta casa? : is this house yours?⟩

tuyo², -ya *pron* **1** : yours ⟨ése es el tuyo : that one is yours⟩ ⟨trae la tuya : bring your own⟩ **2 los tuyos** : your relations, your friends ⟨¿vendrán los tuyos? : are your folks coming?⟩

tweed [ˈtwið] *nm* : tweed

U

u¹ *nf* : twenty-second letter of the Spanish alphabet

u² *conj (used instead of* **o** *before words beginning with* o- *or* ho-*)* : or

ualabí *nm* : wallaby

uapití *nm* : American elk, wapiti

ubicación *nf, pl* **-ciones** : location, position

ubicar {72} *vt* **1** SITUAR : to place, to put, to position **2** LOCALIZAR : to locate, to find — **ubicarse** *vr* **1** LOCALIZARSE : to be placed, to be located **2** SITUARSE : to position oneself

ubicuidad *nf* OMNIPRESENCIA : ubiquity

ubicuo, -cua *adj* OMNIPRESENTE : ubiquitous

ubre *nf* : udder

ucraniano¹, -na *adj & n* : Ukrainian

ucraniano² *nm* : Ukrainian (language)

Ud., Uds. → **usted**

ufanarse *vr* ~ **de** : to boast about, to pride oneself on

ufano, -na *adj* **1** ORGULLOSO : proud **2** : self-satisfied, smug

ugandés, -desa *adj & n, mpl* **-deses** : Ugandan

ukelele *nm* : ukulele

úlcera *nf* : ulcer — **ulceroso, -sa** *adj*

ulcerar *vt* : to ulcerate — **ulcerarse** *vr* — **ulceración** *nf*

ulceroso, -sa *adj* : ulcerous

ulterior *adj* : later, subsequent — **ulteriormente** *adv*

últimamente *adv* : lately, recently

ultimar *vt* **1** CONCLUIR : to complete, to finish, to finalize **2** MATAR : to kill

ultimátum *nm, pl* **-tums** : ultimatum

último, -ma *adj* **1** : last, final ⟨la última galleta : the last cookie⟩ ⟨en último caso : as a last resort⟩ **2** : last, latest, most recent ⟨su último viaje a España : her last trip to Spain⟩ ⟨en los últimos años : in recent years⟩ **3 por** ~ : finally

ultrajar *vt* INSULTAR : to offend, to outrage, to insult

ultraje *nm* INSULTO : outrage, insult

ultramar *nm* **de** ~ *or* **en** ~ : overseas, abroad

ultranza *nf* **1 a** ~ : to the extreme ⟨lo defendió a ultranza : she defended him fiercely⟩ **2 a** ~ : extreme, out-and-out ⟨perfeccionismo a ultranza : rabid perfectionism⟩

ultrarrojo, -ja *adj* : infrared

ultravioleta *adj* : ultraviolet

ulular *vi* **1** : to hoot **2** : to howl, to wail

ululato *nm* : hoot (of an owl), wail (of a person)

umbilical *adj* : umbilical ⟨cordón umbilical : umbilical cord⟩

umbral *nm* : threshold, doorstep

un¹ *adj* → **uno¹**

un², una *art, mpl* **unos 1** : a, an **2 unos** *or* **unas** *pl* : some, a few ⟨hace unas semanas : a few weeks ago⟩ **3 unos** *or* **unas** *pl* : about, approximately ⟨unos veinte años antes : about twenty years before⟩

unánime *adj* : unanimous — **unánimemente** *adv*

unanimidad *nf* **1** : unanimity **2 por** ~ : unanimously

unción *nf, pl* **-ciones** : unction

uncir {83} *vt* : to yoke

undécimo¹, -ma *adj* : eleventh

undécimo², -ma *n* : eleventh (in a series)

ungir {35} *vt* : to anoint

ungüento *nm* : ointment, salve

únicamente *adv* : only, solely

unicelular *adj* : unicellular

único¹, -ca *adj* **1** : only, sole **2** : unique, extraordinary

único², -ca *n* : only one ⟨los únicos que vinieron : the only ones who showed up⟩

unicornio *nm* : unicorn

unidad *nf* **1** : unity **2** : unit

unidireccional *adj* : unidirectional

unido, -da *adj* **1** : joined, united **2** : close ⟨unos amigos muy unidos : very close friends⟩

unificar {72} *vt* : to unify — **unificación** *nf*

uniformado, -da *adj* : uniformed

uniformar *vt* ESTANDARIZAR : to standardize, to make uniform

uniforme¹ *adj* : uniform — **uniformemente** *adv*

uniforme² *nm* : uniform

uniformidad *nf* : uniformity

unilateral *adj* : unilateral — **unilateralmente** *adv*

unión *nf, pl* **uniones 1** : union **2** JUNTURA : joint, coupling

unir *vt* **1** JUNTAR : to unite, to join, to link **2** COMBINAR : to combine, to blend — **unirse** *vr* **1** : to join together **2** : to combine, to mix together **3** ~ **a** : to join ⟨se unieron al grupo : they joined the group⟩

unísono *nm* : unison ⟨al unísono : in unison⟩

unitario, -ria *adj* : unitary, unit ⟨precio unitario : unit price⟩

universal *adj* : universal — **universalmente** *adv*

universidad *nf* : university

universitario¹, -ria *adj* : university, college

universitario², -ria *n* : university student, college student

universo *nm* : universe

unja, etc. → **ungir**

uno¹, una *adj* ⟨**un** *before masculine singular nouns*⟩ : one ⟨una silla : one chair⟩ ⟨tiene treinta y un años : he's thirty-one years old⟩ ⟨el tomo uno : volume one⟩

uno² *nm* : one, number one

uno³, una *pron* **1** : one (number) ⟨uno por uno : one by one⟩ ⟨es la una : it's one o'clock⟩ **2** : one (person or thing) ⟨una es mejor que las otras : one (of them) is better than the others⟩ ⟨hacerlo uno mismo : to do it oneself⟩ **3 unos, unas** *pl* : some (ones), some people **4 uno y otro** : both **5 unos y otros** : all of them **6 el uno al otro** : one another, each other ⟨se enseñaron los unos a los otros : they taught each other⟩

untar *vt* **1** : to anoint **2** : to smear, to grease **3** : to bribe

unza, etc. → **uncir**

uña *nf* **1** : fingernail, toenail **2** : claw, hoof, stinger

uranio *nm* : uranium

Urano *nm* : Uranus

urbanidad *nf* : urbanity, courtesy

urbanización *nf, pl* **-ciones** : housing development, residential area

urbanizar {21} *vt* : to develop (an area)

urbano, -na *adj* **1** : urban **2 CORTÉS** : urbane, polite

urbe *nf* : large city, metropolis

urdimbre *nf* : warp (in a loom)

urdu *nm* : Urdu

uretra *nf* : urethra

urgencia *nf* **1** : urgency **2 EMERGENCIA** : emergency

urgente *adj* : urgent — **urgentemente** *adv*

urgir {35} *v impers* : to be urgent, to be pressing ⟨me urge localizarlo : I urgently need to find him⟩ ⟨el tiempo urge : time is running out⟩

urinario¹, -ria *adj* : urinary

urinario² *nm* : urinal (place)

urja, etc. → **urgir**

urna *nf* **1** : urn **2** : ballot box ⟨acudir a las urnas : to go to the polls⟩

urogallo *nm* : grouse (bird)

urraca *nf* **1** : magpie **2 urraca de América** : blue jay

urticaria *nf* : hives

uruguayo, -ya *adj & n* : Uruguayan

usado, -da *adj* **1** : used, secondhand **2** : worn, worn-out

usanza *nf* : custom, usage

usar *vt* **1 EMPLEAR, UTILIZAR** : to use, to make use of **2 CONSUMIR** : to consume, to use (up) **3 LLEVAR** : to wear **4 de usar y tirar** : disposable — **usarse** *vr* **1** : to be used **2** : to be in fashion

uso *nm* **1 EMPLEO, UTILIZACIÓN** : use ⟨de uso personal : for personal use⟩ ⟨hacer uso de : to make use of⟩ **2** : wear ⟨uso y desgaste : wear and tear⟩ **3 USANZA** : custom, usage, habit ⟨al uso de : in the manner of, in the style of⟩

usted *pron* (*formal form of address in most countries; often written as* **Ud.** *or* **Vd.**) : you **2 ustedes** *pl* (*often written as* **Uds.** *or* **Vds.**) : you, all of you

usual *adj* : usual, common, normal ⟨poco usual : not very common⟩ — **usualmente** *adv*

usuario, -ria *n* : user

usura *nf* : usury — **usurario, -ria** *adj*

usurero, -ra *n* : usurer

usurpador, -dora *n* : usurper

usurpar *vt* : to usurp — **usurpación** *nf*

utensilio *nm* : utensil, tool

uterino, -na *adj* : uterine

útero *nm* : uterus, womb

útil *adj* : useful, handy, helpful

útiles *nmpl* : implements, tools

utilidad *nf* **1** : utility, usefulness **2 utilidades** *nfpl* : profits

utilitario, -ria *adj* : utilitarian

utilizable *adj* : usable, fit for use

utilización *nf, pl* **-ciones** : utilization, use

utilizar {21} *vt* : to use, to utilize

útilmente *adv* : usefully

utopía *nf* : utopia

utópico, -ca *adj* : utopian

uva *nf* : grape

uvular *adj* : uvular

V

v *nf* : twenty-third letter of the Spanish alphabet

va → **ir**

vaca *nf* : cow

vacación *nf, pl* **-ciones** **1** : vacation ⟨dos semanas de vacaciones : two weeks of vacation⟩ **2 estar de vacaciones** : to be on vacation **3 irse de vacaciones** : to go on vacation

vacacionar *vi Mex* : to vacation

vacacionista *nmf CA, Mex* : vacationer

vacante¹ *adj* : vacant, empty

vacante² *nf* : vacancy (for a job)

vaciado *nm* : cast, casting ⟨vaciado de yeso : plaster cast⟩

vaciar {85} *vt* **1** : to empty, to empty out, to drain **2 AHUECAR** : to hollow out **3** : to cast (in a mold) — *vi* ~ **en** : to flow into, to empty into

vacilación *nf, pl* **-ciones** : hesitation, vacillation

vacilante *adj* **1** : hesitant, unsure **2** : shaky, unsteady **3** : flickering

vacilar *vi* **1** : to hesitate, to vacillate, to waver **2** : to be unsteady, to wobble **3** : to flicker **4 fam** : to joke, to fool around

vacío¹, -cía *adj* **1** : vacant **2** : empty **3** : meaningless

vacío² *nm* **1** : emptiness, void **2** : space, gap **3** : vacuum **4 hacerle el vacío a alguien** : to ostracize someone, to give someone the cold shoulder

vacuidad *nf* : vacuity, vacuousness

vacuna *nf* : vaccine
vacunación *nf, pl* **-ciones** INOCU-LACIÓN : vaccination, inoculation
vacunar *vt* INOCULAR : to vaccinate, to inoculate
vacuno¹, -na *adj* : bovine ⟨ganado vacuno : beef cattle⟩
vacuno² *nm* : bovine
vacuo, -cua *adj* : empty, shallow, inane
vadear *vt* : to ford, to wade across
vado *nm* : ford
vagabundear *vi* : to wander, to roam about
vagabundo¹, -da *adj* **1** ERRANTE : wandering **2** : stray
vagabundo², -da *n* : vagrant, bum, vagabond
vagamente *adv* : vaguely
vagancia *nf* **1** : vagrancy **2** PEREZA : laziness, idleness
vagar {52} *vi* ERRAR : to roam, to wander
vagina *nf* : vagina — **vaginal** *adj*
vago¹, -ga *adj* **1** : vague **2** PEREZOSO : lazy, idle
vago², -ga *n* **1** : idler, loafer **2** VAGA-BUNDO : vagrant, bum
vagón *nm, pl* **vagones** : car (of a train)
vague, etc. → vagar
vaguear *vi* **1** : to loaf, to lounge around **2** VAGAR : to wander
vaguedad *nf* : vagueness
vahído, etc. → valer
vaho *nm* **1** : breath **2** : vapor, steam (on glass, etc.)
vaina *nf* **1** : sheath, scabbard **2** : pod (of a pea or bean) **3** *fam* : nuisance, bother
vainilla *nf* : vanilla
vaivén *nm, pl* **vaivenes 1** : swinging, swaying, rocking **2** : change, fluctuation ⟨los vaivenes de la vida : life's ups and downs⟩
vajilla *nf* : dishes *pl*, set of dishes
valdrá, etc. → valer
vale *nm* **1** : voucher **2** PAGARÉ : promissory note, IOU
valedero, -ra *adj* : valid
valentía *nf* : courage, valor
valer {84} *vt* **1** : to be worth ⟨valen una fortuna : they're worth a fortune⟩ ⟨no vale protestar : there's no point in protesting⟩ ⟨valer la pena : to be worth the trouble⟩ **2** : to cost ⟨¿cuánto vale? : how much does it cost?⟩ **3** : to earn, to gain ⟨le valió una reprimenda : it earned him a reprimand⟩ **4** : to protect, to aid ⟨¡válgame Dios! : God help me!⟩ **5** : to be equal to — *vi* **1** : to have value ⟨sus consejos no valen para nada : his advice is worthless⟩ **2** : to be valid, to count ⟨¡eso no vale! : that doesn't count!⟩ **3 hacerse valer** : to assert oneself **4 más vale** : it's better ⟨más vale que te vayas : you'd better go⟩ — **valerse** *vr* **1 ~ de** : to take advantage of **2 valerse solo** *or* **valerse por sí mismo** : to look after oneself **3** *Mex* : to be fair ⟨no se vale : it's not fair⟩

valeroso, -sa *adj* : brave, valiant
valet [ˈbalet, -ˈle] *nm* : jack (in playing cards)
valga, etc. → valer
valía *nf* : value, worth
validar *vt* : to validate — **validación** *nf*
validez *nf* : validity
válido, -da *adj* : valid
valiente *adj* **1** : brave, valiant **2** (*used ironically*) : fine, great ⟨¡valiente amiga! : what a fine friend!⟩ — **valientemente** *adv*
valija *nf* : suitcase, valise
valioso, -sa *adj* PRECIOSO : valuable, precious
valla *nf* **1** : fence, barricade **2** : hurdle (in sports) **3** : obstacle, hindrance
vallar *vt* : to fence, to put a fence around
valle *nm* : valley, vale
valor *nm* **1** : value, worth, importance **2** CORAJE : courage, valor **3 valores** *nmpl* : values, principles **4 valores** *nmpl* : securities, bonds **5 sin ~** : worthless
valoración *nf, pl* **-ciones 1** EVALUA-CIÓN : valuation, appraisal, assessment **2** APRECIACIÓN : appreciation
valorar *vt* **1** EVALUAR : to evaluate, to appraise, to assess **2** APRECIAR : to value, to appreciate
valorizarse {21} *vr* : to appreciate, to increase in value — **valorización** *nf*
vals *nm* : waltz
valsar *vi* : to waltz
valuación *nf, pl* **-ciones** : valuation, appraisal
valuar {3} *vt* : to value, to appraise, to assess
válvula *nf* **1** : valve **2 válvula reguladora** : throttle
vamos → ir
vampiro *nm* : vampire
van → ir
vanadio *nm* : vanadium
vanagloriarse *vr* : to boast, to brag
vanamente *adv* : vainly, in vain
vandalismo *nm* : vandalism
vándalo *nm* : vandal — **vandalismo** *nm*
vanguardia *nf* **1** : vanguard **2** : avantegarde **3 a la vanguardia** : at the forefront
vanidad *nf* : vanity
vanidoso, -sa *adj* PRESUMIDO : vain, conceited
vano, -na *adj* **1** INÚTIL : vain, useless **2** : vain, worthless ⟨vanas promesas : empty promises⟩ **3 en ~** : in vain, of no avail
vapor *nm* **1** : vapor, steam **2** : steamer, steamship **3 al vapor** : steamed
vaporizador *nm* : vaporizer
vaporizar {21} *vt* : to vaporize — **vaporizarse** *vr* — **vaporización** *nf*
vaporoso, -sa *adj* **1** : vaporous **2** : sheer, airy
vapulear *vt* : to beat, to thrash
vaquero¹, -ra *adj* : cowboy ⟨pantalón vaquero : jeans⟩

vaquero², **-ra** *n* : cowboy *m*, cowgirl *f*
vaqueros *nmpl* JEANS : jeans
vaquilla *nf* : heifer
vara *nf* **1** : pole, stick, rod **2** : staff (of office) **3** : lance, pike (in bullfighting) **4** : yardstick **5 vara de oro** : golden-rod
varado, -da *adj* **1** : beached, aground **2** : stranded
varar *vt* : to beach (a ship), to strand — *vi* : to run aground
variable *adj & n* : variable — **variabilidad** *nf*
variación *nf, pl* **-ciones** : variation
variado, -da *adj* : varied, diverse
variante *adj & nf* : variant
varianza *nf* : variance
variar {85} *vt* **1** : to change, to alter **2** : to diversify — *vi* **1** : to vary, to change **2 variar de opinión** : to change one's mind
varicela *nf* : chicken pox
varices *or* **várices** *nfpl* : varicose veins
varicoso, -sa *adj* : varicose
variedad *nf* DIVERSIDAD : variety, diversity
varilla *nf* **1** : rod, bar **2** : spoke (of a wheel) **3** : rib (of an umbrella)
vario, -ria *adj* **1** : varied, diverse **2** : variegated, motley **3** : changeable **4 varios, varias** *pl* : various, several
variopinto, -ta *adj* : diverse, assorted, motley
varita *nf* : wand ⟨varita mágica : magic wand⟩
varón *nm, pl* **varones 1** HOMBRE : man, male **2** NIÑO : boy
varonil *adj* **1** : masculine, manly **2** : mannish
vas → **ir**
vasallo *nm* : vassal — **vasallaje** *nm*
vasco¹, -ca *adj & n* : Basque
vasco² *nm* : Basque (language)
vascular *adj* : vascular
vasija *nf* : container, vessel
vaso *nm* **1** : glass, tumbler **2** : glassful **3** : vessel ⟨vaso sanguíneo : blood vessel⟩
vástago *nm* **1** : offspring, descendant **2** : shoot (of a plant)
vastedad *nf* : vastness, immensity
vasto, -ta *adj* : vast, immense
vataje *nm* : wattage
vaticinar *vt* : to predict, to foretell
vaticinio *nm* : prediction, prophecy
vatio *nm* : watt
vaya, etc. → **ir**
Vd., Vds. → **usted**
ve, etc. → **ir, ver**
vea, etc. → **ver**
vecinal *adj* : local
vecindad *nf* **1** : neighborhood, vicinity **2 casa de vecindad** : tenement
vecindario *nm* **1** : neighborhood, area **2** : residents *pl*
vecino, -na *n* **1** : neighbor **2** : resident, inhabitant
veda *nf* **1** PROHIBICIÓN : prohibition **2** : closed season (for hunting or fishing)

vedar *vt* **1** : to prohibit, to ban **2** IMPEDIR : to impede, to prevent
vega *nf* : fertile lowland
vegetación *nf, pl* **-ciones 1** : vegetation **2 vegetaciones** *nfpl* : adenoids
vegetal *adj & nm* : vegetable, plant
vegetar *vi* : to vegetate
vegetarianismo *nm* : vegetarianism
vegetariano, -na *adj & n* : vegetarian
vegetativo, -va *adj* : vegetative
vehemente *adj* : vehement — **vehemencia** *nf*
vehículo *nm* : vehicle — **vehicular** *adj*
veía, etc. → **ver**
veinte *adj & nm* : twenty
veinteavo¹, -va *adj* : twentieth
veinteavo² *nm* : twentieth (fraction)
veintena *nf* : group of twenty, score ⟨una veintena de participantes : about twenty participants⟩
vejación *nf, pl* **-ciones** : ill-treatment, humiliation
vejar *vt* : to mistreat, to ridicule, to harass
vejete *nm* : old fellow, codger
vejez *nf* : old age
vejiga *nf* **1** : bladder **2** AMPOLLA : blister
vela *nf* **1** VIGILIA : wakefulness ⟨pasé la noche en vela : I stayed awake all night⟩ **2** : watch, vigil, wake **3** : candle **4** : sail
velada *nf* : evening party, soirée
velado, -da *adj* **1** : veiled, hidden **2** : blurred **3** : muffled
velador¹, -dora *n* : guard, night watchman
velador² *nm* **1** : candlestick **2** : night table
velar *vt* **1** : to hold a wake over **2** : to watch over, to sit up with **3** : to blur, to expose (a photo) **4** : to veil, to conceal — *vi* **1** : to stay awake **2** ~ **por** : to watch over, to look after
velatorio *nm* VELORIO : wake (for the dead)
veleidad *nf* **1** : fickleness **2** : whim, caprice
veleidoso, -sa *adj* : fickle, capricious
velero *nm* **1** : sailing ship **2** : sailboat
veleta *nf* : weather vane
vello *nm* **1** : body hair **2** : down, fuzz
vellocino *nm* : fleece
vellón *nm, pl* **vellones 1** : fleece, sheepskin **2** PRi : nickel (coin)
vellosidad *nf* : downiness, hairiness
velloso, -sa *adj* : downy, fluffy, hairy
velo *nm* : veil
velocidad *nf* **1** : speed, velocity ⟨velocidad máxima : speed limit⟩ **2** MARCHA : gear (of an automobile)
velocímetro *nm* : speedometer
velocista *nmf* : sprinter
velorio *nm* VELATORIO : wake (for the dead)
velour *nm* : velour, velours
veloz *adj, pl* **veloces** : fast, quick, swift — **velozmente** *adv*
ven → **venir**

vena *nf* **1** : vein ⟨vena yugular : jugular vein⟩ **2** : vein, seam, lode **3** : grain (of wood) **4** : style ⟨en vena lírica : in a lyrical vein⟩ **5** : strain, touch ⟨una vena de humor : a touch of humor⟩ **6** : mood

venado *nm* **1** : deer **2** : venison

venal *adj* : venal — **venalidad** *nf*

vencedor, -dora *n* : winner, victor

vencejo *nm* : swift (bird)

vencer {86} *vt* **1** DERROTAR : to vanquish, to defeat **2** SUPERAR : to overcome, to surmount — *vi* **1** GANAR : to win, to triumph **2** CADUCAR : to expire ⟨el plazo vence el jueves : the deadline is Thursday⟩ **3** : to fall due, to mature — **vencerse** *vr* **1** DOMINARSE : to control oneself **2** : to break, to collapse

vencido, -da *adj* **1** : defeated **2** : expired **3** : due, payable **4** darse por vencido : to give up

vencimiento *nm* **1** : defeat **2** : expiration **3** : maturity (of a loan)

venda *nf* : bandage

vendaje *nm* : bandage, dressing

vendar *vt* **1** : to bandage **2** vendar los ojos : to blindfold

vendaval *nm* : gale, strong wind

vendedor, -dora *n* : salesperson, salesman *m*, saleswoman *f*

vender *vt* **1** : to sell **2** : to sell out, to betray — **venderse** *vr* **1** : to be sold ⟨se vende : for sale⟩ **2** : to sell out

vendetta *nf* : vendetta

vendible *adj* : salable, marketable

vendimia *nf* : grape harvest

vendrá, etc. → venir

veneno *nm* **1** : poison **2** : venom

venenoso, -sa *adj* : poisonous, venomous

venerable *adj* : venerable

veneración *nf, pl* **-ciones** : veneration, reverence

venerar *vt* : to venerate, to revere

venéreo, -rea *adj* : venereal

venero *nm* **1** VENA : seam, lode, vein **2** MANANTIAL : spring **3** FUENTE : origin, source

venezolano, -na *adj & n* : Venezuelan

venga, etc. → venir

vengador, -dora *n* : avenger

venganza *nf* : vengeance, revenge

vengar {52} *vt* : to avenge — **vengarse** *vr* : to get even, to revenge oneself

vengativo, -va *adj* : vindictive, vengeful

vengue, etc. → vengar

venia *nf* **1** PERMISO : permission, leave **2** PERDÓN : pardon **3** : bow (of the head)

venial *adj* : venial

venida *nf* **1** LLEGADA : arrival, coming **2** REGRESO : return **3** idas y venidas : comings and goings

venidero, -ra *adj* : coming, future

venir {87} *vi* **1** : to come ⟨lo vi venir : I saw him coming⟩ ⟨¡venga! : come on!⟩ **2** : to arrive ⟨vinieron en coche : they came by car⟩ **3** : to come, to originate ⟨sus zapatos vienen de Italia : her shoes

are from Italy⟩ **4** : to come, to be available ⟨viene envuelto en plástico : it comes wrapped in plastic⟩ **5** : to come back, to return **6** : to affect, to overcome ⟨me vino un vahído : a dizzy spell came over me⟩ **7** : to fit ⟨te viene un poco grande : it's a little big for you⟩ **8** (*with the present participle*) : to have been ⟨viene entrenando diariamente : he's been training daily⟩ **9 ~ a** (*with the infinitive*) : to end up, to turn out ⟨viene a ser lo mismo : it comes out the same⟩ **10** que viene : coming, next ⟨el año que viene : next year⟩ **11** venir bien : to be suitable, to be just right — **venirse** *vr* **1** : to come, to arrive **2** : to come back **3** venirse abajo : to fall apart, to collapse

venta *nf* **1** : sale **2** venta al por menor *or* venta al detalle : retail sales

ventaja *nf* **1** : advantage **2** : lead, head start **3** ventajas *nfpl* : perks, extras

ventajoso, -sa *adj* **1** : advantageous **2** : profitable — **ventajosamente** *adv*

ventana *nf* **1** : window (of a building) **2** ventana de la nariz : nostril

ventanal *nm* : large window

ventanilla *nf* **1** : window (of a vehicle or airplane) **2** : ticket window, box office

ventero, -ra *n* : innkeeper

ventilación *nf, pl* **-ciones** : ventilation

ventilador *nm* **1** : ventilator **2** : fan

ventilar *vt* **1** : to ventilate, to air out **2** : to air, to discuss **3** : to make public, to reveal — **ventilarse** *vr* : to get some air

ventisca *nf* : snowstorm, blizzard

ventisquero *nm* : snowdrift

ventosear *vi* : to break wind

ventosidad *nf* : wind, flatulence

ventoso, -sa *adj* : windy

ventrículo *nm* : ventricle

ventrílocuo, -cua *n* : ventriloquist

ventriloquia *nf* : ventriloquism

ventura *nf* **1** : fortune, luck, chance **2** : happiness **3** a la ventura : at random, as it comes

venturoso, -sa *adj* **1** AFORTUNADO : fortunate, lucky **2** : successful

Venus *nm* : Venus

venza, etc. → vencer

ver[1] {88} *vt* **1** : to see ⟨vimos la película : we saw the movie⟩ **2** ENTENDER : to understand ⟨ya lo veo : now I get it⟩ **3** EXAMINAR : to examine, to look into ⟨lo veré : I'll take a look at it⟩ **4** JUZGAR : to see, to judge ⟨a mi manera de ver : to my way of thinking⟩ **5** VISITAR : to meet with, to visit **6** AVERIGUAR : to find out **7** a ver *or* vamos a ver : let's see — *vi* **1** : to see **2** ENTERARSE : to learn, to find out **3** ENTENDER : to understand — **verse** *vr* **1** HALLARSE : to find oneself **2** PARECER : to look, to appear **3** ENCONTRARSE : to see each other, to meet

ver[2] *nm* **1** : looks *pl*, appearance **2** : opinion ⟨a mi ver : in my view⟩

vera *nf* : side ⟨a la vera del camino : alongside the road⟩
veracidad *nf* : truthfulness, veracity
veranda *nf* : veranda
veraneante *nmf* : summer vacationer
veranear *vi* : to spend the summer
veraniego, -ga *adj* 1 ESTIVAL : summer ⟨el sol veraniego : the summer sun⟩ 2 : summery
verano *nm* : summer
veras *nfpl* **de** ~ : really, truly
veraz *adj, pl* **veraces** : truthful, veracious
verbal *adj* : verbal — **verbalmente** *adv*
verbalizar {21} *vt* : to verbalize, to express
verbena *nf* 1 FIESTA : festival, fair 2 : verbena, vervain
verbigracia *adv* : for example
verbo *nm* : verb
verborrea *nf* : verbiage
verbosidad *nf* : verbosity, wordiness
verboso, -sa *adj* : verbose, wordy
verdad *nf* 1 : truth 2 **de** ~ : really, truly 3 ¿**verdad**? : right?, isn't that so?
verdaderamente *adv* : really, truly
verdadero, -dera *adj* 1 REAL, VERÍDICO : true, real 2 AUTÉNTICO : genuine
verde[1] *adj* 1 : green (in color) 2 : green, unripe 3 : inexperienced, green 4 : dirty, risqué
verde[2] *nm* : green
verdear *vi* : to turn green, to become verdant
verdín *nm, pl* **verdines** : slime, scum
verdor *nm* 1 : greenness 2 : verdure
verdoso, -sa *adj* : greenish
verdugo *nm* 1 : executioner, hangman 2 : tyrant
verdugón *nm, pl* **-gones** : welt, wheal
verdura *nf* : vegetable(s), green(s)
vereda *nf* 1 SENDA : path, trail 2 : sidewalk, pavement
veredicto *nm* : verdict
verga *nf* : spar, yard (of a ship)
vergonzoso, -sa *adj* 1 : disgraceful, shameful 2 : bashful, shy — **vergonzosamente** *adv*
vergüenza *nf* 1 : disgrace, shame 2 : embarrassment 3 : bashfulness, shyness
vericueto *nm* : rough terrain
verídico, -ca *adj* 1 REAL, VERDADERO : true, real 2 VERAZ : truthful
verificación *nf, pl* **-ciones** 1 : verification 2 : testing, checking
verificador, -dora *n* : inspector, tester
verificar {72} *vt* 1 : to verify, to confirm 2 : to test, to check 3 : to carry out, to conduct — **verificarse** *vr* 1 : to take place, to occur 2 : to come true
verja *nf* 1 : rails *pl* (of a fence) 2 : grating, grille 3 : gate
vermut *nm, pl* **vermuts** : vermouth
vernáculo, -la *adj* : vernacular
vernal *adj* : vernal, spring
verosímil *adj* 1 : probable, likely 2 : credible, realistic

verosimilitud *nf* 1 : probability, likeliness 2 : verisimilitude
verraco *nm* : boar
verruga *nf* : wart
versado, -da *adj* ~ **en** : versed in, knowledgeable about
versar *vi* ~ **sobre** : to deal with, to be about
versátil *adj* 1 : versatile 2 : fickle
versatilidad *nf* 1 : versatility 2 : fickleness
versículo *nm* : verse (in the Bible)
versión *nf, pl* **versiones** 1 : version 2 : translation
verso *nm* : verse
versus *prep* : versus, against
vértebra *nf* : vertebra — **vertebral** *adj*
vertebrado[1], **-da** *adj* : vertebrate
vertebrado[2] *nm* : vertebrate
vertedero *nm* 1 : garbage dump 2 DESAGÜE : drain, outlet
verter {56} *vt* 1 : to pour 2 : to spill, to shed 3 : to empty out 4 : to express, to voice 5 : to translate, to render — *vi* : to flow
vertical *adj & nf* : vertical — **verticalmente** *adv*
vértice *nm* : vertex, apex
vertido *nm* : spilling, spill
vertiente *nf* 1 : slope 2 : aspect, side, element
vertiginoso, -sa *adj* : vertiginous — **vertiginosamente** *adv*
vértigo *nm* : vertigo, dizziness
vesícula *nf* 1 : vesicle 2 **vesícula biliar** : gallbladder
vesicular *adj* : vesicular
vestíbulo *nm* : vestibule, hall, lobby, foyer
vestido *nm* 1 : dress, costume, clothes *pl* 2 : dress (garment)
vestidor *nm* : dressing room
vestiduras *nfpl* 1 : clothing, raiment, regalia 2 **or vestiduras sacerdotales** : vestments
vestigio *nm* : vestige, sign, trace
vestimenta *nf* ROPA : clothing, clothes *pl*
vestir {54} *vt* 1 : to dress, to clothe 2 LLEVAR : to wear 3 ADORNAR : to decorate, to dress up — *vi* 1 : to dress ⟨vestir bien : to dress well⟩ 2 : to look good, to suit the occasion — **vestirse** *vr* 1 : to get dressed 2 ~ **de** : to dress up as ⟨se vistieron de soldados : they dressed up as soldiers⟩ 3 ~ **de** : to wear, to dress in
vestuario *nm* 1 : wardrobe 2 : dressing room, locker room
veta *nf* 1 : grain (in wood) 2 : vein, seam, lode 3 : trace, streak ⟨una veta de terco : a stubborn streak⟩
vetar *vt* : to veto
veteado, -da *adj* : streaked, veined
veterano, -na *adj & n* : veteran
veterinaria *nf* : veterinary medicine
veterinario[1], **-ria** *adj* : veterinary
veterinario[2], **-ria** *n* : veterinarian

veto *nm* : veto

vetusto, -ta *adj* ANTIGUO : ancient, very old

vez *nf, pl* **veces 1** : time, occasion ⟨a la vez : at the same time⟩ ⟨a veces : at times, occasionally⟩ ⟨de vez en cuando : from time to time⟩ **2** (*with numbers*) : time ⟨una vez : once⟩ ⟨de una vez : all at once⟩ ⟨de una vez para siempre : once and for all⟩ ⟨dos veces : twice⟩ **3** : turn ⟨a su vez : in turn⟩ ⟨en vez de : instead of⟩ ⟨hacer las veces de : to act as, to stand in for⟩

vía¹ *nf* **1** RUTA, CAMINO : road, route, way ⟨Vía Láctea : Milky Way⟩ **2** MEDIO : means, way ⟨por vía oficial : through official channels⟩ **3** : track, line (of a railroad) **4** : tract, passage ⟨por vía oral : orally⟩ **5 en vías de** : in the process of ⟨en vías de solución : on the road to a solution⟩ **6 por ∼** : by (in transportation) ⟨por vía aérea : by air, airmail⟩

vía² *prep* : via

viable *adj* : viable, feasible — **viabilidad** *nf*

viaducto *nm* : viaduct

viajante *mf* : traveling salesman, traveling saleswoman

viajar *vi* : to travel, to journey

viaje *nm* : trip, journey ⟨viaje de negocios : business trip⟩

viajero¹, -ra *adj* : traveling

viajero², -ra *n* **1** : traveler **2** PASAJERO : passenger

vial *adj* : road, traffic

viático *nm* : travel allowance, travel expenses *pl*

víbora *nf* : viper

vibración *nf, pl* **-ciones** : vibration

vibrador *nm* : vibrator

vibrante *adj* **1** : vibrant **2** : vibrating

vibrar *vi* : to vibrate

vibratorio, -ria *adj* : vibratory

vicario, -ria *n* : vicar

vicealmirante *nmf* : vice admiral

vicepresidente, -ta *n* : vice president — **vicepresidencia** *nf*

viceversa *adv* : vice versa, conversely

viciado, -da *adj* : stuffy, close

viciar *vt* **1** : to corrupt **2** : to invalidate **3** FALSEAR : to distort **4** : to pollute, to adulterate

vicio *nm* **1** : vice, depravity **2** : bad habit **3** : defect, blemish

vicioso, -sa *adj* : depraved, corrupt

vicisitud *nf* : vicissitude

víctima *nf* : victim

victimario, -ria *n* ASESINO : killer, murderer

victimizar {21} *vt Arg, Mex* : to victimize

victoria *nf* : victory — **victorioso, -sa** *adj* — **victoriosamente** *adv*

victoriano, -na *adj* : Victorian

vid *nf* **1** : vine, grapevine

vida *nf* **1** : life ⟨la vida cotidiana : everyday life⟩ **2** : life span, lifetime **3** BIOGRAFÍA : biography, life **4** : way of life, lifestyle **5** : livelihood ⟨ganarse la vida : to earn one's living⟩ **6** VIVEZA : liveliness **7 media vida** : half-life

vidente *nmf* **1** : psychic, clairvoyant **2** : sighted person

video *or* **vídeo** *nm* : video

videocasete *or* **videocassette** *nm* : videocassette

videocasetera *or* **videocassettera** *nf* : videocassette recorder, VCR

videocinta *nf* : videotape

videograbar *vt* : to videotape

vidriado *nm* : glaze

vidriar *vt* : to glaze (pottery, tile, etc.)

vidriera *nf* **1** : stained-glass window **2** : glass door or window **3** : store window

vidriero, -ra *n* : glazier

vidrio *nm* **1** : glass, piece of glass **2** : windowpane

vidrioso, -sa *adj* **1** : brittle, fragile **2** : slippery **3** : glassy, glazed (of eyes) **4** : touchy, delicate

vieira *nf* **1** : scallop **2** : scallop shell

viejo¹, -ja *adj* **1** ANCIANO : old, elderly **2** ANTIGUO : former, longstanding ⟨viejas tradiciones : old traditions⟩ ⟨viejos amigos : old friends⟩ **3** GASTADO : old, worn, worn-out

viejo², -ja *n* ANCIANO : old man *m*, old woman *f*

viene, etc. → **venir**

viento *nm* **1** : wind **2 hacer viento** : to be windy **3 contra viento y marea** : against all odds **4 viento alisio** : trade wind **5 viento en popa** : splendidly, successfully

vientre *nm* **1** : abdomen, belly **2** : womb **3** : bowels *pl*

viernes *nms & pl* : Friday

vierte, etc. → **verter**

vietnamita¹ *adj & nmf* : Vietnamese

vietnamita² *nm* : Vietnamese (language)

viga *nf* **1** : beam, rafter, girder **2 viga voladiza** : cantilever

vigencia *nf* **1** : validity **2** : force, effect ⟨entrar en vigencia : to go into effect⟩

vigente *adj* : valid, in force

vigésimo¹, -ma *adj* : twentieth, twenty- ⟨la vigésima segunda edición : the twenty-second edition⟩

vigésimo², -ma *n* : twentieth, twenty- (in a series)

vigía *nmf* : lookout

vigilancia *nf* : vigilance, watchfulness ⟨bajo vigilancia : under surveillance⟩

vigilante¹ *adj* : vigilant, watchful

vigilante² *nmf* : watchman, guard

vigilar *vt* **1** CUIDAR : to look after, to keep an eye on **2** GUARDAR : to watch over, to guard — *vi* **1** : to be watchful **2** : to keep watch

vigilia *nf* **1** VELA : wakefulness **2** : night work **3** : vigil (in religion)

vigor *nm* **1** : vigor, energy, strength **2** VIGENCIA : force, effect

vigorizante *adj* : invigorating

vigorizar {21} *vt* : to strengthen, to invigorate

vigoroso, -sa *adj* : vigorous — **vigorosamente** *adv*

VIH *nm* (virus de inmunodeficiencia humana) : HIV

vikingo, -ga *adj & n* : Viking

vil *adj* : vile, despicable

vileza *nf* **1** : vileness **2** : despicable action, villainy

vilipendiar *vt* : to vilify, to revile

villa *nf* **1** : town, village **2** :

villancico *nm* : carol, Christmas carol

villano, -na *n* **1** : villain **2** : peasant

vilo *nm* **1 en ~** : in the air **2 en ~** : uncertain, in suspense

vinagre *nm* : vinegar

vinagrera *nf* : cruet (for vinegar)

vinatería *nf* : wine shop

vinculación *nf*, *pl* **-ciones 1** : linking **2** RELACIÓN : bond, link, connection

vincular *vt* CONECTAR, RELACIONAR : to tie, to link, to connect

vínculo *nm* LAZO : tie, link, bond

vindicación *nf*, *pl* **-ciones** : vindication

vindicar *vt* **1** : to vindicate **2** : to avenge

vinilo *nm* : vinyl

vino¹, etc. → **venir**

vino² *nm* : wine

viña *nf* : vineyard

viñedo *nm* : vineyard

vio, etc. → **ver**

viola *nf* : viola

violación *nf*, *pl* **-ciones 1** : violation, offense **2** : rape

violador¹, -dora *n* : violator, offender

violador² *nm* : rapist

violar *vt* **1** : to rape **2** : to violate (a law or right) **3** PROFANAR : to desecrate

violencia *nf* : violence

violentamente *adv* : by force, violently

violentar *vt* **1** FORZAR : to break open, to force **2** : to distort (words or ideas) — **violentarse** *vr* : to force oneself

violento, -ta *adj* **1** : violent **2** EMBARAZOSO, INCÓMODO : awkward, embarassing

violeta¹ *adj & nm* : violet (color)

violeta² *nf* : violet (flower)

violín *nm*, *pl* **-lines** : violin

violinista *nmf* : violinist

violonchelista *nmf* : cellist

violonchelo *nm* : cello, violoncello

VIP *nmf*, *pl* **VIPs** : VIP

vira *nf* : welt (of a shoe)

virago *nf* : virago, shrew

viraje *nm* **1** : turn, swerve **2** : change

viral *adj* : viral

virar *vi* : to tack, to turn, to veer

virgen¹ *adj* : virgin ⟨lana virgen : virgin wool⟩

virgen² *nmf*, *pl* **vírgenes** : virgin ⟨la Santísima Virgen : the Blessed Virgin⟩

virginal *adj* : virginal, chaste

virginidad *nf* : virginity

Virgo *nmf* : Virgo

vírico, -ca *adj* : viral

viril *adj* : virile — **virilidad** *nf*

virrey, -rreina *n* : viceroy *m*, vicereine *f*

virtual *adj* : virtual — **virtualmente** *adv*

virtud *nf* **1** : virtue **2 en virtud de** : by virtue of

virtuosismo *nm* : virtuosity

virtuoso¹, -sa *adj* : virtuous — **virtuosamente** *adv*

virtuoso², -sa *n* : virtuoso

viruela *nf* **1** : smallpox **2** : pockmark

virulencia *nf* : virulence

virulento, -ta *adj* : virulent

virus *nm* : virus

viruta *nf* : shaving

visa *nf* : visa

visado *nm* *Spain* : visa

visaje *nm* : face, grimace ⟨hacer visajes : to make faces⟩

visceral *adj* : visceral

vísceras *nfpl* : viscera, entrails

visconde, -desa *n* : viscount *m*, viscountess *f*

viscosidad *nf* : viscosity

viscoso, -sa *adj* : viscous

visera *nf* : visor

visibilidad *nf* : visibility

visible *adj* : visible — **visiblemente** *adv*

visión *nf*, *pl* **visiones 1** : vision, eyesight **2** : view, perspective **3** : vision, illusion ⟨ver visiones : to be seeing things⟩

visionario, -ria *adj & n* : visionary

visita *nf* **1** : visit, call **2** : visitor **3 ir de visita** : to go visiting

visitador, -dora *n* : visitor, frequent caller

visitante¹ *adj* : visiting

visitante² *nmf* : visitor

visitar *vt* : to visit

vislumbrar *vt* **1** : to discern, to make out **2** : to begin to see, to have an inkling of

vislumbre *nf* : glimmer, gleam

viso *nm* **1** APARIENCIA : appearance ⟨tener visos de : to seem, to show signs of⟩ **2** DESTELLO : glint, gleam **3** : sheen, iridescence

visón *nm*, *pl* **visones** : mink

víspera *nf* **1** : eve, day before **2** **vísperas** *nfpl* : vespers

vista *nf* **1** VISIÓN : vision, eyesight **2** MIRADA : look, gaze, glance **3** PANORAMA : view, vista, panorama **4** : hearing (in court) **5 a primera vista** : at first sight **6 en vista de** : in view of **7 hacer la vista gorda** : to turn a blind eye **8 ¡hasta la vista!** : so long!, see you! **9 perder de vista** : to lose sight of **10 punto de vista** : point of view

vistazo *nm* : glance, look

viste, etc. → **ver¹, vestir**

visto¹ *pp* → **ver**

visto², -ta *adj* **1** : obvious, clear **2** : in view of, considering **3 estar bien visto** : to be approved of **4 estar mal visto** : to be frowned upon **5 por lo visto** : apparently **6 nunca visto** : unheard-of **7 visto que** : since, given that

visto³ *nm* **visto bueno** : approval

vistoso, -sa *adj* : colorful, bright
visual *adj* : visual — **visualmente** *adv*
visualización *nf, pl* **-ciones** : visualization
visualizar {21} *vt* **1** : to visualize **2** : to display (on a screen)
vital *adj* **1** : vital **2** : lively, dynamic
vitalicio, -cia *adj* : life, lifetime
vitalidad *nf* : vitality
vitamina *nf* : vitamin
vitamínico, -ca *adj* : vitamin ⟨complejos vitamínicos : vitamin compounds⟩
vitorear *vt* : to cheer, to acclaim
vitral *nm* : stained-glass window
vítreo, -rea *adj* : vitreous, glassy
vitrina *nf* **1** : showcase, display case **2** : store window
vitriolo *nm* : vitriol
vituperar *vt* : to condemn, to vituperate against
vituperio *nm* : vituperation, censure
viudez *nf* : widowerhood, widowhood
viudo, -da *n* : widower *m*, widow *f*
vivacidad *nf* VIVEZA : vivacity, liveliness
vivamente *adv* **1** : in a lively manner **2** : vividly **3** : strongly, acutely ⟨lo recomendamos vivamente : we strongly recommend it⟩
vivaque *nm* : bivouac
vivaquear *vi* : to bivouac
vivar *vi* : to cheer
vivaz *adj, pl* **vivaces 1** : lively, vivacious **2** : clever, sharp **3** : perennial
víveres *nmpl* : provisions, supplies, food
vivero *nm* **1** : nursery (for plants) **2** : hatchery, fish farm
viveza *nf* **1** VIVACIDAD : liveliness **2** BRILLO : vividness, brightness **3** ASTUCIA : cleverness, sharpness
vívido, -da *adj* : vivid, lively
vividor, -dora *n* : sponger, parasite
vivienda *nf* **1** : housing **2** MORADA : dwelling, home
viviente *adj* : living
vivificar {72} *vt* : to vivify, to give life to
vivir¹ *vi* **1** : to live, to be alive **2** SUBSISTIR : to subsist, to make a living **3** RESIDIR : to reside **4** : to spend one's life ⟨vive para trabajar : she lives to work⟩ **5** ~ **de** : to live on — *vt* **1** : to live ⟨vivir su vida : to live one's life⟩ **2** EXPERIMENTAR : to go through, to experience
vivir² *nm* **1** : life, lifestyle **2 de mal vivir** : disreputable
vivisección *nf, pl* **-ciones** : vivisection
vivo, -va *adj* **1** : alive **2** INTENSO : vivid, bright, intense **3** ANIMADO : lively, vivacious **4** ASTUTO : sharp, clever **5 en** ~ : live ⟨transmisión en vivo : live broadcast⟩ **6 al rojo vivo** : red-hot
vizconde, -desa *n* : viscount *m*, viscountess *f*
vocablo *nm* PALABRA : word
vocabulario *nm* : vocabulary
vocación *nf, pl* **-ciones** : vocation
vocacional *adj* : vocational
vocal¹ *adj* : vocal

vocal² *nmf* : member (of a committee, board, etc.)
vocal³ *nf* : vowel
vocalista *nmf* CANTANTE : singer, vocalist
vocalizar {21} *vi* : to vocalize
vocear *v* : to shout
vocerío *nm* : clamor, shouting
vocero, -ra *n* PORTAVOZ : spokesperson, spokesman *m*, spokeswoman *f*
vociferante *adj* : vociferous
vociferar *vi* GRITAR : to shout, to yell
vodevil *nm* : vaudeville
vodka *nm* : vodka
voladizo¹, -za *adj* : projecting
voladizo² *nm* : projection
volador, -dora *adj* : flying
volando *adv* : quickly, in a hurry
volante¹ *adj* : flying
volante² *nm* **1** : steering wheel **2** FOLLETO : flier, circular **3** : shuttlecock **4** : flywheel **5** : balance wheel (of a watch) **6** : ruffle, flounce
volar {19} *vi* **1** : to fly **2** CORRER : to hurry, to rush ⟨el tiempo vuela : time flies⟩ ⟨pasar volando : to fly past⟩ **3** DIVULGARSE : to spread ⟨unos rumores volaban : rumors were spreading around⟩ **4** DESAPARECER : to disappear ⟨el dinero ya voló : the money's already gone⟩ — *vt* **1** : to blow up, to demolish **2** : to irritate
volátil *adj* : volatile — **volatilidad** *nf*
volatilizar {21} *vt* : to volatilize — **volatilizarse** *vr*
volcán *nm, pl* **volcanes** : volcano
volcánico, -ca *adj* : volcanic
volcar {82} *vt* **1** : to upset, to knock over, to turn over **2** : to empty out **3** : to make dizzy **4** : to cause a change of mind in **5** : to irritate — *vi* : to overturn, to tip over **6** : to capsize — **volcarse** *vr* **1** : to overturn **2** : to do one's utmost
volea *nf* : volley (in sports)
volear *vi* : to volley (in sports)
voleibol *nm* : volleyball
voleo *nm* **al voleo** : haphazardly, at random
volframio *nm* : wolfram, tungsten
volición *nf, pl* **-ciones** : volition
volqué, etc. → **volcar**
voltaje *nm* : voltage
voltear *vt* **1** : to turn over, to turn upside down **2** : to reverse, to turn inside out **3** : to turn ⟨voltear la cara : to turn one's head⟩ **4** : to knock down — *vi* **1** : to roll over, to do somersaults **2** : to turn ⟨volteó a la izquierda : he turned left⟩ — **voltearse** *vr* **1** : to turn around **2** : to change one's allegiance
voltereta *nf* : somersault, tumble
voltio *nm* : volt
volubilidad *nf* : fickleness, changeableness
voluble *adj* : fickle, changeable
volumen *nm, pl* **-lúmenes 1** TOMO : volume, book **2** : capacity, size, bulk **3** CANTIDAD : amount ⟨el volumen de

ventas : the volume of sales⟩ 4 : volume, loudness
voluminoso, -sa *adj* : voluminous, massive, bulky
voluntad *nf* 1 : will, volition 2 DESEO
: desire, wish 3 INTENCIÓN : intention
4 **a voluntad** : at will 5 **buena volun-**
tad : good will 6 **mala voluntad** : ill
will 7 **fuerza de voluntad** : willpower
voluntario¹, -ria *adj* : voluntary — **vol-**
untariamente *adv*
voluntario², -ria *n* : volunteer
voluntarioso, -sa *adj* 1 : stubborn 2
: willing, eager
voluptuosidad *nf* : voluptuousness
voluptuoso, -sa *adj* : voluptuous —
voluptuosamente *adv*
voluta *nf* : spiral, column (of smoke)
volver {89} *vi* 1 : to return, to come or
go back ⟨volver a casa : to return
home⟩ 2 : to revert ⟨volver al tema : to
get back to the subject⟩ 3 **~ a** : to do
again ⟨volvieron a llamar : they called
again⟩ 4 **volver en sí** : to come to, to
regain consciousness — *vt* 1 : to turn,
to turn over, to turn inside out 2 : to
return, to repay, to restore 3 : to cause,
to make ⟨la volvía loca : it was driving
her crazy⟩ — **volverse** *vr* 1 : to become ⟨se volvió deprimido : he became
depressed⟩ 2 : to turn around
vomitar *vi* : to vomit — *vt* 1 : to vomit
2 : to spew out (lava, etc.)
vómito *nm* 1 : vomiting 2 : vomit
voracidad *nf* : voracity
vorágine *nf* : whirlpool, maelstrom
voraz *adj, pl* **voraces** : voracious — **vo-**
razmente *adv*
vórtice *nm* 1 : whirlpool, vortex 2 TOR-
BELLINO : whirlwind
vos *pron* (*in some regions of Latin America*) : you
vosear *vt* : to address as *vos*
vosotros, -tras *pron pl Spain* 1 : you,
yourselves 2 : ye
votación *nf, pl* **-ciones** : vote, voting
votante *nmf* : voter
votar *vi* : to vote — *vt* : to vote for
votivo, -va *adj* : votive
voto *nm* 1 : vote 2 : vow (in religion)
3 **votos** *nmpl* : good wishes
voy → ir
voz *nf, pl* **voces** 1 : voice 2 : opinion,
say 3 GRITO : shout, yell 4 : sound 5
VOCABLO : word, term 6 : rumor 7 **a**

voz en cuello : at the top of one's lungs
8 **dar voces** : to shout 9 **en voz alta**
: aloud, in a loud voice 10 **en voz baja**
: softly, in a low voice
vudú *nm* : voodoo
vuelco *nm* : upset, overturning ⟨me dio
un vuelco el corazón : my heart
skipped a beat⟩
vuela, etc. → volar
vuelca, vuelque etc. → volcar
vuelo *nm* 1 : flight, flying ⟨alzar el vuelo : to take flight⟩ 2 : flight (of an aircraft) ⟨vuelo espacial : space flight⟩ 3
: flare, fullness (of clothing) 4 **al vue-**
lo : on the wing
vuelta *nf* 1 GIRO : turn ⟨se dio la vuelta
: he turned around⟩ 2 REVOLUCIÓN
: circle, revolution ⟨dio la vuelta al
mundo : she went around the world⟩
⟨las ruedas daban vueltas : the wheels
were spinning⟩ 3 : flip, turn ⟨le dio la
vuelta : she flipped it over⟩ 4 : bend,
curve ⟨a la vuelta de la esquina
: around the corner⟩ 5 REGRESO : return ⟨de ida y vuelta : round trip⟩ ⟨a
vuelta de correo : return mail⟩ 6
: round, lap (in sports or games) 7
PASEO : walk, drive, ride ⟨dio una
vuelta : he went for a walk⟩ 8 DORSO,
REVÉS : back, other side ⟨a la vuelta
: on the back⟩ 9 : cuff (of pants) 10
darle vueltas : to think over 11 **estar**
de vuelta : to be back
vuelto *pp* → **volver**
vuelve, etc. → volver
vuestro¹, -stra *adj Spain* : your, of yours
⟨vuestros coches : your cars⟩ ⟨una
amiga vuestra : a friend of yours⟩
vuestro², -stra *pron Spain*, (*with definite
article*) : yours ⟨la vuestra es más
grande : yours is bigger⟩ ⟨esos son los
vuestros : those are yours⟩
vulcanizar {21} *vt* : to vulcanize
vulgar *adj* 1 : common 2 : vulgar
vulgaridad *nf* : vulgarity
vulgarismo *nm* : vulgarism
vulgarizar {21} *vt* : to vulgarize, to popularize
vulgarmente *adv* : vulgarly, popularly
vulgo *nm* **el vulgo** : the masses, common people
vulnerable *adj* : vulnerable — **vulnera-**
bilidad *nf*
vulnerar *vt* 1 : to injure, to damage
(one's reputation or honor) 2 : to violate, to break (a law or contract)

W

w *nf* : twenty-fourth letter of the Spanish alphabet
wafle *nm* : waffle
waflera *nf* : waffle iron

wapití *nm* : wapiti, elk
whisky *nm, pl* **whiskys** *or* **whiskies**
: whiskey
wigwam *nm* : wigwam

X

x *nf* : twenty-fifth letter of the Spanish alphabet
xenofobia *nf* : xenophobia
xenófobo¹, -ba *adj* : xenophobic

xenófobo², -ba *n* : xenophobe
xenón *nm* : xenon
xerocopiar *vt* : to photocopy, to xerox
xilófono *nm* : xylophone

Y

y¹ *nf* : twenty-sixth letter of the Spanish alphabet
y² *conj* (**e** *before words beginning with i- or hi-*) **1** : and ⟨mi hermano y yo : my brother and I⟩ ⟨¿y los demás? : and (what about) the others?⟩ **2** (*used in numbers*) ⟨cincuenta y cinco : fifty-five⟩ **3** *fam* : well ⟨y por supuesto : well, of course⟩
ya *adv* **1** : already ⟨ya terminó : she's finished already⟩ **2** : now, right now ⟨hazlo ya! : do it now!⟩ ⟨ya mismo : right away⟩ **3** : later, soon ⟨ya iremos : we'll go later on⟩ **4** : no longer, anymore ⟨ya no fuma : he no longer smokes⟩ **5** (*used for emphasis*) ⟨¡ya lo sé! : I know!⟩ ⟨ya lo creo : of course⟩ **6 no ya** : not only ⟨no ya lloran sino gritan : they're not only crying but screaming⟩ **7 ya que** : now that, since ⟨ya que sabe la verdad : now that she knows the truth⟩
ya² *conj* **ya . . . ya** : whether . . . or, first . . . then ⟨ya le gusta, ya no : first he likes it, then he doesn't⟩
yac *nm* : yak
yacer {90} *vi* : to lie ⟨en esta tumba yacen sus abuelos : his grandparents lie in this grave⟩
yacimiento *nm* : bed, deposit ⟨yacimiento petrolífero : oil field⟩
yaga, etc. → yacer
yanqui *adj & nmf* : Yankee
yarda *nf* : yard
yate *nm* : yacht
yaz, yazca, yazga etc. → yacer
yedra *nf* : ivy
yegua *nf* : mare
yelmo *nm* : helmet
yema *nf* **1** : bud, shoot **2** : yolk (of an egg) **3 yema del dedo** : fingertip
yemenita *adj & nmf* : Yemenite
yen *nm* : yen (currency)
yendo → ir

yerba *nf* **1** *or* **yerba mate** : maté **2 →** hierba
yerga, yergue etc. → erguir
yermo¹, -ma *adj* : barren, deserted
yermo² *nm* : wasteland
yerno *nm* : son-in-law
yerra, etc. → errar
yerro *nm* : blunder, mistake
yerto, -ta *adj* : rigid, stiff
yesca *nf* : tinder
yeso *nm* **1** : plaster **2** : gypsum
yo¹ *nm* : ego, self
yo² *pron* **1** : I **2** : me ⟨todos menos yo : everyone except me⟩ ⟨tan bajo como yo : as short as me⟩ **3 soy yo** : it is I, it's me
yodado, -da *adj* : iodized
yodo *nm* : iodine
yoduro *nm* : iodide
yoga *nm* : yoga
yogui *nm* : yogi
yogurt *or* **yogur** *nm* : yogurt
yola *nf* : yawl
yoyo *or* **yoyó** *nm* : yo-yo
yuca *nf* **1** : yucca (plant) **2** : cassava, manioc
yucateco¹, -ca *adj* : of or from the Yucatán
yucateco², -ca *n* : person from the Yucatán
yudo → judo
yugo *nm* : yoke
yugoslavo, -va *adj & n* : Yugoslavian
yugular *adj* : jugular ⟨vena yugular : jugular vein⟩
yungas *nfpl Bol, Chile, Peru* : warm tropical valleys
yunque *nm* : anvil
yunta *nf* : yoke, team (of oxen)
yuppy *nmf, pl* **yuppies** : yuppie
yute *nm* : jute
yuxtaponer {60} *vt* : to juxtapose — **yuxtaposición** *nf*

Z

z *nf* : twenty-seventh letter of the Spanish alphabet
zacate *nm CA, Mex* **1** : grass, forage **2** : hay
zafacón *nm, pl* **-cones** *Car* : wastebasket
zafar *vt* : to loosen, to untie — **zafarse**

vr **1** : to loosen up, to come undone **2** : to get free of
zafio, -fia *adj* : coarse, crude
zafiro *nm* : sapphire
zaga *nf* **1** : defense (in sports) **2 a la zaga** *or* **en** ~ : behind, in the rear
zaguán *nm* : paddle (of a canoe)

zaguán *nm, pl* **zaguanes** : front hall, vestibule
zaherir {76} *vt* **1** : to criticize sharply **2** : to wound, to mortify
zahones *nmpl* : chaps
zaino, -na *adj* : chestnut (color)
zalamería *nf* : flattery, sweet talk
zalamero¹, -ra *adj* : flattering, fawning
zalamero², -ra *n* : flatterer
zambiano, -na *adj & nmf* : Zambian
zambullida *nf* : dive, plunge
zambullirse {38} *vr* : to dive, to plunge
zanahoria *nf* : carrot
zancada *nf* : stride, step
zancadilla *nf* **1** : trip, stumble **2** *fam* : trick, ruse
zancos *nmpl* : stilts
zancuda *nf* : wading bird
zancudo *nm* MOSQUITO : mosquito
zángano *nm* : drone, male bee
zanja *nf* : ditch, trench
zanjar *vt* ACLARAR : to settle, to clear up, to resolve
zapallo *nm* *Arg, Chile, Peru, Uru* : pumpkin
zapapico *nm* : pickax
zapata *nf* : brake shoe
zapatería *nf* **1** : shoemaker's, shoe factory **2** : shoe store
zapatero¹, -ra *adj* : dry, tough, poorly cooked
zapatero², -ra *n* : shoemaker, cobbler
zapatilla *nf* **1** PANTUFLA : slipper **2** *or* **zapatilla de deporte** : sneaker
zapato *nm* : shoe
zar, zarina *n* : czar *m*, czarina *f*
zarandear *vt* **1** : to sift, to sieve **2** : to shake, to jostle, to jiggle
zarapito *nm* : curlew
zarcillo *nm* **1** : earring **2** : tendril (of a plant)
zarigüeya *nf* : opossum
zarista *adj & nmf* : czarist
zarpa *nf* : paw
zarpar *vi* : to set sail, to raise anchor
zarza *nf* : bramble, blackberry bush
zarzamora *nf* **1** : blackberry **2** : bramble, blackberry bush

zarzaparrilla *nf* : sarsaparilla
zepelín *nm, pl* **-lines** : zeppelin
zigoto *nm* : zygote
zigzag *nm, pl* **zigzags** *or* **zigzagues** : zigzag
zigzaguear *vi* : to zigzag
zimbabuense *adj & nmf* : Zimbabwean
zinc *nm* : zinc
zinnia *nf* : zinnia
zíper *nm* *CA, Mex* : zipper
zircón *nm, pl* **zircones** : zircon
zócalo *nm* *Mex* : main square
zodíaco *or* **zodiaco** *nm* : zodiac — **zodíacal** *adj*
zombi *or* **zombie** *nmf* : zombie
zona *nf* : zone, district, area
zonzo¹, -za *adj* : stupid, silly
zonzo², -za *n* : idiot, nitwit
zoo *nm* : zoo
zoología *nf* : zoology
zoológico¹, -ca *adj* : zoological
zoológico² *nm* : zoo
zoólogo, -ga *n* : zoologist
zoom *nm* : zoom lens
zopilote *nm* *CA, Mex* : buzzard
zoquete *nmf* *fam* : oaf, blockhead
zorrillo *nm* MOFETA : skunk
zorro¹, -rra *adj* : sly, crafty
zorro², -rra *n* **1** : fox, vixen **2** : sly crafty person
zorzal *nm* : thrush
zozobra *nf* : anxiety, worry
zozobrar *vi* : to capsize
zueco *nm* : clog (shoe)
zulú¹ *adj & nmf* : Zulu
zulú² *nm* : Zulu (language)
zumaque *nm* : sumac
zumbar *vi* : to buzz, to hum — *vt* *fam* **1** : to hit, to thrash **2** : to make fun of
zumbido *nm* : buzzing, humming
zumo *nm* JUGO : juice
zurcir {83} *vt* : to darn, to mend
zurdo¹, -da *adj* : left-handed
zurdo², -da *n* : left-handed person
zurza, etc. → **zurcir**
zutano, -na → **fulano**

English–Spanish Dictionary

A

a¹ ['eɪ] *n, pl* **a's** *or* **as** ['eɪz] : primera letra del alfabeto inglés

a² [ə, 'eɪ] *art* (**an** /ən, 'æn/ before vowel or silent *h*) **1** : un *m*, una *f* ⟨a house : una casa⟩ ⟨half an hour : media hora⟩ ⟨what a surprise! : ¡qué sorpresa!⟩ **2** PER : por, a la, al ⟨30 kilometers an hour : 30 kilómetros por hora⟩ ⟨twice a month : dos veces al mes⟩

aardvark ['ɑrd,vɑrk] *n* : oso *m* hormiguero

aback [ə'bæk] *adv* **1** : por sorpresa **2 to be taken aback** : quedarse desconcertado

abacus ['æbəkəs] *n, pl* **abaci** ['æbə,saɪ, -,kiː] *or* **abacuses** : ábaco *m*

abaft [ə'bæft] *adv* : a popa

abalone [,æbə'loːni] *n* : abulón *m*, oreja *f* marina

abandon¹ [ə'bændən] *vt* **1** DESERT, FORSAKE : abandonar, desamparar (a alguien), desertar de (algo) **2** GIVE UP, SUSPEND : renunciar a, suspender ⟨he abandoned the search : suspendió la búsqueda⟩ **3** EVACUATE, LEAVE : abandonar, evacuar, dejar ⟨to abandon ship : abandonar el buque⟩ **4 to abandon oneself** : entregarse, abandonarse

abandon² *n* : desenfreno *m* ⟨with wild abandon : desenfrenadamente⟩

abandoned [ə'bændənd] *adj* **1** DESERTED : abandonado **2** UNRESTRAINED : desenfrenado, desinhibido

abandonment [ə'bændənmənt] *n* : abandono *m*, desamparo *m*

abase [ə'beɪs] *vt* **abased; abasing** : degradar, humillar, rebajar

abash [ə'bæʃ] *vt* : avergonzar, abochornar

abashed [ə'bæʃt] *adj* : avergonzado

abate [ə'beɪt] *vi* **abated; abating** : amainar, menguar, disminuir

abattoir ['æbə,twɑr] *n* : matadero *m*

abbess ['æbəs, -,bɛs, -bəs] *n* : abadesa *f*

abbey ['æbi] *n, pl* **-beys** : abadía *f*

abbot ['æbət] *n* : abad *m*

abbreviate [ə'briːvi,eɪt] *vt* **-ated; -ating** : abreviar

abbreviation [ə,briːvi'eɪʃən] *n* : abreviación *f*, abreviatura *f*

ABC's [,eɪ,biː'siːz] *npl* : abecé *m*

abdicate ['æbdɪ,keɪt] *v* **-cated; -cating** : abdicar

abdication [,æbdɪ'keɪʃən] *n* : abdicación *f*

abdomen ['æbdəmən, æb'doːmən] *n* : abdomen *m*, vientre *m*

abdominal [æb'dɑmənəl] *adj* : abdominal — **abdominally** *adv*

abduct [æb'dʌkt] *vt* : raptar, secuestrar

abduction [æb'dʌkʃən] *n* : rapto *m*, secuestro *m*

abductor [æb'dʌktər] *n* : raptor *m*, -tora *f*; secuestrador *m*, -dora *f*

abed [ə'bɛd] *adv & adj* : en cama

aberrant [æ'bɛrənt, 'æbərənt] *adj* **1** ABNORMAL : anormal, aberrante **2** ATYPICAL : anómalo, atípico

aberration [,æbə'reɪʃən] *n* **1** : aberración *f* **2** DERANGEMENT : perturbación *f* mental

abet [ə'bɛt] *vt* **abetted; abetting** ASSIST : ayudar ⟨to aid and abet : ser cómplice de⟩

abeyance [ə'beɪənts] *n* : desuso *m*, suspensión *f*

abhor [əb'hɔr, æb-] *vt* **-horred; -horring** : abominar, aborrecer

abhorrence [əb'hɔrənts, æb-] *n* : aborrecimiento *m*, odio *m*

abhorrent [əb'hɔrənt, æb-] *adj* : abominable, aborrecible, odioso

abide [ə'baɪd] *v* **abode** [ə'boːd] *or* **abided; abiding** *vt* STAND : soportar, tolerar ⟨I can't abide them : no los puedo ver⟩ — *vi* **1** ENDURE : quedar, permanecer **2** DWELL : morar, residir **3 to abide by** : atenerse a

ability [ə'bɪləti] *n, pl* **-ties 1** CAPABILITY : aptitud *f*, capacidad *f*, facultad *f* **2** COMPETENCE : competencia *f* **3** TALENT : talento *m*, don *m*, habilidad *f*

abject ['æb,dʒɛkt, æb'-] *adj* **1** WRETCHED : miserable, desdichado **2** HOPELESS : abatido, desesperado **3** SERVILE : servil ⟨abject flattery : halagos serviles⟩ — **abjectly** *adv*

abjure [æb'dʒʊr] *vt* **-jured; -juring** : abjurar de

ablaze [ə'bleɪz] *adj* **1** BURNING : ardiendo, en llamas **2** RADIANT : resplandeciente, radiante

able ['eɪbəl] *adj* **abler; ablest 1** CAPABLE : capaz, hábil **2** COMPETENT : competente

ablution [ə'bluːʃən] *n* : ablución *f* ⟨to perform one's ablutions : lavarse⟩

ably ['eɪbəli] *adv* : hábilmente, eficientemente

abnormal [æb'nɔrməl] *adj* : anormal — **abnormally** *adv*

abnormality [,æbnɔr'mæləti, -nɔr-] *n, pl* **-ties** : anormalidad *f*

aboard¹ [ə'bord] *adv* : a bordo

aboard² *prep* : a bordo de

abode¹ → **abide**

abode² [ə'boːd] *n* : morada *f*, residencia *f*, vivienda *f*

abolish [ə'bɑlɪʃ] *vt* : abolir, suprimir

abolition [,æbə'lɪʃən] *n* : abolición *f*, supresión *f*

abominable [ə'bɑmənəbəl] *adj* DETESTABLE : abominable, aborrecible, espantoso

abominate [ə'bɑmə,neɪt] *vt* **-nated; -nating** : abominar, aborrecer

abomination [ə,bɑmə'neɪʃən] *n* : abominación *f*

aboriginal [,æbə'rɪdʒənəl] *adj* : aborigen, indígena

aborigine [,æbə'rɪdʒəni] *n* NATIVE : aborigen *mf*, indígena *mf*

abort [ə'bɔrt] vt 1 : abortar (en medicina) 2 CALL OFF : suspender, abandonar — vi : abortar, hacerse un aborto

abortion [ə'bɔrʃən] n : aborto m

abortive [ə'bɔrtɪv] adj UNSUCCESSFUL : fracasado, frustrado, malogrado

abound [ə'baʊnd] vi to abound in : abundar en, estar lleno de

about[1] [ə'baʊt] adv 1 APPROXIMATELY : aproximadamente, casi, más o menos 2 AROUND : por todas partes, alrededor ⟨the children are running about : los niños están corriendo por todas partes⟩ 3 to be about to : estar a punto de 4 to be up and about : estar levantado

about[2] prep 1 AROUND : alrededor de 2 CONCERNING : de, acerca de, sobre ⟨he always talks about politics : siempre habla de política⟩

above[1] [ə'bʌv] adv 1 OVERHEAD : por encima, arriba 2 : más arriba ⟨as stated above : como se indica más arriba⟩

above[2] adj : anterior, antedicho ⟨for the above reasons : por las razones antedichas⟩

above[3] prep 1 OVER : encima de, arriba de, sobre 2 : superior a, por encima de ⟨he's above those things : él está por encima de esas cosas⟩ 3 : más de, superior a ⟨he earns above $50,000 : gana más de $50,000⟩ ⟨a number above 10 : un número superior a 10⟩ 4 above all : sobre todo

aboveboard[1] [ə'bʌv₁bord, -₁bord] adv open and aboveboard : sin tapujos

aboveboard[2] adj : legítimo, sincero

abrade [ə'breɪd] vt abraded; abrading 1 ERODE : erosionar, corroer 2 SCRAPE : escoriar, raspar

abrasion [ə'breɪʒən] n 1 SCRAPE, SCRATCH : raspadura f, rasguño m 2 EROSION : erosión f

abrasive[1] [ə'breɪsɪv] adj 1 ROUGH : abrasivo, áspero 2 BRUSQUE, IRRITATING : brusco, irritante

abrasive[2] n : abrasivo m

abreast [ə'brɛst] adv 1 : en fondo, al lado ⟨to march three abreast : marchar de tres en fondo⟩ 2 to keep abreast : mantenerse al día

abridge [ə'brɪʤ] vt abridged; abridging : compendiar, resumir

abridgment or **abridgement** [ə'brɪʤmənt] n : compendio m, resumen m

abroad [ə'brɔd] adv 1 ABOUT, WIDELY : por todas partes, en todas direcciones ⟨the news spread abroad : la noticia corrió por todas partes⟩ 2 OVERSEAS : en el extranjero, en el exterior

abrogate ['æbrə₁geɪt] vt -gated; -gating : abrogar

abrupt [ə'brʌpt] adj 1 SUDDEN : abrupto, repentino, súbito 2 BRUSQUE, CURT : brusco, cortante — **abruptly** adv

abscess ['æb₁sɛs] n : absceso m

abscond [æb'skand] vi : huir, fugarse

absence ['æbsənts] n 1 : ausencia f (de una persona) 2 LACK : falta f, carencia f

absent[1] [æb'sɛnt] vt to absent oneself : ausentarse

absent[2] ['æbsənt] adj : ausente

absentee [₁æbsən'tiː] n : ausente mf

absentminded [₁æbsənt'maɪndəd] adj : distraído, despistado

absentmindedly [₁æbsənt'maɪndədli] adv : distraídamente

absentmindedness [₁æbsənt'maɪndədnəs] n : distracción f, despiste m

absolute ['æbsə₁luːt, ₁æbsə'luːt] adj 1 COMPLETE, PERFECT : completo, pleno, perfecto 2 UNCONDITIONAL : absoluto, incondicional 3 DEFINITE : categórico, definitivo

absolutely ['æbsə₁luːtli, ₁æbsə'luːtli] adv 1 COMPLETELY : completamente, absolutamente 2 CERTAINLY : desde luego ⟨do you agree? absolutely! : ¿estás de acuerdo? ¡desde luego!⟩

absolution [₁æbsə'luːʃən] n : absolución f

absolutism ['æbsə₁luː₁tɪzəm] n : absolutismo m

absolve [əb'zalv, æb-, -'salv] vt -solved; -solving : absolver, perdonar

absorb [əb'zɔrb, æb-, -'sɔrb] vt 1 : absorber, embeber (un líquido), amortiguar (un golpe, la luz) 2 ENGROSS : absorber 3 ASSIMILATE : asimilar

absorbed [əb'zɔrbd, æb-, -'sɔrbd] adj ENGROSSED : absorto, ensimismado

absorbency [əb'zɔrbəntsi, æb-, -'sɔr-] n : absorbencia f

absorbent [əb'zɔrbənt, æb-, -'sɔr-] adj : absorbente

absorbing [əb'zɔrbɪŋ, æb-, -'sɔr-] adj : absorbente, fascinante

absorption [əb'zɔrpʃən, æb-, -'sɔrp-] n 1 : absorción f 2 CONCENTRATION : concentración f

abstain [əb'steɪn, æb-] vi : abstenerse

abstainer [əb'steɪnər, æb-] n : abstemio m, -mia f

abstemious [æb'stiːmiəs] adj : abstemio, sobrio — **abstemiously** adv

abstention [əb'stɛntʃən, æb-] n : abstención f

abstinence ['æbstənənts] n : abstinencia f

abstract[1] [æb'strækt, 'æb₁-] vt 1 EXTRACT : abstraer, extraer 2 SUMMARIZE : compendiar, resumir

abstract[2] adj : abstracto — **abstractly** [æb'stræktli, 'æb₁-] adv

abstract[3] ['æb₁strækt] n : resumen m, compendio m, sumario m

abstraction [æb'strækʃən] n 1 : abstracción f, idea f abstracta 2 ABSENTMINDEDNESS : distracción f

abstruse [əb'struːs, æb-] adj : abstruso, recóndito — **abstrusely** adv

absurd [əb'sərd, -'zərd] adj : absurdo, ridículo, disparatado — **absurdly** adv

absurdity [əb'sərdəti, -'zər-] *n*, *pl* **-ties 1**
: absurdo *m* **2** NONSENSE : disparate
m, despropósito *m*

abundance [ə'bʌndənts] *n* : abundancia
f

abundant [ə'bʌndənt] *adj* : abundante,
cuantioso, copioso

abundantly [ə'bʌndəntli] *adv* : abundantemente, en abundancia

abuse¹ [ə'bju:z] *vt* **abused; abusing 1**
MISUSE : abusar de **2** MISTREAT : maltratar **3** REVILE : insultar, injuriar,
denostar

abuse² [ə'bju:s] *n* **1** MISUSE : abuso *m*
2 MISTREATMENT : abuso *m*, maltrato
m **3** INSULTS : insultos *mpl*, impro-
perios *mpl* ⟨a string of abuse : una serie
de improperios⟩

abuser [ə'bju:zər] *n* : abusador *m*, -dora
f

abusive [ə'bju:sɪv] *adj* **1** ABUSING : abusivo **2** INSULTING : ofensivo, injurioso,
insultante — **abusively** *adv*

abut [ə'bʌt] *v* **abutted; abutting** *vt* : bordear — *vi* **to abut on** : colindar con

abutment [ə'bʌtmənt] *n* **1** BUTTRESS
: contrafuerte *m*, estribo *m* **2** CLOSE-
NESS : contigüidad *f*

abysmal [ə'bɪzməl] *adj* **1** DEEP : abismal, insondable **2** TERRIBLE : atroz,
desastroso

abysmally [ə'bɪzməli] *adv* : desastrosa-
mente, terriblemente

abyss [ə'bɪs, 'æbɪs] *n* : abismo *m*, sima
f

acacia [ə'keɪʃə] *n* : acacia *f*

academic¹ [ˌækə'dɛmɪk] *adj* **1** : académico **2** THEORETICAL : teórico —
academically [-mɪkli] *adv*

academic² *n* : académico *m*, -ca *f*

academician [ˌækədə'mɪʃən] *n* → **academic**

academy [ə'kædəmi] *n*, *pl* **-mies** : academia *f*

acanthus [ə'kænθəs] *n* : acanto *m*

accede [æk'si:d] *vi* **-ceded; -ceding 1**
AGREE : acceder, consentir **2** ASCEND
: subir, ascender ⟨he acceded to the
throne : subió al trono⟩

accelerate [ɪk'sɛləˌreɪt, æk-] *v* **-ated;
-ating** *vt* : acelerar, apresurar — *vi*
: acelerar (dícese de un carro)

acceleration [ɪkˌsɛləˈreɪʃən, æk-] *n*
: aceleración *f*

accelerator [ɪk'sɛləˌreɪtər, æk-] *n* : acelerador *m*

accent¹ ['ækˌsɛnt, æk'sɛnt] *vt* : acentuar

accent² ['ækˌsɛnt, -sənt] *n* **1** : acento *m*
2 EMPHASIS, STRESS : énfasis *m*, acento *m*

accentuate [ɪk'sɛntʃuˌeɪt, æk-] *vt* **-ated;
-ating** : acentuar, poner énfasis en

accept [ɪk'sɛpt, æk-] *vt* **1** : aceptar **2** AC-
KNOWLEDGE : admitir, reconocer

acceptability [ɪkˌsɛptə'bɪləti, æk-] *n*
: aceptabilidad *f*

acceptable [ɪk'sɛptəbəl, æk-] *adj*
: aceptable, admisible — **acceptably**
[-bli] *adv*

acceptance [ɪk'sɛptənts, æk-] *n* : aceptación *f*, aprobación *f*

access¹ ['ækˌsɛs] *vt* : obtener acceso a,
entrar a

access² *n* : acceso *m*

accessibility [ɪkˌsɛsə'bɪləti] *n*, *pl* **-ties**
: accesibilidad *f*

accessible [ɪk'sɛsəbəl, æk-] *adj* : accesible, asequible

accession [ɪk'sɛʃən, æk-] *n* **1** : ascenso
f, subida *f* (al trono, etc.) **2** ACQUISI-
TION : adquisición *f*

accessory¹ [ɪk'sɛsəri, æk-] *adj* : auxiliar

accessory² *n*, *pl* **-ries 1** : accesorio *m*,
complemento *m* **2** ACCOMPLICE : cómplice *mf*

accident ['æksədənt] *n* **1** MISHAP : accidente *m* **2** CHANCE : casualidad *f*

accidental [ˌæksə'dɛntəl] *adj* : accidental, casual, imprevisto, fortuito

accidentally [ˌæksə'dɛntəli, -'dɛntli] *adv*
1 BY CHANCE : por casualidad **2** UN-
INTENTIONALLY : sin querer, involuntariamente

acclaim¹ [ə'kleɪm] *vt* : aclamar, elogiar

acclaim² *n* : aclamación *f*, elogio *m*

acclamation [ˌæklə'meɪʃən] *n* : aclamación *f*

acclimate ['æklə,meɪt, ə'klaɪmət] → **acclimatize**

acclimatize [ə'klaɪmə,taɪz] *v* **-tized;
-tizing** *vt* **1** : aclimatar **2 to acclimatize oneself** : aclimatarse

accolade ['ækə,leɪd, -,lɑd] *n* **1** PRAISE
: elogio *m* **2** AWARD : galardón *m*

accommodate [ə'kɑmə,deɪt] *vt* **-dated;
-dating 1** ADAPT : acomodar, adaptar
2 SATISFY : tener en cuenta, satisfacer
3 HOLD : dar cabida a, tener cabida
para

accommodation [əˌkɑmə'deɪʃən] *n* **1**
: adaptación *f*, adecuación *f* **2 accommodations** *npl* LODGING : alojamiento *m*, hospedaje *m*

accompaniment [ə'kʌmpənəmənt,
-'kʌm-] *n* : acompañamiento *m*

accompanist [ə'kʌmpənɪst, -'kʌm-] *n*
: acompañante *mf*

accompany [ə'kʌmpəni, -'kʌm-] *vt*
-nied; -nying : acompañar

accomplice [ə'kɑmpləs, -'kʌm-] *n* : cómplice *mf*

accomplish [ə'kɑmplɪʃ, -'kʌm-] *vt* : efectuar, realizar, lograr, llevar a cabo

accomplished [ə'kɑmplɪʃt, -'kʌm-] *adj*
: consumado, logrado

accomplishment [ə'kɑmplɪʃmənt,
-'kʌm-] *n* **1** ACHIEVEMENT : logro *m*,
éxito *m* **2** SKILL : destreza *f*, habilidad
f

accord¹ [ə'kɔrd] *vt* **1** GRANT : conceder,
otorgar — *vi* **to accord with** : concordar con, conformarse con

accord² *n* **1** AGREEMENT : acuerdo *m*,
convenio *m* **2** VOLITION : voluntad *f*

⟨on one's own accord : voluntaria-
mente, de motu proprio⟩

accordance [əˈkɔrdənts] n 1 ACCORD
: acuerdo m, conformidad f 2 **in accordance with** : conforme a, según, de
acuerdo con

accordingly [əˈkɔrdɪŋli] adv 1 CORRE-
SPONDINGLY : en consecuencia 2
CONSEQUENTLY : por consiguiente,
por lo tanto

according to [əˈkɔrdɪŋ] prep : según, de
acuerdo con, conforme a

accordion [əˈkɔrdiən] n : acordeón m

accordionist [əˈkɔrdiənɪst] n : acordeonista mf

accost [əˈkɔst] vt : abordar, dirigirse a

account¹ [əˈkaʊnt] vt : considerar, estimar ⟨he accounts himself lucky : se
considera afortunado⟩ — vi to **account for** : dar cuenta de, explicar

account² n 1 : cuenta f ⟨savings account
: cuenta de ahorros⟩ 2 EXPLANATION
: versión f, explicación f 3 REPORT : relato m, informe m 4 IMPORTANCE : importancia f ⟨to be of no account : no
tener importancia⟩ 5 **on account of**
BECAUSE OF : a causa de, debido a, por
6 **on no account** : de ninguna manera

accountability [əˌkaʊntəˈbɪləti] n : responsabilidad f

accountable [əˈkaʊntəbəl] adj : responsable

accountant [əˈkaʊntənt] n : contador m,
-dora f; contable mf Spain

accounting [əˈkaʊntɪŋ] n : contabilidad
f

accoutrements or **accouterments** [ə-
ˈkuːtrəmənts, -ˈkuːtər-] npl 1 EQUIP-
MENT : equipo m, avíos mpl 2 ACCES-
SORIES : accesorios mpl 3 TRAPPINGS
: símbolos mpl ⟨the accoutrements of
power : los símbolos del poder⟩

accredit [əˈkrɛdət] vt : acreditar, autorizar

accreditation [əˌkrɛdəˈteɪʃən] n : acreditación f, homologación f

accretion [əˈkriːʃən] n 1 : acrecentamiento m (proceso) 2 : acreción f,
acrecencia f (producto)

accrual [əˈkruːəl] n : incremento m, acumulación f

accrue [əˈkruː] vi -**crued**; -**cruing** : acumularse, aumentarse

accumulate [əˈkjuːmjəˌleɪt] v -**lated**;
-**lating** vt : acumular, amontonar — vi
: acumularse, amontonarse

accumulation [əˌkjuːmjəˈleɪʃən] n : acumulación f, amontonamiento m

accuracy [ˈækjərəsi] n : exactitud f, precisión f

accurate [ˈækjərət] adj : exacto, correcto, fiel, preciso — **accurately** adv

accusation [ˌækjəˈzeɪʃən] n : acusación
f

accusatory [əˈkjuːzəˌtori] adj : acusatorio

accuse [əˈkjuːz] vt -**cused**; -**cusing**
: acusar, delatar, denunciar

accused [əˈkjuːzd] ns & pl DEFENDANT
: acusado m, -da f

accuser [əˈkjuːzər] n : acusador m, -dora
f

accustom [əˈkʌstəm] vt : acostumbrar,
habituar

ace [ˈeɪs] n : as m

acerbic [əˈsərbɪk, æ-] adj : acerbo, mordaz

acetate [ˈæsəˌteɪt] n : acetato m

acetic [əˈsiːtɪk] adj : acético

acetone [ˈæsəˌtoːn] n : acetona f

acetylene [əˈsɛtəˌliːn, -ˌtəˌliːn] n : acetileno m

ache¹ [ˈeɪk] vi **ached**; **aching** 1 : doler
2 **to ache for** : anhelar, ansiar

ache² n : dolor m

achieve [əˈtʃiːv] vt **achieved**; **achieving**
: lograr, alcanzar, conseguir, realizar

achievement [əˈtʃiːvmənt] n : logro m,
éxito m, realización f

acid¹ [ˈæsəd] adj 1 SOUR : ácido, agrio
2 CAUSTIC, SHARP : acerbo, mordaz —
acidly adv

acid² n : ácido m

acidic [əˈsɪdɪk, æ-] adj : ácido

acidity [əˈsɪdəti, æ-] n, pl -**ties** : acidez f

acknowledge [ɪkˈnɑlɪʤ, æk-] vt -**edged**;
-**edging** 1 ADMIT : reconocer, admitir
2 RECOGNIZE : reconocer 3 **to acknowledge receipt of** : acusar recibo
de

acknowledgment [ɪkˈnɑlɪʤmənt, æk-] n
1 RECOGNITION : reconocimiento m 2
THANKS : agradecimiento m

acme [ˈækmi] n : colmo m, apogeo m,
cúspide f

acne [ˈækni] n : acné m

acolyte [ˈækəˌlaɪt] n : acólito m

acorn [ˈeɪˌkɔrn, -kərn] n : bellota f

acoustic [əˈkuːstɪk] or **acoustical**
[-stɪkəl] adj : acústico — **acoustically**
adv

acoustics [əˈkuːstɪks] ns & pl : acústica
f

acquaint [əˈkweɪnt] vt 1 INFORM : enterar, informar 2 FAMILIARIZE : familiarizar 3 **to be acquainted with**
: conocer a (una persona), estar al tanto de (un hecho)

acquaintance [əˈkweɪntənts] n 1
KNOWLEDGE : conocimiento m 2
: conocido m, -da f ⟨friends and ac-
quaintances : amigos y conocidos⟩

acquiesce [ˌækwiˈɛs] vi -**esced**; -**escing**
: consentir, conformarse

acquiescence [ˌækwiˈɛsənts] n : consentimiento m, aquiescencia f

acquire [əˈkwaɪr] vt -**quired**; -**quiring**
: adquirir, obtener

acquisition [ˌækwəˈzɪʃən] n : adquisición f

acquisitive [əˈkwɪzətɪv] adj : adquisitivo, codicioso

acquit [əˈkwɪt] vt -**quitted**; -**quitting** 1
: absolver, exculpar 2 **to acquit oneself** : comportarse, defenderse

acquittal [əˈkwɪtəl] n : absolución f, exculpación f

acre ['eɪkər] n : acre m

acreage ['eɪkərɪʤ] n : superficie f en acres

acrid ['ækrəd] adj 1 BITTER : acre 2 CAUSTIC : acre, mordaz — **acridly** adv

acrimonious [ˌækrə'moːniəs] adj : áspero, cáustico, sarcástico

acrimony ['ækrəˌmoːni] n, pl -nies : acrimonia f

acrobat ['ækrəˌbæt] n : acróbata mf, saltimbanqui m

acrobatic [ˌækrə'bætɪk] adj : acrobático

acrobatics [ˌækrə'bætɪks] ns & pl : acrobacia f

acronym ['ækrəˌnɪm] n : acrónimo m

across[1] [ə'krɔs] adv 1 CROSSWISE : al través 2 : a través, del otro lado ⟨he's already across : ya está del otro lado⟩ 3 : de ancho ⟨40 feet across : 40 pies de ancho⟩

across[2] prep 1 : al otro lado de ⟨across the street : al otro lado de la calle⟩ 2 : a través de ⟨a log across the road : un tronco a través del camino⟩

acrylic [ə'krɪlɪk] n : acrílico m

act[1] ['ækt] vi 1 PERFORM : actuar, interpretar 2 FEIGN, PRETEND : fingir, simular 3 BEHAVE : comportarse 4 FUNCTION : actuar, servir, funcionar 5 : tomar medidas ⟨he acted to save the business : tomó medidas para salvar el negocio⟩ 6 to act as : servir de, hacer

act[2] n 1 DEED : acto m, hecho m, acción f 2 DECREE : ley f, decreto m 3 : acto m (en una obra de teatro), número m (en un espectáculo) 4 PRETENSE : fingimiento m

action ['ækʃən] n 1 DEED : acción f, acto m, hecho m 2 BEHAVIOR : actuación f, comportamiento m 3 LAWSUIT : demanda f 4 MOVEMENT : movimiento m 5 COMBAT : combate m 6 PLOT : acción f, trama f 7 MECHANISM : mecanismo m

activate ['æktəˌveɪt] vt -vated; -vating : activar

activation [ˌæktə'veɪʃən] n : activación f

active ['æktɪv] adj 1 MOVING : activo, en movimiento 2 LIVELY : vigoroso, enérgico 3 : en actividad ⟨an active volcano : un volcán en actividad⟩ 4 OPERATIVE : vigente

actively ['æktɪvli] adv : activamente, enérgicamente

activist ['æktɪvɪst] n : activista mf — **activist** adj

activity [æk'tɪvəti] n, pl -ties 1 MOVEMENT : actividad f, movimiento m 2 VIGOR : vigor m, energía f 3 OCCUPATION : actividad f, ocupación f

actor ['æktər] n : actor m, artista mf

actress ['æktrəs] n : actriz f

actual ['æktʃuəl] adj : real, verdadero

actuality [ˌæktʃu'æləti] n, pl -ties : realidad f

actually ['æktʃuəli, -ʃəli] adv : realmente, en realidad

actuary ['æktʃuˌeri] n, pl -aries : actuario m, -ria f de seguros

acumen [ə'kjuːmən] n : perspicacia f

acupuncture ['ækjuˌpʌŋktʃər] n : acupuntura f

acute [ə'kjuːt] adj acuter; acutest 1 SHARP : agudo 2 PERCEPTIVE : perspicaz, sagaz 3 KEEN : fino, muy desarrollado, agudo ⟨an acute sense of smell : un fino olfato⟩ 4 SEVERE : grave 5 acute angle : ángulo m agudo

acutely [ə'kjuːtli] adv : intensamente ⟨to be acutely aware : estar perfectamente consciente⟩

acuteness [ə'kjuːtnəs] n : agudeza f

ad ['æd] → advertisement

adage ['ædɪʤ] n : adagio m, refrán m, dicho m

adamant ['ædəmənt, -ˌmænt] adj : firme, categórico, inflexible — **adamantly** adv

Adam's apple ['ædəmz] n : nuez f de Adán

adapt [ə'dæpt] vt : adaptar, ajustar — vi : adaptarse

adaptability [əˌdæptə'bɪləti] n : adaptabilidad f, flexibilidad f

adaptable [ə'dæptəbəl] adj : adaptable, amoldable

adaptation [ˌæˌdæp'teɪʃən, -dəp-] n 1 : adaptación f, modificación f 2 VERSION : versión f

adapter [ə'dæptər] n : adaptador m

add ['æd] vt 1 : añadir, agregar ⟨to add a comment : añadir una observación⟩ 2 : sumar ⟨add these numbers : suma estos números⟩ — vi : sumar (en total)

adder ['ædər] n : víbora f

addict[1] [ə'dɪkt] vt : causar adicción en

addict[2] ['ædɪkt] n 1 : adicto m, -ta f 2 **drug addict** : drogadicto m, -ta f; toxicómano m, -na f

addiction [ə'dɪkʃən] n 1 : adicción f, dependencia f 2 **drug addiction** : drogadicción f

addictive [ə'dɪktɪv] adj : adictivo

addition [ə'dɪʃən] n 1 : adición f, añadidura f 2 **in ~** : además, también

additional [ə'dɪʃənəl] adj : extra, adicional, de más

additionally [ə'dɪʃənəli] adv : además, adicionalmente

additive ['ædətɪv] n : aditivo m

addle ['ædəl] vt -dled; -dling : confundir, enturbiar

address[1] [ə'drɛs] vt 1 : dirigirse a, pronunciar un discurso ante ⟨to address a jury : dirigirse a un jurado⟩ 2 : dirigir, ponerle la dirección a ⟨to address a letter : dirigir una carta⟩

address[2] ['ædrɛs, ˌæˌdrɛs] n 1 SPEECH : discurso m, alocución f 2 : dirección f (de una residencia, etc.)

addressee [ˌæˌdrɛ'siː, ə-] n : destinatario m, -ria f

adduce [ə-'du:s, 'dju:s] *vt* **-duced; -ducing** : aducir

adenoids ['æd,nɔɪd, -dən,ɔɪd] *npl* : adenoides *fpl*

adept [ə'dɛpt] *adj* : experto, hábil — **adeptly** *adv*

adequacy ['ædɪkwəsi] *n, pl* **-cies** : cantidad *f* suficiente

adequate ['ædɪkwət] *adj* **1** SUFFICIENT : adecuado, suficiente **2** ACCEPTABLE, PASSABLE : adecuado, aceptable

adequately ['ædɪkwətli] *adv* : suficientemente, apropiadamente

adhere [æd'hɪr, əd-] *vi* **-hered; -hering 1** STICK : pegarse, adherirse **2 to adhere to** : adherirse a (una política, etc.), cumplir con (una promesa)

adherence [æd'hɪrənts, əd-] *n* : adhesión *f*, adherencia *f*, observancia *f* (de una ley, etc.)

adherent¹ [æd'hɪrənt, əd-] *adj* : adherente, adhesivo, pegajoso

adherent² *n* : adepto *m*, -ta *f*; partidario *m*, -ria *f*

adhesion [æd'hi:ʒən, əd-] *n* : adhesión *f*

adhesive¹ [æd'hi:sɪv, əd-, -zɪv] *adj* : adhesivo

adhesive² *n* : adhesivo *m*, pegamento *m*

adjacent [ə'dʒeɪsənt] *adj* : adyacente, colindante, contiguo

adjective ['ædʒɪktɪv] *n* : adjetivo *m* — **adjectival** [,ædʒɪk'taɪvəl] *adj*

adjoin [ə'dʒɔɪn] *vt* : lindar con, colindar con

adjoining [ə'dʒɔɪnɪŋ] *adj* : contiguo, colindante

adjourn [ə'dʒərn] *vt* : levantar, suspender ⟨the meeting is adjourned : se levanta la sesión⟩ — *vi* : aplazarse

adjournment [ə'dʒərnmənt] *n* : suspensión *f*, aplazamiento *m*

adjudicate [ə'dʒu:dɪ,keɪt] *vt* **-cated; -cating** : juzgar, arbitrar

adjudication [ə,dʒu:dɪ'keɪʃən] *n* **1** JUDGING : arbitrio *m* (judicial) **2** JUDGMENT : fallo *m*

adjunct ['æ,dʒʌŋkt] *n* : adjunto *m*, complemento *m*

adjust [ə'dʒʌst] *vt* : ajustar, arreglar, regular — *vi* **to adjust to** : adaptarse a

adjustable [ə'dʒʌstəbəl] *adj* : ajustable, regulable, graduable

adjustment [ə'dʒʌstmənt] *n* : ajuste *m*, modificación *f*

ad-lib¹ ['æd'lɪb] *v* **-libbed; -libbing** : improvisar

ad-lib² *adj* : improvisado

administer [æd'mɪnəstər, əd-] *vt* : administrar

administration [æd,mɪnə'streɪʃən, əd-] *n* **1** MANAGING : administración *f*, dirección *f* **2** GOVERNMENT, MANAGEMENT : administración *f*, gobierno *m*

administrative [æd'mɪnə,streɪtɪv, əd-] *adj* : administrativo — **administratively** *adv*

administrator [æd'mɪnə,streɪtər, əd-] *n* : administrador *m*, -dora *f*

admirable ['ædmərəbəl] *adj* : admirable, loable — **admirably** *adv*

admiral ['ædmərəl] *n* : almirante *mf*

admiration [,ædmə'reɪʃən] *n* : admiración *f*

admire [æd'maɪr] *vt* **-mired; -miring** : admirar

admirer [æd'maɪrər] *n* : admirador *m*, -dora *f*

admiring [æd'maɪrɪŋ] *adj* : admirativo, de admiración

admiringly [æd'maɪrɪŋli] *adv* : con admiración

admissible [æd'mɪsəbəl] *adj* : admisible, aceptable

admission [æd'mɪʃən] *n* **1** ADMITTANCE : entrada *f*, admisión *f* **2** ACKNOWLEDGMENT : reconocimiento *m*, admisión *f*

admit [æd'mɪt, əd-] *vt* **-mitted; -mitting 1** : admitir, dejar entrar ⟨the museum admits children : el museo deja entrar a los niños⟩ **2** ACKNOWLEDGE : reconocer, admitir

admittance [æd'mɪtənts, əd-] *n* : admisión *f*, entrada *f*, acceso *m*

admittedly [æd'mɪtədli, əd-] *adv* : la verdad es que, lo cierto es que ⟨admittedly we went too fast : la verdad es que fuimos demasiado de prisa⟩

admonish [æd'mɑnɪʃ, əd-] *vt* : amonestar, reprender

admonition [,ædmə'nɪʃən] *n* : admonición *f*

ado [ə'du:] *n* **1** FUSS : ruido *m*, alboroto *m* **2** TROUBLE : dificultad *f*, lío *m* **3 without further ado** : sin más preámbulos

adobe [ə'do:bi] *n* : adobe *m*

adolescence [,ædəl'ɛsənts] *n* : adolescencia *f*

adolescent¹ [,ædəl'ɛsənt] *adj* : adolescente, de adolescencia

adolescent² *n* : adolescente *mf*

adopt [ə'dɑpt] *vt* : adoptar

adoption [ə'dɑpʃən] *n* : adopción *f*

adoptive [ə'dɑptɪv] *adj* : adoptivo

adorable [ə'dorəbəl] *adj* : adorable, encantador

adorably [ə'dorəbli] *adv* : de manera adorable

adoration [,ædə'reɪʃən] *n* : adoración *f*

adore [ə'dor] *vt* **adored; adoring 1** WORSHIP : adorar **2** LOVE : querer, adorar **3** LIKE : encantarle (algo a uno), gustarle mucho (algo a uno) ⟨I adore your new dress : me encanta tu vestido nuevo⟩

adorn [ə'dorn] *vt* : adornar, ornar, engalanar

adornment [ə'dornmənt] *n* : adorno *m*, decoración *f*

adrenaline [ə'drɛnələn] *n* : adrenalina *f*

adrift [ə'drɪft] *adj & adv* : a la deriva

adroit [ə'drɔɪt] *adj* : diestro, hábil — **adroitly** *adv*

adroitness [ə'drɔɪtnəs] *n* : destreza *f*, habilidad *f*

adult[1] [ə'dʌlt, 'æ,dʌlt] *adj* : adulto
adult[2] *n* : adulto *m*, -ta *f*
adulterate [ə'dʌltə,reɪt] *vt* -ated; -ating : adulterar
adulterous [ə'dʌltərəs] *adj* : adúltero
adultery [ə'dʌltəri] *n, pl* -teries : adulterio *m*
adulthood[ə'dʌlt,hʊd] *n* : adultez *f*, edad *f* adulta
advance[1] [æd'vænts, əd-] *v* -vanced; -vancing *vt* 1 : avanzar, adelantar ⟨to advance troops : avanzar las tropas⟩ 2 PROMOTE : ascender, promover 3 PROPOSE : proponer, presentar 4 : adelantar, anticipar ⟨they advanced me next month's salary : me adelantaron el sueldo del próximo mes⟩ — *vi* 1 PROCEED : avanzar, adelantarse 2 PROGRESS : progresar
advance[2] *adj* : anticipado ⟨advance notice : previo aviso⟩
advance[3] *n* 1 PROGRESSION : avance *m* 2 PROGRESS : adelanto *m*, mejora *f*, progreso *m* 3 RISE : aumento *m*, alza *f* 4 LOAN : anticipo *m*, préstamo *m* 5 in ~ : por adelantado
advanced [æd'væntst, əd-] *adj* 1 DEVELOPED : avanzado, desarrollado 2 PRECOCIOUS : adelantado, precoz 3 HIGHER : superior
advancement [æd'væntsmənt, əd-] *n* 1 FURTHERANCE : fomento *m*, adelantamiento *m*, progreso *m* 2 PROMOTION : ascenso *m*
advantage [əd'væntɪdʒ, æd-] *n* 1 SUPERIORITY : ventaja *f*, superioridad *f* 2 GAIN : provecho *m*, partido *m* 3 to take advantage of : aprovecharse de
advantageous [,æd,væn'teɪdʒəs, -vən-] *adj* : ventajoso, provechoso — **advantageously** *adv*
advent ['æd,vɛnt] *n* 1 **Advent** : Adviento *m* 2 ARRIVAL : advenimiento *m*, venida *f*
adventure [æd'vɛntʃər, əd-] *n* : aventura *f*
adventurer [æd'vɛntʃərər, əd-] *n* : aventurero *m*, -ra *f*
adventurous [æd'vɛntʃərəs, əd-] *adj* : intrépido, aventurero ⟨an adventurous traveler : un viajero intrépido⟩ 2 RISKY : arriesgado, aventurado
adverb ['æd,vərb] *n* : adverbio *m* — **adverbial** [æd'vərbiəl] *adj*
adversary ['ædvər,sɛri] *n, pl* -saries : adversario *m*, -ria *f*
adverse [æd'vərs, 'æd,] *adj* 1 OPPOSING : opuesto, contrario 2 UNFAVORABLE : adverso, desfavorable — **adversely** *adv*
adversity [æd'vərsəti, əd-] *n, pl* -ties : adversidad *f*
advertise ['ædvər,taɪz] *v* -tised; -tising *vt* : anunciar, hacerle publicidad a — *vi* : hacer publicidad, hacer propaganda
advertisement ['ædvər,taɪzmənt; æd 'vərtəzmənt] *n* : anuncio *m*

advertiser ['ædvər,taɪzər] *n* : anunciante *mf*
advertising ['ædvər,taɪzɪŋ] *n* : publicidad *f*, propaganda *f*
advice [æd'vaɪs] *n* : consejo *m*, recomendación *f* ⟨take my advice : sigue mis consejos⟩
advisability [æd,vaɪzə'bɪləti, əd-] *n* : conveniencia *f*
advisable [æd'vaɪzəbəl, əd-] *adj* : aconsejable, recomendable, conveniente
advise [æd'vaɪz, əd-] *v* -vised; -vising *vt* 1 COUNSEL : aconsejar, asesorar 2 RECOMMEND : recomendar 3 INFORM : informar, notificar — *vi* : dar consejo
adviser *or* **advisor** [æd'vaɪzər, əd-] *n* : consejero *m*, -ra *f*; asesor *m*, -sora *f*
advisory [æd'vaɪzəri, əd-] *adj* 1 : consultivo 2 in an advisory capacity : como asesor
advocacy ['ædvəkəsi] *n* : promoción *f*, apoyo *m*
advocate[1] ['ædvə,keɪt] *vt* -cated; -cating : recomendar, abogar por, ser partidario de
advocate[2] ['ædvəkət] *n* : defensor *m*, -sora *f*; partidario *m*, -ria *f*
adze ['ædz] *n* : azuela *f*
aeon ['i:ən, 'i:,ɑn] *n* : eón *m*, siglo *m*, eternidad *f*
aerate ['ær,eɪt] *vt* -ated; -ating : gasear (un líquido), oxigenar (la sangre)
aerial[1] ['æriəl] *adj* : aéreo
aerial[2] *n* : antena *f*
aerie ['æri, 'ɪri, 'ɛiəri] *n* : aguilera *f*
aerobic [,ær'o:bɪk] *adj* : aerobio, aeróbico ⟨aerobic exercises : ejercicios aeróbicos⟩
aerobics [,ær'o:bɪks] *ns & pl* : aeróbic *m*
aerodynamic [,ærो:daɪ'næmɪk] *adj* : aerodinámico — **aerodynamically** [-mɪkli] *adv*
aerodynamics [,ærो:daɪ'næmɪks] *n* : aerodinámica *f*
aeronautical [,ærə'nɔtɪkəl] *adj* : aeronáutico
aeronautics [,ærə'nɔtɪks] *n* : aeronáutica *f*
aerosol ['ærə,sɔl] *n* : aerosol *m*
aerospace[1] ['ærो,speɪs] *adj* : aeroespacial
aerospace[2] *n* : espacio *m*
aesthetic [ɛs'θɛtɪk] *adj* : estético — **aesthetically** [-tɪkli] *adv*
aesthetics [ɛs'θɛtɪks] *n* : estética *f*
afar [ə'fɑr] *adv* : lejos, a lo lejos
affability [,æfə'bɪləti] *n* : afabilidad *f*
affable ['æfəbəl] *adj* : afable — **affably** *adv*
affair [ə'fær] *n* 1 MATTER : asunto *m*, cuestión *f*, caso *m* 2 EVENT : ocasión *f*, acontecimiento *m* 3 LIAISON : amorío *m*, aventura *f* 4 business affairs : negocios *mpl* 5 current affairs : actualidades *fpl*
affect [ə'fɛkt, æ-] *vt* 1 INFLUENCE, TOUCH : afectar, tocar 2 FEIGN : fingir

affectation [ˌæˌfɛkˈteɪʃən] n : afectación f

affected [əˈfɛktəd, æ-] adj **1** FEIGNED : afectado, fingido **2** MOVED : conmovido

affecting [əˈfɛktɪŋ, æ-] adj : conmovedor

affection [əˈfɛkʃən] n : afecto m, cariño m

affectionate [əˈfɛkʃənət] adj : afectuoso, cariñoso — **affectionately** adv

affidavit [ˌæfəˈdeɪvət, ˈæfə-] n : declaración f jurada, affidávit m

affiliate[1] [əˈfɪliˌeɪt] v -ated; -ating vt : afiliar, asociar ⟨to be affiliated with : estar afiliado a⟩

affiliate[2] [əˈfɪliət] n : afiliado m, -da f (persona), filial f (organización)

affiliation [ə,fɪliˈeɪʃən] n : afiliación f, filiación f

affinity [əˈfɪnəti] n, pl -ties : afinidad f

affirm [əˈfərm] vt : afirmar, aseverar, declarar

affirmation [ˌæfərˈmeɪʃən] n : afirmación f, aserto m, declaración f

affirmative[1] [əˈfərmətɪv] adj : afirmativo ⟨affirmative action : acción afirmativa⟩

affirmative[2] n **1** : afirmativa f **2 to answer in the affirmative** : responder afirmativamente, dar una respuesta afirmativa

affix [əˈfɪks] vt : fijar, poner, pegar

afflict [əˈflɪkt] vt **1** : afligir, aquejar **2 to be afflicted with** : padecer de, sufrir de

affliction [əˈflɪkʃən] n **1** TRIBULATION : aflicción f, tribulación f **2** AILMENT : enfermedad f, padecimiento m

affluence [ˈæˌfluːənts; æˈfluː-, ə-] n : afluencia f, abundancia f, prosperidad f

affluent [ˈæˌfluːənt; æˈfluː-, ə-] adj : próspero, adinerado

afford [əˈford] vt **1** : tener los recursos para, permitirse el lujo de ⟨I can afford it : puedo permitírmelo, tengo con que comprarlo⟩ **2** PROVIDE : ofrecer, proporcionar, dar

affront[1] [əˈfrʌnt] vt : afrentar, insultar, ofender

affront[2] n : afrenta f, insulto m, ofensa f

Afghan [ˈæf,gæn, -gən] n : afgano m, -na f — **Afghan** adj

afire [əˈfaɪr] adj : ardiendo, en llamas

aflame [əˈfleɪm] adj : llameante, en llamas

afloat [əˈfloːt] adv & adj : a flote

afoot [əˈfʊt] adj **1** WALKING : a pie, andando **2** UNDER WAY : en marcha ⟨something suspicious is afoot : algo sospechoso se está tramando⟩

aforementioned [əˈforˈmenˌtʃənd] adj : antedicho, susodicho

aforesaid [əˈforˌsɛd] adj : antes mencionado, antedicho

afraid [əˈfreɪd] adj **1 to be afraid** : tener miedo **2 to be afraid that** : temerse que ⟨I'm afraid not : me temo que no⟩

afresh [əˈfrɛʃ] adv **1** : de nuevo, otra vez **2 to start afresh** : volver a empezar

African [ˈæfrɪkən] n : africano m, -na f — **African** adj

Afro–American[1] [ˌæfroˈmɛrɪkən] adj : afroamericano m, -na f

Afro–American[2] n : afroamericano

aft [ˈæft] adv : a popa

after[1] [ˈæftər] adv **1** AFTERWARD : después **2** BEHIND : detrás, atrás

after[2] adj : posterior, siguiente ⟨in after years : en los años posteriores⟩

after[3] conj : después de, después de que ⟨after we ate : después de que comimos, después de comer⟩

after[4] prep **1** FOLLOWING : después de, tras ⟨after Saturday : después del sábado⟩ ⟨day after day : día tras día⟩ **2** BEHIND : tras de, después de ⟨I ran after the dog : corrí tras del perro⟩ **3** CONCERNING : por ⟨they asked after you : preguntaron por ti⟩ **4 after all** : después de todo

aftereffect [ˈæftərɪˌfɛkt] n : efecto m secundario

afterlife [ˈæftərˌlaɪf] n : vida f venidera, vida f después de la muerte

aftermath [ˈæftərˌmæθ] n : consecuencias fpl, resultados mpl

afternoon [ˌæftərˈnuːn] n : tarde f

aftertaste [ˈæftərˌteɪst] n : resabio m, regusto m

afterthought [ˈæftərˌθɔt] n : ocurrencia f tardía, idea f tardía

afterward [ˈæftərwərd] or **afterwards** [-wərdz] adv : después, luego ⟨soon afterward : poco después⟩

again [əˈgɛn, -ˈgɪn] adv **1** ANEW, OVER : de nuevo, otra vez **2** BESIDES : además **3 then again** : por otra parte ⟨I may stay, then again I may not : puede ser que me quede, por otra parte, puede que no⟩

against [əˈgɛnst, -ˈgɪnst] prep **1** TOUCHING : contra ⟨against the wall : contra la pared⟩ **2** OPPOSING : contra, en contra de ⟨I will vote against the proposal : votaré en contra de la propuesta⟩ ⟨against the grain : a contrapelo⟩

agape [əˈgeɪp] adj : boquiabierto

agate [ˈægət] n : ágata f

age[1] [ˈeɪdʒ] vi **aged**; **aging** : envejecer, madurar

age[2] n **1** : edad f ⟨ten years of age : diez años de edad⟩ ⟨to be of age : ser mayor de edad⟩ **2** PERIOD : era f, siglo m, época f **3 old age** : vejez f **4 ages** npl : siglos mpl, eternidad f

aged adj **1** [ˈeɪdʒəd, ˈeɪdʒd] OLD : anciano, viejo, vetusto **2** [ˈeɪdʒd] (indicating a specified age) ⟨a girl aged 10 : una niña de 10 años de edad⟩

ageless [ˈeɪdʒləs] adj **1** YOUTHFUL : eternamente joven **2** TIMELESS : eterno, perenne

agency [ˈeɪdʒəntsi] n, pl -cies **1** : agencia f, oficina f ⟨travel agency : agencia de viajes⟩ **2 through the agency of :** a través de, por medio de

agenda [ə'ʤɛndə] *n* : agenda *f*, orden *m* del día

agent ['eɪʤənt] *n* **1** MEANS : agente *m*, medio *m*, instrumento *m* **2** REPRESENTATIVE : agente *mf*, representante *mf*

aggravate ['ægrə,veɪt] *vt* -**vated**; -**vating 1** WORSEN : agravar, empeorar **2** ANNOY : irritar, exasperar

aggravation [,ægrə'veɪʃən] *n* **1** WORSENING : empeoramiento *m* **2** ANNOYANCE : molestia *f*, irritación *f*, exasperación *f*

aggregate[1] ['ægrɪ,geɪt] *vt* -**gated**; -**gating** : juntar, sumar

aggregate[2] ['ægrɪgət] *adj* : total, global, conjunto

aggregate[3] ['ægrɪgət] *n* **1** CONGLOMERATE : agregado *m*, conglomerado *m* **2** WHOLE : total *m*, conjunto *m*

aggression [ə'grɛʃən] *n* **1** ATTACK : agresión *f* **2** AGGRESSIVENESS : agresividad *f*

aggressive [ə'grɛsɪv] *adj* : agresivo — **aggressively** *adv*

aggressiveness [ə'grɛsɪvnəs] *n* : agresividad *f*

aggressor [ə'grɛsər] *n* : agresor *m*, -sora *f*

aggrieved [ə'gri:vd] *adj* : ofendido, herido

aghast [ə'gæst] *adj* : espantado, aterrado, horrorizado

agile ['æʤəl] *adj* : ágil

agility [ə'ʤɪləti] *n, pl* -**ties** : agilidad *f*

agitate ['æʤə,teɪt] *v* -**tated**; -**tating** *vt* **1** SHAKE : agitar **2** UPSET : inquietar, perturbar — *vi* **to agitate against :** hacer campaña en contra de

agitation [,æʤə'teɪʃən] *n* : agitación *f*, inquietud *f*

agitator ['æʤə,teɪtər] *n* : agitador *m*, -dora *f*

agnostic [æg'nɑstɪk] *n* : agnóstico *m*, -ca *f*

ago [ə'go:] *adv* : hace ⟨two years ago : hace dos años⟩ ⟨long ago : hace tiempo, hace mucho tiempo⟩

agog [ə'gɑg] *adj* : ansioso, curioso

agonize ['ægə,naɪz] *vi* -**nized**; -**nizing** : tormentarse, angustiarse

agonizing ['ægə,naɪzɪŋ] *adj* : angustioso, terrible — **agonizingly** [-zɪŋli] *adv*

agony ['ægəni] *n, pl* -**nies 1** PAIN : dolor *m* **2** ANGUISH : angustia *f*

agrarian [ə'grɛriən] *adj* : agrario

agree [ə'gri:] *v* -**greed**; -**greeing** *vt* ACKNOWLEDGE : estar de acuerdo ⟨he agreed that I was right : estuvo de acuerdo en que tenía razón⟩ — *vi* **1** CONCUR : estar de acuerdo **2** CONSENT : ponerse de acuerdo **3** TALLY : concordar **4 to agree with :** sentarle bien (a alguien) ⟨this climate agrees with me : este clima me sienta bien⟩

agreeable [ə'gri:əbəl] *adj* **1** PLEASING : agradable, simpático **2** WILLING : dispuesto **3** AGREEING : de acuerdo, conforme

agreeably [ə'gri:əbli] *adv* : agradablemente

agreement [ə'gri:mənt] *n* **1** : acuerdo *m*, conformidad *f* ⟨in agreement with : de acuerdo con⟩ **2** CONTRACT, PACT : acuerdo *m*, pacto *m*, convenio *m* **3** CONCORD, HARMONY : concordia *f*

agriculture ['ægrɪ,kʌltʃər] *n* : agricultura *f* — **agricultural** [,ægrɪ'kʌltʃərəl] *adj*

aground [ə'graʊnd] *adj* : encallado, varado

ahead [ə'hɛd] *adv* **1** : al frente, delante, adelante ⟨he walked ahead : caminó delante⟩ **2** BEFOREHAND : con antelación, con antelación **3** LEADING : a la delantera **4 to get ahead :** adelantar, progresar

ahead of *prep* **1** : al frente de, delante de, antes de **2 to get ahead of :** adelantarse a

ahoy [ə'hɔɪ] *interj* **ship ahoy! :** ¡barco a la vista!

aid[1] ['eɪd] *vt* : ayudar, auxiliar

aid[2] *n* **1** HELP : ayuda *f*, asistencia *f* **2** ASSISTANT : asistente *mf*

aide ['eɪd] *n* : ayudante *mf*

AIDS ['eɪdz] *n* : SIDA *m*, sida *m*

ail ['eɪl] *vt* : molestar, afligir — *vi* : sufrir, estar enfermo

aileron ['eɪlə,rɑn] *n* : alerón *m*

ailment ['eɪlmənt] *n* : enfermedad *f*, dolencia *f*, achaque *m*

aim[1] ['eɪm] *vt* **1** : apuntar (un arma), dirigir (una observación) **2** INTEND : proponerse, querer ⟨he aims to do it tonight : se propone hacerlo esta noche⟩ — *vi* **1** POINT : apuntar **2 to aim at :** aspirar a

aim[2] *n* **1** MARKSMANSHIP : puntería *f* **2** GOAL : propósito *m*, objetivo *m*, fin *m*

aimless ['eɪmləs] *adj* : sin rumbo, sin objeto

aimlessly ['eɪmləsli] *adv* : sin rumbo, sin objeto

air[1] ['ær] *vt* **1** : airear, ventilar ⟨to air out a mattress : airear un colchón⟩ **2** EXPRESS : airear, manifestar, comunicar **3** BROADCAST : transmitir, emitir

air[2] *n* **1** : aire *m* **2** MELODY : aire *m* **3** APPEARANCE : aire *m*, aspecto *m* **4 airs** *npl* : aires *mpl*, afectación *f* **5 by ~** : por avión (dícese de una carta), en avión (dícese de una persona) **6 to be on the air :** estar en el aire, estar emitiendo

airborne ['ær,bɔrn] *adj* **1** : aerotransportado ⟨airborne troops : tropas aerotransportadas⟩ **2** FLYING : volando, en el aire

air-condition [,ærkən'dɪʃən] *vt* : climatizar, condicionar con el aire

air conditioner [,ærkən'dɪʃənər] *n* : acondicionador *m* de aire

air–conditioning [ˌærkənˈdɪʃənɪŋ] *n* : aire *m* acondicionado

aircraft [ˈærˌkræft] *ns & pl* **1** : avión *m*, aeronave *f* **2 aircraft carrier** : portaaviones *m*

airfield [ˈærˌfiːld] *n* : aeródromo *m*, campo *m* de aviación

air force *n* : fuerza *f* aérea

airlift [ˈærˌlɪft] *n* : puente *m* aéreo, transporte *m* aéreo

airline [ˈærˌlaɪn] *n* : aerolínea *f*, línea *f* aérea

airliner [ˈærˌlaɪnər] *n* : avión *m* de pasajeros

airmail¹ [ˈærˌmeɪl] *vt* : enviar por vía aérea

airmail² *n* : correo *m* aéreo

airman [ˈærmən] *n*, *pl* **-men** [-mən, -ˌmɛn] **1** AVIATOR : aviador *m*, -dora *f* **2** : soldado *m* de la fuerza aérea

airplane [ˈærˌpleɪn] *n* : avión *m*

airport [ˈærˌport] *n* : aeropuerto *m*

airship [ˈærˌʃɪp] *n* : dirigible *m*, zepelín *m*

airstrip [ˈærˌstrɪp] *n* : pista *f* de aterrizaje

airtight [ˈærˈtaɪt] *adj* : hermético, herméticamente cerrado

airwaves [ˈærˌweɪvz] *npl* : radio *m*, televisión *f*

airy [ˈæri] *adj* **airier** [-iər]; **-est** **1** DELICATE, LIGHT : delicado, ligero **2** BREEZY : aireado, bien ventilado

aisle [ˈaɪl] *n* : pasillo *m*, nave *f* lateral (de una iglesia)

ajar [əˈdʒɑr] *adj* : entreabierto, entornado

akimbo [əˈkɪmbo] *adj & adv* : en jarras

akin [əˈkɪn] *adj* **1** RELATED : emparentado **2** SIMILAR : semejante, parecido

alabaster [ˈæləˌbæstər] *n* : alabastro *m*

alacrity [əˈlækrəti] *n* : presteza *f*, prontitud *f*

alarm¹ [əˈlɑrm] *vt* **1** WARN : alarmar, alertar **2** FRIGHTEN : asustar

alarm² *n* **1** WARNING : alarma *f*, alerta *f* **2** APPREHENSION, FEAR : aprensión *f*, inquietud *f*, temor *m* **3 alarm clock** : despertador *m*

alarming [əˈlɑrmɪŋ] *adj* : alarmante

alas [əˈlæs] *interj* : ¡ay!

Albanian [ælˈbeɪniən] *n* : albanés *m*, -nesa *f* — **Albanian** *adj*

albatross [ˈælbəˌtrɔs] *n*, *pl* **-tross** or **-trosses** : albatros *m*

albeit [ɔlˈbiːət, æl-] *conj* : aunque

albino [ælˈbaɪno] *n*, *pl* **-nos** : albino *m*, -na *f*

album [ˈælbəm] *n* : álbum *m*

albumen [ælˈbjuːmən] *n* **1** : clara *f* de huevo **2** → **albumin**

albumin [ælˈbjuːmən] *n* : albúmina *f*

alchemist [ˈælkəmɪst] *n* : alquimista *mf*

alchemy [ˈælkəmi] *n*, *pl* **-mies** : alquimia *f*

alcohol [ˈælkəˌhɔl] *n* **1** ETHANOL : alcohol *m*, etanol *m* **2** LIQUOR : alcohol *m*, bebidas *fpl* alcohólicas

alcoholic¹ [ˌælkəˈhɔlɪk] *adj* : alcohólico

alcoholic² *n* : alcohólico *m*, -ca *f*

alcoholism [ˈælkəhəˌlɪzəm] *n* : alcoholismo *m*

alcove [ˈælˌkoːv] *n* : nicho *m*, hueco *m*

alderman [ˈɔldərmən] *n*, *pl* **-men** [-mən, -ˌmɛn] : concejal *mf*

ale [ˈeɪl] *n* : cerveza *f*

alert¹ [əˈlərt] *vt* : alertar, poner sobre aviso

alert² *adj* **1** WATCHFUL : alerta, vigilante **2** QUICK : listo, vivo

alert³ *n* : alerta *f*, alarma *f*

alertly [əˈlərtli] *adv* : con listeza

alertness [əˈlərtnəs] *n* **1** WATCHFULNESS : vigilancia *f* **2** ASTUTENESS : listeza *f*, viveza *f*

alfalfa [ælˈfælfə] *n* : alfalfa *f*

alga [ˈælgə] *n*, *pl* **-gae** [ˈælˌdʒi:] : alga *f*

algebra [ˈældʒəbrə] *n* : álgebra *m*

algebraic [ˌældʒəˈbreɪk] *adj* : algebraico — **algebraically** [-ɪkli] *adv*

Algerian [ælˈdʒɪriən] *n* : argelino *m*, -na *f* — **Algerian** *adj*

algorithm [ˈælgəˌrɪðəm] *n* : algoritmo *m*

alias¹ [ˈeɪliəs] *adv* : alias

alias² *n* : alias *m*

alibi¹ [ˈæləˌbaɪ] *vi* : ofrecer una coartada

alibi² *n* **1** : coartada *f* **2** EXCUSE : pretexto *m*, excusa *f*

alien¹ [ˈeɪliən] *adj* **1** STRANGE : ajeno, extraño **2** FOREIGN : extranjero, foráneo **3** EXTRATERRESTRIAL : extraterrestre

alien² *n* **1** FOREIGNER : extranjero *m*, -ra *f*; forastero *m*, -ra *f* **2** EXTRATERRESTRIAL : extraterrestre *mf*

alienate [ˈeɪliəˌneɪt] *vt* **-ated; -ating** **1** ESTRANGE : alienar, enajenar **2 to alienate oneself** : alejarse, distanciarse

alienation [ˌeɪliəˈneɪʃən] *n* : alienación *f*, enajenación *f*

alight [əˈlaɪt] *vi* **1** DISMOUNT : bajarse, apearse **2** LAND : posarse, aterrizar

align [əˈlaɪn] *vt* : alinear

alignment [əˈlaɪnmənt] *n* : alineación *f*, alineamiento *m*

alike¹ [əˈlaɪk] *adv* : igual, del mismo modo

alike² *adj* : igual, semejante, parecido

alimentary [ˌæləˈmɛntəri] *adj* **1** : alimenticio **2 alimentary canal** : tubo *m* digestivo

alimony [ˈæləˌmoːni] *n*, *pl* **-nies** : pensión *f* alimenticia

alive [əˈlaɪv] *adj* **1** LIVING : vivo, viviente **2** LIVELY : animado, activo **3** ACTIVE : vigente, en uso **4** AWARE : consciente ⟨alive to the danger : consciente del peligro⟩

alkali [ˈælkəˌlaɪ] *n*, *pl* **-lies** [-ˌlaɪz] or **-lis** [-ˌlaɪz] : álcali *m*

alkaline [ˈælkələn, -ˌlaɪn] *adj* : alcalino

all¹ [ˈɔl] *adv* **1** COMPLETELY : todo, completamente **2** : igual ⟨the score is 14 all : 14 iguales, están empatados a 14⟩

3 all the better : tanto mejor **4 all the more** : aún más, todavía más

all² adj : todo ⟨all the children : todos los niños⟩ ⟨in all likelihood : con toda probabilidad, con la mayor probabilidad⟩

all³ pron **1** : todo, -da ⟨they ate it all : lo comieron todo⟩ ⟨that's all : eso es todo⟩ ⟨enough for all : suficiente para todos⟩ **2 all in all** : en general **3 not at all** (*in negative constructions*) : en absoluto, para nada

Allah ['ɑlɑ, ɑ'lɑ] n : Alá m

all–around [ˌɔlə'raʊnd] adj : completo, amplio

allay [ə'leɪ] vt **1** ALLEVIATE : aliviar, mitigar **2** CALM : aquietar, calmar

allegation [ˌælɪ'geɪʃən] n : alegato m, acusación f

allege [ə'lɛʤ] vt **-leged; -leging 1** : alegar, afirmar **2 to be alleged** : decirse, pretenderse ⟨she is alleged to be wealthy : se dice que es adinerada⟩

alleged [ə'lɛʤd, ə'lɛʤəd] adj : presunto, supuesto

allegedly [ə'lɛʤədli] adv : supuestamente, según se alega

allegiance [ə'liːʤənts] n : lealtad f, fidelidad f

allegorical [ˌælə'gɔrɪkəl] adj : alegórico

allegory ['ælə,gori] n, pl **-ries** : alegoría f

alleluia [ˌɑlə'luːjə, ˌæ-] → **hallelujah**

allergen ['ælərʤən] n : alérgeno m

allergic [ə'lərʤɪk] adj : alérgico

allergy ['ælərʤi] n, pl **-gies** : alergia f

alleviate [ə'liːviˌeɪt] vt **-ated; -ating** : aliviar, mitigar, paliar

alleviation [ə,liːvi'eɪʃən] n : alivio m

alley ['æli] n, pl **-leys 1** : callejón m **2 bowling alley** : bolera f

alliance [ə'laɪənts] n : alianza f, coalición f

alligator ['ælə,geɪtər] n : caimán m

alliteration [ə,lɪtə'reɪʃən] n : aliteración f

allocate ['ælə,keɪt] vt **-cated; -cating** : asignar, adjudicar

allocation [ˌælə'keɪʃən] n : asignación f, reparto m, distribución f

allot [ə'lɑt] vt **-lotted; -lotting** : repartir, distribuir, asignar

allotment [ə'lɑtmənt] n : reparto m, asignación f, distribución f

allow [ə'laʊ] vt **1** PERMIT : permitir, dejar **2** ALLOT : conceder, dar **3** ADMIT, CONCEDE : admitir, conceder — vi **to allow for** : tener en cuenta

allowable [ə'laʊəbəl] adj **1** PERMISSIBLE : permisible, lícito **2** : deducible ⟨allowable expenditure : gasto deducible⟩

allowance [ə'laʊənts] n **1** : complemento m (para gastos, etc.), mesada f (para niños) **2 to make allowance(s)** : tener en cuenta, disculpar

alloy ['æ,lɔɪ] n : aleación f

all–purpose ['ɔl'pərpəs] adj : multiuso ⟨all-purpose flour : harina común⟩

all right¹ adv **1** YES : sí, por supuesto **2** WELL : bien ⟨I did all right : me fue bien⟩ **3** DEFINITELY : bien, ciertamente, sin duda ⟨he's sick all right : está bien enfermo⟩

all right² adj **1** OK : bien ⟨are you all right? : ¿estás bien?⟩ **2** SATISFACTORY : bien, bueno ⟨your work is all right : tu trabajo es bueno⟩

all–round [ˌɔl'raʊnd] → **all–around**

allspice ['ɔlspaɪs] n : pimienta f de Jamaica

allude [ə'luːd] vi **-luded; -luding** : aludir, referirse

allure¹ [ə'lʊr] vt **-lured; -luring** : cautivar, atraer

allure² [ə'lʊr] n : atractivo m, encanto m

allusion [ə'luːʒən] n : alusión f

ally¹ [ə'laɪ, 'æ,laɪ] vi **-lied; -lying** : aliarse

ally² ['æ,laɪ, ə'laɪ] n : aliado m, -da f

almanac ['ɔlmə,næk, 'æl-] n : almanaque m

almighty [ɔl'maɪti] adj : omnipotente, todopoderoso

almond ['ɑmənd, 'ɑl-, 'æ-, 'æl-] n : almendra f

almost ['ɔl,moːst, ɔl'moːst] adv : casi, prácticamente

alms ['ɑmz, 'ɑlmz, 'ælmz] ns & pl : limosna f, caridad f

aloe ['æloː] n : áloe m

aloft [ə'lɔft] adv : en alto, en el aire

alone¹ [ə'loːn] adv : sólo, solamente, únicamente

alone² adj : solo ⟨they're alone in the house : están solos en la casa⟩

along¹ [ə'lɔŋ] adv **1** FORWARD : adelante ⟨farther along : más adelante⟩ ⟨move along! : ¡circulen, por favor!⟩ **2 to bring along** : traer **3 ~ with** : con, junto con **4 all along** : desde el principio

along² prep **1** : por, a lo largo de ⟨along the coast : a lo largo de la costa⟩ **2** : en, en el curso de, por ⟨along the way : en el curso del viaje⟩

alongside¹ [ə,lɔŋ'saɪd] adv : al costado, al lado

alongside² or **alongside of** prep : junto a, al lado de

aloof [ə'luːf] adj : distante, reservado

aloofness [ə'luːfnəs] n : reserva f, actitud f distante

aloud [ə'laʊd] adv : en voz alta

alpaca [æl'pækə] n : alpaca f

alphabet ['ælfə,bɛt] n : alfabeto m

alphabetical [ˌælfə'bɛtɪkəl] or **alphabetic** [-'bɛtɪk] adj : alfabético — alphabetically [-tɪkli] adv

alphabetize ['ælfəbə,taɪz] vt **-ized; -izing** : alfabetizar, poner en orden alfabético

alpine ['æl,paɪn] adj : alpino

already [ɔl'rɛdi] adv : ya

also ['ɔl,soː] adv : también, además

altar ['ɔltər] n : altar m

alter ['ɔltər] vt : alterar, cambiar, modificar

alteration [ˌɔltəˈreɪʃən] n : alteración f, cambio m, modificación f

altercation [ˌɔltərˈkeɪʃən] n : altercado m, disputa f

alternate¹ [ˈɔltərˌneɪt] v -nated; -nating : alternar

alternate² [ˈɔltərnət] adj 1 : alterno ⟨alternate cycles of inflation and depression : ciclos alternos de inflación y depresión⟩ 2 : uno sí y otro no ⟨he cooks on alternate days : cocina un día sí y otro no⟩

alternate³ [ˈɔltərnət] n : suplente mf; sustituto m, -ta f

alternately [ˈɔltərnətli] adv : alternativamente, por turno

alternating current [ˈɔltərˌneɪtɪŋ] n : corriente f alterna

alternation [ˌɔltərˈneɪʃən] n : alternación f, rotación f

alternative¹ [ɔlˈtərnətɪv] adj : alternativo

alternative² n : alternativa f

alternator [ˈɔltərˌneɪtər] n : alternador m

although [ɔlˈðoː] conj : aunque, a pesar de que

altitude [ˈæltəˌtuːd, -ˌtjuːd] n : altitud f, altura f

alto [ˈælˌtoː] n, pl -tos : alto mf, contralto mf

altogether [ˌɔltəˈgɛðər] adv 1 COMPLETELY : completamente, totalmente, del todo 2 ON THE WHOLE : en suma, en general

altruism [ˈæltruˌɪzəm] n : altruismo m

altruistic [ˌæltruˈɪstɪk] adj : altruista — altruistically [-tɪkli] adv

alum [ˈæləm] n : alumbre m

aluminum [əˈluːmənəm] n : aluminio m

alumna [əˈlʌmnə] n, pl -nae [-ˌniː] : exalumna f

alumnus [əˈlʌmnəs] n, pl -ni [-ˌnaɪ] : exalumno m

always [ˈɔlwiz, -ˌweɪz] adv 1 INVARIABLY : siempre, invariablemente 2 FOREVER : para siempre

am → be

amalgam [əˈmælgəm] n : amalgama f

amalgamate [əˈmælgəˌmeɪt] vt -ated; -ating : amalgamar, unir, fusionar

amalgamation [əˌmælgəˈmeɪʃən] n : fusión f, unión f

amaryllis [ˌæməˈrɪləs] n : amarilis f

amass [əˈmæs] vt : amasar, acumular

amateur [ˈæmətʃər, -tər, -ˌtur, -ˌtjur] n 1 : amateur mf 2 BEGINNER : principiante mf; aficionado m, -da f

amateurish [ˈæməˌtʃɜriʃ, -ˌtəːr-, -ˌtur-, -ˌtjur-] adj : amateur, inexperto

amaze [əˈmeɪz] vt amazed; amazing : asombrar, maravillar, pasmar

amazement [əˈmeɪzmənt] n : asombro m, sorpresa f

amazing [əˈmeɪzɪŋ] adj : asombroso, sorprendente — amazingly [-zɪŋli] adv

Amazon [ˈæməˌzɑn] n : amazona f (en mitología)

Amazonian [ˌæməˈzoːniən] adj : amazónico

ambassador [æmˈbæsədər] n : embajador m, -dora f

amber [ˈæmbər] n : ámbar m

ambergris [ˈæmbərˌgrɪs, -ˌgriːs] n : ámbar m gris

ambidextrous [ˌæmbɪˈdɛkstrəs] adj : ambidextro — ambidextrously adv

ambience or ambiance [ˈæmbiənts, ˈɑmbiˌɑnts] n : ambiente m, atmósfera f

ambiguity [ˌæmbəˈgjuːəti] n, pl -ties : ambigüedad f

ambiguous [æmˈbɪgjuəs] adj : ambiguo

ambition [æmˈbɪʃən] n : ambición f

ambitious [æmˈbɪʃəs] adj : ambicioso — ambitiously adv

ambivalence [æmˈbɪvələnts] n : ambivalencia f

ambivalent [æmˈbɪvələnt] adj : ambivalente

amble¹ [ˈæmbəl] vi -bled; -bling : ir tranquilamente, pasearse despreocupadamente

amble² n : paseo m tranquilo

ambulance [ˈæmbjələnts] n : ambulancia f

ambush¹ [ˈæmˌbuʃ] vt : emboscar

ambush² n : emboscada f, celada f

ameliorate [əˈmiːljəˌreɪt] v -rated; -rating IMPROVE : mejorar

amelioration [əˌmiːljəˈreɪʃən] n : mejora f

amen [ˈeɪˈmɛn, ˈɑ-] interj : amén

amenable [əˈmiːnəbəl, -ˈmɛ-] adj RESPONSIVE : susceptible, receptivo, sensible

amend [əˈmɛnd] vt 1 IMPROVE : mejorar, enmendar 2 CORRECT : enmendar, corregir

amendment [əˈmɛndmənt] n : enmienda f

amends [əˈmɛndz] ns & pl : compensación f, reparación f, desagravio m

amenity [əˈmɛnəti, -ˈmiː-] n, pl -ties 1 PLEASANTNESS : lo agradable, amenidad f 2 amenities npl : servicios mpl, comodidades fpl

American [əˈmɛrɪkən] n : americano m, -na f — American adj

American Indian n : indio m (americano), india f (americana)

amethyst [ˈæməθəst] n : amatista f

amiability [ˌeɪmiːəˈbɪləti] n : amabilidad f, afabilidad f

amiable [ˈeɪmiːəbəl] adj : amable, afable — amiably [-bli] adv

amicable [ˈæmɪkəbəl] adj : amigable, amistoso, cordial — amicably [-bli] adv

amid [əˈmɪd] or amidst [əˈmɪdst] prep : en medio de, entre

amino acid [əˈmiːno] n : aminoácido m

amiss¹ [əˈmɪs] adv : mal, fuera de lugar ⟨to take amiss : tomar a mal, llevar a mal⟩

amiss² adj 1 WRONG : malo, inoportuno 2 there's something amiss : pasa algo, algo anda mal

ammeter [ˈæˌmiːtər] n : amperímetro m

ammonia [ə'moːnjə] *n* : amoníaco *m*

ammunition [ˌæmjə'nɪʃən] *n* **1** : municiones *fpl* **2** ARGUMENTS : argumentos *mpl*

amnesia [æm'niːʒə] *n* : amnesia *f*

amnesty ['æmnəsti] *n, pl* **-ties** : amnistía *f*

amoeba [ə'miːbə] *n, pl* **-bas** *or* **-bae** [-ˌbiː] : ameba *f*

amoebic [ə'miːbɪk] *adj* : amébico *m*

amok [ə'mʌk, -'mɑk] *adv* **to run amok** : correr a ciegas, enloquecerse, desbocarse (dícese de la economía, etc.)

among [ə'mʌŋ] *prep* : entre

amoral [eɪ'mɔrəl] *adj* : amoral

amorous ['æmərəs] *adj* **1** PASSIONATE : enamoradizo, apasionado **2** ENAMORED : enamorado **3** LOVING : amoroso, cariñoso

amorously ['æmərəsli] *adv* : con cariño

amorphous [ə'mɔrfəs] *adj* : amorfo, informe

amortize ['æmərˌtaɪz, ə'mɔr-] *vt* **-tized; -tizing** : amortizar

amount[1] [ə'maʊnt] *vi* **to amount to 1** : equivaler a, significar ⟨that amounts to treason : eso equivale a la traición⟩ **2** : ascender (a) ⟨my debts amount to $2000 : mis deudas ascienden a $2000⟩

amount[2] *n* : cantidad *f*, suma *f*

ampere ['æmˌpɪr] *n* : amperio *m*

ampersand ['æmpərˌsænd] *n* : el signo &

amphetamine [æm'fɛtəˌmiːn] *n* : anfetamina *f*

amphibian [æm'fɪbiən] *n* : anfibio *m*

amphibious [æm'fɪbiəs] *adj* : anfibio

amphitheater ['æmfəˌθiːətər] *n* : anfiteatro *m*

ample ['æmpəl] *adj* **-pler; -plest 1** LARGE, SPACIOUS : amplio, extenso, grande **2** ABUNDANT : abundante, generoso

amplifier ['æmpləˌfaɪər] *n* : amplificador *m*

amplify ['æmpləˌfaɪ] *vt* **-fied; -fying** : amplificar

amply ['æmpli] *adv* : ampliamente, abundantemente, suficientemente

amputate ['æmpjəˌteɪt] *vt* **-tated; -tating** : amputar

amputation [ˌæmpjə'teɪʃən] *n* : amputación *f*

amuck [ə'mʌk] → **amok**

amulet ['æmjələt] *n* : amuleto *m*, talismán *m*

amuse [ə'mjuːz] *vt* **amused; amusing 1** ENTERTAIN : entretener, distraer **2** : hacer reír, divertir ⟨the joke amused us : la broma nos hizo reír⟩

amusement [ə'mjuːzmənt] *n* **1** ENTERTAINMENT : diversión *f*, entretenimiento *m*, pasatiempo *m* **2** LAUGHTER : risa *f*

an *art* → **a**[2]

anachronism [ə'nækrəˌnɪzəm] *n* : anacronismo *m*

anachronistic [əˌnækrə'nɪstɪk] *adj* : anacrónico

anaconda [ˌænə'kɑndə] *n* : anaconda *f*

anagram ['ænəˌgræm] *n* : anagrama *m*

anal ['eɪnəl] *adj* : anal

analgesic [ˌænəl'dʒiːzɪk, -sɪk] *n* : analgésico *m*

analog ['ænəˌlɔg] *adj* : analógico

analogical [ˌænəl'ɑdʒɪkəl] *adj* : analógico — **analogically** [-kli] *adv*

analogous [ə'næləgəs] *adj* : análogo

analogy [ə'nælədʒi] *n, pl* **-gies** : analogía *f*

analysis [ə'næləsəs] *n, pl* **-yses** [-ˌsiːz] **1** : análisis *m* **2** PSYCHOANALYSIS : psicoanálisis *m*

analyst ['ænəlɪst] *n* **1** : analista *mf* **2** PSYCHOANALYST : psicoanalista *mf*

analytic [ˌænəl'ɪtɪk] *or* **analytical** [-tɪkəl] *adj* : analítico — **analytically** [-tɪkli] *adv*

analyze ['ænəˌlaɪz] *vt* **-lyzed; -lyzing** : analizar

anarchic [æ'nɑrkɪk] *adj* : anárquico — **anarchically** [-kɪkli] *adv*

anarchism ['ænərˌkɪzəm, -nɑr-] *n* : anarquismo *m*

anarchist ['ænərkɪst, -nɑr-] *n* : anarquista *mf*

anarchy ['ænərki, -nɑr-] *n* : anarquía *f*

anathema [ə'næθəmə] *n* : anatema *m*

anatomic [ˌænə'tɑmɪk] *or* **anatomical** [-mɪkəl] *adj* : anatómico — **anatomically** [-mɪkli] *adv*

anatomy [ə'nætəmi] *n, pl* **-mies** : anatomía *f*

ancestor ['ænˌsɛstər] *n* : antepasado *m*, -da *f*; antecesor *m*, -sora *f*

ancestral [æn'sɛstrəl] *adj* : ancestral, de los antepasados

ancestry ['ænˌsɛstri] *n* **1** DESCENT : ascendencia *f*, linaje *m*, abolengo *m* **2** ANCESTORS : antepasados *mpl*, -das *fpl*

anchor[1] ['æŋkər] *vt* **1** MOOR : anclar, fondear **2** FASTEN : sujetar, asegurar, fijar

anchor[2] *n* **1** : ancla *f* **2** : presentador *m*, -dora *f* (en televisión)

anchorage ['æŋkərɪdʒ] *n* : anclaje *m*

anchovy ['ænˌtʃoːvi, æn'tʃo-] *n, pl* **-vies** *or* **-vy** : anchoa *f*

ancient ['eɪntʃənt] *adj* **1** : antiguo ⟨ancient history : historia antigua⟩ **2** OLD : viejo

ancients ['eɪntʃənts] *npl* : los antiguos *mpl*

and ['ænd] *conj* **1** : y (e before words beginning with i- or hi-) ⟨ham and eggs : huevos con jamón⟩ **3** : a ⟨go and see : ve a ver⟩ **4** : de ⟨try and finish it soon : trata de terminarlo pronto⟩

Andalusian [ˌændə'luːʒən] *n* : andaluz *m*, -luza *f* — **Andalusian** *adj*

Andean ['ændiən] *adj* : andino

andiron ['ænˌdaɪərn] *n* : morillo *m*

Andorran [æn'dɔrən] *n* : andorrano *m*, -na *f* — **Andorran** *adj*

androgynous [æn'drɑdʒənəs] *adj* : andrógino

anecdotal [ˌænɪk'doːtəl] *adj* : anecdótico

anecdote [ˈænɪkˌdoːt] n : anécdota f

anemia [əˈniːmiə] n : anemia f

anemic [əˈniːmɪk] adj : anémico

anemone [əˈnɛməni] n : anémona f

anesthesia [ˌænəsˈθiːʒə] n : anestesia f

anesthetic¹ [ˌænəsˈθɛtɪk] adj : anestésico

anesthetic² n : anestésico m

anesthetist [əˈnɛsθətɪst] n : anestesista mf

anesthetize [əˈnɛsθəˌtaɪz] vt -tize; -tized : anestesiar

aneurysm [ˈænjəˌrɪzəm] n : aneurisma mf

anew [əˈnuː, -ˈnjuː] adv : de nuevo, otra vez, nuevamente

angel [ˈeɪndʒəl] n : ángel m

angelic [ænˈdʒɛlɪk] or angelical [-lɪkəl] adj : angélico, angelical — angelically [-lɪkli] adv

anger¹ [ˈæŋgər] vt : enojar, enfadar

anger² n : enojo m, enfado m, ira f, cólera f, rabia f

angina [ænˈdʒaɪnə] n : angina f

angle¹ [ˈæŋgəl] v angled; angling vt DIRECT, SLANT : orientar, dirigir — vi FISH : pescar (con caña)

angle² n 1 : ángulo m 2 POINT OF VIEW : perspectiva f, punto m de vista

angler [ˈæŋglər] n : pescador m, -dora f

Anglican [ˈæŋglɪkən] n : anglicano m, -na f — Anglican adj

Anglo–Saxon [ˌæŋgloˈsæksən] adj : anglosajón

Anglo–Saxon² n : anglosajón m, -jona f

Angolan [æŋˈgoːlən, æn-] n : angoleño m, -ña f — Angolan adj

angora [æŋˈgorə, æn-] n : angora f

angrily [ˈæŋgrəli] adv : furiosamente, con ira

angry [ˈæŋgri] adj -grier; -est : enojado, enfadado, furioso

anguish [ˈæŋgwɪʃ] n : angustia f, congoja f

anguished [ˈæŋgwɪʃt] adj : angustiado, acongojado

angular [ˈæŋgjələr] adj : angular (dícese de las formas), anguloso (dícese de las caras)

animal [ˈænəməl] n 1 : animal m 2 BRUTE : bruto m, -ta f

animate¹ [ˈænəˌmeɪt] vt -mated; -mating : animar

animate² [ˈænəmət] adj : animado

animated [ˈænəˌmeɪtəd] adj 1 LIVELY : animado, vivo, vivaz 2 animated cartoon : dibujos mpl animados

animation [ˌænəˈmeɪʃən] n : animación f

animosity [ˌænəˈmɑsəti] n, pl -ties : animosidad f, animadversión f

anise [ˈænəs] n : anís m

aniseed [ˈænəsˌsiːd] n : anís m, semilla f de anís

ankle [ˈæŋkəl] n : tobillo m

anklebone [ˈæŋkəlˌboːn] n : taba f

annals [ˈænəlz] npl : anales mpl, crónica f

anneal [əˈniːl] vt 1 TEMPER : templar 2 STRENGTHEN : fortalecer

annex¹ [əˈnɛks, ˈæˌnɛks] vt : anexar

annex² [ˈæˌnɛks, -nɪks] n : anexo m, anejo m

annexation [ˌæˌnɛkˈseɪʃən] n : anexión f

annihilate [əˈnaɪəˌleɪt] vt -lated; -lating : aniquilar

annihilation [əˌnaɪəˈleɪʃən] n : aniquilación f, aniquilamiento m

anniversary [ˌænəˈvərsəri] n, pl -ries : aniversario m

annotate [ˈænəˌteɪt] vt -tated; -tating : anotar

annotation [ˌænəˈteɪʃən] n : anotación f

announce [əˈnaʊnts] vt -nounced; -nouncing : anunciar

announcement [əˈnaʊntsmənt] n : anuncio m

announcer [əˈnaʊntsər] n : anunciador m, -dora f; comentarista mf; locutor m, -tora f

annoy [əˈnɔɪ] vt : molestar, fastidiar, irritar

annoyance [əˈnɔɪənts] n 1 IRRITATION : irritación f, fastidio m 2 NUISANCE : molestia f, fastidio m

annoying [əˈnɔɪɪŋ] adj : molesto, fastidioso, engorroso — annoyingly [-ɪŋli] adv

annual¹ [ˈænjuəl] adj : anual — annually adv

annual² n 1 : planta f anual 2 YEARBOOK : anuario m

annuity [əˈnuːəti] n, pl -ties : anualidad f

annul [əˈnʌl] vt annulled; annulling : anular, invalidar

annulment [əˈnʌlmənt] n : anulación f

anode [ˈæˌnoːd] n : ánodo m

anoint [əˈnɔɪnt] vt : ungir

anomalous [əˈnɑmələs] adj : anómalo

anomaly [əˈnɑməli] n, pl -lies : anomalía f

anonymity [ˌænəˈnɪməti] n : anonimato m

anonymous [əˈnɑnəməs] adj : anónimo — anonymously adv

anorexia [ˌænəˈrɛksiə] n : anorexia f

anorexic [ˌænəˈrɛksɪk] adj : anoréxico

another¹ [əˈnʌðər] adj : otro

another² pron : otro, otra

answer¹ [ˈæntsər] vt 1 : contestar (a), responder a ⟨to answer the telephone : contestar el teléfono⟩ 2 FULFILL : satisfacer 3 to answer for : ser responsable de, pagar por ⟨she'll answer for that mistake : pagará por ese error⟩ — vi : contestar, responder

answer² n 1 REPLY : respuesta f, contestación f 2 SOLUTION : solución f

answerable [ˈæntsərəbəl] adj : responsable

ant [ˈænt] n : hormiga f

antacid [æntˈæsəd, ˈæntˌtæ-] n : antiácido m

antagonism [ænˈtægəˌnɪzəm] n : antagonismo m, hostilidad f

antagonist [ænˈtægənɪst] n : antagonista mf

antagonistic [æn‚tægə'nıstık] *adj* : antagonista, hostil

antagonize [æn'tægə‚naız] *vt* **-nized; -nizing** : antagonizar

antarctic [ænt'arktık, -'arţık] *adj* : antártico

antarctic circle *n* : círculo *m* antártico

anteater ['ænt‚i:ţər] *n* : oso *m* hormiguero

antebellum [‚æntı'bɛləm] *adj* : prebélico

antecedent¹ [‚æntə'si:dənt] *adj* : antecedente, precedente

antecedent² *n* : antecedente *mf*; precursor *m*, -sora *f*

antelope ['æntə‚lo:p] *n*, *pl* **-lope** or **-lopes** : antílope *m*

antenna [æn'tenə] *n*, *pl* **-nae** [-‚ni:, -‚naı] or **-nas** : antena *f*

anterior [æn'tıriər] *adj* : anterior

anthem ['ænθəm] *n* : himno *m* ⟨national anthem : himno nacional⟩

anther ['ænθər] *n* : antera *f*

anthill ['ænt‚hıl] *n* : hormiguero *m*

anthology [æn'θalədʒi] *n*, *pl* **-gies** : antología *f*

anthracite ['ænθrə‚saıt] *n* : antracita *f*

anthropoid¹ ['ænθrə‚pɔıd] *adj* : antropoide

anthropoid² *n* : antropoide *mf*

anthropological [‚ænθrəpə'ladʒıkəl] *adj* : antropológico

anthropologist [‚ænθrə'palədʒıst] *n* : antropólogo *m*, -ga *f*

anthropology [‚ænθrə'palədʒi] *n* : antropología *f*

antiabortion [‚æntiə'bɔrʃən, ‚æntaı-]*adj* : antiaborto

antiaircraft [‚ænti'ær‚kræft, ‚æntaı-] *adj* : antiaéreo

anti–American [‚æntiə'merıkən, ‚æntaı-] *adj* : antiamericano

antibiotic¹ [‚æntibaı'atık, ‚æntaı-, -bi-] *adj* : antibiótico

antibiotic² *n* : antibiótico *m*

antibody ['ænti‚badi] *n*, *pl* **-bodies** : anticuerpo *m*

antic¹ ['æntık] *adj* : extravagante, juguetón

antic² *n* : payasada *f*, travesura *f*

anticipate [æn'tısə‚peıt] *vt* **-pated; -pating** 1 FORESEE : anticipar, prever 2 EXPECT : esperar, contar con

anticipation [æn‚tısə'peıʃən] *n* 1 FORESIGHT : previsión *f* 2 EXPECTATION : anticipación *f*, expectación *f*, esperanza *f*

anticipatory [æn'tısəpə‚tori] *adj* : en anticipación, en previsión

anticlimactic [‚æntiklaı'mæktık] *adj* : anticlimático, decepcionante

anticlimax [‚ænti'klaı‚mæks] *n* : anticlímax *m*

anticommunism [‚ænti'kamjə‚nızəm, ‚æntaı-] *n* : anticomunismo *m*

anticommunist¹ [‚ænti'kamjənıst, ‚æntaı-] *adj* : anticomunista

anticommunist² *n* : anticomunista *mf*

antidemocratic [‚ænti‚dɛmə'krætık, ‚æntaı-] *adj* : antidemocrático

antidepressant [‚æntidi'prɛsənt] *n* : antidepresivo *m* — **antidepressant** *adj*

antidote ['æntı‚do:t] *n* : antídoto *m*

antidrug [‚ænti'drʌg, ‚æntaı-; 'ænti‚drʌg, 'æntaı-] *adj* : antidrogas

antifascist [‚ænti'fæʃıst, ‚æntaı-] *adj* : antifascista

antifeminist [‚ænti'femənıst, ‚æntaı-] *adj* : antifeminista

antifreeze ['ænti‚fri:z] *n* : anticongelante *m*

antigen ['æntıdʒən, -‚dʒɛn] *n* : antígeno *m*

antihistamine [‚ænti'hıstə‚mi:n, -mən] *n* : antihistamínico *m*

anti–imperialism [‚æntiım'pıriə‚lızəm, ‚æntaı-] *n* : antiimperialismo *m*

anti–imperialist [‚æntiım'pıriəlıst, ‚æntaı-] *n* : antiimperialista

anti–inflammatory [‚æntiın'flæmətori] *adj* : antiinflamatorio

anti–inflationary [‚æntiın'fleıʃə‚neri, ‚æntaı-] *adj* : antiinflacionario

antimony ['æntə‚mo:ni] *n* : antimonio *m*

antipathy [æn'tıpəθi] *n*, *pl* **-thies** : antipatía *f*, aversión *f*

antiperspirant [‚ænti'pərspərənt, ‚æntaı-] *n* : antitranspirante *m*

antiquarian¹ [‚æntə'kweriən] *adj* : antiguo, anticuario ⟨an antiquarian book : un libro antiguo⟩

antiquarian² *n* : anticuario *m*, -ria *f*

antiquary ['æntə‚kweri] *n* → **antiquarian²**

antiquated ['æntə‚kweıţəd] *adj* : anticuado, pasado de moda

antique¹ [æn'ti:k] *adj* 1 OLD : antiguo, de época ⟨an antique mirror : un espejo antiguo⟩ 2 OLD-FASHIONED : anticuado, pasado de moda

antique² *n* : antigüedad *f*

antiquity [æn'tıkwəţi] *n*, *pl* **-ties** : antigüedad

antirevolutionary [‚ænti‚revə'lu:ʃə‚neri, ‚æntaı-] *adj* : antirrevolucionario

anti–Semitic [‚æntisə'mıţık, ‚æntaı-] *adj* : antisemita

anti–Semitism [‚ænti'semə‚tızəm, ‚æntaı-] *n* : antisemitismo *m*

antiseptic¹ [‚ænti'sepţık] *adj* : antiséptico — **antiseptically** [-tıkli] *adv*

antiseptic² *n* : antiséptico *m*

antismoking [‚ænti'smo:kıŋ, ‚æntaı-] *adj* : antitabaco

antisocial [‚ænti'so:ʃəl, ‚æntaı-] *adj* 1 : antisocial 2 UNSOCIABLE : poco sociable

antitheft [‚ænti'θeft, ‚æntaı-] *adj* : antirrobo

antithesis [æn'tıθəsıs] *n*, *pl* **-eses** [-‚si:z] : antítesis *f*

antitoxin [‚ænti'taksən, ‚æntaı-] *n* : antitoxina *f*

antitrust [‚ænti'trʌst, ‚æntaı-] *adj* : antimonopolista

antler ['æntlər] *n* : asta *f*, cuerno *m*

antonym ['æntə,nɪm] n : antónimo m

anus ['eɪnəs] n : ano m

anvil ['ænvəl, -vɪl] n : yunque m

anxiety [æŋk'zaɪəti] n, pl -eties 1 UN-EASINESS : inquietud f, preocupación f, ansiedad f 2 APPREHENSION : ansiedad f, angustia f

anxious ['æŋkʃəs] adj 1 WORRIED : inquieto, preocupado, ansioso 2 WORRISOME : preocupante, inquietante 3 EAGER : ansioso, deseoso

anxiously ['æŋkʃəsli] adv : con inquietud, con ansiedad

any¹ ['eni] adv 1 : algo ⟨is it any better? : ¿está algo mejor?⟩ 2 : para nada ⟨it is not any good : no sirve para nada⟩

any² adj 1 : alguno ⟨is there any doubt? : ¿hay alguna duda?⟩ ⟨call me if you have any questions : llámeme si tiene alguna pregunta⟩ 2 : cualquier ⟨I can answer any question : puedo responder a cualquier pregunta⟩ 3 : todo ⟨in any case : en todo caso⟩ 4 : ningún ⟨he would not accept it under any circumstances : no lo aceptaría bajo ninguna circunstancia⟩

any³ pron 1 : alguno m, -na f ⟨are there any left? : ¿quedan algunos?⟩ 2 : ninguno m, -na f ⟨I don't want any : no quiero ninguno⟩

anybody ['eni,bʌdi, -,bɑ-] → anyone

anyhow ['eni,haʊ] adv 1 HAPHAZARDLY : de cualquier manera 2 IN ANY CASE : de todos modos, en todo caso

anymore [,eni'mor] adv 1 : ya, ya más ⟨he doesn't dance anymore : ya no baila más⟩ 2 : todavía ⟨do they sing anymore? : ¿cantan todavía?⟩

anyone ['eni,wʌn] pron 1 : alguien ⟨is anyone here? : ¿hay alguien aquí?⟩ ⟨if anyone wants to come : si alguno quiere venir⟩ 2 : cualquiera ⟨anyone can play : cualquiera puede jugar⟩ 3 : nadie ⟨I don't want anyone here : no quiero a nadie aquí⟩

anyplace ['eni,pleɪs] → anywhere

anything ['eni,θɪŋ] pron 1 : algo, alguna cosa ⟨do you want anything? : ¿quieres algo?, ¿quieres alguna cosa?⟩ 2 : nada ⟨hardly anything : casi nada⟩ 3 : cualquier cosa ⟨I eat anything : como de todo⟩

anytime ['eni,taɪm] adv : en cualquier momento, a cualquier hora, cuando sea

anyway ['eni,weɪ] → anyhow

anywhere ['eni,ʰwer] adv 1 : en algún sitio, en alguna parte ⟨do you see it anywhere? : ¿lo ves en alguna parte?⟩ 2 : en ningún sitio, por ninguna parte ⟨I can't find it anywhere : no puedo encontrarlo por ninguna parte⟩ 3 : en cualquier parte, dondequiera, donde sea ⟨put it anywhere : ponlo dondequiera⟩

aorta [eɪ'ɔrtə] n, pl -tas or -tae [-ṭi, -,taɪ] : aorta f

Apache [ə'pætʃi] n, pl Apache or Apaches : apache mf

apart [ə'pɑrt] adv 1 SEPARATELY : aparte, separadamente 2 ASIDE : aparte, a un lado 3 to fall apart : deshacerse, hacerse pedazos 4 to take apart : desmontar, desmantelar

apartheid [ə'pɑr,teɪt, -,taɪt] n : apartheid m

apartment [ə'pɑrtmənt] n : apartamento m, departamento m, piso m Spain

apathetic [,æpə'θɛtɪk] adj : apático, indiferente — apathetically [-tɪkli] adv

apathy ['æpəθi] n : apatía f, indiferencia f

ape¹ ['eɪp] vt aped; aping : imitar, remedar

ape² n : simio m; mono m, -na f

aperitif [ə,perɑ'ti:f] n : aperitivo m

aperture ['æpərtʃər, -,tʃʊr] n : abertura f, rendija f, apertura f (en fotografía)

apex ['eɪ,pɛks] n, pl apexes or apices ['eɪpə,si:z, 'æ-] : ápice m, cúspide f, cima f

aphid ['eɪfɪd, 'æ-] n : áfido m

aphorism ['æfə,rɪzəm] n : aforismo m

aphrodisiac [,æfrə'di:zi,æk, -'dɪ-] n : afrodisíaco m

apiary ['eɪpi,eri] n, pl -aries : apiario m, colmenar m

apiece [ə'pi:s] adv : cada uno

aplenty [ə'plɛnti] adj : en abundancia

aplomb [ə'plɑm, -'plʌm] n : aplomo m

apocalypse [ə'pɑkə,lɪps] n : apocalipsis m

apocalyptic [ə,pɑkə'lɪptɪk] adj : apocalíptico

apocrypha [ə'pɑkrəfə] n : textos mpl apócrifos

apocryphal [ə'pɑkrəfəl] adj : apócrifo

apologetic [ə,pɑlə'dʒɛtɪk] adj : lleno de disculpas

apologetically [ə,pɑlə'dʒɛtɪkli] adv : disculpándose, con aire de disculpas

apologize [ə'pɑlə,dʒaɪz] vi -gized; -gizing : disculparse, pedir perdón

apology [ə'pɑlədʒi] n, pl -gies : disculpa f, excusa f

apoplectic [,æpə'plɛktɪk] adj : apopléctico

apoplexy ['æpə,plɛksi] n : apoplejía f

apostasy [ə'pɑstəsi] n, pl -sies : apostasía f

apostate [ə'pɑs,teɪt] n, pl -tes : apóstata mf

apostle [ə'pɑsəl] n : apóstol m

apostolic [,æpə'stɑlɪk] adj : apostólico

apostrophe [ə'pɑstrə,fi:] n : apóstrofo m (ortográfico)

apothecary [ə'pɑθə,keri] n, pl -caries : boticario m, -ria f

appall [ə'pɔl] vt : consternar, horrorizar

apparatus [,æpə'ræṭəs, -'reɪ-] n, pl -tuses or -tus : aparato m, equipo m

apparel [ə'pærəl] n : atavío m, ropa f

apparent [ə'pærənt] adj 1 VISIBLE : visible 2 OBVIOUS : claro, evidente, manifiesto 3 SEEMING : aparente, ostensible

apparently [ə'pærəntli] *adv* : aparentemente, al parecer

apparition [ˌæpə'rɪʃən] *n* : aparición *f*, visión *f*

appeal[1] [ə'pi:l] *vi* 1 : apelar ⟨to appeal a decision : apelar contra una decisión⟩ — *vi* 1 **to appeal for** : pedir, solicitar 2 **to appeal to** : atraer a ⟨that doesn't appeal to me : eso no me atrae⟩

appeal[2] *n* 1 : apelación *f* (en derecho) 2 PLEA : ruego *m*, súplica *f* 3 ATTRACTION : atracción *f*, atractivo *m*, interés *m*

appear [ə'pɪr] *vi* 1 : aparecer, aparecerse, presentarse ⟨he suddenly appeared : apareció de repente⟩ 2 COME OUT : aparecer, salir, publicarse 3 : comparecer (ante el tribunal), actuar (en el teatro) 4 SEEM : parecer

appearance [ə'pɪrən(t)s] *n* 1 APPEARING : aparición *f*, presentación *f*, comparecencia *f* (ante un tribunal), publicación *f* (de un libro) 2 LOOK : apariencia *f*, aspecto *m*

appease [ə'pi:z] *vt* -peased; -peasing 1 CALM, PACIFY : aplacar, apaciguar, sosegar 2 SATISFY : satisfacer, mitigar

appeasement [ə'pi:zmənt] *n* : aplacamiento *m*, apaciguamiento *m*

append [ə'pɛnd] *vt* : agregar, añadir, adjuntar

appendage [ə'pɛndɪdʒ] *n* 1 ADDITION : apéndice *m*, añadidura *f* 2 LIMB : miembro *m*, extremidad *f*

appendectomy [ˌæpən'dɛktəmi] *n, pl* -mies : apendicectomía *f*

appendicitis [ə,pɛndə'saɪtəs] *n* : apendicitis *f*

appendix [ə'pɛndɪks] *n, pl* -dixes *or* -dices [-də,si:z] : apéndice *m*

appetite ['æpə,taɪt] *n* 1 CRAVING : apetito *m*, deseo *m*, ganas *fpl* 2 PREFERENCE : gusto *m*, preferencia *f* ⟨the cultural appetites of today : los gustos culturales de hoy⟩

appetizer ['æpə,taɪzər] *n* : aperitivo *m*, entremés *m*, botana *f Mex*, tapa *f Spain*

appetizing ['æpə,taɪzɪŋ] *adj* : apetecible, apetitoso — **appetizingly** [-zɪŋli] *adv*

applaud [ə'plɔd] *v* : aplaudir

applause [ə'plɔz] *n* : aplauso *m*

apple ['æpəl] *n* : manzana *f*

appliance [ə'plaɪən(t)s] *n* 1 : aparato *m* 2 **household appliance** : electrodoméstico *m*, aparato *m* electrodoméstico

applicability [ˌæplɪkə'bɪləti, ə,plɪkə-] *n* : aplicabilidad *f*

applicable ['æplɪkəbəl, ə'plɪkə-] *adj* : aplicable, pertinente

applicant ['æplɪkənt] *n* : solicitante *mf*, aspirante *mf*, postulante *mf*; candidato *m*, -ta *f*

application [ˌæplə'keɪʃən] *n* 1 USE : aplicación *f*, empleo *m*, uso *m* 2 DILIGENCE : aplicación *f*, diligencia *f*, dedicación *f* 3 REQUEST : solicitud *f*, petición *f*, demanda *f*

applicator ['æplə,keɪtər] *n* : aplicador *m*

appliqué[1] [ˌæplɪ'keɪ] *vt* : decorar con apliques

appliqué[2] *n* : aplique *m*

apply [ə'plaɪ] *v* -plied; -plying *vt* 1 : aplicar (una sustancia, los frenos, el conocimiento) 2 **to apply oneself** : dedicarse, aplicarse — *vi* 1 : aplicarse, referirse ⟨the rules apply to everyone : las reglas se aplican a todos⟩ 2 **to apply for** : solicitar, pedir

appoint [ə'pɔɪnt] *vt* 1 NAME : nombrar, designar 2 FIX, SET : fijar, señalar, designar ⟨to appoint a date : fijar una fecha⟩ 3 EQUIP : equipar ⟨a well-appointed office : una oficina bien equipada⟩

appointee [ə,pɔɪn'ti:, ˌæ-] *n* : persona *f* designada

appointment [ə'pɔɪntmənt] *n* 1 APPOINTING : nombramiento *m*, designación *f* 2 ENGAGEMENT : cita *f*, hora *f* 3 POST : puesto *m*

apportion [ə'pɔrʃən] *vt* : distribuir, repartir

apportionment [ə'pɔrʃənmənt] *n* : distribución *f*, repartición *f*, reparto *m*

apposite ['æpəzət] *adj* : apropiado, oportuno, pertinente — **appositely** *adv*

appraisal [ə'preɪzəl] *n* : evaluación *f*, valoración *f*, tasación *f*, apreciación *f*

appraise [ə'preɪz] *vt* -praised; -praising : evaluar, valorar, tasar, apreciar

appraiser [ə'preɪzər] *n* : tasador *m*, -dora *f*

appreciable [ə'pri:ʃəbəl, -'prɪʃiə-] *adj* : apreciable, sensible, considerable — **appreciably** [-bli] *adv*

appreciate [ə'pri:ʃi,eɪt, -'prɪ-] *v* -ated; -ating *vt* 1 VALUE : apreciar, valorar 2 : agradecer ⟨we appreciate his frankness : agradecemos su franqueza⟩ 3 UNDERSTAND : darse cuenta de, entender — *vi* : apreciarse, valorizarse

appreciation [ə,pri:ʃi'eɪʃən, -,prɪ-] *n* 1 GRATITUDE : agradecimiento *m*, reconocimiento *m* 2 VALUING : apreciación *f*, valoración *f*, estimación *f* ⟨art appreciation : apreciación artística⟩ 3 UNDERSTANDING : comprensión *f*, entendimiento *m*

appreciative [ə'pri:ʃətɪv, -'prɪ-; ə'pri:ʃiˌeɪ-] *adj* 1 : apreciativo ⟨an appreciative audience : un público apreciativo⟩ 2 GRATEFUL : agradecido 3 ADMIRING : de admiración

apprehend [ˌæprɪ'hɛnd] *vt* 1 ARREST : aprehender, detener, arrestar 2 DREAD : temer 3 COMPREHEND : comprender, entender

apprehension [ˌæprɪ'hɛntʃən] *n* 1 ARREST : arresto *m*, detención *f*, aprehensión *f* 2 ANXIETY : aprensión *f*, ansiedad *f*, temor *m* 3 UNDERSTANDING : comprensión *f*, percepción *f*

apprehensive [ˌæprɪ'hɛntsɪv] *adj* : aprensivo, inquieto — **apprehensively** *adv*

apprentice[1] [ə'prɛntɪs] vt **-ticed; -ticing** : colocar de aprendiz

apprentice[2] n : aprendiz m, -diza f

apprenticeship [ə'prɛntɪs,ʃɪp] n : aprendizaje f

apprise [ə'praɪz] vt **-prised; -prising** : informar, avisar

approach[1] [ə'pro:tʃ] vt **1** NEAR : acercarse a **2** APPROXIMATE : aproximarse a **3** : abordar, dirigirse a ⟨I approached my boss with the proposal : me dirigí a mi jefe con la propuesta⟩ **4** TACKLE : abordar, enfocar, considerar — vi : acercarse, aproximarse

approach[2] n **1** NEARING : acercamiento m, aproximación f **2** POSITION : enfoque m, planteamiento f **3** OFFER : propuesta, oferta f **4** ACCESS : acceso m, vía f de acceso

approachable [ə'pro:tʃəbəl] adj : accesible, asequible

approbation [ˌæprə'beɪʃən] n : aprobación f

appropriate[1] [ə'pro:pri,eɪt] vt **-ated; -ating 1** SEIZE : apropiarse de **2** ALLOCATE : destinar, asignar

appropriate[2] [ə'pro:priət] adj : apropiado, adecuado, idóneo — **appropriately** adv

appropriateness [ə'pro:priətnəs] n : idoneidad f, propiedad f

appropriation [ə,pro:pri'eɪʃən] n **1** SEIZURE : apropiación f **2** ALLOCATION : asignación f

approval [ə'pru:vəl] n **1** : aprobación f, visto m bueno **2 on approval** : a prueba

approve [ə'pru:v] vt **-proved; -proving 1** : aprobar, sancionar, darle el visto bueno a **2 to approve of** : consentir en, aprobar ⟨he doesn't approve of smoking : está en contra del tabaco⟩

approximate[1] [ə'praks,meɪt] vt **-mated; -mating** : aproximarse a, acercarse a

approximate[2] [ə'praksəmət] adj : aproximado

approximately [ə'praksəmətli] adv : aproximadamente, más o menos

approximation [ə,praksə'meɪʃən] n : aproximación f

appurtenance [ə'pərtənənts] n : accesorio m

apricot ['æprə,kɑt, 'eɪ-] n : albaricoque m, chabacano m Mex

April ['eɪprəl] n : abril m

apron ['eɪprən] n : delantal m, mandil m

apropos[1] [ˌæprə'po:, 'æprə,po:] adv : a propósito

apropos[2] adj : pertinente, oportuno, acertado

apropos of prep : a propósito de

apt ['æpt] adj **1** FITTING : apto, apropiado, acertado, oportuno **2** LIABLE : propenso, inclinado **3** CLEVER, QUICK : listo, despierto

aptitude ['æptə,tu:d, -'tju:d] n **1** : aptitud f, capacidad f ⟨aptitude test : prueba de aptitud⟩ **2** TALENT : talento m, facilidad f

aptly ['æptli] adv : acertadamente

aqua ['ækwə, 'a-] n : color m aguamarina

aquarium [ə'kwæriəm] n, pl **-iums** or **-ia** [-iə] : acuario m

Aquarius [ə'kwæriəs] n : Acuario mf

aquatic [ə'kwɑtɪk, -'kwæ-] adj : acuático

aqueduct ['ækwə,dʌkt] n : acueducto m

aqueous ['ækwiəs, 'æk-] adj : acuoso

aquiline ['ækwə,laɪn, -lən] adj : aguileño

Arab[1] ['ærəb] adj : árabe

Arab[2] n : árabe mf

arabesque [ˌærə'bɛsk] n : arabesco m

Arabian[1] [ə'reɪbiən] adj : árabe

Arabian[2] n → **Arab**[2]

Arabic[1] ['ærəbɪk] adj : árabe

Arabic[2] n : árabe m (idioma)

arable ['ærəbəl] adj : arable, cultivable

arbiter ['arbətər] n : árbitro m, -tra f

arbitrary ['arbə,treri] adj : arbitrario — **arbitrarily** [ˌarbə'trerəli] adv

arbitrate ['arbə,treɪt] v **-trated; -trating** : arbitrar

arbitration [ˌarbə'treɪʃən] n : arbitraje m

arbitrator ['arbə,treɪtər] n : árbitro m, -tra f

arbor ['arbər] n : cenador m, pérgola f

arboreal [ar'boriəl] adj : arbóreo

arc[1] ['ark] vi **arced; arcing** : formar un arco

arc[2] n : arco m

arcade [ar'keɪd] n **1** ARCHES : arcada f **2** MALL : galería f comercial

arcane [ar'keɪn] adj : arcano, secreto, misterioso

arch[1] ['artʃ] vt : arquear, enarcar — vi : formar un arco, arquearse

arch[2] adj **1** CHIEF : principal **2** MISCHIEVOUS : malicioso, pícaro

arch[3] n : arco m

archaeological [ˌarkiə'ladʒɪkəl] adj : arqueológico

archaeologist [ˌarki'alədʒɪst] n : arqueólogo m, -ga f

archaeology or **archeology** [ˌarki'alədʒi] n : arqueología f

archaic [ar'keɪk] adj : arcaico — **archaically** [-ɪkli] adv

archangel ['ark,eɪndʒəl] n : arcángel m

archbishop [artʃ'bɪʃəp] n : arzobispo m

archdiocese [artʃ'daɪəsəs, -,si:z, -,sis] n : archidiócesis f

archer ['artʃər] n : arquero m, -ra f

archery ['artʃəri] n : tiro m al arco

archetypal [ˌarki'taɪpəl] adj : arquetípico

archetype ['arkɪ,taɪp] n : arquetipo m

archipelago [ˌarkə'pelə,go:, ˌartʃə-] n, pl **-goes** or **-gos** [-go:z] : archipiélago m

architect ['arkə,tɛkt] n : arquitecto m, -ta f

architectural [ˌarkə'tɛktʃərəl] adj : arquitectónico — **architecturally** adv

architecture ['arkə,tɛktʃər] n : arquitectura f

archive ['ar,kaɪv] n or **archives** ['ar,kaɪvz] npl : archivo m

archivist [ˈɑrkəvɪst, -ˌkaɪ-] n : archivero m, -ra f; archivista mf

archway [ˈɑrtʃˌweɪ] n : arco m, pasadizo m abovedado

arctic [ˈɑrktɪk, ˈɑrt̬-] adj 1 : ártico ⟨arctic regions : zonas árticas⟩ 2 FRIGID : glacial

arctic circle n : círculo m ártico

ardent [ˈɑrdənt] adj 1 PASSIONATE : ardiente, fogoso, apasionado 2 FERVENT : ferviente, fervoroso — **ardently** adv

ardor [ˈɑrdər] n : ardor m, pasión f, fervor m

arduous [ˈɑrdʒuəs] adj : arduo, duro, riguroso — **arduously** adv

arduousness [ˈɑrdʒuəsnəs] n : dureza f, rigor m

are → be

area [ˈæriə] n 1 SURFACE : área f, superficie f 2 REGION : área f, región f, zona f 3 FIELD : área f, terreno m, campo m (de conocimiento)

area code n : código m de la zona, prefijo m Spain

arena [əˈriːnə] n 1 : arena f, estadio m ⟨sports arena : estadio deportivo⟩ 2 : arena f, ruedo m ⟨the political arena : el ruedo político⟩

Argentine [ˈɑrdʒənˌtaɪn, -ˌtiːn] or **Argentinean** or **Argentinian** [ˌɑrdʒənˈtɪniən] n : argentino m, -na f — **Argentine** or **Argentinean** or **Argentinian** adj

argon [ˈɑrˌgɑn] n : argón m

argot [ˈɑrgət, -ˌgoː] n : argot m

arguable [ˈɑrgjuəbəl] adj : discutible

argue [ˈɑrgjuː] v -gued; -guing vi 1 REASON : argüir, argumentar, razonar 2 DISPUTE : discutir, pelear(se), alegar — vt 1 SUGGEST : sugerir 2 MAINTAIN : alegar, argüir, sostener 3 DISCUSS : discutir, debatir

argument [ˈɑrgjəmənt] n 1 REASONING : argumento m, razonamiento m 2 DISCUSSION : discusión f, debate m 3 QUARREL : pelea f, riña f, disputa f

argumentative [ˌɑrgjəˈmɛntət̬ɪv] adj : discutidor

argyle [ˈɑrˌgaɪl] n : diseño m de rombos

aria [ˈɑriə] n : aria f

arid [ˈærəd] adj : árido

aridity [əˈrɪdət̬i, æ-] n : aridez f

Aries [ˈɛriːz, -iˌiːz] n : Aries mf

arise [əˈraɪz] vi **arose** [əˈroːz]; **arisen** [əˈrɪzən]; **arising** 1 ASCEND : ascender, subir, elevarse 2 ORIGINATE : originarse, surgir, presentarse 3 GET UP : levantarse

aristocracy [ˌærəˈstɑkrəsi] n, pl -cies : aristocracia f

aristocrat [əˈrɪstəˌkræt] n : aristócrata mf

aristocratic [əˌrɪstəˈkræt̬ɪk] adj : aristocrático, noble

arithmetic[1] [ˈærɪθˌmɛt̬ɪk] or **arithmetical** [-t̬ɪkəl] adj : aritmético

arithmetic[2] [əˈrɪθməˌtɪk] n : aritmética f

ark [ˈɑrk] n : arca f

arm[1] [ˈɑrm] vt : armar — vi : armarse

arm[2] n 1 : brazo m (del cuerpo o de un sillón), manga f (de una prenda) 2 BRANCH : rama f, sección f 3 WEAPON : arma f ⟨to take up arms : tomar las armas⟩ 4 → **coat of arms**

armada [ɑrˈmɑdə, -ˈmeɪ-] n : armada f, flota f

armadillo [ˌɑrməˈdɪlo] n, pl -los : armadillo m

armament [ˈɑrməmənt] n : armamento m

armchair [ˈɑrmˌtʃɛr] n : butaca f, sillón m

armed [ˈɑrmd] adj 1 : armado ⟨armed robbery : robo a mano armada⟩ 2 **armed forces** : fuerzas fpl armadas

Armenian [ɑrˈmiːniən] n : armenio m, -nia f — **Armenian** adj

armistice [ˈɑrməstɪs] n : armisticio m

armor [ˈɑrmər] n : armadura f, coraza f

armored [ˈɑrmərd] adj : blindado, acorazado

armory [ˈɑrməri] n, pl -mories : arsenal m (almacén), armería f (museo), fábrica f de armas

armpit [ˈɑrmˌpɪt] n : axila f, sobaco m

army [ˈɑrmi] n, pl -mies 1 : ejército m (militar) 2 MULTITUDE : legión f, multitud f, ejército m

aroma [əˈroːmə] n : aroma f

aromatic [ˌærəˈmæt̬ɪk] adj : aromático

around[1] [əˈraʊnd] adv 1 : de circunferencia ⟨a tree three feet around : un árbol de tres pies de circunferencia⟩ 2 : alrededor, a la redonda ⟨for miles around : por millas a la redonda⟩ ⟨all around : por todos lados, todo alrededor⟩ 3 : por ahí ⟨they're somewhere around : deben estar por ahí⟩ 4 APPROXIMATELY : más o menos, aproximadamente ⟨around 5 o'clock : a eso de las 5⟩ 5 **to turn around** : darse la vuelta, voltearse

around[2] prep 1 SURROUNDING : alrededor de, en torno a 2 THROUGH : por, en ⟨he traveled around Mexico : viajó por México⟩ ⟨around the house : en casa⟩ 3 : a la vuelta de ⟨around the corner : a la vuelta de la esquina⟩ 4 NEAR : alrededor de, cerca de

arousal [əˈraʊzəl] n : excitación f

arouse [əˈraʊz] vt **aroused**; **arousing** 1 AWAKE : despertar 2 EXCITE : despertar, suscitar, excitar

arraign [əˈreɪn] vt : hacer comparecer (ante un tribunal)

arraignment [əˈreɪnmənt] n : orden m de comparecencia, acusación f

arrange [əˈreɪndʒ] vt -ranged; -ranging 1 ORDER : arreglar, poner en orden, disponer 2 SETTLE : arreglar, fijar, concertar 3 ADAPT : arreglar, adaptar

arrangement [əˈreɪndʒmənt] n 1 ORDER : arreglo m, orden m 2 ARRANGING : disposición f ⟨floral arrangement : arreglo floral⟩ 3 AGREEMENT : arreglo m, acuerdo m, convenio m 4 **arrange-**

ments *npl* : preparativos *mpl*, planes *mpl*

array¹ [ə'reɪ] *vt* **1** ORDER : poner en orden, presentar, formar **2** GARB : vestir, ataviar, engalanar

array² *n* **1** ORDER : orden *m*, formación *f* **2** ATTIRE : atavío *m*, galas *mpl* **3** RANGE, SELECTION : selección *f*, serie *f*, gama *f* ⟨an array of problems : una serie de problemas⟩

arrears [ə'rɪrz] *npl* : atrasos *mpl* ⟨to be in arrears : estar atrasado en los pagos⟩

arrest¹ [ə'rɛst] *vt* **1** APPREHEND : arrestar, detener **2** CHECK, STOP : detener, parar

arrest² *n* **1** APPREHENSION : arresto *m*, detención *f* ⟨under arrest : detenido⟩ **2** STOPPING : paro *m*

arrival [ə'raɪvəl] *n* : llegada *f*, venida *f*, arribo *m*

arrive [ə'raɪv] *vi* -**rived**; -**riving** **1** COME : llegar, arribar **2** SUCCEED : triunfar, tener éxito

arrogance [ˈærəgənts] *n* : arrogancia *f*, soberbia *f*, altanería *f*, altivez *f*

arrogant [ˈærəgənt] *adj* : arrogante, soberbio, altanero, altivo — **arrogantly** *adv*

arrogate [ˈærəˌgeɪt] *vt* -**gated**; -**gating** to **arrogate to oneself** : arrogarse

arrow [ˈæro] *n* : flecha *f*

arrowhead [ˈæroˌhɛd] *n* : punta *f* de flecha

arroyo [ə'rɔɪo] *n* : arroyo *m*

arsenal [ˈɑrsənəl] *n* : arsenal *m*

arsenic [ˈɑrsənɪk] *n* : arsénico *m*

arson [ˈɑrsən] *n* : incendio *m* premeditado

arsonist [ˈɑrsənɪst] *n* : incendiario *m*, -ria *f*; pirómano *m*, -na *f*

art [ˈɑrt] *n* **1** : arte *m* **2** SKILL : destreza *f*, habilidad *f*, maña *f* **3 arts** *npl* : letras *fpl* (en la educación) **4 fine arts** : bellas artes *fpl*

arterial [ɑr'tɪriəl] *adj* : arterial

arteriosclerosis [ɑr,tɪriosklə'rosɪs] *n* : arteriosclerosis *f*

artery [ˈɑrtəri] *n*, *pl* -**teries** **1** : arteria *f* **2** THOROUGHFARE : carretera *f* principal, arteria *f*

artesian well [ɑr'ti:ʒən] *n* : pozo *m* artesiano

artful [ˈɑrtfəl] *adj* **1** INGENIOUS : ingenioso, diestro **2** CRAFTY : astuto, taimado, ladino, artero — **artfully** *adv*

arthritic [ɑr'θrɪtɪk] *adj* : artrítico

arthritis [ɑr'θraɪtəs] *n*, *pl* -**tides** [ɑr-'θrɪtə,di:z] : artritis *f*

arthropod [ˈɑrθrə,pɑd] *n* : artrópodo *m*

artichoke [ˈɑrtə,tʃo:k] *n* : alcachofa *f*

article [ˈɑrtɪkəl] *n* **1** ITEM : artículo *m*, objeto *m* **2** ESSAY : artículo *m* **3** CLAUSE : artículo *m*, cláusula *f* **4** : artículo *m* ⟨definite article : artículo determinado⟩

articulate¹ [ɑr'tɪkjə,leɪt] *vt* -**lated**; -**lating** **1** UTTER : articular, enunciar, expresar **2** CONNECT : articular (en anatomía)

articulate² [ɑr'tɪkjələt] *adj* to be **articulate** : poder articular palabras, expresarse bien

articulately [ɑr'tɪkjələtli] *adv* : elocuentemente, con fluidez

articulateness [ɑr'tɪkjələtnəs] *n* : elocuencia *f*, fluidez *f*

articulation [ɑr,tɪkjə'leɪʃən] *n* **1** JOINT : articulación *f* **2** UTTERANCE : articulación *f*, declaración *f* **3** ENUNCIATION : articulación *f*, pronunciación *f*

artifact [ˈɑrtə,fækt] *n* : artefacto *m*

artifice [ˈɑrtəfəs] *n* : artificio *m*

artificial [,ɑrtə'fɪʃəl] *adj* **1** SYNTHETIC : artificial, sintético **2** FEIGNED : artificial, falso, afectado

artificially [,ɑrtə'fɪʃəli] *adv* : artificialmente, con afectación

artillery [ɑr'tɪləri] *n*, *pl* -**leries** : artillería *f*

artisan [ˈɑrtəzən, -sən] *n* : artesano *m*, -na *f*

artist [ˈɑrtɪst] *n* : artista *mf*

artistic [ɑr'tɪstɪk] *adj* : artístico — **artistically** [-tɪkli] *adv*

artistry [ˈɑrtəstri] *n* : maestría *f*, arte *m*

artless [ˈɑrtləs] *adj* : sencillo, natural, ingenuo, cándido — **artlessly** *adv*

artlessness [ˈɑrtləsnəs] *n* : ingenuidad *f*, candidez *f*

arty [ˈɑrti] *adj* **artier**; -**est** : pretenciosamente artístico

as¹ [ˈæz] *adv* **1** : tan, tanto ⟨this one's not as difficult : éste no es tan difícil⟩ **2** : como ⟨some trees, as oak and pine : algunos árboles, como el roble y el pino⟩

as² *conj* **1** LIKE : como, igual que **2** WHEN, WHILE : cuando, mientras, a la vez que **3** BECAUSE : porque **4** THOUGH : aunque, por más que ⟨strange as it may appear : por extraño que parezca⟩ **5 as is** : tal como está

as³ *prep* **1** : de ⟨I met her as a child : la conocí de pequeña⟩ **2** LIKE : como ⟨behave as a man : compórtate como un hombre⟩

as⁴ *pron* : que ⟨in the same building as my brother : en el mismo edificio que mi hermano⟩

asbestos [æz'bɛstəs, æs-] *n* : asbesto *m*, amianto *m*

ascend [ə'sɛnd] *vi* : ascender, subir — *vt* : subir, subir a, escalar

ascendancy [ə'sɛndəntsi] *n* : ascendiente *m*, predominio *m*

ascendant¹ [ə'sɛndənt] *adj* **1** RISING : ascendente **2** DOMINANT : superior, dominante

ascendant² *n* to be in the **ascendant** : estar en alza, ir ganando predominio

ascension [ə'sɛntʃən] *n* : ascensión *f*

ascent [ə'sɛnt] *n* **1** RISE : ascensión *f*, subida *f*, ascenso *m* **2** SLOPE : cuesta *f*, pendiente *f*

ascertain [,æsər'teɪn] *vt* : determinar, establecer, averiguar

ascertainable [,æsər'teɪnəbəl] *adj* : determinable, averiguable

ascetic[1] [ə'sɛtɪk] *adj* : ascético
ascetic[2] *n* : asceta *mf*
asceticism [ə'sɛtə,sɪzəm] *n* : ascetismo *m*
ascribable [ə'skraɪbəbəl] *adj* : atribuible, imputable
ascribe [ə'skraɪb] *vt* **-cribed; -cribing** : atribuir, imputar
aseptic [eɪ'sɛptɪk] *adj* : aséptico
asexual [,eɪ'sɛkʃʊəl] *adj* : asexual
as for *prep* CONCERNING : en cuanto a, respecto a, para
ash ['æʃ] *n* **1** : ceniza *f* ⟨to reduce to ashes : reducir a cenizas⟩ **2** : fresno *m* (árbol)
ashamed [ə'ʃeɪmd] *adj* : avergonzado, abochornado, apenado — **ashamedly** [ə'ʃeɪmədli] *adv*
ashen ['æʃən] *adj* : lívido, ceniciento, pálido
ashore [ə'ʃor] *adv* **1** : en tierra **2 to go ashore** : desembarcar
ashtray ['æʃ,treɪ] *n* : cenicero *m*
Asian[1] ['eɪʒən, -ʃən] *adj* : asiático
Asian[2] *n* : asiático *m*, -ca *f*
aside [ə'saɪd] *adv* **1** : a un lado ⟨to step aside : hacerse a un lado⟩ **2** : de lado, aparte ⟨jesting aside : bromas aparte⟩ **3 to set aside** : guardar, apartar, reservar
aside from *prep* **1** BESIDES : además de **2** EXCEPT : aparte de, menos
as if *conj* : como si
asinine ['æsən,aɪn] *adj* : necio, estúpido
ask ['æsk] *vt* **1** : preguntar ⟨ask him if he's coming : pregúntale si viene⟩ **2** REQUEST : pedir, solicitar ⟨to ask a favor : pedir un favor⟩ **3** INVITE : invitar — *vi* **1** INQUIRE : preguntar ⟨I asked about her children : pregunté por sus niños⟩ **2** REQUEST : pedir ⟨we asked for help : pedimos ayuda⟩
askance [ə'skænts] *adv* **1** SIDELONG : de reojo, de soslayo **2** SUSPICIOUSLY : con recelo, con desconfianza
askew [ə'skju] *adj* : torcido, ladeado
asleep [ə'sli:p] *adj* **1** : dormido, durmiendo **2 to fall asleep** : quedarse dormido
as of *prep* : desde, a partir de
asparagus [ə'spærəgəs] *n* : espárrago *m*
aspect ['æ,spɛkt] *n* : aspecto *m*
aspen ['æspən] *n* : álamo *m* temblón
asperity [æ'spɛrəṭi, ə-] *n*, *pl* **-ties** : aspereza *f*
aspersion [ə'spərʒən] *n* : difamación *f*, calumnia *f*
asphalt ['æs,fɔlt] *n* : asfalto *m*
asphyxia [æs'fɪksiə, ə-] *n* : asfixia *f*
asphyxiate [æs'fɪksi,eɪt] *v* **-ated; -ating** *vt* : asfixiar — *vi* : asfixiarse
asphyxiation [æ,sfɪksi'eɪʃən] *n* : asfixia *f*
aspirant ['æspərənt, ə'spaɪrənt] *n* : aspirante *mf*, pretendiente *mf*
aspiration [,æspə'reɪʃən] *n* **1** DESIRE : aspiración *f*, anhelo *m*, ambición *f* **2** BREATHING : aspiración *f*

aspire [ə'spaɪr] *vi* **-pired; -piring** : aspirar
aspirin ['æsprən, 'æspə-] *n*, *pl* **aspirin** *or* **aspirins** : aspirina *f*
ass ['æs] *n* **1** : asno *m* **2** IDIOT : imbécil *mf*, idiota *mf*
assail [ə'seɪl] *vt* : atacar, asaltar
assailant [ə'seɪlənt] *n* : asaltante *mf*, atacante *mf*
assassin [ə'sæsən] *n* : asesino *m*, -na *f*
assassinate [ə'sæsən,eɪt] *vt* **-nated; -nating** : asesinar
assassination [ə,sæsən'eɪʃən] *n* : asesinato *m*
assault[1] [ə'sɔlt] *vt* : atacar, asaltar, agredir
assault[2] *n* : ataque *m*, asalto *m*, agresión *f*
assay[1] [æ'seɪ, 'æ,seɪ] *vt* : ensayar
assay[2] ['æ,seɪ, æ'seɪ] *n* : ensayo *m*
assemble [ə'sɛmbəl] *v* **-bled; -bling** *vt* **1** GATHER : reunir, recoger, juntar **2** CONSTRUCT : ensamblar, montar, construir — *vi* : reunirse, congregarse
assembly [ə'sɛmbli] *n*, *pl* **-blies 1** MEETING : reunión *f* **2** CONSTRUCTING : ensamblaje *m*, montaje *m*
assemblyman [ə'sɛmblimən] *n*, *pl* **-men** [-mən, -,mɛn] : asambleísta *m*
assemblywoman [ə'sɛmbli,wʊmən] *n*, *pl* **-women** [-,wɪmən] : asambleísta *f*
assent[1] [ə'sɛnt] *vi* : asentir, consentir
assent[2] *n* : asentimiento *m*, aprobación *f*
assert [ə'sərt] *vt* **1** AFFIRM : afirmar, aseverar, mantener **2 to assert oneself** : imponerse, hacerse valer
assertion [ə'sərʃən] *n* : afirmación *f*, aseveración *f*, aserto *m*
assertive [ə'sərṭɪv] *adj* : firme, enérgico
assertiveness [ə'sərṭɪvnəs] *n* : seguridad *f* en sí mismo
assess [ə'sɛs] *vt* **1** IMPOSE : gravar (un impuesto), imponer **2** EVALUATE : evaluar, valorar, aquilatar
assessment [ə'sɛsmənt] *n* : evaluación *f*, valoración *f*
assessor [ə'sɛsər] *n* : evaluador *m*, -dora *f*; tasador *m*, -dora *f*
asset ['æ,sɛt] *n* **1** : ventaja *f*, recurso *m* **2 assets** *npl* : bienes *mpl*, activo *m* ⟨assets and liabilities : activo y pasivo⟩
assiduous [ə'sɪdʒʊəs] *adj* : diligente, aplicado, asiduo — **assiduously** *adv*
assign [ə'saɪn] *vt* **1** APPOINT : designar, nombrar **2** ALLOT : asignar, señalar **3** ATTRIBUTE : atribuir, dar, conceder
assignment [ə'saɪnmənt] *n* **1** TASK : función *f*, tarea *f*, misión *f* **2** HOMEWORK : tarea *f*, asignación *f* PRi, deberes *mpl* Spain **3** APPOINTMENT : nombramiento *m* **4** ALLOCATION : asignación *f*
assimilate [ə'sɪmə,leɪt] *v* **-lated; -lating** *vt* : asimilar — *vi* : adaptarse, integrarse
assimilation [ə,sɪmə'leɪʃən] *n* : asimilación *f*
assist[1] [ə'sɪst] *vt* : asistir, ayudar
assist[2] *n* : asistencia *f*, contribución *f*

assistance [ə'sɪstənts] n : asistencia f, ayuda f, auxilio m

assistant [ə'sɪstənt] n : ayudante mf, asistente mf

associate¹ [ə'so:ʃi‚eɪt, -si-] v -ated; -ating vt 1 CONNECT, RELATE : asociar, relacionar 2 to be associated with : estar relacionado con, estar vinculado a — vi to associate with : relacionarse con, frecuentar

associate² [ə'so:ʃiət, -siət] n : asociado m, -da f; colega mf; socio m, -cia f

association [ə‚so:ʃi'eɪʃən, -si-] n 1 ORGANIZATION : asociación f, sociedad f 2 RELATIONSHIP : asociación f, relación f

as soon as conj : en cuanto, tan pronto como

assorted [ə'sɔrtəd] adj : surtido

assortment [ə'sɔrtmənt] n : surtido m, variedad f, colección f

assuage [ə'sweɪʤ] vt -suaged; -suaging 1 EASE : aliviar, mitigar 2 CALM : calmar, aplacar 3 SATISFY : saciar, satisfacer

assume [ə'su:m] vt -sumed; -suming 1 SUPPOSE : suponer, asumir 2 UNDERTAKE : asumir, encargarse de 3 TAKE ON : adquirir, adoptar, tomar ⟨to assume importance : tomar importancia⟩ 4 FEIGN : adoptar, afectar, simular

assumption [ə'sʌmpʃən] n : asunción f, presunción f

assurance [ə'ʃʊrənts] n 1 CERTAINTY : certidumbre f, certeza f 2 CONFIDENCE : confianza f, aplomo m, seguridad f

assure [ə'ʃʊr] vt -sured; -suring : asegurar, garantizar ⟨I assure you that I'll do it : te aseguro que lo haré⟩

assured [ə'ʃʊrd] adj 1 CERTAIN : seguro, asegurado 2 CONFIDENT : confiado, seguro de sí mismo

aster ['æstər] n : aster m

asterisk ['æstə‚rɪsk] n : asterisco m

astern [ə'stərn] adv 1 BEHIND : detrás, a popa 2 BACKWARDS : hacia atrás

asteroid ['æstə‚rɔɪd] n : asteroide m

asthma ['æzmə] n : asma m

asthmatic [æz'mætɪk] adj : asmático

as though → as if

astigmatism [ə'stɪgmə‚tɪzəm] n : astigmatismo m

as to prep 1 ABOUT : sobre, acerca de 2 → according to

astonish [ə'stɑnɪʃ] vt : asombrar, sorprender, pasmar

astonishing [ə'stɑnɪʃɪŋ] adj : asombroso, sorprendente, increíble — **astonishingly** adv

astonishment [ə'stɑnɪʃmənt] n : asombro m, estupefacción f, sorpresa f

astound [ə'staʊnd] vt : asombrar, pasmar, dejar estupefacto

astounding [ə'staʊndɪŋ] adj : asombroso, pasmoso — **astoundingly** adv

astraddle [ə'strædəl] adv : a horcajadas

astral ['æstrəl] adj : astral

astray [ə'streɪ] adv & adj : perdido, extraviado, descarriado

astride [ə'straɪd] adv : a horcajadas

astringency [ə'strɪnʤəntsi] n : astringencia f

astringent¹ [ə'strɪnʤənt] adj : astringente

astringent² n : astringente m

astrologer [ə'strɑləʤər] n : astrólogo m, -ga f

astrological [‚æstrə'lɑʤɪkəl] adj : astrológico

astrology [ə'strɑləʤi] n : astrología f

astronaut ['æstrə‚nɔt] n : astronauta mf

astronautic [‚æstrə'nɔtɪk] or **astronautical** [-tɪkəl] adj : astronáutico

astronautics [‚æstrə'nɔtɪks] ns & pl : astronáutica f

astronomer [ə'strɑnəmər] n : astrónomo m, -ma f

astronomical [‚æstrə'nɑmɪkəl] adj 1 : astronómico 2 ENORMOUS : astronómico, enorme, gigantesco

astronomy [ə'strɑnəmi] n, pl -mies : astronomía f

astute [ə'stu:t, -'stju:t] adj : astuto, sagaz, perspicaz — **astutely** adv

astuteness [ə'stu:tnəs, -'stju:t-] n : astucia f, sagacidad f, perspicacia f

asunder [ə'sʌndər] adv : en dos, en pedazos ⟨to tear asunder : hacer pedazos⟩

as well as¹ conj : tanto como

as well as² prep BESIDES : además de, aparte de

as yet adv : aún, todavía

asylum [ə'saɪləm] n 1 REFUGE : refugio m, santuario m, asilo m 2 insane asylum : manicomio m

asymmetrical [‚eɪsə'mɛtrɪkəl] or **asymmetric** [-'mɛtrɪk] adj : asimétrico

asymmetry [‚eɪ'sɪmətri] n : asimetría f

at ['æt] prep 1 : en ⟨at the top : en lo alto⟩ ⟨at peace : en paz⟩ ⟨at Ann's house : en casa de Ana⟩ 2 : a ⟨at the rear : al fondo⟩ ⟨at 10 o'clock : a las diez⟩ 3 : por ⟨at last : por fin⟩ ⟨to be surprised at something : sorprenderse por algo⟩ 4 : de ⟨he's laughing at you : está riéndose de ti⟩ 5 : para ⟨you're good at this : eres bueno para esto⟩

at all adv : en absoluto, para nada

ate → eat

atheism ['eɪθi‚ɪzəm] n : ateísmo m

atheist ['eɪθiɪst] n : ateo m, atea f

atheistic [‚eɪθi'ɪstɪk] adj : ateo

athlete ['æθ‚li:t] n : atleta mf

athletic [æθ'lɛtɪk] adj : atlético

athletics [æθ'lɛtɪks] ns & pl : atletismo m

Atlantic [ət'læntɪk, æt-] adj : atlántico

atlas ['ætləs] n : atlas m

ATM [‚eɪ‚ti:'ɛm] n : cajero m automático

atmosphere ['ætmə‚sfɪr] n 1 AIR : atmósfera f 2 AMBIENCE : ambiente m, atmósfera f, clima m

atmospheric [‚ætmə'sfɪrɪk, -'sfɛr-] adj : atmosférico — **atmospherically** [-ɪkli] adv

atoll [ˈæˌtɔl, ˈeɪ-, -ˌtal] n : atolón m
atom [ˈætəm] n 1 : átomo m 2 SPECK : ápice m, pizca f
atomic [əˈtamɪk] adj : atómico
atomic bomb n : bomba f atómica
atomizer [ˈætəˌmaɪzər] n : atomizador m, pulverizador m
atone [əˈtoːn] vt **atoned; atoning to atone for** : expiar
atonement [əˈtoːnmənt] n : expiación f, desagravio m
atop¹ [əˈtap] adj : encima
atop² prep : encima de, sobre
atrium [ˈeɪtriəm] n, pl **atria** [-triə] or **atriums** 1 : atrio m 2 : aurícula f (del corazón)
atrocious [əˈtroːʃəs] adj : atroz — **atrociously** adv
atrocity [əˈtrasəti] n, pl **-ties** : atrocidad f
atrophy¹ [ˈætrəfi] vt **-phied; -phying** : atrofiar
atrophy² n, pl **-phies** : atrofia f
attach [əˈtætʃ] vt 1 FASTEN : sujetar, atar, amarrar, pegar 2 JOIN : juntar, adjuntar 3 ATTRIBUTE : dar, atribuir ⟨I attached little importance to it : le di poca importancia⟩ 4 SEIZE : embargar 5 **to become attached to someone** : encariñarse con alguien
attaché [ˌætæˈʃeɪ, ˌæˌtæ-, ə-, ˌtæ-] n : agregado m, -da f
attachment [əˈtætʃmənt] n 1 ACCESSORY : accesorio m 2 CONNECTION : conexión f, acoplamiento m 3 FONDNESS : apego m, cariño m, afición f
attack¹ [əˈtæk] vt 1 ASSAULT : atacar, asaltar, agredir 2 TACKLE : acometer, combatir, enfrentarse con
attack² n 1 : ataque m, asalto m, acometida f ⟨to launch an attack : lanzar un ataque⟩ 2 : ataque m, crisis f ⟨heart attack : ataque cardíaco, infarto⟩ ⟨attack of nerves : crisis nerviosa⟩
attacker [əˈtækər] n : asaltante mf
attain [əˈteɪn] vt 1 ACHIEVE : lograr, conseguir, alcanzar, realizar 2 REACH : alcanzar, llegar a
attainable [əˈteɪnəbəl] adj : alcanzable, realizable, asequible
attainment [əˈteɪnmənt] n : logro m, consecución f, realización f
attempt¹ [əˈtempt] vt : intentar, tratar de
attempt² n : intento m, tentativa f
attend [əˈtend] vt 1 : asistir a ⟨to attend a meeting : asistir a una reunión⟩ 2 : atender, ocuparse de, cuidar ⟨to attend a patient : atender a un paciente⟩ 3 HEED : atender a, hacer caso de 4 ACCOMPANY : acompañar
attendance [əˈtendənts] n 1 ATTENDING : asistencia f 2 TURNOUT : concurrencia f
attendant¹ [əˈtendənt] adj : concomitante, inherente
attendant² n : asistente mf, acompañante mf, guarda mf

attention [əˈtenʧən] n 1 : atención f 2 **to pay attention** : prestar atención, hacer caso 3 **to stand at attention** : estar firme
attentive [əˈtentɪv] adj : atento — **attentively** adv
attentiveness [əˈtentɪvnəs] n 1 THOUGHTFULNESS : cortesía f, consideración f 2 CONCENTRATION : atención f, concentración f
attest [əˈtest] vt : atestiguar, dar fe de
attestation [ˌæˌtsˈteɪʃən] n : testimonio m
attic [ˈætɪk] n : ático m, desván m, buhardilla f
attire¹ [əˈtaɪr] vt **-tired; -tiring** : ataviar
attire² n : atuendo m, atavío m
attitude [ˈætəˌtuːd, -ˌtjuːd] n 1 FEELING : actitud f 2 POSTURE : postura f
attorney [əˈtərni] n, pl **-neys** : abogado m, -da f
attract [əˈtrækt] vt 1 : atraer 2 **to attract attention** : llamar la atención
attraction [əˈtrækʃən] n : atracción f, atractivo m
attractive [əˈtræktɪv] adj : atractivo, atrayente
attractively [əˈtræktɪvli] adv : de manera atractiva, de buen gusto, hermosamente
attractiveness [əˈtræktɪvnəs] n : atractivo m
attributable [əˈtrɪbjutəbəl] adj : atribuible, imputable
attribute¹ [əˈtrɪˌbjuːt] vt **-tributed; -tributing** : atribuir
attribute² [ˈætrəˌbjuːt] n : atributo m, cualidad f
attribution [ˌætrəˈbjuːʃən] n : atribución f
attune [əˈtuːn, -ˈtjuːn] vt **-tuned; -tuning** 1 ADAPT : adaptar, adecuar 2 **to be attuned to** : estar en armonía con
atypical [ˌeɪˈtɪpɪkəl] adj : atípico
auburn [ˈɔbərn] adj : castaño rojizo
auction¹ [ˈɔkʃən] vt : subastar, rematar
auction² n : subasta f, remate m
auctioneer [ˌɔkʃəˈnɪr] n : subastador m, -dora f; rematador m, -dora f
audacious [ɔˈdeɪʃəs] adj : audaz, atrevido
audacity [ɔˈdæsəti] n, pl **-ties** : audacia f, atrevimiento m, descaro m
audible [ˈɔdəbəl] adj : audible — **audibly** [-bli] adv
audience [ˈɔdiənts] n 1 INTERVIEW : audiencia f 2 PUBLIC : audiencia f, público m, auditorio m, espectadores mpl
audio¹ [ˈɔdiˌoː] adj : de sonido, de audio
audio² n : audio m
audiovisual [ˌɔdioˈvɪʒuəl] adj : audiovisual
audit¹ [ˈɔdət] vt 1 : auditar (finanzas) 2 : asistir como oyente a (una clase o un curso)
audit² n : auditoría f
audition¹ [ɔˈdɪʃən] vi : hacer una audición

audition[2] *n* : audición *f*

auditor ['ɔdətər] *n* 1 : auditor *m*, -tora *f* (de finanzas) 2 STUDENT : oyente *mf*

auditorium [,ɔdə'toriəm] *n, pl* **-riums** *or* **-ria** [-riə] : auditorio *m*, sala *f*

auditory ['ɔdə,tori] *adj* : auditivo

auger ['ɔgər] *n* : taladro *m*, barrena *f*

augment [ɔg'mɛnt] *vt* : aumentar, incrementar

augmentation [,ɔgmən'teɪʃən] *n* : aumento *m*, incremento *m*

augur[1] ['ɔgər] *vt* : augurar, presagiar — *vi* **to augur well** : ser de buen agüero

augur[2] *n* : augur *m*

augury ['ɔgjuri, -gər-] *n, pl* **-ries** : augurio *m*, presagio *m*, agüero *m*

august [ɔ'gʌst] *adj* : augusto

August ['ɔgəst] *n* : agosto *m*

auk ['ɔk] *n* : alca *f*

aunt ['ænt, 'ant] *n* : tía *f*

aura ['ɔrə] *n* : aura *f*

aural ['ɔrəl] *adj* : auditivo

auricle ['ɔrɪkəl] *n* : aurícula *f*

aurora borealis [ə'rorə,bori'æləs] *n* : aurora *f* boreal

auspices ['ɔspəsəz, -,si:z] *npl* : auspicios *mpl*

auspicious [ɔ'spɪʃəs] *adj* : prometedor, propicio, de buen augurio

austere [ɔ'stɪr] *adj* : austero, severo, adusto — **austerely** *adv*

austerity [ɔ'stɛrəti] *n, pl* **-ties** : austeridad *f*

Australian [ɔ'streɪljən] *n* : australiano *m*, -na *f* — **Australian** *adj*

Austrian ['ɔstriən] *n* : austriaco *m*, -ca *f* — **Austrian** *adj*

authentic [ə'θɛntɪk, ɔ-] *adj* : auténtico, genuino — **authentically** [-tɪkli] *adv*

authenticate [ə'θɛntɪ,keɪt, ɔ-] *vt* **-cated; -cating** : autenticar, autentificar

authenticity [ɔ,θɛn'tɪsəti] *n* : autenticidad *f*

author ['ɔθər] *n* 1 WRITER : escritor *m*, -tora *f*; autor *m*, -tora *f* 2 CREATOR : autor *m*, -tora *f*; creador *m*, -dora *f*; artífice *mf*

authoritarian [ɔ,θɔrə'tɛriən, ə-] *adj* : autoritario

authoritative [ə'θɔrə,teɪtɪv, ɔ-] *adj* 1 RELIABLE : fidedigno, autorizado 2 DICTATORIAL : autoritario, dictatorial, imperioso

authoritatively [ə'θɔrə,teɪtɪvli, ɔ-] *adv* 1 RELIABLY : con autoridad 2 DICTATORIALLY : de manera autoritaria

authority [ə'θɔrəti, ɔ-] *n, pl* **-ties** 1 EXPERT : autoridad *f*; experto *m*, -ta *f* 2 POWER : autoridad *f*, poder *m* 3 AUTHORIZATION : autorización *f*, licencia *f* 4 **the authorities** : las autoridades 5 **on good authority** : de buena fuente

authorization [,ɔθərə'zeɪʃən] *n* : autorización *f*

authorize ['ɔθə,raɪz] *vt* **-rized; -rizing** : autorizar, facultar

authorship ['ɔθər,ʃɪp] *n* : autoría *f*

autism ['ɔ,tɪzəm] *n* : autismo *m*

autistic [ɔ'tɪstɪk] *adj* : autista

auto ['ɔto] → **automobile**

autobiographical [,ɔto,baɪə'græfɪkəl] *adj* : autobiográfico

autobiography [,ɔtobaɪ'agrəfi] *n, pl* **-phies** : autobiografía *f*

autocracy [ɔ'takrəsi] *n, pl* **-cies** : autocracia *f*

autocrat ['ɔtə,kræt] *n* : autócrata *mf*

autocratic [,ɔtə'krætɪk] *adj* : autocrático — **autocratically** [-tɪkli] *adv*

autograph[1] ['ɔtə,græf] *vt* : autografiar

autograph[2] *n* : autógrafo *m*

automaker ['ɔto,meɪkər] *n* : fabricante *mf* de autos, automotriz *f*

automate ['ɔtə,meɪt] *vt* **-mated; -mating** : automatizar

automatic [,ɔtə'mætɪk] *adj* : automático — **automatically** [-tɪkli] *adv*

automation [,ɔtə'meɪʃən] *n* : automatización *f*

automaton [ɔ'tamə,tan] *n, pl* **-atons** *or* **-ata** [-tə, -,ta] : autómata *m*

automobile [,ɔtəmo'bi:l, -'mo:,bi:l] *n* : automóvil *m*, auto *m*, carro *m*, coche *m*

automotive [,ɔtə'mo:tɪv] *adj* : automotor

autonomous [ɔ'tanəməs] *adj* : autónomo — **autonomously** *adv*

autonomy [ɔ'tanəmi] *n, pl* **-mies** : autonomía *f*

autopsy ['ɔ,tapsi, -təp-] *n, pl* **-sies** : autopsia *f*

autumn ['ɔtəm] *n* : otoño *m*

autumnal [ɔ'tʌmnəl] *adj* : otoñal

auxiliary[1] [ɔg'zɪljəri, -'zɪləri] *adj* : auxiliar

auxiliary[2] *n, pl* **-ries** : auxiliar *mf*, ayudante *mf*

avail[1] [ə'veɪl] *vt* **to avail oneself** : aprovecharse, valerse

avail[2] *n* 1 : provecho *m*, utilidad *f* 2 **to no avail** : en vano 3 **to be of no avail** : no servir de nada, ser inútil

availability [ə,veɪlə'bɪləti] *n, pl* **-ties** : disponibilidad *f*

available [ə'veɪləbəl] *adj* : disponible

avalanche ['ævə,læntʃ] *n* : avalancha *f*, alud *m*

avarice ['ævərəs] *n* : avaricia *f*, codicia *f*

avaricious [,ævə'rɪʃəs] *adj* : avaricioso, codicioso

avenge [ə'vɛndʒ] *vt* **ávenged; avenging** : vengar

avenger [ə'vɛndʒər] *n* : vengador *m*, -dora *f*

avenue ['ævə,nu:, -,nju:] *n* 1 : avenida *f* 2 MEANS : vía *f*, camino *m*

average[1] ['ævrɪdʒ, 'ævə-] *vt* **-aged; -aging** 1 : hacer un promedio de ⟨he averages 8 hours a day : hace un promedio de 8 horas diarias⟩ 2 : calcular el promedio de, promediar (en matemáticas)

average[2] *adj* 1 MEAN : medio ⟨the average temperature : la temperatura media⟩ 2 ORDINARY : común, ordinario ⟨the average man : el hombre común⟩

average³ n : promedio m
averse [ə'vərs] adj : reacio, opuesto
aversion [ə'vərʒən] n : aversión f
avert [ə'vərt] vt **1** : apartar, desviar ⟨he
averted his eyes from the scene : apartó
los ojos de la escena⟩ **2** AVOID, PRE-
VENT : evitar, prevenir
aviary ['eɪviˌɛri] n, pl **-aries** : pajarera f
aviation [ˌeɪvi'eɪʃən] n : aviación f
aviator ['eɪviˌeɪtər] n : aviador m, -dora
f
avid ['ævɪd] adj **1** GREEDY : ávido, codicioso **2** ENTHUSIASTIC : ávido, entusiasta, ferviente — **avidly** adv
avocado [ˌævə'kɑdo, ˌɑvə-] n, pl **-dos**
: aguacate m, palta f
avocation [ˌævə'keɪʃən] n : pasatiempo
m, afición f
avoid [ə'vɔɪd] vt **1** SHUN : evitar, eludir
2 FORGO : evitar, abstenerse de ⟨I always avoided gossip : siempre evitaba
los chismes⟩ **3** EVADE : evitar ⟨if I can
avoid it : si puedo evitarlo⟩
avoidable [ə'vɔɪdəbəl] adj : evitable
avoidance [ə'vɔɪdəns] n : el evitar
avoirdupois [ˌævərdə'pɔɪz] n : sistema m
inglés de pesos y medidas
avow [ə'vaʊ] vt : reconocer, confesar
avowal [ə'vaʊəl] n : reconocimiento m,
confesión f
await [ə'weɪt] vt : esperar
awake¹ [ə'weɪk] v **awoke** [ə'wo:k]; **awok-
en** [ə'wo:kən] or **awaked**; **awaking**
: despertar
awake² adj : despierto
awaken [ə'weɪkən] → **awake¹**
award¹ [ə'wɔrd] vt : otorgar, conceder,
conferir
award² n **1** PRIZE : premio m, galardón
m **2** MEDAL : condecoración f
aware [ə'wær] adj : consciente ⟨to be
aware of : darse cuenta de, estar consciente de⟩
awareness [ə'wærnəs] n : conciencia f,
conocimiento m
awash [ə'wɔʃ] adj : inundado
away¹ [ə'weɪ] adv **1** : de aquí ⟨go away!
: ¡fuera de aquí!, ¡vete!⟩ **2** : de distancia ⟨10 miles away : 10 millas de distancia, queda a 10 millas⟩ **3 far away**
: lejos, a lo lejos **4 right away** : en segui-

da, ahora mismo **5 to be away** : estar
ausente, estar de viaje **6 to give away**
: regalar (una posesión), revelar (un secreto) **7 to go away** : irse, largarse **8
to put away** : guardar **9 to turn away**
: volver la cara
away² n **1** ABSENT : ausente ⟨away for
the week : ausente por la semana⟩ **2
away game** : partido m que se juega
fuera
awe¹ ['ɔ] vt **awed**; **awing** : abrumar,
impresionar
awe² n : asombro m
awesome ['ɔsəm] adj **1** IMPOSING : imponente, formidable **2** AMAZING
: asombroso
awestruck ['ɔˌstrʌk] adj : asombrado
awful ['ɔfəl] adj **1** AWESOME : asombroso **2** DREADFUL : horrible, terrible,
atroz **3** ENORMOUS : enorme, tremendo ⟨an awful lot of people : muchísima gente, la mar de gente⟩
awfully ['ɔfli] adv **1** EXTREMELY : terriblemente, extremadamente **2** BAD-
LY : muy mal, espantosamente
awhile [ə'hwaɪl] adv : un rato, algún
tiempo
awkward ['ɔkwərd] adj **1** CLUMSY : torpe, desmañado **2** EMBARRASSING : embarazoso, delicado — **awkwardly** adv
awkwardness ['ɔkwərdnəs] n **1** CLUM-
SINESS : torpeza f **2** INCONVENIENCE
: incomodidad f
awl ['ɔl] n : punzón m
awning ['ɔnɪŋ] n : toldo m
awry [ə'raɪ] adj **1** ASKEW : torcido **2 to
go awry** : salir mal, fracasar
ax or **axe** ['æks] n : hacha f
axiom ['æksiəm] n : axioma m
axiomatic [ˌæksiə'mætɪk] adj : axiomático
axis ['æksɪs] n, pl **axes** [-ˌsi:z] : eje m
axle ['æksəl] n : eje m
aye¹ ['aɪ] adv : sí
aye² n : sí m
azalea [ə'zeɪljə] n : azalea f
azimuth ['æzəməθ] n : azimut m, acimut
m
Aztec ['æzˌtɛk] n : azteca mf
azure¹ ['æʒər] adj : azur, celeste
azure² n : azur m

B

b ['bi:] n, pl **b's** or **bs** ['bi:z] : segunda letra del alfabeto inglés
babble¹ ['bæbəl] vi **-bled; -bling 1** PRAT-
TLE : balbucear **2** CHATTER : charlatanear, parlotear fam **3** MURMUR
: murmurar
babble² n : balbuceo m (de bebé), parloteo m (de adultos), murmullo m (de
voces, de un arroyo)
babe ['beɪb] n → **baby³**
babel ['beɪbəl, 'bæ-] n : babel f, caos m

baboon [bæ'bu:n] n : babuino m
baby¹ ['beɪbi] vt **-bied; -bying** : mimar,
consentir
baby² adj **1** : de niño ⟨a baby carriage
: un cochecito⟩ ⟨baby talk : habla in-
fantil⟩ **2** TINY : pequeño, minúsculo
baby³ n, pl **-bies** : bebé m; niño m, -ña
f
babyhood ['beɪbiˌhʊd] n : niñez f,
primera infancia f
babyish ['beɪbiɪʃ] adj : infantil, pueril

baby–sit ['beɪbiˌsɪt] *vi* **-sat** [-ˌsæt];
-sitting : cuidar niños, hacer de canguro *Spain*
baby–sitter ['beɪbiˌsɪtər] *n* : niñero *m*,
-ra *f*; canguro *mf Spain*
baccalaureate [ˌbækəˈlɔriət] *n* : licenciatura *f*
bachelor ['bætʃələr] *n* 1 : soltero *m* 2
: licenciado *m*, -da *f* ⟨bachelor of arts
degree : licenciatura en filosofía y le-
tras⟩
bacillus [bəˈsɪləs] *n, pl* **-li** [-ˌlaɪ] : bacilo
m
back¹ ['bæk] *vt* 1 *or* **to back up** SUPPORT
: apoyar, respaldar 2 *or* **to back up** RE-
VERSE : darle marcha atrás a (un vehículo) 3 : estar detrás de, formar el
fondo de ⟨trees back the garden : unos
árboles están detrás del jardín⟩ — *vi* 1
or **to back up** : retroceder 2 **to back
away** : echarse atrás 3 **to back down**
or **to back out** : volverse atrás, echarse
para atrás
back² *adv* 1 : atrás, hacia atrás, detrás
⟨to move back : moverse atrás⟩ ⟨back
and forth : de acá para allá⟩ 2 AGO
: atrás, antes, ya ⟨some years back
: unos años atrás, ya unos años⟩ ⟨10
months back : hace diez meses⟩ 3 : de
vuelta, de regreso ⟨we're back : estamos de vuelta⟩ ⟨she ran back : volvió
corriendo⟩ ⟨to call back : llamar de
nuevo⟩
back³ *adj* 1 REAR : de atrás, posterior,
trasero 2 OVERDUE : atrasado 3 **back
pay** : atrasos *mpl*
back⁴ *n* 1 : espalda *f* (de un ser humano),
lomo *m* (de un animal) 2 : respaldo *m*
(de una silla), espalda *f* (de ropa) 3 RE-
VERSE : reverso *m*, dorso *m*, revés *m* 4
REAR : fondo *m*, parte *f* de atrás 5 : defensa *mf* (en deportes)
backache ['bækˌeɪk] *n* : dolor *m* de espalda
backbite ['bækˌbaɪt] *v* **-bit** [-ˌbɪt]; **-bitten**
[-ˌbɪtən]; **-biting** *vt* : calumniar, hablar
mal de — *vi* : murmurar
backbiter ['bækˌbaɪtər] *n* : calumniador
m, -dora *f*
backbone ['bækˌboːn] *n* 1 : columna *f*
vertebral 2 FIRMNESS : firmeza *f*,
carácter *m*
backdrop ['bækˌdrɑp] *n* : telón *m* de fondo
backer ['bækər] *n* 1 SUPPORTER : partidario *m*, -ria *f* 2 SPONSOR : patrocinador *m*, -dora *f*
backfire¹ ['bækˌfaɪr] *vi* **-fired; -firing** 1
: petardear (dícese de un automóvil) 2
FAIL : fallar, salir el tiro por la culata
backfire² *n* : petardeo *m*, explosión *f*
background ['bækˌgraʊnd] *n* 1 : fondo
m (de un cuadro, etc.), antecedentes
mpl (de una situación) 2 EXPERIENCE,
TRAINING : experiencia *f* profesional,
formación *f*
backhand¹ ['bækˌhænd] *adv* : de revés,
con el revés

backhand² *n* : revés *m*
backhanded ['bækˌhændəd] *adj* 1
: dado con el revés, de revés 2 INDI-
RECT : indirecto, ambiguo
backing ['bækɪŋ] *n* 1 SUPPORT : apoyo
m, respaldo *m* 2 REINFORCEMENT : refuerzo *m* 3 SUPPORTERS : partidarios
mpl, -rias *fpl*
backlash ['bækˌlæʃ] *n* : reacción *f* vio-
lenta
backlog ['bækˌlɔg] *n* : atraso *m*, trabajo
m acumulado
backpack¹ ['bækˌpæk] *vi* : viajar con
mochila
backpack² *n* : mochila *f*
backrest ['bækˌrest] *n* : respaldo *m*
backside ['bækˌsaɪd] *n* : trasero *m*
backslide ['bækˌslaɪd] *vi* **-slid** [-ˌslɪd];
-slid *or* **-slidden** [-ˌslɪdən]; **-sliding** : recaer, reincidir
backstage [ˌbækˈsteɪdʒ, 'bækˌ-] *adv &
adj* : entre bastidores
backtrack ['bækˌtræk] *vi* : dar marcha
atrás, volverse atrás
backup ['bækˌʌp] *n* 1 SUPPORT : respaldo *m*, apoyo *m* 2 : copia *f* de seguridad (para computadoras)
backward¹ ['bækwərd] *or* **backwards**
[-wərdz] *adv* 1 : hacia atrás 2 : de espaldas ⟨he fell backwards : se cayó de
espaldas⟩ 3 : al revés ⟨you're doing it
backwards : lo estás haciendo al revés⟩
4 **to bend over backwards** : hacer todo
lo posible
backward² *adj* 1 : hacia atrás ⟨a backward glance : una mirada hacia atrás⟩
2 RETARDED : retrasado 3 SHY : tímido 4 UNDERDEVELOPED : atrasado
backwardness ['bækwərdnəs] *n* : atraso *m* (dícese de una región), retraso *m*
(dícese de una persona)
backwoods [ˌbækˈwʊdz] *npl* : monte *m*,
región *f* alejada
bacon ['beɪkən] *n* : tocino *m*, tocineta *f*
Col, Ven, bacon *m Spain*
bacterial [bækˈtɪriəl] *adj* : bacteriano
bacteriologist [bækˌtɪriˈɑlədʒɪst] *n* : bacteriólogo *m*, -ga *f*
bacteriology [bækˌtɪriˈɑlədʒi] *n* : bacteriología *f*
bacterium [bækˈtɪriəm] *n, pl* **-ria** [-iə]
: bacteria *f*
bad¹ ['bæd] *adv* → **badly**
bad² *adj* 1 : malo 2 ROTTEN : podrido
3 SERIOUS, SEVERE : grave 4 DEFEC-
TIVE : defectuoso ⟨a bad check : un
cheque sin fondos⟩ 5 HARMFUL : perjudicial 6 CORRUPT, EVIL : malo, corrompido 7 NAUGHTY : travieso 8
from bad to worse : de mal en peor 9
too bad! : ¡qué lástima!
bad³ *n* : lo malo ⟨the good and the bad
: lo bueno y lo malo⟩
bade → **bid**
badge ['bædʒ] *n* : insignia *f*, botón *m*,
chapa *f*
badger¹ ['bædʒər] *vt* : fastidiar, acosar,
importunar

badger[2] *n* : tejón *m*

badly ['bædli] *adv* **1** PERPLEX-LY : mal **2** URGENT-LY : mucho, con urgencia **3** SEVERE-LY : gravemente

badminton [,bæd,mɪntən, -,mɪt-] *n* : bádminton *m*

badness ['bædnəs] *n* : maldad *f*

baffle[1] ['bæfəl] *vt* -**fled**; -**fling** **1** PERPLEX : desconcertar, confundir **2** FRUS-TRATE : frustrar

baffle[2] *n* : deflector *m*, bafle *m* (acústi-co)

bafflement ['bæfəlmənt] *n* : desconcier-to *m*, confusión *f*

bag[1] ['bæg] *v* **bagged**; **bagging** *vi* SAG : formar bolsas — *vt* **1** : ensacar, pon-er en una bolsa **2** : cobrar (en la caza), cazar

bag[2] *n* **1** : bolsa *f*, saco *m* **2** HANDBAG : cartera *f*, bolso *m*, bolsa *f Mex* **3** SUIT-CASE : maleta *f*, valija *f*

bagatelle [,bægə'tɛl] *n* : bagatela *f*

bagel ['beɪgəl] *n* : rosquilla *f* de pan

baggage ['bægɪdʒ] *n* : equipaje *m*

baggy ['bægi] *adj* -**gier**; -**est** : holgado, ancho

bagpipe ['bæg,paɪp] *n or* **bagpipes** ['bæg,paɪps] *npl* : gaita *f*

bail[1] ['beɪl] *vt* **1** : achicar (agua de un bote) **2 to bail out** : poner en libertad (de una cárcel) bajo fianza **3 to bail out** EXTRICATE : sacar de apuros

bail[2] *n* : fianza *f*, caución *f*

bailiff ['beɪləf] *n* : alguacil *mf*

bailiwick ['beɪli,wɪk] *n* : dominio *m*

bailout ['beɪl,aʊt] *n* : rescate *m* (finan-ciero)

bait[1] ['beɪt] *vt* **1** : cebar (un anzuelo o cepo) **2** HARASS : acosar

bait[2] *n* : cebo *m*, carnada *f*

bake[1] ['beɪk] *vt* **baked**; **baking** : horn-ear, hacer al horno

bake[2] *n* : fiesta con platos hechos al horno

baker ['beɪkər] *n* : panadero *m*, -ra *f*

baker's dozen *n* : docena *f* de fraile

bakery ['beɪkəri] *n, pl* -**ries** : panadería *f*

bakeshop ['beɪk,ʃap] *n* : pastelería *f*, panadería *f*

baking powder *n* : levadura *f* en polvo

baking soda → **sodium bicarbonate**

balance[1] ['bæləns] *v* -**anced**; -**ancing** *vt* **1** : hacer el balance de (una cuenta) ⟨to balance the books : cuadrar las cuen-tas⟩ **2** EQUALIZE : balancear, equili-brar **3** HARMONIZE : armonizar — *vi* : balancearse

balance[2] *n* **1** SCALES : balanza *f*, bás-cula *f* **2** COUNTERBALANCE : contrapeso *m* **3** EQUILIBRIUM : equilibrio *m* **4** REMAINDER : balance *m*, resto *m*

balanced ['bæləntst] *adj* : equilibrado, balanceado

balcony ['bælkəni] *n, pl* -**nies** **1** : bal-cón *m*, terraza *f* (de un edificio) **2** : galería *f* (de un teatro)

bald ['bɔld] *adj* **1** : calvo, pelado, pelón **2** PLAIN : simple, puro ⟨the bald truth : la pura verdad⟩

balding ['bɔldɪŋ] *adj* : quedándose cal-vo

baldly ['bɔldli] *adv* : sin reparos, sin rodeos, francamente

baldness ['bɔldnəs] *n* : calvicie *f*

bale[1] ['beɪl] *vt* **baled**; **baling** : empacar, hacer balas de

bale[2] *n* : bala *f*, fardo *m*, paca *f*

baleful ['beɪlfəl] *adj* **1** DEADLY : mortífero **2** SINISTER : siniestro, fu-nesto, torvo ⟨a baleful glance : una mi-rada torva⟩

balk[1] ['bɔk] *vt* : obstaculizar, impedir — *vi* **1** : plantarse *fam* (dícese de un ca-ballo, etc.) **2 to balk at** : resistarse a, mostrarse reacio a

balk[2] *n* : obstáculo *m*

Balkan ['bɔlkən] *adj* : balcánico

balky ['bɔki] *adj* **balkier**; -**est** : reacio, obstinado, terco

ball[1] ['bɔl] *vt* : apelotonar, ovillar

ball[2] *n* **1** : pelota *f*, bola *f*, balón *m*, ovi-llo *m* (de lana) **2** : juego *m* con pelota o bola **3** DANCE : baile *m*, baile *m* de etiqueta

ballad ['bæləd] *n* : romance *m*, balada *f*

balladeer [,bælə'dɪr] *n* : cantante *mf* de baladas

ballast[1] ['bæləst] *vt* : lastrar

ballast[2] *n* : lastre *m*

ball bearing *n* : cojinete *m* de bola

ballerina [,bælə'ri:nə] *n* : bailarina *f*

ballet [bæ'leɪ, 'bæ,leɪ] *n* : ballet *m*

ballistic [bə'lɪstɪk] *adj* : balístico

ballistics [bə'lɪstɪks] *ns & pl* : balística *f*

balloon[1] [bə'lu:n] *vi* **1** : viajar en globo **2** SWELL : hincharse, inflarse

balloon[2] *n* : globo *m*

balloonist [bə'lu:nɪst] *n* : aeróstata *mf*

ballot[1] ['bælət] *vi* : votar

ballot[2] *n* **1** : papeleta *f* (de voto) **2** BAL-LOTING : votación *f* **3** VOTE : voto *m*

ballpoint pen ['bɔl,pɔɪnt] *n* : bolígrafo *m*

ballroom ['bɔl,ru:m, -,rʊm] *n* : sala *f* de baile

ballyhoo ['bæli,hu:] *n* : propaganda *f*, publicidad *f*, bombo *m fam*

balm ['bam, 'balm] *n* : bálsamo *m*, ungüento *m*

balmy ['bami, 'bal-] *adj* **balmier**; -**est** **1** MILD : templado, agradable **2** SOOTH-ING : balsámico **3** CRAZY : chiflado *fam*, chalado *fam*

baloney [bə'lo:ni] *n* NONSENSE : ton-terías *fpl*, estupideces *fpl*

balsa ['bɔlsə] *n* : balsa *f*

balsam ['bɔlsəm] *n* **1** : bálsamo *m* **2 or balsam fir** : abeto *m* balsámico

Baltic ['bɔltɪk] *adj* : báltico

baluster ['bæləstər] *n* : balaustre *m*

balustrade [,bælə,streɪd] *n* : balaustra-da *f*

bamboo [bæm'bu:] *n* : bambú *m*

bamboozle [bæm'bu:zəl] *vt* -**zled**; -**zling** : engañar, embaucar

ban¹ ['bæn] *vt* banned; banning : prohibir, proscribir

ban² *n* : prohibición *f*, proscripción *f*

banal [bə'nɑl, bə'næl, 'beɪnəl] *adj* : banal, trivial

banality [bə'næləti] *n*, *pl* -ties : banalidad *f*, trivialidad *f*

banana [bə'nænə] *n* : banano *m*, plátano *m*, banana *f*, cambur *m* Ven, guineo *m* Car

band¹ ['bænd] *vt* **1** BIND : fajar, atar **2 to band together** : unirse, juntarse

band² *n* **1** STRIP : banda *f*, cinta *f* (de un sombrero, etc.) **2** STRIPE : franja *f* **3** : banda *f* (de radiofrecuencia) **4** RING : anillo *m* **5** GROUP : banda *f*, grupo *m*, conjunto *m* ⟨jazz band : conjunto de jazz⟩

bandage¹ ['bændɪdʒ] *vt* -daged; -daging : vendar

bandage² *n* : vendaje *m*, venda *f*

bandanna *or* **bandana** [bæn'dænə] *n* : pañuelo *m* (de colores)

bandit ['bændət] *n* : bandido *m*, -da *f*; bandolero *m*, -ra *f*

banditry ['bændətri] *n* : bandolerismo *m*, bandidaje *m*

bandstand ['bænd,stænd] *n* : quiosco *m* de música

bandwagon ['bænd,wægən] *n* **1** : carroza *f* de músicos **2 to jump on the bandwagon** : subirse al carro, seguir la moda

bandy¹ ['bændi] *vt* -died; -dying **1** EXCHANGE : intercambiar **2 to bandy about** : circular, propagar

bandy² *adj* : arqueado, torcido ⟨bandy-legged : de piernas arqueadas⟩

bane ['beɪn] *n* **1** POISON : veneno *m* **2** RUIN : ruina *f*, pesadilla *f*

baneful ['beɪnfəl] *adj* : nefasto, funesto

bang¹ ['bæŋ] *vt* **1** STRIKE : golpear, darse ⟨he banged his elbow against the door : se dio con el codo en la puerta⟩ **2** SLAM : cerrar (la puerta) con un portazo — *vi* **1** SLAM : cerrarse con un golpe **2 to bang on** : aporrear, golpear ⟨she was banging on the table : aporreaba la mesa⟩

bang² *adv* : directamente, exactamente

bang³ *n* **1** BLOW : golpe *m*, porrazo *m*, trancazo *m* **2** EXPLOSION : explosión *f*, estallido *m* **3** SLAM : portazo *m* **4 bangs** *npl* : flequillo *m*, fleco *m*

Bangladeshi [,bɑŋglə'deʃi, ,bæŋ-, ,bʌŋ-, -'deɪ-] *n* : bangladesí *mf* — **Bangladeshi** *adj*

bangle ['bæŋgəl] *n* : brazalete *m*, pulsera *f*

banish ['bænɪʃ] *vt* **1** EXILE : desterrar, exiliar **2** EXPEL : expulsar

banishment ['bænɪʃmənt] *n* **1** EXILE : destierro *m*, exilio *m* **2** EXPULSION : expulsión *f*

banister ['bænəstər] *n* **1** BALUSTER : balaustre *m* **2** HANDRAIL : pasamanos *m*, barandilla *f*, barandal *m*

banjo ['bæn,dʒo] *n*, *pl* -jos : banjo *m*

bank¹ ['bæŋk] *vt* **1** TILT : peraltar (una carretera), ladear (un avión) **2** HEAP : amontonar **3** : cubrir (un fuego) **4** : depositar (dinero en un banco) — *vi* **1** : ladearse (dícese de un avión) **2** : tener una cuenta (en un banco) **3 to bank on** : contar con

bank² *n* **1** MASS : montón *m*, montículo *m*, masa *f* **2** : orilla *f*, ribera *f* (de un río) **3** : peralte *m* (de una carretera) **4** : banco *m* ⟨World Bank : Banco Mundial⟩ ⟨banco de sangre : blood bank⟩

bankbook ['bæŋk,bʊk] *n* : libreta *f* bancaria, libreta *f* de ahorros

banker ['bæŋkər] *n* : banquero *m*, -ra *f*

banking ['bæŋkɪŋ] *n* : banca *f*

bankrupt¹ ['bæŋ,krʌpt] *vt* : hacer quebrar, llevar a la quiebra, arruinar

bankrupt² *adj* **1** : en bancarrota, en quiebra **2 ~ of** LACKING : carente de, falto de

bankrupt³ *n* : fallido *m*, -da *f*; quebrado *m*, -da *f*

bankruptcy ['bæŋ,krʌptsi] *n*, *pl* -cies : ruina *f*, quiebra *f*, bancarrota *f*

banner¹ ['bænər] *adj* : excelente

banner² *n* : estandarte *m*, bandera *f*

banns ['bænz] *npl* : amonestaciones *fpl*

banquet¹ ['bæŋkwət] *vi* : celebrar un banquete

banquet² *n* : banquete *m*

banter¹ ['bæntər] *vi* : bromear, hacer bromas

banter² *n* : bromas *fpl*

baptism ['bæp,tɪzəm] *n* : bautismo *m*

baptismal [bæp'tɪzməl] *adj* : bautismal

Baptist ['bæptɪst] *n* : bautista *mf* — **Baptist** *adj*

baptize [bæp'taɪz, 'bæp,taɪz] *vt* -tized; -tizing : bautizar

bar¹ ['bɑr] *vt* barred; barring **1** OBSTRUCT : obstruir, bloquear **2** EXCLUDE : excluir **3** PROHIBIT : prohibir **4** SECURE : atrancar, asegurar ⟨bar the door! : ¡atranca la puerta!⟩

bar² *n* **1** : barra *f*, barrote *m* (de una ventana), tranca *f* (de una puerta) **2** BARRIER : barrera *f*, obstáculo *m* **3** LAW : abogacía *f* **4** STRIPE : franja *f* **5** COUNTER : mostrador *m*, barra *f* **6** TAVERN : bar *m*, taberna *f*

bar³ *prep* : excepto, con excepción de **2 bar none** : sin excepción

barb ['bɑrb] *n* **1** POINT : púa *f*, lengüeta *f* **2** GIBE : pulla *f*

barbarian¹ [bɑr'bæriən] *adj* **1** : bárbaro **2** CRUDE : tosco, bruto

barbarian² *n* : bárbaro *m*, -ra *f*

barbaric [bɑr'bærɪk] *adj* **1** PRIMITIVE : primitivo **2** CRUEL : brutal, cruel

barbarity [bɑr'bærəti] *n*, *pl* -ties : barbaridad *f*

barbarous ['bɑrbərəs] *adj* **1** UNCIVILIZED : bárbaro **2** MERCILESS : despiadado, cruel

barbarously ['bɑrbərəsli] *adv* : bárbaramente

barbecue[1] ['barbɪˌkju:] *vt* **-cued; -cuing** : asar a la parrilla

barbecue[2] *n* : barbacoa *f*, parrillada *f*

barbed ['barbd] *adj* **1** : con púas ⟨barbed wire : alambre de púas⟩ **2** BITING : mordaz

barber ['barbər] *n* : barbero *m*

barbiturate [bar'bɪtʃərət] *n* : barbitúrico *m*

bard ['bard] *n* : bardo *m*

bare[1] ['bær] *vt* **bared; baring** : desnudar

bare[2] *adj* **1** NAKED : desnudo **2** EXPOSED : descubierto, sin protección **3** EMPTY : desprovisto, vacío **4** MINIMUM : mero, mínimo ⟨the bare necessities : las necesidades mínimas⟩ **5** PLAIN : puro, sencillo

bareback ['bærˌbæk] *or* **barebacked** [-ˌbækt] *adv & adj* : a pelo

barefaced ['bærˌfeɪst] *adj* : descarado

barefoot ['bærˌfʊt] *or* **barefooted** [-ˌfʊtəd] *adv & adj* : descalzo

bareheaded ['bærˌhɛdəd] *adv & adj* : sin sombrero, con la cabeza descubierta

barely ['bærli] *adv* : apenas, por poco

bareness ['bærnəs] *n* : desnudez *f*

bargain[1] ['bargən] *vi* HAGGLE : regatear, negociar — *vt* BARTER : trocar, cambiar

bargain[2] *n* **1** AGREEMENT : acuerdo *m*, convenio *m* ⟨to strike a bargain : cerrar un trato⟩ **2** ganga *f* ⟨bargain price : precio de ganga⟩

barge[1] ['bardʒ] *vi* **barged; barging 1** : mover con torpeza **2 to barge in** : entrometerse, interrumpir

barge[2] *n* : barcaza *f*, gabarra *f*

bar graph *n* : gráfico *m* de barras

baritone ['bærəˌto:n] *n* : barítono *m*

barium ['bæriəm] *n* : bario *m*

bark[1] ['bark] *vi* : ladrar — *vt or* **to bark out** : gritar ⟨to bark out an order : dar una orden a gritos⟩

bark[2] *n* **1** : ladrido *m* (de un perro) **2** : corteza *f* (de un árbol) **3** *or* **barque** : tipo de embarcación con velas de proa y popa

barley ['barli] *n* : cebada *f*

barn ['barn] *n* : granero *m* (para cosechas), establo *m* (para ganado)

barnacle ['barnɪkəl] *n* : percebe *m*

barnyard ['barnˌjard] *n* : corral *m*

barometer [bə'ramətər] *n* : barómetro *m*

barometric [ˌbærə'mɛtrɪk] *adj* : barométrico

baron ['bærən] *n* **1** : barón *m* **2** TYCOON : magnate *mf*

baroness ['bærənɪs, -nəs, -ˌnɛs] *n* : baronesa *f*

baronet [ˌbærə'nɛt, 'bærənət] *n* : baronet *m*

baronial [bə'ro:niəl] *adj* **1** : de barón **2** STATELY : señorial, majestuoso

baroque [bə'ro:k, -'rak] *adj* : barroco

barracks ['bærəks] *ns & pl* : cuartel *m*

barracuda [ˌbærə'ku:də] *n, pl* **-da** *or* **-das** : barracuda *f*

barrage [bə'raʒ, -'radʒ] *n* **1** : descarga *f* (de artillería) **2** DELUGE : aluvión *m* ⟨a barrage of questions : un aluvión de preguntas⟩

barred ['bard] *adj* : excluido, prohibido

barrel[1] ['bærəl] *v* **-reled** *or* **-relled; -reling** *or* **-relling** *vt* : embarrilar — *vi* : ir disparado

barrel[2] *n* **1** : barril *m*, tonel *m* **2** : cañón *m* (de un arma de fuego), cilindro *m* (de una cerradura)

barren ['bærən] *adj* **1** STERILE : estéril (dícese de las plantas o la mujer), árido (dícese del suelo) **2** DESERTED : yermo, desierto

barrette [ba'rɛt, bə-] *n* : pasador *m*, broche *m* para el cabello

barricade[1] ['bærəˌkeɪd, ˌbærə'-] *vt* **-caded; -cading** : cerrar con barricadas

barricade[2] *n* : barricada *f*

barrier ['bæriər] *n* **1** : barrera *f* **2** OBSTACLE : obstáculo *m*, impedimento *m*

barring ['barɪŋ] *prep* : excepto, salvo, a excepción de

barrio ['bario, 'bær-] *n* : barrio *m*

barroom ['barˌru:m, -ˌrʊm] *n* : bar *m*

barrow ['bærˌo:] → **wheelbarrow**

bartender ['barˌtɛndər] *n* : camarero *m*, -ra *f*; barman *m*

barter[1] ['bartər] *vt* : cambiar, trocar

barter[2] *n* : trueque *m*, permuta *f*

basalt [bə'sɔlt, 'beɪˌ-] *n* : basalto *m*

base[1] ['beɪs] *vt* **based; basing** : basar, fundamentar, establecer

base[2] *adj* **baser; basest 1** : de baja ley (dícese de un metal) **2** CONTEMPTIBLE : vil, despreciable

base[3] *n, pl* **bases** : base *f*

baseball ['beɪsˌbɔl] *n* : beisbol *m*, béisbol *m*

baseless ['beɪsləs] *adj* : infundado

basely ['beɪsli] *adv* : vilmente

basement ['beɪsmənt] *n* : sótano *m*

baseness ['beɪsnəs] *n* : vileza *f*, bajeza *f*

bash[1] ['bæʃ] *vt* : golpear violentamente

bash[2] *n* **1** BLOW : golpe *m*, porrazo *m*, madrazo *m* Mex fam **2** PARTY : fiesta *f*, juerga *f* fam

bashful ['bæʃfəl] *adj* : tímido, vergonzoso, penoso

bashfulness ['bæʃfəlnəs] *n* : timidez *f*

basic[1] ['beɪsɪk] *adj* **1** FUNDAMENTAL : básico, fundamental **2** RUDIMENTARY : básico, elemental **3** : básico (en química)

basic[2] *n* : fundamento *m*, rudimento *m*

basically ['beɪsɪkli] *adv* : fundamentalmente

basil ['beɪzəl, 'bæzəl] *n* : albahaca *f*

basilica [bə'sɪlɪkə] *n* : basílica *f*

basin ['beɪsən] *n* **1** WASHBOWL : palangana *f*, lavamanos *m*, lavabo *m* **2** : cuenca *f* (de un río)

basis ['beɪsəs] *n, pl* **bases** [-ˌsi:z] **1** BASE : base *f*, pilar *m* **2** FOUNDATION : fundamento *m*, base *f* **3 on a weekly basis** : semanalmente

bask ['bæsk] *vi* : disfrutar, deleitarse ⟨to bask in the sun : disfrutar del sol⟩

basket ['bæskət] *n* : cesta *f*, cesto *m*, canasta *f*

basketball ['bæskət,bɔl] *n* : baloncesto *m*, basquetbol *m*

bas–relief [,bɑ:rɪ'li:f] *n* : bajorrelieve *m*

bass¹ ['bæs] *n*, *pl* **bass** *or* **basses** : róbalo *m* (pesca)

bass² ['beɪs] *n* : bajo *m* (tono, voz, cantante)

bass drum *n* : bombo *m*

basset hound ['bæsət,haʊnd] *n* : basset *m*

bassinet [,bæsə'nɛt] *n* : moisés *m*, cuna *f*

bassist ['beɪsɪst] *n* : bajista *mf*

bassoon [bə'su:n, bæ-] *n* : fagot *m*

bass viol ['beɪs'vaɪəl, -,o:l] → **double bass**

bastard¹ ['bæstərd] *adj* : bastardo

bastard² *n* : bastardo *m*, -da *f*

bastardize ['bæstər,daɪz] *vt* -ized; -izing DEBASE : degradar, envilecer

baste ['beɪst] *vt* basted; basting 1 STITCH : hilvanar 2 : bañar (con su jugo durante la cocción)

bastion ['bæstʃən] *n* : bastión *m*, baluarte *m*

bat¹ ['bæt] *vt* batted; batting 1 HIT : batear 2 without batting an eye : sin pestañear

bat² *n* 1 : murciélago *m* (animal) 2 : bate *m* ⟨baseball bat : bate de beisbol⟩

batch ['bætʃ] *n* : hornada *f*, tanda *f*, grupo *m*, cantidad *f*

bate ['beɪt] *vt* bated; bating 1 : aminorar, reducir 2 with bated breath : con ansiedad, aguantando la respiración

bath ['bæθ, 'bɑθ] *n*, *pl* **baths** ['bæðz, 'bæθs, 'baðz, 'baθs] 1 BATHING : baño *m* ⟨to take a bath : bañarse⟩ 2 : baño *m* (en fotografía, etc.) 3 BATHROOM : baño *m*, cuarto *m* de baño 4 SPA : balneario *m* 5 LOSS : pérdida *f*

bathe ['beɪð] *v* bathed; bathing *vt* 1 WASH : bañar, lavar 2 SOAK : poner en remojo 3 FLOOD : inundar ⟨to bathe with light : inundar de luz⟩ — *vi* : bañarse, ducharse

bather ['beɪðər] *n* : bañista *mf*

bathrobe ['bæθ,ro:b] *n* : bata *f* (de baño)

bathroom ['bæθ,ru:m, -,rʊm] *n* : baño *m*, cuarto *m* de baño

bathtub ['bæθ,tʌb] *n* : bañera *f*, tina *f* (de baño)

batiste [bə'ti:st] *n* : batista *f*

baton [bə'tɑn] *n* : batuta *f*, bastón *m*

battalion [bə'tæljən] *n* : batallón *m*

batten ['bætən] *vt* to batten down the hatches : cerrar las escotillas

batter¹ ['bætər] *vt* 1 BEAT : aporrear, golpear 2 MISTREAT : maltratar

batter² *n* 1 : masa *f* para rebozar 2 HITTER : bateador *m*, -dora *f*

battering ram *n* : ariete *m*

battery ['bætəri] *n*, *pl* -teries 1 : lesiones *fpl* ⟨assault and battery : agresión con

lesiones⟩ 2 ARTILLERY : batería *f* 3 : batería *f*, pila *f* (de electricidad) 4 SERIES : serie *f*

batting ['bætɪŋ] *n* 1 *or* cotton batting : algodón *m* en láminas 2 : bateo *m* (en beisbol)

battle¹ ['bætəl] *vi* -tled; -tling : luchar, pelear

battle² *n* : batalla *f*, lucha *f*, pelea *f*

battle–ax ['bætəl,æks] *n* : hacha *f* de guerra

battlefield ['bætəl,fi:ld] *n* : campo *m* de batalla

battlements ['bætəlmənts] *npl* : almenas *fpl*

battleship ['bætəl,ʃɪp] *n* : acorazado *m*

batty ['bæti] *adj* -tier; -est : chiflado *fam*, chalado *fam*

bauble ['bɔbəl] *n* : chuchería *f*, baratija *f*

Bavarian [bə'veriən] *n* : bávaro *m*, -ra *f* — **Bavarian** *adj*

bawdiness ['bɔdinəs] *n* : picardía *f*

bawdy ['bɔdi] *adj* **bawdier; -est** : subido de tono, verde, colorado *Mex*

bawl¹ ['bɔl] *vi* : llorar a gritos

bawl² *n* : grito *m*, alarido *m*

bawl out *vt* SCOLD : regañar

bay¹ ['beɪ] *vi* HOWL : aullar

bay² *adj* : castaño, zaino (dícese de los caballos)

bay³ *n* 1 : bahía *f* ⟨Bay of Campeche : Bahía de Campeche⟩ 2 *or* bay horse : caballo *m* castaño 3 LAUREL : laurel *m* 4 HOWL : aullido *m* 5 : saliente *m* ⟨bay window : ventana en saliente⟩ 6 COMPARTMENT : área *f*, compartimento *m* 7 at ~ : acorralado

bayberry ['beɪ,bɛri] *n*, *pl* -ries : arrayán *m* brabántico

bayonet¹ [,beɪə'nɛt, 'beɪə,nɛt] *vt* -neted; -neting : herir *o* matar) con bayoneta

bayonet² *n* : bayoneta *f*

bayou ['baɪ,u:, -,o:] *n* : pantano *m*

bazaar [bə'zɑr] *n* 1 : bazar *m* 2 SALE : venta *f* benéfica

bazooka [bə'zu:kə] *n* : bazuca *f*

be ['bi:] *v* was ['wɑz, 'wɑz]; were ['wər]; been ['bɪn]; being; am ['æm]; is ['ɪz]; are ['ɑr] *vi* 1 (*expressing equality*) : ser ⟨José is a doctor : José es doctor⟩ ⟨I'm Ann's sister : soy la hermana de Ana⟩ 2 (*expressing quality*) : ser ⟨the tree is tall : el árbol es alto⟩ ⟨you're silly! : ¡eres tonto!⟩ 3 (*expressing origin or possession*) : ser ⟨she's from Managua : es de Managua⟩ ⟨it's mine : es mío⟩ 4 (*expressing location*) : estar ⟨my mother is at home : mi madre está en casa⟩ ⟨the cups are on the table : las tazas están en la mesa⟩ 5 (*expressing existence*) : ser, existir ⟨to be or not to be : ser, o no ser⟩ ⟨I think, therefore I am : pienso, luego existo⟩ 6 (*expressing a state of being*) : estar, tener ⟨how are you? : ¿cómo estás?⟩ ⟨I'm cold : tengo frío⟩ ⟨she's 10 years old : tiene 10 años⟩ ⟨they're both sick : están enfermos los dos⟩ — *v impers* **1** (*indicating time*) : ser ⟨it's eight o'clock : son las ocho⟩ ⟨it's Friday : hoy es viernes⟩ **2** (*indicating a condition*) : hacer, estar ⟨it's sunny : hace sol⟩ ⟨it's very dark outside : está bien oscuro afuera⟩ — *v aux* **1** (*expressing progression*) : estar ⟨what are you doing?—I'm working : ¿qué haces?—estoy trabajando⟩ **2** (*expressing occurrence*) : ser ⟨it was finished yesterday : fue acabado ayer, se acabó ayer⟩ ⟨it was cooked in the oven : se cocinó en el horno⟩ **3** (*expressing possibility*) : poderse ⟨can she be trusted? : ¿se puede confiar en ella?⟩ **4** (*expressing obligation*) : deber ⟨you are to stay here : debes quedarte aquí⟩ ⟨he was to come yesterday : se esperaba que viniese ayer⟩

beach¹ [ˈbiːʃ] *vt* : hacer embarrancar, hacer varar, hacer encallar

beach² *n* : playa *f*

beachcomber [ˈbiːʃˌkoːmər] *n* : raquero *m*, -ra *f*

beachhead [ˈbiːʃˌhɛd] *n* : cabeza *f* de playa

beacon [ˈbiːkən] *n* : faro *m*

bead¹ [ˈbiːd] *vi* : formarse en gotas

bead² *n* **1** : cuenta *f* **2** DROP : gota *f* **3 beads** *npl* NECKLACE : collar *m*

beady [ˈbiːdi] *adj* **beadier; -est 1** : de forma de cuenta **2 beady eyes** : ojos *mpl* pequeños y brillantes

beagle [ˈbiːgəl] *n* : beagle *m*

beak [ˈbiːk] *n* : pico *m*

beaker [ˈbiːkər] *n* **1** CUP : taza *f* alta **2** : vaso *m* de precipitados (en un laboratorio)

beam¹ [ˈbiːm] *vi* **1** SHINE : brillar **2** SMILE : sonreír radiantemente — *vt* BROADCAST : transmitir, emitir

beam² *n* **1** : viga *f*, barra *f* **2** RAY : rayo *m*, haz *m* de luz **3** : haz *m* de radiofaro (para guiar pilotos, etc.)

bean [ˈbiːn] *n* **1** : habichuela *f*, frijol *m* **2 broad bean** : haba *f* **3 string bean** : judía *f*

bear¹ [ˈbær] *v* **bore** [ˈbor]; **borne** [ˈbɔrn]; **bearing** *vt* **1** CARRY : llevar, portar **2** : dar a luz a (un niño) **3** PRODUCE : dar (frutas, cosechas) **4** ENDURE, SUPPORT : soportar, resistir, aguantar — *vi* **1** TURN : doblar, dar la vuelta ⟨bear right : doble a la derecha⟩ **2 to bear up** : resistir

bear² *n, pl* **bears** *or* **bear** : oso *m*, osa *f*

bearable [ˈbærəbəl] *adj* : soportable

beard [ˈbird] *n* **1** : barba *f* **2** : arista *f* (de plantas)

bearded [ˈbirdəd] *adj* : barbudo, de barba

bearer [ˈbærər] *n* : portador *m*, -dora *f*

bearing [ˈbæriŋ] *n* **1** CONDUCT, MANNERS : comportamiento *m*, modales *mpl* **2** SUPPORT : soporte *m* **3** SIGNIFICANCE : relación *f*, importancia *f* ⟨to have no bearing on : no tener nada que ver con⟩ **4** : cojinete *m*, rodamiento *m*

(de una máquina) **5** COURSE, DIRECTION : dirección *f*, rumbo *m* ⟨to get one's bearings : orientarse⟩

beast [ˈbiːst] *n* **1** : bestia *f*, fiera *f* ⟨beast of burden : animal de carga⟩ **2** BRUTE : bruto *m*, -ta *f*; bestia *mf*

beastly [ˈbiːstli] *adj* : detestable, repugnante

beat¹ [ˈbiːt] *v* **beat; beaten** [ˈbiːtən] *or* **beat; beating** *vt* **1** STRIKE : golpear, pegar, darle una paliza (a alguien) **2** DEFEAT : vencer, derrotar **3** AVOID : anticiparse a, evitar ⟨to beat the crowd : evitar el gentío⟩ **4** MASH, WHIP : batir — *vi* THROB : palpitar, latir

beat² *adj* EXHAUSTED : derrengado, muy cansado ⟨I'm beat! : ¡estoy molido!⟩

beat³ *n* **1** : golpe *m*, redoble *m* (de un tambor), latido *m* (del corazón) **2** RHYTHM : ritmo *m*, tiempo *m*

beater [ˈbiːtər] *n* **1** : batidor *m*, -dora *f* **2** EGGBEATER : batidor *m*

beatific [ˌbiːəˈtɪfɪk] *adj* : beatífico

beatitude [biˈætəˌtuːd] *n* **1** : beatitud *f* **2 the Beatitudes** : las bienaventuranzas

beau [ˈboː] *n, pl* **beaux** *or* **beaus** : pretendiente *m*, galán *m*

beautification [ˌbjuːtəfəˈkeɪʃən] *n* : embellecimiento *m*

beautiful [ˈbjuːtɪfəl] *adj* : hermoso, bello, lindo, precioso

beautifully [ˈbjuːtɪfəli] *adv* **1** ATTRACTIVELY : hermosamente **2** EXCELLENTLY : maravillosamente, excelentemente

beauty [ˈbjuːti] *n, pl* **-ties** : belleza *f*, hermosura *f*, beldad *f*

beauty shop *or* **beauty salon** *n* : salón *m* de belleza

beaver [ˈbiːvər] *n* : castor *m*

because [biˈkʌz, -ˈkɔz] *conj* : porque

because of *prep* : por, a causa de, debido a

beck [ˈbɛk] *n* **to be at the beck and call of** : estar a la entera disposición de, estar sometido a la voluntad de

beckon [ˈbɛkən] *vi* **to beckon to someone** : hacerle señas a alguien

become [biˈkʌm] *v* **-came** [-ˈkeɪm]; **-come; -coming** *vi* : hacerse, volverse, ponerse ⟨he became famous : se hizo famoso⟩ ⟨to become sad : ponerse triste⟩ ⟨to become accustomed to : acostumbrarse a⟩ — *vt* **1** BEFIT : ser apropiado para **2** SUIT : favorecer, quedarle bien (a alguien) ⟨that dress becomes you : ese vestido te favorece⟩

becoming [biˈkʌmɪŋ] *adj* **1** SUITABLE : apropiado **2** FLATTERING : favorecedor

bed¹ [ˈbɛd] *v* **bedded; bedding** *vt* : acostar — *vi* : acostarse

bed² *n* **1** : cama *f*, lecho *m* **2** : cauce *m* (de un río), fondo *m* (del mar) **3** : arriate *m* (para plantas) **4** LAYER, STRATUM : estrato *m*, capa *f*

bedbug [ˈbɛdˌbʌɡ] n : chinche f
bedclothes [ˈbɛdˌkloːðz, -ˌkloːz] npl : ropa f de cama, sábanas fpl
bedding [ˈbɛdɪŋ] n 1 → **bedclothes** 2 : cama f (para animales)
bedeck [bɪˈdɛk] vt : adornar, engalanar
bedevil [bɪˈdɛvəl] vt -iled or -illed; -iling or -illing : acosar, plagar
bedlam [ˈbɛdləm] n : locura f, caos m, alboroto m
bedraggled [bɪˈdræɡəld] adj : desaliñado, despeinado
bedridden [ˈbɛdˌrɪdən] adj : postrado en cama
bedrock [ˈbɛdˌrɑk] n : lecho m de roca
bedroom [ˈbɛdˌruːm, -ˌrʊm] n : dormitorio m, habitación f, pieza f, recámara f Col, Mex, Pan
bedspread [ˈbɛdˌsprɛd] n : cubrecama m, colcha f, cobertor m
bee [ˈbiː] n 1 : abeja f (insecto) 2 GATHERING : círculo m, reunión f
beech [ˈbiːtʃ] n, pl **beeches** or **beech** : haya f
beechnut [ˈbiːtʃˌnʌt] n : hayuco m
beef¹ [ˈbiːf] vt **to beef up** : fortalecer, reforzar — vi COMPLAIN : quejarse
beef² n, pl **beefs** [ˈbiːfs] or **beeves** [ˈbiːvz] : carne f de vaca, carne f de res CA, Mex
beefsteak [ˈbiːfˌsteɪk] n : filete m, bistec m
beehive [ˈbiːˌhaɪv] n : colmena f
beekeeper [ˈbiːˌkiːpər] n : apicultor m, -tora f
beeline [ˈbiːˌlaɪn] n **to make a beeline for** : ir derecho a, ir directo hacia
been → **be**
beep¹ [ˈbiːp] v : pitar
beep² n : pitido m
beeper [ˈbiːpər] n : busca m, buscapersonas m
beer [ˈbɪr] n : cerveza f
beeswax [ˈbiːzˌwæks] n : cera f de abejas
beet [ˈbiːt] n : remolacha f, betabel m Mex
beetle [ˈbiːtəl] n : escarabajo m
befall [bɪˈfɔl] v -fell [-ˈfɛl]; -fallen [-ˈfɔlən] vt : sucederle a, acontecerle a — vi : acontecer
befit [bɪˈfɪt] vt -fitted; -fitting : convenir a, ser apropiado para
before¹ [bɪˈfor] adv 1 : antes ⟨before and after : antes y después⟩ 2 : anterior ⟨the month before : el mes anterior⟩
before² conj : antes que ⟨he would die before surrendering : moriría antes que rendirse⟩
before³ prep 1 : antes de ⟨before eating : antes de comer⟩ 2 : delante de, ante ⟨I stood before the house : estaba parada delante de la casa⟩ ⟨before the judge : ante el juez⟩
beforehand [bɪˈforˌhænd] adv : antes, por adelantado, de antemano, con anticipación
befriend [bɪˈfrɛnd] vt : hacerse amigo de

befuddle [bɪˈfʌdəl] vt -dled; -dling : aturdir, ofuscar, confundir
beg [ˈbɛɡ] v **begged; begging** vt : pedir, mendigar, suplicar ⟨I begged him to go : le supliqué que fuera⟩ — vi : mendigar, pedir limosna
beget [bɪˈɡɛt] vt -got [-ˈɡɑt]; -gotten [-ˈɡɑtən] or -got; -getting : engendrar
beggar [ˈbɛɡər] n : mendigo m, -ga f; pordiosero m, -ra f
begin [bɪˈɡɪn] v -gan [-ˈɡæn]; -gun [-ˈɡʌn]; -ginning vt : empezar, comenzar, iniciar — vi 1 START : empezar, comenzar, iniciarse 2 ORIGINATE : nacer, originarse 3 **to begin with** : en primer lugar, para empezar
beginner [bɪˈɡɪnər] n : principiante mf
beginning [bɪˈɡɪnɪŋ] n : principio m, comienzo m
begone [biˈɡɔn] interj : ¡fuera de aquí!
begonia [bɪˈɡoːnjə] n : begonia f
begrudge [bɪˈɡrʌdʒ] vt -grudged; -grudging 1 : dar de mala gana 2 ENVY : envidiar, resentir
beguile [bɪˈɡaɪl] vt -guiled; -guiling 1 DECEIVE : engañar 2 AMUSE : divertir, entretener
behalf [bɪˈhæf, -ˈhaf] n 1 : favor m, beneficio m, parte f 2 **on behalf of** or **in behalf of** : de parte de, en nombre de
behave [bɪˈheɪv] vi -haved; -having : comportarse, portarse
behavior [bɪˈheɪvjər] n : comportamiento m, conducta f
behead [bɪˈhɛd] vt : decapitar
behest [bɪˈhɛst] n 1 : mandato m, orden f 2 **at the behest of** : a instancia de
behind¹ [bɪˈhaɪnd] adv : atrás, detrás ⟨to fall behind : quedarse atrás⟩
behind² prep 1 : atrás de, detrás de, tras ⟨behind the house : detrás de la casa⟩ ⟨one behind another : uno tras otro⟩ 2 : atrasado con, después de ⟨behind schedule : atrasado con el trabajo⟩ ⟨I arrived behind the others : llegué después de los otros⟩ 3 SUPPORTING : en apoyo de, detrás
behind³ [bɪˈhaɪnd, ˈbiːˌhaɪnd] n : trasero m
behold [bɪˈhoːld] vt -held; -holding : contemplar
beholder [bɪˈhoːldər] n : observador m, -dora f
behoove [bɪˈhuːv] vt -hooved; -hooving : convenirle a, corresponderle a ⟨it behooves us to help him : nos conviene ayudarlo⟩
beige¹ [ˈbeɪʒ] adj : beige
beige² n : beige m
being [ˈbiːɪŋ] n 1 EXISTENCE : ser m, existencia f 2 CREATURE : ser m, ente m
belabor [bɪˈleɪbər] vt **to belabor the point** : extenderse sobre el tema
belated [bɪˈleɪtəd] adj : tardío, retrasado
belch¹ [ˈbɛltʃ] vi 1 BURP : eructar 2 EXPEL : expulsar, arrojar
belch² n : eructo m

beleaguer [bɪˈliːɡər] vt **1** BESIEGE : asediar, sitiar **2** HARASS : fastidiar, molestar

belfry [ˈbɛlfrɪ] n, pl **-fries** : campanario m

Belgian [ˈbɛldʒən] n : belga mf — **Belgian** adj

belie [bɪˈlaɪ] vt **-lied; -lying 1** MISREPRESENT : falsear, ocultar **2** CONTRADICT : contradecir, desmentir

belief [bəˈliːf] n **1** TRUST : confianza f **2** CONVICTION : creencia f, convicción f **3** FAITH : fe f

believable [bəˈliːvəbəl] adj : verosímil, creíble

believe [bəˈliːv] v **-lieved; -lieving** : creer

believer [bəˈliːvər] n **1** : creyente mf **2** : partidario m, -ria f; entusiasta mf ⟨she's a great believer in vitamins : ella es una gran partidaria de las vitaminas⟩

belittle [bɪˈlɪtəl] vt **-littled; -littling 1** DISPARAGE : menospreciar, denigrar, rebajar **2** MINIMIZE : minimizar, quitar importancia a

Belizean [bəˈliːzɪən] n : beliceño m, -ña f — **Belizean** adj

bell¹ [ˈbɛl] vt : ponerle un cascabel a

bell² n : campana f, cencerro m (para una vaca o cabra), cascabel m (para un gato), timbre m (de teléfono, de la puerta)

belle [ˈbɛl] n : belleza f, beldad f

bellhop [ˈbɛlˌhɑp] n : botones m

bellicose [ˈbɛlɪˌkoːs] adj : belicoso m — **bellicosity** [ˌbɛlɪˈkɑsəṭi] n

belligerence [bəˈlɪdʒərənts] n : agresividad f, beligerancia f

belligerent¹ [bəˈlɪdʒərənt] adj : agresivo, beligerante

belligerent² n : beligerante mf

bellow¹ [ˈbɛˌloː] vi : bramar, mugir — vt : gritar

bellow² n : bramido m, grito m

bellows [ˈbɛˌloːz] ns & pl : fuelle m

bellwether [ˈbɛlˌwɛðər] n : líder mf

belly¹ [ˈbɛli] vi **-lied; -lying** SWELL : hincharse, inflarse

belly² n, pl **-lies** : abdomen m, vientre m, barriga f, panza f

belong [bɪˈlɔŋ] vi **1** : pertenecer (a), ser propiedad (de) ⟨it belongs to her : pertenece a ella, es suyo, es de ella⟩ **2** : ser parte (de), ser miembro (de) ⟨he belongs to the club : es miembro del club⟩ **3** : deber estar, ir ⟨your coat belongs in the closet : tu abrigo va en el ropero⟩

belongings [bɪˈlɔŋɪŋz] npl : pertenencias fpl, efectos mpl personales

beloved¹ [bɪˈlʌvd, -ˈlʌvəd] adj : querido, amado

beloved² n : amado m, -da f; enamorado m, -da f; amor m

below¹ [bɪˈloː] adv : abajo

below² prep **1** : abajo de, debajo de ⟨below the window : debajo de la ventana⟩ **2** : por debajo de, bajo ⟨below average : por debajo del promedio⟩ ⟨5 degrees below zero : 5 grados bajo cero⟩

belt¹ [ˈbɛlt] vt **1** : ceñir con un cinturón, ponerle un cinturón a **2** THRASH : darle una paliza a, darle un trancazo a

belt² n **1** : cinturón m, cinto m (para el talle) **2** BAND, STRAP : cinta f, correa f, banda f Mex **3** AREA : frente m, zona f

beltway [ˈbɛltˌweɪ] n : carretera f de circunvalación; periférico m CA, Mex; libramiento m Mex

bemoan [bɪˈmoːn] vt : lamentarse de

bemuse [bɪˈmjuːz] vt **-mused; -musing 1** BEWILDER : confundir, desconcertar **2** ENGROSS : absorber

bench [ˈbɛntʃ] n **1** SEAT : banco m, escaño m, banca f **2** : estrado m (de un juez) **3** COURT : tribunal m

bend¹ [ˈbɛnd] v **bent** [ˈbɛnt]; **bending** vt : torcer, doblar, curvar, flexionar — vi **1** : torcerse, agacharse ⟨to bend over : inclinarse⟩ **2** TURN : torcer, hacer una curva

bend² n **1** TURN : vuelta f, recodo m **2** CURVE : curva f, ángulo m, codo m

beneath¹ [bɪˈniːθ] adv : bajo, abajo, debajo

beneath² prep : bajo de, abajo de, por debajo de

benediction [ˌbɛnəˈdɪkʃən] n : bendición f

benefactor [ˈbɛnəˌfæktər] n : benefactor m, -tora f

beneficence [bəˈnɛfəsənts] n : beneficencia f

beneficent [bəˈnɛfəsənt] adj : benéfico, caritativo

beneficial [ˌbɛnəˈfɪʃəl] adj : beneficioso, provechoso — **beneficially** adv

beneficiary [ˌbɛnəˈfɪʃiˌɛri, -ˈfɪʃəri] n, pl **-ries** : beneficiario m, -ria f

benefit¹ [ˈbɛnəfɪt] vt : beneficiar — vi : beneficiarse

benefit² n **1** ADVANTAGE : beneficio m, ventaja f, provecho m **2** AID : asistencia f, beneficio m **3** : función f benéfica (para recaudar fondos)

benevolence [bəˈnɛvələnts] n : bondad f, benevolencia f

benevolent [bəˈnɛvələnt] adj : benévolo, bondadoso — **benevolently** adv

Bengali [bɛnˈɡɑli, bɛŋ-] n **1** : bengalí mf **2** : bengalí m (idioma) — **Bengali** adj

benign [bɪˈnaɪn] adj **1** GENTLE, KIND : benévolo, amable **2** FAVORABLE : propicio, favorable **3** MILD : benigno ⟨a benign tumor : un tumor benigno⟩

Beninese [bəˌniːˈniːz, -ˌniː-, -ˈniːs, bnɪ-] : beninés m, -nesa f — **Beninese** adj

bent [ˈbɛnt] n : aptitud f, inclinación f

benumb [bɪˈnʌm] vt : entumecer

benzene [ˈbɛnˌziːn] n : benceno m

bequeath [bɪˈkwiːθ, -ˈkwiːð] vt : legar, dejar en testamento

bequest [bɪˈkwɛst] n : legado m

berate [bɪˈreɪt] vt **-rated; -rating** : reprender, regañar

bereaved [bɪˈriːvd] adj : que está de luto, afligido (por la muerte de alguien)

bereaved² *n* **the bereaved** : los deudos del difunto (o de la difunta)
bereavement [bɪˈriːvmənt] *n* **1** SORROW : dolor *m*, pesar *m* **2** LOSS : pérdida *f*
bereft [bɪˈrɛft] *adj* : privado, desprovisto
beret [bəˈreɪ] *n* : boina *f*
beriberi [ˌbɛriˈbɛri] *n* : beriberi *m*
berm [ˈbərm] *n* : arcén *m*
berry [ˈbɛri] *n*, *pl* **-ries** : baya *f*
berserk [bərˈsərk, -ˈzərk] *adj* **1** : enloquecido **2 to go berserk** : volverse loco
berth¹ [ˈbərθ] *vi* : atracar
berth² *n* **1** DOCK : atracadero *m* **2** ACCOMMODATION : litera *f*, camarote *m* **3** POSITION : trabajo *m*, puesto *m*
beryl [ˈbɛrəl] *n* : berilo *m*
beseech [bɪˈsiːtʃ] *vt* **-seeched** *or* **-sought** [-ˈsɔt]; **-seeching** : suplicar, implorar, rogar
beset [bɪˈsɛt] *vt* **-set; -setting 1** HARASS : acosar **2** SURROUND : rodear
beside [bɪˈsaɪd] *prep* : al lado de, junto a
besides¹ [bɪˈsaɪdz] *adv* **1** ALSO : además, también, aparte **2** MOREOVER : además, por otra parte
besides² *prep* **1** : además de, aparte de ⟨six others besides you : seis otros además de ti⟩ **2** EXCEPT : excepto, fuera de, aparte de
besiege [bɪˈsiːdʒ] *vt* **-sieged; -sieging** : asediar, sitiar, cercar
besmirch [bɪˈsmərtʃ] *vt* : ensuciar, mancillar
best¹ [ˈbɛst] *vt* : superar, ganar a
best² *adv* (*superlative of* **well**) : mejor ⟨as best I can : lo mejor que puedo⟩
best³ *adj* (*superlative of* **good**) : mejor ⟨my best friend : mi mejor amigo⟩
best⁴ *n* **1 the best** : lo mejor, el mejor, la mejor, los mejores, las mejores **2 at ~** : a lo más **3 to do one's best** : hacer todo lo posible
bestial [ˈbɛstʃəl, ˈbiːs-] *adj* **1** : bestial **2** BRUTISH : brutal, salvaje
best man *n* : padrino *m*
bestow [bɪˈstoː] *vt* : conferir, otorgar, conceder
bestowal [bɪˈstoːəl] *n* : concesión *f*, otorgamiento *m*
bet¹ [ˈbɛt] *vt* **bet; betting** *vt* : apostar — *vi* **to bet on** : apostarle a
bet² *n* : apuesta *f*
betoken [bɪˈtoːkən] *vt* : denotar, ser indicio de
betray [bɪˈtreɪ] *vt* **1** : traicionar ⟨to betray one's country : traicionar uno a su patria⟩ **2** DIVULGE, REVEAL : delatar, revelar ⟨to betray a secret : revelar un secreto⟩
betrayal [bɪˈtreɪəl] *n* : traición *f*, delación *f*, revelación *f* ⟨betrayal of trust : abuso de confianza⟩
betrothal [bɪˈtroːðəl, -ˈtroː-] *n* : esponsales *mpl*, compromiso *m*
betrothed [bɪˈtroːðd, -ˈtroːθt] *n* FIANCÉ : prometido *m*, -da *f*

better¹ [ˈbɛtər] *vt* **1** IMPROVE : mejorar **2** SURPASS : superar
better² *adv* (*comparative of* **well**) **1** : mejor **2** MORE : más ⟨better than 50 miles : más de 50 millas⟩
better³ *adj* (*comparative of* **good**) **1** : mejor ⟨the weather is better today : hace mejor tiempo hoy⟩ ⟨I was sick, but now I'm better : estuve enfermo, pero ahora estoy mejor⟩ **2** : mayor ⟨the better part of a month : la mayor parte de un mes⟩
better⁴ *n* **1** : el mejor, la mejor ⟨the better of the two : el mejor de los dos⟩ **2 to get the better of** : vencer a, quedar por encima de, superar
betterment [ˈbɛtərmənt] *n* : mejoramiento *m*, mejora *f*
bettor *or* **better** [ˈbɛtər] *n* : apostador *m*, -dora *f*
between¹ [bɪˈtwiːn] *adv* **1** : en medio, por lo medio **2 in ~** : intermedio
between² *prep* : entre
bevel¹ [ˈbɛvəl] *vt* **-eled** *or* **-elled; -eling** *or* **-elling** *vt* : biselar — *vi* INCLINE : inclinarse
bevel² *n* : bisel *m*
beverage [ˈbɛvərɪdʒ, ˈbɛvrə-] *n* : bebida *f*
bevy [ˈbɛvi] *n*, *pl* **bevies** : grupo *m* (de personas), bandada *f* (de pájaros)
bewail [bɪˈweɪl] *vt* : lamentarse de, llorar
beware [bɪˈwær] *vi* **to beware of** : tener cuidado con ⟨beware of the dog! : ¡cuidado con el perro!⟩ — *vt* : guardarse de, cuidarse de
bewilder [bɪˈwɪldər] *vt* : desconcertar, dejar perplejo
bewilderment [bɪˈwɪldərmənt] *n* : desconcierto *m*, perplejidad *f*
bewitch [bɪˈwɪtʃ] *vt* **1** : hechizar, embrujar **2** CHARM : cautivar, encantar
bewitchment [bɪˈwɪtʃmənt] *n* : hechizo *m*
beyond¹ [bɪˈjɑnd] *adv* **1** FARTHER, LATER : más allá, más lejos (en el espacio), más adelante (en el tiempo) **2** MORE : más ⟨$50 and beyond : $50 o más⟩
beyond² *n* **the beyond** : el más allá, lo desconocido
beyond³ *prep* **1** : más allá de ⟨beyond the frontier : más allá de la frontera⟩ **2** : fuera de ⟨beyond one's reach : fuera de su alcance⟩ **3** BESIDES : además de
biannual [ˌbaɪˈænjuəl] *adj* : bianual — **biannually** *adv*
bias¹ [ˈbaɪəs] *vt* **-ased** *or* **-assed; -asing** *or* **-assing 1** : predisponer, sesgar, influir en, afectar **2 to be biased against** : tener prejuicio contra
bias² *n* **1** : sesgo *m*, bies *m* (en la costura) **2** PREJUDICE : prejuicio *m* **3** TENDENCY : inclinación *f*, tendencia *f*
biased [ˈbaɪəst] *adj* : tendencioso, parcial
bib [ˈbɪb] *n* **1** : peto *m* **2** : babero *m* (para niños)
Bible [ˈbaɪbəl] *n* : Biblia *f*
biblical [ˈbɪblɪkəl] *adj* : bíblico

bibliographer [ˌbɪbliˈagrəfər] n : bibliógrafo m, -fa f

bibliographic [ˌbɪbliəˈgræfɪk] adj : bibliográfico

bibliography [ˌbɪbliˈagrəfi] n, pl **-phies** : bibliografía f

bicameral [ˌbaɪˈkæmərəl] adj : bicameral

bicarbonate [ˌbaɪˈkarbənət, -ˌneɪt] n : bicarbonato m

bicentennial [ˌbaɪsɛnˈtɛniəl] n : bicentenario m

biceps [ˈbaɪˌsɛps] ns & pl : bíceps m

bicker[1] [ˈbɪkər] vi : pelear, discutir, reñir

bicker[2] [ˈbɪkər] n : pelea f, riña f, discusión f

bicuspid [baɪˈkʌspɪd] n : premolar m, diente m bicúspide

bicycle[1] [ˈbaɪsɪkəl, -ˌsɪ-] vi **-cled; -cling** : ir en bicicleta

bicycle[2] n : bicicleta f

bicycling [ˈbaɪsɪkəlɪŋ] n : ciclismo m

bicyclist [ˈbaɪsɪkəlɪst] n : ciclista mf

bid[1] [ˈbɪd] vt **bade** [ˈbæd, ˈbeɪd] or **bid; bidden** [ˈbɪdən] or **bid; bidding** **1** ORDER : pedir, mandar **2** INVITE : invitar **3** SAY : dar, decir ⟨to bid good evening : dar las buenas noches⟩ ⟨to bid farewell to : decir adiós a⟩ **4** : ofrecer (en una subasta), declarar (en juegos de cartas)

bid[2] n **1** OFFER : oferta f (en una subasta), declaración f (en juegos de cartas) **2** INVITATION : invitación f **3** ATTEMPT : intento m, tentativa f

bidder [ˈbɪdər] n : postor m, -tora f

bide [ˈbaɪd] v **bode** [ˈboːd] or **bided; bided; biding** vt : esperar, aguardar ⟨to bide one's time : esperar el momento oportuno⟩ — vi DWELL : morar, vivir

biennial [baɪˈɛniəl] adj : bienal — **biennially** adv

bier [ˈbɪr] n **1** STAND : andas fpl **2** COFFIN : ataúd m, féretro m

bifocals [ˈbaɪˌfoːkəlz] npl : lentes mpl bifocales, bifocales mpl

big [ˈbɪg] adj **bigger; biggest 1** LARGE : grande **2** PREGNANT : embarazada **3** IMPORTANT, MAJOR : importante, grande ⟨a big decision : una gran decisión⟩ **4** POPULAR : popular, famoso, conocido

bigamist [ˈbɪgəmɪst] n : bígamo m, -ma f

bigamous [ˈbɪgəməs] adj : bígamo

bigamy [ˈbɪgəmi] n : bigamia f

Big Dipper → **dipper**

bighorn [ˈbɪgˌhɔrn] n, pl **-horn** or **-horns** or **bighorn sheep** : oveja f salvaje de las montañas

bight [ˈbaɪt] n : bahía f, ensenada f, golfo m

bigot [ˈbɪgət] n : intolerante mf

bigoted [ˈbɪgətəd] adj : intolerante, prejuiciado, fanático

bigotry [ˈbɪgətri] n, pl **-tries** : intolerancia f

big shot n : pez m gordo fam, mandamás mf

bigwig [ˈbɪgˌwɪg] → **big shot**

bike [ˈbaɪk] n **1** : bicicleta f, bici f fam **2** : motocicleta f, moto f

bikini [bəˈkiːni] n : bikini m

bilateral [baɪˈlætərəl] adj : bilateral — **bilaterally** adv

bile [ˈbaɪl] n **1** : bilis f **2** IRRITABILITY : mal genio m

bilingual [baɪˈlɪŋgwəl] adj : bilingüe

bilious [ˈbɪliəs] adj **1** : bilioso **2** IRRITABLE : bilioso, colérico

bilk [ˈbɪlk] vt : burlar, estafar, defraudar

bill[1] [ˈbɪl] vt : pasarle la cuenta a — vi : acariciar ⟨to bill and coo : acariciarse⟩

bill[2] n **1** LAW : proyecto m de ley, ley f **2** INVOICE : cuenta f, factura f **3** POSTER : cartel m **4** PROGRAM : programa m (del teatro) **5** : billete m ⟨a five-dollar bill : un billete de cinco dólares⟩ **6** BEAK : pico m

billboard [ˈbɪlˌbord] n : cartelera f

billet[1] [ˈbɪlət] vt : acuartelar, alojar

billet[2] n : alojamiento m

billfold [ˈbɪlˌfoːld] n : billetera f, cartera f

billiards [ˈbɪljərdz] n : billar m

billion [ˈbɪljən] n, pl **billions** or **billion** : mil millones mpl

billow[1] [ˈbɪloː] vi : hincharse, inflarse

billow[2] n **1** WAVE : ola f **2** CLOUD : nube f ⟨a billow of smoke : un nube de humo⟩

billowy [ˈbɪloːwi] adj : ondulante

billy goat [ˈbɪliˌgoːt] n : macho m cabrío

bin [ˈbɪn] n : cubo m, cajón m

binary [ˈbaɪnəri, -ˌneri] adj : binario m

bind [ˈbaɪnd] vt **bound** [ˈbaʊnd], **binding 1** TIE : atar, amarrar **2** OBLIGATE : obligar **3** UNITE : aglutinar, ligar, unir **4** BANDAGE : vendar **5** : encuadernar (un libro)

binder [ˈbaɪndər] n **1** FOLDER : carpeta f **2** : encuadernador m, -dora f (de libros)

binding [ˈbaɪndɪŋ] n **1** : encuadernación f (de libros) **2** COVER : cubierta f, forro m

binge [ˈbɪndʒ] n : juerga f, parranda f fam

bingo [ˈbɪŋˌgoː] n, pl **-gos** : bingo m

binocular [baɪˈnakjələr, bə-] adj : binocular

binoculars [bəˈnakjələrz, baɪ-] npl : binoculares mpl

biochemical[1] [ˌbaɪoˈkɛmɪkəl] adj : bioquímico

biochemical[2] n : bioquímico m

biochemist [ˌbaɪoˈkɛmɪst] n : bioquímico m, -ca f

biochemistry [ˌbaɪoˈkɛməstri] n : bioquímica f

biodegradable [ˌbaɪodɪˈgreɪdəbəl] adj : biodegradable

biodegradation [ˌbaɪodɛgrəˈdeɪʃən] n : biodegradación f

biodegrade [ˌbaɪodɪˈgreɪd] vi **-graded; -grading** : biodegradarse

biodiversity [,baɪodəˈvərsəti, -daɪ-] n, pl
-ties : bioversidad f
biographer [baɪˈagrəfər] n : biógrafo m,
-fa f
biographical [,baɪəˈgræfɪkəl] adj : biográfico
biography [baɪˈagrəfi, bi:-] n, pl **-phies**
: biografía f
biologic [,baɪəˈladʒɪk] or **biological**
[-dʒɪkəl] adj : biológico
biologist [baɪˈaladʒɪst] n : biólogo m, -ga
f
biology [baɪˈaladʒi] n : biología f
biophysical [,baɪoˈfɪzɪkəl] adj : biofísico
biophysicist [,baɪoˈfɪzəsɪst] n : biofísico
m, -ca f
biophysics [,baɪoˈfɪzɪks] ns & pl : biofísica f
biopsy [ˈbaɪ,apsi] n, pl **-sies** : biopsia f
biosphere [ˈbaɪə,sfɪr] n : biosfera f, biósfera f
biotechnology [,baɪotɛkˈnaladʒi] n : biotecnología f
biotic [baɪˈatɪk] adj : biótico
bipartisan [baɪˈpartəzən, -sən] adj : bipartidista, de dos partidas
biped [ˈbaɪ,pɛd] n : bípedo m
birch [ˈbərtʃ] n : abedul m
bird [ˈbərd] n : pájaro m (pequeño), ave
f (grande)
birdbath [ˈbərd,bæθ, -,baθ] n : pila f para
pájaros
bird dog n : perro m, -rra f de caza
bird of prey n : ave f rapaz, ave f de presa
birdseed [ˈbərd,si:d] n : alpiste m
bird's-eye [ˈbərdz,aɪ] adj 1 : visto desde arriba ⟨bird's-eye view : vista aérea⟩
2 CURSORY : rápido, somero
birth [ˈbərθ] n 1 : nacimiento m, parto
m 2 ORIGIN : origen m, nacimiento m
birthday [ˈbərθ,deɪ] n : cumpleaños m,
aniversario m
birthmark [ˈbərθ,mark] n : mancha f de
nacimiento
birthplace [ˈbərθ,pleɪs] n : lugar m de
nacimiento
birthrate [ˈbərθ,reɪt] n : índice m de natalidad
birthright [ˈbərθ,raɪt] n : derecho m de
nacimiento
biscuit [ˈbɪskət] n : bizcocho m
bisect [ˈbaɪ,sɛkt, ,baɪ-] v : bisecar
bisexual [,baɪˈsɛkʃuəl] adj : bisexual
bishop [ˈbɪʃəp] n 1 : obispo m 2 : alfil
m (en ajedrez)
bismuth [ˈbɪzməθ] n : bismuto m
bison [ˈbaɪzən, -sən] ns & pl : bisonte m
bistro [ˈbi:stro, ˈbɪs-] n, pl **-tros** : bar m,
restaurante m pequeño
bit [ˈbɪt] n 1 FRAGMENT, PIECE : pedazo m, trozo m ⟨a bit of luck : un poco
de suerte⟩ 2 : freno m, bocado m (de
una brida) 3 : broca f (de un taladro)
4 : bit m (de información)
bitch¹ [ˈbɪtʃ] vi COMPLAIN : quejarse,
reclamar

bitch² n : perra f
bite¹ [ˈbaɪt] v **bit** [ˈbɪt]; **bitten** [ˈbɪtən];
biting vt 1 : morder 2 STING : picar 3
PUNCTURE : punzar, pinchar 4 GRIP
: agarrar — vi 1 : morder ⟨that dog
bites : ese perro muerde⟩ 2 STING
: picar (dícese de un insecto), cortar
(dícese del viento) 3 : picar ⟨the fish
are biting now : ya están picando los
peces⟩ 4 GRAB : agarrarse
bite² n 1 BITING : mordisco m, dentellada f 2 SNACK : bocado m ⟨a bite to
eat : algo de comer⟩ 3 : picadura f (de
un insecto), mordedura f (de un animal) 4 SHARPNESS : mordacidad f, penetración f
biting adj 1 PENETRATING : cortante,
penetrante 2 CAUSTIC : mordaz, sarcástico
bitter [ˈbɪtər] adj 1 ACRID : amargo, acre
2 PENETRATING : cortante, penetrante
⟨bitter cold : frío glacial⟩ 3 HARSH
: duro, amargo ⟨to the bitter end : hasta el final⟩ 4 INTENSE, RELENTLESS
: intenso, extremo, implacable ⟨bitter
hatred : odio implacable⟩
bitterly [ˈbɪtərli] adv : amargamente
bitterness [ˈbɪtərnəs] n : amargura f
bittersweet [ˈbɪtər,swi:t] adj : agridulce
bivalve [ˈbaɪ,vælv] n : bivalvo m — **bivalve** adj
bivouac¹ [ˈbɪvə,wæk, ˈbɪv,wæk] vi
-ouacked; **-ouacking** : acampar, vivaquear
bivouac² n : vivaque m
bizarre [bəˈzar] adj : extraño, singular,
estrafalario, estrambótico — **bizarrely**
adv
blab [ˈblæb] vi **blabbed**; **blabbing** : parlotear fam, cotorrear fam
black¹ [ˈblæk] vt : ennegrecer
black² adj 1 : negro (color, raza) 2
SOILED : sucio 3 DARK : oscuro, negro
4 WICKED : malvado, perverso, malo 5
GLOOMY : negro, sombrío, deprimente
black³ n 1 : negro m (color) 2 : negro
m, -gra f (persona)
black-and-blue [,blækənˈblu:] adj
: amoratado
blackball [ˈblæk,bɔl] vt 1 OSTRACIZE
: hacerle el vacío a, aislar 2 BOYCOTT
: boicotear
blackberry [ˈblæk,beri] n, pl **-ries** : mora
f
blackbird [ˈblæk,bərd] n : mirlo m
blackboard [ˈblæk,bord] n : pizarra f,
pizarrón m
blacken [ˈblækən] vt 1 BLACK : ennegrecer 2 DEFAME : deshonrar,
difamar, manchar
blackhead [ˈblæk,hɛd] n : espinilla f,
punto m negro
black hole n : agujero m negro
blackjack [ˈblæk,dʒæk] n 1 : cachiporra
f (arma) 2 : veintiuna f (juego de cartas)
blacklist¹ [ˈblæk,lɪst] vt : poner en la lista
negra

blacklist² *n* : lista *f* negra
blackmail¹ ['blæk,meɪl] *vt* : chantajear, hacer chantaje a
blackmail² *n* : chantaje *m*
blackmailer ['blæk,meɪlər] *n* : chantajista *mf*
blackout ['blæk,aʊt] *n* 1 : apagón *m* (de poder eléctrico) 2 FAINT : desmayo *m*, desvanecimiento *m*
black out *vt* : dejar sin luz — *vi* FAINT : perder el conocimiento, desmayarse
blacksmith ['blæk,smɪθ] *n* : herrero *m*
blacktop ['blæk,tɑp] *n* : asfalto *m*
bladder ['blædər] *n* : vejiga *f*
blade ['bleɪd] *n* : hoja *f* (de un cuchillo), cuchilla *f* (de un patín), pala *f* (de un remo o una hélice), brizna *f* (de hierba)
blamable ['bleɪməbəl] *adj* : culpable
blame¹ ['bleɪm] *vt* **blamed; blaming** : culpar, echar la culpa a
blame² *n* : culpa *f*
blameless ['bleɪmləs] *adj* : intachable, sin culpa, inocente — **blamelessly** *adv*
blameworthiness ['bleɪm,wərðinəs] *n* : culpa *f*, culpabilidad *f*
blameworthy ['bleɪm,wərði] *adj* : culpable, reprochable, censurable
blanch ['blæntʃ] *vt* WHITEN : blanquear — *vi* PALE : palidecer
bland ['blænd] *adj* : soso, insulso, desabrido ⟨a bland smile : una sonrisa insulsa⟩ ⟨a bland diet : una dieta fácil de digerir⟩
blandishments ['blændɪʃmənts] *npl* : lisonjas *fpl*, halagos *mpl*
blandly ['blændli] *adv* : de manera insulsa
blandness ['blændnəs] *n* : lo insulso, lo desabrido
blank¹ ['blæŋk] *vt* OBLITERATE : borrar
blank² *adj* 1 DAZED : perplejo, desconcertado 2 EXPRESSIONLESS : sin expresión, inexpresivo 3 : en blanco (dícese de un papel), liso (dícese de una pared) 4 EMPTY : vacío, en blanco ⟨a blank stare : una mirada vacía⟩ ⟨his mind went blank : se quedó en blanco⟩
blank³ *n* 1 SPACE : espacio *m* en blanco 2 FORM : formulario *m* 3 CARTRIDGE : cartucho *m* de fogueo 4 *or* **blank key** : llave *f* ciega
blanket¹ ['blæŋkət] *vt* : cubrir
blanket² *adj* : global
blanket³ *n* : manta *f*, cobija *f*, frazada *f*
blankly ['blæŋkli] *adv* : sin comprender
blankness ['blæŋknəs] *n* 1 PERPLEXITY : desconcierto *m*, perplejidad *f* 2 EMPTINESS : vacío *m*, vacuidad *f*
blare¹ ['blær] *vi* **blared; blaring** : resonar
blare² *n* : estruendo *m*
blarney ['blɑrni] *n* : labia *f fam*
blasé [blɑ'zeɪ] *adj* : displicente, indiferente
blaspheme [blæs'fiːm, 'blæs,-] *vi* **-phemed; -pheming** : blasfemar
blasphemer [blæs'fiːmər, 'blæs,-] *n* : blasfemo *m*, -ma *f*

blasphemous ['blæsfəməs] *adj* : blasfemo
blasphemy ['blæsfəmi] *n, pl* **-mies** : blasfemia *f*
blast¹ ['blæst] *vt* 1 BLOW UP : volar, hacer volar 2 ATTACK : atacar, arremeter contra
blast² *n* 1 GUST : ráfaga *f* 2 EXPLOSION : explosión *f*
blast–off ['blæst,ɔf] *n* : despegue *m*
blast off *vi* : despegar
blatant ['bleɪtənt] *adj* : descarado — **blatantly** ['bleɪtəntli] *adv*
blaze¹ ['bleɪz] *v* **blazed; blazing** *vi* SHINE : arder, brillar, resplandecer — *vt* MARK : marcar, señalar ⟨to blaze a trail : abrir un camino⟩
blaze² *n* 1 FIRE : fuego *m* 2 BRIGHTNESS : resplandor *m*, brillantez *f* 3 OUTBURST : arranque *m* ⟨a blaze of anger : un arranque de cólera⟩ 4 DISPLAY : alarde *m*, llamarada *f* ⟨a blaze of color : un derroche de color⟩
blazer ['bleɪzər] *n* : chaqueta *f* deportiva, blazer *m*
bleach¹ ['bliːtʃ] *vt* : blanquear, decolorar
bleach² *n* : lejía *f*, blanqueador *m*
bleachers ['bliːtʃərz] *ns & pl* : gradas *fpl*, tribuna *f* descubierta
bleak ['bliːk] *adj* 1 DESOLATE : inhóspito, sombrío, desolado 2 DEPRESSING : deprimente, triste, sombrío
bleakly ['bliːkli] *adv* : sombríamente
bleakness ['bliːknəs] *n* : lo inhóspito, lo sombrío
blear ['blɪr] *adj* : empañado, nublado
bleary ['blɪri] *adj* 1 : adormilada, fatigado 2 **bleary–eyed** : con los ojos nublados
bleat¹ ['bliːt] *vi* : balar
bleat² *n* : balido *m*
bleed ['bliːd] *v* **bled** ['blɛd]; **bleeding** *vi* 1 : sangrar 2 GRIEVE : sufrir, afligirse 3 EXUDE : exudar (dícese de una planta), correrse (dícese de los colores) — *vt* 1 : sangrar (a una persona), purgar (frenos) 2 **to bleed someone dry** : sacarle todo el dinero a alguien
blemish¹ ['blɛmɪʃ] *vt* : manchar, marcar
blemish² *n* : imperfección *f*, mancha *f*, marca *f*
blend¹ ['blɛnd] *vt* 1 MIX : mezclar 2 COMBINE : combinar, aunar
blend² *n* : mezcla *f*, combinación *f*
blender ['blɛndər] *n* : licuadora *f*
bless ['blɛs] *vt* **blessed** ['blɛst]; **blessing** 1 CONSECRATE : bendecir, consagrar 2 : bendecir ⟨may God bless you! : ¡que Dios te bendiga!⟩ 3 **to bless with** : dotar de 4 **to bless oneself** : santiguarse
blessed ['blɛsəd] *or* **blest** ['blɛst] *adj* : bienaventurado, bendito, dichoso
blessedly ['blɛsədli] *adv* : felizmente, alegremente, afortunadamente
blessing ['blɛsɪŋ] *n* 1 APPROVAL : aprobación *f*, consentimiento *m*

blew → blow

blight¹ ['blaɪt] *vt* : arruinar, infestar

blight² *n* **1** : añublo *m* **2** PLAGUE : peste *f*, plaga *f* **3** DECAY : deterioro *m*, ruina *f*

blimp ['blɪmp] *n* : dirigible *m*

blind¹ ['blaɪnd] *vt* **1** : cegar, dejar ciego **2** DAZZLE : deslumbrar

blind² *adj* **1** SIGHTLESS : ciego **2** IN-SENSITIVE : ciego, insensible, sin razón **3** CLOSED : sin salida ⟨blind alley : callejón sin salida⟩

blind³ *n* **1** : persiana *f* (para una ventana) **2** COVER : escondite *m*, escondrijo *m*

blinders ['blaɪndərz] *npl* : anteojeras *fpl*

blindfold¹ ['blaɪnd,fo:ld] *vt* : vendar los ojos

blindfold² *n* : venda *f* (para los ojos)

blinding ['blaɪndɪŋ] *adj* : enceguecedor, cegador ⟨with blinding speed : con una rapidez inusitada⟩

blindly ['blaɪndli] *adv* : a ciegas, ciegamente

blindness ['blaɪndnəs] *n* : ceguera *f*

blink¹ ['blɪŋk] *vi* **1** WINK : pestañear, parpadear **2** : brillar intermitentemente

blink² *n* : pestañeo *m*, parpadeo *m*

blinker ['blɪŋkər] *n* : intermitente *m*, direccional *f*

bliss ['blɪs] *n* **1** HAPPINESS : dicha *f*, felicidad *f* absoluta **2** PARADISE : paraíso *m*

blissful ['blɪsfəl] *adj* : dichoso, feliz — **blissfully** *adv*

blister¹ ['blɪstər] *vi* : ampollarse

blister² *n* : ampolla *f* (en la piel o una superficie), burbuja *f* (en una superficie)

blithe ['blaɪθ, 'blaɪð] *adj* **blither; blithest 1** CAREFREE : despreocupado **2** CHEERFUL : alegre, risueño — **blithely** *adv*

blitz¹ ['blɪts] *vt* **1** BOMBARD : bombardear **2** : atacar con rapidez

blitz² *n* **1** : bombardeo *m* aéreo **2** CAMPAIGN : ataque *m*, acometida *f*

blizzard ['blɪzərd] *n* : tormenta *f* de nieve, ventisca *f*

bloat ['blo:t] *vi* : hincharse, inflarse

blob ['blɑb] *n* : gota *f*, mancha *f*, borrón *m*

bloc ['blɑk] *n* : bloque *m*

block¹ ['blɑk] *vt* **1** OBSTRUCT : obstruir, bloquear **2** CLOG : atascar, atorar

block² *n* **1** PIECE : bloque *m* ⟨building blocks : cubos de construcción⟩ ⟨auction block : plataforma de subastas⟩ ⟨starting block : taco de salida⟩ **2** OB-STRUCTION : obstrucción *f*, bloqueo *m* **3** : cuadra *f*, manzana *f* (de edificios) ⟨to go around the block : dar la vuelta a la cuadra⟩ **4** BUILDING : edificio *m* (de apartamentos, oficinas, etc.) **5** GROUP, SERIES : serie *f*, grupo *m* ⟨a block of tickets : una serie de entradas⟩ **6 block and tackle** : aparejo *m* de poleas

blockade¹ [blɑ'keɪd] *vt* **-aded; -ading** : bloquear

blockade² *n* : bloqueo *m*

blockage ['blɑkɪdʒ] *n* : bloqueo *m*, obstrucción *f*

blockhead ['blɑk,hɛd] *n* : bruto *m*, -ta *f*; estúpido *m*, -da *f*

blond¹ *or* **blonde** ['blɑnd] *adj* : rubio, güero *Mex*, claro (dícese de la madera)

blond² *or* **blonde** *n* : rubio *m*, -bia *f*; güero *m*, -ra *f Mex*

blood ['blʌd] *n* **1** : sangre *f* **2** LIFEBLOOD : vida *f*, alma *f* **3** LINEAGE : linaje *m*, sangre *f*

blood bank *n* : banco *m* de sangre

bloodcurdling ['blʌd,kərdəlɪŋ] *adj* : espeluznante, aterrador

blooded ['blʌdəd] *adj* : de sangre ⟨cold-blooded animal : animal de sangre fría⟩

bloodhound ['blʌd,haʊnd] *n* : sabueso *m*

bloodless ['blʌdləs] *adj* **1** : incruento, sin derramamiento de sangre **2** LIFE-LESS : desanimado, insípido, sin vida

bloodmobile ['blʌdmo,bi:l] *n* : unidad *f* móvil para donantes de sangre

blood pressure *n* : tensión *f*, presión *f* (arterial)

bloodshed ['blʌd,ʃɛd] *n* : derramamiento *m* de sangre

bloodshot ['blʌd,ʃɑt] *adj* : inyectado de sangre

bloodstain ['blʌd,steɪn] *n* : mancha *f* de sangre

bloodstained ['blʌd,steɪnd] *adj* : manchado de sangre

bloodstream ['blʌd,stri:m] *n* : torrente *m* sanguíneo, corriente *f* sanguínea

bloodsucker ['blʌd,sʌkər] *n* : sanguijuela *f*

bloodthirsty ['blʌd,θərsti] *adj* : sanguinario

blood vessel *n* : vaso *m* sanguíneo

bloody ['blʌdi] *adj* **bloodier; -est** : ensangrentado, sangriento

bloom¹ ['blu:m] *vi* **1** FLOWER : florecer **2** MATURE : madurar

bloom² *n* **1** FLOWER : flor *f* ⟨to be in bloom : estar en flor⟩ **2** FLOWERING : floración *f* ⟨in full bloom : en plena floración⟩ **3** : rubor *m* (de la tez) ⟨in the bloom of youth : en plena juventud, en la flor de la vida⟩

bloomers ['blu:mərz] *npl* : bombachos *mpl*

blooper ['blu:pər] *n* : metedura *f* de pata *fam*

blossom¹ ['blɑsəm] *vi* : florecer, dar flor

blossom² *n* : flor *f*

blot¹ ['blɑt] *vt* **blotted; blotting 1** SPOT : emborronar, borronear **2** DRY : secar

blot² *n* **1** STAIN : mancha *f*, borrón *m* **2** BLEMISH : mancha *f*, tacha *f*

blotch¹ ['blɑtʃ] *vt* : emborronar, borronear

blotch² *n* : mancha *f*, borrón *m*

blotchy ['blɑtʃi] *adj* **blotchier; -est** : lleno de manchas

blotter ['blɑɾər] *n* : hoja *f* de papel secante, secante *m*

blouse ['blaʊs, 'blaʊz] *n* : blusa *f*

blow[1] ['bloː] *v* **blew** ['bluː]; **blown** ['bloːn]; **blowing** *vi* **1** : soplar, volar ⟨the wind is blowing hard : el viento está soplando con fuerza⟩ ⟨it blew out the door : voló por la puerta⟩ ⟨the window blew shut : se cerró la ventana⟩ **2** SOUND : sonar ⟨the whistle blew : sonó el silbato⟩ **3 to blow out** : fundirse (dícese de un fusible eléctrico), reventarse (dícese de una llanta) **4 to blow off** : dejar plantado (a alguien), flatar a (una cita, etc.) — *vt* **1** : soplar, echar ⟨to blow smoke : echar humo⟩ **2** SOUND : tocar, sonar **3** SHAPE : soplar, dar forma a ⟨to blow glass : soplar vidrio⟩ **4** BUNGLE : echar a perder

blow[2] *n* **1** PUFF : soplo *m*, soplido *m* **2** GALE : vendaval *f* **3** HIT, STROKE : golpe *m* **4** CALAMITY : golpe *m*, desastre *m* **5 to come to blows** : llegar a las manos

blower ['bloːər] *n* FAN : ventilador *m*

blowout ['bloːˌaʊt] *n* : reventón *m*

blowtorch ['bloːˌtɔrtʃ] *n* : soplete *m*

blow up *vi* EXPLODE : estallar, hacer explosión — *vt* BLAST : volar, hacer volar

blubber[1] ['blʌbər] *vi* : lloriquear

blubber[2] *n* : esperma *f* de ballena

bludgeon ['blʌdʒən] *vt* : aporrear

blue[1] ['bluː] *adj* **bluer**; **bluest** **1** : azul **2** MELANCHOLY : melancólico, triste

blue[2] *n* : azul *m*

blueberry ['bluːˌbɛri] *n*, *pl* **-ries** : arándano *m*

bluebird ['bluːˌbərd] *n* : azulejo *m*

blue cheese *n* : queso *m* azul

blueprint ['bluːˌprɪnt] *n* **1** : plano *m*, proyecto *m*, cianotipo *m* **2** PLAN : anteproyecto *m*, programa *m*

blues ['bluːz] *npl* **1** DEPRESSION : depresión *f*, melancolía *f* **2** : blues *m* ⟨to sing the blues : cantar blues⟩

bluff[1] ['blʌf] *vi* : hacer un farol, blofear *Col, Mex*

bluff[2] *adj* **1** STEEP : escarpado **2** FRANK : campechano, franco, directo

bluff[3] *n* **1** : farol *m*, blof *m* *Col, Mex* **2** CLIFF : acantilado *m*, risco *m*

bluing *or* **blueing** ['bluːɪŋ] *n* : añil *m*, azulete *m*

bluish ['bluːɪʃ] *adj* : azulado

blunder[1] ['blʌndər] *vi* **1** STUMBLE : tropezar, dar traspiés **2** ERR : cometer un error, tropezar, meter la pata *fam*

blunder[2] *n* : error *m*, fallo *m* garrafal, metedura *f* de pata *fam*

blunderbuss ['blʌndərˌbʌs] *n* : trabuco *m*

blunt[1] ['blʌnt] *vt* : despuntar (aguja o lápiz), desafilar (cuchillo o tijeras), suavizar (crítica)

blunt[2] *adj* **1** DULL : desafilado, despuntado **2** DIRECT : directo, franco, categórico

bluntly ['blʌntli] *adv* : sin rodeos, francamente, bruscamente

bluntness ['blʌntnəs] *n* **1** DULLNESS : falta *f* de filo, embotadura *f* **2** FRANKNESS : franqueza *f*

blur[1] ['blər] *vt* **blurred**; **blurring** : desdibujar, hacer borroso

blur[2] *n* **1** SMEAR : mancha *f*, borrón *m* **2** : aspecto *m* borroso ⟨everything was just a blur : todo se volvió borroso⟩

blurb ['blərb] *n* : propaganda *f*, nota *f* publicitaria

blurry ['bləri] *adj* : borroso

blurt ['blərt] *vt* : espetar, decir impulsivamente

blush[1] ['blʌʃ] *vi* : ruborizarse, sonrojarse, hacerse colorado

blush[2] *n* : rubor *m*, sonrojo *m*

bluster[1] ['blʌstər] *vi* **1** BLOW : soplar con fuerza **2** BOAST : fanfarronear, echar bravatas

bluster[2] *n* : fanfarronada *f*, bravatas *fpl*

blustery ['blʌstəri] *adj* : borrascoso, tempestuoso

boa ['boːə] *n* : boa *f*

boar ['bor] *n* : cerdo *m* macho, verraco *m*

board[1] ['bord] *vt* **1** : embarcarse en, subir a bordo de (una nave o un avión), subir a (un tren o carro) **2** LODGE : hospedar, dar hospedaje con comidas a **3 to board up** : cerrar con tablas

board[2] *n* **1** PLANK : tabla *f*, tablón *m* **2** : tablero *m* ⟨chessboard : tablero de ajedrez⟩ **3** MEALS : comida *f* ⟨board and lodging : comida y alojamiento⟩ **4** COMMITTEE, COUNCIL : junta *f*, consejo *m*

boarder ['bordər] *n* LODGER : huésped *m*, -peda *f*

boardinghouse ['bordɪŋˌhaʊs] *n* : casa *f* de huéspedes

boarding school *n* : internado *m*

boardwalk ['bordˌwɔk] *n* : paseo *m* marítimo

boast[1] ['boːst] *vi* : alardear, presumir, jactarse

boast[2] *n* : jactancia *f*, alarde *m*

boaster ['boːstər] *n* : presumido *m*, -da *f*; fanfarrón *m*, -rrona *f fam*

boastful ['boːstfəl] *adj* : jactancioso, fanfarrón *fam*

boastfully ['boːstfəli] *adv* : de manera jactanciosa

boat[1] ['boːt] *vt* : transportar en barco, poner a bordo

boat[2] *n* : barco *m*, embarcación *f*, bote *m*, barca *f*

boatman ['boːtmən] *n*, *pl* **-men** [-mən, -ˌmɛn] : barquero *m*

boatswain ['boːsən] *n* : contramaestre *m*

bob[1] ['bɑb] *v* **bobbed**; **bobbing** *vi* **1** : balancearse, mecerse ⟨to bob up and down : subir y bajar⟩ **2** APPEAR : presentarse, surgir — *vt* **1** : inclinar (la cabeza o el cuerpo) **2** CUT : cortar, recortar ⟨she bobbed her hair : se cortó el pelo⟩

bob² [ˈbɑb] *n* **1** : inclinación *f* (de la cabeza, del cuerpo), sacudida *f* **2** FLOAT : flotador *m*, corcho *m* (de pesca) **3** : pelo *m* corto

bobbin [ˈbɑbən] *n* : bobina *f*, carrete *m*

bobby pin [ˈbɑbiˌpɪn] *n* : horquilla *f*

bobcat [ˈbɑbˌkæt] *n* : lince *m* rojo

bobolink [ˈbɑbəˌlɪŋk] *n* : tordo *m* arrocero

bobsled [ˈbɑbˌslɛd] *n* : bobsleigh *m*

bobwhite [ˈbɑbˈʰwaɪt] *n* : codorniz *f* (del Nuevo Mundo)

bode¹ [ˈboːd] *v* **boded; boding** *vt* : presagiar, augurar — *vi* **to bode well** : ser de buen agüero

bode² → **bide**

bodice [ˈbɑdəs] *n* : corpiño *m*

bodied [ˈbɑdid] *adj* : de cuerpo ⟨lean-bodied : de cuerpo delgado⟩ ⟨able-bodied : no discapacitado⟩

bodiless [ˈbɑdiləs, ˈbɑdələs] *adj* : incorpóreo

bodily¹ [ˈbɑdəli] *adv* : en peso ⟨to lift someone bodily : levantar a alguien en peso⟩

bodily² *adj* : corporal, del cuerpo ⟨bodily harm : daños corporales⟩

body [ˈbɑdi] *n, pl* **bodies** *n* **1** : cuerpo *m*, organismo *m* **2** CORPSE : cadáver *m* **3** PERSON : persona *f*, ser *m* humano **4** : nave *f* (de una iglesia), carrocería (de un automóvil), fuselaje *m* (de un avión), casco *m* (de una nave) **5** COLLECTION, MASS : conjunto *m*, grupo *m*, masa *f* ⟨in a body : todos juntos, en masa⟩ **6** ORGANIZATION : organismo *m*, organización *f*

bodyguard [ˈbɑdiˌgɑrd] *n* : guardaespaldas *mf*

bog¹ [ˈbɑg, ˈbɔg] *n* : lodazal *m*, ciénaga *f*, cenagal *m*

bog² *vi* **bogged; bogging** : empantanar, inundar ⟨to get bogged down : empantanarse⟩

bogey [ˈbʊgi, ˈboː-] *n, pl* **-geys** : terror *m*, coco *m* fam

boggle [ˈbɑgəl] *vi* **-gled; -gling** : quedarse atónito, quedarse pasmado ⟨the mind boggles : ¡es increíble!⟩

boggy [ˈbɑgi, ˈbɔ-] *adj* **boggier; -est** : cenagoso

bogus [ˈboːgəs] *adj* : falso, fingido, falaz

bohemian [boːˈhiːmiən] *n* : bohemio *m*, -mia *f* — **bohemian** *adj*

boil¹ [ˈbɔɪl] *vi* **1** : hervir **2 to make one's blood boil** : hervirle la sangre a uno — *vt* **1** : hervir, hacer hervir ⟨to boil water : hervir agua⟩ **2** : cocer, hervir ⟨to boil potatoes : cocer papas⟩

boil² *n* **1** BOILING : hervor *m* **2** : furúnculo *m*, divieso *m* (en medicina)

boiler [ˈbɔɪlər] *n* : caldera *f*

boisterous [ˈbɔɪstərəs] *adj* : bullicioso, escandaloso — **boisterously** *adv*

bold [ˈboːld] *adj* **1** COURAGEOUS : valiente **2** INSOLENT : insolente, descarado **3** DARING : atrevido, audaz — **boldly** *adv*

boldface [ˈboːldˌfeɪs] *or* **boldface type** *n* : negrita *f*

boldness [ˈboːldnəs] *n* **1** COURAGE : valor *m*, coraje *m* **2** INSOLENCE : atrevimiento *m*, insolencia *f*, descaro *m* **3** DARING : audacia *f*

bolero [bəˈlɛroː] *n, pl* **-ros** : bolero *m*

Bolivian [bəˈlɪviən] *n* : boliviano *m*, -na *f* — **Bolivian** *adj*

boll [ˈboːl] *n* : cápsula *f* (del algodón)

boll weevil *n* : gorgojo *m* del algodón

bologna [bəˈloːni] *n* : salchicha *f* ahumada

bolster¹ [ˈboːlstər] *vt* **-stered; -stering** : reforzar, reafirmar ⟨to bolster morale : levantar la moral⟩

bolster² *n* : cabezal *m*, almohadón *m*

bolt¹ [ˈboːlt] *vt* **1** : atornillar, sujetar con pernos ⟨bolted to the floor : sujetado con pernos al suelo⟩ **2** : cerrar con pestillo, echar el cerrojo a ⟨to bolt the door : echar el cerrojo a la puerta⟩ **3 to bolt down** : engullir ⟨she bolted down her dinner : engulló su comida⟩ — *vi* : echar a correr, salir corriendo ⟨he bolted from the room : salió corriendo de la sala⟩

bolt² *n* **1** LATCH : pestillo *m*, cerrojo *m* **2** : tornillo *m*, perno *m* ⟨nuts and bolts : tuercas y tornillos⟩ **3** : rollo *m* ⟨a bolt of cloth : un rollo de tela⟩ **4** lightning bolt : relámpago *m*, rayo *m*

bomb¹ [ˈbɑm] *vt* : bombardear

bomb² *n* : bomba *f*

bombard [bɑmˈbɑrd, bəm-] *vt* : bombardear

bombardier [ˌbɑmbəˈdɪr] *n* : bombardero *m*, -ra *f*

bombardment [bɑmˈbɑrdmənt] *n* : bombardeo *m*

bombast [ˈbɑmˌbæst] *n* : grandilocuencia *f*, ampulosidad *f*

bombastic [bɑmˈbæstɪk] *adj* : grandilocuente, ampuloso, bombástico

bomber [ˈbɑmər] *n* : bombardero *m*

bombproof [ˈbɑmˌpruːf] *adj* : a prueba de bombas

bombshell [ˈbɑmˌʃɛl] *n* : bomba *f* ⟨a political bombshell : una bomba política⟩

bona fide [ˈboːnəˌfaɪd, ˈbɑ-; ˌboːnəˈfaɪdi] *adj* **1** : de buena fe ⟨a bona fide offer : una oferta de buena fe⟩ **2** GENUINE : genuino, auténtico

bonanza [bəˈnænzə] *n* : bonanza *f*

bonbon [ˈbɑnˌbɑn] *n* : bombón *m*

bond¹ [ˈbɑnd] *vt* **1** INSURE : dar fianza a, asegurar **2** STICK : adherir, pegar — *vi* : adherirse, pegarse

bond² *n* **1** LINK, TIE : vínculo *m*, lazo *m* **2** BAIL : fianza *f*, caución *f* **3** : bono *m* ⟨stocks and bonds : acciones y bonos⟩ **4 bonds** *npl* FETTERS : cadenas *fpl*

bondage [ˈbɑndɪdʒ] *n* : esclavitud *f*

bondholder [ˈbɑndˌhoːldər] *n* : tenedor *m*, -dora *f* de bonos

bondsman [ˈbɑndzmən] *n, pl* **-men** [-mən, -ˌmɛn] **1** SLAVE : esclavo *m* **2** SURETY : fiador *m*, -dora *f*

bone¹ [ˈboːn] *vt* **boned; boning** : deshuesar

bone[2] *n* : hueso *m*

boneless ['boːnləs] *adj* : sin huesos, sin espinas

boner ['boːnər] *n* : metedura *f* de pata, metida *f* de pata

bonfire ['bɑn,faɪr] *n* : hoguera *f*, fogata *f*, fogón *m*

bonito [bə'niːṭo] *n, pl* -**tos** *or* -**to** : bonito *m*

bonnet ['bɑnət] *n* : sombrero *m* (de mujer), gorra *f* (de niño)

bonus ['boːnəs] *n* 1 : prima *f*, bonificación *f* (pagado al empleado) 2 ADVANTAGE, BENEFIT : beneficio *m*, provecho *m*

bony ['boːni] *adj* **bonier; -est** : huesudo

boo[1] ['buː] *vt* : abuchear

boo[2] *n, pl* **boos** : abucheo *m*

booby ['buːbi] *n, pl* -**bies** : bobo *m*, -ba *f*; tonto *m*, -ta *f*

book[1] -['bʊk] *vt* : reservar ⟨to book a flight : reservar un vuelo⟩

book[2] *n* 1 : libro *m* 2 **the Book** : la Biblia 3 **by the book** : según las reglas

bookcase ['bʊk,keɪs] *n* : estantería *f*, librero *m* Mex

bookend ['bʊk,ɛnd] *n* : sujetalibros *m*

bookie ['bʊki] → **bookmaker**

bookish ['bʊkɪʃ] *adj* : libresco

bookkeeper ['bʊk,kiːpər] *n* : tenedor *m*, -dora *f* de libros; contable *mf* Spain

bookkeeping ['bʊk,kiːpɪŋ] *n* : contabilidad *f*, teneduría *f* de libros

booklet ['bʊklət] *n* : folleto *m*

bookmaker ['bʊk,meɪkər] *n* : corredor *m*, -dora *f* de apuestas

bookmark ['bʊk,mɑrk] *n* : señalador *m* de libros, marcador *m* de libros

bookseller ['bʊk,slər] *n* : librero *m*, -ra *f*

bookshelf ['bʊk,ʃɛlf] *n, pl* -**shelves** 1 : estante *m* 2 **bookshelves** *npl* : estantería *f*

bookstore ['bʊk,stor] *n* : librería *f*

bookworm ['bʊk,wərm] *n* : ratón *m* de biblioteca *fam*

boom[1] ['buːm] *vi* 1 THUNDER : tronar, resonar 2 FLOURISH, PROSPER : estar en auge, prosperar

boom[2] *n* 1 BOOMING : bramido *m*, estruendo *m* 2 FLOURISHING : auge *m* ⟨population boom : auge de población⟩

boomerang ['buːmə,ræŋ] *n* : bumerán *m*

boon[1] ['buːn] *adj* **boon companion** : amigo *m*, -ga *f* del alma

boon[2] *n* : ayuda *f*, beneficio *m*, adelanto *m*

boondocks ['buːn,dɑks] *npl* : área *f* rural remota, región *f* alejada

boor ['bʊr] *n* : grosero *m*, -ra *f*

boorish ['bʊrɪʃ] *adj* : grosero

boost[1] ['buːst] *vt* 1 LIFT : levantar, alzar 2 INCREASE : aumentar, incrementar 3 PROMOTE : promover, fomentar, hacer publicidad por

boost[2] *n* 1 THRUST : impulso *m*, empujón *m* 2 ENCOURAGEMENT : estímulo *m*, aliento *m* 3 INCREASE : aumento *m*, incremento *m*

booster ['buːstər] *n* 1 SUPPORTER : partidario *m*, -ria *f* 2 **booster rocket** : cohete *m* propulsor 3 **booster shot** : vacuna *f* de refuerzo

boot[1] ['buːt] *vt* KICK : dar una patada a, patear

boot[2] *n* 1 : bota *f*, botín *m* 2 KICK : puntapié *m*, patada *f*

bootee *or* **bootie** ['buːṭi] *n* : botita *f*, botín *m*

booth ['buːθ] *n, pl* **booths** ['buːðz, 'buːθs] : cabina *f* (de teléfono, de votar), caseta *f* (de información), barraca *f* (a una feria)

bootlegger ['buːt,lɛgər] *n* : contrabandista *mf* del alcohol

booty ['buːṭi] *n, pl* -**ties** : botín *m*

booze ['buːz] *n fam* : alcohol *m*

borax ['bɔr,æks] *n* : bórax *m*

border[1] ['bɔrdər] *vt* 1 EDGE : ribetear, bordear 2 BOUND : limitar con, lindar con — *vi* VERGE : rayar, lindar ⟨that borders on absurdity : eso raya en el absurdo⟩

border[2] *n* 1 EDGE : borde *m*, orilla *f* 2 TRIM : ribete *m* 3 FRONTIER : frontera *f*

bore[1] ['bor] *vt* **bored; boring** 1 PIERCE : taladrar, perforar ⟨to bore metals : taladrar metales⟩ 2 OPEN : hacer, abrir ⟨to bore a tunnel : abrir un túnel⟩ 3 WEARY : aburrir

bore[2] → **bear**[1]

bore[3] *n* 1 : pesado *m*, -da *f* (persona aburrida) 2 TEDIOUSNESS : pesadez *f*, lo aburrido 3 DIAMETER : calibre *m*

boredom ['bordəm] *n* : aburrimiento *m*

boring ['borɪŋ] *adj* : aburrido, pesado

born ['bɔrn] *adj* 1 : nacido 2 : nato ⟨she's a born singer : es una cantante nata⟩ ⟨he's a born leader : nació para mandar⟩

borne *pp* → **bear**[1]

boron ['bor,ɑn] *n* : boro *m*

borough ['bəro] *n* : distrito *m* municipal

borrow ['bɑro] *vt* 1 : pedir prestado, tomar prestado 2 APPROPRIATE : apropiarse de, adoptar

borrower ['bɑrəwər] *n* : prestatario *m*, -ria *f*

Bosnian ['bɑzniən, 'bɔz-] *n* : bosnio *m*, -nia *f* — **Bosnian** *adj*

bosom[1] ['bʊzəm, 'buː-] *adj* : íntimo

bosom[2] *n* 1 CHEST : pecho *m* 2 BREAST : pecho *m*, seno *m* 3 CLOSENESS : seno *m* ⟨in the bosom of her family : en el seno de su familia⟩

bosomed ['bʊzəmd, 'buː-] *adj* : con busto ⟨big-bosomed : con mucho busto⟩

boss[1] ['bɔs] *vt* 1 SUPERVISE : dirigir, supervisar 2 **to boss around** : mandonear *fam*, mangonear *fam*

boss[2] *n* : jefe *m*, -fa *f*; patrón *m*, -trona *f*

bossy ['bɔsi] *adj* **bossier; -est** : mandón *fam*, autoritario, dominante

botanist ['bɑtənɪst] *n* : botánico *m*, -ca *f*

botany ['bɑtəni] *n* : botánica *f* — **botanical** [bə'tænɪkəl] *adj*

botch[1] ['bɑtʃ] *vt* : hacer una chapuza de, estropear

botch[2] *n* : chapuza *f*

both[1] ['boːθ] *adj* : ambos, los dos, las dos ⟨both books : ambos libros, los dos libros⟩

both[2] *conj* : tanto como ⟨both Ann and her mother are tall : tanto Ana como su madre son altas⟩

both[3] *pron* : ambos *m*, -bas *f*; los dos, las dos

bother[1] ['bɑðər] *vt* **1** IRK : preocupar ⟨nothing's bothering me : nada me preocupa⟩ ⟨what's bothering him? : ¿qué le pasa?⟩ **2** PESTER : molestar, fastidiar — *vi* **to bother to** : molestarse en, tomar la molestia de

bother[2] *n* **1** TROUBLE : molestia *f*, problemas *mpl* **2** ANNOYANCE : molestia *f*, fastidio *m*

bothersome ['bɑðərsəm] *adj* : molesto, fastidioso

bottle[1] ['bɑtəl] *vt* **bottled; bottling** : embotellar, envasar

bottle[2] *n* : botella *f*, frasco *m*

bottleneck ['bɑtəl,nɛk] *n* **1** : cuello *m* de botella (en un camino) **2** : embotellamiento *m*, atasco *m* (de tráfico) **3** OBSTACLE : obstáculo *m*

bottom[1] ['bɑtəm] *adj* : más bajo, inferior, de abajo

bottom[2] *n* **1** : fondo *m* (de una caja, de una taza, del mar), pie *m* (de una escalera, una página, una montaña), asiento *m* (de una silla), parte *f* de abajo (de una pila) **2** CAUSE : origen *m*, causa *f* ⟨to get to the bottom of : llegar al fondo de⟩ **3** BUTTOCKS : trasero *m*, nalgas *fpl*

bottomless ['bɑtəmləs] *adj* : sin fondo, sin límites

botulism ['bɑtʃə,lɪzəm] *n* : botulismo *m*

boudoir [bə'dwɑr, bu-; 'buː,-, 'bu-] *n* : tocador *m*

bough ['baʊ] *n* : rama *f*

bought → **buy**[1]

bouillon ['buː,jɑn; 'bʊl,jɑn, -jən] *n* : caldo *m*

boulder ['boːldər] *n* : canto *m* rodado, roca *f* grande

boulevard ['bʊlə,vɑrd, 'buː-] *n* : bulevar *m*, boulevard *m*

bounce[1] ['baʊnts] *v* **bounced; bouncing** *vt* : hacer rebotar — *vi* : rebotar

bounce[2] *n* : rebote *m*

bouncy ['baʊntsi] *adj* **bouncier; -est 1** LIVELY : vivo, exuberante, animado **2** RESILIENT : elástico, flexible **3** : que rebota (dícese de una pelota)

bound[1] ['baʊnd] *vt* : delimitar, rodear — *vi* LEAP : saltar, dar brincos

bound[2] *adj* **1** OBLIGED : obligado **2** : encuadernado, empastado ⟨a book bound in leather : un libro encuadernado en cuero⟩ **3** DETERMINED : de-

cidido, empeñado **4 to be bound to** : ser seguro que, tener que, no caber duda que ⟨it was bound to happen : tenía que suceder⟩ **5 bound for** : con rumbo a ⟨bound for Chicago : con rumbo a Chicago⟩ ⟨to be homeward bound : ir camino a casa⟩

bound[3] *n* **1** LIMIT : límite *m* **2** LEAP : salto *m*, brinco *m*

boundary ['baʊndri, -dəri] *n*, *pl* **-aries** : límite *m*, línea *f* divisoria, linde *mf*

boundless ['baʊndləs] *adj* : sin límites, infinito

bounteous ['baʊntiəs] *adj* **1** GENEROUS : generoso **2** ABUNDANT : copioso, abundante — **bounteously** *adv*

bountiful ['baʊntɪfəl] *adj* **1** GENEROUS, LIBERAL : munificente, pródigo, generoso **2** ABUNDANT : copioso, abundante

bounty ['baʊnti] *n*, *pl* **-ties 1** GENEROSITY : generosidad *f*, munificencia *f* **2** REWARD : recompensa *f*

bouquet [boː'keɪ, buː-] *n* **1** : ramo *m*, ramillete *m* **2** FRAGRANCE : bouquet *m*, aroma *m*

bourbon ['bərbən, 'bʊr-] *n* : bourbon *m*, whisky *m* americano

bourgeois[1] ['bʊrʒ,wɑ, bʊrʒ'wɑ] *adj* : burgués

bourgeois[2] *n* : burgués *m*, -guesa *f*

bourgeoisie [,bʊrʒ,wɑ'zi] *n* : burguesía *f*

bout ['baʊt] *n* **1** : encuentro *m*, combate *m* (en deportes) **2** ATTACK : ataque *m* (de una enfermedad) **3** PERIOD, SPELL : período *m* (de actividad)

boutique [buː'tiːk] *n* : boutique *f*

bovine[1] ['boː,vaɪn, -,viːn] *adj* : bovino, vacuno

bovine[2] *n* : bovino *m*

bow[1] ['baʊ] *vi* **1** : hacer una reverencia, inclinarse **2** SUBMIT : ceder, resignarse, someterse — *vt* **1** LOWER : inclinar, bajar **2** BEND : doblar

bow[2] ['baʊ] *n* **1** BOWING : reverencia *f*, inclinación *f* **2** : proa *f* (de un barco)

bow[3] ['boː] *vi* CURVE : arquearse, doblarse

bow[4] ['boː] *n* **1** ARCH, CURVE : arco *m*, curva *f* **2** : arco *m* (arma o vara para tocar varios instrumentos de música) **3** : lazo *m*, moño *m* ⟨to tie a bow : hacer un moño⟩

bowels ['baʊəls] *npl* **1** INTESTINES : intestinos *mpl* **2** : entrañas *fpl* ⟨in the bowels of the earth : en las entrañas de la tierra⟩

bower ['baʊər] *n* : enramada *f*

bowl[1] ['boːl] *vi* : jugar a los bolos

bowl[2] *n* : tazón *m*, cuenco *m*

bowler ['boːlər] *n* : jugador *m*, -dora *f* de bolos

bowling ['boːlɪŋ] *n* : bolos *mpl*

box[1] ['bɑks] *vt* **1** PACK : empaquetar, embalar, encajonar **2** SLAP : bofetear, cachetear — *vi* : boxear

box[2] *n* **1** CONTAINER : caja *f*, cajón *m* **2** COMPARTMENT : compartimiento *m*, palco *m* (en el teatro) **3** SLAP : bofetada *f*, cachetada *f* **4** : boj *m* (planta)

boxcar ['bɑks,kɑr] *n* : vagón *m* de carga, furgón *m*

boxer ['bɑksər] *n* : boxeador *m*, -dora *f*

boxing ['bɑksɪŋ] *n* : boxeo *m*

box office *n* : taquilla *f*, boletería *f*

boxwood ['bɑks,wʊd] *n* : boj *m*

boy ['bɔɪ] *n* **1** : chico *m*, muchacho *m* **2** *or* **little boy** : niño *m*, chico *m* **3** SON : hijo *m*

boycott[1] ['bɔɪ,kɑt] *vt* : boicotear

boycott[2] *n* : boicot *m*

boyfriend ['bɔɪ,frɛnd] *n* **1** FRIEND : amigo *m* **2** SWEETHEART : novio *m*

boyhood ['bɔɪ,hʊd] *n* : niñez *f*

boyish ['bɔɪʃ] *adj* : de niño, juvenil

bra ['brɑ] → **brassiere**

brace[1] ['breɪs] *v* **braced; bracing** *vt* **1** PROP UP, SUPPORT : apuntalar, apoyar, sostener **2** INVIGORATE : vigorizar **3** REINFORCE : reforzar — *vi* **to brace oneself** PREPARE : prepararse

brace[2] *n* **1** : berbiquí *m* ⟨brace and bit : berbiquí y barrena⟩ **2** CLAMP, REINFORCEMENT : abrazadera *f*, refuerzo *m* **3** : llave *f* (signo de puntuación) **4 braces** *npl* : aparatos *mpl* (de ortodoncia), frenos *mpl* Mex

bracelet ['breɪslət] *n* : brazalete *m*, pulsera *f*

bracken ['brækən] *n* : helecho *m*

bracket[1] ['brækət] *vt* **1** SUPPORT : asegurar, apuntalar **2** : poner entre corchetes **3** CATEGORIZE, GROUP : catalogar, agrupar

bracket[2] *n* **1** SUPPORT : soporte *m* **2** : corchete *m* (marca de puntuación) **3** CATEGORY, CLASS : clase *f*, categoría *f*

brackish ['brækɪʃ] *adj* : salobre

brad ['bræd] *n* : clavo *m* con cabeza pequeña, clavito *m*

brag[1] ['bræg] *vi* **bragged; bragging** : alardear, fanfarronear, jactarse

brag[2] *n* : alarde *m*, jactancia *f*, fanfarronada *f*

braggart ['brægərt] *n* : fanfarrón *m*, -rrona *f* fam; jactancioso *m*, -sa *f*

braid[1] ['breɪd] *vt* : trenzar

braid[2] *n* : trenza *f*

braille ['breɪl] *n* : braille *m*

brain[1] ['breɪn] *vt* : romper la crisma a, aplastar el cráneo a

brain[2] *n* **1** : cerebro *m* **2 brains** *npl* INTELLECT : inteligencia *f*, sesos *mpl*

brainless ['breɪnləs] *adj* : estúpido, tonto

brainstorm ['breɪn,stɔrm] *n* : idea *f* brillante, idea *f* genial

brainy ['breɪni] *adj* **brainier; -est** : inteligente, listo

braise ['breɪz] *vt* **braised; braising** : cocer a fuego lento, estofar

brake[1] ['breɪk] *v* **braked; braking** : frenar

brake[2] *n* : freno *m*

bramble ['bræmbəl] *n* : zarza *f*, zarzamora *f*

bran ['bræn] *n* : salvado *m*

branch[1] ['bræntʃ] *vi* **1** : echar ramas (dícese de una planta) **2** DIVERGE : ramificarse, separarse

branch[2] *n* **1** : rama *f* (de una planta) **2** EXTENSION : ramal *m* (de un camino, un ferrocarril, un río), rama *f* (de una familia o un campo de estudiar), sucursal *f* (de una empresa), agencia *f* (del gobierno)

brand[1] ['brænd] *vt* **1** : marcar (ganado) **2** LABEL : tachar, tildar ⟨they branded him as a liar : lo tacharon de mentiroso⟩

brand[2] *n* **1** : marca *f* (de ganado) **2** STIGMA : estigma *m* **3** MAKE : marca *f* ⟨brand name : marca de fábrica⟩

brandish ['brændɪʃ] *vt* : blandir

brand–new ['brænd'nu:, -'nju:] *adj* : nuevo, flamante

brandy ['brændi] *n, pl* **-dies** : brandy *m*

brash ['bræʃ] *adj* **1** IMPULSIVE : impulsivo, impetuoso **2** BRAZEN : excesivamente desenvuelto, descarado

brass ['bræs] *n* **1** : latón *m* **2** GALL, NERVE : descaro *m*, cara *f* fam **3** OFFICERS : mandamases *mpl* fam

brassiere [brə'zɪr, brɑ-] *n* : sostén *m*, brasier *m* Col, Mex

brassy ['bræsi] *adj* **brassier; -est** : dorado

brat ['bræt] *n* : mocoso *m*, -sa *f*; niño *m* mimado, niña *f* mimada

bravado [brə'vɑdo] *n, pl* **-does** *or* **-dos** : bravuconadas *fpl*, bravatas *fpl*

brave[1] ['breɪv] *vt* **braved; braving** : afrontar, hacer frente a

brave[2] *adj* **braver; bravest** : valiente, valeroso — **bravely** *adv*

brave[3] *n* : guerrero *m* indio

bravery ['breɪvəri] *n* : valor *m*, valentía *f*

bravo ['brɑ,vo:] *n, pl* **-vos** : bravo *m*

brawl[1] ['brɔl] *vi* : pelearse, pegarse

brawl[2] *n* : pelea *f*, reyerta *f*

brawn ['brɔn] *n* : fuerza *f* muscular

brawny ['brɔni] *adj* **brawnier; -est** : musculoso

bray[1] ['breɪ] *vi* : rebuznar

bray[2] *n* : rebuzno *m*

brazen ['breɪzən] *adj* **1** : de latón **2** BOLD : descarado, directo

brazenly ['breɪzənli] *adv* : descaradamente, insolentemente

brazenness ['breɪzənnəs] *n* : descaro *m*, atrevimiento *m*

brazier ['breɪʒər] *n* : brasero *m*

Brazilian [brə'zɪljən] *n* : brasileño *m*, -ña *f* — **Brazilian** *adj*

Brazil nut [brə'zɪl,nʌt] *n* : nuez *f* de Brasil

breach[1] ['bri:tʃ] *vt* **1** PENETRATE : abrir una brecha en, penetrar **2** VIOLATE : infringir, violar

breach[2] *n* **1** VIOLATION : infracción *f*, violación *f* ⟨breach of trust : abuso de confianza⟩ **2** GAP, OPENING : brecha *f*

bread[1] ['brɛd] *vt* : empanar
bread[2] *n* : pan *m*
breadth ['brɛtθ] *n* : ancho *m*, anchura *f*
breadwinner ['brɛd,wɪnər] *n* : sostén *m* de la familia
break[1] ['breɪk] *v* **broke** ['bro:k]; **broken** ['bro:kən]; **breaking** *vt* 1 SMASH : romper, quebrar 2 VIOLATE : infringir, violar, romper 3 SURPASS : batir, superar 4 CRUSH, RUIN : arruinar, deshacer, destrozar ⟨to break one's spirit : quebrantar su espíritu⟩ 5 : dar, comunicar ⟨to break the news : dar las noticias⟩ 6 INTERRUPT : cortar, interrumpir — *vi* 1 : romperse, quebrarse ⟨my calculator broke : se me rompió la calculadora⟩ 2 DISPERSE : dispersarse, despejarse 3 : estallar (dícese de una tormenta), romper (dícese del día) 4 CHANGE : cambiar (dícese del tiempo o de la voz) 5 DECREASE : bajar ⟨my fever broke : me bajó la fiebre⟩ 6 : divulgarse, revelarse ⟨the news broke : la noticia se divulgó⟩ 7 **to break into** : forzar, abrir 8 **to break out of** : escaparse de 9 **to break through** : penetrar
break[2] *n* 1 : ruptura *f*, rotura *f*, fractura *f* (de un hueso), claro *m* (entre las nubes), cambio *m* (del tiempo) 2 CHANCE : oportunidad *f* ⟨a lucky break : un golpe de suerte⟩ 3 REST : descanso *m* ⟨to take a break : tomar(se) un descanso⟩
breakable ['breɪkəbəl] *adj* : quebradizo, frágil
breakage ['breɪkɪdʒ] *n* 1 BREAKING : rotura *f* 2 DAMAGE : destrozos *mpl*, daños *mpl*
breakdown ['breɪk,daʊn] *n* 1 : avería *f* (de máquinas), interrupción *f* (de comunicaciones), fracaso *m* (de negociaciones) 2 ANALYSIS : análisis *m*, desglose *m* 3 or **nervous breakdown** : crisis *f* nerviosa
break down *vi* 1 : estropearse, descomponerse ⟨the machine broke down : la máquina se descompuso⟩ 2 FAIL : fracasar 3 CRY : echarse a llorar — *vt* 1 DESTROY : derribar, echar abajo 2 OVERCOME : vencer (la resistencia), disipar (sospechas) 3 ANALYZE : analizar, descomponer
breaker ['breɪkər] *n* 1 WAVE : ola *f* grande 2 : interruptor *m* automático (de electricidad)
breakfast[1] ['brɛkfəst] *vi* : desayunar
breakfast[2] *n* : desayuno *m*
breakneck ['breɪk,nɛk] *adj* **at breakneck speed** : a una velocidad vertiginosa
break out *vi* 1 : salirse ⟨she broke out in spots : le salieron granos⟩ 2 ERUPT : estallar (dícese de una guerra, de la violencia, etc.) 3 ESCAPE : fugarse, escaparse
breakup ['breɪk,əp] *n* 1 DIVISION : desintegración *f* 2 : ruptura *f*

break up *vt* 1 DIVIDE : dividir 2 : disolver (una muchedumbre, una pelea, etc.) — *vi* 1 BREAK : romperse 2 SEPARATE : deshacerse, separarse ⟨I broke up with him : terminé con él⟩
breast ['brɛst] *n* 1 : pecho *m*, seno *m* (de una mujer) 2 CHEST : pecho *m*
breastbone ['brɛst,bo:n] *n* : esternón *m*
breast–feed ['brɛst,fi:d] *vt* **-fed** [-,fɛd]; **-feeding** : amamantar, darle de mamar (a un niño)
breath ['brɛθ] *n* 1 BREATHING : aliento *m* ⟨to hold one's breath : aguantar la respiración⟩ 2 BREEZE : soplo *m* ⟨a breath of fresh air : un soplo de aire fresco⟩
breathe ['bri:ð] *v* **breathed; breathing** *vi* 1 : respirar 2 LIVE : vivir, respirar — *vt* 1 : respirar, aspirar ⟨to breathe fresh air : respirar el aire fresco⟩ 2 UTTER : decir ⟨I won't breathe a word of this : no diré nada de esto⟩
breathless ['brɛθləs] *adj* : sin aliento, jadeante
breathlessly ['brɛθləsli] *adv* : entrecortadamente, jadeando
breathlessness ['brɛθləsnəs] *n* : dificultad *f* al respirar
breathtaking ['brɛθ,teɪkɪŋ] *adj* IMPRESSIVE : impresionante, imponente
breeches ['brɪtʃəz, 'bri:-] *npl* : pantalones *mpl*, calzones *mpl*, bombachos *mpl*
breed[1] ['bri:d] *v* **bred** ['brɛd]; **breeding** *vt* 1 : criar (animales) 2 ENGENDER : engendrar, producir ⟨familiarity breeds contempt : la confianza hace perder el respeto⟩ 3 RAISE, REAR : criar, educar — *vi* REPRODUCE : reproducirse
breed[2] *n* 1 : variedad *f* (de plantas), raza *f* (de animales) 2 CLASS : clase *f*, tipo *m*
breeder ['bri:dər] *n* : criador *m*, -dora *f* (de animales); cultivador *m*, -dora *f* (de plantas)
breeze[1] ['bri:z] *vi* **breezed; breezing** : pasar con ligereza ⟨to breeze in : entrar como si nada⟩
breeze[2] *n* : brisa *f*, soplo *m* (de aire)
breezy ['bri:zi] *adj* **breezier; -est** 1 AIRY, WINDY : aireado, ventoso 2 LIVELY : animado, alegre 3 NONCHALANT : despreocupado
brethren → **brother**
brevity ['brɛvəti] *n, pl* **-ties** : brevedad *f*, concisión *f*
brew[1] ['bru:] *vt* 1 : fabricar, elaborar (cerveza) 2 FOMENT : tramar, maquinar, fomentar — *vi* 1 : fabricar cerveza 2 : amenazar ⟨a storm is brewing : una tormenta amenaza⟩
brew[2] *n* 1 BEER : cerveza *f* 2 POTION : brebaje *m*
brewer ['bru:ər] *n* : cervecero *m*, -ra *f*
brewery ['bru:əri, 'bruri] *n, pl* **-eries** : cervecería *f*
briar ['braɪər] → **brier**

bribe[1] [ˈbraɪb] *vt* **bribed; bribing** : sobornar, cohechar, coimear *Arg, Chile, Peru*

bribe[2] *n* : soborno *m*, cohecho *m*, coima *f Arg, Chile, Peru*, mordida *f CA, Mex*

bribery [ˈbraɪbəri] *n, pl* **-eries** : soborno *m*, cohecho *m*, coima *f*, mordida *f CA, Mex*

bric-a-brac [ˈbrɪkəˌbræk] *npl* : baratijas *fpl*, chucherías *fpl*

brick[1] [ˈbrɪk] *vt* **to brick up** : tabicar, tapiar

brick[2] *n* : ladrillo *m*

bricklayer [ˈbrɪkˌleɪər] *n* : albañil *mf*

bricklaying [ˈbrɪkˌleɪɪŋ] *n* : albañilería *f*

bridal [ˈbraɪdəl] *adj* : nupcial, de novia *f*

bride [ˈbraɪd] *n* : novia *f*

bridegroom [ˈbraɪdˌgruːm] *n* : novio *m*

bridesmaid [ˈbraɪdzˌmeɪd] *n* : dama *f* de honor

bridge[1] [ˈbrɪdʒ] *vt* **bridged; bridging 1** : tender un puente sobre **2 to bridge the gap** : salvar las diferencias

bridge[2] *n* **1** : puente *m* **2** : caballete *m* (de la nariz) **3** : puente *m* de mando (de un barco) **4 DENTURE** : puente *m* (dental) **5** : bridge *m* (juego de naipes)

bridle[1] [ˈbraɪdəl] *v* **-dled; -dling** *vt* **1** : embridar (un caballo) **2 RESTRAIN** : refrenar, dominar, contener — *vi* **to bridle at** : molestarse por, picarse por

bridle[2] *n* : brida *f*

brief[1] [ˈbriːf] *vt* : dar órdenes a, instruir

brief[2] *adj* : breve, sucinto, conciso

brief[3] *n* **1** : resumen *m*, sumario *m* **2 briefs** *npl* : calzoncillos *mpl*

briefcase [ˈbriːfˌkeɪs] *n* : portafolio *m*, maletín *m*

briefly [ˈbriːfli] *adv* : brevemente, por poco tiempo ⟨to speak briefly : discursar en pocas palabras⟩

brier [ˈbraɪər] *n* **1 BRAMBLE** : zarza *f*, rosal *m* silvestre **2 HEATH** : brezo *m* veteado

brig [ˈbrɪg] *n* **1** : bergantín *m* (barco) **2** : calabozo *m* (en un barco)

brigade [brɪˈgeɪd] *n* : brigada *f*

brigadier general [ˌbrɪgəˈdɪr] *n* : general *m* de brigada

brigand [ˈbrɪgənd] *n* : bandolero *m*, -ra *f*; forajido *m*, -da *f*

bright [ˈbraɪt] *adj* **1** : brillante (dícese del sol, de los ojos), vivo (dícese de un color), claro, fuerte **2 CHEERFUL** : alegre, animado ⟨bright and early : muy temprano⟩ **3 INTELLIGENT** : listo, inteligente ⟨a bright idea : una idea luminosa⟩

brighten [ˈbraɪtən] *vt* **1 ILLUMINATE** : iluminar **2 ENLIVEN** : alegrar, animar — *vi* **1** : hacerse más brillante **2 to brighten up** : animarse, alegrarse, mejorar

brightly [ˈbraɪtli] *adv* : vivamente, intensamente, alegremente

brightness [ˈbraɪtnəs] *n* **1 LUMINOSITY** : luminosidad *f*, brillantez *f*, resplandor *m*, brillo *m* **2 CHEERFULNESS** : alegría *f*, ánimo *m*

brilliance [ˈbrɪljənts] *n* **1 BRIGHTNESS** : resplandor *m*, fulgor *m*, brillo *m*, brillantez *f* **2 INTELLIGENCE** : inteligencia *f*, brillantez *f*

brilliancy [ˈbrɪljəntsi] → **brilliance**

brilliant [ˈbrɪljənt] *adj* : brillante

brilliantly [ˈbrɪljəntli] *adv* : brillantemente, con brillantez

brim[1] [ˈbrɪm] *vi* **brimmed; brimming 1** *or* **to brim over** : desbordarse, rebosar **2 to brim with tears** : llenarse de lágrimas

brim[2] *n* **1** : ala *f* (de un sombrero) **2** : borde *m* (de una taza o un vaso)

brimful [ˈbrɪmˈful] *adj* : lleno hasta el borde, repleto, rebosante

brimless [ˈbrɪmləs] *adj* : sin ala

brimstone [ˈbrɪmˌstoːn] *n* : azufre *m*

brindled [ˈbrɪndəld] *adj* : manchado, pinto

brine [ˈbraɪn] *n* **1** : salmuera *f*, escabeche *m* (para encurtir) **2 OCEAN** : océano *m*, mar *m*

bring [ˈbrɪŋ] *vt* **brought; bringing 1 CARRY** : traer ⟨bring me some coffee : tráigame un café⟩ **2 PRODUCE** : traer, producir, conseguir ⟨his efforts will bring him success : sus esfuerzos le conseguirán el éxito⟩ **3 PERSUADE** : convencer, persuadir **4 YIELD** : rendir, alcanzar, venderse por ⟨to bring a good price : alcanzar un precio alto⟩ **5 to bring to an end** : terminar (con) **6 to bring to light** : sacar a la luz

bring about *vt* : ocasionar, provocar, determinar

bring forth *vt* **PRODUCE** : producir

bring out *vt* : sacar, publicar (un libro, etc.)

bring to *vt* **REVIVE** : resucitar

bring up *vt* **1 REAR** : criar **2 MENTION** : sacar, mencionar

brininess [ˈbraɪnɪnəs] *n* : salinidad *f*

brink [ˈbrɪŋk] *n* : borde *m*

briny [ˈbraɪni] *adj* **brinier; -est** : salobre

briquette *or* **briquet** [brɪˈkɛt] *n* : briqueta *f*

brisk [ˈbrɪsk] *adj* **1 LIVELY** : rápido, enérgico, brioso **2 INVIGORATING** : fresco, estimulante

brisket [ˈbrɪskət] *n* : falda *f*

briskly [ˈbrɪskli] *adv* : rápidamente, enérgicamente, con brío

briskness [ˈbrɪsknəs] *n* : brío *m*, rapidez *f*

bristle[1] [ˈbrɪsəl] *vi* **-tled; -tling 1** : erizarse, ponerse de punta **2** : enfurecerse, enojarse ⟨she bristled at the suggestion : se enfureció ante tal sugerencia⟩ **3** : estar plagado, estar repleto ⟨a city bristling with tourists : una ciudad repleta de turistas⟩

bristle[2] *n* : cerda *f* (de un animal), pelo *m* (de una planta)

bristly [ˈbrɪsəli] *adj* **bristlier; -est** : áspero y erizado

British[1] [ˈbrɪtɪʃ] *adj* : británico

British[2] *n* **the British** *npl* : los británicos

brittle ['brɪtəl] *adj* **-tler; -tlest** : frágil, quebradizo

brittleness ['brɪtəlnəs] *n* : fragilidad *f*

broach ['broːtʃ] *vt* BRING UP : mencionar, abordar, sacar

broad ['brɔd] *adj* **1** WIDE : ancho **2** SPACIOUS : amplio, extenso **3** FULL : pleno ⟨in broad daylight : en pleno día⟩ **4** OBVIOUS : claro, evidente **5** TOLERANT : tolerante, liberal **6** GENERAL : general **7** ESSENTIAL : principal, esencial ⟨the broad outline : los rasgos esenciales⟩

broadcast¹ ['brɔd,kæst] *vt* **-cast; -casting 1** SCATTER : esparcir, diseminar **2** CIRCULATE, SPREAD : divulgar, difundir, propagar **3** TRANSMIT : transmitir, emitir

broadcast² *n* **1** TRANSMISSION : transmisión *f*, emisión *f* **2** PROGRAM : programa *m*, emisión *f*

broadcaster ['brɔd,kæstər] *n* : presentador *m*, -dora *f*; locutor *m*, -tora *f*

broadcloth ['brɔd,klɔθ] *n* : paño *m* fino

broaden ['brɔdən] *vt* : ampliar, ensanchar — *vi* : ampliarse, ensancharse

broadloom ['brɔd,luːm] *adj* : tejido en telar ancho

broadly ['brɔdli] *adv* **1** GENERALLY : en general, aproximadamente **2** WIDELY : extensivamente

broad–minded ['brɔd'maɪndəd] *adj* : tolerante, de amplias miras

broad–mindedness ['brɔd'maɪndədnəs] *n* : tolerancia *f*

broadside ['brɔd,saɪd] *n* **1** VOLLEY : andanada *f* **2** ATTACK : ataque *m*, invectiva *f*, andanada *f*

brocade [bro'keɪd] *n* : brocado *m*

broccoli ['brɑkəli] *n* : brócoli *m*, brécol *m*

brochure [bro'ʃʊr] *n* : folleto *m*

brogue ['broːg] *n* : acento *m* irlandés

broil¹ ['brɔɪl] *vt* : asar a la parrilla

broil² *n* : asado *m*

broiler ['brɔɪlər] *n* **1** GRILL : parrilla *f* **2** : pollo *m* para asar

broke¹ ['broːk] → **break¹**

broke² *adj* : pelado, arruinado ⟨to go broke : arruinarse, quebrar⟩

broken ['broːkən] *adj* **1** DAMAGED, SHATTERED : roto, quebrado, fracturado **2** IRREGULAR, UNEVEN : accidentado, irregular, recortado **3** VIOLATED : roto, quebrantado **4** INTERRUPTED : interrumpido, discontinuo **5** CRUSHED : abatido, quebrantado ⟨a broken man : un hombre destrozado⟩ **6** IMPERFECT : mal ⟨to speak broken English : hablar el inglés con dificultad⟩

brokenhearted [,broːkən'hɑrtəd] *adj* : descorazonado, desconsolado

broker¹ ['broːkər] *vt* : hacer corretaje de

broker² *n* **1** : agente *mf*; corredor *m*, -dora *f* **2** → **stockbroker**

brokerage ['broːkərɪdʒ] *n* : corretaje *m*, agencia *f* de corredores

bromine ['broː,miːn] *n* : bromo *m*

bronchitis [brɑn'kaɪtəs, brɑŋ-] *n* : bronquitis *f*

bronze¹ ['brɑnz] *vt* **bronzed; bronzing** : broncear

bronze² *n* : bronce *m*

brooch ['broːtʃ, 'bruːtʃ] *n* : broche *m*, prendedor *m*

brood¹ ['bruːd] *vt* **1** INCUBATE : empollar, incubar **2** PONDER : sopesar, considerar — *vi* **1** INCUBATE : empollar **2** REFLECT : rumiar, reflexionar **3** WORRY : ponerse melancólico, inquietarse

brood² *adj* : de cría

brood³ *n* : nidada *f* (de pájaros), camada *f* (de mamíferos)

brooder ['bruːdər] *n* **1** THINKER : pensador *m*, -dora *f* **2** INCUBATOR : incubadora *f*

brook¹ ['brʊk] *vt* TOLERATE : tolerar, admitir

brook² *n* : arroyo *m*

broom ['bruːm, 'brʊm] *n* **1** : retama *f*, hiniesta *f* **2** : escoba *f* (para barrer)

broomstick ['bruːm,stɪk, 'brʊm-] *n* : palo *m* de escoba

broth ['brɔθ] *n, pl* **broths** ['brɔθs, 'brɔðz] : caldo *m*

brothel ['brɑθəl, 'brɔ-] *n* : burdel *m*

brother ['brʌðər] *n, pl* **brothers** *also* **brethren** ['brɔðrən, -ðərn] **1** : hermano *m* **2** KINSMAN : pariente *m*, familiar *m*

brotherhood ['brʌðər,hʊd] *n* **1** FELLOWSHIP : fraternidad *f* **2** ASSOCIATION : hermandad *f*

brother–in–law ['brʌðərɪn,lɔ] *n, pl* **brothers–in–law** : cuñado *m*

brotherly ['brʌðərli] *adj* : fraternal

brought → **bring**

brow ['braʊ] *n* **1** EYEBROW : ceja *f* **2** FOREHEAD : frente *f* **3** : cima *f* ⟨the brow of a hill : la cima de una colina⟩

browbeat ['braʊ,biːt] *vt* **-beat; -beaten** [-,biːtən] *or* **-beat; -beating** : intimidar

brown¹ ['braʊn] *vt* **1** : dorar (en cocina) **2** TAN : broncear — *vi* **1** : dorarse (en cocina) **2** TAN : broncearse

brown² *adj* : marrón, café, castaño (dícese del pelo), moreno (dícese de la piel)

brown³ *n* : marrón *m*, café *m*

brownish ['braʊnɪʃ] *adj* : pardo

browse ['braʊz] *vi* **browsed; browsing 1** GRAZE : pacer **2** LOOK : mirar, echar un vistazo

bruin ['bruːɪn] *n* BEAR : oso *m*

bruise¹ ['bruːz] *vt* **bruised; bruising 1** : contusionar, machucar, magullar (a una persona) **2** DAMAGE : magullar, dañar (frutas) **3** CRUSH : majar **4** HURT : herir (los sentimientos)

bruise² *n* : moretón *m*, cardenal *m*, magulladura *f* (dícese de frutas)

brunch ['brʌntʃ] *n* : combinación *f* de desayuno y almuerzo

brunet¹ *or* **brunette** [bru'nɛt] *adj* : moreno

brunet² *or* **brunette** *n* : moreno *m*, -na *f*

brunt [ˈbrʌnt] *n* **to bear the brunt of** : llevar el peso de, aguantar el mayor impacto de

brush¹ [ˈbrʌʃ] *vt* **1** : cepillar ⟨to brush one's teeth : cepillarse uno los dientes⟩ **2** SWEEP : barrer, quitar·con un cepillo **3** GRAZE : rozar **4 to brush off** DISREGARD : hacer caso omiso de, ignorar — *vi* **to brush up on** : repasar, refrescar, dar un repaso a

brush² *n* **1** *or* **brushwood** [ˈbrʌʃˌwʊd] : broza *f* **2** SCRUB, UNDERBRUSH : maleza *f* **3** : cepillo *m*, pincel *m* (de artista), brocha *f* (de pintor) **4** TOUCH : roce *m* **5** SKIRMISH : escaramuza *f*

brush–off [ˈbrʌʃˌɔf] *n* **to give the brush–off to** : dar calabazas a

brusque [ˈbrʌsk] *adj* : brusco — **brusquely** *adv*

brussels sprout [ˈbrʌsəlzˌspraʊt] *n* : col *f* de Bruselas

brutal [ˈbruːt̬əl] *adj* : brutal, cruel, salvaje — **brutally** *adv*

brutality [bruːˈtæl̬ət̬i] *n, pl* **-ties** : brutalidad *f*

brutalize [ˈbruːt̬əlˌaɪz] *vt* **-ized; -izing** : brutalizar, maltratar

brute¹ [ˈbruːt] *adj* : bruto ⟨brute force : fuerza bruta⟩

brute² *n* **1** BEAST : bestia *f*, animal *m* **2** : bruto *m*, -ta *f*; bestia *mf* (persona)

brutish [ˈbruːt̬ɪʃ] *adj* **1** : de animal **2** CRUEL : brutal, salvaje **3** STUPID : bruto, estúpido

bubble¹ [ˈbʌbəl] *vi* **-bled; -bling** : burbujear ⟨to bubble over with joy : rebosar de alegría⟩

bubble² *n* : burbuja *f*

bubbly [ˈbʌbəli] *adj* **bubblier; -est 1** BUBBLING : burbujeante **2** LIVELY : vivaz, lleno de vida

bubonic plague [buːˈbɑnɪk, ˈbjuː-] *n* : peste *f* bubónica

buccaneer [ˌbʌkəˈnɪr] *n* : bucanero *m*

buck¹ [ˈbʌk] *vi* **1** : corcovear (dícese de un caballo o un burro) **2** JOLT : dar sacudidas **3 to buck against** : resistirse a, rebelarse contra **4 to buck up** : animarse, levantar el ánimo — *vt* OPPOSE : oponerse a, ir en contra de

buck² *n, pl* **buck** *or* **bucks 1** : animal *m* macho, ciervo *m* (macho) **2** DOLLAR : dólar *m* **3 to pass the buck** *fam* : pasar la pelota *fam*

bucket [ˈbʌkət] *n* : balde *m*, cubo *m*, cubeta *f Mex*

bucketful [ˈbʌkətˌfʊl] *n* : balde *m* lleno

buckle¹ [ˈbʌkəl] *v* **-led; -ling** *vt* **1** FASTEN : abrochar **2** BEND, TWIST : combar, torcer — *vi* **1** BEND, TWIST : combarse, torcerse, doblarse (dícese de las rodillas) **2 to buckle down** : ponerse a trabajar con esmero **3 to buckle up** : abrocharse

buckle² *n* **1** : hebilla *f* **2** TWISTING : torcedura *f*

buckshot [ˈbʌkˌʃɑt] *n* : perdigón *m*

buckskin [ˈbʌkˌskɪn] *n* : gamuza *f*

bucktooth [ˈbʌkˌtuːθ] *n* : diente *m* saliente, diente *m* salido

buckwheat [ˈbʌkˌʍiːt] *n* : trigo *m* rubión, alforfón *m*

bucolic [bjuːˈkɑlɪk] *adj* : bucólico

bud¹ [ˈbʌd] *v* **budded; budding** *vt* GRAFT : injertar — *vi* : brotar, hacer brotes

bud² *n* : brote *m*, yema *f*, capullo *m* (de una flor)

Buddhism [ˈbuːˌdɪzəm, ˈbʊ-] *n* : budismo *m*

Buddhist [ˈbuːdɪst, ˈbʊ-] : budista *mf* — **Buddhist** *adj*

buddy [ˈbʌdi] *n, pl* **-dies** : amigo *m*, -ga *f*; compinche *mf fam*; cuate *m*, -ta *f Mex fam*

budge [ˈbʌdʒ] *vi* **budged; budging 1** MOVE : moverse, desplazarse **2** YIELD : ceder

budget¹ [ˈbʌdʒət] *vt* : presupuestar (gastos), asignar (dinero) — *vi* : presupuestar, planear el presupuesto

budget² *n* : presupuesto

budgetary [ˈbʌdʒəˌt̬eri] *adj* : presupuestario

buff¹ [ˈbʌf] *vt* POLISH : pulir, sacar brillo a, lustrar

buff² *adj* : beige, amarillento

buff³ *n* **1** : beige *m*, amarillento *m* **2** ENTHUSIAST : aficionado *m*, -da *f*; entusiasta *mf*

buffalo [ˈbʌfəˌloː] *n, pl* **-lo** *or* **-loes 1** : búfalo *m* **2** BISON : bisonte *m*

buffer [ˈbʌfər] *n* **1** BARRIER : barrera *f* ⟨buffer state : estado tapón⟩ **2** SHOCK ABSORBER : amortiguador *m*

buffet¹ [ˈbʌfət] *vt* : golpear, zarandear, sacudir

buffet² *n* BLOW : golpe *m*

buffet³ [ˌbʌˈfeɪ, ˌbuː-] *n* **1** : bufete *m*, bufé *m* (comida) **2** SIDEBOARD : aparador *m*

buffoon [ˌbʌˈfuːn] *n* : bufón *m*, -fona *f*; payaso *m*, -sa *f*

buffoonery [ˌbʌˈfuːnəri] *n, pl* **-eries** : bufonada *f*, payasada *f*

bug¹ [ˈbʌg] *vt* **bugged; bugging 1** PESTER : fastidiar, molestar **2** : ocultar micrófonos en

bug² *n* **1** INSECT : bicho *m*, insecto *m* **2** DEFECT : defecto *m*, falla *f*, problema *m* **3** GERM : microbio *m*, virus *m* **4** MICROPHONE : micrófono *m*

bugaboo [ˈbʌgəˌbuː] → **bogey**

bugbear [ˈbʌgˌbær] *n* : pesadilla *f*, coco *m*

buggy [ˈbʌgi] *n, pl* **-gies** : calesa *f* (tirada por caballos), cochecito *m* (para niños)

bugle [ˈbjuːgəl] *n* : clarín *m*, corneta *f*

bugler [ˈbjuːgələr] *n* : corneta *mf*

build¹ [ˈbɪld] *v* **built** [ˈbɪlt]; **building** *vt* **1** CONSTRUCT : construir, edificar, ensamblar, levantar **2** DEVELOP : desarrollar, elaborar, forjar **3** INCREASE : incrementar, aumentar — *vi* **to build up** : aumentar, intensificar

build² *n* PHYSIQUE : físico *m*, complexión *f*

builder ['bɪldər] *n* : constructor *m*, -tora *f*; contratista *mf*

building ['bɪldɪŋ] *n* **1** EDIFICE : edificio *m* **2** CONSTRUCTION : construcción *f*

built–in ['bɪlt'ɪn] *adj* **1** : empotrado ⟨built-in cabinets : armarios empotrados⟩ **2** INHERENT : incorporado, intrínseco

bulb ['bʌlb] *n* **1** : bulbo *m* (de una planta), cabeza *f* (de ajo), cubeta *f* (de un termómetro) **2** LIGHTBULB : bombilla *f*, foco *m*, bombillo *m* CA, Col, Ven

bulbous ['bʌlbəs] *adj* : bulboso

Bulgarian [bʌl'gæriən, bʊl-] *n* **1** : búlgaro *m*, -ra *f* **2** : búlgaro *m* (idioma) — **Bulgarian** *adj*

bulge[1] ['bʌldʒ] *vi* **bulged; bulging** : abultar, sobresalir

bulge[2] *n* : bulto *m*, protuberancia *f*

bulk[1] ['bʌlk] *vt* : hinchar — *vi* EXPAND, SWELL : ampliarse, hincharse

bulk[2] *n* **1** SIZE, VOLUME : volumen *m*, tamaño *m* **2** FIBER : fibra *f* **3** MASS : mole *f* **4 the bulk of** : la mayor parte de **5 in ~** : en grandes cantidades

bulkhead ['bʌlk,hɛd] *n* : mamparo *m*

bulky ['bʌlki] *adj* **bulkier; -est** : voluminoso, grande

bull[1] ['bʊl] *adj* : macho

bull[2] *n* **1** : toro *m*, macho *m* (de ciertas especies) **2** : bula *f* (papal) **3** DECREE : decreto *m*, edicto *m*

bulldog ['bʊl,dɔg] *n* : bulldog *m*

bulldoze ['bʊl,do:z] *vt* **-dozed; -dozing** **1** LEVEL : nivelar (el terreno), derribar (un edificio) **2** FORCE : forzar ⟨he bulldozed his way through : se abrió paso a codazos⟩

bulldozer ['bʊl,do:zər] *n* : bulldozer *m*

bullet ['bʊlət] *n* : bala *f*

bulletin ['bʊlətən, -lətən] *n* **1** NOTICE : comunicado *m*, anuncio *m*, boletín *m* **2** NEWSLETTER : boletín *m* (informativo)

bulletin board *n* : tablón *m* de anuncios

bulletproof ['bʊlət,pru:f] *adj* : antibalas, a prueba de balas

bullfight ['bʊl,faɪt] *n* : corrida *f* (de toros)

bullfighter ['bʊl,faɪtər] *n* : torero *m*, -ra *f*; matador *m*

bullfrog ['bʊl,frɔg] *n* : rana *f* toro

bullheaded ['bʊl'hɛdəd] *adj* : testarudo

bullion ['bʊljən] *n* : oro *m* en lingotes, plata *f* en lingotes

bullock ['bʊlək] *n* **1** STEER : buey *m*, toro *m* castrado **2** : toro *m* joven, novillo *m*

bull's–eye ['bʊlz,aɪ] *n, pl* **bull's–eyes** : diana *f*, blanco *m*

bully[1] ['bʊli] *vt* **-lied; -lying** : intimidar, amedrentar, mangonear

bully[2] *n, pl* **-lies** : matón *m*; bravucón *m*, -cona *f*

bulrush ['bʊl,rʌʃ] *n* : especie *f* de junco

bulwark ['bʊl,wərk, -,wɔrk; 'bʌl,wərk] *n* : baluarte *m*, bastión *f*

bum[1] ['bʌm] *v* **bummed; bumming** *vi* **to bum around** : vagabundear, vagar — *vt* : gorronear *fam*, sablear *fam*

bum[2] *adj* : inútil, malo ⟨a bum rap : una acusación falsa⟩

bum[3] *n* **1** LOAFER : vago *m*, -ga *f* **2** HOBO, TRAMP : vagabundo *m*, -da *f*

bumblebee ['bʌmbəl,bi:] *n* : abejorro *m*

bump[1] ['bʌmp] *vt* : chocar contra, golpear contra, dar ⟨to bump one's head : darse (un golpe) en la cabeza⟩ — *vi* **to bump into** MEET : encontrarse con, tropezarse con

bump[2] *n* **1** BULGE : bulto *m*, protuberancia *f* **2** IMPACT : golpe *m*, choque *m* **3** JOLT : sacudida *f*

bumper[1] ['bʌmpər] *adj* : extraordinario, récord ⟨a bumper crop : una cosecha abundante⟩

bumper[2] *n* : parachoques *mpl*

bumpkin ['bʌmpkən] *n* : palurdo *m*, -da *f*

bumpy ['bʌmpi] *adj* **bumpier; -est** : desigual, lleno de baches (dícese de un camino), agitado (dícese de un vuelo en avión)

bun ['bʌn] *n* : bollo *m*

bunch[1] ['bʌntʃ] *vt* : agrupar, amontonar — *vi* **to bunch up** : amontonarse, agruparse, fruncirse (dícese de una tela)

bunch[2] *n* : grupo *m*, montón *m*, ramo *m* (de flores)

bundle[1] ['bʌndəl] *vt* **-dled; -dling** : liar, atar

bundle[2] *n* **1** : fardo *m*, atado *m*, bulto *m*, haz *m* (de palos) **2** PARCEL : paquete *m* **3** LOAD : montón *m* ⟨a bundle of money : un montón de dinero⟩

bungalow ['bʌŋgə,lo:] *n* : tipo de casa de un solo piso

bungle[1] ['bʌŋgəl] *vt* **-gled; -gling** : echar a perder, malograr

bungle[2] *n* : chapuza *f*, desatino *m*

bungler ['bʌŋgələr] *n* : chapucero *m*, -ra *f*; inepto *m*, -ta *f*

bunion ['bʌnjən] *n* : juanete *m*

bunk[1] ['bʌŋk] *vi* : dormir (en una litera)

bunk[2] *n* **1** *or* **bunk bed** : litera *f* **2** NONSENSE : tonterías *fpl*, bobadas *fpl*

bunker ['bʌŋkər] *n* **1** : carbonera *f* (en un barco) **2** SHELTER : búnker *m*

bunny ['bʌni] *n, pl* **-nies** : conejo *m*, -ja *f*

buoy[1] ['bu:i, 'bɔɪ] *vt* **to buoy up** **1** : mantener a flote **2** CHEER, HEARTEN : animar, levantar el ánimo a

buoy[2] *n* : boya *f*

buoyancy ['bɔɪənʧ,si, 'bu:jən-] *n* **1** : flotabilidad *f* **2** OPTIMISM : confianza *f*, optimismo *m*

buoyant ['bɔɪənt, 'bu:jənt] *adj* : boyante, flotante

bur *or* **burr** ['bər] *n* : abrojo *m* (de una planta)

burden[1] ['bərdən] *vt* : cargar, oprimir

burden[2] *n* : carga *f*, peso *m*

burdensome ['bərdənsəm] *adj* : oneroso

burdock ['bər,dɑk] *n* : bardana *f*

bureau ['bjʊro] *n* **1** CHEST OF DRAWERS : cómoda *f* **2** DEPARTMENT : departamento *m* (del gobierno) **3** AGENCY

: agencia *f* ⟨travel bureau : agencia de viajes⟩

bureaucracy [bjʊ'rɑkrəsi] *n, pl* **-cies** : burocracia *f*

bureaucrat ['bjʊrə,kræt] *n* : burócrata *mf*

bureaucratic [,bjʊrə'krætɪk] *adj* : burocrático

burgeon ['bərdʒən] *vi* : florecer, retoñar, crecer

burglar ['bərglər] *n* : ladrón *m*, -drona *f*

burglarize ['bərglə,raɪz] *vt* **-ized; -izing** : robar

burglary ['bərgləri] *n, pl* **-glaries** : robo *m*

burgle ['bərgəl] *vt* **-gled; -gling** : robar

burgundy ['bərgəndi] *n, pl* **-dies** : borgoña *m*, vino *m* de Borgoña

burial ['bɛriəl] *n* : entierro *m*, sepelio *m*

burlap ['bər,læp] *n* : arpillera *f*

burlesque¹ [bər'lɛsk] *vt* **-lesqued; -lesquing** : parodiar

burlesque² *n* **1** PARODY : parodia *f* **2** REVUE : revista *f* (musical)

burly ['bərli] *adj* **-lier; -liest** : fornido, corpulento, musculoso

Burmese [,bər'mi:z, -'mi:s] *n* : birmano *m*, -na *f* — **Burmese** *adj*

burn¹ ['bərn] *v* **burned** ['bərnd, 'bərnt] *or* **burnt** ['bərnt]; **burning** *vt* **1** : quemar, incendiar ⟨to burn a building : incendiar un edificio⟩ ⟨I burned my hand : me quemé la mano⟩ **2** CONSUME : usar, gastar, consumir — *vi* **1** : arder (dícese de un fuego o un edificio), quemarse (dícese de la comida, etc.) **2** : estar prendido, estar encendido ⟨we left the lights burning : dejamos las luces encendidas⟩ **3 to burn out** : consumirse, apagarse **4 to burn with** : arder de ⟨he was burning with jealousy : ardía de celos⟩

burn² *n* : quemadura *f*

burner ['bərnər] *n* : quemador *m*

burnish ['bərnɪʃ] *vt* : bruñir

burp¹ ['bərp] *vi* : eructar — *vt* : hacer eructar

burp² *n* : eructo *m*

burr → **bur**

burro ['bərro, 'bʊr-] *n, pl* **-os** : burro *m*

burrow¹ ['bərro] *vi* **1** : cavar, hacer una madriguera **2 to burrow into** : hurgar en — *vt* : cavar, excavar

burrow² *n* : madriguera *f*, conejera *f* (de un conejo)

bursar ['bərsər] *n* : administrador *m*, -dora *f*

bursitis [bər'saɪtəs] *n* : bursitis *f*

burst¹ ['bərst] *v* **burst; bursting** *vi* **1** : reventarse (dícese de una llanta o un globo), estallar (dícese de obuses o fuegos artificiales), romperse (dícese de un dique) **2 to burst in** : irrumpir en **3 to burst into** : empezar a, echar a ⟨to burst into tears : echarse a llorar⟩ — *vt* : reventar

burst² *n* **1** EXPLOSION : estallido *m*, explosión *f*, reventón *m* (de una llanta) **2** OUTBURST : arranque *m* (de actividad,

de velocidad), arrebato *m* (de ira), salva *f* (de aplausos)

Burundian [bʊ'ru:ndiən, -'rʊn-] *n* : burundés *m*, -desa *f* — **Burundian** *adj*

bury ['bɛri] *vt* **buried; burying** **1** INTER : enterrar, sepultar **2** HIDE : esconder, ocultar **3 to bury oneself in** : enfrascarse en

bus¹ ['bʌs] *v* **bused** *or* **bussed** ['bʌst]; **busing** *or* **bussing** ['bʌsɪŋ] *vt* : transportar en autobús — *vi* : viajar en autobús

bus² *n* : autobús *m*, bus *m*, camión *m* *Mex*, colectivo *m* *Arg, Bol, Peru*

busboy ['bʌs,bɔɪ] *n* : ayudante *mf* de camarero

bush ['bʊʃ] *n* **1** SHRUB : arbusto *m*, mata *f* **2** THICKET : maleza *f*, matorral *m*

bushel ['bʊʃəl] *n* : medida *f* de áridos igual a 35.24 litros

bushing ['bʊʃɪŋ] *n* : cojinete *m*

bushy ['bʊʃi] *adj* **bushier; -est** : espeso, poblado ⟨bushy eyebrows : cejas pobladas⟩

busily ['bɪzəli] *adv* : afanosamente, diligentemente

business ['bɪznəs, -nəz] *n* **1** OCCUPATION : ocupación *f*, oficio *m* **2** DUTY, MISSION : misión *f*, deber *m*, responsabilidad *f* **3** ESTABLISHMENT, FIRM : empresa *f*, firma *f*, negocio *m*, comercio *m* **4** COMMERCE : negocios *mpl*, comercio *m* **5** AFFAIR, MATTER : asunto *m*, cuestión *f*, cosa *f* ⟨it's none of your business : no es asunto tuyo⟩

businessman ['bɪznəs,mæn, -nəz-] *n, pl* **-men** [-mən, -,mɛn] : empresario *m*, hombre *m* de negocios

businesswoman ['bɪznəs,wʊmən, -nəz-] *n, pl* **-women** [-,wɪmən] : empresaria *f*, mujer *f* de negocios

bust¹ ['bʌst] *vt* **1** BREAK, SMASH : romper, quebrar, destrozar **2** TAME : domar, amansar (un caballo) — *vi* **1** : romperse, estropearse

bust² *n* **1** : busto *m* (en la escultura) **2** BREASTS : pecho *m*, senos *mpl*, busto *m*

bustle¹ ['bʌsəl] *vi* **-tled; -tling to bustle about** : ir y venir, trajinar, ajetrearse

bustle² *n* **1** *or* **hustle and bustle** : bullicio *m*, ajetreo *m* **2** : polisón *m* (en la ropa feminina)

busy¹ ['bɪzi] *vt* **busied; busying to busy oneself with** : ocuparse con, ponerse a, entretenerse con

busy² *adj* **busier; -est** **1** OCCUPIED : ocupado, atareado ⟨he's busy working : está ocupado en su trabajo⟩ ⟨the telephone was busy : el teléfono estaba ocupado⟩ **2** BUSTLING : concurrido, animado ⟨a busy street : una calle concurrida, una calle con mucho tránsito⟩

busybody ['bɪzi,bɑdi] *n, pl* **-bodies** : entrometido *m*, -da *f*; metiche *mf fam*; metomentodo *mf*

but¹ ['bʌt] *conj* **1** THAT : que ⟨there is no doubt but he is lazy : no cabe duda que sea perezoso⟩ **2** WITHOUT : sin que **3** NEVERTHELESS : pero, no obstante, sin embargo ⟨I called her but she didn't answer : la llamé pero no contestó⟩ **4** YET : pero ⟨he was poor but proud : era pobre pero orgulloso⟩

but² *prep* EXCEPT : excepto, menos ⟨everyone but Carlos : todos menos Carlos⟩ ⟨the last but one : el penúltimo⟩

butcher¹ ['bʊtʃər] *vt* **1** SLAUGHTER : matar (animales) **2** KILL : matar, asesinar, masacrar **3** BOTCH : estropear, hacer una chapuza

butcher² *n* **1** : carnicero *m*, -ra *f* **2** KILLER : asesino *m*, -na *f* **3** BUNGLER : chapucero *m*, -ra *f*

butler ['bʌtlər] *n* : mayordomo *m*

butt¹ ['bʌt] *vt* **1** : embestir (con los cuernos), darle un cabezazo a **2** ABUT : colindar con, bordear — *vi* **to butt in 1** INTERRUPT : interrumpir **2** MEDDLE : entrometerse, meterse

butt² *n* **1** BUTTING : embestida *f* (de cuernos), cabezazo *m* **2** TARGET : blanco *m* ⟨the butt of their jokes : el blanco de sus bromas⟩ **3** BOTTOM, END : extremo *m*, culata *f* (de un rifle), colilla *f* (de un cigarrillo)

butte ['bju:t] *n* : colina *f* empinada y aislada

butter¹ ['bʌtər] *vt* **1** : untar con mantequilla **2 to butter up** : halagar

butter² *n* : mantequilla *f*

buttercup ['bʌtər,kʌp] *n* : ranúnculo *m*

butterfat ['bʌtər,fæt] *n* : grasa *f* de la leche

butterfly ['bʌtər,flaɪ] *n, pl* **-flies** : mariposa *f*

buttermilk ['bʌtər,mɪlk] *n* : suero *m* de la leche

butternut ['bʌtər,nʌt] *n* : nogal *m* ceniciento (árbol)

butterscotch ['bʌtər,skatʃ] *n* : caramelo *m* duro hecho con mantequilla

buttery ['bʌtəri] *adj* : mantecoso

buttocks ['bʌtəks, -,taks] *npl* : nalgas *fpl*, trasero *m*

button¹ ['bʌtən] *vt* : abrochar, abotonar — *vi* : abrocharse, abotonarse

button² *n* : botón *m*

buttonhole¹ ['bʌtən,ho:l] *vt* **-holed; -holing** : acorralar

buttonhole² *n* : ojal *m*

buttress¹ ['bʌtrəs] *vt* : apoyar, reforzar

buttress² *n* **1** : contrafuerte *m* (en la arquitectura) **2** SUPPORT : apoyo *m*, sostén *m*

buxom ['bʌksəm] *adj* : con mucho busto, con mucho pecho

buy¹ ['baɪ] *vt* **bought** ['bɔt]; **buying** : comprar

buy² *n* BARGAIN : compra *f*, ganga *f*

buyer ['baɪər] *n* : comprador *m*, -dora *f*

buzz¹ ['bʌz] *vi* : zumbar (dícese de un insecto), sonar (dícese de un teléfono o un despertador)

buzz² *n* **1** : zumbido *m* (de insectos) **2** : murmullo *m*, rumor *m* (de voces)

buzzard ['bʌzərd] *n* VULTURE : buitre *m*, zopilote *m* CA, Mex

buzzer ['bʌzər] *n* : timbre *m*, chicharra *f*

buzzword ['bʌz,wərd] *n* : palabra *f* de moda

by¹ ['baɪ] *adv* **1** NEAR : cerca ⟨he lives close by : vive muy cerca⟩ **2 to stop by** : pasar por casa, hacer una visita **3 to go by** : pasar ⟨they rushed by : pasaron corriendo⟩ **4 to put by** : reservar, poner a un lado **5 by and by** : poco después, dentro de poco **6 by and large** : en general

by² *prep* **1** NEAR : cerca de, al lado de, junto a **2** VIA : por ⟨she left by the door : salió por la puerta⟩ **3** PAST : por, por delante de ⟨they walked by him : pasaron por delante de él⟩ **4** DURING : de, durante ⟨by night : de noche⟩ **5** (*in expressions of time*) : para ⟨we'll be there by ten : estaremos allí para las diez⟩ ⟨by then : para entonces⟩ **6** (*indicating cause or agent*) : por, de, a ⟨built by the Romans : construido por los romanos⟩ ⟨a book by Borges : un libro de Borges⟩ ⟨made by hand : hecho a mano⟩

by and by *adv* : dentro de poco

bygone¹ ['baɪ,gɔn] *adj* : pasado

bygone² *n* **let bygones be bygones** : lo pasado, pasado está

bylaw *or* **byelaw** ['baɪ,lɔ] *n* : norma *f*, reglamento *m*

by-line ['baɪ,laɪn] *n* : data *f*

bypass¹ ['baɪ,pæs] *vt* : evitar

bypass² *n* **1** BELTWAY : carretera *f* de circunvalación **2** DETOUR : desvío *m*

by-product ['baɪ,pradəkt] *n* : subproducto *m*, producto *m* derivado

bystander ['baɪ,stændər] *n* : espectador *m*, -dora *f*

byte ['baɪt] *n* : byte *m*

byway ['baɪ,weɪ] *n* : camino *m* (apartado), carretera *f* secundaria

byword ['baɪ,wərd] *n* **1** PROVERB : proverbio *m*, refrán *m* **2 to be a byword for** : estar sinónimo de

C

c ['si:] n, pl c's or cs : tercera letra del alfabeto inglés

cab ['kæb] n 1 TAXI : taxi m 2 : cabina f (de un camión o una locomotora) 3 CARRIAGE : coche m de caballos

cabal [kə'bɑl, -'bæl] n 1 INTRIGUE, PLOT : conspiración f, complot m, intriga f 2 : grupo m de conspiradores

cabaret [,kæbə'reɪ] n : cabaret m

cabbage ['kæbɪʤ] n : col f, repollo m

cabbie or cabby ['kæbi] n : taxista mf

cabin ['kæbən] n 1 HUT : cabaña f, choza f, barraca f 2 STATEROOM : camarote m 3 : cabina f (de un automóvil o avión)

cabinet ['kæbnət] n 1 CUPBOARD : armario m 2 : gabinete m, consejo m de ministros 3 medicine cabinet : botiquín m

cabinetmaker ['kæbnət,meɪkər] n : ebanista mf

cabinetmaking ['kæbnət,meɪkɪŋ] n : ebanistería f

cable¹ ['keɪbəl] vt -bled; -bling : enviar un cable, telegrafiar

cable² n 1 : cable m (para colgar o sostener algo) 2 : cable m eléctrico 3 → cablegram

cablegram ['keɪbəl,græm] n : telegrama m, cable m

caboose [kə'bu:s] n : furgón m de cola, cabús m Mex

cabstand ['kæb,stænd] n : parada f de taxis

cacao [kə'kaʊ, -'keɪo] n, pl cacaos : cacao m

cache¹ ['kæʃ] vt cached; caching : esconder, guardar en un escondrijo

cache² n 1 : escondite m, escondrijo m ⟨cache of weapons : escondite de armas⟩ 2 : cache m ⟨cache memory : memoria cache⟩

cachet [kæ'ʃeɪ] n : caché m, prestigio m

cackle¹ ['kækəl] vi -led; -ling 1 CLUCK : cacarear 2 : reírse o carcajearse estridentemente ⟨he was cackling with delight : estaba carcajeándose de gusto⟩

cackle² n 1 : cacareo m (de una polla) 2 LAUGH : risa f estridente

cacophony [kæ'kɑfəni, -'kɔ-] n, pl -nies : cacofonía f

cactus ['kæktəs] n, pl cacti [-,taɪ] or -tuses : cacto m, cactus m

cadaver [kə'dævər] n : cadáver m

cadaverous [kə'dævərəs] adj : cadavérico

caddie¹ or caddy ['kædi] vi caddied; caddying : trabajar de caddie, hacer de caddie

caddie² or caddy n, pl -dies : caddie mf

caddy ['kædi] n, pl -dies : cajita f para té

cadence ['keɪdənts] n : cadencia f, ritmo m

cadenced ['keɪdəntst] adj : cadencioso, rítmico

cadet [kə'dɛt] n : cadete mf

cadmium ['kædmiəm] n : cadmio m

cadre ['kæ,dreɪ, 'kɑ-, -,dri:] n : cuadro m (de expertos)

café [kæ'feɪ, kə-] n : café m, cafetería f

cafeteria [,kæfə'tɪriə] n : cafetería f, restaurante m de autoservicio

caffeine [kæ'fi:n] n : cafeína f

cage¹ ['keɪʤ] vt caged; caging : enjaular

cage² n : jaula f

cagey ['keɪʤi] adj -gier; -est 1 CAUTIOUS : cauteloso, reservado 2 SHREWD : astuto, vivo — cagily [-ʤəli] adv

caisson ['keɪ,sɑn, -sən] n 1 : cajón m de municiones 2 : cajón m hidráulico

cajole [kə'ʤo:l] vt -joled; -joling : engatusar

cajolery [kə'ʤo:ləri] n : engatusamiento m

cake¹ ['keɪk] v caked; caking vt : cubrir ⟨caked with mud : cubierto de barro⟩ — vi : endurecerse

cake² n 1 : torta f, bizcocho m, pastel m 2 : pastilla f (de jabón) 3 to take the cake : llevarse la palma, ser el colmo

calabash ['kælə,bæʃ] n : calabaza f

calamari [,kɑlə'mɑri] ns & pl : calamares mpl

calamine ['kælə,maɪn] n : calamina f ⟨calamine lotion : loción de calamina⟩

calamitous [kə'læmətəs] adj : desastroso, catastrófico, calamitoso — calamitously adv

calamity [kə'læməti] n, pl -ties : desastre m, desgracia f, calamidad f

calcium ['kælsiəm] n : calcio m

calcium carbonate ['kɑrbə,neɪt, -nət] n : carbonato m de calcio

calculable ['kælkjələbəl] adj : calculable, computable

calculate ['kælkjə,leɪt] v -lated; -lating vt 1 COMPUTE : calcular, computar 2 ESTIMATE : calcular, creer 3 INTEND : planear, tener la intención de ⟨I calculated on spending $100 : planeaba gastar $100⟩ — vi : calcular, hacer cálculos

calculated ['kælkjə,leɪtəd] adj 1 ESTIMATED : calculado 2 DELIBERATE : intencional, premeditado, deliberado

calculating ['kælkjə,leɪtɪŋ] adj SHREWD : calculador, astuto

calculation [,kælkjə'leɪʃən] n : cálculo m

calculator ['kælkjə,leɪtər] n : calculadora f

calculus ['kælkjələs] n, pl -li [-,laɪ] 1 : cálculo m ⟨differential calculus : cálculo diferencial⟩ 2 TARTAR : sarro m (dental)

caldron ['kɔldrən] → cauldron

calendar ['kæləndər] n 1 : calendario m 2 SCHEDULE : calendario m, programa m, agenda f

calf ['kæf, 'kaf] n, pl **calves** ['kævz, 'kavz] **1** : becerro m, -rra f; ternero m, -ra f (de vacunos) **2** : cría f (de otros mamíferos) **3** : pantorrilla f (de la pierna)

calfskin ['kæf,skɪn] n : piel f de becerro

caliber or **calibre** ['kæləbər] n **1** : calibre m ⟨a .38 caliber gun : una pistola de calibre .38⟩ **2** ABILITY : calibre m, valor m, capacidad f

calibrate ['kælə,breɪt] vt **-brated; -brating** : calibrar (armas), graduar (termómetros)

calibration [,kælə'breɪʃən] n : calibrado m, calibración f

calico ['kælɪ,ko] n, pl **-coes** or **-cos** **1** : calicó m, percal m **2** or **calico cat** : gato m manchado

calipers ['kæləpərz] npl : calibrador m

caliph or **calif** ['keɪləf, 'kæ-] n : califa m

calisthenics [,kæləs'θenɪks] ns & pl : calistenia f

calk ['kɔk] → **caulk**

call[1] ['kɔl] vi **1** CRY, SHOUT : gritar, vociferar **2** VISIT : hacer (una) visita, visitar **3** to call for : exigir, requerir, necesitar ⟨it calls for patience : requiere mucha paciencia⟩ — vt **1** SUMMON : llamar, convocar **2** TELEPHONE : llamar por teléfono, telefonear **3** NAME : llamar, apodar

call[2] n **1** SHOUT : grito m, llamada f **2** : grito m (de un animal), reclamo m (de un pájaro) **3** SUMMONS : llamada f **4** DEMAND : llamado m, petición f **5** VISIT : visita f **6** DECISION : decisión f (en deportes) **7** or **telephone call** : llamada f (telefónica)

call down vt REPRIMAND : reprender, reñir

caller ['kɔlər] n **1** VISITOR : visita f **2** : persona f que llama (por teléfono)

calligraphy [kə'lɪgrəfi] n, pl **-phies** : caligrafía f

calling ['kɔlɪŋ] n : vocación f, profesión f

calliope [kə'laɪə,pi:, 'kæli,o:p] n : órgano m de vapor

call off vt CANCEL : cancelar, suspender

callous[1] ['kæləs] vt : encallecer

callous[2] adj **1** CALLUSED : calloso, encallecido **2** UNFEELING : insensible, desalmado, cruel

callously ['kæləsli] adv : cruelmente, insensiblemente

callousness ['kæləsnəs] n : insensibilidad f, crueldad f

callow ['kælo] adj : inexperto, inmaduro

callus ['kæləs] n : callo m

callused ['kæləst] adj : encallecido, calloso

calm[1] ['kam, 'kalm] vt : tranquilizar, calmar, sosegar — vi : tranquilizarse, calmarse ⟨calm down! : ¡tranquilízate!⟩

calm[2] adj **1** TRANQUIL : calmo, tranquilo, sereno, ecuánime **2** STILL : en calma (dícese del mar), sin viento (dícese del aire)

calm[3] n : tranquilidad f, calma f

calmly ['kamli, 'kalm-] adv : con calma, tranquilamente

calmness ['kamnəs, 'kalm-] n : calma f, tranquilidad f

caloric [kə'lɔrɪk] adj : calórico (dícese de los alimentos), calorífico (dícese de la energía)

calorie ['kæləri] n : caloría f

calumniate [kə'lʌmni,eɪt] vt **-ated; -ating** : calumniar, difamar

calumny ['kæləmni] n, pl **-nies** : calumnia f, difamación f

calve ['kæv, 'kav] vi **calved; calving** : parir (dícese de los mamíferos)

calves → **calf**

calypso [kə'lɪp,so:] n, pl **-sos** : calipso m

calyx ['keɪlɪks, 'kæ-] n, pl **-lyxes** or **-lyces** [-lə,si:z] : cáliz m

cam ['kæm] n : leva f

camaraderie [,kam'radəri, ,kæm-; ,kamə'ra-] n : compañerismo m, camaradería f

Cambodian [kæm'bo:diən] n : camboyano m, -na f — **Cambodian** adj

came → **come**

camel ['kæməl] n : camello m

camellia [kə'mi:ljə] n : camelia f

cameo ['kæmi,o:] n, pl **-eos** **1** : camafeo m **2** or **cameo performance** : actuación f especial

camera ['kæmrə, 'kæmərə] n : cámara f, máquina f fotográfica

Cameroonian [,kæmə'ru:niən] n : camerunés m, -nesa f

camouflage[1] ['kæmə,flaʒ, -,flaʤ] vt **-flaged; -flaging** : camuflajear, camuflar

camouflage[2] n : camuflaje m

camp[1] ['kæmp] vi : acampar, ir de camping

camp[2] n **1** : campamento m **2** FACTION : campo m, bando m ⟨in the same camp : del mismo bando⟩ **3** to pitch camp : acampar, poner el campamento **4** to break camp : levantar el campamento

campaign[1] [kæm'peɪn] vi : hacer (una) campaña

campaign[2] n : campaña f

campanile [,kæmpə'ni:,li:, -'ni:l] n, pl **-niles** or **-nili** [-'ni:,li:] : campanario m

camper ['kæmpər] n **1** : campista mf (persona) **2** : cámper m (vehículo)

campground ['kæmp,graʊnd] n : campamento m, camping m

camphor ['kæmpfər] n : alcanfor m

campsite ['kæmp,saɪt] n : campamento m, camping m

campus ['kæmpəs] n : campus m, recinto m universitario

can[1] ['kæn] v aux, past **could** ['kʊd]; present s & pl **can 1** : poder ⟨could you help me? : ¿podría ayudarme?⟩ **2** : saber ⟨she can't drive yet : todavía no sabe manejar⟩ **3** MAY : poder, tener permiso para ⟨can I sit down? : ¿puedo sentarme?⟩ **4** : poder ⟨it can't be! : ¡no

puede ser!⟩ ⟨where can they be?
: ¿dónde estarán?⟩
can² [ˈkæn] *vt* **canned; canning** 1 : enlatar, envasar ⟨to can tomatoes : enlatar tomates⟩ 2 DISMISS, FIRE : despedir, echar
can³ *n* : lata *f*, envase *m*, cubo *m* ⟨a can
of beer : una lata de cerveza⟩ ⟨garbage
can : cubo de basura⟩
Canadian [kəˈneɪdiən] *n* : canadiense *mf*
— **Canadian** *adj*
canal [kəˈnæl] *n* 1 : canal *m*, tubo *m* ⟨ali-
mentary canal : tubo digestivo⟩ 2
: canal *m* ⟨Panama Canal : Canal de
Panamá⟩
canapé [ˈkænəpi, -ˌpeɪ] *n* : canapé *m*
canary [kəˈnɛri] *n, pl* **-naries** : canario
m
cancel [ˈkæntsəl] *vt* **-celed** *or* **-celled;**
-celing *or* **-celling** : cancelar
cancellation [ˌkæntsəˈleɪʃən] *n* : cancelación *f*
cancer [ˈkænsər] *n* : cáncer *m*
Cancer *n* : Cáncer *mf*
cancerous [ˈkæntsərəs] *adj* : canceroso
candelabrum [ˌkændəˈlɑbrəm, -ˈlæ-] *or*
candelabra [-brə] *n, pl* **-bra** *or* **-bras**
: candelabro *m*
candid [ˈkændɪd] *adj* 1 FRANK : franco,
sincero, abierto 2 : natural, espontáneo (en la fotografía)
candidacy [ˈkændədəsi] *n, pl* **-cies**
: candidatura *f*
candidate [ˈkændəˌdeɪt, -dət] *n* : candidato *m*, -ta *f*
candidly [ˈkændɪdli] *adv* : con franqueza
candied [ˈkændid] *adj* : confitado
candle [ˈkændəl] *n* : vela *f*, candela *f*,
cirio *m* (ceremonial)
candlestick [ˈkændəlˌstɪk] *n* : candelero
m
candor [ˈkændər] *n* : franqueza *f*
candy [ˈkændi] *n, pl* **-dies** : dulce *m*,
caramelo *m*
cane¹ [ˈkeɪn] *vt* **caned; caning** 1
: tapizar (muebles) con mimbre 2
FLOG : azotar con una vara
cane² *n* 1 : bastón *m* (para andar), vara
f (para castigar) 2 REED : caña *f*, mimbre *m* (para muebles)
canine¹ [ˈkeɪˌnaɪn] *adj* : canino
canine² *n* 1 DOG : canino *m*; perro *m*,
-rra *f* 2 *or* **canine tooth** : colmillo *m*,
diente *m* canino
canister [ˈkænəstər] *n* : lata *f*, bote *m*
canker [ˈkæŋkər] *n* : úlcera *f* bucal
cannery [ˈkænəri] *n, pl* **-ries** : fábrica *f*
de conservas
cannibal [ˈkænəbəl] *n* : caníbal *mf*; antropófago *m*, -ga *f*
cannibalism [ˈkænəbəˌlɪzəm] *n* : canibalismo *m*, antropofagia *f*
cannibalize [ˈkænəbəˌlaɪz] *vt* **-ized;**
-izing : canibalizar
cannily [ˈkænəli] *adv* : astutamente,
sagazmente
cannon [ˈkænən] *n, pl* **-nons** *or* **-non**
: cañón *m*

cannot (can not) [ˈkænˌɑt, kəˈnɑt] →
can¹
canny [ˈkæni] *adj* **-nier; -est** SHREWD
: astuto, sagaz
canoe¹ [kəˈnuː] *vi* **-noed; -noeing** : ir en
canoa
canoe² *n* : canoa *f*, piragua *f*
canon [ˈkænən] *n* 1 : canon *m* ⟨canon
law : derecho canónico⟩ 2 WORKS
: canon *m* ⟨the canon of American literature : el canon de la literatura amer-
icana⟩ 3 : canónigo *m* (de una catedral) 4 STANDARD : canon *m*, norma *f*
canonical [kəˈnɑnɪkəl] *adj* : canónico
canonize [ˈkænəˌnaɪz] *vt* **-ized; -izing**
: canonizar
canopy [ˈkænəpi] *n, pl* **-pies** : dosel *m*,
toldo *m*
cant¹ [ˈkænt] *vt* TILT : ladear, inclinar —
vi 1 SLANT : ladearse, inclinarse, escorar (dícese de un barco) 2 : hablar in-
sinceramente
cant² *n* 1 SLANT : plano *m* inclinado 2
JARGON : jerga *f* 3 : palabras *fpl* insin-
ceras
can't [ˈkænt, ˈkɑnt] (*contraction of* **can**
not) → **can¹**
cantaloupe [ˈkæntəlˌoːp] *n* : melón *m*,
cantalupo *m*
cantankerous [kænˈtæŋkərəs] *adj* : irritable, irascible — **cantankerously** *adv*
cantankerousness [kænˈtæŋkərəsnəs]
n : irritabilidad *f*, irascibilidad *f*
cantata [kənˈtɑtə] *n* : cantata *f*
canteen [kænˈtiːn] *n* 1 FLASK : cantimplora *f* 2 CAFETERIA : cantina *f*, comé-
dor *m* 3 : club *m* para actividades sociales y recreativas
canter¹ [ˈkæntər] *vi* : ir a medio galope
canter² *n* : medio galope *m*
cantilever [ˈkæntəˌliːvər, -ˌlɛvər] *n* 1
: viga *f* voladiza 2 **cantilever bridge**
: puente *m* voladizo
canto [ˈkænˌtoː] *n, pl* **-tos** : canto *m*
canton [ˈkæntən, -ˌtɑn] *n* : cantón *m*
Cantonese [ˌkæntənˈiːz, -ˈiːs] *n* 1 : cantonés *m*, -nesa *f* 2 : cantonés *m* (idioma) — **Cantonese** *adj*
cantor [ˈkæntər] *n* : solista *mf*
canvas [ˈkænvəs] *n* 1 : lona *f* 2 SAILS
: velas *fpl* (de un barco) 3 : lienzo *m*,
tela *f* (de pintar) 4 PAINTING : pintura
f, óleo *m*, cuadro *m*
canvass¹ [ˈkænvəs] *vt* 1 SOLICIT : solicitar votos o pedidos de, hacer campaña
entre 2 SOUND OUT : sondear (opiniones, etc.)
canvass² *n* SURVEY : sondeo *m*, encuesta *f*
canyon [ˈkænjən] *n* : cañón *m*
cap¹ [ˈkæp] *vt* **capped; capping** 1 COV-
ER : tapar (un recipiente), enfundar (un
diente), cubrir (una montaña) 2 CLI-
MAX : coronar, ser el punto culminante
de ⟨to cap it all off : para colmo⟩ 3
LIMIT : limitar, poner un tope a
cap² *n* 1 : gorra *f*, gorro *m*, cachucha *f*
Mex ⟨baseball cap : gorra de béisbol⟩

2 COVER, TOP : tapa f, tapón m (de botellas), corcholata f Mex 3 LIMIT : tope m, límite m

capability [ˌkeɪpəˈbɪləti] n, pl **-ties** : capacidad f, habilidad f, competencia f

capable [ˈkeɪpəbəl] adj : competente, capaz, hábil — **capably** [-bli] adv

capacious [kəˈpeɪʃəs] adj : amplio, espacioso, de gran capacidad

capacity[1] [kəˈpæsəti] adj : completo, total ⟨a capacity crowd : un lleno completo⟩

capacity[2] n, pl **-ties** 1 ROOM, SPACE : capacidad f, cabida f, espacio m 2 CAPABILITY : habilidad f, competencia f 3 FUNCTION, ROLE : calidad f, función f ⟨in his capacity as ambassador : en su calidad de embajador⟩

cape [ˈkeɪp] n 1 : capa f 2 : cabo m ⟨Cape Horn : el Cabo de Hornos⟩

caper[1] [ˈkeɪpər] vi : dar saltos, correr y brincar

caper[2] n 1 : alcaparra f ⟨olives and capers : aceitunas y alcaparras⟩ 2 ANTIC, PRANK : broma f, travesura f 3 LEAP : brinco m, salto m

Cape Verdean [ˈkeɪpˈvərdiən] n : caboverdiano m, -na f — **Cape Verdean** adj

capful [ˈkæpˌfʊl] n : tapa f, tapita f

capillary[1] [ˈkæpəˌleri] adj : capilar

capillary[2] n, pl **-ries** : capilar m

capital[1] [ˈkæpətəl] adj 1 : capital ⟨capital punishment : pena capital⟩ 2 : mayúsculo (dícese de las letras) 3 : de capital ⟨capital assets : activo fijo⟩ ⟨capital gain : ganancia de capital, plusvalía⟩ 4 EXCELLENT : excelente, estupendo

capital[2] n 1 or **capital city** : capital f, sede f del gobierno 2 WEALTH : capital m 3 or **capital letter** : mayúscula f 4 : capitel m (de una columna)

capitalism [ˈkæpətəlˌɪzəm] n : capitalismo m

capitalist[1] [ˈkæpətəlɪst] or **capitalistic** [ˌkæpətəlˈɪstɪk] adj : capitalista

capitalist[2] n : capitalista mf

capitalization [ˌkæpətələˈzeɪʃən] n : capitalización f

capitalize [ˈkæpətəlˌaɪz] v -ized; -izing vt 1 FINANCE : capitalizar, financiar 2 : escribir con mayúscula — vi to **capitalize on** : sacar partido de, aprovechar

capitol [ˈkæpətəl] n : capitolio m

capitulate [kəˈpɪtʃəˌleɪt] vi -lated; -lating : capitular

capitulation [kəˌpɪtʃəˈleɪʃən] n : capitulación f

capon [ˈkeɪˌpɑn, -pən] n : capón m

cappuccino [ˌkɑpəˈtʃiːnoː] n : capuchino m (café)

caprice [kəˈpriːs] n : capricho m, antojo m

capricious [kəˈprɪʃəs, -ˈpriː-] adj : caprichoso — **capriciously** adv

Capricorn [ˈkæpriˌkɔrn] n : Capricornio mf

capsize [ˈkæpˌsaɪz, kæpˈsaɪz] v -sized; -sizing vi : volcar, volcarse — vt : hacer volcar

capstan [ˈkæpstən, -ˌstæn] n : cabrestante m

capsule [ˈkæpsəl, -ˌsuːl] n 1 : cápsula f (en la farmacéutica y botánica) 2 **space capsule** : cápsula f espacial

captain[1] [ˈkæptən] vt : capitanear

captain[2] n 1 : capitán m, -tana f 2 HEADWAITER : jefe m, -fa f de comedor 3 **captain of industry** : magnate mf

caption[1] [ˈkæpʃən] vt : ponerle una leyenda a (una ilustración), titular (un artículo), subtitular (una película)

caption[2] n 1 HEADING : titular m, encabezamiento m 2 : leyenda f (al pie de una ilustración) 3 SUBTITLE : subtítulo m

captivate [ˈkæptəˌveɪt] vt -vated; -vating CHARM : cautivar, hechizar, encantar

captivating [ˈkæptəˌveɪtɪŋ] adj : cautivador, hechicero, encantador

captive[1] [ˈkæptɪv] adj : cautivo

captive[2] n : cautivo m, -va f

captivity [kæpˈtɪvəti] n : cautiverio m

captor [ˈkæptər] n : captor m, -tora f

capture[1] [ˈkæpʃər] vt -tured; -turing 1 SEIZE : capturar, apresar 2 CATCH : captar ⟨to capture one's interest : captar el interés de uno⟩

capture[2] n : captura f, apresamiento m

car [ˈkɑr] n 1 AUTOMOBILE : automóvil m, coche m, carro m 2 : vagón m, coche m (de un tren) 3 : cabina f (de un ascensor)

carafe [kəˈræf, -ˈrɑf] n : garrafa f

caramel [ˈkɑrməl, ˈkærəməl, -ˌmɛl] n 1 : caramelo m, azúcar f quemada 2 or **caramel candy** : caramelo m, dulce m de leche

carat [ˈkærət] n : quilate m

caravan [ˈkærəˌvæn] n : caravana f

caraway [ˈkærəˌweɪ] n : alcaravea f

carbine [ˈkɑrˌbaɪn, -ˌbiːn] n : carabina f

carbohydrate [ˌkɑrboˈhaɪˌdreɪt, -drət] n : carbohidrato m, hidrato m de carbono

carbon [ˈkɑrbən] n 1 : carbono m 2 → **carbon paper** 3 → **carbon copy**

carbonated [ˈkɑrbəˌneɪtəd] adj : carbonatado (dícese del agua), gaseoso (dícese de las bebidas)

carbon copy n 1 : copia f al carbón 2 DUPLICATE : duplicado m, copia f exacta

carbon paper n : papel m carbón

carbuncle [ˈkɑrˌbʌŋkəl] n : carbunco m

carburetor [ˈkɑrbəˌreɪtər, -bjə-] n : carburador m

carcass [ˈkɑrkəs] n : cuerpo m (de un animal muerto)

carcinogen [kɑrˈsɪnədʒən, ˈkɑrsənəˌdʒɛn] n : carcinógeno m, cancerígeno m

carcinogenic [ˌkɑrsənoˈdʒɛnɪk] adj : carcinogénico

carcinoma [ˌkɑrsəˈnoːmə] n : carcinoma

card¹ ['kɑrd] *vt* : cardar (fibras)
card² *n* **1** : carta *f*, naipe *m* ⟨to play cards : jugar a las cartas⟩ ⟨a deck of cards : una baraja⟩ **2** : tarjeta *f* ⟨birthday card : tarjeta de cumpleaños⟩ ⟨business card : tarjeta (de visita)⟩
cardboard ['kɑrd,bord] *n* : cartón *m*, cartulina *f*
cardiac ['kɑrdi,æk] *adj* : cardíaco, cardiaco
cardigan ['kɑrdɪgən] *n* : cárdigan *m*, chaqueta *f* de punto
cardinal¹ ['kɑrdənəl] *adj* FUNDAMENTAL : cardinal, fundamental
cardinal² *n* : cardenal *m*
cardinal number *n* : número *m* cardinal
cardinal point *n* : punto *m* cardinal
cardiologist [,kɑrdi'ɑlədʒɪst] *n* : cardiólogo *m*, -ga *f*
cardiology [,kɑrdi'ɑlədʒi] *n* : cardiología *f*
cardiovascular [,kɑrdio'væskjələr] *adj* : cardiovascular
care¹ ['kær] *v* **cared; caring** *vi* **1** : importarle a uno ⟨they don't care : no les importa⟩ **2** : preocuparse, inquietarse ⟨she cares about the poor : se preocupa por los pobres⟩ **3** to care for TEND : cuidar (de), atender, encargarse de **4** to care for CHERISH : querer, sentir cariño por **5** to care for LIKE : gustarle (algo a uno) ⟨I don't care for your attitude : tu actitud no me agrada⟩ — *vt* WISH : desear, querer ⟨if you care to go : si deseas ir⟩
care² *n* **1** ANXIETY : inquietud *f*, preocupación *f* **2** CAREFULNESS : cuidado *m*, atención *f* ⟨handle with care : manejar con cuidado⟩ **3** CHARGE : cargo *m*, cuidado *m* **4** to take care of : cuidar (de), atender, encargarse de
careen [kə'ri:n] *vi* **1** SWAY : oscilar, balancearse **2** CAREER : ira toda velocidad
career¹ [kə'rir] *vi* : ir a toda velocidad
career² *n* VOCATION : vocación *f*, profesión *f*, carrera *f*
carefree ['kær,fri:, ,kær'-] *adj* : despreocupado
careful ['kærfəl] *adj* **1** CAUTIOUS : cuidadoso, cauteloso **2** PAINSTAKING : cuidadoso, esmerado, meticuloso
carefully ['kærfəli] *adv* : con cuidado, cuidadosamente
carefulness ['kærfəlnəs] *n* **1** CAUTION : cuidado *m*, cautela *f* **2** METICULOUSNESS : esmero *m*, meticulosidad *f*
caregiver ['kær,gɪvər] *n* : persona *f* que cuida a niños o enfermos
careless ['kærləs] *adj* : descuidado, negligente — **carelessly** *adv*
carelessness ['kærləsnəs] *n* : descuido *m*, negligencia *f*
caress¹ [kə'rɛs] *vt* : acariciar
caress² *n* : caricia *f*
caret ['kærət] *n* : signo *m* de intercalación
caretaker ['kær,teɪkər] *n* : conserje *mf*; velador *m*, -dora *f*

cargo ['kɑr,go:] *n*, *pl* **-goes** *or* **-gos** : cargamento *m*, carga *f*
Caribbean [kærə'bi:ən, kə'rɪbiən] *adj* : caribeño ⟨the Caribbean Sea : el mar Caribe⟩
caribou ['kærə,bu:] *n*, *pl* **-bou** *or* **-bous** : caribú *m*
caricature¹ ['kærɪkə,tʃur] *vt* **-tured; -turing** : caricaturizar
caricature² *n* : caricatura *f*
caricaturist ['kærɪkə,tʃurɪst] *n* : caricaturista *mf*
caries ['kær,i:z] *ns & pl* : caries *f*
carillon ['kærə,lɑn] *n* : carillón *m*
carmine ['kɑrmən, -,maɪn] *n* : carmín *m*
carnage ['kɑrnɪdʒ] *n* : matanza *f*, carnicería *f*
carnal ['kɑrnəl] *adj* : carnal
carnation [kɑr'neɪʃən] *n* : clavel *m*
carnival ['kɑrnəvəl] *n* : carnaval *m*, feria *f*
carnivore ['kɑrnə,vor] *n* : carnívoro *m*
carnivorous [kɑr'nɪvərəs] *adj* : carnívoro
carol¹ ['kærəl] *vi* **-oled** *or* **-olled; -oling** *or* **-olling** : cantar villancicos
carol² *n* : villancico *m*
caroler *or* **caroller** ['kærələr] *n* : persona *f* que canta villancicos
carom¹ ['kærəm] *vi* **1** REBOUND : rebotar ⟨the bullet caromed off the wall : la bala rebotó contra el muro⟩ **2** : hacer carambola (en billar)
carom² *n* : carambola *f*
carouse [kə'rauz] *vt* **-roused; -rousing** : irse de parranda, irse de juerga
carousel *or* **carrousel** [,kærə'sɛl, 'kærə,-] *n* : carrusel *m*, tiovivo *m*
carouser [kə'rauzər] *n* : juerguista *mf*
carp¹ ['kɑrp] *vi* **1** COMPLAIN : quejarse **2** to carp at : criticar
carp² *n*, *pl* **carp** *or* **carps** : carpa *f*
carpel ['kɑrpəl] *n* : carpelo *m*
carpenter ['kɑrpəntər] *n* : carpintero *m*, -ra *f*
carpentry ['kɑrpəntri] *n* : carpintería *f*
carpet¹ ['kɑrpət] *vt* : alfombrar
carpet² *n* : alfombra *f*
carpeting ['kɑrpətɪŋ] *n* : alfombrado *m*
carport ['kɑr,port] *n* : cochera *f*, garaje *m* abierto
carriage ['kærɪdʒ] *n* **1** TRANSPORT : transporte *m*, porte *m*, postura *f* **3** horse-drawn carriage : carruaje *m*, coche *m* **4** baby carriage : cochecito *m*
carrier ['kæriər] *n* **1** : transportista *mf*, empresa *f* de transportes **2** : portador *m*, -dora *f* (de una enfermedad) **3** aircraft carrier : portaaviones *m*
carrier pigeon *n* : paloma *f* mensajera
carrion ['kæriən] *n* : carroña *f*
carrot ['kærət] *n* : zanahoria *f*
carry ['kæri] *v* **-ried; -rying** *vt* **1** TRANSPORT : llevar, cargar, transportar (cargamento), conducir (electricidad), portar (un virus) ⟨to carry a bag : cargar una bolsa⟩ ⟨to carry money : llevar dinero encima, traer dinero consi-

go) **2** BEAR : soportar, aguantar, resistir (peso) **3** STOCK : vender, tener en abasto **4** ENTAIL : llevar, implicar, acarrear **5** WIN : ganar (una elección o competición), aprobar (una moción) **6 to carry oneself** : portarse, comportarse ⟨he carried himself honorably : se comportó dignamente⟩ — vi : oírse, proyectarse ⟨her voice carries well : su voz se puede oír desde lejos⟩

carryall [ˈkæriˌɔl] n : bolsa f de viaje

carry away vt **to get carried away** : exaltarse, entusiasmarse

carry on vt CONDUCT : realizar, ejercer, mantener ⟨to carry on research : realizar investigaciones⟩ ⟨to carry on a correspondence : mantener una correspondencia⟩ — vi **1** : portarse de manera escandalosa o inapropiada ⟨it's embarrassing how he carries on : su manera de comportarse da vergüenza⟩ **2** CONTINUE : seguir, continuar

carry out vt **1** PERFORM : llevar a cabo, realizar **2** FULFILL : cumplir

cart¹ [ˈkɑrt] vt : acarrear, llevar

cart² n : carreta f, carro m

cartel [kɑrˈtɛl] n : cártel m

cartilage [ˈkɑrtəlɪdʒ] n : cartílago m

cartilaginous [ˌkɑrtəlˈædʒənəs] adj : cartilaginoso

cartographer [kɑrˈtɑgrəfər] n : cartógrafo m, -fa f

cartography [kɑrˈtɑgrəfi] n : cartografía f

carton [ˈkɑrtən] n : caja f de cartón

cartoon [kɑrˈtuːn] n **1** : chiste m (gráfico), caricatura f ⟨a political cartoon : un chiste político⟩ **2** COMIC STRIP : tira f cómica, historieta f **3 or animated cartoon** : dibujo m animado

cartoonist [kɑrˈtuːnɪst] n : caricaturista mf, dibujante mf (de chistes)

cartridge [ˈkɑrtrɪdʒ] n : cartucho m

carve [ˈkɑrv] vt carved; carving **1** : tallar (madera), esculpir (piedra), grabar ⟨he carved his name in the bark : grabó su nombre en la corteza⟩ **2** SLICE : cortar, trinchar (carne)

cascade¹ [kæsˈkeɪd] vi -caded; -cading : caer en cascada

cascade² n : cascada f, salto m de agua

case¹ [ˈkeɪs] vt cased; casing **1** BOX, PACK : embalar, encajonar **2** INSPECT : observar, inspeccionar (antes de cometer un delito)

case² n **1** : caso m ⟨an unusual case : un caso insólito⟩ ⟨ablative case : caso ablativo⟩ ⟨a case of the flu : un caso de gripe⟩ **2** BOX : caja f **3** CONTAINER : funda f, estuche m **4 in any case** : de todos modos, en cualquier caso **5 in case** : como precaución ⟨just in case : por si acaso⟩ **6 in case of** : en caso de

casement [ˈkeɪsmənt] n : ventana f con bisagras

cash¹ [ˈkæʃ] vt : convertir en efectivo, cobrar, cambiar (un cheque)

cash² n : efectivo m, dinero m en efectivo

cashew [ˈkæˌʃuː, kəˈʃuː] n : anacardo m

cashier¹ [kæˈʃɪr] vt : destituir, despedir

cashier² n : cajero m, -ra f

cashmere [ˈkæʒˌmɪr, ˈkæʃ-] n : cachemir m

casino [kəˈsiːˌnoː] n, pl **-nos** : casino m

cask [ˈkæsk] n : tonel m, barrica f, barril m

casket [ˈkæskət] n COFFIN : ataúd m, féretro m

cassava [kəˈsɑvə] n : mandioca f, yuca f

casserole [ˈkæsəˌroːl] n **1** : cazuela f **2** : guiso m, guisado m ⟨tuna casserole : guiso de atún⟩

cassette [kəˈsɛt, kæ-] n : cassette mf

cassock [ˈkæsək] n : sotana f

cast¹ [ˈkæst] vt cast; casting **1** THROW : tirar, echar, arrojar ⟨die the is cast : la suerte está echada⟩ **2** : depositar (un voto) **3** : asignar (papeles en una obra de teatro) **4** MOLD : moldear, fundir, vaciar **5 to cast off** ABANDON : desamparar, abandonar

cast² n **1** THROW : lance m, lanzamiento m **2** APPEARANCE : aspecto m, forma f **3** : elenco m, reparto m (de una obra de teatro) **4 plaster cast** : molde m de yeso, escayola f

castanets [ˌkæstəˈnɛts] npl : castañuelas fpl

castaway¹ [ˈkæstəˌweɪ] adj : náufrago

castaway² n : náufrago m, -ga f

caste [ˈkæst] n : casta f

caster [ˈkæstər] n : ruedita f (de un mueble)

castigate [ˈkæstəˌgeɪt] vt -gated; -gating : castigar severamente, censurar, reprobar

Castilian [kæˈstɪljən] n **1** : castellano m, -na f **2** : castellano m (idioma) — **Castilian** adj

cast iron n : hierro m fundido

castle [ˈkæsəl] n **1** : castillo m **2** : torre f (en ajedrez)

cast-off [ˈkæstˌɔf] adj : desechado

castoff [ˈkæstˌɔf] n : desecho m

castrate [ˈkæsˌtreɪt] vt -trated; -trating : castrar

castration [kæˈstreɪʃən] n : castración f

casual [ˈkæʒuəl] adj **1** FORTUITOUS : casual, fortuito **2** INDIFFERENT : indiferente, despreocupado **3** INFORMAL : informal — **casually** [ˈkæʒuəli, ˈkæʒəli] adv

casualness [ˈkæʒuəlnəs] n **1** FORTUITOUSNESS : casualidad f **2** INDIFFERENCE : indiferencia f, despreocupación f **3** INFORMALITY : informalidad f

casualty [ˈkæʒuəlti, ˈkæʒəl-] n, pl **-ties 1** ACCIDENT : accidente m serio, desastre m **2** VICTIM : víctima f; baja f, herido m, -da f

cat [ˈkæt] n : gato m, -ta f

cataclysm [ˈkætəˌklɪzəm] n : cataclismo m

cataclysmal [ˌkætəˈklɪzməl] *or* **cataclysmic** [ˌkætəˈklɪzmɪk] *adj* : catastrófico

catacombs [ˈkætəˌkoːmz] *npl* : catacumbas *fpl*

Catalan [ˈkætələn, -ˌlæn] *n* **1** : catalán *m*, catalana *f* **2** : catalán *m* (idioma) — **Catalan** *adj*

catalog¹ *or* **catalogue** [ˈkætəˌlɔg] *vt* **-loged** *or* **-logued; -loging** *or* **-loguing** : catalogar

catalog² *n* : catálogo *m*

catalyst [ˈkætələst] *n* : catalizador *m*

catalytic [ˌkætəlˈɪtɪk] *adj* : catalítico

catamaran [ˌkætəməˈræn, ˈkætəməˌræn] *n* : catamarán *m*

catapult¹ [ˈkætəˌpʌlt, -ˌpult] *vt* : catapultar

catapult² *n* : catapulta *f*

cataract [ˈkætəˌrækt] *n* : catarata *f*

catarrh [kəˈtɑr] *n* : catarro *m*

catastrophe [kəˈtæstrəˌfiː] *n* : catástrofe *f*

catastrophic [ˌkætəˈstrɑfɪk] *adj* : catastrófico — **catastrophically** [-fɪkli] *adv*

catcall [ˈkætˌkɔl] *n* : rechifla *f*, abucheo *m*

catch¹ [ˈkætʃ, ˈkɛtʃ] *v* **caught** [ˈkɔt]; **catching** *vt* **1** CATCHING, TRAP : capturar, agarrar, atrapar, coger **2** : agarrar, pillar *fam*, tomar de sorpresa ⟨they caught him red-handed : lo pillaron con las manos en la masa⟩ **3** GRASP : agarrar, captar **4** ENTANGLE : enganchar, enredar **5** : tomar (un tren, etc.) **6** : contagiarse de ⟨to catch a cold : contagiarse de un resfriado, resfriarse⟩ — *vi* **1** GRASP : agarrar **2** HOOK : engancharse **3** IGNITE : prender, agarrar

catch² *n* **1** CATCHING : captura *f*, atrapada *f*, parada *f* (de una pelota) **2** : redada *f* (de pescado), presa *f* (de caza) ⟨he's a good catch : es un buen partido⟩ **3** LATCH : pestillo *m*, pasador *m* **4** DIFFICULTY, TRICK : problema *m*, trampa *f*, truco *m*

catcher [ˈkætʃər, ˈkɛ-] *n* : cácher *mf*; receptor *m*, -tora *f* (en béisbol)

catching [ˈkætʃɪŋ, ˈkɛ-] *adj* : contagioso

catchup [ˈkætʃəp, ˈkɛ-] → **ketchup**

catchword [ˈkætʃˌwərd, ˈkɛtʃ-] *n* : eslogan *m*, lema *m*

catchy [ˈkætʃi, ˈkɛ-] *adj* **catchier; -est** : pegajoso ⟨a catchy song : una canción pegajosa⟩

catechism [ˈkætəˌkɪzəm] *n* : catecismo *m*

categorical [ˌkætəˈgɔrɪkəl] *adj* : categórico, absoluto, rotundo — **categorically** [-kli] *adv*

categorize [ˈkætɪgəˌraɪz] *vt* **-rized; -rizing** : clasificar, catalogar

category [ˈkætəˌgori] *n, pl* **-ries** : categoría *f*, género *m*, clase *f*

cater [ˈkeɪtər] *vi* **1** : proveer alimentos (para fiestas, bodas, etc.) **2 to cater to** : atender a ⟨to cater to all tastes : atender a todos los gustos⟩

catercorner¹ [ˈkæti̬ˌkɔrnər, ˈkætə-, ˈkɪti̬-] *or* **cater-cornered** [-ˌkɔrnərd] *adv* : diagonalmente, en diagonal

catercorner² *or* **cater-cornered** *adj* : diagonal

caterer [ˈkeɪtərər] *n* : proveedor *m*, -dora *f* de comida

caterpillar [ˈkætərˌpɪlər] *n* : oruga *f*

catfish [ˈkætˌfɪʃ] *n* : bagre *m*

catgut [ˈkætˌgʌt] *n* : cuerda *f* de tripa

catharsis [kəˈθɑrsɪs] *n, pl* **catharses** [-ˌsiːz] : catarsis *f*

cathartic¹ [kəˈθɑrtɪk] *adj* : catártico

cathartic² *n* : purgante *m*

cathedral [kəˈθiːdrəl] *n* : catedral *f*

catheter [ˈkæθətər] *n* : catéter *m*, sonda *f*

cathode [ˈkæˌθoːd] *n* : cátodo *m*

catholic [ˈkæθəlɪk] *adj* **1** BROAD, UNIVERSAL : liberal, universal **2 Catholic** : católico

Catholic *n* : católico *m*, -ca *f*

Catholicism [kəˈθɑləˌsɪzəm] *n* : catolicismo *m*

catlike [ˈkætˌlaɪk] *adj* : gatuno, felino

catnap¹ [ˈkætˌnæp] *vi* **-napped; -napping** : tomarse una siestecita

catnap² *n* : siesta *f* breve, siestecita *f*

catnip [ˈkætˌnɪp] *n* : nébeda *f*

catsup [ˈkætʃəp, ˈkætsəp] → **ketchup**

cattail [ˈkætˌteɪl] *n* : espadaña *f*, anea *f*

cattiness [ˈkætinəs] *n* : malicia *f*

cattle [ˈkætəl] *npl* : ganado *m*, reses *fpl*

cattleman [ˈkætəlmən, -ˌmæn] *n, pl* **-men** [-mən, -ˌmɛn] : ganadero *m*

catty [ˈkæti] *adj* **-tier; -est** : malicioso, malintencionado

catwalk [ˈkætˌwɔk] *n* : pasarela *f*

Caucasian¹ [kɔˈkeɪʒən] *adj* : caucásico

Caucasian² *n* : caucásico *m*, -ca *f*

caucus [ˈkɔkəs] *n* : junta *f* de políticos

caught → **catch**

cauldron [ˈkɔldrən] *n* : caldera *f*

cauliflower [ˈkɑlɪˌflaʊər, ˈko-] *n* : coliflor *f*

caulk¹ [ˈkɔk] *vt* : calafatear (un barco), enmasillar (una grieta)

caulk² *n* : masilla *f*

causal [ˈkɔzəl] *adj* : causal

causality [kɔˈzæləti] *n* : causalidad *f*

cause¹ [ˈkɔz] *vt* **caused; causing** : causar, provocar, ocasionar

cause² *n* **1** ORIGIN : causa *f*, origen *m* **2** REASON : causa *f*, razón *f*, motivo *m* **3** LAWSUIT : litigio *m*, pleito *m* **4** MOVEMENT : causa *f*, movimiento *m*

causeless [ˈkɔzləs] *adj* : sin causa

causeway [ˈkɔzˌweɪ] *n* : camino *m* elevado

caustic [ˈkɔstɪk] *adj* **1** CORROSIVE : cáustico, corrosivo **2** BITING : mordaz, sarcástico

cauterize [ˈkɔtəˌraɪz] *vt* **-ized; -izing** : cauterizar

caution¹ [ˈkɔʃən] *vt* : advertir

caution² *n* **1** WARNING : advertencia *f*, aviso *m* **2** CARE, PRUDENCE : precaución *f*, cuidado *m*, cautela *f*

cautionary ['kɔʃə,nɛri] *adv* : admonitorio ⟨cautionary tale : cuento moral⟩

cautious ['kɔʃəs] *adj* : cauteloso, cuidadoso, precavido

cautiously ['kɔʃəsli] *adv* : cautelosamente, con precaución

cautiousness ['kɔʃəsnəs] *n* : cautela *f*, precaución *f*

cavalcade [,kævəl'keɪd, 'kævəl,-] *n* 1 : cabalgata *f* 2 SERIES : serie *f*

cavalier[1] [,kævə'lɪr] *adj* : altivo, desdeñoso — **cavalierly** *adv*

cavalier[2] *n* : caballero *m*

cavalry ['kævəlri] *n*, *pl* **-ries** : caballería *f*

cave[1] ['keɪv] *vi* **caved; caving** *or* **to cave in** : derrumbarse

cave[2] *n* : cueva *f*

cavern ['kævərn] *n* : caverna *f*

cavernous ['kævərnəs] *adj* : cavernoso — **cavernously** *adv*

caviar *or* **caviare** ['kævi,ɑr, 'kɑ-] *n* : caviar *m*

cavity ['kævəti] *n*, *pl* **-ties** 1 HOLE : cavidad *f*, hueco *m* 2 CARIES : caries *f*

cavort [kə'vɔrt] *vi* : brincar, hacer cabriolas

caw[1] ['kɔ] *vi* : graznar

caw[2] *n* : graznido *m*

cayenne pepper [,kaɪ'ɛn, ,keɪ-] *n* : pimienta *f* cayena, pimentón *m*

CD [,si:'di:] *n* : CD *m*, disco *m* compacto

CD–ROM [,si:,di:'rɑm] *n* : CD-ROM *m*

cease ['si:s] *v* **ceased; ceasing** *vt* : dejar de ⟨they ceased bickering : dejaron de discutir⟩ — *vi* : cesar, pasarse

ceaseless ['si:sləs] *adj* : incesante, continuo

cedar ['si:dər] *n* : cedro *m*

cede ['si:d] *vt* **ceded; ceding** : ceder, conceder

ceiling ['si:lɪŋ] *n* 1 : techo *m*, cielo *m* raso 2 LIMIT : límite *m*, tope *m*

celebrant ['sɛləbrənt] *n* : celebrante *mf*, oficiante *mf*

celebrate ['sɛlə,breɪt] *v* **-brated; -brating** *vt* 1 : celebrar, oficiar ⟨to celebrate Mass : celebrar la misa⟩ 2 : celebrar, festejar ⟨we're celebrating our anniversary : estamos celebrando nuestro aniversario⟩ 3 EXTOL : alabar, ensalzar, exaltar — *vi* : estar de fiesta, divertirse

celebrated ['sɛlə,breɪtəd] *adj* : célebre, famoso, renombrado

celebration [,sɛlə'breɪʃən] *n* : celebración *f*, festejos *mpl*

celebrity [sə'lɛbrəti] *n*, *pl* **-ties** 1 RENOWN : fama *f*, renombre *m*, celebridad *f* 2 PERSONALITY : celebridad *f*, personaje *m*

celery ['sɛləri] *n*, *pl* **-eries** : apio *m*

celestial [sə'lɛstʃəl, -'lɪstiəl] *adj* 1 : celeste 2 HEAVENLY : celestial, paradisiaco

celibacy ['sɛləbəsi] *n* : celibato *m*

celibate[1] ['sɛləbət] *adj* : célibe

celibate[2] *n* : célibe *mf*

cell ['sɛl] *n* 1 : célula *f* (de un organismo) 2 : celda *f* (en una cárcel, etc.) 3 : elemento *m* (de una pila)

cellar ['sɛlər] *n* 1 BASEMENT : sótano *m* 2 : bodega *f* (de vinos)

cellist ['tʃɛlɪst] *n* : violonchelista *mf*

cello ['tʃɛ,lo:] *n*, *pl* **-los** : violonchelo *m*

cellophane ['sɛlə,feɪn] *n* : celofán *m*

cell phone *n* : teléfono *m* celular

cellular ['sɛljələr] *adj* : celular

celluloid ['sɛljə,lɔɪd] *n* : celuloide *m*

cellulose ['sɛljə,lo:s] *n* : celulosa *f*

Celsius ['sɛlsiəs] *adj* : centígrado ⟨100 degrees Celsius : 100 grados centígrados⟩

Celt ['kɛlt, 'sɛlt] *n* : celta *mf*

Celtic[1] ['kɛltɪk, 'sɛl-] *adj* : celta

Celtic[2] *n* : celta *m*

cement[1] [sɪ'mɛnt] *vi* : unir o cubrir algo con cemento, cementar

cement[2] *n* 1 : cemento *m* 2 GLUE : pegamento *m*

cemetery ['sɛmə,teri] *n*, *pl* **-teries** : cementerio *m*, panteón *m*

censer ['sɛnsər] *n* : incensario *m*

censor[1] ['sɛnsər] *vt* : censurar

censor[2] *n* : censor *m*, -sora *f*

censorious [sɛn'soriəs] *adj* : de censura, crítico

censorship ['sɛnsər,ʃɪp] *n* : censura *f*

censure[1] ['sɛnʃər] *vt* **-sured; -suring** : censurar, criticar, reprobar — **censurable** [-tʃərəbəl] *adj*

censure[2] *n* : censura *f*, reproche *m* oficial

census ['sɛnsəs] *n* : censo *m*

cent ['sɛnt] *n* : centavo *m*

centaur ['sɛn,tɔr] *n* : centauro *m*

centennial[1] [sɛn'tɛniəl] *adj* : del centenario

centennial[2] *n* : centenario *m*

center[1] ['sɛntər] *vt* 1 : centrar 2 CONCENTRATE : concentrar, fijar, enfocar — *vi* : centrarse, enfocarse

center[2] *n* 1 : centro *m* ⟨center of gravity : centro de gravedad⟩ 2 : centro *m* (en futbol americano), pívot *mf* (en basquetbol)

centerpiece ['sɛntər,pi:s] *n* : centro *m* de mesa

centigrade ['sɛntə,greɪd, 'sɑn-] *adj* : centígrado

centigram ['sɛntə,græm, 'sɑn-] *n* : centigramo *m*

centimeter ['sɛntə,mi:tər, 'sɑn-] *n* : centímetro *m*

centipede ['sɛntə,pi:d] *n* : ciempiés *m*

central ['sɛntrəl] *adj* 1 : céntrico, central ⟨in a central location : en un lugar céntrico⟩ 2 MAIN, PRINCIPAL : central, fundamental, principal

Central American[1] *adj* : centroamericano

Central American[2] *n* : centroamericano *m*, -na *f*

centralization [,sɛntrələ'zeɪʃən] *n* : centralización *f*

centralize ['sɛntrə,laɪz] *vt* **-ized; -izing** : centralizar

centrally [ˈsɛntrəli] *adv* **1 centrally heated** : con calefacción central **2 centrally located** : céntrico, en un lugar céntrico

centre [ˈsɛntər] → **center**

centrifugal [sɛnˈtrɪfɪgəl, -ˈtrɪfɪ-] *adj* : centrífugo

centrifugal force *n* : fuerza *f* centrífuga

century [ˈsɛntʃəri] *n, pl* **-ries** : siglo *m*

ceramic¹ [səˈræmɪk] *adj* : de cerámica

ceramic² *n* **1** : objeto *m* de cerámica, cerámica *f* **2 ceramics** *npl* : cerámica *f*

cereal¹ [ˈsɪriəl] *adj* : cereal

cereal² *n* : cereal *m*

cerebellum [ˌsɛrəˈbɛləm] *n, pl* **-bellums** *or* **-bella** [-ˈbɛlə] : cerebelo *m*

cerebral [səˈriːbrəl, ˈsɛrə-] *adj* : cerebral

cerebral palsy *n* : parálisis *f* cerebral

cerebrum [səˈriːbrəm, ˈsɛrə-] *n, pl* **-brums** *or* **-bra** [-brə] : cerebro *m*

ceremonial¹ [ˌsɛrəˈmoːniəl] *adj* : ceremonial

ceremonial² *n* : ceremonial *m*

ceremonious [ˌsɛrəˈmoːniəs] *adj* **1** FORMAL : ceremonioso, formal **2** CEREMONIAL : ceremonial

ceremony [ˈsɛrəˌmoːni] *n, pl* **-nies** : ceremonia *f*

cerise [səˈriːs] *n* : rojo *m* cereza

certain¹ [ˈsərtən] *adj* **1** DEFINITE : cierto, determinado ⟨a certain percentage : un porcentaje determinado⟩ **2** TRUE : cierto, con certeza ⟨I don't know for certain : no sé exactamente⟩ **3** : cierto, alguno ⟨it has a certain charm : tiene cierta gracia⟩ **4** INEVITABLE : seguro, inevitable **5** ASSURED : seguro, asegurado ⟨she's certain to do well : seguro que le irá bien⟩

certain² *pron* : ciertos *pl*, algunos *pl* ⟨certain of my friends : algunos de mis amigos⟩

certainly [ˈsərtənli] *adv* **1** DEFINITELY : ciertamente, seguramente **2** OF COURSE : por supuesto

certainty [ˈsərtənti] *n, pl* **-ties** : certeza *f*, certidumbre *f*, seguridad *f*

certifiable [ˌsərtəˈfaɪəbəl] *adj* : certificable

certificate [sərˈtɪfɪkət] *n* : certificado *m*, acta *f* ⟨birth certificate : acta de nacimiento⟩

certification [ˌsərtəfəˈkeɪʃən] *n* : certificación *f*

certify [ˈsərtəˌfaɪ] *vt* **-fied; -fying 1** VERIFY : certificar, verificar, confirmar **2** ENDORSE : endosar, aprobar oficialmente

certitude [ˈsərtəˌtuːd, -ˌtjuːd] *n* : certeza *f*, certidumbre *f*

cervical [ˈsərvɪkəl] *adj* **1** : cervical (dícese del cuello) **2** : del cuello del útero

cervix [ˈsərvɪks] *n, pl* **-vices** [-vəˌsiːz] *or* **-vixes 1** NECK : cerviz *f* **2** *or* **uterine cervix** : cuello *m* del útero

cesarean¹ [sɪˈzæriən] *adj* : cesáreo

cesarean² *n* : cesárea *f*

cesium [ˈsiːziəm] *n* : cesio *m*

cessation [sɛˈseɪʃən] *n* : cesación *f*, cese *m*

cesspool [ˈsɛsˌpuːl] *n* : pozo *m* séptico

Chadian [ˈtʃædiən] *n* : chadiano *m*, -na *f* — **Chadian** *adj*

chafe [ˈtʃeɪf] *v* **chafed; chafing** *vi* : enojarse, irritarse — *vt* : rozar

chaff [ˈtʃæf] *n* **1** : barcia *f*, granzas *fpl* **2 to separate the wheat from the chaff** : separar el grano de la paja

chafing dish [ˈtʃeɪfɪŋˌdɪʃ] *n* : escalfador *m*

chagrin¹ [ʃəˈgrɪn] *vt* : desilusionar, avergonzar

chagrin² *n* : desilusión *f*, disgusto *m*

chain¹ [ˈtʃeɪn] *vt* : encadenar

chain² *n* **1** : cadena *f* ⟨steel chain : cadena de acero⟩ ⟨restaurant chain : cadena de restaurantes⟩ **2** SERIES : serie *f* ⟨chain of events : serie de eventos⟩ **3 chains** *npl* FETTERS : grillos *mpl*

chair¹ [ˈtʃɛr] *vt* : presidir, moderar

chair² *n* **1** : silla *f* **2** CHAIRMANSHIP : presidencia *f* **3** → **chairman, chairwoman**

chairman [ˈtʃɛrmən] *n, pl* **-men** [-mən, -ˌmɛn] : presidente *m*

chairmanship [ˈtʃɛrmənˌʃɪp] *n* : presidencia *f*

chairwoman [ˈtʃɛrˌwʊmən] *n, pl* **-women** [-ˌwɪmən] : presidenta *f*

chaise longue [ˈʃeɪzˈlɔŋ] *n, pl* **chaise longues** [-lɔŋ, -ˈlɔŋz] : chaise longue *f*

chalet [ʃæˈleɪ] *n* : chalet *m*, chalé *m*

chalice [ˈtʃælɪs] *n* : cáliz *m*

chalk¹ [ˈtʃɔk] *vt* : escribir con tiza

chalk² *n* **1** LIMESTONE : creta *f*, caliza *f* **2** : tiza *f*, gis *m Mex* (para escribir)

chalkboard [ˈtʃɔkˌbɔrd] → **blackboard**

chalk up *vt* **1** ASCRIBE : atribuir, adscribir **2** SCORE : apuntarse, anotarse (una victoria, etc.)

chalky [ˈtʃɔki] *adj* **chalkier; -est 1** : calcáreo **2** PALE : pálido **3** POWDERY : polvoriento

challenge¹ [ˈtʃælɪndʒ] *vt* **-lenged; -lenging 1** DISPUTE : disputar, cuestionar, poner en duda **2** DARE : desafiar, retar **3** STIMULATE : estimular, incentivar

challenge² *n* : reto *m*, desafío *m*

challenger [ˈtʃælɪndʒər] *n* : retador *m*, -dora *f*; contendiente *mf*

chamber [ˈtʃeɪmbər] *n* **1** ROOM : cámara *f*, sala *f* ⟨the senate chamber : la cámara del senado⟩ **2** : recámara *f* (de un arma de fuego), cámara *f* (de combustión) **3** : cámara *f* ⟨chamber of commerce : cámara de comercio⟩ **4 chambers** *npl or* **judge's chambers** : despacho *m* del juez

chambermaid [ˈtʃeɪmbərˌmeɪd] *n* : camarera *f*

chamber music *n* : música *f* de cámara

chameleon [kəˈmiːljən, -liən] *n* : camaleón *m*

chamois ['ʃæmi] *n, pl* **chamois** [-mi, -miz] : gamuza *f*

champ¹ ['ʧæmp, 'ʃamp] *vi* 1 : masticar ruidosamente 2 **to champ at the bit** : impacientarse, comerle a uno la impaciencia

champ² ['ʧæmp] *n* : campeón *m*, -peona *f*

champagne [ʃæm'peɪn] *n* : champaña *m*, champán *m*

champion¹ ['ʧæmpiən] *vt* : defender, luchar por (una causa)

champion² *n* 1 ADVOCATE, DEFENDER : paladín *m*; campeón *m*, -peona *f*; defensor *m*, -sora *f* 2 WINNER : campeón *m*, -peona *f* ⟨world champion : campeón mundial⟩

championship ['ʧæmpiən,ʃɪp] *n* : campeonato *m*

chance¹ ['ʧænts] *v* **chanced**; **chancing** *vi* 1 HAPPEN : ocurrir por casualidad 2 **to chance upon** : encontrar por casualidad — *vt* RISK : arriesgar

chance² *adj* : fortuito, casual ⟨a chance encounter : un encuentro casual⟩

chance³ *n* 1 FATE, LUCK : azar *m*, suerte *f*, fortuna *f* 2 OPPORTUNITY : oportunidad *f*, ocasión *f* 3 PROBABILITY : probabilidad *f*, posibilidad *f* 4 RISK : riesgo *m* 5 : boleto *m* (de una rifa o lotería) 6 **by chance** : por casualidad

chancellor ['ʧæntsələr] *n* 1 : canciller *m* 2 : rector *m*, -tora *f* (de una universidad)

chancre ['ʃæŋkər] *n* : chancro *m*

chancy ['ʧæntsi] *adj* **chancier**; **-est** : riesgoso, arriesgado

chandelier [,ʃændə'lɪr] *n* : araña *f* de luces

change¹ ['ʧeɪnʤ] *v* **changed**; **changing** *vt* 1 ALTER : cambiar, alterar, modificar 2 EXCHANGE : cambiar de, intercambiar ⟨to change places : cambiar de sitio⟩ — *vi* 1 VARY : cambiar, variar, transformarse ⟨you haven't changed : no has cambiado⟩ 2 **or to change clothes** : cambiarse (de ropa)

change² *n* 1 ALTERATION : cambio *m* 2 : cambio *m*, vuelto *m* ⟨two dollars change : dos dólares de vuelto⟩ 3 COINS : cambio *m*, monedas *fpl*

changeable ['ʧeɪnʤəbəl] *adj* : cambiante, variable

changeless ['ʧeɪnʤləs] *adj* : invariable, constante

changer ['ʧeɪnʤər] *n* 1 : cambiador *m* ⟨record changer : cambiador de discos⟩ 2 **or money changer** : cambista *mf* (de dinero)

channel¹ ['ʧænəl] *vt* **-neled** *or* **-nelled**; **-neling** *or* **-nelling** : encauzar, canalizar

channel² *n* 1 RIVERBED : cauce *m* 2 STRAIT : canal *m*, estrecho *m* ⟨English Channel : Canal de la Mancha⟩ 3 COURSE, MEANS : vía *f*, conducto *m* ⟨the usual channels : las vías normales⟩ 4 : canal *m* (de televisión)

chant¹ ['ʧænt] *v* : salmodiar, cantar

chant² *n* 1 : salmodia *f* 2 **Gregorian chant** : canto *m* gregoriano

Chanukah ['xɑnəkə, 'hɑ-] → **Hanukkah**

chaos ['keɪ,ɑs] *n* : caos *m*

chaotic [keɪ'ɑtɪk] *adj* : caótico — **chaotically** [-tɪkli] *adv*

chap¹ ['ʧæp] *vi* **chapped**; **chapping** : partirse, agrietarse

chap² *n* FELLOW : tipo *m*, hombre *m*

chapel ['ʧæpəl] *n* : capilla *f*

chaperon¹ *or* **chaperone** ['ʃæpə,ro:n] *vt* **-oned**; **-oning** : ir de chaperón, acompañar

chaperon² *or* **chaperone** *n* : chaperón *m*, -rona *f*; acompañante *mf*

chaplain ['ʧæplɪn] *n* : capellán *m*

chapter ['ʧæptər] *n* 1 : capítulo *m* (de un libro) 2 BRANCH : sección *f*, división *f* (de una organización)

char ['ʧɑr] *vt* **charred**; **charring** 1 BURN : carbonizar 2 SCORCH : chamuscar

character ['kærɪktər] *n* 1 LETTER, SYMBOL : carácter *m* ⟨Chinese characters : caracteres chinos⟩ 2 DISPOSITION : carácter *m*, personalidad *f* ⟨of good character : de buena reputación⟩ 3 : tipo *m*, personaje *m* peculiar ⟨he's quite a character! : ¡él es algo serio!⟩ 4 : personaje *m* (ficticio)

characteristic¹ [,kærɪktə'rɪstɪk] *adj* : característico, típico — **characteristically** [-tɪkli] *adv*

characteristic² *n* : característica *f*

characterization [,kærɪktərə'zeɪʃən] *n* : caracterización *f*

characterize ['kærɪktə,raɪz] *vt* **-ized**; **-izing** : caracterizar

charades [ʃə'reɪdz] *ns & pl* : charada *f*

charcoal ['ʧɑr,ko:l] *n* : carbón *m*

chard ['ʧɑrd] → **Swiss chard**

charge¹ ['ʧɑrʤ] *v* **charged**; **charging** *vt* 1 : cargar ⟨to charge the batteries : cargar las pilas⟩ 2 ENTRUST : encomendar, encargar 3 COMMAND : ordenar, mandar 4 ACCUSE : acusar ⟨charged with robbery : acusado de robo⟩ 5 : cargar a una cuenta, comprar a crédito — *vi* 1 : cargar (contra el enemigo) ⟨charge! : ¡a la carga!⟩ 2 : cobrar ⟨they charge too much : cobran demasiado⟩

charge² *n* 1 : carga *f* (eléctrica) 2 BURDEN : carga *f*, peso *m* 3 RESPONSIBILITY : cargo *m*, responsabilidad *f* ⟨to take charge of : hacerse cargo de⟩ 4 ACCUSATION : cargo *m*, acusación *f* 5 COST : costo *m*, cargo *m*, precio *m* 6 ATTACK : carga *f*, ataque *m*

charge card → **credit card**

chargeable ['ʧɑrʤəbəl] *adj* 1 : acusable, perseguible (dícese de un delito) 2 **~ to** : a cargo de (una cuenta)

charger ['ʧɑrʤər] *n* : corcel *m*, caballo *m* (de guerra)

chariot ['ʧæriət] *n* : carro *m* (de guerra)

charisma [kə'rɪzmə] *n* : carisma *m*

charismatic [,kærəz'mætɪk] *adj* : carismático

charitable [ˈtʃærətəbəl] *adj* **1** GENEROUS : caritativo ⟨a charitable organization : una organización benéfica⟩ **2** KIND, UNDERSTANDING : generoso, benévolo, comprensivo — **charitably** [-bli] *adv*

charitableness [ˈtʃærətəbəlnəs] *n* : caridad *f*

charity [ˈtʃærəti] *n, pl* **-ties 1** GENEROSITY : caridad *f* **2** ALMS : caridad *f*, limosna *f* **3** : organización *f* benéfica, obra *f* de beneficencia

charlatan [ˈʃɑrlətən] *n* : charlatán *m*, -tana *f*; farsante *mf*

charley horse [ˈtʃɑrli‚hɔrs] *n* : calambre *m*

charm[1] [ˈtʃɑrm] *vt* : encantar, cautivar, fascinar

charm[2] *n* **1** AMULET : amuleto *m*, talismán *m* **2** ATTRACTION : encanto *m*, atractivo *m* ⟨it has a certain charm : tiene cierto atractivo⟩ **3** : dije *m*, colgante *m* ⟨charm bracelet : pulsera de dijes⟩

charmer [ˈtʃɑrmər] *n* : persona *f* encantadora

charming [ˈtʃɑrmɪŋ] *adj* : encantador, fascinante

chart[1] [ˈtʃɑrt] *vt* **1** : trazar un mapa de, hacer un gráfico de **2** PLAN : trazar, planear ⟨to chart a course : trazar un derrotero⟩

chart[2] *n* **1** MAP : carta *f*, mapa *m* **2** DIAGRAM : gráfico *m*, cuadro *m*, tabla *f*

charter[1] [ˈtʃɑrtər] *vt* **1** : establecer los estatutos de (una organización) **2** RENT : alquilar, fletar

charter[2] *n* **1** STATUTES : estatutos *mpl* **2** CONSTITUTION : carta *f*, constitución *f*

chartreuse [ʃɑrˈtruːz, -ˈtruːs] *n* : color *m* verde-amarillo intenso

chary [ˈtʃæri] *adj* **charier; -est 1** WARY : cauteloso, precavido **2** SPARING : parco

chase[1] [ˈtʃeɪs] *vt* **chased; chasing 1** PURSUE : perseguir, ir a la caza de **2** DRIVE : ahuyentar, echar ⟨he chased the dog from the garden : ahuyentó al perro del jardín⟩ **3** : grabar (metales)

chase[2] *n* **1** PURSUIT : persecución *f*, caza *f* **2 the chase** HUNTING : caza *f*

chaser [ˈtʃeɪsər] *n* **1** PURSUER : perseguidor *m*, -dora *f* **2** : bebida *f* que se toma después de un trago de licor

chasm [ˈkæzəm] *n* : abismo *m*, sima *f*

chassis [ˈtʃæsi, ˈʃæsi] *n, pl* **chassis** [-siz] : chasis *m*, armazón *m*

chaste [ˈtʃeɪst] *adj* **chaster; -est 1** : casto **2** MODEST : modesto, puro **3** AUSTERE : austero, sobrio

chastely [ˈtʃeɪstli] *adv* : castamente

chasten [ˈtʃeɪsən] *vt* : castigar, sancionar

chasteness [ˈtʃeɪstnəs] *n* **1** MODESTY : modestia *f*, castidad *f* **2** AUSTERITY : sobriedad *f*, austeridad *f*

chastise [ˈtʃæs‚taɪz, tʃæsˈ-] *vt* **-tised; -tising 1** REPRIMAND : reprender, corregir, reprobar **2** PUNISH : castigar

chastisement [ˈtʃæs‚taɪzmənt, tʃæsˈtaɪz-, ˈtʃæstəz-] *n* : castigo *m*, corrección *f*

chastity [ˈtʃæstəti] *n* : castidad *f*, decencia *f*, modestia *f*

chat[1] [ˈtʃæt] *vi* **chatted; chatting** : charlar, platicar

chat[2] *n* : charla *f*, plática *f*

château [ʃæˈtoː] *n, pl* **-teaus** [-ˈtoːz] *or* **-teaux** [-ˈtoː, -ˈtoːz] : mansión *f* campestre

chattel [ˈtʃætəl] *n* : bienes *fpl* muebles, enseres *mpl*

chatter[1] [ˈtʃætər] *vi* **1** : castañetear (dícese de los dientes) **2** GAB : parlotear *fam*, cotorrear *fam*

chatter[2] *n* **1** CHATTERING : castañeteo *m* (de dientes) **2** GABBING : parloteo *m fam*, cotorreo *m fam*, cháchara *f fam*

chatterbox [ˈtʃætər‚bɑks] *n* : parlanchín *m*, -china *f*; charlatán *m*, -tana *f*, hablador *m*, -dora *f*

chatty [ˈtʃæti] *adj* **chattier; chattiest 1** TALKATIVE : parlanchín, charlatán **2** CONVERSATIONAL : familiar, conversador ⟨a chatty letter : una carta llena de noticias⟩

chauffeur[1] [ˈʃoːfər, ʃoˈfər] *vi* : trabajar de chofer privado — *vt* : hacer de chofer para

chauffeur[2] *n* : chofer *m* privado

chauvinism [ˈʃoːvə‚nɪzəm] *n* : chauvinismo *m*, patriotería *f*

chauvinist [ˈʃoːvənɪst] *n* : chauvinista *mf*; patriotero *m*, -ra *f*

chauvinistic [‚ʃoːvəˈnɪstɪk] *adj* : chauvinista, patriotero

cheap[1] [ˈtʃiːp] *adv* : barato ⟨to sell cheap : vender barato⟩

cheap[2] *adj* **1** INEXPENSIVE : barato, económico **2** SHODDY : barato, mal hecho **3** STINGY : tacaño, agarrado *fam*, codo *Mex*

cheapen [ˈtʃiːpən] *vt* : degradar, rebajar

cheaply [ˈtʃiːpli] *adv* : barato, a precio bajo

cheapness [ˈtʃiːpnəs] *n* **1** : baratura *f*, precio *m* bajo **2** STINGINESS : tacañería *f*

cheapskate [ˈtʃiːp‚skeɪt] *n* : tacaño *m*, -ña *f*; codo *m*, -da *f Mex*

cheat[1] [ˈtʃiːt] *vt* : defraudar, estafar, engañar — *vi* : hacer trampa

cheat[2] *n* **1** CHEATING : engaño *m*, fraude *m*, trampa *f* **2** → **cheater**

cheater [ˈtʃiːtər] *n* : estafador *m*, -dora *f*; tramposo *m*, -sa *f*

check[1] [ˈtʃek] *vt* **1** HALT : frenar, parar, detener **2** RESTRAIN : refrenar, contener, reprimir **3** VERIFY : verificar, comprobar **4** INSPECT : revisar, chequear, inspeccionar **5** MARK : marcar, señalar **6** : chequear, facturar (maletas, equipaje) **7** CHECKER : marcar con cuadros **8 to check in** : registrarse en un hotel **9 to check out** : irse de un hotel

check² *n* **1** HALT : detención *f* súbita, parada *f* **2** RESTRAINT : control *m*, freno *m* **3** INSPECTION : inspección *f*, verificación *f*, chequeo *m* **4** : cheque *m* ⟨to pay by check : pagar con cheque⟩ **5** VOUCHER : resguardo *m*, comprobante *m* **6** BILL : cuenta *f* (en un restaurante) **7** SQUARE : cuadro *m* **8** MARK : marca *f* **9** : jaque *m* (en ajedrez)

checkbook ['tʃɛk,bʊk] *n* : chequera *f*

checker¹ ['tʃɛkər] *vt* : marcar con cuadros

checker² *n* **1** : pieza *f* (en el juego de damas) **2** : verificador *m*, -dora *f* **3** CASHIER : cajero *m*, -ra *f*

checkerboard ['tʃɛkər,bord] *n* : tablero *m* de damas

checkers ['tʃɛkərz] *n* : damas *fpl*

checkmate¹ ['tʃɛk,meɪt] *vt* -mated; -mating **1** : dar jaque mate a (en ajedrez) **2** THWART : frustrar, arruinar

checkmate² *n* : jaque mate *m*

checkout ['tʃɛk,aʊt] *n or* **checkout counter** : caja *f*

checkpoint ['tʃɛk,pɔɪnt] *n* : puesto *m* de control

checkup ['tʃɛk,ʌp] *n* : examen *m* médico, chequeo *m*

cheddar ['tʃɛdər] *n* : queso *m* Cheddar

cheek ['tʃiːk] *n* **1** : mejilla *f*, cachete *m* **2** IMPUDENCE : insolencia *f*, descaro *m*

cheekbone ['tʃiːk,boːn] *n* : pómulo *m*

cheeky ['tʃiːki] *adj* **cheekier; -est** : descarado, insolente, atrevido

cheep¹ ['tʃiːp] *vi* : piar

cheep² *n* : pío *m*

cheer¹ ['tʃɪr] *vt* **1** ENCOURAGE : alentar, animar **2** GLADDEN : alegrar, levantar el ánimo a **3** ACCLAIM : aclamar, vitorear, echar porras a

cheer² *n* **1** CHEERFULNESS : alegría *f*, buen humor *m*, jovialidad *f* **2** APPLAUSE : aclamación *f*, ovación *f*, aplausos *mpl* ⟨three cheers for the chief! : ¡viva el jefe!⟩ **3** cheers! : ¡salud!

cheerful ['tʃɪrfəl] *adj* : alegre, de buen humor

cheerfully ['tʃɪrfəli] *adv* : alegremente, jovialmente

cheerfulness ['tʃɪrfəlnəs] *n* : buen humor *m*, alegría *f*

cheerily ['tʃɪrəli] *adv* : alegremente

cheeriness ['tʃɪrinəs] *n* : buen humor *m*, alegría *f*

cheerleader ['tʃɪr,liːdər] *n* : porrista *mf*

cheerless ['tʃɪrləs] *adj* BLEAK : triste, sombrío

cheerlessly ['tʃɪrləsli] *adv* : desanimadamente

cheery ['tʃɪri] *adj* **cheerier; -est** : alegre, de buen humor

cheese ['tʃiːz] *n* : queso *m*

cheesecloth ['tʃiːz,klɔθ] *n* : estopilla *f*

cheesy ['tʃiːzi] *adj* **cheesier; -est 1** : a queso **2** : que contiene queso **3** CHEAP : barato, de mala calidad

cheetah ['tʃiːtə] *n* : guepardo *m*

chef ['ʃɛf] *n* : chef *m*

chemical¹ ['kɛmɪkəl] *adj* : químico — **chemically** [-mɪkli] *adv*

chemical² *n* : sustancia *f* química

chemise [ʃəˈmiːz] *n* **1** : camiseta *f*, prenda *f* interior de una pieza **2** : vestido *m* holgado

chemist ['kɛmɪst] *n* : químico *m*, -ca *f*

chemistry ['kɛmɪstri] *n, pl* -**tries** : química *f*

chemotherapy [,kiːmoˈθɛrəpi, ,kɛmo-] *n, pl* -**pies** : quimioterapia *f*

chenille [ʃəˈniːl] *n* : felpilla *f*

cherish ['tʃɛrɪʃ] *vt* **1** VALUE : apreciar, valorar **2** HARBOR : abrigar, albergar

cherry ['tʃɛri] *n, pl* -**ries 1** : cereza *f* (fruta) **2** : cerezo *m* (árbol)

cherub ['tʃɛrəb] *n* **1** *pl* -**ubim** ['tʃɛrə,bɪm, 'tʃɛrə-] ANGEL : ángel *m*, querubín *m* **2** *pl* -**ubs** : niño *m* regordete, niña *f* regordeta

cherubic [tʃəˈruːbɪk] *adj* : querúbico, angelical

chess ['tʃɛs] *n* : ajedrez *m*

chessboard ['tʃɛs,bord] *n* : tablero *m* de ajedrez

chessman ['tʃɛsmən, -,mæn] *n, pl* -**men** [-mən, -,mɛn] : pieza *f* de ajedrez

chest ['tʃɛst] *n* **1** : cofre *m*, baúl *m* **2** : pecho *m* ⟨chest pains : dolores de pecho⟩

chestnut ['tʃɛst,nʌt] *n* **1** : castaña *f* (fruto) **2** : castaño *m* (árbol)

chest of drawers *n* : cómoda *f*

chevron ['ʃɛvrən] *n* : galón *m* (de un oficial militar)

chew¹ ['tʃuː] *vt* : masticar, mascar

chew² *n* : algo que se masca (como tabaco)

chewable ['tʃuːəbəl] *adj* : masticable

chewing gum *n* : goma *f* de mascar, chicle *m*

chewy ['tʃuːi] *adj* **chewier; -est 1** : fibroso (dícese de las carnes o los vegetales) **2** : pegajoso, chicloso (dícese de los dulces)

chic¹ ['ʃiːk] *adj* : chic, elegante, de moda

chic² *n* : chic *m*, elegancia *f*

Chicano [tʃɪˈkɑno] *n* : chicano *m*, -na *f* — **Chicano** *adj*

chick ['tʃɪk] *n* : pollito *m*, -ta *f*; polluelo *m*, -la *f*

chicken ['tʃɪkən] *n* **1** FOWL : pollo *m* **2** COWARD : cobarde *mf*

chickenhearted ['tʃɪkən,hɑrtəd] *n* : miedoso, cobarde

chicken pox *n* : varicela *f*

chickpea ['tʃɪk,piː] *n* : garbanzo *m*

chicle ['tʃɪkəl] *n* : chicle *m* (resina)

chicory ['tʃɪkəri] *n, pl* -**ries 1** : endibia *f* (para ensaladas) **2** : achicoria *f* (aditivo de café)

chide ['tʃaɪd] *vt* **chid** ['tʃɪd] *or* **chided; chid** *or* **chidden** ['tʃɪdən] *or* **chided; chiding** ['tʃaɪdɪŋ] : regañar, reprender

chief¹ ['tʃiːf] *adj* : principal, capital ⟨chief negotiator : negociador en jefe⟩ — **chiefly** *adv*

chief² *n* : jefe *m*, -fa *f*

chieftain ['tʃi:ftən] n : jefe m, -fa f (de una tribu)

chiffon [ʃɪ'fɑn, 'ʃɪ₋-] n : chifón m

chigger ['tʃɪɡər] n : nigua f

chignon ['ʃi:n,jɑn, -,jɔn] n : moño m, chongo m Mex

chilblain ['tʃɪl,bleɪn] n : sabañón m

child ['tʃaɪld] n, pl **children** ['tʃɪldrən] **1** BABY, YOUNGSTER : niño m, -ña f; criatura f **2** OFFSPRING : hijo m, -ja f; progenie f

childbearing[1] ['tʃaɪl,berɪŋ] adj : relativo al parto ⟨of childbearing age : en edad fértil⟩

childbearing[2] → childbirth

childbirth ['tʃaɪld,bərθ] n : parto m

childhood ['tʃaɪld,hʊd] n : infancia f, niñez f

childish ['tʃaɪldɪʃ] adj : infantil, inmaduro — **childishly** adv

childishness ['tʃaɪldɪʃnəs] n : infantilismo m, inmadurez f

childless ['tʃaɪldləs] adj : sin hijos

childlike ['tʃaɪld,laɪk] adj : infantil, inocente ⟨a childlike imagination : una imaginación infantil⟩

childproof ['tʃaɪld,pru:f] adj : a prueba de niños

Chilean ['tʃɪliən, tʃɪ'leɪən] n : chileno m, -na f — **Chilean** adj

chili or **chile** or **chilli** ['tʃɪli] n, pl **chilies** or **chiles** or **chillies** **1** or **chili pepper** : chile m, ají m **2** : chile m con carne

chill[1] ['tʃɪl] v : enfriar

chill[2] adj : frío, gélido ⟨a chill wind : un viento frío⟩

chill[3] n **1** CHILLINESS : fresco m, frío m **2** SHIVER : escalofrío m **3** DAMPER : enfriamiento m, frío m ⟨to cast a chill over : enfriar⟩

chilliness ['tʃɪlinəs] n : frío m, fresco m

chilly ['tʃɪli] adj **chillier**; **-est** : frío ⟨it's chilly tonight : hace frío esta noche⟩

chime[1] ['tʃaɪm] v **chimed**; **chiming** v : hacer sonar (una campana) — vi : sonar una campana, dar campanadas

chime[2] n **1** BELLS : juego m de campanitas sintonizadas, carillón m **2** PEAL : tañido m, campanada f

chime in vi : meterse en una conversación

chimera or **chimaera** [kaɪ'mɪrə, kə-] n : quimera f

chimney ['tʃɪmni] n, pl **-neys** : chimenea f

chimney sweep n : deshollinador m, -dora f

chimp ['tʃɪmp, 'ʃɪmp] → chimpanzee

chimpanzee [,tʃɪm,pæn'zi:, ,ʃɪm-; tʃɪm'pænzi, ʃɪm-] n : chimpancé m

chin ['tʃɪn] n : barbilla f, mentón m, barba f

china ['tʃaɪnə] n **1** PORCELAIN : porcelana f, loza f **2** CROCKERY, TABLEWARE : loza f, vajilla f

chinchilla [tʃɪn'tʃɪlə] n : chinchilla f

Chinese ['tʃaɪ'ni:z, -'ni:s] n **1** : chino m, -na f **2** : chino m (idioma) — **Chinese** adj

chink ['tʃɪŋk] n : grieta f, abertura f

chintz ['tʃɪnts] n : chintz m, chinz m

chip[1] ['tʃɪp] v **chipped**; **chipping** vt : desportillar, desconchar, astillar (madera) — vi : desportillarse, desconcharse, descascararse (dícese de la pintura, etc.)

chip[2] n **1** : astilla f (de madera o vidrio), lasca f (de piedra) ⟨he's a chip off the old block : de tal palo, tal astilla⟩ **2** : bocado m pequeño (en rodajas o rebanadas) ⟨tortilla chips : totopos, tortillitas tostadas⟩ **3** : ficha f (de póker, etc.) **4** NICK : desportilladura f, mella f **5** : chip m ⟨memory chip : chip de memoria⟩

chip in v CONTRIBUTE : contribuir

chipmunk ['tʃɪp,mʌŋk] n : ardilla f listada

chipper ['tʃɪpər] adj : alegre y vivaz

chiropodist [kə'rɑpədɪst, ʃə-] n : podólogo m, -ga f

chiropody [kə'rɑpədi, ʃə-] n : podología f

chiropractic ['kaɪrə,præktɪk] n : quiropráctica f

chiropractor ['kaɪrə,præktər] n : quiropráctico m, -ca f

chirp[1] ['tʃərp] vi : gorjear (dícese de los pájaros), chirriar (dícese de los grillos)

chirp[2] n : gorjeo m (de un pájaro), chirrido m (de un grillo)

chisel[1] ['tʃɪzəl] vt **-eled** or **-elled**; **-eling** or **-elling** **1** : cincelar, tallar, labrar **2** CHEAT : estafar, defraudar

chisel[2] n : cincel m (para piedras y metales), escoplo m (para madera), formón m

chiseler ['tʃɪzələr] n SWINDLER : estafador m, -dora f; fraude mf

chit ['tʃɪt] n : resguardo m, recibo m

chitchat ['tʃɪt,tʃæt] n : cotorreo m, charla f

chivalric [ʃə'vælrɪk] → chivalrous

chivalrous ['ʃɪvəlrəs] adj **1** KNIGHTLY : caballeresco, relativo a la caballería **2** GENTLEMANLY : caballeroso, honesto, cortés

chivalrousness ['ʃɪvəlrəsnəs] n : caballerosidad f, cortesía f

chivalry ['ʃɪvəlri] n, pl **-ries** **1** KNIGHTHOOD : caballería f **2** CHIVALROUSNESS : caballerosidad f, nobleza f, cortesía f

chive ['tʃaɪv] n : cebollino m

chloride ['klor,aɪd] n : cloruro m

chlorinate ['klorə,neɪt] vt **-nated**; **-nating** : clorar

chlorination [,klorə'neɪʃən] n : cloración f

chlorine ['klor,i:n] n : cloro m

chloroform ['klorə,fɔrm] n : cloroformo m

chlorophyll ['klorə,fɪl] n : clorofila f

chock-full ['tʃɑk'fʊl, 'tʃɔk-] adj : colmado, repleto

chocolate ['tʃɑkələt, 'tʃɔk-] n **1** : chocolate m **2** BONBON : bombón m **3** : color m chocolate, marrón m

choice[1] [ˈtʃɔɪs] *adj* **choicer; -est** : selecto, escogido, de primera calidad

choice[2] *n* **1** CHOOSING : elección *f*, selección *f* **2** OPTION : elección *f*, opción *f* ⟨I have no choice : no tengo alternativa⟩ **3** PREFERENCE : preferencia *f*, elección *f* **4** VARIETY : surtido *m*, selección *f* ⟨a wide choice : un gran surtido⟩

choir [ˈkwaɪr] *n* : coro *m*

choirboy [ˈkwaɪrˌbɔɪ] *n* : niño *m* de coro

choke[1] [ˈtʃoːk] *v* **choked; choking** *vt* **1** ASPHYXIATE, STRANGLE : sofocar, asfixiar, ahogar, estrangular **2** BLOCK : tapar, obstruir — *vi* **1** SUFFOCATE : asfixiarse, sofocarse, ahogarse, atragantarse (con comida) **2** CLOG : taparse, obstruirse

choke[2] *n* **1** CHOKING : estrangulación *f* **2** : choke *m* (de un motor)

choker [ˈtʃoːkər] *n* : gargantilla *f*

cholera [ˈkɑlərə] *n* : cólera *m*

cholesterol [kəˈlɛstəˌrɔl] *n* : colesterol *m*

choose [ˈtʃuːz] *v* **chose** [ˈtʃoːz]; **chosen** [ˈtʃoːzən]; **choosing** *vt* **1** SELECT : escoger, elegir ⟨choose only one : escoja sólo uno⟩ **2** DECIDE : decidir ⟨he chose to leave : decidió irse⟩ **3** PREFER : preferir ⟨which one do you choose? : ¿cuál prefiere?⟩ — *vi* : escoger ⟨much to choose from : mucho de donde escoger⟩

choosy *or* **choosey** [ˈtʃuːzi] *adj* **choosier; -est** : exigente, remilgado

chop[1] [ˈtʃɑp] *vt* **chopped; chopping 1** MINCE : picar, cortar, moler (carne) **2 to chop down** : cortar, talar (un árbol)

chop[2] *n* **1** CUT : hachazo *m* (con una hacha), tajo *m* (con una cuchilla), golpe *m* (penetrante) ⟨karate chop : golpe de karate⟩ **2** : chuleta *f* ⟨pork chops : chuletas de cerdo⟩

chopper [ˈtʃɑpər] → **helicopter**

choppy [ˈtʃɑpi] *adj* **choppier; -est 1** : agitado, picado (dícese del mar) **2** DISCONNECTED : incoherente, inconexo

chops [ˈtʃɑps] *npl* **1** : quijada *f*, mandíbula *f*, boca *f* (de una persona) **2 to lick one's chops** : relamerse

chopsticks [ˈtʃɑpˌstɪks] *npl* : palillos *mpl*

choral [ˈkɔrəl] *adj* : coral

chorale [kəˈræl, -ˈrɑl] *n* **1** : coral *f* (composición musical vocal) **2** CHOIR, CHORUS : coral *f*, coro *m*

chord [ˈkɔrd] *n* **1** : acorde *m* (en música) **2** : cuerda *f* (en anatomía o geometría)

chore [ˈtʃor] *n* **1** TASK : tarea *f* rutinaria **2** BOTHER, NUISANCE : lata *f fam*, fastidio *m* **3 chores** *npl* WORK : quehaceres *mpl*, faenas *fpl*

choreograph [ˈkoriəˌgræf] *vt* : coreografiar

choreographer [ˌkoriˈɑgrəfər] *n* : coreógrafo *m*, -fa *f*

choreographic [ˌkoriəˈgræfɪk] *adj* : coreográfico

choreography [ˌkoriˈɑgrəfi] *n, pl* **-phies** : coreografía *f*

chorister [ˈkorəstər] *n* : corista *mf*

chortle[1] [ˈtʃɔrtəl] *vi* **-tled; -tling** : reírse (con satisfacción o júbilo)

chortle[2] *n* : risa *f* (de satisfacción o júbilo)

chorus[1] [ˈkorəs] *vt* : corear

chorus[2] *n* **1** : coro *m* (grupo o composición musical) **2** REFRAIN : coro *m*, estribillo *m*

chose → **choose**

chosen [ˈtʃoːzən] *adj* : elegido, selecto

chow [ˈtʃaʊ] *n* **1** FOOD : comida *f* **2** : chow-chow *m* (perro)

chowder [ˈtʃaʊdər] *n* : sopa *f* de pescado

Christ [ˈkraɪst] *n* **1** : Cristo *m* **2 for Christ's sake** : ¡por Dios!

christen [ˈkrɪsən] *vt* **1** BAPTIZE : bautizar **2** NAME : bautizar con el nombre de

Christendom [ˈkrɪsəndəm] *n* : cristiandad *f*

christening [ˈkrɪsənɪŋ] *n* : bautismo *m*, bautizo *m*

Christian[1] [ˈkrɪstʃən] *adj* : cristiano

Christian[2] *n* : cristiano *m*, -na *f*

Christianity [ˌkrɪstʃiˈænəti, ˌkrɪsˈtʃæ-] *n* : cristianismo *m*

Christian name *n* : nombre *m* de pila

Christmas [ˈkrɪsməs] *n* : Navidad *f* ⟨Christmas season : las Navidades⟩

chromatic [kroˈmætɪk] *adj* : cromático ⟨chromatic scale : escala cromática⟩

chrome [ˈkroːm] *n* : cromo *m* (metal)

chromium [ˈkroːmiəm] *n* : cromo *m* (elemento)

chromosome [ˈkroːməˌsoːm, -ˌzoːm] *n* : cromosoma *m*

chronic [ˈkrɑnɪk] *adj* : crónico — **chronically** [-nɪkli] *adv*

chronicle[1] [ˈkrɑnɪkəl] *vt* **-cled; -cling** : escribir (una crónica o historia)

chronicle[2] *n* : crónica *f*, historia *f*

chronicler [ˈkrɑnɪklər] *n* : historiador *m*, -dora *f*; cronista *mf*

chronological [ˌkrɑnəlˈɑdʒɪkəl] *adj* : cronológico — **chronologically** [-kli] *adv*

chronology [krəˈnɑlədʒi] *n, pl* **-gies** : cronología *f*

chronometer [krəˈnɑmətər] *n* : cronómetro *m*

chrysalis [ˈkrɪsələs] *n, pl* **chrysalides** [krɪˈsæləˌdiːz] *or* **chrysalises** : crisálida *f*

chrysanthemum [krɪˈsænθəməm] *n* : crisantemo *m*

chubbiness [ˈtʃʌbinəs] *n* : gordura *f*

chubby [ˈtʃʌbi] *adj* **-bier; -est** : gordito, regordete, rechoncho

chuck[1] [ˈtʃʌk] *vt* **1** TOSS : tirar, lanzar, aventar *Col, Mex* **2 to chuck under the chin** : hacer la mamola

chuck[2] *n* **1** PAT : mamola *f*, palmada *f* **2** TOSS : lanzamiento *m* **3** *or* **chuck steak** : corte *m* de carne de res

chuckle[1] [ˈtʃʌkəl] *vi* **-led; -ling** : reírse entre dientes

chuckle[2] *n* : risita *f*, risa *f* ahogada

chug[1] ['tʃʌg] *vi* **chugged; chugging** : resoplar, traquetear

chug[2] *n* : resoplido *m*, traqueteo *m*

chum[1] ['tʃʌm] *vi* **chummed; chumming** : ser camaradas, ser cuates *Mex fam*

chum[2] *n* : amigo *m*, -ga *f*; camarada *mf*; compinche *mf fam*

chummy ['tʃʌmi] *adj* **-mier; -est** : amistoso ⟨they're very chummy : son muy amigos⟩

chump ['tʃʌmp] *n* : tonto *m*, -ta *f*; idiota *mf*

chunk ['tʃʌŋk] *n* **1** PIECE : cacho *m*, pedazo *m*, trozo *m* **2** : cantidad *f* grande ⟨a chunk of money : mucho dinero⟩

chunky ['tʃʌŋki] *adj* **chunkier; -est 1** STOCKY : fornido, robusto **2** : que contiene pedazos

church ['tʃərtʃ] *n* **1** : iglesia *f* ⟨to go to church : ir a la iglesia⟩ **2** CHRISTIANS : iglesia *f*, conjunto *m* de fieles cristianos **3** DENOMINATION : confesión *f*, secta *f* **4** CONGREGATION : feligreses *mpl*, fieles *mpl*

churchgoer ['tʃərtʃ,go:ər] *n* : practicante *mf*

churchyard ['tʃərtʃ,jard] *n* : cementerio *m* (junto a una iglesia)

churn[1] ['tʃərn] *vt* **1** : batir (crema), hacer (mantequilla) **2** : agitar con fuerza, revolver — *vi* : agitarse, arremolinarse

churn[2] *n* : mantequera *f*

chute ['ʃu:t] *n* : conducto *m* inclinado, vertedero *m* (para basuras)

chutney ['tʃʌtni] *n, pl* **-neys** : chutney *m*

chutzpah ['hutspə, 'xʊt-, -,spa] *n* : descaro *m*, frescura *f*, cara *f fam*

cicada [sə'keɪdə, -'kɑ-] *n* : cigarra *f*, chicharra *f*

cider ['saɪdər] *n* **1** : jugo *m* (de manzana, etc.) **2 hard cider** : sidra *f*

cigar [sɪ'gɑr] *n* : puro *m*, cigarro *m*

cigarette [,sɪgə'rɛt, 'sɪgə,rɛt] *n* : cigarrillo *m*, cigarro *m*

cilantro [sɪ'lɑntro:, -'læn-] *n* : cilantro *m*

cinch[1] ['sɪntʃ] *vt* **1** : cinchar (un caballo) **2** ASSURE : asegurar

cinch[2] *n* **1** : cincha *f* (para caballos) **2** : algo fácil o seguro ⟨it's a cinch : es bien fácil, es pan comido⟩

cinchona [sɪŋ'ko:nə] *n* : quino *m*

cinder ['sɪndər] *n* **1** EMBER : brasa *f*, ascua *f* **2 cinders** *npl* ASHES : cenizas *fpl*

cinema ['sɪnəmə] *n* : cine *m*

cinematic [,sɪnə'mætɪk] *adj* : cinematográfico

cinnamon ['sɪnəmən] *n* : canela *f*

cipher ['saɪfər] *n* **1** ZERO : cero *m* **2** CODE : cifra *f*, clave *f*

circa ['sərkə] *prep* : alrededor de, hacia ⟨circa 1800 : hacia el año 1800⟩

circle[1] ['sərkəl] *v* **-cled; -cling** *vt* **1** : encerrar en un círculo, poner un círculo alrededor de **2** : girar alrededor de, dar vueltas a ⟨we circled the building twice : le dimos vueltas al edificio dos veces⟩ — *vi* : dar vueltas

circle[2] *n* **1** : círculo *m* **2** CYCLE : ciclo *m* ⟨to come full circle : volver al punto de partida⟩ **3** GROUP : círculo *m*, grupo *m* (social)

circuit ['sərkət] *n* **1** BOUNDARY : circuito *m*, perímetro *m* (de una zona o un territorio) **2** TOUR : circuito *m*, recorrido *m*, tour *m* **3** : circuito *m* (eléctrico) ⟨a short circuit : un cortocircuito⟩

circuitous [,sər'kju:əţəs] *adj* : sinuoso, tortuoso

circuitry ['sərkətri] *n, pl* **-ries** : sistema *m* de circuitos

circular[1] ['sərkjələr] *adj* ROUND : circular, redondo

circular[2] *n* : circular *f*

circulate ['sərkjə,leɪt] *v* **-lated; -lating** *vi* : circular — *vt* **1** : circular (noticias, etc.) **2** DISSEMINATE : hacer circular, divulgar

circulation [,sərkjə'leɪʃən] *n* : circulación *f*

circulatory ['sərkjələ,tori] *adj* : circulatorio

circumcise ['sərkəm,saɪz] *vt* **-cised; -cising** : circuncidar

circumcision [,sərkəm'sɪʒən, 'sərkəm,-] *n* : circuncisión *f*

circumference [sər'kʌmpfrənts] *n* : circunferencia *f*

circumflex ['sərkəm,flɛks] *n* : acento *m* circunflejo

circumlocution [,sərkəmlo:'kju:ʃən] *n* : circunlocución *f*

circumnavigate [,sərkəm'nævə,geɪt] *vt* **-gated; -gating** : circunnavegar

circumscribe ['sərkəm,skraɪb] *vt* **-scribed; -scribing 1** : circunscribir, trazar una figura alrededor de **2** LIMIT : circunscribir, limitar

circumspect ['sərkəm,spɛkt] *adj* : circunspecto, prudente, cauto

circumspection [,sərkəm'spɛkʃən] *n* : circunspección *f*, cautela *f*

circumstance ['sərkəm,stænts] *n* **1** EVENT : circunstancia *f*, acontecimiento *m* **2 circumstances** *npl* SITUATION : circunstancias *fpl*, situación *f* ⟨under the circumstances : dadas las circunstancias⟩ ⟨under no circumstances : de ninguna manera, bajo ningún concepto⟩ **3 circumstances** *npl* : situación *f* económica

circumstantial [,sərkəm'stæntʃəl] *adj* : circunstancial

circumvent [,sərkəm'vɛnt] *vt* : evadir, burlar (una ley o regla), sortear (una responsabilidad o dificultad)

circumvention [,sərkəm'vɛntʃən] *n* : evasión *f*

circus ['sərkəs] *n* : circo *m*

cirrhosis [sə'ro:sɪs] *n, pl* **-rhoses** [-'ro:,si:z] : cirrosis *f*

cirrus ['sɪrəs] *n, pl* **-ri** ['sɪr,aɪ] : cirro *m*

cistern ['sɪstərn] *n* : cisterna *f*, aljibe *m*

citadel ['sɪţədəl, -,dɛl] *n* FORTRESS : ciudadela *f*, fortaleza *f*

citation [saɪˈteɪʃən] n 1 SUMMONS : emplazamiento m, citación f, convocatoria f (judicial) 2 QUOTATION : cita f 3 COMMENDATION : elogio m, mención f (de honor)

cite [ˈsaɪt] vt **cited; citing** 1 ARRAIGN, SUBPOENA : emplazar, citar, hacer comparecer (ante un tribunal) 2 QUOTE : citar 3 COMMEND : elogiar, honrar (oficialmente)

citizen [ˈsɪtəzən] n : ciudadano m, -na f

citizenry [ˈsɪtəzənri] n, pl **-ries** : ciudadanía f, conjunto m de ciudadanos

citizenship [ˈsɪtəzənˌʃɪp] n : ciudadanía f ⟨Nicaraguan citizenship : ciudadanía nicaragüense⟩

citron [ˈsɪtrən] n : cidra f

citrus [ˈsɪtrəs] n, pl **-rus** or **-ruses** : cítrico m

city [ˈsɪti] n, pl **cities** : ciudad f

civic [ˈsɪvɪk] adj : cívico

civics [ˈsɪvɪks] ns & pl : civismo m

civil [ˈsɪvəl] adj 1 : civil ⟨civil law : derecho civil⟩ 2 POLITE : civil, cortés

civilian [səˈvɪljən] n : civil mf ⟨soldiers and civilians : soldados y civiles⟩

civility [səˈvɪləti] n, pl **-ties** : cortesía f, educación f

civilization [ˌsɪvələˈzeɪʃən] n : civilización f

civilize [ˈsɪvəˌlaɪz] vt **-lized; -lizing** : civilizar — **civilized** adj

civil liberties npl : derechos mpl civiles

civilly [ˈsɪvəli] adv : cortésmente

civil rights npl : derechos mpl civiles

civil service n : administración f pública

civil war n : guerra f civil

clack¹ [ˈklæk] vi : tabletear

clack² n : tableteo m

clad [ˈklæd] adj 1 CLOTHED : vestido 2 COVERED : cubierto

claim¹ [ˈkleɪm] vt 1 DEMAND : reclamar, reivindicar ⟨she claimed her rights : reclamó sus derechos⟩ 2 MAINTAIN : afirmar, sostener ⟨they claim it's theirs : sostienen que es suyo⟩

claim² n 1 DEMAND : demanda f, reclamación f 2 DECLARATION : declaración f, afirmación f 3 **to stake a claim** : reclamar, reivindicar

claimant [ˈkleɪmənt] n : demandante mf (ante un juez), pretendiente mf (al trono, etc.)

clairvoyance [klærˈvɔɪənts] n : clarividencia f

clairvoyant¹ [klærˈvɔɪənt] adj : clarividente

clairvoyant² n : clarividente mf

clam [ˈklæm] n : almeja f

clamber [ˈklæmbər] vi : treparse o subirse torpemente

clammy [ˈklæmi] adj **-mier; -est** : húmedo y algo frío

clamor¹ [ˈklæmər] vi : gritar, clamar

clamor² n : clamor m

clamorous [ˈklæmərəs] adj : clamoroso, ruidoso, estrepitoso

clamp¹ [ˈklæmp] vt : sujetar con abrazaderas

clamp² n : abrazadera f

clan [ˈklæn] n : clan m

clandestine [klænˈdɛstɪn] adj : clandestino, secreto

clang¹ [ˈklæŋ] vi : hacer resonar (dícese de un objeto metálico)

clang² n : ruido m metálico fuerte

clangor [ˈklæŋər, -gər] n : estruendo m metálico

clank¹ [ˈklæŋk] vi : producir un ruido metálico seco

clank² n : ruido m metálico seco

clannish [ˈklænɪʃ] adj : exclusivista

clap¹ [ˈklæp] v **clapped; clapping** vt 1 SLAP, STRIKE : golpear ruidosamente, dar una palmada ⟨to clap one's hands : batir palmas, dar palmadas⟩ 2 APPLAUD : aplaudir — vi APPLAUD : aplaudir

clap² n 1 SLAP : palmada f, golpecito m 2 NOISE : ruido m seco ⟨a clap of thunder : un trueno⟩

clapboard [ˈklæbərd, ˈklæpˌbord] n : tabla f de madera (para revestir muros)

clapper [ˈklæpər] n : badajo m (de una campana)

clarification [ˌklærəfəˈkeɪʃən] n : clarificación f

clarify [ˈklærəˌfaɪ] vt **-fied; -fying** 1 EXPLAIN : aclarar 2 : clarificar (un líquido)

clarinet [ˌklærəˈnɛt] n : clarinete m

clarion [ˈklæriən] adj : claro y sonoro

clarity [ˈklærəti] n : claridad f, nitidez f

clash¹ [ˈklæʃ] vi 1 : sonar, chocarse ⟨the cymbals clashed : los platillos sonaron⟩ 2 : chocar, enfrentarse ⟨the students clashed with the police : los estudiantes se enfrentaron con la policía⟩ 3 CONFLICT : estar en conflicto, oponerse 4 : desentonar (dícese de los colores), coincidir (dícese de los datos)

clash² n 1 : ruido m (producido por un choque) 2 CONFLICT, CONFRONTATION : enfrentamiento m, conflicto m, choque m 3 : desentono m (de colores), coincidencia f (de datos)

clasp¹ [ˈklæsp] vt 1 FASTEN : sujetar, abrochar 2 EMBRACE, GRASP : agarrar, sujetar, abrazar

clasp² n 1 FASTENING : broche m, cierre m 2 EMBRACE, SQUEEZE : apretón m, abrazo m

class¹ [ˈklæs] vt : clasificar, catalogar

class² n 1 KIND, TYPE : clase f, tipo m, especie f 2 : clase f, rango m social ⟨the working class : la clase obrera⟩ 3 LESSON : clase f, curso m ⟨English class : clase de inglés⟩ 4 : conjunto m de estudiantes, clase f ⟨the class of '97 : la promoción del 97⟩

classic¹ [ˈklæsɪk] adj : clásico

classic² n : clásico m, obra f clásica

classical [ˈklæsɪkəl] adj : clásico — **classically** [-kli] adv

classicism [ˈklæsəˌsɪzəm] n : clasicismo m

classification [ˌklæsəfəˈkeɪʃən] n : clasificación f

classified [ˈklæsəˌfaɪd] adj 1 : clasificado ⟨classified ads : avisos clasificados⟩ 2 RESTRICTED : confidencial, secreto ⟨classified documents : documentos secretos⟩

classify [ˈklæsəˌfaɪ] vt -fied; -fying : clasificar, catalogar

classless [ˈklæsləs] adj : sin clases

classmate [ˈklæsˌmeɪt] n : compañero m, -ra f de clase

classroom [ˈklæsˌruːm] n : aula f, salón m de clase

clatter[1] [ˈklætər] vi : traquetear, hacer ruido

clatter[2] n : traqueteo m, ruido m, estrépito m

clause [ˈklɔz] n : cláusula f

claustrophobia [ˌklɔstrəˈfoːbiə] n : claustrofobia f

claustrophobic [ˌklɔstrəˈfoːbɪk] adj : claustrofóbico

clavicle [ˈklævɪkəl] n : clavícula f

claw[1] [ˈklɔ] v : arañar

claw[2] n : garra f, uña f (de un gato), pinza f (de un crustáceo)

clay [ˈkleɪ] n : arcilla f, barro m

clayey [ˈkleɪi] adj : arcilloso

clean[1] [ˈkliːn] vt : limpiar, lavar, asear

clean[2] adv : limpio, limpiamente ⟨to play clean : jugar limpio⟩

clean[3] adj 1 : limpio 2 UNADULTERATED : puro 3 IRREPROACHABLE : intachable, sin mancha ⟨to have a clean record : no tener antecedentes penales⟩ 4 DECENT : decente 5 COMPLETE : completo, absoluto ⟨a clean break with the past : un corte radical con el pasado⟩

cleaner [ˈkliːnər] n 1 : limpiador m, -dora f 2 : producto m de limpieza 3 DRY CLEANER : tintorería f (servicio)

cleanliness [ˈklɛnlinəs] n : limpieza f, aseo m

cleanly[1] [ˈkliːnli] adv : limpiamente, con limpieza

cleanly[2] [ˈklɛnli] adj -lier; -est : limpio, pulcro

cleanness [ˈkliːnnəs] n : limpieza f

cleanse [ˈklɛnz] vt cleansed; cleansing : limpiar, purificar

cleanser [ˈklɛnzər] n : limpiador m, purificador m

clear[1] [ˈklɪr] vt 1 CLARIFY : aclarar, clarificar (un líquido) 2 : despejar (una superficie), desatascar (un tubo), desmontar (una selva) ⟨to clear the table : levantar la mesa⟩ ⟨to clear one's throat : carraspear, aclararse la voz⟩ 3 EXONERATE : absolver, limpiar el nombre de 4 EARN : ganar, sacar (una ganancia de) 5 : pasar sin tocar ⟨he cleared the hurdle : saltó por encima de la valla⟩ 6 to clear up RESOLVE : aclarar, resolver, esclarecer — vi 1

DISPERSE : irse, despejarse, disiparse 2 : ser compensado (dícese de un cheque) 3 to clear up : despejar (dícese del tiempo), mejorarse (dícese de una enfermedad)

clear[2] adv : claro, claramente

clear[3] adj 1 BRIGHT : claro, lúcido 2 FAIR : claro, despejado 3 TRANSPARENT : transparente, translúcido 4 EVIDENT, UNMISTAKABLE : evidente, claro, obvio 5 CERTAIN : seguro 6 UNOBSTRUCTED : despejado, libre

clear[4] n 1 in the clear : inocente, libre de toda sospecha 2 in the clear SAFE : fuera de peligro

clearance [ˈklɪrənts] n 1 CLEARING : despeje m 2 SPACE : espacio m (libre), margen m 3 AUTHORIZATION : autorización f, despacho m (de la aduana)

clearing [ˈklɪrɪŋ] n : claro m (de un bosque)

clearly [ˈklɪrli] adv 1 DISTINCTLY : claramente, directamente 2 OBVIOUSLY : obviamente, evidentemente

cleat [ˈkliːt] n 1 : taco m 2 cleats npl : zapatos mpl deportivos (con tacos)

cleavage [ˈkliːvɪʤ] n 1 CLEFT : hendidura f, raja f 2 : escote m (del busto)

cleave[1] [ˈkliːv] vi cleaved [ˈkliːvd] or clove [ˈkloːv]; cleaving ADHERE : adherirse, unirse

cleave[2] vt cleaved; cleaving SPLIT : hender, dividir, partir

cleaver [ˈkliːvər] n : cuchilla f de carnicero

clef [ˈklɛf] n : clave f

cleft [ˈklɛft] n : hendidura f, raja f, grieta f

clemency [ˈklɛməntsi] n : clemencia f

clement [ˈklɛmənt] adj 1 MERCIFUL : clemente, piadoso 2 MILD : clemente, apacible

clench [ˈklɛntʃ] vt 1 CLUTCH : agarrar 2 TIGHTEN : apretar (el puño, los dientes)

clergy [ˈklərʤi] n, pl -gies : clero m

clergyman [ˈklərʤimən] n, pl -men [-mən, -ˌmɛn] : clérigo m

cleric [ˈklɛrɪk] n : clérigo m, -ga f

clerical [ˈklɛrɪkəl] adj 1 : clerical ⟨a clerical collar : un alzacuello⟩ 2 : de oficina ⟨clerical staff : personal de oficina⟩

clerk[1] [ˈklərk, Brit ˈklɑrk] vi : trabajar de oficinista, trabajar de dependiente

clerk[2] n 1 : funcionario m, -ria f (de una oficina gubernamental) 2 : oficinista mf, empleado m, -da f de oficina 3 SALESPERSON : dependiente m, -ta f

clever [ˈklɛvər] adj 1 SKILLFUL : ingenioso, hábil 2 SMART : listo, inteligente, astuto

cleverly [ˈklɛvərli] adv 1 SKILLFULLY : ingeniosamente, hábilmente 2 INTELLIGENTLY : inteligentemente

cleverness [ˈklɛvərnəs] n 1 SKILL : ingenio m, habilidad f 2 INTELLIGENCE : inteligencia f

clew [ˈkluː] → **clue**

cliché [kliˈʃeɪ] n : cliché m, tópico m

click¹ [ˈklɪk] vt 1 : chasquear (los dedos, etc.) ⟨to click one's heels : dar un taconazo⟩ 2 : hacer clic en (un botón, etc.) — vi 1 : hacer clic 2 SNAP : chasquear 3 SUCCEED : tener éxito 4 GET ALONG : congeniar, llevarse bien

click² n : chasquido m (de los dedos, etc.), clic m (de un botón, etc.)

client [ˈklaɪənt] n : cliente m, -ta f

clientele [ˌklaɪənˈtɛl, ˌkliː-] n : clientela f

cliff [ˈklɪf] n : acantilado m, precipicio m, risco m

climate [ˈklaɪmət] n : clima m

climatic [klaɪˈmætɪk, klə-] adj : climático

climax¹ [ˈklaɪˌmæks] vi : llegar al punto culminante, culminar — vt : ser el punto culminante de

climax² n : clímax m, punto m culminante

climb¹ [ˈklaɪm] vt : escalar, trepar a, subir ⟨to climb a mountain : escalar una montaña⟩ — vi 1 RISE : subir, ascender ⟨prices are climbing : los precios están subiendo⟩ 2 : subirse, treparse ⟨to climb up a tree : treparse a un árbol⟩

climb² n : ascenso m, subida f

climber [ˈklaɪmər] n 1 : escalador m, -dora f ⟨a mountain climber : un alpinista⟩ 2 : trepadora f (planta)

clinch¹ [ˈklɪntʃ] vt 1 FASTEN, SECURE : remachar (un clavo), afianzar, abrochar 2 SETTLE : decidir, cerrar ⟨to clinch the title : ganar el título⟩

clinch² n : abrazo m, clinch m (en el boxeo)

clincher [ˈklɪntʃər] n : argumento m decisivo

cling [ˈklɪŋ] vi **clung** [ˈklʌŋ]; **clinging** 1 STICK : adherirse, pegarse 2 : aferrarse, agarrarse ⟨he clung to the railing : se aferró a la barandilla⟩

clinic [ˈklɪnɪk] n : clínica f

clinical [ˈklɪnɪkəl] adj : clínico — **clinically** [-kli] adv

clink¹ [ˈklɪŋk] vi : tintinear

clink² n : tintineo m

clip¹ [ˈklɪp] vt **clipped; clipping** 1 CUT : cortar, recortar 2 HIT : golpear, dar un puñetazo a 3 FASTEN : sujetar (con un clip)

clip² n 1 → **clippers** 2 BLOW : golpe m, puñetazo m 3 PACE : paso m rápido 4 FASTENER : clip m ⟨a paper clip : un sujetapapeles⟩

clipper [ˈklɪpər] n 1 : clíper m (buque de vela) 2 **clippers** npl : tijeras fpl ⟨nail clippers : cortaúñas⟩

clique [ˈkliːk, ˈklɪk] n : grupo m exclusivo, camarilla f (de políticos)

clitoris [ˈklɪtərəs, klɪˈtɔrəs] n, pl **clitorides** [-ˈtɔrəˌdiːz] : clítoris m

cloak¹ [ˈkloːk] vt : encubrir, envolver (en un manto de)

cloak² n : capa f, capote m, manto m ⟨under the cloak of darkness : al amparo de la oscuridad⟩

clobber [ˈklɑbər] vt : dar una paliza a

clock¹ [ˈklɑk] vt : cronometrar

clock² n 1 : reloj m (de pared), cronómetro m (en deportes o competencias) 2 **around the clock** : las veinticuatro horas

clockwise [ˈklɑkˌwaɪz] adv & adj : en la dirección de las manecillas del reloj

clockwork [ˈklɑkˌwərk] n : mecanismo m de relojería

clod [ˈklɑd] n 1 : terrón m 2 OAF : zoquete mf

clog¹ [ˈklɑg] v **clogged; clogging** vt 1 HINDER : estorbar, impedir 2 BLOCK : atascar, tapar — vi : atascarse, taparse

clog² n 1 OBSTACLE : traba f, impedimento m, estorbo m 2 : zueco m (zapato)

cloister¹ [ˈklɔɪstər] vt : enclaustrar

cloister² n : claustro m

clone [ˈkloːn] n 1 : clon m (de un organismo) 2 COPY : copia f, reproducción f

close¹ [ˈkloːz] v **closed; closing** vt : cerrar — vi 1 : cerrarse, cerrar 2 TERMINATE : concluirse, terminar 3 **to close in** APPROACH : acercarse, aproximarse

close² [ˈkloːs] adv : cerca, de cerca

close³ adj **closer; closest** 1 CONFINING : restrictivo, estrecho 2 SECRETIVE : reservado 3 STRICT : estricto, detallado 4 STUFFY : cargado, bochornoso (dícese del tiempo) 5 TIGHT : apretado, entallado, ceñido ⟨it's a close fit : es muy apretado⟩ 6 NEAR : cercano, próximo 7 INTIMATE : íntimo ⟨close friends : amigos íntimos⟩ 8 ACCURATE : fiel, exacto 9 : reñido ⟨a close election : una elección muy reñida⟩

close⁴ [ˈkloːz] n : fin m, final m, conclusión f

closely [ˈkloːsli] adv : cerca, de cerca

closeness [ˈkloːsnəs] n 1 NEARNESS : cercanía f, proximidad f 2 INTIMACY : intimidad f

closet¹ [ˈklɑzət] vt **to be closeted with** : estar encerrado con

closet² n : armario m, guardarropa f, clóset m

closure [ˈkloːʒər] n 1 CLOSING, END : cierre m, clausura f, fin m 2 FASTENER : cierre m

clot¹ [ˈklɑt] v **clotted; clotting** vt : coagular, cuajar — vi : cuajarse, coagularse

clot² n : coágulo m

cloth [ˈklɑθ] n, pl **cloths** [ˈklɑðz, ˈklɑθs] 1 FABRIC : tela f 2 RAG : trapo m 3 TABLECLOTH : mantel m

clothe [ˈkloːð] vt **clothed** or **clad** [ˈklæd]; **clothing** DRESS : vestir, arropar, ataviar

clothes [ˈkloːz, ˈkloːðz] npl 1 CLOTHING : ropa f 2 BEDCLOTHES : ropa f de cama

clothespin [ˈkloːzˌpɪn] n : pinza f (para la ropa)

clothing [ˈkloːðɪŋ] *n* : ropa *f*, indumentaria *f*

cloud¹ [ˈklaʊd] *vt* : nublar, oscurecer — *vi* **to cloud over** : nublarse

cloud² *n* : nube *f*

cloudburst [ˈklaʊdˌbərst] *n* : chaparrón *m*, aguacero *m*

cloudless [ˈklaʊdləs] *adj* : despejado, claro

cloudy [ˈklaʊdi] *adj* **cloudier; -est** : nublado, nuboso

clout¹ [ˈklaʊt] *vt* : bofetear, dar un tortazo a

clout² *n* **1** BLOW : golpe *m*, tortazo *m* *fam* **2** INFLUENCE : influencia *f*, palanca *f* *fam*

clove¹ [ˈkloːv] *n* **1** : diente *m* (de ajo) **2** : clavo *m* (especia)

clove² → **cleave**

cloven hoof [ˈkloːvən] *n* : pezuña *f* hendida

clover [ˈkloːvər] *n* : trébol *m*

cloverleaf [ˈkloːvərˌliːf] *n*, *pl* **-leafs** *or* **-leaves** [-ˌliːvz] : intersección *f* en trébol

clown¹ [ˈklaʊn] *vi* : payasear, bromear ⟨stop clowning around : déjate de payasadas⟩

clown² *n* : payaso *m*, -sa *f*

clownish [ˈklaʊnɪʃ] *adj* **1** : de payaso **2** BOORISH : grosero — **clownishly** *adv*

cloying [ˈklɔɪɪŋ] *adj* : empalagoso, meloso

club¹ [ˈklʌb] *vt* **clubbed; clubbing** : aporrear, dar garrotazos a

club² *n* **1** CUDGEL : garrote *m*, porra *f* **2** : palo *m* ⟨golf club : palo de golf⟩ **3** : trébol *m* (naipe) **4** ASSOCIATION : club *m*

clubfoot [ˈklʌbˌfʊt] *n*, *pl* **-feet** : pie *m* deforme

clubhouse [ˈklʌbˌhaʊs] *n* : sede *f* de un club

cluck¹ [ˈklʌk] *vi* : cloquear, cacarear

cluck² *n* : cloqueo *m*, cacareo *m*

clue¹ [ˈkluː] *vt* **clued; clueing** *or* **cluing** *or* **to clue in** : dar una pista a, informar

clue² *n* : pista *f*, indicio *m*

clump¹ [ˈklʌmp] *vi* **1** : caminar con pisadas fuertes **2** LUMP : agruparse, aglutinarse — *vt* : amontonar

clump² *n* **1** : grupo *m* (de arbustos o árboles), terrón *m* (de tierra) **2** : pisada *f* fuerte

clumsily [ˈklʌmzəli] *adv* : torpemente, sin gracia

clumsiness [ˈklʌmzinəs] *n* : torpeza *f*

clumsy [ˈklʌmzi] *adj* **-sier; -est 1** AWKWARD : torpe, desmañado **2** TACTLESS : carente de tacto, poco delicado

clung → **cling**

clunky [ˈklʌŋki] *adj* : torpe, poco elegante

cluster¹ [ˈklʌstər] *vt* : agrupar, juntar — *vi* : agruparse, apiñarse, arracimarse

cluster² *n* : grupo *m*, conjunto *m*, racimo *m* (de uvas)

clutch¹ [ˈklʌtʃ] *vt* : agarrar, asir — *vi* **to clutch at** : tratar de agarrar

clutch² *n* **1** GRASP, GRIP : agarre *m*, apretón *m* **2** : embrague *m*, clutch *m* (de una máquina) **3** clutches *npl* : garras *fpl* ⟨he fell into their clutches : cayó en sus garras⟩

clutter¹ [ˈklʌtər] *vt* : atiborrar o atestar de cosas, llenar desordenadamente

clutter² *n* : desorden *m*, revoltijo *m*

coach¹ [ˈkoːtʃ] *vt* : entrenar (atletas, artistas), preparar (alumnos)

coach² *n* **1** CARRIAGE : coche *m*, carruaje *m*, carroza *f* **2** : vagón *m* de pasajeros (de un tren) **3** BUS : autobús *m*, ómnibus *m* **4** : pasaje *m* aéreo de segunda clase **5** TRAINER : entrenador *m*, -dora *f*

coagulate [koˈægjəˌleɪt] *v* **-lated; -lating** *vt* : coagular, cuajar — *vi* : coagularse, cuajarse

coal [ˈkoːl] *n* **1** EMBER : ascua *f*, brasa *f* **2** : carbón *m* ⟨a coal mine : una mina de carbón⟩

coalesce [ˌkoːəˈlɛs] *vi* **-alesced; -alescing** : unirse

coalition [ˌkoːəˈlɪʃən] *n* : coalición *f*

coarse [ˈkors] *adj* **coarser; -est 1** : grueso (dícese de la arena o la sal), basto (dícese de las telas), áspero (dícese de la piel) **2** CRUDE, ROUGH : basto, tosco, ordinario **3** VULGAR : grosero — **coarsely** *adv*

coarsen [ˈkorsən] *vt* : hacer áspero o basto — *vi* : volverse áspero o basto

coarseness [ˈkorsnəs] *n* : aspereza *f*, tosquedad *f*

coast¹ [ˈkoːst] *vi* : deslizarse, rodar sin impulso

coast² *n* : costa *f*, litoral *m*

coastal [ˈkoːstəl] *adj* : costero

coaster [ˈkoːstər] *n* : posavasos *m*

coast guard *n* : guardia *f* costera, guardacostas *mpl*

coastline [ˈkoːstˌlaɪn] *n* : costa *f*

coat¹ [ˈkoːt] *vt* : cubrir, revestir, bañar (en un líquido)

coat² *n* **1** : abrigo *m* ⟨a sport coat : una chaqueta, un saco⟩ **2** : pelaje *m* (de animales) **3** LAYER : capa *f*, mano *f* (de pintura)

coating [ˈkoːtɪŋ] *n* : capa *f*

coat of arms *n* : escudo *m* de armas

coax [ˈkoːks] *vt* : engatusar, persuadir

cob [ˈkab] → **corncob**

cobalt [ˈkoːˌbɔlt] *n* : cobalto *m*

cobble [ˈkabəl] *vt* **cobbled; cobbling 1** : fabricar o remendar (zapatos) **2 to cobble together** : improvisar, hacer apresuradamente

cobbler [ˈkablər] *n* **1** SHOEMAKER : zapatero *m*, -ra *f* **2 fruit cobbler** : tarta *f* de fruta

cobblestone [ˈkabəlˌstoːn] *n* : adoquín *m*

cobra [ˈkoːbrə] *n* : cobra *f*

cobweb [ˈkabˌwɛb] *n* : telaraña *f*

coca [ˈkoːkə] *n* : coca *f*

cocaine [ko:'keɪn, 'ko:ˌkeɪn] n : cocaína f

cock¹ ['kɑk] vt 1 : ladear ⟨to cock one's head : ladear la cabeza⟩ 2 : montar, amartillar (un arma de fuego)

cock² n 1 ROOSTER : gallo m 2 FAUCET : grifo m, llave f 3 : martillo m (de un arma de fuego)

cockatoo ['kɑkəˌtu:] n, pl **-toos** : cacatúa f

cockeyed ['kɑkˌaɪd] adj 1 ASKEW : ladeado, torcido, chueco 2 ABSURD : disparatado, absurdo

cockfight ['kɑkˌfaɪt] n : pelea f de gallos

cockiness ['kɑkinəs] n : arrogancia f

cockle ['kɑkəl] n : berberecho m

cockpit ['kɑkˌpɪt] n : cabina f

cockroach ['kɑkˌro:tʃ] n : cucaracha f

cocktail ['kɑkˌteɪl] n 1 : coctel m, cóctel m 2 APPETIZER : aperitivo m

cocky ['kɑki] adj **cockier; -est** : creído, engreído

cocoa ['ko:ˌko:] n 1 CACAO : cacao m 2 : cocoa f, chocolate m (bebida)

coconut ['ko:kəˌnʌt] n : coco m

cocoon [kə'ku:n] n : capullo m

cod ['kɑd] n, pl **cod** : bacalao m

coddle ['kɑdəl] vt **-dled; -dling** : mimar, consentir

code ['ko:d] n 1 : código m ⟨civil code : código civil⟩ 2 : código m, clave f ⟨secret code : clave secreta⟩

codeine ['ko:ˌdi:n] n : codeína f

codex ['ko:ˌdɛks] n, pl **-dexes** [-ˌdɛksəz] or **-dices** [-dəˌsi:z] : códice m

codger ['kɑdʒər] n : viejo m, vejete m

codify ['kɑdəˌfaɪ, 'ko:-] vt **-fied; -fying** : codificar

coeducation [ˌko:ˌɛdʒə'keɪʃən] n : coeducación f, enseñanza f mixta

coeducational [ˌko:ˌɛdʒə'keɪʃənəl] adj : mixto

coefficient [ˌko:ə'fɪʃənt] n : coeficiente m

coerce [ko:'ərs] vt **-erced; -ercing** : coaccionar, forzar, obligar

coercion [ko:'ərʒən, -ʃən] n : coacción f

coercive [ko:'ərsɪv] adj : coactivo

coexist [ˌko:ɪg'zɪst] vi : coexistir

coexistence [ˌko:ɪg'zɪstənts] n : coexistencia f

coffee ['kɔfi] n : café m

coffeepot ['kɔfiˌpɑt] n : cafetera f

coffee table n : mesa f de centro

coffer ['kɔfər] n : cofre m

coffin ['kɔfən] n : ataúd m, féretro m

cog ['kɑg] n : diente m (de una rueda dentada)

cogent ['ko:dʒənt] adj : convincente, persuasivo

cogitate ['kɑdʒəˌteɪt] vi **-tated; -tating** : reflexionar, meditar, discurrir

cogitation [ˌkɑdʒə'teɪʃən] n : reflexión f, meditación f

cognac ['ko:nˌjæk] n : coñac m

cognate ['kɑgˌneɪt] adj : relacionado, afín

cognition [kɑg'nɪʃən] n : cognición f

cognitive ['kɑgnətɪv] adj : cognitivo

cogwheel ['kɑgˌʍi:l] n : rueda f dentada

cohabit [ˌko:'hæbət] vi : cohabitar

cohere [ko:'hɪr] vi **-hered; -hering** 1 ADHERE : adherirse, pegarse 2 : ser coherente o congruente

coherence [ko:'hɪrənts] n : coherencia f, congruencia f

coherent [ko:'hɪrənt] adj : coherente, congruente — **coherently** adv

cohesion [ko:'hi:ʒən] n : cohesión f

cohesive [ko:'hi:sɪv, -zɪv] adj : cohesivo

cohort ['ko:ˌhɔrt] n 1 : cohorte f (de soldados) 2 COMPANION : compañero m, -ra f; colega mf

coiffure [kwɑ'fjʊr] n : peinado m

coil¹ ['kɔɪl] vt : enrollar — vi : enrollarse, enroscarse

coil² n : rollo m (de cuerda, etc.), espiral f (de humo)

coin¹ ['kɔɪn] vt 1 MINT : acuñar (moneda) 2 INVENT : acuñar, crear, inventar ⟨to coin a phrase : como se suele decir⟩

coin² n : moneda f

coincide [ˌko:ɪn'saɪd, 'ko:ɪnˌsaɪd] vi **-cided; -ciding** : coincidir

coincidence [ko:'ɪntsədənts] n : coincidencia f, casualidad f ⟨what a coincidence! : ¡qué casualidad!⟩

coincident [ko:'ɪntsədənt] adj : coincidente, concurrente

coincidental [ko:ˌɪntsə'dɛntəl] adj : casual, accidental, fortuito

coitus ['ko:ətəs] n : coito m

coke ['ko:k] n : coque m

colander ['kɑləndər, 'kʌ-] n : colador m

cold¹ ['ko:ld] adj : frío ⟨it's cold out : hace frío⟩ ⟨a cold reception : una fría recepción⟩ ⟨in cold blood : a sangre fría⟩

cold² n 1 : frío m ⟨to feel the cold : sentir frío⟩ 2 : resfriado m, catarro m ⟨to catch a cold : resfriarse⟩

cold-blooded ['ko:ld'blʌdəd] adj 1 CRUEL : cruel, despiadado 2 : de sangre fría (dícese de los reptiles, etc.)

coldly ['ko:ldli] adv : fríamente, con frialdad

coldness ['ko:ldnəs] n : frialdad f (de una persona o una actitud), frío m (de la temperatura)

coleslaw ['ko:lˌslɔ] n : ensalada f de col

colic ['kɑlɪk] n : cólico m

coliseum [ˌkɑlə'si:əm] n : coliseo m, arena f

collaborate [kə'læbəˌreɪt] vi **-rated; -rating** : colaborar

collaboration [kəˌlæbə'reɪʃən] n : colaboración f

collaborator [kə'læbəˌreɪtər] n 1 COLLEAGUE : colaborador m, -dora f 2 TRAITOR : colaboracionista mf

collage [kə'lɑʒ] n : collage m

collapse¹ [kə'læps] vi **-lapsed; -lapsing** 1 : derrumbarse, desplomarse, hundirse ⟨the building collapsed : el edificio se derrumbó⟩ **2** FALL : desplomarse, caerse ⟨he collapsed on the bed : se desplomó en la cama⟩ ⟨to collapse with laughter : morirse de risa⟩ **3** FAIL : fracasar, quebrar, arruinarse **4** FOLD : plegarse

collapse[2] *n* **1** FALL : derrumbe *m*, desplome *m* **2** BREAKDOWN, FAILURE : fracaso *m*, colapso *m* (físico), quiebra *f* (económica)

collapsible [kəˈlæpsəbəl] *adj* : plegable

collar[1] [ˈkɑlər] *vt* : agarrar, atrapar

collar[2] *n* : cuello *m*

collarbone [ˈkɑlərˌboːn] *n* : clavícula *f*

collate [kəˈleɪt; ˈkɑˌleɪt, ˈkoː-] *vt* **-lated; -lating 1** COMPARE : cotejar, comparar **2** : ordenar, recopilar (páginas)

collateral[1] [kəˈlætərəl] *adj* : colateral

collateral[2] *n* : garantía *f*, fianza *f*, prenda *f*

colleague [ˈkɑˌliːg] *n* : colega *mf*; compañero *m*, -ra *f*

collect[1] [kəˈlɛkt] *vt* **1** GATHER : recopilar, reunir, recoger ⟨she collected her thoughts : puso en orden sus ideas⟩ **2** : coleccionar, juntar ⟨to collect stamps : coleccionar timbres⟩ **3** : cobrar (una deuda), recaudar (un impuesto) **4** DRAW : cobrar, percibir (un sueldo, etc.) — *vi* **1** ACCUMULATE : acumularse, juntarse **2** CONGREGATE : congregarse, reunirse

collect[2] *adv & adj* : por cobrar, a cobro revertido

collectible *or* **collectable** [kəˈlɛktəbəl] *adj* : coleccionable

collection [kəˈlɛkʃən] *n* **1** COLLECTING : colecta *f* (de contribuciones), cobro *m* (de deudas), recaudación *f* (de impuestos) **2** GROUP : colección *f* (de objetos), grupo *m* (de personas)

collective[1] [kəˈlɛktɪv] *adj* : colectivo — **collectively** *adv*

collective[2] *n* : colectivo *m*

collector [kəˈlɛktər] *n* **1** : coleccionista *mf* (de objetos) **2** : cobrador *m*, -dora *f* (de deudas)

college [ˈkɑlɪdʒ] *n* **1** : universidad *f* **2** : colegio *m* (de electores o profesionales)

collegiate [kəˈliːdʒət] *adj* : universitario

collide [kəˈlaɪd] *vi* **-lided; -liding** : chocar, colisionar, estrellarse

collie [ˈkɑli] *n* : collie *mf*

collision [kəˈlɪʒən] *n* : choque *m*, colisión *f*

colloquial [kəˈloːkwiəl] *adj* : coloquial

colloquialism [kəˈloːkwiəˌlɪzəm] *n* : expresión *f* coloquial

collusion [kəˈluːʒən] *n* : colusión *f*

cologne [kəˈloːn] *n* : colonia *f*

Colombian [kəˈlʌmbiən] *n* : colombiano *m*, -na *f* — **Colombian** *adj*

colon[1] [ˈkoːlən] *n, pl* **colons** *or* **cola** [-lə] : colon *m* (de los intestinos)

colon[2] *n, pl* **colons** : dos puntos *mpl* (signo ortográfico)

colonel [ˈkərnəl] *n* : coronel *m*

colonial[1] [kəˈloːniəl] *adj* : colonial

colonial[2] *n* : colono *m*, -na *f*

colonist [ˈkɑlənɪst] *n* : colono *m*, -na *f*; colonizador *m*, -dora *f*

colonization [ˌkɑlənəˈzeɪʃən] *n* : colonización *f*

colonize [ˈkɑləˌnaɪz] *vt* **-nized; -nizing 1** : establecer una colonia en **2** SETTLE : colonizar

colonnade [ˌkɑləˈneɪd] *n* : columnata *f*

colony [ˈkɑləni] *n, pl* **-nies** : colonia *f*

color[1] [ˈkʌlər] *vt* **1** : colorear, pintar **2** INFLUENCE : influir en, influenciar — *vi* BLUSH : sonrojarse, ruborizarse

color[2] *n* **1** : color *m* ⟨primary colors : colores primarios⟩ **2** INTEREST, VIVIDNESS : color *m*, colorido *m* ⟨local color : color local⟩

coloration [ˌkʌləˈreɪʃən] *n* : coloración *f*

color-blind [ˈkʌlərˌblaɪnd] *adj* : daltónico

color blindness *n* : daltonismo *m*

colored [ˈkʌlərd] *adj* **1** : de color (dícese de los objetos) **2** : de color, negro (dícese de las personas)

colorfast [ˈkʌlərˌfæst] *adj* : que no se destiñe

colorful [ˈkʌlərfəl] *adj* **1** : lleno de colorido, de colores vivos **2** PICTURESQUE, STRIKING : pintoresco, llamativo

coloring [ˈkələrɪŋ] *n* **1** : color *m*, colorido *m* **2 food coloring** : colorante *m*

colorless [ˈkʌlərləs] *adj* **1** : incoloro, sin color **2** DULL : soso, aburrido

colossal [kəˈlɑsəl] *adj* : colosal

colossus [kəˈlɑsəs] *n, pl* **-si** [-ˌsaɪ] : coloso *m*

colt [ˈkoːlt] *n* : potro *m*, potranco *m*

column [ˈkɑləm] *n* : columna *f*

columnist [ˈkɑləmnɪst, -ləmɪst] *n* : columnista *mf*

coma [ˈkoːmə] *n* : coma *m*, estado *m* de coma

Comanche [kəˈmæntʃi] *n* : comanche *mf* — **Comanche** *adj*

comatose [ˈkoːməˌtoːs, ˈkɑ-] *adj* : comatoso, en estado de coma

comb[1] [ˈkoːm] *vt* **1** : peinar (el pelo) **2** SEARCH : peinar, rastrear, registrar a fondo

comb[2] *n* **1** : peine *m* **2** : cresta *f* (de un gallo)

combat[1] [kəmˈbæt, ˈkɑmˌbæt] *vt* **-bated** *or* **-batted; -bating** *or* **-batting** : combatir, luchar contra

combat[2] [ˈkɑmˌbæt] *n* : combate *m*, lucha *f*

combatant [kəmˈbætənt] *n* : combatiente *mf*

combative [kəmˈbætɪv] *adj* : combativo

combination [ˌkɑmbəˈneɪʃən] *n* : combinación *f*

combine[1] [kəmˈbaɪn] *v* **-bined; -bining** *vt* : combinar, aunar — *vi* : combinarse, mezclarse

combine[2] [ˈkɑmˌbaɪn] *n* **1** ALLIANCE : alianza *f* comercial o política **2** HARVESTER : cosechadora *f*

combustible [kəm'bʌstəbəl] *adj* : inflamable, combustible

combustion [kəm'bʌstʃən] *n* : combustión *f*

come ['kʌm] *vi* **came** ['keɪm]; **come**; **coming** **1** APPROACH : venir, aproximarse ⟨here they come : acá vienen⟩ **2** ARRIVE : venir, llegar, alcanzar ⟨they came yesterday : vinieron ayer⟩ **3** ORIGINATE : venir, provenir ⟨this wine comes from France : este vino viene de Francia⟩ **4** AMOUNT : llegar, ascender ⟨the investment came to two million : la inversión llegó a dos millones⟩ **5 to come clean** : confesar, desahogar la conciencia **6 to come into** ACQUIRE : adquirir ⟨to come into a fortune : heredar una fortuna⟩ **7 to come off** SUCCEED : tener éxito, ser un éxito **8 to come out** : salir, aparecer, publicarse **9 to come to** REVIVE : recobrar el conocimiento, volver en sí **10 to come to pass** HAPPEN : acontecer **11 to come to terms** : llegar a un acuerdo

comeback ['kʌm,bæk] *n* **1** RETORT : réplica *f*, respuesta *f* **2** RETURN : retorno *m*, regreso *m* ⟨the champion announced his comeback : el campeón anunció su regreso⟩

come back *vi* **1** RETORT : replicar, contestar **2** RETURN : volver ⟨come back here! : ¡vuelve acá!⟩ ⟨that style's coming back : ese estilo está volviendo⟩

comedian [kə'miːdiən] *n* : cómico *m*, -ca *f*; humorista *mf*

comedienne [kə,miːdi'ɛn] *n* : cómica *f*, humorista *f*

comedy ['kɑmədi] *n, pl* **-dies** : comedia *f*

comely ['kʌmli] *adj* **-lier; -est** : bello, bonito

comet ['kɑmət] *n* : cometa *m*

comfort[1] ['kʌmpfərt] *vt* **1** CHEER : confortar, alentar **2** CONSOLE : consolar

comfort[2] *n* **1** CONSOLATION : consuelo *m* **2** WELL-BEING : confort *m*, bienestar *m* **3** CONVENIENCE : comodidad *f* ⟨the comforts of home : las comodidades del hogar⟩

comfortable ['kʌmpfərtəbəl, 'kʌmpftə-] *adj* : cómodo, confortable — **comfortably** ['kʌmpfərtəbli, 'kʌmpftə-] *adv*

comforter ['kʌmpfərtər] *n* QUILT : edredón *m*, cobertor *m*

comic[1] ['kɑmɪk] *adj* : cómico, humorístico

comic[2] *n* **1** COMEDIAN : cómico *m*, -ca *f*; humorista *mf* **2 or comic book** : historieta *f*, cómic *m*

comical ['kɑmɪkəl] *adj* : cómico, gracioso, chistoso

comic strip *n* : tira *f* cómica, historieta *f*

coming ['kʌmɪŋ] *adj* : siguiente, próximo, que viene

comma ['kɑmə] *n* : coma *f*

command[1] [kə'mænd] *vt* **1** ORDER : ordenar, mandar **2** CONTROL, DIRECT : comandar, tener el mando de — *vi* **1** : dar órdenes **2** GOVERN : estar al mando *m*, gobernar

command[2] *n* **1** CONTROL, LEADERSHIP : mando *m*, control *m*, dirección *f* **2** ORDER : orden *f*, mandato *m* **3** MASTERY : maestría *f*, destreza *f*, dominio *m* **4** : tropa *f* asignada a un comandante

commandant ['kɑmən,dɑnt, -,dænt] *n* : comandante *mf*

commandeer [,kɑmən'dɪr] *vt* : piratear, secuestrar (un vehículo, etc.)

commander [kə'mændər] *n* : comandante *mf*

commandment [kə'mændmənt] *n* : mandamiento *m*, orden *f* ⟨the Ten Commandments : los diez mandamientos⟩

commando [kə'mændoː] *n* : comando *m*

commemorate [kə'mɛmə,reɪt] *vt* **-rated; -rating** : conmemorar

commemoration [kə,mɛmə'reɪʃən] *n* : conmemoración *f*

commemorative [kə'mɛmrətɪv, -'mɛmə,reɪtɪv] *adj* : conmemorativo

commence [kə'mɛnts] *v* **-menced; -mencing** *vt* : iniciar, comenzar — *vi* : iniciarse, comenzar

commencement [kə'mɛntsmənt] *n* **1** BEGINNING : inicio *m*, comienzo *m* **2** : ceremonia *f* de graduación

commend [kə'mɛnd] *vt* **1** ENTRUST : encomendar **2** RECOMMEND : recomendar **3** PRAISE : elogiar, alabar

commendable [kə'mɛndəbəl] *adj* : loable, meritorio, encomiable

commendation [,kɑmən'deɪʃən, -,mɛn-] *n* : elogio *m*, encomio *m*

commensurate [kə'mɛntsərət, -'mɛntʃurət] *adj* : proporcionado ⟨commensurate with : en proporción a⟩

comment[1] ['kɑ,mɛnt] *vi* **1** : hacer comentarios **2 to comment on** : comentar, hacer observaciones sobre

comment[2] *n* : comentario *m*, observación *f*

commentary ['kɑmən,tɛri] *n, pl* **-taries** : comentario *m*, crónica *f* (deportiva)

commentator ['kɑmən,teɪtər] *n* : comentarista *mf*, cronista *mf* (de deportes)

commerce ['kɑmərs] *n* : comercio *m*

commercial[1] [kə'mərʃəl] *adj* : comercial — **commercially** *adv*

commercial[2] *n* : comercial *m*

commercialize [kə'mərʃə,laɪz] *vt* **-ized; -izing** : comercializar

commiserate [kə'mɪzə,reɪt] *vi* **-ated; -ating** : compadecerse, consolarse

commiseration [kə,mɪzə'reɪʃən] *n* : conmiseración *f*

commission[1] [kə'mɪʃən] *vt* **1** : nombrar (un oficial) **2** : comisionar, encargar ⟨to commission a painting : encargar una pintura⟩

commission[2] *n* **1** : nombramiento *m* (al grado de oficial) **2** COMMITTEE : comisión *f*, comité *m* **3** COMMITTING : comisión *f*, realización *f* (de un acto) **4** PERCENTAGE : comisión *f* ⟨sales commissions : comisiones de venta⟩

commissioned officer *n* : oficial *mf*

commissioner [kə'mɪʃənər] *n* **1** : comisionado *m*, -da *f*; miembro *m* de una comisión **2** : comisario *m*, -ria *f* (de policía, etc.)

commit [kə'mɪt] *vt* **-mitted; -mitting 1** ENTRUST : encomendar, confiar **2** CONFINE : internar (en un hospital), encarcelar (en una prisión) **3** PERPETRATE : cometer ⟨to commit a crime : cometer un crimen⟩ **4 to commit oneself** : comprometerse

commitment [kə'mɪtmənt] *n* **1** RESPONSIBILITY : compromiso *m*, responsabilidad *f* **2** DEDICATION : dedicación *f*, devoción *f* ⟨commitment to the cause : devoción a la causa⟩

committee [kə'mɪti] *n* : comité *m*

commodious [kə'mo:diəs] *adj* SPACIOUS : amplio, espacioso

commodity [kə'mɑdəti] *n, pl* **-ties** : artículo *m* de comercio, mercancía *f*, mercadería *f*

commodore ['kɑmə,dor] *n* : comodoro *m*

common[1] ['kɑmən] *adj* **1** PUBLIC : común, público ⟨the common good : el bien común⟩ **2** SHARED : común ⟨a common interest : un interés común⟩ **3** GENERAL : común, general ⟨it's common knowledge : todo el mundo lo sabe⟩ **4** ORDINARY : ordinario, común y corriente ⟨the common man : el hombre medio, el hombre de la calle⟩

common[2] *n* **1** : tierra *f* comunal **2 in ~** : en común

common cold *n* : resfriado *m* común

common denominator *n* : denominador *m* común

commoner ['kɑmənər] *n* : plebeyo *m*, -ya *f*

commonly ['kɑmənli] *adv* **1** FREQUENTLY : comúnmente, frecuentemente **2** USUALLY : normalmente

common noun *n* : nombre *m* común

commonplace[1] ['kɑmən,pleɪs] *adj* : común, ordinario

commonplace[2] *n* : cliché *m*, tópico *m*

common sense *n* : sentido *m* común

commonwealth ['kɑmən,wɛlθ] *n* : entidad *f* política ⟨the British Commonwealth : la Mancomunidad Británica⟩

commotion [kə'mo:ʃən] *n* **1** RUCKUS : alboroto *m*, jaleo *m*, escándalo *m* **2** STIR, UPSET : revuelo *m*, conmoción *f*

communal [kə'mju:nəl] *adj* : comunal

commune[1] [kə'mju:n] *vi* **-muned; -muning** : estar en comunión

commune[2] ['kɑ,mju:n, kə'mju:n] *n* : comuna *f*

communicable [kə'mju:nɪkəbəl] *adj* CONTAGIOUS : transmisible, contagioso

communicate [kə'mju:nə,keɪt] *v* **-cated; -cating** *vt* **1** CONVEY : comunicar, expresar, hacer saber **2** TRANSMIT : transmitir (una enfermedad), contagiar — *vi* : comunicarse, expresarse

communication [kə,mju:nə'keɪʃən] *n* : comunicación *f*

communicative [kə'mju:nɪ,keɪtɪv, -kətɪv] *adj* : comunicativo

communion [kə'mju:njən] *n* **1** SHARING : comunión *f* **2 Communion** : comunión *f*, eucaristía *f*

communiqué [kə'mju:nə,keɪ, -,mju:nə'keɪ] *n* : comunicado *m*

communism *or* **Communism** ['kɑmjə,nɪzəm] *n* : comunismo *m*

communist[1] *or* **Communist** ['kɑmjə,nɪst] *adj* : comunista ⟨the Communist Party : el Partido Comunista⟩

communist[2] *or* **Communist** *n* : comunista *mf*

communistic *or* **Communistic** [,kɑmjə'nɪstɪk] *adj* : comunista

community [kə'mju:nəti] *n, pl* **-ties** : comunidad *f*

commute [kə'mju:t] *v* **-muted; -muting** *vt* REDUCE : conmutar, reducir (una sentencia) — *vi* : viajar de la residencia al trabajo

commuter [kə'mju:tər] *n* : persona *f* que viaja diariamente al trabajo

compact[1] [kəm'pækt, 'kɑm,pækt] *vt* : compactar, consolidar, comprimir

compact[2] [kəm'pækt, 'kɑm,pækt] *adj* **1** DENSE, SOLID : compacto, macizo, denso **2** CONCISE : breve, conciso

compact[3] ['kɑm,pækt] *n* **1** AGREEMENT : acuerdo *m*, pacto *m* **2** : polvera *f*, estuche *m* de maquillaje **3** *or* **compact car** : auto *m* compacto

compact disc ['kɑm,pækt'dɪsk] *n* : disco *m* compacto, compact disc *m*

compactly [kəm'pæktli, 'kɑm,pækt-] *adv* **1** DENSELY : densamente, macizamente **2** CONCISELY : concisamente, brevemente

companion [kəm'pænjən] *n* **1** COMRADE : compañero *m*, -ra *f*; acompañante *mf* **2** MATE : pareja *f* (de un zapato, etc.)

companionable [kəm'pænjənəbəl] *adj* : sociable, amigable

companionship [kəm'pænjən,ʃɪp] *n* : compañerismo *m*, camaradería *f*

company ['kʌmpəni] *n, pl* **-nies 1** FIRM : compañía *f*, empresa *f* **2** GROUP : compañía *f* (de actores o soldados) **3** GUESTS : visita *f* ⟨we have company : tenemos visita⟩

comparable ['kɑmpərəbəl] *adj* : comparable, parecido

comparative[1] [kəm'pærətɪv] *adj* RELATIVE : comparativo, relativo — **comparatively** *adv*

comparative[2] *n* : comparativo *m*

compare¹ [kəm'pær] v **-pared; -paring** vt : comparar — vi **to compare with** : poder comparar con, tener comparación con

compare² n : comparación f ⟨beyond compare : sin igual, sin par⟩

comparison [kəm'pærəsən] n : comparación f

compartment [kəm'pɑrtmənt] n : compartimiento m, compartimiento m

compass ['kʌmpəs, 'kam-] n **1** RANGE, SCOPE : alcance m, extensión f, límites mpl **2** : compás m (para trazar circunferencias) **3** : compás m, brújula f ⟨the points of the compass : los puntos cardinales⟩

compassion [kəm'pæʃən] n : compasión f, piedad f, misericordia f

compassionate [kəm'pæʃənət] adj : compasivo

compatibility [kəm,pætə'bɪləti] n : compatibilidad f

compatible [kəm'pætəbəl] adj : compatible, afín

compatriot [kəm'peɪtriət, -'pæ-] n : compatriota mf; paisano m, -na f

compel [kəm'pɛl] vt **-pelled; -pelling** : obligar, compeler

compelling [kəm'pɛliŋ] adj **1** FORCEFUL : fuerte **2** ENGAGING : absorbente **3** PERSUASIVE : persuasivo, convincente

compendium [kəm'pɛndiəm] n, pl **-diums** or **-dia** [-diə] : compendio m

compensate ['kɑmpən,seɪt] v **-sated; -sating** vi **to compensate for** : compensar — vt : indemnizar, compensar

compensation [,kɑmpən'seɪʃən] n : compensación f, indemnización f

compensatory [kəm'pɛntsə,tori] adj : compensatorio

compete [kəm'pi:t] vi **-peted; -peting** : competir, contender, rivalizar

competence ['kɑmpətənts] n : competencia f, aptitud f

competency ['kɑmpətəntsi] → **competence**

competent ['kɑmpətənt] adj : competente, capaz

competition [,kɑmpə'tɪʃən] n : competencia f, concurso m

competitive [kəm'pɛtətɪv] adj : competitivo

competitor [kəm'pɛtətər] n : competidor m, -dora f

compilation [,kɑmpə'leɪʃən] n : recopilación f, compilación f

compile [kəm'paɪl] vt **-piled; -piling** : compilar, recopilar

complacency [kəm'pleɪsəntsi] n : satisfacción f consigo mismo, suficiencia f

complacent [kəm'pleɪsənt] adj : satisfecho de sí mismo, suficiente

complain [kəm'pleɪn] vi **1** GRIPE : quejarse, regañar, rezongar **2** PROTEST : reclamar, protestar

complaint [kəm'pleɪnt] n **1** GRIPE : queja f **2** AILMENT : afección f, dolencia f

3 ACCUSATION : reclamo m, acusación f

complement¹ ['kɑmplə,mɛnt] vt : complementar

complement² ['kɑmpləmənt] n : complemento m

complementary [,kɑmplə'mɛntəri] adj : complementario

complete¹ [kəm'pli:t] vt **-pleted; -pleting 1** : completar, hacer entero ⟨this piece completes the collection : esta pieza completa la colección⟩ **2** FINISH : completar, acabar, terminar ⟨she completed her studies : completó sus estudios⟩

complete² adj **-pleter; -est 1** WHOLE : completo, entero, íntegro **2** FINISHED : terminado, acabado **3** TOTAL : completo, total, absoluto

completely [kəm'pli:tli] adv : completamente, totalmente

completion [kəm'pli:ʃən] n : finalización f, cumplimiento m

complex¹ [kɑm'plɛks, kəm-; 'kɑm,plɛks] adj : complejo, complicado

complex² ['kɑm,plɛks] n : complejo m

complexion [kəm'plɛkʃən] n : cutis m, tez f ⟨of dark complexion : de tez morena⟩

complexity [kəm'plɛksəti, kɑm-] n, pl **-ties** : complejidad f

compliance [kəm'plaɪənts] n : conformidad f ⟨in compliance with the law : conforme a la ley⟩

compliant [kəm'plaɪənt] adj : dócil, sumiso

complicate ['kɑmplə,keɪt] vt **-cated; -cating** : complicar

complicated ['kɑmplə,keɪtəd] adj : complicado

complication [,kɑmplə'keɪʃən] n : complicación f

complicity [kəm'plɪsəti] n, pl **-ties** : complicidad f

compliment¹ ['kɑmplə,mɛnt] vt : halagar, florear Mex

compliment² ['kɑmpləmənt] n **1** : halago m, cumplido m **2 compliments** npl : saludos mpl ⟨give them my compliments : déles saludos de mi parte⟩

complimentary [,kɑmplə'mɛntəri] adj **1** FLATTERING : halagador, halagüeño **2** FREE : de cortesía, gratis

comply [kəm'plaɪ] vi **-plied; -plying** : cumplir, acceder, obedecer

component¹ [kəm'po:nənt, 'kɑm-,po:-] adj : componente

component² n : componente m, elemento m, pieza f

compose [kəm'po:z] vt **-posed; -posing 1** : componer, crear ⟨to compose a melody : componer una melodía⟩ **2** CALM : calmar, serenar ⟨to compose oneself : serenarse⟩ **3** CONSTITUTE : constar, componer ⟨to be composed of : constar de⟩ **4** : componer (un texto a imprimirse)

composer [kəm'po:zər] n : compositor m, -tora f

composite¹ [kəm'pazət, kəm-; 'kam-pazət] *adj* : compuesto (de varias partes)

composite² *n* : compuesto *m*, mezcla *f*

composition [ˌkampə'zɪʃən] *n* **1** MAKE-UP : composición *f* **2** ESSAY : ensayo *m*, trabajo *m*

compost ['kam,po:st] *n* : abono *m* vegetal

composure [kəm'po:ʒər] *n* : compostura *f*, serenidad *f*

compound¹ ['kam'paʊnd, kəm-; 'kam-ˌpaʊnd] *vt* **1** COMBINE, COMPOSE : combinar, componer **2** AUGMENT : agravar, aumentar ⟨to compound a problem : agravar un problema⟩

compound² ['kam,paʊnd; kam'paʊnd, kəm-] *adj* : compuesto ⟨compound interest : interés compuesto⟩

compound³ ['kam,paʊnd] *n* **1** MIXTURE : compuesto *m*, mezcla *f* **2** ENCLOSURE : recinto *m* (de residencias, etc.)

compound fracture *n* : fractura *f* complicada

comprehend [ˌkamprɪ'hend] *vt* **1** UN-DERSTAND : comprender, entender **2** INCLUDE : comprender, incluir, abarcar

comprehensible [ˌkamprɪ'hentsəbəl] *adj* : comprensible

comprehension [ˌkamprɪ'hentʃən] *n* : comprensión *f*

comprehensive [ˌkamprɪ'hentsɪv] *adj* **1** INCLUSIVE : inclusivo, exhaustivo **2** BROAD : extenso, amplio

compress¹ [kəm'pres] *vt* : comprimir

compress² ['kam,pres] *n* : cómpresa *f*

compression [kəm'preʃən] *n* : compresión *f*

compressor [kəm'presər] *n* : compresor *m*

comprise [kəm'praɪz] *vt* **-prised; -prising 1** INCLUDE : comprender, incluir **2** : componerse de, constar de ⟨the installation comprises several buildings : la instalación está compuesta de varios edificios⟩

compromise¹ ['kamprə,maɪz] *v* **-mised; -mising** *vi* : transigir, avenirse — *vt* JEOPARDIZE : comprometer, poner en peligro

compromise² *n* : acuerdo *m* mutuo, compromiso *m*

comptroller [kən'tro:lər, 'kamp,tro:-] *n* : contralor *m*, -lora *f*; interventor *m*, -tora *f*

compulsion [kəm'pʌlʃən] *n* **1** COER-CION : coacción *f* **2** URGE : compulsión *f*, impulso *m*

compulsive [kəm'pʌlsɪv] *adj* : compulsivo

compulsory [kəm'pʌlsəri] *adj* : obligatorio

compunction [kəm'pʌŋkʃən] *n* **1** QUALM : reparo *m*, escrúpulo *m* **2** RE-MORSE : remordimiento *m*

computation [ˌkampjʊ'teɪʃən] *n* : cálculo *m*, cómputo *m*

compute [kəm'pju:t] *vt* **-puted; -puting** : computar, calcular

computer [kəm'pju:tər] *n* : computadora *f*, computador *m*, ordenador *m* Spain

computerize [kəm'pju:tə,raɪz] *vt* **-ized; -izing** : computarizar, informatizar

comrade ['kam,ræd] *n* : camarada *mf*; compañero *m*, -ra *f*

con¹ ['kan] *vt* **conned; conning** SWIN-DLE : estafar, timar

con² *adv* : contra

con³ *n* : contra *m* ⟨the pros and cons : los pros y los contras⟩

concave [kan'keɪv, 'kan,keɪv] *adj* : cóncavo

conceal [kən'si:l] *vt* : esconder, ocultar, disimular

concealment [kən'si:lmənt] *n* : escondimiento *m*, ocultación *f*

concede [kən'si:d] *v* **-ceded; -ceding 1** ALLOW, GRANT : conceder **2** ADMIT : conceder, reconocer ⟨to concede defeat : reconocer la derrota⟩

conceit [kən'si:t] *n* : engreimiento *m*, presunción *f*

conceited [kən'si:təd] *adj* : presumido, engreído, presuntuoso

conceivable [kən'si:vəbəl] *adj* : concebible, imaginable

conceivably [kən'si:vəbli] *adv* : posiblemente, de manera concebible

conceive [kən'si:v] *v* **-ceived; -ceiving** *vi* : concebir, embarazarse — *vt* IMAG-INE : concebir, imaginar

concentrate¹ ['kantsən,treɪt] *v* **-trated; -trating** *vt* : concentrar — *vi* : concentrarse

concentrate² *n* : concentrado *m*

concentration [ˌkantsən'treɪʃən] *n* : concentración *f*

concentric [kən'sɛntrɪk] *adj* : concéntrico

concept ['kan,sɛpt] *n* : concepto *m*, idea *f*

conception [kən'sɛpʃən] *n* **1** : concepción *f* (de un bebé) **2** IDEA : concepto *m*, idea *f*

concern¹ [kən'sərn] *vt* **1** : tratarse de, tener que ver con ⟨the novel concerns a sailor : la novela se trata de un marinero⟩ **2** INVOLVE : concernir, incumbir a, afectar ⟨that does not concern me : eso no me incumbe⟩

concern² *n* **1** AFFAIR : asunto *m* **2** WOR-RY : inquietud *f*, preocupación *f* **3** BUSINESS : negocio *m*

concerned [kən'sərnd] *adj* **1** ANXIOUS : preocupado, ansioso **2** INTERESTED, INVOLVED : interesado, afectado

concerning [kən'sərnɪŋ] *prep* REGARD-ING : con respecto a, acerca de, sobre

concert ['kan,sərt] *n* **1** AGREEMENT : concierto *m*, acuerdo *m* **2** : concierto *m* (musical)

concerted [kən'sərtəd] *adj* : concertado, coordinado ⟨to make a concerted effort : coordinar los esfuerzos⟩

concertina [ˌkantsər'ti:nə] *n* : concertina *f*

concerto [kən'tʃɛrto:] *n, pl* -ti [-ti, -,ti:] *or* -tos : concierto *m* ⟨violin concerto : concierto para violín⟩

concession [kən'sɛʃən] *n* : concesión *f*

conch ['kaŋk, 'kantʃ] *n, pl* **conchs** ['kaŋks] *or* **conches** ['kantʃəz] : caracol *m* (animal), caracola *f* (concha)

conciliatory [kən'sɪliə,tori] *adj* : conciliador, conciliatorio

concise [kən'sais] *adj* : conciso, breve — **concisely** *adv*

conclave ['kan,kleiv] *n* : cónclave *m*

conclude [kən'klu:d] *v* -**cluded**; -**cluding** *vt* 1 END : concluir, finalizar ⟨to conclude a meeting : concluir una reunión⟩ 2 DECIDE : concluir, llegar a la conclusión de — *vi* END : concluir, terminar

conclusion [kən'klu:ʒən] *n* 1 INFERENCE : conclusión *f* 2 END : fin *m*, final *m*

conclusive [kən'klu:sɪv] *adj* : concluyente, decisivo — **conclusively** *adv*

concoct [kən'kakt, kan-] *vt* 1 PREPARE : preparar, confeccionar 2 DEVISE : inventar, tramar

concoction [kən'kakʃən] *n* : invención *f*, mejunje *m*, brebaje *m*

concomitant [kən'kamətənt] *adj* : concomitante

concord ['kan,kord, 'kaŋ-] *n* 1 HARMONY : concordia *f*, armonía *f* 2 AGREEMENT : acuerdo *m*

concordance [kən'kordənts] *n* : concordancia *f*

concourse ['kan,kors] *n* : explanada *f*, salón *m* (para pasajeros)

concrete[1] ['kan'kri:t, 'kan,kri:t] *adj* 1 REAL : concreto ⟨concrete objects : objetos concretos⟩ 2 SPECIFIC : determinado, específico 3 : de concreto, de hormigón ⟨concrete walls : paredes de concreto⟩

concrete[2] ['kan,kri:t, kan'kri:t] *n* : concreto *m*, hormigón *m*

concur [kən'kər] *vi* **concurred**; **concurring** 1 COINCIDE : concurrir, coincidir 2 AGREE : concurrir, estar de acuerdo

concurrent [kən'kərənt] *adj* : concurrente, simultáneo

concussion [kən'kʌʃən] *n* : conmoción *f* cerebral

condemn [kən'dɛm] *vt* 1 CENSURE : condenar, reprobar, censurar 2 : declarar insalubre (alimentos), declarar ruinoso (un edificio) 3 SENTENCE : condenar ⟨condemned to death : condenado a muerte⟩

condemnation [,kan,dɛm'neiʃən] *n* : condena *f*, reprobación *f*

condensation [,kan,dɛn'seiʃən, -dən-] *n* : condensación *f*

condense [kən'dɛnts] *v* -**densed**; -**densing** *vt* 1 ABRIDGE : condensar, resumir 2 : condensar (vapor, etc.) — *vi* : condensarse

condescend [,kandi'sɛnd] *vi* 1 DEIGN : condescender, dignarse 2 **to condescend to someone** : tratar a alguien con condescendencia

condescension [,kandi'sɛntʃən] *n* : condescendencia *f*

condiment ['kandəmənt] *n* : condimento *m*

condition[1] [kən'dɪʃən] *vt* 1 DETERMINE : condicionar, determinar 2 : acondicionar (el pelo o el aire), poner en forma (el cuerpo)

condition[2] *n* 1 STIPULATION : condición *f*, estipulación *f* ⟨on the condition that : a condición de que⟩ 2 STATE : condición *f*, estado *m* ⟨in poor condition : en malas condiciones⟩ 3 **conditions** *npl* : condiciones *fpl*, situación *f* ⟨working conditions : condiciones del trabajo⟩

conditional [kən'dɪʃənəl] *adj* : condicional — **conditionally** *adv*

conditioner [kən'dɪʃənər] *n* : acondicionador *m*

condo ['kando:] → **condominium**

condolence [kən'do:lənts] *n* 1 SYMPATHY : condolencia *f* 2 **condolences** *npl* : pésame *m*

condom ['kandəm] *n* : condón *m*

condominium [,kandə'mɪniəm] *n, pl* -**ums** : condominio *m*

condone [kən'do:n] *vt* -**doned**; -**doning** : aprobar, perdonar, tolerar

condor ['kandər, -,dor] *n* : cóndor *m*

conducive [kən'du:sɪv, -'dju:-] *adj* : propicio, favorable

conduct[1] [kən'dʌkt] *vt* 1 GUIDE : guiar, conducir ⟨to conduct a tour : guiar una visita⟩ 2 DIRECT : conducir, dirigir ⟨to conduct an orchestra : dirigir una orquesta⟩ 3 CARRY OUT : realizar, llevar a cabo ⟨to conduct an investigation : llevar a cabo una investigación⟩ 4 TRANSMIT : conducir, transmitir (calor, electricidad, etc.) 5 **to conduct oneself** BEHAVE : conducirse, comportarse

conduct[2] ['kan,dʌkt] *n* 1 MANAGEMENT : conducción *f*, dirección *f*, manejo *m* ⟨the conduct of foreign affairs : la conducción de asuntos exteriores⟩ 2 BEHAVIOR : conducta *f*, comportamiento *m*

conduction [kən'dʌkʃən] *n* : conducción *f*

conductivity [,kan,dʌk'tɪvəti] *n, pl* -**ties** : conductividad *f*

conductor [kən'dʌktər] *n* 1 : conductor *m*, -tora *f*; revisor *m*, -sora *f* (en un tren); cobrador *m*, -dora *f* (en un bus); director *m*, -tora *f* (de una orquesta) 2 : conductor *m* (de electricidad, etc.)

conduit ['kan,du:ət, -,dʒu:-] *n* : conducto *m*, canal *m*, vía *f*

cone ['ko:n] *n* 1 : piña *f* (fruto de las coníferas) 2 : cono *m* (en geometría) 3 **ice–cream cone** : cono *m*, barquillo *m*, cucurucho *m*

confection [kən'fɛkʃən] *n* : dulce *m*

confectioner [kən'fɛkʃənər] n : confitero m, -ra f

confederacy [kən'fɛdərəsi] n, pl **-cies** : confederación f

confederate¹ [kən'fɛdə,reit] v **-ated; -ating** vt : unir, confederar — vi : confederarse, aliarse

confederate² [kən'fɛdərət] adj : confederado

confederate³ n : cómplice mf; aliado m, -da f

confederation [kən,fɛdə'reiʃən] n : confederación f, alianza f

confer [kən'fər] v **-ferred; -ferring** vt : conferir, otorgar — vi **to confer with** : consultar

conference ['kanfrənts, -fərənts] n : conferencia f ⟨press conference : conferencia de prensa⟩

confess [kən'fɛs] vt : confesar — vi 1 : confesar ⟨the prisoner confessed : el detenido confesó⟩ 2 : confesarse (en religión)

confession [kən'fɛʃən] n : confesión f

confessional [kən'fɛʃənəl] n : confesionario m

confessor [kən'fɛsər] n : confesor m

confetti [kən'fɛti] n : confeti m

confidant ['kanfə,dant, -,dænt] n : confidente mf

confide [kən'faid] v **-fided; -fiding** : confiar

confidence ['kanfədənts] n 1 TRUST : confianza f 2 SELF-ASSURANCE : confianza f en sí mismo, seguridad f en sí mismo 3 SECRET : confidencia f, secreto m

confident ['kanfədənt] adj 1 SURE : seguro 2 SELF-ASSURED : confiado, seguro de sí mismo

confidential [,kanfə'dɛntʃəl] adj : confidencial — **confidentially** [,kanfə'dɛntʃəli] adv

confidently ['kanfədəntli] adv : con seguridad, con confianza

configuration [kən,fiɡjə'reiʃən] n : configuración f

confine [kən'fain] vt **-fined; -fining** 1 LIMIT : confinar, restringir, limitar 2 IMPRISON : recluir, encarcelar, encerrar

confinement [kən'fainmənt] n : confinamiento m, reclusión f, encierro m

confines ['kan,fainz] npl : límites mpl, confines mpl

confirm [kən'fərm] vt 1 RATIFY : ratificar 2 VERIFY : confirmar, verificar 3 : confirmar (en religión)

confirmation [,kanfər'meiʃən] n : confirmación f

confiscate ['kanfə,skeit] vt **-cated; -cating** : confiscar, incautar, decomisar

confiscation [,kanfə'skeiʃən] n : confiscación f, incautación f, decomiso m

conflagration [,kanflə'ɡreiʃən] n : conflagración f

conflict¹ [kən'flikt] vi : estar en conflicto, oponerse

conflict² ['kan,flikt] n : conflicto m ⟨to be in conflict : estar en desacuerdo⟩

confluence ['kan,flu:ənts, kən'flu:ənts] n : confluencia f

conform [kən'fərm] vi 1 ACCORD, COMPLY : ajustarse, adaptarse, conformarse ⟨it conforms with our standards : se ajusta a nuestras normas⟩ 2 CORRESPOND : corresponder, encajar ⟨to conform to the truth : corresponder a la verdad⟩

conformity [kən'fərməti] n, pl **-ties** : conformidad f

confound [kən'faund, kan-] vt : confundir, desconcertar

confront [kən'frʌnt] vt : afrontar, enfrentarse a, encarar

confrontation [,kanfrən'teiʃən] n : enfrentamiento m, confrontación f

confuse [kən'fju:z] vt **-fused; -fusing** 1 PUZZLE : confundir, enturbiar 2 COMPLICATE : confundir, enredar, complicar ⟨to confuse the issue : complicar las cosas⟩

confusing [kən'fju:ziŋ] adj : complicado, que confunde

confusion [kən'fju:ʒən] n 1 PERPLEXITY : confusión f 2 MESS, TURMOIL : confusión f, embrollo m, lío m fam

congeal [kən'dʒi:l] vi 1 FREEZE : congelarse 2 COAGULATE, CURDLE : coagularse, cuajarse

congenial [kən'dʒi:niəl] adj : agradable, simpático

congenital [kən'dʒɛnətəl] adj : congénito

congest [kən'dʒɛst] vt 1 : congestionar (en la medicina) 2 OVERCROWD : abarrotar, atestar, congestionar (el tráfico) — vi : congestionarse

congestion [kən'dʒɛstʃən] n : congestión f

conglomerate¹ [kən'ɡlamərət] adj : conglomerado

conglomerate² [kən'ɡlamərət] n : conglomerado m

conglomeration [kən,ɡlamə'reiʃən] n : conglomerado m, acumulación f

Congolese [,kaŋɡə'li:z, -'li:s] n : congoleño m, -ña f — **Congolese** adj

congratulate [kən'ɡrædʒə,leit, -'ɡrætʃə-] vt **-lated; -lating** : felicitar

congratulation [kən,ɡrædʒə'leiʃən, -,ɡrætʃə-] n : felicitación f ⟨congratulations! : ¡felicidades!, ¡enhorabuena!⟩

congregate ['kaŋɡri,ɡeit] v **-gated; -gating** vt : congregar, reunir — vi : congregarse, reunirse

congregation [,kaŋɡri'ɡeiʃən] n 1 GATHERING : congregación f, fieles mpl (a un servicio religioso) 2 PARISHIONERS : feligreses mpl

congress ['kaŋɡrəs] n : congreso m

congressional [kən'ɡrɛʃənəl, kaŋ-] adj : del congreso

congressman ['kaŋɡrəsmən] n, pl **-men** [-mən, -,mɛn] : congresista m, diputado m

congresswoman ['kɑŋgrəs,wʊmən] *n, pl* **-women** [-,wɪmən] : congresista *f*, diputada *f*

congruence [kən'gru:ənts, 'kɑŋgruənts] *n* : congruencia *f*

congruent [kən'gru:ənt, 'kɑŋgruənt] *adj* : congruente

conic ['kɑnɪk] → **conical**

conical ['kɑnɪkəl] *adj* : cónico

conifer ['kɑnəfər, 'ko:-] *n* : conífera *f*

coniferous [ko:'nɪfərəs, kə-] *adj* : conífero

conjecture¹ [kən'dʒɛktʃər] *v* **-tured; -turing** : conjeturar

conjecture² *n* : conjetura *f*, presunción *f*

conjugal ['kɑndʒɪgəl, kən'dʒu:-] *adj* : conyugal

conjugate ['kɑndʒə,geɪt] *vt* **-gated; -gating** : conjugar

conjugation [,kɑndʒə'geɪʃən] *n* : conjugación *f*

conjunction [kən'dʒʌŋkʃən] *n* : conjunción *f* ⟨in conjunction with : en combinación con⟩

conjure ['kɑndʒər, 'kʌn-] *v* **-jured; -juring** *vt* 1 ENTREAT : rogar, suplicar 2 to conjure up : hacer aparecer (apariciones), evocar (memorias, etc.) — *vi* : practicar la magia

conjurer *or* **conjuror** ['kɑndʒərər, 'kʌn-] *n* : mago *m*, -ga *f*; prestidigitador *m*, -dora *f*

connect [kə'nɛkt] *vi* : conectar, enlazar, empalmar, comunicarse — *vt* 1 JOIN, LINK : conectar, unir, juntar, vincular 2 RELATE : relacionar, asociar (ideas)

connection [kə'nɛkʃən] *n* : conexión *f*, enlace *m* ⟨professional connections : relaciones profesionales⟩

connective [kə'nɛktɪv] *adj* : conectivo, conjuntivo ⟨connective tissue : tejido conjuntivo⟩

connector [kə'nɛktər] *n* : conector *m*

connivance [kə'naɪvənts] *n* : connivencia *f*, complicidad *f*

connive [kə'naɪv] *vi* **-nived; -niving** CONSPIRE, PLOT : actuar en connivencia, confabularse, conspirar

connoisseur [,kɑnə'sur, -'sʊr] *n* : conocedor *m*, -dora *f*; entendido *m*, -da *f*

connotation [,kɑnə'teɪʃən] *n* : connotación *f*

connote [kə'no:t] *vt* **-noted; -noting** : connotar

conquer ['kɑŋkər] *vt* : conquistar, vencer

conqueror ['kɑŋkərər] *n* : conquistador *m*, -dora *f*

conquest ['kɑn,kwɛst, 'kɑŋ-] *n* : conquista *f*

conscience ['kɑntʃənts] *n* : conciencia *f*, consciencia *f* ⟨to have a clear conscience : tener la conciencia limpia⟩

conscientious [,kɑntʃi'ɛntʃəs] *adj* : concienzudo — **conscientiously** *adv*

conscious ['kɑntʃəs] *adj* 1 AWARE : consciente ⟨to become conscious of : darse cuenta de⟩ 2 ALERT, AWAKE : consciente 3 INTENTIONAL : intencional, deliberado

consciously ['kɑntʃəsli] *adv* INTENTIONALLY : intencionalmente, deliberadamente, a propósito

consciousness ['kɑntʃəsnəs] *n* 1 AWARENESS : conciencia *f*, consciencia *f* 2 : conocimiento *m* ⟨to lose consciousness : perder el conocimiento⟩

conscript¹ [kən'skrɪpt] *vt* : reclutar, alistar, enrolar

conscript² ['kɑn,skrɪpt] *n* : conscripto *m*, -ta *f*; recluta *mf*

consecrate ['kɑntsə,kreɪt] *vt* **-crated; -crating** : consagrar

consecration [,kɑntsə'kreɪʃən] *n* : consagración *f*, dedicación *f*

consecutive [kən'sɛkjətɪv] *adj* : consecutivo, seguido ⟨on five consecutive days : cinco días seguidos⟩

consecutively [kən'sɛkjətɪvli] *adv* : consecutivamente

consensus [kən'sɛntsəs] *n* : consenso *m*

consent¹ [kən'sɛnt] *vi* 1 AGREE : acceder, ponerse de acuerdo 2 to consent to do something : consentir en hacer algo

consent² *n* : consentimiento *m*, permiso *m* ⟨by common consent : de común acuerdo⟩

consequence ['kɑntsə,kwɛnts, -kwənts] *n* 1 RESULT : consecuencia *f*, secuela *f* 2 IMPORTANCE : importancia *f*, trascendencia *f*

consequent ['kɑntsəkwənt, -,kwɛnt] *adj* : consiguiente

consequential [,kɑntsə'kwɛntʃəl] *adj* 1 CONSEQUENT : consiguiente 2 IMPORTANT : importante, trascendente, trascendental

consequently ['kɑntsəkwəntli, -,kwɛnt-] *adv* : por consiguiente, por ende, por lo tanto

conservation [,kɑntsər'veɪʃən] *n* : conservación *f*, protección *f*

conservationist [,kɑntsər'veɪʃənɪst] *n* : conservacionista *mf*

conservatism [kən'sərvə,tɪzəm] *n* : conservadurismo *m*

conservative¹ [kən'sərvətɪv] *adj* 1 : conservador 2 CAUTIOUS : moderado, cauteloso ⟨a conservative estimate : un cálculo moderado⟩

conservative² *n* : conservador *m*, -dora *f*

conservatory [kən'sərvə,tori] *n, pl* **-ries** : conservatorio *m*

conserve¹ [kən'sərv] *vt* **-served; -serving** : conservar, preservar

conserve² ['kɑn,sərv] *n* PRESERVES : confitura *f*

consider [kən'sɪdər] *vt* 1 CONTEMPLATE : considerar, pensar en ⟨we'd considered attending : habíamos pensado en asistir⟩ 2 : considerar, tener en cuenta ⟨consider the consequences : considera las consecuencias⟩ 3 JUDGE, REGARD : considerar, estimar

considerable [kən'sıdərəbəl] *adj* : considerable — **considerably** [-bli] *adv*

considerate [kən'sıdərət] *adj* : considerado, atento

consideration [kən,sıdə'reıʃən] *n* : consideración *f* ⟨to take into consideration : tener en cuenta⟩

considering [kən'sıdərıŋ] *prep* : teniendo en cuenta, visto

consign [kən'saın] *vt* **1** COMMIT, ENTRUST : confiar, encomendar **2** TRANSFER : consignar, transferir **3** SEND : consignar, enviar (mercancía)

consignment [kən'saınmənt] *n* **1** : envío *m*, remesa *f* **2 on ~** : en consignación

consist [kən'sıst] *vi* **1** LIE : consistir ⟨success consists in hard work : el éxito consiste en trabajar duro⟩ **2** : constar, componerse ⟨the set consists of 5 pieces : el juego se compone de 5 piezas⟩

consistency [kən'sıstəntsi] *n*, *pl* **-cies** **1** : consistencia *f* (de una mezcla o sustancia) **2** COHERENCE : coherencia *f* **3** UNIFORMITY : regularidad *f*, uniformidad *f*

consistent [kən'sıstənt] *adj* **1** COMPATIBLE : compatible, coincidente ⟨consistent with policy : coincidente con la política⟩ **2** UNIFORM : uniforme, constante, regular — **consistently** [kən'sıstəntli] *adv*

consolation [,kɑntsə'leıʃə n] *n* **1** : consuelo *m* **2 consolation prize** : premio *m* de consolación

console[1] [kən'so:l] *vt* **-soled; -soling** : consolar

console[2] ['kɑn,so:l] *n* : consola *f*

consolidate [kən'sɑlə,deıt] *vt* **-dated; -dating** : consolidar, unir

consolidation [kən,sɑlə'deıʃən] *n* : consolidación *f*

consommé [,kɑntsə'meı] *n* : consomé *m*

consonant [kən'sənənt] *n* : consonante *m*

consort[1] [kən'sərt] *vi* : asociarse, relacionarse, tener trato ⟨to consort with criminals : tener trato con criminales⟩

consort[2] ['kɑn,sɔrt] *n* : consorte *mf*

consortium [kən'sɔrʃəm] *n*, *pl* **-tia** [-ʃə] *or* **-tiums** [-ʃəmz] : consorcio *m*

conspicuous [kən'spıkjuəs] *adj* **1** OBVIOUS : visible, evidente **2** STRIKING : llamativo

conspicuously [kən'spıkjuəsli] *adv* : de manera llamativa

conspiracy [kən'spırəsi] *n*, *pl* **-cies** : conspiración *f*, complot *m*, confabulación *f*

conspirator [kən'spırətər] *n* : conspirador *m*, -dora *f*

conspire [kən'spaır] *vi* **-spired; -spiring** : conspirar, confabular

constable ['kɑntstəbəl, 'kʌntstə-] *n* : agente *mf* de policía (en un pueblo)

constancy ['kɑntstəntsi] *n*, *pl* **-cies** : constancia *f*

constant[1] ['kɑntstənt] *adj* **1** FAITHFUL : leal, fiel **2** INVARIABLE : constante, invariable **3** CONTINUAL : constante, continuo

constant[2] *n* : constante *f*

constantly ['kɑntstəntli] *adv* : constantemente, continuamente

constellation [,kɑntstə'leıʃən] *n* : constelación *f*

consternation [,kɑntstər'neıʃən] *n* : consternación *f*

constipate ['kɑntstə,peıt] *vt* **-pated; -pating** : estreñir

constipation ['kɑntstə'peıʃən] *n* : estreñimiento *m*, constipación *f* (de vientre)

constituency [kən'stıtʃuəntsi] *n*, *pl* **-cies** **1** : distrito *m* electoral **2** : residentes *mpl* de un distrito electoral

constituent[1] [kən'stıtʃuənt] *adj* **1** COMPONENT : constituyente, componente **2** : constituyente, constitutivo ⟨a constituent assembly : una asamblea constituyente⟩

constituent[2] *n* **1** COMPONENT : componente *m* **2** ELECTOR, VOTER : elector *m*, -tora *f*; votante *mf*

constitute ['kɑntstə,tu:t, -,tju:t] *vt* **-tuted; -tuting 1** ESTABLISH : constituir, establecer **2** COMPOSE, FORM : constituir, componer

constitution [,kɑntstə'tu:ʃən, -'tju:-] *n* : constitución *f*

constitutional [,kɑntstə'tu:ʃənəl, -'tju:-] *adj* : constitucional

constitutionality [,kɑntstə,tu:ʃə'næləti, -,tju:-] *n* : constitucionalidad *f*

constrain [kən'streın] *vt* **1** COMPEL : constreñir, obligar **2** CONFINE : constreñir, limitar, restringir **3** RESTRAIN : contener, refrenar

constraint [kən'streınt] *n* : restricción *f*, limitación *f*

constrict [kən'strıkt] *vt* : estrechar, apretar, comprimir

constriction [kən'strıkʃən] *n* : estrechamiento *m*, compresión *f*

construct [kən'strʌkt] *vt* : construir

construction [kən'strʌkʃən] *n* : construcción *f*

constructive [kən'strʌktıv] *adj* : constructivo

construe [kən'stru:] *vt* **-strued; -struing** : interpretar

consul ['kɑntsəl] *n* : cónsul *mf*

consular ['kɑntsələr] *adj* : consular

consulate ['kɑntsələt] *n* : consulado *m*

consult [kən'sʌlt] *vt* : consultar — *vi* **to consult with** : consultar con, solicitar la opinión de

consultant [kən'sʌltənt] *n* : consultor *m*, -tora *f*; asesor *m*, -sora *f*

consultation [,kɑntsəl'teıʃən] *n* : consulta *f*

consumable [kən'su:məbəl] *adj* : consumible

consume [kən'su:m] *vt* **-sumed; -suming** : consumir, usar, gastar

consumer [kənˈsuːmər] *n* : consumidor *m*, -dora *f*

consummate¹ [ˈkɑnsəˌmeɪt] *vt* **-mated; -mating** : consumar

consummate² [kənˈsʌmət, ˈkɑnsə-mət] *adj* : consumado, perfecto

consummation [ˌkɑntsəˈmeɪʃən] *n* : consumación *f*

consumption [kənˈsʌmpʃən] *n* **1** USE : consumo *m*, uso *m* ⟨consumption of electricity : consumo de electricidad⟩ **2** TUBERCULOSIS : tisis *f*, consunción *f*

contact¹ [ˈkɑnˌtækt, kənˈ-] *vt* : ponerse en contacto con, contactar (con)

contact² [ˈkɑnˌtækt] *n* **1** TOUCHING : contacto *m* ⟨to come into contact with : entrar en contacto con⟩ **2** TOUCH : contacto *m*, comunicación *f* ⟨to lose contact with : perder contacto con⟩ **3** CONNECTION : contacto *m* (en negocios) **4** → contact lens

contact lens [ˈkɑnˌtæktˈlenz] *n* : lente *mf* de contacto, pupilente *m Mex*

contagion [kənˈteɪdʒən] *n* : contagio *m*

contagious [kənˈteɪdʒəs] *adj* : contagioso

contain [kənˈteɪn] *vt* **1** : contener **2 to contain oneself** : contenerse

container [kənˈteɪnər] *n* : recipiente *m*, envase *m*

containment [kənˈteɪnmənt] *n* : contención *f*

contaminant [kənˈtæmənənt] *n* : contaminante *m*

contaminate [kənˈtæməˌneɪt] *vt* **-nated; -nating** : contaminar

contamination [kənˌtæməˈneɪʃən] *n* : contaminación *f*

contemplate [ˈkɑntəmˌpleɪt] *v* **-plated; -plating** *vt* **1** VIEW : contemplar **2** PONDER : contemplar, considerar **3** CONSIDER, PROPOSE : proponerse, proyectar, pensar en ⟨to contemplate a trip : pensar en viajar⟩ — *vi* MEDITATE : meditar

contemplation [ˌkɑntəmˈpleɪʃən] *n* : contemplación *f*

contemplative [kənˈtemplətɪv, ˈkɑntəmˌpleɪtɪv] *adj* : contemplativo

contemporaneous [kənˌtempəˈreɪniəs] *adj* → contemporary¹

contemporary¹ [kənˈtempəˌreri] *adj* : contemporáneo

contemporary² *n, pl* **-raries** : contemporáneo *m*, -nea *f*

contempt [kənˈtempt] *n* **1** DISDAIN : desprecio *m*, desdén *m* ⟨to hold in contempt : despreciar⟩ **2** : desacato *m* (ante un tribunal)

contemptible [kənˈtemptəbəl] *adj* : despreciable, vil

contemptuous [kənˈtemptʃuəs] *adj* : despectivo, despreciativo, desdeñoso

contemptuously [kənˈtemptʃuəsli] *adv* : despectivamente, con desprecio

contend [kənˈtend] *vi* **1** STRUGGLE : luchar, lidiar, contender ⟨to contend with a problem : lidiar con un proble-

ma⟩ **2** COMPETE : competir ⟨to contend for a position : competir por un puesto⟩ — *vt* **1** ARGUE, MAINTAIN : argüir, sostener, afirmar ⟨he contended that he was right : afirmó que tenía razón⟩ **2** CONTEST : protestar contra (una decisión, etc.), disputar

contender [kənˈtendər] *n* : contendiente *mf*; aspirante *mf*; competidor *m*, -dora *f*

content¹ [kənˈtent] *vt* SATISFY : contentar, satisfacer

content² *adj* : conforme, contento, satisfecho

content³ *n* CONTENTMENT : contento *m*, satisfacción *f* ⟨to one's heart's content : hasta quedar satisfecho, a más no poder⟩

content⁴ [ˈkɑnˌtent] *n* **1** MEANING : contenido *m*, significado *m* **2** PROPORTION : contenido *m*, proporción *f* ⟨fat content : contenido de grasa⟩ **3 contents** *npl* : contenido *m*, sumario *m* (de un libro) ⟨table of contents : índice de materias⟩

contented [kənˈtentəd] *adj* : conforme, satisfecho ⟨a contented smile : una sonrisa de satisfacción⟩

contentedly [kənˈtentədli] *adv* : con satisfacción

contention [kənˈtentʃən] *n* **1** DISPUTE : disputa *f*, discusión *f* **2** COMPETITION : competencia *f*, contienda *f* **3** OPINION : argumento *m*, opinión *f*

contentious [kənˈtentʃəs] *adj* : disputador, pugnaz, combativo

contentment [kənˈtentmənt] *n* : satisfacción *f*, contento *m*

contest¹ [kənˈtest] *vt* : disputar, cuestionar, impugnar ⟨to contest a will : impugnar un testamento⟩

contest² [ˈkɑnˌtest] *n* **1** STRUGGLE : lucha *f*, contienda *f* **2** GAME : concurso *m*, competencia *f*

contestable [kənˈtestəbəl] *adj* : discutible, cuestionable

contestant [kənˈtestənt] *n* : concursante *mf*; competidor *m*, -dora *f*

context [ˈkɑnˌtekst] *n* : contexto *m*

contiguous [kənˈtɪgjuəs] *adj* : contiguo

continence [ˈkɑntənənts] *n* : continencia *f*

continent¹ [ˈkɑntənənt] *adj* : continente

continent² *n* : continente *m* — **continental** [ˌkɑntənˈentəl] *adj*

contingency [kənˈtɪndʒəntsi] *n, pl* **-cies** : contingencia *f*, eventualidad *f*

contingent¹ [kənˈtɪndʒənt] *adj* **1** POSSIBLE : contingente, eventual **2** ACCIDENTAL : fortuito, accidental **3 to be contingent on** : depender de, estar sujeto a

contingent² *n* : contingente *m*

continual [kənˈtɪnjuəl] *adj* : continuo, constante — **continually** [kənˈtɪnjuəli, -ˈtɪnjəli] *adv*

continuance [kənˈtɪnjuənts] *n* **1** CONTINUATION : continuación *f* **2** DURA-

TION : duración f 3 : aplazamiento m (de un proceso)

continuation [kənˌtɪnjuˈeɪʃən] n : continuación f, prolongación f

continue [kənˈtɪnjuː] v **-tinued; -tinuing** vi 1 CARRY ON : continuar, seguir, proseguir ⟨please continue : continúe, por favor⟩ 2 ENDURE, LAST : continuar, prolongarse, durar 3 RESUME : continuar, reanudarse — vt 1 : continuar, seguir ⟨she continued writing : continuó escribiendo⟩ 2 RESUME : continuar, reanudar 3 EXTEND, PROLONG : continuar, prolongar

continuity [ˌkɑntəˈnuːəti, -ˈnjuː-] n, pl **-ties** : continuidad f

continuous [kənˈtɪnjuəs] adj : continuo — **continuously** adv

contort [kənˈtɔrt] vt : torcer, retorcer, contraer (el rostro) — vi : contraerse, demudarse

contortion [kənˈtɔrʃən] n : contorsión f

contour [ˈkɑnˌtʊr] n 1 OUTLINE : contorno m 2 **contours** npl SHAPE : forma f, curvas fpl 3 **contour map** : mapa m topográfico

contraband [ˈkɑntrəˌbænd] n : contrabando m

contraception [ˌkɑntrəˈsɛpʃən] n : anticoncepción f, contracepción f

contraceptive[1] [ˌkɑntrəˈsɛptɪv] adj : anticonceptivo, contraceptivo

contraceptive[2] n : anticonceptivo m, contraceptivo m

contract[1] [ˈkɑnˌtrækt, 1 usu ˈkɑnˌtrækt] vt 1 : contratar (servicios profesionales) 2 : contraer (una enfermedad, una deuda) 3 TIGHTEN : contraer (un músculo) 4 SHORTEN : contraer (una palabra) — vi : contraerse, reducirse

contract[2] [ˈkɑnˌtrækt] n : contrato m

contraction [kənˈtrækʃən] n : contracción f

contractor [ˈkɑnˌtræktər, kənˈtræk-] n : contratista mf

contractual [kənˈtræktʃuəl] adj : contractual — **contractually** adv

contradict [ˌkɑntrəˈdɪkt] vt : contradecir, desmentir

contradiction [ˌkɑntrəˈdɪkʃən] n : contradicción f

contradictory [ˌkɑntrəˈdɪktəri] adj : contradictorio

contralto [kənˈtrælˌtoː] n, pl **-tos** : contralto m (voz), contralto mf (vocalista)

contraption [kənˈtræpʃən] n DEVICE : aparato m, artefacto m

contrary[1] [ˈkɑnˌtrɛri, 2 often kənˈtrɛri] adj 1 OPPOSITE : contrario, opuesto 2 BALKY, STUBBORN : terco, testarudo 3 **contrary to** : al contrario de, en contra de ⟨contrary to the facts : en contra de los hechos⟩

contrary[2] [ˈkɑnˌtrɛri] n, pl **-traries** 1 OPPOSITE : lo contrario, lo opuesto 2 **on the contrary** : al contrario, todo lo contrario

contrast[1] [kənˈtræst] vi DIFFER : contrastar, diferir — vt COMPARE : contrastar, comparar

contrast[2] [ˈkɑnˌtræst] n : contraste m

contravene [ˌkɑntrəˈviːn] vt **-vened; -vening** : contravenir, infringir

contribute [kənˈtrɪbjət] v **-uted; -uting** vt : contribuir, aportar (dinero, bienes, etc.) — vi : contribuir

contribution [ˌkɑntrəˈbjuːʃən] n : contribución f

contributor [kənˈtrɪbjətər] n : contribuidor m, -dora f; colaborador m, -dora f (en periodismo)

contrite [ˈkɑnˌtraɪt, kənˈtraɪt] adj REPENTANT : contrito, arrepentido

contrition [kənˈtrɪʃən] n : contrición f, arrepentimiento m

contrivance [kənˈtraɪvənts] n 1 DEVICE : aparato m, artefacto m 2 SCHEME : artimaña f, treta f, ardid m

contrive [kənˈtraɪv] vt **-trived; -triving** 1 DEVISE : idear, ingeniar, maquinar 2 MANAGE : lograr, ingeniárselas para ⟨she contrived a way out of the mess : se las ingenió para salir del enredo⟩

control[1] [kənˈtroːl] vt **-trolled; -trolling** : controlar, dominar

control[2] n 1 : control m, dominio m, mando m ⟨to be under control : estar bajo control⟩ 2 RESTRAINT : control m, limitación f ⟨birth control : control natal⟩ 3 : control m, dispositivo m de mando ⟨remote control : control remoto⟩

controllable [kənˈtroːləbəl] adj : controlable

controller [kənˈtroːlər, ˈkɑn-] n 1 → **comptroller** 2 : controlador m, -dora f ⟨air traffic controller : controlador aéreo⟩

controversial [ˌkɑntrəˈvərʃəl, -siəl] adj : controvertido ⟨a controversial decision : una decisión controvertida⟩

controversy [ˈkɑntrəˌvərsi] n, pl **-sies** : controversia f

controvert [ˈkɑntrəˌvərt, ˌkɑntrə-] vt : controvertir, contradecir

contusion [kənˈtuːʒən, -tjuː-] n BRUISE : contusión f, moretón m

conundrum [kəˈnʌndrəm] n RIDDLE : acertijo m, adivinanza f

convalesce [ˌkɑnvəˈlɛs] vi **-lesced; -lescing** : convalecer

convalescence [ˌkɑnvəˈlɛsənts] n : convalecencia f

convalescent[1] [ˌkɑnvəˈlɛsənt] adj : convaleciente

convalescent[2] n : convaleciente mf

convection [kənˈvɛkʃən] n : convección f

convene [kənˈviːn] v **-vened; -vening** vt : convocar — vi : reunirse

convenience [kənˈviːnjənts] n 1 : conveniencia f ⟨at your convenience : cuando le resulte conveniente⟩ 2 AMENITY : comodidad f ⟨modern conveniences : comodidades modernas⟩

convenience store n : tienda f de conveniencia

convenient [kən'vi:njənt] adj : conveniente, cómodo — **conveniently** adv

convent ['kɑnvənt, -,vɛnt] n : convento m

convention [kən'vɛntʃən] n 1 PACT : convención f, convenio m, pacto m ⟨the Geneva Convention : la Convención de Ginebra⟩ 2 MEETING : convención f, congreso m 3 CUSTOM : convención f, convencionalismo m

conventional [kən'vɛntʃənəl] adj : convencional — **conventionally** adv

converge [kən'vərdʒ] vi **-verged; -verging** : converger, convergir

convergence [kən'vərdʒənts] n : convergencia f

convergent [kən'vərdʒənt] adj : convergente

conversant [kən'vərsənt] adj **conversant with** : versado con, experto en

conversation [,kɑnvər'seɪʃən] n : conversación f

conversational [,kɑnvər'seɪʃənəl] adj : familiar ⟨a conversational style : un estilo familiar⟩

converse [kən'vərs] vi **-versed; -versing** : conversar

converse² [kən'vərs, 'kɑn,vərs] adj : contrario, opuesto, inverso

conversely [kən'vərsli, 'kɑn,vərs-] adv : a la inversa

conversion [kən'vərʒən] n 1 CHANGE : conversión f, transformación f, cambio m 2 : conversión f (a una religión)

convert¹ [kən'vərt] vt 1 : convertir (a una religión o un partido) 2 CHANGE : convertir, cambiar — vi : convertirse

convert² ['kɑn,vərt] n : converso m, -sa f

converter or **convertor** [kən'vərtər] n : convertidor m

convertible¹ [kən'vərtəbəl] adj : convertible

convertible² n : convertible m, descapotable m

convex [kɑn'vɛks, 'kɑn,-, kən'-] adj : convexo

convey [kən'veɪ] vt 1 TRANSPORT : transportar, conducir 2 TRANSMIT : transmitir, comunicar, expresar (noticias, ideas, etc.)

conveyance [kən'veɪənts] n 1 TRANSPORT : transporte m, transportación f 2 COMMUNICATION : transmisión f, comunicación f 3 TRANSFER : transferencia f, traspaso m (de una propiedad)

conveyor [kən'veɪər] n : transportador m, -dora f ⟨conveyor belt : cinta transportadora⟩

convict¹ [kən'vɪkt] vt : declarar culpable

convict² ['kɑn,vɪkt] n : preso m, -sa f; presidiario m, -ria f; recluso m, -sa f

conviction [kən'vɪkʃən] n 1 : condena f (de un acusado) 2 BELIEF : convicción f, creencia f

convince [kən'vɪnts] vt **-vinced; -vincing** : convencer

convincing [kən'vɪntsɪŋ] adj : convincente, persuasivo

convincingly [kən'vɪntsɪŋli] adv : de forma convincente

convivial [kən'vɪvjəl, -'vɪviəl] adj : jovial, festivo, alegre

conviviality [kən,vɪvi'æləti] n, pl **-ties** : jovialidad f

convoke [kən'vo:k] vt **-voked; -voking** : convocar

convoluted ['kɑnvə,lu:təd] adj : intrincado, complicado

convoy ['kɑn,vɔɪ] n : convoy m

convulse [kən'vʌls] v **-vulsed; -vulsing** vt : convulsionar — vi : sufrir convulsiones

convulsion [kən'vʌlʃən] n : convulsión f

convulsive [kən'vʌlsɪv] adj : convulsivo — **convulsively** adv

coo¹ ['ku:] vi : arrullar

coo² n : arrullo m (de una paloma)

cook¹ ['kʊk] vi : cocinar — vt 1 : preparar (comida) **2 to cook up** CONCOCT : inventar, tramar

cook² n : cocinero m, -ra f

cookbook ['kʊk,bʊk] n : libro m de cocina

cookery ['kʊkəri] n, pl **-eries** : cocina f

cookie or **cooky** ['kʊki] n, pl **-ies** : galleta f (dulce)

cooking ['kʊkɪŋ] n 1 COOKERY : cocina f 2 : cocción f, cocimiento m ⟨cooking time : tiempo de cocción⟩

cookout ['kʊk,aʊt] n : comida f al aire libre

cool¹ ['ku:l] vt : refrescar, enfriar — vi 1 : refrescarse, enfriarse ⟨the pie is cooling : el pastel se está enfriando⟩ 2 : calmarse, tranquilizarse ⟨his anger cooled : su ira se calmó⟩

cool² adj 1 : fresco, frío ⟨cool weather : tiempo fresco⟩ 2 CALM : tranquilo, sereno 3 ALOOF : frío, distante

cool³ n 1 : fresco m ⟨the cool of the evening : el fresco de la tarde⟩ 2 COMPOSURE : calma f, serenidad f

coolant ['ku:lənt] n : refrigerante m

cooler ['ku:lər] n : nevera f portátil

coolie ['ku:li] n : culí m

coolly ['ku:lli] adv 1 CALMLY : con calma, tranquilamente 2 COLDLY : fríamente, con frialdad

coolness ['ku:lnəs] n 1 : frescura f, frescor m ⟨the coolness of the evening : el frescor de la noche⟩ 2 CALMNESS : tranquilidad f, serenidad f 3 COLDNESS, INDIFFERENCE : frialdad f, indiferencia f

coop¹ ['ku:p, 'kʊp] vt or **to coop up** : encerrar ⟨cooped up in the house : encerrado en la casa⟩

coop² n : gallinero m

co-op ['ko:,ɑp] n → **cooperative²**

cooperate [ko'ɑpə,reɪt] vi **-ated; -ating** : cooperar, colaborar

cooperation [ko͵apə'reɪʃən] n : cooperación f, colaboración f

cooperative[1] [ko'apərət͝ɪv, -'apə͵reɪtɪv] adj : cooperativo

cooperative[2] [ko'apərət͝ɪv] n : cooperativa f

co–opt [ko'apt] vt 1 : nombrar como miembro, cooptar 2 APPROPRIATE : apropiarse de

coordinate[1] [ko'ɔrdən͵eɪt] v -nated; -nating vt : coordinar — vi : coordinarse, combinar, acordar

coordinate[2] [ko'ɔrdənət] adj 1 COORDINATED : coordinado 2 EQUAL : igual, semejante

coordinate[3] [ko'ɔrdənət] n : coordenada f

coordination [ko͵ɔrdən'eɪʃən] n : coordinación f

coordinator [ko'ɔrdən͵eɪtər] n : coordinador m, -dora f

cop ['kɑp] n : police officer

cope ['ko:p] vi **coped; coping** 1 : arreglárselas 2 to cope with : hacer frente a, poder con ⟨I can't cope with all this! : ¡no puedo con todo esto!⟩

copier ['kɑpiər] n : copiadora f, fotocopiadora f

copilot ['ko͵paɪlət] n : copiloto m

copious ['ko:piəs] adj : copioso, abundante — **copiously** adv

copiousness ['ko:piəsnəs] n : abundancia f

copper ['kɑpər] n : cobre m

coppery ['kɑpəri] adj : cobrizo

copra ['ko:prə, 'kɑ-] n : copra f

copse ['kɑps] n THICKET : soto m, matorral m

copulate ['kɑpjə͵leɪt] vi -lated; -lating : copular

copulation [͵kɑpjə'leɪʃən] n : cópula f, relaciones fpl sexuales

copy[1] ['kɑpi] vt **copied; copying** 1 DUPLICATE : hacer una copia de, duplicar, reproducir 2 IMITATE : copiar, imitar

copy[2] n, pl **copies** 1 : copia f, duplicado m (de un documento), reproducción f (de una obra de arte) 2 : ejemplar m (de un libro), número m (de una revista) 3 TEXT : manuscrito m, texto m

copyright[1] ['kɑpi͵raɪt] vt : registrar los derechos de

copyright[2] n : derechos mpl de autor

coral[1] ['kɔrəl] adj : de coral ⟨a coral reef : un arrecife de coral⟩

coral[2] n : coral m

coral snake n : serpiente f de coral

cord ['kɔrd] n 1 ROPE, STRING : cuerda f, cordón m, cordel m 2 : cuerda f, cordón m, médula f (en la anatomía) ⟨vocal cords : cuerdas vocales⟩ 3 : cuerda f ⟨a cord of firewood : una cuerda de leña⟩ 4 or **electric cord** : cable m eléctrico

cordial[1] ['kɔrdʒəl] adj : cordial — **cordially** adv

cordial[2] n : cordial m

cordiality [͵kɔrdʒi'æləti] n : cordialidad f

cordless ['kɔrdləs] adj : inalámbrico

cordon[1] ['kɔrdən] vt **to cordon off** : acordonar

cordon[2] n : cordón m

corduroy ['kɔrdə͵rɔɪ] n 1 : pana f 2 **corduroys** npl : pantalones mpl de pana

core[1] ['kor] vt **cored; coring** : quitar el corazón a (una fruta)

core[2] n 1 : corazón m, centro m (de algunas frutas) 2 CENTER : núcleo m, centro m 3 ESSENCE : núcleo m, meollo m ⟨to the core : hasta la médula⟩

coriander ['kori͵ændər] n : cilantro m

cork[1] ['kɔrk] vt : ponerle un corcho a

cork[2] n : corcho m

corkscrew ['kɔrk͵skru:] n : tirabuzón m, sacacorchos m

cormorant ['kɔrmərənt, -͵rænt] n : cormorán m

corn[1] ['kɔrn] vt : conservar en salmuera ⟨corned beef : carne en conserva⟩

corn[2] n 1 GRAIN : grano m 2 : maíz m, elote m Mex ⟨corn tortillas : tortillas de maíz⟩ 3 : callo m ⟨corn plaster : emplasto para callos⟩

corncob ['kɔrn͵kɑb] n : mazorca f (de maíz), choclo m, elote m CA, Mex

cornea ['kɔrniə] n : córnea f

corner[1] ['kɔrnər] vt 1 TRAP : acorralar, arrinconar 2 MONOPOLIZE : monopolizar, acaparar (un mercado) — vi : tomar una curva, doblar una esquina (en un automóvil)

corner[2] n 1 ANGLE : rincón m, esquina f, ángulo m ⟨the corner of a room : el rincón de una sala⟩ ⟨all corners of the world : todos los rincones del mundo⟩ ⟨to cut corners : atajar, economizar esfuerzos⟩ 2 INTERSECTION : esquina f 3 IMPASSE, PREDICAMENT : aprieto m, impasse m ⟨to be backed into a corner : estar acorralado⟩

cornerstone ['kɔrnər͵sto:n] n : piedra f angular

cornet [kɔr'nɛt] n : corneta f

cornfield ['kɔrn͵fi:ld] n : maizal m; milpa f CA, Mex

cornice ['kɔrnɪs] n : cornisa f

cornmeal ['kɔrn͵mi:l] n : harina f de maíz

cornstalk ['kɔrn͵stɔk] n : tallo m del maíz

cornstarch ['kɔrn͵stɑrtʃ] n : maicena f, almidón m de maíz

cornucopia [͵kɔrnə'ko:piə, -njə-] n : cornucopia f

corolla [kə'rɑlə] n : corola f

corollary ['kɔrə͵lɛri] n, pl -laries : corolario m

corona [kə'ro:nə] n : corona f (del sol)

coronary[1] ['kɔrə͵nɛri] adj : coronario

coronary[2] n, pl -naries 1 : trombosis f coronaria 2 HEART ATTACK : infarto m, ataque m al corazón

coronation [͵kɔrə'neɪʃən] n : coronación f

coroner [ˈkɔrənər] n : médico m forense
corporal¹ [ˈkɔrpərəl] adj : corporal ⟨corporal punishment : castigos corporales⟩
corporal² n : cabo m
corporate [ˈkɔrpərət] adj : corporativo, empresarial
corporation [ˌkɔrpəˈreɪʃən] n : sociedad f anónima, corporación f, empresa f
corporeal [kɔrˈpɔriəl] adj 1 PHYSICAL : corpóreo 2 MATERIAL : material, tangible — **corporeally** adv
corps [ˈkor] n, pl **corps** [ˈkorz] : cuerpo m ⟨medical corps : cuerpo médico⟩ ⟨diplomatic corps : cuerpo diplomático⟩
corpse [ˈkorps] n : cadáver m
corpulence [ˈkɔrpjələnts] n : obesidad f, gordura f
corpulent [ˈkɔrpjələnt] adj : obeso, gordo
corpuscle [ˈkɔrˌpʌsəl] n : corpúsculo m, glóbulo m (sanguíneo)
corral¹ [kəˈræl] vt **-ralled; -ralling** : acorralar, encorralar (ganado)
corral² n : corral m
correct¹ [kəˈrɛkt] vt 1 RECTIFY : corregir, rectificar 2 REPRIMAND : corregir, reprender
correct² adj 1 ACCURATE, RIGHT : correcto, exacto ⟨to be correct : estar en lo cierto⟩ 2 PROPER : correcto, apropiado
correction [kəˈrɛkʃən] n : corrección f
corrective [kəˈrɛktɪv] adj : correctivo
correctly [kəˈrɛktli] adv : correctamente
correctness [kəˈrɛk(t)nəs] n 1 ACCURACY : exactitud f 2 PROPRIETY : corrección f
correlate [ˈkɔrəˌleɪt] vt **-lated; -lating** : relacionar, poner en correlación
correlation [ˌkɔrəˈleɪʃən] n : correlación f
correspond [ˌkɔrəˈspand] vi 1 MATCH : corresponder, concordar, coincidir 2 WRITE : corresponderse, escribirse
correspondence [ˌkɔrəˈspandənts] n : correspondencia f
correspondent [ˌkɔrəˈspandənt] n : corresponsal mf
corresponding [kɔrəˈspandɪŋ, kar-] adj : correspondiente
correspondingly [ˌkɔrəˈspandɪŋli] adv : en consecuencia, de la misma manera
corridor [ˈkɔrədər, -ˌdɔr] n : corredor m, pasillo m
corroborate [kəˈrabəˌreɪt] vt **-rated; -rating** : corroborar
corroboration [kəˌrabəˈreɪʃən] n : corroboración f
corrode [kəˈroːd] v **-roded; -roding** vt : corroer — vi : corroerse
corrosion [kəˈroːʒən] n : corrosión f
corrosive [kəˈroːsɪv] adj : corrosivo
corrugate [ˈkɔrəˌgeɪt] vt **-gated; -gating** : ondular, acanalar, corrugar

corrugated [ˈkɔrəˌgeɪtəd] adj : ondulado, acanalado ⟨corrugated cardboard : cartón ondulado⟩
corrupt¹ [kəˈrʌpt] vt 1 PERVERT : corromper, pervertir, degradar (información) 2 BRIBE : sobornar
corrupt² adj : corrupto, corrompido
corruptible [kəˈrʌptəbəl] adj : corruptible
corruption [kəˈrʌpʃən] n : corrupción f
corsage [kɔrˈsaʒ, -ˈsadʒ] n : ramillete m que se lleva como adorno
corset [ˈkɔrsət] n : corsé m
cortex [ˈkɔrˌteks] n, pl **-tices** [ˈkɔrtəˌsiːz] or **-texes** : corteza f ⟨cerebral cortex : corteza cerebral⟩
cortisone [ˈkɔrtəˌsoːn, -zoːn] n : cortisona f
cosmetic¹ [kazˈmɛtɪk] adj : cosmético
cosmetic² n : cosmético m
cosmic [ˈkazmɪk] adj 1 : cósmico ⟨cosmic ray : rayo cósmico⟩ 2 VAST : grandioso, inmenso, vasto
cosmonaut [ˈkazməˌnɔt] n : cosmonauta mf
cosmopolitan¹ [ˌkazməˈpalətən] adj : cosmopolita
cosmopolitan² n : cosmopolita mf
cosmos [ˈkazməs, -ˌmoːs, -ˌmas] n : cosmos m, universo m
cost¹ [ˈkɔst] v **cost; costing** vt : costar ⟨how much does it cost? : ¿cuánto cuesta?, ¿cuánto vale?⟩ — vi : costar ⟨these cost more : éstos cuestan más⟩
cost² n : costo m, precio m, coste m ⟨cost of living : costo de vida⟩ ⟨victory at all costs : victoria a toda costa⟩
Costa Rican¹ [ˌkɔstəˈriːkən] adj : costarricense
Costa Rican² n : costarricense mf
costly [ˈkɔstli] adj : costoso, caro
costume [ˈkas,tuːm, -ˌtjuːm] n 1 : traje m ⟨national costume : traje típico⟩ 2 : disfraz m ⟨costume party : fiesta de disfraces⟩ 3 OUTFIT : vestimenta f, traje m, conjunto m
cosy [ˈkoːzi] → **cozy**
cot [ˈkat] n : catre m
coterie [ˈkoːtə,ri, ˌkoːtəˈ-] n : tertulia f, círculo m (social)
cottage [ˈkatɪdʒ] n : casita f (de campo)
cottage cheese n : requesón m
cotton [ˈkatən] n : algodón m
cottonmouth [ˈkatən,mauθ] → **moccasin**
cottonseed [ˈkatən,siːd] n : semilla f de algodón
cotton swab → **swab**
cottontail [ˈkatən,teɪl] n : conejo m de cola blanca
couch¹ [ˈkautʃ] vt : expresar, formular ⟨couched in strong language : expresado en lenguaje enérgico⟩
couch² n SOFA : sofá m
couch potato n : haragán m, -gana f; vago m, -ga f
cougar [ˈkuːgər] n : puma m
cough [ˈkɔf] vi : toser

cough² n : tos f
could ['kʊd] → can
council ['kaʊntsəl] n 1 : concejo m ‹city council : concejo municipal, ayuntamiento› 2 MEETING : concejo m, junta f 3 BOARD : consejo m 4 : concilio m (eclesiástico)
councillor or **councilor** ['kaʊntsələr] n : concejal m, -jala f
councilman ['kaʊntsəlmən] n, pl -men [-mən, -ˌmɛn] : concejal m
councilwoman ['kaʊntsəlˌwʊmən] n, pl -women [-ˌwɪmən] : concejala f
counsel¹ ['kaʊntsəl] v -seled or -selled; -seling or -selling vt ADVISE : aconsejar, asesorar, recomendar — vi CONSULT : consultar
counsel² n 1 ADVICE : consejo m, recomendación f 2 CONSULTATION : consulta f 3 counsel ns & pl LAWYER : abogado m, -da f
counselor or **counsellor** ['kaʊntsələr] n : consejero m, -ra f; consultor m, -tora f; asesor m, -sora f
count¹ ['kaʊnt] vt : contar, enumerar — vi 1 : contar ‹to count out loud : contar en voz alta› 2 MATTER : contar, valer, importar ‹that's what counts : eso es lo que cuenta› 3 to count on : contar con
count² n 1 COMPUTATION : cómputo m, recuento m, cuenta f ‹to lose count : perder la cuenta› 2 CHARGE : cargo m ‹two counts of robbery : dos cargos de robo› 3 : conde m (noble)
countable ['kaʊntəbəl] adj : numerable
countdown ['kaʊntˌdaʊn] n : cuenta f atrás
countenance¹ ['kaʊntənənts] vt -nanced; -nancing : permitir, tolerar
countenance² n FACE : semblante m, rostro m
counter¹ ['kaʊntər] vt 1 → counteract 2 OPPOSE : oponerse a, resistir — vi RETALIATE : responder, contraatacar
counter² adv counter to : contrario a, en contra de
counter³ adj : contrario, opuesto
counter⁴ n 1 PIECE : ficha f (de un juego) 2 : mostrador m (de un negocio), ventanilla f (en un banco) 3 : contador m (aparato) 4 COUNTERBALANCE : fuerza f opuesta, contrapeso m
counteract [ˌkaʊntər'ækt] vt : contrarrestar
counterattack ['kaʊntərəˌtæk] n : contraataque m
counterbalance¹ [ˌkaʊntər'bælənts] vt -anced; -ancing : contrapesar
counterbalance² ['kaʊntərˌbælənts] n : contrapeso m
counterclockwise [ˌkaʊntər'klakˌwaɪz] adv & adj : en el sentido opuesto al de las manecillas del reloj
counterfeit¹ ['kaʊntərˌfɪt] vt 1 : falsificar (dinero) 2 PRETEND : fingir, aparentar
counterfeit² adj : falso, inauténtico
counterfeit³ n : falsificación f

counterfeiter ['kaʊntərˌfɪtər] n : falsificador m, -dora f
countermand [ˌkaʊntər'mænd, ˌkaʊntər'-] vt : contramandar
countermeasure ['kaʊntərˌmɛʒər] n : contramedida f
counterpart ['kaʊntərˌpart] n : homólogo m, contraparte f Mex
counterpoint ['kaʊntərˌpɔɪnt] n : contrapunto m
counterproductive [ˌkaʊntərprə'dʌktɪv] adj : contraproducente
counterrevolution [ˌkaʊntərˌrɛvə-'lu:ʃən] n : contrarrevolución f
counterrevolutionary¹ [ˌkaʊntər,rɛvə-'lu:ʃənˌɛri] adj : contrarrevolucionario
counterrevolutionary² n, pl -ries : contrarrevolucionario m, -ria f
countersign ['kaʊntərˌsaɪn] n : contraseña f
countess ['kaʊntɪs] n : condesa f
countless ['kaʊntləs] adj : incontable, innumerable
country¹ ['kʌntri] adj : campestre, rural
country² n, pl -tries 1 NATION : país m, nación f, patria f ‹country of origin : país de origen› ‹love of one's country : amor a la patria› 2 : campo m ‹they left the city for the country : se fueron de la ciudad al campo›
countryman ['kʌntrimən] n, pl -men [-mən, -ˌmɛn] : compatriota mf; paisano m, -na f
countryside ['kʌntriˌsaɪd] n : campo m, campiña f
county ['kaʊnti] n, pl -ties : condado m
coup ['ku:] n, pl coups ['ku:z] 1 : golpe m maestro 2 or coup d'etat : golpe m (de estado), cuartelazo m
coupe ['ku:p] n : cupé m
couple¹ ['kʌpəl] vt -pled; -pling : acoplar, enganchar, conectar
couple² n 1 PAIR : par m ‹a couple of hours : un par de horas, unas dos horas› 2 : pareja f ‹a young couple : una pareja joven›
coupling ['kʌplɪŋ] n : acoplamiento m
coupon ['ku:ˌpan, 'kju:-] n : cupón m
courage ['kərɪʤ] n : valor m, valentía f, coraje m
courageous [kə'reɪʤəs] adj : valiente, valeroso
courier ['kʊriər, 'kəriər] n : mensajero m, -ra f
course¹ ['kors] vi coursed; coursing : correr (a toda velocidad)
course² n 1 PROGRESS : curso m, transcurso m ‹to run its course : seguir su curso› 2 DIRECTION : rumbo m (de un avión), derrota f, derrotero m (de un barco) 3 PATH, WAY : camino m, vía f ‹course of action : línea de conducta› 4 : plato m (de una cena) ‹the main course : el plato principal› 5 : curso m (académico) 6 of course : desde luego, por supuesto ‹yes, of course! : ¡claro que sí!›

court[1] ['kort] vt WOO : cortejar, galantear

court[2] n 1 PALACE : palacio m 2 RETINUE : corte f, séquito m 3 COURTYARD : patio m 4 : cancha f (de tenis, baloncesto, etc.) 5 TRIBUNAL : corte f, tribunal m ⟨the Supreme Court : la Corte Suprema⟩

courteous ['kortiəs] adj : cortés, atento, educado — **courteously** adv

courtesan ['kortəzən, 'kər-] n : cortesana f

courtesy ['kərtəsi] n, pl -sies : cortesía f

courthouse ['kort,haus] n : palacio m de justicia, juzgado m

courtier ['kortiər, 'kortjər] n : cortesano m, -na f

courtly ['kortli] adj -lier; -est : distinguido, elegante, cortés

court–martial[1] ['kort,marʃəl] vt : someter a consejo de guerra

court–martial[2] n, pl **courts–martial** ['korts,marʃəl] : consejo m de guerra

court order n : mandamiento m judicial

courtroom ['kort,ru:m] n : tribunal m, corte f

courtship ['kort,ʃɪp] n : cortejo m, noviazgo m

courtyard ['kort,jard] n : patio m

cousin ['kʌzən] n : primo m, -ma f

couture [ku:'tʊr] n : industria f de la moda ⟨haute couture : alta costura⟩

cove ['ko:v] n : ensenada f, cala f

covenant ['kʌvənənt] n : pacto m, contrato m

cover[1] ['kʌvər] vt 1 : cubrir, tapar ⟨cover your head : tápate la cabeza⟩ ⟨covered with mud : cubierto de lodo⟩ 2 HIDE, PROTECT : cubrir, proteger 3 TREAT : tratar 4 INSURE : asegurar, cubrir

cover[2] n 1 SHELTER : cubierta f, abrigo m, refugio m ⟨to take cover : ponerse a cubierto⟩ ⟨under cover of darkness : al amparo de la oscuridad⟩ 2 LID, TOP : cubierta f, tapa f 3 : cubierta f (de un libro), portada f (de una revista) 4 **covers** npl BEDCLOTHES : ropa f de cama, cobijas fpl, mantas fpl

coverage ['kʌvərɪʤ] n : cobertura f

coverlet ['kʌvərlət] n : cobertor m

covert[1] ['ko:,vərt, 'kʌvərt] adj : encubierto, secreto ⟨covert operations : operaciones encubiertas⟩

covert[2] ['kʌvərt, 'ko:-] n THICKET : espesura f, maleza f

cover–up ['kʌvər,ʌp] n : encubrimiento m (de algo ilícito)

covet ['kʌvət] vt : codiciar

covetous ['kʌvətəs] adj : codicioso

covey ['kʌvi] n, pl **-eys** 1 : bandada f pequeña (de codornices, etc.) 2 GROUP : grupo m

cow[1] ['kau] vt : intimidar, acobardar

cow[2] n : vaca f, hembra f (de ciertas especies)

coward ['kauərd] n : cobarde mf

cowardice ['kauərdɪs] n : cobardía f

cowardly ['kauərdli] adj : cobarde

cowboy ['kau,bɔɪ] n : vaquero m, cowboy m

cower ['kauər] vi : encogerse (de miedo), acobardarse

cowgirl ['kau,gərl] n : vaquera f

cowherd ['kau,hərd] n : vaquero m, -ra f

cowhide ['kau,haid] n : cuero m, piel f de vaca

cowl ['kaul] n : capucha f (de un monje)

cowlick ['kau,lɪk] n : remolino m

cowpuncher ['kau,pʌntʃər] → **cowboy**

cowslip ['kau,slɪp] n : prímula f, primavera f

coxswain ['kaksən, -,swein] n : timonel m

coy ['kɔɪ] adj 1 SHY : tímido, cohibido 2 COQUETTISH : coqueto

coyote [kai'o:ti, 'kai,o:t] n, pl **coyotes** or **coyote** : coyote m

cozy ['ko:zi] adj -zier; -est : acogedor, cómodo

CPU [,si:,pi:'ju:] n (central processing unit) : CPU f

crab ['kræb] n : cangrejo m, jaiba f

crabby ['kræbi] adj -bier; -est : gruñón, malhumorado

crabgrass ['kræb,græs] n : garranchuelo m

crack[1] ['kræk] vi 1 : chasquear, restallar ⟨the whip cracked : el látigo restalló⟩ 2 SPLIT : rajarse, resquebrajarse, agrietarse 3 : quebrarse (dícese de la voz) — vt 1 : restallar, chasquear (un látigo, etc.) 2 SPLIT : rajar, agrietar, resquebrajar 3 BREAK : romper (un huevo), cascar (nueces), forzar (una caja fuerte) 4 SOLVE : resolver, descifrar (un código)

crack[2] adj FIRST-RATE : buenísimo, de primera

crack[3] n 1 : chasquido m, restallido m, estallido m (de un arma de fuego), crujido m (de huesos) ⟨a crack of thunder : un trueno⟩ 2 WISECRACK : chiste m, ocurrencia f, salida f 3 CREVICE : raja f, grieta f, fisura f 4 BLOW : golpe m 5 ATTEMPT : intento m

crackdown ['kræk,daun] n : medidas fpl enérgicas

crack down vt : tomar medidas enérgicas

cracker ['krækər] n : galleta f (de soda, etc.)

crackle[1] ['kræk əl] vi -led; -ling : crepitar, chisporrotear

crackle[2] n : crujido m, chisporroteo m

crackpot ['kræk,pat] n : excéntrico m, -ca f, chiflado m, -da f

crack–up ['kræk,ʌp] n 1 CRASH : choque m, estrellamiento m 2 BREAKDOWN : crisis f nerviosa

crack up vt 1 : estrellar (un vehículo) 2 : hacer reír 3 : elogiar ⟨it isn't all that it's cracked up to be : no es tan bueno como se dice⟩ — vi 1 : estrellarse 2 LAUGH : echarse a reír

cradle¹ ['kreɪdəl] *vt* **-dled; -dling** : acunar, mecer (a un niño)
cradle² *n* : cuna *f*
craft ['kræft] *n* **1** TRADE : oficio *m* ⟨the craft of carpentry : el oficio de carpintero⟩ **2** CRAFTSMANSHIP, SKILL : arte *m*, artesanía *f*, destreza *f* **3** CRAFTINESS : astucia *f*, maña *f* **4** *pl usually* craft BOAT : barco *m*, embarcación *f* **5** *pl usually* craft AIRCRAFT : avión *m*, aeronave *f*
craftiness ['kræftinəs] *n* : astucia *f*, maña *f*
craftsman ['kræftsmən] *n, pl* **-men** [-mən, -ˌmɛn] : artesano *m*, -na *f*
craftsmanship ['kræftsmənˌʃɪp] *n* : artesanía *f*, destreza *f*
crafty ['kræfti] *adj* **craftier; -est** : astuto, taimado
crag ['kræg] *n* : peñasco *m*
craggy ['krægi] *adj* **-gier; -est** : peñascoso
cram ['kræm] *v* **crammed; cramming** *vt* **1** JAM : embutir, meter **2** STUFF : atiborrar, abarrotar ⟨crammed with people : atiborrado de gente⟩ — *vi* : estudiar a última hora, memorizar (para un examen)
cramp¹ ['kræmp] *vt* **1** : dar calambre en **2** RESTRICT : limitar, restringir, entorpecer ⟨to cramp someone's style : cortarle el vuelo a alguien⟩ — *vi or* to cramp up : acalambrarse
cramp² *n* **1** SPASM : calambre *m*, espasmo *m* (de los músculos) **2** cramps *npl* : retorcijones *mpl* ⟨stomach cramps : retorcijones de estómago⟩
cranberry ['krænˌbɛri] *n, pl* **-berries** : arándano *m* (rojo y agrio)
crane¹ ['kreɪn] *vt* **craned; craning** : estirar ⟨to crane one's neck : estirar el cuello⟩
crane² *n* **1** : grulla *f* (ave) **2** : grúa *f* (máquina)
cranial ['kreɪniəl] *adj* : craneal, craneano
cranium ['kreɪniəm] *n, pl* **-niums** *or* **-nia** [-niə] : cráneo *m*
crank¹ ['kræŋk] *vt or* to crank up : arrancar (con una manivela)
crank² *n* **1** : manivela *f*, manubrio *m* **2** ECCENTRIC : excéntrico *m*, -ca *f*
cranky ['kræŋki] *adj* **crankier; -est** : irritable, malhumorado, enojadizo
cranny ['kræni] *n, pl* **-nies** : grieta *f* ⟨every nook and cranny : todos los rincones⟩
crash¹ ['kræʃ] *vi* **1** SMASH : caerse con estrépito, estrellarse **2** COLLIDE : estrellarse, chocar **3** BOOM, RESOUND : retumbar, resonar — *vt* **1** SMASH : estrellar **2** to crash a party : colarse en una fiesta **3** to crash one's car : tener un accidente
crash² *n* **1** DIN : estrépito *m* **2** COLLISION : choque *m*, colisión *f* ⟨car crash : accidente automovilístico⟩ **3** FAILURE : quiebra *f* (de un negocio), crac *m* (de la bolsa)

crass ['kræs] *adj* : grosero, de mal gusto
crate¹ ['kreɪt] *vt* **crated; crating** : empacar en un cajón
crate² *n* : cajón *m* (de madera)
crater ['kreɪtər] *n* : cráter *m*
cravat [krə'væt] *n* : corbata *f*
crave ['kreɪv] *vt* **craved; craving** : ansiar, apetecer, tener muchas ganas de
craven ['kreɪvən] *adj* : cobarde, pusilánime
craving ['kreɪvɪŋ] *n* : ansia *f*, antojo *m*, deseo *m*
crawfish ['krɔˌfɪʃ] → **crayfish**
crawl¹ ['krɔl] *vi* **1** CREEP : arrastrarse, gatear (dícese de un bebé) **2** TEEM : estar plagado
crawl² *n* : paso *m* lento
crayfish ['kreɪˌfɪʃ] *n* **1** : ástaco *m* (de agua dulce) **2** : langostino *m* (de mar)
crayon ['kreɪˌɑn, -ən] *n* : crayón *m*
craze ['kreɪz] *n* : moda *f* pasajera, manía *f*
crazed ['kreɪzd] *adj* : enloquecido
crazily ['kreɪzəli] *adv* : locamente, erráticamente, insensatamente
craziness ['kreɪzinəs] *n* : locura *f*, demencia *f*
crazy ['kreɪzi] *adj* **-zier; -est** **1** INSANE : loco, demente ⟨to go crazy : volverse loco⟩ **2** ABSURD, FOOLISH : loco, insensato, absurdo **3** like crazy : como loco **4** to be crazy about : estar loco por
creak¹ ['kri:k] *vi* : chirriar, rechinar, crujir
creak² *n* : chirrido *m*, crujido *m*
creaky ['kri:ki] *adj* **creakier; -est** : chirriante, que cruje
cream¹ ['kri:m] *vt* **1** BEAT, MIX : batir, mezclar (azúcar y mantequilla, etc.) **2** : preparar (alimentos) con crema
cream² *n* **1** : crema *f* (de leche) **2** LOTION : crema *f*, loción *f* **3** ELITE : crema *f*, elite *f* ⟨the cream of the crop : la crema y nata, lo mejor⟩
creamery ['kri:məri] *n, pl* **-eries** : fábrica *f* de productos lácteos
creamy ['kri:mi] *adj* **creamier; -est** : cremoso
crease¹ ['kri:s] *vt* **creased; creasing** **1** : plegar, poner una raya en (pantalones) **2** WRINKLE : arrugar
crease² *n* : pliegue *m*, doblez *m*, raya *f* (de pantalones)
create [kri'eɪt] *vt* **-ated; -ating** : crear, hacer
creation [kri'eɪʃən] *n* : creación *f*
creative [kri'eɪtɪv] *adj* : creativo, original ⟨creative people : personas creativas⟩ ⟨a creative work : una obra original⟩
creatively [kri'eɪtɪvli] *adv* : creativamente, con originalidad
creativity [ˌkri:eɪ'tɪvəti] *n* : creatividad *f*
creator [kri'eɪtər] *n* : creador *m*, -dora *f*
creature ['kri:tʃər] *n* : ser *m* viviente, criatura *f*, animal *m*

credence ['kri:dənts] n : crédito m
credentials [krɪ'dɛntʃəlz] npl : referencias fpl oficiales, cartas fpl credenciales
credibility [ˌkrɛdə'bɪlət̬i] n : credibilidad f
credible ['krɛdəbəl] adj : creíble
credit¹ ['krɛdɪt] vt 1 BELIEVE : creer, dar crédito a 2 : ingresar, abonar ⟨to credit $100 to an account : ingresar $100 en (una) cuenta⟩ 3 ATTRIBUTE : atribuir ⟨they credit the invention to him : a él se le atribuye el invento⟩
credit² n 1 : saldo m positivo, saldo m a favor (de una cuenta) 2 : crédito m ⟨to buy on credit : comprar a crédito⟩ ⟨credit card : tarjeta de crédito⟩ 3 CREDENCE : crédito m ⟨I gave credit to everything he said : di crédito a todo lo que dijo⟩ 4 RECOGNITION : reconocimiento m 5 : orgullo m, honor m ⟨she's a credit to the school : ella es el orgullo de la escuela⟩
creditable ['krɛdɪt̬əbəl] adj : encomiable, loable — **creditably** [-bli] adv
credit card n : tarjeta de crédito
creditor ['krɛdɪt̬ər] n : acreedor m, -dora f
credo ['kri:do:, 'kreɪ-] n : credo m
credulity [krɪ'du:lət̬i, -'dju:-] n : credulidad f
credulous ['krɛdʒələs] adj : crédulo
creed ['kri:d] n : credo m
creek ['kri:k, 'krɪk] n : arroyo m, riachuelo m
creel ['kri:l] n : nasa f, cesta f (de pescador)
creep¹ ['kri:p] vi **crept** ['krɛpt]; **creeping** 1 CRAWL : arrastrarse, gatear 2 : moverse lentamente o sigilosamente ⟨he crept out of the house : salió sigilosamente de la casa⟩ 3 SPREAD : trepar (dícese de una planta)
creep² n 1 CRAWL : paso m lento 2 : asqueroso m, -sa f 3 **creeps** npl : escalofríos mpl ⟨that gives me the creeps : eso me da escalofríos⟩
creeper ['kri:pər] n : planta f trepadora, trepadora f
creepy ['kri:pi] adj 1 SPOOKY : espeluznante 2 UNPLEASANT : asqueroso
cremate ['kri:ˌmeɪt] vt **-mated; -mating** : cremar
cremation [krɪ'meɪʃən] n : cremación f
Creole ['kri:ˌo:l] n 1 : criollo m, criolla f 2 : criollo m (idioma) — **Creole** adj
creosote ['kri:əˌso:t] n : creosota f
crepe or **crêpe** ['kreɪp] n 1 : crespón m (tela) 2 PANCAKE : crepe mf, crepa f Mex
crescendo [krɪ'ʃɛnˌdo:] n, pl **-dos** or **-does** : crescendo m
crescent ['krɛsənt] n : creciente m
crest ['krɛst] n 1 : cresta f, penacho m (de un ave) 2 PEAK, TOP : cresta f (de una ola), cima f (de una colina) 3 : emblema m (sobre un escudo de armas)
crestfallen ['krɛstˌfɔlən] adj : alicaído, abatido

cretin ['kri:tən] n : cretino m, -na f
crevasse [krɪ'væs] n : grieta f, fisura f
crevice ['krɛvɪs] n : grieta f, hendidura f
crew ['kru:] n 1 : tripulación f (de una nave) 2 TEAM : equipo m (de trabajadores o atletas)
crib ['krɪb] n 1 MANGER : pesebre m 2 GRANARY : granero m 3 : cuna f (de un bebé)
crick ['krɪk] n : calambre m, espasmo m muscular
cricket ['krɪkət] n 1 : grillo m (insecto) 2 : críquet m (juego)
crime ['kraɪm] n 1 : crimen m, delito m ⟨to commit a crime : cometer un delito⟩ 2 : crimen m, delincuencia f ⟨organized crime : crimen organizado⟩
criminal¹ ['krɪmənəl] adj : criminal
criminal² n : criminal mf, delincuente mf
crimp ['krɪmp] vt : ondular, rizar (el pelo), arrugar (una tela, etc.)
crimson ['krɪmzən] n : carmesí m
cringe ['krɪndʒ] vi **cringed; cringing** : encogerse
crinkle¹ ['krɪŋkəl] v **-kled; -kling** : arrugar — vi : arrugarse
crinkle² n : arruga f
crinkly ['krɪŋkəli] adj : arrugado
cripple¹ ['krɪpəl] vt **-pled; -pling** 1 DISABLE : lisiar, dejar inválido 2 INCAPACITATE : inutilizar, incapacitar
cripple² n : lisiado m, -da f
crisis ['kraɪsɪs] n, pl **crises** [-ˌsi:z] : crisis f
crisp¹ ['krɪsp] vt : tostar, hacer crujiente
crisp² adj 1 CRUNCHY : crujiente, crocante 2 FIRM, FRESH : firme, fresco ⟨crisp lettuce : lechuga fresca⟩ 3 LIVELY : vivaz, alegre ⟨a crisp tempo : un ritmo alegre⟩ 4 INVIGORATING : fresco, vigorizante ⟨the crisp autumn air : el fresco aire otoñal⟩ — **crisply** adv
crisp³ n : postre m de fruta (con pedacitos de masa dulce por encima)
crispy ['krɪspi] adj **crispier; -est** : crujiente ⟨crispy potato chips : papitas crujientes⟩
crisscross ['krɪsˌkrɔs] vt : entrecruzar
criterion [kraɪ'tɪriən] n, pl **-ria** [-iə] : criterio m
critic ['krɪt̬ɪk] n 1 : crítico m, -ca f (de las artes) 2 FAULTFINDER : detractor m, -tora f; criticón m, -cona f
critical ['krɪt̬ɪkəl] adj : crítico
critically ['krɪt̬ɪkli] adv : críticamente ⟨critically ill : gravemente enfermo⟩
criticism ['krɪt̬əˌsɪzəm] n : crítica f
criticize ['krɪt̬əˌsaɪz] vt **-cized; -cizing** 1 EVALUATE, JUDGE : criticar, analizar, evaluar 2 CENSURE : criticar, reprobar
critique [krɪ'ti:k] n : crítica f, evaluación f
croak¹ ['kro:k] vi : croar
croak² n : croar m, canto m (de la rana)
Croatian [kro'eɪʃən] n : croata mf — **Croatian** adj

crochet[1] [kro:'ʃeɪ] *v* : tejer al croché
crochet[2] *n* : croché *m*, crochet *m*
crock ['krɑk] *n* : vasija *f* de barro
crockery ['krɑkəri] *n* : vajilla *f* (de barro)
crocodile ['krɑkə,daɪl] *n* : cocodrilo *m*
crocus ['kro:kəs] *n, pl* -cuses : azafrán *m*
croissant [krə'sɑnt] *n* : croissant *m*
crone ['kro:n] *n* : vieja *f* arpía, vieja *f* bruja
crony[1] ['kro:ni] *n, pl* -nies : amigote *m fam*; compinche *mf fam*
crook[1] ['krʊk] *vt* : doblar (el brazo o el dedo)
crook[2] *n* 1 STAFF : cayado *m* (de pastor), báculo *m* (de obispo) 2 THIEF : ratero *m*, -ra *f*; ladrón *m*, -drona *f*
crooked ['krʊkəd] *adj* 1 BENT : chueco, torcido 2 DISHONEST : deshonesto
crookedness ['krʊkədnəs] *n* 1 : lo torcido, lo chueco 2 DISHONESTY : falta *f* de honradez
croon ['kru:n] *v* : cantar suavemente
crop[1] ['krɑp] *v* cropped; cropping *vt* TRIM : recortar, cortar — *vi* to crop up : aparecer, surgir ⟨these problems keep cropping up : estos problemas no cesan de surgir⟩
crop[2] *n* 1 : buche *m* (de un ave o insecto) 2 WHIP : fusta *f* (de jinete) 3 HARVEST : cosecha *f*, cultivo *m*
croquet [kro:'keɪ] *n* : croquet *m*
croquette [kro:'kɛt] *n* : croqueta *f*
cross[1] ['krɔs] *vt* 1 : cruzar, atravesar ⟨to cross the street : cruzar la calle⟩ ⟨several canals cross the city : varios canales atraviesan la ciudad⟩ 2 CANCEL : tachar, cancelar ⟨he crossed his name off the list : tachó su nombre de la planilla⟩ 3 INTERBREED : cruzar (en genética)
cross[2] *adj* 1 : que atraviesa ⟨cross ventilation : ventilación que atraviesa un cuarto⟩ 2 CONTRARY : contrario, opuesto ⟨cross purposes : objetivos opuestos⟩ 3 ANGRY : enojado, de mal humor
cross[3] *n* 1 : cruz *f* ⟨the sign of the cross : la señal de la cruz⟩ 2 : cruza *f* (en biología)
crossbones ['krɔs,bo:nz] *npl* 1 : huesos *mpl* cruzados 2 → skull
crossbow ['krɔs,bo:] *n* : ballesta *f*
crossbreed ['krɔs,bri:d] *vt* -bred [-,brɛd]; -breeding : cruzar
crosscurrent ['krɔs,kərənt] *n* : contracorriente *f*
cross-examination [,krɔsɪg,zæmə'neɪʃən] *n* : repreguntas *fpl*, interrogatorio *m*
cross-examine [,krɔsɪg'zæmən] *vt* -ined; -ining : repreguntar
cross-eyed ['krɔs,aɪd] *adj* : bizco
crossing ['krɔsɪŋ] *n* 1 INTERSECTION : cruce *m*, paso *m* ⟨pedestrian crossing : paso *m* de peatones⟩ 2 VOYAGE : travesía *f* (del mar)

crossly ['krɔsli] *adv* : con enojo, con enfado
cross-reference [,krɔs'rɛfrənts, -'rɛfə-rənts] *n* : referencia *f*, remisión *f*
crossroads ['krɔs,ro:dz] *n* : cruce *m*, encrucijada *f*, crucero *m Mex*
cross section *n* 1 SECTION : corte *m* transversal 2 SAMPLE : muestra *f* representativa ⟨a cross section of the population : una muestra representativa de la población⟩
crosswalk ['krɔs,wɔk] *n* : cruce *m* peatonal, paso *m* de peatones
crossways ['krɔs,weɪz] → **crosswise**
crosswise[1] ['krɔs,waɪz] *adv* : transversalmente, diagonalmente
crosswise[2] *adj* : transversal, diagonal
crossword puzzle ['krɔs,wərd] *n* : crucigrama *m*
crotch ['krɑtʃ] *n* : entrepierna *f*
crotchety ['krɑtʃəti] *adj* CRANKY : malhumorado, irritable, enojadizo
crouch ['kraʊtʃ] *vi* : agacharse, ponerse de cuclillas
croup ['kru:p] *n* : crup *m*
crouton ['kru:,tɑn] *n* : crutón *m*
crow[1] ['kro:] *vi* 1 : cacarear, cantar (como un cuervo) 2 BRAG : alardear, presumir
crow[2] *n* 1 : cuervo *m* (ave) 2 : cantar *m* (del gallo)
crowbar ['kro:,bɑr] *n* : palanca *f*
crowd[1] ['kraʊd] *vi* : aglomerarse, amontonarse — *vt* : atestar, atiborrar, llenar
crowd[2] *n* : multitud *f*, muchedumbre *f*, gentío *m*
crown[1] ['kraʊn] *vt* : coronar
crown[2] *n* : corona *f*
crow's nest *n* : cofa *f*
crucial ['kru:ʃəl] *adj* : crucial, decisivo
crucible ['kru:səbəl] *n* : crisol *m*
crucifix ['kru:sə,fɪks] *n* : crucifijo *m*
crucifixion [,kru:sə'fɪkʃən] *n* : crucifixión *f*
crucify ['kru:sə,faɪ] *vt* -fied; -fying : crucificar
crude ['kru:d] *adj* **cruder; -est** 1 RAW, UNREFINED : crudo, sin refinar ⟨crude oil : petróleo crudo⟩ 2 VULGAR : grosero, de mal gusto 3 ROUGH : tosco, burdo, rudo
crudely ['kru:dli] *adv* 1 VULGARLY : groseramente 2 ROUGHLY : burdamente, de manera rudimentaria
crudity ['kru:dəti] *n, pl* -ties 1 VULGARITY : grosería *f* 2 COARSENESS, ROUGHNESS : tosquedad *f*, rudeza *f*
cruel ['kru:əl] *adj* -eler *or* -eller; -elest *or* -ellest : cruel
cruelly ['kru:əli] *adv* : cruelmente
cruelty ['kru:əlti] *n, pl* -ties : crueldad *f*
cruet ['kru:ɪt] *n* : vinagrera *f*, aceitera *f*
cruise[1] ['kru:z] *vi* **cruised; cruising** 1 : hacer un crucero 2 : navegar o conducir a una velocidad constante ⟨cruising speed : velocidad de crucero⟩
cruise[2] *n* : crucero *m*

cruiser ['kru:zər] n **1** WARSHIP : crucero m, buque m de guerra **2** : patrulla f (de policía)

crumb ['krʌm] n : miga f, migaja f

crumble ['krʌmbəl] v **-bled; -bling** vt : desmigajar, desmenuzar — vi : desmigajarse, desmoronarse, desmenuzarse

crumbly ['krʌmbli] adj : que se desmenuza fácilmente, friable

crumple ['krʌmpəl] v **-pled; -pling** vt RUMPLE : arrugar — vi **1** WRINKLE : arrugarse **2** COLLAPSE : desplomarse

crunch¹ ['krʌntʃ] vt **1** : ronzar (con los dientes) **2** : hacer crujir (con los pies, etc.) — vi : crujir

crunch² n : crujido m

crunchy ['krʌntʃi] adj **crunchier; -est** : crujiente

crusade¹ [kru:'seɪd] vi **-saded; -sading** : hacer una campaña (a favor de o contra algo)

crusade² n **1** : campaña f (de reforma, etc.) **2** Crusade : cruzada f

crusader [kru:'seɪdər] n **1** : cruzado m (en la Edad Media) **2** : campeón m, -peona f (de una causa)

crush¹ ['krʌʃ] vt **1** SQUASH : aplastar, apachurrar **2** GRIND, PULVERIZE : triturar, machacar **3** SUPPRESS : aplastar, suprimir

crush² n **1** CROWD, MOB : gentío m, multitud f, aglomeración f **2** INFATUATION : enamoramiento m

crushing ['krʌʃɪŋ] adj : aplastante, abrumador

crust ['krʌst] n **1** : corteza f, costra f (de pan) **2** : tapa f de masa, pasta f (de un pastel) **3** LAYER : capa f, corteza f ⟨the earth's crust : la corteza terrestre⟩

crustacean [ˌkrʌs'teɪʃən] n : crustáceo m

crusty ['krʌsti] adj **crustier; -est 1** : de corteza dura **2** CROSS, GRUMPY : enojado, malhumorado

crutch ['krʌtʃ] n : muleta f

crux ['krʌks, 'kruks] n, pl **cruxes** : quid m, esencia f, meollo m ⟨the crux of the problem : el quid del problema⟩

cry¹ ['kraɪ] vi **cried; crying 1** SHOUT : gritar ⟨they cried for more : a gritos pidieron más⟩ **2** WEEP : llorar

cry² n, pl **cries 1** SHOUT : grito m **2** WEEPING : llanto m **3** : chillido m (de un animal)

crybaby ['kraɪˌbeɪbi] n, pl **-bies** : llorón m, -rona f

crypt ['krɪpt] n : cripta f

cryptic ['krɪptɪk] adj : enigmático, críptico

crystal ['krɪstəl] n : cristal m

crystalline ['krɪstəlɪn] adj : cristalino

crystallize ['krɪstəˌlaɪz] v **-lized; -lizing** vt : cristalizar, materializar ⟨to crystallize one's thoughts : cristalizar uno sus pensamientos⟩ — vi : cristalizarse

cub ['kʌb] n : cachorro m

Cuban ['kju:bən] n : cubano m, -na f — **Cuban** adj

cubbyhole ['kʌbiˌho:l] n : chiribitil m

cube¹ ['kju:b] vt **cubed; cubing 1** : elevar (un número) al cubo **2** : cortar en cubos

cube² n **1** : cubo m **2 ice cube** : cubito m de hielo **3 sugar cube** : terrón m de azúcar

cubic ['kju:bɪk] adj : cúbico

cubicle ['kju:bɪkəl] n : cubículo m

cuckoo¹ ['ku:ˌku:, 'ku-] adj : loco, chiflado

cuckoo² n, pl **-oos** : cuco m, cuclillo m

cucumber ['kju:ˌkʌmbər] n : pepino m

cud ['kʌd] n **to chew the cud** : rumiar

cuddle ['kʌdəl] v **-dled; -dling** vi : abrazarse tiernamente, acurrucarse — vt : abrazar

cudgel¹ ['kʌdʒəl] vt **-geled** or **-gelled; -geling** or **-gelling** : apalear, aporrear

cudgel² n : garrote m, porra f

cue¹ ['kju:] vt **cued; cuing** or **cueing** : darle el pie a, darle la señal a

cue² n **1** SIGNAL : señal f, pie m (en teatro), entrada f (en música) **2** : taco m (de billar)

cuff¹ ['kʌf] vt : bofetear, cachetear

cuff² n **1** : puño m (de una camisa), vuelta f (de pantalones) **2** SLAP : bofetada f, cachetada f **3 cuffs** npl HANDCUFFS : esposas fpl

cuisine [kwɪ'zi:n] n : cocina f ⟨Mexican cuisine : la cocina mexicana⟩

culinary ['kʌləˌneri, 'kju:lə-] adj : culinario

cull ['kʌl] vt : seleccionar, entresacar

culminate ['kʌlməˌneɪt] vi **-nated; -nating** : culminar

culmination [ˌkʌlmə'neɪʃən] n : culminación f, punto m culminante

culpable ['kʌlpəbəl] adj : culpable

culprit ['kʌlprɪt] n : culpable mf

cult ['kʌlt] n : culto m

cultivate ['kʌltəˌveɪt] vt **-vated; -vating 1** TILL : cultivar, labrar **2** FOSTER : cultivar, fomentar **3** REFINE : cultivar, refinar ⟨to cultivate the mind : cultivar la mente⟩

cultivation [ˌkʌltə'veɪʃən] n **1** : cultivo m ⟨under cultivation : en cultivo⟩ **2** CULTURE, REFINEMENT : cultura f, refinamiento m

cultural ['kʌltʃərəl] adj : cultural — **culturally** adv

culture ['kʌltʃər] n **1** CULTIVATION : cultivo m **2** REFINEMENT : cultura f, educación f, refinamiento m **3** CIVILIZATION : cultura f, civilización f ⟨the Incan culture : la cultura inca⟩

cultured ['kʌltʃərd] adj **1** EDUCATED, REFINED : culto, educado, refinado **2** : de cultivo, cultivado ⟨cultured pearls : perlas de cultivo⟩

culvert ['kʌlvərt] n : alcantarilla f

cumbersome ['kʌmbərsəm] adj : torpe y pesado, difícil de manejar

cumin ['kʌmən] n : comino m

cumulative ['kju:mjələtɪv, -ˌleɪtɪv] adj : acumulativo

cumulus ['kju:mjələs] *n, pl* **-li** [-,laɪ, -,li:] : cúmulo *m*

cunning¹ ['kʌnɪŋ] *adj* **1** CRAFTY : astuto, taimado **2** CLEVER : ingenioso, hábil **3** CUTE : mono, gracioso, lindo

cunning² *n* **1** SKILL : habilidad *f* **2** CRAFTINESS : astucia *f*, maña *f*

cup¹ ['kʌp] *vt* **cupped; cupping** : ahuecar (las manos)

cup² *n* **1** : taza *f* ⟨a cup of coffee : una taza de café⟩ **2** CUPFUL : taza *f* **3** : media pinta *f* (unidad de medida) **4** GOBLET : copa *f* **5** TROPHY : copa *f*, trofeo *m*

cupboard ['kʌbərd] *n* : alacena *f*, armario *m*

cupcake ['kʌp,keɪk] *n* : pastelito *m*

cupful ['kʌp,fʊl] *n* : taza *f*

cupola ['kju:pələ, -,lo:] *n* : cúpula *f*

cur ['kər] *n* : perro *m* callejero, perro *m* corriente *Mex*

curate ['kjʊrət] *n* : cura *m*, párroco *m*

curator ['kjʊr,eɪtər, kjʊ'reɪtər] *n* : conservador *m*, -dora *f* (de un museo); director *m*, -tora *f* (de un zoológico)

curb¹ ['kərb] *vt* : refrenar, restringir, controlar

curb² *n* **1** RESTRAINT : freno *m*, control *m* **2** : borde *m* de la acera

curd ['kərd] *n* : cuajada *f*

curdle ['kərdəl] *v* **-dled; -dling** *vi* : cuajarse — *vt* : cuajar ⟨to curdle one's blood : helarle la sangre a uno⟩

cure¹ ['kjʊr] *vt* **cured; curing 1** HEAL : curar, sanar **2** REMEDY : remediar **3** PROCESS : curar (alimentos, etc.)

cure² *n* **1** RECOVERY : curación *f*, recuperación *f* **2** REMEDY : cura *f*, remedio *m*

curfew ['kər,fju:] *n* : toque *m* de queda

curio ['kjʊri,o:] *n, pl* **-rios** : curiosidad *f*, objeto *m* curioso

curiosity [,kjʊri'ɑsəti] *n, pl* **-ties** : curiosidad *f*

curious ['kjʊriəs] *adj* **1** INQUISITIVE : curioso **2** STRANGE : curioso, raro

curl¹ ['kərl] *vt* **1** : rizar, ondular (el pelo) **2** COIL : enrollar **3** TWIST : torcer ⟨to curl one's lip : hacer una mueca⟩ — *vi* **1** : rizarse, ondularse **2** to curl up : acurrucarse (con un libro, etc.)

curl² *n* **1** RINGLET : rizo *m* **2** COIL : espiral *f*, rosca *f*

curler ['kərlər] *n* : rulo *m*

curlew ['kər,lu:, 'kərl,ju:] *n, pl* **-lews** *or* **-lew** : zarapito *m*

curly ['kərli] *adj* **curlier; -est** : rizado, crespo

currant ['kərənt] *n* **1** : grosella *f* (fruta) **2** RAISIN : pasa *f* de Corinto

currency ['kərənsi] *n, pl* **-cies 1** PREVALENCE, USE : uso *m*, aceptación *f*, difusión *f* ⟨to be in currency : estar en uso⟩ **2** MONEY : moneda *f*, dinero *m*

current¹ ['kərənt] *adj* **1** PRESENT : actual ⟨current events : actualidades⟩ **2** PREVALENT : corriente, común — **currently** *adv*

current² *n* : corriente *f*

curriculum [kə'rɪkjələm] *n, pl* **-la** [-lə] : currículum *m*, currículo *m*, programa *m* de estudio

curriculum vitae ['vi:,taɪ, 'vaɪtiː] *n, pl* **curricula vitae** : currículum *m*, currículo *m*

curry¹ ['kəri] *vt* **-ried; -rying 1** GROOM : almohazar (un caballo) **2** : condimentar con curry **3 to curry favor** : congraciarse (con alguien)

curry² *n, pl* **-ries** : curry *m*

curse¹ ['kərs] *v* **cursed; cursing** *vt* **1** DAMN : maldecir **2** INSULT : injuriar, insultar, decir malas palabras a **3** AFFLICT : afligir — *vi* : maldecir, decir malas palabras

curse² *n* **1** : maldición *f* ⟨to put a curse on someone : echarle una maldición a alguien⟩ **2** AFFLICTION : maldición *f*, aflicción *f*, cruz *f*

cursor ['kərsər] *n* : cursor *m*

cursory ['kərsəri] *adj* : rápido, superficial, somero

curt ['kərt] *adj* : cortante, brusco, seco — **curtly** *adv*

curtail [kər'teɪl] *vt* : acortar, limitar, restringir

curtailment [kər'teɪlmənt] *n* : restricción *f*, limitación *f*

curtain ['kərtən] *n* : cortina *f* (de una ventana), telón *m* (en un teatro)

curtness ['kərtnəs] *n* : brusquedad *f*, sequedad *f*

curtsy¹ *or* **curtsey** ['kərtsi] *vt* **-sied** *or* **-seyed; -sying** *or* **-seying** : hacer una reverencia

curtsy² *or* **curtsey** *n, pl* **-sies** *or* **-seys** : reverencia *f*

curvature ['kərvə,tʃʊr] *n* : curvatura *f*

curve¹ ['kərv] *v* **curved; curving** *vi* : torcerse, describir una curva — *vt* : encorvar

curve² *n* : curva *f*

cushion¹ ['kʊʃən] *vt* **1** : poner cojines o almohadones a **2** SOFTEN : amortiguar, mitigar, suavizar ⟨to cushion a blow : amortiguar un golpe⟩

cushion² *n* **1** : cojín *m*, almohadón *m* **2** PROTECTION : colchón *m*, protección *f*

cusp ['kʌsp] *n* : cúspide *f* (de un diente), cuerno *m* (de la luna)

cuspid ['kʌspɪd] *n* : diente *m* canino, colmillo *m*

custard ['kʌstərd] *n* : natillas *fpl*

custodian [,kʌ'sto:diən] *n* : custodio *m*, -dia *f*; guardián, -diana *f*

custody ['kʌstədi] *n, pl* **-dies** : custodia *f*, cuidado *m* ⟨to be in custody : estar detenido⟩

custom¹ ['kʌstəm] *adj* : a la medida, a la orden

custom² *n* **1** : costumbre *f*, tradición *f* **2 customs** *npl* : aduana *f*

customarily [,kʌstə'merəli] *adv* : habitualmente, normalmente, de costumbre

customary [ˈkʌstəˌmɛri] *adj* **1** TRADI-
TIONAL : tradicional **2** USUAL : habitual, de costumbre
customer [ˈkʌstəmər] *n* : cliente *m*, -ta *f*
custom—made [ˈkʌstəmˈmeɪd] *adj* : hecho a la medida
cut[1] [ˈkʌt] *v* **cut; cutting** *vt* **1** : cortar ⟨to
cut paper : cortar papel⟩ **2** : cortarse
⟨to cut one's finger : cortarse uno el
dedo⟩ **3** TRIM : cortar, recortar ⟨to
have one's hair cut : cortarse el pelo⟩
4 INTERSECT : cruzar, atravesar **5**
SHORTEN : acortar, abreviar **6** REDUCE
: reducir, rebajar ⟨to cut prices : rebajar los precios⟩ **7 to cut one's teeth**
: salirle los dientes a uno — *vi* **1** : cortar, cortarse **2 to cut in** : entrometerse
cut[2] *n* **1** : corte *m* ⟨a cut of meat : un
corte de carne⟩ **2** SLASH : tajo *m*, corte
m, cortadura *f* **3** REDUCTION : rebaja
f, reducción *f* ⟨a cut in the rates : una
rebaja en las tarifas⟩
cute [ˈkjuːt] *adj* **cuter; -est** : mono *fam*,
lindo
cuticle [ˈkjuːtɪkəl] *n* : cutícula *f*
cutlass [ˈkʌtləs] *n* : alfanje *m*
cutlery [ˈkʌtləri] *n* : cubiertos *mpl*
cutlet [ˈkʌtlət] *n* : chuleta *f*
cutter [ˈkʌtər] *n* **1** : cortadora *f* (implemento) **2** : cortador *m*, -dora *f* (persona) **3** : cúter *m* (embarcación)
cutthroat [ˈkʌtˌθroːt] *adj* : despiadado,
desalmado ⟨cutthroat competition
: competencia feroz⟩
cutting[1] [ˈkʌtɪŋ] *adj* **1** : cortante ⟨a cutting wind : un viento cortante⟩ **2** CAUS-
TIC : mordaz

cutting[2] *n* : esqueje *m* (de una planta)
cuttlefish [ˈkʌtəlˌfɪʃ] *n, pl* **-fish** *or*
-fishes : jibia *f*, sepia *f*
cyanide [ˈsaɪəˌnaɪd, -nɪd] *n* : cianuro *m*
cycle[1] [ˈsaɪkəl] *vi* **-cled; -cling** : andar en
bicicleta, ir en bicicleta
cycle[2] *n* **1** : ciclo *m* ⟨life cycle : ciclo de
vida, ciclo vital⟩ **2** BICYCLE : bicicleta
f **3** MOTORCYCLE : motocicleta *f*
cyclic [ˈsaɪklɪk, ˈsɪ-] *or* **cyclical** [-klɪkəl]
adj : cíclico
cyclist [ˈsaɪklɪst] *n* : ciclista *mf*
cyclone [ˈsaɪˌkloːn] *n* **1** : ciclón *m* **2**
TORNADO : tornado *m*
cyclopedia *or* **cyclopaedia** [ˌsaɪklə-
ˈpiːdiə] → **encyclopedia**
cylinder [ˈsɪləndər] *n* : cilindro *m*
cylindrical [səˈlɪndrɪkəl] *adj* : cilíndrico
cymbal [ˈsɪmbəl] *n* : platillo *m*, címbalo
m
cynic [ˈsɪnɪk] *n* : cínico *m*, -ca *f*
cynical [ˈsɪnɪkəl] *adj* : cínico
cynicism [ˈsɪnəˌsɪzəm] *n* : cinismo *m*
cypress [ˈsaɪprəs] *n* : ciprés *m*
Cypriot [ˈsɪpriət, -ˌɑt] *n* : chipriota *mf* —
Cypriot *adj*
cyst [ˈsɪst] *n* : quiste *m*
cytoplasm [ˈsaɪtoˌplæzəm] *n* : citoplasma *m*
czar [ˈzɑr, ˈsɑr] *n* : zar *m*
czarina [zɑˈriːnə, sɑ-] *n* : zarina *f*
Czech [ˈtʃɛk] *n* **1** : checo *m*, -ca *f* **2**
: checo (idioma) — **Czech** *adj*
Czechoslovak [ˌtʃɛkoˈsloːˌvɑk, -ˈslovək] *or*
Czechoslovakian [-sloˈvɑkiən, -ˈvæ-] *n*
: checoslovaco *m*, -ca *f* — **Czechoslovak** *or* **Czechoslovakian** *adj*

D

d [ˈdiː] *n, pl* **d's** *or* **ds** [ˈdiːz] : cuarta
letra del alfabeto inglés
dab[1] [ˈdæb] *vt* **dabbed; dabbing** : darle
toques ligeros a, aplicar suavemente
dab[2] *n* **1** BIT : toque *m*, pizca *f*, poco *m*
⟨a dab of ointment : un toque de
ungüento⟩ **2** PAT : toque *m* ligero,
golpecito *m*
dabble [ˈdæbəl] *v* **-bled; -bling** *vt* SPAT-
TER : salpicar — *vi* **1** SPLASH
: chapotear **2** TRIFLE : jugar, interesarse superficialmente
dabbler [ˈdæbələr] *n* : diletante *mf*
dachshund [ˈdɑksˌhʊnt, -ˌhʊnd; ˈdɑk-
sənt, -sənd] *n* : perro *m* salchicha
dad [ˈdæd] *n* : papá *m fam*
daddy [ˈdædi] *n, pl* **-dies** : papi *m fam*
daffodil [ˈdæfəˌdɪl] *n* : narciso *m*
daft [ˈdæft] *adj* : tonto, bobo
dagger [ˈdægər] *n* : daga *f*, puñal *m*
dahlia [ˈdæljə, ˈdɑl-, ˈdeɪl-] *n* : dalia *f*
daily[1] [ˈdeɪli] *adv* : a diario, diariamente
daily[2] *adj* : diario, cotidiano
daily[3] *n, pl* **-lies** : diario *m*, periódico *m*
daintily [ˈdeɪntəli] *adv* : delicadamente,
con delicadeza

daintiness [ˈdeɪntinəs] *n* : delicadeza *f*,
finura *f*
dainty[1] [ˈdeɪnti] *adj* **-tier; -est 1** DELI-
CATE : delicado **2** FASTIDIOUS : remilgado, melindroso **3** DELICIOUS : exquisito, sabroso
dainty[2] *n, pl* **-ties** DELICACY : exquisitez
f, manjar *m*
dairy [ˈdæri] *n, pl* **-ies 1** *or* **dairy store**
: lechería *f* **2** *or* **dairy farm** : granja *f*
lechera
dairymaid [ˈdæriˌmeɪd] *n* : lechera *f*
dairyman [ˈdærimən, -ˌmæn] *n, pl* **-men**
[-mən, -ˌmɛn] : lechero *m*
dais [ˈdeɪəs] *n* : tarima *f*, estrado *m*
daisy [ˈdeɪzi] *n, pl* **-sies** : margarita *f*
dale [ˈdeɪl] *n* : valle *m*
dally [ˈdæli] *vi* **-lied; -lying 1** TRIFLE
: juguetear **2** DAWDLE : entretenerse,
perder tiempo
dalmatian [dælˈmeɪʃən, dɔl-] *n* : dálmata *m*
dam[1] [ˈdæm] *vt* **dammed; damming**
: represar, embalsar
dam[2] *n* **1** : represa *f*, dique *m* **2** : madre
f (de animales domésticos)

damage¹ ['dæmɪʤ] *vt* **-aged; -aging** : dañar (un objeto o una máquina), perjudicar (la salud o una reputación)

damage² *n* **1** : daño *m*, perjuicio *m* **2 damages** *npl* : daños y perjuicios *mpl*

damaging ['dæməʤɪŋ] *adj* : perjudicial

damask ['dæməsk] *n* : damasco *m*

dame ['deɪm] *n* LADY : dama *f*, señora *f*

damn¹ ['dæm] *vt* **1** CONDEMN : condenar **2** CURSE : maldecir

damn² *or* **damned** ['dæmd] *adj* : condenado *fam*, maldito *fam*

damn³ *n* : pito *m*, bledo *m*, comino *m* ⟨it's not worth a damn : no vale un pito⟩ ⟨I don't give a damn : me importa un comino⟩

damnable ['dæmnəbəl] *adj* : condenable, detestable

damnation [dæm'neɪʃən] *n* : condenación *f*

damned¹ ['dæmd] *adv* VERY : muy

damned² *adj* **1** → **damnable 2** REMARKABLE : extraordinario

damp¹ ['dæmp] *vt* → **dampen**

damp² *adj* : húmedo

damp³ *n* MOISTURE : humedad *f*

dampen ['dæmpən] *vt* **1** MOISTEN : humedecer **2** DISCOURAGE : desalentar, desanimar

damper ['dæmpər] *n* **1** : regulador *m* de tiro (de una chimenea) **2** : sordina *f* (de un piano) **3 to put a damper on** : desanimar, apagar (el entusiasmo), enfriar

dampness ['dæmpnəs] *n* : humedad *f*

damsel ['dæmzəl] *n* : damisela *f*

dance¹ ['dænts] *v* **danced; dancing** : bailar

dance² *n* : baile *m*

dancer ['dæntsər] *n* : bailarín *m*, -rina *f*

dandelion ['dændəl,aɪən] *n* : diente *m* de león

dandruff ['dændrəf] *n* : caspa *f*

dandy¹ ['dændi] *adj* **-dier; -est** : excelente, magnífico, macanudo *fam*

dandy² *n, pl* **-dies 1** FOP : dandi *m* **2** : algo *m* excelente ⟨this new program is a dandy : este programa nuevo es algo excelente⟩

Dane ['deɪn] *n* : danés *m*, -nesa *f*

danger ['deɪnʤər] *n* : peligro *m*

dangerous ['deɪnʤərəs] *adj* : peligroso

dangle ['dæŋgəl] *v* **-gled; -gling** *vi* HANG : colgar, pender — *vt* **1** SWING : hacer oscilar **2** PROFFER : ofrecer (como un incentivo) **3 to keep someone dangling** : dejar a alguien en suspenso

Danish¹ ['deɪnɪʃ] *adj* : danés

Danish² *n* : danés *m* (idioma)

dank ['dæŋk] *adj* : frío y húmedo

dapper ['dæpər] *adj* : pulcro, atildado

dappled ['dæpəld] *adj* : moteado ⟨a dappled horse : un caballo rodado⟩

dare¹ ['dær] *v* **dared; daring** *vi* : osar, atreverse ⟨how dare you! : ¡cómo te atreves!⟩ — *vt* **1** CHALLENGE : desafiar, retar **2 to dare to do something** : atreverse a hacer algo, osar hacer algo

dare² *n* : desafío *m*, reto *m*

daredevil ['dær,dɛvəl] *n* : persona *f* temeraria

daring¹ ['dærɪŋ] *adj* : osado, atrevido, audaz

daring² *n* : arrojo *m*, coraje *m*, audacia *f*

dark ['dɑrk] *adj* **1** : oscuro (dícese del ambiente o de los colores), moreno (dícese del pelo o de la piel) **2** SOMBER : sombrío, triste

darken ['dɑrkən] *vt* **1** DIM : oscurecer **2** SADDEN : entristecer — *vi* : ensombrecerse, nublarse

darkly ['dɑrkli] *adv* **1** DIMLY : oscuramente **2** GLOOMILY : tristemente **3** MYSTERIOUSLY : misteriosamente, enigmáticamente

darkness ['dɑrknəs] *n* : oscuridad *f*, tinieblas *f*

darling¹ ['dɑrlɪŋ] *adj* **1** BELOVED : querido, amado **2** CHARMING : encantador, mono *fam*

darling² *n* **1** BELOVED : querido *m*, -da *f*; amado *m*, -da *f*; cariño *m*, -ña *f* **2** FAVORITE : preferido *m*, -da *f*; favorito *m*, -ta *f*

darn¹ ['dɑrn] *vt* : zurcir

darn² *n* **1** : zurcido *m* **2** → **damn³**

dart¹ ['dɑrt] *vt* THROW : lanzar, tirar — *vi* DASH : lanzarse, precipitarse

dart² *n* **1** : dardo *m* **2 darts** *npl* : juego *m* de dardos

dash¹ ['dæʃ] *vt* **1** SMASH : romper, estrellar **2** HURL : arrojar, lanzar **3** SPLASH : salpicar **4** FRUSTRATE : frustrar **5 to dash off** : hacer (algo) rápidamente — *vi* **1** SMASH : romperse, estrellarse **2** DART : lanzarse, irse apresuradamente

dash² *n* **1** BURST, SPLASH : arranque *m*, salpicadura *f* (de aguas) **2** : guión *m* largo (signo de puntuación) **3** DROP : gota *f*, pizca *f* **4** VERVE : brío *m* **5** RACE : carrera *f* ⟨a 100-meter dash : una carrera de 100 metros⟩ **6 to make a dash for it** : precipitarse (hacia), echarse a correr **7** → **dashboard**

dashboard ['dæʃ,bord] *n* : tablero *m* de instrumentos

dashing ['dæʃɪŋ] *adj* : gallardo, apuesto

data ['deɪtə, 'dæ-, 'dɑ-] *ns & pl* : datos *mpl*, información *f*

database ['deɪtə,beɪs, 'dæ-, 'dɑ-] *n* : base *f* de datos

date¹ ['deɪt] *v* **dated; dating** *vt* **1** : fechar (una carta, etc.), datar (un objeto) ⟨it was dated June 9 : estaba fechada el 9 de junio⟩ **2** : salir con ⟨she's dating my brother : sale con mi hermano⟩ — *vi* : datar

date² *n* **1** : fecha *f* ⟨to date : hasta la fecha⟩ **2** EPOCH, PERIOD : época *f*, período *m* **3** APPOINTMENT : cita *f* **4** COMPANION : acompañante *mf* **5** : dátil *m* (fruta)

dated ['deɪtəd] *adj* OUT-OF-DATE : anticuado, pasado de moda

datum ['deɪtəm, 'dæ-, 'dɑ-] *n, pl* **-ta** [-[ʈə] *or* **-tums** : dato *m*

daub[1] ['dɔb] *vt* : embadurnar

daub[2] *n* : mancha *f*

daughter ['dɔʈər] *n* : hija *f*

daughter–in–law ['dɔʈərɪn,lɔ] *n, pl* **daughters–in–law** : nuera *f*, hija *f* política

daunt ['dɔnt] *vt* : amilanar, acobardar, intimidar

dauntless ['dɔntləs] *adj* : intrépido, impávido

davenport ['dævən,port] *n* : sofá *m*

dawdle ['dɔdəl] *vi* **-dled; -dling** 1 DALLY : demorarse, entretenerse, perder tiempo 2 LOITER : vagar, holgazanear, haraganear

dawn[1] ['dɔn] *vi* 1 : amanecer, alborear, despuntar ⟨Saturday dawned clear and bright : el sábado amaneció claro y luminoso⟩ 2 **to dawn on** : hacerse obvio ⟨it dawned on me that she was right : me di cuenta de que tenía razón⟩

dawn[2] *n* 1 DAYBREAK : amanecer *m*, alba *f* 2 BEGINNING : albor *m*, comienzo *m* ⟨the dawn of history : los albores de la historia⟩ 3 **from dawn to dusk** : de sol a sol

day ['deɪ] *n* 1 : día *m* 2 DATE : fecha *f* 3 TIME : día *m*, tiempo *m* ⟨in olden days : intaño⟩ 4 WORKDAY : jornada *f* laboral

daybreak ['deɪ,breɪk] *n* : alba *f*, amanecer *m*

day care *n* : servicio *m* de guardería infantil

daydream[1] ['deɪ,dri:m] *vi* : soñar despierto, fantasear

daydream[2] *n* : ensueño *m*, ensoñación *f*, fantasía *f*

daylight ['deɪ,laɪt] *n* 1 : luz *f* del día ⟨in broad daylight : a plena luz del día⟩ 2 → **daybreak** 3 → **daytime**

daylight saving time *n* : hora *f* de verano

daytime ['deɪ,taɪm] *n* : horas *fpl* diurnas, día *m*

daze[1] ['deɪz] *vt* **dazed; dazing** 1 STUN : aturdir 2 DAZZLE : deslumbrar, ofuscar

daze[2] *n* 1 : aturdimiento *m* 2 **in a daze** : aturdido, atontado

dazzle[1] ['dæzəl] *vt* **-zled; -zling** : deslumbrar, ofuscar

dazzle[2] *n* : resplandor *m*, brillo *m*

DDT [,di:,di:'ti:] *n* : DDT *m*

deacon ['di:kən] *n* : diácono *m*

dead[1] ['dɛd] *adv* 1 ABRUPTLY : repentinamente, súbitamente ⟨to stop dead : parar en seco⟩ 2 ABSOLUTELY : absolutamente ⟨I'm dead certain : estoy absolutamente seguro⟩ 3 DIRECTLY : justo ⟨dead ahead : justo adelante⟩

dead[2] *adj* 1 LIFELESS : muerto 2 NUMB : entumecido 3 INDIFFERENT : indiferente, frío 4 INACTIVE : inactivo ⟨a dead volcano : un volcán inactivo⟩ 5 : desconectado (dícese del teléfono),

descargado (dícese de una batería) 6 EXHAUSTED : agotado, derrengado, muerto 7 OBSOLETE : obsoleto, muerto ⟨a dead language : una lengua muerta⟩ 8 EXACT : exacto ⟨in the dead center : justo en el blanco⟩

dead[3] *n* 1 **the dead** : los muertos 2 **in the dead of night** : a las altas horas de la noche 3 **in the dead of winter** : en pleno invierno

deadbeat ['dɛd,bi:t] *n* 1 LOAFER : vago *m*, -ga *f*; holgazán *m*, -zana *f* 2 FREELOADER : gorrón *m*, -rrona *f fam*; gorrero *m*, -ra *f fam*

deaden ['dɛdən] *vt* 1 : atenuar (un dolor), entorpecer (sensaciones) 2 DULL : deslustrar 3 DISPIRIT : desanimar 4 MUFFLE : amortiguar, reducir (sonidos)

dead–end ['dɛd'ɛnd] *adj* 1 : sin salida ⟨dead-end street : calle sin salida⟩ 2 : sin futuro ⟨a dead-end job : un trabajo sin porvenir⟩

dead end *n* : callejón *m* sin salida

dead heat *n* : empate *m*

deadline ['dɛd,laɪn] *n* : fecha *f* límite, fecha *f* tope, plazo *m* (determinado)

deadlock[1] ['dɛd,lɑk] *vt* : estancar — *vi* : estancarse, llegar a punto muerto

deadlock[2] *n* : punto muerto, impasse *m*

deadly[1] ['dɛdli] *adv* : extremadamente, sumamente ⟨deadly serious : muy en serio⟩

deadly[2] *adj* **-lier; -est** 1 LETHAL : mortal, letal, mortífero 2 ACCURATE : certero, preciso ⟨a deadly aim : una puntería infalible⟩ 3 CAPITAL : capital ⟨the seven deadly sins : los siete pecados capitales⟩ 4 DULL : funesto, aburrido 5 EXTREME : extremo, absoluto ⟨a deadly calm : una calma absoluta⟩

deadpan[1] ['dɛd,pæn] *adv* : de manera inexpresiva, sin expresión

deadpan[2] *adj* : inexpresivo, impasible

deaf ['dɛf] *adj* : sordo

deafen ['dɛfən] *vt* **-ened; -ening** : ensordecer

deafening ['dɛfənɪŋ] *adj* : ensordecedor

deaf-mute ['dɛf'mju:t] *n* : sordomudo *m*, -da *f*

deafness ['dɛfnəs] *n* : sordera *f*

deal[1] ['di:l] *v* **dealt; dealing** *vt* 1 APPORTION : repartir ⟨to deal justice : repartir la justicia⟩ 2 DISTRIBUTE : repartir, dar (naipes) 3 DELIVER : asestar, propinar ⟨to deal a blow : asestar un golpe⟩ — *vi* 1 : dar, repartir (en juegos de naipes) 2 **to deal in** : comerciar en, traficar con (drogas) 3 **to deal with** CONCERN : tratar de, tener que ver con ⟨the book deals with poverty : el libro trata de la pobreza⟩ 4 **to deal with** HANDLE : tratar (con), encargarse de 5 **to deal with** TREAT : tratar ⟨the judge dealt with him severely : el juez lo trató con severidad⟩ 6 **to deal with** ACCEPT : aceptar (una situación o desgracia)

deal² *n* **1** : reparto *m* (de naipes) **2** AGREEMENT, TRANSACTION : trato *m*, acuerdo *m*, transacción *f* **3** TREATMENT : trato *m* ⟨he got a raw deal : le hicieron una injusticia⟩ **4** BARGAIN : ganga *f*, oferta *f* **5 a good deal** *or* **a great deal** : mucho, una gran cantidad

dealer ['di:lər] *n* : comerciante *mf*, traficante *mf*

dealership ['di:lər,ʃɪp] *n* : concesión *f*

dealings ['di:lɪŋz] *npl* **1** : relaciones *fpl* (personales) **2** TRANSACTIONS : negocios *mpl*, transacciones *fpl*

dean ['di:n] *n* **1** : deán *m* (del clero) **2** : decano *m*, -na *f* (de una facultad o profesión)

dear¹ ['dɪr] *adj* **1** ESTEEMED, LOVED : querido, estimado ⟨a dear friend : un amigo querido⟩ ⟨Dear Sir : Estimado Señor⟩ **2** COSTLY : caro, costoso

dear² *n* : querido *m*, -da *f*; amado *m*, -da *f*

dearly ['dɪrli] *adv* **1** : mucho ⟨I love them dearly : los quiero mucho⟩ **2** : caro ⟨to pay dearly : pagar caro⟩

dearth ['dərθ] *n* : escasez *f*, carestía *f*

death ['dɛθ] *n* **1** : muerte *f*, fallecimiento *m* ⟨to be the death of : matar⟩ **2** FATALITY : víctima *f* (mortal); muerto *m*, -ta *f* **3** END : fin *m* ⟨the death of civilization : el fin de la civilización⟩

deathbed ['dɛθ,bɛd] *n* : lecho *m* de muerte

deathblow ['dɛθ,blo:] *n* : golpe *m* mortal

deathless ['dɛθləs] *adj* : eterno, inmortal

deathly ['dɛθli] *adj* : de muerte, sepulcral (dícese del silencio), cadavérico (dícese de la palidez)

debacle [dɪ'bɑkəl, -'bæ-] *n* : desastre *m*, debacle *m*, fiasco *m*

debar [dɪ'bɑr] *vt* -barred; -barring : excluir, prohibir

debase [dɪ'beɪs] *vt* -based; -basing : degradar, envilecer

debasement [dɪ'beɪsmənt] *n* : degradación *f*, envilecimiento *m*

debatable [dɪ'beɪtəbəl] *adj* : discutible

debate¹ [dɪ'beɪt] *v* -bated; -bating : debatir, discutir

debate² *n* : debate *m*, discusión *f*

debauch [dɪ'bɔtʃ] *vt* : pervertir, corromper

debauchery [dɪ'bɔtʃəri] *n, pl* -eries : libertinaje *m*, disipación *f*, intemperancia *f*

debilitate [dɪ'bɪlə,teɪt] *vt* -tated; -tating : debilitar

debility [dɪ'bɪləti] *n, pl* -ties : debilidad *f*

debit¹ ['dɛbɪt] *vt* : adeudar, cargar, debitar

debit² *n* : débito *m*, cargo *m*, debe *m*

debonair [,dɛbə'nær] *adj* : elegante y desenvuelto, apuesto

debris [də'bri:, deɪ-; 'deɪ,bri:] *n, pl* -bris [-'bri:z, -,bri:z] **1** RUBBLE, RUINS : escombros *mpl*, ruinas *fpl*, restos *mpl* **2** RUBBISH : basura *f*, deshechos *mpl*

debt ['dɛt] *n* **1** : deuda *f* ⟨to pay a debt : saldar una deuda⟩ **2** INDEBTEDNESS : endeudamiento *m*

debtor ['dɛtər] *n* : deudor *m*, -dora *f*

debunk [dɪ'bʌŋk] *vt* DISCREDIT : desacreditar, desprestigiar

debut¹ [deɪ'bju:, 'deɪ,bju:] *vi* : debutar

debut² *n* **1** : debut *m* (de un actor), estreno *m* (de una obra) **2** : debut *m*, presentación *f* (en sociedad)

debutante ['dɛbju,tɑnt] *n* : debutante *f*

decade ['dɛ,keɪd, dɛ'keɪd] *n* : década *f*

decadence ['dɛkədənts] *n* : decadencia *f*

decadent ['dɛkədənt] *adj* : decadente

decaf¹ ['di:,kæf] → **decaffeinated**

decaf² *n* : café *m* descafeinado

decaffeinated [di'kæfə,neɪtəd] *adj* : descafeinado

decal ['di:,kæl, dɪ'kæl] *n* : calcomanía *f*

decamp [dɪ'kæmp] *vi* : irse, largarse *fam*

decant [dɪ'kænt] *vt* : decantar

decanter [dɪ'kæntər] *n* : licorera *f*, garrafa *f*

decapitate [dɪ'kæpə,teɪt] *vt* -tated; -tating : decapitar

decay¹ [dɪ'keɪ] *vi* **1** DECOMPOSE : descomponerse, pudrirse **2** DETERIORATE : deteriorarse **3** : cariarse (dícese de los dientes)

decay² *n* **1** DECOMPOSITION : descomposición *f* **2** DECLINE, DETERIORATION : decadencia *f*, deterioro *m* **3** : caries *f* (de los dientes)

decease¹ [dɪ'si:s] *vi* -ceased; -ceasing : morir, fallecer

decease² *n* : fallecimiento *m*, defunción *f*, deceso *m*

deceit [dɪ'si:t] *n* **1** DECEPTION : engaño *m* **2** DISHONESTY : deshonestidad *f*

deceitful [dɪ'si:tfəl] *adj* : falso, embustero, engañoso, mentiroso

deceitfully [dɪ'si:tfəli] *adv* : con engaño, con falsedad

deceitfulness [dɪ'si:tfəlnəs] *n* : falsedad *f*, engaño *m*

deceive [dɪ'si:v] *vt* -ceived; -ceiving : engañar, burlar

deceiver [dɪ'si:vər] *n* : impostor *m*, -tora *f*

decelerate [dɪ'sɛlə,reɪt] *vi* -ated; -ating : reducir la velocidad, desacelerar

December [dɪ'sɛmbər] *n* : diciembre *m*

decency ['di:sənʦi] *n, pl* -cies : decencia *f*, decoro *m*

decent ['di:sənt] *adj* **1** CORRECT, PROPER : decente, decoroso, correcto **2** CLOTHED : vestido, presentable **3** MODEST : púdico, modesto **4** ADEQUATE : decente, adecuado ⟨decent wages : paga adecuada⟩

decently ['di:səntli] *adv* : decentemente

decentralize [dɪ'sɛntrə,laɪz] *v* -lized [-,laɪzd]; -lizing [-,laɪzɪŋ] *vt* : descentralizar — *vi* : descentralizarse

deception [dɪ'sɛpʃən] *n* : engaño *m*

deceptive [dɪ'sɛptɪv] *adj* : engañoso, falaz — **deceptively** *adv*

decibel ['dɛsəbəl, -ˌbɛl] *n* : decibelio *m*

decide [dɪ'saɪd] *v* **-cided; -ciding** *vt* 1 CONCLUDE : decidir, llegar a la conclusión de ⟨he decided what to do : decidió qué iba a hacer⟩ 2 DETERMINE : decidir, determinar ⟨one blow decided the fight : un solo golpe determinó la pelea⟩ 3 CONVINCE : decidir ⟨her pleas decided me to help : sus súplicas me decidieron a ayudarla⟩ 4 RESOLVE : resolver — *vi* : decidirse

decided [dɪ'saɪdəd] *adj* 1 UNQUESTIONABLE : indudable 2 RESOLUTE : decidido, resuelto — **decidedly** *adv*

deciduous [dɪ'sɪdʒuəs] *adj* : caduco, de hoja caduca

decimal[1] ['dɛsəməl] *adj* : decimal

decimal[2] *n* : número *m* decimal

decipher [dɪ'saɪfər] *vt* : descifrar — **decipherable** [-əbəl] *adj*

decision [dɪ'sɪʒən] *n* : decisión *f*, determinación *f* ⟨to make a decision : tomar una decisión⟩

decisive [dɪ'saɪsɪv] *adj* 1 DECIDING : decisivo ⟨the decisive vote : el voto decisivo⟩ 2 CONCLUSIVE : decisivo, concluyente, contundente ⟨a decisive victory : una victoria contundente⟩ 3 RESOLUTE : decidido, resuelto, firme

decisively [dɪ'saɪsɪvli] *adv* : con decisión, de manera decisiva

decisiveness [dɪ'saɪsɪvnəs] *n* 1 FORCEFULNESS : contundencia *f* 2 RESOLUTION : firmeza *f*, decisión *f*, determinación *f*

deck[1] ['dɛk] *vt* 1 FLOOR : tumbar, derribar ⟨she decked him with one blow : lo tumbó de un solo golpe⟩ 2 **to deck out** : adornar, engalanar

deck[2] *n* 1 : cubierta *f* (de un barco) 2 *or* **deck of cards** : baraja *f* (de naipes)

declaim [dɪ'kleɪm] *v* : declamar

declaration [ˌdɛklə'reɪʃən] *n* : declaración *f*, pronunciamiento *m* (oficial)

declare [dɪ'klær] *vt* **-clared; -claring** : declarar, manifestar ⟨to declare war : declarar la guerra⟩ ⟨they declared their support : manifestaron su apoyo⟩

decline[1] [dɪ'klaɪn] *v* **-clined; -clining** *vi* 1 DESCEND : descender 2 DETERIORATE : deteriorarse, decaer ⟨her health is declining : su salud se está deteriorando⟩ 3 DECREASE : disminuir, decrecer, decaer 4 REFUSE : rehusar — *vt* 1 INFLECT : declinar 2 REFUSE, TURN DOWN : declinar, rehusar

decline[2] *n* 1 DETERIORATION : decadencia *f*, deterioro *m* 2 DECREASE : disminución *f*, descenso *m* 3 SLOPE : declive *m*, pendiente *f*

decode [dɪ'ko:d] *vt* **-coded; -coding** : descifrar (un mensaje), descodificar (una señal)

decoder [dɪ'ko:dər] *n* : descodificador *m*

decompose [ˌdi:kəm'po:z] *v* **-posed; -posing** *vt* 1 BREAK DOWN : descomponer 2 ROT : descomponer, pudrir — *vi* : descomponerse, pudrirse

decomposition [ˌdi:ˌkɑmpə'zɪʃən] *n* : descomposición *f*

decongestant [ˌdi:kən'dʒɛstənt] *n* : descongestionante *m*

decor *or* **décor** [deɪ'kɔr, 'deɪˌkɔr] *n* : decoración *f*

decorate ['dɛkəˌreɪt] *vt* **-rated; -rating** 1 ADORN : decorar, adornar 2 : condecorar ⟨he was decorated for bravery : lo condecoraron por valor⟩

decoration [ˌdɛkə'reɪʃən] *n* 1 ADORNMENT : decoración *f*, adorno *m* 2 : condecoración *f* (militar)

decorative ['dɛkərətɪv, -ˌreɪ-] *adj* : decorativo, ornamental, de adorno

decorator ['dɛkəˌreɪtər] *n* : decorador *m*, -dora *f*

decorum [dɪ'kɔrəm] *n* : decoro *m*

decoy[1] ['di:ˌkɔɪ, dɪ'-] *vt* : atraer (con señuelo)

decoy[2] *n* : señuelo *m*, reclamo *m*, cimbel *m*

decrease[1] [dɪ'kri:s] *v* **-creased; -creasing** *vi* : decrecer, disminuir, bajar — *vt* : reducir, disminuir

decrease[2] ['di:ˌkri:s] *n* : disminución *f*, descenso *m*, bajada *f*

decree[1] [dɪ'kri:] *vt* **-creed; -creeing** : decretar

decree[2] *n* : decreto *m*

decrepit [dɪ'krɛpɪt] *adj* 1 FEEBLE : decrépito, débil 2 DILAPIDATED : deteriorado, ruinoso

decry [dɪ'kraɪ] *vt* **-cried; -crying** : censurar, criticar

dedicate ['dɛdɪˌkeɪt] *vt* **-cated; -cating** 1 : dedicar ⟨she dedicated the book to Carlos : le dedicó el libro a Carlos⟩ 2 : consagrar, dedicar ⟨to dedicate one's life : consagrar uno su vida⟩

dedication [ˌdɛdɪ'keɪʃən] *n* 1 DEVOTION : dedicación *f*, devoción *f* 2 : dedicatoria *f* (de un libro, una canción, etc.) 3 CONSECRATION : dedicación *f*

deduce [dɪ'du:s, -'dju:s] *vt* **-duced; -ducing** : deducir, inferir

deduct [dɪ'dʌkt] *vt* : deducir, descontar, restar

deductible [dɪ'dʌktəbəl] *adj* : deducible

deduction [dɪ'dʌkʃən] *n* : deducción *f*

deed[1] ['di:d] *vt* : ceder, transferir

deed[2] *n* 1 ACT : acto *m*, acción *f*, hecho *m* ⟨a good deed : una buena acción⟩ 2 FEAT : hazaña *f*, proeza *f* 3 TITLE : escritura *f*, título *m*

deem ['di:m] *vt* : considerar, juzgar

deep[1] ['di:p] *adv* : hondo, profundamente ⟨to dig deep : cavar hondo⟩

deep[2] *adj* 1 : hondo, profundo ⟨the deep end : la parte honda⟩ ⟨a deep wound : una herida profunda⟩ 2 WIDE : ancho 3 INTENSE : profundo, intenso 4 DARK : intenso, subido ⟨deep red : rojo subido⟩ 5 LOW : profundo ⟨a deep tone

: un tono profundo⟩ **6** ABSORBED : absorto ⟨deep in thought : absorto en la meditación⟩

deep³ *n* **1 the deep** : lo profundo, el piélago **2 the deep of night** : lo más profundo de la noche

deepen [ˈdiːpən] *vt* **1** : ahondar, profundizar **2** INTENSIFY : intensificar — *vi* **1** : hacerse más profundo **2** INTENSIFY : intensificarse

deeply [ˈdiːpli] *adv* : hondo, profundamente ⟨I'm deeply sorry : lo siento sinceramente⟩

deep-seated [ˈdiːpˈsiːtəd] *adj* : profundamente arraigado, enraizado

deer [ˈdɪr] *ns & pl* : ciervo *m*, venado *m*

deerskin [ˈdɪrˌskɪn] *n* : piel *f* de venado

deface [dɪˈfeɪs] *vt* **-faced; -facing** MAR : desfigurar

defacement [dɪˈfeɪsmənt] *n* : desfiguración *f*

defamation [ˌdɛfəˈmeɪʃən] *n* : difamación *f*

defamatory [dɪˈfæməˌtori] *adj* : difamatorio

defame [dɪˈfeɪm] *vt* **-famed; -faming** : difamar, calumniar

default¹ [dɪˈfɔlt, ˈdiˌfɔlt] *vi* **1** : no cumplir (con una obligación), no pagar **2** : no presentarse (en un tribunal)

default² *n* **1** NEGLECT : omisión *f*, negligencia *f* **2** NONPAYMENT : impago *m*, falta *f* de pago **3 to win by default** : ganar por abandono

defaulter [dɪˈfɔltər] *n* : moroso *m*, -sa *f*; rebelde *mf* (en un tribunal)

defeat¹ [dɪˈfiːt] *vt* **1** FRUSTRATE : frustrar **2** BEAT : vencer, derrotar

defeat² *n* : derrota *f*, rechazo *m* (de legislación), fracaso *m* (de planes, etc.)

defecate [ˈdɛfɪˌkeɪt] *vi* **-cated; -cating** : defecar

defect¹ [dɪˈfɛkt] *vi* : desertar

defect² [ˈdiˌfɛkt, dɪˈfɛkt] *n* : defecto *m*

defection [dɪˈfɛkʃən] *n* : deserción *f*, defección *f*

defective [dɪˈfɛktɪv] *adj* **1** FAULTY : defectuoso **2** DEFICIENT : deficiente

defector [dɪˈfɛktər] *n* : desertor *m*, -tora *f*

defend [dɪˈfɛnd] *vt* : defender

defendant [dɪˈfɛndənt] *n* : acusado *m*, -da *f*; demandado *m*, -da *f*

defender [dɪˈfɛndər] *n* **1** ADVOCATE : defensor *m*, -sora *f* **2** : defensa *mf* (en deportes)

defense [dɪˈfɛns, ˈdiˌfɛns] *n* : defensa *f*

defenseless [dɪˈfɛnsləs] *adj* : indefenso

defensive¹ [dɪˈfɛnsɪv] *adj* : defensivo

defensive² *n* **on the defensive** : a la defensiva

defer [dɪˈfər] *v* **-ferred; -ferring** *vt* POSTPONE : diferir, aplazar, posponer — *vi* **to defer to** : deferir a

deference [ˈdɛfərəns] *n* : deferencia *f*

deferential [ˌdɛfəˈrɛnʃəl] *adj* : respetuoso

deferment [dɪˈfərmənt] *n* : aplazamiento *m*

defiance [dɪˈfaɪənts] *n* : desafío *m*

defiant [dɪˈfaɪənt] *adj* : desafiante, insolente

deficiency [dɪˈfɪʃəntsi] *n, pl* **-cies** : deficiencia *f*, carencia *f*

deficient [dɪˈfɪʃənt] *adj* : deficiente, carente

deficit [ˈdɛfəsɪt] *n* : déficit *m*

defile [dɪˈfaɪl] *vt* **-filed; -filing 1** DIRTY : ensuciar, manchar **2** CORRUPT : corromper **3** DESECRATE, PROFANE : profanar **4** DISHONOR : deshonrar

defilement [dɪˈfaɪlmənt] *n* **1** DESECRATION : profanación *f* **2** CORRUPTION : corrupción *f* **3** CONTAMINATION : contaminación *f*

define [dɪˈfaɪn] *vt* **-fined; -fining 1** BOUND : delimitar, demarcar **2** CLARIFY : aclarar, definir **3** : definir ⟨to define a word : definir una palabra⟩

definite [ˈdɛfənɪt] *adj* **1** CERTAIN : definido, determinado **2** CLEAR : claro, explícito **3** UNQUESTIONABLE : seguro, incuestionable

definite article *n* : artículo *m* definido

definitely [ˈdɛfənɪtli] *adv* **1** DOUBTLESSLY : indudablemente, sin duda **2** DEFINITIVELY : definitivamente, seguramente

definition [ˌdɛfəˈnɪʃən] *n* : definición *f*

definitive [dɪˈfɪnətɪv] *adj* **1** CONCLUSIVE : definitivo, decisivo **2** AUTHORITATIVE : de autoridad, autorizado

deflate [dɪˈfleɪt] *v* **-flated; -flating** *vt* **1** : desinflar (una llanta, etc.) **2** REDUCE : rebajar ⟨to deflate one's ego : bajarle los humos a uno⟩ — *vi* : desinflarse

deflation [dɪˈfleɪʃən] *n* **1** : desinflación *f* (de una llanta, etc.) **2** : deflación *f* (económica)

deflect [dɪˈflɛkt] *vt* : desviar — *vi* : desviarse

defoliant [dɪˈfoːliənt] *n* : defoliante *m*

deforestation [diˌfɔrəˈsteɪʃən] *n* : deforestación *f*, desforestación *f*

deform [dɪˈfɔrm] *vt* : deformar

deformation [ˌdiːˌfɔrˈmeɪʃən] *n* : deformación *f*

deformed [dɪˈfɔrmd] *adj* : deforme

deformity [dɪˈfɔrməti] *n, pl* **-ties** : deformidad *f*

defraud [dɪˈfrɔd] *vt* : estafar, defraudar

defray [dɪˈfreɪ] *vt* : sufragar, costear

defrost [dɪˈfrɔst] *vt* : descongelar, deshelar — *vi* : descongelarse, deshelarse

deft [ˈdɛft] *adj* : hábil, diestro — **deftly** *adv*

defunct [dɪˈfʌŋkt] *adj* **1** DECEASED : difunto, fallecido **2** EXTINCT : extinto, fenecido

defuse [dɪˈfjuːz] *vt* : desactivar ⟨to defuse the situation : reducir las tensiones⟩

defy [dɪˈfaɪ] *vt* **-fied; -fying 1** CHALLENGE : desafiar, retar **2** DISOBEY : desobedecer **3** RESIST : resistir, hacer imposible, hacer inútil

degenerate¹ [dɪ'dʒɛnə,reɪt] *vi* -ated; -ating : degenerar

degenerate² [dɪ'dʒɛnərət] *adj* : degenerado

degeneration [dɪ,dʒɛnə'reɪʃən] *n* : degeneración *f*

degenerative [dɪ'dʒɛnərətɪv] *adj* : degenerative

degradation [,dɛgrə'deɪʃən] *n* : degradación *f*

degrade [dɪ'greɪd] *vt* -graded; -grading 1 : degradar, envilecer 2 to degrade oneself : rebajarse

degrading [dɪ'greɪdɪŋ] *adj* : degradante

degree [dɪ'gri:] *n* 1 EXTENT : grado *m* ⟨a third degree burn : una quemadura de tercer grado⟩ 2 : título *m* (de enseñanza superior) 3 : grado *m* (de un círculo, de la temperatura) 4 by degrees : gradualmente, poco a poco

dehydrate [di'haɪ,dreɪt] *v* -drated; -drating *vt* : deshidratar — *vi* : deshidratarse

dehydration [,di:haɪ'dreɪʃən] *n* : deshidratación *f*

deice [di'aɪs] *vt* -iced; -icing : deshelar, descongelar

deify [ˈdi:ə,faɪ, ˈdeɪ-] *vt* -fied; -fying : deificar

deign [ˈdeɪn] *vi* : dignarse, condescender

deity [ˈdi:əti, ˈdeɪ-] *n, pl* -ties 1 the Deity : Dios *m* 2 GOD, GODDESS : deidad *f*; dios *m*, diosa *f*

dejected [dɪ'dʒɛktəd] *adj* : abatido, desalentado, desanimado

dejection [dɪ'dʒɛkʃən] *n* : abatimiento *m*, desaliento *m*, desánimo *m*

delay¹ [dɪ'leɪ] *vt* 1 POSTPONE : posponer, postergar 2 HOLD UP : retrasar, demorar — *vi* : tardar, demorar

delay² *n* 1 LATENESS : tardanza *f* 2 HOLDUP : demora *f*, retraso *m*

delectable [dɪ'lɛktəbəl] *adj* 1 DELICIOUS : delicioso, exquisito 2 DELIGHTFUL : encantador

delegate¹ [ˈdɛlɪ,geɪt] *v* -gated; -gating : delegar

delegate² [ˈdɛlɪgət, -,geɪt] *n* : delegado *m*, -da *f*

delegation [,dɛlɪ'geɪʃən] *n* : delegación *f*

delete [di'li:t] *vt* -leted; -leting : suprimir, tachar, eliminar

deletion [di'li:ʃən] *n* : supresión *f*, tachadura *f*, eliminación *f*

deli [ˈdɛli] → delicatessen

deliberate¹ [dɪ'lɪbə,reɪt] *v* -ated; -ating *vt* : deliberar sobre, reflexionar sobre, considerar — *vi* : deliberar

deliberate² [dɪ'lɪbərət] *adj* 1 CONSIDERED : reflexionado, premeditado 2 INTENTIONAL : deliberado, intencional 3 SLOW : lento, pausado

deliberately [dɪ'lɪbərətli] *adv* 1 INTENTIONALLY : adrede, a propósito 2 SLOWLY : pausadamente, lentamente

deliberation [dɪ,lɪbə'reɪʃən] *n* 1 CONSIDERATION : deliberación *f*, consideración *f* 2 SLOWNESS : lentitud *f*

delicacy [ˈdɛlɪkəsi] *n, pl* -cies 1 : manjar *m*, exquisitez *f* ⟨caviar is a real delicacy : el caviar es un verdadero manjar⟩ 2 FINENESS : delicadeza *f* 3 FRAGILITY : fragilidad *f*

delicate [ˈdɛlɪkət] *adj* 1 SUBTLE : delicado ⟨a delicate fragrance : una fragancia delicada⟩ 2 DAINTY : delicado, primoroso, fino 3 FRAGILE : frágil 4 SENSITIVE : delicado ⟨a delicate matter : un asunto delicado⟩

delicately [ˈdɛlɪkətli] *adv* : delicadamente, con delicadeza

delicatessen [,dɛlɪkə'tɛsən] *n* : charcutería *f*, fiambrería *f*, salchichonería *f* Mex

delicious [dɪ'lɪʃəs] *adj* : delicioso, exquisito, rico — **deliciously** *adv*

delight¹ [dɪ'laɪt] *vt* : deleitar, encantar — *vi* to delight in : deleitarse con, complacerse en

delight² *n* 1 JOY : placer *m*, deleite *m*, gozo *m* 2 : encanto *m* ⟨your garden is a delight : su jardín es un encanto⟩

delightful [dɪ'laɪtfəl] *adj* : delicioso, encantador

delightfully [dɪ'laɪtfəli] *adv* : de manera encantadora, de maravilla

delineate [dɪ'lɪni,eɪt] *vt* -eated; -eating : delinear, trazar, bosquejar

delinquency [dɪ'lɪŋkwənsi] *n, pl* -cies : delincuencia *f*

delinquent¹ [dɪ'lɪŋkwənt] *adj* 1 : delincuente 2 OVERDUE : vencido y sin pagar, moroso

delinquent² *n* : delincuente *mf* ⟨juvenile delinquent : delincuente juvenil⟩

delirious [dɪ'lɪriəs] *adj* : delirante ⟨delirious with joy : loco de alegría⟩

delirium [dɪ'lɪriəm] *n* : delirio *m*, desvarío *m*

deliver [dɪ'lɪvər] *vt* 1 FREE : liberar, librar 2 DISTRIBUTE, HAND : entregar, repartir 3 : asistir en el parto de (un niño) 4 : pronunciar ⟨to deliver a speech : pronunciar un discurso⟩ 5 PROJECT : despachar, lanzar ⟨he delivered a fast ball : lanzó un pelota rápida⟩ 6 DEAL : propinar, asestar ⟨to deliver a blow : asestar un golpe⟩

deliverance [dɪ'lɪvərənts] *n* : liberación *f*, rescate *m*, salvación *f*

deliverer [dɪ'lɪvərər] *n* RESCUER : libertador *m*, -dora *f*; salvador *m*, -dora *f*

delivery [dɪ'lɪvəri] *n, pl* -eries 1 LIBERATION : liberación *f* 2 : entrega *f*, reparto *m* ⟨cash on delivery : entrega contra reembolso⟩ ⟨home delivery : servicio a domicilio⟩ 3 CHILDBIRTH : parto *m*, alumbramiento *m* 4 SPEECH : expresión *f* oral, modo *m* de hablar 5 THROW : lanzamiento *m*

dell [ˈdɛl] *n* : hondonada *f*, valle *m* pequeño

delta [ˈdɛltə] *n* : delta *m*

delude [di'lu:d] *vt* -luded; -luding 1 : engañar 2 to delude oneself : engañarse

deluge¹ ['dɛl,juːdʒ, -,juːʒ] vt **-uged;
-uging 1** FLOOD : inundar **2** OVER-
WHELM : abrumar ⟨deluged with re-
quests : abrumado de pedidos⟩

deluge² n **1** FLOOD : inundación f **2**
DOWNPOUR : aguacero m **3** BARRAGE
: aluvión m

delusion [di'luːʒən] n **1** : ilusión f
(falsa) **2 delusions of grandeur**
: delirios mpl de grandeza

deluxe [di'lʌks, -'luks] adj : de lujo

delve ['dɛlv] vi **delved; delving 1** DIG
: escarbar **2 to delve into** PROBE
: cavar en, ahondar en

demagogue ['dɛmə,gɑg] n : demagogo
m, demagoga f

demand¹ [di'mænd] vt : demandar, exigir, reclamar

demand² n **1** REQUEST : petición f, pedido m, demanda f ⟨by popular demand : a petición del público⟩ **2** CLAIM
: reclamación f, exigencia f **3** MARKET
: demanda f ⟨supply and demand : la
oferta y la demanda⟩

demanding [di'mændɪŋ] adj : exigente

demarcation [,diː,mɑr'keɪʃən] n : demarcación f, deslinde m

demean [di'miːn] vt : degradar, rebajar

demeanor [di'miːnər] n : comportamiento m, conducta f

demented [di'mɛntəd] adj : demente,
loco

dementia [di'mɛntʃə] n : demencia f

demerit [di'mɛrət] n : demérito m

demigod ['dɛmi,gɑd] n : semidiós
m

demise [di'maɪz] n **1** DEATH : fallecimiento m, deceso m **2** END : hundimiento m, desaparición f (de una institución, etc.)

demitasse ['dɛmi,tæs, -,tɑs] n : taza f pequeña (de café)

demobilization [di,moːbələ'zeɪʃən] n
: desmovilización f

demobilize [di'moːbə,laɪz] vt **-lized;
-lizing** : desmovilizar

democracy [di'mɑkrəsi] n, pl **-cies**
: democracia f

democrat ['dɛmə,kræt] n : demócrata
mf

democratic [,dɛmə'krætɪk] adj : democrático — **democratically** [-tɪkli] adv

demographic [dɛmə'græfɪk] adj : demográfico

demolish [di'mɑlɪʃ] vt **1** RAZE : demoler, derribar, arrasar **2** DESTROY : destruir, destrozar

demolition [,dɛmə'lɪʃən, ,diː-] n : demolición f, derribo m

demon ['diːmən] n : demonio m, diablo
m

demonstrably [di'mɑnɪstrəbli] adv : manifiestamente, claramente

demonstrate ['dɛmən,streɪt] vt **-strated;
-strating 1** SHOW : demostrar **2** PROVE
: probar, demostrar **3** EXPLAIN : explicar, ilustrar

demonstration [,dɛmən'streɪʃən] n **1**
SHOW : muestra f, demostración f **2**
RALLY : manifestación f

demonstrative [di'mɑnɪstrətɪv] adj **1**
EFFUSIVE : efusivo, expresivo,
demostrativo **2** : demostrativo (en
lingüística) ⟨demonstrative pronoun
: pronombre demostrativo⟩

demonstrator ['dɛmən,streɪtər] n **1**
: demostrador m, -dora f (de productos) **2** PROTESTER : manifestante
mf

demoralize [di'mɔrə,laɪz] vt **-ized; -izing**
: desmoralizar

demote [di'moːt] vt **-moted; -moting**
: degradar, bajar de categoría

demotion [di'moːʃən] n : degradación f,
descenso m de categoría

demur [di'mər] vi **-murred; -murring 1**
OBJECT : oponerse **2 to demur at** : ponerle objeciones a (algo)

demure [di'mjur] adj : recatado, modesto — **demurely** adv

den ['dɛn] n **1** LAIR : cubil m, madriguera f **2** HIDEOUT : guarida f **3**
STUDY : estudio m, gabinete m

denature [di'neɪtʃər] vt **-tured; -turing**
: desnaturalizar

denial [di'naɪəl] n **1** REFUSAL : rechazo
m, denegación f, negativa f **2** REPUDI-
ATION : negación f (de una creencia,
etc.), rechazo m

denigrate ['dɛni,greɪt] vt **-grated; -grat-
ing** : denigrar

denim ['dɛnəm] n **1** : tela f vaquera,
mezclilla f Chile, Mex **2 denims** npl →
jeans

denizen ['dɛnəzən] n : habitante mf,
morador m, -dora f

denomination [di,nɑmə'neɪʃən] n **1**
FAITH : confesión f, fe f **2** VALUE : denominación f, valor m (de una moneda)

denominator [di'nɑmə,neɪtər] n : denominador m

denote [di'noːt] vt **-noted; -noting 1** IN-
DICATE, MARK : indicar, denotar, señalar **2** MEAN : significar

denouement [,deɪnuː'mɑ] n : desenlace
m

denounce [di'naʊnts] vt **-nounced;
-nouncing 1** CENSURE : denunciar,
censurar **2** ACCUSE : denunciar,
acusar, delatar

dense ['dɛnts] adj **denser; -est 1** THICK
: espeso, denso ⟨dense vegetation : vegetación densa⟩ ⟨a dense fog : una
niebla espesa⟩ **2** STUPID : estúpido,
burro fam

densely ['dɛntsli] adv **1** THICKLY : densamente **2** STUPIDLY : torpemente

denseness ['dɛntsnəs] n **1** → **density 2**
STUPIDITY : estupidez f

density ['dɛntsəti] n, pl **-ties** : densidad
f

dent¹ ['dɛnt] vt : abollar, mellar

dent² n : abolladura f, mella f

dental ['dɛntəl] adj : dental

dental floss n : hilo m dental

dentifrice ['dɛntəfrɪs] n : dentífrico m, pasta f de dientes
dentist ['dɛntɪst] n : dentista mf
dentistry ['dɛntɪstri] n : odontología f
dentures ['dɛntʃərz] npl : dentadura f postiza
denude [dɪ'nu:d, -'nju:d] vt **-nuded; -nuding** STRIP : desnudar, despojar
denunciation [dɪˌnʌnˌsi'eɪʃən] n : denuncia f, acusación f
deny [dɪ'naɪ] vt **-nied; -nying 1** REFUTE : desmentir, negar **2** DISOWN, REPUDIATE : negar, renegar de **3** REFUSE : denegar **4 to deny oneself** : privarse, sacrificarse
deodorant [di'o:dərənt] n : desodorante m
deodorize [di'o:dəˌraɪz] vt **-ized; -izing** : desodorizar
depart [dɪ'part] vt : salirse de — vi **1** LEAVE : salir, partir, irse **2** DIE : morir
department [dɪ'partmənt] n **1** DIVISION : sección f (de una tienda, una organización, etc.), departamento m (de una empresa, una universidad, etc.), ministerio m (del gobierno) **2** PROVINCE, SPHERE : esfera f, campo m, competencia f
departmental [dɪˌpart'mɛntəl, ˌdi:-] adj : departamental
department store n : grandes almacenes mpl
departure [dɪ'partʃər] n **1** LEAVING : salida f, partida f **2** DEVIATION : desviación f
depend [dɪ'pɛnd] vi **1** RELY : contar (con), confiar (en) ⟨depend on me! : ¡cuenta conmigo!⟩ **2 to depend on** : depender de ⟨success depends on hard work : el éxito depende de trabajar duro⟩ **3 that depends** : según, eso depende
dependable [dɪ'pɛndəbəl] adj : responsable, digno de confianza, fiable
dependence [dɪ'pɛndənts] n : dependencia f
dependency [dɪ'pɛndəntsi] n, pl **-cies** → **dependence 2** : posesión f (de una unidad territorial)
dependent¹ [dɪ'pɛndənt] adj : dependiente
dependent² n : persona f a cargo de alguien
depict [dɪ'pɪkt] vt **1** PORTRAY : representar **2** DESCRIBE : describir
depiction [dɪ'pɪkʃən] n : representación f, descripción f
deplete [dɪ'pli:t] vt **-pleted; -pleting 1** EXHAUST : agotar **2** REDUCE : reducir
depletion [dɪ'pli:ʃən] n **1** EXHAUSTION : agotamiento m **2** REDUCTION : reducción f, disminución f
deplorable [dɪ'plorəbəl] adj **1** CONTEMPTIBLE : deplorable, despreciable **2** LAMENTABLE : lamentable
deplore [dɪ'plor] vt **-plored; -ploring 1** REGRET : deplorar, lamentar **2** CONDEMN : condenar, deplorar

deploy [dɪ'plɔɪ] vt : desplegar
deployment [dɪ'plɔɪmənt] n : despliegue m
deport [dɪ'port] vt **1** EXPEL : deportar, expulsar (de un país) **2 to deport oneself** BEHAVE : comportarse
deportation [ˌdi:ˌpor'teɪʃən] n : deportación f
depose [dɪ'po:z] vt **-posed; -posing** : deponer
deposit¹ [dɪ'pazət] vt **-ited; -iting** : depositar
deposit² n **1** : depósito m (en el banco) **2** DOWN PAYMENT : entrega f inicial **3** : depósito m, yacimiento m (en geología)
deposition [ˌdɛpə'zɪʃən] n TESTIMONY : deposición f
depositor [dɪ'pazətər] n : depositante mf
depository [dɪ'pazəˌtori] n, pl **-ries** : almacén m, depósito m
depot [in sense 1 usu 'dɛˌpo:, 2 usu 'di:-] n **1** STOREHOUSE : almacén m, depósito m **2** STATION, TERMINAL : terminal mf, estación f (de autobuses, ferrocarriles, etc.)
deprave [dɪ'preɪv] vt **-praved; -praving** : depravar, pervertir
depraved [dɪ'preɪvd] adj : depravado, degenerado
depravity [dɪ'prævəti] n, pl **-ties** : depravación f
depreciate [dɪ'pri:ʃiˌeɪt] v **-ated; -ating** vt **1** DEVALUE : depreciar, devaluar **2** DISPARAGE : menospreciar, despreciar — vi : depreciarse, devaluarse
depreciation [dɪˌpri:ʃi'eɪʃən] n : depreciación f, devaluación f
depress [dɪ'prɛs] vt **1** PRESS, PUSH : apretar, presionar, pulsar **2** REDUCE : reducir, hacer bajar (precios, ventas, etc.) **3** SADDEN : deprimir, abatir, entristecer **4** DEVALUE : depreciar
depressant¹ [dɪ'prɛsənt] adj : depresivo
depressant² n : depresivo m
depressed [dɪ'prɛst] adj **1** DEJECTED : deprimido, abatido **2** : deprimido, en crisis (dícese de la economía)
depressing [dɪ'prɛsɪŋ] adj : deprimente, triste
depression [dɪ'prɛʃən] n **1** DESPONDENCY : depresión f, abatimiento m **2** : depresión (en una superficie) **3** RECESSION : depresión f económica, crisis f
deprivation [ˌdɛprə'veɪʃən] n : privación f
deprive [dɪ'praɪv] vt **-prived; -priving** : privar
depth ['dɛpθ] n, pl **depths** ['dɛpθs, 'dɛps] : profundidad f, fondo m ⟨to study in depth : estudiar a fondo⟩ ⟨in the depths of winter : en pleno invierno⟩
deputize ['dɛpjəˌtaɪz] vt **-tized; -tizing** : nombrar como segundo
deputy ['dɛpjuti] n, pl **-ties** : suplente mf, sustituto m, -ta f
derail [dɪ'reɪl] v : descarrilar

derailment [dɪ'reɪlmənt] *n* : descarril-
amiento *m*
derange [dɪ'reɪndʒ] *vt* **-ranged; -ranging**
1 DISARRANGE : desarreglar, desordenar **2** DISTURB, UPSET : trastornar,
perturbar **3** MADDEN : enloquecer,
volver loco
derangement [dɪ'reɪndʒmənt] *n* **1** DIS-
TURBANCE, UPSET : trastorno *m* **2** IN-
SANITY : locura *f*, perturbación *f* mental
derby ['dərbi] *n, pl* **-bies 1** : derby *m*
⟨the Kentucky Derby : el Derby de
Kentucky⟩ **2** : sombrero *m* hongo
deregulate [dɪ'rɛgjʊ,leɪt] *vt* **-lated;
-lating** : desregular
deregulation [di,rɛgjʊ'leɪʃən] *n* : desregulación *f*
derelict¹ ['dɛrə,lɪkt] *adj* **1** ABANDONED
: abandonado, en ruinas **2** REMISS
: negligente, remiso
derelict² *n* **1** : propiedad *f* abandonada
2 VAGRANT : vagabundo *m*, -da *f*
deride [dɪ'raɪd] *vt* **-rided; -riding** : ridiculizar, burlarse de
derision [dɪ'rɪʒən] *n* : escarnio *m*, irrisión *f*, mofa *f*
derisive [dɪ'raɪsɪv] *adj* : burlón
derivation [,dɛrə'veɪʃən] *n* : derivación
f
derivative¹ [dɪ'rɪvətɪv] *adj* **1** DERIVED
: derivado **2** BANAL : carente de originalidad, banal
derivative² *n* : derivado *m*
derive [dɪ'raɪv] *v* **-rived; -riving** *vt* **1** OB-
TAIN : obtener, sacar **2** DEDUCE : de-
ducir, inferir — *vi* : provenir, derivar,
proceder
dermatologist [,dərmə'talədʒɪst] *n* : dermatólogo *m*, -ga *f*
dermatology [,dərmə'talədʒi] *n* : dermatología *f*
derogatory [dɪ'ragə,tori] *adj* : despectivo, despreciativo
derrick ['dɛrɪk] *n* **1** CRANE : grúa *f* **2**
: torre *f* de perforación (sobre un pozo
de petróleo)
descend [dɪ'sɛnd] *vt* : descender, bajar
— *vi* **1** : descender, bajar ⟨he de-
scended from the platform : descendió
del estrado⟩ **2** DERIVE : descender,
provenir **3** STOOP : rebajarse ⟨I de-
scended to his level : me rebajé a su
nivel⟩ **4 to descend upon** : caer sobre, invadir
descendant¹ [dɪ'sɛndənt] *adj* : descendente
descendant² *n* : descendiente *mf*
descent [dɪ'sɛnt] *n* **1** : bajada *f*, descenso *m* ⟨the descent from the mountain
: el descenso de la montaña⟩ **2** AN-
CESTRY : ascendencia *f*, linaje *f* **3**
SLOPE : pendiente *f*, cuesta *f* **4** FALL
: caída *f* **5** ATTACK : incursión *f*, ataque
m
describe [dɪ'skraɪb] *vt* **-scribed; -scrib-
ing** : describir
description [dɪ'skrɪpʃən] *n* : descripción
f

descriptive [dɪ'skrɪptɪv] *adj* : descriptivo ⟨descriptive adjective : adjetivo cal-
ificativo⟩
desecrate ['dɛsɪ,kreɪt] *vt* **-crated; -crat-
ing** : profanar
desecration [,dɛsɪ'kreɪʃən] *n* : profanación *f*
desegregate [dɪ'sɛgrə,geɪt] *vt* **-gated;
-gating** : eliminar la segregación racial
de
desegregation [di,sɛgrə'geɪʃən] *n*
: eliminación *f* de la segregación racial
desert¹ [dɪ'zərt] *vt* : abandonar (una persona o un lugar), desertar de (una
causa, etc.) — *vi* : desertar
desert² ['dɛzərt] *adj* : desierto ⟨a desert
island : una isla desierta⟩
desert³ [dɪ'zərt] *n* **1** ['dɛzərt] : desierto *m* (en geografía) **2** [dɪ'zərt] → **deserts**
deserter [dɪ'zərtər] *n* : desertor *m*, -tora
f
desertion [dɪ'zərʃən] *n* : abandono *m*,
deserción *f* (militar)
deserts [dɪ'zərts] *npl* : merecido *m* ⟨to
get one's just deserts : llevarse uno su
merecido⟩
deserve [dɪ'zərv] *vt* **-served; -serving**
: merecer, ser digno de
deserving [dɪ'zərvɪŋ] *adj* : meritorio
⟨deserving of : digno de⟩
desiccate ['dɛsɪ,keɪt] *vt* **-cated; -cating**
: desecar, deshidratar
design¹ [dɪ'zaɪn] *vt* **1** DEVISE : diseñar,
concebir, idear **2** PLAN : proyectar **3**
SKETCH : trazar, bosquejar
design² *n* **1** PLAN, SCHEME : plan *m*,
proyecto *m* ⟨by design : a propósito,
intencionalmente⟩ **2** SKETCH : diseño
m, bosquejo *m* **3** PATTERN, STYLE
: diseño *m*, estilo *m* **4 designs** *npl* IN-
TENTIONS : propósitos *mpl*, designios
mpl
designate ['dɛzɪg,neɪt] *vt* **-nated; -nat-
ing 1** INDICATE, SPECIFY : indicar, especificar **2** APPOINT : nombrar, designar
designation [,dɛzɪg'neɪʃən] *n* **1** NAM-
ING : designación *f* **2** NAME : denominación *f*, nombre *m* **3** APPOINTMENT
: designación *f*, nombramiento *m*
designer [dɪ'zaɪnər] *n* : diseñador *m*,
-dora *f*
desirability [dɪ,zaɪrə'bɪləti] *n, pl* **-ties 1**
ADVISABILITY : conveniencia *f* **2** AT-
TRACTIVENESS : atractivo *m*
desirable [dɪ'zaɪrəbəl] *adj* **1** ADVISABLE
: conveniente, aconsejable **2** ATTRAC-
TIVE : deseable, atractivo
desire¹ [dɪ'zaɪr] *vt* **-sired; -siring 1**
WANT : desear **2** REQUEST : rogar, solicitar
desire² *n* : deseo *m*, anhelo *m*, ansia *m*
desist [dɪ'sɪst, -'zɪst] *vi* **to desist from**
: desistir de, abstenerse de
desk ['dɛsk] *n* : escritorio *m*, pupitre *m*
(en la escuela)
desktop ['dɛsk,tap] *adj* : de escritorio

desolate[1] [ˈdɛsəˌleɪt, -zə-] *vt* **-lated;**
-lating : devastar, desolar

desolate[2] [ˈdɛsələt, -zə-] *adj* 1 BARREN
: desolado, desierto, yermo 2 DISCON-
SOLATE : desconsolado, desolado

desolation [ˌdɛsəˈleɪʃən, -zə-] *n* : desolación *f*

despair[1] [diˈspær] *vi* : desesperar, perder
las esperanzas

despair[2] *n* : desesperación *f*, desesperanza *f*

desperate [ˈdɛspərət] *adj* 1 HOPELESS
: desesperado, sin esperanzas 2 RASH
: desesperado, precipitado 3 SERIOUS,
URGENT : grave, urgente, apremiante
⟨a desperate need : una necesidad
apremiante⟩

desperately [ˈdɛspərətli] *adv* : desesperadamente, urgentemente

desperation [ˌdɛspəˈreɪʃən] *n* : desesperación *f*

despicable [diˈspɪkəbəl, ˈdɛspɪ-] *adj* : vil,
despreciable, infame

despise [diˈspaɪz] *vt* **-spised; -spising**
: despreciar

despite [dəˈspaɪt] *prep* : a pesar de, aún
con

despoil [diˈspɔɪl] *vt* : saquear

despondency [diˈspɑndənt̬si] *n* : desaliento *m*, desánimo *m*, depresión *f*

despondent [diˈspɑndənt] *adj* : desalentado, desanimado

despot [ˈdɛspət, -ˌpɑt] *n* : déspota *mf*;
tirano *m*, -na *f*

despotic [dɛsˈpɑtɪk] *adj* : despótico

despotism [ˈdɛspəˌtɪzəm] *n* : despotismo
m

dessert [diˈzərt] *n* : postre *m*

destination [ˌdɛstəˈneɪʃən] *n* : destino *m*,
destinación *f*

destined [ˈdɛstənd] *adj* 1 FATED : predestinado 2 BOUND : destinado, con
destino (a), con rumbo (a)

destiny [ˈdɛstəni] *n, pl* **-nies** : destino *m*

destitute [ˈdɛstəˌtuːt, -ˌtjuːt] *adj* 1 LACK-
ING : carente, desprovisto 2 POOR : indigente, en miseria

destitution [ˌdɛstəˈtuːʃən, -ˈtjuː-] *n* : indigencia *f*, miseria *f*

destroy [diˈstrɔɪ] *vt* 1 KILL : matar 2 DE-
MOLISH : destruir, destrozar

destroyer [diˈstrɔɪər] *n* : destructor *m*
(buque)

destructible [diˈstrʌktəbəl] *adj* : destructible

destruction [diˈstrʌkʃən] *n* : destrucción
f, ruina *f*

destructive [diˈstrʌktɪv] *adj* : destructor, destructivo

desultory [ˈdɛsəlˌtori] *adj* 1 AIMLESS
: sin rumbo, sin objeto 2 DISCON-
NECTED : inconexo

detach [diˈtætʃ] *vt* : separar, quitar, desprender

detached [diˈtætʃt] *adj* 1 SEPARATE
: separado, suelto 2 ALOOF : distante,
indiferente 3 IMPARTIAL : imparcial,
objetivo

detachment [diˈtætʃmənt] *n* 1 SEPARA-
TION : separación *f* 2 DETAIL : destacamento *m* (de tropas) 3 ALOOFNESS
: reserva *f*, indiferencia *f* 4 IMPAR-
TIALITY : imparcialidad *f*

detail[1] [diˈteɪl, ˈdiːˌteɪl] *vt* : detallar, exponer en detalle

detail[2] *n* 1 : detalle *m*, pormenor *m* 2
: destacamento *m* (de tropas)

detailed [diˈteɪld, ˈdiːˌteɪld] *adj* : detallado, minucioso

detain [diˈteɪn] *vt* 1 HOLD : detener 2
DELAY : entretener, demorar, retrasar

detect [diˈtɛkt] *vt* : detectar, descubrir

detection [diˈtɛkʃən] *n* : descubrimiento *m*

detective [diˈtɛktɪv] *n* : detective *mf*
⟨private detective : detective privado⟩

detector [diˈtɛktər] *n* : detector *m*

detention [diˈtɛnʃən] *n* : detención *f*

deter [diˈtər] *vt* **-terred; -terring** : disuadir, impedir

detergent [diˈtərdʒənt] *n* : detergente *m*

deteriorate [diˈtiriəˌreɪt] *vi* **-rated; -rat-**
ing : deteriorarse, empeorar

deterioration [diˌtiriəˈreɪʃən] *n* : deterioro *m*, empeoramiento *m*

determinant[1] [diˈtərmənənt] *adj* : determinante

determinant[2] *n* 1 : factor *m* determinante 2 : determinante *m* (en matemáticas)

determination [diˌtərməˈneɪʃən] *n* 1 DE-
CISION : determinación *f*, decisión *f* 2
RESOLUTION : resolución *f*, determinación *f* ⟨with grim determination
: con una firme resolución⟩

determine [diˈtərmən] *vt* **-mined;**
-mining 1 ESTABLISH : determinar,
establecer 2 SETTLE : decidir 3 FIND
OUT : averiguar 4 BRING ABOUT : determinar

determined [diˈtərmənd] *adj* RESOLUTE
: decidido, resuelto

deterrent [diˈtərənt] *n* : medida *f* disua-
siva

detest [diˈtɛst] *vt* : detestar, odiar, aborrecer

detestable [diˈtɛstəbəl] *adj* : detestable,
odioso, aborrecible

dethrone [diˈθroːn] *vt* **-throned; -thron-**
ing : destronar

detonate [ˈdɛtəˌneɪt] *v* **-nated; -nating** *vt*
: hacer detonar — *vi* : detonar, estallar

detonation [ˌdɛtəˈneɪʃən] *n* : detonación
f

detour[1] [ˈdiːˌtʊr, diˈtʊr] *vi* : desviarse

detour[2] *n* : desvío *m*, rodeo *m*

detract [diˈtrækt] *vi* **to detract from**
: restarle valor a, quitarle méritos a

detractor [diˈtræktər] *n* : detractor *m*,
-tora *f*

detriment [ˈdɛtrəmənt] *n* : detrimento
m, perjuicio *m*

detrimental [ˌdɛtrəˈmɛntəl] *adj* : perjudicial — **detrimentally** *adv*

devaluation [diˌvæljuˈeɪʃən] *n* : devaluación *f*

devalue [di'væl,ju:] vt **-ued; -uing** : devaluar, depreciar

devastate ['dɛvə,steɪt] vt **-tated; -tating** : devastar, arrasar, asolar

devastation [,dɛvə'steɪʃən] n : devastación f, estragos mpl

develop [di'vɛləp] vt **1** FORM, MAKE : desarrollar, elaborar, formar **2** : revelar (en fotografía) **3** FOSTER : desarrollar, fomentar **4** EXPLOIT : explotar (recursos), urbanizar (un área) **5** ACQUIRE : adquirir ⟨to develop an interest : adquirir un interés⟩ **6** CONTRACT : contraer (una enfermedad) — vi **1** GROW : desarrollarse **2** ARISE : aparecer, surgir

developed [di'vɛləpt] adj : avanzado, desarrollado

developer [di'vɛləpər] n **1** : inmobiliaria f, urbanizadora f **2** : revelador m (en fotografía)

development [di'vɛləpmənt] n **1** : desarrollo m ⟨physical development : desarrollo físico⟩ **2** : urbanización f (de un área), explotación f (de recursos), creación f (de inventos) **3** EVENT : acontecimiento m, suceso m ⟨to await developments : esperar acontecimientos⟩

deviant ['di:viənt] adj : desviado, anormal

deviate ['di:vi,eɪt] v **-ated; -ating** vi : desviarse, apartarse — vt : desviar

deviation [,di:vi'eɪʃən] n : desviación f

device [di'vaɪs] n **1** MECHANISM : dispositivo m, aparato m, mecanismo m **2** EMBLEM : emblema m

devil¹ ['dɛvəl] vt **-iled** or **-illed; -iling** or **-illing** **1** : sazonar con picante y especias **2** PESTER : molestar

devil² n **1** SATAN : el diablo, Satanás m **2** DEMON : diablo m, demonio m **3** FIEND : persona f diabólica; malvado m, -da f

devilish ['dɛvəlɪʃ] adj : diabólico

devilry ['dɛvəlri] n, pl **-ries** : diabluras fpl, travesuras fpl

devious ['di:viəs] adj **1** CRAFTY : taimado, artero **2** WINDING : tortuoso, sinuoso

devise [di'vaɪz] vt **-vised; -vising** **1** INVENT : idear, concebir, inventar **2** PLOT : tramar

devoid [di'vɔɪd] adj ~ of : carente de, desprovisto de

devote [di'vo:t] vt **-voted; -voting** **1** DEDICATE : consagrar, dedicar ⟨to devote one's life : dedicar uno su vida⟩ **2** **to devote oneself** : dedicarse

devoted [di'vo:təd] adj **1** FAITHFUL : leal, fiel **2 to be devoted to someone** : tenerle mucho cariño a alguien

devotee [,dɛvə'ti:, -'teɪ] n : devoto m, -ta f

devotion [di'vo:ʃən] n **1** DEDICATION : dedicación f, devoción f **2 devotions** PRAYERS : oraciones fpl, devociones fpl

devour [di'vauər] vt : devorar

devout [di'vaut] adj **1** PIOUS : devoto, piadoso **2** EARNEST, SINCERE : sincero, ferviente — **devoutly** adv

devoutness [di'vautnəs] n : devoción f, piedad f

dew ['du:, 'dju:] n : rocío m

dewlap ['du:,læp, 'dju-] n : papada f

dew point n : punto m de condensación

dewy ['du:i, 'dju:i] adj **dewier; -est** : cubierto de rocío

dexterity [dɛk'stɛrəti] n, pl **-ties** : destreza f, habilidad f

dexterous ['dɛkstrəs] adj : diestro, hábil

dexterously ['dɛkstrəsli] adv : con destreza, con habilidad, hábilmente

dextrose ['dɛk,stro:s] n : dextrosa f

diabetes [,daɪə'bi:,ti:z] n : diabetes f

diabetic¹ [,daɪə'bɛtɪk] adj : diabético

diabetic² n : diabético m, -ca f

diabolic [,daɪə'balɪk] or **diabolical** [-lɪkəl] adj : diabólico, satánico

diacritical mark [,daɪə'krɪtɪkəl] n : signo m diacrítico

diadem ['daɪə,dɛm, -dəm] n : diadema f

diagnose ['daɪɪg,no:s, ,daɪɪg'no:s] vt **-nosed; -nosing** : diagnosticar

diagnosis [,daɪɪg'no:sɪs] n, pl **-noses** [-'no:,si:z] : diagnóstico m

diagnostic [,daɪɪg'nastɪk] adj : diagnóstico

diagonal¹ [daɪ'ægənəl] adj : diagonal, en diagonal

diagonal² n : diagonal f

diagonally [daɪ'ægənəli] adv : diagonalmente, en diagonal

diagram¹ ['daɪə,græm] vt **-gramed** or **-grammed; -graming** or **-gramming** : hacer un diagrama de

diagram² n : diagrama m, gráfico m, esquema m

dial¹ ['daɪl] v **dialed** or **dialled; dialing** or **dialling** : marcar, discar

dial² n : esfera f (de un reloj), dial m (de un radio), disco m (de un teléfono)

dialect ['daɪə,lɛkt] n : dialecto m

dialogue ['daɪə,lɔg] n : diálogo m

diameter [daɪ'æmətər] n : diámetro m

diamond ['daɪmənd, 'daɪə-] n **1** : diamante m, brillante m ⟨a diamond necklace : un collar de brillantes⟩ **2** : rombo m, forma f de rombo **3** : diamante m (en naipes) **4** INFIELD : cuadro m, diamante m (en béisbol)

diaper ['daɪpər, 'daɪə-] n : pañal m

diaphragm ['daɪə,fræm] n : diafragma m

diarrhea [,daɪə'ri:ə] n : diarrea f

diary ['daɪəri] n, pl **-ries** : diario m

diatribe ['daɪə,traɪb] n : diatriba f

dice¹ ['daɪs] vt **diced; dicing** : cortar en cubos

dice² ns & pl **1** → **die²** **2** : dados mpl (juego)

dicker ['dɪkər] vt : regatear

dictate ['dɪk,teɪt, dɪk'teɪt] v **-tated; -tating** vt **1** : dictar ⟨to dictate a letter : dictar una carta⟩ **2** ORDER : mandar, ordenar — vi : dar órdenes

dictate² ['dɪk,teɪt] n 1 : mandato m, orden f 2 **dictates** npl : dictados mpl ⟨the dictates of conscience : los dictados de la conciencia⟩

dictation [dɪk'teɪʃən] n : dictado m

dictator ['dɪk,teɪtər] n : dictador m, -dora f

dictatorial [,dɪktə'toriəl] adj : dictatorial — **dictatorially** adv

dictatorship [dɪk'teɪtər,ʃɪp, 'dɪk,-] n : dictadura f

diction ['dɪkʃən] n 1 : lenguaje m, estilo m 2 ENUNCIATION : dicción f, articulación f

dictionary ['dɪkʃə,neri] n, pl -naries : diccionario m

did → do

didactic [daɪ'dæktɪk] adj : didáctico

die¹ ['daɪ] vi **died**; **dying** ['daɪɪŋ] 1 : morir 2 CEASE : morir, morirse ⟨a dying civilization : una civilización moribunda⟩ 3 STOP : apagarse, dejar de funcionar ⟨the motor died : el motor se apagó⟩ 4 to die down SUBSIDE : amainar, disminuir 5 to die out : extinguirse 6 to be dying for or to be dying to : morirse por ⟨I'm dying to leave : me muero por irme⟩

die² ['daɪ] n, pl **dice** ['daɪs] : dado m

die³ n, pl **dies** ['daɪz] 1 STAMP : troquel m, cuño m 2 MOLD : matriz f, molde m

diesel ['di:zəl, -səl] n : diesel m

diet¹ ['daɪət] vi : ponerse a régimen, hacer dieta

diet² n : régimen m, dieta f

dietary ['daɪə,teri] adj : alimenticio, dietético

dietitian or **dietician** [,daɪə'tɪʃən] n : dietista mf

differ ['dɪfər] vi **-fered**; **-ferring** 1 : diferir, diferenciarse 2 VARY : variar 3 DISAGREE : discrepar, diferir, no estar de acuerdo

difference ['dɪfrənts, 'dɪfərənts] n : diferencia f

different ['dɪfrənt, 'dɪfərənt] adj : distinto, diferente

differentiate [,dɪfə'rentʃi,eɪt] v **-ated**; **-ating** vt 1 : hacer diferente 2 DISTINGUISH : distinguir, diferenciar — vi : distinguir

differentiation [,dɪfə,rentʃi'eɪʃən] n : diferenciación f

differently ['dɪfrəntli, 'dɪfərənt-] adv : de otra manera, de otro modo, distintamente

difficult ['dɪfɪ,kʌlt] adj : difícil

difficulty ['dɪfɪ,kʌlti] n, pl **-ties** 1 : dificultad f 2 PROBLEM : problema f, dificultad f

diffidence ['dɪfədənts] n 1 SHYNESS : retraimiento m, timidez f, apocamiento m 2 RETICENCE : reticencia f

diffident ['dɪfədənt] adj 1 SHY : tímido, apocado, inseguro 2 RESERVED : reservado

diffuse¹ [dɪ'fju:z] v **-fused**; **-fusing** vt : difundir, esparcir — vi : difundirse, esparcirse

diffuse² [dɪ'fju:s] adj 1 WORDY : prolijo, verboso 2 WIDESPREAD : difuso

diffusion [dɪ'fju:ʒən] n : difusión f

dig¹ ['dɪg] v **dug** ['dʌg]; **digging** vt 1 : cavar, excavar ⟨to dig a hole : cavar un hoyo⟩ 2 EXTRACT : sacar ⟨to dig up potatoes : sacar papas del suelo⟩ 3 POKE, THRUST : clavar, hincar ⟨he dug me in the ribs : me dio un codazo en las costillas⟩ 4 to dig up DISCOVER : descubrir, sacar a luz — vi : cavar, excavar

dig² n 1 POKE : codazo m 2 GIBE : pulla f 3 EXCAVATION : excavación f

digest¹ ['daɪ,dʒest, dɪ-] vt 1 ASSIMILATE : digerir, asimilar 2 : digerir (comida) 3 SUMMARIZE : compendiar, resumir

digest² ['daɪ,dʒest] n : compendio m, resumen m

digestible [daɪ'dʒestəbəl, dɪ-] adj : digerible

digestion [daɪ'dʒestʃən, dɪ-] n : digestión f

digestive [daɪ'dʒestɪv, dɪ-] adj : digestivo ⟨the digestive system : el sistema digestivo⟩

digit ['dɪdʒət] n 1 NUMERAL : dígito m, número m 2 FINGER, TOE : dedo m

digital ['dɪdʒətəl] adj : digital — **digitally** adv

dignified ['dɪgnə,faɪd] adj : digno, decoroso

dignify ['dɪgnə,faɪ] vt **-fied**; **-fying** : dignificar, honrar

dignitary ['dɪgnə,teri] n, pl **-taries** : dignatario m, -ria f

dignity ['dɪgnəti] n, pl **-ties** : dignidad f

digress [daɪ'gres, də-] vi : desviarse del tema, divagar

digression [daɪ'greʃən, də-] n : digresión f

dike or **dyke** ['daɪk] n : dique m

dilapidated [də'læpə,deɪtəd] adj : ruinoso, desvencijado, destartalado

dilapidation [də,læpə'deɪʃən] n : deterioro m, estado m ruinoso

dilate [daɪ'leɪt, 'daɪ,leɪt] v **-lated**; **-lating** vt : dilatar — vi : dilatarse

dilemma [dɪ'lemə] n : dilema m

dilettante ['dɪlə,tɑnt, -,tænt] n, pl **-tantes** [-,tɑnts, -,tænts] or **-tanti** [,dɪlə'tɑnti, -'tæn-] : diletante mf

diligence ['dɪlədʒənts] n : diligencia f, aplicación f

diligent ['dɪlədʒənt] adj : diligente ⟨a diligent search : una búsqueda minuciosa⟩ — **diligently** adv

dill ['dɪl] n : eneldo m

dillydally ['dɪli,dæli] vi **-lied**; **-lying** : demorarse, perder tiempo

dilute [daɪ'lu:t, də-] vt **-luted**; **-luting** : diluir, aguar

dilution [daɪ'lu:ʃən, də-] n : dilución f

dim¹ ['dɪm] v **dimmed**; **dimming** vt : atenuar (la luz), nublar (la vista), borrar (la memoria), opacar (una superficie) — *vi* : oscurecerse, apagarse

dim² *adj* **dimmer; dimmest 1** FAINT : oscuro, tenue (dícese de la luz), nublado (dícese de la vista), borrado (dícese de la memoria) **2** DULL : deslustrado **3** STUPID : tonto, torpe

dime ['daɪm] *n* : moneda *f* de diez centavos

dimension [də'mɛntʃən, daɪ-] *n* **1** : dimensión *f* **2 dimensions** *npl* EXTENT, SCOPE : dimensiones *fpl*, extensión *f*, medida *f*

diminish [də'mɪnɪʃ] *vt* LESSEN : disminuir, reducir, amainar — *vi* DWINDLE, WANE : menguar, reducirse

diminutive [də'mɪnjʊt̬ɪv] *adj* : diminutivo, minúsculo

dimly ['dɪmli] *adv* : indistintamente, débilmente

dimmer ['dɪmər] *n* : potenciómetro *m*, conmutador *m* de luces (en automóviles)

dimness ['dɪmnəs] *n* : oscuridad *f*, debilidad *f* (de la vista), imprecisión *f* (de la memoria)

dimple ['dɪmpəl] *n* : hoyuelo *m*

din ['dɪn] *n* : estrépito *m*, estruendo *m*

dine ['daɪn] *vi* **dined; dining** : cenar

diner ['daɪnər] *n* **1** : comensal *mf* (persona) **2** : vagón *m* restaurante (en un tren) **3** : cafetería *f*, restaurante *m* barato

dinghy ['dɪŋi, 'dɪŋgi, 'dɪŋki] *n, pl* **-ghies** : bote *m*

dinginess ['dɪndʒinəs] *n* **1** DIRTINESS : suciedad *f* **2** SHABBINESS : lo gastado, lo deslucido

dingy ['dɪndʒi] *adj* **-gier; -est 1** DIRTY : sucio **2** SHABBY : gastado, deslucido

dinner ['dɪnər] *n* : cena *f*, comida *f*

dinosaur ['daɪnə,sɔr] *n* : dinosaurio *m*

dint ['dɪnt] *n* **by dint of** : a fuerza de

diocese ['daɪəsəs, -,siːz, -,siːs] *n, pl* **-ceses** ['daɪəsəsəz] : diócesis *f*

dip¹ ['dɪp] *v* **dipped; dipping** *vt* **1** DUNK, PLUNGE : sumergir, mojar, meter **2** LADLE : servir con cucharón **3** LOWER : bajar, arriar (una bandera) — *vi* **1** DESCEND, DROP : bajar en picada, descender **2** SLOPE : bajar, inclinarse

dip² *n* **1** SWIM : chapuzón *m* **2** DROP : descenso *m*, caída *f* **3** SLOPE : cuesta *f*, declive *m* **4** SAUCE : salsa *f*

diphtheria [dɪf'θɪriə] *n* : difteria *f*

diphthong ['dɪf,θɔŋ] *n* : diptongo *m*

diploma [də'ploːmə] *n, pl* **-mas** : diploma *m*

diplomacy [də'ploːməsi] *n* **1** : diplomacia *f* **2** TACT : tacto *m*, discreción *f*

diplomat ['dɪplə,mæt] *n* **1** : diplomático *m*, **-ca** *f* (en relaciones internacionales) **2** : persona *f* diplomática

diplomatic [,dɪplə'mæt̬ɪk] *adj* : diplomático ⟨diplomatic immunity : inmunidad diplomática⟩

dipper ['dɪpər] *n* **1** LADLE : cucharón *m*, cazo *m* **2 Big Dipper** : Osa *f* Mayor **3 Little Dipper** : Osa *f* Menor

dire ['daɪr] *adj* **direr; direst 1** HORRIBLE : espantoso, terrible, horrendo **2** EXTREME : extremo ⟨dire poverty : pobreza extrema⟩

direct¹ [də'rɛkt, daɪ-] *vt* **1** ADDRESS : dirigir, mandar **2** AIM, POINT : dirigir **3** GUIDE : indicarle el camino (a alguien), orientar **4** MANAGE : dirigir ⟨to direct a film : dirigir una película⟩ **5** COMMAND : ordenar, mandar

direct² *adv* : directamente

direct³ *adj* **1** STRAIGHT : directo **2** FRANK : franco

direct current *n* : corriente *f* continua

direction [də'rɛkʃən, daɪ-] *n* **1** SUPERVISION : dirección *f* **2** INSTRUCTION, ORDER : instrucción *f*, orden *f* **3** COURSE : dirección *f*, rumbo *m* ⟨to change direction : cambiar de dirección⟩ **4 to ask directions** : pedir indicaciones

directional [də'rɛkʃənəl, daɪ-] *adj* : direccional

directive [də'rɛktɪv, daɪ-] *n* : directiva *f*

directly [də'rɛktli, daɪ-] *adv* **1** STRAIGHT : directamente ⟨directly north : directamente al norte⟩ **2** FRANKLY : francamente, justo ⟨directly opposite : justo enfrente⟩ **4** IMMEDIATELY : en seguida, inmediatamente

directness [də'rɛktnəs, daɪ-] *n* : franqueza *f*

director [də'rɛktər, daɪ-] *n* **1** : director *m*, **-tora** *f* **2 board of directors** : junta *f* directiva, directorio *m*

directory [də'rɛktəri, daɪ-] *n, pl* **-ries** : guía *f*, directorio *m* ⟨telephone directory : directorio telefónico⟩

dirge ['dərdʒ] *n* : canto *m* fúnebre

dirigible ['dɪrədʒəbəl, də'rɪdʒə-] *n* : dirigible *m*, zepelín *m*

dirt ['dərt] *n* **1** FILTH : suciedad *f*, mugre *f*, porquería *f* **2** SOIL : tierra *f*

dirtiness ['dərtinəs] *n* : suciedad *f*

dirty¹ ['dərti] *vt* **dirtied; dirtying** : ensuciar, manchar

dirty² *adj* **dirtier; -est 1** SOILED, STAINED : sucio, manchado **2** DISHONEST : sucio, deshonesto ⟨a dirty player : un jugador tramposo⟩ ⟨a dirty trick : una mala pasada⟩ **3** INDECENT : indecente, cochino ⟨a dirty joke : un chiste verde⟩

disability [,dɪsə'bɪlət̬i] *n, pl* **-ties** : minusvalía *f*, discapacidad *f*, invalidez *f*

disable [dɪs'eɪbəl] *vt* **-abled; -abling** : dejar inválido, inutilizar, incapacitar

disabled [dɪs'eɪbəld] *adj* : minusválido, discapacitado

disabuse [,dɪsə'bjuːz] *vt* **-bused; -busing** : desengañar, sacar del error

disadvantage [,dɪsəd'væntɪdʒ] *n* : desventaja *f*

disadvantageous [,dɪs,æd,væn'teɪ-dʒəs] *adj* : desventajoso, desfavorable

disagree [ˌdɪsəˈgriː] vi 1 DIFFER : discrepar, no coincidir 2 DISSENT : disentir, discrepar, no estar de acuerdo
disagreeable [ˌdɪsəˈgriːəbəl] adj : desagradable
disagreement [ˌdɪsəˈgriːmənt] n 1 : desacuerdo m 2 DISCREPANCY : discrepancia f 3 ARGUMENT : discusión f, altercado m, disputa f
disappear [ˌdɪsəˈpɪr] vi : desaparecer, desvanecerse ⟨to disappear from view : perderse de vista⟩
disappearance [ˌdɪsəˈpɪrənts] n : desaparición f
disappoint [ˌdɪsəˈpɔɪnt] vt : decepcionar, defraudar, fallar
disappointing [ˌdɪsəˈpɔɪntɪŋ] adj : decepcionante
disappointment [ˌdɪsəˈpɔɪntmənt] n : decepción f, desilusión f, chasco m
disapproval [ˌdɪsəˈpruːvəl] n : desaprobación f
disapprove [ˌdɪsəˈpruːv] vi -proved; -proving : desaprobar, estar en contra
disapprovingly [ˌdɪsəˈpruːvɪŋli] adv : con desaprobación
disarm [dɪsˈɑrm] vt : desarmar
disarmament [dɪsˈɑrməmənt] n : desarme m ⟨nuclear disarmament : desarme nuclear⟩
disarrange [ˌdɪsəˈreɪndʒ] vt -ranged; -ranging : desarreglar, desordenar
disarray [ˌdɪsəˈreɪ] n : desorden m, confusión f, desorganización f
disaster [dɪˈzæstər] n : desastre m, catástrofe f
disastrous [dɪˈzæstrəs] adj : desastroso
disband [dɪsˈbænd] vt : disolver — vi : disolverse, dispersarse
disbar [dɪsˈbɑr] vt -barred; -barring : prohibir de ejercer la abogacía
disbelief [ˌdɪsbɪˈliːf] n : incredulidad f
disbelieve [ˌdɪsbɪˈliːv] v -lieved; -lieving : no creer, dudar
disburse [dɪsˈbərs] vt -bursed; -bursing : desembolsar
disbursement [dɪsˈbərsmənt] n : desembolso m
disc → **disk**
discard [dɪsˈkɑrd, ˈdɪsˌkɑrd] vt : desechar, deshacerse de, botar — vi : descartarse (en juegos de naipes)
discern [dɪˈsərn, -ˈzərn] vt : discernir, distinguir, percibir
discernible [dɪˈsərnəbəl, -ˈzər-] adj : perceptible, visible
discernment [dɪˈsərnmənt, -ˈzərn-] n : discernimiento m, criterio m
discharge¹ [dɪsˈtʃɑrdʒ, ˈdɪsˌ-] v -charged; -charging 1 UNLOAD : descargar (carga), desembarcar (pasajeros) 2 SHOOT : descargar, disparar 3 FREE : liberar, poner en libertad 4 DISMISS : despedir 5 EMIT : despedir (humo, etc.), descargar (electricidad) 6 : cumplir con (una obligación), saldar (una deuda) — vi 1 : descargarse (dícese de una batería) 2 OOZE : supurar

discharge² [ˈdɪsˌtʃɑrdʒ, dɪsˈ-] n 1 EMISSION : descarga f (de electricidad), emisión f (de gases) 2 DISMISSAL : despido m (del empleo), baja f (del ejército) 3 SECRETION : secreción f
disciple [dɪˈsaɪpəl] n : discípulo m, -la f
discipline¹ [ˈdɪsəplən] vt -plined; -plining 1 PUNISH : castigar, sancionar (a los empleados) 2 CONTROL : disciplinar 3 to discipline oneself : disciplinarse
discipline² n 1 FIELD : disciplina f, campo m 2 TRAINING : disciplina f 3 PUNISHMENT : castigo m 4 SELF-CONTROL : dominio m de sí mismo
disc jockey n : disc jockey mf
disclaim [dɪsˈkleɪm] vt DENY : negar
disclose [dɪsˈkloːz] vt -closed; -closing : revelar, poner en evidencia
disclosure [dɪsˈkloːʒər] n : revelación f
disco [ˈdɪskoː] n 1 → **discotheque** 2 or **disco music** : disco f, música f disco
discolor [dɪsˈkʌlər] vt 1 BLEACH : decolorar 2 FADE : desteñir 3 STAIN : manchar — vi : decolorarse, desteñirse
discoloration [dɪsˌkʌləˈreɪʃən] n 1 FADING : decoloración f 2 STAIN : mancha f
discomfort [dɪsˈkʌmfərt] n 1 PAIN : molestia f, malestar m 2 UNEASINESS : inquietud f
disconcert [ˌdɪskənˈsərt] vt : desconcertar
disconcerting [ˌdɪskənˈsərtɪŋ] adj : desconcertante
disconnect [ˌdɪskəˈnɛkt] vt : desconectar
disconnected [ˌdɪskəˈnɛktəd] adj : inconexo
disconsolate [dɪsˈkɑntsələt] adj : desconsolado
discontent [ˌdɪskənˈtɛnt] n : descontento m
discontented [ˌdɪskənˈtɛntəd] adj : descontento
discontinue [ˌdɪskənˈtɪnˌjuː] vt -ued; -uing : suspender, descontinuar
discontinuity [dɪsˌkɑntəˈnuːəţi, -ˈnjuː-] n, pl -ties : discontinuidad f
discontinuous [ˌdɪskənˈtɪnjəwəs] adj : discontinuo
discord [ˈdɪsˌkɔrd] n 1 STRIFE : discordia f, discordancia f 2 : disonancia f (en música)
discordant [dɪsˈkɔrdənt] adj : discordante, discorde — **discordantly** adv
discotheque [ˈdɪskəˌtɛk, ˌdɪskəˈtɛk] n : discoteca f
discount¹ [ˈdɪsˌkaʊnt, dɪsˈ-] vt 1 REDUCE : descontar, rebajar (precios) 2 DISREGARD : descartar, ignorar
discount² [ˈdɪsˌkaʊnt] n : descuento m, rebaja f
discourage [dɪsˈkərɪdʒ] vt -aged; -aging 1 DISHEARTEN : desalentar, desanimar 2 DISSUADE : disuadir
discouragement [dɪsˈkərɪdʒmənt] n : desánimo m, desaliento m

discouraging [dɪsˈkərədʒɪŋ] *adj* : desalentador

discourse[1] [dɪsˈkors] *vi* **-coursed; -coursing** : disertar, conversar

discourse[2] [ˈdɪsˌkors] *n* **1** TALK : conversación *f* **2** SPEECH, TREATISE : discurso *m*, tratado *m*

discourteous [dɪsˈkərtiəs] *adj* : descortés — **discourteously** *adv*

discourtesy [dɪsˈkərtəsi] *n, pl* **-sies** : descortesía *f*

discover [dɪsˈkʌvər] *vt* : descubrir

discoverer [dɪsˈkʌvərər] *n* : descubridor *m*, -dora *f*

discovery [dɪsˈkʌvəri] *n, pl* **-ries** : descubrimiento *m*

discredit[1] [dɪsˈkrɛdət] *vt* **1** DISBELIEVE : no creer, dudar *f* **2** : desacreditar, desprestigiar, poner en duda ⟨they discredited his research : desacreditaron sus investigaciones⟩

discredit[2] *n* **1** DISREPUTE : descrédito *m*, desprestigio *m* **2** DOUBT : duda *f*

discreet [dɪsˈkriːt] *adj* : discreto — **discreetly** *adv*

discrepancy [dɪsˈkrɛpəntsi] *n, pl* **-cies** : discrepancia *f*

discretion [dɪsˈkrɛʃən] *n* **1** CIRCUMSPECTION : discreción *f*, circunspección *f* **2** JUDGMENT : discernimiento *m*, criterio *m*

discretionary [dɪsˈkrɛʃəˌnɛri] *adj* : discrecional

discriminate [dɪsˈkrɪməˌneɪt] *v* **-nated; -nating** *vt* DISTINGUISH : distinguir, discriminar, diferenciar — *vi* : discriminar ⟨to discriminate against women : discriminar a las mujeres⟩

discrimination [dɪsˌkrɪməˈneɪʃən] *n* **1** PREJUDICE : discriminación *f* **2** DISCERNMENT : discernimiento *m*

discriminatory [dɪsˈkrɪmənəˌtori] *adj* : discriminatorio

discus [ˈdɪskəs] *n, pl* **-cuses** [-kəsəz] : disco *m*

discuss [dɪsˈkʌs] *vt* : hablar de, discutir, tratar (de)

discussion [dɪsˈkʌʃən] *n* : discusión *f*, debate *m*, conversación *f*

disdain[1] [dɪsˈdeɪn] *vt* : desdeñar, despreciar ⟨they disdained to reply : no se dignaron a responder⟩

disdain[2] *n* : desdén *m*

disdainful [dɪsˈdeɪnfəl] *adj* : desdeñoso — **disdainfully** *adv*

disease [dɪˈziːz] *n* : enfermedad *f*, mal *m*, dolencia *f*

diseased [dɪˈziːzd] *adj* : enfermo

disembark [ˌdɪsɪmˈbark] *v* : desembarcar

disembarkation [dɪsˌɛmˌbarˈkeɪʃən] *n* : desembarco *m*, desembarque *m*

disembodied [ˌdɪsɪmˈbadid] *adj* : incorpóreo

disenchant [ˌdɪsɪnˈtʃænt] *vt* : desilusionar, desencantar, desengañar

disenchantment [ˌdɪsɪnˈtʃæntmənt] *n* : desencanto *m*, desilusión *f*

disengage [ˌdɪsɪnˈgeɪdʒ] *vt* **-gaged; -gaging 1** : soltar, desconectar (un mecanismo) **2 to disengage the clutch** : desembragar

disentangle [ˌdɪsɪnˈtæŋgəl] *vt* **-gled; -gling** UNTANGLE : desenredar, desenmarañar

disfavor [dɪsˈfeɪvər] *n* : desaprobación *f*

disfigure [dɪsˈfɪgjər] *vt* **-ured; -uring** : desfigurar (a una persona), afear (un edificio, un área)

disfigurement [dɪsˈfɪgjərmənt] *n* : desfiguración *f*, afeamiento *m*

disfranchise [dɪsˈfrænˌtʃaɪz] *vt* **-chised; -chising** : privar del derecho a votar

disgrace[1] [dɪsˈkreɪs] *vt* **-graced; -gracing** : deshonrar

disgrace[2] *n* **1** DISHONOR : desgracia *f*, deshonra *f* **2** SHAME : vergüenza *f* ⟨he's a disgrace to his family : es una vergüenza para su familia⟩

disgraceful [dɪsˈkreɪsfəl] *adj* : vergonzoso, deshonroso, ignominioso

disgracefully [dɪsˈkreɪsfəli] *adv* : vergonzosamente

disgruntle [dɪsˈgrʌntəl] *vt* **-tled; -tling** : enfadar, contrariar

disguise[1] [dɪsˈkaɪz] *vt* **-guised; -guising 1** : disfrazar, enmascarar (el aspecto) **2** CONCEAL : encubrir, disimular

disguise[2] *n* : disfraz *m*

disgust[1] [dɪsˈkʌst] *vt* : darle asco (a alguien), asquear, repugnar ⟨that disgusts me : eso me da asco⟩

disgust[2] *n* : asco *m*, repugnancia *f*

disgusting [dɪsˈkʌstɪŋ] *adj* : asqueroso, repugnante — **disgustingly** *adv*

dish[1] [ˈdɪʃ] *vt* SERVE : servir

dish[2] *n* **1** : plato *m* ⟨the national dish : el plato nacional⟩ **2** PLATE : plato *m* ⟨to wash the dishes : lavar los platos⟩ **3 serving dish** : fuente *f*

dishcloth [ˈdɪʃˌklɔθ] *n* : paño *m* de cocina (para secar), trapo *m* de fregar (para lavar)

dishearten [dɪsˈhartən] *vt* : desanimar, desalentar

dishevel [dɪˈʃɛvəl] *vt* **-eled** *or* **-elled; -eling** *or* **-elling** : desarreglar, despeinar (el pelo)

disheveled *or* **dishevelled** [dɪˈʃɛvəld] *adj* : despeinado (dícese del pelo), desarreglado, desaliñado

dishonest [dɪˈsanəst] *adj* : deshonesto, fraudulento — **dishonestly** *adv*

dishonesty [dɪˈsanəsti] *n, pl* **-ties** : deshonestidad *f*, falta *f* de honradez

dishonor[1] [dɪˈsanər] *vt* : deshonrar

dishonor[2] *n* : deshonra *f*

dishonorable [dɪˈsanərəbəl] *adj* : deshonroso — **dishonorably** [-bli] *adv*

dishrag [ˈdɪʃˌræg] *n* → **dishcloth**

dishwasher [ˈdɪʃˌwɔʃər] *n* : lavaplatos *m*, lavavajillas *m*

disillusion [ˌdɪsəˈluːʒən] *vt* : desilusionar, desencantar, desengañar

disillusionment [ˌdɪsəˈluːʒənmənt] *n* : desilusión *f*, desencanto *m*

disinclination [dɪsˌɪnklə'neɪʃən, -ˌɪŋ-] *n* : aversión *f*

disinclined [ˌdɪsɪn'klaɪnd] *adv* : poco dispuesto

disinfect [ˌdɪsɪn'fɛkt] *vt* : desinfectar

disinfectant¹ [ˌdɪsɪn'fɛktənt] *adj* : desinfectante

disinfectant² *n* : desinfectante *m*

disinherit [ˌdɪsɪn'hɛrət] *vt* : desheredar

disintegrate [dɪs'ɪntəˌɡreɪt] *v* **-grated; -grating** *vt* : desintegrar, deshacer — *vi* : desintegrarse, deshacerse

disintegration [dɪsˌɪntə'ɡreɪʃən] *n* : desintegración *f*

disinterested [dɪs'ɪntərəstəd, -ˌrɛs-] *adj* **1** INDIFFERENT : indiferente **2** IMPARTIAL : imparcial, desinteresado

disinterestedness [dɪs'ɪntərəstədnəs, -ˌrɛs-] *n* : desinterés *m*

disjointed [dɪs'dʒɔɪntəd] *adj* : inconexo, incoherente

disk *or* **disc** ['dɪsk] *n* : disco *m*

disk drive *n* : unidad *f* de disco

diskette [ˌdɪs'kɛt] *n* : diskette *m*, disquete *m*

dislike¹ [dɪs'laɪk] *vt* **-liked; -liking** : tenerle aversión a (algo), tenerle antipatía (a alguien), no gustarle (algo a uno)

dislike² *n* : aversión *f*, antipatía *f*

dislocate ['dɪsloˌkeɪt, dɪs'lo:-] *vt* **-cated; -cating** : dislocar

dislocation [ˌdɪslo'keɪʃən] *n* : dislocación *f*

dislodge [dɪs'lɑdʒ] *vt* **-lodged; -lodging** : sacar, desalojar, desplazar

disloyal [dɪs'lɔɪəl] *adj* : desleal

disloyalty [dɪs'lɔɪəlti] *n, pl* **-ties** : deslealtad *f*

dismal ['dɪzməl] *adj* **1** GLOOMY : sombrío, lúgubre, tétrico **2** DEPRESSING : deprimente, triste

dismantle [dɪs'mæntəl] *vt* **-tled; -tling** : desmantelar, desmontar, desarmar

dismay¹ [dɪs'meɪ] *vt* : consternar

dismay² *n* : consternación *f*

dismember [dɪs'mɛmbər] *vt* : desmembrar

dismiss [dɪs'mɪs] *vt* **1** : dejar salir, darle permiso (a alguien) para retirarse **2** DISCHARGE : despedir, destituir **3** REJECT : descartar, desechar, rechazar

dismissal [dɪs'mɪsəl] *n* **1** : permiso *m* para retirarse **2** DISCHARGE : despido *m* (de un empleado), destitución *f* (de un funcionario) **3** REJECTION : rechazo *m*

dismount [dɪs'maʊnt] *vi* : desmontar, bajarse, apearse

disobedience [ˌdɪsə'bi:diənts] *n* : desobediencia *f* — **disobedient** [-ənt] *adj*

disobey [ˌdɪsə'beɪ] *v* : desobedecer

disorder¹ [dɪs'ɔrdər] *vt* : desordenar, desarreglar

disorder² *n* **1** DISARRAY : desorden *m* **2** UNREST : disturbios *mpl*, desórdenes *mpl* **3** AILMENT : afección *f*, indisposición *f*, dolencia *f*

disorderly [dɪs'ɔrdərli] *adj* **1** UNTIDY : desordenado, desarreglado **2** UNRULY : indisciplinado, alborotado **3** **disorderly conduct** : conducta *f* escandalosa

disorganization [dɪsˌɔrɡənə'zeɪʃən] *n* : desorganización *f*

disorganize [dɪs'ɔrɡəˌnaɪz] *vt* **-nized; -nizing** : desorganizar

disorient [dɪs'ɔriˌɛnt] *vt* : desorientar

disown [dɪs'o:n] *vt* : renegar de, repudiar

disparage [dɪs'pærɪdʒ] *vt* **-aged; -aging** : menospreciar, denigrar

disparagement [dɪs'pærɪdʒmənt] *n* : menosprecio *m*

disparate ['dɪspərət, dɪs'pærət] *adj* : dispar, diferente

disparity [dɪs'pærəti] *n, pl* **-ties** : disparidad *f*

dispassionate [dɪs'pæʃənət] *adj* : desapasionado, imparcial — **dispassionately** *adv*

dispatch¹ [dɪs'pætʃ] *vt* **1** SEND : despachar, enviar **2** KILL : despachar, matar **3** HANDLE : despachar

dispatch² *n* **1** SENDING : envío *m*, despacho *m* **2** MESSAGE : despacho *m*, reportaje *m* (de un periodista), parte *m* (en el ejército) **3** PROMPTNESS : prontitud *f*, rapidez *f*

dispel [dɪs'pɛl] *vt* **-pelled; -pelling** : disipar, desvanecer

dispensable [dɪ'spɛntsəbəl] *adj* : prescindible

dispensation [ˌdɪspɛn'seɪʃən] *n* EXEMPTION : exención *m*, dispensa *f*

dispense [dɪs'pɛnts] *v* **-pensed; -pensing** *vt* **1** DISTRIBUTE : repartir, distribuir, dar **2** ADMINISTER, BESTOW : administrar (justicia), conceder (favores, etc.) **3** : preparar y despachar (medicamentos) — *vi* **to dispense with** : prescindir de

dispenser [dɪs'pɛntsər] *n* : dispensador *m*, distribuidor *m* automático

dispersal [dɪs'pərsəl] *n* : dispersión *f*

disperse [dɪs'pərs] *v* **-persed; -persing** *vt* : dispersar, diseminar — *vi* : dispersarse

dispersion [dɪ'spərʒən] *n* : dispersión *f*

dispirit [dɪ'spɪrət] *vt* : desalentar, desanimar

displace [dɪs'pleɪs] *vt* **-placed; -placing** **1** : desplazar (un líquido, etc.) **2** REPLACE : reemplazar

displacement [dɪs'pleɪsmənt] *n* **1** : desplazamiento *m* (de personas) **2** REPLACEMENT : sustitución *f*, reemplazo *m*

display¹ [dɪs'pleɪ] *vt* : exponer, exhibir, mostrar

display² *n* **1** : muestra *f*, exposición *f*, alarde *m* **2** : visualizador *m* (de una computadora)

displease [dɪs'pli:z] *vt* **-pleased; -pleasing** : desagradar a, disgustar, contrariar

displeasure [dɪsˈplɛʒər] n : desagrado m
disposable [dɪsˈpoːzəbəl] adj 1 : desechable ⟨disposable diapers : pañales desechables⟩ 2 AVAILABLE : disponible
disposal [dɪsˈpoːzəl] n 1 PLACEMENT : disposición f, colocación f 2 REMOVAL : eliminación f 3 to have at one's disposal : disponer de, tener a su disposición
dispose [dɪsˈpoːz] v -posed; -posing vt 1 ARRANGE : disponer, colocar 2 INCLINE : predisponer — vi 1 to dispose of DISCARD : desechar, deshacerse de 2 to dispose of HANDLE : despachar
disposition [ˌdɪspəˈzɪʃən] n 1 ARRANGEMENT : disposición f 2 TENDENCY : predisposición f, inclinación f 3 TEMPERAMENT : temperamento m, carácter m
dispossess [ˌdɪspəˈzɛs] vt : deposeer
disproportion [ˌdɪsprəˈporʃən] n : desproporción f
disproportionate [ˌdɪsprəˈporʃənət] adj : desproporcionado — **disproportionately** adv
disprove [dɪsˈpruːv] vt -proved; -proving : rebatir, refutar
disputable [dɪsˈpjuːtəbəl, ˈdɪspjʊtəbəl] adj : disputable, discutible
dispute¹ [dɪsˈpjuːt] v -puted; -puting vt 1 QUESTION : discutir, cuestionar 2 OPPOSE : combatir, resistir — vi ARGUE, DEBATE : discutir
dispute² n 1 DEBATE : debate m, discusión f 2 QUARREL : disputa f, discusión f
disqualification [dɪsˌkwɑləfəˈkeɪʃən] n : descalificación f
disqualify [dɪsˈkwɑləˌfaɪ] vt -fied; -fying : descalificar, inhabilitar
disquiet¹ [dɪsˈkwaɪət] vt : inquietar
disquiet² n : ansiedad f, inquietud f
disregard¹ [ˌdɪsrɪˈgɑrd] vt : ignorar, no prestar atención a
disregard² n : indiferencia f
disrepair [ˌdɪsrɪˈpær] n : mal estado m
disreputable [dɪsˈrɛpjʊtəbəl] adj : de mala fama (dícese de una persona o un lugar), vergonzoso (dícese de la conducta)
disreputably [dɪsˈrɛpjʊtəbli] adv : vergonzosamente
disrepute [ˌdɪsrɪˈpjuːt] n : descrédito m, mala fama f, deshonra f
disrespect [ˌdɪsrɪˈspɛkt] n : falta f de respeto
disrespectful [ˌdɪsrɪˈspɛktfəl] adj : irrespetuoso — **disrespectfully** adv
disrobe [dɪsˈroːb] v -robed; -robing vt : desvestir, desnudar — vi : desvestirse, desnudarse
disrupt [dɪsˈrʌpt] vt : trastornar, perturbar
disruption [dɪsˈrʌpʃən] n : trastorno m
disruptive [dɪsˈrʌptɪv] adj : perjudicial, perturbador — **disruptively** adv
dissatisfaction [dɪsˌsætəsˈfækʃən] n : descontento m, insatisfacción f

dissatisfied [dɪsˈsætəsˌfaɪd] adj : descontento, insatisfecho
dissatisfy [dɪsˈsætəsˌfaɪ] vt -fied; -fying : no contentar, no satisfacer
dissect [dɪˈsɛkt] vt : disecar
dissection [dɪˈsɛkʃən] n : disección f
dissemble [dɪˈsɛmbəl] v -bled; -bling vt HIDE : ocultar, disimular — vi PRETEND : fingir, disimular
disseminate [dɪˈsɛməˌneɪt] vt -nated; -nating : diseminar, difundir, divulgar
dissemination [dɪˌsɛməˈneɪʃən] n : diseminación f, difusión f
dissension [dɪˈsɛnʃən] n : disensión f, desacuerdo m
dissent¹ [dɪˈsɛnt] vi : disentir
dissent² n : disentimiento m, disensión f
dissertation [ˌdɪsərˈteɪʃən] n 1 DISCOURSE : disertación f, discurso m 2 THESIS : tesis f
disservice [dɪsˈsɔrvɪs] n : perjuicio m
dissident¹ [ˈdɪsədənt] adj : disidente
dissident² n : disidente mf
dissimilar [dɪˈsɪmələr] adj : distinto, diferente, disímil
dissipate [ˈdɪsəˌpeɪt] vt -pated; -pating 1 DISPERSE : disipar, dispersar 2 SQUANDER : malgastar, desperdiciar, derrochar, disipar
dissipation [ˌdɪsəˈpeɪʃən] n : disipación f, libertinaje m
dissociate [dɪˈsoːʃiˌeɪt, -siˌ-] v -ated [-ˌeɪtəd]; -ating [-ˌeɪtɪŋ] vt : disociar ⟨to disassociate oneself : disociarse⟩ — vi : disociarse
dissociation [dɪˌsoːʃiˈeɪʃən, -siˈ-] n : disociación f
dissolute [ˈdɪsəˌluːt] adj : disoluto
dissolution [ˌdɪsəˈluːʃən] n : disolución f
dissolve [dɪˈzɑlv] v -solved; -solving vt : disolver — vi : disolverse
dissonance [ˈdɪsənənts] n : disonancia f
dissuade [dɪˈsweɪd] vt -suaded; -suading : disuadir
distance¹ [ˈdɪstənts] vt -tanced [-tənst]; -tancing [-təntsɪŋ] to distance oneself : distanciarse
distance² n 1 : distancia f ⟨the distance between two points : la distancia entre dos puntos⟩ ⟨in the distance : a lo lejos⟩ 2 RESERVE : actitud f distante, reserva f ⟨to keep one's distance : guardar las distancias⟩
distant [ˈdɪstənt] adj 1 FAR : distante, lejano 2 REMOTE : distante, lejano, remoto 3 ALOOF : distante, frío
distantly [ˈdɪstəntli] adv 1 LOOSELY : aproximadamente, vagamente 2 COLDLY : fríamente, con frialdad
distaste [dɪsˈteɪst] n : desagrado m, aversión f
distasteful [dɪsˈteɪstfəl] adj : desagradable, de mal gusto
distemper [dɪsˈtɛmpər] n : moquillo m
distend [dɪsˈtɛnd] vt : dilatar, hinchar — vi : dilatarse, hincharse

distill [dɪˈstɪl] *vt* : destilar
distillation [ˌdɪstəˈleɪʃən] *n* : destilación *f*
distiller [dɪˈstɪlər] *n* : destilador *m*, -dora *f*
distillery [dɪˈstɪləri] *n, pl* **-ries** [-riz] : destilería *f*
distinct [dɪˈstɪŋkt] *adj* **1** DIFFERENT : distinto, diferente **2** CLEAR, UNMISTAKABLE : marcado, claro, evidente ⟨a distinct possibility : una clara posibilidad⟩
distinction [dɪˈstɪŋkʃən] *n* **1** DIFFERENTIATION : distinción *f* **2** DIFFERENCE : diferencia *f* **3** EXCELLENCE : distinción *f*, excelencia *f* ⟨a writer of distinction : un escritor destacado⟩
distinctive [dɪˈstɪŋktɪv] *adj* : distintivo, característico — **distinctively** *adv*
distinctiveness [dɪˈstɪŋktɪvnəs] *n* : peculiaridad *f*
distinctly [dɪˈstɪŋktli] *adv* : claramente, con claridad
distinguish [dɪsˈtɪŋgwɪʃ] *vt* **1** DIFFERENTIATE : distinguir, diferenciar **2** DISCERN : distinguir ⟨he distinguished the sound of the piano : distinguió el sonido del piano⟩ **3** **to distinguish oneself** : señalarse, distinguirse — *vi* DISCRIMINATE : distinguir
distinguishable [dɪsˈtɪŋgwɪʃəbəl] *adj* : distinguible
distinguished [dɪsˈtɪŋgwɪʃt] *adj* : distinguido
distort [dɪˈstɔrt] *vt* **1** MISREPRESENT : distorsionar, tergiversar **2** DEFORM : distorsionar, deformar
distortion [dɪˈstɔrʃən] *n* : distorsión *f*, deformación *f*, tergiversación *f*
distract [dɪˈstrækt] *vt* : distraer, entretener
distracted [dɪˈstræktəd] *adj* : distraído
distraction [dɪˈstrækʃən] *n* **1** INTERRUPTION : distracción *f*, interrupción *f* **2** CONFUSION : confusión *f* **3** AMUSEMENT : diversión *f*, entretenimiento *m*, distracción *f*
distraught [dɪˈstrɔt] *adj* : afligido, turbado
distress¹ [dɪˈstrɛs] *vt* : afligir, darle pena (a alguien), hacer sufrir
distress² *n* **1** SORROW : dolor *m*, angustia *f*, aflicción *f* **2** PAIN : dolor *m* **3** **in ~** : en peligro
distressful [dɪˈstrɛsfəl] *adj* : doloroso, penoso
distribute [dɪˈstrɪˌbjuːt, -bjut] *vt* **-uted; -uting** : distribuir, repartir
distribution [ˌdɪstrəˈbjuːʃən] *n* : distribución *f*, reparto *m*
distributive [dɪˈstrɪbjutɪv] *adj* : distributivo
distributor [dɪˈstrɪbjutər] *n* : distribuidor *m*, -dora *f*
district [ˈdɪsˌtrɪkt] *n* **1** REGION : región *f*, zona *f*, barrio *m* (de una ciudad) **2** : distrito *m* (zona política)
distrust¹ [dɪsˈtrʌst] *vt* : desconfiar de

distrust² *n* : desconfianza *f*, recelo *m*
distrustful [dɪsˈtrʌstfəl] *adj* : desconfiado, receloso, suspicaz
disturb [dɪˈstərb] *vt* **1** BOTHER : molestar, perturbar ⟨sorry to disturb you : perdone la molestia⟩ **2** DISARRANGE : desordenar **3** WORRY : inquietar, preocupar **4** **to disturb the peace** : alterar el orden público
disturbance [dɪˈstərbəns] *n* **1** COMMOTION : alboroto *m*, disturbio *m* **2** INTERRUPTION : interrupción *f*
disuse [dɪsˈjuːs] *n* : desuso *m*
ditch¹ [ˈdɪtʃ] *vt* **1** : cavar zanjas en **2** DISCARD : deshacerse de, botar
ditch² *n* : zanja *f*, fosa *f*, cuneta *f* (en una carretera)
dither [ˈdɪðər] *n* **to be in a dither** : estar nervioso, ponerse como loco
ditto [ˈdɪto] *n, pl* **-tos** **1** : lo mismo, ídem *m* **2** **ditto marks** : comillas *fpl*
ditty [ˈdɪti] *n, pl* **-ties** : canción *f* corta y simple
diurnal [daɪˈərnəl] *adj* **1** DAILY : diario, cotidiano **2** : diurno ⟨a diurnal animal : un animal diurno⟩
divan [ˈdaɪˌvæn, dɪˈ-] *n* : diván *m*
dive¹ [ˈdaɪv] *vi* **dived** *or* **dove** [ˈdoːv]; **dived; diving** **1** PLUNGE : tirarse al agua, zambullirse, dar un clavado **2** SUBMERGE : sumergirse **3** DROP : bajar en picada (dícese de un avión), caer en picada
dive² *n* **1** PLUNGE : zambullida *f*, clavado *m* (en el agua) **2** DESCENT : descenso *m* en picada **3** BAR, JOINT : antro *m*
diver [ˈdaɪvər] *n* : saltador *m*, -dora *f*; clavadista *mf*
diverge [dəˈvərdʒ, daɪ-] *vi* **-verged; -verging** **1** SEPARATE : divergir, separarse **2** DIFFER : divergir, discrepar
divergence [dəˈvərdʒəns, daɪ-] *n* : divergencia *f* — **divergent** [-ənt] *adj*
diverse [daɪˈvərs, də-, ˈdaɪˌvərs] *adj* : diverso, variado
diversification [daɪˌvərsəfəˈkeɪʃən, də-] *n* : diversificación *f*
diversify [daɪˈvərsəˌfaɪ, də-] *vt* **-fied; -fying** : diversificar, variar
diversion [daɪˈvərʒən, də-] *n* **1** DEVIATION : desviación *f* **2** AMUSEMENT, DISTRACTION : diversión *f*, distracción *f*, entretenimiento *m*
diversity [daɪˈvərsəti, də-] *n, pl* **-ties** : diversidad *f*
divert [dəˈvərt, daɪ-] *vt* **1** DEFLECT : desviar **2** DISTRACT : distraer **3** AMUSE : divertir, entretener
divest [daɪˈvest, də-] *vt* **1** UNDRESS : desnudar, desvestir **2** **to divest of** : despojar de
divide [dəˈvaɪd] *v* **-vided; -viding** *vt* **1** HALVE : dividir, partir por la mitad **2** SHARE : repartir, dividir **3** : dividir (números) — *vi* : dividirse, dividir (en matemáticas)

dividend [ˈdɪvəˌdɛnd, -dənd] *n* **1** : dividendo *m* (en finanzas) **2** BONUS : beneficio *m*, provecho *m* **3** : dividendo *m* (en matemáticas)

divider [dɪˈvaɪdər] *n* **1** : separador *m* (para ficheros, etc.) **2** *or* **room divider** : mampara *f*, biombo *m*

divination [ˌdɪvəˈneɪʃən] *n* : adivinación *f*

divine¹ [dəˈvaɪn] *adj* **-viner; -est 1** : divino **2** SUPERB : divino, espléndido — **divinely** *adv*

divine² *n* : clérigo *m*, eclesiástico *m*

divinity [dəˈvɪnəti] *n, pl* **-ties** : divinidad *f*

divisible [dɪˈvɪzəbəl] *adj* : divisible

division [dɪˈvɪʒən] *n* **1** DISTRIBUTION : división *f*, reparto *m* ⟨division of labor : distribución del trabajo⟩ **2** PART : división *f*, sección *f* **3** : división *f* (en matemáticas)

divisive [dəˈvaɪsɪv] *adj* : divisivo

divisor [dɪˈvaɪzər] *n* : divisor *m*

divorce¹ [dəˈvors] *v* **-vorced; -vorcing** *vt* : divorciar — *vi* : divorciarse

divorce² *n* : divorcio *m*

divorcé [dɪˌvorˈseɪ, -ˈsiː; -ˈvorˌ-] *n* : divorciado *m*

divorcée [dɪˌvorˈseɪ, -ˈsiː; -ˈvorˌ-] *n* : divorciada *f*

divulge [dəˈvʌldʒ, daɪ-] *vt* **-vulged; -vulging** : revelar, divulgar

dizzily [ˈdɪzəli] *adv* : vertiginosamente

dizziness [ˈdɪzinəs] *n* : mareo *m*, vahído *m*, vértigo *m*

dizzy [ˈdɪzi] *adj* **dizzier; -est 1** : mareado ⟨I feel dizzy : estoy mareado⟩ **2** : vertiginoso ⟨a dizzy speed : una velocidad vertiginosa⟩

DNA [ˌdiˌɛnˈeɪ] *n* : ADN *m*

do [ˈduː] *v* **did** [ˈdɪd]; **done** [ˈdʌn]; **doing; does** [ˈdʌz] *vt* **1** CARRY OUT, PERFORM : hacer, realizar, llevar a cabo ⟨she did her best : hizo todo lo posible⟩ **2** PREPARE : preparar, hacer ⟨do your homework : haz tu tarea⟩ **3** ARRANGE : arreglar, peinar (el pelo) **4 to do in** RUIN : estropear, arruinar **5** KILL : matar, liquidar *fam* — *vi* **1** : hacer ⟨you did well : hiciste bien⟩ **2** FARE : estar, ir, andar ⟨how are you doing? : ¿cómo estás?, ¿cómo te va?⟩ **3** FINISH : terminar ⟨now I'm done : ya terminé⟩ **4** SERVE : servir, ser suficiente, alcanzar ⟨this will do for now : esto servirá por el momento⟩ **5 to do away with** ABOLISH : abolir, suprimir **6 to do away with** KILL : eliminar, matar **7 to do by** TREAT : tratar ⟨he does well by her : él la trata bien⟩ — *v aux* **1** (*used in interrogative sentences and negative statements*) ⟨do you know her? : ¿la conoces?⟩ ⟨I don't like that : a mí no me gusta eso⟩ **2** (*used for emphasis*) ⟨I do hope you'll come : espero que vengas⟩ **3** (*used as a substitute verb to avoid repetition*) ⟨do you speak English? yes, I do : ¿habla inglés? sí⟩

docile [ˈdɑsəl] *adj* : dócil, sumiso

dock¹ [ˈdɑk] *vt* **1** CUT : cortar **2** : descontar dinero de (un sueldo) — *vi* ANCHOR, LAND : fondear, atracar

dock² *n* **1** PIER : atracadero *m* **2** WHARF : muelle *m* **3** : banquillo *m* de los acusados (en un tribunal)

doctor¹ [ˈdɑktər] *vt* **1** TREAT : tratar, curar **2** ALTER : adulterar, alterar, falsificar (un documento)

doctor² *n* **1** : doctor *m*, -tora *f* ⟨Doctor of Philosophy : doctor en filosofía⟩ **2** PHYSICIAN : médico *m*, -ca *f*; doctor *m*, -tora *f*

doctorate [ˈdɑktərət] *n* : doctorado *m*

doctrine [ˈdɑktrɪn] *n* : doctrina *f*

document¹ [ˈdɑkjuˌmɛnt] *vt* : documentar

document² [ˈdɑkjumənt] *n* : documento *m*

documentary¹ [ˌdɑkjuˈmɛntəri] *adj* : documental

documentary² *n, pl* **-ries** : documental *m*

documentation [ˌdɑkjumənˈteɪʃən] *n* : documentación *f*

dodge¹ [ˈdɑdʒ] *v* **dodged; dodging** *vt* : esquivar, eludir, evadir (impuestos) — *vi* : echarse a un lado

dodge² *n* **1** RUSE : truco *m*, treta *f*, artimaña *f* **2** EVASION : regate *m*, evasión *f*

dodo [ˈdoːˌdoː] *n, pl* **-does** *or* **-dos** : dodo *m*

doe [ˈdoː] *n, pl* **does** *or* **doe** : gama *f*, cierva *f*

does → do

doff [ˈdɑf, ˈdɔf] *vt* : quitarse ⟨to doff one's hat : quitarse el sombrero⟩

dog¹ [ˈdɔɡ, ˈdɑɡ] *vt* **dogged; dogging** : seguir de cerca, perseguir, acosar ⟨to dog someone's footsteps : seguir los pasos de alguien⟩ ⟨dogged by bad luck : perseguido por la mala suerte⟩

dog² *n* : perro *m*, -rra *f*

dogcatcher [ˈdɔɡˌkætʃər] *n* : perrero *m*, -ra *f*

dog-eared [ˈdɔɡˌɪrd] *adj* : con las esquinas dobladas

dogged [ˈdɔɡəd] *adj* : tenaz, terco, obstinado

doggy [ˈdɔɡi] *n, pl* **doggies** : perrito *m*, -ta *f*

doghouse [ˈdɔɡˌhaʊs] *n* : casita *f* de perro

dogma [ˈdɔɡmə] *n* : dogma *m*

dogmatic [dɔɡˈmætɪk] *adj* : dogmático

dogmatism [ˈdɔɡməˌtɪzəm] *n* : dogmatismo *m*

dogwood [ˈdɔɡˌwʊd] *n* : cornejo *m*

doily [ˈdɔɪli] *n, pl* **-lies** : pañito *m*

doings [ˈduːɪŋz] *npl* : eventos *mpl*, actividades *fpl*

doldrums [ˈdoːldrəmz, ˈdɑl-] *npl* **1** : zona *f* de las calmas ecuatoriales **2 to be in the doldrums** : estar abatido (dícese de una persona), estar estancado (dícese de una empresa)

dole ['do:l] *n* **1** ALMS : distribución *f* a los necesitados, limosna *f* **2** : subsidios *mpl* de desempleo

doleful ['do:lfəl] *adj* : triste, lúgubre

dolefully ['do:lfəli] *adv* : con pesar, de manera triste

dole out *vt* **doled out; doling out** : repartir

doll ['dɑl, 'dɔl] *n* : muñeco *m*, -ca *f*

dollar ['dɑlər] *n* : dólar *m*

dolly ['dɑli] *n, pl* **-lies** **1** → doll **2** : plataforma *f* rodante

dolphin ['dɑlfən, 'dɔl-] *n* : delfín *m*

dolt ['do:lt] *n* : imbécil *mf*; tonto *m*, -ta *f*

domain [do'meɪn, də-] *n* **1** TERRITORY : dominio *m*, territorio *m* **2** FIELD : campo *m*, esfera *f*, ámbito *m* ⟨the domain of art : el ámbito de las artes⟩

dome ['do:m] *n* : cúpula *f*, bóveda *f*

domestic¹ [də'mɛstɪk] *adj* **1** HOUSEHOLD : doméstico, casero **2** : nacional, interno ⟨domestic policy : política interna⟩ **3** TAME : domesticado

domestic² *n* : empleado *m* doméstico, empleada *f* doméstica

domestically [də'mɛstɪkli] *adv* : domésticamente

domesticate [də'mɛstɪˌkeɪt] *vt* **-cated; -cating** : domesticar

domicile ['dɑməˌsaɪl, 'do:-; 'dɑməsɪl] *n* : domicilio *m*

dominance ['dɑmənənts] *n* : dominio *m*, dominación *f*

dominant ['dɑmənənt] *adj* : dominante

dominate ['dɑməˌneɪt] *v* **-nated; -nating** : dominar

domination [ˌdɑmə'neɪʃən] *n* : dominación *f*

domineer [ˌdɑmə'nɪr] *vt* : dominar sobre, avasallar, tiranizar

Dominican [də'mɪnɪkən] *n* : dominicano *m*, -na *f* — **Dominican** *adj*

dominion [də'mɪnjən] *n* **1** POWER : dominio *m* **2** DOMAIN, TERRITORY : dominio *m*, territorio *m*

domino ['dɑməˌno:] *n, pl* **-noes** *or* **-nos** **1** : dominó *m* **2 dominoes** *npl* : dominó *m* (juego)

don ['dɑn] *vt* **donned; donning** : ponerse

donate ['do:ˌneɪt, do:'-] *vt* **-nated; -nating** : donar, hacer un donativo de

donation [do:'neɪʃən] *n* : donación *f*, donativo *m*

done¹ ['dʌn] → do

done² *adj* **1** FINISHED : terminado, acabado, concluido **2** COOKED : cocinado

donkey ['dɑŋki, 'dʌŋ-] *n, pl* **-keys** : burro *m*, asno *m*

donor ['do:nər] *n* : donante *mf*; donador *m*, -dora *f*

don't ['do:nt] (*contraction of* do not) → do

doodle¹ ['du:dəl] *v* **-dled; -dling** : garabatear

doodle² *n* : garabato *m*

doom¹ ['du:m] *vt* : condenar

doom² *n* **1** JUDGMENT : sentencia *f*, condena *f* **2** DEATH : muerte *f* **3** FATE : destino *m* **4** RUIN : perdición *f*, ruina *f*

door ['dor] *n* : puerta *f*

doorbell ['dorˌbɛl] *n* : timbre *m*

doorknob ['dorˌnɑb] *n* : pomo *m*, perilla *f*

doorman ['dormən] *n, pl* **-men** [-mən, -ˌmɛn] : portero *m*

doormat ['dorˌmæt] *n* : felpudo *m*

doorstep ['dorˌstɛp] *n* : umbral *m*

doorway ['dorˌweɪ] *n* : entrada *f*, portal *m*

dope¹ ['do:p] *vt* **doped; doping** : drogar, narcotizar

dope² *n* **1** DRUG : droga *f*, estupefaciente *m*, narcótico *m* **2** IDIOT : idiota *mf*; tonto *m*, -ta *f* **3** INFORMATION : información *f*

dormant ['dormənt] *adj* : inactivo, latente

dormer ['dormər] *n* : buhardilla *f*

dormitory ['dorməˌtori] *n, pl* **-ries** : dormitorio *m*, residencia *f* de estudiantes

dormouse ['dorˌmaus] *n* : lirón *m*

dorsal ['dorsəl] *adj* : dorsal — **dorsally** *adv*

dory ['dori] *n, pl* **-ries** : bote *m* de fondo plano

dosage ['do:sɪʤ] *n* : dosis *f*

dose¹ ['do:s] *vt* **dosed; dosing** : medicinar

dose² *n* : dosis *f*

dossier ['dɔsˌjeɪ, 'dɑs-] *n* : dossier *m*

dot¹ ['dɑt] *vt* **dotted; dotting** **1** : poner el punto sobre (una letra) **2** SCATTER : esparcir, salpicar

dot² *n* : punto *m* ⟨at six on the dot : a las seis en punto⟩ ⟨dots and dashes : puntos y rayas⟩

dote ['do:t] *vi* **doted; doting** : chochear

double¹ ['dʌbəl] *v* **-bled; -bling** *vt* **1** : doblar, duplicar (una cantidad), redoblar (esfuerzos) **2** FOLD : doblar, plegar **3 to double one's fist** : apretar el puño — *vi* **1** : doblar, duplicarse **2 to double over** : retorcerse

double² *adj* : doble — **doubly** *adv*

double³ *n* : doble *m*

double bass *n* : contrabajo *m*

double–cross [ˌdʌbəl'krɔs] *vt* : traicionar

double–crosser [ˌdʌbəl'krɔsər] *n* : traidor *m*, -dora *f*

double–jointed [ˌdʌbəl'ʤɔɪntəd] *adj* : con articulaciones laxas

double–talk ['dʌbəlˌtɔk] *n* : ambigüedades *fpl*, lenguaje *m* con doble sentido

doubt¹ ['daut] *vt* **1** QUESTION : dudar de, cuestionar **2** DISTRUST : desconfiar de **3** : dudar, creer poco probable ⟨I doubt it very much : lo dudo mucho⟩

doubt² *n* **1** UNCERTAINTY : duda *f*, incertidumbre *f* **2** DISTRUST : desconfianza *f* **3** SKEPTICISM : duda *f*, escepticismo *m*

doubtful ['daʊtfəl] *adj* **.1** QUESTIONABLE : dudoso **2** UNCERTAIN : dudoso, incierto

doubtfully ['daʊtfəli] *adv* : dudosamente, sin estar convencido

doubtless ['daʊtləs] *or* **doubtlessly** *adv* : sin duda

douche¹ ['duːʃ] *vt* **douched; douching** : irrigar

douche² *n* : ducha *f*, irrigación *f*

dough ['doː] *n* : masa *f*

doughnut *or* **donut** ['doːˌnʌt] *n* : rosquilla *f*, dona *f* Mex

doughty ['daʊti] *adj* **-tier; -est** : fuerte, valiente

dour ['daʊər, 'dʊr] *adj* **1** STERN : severo, adusto **2** SULLEN : hosco, taciturno — **dourly** *adv*

douse ['daʊs, 'daʊz] *vt* **doused; dousing 1** DRENCH : empapar, mojar **2** EXTINGUISH : extinguir, apagar

dove¹ ['doːv] → **dive**

dove² ['dʌv] *n* : paloma *f*

dovetail ['dʌvˌteɪl] *vi* : encajar, enlazar

dowdy ['daʊdi] *adj* **dowdier; -est** : sin gracia, poco elegante

dowel ['daʊəl] *n* : clavija *f*

down¹ ['daʊn] *vt* **1** FELL : tumbar, derribar, abatir **2** DEFEAT : derrotar

down² *adv* **1** DOWNWARD : hacia abajo **2 to lie down** : acostarse, echarse **3 to put down (money)** : pagar un depósito (de dinero) **4 to sit down** : sentarse **5 to take down, to write down** : apuntar, anotar

down³ *adj* **1** DESCENDING : de bajada ⟨the down elevator : el ascensor de bajada⟩ **2** REDUCED : reducido, rebajado ⟨attendance is down : la concurrencia ha disminuido⟩ **3** DOWNCAST : abatido, deprimido

down⁴ *n* **1** : plumón *m* **2** : down *m* (en deportes) **3 ups and downs** : altibajos *mpl*

down⁵ *prep* **1** : (hacia) abajo ⟨down the mountain : montaña abajo⟩ ⟨I walked down the stairs : bajé por la escalera⟩ **2** ALONG : por, a lo largo de ⟨we ran down the beach : corrimos por la playa⟩ **3** : a través de ⟨down the years : a través de los años⟩

downcast ['daʊnˌkæst] *adj* **1** SAD : triste, abatido **2 with downcast eyes** : con los ojos bajos, con los ojos mirando al suelo

downfall ['daʊnˌfɔl] *n* : ruina *f*, perdición *f*

downgrade¹ ['daʊnˌgreɪd] *vt* **-graded; -grading** : bajar de categoría

downgrade² *n* : bajada *f*

downhearted ['daʊnˌhɑrtəd] *adj* : desanimado, descorazonado

downhill ['daʊnˌhɪl] *adv & adj* : cuesta abajo

download¹ ['daʊnˌloːd] *vt* : descargar (un archivo)

download² *n* : descarga *f* (de archivos, etc.)

down payment *n* : entrega *f* inicial

downplay ['daʊnˌpleɪ] *vt* : minimizar

downpour ['daʊnˌpor] *n* : aguacero *m*, chaparrón *m*

downright¹ ['daʊnˌraɪt] *adv* THOROUGHLY : absolutamente, completamente

downright² *adj* : patente, manifiesto, absoluto ⟨a downright refusal : un rechazo categórico⟩

downside ['daʊnˌsaɪd] *n* : desventaja *f*

downstairs¹ ['daʊnˌstærz] *adv* : abajo

downstairs² ['daʊnˌstærz] *adj* : del piso de abajo

downstairs³ ['daʊnˌstærz, -ˌstærz] *n* : planta *f* baja

downstream ['daʊnˌstriːm] *adv* : río abajo

down–to–earth [ˌdaʊntuˈərθ] *adj* : práctico, realista

downtown¹ ['daʊnˈtaʊn] *adv* : hacia el centro, al centro, en el centro (de la ciudad)

downtown² *adj* : del centro (de la ciudad) ⟨downtown Chicago : el centro de Chicago⟩

downtown³ [ˌdaʊnˈtaʊn, 'daʊnˌtaʊn] *n* : centro *m* (de la ciudad)

downtrodden ['daʊnˌtrɑdən] *adj* : oprimido

downward ['daʊnwərd] *or* **downwards** [-wərdz] *adv & adj* : hacia abajo

downwind ['daʊnˈwɪnd] *adv & adj* : en la dirección del viento

downy ['daʊni] *adj* **downier; -est 1** : cubierto de plumón, plumoso **2** VELVETY : aterciopelado, velloso

dowry ['daʊri] *n, pl* **-ries** : dote *f*

doze¹ ['doːz] *vi* **dozed; dozing** : dormitar

doze² *n* : sueño *m* ligero, cabezada *f*

dozen ['dʌzən] *n, pl* **dozens** *or* **dozen** : docena *f*

drab ['dræb] *adj* **drabber; drabbest 1** BROWNISH : pardo **2** DULL, LACKLUSTER : monótono, gris, deslustrado

draft¹ ['dræft, 'draft] *vt* **1** CONSCRIPT : reclutar **2** COMPOSE, SKETCH : hacer el borrador de, redactar

draft² *adj* **1** : de barril ⟨draft beer : cerveza de barril⟩ **2** : de tiro ⟨draft horses : caballos de tiro⟩

draft³ *n* **1** HAULAGE : tiro *m* **2** DRINK, GULP : trago *m* **3** OUTLINE, SKETCH : bosquejo *m*, borrador *m*, versión *f* **4** : corriente *f* de aire, chiflón *m*, tiro *m* (de una chimenea) **5** CONSCRIPTION : conscripción *f* **6 bank draft** : giro *m* bancario, letra *f* de cambio

draftee [dræfˈtiː] *n* : recluta *mf*

draftsman ['dræftsmən] *n, pl* **-men** [-mən, -ˌmɛn] : dibujante *mf*

drafty ['dræfti] *adj* **draftier; -est** : con corrientes de aire

drag¹ ['dræg] *v* **dragged; dragging** *vt* **1** HAUL : arrastrar, jalar **2** DREDGE : dragar — *vi* **1** TRAIL : arrastrarse **2** LAG : rezagarse **3** : hacerse pesado, hacerse largo ⟨the day dragged on : el día se hizo largo⟩

drag[2] *n* **1** RESISTANCE : resistencia *f* (aerodinámica) **2** HINDRANCE : traba *f*, estorbo *m* **3** BORE : pesadez *f*, plomo *m fam*

dragnet ['dræg,nɛt] *n* **1** : red *f* barredera (en pesca) **2** : operativo *m* policial de captura

dragon ['drægən] *n* : dragón *m*

dragonfly ['drægən,flaɪ] *n, pl* **-flies** : libélula *f*

drain[1] ['dreɪn] *vt* **1** EMPTY : vaciar, drenar **2** EXHAUST : agotar, consumir — *vi* **1** : escurrir, escurrirse ⟨the dishes are draining : los platos están escurriéndose⟩ **2** EMPTY : desaguar **3 to drain away** : irse agotando

drain[2] *n* **1** : desagüe *m* **2** SEWER : alcantarilla *f* **3** GRATING : sumidero *m*, resumidero *m*, rejilla *f* **4** EXHAUSTION : agotamiento *m*, disminución *f* (de energía, etc.) ⟨to be a drain on : agotar, consumir⟩ **5 to throw down the drain** : tirar por la ventana

drainage ['dreɪnɪʤ] *n* : desagüe *m*, drenaje *m*

drainpipe ['dreɪn,paɪp] *n* : tubo *m* de desagüe, caño *m*

drake ['dreɪk] *n* : pato *m* (macho)

drama ['drɑmə, 'dræ-] *n* **1** THEATER : drama *m*, teatro *m* **2** PLAY : obra *f* de teatro, drama *m*

dramatic [drə'mætɪk] *adj* : dramático — **dramatically** [-tɪkli] *adv*

dramatist ['dræmətɪst, 'drɑ-] *n* : dramaturgo *m*, -ga *f*

dramatization [,dræmətə'zeɪʃən, ,drɑ-] *n* : dramatización *f*

dramatize ['dræmə,taɪz, 'drɑ-] *vt* **-tized; -tizing** : dramatizar

drank → **drink**

drape[1] ['dreɪp] *vt* **draped; draping** **1** COVER : cubrir (con tela) **2** HANG : drapear, disponer los pliegues de

drape[2] *n* **1** HANG : caída *f* **2 drapes** *npl* : cortinas *fpl*

drapery ['dreɪpəri] *n, pl* **-eries** **1** CLOTH : pañería *f*, tela *f* para cortinas **2 draperies** *fpl* : cortinas *fpl*

drastic ['dræstɪk] *adj* **1** HARSH, SEVERE : drástico, severo **2** EXTREME : radical, excepcional — **drastically** [-tɪkli] *adv*

draught ['dræft, 'drɑft] *n* → **draft**[3]

draughty ['drɑfti] → **drafty**

draw[1] ['drɔ] *v* **drew** ['dru:]; **drawn** ['drɔn]; **drawing** *vt* **1** PULL : tirar de, jalar, correr (cortinas) **2** ATTRACT : atraer **3** PROVOKE : provocar, suscitar **4** INHALE : aspirar ⟨to draw breath : respirar⟩ **5** EXTRACT : sacar, extraer **6** TAKE : sacar ⟨to draw a number : sacar un número⟩ **7** COLLECT : cobrar, percibir (un sueldo, etc.) **8** BEND : tensar (un arco) **9** TIE : empatar (en deportes) **10** SKETCH : dibujar, trazar **11** FORMULATE : sacar, formular, llegar a ⟨to draw a conclusion : llegar a

una conclusión⟩ **12 to draw out** : hacer hablar (sobre algo), hacer salir de sí mismo **13 to draw up** DRAFT : redactar — *vi* **1** SKETCH : dibujar **2** TUG : tirar, jalar **3 to draw near** : acercarse **4 to draw to a close** : terminar, finalizar **5 to draw up** STOP : parar

draw[2] *n* **1** DRAWING, RAFFLE : sorteo *m* **2** TIE : empate *m* **3** ATTRACTION : atracción *f* **4** PUFF : chupada *f* (de un cigarrillo, etc.)

drawback ['drɔ,bæk] *n* : desventaja *f*, inconveniente *m*

drawbridge ['drɔ,brɪʤ] *n* : puente *m* levadizo

drawer ['drɔr, 'drɔər] *n* **1** ILLUSTRATOR : dibujante *mf* **2** : gaveta *f*, cajón *m* (en un mueble) **3 drawers** *npl* UNDERPANTS : calzones *mpl*

drawing ['drɔɪŋ] *n* **1** LOTTERY : sorteo *m*, lotería *f* **2** SKETCH : dibujo *m*, bosquejo *m*

drawl[1] ['drɔl] *vi* : hablar arrastrando las palabras

drawl[2] *n* : habla *f* lenta y con vocales prolongadas

dread[1] ['drɛd] *vt* : tenerle pavor a, temer

dread[2] *adj* : pavoroso, aterrado

dread[3] *n* : pavor *m*, temor *m*

dreadful ['drɛdfəl] *adj* **1** DREAD : pavoroso **2** TERRIBLE : espantoso, atroz, terrible — **dreadfully** *adv*

dream[1] ['dri:m] *v* **dreamed** ['drɛmpt, 'dri:md] *or* **dreamt** ['drɛmpt]; **dreaming** *vi* **1** : soñar ⟨to dream about : soñar con⟩ **2** FANTASIZE : fantasear — *vt* **1** : soñar **2** IMAGINE : imaginarse **3 to dream up** : inventar, idear

dream[2] *n* **1** : sueño *m*, ensueño *m* **2 bad dream** NIGHTMARE : pesadilla *f*

dreamer ['dri:mər] *n* : soñador *m*, -dora *f*

dreamlike ['dri:m,laɪk] *adj* : de ensueño

dreamy ['dri:mi] *adj* **dreamier; -est** **1** DISTRACTED : soñador, distraído **2** DREAMLIKE : de ensueño **3** MARVELOUS : maravilloso

drearily ['drɪrəli] *adv* : sombríamente

dreary ['drɪri] *adj* **-rier; -est** : deprimente, lóbrego, sombrío

dredge[1] ['drɛʤ] *vt* **dredged; dredging** **1** DIG : dragar **2** COAT : espolvorear, enharinar

dredge[2] *n* : draga *f*

dredger ['drɛʤər] *n* : draga *f*

dregs ['drɛgz] *npl* **1** LEES : posos *mpl*, heces *fpl* (de un líquido) **2** : heces *fpl*, escoria *f* ⟨the dregs of society : la escoria de la sociedad⟩

drench ['drɛntʃ] *vt* : empapar, mojar, calar

dress[1] ['drɛs] *vt* **1** CLOTHE : vestir **2** DECORATE : decorar, adornar **3** : preparar (pollo o pescado), aliñar (ensalada) **4** : curar, vendar (una herida) **5** FERTILIZE : abonar (la tierra) — *vi* **1** : vestirse **2 to dress up** : ataviarse, engalanarse, ponerse de etiqueta

dress² *n* **1** APPAREL : indumentaria *f*, ropa *f* **2** : vestido *m*, traje *m* (de mujer)

dresser ['drɛsər] *n* : cómoda *f* con espejo

dressing ['drɛsɪŋ] *n* **1** : vestirse *m* **2** : aderezo *m*, aliño *m* (de ensalada), relleno *m* (de pollo) **3** BANDAGE : vendaje *m*, gasa *f*

dressmaker ['drɛs,meɪkər] *n* : modista *mf*

dressmaking ['drɛs,meɪkɪŋ] *n* : costura *f*

dressy ['drɛsi] *adj* **dressier; -est** : de mucho vestir, elegante

drew → **draw**

dribble¹ ['drɪbəl] *vi* **-bled; -bling 1** DRIP : gotear **2** DROOL : babear **3** : driblar (en basquetbol)

dribble² *n* **1** TRICKLE : goteo *m*, hilo *m* **2** DROOL : baba *f* **3** : drible *m* (en basquetbol)

drier → **dry²**, **dryer**

driest *adj* → **dry²**

drift¹ ['drɪft] *vi* **1** : dejarse llevar por la corriente, ir a la deriva (dícese de un bote), ir sin rumbo (dícese de una persona) **2** ACCUMULATE : amontonarse, acumularse, apilarse

drift² *n* **1** DRIFTING : deriva *f* **2** HEAP, MASS : montón *m* (de arena, etc.), ventisquero *m* (de nieve) **3** MEANING : sentido *m*

drifter ['drɪftər] *n* : vagabundo *m*, -da *f*

driftwood ['drɪft,wʊd] *n* : madera *f* flotante

drill¹ ['drɪl] *vt* **1** BORE : perforar, taladrar **2** INSTRUCT : instruir por repetición — *vi* **1** TRAIN : entrenarse **2** to drill for oil : perforar en busca de petróleo

drill² *n* **1** : taladro *m*, barrena *f* **2** EXERCISE, PRACTICE : ejercicio *m*, instrucción *f*

drily → **dryly**

drink¹ ['drɪŋk] *v* **drank** ['dræŋk]; **drunk** ['drʌŋk] *or* **drank; drinking** *vt* **1** IMBIBE : beber, tomar **2** to drink up ABSORB : absorber — *vi* **1** : beber **2** : beber alcohol, tomar

drink² *n* **1** : bebida *f* **2** : bebida *f* alcohólica

drinkable ['drɪŋkəbəl] *adj* : potable

drinker ['drɪŋkər] *n* : bebedor *m*, -dora *f*

drip¹ ['drɪp] *vi* **dripped; dripping** : gotear, chorrear

drip² *n* **1** DROP : gota *f* **2** DRIPPING : goteo *m*

drive¹ ['draɪv] *v* **drove** ['droːv]; **driven** ['drɪvən]; **driving** *vt* **1** IMPEL : impeler, impulsar **2** OPERATE : guiar, conducir, manejar (un vehículo) **3** COMPEL : obligar, forzar **4** : clavar, hincar ⟨to drive a stake : clavar una estaca⟩ **5** *or* **to drive away** : ahuyentar, echar **6** to **drive crazy** : volver loco — *vi* : manejar, conducir ⟨do you know how to drive? : ¿sabes manejar?⟩

drive² *n* **1** RIDE : paseo *m* en coche **2** CAMPAIGN : campaña *f* ⟨fund-raising drive : campaña para recaudar fondos⟩ **3** DRIVEWAY : camino *m* de entrada, entrada *f* **4** TRANSMISSION : transmisión *f* ⟨front-wheel drive : tracción delantera⟩ **5** ENERGY : dinamismo *m*, energía *f* **6** INSTINCT, NEED : instinto *m*, necesidad *f* básica **7** → **disk drive**

drivel ['drɪvəl] *n* : tontería *f*, estupidez *f*

driver ['draɪvər] *n* : conductor *m*, -tora *f*; chofer *m*

driveway ['draɪv,weɪ] *n* : camino *m* de entrada, entrada *f* (para coches)

drizzle¹ ['drɪzəl] *vi* **-zled; -zling** : lloviznar, garuar

drizzle² *n* : llovizna *f*, garúa *f*

droll ['droːl] *adj* : cómico, gracioso, chistoso — **drolly** *adv*

dromedary ['drɑmə,dɛri] *n, pl* **-daries** : dromedario *m*

drone¹ ['droːn] *vi* **droned; droning 1** BUZZ : zumbar **2** MURMUR : hablar con monotonía, murmurar

drone² *n* **1** : zángano *m* (abeja) **2** FREELOADER : gorrón *m*, -rrona *f fam*; parásito *m*, -ta *f* **3** BUZZ, HUM : zumbido *m*, murmullo *m*

drool¹ ['druːl] *vi* : babear

drool² *n* : baba *f*

droop¹ ['druːp] *vi* **1** HANG : inclinarse (dícese de la cabeza), encorvarse (dícese de los escombros), marchitarse (dícese de las flores) **2** FLAG : decaer, flaquear ⟨his spirits drooped : se desanimó⟩

droop² *n* : inclinación *f*, caída *f*

drop¹ ['drɑp] *v* **dropped; dropping** *vt* **1** : dejar caer, soltar ⟨she dropped the glass : se le cayó el vaso⟩ **2** to drop a hint : dejar caer una indirecta **2** SEND : mandar ⟨drop me a line : mándame unas líneas⟩ **3** ABANDON : abandonar, dejar ⟨to drop the subject : cambiar de tema⟩ **4** LOWER : bajar ⟨he dropped his voice : bajó la voz⟩ **5** OMIT : omitir **6** to drop off : dejar — *vi* **1** DRIP : gotear **2** FALL : caer(se) **3** DECREASE, DESCEND : bajar, descender ⟨the wind dropped : amainó el viento⟩ **4** to **drop back** *or* **to drop behind** : rezagarse, quedarse atrás **5** to **drop by** *or* **to drop in** : pasar

drop² *n* **1** : gota *f* (de líquido) **2** DECLINE : caída *f*, bajada *f*, descenso *m* **3** INCLINE : caída *f*, pendiente *f* ⟨a 20-foot drop : una caída de 20 pies⟩ **4** SWEET : pastilla *f*, dulce *m* **5** **drops** *npl* : gotas *fpl* (de medicina)

droplet ['drɑplət] *n* : gotita *f*

dropper ['drɑpər] *n* : gotero *m*, cuentagotas *m*

dross ['drɑs, 'drɔs] *n* : escoria *f*

drought ['draʊt] *n* : sequía *f*

drove¹ → **drive**

drove² ['droːv] *n* : multitud *f*, gentío *m*, manada *f* (de ganado) ⟨in droves : en manada⟩

drown ['draʊn] *vt* **1** : ahogar **2** INUNDATE : anegar, inundar **3 to drown out** : ahogar — *vi* : ahogarse

drowse[1] ['draʊz] *vi* **drowsed; drowsing** DOZE : dormitar

drowse[2] *n* : sueño *m* ligero, cabezada *f*

drowsiness ['draʊzinəs] *n* : somnolencia *f*, adormecimiento *m*

drowsy ['draʊzi] *adj* **drowsier; -est** : somnoliento, soñoliento

drub ['drʌb] *vt* **drubbed; drubbing 1** BEAT, THRASH : golpear, apalear **2** DEFEAT : derrotar por completo

drudge[1] ['drʌdʒ] *vi* **drudged; drudging** : trabajar como esclavo, trabajar duro

drudge[2] *n* : esclavo *m*, -va *f* del trabajo

drudgery ['drʌdʒəri] *n, pl* **-eries** : trabajo *m* pesado

drug[1] ['drʌg] *vt* **drugged; drugging** : drogar, narcotizar

drug[2] *n* **1** MEDICATION : droga *f*, medicina *f*, medicamento *m* **2** NARCOTIC : narcótico *m*, estupefaciente *m*, droga *f*

druggist ['drʌgɪst] *n* : farmacéutico *m*, -ca *f*

drugstore ['drʌg,stor] *n* : farmacia *f*, botica *f*, droguería *f*

drum[1] ['drʌm] *v* **drummed; drumming** *vt* : meter a fuerza ⟨he drummed it into my head : me lo metió en la cabeza a fuerza⟩ — *vi* : tocar el tambor

drum[2] *n* **1** : tambor *m* **2** : bidón *m* ⟨oil drum : bidón de petróleo⟩

drummer ['drʌmər] *n* : baterista *mf*

drumstick ['drʌm,stɪk] *n* **1** : palillo *m* (de tambor), baqueta *f* **2** : muslo *m* de pollo

drunk[1] *pp* → **drink**[1]

drunk[2] ['drʌŋk] *adj* : borracho, embriagado, ebrio

drunk[3] *n* : borracho *m*, -cha *f*

drunkard ['drʌŋkərd] *n* : borracho *m*, -cha *f*

drunken ['drʌŋkən] *adj* : borracho, ebrio ⟨drunken driver : conductor ebrio⟩ ⟨drunken brawl : pleito de borrachos⟩

drunkenly ['drʌŋkənli] *adv* : como un borracho

drunkenness ['drʌŋkənnəs] *n* : borrachera *f*, embriaguez *f*, ebriedad *f*

dry[1] ['draɪ] *v* **dried; drying** *vt* : secar — *vi* : secarse

dry[2] *adj* **drier; driest 1** : seco **2** THIRSTY : sediento **3** : donde la venta de bebidas alcohólicas está prohibida ⟨a dry county : un condado seco⟩ **4** DULL : aburrido, árido **5** : seco (dícese del vino), brut (dícese de la champaña)

dry–clean ['draɪ,kli:n] *v* : limpiar en seco

dry cleaner *n* : tintorería *f* (servicio)

dry cleaning *n* : limpieza *f* en seco

dryer ['draɪər] *n* **1 hair dryer** : secador *m* **2 clothes dryer** : secadora *f*

dry goods *npl* : artículos *mpl* de confección

dry ice *n* : hielo *m* seco

dryly ['draɪli] *adv* : secamente

dryness ['draɪnəs] *n* : sequedad *f*, aridez *f*

dual ['du:əl, 'dju:-] *adj* : doble

dualism ['du:ə,lɪzəm] *n* : dualismo *m*

dub ['dʌb] *vt* **dubbed; dubbing 1** CALL : apodar **2** : doblar (una película), mezclar (una grabación)

dubious ['du:biəs, 'dju:-] *adj* **1** UNCERTAIN : dudoso, indeciso **2** QUESTIONABLE : sospechoso, dudoso, discutible

dubiously ['du:biəsli, 'dju:-] *adv* **1** UNCERTAINLY : dudosamente, con desconfianza **2** SUSPICIOUSLY : de modo sospechoso, con recelo

duchess ['dʌtʃəs] *n* : duquesa *f*

duck[1] ['dʌk] *vt* **1** LOWER : agachar, bajar (la cabeza) **2** PLUNGE : zambullir **3** EVADE : eludir, evadir — *vi* **to duck down** : agacharse

duck[2] *n, pl* **duck** *or* **ducks** : pato *m*, -ta *f*

duckling ['dʌklɪŋ] *n* : patito *m*, -ta *f*

duct ['dʌkt] *n* : conducto *m*

ductile ['dʌktəl] *adj* : dúctil

dude ['du:d, 'dju:d] *n* **1** DANDY : dandi *m*, dandy *m* **2** GUY : tipo *m*

due[1] ['du:, 'dju:] *adv* : justo a, derecho hacia ⟨due north : derecho hacia el norte⟩

due[2] *adj* **1** PAYABLE : pagadero, sin pagar **2** APPROPRIATE : debido, apropiado ⟨after due consideration : con las debidas consideraciones⟩ **3** EXPECTED : esperado ⟨the train is due soon : esperamos el tren muy pronto, el tren debe llegar pronto⟩ **4 due to** : debido a, por

due[3] *n* **1 to give someone his (her) due** : darle a alguien su merecido **2 dues** *npl* : cuota *f*

duel[1] ['du:əl, 'dju:-] *vi* : batirse en duelo

duel[2] *n* : duelo *m*

duet [du'ɛt, dju-] *n* : dúo *m*

due to *prep* : debido a

dug → **dig**

dugout ['dʌg,aʊt] *n* **1** CANOE : piragua *f* **2** SHELTER : refugio *m* subterráneo

duke ['du:k, 'dju:k] *n* : duque *m*

dull[1] ['dʌl] *vt* **1** DIM : opacar, quitar el brillo a, deslustrar **2** BLUNT : embotar (un filo), entorpecer (los sentidos), aliviar (el dolor), amortiguar (sonidos)

dull[2] *adj* **1** STUPID : torpe, lerdo, lento **2** BLUNT : desafilado, despuntado **3** LACKLUSTER : sin brillo, deslustrado **4** BORING : aburrido, soso, pesado — **dully** *adv*

dullness ['dʌlnəs] *n* **1** STUPIDITY : estupidez *f* **2** : embotamiento *m* (de los sentidos) **3** MONOTONY : monotonía *f*, insipidez *f* **4** : falta *f* de brillo **5** BLUNTNESS : falta *f* de filo, embotadura *f*

duly ['du:li, 'dju:-] *adv* PROPERLY : debidamente, a su debido tiempo

dumb ['dʌm] *adj* **1** MUTE : mudo **2** STUPID : estúpido, tonto, bobo — **dumbly** *adv*

dumbbell ['dʌm,bɛl] *n* **1** WEIGHT : pesa *f* **2** : estúpido *m*, -da *f*

dumbfound *or* **dumfound** [,dʌm-'faʊnd] *vt* : dejar atónito, dejar sin habla

dummy ['dʌmi] *n, pl* **-mies 1** SHAM : imitación *f*, sustituto *m* **2** PUPPET : muñeco *m* **3** MANNEQUIN : maniquí *m* **4** IDIOT : tonto *m*, -ta *f*; idiota *mf*

dump¹ ['dʌmp] *vt* : descargar, verter

dump² *n* **1** : vertedero *m*, tiradero *m* Mex **2 down in the dumps** : triste, deprimido

dumpling ['dʌmplɪŋ] *n* : bola *f* de masa hervida

dumpy ['dʌmpi] *adj* **dumpier; -est** : rechoncho, regordete

dun¹ ['dʌn] *vt* **dunned; dunning** : apremiar (a un deudor)

dun² *adj* : pardo (color)

dunce ['dʌns] *n* : estúpido *m*, -da *f*; burro *m*, -rra *f* fam

dune ['du:n, 'dju:n] *n* : duna *f*

dung ['dʌŋ] *n* **1** FECES : excrementos *mpl* **2** MANURE : estiércol *m*

dungaree [,dʌŋgə'ri:] *n* **1** DENIM : tela *f* vaquera, mezclilla *f* Chile, Mex **2 dungarees** *npl* : pantalones *mpl* de trabajo hechos de tela vaquera

dungeon ['dʌndʒən] *n* : mazmorra *f*, calabozo *m*

dunk ['dʌŋk] *vt* : mojar, ensopar

duo ['du:o:, 'dju:-] *n, pl* **duos** : dúo *m*, par *m*

dupe¹ ['du:p, 'dju:p] *vt* **duped; duping** : engañar, embaucar

dupe² *n* : inocentón *m*, -tona *f*; simple *mf*

duplex¹ ['du:,plɛks, 'dju:-] *adj* : doble

duplex² *n* : casa *f* de dos viviendas, dúplex *m*

duplicate¹ ['du:plɪ,keɪt, 'dju:-] *vt* **-cated; -cating 1** COPY : duplicar, hacer copias de **2** REPEAT : repetir, reproducir

duplicate² ['du:plɪkət, 'dju:-] *adj* : duplicado ⟨a duplicate invoice : una factura por duplicado⟩

duplicate³ ['du:plɪkət, 'dju:-] *n* : duplicado *m*, copia *f*

duplication [,du:plɪ'keɪʃən, ,dju:-] *n* **1** DUPLICATING : duplicación *f*, repetición *f* (de esfuerzos) **2** DUPLICATE : copia *f*, duplicado *m*

duplicity [dʊ'plɪsəti, ,dju:-] *n, pl* **-ties** : duplicidad *f*

durability [,dʊrə'bɪləti, ,djʊr-] *n* : durabilidad *f* (de un producto) permanencia *f*

durable ['dʊrəbəl, 'djʊr-] *adj* : duradero

duration [dʊ'reɪʃən, dju-] *n* : duración *f*

duress [dʊ'rɛs, dju-] *n* : coacción *f*

during ['dʊrɪŋ, 'djʊr-] *prep* : durante

dusk ['dʌsk] *n* : anochecer *m*, crepúsculo *m*

dusky ['dʌski] *adj* **duskier; -est** : oscuro (dícese de los colores)

dust¹ ['dʌst] *vt* **1** : quitar el polvo de **2** SPRINKLE : espolvorear

dust² *n* : polvo *m*

duster ['dʌstər] *n* **1** *or* **dust cloth** : trapo *m* de polvo **2** HOUSECOAT : guardapolvo *m* **3 feather duster** : plumero *m*

dustpan ['dʌst,pæn] *n* : recogedor *m*

dusty ['dʌsti] *adj* **dustier; -est** : cubierto de polvo, polvoriento

Dutch¹ ['dʌtʃ] *adj* : holandés

Dutch² *n* **1** : holandés *m* (idioma) **2 the Dutch** *npl* : los holandeses

Dutch treat *n* : invitación o pago a escote

dutiful ['du:tɪfəl, 'dju:-] *adj* : motivado por sus deberes, responsable

duty ['du:ti, 'dju:-] *n, pl* **-ties 1** OBLIGATION : deber *m*, obligación *f*, responsabilidad *f* **2** TAX : impuesto *m*, arancel *m*

DVD [,di:,vi:'di:] *n* : DVD *m*

dwarf¹ ['dwɔrf] *vt* **1** STUNT : arrestar el crecimiento de **2** : hacer parecer pequeño

dwarf² *n, pl* **dwarfs** ['dwɔrfs] *or* **dwarves** ['dwɔrvz] : enano *m*, -na *f*

dwell ['dwɛl] *vi* **dwelled** *or* **dwelt** ['dwɛlt]; **dwelling 1** RESIDE : residir, morar, vivir **2 to dwell on** : pensar demasiado en, insistir en

dweller ['dwɛlər] *n* : habitante *mf*

dwelling ['dwɛlɪŋ] *n* : morada *f*, vivienda *f*, residencia *f*

dwindle ['dwɪndəl] *vi* **-dled; -dling** : menguar, reducirse, disminuir

dye¹ ['daɪ] *vt* **dyed; dyeing** : teñir

dye² *n* : tintura *f*, tinte *m*

dying → die

dyke → dike

dynamic [daɪ'næmɪk] *adj* : dinámico

dynamics [daɪ'næmɪks] *npl* : dinámica *f*

dynamite¹ ['daɪnə,maɪt] *vt* **-mited; -miting** : dinamitar

dynamite² *n* : dinamita *f*

dynamo ['daɪnə,mo:] *n, pl* **-mos** : dínamo *m*, generador *m* de electricidad

dynasty ['daɪnəsti, -,næs-] *n, pl* **-ties** : dinastía *f*

dysentery ['dɪsən,teri] *n, pl* **-teries** : disentería *f*

dysfunction [dɪs'fʌŋkʃən] *n* : disfunción *f*

dystrophy ['dɪstrəfi] *n, pl* **-phies 1** : distrofia *f* **2 → muscular dystrophy**

E

e [ˈiː] *n, pl* **e's** *or* **es** [ˈiːz] : quinta letra del alfabeto inglés

each¹ [ˈiːtʃ] *adv* : cada uno, por persona ⟨they cost $10 each : costaron $10 cada uno⟩

each² *adj* : cada ⟨each student : cada estudiante⟩ ⟨each and every one : todos sin excepción⟩

each³ *pron* **1** : cada uno *m*, cada una *f* ⟨each of us : cada uno de nosotros⟩ **2 each other** : el uno al otro, mutuamente ⟨we are helping each other : nos ayudamos el uno al otro⟩ ⟨they love each other : se aman⟩

eager [ˈiːɡər] *adj* **1** ENTHUSIASTIC : entusiasta, ávido, deseoso **2** ANXIOUS : ansioso, impaciente

eagerly [ˈiːɡərli] *adv* : con entusiasmo, ansiosamente

eagerness [ˈiːɡərnəs] *n* : entusiasmo *m*, deseo *m*, impaciencia *f*

eagle [ˈiːɡəl] *n* : águila *f*

ear [ˈɪr] *n* **1** : oído *m*, oreja *f* ⟨inner ear : oído interno⟩ ⟨big ears : orejas grandes⟩ **2 ear of corn** : mazorca *f*, choclo *m*

earache [ˈɪr‚eɪk] *n* : dolor *m* de oído

eardrum [ˈɪr‚drʌm] *n* : tímpano *m*

earl [ˈərl] *n* : conde *m*

earlobe [ˈɪr‚loːb] *n* : lóbulo *m* de la oreja, perilla *f* de la oreja

early¹ [ˈərli] *adv* **earlier; -est** : temprano, pronto ⟨he arrived early : llegó temprano⟩ ⟨as early as possible : lo más pronto posible, cuanto antes⟩ ⟨ten minutes early : diez minutos de adelanto⟩

early² *adj* **earlier; -est 1** *(referring to a beginning)* : primero ⟨the early stages : las primeras etapas⟩ ⟨in early May : a principios de mayo⟩ **2** *(referring to antiquity)* : primitivo, antiguo ⟨early man : el hombre primitivo⟩ ⟨early painting : la pintura antigua⟩ **3** *(referring to a designated time)* : temprano, antes de la hora, prematuro ⟨he was early : llegó temprano⟩ ⟨early fruit : frutas tempraneras⟩ ⟨an early death : una muerte prematura⟩

earmark [ˈɪr‚mɑrk] *vt* : destinar ⟨earmarked funds : fondos destinados⟩

earn [ˈərn] *vt* **1** : ganar ⟨to earn money : ganar dinero⟩ **2** DESERVE : ganarse, merecer

earnest¹ [ˈərnəst] *adj* : serio, sincero

earnest² *n* **in ~** : en serio, de verdad ⟨we began in earnest : empezamos de verdad⟩

earnestly [ˈərnəstli] *adv* **1** SERIOUSLY : con seriedad, en serio **2** FERVENTLY : de todo corazón

earnestness [ˈərnəstnəs] *n* : seriedad *f*, sinceridad *f*

earnings [ˈərnɪŋz] *npl* : ingresos *mpl*, ganancias *fpl*, utilidades *fpl*

earphone [ˈɪr‚foːn] *n* : audífono *m*

earring [ˈɪr‚rɪŋ] *n* : zarcillo *m*, arete *m*, aro *m Arg, Chile, Uru*, pendiente *m Spain*

earshot [ˈɪr‚ʃɑt] *n* : alcance *m* del oído

earth [ˈərθ] *n* **1** LAND, SOIL : tierra *f*, suelo *m* **2 the Earth** : la Tierra

earthen [ˈərθən, -ðən] *adj* : de tierra, de barro

earthenware [ˈərθən‚wær, -ðən-] *n* : loza *f*, vajillas *fpl* de barro

earthly [ˈərθli] *adj* : terrenal, mundano

earthquake [ˈərθ‚kweɪk] *n* : terremoto *m*, temblor *m*

earthworm [ˈərθ‚wərm] *n* : lombriz *f* (de tierra)

earthy [ˈərθi] *adj* **earthier; -est 1** : terroso ⟨earthy colors : colores terrosos⟩ **2** DOWN-TO-EARTH : realista, práctico, llano **3** COARSE, CRUDE : basto, grosero, tosco ⟨earthy jokes : chistes groseros⟩

earwax [ˈɪr‚wæks] *n* → **wax²**

earwig [ˈɪr‚wɪɡ] *n* : tijereta *f*

ease¹ [ˈiːz] *v* **eased; easing** *vt* **1** ALLEVIATE : aliviar, calmar, hacer disminuir **2** LOOSEN, RELAX : aflojar (una cuerda), relajar (tensiones), descargar (tensiones) **3** FACILITATE : facilitar — *vi* : calmarse, relajarse

ease² *n* **1** CALM, RELIEF : tranquilidad *f*, comodidad *f*, desahogo *m* **2** FACILITY : facilidad *f* **3 at ~** : relajado, cómodo ⟨to put someone at ease : tranquilizar a alguien⟩

easel [ˈiːzəl] *n* : caballete *m*

easily [ˈiːzəli] *adv* **1** : fácilmente, con facilidad **2** UNQUESTIONABLY : con mucho, de lejos

easiness [ˈiːzinəs] *n* : facilidad *f*, soltura *f*

east¹ [ˈiːst] *adv* : al este

east² *adj* : este, del este, oriental ⟨east winds : vientos del este⟩

east³ *n* **1** : este *m* **2 the East** : el Oriente

Easter [ˈiːstər] *n* : Pascua *f* (de Resurrección)

easterly [ˈiːstərli] *adv & adj* : del este

eastern [ˈiːstərn] *adj* **1** : Oriental, del Este ⟨Eastern Europe : Europa del Este⟩ **2** : oriental, este

Easterner [ˈiːstərnər] *n* : habitante *mf* del este

eastward [ˈiːstwərd] *adv & adj* : hacia el este

easy [ˈiːzi] *adj* **easier; -est 1** : fácil **2** LENIENT : indulgente

easygoing [‚iːziˈɡoːɪŋ] *adj* : acomodaticio, tolerante, poco exigente

eat [ˈiːt] *v* **ate** [ˈeɪt]; **eaten** [ˈiːtən]; **eating** *vt* **1** : comer **2** CONSUME : consumir, gastar, devorar ⟨expenses ate up profits : los gastos devoraron las ganancias⟩ **3** CORRODE : corroer — *vi* **1** : comer **2 to eat away at** *or* **to eat into** : comerse **3 to eat out** : comer fuera

eatable[1] ['iːtəbəl] *adj* : comestible, comible *fam*

eatable[2] *n* 1 : algo para comer 2 **eatables** *npl* : comestibles *mpl*, alimentos *mpl*

eater ['iːtər] *n* : comedor *m*, -dora *f*

eaves ['iːvz] *npl* : alero *m*

eavesdrop ['iːvzˌdrɑp] *vi* **-dropped; -dropping** : escuchar a escondidas

eavesdropper ['iːvzˌdrɑpər] *n* : persona *f* que escucha a escondidas

ebb[1] ['ɛb] *vi* 1 : bajar, menguar (dícese de la marea) 2 DECLINE : decaer, disminuir

ebb[2] *n* 1 : reflujo *m* (de una marea) 2 DECLINE : decadencia *f*, declive *m*, disminución *f*

ebony[1] ['ɛbəni] *adj* 1 : de ébano 2 BLACK : de color ébano, negro

ebony[2] *n*, *pl* **-nies** : ébano *m*

ebullience [ɪ'buljəns, -'bʌl-] *n* : efervescencia *f*, vivacidad *f*

ebullient [ɪ'buljənt, -'bʌl-] *adj* : efervescente, vivaz

eccentric[1] [ɪk'sɛntrɪk] *adj* 1 : excéntrico ⟨an eccentric wheel : una rueda excéntrica⟩ 2 ODD, SINGULAR : excéntrico, extraño, raro — **eccentrically** [-trɪkli] *adv*

eccentric[2] *n* : excéntrico *m*, -ca *f*

eccentricity [ˌɛkˌsen'trɪsəti] *n*, *pl* **-ties** : excentricidad *f*

ecclesiastic [ɪˌkliːzi'æstɪk] *n* : eclesiástico *m*, clérigo *m*

ecclesiastical [ɪˌkliːzi'æstɪkəl] *or* **ecclesiastic** *adj* : eclesiástico — **ecclesiastically** *adv*

echelon ['ɛʃəˌlɑn] *n* 1 : escalón *m* (de tropas o aviones) 2 LEVEL : nivel *m*, esfera *f*, estrato *m*

echo[1] ['ɛˌkoː] *v* **echoed; echoing** *vi* : hacer eco, resonar — *vt* : repetir

echo[2] *n*, *pl* **echoes** : eco *m*

éclair [eɪ'klær, i-] *n* : pastel *m* relleno de crema

eclectic [ɛ'klɛktɪk, ɪ-] *adj* : ecléctico

eclipse[1] [ɪ'klɪps] *vt* **eclipsed; eclipsing** : eclipsar

eclipse[2] *n* : eclipse *m*

ecological [ˌiːkə'lɑdʒɪkəl, ˌɛkə-] *adj* : ecológico — **ecologically** *adv*

ecologist [i'kɑlədʒɪst, ɛ-] *n* : ecólogo *m*, -ga *f*

ecology [i'kɑlədʒi, ɛ-] *n*, *pl* **-gies** : ecología *f*

economic [ˌiːkə'nɑmɪk, ˌɛkə-] *adj* : económico

economical [ˌiːkə'nɑmɪkəl, ˌɛkə-] *adj* : económico — **economically** *adv*

economics [ˌiːkə'nɑmɪks, ˌɛkə-] *n* : economía *f*

economist [i'kɑnəmɪst] *n* : economista *mf*

economize [i'kɑnəˌmaɪz] *v* **-mized; -mizing** : economizar, ahorrar

economy [i'kɑnəmi] *n*, *pl* **-mies** 1 : economía *f*, sistema *m* económico 2 THRIFT : economía *f*, ahorro *m*

ecosystem ['iːkoˌsɪstəm] *n* : ecosistema *m*

ecru ['ɛˌkruː, 'eɪ-] *n* : color *m* crudo

ecstasy ['ɛkstəsi] *n*, *pl* **-sies** : éxtasis *m*

ecstatic [ɛk'stætɪk, ɪk-] *adj* : extático

ecstatically [ɛk'stætɪkli, ɪk-] *adv* : con éxtasis, con gran entusiasmo

Ecuadoran [ˌɛkwə'dorən] *or* **Ecuadorean** *or* **Ecuadorian** [-'doriən] *n* : ecuatoriano *m*, -na *f* — **Ecuadorean** *or* **Ecuadorian** *adj*

ecumenical [ˌɛkju'mnɪkəl] *adj* : ecuménico

eczema [ɪg'ziːmə, 'ɛgzəmə, 'ɛksə-] *n* : eczema *m*

eddy[1] ['ɛdi] *vi* **eddied; eddying** : arremolinarse, hacer remolinos

eddy[2] *n*, *pl* **-dies** : remolino *m*

edema [ɪ'diːmə] *n* : edema *m*

Eden ['iːdən] *n* : Edén *m*

edge[1] ['ɛdʒ] *v* **edged; edging** *vt* 1 BORDER : bordear, ribetear, orlar 2 SHARPEN : afilar, aguzar 3 *or* **to edge one's way** : avanzar poco a poco 4 **to edge out** : derrotar por muy poco — *vi* ADVANCE : ir avanzando (poco a poco)

edge[2] *n* 1 : filo *m* (de un cuchillo) 2 BORDER : borde *m*, orilla *f*, margen *m* 3 ADVANTAGE : ventaja *f*

edger ['ɛdʒər] *n* : cortabordes *m*

edgewise ['ɛdʒˌwaɪz] *adv* SIDEWAYS : de lado, de canto

edginess ['ɛdʒinəs] *n* : tensión *f*, nerviosismo *m*

edgy ['ɛdʒi] *adj* **edgier; -est** : tenso, nervioso

edible ['ɛdəbəl] *adj* : comestible

edict ['iːˌdɪkt] *n* : edicto *m*, mandato *m*, orden *f*

edification [ˌɛdəfə'keɪʃən] *n* : edificación *f*, instrucción *f*

edifice ['ɛdəfɪs] *n* : edificio *m*

edify ['ɛdəˌfaɪ] *vt* **-fied; -fying** : edificar

edit ['ɛdɪt] *vt* 1 : editar, redactar, corregir 2 *or* **to edit out** DELETE : recortar, cortar

edition [ɪ'dɪʃən] *n* : edición *f*

editor ['ɛdɪtər] *n* : editor *m*, -tora *f*; redactor *m*, -tora *f*

editorial[1] [ˌɛdɪ'toriəl] *adj* 1 : de redacción 2 : editorial ⟨an editorial comment : un comentario editorial⟩

editorial[2] *n* : editorial *m*

editorship ['ɛdɪtərˌʃɪp] *n* : dirección *f*

educable ['ɛdʒəkəbəl] *adj* : educable

educate ['ɛdʒəˌkeɪt] *vt* **-cated; -cating** 1 TEACH : educar, enseñar 2 INSTRUCT : formar, educar, instruir 3 INFORM : informar, concientizar

education [ˌɛdʒə'keɪʃən] *n* : educación *f*

educational [ˌɛdʒə'keɪʃənəl] *adj* 1 : docente, de enseñanza ⟨an educational institution : una institución docente⟩ 2 PEDAGOGICAL : pedagógico 3 INSTRUCTIONAL : educativo, instructivo

educator ['ɛdʒəˌkeɪtər] *n* : educador *m*, -dora *f*

eel ['iːl] *n* : anguila *f*

eerie [ˈɪri] *adj* **-rier; -est 1** SPOOKY : que da miedo, espeluznante **2** GHOSTLY : fantasmagórico

eerily [ˈɪrəli] *adv* : de manera extraña y misteriosa

efface [ɪˈfeɪs, -] *vt* **-faced; -facing** : borrar

effect¹ [ɪˈfɛkt] *vt* **1** CARRY OUT : efectuar, llevar a cabo **2** ACHIEVE : lograr, realizar

effect² *n* **1** RESULT : efecto *m*, resultado *m*, consecuencia *f* ⟨to no effect : sin resultado⟩ **2** MEANING : sentido *m* ⟨something to that effect : algo por el estilo⟩ **3** INFLUENCE : efecto *m*, influencia *f* **4 effects** *npl* BELONGINGS : éfectos *mpl*, pertenencias *fpl* **5 to go into effect** : entrar en vigor **6 in ~** REALLY : en realidad, efectivamente

effective [ɪˈfɛktɪv] *adj* **1** EFFECTUAL : efectivo, eficaz **2** OPERATIVE : vigente — **effectively** *adv*

effectiveness [ɪˈfɛktɪvnəs] *n* : eficacia *f*, efectividad *f*

effectual [ɪˈfɛktʃuəl] *adj* : eficaz, efectivo — **effectually** *adv*

effeminate [əˈfɛmənət] *adj* : afeminado

effervesce [ˌɛfərˈvɛs] *vi* **-vesced; -vescing 1** : estar en efervescencia, burbujear (dícese de líquidos) **2** : estar eufórico, estar muy animado (dícese de las personas)

effervescence [ˌɛfərˈvɛsənts] *n* **1** : efervescencia *f* **2** LIVELINESS : vivacidad *f*

effervescent [ˌɛfərˈvɛsənt] *adj* **1** : efervescente **2** LIVELY, VIVACIOUS : vivaz, animado

effete [ɛˈfiːt, ɪ-] *adj* **1** WORN-OUT : desgastado, agotado **2** DECADENT : decadente **3** EFFEMINATE : afeminado

efficacious [ˌɛfəˈkeɪʃəs] *adj* : eficaz, efectivo

efficacy [ˈɛfɪkəsi] *n, pl* **-cies** : eficacia *f*

efficiency [ɪˈfɪʃəntsi] *n, pl* **-cies** : eficiencia *f*

efficient [ɪˈfɪʃənt] *adj* : eficiente — **efficiently** *adv*

effigy [ˈɛfədʒi] *n, pl* **-gies** : efigie *f*

effluent [ˈɛˌfluːənt, ɛˈfluː-] *n* : efluente *m* — **effluent** *adj*

effort [ˈɛfərt] *n* **1** EXERTION : esfuerzo *m* **2** ATTEMPT : tentativa *f*, intento *m* ⟨it's not worth the effort : no vale la pena⟩

effortless [ˈɛfərtləs] *adj* : fácil, sin esfuerzo

effortlessly [ˈɛfərtləsli] *adv* : sin esfuerzo, fácilmente

effrontery [ɪˈfrʌntəri] *n, pl* **-teries** : insolencia *f*, desfachatez *f*, descaro *m*

effusion [ɪˈfjuːʒən, ɛ-] *n* : efusión *f*

effusive [ɪˈfjuːsɪv, ɛ-] *adj* : efusivo — **effusively** *adv*

egg¹ [ˈɛg] *vt* **to egg on** : incitar, azuzar, provocar

egg² *n* **1** : huevo *m* **2** OVUM : óvulo *m*

eggbeater [ˈɛgˌbiːtər] *n* : batidor *m* (de huevos)

eggnog [ˈɛgˌnɑg] *n* : ponche *m* de huevo, rompope *m* CA, Mex

eggplant [ˈɛgˌplænt] *n* : berenjena *f*

eggshell [ˈɛgˌʃl] *n* : cascarón *m*

ego [ˈiːˌgo] *n, pl* **egos 1** SELF-ESTEEM : amor *m* propio **2** SELF : ego *m*, yo *m*

egocentric [ˌiːgoˈsɛntrɪk] *adj* : egocéntrico

egoism [ˈiːgoˌwɪzəm] *n* : egoísmo *m*

egoist [ˈiːgowɪst] *n* : egoísta *mf*

egoistic [ˌiːgoˈwɪstɪk] *adj* : egoísta

egotism [ˈiːgəˌtɪzəm] *n* : egotismo *m*

egotist [ˈiːgətɪst] *n* : egotista *mf*

egotistic [ˌiːgəˈtɪstɪk] *or* **egotistical** [-ˈtɪstɪkəl] *adj* : egotista — **egotistically** *adv*

egregious [ɪˈgriːdʒəs] *adj* : atroz, flagrante, mayúsculo — **egregiously** *adv*

egress [ˈiːˌgrɛs] *n* : salida *f*

egret [ˈiːgrət, -ˌgrɛt] *n* : garceta *f*

Egyptian [ɪˈdʒɪpʃən] *n* **1** : egipcio *m*, -cia *f* **2** : egipcio *m* (idioma) — **Egyptian** *adj*

eiderdown [ˈaɪdərˌdaun] *n* **1** : plumón *m* **2** COMFORTER : edredón *m*

eight¹ [ˈeɪt] *adj* : ocho

eight² *n* : ocho *m*

eight hundred¹ *adj* : ochocientos

eight hundred² *n* : ochocientos *m*

eighteen¹ [eɪˈtiːn] *adj* : dieciocho

eighteen² *n* : dieciocho *m*

eighteenth¹ [eɪˈtiːnθ] *adj* : decimoctavo

eighteenth² *n* **1** : decimoctavo *m*, -va *f* (en una serie) **2** : dieciochoavo *m*, dieciochoava parte *f*

eighth¹ [ˈeɪtθ] *adj* : octavo

eighth² *n* **1** : octavo *m*, -va *f* (en una serie) **2** : octavo *m*, octava parte *f*

eightieth¹ [ˈeɪtiəθ] *adj* : octogésimo

eightieth² *n* **1** : octogésimo *m*, -ma *f* (en una serie) **2** : ochentavo *m*, ochentava parte *f*

eighty¹ [ˈeɪti] *adj* : ochenta

eighty² *n, pl* **eighties 1** : ochenta *m* **2 the eighties** : los ochenta *mpl*

either¹ [ˈiːðər, ˈaɪ-] *adj* **1** : cualquiera (de los dos) ⟨we can watch either movie : podemos ver cualquiera de las dos películas⟩ **2** : ninguno de los dos ⟨she wasn't in either room : no estaba en ninguna de las dos salas⟩ **3** EACH : cada ⟨on either side of the street : a cada lado de la calle⟩

either² *pron* **1** : cualquiera *mf* (de los dos) ⟨either is fine : cualquiera de los dos está bien⟩ **2** : ninguno *m*, -na *f* (de los dos) ⟨I don't like either : no me gusta ninguno⟩ **3** : algún *m*, alguna *f* ⟨is either of you interested? : ¿está alguno de ustedes (dos) interesado?⟩

either³ *conj* **1** : o, u ⟨either David or Daniel could go : puede ir (o) David o Daniel⟩ **2** : ni ⟨we won't watch either this movie or the other : no veremos ni esta película ni la otra⟩

ejaculate [ɪˈdʒækjəˌleɪt] *v* **-lated; -lating** *vt* **1** : eyacular **2** EXCLAIM : exclamar — *vi* : eyacular

ejaculation [i̱ˌdʒækjə'leɪʃən] *n* **1** : eyaculación *f* (en fisiología) **2** EXCLAMATION : exclamación *f*

eject [i'dʒɛkt] *vt* : expulsar, expeler

ejection [i'dʒɛkʃən] *n* : expulsión *f*

eke ['iːk] *vt* **eked; eking** *or* **to eke out** : ganar a duras penas

elaborate[1] [i'læbə̱ˌreɪt] *v* **-rated; -rating** *vt* : elaborar, idear, desarrollar — *vi* **to elaborate on** : ampliar, entrar en detalles

elaborate[2] [i'læbərət] *adj* **1** DETAILED : detallado, minucioso, elaborado **2** COMPLICATED : complicado, intrincado, elaborado — **elaborately** *adv*

elaboration [i̱ˌlæbə'reɪʃən] *n* : elaboración *f*

elapse [i'læps] *vi* **elapsed; elapsing** : transcurrir, pasar

elastic[1] [i'læstɪk] *adj* : elástico

elastic[2] *n* **1** : elástico *m* **2** RUBBER BAND : goma *f*, gomita *f*, elástico *m*, liga *f*

elasticity [i̱ˌlæs'tɪsət̬i, ̱iːˌlæs-] *n, pl* **-ties** : elasticidad *f*

elate [i'leɪt] *vt* **elated; elating** : alborozar, regocijar

elation [i'leɪʃən] *n* : euforia *f*, júbilo *m*, alborozo *m*

elbow[1] ['ɛlˌboʊ] *vt* : darle un codazo a

elbow[2] *n* : codo *m*

elder[1] ['ɛldər] *adj* : mayor

elder[2] *n* **1 to be someone's elder** : ser mayor que alguien **2** : anciano *m*, -na *f* (de un pueblo o una tribu) **3** : miembro *m* del consejo (en varias religiones)

elderberry ['ɛldərˌbɛri] *n, pl* **-berries** : baya *f* de saúco (fruta), saúco *m* (árbol)

elderly ['ɛldərli] *adj* : mayor, de edad, anciano

eldest ['ɛldəst] *adj* : mayor, de más edad

elect[1] [i'lɛkt] *vt* : elegir

elect[2] *adj* : electo ⟨the president-elect : el presidente electo⟩

elect[3] *npl* **the elect** : los elegidos *mpl*

election [i'lɛkʃən] *n* : elección *f*

elective[1] [i'lɛktɪv] *adj* **1** : electivo **2** OPTIONAL : facultativo, optativo

elective[2] *n* : asignatura *f* electiva

elector [i'lɛktər] *n* : elector *m*, -tora *f*

electoral [i'lɛktərəl] *adj* : electoral

electorate [i'lɛktərət] *n* : electorado *m*

electric [i'lɛktrɪk] *adj* **1** *or* **electrical** [-trɪkəl] : eléctrico **2** THRILLING : electrizante, emocionante

electrician [i̱ˌlɛk'trɪʃən] *n* : electricista *mf*

electricity [i̱ˌlɛk'trɪsət̬i] *n, pl* **-ties 1** : electricidad *f* **2** CURRENT : corriente *m* eléctrica

electrification [i̱ˌlɛktrəfə'keɪʃən] *n* : electrificación *f*

electrify [i'lɛktrəˌfaɪ] *vt* **-fied; -fying 1** : electrificar **2** THRILL : electrizar, emocionar

electrocardiogram [i̱ˌlɛktro'kɑrdiəˌgræm] *n* : electrocardiograma *m*

electrocardiograph [i̱ˌlɛktro'kɑrdiəˌgræf] *n* : electrocardiógrafo *m*

electrocute [i'lɛktrəˌkjuːt] *vt* **-cuted; -cuting** : electrocutar

electrocution [i̱ˌlɛktrə'kjuːʃən] *n* : electrocución *f*

electrode [i'lɛkˌtroːd] *n* : electrodo *m*

electrolysis [i̱ˌlɛk'trɑləsɪs] *n* : electrólisis *f*

electrolyte [i'lɛktrəˌlaɪt] *n* : electrolito *m*

electromagnet [i̱ˌlɛktro'mægnət] *n* : electroimán *m*

electromagnetic [i̱ˌlɛktromæg'nɪt̬ɪk] *adj* : electromagnético — **electromagnetically** [-t̬ɪkli] *adv*

electromagnetism [i̱ˌlɛktro'mægnəˌtɪzəm] *n* : electromagnetismo *m*

electron [i'lɛkˌtrɑn] *n* : electrón *m*

electronic [i̱ˌlɛk'trɑnɪk] *adj* : electrónico — **electronically** [-nɪkli] *adv*

electronic mail *n* : correo *m* electrónico

electronics [i̱ˌlɛk'trɑnɪks] *n* : electrónica *f*

electroplate [i'lɛktrəˌpleɪt] *vt* **-plated; plating** : galvanizar mediante electrólisis

elegance ['ɛlɪgənts] *n* : elegancia *f*

elegant ['ɛlɪgənt] *adj* : elegante — **elegantly** *adv*

elegy ['ɛlədʒi] *n, pl* **-gies** : elegía *f*

element ['ɛləmənt] *n* **1** COMPONENT : elemento *m*, factor *m* **2** : elemento *m* (en la química) **3** MILIEU : elemento *m*, medio *m* ⟨to be in one's element : estar en su elemento⟩ **4 elements** *npl* RUDIMENTS : elementos *mpl*, rudimentos *mpl*, bases *fpl* **5 the elements** WEATHER : los elementos *mpl*

elemental [ˌɛlə'mɛntəl] *adj* **1** BASIC : elemental, primario **2** : elemental (dícese de los elementos químicos)

elementary [ˌɛlə'mɛntri] *adj* **1** SIMPLE : elemental, simple, fundamental **2** : de enseñanza primaria

elementary school *n* : escuela *f* primaria

elephant ['ɛləfənt] *n* : elefante *m*, -ta *f*

elevate ['ɛləˌveɪt] *vt* **-vated; -vating 1** RAISE : elevar, levantar, alzar **2** EXALT, PROMOTE : elevar, exaltar, ascender **3** ELATE : alborozar, regocijar

elevation [ˌɛlə'veɪʃən] *n* **1** : elevación *f* **2** ALTITUDE : altura *f*, altitud *f* **3** PROMOTION : ascenso *m*

elevator ['ɛləˌveɪt̬ər] *n* : ascensor *m*, elevador *m*

eleven[1] [i'lɛvən] *adj* : once

eleven[2] *n* : once *m*

eleventh[1] [ɪ'lɛvənθ] *adj* : undécimo

eleventh[2] *n* **1** : undécimo *m*, -ma *f* (en una serie) **2** : onceavo *m*, onceava parte *f*

elf ['ɛlf] *n, pl* **elves** ['ɛlvz] : elfo *m*, geniecillo *m*, duende *m*

elfin ['ɛlfən] *adj* **1** : de elfo, menudo **2** ENCHANTING, MAGIC : mágico, encantador

elfish ['ɛlfɪʃ] *adj* **1** : de elfo **2** MISCHIEVOUS : travieso

elicit [ɪ'lɪsət] *vt* : provocar

eligibility [ˌɛləʤəˈbɪləʧi] n, pl **-ties** : elegibilidad f

eligible [ˈɛlɪʤəbəl] adj **1** QUALIFIED : elegible **2** SUITABLE : idóneo

eliminate [ɪˈlɪməˌneɪt] vt **-nated; -nating** : eliminar

elimination [ɪˌlɪməˈneɪʃən] n : eliminación f

elite [eɪˈliːt, i-] n : elite f

elixir [ɪˈlɪksər] n : elixir m

elk [ˈɛlk] n : alce m (de Europa), uapití m (de América)

ellipse [ɪˈlɪps, -] n : elipse f

ellipsis [ɪˈlɪpsəs, -] n, pl **-lipses** [-ˌsiːz] **1** : elipsis f **2** : puntos mpl suspensivos (en la puntuación)

elliptical [ɪˈlɪptɪkəl, -] or **elliptic** [-tɪk] adj : elíptico

elm [ˈɛlm] n : olmo m

elocution [ˌɛləˈkjuːʃən] n : elocución f

elongate [iˈlɔŋˌgeɪt] vt **-gated; -gating** : alargar

elongation [ˌiːˌlɔŋˈgeɪʃən] n : alargamiento m

elope [iˈloːp] vi **eloped; eloping** : fugarse

elopement [iˈloːpmənt] n : fuga f

eloquence [ˈɛləkwənts] n : elocuencia f

eloquent [ˈɛləkwənt] adj : elocuente — **eloquently** adv

El Salvadoran [ˌɛlˌsælvəˈdorən] n : salvadoreño m, -ña f — **El Salvadoran** adj

else[1] [ˈɛls] adv **1** DIFFERENTLY : de otro modo, de otra manera ⟨how else? : ¿de qué otro modo?⟩ **2** ELSEWHERE : de otro sitio, de otro lugar ⟨where else? : ¿en qué otro sitio?⟩ **3 or else** OTHERWISE : si no, de lo contrario

else[2] adj **1** OTHER : otro ⟨anyone else : cualquier otro⟩ ⟨everyone else : todos los demás⟩ ⟨nobody else : ningún otro, nadie más⟩ ⟨somebody else : otra persona⟩ **2** MORE : más ⟨nothing else : nada más⟩ ⟨what else? : ¿qué más?⟩

elsewhere [ˈɛlsˌʰwɛr] adv : en otra parte, en otro sitio, en otro lugar

elucidate [iˈluːsəˌdeɪt] vt **-dated; -dating** : dilucidar, elucidar, esclarecer

elucidation [iˌluːsəˈdeɪʃən] n : elucidación f, esclarecimiento m

elude [iˈluːd] vt **eluded; eluding** : eludir, evadir

elusive [iˈluːsɪv] adj **1** EVASIVE : evasivo, esquivo **2** SLIPPERY : huidizo, escurridizo **3** FLEETING, INTANGIBLE : impalpable, fugaz

elusively [iˈluːsɪvli] adv : de manera esquiva

elves → elf

emaciate [iˈmeɪʃiˌeɪt] vt **-ated; -ating** : enflaquecer

emaciation [iˌmeɪsiˈeɪʃən, -ʃi-] n : enflaquecimiento m, escualidez f, delgadez f extrema

e–mail [ˈiːˌmeɪl] n : e-mail m

emanate [ˈɛməˌneɪt] v **-nated; -nating** vi : emanar, provenir, proceder — vt : emanar

emanation [ˌɛməˈneɪʃən] n : emanación f

emancipate [iˈmæntsəˌpeɪt] vt **-pated; -pating** : emancipar

emancipation [iˌmæntsəˈpeɪʃən] n : emancipación f

emasculate [iˈmæskjəˌleɪt] vt **-lated; -lating** **1** CASTRATE : castrar, emascular **2** WEAKEN : debilitar

embalm [ɪmˈbɑm, ɛm-, -ˈbɑlm] vt : embalsamar

embankment [ɪmˈbæŋkmənt, ɛm-] n : terraplén m, muro m de contención

embargo[1] [ɪmˈbɑrgo, ɛm-] vt **-goed; -going** : imponer un embargo sobre

embargo[2] n, pl **-goes** : embargo m

embark [ɪmˈbɑrk, ɛm-] vi **1** : embarcar — vi **1** : embarcar **2 to embark on** START : emprender, embarcarse en

embarkation [ˌɛmˌbɑrˈkeɪʃən] n : embarque m, embarco m

embarrass [ɪmˈbærəs, ɛm-] vt : avergonzar, abochornar

embarrassing [ɪmˈbærəsɪŋ, ɛm-] adj : embarazoso, violento

embarrassment [ɪmˈbærəsmənt, ɛm-] n : vergüenza f, pena f

embassy [ˈɛmbəsi] n, pl **-sies** : embajada f

embed [ɪmˈbɛd, ɛm-] vt **-bedded; -bedding** : incrustar, empotrar, grabar (en la memoria)

embellish [ɪmˈbɛlɪʃ, ɛm-] vt : adornar, embellecer

embellishment [ɪmˈbɛlɪʃmənt, ɛm-] n : adorno m

ember [ˈɛmbər] n : ascua f, brasa f

embezzle [ɪmˈbɛzəl, ɛm-] vt **-zled; -zling** : desfalcar, malversar

embezzlement [ɪmˈbɛzəlmənt, ɛm-] n : desfalco m, malversación f

embezzler [ɪmˈbɛzələr, ɛm-] n : desfalcador m, -dora f; malversador m, -dora f

embitter [ɪmˈbɪtər, ɛm-] vt : amargar

emblem [ˈɛmbləm] n : emblema m, símbolo m

emblematic [ˌɛmbləˈmætɪk] adj : emblemático, simbólico

embodiment [ɪmˈbɑdimənt, ɛm-] n : encarnación f, personificación f

embody [ɪmˈbɑdi, ɛm-] vt **-bodied; -bodying** : encarnar, personificar

emboss [ɪmˈbɑs, ɛm-, -ˈbɔs] vt : repujar, grabar en relieve

embrace[1] [ɪmˈbreɪs, ɛm-] vt **-braced; -bracing** **1** HUG : abrazar **2** ADOPT, TAKE ON : adoptar, aceptar **3** INCLUDE : abarcar, incluir

embrace[2] n : abrazo m

embroider [ɪmˈbrɔɪdər, ɛm-] vt : bordar (una tela), adornar (una historia)

embroidery [ɪmˈbrɔɪdəri, ɛm-] n, pl **-deries** : bordado m

embroil [ɪmˈbrɔɪl, ɛm-] vt : embrollar, enredar

embryo [ˈɛmbriˌoː] n, pl **embryos** : embrión m

embryonic [ˌɛmbri'ɑnɪk] *adj* : embrionario

emend [i'mɛnd] *vt* : enmendar, corregir

emendation [ˌiːˌmɛn'deɪʃən] *n* : enmienda *f*

emerald¹ ['ɛmrəld, 'ɛmə-] *adj* : verde esmeralda

emerald² *n* : esmeralda *f*

emerge [i'mərdʒ] *vi* **emerged; emerging**
: emerger, salir, aparecer, surgir

emergence [i'mərdʒənts] *n* : aparición *f*,
surgimiento *m*

emergency [i'mərdʒəntsi] *n, pl* **-cies**
: emergencia *f*

emergent [i'mərdʒənt] *adj* : emergente

emery ['ɛməri] *n, pl* **-eries** : esmeril *m*

emetic¹ [i'mɛtɪk] *adj* : vomitivo, emético

emetic² *n* : vomitivo *m*, emético *m*

emigrant ['ɛmɪgrənt] *n* : emigrante *mf*

emigrate ['ɛmə,greɪt] *vi* **-grated; -grat-
ing** : emigrar

emigration [ˌɛmə'greɪʃən] *n* : emigración *f*

eminence ['ɛmənənts] *n* **1** PROMINENCE
: eminencia *f*, prestigio *m*, renombre *m*
2 DIGNITARY : eminencia *f*, dignatario
m, -ria *f* ⟨Your Eminence : Su Emi-
nencia⟩

eminent ['ɛmənənt] *adj* : eminente, ilustre

eminently ['ɛmənəntli] *adv* : sumamente

emissary ['ɛmə,sɛri] *n, pl* **-saries** : emis-
ario *m*, -ria *f*

emission [i'mɪʃən] *n* : emisión *f*

emit [i'mɪt] *vt* **emitted; emitting** : emitir, despedir, producir

emote [i'mo:t] *vi* **emoted; emoting** : exteriorizar las emociones

emotion [i'mo:ʃən] *n* : emoción *f*, sentimiento *m*

emotional [i'mo:ʃənəl] *adj* **1** : emocional, afectivo ⟨an emotional reaction
: una reacción emocional⟩ **2** MOVING
: emocionante, emotivo, conmovedor

emotionally [i'mo:ʃənəli] *adv* : emocionalmente

empathy ['ɛmpəθi] *n* : empatía *f*

emperor ['ɛmpərər] *n* : emperador *m*

emphasis ['ɛmfəsɪs] *n, pl* **-phases** [-ˌsiːz]
: énfasis *m*, hincapié *m*

emphasize ['ɛmfə,saɪz] *vt* **-sized; -siz-
ing** : enfatizar, destacar, subrayar,
hacer hincapié en

emphatic [ɪm'fætɪk, ɛm-] *adj* : enfático,
enérgico, categórico — **emphatically**
[-ɪkli] *adv*

empire ['ɛm,paɪr] *n* : imperio *m*

empirical [ɪm'pɪrɪkəl, ɛm-] *adj* : empírico — **empirically** [-ɪkli] *adv*

employ¹ [ɪm'plɔɪ, ɛm-] *vt* **1** USE : usar,
utilizar **2** HIRE : contratar, emplear **3**
OCCUPY : ocupar, dedicar, emplear

employ² [ɪm'plɔɪ, ɛm-; 'ɪm,-, 'ɛm,-] *n* **1**
: puesto *m*, cargo *m*, ocupación *f* **2 to
be in the employ of** : estar al servicio
de, trabajar para

employee [ɪm,plɔɪ'iː, ɛm-, -'plɔɪˌiː] *n*
: empleado *m*, -da *f*

employer [ɪm'plɔɪər, ɛm-] *n* : patrón *m*,
-trona *f*; empleador *m*, -dora *f*

employment [ɪm'plɔɪmənt, ɛm-] *n* : trabajo *m*, empleo *m*

empower [ɪm'paʊər, ɛm-] *vt* : facultar,
autorizar, conferirle poder a

empowerment [ɪm'paʊərmənt, ɛm-] *n*
: autorización *f*

empress ['ɛmprəs] *n* : emperatriz *f*

emptiness ['ɛmptinəs] *n* : vacío *m*,
vacuidad *f*

empty¹ ['ɛmpti] *v* **-tied; -tying** *vt* : vaciar
— *vi* : desaguar (dícese de un río)

empty² *adj* **emptier; -est 1** : vacío **2** VA-
CANT : desocupado, libre **3** MEANING-
LESS : vacío, hueco, vano

empty–handed [ˌɛmpti'hændəd] *adj*
: con las manos vacías

empty–headed [ˌɛmpti'hɛdəd] *adj*
: cabeza hueca, tonto

emu ['iːˌmjuː] *n* : emú *m*

emulate ['ɛmjə,leɪt] *vt* **-lated; -lating**
: emular

emulation [ˌɛmjə'leɪʃən] *n* : emulación *f*

emulsifier [i'mʌlsə,faɪər] *n* : emulsionante *m*

emulsify [i'mʌlsə,faɪ] *vt* **-fied; -fying**
: emulsionar

emulsion [i'mʌlʃən] *n* : emulsión *f*

enable [i'neɪbəl, ɛ-] *vt* **-abled; -abling 1**
EMPOWER : habilitar, autorizar, facul-
tar **2** PERMIT : hacer posible, posibilitar, permitir

enact [i'nækt, ɛ-] *vt* **1** : promulgar (un
ley o decreto) **2** : representar (un papel en el teatro)

enactment [i'næktmənt, ɛ-] *n* : promulgación *f*

enamel¹ [i'næməl] *vt* **-eled** *or* **-elled; -el-
ing** *or* **-elling** : esmaltar

enamel² *n* : esmalte *m*

enamor [i'næmər] *vt* **1** : enamorar **2 to
be enamored of** : estar enamorado de
(una persona), estar entusiasmado con
(algo)

encamp [ɪn'kæmp, ɛn-] *vi* : acampar

encampment [ɪn'kæmpmənt, ɛn-] *n*
: campamento *m*

encase [ɪn'keɪs, ɛn-] *vt* **-cased; -casing**
: encerrar, revestir

encephalitis [ɪnˌsɛfə'laɪtəs, ɛn-] *n, pl*
-litides [-'lɪtəˌdiːz] : encefalitis *f*

enchant [ɪn'tʃænt, ɛn-] *vt* **1** BEWITCH
: hechizar, encantar, embrujar **2**
CHARM, FASCINATE : cautivar, fascinar, encantar

enchanting [ɪn'tʃæntɪŋ, ɛn-] *adj* : encantador

enchanter [ɪn'tʃæntər, ɛn-] *n* SORCERER
: mago *m*, encantador *m*

enchantment [ɪn'tʃæntmənt, ɛn-] *n* **1**
SPELL : encanto *m*, hechizo *m* **2**
CHARM : encanto *m*

enchantress [ɪn'tʃæntrəs, ɛn-] *n* **1** SOR-
CERESS : maga *f*, hechicera *f* **2**
CHARMER : mujer *f* cautivadora

encircle [ɪn'sərkəl, ɛn-] *vt* **-cled; -cling**
: rodear, ceñir, cercar

enclose [ɪn'kloːz, ɛn-] vt **-closed;**
-closing 1 SURROUND : encerrar, cercar, rodear **2** INCLUDE : incluir, adjuntar, acompañar ⟨please find enclosed : le enviamos adjunto⟩
enclosure [ɪn'kloːʒər, ɛn-] n **1** ENCLOS-
ING : encierro m **2** : cercado m (de terreno), recinto m ⟨an enclosure for the
press : un recinto para la prensa⟩ **3** AD-
JUNCT : anexo m (con una carta), documento m adjunto
encode [ɪn'koːd, ɛn-] vt : cifrar (mensajes, etc.), codificar (en informática)
encompass [ɪn'kʌmpəs, ɛn-, -'kɑm-] vt
1 SURROUND : circundar, rodear **2** IN-
CLUDE : abarcar, comprender
encore [ˈɑnˌkor] n : bis m, repetición f
encounter[1] [ɪn'kaʊntər, ɛn-] vt **1** MEET
: encontrar, encontrarse con, toparse
con, tropezar con **2** FIGHT : combatir,
luchar contra
encounter[2] n : encuentro m
encourage [ɪn'kəriʤ, ɛn-] vt **-aged;**
-aging 1 HEARTEN, INSPIRE : animar,
alentar **2** FOSTER : fomentar, promover
encouragement [ɪn'kəriʤmənt, ɛn-] n
: ánimo m, aliento m
encouraging [ɪn'kərəʤɪŋ, ɛn-] adj
: alentador, esperanzador
encroach [ɪn'kroːʧ, ɛn-] vi **to encroach
on** : invadir, abusar (derechos), quitar
(tiempo)
encroachment [ɪn'kroːʧmənt, ɛn-] n
: invasión f, usurpación f
encrust [ɪn'krʌst, ɛn-] vt **1** : recubrir con
una costra **2** INLAY : incrustar ⟨en-
crusted with gems : incrustado de
gemas⟩
encumber [ɪn'kʌmbər, ɛn-] vt **1** BLOCK
: obstruir, estorbar **2** BURDEN : cargar, gravar
encumbrance [ɪn'kʌmbrənts, ɛn-] n : estorbo m, carga f, gravamen m
encyclopedia [ɪnˌsaɪkləˈpiːdiə, ɛn-] n
: enciclopedia f
encyclopedic [ɪnˌsaɪkləˈpiːdɪk, ɛn-] adj
: enciclopédico
end[1] [ˈɛnd] vt **1** STOP : terminar, poner
fin a **2** CONCLUDE : concluir, terminar
— vi : terminar(se), acabar, con-
cluir(se)
end[2] n **1** EXTREMITY : extremo m, final
m, punta f **2** CONCLUSION : fin m, final m **3** AIM : fin m
endanger [ɪn'deɪnʤər, ɛn-] vt : poner en
peligro
endear [ɪn'dɪr, ɛn-] vi **to endear oneself
to** : ganarse la simpatía de, granjearse
el cariño de
endearment [ɪn'dɪrmənt, ɛn-] n : expresión f de cariño
endeavor[1] [ɪn'dɛvər, ɛn-] vi : intentar,
esforzarse por ⟨he endeavored to improve his work : intentó por mejorar
su trabajo⟩
endeavor[2] n : intento m, esfuerzo m
endemic [ɛn'dɛmɪk, ɪn-] adj : endémico

ending [ˈɛndɪŋ] n **1** CONCLUSION : final
m, desenlace m **2** SUFFIX : sufijo m,
terminación f
endive [ˈɛnˌdaɪv, ˌɑn'diːv] n : endibia f,
endivia f
endless [ˈɛndləs] adj **1** INTERMINABLE
: interminable, inacabable, sin fin **2**
INNUMERABLE : innumerable, incontable
endlessly [ˈɛndləsli] adv : interminablemente, eternamente, sin parar
endocrine [ˈɛndəkrən, -ˌkraɪn, -ˌkriːn]
adj : endocrino
endorse [ɪn'dors, ɛn-] vt **-dorsed;**
-dorsing 1 SIGN : endosar, firmar **2**
APPROVE : aprobar, sancionar
endorsement [ɪn'dorsmənt, ɛn-] n **1**
SIGNATURE : endoso m, firma f **2** AP-
PROVAL : aprobación f, aval m
endow [ɪn'daʊ, ɛn-] vt : dotar
endowment [ɪn'daʊmənt, ɛn-] n **1**
FUNDING : dotación f **2** DONATION
: donación f, legado m **3** ATTRIBUTE,
GIFT : atributo m, dotes fpl
endurable [ɪn'dʊrəbəl, ɛn-, -'djʊr-] adj
: tolerable, soportable
endurance [ɪn'dʊrənts, ɛn-, -'djʊr-] n
: resistencia f, aguante m
endure [ɪn'dʊr, ɛn-, -'djʊr] v **-dured;**
-during vt **1** BEAR : resistir, soportar,
aguantar **2** TOLERATE : tolerar, soportar — vi LAST : durar, perdurar
enema [ˈɛnəmə] n : enema m, lavativa f
enemy [ˈɛnəmi] n, pl **-mies** : enemigo m,
-ga f
energetic [ˌɛnərˈʤɛtɪk] adj : enérgico,
vigoroso — **energetically** [-tɪkli] adv
energize [ˈɛnərˌʤaɪz] vt **-gized; -gizing**
1 ACTIVATE : activar **2** INVIGORATE
: vigorizar
energy [ˈɛnərʤi] n, pl **-gies 1** VITALITY
: energía f, vitalidad f **2** EFFORT : esfuerzo m, energías fpl **3** POWER : energía f ⟨atomic energy : energía atómi-
ca⟩
enervate [ˈɛnərˌveɪt] vt **-vated; -vating**
: enervar, debilitar
enfold [ɪn'foːld, ɛn-] vt : envolver
enforce [ɪn'fors, ɛn-] vt **-forced; -forcing**
1 : hacer respetar, hacer cumplir (una
ley, etc.) **2** IMPOSE : imponer ⟨to enforce obedience : imponer la obedien-
cia⟩
enforcement [ɪn'forsmənt, ɛn-] n : imposición f
enfranchise [ɪn'frænˌʧaɪz, ɛn-] vt
-chised; -chising : conceder el voto a
enfranchisement [ɪn'frænˌʧaɪzmənt,
ɛn-] n : concesión f del voto
engage [ɪn'geɪʤ, ɛn-] v **-gaged; -gaging**
vt **1** ATTRACT : captar, atraer, llamar
⟨to engage one's attention : captar la
atención⟩ **2** MESH : engranar ⟨to engage the clutch : embragar⟩ **3** COMMIT
: comprometer ⟨to get engaged : com-
prometerse⟩ **4** HIRE : contratar **5**
: entablar combate con (un enemigo)

— *vi* **1** PARTICIPATE : participar **2 to engage in combat** : entrar en combate

engagement [ɪnˈɡeɪdʒmənt, ɛn-] *n* **1** APPOINTMENT : cita *f*, hora *f* **2** BETROTHAL : compromiso *m*

engaging [ɪnˈɡeɪdʒɪŋ, ɛn-] *adj* : atractivo, encantador, interesante

engender [ɪnˈdʒɛndər, ɛn-] *vt* -dered; -dering : engendrar

engine [ˈɛndʒən] *n* **1** MOTOR : motor *m* **2** LOCOMOTIVE : locomotora *f*, máquina *f*

engineer¹ [ˌɛndʒəˈnɪr] *vt* **1** : diseñar, construir (un sistema, un mecanismo, etc.) **2** CONTRIVE : maquinar, tramar, fraguar

engineer² *n* **1** : ingeniero *m*, -ra *f* **2** : maquinista *mf* (de locomotoras)

engineering [ˌɛndʒəˈnɪrɪŋ] *n* : ingeniería *f*

English¹ [ˈɪŋɡlɪʃ, ˈɪŋlɪʃ] *adj* : inglés

English² *n* **1** : inglés *m* (idioma) **2 the English** : los ingleses

Englishman [ˈɪŋɡlɪʃmən, ˈɪŋlɪʃ-] *n, pl* -men [-mən, -ˌmɛn] : inglés *m*

Englishwoman [ˈɪŋɡlɪʃˌwʊmən, ˈɪŋlɪʃ-] *n, pl* -women [-ˌwɪmən] : inglesa *f*

engrave [ɪnˈɡreɪv, ɛn-] *vt* -graved; -graving : grabar

engraver [ɪnˈɡreɪvər, ɛn-] *n* : grabador *m*, -dora *f*

engraving [ɪnˈɡreɪvɪŋ, ɛn-] *n* : grabado *m*

engross [ɪnˈɡroːs, ɛn-] *vt* : absorber

engrossed [ɪnˈɡroːst, ɛn-] *adj* : absorto

engrossing [ɪnˈɡroːsɪŋ, ɛn-] *adj* : fascinante, absorbente

engulf [ɪnˈɡʌlf, ɛn-] *vt* : envolver, sepultar

enhance [ɪnˈhænts, ɛn-] *vt* -hanced; -hancing : realzar, aumentar, mejorar

enhancement [ɪnˈhæntsmənt, ɛn-] *n* : mejora *f*, realce *m*, aumento *m*

enigma [ɪˈnɪɡmə] *n* : enigma *m*

enigmatic [ˌɛnɪɡˈmætɪk, ˌiː-nɪɡ-] *adj* : enigmático — **enigmatically** [-tɪkli] *adv*

enjoin [ɪnˈdʒɔɪn, ɛn-] *vt* **1** COMMAND : ordenar, imponer **2** FORBID : prohibir, vedar

enjoy [ɪnˈdʒɔɪ, ɛn-] *vt* **1** : disfrutar, gozar ⟨did you enjoy the book? : ¿te gustó el libro?⟩ ⟨to enjoy good health : gozar de buena salud⟩ **2 to enjoy oneself** : divertirse, pasarlo bien

enjoyable [ɪnˈdʒɔɪəbəl, ɛn-] *adj* : agradable, placentero, divertido

enjoyment [ɪnˈdʒɔɪmənt, ɛn-] *n* : placer *m*, goce *m*, disfrute *m*, deleite *m*

enlarge [ɪnˈlɑrdʒ, ɛn-] *v* -larged; -larging *vt* **1** : extender, agrandar, ampliar — *vi* **1** : ampliarse **2 to enlarge upon** : extenderse sobre, entrar en detalles sobre

enlargement [ɪnˈlɑrdʒmənt, ɛn-] *n* : expansión *f*, ampliación *f* (dícese de fotografías)

enlarger [ɪnˈlɑrdʒər, ɛn-] *n* : ampliadora *f*

enlighten [ɪnˈlaɪtən, ɛn-] *vt* : iluminar, aclarar

enlightenment [ɪnˈlaɪtənmənt, ɛn-] *n* **1** : ilustración *f* ⟨the Enlightenment : la Ilustración⟩ **2** CLARIFICATION : aclaración *f*

enlist [ɪnˈlɪst, ɛn-] *vt* **1** ENROLL : alistar, reclutar **2** SECURE : conseguir ⟨to enlist the support of : conseguir el apoyo de⟩ — *vi* : alistarse

enlisted man [ɪnˈlɪstəd, ɛn-] *n* : soldado *m* raso

enlistment [ɪnˈlɪstmənt, ɛn-] *n* : alistamiento *m*, reclutamiento *m*

enliven [ɪnˈlaɪvən, ɛn-] *vt* : animar, alegrar, darle vida a

enmity [ˈɛnməti] *n, pl* -ties : enemistad *f*, animadversión *f*

ennoble [ɪˈnoːbəl, ɛ-] *vt* -bled; -bling : ennoblecer

ennui [ˌɑnˈwiː] *n* : hastío *m*, tedio *m*, fastidio *m*, aburrimiento *m*

enormity [ɪˈnɔrməti] *n, pl* -ties **1** ATROCITY : atrocidad *f*, barbaridad *f* **2** IMMENSITY : enormidad *f*, inmensidad *f*

enormous [ɪˈnɔrməs] *adj* : enorme, inmenso, tremendo — **enormously** *adv*

enough¹ [ɪˈnʌf] *adv* **1** : bastante, suficientemente **2 fair enough!** : ¡está bien!, ¡de acuerdo! **3 strangely enough** : por extraño que parezca **4 sure enough** : en efecto, sin duda alguna **5 well enough** : muy bien, bastante bien

enough² *adj* : bastante, suficiente ⟨do we have enough chairs? : ¿tenemos suficientes sillas?⟩

enough³ *pron* : (lo) suficiente, (lo) bastante ⟨enough to eat : lo suficiente para comer⟩ ⟨it's not enough : no basta⟩ ⟨I've had enough! : ¡estoy harto!, ¡está bueno ya!⟩

enquire [ɪnˈkwaɪr, ɛn-] **enquiry** [ˈɪnˌkwaɪri, ˈɛn-, -kwəri; ɪnˈkwaɪri, ɛn-] → **inquire, inquiry**

enrage [ɪnˈreɪdʒ, ɛn-] *vt* -raged; -raging : enfurecer, encolerizar

enraged [ɪnˈreɪdʒd, ɛn-] *adj* : enfurecido, furioso

enrich [ɪnˈrɪtʃ, ɛn-] *vt* : enriquecer

enrichment [ɪnˈrɪtʃmənt, ɛn-] *n* : enriquecimiento *m*

enroll *or* **enrol** [ɪnˈroːl, ɛn-] *v* -rolled; -rolling *vt* : matricular, inscribir — *vi* : matricularse, inscribirse

enrollment [ɪnˈroːlmənt, ɛn-] *n* : matrícula *f*, inscripción *f*

en route [ɑnˈruːt, ɛnˈraʊt] *adv* : de camino, por el camino

ensconce [ɪnˈskɑnts, ɛn-] *vt* -sconced; -sconcing : acomodar, instalar, establecer cómodamente

ensemble [ɑnˈsɑmbəl] *n* : conjunto *m*

enshrine [ɪnˈʃraɪn, ɛn-] *vt* -shrined; -shrining : conservar religiosamente, preservar

ensign [ˈɛnsən, ˈɛnˌsaɪn] *n* **1** FLAG : enseña *f*, pabellón *m* **2** : alférez *mf* (de fragata)

enslave [ɪnˈsleɪv, ɛn-] vt **-slaved; -slaving** : esclavizar

enslavement [ɪnˈsleɪvmənt, ɛn-] n : esclavización f

ensnare [ɪnˈsnær, ɛn-] vt **-snared; -snaring** : atrapar

ensue [ɪnˈsuː, ɛn-] vi **-sued; -suing** : seguir, resultar

ensure [ɪnˈʃʊr, ɛn-] vt **-sured; -suring** : asegurar, garantizar

entail [ɪnˈteɪl, ɛn-] vt : implicar, suponer, conllevar

entangle [ɪnˈtæŋɡəl, ɛn-] vt **-gled; -gling** : enredar

entanglement [ɪnˈtæŋɡəlmənt, ɛn-] n : enredo m

enter [ˈɛntər] vt **1** : entrar en, entrar a **2** BEGIN : entrar en, comenzar, iniciar **3** RECORD : anotar, inscribir, dar entrada a ⟨to enter data : introducir datos⟩ **4** JOIN : entrar en, alistarse en, hacerse socio de — vi **1** : entrar **2 to enter into** : entrar en, firmar (un acuerdo), entablar (negociaciones, etc.)

enterprise [ˈɛntərˌpraɪz] n **1** UNDERTAKING : empresa f **2** BUSINESS : empresa f, firma f **3** INITIATIVE : iniciativa f, empuje m

enterprising [ˈɛntərˌpraɪzɪŋ] adj : emprendedor

entertain [ˌɛntərˈteɪn] vt **1** : recibir, agasajar ⟨to entertain guests : tener invitados⟩ **2** CONSIDER : considerar, contemplar **3** AMUSE : entretener, divertir

entertainer [ˌɛntərˈteɪnər] n : artista mf

entertaining [ˌɛntərˈteɪnɪŋ] adj : entretenido, divertido

entertainment [ˌɛntərˈteɪnmənt] n : entretenimiento m, diversión f

enthrall or **enthral** [ɪnˈθrɔl, ɛn-] vt **-thralled; -thralling** : cautivar, embelesar

enthuse [ɪnˈθuiz, ɛn-] v **-thused; -thusing** vt **1** EXCITE : entusiasmar **2** : decir con entusiasmo — vi **to enthuse over** : hablar con entusiasmo sobre

enthusiasm [ɪnˈθuːziˌæzəm, ɛn-, -ˈθjuː-] n : entusiasmo m

enthusiast [ɪnˈθuːziˌæst, ɛn-, -ˈθjuː-, -əst] n : entusiasta mf; aficionado m, -da f

enthusiastic [ɪnˌθuːziˈæstɪk, ɛn-, -ˌθjuː-] adj : entusiasta, aficionado

enthusiastically [ɪnˌθuːziˈæstɪkli, ɛn-, -ˌθjuː-] adv : con entusiasmo

entice [ɪnˈtaɪs, ɛn-] vt **-ticed; -ticing** : atraer, tentar

enticement [ɪnˈtaɪsmənt, ɛn-] n : tentación f, atracción f, señuelo m

entire [ɪnˈtaɪr, ɛn-] adj : entero, completo

entirely [ɪnˈtaɪrli, ɛn-] adv : completamente, totalmente

entirety [ɪnˈtaɪrti, ɛn-, -ˈtaɪrəti] n, pl **-ties** : totalidad f

entitle [ɪnˈtaɪtəl, ɛn-] vt **-tled; -tling 1** NAME : titular, intitular **2** : dar derecho a ⟨it entitles you to enter free : le

da derecho a entrar gratis⟩ **3 to be entitled to** : tener derecho a

entitlement [ɪnˈtaɪtəlmənt, ɛn-] n RIGHT : derecho m

entity [ˈɛntəti] n, pl **-ties** : entidad f, ente m

entomologist [ˌɛntəˈmɑlədʒɪst] n : entomólogo m, -ga f

entomology [ˌɛntəˈmɑlədʒi] n : entomología f

entourage [ˌɑntuˈrɑʒ] n : séquito m

entrails [ˈɛnˌtreɪlz, -trəlz] npl : entrañas fpl, vísceras fpl

entrance¹ [ɪnˈtræns, ɛn-] vt **-tranced; -trancing** : encantar, embelesar, fascinar

entrance² [ˈɛntrənts] n **1** ENTERING : entrada f ⟨to make an entrance : entrar en escena⟩ **2** ENTRY : entrada f, puerta f **3** ADMISSION : entrada f, ingreso m ⟨entrance examination : examen de ingreso⟩

entrant [ˈɛntrənt] n : candidato m, -ta f (en un examen); participante mf (en un concurso)

entrap [ɪnˈtræp, ɛn-] vt **-trapped; -trapping** : atrapar, entrampar, hacer caer en una trampa

entrapment [ɪnˈtræpmənt, ɛn-] n : captura f

entreat [ɪnˈtriːt, ɛn-] vt : suplicar, rogar

entreaty [ɪnˈtriːti, ɛn-] n, pl **-treaties** : ruego m, súplica f

entrée or **entree** [ˈɑnˌtreɪ, ˌɑn'-] n : plato m principal

entrench [ɪnˈtrentʃ, ɛn-] vt **1** FORTIFY : atrincherar (una posición militar) **2** : consolidar, afianzar ⟨firmly entrenched in his job : afianzado en su puesto⟩

entrepreneur [ˌɑntrəprəˈnər, -ˈnjʊr] n : empresario m, -ria f

entrust [ɪnˈtrʌst, ɛn-] vt : confiar, encomendar

entry [ˈɛntri] n, pl **-tries 1** ENTRANCE : entrada f **2** NOTATION : entrada f, anotación f

entwine [ɪnˈtwaɪn, ɛn-] vt **-twined; -twining** : entrelazar, entretejer, entrecruzar

enumerate [ɪˈnuːməˌreɪt, ɛ-, -ˈnjuː-] vt **-ated; -ating 1** LIST : enumerar **2** COUNT : contar, enumerar

enumeration [ɪˌnuːməˈreɪʃən, ɛ-, -ˌnjuː-] n : enumeración f, lista f

enunciate [iˈnʌnsiˌeɪt, ɛ-] vt **-ated; -ating 1** STATE : enunciar, decir **2** PRONOUNCE : articular, pronunciar

enunciation [iˌnʌnsiˈeɪʃən, ɛ-] n **1** STATEMENT : enunciación f, declaración f **2** ARTICULATION : articulación f, pronunciación f, dicción f

envelop [ɪnˈvləp, ɛn-] vt : envolver, cubrir

envelope [ˈɛnvəˌloːp, ˈɑn-] n : sobre m

enviable [ˈɛnviəbəl] adj : envidiable

envious [ˈɛnviəs] adj : envidioso — **enviously** adv

environment [ɪn'vaɪrənmənt, ɛn-, -'vaɪərn-] n : medio m (ambiente), ambiente m, entorno m

environmental [ɪn,vaɪrən'mɛntəl, ɛn-, -,vaɪərn-] adj : ambiental

environmentalist [ɪn,vaɪrən'mɛntəlɪst, ɛn-, -,vaɪərn-] n : ecologista mf

environs [ɪn'vaɪrənz, ɛn-, -'vaɪərnz] npl : alrededores mpl, entorno m, inmediaciones fpl

envisage [ɪn'vɪzɪdʒ, ɛn-] vt -aged; -aging 1 IMAGINE : imaginarse, concebir 2 FORESEE : prever

envision [ɪn'vɪʒən, ɛn-] vt : imaginar

envoy ['ɛn,vɔɪ, 'ɑn-] n : enviado m, -da f

envy¹ ['ɛnvi] vt -vied; -vying : envidiar

envy² n, pl **envies** : envidia f

enzyme ['ɛn,zaɪm] n : enzima f

eon ['i:ən, i:,ɑn] → aeon

epaulet [,ɛpə'lɛt] n : charretera f

ephemeral [ɪ'fɛmərəl, -'fi:-] adj : efímero, fugaz

epic¹ ['ɛpɪk] adj : épico

epic² n : poema m épico, epopeya f

epicure ['ɛpɪ,kjʊr] n : epicúreo m, -rea f; gastrónomo m, -ma f

epicurean [,ɛpɪkjʊ'ri:ən, -'kjʊriən] adj : epicúreo

epidemic¹ [,ɛpə'dɛmɪk] adj : epidémico

epidemic² n : epidemia f

epidermis [,ɛpə'dərməs] n : epidermis f

epigram ['ɛpə,ɡræm] n : epigrama m

epilepsy ['ɛpə,lɛpsi] n, pl -sies : epilepsia f

epileptic¹ [,ɛpə'lɛptɪk] adj : epiléptico

epileptic² n : epiléptico m, -ca f

epilogue ['ɛpə,lɔɡ, -,lɑɡ] n : epílogo m

epiphany [ɪ'pɪfəni] n, pl -nies 1 **Epiphany** : Epifanía f 2 **to have an epiphany** : tener una revelación

episcopal [ɪ'pɪskəpəl] adj : episcopal

Episcopalian [ɪ,pɪskə'peɪljən] n : episcopalista mf; episcopaliano m, -na f

episode ['ɛpə,so:d] n : episodio m

episodic [,ɛpə'sɑdɪk] adj : episódico

epistle [ɪ'pɪsəl] n : epístola f, carta f

epitaph ['ɛpə,tæf] n : epitafio m

epithet ['ɛpə,θɛt, -θət] n : epíteto m

epitome [ɪ'pɪtəmi] n 1 SUMMARY : epítome m, resumen m 2 EMBODIMENT : personificación f

epitomize [ɪ'pɪtə,maɪz] vt -mized; -mizing 1 SUMMARIZE : resumir 2 EMBODY : ser la personificación de, personificar

epoch ['ɛpək, 'ɛ,pɑk, 'i:,pɑk] n : época f, era f

epoxy [ɪ'pɑksi] n, pl **epoxies** : resina f epoxídica

equable ['ɛkwəbəl, 'i:-] adj 1 CALM, STEADY : ecuánime 2 UNIFORM : estable (dícese de la temperatura), constante (dícese del clima), uniforme

equably ['ɛkwəbli, 'i:-] adv : con ecuanimidad

equal¹ ['i:kwəl] vt equaled or equalled; equaling or equalling 1 : ser igual a

⟨two plus three equals five : dos más tres es igual a cinco⟩ 2 MATCH : igualar

equal² adj 1 SAME : igual 2 ADEQUATE : adecuado, capaz

equal³ n : igual mf

equality [ɪ'kwɑləti] n, pl -ties : igualdad f

equalize ['i:kwə,laɪz] vt -ized; -izing : igualar, equiparar

equally ['i:kwəli] adv : igualmente, por igual

equanimity [,i:kwə'nɪməti, ,ɛ-] n, pl -ties : ecuanimidad f

equate [ɪ'kweɪt] vt equated; equating : equiparar, identificar

equation [ɪ'kweɪʒən] n : ecuación f

equator [ɪ'kweɪtər] n : ecuador m

equatorial [,i:kwə'tori:əl, ,ɛ-] adj : ecuatorial

equestrian¹ [ɪ'kwɛstri:ən, ɛ-] adj : ecuestre

equestrian² n : jinete mf, caballista mf

equilateral [,i:kwə'lætərəl, ,ɛ-] adj : equilátero

equilibrium [,i:kwə'lɪbri:əm, ,ɛ-] n, pl -riums or -ria : equilibrio m

equine ['i:,kwaɪn, 'ɛ-] adj : equino, hípico

equinox ['i:kwə,nɑks, 'ɛ-] n : equinoccio m

equip [ɪ'kwɪp] vt equipped; equipping 1 FURNISH : equipar 2 PREPARE : preparar

equipment [ɪ'kwɪpmənt] n : equipo m

equitable ['ɛkwətəbəl] adj : equitativo, justo, imparcial

equity ['ɛkwəti] n, pl -ties 1 FAIRNESS : equidad f, imparcialidad f 2 VALUE : valor m líquido

equivalence [ɪ'kwɪvələnts] n : equivalencia f

equivalent¹ [ɪ'kwɪvələnt] adj : equivalente

equivalent² n : equivalente m

equivocal [ɪ'kwɪvəkəl] adj 1 AMBIGUOUS : equívoco, ambiguo 2 QUESTIONABLE : incierto, dudoso, sospechoso

equivocate [ɪ'kwɪvə,keɪt] vi -cated; -cating : usar lenguaje equívoco, andarse con evasivas

equivocation [ɪ,kwɪvə'keɪʃən] n : evasiva f, subterfugio m

era ['ɪrə, 'ɛrə, 'i:rə] n : era f, época f

eradicate [ɪ'rædə,keɪt] vt -cated; -cating : erradicar

erase [ɪ'reɪs] vt erased; erasing : borrar

eraser [ɪ'reɪsər] n : goma f de borrar, borrador m

erasure [ɪ'reɪʃər] n : tachadura f

ere¹ ['ɛr] conj : antes de que

ere² prep 1 : antes de 2 **ere long** : dentro de poco

erect¹ [ɪ'rɛkt] vt 1 CONSTRUCT : erigir, construir 2 RAISE : levantar 3 ESTABLISH : establecer

erect² adj : erguido, derecho, erecto

erection [ɪ'rɛkʃən] n 1 : erección f (en fisiología) 2 BUILDING : construcción f

ergonomics [ˌərgə'namɪks] npl : ergonomía f

ermine ['ərmən] n : armiño m

erode [ɪ'ro:d] vt **eroded; eroding** : erosionar (el suelo), corroer (metales)

erosion [ɪ'ro:ʒən] n : erosión f, corrosión f

erotic [ɪ'ratɪk] adj : erótico — **erotically** [-t̬ɪkli] adv

eroticism [ɪ'rat̬əˌsɪzəm] n : erotismo m

err ['ɛr, 'ər] vi : cometer un error, equivocarse, errar

errand ['ɛrənd] n : mandado m, encargo m, recado m Spain ⟨an errand of mercy : una misión de caridad⟩

errant ['ɛrənt] adj 1 WANDERING : errante 2 ASTRAY : descarriado

erratic [ɪ'ræt̬ɪk] adj 1 INCONSISTENT : errático, irregular, inconsistente 2 ECCENTRIC : excéntrico, raro

erratically [ɪ'ræt̬ɪkli] adv : erráticamente, de manera irregular

erroneous [ɪ'ro:niəs, ɛ-] adj : erróneo — **erroneously** adv

error ['ɛrər] n : error m, equivocación f ⟨to be in error : estar equivocado⟩

ersatz ['ɛrˌsats, 'ərˌsæts] adj : artificial, sustituto

erstwhile ['ərstˌhwaɪl] adj : antiguo

erudite ['ɛrəˌdaɪt, 'ɛrju-] adj : erudito, letrado

erudition [ˌɛrə'dɪʃən, ˌɛrju-] n : erudición f

erupt [ɪ'rʌpt] vi 1 : hacer erupción (dícese de un volcán o un sarpullido) 2 : estallar (dícese de la cólera o la violencia)

eruption [ɪ'rʌpʃən] n : erupción f, estallido m

eruptive [ɪ'rʌptɪv] adj : eruptivo

escalate ['ɛskəˌleɪt] v **-lated; -lating** vt : intensificar (un conflicto), aumentar (precios) — vi : intensificarse, aumentarse

escalation [ˌɛskə'leɪʃən] n : intensificación f, escalada f, aumento m, subida f

escalator ['ɛskəˌleɪt̬ər] n : escalera f mecánica

escapade ['ɛskəˌpeɪd] n : aventura f

escape¹ [ɪ'skeɪp, ɛ-] v **-caped; -caping** vt : escaparse de, librarse de, evitar — vi : escaparse, fugarse, huir

escape² n 1 FLIGHT : fuga f, huida f, escapada f 2 LEAKAGE : escape m, fuga f 3 : escapatoria f, evasión f ⟨to have no escape : no tener escapatoria⟩ ⟨escape from reality : evasión de la realidad⟩

escapee [ɪˌskeɪ'pi:, ˌɛ-] n : fugitivo m, -va f

escarole ['ɛskəˌro:l] n : escarola f

escarpment [ɪs'kɑrpmənt, ɛs-] n : escarpa f, escarpadura f

eschew [ɛ'ʃu:, ɪs'tʃu:] vt : evitar, rehuir, abstenerse de

escort¹ [ɪ'skɔrt, ɛ-] vt : escoltar ⟨to escort a ship : escoltar un barco⟩ 2 ACCOMPANY : acompañar

escort² ['ɛsˌkɔrt] n 1 : escolta f ⟨armed escort : escolta armada⟩ 2 COMPANION : acompañante mf; compañero m, -ra f

escrow ['ɛsˌkro:] n **in escrow** : en depósito, en custodia de un tercero

Eskimo ['ɛskəˌmo:] n 1 : esquimal mf 2 : esquimal m (idioma) — **Eskimo** adj

esophagus [ɪ'safəgəs, i:-] n, pl **-gi** [-ˌgaɪ, -ˌdʒaɪ] : esófago m

esoteric [ˌɛsə'tɛrɪk] adj : esotérico, hermético

especially [ɪ'spɛʃəli] adv : especialmente, particularmente

espionage ['ɛspiəˌnaʒ, -ˌnɑdʒ] n : espionaje m

espouse [ɪ'spaʊz, ɛ-] vt **espoused; espousing** 1 MARRY : casarse con 2 ADOPT, ADVOCATE : apoyar, adherirse a, adoptar

espresso ['ɛspreˌso:] n, pl **-sos** : café m exprés

essay¹ ['ɛseɪ, 'ɛˌseɪ] vt : intentar, tratar

essay² ['ɛˌseɪ] n 1 COMPOSITION : ensayo m, trabajo m 2 ATTEMPT : intento m

essayist ['ɛˌseɪɪst] n : ensayista mf

essence ['ɛsənts] n 1 CORE : esencia f, núcleo m, meollo m ⟨in essence : esencialmente⟩ 2 EXTRACT : esencia f, extracto m 3 PERFUME : esencia f, perfume m

essential¹ [ɪ'sɛntʃəl] adj : esencial, imprescindible, fundamental — **essentially** adv

essential² n : elemento m esencial, lo imprescindible

establish [ɪ'stæblɪʃ, ɛ-] vt 1 FOUND : establecer, fundar 2 SET UP : establecer, instaurar, instituir 3 PROVE : demostrar, probar

establishment [ɪ'stæblɪʃmənt, ɛ-] n 1 ESTABLISHING : establecimiento m, fundación f, instauración f 2 BUSINESS : negocio m, establecimiento m 3 **the Establishment** : la clase dirigente

estate [ɪ'steɪt, ɛ-] n 1 POSSESSIONS : bienes mpl, propiedad f, patrimonio m 2 PROPERTY : hacienda f, finca f, propiedad f

esteem¹ [ɪ'sti:m, ɛ-] vt : estimar, apreciar

esteem² n : estima f, aprecio m

ester ['ɛstər] n : éster m

esthetic [ɛs'θɛt̬ɪk] → **aesthetic**

estimable ['ɛstəməbəl] adj : estimable

estimate¹ ['ɛstəˌmeɪt] vt **-mated; -mating** : calcular, estimar

estimate² ['ɛstəmət] n 1 : cálculo m aproximado ⟨to make an estimate : hacer un cálculo⟩ 2 ASSESSMENT : valoración f, estimación f

estimation [ˌɛstə'meɪʃən] n 1 JUDGMENT : juicio m, opinión f ⟨in my estimation : en mi opinión, según mis cálculos⟩ 2 ESTEEM : estima f, aprecio m

estimator [ˈɛstəˌmeɪtər] *n* : tasador *m*, -dora *f*

Estonian [ɛˈstoːniən] *n* : estonio *m*, -nia *f* — **Estonian** *adj*

estrange [ɪˈstreɪndʒ, ɛ-] *vt* **-tranged; -tranging** : enajenar, apartar, alejar

estrangement [ɪˈstreɪndʒmənt, ɛ-] *n* : alejamiento *m*, distanciamiento *m*

estrogen [ˈɛstrədʒən] *n* : estrógeno *m*

estrus [ˈɛstrəs] *n* : celo *m*

estuary [ˈɛstʃuˌwɛri] *n, pl* **-aries** : estuario *m*, -ría *f*

et cetera [ɛtˈsɛtərə, -ˈsɛtrə] : etcétera

etch [ˈɛtʃ] *v* : grabar al aguafuerte

etching [ˈɛtʃɪŋ] *n* : aguafuerte *m*, grabado *m* al aguafuerte

eternal [ɪˈtərnəl, iː-] *adj* **1** EVERLASTING : eterno **2** INTERMINABLE : constante, incesante

eternally [ɪˈtərnəli, iː-] *adv* : eternamente, para siempre

eternity [ɪˈtərnəti, iː-] *n, pl* **-ties** : eternidad *f*

ethane [ˈɛˌθeɪn] *n* : etano *m*

ethanol [ˈɛθəˌnɔl, -ˌnoːl] *n* : etanol *m*

ether [ˈiːθər] *n* : éter *m*

ethereal [ɪˈθɪriəl, iː-] *adj* **1** CELESTIAL : etéreo, celeste **2** DELICATE : delicado

ethical [ˈɛθɪkəl] *adj* : ético — **ethically** *adv*

ethics [ˈɛθɪks] *ns & pl* **1** : ética *f* **2** MORALITY : ética *f*, moral *f*, moralidad *f*

Ethiopian [ˌiːθiˈoːpiən] *n* : etíope *mf* — **Ethiopian** *adj*

ethnic [ˈɛθnɪk] *adj* : étnico

ethnologist [ɛθˈnɑlədʒɪst] *n* : etnólogo *m*, -ga *f*

ethnology [ɛθˈnɑlədʒi] *n* : etnología *f*

etiquette [ˈɛtɪkət, -ˌkɛt] *n* : etiqueta *f*, protocolo *m*

etymological [ˌɛtəməˈlɑdʒɪkəl] *adj* : etimológico

etymology [ˌɛtəˈmɑlədʒi] *n, pl* **-gies** : etimología *f*

eucalyptus [ˌjuːkəˈlɪptəs] *n, pl* **-ti** [-ˌtaɪ] *or* **-tuses** [-təsəz] : eucalipto *m*

Eucharist [ˈjuːkərɪst] *n* : Eucaristía *f*

eulogize [ˈjuːləˌdʒaɪz] *vt* **-gized; -gizing** : elogiar, encomiar

eulogy [ˈjuːlədʒi] *n, pl* **-gies** : elogio *m*, encomio *m*, panegírico *m*

eunuch [ˈjuːnək] *n* : eunuco *m*

euphemism [ˈjuːfəˌmɪzəm] *n* : eufemismo *m*

euphemistic [ˌjuːfəˈmɪstɪk] *adj* : eufemístico

euphony [ˈjuːfəni] *n, pl* **-nies** : eufonía *f*

euphoria [juˈforiə] *n* : euforia *f*

euphoric [juˈforɪk] *adj* : eufórico

European [ˌjʊrəˈpiːən] *n* : europeo *m*, europea *f* — **European** *adj*

euthanasia [ˌjuːθəˈneɪʒə, -ʒiə] *n* : eutanasia *f*

evacuate [ɪˈvækjuˌeɪt] *v* **-ated; -ating** *vt* VACATE : evacuar, desalojar — *vi* WITHDRAW : retirarse

evacuation [ɪˌvækjuˈeɪʃən] *n* : evacuación *f*, desalojo *m*

evade [ɪˈveɪd] *vt* **evaded; evading** : evadir, eludir, esquivar

evaluate [ɪˈvæljuˌeɪt] *vt* **-ated; -ating** : evaluar, valorar, tasar

evaluation [ɪˌvæljuˈeɪʃən] *n* : evaluación *f*, valoración *f*, tasación *f*

evangelical [ˌiːˌvænˈdʒɛlɪkəl, ˌɛvən-] *adj* : evangélico

evangelist [ɪˈvændʒəlɪst] *n* **1** : evangelista *m* **2** PREACHER : predicador *m*, -dora *f*

evaporate [ɪˈvæpəˌreɪt] *vi* **-rated; -rating** **1** VAPORIZE : evaporar **2** VANISH : evaporarse, desvanecerse, esfumarse

evaporation [ɪˌvæpəˈreɪʃən] *n* : evaporación *f*

evasion [ɪˈveɪʒən] *n* : evasión *f*

evasive [ɪˈveɪsɪv] *adj* : evasivo

evasiveness [ɪˈveɪsɪvnəs] *n* : carácter *m* evasivo

eve [ˈiːv] *n* **1** : víspera *f* ⟨on the eve of the festivities : en vísperas de las festividades⟩ **2** → **evening**

even¹ [ˈiːvən] *vt* **1** LEVEL : allanar, nivelar, emparejar **2** EQUALIZE : igualar, equilibrar — *vi* **to even out** : nivelarse, emparejarse

even² *adv* **1** : hasta, incluso ⟨even a child can do it : hasta un niño puede hacerlo⟩ ⟨he looked content, even happy : se le veía satisfecho, incluso feliz⟩ **2** (*in negative constructions*) : ni siquiera ⟨he didn't even try : ni siquiera lo intentó⟩ **3** (*in comparisons*) : aún, todavía ⟨even better : aún mejor, todavía mejor⟩ **4 even if** : aunque **5 even so** : aun así **6 even though** : aun cuando, a pesar de que

even³ *adj* **1** SMOOTH : uniforme, liso, parejo **2** FLAT : plano, llano **3** EQUAL : igual, igualado ⟨an even score : un marcador igualado⟩ **4** REGULAR : regular, constante ⟨an even pace : un ritmo constante⟩ **5** EXACT : exacto, justo **6** : par ⟨even number : número par⟩ **7 to be even** : estar en paz, estar a mano **8 to get even** : desquitarse, vengarse

evening [ˈiːvnɪŋ] *n* : tarde *f*, noche *f* ⟨in the evening : por la noche⟩

evenly [ˈiːvənli] *adv* **1** UNIFORMLY : de modo uniforme, de manera constante **2** FAIRLY : igualmente, equitativamente

evenness [ˈiːvənnəs] *n* : uniformidad *f*, igualdad *f*, regularidad *f*

event [ɪˈvɛnt] *n* **1** : acontecimiento *m*, suceso *m*, prueba *f* (en deportes) **2 in the event that** : en caso de que

eventful [ɪˈvɛntfəl] *adj* : lleno de incidentes, memorable

eventual [ɪˈvɛntʃuəl] *adj* : final, consiguiente

eventuality [ɪˌvɛntʃuˈæləti] *n, pl* **-ties** : eventualidad *f*

eventually [ɪˈvɛntʃuəli] *adv* : al fin, con el tiempo, algún día

ever ['ɛvər] *adv* **1** ALWAYS : siempre ⟨as ever : como siempre⟩ ⟨ever since : desde entonces⟩ **2** (*in questions*) : alguna vez, algún día ⟨have you ever been to Mexico? : ¿has estado en México alguna vez?⟩ **3** (*in negative constructions*) : nunca ⟨doesn't he ever work? : ¿es que nunca trabaja?⟩ ⟨nobody ever helps me : nadie nunca me ayuda⟩ **4** (*in comparisons*) : nunca ⟨better than ever : mejor que nunca⟩ **5** (*as intensifier*) ⟨I'm ever so happy! : ¡estoy tan y tan feliz!⟩ ⟨he looks ever so angry : parece estar muy enojado⟩

evergreen¹ ['ɛvər,gri:n] *adj* : de hoja perenne

evergreen² *n* : planta *f* de hoja perenne

everlasting [,ɛvər'læstɪŋ] *adj* : eterno, perpetuo, imperecedero

evermore [,ɛvər'mor] *adv* : eternamente

every ['ɛvri] *adj* **1** EACH : cada ⟨every time : cada vez⟩ ⟨every other house : cada dos casas⟩ **2** ALL : todo ⟨every month : todos los meses⟩ ⟨every woman : toda mujer, todas las mujeres⟩ **3** COMPLETE : pleno, entero ⟨to have every confidence : tener plena confianza⟩

everybody ['ɛvri,bɑdi, -,bʌ-] *pron* : todos *mpl*, -das *fpl*; todo el mundo

everyday [,ɛvri'deɪ, 'ɛvri,-] *adj* : cotidiano, diario, corriente ⟨everyday clothes : ropa de todos los días⟩

everyone ['ɛvri,wʌn] → everybody

everything ['ɛvri,θɪŋ] *pron* : todo

everywhere ['ɛvri,ʍwer] *adv* : en todas partes, por todas partes, dondequiera ⟨I looked everywhere : busqué en todas partes⟩ ⟨everywhere we go : dondequiera que vayamos⟩

evict [ɪ'vɪkt] *vt* : desalojar, desahuciar

eviction [ɪ'vɪkʃən] *n* : desalojo *m*, desahucio *m*

evidence ['ɛvədənts] *n* **1** INDICATION : indicio *m*, señal *m* ⟨to be in evidence : estar a la vista⟩ **2** PROOF : evidencia *f*, prueba *f* **3** TESTIMONY : testimonio *m*, declaración *f* ⟨to give evidence : declarar como testigo, prestar declaración⟩

evident ['ɛvidənt] *adj* : evidente, patente, manifiesto

evidently ['ɛvidəntli, ,ɛvi'dɛntli] *adv* **1** CLEARLY : claramente, obviamente **2** APPARENTLY : aparentemente, evidentemente, al parecer

evil¹ ['i:vəl, -,vɪl] *adj* **eviler** *or* **eviller**; **evilest** *or* **evillest 1** WICKED : malvado, malo, maligno **2** HARMFUL : nocivo, dañino, pernicioso **3** UNPLEASANT : desagradable ⟨an evil odor : un olor horrible⟩

evil² *n* **1** WICKEDNESS : mal *m*, maldad *f* **2** MISFORTUNE : desgracia *f*, mal *m*

evildoer [,i:vəl'du:ər, 'i:vil-] *n* : malvado *m*, -da *f*

evince [ɪ'vɪnts] *vt* **evinced; evincing** : mostrar, manifestar, revelar

eviscerate [ɪ'vɪsə,reɪt] *vt* **-ated; -ating** : eviscerar, destripar (un pollo, etc.)

evocation [,i:vo'keɪʃən, ,ɛ-] *n* : evocación *f*

evocative [i'vɑkətɪv] *adj* : evocador

evoke [i'vo:k] *vt* **evoked; evoking** : evocar, provocar

evolution [,ɛvə'lu:ʃən, ,i:-] *n* : evolución *f*, desarrollo *m*

evolutionary [,ɛvə'lu:ʃə,nɛri, ,i:-] *adj* : evolutivo

evolve [i'vɑlv] *vi* **evolved; evolving** : evolucionar, desarrollarse

ewe ['ju:] *n* : oveja *f*

exacerbate [ɪg'zæsər,beɪt] *vt* **-bated; -bating** : exacerbar

exact¹ [ɪg'zækt, ɛ-] *vt* : exigir, imponer, arrancar

exact² *adj* : exacto, preciso — **exactly** *adv*

exacting [ɪ'zæktɪŋ, ɛg-] *adj* : exigente, riguroso

exactitude [ɪg'zæktə,tu:d, ɛg-, -,tju:d] *n* : exactitud *f*, precisión *f*

exaggerate [ɪg'zædʒə,reɪt, ɛg-] *v* **-ated; -ating** : exagerar

exaggerated [ɪg'zædʒə,reɪtəd, ɛg-] : exagerado — **exaggeratedly** *adv*

exaggeration [ɪg,zædʒə'reɪʃən, ɛg-] *n* : exageración *f*

exalt [ɪg'zɔlt, ɛg-] *vt* : exaltar, ensalzar, glorificar

exaltation [,ɛg,zɔl'teɪʃən, ,ɛk,sɔl-] *n* : exaltación *f*

exam [ɪg'zæm, ɛg-] → examination

examination [ɪg,zæmə'neɪʃən, ɛg-] *n* **1** TEST : examen *m* **2** INSPECTION : inspección *f*, revisión *f* **3** INVESTIGATION : examen *m*, estudio *m*

examine [ɪg'zæmən, ɛg-] *vt* **-ined; -ining 1** TEST : examinar **2** INSPECT : inspeccionar, revisar **3** STUDY : examinar

example [ɪg'zæmpəl, ɛg-] *n* : ejemplo *m* ⟨for example : por ejemplo⟩ ⟨to set an example : dar ejemplo⟩

exasperate [ɪg'zæspə,reɪt, ɛg-] *vt* **-ated; -ating** : exasperar, sacar de quicio

exasperation [ɪg,zæspə'reɪʃən, ɛg-] *n* : exasperación *f*

excavate ['ɛkskə,veɪt] *vt* **-vated; -vating** : excavar

excavation [,ɛkskə'veɪʃən] *n* : excavación *f*

exceed [ɪk'si:d, ɛk-] *vt* **1** SURPASS : ceder, rebasar, sobrepasar **2** : exceder de, sobrepasar ⟨not exceeding two months : que no exceda de dos meses⟩

exceedingly [ɪk'si:dɪŋli, ɛk-] *adv* : extremadamente, sumamente

excel [ɪk'sɛl, ɛk-] *v* **-celled; -celling** *vi* : sobresalir, descollar, lucirse — *vt* : superar

excellence ['ɛksələnts] *n* : excelencia *f*

excellency ['ɛksələntsi] *n, pl* **-cies** : excelencia *f* ⟨His Excellency : Su Excelencia⟩

excellent ['ɛksələnt] *adj* : excelente, sobresaliente — **excellently** *adv*

except[1] [ɪkˈsɛpt] *vt* : exceptuar, excluir

except[2] *conj* : pero, si no fuera por

except[3] *prep* : excepto, menos, salvo ⟨everyone except Carlos : todos menos Carlos⟩

exception [ɪkˈsɛpʃən] *n* **1** : excepción *f* **2 to take exception to** : ofenderse por, objetar a

exceptional [ɪkˈsɛpʃənəl] *adj* : excepcional, extraordinario — **exceptionally** *adv*

excerpt[1] [ɛkˈsərpt, ɛgˈzərpt, ˈɛk-, ˈg-] *vt* : escoger, seleccionar

excerpt[2] [ˈɛkˌsərpt, ˈɛgˌzərpt] *n* : pasaje *m*, selección *f*

excess[1] [ˈɛkˌsɛs, ɪkˈsɛs] *adj* **1** : excesivo, de sobra ⟨excess baggage : exceso *m* de equipaje⟩

excess[2] [ɪkˈsɛs, ˈɛkˌsɛs] *n* **1** SUPERFLUITY : exceso *m*, superfluidad *f* ⟨an excess of energy : un exceso de energía⟩ **2** SURPLUS : excedente *m*, sobrante *m* ⟨in excess of : superior a⟩

excessive [ɪkˈsɛsɪv, ɛk-] *adj* : excesivo, exagerado, desmesurado — **excessively** *adv*

exchange[1] [ɪksˈtʃeɪndʒ, ɛks-; ˈɛksˌtʃeɪndʒ] *vt* **-changed; -changing** : cambiar, intercambiar, canjear

exchange[2] *n* **1** : cambio *m*, intercambio *m*, canje *m* **2 stock exchange** : bolsa *f* (de valores)

exchangeable [ɪksˈtʃeɪndʒəbəl, ɛks-] *adj* : canjeable

excise[1] [ˈɛkˌsaɪz, ɛk-] *vt* **-cised; -cising** : extirpar

excise[2] [ˈɛkˌsaɪz] *n* **excise tax** : impuesto *m* interno, impuesto *m* sobre el consumo

excision [ɪkˈsɪʒən, ɛk-] *n* : extirpación *f*, excisión *f*

excitability [ɪkˌsaɪtəˈbɪləti, ɛk-] *n* : excitabilidad *f*

excitable [ɪkˈsaɪtəbəl, ɛk-] *adj* : excitable

excitation [ˌɛkˌsaɪˈteɪʃən] *n* : excitación *f*

excite [ɪkˈsaɪt] *vt* **-cited; -citing 1** AROUSE, STIMULATE : excitar, mover, estimular **2** ANIMATE : entusiasmar, animar **3** EVOKE, PROVOKE : provocar, despertar, suscitar ⟨to excite curiosity : despertar la curiosidad⟩

excited [ɪkˈsaɪtəd, ɛk-] *adj* **1** STIMULATED : excitado, estimulado **2** ENTHUSIASTIC : entusiasmado, emocionado

excitedly [ɪkˈsaɪtədli, ɛk-] *adv* : con excitación, con entusiasmo

excitement [ɪkˈsaɪtmənt, ɛk-] *n* **1** ENTHUSIASM : entusiasmo *m*, emoción *f* **2** AGITATION : agitación *f*, alboroto *m*, conmoción *f* **3** AROUSAL : excitación *f*

exciting [ɪkˈsaɪtɪŋ, ɛk-] *adj* **1** : emocionante **2** AROUSING : excitante

exclaim [ɪksˈkleɪm, ɛks-] *v* : exclamar

exclamation [ˌɛkskləˈmeɪʃən] *n* : exclamación *f*

exclamation point *n* : signo *m* de admiración

exclamatory [ɪksˈklæməˌtori, ɛks-] *adj* : exclamativo

exclude [ɪksˈkluːd, ɛks-] *vt* **-cluded; -cluding 1** BAR : excluir, descartar, no admitir **2** EXPEL : expeler, expulsar

exclusion [ɪksˈkluːʒən, ɛks-] *n* : exclusión *f*

exclusive[1] [ɪksˈkluːsɪv, ɛks-] *adj* **1** SOLE : exclusivo, único **2** SELECT : exclusivo, selecto

exclusive[2] *n* : exclusiva *f*

exclusively [ɪksˈkluːsɪvli, ɛks-] *adv* : exclusivamente, únicamente

exclusiveness [ɪksˈkluːsɪvnəs, ɛks-] *n* : exclusividad *f*

excommunicate [ˌɛkskəˈmjuːnəˌkeɪt] *vt* **-cated; -cating** : excomulgar

excommunication [ˌɛkskəˌmjuːnəˈkeɪʃən] *n* : excomunión *f*

excrement [ˈɛkskrəmənt] *n* : excremento *m*

excrete [ɪkˈskriːt, ɛk-] *vt* **-creted; -creting** : excretar

excretion [ɪkˈskriːʃən, ɛk-] *n* : excreción *f*

excruciating [ɪkˈskruːʃiˌeɪtɪŋ, ɛk-] *adj* : insoportable, atroz, terrible — **excruciatingly** *adv*

exculpate [ˈɛkskəlˌpeɪt] *vt* **-pated; -pating** : exculpar

excursion [ɪkˈskərʒən, ɛk-] *n* **1** OUTING : excursión *f*, paseo *m* **2** DIGRESSION : digresión *f*

excuse[1] [ɪkˈskjuːz, ɛk-] *vt* **-cused; -cusing 1** PARDON : disculpar, perdonar ⟨excuse me : con permiso, perdóneme, perdón⟩ **2** EXEMPT : eximir, disculpar **3** JUSTIFY : excusar, justificar

excuse[2] [ɪkˈskjuːs, ɛk-] *n* **1** JUSTIFICATION : excusa *f*, justificación *f* **2** PRETEXT : pretexto *m* **3 to make one's excuses to someone** : pedirle disculpas a alguien

execute [ˈɛksɪˌkjuːt] *vt* **-cuted; -cuting 1** CARRY OUT : ejecutar, llevar a cabo, desempeñar **2** ENFORCE : ejecutar, cumplir (un testamento, etc.) **3** KILL : ejecutar, ajusticiar

execution [ˌɛksɪˈkjuːʃən] *n* **1** PERFORMANCE : ejecución *f*, desempeño *m* **2** IMPLEMENTATION : cumplimiento *m* **3** : ejecución *f* (por un delito)

executioner [ˌɛksɪˈkjuːʃənər] *n* : verdugo *m*

executive[1] [ɪgˈzɛkjətɪv, ɛg-] *adj* : ejecutivo

executive[2] *n* : ejecutivo *m*, -va *f*

executor [ɪgˈzɛkjətər, ɛg-] *n* : albacea *m*, testamentario *m*

executrix [ɪgˈzɛkjəˌtrɪks, ɛg-] *n, pl* **executrices** [-ˌzɛkjəˈtraɪˌsiːz] *or* **executrixes** [-ˈzɛkjəˌtrɪksəz] : albacea *f*, testamentaria *f*

exemplary [ɪgˈzɛmpləri, ɛg-] *adj* : ejemplar

exemplify [ɪgˈzɛmpləˌfaɪ, ɛg-] *vt* **-fied; -fying** : ejemplificar, ilustrar, demostrar

exempt[1] [ɪg'zɛmpt, ɛg-] vt : eximir, dispensar, exonerar

exempt[2] adj : exento, eximido

exemption [ɪg'zɛmpʃən, ɛg-] n : exención f

exercise[1] ['ɛksər,saɪz] v -cised; -cising vt 1 : ejercitar (el cuerpo) 2 USE : ejercer, hacer uso de — vi : hacer ejercicio

exercise[2] n 1 : ejercicio m 2 **exercises** npl WORKOUT : ejercicios mpl físicos 3 **exercises** npl CEREMONY : ceremonia f

exert [ɪg'zərt, ɛg-] vt 1 : ejercer, emplear 2 **to exert oneself** : esforzarse

exertion [ɪg'zərʃən, ɛg-] n 1 USE : ejercicio m (de autoridad, etc.), uso m (de fuerza, etc.) 2 EFFORT : esfuerzo m, empeño m

exhalation [,ɛksə'leɪʃən, ,ɛkshə-] n : exhalación f, espiración f

exhale [ɛks'heɪl] v -haled; -haling vt 1 : exhalar, espirar 2 EMIT : exhalar, despedir, emitir — vi : espirar

exhaust[1] [ɪg'zɔst, ɛg-] vt 1 DEPLETE : agotar 2 TIRE : cansar, fatigar, agotar 3 EMPTY : vaciar

exhaust[2] n 1 **exhaust fumes** : gases mpl de escape 2 **exhaust pipe** : tubo m de escape 3 **exhaust system** : sistema m de escape

exhausted [ɪg'zɔstəd, ɛg-] adj : agotado, derrengado

exhausting [ɪg'zɔstɪŋ, ɛg-] adj : extenuante, agotador

exhaustion [ɪg'zɔstʃən, ɛg-] n : agotamiento m

exhaustive [ɪg'zɔstɪv, ɛg-] adj : exhaustivo

exhibit[1] [ɪg'zɪbət, ɛg-] vt 1 DISPLAY : exhibir, exponer 2 PRODUCE, SHOW : mostrar, presentar

exhibit[2] n 1 OBJECT : objeto m expuesto 2 EXHIBITION : exposición f, exhibición f 3 EVIDENCE : prueba f instrumental

exhibition [,ɛksə'bɪʃən] n 1 : exposición f, exhibición f 2 **to make an exhibition of oneself** : dar el espectáculo, hacer el ridículo

exhibitor [ɪg'zɪbətər] n : expositor m, -tora f

exhilarate [ɪg'zɪlə,reɪt, ɛg-] vt -rated; -rating : alegrar, levantar el ánimo de

exhilaration [ɪg,zɪlə'reɪʃən, ɛg-] n : alegría f, regocijo m, júbilo m

exhort [ɪg'zɔrt, ɛg-] vt : exhortar

exhortation [,ɛk,sɔr'teɪʃən, -sər-; ,ɛg-,zɔr-] n : exhortación f

exhumation [,ɛksju'meɪʃən, -hju-; ,ɛgzu-, -zju-] n : exhumación f

exhume [ɪg'zu:m, -'zju:m; ɪks'ju:m, -'hju:m] vt -humed; -huming : exhumar, desenterrar

exigencies ['ɛksɪʤən,siz, ɪg'zɪʤən,si:z] npl : exigencias fpl

exile[1] ['ɛg,zaɪl, 'ɛk,saɪl] vt exiled; exiling : exiliar, desterrar

exile[2] n 1 BANISHMENT : exilio m, destierro m 2 OUTCAST : exiliado m, -da f; desterrado m, -da f

exist [ɪg'zɪst, ɛg-] vi 1 BE : existir 2 LIVE : subsistir, vivir

existence [ɪg'zɪstənts, ɛg-] n : existencia f

existent [ɪg'zɪstənt, ɛg-] adj : existente

existing [ɪg'zɪstɪŋ, ɛg-] adj : existente

exit[1] ['ɛgzət, 'ɛksət] vi : salir, hacer mutis (en el teatro) — vt : salir de

exit[2] n 1 DEPARTURE : salida f, partida f 2 EGRESS : salida f ⟨emergency exit : salida de emergencia⟩

exodus ['ɛksədəs] n : éxodo m

exonerate [ɪg'zɑnə,reɪt, ɛg-] vt -ated; -ating : exonerar, disculpar, absolver

exoneration [ɪg,zɑnə'reɪʃən, ɛg-] n : exoneración f

exorbitant [ɪg'zɔrbətənt, ɛg-] adj : exorbitante, excesivo

exorcise ['ɛk,sɔr,saɪz, -sər-] vt -cised; -cising : exorcizar

exorcism ['ɛksɔr,sɪzəm] n : exorcismo m

exotic[1] [ɪg'zɑtɪk, ɛg-] adj : exótico — **exotically** [-ɪkli] adv

exotic[2] n : planta f exótica

expand [ɪk'spænd, ɛk-] vt 1 ENLARGE : expandir, dilatar, aumentar, ampliar 2 EXTEND : extender — vi 1 ENLARGE : ampliarse, extenderse 2 : expandirse, dilatarse (dícese de los metales, gases, etc.)

expanse [ɪk'spænts, ɛk-] n : extensión f

expansion [ɪk'spænʃən, ɛk-] n 1 ENLARGEMENT : expansión f, ampliación f 2 EXPANSE : extensión f

expansive [ɪk'spæntsɪv, ɛk-] adj 1 : expansivo 2 OUTGOING : expansivo, comunicativo 3 AMPLE : ancho, amplio — **expansiveness** adv

expansiveness [ɪk'spæntsɪvnəs, ɛk-] n : expansibilidad f

expatriate[1] [ɛks'peɪtri,eɪt] vt -ated; -ating : expatriar

expatriate[2] [ɛks'peɪtriət, -,eɪt] adj : expatriado

expatriate[3] [ɛks'peɪtriət, -,eɪt] n : expatriado m, -da f

expect [ɪk'spkt, ɛk-] vt 1 SUPPOSE : suponer, imaginarse 2 ANTICIPATE : esperar 3 COUNT ON, REQUIRE : contar con, esperar — vi **to be expecting** : estar embarazada

expectancy [ɪk'spɛktəntsi, ɛk-] n, pl -cies : expectativa f, esperanza f

expectant [ɪk'spɛktənt, ɛk-] adj 1 ANTICIPATING : expectante 2 EXPECTING : futuro ⟨expectant mother : futura madre⟩

expectantly [ɪk'spɛktəntli, ɛk-] adv : con expectación

expectation [,ɛk,spɛk'teɪʃən] n 1 ANTICIPATION : expectación f 2 EXPECTANCY : expectativa f

expedient[1] [ɪk'spi:diənt, ɛk-] adj : conveniente, oportuno

expedient[2] n : expediente m, recurso m

expédite [ˈɛkspəˌdaɪt] *vt* **-dited; -diting** **1** FACILITATE : facilitar, dar curso a **2** HASTEN : acelerar

expedition [ˌɛkspəˈdɪʃən] *n* : expedición *f*

expeditious [ˌɛkspəˈdɪʃəs] *adj* : pronto, rápido

expel [ɪkˈspɛl, ɛk-] *vt* **-pelled; -pelling** : expulsar, expeler

expend [ɪkˈspɛnd, ɛk-] *vt* **1** DISBURSE : gastar, desembolsar **2** CONSUME : consumir, agotar

expendable [ɪkˈspɛndəbəl, ɛk-] *adj* : prescindible

expenditure [ɪkˈspɛndɪtʃər, ɛk-, -ˌtʃur] *n* : gasto *m*

expense [ɪkˈspɛns, ɛk-] *n* **1** COST : gasto *m* **2** **expenses** *npl* : gastos *mpl*, expensas *fpl* **3 at the expense of** : a expensas de

expensive [ɪkˈspɛnsɪv, ɛk-] *adj* : costoso, caro — **expensively** *adv*

experience[1] [ɪkˈspɪriənts, ɛk-] *vt* **-enced; -encing** : experimentar (sentimientos), tener (dificultades), sufrir (una pérdida)

experience[2] *n* : experiencia *f*

experienced [ɪkˈspɪriəntst, ɛk-] *adj* : con experiencia, experimentado

experiment[1] [ɪkˈspɛrəmənt, ɛk-, -ˈspɪr-] *vi* : experimentar, hacer experimentos

experiment[2] *n* : experimento *m*

experimental [ɪkˌspɛrəˈmɛntəl, ɛk-, -ˌspɪr-] *adj* : experimental — **experimentally** *adv*

experimentation [ɪkˌspɛrəmənˈteɪʃən, ɛk-, -ˌspɪr-] *n* : experimentación *f*

expert[1] [ˈɛkˌspɔrt, ɛkˈspɔrt] *adj* : experto, de experto, pericial (dícese de un testigo) — **expertly** *adv*

expert[2] [ˈɛkˌspɔrt] *n* : experto *m*, -ta *f*; perito *m*, -ta *f*; especialista *mf*

expertise [ˌɛkspərˈtiːz] *n* : pericia *f*, competencia *f*

expiate [ˈɛkspiˌeɪt] *vt* **-ated; -ating** : expiar

expiation [ˌɛkspiˈeɪʃən] *n* : expiación *f*

expiration [ˌɛkspəˈreɪʃən] *n* **1** EXHALATION : exhalación *f*, espiración *f* **2** DEATH : muerte *f* **3** TERMINATION : vencimiento *m*, caducidad *f*

expire [ɪkˈspaɪr, ɛk-] *vi* **-pired; -piring** **1** EXHALE : espirar **2** DIE : expirar, morir **3** TERMINATE : caducar, vencer

explain [ɪkˈspleɪn, ɛk-] *vt* : explicar

explanation [ˌɛkspləˈneɪʃən] *n* : explicación *f*

explanatory [ɪkˈsplænəˌtori, ɛk-] *adj* : explicativo, aclaratorio

expletive [ˈɛksplətɪv] *n* : improperio *m*, palabrota *f* *fam*, grosería *f*

explicable [ɛkˈsplɪkəbəl, ˈɛkˌsplɪ-] *adj* : explicable

explicit [ɪkˈsplɪsət, ɛk-] *adj* : explícito, claro, categórico, rotundo — **explicitly** *adv*

explicitness [ɪkˈsplɪsətnəs, ɛk-] *n* : claridad *f*, carácter *m* explícito

explode [ɪkˈsploːd, ɛk-] *v* **-ploded; -ploding** *vt* **1** BURST : hacer explosionar, hacer explotar **2** REFUTE : rebatir, refutar, desmentir — *vi* **1** BURST : explotar, estallar, reventar **2** SKYROCKET : dispararse

exploit[1] [ɪkˈsplɔɪt, ɛk-] *vt* : explotar, aprovecharse de

exploit[2] [ˈɛkˌsplɔɪt] *n* : hazaña *f*, proeza *f*

exploitation [ˌɛkˌsplɔɪˈteɪʃən] *n* : explotación *f*

exploration [ˌɛkspləˈreɪʃən] *n* : exploración *f*

exploratory [ɪkˈsplɔrəˌtori, ɛk-] *adj* : exploratorio

explore [ɪkˈsplor, ɛk-] *vt* **-plored; -ploring** : explorar, investigar, examinar

explorer [ɪkˈsplɔrər, ɛk-] *n* : explorador *m*, -dora *f*

explosion [ɪkˈsploːʒən, ɛk-] *n* : explosión *f*, estallido *m*

explosive[1] [ɪkˈsploːsɪv, ɛk-] *adj* : explosivo, fulminante — **explosively** *adv*

explosive[2] *n* : explosivo *m*

exponent [ɪkˈspoːnənt, ˈɛkˌspoː-] *n* **1** : exponente *m* **2** ADVOCATE : defensor *m*, -sora *f*; partidario *m*, -ria *f*

exponential [ˌɛkspoˈnɛntʃəl] *adj* : exponencial — **exponentially** *adv*

export[1] [ɛkˈsport, ˈɛkˌsport] *vt* : exportar

export[2] [ˈɛkˌsport] *n* **1** : artículo *m* de exportación **2** → **exportation**

exportation [ˌɛkˌsporˈteɪʃən] *n* : exportación *f*

exporter [ɛkˈsportər, ˈɛkˌspor-] *n* : exportador *m*, -dora *f*

expose [ɪkˈspoːz, ɛk-] *vt* **-posed; -posing** **1** : exponer (al peligro, a los elementos, a una enfermedad) **2** : exponer (una película a la luz) **3** DISCLOSE : descubrir, revelar, poner en evidencia **4** UNMASK : desenmascarar

exposé *or* **expose** [ˌɛkspoˈzeɪ] *n* : exposición *f* (de hechos), revelación *f* (de un escándalo)

exposed [ɪkˈspoːzd, ɛk-] *adj* : descubierto, sin protección

exposition [ˌɛkspəˈzɪʃən] *n* : exposición *f*

exposure [ɪkˈspoːʒər, ɛk-] *n* **1** : exposición *f* **2** CONTACT : exposición *f*, experiencia *f*, contacto *m* **3** UNMASKING : desenmascaramiento *m* **4** ORIENTATION : orientación *f* ⟨a room with a northern exposure : una sala orientada al norte⟩

expound [ɪkˈspaʊnd, ɛk-] *vt* : exponer, explicar — *vi* : hacer comentarios detallados

express[1] [ɪkˈsprɛs, ɛk-] *vt* **1** SAY : expresar, comunicar **2** SHOW : expresar, manifestar, externar *Mex* **3** SQUEEZE : exprimir ⟨to express the juice from a lemon : exprimir el jugo de un limón⟩

express[2] *adv* : por correo exprés, por correo urgente

express³ *adj* **1** EXPLICIT : expreso, manifiesto **2** SPECIFIC : específico ⟨for that express purpose : con ese fin específico⟩ **3** RAPID : expreso, rápido

express⁴ *n* **1** : correo *m* exprés, correo *m* urgente **2** : expreso *m* (tren)

expression [ɪkˈsprɛʃən, ɛk-] *n* **1** UTTERANCE : expresión *f* ⟨freedom of expression : libertad de expresión⟩ **2** : presión *f* (en la matemática) **3** PHRASE : frase *f*, expresión *f* **4** LOOK : expresión *f*, cara *f*, gesto *m* ⟨with a sad expression : con un gesto de tristeza⟩

expressionless [ɪkˈsprɛʃənləs, ɛk-] *adj* : inexpresivo

expressive [ɪkˈsprɛsɪv, ɛk-] *adj* : expresivo

expressway [ɪkˈsprɛsˌweɪ, ɛk-] *n* : autopista *f*

expulsion [ɪkˈspʌlʃən, ɛk-] *n* : expulsión *f*

expurgate [ˈɛkspərˌɡeɪt] *vt* **-gated; -gating** : expurgar

exquisite [ɛkˈskwɪzət, ˈɛkˌskwɪ-] *adj* **1** FINE : exquisito, delicado, primoroso **2** INTENSE : intenso, extremo

extant [ˈɛkstənt, ɛkˈstænt] *adj* : existente

extemporaneous [ɛkˌstɛmpəˈreɪniəs] *adj* : improvisado — **extemporaneously** *adv*

extend [ɪkˈstɛnd, ɛk-] *vt* **1** STRETCH : extender, tender **2** PROLONG : prolongar, prorrogar **3** ENLARGE : agrandar, ampliar, aumentar **4** PROFFER : extender, dar, ofrecer — *vi* : extenderse

extended [ɪkˈstɛndəd, ɛk-] *adj* LENGTHY : prolongado, largo

extension [ɪkˈstɛnʃən, ɛk-] *n* **1** EXTENDING : extensión *f*, ampliación *f*, prórroga *f*, prolongación *f* **2** ANNEX : ampliación *f*, anexo *m* **3** : extensión *f* (de teléfono)

extensive [ɪkˈstɛnsɪv, ɛk-] *adj* : extenso, vasto, amplio — **extensively** *adv*

extent [ɪkˈstɛnt, ɛk-] *n* **1** SIZE : extensión *f*, magnitud *f* **2** DEGREE, SCOPE : alcance *m*, grado *m* ⟨to a certain extent : hasta cierto punto⟩

extenuate [ɪkˈstɛnjəˌweɪt, ɛk-] *vt* **-ated; -ating** : atenuar, aminorar, mitigar ⟨extenuating circumstances : circunstancias atenuantes⟩

extenuation [ɪkˌstɛnjəˈweɪʃən, ɛk-] *n* : atenuación *f*, aminoración *f*

exterior¹ [ɛkˈstɪriər] *adj* : exterior

exterior² *n* : exterior *m*

exterminate [ɪkˈstərməˌneɪt, ɛk-] *vt* **-nated; -nating** : exterminar

extermination [ɪkˌstərməˈneɪʃən, ɛk-] *n* : exterminación *f*, exterminio *m*

exterminator [ɪkˈstərməˌneɪtər, ɛk-] *n* : exterminador *m*, -dora *f*

external [ɪkˈstərnəl, ɛk-] *adj* : externo, exterior — **externally** *adv*

extinct [ɪkˈstɪŋkt, ɛk-] *adj* : extinto

extinction [ɪkˈstɪŋkʃən, ɛk-] *n* : extinción *f*

extinguish [ɪkˈstɪŋwɪʃ, ɛk-] *vt* : extinguir, apagar

extinguisher [ɪkˈstɪŋwɪʃər, ɛk-] *n* : extinguidor *m*, extintor *m*

extirpate [ˈɛkstərˌpeɪt] *vt* **-pated; -pating** : extirpar, exterminar

extol [ɪkˈstoːl, ɛk-] *vt* **-tolled; -tolling** : exaltar, ensalzar, alabar

extort [ɪkˈstort, ɛk-] *vt* : extorsionar

extortion [ɪkˈstorʃən, ɛk-] *n* : extorsión *f*

extra¹ [ˈɛkstrə] *adv* : extra, más, extremadamente, super ⟨extra special : super especial⟩

extra² *adj* **1** ADDITIONAL : adicional, suplementario, de más **2** SUPERIOR : superior

extra³ *n* : extra *m*

extract¹ [ɪkˈstrækt, ɛk-] *vt* : extraer, sacar

extract² [ˈɛkˌstrækt] *n* **1** EXCERPT : pasaje *m*, selección *f*, trozo *m* **2** : extracto *m* ⟨vanilla extract : extracto de vainilla⟩

extraction [ɪkˈstrækʃən, ɛk-] *n* : extracción *f*

extractor [ɪkˈstræktər, ɛk-] *n* : extractor *m*

extracurricular [ˌɛkstrəkəˈrɪkjələr] *adj* : extracurricular

extradite [ˈɛkstrəˌdaɪt] *vt* **-dited; -diting** : extraditar

extradition [ˌɛkstrəˈdɪʃən] *n* : extradición *f*

extramarital [ˌɛkstrəˈmærətəl] *adj* : extramatrimonial

extraneous [ɛkˈstreɪniəs] *adj* **1** OUTSIDE : extrínseco, externo **2** SUPERFLUOUS : superfluo, ajeno — **extraneously** *adv*

extraordinary [ɪkˈstrordən̩ˌɛri, ˌɛkstrəˈord-] *adj* : extraordinario, excepcional — **extraordinarily** [ɪkˌstrordən̩ˈɛrəli, ˌɛkstrəˌord-] *adv*

extrasensory [ˌɛkstrəˈsɛntsəri] *adj* : extrasensorial

extraterrestrial¹ [ˌɛkstrətəˈrɛstriəl] *adj* : extraterrestre

extraterrestrial² *n* : extraterrestre *mf*

extravagance [ɪkˈstrævɪɡənts, ɛk-] *n* **1** EXCESS : exceso *m*, extravagancia *f* **2** WASTEFULNESS : derroche *m*, despilfarro *m* **3** LUXURY : lujo *m*

extravagant [ɪkˈstrævɪɡənt, ɛk-] *adj* **1** EXCESSIVE : excesivo, extravagante **2** WASTEFUL : despilfarrador, derrochador, gastador **3** EXORBITANT : costoso, exorbitante

extravagantly [ɪkˈstrævɪɡəntli, ɛk-] *adv* **1** LAVISHLY : a lo grande **2** EXCESSIVELY : exageradamente, desmesuradamente

extravaganza [ɪkˌstrævəˈɡænzə, ɛk-] *n* : gran espectáculo *m*

extreme¹ [ɪkˈstriːm, ɛk-] *adj* **1** UTMOST : extremo, sumo ⟨of extreme importance : de suma importancia⟩ **2** INTENSE : intenso, extremado ⟨extreme cold : frío extremado⟩ **3** EXCESSIVE : excesivo, extremo ⟨extreme views : opiniones extremas⟩ ⟨extreme measures : medidas excepcionales, medidas drásticas⟩ **4** OUTERMOST : extremo ⟨the extreme north : el norte extremo⟩

extreme² *n* **1** : extremo *m* **2 in the extreme** : en extremo, en sumo grado

extremely [ɪk'stri:mli, ɛk-] *adv* : sumamente, extremadamente, terriblemente

extremist [ɪk'stri:mɪst, ɛk-] *n* : extremista *mf* — **extremist** *adj*

extremity [ɪk'strɛməti, ɛk-] *n, pl* **-ties 1** EXTREME : extremo *m* **2 extremities** *npl* LIMBS : extremidades *fpl*

extricate ['ɛkstrə,keɪt] *vt* **-cated; -cating** : librar, sacar

extrinsic [ɪk'strɪnzɪk, -'strɪntsɪk] *adj* : extrínseco

extrovert ['ɛkstrə,vərt] *n* : extrovertido *m*, -da *f*

extroverted ['ɛkstrə,vərtəd] *adj* : extrovertido

extrude [ɪk'stru:d, ɛk-] *vt* **-truded; -truding** : extrudir, expulsar

exuberance [ɪg'zu:bərənts, ɛg-] *n* **1** JOYOUSNESS : euforia *f*, exaltación *f* **2** VIGOR : exuberancia *f*, vigor *m*

exuberant [ɪg'zu:bərənt, ɛg-] *adj* **1** JOYOUS : eufórico **2** LUSH : exuberante — **exuberantly** *adv*

exude [ɪg'zu:d, ɛg-] *vt* **-uded; -uding 1** OOZE : rezumar, exudar **2** EMANATE : emanar, irradiar

exult [ɪg'zʌlt, ɛg-] *vi* : exultar, regocijarse

exultant [ɪg'zʌltənt, ɛg-] *adj* : exultante, jubiloso — **exultantly** *adv*

exultation [,ɛksəl'teɪʃən, ,ɛgzəl-] *n* : exultación *f*, júbilo *m*, alborozo *m*

eye¹ ['aɪ] *vt* **eyed; eyeing** *or* **eying** : mirar, observar

eye² *n* **1** : ojo *m* **2** VISION : visión *f*, vista *f*, ojo *m* ⟨a good eye for bargains : un buen ojo para las gangas⟩ **3** GLANCE : mirada *f*, ojeada *f* **4** ATTENTION : atención *f* ⟨to catch one's eye : llamar la atención⟩ **5** POINT OF VIEW : punto *m* de vista ⟨in the eyes of the law : según la ley⟩ **6** : ojo *m* (de una aguja, una papa, una tormenta)

eyeball ['aɪ,bɔl] *n* : globo *m* ocular

eyebrow ['aɪ,braʊ] *n* : ceja *f*

eyedropper ['aɪ,drɑpər] *n* : cuentagotas *f*

eyeglasses ['aɪ,glæsəz] *npl* : anteojos *mpl*, lentes *mpl*, espejuelos *mpl*, gafas *fpl*

eyelash ['aɪ,læʃ] *n* : pestaña *f*

eyelet ['aɪlət] *n* : ojete *m*

eyelid ['aɪ,lɪd] *n* : párpado *m*

eye-opener ['aɪ,o:pənər] *n* : revelación *f*, sorpresa *f*

eye-opening ['aɪ,o:pənɪŋ] *adj* : revelador

eyepiece ['aɪ,pi:s] *n* : ocular *m*

eyesight ['aɪ,saɪt] *n* : vista *f*, visión *f*

eyesore ['aɪ,sor] *n* : monstruosidad *f*, adefesio *m*

eyestrain ['aɪ,streɪn] *n* : fatiga *f* visual, vista *f* cansada

eyetooth ['aɪ,tu:θ] *n* : colmillo *m*

eyewitness ['aɪ'wɪtnəs] *n* : testigo *mf* ocular, testigo *mf* presencial

eyrie ['aɪri] → **aerie**

F

f ['ɛf] *n, pl* **f's** *or* **fs** ['ɛfs] : sexta letra del alfabeto inglés

fable ['feɪbəl] *n* : fábula *f*

fabled ['feɪbəld] *adj* : legendario, fabuloso

fabric ['fæbrɪk] *n* **1** MATERIAL : tela *f*, tejido *m* **2** STRUCTURE : estructura *f* ⟨the fabric of society : la estructura de la sociedad⟩

fabricate ['fæbrɪ,keɪt] *vt* **-cated; -cating 1** CONSTRUCT, MANUFACTURE : construir, fabricar **2** INVENT : inventar (excusas o mentiras)

fabrication [,fæbrɪ'keɪʃən] *n* **1** LIE : mentira *f*, invención *f* **2** MANUFACTURE : fabricación *f*

fabulous ['fæbjələs] *adj* **1** LEGENDARY : fabuloso, legendario **2** INCREDIBLE : increíble, fabuloso ⟨fabulous wealth : riqueza fabulosa⟩ **3** WONDERFUL : magnífico, estupendo, fabuloso — **fabulously** *adv*

facade ['fə'sɑd] *n* : fachada *f*

face¹ ['feɪs] *v* **faced; facing** *vt* **1** LINE : recubrir (una superficie), forrar (ropa) **2** CONFRONT : enfrentarse a, afrontar, hacer frente a ⟨to face the

music : afrontar las consecuencias⟩ ⟨to face the facts : aceptar la realidad⟩ **3** : estar de cara a, estar enfrente de ⟨she's facing her brother : está de cara a su hermano⟩ **4** OVERLOOK : dar a — *vi* : mirar (hacia), estar orientado (a)

face² *n* **1** : cara *f*, rostro *m* ⟨he told me to my face : me lo dijo a la cara⟩ **2** EXPRESSION : cara *f*, expresión *f* ⟨to pull a long face : poner mala cara⟩ **3** GRIMACE : mueca *f* ⟨to make faces : hacer muecas⟩ **4** APPEARANCE : fisonomía *f*, aspecto *m* ⟨the face of society : la fisonomía de la sociedad⟩ **5** EFFRONTERY : desfachatez *f* **6** PRESTIGE : prestigio *m* ⟨to lose face : desprestigiarse⟩ **7** FRONT, SIDE : cara *f* (de una moneda), esfera *f* (de un reloj), fachada *f* (de un edificio), pared *f* (de una montaña) **8** SURFACE : superficie *f*, faz *f* (de la tierra), cara *f* (de la luna) **9 in the face of** DESPITE : en medio de, en visto de, ante

facedown ['feɪs,daʊn] *adv* : boca abajo

faceless ['feɪsləs] *adj* ANONYMOUS : anónimo

face–lift ['feɪs,lɪft] *n* **1** : estiramiento *m*

facial 2 RENOVATION : renovación f, remozamiento m

facet ['fæsət] n 1 : faceta f (de una piedra) 2 ASPECT : faceta f, aspecto m

facetious [fə'si:ʃəs] adj : gracioso, burlón, bromista

facetiously [fə'si:ʃəsli] adv : en tono de burla

facetiousness [fə'si:ʃəsnəs] n : jocosidad f

face-to-face adv & adj : cara a cara

faceup ['feɪs'ʌp] adv : boca arriba

face value n : valor m nominal

facial[1] ['feɪʃəl] adj : de la cara, facial

facial[2] n : tratamiento m facial, limpieza f de cutis

facile ['fæsəl] adj SUPERFICIAL : superficial, simplista

facilitate [fə'sɪlə,teɪt] vt **-tated; -tating** : facilitar

facility [fə'sɪləti] n, pl **-ties** 1 EASE : facilidad f 2 CENTER, COMPLEX : centro m, complejo m 3 **facilities** npl AMENITIES : comodidades fpl, servicios mpl

facing ['feɪsɪŋ] n 1 LINING : entretela f (de una prenda) 2 : revestimiento m (de un edificio)

facsimile [fæk'sɪməli] n : facsímile m, facsímil m

fact ['fækt] n 1 : hecho m ⟨as a matter of fact : de hecho⟩ 2 INFORMATION : información f, datos mpl ⟨facts and figures : datos y cifras⟩ 3 REALITY : realidad f ⟨in fact : en realidad⟩

faction ['fækʃən] n : facción m, bando m

factional ['fækʃənəl] adj : entre facciones

factious ['fækʃəs] adj : faccioso, contencioso

factitious [fæk'tɪʃəs] adj : artificial, facticio

factor ['fæktər] n : factor m

factory ['fæktəri] n, pl **-ries** : fábrica f

factual ['fæktʃuəl] adj : basado en hechos, objetivo

factually ['fæktʃuəli] adv : en cuanto a los hechos

faculty ['fækəlti] n, pl **-ties** 1 : facultad f ⟨the faculty of sight : las facultades visuales, el sentido de la vista⟩ 2 APTITUDE : aptitud f, facilidad f 3 TEACHERS : cuerpo m docente

fad ['fæd] n : moda f pasajera, manía f

fade ['feɪd] v **faded; fading** vi 1 WITHER : debilitarse (dícese de las personas), marchitarse (dícese de las flores y las plantas) 2 DISCOLOR : desteñirse, decolorarse 3 DIM : apagarse (dícese de la luz), perderse (dícese de los sonidos), fundirse (dícese de las imágenes) 4 VANISH : desvanecerse, decaer — vt DISCOLOR : desteñir

fag ['fæg] vt **fagged; fagging** EXHAUST : cansar, fatigar

fagot or **faggot** ['fægət] n : haz m de leña

Fahrenheit ['færən,haɪt] adj : Fahrenheit

fail[1] ['feɪl] vi 1 WEAKEN : fallar, deteriorarse 2 STOP : fallar, detenerse ⟨his heart failed : le falló el corazón⟩ 3 : fracasar, fallar ⟨her plan failed : su plan fracasó⟩ ⟨the crops failed : se perdió la cosecha⟩ 4 : quebrar ⟨a business about to fail : una empresa a punto de quebrar⟩ 5 **to fail in** : faltar a, no cumplir con ⟨to fail in one's duties : faltar a sus deberes⟩ — vt 1 FLUNK : reprobar (un examen) 2 : fallar ⟨words fail me : las palabras me fallan, no encuentro palabras⟩ 3 DISAPPOINT : fallar, decepcionar ⟨don't fail me! : ¡no me falles!⟩

fail[2] n : fracaso m

failing ['feɪlɪŋ] n : defecto m

failure ['feɪljər] n 1 : fracaso m, malogro m ⟨crop failure : pérdida de la cosecha⟩ ⟨heart failure : insuficiencia cardíaca⟩ ⟨engine failure : falla mecánica⟩ 2 BANKRUPTCY : bancarrota f, quiebra f 3 : fracaso m (persona) ⟨he was a failure as a manager : como gerente, fue un fracaso⟩

faint[1] ['feɪnt] vi : desmayarse

faint[2] adj 1 COWARDLY, TIMID : cobarde, tímido 2 DIZZY : mareado ⟨faint with hunger : desfallecido de hambre⟩ 3 SLIGHT : leve, ligero, vago ⟨I haven't the faintest idea : no tengo la más mínima idea⟩ 4 INDISTINCT : tenue, indistinto, apenas perceptible

faint[3] n : desmayo m

fainthearted ['feɪnt'hɑrtəd] adj : cobarde, pusilánime

faintly ['feɪntli] adv : débilmente, ligeramente, levemente

faintness ['feɪntnəs] n 1 INDISTINCTNESS : lo débil, falta f de claridad 2 FAINTING : desmayo m, desfallecimiento m

fair[1] ['fær] adj 1 ATTRACTIVE, BEAUTIFUL : bello, hermoso, atractivo 2 (relating to weather) : bueno, despejado ⟨fair weather : tiempo despejado⟩ 3 JUST : justo, imparcial 4 ALLOWABLE : permisible 5 BLOND, LIGHT : rubio (dícese del pelo), blanco (dícese de la tez) 6 ADEQUATE : bastante, adecuado ⟨fair to middling : mediano, regular⟩ 7 **fair game** : presa f fácil 8 **to play fair** : jugar limpio

fair[2] n : feria f

fairground ['fær,graʊnd] n : parque m de diversiones

fairly ['færli] adv 1 IMPARTIALLY : imparcialmente, limpiamente, equitativamente 2 QUITE : bastante 3 MODERATELY : medianamente

fairness ['færnəs] n 1 IMPARTIALITY : imparcialidad f, justicia f 2 LIGHTNESS : blancura f (de la piel), lo rubio (del pelo)

fairy ['færi] n, pl **fairies** 1 : hada f 2 **fairy tale** : cuento m de hadas

fairyland ['færi,lænd] n 1 : país m de las hadas 2 : lugar m encantador

faith ['feɪθ] n, pl **faiths** ['feɪθs, 'feɪðz] 1 BELIEF : fe f 2 ALLEGIANCE : lealtad f 3 CONFIDENCE, TRUST : confianza f, fe f 4 RELIGION : religión f

faithful ['feɪθfəl] adj : fiel — **faithfully** adv

faithfulness ['feɪθfəlnəs] n : fidelidad f

faithless ['feɪθləs] adj 1 DISLOYAL : desleal 2 : infiel (en la religión) — **faithlessly** adv

faithlessness ['feɪθləsnəs] n : deslealtad f

fake¹ ['feɪk] v **faked; faking** vt 1 FALSIFY : falsificar, falsear 2 FEIGN : fingir — vi 1 PRETEND : fingir 2 : hacer un engaño, hacer una finta (en deportes)

fake² adj : falso, fingido, postizo

fake³ n 1 IMITATION : imitación f, falsificación f 2 IMPOSTOR : impostor m, -tora f; charlatán m, -tana f; farsante mf 3 FEINT : engaño m, finta f (en deportes)

faker ['feɪkər] n : impostor m, -tora f; charlatán m, -tana f; farsante mf

fakir [fə'kɪr, 'feɪkər] n : faquir m

falcon ['fælkən, 'fɔl-] n : halcón m

falconry ['fælkənri, 'fɔl-] n : cetrería f

fall¹ ['fɔl] vi **fell** ['fɛl]; **falling** 1 : caer, caerse ⟨to fall out of bed : caer de la cama⟩ ⟨to fall down : caerse⟩ 2 HANG : caer, DESCEND : caer (dícese de la lluvia o de la noche), bajar (dícese de los precios), descender (dícese de la temperatura) 4 : caer (a un enemigo), rendirse ⟨the city fell : la ciudad se rindió⟩ 5 OCCUR : caer ⟨Christmas falls on a Friday : la Navidad cae en viernes⟩ 6 **to fall asleep** : dormirse, quedarse dormido 7 **to fall from grace** SIN : perder la gracia 8 **to fall sick** : caer enfermo, enfermarse 9 **to fall through** : fracasar, caer en la nada 10 **to fall to** : tocar a, corresponder a ⟨the task fell to him : le tocó hacerlo⟩

fall² n 1 TUMBLE : caída f ⟨to break one's fall : frenar uno su caída⟩ ⟨a fall of three feet : una caída de tres pies⟩ 2 FALLING : derrumbe m (de rocas), aguacero m (de lluvia), nevada f (de nieve), bajada f (de precios), disminución f (de cantidades) 3 AUTUMN : otoño m 4 DOWNFALL : caída f, ruina f 5 **falls** npl WATERFALL : cascada f, catarata f

fallacious [fə'leɪʃəs] adj : erróneo, engañoso, falaz

fallacy ['fæləsi] n, pl **-cies** : falacia f

fall back vi 1 RETREAT : retirarse, replegarse 2 **to fall back on** : recurrir a

fall guy n SCAPEGOAT : chivo m expiatorio

fallible ['fæləbəl] adj : falible

fallout ['fɔl,aʊt] n 1 : lluvia f radioactiva 2 CONSEQUENCES : secuelas fpl, consecuencias fpl

fallow¹ ['fælo] vt : barbechar

fallow² adj **to lie fallow** : estar en barbecho

fallow³ n : barbecho m

false ['fɔls] adj **falser; falsest** 1 UNTRUE : falso 2 ERRONEOUS : erróneo, equivocado 3 FAKE : falso, postizo 4 UNFAITHFUL : infiel 5 FRAUDULENT : fraudulento ⟨under false pretenses : por fraude⟩

falsehood ['fɔls,hʊd] n : mentira f, falsedad f

falsely ['fɔlsli] adv : falsamente, con falsedad

falseness ['fɔlsnəs] n : falsedad f

falsetto [fɔl'sɛto:] n, pl **-tos** : falsete m

falsification [,fɔlsəfə'keɪʃən] n : falsificación f, falseamiento m

falsify ['fɔlsə,faɪ] vt **-fied; -fying** : falsificar, falsear

falsity ['fɔlsəti] n, pl **-ties** : falsedad f

falter ['fɔltər] vi **-tered; -tering** 1 TOTTER : tambalearse 2 STAMMER : titubear, tartamudear 3 WAVER : vacilar

faltering ['fɔltərɪŋ] adj : titubeante, vacilante

fame ['feɪm] n : fama f

famed ['feɪmd] adj : famoso, célebre, afamado

familial [fə'mɪljəl, -liəl] adj : familiar

familiar¹ [fə'mɪljər] adj 1 KNOWN : familiar, conocido ⟨to be familiar with : estar familiarizado con⟩ 2 INFORMAL : familiar, informal 3 INTIMATE : íntimo, de confianza 4 FORWARD : confianzudo, atrevido — **familiarly** adv

familiar² n : espíritu m guardián

familiarity [fə,mɪli'ærəti, -,mɪl'jær-] n, pl **-ties** 1 KNOWLEDGE : conocimiento m, familiaridad f 2 INFORMALITY, INTIMACY : confianza f, familiaridad f 3 FORWARDNESS : exceso m de confianza, descaro m

familiarize [fə'mɪljə,raɪz] vt **-ized; -izing** 1 : familiarizar 2 **to familiarize oneself** : familiarizarse

family ['fæmli, 'fæmə-] n, pl **-lies** : familia f

family room n : living m, sala f (informal)

family tree n : árbol m genealógico

famine ['fæmən] n : hambre f, hambruna f

famish ['fæmɪʃ] vi **to be famished** : estar famélico, estar hambriento, morir de hambre fam

famous ['feɪməs] adj : famoso

famously ['feɪməsli] adv **to get on famously** : llevarse de maravilla

fan¹ ['fæn] n, v **fanned; fanning** 1 : abanicar (a una persona), avivar (un fuego) 2 STIMULATE : avivar, estimular

fan² n 1 : ventilador m, abanico m 2 ADMIRER, ENTHUSIAST : aficionado m, -da f; entusiasta mf; admirador m, -dora f

fanatic¹ [fə'nætɪk] or **fanatical** [-tɪ-kəl] adj : fanático

fanatic² n : fanático m, -ca f

fanaticism [fə'nætə,sızəm] *n* : fanatismo *m*

fanciful ['fænsıfəl] *adj* **1** CAPRICIOUS : caprichoso, fantástico, extravagante **2** IMAGINATIVE : imaginativo — **fancifully** *adv*

fancy[1] ['fænsi] *vt* **-cied; -cying 1** IMAGINE : imaginarse, figurarse ⟨fancy that! : ¡figúrate!, ¡imagínate!⟩ **2** CRAVE : apetecer, tener ganas de

fancy[2] *adj* **-cier; -est 1** ELABORATE : elaborado **2** LUXURIOUS : lujoso, elegante — **fancily** ['fænsəli] *adv*

fancy[3] *n, pl* **-cies 1** LIKING : gusto *m*, afición *f* **2** WHIM : antojo *m*, capricho *m* **3** IMAGINATION : fantasía *f*, imaginación *f*

fandango [fæn'dæŋgo] *n, pl* **-gos** : fandango *m*

fanfare ['fæn,fær] *n* : fanfarria *f*

fang ['fæŋ] *n* : colmillo *m* (de un animal), diente *m* (de una serpiente)

fanlight ['fæn,laıt] *n* : tragaluz *m*

fantasia [fæn'teɪʒə, -ziə; ,fæntə-'zi:ə] *n* : fantasía *f*

fantasize ['fæntə,saız] *vi* **-sized; -sizing** : fantasear

fantastic [fæn'tæstık] *adj* **1** UNBELIEVABLE : fantástico, increíble, extraño **2** ENORMOUS : fabuloso, inmenso ⟨fantastic sums : sumas fabulosas⟩ **3** WONDERFUL : estupendo, fantástico, bárbaro *fam*, macanudo *fam* — **fantastically** [-tıklı] *adv*

fantasy ['fæntəsi] *n, pl* **-sies** : fantasía *f*

far[1] ['fɑr] *adv* **farther** ['fɑrðər] *or* **further** ['fər-]; **farthest** *or* **furthest** [-ðəst] **1** : lejos ⟨far from here : lejos de aquí⟩ ⟨to go far : llegar lejos⟩ ⟨as far as Chicago : hasta Chicago⟩ ⟨far away : a lo lejos⟩ **2** MUCH : muy, mucho ⟨far bigger : mucho más grande⟩ ⟨far superior : muy superior⟩ ⟨it's by far the best : es con mucho el mejor⟩ **3** (*expressing degree or extent*) ⟨the results are far off : salieron muy inexactos los resultados⟩ ⟨to go so far as : decir tanto como⟩ ⟨to go far enough : tener el alcance necesario⟩ **4** (*expressing progress*) ⟨the work is far advanced : el trabajo está muy avanzado⟩ ⟨to take (something) too far : llevar (algo) demasiado lejos⟩ **5 far and wide** : por todas partes **6 far from it!** : ¡todo lo contrario! **7 so far** : hasta ahora, todavía

far[2] *adj* **farther** *or* **further**; **farthest** *or* **furthest 1** REMOTE : lejano, remoto ⟨the Far East : el Lejano Oriente, el Extremo Oriente⟩ ⟨a far country : un país lejano⟩ **2** LONG : largo ⟨a far journey : un viaje largo⟩ **3** EXTREME : extremo ⟨the far right : la extrema derecha⟩ ⟨at the far end of the room : en el otro extremo de la sala⟩

faraway ['fɑrə,weı] *adj* : remoto, lejano

farce ['fɑrs] *n* : farsa *f*

farcical ['fɑrsıkəl] *adj* : absurdo, ridículo

fare[1] ['fær] *vi* **fared; faring** : ir, salir ⟨how did you fare? : ¿cómo te fue?⟩

fare[2] *n* **1** : pasaje *m*, billete *m*, boleto *m* ⟨half fare : medio pasaje⟩ **2** FOOD : comida *f*

farewell[1] ['fær'wɛl] *adj* : de despedida

farewell[2] *n* : despedida *f*

far-fetched ['fɑr'fɛtʃt] *adj* : improbable, exagerado

farina [fə'ri:nə] *n* : harina *f*

farm[1] ['fɑrm] *vt* **1** : cultivar, labrar **2** : criar (animales) — *vi* : ser agricultor

farm[2] *n* : granja *f*, hacienda *f*, finca *f*, estancia *f*

farmer ['fɑrmər] *n* : agricultor *m*, granjero *m*

farmhand ['fɑrm,hænd] *n* : peón *m*

farmhouse ['fɑrm,haʊs] *n* : granja *f*, vivienda *f* del granjero, casa *f* de hacienda

farming ['fɑrmıŋ] *n* : labranza *f*, cultivo *m*, crianza *f* (de animales)

farmland ['fɑrm,lænd] *n* : tierras *fpl* de labranza

farmyard ['fɑrm,jɑrd] *n* : corral *m*

far-off ['fɑr,ɔf, -'ɔf] *adj* : remoto, distante, lejano

far-reaching ['fɑr'ri:tʃıŋ] *adj* : de gran alcance

farsighted ['fɑr,saıtəd] *adj* **1** : hipermétrope **2** JUDICIOUS : con visión de futuro, previsor, precavido

farsightedness ['fɑr,saıtədnəs] *n* **1** : hipermetropía *f* **2** PRUDENCE : previsión *f*

farther[1] ['fɑrðər] *adv* **1** AHEAD : más lejos (en el espacio), más adelante (en el tiempo) **2** MORE : más

farther[2] *adj* : más lejano, más remoto

farthermost ['fɑrðər,mo:st] *adj* : (el) más lejano

farthest[1] ['fɑrðəst] *adv* **1** : lo más lejos ⟨I jumped farthest : salté lo más lejos⟩ **2** : lo más avanzado ⟨he progressed farthest : progresó al punto más avanzado⟩ **3** : más ⟨the farthest developed : el plan más desarrollado⟩

farthest[2] *adj* : más lejano

fascicle ['fæsıkəl] *n* : fascículo *m*

fascinate ['fæsən,eıt] *vt* **-nated; -nating** : fascinar, cautivar

fascinating ['fæsən,eıtıŋ] *adj* : fascinante

fascination [,fæsən'eıʃən] *n* : fascinación *f*

fascism ['fæʃ,ızəm] *n* : fascismo *m*

fascist[1] ['fæʃıst] *adj* : fascista

fascist[2] *n* : fascista *mf*

fashion[1] ['fæʃən] *vt* : formar, moldear

fashion[2] *n* **1** MANNER : manera *f*, modo *m* **2** CUSTOM : costumbre *f* **3** STYLE : moda *f*

fashionable ['fæʃənəbəl] *adj* : de moda, chic

fashionably ['fæʃənəbli] *adv* : a la moda

fast[1] ['fæst] *vi* : ayunar

fast[2] *adv* **1** SECURELY : firmemente, seguramente ⟨to hold fast : agarrarse bien⟩ **2** RAPIDLY : rápidamente, rápido, de prisa **3 to run fast** : ir adelantado (dícese de un reloj) **4** SOUNDLY : profundamente ⟨fast asleep : profundamente dormido⟩

fast³ *adj* **1** SECURE : firme, seguro ⟨to make fast : amarrar (un barco)⟩ **2** FAITHFUL : leal ⟨fast friends : amigos leales⟩ **3** RAPID : rápido, veloz **4** : adelantado ⟨my watch is fast : tengo el reloj adelantado⟩ **5** DEEP : profundo ⟨a fast sleep : un sueño profundo⟩ **6** COLORFAST : inalterable, que no destiñe **7** DISSOLUTE : extravagante, disipado, disoluto

fast⁴ *n* : ayuno *m*

fasten [ˈfæsən] *vt* **1** ATTACH : sujetar, atar **2** FIX : fijar ⟨to fasten one's eyes on : fijar los ojos en⟩ **3** SECURE : abrochar (ropa o cinturones), atar (cordones), cerrar (una maleta) — *vi* : abrocharse, cerrar

fastener [ˈfæsənər] *n* : cierre *m*, sujetador *m*

fastening [ˈfæsənɪŋ] *n* : cierre *m*, sujetador *m*

fast food *n* : comida *f* rápida

fastidious [fæsˈtɪdiəs] *adj* : quisquilloso, exigente — **fastidiously** *adv*

fat¹ [ˈfæt] *adj* **fatter; fattest 1** OBESE : gordo, obeso **2** THICK : grueso

fat² *n* : grasa *f*

fatal [ˈfeɪtəl] *adj* **1** DEADLY : mortal **2** ILL-FATED : malhadado, fatal **3** MOMENTOUS : fatídico

fatalism [ˈfeɪtəlˌɪzəm] *n* : fatalismo *m*

fatalist [ˈfeɪtəlɪst] *n* : fatalista *mf*

fatalistic [ˌfeɪtəlˈɪstɪk] *adj* : fatalista

fatality [feɪˈtæləti, fə-] *n, pl* **-ties** : víctima *f* mortal

fatally [ˈfeɪtəli] *adv* : mortalmente

fate [ˈfeɪt] *n* **1** DESTINY : destino *m* **2** END, LOT : final *m*, suerte *f*

fated [ˈfeɪtəd] *adj* : predestinado

fateful [ˈfeɪtfəl] *adj* **1** MOMENTOUS : fatídico, aciago **2** PROPHETIC : profético — **fatefully** *adv*

father¹ [ˈfɑðər] *vt* : engendrar

father² *n* **1** : padre *m* ⟨my father and my mother : mi padre y mi madre⟩ ⟨Father Smith : el padre Smith⟩ **2 the Father** GOD : el Padre, Dios *m*

fatherhood [ˈfɑðərˌhʊd] *n* : paternidad *f*

father-in-law [ˈfɑðərɪnˌlɔ] *n, pl* **fathers-in-law** : suegro *m*

fatherland [ˈfɑðərˌlænd] *n* : patria *f*

fatherless [ˈfɑðərləs] *adj* : huérfano de padre, sin padre

fatherly [ˈfɑðərli] *adj* : paternal

fathom¹ [ˈfæðəm] *vt* UNDERSTAND : entender, comprender

fathom² *n* : braza *f*

fatigue¹ [fəˈtiːg] *vt* **-tigued; -tiguing** : fatigar, cansar

fatigue² *n* : fatiga *f*

fatness [ˈfætnəs] *n* : gordura *f* (de una persona o un animal), grosor *m* (de un objeto)

fatten [ˈfætən] *vt* : engordar, cebar

fatty [ˈfæti] *adj* **fattier; -est** : graso, grasoso, adiposo (dícese de los tejidos)

fatuous [ˈfætʃuəs] *adj* : necio, fatuo — **fatuously** *adv*

faucet [ˈfɔsət] *n* : llave *f*, canilla *f Arg, Uru*, grifo *m*

fault¹ [ˈfɔlt] *vt* : encontrar defectos a

fault² *n* **1** SHORTCOMING : defecto *m*, falta *f* **2** DEFECT : falta *f*, defecto *m*, falla *f* **3** BLAME : culpa *f* **4** FRACTURE : falla *f* (geológica)

faultfinder [ˈfɔltˌfaɪndər] *n* : criticón *m*, -cona *f*

faultfinding [ˈfɔltˌfaɪndɪŋ] *n* : crítica *f*

faultless [ˈfɔltləs] *adj* : sin culpa, sin imperfecciones, impecable

faultlessly [ˈfɔltləsli] *adv* : impecablemente, perfectamente

faulty [ˈfɔlti] *adj* **faultier; -est** : defectuoso, imperfecto — **faultily** [ˈfɔltəli] *adv*

fauna [ˈfɔnə] *n* : fauna *f*

faux [ˈfoː] *adj* : de imitación

faux pas [ˌfoːˈpɑ] *n, pl* **faux pas** [*same or* -ˈpɑz] : metedura *f* de pata *fam*

favor¹ [ˈfeɪvər] *vt* **1** SUPPORT : estar a favor de, ser partidario de, apoyar **2** OBLIGE : hacerle un favor a **3** PREFER : preferir **4** RESEMBLE : parecerse a, salir a

favor² *n* : favor *m* ⟨in favor of : a favor de⟩ ⟨an error in his favor : un error a su favor⟩

favorable [ˈfeɪvərəbəl] *adj* : favorable, propicio

favorably [ˈfeɪvərəbli] *adv* : favorablemente, bien

favorite¹ [ˈfeɪvərət] *adj* : favorito, preferido

favorite² *n* : favorito *m*, -ta *f*; preferido *m*, -da *f*

favoritism [ˈfeɪvərəˌtɪzəm] *n* : favoritismo *m*

fawn¹ [ˈfɔn] *vi* : adular, lisonjear

fawn² *n* : cervato *m*

fax [ˈfæks] *n* : facsímil *m*, facsímile *m*

faze [ˈfeɪz] *vt* **fazed; fazing** : desconcertar, perturbar

fear¹ [ˈfɪr] *vt* : temer, tener miedo de — *vi* : temer

fear² *n* : miedo *m*, temor *m* ⟨for fear of : por temor a⟩

fearful [ˈfɪrfəl] *adj* **1** FRIGHTENING : espantoso, aterrador, horrible **2** FRIGHTENED : temeroso, miedoso

fearfully [ˈfɪrfəli] *adv* **1** EXTREMELY : extremadamente, terriblemente **2** TIMIDLY : con temor

fearless [ˈfɪrləs] *adj* : intrépido, impávido

fearlessly [ˈfɪrləsli] *adv* : sin temor

fearlessness [ˈfɪrləsnəs] *n* : intrepidez *f*, impavidez *f*

fearsome [ˈfɪrsəm] *adj* : aterrador

feasibility [ˌfiːzəˈbɪləti] *n* : viabilidad *f*, factibilidad *f*

feasible [ˈfiːzəbəl] *adj* : viable, factible, realizable

feast[1] [ˈfiːst] vi : banquetear — vt 1 : agasajar, festejar 2 **to feast one's eyes on** : regalarse la vista con

feast[2] n 1 BANQUET : banquete m, festín m 2 FESTIVAL : fiesta f

feat [ˈfiːt] n : proeza f, hazaña f

feather[1] [ˈfɛðər] vt 1 : emplumar 2 **to feather one's nest** : hacer su agosto

feather[2] n 1 : pluma f 2 **a feather in one's cap** : un triunfo personal

feathered [ˈfɛðərd] adj : con plumas

feathery [ˈfɛðəri] adj 1 DOWNY : plumoso 2 LIGHT : liviano

feature[1] [ˈfiːtʃər] v -tured; -turing vt 1 IMAGINE : imaginarse 2 PRESENT : presentar — vi : figurar

feature[2] n 1 CHARACTERISTIC : característica f, rasgo m 2 : largometraje m (en el cine), artículo m (en un periódico), documental m (en la televisión) 3 **features** npl : rasgos mpl, facciones fpl ⟨delicate features : facciones delicadas⟩

February [ˈfɛbjuˌri, ˈfɛbu-, ˈfɛbru-] n : febrero m

fecal [ˈfiːkəl] adj : fecal

feces [ˈfiːˌsiːz] npl : heces fpl, excrementos mpl

feckless [ˈfɛkləs] adj : irresponsable

fecund [ˈfɛkənd, ˈfiː-] adj : fecundo

fecundity [frˈkʌndəti, fɛ-] n : fecundidad f

federal [ˈfɛdərəl, -drəl] adj : federal

federalism [ˈfɛdrəˌlɪzəm, -dərə-] n : federalismo m

federalist[1] [ˈfɛdrəlɪst, -dərə-] n : federalista

federalist[2] n : federalista mf

federate [ˈfɛdəˌreɪt] vt -ated; -ating : federar

federation [ˌfɛdəˈreɪʃən] n : federación f

fedora [frˈdorə] n : sombrero m flexible de fieltro

fed up adj : harto

fee [ˈfiː] n 1 : honorarios mpl (a un médico, un abogado, etc.) 2 **entrance fee** : entrada f

feeble [ˈfiːbəl] adj -bler; -blest 1 WEAK : débil, endeble 2 INEFFECTIVE : flojo, pobre, poco convincente

feebleminded [ˌfiːbəlˈmaɪndəd] adj 1 : débil mental 2 FOOLISH, STUPID : imbécil, tonto

feebleness [ˈfiːbəlnəs] n : debilidad f

feebly [ˈfiːbli] adv : débilmente

feed[1] [ˈfiːd] v fed [ˈfɛd]; feeding vt 1 : dar de comer a, nutrir, alimentar (a una persona) 2 : alimentar (un fuego o una máquina), proveer (información), introducir (datos) — vi : comer, alimentarse

feed[2] n 1 NOURISHMENT : alimento m 2 FODDER : pienso m

feedback [ˈfiːdˌbæk] n 1 : realimentación f (electrónica) 2 RESPONSE : reacción f

feeder [ˈfiːdər] n : comedero m (para animales)

feel[1] [ˈfiːl] v felt [ˈfɛlt]; feeling vi 1 : tirse, encontrarse ⟨I feel tired : me siento cansada⟩ ⟨he feels hungry : tiene hambre⟩ ⟨she feels like a fool : se siente como una idiota⟩ ⟨to feel like doing something : tener ganas de hacer algo⟩ 2 SEEM : parecer ⟨it feels like spring : parece primavera⟩ 3 THINK : parecerse, opinar, pensar ⟨how does he feel about that? : ¿qué opina él de eso?⟩ — vt 1 TOUCH : tocar, palpar 2 SENSE : sentir ⟨to feel the cold : sentir el frío⟩ 3 CONSIDER : sentir, creer, considerar ⟨to feel (it) necessary : creer necesario⟩

feel[2] n 1 SENSATION, TOUCH : sensación f, tacto m 2 ATMOSPHERE : ambiente m, atmósfera f 3 **to have a feel for** : tener un talento especial para

feeler [ˈfiːlər] n : antena f, tentáculo m

feeling [ˈfiːlɪŋ] n 1 SENSATION : sensación f, sensibilidad f 2 EMOTION : sentimiento m 3 OPINION : opinión f 4 **feelings** npl SENSIBILITIES : sentimientos mpl ⟨to hurt someone's feelings : herir los sentimientos de alguien⟩

feet → **foot**

feign [ˈfeɪn] vt : simular, aparentar, fingir

feint[1] [ˈfeɪnt] vi : fintar, fintear

feint[2] n : finta f

feldspar [ˈfɛldˌspɑr] n : feldespato m

felicitate [frˈlɪsəˌteɪt] vt -tated; -tating : felicitar, congratular

felicitation [frˌlɪsəˈteɪʃən] n : felicitación f

felicitous [frˈlɪsətəs] adj : acertado, oportuno

feline[1] [ˈfiːˌlaɪn] adj : felino

feline[2] n : felino m, -na f

fell[1] [ˈfɛl] vt : talar (un árbol), derribar (a una persona)

fell[2] → **fall**

fellow [ˈfɛˌloː] n 1 COMPANION : compañero m, -ra f; camarada mf 2 ASSOCIATE : socio m, -cia f 3 MAN : tipo m, hombre m

fellowman [ˌfɛloːˈmæn] n, pl **-men** : prójimo m, semejante m

fellowship [ˈfɛloːˌʃɪp] n 1 COMPANIONSHIP : camaradería f, compañerismo m 2 ASSOCIATION : fraternidad f 3 GRANT : beca f (de investigación)

felon [ˈfɛlən] n : malhechor m, -chora f; criminal mf

felonious [fəˈloːniəs] adj : criminal

felony [ˈfɛləni] n, pl **-nies** : delito m grave

felt[1] [ˈfɛlt] n : fieltro m

felt[2] → **feel**

female[1] [ˈfiːˌmeɪl] adj : femenino

female[2] n 1 : hembra f (de animal) 2 WOMAN : mujer f

feminine [ˈfɛmənən] adj : femenino

femininity [ˌfɛməˈnɪnəti] n : feminidad f, feminidad f

feminism [ˈfɛməˌnɪzəm] n : feminismo m

feminist[1] [ˈfɛmənɪst] adj : feminista

feminist[2] n : feminista mf

femoral ['fɛmərəl] *adj* : femoral
femur ['fi:mər] *n, pl* **femurs** *or* **femora** ['fɛmərə] : fémur *m*
fence[1] ['fɛnts] *v* **fenced; fencing** *vt* : vallar, cercar — *vi* : hacer esgrima
fence[2] *n* : cerca *f*, valla *f*, cerco *m*
fencer ['fɛntsər] *n* : esgrimista *mf*; esgrimidor *m*, -dora *f*
fencing ['fɛntsɪŋ] *n* **1** : esgrima *m* (deporte) **2** : materiales *mpl* para cercas **3** ENCLOSURE : cercado *m*
fend ['fɛnd] *vt* **to fend off** : rechazar (un enemigo), parar (un golpe), eludir (una pregunta) — *vi* **to fend for oneself** : arreglárselas sólo, valerse por sí mismo
fender ['fɛndər] *n* : guardabarros *mpl*, salpicadera *f Mex*
fennel ['fɛnəl] *n* : hinojo *m*
ferment[1] [fər'mɛnt] *v* : fermentar
ferment[2] ['fər,mɛnt] *n* **1** : fermento *m* (en la química) **2** TURMOIL : agitación *f*, conmoción *f*
fermentation [,fərmən'teɪʃən, -,mɛn-] *n* : fermentación *f*
fern ['fərn] *n* : helecho *m*
ferocious [fə'ro:ʃəs] *adj* : feroz — **ferociously** *adv*
ferociousness [fə'ro:ʃəsnəs] *n* : ferocidad *f*
ferocity [fə'rɑsəti] *n* : ferocidad *f*
ferret[1] ['fɛrət] *vi* SNOOP : hurgar, husmear — *vt* **to ferret out** : descubrir
ferret[2] *n* : hurón *m*
ferric ['fɛrɪk] *or* **ferrous** ['fɛrəs] *adj* : férrico
Ferris wheel ['fɛrɪs] *n* : noria *f*
ferry[1] ['fɛri] *vt* **-ried; -rying** : llevar, transportar
ferry[2] *n, pl* **-ries** : transbordador *m*, ferry *m*
ferryboat ['fɛri,bo:t] *n* : transbordador *m*, ferry *m*
fertile ['fərtəl] *adj* : fértil, fecundo
fertility [fər'tɪləti] *n* : fertilidad *f*
fertilization [,fərtələ'zeɪʃən] *n* : fertilización *f* (del suelo), fecundación (de un huevo)
fertilize ['fərtəl,aɪz] *vt* **-ized; -izing 1** : fecundar (un huevo) **2** : fertilizar, abonar (el suelo)
fertilizer ['fərtəl,aɪzər] *n* : fertilizante *m*, abono *m*
fervent ['fərvənt] *adj* : ferviente, fervoroso, ardiente — **fervently** *adv*
fervid ['fərvɪd] *adj* : ardiente, apasionado — **fervidly** *adv*
fervor ['fərvər] *n* : fervor *m*, ardor *m*
fester ['fɛstər] *vi* : enconarse, supurar
festival ['fɛstəvəl] *n* : fiesta *f*, festividad *f*, festival *m*
festive ['fɛstɪv] *adj* : festivo — **festively** *adv*
festivity [fɛs'tɪvəti] *n, pl* **-ties** : festividad *f*, celebración *f*
festoon[1] [fɛs'tu:n] *vt* : adornar, engalanar
festoon[2] *n* GARLAND : guirnalda *f*
fetal ['fi:təl] *adj* : fetal

fetch ['fɛtʃ] *vt* **1** BRING : traer, recoger, ir a buscar **2** REALIZE : realizar, venderse por ⟨the jewelry fetched $10,000 : las joyas se vendieron por $10,000⟩
fetching ['fɛtʃɪŋ] *adj* : atractivo, encantador
fête[1] ['feɪt, 'fɛt] *vt* **fêted; fêting** : festejar, agasajar
fête[2] *n* : fiesta *f*
fetid ['fɛtəd] *adj* : fétido
fetish ['fɛtɪʃ] *n* : fetiche *m*
fetlock ['fɛt,lɑk] *n* : espolón *m*
fetter ['fɛtər] *vt* : encadenar, poner grillos a
fetters ['fɛtərz] *npl* : grillos *mpl*, grilletes *mpl*, cadenas *fpl*
fettle ['fɛtəl] *n* **in fine fettle** : en buena forma, en plena forma
fetus ['fi:təs] *n* : feto *m*
feud[1] ['fju:d] *vi* : pelear, contender
feud[2] *n* : contienda *f*, enemistad *f* (heredada)
feudal ['fju:dəl] *adj* : feudal
feudalism ['fju:dəl,ɪzəm] *n* : feudalismo *m*
fever ['fi:vər] *n* : fiebre *f*, calentura *f*
feverish ['fi:vərɪʃ] *adj* **1** : afiebrado, con fiebre, febril **2** FRANTIC : febril, frenético
few[1] ['fju:] *adj* : pocos ⟨with few exceptions : con pocas excepciones⟩ ⟨a few times : varias veces⟩
few[2] *pron* **1** : pocos ⟨few of them were ready : pocos estaban listos⟩ **2 a few** : algunos, unos cuantos **3 few and far between** : contados
fewer ['fju:ər] *pron* : menos ⟨the fewer the better : cuantos menos mejor⟩
fez ['fɛz] *n, pl* **fezzes** : fez *m*
fiancé [,fi:,ɑn'seɪ, ,fi:'ɑn,seɪ] *n* : prometido *m*, novio *m*
fiancée [,fi:,ɑn'seɪ, ,fi:'ɑn,seɪ] *n* : prometida *f*, novia *f*
fiasco [fi'æs,ko:] *n, pl* **-coes** : fiasco *m*, fracaso *m*
fiat ['fi:,ɑt, -,æt, -ət; 'faɪət, -,æt] *n* : decreto *m*, orden *f*
fib[1] ['fɪb] *vi* **fibbed; fibbing** : decir mentirillas
fib[2] *n* : mentirilla *f*, bola *f fam*
fibber ['fɪbər] *n* : mentirosillo *m*, -lla *f*; cuentista *mf fam*
fiber *or* **fibre** ['faɪbər] *n* : fibra *f*
fiberboard ['faɪbər,bord] *n* : cartón *m* madera
fiberglass ['faɪbər,glæs] *n* : fibra *f* de vidrio
fibrillate ['fɪbrə,leɪt, 'faɪ-] *vi* **-lated; -lating** : fibrilar
fibrillation [,fɪbrə'leɪʃən, ,faɪ-] *n* : fibrilación *f*
fibrous ['faɪbrəs] *adj* : fibroso
fibula ['fɪbjələ] *n, pl* **-lae** [-,li:, -,laɪ] *or* **-las** : peroné *m*
fickle ['fɪkəl] *adj* : inconstante, voluble, veleidoso
fickleness ['fɪkəlnəs] *n* : volubilidad *f*, inconstancia *f*, veleidad *f*

fiction [ˈfɪkʃən] *n* : ficción *f*
fictional [ˈfɪkʃənəl] *adj* : ficticio
fictitious [fɪkˈtɪʃəs] *adj* **1** IMAGINARY : ficticio, imaginario **2** FALSE : falso, ficticio
fiddle¹ [ˈfɪdəl] *vi* **-dled; -dling 1** : tocar el violín **2 to fiddle with** : juguetear con, toquetear
fiddle² *n* : violín *m*
fiddler [ˈfɪdlər, ˈfɪdələr] *n* : violinista *mf*
fiddlesticks [ˈfɪdəlˌstɪks] *interj* : ¡tonterías!
fidelity [fəˈdɛləti, faɪ-] *n*, *pl* **-ties** : fidelidad *f*
fidget¹ [ˈfɪdʒət] *vi* **1** : moverse, estarse inquieto **2 to fidget with** : juguetear con
fidget² *n* **1** : persona *f* inquieta **2 fidgets** *npl* RESTLESSNESS : inquietud *f*
fidgety [ˈfɪdʒəti] *adj* : inquieto
fiduciary¹ [fəˈduːʃiˌɛri, -ˈdjuː-, -ʃəri] *adj* : fiduciario
fiduciary² *n*, *pl* **-ries** : fiduciario *m*, -ria *f*
field¹ [ˈfiːld] *vt* : interceptar y devolver (una pelota), presentar (un candidato), sortear (una pregunta)
field² *adj* : de campaña, de campo ⟨field hospital : hospital de campaña⟩ ⟨field goal : gol de campo⟩ ⟨field trip : viaje de estudio⟩
field³ *n* **1** : campo *m* (de cosechas, de batalla, de magnetismo) **2** : campo *m*, cancha *f* (en deportes) **3** : campo *m* (de trabajo), esfera *f* (de actividades)
fielder [ˈfiːldər] *n* : jugador *m*, -dora *f* de campo; fildeador *m*, -dora *f*
field glasses *n* : binoculares *mpl*, gemelos *mpl*
fiend [ˈfiːnd] *n* **1** DEMON : demonio *m* **2** EVILDOER : persona *f* maligna; malvado *m*, -da *f* **3** FANATIC : fanático *m*, -ca *f*
fiendish [ˈfiːndɪʃ] *adj* : diabólico —
fiendishly *adv*
fierce [ˈfɪrs] *adj* **fiercer; -est 1** FEROCIOUS : fiero, feroz **2** HEATED : acalorado **3** INTENSE : intenso, violento, fuerte — **fiercely** *adv*
fierceness [ˈfɪrsnəs] *n* **1** FEROCITY : ferocidad *f*, fiereza *f* **2** INTENSITY : intensidad *f*, violencia *f*
fieriness [ˈfaɪərinəs] *n* : pasión *f*, ardor *m*
fiery [ˈfaɪəri] *adj* **fierier; -est 1** BURNING : ardiente, llameante **2** GLOWING : encendido **3** PASSIONATE : acalorado, ardiente, fogoso
fiesta [fiˈɛstə] *n* : fiesta *f*
fife [ˈfaɪf] *n* : pífano *m*
fifteen¹ [fɪfˈtiːn] *adj* : quince
fifteen² *n* : quince *m*
fifteenth¹ [fɪfˈtiːnθ] *adj* : decimoquinto
fifteenth² *n* **1** : decimoquinto *m*, -ta *f* (en una serie) **2** : quinceavo *m*, quinceava parte *f*
fifth¹ [ˈfɪfθ] *adj* : quinto

fifth² *n* **1** : quinto *m*, -ta *f* (en una serie) **2** : quinto *m*, quinta parte *f* **3** : quinta *f* (en la música)
fiftieth¹ [ˈfɪftiəθ] *adj* : quincuagésimo
fiftieth² *n* **1** : quincuagésimo *m*, -ma *f* (en una serie) **2** : cincuentavo *m*, cincuentava parte *f*
fifty¹ [ˈfɪfti] *adj* : cincuenta
fifty² *n*, *pl* **-ties** : cincuenta *m*
fifty–fifty¹ [ˌfɪftiˈfɪfti] *adv* : a medias, mitad y mitad
fifty–fifty² *adj* **to have a fifty–fifty chance** : tener un cincuenta por ciento de posibilidades
fig [ˈfɪg] *n* : higo *m*
fight¹ [ˈfaɪt] *v* **fought** [ˈfɔt]; **fighting** *vi* : luchar, combatir, pelear — *vt* : luchar contra, combatir contra
fight² *n* **1** COMBAT : lucha *f*, pelea *f*, combate *m* **2** MATCH : pelea *f*, combate *m* (en boxeo) **3** QUARREL : disputa *f*, pelea *f*, pleito *m*
fighter [ˈfaɪtər] *n* **1** COMBATANT : luchador *m*, -dora *f*; combatiente *mf* **2** BOXER : boxeador *m*, -dora *f*
figment [ˈfɪgmənt] *n* **figment of the imagination** : producto *m* de la imaginación
figurative [ˈfɪgjərətɪv, -gə-] *adj* : figurado, metafórico
figuratively [ˈfɪgjərətɪvli, -gə-] *adv* : en sentido figurado, de manera metafórica
figure¹ [ˈfɪgjər, -gər] *v* **-ured; -uring** *vt* **1** CALCULATE : calcular **2** ESTIMATE : figurarse, calcular ⟨he figured it was possible : se figuró que era posible⟩ — *vi* **1** FEATURE, STAND OUT : figurar, destacar **2 that figures!** : ¡obvio!, ¡no me extraña nada!
figure² *n* **1** DIGIT : número *m*, cifra *f* **2** PRICE : precio *m*, cifra *f* **3** PERSONAGE : figura *f*, personaje *m* **4** : figura *f*, tipo *m*, físico *m* ⟨to have a good figure : tener buen tipo, tener un buen físico⟩ **5** DESIGN, OUTLINE : figura *f* **6 figures** *npl* : aritmética *f*
figurehead [ˈfɪgjərˌhɛd, -gər-] *n* : testaferro *m*, líder *mf* sin poder
figure of speech *n* : figura *f* retórica, figura *f* de hablar
figure out *vt* **1** UNDERSTAND : entender **2** RESOLVE : resolver (un problema, etc.)
figurine [ˌfɪgjəˈriːn] *n* : estatuilla *f*
Fijian [ˈfiːdʒiən, fɪˈdʒiːən] *n* : fijiano *m*, -na *f* — **Fijian** *adj*
filament [ˈfɪləmənt] *n* : filamento *m*
filbert [ˈfɪlbərt] *n* : avellana *f*
filch [ˈfɪltʃ] *vt* : hurtar, birlar *fam*
file¹ [ˈfaɪl] *v* **filed; filing** *vt* **1** CLASSIFY : clasificar **2** : archivar (documentos) **3** SUBMIT : presentar ⟨to file charges : presentar cargos⟩ **4** SMOOTH : limar — *vi* : desfilar, entrar (o salir) en fila
file² *n* **1** : lima *f* ⟨nail file : lima de uñas⟩ **2** DOCUMENTS : archivo *m* **3** LINE : fila *f*

filial ['fɪliəl, 'fɪljəl] *adj* : filial
filibuster[1] ['fɪlə,bʌstər] *vi* : practicar el obstruccionismo
filibuster[2] *n* : obstruccionismo *m*
filibusterer ['fɪlə,bʌstərər] *n* : obstruccionista *mf*
filigree ['fɪlə,gri:] *n* : filigrana *f*
Filipino ['fɪlə'pi:no:] *n* : filipino *m*, -na *f* — **Filipino** *adj*
fill[1] ['fɪl] *vt* 1 : llenar, ocupar ⟨to fill a cup : llenar una taza⟩ ⟨to fill a room : ocupar una sala⟩ 2 STUFF : rellenar 3 PLUG : tapar, rellenar, empastar (un diente) 4 SATISFY : cumplir con, satisfacer 5 *or* to fill out : llenar, re- llenar ⟨to fill out a form : rellenar un formulario⟩
fill[2] *n* 1 FILLING, STUFFING : relleno *m* 2 to eat one's fill : comer lo suficiente 3 to have one's fill of : estar harto de
filler ['fɪlər] *n* : relleno *m*
fillet[1] ['fɪlət, fɪ'leɪ, 'fɪ,leɪ] *vt* : cortar en filetes
fillet[2] *n* : filete *m*
fill in *vt* INFORM : informar, poner al corriente — *vi* to fill in for : reemplazar a
filling ['fɪlɪŋ] *n* 1 : relleno *m* 2 : empaste *m* (de un diente)
filling station → gas station
filly ['fɪli] *n*, *pl* -lies : potra *f*, potranca *f*
film[1] ['fɪlm] *vt* : filmar — *vi* : rodar
film[2] *n* 1 COATING : capa *f*, película *f* 2 : película *f* (fotográfica) 3 MOVIE : película *f*, filme *m*
filmmaker ['fɪlm,meɪkər] *n* : cineasta *mf*
filmy ['fɪlmi] *adj* filmier; -est 1 GAUZY : diáfano, vaporoso 2 : cubierto de una película
filter[1] ['fɪltər] *vt* : filtrar
filter[2] *n* : filtro *m*
filth ['fɪlθ] *n* : mugre *f*, porquería *f*, roña *f*
filthiness ['fɪlθinəs] *n* : suciedad *f*
filthy ['fɪlθi] *adj* filthier; -est 1 DIRTY : mugriento, sucio 2 OBSCENE : obsceno, indecente
filtration [fɪl'treɪʃən] *n* : filtración *f*
fin ['fɪn] *n* 1 : aleta *f* 2 : alerón *m* (de un automóvil o un avión)
finagle [fə'neɪgəl] *vt* -gled; -gling : arreglárselas para conseguir
final[1] ['faɪnəl] *adj* 1 DEFINITIVE : definitivo, final, inapelable 2 ULTIMATE : final 3 LAST : último, final
final[2] *n* 1 : final *f* (en deportes) 2 finals *npl* : exámenes *mpl* finales
finale [fɪ'næli, -'nɑ-] *n* : final *m* ⟨grand finale : final triunfal⟩
finalist ['faɪnəlɪst] *n* : finalista *mf*
finality [faɪ'næləti, fə-] *n*, *pl* -ties : finalidad *f*
finalize ['faɪnəl,aɪz] *vt* -ized; -izing : finalizar
finally ['faɪnəli] *adv* 1 LASTLY : por último, finalmente 2 EVENTUALLY : por fin, al final 3 DEFINITIVELY : definitivamente

finance[1] [fə'nænts, 'faɪ,nænts] *vt* -nanced; -nancing : financiar
finance[2] *n* 1 : finanzas *fpl* 2 finances *npl* RESOURCES : recursos *mpl* financieros
financial [fə'næntʃəl, faɪ-] *adj* : financiero, económico
financially [fə'næntʃəli, faɪ-] *adv* : económicamente
financier [,fɪnən'sɪr, ,faɪ,næn-] *n* : financiero *m*, -ra *f*; financista *mf*
financing [fə'næntsɪŋ, 'fæɪ,næntsɪŋ] *n* : financiación *f*, financiamiento *m*
finch ['fɪntʃ] *n* : pinzón *m*
find[1] ['faɪnd] *vt* found ['faʊnd]; finding 1 LOCATE : encontrar, hallar ⟨I can't find it : no lo encuentro⟩ ⟨to find one's way : encontrar el camino, orientarse⟩ 2 DISCOVER, REALIZE : descubrir, darse cuenta de ⟨he found it difficult : descubrió que era difícil⟩ 3 DECLARE : declarar, hallar ⟨they found him guilty : lo declararon culpable⟩
find[2] *n* : hallazgo *m*
finder ['faɪndər] *n* : descubridor *m*, -dora *f*
finding ['faɪndɪŋ] *n* 1 FIND : hallazgo *m* 2 findings *npl* : conclusiones *fpl*
find out *vt* DISCOVER : descubrir, averiguar — *vi* LEARN : enterarse
fine[1] ['faɪn] *vt* fined; fining : multar
fine[2] *adj* finer; -est 1 PURE : puro (dícese del oro y de la plata) 2 THIN : fino, delgado 3 : fino ⟨fine sand : arena fina⟩ 4 SMALL : pequeño, minúsculo ⟨fine print : letras minúsculas⟩ 5 SUBTLE : sutil, delicado 6 EXCELLENT : excelente, magnífico, selecto 7 FAIR : bueno ⟨it's a fine day : hace buen tiempo⟩ 8 EXQUISITE : exquisito, delicado, fino ⟨fine arts : bellas artes *fpl*⟩
fine[3] *n* : multa *f*
finely ['faɪnli] *adv* 1 EXCELLENTLY : con arte 2 ELEGANTLY : elegantemente 3 PRECISELY : con precisión 4 to chop finely : picar muy fino, picar en trozos pequeños
fineness ['faɪnnəs] *n* 1 EXCELLENCE : excelencia *f* 2 ELEGANCE : elegancia *f*, refinamiento *m* 3 DELICACY : delicadeza *f*, lo fino 4 PRECISION : precisión *f* 5 SUBTLETY : sutileza *f* 6 PURITY : ley *f* (de oro y plata)
finery ['faɪnəri] *n* : galas *fpl*, adornos *mpl*
finesse[1] [fə'nɛs] *vt* -nessed; -nessing : ingeniar
finesse[2] *n* 1 REFINEMENT : refinamiento *m*, finura *f* 2 TACT : delicadeza *f*, tacto *m*, diplomacia *f* 3 CRAFTINESS : astucia *f*
finger[1] ['fɪŋgər] *vt* 1 HANDLE : tocar, toquetear 2 ACCUSE : acusar, delatar
finger[2] *n* : dedo *m*
fingerling ['fɪŋgərlɪŋ] *n* : pez *m* pequeño y joven
fingernail ['fɪŋgər,neɪl] *n* : uña *f*
fingerprint[1] ['fɪŋgər,prɪnt] *vt* : tomar las huellas digitales a

fingerprint[2] *n* : huella *f* digital

fingertip ['fɪŋgər,tɪp] *n* : punta *f* del dedo, yema *f* del dedo

finicky ['fɪnɪki] *adj* : maniático, melindroso, mañoso

finish[1] ['fɪnɪʃ] *vt* **1** COMPLETE : acabar, terminar **2** : aplicar un acabado a (muebles, etc.)

finish[2] *n* **1** END : fin *m*, final *m* **2** REFINEMENT : refinamiento *m* **3** : acabado *m* ⟨a glossy finish : un acabado brillante⟩

finite ['faɪ,naɪt] *adj* : finito

fink ['fɪŋk] *n* : mequetrefe *mf fam*

Finn ['fɪn] *n* : finlandés *m*, -desa *f*

Finnish[1] ['fɪnɪʃ] *adj* : finlandés

Finnish[2] *n* : finlandés *m* (idioma)

fiord ['fi'ɔrd] → **fjord**

fir ['fər] *n* : abeto *m*

fire[1] ['faɪr] *vt* **fired; firing 1** IGNITE, KINDLE : encender **2** ENLIVEN : animar, avivar **3** DISMISS : despedir **4** SHOOT : disparar **5** BAKE : cocer (cerámica)

fire[2] *n* **1** : fuego *m* **2** BURNING : incendio *m* ⟨fire alarm : alarma contra incendios⟩ ⟨to be on fire : estar en llamas⟩ **3** ENTHUSIASM : ardor *m*, entusiasmo *m* **4** SHOOTING : disparos *mpl*, fuego *m*

firearm ['faɪr,ɑrm] *n* : arma *f* de fuego

fireball ['faɪr,bɔl] *n* **1** : bola *f* de fuego **2** METEOR : bólido *m*

firebreak ['faɪr,breɪk] *n* : cortafuegos *m*

firebug ['faɪr,bʌg] *n* : pirómano *m*, -na *f*; incendiario *m*, -ria *f*

firecracker ['faɪr,krækər] *n* : petardo *m*

fire escape *n* : escalera *f* de incendios

firefighter ['faɪr,faɪtər] *n* : bombero *m*, -ra *f*

firefly ['faɪr,flaɪ] *n, pl* **-flies** : luciérnaga *f*

fireman ['faɪrmən] *n, pl* **-men** [-mən, -,mɛn] **1** FIREFIGHTER : bombero *m*, -ra *f* **2** STOKER : fogonero *m*, -ra *f*

fireplace ['faɪr,pleɪs] *n* : hogar *m*, chimenea *f*

fireproof[1] ['faɪr,pru:f] *vt* : hacer incombustible

fireproof[2] *adj* : incombustible, ignífugo

fireside ['faɪr,saɪd] *adj* : informal ⟨fireside chat : charla informal⟩

fireside[2] *n* **1** HEARTH : chimenea *f*, hogar *m* **2** HOME : hogar *m*, casa *f*

firewall ['faɪr,wɔl] *n* : cortafuegos *m*

firewood ['faɪr,wʊd] *n* : leña *f*

fireworks ['faɪr,wərks] *npl* : fuegos *mpl* artificiales, pirotecnia *f*

firm[1] ['fərm] *vt or* **to firm up** : endurecer

firm[2] *adj* **1** VIGOROUS : fuerte, vigoroso **2** SOLID, UNYIELDING : firme, duro, sólido **3** UNCHANGING : firme, inalterable **4** RESOLUTE : firme, resuelto

firm[3] *n* : empresa *f*, firma *f*, compañía *f*

firmament ['fərməmənt] *n* : firmamento *m*

firmly ['fərmli] *adv* : firmemente

firmness ['fərmnəs] *n* : firmeza *f*

first[1] ['fərst] *adv* **1** : primero ⟨finish your homework first : primero termina tu tarea⟩ ⟨first and foremost : ante todo⟩ ⟨first of all : en primer lugar⟩ **2** : por primera vez ⟨I saw it first in Boston : lo vi por primera vez en Boston⟩

first[2] *adj* **1** : primero ⟨the first time : la primera vez⟩ ⟨at first sight : a primera vista⟩ ⟨in the first place : en primer lugar⟩ ⟨the first ten applicants : los diez primeros candidatos⟩ **2** FOREMOST : principal, primero ⟨first tenor : tenor principal⟩

first[3] *n* **1** : primero *m*, -ra *f* **2** *or* **first gear** : primera *f* **3** **at ~** : al principio

first aid *n* : primeros auxilios *mpl*

first-class[1] ['fərst'klæs] *adv* : en primera ⟨to travel first-class : viajar en primera⟩

first-class[2] *adj* : de primera

first class *n* : primera clase *f*

firsthand[1] ['fərst'hænd] *adv* : directamente

firsthand[2] *adj* : de primera mano

first lieutenant *n* : teniente *mf*; teniente primero *m*, teniente primera *f*

firstly ['fərstli] *adv* : primeramente, principalmente, en primer lugar

first-rate[1] ['fərst'reɪt] *adv* : muy bien

first-rate[2] *adj* : de primera, de primera clase

first sergeant *n* : sargento *mf*

firth ['fərθ] *n* : estuario *m*

fiscal ['fɪskəl] *adj* : fiscal — **fiscally** *adv*

fish[1] ['fɪʃ] *vi* : pescar **2 to fish for** SEEK : buscar, rebuscar ⟨to fish for compliments : andar a la caza de cumplidos⟩ — *vt* : pescar

fish[2] *n, pl* **fish** *or* **fishes** : pez *m* (vivo), pescado *m* (para comer)

fisherman ['fɪʃərmən] *n, pl* **-men** [-mən, -,mɛn] : pescador *m*, -dora *f*

fishery ['fɪʃəri] *n, pl* **-eries 1** → **fishing 2** : zona *f* pesquera, pesquería *f*

fishhook ['fɪʃ,hʊk] *n* : anzuelo *m*

fishing ['fɪʃɪŋ] *n* : pesca *f*, industria *f* pesquera

fishing pole *n* : caña *f* de pescar

fish market *n* : pescadería *f*

fishy ['fɪʃi] *adj* **fishier; -est 1** : a pescado ⟨a fishy taste : un sabor a pescado⟩ **2** QUESTIONABLE : dudoso, sospechoso ⟨there's something fishy going on : aquí hay gato encerrado⟩

fission ['fɪʃən, -ʒən] *n* : fisión *f*

fissure ['fɪʃər] *n* : fisura *f*, hendidura *f*

fist ['fɪst] *n* : puño *m*

fistful ['fɪst,fʊl] *n* : puñado *m*

fisticuffs ['fɪstɪ,kʌfs] *npl* : lucha *f* a puñetazos

fit[1] ['fɪt] *v* **fitted; fitting** *vt* **1** MATCH : corresponder a, coincidir con ⟨the punishment fits the crime : el castigo corresponde al crimen⟩ **2** : quedar ⟨the dress doesn't fit me : el vestido no me queda⟩ **3** GO : caber, encajar en ⟨her key fits the lock : su llave encaja en la cerradura⟩ **4** INSERT, INSTALL : poner, colocar **5** ADAPT : adecuar, ajustar, adaptar **6** *or* **to fit out** EQUIP : equipar

433

— **vi 1** : quedar, entallar ⟨these pants don't fit : estos pantalones no me quedan⟩ **2** CONFORM : encajar, cuadrar **3 to fit in** : encajar, estar integrado

fit² *adj* **fitter; fittest 1** SUITABLE : adecuado, apropiado, conveniente **2** QUALIFIED : calificado, competente **3** HEALTHY : sano, en forma

fit³ *n* **1** ATTACK : ataque *m*, acceso *m*, arranque *m* **2 to be a good fit** : quedar bien **3 to be a tight fit** : ser muy entallado (de ropa), estar apretado (de espacios)

fitful [ˈfɪtfəl] *adj* : irregular, intermitente — **fitfully** *adv*

fitness [ˈfɪtnəs] *n* **1** HEALTH : salud *f*, buena forma *f* (física) **2** SUITABILITY : idoneidad *f*

fitting¹ [ˈfɪtɪŋ] *adj* : adecuado, apropiado

fitting² *n* : accesorio *m*

five¹ [ˈfaɪv] *adj* : cinco

five² *n* : cinco *m*

five hundred¹ *adj* : quinientos

five hundred² *n* : quinientos *m*

fix¹ [ˈfɪks] *vt* **1** ATTACH, SECURE : sujetar, asegurar, fijar **2** ESTABLISH : concretar, establecer **3** REPAIR : arreglar, reparar **4** PREPARE : preparar ⟨to fix dinner : preparar la cena⟩ **5** : arreglar, amañar ⟨to fix a race : arreglar una carrera⟩ **6** RIVET : fijar (los ojos, la mirada, etc.)

fix² *n* **1** PREDICAMENT : aprieto *m*, apuro *m* **2** : posición *f* ⟨to get a fix on : establecer la posición de⟩

fixate [ˈfɪkˌseɪt] *v* **-ated; -ating** : obsesionarse

fixation [fɪkˈseɪʃən] *n* : fijación *f*, obsesión *f*

fixed [ˈfɪkst] *adj* **1** STATIONARY : estacionario, inmóvil **2** UNCHANGING : fijo, inalterable **3** INTENT : fijo ⟨a fixed stare : una mirada fija⟩ **4 to be comfortably fixed** : estar en posición acomodada

fixedly [ˈfɪksədli] *adv* : fijamente

fixedness [ˈfɪksədnəs, ˈfɪkst-] *n* : rigidez *f*

fixture [ˈfɪkstʃər] *n* **1** : parte *f* integrante, elemento *m* fijo **2 fixtures** *npl* : instalaciones *fpl* (de una casa)

fizz¹ [ˈfɪz] *vi* : burbujear

fizz² *n* : efervescencia *f*, burbujeo *m*

fizzle¹ [ˈfɪzəl] *vi* **-zled; -zling 1** FIZZ : burbujear **2** FAIL : fracasar

fizzle² *n* : fracaso *m*, fiasco *m*

fjord [fiˈɔrd] *n* : fiordo *m*

flab [ˈflæb] *n* : gordura *f*

flabbergast [ˈflæbərˌgæst] *vt* : asombrar, pasmar, dejar atónito

flabby [ˈflæbi] *adj* **-bier; -est** : blando, fofo, aguado *CA, Col, Mex*

flaccid [ˈflæksəd, ˈflæsəd] *adj* : fláccido

flag¹ [ˈflæg] *vi* **flagged; flagging 1** : hacer señales con banderas **2** WEAKEN : flaquear, desfallecer

flag² *n* : bandera *f*, pabellón *m*, estandarte *m*

flagon [ˈflægən] *n* : jarra *f* grande

flagpole [ˈflægˌpoːl] *n* : asta *f*, mástil *m*

flagrant [ˈfleɪgrənt] *adj* : flagrante — **flagrantly** *adv*

flagship [ˈflægˌʃɪp] *n* : buque *m* insignia

flagstaff [ˈflægˌstæf] → **flagpole**

flagstone [ˈflægˌstoːn] *n* : losa *f*, piedra *f*

flail¹ [ˈfleɪl] *vt* **1** : trillar (grano) **2** : sacudir, agitar (los brazos)

flail² *n* : mayal *m*

flair [ˈflær] *n* : don *m*, facilidad *f*

flak [ˈflæk] *ns & pl* **1** : fuego *m* antiaéreo **2** CRITICISM : críticas *fpl*

flake¹ [ˈfleɪk] *vi* **flaked; flaking** : desmenuzarse, pelarse (dícese de la piel)

flake² *n* : copo *m* (de nieve), escama *f* (de la piel), astilla *f* (de madera)

flamboyance [flæmˈbɔɪənts] *n* : extravagancia *f*, rimbombancia *f*

flamboyant [flæmˈbɔɪənt] *adj* : exuberante, extravagante, rimbombante

flame¹ [ˈfleɪm] *vi* **flamed; flaming 1** BLAZE : arder, llamear **2** GLOW : brillar, encenderse

flame² *n* BLAZE : llama *f* ⟨to burst into flames : estallar en llamas⟩ ⟨to go up in flame : incendiarse⟩

flamethrower [ˈfleɪmˌθroːər] *n* : lanzallamas *m*

flamingo [fləˈmɪŋgo] *n*, *pl* **-gos** : flamenco *m*

flammable [ˈflæməbəl] *adj* : inflamable, flamable

flange [ˈflændʒ] *n* : reborde *m*, pestaña *f*

flank¹ [ˈflæŋk] *vt* **1** : flanquear (para defender o atacar) **2** BORDER, LINE : bordear

flank² *n* : ijada *f* (de un animal), costado *m* (de una persona), falda *f* (de una colina), flanco *m* (de un cuerpo de soldados)

flannel [ˈflænəl] *n* : franela *f*

flap¹ [ˈflæp] *v* **flapped; flapping** *vi* **1** : aletear ⟨the bird was flapping (its wings) : el pájaro aleteaba⟩ **2** FLUTTER : ondear, agitarse — *vt* : batir, agitar

flap² *n* **1** FLAPPING : aleteo *m*, aletazo *m* (de alas) **2** : soplada *f* (de un sobre), hoja *f* (de una mesa), faldón *m* (de una chaqueta)

flapjack [ˈflæpˌdʒæk] → **pancake**

flare¹ [ˈflær] *vi* **flared; flaring 1** FLAME, SHINE : llamear, brillar **2 to flare up** : estallar, explotar (de cólera)

flare² *n* **1** FLASH : destello *m* **2** SIGNAL : (luz *f* de) bengala *f* **3 solar flare** : erupción *f* solar

flash¹ [ˈflæʃ] *vi* **1** SHINE, SPARKLE : destellar, brillar, relampaguear **2** : pasar como un relámpago ⟨an idea flashed through my mind : una idea me cruzó la mente como un relámpago⟩ — *vt* : despedir, lanzar (una luz), transmitir (un mensaje)

flash² adj SUDDEN : repentino
flash³ n 1 : destello m (de luz), fogonazo m (de una explosión) 2 **flash of lightning** : relámpago m 3 **in a flash** : de repente, de un abrir y cerrar los ojos
flashback ['flæʃˌbæk] n : flashback m
flashiness ['flæʃinəs] n : ostentación f
flashlight ['flæʃˌlaɪt] n : linterna f
flashy ['flæʃi] adj **flashier; -est** : llamativo, ostentoso
flask ['flæsk] n : frasco m
flat¹ ['flæt] vt **flatted; flatting** 1 FLATTEN : aplanar, achatar 2 : bajar de tono (en música)
flat² adv 1 EXACTLY : exactamente ⟨in ten minutes flat : en diez minutos exactos⟩ 2 : desafinado, demasiado bajo (en la música)
flat³ adj **flatter; flattest** 1 EVEN, LEVEL : plano, llano 2 SMOOTH : liso 3 DEFINITE : categórico, rotundo, explícito ⟨a flat refusal : una negativa categórica⟩ 4 DULL : aburrido, soso, monótono (dícese de la voz) 5 DEFLATED : desinflado, pinchado, ponchado Mex 6 : bemol (en música) ⟨to sing flat : cantar desafinado⟩
flat⁴ n 1 PLAIN : llano m, terreno m llano 2 : bemol m (en la música) 3 APARTMENT : apartamento m, departamento m 4 or **flat tire** : pinchazo m, ponchadura f Mex
flatbed ['flætˌbɛd] n : camión m de plataforma
flatcar ['flætˌkɑr] n : vagón m abierto
flatfish ['flætˌfɪʃ] n : platija f
flat-footed ['flætˌfʊtəd, ˌflæt'-] adj : de pies planos
flatly ['flætli] adv DEFINITELY : categóricamente, rotundamente
flatness ['flætnəs] n 1 EVENNESS : lo llano, lisura f, uniformidad f 2 DULLNESS : monotonía f
flat-out ['flæt'aʊt] adj 1 : frenético, a toda máquina ⟨a flat-out effort : un esfuerzo frenético⟩ 2 CATEGORICAL : descarado, rotundo, categórico
flatten ['flætən] vt : aplanar, achatar
flatter ['flætər] vt 1 OVERPRAISE : adular 2 COMPLIMENT : halagar 3 : favorecer ⟨the photo flatters you : la foto te favorece⟩
flatterer ['flætərər] n : adulador m, -dora f
flattering ['flætərɪŋ] adj 1 COMPLIMENTARY : halagador 2 BECOMING : favorecedor
flattery ['flætəri] n, pl **-ries** : halagos mpl
flatulence ['flætʃələnts] n : flatulencia f, ventosidad f
flatulent ['flætʃələnt] adj : flatulento
flatware ['flætˌwær] n : cubertería f, cubiertos mpl
flaunt¹ ['flɔnt] vt : alardear, hacer alarde de
flaunt² n : alarde m, ostentación f
flavor¹ ['fleɪvər] vt : dar sabor a, sazonar

flavor² n 1 : gusto m, sabor m 2 FLAVORING : sazón f, condimento m
flavorful ['fleɪvərfəl] adj : sabroso
flavoring ['fleɪvərɪŋ] n : condimento m, sazón f
flavorless ['fleɪvərləs] adj : sin sabor
flaw ['flɔ] n : falla f, defecto m, imperfección f
flawed ['flɔd] adj : imperfecto, con defectos
flawless ['flɔləs] adj : impecable, perfecto — **flawlessly** adv
flax ['flæks] n : lino m
flaxen ['flæksən] adj : rubio, blondo (dícese del pelo)
flay ['fleɪ] vt 1 SKIN : desollar, despellejar 2 VILIFY : criticar con dureza, vilipendiar
flea ['fli:] n : pulga f
fleck¹ ['flɛk] vt : salpicar
fleck² n : mota f, pinta f
fledgling ['flɛdʒlɪŋ] n : polluelo m, pollito m
flee ['fli:] v **fled** ['flɛd]; **fleeing** vi : huir, escapar(se) — vt : huir de
fleece¹ ['fli:s] vt **fleeced; fleecing** 1 SHEAR : esquilar, trasquilar 2 SWINDLE : estafar, defraudar
fleece² n : lana f, vellón m
fleet¹ ['fli:t] vi : moverse con rapidez
fleet² adj SWIFT : rápido, veloz
fleet³ n : flota f
fleet admiral n : almirante mf
fleeting ['fli:tɪŋ] adj : fugaz, breve
flesh ['flɛʃ] n 1 : carne f (de seres humanos y animales) 2 : pulpa f (de frutas)
flesh out vt : desarrollar, darle cuerpo a
fleshy ['flɛʃi] adj **fleshier; -est** : gordo (dícese de las personas), carnoso (dícese de la fruta)
flew → fly
flex ['flɛks] vt : doblar, flexionar
flexibility [ˌflɛksə'bɪləti] n, pl **-ties** : flexibilidad f, elasticidad f
flexible ['flɛksəbəl] adj : flexible — **flexibly** [-bli] adv
flick¹ ['flɪk] vt : dar un capirotazo a (con el dedo) ⟨to flick a switch : darle al interruptor⟩ — vi 1 FLIT : revolotear 2 **to flick through** : hojear (un libro)
flick² n : coletazo m (de una cola), capirotazo m (de un dedo)
flicker¹ ['flɪkər] vi 1 FLUTTER : revolotear, aletear 2 BLINK, TWINKLE : parpadear, titilar
flicker² n 1 : parpadeo m, titileo m 2 HINT, TRACE : indicio m, rastro m ⟨a flicker of hope : un rayo de esperanza⟩
flier ['flaɪər] n 1 AVIATOR : aviador m, -dora f 2 CIRCULAR : folleto m publicitario, circular f
flight ['flaɪt] n 1 : vuelo m (de aves o aviones), trayectoria f (de proyectiles) 2 TRIP : vuelo m 3 FLOCK, SQUADRON : bandada f (de pájaros), escuadrilla f (de aviones) 4 ESCAPE : huida f, fuga

f **5 flight of fancy** : ilusiones *fpl*, fantasía *f* **6 flight of stairs** : tramo *m*

flight attendant *n* : auxiliar *mf* de vuelo

flightless ['flaɪtləs] *adj* : no volador

flighty ['flaɪti] *adj* **flightier; -est** : caprichoso, frívolo

flimsy ['flɪmzi] *adj* **flimsier; -est** **1** LIGHT, THIN : ligero, fino **2** WEAK : endeble, poco sólido **3** IMPLAUSIBLE : pobre, flojo, poco convincente ⟨a flimsy excuse : una excusa floja⟩

flinch ['flɪntʃ] *vi* **1** WINCE : estremecerse **2** RECOIL : recular, retroceder

fling¹ ['flɪŋ] *vt* **flung** ['flʌŋ]; **flinging 1** THROW : lanzar, tirar, arrojar **2 to fling oneself** : lanzarse, tirarse, precipitarse

fling² *n* **1** THROW : lanzamiento *m* **2** ATTEMPT : intento *m* **3** AFFAIR : aventura *f* **4** BINGE : juerga *f*

flint ['flɪnt] *n* : pedernal *m*

flinty ['flɪnti] *adj* **flintier; -est** : de pedernal **2** STERN, UNYIELDING : severo, inflexible

flip¹ ['flɪp] *v* **flipped; flipping** *vt* **1** TOSS : tirar ⟨to flip a coin : echar a cara o cruz⟩ **2** OVERTURN : dar la vuelta a, voltear — *vi* **1** : moverse bruscamente **2 to flip through** : hojear (un libro)

flip² *adj* : insolente, descarado

flip³ *n* **1** FLICK : capirotazo *m*, golpe *m* ligero **2** SOMERSAULT : voltereta *f*

flip-flop ['flɪp,flɑp] *n* **1** REVERSAL : giro *m* radical **2** THONG : chancla *f*, chancleta *f*

flippancy ['flɪpəntsi] *n, pl* **-cies** : ligereza *f*, falta *f* de seriedad

flippant ['flɪpənt] *adj* : ligero, frívolo, poco serio

flipper ['flɪpər] *n* : aleta *f*

flirt¹ ['flərt] *vi* **1** : coquetear, flirtear **2** TRIFLE : jugar ⟨to flirt with death : jugar con la muerte⟩

flirt² *n* : coqueto *m*, -ta *f*

flirtation [,flər'teɪʃən] *n* : devaneo *m*, coqueteo *m*

flirtatious [,flər'teɪʃəs] *adj* : insinuante, coqueto

flit ['flɪt] *vi* **flitted; flitting 1** : revolotear **2 to flit about** : ir y venir rápidamente

float¹ ['floːt] *vi* **1** : flotar **2** WANDER : vagar, errar — *vt* **1** : poner a flote, hacer flotar (un barco) **2** LAUNCH : hacer flotar (una empresa) **3** ISSUE : emitir (acciones en la bolsa)

float² *n* **1** : flotador *m*, corcho *m* (para pescar) **2** BUOY : boya *f* **3** : carroza *f* (en un desfile)

floating ['floːtɪŋ] *adj* : flotante

flock¹ ['flɑk] *vi* **1** : moverse en rebaño **2** CONGREGATE : congregarse, reunirse

flock² *n* : rebaño *m* (de ovejas), bandada *f* (de pájaros)

floe ['floː] *n* : témpano *m* de hielo

flog ['flɑg] *vt* **flogged; flogging** : azotar, fustigar

flood¹ ['flʌd] *vt* : inundar, anegar

flood² *n* **1** INUNDATION : inundación *f* **2** TORRENT : avalancha *f*, diluvio *m*, torrente *m* ⟨a flood of tears : un mar de lágrimas⟩

floodlight ['flʌd,laɪt] *n* : foco *m*

floodwater ['flʌd,wɔtər] *n* : crecida *f*, creciente *f*

floor¹ ['flor] *vt* **1** : solar, poner suelo a (una casa o una sala) **2** KNOCK DOWN : derribar, echar al suelo **3** NONPLUS : desconcertar, confundir, dejar perplejo

floor² *n* **1** : suelo *m*, piso *m* ⟨dance floor : pista de baile⟩ **2** STORY : piso *m*, planta *f* ⟨ground floor : planta baja⟩ ⟨second floor : primer piso⟩ **3** : mínimo *m* (de sueldos, precios, etc.)

floorboard ['flor,bord] *n* : tabla *f* del suelo, suelo *m*, piso *m*

flooring ['florɪŋ] *n* : entarimado *m*

flop¹ ['flɑp] *vi* **flopped; flopping 1** FLAP : golpearse, agitarse **2** COLLAPSE : dejarse caer, desplomarse **3** FAIL : fracasar

flop² *n* **1** FAILURE : fracaso *m* **2 to take a flop** : caerse

floppy ['flɑpi] *adj* **-pier; -est 1** : blando, flexible **2 floppy disk** : diskette *m*, disquete *m*

flora ['florə] *n* : flora *f*

floral ['florəl] *adj* : floral, floreado

florid ['florəd] *adj* **1** FLOWERY : florido **2** REDDISH : rojizo

florist ['florɪst] *n* : florista *mf*

floss¹ ['flɔs] *vi* : limpiarse los dientes con hilo dental

floss² *n* **1** : hilo *m* de seda (de bordar) **2** → **dental floss**

flotation [floˈteɪʃən] *n* : flotación *f*

flotilla [floˈtɪlə] *n* : flotilla *f*

flotsam ['flɑtsəm] *n* **1** : restos *mpl* flotantes (en el mar) **2 flotsam and jetsam** : desechos *mpl*, restos *mpl*

flounce¹ ['flaʊnts] *vi* **flounced; flouncing** : moverse haciendo aspavientos ⟨she flounced into the room : entró en la sala haciendo aspavientos⟩

flounce² *n* **1** RUFFLE : volante *m* **2** FLOURISH : aspaviento *m*

flounder¹ ['flaʊndər] *vi* **1** STRUGGLE : forcejear **2** STUMBLE : no saber qué hacer o decir, perder el hilo (en un discurso)

flounder² *n, pl* **flounder** *or* **flounders** : platija *f*

flour¹ ['flaʊər] *vt* : enharinar

flour² *n* : harina *f*

flourish¹ ['flərɪʃ] *vi* THRIVE : florecer, prosperar, crecer (dícese de las plantas) — *vt* BRANDISH : blandir

flourish² *n* : floritura *f*, floreo *m*

flourishing ['flərɪʃɪŋ] *adj* : floreciente, próspero

flout ['flaʊt] *vt* : desacatar, burlarse de

flow¹ ['floː] *vi* **1** COURSE : fluir, manar, correr **2** CIRCULATE : circular, correr ⟨traffic is flowing smoothly : el tránsito está circulando con fluidez⟩

flow[2] *n* **1** FLOWING : flujo *m*, circulación *f* **2** STREAM : corriente *f*, chorro *m*

flower[1] ['flaʊər] *vi* : florecer, florear

flower[2] *n* : flor *f*

flowered ['flaʊərd] *adj* : florido, floreado

floweriness ['flaʊərinəs] *n* : floritura *f*

flowering[1] ['flaʊərɪŋ] *adj* : floreciente

flowering[2] *n* : floración *f*, florecimiento *m*

flowerpot ['flaʊər‚pɑt] *n* : maceta *f*, tiesto *m*, macetero *m*

flowery ['flaʊəri] *adj* **1** : florido **2** FLOWERED : floreado, de flores

flowing → flow

flown → fly

flu ['flu:] *n* : gripe *f*, gripa *f* Col, Mex

fluctuate ['flʌktʃʊ‚eɪt] *vi* **-ated; -ating** : fluctuar

fluctuation [‚flʌktʃʊ'eɪʃən] *n* : fluctuación *f*

flue ['flu:] *n* : tiro *m*, salida *f* de humos

fluency ['flu:əntsi] *n* : fluidez *f*, soltura *f*

fluent ['flu:ənt] *adj* : fluido

fluently ['flu:əntli] *adv* : con soltura, con fluidez

fluff[1] ['flʌf] *vt* **1** : mullir ⟨to fluff up the pillows : mullir las almohadas⟩ **2** BUNGLE : echar a perder, equivocarse

fluff[2] *n* **1** FUZZ : pelusa *f* **2** DOWN : plumón *m*

fluffy ['flʌfi] *adj* **fluffier; -est 1** DOWNY : lleno de pelusa, velloso **2** SPONGY : esponjoso

fluid[1] ['flu:ɪd] *adj* : fluido

fluid[2] *n* : fluido *m*, líquido *m*

fluidity [flu'ɪdəṭi] *n* : fluidez *f*

fluid ounce *n* : onza *f* líquida (29.57 mililitros)

fluke ['flu:k] *n* : golpe *m* de suerte, chiripa *f*, casualidad *f*

flung → fling

flunk ['flʌŋk] *vt* FAIL : reprobar — *vi* : salir reprobando

fluorescence [‚flʊr'esənts, ‚flɔr-] *n* : fluorescencia *f*

fluorescent [‚flʊr'esənt, ‚flɔr-] *adj* : fluorescente

fluoridate ['flʊrə‚deɪt, 'flʊr-] *vt* **-dated; -dating** : fluorizar

fluoridation [‚flʊrə'deɪʃən, ‚flʊr-] *n* : fluorización *f*, fluoración *f*

fluoride ['flʊr‚aɪd, 'flʊr-] *n* : fluoruro *m*

fluorine ['flʊr‚i:n] *n* : flúor *m*

fluorocarbon [‚flʊro'kɑrbən, ‚flʊr-] *n* : fluorocarbono *m*

flurry ['flʌri] *n, pl* **-ries 1** GUST : ráfaga *f* **2** SNOWFALL : nevisca *f* **3** BUSTLE : frenesí *m*, bullicio *m* **4** BARRAGE : aluvión *m*, oleada *f* ⟨a flurry of questions : un aluvión de preguntas⟩

flush[1] ['flʌʃ] *vt* **1** : limpiar con agua ⟨to flush the toilet : jalar la cadena⟩ **2** RAISE : hacer salir, levantar (en la caza) — *vi* BLUSH : ruborizarse, sonrojarse

flush[2] *adv* : al mismo nivel, a ras

flush[3] *adj* **1** *or* **flushed** ['flʌʃt] : colorado, rojo, encendido (dícese de la cara) **2** FILLED : lleno a rebosar **3** ABUNDANT : copioso, abundante **4** AFFLUENT : adinerado **5** ALIGNED, SMOOTH : alineado, liso **6** flush against : pegado a, contra

flush[4] *n* **1** FLOW, JET : chorro *m*, flujo *m* rápido **2** SURGE : arrebato *m*, arranque *m* ⟨a flush of anger : un arrebato de cólera⟩ **3** BLUSH : rubor *m*, sonrojo *m* **4** GLOW : resplandor *m*, flor *f* ⟨the flush of youth : la flor de la juventud⟩ ⟨in the flush of victory : en la euforia del triunfo⟩

fluster[1] ['flʌstər] *vt* : poner nervioso, aturdir

fluster[2] *n* : agitación *f*, confusión *f*

flute ['flu:t] *n* : flauta *f*

fluted ['flu:ṭəd] *adj* **1** GROOVED : estriado, acanalado **2** WAVY : ondulado

fluting ['flu:ṭɪŋ] *n* : estrías *fpl*

flutist ['flu:ṭɪst] *n* : flautista *mf*

flutter[1] ['flʌṭər] *vi* **1** : revolotear (dícese de un pájaro), ondear (dícese de una bandera), palpitar con fuerza (dícese del corazón), revolotear — *vt* **2 to flutter about** : ir y venir, revolotear — *vt* : sacudir, batir

flutter[2] *n* **1** FLUTTERING : revoloteo *m*, aleteo *m* **2** COMMOTION, STIR : revuelo *m*, agitación *f*

flux ['flʌks] *n* **1** : flujo *m* (en física y medicina) **2** CHANGE : cambio *m* ⟨to be in a state of flux : estar cambiando continuamente⟩

fly[1] ['flaɪ] *v* **flew** ['flu:]; **flown** ['flo:n]; **flying** *vi* **1** : volar (dícese de los pájaros, etc.) **2** TRAVEL : volar (dícese de los aviones), ir en avión (dícese de los pasajeros) **3** FLOAT : flotar, ondear **4** FLEE : huir, escapar **5** RUSH : correr, irse volando **6** PASS : pasar (volando) ⟨how time flies! : ¡cómo pasa el tiempo!⟩ **7 to fly open** : abrir de golpe — *vt* : pilotar (un avión), hacer volar (una cometa)

fly[2] *n, pl* **flies 1** : mosca *f* ⟨to drop like flies : caer como moscas⟩ **2** : bragueta *f* (de pantalones, etc.)

flyer → flier

flying saucer *n* : platillo *m* volador

flypaper ['flaɪ‚peɪpər] *n* : papel *m* matamoscas

flyspeck ['flaɪ‚spɛk] *n* **1** : excremento *m* de mosca **2** SPECK : motita *f*, puntito *m*

flyswatter ['flaɪ‚swɑṭər] *n* : matamoscas *m*

flywheel ['flaɪ‚hwi:l] *n* : volante *m*

foal[1] ['fo:l] *vi* : parir

foal[2] *n* : potro *m*, -tra *f*

foam[1] ['fo:m] *vi* : hacer espuma

foam[2] *n* : espuma *f*

foamy ['fo:mi] *adj* **foamier; -est** : espumoso

focal ['fo:kəl] *adj* **1** : focal, central **2 focal point** : foco *m*, punto *m* de referencia

fo'c'sle ['fo:ksəl] → forecastle

focus¹ ['foːkəs] v **-cused** or **-cussed**; **-cusing** or **-cussing** vt **1** : enfocar (un instrumento) **2** CONCENTRATE : concentrar, centrar — vi : enfocar, fijar la vista

focus² n, pl **-ci** ['foːˌsaɪ, -ˌkaɪ] **1** : foco m ⟨to be in focus : estar enfocado⟩ **2** FOCUSING : enfoque m **3** CENTER : centro m, foco m

fodder ['fɑdər] n : pienso m, forraje m

foe ['foː] n : enemigo m, -ga f

fog¹ ['fɔg, 'fɑg] v **fogged**; **fogging** vt : empañar — vi **to fog up** : empañarse

fog² n : niebla f, neblina f

foggy ['fɔgi, 'fɑ-] adj **foggier**; **-est** : nebuloso, brumoso

foghorn ['fɔgˌhɔrn, 'fɑg-] n : sirena f de niebla

fogy ['foːgi] n, pl **-gies** : carca mf fam, persona f chapada a la antigua

foible ['fɔɪbəl] n : flaqueza f, debilidad f

foil¹ ['fɔɪl] vt : frustrar, hacer fracasar

foil² n **1** : lámina f de metal, papel m de aluminio **2** CONTRAST : contraste m, complemento m **3** SWORD : florete m (en esgrima)

foist ['fɔɪst] vt : encajar, endilgar fam, colocar

fold¹ ['foːld] vt **1** BEND : doblar, plegar **2** CLASP : cruzar (brazos), enlazar (manos), plegar (alas) **3** EMBRACE : estrechar, abrazar **4 to fold in** : incorporar ⟨fold in the cream : incorpore la crema⟩ — vi **1** FAIL : fracasar **2 to fold up** : doblarse, plegarse

fold² n **1** SHEEPFOLD : redil m (para ovejas) **2** FLOCK : rebaño m ⟨to return to the fold : volver al redil⟩ **3** CREASE : pliegue m, doblez m

folder ['foːldər] n **1** CIRCULAR : circular f, folleto m **2** BINDER : carpeta f

foliage ['foːliɪʤ, -liɪʤ] n : follaje m

folio ['foːliˌoː] n, pl **-lios** : folio m

folk¹ ['foːk] adj : popular, folklórico ⟨folk customs : costumbres populares⟩ ⟨folk dance : danza folklórica⟩

folk² n, pl **folk** or **folks 1** PEOPLE : gente f **2 folks** npl : familia f, padres mpl

folklore ['foːkˌlor] n : folklore m

folklorist ['foːkˌlorɪst] n : folklorista mf

folksy ['foːksi] adj **folksier**; **-est** : campechano

follicle ['fɑlɪkəl] n : folículo m

follow ['fɑloː] vt **1** : seguir ⟨follow the guide : siga al guía⟩ ⟨she followed the road : siguió el camino, continuó por el camino⟩ **2** PURSUE : perseguir, seguir **3** OBEY : seguir, cumplir, observar **4** UNDERSTAND : entender — vi **1** : seguir **2** UNDERSTAND : entender **3 it follows that . . .** : se deduce que . . .

follower ['fɑloər] n : seguidor m, -dora f

following¹ ['fɑloɪŋ] adj NEXT : siguiente

following² n FOLLOWERS : seguidores mpl

following³ prep AFTER : después de

follow through vi **to follow through with** : continuar con, realizar

follow up vt : seguir (una sugerencia, etc.), investigar (una huella)

folly ['fɑli] n, pl **-lies** : locura f, desatino m

foment [foˈmɛnt] vt : fomentar

fond ['fɑnd] adj **1** LOVING : cariñoso, tierno **2** PARTIAL : aficionado **3** FERVENT : ferviente, fervoroso

fondle ['fɑndəl] vt **-dled**; **-dling** : acariciar

fondly ['fɑndli] adv : cariñosamente, afectuosamente

fondness ['fɑndnəs] n **1** LOVE : cariño m **2** LIKING : afición f

fondue ['fɑnˌduː, -ˈdjuː] n : fondue f

font ['fɑnt] n **1** or **baptismal font** : pila f bautismal **2** FOUNTAIN : fuente f

food ['fuːd] n : comida f, alimento m

food chain n : cadena f alimenticia

foodstuffs ['fuːdˌstʌfs] npl : comestibles mpl

fool¹ ['fuːl] vi **1** JOKE : bromear, hacer el tonto **2** TOY : jugar, juguetear ⟨don't fool with the computer : no juegues con la computadora⟩ **3 to fool around** : perder el tiempo ⟨he fools around instead of working : pierde el tiempo en vez de trabajar⟩ — vt DECEIVE : engañar, burlar

fool² n **1** IDIOT : idiota mf; tonto m, -ta f; bobo m, -ba f **2** JESTER : bufón m, -fona f

foolhardiness ['fuːlˌhardinəs] n : imprudencia f

foolhardy ['fuːlˌhardi] adj RASH : imprudente, temerario, precipitado

foolish ['fuːlɪʃ] adj **1** STUPID : insensato, estúpido **2** SILLY : idiota, tonto

foolishly ['fuːlɪʃli] adv : tontamente

foolishness ['fuːlɪʃnəs] n : insensatez f, estupidez f, tontería f

foolproof ['fuːlˌpruːf] adj : infalible

foot ['fʊt] n, pl **feet** ['fiːt] : pie m

footage ['fʊtɪʤ] n : medida f en pies, metraje m (en el cine)

football ['fʊtˌbɔl] n : futbol m americano, fútbol m americano

footbridge ['fʊtˌbrɪʤ] n : pasarela f, puente m peatonal

foothills ['fʊtˌhɪlz] npl : estribaciones fpl

foothold ['fʊtˌhoːld] n **1** : punto m de apoyo **2 to gain a foothold** : afianzarse en una posición

footing ['fʊtɪŋ] n **1** BALANCE : equilibrio m **2** FOOTHOLD : punto m de apoyo **3** BASIS : base f ⟨on an equal footing : en igualdad⟩

footlights ['fʊtˌlaɪts] npl : candilejas fpl

footlocker ['fʊtˌlɑkər] n : baúl m pequeño, cofre m

footloose ['fʊtˌluːs] adj : libre y sin compromiso

footman ['fʊtmən] n, pl **-men** [-mən, -ˌmɛn] : lacayo m

footnote ['fʊtˌnoːt] n : nota f al pie de la página

footpath ['fʊtˌpæθ] n : sendero m, senda f, vereda f

footprint ['fʊt‚prɪnt] n : huella f
footrace ['fʊt‚reɪs] n : carrera f pedestre
footrest ['fʊt‚rest] n : apoyapiés m, reposapiés m
footstep ['fʊt‚step] n **1** STEP : paso m **2** FOOTPRINT : huella f
footstool ['fʊt‚stu:l] n : taburete m, escabel m
footwear ['fʊt‚wær] n : calzado m
footwork ['fʊt‚wərk] n : juego m de piernas, juego m de pies
fop ['fɑp] n : petimetre m, dandi m
for¹ ['fɔr] conj : puesto que, porque
for² prep **1** (indicating purpose) : para, de ⟨clothes for children : ropa para niños⟩ ⟨it's time for dinner : es la hora de comer⟩ **2** BECAUSE OF : por ⟨for fear of : por miedo de⟩ **3** (indicating a recipient) : para, por ⟨a gift for you : un regalo para ti⟩ **4** (indicating support) : por ⟨he fought for his country : luchó por su patria⟩ **5** (indicating a goal) : por, para ⟨a cure for cancer : una cura para el cáncer⟩ ⟨for your own good : por tu propio bien⟩ **6** (indicating correspondence or exchange) : por, para ⟨I bought it for $5 : lo compré por $5⟩ ⟨a lot of trouble for nothing : mucha molestia para nada⟩ **7** AS FOR : para, con respecto a **8** (indicating duration) : durante, por ⟨he's going for two years : se va por dos años⟩ ⟨I spoke for ten minutes : hablé (durante) diez minutos⟩ ⟨she has known it for three months : lo sabe desde hace tres meses⟩
forage¹ ['fɔrɪdʒ] v **-aged; -aging** vi : hurgar (en busca de alimento) — vt : buscar (provisiones)
forage² n : forraje m
foray ['fɔr‚eɪ] n : incursión f
forbear¹ [fɔr'bær] vi **-bore** [-'bor]; **-borne** [-'born]; **-bearing 1** ABSTAIN : abstenerse **2** : tener paciencia
forbear² → forebear
forbearance [fɔr'bærənts] n **1** ABSTAINING : abstención f **2** PATIENCE : paciencia f
forbid [fər'bɪd] vt **-bade** [-'bæd, -'beɪd]; **-bidden** [-'bɪdən]; **-bidding 1** PROHIBIT : prohibir **2** PREVENT : impedir
forbidding [fər'bɪdɪŋ] adj **1** IMPOSING : imponente **2** DISAGREEABLE : desagradable, ingrato **3** GRIM : severo
force¹ ['fɔrs] vt **forced; forcing 1** COMPEL : obligar, forzar **2** : forzar ⟨to force open the window : forzar la ventana⟩ ⟨to force a lock : forzar una cerradura⟩ **3** IMPOSE : imponer, obligar
force² n **1** : fuerza f **2** by force : por la fuerza **3** in force : en vigor, en vigencia
forced ['fɔrst] adj : forzado, forzoso
forceful ['fɔrsfəl] adj : fuerte, energético, contundente
forcefully ['fɔrsfəli] adv : con energía, con fuerza
forcefulness ['fɔrsfəlnəs] n : contundencia f, fuerza f

forceps ['fɔrsəps, -‚seps] ns & pl : fórceps m
forcible ['fɔrsəbəl] adj **1** FORCED : forzoso **2** CONVINCING : contundente, convincente — **forcibly** [-bli] adv
ford¹ ['fɔrd] vt : vadear
ford² n : vado m
fore¹ ['fɔr] adv **1** FORWARD : hacia adelante **2** fore and aft : de popa a proa
fore² adj **1** FORWARD : delantero, de adelante **2** FORMER : anterior
fore³ n **1** : frente m, delantera f **2** to come to the fore : empezar a destacar, saltar a primera plana
fore-and-aft ['fɔrən'æft, -ənd-] adj : longitudinal
forearm ['fɔr‚ɑrm] n : antebrazo m
forebear ['fɔr‚bær] n : antepasado m, -da
foreboding [fɔr'bodɪŋ] n : premonición f, presentimiento m
forecast¹ ['fɔr‚kæst] vt **-cast; -casting** : pronosticar, predecir
forecast² n : predicción f, pronóstico m
forecastle ['fo:ksəl] n : castillo m de proa
foreclose [fɔr'kloz] vt **-closed; -closing** : ejecutar (una hipoteca)
forefather ['fɔr‚fɑðər] n : antepasado m, ancestro m
forefinger ['fɔr‚fɪŋgər] n : índice m, dedo m índice
forefoot ['fɔr‚fʊt] n : pata f delantera
forefront ['fɔr‚frʌnt] n : frente m, vanguardia f ⟨in the forefront : a la vanguardia⟩
forego [fɔr'go:] vt **-went; -gone; -going 1** PRECEDE : preceder **2** → forgo
foregoing [fɔr'go:ɪŋ] adj : precedente, anterior
foregone [fɔr'gɔn] adj : previsto ⟨a foregone conclusion : un resultado inevitable⟩
foreground ['fɔr‚graʊnd] n : primer plano m
forehand¹ ['fɔr‚hænd] adj : directo, derecho
forehand² n : golpe m del derecho
forehead ['fɔrəd, 'fɔr‚hed] n : frente f
foreign ['fɔrən] adj **1** : extranjero, exterior ⟨foreign countries : países extranjeros⟩ ⟨foreign trade : comercio exterior⟩ **2** ALIEN : ajeno, extraño ⟨foreign to their nature : ajeno a su carácter⟩ ⟨a foreign body : un cuerpo extraño⟩
foreigner ['fɔrənər] n : extranjero m, -ra f
foreknowledge [fɔr'nɑlɪdʒ] n : conocimiento m previo
foreleg ['fɔr‚leg] n : pata f delantera
foreman ['fɔrmən] n, pl **-men** [-mən, -‚men] : capataz mf ⟨foreman of the jury : presidente del jurado⟩
foremost¹ ['fɔr‚most] adv : en primer lugar
foremost² adj : más importante, principal, grande
forenoon ['fɔr‚nu:n] n : mañana m

forensic [fəˈrɛntsɪk] *adj* **1** RHETORICAL : retórico, de argumentación **2** : forense ⟨forensic medicine : medicina forense⟩

foreordain [ˌfororˈdeɪn] *vt* : predestinar, predeterminar

forequarter [ˈforˌkwɔrtər] *n* : cuarto *m* delantero

forerunner [ˈforˌrʌnər] *n* : precursor *m*, -sora *f*

foresee [forˈsiː] *vt* **-saw; -seen; -seeing** : prever

foreseeable [forˈsiːəbəl] *adj* : previsible ⟨in the foreseeable future : en el futuro inmediato⟩

foreshadow [forˈʃædoː] *vt* : anunciar, prefigurar

foresight [ˈforˌsaɪt] *n* : previsión *f*

foresighted [ˈforˌsaɪtəd] *adj* : previsto

forest [ˈforəst] *n* : bosque *m* (en zonas templadas), selva *f* (en zonas tropicales)

forestall [forˈstɔl] *vt* **1** PREVENT : prevenir, impedir **2** PREEMPT : adelantarse a

forested [ˈforəstəd] *adj* : arbolado

forester [ˈforəstər] *n* : silvicultor *m*, -tora *f*

forestland [ˈforəstˌlænd] *n* : zona *f* boscosa

forest ranger → **ranger**

forestry [ˈforəstri] *n* : silvicultura *f*, ingeniería *f* forestal

foreswear → **forswear**

foretaste¹ [ˈforˌteɪst] *vt* **-tasted; -tasting** : anticipar

foretaste² *n* : anticipo *m*

foretell [forˈtɛl] *vt* **-told; -telling** : predecir, pronosticar, profetizar

forethought [ˈforˌθɔt] *n* : previsión *f*, reflexión *f* previa

forever [fərˈɛvər] *adv* **1** PERPETUALLY : para siempre, eternamente **2** CONTINUALLY : siempre, constantemente

forevermore [fərˌɛvərˈmor] *adv* : por siempre jamás

forewarn [forˈwɔrn] *vt* : prevenir, advertir

foreword [ˈforwərd] *n* : prólogo *m*

forfeit¹ [ˈforfət] *vt* : perder el derecho a

forfeit² *n* **1** FINE, PENALTY : multa *f* **2** : prenda *f* (en un juego)

forge¹ [ˈforʤ] *v* **forged; forging** *vt* **1** : forjar (metal o un plan) **2** COUNTERFEIT : falsificar — *vi* **to forge ahead** : avanzar, seguir adelante

forge² *n* : forja *f*

forger [ˈforʤər] *n* : falsificador *m*, -dora *f*

forgery [ˈforʤəri] *n, pl* **-eries** : falsificación *f*

forget [fərˈgɛt] *v* **-got** [-ˈgɑt]; **-gotten** [-ˈgɑtən] *or* **-got; -getting** *vt* : olvidar — *vi* **to forget about** : olvidarse de, no acordarse de

forgetful [fərˈgɛtfəl] *adj* : olvidadizo

forget–me–not [fərˈgɛtmiˌnɑt] *n* : nomeolvides *mf*

forgettable [fərˈgɛtəbəl] *adj* : poco memorable

forgivable [fərˈgɪvəbəl] *adj* : perdonable

forgive [fərˈgɪv] *vt* **-gave** [-ˈgeɪv]; **-given** [-ˈgɪvən]; **-giving** : perdonar

forgiveness [fərˈgɪvnəs] *n* : perdón *m*

forgiving [fərˈgɪvɪŋ] *adj* : indulgente, comprensivo, clemente

forgo *or* **forego** [forˈgoː] *vt* **-went; -gone; -going** : privarse de, renunciar a

fork¹ [ˈfork] *vi* : ramificarse, bifurcarse — *vt* **1** : levantar (con un tenedor, una horca, etc.) **2 to fork over** : desembolsar

fork² *n* **1** : tenedor *m* (utensilio de cocina) **2** PITCHFORK : horca *f*, horquilla *f* **3** : bifurcación *f* (de un río o camino), horqueta *f* (de un árbol)

forked [ˈforkt, ˈforkəd] *adj* : bífido, ahorquillado

forklift [ˈforkˌlɪft] *n* : carretilla *f* elevadora

forlorn [fərˈlorn] *adj* **1** DESOLATE : abandonado, desolado, desamparado **2** SAD : triste **3** DESPERATE : desesperado

forlornly [fərˈlornli] *adv* **1** SADLY : con tristeza **2** HALFHEARTEDLY : sin ánimo

form¹ [ˈform] *vt* **1** FASHION, MAKE : formar **2** DEVELOP : moldear, desarrollar **3** CONSTITUTE : constituir, formar **4** ACQUIRE : adquirir (un hábito), formar (una idea) — *vi* : tomar forma, formarse

form² *n* **1** SHAPE : forma *f*, figura *f* **2** MANNER : manera *f*, forma *f* **3** DOCUMENT : formulario *m* **4** : forma *f* ⟨in good form : en buena forma⟩ ⟨true to form : en forma consecuente⟩ **5** MOLD : molde *m* **6** KIND, VARIETY : clase *f*, tipo *m* **7** : forma *f* (en gramática) ⟨plural forms : formas plurales⟩

formal¹ [ˈforməl] *adj* **1** CEREMONIOUS : formal, de etiqueta, ceremonioso **2** OFFICIAL : formal, oficial, de forma

formal² *n* **1** BALL : baile *m* formal, baile *m* de etiqueta **2** *or* **formal dress** : traje *m* de etiqueta

formaldehyde [forˈmældəˌhaɪd] *n* : formaldehído *m*

formality [forˈmæləti] *n, pl* **-ties** : formalidad *f*

formalize [ˈforməˌlaɪz] *vt* **-ized; -izing** : formalizar

formally [ˈforməli] *adv* : formalmente

format¹ [ˈforˌmæt] *vt* **-matted; -matting** : formatear

format² *n* : formato *m*

formation [forˈmeɪʃən] *n* **1** FORMING : formación *f* **2** SHAPE : forma *f* **3 in formation** : en formación

formative [ˈformətɪv] *adj* : formativo

former [ˈformər] *adj* **1** PREVIOUS : antiguo, anterior ⟨the former president : el antiguo presidente⟩ **2** : primero (de dos)

formerly [ˈformərli] *adv* : anteriormente, antes

formidable ['fɔrmədəbəl, fɔr'mɪdə-] *adj* : formidable — **formidably** *adv*

formless ['fɔrmləs] *adj* : informe, amorfo

formula ['fɔrmjələ] *n, pl* **-las** *or* **-lae** [-,liː, -,laɪ] **1** : fórmula *f* **2 baby formula** : preparado *m* para biberón

formulate ['fɔrmjə,leɪt] *vt* **-lated; -lating** : formular, hacer

formulation [,fɔrmjə'leɪʃən] *n* : formulación *f*

fornicate ['fɔrnə,keɪt] *vi* **-cated; -cating** : fornicar

fornication [,fɔrnə'keɪʃən] *n* : fornicación *f*

forsake [fər'seɪk] *vt* **-sook** [-'sʊk]; **-saken** [-'seɪkən]; **-saking 1** ABANDON : abandonar, desamparar **2** RELINQUISH : renunciar a

forswear [fɔr'swær] *v* **-swore; -sworn; -swearing** *vt* RENOUNCE : renunciar a — *vi* : perjurar

forsythia [fər'sɪθiə] *n* : forsitia *f*

fort ['fɔrt] *n* **1** STRONGHOLD : fuerte *m*, fortaleza *f*, fortín *m* **2** BASE : base *f* militar

forte ['fɔrt, 'fɔr,teɪ] *n* : fuerte *m*

forth ['fɔrθ] *adv* **1** : adelante ⟨from this day forth : de hoy en adelante⟩ **2 and so forth** : etcétera

forthcoming [forθ'kʌmɪŋ, 'forθ-] *adj* **1** COMING : próximo **2** DIRECT, OPEN : directo, franco, comunicativo

forthright ['forθ,raɪt] *adj* : directo, franco — **forthrightly** *adv*

forthrightness ['forθ,raɪtnəs] *n* : franqueza *f*

forthwith [forθ'wɪθ, -'wɪð] *adv* : inmediatamente, en el acto, enseguida

fortieth[1] [fɔrtiəθ] *adj* : cuadragésimo

fortieth[2] *n* **1** : cuadragésimo *m*, -ma *f* (en una serie) **2** : cuarentavo *m*, cuarentava parte *f*

fortification [,fɔrtəfə'keɪʃən] *n* : fortificación *f*

fortify ['fɔrtə,faɪ] *vt* **-fied; -fying** : fortificar

fortitude ['fɔrtə,tuːd, -,tjuːd] *n* : fortaleza *f*, valor *m*

fortnight ['fort,naɪt] *n* : quince días *mpl*, dos semanas *fpl*

fortnightly[1] ['fort,naɪtli] *adv* : cada quince días

fortnightly[2] *adj* : quincenal

fortress ['fɔrtrəs] *n* : fortaleza *f*

fortuitous [fɔr'tuːətəs, -'tjuː-] *adj* : fortuito, accidental

fortunate ['fɔrtʃənət] *adj* : afortunado

fortunately ['fɔrtʃənətli] *adv* : afortunadamente, con suerte

fortune ['fɔrtʃən] *n* **1** : fortuna *f* ⟨to seek one's fortune : buscar uno su fortuna⟩ **2** LUCK : suerte *f*, fortuna *f* **3** DESTINY, FUTURE : destino *m*, buenaventura *f* **4** : dineral *m*, platal *m* ⟨she spent a fortune : se gastó un dineral⟩

fortune–teller ['fɔrtʃən,tɛlər] *n* : adivino *m*, -na *f*

fortune–telling ['fɔrtʃən,tɛlɪŋ] *n* : adivinación *f*

forty[1] ['fɔrti] *adj* : cuarenta

forty[2] *n, pl* **forties** : cuarenta *m*

forum ['fɔrəm] *n, pl* **-rums** : foro *m*

forward[1] ['fɔrwərd] *vt* **1** PROMOTE : promover, adelantar, fomentar **2** SEND : remitir, enviar

forward[2] *adv* **1** : adelante, hacia adelante ⟨to go forward : irse adelante⟩ **2 from this day forward** : de aquí en adelante

forward[3] *adj* **1** : hacia adelante, delantero **2** BRASH : atrevido, descarado

forward[4] *n* : delantero *m*, -ra *f* (en deportes)

forwarder ['fɔrwərdər] *n* : agencia *f* de transportes, agente *mf* expedidor

forwardness ['fɔrwərdnəs] *n* : atrevimiento *m*, descaro *m*

forwards ['fɔrwərdz] *adv* → **forward[2]**

fossil[1] ['fɑsəl] *adj* : fósil

fossil[2] *n* : fósil *m*

fossilize ['fɑsə,laɪz] *vt* **-ized; -izing** : fosilizar — *vi* : fosilizarse

foster[1] ['fɑstər] *vt* : promover, fomentar

foster[2] *adj* : adoptivo ⟨foster child : niño adoptivo⟩

fought → **fight**

foul[1] ['faʊl] *vi* : cometer faltas (en deportes) — *vt* **1** DIRTY, POLLUTE : contaminar, ensuciar **2** TANGLE : enredar

foul[2] *adv* → **foully 1** : contra las reglas

foul[3] *adj* **1** REPULSIVE : asqueroso, repugnante **2** CLOGGED : atascado, obstruido **3** TANGLED : enredado **4** OBSCENE : obsceno **5** BAD : malo ⟨foul weather : mal tiempo⟩ **6** : antirreglamentario (en deportes)

foul[4] *n* : falta *f*, faul *m*

foully ['faʊli] *adv* : asquerosamente

foulmouthed ['faʊl,mæʊ:ðd, -,maʊθt] *adj* : malhablado

foulness ['faʊlnəs] *n* **1** DIRTINESS : suciedad *f* **2** INCLEMENCY : inclemencia *f* **3** OBSCENITY : obscenidad *f*, grosería *f*

foul play *n* : actos *mpl* criminales

foul–up ['faʊl,ʌp] *n* : lío *m*, confusión *f*, desastre *m*

foul up *vt* SPOIL : estropear, arruinar — *vi* BUNGLE : echar todo a perder

found[1] → **find**

found[2] ['faʊnd] *vt* : fundar, establecer

foundation [faʊn'deɪʃən] *n* **1** FOUNDING : fundación *f* **2** BASIS : fundamento *m*, base *f* **3** INSTITUTION : fundación *f* **4** : cimientos *mpl* (de un edificio)

founder[1] ['faʊndər] *vi* SINK : hundirse, irse a pique

founder[2] *n* : fundador *m*, -dora *f*

founding ['faʊndɪŋ] *adj* : fundador ⟨the founding fathers : los fundadores⟩

foundling ['faʊndlɪŋ] *n* : expósito *m*, -ta *f*

foundry ['faʊndri] *n, pl* **-dries** : fundición *f*

fount ['faʊnt] *n* SOURCE : fuente *f*, origen *m*

fountain ['faʊntən] *n* **1** SPRING : fuente *f*, manantial *m* **2** SOURCE : fuente *f*, origen *m* **3** JET : chorro *m* (de agua), surtidor *m*

fountain pen *n* : pluma *f* fuente

four[1] ['for] *adj* : cuatro

four[2] *n* **1** : cuatro *m* **2 on all fours** : a gatas

fourfold ['for,fo:ld, -'fo:ld] *adj* : cuadruple

four hundred[1] *adj* : cuatrocientos

four hundred[2] *n* : cuatrocientos *m*

fourscore ['for'skor] *adj* EIGHTY : ochenta

fourteen [for'ti:n] *adj* : catorce

fourteen[2] *n* : catorce *m*

fourteenth[1] [for'ti:nθ] *adj* : decimocuarto

fourteenth[2] *n* **1** : decimocuarto *m*, -ta *f* (en una serie) **2** : catorceavo, catorceava parte *f*

fourth[1] ['forθ] *adj* : cuarto

fourth[2] *n* **1** : cuarto *m*, -ta *f* (en una serie) **2** : cuarto *m*, cuarta parte *f*

fowl ['faʊl] *n, pl* **fowl** *or* **fowls 1** BIRD : ave *f* **2** CHICKEN : pollo *m*

fox[1] ['fɑks] *vt* **1** TRICK : engañar **2** BAFFLE : confundir

fox[2] *n, pl* **foxes** : zorro *m*, -ra *f*

foxglove ['fɑks,glʌv] *n* : dedalera *f*, digital *f*

foxhole ['fɑks,ho:l] *n* : hoyo *m* para atrincherarse, trinchera *f* individual

foxy ['fɑksi] *adj* **foxier; -est** SHREWD : astuto

foyer ['fɔɪər, 'fɔɪ,jeɪ] *n* : vestíbulo *m*

fracas ['freɪkəs, 'fræ-] *n, pl* **-cases** [-kəsəz] : altercado *m*, pelea *f*, reyerta *f*

fraction ['frækʃən] *n* **1** : fracción *f*, quebrado *m* **2** PORTION : porción *f*, parte *f*

fractional ['frækʃənəl] *adj* **1** : fraccionario **2** TINY : minúsculo, mínimo, insignificante

fractious ['frækʃəs] *adj* **1** UNRULY : rebelde **2** IRRITABLE : malhumorado, irritable

fracture[1] ['fræktʃər] *vt* **-tured; -turing** : fracturar

fracture[2] *n* **1** : fractura *f* (de un hueso) **2** CRACK : fisura *f*, grieta *f*, falla *f* (geológica)

fragile ['frædʒəl, -,dʒaɪl] *adj* : frágil

fragility [frə'dʒɪləti] *n, pl* **-ties** : fragilidad *f*

fragment[1] ['fræg,mɛnt] *vt* : fragmentar — *vi* : fragmentarse, hacerse añicos

fragment[2] ['frægmənt] *n* : fragmento *m*, trozo *m*, pedazo *m*

fragmentary ['frægmən,tɛri] *adj* : fragmentario, incompleto

fragmentation [,frægmən'teɪʃən, -,mn-] *n* : fragmentación *f*

fragrance ['freɪgrənts] *n* : fragancia *f*, aroma *m*

fragrant ['freɪgrənt] *adj* : fragante, aromático — **fragrantly** *adv*

frail ['freɪl] *adj* : débil, delicado

frailty ['freɪlti] *n, pl* **-ties** : debilidad *f*, flaqueza *f*

frame[1] ['freɪm] *vt* **framed; framing 1** FORMULATE : formular, elaborar **2** BORDER : enmarcar, encuadrar **3** INCRIMINATE : incriminar

frame[2] *n* **1** BODY : cuerpo *m* **2** : armazón *f* (de un edificio, un barco, o un avión), bastidor *m* (de un automóvil), cuadro *m* (de una bicicleta), marco *m* (de un cuadro, una ventana, una puerta, etc.) **3 frames** *npl* : armazón *mf*, montura *f* (para anteojos) **4 frame of mind** : estado *m* de ánimo

framework ['freɪm,wərk] *n* **1** SKELETON, STRUCTURE : armazón *f*, estructura *f* **2** BASIS : marco *m*

franc ['fræŋk] *n* : franco *m*

franchise ['fræn,tʃaɪz] *n* **1** LICENSE : licencia *f* exclusiva, concesión *f* (en comercio) **2** SUFFRAGE : sufragio *m*

franchisee [,fræn,tʃaɪ'zi:, -'tʃə-] *n* : concesionario *m*, -ria *f*

Franciscan [fræn'sɪskən] *n* : franciscano *m*, -na *f* — **Franciscan** *adj*

frank[1] ['fræŋk] *vt* : franquear

frank[2] *adj* : franco, sincero, cándido — **frankly** *adv*

frank[3] *n* : franqueo *m* (de correo)

frankfurter ['fræŋkfərtər, -,fər-] *or* **frankfurt** [-fərt] *n* : salchicha *f* (de Frankfurt, de Viena), perro *m* caliente

frankincense ['fræŋkən,sɛnts] *n* : incienso *m*

frankness ['fræŋknəs] *n* : franqueza *f*, sinceridad *f*, candidez *f*

frantic ['fræntɪk] *adj* : frenético, desesperado — **frantically** *adv*

fraternal [frə'tərnəl] *adj* : fraterno, fraternal

fraternity [frə'tərnəti] *n, pl* **-ties** : fraternidad *f*

fraternization [,frætərnə'zeɪʃən] *n* : fraternización *f*, confraternización *f*

fraternize ['frætər,naɪz] *vi* **-nized; -nizing** : fraternizar, confraternizar

fratricidal [,frætrə'saɪdəl] *adj* : fratricida

fratricide ['frætrə,saɪd] *n* : fratricidio *m*

fraud ['frɔd] *n* **1** DECEPTION, SWINDLE : fraude *m*, estafa *f*, engaño *m* **2** IMPOSTOR : impostor *m*, -tora *f*; farsante *mf*

fraudulent ['frɔdʒələnt] *adj* : fraudulento — **fraudulently** *adv*

fraught ['frɔt] *adj* **fraught with** : lleno de, cargado de

fray[1] ['freɪ] *vt* **1** WEAR : desgastar, deshilachar **2** IRRITATE : crispar, irritar (los nervios) — *vi* : desgastarse, deshilacharse

fray[2] *n* : pelea *f* ⟨to join the fray : salir a la palestra⟩ ⟨to return to the fray : volver a la carga⟩

frazzle[1] ['fræzəl] *vt* **-zled; -zling 1** FRAY : desgastar, deshilachar **2** EXHAUST : agotar, fatigar

frazzle[2] *n* EXHAUSTION : agotamiento *m*

freak ['fri:k] *n* **1** ODDITY : ejemplar *m* anormal, fenómeno *m*, rareza *f* **2** ENTHUSIAST : entusiasta *mf*

freakish ['fri:kɪʃ] *adj* : extraño, estrafalario, raro

freak out *vi* : ponerse como loco — *vt* : darle un ataque (a alguien)

freckle[1] ['frɛkəl] *vi* **-led; -ling** : cubrirse de pecas

freckle[2] *n* : peca *f*

free[1] ['fri:] *vt* **freed; freeing 1** LIBERATE : libertar, liberar, poner en libertad **2** RELIEVE, RID : librar, eximir **3** RELEASE, UNTIE : desatar, soltar **4** UNCLOG : desatascar, destapar

free[2] *adv* **1** FREELY : libremente **2** GRATIS : gratuitamente, gratis

free[3] *adj* **freer; freest 1** : libre ⟨free as a bird : libre como un pájaro⟩ **2** EXEMPT : libre ⟨tax-free : libre de impuestos⟩ **3** GRATIS : gratuito, gratis **4** VOLUNTARY : espontáneo, voluntario, libre **5** UNOCCUPIED : desocupado, libre **6** LOOSE : suelto

freebooter ['fri:,bu:t̬ər] *n* : pirata *mf*

freeborn ['fri:'bɔrn] *adj* : nacido libre

freedom ['fri:dəm] *n* : libertad *f*

free-for-all ['fri:fər,ɔl] *n* : pelea *f*, batalla *f* campal

freelance[1] ['fri:,lænts] *vi* **-lanced; -lancing** : trabajar por cuenta propia

freelance[2] *adj* : por cuenta propia, independiente

freeload ['fri:,lo:d] *vi* : gorronear *fam*, gorrear *fam*

freeloader ['fri:,lo:dər] *n* : gorrón *m*, -rrona *f*; gorrero *m*, -ra *f*; vividor *m*, -dora *f*

freely ['fri:li] *adv* **1** FREE : libremente **2** GRATIS : gratis, gratuitamente

freestanding ['fri:'stændɪŋ] *adj* : de pie, no empotrado, independiente

freeway ['fri:,weɪ] *n* : autopista *f*

freewill ['fri:,wɪl] *adj* : de propia voluntad

free will *n* : libre albedrío *m*, propia voluntad *f*

freeze[1] ['fri:z] *v* **froze** ['fro:z]; **frozen** ['fro:zən]; **freezing** *vi* **1** : congelarse, helarse ⟨the water froze in the lake : el agua se congeló en el lago⟩ ⟨my blood froze : se me heló la sangre⟩ ⟨I'm freezing : me estoy helando⟩ **2** STOP : quedarse inmóvil — *vt* : helar, congelar (líquidos), congelar (alimentos, precios, activos)

freeze[2] *n* **1** FROST : helada *f* **2** FREEZING : congelación *f*, congelamiento *m*

freeze-dried ['fri:z'draɪd] *adj* : liofilizado

freeze-dry ['fri:z'draɪ] *vt* **-dried; -drying** : liofilizar

freezer ['fri:zər] *n* : congelador *m*

freezing ['fri:zɪŋ] *adj* : helando ⟨it's freezing! : ¡hace un frío espantoso!⟩

freezing point *n* : punto *m* de congelación

freight[1] ['freɪt] *vt* : enviar como carga

freight[2] *n* **1** SHIPPING, TRANSPORT : transporte *m*, porte *m*, flete *m* **2** GOODS : mercancías *fpl*, carga *f*

freighter ['freɪt̬ər] *n* : carguero *m*, buque *m* de carga

French[1] ['frɛntʃ] *adj* : francés

French[2] *n* **1** : francés *m* (idioma) **2** **the French** *npl* : los franceses

french fries ['frɛntʃ,fraɪz] *npl* : papas *fpl* fritas

Frenchman ['frɛntʃmən] *n, pl* **-men** [-mən, -,mɛn] : francés *m*

Frenchwoman ['frɛntʃ,wumən] *n, pl* **-women** [-,wɪmən] : francesa *f*

frenetic [frɪ'nɛt̬ɪk] *adj* : frenético — **frenetically** [-t̬ɪkli] *adv*

frenzied ['frɛnzid] *adj* : frenético

frenzy ['frɛnzi] *n, pl* **-zies** : frenesí *m*

frequency ['fri:kwəntsi] *n, pl* **-cies** : frecuencia *f*

frequent[1] [fri'kwɛnt, 'fri:kwənt] *vt* : frecuentar

frequent[2] ['fri:kwənt] *adj* : frecuente — **frequently** *adv*

fresco ['frɛs,ko:] *n, pl* **-coes** : fresco *m*

fresh ['frɛʃ] *adj* **1** : dulce ⟨freshwater : agua dulce⟩ **2** PURE : puro **3** : fresco ⟨fresh fruits : frutas frescas⟩ **4** CLEAN, NEW : limpio, nuevo ⟨fresh clothes : ropa limpia⟩ ⟨fresh evidence : evidencia nueva⟩ **5** REFRESHED : fresco, descansado **6** IMPERTINENT : descarado, impertinente

freshen ['frɛʃən] *vt* : refrescar, arreglar — *vi* **to freshen up** : arreglarse, lavarse

freshet ['frɛʃət] *n* : arroyo *m* desbordado

freshly ['frɛʃli] *adv* : recientemente, recién

freshman ['frɛʃmən] *n, pl* **-men** [-mən, -,mɛn] : estudiante *mf* de primer año universitario

freshness ['frɛʃnəs] *n* : frescura *f*

freshwater ['frɛʃ,wɔt̬ər] *n* : agua *f* dulce

fret[1] ['frɛt] *vi* **fretted; fretting** : preocuparse, inquietarse

fret[2] *n* **1** VEXATION : irritación *f*, molestia *f* **2** WORRY : preocupación *f* **3** : traste *m* (de un instrumento musical)

fretful ['frɛtfəl] *adj* : fastidioso, quejoso, neurótico

fretfully ['frɛtfəli] *adv* : ansiosamente, fastidiosamente, inquieto

fretfulness ['frɛtfəlnəs] *n* : inquietud *f*, irritabilidad *f*

friable ['fraɪəbəl] *adj* : friable, pulverizable

friar ['fraɪər] *n* : fraile *m*

fricassee[1] ['frɪkə,si:, ,frɪkə'si:] *vt* **-seed; -seeing** : cocinar al fricasé

fricassee[2] *n* : fricasé *m*

friction ['frɪkʃən] *n* **1** RUBBING : fricción *f* **2** CONFLICT : fricción *f*, roce *m*

Friday ['fraɪ,deɪ, -di] *n* : viernes *m*

fridge ['frɪdʒ] → **refrigerator**

friend ['frɛnd] *n* : amigo *m*, -ga *f*

friendless ['frɛndləs] *adj* : sin amigos

friendliness ['frɛndlinəs] *n* : simpatía *f*, amabilidad *f*

friendly ['frɛndli] *adj* **-lier; -est 1** : simpático, amable, de amigo ⟨a friendly child : un niño simpático⟩ ⟨friendly advice : consejo de amigo⟩ **2** : agradable, acogedor ⟨a friendly atmosphere : un ambiente agradable⟩ **3** GOOD-NA-TURED : amigable, amistoso ⟨friendly competition : competencia amistosa⟩

friendship ['frɛnd‚ʃɪp] *n* : amistad *f*

frieze ['fri:z] *n* : friso *m*

frigate ['frɪgət] *n* : fragata *f*

fright ['fraɪt] *n* : miedo *m*, susto *m*

frighten ['fraɪtən] *vt* : asustar, espantar

frightened ['fraɪtənd] *adj* : asustado, temeroso

frightening ['fraɪtənɪŋ] *adj* : espantoso, aterrador

frightful ['fraɪtfəl] *adj* **1** → frightening **2** TREMENDOUS : espantoso, tremendo

frightfully ['fraɪtfəli] *adv* : terriblemente, tremendamente

frigid ['frɪʤɪd] *adj* : glacial, extremadamente frío

frigidity [frɪ'ʤɪdəti] *n* **1** COLDNESS : frialdad *f* **2** : frigidez *f* (sexual)

frill ['frɪl] *n* **1** RUFFLE : volante *m* **2** EM-BELLISHMENT : floritura *f*, adorno *m*

frilly ['frɪli] *adj* **frillier; -est 1** RUFFLY : con volantes **2** OVERDONE : recargado

fringe[1] ['frɪnʤ] *vt* **fringed; fringing** : orlar, bordear

fringe[2] *n* **1** BORDER : fleco *m*, orla *f* **2** EDGE : periferia *f*, margen *m* **3** fringe benefits : incentivos *mpl*, extras *mpl*

frisk ['frɪsk] *vi* FROLIC : retozar, juguetear — *vt* SEARCH : cachear, registrar

friskiness ['frɪskinəs] *n* : vivacidad *f*

frisky ['frɪski] *adj* **friskier; -est** : retozón, juguetón

fritter[1] ['frɪtər] *vt* : desperdiciar, malgastar ⟨I frittered away the money : malgasté el dinero⟩

fritter[2] *n* : buñuelo *m*

frivolity [frɪ'vɑləti] *n*, *pl* **-ties** : frivolidad *f*

frivolous ['frɪvələs] *adj* : frívolo, de poca importancia

frivolously ['frɪvələsli] *adv* : frívolamente, a la ligera

frizz[1] ['frɪz] *vi* : rizarse, encresparse, ponerse chino *Mex*

frizz[2] *n* : rizos *mpl* muy apretados

frizzy ['frɪzi] *adj* **frizzier; -est** : rizado, crespo, chino *Mex*

fro ['fro:] *adv* **to and fro** : de aquí para allá, de un lado para otro

frock ['frɑk] *n* DRESS : vestido *m*

frog ['frɔg, 'frɑg] *n* **1** : rana *f* **2** FAS-TENER : alamar *m* **3 to have a frog in one's throat** : tener carraspera

frogman ['frɔg‚mæn, 'frɑg-, -mən] *n*, *pl* **-men** [-mən, -‚mɛn] : hombre *m* rana, submarinista *mf*

frolic[1] ['frɑlɪk] *vi* **-icked; -icking** : retozar, juguetear

frolic[2] *n* FUN : diversión *f*

frolicsome ['frɑlɪksəm] *adj* : juguetón

from ['frʌm, 'frɑm] *prep* **1** (*indicating a starting point*) : desde, de, a partir de ⟨from Cali to Bogota : de Cali a Bogotá⟩ ⟨where are you from? : ¿de dónde eres?⟩ ⟨from that time onward : desde entonces⟩ ⟨from tomorrow : a partir de mañana⟩ **2** (*indicating a source or sender*) : de ⟨a letter from my friend : una carta de mi amiga⟩ ⟨a quote from Shakespeare : una cita de Shakespeare⟩ **3** (*indicating distance*) : de ⟨10 feet from the entrance : a 10 pies de la entrada⟩ **4** (*indicating a cause*) : de ⟨red from crying : rojos de llorar⟩ ⟨he died from the cold : murió del frío⟩ **5** OFF, OUT OF : de ⟨she took it from the drawer : lo sacó del cajón⟩ **6** (*with adverbs or adverbial phrases*) : de, desde ⟨from above : desde arriba⟩ ⟨from among : de entre⟩

frond ['frɑnd] *n* : fronda *f*, hoja *f*

front[1] ['frʌnt] *vi* FACE : dar, estar orientado ⟨the house fronts north : la casa da al norte⟩ **2** : servir de pantalla ⟨he fronts for his boss : sirve de pantalla para su jefe⟩

front[2] *adj* : delantero, de adelante, primero ⟨the front row : la primera fila⟩

front[3] *n* **1** : frente *m*, parte *f* de adelante, delantera *f* ⟨the front of the class : el frente de la clase⟩ ⟨at the front of the train : en la parte delantera del tren⟩ **2** AREA, ZONE : frente *m*, zona *f* ⟨the Eastern front : el frente oriental⟩ ⟨on the educational front : en el frente de la enseñanza⟩ **3** FACADE : fachada *f* (de un edificio o una persona) **4** : frente *m* (en meteorología)

frontage ['frʌntɪʤ] *n* : fachada *f*, frente *m*

frontal ['frʌntəl] *adj* : frontal, de frente

frontier [‚frʌn'tɪr] *n* : frontera *f*

frontiersman [‚frʌn'tɪrzmən] *n*, *pl* **-men** [-mən, -‚mɛn] : hombre *m* de la frontera

frontispiece ['frʌntəs‚pi:s] *n* : frontispicio *m*

frost[1] ['frɔst] *vt* **1** FREEZE : helar **2** ICE : escarchar (pasteles)

frost[2] *n* **1** : helada *f* (en meteorología) **2** : escarcha *f* ⟨frost on the window : escarcha en la ventana⟩

frostbite ['frɔst‚baɪt] *n* : congelación *f*

frostbitten ['frɔst‚bɪtən] *adj* : congelado (dícese de una persona), quemado (dícese de una planta)

frosting ['frɔstɪŋ] *n* ICING : glaseado *m*, betún *m* *Mex*

frosty ['frɔsti] *adj* **frostier; -est 1** CHILLY : helado, frío **2** COOL, UN-FRIENDLY : frío, glacial

froth ['frɔθ] *n*, *pl* **froths** ['frɔθs, 'frɔðz] : espuma *f*

frothy ['frɔθi] *adj* **frothier; -est** : espumoso

frown[1] ['fraʊn] *vi* **1** : fruncir el ceño, fruncir el entrecejo **2 to frown at** : mirar (algo) con ceño, mirar (a alguien) con ceño

frown[2] *n* : ceño *m* (fruncido)

frowsy *or* **frowzy** ['fraʊzi] *adj* **frowsier** *or* **frowzier; -est** : desaliñado, desaseado

froze → **freeze**

frozen → **freeze**

frugal ['fru:gəl] *adj* : frugal, ahorrativo, parco — **frugally** *adv*

frugality [fru'gæləṭi] *n* : frugalidad *f*

fruit[1] ['fru:t] *vi* : dar fruto

fruit[2] *n* **1** : fruta *f* (término genérico), fruto *m* (término particular) **2 fruits** *npl* REWARDS : frutos *mpl* ⟨the fruits of his labor : los frutos de su trabajo⟩

fruitcake ['fru:t,keɪk] *n* : pastel *m* de frutas

fruitful ['fru:tfəl] *adj* : fructífero, provechoso

fruition [fru'ʃən] *n* **1** : cumplimiento *m*, realización *f* **2 to bring to fruition** : realizar

fruitless ['fru:tləs] *adj* : infructuoso, inútil — **fruitlessly** *adv*

fruity ['fru:ṭi] *adj* **fruitier; -est** : (con sabor) a fruta

frumpy ['frʌmpi] *adj* **frumpier; -est** : anticuado y sin atractivo

frustrate ['frʌs,treɪt] *vt* **-trated; -trating** : frustrar

frustrating ['frʌs,treɪtɪŋ] *adj* : frustrante — **frustratingly** *adv*

frustration [,frʌs'treɪʃən] *n* : frustración *f*

fry[1] ['fraɪ] *vt* **fried; frying** : freír

fry[2] *n, pl* **fries** **1** : fritura *f*, plato *m* frito **2** : fiesta *f* en que se sirven frituras **3** *pl* **fry** : alevín *m* (pez)

frying pan *n* : sartén *mf*

fuchsia ['fju:ʃə] *n* **1** : fucsia *f* (planta) **2** : fucsia *m* (color)

fuddle ['fʌdəl] *vt* **-dled; -dling** : confundir, atontar

fuddy-duddy ['fʌdi,dʌdi] *n, pl* **-dies** : persona *f* chapada a la antigua, carca *mf*

fudge[1] ['fʌdʒ] *vt* **fudged; fudging 1** FALSIFY : amañar, falsificar **2** DODGE : esquivar

fudge[2] *n* : dulce *m* blando de chocolate y leche

fuel[1] ['fju:əl] *vt* **-eled** *or* **-elled; -eling** *or* **-elling 1** : abastecer de combustible **2** STIMULATE : estimular

fuel[2] *n* : combustible *m*, carburante *m* (para motores)

fugitive[1] ['fju:dʒəṭɪv] *adj* **1** RUNAWAY : fugitivo **2** FLEETING : efímero, pasajero, fugaz

fugitive[2] *n* : fugitivo *m*, -va *f*

fugue ['fju:g] *n* : fuga *f*

fulcrum ['fʊlkrəm, 'fʌl-] *n, pl* **-crums** *or* **-cra** [-krə] : fulcro *m*

fulfill *or* **fulfil** [fʊl'fɪl] *vt* **-filled; -filling 1** PERFORM : cumplir con, realizar, llevar a cabo **2** SATISFY : satisfacer

fulfillment [fʊl'fɪlmənt] *n* **1** PERFORMANCE : cumplimiento *m*, ejecución *f* **2** SATISFACTION : satisfacción *f*, realización *f*

full[1] ['fʊl] *adv* **1** VERY : muy ⟨full well : muy bien, perfectamente⟩ **2** ENTIRELY : completamente ⟨she swung full around : giró completamente⟩ **3** DIRECTLY : de lleno, directamente ⟨he looked me full in the face : me miró directamente a la cara⟩

full[2] *adj* **1** FILLED : lleno **2** COMPLETE : completo, detallado **3** MAXIMUM : todo, pleno ⟨at full speed : a toda velocidad⟩ ⟨in full bloom : en plena flor⟩ **4** PLUMP : redondo, llenito *fam*, regordete *fam* ⟨a full face : una cara redonda⟩ ⟨a full figure : un cuerpo llenito⟩ **5** AMPLE : amplio ⟨a full skirt : una falda amplia⟩

full[3] *n* **1 to pay in full** : pagar en su totalidad **2 to the full** : al máximo

full-fledged ['fʊl'flɛdʒd] *adj* : hecho y derecho

fullness ['fʊlnəs] *n* **1** ABUNDANCE : plenitud *f*, abundancia *f* **2** : amplitud *f* (de una falda)

fully ['fʊli] *adv* **1** COMPLETELY : completamente, totalmente **2** : al menos, por lo menos ⟨fully half of them : al menos la mitad de ellos⟩

fulsome ['fʊlsəm] *adj* : excesivo, exagerado, efusivo

fumble[1] ['fʌmbəl] *v* **-bled; -bling** *vt* **1** : dejar caer, fumblear **2 to fumble one's way** : ir a tientas — *vi* **1** GROPE : hurgar, tantear **2 to fumble with** : manejar con torpeza

fumble[2] *n* : fumble *m* (en futbol americano)

fume[1] ['fju:m] *vi* **fumed; fuming 1** SMOKE : echar humo, humear **2** : estar furioso

fume[2] *n* : gas *m*, humo *m*, vapor *m*

fumigate ['fju:mə,geɪt] *vt* **-gated; -gating** : fumigar

fumigation [,fju:mə'geɪʃən] *n* : fumigación *m*

fun[1] ['fʌn] *adj* : divertido, entretenido

fun[2] *n* **1** AMUSEMENT : diversión *f*, entretenimiento *m* **2** ENJOYMENT : disfrute *m* **3 to have fun** : divertirse **4 to make fun of** : reírse de, burlarse de

function[1] ['fʌŋkʃən] *vi* : funcionar, desempeñarse, servir

function[2] *n* **1** PURPOSE : función *f* **2** GATHERING : reunión *f* social, recepción *f* **3** CEREMONY : ceremonia *f*, acto *m*

functional ['fʌŋkʃənəl] *adj* : funcional — **functionally** *adv*

functionary ['fʌŋkʃə,neri] *n, pl* **-aries** : funcionario *m*, -ria *f*

fund[1] ['fʌnd] *vt* : financiar

fund[2] *n* **1** SUPPLY : reserva *f*, cúmulo *m* **2** : fondo *m* ⟨investment fund : fondo de inversiones⟩ **3 funds** *npl* RESOURCES : fondos *mpl*

fundamental[1] [ˌfʌndəˈmɛntəl] *adj* **1** BASIC : fundamental, básico **2** PRINCIPAL : esencial, principal **3** INNATE : innato, intrínseco

fundamental[2] *n* : fundamento *m*

fundamentalism [ˌfʌndəˈmɛntəlˌizəm] *n* : integrismo *m*, fundamentalismo *m*

fundamentalist [ˌfʌndəˈmɛntəlıst] *n* : integrista *mf*, fundamentalista *mf* — **fundamentalist** *adj*

fundamentally [ˌfʌndəˈmɛntəli] *adv* : fundamentalmente, básicamente

funding [ˈfʌndıŋ] *n* : financiación *f*

fund–raiser [ˈfʌndˌreızər] *n* : función *f* para recaudar fondos

funeral[1] [ˈfjuːnərəl] *adj* **1** : funeral, funerario, fúnebre ⟨funeral procession : cortejo fúnebre⟩ **2 funeral home** : funeraria *f*

funeral[2] *n* : funeral *m*, funerales *mpl*

funereal [fjuːˈnıriəl] *adj* : fúnebre

fungal [ˈfʌŋgəl] *adj* : de hongos, micótico

fungicidal [ˌfʌndʒəˈsaıdəl, ˌfʌŋgə-] *adj* : fungicida

fungicide [ˈfʌndʒəˌsaıd, ˈfʌŋgə-] *n* : fungicida *m*

fungous [ˈfʌŋgəs] *adj* : fungoso

fungus [ˈfʌŋgəs] *n*, *pl* **fungi** [ˈfʌnˌdʒaı, ˈfʌŋˌgaı] : hongo *m*

funk [ˈfʌŋk] *n* **1** FEAR : miedo *m* **2** DEPRESSION : depresión *f*

funky [ˈfʌŋki] *adj* **funkier; -est** ODD, QUAINT : raro, extraño, original

funnel[1] [ˈfʌnəl] *vt* **-neled;** or **-neling** CHANNEL : canalizar, encauzar

funnel[2] *n* **1** : embudo *m* **2** SMOKESTACK : chimenea *f* (de un barco o vapor)

funnies [ˈfʌniz] *npl* : tiras *fpl* cómicas

funny [ˈfʌni] *adj* **funnier; -est 1** AMUSING : divertido, cómico **2** STRANGE : extraño, raro

fur[1] [ˈfər] *adj* : de piel

fur[2] *n* **1** : pelaje *m*, piel *f* **2** : prenda *f* de piel

furbish [ˈfərbıʃ] *vt* : pulir, limpiar

furious [ˈfjuriəs] *adj* **1** ANGRY : furioso **2** FRANTIC : violento, frenético, vertiginoso (dícese de la velocidad)

furiously [ˈfjuriəsli] *adv* **1** ANGRILY : furiosamente **2** FRANTICALLY : frenéticamente

furlong [ˈfərˌlɔŋ] *n* : estadio *m* (201.2 m)

furlough[1] [ˈfərˌloː] *vt* : dar permiso a, dar licencia a

furlough[2] *n* LEAVE : permiso *m*, licencia *f*

furnace [ˈfərnəs] *n* : horno *m*

furnish [ˈfərnıʃ] *vt* **1** SUPPLY : proveer, suministrar **2** : amueblar ⟨furnished apartment : departamento amueblado⟩

furnishings [ˈfərnıʃıŋz] *npl* **1** ACCESSORIES : accesorios *mpl* **2** FURNITURE : muebles *mpl*, mobiliario *m*

furniture [ˈfərnıtʃər] *n* : muebles *mpl*, mobiliario *m*

furor [ˈfjurˌɔr, -ər] *n* **1** RAGE : furia *f*, rabia *f* **2** UPROAR : escándalo *m*, jaleo *m*, alboroto *m*

furrier [ˈfjuriər] *n* : peletero *m*, -ra *f*

furrow[1] [ˈfəroː] *vt* **1** : surcar **2 to furrow one's brow** : fruncir el ceño

furrow[2] *n* **1** GROOVE : surco *m* **2** WRINKLE : arruga *f*, surco *m*

furry [ˈfəri] *adj* **furrier; -est** : peludo (dícese de un animal), peluche (dícese de un objeto)

further[1] [ˈfərðər] *vt* : promover, fomentar

further[2] *adv* **1** FARTHER : más lejos, más adelante **2** MOREOVER : además **3** MORE : más ⟨I'll consider it further in the morning : lo consideraré más en la mañana⟩

further[3] *adj* **1** FARTHER : más lejano **2** ADDITIONAL : adicional, más

furtherance [ˈfərðərəns] *n* : promoción *f*, fomento *m*, adelantamiento *m*

furthermore [ˈfərðərˌmor] *adv* : además

furthermost [ˈfərðərˌmost] *adv* : más lejano, más distante

furthest [ˈfərðəst] → **farthest**[1], **farthest**[2]

furtive [ˈfərtıv] *adj* : furtivo, sigiloso — **furtively** *adv*

furtiveness [ˈfərtıvnəs] *n* STEALTH : sigilo *m*

fury [ˈfjuri] *n*, *pl* **-ries 1** RAGE : furia *f*, ira *f* **2** VIOLENCE : furia *f*, furor *m*

fuse[1] [ˈfjuːz] or **fuze** *vt* **fused** or **fuzed; fusing** or **fuzing** : equipar con un fusible

fuse[2] *v* **fused; fusing** *vt* **1** SMELT : fundir **2** MERGE : fusionar, fundir — *vi* : fundirse, fusionarse

fuse[3] *n* : fusible *m*

fuselage [ˈfjuːsəˌlɑʒ, -zə-] *n* : fuselaje *m*

fusillade [ˈfjuːsəˌlɑd, -ˌleıd, ˌfjuːsə'-, -zə-] *n* : descarga *f* de fusilería

fusion [ˈfjuːʒən] *n* : fusión *f*

fuss[1] [ˈfʌs] *vi* **1** WORRY : preocuparse **2 to fuss with** : juguetear con, toquetear **3 to fuss over** : mimar

fuss[2] *n* **1** COMMOTION : alboroto *m*, escándalo *m* **2** ATTENTION : atenciones *fpl* **3** COMPLAINT : quejas *fpl*

fussbudget [ˈfʌsˌbʌdʒət] *n* : quisquilloso *m*, -sa *f*; melindroso *m*, -sa *f*

fussiness [ˈfʌsinəs] *n* **1** IRRITABILITY : irritabilidad *f* **2** ORNATENESS : lo recargado **3** METICULOUSNESS : meticulosidad *f*

fussy [ˈfʌsi] *adj* **fussier; -est 1** IRRITABLE : irritable, nervioso **2** OVERELABORATE : recargado **3** METICULOUS : meticuloso **4** FASTIDIOUS : quisquilloso, exigente

futile [ˈfjuːtəl, ˈfjuːˌtaıl] *adj* : inútil, vano

futility [fjuːˈtıləti] *n*, *pl* **-ties** : inutilidad *f*

future[1] [ˈfjuːˈtʃər] *adj* : futuro

future[2] *n* : futuro *m*

futuristic [ˌfjuːˈtʃəˈrıstık] *adj* : futurista

fuze → **fuse**[1]

fuzz ['fʌz] n : pelusa f
fuzziness ['fʌzinəs] n 1 DOWNINESS : vellosidad f 2 INDISTINCTNESS : falta f de claridad

fuzzy ['fʌzi] adj **fuzzier; -est 1** FLUFFY, FURRY : con pelusa, peludo **2** INDISTINCT : indistinto ⟨a fuzzy image : una imagen borrosa⟩

G

g ['dʒiː] n, pl **g's** or **gs** ['dʒiːz] : séptima letra del alfabeto inglés
gab¹ ['gæb] vi **gabbed; gabbing** : charlar, cotorrear fam, parlotear fam
gab² n CHATTER : cotorreo m fam, parloteo m fam
gabardine ['gæbər,diːn] n : gabardina f
gabby ['gæbi] adj **gabbier; -est** : hablador, parlanchín
gable ['geɪbəl] n : hastial m, aguilón m
Gabonese [,gæbə'niːz, -'niːs] n : gabonés m, -nesa f — **Gabonese** adj
gad ['gæd] vi **gadded; gadding** WANDER : deambular, vagar, callejear
gadfly ['gæd,flaɪ] n, pl **-flies 1** : tábano m (insecto) **2** FAULTFINDER : criticón m, -cona f fam
gadget ['gædʒət] n : artilugio m, aparato m
gadgetry ['gædʒətri] n : artilugios mpl, aparatos mpl
Gaelic ['geɪlɪk, 'gæ] n : gaélico m (idioma) — **Gaelic** adj
gaff ['gæf] n 1 : garfio m 2 → **gaffe**
gaffe ['gæf] n : metedura f de pata fam
gag¹ ['gæg] v **gagged; gagging** vt : amordazar ⟨to tie up and gag : atar y amordazar⟩ — vi 1 CHOKE : atragantarse 2 RETCH : hacer arcadas
gag² n 1 : mordaza f (para la boca) 2 JOKE : chiste m
gage → **gauge**
gaggle ['gægəl] n : bandada f, manada f (de gansos)
gaiety ['geɪəti] n, pl **-eties 1** MERRYMAKING : juerga f 2 MERRIMENT : alegría f, regocijo m
gaily ['geɪli] adv : alegremente
gain¹ ['geɪn] vt 1 ACQUIRE, OBTAIN : ganar, obtener, adquirir, conseguir ⟨to gain knowledge : adquirir conocimientos⟩ ⟨to gain a victory : obtener una victoria⟩ 2 REACH : alcanzar, llegar a 3 INCREASE : ganar, aumentar ⟨to gain weight : aumentar de peso⟩ 4 : adelantarse, ganar ⟨the watch gains two minutes a day : el reloj se adelanta dos minutos por día⟩ — vi 1 PROFIT : beneficiarse 2 INCREASE : aumentar
gain² n 1 PROFIT : beneficio m, ganancia f, lucro m, provecho m 2 INCREASE : aumento m
gainful ['geɪnfəl] adj : lucrativo, beneficioso, provechoso ⟨gainful employment : trabajo remunerado⟩
gait ['geɪt] n : paso m, andar m, manera f de caminar
gal ['gæl] n : muchacha f
gala¹ ['geɪlə, 'gæ-, 'gɑ-] adj : de gala

gala² n : gala f, fiesta f
galactic [gə'læktɪk] adj : galáctico
galaxy ['gæləksi] n, pl **-axies** : galaxia f
gale ['geɪl] n 1 WIND : vendaval f, viento m fuerte 2 **gales of laughter** : carcajadas fpl
gall¹ ['gɔl] vt 1 CHAFE : rozar 2 IRRITATE, VEX : irritar, molestar
gall² n 1 BILE : bilis f, hiel f 2 INSOLENCE : audacia f, insolencia f, descaro m 3 SORE : rozadura f (de un caballo) 4 : agalla f (de una planta)
gallant ['gælənt] adj 1 BRAVE : valiente, gallardo 2 CHIVALROUS, POLITE : galante, cortés
gallantry ['gæləntri] n, pl **-ries** : galantería f, caballerosidad f
gallbladder ['gɔl,blædər] n : vesícula f biliar
galleon ['gæljən] n : galeón m
gallery ['gæləri] n, pl **-leries 1** BALCONY : galería f (para espectadores) 2 CORRIDOR : pasillo m, galería f, corredor m 3 : galería f (para exposiciones)
galley ['gæli] n, pl **-leys** : galera f
gallium ['gæliəm] n : galio m
gallivant ['gælə,vænt] vi : callejear
gallon ['gælən] n : galón m
gallop¹ ['gæləp] vi : galopar
gallop² n : galope m
gallows ['gæ,loːz] n, pl **-lows** or **-lowses** [-,loːzəz] : horca f
gallstone ['gɔl,stoːn] n : cálculo m biliar
galore [gə'lor] adj : en abundancia ⟨bargains galore : muchísimas gangas⟩
galoshes [gə'lɑʃəz] npl : galochas fpl, chanclos mpl
galvanize ['gælvən,aɪz] vt **-nized; -nizing 1** STIMULATE : estimular, excitar, impulsar 2 : galvanizar (metales)
Gambian ['gæmbiən] n : gambiano m, -na f — **Gambian** adj
gambit ['gæmbɪt] n 1 : gambito m (en ajedrez) 2 STRATAGEM : estratagema f, táctica f
gamble¹ ['gæmbəl] v **-bled; -bling** vi : jugar, arriesgarse — vt 1 BET, WAGER : apostar, jugar 2 RISK : arriesgar
gamble² n 1 BET : apuesta f 2 RISK : riesgo m
gambler ['gæmbələr] n : jugador m, -dora f
gambling ['gæmbəlɪŋ] n : juego m
gambol ['gæmbəl] vi **-boled** or **-bolled; -boling** or **-bolling** FROLIC : retozar, juguetear
game¹ ['geɪm] adj 1 READY : listo, dispuesto ⟨we're game for anything : es-

tamos listos para lo que sea〉 2 LAME : cojo

game² *n* **1** AMUSEMENT : juego *m*, diversión *f* **2** CONTEST : juego *m*, partido *m*, concurso *m* **3** : caza *f* 〈big game : caza mayor〉

gamecock ['geɪm,kɑk] *n* : gallo *m* de pelea

gamekeeper ['geɪm,ki:pər] *n* : guardabosque *mf*

gamely ['geɪmli] *adv* : animosamente

gamma ray ['gæmə] *n* : rayo *m* gamma

gamut ['gæmət] *n* : gama *f*, espectro *m* 〈to run the gamut : pasar por toda la gama〉

gamy *or* **gamey** ['geɪmi] *adj* **gamier; -est** : con sabor de animal de caza, fuerte

gander ['gændər] *n* **1** : ganso *m* (animal) **2** GLANCE : mirada *f*, vistazo *m*, ojeada *f*

gang¹ ['gæŋ] *vi* **to gang up** : agruparse, unirse

gang² *n* : banda *f*, pandilla *f*

gangling ['gæŋgliŋ] *adj* LANKY : larguirucho *fam*

ganglion ['gæŋgliən] *n, pl* **-glia** [-gliə] : ganglio *m*

gangplank ['gæŋ,plæŋk] *n* : pasarela *f*

gangrene ['gæŋ,gri:n, 'gæn-; gæŋ'-, gæn'-] *n* : gangrena *f*

gangrenous ['gæŋgrənəs] *adj* : gangrenoso

gangster ['gæŋstər] *n* : gángster *mf*

gangway ['gæŋ,weɪ] *n* **1** : pasarela *f* **2 gangway!** : ¡abran paso!

gap ['gæp] *n* **1** BREACH, OPENING : espacio *m*, brecha *f*, abertura *f* **2** GORGE : desfiladero *m*, barranco *m* **3** : laguna *f* 〈a gap in my education : una laguna en mi educación〉 **4** INTERVAL : pausa *f*, intervalo *m* **5** DISPARITY : brecha *f*, disparidad *f*

gape¹ ['geɪp] *vi* **gaped; gaping 1** OPEN : abrirse, estar abierto **2** STARE : mirar fijamente con la boca abierta, mirar boquiabierto

gape² *n* **1** OPENING : abertura *f*, brecha *f* **2** STARE : mirada *f* boquiabierta

garage¹ [gə'rɑʒ, -'rɑdʒ] *vt* **-raged; -raging** : dejar en un garaje

garage² *n* : garaje *m*, cochera *f*

garb¹ ['gɑrb] *vt* : vestir, ataviar

garb² *n* : vestimenta *f*, atuendo *f*

garbage ['gɑrbɪdʒ] *n* : basura *f*, desechos *mpl*

garbageman ['gɑrbɪdʒmən] *n, pl* **-men** [-mən, -,mɛn] : basurero *m*

garble ['gɑrbəl] *vt* **-bled; -bling** : tergiversar, distorsionar

garbled ['gɑrbəld] *adj* : incoherente, incomprensible

garden¹ ['gɑrdən] *vi* : trabajar en el jardín

garden² *n* : jardín *m*

gardener ['gɑrdənər] *n* : jardinero *m*, -ra *f*

gardenia [gɑr'di:njə] *n* : gardenia *f*

gardening ['gɑrdənɪŋ] *n* : jardinería *f*

gargantuan [gɑr'gæntʃuən] *adj* : gigantesco, colosal

gargle¹ ['gɑrgəl] *vi* **-gled; -gling** : hacer gárgaras, gargarizar

gargle² *n* : gárgara *f*

gargoyle ['gɑr,gɔɪl] *n* : gárgola *f*

garish ['gærɪʃ] *adj* GAUDY : llamativo, chillón, charro — **garishly** *adv*

garland¹ ['gɑrlənd] *vt* : adornar con guirnaldas

garland² *n* : guirnalda *f*

garlic ['gɑrlɪk] *n* : ajo *m*

garment ['gɑrmənt] *n* : prenda *f*

garner ['gɑrnər] *vt* : recoger, cosechar

garnet ['gɑrnət] *n* : granate *m*

garnish¹ ['gɑrnɪʃ] *vt* : aderezar, guarnecer

garnish² *n* : aderezo *m*, guarnición *f*

garret ['gærət] *n* : buhardilla *f*, desván *m*

garrison¹ ['gærəsən] *vt* **1** QUARTER : acuartelar (tropas) **2** OCCUPY : guarnecer, ocupar (con tropas)

garrison² *n* **1** : guarnición *f* (ciudad) **2** FORT : fortaleza *f*, poste *m* militar

garrulous ['gærələs] *adj* : charlatán, parlanchín, garlero *Col fam*

garter ['gɑrtər] *n* : liga *f*

gas¹ ['gæs] *v* **gassed; gassing** *vt* : gasear — *vi* **to gas up** : llenar el tanque con gasolina

gas² *n, pl* **gases** ['gæsəz] **1** : gas *m* 〈tear gas : gas lacrimógeno〉 **2** GASOLINE : gasolina *f*

gaseous ['gæʃəs, 'gæsiəs] *adj* : gaseoso

gash¹ ['gæʃ] *vt* : hacer un tajo en, cortar

gash² *n* : cuchillada *f*, tajo *m*

gasket ['gæskət] *n* : junta *f*

gas mask *n* : máscara *f* antigás

gasoline ['gæsə,li:n, ,gæsə'-] *n* : gasolina *f*, nafta *f*

gasp¹ ['gæsp] *vi* **1** : boquear 〈to gasp with surprise : gritar de asombro〉 **2** PANT : jadear, respirar con dificultad

gasp² *n* **1** : boqueada *f* 〈a gasp of surprise : un grito sofocado〉 **2** PANTING : jadeo *m*

gas station *n* : estación *f* de servicio, gasolinera *f*

gastric ['gæstrɪk] *adj* : gástrico 〈gastric juice : jugo gástrico〉

gastronomic [,gæstrə'nɑmɪk] *adj* : gastronómico

gastronomy [gæs'trɑnəmi] *n* : gastronomía *f*

gate ['geɪt] *n* : portón *m*, verja *f*, puerta *f*

gatekeeper ['geɪt,ki:pər] *n* : guarda *mf*; guardián *m*, -diana *f*

gateway ['geɪt,weɪ] *n* : puerta *f* (de acceso), entrada *f*

gather ['gæðər] *vt* **1** ASSEMBLE : juntar, recoger, reunir **2** HARVEST : recoger, cosechar **3** : fruncir (una tela) **4** INFER : deducir, suponer

gathering ['gæðərɪŋ] *n* : reunión *f*

gauche ['goːʃ] *adj* : torpe, falto de tacto

gaudy ['gɔdi] *adj* **gaudier; -est** : chillón, llamativo

gauge¹ ['geɪʤ] *vt* **gauged; gauging 1** MEASURE : medir **2** ESTIMATE, JUDGE : estimar, evaluar, juzgar

gauge² *n* **1** : indicador *m* ⟨pressure gauge : indicador de presión⟩ **2** CALIBER : calibre *m* **3** INDICATION : indicio *m*, muestra *f*

gaunt ['gɔnt] *adj* : demacrado, enjuto, descarnado

gauntlet ['gɔntlət] *n* : guante *m* ⟨to run the gauntlet of : exponerse a⟩

gauze ['gɔz] *n* : gasa *f*

gauzy ['gɔzi] *adj* **gauzier; -est** : diáfano, vaporoso

gave → **give**

gavel ['gævəl] *n* : martillo *m* (de un juez, un subastador, etc.)

gawk ['gɔk] *vi* GAPE : mirar boquiabierto

gawky ['gɔki] *adj* **gawkier; -est** : desmañado, torpe, desgarbado

gay ['geɪ] *adj* **1** MERRY : alegre **2** BRIGHT, COLORFUL : vistoso, vivo **3** HOMOSEXUAL : homosexual

gaze¹ ['geɪz] *vi* **gazed; gazing** : mirar (fijamente)

gaze² *n* : mirada *f* (fija)

gazelle [gə'zɛl] *n* : gacela *f*

gazette [gə'zɛt] *n* : gaceta *f*

gazetteer [ˌgæzə'tɪr] *n* : diccionario *m* geográfico

gear¹ ['gɪr] *vt* ADAPT, ORIENT : adaptar, ajustar, orientar ⟨a book geared to children : un libro adaptado a los niños⟩ — *vi* **to gear up** : prepararse

gear² *n* **1** CLOTHING : ropa *f* **2** BELONGINGS : efectos *mpl* personales **3** EQUIPMENT, TOOLS : equipo *m*, aparejo *m*, herramientas *fpl* ⟨fishing gear : aparejo de pescar⟩ ⟨landing gear : tren de aterrizaje⟩ **4** COGWHEEL : rueda *f* dentada **5** : marcha *f*, velocidad *f* (de un vehículo) ⟨to put in gear : poner en marcha⟩ ⟨to change gear(s) : cambiar de velocidad⟩

gearshift ['gɪr,ʃɪft] *n* : palanca *f* de cambio, palanca *f* de velocidad

geek ['giːk] *n fam* : intelectual *mf*

geese → **goose**

Geiger counter ['gaɪgər,kaʊntər] *n* : contador *m* Geiger

gel ['ʤɛl] *n* : gel *m*

gelatin ['ʤɛlətən] *n* : gelatina *f*

gem ['ʤɛm] *n* : joya *f*, gema *f*, alhaja *f*

Gemini ['ʤɛmə,naɪ] *n* : Géminis *mf*

gemstone ['ʤɛm,stoːn] *n* : piedra *f* (semipreciosa o preciosa), gema *f*

gender ['ʤɛndər] *n* **1** SEX : sexo *m* **2** : género *m* (en la gramática)

gene ['ʤiːn] *n* : gen *m*, gene *m*

genealogical [ˌʤiːniə'lɑʤɪkəl] *adj* : genealógico

genealogy [ˌʤiːni'ɑləʤi, ˌʤɛ-, -'æ-] *n, pl* **-gies** : genealogía *f*

genera → **genus**

general¹ ['ʤɛnrəl, 'ʤɛnə-] *adj* : general ⟨in general : en general, por lo general⟩

general² *n* : general *mf*

generality [ˌʤɛnə'ræləti] *n, pl* **-ties** : generalidad *f*

generalization [ˌʤɛnrələ'zeɪʃən, ˌʤɛnərə-] *n* : generalización *f*

generalize ['ʤɛnrə,laɪz, 'ʤɛnərə-] *v* **-ized; -izing** : generalizar

generally ['ʤɛnrəli, 'ʤɛnərə-] *adv* : generalmente, por lo general, en general

generate ['ʤɛnə,reɪt] *vt* **-ated; -ating** : generar, producir

generation [ˌʤɛnə'reɪʃən] *n* : generación *f*

generator ['ʤɛnə,reɪtər] *n* : generador *m*

generic [ʤə'nɛrɪk] *adj* : genérico

generosity [ˌʤɛnə'rɑsəti] *n, pl* **-ties** : generosidad *f*

generous ['ʤɛnərəs] *adj* **1** OPENHANDED : generoso, dadivoso, desprendido **2** ABUNDANT, AMPLE : abundante, amplio, generoso — **generously** *adv*

genetic [ʤə'nɛtɪk] *adj* : genético — **genetically** [-tɪkli] *adv*

geneticist [ʤə'nɛtəsɪst] *n* : genetista *mf*

genetics [ʤə'nɛtɪks] *n* : genética *f*

genial ['ʤiːniəl] *adj* GRACIOUS : simpático, cordial, afable — **genially** *adv*

geniality [ˌʤiːni'æləti] *n* : simpatía *f*, afabilidad *f*

genie ['ʤiːni] *n* : genio *m*

genital ['ʤɛnətəl] *adj* : genital

genitals ['ʤɛnətəlz] *npl* : genitales *mpl*

genius ['ʤiːnjəs] *n* : genio *m*

genocide ['ʤɛnə,saɪd] *n* : genocidio *m*

genre ['ʒɑnrə, 'ʒɑr] *n* : género *m*

genteel [ʤɛn'tiːl] *adj* : cortés, fino, refinado

gentile¹ ['ʤɛn,taɪl] *adj* : gentil

gentile² *n* : gentil *m*

gentility [ʤɛn'tɪləti] *n, pl* **-ties 1** : nobleza *f* (de nacimiento) **2** POLITENESS, REFINEMENT : cortesía *f*, refinamiento *m*

gentle ['ʤɛntəl] *adj* **-tler; -tlest 1** NOBLE : bien nacido, noble **2** DOCILE : dócil, manso **3** KINDLY : bondadoso, amable **4** MILD : suave, apacible ⟨a gentle breeze : una brisa suave⟩ **5** SOFT : suave (dícese de un sonido), ligero (dícese del tacto) **6** MODERATE : moderado, gradual ⟨a gentle slope : una cuesta gradual⟩

gentleman ['ʤɛntəlmən] *n, pl* **-men** [-mən, -ˌmɛn] : caballero *m*, señor *m*

gentlemanly ['ʤɛntəlmənli] *adj* : caballeroso

gentleness ['ʤɛntəlnəs] *n* : delicadeza *f*, suavidad *f*, ternura *f*

gentlewoman ['ʤɛntəl,wʊmən] *n, pl* **-women** [-,wɪmən] : dama *f*, señora *f*

gently ['ʤɛntli] *adv* **1** CAREFULLY, SOFTLY : con cuidado, suavemente, ligeramente **2** KINDLY : amablemente, con delicadeza

gentry ['ʤentri] *n*, *pl* **-tries** : aristocracia *f*

genuflect ['ʤenjʊ,flɛkt] *vi* : doblar la rodilla, hacer una genuflexión

genuflection [,ʤenju'flɛkʃən] *n* : genuflexión *f*

genuine ['ʤenjuwən] *adj* **1** AUTHENTIC, REAL : genuino, verdadero, auténtico **2** SINCERE : sincero — **genuinely** *adv*

genus ['ʤi:nəs] *n*, *pl* **genera** ['ʤɛ-nərə] : género *m*

geographer [ʤi'agrəfər] *n* : geógrafo *m*, -fa *f*

geographical [,ʤi:ə'græfɪkəl] *or* **geographic** [-fɪk] *adj* : geográfico — **geographically** [-fɪkli] *adv*

geography [ʤi'agrəfi] *n*, *pl* **-phies** : geografía *f*

geologic [,ʤi:ə'laʤɪk] *or* **geological** [-ʤɪkəl] *adj* : geológico — **geologically** [-ʤɪkli] *adv*

geologist [ʤi'aləʤɪst] *n* : geólogo *m*, -ga *f*

geology [ʤi'aləʤi] *n* : geología *f*

geometric [,ʤi:ə'mɛtrɪk] *or* **geometrical** [-trɪkəl] *adj* : geométrico

geometry [ʤi'amətri] *n*, *pl* **-tries** : geometría *f*

geopolitical [,ʤi:opə'lɪtɪkəl] *adj* : geopolítico

Georgian ['ʤorʤən] *n* **1** : georgiano *m* (idioma) **2** : georgiano *m*, -na *f* — **Georgian** *adj*

geranium [ʤə'reɪniəm] *n* : geranio *m*

gerbil ['ʤərbəl] *n* : jerbo *m*, gerbo *m*

geriatric [,ʤɛri'ætrɪk] *adj* : geriátrico

geriatrics [,ʤɛri'ætrɪks] *n* : geriatría *f*

germ ['ʤərm] *n* **1** MICROORGANISM : microbio *m*, germen *m* **2** BEGINNING : germen *m*, principio *m* ⟨the germ of a plan : el germen de un plan⟩

German ['ʤərmən] *n* **1** : alemán *m*, -mana *f* **2** : alemán *m* (idioma) — **German** *adj*

germane [ʤər'meɪn] *adj* : relevante, pertinente

Germanic[1] [ʤər'mænɪk] *adj* : germánico, alemán

Germanic[2] *n* : germánico *m* (idioma)

germanium [ʤər'meɪniəm] *n* : germanio *m*

germ cell *n* : célula *f* germen

germicide ['ʤərmə,saɪd] *n* : germicida *m*

germinate ['ʤərmə,neɪt] *v* **-nated; -nating** *vi* : germinar — *vt* : hacer germinar

germination [,ʤərmə'neɪʃən] *n* : germinación *f*

gerund ['ʤɛrənd] *n* : gerundio *m*

gestation [ʤɛ'steɪʃən] *n* : gestación *f*

gesture[1] ['ʤɛsʧər] *vi* **-tured; -turing** : gesticular, hacer gestos

gesture[2] *n* **1** : gesto *m*, ademán *m* **2** SIGN, TOKEN : gesto *m*, señal *f* ⟨a gesture of friendship : una señal de amistad⟩

get ['gɛt] *v* **got** ['gat]; **got** *or* **gotten** ['gatən]; **getting** *vt* **1** OBTAIN : conseguir, obtener, adquirir **2** RECEIVE : recibir ⟨to get a letter : recibir una carta⟩ **3** EARN : ganar ⟨he gets $10 an hour : gana $10 por hora⟩ **4** FETCH : traer ⟨get me my book : tráigame el libro⟩ **5** CATCH : tomar (un tren, etc.), agarrar (una pelota, una persona, etc.) **6** CONTRACT : contagiarse de, contraer ⟨she got the measles : le dio el sarampión⟩ **7** PREPARE : preparar (una comida) **8** PERSUADE : persuadir, mandar a hacer ⟨I got him to agree : logré convencerlo⟩ **9** (*to cause to be*) ⟨to get one's hair cut : cortarse el pelo⟩ **10** UNDERSTAND : entender ⟨now I get it! : ¡ya entiendo!⟩ **11** **to have got** : tener ⟨I've got a headache : tengo un dolor de cabeza⟩ **12** **to have got to** : tener que ⟨you've got to come : tienes que venir⟩ — *vi* **1** BECOME : ponerse, volverse, hacerse ⟨to get angry : ponerse furioso, enojarse⟩ **2** GO, MOVE : ir, avanzar ⟨he didn't get far : no avanzó mucho⟩ **3** ARRIVE : llegar ⟨to get home : llegar a casa⟩ **4** **to get to be** : llegar a ser ⟨she got to be the director : llegó a ser directora⟩ **5** **to get ahead** : adelantarse, progresar **6** **to get along** : llevarse bien (con alguien), congeniar **7** **to get by** : arreglárselas **8** **to get over** OVERCOME : superar, consolarse de **9** **to get together** MEET : reunirse **10** **to get up** : levantarse

getaway ['gɛtə,weɪ] *n* ESCAPE : fuga *f*, huida *f*, escapada *f*

geyser ['gaɪzər] *n* : géiser *m*

Ghanaian [gɑniən, 'gæ-] *n* : ghanés *m*, -nesa *f* — **Ghanaian** *adj*

ghastly ['gæstli] *adj* **-lier; -est** **1** HORRIBLE : horrible, espantoso **2** PALE : pálido, cadavérico

gherkin ['gərkən] *n* : pepinillo *m*

ghetto ['gɛto] *n*, *pl* **-tos** *or* **-toes** : gueto *m*

ghost ['goːst] *n* **1** : fantasma *f*, espectro *m* **2** **the Holy Ghost** : el Espíritu Santo

ghostly ['goːstli] *adv* : fantasmal

ghoul ['guːl] *n* **1** : demonio *m* necrófago **2** : persona *f* de gustos macabros

GI [,ʤi:'aɪ] *n*, *pl* **GI's** *or* **GIs** : soldado *m* estadounidense

giant[1] ['ʤaɪənt] *adj* : gigante, gigantesco, enorme

giant[2] *n* : gigante *m*, -ta *f*

gibberish ['ʤɪbərɪʃ] *n* : galimatías *m*, jerigonza *f*

gibbon ['gɪbən] *n* : gibón *m*

gibe[1] ['ʤaɪb] *vi* **gibed; gibing** : mofarse, burlarse

gibe[2] *n* : pulla *f*, burla *f*, mofa *f*

giblets ['ʤɪbləts] *npl* : menudos *mpl*, menudencias *fpl*

giddiness ['gɪdinəs] *n* **1** DIZZINESS : vértigo *m*, mareo *m* **2** SILLINESS : frivolidad *f*, estupidez *f*

giddy ['gɪdi] *adj* **-dier; -est 1** DIZZY : mareado, vertiginoso **2** FRIVOLOUS, SILLY : frívolo, tonto

gift ['gɪft] *n* **1** TALENT : don *m*, talento *m*, dotes *fpl* **2** PRESENT : regalo *m*, obsequio *m*

gifted ['gɪftəd] *adj* TALENTED : talentoso

gig ['gɪg] *vi* : trabajo *m* (de duración limitada) ⟨to play a gig : tocar en un concierto⟩

gigabyte ['dʒɪgə,baɪt, 'gɪ-] *n* : gigabyte *m*

gigantic [dʒaɪ'gæntɪk] *adj* : gigantesco, enorme, colosal

giggle¹ ['gɪgəl] *vi* **-gled; -gling** : reírse tontamente

giggle² *n* : risita *f*, risa *f* tonta

gild ['gɪld] *vt* **gilded** *or* **gilt** ['gɪlt]; **gilding** : dorar

gill¹ ['gɪl] *n* : agalla *f*, branquia *f*

gilt¹ ['gɪlt] *adj* : dorado

gilt² *n* : dorado *m*

gimlet ['gɪmlət] *n* **1** : barrena *f* (herramienta) **2** : bebida *f* de vodka o ginebra y limón

gimmick ['gɪmɪk] *n* **1** GADGET : artilugio *m* **2** CATCH : engaño *m*, trampa *f* **3** SCHEME, TRICK : ardid *m*, truco *m*

gin ['dʒɪn] *n* **1** : desmotadora *f* (de algodón) **2** : ginebra *f* (bebida alcohólica)

ginger ['dʒɪndʒər] *n* : jengibre *m*

ginger ale *n* : ginger ale *m*, gaseosa *f* de jengibre

gingerbread ['dʒɪndʒər,brɛd] *n* : pan *m* de jengibre

gingerly ['dʒɪndʒərli] *adv* : con cuidado, cautelosamente

gingham ['gɪŋəm] *n* : guinga *f*

ginseng ['dʒɪn,sɪŋ, -,sɛŋ] *n* : ginseng *m*

giraffe [dʒə'ræf] *n* : jirafa *f*

gird ['gərd] *vt* **girded** *or* **girt** ['gərt]; **girding 1** BIND : ceñir, atar **2** ENCIRCLE : rodear **3** to gird oneself : prepararse

girder ['gərdər] *n* : viga *f*

girdle¹ ['gərdəl] *vt* **-dled; -dling 1** GIRD : ceñir, atar **2** SURROUND : rodear, circundar

girdle² *n* : faja *f*

girl ['gərl] *n* **1** : chica *f*, muchacha *f* **2** *or* **little girl** : niña *f*, chica *f* **3** SWEETHEART : novia *f* **4** DAUGHTER : hija *f*

girlfriend ['gərl,frɛnd] *n* : novia *f*, amiga *f*

girlhood ['gərl,hʊd] *n* : niñez *f*, juventud *f* (de una muchacha)

girlish ['gərlɪʃ] *adj* : de niña

girth ['gərθ] *n* **1** : circunferencia *f* (de un árbol, etc.), cintura *f* (de una pérsona) **2** CINCH : cincha *f* (para caballos, etc.)

gist ['dʒɪst] *n* : quid *m*, meollo *m*

give¹ ['gɪv] *v* **gave** ['geɪv]; **given** ['gɪvən]; **giving** *vt* **1** HAND, PRESENT : dar, regalar, obsequiar ⟨give it to me : dámelo⟩ ⟨they gave him a gold watch : le regalaron un reloj de oro⟩ **2** PAY : dar, pagar ⟨I'll give you $10 for this one : te daré $10 por éste⟩ **3** UTTER : dar, pronunciar ⟨to give a shout : dar un grito⟩ ⟨to give a speech : pronunciar un

discurso⟩ ⟨to give a verdict : dictar sentencia⟩ **4** PROVIDE : dar ⟨to give one's word : dar uno su palabra⟩ ⟨to give a party : dar una fiesta⟩ **5** CAUSE : dar, causar, ocasionar ⟨to give trouble : causar problemas⟩ ⟨to give someone to understand : darle a entender a alguien⟩ **6** GRANT : dar, otorgar ⟨to give permission : dar permiso⟩ — *vi* **1** : hacer regalos ⟨to give to charity⟩ **2** YIELD : ceder, romperse ⟨it gave under the weight of the crowd : cedió bajo el peso de la muchedumbre⟩ **3** to give in *or* to give up SURRENDER : rendirse, entregarse **4** to give out : agotarse, acabarse ⟨the supplies gave out : las provisiones se agotaron⟩

give² *n* FLEXIBILITY : flexibilidad *f*, elasticidad *f*

giveaway ['gɪvə,weɪ] *n* **1** : revelación *f* involuntaria **2** GIFT : regalo *m*, obsequio *m*

given ['gɪvən] *adj* **1** INCLINED : dado, inclinado ⟨he's given to quarreling : es muy dado a discutir⟩ **2** SPECIFIC : dado, determinado ⟨at a given time : en un momento dado⟩

given name *n* : nombre *m* de pila

give up *vt* : dejar, renunciar a, abandonar ⟨to give up smoking : dejar de fumar⟩

gizzard ['gɪzərd] *n* : molleja *f*

glacial ['gleɪʃəl] *adj* : glacial — **glacially** *adv*

glacier ['gleɪʃər] *n* : glaciar *m*

glad ['glæd] *adj* **gladder; gladdest 1** PLEASED : alegre, contento ⟨she was glad I came : se alegró de que haya venido⟩ ⟨glad to meet you! : ¡mucho gusto!⟩ **2** HAPPY, PLEASING : feliz, agradable ⟨glad tidings : buenas nuevas⟩ **3** WILLING : dispuesto, gustoso ⟨I'll be glad to do it : lo haré con mucho gusto⟩

gladden ['glædən] *vt* : alegrar

glade ['gleɪd] *n* : claro *m*

gladiator ['glædi,eɪtər] *n* : gladiador *m*

gladiolus [,glædi'o:ləs] *n, pl* **-li** [-li, -,laɪ] : gladiolo *m*, gladíolo *m*

gladly ['glædli] *adv* : con mucho gusto

gladness ['glædnəs] *n* : alegría *f*, gozo *m*

glamor *or* **glamour** ['glæmər] *n* : atractivo *m*, hechizo *m*, encanto *m*

glamorous ['glæmərəs] *adj* : atractivo, encantador

glance¹ ['glænʦ] *vi* **glanced; glancing 1** RICOCHET : rebotar ⟨it glanced off the wall : rebotó en la pared⟩ **2** to glance at : mirar, echar un vistazo a **3** to glance away : apartar los ojos

glance² *n* : mirada *f*, vistazo *m*, ojeada *f*

gland ['glænd] *n* : glándula *f*

glandular ['glændʒʊlər] *adj* : glandular

glare¹ ['glær] *vi* **glared; glaring 1** SHINE : brillar, relumbrar **2** STARE : mirar con ira, lanzar una mirada feroz

glare[2] *n* **1** BRIGHTNESS : resplandor *m*, luz *f* deslumbrante **2** : mirada *f* feroz

glaring ['glærɪŋ] *adj* **1** BRIGHT : deslumbrante, brillante **2** FLAGRANT, OBVIOUS : flagrante, manifiesto ⟨a glaring error : un error que salta a la vista⟩

glass ['glæs] *n* **1** : vidrio *m*, cristal *m* ⟨stained glass : vidrio de color⟩ **2** : vaso *m* ⟨a glass of milk : un vaso de leche⟩ **3 glasses** *npl* SPECTACLES : gafas *fpl*, anteojos *mpl*, lentes *mpl*, espejuelos *mpl*

glassblowing ['glæs,blo:ɪŋ] *n* : soplado *m* del vidrio

glassful ['glæs,ful] *n* : vaso *m*, copa *f*

glassware ['glæs,wær] *n* : cristalería *f*

glassy ['glæsi] *adj* **glassier; -est 1** VITREOUS : vítreo **2** : vidrioso ⟨glassy eyes : ojos vidriosos⟩

glaucoma [glaʊˈkoːmə, glɔ-] *n* : glaucoma *m*

glaze[1] ['gleɪz] *vt* **glazed; glazing 1** : ponerle vidrios a (una ventana, etc.) **2** : vidriar (cerámica) **3** : glasear (papel, verduras, etc.)

glaze[2] *n* : vidriado *m*, glaseado *m*, barniz *m*

glazier ['gleɪʒər] *n* : vidriero *m*, -ra *f*

gleam[1] ['gli:m] *vi* : brillar, destellar, relucir

gleam[2] *n* **1** LIGHT : luz *f* (oscura) **2** GLINT : destello *m* **3** GLIMMER : rayo *m*, vislumbre *f* ⟨a gleam of hope : un rayo de esperanza⟩

glean ['gli:n] *vt* : recoger, espigar

glee ['gli:] *n* : alegría *f*, júbilo *m*, regocijo *m*

gleeful ['gli:fəl] *adj* : lleno de alegría

glen ['glɛn] *n* : cañada *f*

glib ['glɪb] *adj* **glibber; glibbest 1** : simplista ⟨a glib reply : una respuesta simplista⟩ **2** : con mucha labia (dícese de una persona)

glibly ['glɪbli] *adv* : con mucha labia

glide[1] ['glaɪd] *vi* **glided; gliding** : deslizarse (en una superficie), planear (en el aire)

glide[2] *n* : planeo *m*

glider ['glaɪdər] *n* **1** : planeador *m* (aeronave) **2** : mecedor *m* (tipo de columpio)

glimmer[1] ['glɪmər] *vi* : brillar con luz trémula

glimmer[2] *n* **1** : luz *f* trémula, luz *f* tenue **2** GLEAM : rayo *m*, vislumbre *f* ⟨a glimmer of understanding : un rayo de entendimiento⟩

glimpse[1] ['glɪmps] *vt* **glimpsed; glimpsing** : vislumbrar, entrever

glimpse[2] *n* : mirada *f* breve ⟨to catch a glimpse of : alcanzar a ver, vislumbrar⟩

glint[1] ['glɪnt] *vi* GLEAM, SPARKLE : destellar, fulgurar

glint[2] *n* **1** SPARKLE : destello *m*, centelleo *m* **2 to have a glint in one's eye** : chispearle los ojos a uno

glisten[1] ['glɪsən] *vi* : brillar, centellear

glisten[2] *n* : brillo *m*, centelleo *m*

glitch ['glɪtʃ] *n* **1** MALFUNCTION : mal funcionamiento *m* **2** SNAG : problema *m*, complicación *f*

glitter[1] ['glɪtər] *vi* **1** SPARKLE : destellar, relucir, brillar **2** FLASH : relampaguear ⟨his eyes glittered in anger : le relampagueaban los ojos de ira⟩

glitter[2] *n* **1** BRIGHTNESS : brillo *m* **2** : purpurina *f* (para decoración)

glitz ['glɪts] *n* : oropel *m*

gloat ['glo:t] *vi* **to gloat over** : regodearse en

glob ['glɑb] *n* : plasta *f*, masa *f*, grumo *m*

global ['glo:bəl] *adj* **1** SPHERICAL : esférico **2** WORLDWIDE : global, mundial — **globally** *adv*

globe ['glo:b] *n* **1** SPHERE : esfera *f*, globo *m* **2** EARTH : globo *m*, Tierra *f* **3** : globo *m* terráqueo (modelo de la Tierra)

globe–trotter ['glo:b,trɑtər] *n* : trotamundos *mf*

globular ['glɑbjələr] *adj* : globular

globule ['glɑ,bju:l] *n* : glóbulo *m*

gloom ['glu:m] *n* **1** DARKNESS : penumbra *f*, oscuridad *f* **2** MELANCHOLY : melancolía *f*, tristeza *f*

gloomily ['glu:məli] *adv* : tristemente

gloomy ['glu:mi] *adj* **gloomier; -est 1** DARK : oscuro, tenebroso ⟨gloomy weather : tiempo gris⟩ **2** MELANCHOLY : melancólico **3** PESSIMISTIC : pesimista **4** DEPRESSING : deprimente, lúgubre

glorification [,glorəfəˈkeɪʃən] *n* : glorificación *f*

glorify ['glorə,faɪ] *vt* **-fied; -fying** : glorificar

glorious ['gloriəs] *adj* **1** ILLUSTRIOUS : glorioso, ilustre **2** MAGNIFICENT : magnífico, espléndido, maravilloso — **gloriously** *adv*

glory[1] ['glori] *vi* **-ried; -rying** EXULT : exultar, regocijarse

glory[2] *n*, *pl* **-ries 1** RENOWN : gloria *f*, fama *f*, honor *m* **2** PRAISE : gloria *f* ⟨glory to God : gloria a Dios⟩ **3** MAGNIFICENCE : magnificencia *f*, esplendor *m*, gloria *f* **4 to be in one's glory** : estar uno en su gloria

gloss[1] ['glɔs, 'glɑs] *vt* **1** EXPLAIN : glosar, explicar **2** POLISH : lustrar, pulir **3 to gloss over** : quitarle importancia a, minimizar

gloss[2] *n* **1** SHINE : lustre *m*, brillo *m* **2** EXPLANATION : glosa *f*, explicación *f* breve **3** → **glossary**

glossary ['glɔsəri, 'glɑ-] *n*, *pl* **-ries** : glosario *m*

glossy ['glɔsi, 'glɑ-] *adj* **glossier; -est** : brillante, lustroso, satinado (dícese del papel)

glove ['glʌv] *n* : guante *m*

glow[1] ['glo:] *vi* **1** SHINE : brillar, resplandecer **2** BRIM : rebosar ⟨to glow with health : rebosar de salud⟩

glow² n **1** BRIGHTNESS : resplandor m, brillo m, luminosidad f **2** FEELING : sensación f (de bienestar), oleada f (de sentimiento) **3** INCANDESCENCE : incandescencia f

glower ['glauər] vi : fruncir el ceño

glowworm ['glo:ˌwərm] n : luciérnaga f

glucose ['glu:ˌko:s] n : glucosa f

glue¹ ['glu:] vt glued; gluing or glueing : pegar, encolar

glue² n : pegamento m, cola f

gluey ['glu:i] adj gluier; -est : pegajoso

glum ['glʌm] adj glummer; glummest **1** SULLEN : hosco, sombrío **2** DREARY, GLOOMY : sombrío, triste, melancólico

glut¹ ['glʌt] vt glutted; glutting **1** SATIATE : saciar, hartar **2** : inundar (el mercado)

glut² n : exceso m, superabundancia f

glutinous ['glu:tənəs] adj STICKY : pegajoso, glutinoso

glutton ['glʌtən] n : glotón m, -tona f

gluttonous ['glʌtənəs] adj : glotón

gluttony ['glʌtəni] n, pl -tonies : glotonería f, gula f

gnarled ['nɑrld] adj **1** KNOTTY : nudoso **2** TWISTED : retorcido

gnash ['næʃ] vt : hacer rechinar (los dientes)

gnat ['næt] n : jején m

gnaw ['nɔ] vt : roer

gnome ['no:m] n : gnomo m

gnu ['nu:, 'nju:] n, pl gnu or gnus : ñu m

go¹ ['go:] v went ['wɛnt]; gone ['gɔn, 'gɑn]; going; goes ['go:z] vi **1** PROCEED : ir ⟨to go slow : ir despacio⟩ ⟨to go shopping : ir de compras⟩ **2** LEAVE : irse, marcharse, salir ⟨let's go! : ¡vámonos!⟩ ⟨the train went on time : el tren salió a tiempo⟩ **3** DISAPPEAR : desaparecer, pasarse, irse ⟨her fear is gone : se le ha pasado el miedo⟩ ⟨my pen is gone! : ¡mi pluma desapareció!⟩ **4** EXTEND : ir, extenderse, llegar ⟨this road goes to the river : este camino se extiende hasta el río⟩ ⟨to go from top to bottom : ir de arriba abajo⟩ **5** FUNCTION : funcionar, marchar ⟨the car won't go : el coche no funciona⟩ ⟨to get something going : poner algo en marcha⟩ **6** SELL : venderse ⟨it goes for $15 : se vende por $15⟩ **7** PROGRESS : ir, andar, seguir ⟨my exam went well : me fue bien en el examen⟩ ⟨how did the meeting go? : ¿qué tal la reunión?⟩ **8** BECOME : volverse, quedarse ⟨he's going crazy : está volviéndose loco⟩ ⟨the tire went flat : la llanta se desinfló⟩ **9** FIT : caber ⟨it will go through the door : cabe por la puerta⟩ **10** anything goes! : ¡todo vale! **11** to go : faltar ⟨only 10 days to go : faltan sólo 10 días⟩ **12** to go back on : faltar uno a (su promesa) **13** to go bad SPOIL : estropearse, echarse a perder **14** to go for : interesarse uno en, gustarle a uno (algo, alguien) ⟨I don't go for that : eso no me interesa⟩ **15** to go off EXPLODE : estallar **16** to go with MATCH : armonizar con, hacer juego con — v aux to be going to : ir a ⟨I'm going to write a letter : voy a escribir una carta⟩ ⟨it's not going to last : no va a durar⟩

go² n, pl goes **1** ATTEMPT : intento m ⟨to have a go at : intentar, probar⟩ **2** SUCCESS : éxito m **3** ENERGY : energía f, empuje m ⟨to be on the go : no parar, no descansar⟩

goad¹ ['go:d] vt : aguijonear (un animal), incitar (a una persona)

goad² n : aguijón m

goal ['go:l] n **1** : gol m (en deportes) ⟨to score a goal : anotar un gol⟩ **2** or goalposts : portería f **3** AIM, OBJECTIVE : meta m, objetivo m

goalie ['go:li] → goalkeeper

goalkeeper ['go:lˌki:pər] n : portero m, -ra f; guardameta mf; arquero m, -ra f

goaltender ['go:lˌtɛndər] → goalkeeper

goat ['go:t] n **1** : cabra f (hembra) **2** billy goat : macho m cabrío, chivo m

goatee [go:'ti:] n : barbita f de chivo, piocha f Mex

goatskin ['go:tˌskɪn] n : piel f de cabra

gob ['gɑb] n : masa f, grumo m

gobble ['gɑbəl] v -bled; -bling vt to gobble up : tragar, engullir — vi : hacer ruidos de pavo

gobbledygook ['gɑbəldiˌguk, -ˌgu:k] n : jerigonza f

go-between ['go:bɪˌtwi:n] n : intermediario m, -ria f; mediador m, -dora f

goblet ['gɑblət] n : copa f

goblin ['gɑblən] n : duende m, trasgo m

god ['gɑd, 'gɔd] n **1** : dios m **2** God : Dios m

godchild ['gɑdˌtʃaɪld, 'gɔd-] n, pl -children : ahijado m, -da f

goddess ['gɑdəs, 'gɔ-] n : diosa f

godfather ['gɑdˌfɑðər, 'gɔd-] n : padrino m

godless ['gɑdləs, 'gɔd-] adj : ateo

godlike ['gɑdˌlaɪk, 'gɔd-] adj : divino

godly ['gɑdli, 'gɔd-] adj -lier; -est **1** DIVINE : divino **2** DEVOUT, PIOUS : piadoso, devoto, beato

godmother ['gɑdˌmʌðər, 'gɔd-] n : madrina f

godparents ['gɑdˌpærənts, 'gɔd-] npl : padrinos mpl

godsend ['gɑdˌsɛnd, 'gɔd-] n : bendición f, regalo m divino

goes → go

go-getter ['go:ˌgɛtər] n : persona f ambiciosa, buscavidas mf fam

goggle ['gɑgəl] vi -gled; -gling : mirar con ojos desorbitados

goggles ['gɑgəlz] npl : gafas fpl (protectoras), anteojos mpl

goings-on [ˌgo:ɪŋz'ɑn, -'ɔn] npl : sucesos mpl, ocurrencias fpl

goiter ['gɔɪtər] n : bocio m

gold ['go:ld] n : oro m

golden ['go:ldən] adj **1** : (hecho) de oro **2** : dorado, de color oro ⟨golden hair

: pelo rubio⟩ **3** FLOURISHING, PROS-PEROUS : dorado, próspero ⟨golden years : años dorados⟩ **4** FAVORABLE : favorable, excelente ⟨a golden opportunity : una excelente oportunidad⟩

goldenrod ['goːldən,rɑd] *n* : vara *f* de oro

golden rule *n* : regla *f* de oro

goldfinch ['goːld,fɪntʃ] *n* : jilguero *m*

goldfish ['goːld,fɪʃ] *n* : pez *m* de colores

goldsmith ['goːld,smɪθ] *n* : orífice *mf*, orfebre *mf*

golf¹ ['gɑlf, 'gɔlf] *vi* : jugar (al) golf

golf² *n* : golf *m*

golfer ['gɑlfər, 'gɔl-] *n* : golfista *mf*

gondola ['gɑndələ, gɑn'doːlə] *n* : góndola *f*

gone ['gɔn] *adj* **1** DEAD : muerto **2** PAST : pasado, ido **3** LOST : perdido, desaparecido **4** to be far gone : estar muy avanzado **5** to be gone on : estar loco por

goner ['gɔnər] *n* to be a goner : estar en las últimas

gong ['gɔŋ, 'gɑŋ] *n* : gong *m*

gonorrhea [,gɑnə'riːə] *n* : gonorrea *f*

good¹ ['gʊd] *adv* **1** (*used as an intensifier*) : bien ⟨a good strong rope : una cuerda bien fuerte⟩ **2** WELL : bien

good² *adj* **better** ['bɛtər]; **best** ['bɛst] **1** PLEASANT : bueno, agradable ⟨good news : buenas noticias⟩ ⟨to have a good time : divertirse⟩ **2** BENEFICIAL : bueno, beneficioso ⟨good for a cold : beneficioso para los resfriados⟩ ⟨it's good for you : es bueno para uno⟩ **3** FULL : completo, entero ⟨a good hour : una hora entera⟩ **4** CONSIDERABLE : bueno, bastante ⟨a good many people : muchísima gente, un buen número de gente⟩ **5** ATTRACTIVE, DESIRABLE : bueno, bien ⟨a good salary : un buen sueldo⟩ ⟨to look good : quedar bien⟩ **6** KIND, VIRTUOUS : bueno, amable ⟨she's a good person : es buena gente⟩ ⟨that's good of you! : ¡qué amable!⟩ ⟨good deeds : buenas obras⟩ **7** SKILLED : bueno, hábil ⟨to be good at : tener facilidad para⟩ **8** SOUND : bueno, sensato ⟨good advice : buenos consejos⟩ **9** (*in greetings*) : bueno ⟨good morning : buenos días⟩ ⟨good afternoon (evening) : buenas tardes⟩ ⟨good night : buenas noches⟩

good³ *n* **1** RIGHT : bien *m* ⟨to do good : hacer el bien⟩ **2** GOODNESS : bondad *f* **3** BENEFIT : bien *m*, provecho *m* ⟨it's for your own good : es por su propio bien⟩ **4 goods** *npl* PROPERTY : bienes *mpl* personales, posesiones *fpl* **5 goods** *npl* WARES : mercancía *f*, mercadería *f*, artículos *mpl* **6 for** ~ : para siempre

good–bye *or* **good–by** [gʊd'baɪ] *n* : adiós *m*

good–for–nothing ['gʊdfər,nʌθɪŋ] *n* : inútil *mf*; haragán *m*, -gana *f*; holgazán *m*, -zana *f*

Good Friday *n* : Viernes *m* Santo

good–hearted ['gʊd'hɑrtəd] *adj* : bondadoso, benévolo, de buen corazón

good–looking ['gʊd'lʊkɪŋ] *adj* : bello, bonito, guapo

goodly ['gʊdli] *adj* **-lier; -est** : considerable, importante ⟨a goodly number : un número considerable⟩

good–natured ['gʊd'neɪtʃərd] *adj* : amigable, amistoso, bonachón *fam*

goodness ['gʊdnəs] *n* **1** : bondad *f* **2 thank goodness!** : ¡gracias a Dios!, ¡menos mal!

good–tempered ['gʊd'tɛmpərd] *adj* : de buen genio

goodwill [,gʊd'wɪl] *n* **1** BENEVOLENCE : benevolencia *f*, buena voluntad *f* **2** : buen nombre *m* (de comercios), renombre *m* comercial

goody ['gʊdi] *n, pl* **goodies** : cosa *f* rica para comer, golosina *f*

gooey ['guːi] *adj* **gooier; gooiest** : pegajoso

goof¹ ['guːf] *vi* **1 to goof off** : holgazanear **2 to goof around** : hacer tonterías **3 to goof up** BLUNDER : cometer un error

goof² *n* **1** : bobo *m*, -ba *f*; tonto *m*, -ta *f* **2** BLUNDER : error *m*, planchazo *m fam*

goofy ['guːfi] *adj* **goofier; -est** SILLY : tonto, bobo

goose ['guːs] *n, pl* **geese** ['giːs] : ganso *m*, -sa *f*; ánsar *m*; oca *f*

gooseberry ['guːs,bɛri, 'guːz-] *n, pl* **-berries** : grosella *f* espinosa

goose bumps *npl* : carne *f* de gallina

gooseflesh ['guːs,flɛʃ] → **goose bumps**

goose pimples → **goose bumps**

gopher ['goːfər] *n* : taltuza *f*

gore¹ ['gor] *vt* **gored; goring** : cornear

gore² *n* BLOOD : sangre *f*

gorge¹ ['gordʒ] *vt* **gorged; gorging** **1** SATIATE : saciar, hartar **2 to gorge oneself** : hartarse, atiborrarse, atracarse *fam*

gorge² *n* RAVINE : desfiladero *m*

gorgeous ['gordʒəs] *adj* : hermoso, espléndido, magnífico

gorilla [gə'rɪlə] *n* : gorila *m*

gory ['gori] *adj* **gorier; -est** BLOODY : sangriento

gosling ['gɑzlɪŋ, 'gɔz-] *n* : ansarino *m*

gospel ['gɑspəl] *n* **1** *or* **Gospel** : evangelio *m* ⟨the four Gospels : los cuatro evangelios⟩ **2 the gospel truth** : el evangelio, la pura verdad

gossamer ['gɑsəmər, 'gɑzə-] *adj* : tenue, sutil ⟨gossamer wings : alas tenues⟩

gossip¹ ['gɑsɪp] *vi* : chismear, contar chismes

gossip² *n* **1** : chismoso *m*, -sa *f* (persona) **2** RUMOR : chisme *m*, rumor *m*

gossipy ['gɑsɪpi] *adj* : chismoso

got → **get**

Gothic ['gɑθɪk] *adj* : gótico

gotten → **get**

gouge¹ ['gaʊdʒ] *vt* **gouged; gouging** **1** : excavar, escoplear (con una gubia) **2** SWINDLE : estafar, extorsionar

gouge² *n* 1 CHISEL : gubia *f*, formón *m* 2 GROOVE : ranura *f*, hoyo *m* (hecho por un formón)

goulash [ˈguːˌlɑʃ, -ˌlæʃ] *n* : estofado *m*, guiso *m* al estilo húngaro

gourd [ˈgord, ˈgʊrd] *n* : calabaza *f*

gourmand [ˈgʊrˌmɑnd] *n* 1 GLUTTON : glotón *m*, -tona *f* 2 → **gourmet**

gourmet [ˈgʊrˌmeɪ, gʊrˈmeɪ] *n* : gourmet *mf*; gastrónomo *m*, -ma *f*

gout [ˈgaʊt] *n* : gota *f*

govern [ˈgʌvərn] *vt* 1 RULE : gobernar 2 CONTROL, DETERMINE : determinar, controlar, guiar 3 RESTRAIN : dominar (las emociones, etc.) — *vi* : gobernar

governess [ˈgʌvərnəs] *n* : institutriz *f*

government [ˈgʌvərmənt] *n* : gobierno *m*

governmental [ˌgʌvərˈmɛntəl] *adj* : gubernamental, gubernativo

governor [ˈgʌvənər, ˈgʌvərnər] *n* 1 : gobernador *m*, -dora *f* (de un estado, etc.) 2 : regulador *m* (de una máquina)

governorship [ˈgʌvənərˌʃɪp, ˈgʌvərnər-] *n* : cargo *m* de gobernador

gown [ˈgaʊn] *n* 1 : vestido *m* ⟨evening gown : traje *m* de fiesta⟩ 2 : toga *f* (de magistrados, clérigos, etc.)

grab¹ [ˈgræb] *v* grabbed; grabbing *vt* SNATCH : agarrar, arrebatar — *vi* : agarrarse

grab² *n* 1 to make a grab for : tratar de agarrar 2 up for grabs : disponible, libre

grace¹ [ˈgreɪs] *vi* graced; gracing 1 HONOR : honrar 2 ADORN : adornar, embellecer

grace² *n* 1 : gracia *f* ⟨by the grace of God : por la gracia de Dios⟩ 2 BLESSING : bendición *f* (de la mesa) 3 RESPITE : plazo *m*, gracia *f* ⟨a five days' grace (period) : un plazo de cinco días⟩ 4 GRACIOUSNESS : gentileza *f*, cortesía *f* 5 ELEGANCE : elegancia *f*, gracia *f* 6 to be in the good graces of : estar en buenas relaciones con 7 with good grace : de buena gana

graceful [ˈgreɪsfəl] *adj* : lleno de gracia, garboso, grácil

gracefully [ˈgreɪsfəli] *adv* : con gracia, con garbo

gracefulness [ˈgreɪsfəlnəs] *n* : gracilidad *f*, apostura *f*, gallardía *f*

graceless [ˈgreɪsləs] *adj* 1 DISCOURTEOUS : descortés 2 CLUMSY, INELEGANT : torpe, desgarbado, poco elegante

gracious [ˈgreɪʃəs] *adj* : cortés, gentil, cordial

graciously [ˈgreɪʃəsli] *adv* : gentilmente

graciousness [ˈgreɪʃəsnəs] *n* : gentileza *f*

gradation [greɪˈdeɪʃən, grə-] *n* : gradación *f*

grade¹ [ˈgreɪd] *vt* graded; grading 1 SORT : clasificar 2 LEVEL : nivelar 3 : calificar (exámenes, alumnos)

grade² *n* 1 QUALITY : categoría *f*, calidad *f* 2 RANK : grado *m*, rango *m* (mil-

itar) 3 YEAR : grado *m*, curso *m*, año *m* ⟨sixth grade : el sexto grado⟩ 4 MARK : nota *f*, calificación *f* (en educación) 5 SLOPE : cuesta *f*, pendiente *f*, gradiente *f*

grade school → **elementary school**

gradient [ˈgreɪdiənt] *n* : gradiente *f*

gradual [ˈgrædʒuəl] *adj* : gradual, paulatino

gradually [ˈgrædʒuəli, ˈgrædʒəli] *adv* : gradualmente, poco a poco

graduate¹ [ˈgrædʒuˌeɪt] *v* -ated; -ating *vi* : graduarse, licenciarse — *vt* : graduar ⟨a graduated thermometer : un termómetro graduado⟩

graduate² [ˈgrædʒuət] *adj* : de postgrado ⟨graduate course : curso de postgrado⟩

graduate³ *n* 1 : licenciado *m*, -da *f*; graduado *m*, -da *f* (de la universidad) 2 : bachiller *mf* (de la escuela secundaria)

graduate student *n* : postgraduado *m*, -da *f*

graduation [ˌgrædʒuˈeɪʃən] *n* : graduación *f*

graffiti [grəˈfiːti, græ-] *npl* : pintadas *fpl*, graffiti *mpl*

graft¹ [ˈgræft] *vt* : injertar

graft² *n* 1 : injerto *m* ⟨skin graft : injerto cutáneo⟩ 2 CORRUPTION : soborno *m* (político), ganancia *f* ilegal

grain [ˈgreɪn] *n* 1 : grano *m* ⟨a grain of corn : un grano de maíz⟩ ⟨like a grain of sand : como grano de arena⟩ 2 CEREALS : cereales *mpl* 3 : veta *f*, vena *f*, grano *m* (de madera) 4 SPECK, TRACE : pizca *f*, ápice *m* ⟨a grain of truth : una pizca de verdad⟩ 5 grano *m* (unidad de peso)

gram [ˈgræm] *n* : gramo *m*

grammar [ˈgræmər] *n* : gramática *f*

grammar school → **elementary school**

grammatical [grəˈmætɪkəl] *adj* : gramatical — **grammatically** [-kli] *adv*

granary [ˈgreɪnəri, ˈgræ-] *n, pl* -ries : granero *m*

grand [ˈgrænd] *adj* 1 FOREMOST : grande 2 IMPRESSIVE : impresionante, magnífico ⟨a grand view : una vista magnífica⟩ 3 LAVISH : grandioso, suntuoso, lujoso ⟨to live in a grand manner : vivir a lo grande⟩ 4 FABULOUS : fabuloso, magnífico ⟨to have a grand time : pasarlo estupendamente, pasarlo en grande⟩ 5 grand total : total *m*, suma *f* total

grandchild [ˈgrænˌtʃaɪld] *n, pl* -children : nieto *m*, -ta *f*

granddaughter [ˈgrændˌdɔtər] *n* : nieta *f*

grandeur [ˈgrændʒər] *n* : grandiosidad *f*, esplendor *m*

grandfather [ˈgrændˌfɑðər] *n* : abuelo *m*

grandiose [ˈgrændiˌoːs, ˌgrændiˈ-] *adj* 1 IMPOSING : imponente, grandioso 2 POMPOUS : pomposo, presuntuoso

grandma [ˈgræmˌmɑ, -ˌmɔ] *n* : abuelita *f*, nana *f*

grandmother ['grænd,mʌðər] *n* : abuela *f*

grandpa ['græm,pɑ, -,pɔ] *n* : abuelito *m*

grandparents ['grænd,pærənts] *npl* : abuelos *mpl*

grandson ['grænd,sʌn] *n* : nieto *m*

grandstand ['grænd,stænd] *n* : tribuna *f*

granite ['grænɪt] *n* : granito *m*

grant¹ ['grænt] *vt* 1 ALLOW : conceder ⟨to grant a request : conceder una petición⟩ 2 BESTOW : conceder, dar, otorgar ⟨to grant a favor : otorgar un favor⟩ 3 ADMIT : reconocer, admitir ⟨I'll grant that he's clever : reconozco que es listo⟩ 4 to take for granted : dar (algo) por sentado

grant² *n* 1 GRANTING : concesión *f*, otorgamiento *m* 2 SCHOLARSHIP : beca *f* 3 SUBSIDY : subvención *f*

granular ['grænjələr] *adj* : granular

granulated ['grænjʊ,leɪt̬əd] *adj* : granulado

grape ['greɪp] *n* : uva *f*

grapefruit ['greɪp,fru:t] *n* : toronja *f*, pomelo *m*

grapevine ['greɪp,vaɪn] *n* 1 : vid *f*, parra *f* 2 through the grapevine : por vías secretas ⟨I heard it through the grapevine : me lo contaron⟩

graph ['græf] *n* : gráfica *f*, gráfico *m*

graphic ['græfɪk] *adj* 1 VIVID : vívido, gráfico 2 graphic arts : artes gráficas

graphically ['græfɪkli] *adv* : gráficamente

graphite ['græ,faɪt] *n* : grafito *m*

grapnel ['græpnəl] *n* : rezón *m*

grapple ['græpəl] *v* -pled; -pling *vt* GRIP : agarrar (con un garfio) — *vi* STRUGGLE : forcejear, luchar (con un problema, etc.)

grasp¹ ['græsp] *vt* 1 GRIP, SEIZE : agarrar, asir 2 COMPREHEND : entender, comprender — *vi* to grasp at : aprovechar

grasp² *n* 1 GRIP : agarre *m* 2 CONTROL : control *m*, garras *fpl* 3 REACH : alcance *m* ⟨within your grasp : a su alcance⟩ 4 UNDERSTANDING : comprensión *f*, entendimiento *m*

grass ['græs] *n* 1 : hierba *f* (planta) 2 PASTURE : pasto *m*, zacate *m* CA, Mex 3 LAWN : césped *m*, pasto *m*

grasshopper ['græs,hɑpər] *n* : saltamontes *m*

grassland ['græs,lænd] *n* : pradera *f*

grassy ['græsi] *adj* grassier; -est : cubierto de hierba

grate¹ ['greɪt] *v* grated; -ing *vt* 1 : rallar (en cocina) 2 SCRAPE : rascar 3 to grate one's teeth : hacer rechinar los dientes — *vi* 1 RASP, SQUEAK : chirriar 2 IRRITATE : irritar ⟨to grate on one's nerves : crisparle los nervios a uno⟩

grate² *n* 1 : parrilla *f* (para cocinar) 2 GRATING : reja *f*, rejilla *f*, verja *f* (en una ventana)

grateful ['greɪtfəl] *adj* : agradecido

gratefully ['greɪtfəli] *adv* : con agradecimiento

gratefulness ['greɪtfəlnəs] *n* : gratitud *f*, agradecimiento *m*

grater ['greɪt̬ər] *n* : rallador *m*

gratification [,græt̬əfə'keɪʃən] *n* : gratificación *f*

gratify ['græt̬ə,faɪ] *vt* -fied; -fying 1 PLEASE : complacer 2 SATISFY : satisfacer, gratificar

grating ['greɪt̬ɪŋ] *n* : reja *f*, rejilla *f*

gratis¹ ['græt̬əs, 'greɪ-] *adv* : gratis, gratuitamente

gratis² *adj* : gratis, gratuito

gratitude ['græt̬ə,tu:d, -,tju:d] *n* : gratitud *f*, agradecimiento *m*

gratuitous [grə'tu:ət̬əs] *adj* : gratuito

gratuity [grə'tu:ət̬i] *n*, *pl* -ities TIP : propina *f*

grave¹ ['greɪv] *adj* graver; -est 1 IMPORTANT : grave, de mucha gravedad 2 SERIOUS, SOLEMN : grave, serio

grave² *n* : tumba *f*, sepultura *f*

gravel ['grævəl] *n* : grava *f*, gravilla *f*

gravelly ['grævəli] *adj* 1 : de grava 2 HARSH : áspero (dícese de la voz)

gravely ['greɪvli] *adv* : gravemente

gravestone ['greɪv,sto:n] *n* : lápida *f*

graveyard ['greɪv,jɑrd] *n* CEMETERY : cementerio *m*, panteón *m*, camposanto *m*

gravitate ['grævə,teɪt] *vi* -tated; -tating : gravitar

gravitation [,grævə'teɪʃən] *n* : gravitación *f*

gravitational [,grævə'teɪʃənəl] *adj* : gravitacional

gravity ['grævət̬i] *n*, *pl* -ties 1 SERIOUSNESS : gravedad *f*, seriedad *f* 2 : gravedad *f* ⟨the law of gravity : la ley de la gravedad⟩

gravy ['greɪvi] *n*, *pl* -vies : salsa *f* (preparada con el jugo de la carne asada)

gray¹ ['greɪ] *vt* : hacer gris — *vi* : encanecer, ponerse gris

gray² *adj* 1 : gris (dícese del color) 2 : cano, canoso ⟨gray hair : pelo canoso⟩ ⟨to go gray : volverse cano⟩ 3 DISMAL, GLOOMY : gris, triste

gray³ *n* : gris *m*

grayish ['greɪɪʃ] *adj* : grisáceo

graze ['greɪz] *v* grazed; grazing *vi* : pastar, pacer — *vt* 1 : pastorear (ganado) 2 BRUSH : rozar 3 SCRATCH : raspar

grease¹ ['gri:s, 'gri:z] *vt* greased; greasing : engrasar, lubricar

grease² ['gri:s] *n* : grasa *f*

greasy ['gri:si, -zi] *adj* greasier; -est 1 : grasiento 2 OILY : grasa, grasoso

great ['greɪt] *adj* 1 LARGE : grande ⟨a great mountain : una montaña grande⟩ ⟨a great crowd : una gran muchedumbre⟩ 2 INTENSE : intenso, fuerte, grande ⟨great pain : gran dolor⟩ 3 EMINENT : grande, eminente, distinguido ⟨a great poet : un gran poeta⟩ 4 EXCELLENT, TERRIFIC : excelente, estupendo, fabuloso ⟨to have a great time : pasarlo en grande⟩ **5 a great while** : mucho tiempo

great–aunt [ˌgreɪt'ænt, -'ant] *n* : tía *f* abuela

greater ['greɪtər] (*comparative of* **great**) : mayor

greatest ['greɪtəst] (*superlative of* **great**) : el mayor, la mayor

great–grandchild [ˌgreɪt'grænd-ˌtʃaɪld] *n, pl* **-children** [-ˌtʃɪldrən] : bisnieto *m*, -ta *f*

great–grandfather [ˌgreɪt'grænd-ˌfɑðər] *n* : bisabuelo *m*

great–grandmother [ˌgreɪt'grænd-ˌmʌðər] *n* : bisabuela *f*

greatly ['greɪtli] *adv* **1** MUCH : mucho, sumamente ⟨to be greatly improved : haber mejorado mucho⟩ **2** VERY : muy ⟨greatly superior : muy superior⟩

greatness ['greɪtnəs] *n* : grandeza *f*

great–uncle [ˌgreɪt'ʌŋkəl] *n* : tío *m* abuelo

grebe ['griːb] *n* : somorgujo *m*

greed ['griːd] *n* **1** AVARICE : avaricia *f*, codicia *f* **2** GLUTTONY : glotonería *f*, gula *f*

greedily ['griːdəli] *adv* : con avaricia, con gula

greediness ['griːdinəs] → **greed**

greedy ['griːdi] *adj* **greedier; -est 1** AVARICIOUS : codicioso, avaricioso **2** GLUTTONOUS : glotón

Greek ['griːk] *n* **1** : griego *m*, -ga *f* **2** : griego *m* (idioma) — **Greek** *adj*

green¹ ['griːn] *adj* **1** : verde (dícese del color) **2** UNRIPE : verde, inmaduro **3** INEXPERIENCED : verde, novato

green² *n* **1** : verde *m* **2 greens** *npl* VEGETABLES : verduras *fpl*

greenery ['griːnəri] *n, pl* **-eries** : plantas *fpl* verdes, vegetación *f*

greenhorn ['griːnˌhɔrn] *n* : novato *m*, -ta *f*

greenhouse ['griːnˌhaʊs] *n* : invernadero *m*

greenhouse effect : efecto *m* invernadero

greenish ['griːnɪʃ] *adj* : verdoso

Greenlander ['griːnləndər, -ˌlæn-] *n* : groenlandés *m*, -desa *f*

greenness ['griːnnəs] *n* **1** : verdor *m* **2** INEXPERIENCE : inexperiencia *f*

green thumb *n* **to have a green thumb** : tener buena mano para las plantas

greet ['griːt] *vt* **1** : saludar ⟨to greet a friend : saludar a un amigo⟩ **2** : acoger, recibir ⟨they greeted him with boos : lo recibieron con abucheos⟩

greeting ['griːtɪŋ] *n* **1** : saludo *m* **2 greetings** *npl* REGARDS : saludos *mpl*, recuerdos *mpl*

gregarious [grɪ'gæriəs] *adj* : gregario (dícese de los animales), sociable (dícese de las personas) — **gregariously** *adv*

gregariousness [grɪ'gæriəsnəs] *n* : sociabilidad *f*

gremlin ['gremlən] *n* : duende *m*

grenade [grə'neɪd] *n* : granada *f*

Grenadian [grə'neɪdiən] *n* : granadino *m*, -na *f* — **Grenadian** *adj*

grew → **grow**

grey → **gray**

greyhound ['greɪˌhaʊnd] *n* : galgo *m*

grid ['grɪd] *n* **1** GRATING : rejilla *f* **2** NETWORK : red *f* (de electricidad, etc.) **3** : cuadriculado *m* (de un mapa)

griddle ['grɪdəl] *n* : plancha *f*

griddle cake → **pancake**

gridiron ['grɪdˌaɪərn] *n* **1** GRILL : parrilla *f* **2** : campo *m* de futbol americano

gridlock ['grɪdˌlɑk] *n* : atasco *m* completo (de una red de calles)

grief ['griːf] *n* **1** SORROW : dolor *m*, pena *f* **2** ANNOYANCE, TROUBLE : problemas *mpl*, molestia *f*

grievance ['griːvəns] *n* COMPLAINT : queja *f*

grieve ['griːv] *v* **grieved; grieving** *vt* DISTRESS : afligir, entristecer, apenar — *vi* **1** : sufrir, afligirse **2 to grieve for** *or* **to grieve over** : llorar, lamentar

grievous ['griːvəs] *adj* **1** OPPRESSIVE : gravoso, opresivo, severo **2** GRAVE, SERIOUS : grave, severo, doloroso

grievously ['griːvəsli] *adv* : gravemente, de gravedad

grill¹ ['grɪl] *vt* **1** : asar (a la parrilla) **2** INTERROGATE : interrogar

grill² *n* **1** : parrilla *f* (para cocinar) **2** : parrillada *f* (comida) **3** RESTAURANT : grill *m*

grille *or* **grill** ['grɪl] *n* : reja *f*, enrejado *m*

grim ['grɪm] *adj* **grimmer; grimmest 1** CRUEL : cruel, feroz **2** STERN : adusto, severo ⟨a grim expression : un gesto severo⟩ **3** GLOOMY : sombrío, deprimente **4** SINISTER : macabro, siniestro **5** UNYIELDING : inflexible, persistente ⟨with grim determination : con una voluntad de hierro⟩

grimace¹ ['grɪməs, grɪ'meɪs] *vi* **-maced; -macing** : hacer muecas

grimace² *n* : mueca *f*

grime ['graɪm] *n* : mugre *f*, suciedad *f*

grimly ['grɪmli] *adv* **1** STERNLY : severamente **2** RESOLUTELY : inexorablemente

grimy ['graɪmi] *adj* **grimier; -est** : mugriento, sucio

grin¹ ['grɪn] *vi* **grinned; grinning** : sonreír abiertamente

grin² *n* : sonrisa *f* abierta

grind¹ ['graɪnd] *v* **ground** ['graʊnd]; **grinding** *vt* **1** CRUSH : moler, machacar, triturar **2** SHARPEN : afilar **3** POLISH : pulir, esmerilar (lentes, espejos) **4 to grind one's teeth** : rechinarle los dientes a uno **5 to grind down** OPPRESS : oprimir, agobiar — *vi* **1** : funcionar con dificultad, rechinar ⟨to grind to a halt : pararse poco a poco, llegar a un punto muerto⟩ **2** STUDY : estudiar mucho

grind[2] n : trabajo m pesado ⟨the daily grind : la rutina diaria⟩

grinder ['graɪndər] n : molinillo m ⟨coffee grinder : molinillo de café⟩

grindstone ['graɪndˌstoːn] n : piedra m de afilar

grip[1] ['grɪp] vt **gripped; gripping** **1** GRASP : agarrar, asir **2** HOLD, INTEREST : captar el interés de

grip[2] n **1** GRASP : agarre m, asidero m ⟨to have a firm grip on something : agarrarse bien de algo⟩ **2** CONTROL, HOLD : control m, dominio m ⟨to lose one's grip on : perder el control de⟩ ⟨inflation tightened its grip on the economy : la inflación se afianzó en su dominio de la economía⟩ **3** UNDERSTANDING : comprensión f, entendimiento m ⟨to come to grips with : llegar a entender⟩ **4** HANDLE : asidero m, empuñadura f (de un arma)

gripe[1] ['graɪp] v **griped; griping** vt IRRITATE, VEX : irritar, fastidiar, molestar — vi COMPLAIN : quejarse, rezongar

gripe[2] n : queja f

grippe ['grɪp] n : influenza f, gripe f, gripa f Col, Mex

grisly ['grɪzli] adj **-lier; -est** : horripilante, horroroso, truculento

grist ['grɪst] n : molienda f ⟨it's all grist for the mill : todo ayuda, todo es provechoso⟩

gristle ['grɪsəl] n : cartílago m

gristly ['grɪsli] adj **-tlier; -est** : cartilaginoso

grit[1] ['grɪt] vt **gritted; gritting** : hacer rechinar (los dientes, etc.)

grit[2] n **1** SAND : arena f **2** GRAVEL : grava f **3** COURAGE : valor m, coraje m **4** **grits** npl : sémola f de maíz

gritty ['grɪti] adj **-tier; -est 1** : arenoso ⟨a gritty surface : una superficie arenosa⟩ **2** PLUCKY : valiente

grizzled ['grɪzəld] adj : entrecano

grizzly bear ['grɪzli] n : oso m pardo

groan[1] ['groːn] vi **1** MOAN : gemir, quejarse **2** CREAK : crujir

groan[2] n **1** MOAN : gemido m, quejido m **2** CREAK : crujido m

grocer ['groːsər] n : tendero m, -ra f

grocery ['groːsəri, -ʃəri] n, pl **-ceries 1** or **grocery store** : tienda f de comestibles, tienda f de abarrotes **2** **groceries** npl : comestibles mpl, abarrotes mpl

groggy ['grɑgi] adj **-gier; -est** : atontado, grogui, tambaleante

groin ['grɔɪn] n : ingle f

grommet ['grɑmət, 'grʌm-] n : arandela f

groom[1] ['gruːm, 'grʊm] vt **1** : cepillar, almohazar (an animal) **2** : arreglar, cuidar ⟨well-groomed : bien arreglado⟩ **3** PREPARE : preparar

groom[2] n **1** : mozo m, -za f de cuadra **2** BRIDEGROOM : novio m

groove[1] ['gruːv] vt **grooved; grooving** : acanalar, hacer ranuras en, surcar

groove[2] n **1** FURROW, SLOT : ranura f, surco m **2** RUT : rutina f

grope ['groːp] v **groped; groping** vi : andar a tientas, tantear ⟨he groped for the switch : buscó el interruptor a tientas⟩ — vt **to grope one's way** : avanzar a tientas

gross[1] ['groːs] vt : tener entrada bruta de, recaudar en bruto

gross[2] adj **1** FLAGRANT : flagrante, grave ⟨a gross error : un error flagrante⟩ ⟨a gross injustice : una injusticia grave⟩ **2** FAT : muy gordo, obeso **3** : bruto ⟨gross national product : producto nacional bruto⟩ **4** COARSE, VULGAR : grosero, basto

gross[3] n **1** pl **gross** : gruesa f (12 docenas) **2** or **gross income** : ingresos mpl brutos

grossly ['groːsli] adv **1** EXTREMELY : extremadamente ⟨grossly unfair : totalmente injusto⟩ **2** CRUDELY : groseramente

grotesque [groː'tɛsk] adj : grotesco

grotesquely [groː'tɛskli] adv : de forma grotesca

grotto ['grɑtoː] n, pl **-toes** : gruta f

grouch[1] ['graʊtʃ] vi : refunfuñar, rezongar

grouch[2] n **1** COMPLAINT : queja f **2** GRUMBLER : gruñón m, -ñona f; cascarrabias mf fam

grouchy ['graʊtʃi] adj **grouchier; -est** : malhumorado, gruñón

ground[1] ['graʊnd] vt **1** BASE : fundar, basar **2** INSTRUCT : enseñar los conocimientos básicos a ⟨to be well grounded in : ser muy entendido en⟩ **3** : conectar a tierra (un aparato eléctrico) **4** : varar, hacer encallar (un barco) **5** : restringir (un avión o un piloto) a la tierra

ground[2] n **1** EARTH, SOIL : suelo m, tierra f ⟨to dig (in) the ground : cavar la tierra⟩ ⟨to fall to the ground : caerse al suelo⟩ **2** LAND, TERRAIN : terreno m ⟨hilly ground : terreno alto⟩ ⟨to lose ground : perder terreno⟩ **3** BASIS, REASON : razón f, motivo m ⟨grounds for complaint : motivos de queja⟩ **4** BACKGROUND : fondo m **5** FIELD : campo m, plaza f ⟨parade ground : plaza de armas⟩ **6** : tierra f (para electricidad) **7** **grounds** npl PREMISES : recinto m, terreno m **8** **grounds** npl DREGS : posos mpl (de café)

ground[3] → **grind**

groundhog ['graʊndˌhɔg] n : marmota f (de América)

groundless ['graʊndləs] adj : infundado

groundwork ['graʊndˌwərk] n **1** FOUNDATION : fundamento m, base f **2** PREPARATION : trabajo m preparatorio

group[1] ['gruːp] vt : agrupar

group[2] n : grupo m, agrupación f, conjunto m, compañía f

grouper ['gru:pər] *n* : mero *m*

grouse¹ ['graʊs] *vi* **groused; grousing** : quejarse, rezongar, refunfuñar

grouse² *n, pl* **grouse** *or* **grouses** : urogallo *m* (ave)

grout ['graʊt] *n* : lechada *f*

grove ['gro:v] *n* : bosquecillo *m*, arboleda *f*, soto *m*

grovel ['grʌvəl, 'grɑ-] *vi* **-eled** *or* **-elled; -eling** *or* **-elling** 1 CRAWL : arrastrarse 2 : humillarse, postrarse ⟨to grovel before someone : postrarse ante alguien⟩

grow ['gro:] *v* **grew** ['gru:]; **grown** ['gro:n]; **growing** *vi* 1 : crecer ⟨palm trees grow on the islands : las palmas crecen en las islas⟩ ⟨my hair grows very fast : mi pelo crece muy rápido⟩ 2 DEVELOP, MATURE : desarrollarse, madurar 3 INCREASE : crecer, aumentar 4 BECOME : hacerse, volverse, ponerse ⟨she was growing angry : se estaba poniendo furiosa⟩ ⟨to grow dark : oscurecerse⟩ 5 to grow up : hacerse mayor ⟨grow up! : ¡no seas niño!⟩ — *vt* 1 CULTIVATE, RAISE : cultivar 2 : dejar crecer ⟨to grow one's hair : dejarse crecer el pelo⟩

grower ['gro:ər] *n* : cultivador *m*, -dora *f*

growl¹ ['graʊl] *vi* : gruñir (dícese de un animal), refunfuñar (dícese de una persona)

growl² *n* : gruñido *m*

grown–up¹ ['gro:n,ʌp] *adj* : adulto, mayor

grown–up² *n* : adulto *m*, -ta *f*; persona *f* mayor

growth ['gro:θ] *n* 1 : crecimiento *m* ⟨to stunt one's growth : detener el crecimiento⟩ 2 INCREASE : aumento *m*, crecimiento *m*, expansión *f* 3 DEVELOPMENT : desarrollo *m* ⟨economic growth : desarrollo económico⟩ ⟨a five days' growth of beard : una barba de cinco días⟩ 4 LUMP, TUMOR : bulto *m*, tumor *m*

grub¹ ['grʌb] *vi* **grubbed; grubbing** 1 DIG : escarbar 2 RUMMAGE : hurgar, buscar 3 DRUDGE : trabajar duro

grub² *n* 1 : larva *f* ⟨beetle grub : larva del escarabajo⟩ 2 DRUDGE : esclavo *m*, -va *f* del trabajo 3 FOOD : comida *f*

grubby ['grʌbi] *adj* **grubbier; -est** : mugriento, sucio

grudge¹ ['grʌdʒ] *vt* **grudged; grudging** : resentir, envidiar

grudge² *n* : rencor *m*, resentimiento *m* ⟨to hold a grudge : guardar rencor⟩

grueling *or* **gruelling** ['gru:lɪŋ, 'gru:ə-] *adj* : extenuante, agotador, duro

gruesome ['gru:səm] *adj* : horripilante, truculento, horroroso

gruff ['grʌf] *adj* 1 BRUSQUE : brusco ⟨a gruff reply : una respuesta brusca⟩ 2 HOARSE : ronco — **gruffly** *adv*

grumble¹ ['grʌmbəl] *vi* **-bled; -bling** 1 COMPLAIN : refunfuñar, rezongar, quejarse 2 RUMBLE : hacer un ruido sordo, retumbar (dícese del trueno)

grumble² *n* 1 COMPLAINT : queja *f* 2 RUMBLE : ruido *m* sordo, estruendo *m*

grumbler ['grʌmbələr] *n* : gruñón *m*, -ñona *f*

grumpy ['grʌmpi] *adj* **grumpier; -est** : malhumorado, gruñón

grungy ['grʌndʒi] *adj* : sucio

grunt¹ ['grʌnt] *vi* : gruñir

grunt² *n* : gruñido *m*

guacamole [ˌgwɑkəˈmo:li] *n* : guacamole *m*, guacamol *m*

guarantee¹ [ˌgærənˈti:] *vt* **-teed; -teeing** 1 PROMISE : asegurar, prometer 2 : poner bajo garantía, garantizar (un producto o servicio)

guarantee² *n* 1 PROMISE : garantía *f*, promesa *f* ⟨lifetime guarantee : garantía de por vida⟩ 2 → **guarantor**

guarantor [ˌgærənˈtor] *n* : garante *mf*; fiador *m*, -dora *f*

guaranty [ˌgærənˈti:] → **guarantee**

guard¹ ['gɑrd] *vt* 1 DEFEND, PROTECT : defender, proteger 2 : guardar, vigilar, custodiar ⟨to guard the frontier : vigilar la frontera⟩ ⟨she guarded my secret well : guardó bien mi secreto⟩ — *vi* to guard against : protegerse contra, evitar

guard² *n* 1 WATCHMAN : guarda *mf* ⟨security guard : guarda de seguridad⟩ 2 VIGILANCE : guardia *f*, vigilancia *f* ⟨to be on guard : estar en guardia⟩ ⟨to let one's guard down : bajar la guardia⟩ 3 SAFEGUARD : salvaguardia *f*, dispositivo *m* de seguridad (en una máquina) 4 PRECAUTION : precaución *f*, protección *f*

guardhouse ['gɑrd,haʊs] *n* : cuartel *m* de la guardia

guardian ['gɑrdiən] *n* 1 PROTECTOR : guardián *m*, -diana *f*; custodio *m*, -dia *f* 2 : tutor *m*, -tora *f* (de un niño)

guardianship ['gɑrdiən,ʃɪp] *n* : custodia *f*, tutela *f*

Guatemalan [ˌgwɑtəˈmɑlən] *n* : guatemalteco *m*, -ca *f* — **Guatemalan** *adj*

guava ['gwɑvə] *n* : guayaba *f*

gubernatorial [ˌguːbərnəˈtoriəl, ˌgjuː-] *adj* : del gobernador

guerrilla *or* **guerilla** [gəˈrɪlə] *n* : guerrillero *m*, -ra *f*

guess¹ ['gɛs] *vt* 1 CONJECTURE : adivinar, conjeturar ⟨guess what happened! : ¡adivina lo que pasó!⟩ 2 SUPPOSE : pensar, creer, suponer ⟨I guess so : supongo que sí⟩ 3 : adivinar correctamente, acertar ⟨to guess the answer : acertar la respuesta⟩ — *vi* : adivinar

guess² *n* : conjetura *f*, suposición *f*

guesswork ['gɛs,wərk] *n* : suposiciones *fpl*, conjeturas *fpl*

guest ['gɛst] *n* : huésped *mf*; invitado *m*, -da *f*

guffaw¹ [gəˈfɔ] *vi* : reírse a carcajadas, carcajearse *fam*

guffaw² [gəˈfɔ, ˈgʌ,fɔ] *n* : carcajada *f*, risotada *f*

guidance ['gaɪdənts] *n* : orientación *f*, consejos *mpl*

guide¹ ['gaɪd] *vt* **guided; guiding 1** DIRECT, LEAD : guiar, dirigir, conducir **2** ADVISE, COUNSEL : aconsejar, orientar

guide² *n* : guía *f*

guidebook ['gaɪd,bʊk] *n* : guía *f* (para viajeros)

guideline ['gaɪd,laɪn] *n* : pauta *f*, directriz *f*

guild ['gɪld] *n* : gremio *m*, sindicato *m*, asociación *f*

guile ['gaɪl] *n* : astucia *f*, engaño *m*

guileless ['gaɪlləs] *adj* : inocente, cándido, sin malicia

guillotine¹ ['gɪlə,ti:n, ,gi:jə,-] *vt* **-tined; -tining** : guillotinar

guillotine² *n* : guillotina *f*

guilt ['gɪlt] *n* : culpa *f*, culpabilidad *f*

guilty ['gɪlti] *adj* **guiltier; -est** : culpable

guinea fowl ['gɪni] *n* : gallina *f* de Guinea

guinea pig *n* : conejillo *m* de Indias, cobaya *f*

guise ['gaɪz] *n* : apariencia *f*, aspecto *m*, forma *f*

guitar [gə'tɑr, gɪ-] *n* : guitarra *f*

guitarist [gə'tɑrɪst, gɪ-] *n* : guitarrista *mf*

gulch ['gʌltʃ] *n* : barranco *m*, quebrada *f*

gulf ['gʌlf] *n* **1** : golfo *m* ⟨the Gulf of Mexico : el Golfo de México⟩ **2** GAP : brecha *f* ⟨the gulf between generations : la brecha entre las generaciones⟩ **3** CHASM : abismo *m*

gull ['gʌl] *n* : gaviota *f*

gullet ['gʌlət] *n* : garganta *f*

gullible ['gʌlɪbəl] *adj* : crédulo

gully ['gʌli] *n, pl* **-lies** : barranco *m*, hondonada *f*

gulp¹ ['gʌlp] *vt* **1** : engullir, tragar ⟨he gulped down the whiskey : engulló el whisky⟩ **2** SUPPRESS : suprimir, reprimir, tragar ⟨to gulp down a sob : reprimir un sollozo⟩ — *vi* : tragar saliva, tener un nudo en la garganta

gulp² *n* : trago *m*

gum ['gʌm] *n* **1** CHEWING GUM : goma *f* de mascar, chicle *m* **2 gums** *npl* : encías *fpl*

gumbo ['gʌm,bo:] *n* : sopa *f* de quingombó

gumdrop ['gʌm,drɑp] *n* : pastilla *f* de goma

gummy ['gʌmi] *adj* **gummier; -est** : gomoso

gumption ['gʌmpʃən] *n* : iniciativa *f*, agallas *fpl fam*

gun¹ ['gʌn] *vt* **gunned; gunning 1** *or* **to gun down** : matar a tiros, asesinar **2** : acelerar (rápidamente) ⟨to gun the engine : acelerar el motor⟩

gun² *n* **1** CANNON : cañón *m* **2** FIREARM : arma *f* de fuego **3** SPRAY GUN : pistola *f* **4 to jump the gun** : adelantarse, salir antes de tiempo

gunboat ['gʌn,bo:t] *n* : cañonero *m*

gunfight ['gʌn,faɪt] *n* : tiroteo *m*, balacera *f*

gunfire ['gʌn,faɪr] *n* : disparos *mpl*

gunman ['gʌnmən] *n, pl* **-men** [-mən, -,mɛn] : pistolero *m*, gatillero *m* Mex

gunner ['gʌnər] *n* : artillero *m*, -ra *f*

gunnysack ['gʌni,sæk] *n* : saco *m* de yute

gunpowder ['gʌn,paʊdər] *n* : pólvora *f*

gunshot ['gʌn,ʃɑt] *n* : disparo *m*, tiro *m*, balazo *m*

gunwale ['gʌnəl] *n* : borda *f*

guppy ['gʌpi] *n, pl* **-pies** : lebistes *m*

gurgle¹ ['gərgəl] *vi* **-gled; -gling 1** : borbotar, gorgotear (dícese de un líquido) **2** : gorjear (dícese de un niño)

gurgle² *n* **1** : borboteo *m*, gorgoteo *m* (de un líquido) **2** : gorjeo *m* (de un niño)

gush ['gʌʃ] *vi* **1** SPOUT : surgir, salir a chorros, chorrear **2** : hablar con entusiasmo efusivo ⟨she gushed with praise : se deshizo en elogios⟩

gust ['gʌst] *n* : ráfaga *f*, racha *f*

gusto ['gʌs,to:] *n, pl* **gustoes** : entusiasmo *m* ⟨with gusto : con deleite, con ganas⟩

gusty ['gʌsti] *adj* **gustier; -est** : racheado

gut¹ ['gʌt] *vt* **gutted; gutting 1** EVISCERATE : destripar (un pollo, etc.), limpiar (un pescado) **2** : destruir el interior de (un edificio)

gut² *n* **1** INTESTINE : intestino *m* **2 guts** *npl* INNARDS : tripas *fpl fam*, entrañas *fpl* **3 guts** *npl* COURAGE : valentía *f*, agallas *fpl*

gutter ['gʌtər] *n* **1** : canal *mf*, canaleta *f* (de un techo) **2** : cuneta *f*, arroyo *m* (de una calle)

guttural ['gʌtərəl] *adj* : gutural

guy ['gaɪ] *n* **1** *or* **guyline** : cuerda *f* tensora, cable *m* **2** FELLOW : tipo *m*, hombre *m*

guzzle ['gʌzəl] *vt* **-zled; -zling** : chupar, tragarse

gym ['dʒɪm] → **gymnasium**

gymnasium [dʒɪm'neɪziəm, -ʒəm] *n, pl* **-siums** *or* **-sia** [-zi:ə, -ʒə] : gimnasio *m*

gymnast ['dʒɪmnəst, -,næst] *n* : gimnasta *mf*

gymnastic [dʒɪm'næstɪk] *adj* : gimnástico

gymnastics [dʒɪm'næstɪks] *ns & pl* : gimnasia *f*

gynecologist [,gaɪnə'kɑlədʒɪst, ,dʒɪnə-] *n* : ginecólogo *m*, -ga *f*

gynecology [,gaɪnə'kɑlədʒi, ,dʒɪnə-] *n* : ginecología *f*

gyp¹ ['dʒɪp] *vt* **gypped; gypping** : estafar, timar

gyp² *n* **1** SWINDLER : estafador *m*, -dora *f* **2** FRAUD, SWINDLE : estafa *f*, timo *m* *fam*

gypsum ['dʒɪpsəm] *n* : yeso *m*

Gypsy ['dʒɪpsi] *n, pl* **-sies** : gitano *m*, -na *f*

gyrate ['dʒaɪ,reɪt] *vi* **-rated; -rating** : girar, rotar

gyration [dʒaɪ'reɪʃən] *n* : giro *m*, rotación *f*

gyroscope ['dʒaɪrə,sko:p] *n* : giroscopio *m*, giróscopo *m*

H

h ['eɪtʃ] n, pl h's or hs ['eɪtʃəz] : octava letra del alfabeto inglés

ha ['hɑ] interj : ¡ja!

haberdashery ['hæbər,dæʃəri] n, pl -eries : tienda f de ropa para caballeros

habit ['hæbɪt] n 1 CUSTOM : hábito m, costumbre f 2 : hábito m (de un monje o una religiosa) 3 ADDICTION : dependencia f, adicción f

habitable ['hæbɪtəbəl] adj : habitable

habitat ['hæbɪ,tæt] n : hábitat m

habitation [,hæbɪ'teɪʃən] n 1 OCCUPANCY : habitación f 2 RESIDENCE : residencia f, morada f

habit–forming ['hæbɪt,fɔrmɪŋ] adj : que crea dependencia

habitual [hə'bɪtʃuəl] adj 1 CUSTOMARY : habitual, acostumbrado 2 INVETERATE : incorregible, empedernido — habitually adv

habituate [hə'bɪtʃu,eɪt] vt -ated; -ating : habituar, acostumbrar

hack¹ ['hæk] vt : cortar, tajear (a hachazos, etc.) ⟨to hack one's way : abrirse paso⟩ — vi 1 : hacer tajos 2 COUGH : toser

hack² n 1 CHOP : hachazo m, tajo m 2 HORSE : caballo m de alquiler 3 WRITER : escritor m, -tora f a sueldo; escritorzuelo m, -la f 4 COUGH : tos f seca

hackles ['hækəlz] npl 1 : pluma f erizada (de un ave), pelo m erizado (de un perro, etc.) 2 to get one's hackles up : ponerse furioso

hackney ['hækni] n, pl -neys : caballo m de silla, caballo m de tiro

hackneyed ['hæknid] adj TRITE : trillado, gastado

hacksaw ['hæk,sɔ] n : sierra f para metales

had → have

haddock ['hædək] ns & pl : eglefino m

hadn't ['hædənt] (contraction of had not) → have

haft ['hæft] n : mango m, empuñadura f

hag ['hæg] n 1 WITCH : bruja f, hechicera f 2 CRONE : vieja f fea

haggard ['hægərd] adj : demacrado, macilento — haggardly adv

haggle ['hægəl] vi -gled; -gling : regatear

ha–ha [,hɑ'hɑ, 'hɑ'hɑ] interj : ¡ja, ja!

hail¹ ['heɪl] vt 1 GREET : saludar 2 SUMMON : llamar ⟨to hail a taxi : llamar un taxi⟩ — vi : granizar (en meteorología)

hail² n 1 : granizo m 2 BARRAGE : aluvión m, lluvia f

hail³ interj : ¡salve!

hailstone ['heɪl,stoːn] n : granizo m, piedra f de granizo

hailstorm ['heɪl,stɔrm] n : granizada f

hair ['hær] n 1 : pelo m, cabello m ⟨to get one's hair cut : cortarse el pelo⟩ 2 : vello m (en las piernas, etc.)

hairbreadth ['hær,brɛdθ] or hairsbreadth ['hærz-] n by a hairbreadth : por un pelo

hairbrush ['hær,brʌʃ] n : cepillo m (para el pelo)

haircut ['hær,kʌt] n : corte m de pelo

hairdo ['hær,duː] n, pl -dos : peinado m

hairdresser ['hær,drɛsər] n : peluquero m, -ra f

hairiness ['hærinəs] n : vellosidad f

hairless ['hærləs] adj : sin pelo, calvo, pelón

hairline ['hær,laɪn] n 1 : línea f delgada 2 : nacimiento m del pelo ⟨to have a receding hairline : tener entradas⟩

hairpin ['hær,pɪn] n : horquilla f

hair–raising ['hær,reɪzɪŋ] adj : espeluznante

hair spray n : laca f, fijador m (para el pelo)

hairstyle ['hær,staɪl] n : peinado m

hairy ['hæri] adj hairier; -est : peludo, velludo

Haitian ['heɪʃən, 'heɪtiən] n : haitiano m, -na f — Haitian adj

hake ['heɪk] n : merluza f

hale¹ ['heɪl] vt haled; haling : arrastrar, halar ⟨to hale to court : arrastrar al tribunal⟩

hale² adj : saludable, robusto

half¹ ['hæf, 'haf] adv : medio, a medias ⟨half cooked : medio cocido⟩

half² adj : medio, a medias ⟨a half hour : una media hora⟩ ⟨a half truth : una verdad a medias⟩

half³ n, pl halves ['hævz, 'havz] 1 : mitad f ⟨half of my friends : la mitad de mis amigos⟩ ⟨in half : por la mitad⟩ 2 : tiempo m (en deportes)

half brother n : medio hermano m, hermanastro m

halfhearted ['hæf'hɑrtəd] adj : sin ánimo, poco entusiasta

halfheartedly ['hæf'hɑrtədli] adv : con poco entusiasmo, sin ánimo

half–life ['hæf,laɪf] n, pl half–lives : media vida f

half sister n : media hermana f, hermanastra f

halfway¹ ['hæf'weɪ] adv : a medio camino, a mitad de camino

halfway² adj : medio, intermedio ⟨a halfway point : un punto intermedio⟩

half–wit ['hæf,wɪt] n : tonto m, -ta f; imbécil mf

half–witted ['hæf,wɪtəd] adj : estúpido

halibut ['hæləbət] ns & pl : halibut m

hall ['hɔl] n 1 BUILDING : residencia f estudiantil, facultad f (de una universidad) 2 VESTIBULE : entrada f, vestíbulo m, zaguán m 3 CORRIDOR : corredor m, pasillo m 4 AUDITORIUM : sala f, salón m ⟨concert hall : sala de conciertos⟩ 5 city hall : ayuntamiento m

hallelujah [,hælə'luːjə, -,hɑ-] interj : ¡aleluya!

hallmark ['hɔl,mɑrk] *n* : sello *m* (distintivo)

hallow ['hæ,lo:] *vt* : santificar, consagrar

hallowed ['hæ,lo:d, 'hæ,lo:əd, 'hɑ,lo:d] *adj* : sagrado

Halloween [,hælə'wi:n, ,hɑ-] *n* : víspera *f* de Todos los Santos

hallucinate [hə'lu:sən,eɪt] *vi* **-nated; -nating** : alucinar

hallucination [hə,lu:sən'eɪʃən] *n* : alucinación *f*

hallucinatory [hə'lu:sənə,tori] *adj* : alucinante

hallucinogen [hə'lu:sənʤən] *n* : alucinógeno *m*

hallucinogenic [hə,lu:sənə'ʤɛnɪk] *adj* : alucinógeno

hallway ['hɔl,weɪ] *n* **1** ENTRANCE : entrada *f* **2** CORRIDOR : corredor *m*, pasillo *m*

halo ['heɪ,lo:] *n, pl* **-los** *or* **-loes** : aureola *f*, halo *m*

halt[1] ['hɔlt] *vi* : detenerse, pararse — *vt* **1** STOP : detener, parar (a una persona) **2** INTERRUPT : interrumpir (una actividad)

halt[2] *n* **1** : alto *m*, parada *f* **2 to come to a halt** : pararse, detenerse

halter ['hɔltər] *n* **1** : cabestro *m*, ronzal *m* (para un animal) **2** : blusa *f* sin espalda

halting ['hɔltɪŋ] *adj* HESITANT : vacilante, titubeante — **haltingly** *adv*

halve ['hæv, 'hɑv] *vt* **halved; halving 1** DIVIDE : partir por la mitad **2** REDUCE : reducir a la mitad

halves → **half**

ham ['hæm] *n* **1** : jamón *m* **2** *or* **ham actor** : comicastro *m*, -tra *f* **3** *or* **ham radio operator** : radioaficionado *m*, -da *f* **4 hams** *npl* HAUNCHES : ancas *fpl*

hamburger ['hæm,bərgər] *or* **hamburg** [-,bərg] *n* **1** : carne *f* molida **2** : hamburguesa *f* (emparedado)

hamlet ['hæmlət] *n* VILLAGE : aldea *f*, poblado *m*

hammer[1] ['hæmər] *vt* **1** STRIKE : clavar, golpear **2** NAIL : clavar, martillar **3 to hammer out** NEGOTIATE : elaborar, negociar, llegar a — *vi* : martillar, golpear

hammer[2] *n* **1** : martillo *m* **2** : percusor *m*, percutor *m* (de un arma de fuego)

hammock ['hæmək] *n* : hamaca *f*

hamper[1] ['hæmpər] *vt* : obstaculizar, dificultar

hamper[2] *n* : cesto *m*, canasta *f*

hamster ['hæmpstər] *n* : hámster *m*

hamstring ['hæm,strɪŋ] *vt* **-strung** [-,strʌŋ]; **-stringing 1** : cortarle el tendón del corvejón a (un animal) **2** INCAPACITATE : incapacitar, inutilizar

hand[1] ['hænd] *vt* : pasar, dar, entregar

hand[2] *n* **1** : mano *f* ⟨made by hand : hecho a mano⟩ **2** POINTER : manecilla *f*, aguja *f* (de un reloj o instrumento) **3** SIDE : lado *m* ⟨on the other hand : por otro lado⟩ **4** HANDWRITING : letra *f*, escritura *f* **5** APPLAUSE : aplauso *m* **6** : mano *f*, cartas *fpl* (en juegos de naipes)

7 WORKER : obrero *m*, -ra *f*; trabajador *m*, -dora *f* **8 to ask for someone's hand (in marriage)** : pedir la mano de alguien **9 to lend a hand** : echar una mano

handbag ['hænd,bæg] *n* : cartera *f*, bolso *m*, bolsa *f* Mex

handball ['hænd,bɔl] *n* : frontón *m*, pelota *f*

handbill ['hænd,bɪl] *n* : folleto *m*, volante *m*

handbook ['hænd,bʊk] *n* : manual *m*

handcuff ['hænd,kʌf] *vt* : esposar, ponerle esposas (a alguien)

handcuffs ['hænd,kʌfs] *npl* : esposas *fpl*

handful ['hænd,fʊl] *n* : puñado *m*

handgun ['hænd,gʌn] *n* : pistola *f*, revólver *m*

handheld ['hænd,hɛld] *adj* : de mano

handicap[1] ['hændi,kæp] *vt* **-capped; -capping 1** : asignar un handicap a (en deportes) **2** HAMPER : obstaculizar, poner en desventaja

handicap[2] *n* **1** DISABILITY : minusvalía *f*, discapacidad *f* **2** DISADVANTAGE : desventaja *f*, handicap *m* (en deportes)

handicapped ['hændi,kæpt] *adj* DISABLED : minusválido, discapacitado

handicraft ['hændi,kræft] *n* : artesanía *f*

handily ['hændəli] *adv* EASILY : fácilmente, con facilidad

handiwork ['hændi,wərk] *n* **1** WORK : trabajo *m* **2** CRAFTS : artesanías *fpl*

handkerchief ['hæŋkərʧəf, -,ʧiːf] *n, pl* **-chiefs** : pañuelo *m*

handle[1] ['hændəl] *v* **-dled; -dling** *vt* **1** TOUCH : tocar **2** MANAGE : tratar, manejar, despachar **3** SELL : comerciar con, vender — *vi* : responder, conducirse ⟨dícese de un vehículo⟩

handle[2] *n* : asa *m*, asidero *m*, mango *m* (de un cuchillo, etc.), pomo *m* (de una puerta), tirador *m* (de un cajón)

handlebars ['hændəl,bɑrz] *npl* : manubrio *m*, manillar *m*

handler ['hændələr] *n* : cuidador *m*, -dora *f*

handling ['hændlɪŋ] *n* **1** MANAGEMENT : manejo *m* **2** TOUCHING : manoseo *m* **3 shipping and handling** : porte *m*, transporte *m*

handmade ['hænd,meɪd] *adj* : hecho a mano

hand-me-downs ['hændmi,daʊnz] *npl* : ropa *f* usada

handout ['hænd,aʊt] *n* **1** AID : dádiva *f*, limosna *f* **2** LEAFLET : folleto *m*

handpick ['hænd'pɪk] *vt* : seleccionar con cuidado

handrail ['hænd,reɪl] *n* : pasamanos *m*, barandilla *f*, barandal *m*

handsaw ['hænd,sɔ] *n* : serrucho *m*

hands down *adv* **1** EASILY : con facilidad **2** UNQUESTIONABLY : con mucho, de lejos

handshake ['hænd,ʃeɪk] *n* : apretón *m* de manos

handsome ['hæntsəm] *adj* **-somer; -est** **1** ATTRACTIVE : apuesto, guapo, atractivo **2** GENEROUS : generoso **3** SIZABLE : considerable

handsomely ['hæntsəmli] *adv* **1** ELEGANTLY : elegantemente **2** GENEROUSLY : con generosidad

handspring ['hænd,sprɪŋ] *n* : voltereta *f*

handstand ['hænd,stænd] *n* **to do a handstand** : pararse de manos

hand–to–hand ['hændtə'hænd] *adj* : cuerpo a cuerpo

handwriting ['hænd,raɪtɪŋ] *n* : letra *f*, escritura *f*

handwritten ['hænd,rɪtən] *adj* : escrito a mano

handy ['hændi] *adj* **handier; -est** **1** NEARBY : a mano, cercano **2** USEFUL : útil, práctico **3** DEXTEROUS : hábil

hang[1] ['hæŋ] *v* **hung** ['hʌŋ]; **hanging** *vt* **1** SUSPEND : colgar, tender, suspender **2** *past tense often* **hanged** EXECUTE : colgar, ahorcar **3 to hang one's head** : bajar la cabeza — *vi* **1** FALL : caer (dícese de las telas y la ropa) **2** DANGLE : colgar **3** HOVER : flotar, sostenerse en el aire **4** : ser ahorcado **5** DROOP : inclinarse **6 to hang up** : colgar ⟨he hung up on me : me colgó⟩

hang[2] *n* **1** DRAPE : caída *f* **2 to get the hang of something** : agarrarle la onda a algo

hangar ['hæŋər, 'hæŋgər] *n* : hangar *m*

hanger ['hæŋər] *n* : percha *f*, gancho *m* (para ropa)

hangman ['hæŋmən] *n*, *pl* **-men** [-mən, -,mɛn] : verdugo *m*

hangnail ['hæŋ,neɪl] *n* : padrastro *m*

hangout ['hæŋ,aʊt] *n* : lugar *m* popular, sitio *m* muy frecuentado

hangover ['hæŋ,o:vər] *n* : resaca *f*

hank ['hæŋk] *n* : madeja *f*

hanker ['hæŋkər] *vi* **to hanker for** : tener ansias de, tener ganas de

hankering ['hæŋkərɪŋ] *n* : ansia *f*, anhelo *m*

hansom ['hæntsəm] *n* : coche *m* de caballos

Hanukkah ['xɑnəkə, 'hɑ-] *n* : Januká, Hanukkah

haphazard [hæp'hæzərd] *adj* : casual, fortuito, al azar — **haphazardly** *adv*

hapless ['hæpləs] *adj* UNFORTUNATE : desafortunado, desventurado — **haplessly** *adv*

happen ['hæpən] *vi* **1** OCCUR : pasar, ocurrir, suceder, tener lugar **2** BEFALL : pasar, acontecer ⟨what happened to her? : ¿qué le ha pasado?⟩ **3** CHANCE : resultar, ocurrir por casualidad ⟨it happened that I wasn't home : resulta que estaba fuera de casa⟩ ⟨he happens to be right : da la casualidad de que tiene razón⟩

happening ['hæpənɪŋ] *n* : suceso *m*, acontecimiento *m*

happiness ['hæpinəs] *n* : felicidad *f*, dicha *f*

happy ['hæpi] *adj* **-pier; -est** **1** JOYFUL : feliz, contento, alegre **2** FORTUNATE : afortunado, feliz — **happily** [-pəli] *adv*

happy–go–lucky ['hæpigo:'lʌki] *adj* : despreocupado

harangue[1] [hə'ræŋ] *vt* **-rangued; -ranguing** : arengar

harangue[2] *n* : arenga *f*

harass [hə'ræs, 'hærəs] *vt* **1** BESIEGE, HOUND : acosar, asediar, hostigar **2** ANNOY : molestar

harassment [hə'ræsmənt, 'hærəsmənt] *n* : acoso *m*, hostigamiento *m* ⟨sexual harrassment : acoso sexual⟩

harbinger ['hɑrbɪndʒər] *n* **1** HERALD : heraldo *m*, precursor *m* **2** OMEN : presagio *m*

harbor[1] ['hɑrbər] *vt* **1** SHELTER : dar refugio a, albergar **2** CHERISH, KEEP : abrigar, guardar, albergar ⟨to harbor doubts : guardar dudas⟩

harbor[2] *n* **1** REFUGE : refugio *m* **2** PORT : puerto *m*

hard[1] ['hɑrd] *adv* **1** FORCEFULLY : fuerte, con fuerza ⟨the wind blew hard : el viento sopló fuerte⟩ **2** STRENUOUSLY : duro, mucho ⟨to work hard : trabajar duro⟩ **3 to take something hard** : tomarse algo muy mal, estar muy afectado por algo

hard[2] *adj* **1** FIRM, SOLID : duro, firme, sólido **2** DIFFICULT : difícil, arduo **3** SEVERE : severo, duro ⟨a hard winter : un invierno severo⟩ **4** UNFEELING : insensible, duro **5** DILIGENT : diligente ⟨to be a hard worker : ser muy trabajador⟩ **6 hard liquor** : bebidas *fpl* fuertes **7 hard water** : agua *f* dura

hardcover ['hɑrd,kʌvər] *adj* : de pasta dura, de tapa dura

hard disk *n* : disco *m* duro

hard drive → **hard disk**

harden ['hɑrdən] *vt* : endurecer

hardheaded [,hɑrd'hɛdəd] *adj* **1** STUBBORN : testarudo, terco **2** REALISTIC : realista, práctico — **hardheadedly** *adv*

hard–hearted [,hɑrd'hɑrtəd] *adj* : despiadado, insensible — **hard–heartedly** *adv*

hard–heartedness [,hɑrd'hɑrtədnəs] *n* : dureza *f* de corazón

hardly ['hɑrdli] *adv* **1** SCARCELY : apenas, casi ⟨I hardly knew her : apenas la conocía⟩ ⟨hardly ever : casi nunca⟩ **2** NOT : difícilmente, poco, no ⟨they can hardly blame me! : ¡difícilmente pueden echarme la culpa!⟩ ⟨it's hardly likely : es poco probable⟩

hardness ['hɑrdnəs] *n* **1** FIRMNESS : dureza *f* **2** DIFFICULTY : dificultad *f* **3** SEVERITY : severidad *f*

hardship ['hɑrd,ʃɪp] *n* : dificultad *f*, privación *f*

hardware ['hɑrd,wær] *n* **1** TOOLS : ferretería *f* **2** : hardware *m* (de una computadora)

hardwood ['hɑrd,wʊd] *n* : madera *f* dura, madera *f* noble

hardworking ['hɑrd'wərkıŋ] *adj* : trabajador

hardy ['hɑrdi] *adj* -**dier; -est** : fuerte, robusto, resistente (dícese de las plantas) — **hardily** [-dəli] *adv*

hare ['hær] *n, pl* **hare** *or* **hares** : liebre *f*

harebrained ['hær,breınd] *adj* : estúpido, absurdo, disparatado

harelip ['hær,lıp] *n* : labio *m* leporino

harem ['hærəm] *n* : harén *m*

hark ['hɑrk] *vi* 1 (*used only in the imperative*) LISTEN : escuchar 2 **hark back** RETURN : volver 3 **hark back** RECALL : recordar

harlequin ['hɑrlıkən, -kwən] *n* : arlequín *m*

harm[1] ['hɑrm] *vt* : hacerle daño a, perjudicar

harm[2] *n* : daño *m*, perjuicio *m*

harmful ['hɑrmfəl] *adj* : dañino, perjudicial — **harmfully** *adv*

harmless ['hɑrmləs] *adj* : inofensivo, inocuo — **harmlessly** *adv*

harmlessness ['hɑrmləsnəs] *n* : inocuidad *f*

harmonic [hɑr'mɑnık] *adj* : armónico — **harmonically** [-nıkli] *adv*

harmonica [hɑr'mɑnıkə] *n* : armónica *f*

harmonious [hɑr'mo:niəs] *adj* : armonioso — **harmoniously** *adv*

harmonize ['hɑrmə,naız] *v* -**nized; -nizing** : armonizar

harmony ['hɑrməni] *n, pl* -**nies** : armonía *f*

harness[1] ['hɑrnəs] *vt* 1 : enjaezar (un animal) 2 UTILIZE : utilizar, aprovechar

harness[2] *n* : arreos *mpl*, guarniciones *fpl*, arnés *m*

harp[1] ['hɑrp] *vi* **to harp on** : insistir sobre, machacar sobre

harp[2] *n* : arpa *f*

harpist ['hɑrpıst] *n* : arpista *mf*

harpoon[1] [hɑr'pu:n] *vt* : arponear

harpoon[2] *n* : arpón *m*

harpsichord ['hɑrpsı,kɔrd] *n* : clavicémbalo *m*

harrow[1] ['hær,o:] *vt* 1 CULTIVATE : gradar, labrar (la tierra) 2 TORMENT : atormentar

harrow[2] *n* : grada *f*, rastra *f*

harry ['hæri] *vt* -**ried; -rying** HARASS : acosar, hostigar

harsh ['hɑrʃ] *adj* 1 ROUGH : áspero 2 SEVERE : duro, severo 3 : discordante (dícese de los sonidos) — **harshly** *adv*

harshness ['hɑrʃnəs] *n* 1 ROUGHNESS : aspereza *f* 2 SEVERITY : dureza *f*, severidad *f*

harvest[1] ['hɑrvəst] *v* : cosechar

harvest[2] *n* 1 HARVESTING : siega *f*, recolección *f* 2 CROP : cosecha *f*

harvester ['hɑrvəstər] *n* : segador *m*, -dora *f*; cosechadora *f* (máquina)

has → **have**

hash[1] ['hæʃ] *vt* 1 MINCE : picar 2 **to hash over** DISCUSS : discutir, repasar

hash[2] *n* 1 : picadillo *m* (comida) 2 JUMBLE : revoltijo *m*, fárrago *m*

hasn't ['hæzənt] (*contraction of* **has not**) → **has**

hasp ['hæsp] *n* : picaporte *m*, pestillo *m*

hassle[1] ['hæsəl] *vt* -**sled; -sling** : fastidiar, molestar

hassle[2] *n* 1 ARGUMENT : discusión *f*, disputa *f*, bronca *f* 2 FIGHT : pelea *f*, riña *f* 3 BOTHER, TROUBLE : problemas *mpl*, lío *m*

hassock ['hæsək] *n* 1 CUSHION : almohadón *m*, cojín *m* 2 FOOTSTOOL : escabel *m*

haste ['heıst] *n* 1 : prisa *f*, apuro *m* 2 **to make haste** : darse prisa, apurarse

hasten ['heısən] *vt* : acelerar, precipitar — *vi* : apresurarse, apurarse

hasty ['heısti] *adj* **hastier; -est** 1 HURRIED, QUICK : rápido, apresurado, apurado 2 RASH : precipitado — **hastily** [-təli] *adv*

hat ['hæt] *n* : sombrero *m*

hatch[1] ['hæʧ] *vt* 1 : incubar, empollar (huevos) 2 : idear, tramar — *vi* : salir del cascarón

hatch[2] *n* : escotilla *f*

hatchery ['hæʧəri] *n, pl* -**ries** : criadero *m*

hatchet ['hæʧət] *n* : hacha *f*

hatchway ['hæʧ,weı] *n* : escotilla *f*

hate[1] ['heıt] *vt* **hated; hating** : odiar, aborrecer, detestar

hate[2] *n* : odio *m*

hateful ['heıtfəl] *adj* : odioso, aborrecible, detestable — **hatefully** *adv*

hatred ['heıtrəd] *n* : odio *m*

hatter ['hætər] *n* : sombrerero *m*, -ra *f*

haughtiness ['hɔtinəs] *n* : altanería *f*, altivez *f*

haughty ['hɔti] *adj* -**tier; -est** : altanero, altivo — **haughtily** [-təli] *adv*

haul[1] ['hɔl] *vt* 1 DRAG, PULL : arrastrar, jalar 2 TRANSPORT : transportar

haul[2] *n* 1 PULL : tirón *m*, jalón *m* 2 CATCH : redada *f* 3 JOURNEY : viaje *m*, trayecto *m* ⟨it's a long haul : es un trayecto largo⟩

haulage ['hɔlıʤ] *n* : transporte *m*, tiro *m*

hauler ['hɔlər] *n* : transportista *mf*

haunch ['hɔnʧ] *n* 1 HIP : cadera *f* 2 **haunches** *npl* HINDQUARTERS : ancas *fpl*, cuartos *mpl* traseros

haunt[1] ['hɔnt] *vt* 1 : aparecer en (dícese de un fantasma) 2 FREQUENT : frecuentar, rondar 3 PREOCCUPY : perseguir, obsesionar

haunt[2] *n* : guarida *f* (de animales o ladrones), lugar *m* predilecto

haunting ['hɔntıŋ] *adj* : obsesionante, evocador — **hauntingly** *adv*

haute ['o:t] *adj* 1 : de moda, de categoría 2 **haute couture** [,o:tku'tur] : alta costura *f* 3 **haute cuisine** [,o:tkwı'zi:n] : alta cocina *f*

have ['hæv, *in sense 3 as an auxiliary verb usu* 'həf] *v* **had** ['hæd]; **having; has** ['hæz, *in sense 3 as an auxiliary verb usu* 'həs] *vt* 1 POSSESS : tener ⟨do you have change? : ¿tienes cambio?⟩ **2** EXPERI-ENCE, UNDERGO : tener, experimentar, sufrir ⟨I have a toothache : tengo un dolor de muelas⟩ **3** INCLUDE : tener, incluir ⟨April has 30 days : abril tiene 30 días⟩ **4** CONSUME : comer, tomar **5** RECEIVE : tener, recibir ⟨he had my permission : tenía mi permiso⟩ **6** ALLOW : permitir, dejar ⟨I won't have it! : ¡no lo permitiré!⟩ **7** HOLD : hacer ⟨to have a party : dar una fiesta⟩ ⟨to have a meeting : convocar una reunión⟩ **8** HOLD : tener ⟨he had me in his power : me tenía en su poder⟩ **9** BEAR : tener (niños) **10** (*indicating causation*) ⟨she had a dress made : mandó hacer un vestido⟩ ⟨to have one's hair cut : cortarse el pelo⟩ — *v aux* **1** : haber ⟨she has been very busy : ha estado muy ocupada⟩ ⟨I've lived here three years : hace tres años que vivo aquí⟩ **2** (*used in tags*) ⟨you've finished, haven't you? : ha terminado, ¿no?⟩ **3 to have to** : deber, tener que ⟨we have to leave : tenemos que salir⟩

haven [ˈheɪvən] *n* : refugio *m*

havoc [ˈhævək] *n* **1** DESTRUCTION : estragos *mpl*, destrucción *f* **2** CHAOS, DISORDER : desorden *m*, caos *m*

Hawaiian¹ [həˈwaɪən] *adj* : hawaiano

Hawaiian² *n* : hawaiano *m*, -na *f*

hawk¹ [ˈhɔk] *vt* : pregonar, vender (mercancías) en la calle

hawk² *n* : halcón *m*

hawker [ˈhɔkər] *n* : vendedor *m*, -dora *f* ambulante

hawthorn [ˈhɔˌθɔrn] *n* : espino *m*

hay [ˈheɪ] *n* : heno *m*

hay fever *n* : fiebre *f* del heno

hayloft [ˈheɪˌlɔft] *n* : pajar *m*

hayseed [ˈheɪˌsiːd] *n* : palurdo *m*, -da *f*

haystack [ˈheɪˌstæk] *n* : almiar *m*

haywire [ˈheɪˌwaɪr] *adj* : descompuesto, desbaratado ⟨to go haywire : estropearse⟩

hazard¹ [ˈhæzərd] *vt* : arriesgar, aventurar

hazard² *n* **1** DANGER : peligro *m*, riesgo *m* **2** CHANCE : azar *m*

hazardous [ˈhæzərdəs] *adj* : arriesgado, peligroso

haze¹ [ˈheɪz] *vt* **hazed; hazing** : abrumar, acosar

haze² *n* : bruma *f*, neblina *f*

hazel [ˈheɪzəl] *n* **1** : avellano *m* (árbol) **2** : color *m* avellana

hazelnut [ˈheɪzəlˌnʌt] *n* : avellana *f*

haziness [ˈheɪzinəs] *n* **1** MISTINESS : nebulosidad *f* **2** VAGUENESS : vaguedad *f*

hazy [ˈheɪzi] *adj* **hazier; -est 1** MISTY : brumoso, neblinoso, nebuloso **2** VAGUE : vago, confuso

he [ˈhiː] *pron* : él

head¹ [ˈhɛd] *vt* **1** LEAD : encabezar **2** DIRECT : dirigir — *vi* : dirigirse

head² *adj* MAIN : principal ⟨the head office : la oficina central, la sede⟩

head³ *n* **1** : cabeza *f* ⟨from head to foot : de pies a cabeza⟩ **2** MIND : mente *f*, cabeza *f* **3** TIP, TOP : cabeza *f* (de un clavo, un martillo, etc.), cabecera *f* (de una mesa o un río), punta *f* (de una flecha), flor *m* (de un repollo, etc.), encabezamiento *m* (de una carta, etc.), espuma *f* (de cerveza) **4** DIRECTOR, LEADER : director *m*, -tora *f*; jefe *m*, -fa *f*; cabeza *f* (de una familia) **5** : cara *f* (de una moneda) ⟨heads or tails : cara o cruz⟩ **6** : cabeza *f* ⟨500 head of cattle : 500 cabezas de ganado⟩ ⟨$10 a head : $10 por cabeza⟩ **7 to come to a head** : llegar a un punto crítico

headache [ˈhɛdˌeɪk] *n* : dolor *m* de cabeza, jaqueca *f*

headband [ˈhɛdˌbænd] *n* : cinta *f* del pelo

headdress [ˈhɛdˌdrɛs] *n* : tocado *m*

headfirst [ˈhɛdˈfərst] *adv* : de cabeza

headgear [ˈhɛdˌgɪr] *n* : gorro *m*, casco *m*, sombrero *m*

heading [ˈhɛdɪŋ] *n* **1** DIRECTION : dirección *f* **2** TITLE : encabezamiento *m*, título *m* **3** : membrete *m* (de una carta)

headland [ˈhɛdlənd, -ˌlænd] *n* : cabo *m*

headlight [ˈhɛdˌlaɪt] *n* : faro *m*, foco *m*, farol *m* Mex

headline [ˈhɛdˌlaɪn] *n* : titular *m*

headlong¹ [ˈhɛdˈlɔŋ] *adv* **1** HEADFIRST : de cabeza **2** HASTILY : precipitadamente

headlong² [ˈhɛdˌlɔŋ] *adj* : precipitado

headmaster [ˈhɛdˌmæstər] *n* : director *m*

headmistress [ˈhɛdˌmɪstrəs, -ˈmɪs-] *n* : directora *f*

head-on [ˈhɛdˈɑn, -ˈɔn] *adv & adj* : de frente

headphones [ˈhɛdˌfoːnz] *npl* : audífonos *mpl*, cascos *mpl*

headquarters [ˈhɛdˌkwɔrtərz] *ns & pl* **1** SEAT : oficina *f* central, sede *f* **2** : cuartel *m* general (de los militares)

headrest [ˈhɛdˌrɛst] *n* : apoyacabezas *m*

headship [ˈhɛdˌʃɪp] *n* : dirección *f*

head start *n* : ventaja *f*

headstone [ˈhɛdˌstoːn] *n* : lápida *f*

headstrong [ˈhɛdˈstrɔŋ] *adj* : testarudo, obstinado, empecinado

headwaiter [ˈhɛdˈweɪtər] *n* : jefe *m*, -fa *f* de comedor

headwaters [ˈhɛdˌwɔtərz, -ˌwɑ-] *npl* : cabecera *f*

headway [ˈhɛdˌweɪ] *n* : progreso *m* ⟨to make headway against : avanzar contra⟩

heady [ˈhɛdi] *adj* **headier; -est 1** INTOXICATING : embriagador, excitante **2** SHREWD : astuto, sagaz

heal [ˈhiːl] *vt* : curar, sanar — *vi* **1** : sanar, curarse **2 to heal up** : cicatrizarse

healer [ˈhiːlər] *n* **1** : curandero *m*, -dera *f* **2** : curador *m*, -dora *f* (cosa)

health [ˈhɛlθ] *n* : salud *f*

healthful [ˈhɛlθfəl] *adj* : saludable, salubre — **healthfully** *adv*

healthy [ˈhɛlθi] *adj* **healthier; -est** : sano, bien — **healthily** [-θəli] *adv*

heap¹ [ˈhiːp] *vt* **1** PILE : amontonar, apilar **2** SHOWER : colmar

heap² *n* : montón *m*, pila *f*

hear [ˈhɪr] *v* **heard** [ˈhərd]; **hearing** *vt* **1** : oír ⟨do you hear me? : ¿me oyes?⟩ **2** HEED : oír, prestar atención a **3** LEARN : oír, enterarse de — *vi* **1** : oír ⟨to hear about : oír hablar de⟩ **2 to hear from** : tener noticias de

hearing [ˈhɪrɪŋ] *n* **1** : oído *m* ⟨hard of hearing : duro de oído⟩ **2** : vista *f* (en un tribunal) **3** ATTENTION : consideración *f*, oportunidad *f* de expresarse **4** EARSHOT : alcance *m* del oído

hearing aid *n* : audífono *m*

hearken [ˈhɑrkən] *vt* : escuchar

hearsay [ˈhɪrˌseɪ] *n* : rumores *mpl*

hearse [ˈhərs] *n* : coche *m* fúnebre

heart [ˈhɑrt] *n* **1** : corazón *m* **2** CENTER, CORE : corazón *m*, centro *m* ⟨the heart of the matter : el meollo del asunto⟩ **3** FEELINGS : corazón *m*, sentimientos *mpl* ⟨a broken heart : un corazón destrozado⟩ ⟨to have a good heart : tener buen corazón⟩ ⟨to take something to heart : tomarse algo a pecho⟩ **4** COURAGE : valor *m*, corazón *m* ⟨to take heart : animarse, cobrar ánimos⟩ **5** hearts *npl* : corazones *mpl* (en juegos de naipes) **6 by heart** : de memoria

heartache [ˈhɑrtˌeɪk] *n* : pena *f*, angustia *f*

heart attack *n* : infarto *m*, ataque *m* al corazón

heartbeat [ˈhɑrtˌbiːt] *n* : latido *m* (del corazón)

heartbreak [ˈhɑrtˌbreɪk] *n* : congoja *f*, angustia *f*

heartbreaking [ˈhɑrtˌbreɪkɪŋ] *adj* : desgarrador, que parte el corazón

heartbroken [ˈhɑrtˌbroːkən] *adj* : desconsolado, destrozado

heartburn [ˈhɑrtˌbərn] *n* : acidez *f* estomacal

hearten [ˈhɑrtən] *vt* : alentar, animar

heartfelt [ˈhɑrtˌfɛlt] *adj* : sentido

hearth [ˈhɑrθ] *n* : hogar *m*, chimenea *f*

heartily [ˈhɑrtəli] *adv* **1** ENTHUSIASTICALLY : de buena gana, con entusiasmo **2** TOTALLY : totalmente, completamente

heartless [ˈhɑrtləs] *adj* : desalmado, despiadado, cruel

heartsick [ˈhɑrtˌsɪk] *adj* : abatido, desconsolado

heartstrings [ˈhɑrtˌstrɪŋz] *npl* : fibras *fpl* del corazón

heartwarming [ˈhɑrtˌwɔrmɪŋ] *adj* : conmovedor, emocionante

hearty [ˈhɑrti] *adj* **heartier; -est** CORDIAL, WARM : cordial, caluroso **2** STRONG : fuerte ⟨to have a hearty appetite : ser de buen comer⟩ **3** SUBSTANTIAL : abundante, sustancioso ⟨a

hearty breakfast : un desayuno abundante⟩

heat¹ [ˈhiːt] *vt* : calentar

heat² *n* **1** WARMTH : calor *m* **2** HEATING : calefacción *f* **3** EXCITEMENT : calor *m*, entusiasmo *m* ⟨in the heat of the moment : en el calor del momento⟩ **4** ESTRUS : celo *m*

heated [ˈhiːtəd] *adj* **1** WARMED : calentado **2** IMPASSIONED : acalorado, apasionado

heater [ˈhiːtər] *n* : calentador *m*, estufa *f*, calefactor *m*

heath [ˈhiːθ] *n* **1** MOOR : brezal *m*, páramo *m* **2** HEATHER : brezo *m*

heathen¹ [ˈhiːðən] *adj* : pagano

heathen² *n*, *pl* **-thens** *or* **-then** : pagano *m*, -na *f*; infiel *mf*

heather [ˈhɛðər] *n* : brezo *m*

heave¹ [ˈhiːv] *v* **heaved** *or* **hove** [ˈhoːv]; **heaving** *vt* **1** LIFT, RAISE : levantar con esfuerzo **2** HURL : lanzar, tirar **3 to heave a sigh** : echar un suspiro, suspirar — *vi* **1** : subir y bajar, palpitar (dícese del pecho) **2 to heave up** RISE : levantarse

heave² *n* **1** EFFORT : gran esfuerzo *m* (para levantar algo) **2** THROW : lanzamiento *m*

heaven [ˈhɛvən] *n* **1** : cielo *m* ⟨for heaven's sake : por Dios⟩ **2 heavens** *npl* SKY : cielo *m* ⟨the heavens opened up : empezó a llover a cántaros⟩

heavenly [ˈhɛvənli] *adj* **1** : celestial, celeste **2** DELIGHTFUL : divino, encantador

heavily [ˈhɛvəli] *adv* **1** : pesadamente, con mucho peso **2** LABORIOUSLY : trabajosamente, penosamente **3** : mucho

heaviness [ˈhɛvinəs] *n* : peso *m*, pesadez *f*

heavy [ˈhɛvi] *adj* **heavier; -est** **1** WEIGHTY : pesado **2** DENSE, THICK : denso, espeso, grueso **3** BURDENSOME : oneroso, gravoso **4** PROFOUND : profundo **5** SLUGGISH : lento, tardo **6** STOUT : corpulento **7** SEVERE : severo, duro, fuerte

heavy–duty [ˈhɛviˈduːti, -ˈdjuː-] *adj* : muy resistente, fuerte

heavyweight [ˈhɛviˌweɪt] *n* : peso *m* pesado (en deportes)

Hebrew¹ [ˈhiːˌbruː] *adj* : hebreo

Hebrew² *n* **1** : hebreo *m*, -brea *f* **2** : hebreo *m* (idioma)

heck [ˈhɛk] *n* : ¡caramba!, ¡caray! ⟨a heck of a lot : un montón⟩ ⟨what the heck is . . . ? : ¿que diablos es . . . ?⟩

heckle [ˈhɛkəl] *vt* **-led; -ling** : interrumpir (a un orador)

hectare [ˈhɛkˌtær] *n* : hectárea *f*

hectic [ˈhɛktɪk] *adj* : agitado, ajetreado — **hectically** [-tɪkli] *adv*

he'd [ˈhiːd] (*contraction of* **he had** *or* **he would**) → **have**, **would**

hedge¹ [ˈhɛdʒ] *v* **hedged; hedging** *vt* **1** : cercar con un seto **2 to hedge one's bet** : cubrirse — *vi* **1** : dar rodeos, contestar con evasivas **2 to hedge against** : cubrirse contra, protegerse contra

hedge² *n* **1** : seto *m* vivo **2** SAFEGUARD : salvaguardia *f*, protección *f*

hedgehog ['hɛʤ,hɑg, -,hɔg] *n* : erizo *m*

heed¹ ['hi:d] *vt* : prestar atención a, hacer caso de

heed² *n* : atención *f*

heedless ['hi:dləs] *adj* : descuidado, despreocupado, inconsciente ⟨to be heedless of : hacer caso omiso de⟩ — **heedlessly** *adv*

heel¹ ['hi:l] *vi* : inclinarse

heel² *n* : talón *m* (del pie), tacón *m* (de calzado)

heft ['hɛft] *vt* : sopesar

hefty ['hɛfti] *adj* **heftier; -est** : robusto, fornido, pesado

hegemony [hɪ'ʤɛməni] *n, pl* **-nies** : hegemonía *f*

heifer ['hɛfər] *n* : novilla *f*

height ['haɪt] *n* **1** PEAK : cumbre *f*, cima *f*, punto *m* alto ⟨at the height of her career : en la cumbre de su carrera⟩ ⟨the height of stupidity : el colmo de la estupidez⟩ **2** TALLNESS : estatura *f* (de una persona), altura *f* (de un objeto) **3** ALTITUDE : altura *f*

heighten ['haɪtən] *vt* **1** : hacer más alto **2** INTENSIFY : aumentar, intensificar — *vi* : aumentarse, intensificarse

heinous ['heɪnəs] *adj* : atroz, abominable, nefando

heir ['ær] *n* : heredero *m*, -ra *f*

heiress ['ærəs] *n* : heredera *f*

heirloom ['ær,lu:m] *n* : reliquia *f* de familia

held → **hold**

helicopter ['hɛlə,kɑptər] *n* : helicóptero *m*

helium ['hi:liəm] *n* : helio *m*

helix ['hi:lɪks] *n, pl* **helices** ['hɛlə,si:z, 'hi:-] *or* **helixes** ['hi:lɪksəz] : hélice *f*

hell ['hɛl] *n* : infierno *m*

he'll ['hi:l, 'hɪl] (*contraction of* **he shall** *or* **he will**) → **shall, will**

hellish ['hɛlɪʃ] *adj* : horroroso, infernal

hello [hə'lo:, hɛ-] *interj* : ¡hola!

helm ['hɛlm] *n* **1** : timón *m* **2 to take the helm** : tomar el mando

helmet ['hɛlmət] *n* : casco *m*

help¹ ['hɛlp] *vt* **1** AID, ASSIST : ayudar, auxiliar, socorrer, asistir **2** ALLEVIATE : aliviar **3** SERVE : servir ⟨help yourself! : ¡sírvete!⟩ **4** AVOID : evitar ⟨it can't be helped : no lo podemos evitar, no hay más remedio⟩ ⟨I couldn't help smiling : no pude menos que sonreír⟩

help² *n* **1** ASSISTANCE : ayuda *f* ⟨help! : ¡socorro!, ¡auxilio!⟩ **2** STAFF : personal *m* (en una oficina), servicio *m* doméstico

helper ['hɛlpər] *n* : ayudante *mf*

helpful ['hɛlpfəl] *adj* **1** OBLIGING : servicial, amable, atento **2** USEFUL : útil, práctico — **helpfully** *adv*

helpfulness ['hɛlpfəlnəs] *n* **1** KINDNESS : bondad *f*, amabilidad *f* **2** USEFULNESS : utilidad *f*

helping ['hɛlpɪŋ] *n* : porción *f*

helpless ['hɛlpləs] *adj* **1** POWERLESS : incapaz, impotente **2** DEFENSELESS : indefenso

helplessly ['hɛlpləsli] *adv* : en vano, inútilmente

helplessness ['hɛlpləsnəs] *n* POWERLESSNESS : incapacidad *f*, impotencia *f*

helter–skelter [,hɛltər'skɛltər] *adv* : atropelladamente, precipitadamente

hem¹ ['hɛm] *vt* **hemmed; hemming 1** : dobladillar **2 to hem in** : encerrar

hem² *n* : dobladillo *m*, bastilla *f*

hemisphere ['hɛmə,sfɪr] *n* : hemisferio *m*

hemispheric [,hɛmə'sfɪrɪk, -'sfɛr-] *or* **hemispherical** [-ɪkəl] *adj* : hemisférico

hemlock ['hɛm,lɑk] *n* : cicuta *f*

hemoglobin ['hi:mə,glo:bən] *n* : hemoglobina *f*

hemophilia [,hi:mə'fɪliə] *n* : hemofilia *f*

hemorrhage¹ ['hɛmərɪʤ] *vi* **-rhaged; -rhaging** : sufrir una hemorragia

hemorrhage² *n* : hemorragia *f*

hemorrhoids ['hɛmə,rɔɪdz, 'hɛm-,rɔɪdz] *npl* : hemorroides *fpl*, almorranas *fpl*

hemp ['hɛmp] *n* : cáñamo *m*

hen ['hɛn] *n* : gallina *f*

hence ['hɛnts] *adv* **1** : de aquí, de ahí ⟨10 years hence : de aquí a 10 años⟩ ⟨a dog bit me, hence my dislike of animals : un perro me mordió, de ahí mi aversión a los animales⟩ **2** THEREFORE : por lo tanto, por consiguiente

henceforth ['hɛnts,forθ, ,hɛnts'-] *adv* : de ahora en adelante

henchman ['hɛntʃmən] *n, pl* **-men** [-mən, -,mɛn] : secuaz *mf*, esbirro *m*

henpeck ['hɛn,pɛk] *vt* : dominar (al marido)

hepatitis [,hɛpə'taɪtəs] *n, pl* **-titides** [-'tɪtə,di:z] : hepatitis *f*

her¹ ['hər] *adj* : su, sus, de ella ⟨her house : su casa, la casa de ella⟩

her² ['hər, ər] *pron* **1** (*used as direct object*) : la ⟨I saw her yesterday : la vi ayer⟩ **2** (*used as indirect object*) : le, se ⟨he gave her the book : le dio el libro⟩ ⟨he sent it to her : se lo mandó⟩ **3** (*used as object of a preposition*) : ella ⟨we did it for her : lo hicimos por ella⟩ ⟨taller than her : más alto que ella⟩

herald¹ ['hɛrəld] *vt* ANNOUNCE : anunciar, proclamar

herald² *n* **1** MESSENGER : heraldo *m* **2** HARBINGER : precursor *m*

heraldic [he'rældɪk, hə-] *adj* : heráldico

heraldry ['hɛrəldri] *n, pl* **-ries** : heráldica *f*

herb ['ərb, 'hərb] *n* : hierba *f*

herbal ['ərbəl, 'hər-] *adj* : herbario

herbicide ['ərbə,saɪd, 'hər-] *n* : herbicida *m*

herbivore ['ərbə,vor, 'hər-] *n* : herbívoro *m*

herbivorous [,ər'bɪvərəs, ,hər-] *adj* : herbívoro

herculean [,hərkjə'li:ən, ,hər'kju:-liən] *adj* : herculéo, sobrehumano

herd[1] [ˈhərd] *vt* : reunir en manada, conducir en manada — *vi* : ir en manada (dícese de los animales), apiñarse (dícese de la gente)

herd[2] *n* : manada *f*

herder [ˈhərdər] → **herdsman**

herdsman [ˈhərdzmən] *n, pl* **-men** [-mən, -ˌmɛn] : vaquero *m* (de ganado), pastor *m* (de ovejas)

here[1] [ˈhɪr] *adv* **1** : aquí, acá ⟨come here! : ¡ven acá!⟩ ⟨right here : aquí mismo⟩ **2** NOW : en este momento, ahora, ya ⟨here he comes : ya viene⟩ ⟨here it's three o'clock (already) : ahora son las tres⟩ **3** : en este punto ⟨here we agree : estamos de acuerdo en este punto⟩ **4** here you are! : ¡toma!

hereabouts [ˈhɪrəˌbaʊts] *or* **hereabout** [-ˌbaʊt] *adv* : por aquí (cerca)

hereafter[1] [hɪrˈæftər] *adv* **1** : de aquí en adelante, a continuación **2** : en el futuro

hereafter[2] *n* **the hereafter** : el más allá

hereby [hɪrˈbaɪ] *adv* : por este medio

hereditary [həˈrɛdəˌteri] *adj* : hereditario

heredity [həˈrɛdəti] *n* : herencia *f*

herein [hɪrˈɪn] *adv* : aquí

hereof [hɪrˈʌv] *adv* : de aquí

hereon [hɪrˈɑn, -ˈɔn] *adv* : sobre esto

heresy [ˈhɛrəsi] *n, pl* **-sies** : herejía *f*

heretic [ˈhɛrəˌtɪk] *n* : hereje *mf*

heretical [həˈrɛtɪkəl] *adj* : herético

hereto [hɪrˈtuː] *adv* : a esto

heretofore [ˈhɪrtəˌfor] *adv* HITHERTO : hasta ahora

hereunder [hɪrˈʌndər] *adv* : a continuación, abajo

hereupon [ˈhɪrəˌpɑn, -ˈpɔn] *adv* : con esto, en ese momento

herewith [hɪrˈwɪθ] *adv* : adjunto

heritage [ˈhɛrətɪdʒ] *n* : patrimonio *m* (nacional)

hermaphrodite [hərˈmæfrəˌdaɪt] *n* : hermafrodita *mf*

hermetic [hərˈmɛtɪk] *adj* : hermético — **hermetically** [-tɪkli] *adv*

hermit [ˈhərmət] *n* : ermitaño *m*, -ña *f*; eremita *mf*

hernia [ˈhərniə] *n, pl* **-nias** *or* **-niae** [-niˌiː, -niˌaɪ] : hernia *f*

hero [ˈhiːˌroː, ˈhɪrˌoː] *n, pl* **-roes** **1** : héroe *m* **2** PROTAGONIST : protagonista *mf*

heroic [hɪˈroːɪk] *adj* : heroico — **heroically** [-ɪkli] *adv*

heroics [hɪˈroːɪks] *npl* : actos *mpl* heroicos

heroin [ˈhɛroən] *n* : heroína *f*

heroine [ˈhɛroən] *n* **1** : heroína *f* **2** PROTAGONIST : protagonista *f*

heroism [ˈhɛroˌɪzəm] *n* : heroísmo *m*

heron [ˈhɛrən] *n* : garza *f*

herpes [ˈhərˌpiːz] *n* : herpes *m*

herring [ˈhɛrɪŋ] *n, pl* **-ring** *or* **-rings** : arenque *m*

hers [ˈhərz] *pron* : suyo, -ya; suyos, -yas; de ella ⟨these shoes are hers : estos zapatos son suyos⟩ ⟨hers are bigger : los de ella son más grandes⟩

herself [hərˈsɛlf] *pron* **1** (*used reflexively*) : se ⟨she dressed herself : se vistió⟩ **2** (*used emphatically*) : ella misma ⟨she fixed it herself : lo arregló ella misma, lo arregló por sí sola⟩

hertz [ˈhərts, ˈhrts] *ns & pl* : hercio *m*

he's [ˈhiːz] (*contraction of* **he is** *or* **he has**) → **be, have**

hesitancy [ˈhɛzətəntsi] *n, pl* **-cies** : vacilación *f*, titubeo *m*, indecisión *f*

hesitant [ˈhɛzətənt] *adj* : titubeante, vacilante — **hesitantly** *adv*

hesitate [ˈhɛzəˌteɪt] *vi* **-tated; -tating** : vacilar, titubear

hesitation [ˌhɛzəˈteɪʃən] *n* : vacilación *f*, indecisión *f*, titubeo *m*

heterogeneous [ˌhɛtərəˈdʒiːniəs, -njəs] *adj* : heterogéneo

heterosexual[1] [ˌhɛtəroˈskʃuəl] *adj* : heterosexual

heterosexual[2] *n* : heterosexual *mf*

heterosexuality [ˌhɛtəroˌskʃuˈæləti] *n* : heterosexualidad *f*

hew [ˈhjuː] *v* **hewed; hewed** *or* **hewn** [ˈhjuːn]; **hewing** *vt* **1** CUT : cortar, talar (árboles) **2** SHAPE : labrar, tallar — *vi* CONFORM : conformarse, ceñirse

hex[1] [ˈhɛks] *vt* : hacerle un maleficio (a alguien)

hex[2] *n* : maleficio *m*

hexagon [ˈhɛksəˌgɑn] *n* : hexágono *m*

hexagonal [hɛkˈsægənəl] *adj* : hexagonal

hey [ˈheɪ] *interj* : ¡eh!, ¡oye!

heyday [ˈheɪˌdeɪ] *n* : auge *m*, apogeo *m*

hi [ˈhaɪ] *interj* : ¡hola!

hiatus [haɪˈeɪtəs] *n* **1** : hiato *m* **2** PAUSE : pausa *f*

hibernate [ˈhaɪbərˌneɪt] *vi* **-nated; -nating** : hibernar, invernar

hibernation [ˌhaɪbərˈneɪʃən] *n* : hibernación *f*

hiccup[1] [ˈhɪkəp] *vi* **-cuped; -cuping** : hipar, tener hipo

hiccup[2] *n* : hipo *m* ⟨to have the hiccups : tener hipo⟩

hick [ˈhɪk] *n* BUMPKIN : palurdo *m*, -da *f*

hickory [ˈhɪkəri] *n, pl* **-ries** : nogal *m* americano

hidden [ˈhɪdən] *adj* : oculto

hide[1] [ˈhaɪd] *v* **hid** [ˈhɪd]; **hidden** [ˈhɪdən] *or* **hid; hiding** *vt* **1** CONCEAL : esconder **2** : ocultar ⟨to hide one's motives : ocultar uno sus motivos⟩ **3** SCREEN : tapar, no dejar ver — *vi* : esconderse

hide[2] *n* : piel *f*, cuero *m* ⟨to save one's hide : salvar el pellejo⟩

hide-and-seek [ˈhaɪdəndˈsiːk] *n* **to play hide-and-seek** : jugar a las escondidas

hidebound [ˈhaɪdˌbaʊnd] *adj* : rígido, conservador

hideous [ˈhɪdiəs] *adj* : horrible, horroroso, espantoso — **hideously** *adv*

hideout [ˈhaɪdˌaʊt] *n* : guarida *f*, escondrijo *m*

hierarchical [ˌhaɪəˈrɑrkɪkəl] *adj* : jerárquico

hierarchy ['haɪə,rɑrki] *n, pl* **-chies** : jerarquía *f*

hieroglyphic [,haɪərə'glɪfɪk] *n* : jeroglífico *m*

hi–fi ['haɪ'faɪ] *n* 1 → **high fidelity** 2 : equipo *m* de alta fidelidad

high¹ ['haɪ] *adv* : alto

high² *adj* 1 TALL : alto ⟨a high wall : una pared alta⟩ 2 ELEVATED : alto, elevado ⟨high prices : precios elevados⟩ ⟨high blood pressure : presión alta⟩ 3 GREAT, IMPORTANT : grande, importante, alto ⟨a high number : un número grande⟩ ⟨high society : alta sociedad⟩ ⟨high hopes : grandes esperanzas⟩ 4 : alto (en música) 5 INTOXICATED : borracho, drogado

high³ *n* 1 : récord *m*, punto *m* máximo ⟨to reach an all-time high : batir el récord⟩ 2 : zona *f* de alta presión (en meteorología) 3 *or* **high gear** : directa *f* 4 **on high** : en las alturas

highbrow ['haɪ,braʊ] *n* : intelectual *mf*

higher ['haɪər] *adj* : superior

high fidelity *n* : alta fidelidad *f*

high–flown ['haɪ'floːn] *adj* : altisonante

high–handed ['haɪ'hændəd] *adj* : arbitrario

highlands ['haɪləndz] *npl* : tierras *fpl* altas, altiplano *m*

highlight¹ ['haɪ,laɪt] *vt* 1 EMPHASIZE : destacar, poner en relieve, subrayar 2 : ser el punto culminante de

highlight² *n* : punto *m* culminante

highly ['haɪli] *adv* 1 VERY : muy, sumamente 2 FAVORABLY : muy bien ⟨to speak highly of : hablar muy bien de⟩ ⟨to think highly of : tener en mucho a⟩

highness ['haɪnəs] *n* 1 HEIGHT : altura *f* 2 **Highness** : Alteza *f* ⟨Your Royal Highness : Su Alteza Real⟩

high–pitched ['haɪ'pɪtʃt] *adj* : agudo

high–rise ['haɪ,raɪz] *adj* : alto, de muchas plantas

high school *n* : escuela *f* superior, escuela *f* secundaria

high seas *npl* : alta mar *f*

high–spirited ['haɪ'spɪrətəd] *adj* : vivaz, muy animado, brioso

high–strung [,haɪ'strʌŋ] *adj* : nervioso, excitable

highway ['haɪ,weɪ] *n* : carretera *f*

highwayman ['haɪ,weɪmən] *n, pl* **-men** [-mən, -,mɛn] : salteador *m* (de caminos), bandido *m*

hijack¹ ['haɪ,dʒæk] *vt* : secuestrar

hijack² *n* : secuestro *m*

hijacker ['haɪ,dʒækər] *n* : secuestrador *m*, -dora *f*

hike¹ ['haɪk] *v* **hiked; hiking** *vi* : hacer una caminata — *vt* RAISE : subir

hike² *n* 1 : caminata *f*, excursión *f* 2 INCREASE : subida *f* (de precios)

hiker ['haɪkər] *n* : excursionista *mf*

hilarious [hɪ'læriəs, haɪ-] *adj* : muy divertido, hilarante

hilarity [hɪ'lærəṭi, haɪ-] *n* : hilaridad *f*

hill ['hɪl] *n* 1 : colina *f*, cerro *m* 2 SLOPE : cuesta *f*, pendiente *f*

hillbilly ['hɪl,bɪli] *n, pl* **-lies** : palurdo *m*, -da *f* (de las montañas)

hillock ['hɪlək] *n* : loma *f*, altozano *m*, otero *m*

hillside ['hɪl,saɪd] *n* : ladera *f*, cuesta *f*

hilltop ['hɪl,tɑp] *n* : cima *f*, cumbre *f*

hilly ['hɪli] *adj* **hillier; -est** : montañoso, accidentado

hilt ['hɪlt] *n* : puño *m*, empuñadura *f*

him ['hɪm, əm] *pron* 1 (*used as direct object*) : lo ⟨I found him : lo encontré⟩ 2 (*used as indirect object*) : le, se ⟨we gave him a present : le dimos un regalo⟩ ⟨I sent it to him : se lo mandé⟩ 3 (*used as object of a preposition*) : él ⟨she was thinking of him : pensaba en él⟩ ⟨younger than him : más joven que él⟩

himself [hɪm'sɛlf] *pron* 1 (*used reflexively*) : se ⟨he washed himself : se lavó⟩ 2 (*used emphatically*) : él mismo ⟨he did it himself : lo hizo él mismo, lo hizo por sí solo⟩

hind¹ ['haɪnd] *adj* : trasero, posterior ⟨hind legs : patas traseras⟩

hind² *n* : cierva *f*

hinder ['hɪndər] *vt* : dificultar, impedir, estorbar

Hindi ['hɪndi:] *n* : hindi *m*

hindquarters ['haɪnd,kwɔrtərz] *npl* : cuartos *mpl* traseros

hindrance ['hɪndrəns] *n* : estorbo *m*, obstáculo *m*, impedimento *m*

hindsight ['haɪnd,saɪt] *n* : retrospectiva *f* ⟨with the benefit of hindsight : en retrospectiva, con la perspectiva que da la experiencia⟩

Hindu¹ ['hɪn,du:] *adj* : hindú

Hindu² *n* : hindú *mf*

Hinduism ['hɪndu:,ɪzəm] *n* : hinduismo *m*

hinge¹ ['hɪndʒ] *v* **hinged; hinging** *vt* : unir con bisagras — *vi* **to hinge on** : depender de

hinge² *n* : bisagra *f*, gozne *m*

hint¹ ['hɪnt] *vt* : insinuar, dar a entender — *vi* : soltar indirectas

hint² *n* 1 INSINUATION : insinuación *f*, indirecta *f* 2 TIP : consejo *m*, sugerencia *f* 3 TRACE : pizca *f*, indicio *m*

hinterland ['hɪntər,lænd, -lənd] *n* : interior *m* (de un país)

hip ['hɪp] *n* : cadera *f*

hip–hop ['hɪp,hɑp] *n* : hip-hop *m*

hippie ['hɪpi] *n* : hippie *mf*, hippy *mf*

hippopotamus [,hɪpə'pɑṭəməs] *n, pl* **-muses** *or* **-mi** [-,maɪ] : hipopótamo *m*

hippo ['hɪpo:] *n, pl* **hippos** → **hippopotamus**

hire¹ ['haɪr] *vt* **hired; hiring** 1 EMPLOY : contratar, emplear 2 RENT : alquilar, arrendar

hire² *n* 1 RENT : alquiler *m* ⟨for hire : se alquila⟩ 2 WAGES : paga *f*, sueldo *m* 3 EMPLOYEE : empleado *m*, -da *f*

his¹ ['hɪz, ɪz] *adj* : su, sus, de él ⟨his hat : su sombrero, el sombrero de él⟩

his² *pron* : suyo, -ya; suyos, suyas; de él ⟨the decision is his : la decisión es suya⟩ ⟨it's his, not hers : es de él, no de ella⟩

Hispanic[1] [hɪˈspænɪk] *adj* : hispano, hispánico

Hispanic[2] *n* : hispano *m*, -na *f*; hispánico *m*, -ca *f*

hiss[1] [ˈhɪs] *vi* : sisear, silbar — *vt* : decir entre dientes

hiss[2] *n* : siseo *m*, silbido *m*

historian [hɪˈstɔriən] *n* : historiador *m*, -dora *f*

historic [hɪˈstɔrɪk] *or* **historical** [-ɪkəl] *adj* : histórico — **historically** [-ɪkli] *adv*

history [ˈhɪstəri] *n, pl* **-ries** 1 : historia *f* 2 RECORD : historial *m*

histrionics [ˌhɪstriˈɑnɪks] *ns & pl* : histrionismo *m*

hit[1] [ˈhɪt] *v* **hit; hitting** *vt* 1 STRIKE : golpear, pegar, batear (una pelota) ⟨he hit the dog : le pegó al perro⟩ 2 : chocar contra, dar con, dar en (el blanco) ⟨the car hit a tree : el coche chocó contra un árbol⟩ 3 AFFECT : afectar ⟨the news hit us hard : la noticia nos afectó mucho⟩ 4 ENCOUNTER : tropezar con, toparse con ⟨to hit a snag : tropezar con un obstáculo⟩ 5 REACH : llegar a, alcanzar ⟨the price hit $10 a pound : el precio alcanzó los $10 dólares por libra⟩ ⟨to hit town : llegar a la ciudad⟩ ⟨to hit the headlines : ser noticia⟩ 6 to **hit on** *or* **to hit upon** : dar con — *vi* : golpear

hit[2] *n* 1 BLOW : golpe *m* 2 : impacto *m* (de un arma) 3 SUCCESS : éxito *m*

hitch[1] [ˈhɪtʃ] *vt* 1 : mover con sacudidas 2 ATTACH : enganchar, atar, amarrar 3 → **hitchhike** 4 to **hitch up** : subirse (los pantalones, etc.)

hitch[2] *n* 1 JERK : tirón *m*, jalón *m* 2 OBSTACLE : obstáculo *m*, impedimento *m*, tropiezo *m*

hitchhike [ˈhɪtʃˌhaɪk] *vi* **-hiked; -hiking** : hacer autostop, ir de aventón *Col, Mex fam*

hitchhiker [ˈhɪtʃˌhaɪkər] *n* : autostopista *mf*

hither [ˈhɪðər] *adv* : acá, por aquí

hitherto [ˈhɪðərˌtuː, ˌhɪðər'-] *adv* : hasta ahora

hitter [ˈhɪtər] *n* BATTER : bateador *m*, -dora *f*

HIV [ˌeɪtʃˌaɪˈviː] *n* (*human immunodeficiency virus*) : VIH *m*, virus *m* del sida

hive [ˈhaɪv] *n* 1 : colmena *f* 2 SWARM : enjambre *m* 3 : lugar *m* muy activo ⟨a hive of activity : un hervidero de actividad⟩

hives [ˈhaɪvz] *ns & pl* : urticaria *f*

hoard[1] [ˈhord] *vt* : acumular, atesorar

hoard[2] *n* : tesoro *m*, reserva *f*, provisión *f*

hoarfrost [ˈhorˌfrɔst] *n* : escarcha *f*

hoarse [ˈhors] *adj* **hoarser; -est** : ronco — **hoarsely** *adv*

hoarseness [ˈhorsnəs] *n* : ronquera *f*

hoary [ˈhori] *adj* **hoarier; -est** 1 : cano, canoso 2 OLD : vetusto, antiguo

hoax[1] [ˈhoːks] *vt* : engañar, embaucar, bromear

hoax[2] *n* : engaño *m*, broma *f*

hobble[1] [ˈhɑbəl] *v* **-bled; -bling** *vi* LIMP : cojear, renguear — *vt* : manear (un animal)

hobble[2] *n* 1 LIMP : cojera *f*, rengo *m* 2 : maniota *f* (para un animal)

hobby [ˈhɑbi] *n, pl* **-bies** : pasatiempo *m*, afición *f*

hobgoblin [ˈhɑbˌgɑblən] *n* : duende *m*

hobnail [ˈhɑbˌneɪl] *n* : tachuela *f*

hobnob [ˈhɑbˌnɑb] *vi* **-nobbed; -nobbing** : codearse

hobo [ˈhoːˌboː] *n, pl* **-boes** : vagabundo *m*, -da *f*

hock[1] [ˈhɑk] *vt* PAWN : empeñar

hock[2] *n* **in hock** : empeñado

hockey [ˈhɑki] *n* : hockey *m*

hodgepodge [ˈhɑdʒˌpɑdʒ] *n* : mezcolanza *f*

hoe[1] [ˈhoː] *v* **hoed; hoeing** : azadonar

hoe[2] *n* : azada *f*, azadón *m*

hog[1] [ˈhɔg, ˈhɑg] *vt* **hogged; hogging** : acaparar, monopolizar

hog[2] *n* 1 PIG : cerdo *m*, -da *f* 2 GLUTTON : glotón *m*, -tona *f*

hogshead [ˈhɔgzˌhed, ˈhɑgz-] *n* : tonel *m*

hoist[1] [ˈhɔɪst] *vt* : levantar, alzar, izar (una bandera, una vela)

hoist[2] *n* : grúa *f*

hold[1] [ˈhoːld] *v* **held** [ˈheld]; **holding** *vt* 1 POSSESS : tener ⟨to hold office : ocupar un puesto⟩ 2 RESTRAIN : detener, controlar ⟨to hold one's temper : controlar su mal genio⟩ 3 CLASP, GRASP : agarrar, coger ⟨to hold hands : agarrarse de la mano⟩ 4 : sujetar, mantener ⟨hold this nail for me : sujétame este clavo⟩ 5 CONTAIN : contener, dar cabida a 6 SUPPORT : aguantar, sostener 7 REGARD : considerar, tener ⟨he held me responsible : me consideró responsable⟩ 8 CONDUCT : celebrar (una reunión), realizar (un evento), mantener (una conversación) — *vi* 1 : aguantar, resistir ⟨the rope will hold : la cuerda resistirá⟩ 2 : ser válido, valer ⟨my offer still holds : mi oferta todavía es válida⟩ 3 to **hold forth** : perorar, arengar 4 to **hold to** : mantenerse firme en 5 to **hold with** : estar de acuerdo con

hold[2] *n* 1 GRIP : agarre *m*, llave *f* (en deportes) 2 CONTROL : control *m*, dominio *m* ⟨to get hold of oneself : controlarse⟩ 3 DELAY : demora *f* ⟨to put on hold : suspender temporalmente⟩ 4 : bodega *f* (en un barco o un avión) 5 to **get hold of** : conseguir, localizar

holder [ˈhoːldər] *n* : poseedor *m*, -dora *f*; titular *mf*

holdings [ˈhoːldɪŋz] *npl* : propiedades *fpl*

hold out *vi* 1 LAST : aguantar, durar 2 RESIST : resistir

holdup [ˈhoːldˌʌp] *n* 1 ROBBERY : atraco *m* 2 DELAY : retraso *m*, demora *f*

hold up *vt* 1 ROB : robarle (a alguien), atracar, asaltar 2 DELAY : retrasar

hole [ˈhoːl] *n* : agujero *m*, hoyo *m*

holiday ['hɑlə,deɪ] n 1 : día m feriado, fiesta f 2 VACATION : vacaciones fpl

holiness ['hoːlinəs] n 1 : santidad f 2 His Holiness : Su Santidad

holistic [hoːˈlɪstɪk] adj : holístico

holler¹ ['hɑlər] vi : gritar, chillar

holler² n : grito m, chillido m

hollow¹ ['hɑ,loː] vt or to hollow out : ahuecar

hollow² adj -lower; -est 1 : hueco, hundido (dícese de las mejillas, etc.), cavernoso (dícese de un sonido) 2 EMPTY, FALSE : vacío, falso

hollow³ n 1 CAVITY : hueco m, depresión f, cavidad f 2 VALLEY : hondonada f, valle m

hollowness ['hɑ,loːnəs] n 1 HOLLOW : hueco m, cavidad f 2 FALSENESS : falsedad f 3 EMPTINESS : vacuidad f

holly ['hɑli] n, pl -lies : acebo m

hollyhock ['hɑli,hɑk] n : malvarrosa f

holocaust ['hɑlə,kɔst, 'hoː-, 'hɔ-] n : holocausto m

hologram ['hoːlə,græm, 'hɑ-] n : holograma m

holster ['hoːlstər] n : pistolera f

holy ['hoːli] adj -lier; -est : santo, sagrado

Holy Ghost → Holy Spirit

Holy Spirit n the Holy Spirit : el Espíritu Santo

homage ['ɑmɪʤ, 'hɑ-] n : homenaje m

home ['hoːm] n 1 : casa f, hogar m, domicilio m ⟨to feel at home : sentirse en casa⟩ 2 INSTITUTION : residencia f, asilo m

homecoming ['hoːm,kʌmɪŋ] n : regreso m (a casa)

homegrown ['hoːm'groːn] adj 1 : de cosecha propia 2 LOCAL : local

homeland ['hoːm,lænd] n : patria f, tierra f natal, terruño m

homeless ['hoːmləs] adj : sin hogar, sin techo

homely ['hoːmli] adj -lier; -est 1 DOMESTIC : casero, hogareño 2 UGLY : feo, poco atractivo

homemade ['hoːm'meɪd] adj : casero, hecho en casa

homemaker ['hoːm,meɪkər] n : ama f de casa, persona f que se ocupa de la casa

home plate n : base f del bateador

home run n : jonrón m

homesick ['hoːm,sɪk] adj : nostálgico ⟨to be homesick : echar de menos a la familia⟩

homesickness ['hoːm,sɪknəs] n : nostalgia f, morriña f

homespun ['hoːm,spʌn] adj : simple, sencillo

homestead ['hoːm,stɛd] n : estancia f, hacienda f

homeward¹ ['hoːmwərd] or homewards [-wərdz] adv : de vuelta a casa, hacia casa

homeward² adj : de vuelta, de regreso

homework ['hoːm,wərk] n : tarea f, deberes mpl Spain, asignación f PRi

homey ['hoːmi] adj homier; -est : hogareño

homicidal [,hɑmə'saɪdəl, ,hoː-] adj : homicida

homicide ['hɑmə,saɪd, 'hoː-] n : homicidio m

hominy ['hɑməni] n : maíz m descascarillado

homogeneity [,hoːmədʒə'niːəti, -'neɪ-] n, pl -ties : homogeneidad f

homogeneous [,hoːmə'dʒiːniəs, -njəs] adj : homogéneo — homogeneously adv

homogenize [hoːˈmɑdʒə,naɪz, hə-] vt -nized; -nizing : homogeneizar

homograph ['hɑmə,græf, 'hoː-] n : homógrafo m

homologous [hoːˈmɑləgəs, hə-] adj : homólogo

homonym ['hɑmə,nɪm, 'hoː-] n, pl -nims : homónimo m

homophone ['hɑmə,foːn, 'hoː-] n : homófono m

homosexual¹ [,hoːmə'sɛkʃuəl] adj : homosexual

homosexual² n : homosexual mf

homosexuality [,hoːmə,sɛkʃu'æləti] n : homosexualidad f

honcho ['hɑn,ʧoː] n : pez m gordo ⟨the head honcho : el jefe⟩

Honduran [hɑn'durən, -'djur-] n : hondureño m, -ña f — Honduran adj

hone ['hoːn] vt honed; honing : afilar

honest ['ɑnəst] adj : honesto, honrado — honestly adv

honesty ['ɑnəsti] n, pl -ties : honestidad f, honradez f

honey ['hʌni] n, pl -eys : miel f

honeybee ['hʌni,biː] n : abeja f

honeycomb ['hʌni,koːm] n : panal m

honeymoon¹ ['hʌni,muːn] vi : pasar la luna de miel

honeymoon² n : luna f de miel

honeysuckle ['hʌni,sʌkəl] n : madreselva f

honk¹ ['hɑŋk, 'hɔŋk] vi 1 : graznar (dícese del ganso) 2 : tocar la bocina (dícese de un vehículo), pitar

honk² n : graznido m (del ganso), bocinazo m (de un vehículo)

honor¹ ['ɑnər] vt 1 RESPECT : honrar 2 : cumplir con ⟨to honor one's word : cumplir con su palabra⟩ 3 : aceptar (un cheque, etc.)

honor² n 1 : honor m ⟨in honor of : en honor de⟩ 2 honors npl AWARDS : honores mpl, condecoraciones fpl 3 Your Honor : Su Señoría

honorable ['ɑnərəbəl] adj : honorable, honroso — honorably [-bli] adv

honorary ['ɑnə,rɛri] adj : honorario

hood ['hʊd] n 1 : capucha f 2 : capó m, bonete m Car (de un automóvil)

hooded ['hʊdəd] adj : encapuchado

hoodlum ['hʊdləm, 'huː,d-] n THUG : maleante mf, matón m

hoodwink ['hʊd,wɪŋk] vt : engañar

hoof [ˈhʊf, ˈhuːf] *n*, *pl* **hooves** [ˈhʊvz, ˈhuːvz] *or* **hoofs** : pezuña *f*, casco *m*
hoofed [ˈhʊft, ˈhuːft] *adj* : ungulado
hook¹ [ˈhʊk] *vt* : enganchar — *vi* : abrocharse, engancharse
hook² *n* : gancho *m*, percha *f*
hooked [ˈhʊkt] *adj* **1** : en forma de gancho **2 to be hooked on** : estar enganchado a
hooker [ˈhʊkər] *n* : prostituta *f*, fulana *f* *fam*
hookworm [ˈhʊk,wərm] *n* : anquilostoma *m*
hooligan [ˈhuːlɪɡən] *n* : gamberro *m*, -rra *f*
hoop [ˈhuːp] *n* : aro *m*
hooray [hʊˈreɪ] → **hurrah**
hoot¹ [ˈhuːt] *vi* **1** SHOUT : gritar ‹to hoot with laughter› : morirse de risa, reírse a carcajadas› **2** : ulular (dícese de un búho), tocar la bocina (dícese de un vehículo), silbar (dícese de un tren o un barco)
hoot² *n* **1** : ululato *m* (de un búho), silbido *m* (de un tren), bocinazo *m* (de un vehículo) **2** GUFFAW : carcajada *f*, risotada *f* **3 I don't give a hoot** : me vale un comino, me importa un pito
hop¹ [ˈhɑp] *v* **hopped; hopping** : brincar, saltar
hop² *n* **1** LEAP : salto *m*, brinco *m* **2** FLIGHT : vuelo *m* corto **3** : lúpulo *m* (planta)
hope¹ [ˈhoːp] *v* **hoped; hoping** *vi* : esperar — *vt* : esperar que ‹we hope she comes› : esperamos que venga› ‹I hope not› : espero que no›
hope² *n* : esperanza *f*
hopeful [ˈhoːpfəl] *adj* : esperanzado — **hopefully** *adv*
hopeless [ˈhoːpləs] *adj* **1** DESPAIRING : desesperado **2** IMPOSSIBLE : imposible ‹a hopeless case› : un caso perdido›
hopelessly [ˈhoːpləsli] *adv* **1** : sin esperanzas, desesperadamente **2** COMPLETELY : totalmente, completamente **3** IMPOSSIBLY : imposiblemente
hopelessness [ˈhoːpləsnəs] *n* : desesperanza *f*
hopper [ˈhɑpər] *n* : tolva *f*
hopscotch [ˈhɑp,skɑt͡ʃ] *n* : tejo *m*
horde [ˈhɔrd] *n* : horda *f*, multitud *f*
horizon [həˈraɪzən] *n* : horizonte *m*
horizontal [ˌhɔrəˈzɑntəl] *adj* : horizontal — **horizontally** *adv*
hormone [ˈhɔr,moːn] *n* : hormona *f* — **hormonal** [hɔrˈmoːnəl] *adj*
horn [ˈhɔrn] *n* **1** : cuerno *m* (de un toro, una vaca, etc.) **2** : cuerno *m*, trompa *f* (instrumento musical) **3** : bocina *f*, claxon *m* (de un vehículo)
horned [ˈhɔrnd, ˈhɔrnəd] *adj* : cornudo, astado, con cuernos
hornet [ˈhɔrnət] *n* : avispón *m*
horny [ˈhɔrni] *adj* **hornier; -est 1** CALLOUS : calloso **2** LUSTFUL *fam* : caliente *fam*
horoscope [ˈhɔrə,skoːp] *n* : horóscopo *m*

horrendous [həˈrɛndəs] *adj* : horrendo, horroroso, atroz
horrible [ˈhɔrəbəl] *adj* : horrible, espantoso, horroroso — **horribly** [-bli] *adv*
horrid [ˈhɔrɪd] *adj* : horroroso, horrible — **horridly** *adv*
horrific [həˈrɪfɪk] *adj* : terrorífico, horroroso
horrify [ˈhɔrə,faɪ] *vt* -**fied; -fying** : horrorizar
horrifying [ˈhɔrə,faɪɪŋ] *adj* : horripilante, horroroso
horror [ˈhɔrər] *n* : horror *m*
hors d'oeuvre [ɔrˈdərv] *n*, *pl* **hors d'oeuvres** [-ˈdərvz] : entremés *m*
horse [ˈhɔrs] *n* : caballo *m*
horseback [ˈhɔrs,bæk] *n* **on ~** : a caballo
horse chestnut *n* : castaña *f* de Indias
horsefly [ˈhɔrs,flaɪ] *n*, *pl* **-flies** : tábano *m*
horsehair [ˈhɔrs,hær] *n* : crin *f*
horseman [ˈhɔrsmən] *n*, *pl* **-men** [-mən, -ˌmɛn] : jinete *m*, caballista *m*
horsemanship [ˈhɔrsmən,ʃɪp] *n* : equitación *f*
horseplay [ˈhɔrs,pleɪ] *n* : payasadas *fpl*
horsepower [ˈhɔrs,paʊər] *n* : caballo *m* de fuerza
horseradish [ˈhɔrs,rædɪʃ] *n* : rábano *m* picante
horseshoe [ˈhɔrs,ʃuː] *n* : herradura *f*
horsewhip [ˈhɔrs,hwɪp] *vt* -**whipped; -whipping** : azotar, darle fuetazos (a alguien)
horsewoman [ˈhɔrs,wʊmən] *n*, *pl* **-women** [-ˌwɪmən] : amazona *f*, jinete *f*, caballista *f*
horsey *or* **horsy** [ˈhɔrsi] *adj* **horsier; -est** : relacionado a los caballos, caballar
horticultural [ˌhɔrtəˈkʌlt͡ʃərəl] *adj* : hortícola
horticulture [ˈhɔrtə,kʌlt͡ʃər] *n* : horticultura *f*
hose¹ [ˈhoːz] *vt* **hosed; hosing** : regar o lavar con manguera
hose² *n* **1** *pl* **hose** SOCKS : calcetines *mpl*, medias *fpl* **2** *pl* **hose** STOCKINGS : medias *fpl* **3** *pl* **hoses** : manguera *f*, manga *f*
hosiery [ˈhoː,ʒəri, ˈhoːʒə-] *n* : calcetería *f*, medias *fpl*
hospice [ˈhɑspəs] *n* : hospicio *m*
hospitable [hɑˈspɪtəbəl, ˈhɑs,pɪ-] *adj* : hospitalario — **hospitably** [-bli] *adv*
hospital [ˈhɑs,pɪtəl] *n* : hospital *m*
hospitality [ˌhɑspəˈtæləti] *n*, *pl* **-ties** : hospitalidad *f*
hospitalization [ˌhɑs,pɪtələˈzeɪʃən] *n* : hospitalización *f*
hospitalize [ˈhɑs,pɪtəl,aɪz] *vt* -**ized; -izing** : hospitalizar
host¹ [ˈhoːst] *vt* : presentar (un programa de televisión, etc.)
host² *n* **1** : anfitrión *m*, -triona *f* (en la casa, a un evento); presentador *m*, -dora *f* (de un programa de televisión, etc.) **2** *or* **host organism** : huésped *m*

3 TROOPS : huestes *fpl* **4** MULTITUDE : multitud *f* ⟨for a host of reasons : por muchas razones⟩ **5** EUCHARIST : hostia *f*, Eucaristía *f*

hostage ['hɑstɪʤ] *n* : rehén *m*

hostel ['hɑstəl] *n* : albergue *m* juvenil

hostess ['ho:stɪs] *n* : anfitriona *f* (en la casa), presentadora *f* (de un programa)

hostile ['hɑstəl, -,taɪl] *adj* : hostil — **hostilely** *adv*

hostility [hɑs'tɪləti] *n, pl* **-ties** : hostilidad *f*

hot ['hɑt] *adj* **hotter; hottest** **1** : caliente, cálido, caluroso ⟨hot water : agua caliente⟩ ⟨a hot climate : un clima cálido⟩ ⟨a hot day : un día caluroso⟩ **2** ARDENT, FIERY : ardiente, acalorado ⟨to have a hot temper : tener mal genio⟩ **3** SPICY : picante **4** FRESH : reciente, nuevo ⟨hot news : noticias de última hora⟩ **5** EAGER : ávido **6** STOLEN : robado

hot air *n* : palabrería *f*

hotbed ['hɑt,bɛd] *n* **1** : semillero *m* (de plantas) **2** : hervidero *m*, semillero *m* (de crimen, etc.)

hot dog *n* : perro *m* caliente

hotel [ho:'tɛl] *n* : hotel *m*

hothead ['hɑt,hɛd] *n* : exaltado *m*, -da *f*

hotheaded ['hɑt'hɛdəd] *adj* : exaltado

hothouse ['hɑt,haʊs] *n* : invernadero *m*

hot plate *n* : placa *f* (de cocina)

hot rod *n* : coche *m* con motor modificado

hot water *n* **to get into hot water** : meterse en un lío

hound¹ ['haʊnd] *vt* : acosar, perseguir

hound² *n* : perro *m* (de caza)

hour ['aʊər] *n* : hora *f*

hourglass ['aʊər,glæs] *n* : reloj *m* de arena

hourly ['aʊərli] *adv & adj* : cada hora, por hora

house¹ ['haʊz] *vt* **housed; housing** : albergar, alojar, hospedar

house² ['haʊs] *n, pl* **houses** ['haʊzəz, -səz] **1** HOME : casa *f* **2** : cámara *f* (del gobierno) **3** BUSINESS : casa *f*, empresa *f*

houseboat ['haʊs,bo:t] *n* : casa *f* flotante

housebroken ['haʊs,bro:kən] *adj* : enseñado

housefly ['haʊs,flaɪ] *n, pl* **-flies** : mosca *f* común

household¹ ['haʊs,ho:ld] *adj* **1** DOMESTIC : doméstico, de casa **2** FAMILIAR : conocido por todos

household² *n* : casa *f*, familia *f*

householder ['haʊs,ho:ldər] *n* : dueño *m*, -ña *f* de casa

housekeeper ['haʊs,ki:pər] *n* : ama *f* de llaves

housekeeping ['haʊs,ki:pɪŋ] *n* : gobierno *m* de la casa, quehaceres *mpl* domésticos

housemaid ['haʊs,meɪd] *n* : criada *f*, mucama *f*, muchacha *f*, sirvienta *f*

housewarming ['haʊs,wɔrmɪŋ] *n* : fiesta *f* de estreno de una casa

housewife ['haʊs,waɪf] *n, pl* **-wives** : ama *f* de casa

housework ['haʊs,wərk] *n* : faenas *fpl* domésticas, quehaceres *mpl* domésticos

housing ['haʊzɪŋ] *n* **1** HOUSES : vivienda *f* **2** COVERING : caja *f* protectora

hove → **heave**

hovel ['hʌvəl, 'hɑ-] *n* : casucha *f*, tugurio *m*

hover ['hʌvər, 'hɑ-] *vi* **1** : cernerse, sostenerse en el aire **2 to hover about** : rondar

how ['haʊ] *adv* **1** : cómo ⟨how are you? : ¿cómo estás?⟩ ⟨I don't know how to fix it : no se cómo arreglarlo⟩ **2** : qué ⟨how beautiful! : ¡qué bonito!⟩ **3** : cuánto ⟨how old are you? : ¿cuántos años tienes?⟩ **4 how about...?** : ¿qué te parece...?

however¹ [haʊ'ɛvər] *adv* **1** : por mucho que, por más que ⟨however hot it is : por mucho calor que haga⟩ **2** NEVERTHELESS : sin embargo, no obstante

however² *conj* : comoquiera que, de cualquier manera que

howl¹ ['haʊl] *vi* : aullar

howl² *n* : aullido *m*, alarido *m*

hub ['hʌb] *n* **1** CENTER : centro *m* **2** : cubo *m* (de una rueda)

hubbub ['hʌ,bʌb] *n* : algarabía *f*, alboroto *m*, jaleo *m*

hubcap ['hʌb,kæp] *n* : tapacubos *m*

huckster ['hʌkstər] *n* : buhonero *m*, -ra *f*; vendedor *m*, -dora *f* ambulante

huddle¹ ['hʌdəl] *vi* **-dled; -dling** **1** : apiñarse, amontonarse **2 to huddle together** : acurrucarse

huddle² *n* : grupo *m* (cerrado) ⟨to go into a huddle : conferenciar en secreto⟩

hue ['hju:] *n* : color *m*, tono *m*

huff ['hʌf] *n* : enojo *m*, enfado *m* ⟨to be in a huff : estar enojado⟩

huffy ['hʌfi] *adj* **huffier; -est** : enojado, enfadado

hug¹ ['hʌg] *vt* **hugged; hugging** **1** EMBRACE : abrazar **2** : ir pegado a ⟨the road hugs the river : el camino está pegado al río⟩

hug² *n* : abrazo *m*

huge ['hju:ʤ] *adj* **huger; hugest** : inmenso, enorme — **hugely** *adv*

hulk ['hʌlk] *n* **1** : persona *f* fornida **2** : casco *m* (barco), armatoste *m* (edificio, etc.)

hulking ['hʌlkɪŋ] *adj* : grandote *fam*, pesado

hull¹ ['hʌl] *vt* : pelar

hull² *n* **1** HUSK : cáscara *f* **2** : casco *m* (de un barco, un avión, etc.)

hullabaloo ['hʌləbə,lu:] *n, pl* **-loos** : alboroto *m*, jaleo *m*

hum¹ ['hʌm] *v* **hummed; humming** *vi* **1** BUZZ : zumbar **2** : estar muy activo, moverse ⟨to hum with activity : bullir de actividad⟩ — *vt* : tararear (una melodía)

hum² *n* : zumbido *m*, murmullo *m*

human¹ [ˈhjuːmən, ˈjuː-] *adj* : humano — **humanly** *adv*

human² *n* : ser *m* humano

humane [hjuːˈmeɪn, juː-] *adj* : humano, humanitario — **humanely** *adv*

humanism [ˈhjuːmə,nɪzəm, ˈjuː-] *n* : humanismo *m*

humanist¹ [ˈhjuːmənɪst, ˈjuː-] *n* : humanista *mf*

humanist² *or* **humanistic** [,hjuːmə-ˈnɪstɪk, ,juː-] *adj* : humanístico

humanitarian [hjuː,mænəˈtriən, juː-] *adj* : humanitario

humanitarian² *n* : humanitario *m*, -ria *f*

humanity [hjuːˈmænəti, juː-] *n*, *pl* **-ties** : humanidad *f*

humankind [ˈhjuːmənˈkaɪnd, ˈjuː-] *n* : género *m* humano

humble¹ [ˈhʌmbəl] *vt* **-bled; -bling 1** : humillar **2 to humble oneself** : humillarse

humble² *adj* **-bler; -blest** : humilde, modesto — **humbly** [ˈhʌmbli] *adv*

humbug [ˈhʌm,bʌg] *n* **1 FRAUD** : charlatán *m*, -tana *f*; farsante *mf* **2 NONSENSE** : patrañas *fpl*, tonterías *fpl*

humdrum [ˈhʌm,drʌm] *adj* : monótono, rutinario

humid [ˈhjuːməd, ˈjuː-] *adj* : húmedo

humidifier [hjuːˈmɪdə,faɪər, juː-] *n* : humidificador *m*

humidify [hjuːˈmɪdə,faɪ, juː-] *vt* **-fied; -fying** : humidificar

humidity [hjuːˈmɪdəti, juː-] *n*, *pl* **-ties** : humedad *f*

humiliate [hjuːˈmɪli,eɪt, juː-] *vt* **-ated; -ating** : humillar

humiliating [hjuːˈmɪli,eɪtɪŋ, juː-] *adj* : humillante

humiliation [hjuː,mɪliˈeɪʃən, juː-] *n* : humillación *f*

humility [hjuːˈmɪləti, juː-] *n* : humildad *f*

hummingbird [ˈhʌmɪŋ,bərd] *n* : colibrí *m*, picaflor *m*

hummock [ˈhʌmək] *n* : montículo *m*

humor¹ [ˈhjuːmər, ˈjuː-] *vt* : seguir el humor a, complacer

humor² *n* : humor *m*

humorist [ˈhjuːmərɪst, ˈjuː-] *n* : humorista *mf*

humorless [ˈhjuːmərləs, ˈjuː-] *adj* : sin sentido del humor ⟨a humorless smile : una sonrisa forzada⟩

humorous [ˈhjuːmərəs, ˈjuː-] *adj* : humorístico, cómico — **humorously** *adv*

hump [ˈhʌmp] *n* : joroba *f*, giba *f*

humpback [ˈhʌmp,bæk] *n* **1 HUMP** : joroba *f*, giba *f* **2 HUNCHBACK** : jorobado *m*, -da *f*; giboso *m*, -sa *f*

humpbacked [ˈhʌmp,bækt] *adj* : jorobado, giboso

humus [ˈhjuːməs, ˈjuː-] *n* : humus *m*

hunch¹ [ˈhʌntʃ] *vt* : encorvar — *vi* *or* **to hunch up** : encorvarse

hunch² *n* **PREMONITION** : presentimiento *m*

hunchback [ˈhʌntʃ,bæk] *n* **1 HUMP** : joroba *f*, giba *f* **2 HUMPBACK** : jorobado *m*, -da *f*; giboso *m*, -sa *f*

hunchbacked [ˈhʌntʃ,bækt] *adj* : jorobado, giboso

hundred¹ [ˈhʌndrəd] *adj* : cien, ciento

hundred² *n*, *pl* **-dreds** *or* **-dred** : ciento *m*

hundredth¹ [ˈhʌndrədθ] *adj* : centésimo

hundredth² *n* **1** : centésimo *m*, -ma *f* (en una serie) **2** : centésimo *m*, centésima parte *f*

hung → hang

Hungarian [hʌŋˈgæriən] *n* **1** : húngaro *m*, -ra *f* **2** : húngaro *m* (idioma) — **Hungarian** *adj*

hunger¹ [ˈhʌŋgər] *vi* **1** : tener hambre **2 to hunger for** : ansiar, anhelar

hunger² *n* : hambre *f*

hungrily [ˈhʌŋgrəli] *adv* : ávidamente

hungry [ˈhʌŋgri] *adj* **-grier; -est 1** : hambriento **2 to be hungry** : tener hambre

hunk [ˈhʌŋk] *n* : trozo *m*, pedazo *m*

hunt¹ [ˈhʌnt] *vt* **1 PURSUE** : cazar **2 to hunt for** : buscar

hunt² *n* **1 PURSUIT** : caza *f*, cacería *f* **2 SEARCH** : búsqueda *f*, busca *f*

hunter [ˈhʌntər] *n* : cazador *m*, -dora *f*

hunting [ˈhʌntɪŋ] *n* : caza *f* ⟨to go hunting : ir de caza⟩

hurdle¹ [ˈhərdəl] *vt* **-dled; -dling** : saltar, salvar (un obstáculo)

hurdle² *n* : valla *f* (en deportes), obstáculo *m*

hurl [ˈhərl] *vt* : arrojar, tirar, lanzar

hurrah [huˈrɑ, -ˈrɔ] *interj* : ¡hurra!

hurricane [ˈhərə,keɪn] *n* : huracán *m*

hurried [ˈhərid] *adj* : apresurado, precipitado

hurriedly [ˈhərədli] *adv* : apresuradamente, de prisa

hurry¹ [ˈhəri] *v* **-ried; -rying** *vi* : apurarse, darse prisa, apresurarse — *vt* : apurar, darle prisa (a alguien)

hurry² *n* : prisa *f*, apuro *f*

hurt¹ [ˈhərt] *v* **hurt; hurting** *vt* **1 INJURE** : hacer daño a, herir, lastimar ⟨to hurt oneself : hacerse daño⟩ **2 DISTRESS, OFFEND** : hacer sufrir, ofender, herir — *vi* : doler ⟨my foot hurts : me duele el pie⟩

hurt² *n* **1 INJURY** : herida *f* **2 DISTRESS, PAIN** : dolor *m*, pena *f*

hurtful [ˈhərtfəl] *adj* : hiriente, doloroso

hurtle [ˈhərtəl] *vi* **-tled; -tling** : lanzarse, precipitarse

husband¹ [ˈhʌzbənd] *vt* : economizar, bien administrar

husband² *n* : esposo *m*, marido *m*

husbandry [ˈhʌzbəndri] *n* **1 MANAGEMENT, THRIFT** : economía *f*, buena administración *f* **2 AGRICULTURE** : agricultura *f* ⟨animal husbandry : cría de animales⟩

hush¹ [ˈhʌʃ] *vt* **1 SILENCE** : hacer callar, acallar **2 CALM** : calmar, apaciguar

hush² *n* : silencio *m*

hush–hush [ˈhʌʃˈhʌʃ, ˌhʌʃˈhʌʃ] *adj* : muy secreto, confidencial

husk¹ [ˈhʌsk] *vt* : descascarar

husk² *n* : cáscara *f*

huskily [ˈhʌskəli] *adv* : con voz ronca

husky¹ [ˈhʌski] *adj* **-kier; -est 1** HOARSE : ronco **2** BURLY : fornido

husky² *n, pl* **-kies** : perro *m*, -rra *f* esquimal

hustle¹ [ˈhəsəl] *v* **-tled; -tling** *vt* : darle prisa (a alguien), apurar ⟨they hustled me in : me hicieron entrar a empujones⟩ — *vi* : apurarse, ajetrearse

hustle² *n* BUSTLE : ajetreo *m*

hut [ˈhʌt] *n* : cabaña *f*, choza *f*, barraca *f*

hutch [ˈhʌtʃ] *n* **1** CUPBOARD : alacena *f* **2** rabbit hutch : conejera *f*

hyacinth [ˈhaɪəˌsɪnθ] *n* : jacinto *m*

hybrid¹ [ˈhaɪbrɪd] *adj* : híbrido

hybrid² *n* : híbrido *m*

hydrant [ˈhaɪdrənt] *n* : boca *f* de riego, hidrante *m* CA, Col ⟨fire hydrant : boca de incendios⟩

hydraulic [haɪˈdrɔlɪk] *adj* : hidráulico — **hydraulically** *adv*

hydrocarbon [ˌhaɪdroˈkɑrbən] *n* : hidrocarburo *m*

hydrochloric acid [ˌhaɪdroˈklorɪk] *n* : ácido *m* clorhídrico

hydroelectric [ˌhaɪdroɪˈlɛktrɪk] *adj* : hidroeléctrico

hydrogen [ˈhaɪdrədʒən] *n* : hidrógeno *m*

hydrogen bomb *n* : bomba *f* de hidrógeno

hydrogen peroxide *n* : agua *f* oxigenada, peróxido *m* de hidrógeno

hydrophobia [ˌhaɪdrəˈfoːbiə] *n* : hidrofobia *f*, rabia *f*

hydroplane [ˈhaɪdrəˌpleɪn] *n* : hidroplano *m*

hyena [haɪˈiːnə] *n* : hiena *f*

hygiene [ˈhaɪˌdʒiːn] *n* : higiene *f*

hygienic [haɪˈdʒɛnɪk, -ˈdʒiː-; ˌhaɪ-dʒiˈnɪk] *adj* : higiénico — **hygienically** [-nɪkli] *adv*

hygienist [haɪˈdʒiːnɪst, -ˈdʒɛ-; ˈhaɪ-ˌdʒiː-] *n* : higienista *mf*

hygrometer [haɪˈgrɑmətər] *n* : higrómetro *m*

hymn [ˈhɪm] *n* : himno *m*

hymnal [ˈhɪmnəl] *n* : himnario *m*

hype [ˈhaɪp] *n* : bombo *m* publicitario

hyperactive [ˌhaɪpərˈæktɪv] *adj* : hiperactivo

hyperactivity [ˌhaɪpərˌækˈtɪvəti] *n, pl* **-ties** : hiperactividad *f*

hyperbole [haɪˈpərbəli] *n* : hipérbole *f*

hyperbolic [ˌhaɪpərˈbɑlɪk] *adj* : hiperbólico

hypercritical [ˌhaɪpərˈkrɪtəkəl] *adj* : hipercrítico

hypersensitivity [ˌhaɪpərˌsɛnˌsəˈtɪ-vəti] *n* : hipersensibilidad *f*

hypertension [ˈhaɪpərˌtɛntʃən] *n* : hipertensión *f*

hyphen [ˈhaɪfən] *n* : guión *m*

hyphenate [ˈhaɪfənˌeɪt] *vt* **-ated; -ating** : escribir con guión

hypnosis [hɪpˈnoːsɪs] *n, pl* **-noses** [-ˌsiːz] : hipnosis *f*

hypnotic [hɪpˈnɑtɪk] *adj* : hipnótico, hipnotizador

hypnotism [ˈhɪpnəˌtɪzəm] *n* : hipnotismo *m*

hypnotize [ˈhɪpnəˌtaɪz] *vt* **-tized; -tizing** : hipnotizar

hypochondria [ˌhaɪpəˈkɑndriə] *n* : hipocondría *f*

hypochondriac [ˌhaɪpəˈkɑndriˌæk] *n* : hipocondríaco *m*, -ca *f*

hypocrisy [hɪpˈɑkrəsi] *n, pl* **-sies** : hipocresía *f*

hypocrite [ˈhɪpəˌkrɪt] *n* : hipócrita *mf*

hypocritical [ˌhɪpəˈkrɪtɪkəl] *adj* : hipócrita

hypodermic¹ [ˌhaɪpəˈdərmɪk] *adj* : hipodérmico

hypodermic² *n* : aguja *f* hipodérmica

hypotenuse [haɪˈpɑtənˌuːs, -ˌuːz, -ˌjuːs, -ˌjuːz] *n* : hipotenusa *f*

hypothesis [haɪˈpɑθəsɪs] *n, pl* **-eses** [-ˌsiːz] : hipótesis *f*

hypothetical [ˌhaɪpəˈθɛtɪkəl] *adj* : hipotético — **hypothetically** [-ɪkli] *adv*

hysteria [hɪsˈtɛriə, -tɪr-] *n* : histeria *f*, histerismo *m*

hysterical [hɪsˈtɛrɪkəl] *adj* : histérico — **hysterically** [-ɪkli] *adv*

hysterics [hɪsˈtɛrɪks] *n* : histeria *f*, histerismo *m*

I

i [ˈaɪ] *n, pl* **i's** *or* **is** [ˈaɪz] : novena letra del alfabeto inglés

I [ˈaɪ] *pron* : yo

Iberian [aɪˈbɪriən] *adj* : ibérico

ibis [ˈaɪbəs] *n, pl* **ibis** *or* **ibis** *or* **ibises** : ibis *f*

ice¹ [ˈaɪs] *v* **iced; icing** *vt* **1** FREEZE : congelar, helar **2** CHILL : enfriar **3 to ice a cake** : escarchar un pastel — *vi* : helarse, congelarse

ice² *n* **1** : hielo *m* **2** SHERBET : sorbete *m*, nieve *f* Cuba, Mex, PRi

iceberg [ˈaɪsˌbərg] *n* : iceberg *m*

icebox [ˈaɪsˌbɑks] *n* → **refrigerator**

icebreaker [ˈaɪsˌbreɪkər] *n* : rompehielos *m*

ice cap *n* : casquete *m* glaciar

ice–cold [ˈaɪsˈkoːld] *adj* : helado

ice cream *n* : helado *m*, mantecado *m* PRi

Icelander [ˈaɪsˌlændər, -lən-] *n* : islandés *m*, -desa *f*

Icelandic¹ [aɪsˈlændɪk] *adj* : islandés

Icelandic² n : islandés m (idioma)
ice–skate ['aɪs,skeɪt] vi **-skated; -skating** : patinar
ice skater n : patinador m, -dora f
ichthyology [,ɪkthi'ɑlədʒi] n : ictiología f
icicle ['aɪ,sɪkəl] n : carámbano m
icily ['aɪsəli] adv : fríamente, con frialdad ⟨he stared at me icily : me fijó la mirada con mucha frialdad⟩
icing ['aɪsɪŋ] n : glaseado m, betún m Mex
icon ['aɪ,kɑn, -kən] n : icono m
iconoclasm [aɪ'kɑnə,klæzəm] n : iconoclasia f
iconoclast [aɪ'kɑnə,klæst] n : iconoclasta mf
icy ['aɪsi] adj **icier; -est 1** : cubierto de hielo ⟨an icy road : una carretera cubierta de hielo⟩ **2** FREEZING : helado, gélido, glacial **3** ALOOF : frío, distante
id ['ɪd] n : id m
I'd ['aɪd] (contraction of **I should** or **I would**) → should, would
idea [aɪ'diːə] n : idea f
ideal¹ [aɪ'diːəl] adj : ideal
ideal² n : ideal m
idealism [aɪ'diːə,lɪzəm] n : idealismo m
idealist [aɪ'diːəlɪst] n : idealista mf
idealistic [aɪ,diːə'lɪstɪk] adj : idealista
idealistically [aɪ,diːə'lɪstɪkli] adv : con idealismo
idealization [aɪ,diːəlɪ'zeɪʃən] n : idealización f
idealize [aɪ'diːə,laɪz] vt **-ized; -izing** : idealizar
ideally [aɪ'diːəli] adv : perfectamente
identical [aɪ'dɛntɪkəl] adj : idéntico — **identically** [-tɪkli] adv
identifiable [aɪ,dɛntə'faɪəbəl] adj : identificable
identification [aɪ,dɛntəfə'keɪʃən] n **1** : identificación f **2 identification card** : carnet m, cédula f de identidad, identificación f
identify [aɪ'dɛntə,faɪ] v **-fied; -fying** vt : identificar — vi **to identify with** : identificarse con
identity [aɪ'dɛntəti] n, pl **-ties** : identidad f
ideological [,aɪdiə'lɑdʒɪkəl, ,ɪ-] adj : ideológico — **ideologically** [-dʒɪkli] adv
ideology [,aɪdi'ɑlədʒi, ,ɪ-] n, pl **-gies** : ideología f
idiocy ['ɪdiəsi] n, pl **-cies 1** : idiotez f **2** NONSENSE : estupidez f, tontería f
idiom ['ɪdiəm] n **1** LANGUAGE : lenguaje m **2** EXPRESSION : modismo m, expresión f idiomática
idiomatic [,ɪdiə'mætɪk] adj : idiomático
idiosyncrasy [,ɪdio'sɪŋkrəsi] n, pl **-sies** : idiosincrasia f
idiosyncratic [,ɪdiosɪn'krætɪk] adj : idiosincrásico — **idiosyncratically** [-tɪkli] adv
idiot ['ɪdiət] n **1** : idiota mf (en medicina) **2** FOOL : idiota mf; tonto m, -ta f; imbécil mf fam

idiotic [,ɪdi'ɑtɪk] adj : estúpido, idiota
idiotically [,ɪdi'ɑtɪkli] adv : estúpidamente
idle¹ ['aɪdəl] v **idled; idling** vi **1** LOAF : holgazanear, flojear, haraganear **2** : andar al ralentí (dícese de un automóvil), marchar en vacío (dícese de una máquina) — vt : dejar sin trabajo
idle² adj **idler; idlest 1** VAIN : frívolo, vano, infundado ⟨idle curiosity : pura curiosidad⟩ **2** INACTIVE : inactivo, parado, desocupado **3** LAZY : holgazán, haragán, perezoso
idleness ['aɪdəlnəs] n **1** INACTIVITY : inactividad f, ociosidad f **2** LAZINESS : holgazanería f, flojera f, pereza f
idler ['aɪdələr] n : haragán m, -gana f; holgazán m, -zana f
idly ['aɪdəli] adv : ociosamente
idol ['aɪdəl] n : ídolo m
idolater or **idolator** [aɪ'dɑlətər] n : idólatra mf
idolatrous [aɪ'dɑlətrəs] adj : idólatra
idolatry [aɪ'dɑlətri] n, pl **-tries** : idolatría f
idolize ['aɪdəlaɪz] vt **-ized; -izing** : idolatrar
idyll ['aɪdəl] n : idilio m
idyllic [aɪ'dɪlɪk] adj : idílico
if ['ɪf] conj **1** : si ⟨I would do it if I could : lo haría si pudiera⟩ ⟨if so : si es así⟩ ⟨as if : como si⟩ ⟨if I were you : yo que tú⟩ **2** WHETHER : si ⟨I don't know if they're ready : no sé si están listos⟩ **3** THOUGH : aunque, si bien ⟨it's pretty, if somewhat old-fashioned : es lindo aunque algo anticuado⟩
igloo ['ɪ,gluː] n, pl **-loos** : iglú m
ignite [ɪg'naɪt] v **-nited; -niting** vt : prenderle fuego a, encender — vi : prender, encenderse
ignition [ɪg'nɪʃən] n **1** IGNITING : ignición f, encendido m **2** or **ignition switch** : encendido m, arranque m ⟨to turn on the ignition : arrancar el motor⟩
ignoble [ɪg'noːbəl] adj : innoble — **ignobly** adv
ignominious [,ɪgnə'mɪniəs] adj : ignominioso, deshonroso — **ignominiously** adv
ignominy ['ɪgnə,mɪni] n, pl **-nies** : ignominia f
ignoramus [,ɪgnə'reɪməs] n : ignorante mf; bestia mf; bruto m, -ta f
ignorance ['ɪgnərəns] n : ignorancia f
ignorant ['ɪgnərənt] adj **1** : ignorante **2 to be ignorant of** : no ser consciente de, desconocer, ignorar
ignorantly ['ɪgnərəntli] adv : ignorantemente, con ignorancia
ignore [ɪg'nor] vt **-nored; -noring** : ignorar, hacer caso omiso de, no hacer caso de
iguana [ɪ'gwɑnə] n : iguana f, garrobo f CA
ilk ['ɪlk] n : tipo m, clase f, índole f
ill¹ ['ɪl] adv **worse** ['wərs]; **worst** ['wərst] : mal ⟨to speak ill of : hablar mal de⟩

⟨he can ill afford to fail : mal puede permitirse el lujo de fracasar⟩

ill² *adj* **worse; worst 1** SICK : enfermo **2** BAD : malo ⟨ill luck : mala suerte⟩

ill³ *n* **1** EVIL : mal *m* **2** MISFORTUNE : mal *m*, desgracia *f* **3** AILMENT : enfermedad *f*

I'll [ˈaɪl] (*contraction of* I shall *or* I will) → shall, will

illegal [ɪˈliːgəl] *adj* : ilegal — **illegally** *adv*

illegality [ɪliˈgæləti] *n* : ilegalidad *f*

illegibility [ɪˌlɛdʒəˈbɪləti] *n, pl* **-ties** : ilegibilidad *f*

illegible [ɪˈlɛdʒəbəl] *adj* : ilegible — **illegibly** [-bli] *adv*

illegitimacy [ˌɪlɪˈdʒɪtəməsi] *n* : ilegitimidad *f*

illegitimate [ˌɪlɪˈdʒɪtəmət] *adj* **1** BASTARD : ilegítimo, bastardo **2** UNLAWFUL : ilegítimo, ilegal — **illegitimately** *adv*

ill-fated [ˈɪlˈfeɪtəd] *adj* : malhadado, infortunado, desventurado

illicit [ɪˈlɪsət] *adj* : ilícito — **illicitly** *adv*

illiteracy [ɪˈlɪtərəsi] *n, pl* **-cies** : analfabetismo *m*

illiterate¹ [ɪˈlɪtərət] *adj* : analfabeto

illiterate² *n* : analfabeto *m*, -ta *f*

ill-mannered [ˈɪlˈmanərd] *adj* : descortés, maleducado

ill-natured [ˈɪlˈneɪtʃərd] *adj* : desagradable, de mal genio

ill-naturedly [ˌɪlˈneɪtʃərdli] *adv* : desagradablemente

illness [ˈɪlnəs] *n* : enfermedad *f*

illogical [ɪˈlɑːdʒɪkəl] *adj* : ilógico — **illogically** [-kli] *adv*

ill-tempered [ˌɪlˈtempərd] → **ill-natured**

ill-treat [ˌɪlˈtriːt] *vt* : maltratar

ill-treatment [ˌɪlˈtriːtmənt] *n* : maltrato *m*

illuminate [ɪˈluːməˌneɪt] *vt* **-nated; -nating 1** : iluminar, alumbrar **2** ELUCIDATE : esclarecer, elucidar

illumination [ɪˌluːməˈneɪʃən] *n* **1** LIGHTING : iluminación *f*, luz *f* **2** ELUCIDATION : esclarecimiento *m*, elucidación *f*

ill-use [ˈɪlˈjuːz] → **ill-treat**

illusion [ɪˈluːʒən] *n* : ilusión *f*

illusory [ɪˈluːsəri, -zəri] *adj* : engañoso, ilusorio

illustrate [ˈɪləsˌtreɪt] *v* **-trated; -trating** : ilustrar

illustration [ˌɪləˈstreɪʃən] *n* **1** PICTURE : ilustración *f* **2** EXAMPLE : ejemplo *m*, ilustración *f*

illustrative [ɪˈlʌstrətɪv, ˈɪləˌstreɪtɪv] *adj* : ilustrativo — **illustratively** *adv*

illustrator [ˈɪləˌstreɪtər] *n* : ilustrador *m*, -dora *f*; dibujante *mf*

illustrious [ɪˈlʌstriəs] *adj* : ilustre, eminente, glorioso

illustriousness [ɪˈlʌstriəsnəs] *n* : eminencia *f*, prestigio *m*

ill will *n* : animosidad *f*, malquerencia *f*, mala voluntad *f*

I'm [ˈaɪm] (*contraction of* I am) → be

image¹ [ˈɪmɪdʒ] *vt* **-aged; -aging** : imaginar, crear una imagen de

image² *n* : imagen *f*

imagery [ˈɪmɪdʒri] *n, pl* **-eries 1** IMAGES : imágenes *fpl* **2** : imaginería *f* (en el arte)

imaginable [ɪˈmædʒənəbəl] *adj* : imaginable — **imaginably** [-bli] *adv*

imaginary [ɪˈmædʒəˌneri] *adj* : imaginario

imagination [ɪˌmædʒəˈneɪʃən] *n* : imaginación *f*

imaginative [ɪˈmædʒənətɪv, -əˌneɪtɪv] *adj* : imaginativo — **imaginatively** *adv*

imagine [ɪˈmædʒən] *vt* **-ined; -ining** : imaginar(se)

imbalance [ɪmˈbælənts] *n* : desajuste *m*, desbalance *m*, desequilibrio *m*

imbecile¹ [ˈɪmbəsəl, -ˌsɪl] *or* **imbecilic** [ˌɪmbəˈsɪlɪk] *adj* : imbécil, estúpido

imbecile² *n* **1** : imbécil *mf* (en medicina) **2** FOOL : idiota *mf*; imbécil *mf fam*; estúpido *m*, -da *f*

imbecility [ˌɪmbəˈsɪləti] *n, pl* **-ties** : imbecilidad *f*

imbibe [ɪmˈbaɪb] *v* **-bibed; -bibing** *vt* **1** DRINK : beber **2** ABSORB : absorber, embeber — *vi* : beber

imbue [ɪmˈbjuː] *vt* **-bued; -buing** : imbuir

imitate [ˈɪməˌteɪt] *vt* **-tated; -tating** : imitar, remedar

imitation¹ [ˌɪməˈteɪʃən] *adj* : de imitación, artificial

imitation² *n* : imitación *f*

imitative [ˈɪməˌteɪtɪv] *adj* : imitativo, imitador, poco original

imitator [ˈɪməˌteɪtər] *n* : imitador *m*, -dora *f*

immaculate [ɪˈmækjələt] *adj* **1** PURE : inmaculado, puro **2** FLAWLESS : impecable, intachable — **immaculately** *adv*

immaterial [ˌɪməˈtɪriəl] *adj* **1** INCORPOREAL : incorpóreo **2** UNIMPORTANT : irrelevante, sin importancia

immature [ˌɪməˈtʃʊr, -ˈtjʊr, -ˈtʊr] *adj* : inmaduro, verde (dícese de la fruta)

immaturity [ˌɪməˈtʃʊrəti, -ˈtjʊr-, -ˈtʊr-] *n, pl* **-ties** : inmadurez *f*, falta *f* de madurez

immeasurable [ɪˈmeʒərəbəl] *adj* : inconmensurable, incalculable — **immeasurably** [-bli] *adv*

immediacy [ɪˈmiːdiəsi] *n* : inmediatez *f*

immediate [ɪˈmiːdiət] *adj* **1** INSTANT : inmediato, instantáneo ⟨immediate relief : alivio instantáneo⟩ **2** DIRECT : inmediato, directo ⟨the immediate cause of death : la causa directa de la muerte⟩ **3** URGENT : urgente, apremiante **4** CLOSE : cercano, próximo ⟨her immediate family : sus familiares más cercanos⟩ ⟨in the immediate vicinity : en los alrededores, en las inmediaciones⟩

immediately [ɪˈmiːdiətli] *adv* : inmediatamente, enseguida

immemorial [ˌɪməˈmoriəl] *adj* : inmemorial

immense [ɪˈmɛnts] *adj* : inmenso, enorme — **immensely** *adv*

immensity [ɪˈmɛntsəti] *n, pl* **-ties** : inmensidad *f*

immerse [ɪˈmərs] *vt* **-mersed; -mersing** 1 SUBMERGE : sumergir 2 **to immerse oneself in** : enfrascarse en

immersion [ɪˈmərʒən] *n* 1 : inmersión *f* (en un líquido) 2 : enfrascamiento *m* (en una actividad)

immigrant [ˈɪmɪgrənt] *n* : inmigrante *mf*

immigrate [ˈɪməˌgreɪt] *vi* **-grated; -grating** : inmigrar

immigration [ˌɪməˈgreɪʃən] *n* : inmigración *f*

imminence [ˈɪmənənts] *n* : inminencia *f*

imminent [ˈɪmənənt] *adj* : inminente — **imminently** *adv*

immobile [ɪmˈoːbəl] *adj* 1 FIXED, IMMOVABLE : inmovible, fijo 2 MOTIONLESS : inmóvil

immobility [ˌɪmoːˈbɪləti] *n, pl* **-ties** : inmovilidad *f*

immobilize [ɪˈmoːbəˌlaɪz] *vt* **-lized; -lizing** : inmovilizar, paralizar

immoderate [ɪˈmɑdərət] *adj* : inmoderado, desmesurado, desmedido, excesivo — **immoderately** *adv*

immodest [ɪˈmɑdəst] *adj* 1 INDECENT : inmodesto, indecente, impúdico 2 CONCEITED : inmodesto, presuntuoso, engreído — **immodestly** *adv*

immodesty [ɪˈmɑdəsti] *n* : inmodestia *f*

immoral [ɪˈmɔrəl] *adj* : inmoral

immorality [ˌɪmɔˈræləti, ˌɪmə-] *n, pl* **-ties** : inmoralidad *f*

immorally [ɪˈmɔrəli] *adv* : de manera inmoral

immortal[1] [ɪˈmɔrtəl] *adj* : inmortal

immortal[2] *n* : inmortal *mf*

immortality [ˌɪˌmɔrˈtæləti] *n* : inmortalidad *f*

immortalize [ɪˈmɔrtəˌlaɪz] *vt* **-ized; -izing** : inmortalizar

immovable [ɪˈmuːvəbəl] *adj* 1 FIXED : fijo, invoible 2 UNYIELDING : inflexible

immune [ɪˈmjuːn] *adj* 1 : inmune ⟨immune to smallpox : inmune a la viruela⟩ 2 EXEMPT : exento, inmune

immune system *n* : sistema *m* de inmunológico

immunity [ɪˈmjuːnəti] *n, pl* **-ties** 1 : inmunidad *f* 2 EXEMPTION : exención *f*

immunization [ˌɪmjunəˈzeɪʃən] *n* : inmunización *f*

immunize [ˈɪmjʊˌnaɪz] *vt* **-nized; -nizing** : inmunizar

immunology [ˌɪmjʊˈnɑlədʒi] *n* : inmunología *f*

immutable [ɪˈmjuːtəbəl] *adj* : inmutable

imp [ˈɪmp] *n* RASCAL : diablillo *m*; pillo *m*, -lla *f*

impact[1] [ɪmˈpækt] *vt* 1 STRIKE : chocar con, impactar 2 AFFECT : afectar, impactar, impresionar — *vi* 1 STRIKE : hacer impacto, golpear 2 **to impact on** : tener un impacto sobre

impact[2] [ˈɪmˌpækt] *n* 1 COLLISION : impacto *m*, choque *m*, colisión *f* 2 EFFECT : efecto *m*, impacto *m*, consecuencias *fpl*

impacted [ɪmˈpæktəd] *adj* : impactado, incrustado (de los dientes)

impair [ɪmˈpær] *vt* : perjudicar, dañar, afectar

impairment [ɪmˈpærmənt] *n* : perjuicio *m*, daño *m*

impala [ɪmˈpɑlə, -ˈpæ-] *n, pl* **impalas** or **impala** : impala *m*

impale [ɪmˈpeɪl] *vt* **-paled; -paling** : empalar

impanel [ɪmˈpænəl] *vt* **-eled** or **-elled; eling** or **-elling** : elegir (un jurado)

impart [ɪmˈpɑrt] *vt* 1 CONVEY : impartir, dar, conferir 2 DISCLOSE : revelar, divulgar

impartial [ɪmˈpɑrʃəl] *adj* : imparcial — **impartially** *adv*

impartiality [ɪmˌpɑrʃiˈæləti] *n, pl* **-ties** : imparcialidad *f*

impassable [ɪmˈpæsəbəl] *adj* : infranqueable, intransitable — **impassably** [-bli] *adv*

impasse [ˈɪmˌpæs] *n* 1 DEADLOCK : impasse *m*, punto *m* muerto 2 DEAD END : callejón *m* sin salida

impassioned [ɪmˈpæʃənd] *adj* : apasionado, vehemente

impassive [ɪmˈpæsɪv] *adj* : impasible, indiferente

impassively [ɪmˈpæsɪvli] *adv* : impasiblemente, sin emoción

impatience [ɪmˈpeɪʃənts] *n* : impaciencia *f*

impatient [ɪmˈpeɪʃənt] *adj* : impaciente — **impatiently** *adv*

impeach [ɪmˈpiːtʃ] *vt* : destituir (a un funcionario) de su cargo

impeachment [ɪmˈpiːtʃmənt] *n* 1 ACCUSATION : acusación *f* 2 DISMISSAL : destitución *f*

impeccable [ɪmˈpɛkəbəl] *adj* : impecable — **impeccably** [-bli] *adv*

impecunious [ˌɪmpɪˈkjuːniəs] *adj* : falto de dinero

impede [ɪmˈpiːd] *vt* **-peded; -peding** : impedir, dificultar, obstaculizar

impediment [ɪmˈpɛdəmənt] *n* 1 HINDRANCE : impedimento *m*, obstáculo *m* 2 **speech impediment** : defecto *m* del habla

impel [ɪmˈpɛl] *vt* **-pelled; -pelling** : impeler

impend [ɪmˈpɛnd] *vi* : ser inminente

impenetrable [ɪmˈpɛnətrəbəl] *adj* 1 : impenetrable ⟨an impenetrable forest : una selva impenetrable⟩ 2 INSCRUTABLE : incomprensible, inescrutable, impenetrable — **impenetrably** [-bli] *adv*

impenitent [ɪmˈpɛnətənt] *adj* : impenitente

imperative¹ [ɪm'perətɪv] *adj* **1** AUTHOR-ITATIVE : imperativo, imperioso **2** NECESSARY : imprescindible — **imperatively** *adv*

imperative² *n* : imperativo *m*

imperceptible [ˌɪmpər'sɛptəbəl] *adj* : imperceptible — **imperceptibly** [-bli] *adv*

imperfect [ɪm'pərfɪkt] *adj* : imperfecto, defectuoso — **imperfectly** *adv*

imperfection [ˌɪmpər'fɪkʃən] *n* : imperfección *f*, defecto *m*

imperial [ɪm'pɪriəl] *adj* **1** : imperial **2** SOVEREIGN : soberano **3** IMPERIOUS : imperioso, señorial

imperialism [ɪm'pɪriəˌlɪzəm] *n* : imperialismo *m*

imperialist¹ [ɪm'pɪriəlɪst] *adj* : imperialista

imperialist² *n* : imperialista *mf*

imperialistic [ɪmˌpɪriəʔ'lɪstɪk] *adj* : imperialista

imperil [ɪm'perəl] *vt* -iled *or* -illed; -iling *or* -illing : poner en peligro

imperious [ɪm'pɪriəs] *adj* : imperioso — **imperiously** *adv*

imperishable [ɪm'perɪʃəbəl] *adj* : imperecedero

impermanent [ɪm'pərmənənt] *adj* : pasajero, inestable, efímero — **impermanently** *adv*

impermeable [ɪm'pərmiəbəl] *adj* : impermeable

impersonal [ɪm'pərsənəl] *adj* : impersonal — **impersonally** *adv*

impersonate [ɪm'pərsənˌeɪt] *vt* -ated; -ating : hacerse pasar por, imitar

impersonation [ɪmˌpərsən'eɪʃən] *n* : imitación *f*

impersonator [ɪm'pərsənˌeɪtər] *n* : imitador *m*, -dora *f*

impertinence [ɪm'pərtənənts] *n* : impertinencia *f*

impertinent [ɪm'pərtənənt] *adj* **1** IR-RELEVANT : impertinente, irrelevante **2** INSOLENT : impertinente, insolente

impertinently [ɪm'pərtənəntli] *adv* : con impertinencia, impertinentemente

imperturbable [ˌɪmpər'tərbəbəl] *adj* : imperturbable

impervious [ɪm'pərviəs] *adj* **1** IMPENE-TRABLE : impermeable **2** INSENSITIVE : insensible ⟨impervious to criticism : insensible a la crítica⟩

impetuosity [ɪmˌpɛtʃu'ɑsəti] *n*, *pl* -ties : impetuosidad *f*

impetuous [ɪm'pɛtʃuəs] *adj* : impetuoso, impulsivo

impetuously [ɪm'pɛtʃuəsli] *adv* : de manera impulsiva, impetuosamente

impetus [ˈɪmpətəs] *n* : ímpetu *m*, impulso *m*

impiety [ɪm'paɪəti] *n*, *pl* -ties : impiedad *f*

impinge [ɪm'pɪndʒ] *vi* -pinged; -pinging **1 to impinge on** AFFECT : afectar a, incidir en **2 to impinge on** VIOLATE : violar, vulnerar

impious [ˈɪmpiəs, ɪm'paɪəs] *adj* : impío, irreverente

impish [ˈɪmpɪʃ] *adj* MISCHIEVOUS : pícaro, travieso

impishly [ˈɪmpɪʃli] *adv* : con picardía

implacable [ɪm'plækəbəl] *adj* : implacable — **implacably** [-bli] *adv*

implant¹ [ɪm'plænt] *vt* **1** INCULCATE, IN-STILL : inculcar, implantar **2** INSERT : implantar, insertar

implant² [ˈɪmˌplænt] *n* : implante *m* (de pelo), injerto *m* (de piel)

implantation [ˌɪmˌplæn'teɪʃən] *n* : implantación *f*

implausibility [ɪmˌplɔzə'bɪləti] *n*, *pl* -ties : inverosimilitud *f*

implausible [ɪm'plɔzəbəl] *adj* : inverosímil, poco convincente

implement¹ [ˈɪmplə,mnt] *vt* : poner en práctica, implementar

implement² [ˈɪmpləmənt] *n* : utensilio *m*, instrumento *m*, implemento *m*

implementation [ˌɪmpləmən'teɪʃən] *n* : implementación *f*, ejecución *f*, cumplimiento *m*

implicate [ˈɪmplə,keɪt] *vt* -cated; -cating : implicar, involucrar

implication [ˌɪmplə'keɪʃən] *n* **1** CONSE-QUENCE : implicación *f*, consecuencia *f* **2** INFERENCE : insinuación *f*, inferencia *f*

implicit [ɪm'plɪsət] *adj* **1** IMPLIED : implícito, tácito **2** ABSOLUTE : absoluto, completo ⟨implicit faith : fe ciega⟩ — **implicitly** *adv*

implied [ɪm'plaɪd] *adj* : implícito, tácito

implode [ɪm'ploːd] *vi* -ploded; -ploding : implosionar

implore [ɪm'plor] *vt* -plored; -ploring : implorar, suplicar

implosion [ɪm'ploːʒən] *n* : implosión *f*

imply [ɪm'plaɪ] *vt* -plied; -plying **1** SUG-GEST : insinuar, dar a entender **2** IN-VOLVE : implicar, suponer ⟨rights imply obligations : los derechos implican unas obligaciones⟩

impolite [ˌɪmpə'laɪt] *adj* : descortés, maleducado

impoliteness [ˌɪmpə'laɪtnəs] *n* : descortesía *f*, falta *f* de educación

impolitic [ɪm'pɑlə,tɪk] *adj* : imprudente, poco político

imponderable¹ [ɪm'pɑndərəbəl] *adj* : imponderable

imponderable² *n* : imponderable *m*

import¹ [ɪm'port] *vt* **1** SIGNIFY : significar **2** : importar ⟨to import foreign cars : importar autos extranjeros⟩

import² [ˈɪmˌport] *n* **1** SIGNIFICANCE : importancia *f*, significación *f* **2** → **importation**

importance [ɪm'portənts] *n* : importancia *f*

important [ɪm'portənt] *adj* : importante

importantly [ɪm'portəntli] *adv* **1** : con importancia **2 more importantly** : lo que es más importante

importation [ˌɪmˌpor'teɪʃən] *n* : importación *f*

importer [ɪm'portər] *n* : importador *m*, -dora *f*

importunate [ɪmˈpɔrtʃənət] *adj* : importuno, insistente

importune [ˌɪmpərˈtuːn, -ˈtjuːn; ɪmˈpɔrtʃən] *vt* **-tuned; -tuning** : importunar, implorar

impose [ɪmˈpoːz] *v* **-posed; -posing** *vt* : imponer ⟨to impose a tax : imponer un impuesto⟩ — *vi* **to impose on** : abusar de, molestar ⟨to impose on her kindness : abusar de su bondad⟩

imposing [ɪmˈpoːzɪŋ] *adj* : imponente, impresionante

imposition [ˌɪmpəˈzɪʃən] *n* : imposición *f*

impossibility [ɪmˌpɑsəˈbɪləti] *n, pl* **-ties** : imposibilidad *f*

impossible [ɪmˈpɑsəbəl] *adj* **1** : imposible ⟨an impossible task : una tarea imposible⟩ ⟨to make life impossible for : hacerle la vida imposible a⟩ **2** UN-ACCEPTABLE : inaceptable

impossibly [ɪmˈpɑsəbli] *adv* : imposiblemente, increíblemente

impostor *or* **imposter** [ɪmˈpɑstər] *n* : impostor *m*, -tora *f*

impotence [ˈɪmpətənts] *n* : impotencia *f*

impotency [ˈɪmpətənsi] → **impotence**

impotent [ˈɪmpətənt] *adj* : impotente

impound [ɪmˈpaʊnd] *vt* : incautar, embargar, confiscar

impoverish [ɪmˈpɑvərɪʃ] *vt* : empobrecer

impoverishment [ɪmˈpɑvərɪʃmənt] *n* : empobrecimiento *m*

impracticable [ɪmˈpræktɪkəbəl] *adj* : impracticable

impractical [ɪmˈpræktɪkəl] *adj* : poco práctico

imprecise [ˌɪmprɪˈsaɪs] *adj* : impreciso

imprecisely [ˌɪmprɪˈsaɪsli] *adv* : con imprecisión

impreciseness [ˌɪmprɪˈsaɪsnəs] → **imprecision**

imprecision [ˌɪmprɪˈsɪʒən] *n* : imprecisión *f*, falta de precisión *f*

impregnable [ɪmˈprɛgnəbəl] *adj* : inexpugnable, impenetrable, inconquistable

impregnate [ɪmˈprɛgˌneɪt] *vt* **-nated; -nating 1** FERTILIZE : fecundar **2** PERMEATE, SATURATE : impregnar, empapar, saturar

impresario [ˌɪmprəˈsɑriˌo, -ˈsær-] *n, pl* **-rios** : empresario *m*, -ria *f*

impress [ɪmˈprɛs] *vt* **1** IMPRINT : imprimir, estampar **2** : impresionar, causar impresión a ⟨I was not impressed : no me hizo buena impresión⟩ **3 to impress (something) on someone** : recalcarle (algo) a alguien — *vi* : impresionar, hacer una impresión

impression [ɪmˈprɛʃən] *n* **1** IMPRINT : marca *f*, huella *f*, molde *m* (de los dientes) **2** EFFECT : impresión *f*, efecto *m*, impacto *m* **3** PRINTING : impresión *f* **4** NOTION : impresión *f*, noción *f*

impressionable [ɪmˈprɛʃənəbəl] *adj* : impresionable

impressionism [ɪmˈprɛʃəˌnɪzəm] *n* : impresionismo *m*

impressionist [ɪmˈprɛʃənɪst] *n* : impresionista *mf* — **impressionist** *adj*

impressive [ɪmˈprɛsɪv] *adj* : impresionante — **impressively** *adv*

impressiveness [ɪmˈprɛsɪvnəs] *n* : calidad de ser impresionante

imprint¹ [ɪmˈprɪnt, ˈɪmˌ-] *vt* : imprimir, estampar

imprint² [ˈɪmˌprɪnt] *n* : marca *f*, huella *f*

imprison [ɪmˈprɪzən] *vt* **1** JAIL : encarcelar, aprisionar **2** CONFINE : recluir, encerrar

imprisonment [ɪmˈprɪzənmənt] *n* : encarcelamiento *m*

improbability [ɪmˌprɑbəˈbɪləti] *n, pl* **-ties** : improbabilidad *f*, inverosimilitud *f*

improbable [ɪmˈprɑbəbəl] *adj* : improbable, inverosímil

impromptu¹ [ɪmˈprɑmpˌtuː, -ˌtjuː] *adv* : sin preparación, espontáneamente

impromptu² *adj* : espontáneo, improvisado

impromptu³ *n* : improvisación *f*

improper [ɪmˈprɑpər] *adj* **1** INCORRECT : incorrecto, impropio **2** INDECOROUS : indecoroso

improperly [ɪmˈprɑpərli] *adv* : incorrectamente, indebidamente

impropriety [ˌɪmprəˈpraɪəti] *n, pl* **-eties 1** INDECOROUSNESS : indecoro *m*, falta *f* de decoro **2** ERROR : impropiedad *f*, incorrección *f*

improve [ɪmˈpruːv] *v* **-proved; -proving** : mejorar

improvement [ɪmˈpruːvmənt] *n* : mejoramiento *m*, mejora *f*

improvidence [ɪmˈprɑvədənts] *n* : imprevisión *f*

improvisation [ɪmˌprɑvəˈzeɪʃən, ˌɪmprəvə-] *n* : improvisación *f*

improvise [ˈɪmprəˌvaɪz] *v* **-vised; -vising** : improvisar

imprudence [ɪmˈpruːdənts] *n* : imprudencia *f*, indiscreción *f*

imprudent [ɪmˈpruːdənt] *adj* : imprudente, indiscreto

impudence [ˈɪmpjədənts] *n* : insolencia *f*, descaro *m*

impudent [ˈɪmpjədənt] *adj* : insolente, descarado — **impudently** *adv*

impugn [ɪmˈpjuːn] *vt* : impugnar

impulse [ˈɪmˌpʌls] *n* **1** : impulso *m* **2 on impulse** : sin reflexionar

impulsive [ɪmˈpʌlsɪv] *adj* : impulsivo — **impulsively** *adv*

impulsiveness [ɪmˈpʌlsɪvnəs] *n* : impulsividad *f*

impunity [ɪmˈpjuːnəti] *n* **1** : impunidad *f* **2 with impunity** : impunemente

impure [ɪmˈpjʊr] *adj* **1** : impuro ⟨impure thoughts : pensamientos impuros⟩ **2** CONTAMINATED : con impurezas, impuro

impurity [ɪmˈpjʊrəti] *n, pl* **-ties** : impureza *f*

impute [ɪmˈpjuːt] *vt* **-puted; -puting** AT-TRIBUTE : imputar, atribuir

in¹ [ˈɪn] *adv* **1** INSIDE : dentro, adentro ⟨let's go in : vamos adentro⟩ **2** HAR-VESTED : recogido ⟨the crops are in : las cosechas ya están recogidas⟩ **3 to be in** : estar ⟨is Linda in? : ¿está Linda?⟩ **4 to be in** : estar en poder ⟨the De-mocrats are in : los demócratas están en el poder⟩ **5 to be in for** : ser obje-to de, estar a punto de ⟨they're in for a treat : los van a agasajar⟩ ⟨he's in for a surprise : se va a llevar una sorpre-sa⟩ **6 to be in on** : participar en, tomar parte en

in² *adj* **1** INSIDE : interior ⟨the in part : la parte interior⟩ **2** FASHIONABLE : de moda

in³ *prep* **1** (*indicating location or posi-tion*) ⟨in the lake : en el lago⟩ ⟨a pain in the leg : un dolor en la pierna⟩ ⟨in the sun : al sol⟩ ⟨in the rain : bajo la lluvia⟩ ⟨the best restaurant in Buenos Aires : el mejor restaurante de Buenos Aires⟩ **2** INTO : en, a ⟨he broke it in pieces : lo rompió en pedazos⟩ ⟨she went in the house : se metió a la casa⟩ **3** DURING : por, durante ⟨in the after-noon : por la tarde⟩ **4** WITHIN : den-tro de ⟨I'll be back in a week : vuelvo dentro de una semana⟩ **5** (*indicating manner*) : en, con, de ⟨in Spanish : en español⟩ ⟨written in pencil : escrito con lápiz⟩ ⟨in this way : de esta man-era⟩ **6** (*indicating states or circum-stances*) ⟨to be in luck : tener suerte⟩ ⟨to be in love : estar enamorado⟩ ⟨to be in a hurry : tener prisa⟩ **7** (*indicat-ing purpose*) : en ⟨in reply : en re-spuesta, como réplica⟩

in⁴ *n* **ins and outs** : pormenores *mpl*

inability [ˌɪnəˈbɪləti] *n, pl* **-ties** : inca-pacidad *f*

inaccessibility [ˌɪnɪkˌsɛsəˈbɪləti] *n, pl* **-ties** : inaccesibilidad *f*

inaccessible [ˌɪnɪkˈsɛsəbəl] *adj* : inac-cesible

inaccuracy [ɪnˈækjərəsi] *n, pl* **-cies 1** : inexactitud *f* **2** MISTAKE : error *m*

inaccurate [ɪnˈækjərət] *n* : inexacto, erróneo, incorrecto

inaccurately [ɪnˈækjərətli] *adv* : inco-rrectamente, con inexactitud

inaction [ɪnˈækʃən] *n* : inactividad *f*, in-acción *f*

inactive [ɪnˈæktɪv] *adj* : inactivo

inactivity [ˌɪnˌækˈtɪvəti] *n, pl* **-ties** : in-actividad *f*, ociosidad *f*

inadequacy [ɪnˈædɪkwəsi] *n, pl* **-cies 1** INSUFFICIENCY : insuficiencia *f* **2** IN-COMPETENCE : ineptitud *f*, incompe-tencia *f*

inadequate [ɪnˈædɪkwət] *adj* **1** INSUF-FICIENT : insuficiente, inadecuado **2** INCOMPETENT : inepto, incompetente

inadmissible [ˌɪnædˈmɪsəbəl] *adj* : inad-misible

inadvertent [ˌɪnədˈvərtənt] *adj* : inad-vertido, involuntario — **inadvertently** *adv*

inadvisable [ˌɪnædˈvaɪzəbəl] *adj* : de-saconsejable

inalienable [ɪnˈeɪljənəbəl, -ˈeɪliənə-] *adj* : inalienable

inane [ɪˈneɪn] *adj* **inaner; -est** : estúpi-do, idiota, necio

inanimate [ɪnˈænəmət] *adj* : inanimado, exánime

inanity [ɪˈnænəti] *n, pl* **-ties 1** STUPIDI-TY : estupidez *f* **2** NONSENSE : idiotez *f*, disparate *m*

inapplicable [ɪnˈæplɪkəbəl, ˌɪnəˈplɪkə-bəl] *adj* IRRELEVANT : inaplicable, ir-relevante

inappreciable [ˌɪnəˈpriːʃəbəl] *adj* : ina-preciable, imperceptible

inappropriate [ˌɪnəˈproʊpriət] *adj* : in-apropiado, inadecuado, impropio

inappropriateness [ˌɪnəˈproʊpriətnəs] *n* : lo inapropiado, impropiedad *f*

inapt [ɪnˈæpt] *adj* **1** UNSUITABLE : in-adecuado, inapropiado **2** INEPT : in-epto

inarticulate [ˌɪnɑrˈtɪkjələt] *adj* : inarti-culado, incapaz de expresarse

inarticulately [ˌɪnɑrˈtɪkjələtli] *adv* : inar-ticuladamente

inasmuch as [ˌɪnæzˈmʌtʃˌæz] *conj* : ya que, dado que, puesto que

inattention [ˌɪnəˈtɛntʃən] *n* : falta *f* de atención, distracción *f*

inattentive [ˌɪnəˈtɛntɪv] *adj* : distraído, despistado

inattentively [ˌɪnəˈtɛntɪvli] *adv* : distraí-damente, sin prestar atención

inaudible [ɪnˈɔdəbəl] *adj* : inaudible

inaudibly [ɪnˈɔdəbli] *adv* : de forma in-audible

inaugural¹ [ɪˈnɔɡjərəl, -ɡərəl] *adj* : inau-gural, de investidura

inaugural² *n* **1** *or* **inaugural address** : discurso *m* de investidura **2** INAU-GURATION : investidura *f* (de una per-sona)

inaugurate [ɪˈnɔɡjəˌreɪt, -ɡə-] *vt* **-rated; -rating 1** BEGIN : inaugurar **2** INDUCT : investir ⟨to inaugurate the president : investir al presidente⟩

inauguration [ɪˌnɔɡjəˈreɪʃən, -ɡə-] *n* **1** : inauguración *f* (de un edificio, un sis-tema, etc.) **2** : investidura *f* (de una per-sona)

inauspicious [ˌɪnɔˈspɪʃəs] *adj* : desfa-vorable, poco propicio

inborn [ˈɪnˌbɔrn] *adj* **1** CONGENITAL, IN-NATE : innato, congénito **2** HEREDI-TARY : hereditario

inbred [ˈɪnˌbrɛd] *adj* **1** : engendrado por endogamia **2** INNATE : innato

inbreed [ˈɪnˌbriːd] *vt* **-bred; -breeding** : engendrar por endogamia

inbreeding [ˈɪnˌbriːdɪŋ] *n* : endogamia *f*

Inca [ˈɪŋkə] *n* : inca *mf*

incalculable [ɪnˈkælkjələbəl] *adj* : incal-culable — **incalculably** [-bli] *adv*

incandescence [ˌɪnkən'dɛsənts] n : incandescencia f

incandescent [ˌɪnkən'dɛsənt] adj 1 : incandescente 2 BRILLIANT : brillante

incantation [ˌɪnˌkæn'teɪʃən] n : conjuro m, ensalmo m

incapable [ɪn'keɪpəbəl] adj : incapaz

incapacitate [ˌɪnkə'pæsəˌteɪt] vt -tated; -tating : incapacitar

incapacity [ˌɪnkə'pæsəti] n, pl -ties : incapacidad f

incarcerate [ɪn'kɑrsəˌreɪt] vt -ated; -ating : encarcelar

incarceration [ɪnˌkɑrsə'reɪʃən] n : encarcelamiento m, encarcelación f

incarnate¹ [ɪn'kɑrˌneɪt] vt -nated; -nating : encarnar

incarnate² [ɪn'kɑrnət, -ˌneɪt] adj : encarnado

incarnation [ˌɪnˌkɑr'neɪʃən] n : encarnación f

incendiary¹ [ɪn'sɛndiˌri] adj : incendiario

incendiary² n, pl -aries : incendiario m, -ria f; pirómano m, -na f

incense¹ [ɪn'sɛnts] vt -censed; -censing : indignar, enfadar, enfurecer

incense² ['ɪnˌsɛnts] n : incienso m

incentive [ɪn'sɛntɪv] n : incentivo m, aliciente m, motivación f, acicate m

inception [ɪn'sɛpʃən] n : comienzo m, principio m

incessant [ɪn'sɛsənt] adj : incesante, continuo — **incessantly** adv

incest ['ɪnˌsɛst] n : incesto m

incestuous [ɪn'sɛstʃʊəs] adj : incestuoso

inch¹ ['ɪntʃ] v : avanzar poco a poco

inch² n 1 : pulgada f 2 **every inch** : absoluto, seguro ⟨every inch a winner : un seguro ganador⟩ 3 **within an inch of** : a punto de

incidence ['ɪntsədənts] n 1 FREQUENCY : frecuencia f, índice m ⟨a high incidence of crime : un alto índice de crímenes⟩ 2 **angle of incidence** : ángulo m de incidencia

incident¹ ['ɪntsədənt] adj : incidente

incident² n : incidente m, incidencia f, episodio m (en una obra de ficción)

incidental¹ [ˌɪntsə'dɛntəl] adj 1 SECONDARY : incidental, secundario 2 ACCIDENTAL : casual, fortuito

incidental² n 1 : algo incidental 2 **incidentals** npl : imprevistos mpl

incidentally [ˌɪntsə'dɛntəli, -'dɛntli] adv 1 BY CHANCE : incidentalmente, casualmente 2 BY THE WAY : a propósito, por cierto

incinerate [ɪn'sɪnəˌreɪt] vt -ated; -ating : incinerar

incinerator [ɪn'sɪnəˌreɪtər] n : incinerador m

incipient [ɪn'sɪpiənt] adj : incipiente, naciente

incise [ɪn'saɪz] vt -cised; -cising 1 ENGRAVE : grabar, cincelar, inscribir 2 : hacer una incisión en

incision [ɪn'sɪʒən] n : incisión f

incisive [ɪn'saɪsɪv] adj : incisivo, penetrante

incisively [ɪn'saɪsɪvli] adv : con agudeza

incisor [ɪn'saɪzər] n : incisivo m

incite [ɪn'saɪt] vt -cited; -citing : incitar, instigar

incitement [ɪn'saɪtmənt] n : incitación f

inclemency [ɪn'klɛmənsti] n, pl -cies : inclemencia f

inclement [ɪn'klɛmənt] adj : inclemente, tormentoso

inclination [ˌɪnklə'neɪʃən] n 1 PROPENSITY : inclinación f, tendencia f 2 DESIRE : deseo m, ganas fpl 3 BOW : inclinación f

incline¹ [ɪn'klaɪn] v -clined; -clining vi 1 SLOPE : inclinarse 2 TEND : inclinarse, tender ⟨he is inclined to be late : tiende a llegar tarde⟩ — vt 1 LOWER : inclinar, bajar ⟨to incline one's head : bajar la cabeza⟩ 2 SLANT : inclinar 3 PREDISPOSE : predisponer

incline² ['ɪnˌklaɪn] n : inclinación f, pendiente f

inclined [ɪn'klaɪnd] adj 1 SLOPING : inclinado 2 PRONE : prono, dispuesto, dado

inclose, inclosure → **enclose, enclosure**

include [ɪn'kluːd] vt -cluded; -cluding : incluir, comprender

inclusion [ɪn'kluːʒən] n : inclusión f

inclusive [ɪn'kluːsɪv] adj : inclusivo

incognito [ˌɪnˌkɑg'niːˌto, ɪn'kɑgnəˌto] adv & adj : de incógnito

incoherence [ˌɪnko'hɪrənts, -'hɛr-] n : incoherencia f

incoherent [ˌɪnko'hɪrənt, -'hɛr-] adj : incoherente — **incoherently** adv

incombustible [ˌɪnkəm'bʌstəbəl] adj : incombustible

income ['ɪnˌkʌm] n : ingresos mpl, entradas fpl

income tax n : impuesto m sobre la renta

incoming ['ɪnˌkʌmɪŋ] adj 1 ARRIVING : que se recibe (dícese del correo), que llega (dícese de las personas), ascendente (dícese de la marea) 2 NEW : nuevo, entrante ⟨the incoming president : el nuevo presidente⟩ ⟨the incoming year : el año entrante⟩

incommunicado [ˌɪnkəˌmjuːnə'kɑdo] adj : incomunicado

incomparable [ɪn'kɑmpərəbəl] adj : incomparable, sin igual

incompatible [ˌɪnkəm'pæṭəbəl] adj : incompatible

incompetence [ɪn'kɑmpəṭənts] n : incompetencia f, impericia f, ineptitud f

incompetent [ɪn'kɑmpəṭənt] adj : incompetente, inepto, incapaz

incomplete [ˌɪnkəm'pliːt] adj : incompleto — **incompletely** adv

incomprehensible [ˌɪnˌkɑmpri'hɛntsəbəl] adj : incomprensible

inconceivable [ˌɪnkən'siːvəbəl] adj 1 INCOMPREHENSIBLE : incomprensible 2 UNBELIEVABLE : inconcebible, increíble

inconceivably [ˌɪnkən'siːvəbli] *adv* : inconcebiblemente, increíblemente
inconclusive [ˌɪnkən'kluːsɪv] *adj* : inconcluyente, no decisivo
incongruity [ˌɪnkən'gruːəti, -ˌkɑn-] *n, pl* **-ties** : incongruencia *f*
incongruous [ɪn'kɑŋgruəs] *adj* : incongruente, inapropiado, fuera de lugar
incongruously [ɪn'kɑŋgruəsli] *adv* : de manera incongruente, inapropiadamente
inconsequential [ˌɪnˌkɑnsə'kwentʃəl] *adj* : intrascendente, de poco importancia
inconsiderable [ˌɪnkən'sɪdərəbəl] *adj* : insignificante
inconsiderate [ˌɪnkən'sɪdərət] *adj* : desconsiderado, sin consideración — **inconsiderately** *adv*
inconsistency [ˌɪnkən'sɪstəntsi] *n, pl* **-cies** : inconsecuencia *f*, inconsistencia *f*
inconsistent [ˌɪnkən'sɪstənt] *adj* : inconsecuente, inconsistente
inconsolable [ˌɪnkən'soːləbəl] *adj* : inconsolable — **inconsolably** [-bli] *adv*
inconspicuous [ˌɪnkən'spɪkjuəs] *adj* : discreto, no conspicuo, que no llama la atención
inconspicuously [ˌɪnkən'spɪkjuəsli] *adv* : discretamente, sin llamar la atención
incontestable [ˌɪnkən'testəbəl] *adj* : incontestable, indiscutible — **incontestably** [-bli] *adv*
incontinence [ɪn'kɑntənənts] *n* : incontinencia *f*
incontinent [ɪn'kɑntənənt] *adj* : incontinente
inconvenience¹ [ˌɪnkən'viːnjənts] *vt* **-nienced; -niencing** : importunar, incomodar, molestar
inconvenience² *n* : incomodidad *f*, molestia *f*
inconvenient [ˌɪnkən'viːnjənt] *adj* : inconveniente, importuno, incómodo — **inconveniently** *adv*
incorporate [ɪn'kɔrpəˌreɪt] *vt* **-rated; -rating** **1** INCLUDE : incorporar, incluir **2** : incorporar, constituir en sociedad (dícese de un negocio)
incorporation [ɪnˌkɔrpə'reɪʃən] *n* : incorporación *f*
incorporeal [ˌɪnˌkɔr'poriəl] *adj* : incorpóreo
incorrect [ˌɪnkə'rekt] *adj* **1** INACCURATE : incorrecto **2** WRONG : equivocado, erróneo **3** IMPROPER : impropio — **incorrectly** *adv*
incorrigible [ɪn'kɔrədʒəbəl] *adj* : incorregible
incorruptible [ˌɪnkə'rʌptəbəl] *adj* : incorruptible
increase¹ [ɪn'kriːs, 'ɪnˌkriːs] *v* **-creased; -creasing** *vi* GROW : aumentar, crecer, subir (dícese de los precios) — *vt* AUGMENT : aumentar, acrecentar
increase² ['ɪnˌkriːs, ɪn'kriːs] *n* : aumento *m*, incremento *m*, subida *f* (de precios)

increasing [ɪn'kriːsɪŋ, 'ɪnˌkriːsɪŋ] *adj* : creciente
increasingly [ɪn'kriːsɪŋli] *adv* : cada vez más
incredible [ɪn'kredəbəl] *adj* : increíble — **incredibly** [-bli] *adv*
incredulity [ˌɪnkrɪ'duːləti, -'djuː-] *n* : incredulidad *f*
incredulous [ɪn'kredʒələs] *adj* : incrédulo, escéptico
incredulously [ɪn'kredʒələsli] *adv* : con incredulidad
increment ['ɪŋkrəmənt, 'ɪn-] *n* : incremento *m*, aumento *m*
incremental [ˌɪŋkrə'mentəl, ˌɪn-] *adj* : de incremento
incriminate [ɪn'krɪməˌneɪt] *vt* **-nated; -nating** : incriminar
incrimination [ɪnˌkrɪmə'neɪʃən] *n* : incriminación *f*
incriminatory [ɪn'krɪmənəˌtori] *adj* : incriminatorio
incubate ['ɪŋkjuˌbeɪt, 'ɪn-] *v* **-bated; -bating** *vt* : incubar, empollar — *vi* : incubar(se), empollar
incubation [ˌɪŋkju'beɪʃən, ˌɪn-] *n* : incubación *f*
incubator ['ɪŋkjuˌbeɪtər, 'ɪn-] *n* : incubadora *f*
inculcate [ɪn'kʌlˌkeɪt, 'ɪnˌkʌl-] *vt* **-cated; -cating** : inculcar
incumbency [ɪn'kʌmbəntsi] *n, pl* **-cies** **1** OBLIGATION : incumbencia *f* **2** : mandato *m* (en la política)
incumbent¹ [ɪn'kʌmbənt] *adj* : obligatorio
incumbent² *n* : titular *mf*
incur [ɪn'kər] *vt* **incurred; incurring** : provocar (al enojo), incurrir en (gastos, obligaciones)
incurable [ɪn'kjurəbəl] *adj* : incurable, sin remedio
incursion [ɪn'kərʒən] *n* : incursión *f*
indebted [ɪn'detəd] *adj* **1** : endeudado **2 to be indebted to** : estar en deuda con, estarle agradecido a
indebtedness [ɪn'detədnəs] *n* : endeudamiento *m*
indecency [ɪn'diːsəntsi] *n, pl* **-cies** : indecencia *f*
indecent [ɪn'diːsənt] *adj* : indecente — **indecently** *adv*
indecipherable [ˌɪndɪ'saɪfərəbəl] *adj* : indescifrable
indecision [ˌɪndɪ'sɪʒən] *n* : indecisión *f*, irresolución *f*
indecisive [ˌɪndɪ'saɪsɪv] *adj* **1** INCONCLUSIVE : indeciso, que no es decisivo **2** IRRESOLUTE : indeciso, irresoluto, vacilante **3** INDEFINITE : indefinido — **indecisively** *adv*
indecorous [ɪn'dekərəs, ˌɪndɪ'korəs] *adj* : indecoroso — **indecorously** *adv*
indecorousness [ɪn'dkərəsnəs, ˌɪndɪ'korəs-] *n* : indecoro *m*
indeed [ɪn'diːd] *adv* **1** TRULY : verdaderamente, de veras **2** (*used as intensifier*) ⟨thank you very much indeed

: muchísimas gracias⟩ **3** OF COURSE
: claro, por supuesto
indefatigable [ˌɪndɪˈfætɪɡəbəl] *adj* : incansable, infatigable — **indefatigably**
[-bli] *adv*
indefensible [ˌɪndɪˈfɛntsəbəl] *adj* **1** VUL-
NERABLE : indefendible, vulnerable **2**
INEXCUSABLE : inexcusable
indefinable [ˌɪndɪˈfaɪnəbəl] *adj* : indefinible
indefinite [ɪnˈdɛfənət] *adj* **1** : indefinido,
indeterminado ⟨indefinite pronouns
: pronombres indefinidos⟩ **2** VAGUE
: vago, impreciso
indefinitely [ɪnˈdɛfənətli] *adv* : indefinidamente, por un tiempo indefinido
indelible [ɪnˈdɛləbəl] *adj* : indeleble, imborrable — **indelibly** [-bli] *adv*
indelicacy [ɪnˈdɛləkəsi] *n* : falta *f* de delicadeza
indelicate [ɪnˈdɛlɪkət] *adj* **1** IMPROPER
: indelicado, indecoroso **2** TACTLESS
: indiscreto, falto de tacto
indemnify [ɪnˈdɛmnəˌfaɪ] *vt* -**fied**; -**fying**
1 INSURE : asegurar **2** COMPENSATE
: indemnizar, compensar
indemnity [ɪnˈdɛmnəti] *n, pl* -**ties** **1** IN-
SURANCE : indemnidad *f* **2** COMPEN-
SATION : indemnización *f*
indent [ɪnˈdɛnt] *vt* : sangrar (un párrafo)
indentation [ˌɪnˌdɛnˈteɪʃən] *n* **1** NOTCH
: muesca *f*, mella *f* **2** INDENTING : sangría *f* (de un párrafo)
indenture[1] [ɪnˈdɛntʃər] *vt* -**tured**; -**turing**
: ligar por contrato
indenture[2] *n* : contrato de aprendizaje
independence [ˌɪndəˈpɛndənts] *n* : independencia *f*
Independence Day *n* : día *m* de la Independencia (4 de julio en los EE.UU.)
independent[1] [ˌɪndəˈpɛndənt] *adj* : independiente — **independently** *adv*
independent[2] *n* : independiente *mf*
indescribable [ˌɪndɪˈskraɪbəbəl] *adj* : indescriptible, incalificable — **inde-
scribably** [-bli] *adv*
indestructibility [ˌɪndɪˌstrʌktəˈbɪləti] *n*
: indestructibilidad *f*
indestructible [ˌɪndɪˈstrʌktəbəl] *adj* : indestructible
indeterminate [ˌɪndɪˈtərmənət] *adj* **1**
VAGUE : vago, impreciso, indeterminado **2** INDEFINITE : indeterminado,
indefinido
index[1] [ˈɪnˌdɛks] *vt* **1** : ponerle un índice
a (un libro o una revista) **2** : incluir en
un índice ⟨all proper names are in-
dexed : todos los nombres propios están incluidos en el índice⟩ **3** INDICATE
: indicar, señalar **4** REGULATE : indexar, indiciar ⟨to index prices : indiciar los precios⟩
index[2] *n, pl* -**dexes** *or* -**dices** [ˈɪndəˌsiːz]
1 : índice *m* (de un libro, de precios) **2**
INDICATION : indicio *m*, índice *m*, señal
f ⟨an index of her character : una señal
de su carácter⟩

index finger *n* FOREFINGER : dedo *m*
índice
Indian [ˈɪndiən] *n* **1** : indio *m*, -dia *f* **2**
→ **American Indian** — **Indian** *adj*
indicate [ˈɪndəˌkeɪt] *vt* -**cated**; -**cating 1**
POINT OUT : indicar, señalar **2** SHOW,
SUGGEST : ser indicio de, ser señal de
3 EXPRESS : expresar, señalar **4** REG-
ISTER : marcar, poner (una medida,
etc.)
indication [ˌɪndəˈkeɪʃən] *n* : indicio *m*,
señal *f*
indicative [ɪnˈdɪkətɪv] *adj* : indicativo
indicator [ˈɪndəˌkeɪtər] *n* : indicador *m*
indict [ɪnˈdaɪt] *vt* : acusar, procesar (por
un crimen)
indictment [ɪnˈdaɪtmənt] *n* : acusación *f*
indifference [ɪnˈdɪfrənts, -ˈdɪfə-] *n* : indiferencia *f*
indifferent [ɪnˈdɪfrənt, -ˈdɪfə-] *adj* **1** UN-
CONCERNED : indiferente **2** MEDI-
OCRE : mediocre
indifferently [ɪnˈdɪfrəntli, -ˈdɪfə-] *adv* **1**
: con indiferencia, indiferentemente **2**
SO-SO : de modo regular, más o menos
indigence [ˈɪndɪdʒənts] *n* : indigencia *f*
indigenous [ɪnˈdɪdʒənəs] *adj* : indígena,
nativo
indigent [ˈɪndɪdʒənt] *adj* : indigente, pobre
indigestible [ˌɪndaɪˈdʒɛstəbəl, -dɪ-] *adj*
: difícil de digerir
indigestion [ˌɪndaɪˈdʒɛstʃən, -dɪ-] *n* : indigestión *f*, empacho *m*
indignant [ɪnˈdɪɡnənt] *adj* : indignado
indignantly [ɪnˈdɪɡnəntli] *adv* : con indignación
indignation [ˌɪndɪɡˈneɪʃən] *n* : indignación *f*
indignity [ɪnˈdɪɡnəti] *n, pl* -**ties** : indignidad *f*
indigo [ˈɪndɪˌɡoː] *n, pl* -**gos** *or* -**goes**
: añil *m*, índigo *m*
indirect [ˌɪndəˈrɛkt, -daɪ-] *adj* : indirecto — **indirectly** *adv*
indiscernible [ˌɪndɪˈsərnəbəl, -ˈzər-] *adj*
: imperceptible
indiscreet [ˌɪndɪˈskriːt] *adj* : indiscreto,
imprudente — **indiscreetly** *adv*
indiscretion [ˌɪndɪˈskrɛʃən] *n* : indiscreción *f*, imprudencia *f*
indiscriminate [ˌɪndɪˈskrɪmənət] *adj* : in-
discriminada
indiscriminately [ˌɪndɪˈskrɪmənətli] *adv*
: sin discriminación, sin discernimiento
indispensable [ˌɪndɪˈspɛntsəbəl] *adj*
: indispensable, necesario, imprescindible — **indispensably** [-bli] *adv*
indisposed [ˌɪndɪˈspoːzd] *adj* **1** ILL : indispuesto, enfermo **2** AVERSE, DISIN-
CLINED : opuesto, reacio ⟨to be indisposed toward working : no tener ganas
de trabajar⟩
indisputable [ˌɪndɪˈspjuːtəbəl, ɪnˈdɪs-
pjuːtə-] *adj* : indiscutible, incuestionable, incontestable — **indisputably**
[-bli] *adv*

indistinct [ˌɪndɪˈstɪŋkt] *adj* : indistinto — **indistinctly** *adv*

indistinctness [ˌɪndɪˈstɪŋktnəs] *n* : falta *f* de claridad

indistinguishable [ˌɪndɪˈstɪŋgwɪʃəbəl] *adj* : indistinguible

individual¹ [ˌɪndəˈvɪdʒʊəl] *adj* **1** PERSONAL : individual, personal ⟨individual traits : características personales⟩ **2** SEPARATE : individual, separado **3** PARTICULAR : particular, propio

individual² *n* : individuo *m*

individualism [ˌɪndəˈvɪdʒəwəˌlɪzəm] *n* : individualismo *m*

individualist [ˌɪndəˈvɪdʒʊəlɪst] *n* : individualista *mf*

individuality [ˌɪndəˌvɪdʒʊˈæləti] *n, pl* **-ties** : individualidad *f*

individually [ˌɪndəˈvɪdʒʊəli, -dʒəli] *adv* : individualmente

indivisible [ˌɪndɪˈvɪzəbəl] *adj* : indivisible

indoctrinate [ɪnˈdɑktrəˌneɪt] *vt* **-nated; -nating 1** TEACH : enseñar, instruir **2** PROPAGANDIZE : adoctrinar

indoctrination [ɪnˌdɑktrəˈneɪʃən] *n* : adoctrinamiento *m*

indolence [ˈɪndələnts] *n* : indolencia *f*

indolent [ˈɪndələnt] *adj* : indolente

indomitable [ɪnˈdɑmətəbəl] *adj* : invencible, indomable, indómito — **indomitably** [-bli] *adv*

Indonesian [ˌɪndoˈniːʒən, -ʃən] *n* : indonesio *m*, -sia *f* — **Indonesian** *adj*

indoor [ɪnˈdor] *adj* : interior (dícese de las plantas), para estar en casa (dícese de la ropa), cubierto (dícese de las piscinas, etc.), bajo techo (dícese de los deportes)

indoors [ˈɪnˈdorz] *adv* : adentro, dentro

indubitable [ɪnˈduːbətəbəl, -ˈdjuː-] *adj* : indudable, incuestionable, indiscutible

indubitably [ɪnˈduːbətəbli, -ˈdjuː-] *adv* : indudablemente

induce [ɪnˈduːs, -ˈdjuːs] *vt* **-duced; -ducing 1** PERSUADE : persuadir, inducir **2** CAUSE : inducir, provocar ⟨to induce labor : provocar un parto⟩

inducement [ɪnˈduːsmənt, -ˈdjuːs-] *n* **1** INCENTIVE : incentivo *m*, aliciente *m* **2** : inducción *f*, provocación *f* (de un parto)

induct [ɪnˈdʌkt] *vt* **1** INSTALL : instalar, investir **2** ADMIT : admitir (como miembro) **3** CONSCRIPT : reclutar (al servicio militar)

inductee [ˌɪnˌdʌkˈtiː] *n* : recluta *mf*, conscripto *m*, -ta *f*

induction [ɪnˈdʌkʃən] *n* **1** INTRODUCTION : iniciación *f*, introducción *f* **2** : inducción *f* (en la lógica o la electricidad)

inductive [ɪnˈdʌktɪv] *adj* : inductivo

indulge [ɪnˈdʌldʒ] *v* **-dulged; -dulging 1** GRATIFY : gratificar, satisfacer **2** SPOIL : consentir, mimar — *vi* **to indulge in** : permitirse

indulgence [ɪnˈdʌldʒənts] *n* **1** SATISFYING : satisfacción *f*, gratificación *f* **2** HUMORING : complacencia *f*, indulgencia *f* **3** SPOILING : consentimiento *m* **4** : indulgencia *f* (en la religión)

indulgent [ɪnˈdʌldʒənt] *adj* : indulgente, consentido — **indulgently** *adv*

industrial [ɪnˈdʌstriəl] *adj* : industrial — **industrially** *adv*

industrialist [ɪnˈdʌstriəlɪst] *n* : industrial *mf*

industrialization [ɪnˌdʌstriələˈzeɪʃən] *n* : industrialización *f*

industrialize [ɪnˈdʌstriəˌlaɪz] *vt* **-ized; -izing** : industrializar

industrious [ɪnˈdʌstriəs] *adj* : diligente, industrioso, trabajador

industriously [ɪnˈdʌstriəsli] *adv* : con diligencia, con aplicación

industriousness [ɪnˈdʌstriəsnəs] *n* : diligencia *f*, aplicación *f*

industry [ˈɪndəstri] *n, pl* **-tries 1** DILIGENCE : diligencia *f*, aplicación *f* **2** : industria *f* ⟨the steel industry : la industria siderúrgica⟩

inebriated [ɪˈniːbriˌeɪtəd] *adj* : ebrio, embriagado

inebriation [ɪˌniːbriˈeɪʃən] *n* : ebriedad *f*, embriaguez *f*

ineffable [ɪnˈɛfəbəl] *adj* : inefable — **ineffably** [-bli] *adv*

ineffective [ˌɪnɪˈfɛktɪv] *adj* **1** INEFFECTUAL : ineficaz, inútil **2** INCAPABLE : incompetente, ineficiente, incapaz

ineffectively [ˌɪnɪˈfɛktɪvli] *adv* : ineficazmente, infructuosamente

ineffectual [ˌɪnɪˈfɛktʃʊəl] *adj* : inútil, ineficaz — **ineffectually** *adv*

inefficiency [ˌɪnɪˈfɪʃəntsi] *n, pl* **-cies** : ineficiencia *f*, ineficacia *f*

inefficient [ˌɪnɪˈfɪʃənt] *adj* **1** : ineficiente, ineficaz **2** INCAPABLE, INCOMPETENT : incompetente, incapaz — **inefficiently** *adv*

inelegance [ɪnˈɛləgənts] *n* : inelegancia *f*

inelegant [ɪnˈɛləgənt] *adj* : inelegante, poco elegante

ineligibility [ɪnˌɛlədʒəˈbɪləti] *n* : inelegibilidad *f*

ineligible [ɪnˈɛlədʒəbəl] *adj* : inelegible

inept [ɪˈnɛpt] *adj* : inepto ⟨inept at : incapaz para⟩

ineptitude [ɪˈnɛptəˌtuːd, -ˌtjuːd] *n* : ineptitud *f*, incompetencia *f*, incapacidad *f*

inequality [ˌɪnɪˈkwɑləti] *n, pl* **-ties** : desigualdad *f*

inert [ɪˈnərt] *adj* **1** INACTIVE : inerte, inactivo **2** SLUGGISH : lento

inertia [ɪˈnərʃə] *n* : inercia *f*

inescapable [ˌɪnɪˈskeɪpəbəl] *adj* : inevitable, ineludible — **inescapably** [-bli] *adv*

inessential [ˌɪnɪˈsɛntʃəl] *adj* : que no es esencial, innecesario

inestimable [ɪnˈɛstəməbəl] *adj* : inestimable, inapreciable

inevitability [ɪnˌɛvətə'bɪləti] *n, pl* **-ties** : inevitabilidad *f*
inevitable [ɪn'ɛvətəbəl] *adj* : inevitable — **inevitably** [-bli] *adv*
inexact [ˌɪnɪg'zækt] *adj* : inexacto
inexactly [ˌɪnɪg'zæktli] *adv* : sin exactitud
inexcusable [ˌɪnɪk'skjuːzəbəl] *adj* : inexcusable, imperdonable — **inexcusably** [-bli] *adv*
inexhaustible [ˌɪnɪg'zɔstəbəl] *adj* **1** INDEFATIGABLE : infatigable, incansable **2** ENDLESS : inagotable — **inexhaustibly** [-bli] *adv*
inexorable [ɪn'ɛksərəbəl] *adj* : inexorable — **inexorably** [-bli] *adv*
inexpensive [ˌɪnɪk'spɛntsɪv] *adj* : barato, económico
inexperience [ˌɪnɪk'spɪriənts] *n* : inexperiencia *f*
inexperienced [ˌɪnɪk'spɪriəntst] *adj* : inexperto, novato
inexplicable [ˌɪnɪk'splɪkəbəl] *adj* : inexplicable — **inexplicably** [-bli] *adv*
inexpressible [ˌɪnɪk'sprɛsəbəl] *adj* : inexpresable, inefable
inextricable [ˌɪnɪk'strɪkəbəl, ɪ'nɛk-ˌstrɪ-] *adj* : inextricable — **inextricably** [-bli] *adv*
infallibility [ɪnˌfælə'bɪləti] *n* : infalibilidad *f*
infallible [ɪn'fæləbəl] *adj* : infalible — **infallibly** [-bli] *adv*
infamous ['ɪnfəməs] *adj* : infame — **infamously** *adv*
infamy ['ɪnfəmi] *n, pl* **-mies** : infamia *f*
infancy ['ɪnfəntsi] *n, pl* **-cies** : infancia *f*
infant ['ɪnfənt] *n* : bebé *m*; niño *m*, -ña *f*
infantile ['ɪnfən,taɪl, -təl, -,tiːl] *adj* : infantil, pueril
infantile paralysis → poliomyelitis
infantry ['ɪnfəntri] *n, pl* **-tries** : infantería *f*
infatuated [ɪn'fæt∫uˌeɪtəd] *adj* to be **infatuated with** : estar encaprichado con
infatuation [ɪnˌfæt∫u'eɪ∫ən] *n* : encaprichamiento *m*, enamoramiento *m*
infect [ɪn'fɛkt] *vt* : infectar, contagiar
infection [ɪn'fɛk∫ən] *n* : infección *f*, contagio *m*
infectious [ɪn'fɛk∫əs] *adj* : infeccioso, contagioso
infer [ɪn'fər] *vt* **inferred; inferring 1** DEDUCE : deducir, inferir **2** SURMISE : concluir, suponer, tener entendido **3** IMPLY : sugerir, insinuar
inference ['ɪnfərənts] *n* : deducción *f*, inferencia *f*, conclusión *f*
inferior[1] [ɪn'fɪriər] *adj* : inferior, malo
inferior[2] *n* : inferior *mf*
inferiority [ɪnˌfɪri'ɔrəti] *n, pl* **-ties** : inferioridad *f* ⟨inferiority complex : complejo de inferioridad⟩
infernal [ɪn'fərnəl] *adj* **1** : infernal ⟨infernal fires : fuegos infernales⟩ **2** DIABOLICAL : infernal, diabólico **3** DAMNABLE : maldito, condenado
inferno [ɪn'fərˌnoː] *n, pl* **-nos** : infierno *m*

infertile [ɪn'fərtəl, -ˌtaɪl] *adj* : estéril, infecundo
infertility [ˌɪnfər'tɪləti] *n* : esterilidad *f*, infecundidad *f*
infest [ɪn'fɛst] *vt* : infestar, plagar
infestation [ˌɪnˌfɛs'teɪ∫ən] *n* : infestación *f*, plaga *f*
infidel ['ɪnfədəl, -ˌdɛl] *n* : infiel *mf*
infidelity [ˌɪnfə'dɛləti, -faɪ-] *n, pl* **-ties 1** UNFAITHFULNESS : infidelidad *f* **2** DISLOYALTY : deslealtad *f*
infield ['ɪnˌfiːld] *n* : cuadro *m*, diamante *m*
infiltrate [ɪn'fɪlˌtreɪt, 'ɪnfɪl-] *v* **-trated; -trating** *vt* : infiltrar — *vi* : infiltrarse
infiltration [ˌɪnfɪl'treɪ∫ən] *n* : infiltración *f*
infinite ['ɪnfənət] *adj* **1** LIMITLESS : infinito, sin límites **2** VAST : infinito, vasto, extenso
infinitely ['ɪnfənətli] *adv* : infinitamente
infinitesimal [ˌɪnˌfɪnə'tɛsəməl] *adj* : infinitésimo, infinitesimal — **infinitesimally** *adv*
infinitive [ɪn'fɪnətɪv] *n* : infinitivo *m*
infinity [ɪn'fɪnəti] *n, pl* **-ties 1** : infinito *m* (en matemáticas, etc.) **2** : infinidad *f* ⟨an infinity of stars : una infinidad de estrellas⟩
infirm [ɪn'fərm] *adj* **1** FEEBLE : enfermizo, endeble **2** INSECURE : inseguro
infirmary [ɪn'fərməri] *n, pl* **-ries** : enfermería *f*, hospital *m*
infirmity [ɪn'fərməti] *n, pl* **-ties 1** FRAILTY : debilidad *f*, endeblez *f* **2** AILMENT : enfermedad *f*, dolencia *f* ⟨the infirmities of age : los achaques de la vejez⟩
inflame [ɪn'fleɪm] *v* **-flamed; -flaming** *vt* **1** KINDLE : inflamar, encender **2** : inflamar (una herida) **3** STIR UP : encender, provocar, inflamar — *vi* : inflamarse
inflammable [ɪn'flæməbəl] *adj* **1** FLAMMABLE : inflamable **2** IRASCIBLE : irascible, explosivo
inflammation [ˌɪnflə'meɪ∫ən] *n* : inflamación *f*
inflammatory [ɪn'flæməˌtori] *adj* : inflamatorio, incendiario
inflatable [ɪn'fleɪtəbəl] *adj* : inflable
inflate [ɪn'fleɪt] *vt* **-flated; -flating** : inflar, hinchar
inflation [ɪn'fleɪ∫ən] *n* : inflación *f*
inflationary [ɪn'fleɪ∫əˌnɛri] *adj* : inflacionario, inflacionista
inflect [ɪn'flɛkt] *vt* **1** CONJUGATE, DECLINE : conjugar, declinar **2** MODULATE : modular (la voz)
inflection [ɪn'flɛk∫ən] *n* : inflexión *f*
inflexibility [ɪnˌflɛksə'bɪləti] *n, pl* **-ties** : inflexibilidad *f*
inflexible [ɪn'flɛksɪbəl] *adj* : inflexible
inflict [ɪn'flɪkt] *vt* **1** : infligir, causar, imponer **2** to **inflict oneself on** : imponer uno su presencia (a alguien)
infliction [ɪn'flɪk∫ən] *n* : imposición *f*

influence[1] ['ɪn,flu:ənts, ɪn'flu:ənts] *vt* **-enced; -encing** : influenciar, influir en

influence[2] *n* **1** : influencia *f*, influjo *m* ⟨to exert influence over : ejercer influencia sobre⟩ ⟨the influence of gravity : el influjo de la gravedad⟩ **2 under the influence** : bajo la influencia del alcohol, embriagado

influential [,ɪnflu'entʃəl] *adj* : influyente

influenza [,ɪnflu'enzə] *n* : gripe *f*, influenza *f*, gripa *f* Col, Mex

influx ['ɪn,flʌks] *n* : afluencia *f* (de gente), entrada *f* (de mercancías), llegada *f* (de ideas)

inform [ɪn'fɔrm] *vt* : informar, notificar, avisar — *vi* **to inform on** : delatar, denunciar

informal [ɪn'fɔrməl] *adj* **1** UNCEREMONIOUS : sin ceremonia, sin etiqueta **2** CASUAL : informal, familiar (dícese del lenguaje) **3** UNOFFICIAL : extraoficial

informality [,ɪnfɔr'mæləti, -fər-] *n, pl* **-ties** : informalidad *f*, familiaridad *f*, falta *f* de ceremonia

informally [ɪn'fɔrməli] *adv* : sin ceremonias, de manera informal, informalmente

informant [ɪn'fɔrmənt] *n* : informante *mf*; informador *m*, -dora *f*

information [,ɪnfər'meɪʃən] *n* : información *f*

informative [ɪn'fɔrmətɪv] *adj* : informativo, instructivo

informer [ɪn'fɔrmər] *n* : informante *mf*; informador *m*, -dora *f*

infraction [ɪn'frækʃən] *n* : infracción *f*, violación *f*, transgresión *f*

infrared [,ɪnfrə'red] *adj* : infrarrojo

infrastructure ['ɪnfrə,strʌktʃər] *n* : infraestructura *f*

infrequent [ɪn'fri:kwənt] *adj* : infrecuente, raro

infrequently [ɪn'fri:kwəntli] *adv* : raramente, con poca frecuencia

infringe [ɪn'frɪndʒ] *v* **-fringed; -fringing** *vt* : infringir, violar — *vi* **to infringe on** : abusar de, violar

infringement [ɪn'frɪndʒmənt] *n* **1** VIOLATION : violación *f* (de la ley), incumplimiento *m* (de un contrato) **2** ENCROACHMENT : usurpación *f* (de derechos, etc.)

infuriate [ɪn'fjuri,eɪt] *vt* **-ated; -ating** : enfurecer, poner furioso

infuriating [ɪn'fjuri,eɪtɪŋ] *adj* : indignante, exasperante

infuse [ɪn'fju:z] *vt* **-fused; -fusing 1** INSTILL : infundir **2** STEEP : hacer una infusión de

infusion [ɪn'fju:ʒən] *n* : infusión *f*

ingenious [ɪn'dʒi:njəs] *adj* : ingenioso — **ingeniously** *adv*

ingenue *or* **ingénue** ['andʒə,nu:, 'æn-; 'æʒə-, 'a-] *n* : ingenua *f*

ingenuity [,ɪndʒə'nu:əti, -'nju:-] *n, pl* **-ties** : ingenio

ingenuous [ɪn'dʒenjuəs] *adj* **1** FRANK : cándido, franco **2** NAIVE : ingenuo — **ingenuously** *adv*

ingenuousness [ɪn'dʒenjuəsnəs] *n* **1** FRANKNESS : candidez *f*, candor *m* **2** NAIVETÉ : ingenuidad *f*

ingest [ɪn'dʒest] *vt* : ingerir

ingestion [ɪn'dʒestʃən] *n* : ingestión *f*

inglorious [ɪn'glori̇əs] *adj* : deshonroso, ignominioso

ingot ['ɪŋgət] *n* : lingote *m*

ingrained [ɪn'greɪnd] *adj* : arraigado

ingrate ['ɪn,greɪt] *n* : ingrato *m*, -ta *f*

ingratiate [ɪn'greɪʃi,eɪt] *vt* **-ated; -ating** : conseguir la benevolencia de ⟨to ingratiate oneself with someone : congraciarse con alguien⟩

ingratiating [ɪn'greɪʃi,eɪtɪŋ] *adj* : halagador, zalamero, obsequioso

ingratitude [ɪn'grætə,tu:d, -,tju:d] *n* : ingratitud *f*

ingredient [ɪn'gri:diənt] *n* : ingrediente *m*, componente *m*

ingrown ['ɪn,gro:n] *adj* **1** : crecido hacia adentro **2 ingrown toenail** : uña *f* encarnada

inhabit [ɪn'hæbət] *vt* : vivir en, habitar, ocupar

inhabitable [ɪn'hæbətəbəl] *adj* : habitable

inhabitant [ɪn'hæbətənt] *n* : habitante *mf*

inhalant [ɪn'heɪlənt] *n* : inhalante *m*

inhalation [,ɪnhə'leɪʃən, ,ɪnə-] *n* : inhalación *f*

inhale [ɪn'heɪl] *v* **-haled; -haling** *vt* : inhalar, aspirar — *vi* : inspirar

inhaler [ɪn'heɪlər] *n* : inhalador *m*

inhere [ɪn'hɪr] *vi* **-hered; -hering** : ser inherente

inherent [ɪn'hɪrənt, -'her-] *adj* : inherente, intrínseco — **inherently** *adv*

inherit [ɪn'herət] *vt* : heredar

inheritance [ɪn'herətənts] *n* : herencia *f*

inheritor [ɪn'herətər] *n* : heredero *m*, -da *f*

inhibit [ɪn'hɪbət] *vt* IMPEDE : inhibir, impedir

inhibition [,ɪnhə'bɪʃən, ,ɪnə-] *n* : inhibición *f*, cohibición *f*

inhuman [ɪn'hju:mən, -'ju:-] *adj* : inhumano, cruel — **inhumanly** *adv*

inhumane [,ɪnhju'meɪn, -'ju-] *adj* INHUMAN : inhumano, cruel

inhumanity [,ɪnhju'mænəti, -ju-] *n, pl* **-ties** : inhumanidad *f*, crueldad *f*

inimical [ɪ'nɪmɪkəl] *adj* **1** UNFAVORABLE : adverso, desfavorable **2** HOSTILE : hostil — **inimically** *adv*

inimitable [ɪ'nɪmətəbəl] *adj* : inimitable

iniquitous [ɪ'nɪkwətəs] *adj* : inicuo, malvado

iniquity [ɪ'nɪkwəti] *n, pl* **-ties** : iniquidad *f*

initial[1] [ɪ'nɪʃəl] *vt* **-tialed** *or* **-tialled; -tialing** *or* **-tialling** : poner las iniciales a, firmar con las iniciales

initial[2] *adj* : inicial, primero — **initially** *adv*

initial³ *n* : inicial *f*

initiate¹ [ɪ'nɪʃiˌeɪt] *vt* **-ated; -ating 1** BEGIN : comenzar, iniciar **2** INDUCT : instruir **3** INTRODUCE : introducir, instruir

initiate² [ɪ'nɪʃiət] *n* : iniciado *m*, -da *f*

initiation [ɪˌnɪʃi'eɪʃən] *n* : iniciación *f*

initiative [ɪ'nɪʃətɪv] *n* : iniciativa *f*

initiatory [ɪ'nɪʃiəˌtori] *adj* **1** INTRODUCTORY : introductorio **2** : de iniciación ⟨initiatory rites : ritos de iniciación⟩

inject [ɪn'dʒɛkt] *vt* : inyectar

injection [ɪn'dʒɛkʃən] *n* : inyección *f*

injudicious [ˌɪndʒu'dɪʃəs] *adj* : imprudente, indiscreto, poco juicioso

injunction [ɪn'dʒʌŋkʃən] *n* **1** ORDER : orden *f*, mandato *m* **2** COURT ORDER : mandamiento *m* judicial

injure ['ɪndʒər] *vt* **-jured; -juring 1** WOUND : herir, lesionar **2** HURT : lastimar, dañar, herir **3 to injure oneself** : hacerse daño

injurious [ɪn'dʒʊriəs] *adj* : perjudicial ⟨injurious to one's health : perjudicial a la salud⟩

injury ['ɪndʒəri] *n, pl* **-ries 1** WRONG : mal *m*, injusticia *f* **2** DAMAGE, HARM : herida *f*, daño *m*, perjuicio *m*

injustice [ɪn'dʒʌstəs] *n* : injusticia *f*

ink¹ ['ɪŋk] *vt* : entintar

ink² *n* : tinta *f*

inkling ['ɪŋklɪŋ] *n* : presentimiento *m*, indicio *m*, sospecha *f*

inkwell ['ɪŋkˌwɛl] *n* : tintero *m*

inky ['ɪŋki] *adj* **1** : manchado de tinta **2** BLACK : negro, impenetrable ⟨inky darkness : negra oscuridad⟩

inland¹ ['ɪnˌlænd, -lənd] *adv* : hacia el interior, tierra adentro

inland² *adj* : interior

inland³ *n* : interior *m*

in–law ['ɪnˌlɔ] *n* **1** : pariente *m* político **2 in–laws** *npl* : suegros *mpl*

inlay¹ [ɪn'leɪ, 'ɪnˌleɪ] *vt* **-laid** [-'leɪd, -ˌleɪd], **-laying** : incrustar, taracear

inlay² ['ɪnˌleɪ] *n* **1** : incrustación *f* **2** : empaste *m* (de un diente)

inlet ['ɪnˌlɛt, -lət] *n* : cala *f*, ensenada *f*

inmate ['ɪnˌmeɪt] *n* : paciente *mf* (en un hospital); preso *m*, -sa *f* (en una prisión); interno *m*, -na *f* (en un asilo)

in memoriam [ˌɪnmə'moriəm] *prep* : en memoria de

inmost ['ɪnˌmoːst] → **innermost**

inn ['ɪn] *n* **1** : posada *f*, hostería *f*, fonda *f* **2** TAVERN : taberna *f*

innards ['ɪnərdz] *npl* : entrañas *fpl*, tripas *fpl fam*

innate [ɪ'neɪt] *adj* **1** INBORN : innato **2** INHERENT : inherente

inner ['ɪnər] *adj* : interior, interno

innermost ['ɪnərˌmoːst] *adj* : más íntimo, más profundo

innersole ['ɪnərˌsoːl] → **insole**

inning ['ɪnɪŋ] *n* : entrada *f*

innkeeper ['ɪnˌkiːpər] *n* : posadero *m*, -ra *f*

innocence ['ɪnəsənts] *n* : inocencia *f*

innocent¹ ['ɪnəsənt] *adj* : inocente — **innocently** *adv*

innocent² *n* : inocente *mf*

innocuous [ɪ'nɑkjəwəs] *adj* **1** HARMLESS : inocuo **2** INOFFENSIVE : inofensivo

innovate ['ɪnəˌveɪt] *vi* **-vated; -vating** : innovar

innovation [ˌɪnə'veɪʃən] *n* : innovación *f*, novedad *f*

innovative ['ɪnəˌveɪtɪv] *adj* : innovador

innovator ['ɪnəˌveɪtər] *n* : innovador *m*, -dora *f*

innuendo [ˌɪnju'ɛndo] *n, pl* **-dos** *or* **-does** : insinuación *f*, indirecta *f*

innumerable [ɪ'nuːmərəbəl, -'njuː-] *adj* : innumerable

inoculate [ɪ'nɑkjəˌleɪt] *vt* **-lated; -lating** : inocular

inoculation [ɪˌnɑkjə'leɪʃən] *n* : inoculación *f*

inoffensive [ˌɪnə'fɛntsɪv] *adj* : inofensivo

inoperable [ɪn'ɑpərəbəl] *adj* : inoperable

inoperative [ɪn'ɑpərətɪv, -ˌreɪ-] *adj* : inoperante

inopportune [ɪnˌɑpər'tuːn, -'tjuːn] *adj* : inoportuno — **inopportunely** *adv*

inordinate [ɪn'ɔrdənət] *adj* : excesivo, moderado, desmesurado — **inordinately** *adv*

inorganic [ˌɪnɔr'gænɪk] *adj* : inorgánico

inpatient ['ɪnˌpeɪʃənt] *n* : paciente *mf* hospitalizado

input¹ ['ɪnˌpʊt] *vt* **inputted** *or* **input; inputting** : entrar (datos, información)

input² *n* **1** CONTRIBUTION : aportación *f*, contribución *f* **2** ENTRY : entrada *f* (de datos) **3** ADVICE, OPINION : consejos *mpl*, opinión *f*

inquest ['ɪnˌkwɛst] *n* INQUIRY, INVESTIGATION : investigación *f*, averiguación *f*, pesquisa *f* (judicial)

inquire [ɪn'kwaɪr] *v* **-quired; -quiring** *vt* : preguntar, informarse de, inquirir ⟨he inquired how to get in : preguntó como entrar⟩ — *vi* **1** ASK : preguntar, informarse ⟨to inquire about : informarse sobre⟩ ⟨to inquire after (someone) : preguntar por (alguien)⟩ **2 to inquire into** INVESTIGATE : investigar, inquirir sobre

inquiringly [ɪn'kwaɪrɪŋli] *adv* : inquisitivamente

inquiry ['ɪnˌkwaɪri, ɪn'kwaɪri; 'ɪnkwəri, 'ɪŋ-] *n, pl* **-ries 1** QUESTION : pregunta *f* ⟨to make inquiries about : pedir información sobre⟩ **2** INVESTIGATION : investigación *f*, indagación *f*, pesquisa *f*

inquisition [ˌɪnkwə'zɪʃən, ˌɪŋ-] *n* **1** : inquisición *f*, interrogatorio *m*, investigación *f* **2 the Inquisition** : la Inquisición *f*

inquisitive [ɪn'kwɪzətɪv] *adj* : inquisidor, inquisitivo, curioso — **inquisitively** *adv*

inquisitiveness [ɪnˈkwɪzətɪvnəs] n : curiosidad f

inquisitor [ɪnˈkwɪzətər] n : inquisidor m, -dora f; interrogador m, -dora f

inroad [ˈɪnˌroːd] n 1 ENCROACHMENT, INVASION : invasión f, incursión f 2 to make inroads into : ocupar parte de (un tiempo), agotar parte de (ahorros, recursos), invadir (un territorio)

insane [ɪnˈseɪn] adj 1 MAD : loco, demente ⟨to go insane : volverse loco⟩ 2 ABSURD : absurdo, insensato ⟨an insane scheme : un proyecto insensato⟩

insanely [ɪnˈseɪnli] adv : como un loco ⟨insanely suspicious : con aire de recelo⟩

insanity [ɪnˈsænəti] n, pl -ties 1 MADNESS : locura f 2 FOLLY : locura f, insensatez f

insatiable [ɪnˈseɪʃəbəl] adj : insaciable — **insatiably** [-bli] adv

inscribe [ɪnˈskraɪb] vt -scribed; -scribing 1 ENGRAVE : inscribir, grabar 2 ENROLL : inscribir 3 DEDICATE : dedicar (un libro)

inscription [ɪnˈskrɪpʃən] n : inscripción f (en un monumento), dedicación f (en un libro), leyenda f (de una ilustración, etc.)

inscrutable [ɪnˈskruːtəbəl] adj : inescrutable, misterioso — **inscrutably** [-bli] adv

inseam [ˈɪnˌsiːm] n : entrepierna f

insect [ˈɪnˌsɛkt] n : insecto m

insecticidal [ɪnˌsɛktəˈsaɪdəl] adj : insecticida

insecticide [ɪnˈsɛktəˌsaɪd] n : insecticida m

insecure [ˌɪnsɪˈkjʊr] adj : inseguro, poco seguro — **insecurely** adv

insecurely [ˌɪnsɪˈkjʊrli] adv : inseguramente

insecurity [ˌɪnsɪˈkjʊrəti] n, pl -ties : inseguridad f

inseminate [ɪnˈsɛməˌneɪt] vt -nated; -nating : inseminar

insemination [ɪnˌsɛməˈneɪʃən] n : inseminación f

insensibility [ɪnˌsɛntsəˈbɪləti] n, pl -ties : insensibilidad f

insensible [ɪnˈsɛntsəbəl] adj 1 UNCONSCIOUS : inconsciente, sin conocimiento 2 NUMB : insensible, entumecido 3 UNAWARE : inconsciente

insensitive [ɪnˈsɛntsətɪv] adj : insensible

insensitivity [ɪnˌsɛntsəˈtɪvəti] n, pl -ties : insensibilidad f

inseparable [ɪnˈsɛpərəbəl] adj : inseparable

insert[1] [ɪnˈsərt] vt 1 : insertar, introducir, poner, meter ⟨insert your key in the lock : mete tu llave en la cerradura⟩ 2 INTERPOLATE : interpolar, intercalar

insert[2] [ˈɪnˌsərt] n : inserción f, hoja f insertada (en una revista, etc.)

insertion [ɪnˈsərʃən] n : inserción f

inset [ˈɪnˌsɛt] n : página f intercalada (en un libro), entredós m (de encaje en la ropa)

inshore[1] [ˈɪnˈʃor] adv : hacia la costa

inshore[2] adj : cercano a la costa, costero ⟨inshore fishing : pesca costera⟩

inside[1] [ɪnˈsaɪd, ˈɪnˌsaɪd] adv : adentro, dentro ⟨to run inside : correr para adentro⟩ ⟨inside and out : por dentro y por fuera⟩

inside[2] adj 1 : interior, de adentro, de dentro ⟨the inside lane : el carril interior⟩ 2 : confidencial ⟨inside information : información confidencial⟩

inside[3] n 1 : interior m, parte f de adentro 2 insides npl BELLY, GUTS : tripas fpl fam 3 inside out : al revés

inside[4] prep 1 INTO : al interior de 2 WITHIN : dentro de 3 (referring to time) : en menos de ⟨inside an hour : en menos de una hora⟩

inside of prep INSIDE : dentro de

insider [ɪnˈsaɪdər] n : persona f enterada

insidious [ɪnˈsɪdiəs] adj : insidioso — **insidiously** adv

insidiousness [ɪnˈsɪdiəsnəs] n : insidia f

insight [ˈɪnˌsaɪt] n : perspicacia f, penetración f

insightful [ɪnˈsaɪtfəl] adj : perspicaz

insignia [ɪnˈsɪɡniə] or **insigne** [-niː] n, pl -nia or -nias : insignia f, enseña f

insignificance [ˌɪnsɪɡˈnɪfɪkənts] n : insignificancia f

insignificant [ˌɪnsɪɡˈnɪfɪkənt] adj : insignificante

insincere [ˌɪnsɪnˈsɪr] adj : insincero, poco sincero

insincerely [ˌɪnsɪnˈsɪrli] adv : con poca sinceridad

insincerity [ˌɪnsɪnˈsɛrəti, -ˈsɪr-] n, pl -ties : insinceridad f

insinuate [ɪnˈsɪnjuˌeɪt] vt -ated; -ating : insinuar

insinuation [ɪnˌsɪnjuˈeɪʃən] n : insinuación f

insipid [ɪnˈsɪpəd] adj : insípido

insist [ɪnˈsɪst] v : insistir

insistence [ɪnˈsɪstənts] n : insistencia f

insistent [ɪnˈsɪstənt] adj : insistente — **insistently** adv

insofar as conj : en la medida en que, en tanto que, en cuanto a

insole [ˈɪnˌsoːl] n : plantilla f

insolence [ˈɪntsələnts] n : insolencia f

insolent [ˈɪntsələnt] adj : insolente

insolubility [ɪnˌsɑljuˈbɪləti] n : insolubilidad f

insoluble [ɪnˈsɑljubəl] adj : insoluble

insolvency [ɪnˈsɑlvəntsi] n, pl -cies : insolvencia f

insolvent [ɪnˈsɑlvənt] adj : insolvente

insomnia [ɪnˈsɑmniə] n : insomnio m

insomuch as [ˌɪnsoˈmʌtʃæz] → **inasmuch as**

insomuch that conj SO : así que, de manera que

inspect [ɪnˈspɛkt] vt : inspeccionar, examinar, revisar

inspection [ɪnˈspɛkʃən] n : inspección f, examen m, revisión f, revista f (de tropas)

inspector [ɪn'spɛktər] *n* : inspector *m*, -tora *f*

inspiration [,ɪnspə'reɪʃən] *n* : inspiración *f*

inspirational [,ɪnspə'reɪʃənəl] *adj* : inspirador

inspire [ɪn'spaɪr] *v* **-spired; -spiring** *vt* **1** INHALE : inhalar, aspirar **2** STIMULATE : estimular, animar, inspirar **3** INSTILL : inspirar, infundir — *vi* : inspirar

instability [,ɪnstə'bɪləṭi] *n, pl* **-ties** : inestabilidad *f*

install [ɪn'stɔl] *vt* **-stalled; -stalling 1** : instalar ⟨to install the new president : instalar el presidente nuevo⟩ ⟨to install a fan : montar un abanico⟩ **2** to **install oneself** : instalarse

installation [,ɪnstə'leɪʃən] *n* : instalación *f*

installment [ɪn'stɔlmənt] *n* **1** : plazo *m*, cuota *f* ⟨to pay in four installments : pagar a cuatro plazos⟩ **2** : entrega *f* (de una publicación o telenovela) **3** INSTALLATION : instalación *f*

instance [ˈɪnstənts] *n* **1** INSTIGATION : instancia *f* **2** EXAMPLE : ejemplo *m* ⟨for instance : por ejemplo⟩ **3** OCCASION : instancia *f*, caso *m*, ocasión *f* ⟨he prefers, in this instance, to remain anonymous : en este caso prefiere quedarse anónimo⟩

instant¹ [ˈɪnstənt] *adj* **1** IMMEDIATE : inmediato, instantáneo ⟨an instant reply : una respuesta inmediata⟩ **2** : instantáneo ⟨instant coffee : café instantáneo⟩

instant² *n* : momento *m*, instante *m*

instantaneous [,ɪnstən'teɪniəs] *adj* : instantáneo

instantaneously [,ɪnstən'teɪniəsli] *adv* : instantáneamente, al instante

instantly [ˈɪnstəntli] *adv* : al instante, instantáneamente

instead [ɪn'stɛd] *adv* **1** : en cambio, en lugar de eso, en su lugar ⟨Dad was going, but Mom went instead : papá iba a ir, pero mamá fue en su lugar⟩ **2** RATHER : al contrario

instead of *prep* : en vez de, en lugar de

instep [ˈɪn,stɛp] *n* : empeine *m*

instigate [ˈɪnstə,geɪt] *vt* **-gated; -gating** INCITE, PROVOKE : instigar, incitar, provocar, fomentar

instigation [,ɪnstə'geɪʃən] *n* : instancia *f*, incitación *f*

instigator [ˈɪnstə,geɪtər] *n* : instigador *m*, -dora *f*; incitador *m*, -dora *f*

instill [ɪn'stɪl] *vt* **-stilled; -stilling** : inculcar, infundir

instinct [ˈɪn,stɪŋkt] *n* **1** TALENT : instinto *m*, don *m* ⟨an instinct for the right word : un don para escoger la palabra apropiada⟩ **2** : instinto *m* ⟨maternal instincts : instintos maternales⟩

instinctive [ɪn'stɪŋktɪv] *adj* : instintivo

instinctively [ɪn'stɪŋktɪvli] *adv* : instintivamente, por instinto

instinctual [ɪn'stɪŋktʃʊəl] *adj* : instintivo

institute¹ [ˈɪnstə,tuːt, -,tjuːt] *vt* **-tuted; -tuting 1** ESTABLISH : establecer, instituir, fundar **2** INITIATE : iniciar, empezar, entablar

institute² *n* : instituto *m*

institution [,ɪnstə'tuːʃən, -'tjuː-] *n* **1** ESTABLISHING : institución *f*, establecimiento *m* **2** CUSTOM : institución *f*, tradición *f* ⟨the institution of marriage : la institución del matrimonio⟩ **3** ORGANIZATION : institución *f*, organismo *m* **4** ASYLUM : asilo *m*

institutional [,ɪnstə'tuːʃənəl, -'tjuː-] *adj* : institucional

institutionalize [,ɪnstə'tuːʃənə,laɪz, -'tjuː-] *vt* **-ized; -izing 1** : institucionalizar ⟨institutionalized values : valores institucionalizados⟩ **2** : internar ⟨institutionalized orphans : huérfanos internados⟩

instruct [ɪn'strʌkt] *vt* **1** TEACH, TRAIN : instruir, adiestrar, enseñar **2** COMMAND : mandar, ordenar, dar instrucciones a

instruction [ɪn'strʌkʃən] *n* **1** TEACHING : instrucción *f*, enseñanza *f* **2** COMMAND : orden *f*, instrucción *f* **3** **instructions** *npl* DIRECTIONS : instrucciones *fpl*, modo *m* de empleo

instructional [ɪn'strʌkʃənəl] *adj* : instructivo, educativo

instructive [ɪn'strʌktɪv] *adj* : instructivo

instructor [ɪn'strʌktər] *n* : instructor *m*, -tora *f*

instrument [ˈɪnstrəmənt] *n* : instrumento *m*

instrumental [,ɪnstrə'mɛntəl] *adj* : instrumental

instrumentalist [,ɪnstrə'mɛntəlɪst] *n* : instrumentista *mf*

insubordinate [,ɪnsə'bɔrdənət] *adj* : insubordinado

insubordination [,ɪnsə,bɔrdən'eɪʃən] *n* : insubordinación *f*

insubstantial [,ɪnsəb'stæntʃəl] *adj* : insustancial, poco nutritivo (dícese de una comida), poco sólido (dícese de una estructura o un argumento)

insufferable [ɪn'sʌfərəbəl] *adj* UNBEARABLE : insufrible, intolerable, inaguantable, insoportable — **insufferably** [-bli] *adv*

insufficiency [,ɪnsə'fɪʃəntsi] *n, pl* **-cies** : insuficiencia *f*

insufficient [,ɪnsə'fɪʃənt] *adj* : insuficiente — **insufficiently** *adv*

insular [ˈɪnsʊlər, -sjʊ-] *adj* **1** : isleño (dícese de la gente), insular (dícese del clima) ⟨insular residents : residentes de la isla⟩ **2** NARROW-MINDED : de miras estrechas

insularity [,ɪnsʊ'lærəṭi, -sjʊ-] *n* : insularidad *f*

insulate [ˈɪnsə,leɪt] *vt* **-lated; -lating** : aislar

insulation [,ɪnsə'leɪʃən] *n* : aislamiento *m*

insulator [ˈɪnsə,leɪtər] *n* : aislador *m* (pieza), aislante *m* (material)

insulin [ˈɪnt̬sələn] n : insulina f

insult¹ [ɪnˈsʌlt] vt : insultar, ofender, injuriar

insult² [ˈɪnˌsʌlt] n : insulto m, injuria f, agravio m

insulting [ɪnˈsʌltɪŋ] adj : ofensivo, injurioso, insultante

insultingly [ɪnˈsʌltɪŋli] adv : ofensivamente, de manera insultante

insuperable [ɪnˈsuːpərəbəl] adj : insuperable — **insuperably** [-bli] adv

insurable [ɪnˈʃʊrəbəl] adj : asegurable

insurance [ɪnˈʃʊrənts, ˈɪnˌʃʊr-] n : seguro m ⟨life insurance : seguro de vida⟩ ⟨insurance company : compañía de seguros⟩

insure [ɪnˈʃʊr] vt **-sured; -suring** **1** UNDERWRITE : asegurar **2** ENSURE : asegurar, garantizar

insured [ɪnˈʃʊrd] n : asegurado m, -da f

insurer [ɪnˈʃʊrər] n : asegurador m, -dora f

insurgent¹ [ɪnˈsərdʒənt] adj : insurgente

insurgent² n : insurgente mf

insurmountable [ˌɪnsərˈmaʊnt̬əbəl] adj : insuperable, insalvable — **insurmountably** [-bli] adv

insurrection [ˌɪnsəˈrɛkʃən] n : insurrección f, levantamiento m, alzamiento m

intact [ɪnˈtækt] adj : intacto

intake [ˈɪnˌteɪk] n **1** OPENING : entrada f, toma f ⟨fuel intake : toma de combustible⟩ **2** : entrada f (de agua o aire), consumo m (de sustancias nutritivas) **3** intake of breath : inhalación f

intangible [ɪnˈtændʒəbəl] adj : intangible, impalpable — **intangibly** [-bli] adv

integer [ˈɪnt̬ɪdʒər] n : entero m

integral [ˈɪnt̬ɪɡrəl] adj : integral, esencial

integrate [ˈɪnt̬əˌɡreɪt] v **-grated; -grating** vt **1** UNITE : integrar, unir **2** DESEGREGATE : eliminar la segregación de — vi : integrarse

integration [ˌɪnt̬əˈɡreɪʃən] n : integración f

integrity [ɪnˈtɛɡrət̬i] n : integridad f

intellect [ˈɪnt̬əlˌɛkt] n : intelecto m, inteligencia f, capacidad f intelectual

intellectual¹ [ˌɪnt̬əˈlɛktʃuəl] adj : intelectual — **intellectually** adv

intellectual² n : intelectual mf

intellectualism [ˌɪnt̬əˈlɛktʃuəˌlɪzəm] n : intelectualismo m

intelligence [ɪnˈtɛlədʒənts] n **1** : inteligencia f **2** INFORMATION, NEWS : inteligencia f, información f, noticias fpl

intelligent [ɪnˈtɛlədʒənt] adj : inteligente — **intelligently** adv

intelligentsia [ɪnˌtɛləˈdʒɛntsiə, -ˈɡɛn-] ns & pl : intelectualidad f

intelligibility [ɪnˌtɛlədʒəˈbɪlət̬i] n : inteligibilidad f

intelligible [ɪnˈtɛlədʒəbəl] adj : inteligible, comprensible — **intelligibly** [-bli] adv

intemperance [ɪnˈtɛmpərənts] n : inmoderación f, intemperancia f

intemperate [ɪnˈtɛmpərət] adj : excesivo, inmoderado, desmedido

intend [ɪnˈtɛnd] vt **1** MEAN : querer decir ⟨that's not what I intended : eso no es lo que quería decir⟩ **2** PLAN : tener planeado, proyectar, proponerse ⟨I intend to finish by Thursday : me propongo acabar para el jueves⟩

intended [ɪnˈtɛndəd] adj **1** PLANNED : previsto, proyectado **2** INTENTIONAL : intencional, deliberado

intense [ɪnˈtɛnts] adj **1** EXTREME : intenso, extremo ⟨intense pain : dolor intenso⟩ **2** : profundo, intenso ⟨to my intense relief : para mi alivio profundo⟩ ⟨intense enthusiasm : entusiasmo ardiente⟩

intensely [ɪnˈtɛntsli] adv : sumamente, profundamente, intensamente

intensification [ɪnˌtɛntsəfəˈkeɪʃən] n : intensificación f

intensify [ɪnˈtɛntsəˌfaɪ] v **-fied; -fying** vt **1** STRENGTHEN : intensificar, redoblar ⟨to intensify one's efforts : redoblar unos sus esfuerzos⟩ **2** SHARPEN : intensificar, agudizar (dolor, ansiedad) — vi : intensificarse, hacerse más intenso

intensity [ɪnˈtɛntsət̬i] n, pl **-ties** : intensidad f

intensive [ɪnˈtɛntsɪv] adj : intensivo — **intensively** adv

intent¹ [ɪnˈtɛnt] adj **1** FIXED : concentrado, fijo ⟨an intent stare : una mirada fija⟩ **2** intent on or intent upon : resuelto a, atento a

intent² n **1** PURPOSE : intención f, propósito m **2** for all intents and purposes : a todos los efectos, prácticamente

intention [ɪnˈtɛntʃən] n : intención f, propósito m

intentional [ɪnˈtɛntʃənəl] adj : intencional, deliberado

intentionally [ɪnˈtɛntʃənəli] adv : a propósito, adrede

intently [ɪnˈtɛntli] adv : atentamente, fijamente

inter [ɪnˈtər] vt **-terred; -terring** : enterrar, inhumar

interact [ˌɪnt̬ərˈækt] vi : interactuar, actuar recíprocamente, relacionarse

interaction [ˌɪnt̬ərˈækʃən] n : interacción f, interrelación f

interactive [ˌɪnt̬ərˈæktɪv] adj : interactivo

interbreed [ˌɪnt̬ərˈbriːd] v **-bred; -breeding** vt : cruzar — vi : cruzarse

intercalate [ɪnˈtərkəˌleɪt] vt **-lated; -lating** : intercalar

intercede [ˌɪnt̬ərˈsiːd] vi **-ceded; -ceding** : interceder

intercept [ˌɪnt̬ərˈsɛpt] vt : interceptar

interception [ˌɪnt̬ərˈsɛpʃən] n : intercepción f

intercession [ˌɪnt̬ərˈsɛʃən] n : intercesión f

interchange¹ [ˌɪntərˈtʃeɪndʒ] vt
-changed; -changing : intercambiar
interchange² [ˈɪntərˌtʃeɪndʒ] n 1 EX-
CHANGE : intercambio m, cambio m 2
JUNCTION : empalme m, enlace m de
carreteras
interchangeable [ˌɪntərˈtʃeɪndʒəbəl] adj
: intercambiable
intercity [ˈɪntərˌsɪti] adj : interurbano
intercollegiate [ˌɪntərkəˈliːdʒət, -dʒiət]
adj : interuniversitario
interconnect [ˌɪntərkəˈnɛkt] vt 1
: conectar, interconectar (en tecnología) 2 RELATE : interrelacionar —
vi 1 : conectar 2 : interrelacionarse
intercontinental [ˌɪntərˌkantənˈnɛtəl]
adj : intercontinental
intercourse [ˈɪntərˌkors] n 1 RELATIONS
: relaciones fpl, trato m 2 COPULATION
: acto m sexual, relaciones fpl sexuales,
coito m
interdenominational [ˌɪntərdɪˌnamə-
ˈneɪʃənəl] adj : interconfesional
interdepartmental [ˌɪntərdɪˌpart-
ˈmɛntəl, -ˌdi:-] adj : interdepartamental
interdependence [ˌɪntərdɪˈpɛndən̩ts] n
: interdependencia f
interdependent [ˌɪntərdɪˈpɛndənt] adj
: interdependiente
interdict [ˌɪntərˈdɪkt] vt 1 PROHIBIT
: prohibir 2 : cortar (las líneas de comunicación o provisión del enemigo)
interest¹ [ˈɪntrəst, -təˌrɛst] vt : interesar
interest² n 1 SHARE, STAKE : interés m,
participación f 2 BENEFIT : provecho
m, beneficio m, interés m ⟨in the public interest : en el interés público⟩ 3
CHARGE : interés m, cargo m ⟨com-
pound interest : interés compuesto⟩ 4
CURIOSITY : interés m, curiosidad f 5
COLOR : color m, interés m ⟨places of
local interest : lugares de color local⟩
6 HOBBY : afición f
interesting [ˈɪntrəstɪŋ, -təˌrɛstɪŋ] adj : interesante — **interestingly** adv
interface [ˈɪntərˌfeɪs] n 1 : punto m de
contacto ⟨oil-water interface : punto
de contacto entre el agua y el aceite⟩
2 : interfaz f (de una computadora), interfase f
interfere [ˌɪntərˈfɪr] vi -fered; -fering 1
INTERPOSE : interponerse, hacer interferencia ⟨to interfere with a play : obstruir una jugada⟩ 2 MEDDLE : entrometerse, interferir, intervenir 3 to
interfere with DISRUPT : afectar (una
actividad), interferir (la radiotransmi-
sión) 4 to interfere with TOUCH : tocar ⟨someone interfered with my papers : alguien tocó mis papeles⟩
interference [ˌɪntərˈfɪrən̩ts] n : interferencia f, intromisión f
intergalactic [ˌɪntərgəˈlæktɪk] adj : intergaláctico
intergovernmental [ˌɪntərˌgʌvərˈmɛntəl,
-vərn-] adj : intergubernamental
interim¹ [ˈɪntərəm] adj : interino, provisional

interim² n 1 : interín m, intervalo m 2
in the interim : en el interín, mientras
tanto
interior¹ [ɪnˈtɪriər] adj : interior
interior² n : interior m
interject [ˌɪntərˈdʒɛkt] vt : interponer,
agregar
interjection [ˌɪntərˈdʒɛkʃən] n 1 : interjección f (en lingüística) 2 EXCLAMA-
TION : exclamación f 3 INTERPOSI-
TION, INTERRUPTION : interposición f,
interrupción f
interlace [ˌɪntərˈleɪs] vt -laced; -lacing 1
INTERWEAVE : entrelazar 2 INTER-
SPERSE : intercalar
interlock [ˌɪntərˈlak] vt 1 UNITE : trabar,
unir 2 ENGAGE, MESH : engranar — vi
: entrelazarse, trabarse
interloper [ˌɪntərˈloˌpər] n 1 INTRUDER
: intruso m, -sa f 2 MEDDLER : entrometido m, -da f
interlude [ˈɪntərˌluːd] n 1 INTERVAL : intervalo m, intermedio m (en el teatro)
2 : interludio m (en música)
intermarriage [ˌɪntərˈmærɪdʒ] n 1 : matrimonio m mixto (entre miembros de
distintas razas o religiones) 2 : matrimonio m entre miembros del mismo
grupo
intermarry [ˌɪntərˈmæri] vi -married;
-marrying 1 : casarse (con miembros
de otros grupos) 2 : casarse entre sí
(con miembros del mismo grupo)
intermediary¹ [ˌɪntərˈmiːdiˌeri] adj : intermediario
intermediary² n, pl -aries : intermediario m, -ria f
intermediate¹ [ˌɪntərˈmiːdiət] adj : intermedio
intermediate² n GO-BETWEEN : intermediario m, -ria f; mediador m, -dora f
interment [ɪnˈtərmənt] n : entierro m
interminable [ɪnˈtərmənəbəl] adj : interminable, constante — **interminably**
[-bli] adv
intermingle [ˌɪntərˈmɪŋgəl] vt -mingled;
-mingling : entremezclar, mezclar —
vi : entremezclarse
intermission [ˌɪntərˈmɪʃən] n : intermisión f, intervalo m, intermedio m
intermittent [ˌɪntərˈmɪtənt] adj : intermitente — **intermittently** adv
intermix [ˌɪntərˈmɪks] vt : entremezclar
intern¹ [ˈɪnˌtərn, ɪnˈtərn] vt : confinar
(durante la guerra) — vi : servir de interno, hacer las prácticas
intern² [ˈɪnˌtərn] n : interno m, -na f
internal [ɪnˈtərnəl] adj : interno, interi-
or ⟨internal bleeding : hemorragia in-
terna⟩ ⟨internal affairs : asuntos inte-
riores, asuntos domésticos⟩ —
internally adv
international [ˌɪntərˈnæʃənəl] adj : internacional — **internationally** adv
internationalize [ˌɪntərˈnæʃənəˌlaɪz] vt
-ized; -izing : internacionalizar
internee [ˌɪnˌtərˈniː] n : interno m, -na f
Internet [ˈɪntərˌnɛt] n : Internet mf

internist [ˈɪnˌtərnɪst] *n* : internista *mf*

interpersonal [ˌɪntərˈpərsənəl] *adj* : interpersonal

interplay [ˈɪntərˌpleɪ] *n* : interacción *f*, juego *m*

interpolate [ɪnˈtərpəˌleɪt] *vt* **-lated;** **-lating** : interpolar

interpose [ˌɪntərˈpoːz] *v* **-posed; -posing** *vt* : interponer, interrumpir con — *vi* : interponerse

interposition [ˌɪntərpəˈzɪʃən] *n* : interposición *f*

interpret [ɪnˈtərprət] *vt* : interpretar

interpretation [ɪnˌtərprəˈteɪʃən] *n* : interpretación *f*

interpretative [ɪnˈtərprəˌteɪtɪv] *adj* : interpretativo

interpreter [ɪnˈtərprətər] *n* : intérprete *mf*

interpretive [ɪnˈtərprətɪv] *adj* : interpretativo

interracial [ˌɪntərˈreɪʃəl] *adj* : interracial

interrelate [ˌɪntəriˈleɪt] *v* **-related;** **-relating** : interrelacionar

interrelationship [ˌɪntəriˈleɪʃənˌʃɪp] *n* : interrelación *f*

interrogate [ɪnˈtɛrəˌgeɪt] *vt* **-gated;** **-gating** : interrogar, someter a un interrogatorio

interrogation [ɪnˌtɛrəˈgeɪʃən] *n* : interrogación *f*

interrogative¹ [ˌɪntəˈrɑgətɪv] *adj* : interrogativo

interrogative² *n* : interrogativo *m*

interrogator [ɪnˈtɛrəˌgeɪtər] *n* : interrogador *m*, -dora *f*

interrogatory [ˌɪntəˈrɑgəˌtori] *adj* → **interrogative¹**

interrupt [ˌɪntəˈrʌpt] *v* : interrumpir

interruption [ˌɪntəˈrʌpʃən] *n* : interrupción *f*

intersect [ˌɪntərˈsɛkt] *vt* : cruzar, cortar — *vi* : cruzarse (dícese de los caminos), intersectarse (dícese de las líneas o figuras), cortarse

intersection [ˌɪntərˈsɛkʃən] *n* : intersección *f*, cruce *m*

intersperse [ˌɪntərˈspərs] *vt* **-spersed;** **-spersing** : intercalar, entremezclar

interstate [ˌɪntərˈsteɪt] *adj* : interestatal

interstellar [ˌɪntərˈstɛlər] *adj* : interestelar

interstice [ɪnˈtərstəs] *n, pl* **-stices** [-stə-ˌsiːz, -stəsəz] : intersticio *m*

intertwine [ˌɪntərˈtwaɪn] *vi* **-twined;** **-twining** : entrelazarse

interval [ˈɪntərvəl] *n* : intervalo *m*

intervene [ˌɪntərˈviːn] *vi* **-vened;** **-vening** **1** ELAPSE : transcurrir, pasar ⟨the intervening years : los años intermediarios⟩ **2** INTERCEDE : intervenir, interceder, mediar

intervention [ˌɪntərˈvɛntʃən] *n* : intervención *f*

interview¹ [ˈɪntərˌvjuː] *vt* : entrevistar — *vi* : hacer entrevistas

interview² *n* : entrevista *f*

interviewer [ˈɪntərˌvjuːər] *n* : entrevistador *m*, -dora *f*

interweave [ˌɪntərˈwiːv] *v* **-wove** [-ˈwoːv]; **-woven** [-ˈwoːvən]; **-weaving** *vt* : entretejer, entrelazar — *vi* INTERTWINE : entrelazarse, entretejerse

interwoven [ˌɪntərˈwoːvən] *adj* : entretejido

intestate [ɪnˈtɛsˌteɪt, -tət] *adj* : intestado

intestinal [ɪnˈtɛstənəl] *adj* : intestinal

intestine [ɪnˈtɛstən] *n* **1** : intestino *m* **2** **small intestine** : intestino *m* delgado **3** **large intestine** : intestino *m* grueso

intimacy [ˈɪntəməsi] *n, pl* **-cies** **1** CLOSENESS : intimidad *f* **2** FAMILIARITY : familiaridad *f*

intimate¹ [ˈɪntəˌmeɪt] *vt* **-mated; -mating** : insinuar, dar a entender

intimate² [ˈɪntəmət] *adj* **1** CLOSE : íntimo, de confianza ⟨intimate friends : amigos íntimos⟩ **2** PRIVATE : íntimo, privado ⟨intimate clubs : clubes íntimos⟩ **3** INNERMOST, SECRET : íntimo, secreto ⟨intimate fantasies : fantasías secretas⟩

intimate³ *n* : amigo *m* íntimo, amiga *f* íntima

intimidate [ɪnˈtɪməˌdeɪt] *vt* **-dated;** **-dating** : intimidar

intimidation [ɪnˌtɪməˈdeɪʃən] *n* : intimidación *f*

into [ˈɪnˌtuː] *prep* **1** (*indicating motion*) : en, a, contra, dentro de ⟨she got into bed : se metió en la cama⟩ ⟨to get into a plane : subir a un avión⟩ ⟨he crashed into the wall : chocó contra la pared⟩ ⟨looking into the sun : mirando al sol⟩ **2** (*indicating state or condition*) : a, en ⟨to burst into tears : echarse a llorar⟩ ⟨the water turned into ice : el agua se convirtió en hielo⟩ ⟨to translate into English : traducir al inglés⟩ **3** (*indicating time*) ⟨far into the night : hasta bien entrada la noche⟩ ⟨he's well into his eighties : tiene los ochenta bien cumplidos⟩ **4** (*in mathematics*) ⟨3 into 12 is 4 : 12 dividido por 3 es 4⟩

intolerable [ɪnˈtɑlərəbəl] *adj* : intolerable — **intolerably** [-bli] *adv*

intolerance [ɪnˈtɑlərənts] *n* : intolerancia *f*

intolerant [ɪnˈtɑlərənt] *adj* : intolerante

intonation [ˌɪntoˈneɪʃən] *n* : entonación *f*

intone [ɪnˈtoːn] *vt* **-toned; -toning** : entonar

intoxicant [ɪnˈtɑksɪkənt] *n* : bebida *f* alcohólica

intoxicate [ɪnˈtɑksəˌkeɪt] *vt* **-cated;** **-cating** : emborrachar, embriagar

intoxicated [ɪnˈtɑksəˌkeɪtəd] *adj* : borracho, embriagado

intoxicating [ɪnˈtɑksəˌkeɪtɪŋ] *adj* : embriagador

intoxication [ɪnˌtɑksəˈkeɪʃən] *n* : embriaguez *f*

intractable [ɪnˈtræktəbəl] *adj* : obstinado, intratable

intramural [ˌɪntrəˈmjurəl] *adj* : interno, dentro de la universidad

intransigence [ɪnˈtrænʦəʤənʦ, -ˈtræn-zə-] *n* : intransigencia *f*

intransigent [ɪnˈtrænʦəʤənt, -ˈtrænzə-] *adj* : intransigente

intransitive [ɪnˈtrænʦətɪv, -ˈtrænzə-] *adj* : intransitivo

intravenous [ˌɪntrəˈviːnəs] *adj* : intravenoso — **intravenously** *adv*

intrepid [ɪnˈtrepəd] *adj* : intrépido

intricacy [ˈɪntrɪkəsi] *n, pl* **-cies** : complejidad *f*, lo intrincado

intricate [ˈɪntrɪkət] *adj* : intrincado, complicado — **intricately** *adv*

intrigue[1] [ɪnˈtriːg] *v* **-trigued; -triguing** : intrigar

intrigue[2] [ˈɪnˌtriːg, ɪnˈtriːg] *n* : intriga *f*

intriguing [ɪnˈtriːgɪŋ] *adj* : intrigante, fascinante

intrinsic [ɪnˈtrɪnzɪk, -ˈtrɪnsɪk] *adj* : intrínseco, esencial — **intrinsically** [-zɪkli, -sɪ-] *adv*

introduce [ˌɪntrəˈduːs, -ˈdjuːs] *vt* **-duced; -ducing** 1 : presentar ⟨let me introduce my father : permítame presentar a mi padre⟩ 2 : introducir (algo nuevo), lanzar (un producto), presentar (una ley), proponer (una idea o un tema)

introduction [ˌɪntrəˈdʌkʃən] *n* : introducción *f*, presentación *f*

introductory [ˌɪntrəˈdʌktəri] *adj* : introductorio, preliminar, de introducción

introspection [ˌɪntrəˈspekʃən] *n* : introspección *f*

introspective [ˌɪntrəˈspektɪv] *adj* : introspectivo — **introspectively** *adv*

introvert [ˈɪntrəˌvərt] *n* : introvertido *m*, -da *f*

introverted [ˈɪntrəˌvərtəd] *adj* : introvertido

intrude [ɪnˈtruːd] *v* **-truded; -truding** *vi* 1 INTERFERE : inmiscuirse, entrometerse 2 DISTURB, INTERRUPT : molestar, estorbar, interrumpir — *vt* : introducir por fuerza

intruder [ɪnˈtruːdər] *n* : intruso *m*, -sa *f*

intrusion [ɪnˈtruːʒən] *n* : intrusión *f*

intrusive [ɪnˈtruːsɪv] *adj* : intruso

intuit [ɪnˈtuːɪt, -ˈtjuː-] *vt* : intuir

intuition [ˌɪntuˈɪʃən, -tju-] *n* : intuición *f*

intuitive [ɪnˈtuːəṭɪv, -ˈtjuː-] *adj* : intuitivo — **intuitively** *adv*

inundate [ˈɪnənˌdeɪt] *vt* **-dated; -dating** : inundar

inundation [ˌɪnənˈdeɪʃən] *n* : inundación *f*

inure [ɪˈnʊr, -ˈnjʊr] *vt* **-ured; -uring** : acostumbrar, habituar

invade [ɪnˈveɪd] *vt* **-vaded; -vading** : invadir

invader [ɪnˈveɪdər] *n* : invasor *m*, -sora *f*

invalid[1] [ɪnˈvæləd] *adj* : inválido, nulo

invalid[2] [ˈɪnvələd] *adj* : inválido, discapacitado

invalid[3] [ˈɪnvələd] *n* : inválido *m*, -da *f*

invalidate [ɪnˈvæləˌdeɪt] *vt* **-dated; -dating** : invalidar

invalidity [ˌɪnvəˈlɪdəṭi] *n, pl* **-ties** : invalidez *f*, falta de validez *f*

invaluable [ɪnˈvæljəbəl, -ˈvæljuə-] *adj* : invalorable, inestimable, inapreciable

invariable [ɪnˈværiəbəl] *adj* : invariable, constante — **invariably** [-bli] *adv*

invasion [ɪnˈveɪʒən] *n* : invasión *f*

invasive [ɪnˈveɪsɪv] *adj* : invasivo

invective [ɪnˈvektɪv] *n* : invectiva *f*, improperio *m*, vituperio *m*

inveigh [ɪnˈveɪ] *vi* to **inveigh against** : arremeter contra, lanzar invectivas contra

inveigle [ɪnˈveɪgəl, -ˈviː-] *vt* **-gled; -gling** : engatusar, embaucar, persuadir con engaños

invent [ɪnˈvent] *vt* : inventar

invention [ɪnˈventʃən] *n* : invención *f*, invento *m*

inventive [ɪnˈventɪv] *adj* : inventivo

inventiveness [ɪnˈventɪvnəs] *n* : ingenio *m*, inventiva *f*

inventor [ɪnˈventər] *n* : inventor *m*, -tora *f*

inventory[1] [ˈɪnvənˌtɔri] *vt* **-ried; -rying** : inventariar

inventory[2] *n, pl* **-ries** 1 LIST : inventario *m* 2 STOCK : existencias *fpl*

inverse[1] [ɪnˈvərs, ˈɪnˌvərs] *adj* : inverso — **inversely** *adv*

inverse[2] *n* : inverso *m*

inversion [ɪnˈvərʒən] *n* : inversión *f*

invert [ɪnˈvərt] *vt* : invertir

invertebrate[1] [ɪnˈvərtəbrət, -ˌbreɪt] *adj* : invertebrado

invertebrate[2] *n* : invertebrado *m*

invest [ɪnˈvest] *v* 1 AUTHORIZE : investir, autorizar 2 CONFER : conferir 3 : invertir, dedicar ⟨he invested his savings in stocks : invirtió sus ahorros en acciones⟩ ⟨to invest one's time : dedicar uno su tiempo⟩

investigate [ɪnˈvestəˌgeɪt] *v* **-gated; -gating** : investigar

investigation [ɪnˌvestəˈgeɪʃən] *n* : investigación *f*, estudio *m*

investigative [ɪnˈvestəˌgeɪtɪv] *adj* : investigador

investigator [ɪnˈvestəˌgeɪtər] *n* : investigador *m*, -dora *f*

investiture [ɪnˈvestəˌtʃʊr, -tʃər] *n* : investidura *f*

investment [ɪnˈvestmənt] *n* : inversión *f*

investor [ɪnˈvestər] *n* : inversor *m*, -sora *f*; inversionista *mf*

inveterate [ɪnˈveṭərət] *adj* 1 DEEP-SEATED : inveterado, enraizado 2 HABITUAL : empedernido, incorregible

invidious [ɪnˈvɪdiəs] *adj* 1 OBNOXIOUS : repugnante, odioso 2 UNJUST : injusto — **invidiously** *adv*

invigorate [ɪnˈvɪgəˌreɪt] *vt* **-rated; -rating** : vigorizar, animar

invigorating [ɪnˈvɪgəˌreɪtɪŋ] *adj* : vigorizante, estimulante

invigoration [ɪnˌvɪgəˈreɪʃən] *n* : animación *f*

invincibility [ɪnˌvɪnʦəˈbɪləṭi] *n* : invencibilidad *f*

invincible [ɪnˈvɪntsəbəl] *adj* : invencible — **invincibly** [-bli] *adv*

inviolable [ɪnˈvaɪələbəl] *adj* : inviolable

inviolate [ɪnˈvaɪələt] *adj* : inviolado, puro

invisibility [ɪnˌvɪzəˈbɪləti] *n* : invisibilidad *f*

invisible [ɪnˈvɪzəbəl] *adj* : invisible — **invisibly** [-bli] *adv*

invitation [ˌɪnvəˈteɪʃən] *n* : invitación *f*

invite [ɪnˈvaɪt] *vt* **-vited; -viting 1** ATTRACT : atraer, tentar ⟨a book that invites interest : un libro que atrae el interés⟩ **2** PROVOKE : provocar, buscar ⟨to invite trouble : buscarse problemas⟩ **3** ASK : invitar ⟨we invited them for dinner : los invitamos acenar⟩ **4** SOLICIT : solicitar, buscar (preguntas, comentarios, etc.)

inviting [ɪnˈvaɪtɪŋ] *adj* : atractivo, atrayente

invocation [ˌɪnvəˈkeɪʃən] *n* : invocación *f*

invoice[1] [ˈɪnˌvɔɪs] *vt* **-voiced; -voicing** : facturar

invoice[2] *n* : factura *f*

invoke [ɪnˈvoːk] *vt* **-voked; -voking 1** : invocar, apelar a ⟨she invoked our aid : apeló a nuestra ayuda⟩ **2** CITE : invocar, citar ⟨to invoke a precedent : invocar un precedente⟩ **3** CONJURE UP : hacer aparecer, invocar

involuntary [ɪnˈvɑlənˌteri] *adj* : involuntario — **involuntarily** [ɪnˌvɑlənˈtrəli] *adv*

involve [ɪnˈvɑlv] *vt* **-volved; -volving 1** ENGAGE : ocupar (con una tarea, etc.) **2** IMPLICATE : involucrar, enredar, implicar ⟨to be involved in a crime : estar involucrado en un crimen⟩ **3** CONCERN : concernir, afectar **4** CONNECT : conectar, relacionar **5** ENTAIL, INCLUDE : suponer, incluir, consistir *en* ⟨what does the job involve? : ¿en qué consiste el trabajo?⟩ **6 to be involved with someone** : tener una relación (amorosa) con alguien

involved [ɪnˈvɑlvd] *adj* **1** COMPLEX, INTRICATE : complicado, complejo **2** CONCERNED : interesado, afectado

involvement [ɪnˈvɑlvmənt] *n* **1** PARTICIPATION : participación *f*, complicidad *f* **2** RELATIONSHIP : relación *f*

invulnerable [ɪnˈvʌlnərəbəl] *adj* : invulnerable

inward[1] [ˈɪnwərd] *or* **inwards** [-wərdz] *adv* : hacia adentro, hacia el interior

inward[2] *adj* INSIDE : interior, interno

inwardly [ˈɪnwərdli] *adv* **1** MENTALLY, SPIRITUALLY : por dentro **2** INTERNALLY : internamente, interiormente **3** PRIVATELY : para sus adentros, para sí

iodide [ˈaɪəˌdaɪd] *n* : yoduro *m*

iodine [ˈaɪəˌdaɪn, -dən] *n* : yodo *m*, tintura *f* de yodo

iodize [ˈaɪəˌdaɪz] *vt* **-dized; -dizing** : yodar

ion [ˈaɪən, ˈaɪˌɑn] *n* : ion *m*

ionic [aɪˈɑnɪk] *adj* : iónico

ionize [ˈaɪəˌnaɪz] *v* **ionized; ionizing** : ionizar

ionosphere [aɪˈɑnəˌsfɪr] *n* : ionosfera *f*

iota [aɪˈoːtə] *n* : pizca *f*, ápice *m*

IOU [ˌaɪˌoːˈjuː] *n* : pagaré *m*, vale *m*

IPA [ˌaɪˌpiːˈeɪ] *n* International Phonetic Alphabet : AFI *m*

IQ [ˌaɪˈkjuː] *n* (intelligence quotient) : CI *m*, coeficiente *m* intelectual

Iranian [ɪˈreɪniən, -ˈræ-, -ˈrɑ-; aɪˈ-] *n* : iraní *mf* — **Iranian** *adj*

Iraqi [ɪˈrɑki] *n* : iraquí *mf* — **Iraqi** *adj*

irascibility [ɪˌræsəˈbɪləti] *n* : irascibilidad *f*

irascible [ɪˈræsəbəl] *adj* : irascible

irate [aɪˈreɪt] *adj* : furioso, airado, iracundo — **irately** *adv*

ire [ˈaɪr] *n* : ira *f*, cólera *f*

iridescence [ˌɪrəˈdɛsənts] *n* : iridiscencia *f*

iridescent [ˌɪrəˈdɛsənt] *adj* : iridiscente

iridium [ɪˈrɪdiəm] *n* : iridio *m*

iris [ˈaɪrəs] *n*, *pl* **irises** *or* **irides** [ˈaɪrəˌdiːz, ˈɪr-] **1** : iris *m* (del ojo) **2** : lirio *m* (planta)

Irish[1] [ˈaɪrɪʃ] *adj* : irlandés

Irish[2] **1** : irlandés *m* (idioma) **2 the Irish** *npl* : los irlandeses

Irishman [ˈaɪrɪʃmən] *n*, *pl* **-men** : irlandés *m*

Irishwoman [ˈaɪrɪʃˌwʊmən] *n*, *pl* **-women** : irlandesa *f*

irk [ˈərk] *vt* : fastidiar, irritar, preocupar

irksome [ˈərksəm] *adj* : irritante, fastidioso — **irksomely** *adv*

iron[1] [ˈaɪərn] *v* : planchar

iron[2] *n* **1** : hierro *m*, fierro *m* ⟨a will of iron : una voluntad de hierro, una voluntad férrea⟩ **2** : plancha *f* (para planchar la ropa)

ironclad [ˈaɪərnˌklæd] *adj* **1** : acorazado, blindado **2** STRICT : riguroso, estricto

ironic [aɪˈrɑnɪk] *or* **ironical** [-nɪkəl] *adj* : irónico — **ironically** [-kli] *adv*

ironing [ˈaɪərnɪŋ] *n* **1** PRESSING : planchada *f* **2** : ropa *f* para planchar

ironing board *n* : tabla *f* (de planchar)

ironwork [ˈaɪərnˌwərk] *n* **1** : obra *f* de hierro **2 ironworks** *npl* : fundición *f*

ironworker [ˈaɪərnˌwərkər] *n* : fundidor *m*, -dora *f*

irony [ˈaɪrəni] *n*, *pl* **-nies** : ironía *f*

irradiate [ɪˈreɪdiˌeɪt] *vt* **-ated; -ating** : irradiar, radiar

irradiation [ɪˌreɪdiˈeɪʃən] *n* : irradiación *f*, radiación *f*

irrational [ɪˈræʃənəl] *adj* : irracional — **irrationally** *adv*

irrationality [ɪˌræʃəˈnæləti] *n*, *pl* **-ties** : irracionalidad *f*

irreconcilable [ˌɪˌrɛkənˈsaɪləbəl] *adj* : irreconciliable

irrecoverable [ˌɪrɪˈkʌvərəbəl] *adj* : irrecuperable — **irrecoverably** [-bli] *adv*

irredeemable [ˌɪrɪˈdiːməbəl] *adj* **1** : irredimible (dícese de un bono) **2** HOPELESS : irremediable, irreparable

irreducible [ˌɪrɪˈduːsəbəl, -ˈdjuː-] *adj* : irreducible — **irreducibly** [-bli] *adv*

irrefutable [ˌɪrɪˈfjuːtəbəl, ɪrˈrɛfjə-] *adj* : irrefutable

irregular[1] [ɪˈrɛgjələr] *adj* : irregular — **irregularly** *adv*

irregular[2] *n* **1** : soldado *m* irregular **2 irregulars** *npl* : artículos *mpl* defectuosos

irregularity [ɪˌrɛgjəˈlærəti] *n, pl* **-ties** : irregularidad *f*

irrelevance [ɪˈrɛləvənts] *n* : irrelevancia *f*

irrelevant [ɪˈrɛləvənt] *adj* : irrelevante

irreligious [ˌɪrɪˈlɪdʒəs] *adj* : irreligioso

irreparable [ɪˈrɛpərəbəl] *adj* : irreparable

irreplaceable [ˌɪrɪˈpleɪsəbəl] *adj* : irreemplazable, insustituible

irrepressible [ˌɪrɪˈprɛsəbəl] *adj* : incontenible, incontrolable

irreproachable [ɪrɪˈproːtʃəbəl] *adj* : irreprochable, intachable

irresistible [ˌɪrɪˈzɪstəbəl] *adj* : irresistible — **irresistibly** [-bli] *adv*

irresolute [ɪˈrɛzəˌluːt] *adj* : irresoluto, indeciso

irresolutely [ɪˈrɛzəˌluːtli, -ˌrɛzəˈluːt-] *adv* : de manera indecisa

irresolution [ɪˌrɛzəˈluːʃən] *n* : irresolución *f*

irrespective of [ˌɪrɪˈspɛktɪvəv] *prep* : sin tomar en consideración, sin tener en cuenta

irresponsibility [ˌɪrɪˌspɑntsəˈbɪləti] *n, pl* **-ties** : irresponsabilidad *f*, falta *f* de responsabilidad

irresponsible [ˌɪrɪˈspɑntsəbəl] *adj* : irresponsable — **irresponsibly** [-bli] *adv*

irretrievable [ˌɪrɪˈtriːvəbəl] *adj* IRRECOVERABLE : irrecuperable

irreverence [ɪˈrɛvərənts] *n* : irreverencia *f*, falta *f* de respeto

irreverent [ɪˈrɛvərənt] *adj* : irreverente, irrespetuoso

irreversible [ˌɪrɪˈvərsəbəl] *adj* : irreversible

irrevocable [ɪˈrɛvəkəbəl] *adj* : irrevocable — **irrevocably** [-bli] *adv*

irrigate [ˈɪrəˌgeɪt] *vt* **-gated; -gating** : irrigar, regar

irrigation [ˌɪrəˈgeɪʃən] *n* : irrigación *f*, riego *m*

irritability [ˌɪrətəˈbɪləti] *n, pl* **-ties** : irritabilidad *f*

irritable [ˈɪrətəbəl] *adj* : irritable, colérico

irritably [ˈɪrətəbli] *adv* : con irritación

irritant[1] [ˈɪrətənt] *adj* : irritante

irritant[2] *n* : agente *m* irritante

irritate [ˈɪrəˌteɪt] *vt* **-tated; -tating** **1** ANNOY : irritar, molestar **2** : irritar (en medicina)

irritating [ˈɪrəˌteɪtɪŋ] *adj* : irritante

irritatingly [ˈɪrəˌteɪtɪŋli] *adv* : de modo irritante, fastidiosamente

irritation [ˌɪrəˈteɪʃən] *n* : irritación *f*

is → be

Islam [ɪsˈlɑm, ɪz-, -ˈlæm; ˈɪsˌlɑm, ˈɪz-, -ˌlæm] *n* : el Islam

Islamic [ɪsˈlɑmɪk, ɪz-, -ˈlæ-] *adj* : islámico

island [ˈaɪlənd] *n* : isla *f*

islander [ˈaɪləndər] *n* : isleño *m*, -ña *f*

isle [ˈaɪl] *n* : isla *f*, islote *m*

islet [ˈaɪlət] *n* : islote *m*

isolate [ˈaɪsəˌleɪt] *vt* **-lated; -lating** : aislar

isolated [ˈaɪsəˌleɪtəd] *adj* : aislado, solo

isolation [ˌaɪsəˈleɪʃən] *n* : aislamiento *m*

isometric [ˌaɪsəˈmɛtrɪk] *adj* : isométrico

isometrics [ˌaɪsəˈmɛtrɪks] *ns & pl* : isometría *f*

isosceles [aɪˈsɑsəˌliːz] *adj* : isósceles

isotope [ˈaɪsəˌtoːp] *n* : isótopo *m*

Israeli [ɪzˈreɪli] *n* : israelí *mf* — **Israeli** *adj*

issue[1] [ˈɪˌʃuː] *v* **-sued; -suing** *vi* **1** EMERGE : emerger, salir, fluir **2** DESCEND : descender (dícese de los padres o antepasados específicos) **3** EMANATE, RESULT : emanar, surgir, resultar — *vt* **1** EMIT : emitir **2** DISTRIBUTE : emitir, distribuir ⟨to issue a new stamp : emitir un sello nuevo⟩ **3** PUBLISH : publicar

issue[2] *n* **1** EMERGENCE, FLOW : emergencia *f*, flujo *m* **2** PROGENY : descendencia *f*, progenie *f* **3** OUTCOME, RESULT : desenlace *m*, resultado *m*, consecuencia *f* **4** MATTER, QUESTION : asunto *m*, cuestión *f* **5** PUBLICATION : publicación *f*, distribución *f*, emisión *f* **6** : número *m* (de un periódico o una revista)

isthmus [ˈɪsməs] *n* : istmo *m*

it [ˈɪt] *pron* **1** (*as subject; generally omitted*) : él, ella, ello ⟨it's a big building : es un edificio grande⟩ ⟨who was it? : ¿quién era?⟩ **2** (*as indirect object*) ⟨I'll give it some water : voy a darle agua⟩ **3** (*as direct object*) : lo, la ⟨give it to me : dámelo⟩ **4** (*as object of a preposition; generally omitted*) : él, ella, ello ⟨behind it : detrás, detrás de él⟩ **5** (*in impersonal constructions*) ⟨it's raining : está lloviendo⟩ ⟨it's 8 o'clock : son las ocho⟩ **6** (*as the implied subject or object of a verb*) ⟨it is necessary to study : es necesario estudiar⟩ ⟨to give it all one's got : dar lo mejor de sí⟩

Italian [ɪˈtæljən, aɪ-] *n* **1** : italiano *m*, -na *f* **2** : italiano *m* (idioma) — **Italian** *adj*

italic[1] [ɪˈtælɪk, aɪ-] *adj* : en cursiva, en bastardilla

italic[2] *n* : cursiva *f*, bastardilla *f*

italicize [ɪˈtæləˌsaɪz, aɪ-] *vt* **-cized; -cizing** : poner en cursiva

itch[1] [ˈɪtʃ] *vi* **1** : picar ⟨her arm itched : le pica el brazo⟩ **2** : morirse ⟨they were itching to go outside : se morían por salir⟩ — *vt* : dar picazón, hacer picar

itch² *n* **1** ITCHING : picazón *f*, picor *m*, comezón *f* **2** RASH : sarpullido *m*, erupción *f* **3** DESIRE : ansia *f*, deseo *m*

itchy ['ɪtʃi] *adj* **itchier; -est** : que pica, que da comezón

it'd ['ɪtəd] (*contraction of* **it had** *or* **it would**) → **have, would**

item ['aɪtəm] *n* **1** OBJECT : artículo *m*, pieza *f* ⟨item of clothing : prenda de vestir⟩ **2** : punto *m* (en una agenda), número *m* (en el teatro), ítem *m* (en un documento) **3 news item** : noticia *f*

itemize ['aɪtə,maɪz] *vt* **-ized; -izing** : detallar, enumerar, listar

itinerant [aɪ'tɪnərənt] *adj* : itinerante, ambulante

itinerary [aɪ'tɪnə,rɛri] *n, pl* **-aries** : itinerario *m*

it'll ['ɪtəl] (*contraction of* **it shall** *or* **it will**) → **shall, will**

its ['ɪts] *adj* : su, sus ⟨its kennel : su perrera⟩ ⟨a city and its inhabitants : una ciudad y sus habitantes⟩

it's ['ɪts] (*contraction of* **it is** *or* **it has**) → **be, have**

itself [ɪt'sɛlf] *pron* **1** (*used reflexively*) : se ⟨the cat gave itself a bath : el gato se bañó⟩ **2** (*used for emphasis*) : (él) mismo, (ella) misma, sí (mismo), solo ⟨he is courtesy itself : es la misma cortesía⟩ ⟨in and of itself : por sí mismo⟩ ⟨it opened by itself : se abrió solo⟩

IUD [,aɪju'di:] *n* **intrauterine** device : DIU *m*, dispositivo *m* intrauterino

I've ['aɪv] (*contraction of* **I have**) → **have**

ivory ['aɪvəri] *n, pl* **-ries 1** : marfil *m* **2** : color *m* de marfil

ivy ['aɪvi] *n, pl* **ivies 1** : hiedra *f*, yedra *f* **2** → **poison ivy**

J

j ['dʒeɪ] *n, pl* **j's** *or* **js** ['dʒeɪz] : décima letra del alfabeto inglés

jab¹ ['dʒæb] *v* **jabbed; jabbing** *vt* **1** PUNCTURE : clavar, pinchar **2** POKE : dar, golpear (con la punta de algo) ⟨he jabbed me in the ribs : me dio un codazo en las costillas⟩ — *vi* **to jab at** : dar, golpear

jab² *n* **1** PRICK : pinchazo *m* **2** POKE : golpe *m* abrupto

jabber¹ ['dʒæbər] *v* : farfullar

jabber² *n* : galimatías *m*, farfulla *f*

jack¹ ['dʒæk] *vt* **to jack up 1** : levantar (con un gato) **2** INCREASE : subir, aumentar

jack² *n* **1** : gato *m*, cric *m* ⟨hydraulic jack : gato hidráulico⟩ **2** FLAG : pabellón *m* **3** SOCKET : enchufe *m* hembra **4** : jota *f*, valet *m* ⟨jack of hearts : jota de corazones⟩ **5 jacks** *npl* : cantillos *mpl*

jackal ['dʒækəl] *n* : chacal *m*

jackass ['dʒæk,æs] *n* : asno *m*, burro *m*

jacket ['dʒækət] *n* **1** : chaqueta *f* **2** COVER : sobrecubierta *f* (de un libro), carátula *f* (de un disco)

jackhammer ['dʒæk,hæmər] *n* : martillo *m* neumático

jack-in-the-box ['dʒækɪndə,baks] *n* : caja *f* de sorpresa

jackknife¹ ['dʒæk,naɪf] *vi* **-knifed; -knifing** : doblarse como una navaja, plegarse

jackknife² *n* : navaja *f*

jack-of-all-trades *n* : persona *f* que sabe un poco de todo, persona *f* de muchos oficios

jack-o'-lantern ['dʒækə,læntərn] *n* : linterna *f* hecha de una calabaza

jackpot ['dʒæk,pat] *n* **1** : primer premio *m*, gordo *m* **2** **to hit the jackpot** : sacarse la lotería, sacarse el gordo

jackrabbit ['dʒæk,ræbət] *n* : liebre *f* grande de Norteamérica

jade ['dʒeɪd] *n* : jade *m*

jaded ['dʒeɪdəd] *adj* **1** TIRED : agotado **2** BORED : hastiado

jagged ['dʒægəd] *adj* : dentado, mellado

jaguar ['dʒæg,war, 'dʒægju,war] *n* : jaguar *m*

jai alai ['haɪ,laɪ] *n* : jai alai *m*, pelota *f* vasca

jail¹ ['dʒeɪl] *vt* : encarcelar

jail² *n* : cárcel *f*

jailbreak ['dʒeɪl,breɪk] *n* : fuga *f*, huida *f* (de la cárcel)

jailer *or* **jailor** ['dʒeɪlər] *n* : carcelero *m*, -ra *f*

jalapeño [,halə'peɪnjo, ,hæ-, -'pi:no] *n* : jalapeño *m*

jalopy [dʒə'lapi] *n, pl* **-lopies** : cacharro *m fam*, carro *m* destartalado

jalousie ['dʒæləsi] *n* : celosía *f*

jam¹ ['dʒæm] *v* **jammed; jamming** *vt* **1** CRAM : apiñar, embutir **2** BLOCK : atascar, atorar **3 to jam on the brakes** : frenar en seco — *vi* STICK : atascarse, atrancarse

jam² *n* **1** *or* **traffic jam** : atasco *m*, embotellamiento *m* (de tráfico) **2** PREDICAMENT : lío *m*, aprieto *m*, apuro *m* **3** : mermelada *f* ⟨strawberry jam : mermelada de fresa⟩

Jamaican [dʒə'meɪkən] *n* : jamaiquino *m*, -na *f*; jamaicano *m*, -na *f* — **Jamaican** *adj*

jamb ['dʒæm] *n* : jamba *f*

jamboree [,dʒæmbə'ri:] *n* : fiesta *f* grande

jangle¹ ['dʒæŋgəl] *v* **-gled; -gling** *vi* : hacer un ruido metálico — *vt* **1** : hacer sonar **2 to jangle one's nerves** : irritar, crispar

jangle² *n* : ruido *m* metálico

janitor ['dʒænətər] *n* : portero *m*, -ra *f*; conserje *mf*

January ['dʒænju,ɛri] *n* : enero *m*

Japanese [,dʒæpə'ni:z, -'ni:s] *n* **1**

: japonés *m*, -nesa *f* **2** : japonés *m* (idioma) — **Japanese** *adj*

jar¹ ['dʒɑr] *v* **jarred; jarring** *vi* **1** GRATE : chirriar **2** CLASH : desentonar **3** SHAKE : sacudirse **4 to jar on** : crispar, enervar — *vt* JOLT : sacudir

jar² *n* **1** GRATING : chirrido *m* **2** JOLT : vibración *f*, sacudida *f* **3** : tarro *m*, bote *m*, pote *m* ⟨a jar of honey : un tarro de miel⟩

jargon ['dʒɑrgən] *n* : jerga *f*

jasmine ['dʒæzmən] *n* : jazmín *m*

jasper ['dʒæspər] *n* : jaspe *m*

jaundice ['dʒɔndɪs] *n* : ictericia *f*

jaundiced ['dʒɔndɪst] *adj* **1** : ictérico **2** EMBITTERED, RESENTFUL : amargado, resentido, negativo ⟨with a jaundiced eye : con una actitud de cinismo⟩

jaunt ['dʒɔnt] *n* : excursión *f*, paseo *m*

jauntily ['dʒɔntəli] *adv* : animadamente

jauntiness ['dʒɔntinəs] *n* : animación *f*, vivacidad *f*

jaunty ['dʒɔnti] *adj* **-tier; -est 1** SPRIGHTLY : animado, alegre **2** RAKISH : desenvuelto, desenfadado

Javanese [ˌdʒævə'ni:z, ˌdʒɑ-, -'ni:s] *n* **1** : javanés *m* (idioma) **2** : javanés *m*, -nesa *f* — **Javanese** *adj*

javelin ['dʒævələn] *n* : jabalina *f*

jaw¹ ['dʒɔ] *vi* GAB : cotorrear *fam*, parlotear *fam*

jaw² *n* **1** : mandíbula *f*, quijada *f* **2** : mordaza *f* (de una herramienta) **3 the jaws of death** : las garras *f* de la muerte

jawbone ['dʒɔˌbo:n] *n* : mandíbula *f*

jay ['dʒeɪ] *n* : arrendajo *m*, chara *f Mex*, azulejo *m Mex*

jaybird ['dʒeɪˌbərd] → **jay**

jaywalk ['dʒeɪˌwɔk] *vi* : cruzar la calle sin prudencia

jaywalker ['dʒeɪˌwɔkər] *n* : peatón *m* imprudente

jazz¹ ['dʒæz] *vt* **to jazz up** : animar, alegrar

jazz² *n* : jazz *m*

jazzy ['dʒæzi] *adj* **jazzier; -est 1** : con ritmo de jazz **2** FLASHY, SHOWY : llamativo, ostentoso

jealous ['dʒɛləs] *adj* : celoso, envidioso — **jealously** *adv*

jealousy ['dʒɛləsi] *n* : celos *mpl*, envidia *f*

jeans ['dʒi:nz] *npl* : jeans *mpl*, vaqueros *mpl*

jeep ['dʒi:p] *n* : jeep *m*

jeer¹ ['dʒɪr] *vi* **1** BOO : abuchear **2** SCOFF : mofarse, burlarse — *vt* RIDICULE : mofarse de, burlarse de

jeer² *n* **1** : abucheo *m* **2** TAUNT : mofa *f*, burla *f*

Jehovah [dʒɪ'ho:və] *n* : Jehová *m*

jell ['dʒɛl] *vi* **1** SET : gelificarse, cuajar **2** FORM : cuajar, formarse (una idea, etc.)

jelly¹ ['dʒɛli] *v* **jellied; jellying** *vi* **1** JELL : gelificarse, cuajar **2** : hacer jalea — *vt* : gelificar

jelly² *n*, *pl* **-lies 1** : jalea *f* **2** GELATIN : gelatina *f*

jellyfish ['dʒɛliˌfɪʃ] *n* : medusa *f*

jeopardize ['dʒɛpərˌdaɪz] *vt* **-dized; -dizing** : arriesgar, poner en peligro

jeopardy ['dʒɛpərdi] *n* : peligro *m*, riesgo *m*

jerk¹ ['dʒərk] *vt* **1** JOLT : sacudir **2** TUG, YANK : darle un tirón a — *vi* JOLT : dar sacudidas ⟨the train jerked along : el tren iba moviéndose a sacudidas⟩

jerk² *n* **1** TUG : tirón *m*, jalón *m* **2** JOLT : sacudida *f* brusca **3** FOOL : estúpido *m*, -da *f*; idiota *mf*

jerkin ['dʒərkən] *n* : chaqueta *f* sin mangas, chaleco *m*

jerky ['dʒərki] *adj* **jerkier; -est 1** : espasmódico (dícese de los movimientos) **2** CHOPPY : inconexo (dícese de la prosa) — **jerkily** [-kəli] *adv*

jerry–built ['dʒɛriˌbɪlt] *adj* : mal construido, chapucero

jersey ['dʒərzi] *n*, *pl* **-seys** : jersey *m*

jest¹ ['dʒɛst] *vi* : bromear

jest² *n* : broma *f*, chiste *m*

jester ['dʒɛstər] *n* : bufón *m*, -fona *f*

Jesuit ['dʒɛzuət] *n* : jesuita *m* — **Jesuit** *adj*

Jesus ['dʒi:zəs, -zəz] *n* **1** : Jesús *m* **2 Jesus Christ** : Jesucristo *m* **3 Jesus (Christ)!** *fam* : ¡por Dios!

jet¹ ['dʒɛt] *v* **jetted; jetting** *vt* SPOUT : arrojar a chorros — *vi* **1** GUSH : salir a chorros, chorrear **2** FLY : viajar en avión, volar

jet² *n* **1** STREAM : chorro *m* **2 or jet airplane** : avión *m* a reacción, reactor *m* **3** : azabache *m* (mineral) **4 jet engine** : reactor *m*, motor *m* a reacción **5 jet lag** : desajuste *m* de horario (debido a un vuelo largo)

jet–propelled *adj* : a reacción

jetsam ['dʒɛtsəm] *n* **flotsam and jetsam** : restos *mpl*, desechos *mpl*

jettison ['dʒɛtəsən] *vt* **1** : echar al mar **2** DISCARD : desechar, deshacerse de

jetty ['dʒɛti] *n*, *pl* **-ties 1** PIER, WHARF : desembarcadero *m*, muelle *m* **2** BREAKWATER : malecón *m*, rompeolas *m*

Jew ['dʒu:] *n* : judío *m*, -día *f*

jewel ['dʒu:əl] *n* **1** : joya *f*, alhaja *f* **2** GEM : piedra *f* preciosa, gema *f* **3** : rubí *m* (de un reloj) **4** TREASURE : joya *f*, tesoro *m*

jeweler *or* **jeweller** ['dʒu:ələr] *n* : joyero *m*, -ra *f*

jewelry ['dʒu:əlri] *n* : joyas *fpl*, alhajas *fpl*

Jewish ['dʒu:ɪʃ] *adj* : judío

jib ['dʒɪb] *n* : foque *m* (de un barco)

jibe ['dʒaɪb] *vi* **jibed; jibing** AGREE : concordar

jiffy ['dʒɪfi] *n*, *pl* **-fies** : santiamén *m*, segundo *m*, momento *m*

jig¹ ['dʒɪg] *vi* **jigged; jigging** : bailar la giga

jig² *n* **1** : giga *f* **2 the jig is up** : se acabó la fiesta

jigger ['dʒɪgər] *n* : medida de 1 a 2 onzas (para licores)

jiggle[1] ['dʒɪgəl] v **-gled; -gling** vt : agitar o sacudir ligeramente — vi : agitarse, vibrar

jiggle[2] n : sacudida f, vibración f

jigsaw ['dʒɪg,sɔ] n **1** : sierra f de vaivén **2 jigsaw puzzle** : rompecabezas m

jilt ['dʒɪlt] vt : dejar plantado, dar calabazas a

jimmy[1] ['dʒɪmi] vt **-mied; -mying** : forzar con una palanqueta

jimmy[2] n, pl **-mies** : palanqueta f

jingle[1] ['dʒɪŋgəl] v **-gled; -gling** vi : tintinear — vt : hacer sonar

jingle[2] n **1** TINKLE : tintineo m, retintín m **2** : canción f rimada

jingoism ['dʒɪŋgo,ɪzəm] n : jingoísmo m, patriotería f

jingoistic [,dʒɪŋgo'ɪstɪk] or **jingoist** ['dʒɪŋgoɪst] adj : jingoísta, patriotero

jinx[1] ['dʒɪŋks] vt : traer mala suerte a, salar CoRI, Mex

jinx[2] n **1** : cenizo m, -za f **2 to put a jinx on** : echarle el mal de ojo a

jitters ['dʒɪtərz] npl : nervios mpl ⟨he got the jitters : se puso nervioso⟩

jittery ['dʒɪtəri] adj : nervioso

job ['dʒab] n **1** : trabajo m ⟨he did odd jobs for her : le hizo algunos trabajos⟩ **2** CHORE, TASK : tarea f, quehacer m **3** EMPLOYMENT : trabajo m, empleo m, puesto m

jobber ['dʒabər] n MIDDLEMAN : intermediario m, -ria f

jock ['dʒak] n : deportista mf, atleta mf

jockey[1] ['dʒaki] v **-eyed; -eying** vt **1** MANIPULATE : manipular **2** MANEUVER : maniobrar — vi **to jockey for position** : maniobrar para conseguir algo

jockey[2] n, pl **-eys** : jockey mf

jocose [dʒo'ko:s] adj : jocoso

jocular ['dʒakjulər] adj : jocoso — **jocularly** adv

jocularity [,dʒakju'lærəti] n : jocosidad f

jodhpurs ['dʒadpərz] npl : pantalones mpl de montar

jog[1] ['dʒag] v **jogged; jogging** vt **1** NUDGE : dar, empujar, codear **2 to jog one's memory** : refrescar la memoria — vi **1** RUN : correr despacio, trotar, hacer footing (como ejercicio) **2** TRUDGE : andar a trote corto

jog[2] n **1** PUSH, SHAKE : empujoncito m, sacudida f leve **2** TROT : trote m corto, footing m (en deportes) **3** TWIST : recodo m, vuelta f, curva f

jogger ['dʒagər] n : persona f que hace footing

join ['dʒɔɪn] vt **1** CONNECT, LINK : unir, juntar ⟨to join in marriage : unir en matrimonio⟩ **2** ADJOIN : lindar con, colindar con **3** MEET : reunirse con, encontrarse con ⟨we joined them for lunch : nos reunimos con ellos para almorzar⟩ **4** : hacerse socio de (una organización), afiliarse a (un partido), entrar en (una empresa) — vi **1** UNITE : unirse **2** MERGE : empalmar (dícese de las carreteras), confluir (dícese de

los ríos) **3 to join up** : hacerse socio, enrolarse

joiner ['dʒɔɪnər] n **1** CARPENTER : carpintero m, -ra f **2** : persona f que se une a varios grupos

joint[1] ['dʒɔɪnt] adj : conjunto, colectivo, mutuo ⟨a joint effort : un esfuerzo conjunto⟩ — **jointly** adv

joint[2] n **1** : articulación f, coyuntura f ⟨out of joint : dislocado⟩ **2** ROAST : asado m **3** JUNCTURE : juntura f, unión f **4** DIVE : antro m, tasca f

joist ['dʒɔɪst] n : viga f

joke[1] ['dʒo:k] vi **joked; joking** : bromear

joke[2] n **1** STORY : chiste m **2** PRANK : broma f

joker ['dʒo:kər] n **1** PRANKSTER : bromista mf **2** : comodín m (en los naipes)

jokingly ['dʒo:kɪŋli] adv : en broma

jollity ['dʒaləti] n, pl **-ties** MERRIMENT : alegría f, regocijo m

jolly ['dʒali] adj **-lier; -est** : alegre, jovial

jolt[1] ['dʒo:lt] vi **1** JERK : dar tumbos, dar sacudidas — vt : sacudir

jolt[2] n **1** JERK : sacudida f brusca **2** SHOCK : golpe m (emocional)

jonquil ['dʒankwɪl] n : junquillo m

Jordanian [dʒɔr'deɪniən] n : jordano m, -na f — **Jordanian** adj

josh ['dʒaʃ] vt TEASE : tomarle el pelo (a alguien) — vi JOKE : bromear

jostle ['dʒasəl] v **-tled; -tling** vi **1** SHOVE : empujar, dar empellones **2** CONTEND : competir — vt **1** SHOVE : empujar **2 to jostle one's way** : abrirse paso a empellones

jot[1] ['dʒat] vt **jotted; jotting** : anotar, apuntar ⟨jot it down : apúntalo⟩

jot[2] n BIT : ápice m, jota f, pizca f

jounce[1] ['dʒaʊnts] v **jounced; jouncing** vt JOLT : sacudir — vi : dar tumbos, dar sacudidas

jounce[2] n JOLT : sacudida f, tumbo m

journal ['dʒərnəl] n **1** DIARY : diario m **2** PERIODICAL : revista f, publicación f periódica **3** NEWSPAPER : periódico m, diario m

journalism ['dʒərnəl,ɪzəm] n : periodismo m

journalist ['dʒərnəlɪst] n : periodista mf

journalistic [,dʒərnəl'ɪstɪk] adj : periodístico

journey[1] ['dʒərni] vi **-neyed; -neying** : viajar

journey[2] n, pl **-neys** : viaje m

journeyman ['dʒərnimən] n, pl **-men** [-mən, -,mɪn] : oficial m

joust[1] ['dʒaʊst] vi : justar

joust[2] n : justa f

jovial ['dʒo:viəl] adj : jovial — **jovially** adv

joviality [,dʒo:vi'æləti] n : jovialidad f

jowl ['dʒaʊl] n **1** JAW : mandíbula f **2** CHEEK : mejilla f, cachete m

joy ['dʒɔɪ] n **1** HAPPINESS : gozo m, alegría f, felicidad f **2** DELIGHT : placer m, deleite m ⟨the child is a real joy : el niño es un verdadero placer⟩

joyful ['dʒɔɪfəl] adj : gozoso, alegre, feliz — joyfully adv

joyless ['dʒɔɪləs] adj : sin alegría, triste

joyous ['dʒɔɪəs] adj : alegre, feliz, eufórico — joyously adv

joyousness ['dʒɔɪəsnəs] n : alegría f, felicidad f, euforia f

joyride ['dʒɔɪˌraɪd] n : paseo m temerario e irresponsable (en coche)

joystick ['dʒɔɪˌstɪk] n : joystick m

jubilant ['dʒuːbələnt] adj : jubiloso, alborozado — jubilantly adv

jubilation [ˌdʒuːbə'leɪʃən] n : júbilo m

jubilee ['dʒuːbəˌliː] n 1 : quincuagésimo aniversario m 2 CELEBRATION : celebración f, festejos mpl

Judaic [dʒu'deɪɪk] adj : judaico

Judaism ['dʒuːdəˌɪzəm, 'dʒuːˌdiː-, 'dʒuː-ˌdeɪ-] n : judaísmo m

judge¹ ['dʒʌdʒ] vt judged; judging 1 ASSESS : evaluar, juzgar 2 DEEM : juzgar, considerar 3 TRY : juzgar (ante el tribunal) 4 judging by : a juzgar por

judge² n 1 : juez mf, jueza f 2 to be a good judge of : saber juzgar a, entender mucho de

judgment or judgement ['dʒʌdʒ-mənt] n 1 RULING : fallo m, sentencia f 2 OPINION : opinión f 3 DISCERNMENT : juicio m, discernimiento m

judgmental [ˌdʒʌdʒ'mntəl] adj : crítico — judgmentally adv

judicature ['dʒuːdɪkəˌtʃur] n : judicatura f

judicial [dʒu'dɪʃəl] adj : judicial — judicially adv

judiciary¹ [dʒu'dɪʃiˌri, -'dɪʃəri] adj : judicial

judiciary² n 1 JUDICATURE : judicatura f 2 : poder m judicial

judicious [dʒu'dɪʃəs] adj SOUND, WISE : juicioso, sensato — judiciously adv

judo ['dʒuːˌdoː] n : judo m

jug ['dʒʌg] n 1 : jarra f, jarro m, cántaro m 2 JAIL : cárcel f, chirona f fam

juggernaut ['dʒʌgərˌnɔt] n : gigante m, fuerza f irresistible ⟨a political juggernaut : un gigante político⟩

juggle ['dʒʌgəl] v -gled; -gling vt 1 : hacer juegos malabares con 2 MANIPULATE : manipular, jugar con — vi : hacer juegos malabares

juggler ['dʒʌgələr] n : malabarista mf

jugular ['dʒʌgjələr] adj : yugular ⟨jugular vein : vena yugular⟩

juice ['dʒuːs] n 1 : jugo m (de carne, de frutas) m, zumo m (de frutas) 2 ELECTRICITY : electricidad f, luz f

juicer ['dʒuːsər] n : exprimidor m

juiciness ['dʒuːsinəs] n : jugosidad f

juicy ['dʒuːsi] adj juicier, -est 1 SUCCULENT : jugoso, suculento 2 PROFITABLE : jugoso, lucrativo 3 RACY : picante

jukebox ['dʒuːkˌbaks] n : rocola f, máquina f de discos

julep ['dʒuːləp] n : bebida f hecha con whisky americano y menta

July [dʒu'laɪ] n : julio m

jumble¹ ['dʒʌmbəl] vt -bled; -bling : mezclar, revolver

jumble² n : revoltijo m, fárrago m, embrollo m

jumbo¹ ['dʒʌmˌboː] adj : gigante, enorme, de tamaño extra grande

jumbo² n, pl -bos : coloso m, cosa f de tamaño extra grande

jump¹ ['dʒʌmp] vi 1 LEAP : saltar, brincar 2 START : levantarse de un salto, sobresaltarse 3 MOVE, SHIFT : moverse, pasar ⟨to jump from job to job : pasar de un empleo a otro⟩ 4 INCREASE, RISE : dar un salto, aumentarse de golpe, subir bruscamente 5 BUSTLE : animarse, ajetrearse 6 to jump to conclusions : sacar conclusiones precipitadas — vt 1 : saltar ⟨to jump a fence : saltar una valla⟩ 2 SKIP : saltarse 3 ATTACK : atacar, asaltar 4 to jump the gun : precipitarse

jump² n 1 LEAP : salto m 2 START : sobresalto m, respingo m 3 INCREASE : subida f brusca, aumento m 4 ADVANTAGE : ventaja f ⟨we got the jump on them : le llevamos la ventaja⟩

jumper ['dʒʌmpər] n 1 : saltador m, -dora f (en deportes) 2 : jumper m, vestido m sin mangas

jumpy ['dʒʌmpi] adj jumpier; -est : asustadizo, nervioso

junction ['dʒʌŋkʃən] n 1 JOINING : unión f 2 : cruce m (de calles), empalme m (de un ferrocarril), confluencia f (de ríos)

juncture ['dʒʌŋktʃər] n 1 UNION : juntura f, unión f 2 MOMENT, POINT : coyuntura f ⟨at this juncture : en esta coyuntura, en este momento⟩

June ['dʒuːn] n : junio m

jungle ['dʒʌŋgəl] n : jungla f, selva f

junior¹ ['dʒuːnjər] adj 1 YOUNGER : más joven ⟨John Smith, Junior : John Smith, hijo⟩ 2 SUBORDINATE : subordinado, subalterno

junior² n 1 : persona f de menor edad ⟨she's my junior : es menor que yo⟩ 2 SUBORDINATE : subalterno m, -na f; subordinado m, -da f 3 : estudiante mf de penúltimo año

juniper ['dʒuːnəpər] n : enebro m

junk¹ ['dʒʌŋk] vt : echar a la basura

junk² n 1 RUBBISH : desechos mpl, desperdicios mpl 2 STUFF : trastos mpl fam, cachivaches mpl fam 3 piece of junk : cacharro m, porquería f

junket ['dʒʌŋkət] n : viaje m (pagado con dinero público)

junta ['hʊntə, 'dʒʌn-, 'hʌn-] n : junta f militar

Jupiter ['dʒuːpətər] n : Júpiter m

jurisdiction [ˌdʒurəs'dɪkʃən] n : jurisdicción f

jurisprudence [ˌdʒurəs'pruːdənts] n : jurisprudencia f

jurist ['dʒurɪst] n : jurista mf; magistrado m, -da f

juror ['dʒʊrər] *n* : jurado *m*, -da *f*

jury ['dʒʊri] *n, pl* **-ries** : jurado *m*

just¹ ['dʒʌst] *adv* **1** EXACTLY : justo, precisamente, exactamente **2** POSSIBLY : posiblemente ⟨it just might work : tal vez resulte⟩ **3** BARELY : justo, apenas ⟨just in time : justo a tiempo⟩ **4** ONLY : sólo, solamente, nada más ⟨just us : sólo nosotros⟩ **5** QUITE : muy, simplemente ⟨it's just horrible! : ¡qué horrible!⟩ **6 to have just (done something)** : acabar de (hacer algo) ⟨he just called : acaba de llamar⟩

just² *adj* : justo — **justly** *adv*

justice ['dʒʌstɪs] *n* **1** : justicia *f* **2** JUDGE : juez *mf*, jueza *f*

justification [ˌdʒʌstəfə'keɪʃən] *n* : justificación *f*

justify ['dʒʌstəˌfaɪ] *vt* **-fied; -fying** : justificar — **justifiable** [ˌdʒʌstə'faɪəbəl] *adj*

jut ['dʒʌt] *vi* **jutted; jutting** : sobresalir

jute ['dʒuːt] *n* : yute *m*

juvenile¹ ['dʒuːvəˌnaɪl, -vənəl] *adj* **1** : juvenil ⟨juvenile delinquent : delincuente juvenil⟩ ⟨juvenile court : tribunal de menores⟩ **2** CHILDISH : infantil

juvenile² *n* : menor *mf*

juxtapose ['dʒʌkstəˌpoːz] *vt* **-posed; -posing** : yuxtaponer

juxtaposition [ˌdʒʌkstəpə'zɪʃən] *n* : yuxtaposición *f*

K

k ['keɪ] *n, pl* **k's** *or* **ks** ['keɪz] : undécima letra del alfabeto inglés

kaiser ['kaɪzər] *n* : káiser *m*

kale ['keɪl] *n* : col *f* rizada

kaleidoscope [kə'laɪdəˌskoːp] *n* : calidoscopio *m*

kamikaze [ˌkɑmɪ'kɑzi] *n* : kamikaze *m* — **kamikaze** *adj*

kangaroo [ˌkæŋgə'ruː] *n, pl* **-roos** : canguro *m*

kaolin ['keɪələn] *n* : caolín *m*

karaoke [ˌkæri'oːki] *n* : karaoke *m*

karat ['kærət] *n* : quilate *m*

karate [kə'rɑti] *n* : karate *m*

katydid ['keɪtiˌdɪd] *n* : saltamontes *m*

kayak ['kaɪˌæk] *n* : cayac *m*, kayak *m*

keel¹ ['kiːl] *vi* to keel over : volcar (dícese de un barco), desplomarse (dícese de una persona)

keel² *n* : quilla *f*

keen ['kiːn] *adj* **1** SHARP : afilado, filoso ⟨a keen blade : una hoja afilada⟩ **2** PENETRATING : cortante, penetrante ⟨a keen wind : un viento cortante⟩ **3** ENTHUSIASTIC : entusiasta **4** ACUTE : agudo, fino ⟨keen hearing : oído fino⟩ ⟨keen intelligence : inteligencia aguda⟩

keenly ['kiːnli] *adv* **1** ENTHUSIASTICALLY : con entusiasmo **2** INTENSELY : vivamente, profundamente ⟨keenly aware of : muy consciente de⟩

keenness ['kiːnnəs] *n* **1** SHARPNESS : lo afilado, lo filoso **2** ENTHUSIASM : entusiasmo *m* **3** ACUTENESS : agudeza *f*

keep¹ ['kiːp] *v* **kept** ['kɛpt]; **keeping** *vt* **1** : cumplir (la palabra a uno), acudir a (una cita) **2** OBSERVE : observar (una fiesta) **3** GUARD : guardar, cuidar **4** CONTINUE : mantener ⟨to keep silence : mantener silencio⟩ **5** SUPPORT : mantener (una familia) **6** RAISE : criar (animales) **7** : llevar, escribir (un diario, etc.) **8** RETAIN : guardar, conservar, quedarse con **9** STORE : guardar **10** DETAIN : hacer quedar, detener **11** PRESERVE : guardar ⟨to keep a secret : guardar un secreto⟩ — *vi* **1** : conservarse (dícese de los alimentos) **2** CONTINUE : seguir, no dejar ⟨he keeps on pestering us : no deja de molestarnos⟩ **3 to keep from** : abstenerse de ⟨I couldn't keep from laughing : no podía contener la risa⟩

keep² *n* **1** TOWER : torreón *m* (de un castillo), torre *f* del homenaje **2** SUSTENANCE : manutención *f*, sustento *m* **3 for keeps** : para siempre

keeper ['kiːpər] *n* **1** : guarda *mf* (en un zoológico); conservador *m*, -dora *f* (en un museo) **2** GAMEKEEPER : guardabosque *mf*

keeping ['kiːpɪŋ] *n* **1** CONFORMITY : conformidad *f*, acuerdo *m* ⟨in keeping with : de acuerdo con⟩ **2** CARE : cuidado *m* ⟨in the keeping of : al cuidado de⟩

keepsake ['kiːpˌseɪk] *n* : recuerdo *m*

keep up *vt* CONTINUE, MAINTAIN : mantener, seguir con — *vi* **1** : mantenerse al corriente ⟨he kept up with the news : se mantenía al tanto de las noticias⟩ **2** CONTINUE : continuar **3 to keep up with someone** : mantener contacto con alguien

keg ['kɛg] *n* : barril *m*

kelp ['kɛlp] *n* : alga *f* marina

ken ['kɛn] *n* **1** SIGHT : vista *f*, alcance *m* de la vista **2** UNDERSTANDING : comprensión *f*, alcance *m* del conocimiento ⟨it's beyond his ken : no lo puede entender⟩

kennel ['kɛnəl] *n* : caseta *f* para perros, perrera *f*

Kenyan ['kɛnjən, 'kiːn-] *n* : keniano *m*, -na *f* — **Kenyan** *adj*

kept → keep

kerchief ['kərtʃəf, -ˌtʃiːf] *n* : pañuelo *m*

kernel ['kərnəl] *n* **1** : almendra *f* (de semillas y nueces) **2** : grano *m* (de cereales) **3** CORE : meollo *m* ⟨a kernel of truth : un fondo de verdad⟩

kerosene *or* **kerosine** ['kɛrəˌsiːn, ˌkɛrə'-] *n* : queroseno *m*, kerosén *m*, kerosene *m*

ketchup ['kɛtʃəp, 'kæ-] n : salsa f catsup

kettle ['kɛtəl] n 1 : hervidor m, pava f Arg, Bol, Chile 2 → teakettle

kettledrum ['kɛtəl,drʌm] n : timbal m

key¹ ['ki:] vt 1 ATTUNE : adaptar, adecuar 2 to key up : poner nervioso, inquietar

key² adj : clave, fundamental

key³ n 1 : llave f 2 SOLUTION : clave f, soluciones fpl 3 : tecla f (de un piano o una máquina) 4 : tono m, tonalidad f (en la música) 5 ISLET, REEF : cayo m, islote m

keyboard ['ki:,bord] n : teclado m

keyhole ['ki:,ho:l] n : bocallave f, ojo m (de una cerradura)

keynote¹ ['ki:,no:t] vt -noted; -noting 1 : establecer la tónica de (en música) 2 : pronunciar el discurso principal de

keynote² n 1 : tónica f (en música) 2 : idea f fundamental

keystone ['ki:,sto:n] n : clave f, dovela f

keystroke ['ki:,stro:k] n : pulsación f (de tecla)

khaki ['kæki, 'kɑ-] n : caqui m

khan ['kɑn, 'kæn] n : kan m

kibbutz [kə'buts, -'bu:ts] n, pl -butzim [-,bu'si:m, -,bu:t-] : kibutz m

kibitz ['kɪbɪts] vi : dar consejos molestos

kibitzer ['kɪbɪtsər, kə'bɪt-] n : persona f que da consejos molestos

kick¹ ['kɪk] vi 1 : dar patadas (dícese de una persona), cocear (dícese de un animal) 2 PROTEST : patalear, protestar 3 RECOIL : dar un culatazo (dícese de un arma de fuego) — vt : patear, darle una patada (a alguien)

kick² n 1 : patada f, puntapié m, coz f (de un animal) 2 RECOIL : culatazo m (de un arma de fuego) 3 fuerza f (a drink with a kick : una bebida fuerte)

kicker ['kɪkər] n : pateador m, -dora f (en deportes)

kickoff ['kɪk,ɔf] n : saque m (inicial)

kick off vi 1 : hacer el saque inicial (en deportes) 2 BEGIN : empezar — vt : empezar

kid¹ ['kɪd] v kidded; kidding vt 1 FOOL : engañar 2 TEASE : tomarle el pelo (a alguien) — vi JOKE : bromear ⟨I'm only kidding : lo digo en broma⟩

kid² n 1 : chivo m, -va f; cabrito m, -ta f 2 CHILD : chico m, -ca f; niño m, -ña f

kidder ['kɪdər] n : bromista mf

kiddingly ['kɪdɪŋli] adv : en broma

kidnap ['kɪd,næp] vt -napped or -naped [-,næpt], -napping or -naping [-,næpɪŋ] : secuestrar, raptar

kidnapper or **kidnaper** ['kɪd,næpər] n : secuestrador m, -dora f; raptor m, -tora f

kidnapping ['kɪd,næpɪŋ] n : secuestro m

kidney ['kɪdni] n, pl -neys : riñón m

kidney bean n : frijol m

kill¹ ['kɪl] vt 1 : matar 2 END : acabar con, poner fin a 3 to kill time : matar el tiempo

kill² n 1 KILLING : matanza f 2 PREY : presa f

killer ['kɪlər] n : asesino m, -na f

killjoy ['kɪl,dʒɔɪ] n : aguafiestas mf

kiln ['kɪl, 'kɪln] n : horno m

kilo ['ki:,lo:] n, pl -los : kilo m

kilobyte ['kɪlə,baɪt] n : kilobyte m

kilocycle ['kɪlə,saɪkəl] n : kilociclo m

kilogram ['kɪlə,græm, 'ki:-] n : kilogramo m

kilohertz ['kɪlə,hərts] n : kilohertzio m

kilometer [kɪ'lɑmətər, 'kɪlə,mi:-] n : kilómetro m

kilowatt ['kɪlə,wɑt] n : kilovatio m

kilt ['kɪlt] n : falda f escocesa

kilter ['kɪltər] n 1 ORDER : buen estado m 2 out of kilter : descompuesto, estropeado

kimono [kə'mo:no, -nə] n, pl -nos : kimono m, quimono m

kin ['kɪn] n : familiares mpl, parientes mpl

kind¹ ['kaɪnd] adj : amable, bondadoso, benévolo

kind² n 1 ESSENCE : esencia f ⟨a difference in degree, not in kind : una diferencia cuantitativa y no cualitativa⟩ 2 CATEGORY : especie f, género m 3 TYPE : clase f, tipo m, índole f

kindergarten ['kɪndər,gɑrtən, -dən] n : kinder m, kindergarten m, jardín m de infantes, jardín m de niños Mex

kindhearted [,kaɪnd'hɑrtəd] adj : bondadoso, de buen corazón

kindle ['kɪndəl] v -dled; -dling vt 1 IGNITE : encender 2 AROUSE : despertar, suscitar — vi : encenderse

kindliness ['kaɪndlinəs] n : bondad f

kindling ['kɪndlɪŋ, 'kɪndlən] n : astillas fpl, leña f

kindly¹ ['kaɪndli] adv 1 AMIABLY : amablemente, bondadosamente 2 COURTEOUSLY : cortésmente, con cortesía ⟨we kindly ask you not smoke : le rogamos que no fumen⟩ 3 PLEASE : por favor 4 to take kindly to : aceptar de buena gana

kindly² adj -lier; -est : bondadoso, amable

kindness ['kaɪndnəs] n : bondad f

kind of adv SOMEWHAT : un tanto, algo

kindred¹ ['kɪndrəd] adj SIMILAR : similar, afín ⟨kindred spirits : almas gemelas⟩

kindred² n 1 FAMILY : familia f, parentela f 2 → kin

kinfolk ['kɪn,fo:k] or **kinfolks** [-,fo:ks] npl → kin

king ['kɪŋ] n : rey m

kingdom ['kɪŋdəm] n : reino m

kingfisher ['kɪŋ,fɪʃər] n : martín m pescador

kingly ['kɪŋli] adj -lier; -est : regio, real

king-size ['kɪŋ,saɪz] or **king-sized** [-,saɪzd] adj : de tamaño muy grande, extra largo (dícese de cigarrillos)

kink ['kɪŋk] n 1 : rizo m (en el pelo), vuelta f (en una cuerda) 2 CRAMP

: calambre m ⟨to have a kink in the neck : tener tortícolis⟩

kinky ['kɪŋki] *adj* **-kier; -est** : rizado (dícese del pelo), enroscado (dícese de una cuerda)

kinship ['kɪn,ʃɪp] *n* : parentesco *m*

kinsman ['kɪnzmən] *n, pl* **-men** [-mən, -,men] : familiar *m*, pariente *m*

kinswoman ['kɪnz,wʊmən] *n, pl* **-women** [-,wɪmən] : familiar *f*, pariente *f*

kiosk ['ki:,ɑsk] *n* : quiosco *m*

kipper ['kɪpər] *n* : arenque *m* ahumado

kiss¹ ['kɪs] *vt* : besar — *vi* : besarse

kiss² *n* : beso *m*

kit ['kɪt] *n* **1** SET : juego *m*, kit *m* **2** CASE : estuche *m*, caja *f* **3 first–aid kit** : botiquín *m* **4 tool kit** : caja *f* de herramientas **5 travel kit** : neceser *m*

kitchen ['kɪtʃən] *n* : cocina *f*

kite ['kaɪt] *n* **1** : milano *m* (ave) **2** : cometa *f*, papalote *m Mex* ⟨to fly a kite : hacer volar una cometa⟩

kith ['kɪθ] *n* : amigos *mpl* ⟨kith and kin : amigos y parientes⟩

kitten ['kɪtən] *n* : gatito *m*, -ta *f*

kitty ['kɪti] *n, pl* **-ties 1** FUND, POOL : bote *m*, fondo *m* común **2** CAT : gato *m*, gatito *m*

kitty–corner ['kɪti,kɔrnər] *or* **kitty–cornered** [-nərd] → **catercorner**

kiwi ['ki:,wi:] *n* : kiwi *m*

kleptomania [,klɛptə'meɪniə] *n* : cleptomanía *f*

kleptomaniac [,klɛptə'meɪni,æk] *n* : cleptómano *m*, -na *f*

knack ['næk] *n* : maña *f*, facilidad *f*

knapsack ['næp,sæk] *n* : mochila *f*, morral *m*

knave ['neɪv] *n* : bellaco *m*, pícaro *m*

knead ['ni:d] *vt* **1** : amasar, sobar **2** MASSAGE : masajear

knee ['ni:] *n* : rodilla *f*

kneecap ['ni:,kæp] *n* : rótula *f*

kneel ['ni:l] *vi* **knelt** ['nɛlt] *or* **kneeled** ['ni:ld]; **kneeling** : arrodillarse, ponerse de rodillas

knell ['nɛl] *n* : doble *m*, toque *m* ⟨death knell : toque de difuntos⟩

knew → **know**

knickers ['nɪkərz] *npl* : pantalones *mpl* bombachos de media pierna

knickknack ['nɪk,næk] *n* : chuchería *f*, baratija *f*

knife¹ ['naɪf] *vt* **knifed** ['naɪft]; **knifing** : acuchillar, apuñalar

knife² *n, pl* **knives** ['naɪvz] : cuchillo *m*

knight¹ ['naɪt] *vt* : conceder el título de *Sir* a

knight² *n* **1** : caballero *m* ⟨knight errant : caballero andante⟩ **2** : caballo *m* (en ajedrez) **3** : uno que tiene el título de *Sir*

knighthood ['naɪt,hʊd] *n* **1** : caballería *f* **2** : título *m* de *Sir*

knightly ['naɪtli] *adj* : caballeresco

knit ['nɪt] *v* **knit** *or* **knitted** ['nɪtəd]; **knitting** *vt* **1** UNITE : unir, enlazar **2** : tejer ⟨to knit a sweater : tejer un suéter⟩ **3**

to knit one's brows : fruncir el ceño — *vi* **1** : tejer **2** : soldarse (dícese de los huesos)

knit² *n* : prenda *f* tejida

knitter ['nɪtər] *n* : tejedor *m*, -dora *f*

knob ['nɑb] *n* **1** LUMP : bulto *m*, protuberancia *f* **2** HANDLE : perilla *f*, tirador *m*, botón *m*

knobbed ['nɑbd] *adj* **1** KNOTTY : nudoso **2** : que tiene perilla o botón

knobby ['nɑbi] *adj* **knobbier; -est 1** KNOTTY : nudoso **2 knobby knees** : rodillas *fpl* huesudas

knock¹ ['nɑk] *vt* **1** HIT, RAP : golpear, golpetear **2** : hacer chocar ⟨they knocked heads : se dieron en la cabeza⟩ **3** CRITICIZE : criticar — *vi* **1** RAP : dar un golpe, llamar (a la puerta) **2** COLLIDE : darse, chocar

knock² *n* : golpe *m*, llamada *f* (a la puerta), golpeteo *m* (de un motor)

knock down *vt* : derribar, echar al suelo

knocker ['nɑkər] *n* : aldaba *f*, llamador *m*

knock–kneed ['nɑk'ni:d] *adj* : patizambo

knockout ['nɑk,aʊt] *n* : nocaut *m*, knockout *m* (en deportes)

knock out *vt* : dejar sin sentido, poner fuera de combate (en el boxeo)

knoll ['no:l] *n* : loma *f*, otero *m*, montículo *m*

knot¹ ['nɑt] *v* **knotted; knotting** *vt* : anudar — *vi* : anudarse

knot² *n* **1** : nudo *m* (en cordel o madera), nódulo *m* (en los músculos) **2** CLUSTER : grupo *m* **3** : nudo *m* (unidad de velocidad)

knotty ['nɑti] *adj* **-tier; -est 1** GNARLED : nudoso **2** COMPLEX : espinoso, enredado, complejo

know ['no:] *v* **knew** ['nu:, 'nju:]; **known** ['no:n]; **knowing** *vt* **1** : saber ⟨he knows the answer : sabe la respuesta⟩ **2** : conocer (a una persona, un lugar) ⟨do you know Julia? : ¿conoces a Julia?⟩ **3** RECOGNIZE : reconocer **4** DISCERN, DISTINGUISH : distinguir, discernir **5 to know how to** : saber ⟨I don't know how to dance : no sé bailar⟩ — *vi* : saber

knowable ['no:əbəl] *adj* : conocible

knowing ['no:ɪŋ] *adj* **1** KNOWLEDGEABLE : informado ⟨a knowing look : una mirada de complicidad⟩ **2** ASTUTE : astuto **3** DELIBERATE : deliberado, intencional

knowingly ['no:ɪŋli] *adv* **1** : con complicidad ⟨she smiled knowingly : sonrió con una mirada de complicidad⟩ **2** DELIBERATELY : a sabiendas, adrede, a propósito

know–it–all ['no:ɪt,ɔl] *n* : sabelotodo *mf fam*

knowledge ['nɑlɪʤ] *n* **1** AWARENESS : conocimiento *m* **2** LEARNING : conocimientos *mpl*, saber *m*

knowledgeable ['nɑlɪʤəbəl] *adj* : informado, entendido, enterado

known ['noːn] *adj* : conocido, familiar

knuckle ['nʌkəl] *n* : nudillo *m*

koala [koˈwɑlə] *n* : koala *m*

kohlrabi [ˌkoːlˈrɑbi, -ˈræ-] *n, pl* **-bies** : colinabo *m*

Koran [kəˈrɑn, -ˈræn] *n* **the Koran** : el Corán

Korean [kəˈriːən] *n* **1** : coreano *m*, -na *f* **2** : coreano *m* (idioma) — **Korean** *adj*

kosher ['koːʃər] *adj* : aprobado por la ley judía

kowtow [ˌkaʊˈtaʊ, ˈkaʊˌtaʊ] *vi* **to kowtow to** : humillarse ante, doblegarse ante

krypton ['krɪpˌtɑn] *n* : criptón *m*

kudos ['kjuːˌdɑs, 'kuː-, -ˌdoːz] *n* : fama *f*, renombre *f*

kumquat ['kʌmˌkwɑt] *n* : naranjita *f* china

Kurd ['kʊrd, 'kərd] *n* : kurdo *m*, -da *f*

Kurdish ['kʊrdɪʃ, 'kər-] *adj* : kurdo

Kuwaiti [kuˈweɪti] *n* : kuwaití *mf* — **Kuwaiti** *adj*

L

l ['ɛl] *n, pl* **l's** *or* **ls** ['ɛlz] : duodécima letra del alfabeto inglés

lab ['læb] → **laboratory**

label¹ ['leɪbəl] *vt* **-beled** *or* **-belled**; **-beling** *or* **-belling** **1** : etiquetar, poner etiqueta a **2** BRAND, CATEGORIZE : calificar, tildar, tachar ⟨they labeled him as a fraud : lo calificaron de farsante⟩

label² *n* **1** : etiqueta *f*, rótulo *m* **2** DESCRIPTION : calificación *f*, descripción *f* **3** BRAND : marca *f*

labial ['leɪbiəl] *adj* : labial

labor¹ ['leɪbər] *vi* **1** WORK : trabajar **2** STRUGGLE : avanzar penosamente (dícese de una persona), funcionar con dificultad (dícese de un motor) **3** **to labor under a delusion** : hacerse ilusiones, tener una falsa impresión — *vt* BELABOR : insistir en, extenderse sobre

labor² *n* **1** EFFORT, WORK : trabajo *m*, esfuerzos *mpl* **2** : parto *m* ⟨to be in labor : estar de parto⟩ **3** TASK : tarea *f*, labor *m* **4** WORKERS : mano *f* de obra

laboratory ['læbrəˌtori, ləˈbɔrə-] *n, pl* **-ries** : laboratorio *m*

Labor Day *n* : Día *m* del Trabajo

laborer ['leɪbərər] *n* : peón *m*; trabajador *m*, -dora *f*

laborious [ləˈboriəs] *adj* : laborioso, difícil

laboriously [ləˈboriəsli] *adv* : laboriosamente, trabajosamente

labor union → **union**

labyrinth ['læbəˌrɪnθ] *n* : laberinto *m*

lace¹ ['leɪs] *vt* **laced**; **lacing** **1** TIE : acordonar, atar los cordones de **2** : adornar de encaje ⟨I laced the dress in white : adorné el vestido de encaje blanco⟩ **3** SPIKE : echar licor a

lace² *n* **1** : encaje *m* **2** SHOELACE : cordón *m* (de zapatos), agujeta *f* Mex

lacerate ['læsəˌreɪt] *vt* **-ated**; **-ating** : lacerar

laceration [ˌlæsəˈreɪʃən] *n* : laceración *f*

lack¹ ['læk] *vt* : carecer de, no tener ⟨she lacks patience : carece de paciencia⟩ — *vi* : faltar ⟨they lack for nothing : no les falta nada⟩

lack² *n* : falta *f*, carencia *f*

lackadaisical [ˌlækəˈdeɪzɪkəl] *adj* : apático, indiferente, lánguido — **lackadaisically** [-kli] *adv*

lackey ['læki] *n, pl* **-eys** **1** FOOTMAN : lacayo *m* **2** TOADY : adulador *m*, -dora *f*

lackluster ['lækˌlʌstər] *adj* **1** DULL : sin brillo, apagado, deslustrado **2** MEDIOCRE : deslucido, mediocre

laconic [ləˈkɑnɪk] *adj* : lacónico — **laconically** [-nɪkli] *adv*

lacquer¹ ['lækər] *vt* : laquear, pintar con laca

lacquer² *n* : laca *f*

lacrosse [ləˈkrɔs] *n* : lacrosse *f*

lactic acid ['læktɪk] *n* : ácido *m* láctico

lacuna [ləˈkuːnə, -ˈkjuː-] *n, pl* **-nae** [-ˌniː, -ˌnaɪ] *or* **-nas** : laguna *f*

lacy ['leɪsi] *adj* **lacier**; **-est** : de encaje, como de encaje

lad ['læd] *n* : muchacho *m*, niño *m*

ladder ['lædər] *n* : escalera *f*

laden ['leɪdən] *adj* : cargado

ladle¹ ['leɪdəl] *vt* **-dled**; **-dling** : servir con cucharón

ladle² *n* : cucharón *m*, cazo *m*

lady ['leɪdi] *n, pl* **-dies** **1** : señora *f*, dama *f* **2** WOMAN : mujer *f*

ladybird ['leɪdiˌbɔrd] → **ladybug**

ladybug ['leɪdiˌbʌg] *n* : mariquita *f*

lag¹ ['læg] *vi* **lagged**; **lagging** : quedarse atrás, retrasarse, rezagarse

lag² *n* **1** DELAY : retraso *m*, demora *f* **2** INTERVAL : lapso *m*, intervalo *m*

lager ['lɑgər] *n* : cerveza *f* rubia

laggard¹ ['lægərd] *adj* : retardado, retrasado

laggard² *n* : rezagado *m*, -da *f*

lagoon [ləˈguːn] *n* : laguna *f*

laid → **lay¹**

laid-back ['leɪdˈbæk] *adj* : tranquilo, relajado

lain *pp* → **lie¹**

lair ['lær] *n* : guarida *f*, madriguera *f*

laissez-faire [ˌlɛˌseɪˈfær, ˌleɪˌzeɪ-] *n* : liberalismo *m* económico

laity ['leɪəti] *n* **the laity** : los laicos, el laicado

lake ['leɪk] *n* : lago *m*

lama ['lɑmə] *n* : lama *m*

lamb ['læm] *n* **1** : cordero *m*, borrego *m* (animal) **2** : carne *f* de cordero

lambaste [læm'beɪst] *or* **lambast** [-'bæst] *vt* -**basted; -basting 1** BEAT, THRASH : golpear, azotar, darle una paliza (a alguien) **2** CENSURE : arremeter contra, censurar

lame¹ [leɪm] *vt* **lamed; laming** : lisiar, hacer cojo

lame² *adj* **lamer; lamest 1** : cojo, renco, rengo **2** WEAK : pobre, débil, poco convincente ⟨a lame excuse : una excusa débil⟩

lamé [lɑ'meɪ, læ-] *n* : lamé *m*

lame duck *n* : persona *f* sin poder ⟨a lame-duck President : un presidente saliente⟩

lamely [leɪmli] *adv* : sin convicción

lameness [leɪmnəs] *n* **1** : cojera *f*, renquera *f* **2** : falta *f* de convicción, debilidad *f*, pobreza *f* ⟨the lameness of her response : la pobreza de su respuesta⟩

lament¹ [lə'mɛnt] *vt* **1** MOURN : llorar, llorar por **2** DEPLORE : lamentar, deplorar — *vi* : llorar

lament² *n* : lamento *m*

lamentable [læmən̩təbəl, lə'mɛntə-] *adj* : lamentable, deplorable — **lamentably** [-bli] *adv*

lamentation [,læmən'teɪʃən] *n* : lamentación *f*, lamento *m*

laminate¹ [læmə,neɪt] *vt* -**nated; -nating** : laminar

laminate² [læmənət] *n* : laminado *m*

laminated [læmə,neɪt̬əd] *adj* : laminado

lamp [læmp] *n* : lámpara *f*

lampoon¹ [læm'pu:n] *vt* : satirizar

lampoon² *n* : sátira *f*

lamprey [læmpri] *n, pl* -**preys** : lamprea *f*

lance¹ [lænts] *vt* **lanced; lancing** : abrir con lanceta, sajar

lance² *n* : lanza *f*

lance corporal *n* : cabo *m* interino, soldado *m* de primera clase

lancet [læntsət] *n* : lanceta *f*

land¹ [lænd] *vt* **1** : desembarcar (pasajeros de un barco), hacer aterrizar (un avión) **2** CATCH : pescar, sacar (un pez) del agua **3** GAIN, SECURE : conseguir, ganar ⟨to land a job : conseguir empleo⟩ **4** DELIVER : dar, asestar ⟨he landed a punch : asestó un puñetazo⟩ — *vi* **1** : aterrizar, tomar tierra, atracar ⟨the plane just landed : el avión acaba de aterrizar⟩ ⟨the ship landed an hour ago : el barco atracó hace una hora⟩ **2** ALIGHT : posarse, aterrizar ⟨to land on one's feet : caer de pie⟩

land² *n* **1** GROUND : tierra *f* ⟨dry land : tierra firme⟩ **2** TERRAIN : terreno *m* **3** NATION : país *m*, nación *f* **4** DOMAIN : mundo *m*, dominio *m* ⟨the land of dreams : el mundo de los sueños⟩

landfill [lænd,fɪl] *n* : vertedero *m* (de basuras)

landing [lændɪŋ] *n* **1** : aterrizaje *m* (de aviones), desembarco *m* (de barcos) **2** : descansillo *m* (de una escalera)

landing field *n* : campo *m* de aterrizaje

landing strip → airstrip

landlady [lænd,leɪdi] *n, pl* -**dies** : casera *f*, dueña *f*, arrendadora *f*

landless [lændləs] *adj* : sin tierra

landlocked [lænd,lɑkt] *adj* : sin salida al mar

landlord [lænd,lɔrd] *n* : dueño *m*, casero *m*, arrendador *m*

landlubber [lænd,lʌbər] *n* : marinero *m* de agua dulce

landmark [lænd,mɑrk] *n* **1** : señal *f* (geográfica), punto *m* de referencia **2** MILESTONE : hito *m* ⟨a landmark in our history : un hito en nuestra historia⟩ **3** MONUMENT : monumento *m* histórico

landowner [lænd,oːnər] *n* : hacendado *m*, -da *f*; terrateniente *mf*

landscape¹ [lænd,skeɪp] *vt* -**scaped; -scaping** : ajardinar

landscape² *n* : paisaje *m*

landslide [lænd,slaɪd] *n* **1** : desprendimiento *m* de tierras, derrumbe *m* **2** **landslide victory** : victoria *f* arrolladora

landward [lændwərd] *adv* : en dirección de la tierra, hacia tierra

lane [leɪn] *n* **1** PATH, WAY : camino *m*, sendero *m* **2** : carril *m* (de una carretera)

language [læŋgwɪʤ] *n* **1** : idioma *m*, lengua *f* ⟨the English language : el idioma inglés⟩ **2** : lenguaje *m* ⟨body language : lenguaje corporal⟩

languid [læŋgwɪd] *adj* : lánguido — **languidly** *adv*

languish [læŋgwɪʃ] *vi* **1** WEAKEN : languidecer, debilitarse **2** PINE : consumirse, suspirar (por) ⟨to languish for love : suspirar por el amor⟩ ⟨he languished in prison : estuvo pudriéndose en la cárcel⟩

languor [læŋgər] *n* : languidez *f*

languorous [læŋgərəs] *adj* : lánguido — **languorously** *adv*

lank [læŋk] *adj* **1** THIN : delgado, larguirucho *fam* **2** LIMP : lacio

lanky [læŋki] *adj* **lankier; -est** : delgado, larguirucho *fam*

lanolin [lænəlɪn] *n* : lanolina *f*

lantern [læntərn] *n* : linterna *f*, farol *m*

Laotian [leɪ'oːʃən, 'lauʃən] *n* : laosiano *m*, -na *f* — **Laotian** *adj*

lap¹ [læp] *v* **lapped; lapping** *vt* **1** FOLD : plegar, doblar **2** WRAP : envolver **3** : lamer, besar ⟨waves were lapping the shore : las olas lamían la orilla⟩ **4** **to lap up** : beber a lengüetadas (como un gato) — *vi* OVERLAP : traslaparse

lap² *n* **1** : falda *f*, regazo *m* (del cuerpo) **2** OVERLAP : traslapo *m* **3** : vuelta *f* (en deportes) **4** STAGE : etapa *f* (de un viaje)

lapdog [læp,dɔg] *n* : perro *m* faldero

lapel [lə'pɛl] *n* : solapa *f*

lapp [læp] *n* : lapón *m*, -pona *f* — **Lapp** *adj*

lapse¹ [læps] *vi* **lapsed; lapsing 1** FALL, SLIP : caer ⟨to lapse into bad habits : caer en malos hábitos⟩ ⟨to lapse into unconsciousness : perder el conocimiento⟩ ⟨to lapse into silence : quedarse callado⟩ **2** FADE : decaer, desvanecerse ⟨her dedication lapsed : su dedicación se desvaneció⟩ **3** CEASE : cancelarse, perderse **4** ELAPSE : transcurrir, pasar **5** EXPIRE : caducar

lapse² n **1** SLIP : lapsus m, desliz m, falla f ⟨a lapse of memory : una falla de memoria⟩ **2** INTERVAL : lapso m, intervalo m, período m **3** EXPIRATION : caducidad f

laptop¹ [ˈlæpˌtɑp] adj : portátil, laptop

laptop² n : laptop m

larboard [ˈlɑrbərd] n : babor m

larcenous [ˈlɑrsənəs] adj : de robo

larceny [ˈlɑrsəni] n, pl **-nies** : robo m, hurto m

larch [ˈlɑrtʃ] n : alerce f

lard [ˈlɑrd] n : manteca f de cerdo

larder [ˈlɑrdər] n : despensa f, alacena f

large [ˈlɑrdʒ] adj **larger; largest 1** BIG : grande **2** COMPREHENSIVE : amplio, extenso **3 by and large** : por lo general

largely [ˈlɑrdʒli] adv : en gran parte, en su mayoría

largeness [ˈlɑrdʒnəs] n : lo grande

largesse or **largess** [lɑrˈʒɛs, -ˈdʒɛs] n : generosidad f, largueza f

lariat [ˈlæriət] n : lazo m

lark [ˈlɑrk] n **1** FUN : diversión f ⟨what a lark! : ¡qué divertido!⟩ **2** : alondra f (pájaro)

larva [ˈlɑrvə] n, pl **-vae** [-ˌviː, -ˌvaɪ] : larva f — **larval** [-vəl] adj

laryngitis [ˌlærənˈdʒaɪtəs] n : laringitis f

larynx [ˈlærɪŋks] n, pl **-rynges** [ləˈrɪnˌdʒiːz] or **-ynxes** [ˈlærɪŋksəz] : laringe f

lasagna [ləˈzɑnjə] n : lasaña f

lascivious [ləˈsɪviəs] adj : lascivo

lasciviousness [ləˈsɪviəsnəs] n : lascivia f, lujuria f

laser [ˈleɪzər] n : láser m

laser disc n : disco m láser

lash¹ [ˈlæʃ] vt **1** WHIP : azotar **2** BIND : atar, amarrar

lash² n **1** WHIP : látigo m **2** STROKE : latigazo m **3** EYELASH : pestaña f

lass [ˈlæs] or **lassie** [ˈlæsi] n : muchacha f, chica f

lassitude [ˈlæsəˌtuːd, -ˌtjuːd] n : lasitud f

lasso¹ [ˈlæˌsoː, læˈsuː] vt : lazar

lasso² n, pl **-sos** or **-soes** : lazo m, reata f Mex

last¹ [ˈlæst] vi **1** CONTINUE : durar ⟨how long will it last? : ¿cuánto durará?⟩ **2** ENDURE : aguantar, durar **3** SURVIVE : durar, sobrevivir **4** SUFFICE : durar, bastar — vt **1** : durar ⟨it will last a lifetime : durará toda la vida⟩ **2 to last out** : aguantar

last² adv **1** : en último lugar, al último ⟨we came in last : llegamos en último lugar⟩ **2** : por última vez, la última vez ⟨I saw him last in Bogota : lo vi por última vez en Bogotá⟩ **3** FINALLY : por último, en conclusión

last³ adj **1** FINAL : último, final **2** PREVIOUS : pasado ⟨last year : el año pasado⟩

last⁴ n **1** : el último, la última, lo último ⟨at last : por fin, al fin, finalmente⟩ **2** : horma f (de zapatero)

lasting [ˈlæstɪŋ] adj : perdurable, duradero, estable

lastly [ˈlæstli] adv : por último, finalmente

latch¹ [ˈlætʃ] vt : cerrar con picaporte

latch² n : picaporte m, pestillo m, pasador m

late¹ [ˈleɪt] adv **later; latest 1** : tarde ⟨to arrive late : llegar tarde⟩ ⟨to sleep late : dormir hasta tarde⟩ **2** : a última hora, a finales ⟨late in the month : a finales del mes⟩ **3** RECENTLY : recién, últimamente ⟨as late as last year : todavía en el año pasado⟩

late² adj **later; latest 1** TARDY : tardío, de retraso ⟨to be late : llegar tarde⟩ **2** : avanzado ⟨because of the late hour : a causa de la hora avanzada⟩ **3** DECEASED : difunto, fallecido **4** RECENT : reciente, último ⟨our late quarrel : nuestra última pelea⟩

latecomer [ˈleɪtˌkʌmər] n : rezagado m, -da f

lately [ˈleɪtli] adv : recientemente, últimamente

lateness [ˈleɪtnəs] n **1** DELAY : retraso m, atraso m, tardanza f **2** : lo avanzado (de la hora)

latent [ˈleɪtənt] adj : latente — **latently** adv

lateral [ˈlætərəl] adj : lateral — **laterally** adv

latex [ˈleɪˌtɛks] n, pl **-tices** [ˈleɪtəˌsiːz, ˈlætə-] or **-texes** : látex m

lath [ˈlæθ, ˈlæð] n, pl **laths** or **lath** : listón m

lathe [ˈleɪð] n : torno m

lather¹ [ˈlæðər] vt : enjabonar — vi : espumar, hacer espuma

lather² n : espuma f (de jabón) **2** : sudor m (de caballo) **3 to get into a lather** : ponerse histérico

Latin¹ adj : latino

Latin² n **1** : latín m (idioma) **2** → **Latin American**

Latin–American [ˈlætənəˈmrikən] adj : latinoamericano

Latin American n : latinoamericano m, -na f

latitude [ˈlætəˌtuːd, -ˌtjuːd] n : latitud f

latrine [ləˈtriːn] n : letrina f

latte [ˈlɑˌteɪ] n : café m con leche

latter¹ [ˈlætər] adj **1** SECOND : segundo **2** LAST : último

latter² pron **the latter** : éste, ésta, éstos pl, éstas pl

lattice [ˈlætəs] n : enrejado m, celosía f

Latvian [ˈlætviən] n : letón m, -tona f — **Latvian** adj

laud¹ [ˈlɔd] vt : alabar, loar

laud² n : alabanza f, loa f

laudable ['lɔdəbəl] *adj* : loable — **laudably** [-bli] *adv*

laugh[1] ['læf] *vi* : reír, reírse

laugh[2] *n* **1** LAUGHTER : risa *f* **2** JOKE : chiste *m*, broma *f* ⟨he did it for a laugh : lo hizo en broma, lo hizo para divertirse⟩

laughable ['læfəbəl] *adj* : risible, de risa

laughingstock ['læfiŋ,stɑk] *n* : hazmerreír *m*

laughter ['læftər] *n* : risa *f*, risas *fpl*

launch[1] ['lɔntʃ] *vt* **1** HURL : lanzar **2** : botar (un barco) **3** START : iniciar, empezar

launch[2] *n* **1** : lancha *f* (bote) **2** LAUNCHING : lanzamiento *m*

launder ['lɔndər] *vt* : lavar y planchar (ropa) **2** : blanquear, lavar (dinero)

launderer ['lɔndərər] *n* : lavandero *m*, -ra *f*

laundress ['lɔndrəs] *n* : lavandera *f*

laundry ['lɔndri] *n, pl* **laundries 1** : ropa *f* sucia, ropa *f* para lavar ⟨to do the laundry : lavar la ropa⟩ **2** : lavandería *f* (servicio de lavar)

laureate ['lɔriət] *n* : laureado *m*, -da *f* ⟨poet laureate : poeta laureado⟩

laurel ['lɔrəl] *n* **1** : laurel *m* (planta) **2 laurels** *npl* : laureles *mpl* ⟨to rest on one's laurels : dormirse uno en sus laureles⟩

lava ['lɑvə, 'læ-] *n* : lava *f*

lavatory ['lævə,tori] *n, pl* **-ries** : baño *m*, cuarto *m* de baño

lavender ['lævəndər] *n* : lavanda *f*, espliego *m*

lavish[1] ['lævɪʃ] *vt* : prodigar (a), colmar (de)

lavish[2] *adj* **1** EXTRAVAGANT : pródigo, generoso, derrochador **2** ABUNDANT : abundante **3** LUXURIOUS : lujoso, espléndido

lavishly ['lævɪʃli] *adv* : con generosidad, espléndidamente ⟨to live lavishly : vivir a lo grande⟩

lavishness ['lævɪʃnəs] *n* : generosidad *f*, esplendidez *f*

law ['lɔ] *n* **1** : ley *f* ⟨to break the law : violar la ley⟩ **2** : derecho *m* ⟨criminal law : derecho criminal⟩ **3** : abogacía *f* ⟨to practice law : ejercer la abogacía⟩

law–abiding ['lɔə,baɪdɪŋ] *adj* : observante de la ley

lawbreaker ['lɔ,breɪkər] *n* : infractor *m*, -tora *f* de la ley

lawful ['lɔfəl] *adj* : legal, legítimo, lícito — **lawfully** *adv*

lawgiver ['lɔ,gɪvər] *n* : legislador *m*, -dora *f*

lawless ['lɔləs] *adj* : anárquico, ingobernable — **lawlessly** *adv*

lawlessness ['lɔləsnəs] *n* : anarquía *f*, desorden *m*

lawmaker ['lɔ,meɪkər] *n* : legislador *m*, -dora *f*

lawman ['lɔmən] *n, pl* **-men** [-mən, -,mɛn] : agente *m* del orden

lawn ['lɔn] *n* : césped *m*, pasto *m*

lawn mower *n* : cortadora *f* de césped

lawsuit ['lɔ,su:t] *n* : pleito *m*, litigio *m*, demanda *f*

lawyer ['lɔɪər, 'lɔjər] *n* : abogado *m*, -da *f*

lax ['læks] *adj* : laxo, relajado — **laxly** *adv*

laxative ['læksətɪv] *n* : laxante *m*

laxity ['læksəti] *n* : relajación *f*, descuido *m*, falta *f* de rigor

lay[1] ['leɪ] *vt* **laid** ['leɪd]; **laying 1** PLACE, PUT : poner, colocar ⟨she laid it on the table : lo puso en la mesa⟩ ⟨to lay eggs : poner huevos⟩ **2** : hacer ⟨to lay a bet : hacer una apuesta⟩ **3** IMPOSE : imponer ⟨to lay a tax : imponer un impuesto⟩ ⟨to lay the blame on : echarle la culpa a⟩ **4 to lay out** PRESENT : presentar, exponer ⟨he laid out his plan : presentó su proyecto⟩ **5 to lay out** DESIGN : diseñar (el trazado de)

lay[2] → **lie**[1]

lay[3] *adj* SECULAR : laico, lego

lay[4] *n* **1** : disposición *f*, configuración *f* ⟨the lay of the land : la configuración del terreno⟩ **2** BALLAD : romance *m*, balada *f*

layer ['leɪər] *n* **1** : capa *f* (de pintura, etc.), estrato *m* (de roca) **2** : gallina *f* ponedora

layman ['leɪmən] *n, pl* **-men** [-mən, -,mɛn] : laico *m*, lego *m*

layoff ['leɪ,ɔf] *n* : despido *m*

lay off *vt* : despedir

layout ['leɪ,aʊt] *n* : disposición *f*, distribución *f* (de una casa, etc.), trazado *m* (de una ciudad)

lay up *vt* **1** STORE : guardar, almacenar **2 to be laid up** : estar enfermo, tener que guardar cama

laywoman ['leɪ,wumən] *n, pl* **-women** [-,wimən] : laica *f*, lega *f*

laziness ['leɪzinəs] *n* : pereza *f*, flojera *f*

lazy ['leɪzi] *adj* **-zier; -est** : perezoso, holgazán — **lazily** ['leɪzɪli] *adv*

leach ['li:tʃ] *vt* : filtrar

lead[1] ['li:d] *vt* **led** ['lɛd]; **leading 1** GUIDE : conducir, llevar, guiar **2** DIRECT : dirigir **3** HEAD : encabezar, ir al frente de **4 to lead to** : resultar en, llevar a ⟨it only leads to trouble : sólo resulta en problemas⟩

lead[2] *n* : delantera *f*, primer lugar *m* ⟨to take the lead : tomar la delantera⟩

lead[3] ['lɛd] *n* **1** : plomo *m* (metal) **2** : mina *f* (de lápiz) **3 lead poisoning** : saturnismo *m*

leaden ['lɛdən] *adj* **1** : plomizo ⟨a leaden sky : un ciel plomizo⟩ **2** HEAVY : pesado

leader ['li:dər] *n* : jefe *m*, -fa *f*; líder *mf*; dirigente *mf*; gobernante *mf*

leadership ['li:dər,ʃɪp] *n* : mando *m*, dirección *f*

leaf[1] ['li:f] *vi* **1** : echar hojas (dícese de un árbol) **2 to leaf through** : hojear (un libro)

leaf² *n, pl* **leaves** [ˈliːvz] **1** : hoja *f* (de plantas o libros) **2 to turn over a new leaf** : hacer borrón y cuenta nueva

leafless [ˈliːfləs] *adj* : sin hojas, pelado

leaflet [ˈliːflət] *n* : folleto *m*

leafy [ˈliːfi] *adj* **leafier; -est** : frondoso

league¹ [ˈliːg] *v* **leagued; leaguing** *vt* : aliar, unir — *vi* : aliarse, unirse

league² *n* **1** : legua *f* (medida de distancia) **2** ASSOCIATION : alianza *f*, sociedad *f*, liga *f*

leak¹ [ˈliːk] *vt* **1** : perder, dejar escapar (un líquido o un gas) **2** : filtrar (información) — *vi* : gotear, escaparse, fugarse (dícese de un líquido o un gas) **2** : hacer agua (dícese de un bote) **3** : filtrarse, divulgarse (dícese de información)

leak² *n* **1** HOLE : agujero *m* (en recipientes), gotera *f* (en un tejado) **2** ESCAPE : fuga *f*, escape *m* **3** : filtración *f* (de información)

leakage [ˈliːkɪdʒ] *n* : escape *m*, fuga *f*

leaky [ˈliːki] *adj* **leakier; -est** : agujereado (dícese de un recipiente), que hace agua (dícese de un bote), con goteras (dícese de un tejado)

lean¹ [ˈliːn] *vi* **1** BEND : inclinarse, ladearse **2** RECLINE : reclinarse **3** RELY : apoyarse (en), depender (de) **4** INCLINE, TEND : inclinarse, tender — *vt* : apoyar

lean² *adj* **1** THIN : delgado, flaco **2** : sin grasa, magro (dícese de la carne)

leanness [ˈliːnnəs] *n* : delgadez *f*

lean-to [ˈliːˌtuː] *n* : cobertizo *m*

leap¹ [ˈliːp] *vi* **leaped** [ˈliːpt, ˈlɛpt] *or* **leapt; leaping** : saltar, brincar

leap² *n* : salto *m*, brinco *m*

leap year *n* : año *m* bisiesto

learn [ˈlərn] *vt* **1** : aprender ⟨to learn to sing : aprender a cantar⟩ **2** MEMORIZE : aprender de memoria **3** DISCOVER : saber, enterarse de — *vi* **1** : aprender ⟨to learn from experience : aprender por experiencia⟩ **2** FIND OUT : enterarse, saber

learned [ˈlərnəd] *adj* : erudito

learner [ˈlərnər] *n* : principiante *mf*, estudiante *mf*

learning [ˈlərnɪŋ] *n* : erudición *f*, saber *m*

lease¹ [ˈliːs] *vt* **leased; leasing** : arrendar

lease² *n* : contrato *m* de arrendamiento

leash¹ [ˈliːʃ] *vt* : atraillar (un animal)

leash² *n* : traílla *f*

least¹ [ˈliːst] *adv* : menos ⟨when least expected : cuando menos se espera⟩

least² *adj* (*superlative of* **little**) : menor, más mínimo

least³ *n* **1** : lo menos ⟨at least : por lo menos⟩ **2 to say the least** : por no decir más

leather [ˈlɛðər] *n* : cuero *m*

leathery [ˈlɛðəri] *adj* : curtido (dícese de la piel), correoso (dícese de la carne)

leave¹ [ˈliːv] *v* **left** [ˈlɛft]; **leaving** *vt* **1** BEQUEATH : dejar, legar **2** DEPART : dejar, salir(se) de **3** ABANDON : abandonar, dejar **4** FORGET : dejar, olvidarse de ⟨I left the books at the library : dejé los libros en la biblioteca⟩ **5 to be left** : quedar ⟨it's all I have left : es todo lo que me queda⟩ **6 to be left over** : sobrar **7 to leave out** : omitir, excluir — *vi* : irse, salir, partir, marcharse ⟨she left yesterday morning : se fue ayer por la mañana⟩

leave² *n* **1** PERMISSION : permiso *m* ⟨by your leave : con su permiso⟩ **2** *or* **leave of absence** : permiso *m*, licencia *f* ⟨maternity leave : licencia por maternidad⟩ **3 to take one's leave** : despedirse

leaven [ˈlɛvən] *n* : levadura *f*

leaves → **leaf²**

leaving [ˈliːvɪŋ] *n* **1** : salida *f*, partida *f* **2 leavings** *npl* : restos *mpl*, sobras *fpl*

Lebanese [ˌlɛbəˈniːz, -ˈniːs] *n* : libanés *m*, -nesa *f* — **Lebanese** *adj*

lecherous [ˈlɛtʃərəs] *adj* : lascivo, libidinoso — **lecherously** *adv*

lechery [ˈlɛtʃəri] *n* : lascivia *f*, lujuria *f*

lecture¹ [ˈlɛktʃər] *v* **-tured; -turing** *vi* : dar clase, dictar clase, dar una conferencia — *vt* SCOLD : sermonear, echar una reprimenda a, regañar

lecture² *n* **1** : conferencia *f* **2** REPRIMAND : reprimenda *f*

lecturer [ˈlɛktʃərər] *n* **1** SPEAKER : conferenciante *mf* **2** TEACHER : profesor *m*, -sora *f*

led → **lead¹**

ledge [ˈlɛdʒ] *n* : repisa *f* (de una pared), antepecho *m* (de una ventana), saliente *m* (de una montaña)

ledger [ˈlɛdʒər] *n* : libro *m* mayor, libro *m* de contabilidad

lee¹ [ˈliː] *adj* : de sotavento

lee² *n* : sotavento *m*

leech [ˈliːtʃ] *n* : sanguijuela *f*

leek [ˈliːk] *n* : puerro *m*

leer¹ [ˈlɪr] *vi* : mirar con lascivia

leer² *n* : mirada *f* lasciva

leery [ˈlɪri] *adj* : receloso

lees [ˈliːz] *npl* : posos *mpl*, heces *fpl*

leeward¹ [ˈliːwərd, ˈluːərd] *adj* : de sotavento

leeward² *n* : sotavento *m*

leeway [ˈliːˌweɪ] *n* : libertad *f*, margen *m*

left¹ [ˈlɛft] *adv* : hacia la izquierda

left² → **leave¹**

left³ *adj* : izquierdo

left⁴ *n* : izquierda *f* ⟨on the left : a la izquierda⟩

left-hand [ˈlɛftˈhand] *adj* **1** : de la izquierda **2** → **left-handed**

left-handed [ˈlɛftˈhandəd] *adj* **1** : zurdo (dícese de una persona) **2** : con doble sentido ⟨a left-handed compliment : un cumplido a medias⟩

leftist [ˈlɛftɪst] *n* : izquierdista *mf* — **leftist** *adj*

leftover [ˈlɛftˌoːvər] *adj* : sobrante, que sobra

leftovers ['lɛft,oːvərz] *npl* : restos *mpl*, sobras *fpl*

left wing *n* **the left wing** : la izquierda

left-winger ['lɛft'wɪŋər] *n* : izquierdista *mf*

leg ['lɛg] *n* **1** : pierna *f* (de una persona, de carne, de ropa), pata *f* (de un animal, de muebles) **2** STAGE : etapa *f* (de un viaje), vuelta *f* (de una carrera)

legacy ['lɛgəsi] *n, pl* **-cies** : legado *m*, herencia *f*

legal ['liːgəl] *adj* **1** : legal, jurídico ⟨legal advisor : asesor jurídico⟩ ⟨the legal profession : la abogacía⟩ **2** LAWFUL : legítimo, legal

legalistic [,liːgə'lɪstɪk] *adj* : legalista

legality [li'gæləti] *n, pl* **-ties** : legalidad *f*

legalize ['liːgə,laɪz] *vt* **-ized; -izing** : legalizar

legally ['liːgəli] *adv* : legalmente

legate ['lɛgət] *n* : legado *m*

legation [lɪ'geɪʃən] *n* : legación *f*

legend ['lɛdʒənd] *n* **1** STORY : leyenda *f* **2** INSCRIPTION : leyenda *f*, inscripción *f* **3** : signos *mpl* convencionales (en un mapa)

legendary ['lɛdʒən,dɛri] *adj* : legendario

legerdemain [,lɛdʒərdə'meɪn] → **sleight of hand**

leggings ['lɛgɪnz, 'lɛgənz] *npl* : mallas *fpl*

legibility [,lɛdʒə'bɪləti] *n* : legibilidad *f*

legible ['lɛdʒəbəl] *adj* : legible

legibly ['lɛdʒəbli] *adv* : de manera legible

legion ['liːdʒən] *n* : legión *f*

legionnaire [,liːdʒə'nær] *n* : legionario *m*, -ria *f*

legislate ['lɛdʒəs,leɪt] *vi* **-lated; -lating** : legislar

legislation [,lɛdʒəs'leɪʃən] *n* : legislación *f*

legislative ['lɛdʒəs,leɪtɪv] *adj* : legislativo, legislador

legislator ['lɛdʒəs,leɪtər] *n* : legislador *m*, -dora *f*

legislature ['lɛdʒəs,leɪtʃər] *n* : asamblea *f* legislativa

legitimacy [lɪ'dʒɪtəməsi] *n* : legitimidad *f*

legitimate [lɪ'dʒɪtəmət] *adj* **1** VALID : legítimo, válido, justificado **2** LAWFUL : legítimo, legal

legitimately [lɪ'dʒɪtəmətli] *adv* : legítimamente

legitimize [lɪ'dʒɪtə,maɪz] *vt* **-mized; -mizing** : legitimar, hacer legítimo

legume ['lɛ,gjuːm, lɪ'gjuːm] *n* : legumbre *f*

leisure ['liːʒər, 'lɛ-] *n* **1** : ocio *m*, tiempo *m* libre ⟨a life of leisure : una vida de ocio⟩ **2 to take one's leisure** : reposar **3 at your leisure** : cuando te venga bien, cuando tengas tiempo

leisurely ['liːʒərli, 'lɛ-] *adj & adv* : lento, sin prisas

lemming ['lɛmɪŋ] *n* : lemming *m*

lemon ['lɛmən] *n* : limón *m*

lemonade [,lɛmə'neɪd] *n* : limonada *f*

lemony ['lɛməni] *adj* : a limón

lend ['lɛnd] *vt* **lent** ['lɛnt]; **lending 1** : prestar ⟨to lend money : prestar dinero⟩ **2** GIVE : dar ⟨it lends force to his criticism : da fuerza a su crítica⟩ **3 to lend oneself to** : prestarse a

length ['lɛŋkθ] *n* **1** : longitud *f*, largo *m* ⟨10 feet in length : 10 pies de largo⟩ **2** DURATION : duración *f* **3** : trozo *m* (de madera), corte *m* (de tela) **4 to go to any lengths** : hacer todo lo posible **5 at ~** : extensamente ⟨to speak at length : hablar largo y tendido⟩

lengthen ['lɛŋkθən] *vt* **1** : alargar ⟨can they lengthen the dress? : ¿se puede alargar el vestido?⟩ **2** EXTEND, PROLONG : prolongar, extender — *vi* : alargarse, crecer ⟨the days are lengthening : los días están creciendo⟩

lengthways ['lɛŋkθ,weɪz] → **lengthwise**

lengthwise ['lɛŋkθ,waɪz] *adv* : a lo largo, longitudinalmente

lengthy ['lɛŋkθi] *adj* **lengthier; -est 1** OVERLONG : largo y pesado **2** EXTENDED : prolongado, largo

leniency ['liːniənsi] *n, pl* **-cies** : lenidad *f*, indulgencia *f*

lenient ['liːniənt] *adj* : indulgente, poco severo

leniently ['liːniəntli] *adv* : con lenidad, con indulgencia

lens ['lɛnz] *n* **1** : cristalino *m* (del ojo) **2** : lente *mf* (de un instrumento o una cámara) **3** → **contact lens**

lent → **lend**

Lent ['lɛnt] *n* : Cuaresma *f*

lentil ['lɛntəl] *n* : lenteja *f*

Leo ['liːoː] *n* : Leo *mf*

leopard ['lɛpərd] *n* : leopardo *m*

leotard ['liːə,tɑrd] *n* : leotardo *m*, malla *f*

leper ['lɛpər] *n* : leproso *m*, -sa *f*

leprechaun ['lɛprə,kɑn] *n* : duende *m* (irlandés)

leprosy ['lɛprəsi] *n* : lepra *f* — **leprous** ['lɛprəs] *adj*

lesbian[1] ['lɛzbiən] *adj* : lesbiano

lesbian[2] *n* : lesbiana *f*

lesbianism ['lɛzbiə,nɪzəm] *n* : lesbianismo *m*

lesion ['liːʒən] *n* : lesión *f*

less[1] ['lɛs] *adv* (*comparative of* **little**[1]) : menos ⟨the less you know, the better : cuanto menos sepas, mejor⟩ ⟨less and less : cada vez menos⟩

less[2] *adj* (*comparative of* **little**[2]) : menos ⟨less than three : menos de tres⟩ ⟨less money : menos dinero⟩ ⟨nothing less than perfection : nada menos que la perfección⟩

less[3] *pron* : menos ⟨I'm earning less : estoy ganando menos⟩

less[4] *prep* : menos ⟨one month less two days : un mes menos dos días⟩

lessee [lɛ'siː] *n* : arrendatario *m*, -ria *f*

lessen ['lɛsən] *vt* : disminuir, reducir — *vi* : disminuir, reducirse

lesser [ˈlɛsər] *adj* : menor ⟨to a lesser degree : en menor grado⟩

lesson [ˈlɛsən] *n* **1** CLASS : clase *f*, curso *m* **2** : lección *f* ⟨the lessons of history : las lecciones de la historia⟩

lessor [ˈlɛˌsɔr, ˈlɛsˌɔr] *n* : arrendador *m*, -dora *f*

lest [ˈlɛst] *conj* : para (que) no ⟨lest we forget : para que no olvidemos⟩

let [ˈlɛt] *vt* let; letting **1** ALLOW : dejar, permitir ⟨let me see it : déjame verlo⟩ **2** MAKE : hacer ⟨let me know : házmelo saber, avísame⟩ ⟨let them wait : que esperen, haz que esperen⟩ **3** RENT : alquilar **4** (*used in the first person plural imperative*) ⟨let's go! : ¡vamos!, ¡vámonos!⟩ ⟨let us pray : oremos⟩ **5 to let down** DISAPPOINT : fallar **6 to let off** FORGIVE : perdonar **7 to let out** REVEAL : revelar **8 to let up** ABATE : amainar, disminuir ⟨the pace never lets up : el ritmo nunca disminuye⟩

letdown *n* : chasco *m*, decepción *f*

lethal [ˈliːθəl] *adj* : letal — **lethally** *adv*

lethargic [lɪˈθɑrdʒɪk] *adj* : letárgico

lethargy [ˈlɛθərdʒi] *n* : letargo *m*

let on *vi* **1** ADMIT : reconocer ⟨don't let on! : ¡no digas nada!⟩ **2** PRETEND : fingir

let's [ˈlɛts] (*contraction of* let us) → let

letter[1] [ˈlɛtər] *vt* : marcar con letras, inscribir letras en

letter[2] *n* **1** : letra *f* (del alfabeto) **2** : carta *f* ⟨a letter to my mother : una carta a mi madre⟩ **3 letters** *npl* ARTS : letras *fpl* **4 to the letter** : al pie de la letra

lettering [ˈlɛtərɪŋ] *n* : letra *f*

lettuce [ˈlɛtəs] *n* : lechuga *f*

leukemia [luːˈkiːmiə] *n* : leucemia *f*

levee [ˈlɛvi] *n* : dique *m*

level[1] [ˈlɛvəl] *vt* -eled *or* -elled; -eling *or* -elling **1** FLATTEN : nivelar, aplanar **2** AIM : apuntar (una pistola), dirigir (una acusación) **3** RAZE : rasar, arrasar

level[2] *adj* **1** EVEN : llano, plano, parejo **2** CALM : tranquilo ⟨to keep a level head : no perder la cabeza⟩

level[3] *n* : nivel *m*

leveler [ˈlɛvələr] *n* : nivelador *m*, -dora *f*

levelheaded [ˈlɛvəlˈhɛdəd] *adj* : sensato, equilibrado

levelly [ˈlɛvəli] *adv* CALMLY : con ecuanimidad *f*, con calma

levelness [ˈlɛvəlnəs] *n* : uniformidad *f*

lever [ˈlɛvər, ˈliː-] *n* : palanca *f*

leverage [ˈlɛvərɪdʒ, ˈliː-] *n* **1** : apalancamiento *m* (en física) **2** INFLUENCE : influencia *f*, palanca *f fam*

leviathan [lɪˈvaɪəθən] *n* : leviatán *m*, gigante *m*

levity [ˈlɛvəti] *n* : ligereza *f*, frivolidad *f*

levy[1] [ˈlɛvi] *vt* levied; levying **1** IMPOSE : imponer, exigir, gravar (un impuesto) **2** COLLECT : recaudar (un impuesto)

levy[2] *n*, *pl* levies : impuesto *m*, gravamen *m*

lewd [ˈluːd] *adj* : lascivo — **lewdly** *adv*

lewdness [ˈluːdnəs] *n* : lascivia *f*

lexical [ˈlɛksɪkəl] *adj* : léxico

lexicographer [ˌlɛksəˈkɑɡrəfər] *n* : lexicógrafo *m*, -fa *f*

lexicographical [ˌlɛksəkoˈɡræfɪkəl] *or* **lexicographic** [-ˈɡræfɪk] *adj* : lexicográfico

lexicography [ˌlɛksəˈkɑɡrəfi] *n* : lexicografía *f*

lexicon [ˈlɛksɪˌkɑn] *n*, *pl* -ica [-kə] *or* -icons : léxico *m*, lexicón *m*

liability [ˌlaɪəˈbɪləti] *n*, *pl* -ties **1** RESPONSIBILITY : responsabilidad *f* **2** SUSCEPTIBILITY : propensión *f* **3** DRAWBACK : desventaja *f* **4 liabilities** *npl* DEBTS : deudas *fpl*, pasivo *m*

liable [ˈlaɪəbəl] *adj* **1** RESPONSIBLE : responsable **2** SUSCEPTIBLE : propenso **3** PROBABLE : probable ⟨it's liable to happen : es probable que suceda⟩

liaison [ˈliːəˌzɑn, liˈeɪ-] *n* **1** CONNECTION : enlace *m*, relación *f* **2** AFFAIR : amorío *m*, aventura *f*

liar [ˈlaɪər] *n* : mentiroso *m*, -sa *f*; embustero *m*, -ra *f*

libel[1] [ˈlaɪbəl] *vt* -beled *or* -belled; -beling *or* -belling : difamar, calumniar

libel[2] *n* : difamación *f*, calumnia *f*

libeler [ˈlaɪbələr] *n* : difamador *m*, -dora *f*; calumniador *m*, -dora *f*; libelista *mf*

libelous *or* **libellous** [ˈlaɪbələs] *adj* : difamatorio, calumnioso, injurioso

liberal[1] [ˈlɪbrəl, ˈlɪbərəl] *adj* **1** TOLERANT : liberal, tolerante **2** GENEROUS : generoso **3** ABUNDANT : abundante **4 liberal arts** : humanidades *fpl*, artes *fpl* liberales

liberal[2] *n* : liberal *mf*

liberalism [ˈlɪbrəˌlɪzəm, ˈlɪbərə-] *n* : liberalismo *m*

liberality [ˌlɪbəˈræləti] *n*, *pl* -ties : liberalidad *f*, generosidad *f*

liberalize [ˈlɪbrəˌlaɪz, ˈlɪbərə-] *vt* -ized; -izing : liberalizar

liberally [ˈlɪbrəli, ˈlɪbərə-] *adv* **1** GENEROUSLY : generosamente **2** ABUNDANTLY : abundantemente **3** FREELY : libremente

liberate [ˈlɪbəˌreɪt] *vt* -ated; -ating : liberar, libertar

liberation [ˌlɪbəˈreɪʃən] *n* : liberación *f*

liberator [ˈlɪbəˌreɪtər] *n* : libertador *m*, -dora *f*

Liberian [laɪˈbɪriən] *n* : liberiano *m*, -na *f* — **Liberian** *adj*

libertine [ˈlɪbərˌtiːn] *n* : libertino *m*, -na *f*

liberty [ˈlɪbərti] *n*, *pl* -ties **1** : libertad *f* **2 to take the liberty of** : tomarse la libertad de **3 to take liberties with** : tomarse confianzas con, tomarse libertades con

libido [ləˈbiːdoː, -ˈbaɪ-] *n*, *pl* -dos : libido *f* — **libidinous** [ləˈbɪdənəs] *adj*

Libra [ˈliːbrə] *n* : Libra *mf*

librarian [laɪˈbreriən] *n* : bibliotecario *m*, -ria *f*

library [ˈlaɪˌbreri] *n*, *pl* -braries : biblioteca *f*

librettist [lɪˈbrɛtɪst] n : libretista mf
libretto [lɪˈbrɛto] n, pl **-tos** or **-ti** [-ˌtiː] : libreto m
Libyan [ˈlɪbiən] n : libio m, -bia f — **Libyan** adj
lice → **louse**
license¹ [ˈlaɪsənts] vt **licensed; licensing** : licenciar, autorizar, dar permiso a
license² or **licence** n **1** PERMISSION : licencia f, permiso m **2** PERMIT : licencia f, carnet m Spain ⟨driver's license : licencia de conducir⟩ **3** FREEDOM : libertad f **4** LICENTIOUSNESS : libertinaje m
licentious [laɪˈsɛntʃəs] adj : licencioso, disoluto — **licentiously** adv
licentiousness [laɪˈsɛntʃəsnəs] n : libertinaje m
lichen [ˈlaɪkən] n : liquen m
licit [ˈlɪsət] adj : lícito
lick¹ [ˈlɪk] vt **1** : lamer **2** BEAT : darle una paliza (a alguien)
lick² n **1** : lamida f, lengüetada f ⟨a lick of paint : una mano de pintura⟩ **2** BIT : pizca f, ápice m **3 a lick and a promise** : una lavada a la carrera
licorice [ˈlɪkərɪʃ, -rəs] n : regaliz m, dulce m de regaliz
lid [ˈlɪd] n **1** COVER : tapa f **2** EYELID : párpado m
lie¹ [ˈlaɪ] vi **lay** [ˈleɪ]; **lain** [ˈleɪn]; **lying** [ˈlaɪɪŋ] **1** : acostarse, echarse ⟨I lay down : me acosté⟩ **2** : estar, estar situado, encontrarse ⟨the book lay on the table : el libro estaba en la mesa⟩ ⟨the city lies to the south : la ciudad se encuentra al sur⟩ **3** CONSIST : consistir **4 to lie in** : residir en ⟨the power lies in the people : el poder reside en el pueblo⟩
lie² vi **lied; lying** [ˈlaɪɪŋ] : mentir
lie³ n **1** UNTRUTH : mentira f ⟨to tell lies : decir mentiras⟩ **2** POSITION : posición f
liege [ˈliːdʒ] n : señor m feudal
lien [ˈliːn, ˈliːən] n : derecho m de retención
lieutenant [luˈtɛnənt] n : teniente mf
lieutenant colonel n : teniente mf coronel
lieutenant commander n : capitán m, -tana f de corbeta
lieutenant general n : teniente mf general
life [ˈlaɪf] n, pl **lives** [ˈlaɪvz] **1** : vida f ⟨plant life : la vida vegetal⟩ **2** EXISTENCE : vida f, existencia f **3** BIOGRAPHY : biografía f, vida f **4** DURATION : duración f, vida f **5** LIVELINESS : vivacidad f, animación f
lifeblood [ˈlaɪfˌblʌd] n : parte f vital, sustento m
lifeboat [ˈlaɪfˌboːt] n : bote m salvavidas
lifeguard [ˈlaɪfˌɡɑrd] n : socorrista mf, salvavidas mf
lifeless [ˈlaɪfləs] adj : sin vida, muerto
lifelike [ˈlaɪfˌlaɪk] adj : que parece vivo, natural, verosímil

lifelong [ˈlaɪfˌlɔŋ] adj : de toda la vida ⟨a lifelong friend : un amigo de toda la vida⟩
life preserver n : salvavidas m
lifesaver [ˈlaɪfˌseɪvər] n **1** : salvación f **2** → **lifeguard**
lifesaving [ˈlaɪfˌseɪvɪŋ] n : socorrismo m
lifestyle [ˈlaɪfˌstaɪl] n : estilo m de vida
lifetime [ˈlaɪfˌtaɪm] n : vida f, curso m de la vida
lift¹ [ˈlɪft] vt **1** RAISE : levantar, alzar, subir **2** END : levantar ⟨to lift a ban : levantar una prohibición⟩ — vi **1** RISE : levantarse, alzarse **2** CLEAR UP : despejar ⟨the fog lifted : se disipó la niebla⟩
lift² n **1** LIFTING : levantamiento m, alzamiento m **2** BOOST : impulso m, estímulo m **3 to give someone a lift** : llevar en coche a alguien
liftoff [ˈlɪftˌɔf] n : despegue m
ligament [ˈlɪɡəmənt] n : ligamento m
ligature [ˈlɪɡəˌtʃʊr, -tʃər] n : ligadura f
light¹ [ˈlaɪt] v **lit** [ˈlɪt] or **lighted; lighting** vt **1** ILLUMINATE : iluminar, alumbrar **2** IGNITE : encender, prenderle fuego a — vi : encenderse, prender
light² vi **lighted** or **lit** [ˈlɪt]; **lighting 1** LAND, SETTLE : posarse **2** DISMOUNT : bajarse, apearse
light³ [ˈlaɪt] adv **1** LIGHTLY : suavemente, ligeramente **2 to travel light** : viajar con poco equipaje
light⁴ adj **1** LIGHTWEIGHT : ligero, liviano, poco pesado **2** EASY : fácil, ligero, liviano ⟨light reading : lectura fácil⟩ ⟨light work : trabajo liviano⟩ **3** GENTLE, MILD : fino, suave, leve ⟨a light breeze : una brisa suave⟩ ⟨a light rain : una lluvia fina⟩ **4** FRIVOLOUS : de poca importancia, superficial **5** BRIGHT : bien iluminado, claro **6** PALE : claro (dícese de los colores), rubio (dícese del pelo)
light⁵ n **1** ILLUMINATION : luz f **2** DAYLIGHT : luz f del día **3** DAWN : amanecer m, madrugada f **4** LAMP : lámpara f ⟨to turn on off the light : apagar la luz⟩ **5** ASPECT : aspecto m ⟨in a new light : con otros ojos⟩ ⟨in the light of : en vista de, a la luz de⟩ **6** MATCH : fósforo m, cerillo m **7 to bring to light** : sacar a (la) luz
lightbulb [ˈlaɪtˌbʌlb] n : bombilla f, foco m, bombillo m CA, Col, Ven
lighten [ˈlaɪtən] vt **1** ILLUMINATE : iluminar, dar más luz a **2** : aclararse (el pelo) **3** : aligerar (una carga, etc.) **4** RELIEVE : aliviar ⟨it lightened his heart : alegró su corazón⟩
lighter [ˈlaɪtər] n : encendedor m
lighthearted [ˈlaɪtˈhɑrtəd] adj : alegre, despreocupado, desenfadado — **lightheartedly** adv
lightheartedness [ˈlaɪtˈhɑrtədnəs] n : desenfado m, alegría f
lighthouse [ˈlaɪtˌhaʊs] n : faro m

lighting ['laɪtɪŋ] n : iluminación f
lightly ['laɪtli] adv 1 GENTLY : suavemente 2 SLIGHTLY : ligeramente 3 FRIVOLOUSLY : a la ligera 4 to let off lightly : tratar con indulgencia
lightness ['laɪtnəs] n 1 BRIGHTNESS : luminosidad f, claridad f 2 GENTLENESS : ligereza f, suavidad f, delicadeza f 3 : ligereza f, liviandad f (de peso)
lightning ['laɪtnɪŋ] n : relámpago m, rayo m
lightning bug → firefly
lightproof ['laɪt,pru:f] adj : impenetrable por la luz, opaco
lightweight ['laɪt'weɪt] adj : ligero, liviano, de poco peso
light-year ['laɪt,jɪr] n : año m luz
lignite ['lɪg,naɪt] n : lignito m
likable or **likeable** ['laɪkəbəl] adj : simpático, agradable
like[1] ['laɪk] v **liked; liking** vt 1 : agradar, gustarle (algo a uno) ⟨he likes rice : le gusta el arroz⟩ ⟨she doesn't like flowers : a ella no le gustan las flores⟩ ⟨I like you : me caes bien⟩ 2 WANT : quérer, desear ⟨I'd like a hamburger : quiero una hamburguesa⟩ ⟨he would like more help : le gustaría tener más ayuda⟩ — vi : querer ⟨do as you like : haz lo que quieras⟩
like[2] adj : parecido, semejante, similar
like[3] n 1 PREFERENCE : preferencia f, gusto m 2 the like : cosa f parecida, cosas fpl por el estilo ⟨I've never seen the like : nunca he visto cosa parecida⟩
like[4] conj 1 AS IF : como si ⟨they looked at me like I was crazy : se me quedaron mirando como si estuviera loca⟩ 2 AS : como, igual que ⟨she doesn't love you like I do : ella no te quiere como yo⟩
like[5] prep 1 : como, parecido a ⟨she acts like my mother : se comporta como mi madre⟩ ⟨he looks like me : se parece a mí⟩ 2 : propio de, típico de ⟨that's just like her : eso es muy típico de ella⟩ 3 : como ⟨animals like cows : animales como vacas⟩ 4 like this, like that : así ⟨do it like that : hazlo así⟩
likelihood ['laɪkli,hʊd] n : probabilidad f ⟨in all likelihood : con toda probabilidad⟩
likely[1] ['laɪkli] adv : probablemente ⟨most likely he's sick : lo más probable es que esté enfermo⟩ ⟨they're likely to come : es probable que vengan⟩
likely[2] adj -lier; -est 1 PROBABLE : probable ⟨to be likely to : ser muy probable que⟩ 2 SUITABLE : apropiado, adecuado 3 BELIEVABLE : verosímil, creíble 4 PROMISING : prometedor
liken ['laɪkən] vt : comparar
likeness ['laɪknəs] n 1 SIMILARITY : semejanza f, parecido m 2 PORTRAIT : retrato m
likewise ['laɪk,waɪz] adv 1 SIMILARLY : de la misma manera, asimismo 2 ALSO : también, además, asimismo

liking ['laɪkɪŋ] n 1 FONDNESS : afición f (por una cosa), simpatía f (por una persona) 2 TASTE : gusto m ⟨is it to your liking? : ¿te gusta?⟩
lilac ['laɪlək, -,læk, -,lɑk] n : lila f
lilt ['lɪlt] n : cadencia f, ritmo m alegre
lily ['lɪli] n, pl **lilies** 1 : lirio m, azucena f 2 **lily of the valley** : lirio m de los valles, muguete m
lima bean ['laɪmə] n : frijol m de media luna
limb ['lɪm] n 1 APPENDAGE : miembro m, extremidad f 2 BRANCH : rama f
limber[1] ['lɪmbər] vi or to limber up : calentarse, prepararse
limber[2] : ágil (dícese de las personas), flexible (dícese de los objetos)
limbo ['lɪm,bo:] n, pl -bos 1 : limbo m (en la religión) 2 OBLIVION : olvido m ⟨the project is in limbo : el proyecto ha caído en el olvido⟩
lime ['laɪm] n 1 : cal f (óxido) 2 : lima f (fruta), limón m verde Mex
limelight ['laɪm,laɪt] n to be in the limelight : ser el centro de atención, estar en el candelero
limerick ['lɪmərɪk] n : poema m jocoso de cinco versos
limestone ['laɪm,sto:n] n : piedra f caliza, caliza f
limit[1] ['lɪmət] vt : limitar, restringir
limit[2] n 1 MAXIMUM : límite m, máximo m ⟨speed limit : límite de velocidad⟩ 2 **limits** npl : límites mpl, confines mpl ⟨city limits : límites de la ciudad⟩ 3 that's the limit! : ¡eso es el colmo!
limitation [,lɪmə'teɪʃən] n : limitación f, restricción f
limited ['lɪmətəd] adj : limitado, restringido
limitless ['lɪmətləs] adj : ilimitado, sin límites
limousine ['lɪmə,zi:n, ,lɪmə'-] n : limusina f
limp[1] ['lɪmp] vi : cojear
limp[2] adj 1 FLACCID : fláccido 2 LANK : lacio (dícese del pelo) 3 WEAK : débil ⟨to feel limp : sentirse desfallecer, sentirse sin fuerzas⟩
limp[3] n : cojera f
limpid ['lɪmpəd] adj : límpido, claro
limply ['lɪmpli] adv : sin fuerzas
limpness ['lɪmpnəs] n : flaccidez f, debilidad f
linden ['lɪndən] n : tilo m
line[1] ['laɪn] v **lined; lining** vt 1 : forrar, cubrir ⟨to line a dress : forrar un vestido⟩ ⟨to line the walls : cubrir las paredes⟩ 2 MARK : rayar, trazar líneas en 3 BORDER : bordear 4 ALIGN : alinear — vi to line up : ponerse in fila, hacer cola
line[2] n 1 CORD, ROPE : cuerda f 2 WIRE : cable m ⟨power line : cable eléctrico⟩ 3 : línea f (de teléfono) 4 ROW : fila f, hilera f 5 NOTE : nota f, líneas fpl ⟨drop me a line : mándame unas líneas⟩ 6 COURSE : línea f ⟨line of inquiry : línea

de investigación⟩ **7** AGREEMENT : conformidad *f* ⟨to be in line with : ser conforme a⟩ ⟨to fall into line : estar de acuerdo⟩ **8** OCCUPATION : ocupación *f*, rama *f*, especialidad *f* **9** LIMIT : línea *f*, límite *m* ⟨dividing line : línea divisoria⟩ ⟨to draw the line : fijar límites⟩ **10** SERVICE : línea *f* ⟨bus line : línea de autobuses⟩ **11** MARK : línea *f*, arruga *f* (de la cara)

lineage [ˈlɪniɪdʒ] *n* : linaje *m*, abolengo *m*

lineal [ˈlɪniəl] *adj* : en línea directa

lineaments [ˈlɪniəmənts] *npl* : facciones *fpl* (de la cara), rasgos *mpl*

linear [ˈlɪniər] *adj* : lineal

linen [ˈlɪnən] *n* : lino *m*

liner [ˈlaɪnər] *n* **1** LINING : forro *m* **2** SHIP : buque *m*, transatlántico *m*

lineup [ˈlaɪnˌəp] *n* **1** : fila *f* de sospechosos **2** : formación *f* (en deportes) **3** ALIGNMENT : alineación *f*

linger [ˈlɪŋgər] *vi* **1** TARRY : quedarse, entretenerse, rezagarse **2** PERSIST : persistir, sobrevivir

lingerie [ˌlɑndʒəˈreɪ, ˌlænʒəˈriː] *n* : ropa *f* íntima femenina, lencería *f*

lingo [ˈlɪŋgo] *n, pl* **-goes 1** LANGUAGE : idioma *m* **2** JARGON : jerga *f*

linguist [ˈlɪŋgwɪst] *n* : lingüista *mf*

linguistic [lɪŋˈgwɪstɪk] *adj* : lingüístico

linguistics [lɪŋˈgwɪstɪks] *n* : lingüística *f*

liniment [ˈlɪnəmənt] *n* : linimento *m*

lining [ˈlaɪnɪŋ] *n* : forro *m*

link¹ [ˈlɪŋk] *vt* : unir, enlazar, conectar — *vi* to link up : unirse, conectar

link² *n* **1** : eslabón *m* (de una cadena) **2** BOND : conexión *f*, lazo *m*, vínculo *m*

linkage [ˈlɪŋkɪdʒ] *n* : conexión *f*, unión *f*, enlace *m*

linoleum [ləˈnoːliəm] *n* : linóleo *m*

linseed oil [ˈlɪnˌsiːd] *n* : aceite *m* de linaza

lint [ˈlɪnt] *n* : pelusa *f*

lintel [ˈlɪntəl] *n* : dintel *m*

lion [ˈlaɪən] *n* : león *m*

lioness [ˈlaɪənɪs] *n* : leona *f*

lionize [ˈlaɪəˌnaɪz] *vt* **-ized; -izing** : tratar a una persona como muy importante

lip [ˈlɪp] *n* **1** : labio *m* **2** EDGE, RIM : pico *m* (de una jarra), borde *m* (de una taza)

lipreading [ˈlɪpˌriːdɪŋ] *n* : lectura *f* de los labios

lipstick [ˈlɪpˌstɪk] *n* : lápiz *m* de labios, barra *f* de labios

liquefy [ˈlɪkwəˌfaɪ] *v* **-fied; -fying** *vt* : licuar — *vi* : licuarse

liqueur [lɪˈkʊr, -ˈkər, -ˈkjʊr] *n* : licor *f*

liquid¹ [ˈlɪkwəd] *adj* : líquido

liquid² *n* : líquido *m*

liquidate [ˈlɪkwəˌdeɪt] *vt* **-dated; -dating** : liquidar

liquidation [ˌlɪkwəˈdeɪʃən] *n* : liquidación *f*

liquidity [lɪkˈwɪdəti] *n* : liquidez *f*

liquor [ˈlɪkər] *n* : alcohol *m*, bebidas *fpl* alcohólicas, licor *m*

lisp¹ [ˈlɪsp] *vi* : cecear

lisp² *n* : ceceo *m*

lissome [ˈlɪsəm] *adj* **1** FLEXIBLE : flexible **2** LITHE : ágil y grácil

list¹ [ˈlɪst] *vt* **1** ENUMERATE : hacer una lista de, enumerar **2** INCLUDE : poner en una lista, incluir — *vi* : escorar (dícese de un barco)

list² *n* **1** ENUMERATION : lista *f* **2** SLANT : escora *f*, inclinación *f*

listen [ˈlɪsən] *vi* **1** : escuchar, oír **2** to listen to HEED : prestar atención a, hacer caso de, escuchar **3** to listen to reason : atender a razones

listener [ˈlɪsənər] *n* : oyente *mf*, persona *f* que sabe escuchar

listless [ˈlɪstləs] *adj* : lánguido, apático — **listlessly** *adv*

listlessness [ˈlɪstləsnəs] *n* : apatía *f*, languidez *f*, desgana *f*

lit [ˈlɪt] → **light**

litany [ˈlɪtəni] *n, pl* **-nies** : letanía *f*

liter [ˈliːtər] *n* : litro *m*

literacy [ˈlɪtərəsi] *n* : alfabetismo *m*

literal [ˈlɪtərəl] *adj* : literal — **literally** *adv*

literary [ˈlɪtəˌrri] *adj* : literario

literate [ˈlɪtərət] *adj* : alfabetizado

literature [ˈlɪtərəˌtʃʊr, -ˈʃər] *n* : literatura *f*

lithe [ˈlaɪð, ˈlaɪθ] *adj* : ágil y grácil

lithesome [ˈlaɪðsəm, ˈlaɪθ-] → **lissome**

lithium [ˈlɪθiəm] *n* : litio *m*

lithograph [ˈlɪθəˌgræf] *n* : litografía *f*

lithographer [lɪˈθɑgrəfər, ˈlɪθəˌgræfər] *n* : litógrafo *m*, -fa *f*

lithography [lɪˈθɑgrəfi] *n* : litografía *f*

lithosphere [ˈlɪθəˌsfɪr] *n* : litosfera *f*

Lithuanian [ˌlɪθəˈweɪniən] *n* **1** : lituano *m* (idioma) **2** : lituano *m*, -na *f* — **Lithuanian** *adj*

litigant [ˈlɪtɪgənt] *n* : litigante *mf*

litigate [ˈlɪtəˌgeɪt] *vi* **-gated; -gating** : litigar

litigation [ˌlɪtəˈgeɪʃən] *n* : litigio *m*

litmus paper [ˈlɪtməs] *n* : papel *m* de tornasol

litter¹ [ˈlɪtər] *vt* : tirar basura en, ensuciar — *vi* : tirar basura

litter² *n* **1** : camada *f*, cría *f* ⟨a litter of kittens : una cría de gatitos⟩ **2** STRETCHER : camilla *f* **3** RUBBISH : basura *f* **4** : arena *f* higiénica (para gatos)

little¹ [ˈlɪtəl] *adv* less [ˈles]; least [ˈliːst] **1** : poco ⟨she sings very little : canta muy poco⟩ **2** little did I know that . . . : no tenía la menor idea de que . . . **3** as little as possible : lo menos posible

little² *adj* littler or less [ˈles] or lesser [ˈlesər]; littlest or least [ˈliːst] **1** SMALL : pequeño **2** : poco ⟨they speak little Spanish : hablan poco español⟩ ⟨little by little : poco a poco⟩ **3** TRIVIAL : sin importancia, trivial

little³ *n* **1** : poco *m* ⟨little has changed : poco ha cambiado⟩ **2** a little : un poco, algo ⟨it's a little surprising : es algo sorprendente⟩

Little Dipper → **dipper**

liturgical [ləˈtərdʒɪkəl] *adj* : litúrgico — **liturgically** [-kli] *adv*

liturgy [ˈlɪtərd͡ʒi] *n*, *pl* **-gies** : liturgia *f*

livable [ˈlɪvəbəl] *adj* : habitable

live[1] [ˈlɪv] *vi* **lived; living** **1** EXIST : vivir ⟨as long as I live : mientras viva⟩ ⟨to live from day to day : vivir al día⟩ **2** : llevar una vida, vivir ⟨he lived simply : llevó una vida sencilla⟩ **3** SUBSIST : mantenerse, vivir **4** RESIDE : vivir, residir

live[2] [ˈlaɪv] *adj* **1** LIVING : vivo **2** BURNING : encendido ⟨a live coal : una brasa⟩ **3** : con corriente ⟨live wires : cables con corriente⟩ **4** : cargado, sin estallar ⟨a live bomb : una bomba sin estallar⟩ **5** CURRENT : de actualidad ⟨a live issue : un asunto de actualidad⟩ **6** : en vivo, en directo ⟨a live interview : una entrevista en vivo⟩

livelihood [ˈlaɪvliˌhʊd] *n* : sustento *m*, vida *f*, medio *m* de vida

liveliness [ˈlaɪvlinəs] *n* : animación *f*, vivacidad *f*

livelong [ˈlɪvˌlɔŋ] *adj* : entero, completo

lively [ˈlaɪvli] *adj* **-lier; -est** : animado, vivaz, vivo, enérgico

liven [ˈlaɪvən] *vt* : animar — *vi* : animarse

liver [ˈlɪvər] *n* : hígado *m*

livery [ˈlɪvəri] *n*, *pl* **-eries** : librea *f*

lives → **life**

livestock [ˈlaɪvˌstɑk] *n* : ganado *m*

live wire *n* : persona *f* vivaz y muy activa

livid [ˈlɪvəd] *adj* **1** BLACK-AND-BLUE : amoratado **2** PALE : lívido **3** ENRAGED : furioso

living[1] [ˈlɪvɪŋ] *adj* : vivo

living[2] *n* to make a living : ganarse la vida

living room *n* : living *m*, sala *f* de estar

lizard [ˈlɪzərd] *n* : lagarto *m*

llama [ˈlɑmə, ˈjɑ-] *n* : llama *f*

load[1] [ˈloːd] *vt* : cargar, embarcar

load[2] *n* **1** CARGO : carga *f* **2** WEIGHT : peso *m* **3** BURDEN : carga *f*, peso *m* **4** loads *npl* : montón *m*, pila *f*, cantidad *f* ⟨loads of work : un montón de trabajo⟩

loaf[1] [ˈloːf] *vi* : holgazanear, flojear, haraganear

loaf[2] *n*, *pl* **loaves** [ˈloːvz] **1** : pan *m*, pan *m* de molde, barra *f* de pan **2 meat loaf** : pan *m* de carne

loafer [ˈloːfər] *n* : holgazán *m*, -zana *f*; haragán *m*, -gana *f*; vago *m*, -ga *f*

loam [ˈloːm] *n* : marga *f*, suelo *m*

loan[1] [ˈloːn] *vt* : prestar

loan[2] *n* : préstamo *m*, empréstito *m* (del banco)

loath [ˈloːθ, ˈloːð] *adj* : poco dispuesto ⟨I am loath to say it : me resisto a decirlo⟩

loathe [ˈloːð] *vt* **loathed; loathing** : odiar, aborrecer

loathing [ˈloːðɪŋ] *n* : aversión *f*, odio *m*, aborrecimiento *m*

loathsome [ˈloːθsəm, ˈloːð-] *adj* : odioso, repugnante

lob[1] [ˈlɑb] *vt* **lobbed; lobbing** : hacerle un globo (a otro jugador)

lob[2] *n* : globo *m* (en deportes)

lobby[1] [ˈlɑbi] *v* **-bied; -bying** *vt* : presionar, ejercer presión sobre — *vi* to **lobby for** : presionar para (lograr algo)

lobby[2] *n*, *pl* **-bies** **1** FOYER : vestíbulo *m* **2** LOBBYISTS : grupo *m* de presión, lobby *m*

lobbyist [ˈlɑbiɪst] *n* : miembro *m* de un lobby

lobe [ˈloːb] *n* : lóbulo *m*

lobed [ˈloːbd] *adj* : lobulado

lobotomy [ləˈbɑtəmi, loˈ-] *n*, *pl* **-mies** : lobotomía *f*

lobster [ˈlɑbstər] *n* : langosta *f*

local[1] [ˈloːkəl] *adj* : local

local[2] *n* **1** : anestesia *f* local **2 the locals** : los vecinos del lugar, los habitantes

locale [loˈkæl] *n* : lugar *m*, escenario *m*

locality [loˈkæləti] *n*, *pl* **-ties** : localidad *f*

localize [ˈloːkəˌlaɪz] *vt* **-ized; -izing** : localizar

locally [ˈloːkəli] *adv* : en la localidad, en la zona

locate [ˈloːˌkeɪt, loˈkeɪt] *v* **-cated; -cating** *vt* **1** POSITION : situar, ubicar **2** FIND : localizar, ubicar — *vi* SETTLE : establecerse

location [loˈkeɪʃən] *n* **1** POSITION : posición *f*, emplazamiento *m*, ubicación *f* **2** PLACE : lugar *m*, sitio *m*

lock[1] [ˈlɑk] *vt* **1** FASTEN : cerrar **2** CONFINE : encerrar ⟨they locked me in the room : me encerraron en la sala⟩ **3** IMMOBILIZE : bloquear (una rueda) — *vi* **1** : cerrarse (dícese de una puerta) **2** : trabarse, bloquearse (dícese de una rueda)

lock[2] *n* **1** : mechón *m* (de pelo) **2** FASTENER : cerradura *f*, cerrojo *m*, chapa *f* **3** : esclusa *f* (de un canal)

locker [ˈlɑkər] *n* : armario *m*, cajón *m* con llave, lócker *m*

locket [ˈlɑkət] *n* : medallón *m*, guardapelo *m*, relicario *m*

lockjaw [ˈlɑkˌd͡ʒɔ] *n* : tétano *m*

lockout [ˈlɑkˌaʊt] *n* : cierre *m* patronal, lockout *m*

locksmith [ˈlɑkˌsmɪθ] *n* : cerrajero *m*, -ra *f*

lockup [ˈlɑkˌʌp] *n* JAIL : cárcel *f*

locomotion [ˌloːkəˈmoːʃən] *n* : locomoción *f*

locomotive[1] [ˌloːkəˈmoːtɪv] *adj* : locomotor

locomotive[2] *n* : locomotora *f*

locust [ˈloːkəst] *n* **1** : langosta *f*, chapulín *m* CA, Mex **2** CICADA : cigarra *f*, chicharra *f* **3** : acacia *f* blanca (árbol)

locution [loˈkjuːʃən] *n* : locución *f*

lode [ˈloːd] *n* : veta *f*, vena *f*, filón *m*

lodestar [ˈloːdˌstɑr] *n* : estrella *f* polar

lodestone [ˈloːdˌstoːn] *n* : piedra *f* imán

lodge[1] [ˈlɑd͡ʒ] *v* **lodged; lodging** *vt* **1** HOUSE : hospedar, alojar **2** FILE : presentar ⟨to lodge a complaint : presentar una demanda⟩ — *vi* **1** : posarse, meterse ⟨the bullet lodged in the door

: la bala se incrustó en la puerta⟩ 2
STAY : hospedarse, alojarse
lodge² n 1 : pabellón m, casa f de campo ⟨hunting lodge : refugio de caza⟩ 2
: madriguera f (de un castor) 3 : logia
f ⟨Masonic lodge : logia masónica⟩
lodger ['lɑdʒər] n : inquilino m, -na f;
huésped m, -peda f
lodging ['lɑdʒɪŋ] n 1 : alojamiento m 2
lodgings npl ROOMS : habitaciones fpl
loft ['lɔft] n 1 ATTIC : desván m, ático m,
buhardilla f 2 : loft m (en un depósito
comercial) 3 HAYLOFT : pajar m 4
: galería f ⟨choir loft : galería del coro⟩
loftily ['lɔftəli] adv : altaneramente, con
altivez
loftiness ['lɔftinəs] n 1 NOBILITY : nobleza f 2 ARROGANCE : altanería f, arrogancia f 3 HEIGHT : altura f, elevación f
lofty ['lɔfti] adj loftier; -est 1 NOBLE
: noble, elevado 2 HAUGHTY : altivo,
arrogante, altanero 3 HIGH : majestuoso, elevado
log¹ ['lɔg, 'lɑg] vi logged; logging 1 : talar (árboles) 2 RECORD : registrar, anotar 3 to log on : entrar (al sistema) 4
to log off : salir (del sistema)
log² n 1 : tronco m, leño m 2 RECORD
: diario m
logarithm ['lɔgə,rɪðəm, 'lɑ-] n : logaritmo m
logger ['lɔgər, 'lɑ-] n : leñador m, -dora f
loggerhead ['lɔgər,hɛd, 'lɑ-] n 1 : tortuga f boba 2 to be at loggerheads : estar en pugna, estar en desacuerdo
logic ['lɑdʒɪk] n : lógica f — **logical**
['lɑdʒɪkəl] adj — **logically** [-kli] adv
logistic [lə'dʒɪstɪk, lo-] adj : logístico
logistics [lə'dʒɪstɪks, lo-] ns & pl : logística f
logo ['lo,go:] n, pl **logos** [-,go:z] : logotipo m
loin ['lɔɪn] n 1 : lomo m ⟨pork loin
: lomo de cerdo⟩ 2 **loins** npl : lomos
mpl ⟨to gird one's loins : prepararse
para la lucha⟩
loiter ['lɔɪtər] vi : vagar, perder el tiempo
loll ['lɑl] vi 1 SLOUCH : repantigarse 2
IDLE : holgazanear, hacer el vago
lollipop or **lollypop** ['lɑli,pɑp] n : dulce
m en palito, chupete m Chile, Peru,
paleta f CA, Mex
lone ['lo:n] adj 1 SOLITARY : solitario 2
ONLY : único
loneliness ['lo:nlinəs] n : soledad f
lonely ['lo:nli] adj -lier; -est 1 SOLITARY
: solitario, aislado 2 LONESOME : solo
⟨to feel lonely : sentirse muy solo⟩
loner ['lo:nər] n : solitario m, -ria f; recluso m, -sa f
lonesome ['lo:nsəm] adj : solo, solitario
long¹ ['lɔŋ] vi 1 **to long for** : añorar, desear, anhelar 2 **to long to** : anhelar, estar deseando ⟨they longed to see her
: estaban deseando verla, tenían
muchas ganas de verla⟩

long² adv 1 : mucho, mucho tiempo ⟨it
didn't take long : no llevó mucho tiempo⟩ ⟨will it last long? : ¿va a durar mucho?⟩ 2 **all day long** : todo el día 3 **as
long as** or **so long as** : mientras, con
tal que 4 **long before** : mucho antes 5
so long! : ¡hasta luego!, ¡adiós!
long³ adj longer ['lɔŋgər]; longest
['lɔŋgəst] 1 (indicating length)) : largo
⟨the dress is too long : el vestido es demasiado largo⟩ ⟨a long way from : bastante lejos de⟩ ⟨in the long run : a la
larga⟩ 2 (indicating time)) : largo, prolongado ⟨a long illness : una enfermedad prolongada⟩ ⟨a long walk : un
paseo largo⟩ ⟨at long last : por fin⟩ 3
to be long on : estar cargado de
long⁴ n 1 **before long** : dentro de poco
2 **the long and the short** : lo esencial,
lo fundamental
longevity [lɑn'dʒɛvəti] n : longevidad f
longhand ['lɔŋ,hænd] n : escritura f a
mano, escritura f cursiva
longhorn ['lɔŋ,hɔrn] n : longhorn mf
longing ['lɔŋɪŋ] n : vivo deseo m, ansia f,
anhelo m
longingly ['lɔŋɪŋli] adv : ansiosamente,
con ansia
longitude ['lɑndʒə,tu:d, -,tju:d] n : longitud f
longitudinal [,lɑndʒə'tu:dənəl, -'tju:-]
adj : longitudinal — **longitudinally** adv
long-lived ['lɔŋ'lɪvd, -'laɪvd] adj : longevo
longshoreman ['lɔŋ'ʃormən] n, pl **-men**
[-mən, -,mɛn] : estibador m, -dora f
long-standing ['lɔŋ'stændɪŋ] adj : de
larga data
long-suffering ['lɔŋ'sʌfərɪŋ] adj : paciente, sufrido
look¹ ['lʊk] vi 1 GLANCE : mirar ⟨to look
out the window : mirar por la ventana⟩
2 INVESTIGATE : buscar, mirar ⟨look
in the closet : busca en el closet⟩ ⟨look
before you leap : mira lo que haces⟩ 3
SEEM : parecer ⟨he looks happy
: parece estar contento⟩ ⟨I look like my
mother : me parezco a mi madre⟩ 4 to
look after : cuidar, cuidar de 5 **to look
for** EXPECT : esperar 6 **to look for** SEEK
: buscar — vt : mirar
look² n 1 GLANCE : mirada f 2 EXPRESSION : cara f ⟨a look of disapproval : una cara de desaprobación⟩ 3
ASPECT : aspecto m, apariencia f, aire
m 4 **looks** npl : belleza f
lookout ['lʊk,aʊt] n 1 : centinela mf,
vigía mf 2 **to be on the lookout for** : estar al acecho de, andar a la caza de
loom¹ ['lu:m] vi 1 : aparecer, surgir ⟨the
city loomed up in the distance : la ciudad surgió en la distancia⟩ 2 IMPEND
: amenazar, ser inminente 3 **to loom
large** : cobrar mucha importancia
loom² n : telar m
loon ['lu:n] n : somorgujo m, somormujo m
loony or **looney** ['lu:ni] adj -nier; -est
: loco, chiflado fam

loop¹ [ˈluːp] *vt* **1** : hacer lazadas con **2 to loop around** : pasar alrededor de — *vi* **1** : rizar el rizo (dícese de un avión) **2** : serpentear (dícese de una carretera)

loop² *n* **1** : lazada *f* (en hilo o cuerda) **2** BEND : curva *f* **3** CIRCUIT : circuito *m* cerrado **4** : rizo *m* (en la aviación) ⟨to loop the loop : rizar el rizo⟩

loophole [ˈluːpˌhoːl] *n* : escapatoria *f*, pretexto *m*

loose¹ [ˈluːs] *vt* **loosed; loosing 1** RELEASE : poner en libertad, soltar **2** UNTIE : deshacer, desatar **3** DISCHARGE, UNLEASH : descargar, desatar

loose² → **loosely**

loose³ *adj* **looser; -est 1** INSECURE : flojo, suelto, poco seguro ⟨a loose tooth : un diente flojo⟩ **2** ROOMY : suelto, holgado ⟨loose clothing : ropa holgada⟩ **3** OPEN : suelto, abierto ⟨loose soil : suelo suelto⟩ ⟨a loose weave : una tejida abierta⟩ **4** FREE : suelto ⟨to break loose : soltarse⟩ **5** SLACK : flojo, flexible **6** APPROXIMATE : libre, aproximado ⟨a loose translation : una traducción aproximada⟩

loosely [ˈluːsli] *adv* **1** : sin apretar **2** ROUGHLY : aproximadamente, más o menos

loosen [ˈluːsən] *vt* : aflojar

loose–leaf [ˈluːsˈliːf] *adj* : de hojas sueltas

looseness [ˈluːsnəs] *n* **1** : aflojamiento *m*, holgura *f* (de ropa) **2** IMPRECISION : imprecisión *f*

loot¹ [ˈluːt] *vt* : saquear, robar

loot² *n* : botín *m*

looter [ˈluːtər] *n* : saqueador *m*, -dora *f*

lop [ˈlɑp] *vt* **lopped; lopping** : cortar, podar

lope¹ [ˈloːp] *vi* **loped; loping** : correr a paso largo

lope² *n* : paso *m* largo

lopsided [ˈlɑpˌsaɪdəd] *adj* **1** CROOKED : torcido, chueco, ladeado **2** ASYMETRICAL : asimétrico

loquacious [loˈkweɪʃəs] *adj* : locuaz

lord [ˈlɔrd] *n* **1** : señor *m*, noble *m* **2** : lord *m* (en la Gran Bretaña) **3 the Lord** : el Señor **4 good Lord!** : ¡Dios mío!

lordly [ˈlɔrdli] *adj* **-lier; -est** HAUGHTY : arrogante, altanero

lordship [ˈlɔrdˌʃɪp] *n* : señoría *f*

Lord's Supper *n* : Eucaristía *f*

lore [ˈlor] *n* : saber *m* popular, tradición *f*

lose [ˈluːz] *v* **lost** [ˈlɔst]; **losing** [ˈluː-zɪŋ] *vt* **1** : perder ⟨I lost my umbrella : perdí mi paraguas⟩ ⟨to lose blood : perder sangre⟩ ⟨to lose one's voice : quedarse fónico⟩ ⟨to have nothing to lose : no tener nada que perder⟩ ⟨to lose no time : no perder tiempo⟩ ⟨to lose weight : perder peso, adelgazar⟩ ⟨to lose one's temper : perder los estribos, enojarse, enfadarse⟩ ⟨to lose sight of : perder de vista⟩ **2** : costar, hacer perder ⟨the errors lost him his job : los errores le

costaron su empleo⟩ **3** : atrasar ⟨my watch loses 5 minutes a day : mi reloj atrasa 5 minutos por día⟩ **4 to lose oneself** : perderse, ensimismarse — *vi* **1** : perder ⟨we lost to the other team : perdimos contra el otro equipo⟩ **2** : atrasarse ⟨the clock loses time : el reloj se atrasa⟩

loser [ˈluːzər] *n* : perdedor *m*, -dora *f*

loss [ˈlɔs] *n* **1** LOSING : pérdida *f* ⟨loss of memory : pérdida de memoria⟩ ⟨to sell at a loss : vender con pérdida⟩ ⟨to be at a loss to : no saber como⟩ **2** DEFEAT : derrota *f*, juego *m* perdido **3 losses** *npl* DEATHS : muertos *mpl*

lost [ˈlɔst] *adj* **1** : perdido ⟨a lost cause : una causa perdida⟩ ⟨lost in thought : absorto⟩ **2 to get lost** : perderse **3 to make up for lost time** : recuperar el tiempo perdido

lot [ˈlɑt] *n* **1** DRAWING : sorteo *m* ⟨by lot : por sorteo⟩ **2** SHARE : parte *f*, porción *f* **3** FATE : suerte *f* **4** LAND, PLOT : terreno *m*, solar *m*, lote *m*, parcela *f* ⟨parking lot : estacionamiento⟩ **5 a lot of** *or* **lots of** : mucho, un montón de, bastante ⟨lots of books : un montón de libros, muchos libros⟩ ⟨a lot of people : mucha gente⟩

loth [ˈloːθ, ˈloːð] → **loath**

lotion [ˈloːʃən] *n* : loción *f*

lottery [ˈlɑtəri] *n*, *pl* **-teries** : lotería *f*

lotus [ˈloːtəs] *n* : loto *m*

loud¹ [ˈlaʊd] *adv* : alto, fuerte ⟨out loud : en voz alta⟩

loud² *adj* **1** : alto, fuerte ⟨a loud voice : una voz alta⟩ **2** NOISY : ruidoso ⟨a loud party : una fiesta ruidosa⟩ **3** FLASHY : llamativo, chillón

loudly [ˈlaʊdli] *adv* : alto, fuerte, en voz alta

loudness [ˈlaʊdnəs] *n* : volumen *m*, fuerza *f* (del ruido)

loudspeaker [ˈlaʊdˌspiːkər] *n* : altavoz *m*, altoparlante *m*

lounge¹ [ˈlaʊndʒ] *vi* **lounged; lounging** : holgazanear, gandulear

lounge² *n* : salón *m*, sala *f* de estar

louse [ˈlaʊs] *n*, *pl* **lice** [ˈlaɪs] : piojo *m*

lousy [ˈlaʊzi] *adj* **lousier; -est 1** : piojoso, lleno de piojos **2** BAD : pésimo, muy malo

lout [ˈlaʊt] *n* : bruto *m*, patán *m*

louver *or* **louvre** [ˈluːvər] *n* : persiana *f*, listón *m* de persiana

lovable [ˈlʌvəbəl] *adj* : adorable, amoroso, encantador

love¹ [ˈlʌv] *v* **loved; loving** *vt* **1** : querer, amar ⟨I love you : te quiero⟩ **2** ENJOY : encantarle a alguien, ser (muy) aficionado a, gustarle mucho a uno (algo) ⟨she loves flowers : le encantan las flores⟩ ⟨he loves golf : es muy aficionado al golf⟩ ⟨I'd love to go with you : me gustaría mucho acompañarte⟩ — *vi* : querer, amar

love² *n* **1** : amor *m*, cariño *m* ⟨to be in love with : estar enamorado de⟩ ⟨to fall

in love with : enamorarse de⟩ **2** EN-
THUSIASM, INTEREST : amor *m*, afición
m, gusto *m* ⟨love of music : afición a
la música⟩ **3** BELOVED : amor *m*; amado *m*, -da *f*; enamorado *m*, -da *f*
loveless [ˈlʌvləs] *adj* : sin amor
loveliness [ˈlʌvlinəs] *n* : belleza *f*, hermosura *f*
lovelorn [ˈlʌvˌlɔrn] *adj* : herido de amor,
perdidamente enamorado
lovely [ˈlʌvli] *adj* **-lier; -est** : hermoso,
bello, lindo, precioso
lover [ˈlʌvər] *n* : amante *mf* (de personas); aficionado *m*, -da *f* (a alguna actividad)
loving [ˈlʌvɪŋ] *adj* : amoroso, cariñoso
lovingly [ˈlʌvɪŋli] *adv* : cariñosamente
low¹ [ˈloː] *vi* : mugir
low² *adv* : bajo, profundo ⟨to aim low
: apuntar bajo⟩ ⟨to lie low : mantenerse escondido⟩ ⟨to turn the lights
down low : bajar las luces⟩
low³ *adj* **lower** [ˈloːər], **-est** **1** : bajo ⟨a
low building : un edificio bajo⟩ ⟨a low
bow : una profunda reverencia⟩ **2**
SOFT : bajo, suave ⟨in a low voice : en
voz baja⟩ **3** SHALLOW : bajo, poco profundo **4** HUMBLE : humilde, modesto
5 DEPRESSED : deprimido, bajo de
moral **6** INFERIOR : bajo, inferior **7**
UNFAVORABLE : mal ⟨to have a low
opinion of him : tener un mal concepto de él⟩ **8 to be low on** : tener poco
de, estar escaso de
low⁴ *n* **1** : punto *m* bajo ⟨to reach an all-
time low : estar más bajo que nunca⟩
2 *or* **low gear** : primera velocidad *f* **3**
: mugido *m* (de una vaca)
lowbrow [ˈloːˌbraʊ] *n* : persona *f* inculta
lower¹ [ˈloːər] *vt* **1** DROP : bajar ⟨to lower one's voice : bajar la voz⟩ **2** : arriar, bajar ⟨to lower the flag : arriar la
bandera⟩ **3** REDUCE : reducir, bajar **4**
to lower oneself : rebajarse
lower² [ˈloːər] *adj* : inferior, más bajo, de
abajo
lowland [ˈloːlənd, -ˌlænd] *n* : tierras *fpl*
bajas
lowly [ˈloːli] *adj* **-lier; -est** : humilde,
modesto
loyal [ˈlɔɪəl] *adj* : leal, fiel — **loyally** *adv*
loyalist [ˈlɔɪəlɪst] *n* : partidario *m*, -ria *f*
del régimen
loyalty [ˈlɔɪəlti] *n, pl* **-ties** : lealtad *f*, fidelidad *f*
lozenge [ˈlɑzəndʒ] *n* : pastilla *f*
LSD [ˌɛlˌɛsˈdiː] *n* : LSD *m*
lubricant [ˈluːbrɪkənt] *n* : lubricante *m*
lubricate [ˈluːbrɪˌkeɪt] *vt* **-cated; -cating**
: lubricar — **lubrication** [ˌluːbrɪ-
ˈkeɪʃən] *n*
lucid [ˈluːsəd] *adj* : lúcido, claro — **lu-
cidly** *adv*
lucidity [luːˈsɪdəti] *n* : lucidez *f*
luck [ˈlʌk] *n* **1** : suerte *f* **2 to have bad
luck** : tener mala suerte **3 good luck!**
: ¡(buena) suerte!
luckily [ˈlʌkəli] *adv* : afortunadamente,
por suerte

luckless [ˈlʌkləs] *adj* : desafortunado
lucky [ˈlʌki] *adj* **luckier; -est** **1** : afortunado, que tiene suerte ⟨a lucky
woman : una mujer afortunada⟩ **2**
FORTUITOUS : fortuito, de suerte **3** OP-
PORTUNE : oportuno **4** : de (la) suerte
⟨lucky number : número de la suerte⟩
lucrative [ˈluːkrətɪv] *adj* : lucrativo,
provechoso — **lucratively** *adv*
ludicrous [ˈluːdəkrəs] *adj* : ridículo, absurdo — **ludicrously** *adv*
ludicrousness [ˈluːdəkrəsnəs] *n* : ridiculez *f*, absurdo *m*
lug [ˈlʌg] *vt* **lugged; lugging** : arrastrar,
transportar con dificultad
luggage [ˈlʌgɪdʒ] *n* : equipaje *m*
lugubrious [luˈguːbriəs] *adj* : lúgubre —
lugubriously *adv*
lukewarm [ˈluːkˈwɔrm] *adj* **1** TEPID
: tibio **2** HALFHEARTED : poco entusia-
asta
lull¹ [ˈlʌl] *vt* **1** CALM, SOOTHE : calmar,
sosegar **2 to lull to sleep** : arrullar,
adormecer
lull² *n* : calma *f*, pausa *f*
lullaby [ˈlʌləˌbaɪ] *n, pl* **-bies** : canción *f*
de cuna, arrullo *m*, nana *f*
lumber¹ [ˈlʌmbər] *vt* : aserrar (madera)
— *vi* : moverse pesadamente
lumber² *n* : madera *f*
lumberjack [ˈlʌmbərˌdʒæk] *n* : leñador
m, -dora *f*
lumberyard [ˈlʌmbərˌjɑrd] *n* : almacén
m de maderas
luminary [ˈluːməˌneri] *n, pl* **-naries**
: lumbrera *f*, luminaria *f*
luminescence [ˌluːməˈnɛsənts] *n* : luminiscencia *f* — **luminescent** [-ˈnɛs-
ənt] *adj*
luminosity [ˌluːməˈnɑsəti] *n, pl* **-ties**
: luminosidad *f*
luminous [ˈluːmənəs] *adj* : luminoso —
luminously *adv*
lump¹ [ˈlʌmp] *vt or* **to lump together**
: juntar, agrupar, amontonar — *vi*
CLUMP : agruparse, aglutinarse
lump² *n* **1** GLOB : grumo *m* **2** PIECE
: pedazo *m*, trozo *m*, terrón *m* ⟨a lump
of coal : un trozo de carbón⟩, ⟨a lump
of sugar : un terrón de azúcar⟩ **3**
SWELLING : bulto *m*, hinchazón *f*,
protuberancia *f* **4 to have a lump in
one's throat** : tener un nudo en la garganta
lumpy [ˈlʌmpi] *adj* **lumpier; -est 1**
: lleno de grumos (dícese de una salsa)
2 UNEVEN : desigual, disparejo
lunacy [ˈluːnəsi] *n, pl* **-cies** : locura *f*
lunar [ˈluːnər] *adj* : lunar
lunatic¹ [ˈluːnəˌtɪk] *adj* : lunático, loco
lunatic² *n* : loco *m*, -ca *f*
lunch¹ [ˈlʌntʃ] *vi* : almorzar, comer
lunch² *n* : almuerzo *m*, comida *f*, lonche
m
luncheon [ˈlʌntʃən] *n* **1** : comida *f*, almuerzo *m* **2 luncheon meat** : fiambres
fpl

lung ['lʌŋ] *n* : pulmón *m*
lunge[1] ['lʌndʒ] *vi* **lunged; lunging 1**
THRUST : atacar (en la esgrima) **2 to
lunge forward** : arremeter, lanzarse
lunge[2] *n* **1** : arremetida *f*, embestida *f* **2**
: estocada *f* (en la esgrima)
lurch[1] ['lərtʃ] *vi* **1** PITCH : cabecear, dar
bandazos, dar sacudidas **2** STAGGER
: tambalearse
lurch[2] *n* **1** : sacudida *f*, bandazo *m* (de
un vehículo) **2** : tambaleo *m* (de una
persona)
lure[1] ['lʊr] *vt* **lured; luring** : atraer
lure[2] *n* **1** ATTRACTION : atractivo *m* **2**
ENTICEMENT : señuelo *m*, aliciente
m **3** BAIT : cebo *m* artificial (en la
pesca)
lurid ['lʊrəd] *adj* **1** GRUESOME : espeluznante, horripilante **2** SENSA-
TIONAL : sensacionalista, chocante **3**
GAUDY : chillón
lurk ['lərk] *vi* : estar al acecho
luscious ['lʌʃəs] *adj* **1** DELICIOUS : delicioso, exquisito **2** SEDUCTIVE : seductor, cautivador
lush ['lʌʃ] *adj* **1** LUXURIANT : exuberante, lozano **2** LUXURIOUS : suntuoso,
lujoso
lust[1] ['lʌst] *vi* **to lust after** : desear (a una
persona), codiciar (riquezas, etc.)
lust[2] *n* **1** LASCIVIOUSNESS : lujuria *f*, lascivia *f* **2** CRAVING : deseo *m*, ansia *f*,
anhelo *m*
luster *or* **lustre** ['lʌstər] *n* **1** GLOSS,

SHEEN : lustre *m*, brillo *m* **2** SPLEN-
DOR : lustre *m*, esplendor *m*
lusterless ['lʌstərləs] *adj* : deslustrado,
sin brillo
lustful ['lʌstfəl] *adj* : lujurioso, lascivo,
lleno de deseo
lustrous ['lʌstrəs] *adj* : brillante, brilloso, lustroso
lusty ['lʌsti] *adj* **lustier; -est** : fuerte, robusto, vigoroso — **lustily** ['lʌstəli] *adv*
luxuriant [ˌlʌgˈʒʊriənt, ˌlʌkˈʃʊr-] *adj* **1**
: exuberante, lozano (dícese de las
plantas) **2** : abundante y hermoso
(dícese del pelo) — **luxuriantly** *adv*
luxuriate [ˌlʌgˈʒʊriˌeɪt, ˌlʌkˈʃʊr-] *vi*
-ated; -ating 1 : disfrutar **2 to luxuriate in** : deleitarse con
luxurious [ˌlʌgˈʒʊriəs, ˌlʌkˈʃʊr-] *adj* : lujoso, suntuoso — **luxuriously** *adv*
luxury ['lʌkʃəri, 'lʌgʒə-] *n, pl* **-ries** : lujo
m
lye ['laɪ] *n* : lejía *f*
lying → **lie**[1], **lie**[2]
lymph ['lɪmpf] *n* : linfa *f*
lymphatic [lɪmˈfætɪk] *adj* : linfático
lynch ['lɪntʃ] *vt* : linchar
lynx ['lɪŋks] *n, pl* **lynx** *or* **lynxes** : lince
m
lyre ['laɪr] *n* : lira *f*
lyric[1] ['lɪrɪk] *adj* : lírico
lyric[2] *n* **1** : poema *m* lírico **2 lyrics** *npl*
: letra *f* (de una canción)
lyrical ['lɪrɪkəl] *adj* : lírico, elocuente

M

m ['ɛm] *n, pl* **m's** *or* **ms** ['ɛmz] : deci-
motercera letra del alfabeto inglés
ma'am ['mæm] → **madam**
macabre [məˈkɑb, -ˈkɑbər, -ˈkɑbrə] *adj*
: macabro
macadam [məˈkædəm] *n* : macadán *m*
macaroni [ˌmækəˈroːni] *n* : macarrones
mpl
macaroon [ˌmækəˈruːn] *n* : macarrón *m*,
mostachón *m*
macaw [məˈkɔ] *n* : guacamayo *m*
mace ['meɪs] *n* **1** : maza *f* (arma o símbolo) **2** : macis *f* (especia)
machete [məˈʃɛti] *n* : machete *m*
machination [ˌmækəˈneɪʃən, ˌmæʃə-] *n*
: maquinación *f*, intriga *f*
machine[1] [məˈʃiːn] *vt* **-chined; -chining**
: trabajar a máquina
machine[2] *n* **1** : máquina *f* ⟨**machine
shop** : taller de máquinas⟩ ⟨**machine
language** : lenguaje de la máquina⟩ **2**
: aparato *m*, maquinaria *f* (en política)
machine gun *n* : ametralladora *f*
machinery [məˈʃiːnəri] *n, pl* **-eries**
1 : maquinaria *f* **2** WORKS : mecanismo
m
machinist [məˈʃiːnɪst] *n* : maquinista *mf*
machismo [məˈtʃiːzmo] *n* : machismo
m, masculinidad *f*

macho ['mɑtʃo] *adj* : machote, macho
mackerel ['mækərəl] *n, pl* **-el** *or* **-els** : caballa *f*
mackinaw ['mækəˌnɔ] *n* : chaqueta *f* escocesa de lana
mad ['mæd] *adj* **madder; maddest 1** IN-
SANE : loco, demente **2** RABID : rabioso **3** FOOLISH : tonto, insensato **4**
ANGRY : enojado, furioso **5** CRAZY
: loco ⟨I'm mad about you : estoy loco
por ti⟩
Madagascan [ˌmædəˈɡæskən] *n* : malgache *mf* — **Madagascan** *adj*
madam ['mædəm] *n, pl* **mesdames**
[meɪˈdɑm, -ˈdæm] : señora *f*
madcap ['mædˌkæp] *adj* ZANY : alocado, disparatado
madcap[2] *n* : alocado *m*, -da *f*
madden ['mædən] *vt* : enloquecer, enfurecer
maddening ['mædənɪŋ] *adj* : enloquecedor, exasperante ⟨I find it maddena-
ing : me saca de quicio⟩
made → **make**[1]
madhouse ['mædˌhaʊs] *n* : manicomio
m ⟨the office was a madhouse : la oficina parecía una casa de locos⟩
madly ['mædli] *adv* : como un loco, locamente

madman ['mæd,mæn, -mən] *n, pl* **-men** [-mən, -,mɛn] : loco *m*, demente *m*

madness ['mædnəs] *n* : locura *f*, demencia *f*

madwoman ['mæd,wʊmən] *n, pl* **-women** [-,wɪmən] : loca *f*, demente *f*

maelstrom ['meɪlstrəm] *n* : remolino *m*, vorágine *f*

maestro ['maɪ,stro:] *n, pl* **-stros** *or* **-stri** [-,stri:] : maestro *m*

Mafia ['mɑfiə] *n* : Mafia *f*

magazine ['mægə,zi:n] *n* **1** STOREHOUSE : almacén *m*, polvorín *m* (de explosivos) **2** PERIODICAL : revista *f* **3** : cargador *m* (de un arma de fuego)

magenta [mə'dʒɛntə] *n* : magenta *f*, color *m* magenta

maggot ['mægət] *n* : gusano *m*

magic[1] ['mædʒɪk] *or* **magical** ['mædʒɪkəl] *adj* : mágico

magic[2] *n* : magia *f*

magically ['mædʒɪkli] *adv* : mágicamente ⟨they magically appeared : aparecieron como por arte de magia⟩

magician [mə'dʒɪʃən] *n* **1** SORCERER : mago *m*, -ga *f* **2** CONJURER : prestidigitador *m*, -dora *f*; mago *m*, -ga *f*

magistrate ['mædʒə,streɪt] *n* : magistrado *m*, -da *f*

magma ['mægmə] *n* : magma *m*

magnanimity [,mægnə'nɪmət̮i] *n, pl* **-ties** : magnanimidad *f*

magnanimous [mæg'nænəməs] *adj* : magnánimo, generoso — **magnanimously** *adv*

magnate ['mæg,neɪt, -nət] *n* : magnate *mf*

magnesium [mæg'ni:ziəm, -ʒəm] *n* : magnesio *m*

magnet ['mægnət] *n* : imán *m*

magnetic [mæg'nɛt̮ɪk] *adj* : magnético — **magnetically** [-t̮ɪkli] *adv*

magnetic field *n* : campo *m* magnético

magnetism ['mægnə,tɪzəm] *n* : magnetismo *m*

magnetize ['mægnə,taɪz] *vt* **-tized; -tizing 1** : magnetizar, imantar **2** ATTRACT : magnetizar, atraer

magnification [,mægnəfə'keɪʃən] *n* : aumento *m*, ampliación *f*

magnificence [mæg'nɪfəsəns] *n* : magnificencia *f*

magnificent [mæg'nɪfəsənt] *adj* : magnífico — **magnificently** *adv*

magnify ['mægnə,faɪ] *vt* **-fied; -fying 1** ENLARGE : ampliar **2** EXAGGERATE : magnificar, exagerar

magnifying glass *n* : lupa *f*

magnitude ['mægnə,tu:d, -,tju:d] *n* **1** GREATNESS : magnitud *f*, grandeza *f* **2** QUANTITY : cantidad *f* **3** IMPORTANCE : magnitud *f*, envergadura *f*

magnolia [mæg'no:ljə] *n* : magnolia *f* (flor), magnolio *m* (árbol)

magpie ['mæg,paɪ] *n* : urraca *f*

mahogany [mə'hɑgəni] *n, pl* **-nies** : caoba *f*

maid ['meɪd] *n* **1** MAIDEN : doncella *f* **2** *or* **maidservant** ['meɪd,sərvənt] : sirvienta *f*, muchacha *f*, mucama *f*, criada *f*

maiden[1] ['meɪdən] *adj* **1** UNMARRIED : soltera **2** FIRST : primero ⟨maiden voyage : primera travesía⟩

maiden[2] *n* : doncella *f*

maidenhood ['meɪdən,hʊd] *n* : doncellez *f*

maiden name *n* : nombre *m* de soltera

mail[1] ['meɪl] *vt* : enviar por correo, echar al correo

mail[2] *n* **1** : correo *m* ⟨airmail : correo aéreo⟩ **2** : malla *f* ⟨coat of mail : cota de malla⟩

mailbox ['meɪl,bɑks] *n* : buzón *m*

mailman ['meɪl,mæn, -mən] *n, pl* **-men** [-mən, -,mɛn] : cartero *m*

maim ['meɪm] *vt* : mutilar, desfigurar, lisiar

main[1] ['meɪn] *adj* : principal, central ⟨the main office : la oficina central⟩

main[2] *n* **1** HIGH SEAS : alta mar *f* **2** : tubería *f* principal (de agua o gas), cable *m* principal (de un circuito) **3** with might and main : con todas sus fuerzas

mainframe ['meɪn,freɪm] *n* : mainframe *m*, computadora *f* central

mainland ['meɪn,lænd, -lənd] *n* : continente *m*

mainly ['meɪnli] *adv* **1** PRINCIPALLY : principalmente, en primer lugar **2** MOSTLY : principalmente, en la mayor parte

mainstay ['meɪn,steɪ] *n* : pilar *m*, sostén *m* principal

mainstream[1] ['meɪn,stri:m] *adj* : dominante, corriente, convencional

mainstream[2] *n* : corriente *f* principal

maintain [meɪn'teɪn] *vt* **1** SERVICE : dar mantenimiento a (una máquina) **2** PRESERVE : mantener, conservar ⟨to maintain silence : guardar silencio⟩ **3** SUPPORT : mantener, sostener **4** ASSERT : mantener, sostener, afirmar

maintenance ['meɪntənəns] *n* : mantenimiento *m*

maize ['meɪz] *n* : maíz *m*

majestic [mə'dʒɛstɪk] *adj* : majestuoso — **majestically** [-tɪkli] *adv*

majesty ['mædʒəsti] *n, pl* **-ties 1** : majestad *f* ⟨Your Majesty : su Majestad⟩ **2** SPLENDOR : majestuosidad *f*, esplendor *m*

major[1] ['meɪdʒər] *vi* **-jored; -joring** : especializarse

major[2] *adj* **1** GREATER : mayor **2** NOTEWORTHY : mayor, notable **3** SERIOUS : grave **4** : mayor (en la música)

major[3] *n* **1** : mayor *mf*, comandante *mf* (en las fuerzas armadas) **2** : especialidad *f* (universitaria)

Majorcan [mɑ'dʒɔrkən, mə-, -'jɔr-] *n* : mallorquín *m*, -quina *f* — **Majorcan** *adj*

major general *n* : general *mf* de división

majority [mə'ʤɔrəti] n, pl **-ties 1**
ADULTHOOD : mayoría f de edad **2**
: mayoría f, mayor parte f 〈the vast majority : la inmensa mayoría〉

make¹ ['meɪk] v **made** ['meɪd]; **making**
vt **1** CREATE : hacer 〈to make noise
: hacer ruido〉 **2** FASHION, MANUFACTURE : hacer, fabricar 〈she made a
dress : hizo un vestido〉 **3** DEVISE,
FORM : desarrollar, elaborar, formar **4**
CONSTITUTE : hacer, constituir 〈made
of stone : hecho de piedra〉 **5** PREPARE
: hacer, preparar **6** RENDER : hacer,
poner 〈it makes him nervous : lo pone
nervioso〉 〈to make someone happy
: hacer feliz a alguien〉 〈it made me sad
: me dio pena〉 **7** PERFORM : hacer 〈to
make a gesture : hacer un gesto〉 **8**
COMPEL : hacer, forzar, obligar **9**
EARN : ganar 〈to make a living : ganarse la vida〉 — vi **1** HEAD : ir, dirigirse 〈we made for home : nos fuimos
a casa〉 **2 to make do** : arreglárselas **3
to make good** REPAY : pagar **4 to
make good** SUCCEED : tener éxito

make² n BRAND : marca f

make–believe¹ [,meɪkbə'liːv] adj : imaginario

make–believe² n : fantasía f, invención
f 〈a world of make-believe : un mundo de ensueño〉

make out vt **1** WRITE : hacer (un cheque)
2 DISCERN : distinguir, divisar **3** UNDERSTAND : comprender, entender —
vi : arreglárselas 〈how did you make
out? : ¿qué tal te fue?〉

maker ['meɪkər] n : fabricante mf

makeshift ['meɪk,ʃɪft] adj : provisional,
improvisado

makeup ['meɪk,ʌp] n **1** COMPOSITION
: composición f **2** CHARACTER : carácter m, temperamento m **3** COSMETICS
: maquillaje m

make up vt **1** INVENT : inventar **2** : recuperar 〈she made up the time : recuperó las horas perdidas〉 — vi RECONCILE : hacer las paces, reconciliarse

making ['meɪkɪŋ] n **1** : creación f, producción f 〈in the making : en ciernes〉
2 to have the makings of : tener
madera de (dícese de personas), tener
los ingredientes para

maladjusted [,mælə'ʤʌstəd] adj : inadaptado

malady ['mælədi] n, pl **-dies** : dolencia
f, enfermedad f, mal m

malaise [mə'leɪz, mæ-] n : malestar m

malapropism ['mælə,prɑ,pɪzəm] n : uso
m incorrecto y cómico de una palabra

malaria [mə'leriə] n : malaria f, paludismo m

malarkey [mə'lɑrki] n : tonterías fpl, estupideces fpl

Malawian [mə'lɑwiən] n : malauiano m,
-na f — **Malawian** adj

Malay [mə'leɪ, 'meɪ,leɪ] n **1** or **Malayan**
[mə'leɪən, meɪ-] : malayo m,

-ya f **2** : malayo m (idioma) — **Malay**
or **Malayan** adj

Malaysian [mə'leɪʒən, -ʃən] n : malasio
m, -sia f; malaisio m, -sia f — **Malaysian**
adj

male¹ ['meɪl] adj **1** : macho **2** MASCULINE : masculino

male² n : macho m (de animales o plantas), varón m (de personas)

malefactor ['mælə,fæktər] n : malhechor m, -chora f

maleness ['meɪlnəs] n : masculinidad f

malevolence [mə'levələnts] n : malevolencia f

malevolent [mə'levələnt] adj : malévolo

malformation [,mælfɔr'meɪʃən] n : malformación f

malformed [mæl'fɔrmd] adj : mal formado, deforme

malfunction¹ [mæl'fʌŋkʃən] vi : funcionar mal

malfunction² n : mal funcionamiento m

malice ['mælɪs] n **1** : malicia f, malevolencia f **2 with malice aforethought**
: con premeditación

malicious [mə'lɪʃəs] adj : malicioso,
malévolo — **maliciously** adv

malign¹ [mə'laɪn] vt : calumniar, difamar

malign² adj : maligno

malignancy [mə'lɪgnəntsi] n, pl **-cies**
: malignidad f

malignant [mə'lɪgnənt] adj : maligno

malinger [mə'lɪŋgər] vi : fingirse enfermo

malingerer [mə'lɪŋgərər] n : uno que se
finge enfermo

mall ['mɔl] n **1** PROMENADE : alameda
f, paseo m (arbolado) **2** : centro m comercial 〈shopping mall : galería comercial〉

mallard ['mælərd] n, pl **-lard** or **-lards**
: pato m real, ánade mf real

malleable ['mæliəbəl] adj : maleable

mallet ['mælət] n : mazo m

malnourished [mæl'nərɪʃt] adj : desnutrido, malnutrido

malnutrition [,mælnu'trɪʃən, -nju-] n
: desnutrición f, malnutrición f

malodorous [mæl'oːdərəs] adj : maloliente

malpractice [,mæl'præktəs] n : mala
práctica f, negligencia f

malt ['mɔlt] n : malta f

maltreat [mæl'triːt] vt : maltratar

mama or **mamma** ['mɑmə] n : mamá f

mammal ['mæməl] n : mamífero m

mammalian [mə'meɪliən, mæ-] adj
: mamífero

mammary ['mæməri] adj **1** : mamario
2 mammary gland : glándula mamaria

mammogram ['mæmə,græm] n : mamografía f

mammoth¹ ['mæməθ] adj : colosal, gigantesco

mammoth² n : mamut m

man¹ ['mæn] vt **manned; manning** : tripular (un barco o avión), encargarse de
(un servicio)

man[2] *n, pl* **men** ['mɛn] **1** PERSON : hombre *m*, persona *f* **2** MALE : hombre *m* **3** MANKIND : humanidad *f*

manacles ['mænɪkəlz] *npl* HANDCUFFS : esposas *fpl*

manage ['mænɪʤ] *v* **-aged; -aging** *vt* **1** HANDLE : controlar, manejar **2** DIRECT : administrar, dirigir **3** CONTRIVE : lograr, ingeniárselas para — *vi* COPE : arreglárselas

manageable ['mænɪʤəbəl] *adj* : manejable

management ['mænɪʤmənt] *n* **1** DIRECTION : administración *f*, gestión *f*, dirección *f* **2** HANDLING : manejo *m* **3** MANAGERS : dirección *f*, gerencia *f*

manager ['mænɪʤər] *n* : director *m*, -tora *f*; gerente *mf*; administrador *m*, -dora *f*

managerial [,mænə'ʤɪriəl] *adj* : directivo, gerencial

mandarin ['mændərən] *n* **1** : mandarín *m* **2** *or* **mandarin orange** : mandarina *f*

mandate ['mændeɪt] *n* : mandato *m*

mandatory ['mændə,tori] *adj* : obligatorio

mandible ['mændəbəl] *n* : mandíbula *f*

mandolin [,mændə'lɪn, 'mændələn] *n* : mandolina *f*

mane ['meɪn] *n* : crin *f* (de un caballo), melena *f* (de un león o una persona)

maneuver[1] [mə'nu:vər, -'nju:-] *vt* **1** PLACE, POSITION : maniobrar, posicionar, colocar **2** MANIPULATE : manipular, maniobrar — *vi* : maniobrar

maneuver[2] *n* : maniobra *f*

manfully ['mænfəli] *adj* : valientemente

manganese ['mæŋgə,ni:z, -,ni:s] *n* : manganeso *m*

mange ['meɪnʤ] *n* : sarna *f*

manger ['meɪnʤər] *n* : pesebre *m*

mangle ['mæŋgəl] *vt* **-gled; -gling 1** CRUSH, DESTROY : aplastar, despedazar, destrozar **2** MUTILATE : mutilar ⟨to mangle a text : mutilar un texto⟩

mango ['mæŋ,goː] *n, pl* **-goes** : mango *m*

mangrove ['mæŋ,groːv, 'mæŋ-] *n* : mangle *m*

mangy ['meɪnʤi] *adj* **mangier; -est 1** : sarnoso **2** SHABBY : gastado

manhandle ['mæn,hændəl] *vt* **-dled; -dling** : maltratar, tratar con poco cuidado

manhole ['mæn,hoːl] *n* : boca *f* de alcantarilla

manhood ['mæn,hʊd] *n* **1** : madurez *f* (de un hombre) **2** COURAGE, MANLINESS : hombría *f*, valor *m* **3** MEN : hombres *mpl*

manhunt ['mæn,hʌnt] *n* : búsqueda *f* (de un criminal)

mania ['meɪniə, -njə] *n* : manía *f*

maniac ['meɪni,æk] *n* : maníaco *m*, -ca *f*; maniático *m*, -ca *f*

maniacal [mə'naɪəkəl] *adj* : maníaco, maniaco

manicure[1] ['mænə,kjʊr] *vt* **-cured; -curing 1** : hacer la manicura a **2** TRIM : recortar

manicure[2] *n* : manicura *f*

manicurist ['mænə,kjʊrɪst] *n* : manicuro *m*, -ra *f*

manifest[1] ['mænə,fɛst] *vt* : manifestar

manifest[2] *adj* : manifiesto, patente — **manifestly** *adv*

manifestation [,mænəfə'steɪʃən] *n* : manifestación *f*

manifesto [,mænə'fɛs,toː] *n, pl* **-tos** *or* **-toes** : manifiesto *m*

manifold[1] ['mænə,foːld] *adj* : diverso, variado

manifold[2] *n* : colector *m* (de escape)

manipulate [mə'nɪpjə,leɪt] *vt* **-lated; -lating** : manipular

manipulation [mə,nɪpjə'leɪʃən] *n* : manipulación *f*

manipulative [mə'nɪpjə,leɪtɪv, -lətɪv] *adj* : manipulador

mankind ['mæn'kaɪnd, -,kaɪnd] *n* : género *m* humano, humanidad *f*

manliness ['mænlinəs] *n* : hombría *f*, masculinidad *f*

manly ['mænli] *adj* **-lier; -est** : varonil, viril

man-made ['mæn'meɪd] *adj* : artificial ⟨man-made fabrics : telas sintéticas⟩

manna ['mænə] *n* : maná *m*

mannequin ['mænɪkən] *n* **1** DUMMY : maniquí *m* **2** MODEL : modelo *mf*

manner ['mænər] *n* **1** KIND, SORT : tipo *m*, clase *f* **2** WAY : manera *f*, modo *m* **3** STYLE : estilo *m* (artístico) **4** **manners** *npl* CUSTOMS : costumbres *fpl* ⟨Victorian manners : costumbres victorianas⟩ **5** **manners** *npl* ETIQUETTE : modales *mpl*, educación *f*, etiqueta *f* ⟨good manners : buenos modales⟩

mannered ['mænərd] *adj* **1** AFFECTED, ARTIFICIAL : amanerado, afectado **2** **well-mannered** : educado, cortés **3** → **ill-mannered**

mannerism ['mænə,rɪzəm] *n* : peculiaridad *f*, gesto *m* particular

mannerly ['mænərli] *adj* : cortés, bien educado

mannish ['mænɪʃ] *adj* : masculino, hombruno

man-of-war [,mænə'wɔr, -əv'wɔr] *n, pl* **men-of-war** [,mɛn-] WARSHIP : buque *m* de guerra

manor ['mænər] *n* **1** : casa *f* solariega, casa *f* señorial **2** ESTATE : señorío *m*

manpower ['mæn,paʊər] *n* : personal *m*, mano *f* de obra

mansion ['mænʧən] *n* : mansión *f*

manslaughter ['mæn,slɔtər] *n* : homicidio *m* sin premeditación

mantel ['mæntəl] *n* : repisa *f* de chimenea

mantelpiece ['mæntəl,piːs] → **mantel**

mantis ['mæntəs] *n, pl* **-tises** *or* **-tes** ['mæn,tiːz] : mantis *f* religiosa

mantle ['mæntəl] *n* : manto *m*

manual[1] ['mænjʊəl] *adj* : manual — **manually** *adv*

manual[2] *n* : manual *m*

manufacture[1] [ˌmænjə'fækʧər] *vt* **-tured; -turing** : fabricar, manufacturar, confeccionar (ropa), elaborar (comestibles)

manufacture[2] *n* : manufactura *f*, fabricación *f*, confección *f* (de ropa), elaboración *f* (de comestibles)

manufacturer [ˌmænjə'fækʧərər] *n* : fabricante *m*; manufacturero *m*, -ra *f*

manure [mə'nʊr, -'njʊr] *n* : estiércol *m*

manuscript ['mænjəˌskrɪpt] *n* : manuscrito *m*

many[1] ['mɛni] *adj* **more** ['mor]; **most** ['mo:st] : muchos

many[2] *pron* : muchos *pl*, -chas *pl*

map[1] ['mæp] *vt* **mapped; mapping** 1 : trazar el mapa de 2 PLAN : planear, proyectar <to map out a program : planear un programa>

map[2] *n* : mapa *m*

maple ['meɪpəl] *n* : arce *m*

mar ['mar] *vt* **marred; marring** 1 SPOIL : estropear, echar a perder 2 DEFACE : desfigurar

maraschino [ˌmærə'ski:no:, -'ʃi:-] *n, pl* **-nos** : cereza *f* al marrasquino

marathon ['mærəˌθɑn] *n* 1 RACE : maratón *m* 2 CONTEST : competencia *f* de resistencia

maraud [mə'rɔd] *vi* : merodear

marauder [mə'rɔdər] *n* : merodeador *m*, -dora *f*

marble ['marbəl] *n* 1 : mármol *m* 2 : canica *f* <to play marbles : jugar a las canicas>

march[1] ['marʧ] *vi* 1 : marchar, desfilar <they marched past the grandstand : desfilaron ante la tribuna> 2 : caminar con resolución <she marched right up to him : se le acercó sin vacilación>

march[2] *n* 1 MARCHING : marcha *f* 2 PASSAGE : paso *m* (del tiempo) 3 PROGRESS : avance *m*, progreso *m* 4 : marcha *f* (en música)

March ['marʧ] *n* : marzo *m*

marchioness ['marʃənɪs] *n* : marquesa *f*

Mardi Gras ['mardiˌgra] *n* : martes *m* de Carnaval

mare ['mær] *n* : yegua *f*

margarine ['marʤərən] *n* : margarina *f*

margin ['marʤən] *n* : margen *m*

marginal ['marʤənəl] *adj* 1 : marginal 2 MINIMAL : mínimo — **marginally** *adv*

marigold ['mærəˌgo:ld] *n* : maravilla *f*, caléndula *f*

marijuana [ˌmærə'hwɑnə] *n* : marihuana *f*

marina [mə'ri:nə] *n* : puerto *m* deportivo

marinade [ˌmærə'nɑd] *n* : adobo *m*, marinada *f*

marinate ['mærəˌneɪt] *vt* **-nated; -nating** : marinar

marine[1] [mə'ri:n] *adj* 1 : marino <marine life : vida marina> 2 NAUTICAL : náutico, marítimo 3 : de la infantería de marina

marine[2] *n* : soldado *m* de marina

mariner ['mærɪnər] *n* : marinero *m*, marino *m*

marionette [ˌmæriə'nɛt] *n* : marioneta *f*, títere *m*

marital ['mærət̬əl] *adj* 1 : matrimonial 2 **marital status** : estado *m* civil

maritime ['mærəˌtaɪm] *adj* : marítimo

marjoram ['marʤərəm] *n* : mejorana *f*

mark[1] ['mark] *vt* 1 : marcar 2 CHARACTERIZE : caracterizar 3 SIGNAL : señalar 4 NOTICE : prestar atención a, hacer caso de 5 **to mark off** : demarcar, delimitar

mark[2] *n* 1 TARGET : blanco *m* 2 : marca *f*, señal *f* <put a mark where you left off : pon una señal donde terminaste> 3 INDICATION : señal *f*, indicio *m* 4 GRADE : nota *f* 5 IMPRINT : huella *f*, marca *f* 6 BLEMISH : marca *f*, imperfección *f*

marked ['markt] *adj* : marcado, notable — **markedly** ['markədli] *adv*

marker ['markər] *n* : marcador *m*

market[1] ['markət] *vt* : poner en venta, comercializar

market[2] *n* 1 MARKETPLACE : mercado *m* <the open market : el mercado libre> 2 DEMAND : demanda *f*, mercado *m* 3 STORE : tienda *f* 4 → **stock market**

marketable ['markət̬əbəl] *adj* : vendible

marketing ['markət̬ɪŋ] *n* : mercadotecnia *f*, mercadeo *m*

marketplace ['markətˌpleɪs] *n* : mercado *m*

marksman ['marksmən] *n, pl* **-men** [-mən, -ˌmɛn] : tirador *m*

marksmanship ['marksmənˌʃɪp] *n* : puntería *f*

marlin ['marlɪn] *n* : marlín *m*

marmalade ['marməˌleɪd] *n* : mermelada *f*

marmoset ['marməˌsɛt] *n* : tití *m*

marmot ['marmət] *n* : marmota *f*

maroon[1] [mə'ru:n] *vt* : abandonar, aislar

maroon[2] *n* : rojo *m* oscuro, granate *m*

marquee [mar'ki:] *n* : marquesina *f*

marquess ['markwɪs] *or* **marquis** ['markwɪs, mar'ki:] *n, pl* **-quesses** *or* **-quises** [-'ki:z, -'ki:zəz] *or* **-quis** [-'ki:, -'ki:z] : marqués *m*

marquise [mar'ki:z] → **marchioness**

marriage ['mæriʤ] *n* 1 : matrimonio *m* 2 WEDDING : casamiento *m*, boda *f*

marriageable ['mæriʤəbəl] *adj* **of marriageable age** : de edad de casarse

married ['mærid] *adj* 1 : casado 2 **to get married** : casarse

marrow ['mæro:] *n* : médula *f*, tuétano *m*

marry ['mæri] *vt* **-ried; -rying** 1 : casar <the priest married them : el cura los casó> 2 : casarse con <she married John : se casó con John>

Mars ['marz] *n* : Marte *m*

marsh ['marʃ] *n* **1** : pantano *m* **2 salt marsh** : marisma *f*

marshal¹ ['marʃəl] *vt* **-shaled** or **-shalled; -shaling** or **-shalling 1** : poner en orden, reunir **2** USHER : conducir

marshal² *n* **1** : maestro *m* de ceremonias **2** : mariscal *m* (en el ejército); jefe *m*, -fa *f* (de la policía, de los bomberos, etc.)

marshmallow ['marʃˌmɛloː, -ˌmæloː] *n* : malvavisco *m*

marshy ['marʃi] *adj* **marshier; -est** : pantanoso

marsupial [mar'suːpiəl] *n* : marsupial *m*

mart ['mart] *n* MARKET : mercado *m*

marten ['martən] *n, pl* **-ten** or **-tens** : marta *f*

martial ['marʃəl] *adj* : marcial

martin ['martən] *n* **1** SWALLOW : golondrina *f* **2** SWIFT : vencejo *m*

martyr¹ ['martər] *vt* : martirizar

martyr² *n* : mártir *mf*

martyrdom ['martərdəm] *n* : martirio *m*

marvel¹ ['marvəl] *vi* **-veled** or **-velled; -veling** or **-velling** : maravillarse

marvel² *n* : maravilla *f*

marvelous ['marvələs] or **marvellous** *adj* : maravilloso — **marvelously** *adv*

Marxism ['markˌsɪzəm] *n* : marxismo *m*

Marxist¹ ['marksɪst] *adj* : marxista

Marxist² *n* : marxista *mf*

mascara [mæs'kærə] *n* : rímel *m*, rimel *m*

mascot ['mæsˌkɑt, -kət] *n* : mascota *f*

masculine ['mæskjələn] *adj* : masculino

masculinity [ˌmæskjə'lɪnəti] *n* : masculinidad *f*

mash¹ ['mæʃ] *vt* **1** : hacer puré de (papas, etc.) **2** CRUSH : aplastar, majar

mash² *n* **1** FEED : afrecho *m* **2** : malta *f* (para hacer bebidas alcohólicas) **3** PASTE, PULP : papilla *f*, pasta *f*

mask¹ ['mæsk] *vt* **1** CONCEAL, DISGUISE : enmascarar, ocultar **2** COVER : cubrir, tapar

mask² *n* : máscara *f*, careta *f*, mascarilla *f* (de un cirujano o dentista)

masochism ['mæsəˌkɪzəm, 'mæzə-] *n* : masoquismo *m*

masochist ['mæsəˌkɪst, 'mæzə-] *n* : masoquista *mf*

masochistic [ˌmæsə'kɪstɪk, ˌmæzə-] *adj* : masoquista

mason ['meɪsən] *n* **1** BRICKLAYER : albañil *mf* **2** or **stonemason** ['stoˌnˌ-] : mampostero *m*, cantero *m*

masonry ['meɪsənri] *n, pl* **-ries 1** BRICKLAYING : albañería *f* **2** or **stonemasonry** ['stoˌnˌ-] : mampostería *f*

masquerade¹ [ˌmæskə'reɪd] *vi* **-aded; -ading 1** : disfrazarse (de), hacerse pasar (por) **2** : asistir a una mascarada

masquerade² *n* **1** : mascarada *f*, baile *m* de disfraces **2** FACADE : farsa *f*, fachada *f*

mass¹ ['mæs] *vi* : concentrarse, juntarse en masa — *vt* : concentrar

mass² *n* **1** : masa *f* ⟨atomic mass : masa atómica⟩ **2** BULK : mole *f*, volumen *m* **3** MULTITUDE : cantidad *f*, montón *m* (de cosas), multitud *f* (de gente) **4 the masses** : las masas, el pueblo, el populacho

Mass ['mæs] *n* : misa *f*

massacre¹ ['mæsɪkər] *vt* **-cred; -cring** : masacrar

massacre² *n* : masacre *f*

massage¹ [mə'saʒ, -'saʤ] *vt* **-saged; -saging** : masajear

massage² *n* : masaje *m*

masseur [mæ'sər] *n* : masajista *m*

masseuse [mæ'søz, -'suːz] *n* : masajista *f*

massive ['mæsɪv] *adj* **1** BULKY : voluminoso, macizo **2** HUGE : masivo, enorme — **massively** *adv*

mast ['mæst] *n* : mástil *m*, palo *m*

master¹ ['mæstər] *vt* **1** SUBDUE : dominar **2** : llegar a dominar ⟨she mastered French : llegó a dominar el francés⟩

master² *n* **1** TEACHER : maestro *m*, profesor *m* **2** EXPERT : experto *m*, -ta *f* **3** : amo *m* (de animales o esclavos), señor *m* (de la casa) **4 master's degree** : maestría *f*

masterful ['mæstərfəl] *adj* **1** IMPERIOUS : autoritario, imperioso, dominante **2** SKILLFUL : magistral — **masterfully** *adv*

masterly ['mæstərli] *adj* : magistral

mastermind ['mæstərˌmaɪnd] *n* : cerebro *m*, artífice *mf*

masterpiece ['mæstərˌpiːs] *n* : obra *f* maestra

masterwork ['mæstərˌwərk] → **masterpiece**

mastery ['mæstəri] *n* **1** DOMINION : dominio *m*, autoridad *f* **2** SUPERIORITY : superioridad *f* **3** EXPERTISE : maestría *f*

masticate ['mæstəˌkeɪt] *v* **-cated; -cating** : masticar

mastiff ['mæstɪf] *n* : mastín *m*

mastodon ['mæstəˌdɑn] *n* : mastodonte *m*

masturbate ['mæstərˌbeɪt] *v* **-bated; -bating** *vi* : masturbarse — *vt* : masturbar

masturbation [ˌmæstər'beɪʃən] *n* : masturbación *f*

mat¹ ['mæt] *v* **matted; matting** *vt* TANGLE : enmarañar — *vi* : enmarañarse

mat² *n* **1** : estera *f* **2** TANGLE : maraña *f* **3** PAD : colchoneta *f* (de gimnasia) **4** or **matt** or **matte** ['mæt] FRAME : marco *m* (de cartón)

mat³ → **matte**

matador ['mætəˌdɔr] *n* : matador *m*

match¹ ['mæʧ] *vt* **1** PIT : enfrentar, oponer **2** EQUAL, FIT : igualar, corresponder a, coincidir con **3** : combinar con, hacer juego con ⟨her shoes match her dress : sus zapatos hacen juego con su vestido⟩ — *vi* **1** CORRESPOND : concordar, coincidir **2** : hacer juego ⟨with a tie to match : con una corbata que hace juego⟩

match² *n* 1 EQUAL : igual *mf* ⟨he's no match for her : no puede competir con ella⟩ 2 FIGHT, GAME : partido *m*, combate *m* (en boxeo) 3 MARRIAGE : matrimonio *m*, casamiento *m* 4 : fósforo *m*, cerilla *f*, cerillo *m in various countries*⟩ ⟨he lit a match : encendió un fósforo⟩ 5 **to be a good match** : hacer buena pareja (dícese de las personas), hacer juego (dícese de la ropa)

matchless ['mætʃləs] *adj* : sin igual, sin par

matchmaker ['mætʃ,meɪkər] *n* : casamentero *m*, -ra *f*

mate¹ ['meɪt] *v* **mated; mating** *vi* 1 FIT : encajar 2 PAIR : emparejarse 3 (*relating to animals*) : aparearse, copular — *vt* : aparear, acoplar (animales)

mate² *n* 1 COMPANION : compañero *m*, -ra *f*; camarada *mf* 2 : macho *m*, hembra *f* (de animales) 3 : oficial *mf* (de un barco) ⟨first mate : primer oficial⟩ 4 : compañero *m*, -ra *f*; pareja *f* (de un zapato, etc.)

material¹ [mə'tɪriəl] *adj* 1 PHYSICAL : material, físico ⟨the material world : el mundo material⟩ ⟨material needs : necesidades materiales⟩ 2 IMPORTANT : importante, esencial 3 **material evidence** : prueba *f* sustancial

material² *n* 1 : material *m* 2 CLOTH : tejido *m*, tela *f*

materialism [mə'tɪriə,lɪzəm] *n* : materialismo *m*

materialist [mə'tɪriəlɪst] *n* : materialista *mf*

materialistic [mə,tɪriə'lɪstɪk] *adj* : materialista

materialize [mə'tɪriə,laɪz] *v* **-ized; -izing** *vt* : materializar, hacer aparecer — *vi* : materializarse, aparecer

maternal [mə'tərnəl] *adj* MOTHERLY : maternal — **maternally** *adv*

maternity¹ [mə'tərnəti] *adj* : de maternidad ⟨maternity clothes : ropa de futura mamá⟩ ⟨maternity leave : licencia por maternidad⟩

maternity² *n, pl* **-ties** : maternidad *f*

math ['mæθ] → **mathematics**

mathematical [,mæθə'mætɪkəl] *adj* : matemático — **mathematically** *adv*

mathematician [,mæθəmə'tɪʃən] *n* : matemático *m*, -ca *f*

mathematics [,mæθə'mætɪks] *ns & pl* : matemáticas *fpl*, matemática *f*

matinee *or* **matinée** [,mætən'eɪ] *n* : matiné *f*

matriarch ['meɪtri,ɑrk] *n* : matriarca *f*

matriarchy ['meɪtri,ɑrki] *n, pl* **-chies** : matriarcado *m*

matriculate [mə'trɪkjə,leɪt] *v* **-lated; -lating** *vt* : matricular — *vi* : matricularse

matriculation [mə,trɪkjə'leɪʃən] *n* : matrícula *f*, matriculación *f*

matrimony ['mætrə,moːni] *n* : matrimonio *m* — **matrimonial** [,mætrə'moːniəl] *adj*

matrix ['meɪtrɪks] *n, pl* **-trices** ['meɪtrə,siːz, 'mæ-] *or* **-trixes** ['meɪtrɪksəz] : matriz *f*

matron ['meɪtrən] *n* : matrona *f*

matronly ['meɪtrənli] *adj* : de matrona, matronal

matte ['mæt] *adj* : mate, de acabado mate

matter¹ ['mætər] *vi* : importar ⟨it doesn't matter : no importa⟩

matter² *n* 1 QUESTION : asunto *m*, cuestión *f* ⟨a matter of taste : una cuestión de gusto⟩ 2 SUBSTANCE : materia *f*, sustancia *f* 3 **matters** *npl* CIRCUMSTANCES : situación *f*, cosas *fpl* ⟨to make matters worse : para colmo de males⟩ 4 **to be the matter** : pasar ⟨what's the matter? : ¿qué pasa?⟩ 5 **as a matter of fact** : en efecto, en realidad 6 **for that matter** : de hecho 7 **no matter how much** : por mucho que

matter-of-fact ['mætərəv'fækt] *adj* : práctico, realista

mattress ['mætrəs] *n* : colchón *m*

mature¹ [mə'tʊr, -'tjʊr, -'tʃʊr] *vi* **-tured; -turing** 1 : madurar 2 : vencer ⟨when does the loan mature? : ¿cuándo vence el préstamo?⟩

mature² *adj* **-turer; -est** 1 : maduro 2 DUE : vencido

maturity [mə'tʊrəti, -'tjʊr-, -'tʃʊr-] *n* : madurez *f*

maudlin ['mɔdlɪn] *adj* : sensiblero

maul¹ ['mɔl] *vt* 1 BEAT : golpear, pegar 2 MANGLE : mutilar 3 MANHANDLE : maltratar

maul² *n* MALLET : mazo *m*

Mauritanian [,mɔrə'teɪniən] *n* : mauritano *m*, -na *f* — **Mauritanian** *adj*

mausoleum [,mɔsə'liːəm, ,mɔzə-] *n, pl* **-leums** *or* **-lea** ['-liːə] : mausoleo *m*

mauve ['moːv, 'mɔv] *n* : malva *f*

maven *or* **mavin** ['meɪvən] *n* EXPERT : experto *m*, -ta *f*

maverick ['mævrɪk, 'mævə-] *n* 1 : ternero *m* sin marcar 2 NONCONFORMIST : inconformista *mf*, disidente *mf*

mawkish ['mɔkɪʃ] *adj* : sensiblero

maxim ['mæksəm] *n* : máxima *f*

maximize ['mæksə,maɪz] *vt* **-mized; -mizing** : maximizar, llevar al máximo

maximum¹ ['mæksəməm] *adj* : máximo

maximum² *n, pl* **-ma** ['mæksəmə] *or* **-mums** : máximo *m*

may ['meɪ] *v aux, past* **might** ['maɪt] *present s & pl* **may** 1 (*expressing permission*) : poder ⟨you may go : puedes ir⟩ 2 (*expressing possibility or probability*) : poder ⟨you may be right : puede que tengas razón⟩ ⟨it may happen occasionally : puede pasar de vez en cuando⟩ 3 (*expressing desires, intentions, or contingencies*) ⟨may the best man win : que gane el mejor⟩ ⟨I laugh that I may not weep : me río para no llorar⟩ ⟨come what may : pase lo que pase⟩

May ['meɪ] *n* : mayo *m*

Maya ['maɪə] *or* **Mayan** ['maɪən] *n* : maya
mf — **Maya** *or* **Mayan** *adj*

maybe ['meɪbi] *adv* PERHAPS : quizás,
tal vez

mayfly ['meɪˌflaɪ] *n, pl* **-flies** : efímera *f*

mayhem ['meɪˌhɛm, 'meɪəm] *n* **1** MUTI-
LATION : mutilación *f* **2** DEVASTATION
: estragos *mpl*

mayonnaise ['meɪəˌneɪz] *n* : mayonesa *f*

mayor ['meɪər, 'mɛr] *n* : alcalde *m*, -desa
f

mayoral ['meɪərəl, 'mɛrəl] *adj* : de alcalde

maze ['meɪz] *n* : laberinto *m*

me ['mi:] *pron* **1** : me ⟨she called me : me
llamó⟩ ⟨give it to me : dámelo⟩ **2** (*after a preposition*) : mí ⟨for me : para
mí⟩ ⟨with me : conmigo⟩ **3** (*after con-
junctions and verbs*) : yo ⟨it's me : soy
yo⟩ ⟨as big as me : tan grande como
yo⟩ **4** (*emphatic use*) : yo ⟨me, too! : ¡yo
también!⟩ ⟨who, me? : ¿quién, yo?⟩

meadow ['mɛdo:] *n* : prado *m*, pradera
f

meadowland ['mɛdoˌlænd] *n* : pradera *f*

meadowlark ['mɛdoˌlɑrk] *n* : pájaro *m*
cantor con el pecho amarillo

meager *or* **meagre** ['mi:gər] *adj* **1** THIN
: magro, flaco **2** POOR, SCANTY : ex-
iguo, escaso, pobre

meagerly ['mi:gərli] *adv* : pobremente

meagerness ['mi:gərnəs] *n* : escasez *f*,
pobreza *f*

meal ['mi:l] *n* **1** : comida *f* ⟨a hearty meal
: una comida sustanciosa⟩ **2** : harina *f*
(de maíz, etc.)

mealtime ['mi:lˌtaɪm] *n* : hora *f* de comer

mean¹ ['mi:n] *vt* **meant** ['mɛnt]; **meaning** **1** INTEND : querer, pensar, tener
la intención de ⟨I didn't mean to do it
: lo hice sin querer⟩ ⟨what do you mean
to do? : ¿qué piensas hacer?⟩ **2** SIG-
NIFY : querer decir, significar ⟨what
does that mean? : ¿qué quiere decir
eso?⟩ **3** : importar ⟨health means
everything : lo que más importa es la
salud⟩

mean² *adj* **1** HUMBLE : humilde **2** NEG-
LIGIBLE : despreciable ⟨it's no mean
feat : no es poca cosa⟩ **3** STINGY
: mezquino, tacaño **4** CRUEL : malo,
cruel ⟨to be mean to someone : tratar
mal a alguien⟩ **5** AVERAGE, MEDIAN
: medio

mean³ *n* **1** MIDPOINT : término *m* medio
2 AVERAGE : promedio *m*, media *f* aritmética **3** **means** *npl* WAY : medio *m*,
manera *f*, vía *f* **4** **means** *npl* RE-
SOURCES : medios *mpl*, recursos *mpl* **5**
by all means : por supuesto, cómo no
6 **by means of** : por medio de **7** **by no
means** : de ninguna manera, de ningún
modo

meander [mi'ændər] *vi* **-dered; -dering**
1 WIND : serpentear **2** WANDER : vagar, andar sin rumbo fijo

meaning ['mi:nɪŋ] *n* **1** : significado *m*,
sentido *m* ⟨double meaning : doble sen-

tido⟩ **2** INTENT : intención *f*, propósito *m*

meaningful ['mi:nɪŋfəl] *adj* : significativo — **meaningfully** *adv*

meaningless ['mi:nɪŋləs] *adj* : sin sentido

meanness ['mi:nnəs] *n* **1** CRUELTY
: crueldad *f*, mezquindad *f* **2** STINGI-
NESS : tacañería *f*

meantime¹ ['mi:nˌtaɪm] *adv* → **meanwhile¹**

meantime² *n* **1** : interín *m* **2** **in the
meantime** : entretanto, mientras tanto

meanwhile¹ ['mi:nˌʰwaɪl] *adv* : entretanto, mientras tanto

meanwhile² *n* → **meantime²**

measles ['mi:zəlz] *ns & pl* : sarampión
m

measly ['mi:zli] *adj* **-slier; -est** : miserable, mezquino

measurable ['mɛʒərəbəl, 'meɪ-] *adj*
: mensurable — **measurably** [-bli] *adv*

measure¹ ['mɛʒər, 'meɪ-] *v* **-sured;
-suring** : medir ⟨he measured the table
: midió la mesa⟩ ⟨it measures 15 feet
tall : mide 15 pies de altura⟩

measure² *n* **1** AMOUNT : medida *f*, cantidad *f* ⟨in large measure : en gran me-
dida⟩ ⟨a full measure : una cantidad
exacta⟩ ⟨a measure of proficiency
: una cierta competencia⟩ ⟨for good
measure : de ñapa, por añadidura⟩ **2**
DIMENSIONS, SIZE : medida *f*, tamaño
m **3** RULER : regla *f* ⟨tape measure
: cinta métrica⟩ **4** MEASUREMENT
: medida *f* ⟨cubic measure : medida de
capacidad⟩ **5** MEASURING : medición
f **6** **measures** *npl* : medidas *fpl* ⟨secu-
rity measures : medidas de seguridad⟩

measureless ['mɛʒərləs, 'meɪ-] *adj* : inmensurable

measurement ['mɛʒərmənt, 'meɪ-] *n* **1**
MEASURING : medición *f* **2** DIMENSION
: medida *f*

measure up *vi* **to measure up to** : estar
a la altura de

meat ['mi:t] *n* **1** FOOD : comida *f* **2**
: carne *f* ⟨meat and fish : carne y pesca-
do⟩ **3** SUBSTANCE : sustancia *f*, esencia *f* ⟨the meat of the story : la sustancia del cuento⟩

meatball ['mi:tˌbɔl] *n* : albóndiga *f*

meaty ['mi:ti] *adj* **meatier; -est** : con
mucha carne, carnoso

mechanic [mi'kænɪk] *n* : mecánico *m*,
-ca *f*

mechanical [mi'kænɪkəl] *adj* : mecánico — **mechanically** *adv*

mechanics [mi'kænɪks] *ns & pl* **1**
: mecánica *f* ⟨fluid mechanics : la
mecánica de fluidos⟩ **2** MECHANISMS
: mecanismos *mpl*, aspectos *mpl* prác-
ticos

mechanism ['mɛkəˌnɪzəm] *n* : mecanismo *m*

mechanization [ˌmɛkənə'zeɪʃən] *n*
: mecanización *f*

mechanize ['mɛkə,naɪz] *vt* **-nized; -nizing** : mecanizar

medal ['mɛdəl] *n* : medalla *f*, condecoración *f*

medalist ['mɛdəlɪst] *or* **medallist** : medallista *mf*

medallion [mə'dæljən] *n* : medallón *m*

meddle ['mɛdəl] *vi* **-dled; -dling** : meterse, entrometerse

meddler ['mɛdələr] *n* : entrometido *m*, -da *f*

meddlesome ['mɛdəlsəm] *adj* : entrometido

media ['mi:diə] *npl* : medios *mpl* de comunicación

median¹ ['mi:diən] *adj* : medio

median² *n* : valor *m* medio

mediate ['mi:di,eɪt] *vi* **-ated; -ating** : mediar

mediation [,mi:di'eɪʃən] *n* : mediación *f*

mediator ['mi:di,eɪtər] *n* : mediador *m*, -dora *f*

medical ['mɛdɪkəl] *adj* : médico

medicate ['mɛdə,keɪt] *vt* **-cated; -cating** : medicar ⟨medicated powder : polvos medicinales⟩

medication [,mɛdə'keɪʃən] *n* 1 TREATMENT : tratamiento *m*, medicación *f* 2 MEDICINE : medicamento *m* ⟨to be on medication : estar medicado⟩

medicinal [mə'dɪsənəl] *adj* : medicinal

medicine ['mɛdəsən] *n* 1 MEDICATION : medicina *f*, medicamento *m* 2 : medicina *f* ⟨he's studying medicine : estudia medicina⟩

medicine man *n* : hechicero *m*

medieval *or* **mediaeval** [mɪ'di:vəl, ,mi:-, ,m-, -di'i:vəl] *adj* : medieval

mediocre [,mi:di'o:kər] *adj* : mediocre

mediocrity [,mi:di'ɑkrəti] *n, pl* **-ties** : mediocridad *f*

meditate ['mɛdə,teɪt] *vi* **-tated; -tating** : meditar

meditation [,mɛdə'teɪʃən] *n* : meditación *f*

meditative ['mɛdə,teɪtɪv] *adj* : meditabundo

medium¹ ['mi:diəm] *adj* : mediano ⟨of medium height : de estatura mediana, de estatura regular⟩

medium² *n, pl* **-diums** *or* **-dia** ['mi:diə] 1 MEAN : punto *m* medio, término *m* medio ⟨happy medium : justo medio⟩ 2 MEANS : medio *m* 3 SUBSTANCE : medio *m*, sustancia *f* ⟨a viscous medium : un medio viscoso⟩ 4 : medio *m* de comunicación 5 : medio *m* (artístico)

medley ['mɛdli] *n, pl* **-leys** : popurrí *m* (de canciones)

meek ['mi:k] *adj* 1 LONG-SUFFERING : paciente, sufrido 2 SUBMISSIVE : sumiso, dócil, manso

meekly ['mi:kli] *adv* : dócilmente

meekness ['mi:knəs] *n* : mansedumbre *f*, docilidad *f*

meet¹ ['mi:t] *v* **met** ['mɛt]; **meeting** *vt* 1 ENCOUNTER : encontrarse con 2 JOIN : unirse con 3 CONFRONT : enfrentarse a 4 SATISFY : satisfacer, cumplir con ⟨to meet costs : pagar los gastos⟩ 5 : conocer ⟨I met his sister : conocí a su hermana⟩ — *vi* ASSEMBLE : reunirse, congregarse

meet² *n* : encuentro *m*

meeting ['mi:tɪŋ] *n* 1 : reunión *f* ⟨to open the meeting : abrir la sesión⟩ 2 ENCOUNTER : encuentro *m* 3 : entrevista *f* (formal)

meetinghouse ['mi:tɪŋ,haʊs] *n* : iglesia *f* (de ciertas confesiones protestantes)

megabyte ['mɛgə,baɪt] *n* : megabyte *m*

megahertz ['mɛgə,hərts, -,hrts] *n* : megahercio *m*

megaphone ['mɛgə,fo:n] *n* : megáfono *m*

melancholy¹ ['mɛlən,kɑli] *adj* : melancólico, triste, sombrío

melancholy² *n, pl* **-cholies** : melancolía *f*

melanoma [,mɛlə'no:mə] *n, pl* **-mas** : melanoma *m*

meld ['mɛld] *vt* : fusionar, unir — *vi* : fusionar, unirse

melee ['meɪ,leɪ, meɪ'leɪ] *n* BRAWL : reyerta *f*, riña *f*, pelea *f*

meliorate ['mi:ljə,reɪt, 'mi:liə-] → **ameliorate**

mellow¹ ['mɛlo:] *vt* : suavizar, endulzar — *vi* : suavizarse, endulzarse

mellow² *adj* 1 RIPE : maduro 2 MILD : apacible ⟨a mellow character : un carácter apacible⟩ ⟨mellow wines : vinos añejos⟩ 3 : suave, dulce ⟨mellow colors : colores suaves⟩ ⟨mellow tones : tonos dulces⟩

mellowness ['mɛlonəs] *n* : suavidad *f*, dulzura *f*

melodic [mə'lɑdɪk] *adj* : melódico — **melodically** [-dɪkli] *adv*

melodious [mə'lo:diəs] *adj* : melodioso — **melodiously** *adv*

melodiousness [mə'lo:diəsnəs] *n* : calidad *f* de melódico

melodrama ['mɛlə,drɑmə, -,dræ-] *n* : melodrama *m*

melodramatic [,mɛlədrə'mætɪk] *adj* : melodramático — **melodramatically** [-tɪkli] *adv*

melody ['mɛlədi] *n, pl* **-dies** : melodía *f*, tonada *f*

melon ['mɛlən] *n* : melón *m*

melt ['mɛlt] *vt* 1 : derretir, disolver 2 SOFTEN : ablandar ⟨it melted his heart : ablandó su corazón⟩ — *vi* 1 : derretirse, disolverse 2 SOFTEN : ablandarse 3 DISAPPEAR : desvanecerse, esfumarse ⟨the clouds melted away : las nubes se desvanecieron⟩

melting point *n* : punto *m* de fusión

member ['mɛmbər] *n* 1 LIMB : miembro *m* 2 : miembro *m* (de un grupo); socio *m*, -cia *f* (de un club) 3 PART : miembro *m*, parte *f*

membership ['mɛmbər,ʃɪp] *n* 1 : membresía *f* ⟨application for membership

: solicitud de entrada⟩ 2 MEMBERS
: membresía f, miembros mpl, socios
mpl

membrane ['mɛm₁breɪn] n : membrana
f — **membranous** ['mɛmbrə-nəs] adj

memento [mɪ'mɛn₁toː] n, pl **-tos** or **-toes**
: recuerdo m

memo ['mɛmoː] n, pl **memos** : memorándum m

memoirs ['mɛm₁wɑrz] npl : memorias
fpl, autobiografía f

memorabilia [₁mɛmərə'bɪliːə, -'bɪljə] npl
1 : objetos mpl de interés histórico 2
MEMENTOS : recuerdos mpl

memorable ['mɛmərəbəl] adj : memorable, notable — **memorably** [-bli] adv

memorandum [₁mɛmə'rændəm] n, pl
-dums or **-da** [-də] : memorándum m

memorial[1] [mə'moːriəl] adj : conmemorativo

memorial[2] n : monumento m conmemorativo

Memorial Day n : el último lunes de
mayo (observado en Estados Unidos
como día feriado para conmemorar a
los caídos en guerra)

memorialize [mə'moːriə₁laɪz] vt **-ized;
-izing** COMMEMORATE : conmemorar

memorization [₁mɛmərə'zeɪʃən] n
: memorización f

memorize ['mɛmə₁raɪz] vt **-rized; -rizing**
: memorizar, aprender de memoria

memory ['mɛmri, 'mɛmə-] n, pl **-ries** 1
: memoria f ⟨he has a good memory
: tiene buena memoria⟩ 2 RECOLLEC-
TION : recuerdo m 3 COMMEMORA-
TION : memoria f, conmemoración f

men → **man**[2]

menace[1] ['mɛnəs] vt **-aced; -acing** 1
THREATEN : amenazar 2 ENDANGER
: poner en peligro

menace[2] n : amenaza f

menacing ['mɛnəsɪŋ] adj : amenazador,
amenazante

menagerie [mə'nædʒəri, -'næʒəri] n
: colección f de animales salvajes

mend[1] ['mɛnd] vt 1 CORRECT : enmendar, corregir ⟨to mend one's ways
: enmendarse⟩ 2 REPAIR : remendar,
arreglar, reparar — vi HEAL : curarse

mend[2] n : remiendo m

mendicant ['mɛndɪkənt] n BEGGAR
: mendigo m, -ga f

menhaden [mɛn'heɪdən, mən-] ns & pl
: pez m de la misma familia que los
arenques

menial[1] ['miːniəl] adj : servil, bajo

menial[2] n : sirviente m, -ta f

meningitis [₁mɛnən'dʒaɪtəs] n, pl
-gitides [-'dʒɪtə₁diːz] : meningitis f

menopause ['mɛnə₁pɔz] n : menopausia
f

menorah [mə'noːrə] n : candelabro m
(usado en los oficios religiosos judíos)

menstrual ['mɛnstruəl] adj : menstrual

menstruate ['mɛnstru₁eɪt] vi **-ated; -at-
ing** : menstruar

menstruation [₁mɛnstru'eɪʃən] n : menstruación f

mental ['mɛntəl] adj : mental ⟨mental
hospital : hospital psiquiátrico⟩ —
mentally adv

mentality [mɛn'tæləti] n, pl **-ties** : mentalidad f

menthol ['mɛn₁θɔl, -₁θoːl] n : mentol m

mentholated [₁mɛnɪθə₁leɪtəd] adj : men-
tolado

mention[1] ['mɛntʃən] vt : mencionar,
mentar, referirse a ⟨don't mention it!
: ¡de nada!, ¡no hay de qué!⟩

mention[2] n : mención f

mentor ['mɛn₁tɔr, 'mɛntər] n : mentor m

menu ['mɛn₁juː] n 1 : menú m, carta f
(en un restaurante) 2 : menú m (de
computadoras)

meow[1] [miː'aʊ] vi : maullar

meow[2] n : maullido m, miau m

mercantile ['mərkən₁tiːl, -₁taɪl] adj : mercantil

mercenary[1] ['mərsəne₁ri] adj : mercenario

mercenary[2] n, pl **-naries** : mercenario
m, -ria f

merchandise ['mərtʃən₁daɪz, -₁daɪs] n
: mercancía f, mercadería f

merchandiser ['mərtʃən₁daɪzər] n : comerciante mf; vendedor m, -dora f

merchant ['mərtʃənt] n : comerciante mf

merchant marine n : marina f mercante

merciful ['mərsɪfəl] adj : misericordioso,
clemente

mercifully ['mərsɪfli] adv 1 : con misericordia, con compasión 2 FORTU-
NATELY : afortunadamente

merciless ['mərsɪləs] adj : despiadado —
mercilessly adv

mercurial [₁mər'kjʊriəl] adj TEMPERA-
MENTAL : temperamental, volátil

mercury ['mərkjəri] n, pl **-ries** : mercurio m

Mercury n : Mercurio m

mercy ['mərsi] n, pl **-cies** 1 CLEMENCY
: misericordia f, clemencia f 2 BLESS-
ING : bendición f

mere ['mɪr] adj, superlative **merest**
: mero, simple

merely ['mɪrli] adv : solamente, simplemente

merge ['mərdʒ] v **merged; merging** vi
: unirse, fusionarse (dícese de las com-
pañías), confluir (dícese de los ríos, las
calles, etc.) — vt : unir, fusionar, combinar

merger ['mərdʒər] n : unión f, fusión f

meridian [mə'rɪdiən] n : meridiano m

meringue [mə'ræŋ] n : merengue m

merino [mə'riːnoː] n, pl **-nos** 1 : merino
m, -na f 2 or **merino wool** : lana f merino

merit[1] ['mɛrət] vt : merecer, ser digno de

merit[2] n : mérito m, valor m

meritorious [₁mɛrə'toːriəs] adj : meritorio

mermaid ['mər₁meɪd] n : sirena f

merriment ['mɛrɪmənt] n : alegría f, júbilo m, regocijo m

merry ['mɛri] *adj* **-rier; -est** : alegre — **merrily** ['mɛrəli] *adv*

merry–go–round ['mɛrigo,raʊnd] *n* : carrusel *m*, tiovivo *m*

merrymaker ['mɛri,meɪkər] *n* : juerguista *mf*

merrymaking ['mɛri,meɪkɪŋ] *n* : juerga *f*

mesa ['meɪsə] *n* : mesa *f*

mesdames → **madam, Mrs.**

mesh[1] ['mɛʃ] *vi* **1** ENGAGE : engranar (dícese de las piezas mecánicas) **2** TANGLE : enredarse **3** COORDINATE : coordinarse, combinar

mesh[2] *n* **1** : malla *f* ⟨wire mesh : malla metálica⟩ **2** NETWORK : red *f* **3** MESHING : engranaje *m* ⟨in mesh : engranado⟩

mesmerize ['mɛzmə,raɪz] *vt* **-ized; -izing 1** HYPNOTIZE : hipnotizar **2** FASCINATE : cautivar, embelesar, fascinar

mess[1] ['mɛs] *vt* **1** SOIL : ensuciar **2 to mess up** DISARRANGE : desordenar, desarreglar **3 to mess up** BUNGLE : echar a perder — *vi* **1** PUTTER : entretenerse **2** INTERFERE : meterse, entrometerse ⟨don't mess with me : no te metas conmigo⟩

mess[2] *n* **1** : rancho *m* (para soldados, etc.) **2** DISORDER : desorden *m* ⟨your room is a mess : tienes el cuarto hecho un desastre⟩ **3** CONFUSION, TURMOIL : confusión *f*, embrollo *m*, lío *m fam*

message ['mɛsɪʤ] *n* : mensaje *m*, recado *m*

messenger ['mɛsənʤər] *n* : mensajero *m*, -ra *f*

Messiah [mə'saɪə] *n* : Mesías *m*

Messrs. → **Mr.**

messy ['mɛsi] *adj* **messier; -est** UNTIDY : desordenado, sucio

met → **meet**

metabolic [,mɛtə'bɑlɪk] *adj* : metabólico

metabolism [mə'tæbə,lɪzəm] *n* : metabolismo *m*

metabolize [mə'tæbə,laɪz] *vt* **-lized; -lizing** : metabolizar

metal ['mɛtəl] *n* : metal *m*

metallic [mə'tælɪk] *adj* : metálico

metallurgical [,mɛtəl'ərʤɪkəl] *adj* : metalúrgico

metallurgy ['mɛtəl,ərʤi] *n* : metalurgia *f*

metalwork ['mɛtəl,wərk] *n* : objeto *m* de metal

metalworking ['mɛtəl,wərkɪŋ] *n* : metalistería *f*

metamorphosis [,mɛtə'mɔrfəsɪs] *n, pl* **-phoses** [-,siːz] : metamorfosis *f*

metaphor ['mɛtə,fɔr, -fər] *n* : metáfora *f*

metaphoric [,mɛtə'fɔrɪk] *or* **metaphorical** [-ɪkəl] *adj* : metafórico

metaphysical [,mɛtə'fɪzɪkəl] *adj* : metafísico

metaphysics [,mɛtə'fɪzɪks] *n* : metafísica *f*

mete ['miːt] *vt* **meted; meting** ALLOT : repartir, distribuir ⟨to mete out punishment : imponer castigos⟩

meteor ['miːtiər, -,tiːɔr] *n* : meteoro *m*

meteoric [,miːti'ɔrɪk] *adj* : meteórico

meteorite ['miːtiə,raɪt] *n* : meteorito *m*

meteorologic [,miːti,ɔrə'lɑʤɪk] *or* **meteorological** [-'lɑʤɪkəl] *adj* : meteorológico

meteorologist [,miːtiə'rɑləʤɪst] *n* : meteorólogo *m*, -ga *f*

meteorology [,miːtiə'rɑləʤi] *n* : meteorología *f*

meter ['miːtər] *n* **1** : metro *m* ⟨it measures 2 meters : mide 2 metros⟩ **2** : contador *m*, medidor *m* (de electricidad, etc.) ⟨parking meter : parquímetro⟩ **3** : metro *m* (en literatura o música)

methane ['mɛ,θeɪn] *n* : metano *m*

method ['mɛθəd] *n* : método *m*

methodical [mə'θɑdɪkəl] *adj* : metódico — **methodically** *adv*

Methodist ['mɛθədɪst] *n* : metodista *mf* — **Methodist** *adj*

methodology [,mɛθə'dɑləʤi] *n, pl* **-gies** : metodología *f*

meticulous [mə'tɪkjələs] *adj* : meticuloso — **meticulously** *adv*

meticulousness [mə'tɪkjələsnəs] *n* : meticulosidad *f*

metric ['mɛtrɪk] *or* **metrical** [-trɪkəl] *adj* : métrico

metric system *n* : sistema *m* métrico

metronome ['mɛtrə,noːm] *n* : metrónomo *m*

metropolis [mə'trɑpələs] *n* : metrópoli *f*, metrópolis *f*

metropolitan [,mɛtrə'pɑlətən] *adj* : metropolitano

mettle ['mɛtəl] *n* : temple *m*, valor *m* ⟨on one's mettle : dispuesto a mostrar su valía⟩

Mexican ['mɛksɪkən] *n* : mexicano *m*, -na *f* — **Mexican** *adj*

mezzanine ['mɛzə,niːn, ,mɛzə'niːn] *n* **1** : entrepiso *m*, entresuelo *m* **2** : primer piso *m* (de un teatro)

miasma [maɪ'æzmə] *n* : miasma *m*

mica ['maɪkə] *n* : mica *f*

mice → **mouse**

micro ['maɪkro] *adj* : muy pequeño, microscópico

microbe ['maɪ,kro:b] *n* : microbio *m*

microbiology [,maɪkrobaɪ'ɑləʤi] *n* : microbiología *f*

microchip ['maɪkro,ʧɪp] *n* : microchip *m*

microcomputer ['maɪkrokəm,pju:tər] *n* : microcomputadora *f*

microcosm ['maɪkro,kazəm] *n* : microcosmo *m*

microfilm ['maɪkro,fɪlm] *n* : microfilm *m*

micrometer [maɪ'krɑmətər] *n* : micrómetro *m*

micron ['maɪ,krɑn] *n* : micrón *m*

microorganism [,maɪkro'ɔrgə,nɪzəm] *n* : microorganismo *m*, microbio *m*

microphone ['maɪkrə,foːn] n : micrófono m

microprocessor ['maɪkro,prɑ,ssər] n : microprocesador m

microscope ['maɪkrə,skoːp] n : microscopio m

microscopic [,maɪkrə'skɑpɪk] adj : microscópico

microscopy [maɪ'krɑskəpi] n : microscopía f

microwave ['maɪkrə,weɪv] n 1 : microonda f 2 or **microwave oven** : microondas m

mid ['mɪd] adj : medio ⟨mid morning : a media mañana⟩ ⟨in mid-August : a mediados de agosto⟩ ⟨in mid ocean : en alta mar⟩

midair ['mɪd'ær] n **in ~** : en el aire ⟨to catch in midair : agarrar al vuelo⟩

midday ['mɪd,deɪ] n NOON : mediodía m

middle¹ ['mɪdəl] adj 1 CENTRAL : medio, del medio, de en medio 2 INTERMEDIATE : intermedio, mediano ⟨middle age : la mediana edad⟩

middle² n 1 CENTER : medio m, centro m ⟨fold it down the middle : dóblalo por la mitad⟩ 2 **in the middle of** : en medio de (un espacio), a mitad de (una actividad) ⟨in the middle of the month : a mediados del mes⟩

Middle Ages npl : Edad f Media

middle class n : clase f media

middleman ['mɪdəl,mæn] n, pl **-men** [-mən, -,mɛn] : intermediario m, -ria f

middling ['mɪdlɪŋ, -lən] adj 1 MEDIUM, MIDDLE : mediano 2 MEDIOCRE : mediocre, regular

midfielder ['mɪd,fiːldər] n : mediocampista m

midge ['mɪdʒ] n : mosca f pequeña

midget ['mɪdʒət] n 1 : enano m, -na f (persona) 2 : cosa f diminuta

midland ['mɪdlənd, -,lænd] n : región f central (de un país)

midnight ['mɪd,naɪt] n : medianoche f

midpoint ['mɪd,pɔɪnt] n : punto m medio, término m medio

midriff ['mɪd,rɪf] n : diafragma m

midshipman ['mɪd,ʃɪpmən, ,mɪd'ʃɪp-] n, pl **-men** [-mən, -,mɛn] : guardiamarina m

midst¹ ['mɪdst] n : medio m ⟨in our midst : entre nosotros⟩ ⟨in the midst of : en medio de⟩

midst² prep : entre

midstream ['mɪd'striːm, -,striːm] n : medio m de la corriente ⟨in the midstream of his career : en medio de su carrera⟩

midsummer ['mɪd'sʌmər, -,sʌ-] n : pleno verano m

midtown ['mɪd,taʊn] n : centro m (de una ciudad)

midway ['mɪd,weɪ] adv HALFWAY : a mitad de camino

midweek ['mɪd,wiːk] n : medio m de la semana ⟨in midweek : a media semana⟩

midwife ['mɪd,waɪf] n, pl **-wives** [-,waɪvz] : partera f, comadrona f

midwinter ['mɪd'wɪntər, -,wɪn-] n : pleno invierno m

midyear ['mɪd,jɪr] n : medio m del año ⟨at midyear : a mediados del año⟩

mien ['miːn] n : aspecto m, porte m, semblante m

miff ['mɪf] vt : ofender

might¹ ['maɪt] (used to express permission or possibility or as a polite alternative to **may**) → **may** ⟨it might be true : podría ser verdad⟩ ⟨might I speak with Sarah? : ¿se puede hablar con Sarah?⟩

might² n : fuerza f, poder m

mightily ['maɪtəli] adv : con mucha fuerza, poderosamente

mighty¹ ['maɪti] adv VERY : muy ⟨mighty good : muy bueno, buenísimo⟩

mighty² adj **mightier; -est** 1 POWERFUL : poderoso, potente 2 GREAT : grande, imponente

migraine ['maɪ,greɪn] n : jaqueca f, migraña f

migrant ['maɪgrənt] n : trabajador m, -dora f ambulante

migrate ['maɪ,greɪt] vi **-grated; -grating** : emigrar

migration [maɪ'greɪʃən] n : migración f

migratory ['maɪgrə,tori] adj : migratorio

mild ['maɪld] adj 1 GENTLE : apacible, suave ⟨a mild disposition : un temperamento suave⟩ 2 LIGHT : leve, ligero ⟨a mild punishment : un castigo leve, un castigo poco severo⟩ 3 TEMPERATE : templado (dícese del clima) — **mildly** adv

mildew¹ ['mɪl,duː, -,djuː] vi : enmohecerse

mildew² n : moho m

mildness ['maɪldnəs] n : apacibilidad f, suavidad f

mile ['maɪl] n : milla f

mileage ['maɪlɪdʒ] n 1 ALLOWANCE : viáticos mpl (pagados por milla recorrida) 2 : distancia f recorrida (en millas), kilometraje m

milestone ['maɪl,stoːn] n LANDMARK : hito m, jalón m ⟨a milestone in his life : un hito en su vida⟩

milieu [miːl'juː:, -'jø] n, pl **-lieus** or **-lieux** [-'juːz, -'jø] SURROUNDINGS : entorno m, medio m, ambiente m

militant¹ ['mɪlətənt] adj : militante, combativo

militant² n : militante mf

militarism ['mɪlətə,rɪzəm] n : militarismo m

militaristic [,mɪlətə'rɪstɪk] adj : militarista

military¹ ['mɪlə,teri] adj : militar

military² n **the military** : las fuerzas armadas

militia [mə'lɪʃə] n : milicia f

milk¹ ['mɪlk] vt 1 : ordeñar (una vaca, etc.) 2 EXPLOIT : explotar

milk² n : leche f
milkman ['mɪlk,mæn, -mən] n, pl -men [-mən, -,mɛn] : lechero m
milk shake n : batido m, licuado m
milkweed ['mɪlk,wi:d] n : algodoncillo m
milky ['mɪlki] adj milkier; -est : lechoso
Milky Way n : Vía f Láctea
mill¹ ['mɪl] vt : moler (granos), fresar (metales), acordonar (monedas) — vi to mill about : arremolinarse
mill² n 1 : molino m (para moler granos) 2 FACTORY : fábrica f ⟨textile mill : fábrica textil⟩ 3 GRINDER : molinillo m
millennium [mə'lɛniəm] n, pl -nia [-niə] or -niums : milenio m
miller ['mɪlər] n : molinero m, -ra f
millet ['mɪlət] n : mijo m
milligram ['mɪlə,græm] n : miligramo m
milliliter ['mɪlə,li:tər] n : mililitro m
millimeter ['mɪlə,mi:tər] n : milímetro m
milliner ['mɪlənər] n : sombrerero m, -ra f (de señoras)
millinery ['mɪlə,nɛri] n : sombreros mpl de señora
million¹ ['mɪljən] adj a million : un millón de
million² n, pl millions or million : millón m
millionaire [,mɪljə'nær, 'mɪljə,nær] n : millonario m, -ria f
millionth¹ ['mɪljənθ] adj : millonésimo
millionth² n : millonésimo m
millipede ['mɪlə,pi:d] n : milpiés m
millstone ['mɪl,sto:n] n : rueda f de molino, muela f
mime¹ ['maɪm] v mimed; miming vt MIMIC : imitar, remedar — vi PANTOMIME : hacer la mímica
mime² n 1 : mimo mf 2 PANTOMIME : pantomima f
mimeograph ['mɪmiə,græf] n : mimeógrafo m
mimic¹ ['mɪmɪk] vt -icked; -icking : imitar, remedar
mimic² n : imitador m, -dora f
mimicry ['mɪmɪkri] n, pl -ries : mímica f, imitación f
minaret [,mɪnə'rɛt] n : alminar m, minarete m
mince ['mɪnts] v minced; mincing vt 1 CHOP : picar, moler (carne) 2 not to mince one's words : no tener uno pelos en la lengua — vi : caminar de manera afectada
mincemeat ['mɪnts,mi:t] n : mezcla f de fruta picada, sebo, y especias
mind¹ ['maɪnd] vt 1 TEND : cuidar, atender ⟨mind the children : cuida a los niños⟩ 2 OBEY : obedecer 3 : preocuparse por, sentirse molestado por ⟨I don't mind his jokes : sus bromas no me molestan⟩ 4 : tener cuidado con ⟨mind the ladder! : ¡cuidado con la escalera!⟩ — vi 1 OBEY : obedecer 2 CARE : importarle a uno ⟨I don't mind : no me importa, me es igual⟩
mind² n 1 MEMORY : memoria f, recuerdo m ⟨keep it in mind : téngalo en

cuenta⟩ 2 : mente f ⟨the mind and the body : la mente y el cuerpo⟩ 3 INTENTION : intención f, propósito m ⟨to have a mind to do something : tener intención de hacer algo⟩ 4 : razón f ⟨he's out of his mind : está loco⟩ 5 OPINION : opinión f ⟨to change one's mind : cambiar de opinión⟩ 6 INTELLECT : capacidad f intelectual
minded ['maɪndəd] adj 1 (used in combination) ⟨narrow-minded : de mentalidad cerrada⟩ ⟨health-minded : preocupado por la salud⟩ 2 INCLINED : inclinado
mindful ['maɪndfəl] adj AWARE : consciente — mindfully adv
mindless ['maɪndləs] adj 1 SENSELESS : estúpido, sin sentido ⟨mindless violence : violencia sin sentido⟩ 2 HEEDLESS : inconsciente
mindlessly ['maɪndləsli] adv 1 SENSELESSLY : sin sentido 2 HEEDLESSLY : inconscientemente
mine¹ ['maɪn] vt mined; mining 1 : extraer (oro, etc.) 2 : minar (con artefactos explosivos)
mine² n : mina f ⟨gold mine : mina de oro⟩
mine³ pron : mío, mía ⟨that one's mine : ése es el mío⟩ ⟨some friends of mine : unos amigos míos⟩
minefield ['maɪn,fi:ld] n : campo m de minas
miner ['maɪnər] n : minero m, -ra f
mineral ['mɪnərəl] n : mineral m — mineral adj
mineralogy [,mɪnə'rɑlədʒi, -'ræ-] n : mineralogía f
mingle ['mɪŋgəl] v -gled; -gling vt MIX : mezclar — vi 1 MIX : mezclarse 2 CIRCULATE : circular
miniature¹ ['mɪniə,ʧur, 'mɪnɪ,ʧur, -ʧər] adj : en miniatura, diminuto
miniature² n : miniatura f
minibus ['mɪni,bʌs] n : microbús m, pesera f Mex
minicomputer ['mɪnikəm,pju:tər] n : minicomputadora f
minimal ['mɪnəməl] adj : mínimo
minimally ['mɪnəməli] adv : en grado mínimo
minimize ['mɪnə,maɪz] vt -mized; -mizing : minimizar
minimum¹ ['mɪnəməm] adj : mínimo
minimum² n, pl -ma ['mɪnəmə] or -mums : mínimo m
miniseries ['mɪni,sɪri:z] n : miniserie f
miniskirt ['mɪni,skərt] n : minifalda f
minister¹ ['mɪnəstər] vi to minister to : cuidar (de), atender a
minister² n 1 : pastor m, -tora f (de una iglesia) 2 : ministro m, -tra f (en política)
ministerial [,mɪnə'stɪriəl] adj : ministerial
ministry ['mɪnəstri] n, pl -tries 1 : ministerio m (en política) 2 : sacerdocio m (en el catolicismo), clerecía f (en el protestantismo)

minivan ['mɪni,væn] n : minivan f

mink ['mɪŋk] n, pl **mink** or **minks** : visón m

minnow ['mɪno:] n, pl **-nows** : pececillo m de agua dulce

minor[1] ['maɪnər] adj : menor

minor[2] n 1 : menor mf (de edad) 2 : asignatura f secundaria (de estudios)

minority [mə'nɔrəti, maɪ-] n, pl **-ties** : minoría f

minstrel ['mɪntstrəl] n : juglar m, trovador m (en el medioevo)

mint[1] ['mɪnt] vt : acuñar

mint[2] adj : sin usar ⟨in mint condition : como nuevo⟩

mint[3] n 1 : menta f ⟨mint tea : té de menta⟩ 2 : pastilla f de menta 3 : casa f de la moneda ⟨the U.S. Mint : la casa de la moneda de los EE.UU.⟩ 4 FORTUNE : dineral m, fortuna f

minuet [,mɪnju'ɛt] n : minué m

minus[1] ['maɪnəs] n 1 : cantidad f negativa 2 **minus sign** : signo m de menos

minus[2] prep 1 : menos ⟨four minus two : cuatro menos dos⟩ 2 WITHOUT : sin ⟨minus his hat : sin su sombrero⟩

minuscule or **miniscule** ['mɪnəs,kju:l, mɪ'nʌs-] adj : minúsculo

minute[1] [maɪ'nu:t, mɪ-, -'nju:t] adj **-nuter; -est** 1 TINY : diminuto, minúsculo 2 DETAILED : minucioso

minute[2] ['mɪnət] n 1 : minuto m ⟨ten minutes late : diez minutos de retraso⟩ 2 MOMENT : momento m 3 **minutes** npl : actas fpl (de una reunión)

minutely [maɪ'nu:tli, mɪ-, -'nju:t-] adv : minuciosamente

miracle ['mɪrɪkəl] n : milagro m

miraculous [mə'rækjələs] adj : milagroso — **miraculously** adv

mirage [mɪ'rɑ,ʒ, chiefly Brit 'mɪr,ɑ,ʒ] n : espejismo m

mire[1] ['maɪr] vi **mired; miring** : atascarse

mire[2] n 1 MUD : barro m, lodo m 2 : atolladero m ⟨stuck in a mire of debt : agobiado por la deuda⟩

mirror[1] ['mɪrər] vt : reflejar

mirror[2] n : espejo m

mirth ['mərθ] n : alegría f, regocijo m

mirthful ['mərθfəl] adj : alegre, regocijado

misadventure [,mɪsəd'vɛnt͡ʃər] n : malaventura f, desventura f

misanthrope ['mɪsən,θro:p] n : misántropo m, -pa f

misanthropic [,mɪsən'θrɑpɪk] adj : misantrópico

misanthropy [mɪ'sænθrəpi] n : misantropía f

misapprehend [,mɪs,æprə'hɛnd] vt : entender mal

misapprehension [,mɪs,æprə'hɛnt͡ʃən] n : malentendido m

misappropriate [,mɪsə'pro:pri,eɪt] vt **-ated; -ating** : malversar

misbegotten [,mɪsbɪ'gɑtən] adj 1 ILLEGITIMATE : ilegítimo 2 : mal concebido ⟨misbegotten laws : leyes mal concebidas⟩

misbehave [,mɪsbɪ'heɪv] vi **-haved; -having** : portarse mal

misbehavior [,mɪsbɪ'heɪvjər] n : mala conducta f

miscalculate [mɪs'kælkjə,leɪt] v **-lated; -lating** : calcular mal

miscalculation [mɪs,kælkjə'leɪʃən] n : error m de cálculo, mal cálculo m

miscarriage [,mɪs'kærɪd͡ʒ, 'mɪs,kærɪd͡ʒ] n 1 : aborto m 2 FAILURE : fracaso m, malogro m ⟨a miscarriage of justice : una injusticia, un error judicial⟩

miscarry [,mɪs'kæri, 'mɪs,kæri] vi **-ried; -rying** 1 ABORT : abortar 2 FAIL : malograrse, fracasar

miscellaneous [,mɪsə'leɪniəs] adj : misceláneo

miscellany ['mɪsə,leɪni] n, pl **-nies** : miscelánea f

mischance [mɪs't͡ʃænts] n : desgracia f, infortunio m, mala suerte f

mischief ['mɪst͡ʃəf] n : diabluras fpl, travesuras fpl

mischievous ['mɪst͡ʃəvəs] adj : travieso, pícaro

mischievously ['mɪst͡ʃəvəsli] adv : de manera traviesa

misconception [,mɪskən'sɛpʃən] n : concepto m erróneo, idea f falsa

misconduct [mɪs'kɑndəkt] n : mala conducta f

misconstrue [,mɪskən'stru:] vt **-strued; -struing** : malinterpretar

misdeed [mɪs'di:d] n : fechoría f

misdemeanor [,mɪsdɪ'mi:nər] n : delito m menor

miser ['maɪzər] n : avaro m, -ra f; tacaño m, -ña f

miserable ['mɪzərəbəl] adj 1 UNHAPPY : triste, desdichada 2 WRETCHED : miserable, desgraciado ⟨a miserable hut : una choza miserable⟩ 3 UNPLEASANT : desagradable, malo ⟨miserable weather : tiempo malísimo⟩ 4 CONTEMPTIBLE : despreciable, mísero ⟨for a miserable $10 : por unos míseros diez dólares⟩

miserably ['mɪzərəbli] adv 1 SADLY : tristemente 2 WRETCHEDLY : miserablemente, lamentablemente 3 UNFORTUNATELY : desgraciadamente

miserly ['maɪzərli] adj : avaro, tacaño

misery ['mɪzəri] n, pl **-eries** : miseria f, sufrimiento m

misfire [mɪs'faɪr] vi **-fired; -firing** : fallar

misfit ['mɪs,fɪt] n : inadaptado m, -da f

misfortune [mɪs'fɔrt͡ʃən] n : desgracia f, desventura f, infortunio m

misgiving [mɪs'gɪvɪŋ] n : duda f, recelo m

misguided [mɪs'gaɪdəd] adj : desacertado, equivocado, mal informado

mishap ['mɪs,hæp] n : contratiempo m, percance m, accidente m

misinform [,mɪsɪn'fɔrm] vt : informar mal

misinterpret [,mɪsɪn'tərprət] vt : malinterpretar

misinterpretation [ˌmɪsɪnˌtərprəˈteɪ-ʃən] *n* : mala interpretación *f*, malentendido *m*

misjudge [mɪsˈdʒʌdʒ] *vt* **-judged; -judging** : juzgar mal

mislay [mɪsˈleɪ] *vt* **-laid** [-ˈleɪd]; **-laying** : extraviar, perder

mislead [mɪsˈliːd] *vt* **-led** [-ˈlɛd]; **-leading** : engañar

misleading [mɪsˈliːdɪŋ] *adj* : engañoso

mismanage [mɪsˈmænɪdʒ] *vt* **-aged; -aging** : administrar mal

mismanagement [mɪsˈmænɪdʒmənt] *n* : mala administración *f*

misnomer [mɪsˈnoːmər] *n* : nombre *m* inapropiado

misogynist [mɪˈsadʒənɪst] *n* : misógino *m*

misogyny [məˈsadʒəni] *n* : misoginia *f*

misplace [mɪsˈpleɪs] *vt* **-placed; -placing** : extraviar, perder

misprint [ˈmɪsˌprɪnt, mɪsˈ-] *n* : errata *f*, error *m* de imprenta

mispronounce [ˌmɪsprəˈnaʊnts] *vt* **-nounced; -nouncing** : pronunciar mal

mispronunciation [ˌmɪsprəˌnʌntsiˈeɪʃən] *n* : pronunciación *f* incorrecta

misquote [mɪsˈkwoːt] *vt* **-quoted; -quoting** : citar incorrectamente

misread [mɪsˈriːd] *vt* **-read; -reading 1** : leer mal ⟨she misread the sentence : leyó mal la frase⟩ **2** MISUNDERSTAND : malinterpretar ⟨they misread his intention : malinterpretaron su intención⟩

misrepresent [ˌmɪsˌrɛprɪˈzɛnt] *vt* : distorsionar, falsear, tergiversar

misrule¹ [mɪsˈruːl] *vt* **-ruled; -ruling** : gobernar mal

misrule² *n* : mal gobierno *m*

miss¹ [ˈmɪs] *vt* **1** : errar, faltar ⟨to miss the target : no dar en el blanco⟩ **2** : no encontrar, perder ⟨they missed each other : no se encontraron⟩ ⟨I missed the plane : perdí el avión⟩ **3** : echar de menos, extrañar ⟨we miss him a lot : lo echamos de menos de menos⟩ **4** OVERLOOK : pasar por alto, perder (una oportunidad, etc.) **5** AVOID : evitar ⟨they just missed hitting the tree : por muy poco chocan contra el árbol⟩ **6** OMIT : saltarse ⟨he missed breakfast : se saltó el desayuno⟩

miss² *n* **1** : fallo *m* (de un tiro, etc.) **2** FAILURE : fracaso *m* **3** : señorita *f* ⟨Miss Jones called us : nos llamó la señorita Jones⟩ ⟨excuse me, miss : perdone, señorita⟩

missal [ˈmɪsəl] *n* : misal *m*

misshapen [mɪˈʃeɪpən] *adj* : deforme

missile [ˈmɪsəl] *n* **1** : misil *m* ⟨guided missile : misil guiado⟩ **2** PROJECTILE : proyectil *m*

missing [ˈmɪsɪŋ] *adj* **1** ABSENT : ausente ⟨who's missing? : ¿quién falta?⟩ **2** LOST : perdido, desaparecido ⟨missing persons : los desaparecidos⟩

mission [ˈmɪʃən] *n* **1** : misión *f* (mandada por una iglesia) **2** DELEGATION : misión *f*, delegación *f*, embajada *f* **3** TASK : misión *f*

missionary¹ [ˈmɪʃəˌnɛri] *adj* : misionero

missionary² *n, pl* **-aries** : misionero *m*, -ra *f*

missive [ˈmɪsɪv] *n* : misiva *f*

misspell [mɪsˈspɛl] *vt* : escribir mal

misspelling [mɪsˈspɛlɪŋ] *n* : falta *f* de ortografía

misstep [ˈmɪsˌstɛp] *n* : traspié *m*, tropezón *m*

mist [ˈmɪst] *n* **1** HAZE : neblina *f*, niebla *f* **2** SPRAY : rocío *m*

mistake¹ [mɪˈsteɪk] *vt* **-took** [-ˈstʊk]; **-taken** [-ˈsteɪkən]; **-taking 1** MISINTERPRET : malinterpretar **2** CONFUSE : confundir ⟨he mistook her for Clara : la confundió con Clara⟩

mistake² *n* **1** MISUNDERSTANDING : malentendido *m*, confusión *f* **2** ERROR : error *m* ⟨I made a mistake : me equivoqué, cometí un error⟩

mistaken [mɪˈsteɪkən] *adj* **1** WRONG : equivocado — **mistakenly** *adv*

mister [ˈmɪstər] *n* : señor *m* ⟨watch out, mister : cuidado, señor⟩

mistiness [ˈmɪstinəs] *n* : nebulosidad *f*

mistletoe [ˈmɪsəlˌtoː] *n* : muérdago *m*

mistreat [mɪsˈtriːt] *vt* : maltratar

mistreatment [mɪsˈtriːtmənt] *n* : maltrato *m*, abuso *m*

mistress [ˈmɪstrəs] *n* **1** : dueña *f*, señora *f* (de una casa) **2** LOVER : amante *f*

mistrust¹ [mɪsˈtrʌst] *vt* : desconfiar de

mistrust² *n* : desconfianza *f*

mistrustful [mɪsˈtrʌstfəl] *adj* : desconfiado

misty [ˈmɪsti] *adj* **mistier; -est 1** : neblinoso, nebuloso **2** TEARFUL : lloroso

misunderstand [ˌmɪsˌʌndərˈstænd] *vt* **-stood** [-ˈstʊd]; **-standing 1** : entender mal **2** MISINTERPRET : malinterpretar ⟨don't misunderstand me : no me malinterpretes⟩

misunderstanding [ˌmɪsˌʌndərˈstændɪŋ] *n* **1** MISINTERPRETATION : malentendido *m* **2** DISAGREEMENT, QUARREL : disputa *f*, discusión *f*

misuse¹ [mɪsˈjuːz] *vt* **-used; -using 1** : emplear mal **2** ABUSE, MISTREAT : abusar de, maltratar

misuse² [mɪsˈjuːs] *n* **1** : mal empleo *m*, mal uso *m* **2** WASTE : derroche *m*, despilfarro *m* **3** ABUSE : abuso *m*

mite [ˈmaɪt] *n* **1** : ácaro *m* **2** BIT : poco *m* ⟨a mite tired : un poquito cansado⟩

miter or **mitre** [ˈmaɪtər] *n* **1** : mitra *f* (de un obispo) **2** or **miter joint** : inglete *m*

mitigate [ˈmɪtəˌgeɪt] *vt* **-gated; -gating** : mitigar, aliviar

mitigation [ˌmɪtəˈgeɪʃən] *n* : mitigación *f*, alivio *m*

mitosis [maɪˈtoːsɪs] *n, pl* **-toses** [-ˌsiːz] : mitosis *f*

mitt [ˈmɪt] *n* : manopla *f*, guante *m* (de béisbol)

mitten ['mɪtən] n : manopla f, mitón m

mix[1] ['mɪks] vt **1** COMBINE : mezclar **2** STIR : remover, revolver **3 to mix up** CONFUSE : confundir — vi : mezclarse

mix[2] n : mezcla f

mixer ['mɪksər] n **1** : batidora f (de la cocina) **2 cement mixer** : hormigonera f

mixture ['mɪkstʃər] n : mezcla f

mix–up ['mɪks,ʌp] n CONFUSION : confusión f, lío m fam

mnemonic[1] [nɪ'manɪk] adj : mnemónico

moan[1] ['moːn] vi : gemir

moan[2] n : gemido m

moat ['moːt] n : foso m

mob[1] ['mab] vt **mobbed; mobbing 1** ATTACK : atacar en masa **2** HOUND : acosar, rodear

mob[2] n **1** THRONG : multitud f, turba f, muchedumbre f **2** GANG : pandilla f

mobile[1] ['moːbəl, -,biːl, -,baɪl] adj ⟨mobile home : caravana, casa rodante⟩

mobile[2] ['moːbiːl] n : móvil m

mobility [moː'bɪləṭi] n : movilidad f

mobilize ['moːbə,laɪz] vt **-lized; -lizing** : movilizar

moccasin ['makəsən] n **1** : mocasín m **2** or **water moccasin** : serpiente f venenosa de Norteamérica

mocha ['moːkə] n **1** : mezcla f de café y chocolate **2** : color m chocolate

mock[1] ['mak, 'mɔk] vt **1** RIDICULE : burlarse de, mofarse de **2** MIMIC : imitar, remedar (de manera burlona)

mock[2] adj **1** SIMULATED : simulado **2** PHONY : falso

mockery ['makəri, 'mɔ-] n, pl **-eries 1** JEER, TAUNT : burla f, mofa f ⟨to make a mockery of : burlarse de⟩ **2** FAKE : imitación f (burlona)

mockingbird ['makɪŋ,bərd, 'mɔ-] n : sinsonte m

mode ['moːd] n **1** FORM : modo m, forma f **2** MANNER : modo m, manera f, estilo m **3** FASHION : moda f

model[1] ['madəl] v **-eled** or **-elled; -eling** or **-elling** vt SHAPE : modelar — vi : trabajar de modelo

model[2] adj **1** EXEMPLARY : modelo, ejemplar ⟨a model student : un estudiante modelo⟩ **2** MINIATURE : en miniatura

model[3] n **1** PATTERN : modelo m **2** MINIATURE : modelo m, miniatura f **3** EXAMPLE : modelo m, ejemplo m **4** MANNEQUIN : modelo mf **5** DESIGN : modelo m ⟨the '97 model : el modelo '97⟩

modem ['moːdəm, -,dɛm] n : módem m

moderate[1] ['madə,reɪt] v **-ated; -ating** vt : moderar, temperar — vi **1** CALM : moderarse, calmarse **2** : fungir como moderador (en un debate, etc.)

moderate[2] ['madərət] adj : moderado

moderate[3] ['madərət] n : moderado m, -da f

moderately ['madərətli] adv **1** : con moderación **2** FAIRLY : medianamente

moderation [,madə'reɪʃən] n : moderación f

moderator ['madə,reɪtər] n : moderador m, -dora f

modern ['madərn] adj : moderno

modernism ['madər,nɪzəm] n : modernismo m

modernist ['madərnɪst] n : modernista mf — **modernist** adj

modernity [mə'dərnəṭi] n : modernidad f

modernization [,madərnə'zeɪʃən] n : modernización f

modernize ['madər,naɪz] v **-ized; -izing** vt : modernizar — vi : modernizarse

modest ['madəst] adj **1** HUMBLE : modesto **2** DEMURE : recatado, pudoroso **3** MODERATE : modesto, moderado — **modestly** adv

modesty ['madəsti] n : modestia f

modicum ['madɪkəm] n : mínimo m, pizca f

modification [,madəfə'keɪʃən] n : modificación f

modifier ['madə,faɪər] n : modificante m, modificador m

modify ['madə,faɪ] vt **-fied; -fying** : modificar, calificar (en gramática)

modish ['moːdɪʃ] adj STYLISH : a la moda, de moda

modular ['madʒələr] adj : modular

modulate ['madʒə,leɪt] vt **-lated; -lating** : modular

modulation [,madʒə'leɪʃən] n : modulación f

module ['madʒuːl] n : módulo m

mogul ['moːgəl] n : magnate mf; potentado m, -da f

mohair ['moː,hær] n : mohair m

moist ['mɔɪst] adj : húmedo

moisten ['mɔɪsən] vt : humedecer

moistness ['mɔɪstnəs] n : humedad f

moisture ['mɔɪstʃər] n : humedad f

moisturize ['mɔɪstʃə,raɪz] vt **-ized; -izing** : humedecer (el aire), humectar (la piel)

moisturizer ['mɔɪstʃə,raɪzər] n : crema f hidratante, crema f humectante

molar ['moːlər] n : muela f, molar m

molasses [mə'læsəz] n : melaza f

mold[1] ['moːld] vt : moldear, formar (carácter, etc.) — vi : enmohecerse ⟨the bread will mold : el pan se enmohecerá⟩

mold[2] n **1** or **leaf mold** : mantillo m **2** FORM : molde m ⟨to break the mold : romper el molde⟩ **3** FUNGUS : moho m

molder ['moːldər] vi CRUMBLE : desmoronarse

molding ['moːldɪŋ] n : moldura f (en arquitectura)

moldy ['moːldi] adj **moldier; -est** : mohoso

mole ['moːl] n **1** : lunar m (en la piel) **2** : topo m (animal)

molecule ['mɑlɪˌkjuːl] n : molécula f — **molecular** [məˈlɛkjələr] adj

molehill ['moːlˌhɪl] n : topera f

molest [məˈlɛst] vt **1** ANNOY, DISTURB : molestar **2** : abusar (sexualmente)

mollify ['mɑləˌfaɪ] vt **-fied; -fying** : apaciguar, aplacar

mollusk or **mollusc** ['mɑləsk] n : molusco m

mollycoddle ['mɑlɪˌkɑdəl] vt **-dled; -dling** PAMPER : consentir, mimar

molt ['moːlt] vi : mudar, hacer la muda

molten ['moːltən] adj : fundido

mom ['mɑm, 'mʌm] n : mamá f

moment ['moːmənt] n **1** INSTANT : momento m ⟨one moment, please : un momento, por favor⟩ **2** TIME : momento m ⟨at the moment : de momento, actualmente⟩ ⟨from that moment : desde entonces⟩ **3** IMPORTANCE : importancia f ⟨of great moment : de gran importancia⟩

momentarily [ˌmoːmənˈtɛrəli] adv **1** : momentáneamente **2** SOON : dentro de poco, pronto

momentary ['moːmənˌtɛri] adj : momentáneo

momentous [moˈmɛntəs] adj : de suma importancia, fatídico

momentum [moˈmɛntəm] n, pl **-ta** [-tə] or **-tums 1** : momento m (en física) **2** IMPETUS : ímpetu m, impulso m

mommy ['mɑmi, 'mʌ-] n : mami f

monarch ['mɑˌnɑrk, -nərk] n : monarca mf

monarchism ['mɑˌnɑrˌkɪzəm, -nər-] n : monarquismo m

monarchist ['mɑˌnɑrkɪst, -nər-] n : monárquico m, -ca f

monarchy ['mɑˌnɑrki, -nər-] n, pl **-chies** : monarquía f

monastery ['mɑnəˌstɛri] n, pl **-teries** : monasterio m

monastic [məˈnæstɪk] adj : monástico — **monastically** [-tɪkli] adv

Monday ['mʌnˌdeɪ, -di] n : lunes m

monetary ['mɑnəˌtɛri, 'mʌnə-] adj : monetario

money ['mʌni] n, pl **-eys** or **-ies** ['mʌniz] : dinero m, plata f

moneyed ['mʌnid] adj : adinerado

moneylender ['mʌniˌlɛndər] n : prestamista mf

money order n : giro m postal

Mongol ['mɑŋgəl, -ˌgoːl] → **Mongolian**

Mongolian [mɑnˈgoːliən, mɑŋ-] n : mongol m, -gola f — **Mongolian** adj

mongoose ['mɑŋˌguːs, 'mɑŋ-] n, pl **-gooses** : mangosta f

mongrel ['mɑŋgrəl, 'mʌŋ-] n **1** : perro m mestizo, perro m corriente Mex **2** HYBRID : híbrido m

monitor¹ ['mɑnətər] vt : controlar, monitorear

monitor² n **1** : ayudante mf (en una escuela) **2** : monitor m (de una computadora, etc.)

monk ['mʌŋk] n : monje m

monkey¹ ['mʌŋki] vi **-keyed; -keying 1 to monkey around** : hacer payasadas, payasear **2 to monkey with** : juguetear con

monkey² n, pl **-keys** : mono m, -na f

monkeyshines ['mʌŋkiˌʃaɪnz] npl PRANKS : picardías fpl, travesuras fpl

monkey wrench n : llave f inglesa

monocle ['mɑnɪkəl] n : monóculo m

monogamous [məˈnɑgəməs] adj : monógamo

monogamy [məˈnɑgəmi] n : monogamia f

monogram¹ ['mɑnəˌgræm] vt **-grammed; -gramming** : marcar con monograma ⟨monogrammed towels : toallas con monograma⟩

monogram² n : monograma m

monograph ['mɑnəˌgræf] n : monografía f

monolingual [ˌmɑnəˈlɪŋgwəl] adj : monolingüe

monolith ['mɑnəˌlɪθ] n : monolito m

monolithic [ˌmɑnəˈlɪθɪk] adj : monolítico

monologue ['mɑnəˌlɔg] n : monólogo m

monoplane ['mɑnəˌpleɪn] n : monoplano m

monopolize [məˈnɑpəˌlaɪz] vt **-lized; -lizing** : monopolizar

monopoly [məˈnɑpəli] n, pl **-lies** : monopolio m

monosyllabic [ˌmɑnosəˈlæbɪk] adj : monosilábico

monosyllable ['mɑnoˌsɪləbəl] n : monosílabo m

monotheism ['mɑnoθiˌɪzəm] n : monoteísmo m

monotheistic [ˌmɑnoθiˈɪstɪk] adj : monoteísta

monotone ['mɑnəˌtoːn] n : voz f monótona

monotonous [məˈnɑtənəs] adj : monótono — **monotonously** adv

monotony [məˈnɑtəni] n : monotonía f, uniformidad f

monoxide [məˈnɑkˌsaɪd] n : monóxido m

monsoon [mɑnˈsuːn] n : monzón m

monster ['mɑnstər] n : monstruo m

monstrosity [mɑnˈstrɑsəti] n, pl **-ties** : monstruosidad f

monstrous ['mɑnstrəs] adj : monstruoso — **monstrously** adv

montage [mɑnˈtɑʒ] n : montaje m

month ['mʌnθ] n : mes m

monthly¹ ['mʌnθli] adv : mensualmente

monthly² adj : mensual

monthly³ n, pl **-lies** : publicación f mensual

monument ['mɑnjəmənt] n : monumento m

monumental [ˌmɑnjəˈmɛntəl] adj : monumental — **monumentally** adv

moo¹ ['muː] vi : mugir

moo² n : mugido m

mood ['muːd] n : humor m ⟨to be in a good mood : estar de buen humor⟩ ⟨to be in the mood for : tener ganas de⟩ ⟨to be in no mood for : no estar para⟩

moodiness ['muːdinəs] n 1 SADNESS : melancolía f, tristeza f 2 : cambios mpl de humor, carácter m temperamental

moody ['muːdi] adj **moodier; -est** 1 GLOOMY : melancólico, deprimido 2 TEMPERAMENTAL : temperamental, de humor variable

moon ['muːn] n : luna f

moonbeam ['muːnˌbiːm] n : rayo m de luna

moonlight[1] ['muːnˌlaɪt] vi : estar pluriempleado

moonlight[2] n : claro m de luna, luz f de la luna

moonlit ['muːnˌlɪt] adj : iluminado por la luna ⟨a moonlit night : una noche de luna⟩

moonshine ['muːnˌʃaɪn] n 1 MOONLIGHT : luz f de la luna 2 NONSENSE : disparates mpl, tonterías fpl 3 : whisky m destilado ilegalmente

moor[1] ['mʊr, 'mɔr] vt : amarrar

moor[2] n : brezal m, páramo m

Moor ['mʊr] n : moro m, -ra f

mooring ['mʊrɪŋ, 'mɔr-] n DOCK : atracadero m

Moorish ['mʊrɪʃ] adj : moro

moose ['muːs] ns & pl : alce m (norteamericano)

moot ['muːt] adj DEBATABLE : discutible

mop[1] ['mɑp] vt **mopped; mopping** : trapear

mop[2] n : trapeador m

mope ['moːp] vi : andar deprimido, quedar abatido

moped ['moːˌpɛd] n : ciclomotor m

moraine [məˈreɪn] n : morena f

moral[1] ['mɔrəl] adj : moral ⟨moral judgment : juicio moral⟩ ⟨moral support : apoyo moral⟩ — **morally** adv

moral[2] n 1 : moraleja f (de un cuento, etc.) 2 **morals** npl : moral f, moralidad f

morale [məˈræl] n : moral f

moralist ['mɔrəlɪst] n : moralista mf

moralistic [ˌmɔrəˈlɪstɪk] adj : moralista

morality [məˈræləti] n, pl **-ties** : moralidad f

morass [məˈræs] n 1 SWAMP : ciénaga f, pantano m 2 CONFUSION, MESS : lío m fam, embrollo m

moratorium [ˌmɔrəˈtoriəm] n, pl **-riums** or **-ria** [-iə] : moratoria f

moray ['mɔrˌeɪ, məˈreɪ] n : morena f

morbid ['mɔrbɪd] adj 1 : mórbido, morboso (en medicina) 2 GRUESOME : morboso, horripilante

morbidity [mɔrˈbɪdəti] n, pl **-ties** : morbosidad f

more[1] ['mɔr] adv : más ⟨what more can I say? : ¿qué más puedo decir?⟩ ⟨more important : más importante⟩ ⟨once more : una vez más⟩

more[2] n : más ⟨nothing more than that : nada más que eso⟩ ⟨more work : más trabajo⟩

more[3] n : más m ⟨the more you eat, the more you want : cuanto más comes, tanto más quieres⟩

more[4] pron : más ⟨more were found : se encontraron más⟩

moreover [mɔrˈoːvər] adv : además

mores ['mɔrˌeɪz, -iːz] npl CUSTOMS : costumbres fpl, tradiciones fpl

morgue ['mɔrg] n : morgue f

moribund ['mɔrəˌbʌnd] adj : moribundo

Mormon ['mɔrmən] n : mormón m, -mona f — **Mormon** adj

morn ['mɔrn] → **morning**

morning ['mɔrnɪŋ] n : mañana f ⟨good morning! : ¡buenos días!⟩

Moroccan [məˈrɑkən] n : marroquí mf — **Moroccan** adj

moron ['mɔrˌɑn] n 1 : retrasado m, -da f mental 2 DUNCE : estúpido m, -da f; tonto m, -ta f

morose [məˈroːs] adj : hosco, sombrío — **morosely** adv

moroseness [məˈroːsnəs] n : malhumor m

morphine ['mɔrˌfiːn] n : morfina f

morphology [mɔrˈfɑlədʒi] n, pl **-gies** : morfología f

morrow ['mɔroː] n : día m siguiente

Morse code ['mɔrs] n : código m morse

morsel ['mɔrsəl] n 1 BITE : bocado m 2 FRAGMENT : pedazo m

mortal[1] ['mɔrtəl] adj : mortal ⟨mortal blow : golpe mortal⟩ ⟨mortal fear : miedo mortal⟩ — **mortally** adv

mortal[2] n : mortal mf

mortality [mɔrˈtæləti] n : mortalidad f

mortar ['mɔrtər] n 1 : mortero m, molcajete m Mex ⟨mortar and pestle : mortero y maja⟩ 2 : mortero m (mortar shell : granada de mortero) 3 CEMENT : mortero m, argamasa f

mortgage[1] ['mɔrgɪdʒ] vt **-gaged; -gaging** : hipotecar

mortgage[2] n : hipoteca f

mortification [ˌmɔrtəfəˈkeɪʃən] n 1 : mortificación f 2 HUMILIATION : humillación f, vergüenza f

mortify ['mɔrtəˌfaɪ] vt **-fied; -fying** 1 : mortificar (en religión) 2 HUMILIATE : humillar, avergonzar

mortuary ['mɔrtʃəˌwɛri] n, pl **-aries** FUNERAL HOME : funeraria f

mosaic [moːˈzeɪɪk] n : mosaico m

Moslem ['mɑzləm] → **Muslim**

mosque ['mɑsk] n : mezquita f

mosquito [məˈskiːˌtoː] n, pl **-toes** : mosquito m, zancudo m

moss ['mɔs] n : musgo m

mossy ['mɔsi] adj **-ier; -est** : musgoso

most[1] ['moːst] adv : más ⟨the most interesting book : el libro más interesante⟩

most[2] adj 1 : la mayoría de, la mayor parte de ⟨most people : la mayoría de la gente⟩ 2 GREATEST : más (dícese de los números), mayor (dícese de las cantidades) ⟨the most ability : la mayor capacidad⟩

most³ *n* : más *m*, máximo *m* ⟨the most
I can do : lo más que puedo hacer⟩
⟨three weeks at the most : tres semanas
como máximo⟩

most⁴ *pron* : la mayoría, la mayor parte
⟨most will go : la mayoría irá⟩

mostly ['mo:stli] *adv* MAINLY : en su
mayor parte, principalmente

mote ['mo:t] *n* SPECK : mota *f*

motel [mo'tɛl] *n* : motel *m*

moth ['mɔθ] *n* : palomilla *f*, polilla *f*

mother¹ ['mʌðər] *vt* **1** BEAR : dar a luz
a **2** PROTECT : cuidar de, proteger

mother² *n* : madre *f*

motherhood ['mʌðər,hʊd] *n* : maternidad *f*

mother-in-law ['mʌðərɪn,lɔ] *n, pl*
mothers-in-law : suegra *f*

motherland ['mʌðər,lænd] *n* : patria *f*

motherly ['mʌðərli] *adj* : maternal

mother-of-pearl [,mʌðərəv'pərl] *n* : nácar *m*, madreperla *f*

motif [mo'ti:f] *n* : motivo *m*

motion¹ ['mo:ʃən] *vt* : hacerle señas (a
alguien) ⟨she motioned us to come in
: nos hizo señas para que entráramos⟩

motion² *n* **1** MOVEMENT : movimiento
m ⟨to set in motion : poner en marcha⟩
2 PROPOSAL : moción *f* ⟨to second a
motion : apoyar una moción⟩

motionless ['mo:ʃənləs] *adj* : inmóvil,
quieto

motion picture *n* MOVIE : película *f*

motivate ['mo:tə,veɪt] *vt* **-vated; -vating**
: motivar, mover, inducir

motivation [,mo:tə'veɪʃən] *n* : motivación *f*

motive¹ ['mo:tɪv] *adj* : motor ⟨motive
power : fuerza motriz⟩

motive² *n* : motivo *m*, móvil *m*

motley ['mɑtli] *adj* : abigarrado, variopinto

motor¹ ['mo:tər] *vi* : viajar en coche

motor² *n* : motor *m*

motorbike ['mo:tər,baɪk] *n* : motocicleta *f* (pequeña), moto *f*

motorboat ['mo:tər,bo:t] *n* : bote *m* a
motor, lancha *f* motora

motorcar ['mo:tər,kɑr] *n* : automóvil *m*

motorcycle ['mo:tər,saɪkəl] *n* : motocicleta *f*

motorcyclist ['mo:tər,saɪkəlɪst] *n* : motociclista *mf*

motorist ['mo:tərɪst] *n* : automovilista
mf, motorista *mf*

mottle ['mɑtəl] *vt* **-tled; -tling** : manchar,
motear ⟨mottled skin : piel manchada⟩
⟨a mottled surface : una superficie
moteada⟩

motto ['mɑto] *n, pl* **-toes** : lema *m*

mould ['mo:ld] → **mold**

mound ['maʊnd] *n* **1** PILE : montón *m*
2 KNOLL : montículo *m* **3** burial
mound : túmulo *m*

mount¹ ['maʊnt] *vt* **1** : montar a (un caballo), montar en (una bicicleta), subir
a **2** : montar (artillería, etc.) — *vi* IN-
CREASE : aumentar

mount² *n* **1** SUPPORT : soporte *m* **2**
HORSE : caballería *f*, montura *f* **3**
MOUNTAIN : monte *m*, montaña *f*

mountain ['maʊntən] *n* : montaña *f*

mountaineer [,maʊntən'ɪr] *n* : alpinista
mf; montañero *m*, -ra *f*

mountaineering [,maʊntən'ɪrɪŋ] *n* : alpinismo *m*

mountainous ['maʊntənəs] *adj* : montañoso

mountaintop ['maʊntən,tɑp] *n* : cima *f*,
cumbre *f*

mourn ['mɔrn] *vt* : llorar (por), lamentar ⟨to mourn the death of : llorar la
muerte de⟩ — *vi* : llorar, estar de luto

mourner ['mɔrnər] *n* : doliente *mf*

mournful ['mɔrnfəl] *adj* **1** SORROWFUL
: lloroso, plañidero, triste **2** GLOOMY
: deprimente, entristecedor — **mourn-
fully** *adv*

mourning ['mɔrnɪŋ] *n* : duelo *m*, luto *m*

mouse ['maʊs] *n, pl* **mice** ['maɪs]
1 : ratón *m*, -tona *f* **2** : ratón *m* (de una
computadora)

mousetrap ['maʊs,træp] *n* : ratonera *f*

mousse ['mu:s] *n* : mousse *mf*

moustache ['mʌ,stæʃ, mə'stæʃ] → **mustache**

mouth¹ ['maʊð] *vt* **1** : decir con poca sinceridad, repetir sin comprensión **2** : articular en silencio ⟨she mouthed the
words : formó las palabras con los
labios⟩

mouth² ['maʊθ] *n* : boca *f* (de una persona o un animal), entrada *f* (de un
túnel), desembocadura *f* (de un río)

mouthful ['maʊθ,fʊl] *n* : bocado *m* (de
comida), bocanada *f* (de líquido o
humo)

mouthpiece ['maʊθ,pi:s] *n* : boquilla *f*
(de un instrumento musical)

mouthwash ['maʊθ,wɔʃ, -,wɑʃ] *n* : enjuague *m* bucal

movable ['mu:vəbəl] *or* **moveable** *adj*
: movible, móvil

move¹ ['mu:v] *v* **moved; moving** *vi* **1** GO
: ir **2** RELOCATE : mudarse, trasladarse
3 STIR : moverse ⟨don't move! : ¡no te
muevas!⟩ **4** ACT : actuar — *vt* **1**
: mover ⟨move it over there : ponlo
allí⟩ ⟨he kept moving his feet : no de-
jaba de mover los pies⟩ **2** INDUCE,
PERSUADE : inducir, persuadir, mover
3 TOUCH : conmover ⟨it moved him to
tears : lo hizo llorar⟩ **4** PROPOSE : proponer

move² *n* **1** MOVEMENT : movimiento *m*
2 RELOCATION : mudanza *f* (de casa),
traslado *m* **3** STEP : paso *m* ⟨a good
move : un paso acertado⟩

movement ['mu:vmənt] *n* : movimiento
m

mover ['mu:vər] *n* : persona *f* que hace
mudanzas

movie ['mu:vi] *n* **1** : película *f* **2** movies
npl : cine *m*

moving² ['mu:vɪŋ] *adj* **1** : en movimiento ⟨a moving target : un blanco móvil⟩

2 TOUCHING : conmovedor, emocionante

mow[1] ['mo:] vt **mowed; mowed** or **mown** ['mo:n]; **mowing** : cortar (la hierba)

mow[2] ['mau] n : pajar m

mower ['mo:ər] → **lawn mower**

Mr. ['mɪstər] n, pl **Messrs.** ['mɛsərz] : señor m

Mrs. ['mɪsəz, -səs, esp South 'mɪzəz, -zəs] n, pl **Mesdames** [meɪ'dɑm, -'dæm] : señora f

Ms. ['mɪz] n : señora f, señorita f

much[1] ['mʌtʃ] adv **more** ['mor]; **most** ['mo:st] : mucho ⟨I'm much happier : estoy mucho más contenta⟩ ⟨she talks as much as I do : habla tanto como yo⟩

much[2] adj **more; most** : mucho ⟨it has much validity : tiene mucha validez⟩ ⟨too much time : demasiado tiempo⟩

much[3] pron : mucho, -cha ⟨I don't need much : no necesito mucho⟩

mucilage ['mju:səlɪdʒ] n : mucílago m

muck ['mʌk] n **1** MANURE : estiércol m **2** DIRT, FILTH : mugre f, suciedad f **3** MIRE, MUD : barro m, fango m, lodo m

mucous ['mju:kəs] adj : mucoso ⟨mucous membrane : membrana mucosa⟩

mucus ['mju:kəs] n : mucosidad f

mud ['mʌd] n : barro m, fango m, lodo m

muddle[1] ['mʌdəl] v **-dled; -dling** vt **1** CONFUSE : confundir **2** BUNGLE : echar a perder, malograr — vi : andar confundido ⟨to muddle through : arreglárselas⟩

muddle[2] n : confusión f, embrollo m, lío m

muddleheaded [ˌmʌdəl'hɛdəd, 'mʌdəlˌ-] adj CONFUSED : confuso, despistado

muddy[1] ['mʌdi] vt **-died; -dying** : llenar de barro

muddy[2] adj **-dier; -est** : barroso, fangoso, lodoso, enlodado ⟨you're all muddy : estás cubierto de barro⟩

muff[1] ['mʌf] vt BUNGLE : echar a perder, fallar (un tiro, etc.)

muff[2] n : manguito m

muffin ['mʌfən] n : magdalena f, mantecada f Mex

muffle ['mʌfəl] vt **-fled; -fling 1** ENVELOP : cubrir, tapar **2** DEADEN : amortiguar (un sonido)

muffler ['mʌflər] n **1** SCARF : bufanda f **2** : silenciador m, mofle m CA, Mex (de un automóvil)

mug[1] ['mʌg] v **mugged; mugging** vi : posar (con afectación), hacer muecas ⟨mugging for the camera : haciendo muecas para la cámara⟩ — vt ASSAULT : asaltar, atracar

mug[2] n CUP : tazón m

mugger ['mʌgər] n : atracador m, -dora f

mugginess ['mʌginəs] n : bochorno m

muggy ['mʌgi] adj **-gier; -est** : bochornoso

mulatto [mu'lɑto, -'læ-] n, pl **-toes** or **-tos** : mulato m, -ta f

mulberry ['mʌlˌberi] n, pl **-ries** : morera f (árbol), mora f (fruta)

mulch[1] ['mʌltʃ] vt : cubrir con pajote

mulch[2] n : pajote m

mule ['mju:l] n **1** : mula f **2** : obstinado m, -da f; terco m, -ca f

mulish ['mju:lɪʃ] adj : obstinado, terco

mull ['mʌl] vt **to mull over** : reflexionar sobre

mullet ['mʌlət] n, pl **-let** or **-lets** : mújol m, múgil m

multicolored [ˌmʌlti'kʌlərd, ˌmʌltaɪ-] adj : multicolor, abigarrado

multicultural [ˌmʌlti'kʌltʃərəl] adj : multicultural

multifaceted [ˌmʌlti'fæsətəd, ˌmʌltaɪ-] adj : multifacético

multifamily [ˌmʌlti'fæmli, ˌmʌltaɪ-] adj : multifamiliar

multifarious [ˌmʌltə'færiəs] adj DIVERSE : diverso, variado

multilateral [ˌmʌlti'lætərəl, ˌmʌltaɪ-] adj : multilateral

multimedia [ˌmʌlti'mi:diə, ˌmʌltaɪ-] adj : multimedia

multimillionaire [ˌmʌltiˌmiljə'nær, ˌmʌltaɪ-, -'miljəˌnær] adj : multimillonario

multinational [ˌmʌlti'næʃənəl, ˌmʌltaɪ-] adj : multinacional

multiple[1] ['mʌltəpəl] adj : múltiple

multiple[2] n : múltiplo m

multiple sclerosis [sklə'ro:sɪs] n : esclerosis f múltiple

multiplication [ˌmʌltəplə'keɪʃən] n : multiplicación f

multiplicity [ˌmʌltə'plɪsəti] n, pl **-ties** : multiplicidad f

multiplier ['mʌltəˌplaɪər] n : multiplicador m (en matemáticas)

multiply ['mʌltəˌplaɪ] v **-plied; -plying** vt : multiplicar — vi : multiplicarse

multipurpose [ˌmʌlti'pərpəs, ˌmʌltaɪ-] adj : multiuso

multitude ['mʌltəˌtu:d, -ˌtju:d] n **1** CROWD : multitud f, muchedumbre f **2** HOST : multitud f, gran cantidad f ⟨a multitude of ideas : numerosas ideas⟩

multivitamin [ˌmʌlti'vaɪtəmən, ˌmʌltaɪ-] adj : multivitamínico

mum[1] ['mʌm] adj SILENT : callado

mum[2] n → **chrysanthemum**

mumble[1] ['mʌmbəl] v **-bled; -bling** vt : mascullar, musitar — vi : mascullar, hablar entre dientes, murmurar

mumble[2] n **to speak in a mumble** : hablar entre dientes

mummy ['mʌmi] n, pl **-mies** : momia f

mumps ['mʌmps] ns & pl : paperas fpl

munch ['mʌntʃ] v : mascar, masticar

mundane [ˌmʌn'deɪn, 'mʌnˌ-] adj **1** EARTHLY, WORLDLY : mundano, terrenal **2** COMMONPLACE : rutinario, ordinario

municipal [mju'nɪsəpəl] adj : municipal

municipality [mjuˌnɪsə'pæləti] n, pl **-ties** : municipio m

munitions [mju'nɪʃənz] npl : municiones fpl

mural¹ ['mjʊrəl] *adj* : mural
mural² ['mjʊrəlɪst] *n* : mural *m*
murder¹ ['mərdər] *vt* : asesinar, matar —
vi : matar
murder² *n* : asesinato *m*, homicidio *m*
murderer ['mərdərər] *n* : asesino *m*, -na
f; homicida *mf*
murderess ['mərdərɪs, -də,rɛs, -dərəs] *n*
: asesina *f*, homicida *f*
murderous ['mərdərəs] *adj* : asesino,
homicida
murk ['mərk] *n* DARKNESS : oscuridad *f*,
tinieblas *fpl*
murkiness ['mərkinəs] *n* : oscuridad *f*,
tenebrosidad *f*
murky ['mərki] *adj* -kier; -est : oscuro,
tenebroso
murmur¹ ['mərmər] *vi* 1 DRONE : murmurar 2 GRUMBLE : refunfuñar, regañar, rezongar — *vt* MUMBLE : murmurar
murmur² *n* 1 COMPLAINT : queja *f* 2
DRONE : murmullo *m*, rumor *m*
muscle¹ ['mʌsəl] *vi* -cled; -cling : meterse ⟨to muscle in on : meterse por la
fuerza en, entrometerse en⟩
muscle² *n* 1 : músculo *m* 2 STRENGTH
: fuerza *f*
muscular ['mʌskjələr] *adj* 1 : muscular
⟨muscular tissue : tejido muscular⟩ 2
BRAWNY : musculoso
muscular dystrophy *n* : distrofia *f* muscular
musculature ['mʌskjələ,tʃʊr, -tʃər] *n*
: musculatura *f*
muse¹ ['mjuːz] *vi* mused; musing PON-
DER, REFLECT : cavilar, meditar, reflexionar
muse² *n* : musa *f*
museum [mjʊ'ziːəm] *n* : museo *m*
mush ['mʌʃ] *n* 1 : gachas *fpl* (de maíz)
2 SENTIMENTALITY : sensiblería *f*
mushroom¹ ['mʌʃ,ruːm, -,rum] *vi* GROW,
MULTIPLY : crecer rápidamente, multiplicarse
mushroom² *n* : hongo *m*, champiñón *m*,
seta *f*
mushy ['mʌʃi] *adj* mushier; -est 1 SOFT
: blando 2 MAWKISH : sensiblero
music ['mjuːzɪk] *n* : música *f*
musical¹ ['mjuːzɪkəl] *adj* : musical, de
música — **musically** *adv*
musical² *n* : comedia *f* musical
music box *n* : cajita *f* de música
musician [mjʊ'zɪʃən] *n* : músico *m*, -ca
f
musk ['mʌsk] *n* : almizcle *m*
musket ['mʌskət] *n* : mosquete *m*
musketeer [,mʌskə'tɪr] *n* : mosquetero
m
muskrat ['mʌsk,ræt] *n, pl* -rat *or* -rats
: rata *f* almizclera
Muslim¹ ['mʌzləm, 'mʊs-, 'mʊz-] *adj*
: musulmán
Muslim² *n* : musulmán *m*, -mana *f*
muslin ['mʌzlən] *n* : muselina *f*
muss¹ ['mʌs] *vt* : desordenar, despeinar
(el pelo)

muss² *n* : desorden *m*
mussel ['mʌsəl] *n* : mejillón *m*
must¹ ['mʌst] *v aux* 1 (*expressing obligation or necessity*) : deber, tener que
⟨you must stop : debes parar⟩ ⟨we
must obey : tenemos que obedecer⟩ 2
(*expressing probability*) : deber (de),
haber de ⟨you must be tired : debes de
estar cansado⟩ ⟨it must be late : ha de
ser tarde⟩
must² *n* : necesidad *f* ⟨exercise is a must
: el ejercicio es imprescindible⟩
mustache ['mʌ,stæʃ, mʌ'stæʃ] *n* : bigote
m, bigotes *mpl*
mustang ['mʌstæŋ] *n* : mustang *m*
mustard ['mʌstərd] *n* : mostaza *f*
muster¹ ['mʌstər] *vt* 1 ASSEMBLE : reunir 2 **to muster up** : armarse de, cobrar (valor, fuerzas, etc.)
muster² *n* 1 INSPECTION : revista *f* (de
tropas) ⟨it didn't pass muster : no re-
sistió un examen minucioso⟩ 2 COL-
LECTION : colección *f*
mustiness ['mʌstinəs] *n* : lo mohoso
musty ['mʌsti] *adj* mustier; -est : mohoso, que huele a moho, que huele a
encerrado
mutant¹ ['mjuːtənt] *adj* : mutante
mutant² *n* : mutante *m*
mutate ['mjuː,teɪt] *vi* -tated; -tating 1
: mutar (genéticamente) 2 CHANGE
: transformarse
mutation [mjuː'teɪʃən] *n* : mutación *f*
(genética)
mute¹ ['mjuːt] *vt* muted; muting MUF-
FLE : amortiguar, ponerle sordina a (un
instrumento musical)
mute² *adj* muter; mutest : mudo —
mutely *adv*
mute³ *n* 1 : mudo *m*, -da *f* (persona) 2
: sordina *f* (para un instrumento musical)
mutilate ['mjuːtə,leɪt] *vt* -lated; -lating
: mutilar
mutilation [,mjuːtə'leɪʃən] *n* : mutilación
f
mutineer [,mjuːtən'ɪr] *n* : amotinado *m*,
-da *f*
mutinous ['mjuːtənəs] *adj* : amotinado
mutiny¹ ['mjuːtəni] *vi* -nied; -nying
: amotinarse
mutiny² *n, pl* -nies : amotinamiento *m*,
motín *m*
mutt ['mʌt] *n* MONGREL : perro *m* mestizo, perro *m* corriente *Mex*
mutter ['mʌtər] *vi* 1 MUMBLE : mascullar, hablar entre dientes, murmurar
2 GRUMBLE : refunfuñar, regañar, rezongar
mutton ['mʌtən] *n* : carne *f* de carnero
mutual ['mjuːtʃʊəl] *adj* 1 : mutuo ⟨mu-
tual respect : respeto mutuo⟩ 2 COM-
MON : común ⟨a mutual friend : un
amigo común⟩
mutually ['mjuːtʃʊəli, -tʃəli] *adv* 1 : mutuamente ⟨mutually beneficial : mutuamente beneficioso⟩ 2 JOINTLY
: conjuntamente

muzzle¹ ['mʌzəl] vt **-zled; -zling** : ponerle un bozal a (un animal), amordazar

muzzle² n **1** SNOUT : hocico m **2** : bozal m (para un perro, etc.) **3** : boca f (de un arma de fuego)

my¹ ['maɪ] adj : mi ⟨my parents : mis padres⟩

my² interj : ¡caramba!, ¡Dios mío!

myopia [maɪ'o:piə] n : miopía f

myopic [maɪ'o:pɪk, -'a-] adj : miope

myriad¹ ['mɪriəd] adj INNUMERABLE : innumerable

myriad² n : miríada f

myrrh ['mər] n : mirra f

myrtle ['mərtəl] n : mirto m, arrayán m

myself [maɪ'sɛlf] pron **1** (used reflexively) : me ⟨I washed myself : me lavé⟩ **2** (used for emphasis) : yo mismo, yo misma ⟨I did it myself : lo hice yo mismo⟩

mysterious [mɪ'stɪriəs] adj : misterioso — **mysteriously** adv

mysteriousness [mɪ'stɪriəsnəs] n : lo misterioso

mystery ['mɪstəri] n, pl **-teries** : misterio m

mystic¹ ['mɪstɪk] adj : místico

mystic² n : místico m, -ca f

mystical ['mɪstɪkəl] adj : místico — **mystically** adv

mysticism ['mɪstə,sɪzəm] n : misticismo m

mystify ['mɪstə,faɪ] vt **-fied; -fying** : dejar perplejo, confundir

mystique [mɪ'sti:k] n : aura f de misterio

myth ['mɪθ] n : mito m

mythic ['mɪθɪk] adj : mítico

mythical ['mɪθɪkəl] adj : mítico

mythological [ˌmɪθə'lɑdʒɪkəl] adj : mitológico

mythology [mɪ'θɑlədʒi] n, pl **-gies** : mitología f

N

n ['ɛn] n, pl **n's** or **ns** ['ɛnz] : decimocuarta letra del alfabeto inglés

nab ['næb] vt **nabbed; nabbing** : prender, pillar fam, pescar fam

nadir ['neɪdər, 'neɪ,dɪr] n : nadir m, punto m más bajo

nag¹ ['næg] v **nagged; nagging** vi **1** COMPLAIN : quejarse, rezongar **2** to **nag at** HASSLE : molestar, darle (la) lata (a alguien) — vt **1** PESTER : molestar, fastidiar **2** SCOLD : regañar, estarle encima a — n

nag² n **1** GRUMBLER : gruñón m, -ñona f **2** HORSE : jamelgo m

naiad ['neɪəd, 'naɪ-, -,æd] n, pl **-iads** or **-iades** [-ə,di:z] : náyade f

nail¹ ['neɪl] vt : clavar, sujetar con clavos

nail² n **1** FINGERNAIL : uña f ⟨nail file : lima (de uñas)⟩ ⟨nail polish : laca de uñas⟩ **2** : clavo m ⟨to hit the nail on the head : dar en el clavo⟩

naive or **naïve** [nɑ'i:v] adj **-iver; -est 1** INGENUOUS : ingenuo, cándido **2** GULLIBLE : crédulo

naively [nɑ'i:vli] adv : ingenuamente

naïveté [ˌnɑ,i:və'teɪ, nɑ'i:və,-] n : ingenuidad f

naked ['neɪkəd] adj **1** UNCLOTHED : desnudo **2** UNCOVERED : desenvainado (dícese de una espada), pelado (dícese de los árboles), expuesto al aire (dícese de una llama) **3** OBVIOUS, PLAIN : manifiesto, puro, desnudo ⟨the naked truth : la pura verdad⟩ **4** to **the naked eye** : a simple vista

nakedly ['neɪkədli] adv : manifiestamente

nakedness ['neɪkədnəs] n : desnudez f

name¹ ['neɪm] vt **named; naming 1** CALL : llamar, bautizar, ponerle nombre a **2** MENTION : mentar, mencionar, dar el nombre de ⟨they have named a

suspect : han dado el nombre de un sospechoso⟩ **3** APPOINT : nombrar **4** to **name a price** : fijar un precio

name² adj **1** KNOWN : de nombre ⟨name brand : marca conocida⟩ **2** PROMINENT : de renombre, de prestigio

name³ n **1** : nombre m ⟨what is your name? : ¿cómo se llama?⟩ **2** SURNAME : apellido m **3** EPITHET : epíteto m ⟨to call somebody names : llamar a alguien de todo⟩ **4** REPUTATION : fama f, reputación f ⟨to make a name for oneself : darse a conocer, hacerse famoso⟩

nameless ['neɪmləs] adj **1** ANONYMOUS : anónimo **2** INDESCRIBABLE : indecible, indescriptible

namelessly ['neɪmləsli] adv : anónimamente

namely ['neɪmli] adv : a saber

namesake ['neɪm,seɪk] n : tocayo m, -ya f; homónimo m, -ma f

Namibian [nə'mɪbiən] n : namibio m, -bia f — **Namibian** adj

nanny ['næni] n, pl **nannies** : niñera f; nana f CA, Col, Mex, Ven

nap¹ ['næp] vi **napped; napping 1** : dormir, dormir la siesta **2** to **be caught napping** : estar desprevenido

nap² n **1** SLEEP : siesta f ⟨to take a nap : echarse una siesta⟩ **2** FUZZ, PILE : pelo m, pelusa f (de telas)

nape ['neɪp, 'næp] n : nuca f, cerviz f, cogote m

naphtha ['næfθə] n : nafta f

napkin ['næpkən] n : servilleta f

narcissism ['nɑrsə,sɪzəm] n : narcisismo m

narcissist ['nɑrsəsɪst] n : narcisista mf

narcissistic [ˌnɑrsə'sɪstɪk] adj : narcisista

narcissus [nɑr'sɪsəs] n, pl **-cissus** or

-cissuses or -cissi [-'sɪ,saɪ, -,si:] : narciso m

narcotic¹ [nɑr'kɑtɪk] adj : narcótico

narcotic² n : narcótico m, estupefaciente m

narrate ['nær,eɪt] vt -rated; -rating : narrar, relatar

narration [næ'reɪʃən] n : narración f

narrative¹ ['nærətɪv] adj : narrativo

narrative² n : narración f, narrativa f, relato m

narrator ['nær,eɪtər] n : narrador m, -dora f

narrow¹ ['nær,o:] vi : estrecharse, angostarse ⟨the river narrowed : el río se estrechó⟩ — vt 1 : estrechar, angostar 2 LIMIT : restringir, limitar ⟨to narrow the search : limitar la búsqueda⟩

narrow² adj 1 : estrecho, angosto 2 LIMITED : estricto, limitado ⟨in the narrowest sense of the word : en el sentido más estricto de la palabra⟩ 3 to have a narrow escape : escapar por un pelo

narrowly ['næroli] adv 1 BARELY : por poco 2 CLOSELY : de cerca

narrow-minded [,næro'maɪndəd] adj : de miras estrechas

narrowness ['næronəs] n : estrechez f

narrows ['næro:z] npl STRAIT : estrecho m

narwhal ['nɑr,ʰwɑl, 'nɑrwəl] n : narval m

nasal ['neɪzəl] adj : nasal, gangoso ⟨a nasal voice : una voz gangosa⟩

nasally ['neɪzəli] adv 1 : por la nariz 2 : con voz gangosa

nastily ['næstəli] adv : con maldad, cruelmente

nastiness ['næstinəs] n : porquería f

nasturtium [nə'stərʃəm, næ-] n : capuchina f

nasty ['næsti] adj -tier; -est 1 FILTHY : sucio, mugriento 2 OBSCENE : obsceno 3 MEAN, SPITEFUL : malo, malicioso 4 UNPLEASANT : desagradable, feo 5 REPUGNANT : asqueroso, repugnante ⟨a nasty smell : un olor asqueroso⟩

natal ['neɪtəl] adj : natal

nation ['neɪʃən] n : nación f

national¹ ['næʃənəl] adj : nacional

national² n : ciudadano m, -na f; nacional mf

nationalism ['næʃənə,lɪzəm] n : nacionalismo m

nationalist¹ ['næʃənəlɪst] adj : nacionalista

nationalist² n : nacionalista mf

nationalistic [,næʃənə'lɪstɪk] adj : nacionalista

nationality [,næʃə'næləti] n, pl -ties : nacionalidad f

nationalization [,næʃənələ'zeɪʃən] n : nacionalización f

nationalize ['næʃənə,laɪz] vt -ized; -izing : nacionalizar

nationally ['næʃənəli] adv : a escala nacional, a nivel nacional

nationwide ['neɪʃən'waɪd] adj : en toda la nación, por todo el país

native¹ ['neɪtɪv] adj 1 INNATE : innato 2 : natal ⟨her native city : su ciudad natal⟩ 3 INDIGENOUS : indígena, autóctono

native² n 1 ABORIGINE : nativo m, -va f; indígena mf 2 : natural m ⟨he's a native of Mexico : es natural de México⟩

Native American → American Indian

nativity [nə'tɪvəti, neɪ-] n, pl -ties 1 BIRTH : navidad f 2 the Nativity : la Natividad, la Navidad

natty ['næti] adj -tier; -est : elegante, garboso

natural¹ ['nætʃərəl] adj 1 : natural, de la naturaleza ⟨natural woodlands : bosques naturales⟩ ⟨natural childbirth : parto natural⟩ 2 INNATE : innato, natural 3 UNAFFECTED : natural, sin afectación 4 LIFELIKE : natural, vivo

natural² n to be a natural : tener un talento innato (para algo)

natural gas n : gas m natural

natural history n : historia f natural

naturalism ['nætʃərə,lɪzəm] n : naturalismo m

naturalist ['nætʃərəlɪst] n : naturalista mf — **naturalist** adj

naturalistic [,nætʃərə'lɪstɪk] adj : naturalista

naturalization [,nætʃərələ'zeɪʃən] n : naturalización f

naturalize ['nætʃərə,laɪz] vt -ized; -izing : naturalizar

naturally ['nætʃərəli] adv 1 INHERENTLY : naturalmente, intrínsecamente 2 UNAFFECTEDLY : de manera natural 3 OF COURSE : por supuesto, naturalmente

naturalness ['nætʃərəlnəs] n : naturalidad f

natural science n : ciencias fpl naturales

nature ['neɪtʃər] n 1 : naturaleza f ⟨the laws of nature : las leyes de la naturaleza⟩ 2 KIND, SORT : índole f, clase f ⟨things of this nature : cosas de esta índole⟩ 3 DISPOSITION : carácter m, natural m, naturaleza f ⟨it is his nature to be friendly : es de natural simpático⟩ ⟨human nature : la naturaleza humana⟩

naught ['nɔt] n 1 : nada f ⟨to come to naught : reducirse a nada, fracasar⟩ 2 ZERO : cero m

naughtily ['nɔtəli] adv : traviesamente, con malicia

naughtiness ['nɔtinəs] n : mala conducta f, travesuras fpl, malicia f

naughty ['nɔti] adj -tier; -est 1 MISCHIEVOUS : travieso, pícaro 2 RISQUÉ : picante, subido de tono

nausea ['nɔziə, 'nɔʃə] n 1 SICKNESS : náuseas fpl 2 DISGUST : asco m

nauseate ['nɔzi,eɪt, -ʒi-, -si-, -ʃi-] vt -ated; -ating 1 SICKEN : darle náuseas (a alguien) 2 DISGUST : asquear, darle asco (a alguien)

nauseating *adj* : nauseabundo, repugnante

nauseatingly [ˈnɔziˌeɪtɪŋli, -ʒi-, -si-, -ʃi-] *adv* : hasta el punto de dar asco ⟨nauseatingly sweet : tan dulce que da asco⟩

nauseous [ˈnɔʃəs, -ziəs] *adj* **1** SICK : mareado, con náuseas **2** SICKENING : nauseabundo

nautical [ˈnɔtɪkəl] *adj* : náutico

nautilus [ˈnɔtələs] *n, pl* **-luses** *or* **-li** [-ˌlaɪ, -ˌliː] : nautilo *m*

Navajo [ˈnævəˌhoː, ˈnɑ-] *n* : navajo *m*, -ja *f* — **Navajo** *adj*

naval [ˈneɪvəl] *adj* : naval

nave [ˈneɪv] *n* : nave *f*

navel [ˈneɪvəl] *n* : ombligo *m*

navigability [ˌnævɪgəˈbɪləti] *n* : navegabilidad *f*

navigable [ˈnævɪgəbəl] *adj* : navegable

navigate [ˈnævəˌgeɪt] *v* **-gated; -gating** *vi* : navegar — *vt* **1** STEER : gobernar (un barco), pilotar (un avión) **2** : navegar por (un río, etc.)

navigation [ˌnævəˈgeɪʃən] *n* : navegación *f*

navigator [ˈnævəˌgeɪtər] *n* : navegante *mf*

navy [ˈneɪvi] *n, pl* **-vies 1** FLEET : flota *f* **2** : marina *f* de guerra, armada *f* ⟨the United States Navy : la armada de los Estados Unidos⟩ **3** *or* **navy blue** : azul *m* marino

nay[1] [ˈneɪ] *adv* : no

nay[2] *n* : no *m*, voto *m* en contra

Nazi [ˈnɑtsi, ˈnæt-] *n* : nazi *mf*

Nazism [ˈnɑtˌsɪzəm, ˈnæt-] *or* **Naziism** [ˈnɑtsiˌɪzəm, ˈnæt-] *n* : nazismo *m*

Neanderthal man [niˈændərˌθɔl, -ˌtɑl] *n* : hombre *m* de Neanderthal

near[1] [ˈnɪr] *vt* **1** : acercarse a ⟨the ship is nearing port : el barco se está acercando al puerto⟩ **2** : estar a punto de ⟨she is nearing graduation : está a punto de graduarse⟩

near[2] *adv* **1** CLOSE : cerca ⟨my family lives quite near : mi familia vive muy cerca⟩ **2** NEARLY : casi ⟨I came near to finishing : casi terminé⟩

near[3] *adj* **1** CLOSE : cercano, próximo **2** SIMILAR : parecido, semejante

near[4] *prep* : cerca de

nearby[1] [ˈnɪrˌbaɪ, ˈnɪrˌbaɪ] *adv* : cerca

nearby[2] *adj* : cercano

nearly [ˈnɪrli] *adv* **1** ALMOST : casi ⟨nearly asleep : casi dormido⟩ **2** not nearly : ni con mucho, ni mucho menos ⟨it was not nearly so bad as I had expected : no fue ni con mucho tan malo como esperaba⟩

nearness [ˈnɪrnəs] *n* : proximidad *f*

nearsighted [ˈnɪrˌsaɪtəd] *adj* : miope, corto de vista

nearsightedly [ˈnɪrˌsaɪtədli] *adv* : con miopía

nearsightedness [ˈnɪrˌsaɪtədnəs] *n* : miopía *f*

neat [ˈniːt] *adj* **1** CLEAN, ORDERLY : ordenado, pulcro, limpio **2** UNDILUTED : solo, sin diluir **3** SIMPLE, TASTEFUL : sencillo y de buen gusto **4** CLEVER : hábil, ingenioso ⟨a neat trick : un truco ingenioso⟩

neatly [ˈniːtli] *adv* **1** TIDILY : ordenadamente **2** CLEVERLY : ingeniosamente

neatness [ˈniːtnəs] *n* : pulcritud *f*, limpieza *f*, orden *m*

nebula [ˈnɛbjulə] *n, pl* **-lae** [-ˌliː, -ˌlaɪ] : nebulosa *f*

nebulous [ˈnɛbjuləs] *adj* : nebuloso, vago

necessarily [ˌnɛsəˈsɛrəli] *adv* : necesariamente, forzosamente

necessary[1] [ˈnɛsəˌsɛri] *adj* **1** INEVITABLE : inevitable **2** COMPULSORY : necesario, obligatorio **3** ESSENTIAL : imprescindible, preciso, necesario

necessary[2] *n, pl* **-saries** : lo esencial, lo necesario

necessitate [nɪˈsɛsəˌteɪt] *vt* **-tated; -tating** : necesitar, requerir

necessity [nɪˈsɛsəti] *n, pl* **-ties 1** NEED : necesidad *f* **2** REQUIREMENT : requisito *m* indispensable **3** POVERTY : indigencia *f*, necesidad *f* **4** INEVITABILITY : inevitabilidad *f*

neck[1] [ˈnɛk] *vi* : besuquearse

neck[2] *n* **1** : cuello *m* (de una persona), pescuezo *m* (de un animal) **2** COLLAR : cuello *m* **3** : cuello *m* (de una botella), mástil *m* (de una guitarra)

neckerchief [ˈnɛkərtʃəf, -ˌtʃiːf] *n, pl* **-chiefs** [-tʃəfs, -ˌtʃiːfs] : pañuelo *m* (para el cuello), mascada *f* Mex

necklace [ˈnɛkləs] *n* : collar *m*

neckline [ˈnɛkˌlaɪn] *n* : escote *m*

necktie [ˈnɛkˌtaɪ] *n* : corbata *f*

nectar [ˈnɛktər] *n* : néctar *m*

nectarine [ˌnɛktəˈriːn] *n* : nectarina *f*

née *or* **nee** [ˈneɪ] *adj* : de soltera ⟨Mrs. Smith, née Whitman : la señora Smith, de soltera Whitman⟩

need[1] [ˈniːd] *vt* **1** : necesitar ⟨I need your help : necesito su ayuda⟩ ⟨I need money : me falta dinero⟩ **2** REQUIRE : requerir, exigir ⟨that job needs patience : ese trabajo exige paciencia⟩ **3** to need to : tener que ⟨he needs to study : tiene que estudiar⟩ ⟨they need to be scolded : hay que reprenderlos⟩ — *v aux* **1** MUST : tener que, deber ⟨need you shout? : ¿tienes que gritar?⟩ **2** to be needed : hacer falta ⟨you needn't worry : no hace falta que te preocupes, no hay por qué preocuparse⟩

need[2] *n* **1** NECESSITY : necesidad *f* ⟨in case of need : en caso de necesidad⟩ **2** LACK : falta *f* ⟨the need for better training : la falta de mejor capacitación⟩ ⟨to be in need : necesitar⟩ **3** POVERTY : necesidad *f*, indigencia *f* **4** needs *npl* : requisitos *mpl*, carencias *fpl*

needful [ˈniːdfəl] *adj* : necesario

needle[1] [ˈniːdəl] *vt* **-dled; -dling** : pinchar

needle[2] *n* **1** : aguja *f* ⟨to thread a needle : enhebrar una aguja⟩ ⟨knitting

needle : aguja de tejer⟩ **2** POINTER
: aguja *f*, indicador *m*
needlepoint [ˈniːdəlˌpɔint] *n* **1** LACE
: encaje *m* de mano **2** EMBROIDERY
: bordado *m* en cañamazo
needless [ˈniːdləs] *adj* : innecesario
needlessly [ˈniːdləsli] *adv* : sin ninguna
necesidad, innecesariamente
needlework [ˈniːdəlˌwərk] *n* : bordado *m*
needn't [ˈniːdənt] (*contraction of* need
not) → need
needy[1] [ˈniːdi] *adj* **needier; -est** : necesitado
needy[2] *n* **the needy** : los necesitados *mpl*
nefarious [nɪˈfæriəs] *adj* : nefario, nefando, infame
negate [nɪˈgeɪt] *vt* **-gated; -gating 1**
DENY : negar **2** NULLIFY : invalidar,
anular
negation [nɪˈgeɪʃən] *n* : negación *f*
negative[1] [ˈnɛgətɪv] *adj* : negativo
negative[2] *n* **1** : negación *f* (en lingüística) **2** : negativa *f* ⟨to answer in the negative : contestar con una negativa⟩ **3**
: término *m* negativo (en matemáticas)
4 : negativo *m*, imagen *f* en negativo
(en fotografía)
negatively [ˈnɛgətɪvli] *adv* : negativa-
mente
neglect[1] [nɪˈglɛkt] *vt* **1** : desatender, descuidar ⟨to neglect one's health : des-
cuidar la salud⟩ **2** : no cumplir con,
faltar a ⟨to neglect one's obligations
: faltar uno a sus obligaciones⟩ ⟨he neglected to tell me : omitió decírmelo⟩
neglect[2] *n* **1** : negligencia *f*, descuido *m*,
incumplimiento *m* ⟨through neglect
: por negligencia⟩ ⟨neglect of duty : incumplimiento del deber⟩ **2 in a state
of neglect** : abandonado, descuidado
neglectful [nɪˈglɛktfəl] *adj* : descuidado
m
negligee [ˌnɛgləˈʒeɪ] *n* : negligé *m*
negligence [ˈnɛglɪdʒənts] *n* : descuido
m, negligencia *f*
negligent [ˈnɛglɪdʒənt] *adj* : negligente,
descuidado — **negligently** *adv*
negligible [ˈnɛglɪdʒəbəl] *adj* : insignificante, despreciable
negotiable [nɪˈgoːʃəbəl, -ʃiə-] *adj* : negociable
negotiate [nɪˈgoːʃiˌeɪt] *vi* **-ated; -ating** *vi*
: negociar — *vt* **1** : negociar, gestionar
⟨to negotiate a treaty : negociar un tra-
to⟩ **2** : salvar, franquear ⟨they negoti-
ated the obstacles : salvaron los ob-
stáculos⟩ ⟨to negotiate a turn : tomar
una curva⟩
negotiation [nɪˌgoːʃiˈeɪʃən, -siˈeɪ-] *n*
: negociación *f*
negotiator [nɪˈgoːʃiˌeɪtər, -siˌeɪ-] *n* : negociador *m*, -dora *f*
Negro [ˈniːˌgroː] *n, pl* **-groes** : negro *m*,
-gra *f*
neigh[1] [ˈneɪ] *vi* : relinchar
neigh[2] *n* : relincho *m*
neighbor[1] [ˈneɪbər] *vt* : ser vecino de, estar junto a ⟨her house neighbors mine
: su casa está junto a la mía⟩ — *vi* : es-

tar cercano, lindar, colindar ⟨her land
neighbors on mine : sus tierras lindan
con las mías⟩
neighbor[2] *n* **1** : vecino *m*, -na *f* **2 love
thy neighbor** : ama a tu prójimo
neighborhood [ˈneɪbərˌhʊd] *n* **1** : barrio
m, vecindad *f*, vecindario *m* **2 in the
neighborhood of** : alrededor de, cerca
de
neighborly [ˈneɪbərli] *adv* : amable, de
buena vecindad
neither[1] [ˈniːðər, ˈnaɪ-] *adj* : ninguno (de
los dos)
neither[2] *conj* **1** : ni ⟨neither asleep nor
awake : ni dormido ni despierto⟩ **2**
NOR : ni (tampoco) ⟨I'm not asleep—
neither am I : no estoy dormido—ni yo
tampoco⟩
neither[3] *pron* : ninguno
nemesis [ˈnɛməsɪs] *n, pl* **-eses** [-ˌsiːz] **1**
RIVAL : rival *mf* **2** RETRIBUTION : justo castigo *m*
Neoclassical [ˌniːoˈklæsɪkəl] *adj* : neoclásico
neologism [niˈɑləˌdʒɪzəm] *n* : neologismo *m*
neon[1] [ˈniːˌɑn] *adj* : de neón ⟨neon sign
: letrero de neón⟩
neon[2] *n* : neón *m*
neophyte [ˈniːəˌfaɪt] *n* : neófito *m*, -ta *f*
Nepali [nəˈpɑli, -ˈpɑ-, -ˈpæ-] *n* : nepalés
m, -lesa *f* — **Nepali** *adj*
nephew [ˈnɛˌfjuː, *chiefly British* ˈnɛˌvjuː]
n : sobrino *m*
nepotism [ˈnɛpəˌtɪzəm] *n* : nepotismo *m*
Neptune [ˈnɛpˌtuːn, -ˌtjuːn] *n* : Neptuno
m
nerd [ˈnərd] *n* : ganso *m*, -sa *f*
nerve [ˈnərv] *n* **1** : nervio *m* **2** COURAGE
: coraje *m*, valor *m*, fuerza *f* de la voluntad ⟨to lose one's nerve : perder el
valor⟩ **3** AUDACITY, GALL : atrevimiento *m*, descaro *m* ⟨of all the
nerve! : ¡qué descaro!⟩ **4 nerves** *npl*
: nervios *mpl* ⟨a fit of nerves : un ataque
de nervios⟩
nervous [ˈnərvəs] *adj* **1** : nervioso ⟨the
nervous system : el sistema nervioso⟩
2 EXCITABLE : nervioso, excitable ⟨to
get nervous : excitarse, ponerse ner-
vioso⟩ **3** FEARFUL : miedoso, temeroso
nervously [ˈnərvəsli] *adv* : nerviosamente
nervousness [ˈnərvəsnəs] *n* : nerviosismo *m*, nerviosidad *f*, ansiedad *f*
nervy [ˈnərvi] *adj* **nervier; -est 1**
COURAGEOUS : valiente **2** IMPUDENT
: atrevido, descarado, fresco *fam* **3**
NERVOUS : nervioso
nest[1] [ˈnɛst] *vi* : anidar
nest[2] *n* **1** : nido *m* (de un ave), avispero
m (de una avispa), madriguera *f* (de un
animal) **2** REFUGE : nido *m*, refugio *m*
3 SET : juego *m* ⟨a nest of tables : un
juego de mesitas⟩
nestle [ˈnɛsəl] *vi* **-tled; -tling** : acurrucarse, arrimarse cómodamente

net¹ ['nɛt] *vt* **netted; netting 1** CATCH : pescar, atrapar con una red **2** CLEAR : ganar neto ⟨they netted $5000 : ganaron $5000 netos⟩ **3** YIELD : producir neto

net² *adj* : neto ⟨net weight : peso neto⟩ ⟨net gain : ganancia neta⟩

net³ *n* : red *f*, malla *f*

nether ['nɛðər] *adj* **1** : inferior, más bajo **2 the nether regions** : el infierno

nettle¹ ['nɛt̬əl] *vt* **-tled; -tling** : irritar, provocar, molestar

nettle² *n* : ortiga *f*

network ['nɛt̬ˌwərk] *n* **1** SYSTEM : red *f* **2** CHAIN : cadena *f* ⟨a network of supermarkets : una cadena de supermercados⟩

neural ['nʊrəl, 'njʊr-] *adj* : neural

neuralgia [nʊ'rældʒə, njʊ-] *n* : neuralgia *f*

neuritis [nʊ'raɪt̬əs, njʊ-] *n, pl* **-ritides** [-'rɪt̬əˌdiːz] *or* **-ritises** : neuritis *f*

neurological [ˌnʊrə'lɑdʒɪkəl, ˌnjʊr-] *or* **neurologic** [ˌnʊrə'lɑdʒɪk, ˌnjʊr-] *adj* : neurológico

neurologist [nʊ'rɑlədʒɪst, njʊ-] *n* : neurólogo *m*, -ga *f*

neurology [nʊ'rɑlədʒi, njʊ-] *n* : neurología *f*

neurosis [nʊ'roːsɪs, njʊ-] *n, pl* **-roses** [-ˌsiːz] : neurosis *f*

neurotic¹ [nʊ'rɑt̬ɪk, njʊ-] *adj* : neurótico

neurotic² *n* : neurótico *m*, -ca *f*

neuter¹ ['nuːt̬ər, 'njuː-] *vt* : castrar

neuter² *adj* : neutro

neutral¹ ['nuːtrəl, 'njuː-] *adj* **1** IMPARTIAL : neutral, imparcial ⟨to remain neutral : permanecer neutral⟩ **2** : neutro ⟨a neutral color : un color neutro⟩ **3** : neutro (en la química o la electricidad)

neutral² *n* : punto *m* muerto (de un automóvil)

neutrality [nuː'træləti:, njuː-] *n* : neutralidad *f*

neutralization [ˌnuːtrələ'zeɪʃən, ˌnjuː-] *n* : neutralización *f*

neutralize ['nuːtrəˌlaɪz, 'njuː-] *vt* **-ized; -izing** : neutralizar

neutron ['nuːˌtrɑn, 'njuː-] *n* : neutrón *m*

never ['nɛvər] *adv* **1** : nunca, jamás ⟨he never studies : nunca estudia⟩ **2 never again** : nunca más, nunca jamás **3 never mind** : no importa

nevermore [ˌnɛvər'mor] *adv* : nunca más

nevertheless [ˌnɛvərðə'lɛs] *adv* : sin embargo, no obstante

new ['nuː, 'njuː] *adj* **1** : nuevo ⟨a new dress : un vestido nuevo⟩ **2** RECENT : nuevo, reciente ⟨what's new? : ¿qué hay de nuevo?⟩ ⟨a new arrival : un recién llegado⟩ **3** DIFFERENT : nuevo, distinto ⟨this problem is new : este problema es distinto⟩ ⟨new ideas : ideas nuevas⟩ **4 like new** : como nuevo

newborn ['nuːˌbɔrn, 'njuː-] *adj* : recién nacido

newcomer ['nuːˌkʌmər, 'njuː-] *n* : recién llegado *m*, recién llegada *f*

newfangled ['nuːˌfæŋgəld, 'njuː-] *adj* : novedoso

newfound ['nuːˈfaʊnd, 'njuː-] *adj* : recién descubierto

newly ['nuːli, 'njuː-] *adv* : recién, recientemente

newlywed ['nuːliˌwɛd, 'njuː-] *n* : recién casado *m*, -da *f*

new moon *n* : luna *f* nueva

newness ['nuːnəs, 'njuː-] *n* : novedad *f*

news ['nuːz, 'njuːz] *n* : noticias *fpl*

newscast ['nuːzˌkæst, 'njuːz-] *n* : noticiero *m*, informativo *m*

newscaster ['nuːzˌkæstər, 'njuːz-] *n* : presentador *m*, -dora *f*; locutor *m*, -tora *f*

newsletter ['nuːzˌlɛt̬ər, 'njuːz-] *n* : boletín *m* informativo

newsman ['nuːzmən, 'njuːz-, -ˌmæn] *n, pl* **-men** [-mən, -ˌmɛn] : periodista *m*, reportero *m*

newspaper ['nuːzˌpeɪpər, 'njuːz-] *n* : periódico *m*, diario *m*

newspaperman ['nuːzˌpeɪpərˌmæn, 'njuːz-] *n, pl* **-men** [-mən, -ˌmɛn] **1** REPORTER : periodista *m*, reportero *m* **2** : dueño *m* de un periódico

newsprint ['nuːzˌprɪnt, 'njuːz-] *n* : papel *m* de prensa

newsstand ['nuːzˌstænd, 'njuːz-] *n* : quiosco *m*, puesto *m* de periódicos

newswoman ['nuːzˌwʊmən, 'njuːz-] *n, pl* **-women** [-ˌwɪmən] : periodista *f*, reportera *f*

newsworthy ['nuːzˌwərði, 'njuːz-] *adj* : de interés periodístico

newsy ['nuːzi:, 'njuː-] *adj* **newsier; -est** : lleno de noticias

newt ['nuːt, 'njuːt] *n* : tritón *m*

New Testament *n* : Nuevo Testamento *m*

New Year *n* : Año *m* Nuevo

New Year's Day *n* : día *m* del Año Nuevo

New Yorker [nuː'jɔrkər, njuː-] *n* : neoyorquino *m*, -na *f*

New Zealander [nuː'ziːləndər, njuː-] *n* : neozelandés *m*, -desa *f*

next¹ ['nɛkst] *adv* **1** AFTERWARD : después, luego ⟨what will you do next? : ¿qué harás después?⟩ **2** NOW : después, ahora, entonces ⟨next I will sing a song : ahora voy a cantar una canción⟩ **3** : la próxima vez ⟨when next we meet : la próxima vez que nos encontremos⟩

next² *adj* **1** ADJACENT : contiguo, de al lado **2** COMING : que viene, próximo ⟨next Friday : el viernes que viene⟩ **3** FOLLOWING : siguiente ⟨the next year : el año siguiente⟩

next–door ['nɛkstˈdor] *adj* : de al lado

next to¹ *adv* ALMOST : casi, prácticamente ⟨next to impossible : casi imposible⟩

next to² *prep* : junto a, al lado de
nexus [ˈneksəs] *n* : nexo *m*
nib [ˈnɪb] *n* : plumilla *f*
nibble¹ [ˈnɪbəl] *v* **-bled; -bling** *vt* : pellizcar, mordisquear, picar — *vi* : picar
nibble² *n* : mordisco *m*
Nicaraguan [ˌnɪkəˈrɑgwən] *n* : nicaragüense *mf* — **Nicaraguan** *adj*
nice [ˈnaɪs] *adj* **nicer; nicest 1** REFINED : pulido, refinado **2** SUBTLE : fino, sutil **3** PLEASING : agradable, bueno, lindo ⟨nice weather : buen tiempo⟩ **4** RESPECTABLE : bueno, decente **5 nice and** : bien, muy ⟨nice and hot : bien caliente⟩ ⟨nice and slow : despacito⟩
nicely [ˈnaɪsli] *adv* **1** KINDLY : amablemente **2** POLITELY : con buenos modales **3** ATTRACTIVELY : de buen gusto
niceness [ˈnaɪsnəs] *n* : simpatía *f*, amabilidad *f*
nicety [ˈnaɪsəti] *n, pl* **-ties 1** DETAIL, SUBTLETY : sutileza *f*, detalle *m* **2 niceties** *npl* : lujos *mpl*, detalles *mpl*
niche [ˈnɪtʃ] *n* **1** RECESS : nicho *m*, hornacina *f* **2** : nicho *m*, hueco *m* ⟨to make a niche for oneself : hacerse un hueco, encontrarse una buena posición⟩
nick¹ [ˈnɪk] *vt* : cortar, hacer una muesca en
nick² *n* **1** CUT : corte *m*, muesca *f* **2 in the nick of time** : en el momento crítico, justo a tiempo
nickel [ˈnɪkəl] *n* **1** : níquel *m* **2** : moneda *f* de cinco centavos
nickname¹ [ˈnɪkˌneɪm] *vt* **-named; -naming** : apodar
nickname² *n* : apodo *m*, mote *m*, sobrenombre *m*
nicotine [ˈnɪkəˌtiːn] *n* : nicotina *f*
niece [ˈniːs] *n* : sobrina *f*
Nigerian [naɪˈdʒɪriən] *n* : nigeriano *m*, -na *f* — **Nigerian** *adj*
niggardly [ˈnɪgərdli] *adj* : mezquino, tacaño
niggling [ˈnɪgəlɪŋ] *adj* **1** PETTY : insignificante **2** PERSISTENT : constante, persistente ⟨a niggling doubt : una duda constante⟩
nigh¹ [ˈnaɪ] *adv* **1** NEARLY : casi **2 to draw nigh** : acercarse, avecinarse
nigh² *adj* : cercano, próximo
night¹ [ˈnaɪt] *adj* : nocturno, de la noche ⟨the night sky : el cielo nocturno⟩ ⟨night shift : turno de la noche⟩
night² *n* **1** EVENING : noche *f* ⟨at night : de noche⟩ ⟨last night : anoche⟩ ⟨tomorrow night : mañana por la noche⟩ **2** DARKNESS : noche *f*, oscuridad *f* ⟨night fell : cayó la noche⟩
nightclothes [ˈnaɪtˌkloːðz, -ˌkloːz] *npl* : ropa *f* de dormir
nightclub [ˈnaɪtˌklʌb] *n* : cabaret *m*, club *m* nocturno
night crawler [ˈnaɪtˌkrɔlər] *n* EARTHWORM : lombriz *f* (de tierra)
nightfall [ˈnaɪtˌfɔl] *n* : anochecer *m*
nightgown [ˈnaɪtˌgaʊn] *n* : camisón *m* (de noche)

nightingale [ˈnaɪtənˌgeɪl, ˈnaɪtɪŋ-] *n* : ruiseñor *m*
nightly¹ [ˈnaɪtli] *adv* : cada noche, todas las noches
nightly² *adj* : de todas las noches
nightmare [ˈnaɪtˌmær] *n* : pesadilla *f*
nightmarish [ˈnaɪtˌmærɪʃ] *adj* : de pesadilla
night owl *n* : noctámbulo *m*, -la *f*
nightshade [ˈnaɪtˌʃeɪd] *n* : hierba *f* mora
nightshirt [ˈnaɪtˌʃərt] *n* : camisa *f* de dormir
nightstick [ˈnaɪtˌstɪk] *n* : porra *f*
nighttime [ˈnaɪtˌtaɪm] *n* : noche *f*
nihilism [ˈnaɪəˌlɪzəm] *n* : nihilismo *m*
nil [ˈnɪl] *n* : nada *f*, cero *m*
nimble [ˈnɪmbəl] *adj* **-bler; -blest 1** AGILE : ágil **2** CLEVER : hábil, ingenioso
nimbleness [ˈnɪmbəlnəs] *n* : agilidad *f*
nimbly [ˈnɪmbli] *adv* : con agilidad, ágilmente
nincompoop [ˈnɪnkəmˌpuːp, ˈnɪŋ-] *n* FOOL : tonto *m*, -ta *f*; bobo *m*, -ba *f*
nine¹ [ˈnaɪn] *adj* **1** : nueve **2 nine times out of ten** : casi siempre
nine² *n* : nueve *m*
nine hundred¹ *adj* : novecientos
nine hundred² *n* : novecientos *m*
ninepins [ˈnaɪnˌpɪnz] *n* : bolos *mpl*
nineteen¹ [naɪnˈtiːn] *adj* : diecinueve
nineteen² *n* : diecinueve *m*
nineteenth¹ [naɪnˈtiːnθ] *adj* : decimonoveno, decimonono ⟨the nineteenth century : el siglo diecinueve⟩
nineteenth² *n* **1** : decimonoveno *m*, -na *f*; decimonono *m*, -na *f* (en una serie) **2** : diecinueveavo *m*, diecinueveava parte *f*
ninetieth¹ [ˈnaɪntiəθ] *adj* : nonagésimo
ninetieth² *n* **1** : nonagésimo *m*, -ma *f* (en una serie) **2** : noventavo *m*, noventava parte *f*
ninety¹ [ˈnaɪnti] *adj* : noventa
ninety² *n, pl* **-ties** : noventa *m*
ninth¹ [ˈnaɪnθ] *adj* : noveno
ninth² *n* **1** : noveno *m*, -na *f* (en una serie) **2** : noveno *m*, novena parte *f*
ninny [ˈnɪni] *n, pl* **ninnies** FOOL : tonto *m*, -ta *f*; bobo *m*, -ba *f*
nip¹ [ˈnɪp] *vt* **nipped; nipping 1** PINCH : pellizcar **2** BITE : morder, mordisquear **3 to nip in the bud** : cortar de raíz
nip² *n* **1** TANG : sabor *m* fuerte **2** PINCH : pellizco *m* **3** NIBBLE : mordisco *m* **4** SWALLOW : trago *m*, traguito *m* **5 there's a nip in the air** : hace fresco
nipple [ˈnɪpəl] *n* : pezón *m* (de una mujer), tetilla *f* (de un hombre)
nippy [ˈnɪpi] *adj* **-pier; -est 1** SHARP : fuerte, picante **2** CHILLY : frío ⟨it's nippy today : hoy hace frío⟩
nit [ˈnɪt] *n* : liendre *f*
nitrate [ˈnaɪˌtreɪt] *n* : nitrato *m*
nitric acid [ˈnaɪtrɪk] *n* : ácido *m* nítrico
nitrite [ˈnaɪˌtraɪt] *n* : nitrito *m*
nitrogen [ˈnaɪtrədʒən] *n* : nitrógeno *m*
nitroglycerin *or* **nitroglycerine** [ˌnaɪtroˈglɪsərən] *n* : nitroglicerina *f*

nitwit ['nɪt,wɪt] *n* : zonzo *m*, -za *f*; bobo *m*, -ba *f*

no¹ ['no:] *adv* : no ⟨are you leaving? — no : ¿te vas?—no⟩ ⟨no less than : no menos de⟩ ⟨to say no : decir que no⟩ ⟨like it or not : quieras o no quieras⟩

no² *adj* 1 : ninguno ⟨it's no trouble : no es ningún problema⟩ ⟨she has no money : no tiene dinero⟩ 2 (*indicating a small amount*) ⟨we'll be there in no time : llegamos dentro de poco, no tardamos nada⟩ 3 (*expressing a negation*) ⟨he's no liar : no es mentiroso⟩

no³ *n*, *pl* **noes** *or* **nos** ['no:z] 1 DENIAL : no *m* ⟨I won't take no for an answer : no aceptaré un no por respuesta⟩ 2 : voto *f* en contra ⟨the noes have it : se ha rechazado la moción⟩

nobility [no'bɪlət̮i] *n* : nobleza *f*

noble¹ ['no:bəl] *adj* **-bler; -blest** 1 ILLUSTRIOUS : noble, glorioso 2 ARISTOCRATIC : noble 3 STATELY : majestuoso, magnífico 4 LOFTY : noble, elevado ⟨noble sentiments : sentimientos elevados⟩

noble² *n* : noble *m*, aristócrata *mf*

nobleman ['no:bəlmən] *n*, *pl* **-men** [-mən, -,mɛn] : noble *m*, aristócrata *f*

nobleness ['no:bəlnəs] *n* : nobleza *f*

noblewoman ['no:bəl,wumən] *n*, *pl* **-women** [-,wɪmən] : noble *f*, aristócrata *f*

nobly ['no:bli] *adv* : noblemente

nobody¹ ['no:bədi, -,bɑdi] *n*, *pl* **-bodies** : don nadie *m* ⟨he's a mere nobody : es un don nadie⟩

nobody² *pron* : nadie

nocturnal [nɑk'tərnəl] *adj* : nocturno

nocturne ['nɑk,tərn] *n* : nocturno *m*

nod¹ ['nɑd] *v* **nodded; nodding** *vi* 1 : saludar con la cabeza, asentir con la cabeza 2 to nod off : dormirse, quedarse dormido — *vt* : inclinar (la cabeza) ⟨to nod one's head in agreement : asentir con la cabeza⟩

nod² *n* : saludo *m* con la cabeza, señal *m* con la cabeza, señal *m* de asentimiento

node ['no:d] *n* : nudo *m* (de una planta)

nodule ['nɑ,dʒu:l] *n* : nódulo *m*

noel [no'ɛl] *n* 1 CAROL : villancico *m* de Navidad 2 Noel CHRISTMAS : Navidad *f*

noes → **no³**

noise¹ ['nɔɪz] *vt* **noised; noising** : rumorear, publicar

noise² *n* : ruido *m*

noiseless ['nɔɪzləs] *adj* : silencioso, sin ruido

noiselessly ['nɔɪzləsli] *adv* : silenciosamente

noisemaker ['nɔɪz,meɪkər] *n* : matraca *f*

noisiness ['nɔɪzinəs] *n* : ruido *m*

noisome ['nɔɪsəm] *adj* : maloliente, fétido

noisy ['nɔɪzi] *adj* **noisier; -est** : ruidoso — **noisily** ['nɔɪzəli] *adv*

nomad¹ ['no:,mæd] → **nomadic**

nomad² *n* : nómada *mf*

nomadic [no'mædɪk] *adj* : nómada

nomenclature ['no:mən,kleɪtʃər] *n* : nomenclatura *f*

nominal ['nɑmənəl] *adj* 1 : nominal ⟨the nominal head of his party : el jefe nominal de su partido⟩ 2 TRIFLING : insignificante

nominally ['nɑmənəli] *adv* : sólo de nombre, nominalmente

nominate ['nɑmə,neɪt] *vt* **-nated; -nating** 1 PROPOSE : proponer (como candidato), nominar 2 APPOINT : nombrar

nomination [,nɑmə'neɪʃən] *n* 1 PROPOSAL : propuesta *f*, postulación *f* 2 APPOINTMENT : nombramiento *m*

nominative¹ ['nɑmənət̮ɪv] *adj* : nominativo

nominative² *n or* **nominative case** : nominativo *m*

nominee [,nɑmə'ni:] *n* : candidato *m*, -ta *f*

nonaddictive [,nɑnə'dɪktɪv] *adj* : que no crea dependencia

nonalcoholic [,nɑn,ælkə'hɔlɪk] *adj* : sin alcohol, no alcohólico

nonaligned [,nɑnə'laɪnd] *adj* : no alineado

nonbeliever [,nɑnbə'li:vər] *n* : no creyente *mf*

nonbreakable [,nɑn'breɪkəbəl] *adj* : irrompible

nonce ['nɑnts] *n* **for the nonce** : por el momento

nonchalance [,nɑnʃə'lɑnts] *n* : indiferencia *f*, despreocupación *f*

nonchalant [,nɑnʃə'lɑnt] *adj* : indiferente, despreocupado, impasible

nonchalantly [,nɑnʃə'lɑntli] *adv* : con aire despreocupado, con indiferencia

noncombatant [,nɑnkəm'bætənt, -'kɑmbə-] *n* : no combatiente *mf*

noncommissioned officer [,nɑnkə'mɪʃənd] *n* : suboficial *mf*

noncommittal [,nɑnkə'mɪt̮əl] *adj* : evasivo, que no se compromete

nonconductor [,nɑnkən'dʌktər] *n* : aislante *m*

nonconformist [,nɑnkən'fɔrmɪst] *n* : inconformista *mf*, inconforme *mf*

nonconformity [,nɑnkən'fɔrmət̮i] *n* : inconformidad *f*, no conformidad *f*

noncontagious [,nɑnkən'teɪdʒəs] *adj* : no contagioso

nondenominational [,nɑndɪ,nɑmə'neɪʃənəl] *adj* : no sectario

nondescript [,nɑndɪ'skrɪpt] *adj* : anodino, soso

nondiscriminatory [,nɑndɪ'skrɪmənə,tori] *adj* : no discriminatorio

nondrinker [,nɑn'drɪŋkər] *n* : abstemio *m*, -mia *f*

none¹ ['nʌn] *adv* : de ninguna manera, de ningún modo, nada ⟨she was none too happy : no se sintió nada contento⟩ ⟨I'm none the worse for it : no estoy peor por ello⟩ ⟨none too soon : a buena hora⟩

none[2] *pron* : ninguno, ninguna
nonentity [ˌnɑn'ɛntəti] *n, pl* **-ties** : persona *f* insignificante, nulidad *f*
nonessential [ˌnɑn'sɛntʃəl] *adj* : secundario, no esencial
nonessentials [ˌnɑn'sɛntʃəlz] *npl* : cosas *fpl* secundarias, cosas *fpl* accesorias
nonetheless [ˌnʌnðə'lɛs] *adv* : sin embargo, no obstante
nonexistence [ˌnɑnɪg'zɪstənts] *n* : inexistencia *f*
nonexistent [ˌnɑnɪg'zɪstənt] *adj* : inexistente
nonfat [ˌnɑn'fæt] *adj* : sin grasa
nonfattening [ˌnɑn'fætənɪŋ] *adj* : que no engorda
nonfiction [ˌnɑn'fɪkʃən] *n* : no ficción *f*
nonflammable [ˌnɑn'flæməbəl] *adj* : no inflamable
nonintervention [ˌnɑnˌɪntər'vɛntʃən] *n* : no intervención *f*
nonmalignant [ˌnɑnmə'lɪgnənt] *adj* : no maligno, benigno
nonnegotiable [ˌnɑnnɪ'go:ʃəbəl, -ʃiə-] *adj* : no negociable
nonpareil[1] [ˌnɑnpə'rɛl] *adj* : sin parangón, sin par
nonpareil[2] *n* : persona *f* sin igual, cosa *f* sin par
nonpartisan [ˌnɑn'pɑrtəzən, -sən] *adj* : imparcial
nonpaying [ˌnɑn'peɪɪŋ] *adj* : que no paga
nonpayment [ˌnɑn'peɪmənt] *n* : impago *m*, falta *f* de pago
nonperson [ˌnɑn'pərsən] *n* : persona *f* sin derechos
nonplus [ˌnɑn'plʌs] *vt* **-plussed; -plussing** : confundir, desconcertar, dejar perplejo
nonprescription [ˌnɑnprɪ'skrɪpʃən] *adj* : disponible sin receta del médico
nonproductive [ˌnɑnprə'dʌktɪv] *adj* : improductivo
nonprofit [ˌnɑn'prɑfət] *adj* : sin fines lucrativos
nonproliferation [ˌnɑnprəˌlɪfə'reɪʃən] *adj* : no proliferación
nonresident [ˌnɑn'rɛzədənt, -ˌdɛnt] *n* : no residente *mf*
nonscheduled [ˌnɑn'skɛˌdʒu:ld] *adj* : no programado, no regular
nonsectarian [ˌnɑnˌsɛk'tæriən] *adj* : no sectario
nonsense [ˈnɑnˌsɛnts, ˈnɑntsənts] *n* : tonterías *fpl*, disparates *mpl*
nonsensical [nɑn'sɛntsɪkəl] *adj* ABSURD : absurdo, disparatado — **nonsensically** [-kli] *adv*
nonsmoker [ˌnɑn'smo:kər] *n* : no fumador *m*, -dora *f*; persona *f* que no fuma
nonstandard [ˌnɑn'stændərd] *adj* : no regular, no estándar
nonstick [ˌnɑn'stɪk] *adj* : antiadherente
nonstop[1] [ˌnɑn'stɑp] *adv* : sin parar ⟨he talked nonstop : habló sin parar⟩
nonstop[2] *adj* : directo, sin escalas ⟨nonstop flight : vuelo directo⟩

nonsupport [ˌnɑnsə'pɔrt] *n* : falta *f* de manutención
nontaxable [ˌnɑn'tæksəbəl] *adj* : exento de impuestos
nontoxic [ˌnɑn'tɑksɪk] *adj* : no tóxico
nonviolence [ˌnɑn'vaɪlənts, -'vaɪə-] *n* : no violencia *f*
nonviolent [ˌnɑn'vaɪlənt, -'vaɪə-] *adj* : pacífico, no violento
noodle [ˈnu:dəl] *n* : fideo *m*, tallarín *m*
nook [ˈnʊk] *n* : rincón *m*, recoveco *m*, escondrijo *m* ⟨in every nook and cranny : en todos los rincones⟩
noon [ˈnu:n] *n* : mediodía *m*
noonday [ˈnu:nˌdeɪ] *n* : mediodía *m* ⟨the noonday sun : el sol de mediodía⟩
no one *pron* NOBODY : nadie
noontime [ˈnu:nˌtaɪm] *n* : mediodía *m*
noose [ˈnu:s] *n* **1** LASSO : lazo *m* **2** hangman's noose : dogal *m*, soga *f*
nor [ˈnɔr] *conj* : ni ⟨neither good nor bad : ni bueno ni malo⟩ ⟨nor I! : ¡ni yo tampoco!⟩
Nordic [ˈnɔrdɪk] *adj* : nórdico
norm [ˈnɔrm] *n* **1** STANDARD : norma *f*, modelo *m* **2** CUSTOM, RULE : regla *f* general, lo normal
normal [ˈnɔrməl] *adj* : normal — **normally** *adv*
normalcy [ˈnɔrməlsi] *n* : normalidad *f*
normality [nɔr'mæləti] *n* : normalidad *f*
normalize [ˈnɔrməˌlaɪz] *vt* : normalizar
Norse [ˈnɔrs] *adj* : nórdico
north[1] [ˈnɔrθ] *adv* : al norte
north[2] *adj* : norte, del norte ⟨the north coast : la costa del norte⟩
north[3] *n* **1** : norte *m* **2 the North** : el Norte *m*
North American *n* : norteamericano *m*, -na *f* — **North American** *adj*
northbound [ˈnɔrθˌbaʊnd] *adv* : con rumbo al norte
northeast[1] [nɔrθ'i:st] *adv* : hacia el nordeste
northeast[2] *adj* : nordeste, del nordeste
northeast[3] *n* : nordeste *m*, noreste *m*
northeasterly[1] [nɔrθ'i:stərli] *adv* : hacia el nordeste
northeasterly[2] *adj* : nordeste, del nordeste
northeastern [nɔrθ'i:stərn] *adj* : nordeste, del nordeste
northerly[1] [ˈnɔrðərli] *adv* : hacia el norte
northerly[2] *adj* : del norte ⟨a northerly wind : un viento del norte⟩
northern [ˈnɔrðərn] *adj* : norte, norteño, septentrional
Northerner [ˈnɔrðərnər] *n* : norteño *m*, -ña *f*
northern lights → aurora borealis
North Pole : Polo *m* Norte
North Star : estrella *f* polar
northward [ˈnɔrθwərd] *adv & adj* : hacia el norte
northwest[1] [nɔrθ'wɛst] *adv* : hacia el noroeste
northwest[2] *adj* : del noroeste
northwest[3] *n* : noroeste *m*

northwesterly[1] [nɔrθ'wɛstərli] *adv* : hacia el noroeste

northwesterly[2] *adj* : del noroeste

northwestern [nɔrθ'wɛstərn] *adj* : noroeste, del noroeste

Norwegian [nɔr'wiːdʒən] *n* 1 : noruego *m*, -ga *f* 2 : noruego *m* (idioma) — **Norwegian** *adj*

nose[1] ['noːz] *v* **nosed; nosing** *vt* 1 SMELL : olfatear 2 : empujar con el hocico ⟨the dog nosed open the bag : el perro abrió el saco con el hocico⟩ 3 EDGE, MOVE : mover poco a poco — *vi* 1 PRY : entrometerse, meter las narices 2 EDGE : avanzar poco a poco

nose[2] *n* 1 : nariz *f* (de una persona), hocico *m* (de un animal) ⟨to blow one's nose : sonarse las narices⟩ 2 SMELL : olfato *m*, sentido *m* del olfato 3 FRONT : parte *f* delantera, nariz *f* (de un avión), proa *f* (de un barco) 4 to follow one's nose : dejarse guiar por el instinto

nosebleed ['noːz,bliːd] *n* : hemorragia *f* nasal

nosedive ['noːz,daɪv] *n* 1 : descenso *m* en picada (de un avión) 2 : caída *f* súbita (de precios, etc.)

nose–dive ['noːz,daɪv] *vi* : descender en picada, caer en picada

nostalgia [nɑ'stældʒə, nə-] *n* : nostalgia *f*

nostalgic [nɑ'stældʒɪk, nə-] *adj* : nostálgico

nostril ['nɑstrəl] *n* : ventana *f* de la nariz

nostrum ['nɑstrəm] *n* : panacea *f*

nosy *or* **nosey** ['noːzi] *adj* **nosier; -est** : entrometido

not ['nɑt] *adv* 1 (*used to form a negative*) : no ⟨she is not tired : no está cansada⟩ ⟨not to say something would be wrong : no decir nada sería injusto⟩ 2 (*used to replace a negative clause*) : no ⟨are we going or not? : ¿vamos a ir o no?⟩ ⟨of course not! : ¡claro que no!⟩

notable[1] ['noːtəbəl] *adj* 1 NOTEWORTHY : notable, de notar 2 DISTINGUISHED, PROMINENT : distinguido, destacado

notable[2] *n* : persona *f* importante, personaje *m*

notably ['noːtəbli] *adv* : notablemente, particularmente

notarize ['noːtə,raɪz] *vt* **-rized; -rizing** : autenticar, autorizar

notary public ['noːtəri] *n*, *pl* **-ries public** *or* **-ry publics** : notario *m*, -ria *f*; escribano *m*, -na *f*

notation [noː'teɪʃən] *n* 1 NOTE : anotación *f*, nota *f* 2 : notación *f* ⟨musical notation : notación musical⟩

notch[1] ['nɑtʃ] *vt* : hacer una muesca en, cortar

notch[2] *n* : muesca *f*, corte *m*

note[1] ['noːt] *vt* **noted; noting** 1 NOTICE : notar, observar, tomar nota de 2 RECORD : anotar, apuntar

note[2] *n* 1 : nota *f* (musical) 2 COMMENT : nota *f*, comentario *m* 3 LETTER : nota *f*, cartita *f* 4 PROMINENCE : prestigio *m* ⟨a musician of note : un músico destacado⟩ 5 ATTENTION : atención *f* ⟨to take note of : prestar atención a⟩

notebook ['noːt,bʊk] *n* 1 : libreta *f*, cuaderno *m* 2 : notebook *m* (computadora)

noted ['noːtəd] *adj* EMINENT : renombrado, eminente, célebre

noteworthy ['noːt,wərði] *adj* : notable, de notar, de interés

nothing[1] ['nʌθɪŋ] *adv* 1 : de ninguna manera ⟨nothing daunted, we carried on : sin amilanarnos, seguimos adelante⟩ 2 **nothing like** : no . . . en nada ⟨he's nothing like his brother : no se parece en nada a su hermano⟩

nothing[2] *n* 1 NOTHINGNESS : nada *f* 2 ZERO : cero *m* 3 : persona *f* de poca importancia, cero *m* 4 TRIFLE : nimiedad *f*

nothing[3] *pron* : nada ⟨there's nothing better : no hay nada mejor⟩ ⟨nothing else : nada más⟩ ⟨nothing but : solamente⟩ ⟨they mean nothing to me : ellos me son indiferentes⟩

nothingness ['nʌθɪŋnəs] *n* 1 VOID : vacío *m*, nada *f* 2 NONEXISTENCE : inexistencia *f* 3 TRIFLE : nimiedad *f*

notice[1] ['noːtɪs] *vt* **-ticed; -ticing** : notar, observar, advertir, darse cuenta de

notice[2] *n* 1 NOTIFICATION : aviso *m*, notificación *f* 2 ATTENTION : atención *f* ⟨to take notice of : prestar atención a⟩

noticeable ['noːtɪsəbəl] *adj* : evidente, perceptible — **noticeably** [-bli] *adv*

notification [,noːtəfə'keɪʃən] *n* : notificación *f*, aviso *m*

notify ['noːtə,faɪ] *vt* **-fied; -fying** : notificar, avisar

notion ['noːʃən] *n* 1 IDEA : idea *f*, noción *f* 2 WHIM : capricho *m*, antojo *m* 3 **notions** *npl* : artículos *mpl* de mercería

notoriety [,noːtə'raɪəti] *n* : mala fama *f*, notoriedad *f*

notorious [noː'toːriəs] *adj* : de mala fama, célebre, bien conocido

notwithstanding[1] [,nɑtwɪθ'stændɪŋ, -wɪð-] *adv* NEVERTHELESS : no obstante, sin embargo

notwithstanding[2] *conj* : a pesar de que

notwithstanding[3] *prep* : a pesar de, no obstante

nougat ['nuːgət] *n* : turrón *m*

nought ['nɔt, 'nɑt] → **naught**

noun ['naʊn] *n* : nombre *m*, sustantivo *m*

nourish ['nərɪʃ] *vt* 1 FEED : alimentar, nutrir, sustentar 2 FOSTER : fomentar, alentar

nourishing ['nərɪʃɪŋ] *adj* : alimenticio, nutritivo

nourishment ['nərɪʃmənt] *n* : nutrición *f*, alimento *m*, sustento *m*

novel[1] ['nɑvəl] *adj* : original, novedoso

novel² *n* : novela *f*
novelist ['nɑvəlɪst] *n* : novelista *mf*
novelty ['nɑvəlti] *n, pl* **-ties** 1 : novedad *f* 2 **novelties** *npl* TRINKETS : baratijas *fpl*, chucherías *fpl*
November [no'vɛmbər] *n* : noviembre *m*
novice ['nɑvɪs] *n* : novato *m*, -ta *f*; principiante *mf*; novicio *m*, -cia *f*
now¹ ['nɑʊ] *adv* 1 PRESENTLY : ahora, ya, actualmente ⟨from now on : de ahora en adelante⟩ ⟨long before now : ya hace tiempo⟩ ⟨now and then : de vez en cuando⟩ 2 IMMEDIATELY : ahora (mismo), inmediatamente ⟨do it right now! : ¡hazlo ahora mismo!⟩ 3 THEN : ya, entonces ⟨now they were ready : ya estaban listos⟩ 4 *(used to introduce a statement, a question, a command, or a transition)* ⟨now hear this! : ¡presten atención!⟩ ⟨now what do you think of that? : ¿qué piensas de eso?⟩
now² *n (indicating the present time)* ⟨until now : hasta ahora⟩ ⟨by now : ya⟩ ⟨ten years from now : dentro de 10 años⟩
now³ *conj* **now that** : ahora que, ya que
nowadays ['nɑʊə,deɪz] *adv* : hoy en día, actualmente, en la actualidad
nowhere¹ ['no:,ʍwɛr] *adv* 1 : en ninguna parte, a ningún lado ⟨nowhere to be found : en ninguna parte, por ningún lado⟩ ⟨you're going nowhere : no estás yendo a ningún lado, no estás yendo a ninguna parte⟩ 2 **nowhere near** : ni con mucho, nada cerca ⟨it's nowhere near here : no está nada cerca de aquí⟩
nowhere² *n* 1 : ninguna parte *f* 2 **out of nowhere** : de la nada
noxious ['nɑkʃəs] *adj* : nocivo, dañino, tóxico
nozzle ['nɑzəl] *n* : boca *f*
nuance ['nu:,ɑns, 'nju:-] *n* : matiz *m*
nub ['nʌb] *n* 1 KNOB, LUMP : protuberancia *f*, nudo *m* 2 GIST : quid *m*, meollo *m*
nuclear ['nu:kliər, 'nju:-] *adj* : nuclear
nucleus ['nu:kliəs, 'nju:-] *n, pl* **-clei** [-kli,aɪ] : núcleo *m*
nude¹ ['nu:d, 'nju:d] *adj* **nuder; nudest** : desnudo
nude² *n* : desnudo *m*
nudge¹ ['nʌʤ] *vt* **nudged; nudging** : darle con el codo (a alguien)
nudge² *n* : toque *m* que se da con el codo
nudism ['nu:,dɪzəm, 'nju:-] *n* : nudismo *m*
nudist ['nu:dɪst, 'nju:-] *n* : nudista *mf*
nudity ['nu:dəti, 'nju:-] *n* : desnudez *f*
nugget ['nʌgət] *n* : pepita *f*
nuisance ['nu:sənts, 'nju:-] *n* 1 BOTHER : fastidio *m*, molestia *f*, lata *f* 2 PEST : pesado *m*, -da *f fam*
null ['nʌl] *adj* : nulo ⟨null and void : nulo y sin efecto⟩
nullify ['nʌlə,faɪ] *vt* **-fied; -fying** : invalidar, anular
nullity ['nʌləti] *n, pl* **-ties** : nulidad *f*
numb¹ ['nʌm] *vt* : entumecer, adormecer

numb² *adj* : entumecido, dormido ⟨numb with fear : paralizado de miedo⟩
number¹ ['nʌmbər] *vt* 1 COUNT, INCLUDE : contar, incluir 2 : numerar ⟨number the pages : numera las páginas⟩ 3 TOTAL : ascender a, sumar
number² *n* 1 : número *m* ⟨in round numbers : en números redondos⟩ ⟨telephone number : número de teléfono⟩ 2 **a number of** : varios, unos pocos, unos cuantos
numberless ['nʌmbərləs] *adj* : innumerable, sin número
numbness ['nʌmnəs] *n* : entumecimiento *m*
numeral ['nu:mərəl, 'nju:-] *n* : número *m* ⟨Roman numeral : número romano⟩
numerator ['nu:mə,reɪtər, 'nju:-] *n* : numerador *m*
numeric [nʊ'mɛrɪk, nju-] *adj* : numérico
numerical [nʊ'mɛrɪkəl, nju-] *adj* : numérico — **numerically** [-kli] *adv*
numerous ['nu:mərəs, 'nju:-] *adj* : numeroso
numismatics [,nu:məz'mætɪks, ,nju:-] *n* : numismática *f*
numskull ['nʌm,skʌl] *n* : tonto *m*, -ta *f*; mentecato *m*, -ta *f*; zoquete *m fam*
nun ['nʌn] *n* : monja *f*
nuptial ['nʌpʃəl] *adj* : nupcial
nuptials ['nʌpʃəlz] *npl* WEDDING : nupcias *fpl*, boda *f*
nurse¹ ['nərs] *vt* **nursed; nursing** 1 SUCKLE : amamantar 2 : cuidar (de), atender ⟨to nurse the sick : cuidar a los enfermos⟩ ⟨to nurse a cold : curarse de un resfriado⟩
nurse² *n* 1 : enfermero *m*, -ra *f* 2 → nursemaid
nursemaid ['nərs,meɪd] *n* : niñera *f*
nursery ['nərsəri] *n, pl* **-eries** 1 *or* **day nursery** : guardería *f* 2 : vivero *m* (de plantas)
nursing home *n* : hogar *m* de ancianos, clínica *f* de reposo
nurture¹ ['nərtʃər] *vt* **-tured; -turing** 1 FEED, NOURISH : nutrir, alimentar 2 EDUCATE : criar, educar 3 FOSTER : alimentar, fomentar
nurture² *n* 1 UPBRINGING : crianza *f*, educación *f* 2 FOOD : alimento *m*
nut ['nʌt] *n* 1 : nuez *f* 2 : tuerca *f* ⟨nuts and bolts : tuercas y tornillos⟩ 3 LUNATIC : loco *m*, -ca *f*; chiflado *m*, -da *f fam* 4 ENTHUSIAST : fanático *m*, -ca *f*; entusiasta *mf*
nutcracker ['nʌt,krækər] *n* : cascanueces *m*
nuthatch ['nʌt,hætʃ] *n* : trepador *m*
nutmeg ['nʌt,mɛg] *n* : nuez *f* moscada
nutrient ['nu:triənt, 'nju:-] *n* : nutriente *m*, alimento *m* nutritivo
nutriment ['nu:trəmənt, 'nju:-] *n* : nutrimento *m*
nutrition [nʊ'trɪʃən, nju-] *n* : nutrición *f*
nutritional [nʊ'trɪʃənəl, nju-] *adj* : alimenticio
nutritious [nʊ'trɪʃəs, nju-] *adj* : nutritivo, alimenticio

nuts ['nʌts] *adj* **1** FANATICAL : fanático **2** CRAZY : loco, chiflado *fam*

nutshell ['nʌt,ʃɛl] *n* **1** : cáscara *f* de nuez **2 in a nutshell** : en pocas palabras

nutty ['nʌt̬i] *adj* **-tier; -tiest** : loco, chiflado *fam*

nuzzle ['nʌzəl] *v* **-zled; -zling** *vi* NESTLE : acurrucarse, arrimarse — *vt* : acariciar con el hocico

nylon ['naɪ,lɑn] *n* **1** : nilón *m* **2 nylons** *npl* : medias *fpl* de nilón

nymph ['nɪmpf] *n* : ninfa *f*

O

o ['oː] *n, pl* **o's** *or* **os** ['oːz] **1** : decimoquinta letra del alfabeto inglés **2** ZERO : cero *m*

O ['oː] → **oh**

oaf ['oːf] *n* : zoquete *m*; bruto *m*, -ta *f*

oafish ['oːfɪʃ] *adj* : torpe, lerdo

oak ['oːk] *n, pl* **oaks** *or* **oak** : roble *m*

oaken ['oːkən] *adj* : de roble

oar ['or] *n* : remo *m*

oarlock ['or,lɑk] *n* : tolete *m*, escálamo *m*

oasis [oˈeɪsɪs] *n, pl* **oases** [-,siːz] : oasis *m*

oat ['oːt] *n* : avena *f*

oath ['oːθ] *n, pl* **oaths** ['oːðz, 'oːθs] **1** : juramento *m* ⟨to take an oath : prestar juramento⟩ **2** SWEARWORD : mala palabra *f*, palabrota *f*

oatmeal ['oːt,miːl] *n* : avena *f* ⟨instant oatmeal : avena instantánea⟩

obdurate ['ɑbdʊrət, -djʊ-] *adj* : inflexible, firme, obstinado

obedience [oˈbiːdiənts] *n* : obediencia *f*

obedient [oˈbiːdiənt] *adj* : obediente — **obediently** *adv*

obelisk ['ɑbə,lɪsk] *n* : obelisco *m*

obese [oˈbiːs] *adj* : obeso

obesity [oˈbiːsət̬i] *n* : obesidad *f*

obey [oˈbeɪ] *v* **obeyed; obeying** : obedecer ⟨to obey the law : cumplir la ley⟩

obfuscate ['ɑbfə,skeɪt] *vt* **-cated; -cating** : ofuscar, confundir

obituary [oˈbɪtʃu,ɛri] *n, pl* **-aries** : obituario *m*, necrología *f*

object¹ [əbˈdʒɛkt] *vt* : objetar — *vi* : oponerse, poner reparos, hacer objeciones

object² ['ɑbdʒɪkt] *n* **1** : objeto *m* **2** OBJECTIVE, PURPOSE : objetivo *m*, propósito *m* **3** : complemento *m* (en gramática)

objection [əbˈdʒɛkʃən] *n* : objeción *f*

objectionable [əbˈdʒɛkʃənəbəl] *adj* : ofensivo, indeseable — **objectionably** [-bli] *adv*

objective¹ [əbˈdʒɛktɪv] *adj* **1** IMPARTIAL : objetivo, imparcial **2** : de complemento, directo (en gramática)

objective² *n* **1** : objetivo *m* **2** *or* **objective case** : acusativo *m*

objectively [əbˈdʒɛktɪvli] *adv* : objetivamente

objectivity [,ɑb,dʒɛk'tɪvət̬i] *n, pl* **-ties** : objetividad *f*

obligate ['ɑblə,geɪt] *vt* **-gated; -gating** : obligar

obligation [,ɑblə'geɪʃən] *n* : obligación *f*

obligatory [əˈblɪgə,tori] *adj* : obligatorio

oblige [əˈblaɪdʒ] *vt* **obliged; obliging** **1** COMPEL : obligar **2** : hacerle un favor (a alguien), complacer ⟨to oblige a friend : hacerle un favor a un amigo⟩ **3 to be much obliged** : estar muy agradecido

obliging [əˈblaɪdʒɪŋ] *adj* : servicial, complaciente — **obligingly** *adv*

oblique [oˈbliːk] *adj* **1** SLANTING : oblicuo **2** INDIRECT : indirecto — **obliquely** *adv*

obliterate [əˈblɪt̬ə,reɪt] *vt* **-ated; -ating** **1** ERASE : obliterar, borrar **2** DESTROY : destruir, eliminar

obliteration [ə,blɪt̬ə'reɪʃən] *n* : obliteración *f*

oblivion [əˈblɪviən] *n* : olvido *m*

oblivious [əˈblɪviəs] *adj* : inconsciente — **obliviously** *adv*

oblong¹ ['ɑ,blɔŋ] *adj* : oblongo

oblong² *n* : figura *f* oblonga, rectángulo *m*

obnoxious [ɑbˈnɑkʃəs, əb-] *adj* : repugnante, odioso — **obnoxiously** *adv*

oboe ['oː,boː] *n* : oboe *m*

oboist ['oː,boɪst] *n* : oboe *mf*

obscene [ɑbˈsiːn, əb-] *adj* : obsceno, indecente — **obscenely** *adv*

obscenity [ɑbˈsɛnət̬i, əb-] *n, pl* **-ties** : obscenidad *f*

obscure¹ [ɑbˈskjʊr, əb-] *vt* **-scured; -scuring** **1** CLOUD, DIM : oscurecer, nublar **2** HIDE : ocultar

obscure² *adj* **1** DIM : oscuro **2** REMOTE, SECLUDED : recóndito **3** VAGUE : oscuro, confuso, vago **4** UNKNOWN : desconocido ⟨an obscure poet : un poeta desconocido⟩ — **obscurely** *adv*

obscurity [ɑbˈskjʊrət̬i, əb-] *n, pl* **-ties** : oscuridad *f*

obsequious [əbˈsiːkwiəs] *adj* : servil, excesivamente atento

observable [əbˈzərvəbəl] *adj* : observable, perceptible

observance [əbˈzərvənts] *n* **1** FULFILLMENT : observancia *f*, cumplimiento *m* **2** PRACTICE : práctica *f*

observant [əbˈzərvənt] *adj* : observador

observation [,ɑbsər'veɪʃən, -zər-] *n* : observación *f*

observatory [əbˈzərvə,tori] *n, pl* **-ries** : observatorio *m*

observe [əbˈzərv] *v* **-served; -serving** *vt* **1** OBEY : observar, obedecer **2** CELEBRATE : celebrar, guardar (una práctica religiosa) **3** WATCH : observar, mi-

rar **4** REMARK : observar, comentar —
vi LOOK : mirar
observer [ab'zərvər] *n* : observador *m*,
-dora *f*
obsess [əb'sɛs] *vt* : obsesionar
obsession [ab'sɛʃən, əb-] *n* : obsesión *f*
obsessive [ab'sɛsɪv, əb-] *adj* : obsesivo
— **obsessively** *adv*
obsolescence [ˌabsə'lɛsənts] *n* : obsolescencia *f*
obsolescent [ˌabsə'lɛsənt] *adj* : obsolescente ⟨to become obsolescent : caer
en desuso⟩
obsolete [ˌabsə'li:t, 'absə-] *adj* : obsoleto, anticuado
obstacle ['abstɪkəl] *n* : obstáculo *m*, impedimento *m*
obstetric [əb'stɛtrɪk] *or* **obstetrical**
[-trɪkəl] *adj* : obstétrico
obstetrician [ˌabstə'trɪʃən] *n* : obstetra
mf; tocólogo *m*, -ga *f*
obstetrics [əb'stɛtrɪks] *ns & pl* : obstetricia *f*, tocología *f*
obstinacy ['abstənəsi] *n, pl* **-cies** : obstinación *f*, terquedad *f*
obstinate ['abstənət] *adj* : obstinado,
terco — **obstinately** *adv*
obstreperous [əb'strɛpərəs] *adj* **1**
CLAMOROUS : ruidoso, clamoroso **2**
UNRULY : rebelde, indisciplinado
obstruct [əb'strʌkt] *vt* : obstruir, bloquear
obstruction [əb'strʌkʃən] *n* : obstrucción *f*, bloqueo *m*
obstructive [əb'strʌktɪv] *adj* : obstructor
obtain [əb'teɪn] *vt* : obtener, conseguir
— *vi* PREVAIL : imperar, prevalecer
obtainable [əb'teɪnəbəl] *adj* : obtenible,
asequible
obtrude [əb'tru:d] *v* **-truded; -truding** *vt*
1 EXTRUDE : expulsar **2** IMPOSE : imponer — *vi* INTRUDE : inmiscuirse, entrometerse
obtrusive [əb'tru:sɪv] *adj* **1** IMPERTI-
NENT, MEDDLESOME : impertinente,
entrometido **2** PROTRUDING : prominente
obtuse [ab'tu:s, əb-, -'tju:s] *adj* : obtuso, torpe
obtuse angle *n* : ángulo obtuso
obviate ['abvi,eɪt] *vt* **-ated; -ating** : obviar, evitar
obvious ['abviəs] *adj* : obvio, evidente,
manifiesto
obviously ['abviəsli] *adv* **1** CLEARLY
: obviamente, evidentemente **2** OF
COURSE : claro, por supuesto
occasion[1] [ə'keɪʒən] *vt* : ocasionar,
causar
occasion[2] *n* **1** OPPORTUNITY : oportunidad *f*, ocasión *f* **2** CAUSE : motivo *m*,
razón *f* **3** INSTANCE : ocasión *f* **4**
EVENT : ocasión *f*, acontecimiento *m*
5 on ～ : de vez en cuando, ocasionalmente
occasional [ə'keɪʒənəl] *adj* : ocasional
occasionally [ə'keɪʒənəli] *adv* : de vez
en cuando, ocasionalmente

occidental [ˌaksə'dɛntəl] *adj* : oeste, del
oeste, occidental
occult[1] [ə'kʌlt, 'a,kʌlt] *adj* **1** HIDDEN,
SECRET : oculto, secreto **2** ARCANE
: arcano, esotérico
occult[2] *n* the occult : las ciencias ocul-
tas
occupancy ['akjəpəntsi] *n, pl* **-cies**
: ocupación *f*, habitación *f*
occupant ['akjəpənt] *n* : ocupante *mf*
occupation [ˌakjə'peɪʃən] *n* : ocupación
f, profesión *f*, oficio *m*
occupational [ˌakjə'peɪʃənəl] *adj* : ocupacional
occupy ['akjə,paɪ] *vt* **-pied; -pying** : ocupar
occur [ə'kər] *vi* **occurred; occurring 1**
EXIST : encontrarse, existir **2** HAPPEN
: ocurrir, acontecer, suceder, tener lugar **3** : ocurrirse ⟨it occurred to him
that . . . : se le ocurrió que . . . ⟩
occurrence [ə'kərənts] *n* : acontecimiento *m*, suceso *m*, ocurrencia *f*
ocean ['o:ʃən] *n* : océano *m*
oceanic [ˌo:ʃi'ænɪk] *adj* : oceánico
oceanography [ˌo:ʃə'nagrəfi] *n*
: oceanografía *f*
ocelot ['asə,lat, 'o:-] *n* : ocelote *m*
ocher *or* **ochre** ['o:kər] *n* : ocre *m*
o'clock [ə'klak] *adv* (used in telling time)
⟨it's ten o'clock : son las diez⟩ ⟨at six
o'clock : a las seis⟩
octagon ['aktə,gan] *n* : octágono *m*
octagonal [ak'tægənəl] *adj* : octagonal
octave ['aktɪv] *n* : octava *f*
October [ak'to:bər] *n* : octubre *m*
octopus ['aktə,pus, -pəs] *n, pl* **-puses** *or*
-pi [-,paɪ] : pulpo *m*
ocular ['akjələr] *adj* : ocular
oculist ['akjəlɪst] *n* **1** OPHTHALMOLO-
GIST : oftalmólogo *m*, -ga *f*; oculista *mf*
2 OPTOMETRIST : optometrista *mf*
odd ['ad] *adj* **1** : sin pareja, suelto ⟨an
odd sock : un calcetín sin pareja⟩ **2**
UNEVEN : impar ⟨odd numbers
: números impares⟩ **3** : y pico, y tantos ⟨forty odd years ago : hace cuarenta
y pico años⟩ **4** : alguno, uno que otro
⟨odd jobs : algunos trabajos⟩ **5**
STRANGE : extraño, raro
oddball ['ad,bɔl] *n* : excéntrico *m*, -ca *f*;
persona *f* rara
oddity ['adəţi] *n, pl* **-ties** : rareza *f*, cosa
f rara
oddly ['adli] *adv* : de manera extraña
oddness ['adnəs] *n* : rareza *f*, excentricidad *f*
odds ['adz] *npl* **1** CHANCES : probabili-
dades *fpl* **2** : puntos *mpl* de ventaja (de
una apuesta) **3** to be at odds : estar en
desacuerdo
odds and ends *npl* : costillas *fpl*, cosas
fpl sueltas, cachivaches *mpl*
ode ['o:d] *n* : oda *f*
odious ['o:diəs] *adj* : odioso — **odious-
ly** *adv*
odor ['o:dər] *n* : olor *m*
odorless ['o:dərləs] *adj* : inodoro, sin
olor

odorous ['oːdərəs] *adj* : oloroso

odyssey ['ɑdəsi] *n*, *pl* **-seys** : odisea *f*

o'er ['or] → **over**

of ['ʌv, 'əv] *prep* **1** FROM : de ⟨a man of the city : un hombre de la ciudad⟩ **2** (*indicating character or background*) : de ⟨a woman of great ability : una mujer de gran capacidad⟩ **3** (*indicating cause*) : de ⟨he died of the flu : murió de la gripe⟩ **4** BY : de ⟨the works of Shakespeare : las obras de Shakespeare⟩ **5** (*indicating contents, material, or quantity*) : de ⟨a house of wood : una casa de madera⟩ ⟨a glass of water : un vaso de agua⟩ **6** (*indicating belonging or connection*) : de ⟨the front of the house : el frente de la casa⟩ **7** ABOUT : sobre, de ⟨tales of the West : los cuentos del Oeste⟩ **8** (*indicating a particular example*) : de ⟨the city of Caracas : la ciudad de Caracas⟩ **9** FOR : por, a ⟨love of country : amor por la patria⟩ **10** (*indicating time or date*) ⟨five minutes of ten : las diez menos cinco⟩ ⟨the eighth of April : el ocho de abril⟩

off¹ ['ɔf] *adv* **1** (*indicating change of position or state*) ⟨to march off : marcharse⟩ ⟨he dozed off : se puso a dormir⟩ **2** (*indicating distance in space or time*) ⟨some miles off : a varias millas⟩ ⟨the holiday is three weeks off : faltan tres semanas para la fiesta⟩ **3** (*indicating removal*) ⟨the knob came off : se le cayó el pomo⟩ **4** (*indicating termination*) ⟨shut the television off : apaga la televisión⟩ **5** (*indicating suspension of work*) ⟨to take a day off : tomarse un día de descanso⟩ **6 off and on** : de vez en cuando

off² *adj* **1** FARTHER : más remoto, distante ⟨the off side of the building : el lado distante del edificio⟩ **2** STARTED : empezado ⟨to be off on a spree : irse de juerga⟩ **3** OUT : apagado ⟨the light is off : la luz está apagada⟩ **4** CANCELED : cancelado, suspendido **5** INCORRECT : erróneo, incorrecto **6** REMOTE : remoto, lejano ⟨an off chance : una posibilidad remota⟩ **7** FREE : libre ⟨I'm off today : hoy estoy libre⟩ **8 to be well off** : vivir con desahogo, tener bastante dinero

off³ *prep* **1** (*indicating physical separation*) : de ⟨she took it off the table : lo tomó de la mesa⟩ ⟨a shop off the main street : una tienda al lado de la calle principal⟩ **2** : a la costa de, a expensas de ⟨he lives off his sister : vive a expensas de su hermana⟩ **3** (*indicating the suspension of an activity*) ⟨to be off duty : estar libre⟩ ⟨he's off liquor : ha dejado el alcohol⟩ **4** BELOW : por debajo de ⟨he's off his game : está por debajo de su juego normal⟩

offal ['ɔfəl] *n* **1** RUBBISH, WASTE : desechos *mpl*, desperdicios *mpl* **2** VISCERA : vísceras *fpl*, asaduras *fpl*

offend [ə'fɛnd] *vt* **1** VIOLATE : violar, atentar contra **2** HURT : ofender ⟨to be easily offended : ser muy susceptible⟩

offender [ə'fɛndər] *n* : delincuente *mf*; infractor *m*, -tora *f*

offense *or* **offence** [ə'fɛns, 'ɔ,fɛns] *n* **1** INSULT : ofensa *f*, injuria *f*, agravio *m* ⟨to take offense : ofenderse⟩ **2** ASSAULT : ataque *m* **3** ofensiva *f* (en deportes) **4** CRIME, INFRACTION : infracción *f*, delito *m*

offensive¹ [ə'fɛnsɪv, 'ɔ,fɛnt-] *adj* : ofensivo — **offensively** *adv*

offensive² *n* : ofensiva *f*

offer¹ ['ɔfər] *vt* **1** : ofrecer ⟨they offered him the job : le ofrecieron el puesto⟩ **2** PROPOSE : proponer, sugerir **3** SHOW : ofrecer, mostrar ⟨to offer resistance : ofrecer resistencia⟩

offer² *n* : oferta *f*, ofrecimiento *m*, propuesta *f*

offering ['ɔfərɪŋ] *n* : ofrenda *f*

offhand¹ ['ɔf'hænd] *adv* : sin preparación, sin pensarlo

offhand² *adj* **1** IMPROMPTU : improvisado **2** ABRUPT : brusco

office ['ɔfəs] *n* **1** : cargo *m* ⟨to run for office : presentarse como candidato⟩ **2** : oficina *f*, despacho *m*, gabinete *m* (en la casa) ⟨office hours : horas de oficina⟩

officeholder ['ɔfəs,hoːldər] *n* : titular *mf*

officer ['ɔfəsər] *n* **1** *or* **police officer** : policía *mf*, agente *mf* de policía **2** OFFICIAL : oficial *mf*; funcionario *m*, -ria *f*; director *m*, -tora *f* (en una empresa) **3** COMMISSIONED OFFICER : oficial *mf*

official¹ [ə'fɪʃəl] *adj* : oficial — **officially** *adv*

official² *n* : funcionario *m*, -ria *f*; oficial *mf*

officiate [ə'fɪʃi,eɪt] *v* **-ated; -ating** *vi* **1** : arbitrar (en deportes) **2 to officiate at** : oficiar, celebrar — *vt* : arbitrar

officious [ə'fɪʃəs] *adj* : oficioso

offing ['ɔfɪŋ] *n* **in the offing** : en perspectiva

offset ['ɔf,sɛt] *vt* **-set; -setting** : compensar

offshoot ['ɔf,ʃuːt] *n* **1** OUTGROWTH : producto *m*, resultado *m* **2** BRANCH, SHOOT : retoño *m*, rama *f*, vástago *m* (de una planta)

offshore¹ ['ɔf'ʃor] *adv* : a una distancia de la costa

offshore² *adj* **1** : de (la) tierra ⟨an offshore wind : un viento que sopla de tierra⟩ **2** : (de) costa afuera, cercano a la costa ⟨an offshore island : una isla costera⟩

offspring ['ɔf,sprɪŋ] *ns & pl* **1** YOUNG : crías *fpl* (de los animales) **2** PROGENY : prole *f*, progenie *f*

off–white ['ɔf'hwaɪt] *adj* : blancuzco

often ['ɔfən, 'ɔftən] *adv* : muchas veces, a menudo, seguido

oftentimes ['ɔfən,taɪmz, 'ɔftən-] *or* **ofttimes** ['ɔft,taɪmz] → **often**

ogle ['o:gəl] *vt* **ogled; ogling** : comerse con los ojos, quedarse mirando a

ogre ['o:gər] *n* : ogro *m*

oh ['o:] *interj* : ¡oh!, ¡ah!, ¡ay! ⟨oh, of course : ah, por supuesto⟩ ⟨oh no! : ¡ay no!⟩ ⟨oh really? : ¿de veras?⟩

ohm ['o:m] *n* : ohm *m*, ohmio *m*

oil[1] ['ɔɪl] *vt* : lubricar, engrasar, aceitar

oil[2] *n* **1** : aceite *m* **2** PETROLEUM : petróleo *m* **3** *or* **oil painting** : óleo *m*, pintura *f* al óleo **4** *or* **oil paint(s)** : óleo *m*

oilcloth ['ɔɪl,klɔθ] *n* : hule *m*

oiliness ['ɔɪlinəs] *n* : lo aceitoso

oilskin ['ɔɪl,skɪn] *n* : hule *m* **2 oilskins** *npl* : impermeable *m*

oily ['ɔɪli] *adj* **oilier; -est** : aceitoso, grasiento, grasoso ⟨oily fingers : dedos grasientos⟩

ointment ['ɔɪntmənt] *n* : ungüento *m*, pomada *f*

OK[1] [,o:'keɪ] *vt* **OK'd** *or* **okayed** [,o:'keɪd]; **OK'ing** *or* **okaying** APPROVE, AUTHORIZE : dar el visto bueno a, autorizar, aprobar

OK[2] *or* **okay** [,o:'keɪ] *adv* **1** WELL : bien **2** YES : sí, por supuesto

OK[3] *adj* : bien ⟨he's OK : está bien⟩ ⟨it's OK with me : estoy de acuerdo⟩

OK[4] *n* : autorización *f*, visto *m* bueno

okra ['o:krə, *South also* -kri] *n* : quingombó *m*

old[1] ['o:ld] *adj* **1** ANCIENT : antiguo ⟨old civilizations : civilizaciones antiguas⟩ **2** FAMILIAR : viejo ⟨old friends : viejos amigos⟩ ⟨the same old story : el mismo cuento⟩ **3** *(indicating a certain age)* ⟨he's ten years old : tiene diez años (de edad)⟩ **4** AGED : viejo, anciano ⟨an old woman : una anciana⟩ **5** FORMER : antiguo ⟨her old neighborhood : su antiguo barrio⟩ **6** WORN-OUT : viejo, gastado

old[2] *n* **1 the old** : los viejos, los ancianos **2 in the days of old** : antaño, en los tiempos antiguos

olden ['o:ldən] *adj* : de antaño, de antigüedad

old–fashioned ['o:ld'fæʃənd] *adj* : anticuado, pasado de moda

old maid *n* **1** SPINSTER : soltera *f* **2** FUSSBUDGET : maniático *m*, -ca *f*; melindroso *m*, -sa *f*

Old Testament *n* : Antiguo Testamento *m*

old–time ['o:ld'taɪm] *adj* : antiguo

old–timer ['o:ld'taɪmər] *n* **1** VETERAN : veterano *m*, -na *f* **2** *or* **oldster** : anciano *m*, -na *f*

old–world ['o:ld'wərld] *adj* : pintoresco (de antaño)

oleander ['o:li,ændər] *n* : adelfa *f*

oleomargarine [,o:lio'mɑrdʒərən] → **margarine**

olfactory [ɑl'fæktəri, ol-] *adj* : olfativo

oligarchy ['ɑlə,gɑrki, 'o:lə-] *n*, *pl* **-chies** : oligarquía *f*

olive ['ɑlɪv, -ləv] *n* **1** : aceituna *f*, oliva *f* (fruta) **2** : olivo *m* (árbol) **3** *or* **olive green** : color *m* aceituna, verde *m* oliva

Olmec ['ɑl,mɛk, 'o:l-] *n* : olmeca *mf* — **Olmec** *adj*

Olympic [ə'lɪmpɪk, o-] *adj* : olímpico

Olympic Games *npl* : Juegos *mpl* Olímpicos

Olympics [ə'lɪmpɪks, o-] *npl* : olimpiadas *fpl*

Omani [o'mɑni, -'mæ-] *n* : omaní *mf* — **Omani** *adj*

ombudsman ['ɑm,bʊdzmən, ɑm-'bʊdz-] *n*, *pl* **-men** [-mən, -,mɛn] : ombudsman *m*

omelet *or* **omelette** ['ɑmlət, 'ɑmə-] *n* : omelette *mf*, tortilla *f* (de huevo)

omen ['o:mən] *n* : presagio *m*, augurio *m*, agüero *m*

ominous ['ɑmənəs] *adj* : ominoso, agorero, de mal agüero

ominously ['ɑmənəsli] *adv* : de manera amenazadora

omission [o'mɪʃən] *n* : omisión *f*

omit [o'mɪt] *vt* **omitted; omitting 1** LEAVE OUT : omitir, excluir **2** NEGLECT : omitir ⟨they omitted to tell us : omitieron decírnoslo⟩

omnipotence [ɑm'nɪpətənts] *n* : omnipotencia *f* — **omnipotent** [ɑm-'nɪpətənt] *adj*

omnipresent [,ɑmnɪ'prɛzənt] *adj* : omnipresente

omniscient [ɑm'nɪʃənt] *adj* : omnisciente

omnivorous [ɑm'nɪvərəs] *adj* **1** : omnívoro **2** AVID : ávido, voraz

on[1] ['ɑn, 'ɔn] *adv* **1** *(indicating contact with a surface)* ⟨put the top on : pon la tapa⟩ ⟨he has a hat on : lleva un sombrero puesto⟩ **2** *(indicating forward movement)* ⟨from that moment on : a partir de ese momento⟩ ⟨farther on : más adelante⟩ **3** *(indicating operation or an operating position)* ⟨turn the light on : prende la luz⟩

on[2] *adj* **1** *(being in operation)* ⟨the radio is on : el radio está prendido⟩ **2** *(taking place)* ⟨the game is on : el juego ha comenzado⟩ **3 to be on to** : estar enterado de

on[3] *prep* **1** *(indicating position)* : en, sobre, encima de ⟨on the table : en (sobre, encima de) la mesa⟩ ⟨shadows on the wall : sombras en la pared⟩ ⟨on horseback : a caballo⟩ **2** AT, TO : a ⟨on the right : a la derecha⟩ **3** ABOARD, IN : en, a ⟨on the plane : en el avión⟩ ⟨he got on the train : subió al tren⟩ **4** *(indicating time)* ⟨she worked on Saturdays : trabajaba los sábados⟩ ⟨every hour on the hour : a la hora en punto⟩ **5** *(indicating means or agency)* : por ⟨he cut himself on a tin can : se cortó con una lata⟩ ⟨to talk on the telephone : hablar por teléfono⟩ **6** *(indicating a state or process)* : en ⟨on fire : en llamas⟩ ⟨on the increase : en aumento〉 **7** (*indicating connection or membership*) : en 〈on a committee : en una comisión〉 **8** (*indicating an activity*) 〈on vacation : de vacaciones〉 〈on a diet : a dieta〉 **9** ABOUT, CONCERNING : sobre 〈a book on insects : un libro sobre insectos〉 〈reflect on that : reflexiona sobre eso〉

once¹ [ˈwʌnts] *adv* **1** : una vez 〈once a month : una vez al mes〉 〈once and for all : de una vez por todas〉 **2** EVER : alguna vez **3** FORMERLY : antes, anteriormente

once² *adj* FORMER : antiguo

once³ *n* **1** : una vez **2 at ~** SIMULTANEOUSLY : al mismo tiempo, simultáneamente **3 at ~** IMMEDIATELY : inmediatamente, en seguida

once⁴ *conj* : una vez que, tan pronto como

once-over [ˌwʌntsˈoːvər, ˈwʌntsˌ-] *n* **to give someone the once-over** : echarle un vistazo a alguien

oncoming [ˈɑnˌkʌmɪŋ, ˈɔn-] *adj* : que viene

one¹ [ˈwʌn] *adj* **1** (*being a single unit*) : un, una 〈he only wants one apple : sólo quiere una manzana〉 **2** (*being a particular one*) : un, una 〈he arrived early one morning : llegó temprano una mañana〉 **3** (*being the same*) : mismo, misma 〈they're all members of the same team : todos son miembros del mismo equipo〉 **4** SOME : alguno, alguna; un, una 〈I'll see you again some day : algún día te veré otra vez〉 〈at one time or another : en una u otra ocasión〉

one² *n* **1** : uno *m* (número) **2** (*indicating the first of a set or series*) 〈from day one : desde el primer momento〉 **3** (*indicating a single person or thing*) 〈the one (girl) on the right : la de la derecha〉 〈he has the one but needs the other : tiene uno pero necesita el otro〉

one³ *pron* **1** : uno, una 〈one of his friends : una de sus amigas〉 〈one never knows : uno nunca sabe, nunca se sabe〉 〈to cut one's finger : cortarse el dedo〉 **2 one and all** : todos, todo el mundo **3 one another** : el uno al otro, se 〈they love one another : se amaban〉 **4 that one** : aquél, aquella **5 which one?** : ¿cuál?

one-on-one [ˌwʌnɑnˈwʌn, -ɑn-] *adj* : uno a uno — **one-on-one** *adv*

onerous [ˈɑnərəs, ˈoːnə-] *adj* : oneroso, gravoso

oneself [ˌwʌnˈself] *pron* **1** (*used reflexively or for emphasis*) : se, sí mismo, uno mismo 〈to control oneself : controlarse〉 〈to talk to oneself : hablarse a sí mismo〉 〈to do it oneself : hacérselo uno mismo〉 **2 by ~** : solo

one-sided [ˈwʌnˈsaɪdəd] *adj* **1** : de un solo lado **2** LOPSIDED : asimétrico **3** BIASED : parcial, tendencioso **4** UNILATERAL : unilateral

onetime [ˈwʌnˌtaɪm] *adj* FORMER : antiguo

one-way [ˈwʌnˈweɪ] *adj* **1** : de sentido único, de una sola dirección 〈a one-way street : una calle de sentido único〉 **2** : de ida, sencillo 〈a one-way ticket : un boleto de ida〉

ongoing [ˈɑnˌgoːɪŋ] *adj* **1** CONTINUING : en curso, corriente **2** DEVELOPING : en desarrollo

onion [ˈʌnjən] *n* : cebolla *f*

online [ˈɔnˌlaɪn, ˈɑn-] *adj* : en línea

onlooker [ˈɔnˌlʊkər, ˈɑn-] *n* : espectador *m*, -dora *f*; circunstante *mf*

only¹ [ˈoːnli] *adv* **1** MERELY : sólo, solamente, nomás 〈for only two dollars : por tan sólo dos dólares〉 〈only once : sólo una vez, no más de una vez〉 〈I only did it to help : lo hice por ayudar nomás〉 **2** SOLELY : únicamente, sólo, solamente 〈only he knows it : solamente él lo sabe〉 **3** (*indicating a result*) 〈it will only cause him problems : no hará más que crearle problemas〉 **4** If only : ojalá, por lo menos 〈if only it were true! : ¡ojalá sea cierto!〉 〈if he could only dance : si por lo menos pudiera bailar〉

only² *adj* : único 〈an only child : un hijo único〉 〈the only chance : la única oportunidad〉

only³ *conj* BUT : pero 〈I would go, only I'm sick : iría, pero estoy enfermo〉

onset [ˈɑnˌset] *n* : comienzo *m*, llegada *f*

onslaught [ˈɑnˌslɔt, ˈɔn-] *n* : arremetida *f*, embestida *f*, embate *m*

onto [ˈɑnˌtuː, ˈɔn-] *prep* : sobre

onus [ˈoːnəs] *n* : responsabilidad *f*, carga *f*

onward¹ [ˈɑnwərd, ˈɔn-] *or* **onwards** *adv* FORWARD : adelante, hacia adelante

onward² *adj* : hacia adelante

onyx [ˈɑnɪks] *n* : ónix *m*

ooze¹ [ˈuːz] *v* **oozed; oozing** *vi* : rezumar — *vt* **1** : rezumar **2** EXUDE : irradiar, rebosar 〈to ooze confidence : irradiar confianza〉

ooze² *n* SLIME : cieno *m*, limo *m*

opacity [oˈpæsəti] *n, pl* **-ties** : opacidad *f*

opal [ˈoːpəl] *n* : ópalo *m*

opaque [oˈpeɪk] *adj* **1** : opaco **2** UNCLEAR : poco claro

open¹ [ˈoːpən] *vt* : abrir 〈open the door : abre la puerta〉 **2** UNCOVER : destapar **3** UNFOLD : desplegar, abrir **4** CLEAR : abrir (un camino, etc.) **5** INAUGURATE : abrir (una tienda), inaugurar (una exposición, etc.) **6** INITIATE : iniciar, entablar, abrir 〈to open the meeting : abrir la sesión〉 〈to open a discussion : entablar un debate〉 — *vi* **1** : abrirse **2** BEGIN : empezar, comenzar

open² *adj* **1** : abierto 〈an open window : una ventana abierta〉 **2** FRANK : abierto, franco, directo **3** UNCOV-

ERED : descubierto, abierto **4** EX-
TENDED : extendido, abierto ⟨with
open arms : con los brazos abiertos⟩ **5**
UNRESTRICTED : libre, abierto **6** UN-
DECIDED : pendiente, por decidir, sin
resolver ⟨an open question : una
cuestión pendiente⟩ **7** AVAILABLE : vacante, libre ⟨the job is open : el puesto
está vacante⟩

open³ *n* **in the open 1** OUTDOORS : al
aire libre **2** KNOWN : conocido, saca-
do a la luz

open–air [ˈoːpənˌær] *adj* OUTDOOR : al
aire libre

open–and–shut [ˈoːpənəndˈʃʌt] *adj*
: claro, evidente ⟨an open-and-shut
case : un caso muy claro⟩

opener [ˈoːpənər] *n* : destapador *m*,
abrelatas *m*, abridor *m*

openhanded [ˌoːpənˈhændəd] *adj* : generoso, liberal

openhearted [ˌoːpənˈhɑrtəd] *adj* **1**
FRANK : franco, sincero **2** : generoso,
de gran corazón

opening [ˈoːpənɪŋ] *n* **1** BEGINNING
: comienzo *m*, principio *m*, apertura *f*
2 APERTURE : abertura *f*, brecha *f*, claro
m (en el bosque) **3** OPPORTUNITY
: oportunidad *f*

openly [ˈoːpənli] *adv* **1** FRANKLY : abiertamente, francamente **2** PUBLICLY
: públicamente, declaradamente

openness [ˈoːpənnəs] *n* : franqueza *f*

opera [ˈɑprə, ˈɑprə] *n* **1** : ópera *f* **2** →
opus

opera glasses *npl* : gemelos *mpl* de
teatro

operate [ˈɑpəˌreɪt] *v* **-ated; -ating** *vi* **1**
ACT, FUNCTION : operar, funcionar, ac-
tuar **2 to operate on (someone)** : operar a (alguien) — *vt* **1** WORK : operar, manejar, hacer funcionar (una
máquina) **2** MANAGE : manejar, administrar (un negocio)

operatic [ˌɑpəˈrætɪk] *adj* : operístico

operation [ˌɑpəˈreɪʃən] *n* **1** FUNCTION-
ING : funcionamiento *m* **2** USE : uso
m, manejo *m* (de máquinas) **3**
SURGERY : operación *f*, intervención *f*
quirúrgica

operational [ˌɑpəˈreɪʃənəl] *adj* : operacional, de operación

operative [ˈɑpərətɪv, -ˌreɪ-] *adj* **1** OPER-
ATING : vigente, en vigor **2** WORKING
: operativo **3** SURGICAL : quirúrgico

operator [ˈɑpəˌreɪtər] *n* : operador *m*,
-dora *f*

operetta [ˌɑpəˈrɛtə] *n* : opereta *f*

ophthalmologist [ˌɑf,θælˈmɑlədʒɪst,
-θɑl-] *m* *-ga f* : oftalmólogo *m*,

ophthalmology [ˌɑf,θælˈmɑlədʒi,
-θɑl-] *n* : oftalmología *f*

opiate [ˈoːpiət, -piˌeɪt] *n* : opiato *m*

opinion [əˈpɪnjən] *n* : opinión *f*

opinionated [əˈpɪnjəˌneɪtəd] *adj* : testarudo, dogmático

opium [ˈoːpiəm] *n* : opio *m*

opossum [əˈpɑsəm] *n* : zarigüeya *f*, oposum *m*

opponent [əˈpoːnənt] *n* : oponente *mf*;
opositor *m*, -tora *f*; contrincante *mf* (en
deportes)

opportune [ˌɑpərˈtuːn, -ˈtjuːn] *adj*
: oportuno — **opportunely** *adv*

opportunist [ˌɑpərˈtuːnɪst, -ˈtjuː-] *n*
: oportunista *mf*

opportunistic [ˌɑpərtuˈnɪstɪk, -tjuː-] *adj*
: oportunista *mf*

opportunity [ˌɑpərˈtuːnəti, -ˈtjuː-] *n, pl*
-ties : oportunidad *f*, ocasión *f*, chance
m, posibilidades *fpl*

oppose [əˈpoːz] *vt* **-posed; -posing 1** : ir
en contra de, oponerse a ⟨good oppos-
es evil : el bien se opone al mal⟩ **2** COM-
BAT : luchar contra, combatir, resistir

opposite¹ [ˈɑpəzət] *adv* : enfrente

opposite² *adj* **1** FACING : de enfrente
⟨the opposite side : el lado de enfrente⟩
2 CONTRARY : opuesto, contrario ⟨in
opposite directions : en direcciones
contrarias⟩ ⟨the opposite sex : el sexo
opuesto, el otro sexo⟩

opposite³ *n* : lo contrario, lo opuesto

opposite⁴ *prep* : enfrente de, frente a

opposition [ˌɑpəˈzɪʃən] *n* **1** : oposición
f, resistencia *f* **2 in opposition to**
AGAINST : en contra de

oppress [əˈprɛs] *vt* **1** PERSECUTE
: oprimir, perseguir **2** BURDEN
: oprimir, agobiar

oppression [əˈprɛʃən] *n* : opresión *f*

oppressive [əˈprɛsɪv] *adj* **1** HARSH
: opresivo, severo **2** STIFLING : agobiante, sofocante ⟨oppressive heat
: calor sofocante⟩

oppressor [əˈprɛsər] *n* : opresor *m*, -sora
f

opprobrium [əˈproːbriəm] *n* : oprobio *m*

opt [ˈɑpt] *vi* : optar

optic [ˈɑptɪk] *or* **optical** [-tɪkəl] *adj* : óptico

optical disk *n* : disco *m* óptico

optician [ɑpˈtɪʃən] *n* : óptico *m*, -ca *f*

optics [ˈɑptɪks] *npl* : óptica *f*

optimal [ˈɑptəməl] *adj* : óptimo

optimism [ˈɑptəˌmɪzəm] *n* : optimismo
m

optimist [ˈɑptəmɪst] *n* : optimista *mf*

optimistic [ˌɑptəˈmɪstɪk] *adj* : optimista

optimistically [ˌɑptəˈmɪstɪkli] *adv* : con
optimismo, positivamente

optimum¹ [ˈɑptəməm] *adj* → **optimal**

optimum² *n, pl* **-ma** [ˈɑptəmə] : lo óptimo, lo ideal

option [ˈɑpʃən] *n* : opción *f* ⟨she has no
option : no tiene más remedio⟩

optional [ˈɑpʃənəl] *adj* : facultativo, optativo

optometrist [ɑpˈtɑmətrɪst] *n* : optometrista *mf*

optometry [ɑpˈtɑmətri] *n* : optometría *f*

opulence [ˈɑpjələnts] *n* : opulencia *f*

opulent [ˈɑpjələnt] *adj* : opulento

opus [ˈoːpəs] *n, pl* **opera** [ˈoːpərə, ˈɑpə-]
: opus *m*, obra *f* (de música)

or [ˈɔr] *conj* **1** (*indicating an alternative*)
: o (u *before words beginning with o or
ho*) ⟨coffee or tea : café o té⟩ ⟨one day

or another : un día u otro⟩ **2** (*following a negative*) : ni ⟨he didn't have his keys or his wallet : no llevaba ni sus llaves ni su billetera⟩

oracle [ˈɔrəkəl] *n* : oráculo *m*

oral [ˈoral] *adj* : oral — **orally** *adv*

orange [ˈɔrɪndʒ] *n* .1 : naranja *f*, china *f PRi* (fruto) **2** : naranja *m* (color), color *m* de china *PRi*

orangeade [ˌɔrɪndʒˈeɪd] *n* : naranjada *f*

orangutan [əˈræŋəˌtæŋ, -ˈræŋgə-, -ˌtæn] *n* : orangután *m*

oration [əˈreɪʃən] *n* : oración *f*, discurso *m*

orator [ˈɔrətər] *n* : orador *m*, -dora *f*

oratorio [ˌɔrəˈtoriˌoː] *n, pl* **-rios** : oratorio *m*

oratory [ˈɔrəˌtori] *n, pl* **-ries** : oratoria *f*

orb [ˈɔrb] *n* : orbe *m*

orbit[1] [ˈɔrbət] *vt* **1** CIRCLE : girar alrededor de, orbitar **2** : poner en órbita (un satélite, etc.) — *vi* : orbitar

orbit[2] *n* : órbita *f*

orbital [ˈɔrbətəl] *adj* : orbital

orchard [ˈɔrtʃərd] *n* : huerto *m*

orchestra [ˈɔrkəstrə] *n* : orquesta *f*

orchestral [ɔrˈkɛstrəl] *adj* : orquestal

orchestrate [ˈɔrkəˌstreɪt] *vt* **-trated; -trating 1** : orquestar, instrumentar (en música) **2** ORGANIZE : arreglar, organizar

orchestration [ˌɔrkəˈstreɪʃən] *n* : orquestación *f*

orchid [ˈɔrkɪd] *n* : orquídea *f*

ordain [ɔrˈdeɪn] *vt* **1** : ordenar (en religión) **2** DECREE : decretar, ordenar

ordeal [ɔrˈdiːl, ˈɔrˌdiːl] *n* : prueba *f* dura, experiencia *f* terrible

order[1] [ˈɔrdər] *vt* **1** ORGANIZE : arreglar, ordenar, poner en orden **2** COMMAND : ordenar, mandar **3** REQUEST : pedir, encargar ⟨to order a meal : pedir algo de comer⟩ — *vi* : hacer un pedido

order[2] *n* **1** : orden *f* ⟨a religious order : una orden religiosa⟩ **2** COMMAND : orden *f*, mandato *m* ⟨to give an order : dar una orden⟩ **3** REQUEST : orden *f*, pedido *m* ⟨purchase order : orden de compra⟩ **4** ARRANGEMENT : orden *m* ⟨in chronological order : por orden cronológico⟩ **5** DISCIPLINE : orden *f* ⟨law and order : el orden público⟩ **6 in order to** : para **7 out of order** : descompuesto, averiado **8 orders** *npl or* **holy orders** : órdenes *fpl* sagradas

orderliness [ˈɔrdərlinəs] *n* : orden *m*

orderly[1] [ˈɔrdərli] *adj* **1** METHODICAL : ordenado, metódico **2** PEACEFUL : pacífico, disciplinado

orderly[2] *n, pl* **-lies 1** : ordenanza *m* (en el ejército) **2** : camillero *m* (en un hospital)

ordinal [ˈɔrdənəl] *n or* **ordinal number** : ordinal *m*, número *m* ordinal

ordinance [ˈɔrdənənts] *n* : ordenanza *f*, reglamento *m*

ordinarily [ˌɔrdənˈerəli] *adv* : ordinariamente, por lo general

ordinary [ˈɔrdənˌeri] *adj* **1** NORMAL, USUAL : normal, usual **2** AVERAGE : común y corriente, normal **3** MEDIOCRE : mediocre, ordinario

ordination [ˌɔrdənˈeɪʃən] *n* : ordenación *f*

ordnance [ˈɔrdnənts] *n* : artillería *f*

ore [ˈor] *n* : mineral *m* (metalífero), mena *f*

oregano [əˈregəˌnoː] *n* : orégano *m*

organ [ˈɔrgən] *n* **1** : órgano *m* (instrumento) **2** : órgano *m* (del cuerpo) **3** PERIODICAL : publicación *f* periódica, órgano *m*

organic [ɔrˈgænɪk] *adj* : orgánico — **organically** *adv*

organism [ˈɔrgəˌnɪzəm] *n* : organismo *m*

organist [ˈɔrgənɪst] *n* : organista *mf*

organization [ˌɔrgənəˈzeɪʃən] *n* **1** ORGANIZING : organización *f* **2** BODY : organización *f*, organismo *m*

organizational [ˌɔrgənəˈzeɪʃənəl] *adj* : organizativo

organize [ˈɔrgəˌnaɪz] *vt* **-nized; -nizing** : organizar, arreglar, poner en orden

organizer [ˈɔrgəˌnaɪzər] *n* : organizador *m*, -dora *f*

orgasm [ˈɔrˌgæzəm] *n* : orgasmo *m*

orgy [ˈɔrdʒi] *n, pl* **-gies** : orgía *f*

orient [ˈoriˌent] *vt* : orientar

Orient *n* **the Orient** : el Oriente

oriental [ˌoriˈentəl] *adj* : del Oriente, oriental

Oriental *n* : oriental *mf*

orientation [ˌoriənˈteɪʃən] *n* : orientación *f*

orifice [ˈɔrəfəs] *n* : orificio *m*

origin [ˈɔrədʒən] *n* **1** ANCESTRY : origen *m*, ascendencia *f* **2** SOURCE : origen *m*, raíz *f*, fuente *f*

original[1] [əˈrɪdʒənəl] *adj* : original

original[2] *n* : original *m*

originality [əˌrɪdʒəˈnæləti] *n* : originalidad *f*

originally [əˈrɪdʒənəli] *adv* **1** AT FIRST : al principio, originariamente **2** CREATIVELY : originalmente, con originalidad

originate [əˈrɪdʒəˌneɪt] *v* **-nated; -nating** *vt* : originar, iniciar, crear — *vi* **1** BEGIN : originarse, empezar **2** COME : provenir, proceder, derivarse

originator [əˈrɪdʒəˌneɪtər] *n* : creador *m*, -dora *f*; inventor *m*, -tora *f*

oriole [ˈoriˌoːl, -iəl] *n* : oropéndola *f*

ornament[1] [ˈɔrnəmənt] *vt* : adornar, decorar, ornamentar

ornament[2] *n* : ornamento *m*, adorno *m*, decoración *f*

ornamental [ˌɔrnəˈmentəl] *adj* : ornamental, de adorno, decorativo

ornamentation [ˌɔrnəmənˈteɪʃən, -men-] *n* : ornamentación *f*

ornate [ɔrˈneɪt] *adj* : elaborado, recargado

ornery [ˈɔrnəri, ˈɑrnəri] *adj* **ornerier; -est** : de mal genio, malhumorado

ornithologist [ˌɔrnəˈθɑlədʒɪst] *n* : ornitólogo *m*, -ga *f*

ornithology [ˌɔrnəˈθɑləʤi] *n, pl* **-gies** : ornitología *f*

orphan[1] [ˈɔrfən] *vt* : dejar huérfano

orphan[2] *n* : huérfano *m*, -na *f*

orphanage [ˈɔrfənɪʤ] *n* : orfelinato *m*, orfanato *m*

orthodontics [ˌɔrθəˈdɑntɪks] *n* : ortodoncia *f*

orthodontist [ˌɔrθəˈdɑntɪst] *n* : ortodoncista *mf*

orthodox [ˈɔrθəˌdɑks] *adj* : ortodoxo

orthodoxy [ˈɔrθəˌdɑksi] *n, pl* **-doxies** : ortodoxia *f*

orthographic [ˌɔrθəˈgræfɪk] *adj* : ortográfico

orthography [ɔrˈθɑgrəfi] *n, pl* **-phies** SPELLING : ortografía *f*

orthopedic [ˌɔrθəˈpiːdɪk] *adj* : ortopédico

orthopedics [ˌɔrθəˈpiːdɪks] *ns & pl* : ortopedia *f*

orthopedist [ˌɔrθəˈpiːdɪst] *n* : ortopedista *mf*

oscillate [ˈɑsəˌleɪt] *vi* **-lated; -lating** : oscilar

oscillation [ˌɑsəˈleɪʃən] *n* : oscilación *f*

osmosis [ɑzˈmoːsɪs, ɑs-] *n* : ósmosis *f*, osmosis *f*

osprey [ˈɑspri, -ˌpreɪ] *n* : pigargo *m*

ostensible [ɑˈstɛnʦəbəl] *adj* APPARENT : aparente, ostensible — **ostensibly** [-bli] *adv*

ostentation [ˌɑstənˈteɪʃən] *n* : ostentación *f*, boato *m*

ostentatious [ˌɑstənˈteɪʃəs] *adj* : ostentoso — **ostentatiously** *adv*

osteopath [ˈɑstiəˌpæθ] *n* : osteópata *f*

osteopathy [ˌɑstiˈɑpəθi] *n* : osteopatía *f*

osteoporosis [ˌɑstiəpəˈroːsɪs] *n, pl* **-roses** [-ˌsiːz] : osteoporosis *f*

ostracism [ˈɑstrəˌsɪzəm] *n* : ostracismo *m*

ostracize [ˈɑstrəˌsaɪz] *vt* **-cized; -cizing** : condenar al ostracismo, marginar, aislar

ostrich [ˈɑstrɪʧ, ˈɔs-] *n* : avestruz *m*

other[1] [ˈʌðər] *adv* **other than** : aparte de, fuera de

other[2] *adj* : otro ⟨the other boys : los otros muchachos⟩ ⟨smarter than other people : más inteligente que los demás⟩ ⟨on the other hand : por otra parte, por otro lado⟩ ⟨every other day : cada dos días⟩

other[3] *pron* : otro, otra ⟨one in front of the other : uno tras otro⟩ ⟨myself and three others : yo y tres otros, yo y tres más⟩ ⟨somewhere or other : en alguna parte⟩

otherwise[1] [ˈʌðərˌwaɪz] *adv* **1** DIFFERENTLY : de otro modo, de manera distinta ⟨he could not act otherwise : no pudo actuar de manera distinta⟩ **2** : eso aparte, por lo demás ⟨I'm dizzy, but otherwise I'm fine : estoy mareado pero, por lo demás, estoy bien⟩ **3** OR ELSE : de lo contrario, si no ⟨do what I tell you, otherwise you'll be sorry : haz lo que te digo, de lo contrario, te arrepentirás⟩

otherwise[2] *adj* : diferente, distinto ⟨the facts are otherwise : la realidad es diferente⟩

otter [ˈɑtər] *n* : nutria *f*

Ottoman [ˈɑtəmən] *n* **1** : otomano *m*, -na *f* **2** : otomana *f* (mueble) — **Ottoman** *adj*

ouch [ˈauʧ] *interj* : ¡ay!, ¡huy!

ought [ˈɔt] *v aux* : deber ⟨you ought to take care of yourself : deberías cuidarte⟩

oughtn't [ˈɔtənt] (contraction of **ought not**) → **ought**

ounce [ˈaunts] *n* : onza *f*

our [ˈɑr, ˈaur] *adj* : nuestro

ours [ˈaurz, ˈɑrz] *pron* : nuestro, nuestra ⟨a cousin of ours : un primo nuestro⟩

ourselves [ɑrˈsɛlvz, aur-] *pron* **1** (used reflexively) : nos, nosotros ⟨we amused ourselves : nos divertimos⟩ ⟨we were always thinking of ourselves : siempre pensábamos en nosotros⟩ **2** (used for emphasis) : nosotros mismos, nosotras mismas ⟨we did it ourselves : lo hicimos nosotros mismos⟩

oust [ˈaust] *vt* : desbancar, expulsar

ouster [ˈaustər] *n* : expulsión *f* (de un país, etc.), destitución *f* (de un puesto)

out[1] [ˈaut] *vi* : revelarse, hacerse conocido

out[2] *adv* **1** (indicating direction or movement) : para afuera ⟨she opened the door and looked out : abrió la puerta y miró para afuera⟩ **2** (indicating a location away from home or work) : fuera, afuera ⟨to eat out : comer afuera⟩ **3** (indicating loss of control or possession) ⟨they let the secret out : sacaron el secreto a la luz⟩ **4** (indicating completion or discontinuance) ⟨his money ran out : se le acabó el dinero⟩ ⟨to turn out the light : apagar la luz⟩ **5** OUTSIDE : fuera, afuera ⟨out in the garden : afuera en el jardín⟩ **6** ALOUD : en voz alta, en alto ⟨to cry out : gritar⟩

out[3] *adj* **1** EXTERNAL : externo, exterior **2** OUTLYING : alejado, distante ⟨the out islands : las islas distantes⟩ **3** ABSENT : ausente **4** UNFASHIONABLE : fuera de moda **5** EXTINGUISHED : apagado

out[4] *prep* **1** (used to indicate an outward movement) : por ⟨I looked out the window : miré por la ventana⟩ ⟨she ran out the door : corrió por la puerta⟩ **2** → **out of**

out-and-out [ˈautənˈaut] *adj* UTTER : redomado, absoluto

outboard motor [ˈautˌbɔrd] *n* : motor *m* fuera de borde

outbound [ˈautˌbaund] *adj* : que sale, de salida

outbreak [ˈautˌbreɪk] *n* : brote *m* (de una enfermedad), comienzo *m* (de guerra), ola *f* (de violencia), erupción *f* (de granos)

outbuilding ['aʊt,bɪldɪŋ] n : edificio m anexo

outburst ['aʊt,bərst] n : arranque m, arrebato m

outcast ['aʊt,kæst] n : marginado m, -da f; paria mf

outcome ['aʊt,kʌm] n : resultado m, desenlace m, consecuencia f

outcrop ['aʊt,krɑp] n : afloramiento m

outcry ['aʊt,kraɪ] n, pl **-cries** : clamor m, protesta f

outdated [,aʊt'deɪtəd] adj : anticuado, fuera de moda

outdistance [,aʊt'dɪstənts] vt **-tanced; -tancing** : aventajar, dejar atrás

outdo [,aʊt'duː] vt **-did** [-'dɪd], **-done** [-'dʌn], **-doing; -does** [-'dʌz] : superar

outdoor ['aʊt'dor] adj : al aire libre ⟨outdoor sports : deportes al aire libre⟩ ⟨outdoor clothing : ropa de calle⟩

outdoors¹ ['aʊt'dorz] adv : afuera, al aire libre

outdoors² n : aire m libre

outer ['aʊtər] adj 1 : exterior, externo 2 **outer space** : espacio m exterior

outermost ['aʊtər,moːst] adj : más remoto, más exterior, extremo

outfield ['aʊt,fiːld] n **the outfield** : los jardines

outfielder ['aʊt,fiːldər] n : jardinero m, -ra f

outfit¹ ['aʊt,fɪt] vt **-fitted; -fitting** EQUIP : equipar

outfit² n 1 EQUIPMENT : equipo m 2 COSTUME, ENSEMBLE : traje m, conjunto m 3 GROUP : conjunto m

outgo ['aʊt,goː] n, pl **outgoes** : gasto m

outgoing ['aʊt,goːɪŋ] adj 1 OUTBOUND : que sale 2 DEPARTING : saliente ⟨an outgoing president : un presidente saliente⟩ 3 EXTROVERTED : extrovertido, expansivo

outgrow [,aʊt'groː] vt **-grew** [-'gruː], **-grown** [-'groːn]; **-growing** 1 : crecer más que ⟨that tree outgrew all the others : ese árbol creció más que todos los otros⟩ 2 **to outgrow one's clothes** : quedarle pequeña la ropa a uno

outgrowth ['aʊt,groːθ] n 1 OFFSHOOT : brote m, vástago m (de una planta) 2 CONSEQUENCE : consecuencia f, producto m, resultado m

outing ['aʊtɪŋ] n : excursión f

outlandish [aʊt'lændɪʃ] adj : descabellado, muy extraño

outlast [aʊt'læst] vt : durar más que

outlaw¹ ['aʊt,lɔ] vt : hacerse ilegal, declarar fuera de la ley, prohibir

outlaw² n : bandido m, -da f; bandolero m, -ra f; forajido m, -da f

outlay ['aʊt,leɪ] n : gasto m, desembolso m

outlet ['aʊt,lɛt, -lət] n 1 EXIT : salida f, escape m ⟨electrical outlet : toma de corriente⟩ 2 RELIEF : desahogo m 3 MARKET : mercado m, salida f

outline¹ ['aʊt,laɪn] vt **-lined; -lining** 1 SKETCH : diseñar, esbozar, bosquejar

2 DEFINE, EXPLAIN : perfilar, delinear, explicar ⟨she outlined our responsibilities : delineó nuestras responsabilidades⟩

outline² n 1 PROFILE : perfil m, silueta f, contorno m 2 SKETCH : bosquejo m, boceto m 3 SUMMARY : esquema m, resumen m, sinopsis f ⟨an outline of world history : un esquema de la historia mundial⟩

outlive [aʊt'lɪv] vt **-lived; -living** : sobrevivir a

outlook ['aʊt,lʊk] n 1 VIEW : vista f, panorama f 2 POINT OF VIEW : punto m de vista 3 PROSPECTS : perspectivas fpl

outlying ['aʊt,laɪɪŋ] adj : alejado, distante, remoto ⟨the outlying areas : las afueras⟩

outmoded [,aʊt'moːdəd] adj : pasado de moda, anticuado

outnumber [,aʊt'nʌmbər] vt : superar en número a, ser más numeroso de

out of prep 1 (indicating direction or movement from within) : de, por ⟨we ran out of the house : salimos corriendo de la casa⟩ ⟨to look out of the window : mirar por la ventana⟩ 2 (being beyond the limits of) ⟨out of control : fuera de control⟩ ⟨to be out of sight : desaparecer de vista⟩ 3 OF : de ⟨one out of four : uno de cada cuatro⟩ 4 (indicating absence or loss) : sin ⟨out of money : sin dinero⟩ ⟨we're out of matches : nos hemos quedado sin fósforos⟩ 5 BECAUSE OF : por ⟨out of curiosity : por curiosidad⟩ 6 FROM : de ⟨made out of plastic : hecho de plástico⟩

out-of-date [,aʊtəv'deɪt] adj : anticuado, obsoleto, pasado de moda

out-of-door [,aʊtəv'dor] or **out-of-doors** [-'dorz] → outdoor

out-of-doors n → outdoors²

outpatient ['aʊt,peɪʃənt] n : paciente m externo, paciente f externa

outpost ['aʊt,poːst] n : puesto m avanzado

output¹ ['aʊt,pʊt] vt **-putted** or **-put; -putting** : producir

output² n : producción f (de una fábrica), rendimiento m (de una máquina), productividad f (de una persona)

outrage¹ ['aʊt,reɪdʒ] vt **-raged; -raging** 1 INSULT : ultrajar, injuriar 2 INFURIATE : indignar, enfurecer

outrage² n 1 ATROCITY : atropello m, atrocidad f, atentado m 2 SCANDAL : escándalo m 3 ANGER : ira f, furia f

outrageous [,aʊt'reɪdʒəs] adj 1 SCANDALOUS : escandaloso, ofensivo, atroz 2 UNCONVENTIONAL : poco convencional, extravagante 3 EXORBITANT : exorbitante, excesivo ⟨dícese de los precios, etc.⟩

outright¹ [,aʊt'raɪt] adv 1 COMPLETELY : por completo, totalmente ⟨to sell outright : vender por completo⟩ ⟨he refused it outright : lo rechazó rotundamente⟩ 2 DIRECTLY : directamente, sin reserva 3 INSTANTLY : al instante, en el acto

outright² [ˈaʊtˌraɪt] *adj* 1 COMPLETE : completo, absoluto, categórico ⟨an outright lie : una mentira absoluta⟩ 2 : sin reservas ⟨an outright gift : un regalo sin reservas⟩

outset [ˈaʊtˌsɛt] *n* : comienzo *m*, principio *m*

outshine [ˌaʊtˈʃaɪn] *vt* **-shone** [-ˈʃoːn, -ˈʃɑn] *or* **-shined; -shining** : eclipsar

outside¹ [ˌaʊtˈsaɪd, ˈaʊtˌ-] *adv* : fuera, afuera

outside² *adj* 1 : exterior, externo ⟨the outside edge : el borde exterior⟩ ⟨outside influences : influencias externas⟩ 2 REMOTE : remoto ⟨an outside chance : una posibilidad remota⟩

outside³ *n* 1 EXTERIOR : parte *f* de afuera, exterior *m* 2 MOST : máximo *m* ⟨three weeks at the outside : tres semanas como máximo⟩ 3 from the outside : desde afuera, desde fuera

outside⁴ *prep* : fuera de, afuera de ⟨outside my window : fuera de mi ventana⟩ ⟨outside regular hours : fuera del horario normal⟩ ⟨outside the law : afuera de la ley⟩

outside of *prep* 1 → **outside⁴** 2 → **besides²**

outsider [ˌaʊtˈsaɪdər] *n* : forastero *m*, -ra *f*

outskirts [ˈaʊtˌskərts] *npl* : afueras *fpl*, alrededores *mpl*

outsmart [ˌaʊtˈsmɑrt] → **outwit**

outspoken [ˌaʊtˈspoːkən] *adj* : franco, directo

outstanding [ˌaʊtˈstændɪŋ] *adj* 1 UNPAID : pendiente 2 NOTABLE : destacado, notable, excepcional, sobresaliente

outstandingly [ˌaʊtˈstændɪŋli] *adv* : excepcionalmente

outstretched [ˌaʊtˈstrɛtʃt] *adj* : extendido

outstrip [ˌaʊtˈstrɪp] *vt* **-stripped** *or* **-stript** [-ˈstrɪpt]; **-stripping** 1 : aventajar, dejar atrás ⟨he outstripped the other runners : aventajó a los otros corredores⟩ 2 SURPASS : aventajar, sobrepasar

outward¹ [ˈaʊtwərd] *or* **outwards** [-wərdz] *adv* : hacia afuera, hacia el exterior

outward² *adj* 1 : hacia afuera ⟨an outward flow : un flujo hacia afuera⟩ 2 : externo ⟨outward beauty : belleza externa⟩

outwardly [ˈaʊtwərdli] *adv* 1 EXTERNALLY : exteriormente 2 APPARENTLY : aparentemente ⟨outwardly friendly : aparentemente simpático⟩

outwit [ˌaʊtˈwɪt] *vt* **-witted; -witting** : ser más listo que

ova → **ovum**

oval¹ [ˈoːvəl] *adj* : ovalado, oval

oval² *n* : óvalo *m*

ovarian [oˈværiən] *adj* : ovárico

ovary [ˈoːvəri] *n, pl* **-ries** : ovario *m*

ovation [oˈveɪʃən] *n* : ovación *f*

oven [ˈʌvən] *n* : horno *m*

over¹ [ˈoːvər] *adv* 1 (*indicating movement across*) ⟨he flew over to London : voló a Londres⟩ ⟨come on over! : ¡ven acá!⟩ 2 (*indicating an additional amount*) ⟨the show ran 10 minutes over : el espectáculo terminó 10 minutos de tarde⟩ 3 ABOVE, OVERHEAD : por encima 4 AGAIN : otra vez, de nuevo ⟨over and over : una y otra vez⟩ ⟨to start over : volver a empezar⟩ 5 all over EVERYWHERE : por todas partes 6 to fall over : caerse ⟨over⟩ 7 to turn over : poner boca abajo, voltear

over² *adj* 1 HIGHER, UPPER : superior 2 REMAINING : sobrante, que sobra 3 ENDED : terminado, acabado ⟨the work is over : el trabajo está terminado⟩

over³ *prep* 1 ABOVE : encima de, arriba de, sobre ⟨over the fireplace : encima de la chimenea⟩ ⟨the hawk flew over the hills : el halcón voló sobre los cerros⟩ 2 : más de ⟨over $50 : más de $50⟩ 3 ALONG : por, sobre ⟨to glide over the ice : deslizarse sobre el hielo⟩ 4 (*indicating motion through a place or thing*) ⟨they showed me over the house : me mostraron la casa⟩ 5 ACROSS : por encima de, sobre ⟨he jumped over the ditch : saltó por encima de la zanja⟩ 6 UPON : sobre ⟨a cape over my shoulders : una capa sobre los hombros⟩ 7 ON : por ⟨to speak over the telephone : hablar por teléfono⟩ 8 DURING : en, durante ⟨over the past 25 years : durante los últimos 25 años⟩ 9 BECAUSE OF : por ⟨they fought over the money : se pelearon por el dinero⟩

overabundance [ˌoːvərəˈbʌndənts] *n* : superabundancia *f*

overabundant [ˌoːvərəˈbʌndənt] *adj* : superabundante

overactive [ˌoːvərˈæktɪv] *adj* : hiperactivo

overall [ˌoːvərˈɔl] *adj* : total, global, de conjunto

overalls [ˈoːvərˌɔlz] *npl* : overol *m*

overawe [ˌoːvərˈɔ] *vt* **-awed; -awing** : intimidar, impresionar

overbearing [ˌoːvərˈbæriŋ] *adj* : dominante, imperioso, prepotente

overblown [ˌoːvərˈbloːn] *adj* 1 INFLATED : inflado, exagerado 2 BOMBASTIC : grandilocuente, rimbombante

overboard [ˈoːvərˌbord] *adv* : por la borda, al agua

overburden [ˌoːvərˈbərdən] *vt* : sobrecargar, agobiar

overcast [ˈoːvərˌkæst] *adj* CLOUDY : nublado

overcharge [ˌoːvərˈtʃɑrdʒ] *vt* **-charged; -charging** : cobrarle de más (a alguien)

overcoat [ˈoːvərˌkoːt] *n* : abrigo *m*

overcome [ˌoːvərˈkʌm] *v* **-came** [-ˈkeɪm]; **-come; -coming** *vt* 1 CON-

QUER : vencer, derrotar, superar 2
OVERWHELM : abrumar, agobiar — vi
: vencer

overconfidence [ˌoːvərˈkɑnfədənts] n
: exceso m de confianza

overconfident [ˌoːvərˈkɑnfədənt] adj
: demasiado confiado

overcook [ˌoːvərˈkʊk] vt : recocer, cocer
demasiado

overcrowded [ˌoːvərˈkraʊdəd] adj 1
PACKED : abarrotado, atestado de
gente 2 OVERPOPULATED : superpoblado

overdo [ˌoːvərˈduː] vt -did [-ˈdɪd]; -done
[-ˈdʌn]; -doing; -does [-ˈdʌz] 1 : hacer demasiado 2 EXAGGERATE : exagerar 3 OVERCOOK : recocer

overdose [ˈoːvərˌdoːs] n : sobredosis f

overdraft [ˈoːvərˌdræft] n : sobregiro m,
descubierto m

overdraw [ˌoːvərˈdrɔ] vt -drew [-ˈdruː];
-drawn [-ˈdrɔn]; -drawing 1 : sobregirar ⟨my account is overdrawn : tengo
la cuenta en descubierto⟩ 2 EXAG-
GERATE : exagerar

overdue [ˌoːvərˈduː] adj 1 UNPAID : vencido y sin pagar 2 TARDY : de retraso,
tardío

overeat [ˌoːvərˈiːt] vi -ate [-ˈeɪt]; -eaten
[-ˈiːtən]; -eating : comer demasiado

overelaborate [ˌoːvərɪˈlæbərət] adj : recargado

overestimate [ˌoːvərˈɛstəˌmeɪt] vt
-mated; -mating : sobreestimar

overexcited [ˌoːvərɪkˈsaɪtəd] adj : sobreexcitado

overexpose [ˌoːvərɪkˈspoːz] vt -posed;
-posing : sobreexponer

overfeed [ˌoːvərˈfiːd] vt -fed [-ˈfɛd];
-feeding : sobrealimentar

overflow¹ [ˌoːvərˈfloː] vt 1 : desbordar 2
INUNDATE : inundar — vi : desbordarse, rebosar

overflow² [ˈoːvərˌfloː] n 1 : derrame m,
desbordamiento m (de un río) 2 SUR-
PLUS : exceso m, excedente m

overfly [ˌoːvərˈflaɪ] vt -flew [-ˈfluː];
-flown [-ˈfloːn]; -flying : sobrevolar

overgrown [ˌoːvərˈɡroːn] adj 1 : cubierto ⟨overgrown with weeds : cubierto de malas hierbas⟩ 2 : demasiado grande

overhand¹ [ˈoːvərˌhænd] adv : por encima de la cabeza

overhand² adj : por lo alto (tirada)

overhang¹ [ˌoːvərˈhæŋ] v -hung [-ˈhʌŋ];
-hanging vt 1 : sobresalir por encima
de 2 THREATEN : amenazar — vi : sobresalir

overhang² [ˈoːvərˌhæŋ] n : saliente mf

overhaul [ˌoːvərˈhɔl] vt 1 : revisar ⟨to
overhaul an engine : revisar un motor⟩
2 OVERTAKE : adelantar

overhead¹ [ˌoːvərˈhɛd] adv : por encima,
arriba, en lo alto

overhead² [ˈoːvərˌhɛd] adj : de arriba

overhead³ [ˈoːvərˌhɛd] n : gastos mpl
generales

overhear [ˌoːvərˈhɪr] vt -heard; -hearing
: oír por casualidad

overheat [ˌoːvərˈhiːt] vt : recalentar, sobrecalentar, calentar demasiado

overjoyed [ˌoːvərˈdʒɔɪd] adj : rebosante
de alegría

overkill [ˈoːvərˌkɪl] n : exceso m, excedente m

overland¹ [ˈoːvərˌlænd, -lənd] adv : por
tierra

overland² adj : terrestre, por tierra

overlap¹ [ˌoːvərˈlæp] v -lapped; -lapping
vt : traslapar — vi : traslaparse, solaparse

overlap² [ˈoːvərˌlæp] n : traslapo m

overlay¹ [ˌoːvərˈleɪ] vt -laid [-ˈleɪd];
-laying : recubrir, revestir

overlay² [ˈoːvərˌleɪ] n : revestimiento m

overload [ˌoːvərˈloːd] vt : sobrecargar

overlong [ˌoːvərˈlɔŋ] adj : excesivamente largo, largo y pesado

overlook [ˌoːvərˈlʊk] vt 1 INSPECT : inspeccionar, revisar 2 : tener vista a, dar
a ⟨a house overlooking the valley : una
casa que tiene vista al valle⟩ 3 MISS
: pasar por alto 4 EXCUSE : dejar pasar,
disculpar

overly [ˈoːvərli] adv : demasiado

overnight¹ [ˌoːvərˈnaɪt] adv 1 : por la
noche, durante la noche 2 : de la noche
a la mañana ⟨we can't do it overnight
: no podemos hacerlo de la noche a la
mañana⟩

overnight² [ˈoːvərˌnaɪt] adj 1 : de noche
⟨an overnight stay : una estancia de
una noche⟩ ⟨an overnight bag : una
bolsa de viaje⟩ 2 SUDDEN : repentino

overpass [ˈoːvərˌpæs] n : paso m elevado, paso m a desnivel Mex

overpopulated [ˌoːvərˈpɑpjəˌleɪtəd] adj
: sobrepoblado

overpower [ˌoːvərˈpaʊər] vt 1 CON-
QUER, SUBDUE : vencer, superar 2
OVERWHELM : abrumar, agobiar
⟨overpowered by the heat : sofocado
por el calor⟩

overpraise [ˌoːvərˈpreɪz] vt -praised;
-praising : adular

overrate [ˌoːvərˈreɪt] vt -rated; -rating
: sobrevalorar, sobrevaluar

override [ˌoːvərˈraɪd] vt -rode [-ˈroːd];
-ridden [-ˈrɪdən]; -riding 1 : predominar sobre, contar más que ⟨hunger
overrode our manners : el hambre pre-
dominó sobre los modales⟩ 2 ANNUL
: anular, invalidar ⟨to override a veto
: anular un veto⟩

overrule [ˌoːvərˈruːl] vt -ruled; -ruling
: anular (una decisión), desautorizar
(una persona), denegar (un pedido)

overrun [ˌoːvərˈrʌn] v -ran [-ˈræn];
-running 1 INVADE : invadir 2 IN-
FEST : infestar, plagar 3 EXCEED : exceder, rebasar — vi : rebasar el tiempo previsto

overseas¹ [ˌoːvərˈsiːz] adv : en el extranjero ⟨to travel overseas : viajar al
extranjero⟩

overseas² ['o:vər¸si:z] *adj* : extranjero, exterior

oversee [¸o:vər'si:] *vt* -**saw** [-'sɔ]; -**seen** [-'si:n]; -**seeing** SUPERVISE : supervisar

overseer ['o:vər¸si:ər] *n* : supervisor *m*, -sora *f*; capataz *mf*

overshadow [¸o:vər'ʃæ¸do:] *vt* **1** DARKEN : oscurecer, ensombrecer **2** ECLIPSE, OUTSHINE : eclipsar

overshoe ['o:vər¸ʃu:] *n* : chanclo *m*

overshoot [¸o:vər'ʃu:t] *vt* -**shot** [-'ʃɑt]; -**shooting** ⟨to overshoot the mark : pasarse de la raya⟩

oversight ['o:vər¸saɪt] *n* : descuido *m*, inadvertencia *f*

oversleep [¸o:vər'sli:p] *vi* -**slept** [-'slɛpt]; -**sleeping** : no despertarse a tiempo, quedarse dormido

overspread [¸o:vər'sprɛd] *vt* -**spread**; -**spreading** : extenderse sobre

overstaffed [¸o:vər'stæft] *adj* : con exceso de personal

overstate [¸o:vər'steɪt] *vt* -**stated**; -**stating** EXAGGERATE : exagerar

overstatement [¸o:vər'steɪtmənt] *n* : exageración *f*

overstep [¸o:vər'stɛp] *vt* -**stepped**; -**stepping** EXCEED : sobrepasar, traspasar, exceder

overt [o'vərt, 'o:¸vərt] *adj* : evidente, manifiesto, patente

overtake [¸o:vər'teɪk] *vt* -**took** [-'tʊk]; -**taken** [-'teɪkən]; -**taking** : pasar, adelantar, rebasar *Mex*

overthrow¹ [¸o:vər'θro:] *vt* -**threw** [-'θru:]; -**thrown** [-'θro:n]; -**throwing** **1** OVERTURN : dar la vuelta a, volcar **2** DEFEAT, TOPPLE : derrocar, derribar, deponer

overthrow² ['o:vər¸θro:] *n* : derrocamiento *m*, caída *f*

overtime ['o:vər¸taɪm] *n* **1** : horas *fpl* extras (de trabajo) **2** : prórroga *f* (en deportes)

overtly [o'vərtli, 'o:¸vərt-] *adv* OPENLY : abiertamente

overtone ['o:vər¸to:n] *n* **1** : armónico *m* (en música) **2** HINT, SUGGESTION : tinte *m*, insinuación *f*

overture ['o:vər¸tʃur, -¸tʃər] *n* **1** PROPOSAL : propuesta *f* **2** : obertura *f* (en música)

overturn [¸o:vər'tərn] *vt* **1** UPSET : dar la vuelta a, volcar **2** NULLIFY : anular, invalidar — *vi* TURN OVER : volcar, dar un vuelco

overuse [¸o:vər'ju:z] *vt* -**used**; -**using** : abusar de

overview ['o:vər¸vju:] *n* : resumen *m*, visión *f* general

overweening [¸o:vər'wi:nɪŋ] *adj* **1** ARROGANT : arrogante, soberbio **2** IMMODERATE : desmesurado

overweight [¸o:vər'weɪt] *adj* : demasiado gordo, demasiado pesado

overwhelm [¸o:vər'hwɛlm] *vt* **1** CRUSH, DEFEAT : aplastar, arrollar **2** SUBMERGE : inundar, sumergir **3** OVERPOWER : abrumar, agobiar ⟨overwhelmed by remorse : abrumado de remordimiento⟩

overwhelming [¸o:vər'hwɛlmɪŋ] *adj* **1** CRUSHING : abrumador, apabullante **2** SWEEPING : arrollador, aplastante ⟨an overwhelming majority : una mayoría aplastante⟩

overwork [¸o:vər'wərk] *vt* **1** : hacer trabajar demasiado **2** OVERUSE : abusar de — *vi* : trabajar demasiado

overwrought [¸o:vər'rɔt] *adj* : alterado, sobreexcitado

ovoid ['o:¸vɔɪd] *or* **ovoidal** [o'vɔɪdəl] *adj* : ovoide

ovulate ['ɑvjə¸leɪt, 'o:-] *vi* -**lated**; -**lating** : ovular

ovulation [¸ɑvjə'leɪʃən, ¸o:-] *n* : ovulación *f*

ovum ['o:vəm] *n*, *pl* **ova** [-ə] : óvulo *m*

owe ['o:] *vt* **owed**; **owing** : deber ⟨you owe me $10 : me debes $10⟩ ⟨he owes his wealth to his father : le debe su riqueza a su padre⟩

owing to *prep* : debido a

owl ['aʊl] *n* : búho *m*, lechuza *f*, tecolote *m Mex*

own¹ ['o:n] *vt* **1** POSSESS : poseer, tener, ser dueño de **2** ADMIT : reconocer, admitir — *vi* **to own up** : reconocer (algo), admitir (algo)

own² *adj* : propio, personal, particular ⟨his own car : su propio coche⟩

own³ *pron* **my; (your, his/her, our, their); own** : el mío, la mía; el tuyo, la tuya; el suyo, la suya; el nuestro, la nuestra ⟨to each his own : cada uno a lo suyo⟩ ⟨money of my own : mi propio dinero⟩ ⟨to be on one's own : estar solo⟩

owner ['o:nər] *n* : dueño *m*, -ña *f*; propietario *m*, -ria *f*

ownership ['o:nər¸ʃɪp] *n* : propiedad *f*

ox ['ɑks] *n*, *pl* **oxen** ['ɑksən] : buey *m*

oxidation [¸ɑksə'deɪʃən] *n* : oxidación *f*

oxide ['ɑk¸saɪd] *n* : óxido *m*

oxidize ['ɑksə¸daɪz] *vt* -**dized**; -**dizing** : oxidar

oxygen ['ɑksɪdʒən] *n* : oxígeno *m*

oyster ['ɔɪstər] *n* : ostra *f*, ostión *m Mex*

ozone ['o:¸zo:n] *n* : ozono *m*

P

p ['pi:] *n, pl* p's *or* ps ['pi:z] : decimosexta letra del alfabeto inglés

pace¹ ['peɪs] *v* paced; pacing *vi* : caminar, ir y venir — *vt* 1 : caminar por ⟨she paced the floor : caminaba de un lado a otro del cuarto⟩ 2 to pace a runner : marcarle el ritmo a un corredor

pace² *n* 1 STEP : paso *m* 2 RATE : paso *m*, ritmo *m* ⟨to set the pace : marcar el paso, marcar la pauta⟩

pacemaker ['peɪsˌmeɪkər] *n* : marcapasos *m*

pacific [pəˈsɪfɪk] *adj* : pacífico

pacifier ['pæsəˌfaɪər] *n* : chupete *m*, chupón *m*, mamila *f Mex*

pacifism ['pæsəˌfɪzəm] *n* : pacifismo *m*

pacifist ['pæsəfɪst] *n* : pacifista *mf*

pacify ['pæsəˌfaɪ] *vt* -fied; -fying 1 SOOTHE : apaciguar, pacificar 2 : pacificar (un país, una región, etc.)

pack¹ ['pæk] *vt* 1 PACKAGE : empaquetar, embalar, envasar 2 : empacar, meter (en una maleta) ⟨to pack one's bag : hacer la maleta⟩ 3 FILL : llenar, abarrotar ⟨a packed theater : un teatro abarrotado⟩ 4 to pack off SEND : mandar — *vi* : empacar, hacer las maletas

pack² *n* 1 BUNDLE : bulto *m*, fardo *m* 2 BACKPACK : mochila *f* 3 PACKAGE : paquete *m*, cajetilla *f* (de cigarrillos, etc.) 4 : manada *f* (de lobos, etc.), jauría *f* (de perros) ⟨a pack of thieves : una pandilla de ladrones⟩

package¹ ['pækɪdʒ] *vt* -aged; -aging : empaquetar, embalar

package² *n* : paquete *m*, bulto *m*

packaging ['pækɪdʒɪŋ] *n* 1 : embalaje *m* 2 WRAPPING : envoltorio *m*

packer ['pækər] *n* : empacador *m*, -dora *f*

packet ['pækət] *n* : paquete *m*

packing ['pækɪŋ] *n* : embalaje *m*

pact ['pækt] *n* : pacto *m*, acuerdo *m*

pad¹ ['pæd] *vt* padded; padding 1 FILL, STUFF : rellenar, acolchar (una silla, una pared) 2 : meter paja en, rellenar ⟨to pad a speech : rellenar un discurso⟩

pad² *n* 1 CUSHION : almohadilla *f* ⟨a shoulder pad : una hombrera⟩ 2 TABLET : bloc *m* (de papel) 3 *or* lily pad : hoja *f* grande (de un nenúfar) 4 ink pad : tampón *m* 5 launching pad : plataforma *f* (de lanzamiento)

padding ['pædɪŋ] *n* 1 FILLING : relleno *m* 2 : paja *f* (en un discurso, etc.)

paddle¹ ['pædəl] *v* -dled; -dling *vt* 1 : hacer avanzar (una canoa) con canalete 2 HIT : azotar, darle nalgadas a (con una pala o paleta) — *vi* 1 : remar (en una canoa) 2 SPLASH : chapotear, mojarse los pies

paddle² *n* 1 : canalete *m*, zagual *m* (de una canoa, etc.) 2 : pala *f*, paleta *f* (en deportes)

paddock ['pædək] *n* 1 PASTURE : potrero *m* 2 : paddock *m*, cercado *m* (en un hipódromo)

paddy ['pædi] *n, pl* -dies : arrozal *m*

padlock¹ ['pædˌlɑk] *vt* : cerrar con candado

padlock² *n* : candado *m*

pagan¹ ['peɪgən] *adj* : pagano

pagan² *n* : pagano *m*, -na *f*

paganism ['peɪgənˌɪzəm] *n* : paganismo *m*

page¹ ['peɪdʒ] *vt* paged; paging : llamar por altavoz

page² *n* 1 BELLHOP : botones *m* 2 : página *f* (de un libro, etc.)

pageant ['pædʒənt] *n* 1 SPECTACLE : espectáculo *m* 2 PROCESSION : desfile *m*

pageantry ['pædʒəntri] *n* : pompa *f*, fausto *m*

pager ['peɪdʒər] *n* BEEPER : buscapersonas *m*

pagoda [pəˈgoːdə] *n* : pagoda *f*

paid → pay

pail ['peɪl] *n* : balde *m*, cubo *m*, cubeta *f Mex*

pailful ['peɪlˌfʊl] *n* : balde *m*, cubo *m*, cubeta *f Mex*

pain¹ ['peɪn] *vt* : doler

pain² *n* 1 PENALTY : pena *f* ⟨under pain of death : so pena de muerte⟩ 2 SUFFERING : dolor *m*, malestar *m*, pena *f* (mental) 3 pains *npl* EFFORT : esmero *m*, esfuerzo *m* ⟨to take pains : esmerarse⟩

painful ['peɪnfəl] *adj* : doloroso — painfully *adv*

painkiller ['peɪnˌkɪlər] *n* : analgésico *m*

painless ['peɪnləs] *adj* : indoloro, sin dolor

painlessly ['peɪnləsli] *adv* : sin dolor

painstaking ['peɪnˌsteɪkɪŋ] *adj* : esmerado, cuidadoso, meticuloso — painstakingly *adv*

paint¹ ['peɪnt] *v* : pintar

paint² *n* : pintura *f*

paintbrush ['peɪntˌbrʌʃ] *n* : pincel *m* (de un artista), brocha *f* (para pintar casas, etc.)

painter ['peɪntər] *n* : pintor *m*, -tora *f*

painting ['peɪntɪŋ] *n* : pintura *f*

pair¹ ['pær] *vt* : emparejar, poner en parejas — *vi* : emparejarse

pair² *n* : par *m* (de objetos), pareja *f* (de personas o animales) ⟨a pair of scissors : unas tijeras⟩

pajamas [pəˈdʒɑməz, -ˈdʒæ-] *npl* : pijama *m*, piyama *m*

Pakistani [ˌpækɪˈstæni, ˌpɑkɪˈstɑni] *n* : paquistaní *mf* — Pakistani *adj*

pal ['pæl] *n* : amigo *m*, -ga *f*; compinche *mf fam*; chamo *m*, -ma *f Ven fam*; cuate *m*, -ta *f Mex*

palace ['pæləs] *n* : palacio *m*

palatable ['pælətəbəl] *adj* : sabroso

palate ['pælət] *n* 1 : paladar *m* (de la boca) 2 TASTE : paladar *m*, gusto *m*

palatial [pə'leɪʃəl] *adj* : suntuoso, espléndido

palaver [pə'lævər, -'lɑ-] *n* : palabrería *f*

pale¹ ['peɪl] *v* **paled**; **paling** *vi* : palidecer — *vt* : hacer pálido

pale² *adj* **paler**; **palest 1** : pálido ⟨to turn pale : palidecer, ponerse pálido⟩ **2** : claro (dícese de los colores)

paleness ['peɪlnəs] *n* : palidez *f*

paleontologist [ˌpeɪliˌɑn'tɑlədʒɪst] *n* : paleontólogo *m*, -ga *f*

paleontology [ˌpeɪliˌɑn'tɑldʒi] *n* : paleontología *f*

Palestinian [ˌpælə'stɪniən] *n* : palestino *m*, -na *f* — **Palestinian** *adj*

palette ['pælət] *n* : paleta *f* (para mezclar pigmentos)

palisade [ˌpælə'seɪd] *n* **1** FENCE : empalizada *f*, estacada *f* **2** CLIFFS : acantilado *m*

pall¹ ['pɔl] *vi* : perder su sabor, dejar de gustar

pall² *n* **1** : paño *m* mortuorio (sobre un ataúd) **2** COVER : cortina *f* (de humo, etc.) **3 to cast a pall over** : ensombrecer

pallbearer ['pɔlˌbɛrər] *n* : portador *m*, -dora *f* del féretro

pallet ['pælət] *n* **1** BED : camastro *m* **2** PLATFORM : plataforma *f* de carga

palliative ['pæliˌeɪtɪv, 'pæljətɪv] *adj* : paliativo

pallid ['pæləd] *adj* : pálido

pallor ['pælər] *n* : palidez *f*

palm¹ ['pɑm, 'pɑlm] *vt* **1** CONCEAL : escamotear (un naipe, etc.) **2 to palm off** : encajar, endilgar *fam* ⟨he palmed it off on me : me lo endilgó⟩

palm² *n* **1** *or* **palm tree** : palmera *f* **2** : palma *f* (de la mano)

Palm Sunday *n* : Domingo *m* de Ramos

palomino [ˌpælə'miːˌnoː] *n*, *pl* **-nos** : caballo *m* de color dorado

palpable ['pælpəbəl] *adj* : palpable — **palpably** [-bli] *adv*

palpitate ['pælpəˌteɪt] *vi* **-tated**; **-tating** : palpitar

palpitation [ˌpælpə'teɪʃən] *n* : palpitación *f*

palsy ['pɔlzi] *n*, *pl* **-sies 1** : parálisis *f* **2** → **cerebral palsy**

paltry ['pɔltri] *adj* **-trier**; **-est** : mísero, mezquino, insignificante ⟨a paltry excuse : una mala excusa⟩

pampas ['pæmpəz, 'pæmpəs] *npl* : pampa *f*

pamper ['pæmpər] *vt* : mimar, consentir, chiquear *Mex*

pamphlet ['pæmpflət] *n* : panfleto *m*, folleto *m*

pan¹ ['pæn] *vt* **panned**; **panning** CRITICIZE : poner por los suelos — *vi* **to pan for gold** : cribar el oro con batea, lavar oro

pan² *n* **1** : cacerola *f*, cazuela *f* **2 frying pan** : sartén *mf*, freidera *f Mex*

panacea [ˌpænə'siːə] *n* : panacea *f*

Panamanian [ˌpænə'meɪniən] *n* : panameño *m*, -ña *f* — **Panamanian** *adj*

pancake ['pænˌkeɪk] *n* : panqueque *m*

pancreas ['pæŋkriəs, 'pæn-] *n* : páncreas *m*

panda ['pændə] *n* : panda *mf*

pandemonium [ˌpændə'moːniəm] *n* : pandemonio *m*, pandemónium *m*

pander ['pændər] *vi* **to pander to** : satisfacer, complacer (a alguien) ⟨to pander to popular taste : satisfacer el gusto popular⟩

pane ['peɪn] *n* : cristal *m*, vidrio *m*

panel¹ ['pænəl] *vt* **-eled** *or* **-elled**; **-eling** *or* **-elling** : adornar con paneles

panel² *n* **1** : lista *f* de nombres (de un jurado, etc.) **2** GROUP : panel *m*, grupo *m* ⟨discussion panel : panel de discusión⟩ **3** : panel *m* (de una pared, etc.) **4 instrument panel** : tablero *m* de instrumentos

paneling ['pænəlɪŋ] *n* : paneles *mpl*

pang ['pæŋ] *n* : puntada *f*, punzada *f*

panic¹ ['pænɪk] *v* **-icked**; **-icking** *vt* : llenar de pánico — *vi* : ser presa de pánico

panic² *n* : pánico *m*

panicky ['pæniki] *adj* : presa de pánico

panorama [ˌpænə'ræmə, -'rɑ-] *n* : panorama *m*

panoramic [ˌpænə'ræmɪk, -'rɑ-] *adj* : panorámico

pansy ['pænzi] *n*, *pl* **-sies** : pensamiento *m*

pant¹ ['pænt] *vi* : jadear, resoplar

pant² *n* : jadeo *m*, resoplo *m*

pantaloons [ˌpæntə'luːnz] → **pants**

pantheon ['pænˌθiˌɑn, -ən] *n* : panteón *m*

panther ['pænθər] *n* : pantera *f*

panties ['pæntiz] *npl* : calzones *mpl*; pantaletas *fpl Mex, Ven*; bragas *fpl Spain*

pantomime¹ ['pæntəˌmaɪm] *v* **-mimed**; **-miming** *vt* : representar mediante la pantomima — *vi* : hacer la mímica

pantomime² *n* : pantomima *f*

pantry ['pæntri] *n*, *pl* **-tries** : despensa *f*

pants ['pænts] *npl* **1** TROUSERS : pantalón *m*, pantalones *mpl* **2** → **panties**

panty hose ['pænti] *ns & pl* : medias *fpl*, panties *mfpl*, pantimedias *fpl Mex*

pap ['pæp] *n* : papilla *f* (para bebés, etc.)

papa ['pɑpə] *n* : papá *m*

papal ['peɪpəl] *adj* : papal

papaya [pə'paɪə] *n* : papaya *f* (fruta)

paper¹ ['peɪpər] *vt* WALLPAPER : empapelar

paper² *adj* : de papel

paper³ *n* **1** : papel *m* ⟨a piece of paper : un papel⟩ **2** DOCUMENT : papel *m*, documento *m* **3** NEWSPAPER : periódico *m*, diario *m*

paperback ['peɪpərˌbæk] *n* : libro *m* en rústica

paper clip *n* : clip *m*, sujetapapeles *m*

paperweight ['peɪpərˌweɪt] *n* : pisapapeles *m*

paperwork ['peɪpər,wɔrk] n : papeleo m
papery ['peɪpəri] adj : parecido al papel
papier–mâché [,peɪpərmə'ʃeɪ, ,pæ-,pjeɪmæ'ʃeɪ] n : papel m maché
papoose [pæ'puːs, pə-] n : niño m, -ña f de los indios norteamericanos
paprika [pə'priːkə, pæ-] n : pimentón m, paprika f
papyrus [pə'paɪrəs] n, pl **-ruses** or **-ri** [-ri, -,raɪ] : papiro m
par ['pɑr] n 1 VALUE : valor m (nominal), par f ⟨below par : debajo de la par⟩ 2 EQUALITY : igualdad f ⟨to be on a par with : estar al mismo nivel que⟩ 3 : par m (en golf)
parable ['pærəbəl] n : parábola f
parabola [pə'ræbələ] n : parábola f (en matemáticas)
parachute[1] ['pærə,ʃuːt] vi **-chuted; -chuting** : lanzarse en paracaídas
parachute[2] n : paracaídas m
parachutist ['pærə,ʃuːtɪst] n : paracaidista mf
parade[1] [pə'reɪd] vi **-raded; -rading** 1 MARCH : desfilar 2 SHOW OFF : pavonearse, lucirse
parade[2] n 1 PROCESSION : desfile m 2 DISPLAY : alarde m
paradigm ['pærə,daɪm] n : paradigma m
paradise ['pærə,daɪs, -,daɪz] n : paraíso m
paradox ['pærə,dɑks] n : paradoja f
paradoxical [,pærə'dɑksɪkəl] adj : paradójico — **paradoxically** adv
paraffin ['pærəfən] n : parafina f
paragon ['pærə,gɑn, -gən] n : dechado m
paragraph[1] ['pærə,græf] vt : dividir en párrafos
paragraph[2] n : párrafo m, acápite m
Paraguayan [,pærə'gwaɪən, -'gweɪ-] n : paraguayo m, -ya f — **Paraguayan** adj
parakeet ['pærə,kiːt] n : periquito m
paralegal [,pærə'liːgəl] n : asistente mf de abogado
parallel[1] ['pærə,lɛl, -ləl] vt 1 MATCH, RESEMBLE : ser paralelo a, ser análogo a, corresponder con 2 : extenderse en línea paralela con ⟨the road parallels the river : el camino se extiende a lo largo del río⟩
parallel[2] adj : paralelo
parallel[3] n 1 : línea f paralela, superficie f paralela 2 : paralelo m (en geografía) 3 SIMILARITY : paralelismo m, semejanza f
parallelogram [,pærə'lɛlə,græm] n : paralelogramo m
paralysis [pə'ræləsəs] n, pl **-yses** [-,siːz] : parálisis f
paralyze ['pærə,laɪz] vt **-lyzed; -lyzing** : paralizar
parameter [pə'ræmətər] n : parámetro m
paramount ['pærə,maʊnt] adj : supremo ⟨of paramount importance : de suma importancia⟩
paranoia [,pærə'nɔɪə] n : paranoia f

paranoid ['pærə,nɔɪd] adj : paranoico
parapet ['pærəpət, -,pɛt] n : parapeto m
paraphernalia [,pærəfə'neɪljə, -,fər-] ns & pl : parafernalia f
paraphrase[1] ['pærə,freɪz] vt **-phrased; -phrasing** : parafrasear
paraphrase[2] n : paráfrasis f
paraplegic[1] [,pærə'pliːdʒɪk] adj : parapléjico
paraplegic[2] n : parapléjico m, -ca f
parasite ['pærə,saɪt] n : parásito m
parasitic [,pærə'sɪtɪk] adj : parasitario
parasol ['pærə,sɔl] n : sombrilla f, quitasol m, parasol m
paratrooper ['pærə,truːpər] n : paracaidista mf (militar)
parboil ['pɑr,bɔɪl] vt : sancochar, cocer a medias
parcel[1] ['pɑrsəl] vt **-celed** or **-celled; -celing** or **-celling** or **to parcel out** : repartir, parcelar (tierras)
parcel[2] n 1 LOT : parcela f, lote m 2 PACKAGE : paquete m, bulto m
parch ['pɑrtʃ] vt : resecar
parchment ['pɑrtʃmənt] n : pergamino m
pardon[1] ['pɑrdən] vt 1 FORGIVE : perdonar, disculpar ⟨pardon me! : ¡perdone!, ¡disculpe la molestia!⟩ 2 REPRIEVE : indultar (a un delincuente)
pardon[2] n 1 FORGIVENESS : perdón m 2 REPRIEVE : indulto m
pardonable ['pɑrdənəbəl] adj : perdonable, disculpable
pare ['pær] vt **pared; paring** 1 PEEL : pelar 2 TRIM : recortar 3 REDUCE : reducir ⟨he pared it (down) to 50 pages : lo redujo a 50 páginas⟩
parent ['pærənt] n 1 : madre f, padre m 2 **parents** npl : padres mpl
parentage ['pærəntɪdʒ] n : linaje m, abolengo m, origen m
parental [pə'rɛntəl] adj : de los padres
parenthesis [pə'rɛnθəsəs] n, pl **-theses** [-,siːz] : paréntesis m
parenthetic [,pærən'θɛtɪk] or **parenthetical** [-tɪkəl] adj : parentético — **parenthetically** [-tɪkli] adv
parenthood ['pærənt,hʊd] n : paternidad f
parfait [pɑr'feɪ] n : postre m elaborado con frutas y helado
pariah [pə'raɪə] n : paria mf
parish ['pærɪʃ] n : parroquia f
parishioner [pə'rɪʃənər] n : feligrés m, -gresa f
parity ['pærəti] n, pl **-ties** : paridad f
park[1] ['pɑrk] vt : estacionar, parquear, aparcar Spain — vi : estacionarse, parquearse, aparcar Spain
park[2] n : parque m
parka ['pɑrkə] n : parka f
parking ['pɑrkɪŋ] n : estacionamiento m, aparcamiento m Spain
parkway ['pɑrk,weɪ] n : carretera f ajardinada, bulevar m
parley[1] ['pɑrli] vi : parlamentar, negociar

parley² *n*, *pl* **-leys** : negociación *f*, parlamento *m*

parliament ['pɑrləmənt, 'pɑrljə-] *n* : parlamento *m*

parliamentary [ˌpɑrlə'mɛntəri, ˌpɑrljə-] *adj* : parlamentario

parlor ['pɑrlər] *n* **1** : sala *f*, salón *m* (en una casa) **2** : salón *m* ⟨beauty parlor : salón de belleza⟩ **3 funeral parlor** : funeraria *f*

parochial [pə'roːkiəl] *adj* **1** : parroquial **2** PROVINCIAL : pueblerino, de miras estrechas

parody¹ ['pærədi] *vt* **-died; -dying** : parodiar

parody² *n*, *pl* **-dies** : parodia *f*

parole [pə'roːl] *n* : libertad *f* condicional

paroxysm ['pærək،sɪzəm, pə'rɑk-] *n* : paroxismo *m*

parquet ['pɑr،keɪ, pɑr'keɪ] *n* : parquet *m*, parqué *m*

parrakeet → parakeet

parrot ['pærət] *n* : loro *m*, papagayo *m*

parry¹ ['pæri] *v* **-ried; -rying** *vi* : parar un golpe — *vt* EVADE : esquivar (una pregunta, etc.)

parry² *n*, *pl* **-ries** : parada *f*

parsimonious [ˌpɑrsə'moːniəs] *adj* : tacaño, mezquino

parsley ['pɑrsli] *n* : perejil *m*

parsnip ['pɑrsnɪp] *n* : chirivía *f*

parson ['pɑrsən] *n* : pastor *m*, clérigo *m*

parsonage ['pɑrsənɪdʒ] *n* : rectoría *f*, casa *f* del párroco

part¹ ['pɑrt] *vi* **1** SEPARATE : separarse, despedirse ⟨we should part as friends : debemos separarnos amistosamente⟩ **2** OPEN : abrirse ⟨the curtains parted : las cortinas se abrieron⟩ **3 to part with** : deshacerse de — *vt* **1** SEPARATE : separar **2 to part one's hair** : hacerse la raya, peinarse con raya

part² *n* **1** SECTION, SEGMENT : parte *f*, sección *f* **2** PIECE : pieza *f* (de una máquina, etc.) **3** ROLE : papel *m* **4** : raya *f* (del pelo)

partake [pɑr'teɪk, pɑr-] *vi* **-took** [-'tʊk]; **-taken** [-'teɪkən]; **-taking 1 to partake of** CONSUME : comer, beber, tomar **2 to partake in** : participar en (una actividad, etc.)

partial ['pɑrʃəl] *adj* **1** BIASED : parcial, tendencioso **2** INCOMPLETE : parcial, incompleto **3 to be partial to** : ser aficionado a

partiality [ˌpɑrʃi'æləti] *n*, *pl* **-ties** : parcialidad *f*

partially ['pɑrʃəli] *adv* : parcialmente

participant [pər'tɪsəpənt, pɑr-] *n* : participante *mf*

participate [pər'tɪsə،peɪt, pɑr-] *vi* **-pated; -pating** : participar

participation [pər،tɪsə'peɪʃən, pɑr-] *n* : participación *f*

participle ['pɑrtə،sɪpəl] *n* : participio *m*

particle ['pɑrtɪkəl] *n* : partícula *f*

particular¹ [pər'tɪkjələr] *adj* **1** SPECIFIC : particular, en particular ⟨this partic-

ular person : esta persona en particular⟩ **2** SPECIAL : particular, especial ⟨with particular emphasis : con un énfasis especial⟩ **3** FUSSY : exigente, maniático ⟨to be very particular : ser muy especial⟩ ⟨I'm not particular : me da igual⟩

particular² *n* **1** DETAIL : detalle *m*, sentido *m* **2 in particular** : en particular, en especial

particularly [pər'tɪkjələrli] *adv* **1** ESPECIALLY : particularmente, especialmente **2** SPECIFICALLY : específicamente, en especial

partisan ['pɑrtəzən, -sən] *n* **1** ADHERENT : partidario *m*, -ria *f* **2** GUERRILLA : partisano *m*, -na *f*; guerrillero *m*, -ra *f*

partition¹ [pər'tɪʃən, pɑr-] *vt* : dividir ⟨to partition off (a room) : dividir (una habitación) con un tabique⟩

partition² *n* **1** DISTRIBUTION : partición *f*, división *f*, reparto *m* **2** DIVIDER : tabique *m*, mampara *f*, biombo *m*

partly ['pɑrtli] *adv* : en parte, parcialmente

partner ['pɑrtnər] *n* **1** COMPANION : compañero *m*, -ra *f* **2** : pareja *f* (en un juego, etc.) ⟨dancing partner : pareja de baile⟩ **3** SPOUSE : cónyuge *mf* **4** *or* **business partner** : socio *m*, -cia *f*; asociado *m*, -da *f*

partnership ['pɑrtnər،ʃɪp] *n* **1** ASSOCIATION : asociación *f*, compañerismo *m* **2** : sociedad *f* (de negociantes) ⟨to form a partnership : asociarse⟩

part of speech : categoría *f* gramatical

partridge ['pɑrtrɪdʒ] *n*, *pl* **-tridge** *or* **-tridges** : perdiz *f*

party ['pɑrti] *n*, *pl* **-ties 1** : partido *m* (político) **2** PARTICIPANT : parte *f*, participante *mf* **3** GROUP : grupo *m* (de personas) **4** GATHERING : fiesta *f* ⟨to throw a party : dar una fiesta⟩

parvenu ['pɑrvə،nuː, -،njuː] *n* : advenedizo *m*, -za *f*

pass¹ ['pæs] *vi* **1** : pasar, cruzarse ⟨a car passed by : pasó un coche⟩ ⟨we passed in the hallway : nos cruzamos en el pasillo⟩ **2** CEASE : pasarse ⟨the pain passed : se pasó el dolor⟩ **3** ELAPSE : pasar, transcurrir **4** PROCEED : pasar ⟨let me pass : déjame pasar⟩ **5** HAPPEN : pasar, ocurrir **6** : pasar, aprobar (en un examen) **7** RULE : fallar ⟨the jury passed on the case : el jurado falló en el caso⟩ **8** *or* **to pass down** : pasar ⟨the throne passed to his son : el trono pasó a su hijo⟩ **9 to let pass** OVERLOOK : pasar por alto **10 to pass as** : pasar por **11 to pass away** *or* **to pass on** DIE : fallecer, morir — *vt* **1** : pasar por ⟨they passed the house : pasaron por la casa⟩ **2** OVERTAKE : pasar, adelantar **3** SPEND : pasar (tiempo) **4** HAND : pasar ⟨pass me the salt : pásame la sal⟩ **5** : aprobar (un examen, una ley)

pass² n **1** CROSSING, GAP : paso m, desfiladero m, puerto m ⟨mountain pass : puerto de montaña⟩ **2** PERMIT : pase m, permiso m **3** : pase m (en deportes) **4** SITUATION : situación f (difícil) ⟨things have come to a pretty pass! : ¡hasta dónde hemos llegado!⟩

passable ['pæsəbəl] adj **1** ADEQUATE : adecuado, pasable **2** : transitable (dícese de un camino, etc.)

passably ['pæsəbli] adv : pasablemente

passage ['pæsɪdʒ] n **1** PASSING : paso m ⟨the passage of time : el paso del tiempo⟩ **2** PASSAGEWAY : pasillo m (dentro de un edificio), pasaje m (entre edificios) **3** VOYAGE : travesía f (por el mar), viaje m ⟨to grant safe passage : dar un salvoconducto⟩ **4** SECTION : pasaje m (en música o literatura)

passageway ['pæsɪdʒ,weɪ] n : pasillo m, pasadizo m, corredor m

passbook ['pæs,bʊk] n : BANKBOOK : libreta f de ahorros

passé [pæ'seɪ] adj : pasado de moda

passenger ['pæsəndʒər] n : pasajero m, -ra f

passerby [,pæsər'baɪ, 'pæsər,-] n, pl **passersby** : transeúnte mf

passing ['pæsɪŋ] n DEATH : fallecimiento m

passion ['pæʃən] n : pasión f, ardor m

passionate ['pæʃənət] adj **1** IRASCIBLE : irascible, iracundo **2** ARDENT : apasionado, ardiente, ferviente, fogoso

passionately ['pæʃənətli] adv : apasionadamente, fervientemente, con pasión

passive¹ ['pæsɪv] adj : pasivo — **passively** adv

passive² n : voz f pasiva (en gramática)

passivity [pæ'sɪvəti] n : pasividad f

Passover ['pæs,oːvər] n : Pascua f (en el judaísmo)

passport ['pæs,port] n : pasaporte m

password ['pæs,wərd] n : contraseña f

past¹ ['pæst] adv : por delante ⟨he drove past : pasamos en coche⟩

past² adj **1** AGO : hace ⟨10 years past : hace 10 años⟩ **2** LAST : último ⟨the past few months : los últimos meses⟩ **3** BYGONE : pasado ⟨in past times : en tiempos pasados⟩ **4** : pasado (en gramática)

past³ n : pasado m

past⁴ prep **1** BY : por, por delante de ⟨he ran past the house : pasó por la casa corriendo⟩ **2** BEYOND : más allá de ⟨just past the corner : un poco más allá de la esquina⟩ ⟨we went past the exit : pasamos la salida⟩ **3** AFTER : después de ⟨past noon : después del mediodía⟩ ⟨half past two : las dos y media⟩

pasta ['pɑstə, 'pæs-] n : pasta f

paste¹ ['peɪst] vt **pasted; pasting** : pegar (con engrudo)

paste² n **1** : pasta f ⟨tomato paste : pasta de tomate⟩ **2** : engrudo m (para pegar)

pasteboard ['peɪst,bord] n : cartón m, cartulina f

pastel [pæ'stɛl] n : pastel m — **pastel** adj

pasteurization [,pæstʃərə'zeɪʃən, ,pæstjə-] n : pasteurización f

pasteurize ['pæstʃə,raɪz, 'pæstjə-] vt **-ized; -izing** : pasteurizar

pastime ['pæs,taɪm] n : pasatiempo m

pastor ['pæstər] n : pastor m, -tora f

pastoral ['pæstərəl] adj : pastoral

past participle n : participio m pasado

pastry ['peɪstri] n, pl **-ries 1** DOUGH : pasta f, masa f **2** pastries npl : pasteles mpl

pasture¹ ['pæstʃər] v **-tured; -turing** vi GRAZE : pacer, pastar — vt : apacentar, pastar

pasture² n : pastizal m, potrero m, pasto m

pasty ['peɪsti] adj **pastier; -est 1** : pastoso (en consistencia) **2** PALLID : pálido

pat¹ ['pæt] vt **patted; patting** : dar palmaditas a, tocar

pat² adv : de memoria ⟨to have down pat : saberse de memoria⟩

pat³ adj **1** APT : apto, apropiado **2** GLIB : fácil ⟨to stand pat : mantenerse firme⟩

pat⁴ n **1** TAP : golpecito m, palmadita f ⟨a pat on the back : una palmadita en la espalda⟩ **2** CARESS : caricia f **3** : porción f ⟨a pat of butter : una porción de mantequilla⟩

patch¹ ['pætʃ] vt **1** MEND, REPAIR : remendar, parchar, ponerle un parche a **2 to patch together** IMPROVISE : confeccionar, improvisar **3 to patch up** : arreglar ⟨they patched things up : hicieron las paces⟩

patch² n **1** : parche m, remiendo m (para la ropa) ⟨eye patch : parche para el ojo⟩ **2** PIECE : mancha f, trozo m ⟨a patch of sky : un trozo de cielo⟩ **3** PLOT : parcela f, terreno m ⟨cabbage patch : parcela de repollos⟩

patchwork ['pætʃ,wərk] n : labor f de retazos

patchy ['pætʃi] adj **patchier; -est 1** IRREGULAR : irregular, desigual **2** INCOMPLETE : parcial, incompleto

patent¹ ['pætənt] vt : patentar

patent² ['pætənt, 'peɪt-] adj **1** OBVIOUS : patente, evidente **2** ['pæt-] PATENTED : patentado

patent³ ['pætənt] n : patente f

patently ['pætəntli] adv : patentemente, evidentemente

paternal [pə'tərnəl] adj **1** FATHERLY : paternal **2** : paterno ⟨paternal grandfather : abuelo paterno⟩

paternity [pə'tərnəti] n : paternidad f

path ['pæθ, 'pɑθ] n **1** TRACK, TRAIL : camino m, sendero m, senda f **2** COURSE, ROUTE : recorrido m, trayecto m, trayectoria f

pathetic [pə'θɛtɪk] adj : patético — **pathetically** [-tɪkli] adv

pathological [,pæθə'lɑdʒɪkəl] adj : patológico

pathologist [pə'θɑlədʒɪst] *n* : patólogo *m*, -ga *f*

pathology [pə'θɑlədʒi] *n, pl* **-gies** : patología *f*

pathos ['peɪˌθɑs, 'pæ-, -ˌθɔs] *n* : patetismo *m*

pathway ['pæθˌweɪ] *n* : camino *m*, sendero *m*, senda *f*, vereda *f*

patience ['peɪʃənts] *n* : paciencia *f*

patient¹ ['peɪʃənt] *adj* : paciente — **patiently** *adv*

patient² *n* : paciente *mf*

patio ['pæti̱ˌoː] *n, pl* **-tios** : patio *m*

patriarch ['peɪtriˌɑrk] *n* : patriarca *m*

patriarchy ['peɪtriˌɑrki] *n, pl* **-chies** : patriarcado *m*

patrimony ['pætrəˌmoːni] *n, pl* **-nies** : patrimonio *m*

patriot ['peɪtriət] *n* : patriota *mf*

patriotic [ˌpeɪtri'ɑtɪk] *adj* : patriótico — **patriotically** *adv*

patriotism ['peɪtriəˌtɪzəm] *n* : patriotismo *m*

patrol¹ [pə'troːl] *v* **-trolled; -trolling** : patrullar

patrol² *n* : patrulla *f*

patrolman [pə'troːlmən] *n, pl* **-men** [-mən, -ˌmɛn] : policía *mf*, guardia *mf*

patron ['peɪtrən] *n* **1** SPONSOR : patrocinador *m*, -dora *f* **2** CUSTOMER : cliente *m*, -ta *f* **3** *or* **patron saint** : patrono *m*, -na *f*

patronage ['peɪtrənɪdʒ, 'pæ-] *n* **1** SPONSORSHIP : patrocinio *m* **2** CLIENTELE : clientela *f* **3** : influencia *f* (política)

patronize ['peɪtrəˌnaɪz, 'pæ-] *vt* **-ized; -izing 1** SPONSOR : patrocinar **2** : ser cliente de (un negocio) **3** : tratar con condescendencia

patter¹ ['pætər] *vi* **1** TAP : golpetear, tamborilear (dícese de la lluvia) **2 to patter about** : corretear (con pasos ligeros)

patter² *n* **1** TAPPING : golpeteo *m*, tamborileo *m* (de la lluvia), correteo *m* (de pies) **2** CHATTER : palabrería *f*, parloteo *m fam*

pattern¹ ['pætərn] *vt* **1** BASE : basar (en un modelo) **2 to pattern after** : hacer imitación de

pattern² *n* **1** MODEL : modelo *m*, patrón *m* (de costura) **2** DESIGN : diseño *m*, dibujo *m*, estampado *m* (de tela) **3** NORM, STANDARD : pauta *f*, norma *f*, patrón *m*

patty ['pæti] *n, pl* **-ties** : porción *f* de carne picada (u otro alimento) en forma de ruedita ⟨a hamburger patty : una hamburguesa⟩

paucity ['pɔsəti] *n* : escasez *f*

paunch ['pɔntʃ] *n* : panza *f*, barriga *f*

pauper ['pɔpər] *n* : pobre *mf*, indigente *mf*

pause¹ ['pɔz] *vi* **paused; pausing** : hacer una pausa, pararse (brevemente)

pause² *n* : pausa *f*

pave ['peɪv] *vt* **paved; paving** : pavimentar ⟨to pave with stones : empedrar⟩

pavement ['peɪvmənt] *n* : pavimento *m*, empedrado *m*

pavilion [pə'vɪljən] *n* : pabellón *m*

paving ['peɪvɪŋ] → **pavement**

paw¹ ['pɔ] *vt* : tocar, manosear, sobar

paw² *n* : pata *f*, garra *f*, zarpa *f*

pawn¹ ['pɔn] *vt* : empeñar, prendar

pawn² *n* **1** PLEDGE, SECURITY : prenda *f* **2** PAWNING : empeño *m* **3** : peón *m* (en ajedrez)

pawnbroker ['pɔnˌbroːkər] *n* : prestamista *mf*

pawnshop ['pɔnˌʃɑp] *n* : casa *f* de empeños, monte *m* de piedad

pay¹ ['peɪ] *v* **paid** ['peɪd]; **paying** *vt* **1** : pagar (una cuenta, a un empleado, etc.) **2 to pay attention** : poner atención, prestar atención, hacer caso **3 to pay back** : pagar, devolver ⟨she paid them back : les devolvió el dinero⟩ ⟨I'll pay you back for what you did! : ¡me las pagarás!⟩ **4 to pay off** SETTLE : saldar, cancelar (una deuda, etc.) **5 to pay one's respects** : presentar uno sus respetos **6 to pay a visit** : hacer una visita — *vi* : valer la pena ⟨crime doesn't pay : no hay crimen sin castigo⟩

pay² *n* : paga *f*

payable ['peɪəbəl] *adj* DUE : pagadero

paycheck ['peɪˌtʃɛk] *n* : sueldo *m*, cheque *m* del sueldo

payee [peɪ'iː] *n* : beneficiario *m*, -ria *f* (de un cheque, etc.)

payment ['peɪmənt] *n* **1** : pago *m* **2** INSTALLMENT : plazo *m*, cuota *f* **3** REWARD : recompensa *f*

payoff ['peɪˌɔf] *n* **1** REWARD : recompensa *f* **2** PROFIT : ganancia *f* **3** BRIBE : soborno *m*

payroll ['peɪˌroːl] *n* : nómina *f*

PC ['piːˈsiː] *n, pl* **PCs** *or* **PC's** : PC *mf*, computadora *f* personal

pea ['piː] *n* : chícharo *m*, guisante *m*, arveja *f*

peace ['piːs] *n* **1** : paz *f* ⟨peace treaty : tratado de paz⟩ ⟨peace and tranquility : paz y tranquilidad⟩ **2** ORDER : orden *m* (público)

peaceable ['piːsəbəl] *adj* : pacífico — **peaceably** [-bli] *adv*

peaceful ['piːsfəl] *adj* **1** PEACEABLE : pacífico **2** CALM, QUIET : tranquilo, sosegado — **peacefully** *adv*

peacemaker ['piːsˌmeɪkər] *n* : conciliador *m*, -dora *f*; mediador *m*, -dora *f*

peach ['piːtʃ] *n* : durazno *m*, melocotón *m*

peacock ['piːˌkɑk] *n* : pavo *m* real

peak¹ ['piːk] *vi* : alcanzar su nivel máximo

peak² *adj* : máximo

peak³ *n* **1** POINT : punta *f* **2** CREST, SUMMIT : cima *f*, cumbre *f* **3** APEX : cúspide *f*, apogeo *m*, nivel *m* máximo

peaked ['piːkəd] *adj* SICKLY : pálido

peal¹ ['piːl] *vi* : repicar

peal² *n* : repique *m*, tañido *m* (de campanada) ⟨peals of laughter : carcajadas⟩

peanut ['pi:,nʌt] n : maní m, cacahuate m Mex, cacahuete m Spain
pear ['pær] n : pera f
pearl ['pərl] n : perla f
pearly ['pərli] adj **pearlier; -est** : nacarado
peasant ['pɛzənt] n : campesino m, -na f
peat ['pi:t] n : turba f
pebble ['pɛbəl] n : guijarro m, piedrecita f, piedrita f
pecan ['pi:kɑn, -'kæn, 'pi:,kæn] n : pacana f, nuez f Mex
peccadillo [,pɛkə'dɪlo] n, pl **-loes** or **-los** : pecadillo m
peccary ['pɛkəri] n, pl **-ries** : pécari m, pecarí m
peck¹ ['pɛk] vt : picar, picotear
peck² n **1** : medida f de áridos equivalente a 8.810 litros **2** : picotazo m (de un pájaro) ⟨a peck on the cheek : un besito en la mejilla⟩
pectoral ['pɛktərəl] adj : pectoral
peculiar [pɪ'kju:ljər] adj **1** DISTINCTIVE : propio, peculiar, característico ⟨peculiar to this area : propio de esta zona⟩ **2** STRANGE : extraño, raro — **peculiarly** adv
peculiarity [pɪ,kju:li'jærəti, -,kju:li'ær-] n, pl **-ties 1** DISTINCTIVENESS : peculiaridad f **2** ODDITY, QUIRK : rareza f, idiosincrasia f, excentricidad f
pecuniary [pɪ'kju:ni,cri] adj : pecuniario
pedagogical [,pɛdə'gɑdʒɪkəl, -'go:-] adj : pedagógico
pedagogy ['pɛdə,go:dʒi, -,gɑ-] n : pedagogía f
pedal¹ ['pɛdəl] v **-aled** or **-alled; -aling** or **-alling** vi : pedalear — vt : darle a los pedales de
pedal² n : pedal m
pedant ['pɛdənt] n : pedante mf
pedantic [pɪ'dæntɪk] adj : pedante
pedantry ['pɛdəntri] n, pl **-ries** : pedantería f
peddle ['pɛdəl] vt **-dled; -dling** : vender (en las calles)
peddler ['pɛdlər] n : vendedor m, -dora f ambulante; mercachifle m
pedestal ['pɛdəstəl] n : pedestal m
pedestrian¹ [pə'dɛstriən] adj **1** COMMONPLACE : pedestre, ordinario **2** : de peatón, peatonal ⟨pedestrian crossing : paso de peatones⟩
pedestrian² n : peatón m, -tona f
pediatric [,pi:di'ætrɪk] adj : pediátrico
pediatrician [,pi:diə'trɪʃən] n : pediatra mf
pediatrics [,pi:di'ætrɪks] ns & pl : pediatría f
pedigree ['pɛdə,gri:] n **1** FAMILY TREE : árbol m genealógico **2** LINEAGE : pedigrí m (de un animal), linaje m (de una persona)
peek¹ ['pi:k] vi **1** PEEP : espiar, mirar furtivamente — vt **2** GLANCE : echar un vistazo
peek² n **1** : miradita f (furtiva) **2** GLANCE : vistazo m, ojeada f

peel¹ ['pi:l] vt **1** : pelar (fruta, etc.) **2 to peel away** : quitar — vi : pelarse (dícese de la piel), descoharse (dícese de la pintura)
peel² n : cáscara f
peep¹ ['pi:p] vi **1** PEEK : espiar, mirar furtivamente **2** CHEEP : piar **3 to peep out** SHOW : asomarse
peep² n **1** CHEEP : pío m (de un pajarito) **2** GLANCE : vistazo m, ojeada f
peer¹ ['pɪr] vi : mirar detenidamente, mirar con atención
peer² n **1** EQUAL : par m, igual mf **2** NOBLE : noble mf
peerage ['pɪrɪdʒ] n : nobleza f
peerless ['pɪrləs] adj : sin par, incomparable
peeve¹ ['pi:v] vt **peeved; peeving** : fastidiar, irritar, molestar
peeve² n : queja f
peevish ['pi:vɪʃ] adj : quejoso, fastidioso — **peevishly** adv
peevishness ['pi:vɪʃnəs] n : irritabilidad f
peg¹ ['pɛg] vt **pegged; pegging 1** PLUG : tapar (con una clavija) **2** FASTEN, FIX : sujetar (con estaquillas) **3 to peg out** MARK : marcar (con estaquillas)
peg² n : estaquilla f (para clavar), clavija f (para tapar)
pejorative [pɪ'dʒɔrətɪv] adj : peyorativo — **pejoratively** adv
pelican ['pɛlɪkən] n : pelícano m
pellagra [pə'lægrə, -'lei-] n : pelagra f
pellet ['pɛlət] n **1** BALL : bolita f ⟨food pellet : bolita de comida⟩ **2** SHOT : perdigón m
pell-mell ['pɛl'mɛl] adv : desordenadamente, atropelladamente
pelt¹ ['pɛlt] vt **1** THROW : lanzar, tirar (algo a alguien) **2 to pelt with stones** : apedrear — vi BEAT : golpear con fuerza ⟨the rain was pelting down : llovía a cántaros⟩
pelt² n : piel f, pellejo m
pelvic ['pɛlvɪk] adj : pélvico
pelvis ['pɛlvɪs] n, pl **-vises** or **-ves** ['pɛl,vi:z] : pelvis f
pen¹ ['pɛn] vt **penned; penning 1** or **pen in** : encerrar (animales) **2** WRITE : escribir
pen² n **1** CORRAL : corral m, redil m (para ovejas) **2** : pluma f ⟨fountain pen : pluma fuente⟩ ⟨ballpoint pen : bolígrafo⟩
penal ['pi:nəl] adj : penal
penalize ['pi:nəl,aɪz, 'pɛn-] vt **-ized; -izing** : penalizar, sancionar, penar
penalty ['pɛnəlti] n, pl **-ties 1** PUNISHMENT : pena f, castigo m **2** DISADVANTAGE : desventaja f, castigo m, penalty m (en deportes) **3** FINE : multa f
penance ['pɛnənts] n : penitencia f
pence → **penny**
penchant ['pɛntʃənt] n : inclinación f, afición f

pencil¹ ['pɛntsəl] *vt* -ciled *or* -cilled; -ciling *or* -cilling : escribir con lápiz, dibujar con lápiz
pencil² *n* : lápiz *m*
pendant ['pɛndənt] *n* : colgante *m*
pending¹ ['pɛndɪŋ] *adj* : pendiente
pending² *prep* **1** DURING : durante **2** AWAITING : en espera de
pendulum ['pɛndʒələm, -dʒʊləm] *n* : péndulo *m*
penetrate ['pɛnə,treɪt] *vt* -trated; -trating : penetrar
penetrating ['pɛnə,treɪtɪŋ] *adj* : penetrante, cortante
penetration [,pɛnə'treɪʃən] *n* : penetración *f*
penguin ['pɛŋgwɪn, 'pɛn-] *n* : pingüino *m*
penicillin [,pɛnə'sɪlən] *n* : penicilina *f*
peninsula [pə'nɪntsələ, -'nɪntʃʊlə] *n* : península *f*
penis ['pi:nəs] *n, pl* -nes [-,ni:z] *or* -nises : pene *m*
penitence ['pɛnətənts] *n* : arrepentimiento *m*, penitencia *f*
penitent¹ ['pɛnətənt] *adj* : arrepentido, penitente
penitent² *n* : penitente *mf*
penitentiary [,pɛnə'tɛntʃəri] *n, pl* -ries : penitenciaría *f*, prisión *f*, presidio *m*
penmanship ['pɛnmən,ʃɪp] *n* : escritura *f*, caligrafía *f*
pen name *n* : seudónimo *m*
pennant ['pɛnənt] *n* : gallardete *m* (de un barco), banderín *m*
penniless ['pɛniləs] *adj* : sin un centavo
penny ['pɛni] *n, pl* -nies *or* pence ['pɛnts] **1** : penique *m* (del Reino Unido) **2** *pl* -nies CENT : centavo *m* (de los Estados Unidos)
pension¹ ['pɛntʃən] *vt or* to pension off : jubilar
pension² *n* : pensión *m*, jubilación *f*
pensive ['pɛntsɪv] *adj* : pensativo, meditabundo — **pensively** *adv*
pent ['pɛnt] *adj* : encerrado ⟨pent-up feelings : emociones reprimidas⟩
pentagon ['pɛntə,gɑn] *n* : pentágono *m*
pentagonal [pɛn'tægənəl] *adj* : pentagonal
penthouse ['pɛnt,haʊs] *n* : ático *m*, penthouse *m*
penultimate [pɪ'nʌltəmət] *adj* : penúltimo
penury ['pɛnjəri] *n* : penuria *f*, miseria *f*
peon ['pi:,ɑn, -ən] *n, pl* -ons *or* -ones [peɪ'o:ni:z] : peón *m*
peony ['pi:əni] *n, pl* -nies : peonía *f*
people¹ ['pi:pəl] *vt* -pled; -pling : poblar
people² *ns & pl* **1** PEOPLE *npl* : gente *f*, personas *fpl* ⟨people like him : él le cae bien a la gente⟩ ⟨many people : mucha gente, muchas personas⟩ **2** *pl* peoples : pueblo *m* ⟨the Cuban people : el pueblo cubano⟩
pep¹ ['pɛp] *vt* pepped; pepping *or* to pep up : animar
pep² *n* : energía *f*, vigor *m*

pepper¹ ['pɛpər] *vt* **1** : añadir pimienta a **2** RIDDLE : acribillar (a balazos) **3** SPRINKLE : salpicar ⟨peppered with quotations : salpicado de citas⟩
pepper² *n* **1** : pimienta *f* (condimento) **2** : pimiento *m*, pimentón *m* (fruta) **3** → chili
peppermint ['pɛpər,mɪnt] *n* : menta *f*
peppery ['pɛpəri] *adj* : picante
peppy ['pɛpi] *adj* peppier; -est : lleno de energía, vivaz
peptic ['pɛptɪk] *adj* peptic ulcer : úlcera *f* estomacal
per ['pər] *prep* **1** : por ⟨miles per hour : millas por hora⟩ **2** ACCORDING TO : según ⟨per his specifications : según sus especificaciones⟩
per annum [pər'ænəm] *adv* : al año, por año
percale [,pər'keɪl, 'pər-,; ,pər'kæl] *n* : percal *m*
per capita [pər'kæpɪtə] *adv & adj* : per cápita
perceive [pər'si:v] *vt* -ceived; -ceiving **1** REALIZE : percatarse de, concientizarse de, darse cuenta de **2** NOTE : percibir, notar
percent¹ [pər'sɛnt] *adv* : por ciento
percent² *n, pl* -cent *or* -cents **1** : por ciento ⟨10 percent of the population : el 10 por ciento de la población⟩ **2** → percentage
percentage [pər'sɛntɪdʒ] *n* : porcentaje *m*
perceptible [pər'sɛptəbəl] *adj* : perceptible — **perceptibly** [-bli] *adv*
perception [pər'sɛpʃən] *n* **1** : percepción *f* ⟨color perception : la percepción de los colores⟩ **2** INSIGHT : perspicacia *f* **3** IDEA : idea *f*, imagen *f*
perceptive [pər'sɛptɪv] *adj* : perspicaz
perceptively [pər'sɛptɪvli] *adv* : con perspicacia
perch¹ ['pərtʃ] *vi* **1** ROOST : posarse **2** SIT : sentarse (en un sitio elevado) — *vt* PLACE : posar, colocar
perch² *n* **1** ROOST : percha *f* (para los pájaros) **2** *pl* perch *or* perches : perca *f* (pez)
percolate ['pərkə,leɪt] *vi* -lated; -lating : colarse, filtrarse ⟨percolated coffee : café filtrado⟩
percolator ['pərkə,leɪtər] *n* : cafetera *f* de filtro
percussion [pər'kʌʃən] *n* **1** STRIKING : percusión *f* **2** *or* percussion instruments : instrumentos *mpl* de percusión
peremptory [pə'rɛmptəri] *adj* : perentorio
perennial¹ [pə'rɛniəl] *adj* **1** : perenne, vivaz ⟨perennial flowers : flores perennes⟩ **2** RECURRENT : perenne, continuo ⟨a perennial problem : un problema eterno⟩
perennial² *n* : planta *f* perenne, planta *f* vivaz
perfect¹ [pər'fɛkt] *vt* : perfeccionar

perfect² ['pərfɪkt] *adj* : perfecto — **perfectly** *adv*

perfection [pər'fɛkʃən] *n* : perfección *f*

perfectionist [pər'fɛkʃənɪst] *n* : perfeccionista *mf*

perfidious [pər'fɪdiəs] *adj* : pérfido

perforate ['pərfə,reɪt] *vt* -rated; -rating : perforar

perforation [,pərfə'reɪʃən] *n* : perforación *f*

perform [pər'fɔrm] *vt* **1** CARRY OUT : realizar, hacer, desempeñar **2** PRESENT : representar, dar (una obra teatral, etc.) — *vi* : actuar (en una obra teatral), cantar (en una ópera, etc.), tocar (en un concierto, etc.), bailar (en un ballet, etc.)

performance [pər'fɔrmənts] *n* **1** EXECUTION : ejecución *f*, realización *f*, desempeño *m*, rendimiento *m* **2** INTERPRETATION : interpretación *f* ⟨his performance of Hamlet : su interpretación de Hamlet⟩ **3** PRESENTATION : representación *f* (de una obra teatral), función *f*

performer [pər'fɔrmər] *n* : artista *mf*; actor *m*, -triz *f*; intérprete *mf* (de música)

perfume¹ [pər'fju:m, 'pər,-] *vt* -fumed; -fuming : perfumar

perfume² ['pər,fju:m, pər'-] *n* : perfume *m*

perfunctory [pər'fʌŋktəri] *adj* : mecánico, superficial, somero

perhaps [pər'hæps] *adv* : tal vez, quizá, quizás

peril ['pɛrəl] *n* : peligro *m*

perilous ['pɛrələs] *adj* : peligroso — **perilously** *adv*

perimeter [pə'rɪmətər] *n* : perímetro *m*

period ['pɪriəd] *n* **1** : punto *m* (en puntuación) **2** : período *m* ⟨a two-hour period : un período de dos horas⟩ **3** STAGE : época *f* (histórica), fase *f*, etapa *f*

periodic [,pɪri'ɑdɪk] *or* **periodical** [-dɪkəl] *adj* : periódico — **periodically** [-dɪkli] *adv*

periodical [,pɪri'ɑdɪkəl] *n* : publicación *f* periódica, revista *f*

peripheral [pə'rɪfərəl] *adj* : periférico

periphery [pə'rɪfəri] *n, pl* -eries : periferia *f*

periscope ['pɛrə,sko:p] *n* : periscopio *m*

perish ['pɛrɪʃ] *vi* DIE : perecer, morirse

perishable¹ ['pɛrɪʃəbəl] *adj* : perecedero

perishable² *n* : producto *m* perecedero

perjure ['pərdʒər] *vt* -jured; -juring (*used in law*) **to perjure oneself** : perjurar, perjurarse

perjury ['pərdʒəri] *n* : perjurio *m*

perk¹ ['pərk] *vt* **1** : levantar (las orejas, etc.) **2** *or* **to perk up** FRESHEN : arreglar — *vi* **to perk up** : animarse, reanimarse

perk² *n* : extra *m*

perky ['pərki] *adj* **perkier; -est** : animado, alegre, lleno de vida

permanence ['pərmənənts] *n* : permanencia *f*

permanent¹ ['pərmənənt] *adj* : permanente — **permanently** *adv*

permanent² *n* : permanente *f*

permeability [,pərmiə'bɪləti] *n* : permeabilidad *f*

permeable ['pərmiəbəl] *adj* : permeable

permeate ['pərmi,eɪt] *v* -ated; -ating *vt* **1** PENETRATE : penetrar, impregnar **2** PERVADE : penetrar, difundirse por — *vi* : penetrar

permissible [pər'mɪsəbəl] *adj* : permisible, lícito

permission [pər'mɪʃən] *n* : permiso *m*

permissive [pər'mɪsɪv] *adj* : permisivo

permit¹ [pər'mɪt] *vt* -mitted; -mitting : permitir, dejar ⟨weather permitting : si el tiempo lo permite⟩

permit² ['pər,mɪt, pər'-] *n* : permiso *m*, licencia *f*

pernicious [pər'nɪʃəs] *adj* : pernicioso

peroxide [pə'rɑk,saɪd] *n* **1** : peróxido *m* **2** → **hydrogen peroxide**

perpendicular¹ [,pərpən'dɪkjələr] *adj* **1** VERTICAL : vertical **2** : perpendicular ⟨perpendicular lines : líneas perpendiculares⟩ — **perpendicularly** *adv*

perpendicular² *n* : perpendicular *f*

perpetrate ['pərpə,treɪt] *vt* -trated; -trating : perpetrar, cometer (un delito)

perpetrator ['pərpə,treɪtər] *n* : autor *m*, -tora *f* (de un delito)

perpetual [pər'pɛtʃuəl] *adj* **1** EVERLASTING : perpetuo, eterno **2** CONTINUAL : perpetuo, continuo, constante

perpetually [pər'pɛtʃuəli, -tʃəli] *adv* : para siempre, eternamente

perpetuate [pər'pɛtʃu,eɪt] *vt* -ated; -ating : perpetuar

perpetuity [,pərpə'tu:əti, -'tju:-] *n, pl* -ties : perpetuidad *f*

perplex [pər'plɛks] *vt* : dejar perplejo, confundir

perplexed [pər'plɛkst] *adj* : perplejo

perplexity [pər'plɛksəti] *n, pl* -ties : perplejidad *f*, confusión *f*

persecute ['pərsɪ,kju:t] *vt* -cuted; -cuting : perseguir

persecution [,pərsɪ'kju:ʃən] *n* : persecución *f*

perseverance [,pərsə'vɪrənts] *n* : perseverancia *f*

persevere [,pərsə'vɪr] *vi* -vered; -vering : perseverar

Persian ['pərʒən] *n* **1** : persa *mf* **2** : persa *m* (idioma) — **Persian** *adj*

persist [pər'sɪst] *vi* : persistir

persistence [pər'sɪstənts] *n* **1** CONTINUATION : persistencia *f* **2** TENACITY : perseverancia *f*, tenacidad *f*

persistent [pər'sɪstənt] *adj* : persistente — **persistently** *adv*

person ['pərsən] *n* **1** HUMAN, INDIVIDUAL : persona *f*, individuo *m*, ser *m* humano **2** : persona *f* (en gramática) **3 in person** : en persona

personable ['pərsənəbəl] *adj* : agradable

personage [ˈpərsənɪdʒ] n : personaje m
personal [ˈpərsənəl] adj 1 OWN, PRI-
VATE : personal, particular, privado
⟨for personal reasons : por razones per-
sonales⟩ 2 : en persona ⟨to make a personal appearance : presentarse en persona, hacerse acto de presencia⟩ 3
: íntimo, personal ⟨personal hygiene
: higiene personal⟩ 4 INDISCREET,
PRYING : indiscreto, personal
personal computer n : computadora f
personal, ordenador m personal Spain
personal digital assistant n : asistente
m personal digital
personality [ˌpərsənˈæləti] n, pl -ties 1
DISPOSITION : personalidad f, temperamento m 2 CELEBRITY : personalidad f, personaje m, celebridad f
personalize [ˈpərsənəˌlaɪz] vt -ized;
-izing : personalizar
personally [ˈpərsənəli] adv 1 : personalmente, en persona ⟨I'll do it personally : lo haré personalmente⟩ 2
: como persona ⟨personally she's very
amiable : como persona es muy am-
able⟩ 3 : personalmente ⟨personally, I
don't believe it : yo, personalmente, no
me lo creo⟩
personification [pərˌsɑnəfəˈkeɪʃən] n
: personificación f
personify [pərˈsɑnəˌfaɪ] vt -fied; -fying
: personificar
personnel [ˌpərsənˈɛl] n : personal m
perspective [pərˈspɛktɪv] n : perspectiva f
perspicacious [ˌpərspəˈkeɪʃəs] adj : perspicaz
perspiration [ˌpərspəˈreɪʃən] n : transpiración f, sudor m
perspire [pərˈspaɪr] vi -spired; -spiring
: transpirar, sudar
persuade [pərˈsweɪd] vt -suaded; -suad-
ing : persuadir, convencer
persuasion [pərˈsweɪʒən] n : persuasión
f
persuasive [pərˈsweɪsɪv, -zɪv] adj : persuasivo — **persuasively** adv
persuasiveness [pərˈsweɪsɪvnəs, -zɪv-] n
: persuasión f
pert [ˈpərt] adj 1 SAUCY : descarado, impertinente 2 JAUNTY : alegre, animado ⟨a pert little hat : un sombrero co-
queto⟩
pertain [pərˈteɪn] vi 1 BELONG
: pertenecer (a) 2 RELATE : estar relacionado (con)
pertinence [ˈpərtənənts] n : pertinencia
f
pertinent [ˈpərtənənt] adj : pertinente
perturb [pərˈtərb] vt : perturbar
perusal [pəˈruːzəl] n : lectura f cuida-
dosa
peruse [pəˈruːz] vt -rused; -rusing 1
READ : leer con cuidado 2 SCAN
: recorrer con la vista ⟨he perused the
newspaper : echó un vistazo al peri-
ódico⟩

Peruvian [pəˈruːviən] n : peruano m, -na
f — **Peruvian** adj
pervade [pərˈveɪd] vt -vaded; -vading
: penetrar, difundirse por
pervasive [pərˈveɪsɪv, -zɪv] adj : penetrante
perverse [pərˈvərs] adj 1 CORRUPT
: perverso, corrompido 2 STUBBORN
: obstinado, porfiado, terco (sin razón)
— **perversely** adv
perversion [pərˈvərʒən] n : perversión f
perversity [pərˈvərsəti] n, pl -ties 1 COR-
RUPTION : corrupción f 2 STUBBORN-
NESS : obstinación f, terquedad f
pervert[1] [pərˈvərt] vt 1 DISTORT : pervertir, distorsionar 2 CORRUPT : pervertir, corromper
pervert[2] [ˈpərˌvərt] n : pervertido m, -da
f
pesky [ˈpɛski] adj : molestoso, molesto
peso [ˈpeɪˌsoː] n, pl -sos : peso m
pessimism [ˈpɛsəˌmɪzəm] n : pesimismo
m
pessimist [ˈpɛsəmɪst] n : pesimista mf
pessimistic [ˌpɛsəˈmɪstɪk] adj : pesimista
pest [ˈpɛst] n 1 NUISANCE : peste f,
latoso m, -sa f fam ⟨to be a pest : dar
(la) lata⟩ 2 : insecto m nocivo, animal
m nocivo ⟨the squirrels were pests : las
ardillas eran una plaga⟩
pester [ˈpɛstər] vt -tered; -tering : molestar, fastidiar
pesticide [ˈpɛstəˌsaɪd] n : pesticida m
pestilence [ˈpɛstələnts] n : pestilencia f,
peste f
pestle [ˈpɛsəl, ˈpɛstəl] n : mano f de
mortero, mazo m, maja f
pet[1] [ˈpɛt] vt petted; petting : acariciar
pet[2] n 1 : animal m doméstico 2 FA-
VORITE : favorito m, -ta f
petal [ˈpɛtəl] n : pétalo m
petite [pəˈtiːt] adj : pequeña, menuda,
chiquita
petition[1] [pəˈtɪʃən] vt : peticionar
petition[2] n : petición f
petitioner [pəˈtɪʃənər] n : peticionario
m, -ria f
petrify [ˈpɛtrəˌfaɪ] vt -fied; -fying : petrificar
petroleum [pəˈtroːliəm] n : petróleo m
petticoat [ˈpɛtiˌkoːt] n : enagua f, fondo
m Mex
pettiness [ˈpɛtinəs] n 1 INSIGNIFI-
CANCE : insignificancia f 2 MEANNESS
: mezquindad f
petty [ˈpɛti] adj -tier; -est 1 MINOR
: menor ⟨petty cash : dinero para gastos menores⟩ 2 INSIGNIFICANT : insignificante, trivial, nimio 3 MEAN
: mezquino
petty officer n : suboficial mf
petulance [ˈpɛtʃələnts] n : irritabilidad f,
mal genio m
petulant [ˈpɛtʃələnt] adj : irritable, de
mal genio
petunia [pɪˈtuːnjə, -ˈtjuː-] n : petunia f
pew [ˈpjuː] n : banco m (de iglesia)

pewter ['pju:tǝr] *n* : peltre *m*

pH [,pi:'eɪtʃ] *n* : pH *m*

phallic ['fælɪk] *adj* : fálico

phallus ['fæləs] *n, pl* **-li** ['fæ,laɪ] *or* **-luses** : falo *m*

phantasy ['fæntəsi] → **fantasy**

phantom ['fæntəm] *n* : fantasma *m*

pharaoh ['fer,o:, 'feɪ,ro:] *n* : faraón *m*

pharmaceutical [,fɑrmə'su:tɪkəl] *adj* : farmacéutico

pharmacist ['fɑrməsɪst] *n* : farmacéutico *m*, -ca *f*

pharmacology [,fɑrmə'kɑlədʒi] *n* : farmacología *f*

pharmacy ['fɑrməsi] *n, pl* **-cies** : farmacia *f*

pharynx ['færɪŋks] *n, pl* **pharynges** [fə'rɪn,dʒi:z] : faringe *f*

phase¹ ['feɪz] *vt* **phased; phasing 1** SYNCHRONIZE : sincronizar, poner en fase **2** STAGGER : escalonar **3 to phase in** : introducir progresivamente **4 to phase out** : retirar progresivamente, dejar de producir

phase² *n* **1** : fase *f* (de la luna, etc.) **2** STAGE : fase *f*, etapa *f*

pheasant ['fezənt] *n, pl* **-ant** *or* **-ants** : faisán *m*

phenomenal [fɪ'nɑmənəl] *adj* : extraordinario, excepcional

phenomenon [fɪ'nɑmə,nɑn, -nən] *n, pl* **-na** [-nə] *or* **-nons 1** : fenómeno *m* **2** *pl* **-nons** PRODIGY : fenómeno *m*, prodigio *m*

philanthropic [,fɪlən'θrɑpɪk] *adj* : filantrópico

philanthropist [fə'lænθrəpɪst] *n* : filántropo *m*, -pa *f*

philanthropy [fə'lænθrəpi] *n, pl* **-pies** : filantropía *f*

philately [fə'lætəli] *n* : filatelia *f*

philodendron [,fɪlə'dendrən] *n, pl* **-drons** *or* **-dra** [-drə] : arácea *f*

philosopher [fə'lɑsəfər] *n* : filósofo *m*, -fa *f*

philosophic [,fɪlə'sɑfɪk] *or* **philosophical** [-fɪkəl] *adj* : filosófico — **philosophically** [-kli] *adv*

philosophize [fə'lɑsə,faɪz] *vi* **-phized; -phizing** : filosofar

philosophy [fə'lɑsəfi] *n, pl* **-phies** : filosofía *f*

phlebitis [flɪ'baɪtəs] *n* : flebitis *f*

phlegm ['flem] *n* : flema *f*

phlox ['flɑks] *n, pl* **phlox** *or* **phloxes** : polemonio *m*

phobia ['fo:biə] *n* : fobia *f*

phoenix ['fi:nɪks] *n* : fénix *m*

phone¹ ['fo:n] *v* → **telephone¹**

phone² *n* → **telephone²**

phoneme ['fo:,ni:m] *n* : fonema *m*

phonetic [fə'netɪk] *adj* : fonético

phonetics [fə'netɪks] *n* : fonética *f*

phonics ['fɑnɪks] *n* : método *m* fonético de aprender a leer

phonograph ['fo:nə,græf] *n* : fonógrafo *m*, tocadiscos *m*

phony¹ *or* **phoney** ['fo:ni] *adj* **-nier; -est** : falso

phony² *or* **phoney** *n, pl* **-nies** : farsante *mf*; charlatán *m*, -tana *f*

phosphate ['fɑs,feɪt] *n* : fosfato *m*

phosphorescence [,fɑsfə'resənts] *n* : fosforescencia *f*

phosphorescent [,fɑsfə'resənt] *adj* : fosforescente — **phosphorescently** *adv*

phosphorus ['fɑsfərəs] *n* : fósforo *m*

photo ['fo:to:] *n, pl* **-tos** : foto *f*

photocopier ['fo:to,kɑpiər] *n* : fotocopiadora *f*

photocopy¹ ['fo:to,kɑpi] *vt* **-copied; -copying** : fotocopiar

photocopy² *n, pl* **-copies** : fotocopia *f*

photoelectric [,fo:toɪ'lektrɪk] *adj* : fotoeléctrico

photogenic [,fo:tə'dʒenɪk] *adj* : fotogénico

photograph¹ ['fo:tə,græf] *vt* : fotografiar

photograph² *n* : fotografía *f*, foto *f* ⟨to take a photograph of : tomarle una fotografía a, tomar una fotografía de⟩

photographer [fə'tɑgrəfər] *n* : fotógrafo *m*, -fa *f*

photographic [,fo:tə'græfɪk] *adj* : fotográfico — **photographically** [-fɪkli] *adv*

photography [fə'tɑgrəfi] *n* : fotografía *f*

photosynthesis [,fo:to'sɪnθəsɪs] *n* : fotosíntesis *f*

photosynthetic [,fo:tosɪn'θetɪk] *adj* : fotosintético, de fotosíntesis

phrase¹ ['freɪz] *vt* **phrased; phrasing** : expresar

phrase² *n* : frase *f*, locución *f* ⟨to coin a phrase : para decirlo así⟩

phylum ['faɪləm] *n, pl* **-la** [-lə] : phylum *m*

physical¹ ['fɪzɪkəl] *adj* **1** : físico ⟨physical laws : leyes físicas⟩ **2** MATERIAL : material, físico **3** BODILY : físico, córeo — **physically** [-kli] *adv*

physical² *n* CHECKUP : chequeo *m*, reconocimiento *m* médico

physician [fə'zɪʃən] *n* : médico *m*, -ca *f*

physicist ['fɪzəsɪst] *n* : físico *m*, -ca *f*

physics ['fɪzɪks] *ns & pl* : física *f*

physiognomy [,fɪzi'ɑgnəmi] *n, pl* **-mies** : fisonomía *f*

physiological ['fɪziə'lɑdʒɪkəl] *or* **physiologic** [-dʒɪk] *adj* : fisiológico

physiologist [,fɪzi'ɑlədʒɪst] *n* : fisiólogo *m*, -ga *f*

physiology [,fɪzi'ɑlədʒi] *n* : fisiología *f*

physique [fə'zi:k] *n* : físico *m*

pi ['paɪ] *n, pl* **pis** ['paɪz] : pi *f*

pianist [pi'ænɪst, 'pi:ənɪst] *n* : pianista *mf*

piano [pi'æno:] *n, pl* **-anos** : piano *m*

piazza [pi'æzə, -'ɑtsə] *n, pl* **-zas** *or* **-ze** [-'ɑt,seɪ] : plaza *f*

picaresque [,pɪkə'resk, ,pi:-] *adj* : picaresco

picayune [,pɪki'ju:n] *adj* : trivial, nimio, insignificante

piccolo ['pɪkə,lo:] *n, pl* **-los** : flautín *m*

pick¹ ['pɪk] *vt* **1** : picar, labrar (con un pico) ⟨he picked the hard soil : picó la tierra dura⟩ **2** : quitar, sacar (poco a poco) ⟨to pick meat off the bones : quitar pedazos de carne de los huesos⟩ **3** : recoger, arrancar (frutas, flores, etc.) **4** SELECT : escoger, elegir **5** PROVOKE : provocar ⟨to pick a quarrel : buscar pleito, buscar pelea⟩ **6 to pick a lock** : forzar una cerradura **7 to pick someone's pocket** : robarle algo del bolsillo de alguien ⟨someone picked my pocket! : ¡me robaron la cartera del bolsillo!⟩ — *vi* **1** NIBBLE : picar, picotear **2 to pick and choose** : ser exigente **3 to pick at** : tocar, rascarse (una herida, etc.) **4 to pick on** TEASE : mofarse de, atormentar

pick² *n* **1** CHOICE : selección *f* **2** BEST : lo mejor ⟨the pick of the crop : la crema y nata⟩ **3** → pickax

pickax ['pɪk,æks] *n* : pico *m*, zapapico *m*, piqueta *f*

pickerel ['pɪkərəl] *n, pl* **-el** *or* **-els** : lucio *m* pequeño

picket¹ ['pɪkət] *v* : piquetear

picket² *n* **1** STAKE : estaca *f* **2** STRIKER : huelguista *mf*, integrante *mf* de un piquete

pickle¹ ['pɪkəl] *vt* **-led; -ling** : encurtir, escabechar

pickle² *n* **1** BRINE : escabeche *m* **2** GHERKIN : pepinillo *m* (encurtido) **3** JAM, TROUBLE : lío *m*, apuro *m*

pickpocket ['pɪk,pɑkət] *n* : carterista *mf*

pickup ['pɪk,əp] *n* **1** IMPROVEMENT : mejora *f* **2** *or* **pickup truck** : camioneta *f*

pick up *vt* **1** LIFT : levantar **2** TIDY : arreglar, ordenar — *vi* IMPROVE : mejorar

picnic¹ ['pɪk,nɪk] *vi* **-nicked; -nicking** : ir de picnic

picnic² *n* : picnic *m*

pictorial [pɪk'tɔriəl] *adj* : pictórico

picture¹ ['pɪktʃər] *vt* **-tured; -turing 1** DEPICT : representar **2** IMAGINE : imaginarse ⟨can you picture it? : ¿te lo puedes imaginar?⟩

picture² *n* **1** CUADRO : cuadro *m* (pintado o dibujado), ilustración *f*, fotografía *f* **2** DESCRIPTION : descripción *f* **3** IMAGE : imagen *f* ⟨he's the picture of his father : es la viva imagen de su padre⟩ **4** MOVIE : película *f*

picturesque [,pɪktʃə'rɛsk] *adj* : pintoresco

pie ['paɪ] *n* : pastel *m* (con fruta o carne), empanada *f* (con carne)

piebald ['paɪ,bɔld] *adj* : picazo, pío

piece¹ ['pi:s] *vt* **pieced; piecing 1** PATCH : parchar, arreglar **2 to piece together** : construir pieza por pieza

piece² *n* **1** FRAGMENT : trozo *m*, pedazo *m* **2** COMPONENT : pieza *f* ⟨a three-piece suit : un traje de tres piezas⟩ **3** UNIT : pieza *f* ⟨a piece of fruit : una (pieza de) fruta⟩ **4** WORK : obra *f*, pieza *f* (de música, etc.) **5** (*in board games*) : ficha *f*, pieza *f*, figura *f* (en ajedrez)

piecemeal¹ ['pi:s,mi:l] *adv* : poco a poco, por partes

piecemeal² *adj* : hecho poco a poco, poco sistemático

pied ['paɪd] *adj* : pío

pier ['pɪr] *n* **1** : pila *f* (de un puente) **2** WHARF : muelle *m*, atracadero *m*, embarcadero *m* **3** PILLAR : pilar *m*

pierce ['pɪrs] *vt* **pierced; piercing 1** PENETRATE : atravesar, traspasar, penetrar (en) ⟨the bullet pierced his leg : la bala le atravesó la pierna⟩ ⟨to pierce one's heart : traspasarle el corazón a uno⟩ **2** PERFORATE : perforar, agujerear (las orejas, etc.) **3 to pierce the silence** : desgarrar el silencio

piety ['paɪəti] *n, pl* **-eties** : piedad *f*

pig ['pɪg] *n* **1** HOG, SWINE : cerdo *m*, -da *f*; puerco *m*, -ca *f* **2** SLOB : persona *f* desaliñada; cerdo *m*, -da *f* **3** GLUTTON : glotón *m*, -tona *f* **4** *or* **pig iron** : lingote *m* de hierro

pigeon ['pɪdʒən] *n* : paloma *f*

pigeonhole ['pɪdʒən,ho:l] *n* : casilla *f*

pigeon—toed ['pɪdʒən,to:d] *adj* : patituerto

piggish ['pɪgɪʃ] *adj* **1** GREEDY : glotón **2** DIRTY : cochino, sucio

piggyback ['pɪgi,bæk] *adv & adj* : a cuestas

pigheaded ['pɪg,hɛdəd] *adj* : terco, obstinado

piglet ['pɪglət] *n* : cochinillo *m*; lechón *m*, -chona *f*

pigment ['pɪgmənt] *n* : pigmento *m*

pigmentation [,pɪgmən'teɪʃən] *n* : pigmentación *f*

pigmy → **pygmy**

pigpen ['pɪg,pɛn] *n* : chiquero *m*, pocilga *f*

pigsty ['pɪg,staɪ] → **pigpen**

pigtail ['pɪg,teɪl] *n* : coleta *f*, trenza *f*

pike ['paɪk] *n, pl* **pike** *or* **pikes 1** : lucio *m* (pez) **2** LANCE : pica *f* **3** → **turnpike**

pile¹ ['paɪl] *vt* **piled; piling** : amontonar, apilar — *vi* **to pile up** : amontonarse, acumularse

pile² *n* **1** STAKE : pilote *m* **2** HEAP : montón *m*, pila *f* **3** NAP : pelo *m* (de telas)

piles ['paɪlz] *npl* HEMORRHOIDS : hemorroides *fpl*, almorranas *fpl*

pilfer ['pɪlfər] *vt* : robar (cosas pequeñas), ratear

pilgrim ['pɪlgrəm] *n* : peregrino *m*, -na *f*

pilgrimage ['pɪlgrəmɪdʒ] *n* : peregrinación *f*

pill ['pɪl] *n* : pastilla *f*, píldora *f*

pillage¹ ['pɪlɪdʒ] *vt* **-laged; -laging** : saquear

pillage² *n* : saqueo *m*

pillar ['pɪlər] *n* : pilar *m*, columna *f*

pillory ['pɪləri] *n, pl* **-ries** : picota *f*

pillow ['pɪlo:] *n* : almohada *f*

pillowcase ['pɪlo:,keɪs] *n* : funda *f*

pilot¹ ['paɪlət] *vt* : pilotar, pilotear

pilot² *n* : piloto *mf*

pilot light *n* : piloto *m*

pimento [pə'mɛn,to:] → **pimiento**

pimiento [pə'mɛn,to:, -'mjɛn-] n, pl **-tos**
: pimiento m morrón

pimp ['pɪmp] n : proxeneta m

pimple ['pɪmpəl] n : grano m

pimply ['pɪmpəli] adj **-plier; -est** : cubierto de granos

pin¹ ['pɪn] vt **pinned; pinning 1** FASTEN
: prender, sujetar (con alfileres) **2**
HOLD, IMMOBILIZE : inmovilizar, sujetar **3** to pin one's hopes on : poner
sus esperanzas en

pin² n **1** : alfiler m ⟨safety pin : alfiler
de gancho⟩ ⟨a bobby pin : una horqui-
lla⟩ **2** BROOCH : alfiler m, broche m,
prendedor m **3** or **bowling pin** : bolo
m

pinafore ['pɪnə,for] n : delantal m

pincer ['pɪntsər] n **1** CLAW : pinza f (de
una langosta, etc.) **2** **pincers** npl : pinzas fpl, tenazas fpl, tenaza f

pinch¹ ['pɪntʃ] vt **1** : pellizcar ⟨she
pinched my cheek : me pellizcó el ca-
chete⟩ **2** STEAL : robar — vi : apretar
⟨my shoes pinch : me aprietan los za-
patos⟩

pinch² n **1** EMERGENCY : emergencia f
⟨in a pinch : en caso necesario⟩ **2** PAIN
: dolor m, tormento m **3** SQUEEZE : pellizco m (con los dedos) **4** BIT : pizca
f, pellizco m ⟨a pinch of cinnamon : una
pizca de canela⟩

pinch hitter n **1** SUBSTITUTE : sustituto
m, -ta f **2** : bateador m emergente (en
beisbol)

pincushion ['pɪn,kuʃən] n : acerico m,
alfiletero m

pine¹ ['paɪn] vi **pined; pining 1** to pine
away : languidecer, consumirse **2** to
pine for : añorar, suspirar por

pine² n **1** : pino m (árbol) **2** : madera f
de pino

pineapple ['paɪn,æpəl] n : piña f, ananá
m, ananás m

ping-pong ['pɪŋ,paŋ, -,pɔŋ] n : ping-
pong m

pinion¹ ['pɪnjən] vt : sujetar los brazos
de, inmovilizar

pinion² n : piñón m

pink¹ ['pɪŋk] adj : rosa, rosado

pink² n **1** : clavelino m (flor) **2** : rosa m,
rosado m (color) **3** to be in the pink
: estar en plena forma, rebosar de salud

pinkeye ['pɪŋk,aɪ] n : conjuntivitis f agu-
da

pinkish ['pɪŋkɪʃ] adj : rosáceo

pinnacle ['pɪnɪkəl] n **1** : pináculo m (de
un edificio) **2** PEAK : cima f, cumbre f
(de una montaña) **3** ACME : pináculo
m, cúspide f, apogeo m

pinpoint ['pɪn,pɔɪnt] vt : precisar, localizar con precisión

pint ['paɪnt] n : pinta f

pinto ['pɪn,to:] n, pl **pintos** : caballo m
pinto

pinworm ['pɪn,wərm] n : oxiuro m

pioneer¹ ['paɪə'nɪr] vt : promover, iniciar, introducir

pioneer² n : pionero m, -ra f

pious ['paɪəs] adj **1** DEVOUT : piadoso,
devoto **2** SANCTIMONIOUS : beato

piously ['paɪəsli] adv **1** DEVOUTLY : pi-
adosamente **2** SANCTIMONIOUSLY
: santurronamente

pipe¹ ['paɪp] v **piped; piping** vi : hablar
en voz chillona — vt **1** PLAY : tocar (el
caramillo o la flauta) **2** : conducir por
tuberías ⟨to pipe water : transportar el
agua por tubería⟩

pipe² n **1** : caramillo m (instrumento
musical) **2** BAGPIPE : gaita f **3** : tubo
m, caño m ⟨gas pipes : tubería de gas⟩
4 : pipa f (para fumar)

pipeline ['paɪp,laɪn] n **1** : conducto m,
oleoducto m (para petróleo), gasoducto m (para gas) **2** CONDUIT : vía f (de
información, etc.)

piper ['paɪpər] n : músico m, -ca f que
toca el caramillo o la gaita

piping ['paɪpɪŋ] n **1** : música f del
caramillo o de la gaita **2** TRIM : cordoncillo m, ribete m con cordón

piquant ['pi:kənt, 'pɪkwənt] adj **1** SPICY
: picante **2** INTRIGUING : intrigante,
estimulante

pique ['pi:k] v **piqued; piquing 1** IR-
RITATE : picar, irritar **2** AROUSE : despertar (la curiosidad, etc.)

pique² n : pique m, resentimiento m

piracy ['paɪrəsi] n, pl **-cies** : piratería f

piranha [pə'rɑnə, -'rɑnjə, -'rænjə] n : piraña f

pirate¹ ['paɪrət] n : pirata mf

pirate² vt **-rated; -rating** : piratear (software, etc.)

pirouette [,pɪrə'wɛt] n : pirueta f

pis → **pi**

Pisces ['paɪ,si:z, 'pɪ-; 'pɪs,keɪs] n : Piscis
mf

pistachio [pə'stæʃi,o:, -'stɑ-] n, pl **-chios**
: pistacho m

pistil ['pɪstəl] n : pistilo m

pistol ['pɪstəl] n : pistola f

piston ['pɪstən] n : pistón m, émbolo m

pit¹ ['pɪt] v **pitted; pitting** vt **1** : marcar
de hoyos, picar (una superficie) **2**
: deshuesar (una fruta) **3** to pit against
: enfrentar a, oponer a — vi : quedar
marcado

pit² n **1** HOLE : fosa f, hoyo m ⟨a bottomless pit : un pozo sin fondo⟩ **2** MINE
: mina f **3** : foso m ⟨orchestra pit : foso
orquestal⟩ **4** POCKMARK : marca f (en
la cara), cicatriz f de viruela **5** STONE
: hueso m, pepa f (de una fruta) **6** pit
of the stomach : boca f del estómago

pitch¹ ['pɪtʃ] vt **1** SET UP : montar, armar
(una tienda) **2** THROW : lanzar, arrojar **3** ADJUST : dar el tono de (un
discurso, un instrumento musical) —
vi **1** or **pitch forward** FALL : caerse **2**
LURCH : cabecear (dícese de un barco
o un avión), dar bandazos

pitch² n **1** LURCHING : cabezada f,
cabeceo m (de un barco o un avión) **2**
SLOPE : (grado de) inclinación f, pendiente f **3** : tono m (en música) ⟨per-

fect pitch : oído absoluto⟩ **4** THROW
: lanzamiento *m* **5** DEGREE : grado *m*,
nivel *m*, punto *m* ⟨the excitement
reached a high pitch : la excitación
llegó a un punto culminante⟩ **6** *or*
sales pitch : presentación *f* (de un
vendedor) **7** TAR : pez *f*, brea *f*

pitcher ['pɪtʃər] *n* **1** JUG : jarra *f*, jarro
m, cántaro *m*, pichel *m* **2** : lanzador *m*,
-dora *f* (en béisbol, etc.)

pitchfork ['pɪtʃˌfɔrk] *n* : horquilla *f*, horca *f*

piteous ['pɪtiəs] *adj* : lastimoso, lastimero — **piteously** *adv*

pitfall ['pɪtˌfɔl] *n* : peligro *m* (poco obvio), dificultad *f*

pith ['pɪθ] *n* **1** : médula *f* (de una planta) **2** CORE : meollo *m*, entraña *f*

pithy ['pɪθi] *adj* **pithier; -est** : conciso y
sustancioso ⟨pithy comments : comentarios sucintos⟩

pitiable ['pɪtiəbəl] → **pitiful**

pitiful ['pɪtɪfəl] *adj* **1** LAMENTABLE : lastimoso, lastimoso, lamentable **2** CONTEMPTIBLE : despreciable, lamentable
— **pitifully** [-fli] *adv*

pitiless ['pɪtiləs] *adj* : despiadado — **pitilessly** *adv*

pittance ['pɪtənts] *n* : miseria *f*

pituitary [pə'tu:əˌtɛri, -'tju:-] *adj* : pituitario

pity¹ ['pɪti] *vt* **pitied; pitying** : compadecer, compadecerse de

pity² *n*, *pl* **pities** **1** COMPASSION : compasión *f*, piedad *f* **2** SHAME : lástima *f*,
pena *f* ⟨what a pity! : ¡qué lástima!⟩

pivot¹ ['pɪvət] *vi* **1** : girar sobre un eje **2
to pivot on** : girar sobre, depender de

pivot² *n* : pivote *m*

pivotal ['pɪvətəl] *adj* : fundamental, central

pixie *or* **pixy** ['pɪksi] *n*, *pl* **pixies** : elfo
m, hada *f*

pizza ['pi:tsə] *n* : pizza *f*

pizzazz *or* **pizazz** [pə'zæz] *n* **1** GLAMOR
: encanto *m* **2** VITALITY : animación *f*,
vitalidad *f*

placard ['plækɑrd, -ˌkɑrd] *n* POSTER
: cartel *m*, póster *m*, afiche *m*

placate ['pleɪˌkeɪt, 'plæ-] *vt* **-cated;
-cating** : aplacar, apaciguar

place¹ ['pleɪs] *vt* **placed; placing 1** PUT,
SET : poner, colocar **2** SITUATE : situar, ubicar, emplazar ⟨to be well placed
: estar bien situado⟩ ⟨to place in a job
: colocar en un trabajo⟩ **3** IDENTIFY,
RECALL : identificar, ubicar, recordar
⟨I can't place him : no lo ubico⟩ **4 to
place an order** : hacer un pedido

place² *n* **1** SPACE : sitio *m*, lugar *m*
⟨there's no place to sit : no hay sitio
para sentarse⟩ **2** LOCATION, SPOT : lugar *m*, sitio *m*, parte *f* ⟨place of work
: lugar de trabajo⟩ ⟨our summer place
: nuestra casa de verano⟩ ⟨all over the
place : por todas partes⟩ **3** RANK : lugar *m*, puesto *m* ⟨he took first place
: ganó el primer lugar⟩ **4** POSITION : lugar *m* ⟨everything in its place : todo en

su debido lugar⟩ ⟨to feel out of place
: sentirse fuera de lugar⟩ **5** SEAT
: asiento *m*, cubierto *m* (a la mesa) **6**
JOB : puesto *m* **7** ROLE : papel *m*, lugar *m* ⟨to change places : cambiarse los
papeles⟩ **8 to take place** : tener lugar
9 to take the place of : sustituir a

placebo [plə'si:ˌbo:] *n*, *pl* **-bos** : placebo
m

placement ['pleɪsmənt] *n* : colocación *f*

placenta [plə'sɛntə] *n*, *pl* **-tas** *or* **-tae** [-ˌti,
-ˌtaɪ] : placenta *f*

placid ['plæsəd] *adj* : plácido, tranquilo
— **placidly** *adv*

plagiarism ['pleɪdʒəˌrɪzəm] *n* : plagio *m*

plagiarist ['pleɪdʒərɪst] *n* : plagiario *m*,
-ria *f*

plagiarize ['pleɪdʒəˌraɪz] *vt* **-rized;
-rizing** : plagiar

plague¹ ['pleɪg] *vt* **plagued; plaguing 1**
AFFLICT : plagar, afligir **2** HARASS
: acosar, atormentar

plague² *n* **1** : plaga *f* (de insectos, etc.)
2 : peste *f* (en medicina)

plaid¹ ['plæd] *adj* : escocés, de cuadros
⟨a plaid skirt : una falda escocesa⟩

plaid² *n* TARTAN : tela *f* escocesa, tartán
m

plain¹ ['pleɪn] *adj* **1** SIMPLE, UN
ADORNED : liso, sencillo, sin adornos
2 CLEAR : claro ⟨in plain language : en
palabras claras⟩ **3** FRANK : franco,
puro ⟨the plain truth : la pura verdad⟩
4 HOMELY : ordinario, poco atractivo
5 in plain sight : a la vista de todos

plain² *n* : llanura *f*, llano *m*, planicie *f*

plainly ['pleɪnli] *adv* **1** CLEARLY : claramente **2** FRANKLY : francamente, con
franqueza **3** SIMPLY : sencillamente

plaintiff ['pleɪntɪf] *n* : demandante *mf*

plaintive ['pleɪntɪv] *adj* MOURNFUL : lastimero, plañidero

plait¹ ['pleɪt, 'plæt] *vt* **1** PLEAT : plisar **2**
BRAID : trenzar

plait² *n* **1** PLEAT : pliegue *m* **2** BRAID
: trenza *f*

plan¹ ['plæn] *v* **planned; planning** *vt* **1**
: planear, proyectar, planificar ⟨to plan
a trip : planear un viaje⟩ ⟨to plan a city
: planificar una ciudad⟩ **2** INTEND
: tener planeado, proyectar — *vi* : hacer planes

plan² *n* **1** DIAGRAM : plano *m*, esquema
m **2** SCHEME : plan *m*, proyecto *m*, programa *m* ⟨to draw up a plan : elaborar
un proyecto⟩

plane¹ ['pleɪn] *vt* **planed; planing** : cepillar (madera)

plane² *adj* : plano

plane³ *n* **1** : plano *m* (en matemáticas,
etc.) **2** LEVEL : nivel *m* **3** : cepillo *m*
(de carpintero) **4** → **airplane**

planet ['plænət] *n* : planeta *f*

planetarium [ˌplænə'tɛriəm] *n*, *pl* **-iums**
or **-ia** [-iə] : planetario *m*

planetary ['plænəˌtɛri] *adj* : planetario

plank ['plæŋk] *n* **1** BOARD : tablón *m*,
tabla *f* **2** : artículo *m*, punto *m* (de una
plataforma política)

plankton ['plæŋktən] n : plancton m
plant¹ ['plænt] vt 1 : plantar, sembrar
(semillas) ⟨planted with flowers : plantado de flores⟩ 2 PLACE : plantar, colocar ⟨to plant an idea : inculcar una
idea⟩
plant² n 1 : planta f ⟨leafy plants : plantas frondosas⟩ 2 FACTORY : planta f,
fábrica f ⟨hydroelectric plant : planta
hidroeléctrica⟩ 3 MACHINERY : maquinaria f, equipo m
plantain² ['plæntən] n 1 : llantén m (mala
hierba) 2 : plátano m, plátano m macho Mex (fruta)
plantation [plæn'teɪʃən] n : plantación
f, hacienda f ⟨a coffee plantation : un
cafetal⟩
planter ['plæntər] n 1 : hacendado m,
-da f (de una hacienda) 2 FLOWERPOT
: tiesto m, maceta f
plaque ['plæk] n 1 TABLET : placa f 2
: placa f (dental)
plasma ['plæzmə] n : plasma m
plaster¹ ['plæstər] vt 1 : enyesar, revocar (con yeso) 2 COVER : cubrir, llenar
⟨a wall plastered with notices : una
pared cubierta de avisos⟩
plaster² n 1 : yeso m, revoque m (para
paredes, etc.) 2 : escayola f, yeso m (en
medicina) 3 **plaster of Paris** ['pærɪs]
: yeso m mate
plaster cast n : vaciado m de yeso
plasterer ['plæstərər] n : revocador m,
-dora f
plastic¹ ['plæstɪk] adj 1 : de plástico 2
PLIABLE : plástico, flexible 3 **plastic
surgery** : cirugía f plástica
plastic² n : plástico m
plasticity [plæ'stɪsəti] n, pl -ties : plasticidad f
plate¹ ['pleɪt] vt plated; plating : chapar
(en metal)
plate² n 1 PLAQUE, SHEET : placa f ⟨a
steel plate : una placa de acero⟩ 2
UTENSILS : vajilla f (de metal) ⟨silver
plate : vajilla de plata⟩ 3 DISH : plato
m 4 DENTURES : dentadura f postiza
5 ILLUSTRATION : lámina f (en un libro) 6 **license plate** : matrícula f, placa f de matrícula
plateau [plæ'to:] n, pl -teaus or -teaux
[-'to:z] : meseta f
platform ['plæt,fɔrm] n 1 STAGE
: plataforma f, estrado m, tribuna f 2
: andén m (de una estación de ferrocarril) 3 **political platform** : plataforma f política, programa m electoral
plating ['pleɪtɪŋ] n 1 : enchapado m 2
silver plating : plateado m
platinum ['plætənəm] n : platino m
platitude ['plætə,tu:d, -,tju:d] n : lugar
m común, perogrullada f
platonic [plə'tɑnɪk] adj : platónico
platoon [plə'tu:n] n : sección f (en el
ejército)
platter ['plætər] n : fuente f
platypus ['plætɪpəs, -,pʊs] n, pl **platy-
puses** or **platypi** [-,paɪ, -,pi:] : ornitorrinco m

plausibility [,plɔzə'bɪləti] n, pl -ties
: credibilidad f, verosimilitud f
plausible ['plɔzəbəl] adj : creíble, convincente, verosímil — **plausibly** [-bli]
adv
play¹ ['pleɪ] vi 1 : jugar ⟨to play with a
doll : jugar con una muñeca⟩ ⟨to play
with an idea : darle vueltas a una idea⟩
2 FIDDLE, TOY : jugar, juguetear ⟨don't
play with your food : no juegues con
la comida⟩ 3 : tocar ⟨to play in a band
: tocar en un grupo⟩ 4 : actuar (en una
obra de teatro) — vt 1 : jugar (un deporte, etc.), jugar a (un juego), jugar
contra (un contrincante) 2 : tocar
(música o un instrumento) 3 PERFORM
: interpretar, hacer el papel de (un
carácter), representar (una obra de
teatro) ⟨she plays the lead : hace el papel principal⟩ 4 **to play back** : poner
(una grabación) 5 **to play down** : minimizar 6 **to play up** : resaltar
play² n 1 GAME, RECREATION : juego m
⟨children at play : niños jugando⟩ ⟨a
play on words : un juego de palabras⟩
2 ACTION : juego m ⟨the ball is in play
: la pelota está en juego⟩ ⟨to bring into
play : poner en juego⟩ 3 DRAMA : obra
f de teatro, pieza f (de teatro) 4 MOVE-
MENT : juego m (de la luz, una brisa,
etc.) 5 SLACK : juego m ⟨there's not
enough play in the wheel : la rueda no
da lo suficiente⟩
playacting ['pleɪ,æktɪŋ] n : actuación f,
teatro m
player ['pleɪər] n 1 : jugador m, -dora f
(en un juego) 2 ACTOR : actor m, actriz f 3 MUSICIAN : músico m, -ca f
playful ['pleɪfəl] adj 1 FROLICSOME
: juguetón 2 JOCULAR : jocoso — **play-
fully** adv
playfulness ['pleɪfəlnəs] n : lo juguetón,
jocosidad f, alegría f
playground ['pleɪ,graʊnd] n : patio m de
recreo, jardín m para jugar
playhouse ['pleɪ,haʊs] n 1 THEATER
: teatro m 2 : casita f de juguete
playing card n : naipe m, carta f
playmate ['pleɪ,meɪt] n : compañero m,
-ra f de juego
play-off ['pleɪ,ɔf] n : desempate m
playpen ['pleɪ,pɛn] n : corral m (para
niños)
plaything ['pleɪ,θɪŋ] n : juguete m
playwright ['pleɪ,raɪt] n : dramaturgo m,
-ga f
plaza ['plæzə, 'plɑ-] n 1 SQUARE : plaza
f 2 **shopping plaza** MALL : centro m
comercial
plea ['pli:] n 1 : acto m de declararse ⟨he
entered a plea of guilty : se declaró cul-
pable⟩ 2 APPEAL : ruego m, súplica f
plead ['pli:d] v pleaded or pled [pled];
pleading vi 1 : declararse (culpable o
inocente) 2 **to plead for** : suplicar, implorar — vt 1 : alegar, pretextar ⟨he
pleaded illness : pretextó la enfer-
medad⟩ 2 **to plead a case** : defender
un caso

pleasant ['plɛzənt] *adj* : agradable, grato, bueno — **pleasantly** *adv*

pleasantness ['plɛzəntnəs] *n* : lo agradable, amenidad *f*

pleasantries ['plɛzəntriz] *npl* : cumplidos *mpl*, cortesías *fpl* ⟨to exchange pleasantries : intercambiar cumplidos⟩

please¹ ['pli:z] *v* **pleased; pleasing** *vt* 1 GRATIFY : complacer ⟨please yourself! : ¡cómo quieras!⟩ 2 SATISFY : contentar, satisfacer — *vi* 1 SATISFY : complacer, agradar ⟨anxious to please : deseoso de complacer⟩ 2 LIKE : querer ⟨do as you please : haz lo que quieras, haz lo que te parezca⟩

please² *adv* : por favor

pleased ['pli:zd] *adj* : contento, satisfecho, alegre

pleasing ['pli:zɪŋ] *adj* : agradable — **pleasingly** *adv*

pleasurable ['plɛʒərəbəl] *adj* PLEASANT : agradable

pleasure ['plɛʒər] *n* 1 WISH : deseo *m*, voluntad *f* ⟨at your pleasure : cuando guste⟩ 2 ENJOYMENT : placer *m*, disfrute *m*, goce *m* ⟨with pleasure : con mucho gusto⟩ 3 : placer *m*, gusto *m* ⟨it's a pleasure to be here : me da gusto estar aquí⟩ ⟨the pleasures of reading : los placeres de leer⟩

pleat¹ ['pli:t] *vt* : plisar

pleat² *n* : pliegue *m*

plebeian [pli'biən] *adj* : ordinario, plebeyo

pledge¹ ['plɛʤ] *vt* **pledged; pledging** 1 PAWN : empeñar, prendar 2 PROMISE : prometer, jurar

pledge² *n* 1 SECURITY : garantía *f*, prenda *f* 2 PROMISE : promesa *f*

plenteous ['plɛntiəs] *adj* : copioso, abundante

plentiful ['plɛntɪfəl] *adj* : abundante — **plentifully** [-fli] *adv*

plenty ['plɛnti] *n* : abundancia *f* ⟨plenty of time : tiempo de sobra⟩ ⟨plenty of visitors : muchos visitantes⟩

plethora ['plɛθərə] *n* : plétora *f*

pleurisy ['plʊrəsi] *n* : pleuresía *f*

pliable ['plaɪəbəl] *adj* : flexible, maleable

pliant ['plaɪənt] → pliable

pliers ['plaɪərz] *npl* : alicates *mpl*, pinzas *fpl*

plight ['plaɪt] *n* : situación *f* difícil, apuro *m*

plod ['plɑd] *vi* **plodded; plodding** 1 TRUDGE : caminar pesadamente y lentamente 2 DRUDGE : trabajar laboriosamente

plot¹ ['plɑt] *v* **plotted; plotting** *vt* 1 DEVISE : tramar 2 to plot out : trazar, determinar (una posición, etc.) — *vi* CONSPIRE : conspirar

plot² *n* 1 LOT : terreno *m*, parcela *f*, lote *m* 2 STORY : argumento *m* (en el teatro), trama *f* (en un libro, etc.) 3 CONSPIRACY, INTRIGUE : complot *m*, intriga *f*

plotter ['plɑtər] *n* : conspirador *m*, -dora *f*; intrigante *mf*

plow¹ *or* **plough** ['plaʊ] *vt* 1 : arar (la tierra) 2 to plow the seas : surcar los mares

plow² *or* **plough** *n* 1 : arado *m* 2 → snowplow

plowshare ['plaʊˌʃɛr] *n* : reja *f* del arado

ploy ['plɔɪ] *n* : estratagema *f*, maniobra *f*

pluck¹ ['plʌk] *vt* 1 PICK : arrancar 2 : desplumar (un pollo, etc.) — *vi* to pluck at : tirar de

pluck² *n* 1 TUG : tirón *m* 2 COURAGE, SPIRIT : valor *m*, ánimo *m*

plucky ['plʌki] *adj* **pluckier; -est** : valiente, animoso

plug¹ ['plʌg] *vt* **plugged; plugging** 1 BLOCK : tapar 2 PROMOTE : hacerle publicidad a, promocionar 3 to plug in : enchufar

plug² *n* 1 STOPPER : tapón *m* 2 : enchufe *m* (eléctrico) 3 ADVERTISEMENT : publicidad *f*, propaganda *f*

plum ['plʌm] *n* 1 : ciruela *f* (fruta) 2 : color *m* ciruela 3 PRIZE : premio *m*, algo muy atractivo

plumage ['plu:mɪʤ] *n* : plumaje *m*

plumb¹ ['plʌm] *vt* 1 : aplomar ⟨to plumb a wall : aplomar una pared⟩ 2 SOUND : sondear, sondar

plumb² *adv* 1 VERTICALLY : a plomo, verticalmente 2 EXACTLY : justo, exactamente 3 COMPLETELY : completamente, absolutamente ⟨plumb crazy : loco de remate⟩

plumb³ *adj* : a plomo

plumb⁴ *n* *or* **plumb line** : plomada *f*

plumber ['plʌmər] *n* : plomero *m*, -ra *f*; fontanero *m*, -ra *f*

plumbing ['plʌmɪŋ] *n* 1 : plomería *f*, fontanería *f* (trabajo del plomero) 2 PIPES : cañería *f*, tubería *f*

plume ['plu:m] *n* 1 FEATHER : pluma *f* 2 TUFT : penacho *m* (en un sombrero, etc.)

plumed ['plu:md] *adj* : con plumas ⟨white-plumed birds : aves de plumaje blanco⟩

plummet ['plʌmət] *vi* : caer en picada, desplomarse

plump¹ ['plʌmp] *vi* *or* **to plump down** : dejarse caer (pesadamente)

plump² *adv* 1 STRAIGHT : a plomo 2 DIRECTLY : directamente, sin rodeos ⟨he ran plump into the door : dio de cara con la puerta⟩

plump³ *adj* : llenito *fam*, regordete *fam*, rechoncho *fam*

plumpness ['plʌmpnəs] *n* : gordura *f*

plunder¹ ['plʌndər] *vi* : saquear, robar

plunder² *n* : botín *m*

plunderer ['plʌndərər] *n* : saqueador *m*, -dora *f*

plunge¹ ['plʌnʤ] *v* **plunged; plunging** *vt* 1 IMMERSE : sumergir 2 THRUST : hundir, clavar — *vi* 1 DIVE : zambullirse (en el agua) 2 : meterse precipitadamente o violentamente ⟨they plunged into war : se enfrascaron en una guerra⟩ ⟨he plunged into depression : cayó en la depresión⟩ 3 DESCEND : descender en picada ⟨the road plunges dizzily : la calle desciende vertiginosamente⟩

plunge[2] *n* 1 DIVE : zambullida *f* 2 DROP : descenso *m* abrupto ⟨the plunge in prices : el desplome de los precios⟩

plural[1] ['plʊrəl] *adj* : plural

plural[2] *n* : plural *m*

plurality [plʊˈræləti] *n*, *pl* **-ties** : pluralidad *f*

pluralize ['plʊrə,laɪz] *vt* **-ized**; **-izing** : pluralizar

plus[1] ['plʌs] *adj* 1 POSITIVE : positivo ⟨a plus factor : un factor positivo⟩ 2 (*indicating a quantity in addition*) ⟨a grade of C plus : una calificación entre C y B⟩ ⟨a salary of $30,000 plus : un sueldo de más de $30,000⟩

plus[2] *n* 1 *or* **plus sign** : más *m*, signo *m* de más 2 ADVANTAGE : ventaja *f*

plus[3] *prep* : más (en matemáticas)

plus[4] *conj* AND : y

plush[1] ['plʌʃ] *adj* 1 : afelpado 2 LUXURIOUS : lujoso

plush[2] *n* : felpa *f*, peluche *m*

plushy ['plʌʃi] *plushier*; **-est** : lujoso

Pluto ['plu:to] *n* : Plutón *m*

plutocracy [plu:ˈtɑkrəsi] *n*, *pl* **-cies** : plutocracia *f*

plutonium [plu:ˈto:niəm] *n* : plutonio *m*

ply[1] ['plaɪ] *v* **plied**; **plying** *vt* 1 USE, WIELD : manejar ⟨to ply an ax : manejar un hacha⟩ 2 PRACTICE : ejercer ⟨to ply a trade : ejercer un oficio⟩ 3 to ply with questions : acosar con preguntas

ply[2] *n*, *pl* **plies** 1 LAYER : chapa *f* (de madera), capa *f* (de papel) 2 STRAND : cabo *m* (de hilo, etc.)

plywood ['plaɪ,wʊd] *n* : contrachapado *m*

pneumatic [nʊˈmætɪk, njʊ-] *adj* : neumático

pneumonia [nʊˈmo:njə, njʊ-] *n* : pulmonía *f*, neumonía *f*

poach ['po:tʃ] *vt* 1 : cocer a fuego lento ⟨to poach an egg : escalfar un huevo⟩ 2 to poach game : cazar ilegalmente — *vi* : cazar ilegalmente

poacher ['po:tʃər] *n* : cazador *m* furtivo, cazadora *f* furtiva

pock ['pɑk] *n* 1 PUSTULE : pústula *f* 2 → pockmark

pocket[1] ['pɑkət] *vt* 1 : meterse en el bolsillo ⟨he pocketed the pen : se metió la pluma en el bolsillo⟩ 2 STEAL : embolsarse

pocket[2] *n* 1 : bolsillo *m*, bolsa *f Mex* ⟨a coat pocket : el bolsillo de un abrigo⟩ ⟨air pockets : bolsas de aire⟩ 2 CENTER : foco *m*, centro *m* ⟨a pocket of resistance : un foco de resistencia⟩

pocketbook ['pɑkət,bʊk] *n* 1 PURSE : cartera *f*, bolso *m*, bolsa *f Mex* 2 MEANS : recursos *mpl*

pocketknife ['pɑkət,naɪf] *n*, *pl* **-knives** : navaja *f*

pocket–size ['pɑkət'saɪz] *adj* : de bolsillo

pockmark ['pɑk,mɑrk] *n* : cicatriz *f* de viruela, viruela *f*

pod ['pɑd] *n* : vaina *f* ⟨pea pod : vaina de guisantes⟩

podiatrist [pəˈdaɪətrɪst, po-] *n* : podólogo *m*, -ga *f*

podiatry [pəˈdaɪətri, po-] *n* : podología *f*, podiatría *f*

podium ['po:diəm] *n*, *pl* **-diums** *or* **-dia** [-diə] : podio *m*, estrado *m*, tarima *f*

poem ['po:əm] *n* : poema *m*, poesía *f*

poet ['po:ət] *n* : poeta *mf*

poetic [po'ɛtɪk] *or* **poetical** [-tɪkəl] *adj* : poético

poetry ['po:ətri] *n* : poesía *f*

pogrom ['po:grəm, pəˈgrʌm, 'pɑgrəm] *n* : pogrom *m*

poignancy ['pɔɪnjənsi] *n*, *pl* **-cies** : lo conmovedor

poignant ['pɔɪnjənt] *adj* 1 PAINFUL : penoso, doloroso ⟨poignant grief : profundo dolor⟩ 2 TOUCHING : conmovedor, emocionante

poinsettia [pɔɪnˈsɛtiə, -ˈsɛtə] *n* : flor *f* de Nochebuena

point[1] ['pɔɪnt] *vt* 1 SHARPEN : afilar (la punta de) 2 INDICATE : señalar, indicar ⟨to point the way : señalar el camino⟩ 3 AIM : apuntar 4 to point out : señalar, indicar — *vi* 1 to point at : señalar (con el dedo) 2 to point to INDICATE : señalar, indicar

point[2] *n* 1 ITEM : punto *m* ⟨the main points : los puntos principales⟩ 2 QUALITY : cualidad *f* ⟨her good points : sus buenas cualidades⟩ ⟨it's not his strong point : no es su (punto) fuerte⟩ 3 (*indicating a chief idea or meaning*) ⟨it's beside the point : no viene al caso⟩ ⟨to get to the point : ir al grano⟩ ⟨to stick to the point : no salirse del tema⟩ 4 PURPOSE : fin *m*, propósito *m* ⟨there's no point to it : no vale la pena, no sirve para nada⟩ 5 PLACE : punto *m*, lugar *m* ⟨points of interest : puntos interesantes⟩ 6 : punto *m* (en una escala) ⟨boiling point : punto de ebullición⟩ 7 MOMENT : momento *m*, coyuntura *f* ⟨at this point : en este momento⟩ 8 TIP : punta *f* 9 HEADLAND : punta *f*, cabo *m* 10 PERIOD : punto *m* (marca de puntuación) 11 UNIT : punto *m* ⟨he scored 15 points : ganó 15 puntos⟩ ⟨shares fell 10 points : las acciones bajaron 10 enteros⟩ 12 compass points : puntos *mpl* cardinales 13 decimal point : punto *m* decimal, coma *f*

point–blank[1] ['pɔɪnt'blæŋk] *adv* 1 : a quemarropa ⟨to shoot point-blank : disparar a quemarropa⟩ 2 BLUNTLY, DIRECTLY : a bocajarro, sin rodeos, francamente

point–blank[2] *adj* 1 : a quemarropa ⟨point-blank shots : disparos a quemarropa⟩ 2 BLUNT, DIRECT : directo, franco

pointed ['pɔɪntəd] *adj* **1** POINTY : puntiagudo **2** PERTINENT : atinado **3** CONSPICUOUS : marcado, manifiesto

pointedly ['pɔɪntədli] *adv* : intencionadamente, directamente

pointer ['pɔɪntər] *n* **1** STICK : puntero *m* (para maestros, etc.) **2** INDICATOR, NEEDLE : indicador *m*, aguja *f* **3** : perro *m* de muestra **4** HINT, TIP : consejo *m*

pointless ['pɔɪntləs] *adj* : inútil, ocioso, vano ⟨it's pointless to continue : no tiene sentido continuar⟩

point of view *n* : perspectiva *f*, punto *m* de vista

pointy ['pɔɪnti] *adj* : puntiagudo

poise[1] ['pɔɪz] *vt* **poised; poising** BALANCE : equilibrar, balancear

poise[2] *n* : aplomo *m*, compostura *f*

poison[1] ['pɔɪzən] *vt* **1** : envenenar, intoxicar **2** CORRUPT : corromper

poison[2] *n* : veneno *m*

poison ivy *n* : hiedra *f* venenosa

poisonous ['pɔɪzənəs] *adj* : venenoso, tóxico, ponzoñoso

poke[1] ['po:k] *v* **poked; poking** *vt* **1** JAB : golpear (con la punta de algo), dar ⟨he poked me with his finger : me dio con el dedo⟩ **2** THRUST : introducir, asomar ⟨I poked my head out the window : asomé la cabeza por la ventana⟩ — *vi* **1 to poke around** RUMMAGE : hurgar **2 to poke along** DAWDLE : demorarse, entretenerse

poke[2] *n* : golpe *m* abrupto (con la punta de algo)

poker ['po:kər] *n* **1** : atizador *m* (para el fuego) **2** : póker *m*, poker *m* (juego de naipes)

polar ['po:lər] *adj* : polar

polar bear *n* : oso *m* blanco

Polaris [po'lærɪs, -'lar-] → North Star

polarize ['po:lə,raɪz] *vt* **-ized; -izing** : polarizar

pole ['po:l] *n* **1** : palo *m*, poste *m*, vara *f* ⟨telephone pole : poste de teléfonos⟩ **2** : polo *m* ⟨the South Pole : el Polo Sur⟩ **3** : polo *m* (eléctrico o magnético)

Pole ['po:l] *n* : polaco *m*, -ca *f*

polecat ['po:l,kæt] *n, pl* **polecats** *or* **polecat 1** : turón *m* (de Europa) **2** SKUNK : mofeta *f*, zorrillo *m*

polemical [pə'lɛmɪkəl] *adj* : polémico

polemics [pə'lɛmɪks] *ns & pl* : polémica *f*

polestar ['po:l,star] → North Star

police[1] [pə'li:s] *vt* **-liced; -licing** : mantener el orden en ⟨to police the streets : patrullar las calles⟩

police[2] *ns & pl* **1** : policía *f* (organización) **2** POLICE OFFICERS : policías *mfpl*

policeman [pə'li:smən] *n, pl* **-men** [-mən, -,mɛn] : policía *m*

police officer *n* : policía *mf*, agente *mf* de policía

policewoman [pə'li:s,wʊmən] *n, pl* **-women** [-,wɪmən] : policía *f*, mujer *f* policía

policy ['paləsi] *n, pl* **-cies 1** : política *f* ⟨foreign policy : política exterior⟩ **2 or insurance policy** : póliza *f* de seguros, seguro *m*

polio[1] ['po:li,o:] *adj* : de polio ⟨polio vaccine : vacuna contra la polio⟩

polio[2] *n* → **poliomyelitis**

poliomyelitis [,po:li,o:,maɪə'laɪtəs] *n* : poliomielitis *f*, polio *f*

polish[1] ['palɪʃ] *vt* **1** : pulir, lustrar, sacar brillo a ⟨to polish one's nails : pintarse las uñas⟩ **2** REFINE : pulir, perfeccionar

polish[2] *n* **1** LUSTER : brillo *m*, lustre *m* **2** REFINEMENT : refinamiento *m* **3** : betún *m* (para zapatos), cera *f* (para suelos y muebles), esmalte *m* (para las uñas)

Polish[1] ['po:lɪʃ] *adj* : polaco

Polish[2] *n* : polaco *m* (idioma)

polite [pə'laɪt] *adj* **-liter; -est** : cortés, correcto, educado

politely [pə'laɪtli] *adv* : cortésmente, correctamente, con buenos modales

politeness [pə'laɪtnəs] *n* : cortesía *f*

politic ['palə,tɪk] *adj* : diplomático, prudente

political [pə'lɪtɪkəl] *adj* : político — **politically** [-tɪkli] *adv*

politician [,palə'tɪʃən] *n* : político *m*, -ca *f*

politics ['palə,tɪks] *ns & pl* : política *f*

polka ['po:lkə, 'po:kə] *n* : polka *f*

polka dot ['po:kə,dat] *n* : lunar *m* (en un diseño)

poll[1] ['po:l] *vt* **1** : obtener (votos) ⟨she polled over 1000 votes : obtuvo más de 1000 votos⟩ **2** CANVASS : encuestar, sondear — *vi* : obtener votos

poll[2] *n* **1** SURVEY : encuesta *f*, sondeo *m* **2 polls** *npl* : urnas *fpl* ⟨to go to the polls : acudir a las urnas, ir a votar⟩

pollen ['palən] *n* : polen *m*

pollinate ['palə,neɪt] *vt* **-nated; -nating** : polinizar

pollination [,palə'neɪʃən] *n* : polinización *f*

pollster ['po:lstər] *n* : encuestador *m*, -dora *f*

pollutant [pə'lu:tənt] *n* : contaminante *m*

pollute [pə'lu:t] *vt* **-luted; -luting** : contaminar

pollution [pə'lu:ʃən] *n* : contaminación *f*

pollywog *or* **polliwog** ['pali,wɔg] *n* TADPOLE : renacuajo *m*

polo ['po:,lo:] *n* : polo *m*

poltergeist ['po:ltər,gaɪst] *n* : poltergeist *m*, fantasma *m* travieso

polyester ['pali,ɛstər, ,pali'-] *n* : poliéster *m*

polygamous [pə'lɪgəməs] *adj* : polígamo

polygamy [pə'lɪgəmi] *n* : poligamia *f*

polygon ['pali,gan] *n* : polígono *m*

polymer ['paləmər] n : polímero m

Polynesian [,palə'ni:ʒən, -ʃən] n : polinesio m, -sia f — **Polynesian** adj

polyunsaturated [,pali,ʌn'sætʃə-,reɪtəd] adj : poliinsaturado

pomegranate ['pamə,grænət, 'pam-,grænət] n : granada f (fruta)

pommel¹ ['pʌməl] vt → **pummel**

pommel² ['pʌməl, 'pa-] n 1 : pomo m (de una espada) 2 : perilla f (de una silla de montar)

pomp ['pamp] n 1 SPLENDOR : pompa f, esplendor m 2 OSTENTATION : boato m, ostentación f

pom–pom ['pam,pam] n : borla f, pompón m

pomposity [pam'pasəti] n, pl -ties : pomposidad f

pompous ['pampəs] adj : pomposo — **pompously** adv

poncho ['pan,tʃo] n, pl -chos : poncho m

pond ['pand] n : charca f (natural), estanque m (artificial)

ponder ['pandər] vt : reflexionar, considerar — vi to ponder over : reflexionar sobre, sopesar

ponderous ['pandərəs] adj : pesado

pontiff ['pantɪf] n POPE : pontífice m

pontificate [pan'tɪfə,keɪt] vi -cated; -cating : pontificar

pontoon [pan'tu:n] n : pontón m

pony ['poni] n, pl -nies : poni m, poney m, jaca f

ponytail ['po:ni,teɪl] n : cola f de caballo, coleta f

poodle ['pu:dəl] n : caniche m

pool¹ ['pu:l] vt : mancomunar, hacer un fondo común de

pool² n 1 : charca f ⟨a swimming pool : una piscina⟩ 2 PUDDLE : charco m 3 RESERVE, SUPPLY : fondo m común (de recursos), reserva f 4 : billar m (juego)

poor ['pur, 'por] adj 1 : pobre ⟨poor people : los pobres⟩ 2 SCANTY : pobre, escaso ⟨poor attendance : baja asistencia⟩ 3 UNFORTUNATE : pobre ⟨poor thing! : ¡pobrecito!⟩ 4 BAD : malo ⟨to be in poor health : estar mal de salud⟩

poorly ['purli, 'por-] adv : mal

pop¹ ['pap] v popped; popping vi 1 BURST : reventarse, estallar 2 : ir, venir, o aparecer abruptamente ⟨he popped into the house : se metió en la casa⟩ ⟨a menu pops up : aparece un menú⟩ 3 to pop out PROTRUDE : salirse, saltarse ⟨my eyes popped out of my head : se me saltaban los ojos⟩ — vt 1 BURST : reventar 2 : hacer o meter abruptamente ⟨he popped it into his mouth : se lo metió en la boca⟩

pop² adj : popular ⟨pop music : música popular⟩

pop³ n 1 : estallido m pequeño (de un globo, etc.) 2 SODA : refresco m, gaseosa f

popcorn ['pap,kərn] n : palomitas fpl (de maíz)

pope ['po:p] n : papa m ⟨Pope John : el Papa Juan⟩

poplar ['paplər] n : álamo m

poplin ['paplɪn] n : popelín m, popelina f

poppy ['papi] n, pl -pies : amapola f

populace ['papjələs] n 1 MASSES : pueblo m 2 POPULATION : población f

popular ['papjələr] adj 1 : popular ⟨the popular vote : el voto popular⟩ 2 COMMON : generalizado, común ⟨popular beliefs : creencias generalizadas⟩ 3 : popular, de gran popularidad ⟨a popular singer : un cantante popular⟩

popularity [,papjə'lærəti] n : popularidad f

popularize ['papjələ,raɪz] vt -ized; -izing : popularizar

popularly ['papjələrli] adv : popularmente, vulgarmente

populate ['papjə,leɪt] vt -lated; -lating : poblar

population [,papjə'leɪʃən] n : población f

populist ['papjəlɪst] n : populista mf — **populist** adj

populous ['papjələs] adj : populoso

porcelain ['porsələn] n : porcelana f

porch ['portʃ] n : porche m

porcupine ['porkjə,paɪn] n : puerco m espín

pore¹ ['por] vi pored; poring 1 GAZE : mirar (con atención) 2 to pore over : leer detenidamente, estudiar

pore² n : poro m

pork ['pork] n : carne f de cerdo, carne f de puerco

pornographic [,pornə'græfɪk] adj : pornográfico

pornography [por'nagrəfi] n : pornografía f

porous ['porəs] adj : poroso

porpoise ['porpəs] n 1 : marsopa f 2 DOLPHIN : delfín m

porridge ['porɪdʒ] n : sopa f espesa de harina, gachas fpl

port¹ ['port] adj : de babor ⟨on the port side : a babor⟩

port² n 1 HARBOR : puerto m 2 ORIFICE : orificio m (de una válvula, etc.) 3 : puerto m (de una computadora) 4 PORTHOLE : portilla f 5 or port side : babor m (de un barco) 6 : oporto m (vino)

portable ['portəbəl] adj : portátil

portal ['portəl] n : portal m

portend [por'tend] vt : presagiar, augurar

portent ['por,tent] n : presagio m, augurio m

portentous [por'tentəs] adj : profético, que presagia

porter ['portər] n : maletero m, mozo m (de estación)

portfolio [port'fo:li,o] n, pl -lios 1 FOLDER : cartera f (para llevar papeles), carpeta f 2 : cartera f (diplomática) **3** investment **portfolio** : cartera de inversiones

porthole ['port,ho:l] n : portilla f (de un barco), ventanilla f (de un avión)

portico ['port_iko] n, pl **-coes** or **-cos** : pórtico m

portion[1] ['porʃən] vt DISTRIBUTE : repartir

portion[2] n PART, SHARE : porción f, parte f

portly ['portli] adj **-lier; -est** : corpulento

portrait ['portrət, -,treit] n : retrato m

portray [por'trei] vt **1** DEPICT : representar, retratar **2** DESCRIBE : describir **3** PLAY : interpretar (un personaje)

portrayal [por'treiəl] n **1** REPRESENTATION : representación f **2** PORTRAIT : retrato m

Portuguese [,portʃə'gi:z, -'gi:s] n **1** : portugués m, -guesa f (persona) **2** : portugués m (idioma) — **Portuguese** adj

pose[1] ['po:z] v **posed; posing** vt PRESENT : plantear (una pregunta, etc.), representar (una amenaza) — vi **1** : posar (para una foto, etc.) **2 to pose as** : hacerse pasar por

pose[2] n **1** : pose f ⟨to strike a pose : asumir una pose⟩ **2** PRETENSE : pose f, afectación f

posh ['paʃ] adj : elegante, de lujo

position[1] [pə'zɪʃən] vt : colocar, situar, ubicar

position[2] n **1** APPROACH, STANCE : posición f, postura f, planteamiento m **2** LOCATION : posición f, ubicación f **3** STATUS : posición f (en una jerarquía) **4** JOB : puesto m

positive ['pazətɪv] adj **1** DEFINITE : incuestionable, inequívoco ⟨positive evidence : pruebas irrefutables⟩ **2** CONFIDENT : seguro **3** : positivo (en gramática, matemáticas, y física) **4** AFFIRMATIVE : positivo, afirmativo ⟨a positive response : una respuesta positiva⟩

positively ['pazətɪvli] adv **1** FAVORABLY : favorablemente **2** OPTIMISTICALLY : positivamente **3** DEFINITELY : definitivamente, en forma concluyente **4** (used for emphasis) : realmente, verdaderamente ⟨it's positively awful! : ¡es verdaderamente malo!⟩

possess [pə'zɛs] vt **1** HAVE, OWN : poseer, tener **2** SEIZE : apoderarse de ⟨he was possessed by fear : el miedo se apoderó de él⟩

possession [pə'zɛʃən] n **1** POSSESSING : posesión f **2** : posesión f (por un demonio, etc.) **3 possessions** npl PROPERTY : bienes mpl, propiedad f

possessive[1] [pə'zɛsɪv] adj **1** : posesivo (en gramática) **2** JEALOUS : posesivo, celoso

possessive[2] n or **possessive case** : posesivo m

possessor [pə'zɛsər] n : poseedor m, -dora f

possibility [,pasə'bɪləti] n, pl **-ties** : posibilidad f

possible ['pasəbəl] adj : posible

possibly ['pasəbli] adv **1** CONCEIVABLY : posiblemente ⟨it can't possibly be true! : ¡no puede ser!⟩ **2** PERHAPS : quizás, posiblemente

possum ['pasəm] → **opossum**

post[1] ['po:st] vt **1** MAIL : echar al correo, mandar por correo **2** ANNOUNCE : anunciar ⟨they've posted the grades : han anunciado las notas⟩ **3** AFFIX : fijar, poner (noticias, etc.) **4** STATION : apostar **5 to keep (someone) posted** : tener al corriente (a alguien)

post[2] n **1** POLE : poste m, palo m **2** STATION : puesto m **3** CAMP : puesto m (militar) **4** JOB, POSITION : puesto m, empleo m, cargo m

postage ['po:stɪʤ] n : franqueo m

postal ['po:stəl] adj : postal

postcard ['po:st,kard] n : postal f, tarjeta f postal

poster ['po:stər] n : póster m, cartel m, afiche m

posterior[1] [pa'stiriər, po-] adj : posterior

posterior[2] n BUTTOCKS : trasero m, nalgas fpl, asentaderas fpl

posterity [pa'stɛrəti] n : posteridad f

postgraduate[1] [,po:st'græʤuət] adj : de postgrado

postgraduate[2] n : postgraduado m, -da f

posthaste ['po:st'heist] adv : a toda prisa

posthumous ['pasʧəməs] adj : póstumo — **posthumously** adv

postman ['po:stmən, -,mæn] → **mailman**

postmark[1] ['po:st,mark] vt : matasellar

postmark[2] n : matasellos m

postmaster ['po:st,mæstər] n : administrador m, -dora f de correos

postmodern [,po:st'madərn] adj : posmoderno

postmortem [,po:st'mortəm] n : autopsia f

postnatal [,po:st'neitəl] adj : postnatal ⟨postnatal depression : depresión posparto⟩

post office n : correo m, oficina f de correos

postoperative [,po:st'apərətɪv, -,rei-] adj : posoperatorio

postpaid [,po:st'peid] adv : con franqueo pagado

postpone [,po:st'po:n] vt **-poned; -poning** : postergar, aplazar, posponer

postponement [,po:st'po:nmənt] n : postergación f, aplazamiento m

postscript ['po:st,skrɪpt] n : postdata f, posdata f

postulate ['pasʧə,leit] vt **-lated; -lating** : postular

posture[1] ['pasʧər] vi **-tured; -turing** : posar, asumir una pose

posture[2] n : postura f

postwar [,po:st'wor] adj : de (la) posguerra

posy · prairie

posy ['po:zi] *n, pl* **-sies 1** FLOWER : flor *f* **2** BOUQUET : ramo *m*, ramillete *m*
pot¹ ['pɑt] *vt* **potted; potting :** plantar (en una maceta)
pot² *n* **1 :** olla *f* (de cocina) **2 pots and pans :** cacharros *mpl*
potable ['po:təbəl] *adj* : potable
potash ['pɑt,æʃ] *n* : potasa *f*
potassium [pə'tæsiəm] *n* : potasio *m*
potato [pə'teɪto] *n, pl* **-toes :** papa *f*, patata *f* Spain
potato chips *npl* : papas *fpl* fritas (de bolsa)
potbellied ['pɑt,bɛlid] *adj* : panzón, barrigón *fam*
potbelly ['pɑt,bɛli] *n* : panza *f*, barriga *f*
potency ['po:tənsi] *n, pl* **-cies 1** POWER : fuerza *f*, potencia *f* **2** EFFECTIVENESS : eficacia *f*
potent ['po:tənt] *adj* **1** POWERFUL : potente, poderoso **2** EFFECTIVE : eficaz ⟨a potent medicine : una medicina bien fuerte⟩
potential¹ [pə'tɛntʃəl] *adj* : potencial, posible
potential² *n* **1 :** potencial *m* ⟨growth potential : potencial de crecimiento⟩ ⟨a child with potential : un niño que promete⟩ **2 :** potencial *m* (eléctrico) — **potentially** *adv*
potful ['pɑt,fʊl] *n* : contenido *m* de una olla ⟨a potful of water : una olla de agua⟩
pothole ['pɑt,ho:l] *n* : bache *m*
potion ['po:ʃən] *n* : brebaje *m*, poción *f*
potluck ['pɑt,lʌk] *n* **to take potluck :** tomar lo que haya
potpourri [,po:pu'ri:] *n* : popurrí *m*
potshot ['pɑt,ʃɑt] *n* **1 :** tiro *m* al azar ⟨to take potshots at : disparar al azar a⟩ **2** CRITICISM : crítica *f* (hecha al azar)
potter ['pɑtər] *n* : alfarero *m*, -ra *f*
pottery ['pɑtəri] *n, pl* **-teries :** cerámica *f*
pouch ['paʊtʃ] *n* **1** BAG : bolsa *f* pequeña **2 :** bolsa *f* (de un animal)
poultice ['po:ltəs] *n* : emplasto *m*, cataplasma *f*
poultry ['po:ltri] *n* : aves *fpl* de corral
pounce ['paʊnts] *vi* **pounced; pouncing :** abalanzarse
pound¹ ['paʊnd] *vt* **1** CRUSH : machacar, machucar, majar **2** BEAT : golpear, machacar ⟨she pounded the lessons into them : les machacaba las lecciones⟩ ⟨he pounded home his point : les hizo entender su razonamiento⟩ — *vi* **1** BEAT : palpitar (dícese del corazón) **2** RESOUND : retumbar, resonar **3 :** andar con paso pesado ⟨we pounded through the mud : caminamos pesadamente por el barro⟩
pound² *n* **1 :** libra *f* (unidad de peso) **2 :** libra *f* (unidad monetaria) **3 dog pound :** perrera *f*
pour ['por] *vt* **1 :** echar, verter, servir (bebidas) ⟨pour it into a pot : viértalo

en una olla⟩ **2 :** proveer con abundancia ⟨they poured money into it : le invirtieron mucho dinero⟩ **3 to pour out :** dar salida a ⟨he poured out his feelings to her : se desahogó con ella⟩ — *vi* **1** FLOW : manar, fluir, salir ⟨blood was pouring from the wound : la sangre le salía de la herida⟩ **2 it's pouring (outside) :** está lloviendo a cántaros
pout¹ ['paʊt] *vi* : hacer pucheros
pout² *n* : puchero *m*
poverty ['pɑvərti] *n* : pobreza *f*, indigencia *f*
powder¹ ['paʊdər] *vt* **1 :** empolvar ⟨to powder one's face : empolvarse la cara⟩ **2** PULVERIZE : pulverizar
powder² *n* : polvo *m*, polvos *mpl*
powdery ['paʊdəri] *adj* : polvoriento, como polvo
power¹ ['paʊər] *vt* : impulsar, propulsar
power² *n* **1** AUTHORITY : poder *m*, autoridad *f* ⟨executive powers : poderes ejecutivos⟩ **2** ABILITY : capacidad *f*, poder *m* **3 :** potencia *f* (política) ⟨foreign powers : potencias extranjeras⟩ **4** STRENGTH : fuerza *f* **5 :** potencia *f* (en física y matemáticas)
powerful ['paʊərfəl] *adj* : poderoso, potente — **powerfully** *adv*
powerhouse ['paʊər,haʊs] *n* : persona *f* dinámica
powerless ['paʊərləs] *adj* : impotente
power plant *n* : central *f* eléctrica
powwow ['paʊ,waʊ] *n* : conferencia *f*
pox ['pɑks] *n, pl* **pox** *or* **poxes 1** CHICKEN POX : varicela *f* **2** SYPHILIS : sífilis *f*
practicable ['præktɪkəbəl] *adj* : practicable, viable, factible
practical ['præktɪkəl] *adj* : práctico
practicality [,præktɪ'kæləti] *n, pl* **-ties** : factibilidad *f*, viabilidad *f*
practical joke *n* : broma *f* (pesada)
practically ['præktɪkli] *adv* **1 :** de manera práctica **2** ALMOST : casi, prácticamente
practice¹ *or* **practise** ['præktəs] *vt* **-ticed** *or* **-tised; -ticing** *or* **-tising 1 :** practicar ⟨he practiced his German on us : practicó el alemán con nosotros⟩ ⟨to practice politeness : practicar la cortesía⟩ **2 :** ejercer ⟨to practice medicine : ejercer la medicina⟩
practice² *n* **1** USE : práctica *f* ⟨to put into practice : poner en práctica⟩ **2** CUSTOM : costumbre *f* ⟨it's a common practice here : por aquí se acostumbra hacerlo⟩ **3** TRAINING : práctica *f* **4 :** ejercicio *m* (de una profesión)
practitioner [præk'tɪʃənər] *n* **1 :** profesional *mf* **2 general practitioner** : médico *m*, -ca *f*
pragmatic [præg'mætɪk] *adj* : pragmático — **pragmatically** *adv*
pragmatism ['prægmə,tɪzəm] *n* : pragmatismo
prairie ['preri] *n* : pradera *f*, llanura *f*

praise[1] ['preɪz] *vt* **praised; praising** : elogiar, alabar ⟨to praise God : alabar a Dios⟩

praise[2] *n* : elogio *m*, alabanza *f*

praiseworthy ['preɪz,wərði] *adj* : digno de alabanza, loable

prance[1] ['prænts] *vi* **pranced; prancing** **1** : hacer cabriolas, cabriolar ⟨a prancing horse : un caballo haciendo cabriolas⟩ **2** SWAGGER : pavonearse

prance[2] *n* : cabriola *f*

prank ['præŋk] *n* : broma *f*, travesura *f*

prankster ['præŋkstər] *n* : bromista *mf*

prattle[1] ['prætəl] *vt* **-tled; -tling** : parlotear *fam*, cotorrear *fam*, balbucear (como un niño)

prattle[2] *n* : parloteo *m fam*, cotorreo *m fam*, cháchara *f fam*

prawn ['prɔn] *n* : langostino *m*, camarón *m*, gamba *f*

pray ['preɪ] *vt* ENTREAT : rogar, suplicar — *vi* : rezar

prayer ['prɛr] *n* **1** : plegaria *f*, oración *f* ⟨to say one's prayers : orar, rezar⟩ ⟨the Lord's Prayer : el Padrenuestro⟩ **2** PRAYING : rezo *m*, oración *f* ⟨to kneel in prayer : arrodillarse para rezar⟩

praying mantis → mantis

preach ['pri:tʃ] *vi* : predicar — *vt* ADVOCATE : abogar por ⟨to preach cooperation : promover la cooperación⟩

preacher ['pri:tʃər] *n* **1** : predicador *m*, -dora *f* **2** MINISTER : pastor *m*, -tora *f*

preamble ['pri:,æmbəl] *n* : preámbulo *m*

prearrange [,pri:ə'reɪndʒ] *vt* **-ranged; -ranging** : arreglar de antemano

precarious [prɪ'kæriəs] *adj* : precario — **precariously** *adv*

precariousness [prɪ'kæriəsnəs] *n* : precariedad *f*

precaution [prɪ'kɔʃən] *n* : precaución *f*

precautionary [prɪ'kɔʃə,nɛri] *adj* : preventivo, cautelar, precautorio

precede [prɪ'si:d] *v* **-ceded; -ceding** : preceder a

precedence ['prɛsədənts, prɪ'si:dənts] *n* : precedencia *f*

precedent ['prɛsədənt] *n* : precedente *m*

precept ['pri:,sɛpt] *n* : precepto *m*

precinct ['pri:,sɪŋkt] *n* **1** DISTRICT : distrito *m* (policial, electoral, etc.) **2 precincts** *npl* PREMISES : recinto *m*, predio *m*, límites *mpl* (de una ciudad)

precious ['prɛʃəs] *adj* **1** : precioso ⟨precious gems : piedras preciosas⟩ **2** DEAR : querido **3** AFFECTED : afectado

precipice ['prɛsəpəs] *n* : precipicio *m*

precipitate [prɪ'sɪpə,teɪt] *v* **-tated; -tating** *vt* **1** HASTEN, PROVOKE : precipitar, provocar **2** HURL : arrojar **3** : precipitar (en química) — *vi* : precipitarse (en química), condensarse (en meteorología)

precipitation [prɪ,sɪpə'teɪʃən] *n* **1** HASTE : precipitación *f*, prisa *f* **2** : precipitaciones *fpl* (en meteorología)

precipitous [prɪ'sɪpətəs] *adj* **1** HASTY, RASH : precipitado **2** STEEP : escarpa-

do, empinado ⟨a precipitous drop : una caída vertiginosa⟩

précis [preɪ'si:] *n, pl* **précis** [-'si:z] : resumen *m*

precise [prɪ'saɪs] *adj* **1** DEFINITE : preciso, explícito **2** EXACT : exacto, preciso ⟨precise calculations : cálculos precisos⟩ — **precisely** *adv*

preciseness [prɪ'saɪsnəs] *n* : precisión *f*, exactitud *f*

precision [prɪ'sɪʒən] *n* : precisión *f*

preclude [prɪ'klu:d] *vt* **-cluded; -cluding** : evitar, impedir, excluir (una posibilidad, etc.)

precocious [prɪ'koʃəs] *adj* : precoz — **precociously** *adv*

precocity [prɪ'kɑsəti] *n* : precocidad *f*

preconceive [,pri:kən'si:v] *vt* **-ceived; -ceiving** : preconcebir

preconception [,pri:kən'spʃən] *n* : idea *f* preconcebida

precondition [,pri:kən'dɪʃən] *n* : precondición *f*, condición *f* previa

precook [,pri:'kʊk] *vt* : precocinar

precursor [prɪ'kərsər] *n* : precursor *m*, -sora *f*

predator ['prɛdətər] *n* : depredador *m*, -dora *f*

predatory ['prɛdə,tori] *adj* : depredador

predecessor ['prɛdə,sɛsər, 'pri:-] *n* : antecesor *m*, -sora *f*; predecesor *m*, -sora *f*

predestination [,pri:,dɛstə'neɪʃən] *n* : predestinación *f*

predestine [pri:'dɛstən] *vt* **-tined; -tining** : predestinar

predetermine [,pri:dɪ'tərmən] *vt* **-mined; -mining** : predeterminar

predicament [prɪ'dɪkəmənt] *n* : apuro *m*, aprieto *m*

predicate[1] ['prɛdə,keɪt] *vt* **-cated; -cating 1** AFFIRM : afirmar, aseverar **2 to be predicated on** : estar basado en

predicate[2] ['prɛdɪkət] *n* : predicado *m*

predict [prɪ'dɪkt] *vt* : pronosticar, predecir

predictable [prɪ'dɪktəbəl] *adj* : previsible — **predictably** [-bli] *adv*

prediction [prɪ'dɪkʃən] *n* : pronóstico *m*, predicción *f*

predilection [,prɛdəl'ɛkʃən, ,pri:-] *n* : predilección *f*

predispose [,pri:dɪ'spo:z] *vt* **-posed; -posing** : predisponer

predisposition [pri:,dɪspə'zɪʃən] *n* : predisposición *f*

predominance [prɪ'dɑmənənts] *n* : predominio *m*

predominant [prɪ'dɑmənənt] *adj* : predominante — **predominantly** *adv*

predominate [prɪ'dɑmə,neɪt] *vi* **-nated; -nating 1** : predominar (en cantidad) **2** PREVAIL : prevalecer

preeminence [pri:'ɛmənənts] *n* : preeminencia *f*

preeminent [pri:'ɛmənənt] *adj* : preeminente

preeminently [pri:'ɛmənəntli] *adv* : especialmente

preempt [pri'empt] vt 1 APPROPRIATE : apoderarse de, apropiarse de 2 : reemplazar (un programa de televisión, etc.) 3 FORESTALL : adelantarse a (un ataque, etc.)

preen ['pri:n] vt : arreglarse (el pelo, las plumas, etc.)

prefabricated [,pri:'fæbrǝ,keɪtǝd] adj : prefabricado

preface ['prɛfǝs] n : prefacio m, prólogo m

prefatory ['prɛfǝ,tori] adj : preliminar

prefer [pri'fǝr] vt **-ferred; -ferring** 1 : preferir ⟨I prefer coffee : prefiero café⟩ 2 **to prefer charges against** : presentar cargos contra

preferable ['prɛfǝrǝbǝl] adj : preferible

preferably ['prɛfǝrǝbli] adv : preferentemente, de preferencia

preference ['prɛfǝrǝnts, 'prɛfǝr-] : preferencia f, gusto m

preferential [,prɛfǝ'rɛntʃǝl] adj : preferencial, preferente

prefigure [pri'fɪgjǝr] vt **-ured; -uring** FORESHADOW : prefigurar, anunciar

prefix ['pri:,fɪks] n : prefijo m

pregnancy ['prɛgnǝntsi] n, pl **-cies** : embarazo m, preñez f

pregnant ['prɛgnǝnt] adj 1 : embarazada (dícese de una mujer), preñada (dícese de un animal) 2 MEANINGFUL : significativo

preheat [,pri:'hi:t] vt : precalentar

prehensile [pri'hɛntsǝl, -'hɛn,saɪl] adj : prensil

prehistoric [,pri:hɪs'tɔrɪk] or **prehistorical** [-ɪkǝl] adj : prehistórico

prejudge [,pri:'dʒʌdʒ] vt **-judged; -judging** : prejuzgar

prejudice[1] ['prɛdʒǝdǝs] vt **-diced; -dicing** 1 DAMAGE : perjudicar 2 BIAS : predisponer, influir en

prejudice[2] n 1 DAMAGE : perjuicio m (en derecho) 2 BIAS : prejuicio m

prelate ['prɛlǝt] n : prelado m

preliminary[1] [pri'lɪmǝ,nɛri] adj : preliminar

preliminary[2] n, pl **-naries** 1 : preámbulo m, preludio m 2 **preliminaries** npl : preliminares mpl

prelude ['prɛ,lu:d, 'prɛl,ju:d, 'preɪ,lu:d, 'pri:-] n : preludio m

premarital [,pri:'mærǝtǝl] adj : prematrimonial

premature [,pri:mǝ'tʊr, -'tjʊr, -'tʃʊr] adj : prematuro — **prematurely** adv

premeditate [pri'mɛdǝ,teɪt] vt **-tated; -tating** : premeditar

premeditation [pri,mɛdǝ'teɪʃǝn] n : premeditación f

premenstrual [pri'mɛntstrʊǝl] adj : premenstrual

premier[1] [pri'mɪr, -'mjɪr; 'pri:miǝr] adj : principal

premier[2] n PRIME MINISTER : primer ministro m, primera ministra f

premiere[1] [pri'mjɛr, -'mɪr] vt **-miered; -miering** : estrenar

premiere[2] n : estreno m

premise ['prɛmɪs] n 1 : premisa f ⟨the premise of his arguments : la premisa de sus argumentos⟩ 2 **premises** npl : recinto m, local m

premium ['pri:miǝm] n 1 BONUS : prima f 2 SURCHARGE : recargo m ⟨to sell at a premium : vender (algo) muy caro⟩ 3 **insurance premium** : prima f (de seguros) 4 **to set a premium on** : darle un gran valor (a algo)

premonition [,pri:mǝ'nɪʃǝn, ,prɛmǝ-] n : presentimiento m, premonición f

prenatal [,pri:'neɪtǝl] adj : prenatal

preoccupation [pri,akjǝ'peɪʃǝn] n : preocupación f

preoccupied [pri'akjǝ,paɪd] adj : abstraído, ensimismado, preocupado

preoccupy [pri'akjǝ,paɪ] vt **-pied; -pying** : preocupar

preparation [,prɛpǝ'reɪʃǝn] n 1 PREPARING : preparación f 2 MIXTURE : preparado m ⟨a preparation for burns : un preparado para quemaduras⟩ 3 **preparations** npl ARRANGEMENTS : preparativos mpl

preparatory [pri'pærǝ,tori] adj : preparatorio

prepare [pri'pær] v **-pared; -paring** vt : preparar — vi : prepararse

prepay [,pri:'peɪ] vt **-paid; -paying** : pagar por adelantado

preponderance [pri'pandǝrǝnts] n : preponderancia f

preponderant [pri'pandǝrǝnt] adj : preponderante — **preponderantly** adv

preposition [,prɛpǝ'zɪʃǝn] n : preposición f

prepositional [,prɛpǝ'zɪʃǝnǝl] adj : preposicional

prepossessing [,pri:pǝ'zɛsɪŋ] adj : atractivo, agradable

preposterous [pri'pastǝrǝs] adj : absurdo, ridículo

prerequisite[1] [pri'rɛkwǝzǝt] adj : necesario, esencial

prerequisite[2] n : condición f necesario, requisito m previo

prerogative [pri'ragǝtɪv] n : prerrogativa f

presage ['prɛsɪdʒ, pri'seɪdʒ] vt **-saged; -saging** : presagiar

preschool [pri'sku:l] adj : preescolar ⟨preschool students : estudiantes de preescolar⟩

prescribe [pri'skraɪb] vt **-scribed; -scribing** 1 ORDAIN : prescribir, ordenar 2 : recetar (medicinas, etc.)

prescription [pri'skrɪpʃǝn] n : receta f

presence ['prɛzǝnts] n : presencia f

present[1] ['prɛzǝnt] vt 1 INTRODUCE : presentar ⟨to present oneself : presentarse⟩ 2 : presentar (una obra de teatro, etc.) 3 GIVE : entregar (un regalo, etc.), regalar, obsequiar 4 SHOW : presentar, ofrecer ⟨it presents a lovely view : ofrece una vista muy linda⟩

present[2] [prɛzǝnt] adj : actual ⟨present conditions : condiciones actuales⟩

2 : presente ⟨all the students were present : todos los estudiantes estaban presentes⟩

present³ ['prɛzənt] *n* **1** GIFT : regalo *m*, obsequio *m* **2** : presente *m* ⟨at present : en este momento⟩ **3** *or* **present tense** : presente *m*

presentable [prɪ'zɛntəbəl] *adj* : presentable

presentation [ˌpriːˌzɛn'teɪʃən, ˌprɛzən-] *n* : presentación *f* ⟨presentation ceremony : ceremonia de entrega⟩

presentiment [prɪ'zɛntəmənt] *n* : presentimiento *m*, premonición *f*

presently ['prɛzəntli] *adv* **1** SOON : pronto, dentro de poco **2** NOW : actualmente, ahora

present participle *n* : participio *m* presente, participio *m* activo

preservation [ˌprɛzər'veɪʃən] *n* : conservación *f*, preservación *f*

preservative [prɪ'zərvətɪv] *n* : conservante *m*

preserve¹ [prɪ'zərv] *vt* **-served; -serving 1** PROTECT : proteger, preservar **2** : conservar (los alimentos, etc.) **3** MAINTAIN : conservar, mantener

preserve² *n* **1** *or* **preserves** *npl* : conserva *f* ⟨peach preserves : duraznos en conserva⟩ **2** : coto *m* ⟨game preserve : coto de caza⟩

preside [prɪ'zaɪd] *vi* **-sided; -siding 1 to preside over** : presidir ⟨he presided over the meeting : presidió la reunión⟩ **2 to preside over** : supervisar ⟨she presides over the department : dirige el departamento⟩

presidency ['prɛzədən/si] *n, pl* **-cies** : presidencia *f*

president ['prɛzədənt] *n* : presidente *m*, -ta *f*

presidential [ˌprɛzə'dɛntʃəl] *adj* : presidencial

press¹ ['prɛs] *vt* **1** PUSH : apretar **2** SQUEEZE : apretar, prensar (frutas, flores, etc.) **3** IRON : planchar (ropa) **4** URGE : instar, apremiar ⟨he pressed me to come : insistió en que viniera⟩ — *vi* **1** PUSH : apretar ⟨press hard : aprieta con fuerza⟩ **2** CROWD : apiñarse **3** : abrirse paso ⟨I pressed through the crowd : me abrí paso entre el gentío⟩ **4** URGE : presionar

press² *n* **1** CROWD : multitud *f* **2** : imprenta *f*, prensa *f* ⟨to go to press : entrar en prensa⟩ **3** URGENCY : urgencia *f*, prisa *f* **4** PRINTER, PUBLISHER : imprenta *f*, editorial *f* **5 the press** : la prensa ⟨freedom of the press : libertad de prensa⟩

pressing ['prɛsɪŋ] *adj* URGENT : urgente

pressure¹ ['prɛʃər] *vt* **-sured; -suring** : presionar, apremiar

pressure² *n* **1** : presión *f* ⟨to be under pressure : estar bajo presión⟩ **2** → **blood pressure**

pressurize ['prɛʃəˌraɪz] *vt* **-ized; -izing** : presurizar

prestige [prɛ'stiːʒ, -'stiːʤ] *n* : prestigio *m*

prestigious [prɛ'stɪʤəs] *adj* : prestigioso

presto ['prɛsˌtoː] *adv* : de pronto

presumably [prɪ'zuːməbli] *adv* : es de suponer, supuestamente ⟨presumably, he's guilty : supone que es culpable⟩

presume [prɪ'zuːm] *vt* **-sumed; -suming 1** ASSUME, SUPPOSE : suponer, asumir, presumir **2 to presume to** : atreverse a, osar

presumption [prɪ'zʌmpʃən] *n* **1** AUDACITY : atrevimiento *m*, osadía *f* **2** ASSUMPTION : presunción *f*, suposición *f*

presumptuous [prɪ'zʌmptʃuəs] *adj* : descarado, atrevido

presuppose [ˌpriːsə'poːz] *vt* **-posed; -posing** : presuponer

pretend [prɪ'tɛnd] *vt* **1** CLAIM : pretender **2** FEIGN : fingir, simular — *vi* : fingir

pretender [prɪ'tɛndər] *n* : pretendiente *mf* (al trono, etc.)

pretense *or* **pretence** ['priːˌtɛns, prɪ'tɛnts] *n* **1** CLAIM : afirmación *f* (falsa), pretensión *f* **2** FEIGNING : fingimiento *m*, simulación *f* ⟨to make a pretense of doing something : fingir hacer algo⟩ ⟨a pretense of order : una apariencia de orden⟩ **3** PRETEXT : pretexto *m* ⟨under false pretenses : con pretextos falsos, de manera fraudulenta⟩

pretension [prɪ'tɛntʃən] *n* **1** CLAIM : pretensión *f*, afirmación *f* **2** ASPIRATION : aspiración *f*, ambición *f* **3** PRETENTIOUSNESS : pretensiones *fpl*, presunción *f*

pretentious [prɪ'tɛntʃəs] *adj* : pretencioso

pretentiousness [prɪ'tɛntʃəsnəs] *n* : presunción *f*, pretensiones *fpl*

pretext ['priːˌtɛkst] *n* : pretexto *m*, excusa *f*

prettily ['prɪtəli] *adv* : atractivamente

prettiness ['prɪtinəs] *n* : lindeza *f*

pretty¹ ['prɪti] *adv* : bastante, bien ⟨it's pretty obvious : está bien claro⟩ ⟨it's pretty much the same : es más o menos igual⟩

pretty² *adj* **-tier; -est** : bonito, lindo, guapo ⟨a pretty girl : una muchacha guapa⟩ ⟨what a pretty dress! : ¡qué vestido más lindo!⟩

pretzel ['prɛtsəl] *n* : galleta *f* salada (en forma de nudo)

prevail [prɪ'veɪl] *vi* **1** TRIUMPH : prevalecer **2** PREDOMINATE : predominar **3 to prevail upon** : persuadir, convencer ⟨I prevailed upon her to sing : la convencí para que cantara⟩

prevailing [prɪ'veɪlɪŋ] *adj* : imperante, prevaleciente

prevalence ['prɛvələn/s] *n* : preponderancia *f*, predominio *m*

prevalent ['prɛvələnt] *adj* **1** COMMON : común y corriente, general **2** WIDESPREAD : extendido

prevaricate [prɪˈværəˌkeɪt] vi -cated; -cating LIE : mentir

prevarication [prɪˌværəˈkeɪʃən] n : mentira f

prevent [prɪˈvɛnt] vt 1 AVOID : prevenir, evitar ⟨steps to prevent war : medidas para evitar la guerra⟩ 2 HINDER : impedir

preventable [prɪˈvɛntəbəl] adj : evitable

preventative [prɪˈvɛntətɪv] → **preventive**

prevention [prɪˈvɛntʃən] n : prevención f

preventive [prɪˈvɛntɪv] adj : preventivo

preview [ˈpriˌvju] n : preestreno m

previous [ˈpriːviəs] adj : previo, anterior ⟨previous knowledge : conocimientos previos⟩ ⟨the previous day : el día anterior⟩ ⟨in the previous year : en el año pasado⟩

previously [ˈpriːviəsli] adv : antes

prewar [ˌpriˈwɔr] adj : de antes de la guerra

prey [ˈpreɪ] n, pl **preys** : presa f

prey on vt 1 : cazar, alimentarse de ⟨it preys on fish : se alimenta de peces⟩ 2 **to prey on one's mind** : hacer presa en alguien, atormentar a alguien

price¹ [ˈpraɪs] vt **priced; pricing** : poner un precio a

price² n : precio m ⟨peace at any price : la paz a toda costa⟩

priceless [ˈpraɪsləs] adj : inestimable, inapreciable

pricey [ˈpraɪsi] adj : caro

prick¹ [ˈprɪk] vt 1 : pinchar 2 **to prick up one's ears** : levantar las orejas — vi : pinchar

prick² n 1 STAB : pinchazo m ⟨a prick of conscience : un remordimiento⟩ 2 → **pricker**

pricker [ˈprɪkər] n THORN : espina f

prickle¹ [ˈprɪkəl] vi -led; -ling : sentir un cosquilleo, tener un hormigueo

prickle² n 1 : espina f (de una planta) 2 TINGLE : cosquilleo m, hormigueo m

prickly [ˈprɪkəli] adj 1 THORNY : espinoso 2 : que pica ⟨a prickly sensation : un hormigueo⟩

prickly pear n : tuna f

pride¹ [ˈpraɪd] vt **prided; priding** : estar orgulloso de ⟨to pride oneself on : preciarse de, enorgullecerse de⟩

pride² n : orgullo m

priest [ˈpriːst] n : sacerdote m, cura m

priestess [ˈpriːstɪs] n : sacerdotisa f

priesthood [ˈpriːstˌhʊd] n : sacerdocio m

priestly [ˈpriːstli] adj : sacerdotal

prig [ˈprɪg] n : mojigato m, -ta f; gazmoño m, -ña f

prim [ˈprɪm] adj **primmer; primmest** 1 PRISSY : remilgado 2 PRUDISH : mojigato, gazmoño

primarily [praɪˈmɛrəli] adv : principalmente, fundamentalmente

primary¹ [ˈpraɪˌmɛri, ˈpraɪməri] adj 1 FIRST : primario 2 PRINCIPAL : principal 3 BASIC : fundamental

primary² n, pl -**ries** : elección f primaria

primary color n : color m primario

primary school n → **elementary school**

primate n 1 [ˈpraɪˌmeɪt, -mət] : primado m (obispo) 2 [-ˌmeɪt] : primate m (animal)

prime¹ [ˈpraɪm] vt **primed; priming** 1 : cebar ⟨to prime a pump : cebar una bomba⟩ 2 PREPARE : preparar (una superficie para pintar) 3 COACH : preparar (a un testigo, etc.)

prime² adj 1 CHIEF, MAIN : principal, primero 2 EXCELLENT : de primera (categoría), excelente

prime³ n **the prime of one's life** : la flor de la vida

prime minister n : primer ministro m, primera ministra f

primer¹ [ˈpraɪmər] n 1 READER : cartilla f 2 MANUAL : manual m

primer² [ˈpraɪmər] n 1 : cebo m (para explosivos) 2 : base f (de pintura)

prime time n : horas fpl de mayor audiencia

primeval [praɪˈmiːvəl] adj : primitivo, primigenio

primitive [ˈprɪmətɪv] adj : primitivo

primly [ˈprɪmli] adv : mojigatamente

primness [ˈprɪmnəs] n : mojigatería f, gazmoñería f

primordial [praɪˈmɔrdiəl] adj : primordial, fundamental

primp [ˈprɪmp] vi : arreglarse, acicalarse

primrose [ˈprɪmˌroːz] n : primavera f, prímula f

prince [ˈprɪnts] n : príncipe m

princely [ˈprɪntsli] adj : principesco

princess [ˈprɪntsəs, ˈprɪnˌsɛs] n : princesa f

principal¹ [ˈprɪntsəpəl] adj : principal — **principally** adv

principal² n 1 PROTAGONIST : protagonista mf 2 : director m, -tora f (de una escuela) 3 CAPITAL : principal m, capital m (en finanzas)

principality [ˌprɪntsəˈpæləti] n, pl -**ties** : principado m

principle [ˈprɪntsəpəl] n : principio m

print¹ [ˈprɪnt] vt : imprimir (libros, etc.) — vi : escribir con letra de molde

print² n 1 IMPRESSION : marca f, huella f, impresión f 2 : texto m impreso ⟨to be out of print : estar agotado⟩ 3 LETTERING : letra f 4 ENGRAVING : grabado m 5 : copia f (en fotografía) 6 : estampado m (de tela)

printer [ˈprɪntər] n 1 : impresor m, -sora f (persona) 2 : impresora f (máquina)

printing [ˈprɪntɪŋ] n 1 : impresión f (acto) ⟨the third printing : la tercera tirada⟩ 2 : imprenta f (profesión) 3 LETTERING : letras fpl de molde

printing press n : prensa f

print out vt : imprimir (de una computadora)

printout [ˈprɪntˌaʊt] n : copia f impresa (de una computadora)

prior [ˈpraɪər] adj 1 : previo 2 **prior to** : antes de

priority [praɪˈɔrətɪ] n, pl **-ties** : prioridad f

priory [ˈpraɪərɪ] n, pl **-ries** : priorato m

prism [ˈprɪzəm] n : prisma m

prison [ˈprɪzən] n : prisión f, cárcel f

prisoner [ˈprɪzənər] n : preso m, -sa f; recluso m, -sa f ⟨prisoner of war : prisionero de guerra⟩

prissy [ˈprɪsɪ] adj **-sier; -est** : remilgado, melindroso

pristine [ˈprɪsˌtiːn, prɪsˈ-] adj : puro, prístino

privacy [ˈpraɪvəsɪ] n, pl **-cies** : privacidad f

private[1] [ˈpraɪvət] adj **1** PERSONAL : privado, particular ⟨private property : propiedad privada⟩ **2** INDEPENDENT : privado, independiente ⟨private studies : estudios privados⟩ **3** SECRET : secreto **4** SECLUDED : aislado, privado — **privately** adv

private[2] n : soldado m raso

privateer [ˌpraɪvəˈtɪr] n : corsario m

privation [praɪˈveɪʃən] n : privación f

privilege [ˈprɪvlɪʤ, ˈprɪvə-] n : privilegio m

privileged [ˈprɪvlɪʤd, ˈprɪvə-] adj : privilegiado

privy[1] [ˈprɪvɪ] adj to be privy to : estar enterado de

privy[2] n, pl **privies** : excusado m, retrete m (exterior)

prize[1] [ˈpraɪz] vt **prized; prizing** : valorar, apreciar

prize[2] adj **1** : premiado ⟨a prize stallion : un semental premiado⟩ **2** OUTSTANDING : de primera, excepcional

prize[3] n **1** AWARD : premio m ⟨third prize : el tercer premio⟩ **2** joya f, tesoro m ⟨he's a real prize : es un tesoro⟩

prizefighter [ˈpraɪzˌfaɪtər] n : boxeador m, -dora f profesional

prizewinning [ˈpraɪzˌwɪnɪŋ] adj : premiado

pro[1] [ˈproː] adv : a favor

pro[2] adj → **professional**[1]

pro[3] n **1** : pro m ⟨the pros and cons : los pros y los contras⟩ **2** → **professional**[2]

probability [ˌprɑbəˈbɪlətɪ] n, pl **-ties** : probabilidad f

probable [ˈprɑbəbəl] adj : probable — **probably** [-blɪ] adv

probate[1] [ˈproːˌbeɪt] vt **-bated; -bating** : autenticar (un testamento)

probate[2] n : autenticación f (de un testamento)

probation [proːˈbeɪʃən] n **1** : período m de prueba (para un empleado, etc.) **2** : libertad f condicional (para un preso)

probationary [proːˈbeɪʃəˌnerɪ] adj : de prueba

probe[1] [ˈproːb] vt **probed; probing** **1** : sondar (en medicina y tecnología) **2** INVESTIGATE : investigar, sondear

probe[2] n **1** : sonda f (en medicina, etc.) ⟨space probe : sonda espacial⟩ **2** INVESTIGATION : investigación f, sondeo m

probity [ˈproːbətɪ] n : probidad f

problem[1] [ˈprɑbləm] adj : difícil

problem[2] n : problema m

problematic [ˌprɑbləˈmætɪk] or **problematical** [-tɪkəl] adj : problemático

proboscis [prəˈbɑsɪs] n, pl **-cises** also **-cides** [-səˌdiːz] : proboscide f

procedural [prəˈsiːʤərəl] adj : de procedimiento

procedure [prəˈsiːʤər] n : procedimiento m ⟨administrative procedures : trámites administrativos⟩

proceed [proːˈsiːd] vi **1** : proceder ⟨to proceed to do something : proceder a hacer algo⟩ **2** CONTINUE : continuar, proseguir, seguir ⟨he proceeded to the next phase : pasó a la segunda fase⟩ **3** ADVANCE : avanzar ⟨as the conference proceeded : mientras seguía avanzando la conferencia⟩ ⟨the road proceeds south : la calle sigue hacia el sur⟩

proceeding [proːˈsiːdɪŋ] n **1** PROCEDURE : procedimiento m **2 proceedings** npl EVENTS : acontecimientos mpl **3 proceedings** npl MINUTES : actas fpl (de una reunión, etc.)

proceeds [ˈproːˌsiːdz] npl : ganancias fpl

process[1] [ˈprɑˌses, ˈproː-] vt : procesar, tratar

process[2] n, pl **-cesses** [ˈprɑˌsesəz, ˈproː-, -səsəz, -səˌsiːz] **1** : proceso m ⟨the process of elimination : el proceso de eliminación⟩ **2** METHOD : proceso m, método m ⟨manufacturing processes : procesos industriales⟩ **3** : acción f judicial ⟨due process of law : el debido proceso (de la ley)⟩ **4** SUMMONS : citación f **5** PROJECTION : protuberancia f (anatómica) **6 in the process of** : en vías de ⟨in the process of repair : en reparaciones⟩

procession [prəˈseʃən] n : procesión f, desfile m ⟨a funeral procession : un cortejo fúnebre⟩

processional [prəˈseʃənəl] n : himno m para una procesión

processor [ˈprɑˌsesər, ˈproː-, -səsər] n **1** : procesador m (de una computadora) **2 food processor** : procesador m de alimentos

proclaim [proːˈkleɪm] vt : proclamar

proclamation [ˌprɑkləˈmeɪʃən] n : proclamación f

proclivity [proːˈklɪvətɪ] n, pl **-ties** : proclividad f

procrastinate [prəˈkræstəˌneɪt] vi **-nated; -nating** : demorar, aplazar las responsabilidades

procrastination [prəˌkræstəˈneɪʃən] n : aplazamiento m, demora f, dilación f

procreate [ˈproːkriˌeɪt] vi **-ated; -ating** : procrear

procreation [ˌproːkriˈeɪʃən] n : procreación f

proctor[1] [ˈprɑktər] vt : supervisar (un examen)

proctor[2] n : supervisor m, -sora f (de un examen)

procure [prəˈkjʊr] *vt* **-cured; -curing 1**
OBTAIN : procurar, obtener **2** BRING
ABOUT : provocar, lograr, conseguir
procurement [prəˈkjʊrmənt] *n* : obtención *f*
prod¹ [ˈprɑd] *vt* **prodded; prodding 1**
JAB, POKE : pinchar, golpear (con la
punta de algo) **2** GOAD : incitar, estimular
prod² *n* **1** JAB, POKE : golpe *m* (con la
punta de algo), pinchazo *m* **2** STIMULUS : estímulo *m* **3 cattle prod** : picana
f, aguijón *m*
prodigal¹ [ˈprɑdɪɡəl] *adj* SPENDTHRIFT
: pródigo, despilfarrador, derrochador
prodigal² *n* : pródigo *m*, -ga *f*; derrochador *m*, -dora *f*
prodigious [prəˈdɪdʒəs] *adj* **1** MARVELOUS : prodigioso, maravilloso **2**
HUGE : enorme, vasto ⟨prodigious
sums : muchísimo dinero⟩ — **prodigiously** *adv*
prodigy [ˈprɑdədʒi] *n, pl* **-gies** : prodigio
m ⟨child prodigy : niño prodigio⟩
produce¹ [prəˈduːs, -ˈdjuːs] *vt* **-duced;
-ducing 1** EXHIBIT : presentar,
mostrar **2** YIELD : producir **3** CAUSE
: producir, causar **4** CREATE : producir
⟨to produce a poem : escribir un poema⟩ **5** : poner en escena (una obra de
teatro), producir (una película)
produce² [ˈprɑˌduːs, ˈprɑː-, -ˌdjuːs] *n*
: productos *mpl* agrícolas
producer [prəˈduːsər, -ˈdjuː-] *n* : productor *m*, -tora *f*
product [ˈprɑˌdʌkt] *n* : producto *m*
production [prəˈdʌkʃən] *n* : producción
f
productive [prəˈdʌktɪv] *adj* : productivo
productivity [ˌproːˌdʌkˈtɪvəti, ˌprɑ-] *n*
: productividad *f*
profane¹ [proˈfeɪn] *vt* **-faned; -faning**
: profanar
profane² *adj* **1** SECULAR : profano **2** IRREVERENT : irreverente, impío
profanity [proˈfænəti] *n, pl* **-ties 1** IRREVERENCE : irreverencia *f*, impiedad
f **2** : blasfemias *fpl*, obscenidades *fpl*
⟨don't use profanity : no digas blasfemias⟩
profess [prəˈfɛs] *vt* **1** DECLARE : declarar, manifestar **2** CLAIM : pretender
3 : profesar (una religión, etc.)
professedly [prəˈfɛsədli] *adv* **1** OPENLY
: declaradamente **2** ALLEGEDLY
: supuestamente
profession [prəˈfɛʃən] *n* : profesión *f*
professional¹ [prəˈfɛʃənəl] *adj* : profesional — **professionally** *adv*
professional² *n* : profesional *mf*
professionalism [prəˈfɛʃənəˌlɪzəm] *n*
: profesionalismo *m*
professor [prəˈfɛsər] *n* : profesor *m* (universitario), profesora *f* (universitaria);
catedrático *m*, -ca *f*
proffer [ˈprɑfər] *vt* **-fered; -fering** : ofrecer, dar

proficiency [prəˈfɪʃəntsi] *n* : competencia *f*, capacidad *f*
proficient [prəˈfɪʃənt] *adj* : competente,
experto — **proficiently** *adv*
profile [ˈproːˌfaɪl] *n* : perfil *m* ⟨a portrait
in profile : un retrato de perfil⟩ ⟨to
keep a low profile : no llamar la atención, hacerse pasar desapercibido⟩
profit¹ [ˈprɑfət] *vi* : sacar provecho (de),
beneficiarse (de)
profit² *n* **1** ADVANTAGE : provecho *m*,
partido *m*, beneficio *m* **2** GAIN : beneficio *m*, utilidad *f*, ganancia *f* ⟨to make
a profit : sacar beneficios⟩
profitable [ˈprɑfətəbəl] *adj* : rentable, lucrativo — **profitably** [-bli] *adv*
profitless [ˈprɑfətləs] *adj* : infructuoso,
inútil
profligate [ˈprɑflɪɡət, -ˌɡeɪt] *adj* **1** DISSOLUTE : disoluto, licencioso **2** SPENDTHRIFT : despilfarrador, derrochador,
pródigo
profound [prəˈfaʊnd] *adj* : profundo
profoundly [prəˈfaʊndli] *adv* : profundamente, en profundidad
profundity [prəˈfʌndəti] *n, pl* **-ties** : profundidad *f*
profuse [prəˈfjuːs] *adj* **1** COPIOUS : profuso, copioso **2** LAVISH : pródigo —
profusely *adv*
profusion [prəˈfjuːʒən] *n* : abundancia *f*,
profusión *f*
progenitor [proˈdʒɛnətər] *n* : progenitor
m, -tora *f*
progeny [ˈprɑdʒəni] *n, pl* **-nies** : progenie *f*
progesterone [proˈdʒɛstəˌroːn] *n* : progesterona *f*
prognosis [prɑɡˈnoːsɪs] *n, pl* **-noses**
[-ˌsiːz] : pronóstico *m* (médico)
program¹ [ˈproːˌɡræm, -ɡrəm] *vt*
-grammed *or* **-gramed; -gramming** *or*
-graming : programar
program² *n* : programa *m*
programmable [ˈproːˌɡræməbəl] *adj*
: programable
programmer [ˈproːˌɡræmər] *n* : programador *m*, -dora *f*
programming [ˈproːˌɡræmɪŋ] *n* : programación *f*
progress¹ [prəˈɡrɛs] *vi* **1** PROCEED
: progresar, adelantar **2** IMPROVE
: mejorar
progress² [ˈprɑɡrəs, -ˌɡrɛs] *n* **1** ADVANCE : progreso *m*, adelanto *m*,
avance *m* ⟨to make progress : hacer
progresos⟩ **2** BETTERMENT : mejora *f*,
mejoramiento *m*
progression [prəˈɡrɛʃən] *n* **1** ADVANCE
: avance *m* **2** SEQUENCE : desarrollo
m (de eventos)
progressive [prəˈɡrɛsɪv] *adj* **1** : progresista ⟨a progressive society : una sociedad progresista⟩ **2** : progresivo ⟨a
progressive disease : una enfermedad
progresiva⟩ **3** *or* **Progressive** : progresista (en política) **4** : progresivo (en
gramática)

progressively [prə'grɛsɪvli] *adv* : progresivamente, poco a poco

prohibit [pro'hɪbət] *vt* : prohibir

prohibition [ˌproːəˈbɪʃən, ˌproːhə-] *n* : prohibición *f*

prohibitive [pro'hɪbətɪv] *adj* : prohibitivo

project¹ [prə'ʤɛkt] *vt* **1** PLAN : proyectar, planear **2** : proyectar (imágenes, misiles, etc.) — *vi* PROTRUDE : sobresalir, salir

project² ['prɑˌʤɛkt, -ʤɪkt] *n* : proyecto *m*, trabajo *m* (de un estudiante) ⟨research project : proyecto de investigación⟩

projectile [prə'ʤɛktəl, -ˌtaɪl] *n* : proyectil *m*

projection [prə'ʤɛkʃən] *n* **1** PLAN : plan *m*, proyección *f* **2** : proyección *f* (de imágenes, misiles, etc.) **3** PROTRUSION : saliente *m*

projector [prə'ʤɛktər] *n* : proyector *m*

proletarian¹ [ˌproːləˈtɛriən] *adj* : proletario

proletarian² *n* : proletario *m*, -ria *f*

proletariat [ˌproːləˈtɛriət] *n* : proletariado *m*

proliferate [prə'lɪfəˌreɪt] *vi* -ated; -ating : proliferar

proliferation [prəˌlɪfəˈreɪʃən] *n* : proliferación *f*

prolific [prə'lɪfɪk] *adj* : prolífico

prologue ['proːˌlɔg] *n* : prólogo *m*

prolong [prə'lɔŋ] *vt* : prolongar

prolongation [ˌproːˌlɔŋˈgeɪʃən] *n* : prolongación *f*

prom ['prɑm] *n* : baile *m* formal (de un colegio)

promenade¹ [ˌprɑməˈneɪd, -ˈnɑd] *vi* -naded; -nading : pasear, pasearse, dar un paseo

promenade² *n* : paseo *m*

prominence ['prɑmənənts] *n* **1** PROJECTION : prominencia *f* **2** EMINENCE : eminencia *f*, prestigio *m*

prominent ['prɑmənənt] *adj* **1** OUTSTANDING : prominente, destacado **2** PROJECTING : prominente, saliente

prominently ['prɑmənəntli] *adv* : destacadamente, prominentemente

promiscuity [ˌprɑmɪsˈkjuˌəti] *n, pl* -ties : promiscuidad *f*

promiscuous [prə'mɪskjuəs] *adj* : promiscuo — **promiscuously** *adv*

promise¹ ['prɑməs] *v* -ised; -ising : prometer

promise² *n* **1** : promesa *f* ⟨he kept his promise : cumplió su promesa⟩ **2 to show promise** : prometer

promising ['prɑməsɪŋ] *adj* : prometedor

promissory ['prɑməˌsori] *adj* : que promete ⟨a promissory note : un pagaré⟩

promontory ['prɑmənˌtori] *n, pl* -ries : promontorio *m*

promote [prə'moːt] *vt* -moted; -moting **1** : ascender (a un alumno o un empleado) **2** ADVERTISE : promocionar,

hacerle publicidad a **3** FURTHER : promover, fomentar

promoter [prə'moːtər] *n* : promotor *m*, -tora *f*; empresario *m*, -ria *f* (en deportes)

promotion [prə'moːʃən] *n* **1** : ascenso *m* (de un alumno o un empleado) **2** FURTHERING : promoción *f*, fomento *m* **3** ADVERTISING : publicidad *f*, propaganda *f*

promotional [prə'moːʃənəl] *adj* : promocional

prompt¹ ['prɑmpt] *vt* **1** INDUCE : provocar (una cosa), inducir (a una persona) ⟨curiosity prompted me to ask you : la curiosidad me indujo a preguntarle⟩ **2** : apuntar (a un actor, etc.)

prompt² *adj* : pronto, rápido ⟨prompt payment : pago puntual⟩

prompter ['prɑmptər] *n* : apuntador *m*, -dora *f* (en teatro)

promptly ['prɑmptli] *adv* : inmediatamente, rápidamente

promptness ['prɑmptnəs] *n* : prontitud *f*, rapidez *f*

promulgate ['prɑməlˌgeɪt] *vt* -gated; -gating : promulgar

prone ['proːn] *adj* **1** LIABLE : propenso, proclive ⟨accident-prone : propenso a los accidentes⟩ **2** : boca abajo, decúbito prono ⟨in a prone position : en decúbito prono⟩

prong ['prɔŋ] *n* : punta *f*, diente *m*

pronoun ['proːˌnaʊn] *n* : pronombre *m*

pronounce [prə'naʊnts] *vt* -nounced; -nouncing **1** : pronunciar ⟨how do you pronounce your name? : ¿cómo se pronuncia su nombre?⟩ **2** DECLARE : declarar **3 to pronounce sentence** : dictar sentencia, pronunciar un fallo

pronounced [prə'naʊntst] *adj* MARKED : pronunciado, marcado

pronouncement [prə'naʊntsmənt] *n* : declaración *f*

pronunciation [prəˌnʌntsiˈeɪʃən] *n* : pronunciación *f*

proof¹ ['pruːf] *adj* : a prueba ⟨proof against tampering : a prueba de manipulación⟩

proof² *n* : prueba *f*

proofread ['pruːfˌriːd] *v* -read; -reading *vt* : corregir — *vi* : corregir pruebas

proofreader ['pruːfˌriːdər] *n* : corrector *m*, -tora *f* (de pruebas)

prop¹ ['prɑp] *vt* propped; propping **1 to prop against** : apoyar contra **2 to prop up** SUPPORT : apoyar, apuntalar, sostener **3 to prop up** SUSTAIN : alentar (a alguien), darle ánimo (a alguien)

prop² *n* **1** SUPPORT : puntal *m*, apoyo *m*, soporte *m* **2** : accesorio *m* (en teatro)

propaganda [ˌprɑpəˈgændə, ˌproː-] *n* : propaganda *f*

propagandize [ˌprɑpəˈgænˌdaɪz, ˌproː-] *v* -dized; -dizing *vt* : someter a propaganda — *vi* : hacer propaganda

propagate ['prɑpə,geɪt] v **-gated; -gating** vi : propagarse — vt : propagar
propagation [,prɑpə'geɪʃən] n : propagación f
propane ['pro:,peɪn] n : propano m
propel [prə'pɛl] vt **-pelled; -pelling** : impulsar, propulsar, impeler
propellant or **propellent** [prə'pɛlənt] n : propulsor m
propeller [prə'pɛlər] n : hélice f
propensity [prə'pɛntsəti] n, pl **-ties** : propensión f, tendencia f, inclinación f
proper ['prɑpər] adj **1** RIGHT, SUITABLE : apropiado, adecuado **2** : propio, mismo ⟨the city proper : la propia ciudad⟩ **3** CORRECT : correcto **4** GENTEEL : fino, refinado, cortés **5** OWN, SPECIAL : propio ⟨proper name : nombre propio⟩ — **properly** adv
property ['prɑpərti] n, pl **-ties 1** CHARACTERISTIC : característica f, propiedad f **2** POSSESSIONS : propiedad f **3** BUILDING : inmueble m **4** LAND, LOT : terreno m, lote m, parcela f **5** PROP : accesorio m (en teatro)
prophecy ['prɑfəsi] n, pl **-cies** : profecía f, vaticinio m
prophesy ['prɑfə,saɪ] v **-sied; -sying** vt **1** FORETELL : profetizar (como profeta) **2** PREDICT : profetizar, predecir, vaticinar — vi : hacer profecías
prophet ['prɑfət] n : profeta m, profetisa f
prophetic [prə'fɛtɪk] or **prophetical** [-tɪkəl] adj : profético — **prophetically** [-tɪkli] adv
propitiate [pro'pɪʃi,eɪt] vt **-ated; -ating** : propiciar
propitious [prə'pɪʃəs] adj : propicio
proponent [prə'po:nənt] n : defensor m, -sora f; partidario m, -ria f
proportion¹ [prə'porʃən] vt : proporcionar ⟨well-proportioned : de buenas proporciones⟩
proportion² n **1** RATIO : proporción f **2** SYMMETRY : proporción f, simetría f ⟨out of proportion : desproporcionado⟩ **3** SHARE : parte f **4 proportions** npl SIZE : dimensiones fpl
proportional [prə'porʃənəl] adj : proporcional — **proportionally** adv
proportionate [prə'porʃənət] adj : proporcional — **proportionately** adv
proposal [prə'po:zəl] n **1** PROPOSITION : propuesta f, proposición f ⟨marriage proposal : propuesta de matrimonio⟩ **2** PLAN : proyecto m, propuesta f
propose [prə'po:z] v **-posed; -posing** vi : proponer matrimonio — vt **1** INTEND : pensar, proponerse **2** SUGGEST : proponer
proposition [,prɑpə'zɪʃən] n **1** PROPOSAL : proposición f, propuesta f **2** STATEMENT : proposición f
propound [prə'paʊnd] vt : proponer, exponer
proprietary [prə'praɪə,tɛri] adj : propietario, patentado
proprietor [prə'praɪətər] n : propietario m, -ria f
propriety [prə'praɪəti] n, pl **-eties 1** DECORUM : decencia f, decoro m **2 proprieties** npl CONVENTIONS : convenciones fpl, cánones mpl sociales
propulsion [prə'pʌlʃən] n : propulsión f
prosaic [pro'zeɪɪk] adj : prosaico
proscribe [pro'skraɪb] vt **-scribed; -scribing** : proscribir
prose ['pro:z] n : prosa f
prosecute ['prɑsɪ,kjuːt] vt **-cuted; -cuting 1** CARRY OUT : llevar a cabo **2** : procesar, enjuiciar ⟨prosecuted for fraud : procesado por fraude⟩
prosecution [,prɑsɪ'kjuːʃən] n **1** : procesamiento m ⟨the prosecution of forgers : el procesamiento de falsificadores⟩ **2** PROSECUTORS : acusación f ⟨witness for the prosecution : testigo de cargo⟩
prosecutor ['prɑsɪ,kjuːtər] n : acusador m, -dora f; fiscal mf
prospect¹ ['prɑ,spɛkt] vi : prospectar (el terreno) ⟨to prospect for gold : buscar oro⟩
prospect² n **1** VISTA : vista f, panorama m **2** POSSIBILITY : posibilidad f **3** OUTLOOK : perspectiva f **4** : posible cliente m, -ta f ⟨a salesman looking for prospects : un vendedor buscando nuevos clientes⟩
prospective [prə'spɛktɪv, 'prɑ,spɛk-] adj **1** EXPECTANT : futuro ⟨prospective mother : futura madre⟩ **2** POTENTIAL : potencial, posible ⟨prospective employee : posible empleado⟩
prospector ['prɑ,spɛktər, prɑ'spɛk-] n : prospector m, -tora f; explorador m, -dora f
prospectus [prə'spɛktəs] n : prospecto m
prosper ['prɑspər] vi : prosperar
prosperity [prɑ'spɛrəti] n : prosperidad f
prosperous ['prɑspərəs] adj : próspero
prostate ['prɑ,steɪt] n : próstata f
prosthesis [prɑs'θiːsɪs, 'prɑsθə-] n, pl **-theses** [-,siːz] : prótesis f
prostitute¹ ['prɑstə,tuːt, -,tjuːt] vt **-tuted; -tuting 1** : prostituir **2 to prostitute oneself** : prostituirse
prostitute² n : prostituto m, -ta f
prostitution [,prɑstə'tuːʃən, -'tjuː-] n : prostitución f
prostrate¹ ['prɑ,streɪt] vt **-trated; -trating 1** : postrar **2 to prostrate oneself** : postrarse
prostrate² adj : postrado
prostration [prɑ'streɪʃən] n : postración f
protagonist [pro'tægənɪst] n : protagonista mf
protect [prə'tɛkt] vt : proteger
protection [prə'tɛkʃən] n : protección f
protective [prə'tɛktɪv] adj : protector
protector [prə'tɛktər] n **1** : protector m, -tora f (persona) **2** GUARD : protector m (aparato)

protectorate [prə'tɛktərət] *n* : protectorado *m*

protégé ['proːtəˌʒeɪ] *n* : protegido *m*, -da *f*

protein ['proːˌtiːn] *n* : proteína *f*

protest[1] ['proːtɛst] *vt* **1** ASSERT : afirmar, declarar **2** : protestar ⟨they protested the decision : protestaron (por) la decisión⟩ — *vi* **to protest against** : protestar contra

protest[2] ['proːˌtɛst] *n* **1** DEMONSTRATION : manifestación *f* (de protesta) ⟨a public protest : una manifestación pública⟩ **2** COMPLAINT : queja *f*, protesta *f*

Protestant ['prɑtəstənt] *n* : protestante *mf*

Protestantism ['prɑtəstənˌtɪzəm] *n* : protestantismo *m*

protocol ['proːtəˌkɔl] *n* : protocolo *m*

proton ['proːˌtɑn] *n* : protón *m*

protoplasm ['proːtəˌplæzəm] *n* : protoplasma *m*

prototype ['proːtəˌtaɪp] *n* : prototipo *m*

protozoan [ˌproːtəˈzoːən] *n* : protozoario *m*, protozoo *m*

protract [proˈtrækt] *vt* : prolongar

protractor [proˈtræktər] *n* : transportador *m* (instrumento)

protrude [proˈtruːd] *vi* **-truded; -truding** : salir, sobresalir

protrusion [proˈtruːʒən] *n* : protuberancia *f*, saliente *f*

protuberance [proˈtuːbərənts, -ˈtjuː-] *n* : protuberancia *f*

proud ['praʊd] *adj* **1** HAUGHTY : altanero, orgulloso, arrogante **2** orgulloso ⟨she was proud of her work : estaba orgullosa de su trabajo⟩ ⟨too proud to beg : demasiado orgulloso para rogar⟩ **3** GLORIOUS : glorioso — **proudly** *adv*

prove ['pruːv] *v* **proved; proved** *or* **proven** ['pruːvən]; **proving** *vt* **1** TEST : probar **2** DEMONSTRATE : probar, demostrar — *vi* : resultar ⟨it proved effective : resultó efectivo⟩

Provençal [ˌproːvɑnˈsɑl, ˌprɑvən-] *n* **1** : provenzal *mf* **2** : provenzal *m* (idioma) — **Provençal** *adj*

proverb ['prɑˌvərb] *n* : proverbio *m*, refrán *m*

proverbial [prəˈvərbiəl] *adj* : proverbial

provide [prəˈvaɪd] *v* **-vided; -viding** *vt* **1** STIPULATE : estipular **2 to provide with** : proveer de, proporcionar — *vi* **1** : proveer ⟨the Lord will provide : el Señor proveerá⟩ **2 to provide for** SUPPORT : mantener **3 to provide for** ANTICIPATE : hacer previsiones para, prever

provided [prəˈvaɪdəd] *or* **provided that** *conj* : con tal (de) que, siempre que

providence ['prɑvədənts] *n* **1** PRUDENCE : previsión *f*, prudencia *f* **2** *or* **Providence** : providencia *f* ⟨divine providence : la Divina Providencia⟩ **3 Providence** GOD : Providencia *f*

provident ['prɑvədənt] *adj* **1** PRUDENT : previsor, prudente **2** FRUGAL : frugal, ahorrativo

providential [ˌprɑvəˈdɛntʃəl] *adj* : providencial

provider [prəˈvaɪdər] *n* **1** PURVEYOR : proveedor *m*, -dora *f* **2** BREADWINNER : sostén *m* (económico)

providing that → **provided**

province ['prɑvɪnts] *n* **1** : provincia *f* (de un país) ⟨to live in the provinces : vivir en las provincias⟩ **2** FIELD, SPHERE : campo *m*, competencia *f* ⟨it's not in my province : no es de mi competencia⟩

provincial [prəˈvɪntʃəl] *adj* **1** : provincial ⟨provincial government : gobierno provincial⟩ **2** : provinciano, pueblerino ⟨a provincial mentality : una mentalidad provinciana⟩

provision[1] [prəˈvɪʒən] *vt* : aprovisionar, abastecer

provision[2] *n* **1** PROVIDING : provisión *f*, suministro *m* **2** STIPULATION : condición *f*, salvedad *f*, estipulación *f* **3 provisions** *npl* : despensa *f*, víveres *mpl*, provisiones *fpl*

provisional [prəˈvɪʒənəl] *adj* : provisional, provisorio — **provisionally** *adv*

proviso [prəˈvaɪˌzoː] *n*, *pl* **-sos** *or* **-soes** : condición *f*, salvedad *f*, estipulación *f*

provocation [ˌprɑvəˈkeɪʃən] *n* : provocación *f*

provocative [prəˈvɑkətɪv] *adj* : provocador, provocativo ⟨a provocative article : un artículo que hace pensar⟩

provoke [prəˈvoːk] *vt* **-voked; -voking** : provocar

prow ['praʊ] *n* : proa *f*

prowess ['praʊəs] *n* **1** VALOR : valor *m*, valentía *f* **2** SKILL : habilidad *f*, destreza *f*

prowl ['praʊl] *vi* : merodear, rondar — *vt* : rondar por

prowler ['praʊlər] *n* : merodeador *m*, -dora *f*

proximity [prɑkˈsɪməti] *n* : proximidad *f*

proxy ['prɑksi] *n*, *pl* **proxies** **1** : poder *m* (de actuar en nombre de alguien) ⟨by proxy : por poder⟩ **2** AGENT : apoderado *m*, -da *f*; representante *mf*

prude ['pruːd] *n* : mojigato *m*, -ta *f*; gazmoño *m*, -ña *f*

prudence ['pruːdənts] *n* **1** SHREWDNESS : prudencia *f*, sagacidad *f* **2** CAUTION : prudencia *f*, cautela *f* **3** THRIFTINESS : frugalidad *f*

prudent ['pruːdənt] *adj* **1** SHREWD : prudente, sagaz **2** CAUTIOUS, FARSIGHTED : prudente, previsor, precavido **3** THRIFTY : frugal, ahorrativo — **prudently** *adv*

prudery ['pruːdəri] *n*, *pl* **-eries** : mojigatería *f*, gazmoñería *f*

prudish ['pruːdɪʃ] *adj* : mojigato, gazmoño

prune¹ ['pru:n] *vt* **pruned; pruning** : podar (arbustos, etc.), acortar (un texto), recortar (gastos, etc.)

prune² *n* : ciruela *f* pasa

prurient ['prʊriənt] *adj* : lascivo

pry ['praɪ] *v* **pried; prying** *vi* : curiosear, huronear ⟨to pry into other people's business : meterse uno en lo que no le importa⟩ — *vt or* **to pry open** : abrir (con una palanca), apalancar

psalm ['sɑm, 'sɑlm] *n* : salmo *m*

pseudonym ['su:də,nɪm] *n* : seudónimo *m*

psoriasis [sə'raɪəsɪs] *n* : soriasis *f*, psoriasis *f*

psyche ['saɪki] *n* : psique *f*, psiquis *f*

psychedelic¹ [,saɪkə'dɛlɪk] *adj* : psicodélico

psychedelic² *n* : droga *f* psicodélica

psychiatric [,saɪki'ætrɪk] *adj* : psiquiátrico, siquiátrico

psychiatrist [sə'kaɪətrɪst, saɪ-] *n* : psiquiatra *mf*, siquiatra *mf*

psychiatry [sə'kaɪətri, saɪ-] *n* : psiquiatría *f*, siquiatría *f*

psychic¹ ['saɪkɪk] *adj* **1** : psíquico, síquico (en psicología) **2** CLAIRVOYANT : clarividente

psychic² *n* : vidente *mf*, clarividente *mf*

psychoanalysis [,saɪkoə'næləsɪs] *n*, *pl* **-yses** : psicoanálisis *m*, sicoanálisis *m*

psychoanalyst [,saɪko'ænəlɪst] *n* : psicoanalista *mf*, sicoanalista *mf*

psychoanalytic [,saɪko,ænəl'ɪtɪk] *adj* : psicoanalítico, sicoanalítico

psychoanalyze [,saɪko'ænəl,aɪz] *vt* **-lyzed; -lyzing** : psicoanalizar, sicoanalizar

psychological [,saɪkə'lɑʤɪkəl] *adj* : psicológico, sicológico — **psychologically** *adv*

psychologist [saɪ'kɑləʤɪst] *n* : psicólogo *m*, -ga *f*; sicólogo *m*, -ga *f*

psychology [saɪ'kɑləʤi] *n*, *pl* **-gies** : psicología *f*, sicología *f*

psychopath ['saɪkə,pæθ] *n* : psicópata *mf*, sicópata *mf*

psychopathic [,saɪkə'pæθɪk] *adj* : psicopático, sicopático

psychosis [saɪ'ko:sɪs] *n*, *pl* **-choses** [-'ko:,si:z] : psicosis *f*, sicosis *f*

psychosomatic [,saɪkosə'mætɪk] *adj* : psicosomático, sicosomático

psychotherapist [,saɪko'θɛrəpɪst] *n* : psicoterapeuta *mf*, sicoterapeuta *mf*

psychotherapy [,saɪko'θɛrəpi] *n*, *pl* **-pies** : psicoterapia *f*, sicoterapia *f*

psychotic¹ [saɪ'kɑtɪk] *adj* : psicótico, sicótico

psychotic² *n* : psicótico *m*, -ca *f*; sicótico *m*, -ca *f*

puberty ['pju:bərti] *n* : pubertad *f*

pubic ['pju:bɪk] *adj* : pubiano, púbico

public¹ ['pʌblɪk] *adj* : público — **publicly** *adv*

public² *n* : público *m*

publication [,pʌblə'keɪʃən] *n* : publicación *f*

publicist ['pʌbləsɪst] *n* : publicista *mf*

publicity [pə'blɪsəti] *n* : publicidad *f*

publicize ['pʌblə,saɪz] *vt* **-cized; -cizing** : publicitar

public school *n* : escuela *f* pública

publish ['pʌblɪʃ] *vt* : publicar

publisher ['pʌblɪʃər] *n* : casa *f* editorial (compañía); editor *m*, -tora *f* (persona)

publishing ['pʌblɪʃɪŋ] *n* : industria *f* editorial

pucker¹ ['pʌkər] *vt* : fruncir, arrugar — *vi* : arrugarse

pucker² *n* : arruga *f*, frunce *m*, fruncido *m*

pudding ['pʊdɪŋ] *n* : budín *m*, pudín *m*

puddle ['pʌdəl] *n* : charco *m*

pudgy ['pʌʤi] *adj* **pudgier; -est** : regordete *fam*, rechoncho *fam*, gordinflón *fam*

puerile ['pjʊrəl] *adj* : pueril

Puerto Rican¹ [,pwɛrtə'ri:kən, ,portə-] *adj* : puertorriqueño

Puerto Rican² *n* : puertorriqueño *m*, -ña *f*

puff¹ ['pʌf] *vi* **1** BLOW : soplar **2** PANT : resoplar, jadear **3 to puff up** SWELL : hincharse — *vt* **1** BLOW : soplar ⟨to puff smoke : echar humo⟩ **2** INFLATE : inflar, hinchar ⟨to puff out one's cheeks : inflar las mejillas⟩

puff² *n* **1** GUST : soplo *m*, ráfaga *f*, bocanada *f* (de humo) **2** DRAW : chupada *f* (a un cigarrillo) **3** SWELLING : hinchazón *f* **4 cream puff** : pastelito *m* de crema **5 powder puff** : borla *f*

puffy ['pʌfi] *adj* **puffier; -est 1** SWOLLEN : hinchado, inflado **2** SPONGY : esponjoso, suave

pug ['pʌg] *n* **1** : doguillo *m* (perro) **2 or pug nose** : nariz *f* achatada

pugnacious [,pʌg'neɪʃəs] *adj* : pugnaz, agresivo

puke ['pju:k] *vi* **puked; puking** : vomitar, devolver

pull¹ ['pʊl, 'pʌl] *vt* **1** DRAW, TUG : tirar de, jalar **2** EXTRACT : sacar, extraer ⟨to pull teeth : sacar muelas⟩ ⟨to pull a gun on : amenazar a (alguien) con pistola⟩ **3** TEAR : desgarrarse (un músculo, etc.) **4 to pull down** : bajar, echar abajo, derribar (un edificio) **5 to pull in** ATTRACT : atraer (una muchedumbre, etc.) ⟨to pull in votes : conseguir votos⟩ **6 to pull off** REMOVE : sacar, quitar **7 to pull oneself together** : calmarse, tranquilizarse **8 to pull up** RAISE : levantar, subir — *vi* **1** DRAW, TUG : tirar, jalar **2** (indicating movement in a specific direction) ⟨they pulled in front of us : se nos metieron delante⟩ ⟨to pull to a stop : pararse⟩ **3 to pull through** RECOVER : recobrarse, reponerse **4 to pull together** COOPERATE : trabajar juntos, cooperar

pull² *n* **1** TUG : tirón *m*, jalón *m* ⟨he gave it a pull : le dio un tirón⟩ **2** ATTRACTION : atracción *f*, fuerza *f* ⟨the pull of gravity : la fuerza de la gravedad⟩

INFLUENCE : influencia f 4 HANDLE : tirador m (de un cajón, etc.) 5 bell pull : cuerda f

pullet ['pʊlət] n : polla f, gallina f (joven)

pulley ['pʊli] n, pl **-leys** : polea f

pullover ['pʊl,o:vər] n : suéter m

pulmonary ['pʊlmə,nɛri, 'pʌl-] adj : pulmonar

pulp ['pʌlp] n 1 : pulpa f (de una fruta, etc.) 2 MASH : papilla f, pasta f ⟨wood pulp : pasta de papel, pulpa de papel⟩ ⟨to beat to a pulp : hacer papilla (a alguien)⟩ 3 : pulpa f (de los dientes)

pulpit ['pʊl,pɪt] n : púlpito m

pulsate ['pʌl,seɪt] vi **-sated; -sating** 1 BEAT : latir, palpitar 2 VIBRATE : vibrar

pulsation [,pʌl'seɪʃən] n : pulsación f

pulse ['pʌls] n : pulso m

pulverize ['pʌlvə,raɪz] vt **-ized; -izing** : pulverizar

puma ['pu:mə, 'pju:-] n : puma m; león m, leona f (in various countries)

pumice ['pʌməs] n : piedra f pómez

pummel ['pʌməl] vt **-meled; -meling** : aporrear, apalear

pump¹ ['pʌmp] vt 1 : bombear ⟨to pump water : bombear agua⟩ ⟨to pump (up) a tire : inflar una llanta⟩ 2 : mover (una manivela, un pedal, etc.) de arriba abajo ⟨to pump someone's hand : darle un fuerte apretón de manos (a alguien)⟩ 3 **to pump out** : sacar, vaciar (con una bomba)

pump² n 1 : bomba f ⟨water pump : bomba de agua⟩ 2 SHOE : zapato m de tacón

pumpernickel ['pʌmpər,nɪkəl] n : pan m negro de centeno

pumpkin ['pʌmpkɪn, 'pʌŋkən] n : calabaza f, zapallo m Arg, Chile, Peru, Uru

pun¹ ['pʌn] vi **punned; punning** : hacer juegos de palabras

pun² n : juego m de palabras, albur m Mex

punch¹ ['pʌntʃ] vt 1 HIT : darle un puñetazo (a alguien), golpear ⟨she punched him in the nose : le dio un puñetazo en la nariz⟩ 2 PERFORATE : perforar (papel, etc.), picar (un boleto)

punch² n 1 : perforadora f ⟨paper punch : perforadora de papel⟩ 2 BLOW : golpe m, puñetazo m 3 : ponche m ⟨fruit punch : ponche de frutas⟩

punctilious [pəŋk'tɪliəs] adj : puntilloso

punctual ['pʌŋktʃuəl] adj : puntual

punctuality [,pʌŋktʃu'æləti] n : puntualidad f

punctually ['pʌŋktʃuəli] adv : puntualmente, a tiempo

punctuate ['pʌŋktʃu,eɪt] vt **-ated; -ating** : puntuar

punctuation [,pʌŋktʃu'eɪʃən] n : puntuación f

puncture¹ ['pʌŋktʃər] vt **-tured; -turing** : pinchar, punzar, perforar, ponchar Mex

puncture² n : pinchazo m, ponchadura f Mex

pundit ['pʌndɪt] n : experto m, -ta f

pungency ['pʌndʒəntsi] n : acritud f, acrimonia f

pungent ['pʌndʒənt] adj : acre

punish ['pʌnɪʃ] vt : castigar

punishable ['pʌnɪʃəbəl] adj : punible

punishment ['pʌnɪʃmənt] n : castigo m

punitive ['pju:nətɪv] adj : punitivo

punt¹ ['pʌnt] vt : impulsar (un barco) con una pértiga — vi : despejar (en deportes)

punt² n 1 : batea f (barco) 2 : patada f de despeje (en deportes)

puny ['pju:ni] adj **-nier; -est** : enclenque, endeble

pup ['pʌp] n : cachorro m, -rra f (de un perro); cría f (de otros animales)

pupa ['pju:pə] n, pl **-pae** [-pi, -,paɪ] or **-pas** : crisálida f, pupa f

pupil ['pju:pəl] n 1 : alumno m, -na f (de colegio) 2 : pupila f (del ojo)

puppet ['pʌpət] n : títere m, marioneta f

puppy ['pʌpi] n, pl **-pies** : cachorro m, -rra f

purchase¹ ['pərtʃəs] vt **-chased; -chasing** : comprar

purchase² n 1 PURCHASING : compra f, adquisición f 2 : compra f ⟨last-minute purchases : compras de última hora⟩ 3 GRIP : agarre m, asidero m ⟨she got a firm purchase on the wheel : se agarró bien del volante⟩

purchase order n : orden f de compra

pure ['pjʊr] adj **purer; purest** : puro

puree¹ [pjʊ'reɪ, -'ri:] vt **-reed; -reeing** : hacer un puré con

puree² n : puré m

purely ['pjʊrli] adv 1 WHOLLY : puramente, completamente ⟨purely by chance : por pura casualidad⟩ 2 SIMPLY : sencillamente, meramente

purgative ['pərgətɪv] n : purgante m

purgatory ['pərgə,tori] n, pl **-ries** : purgatorio m

purge¹ ['pərdʒ] vt **purged; purging** : purgar

purge² n : purga f

purification [,pjʊrəfə'keɪʃən] n : purificación f

purify ['pjʊrə,faɪ] vt **-fied; -fying** : purificar

puritan ['pjʊrətən] n : puritano m, -na f — **puritan** adj

puritanical [,pjʊrə'tænɪkəl] adj : puritano

purity ['pjʊrəti] n : pureza f

purl¹ ['pərl] v : tejer al revés, tejer del revés

purl² n : punto m del revés

purloin [pər'lɔɪn, 'pər,lɔɪn] vt : hurtar, robar

purple ['pərpəl] n : morado m, color m púrpura

purport [pər'port] vt : pretender ⟨to purport to be : pretender ser⟩

purpose ['pərpəs] n 1 INTENTION : propósito m, intención f ⟨on purpose

: a propósito, adrede⟩ **2** FUNCTION : función *f* **3** RESOLUTION : resolución *f*, determinación *f*

purposeful [ˈpərpəsfəl] *adj* : determinado, decidido, resuelto

purposefully [ˈpərpəsfəli] *adv* : decididamente, resueltamente

purposely [ˈpərpəsli] *adv* : intencionadamente, a propósito, adrede

purr¹ [ˈpər] *vi* : ronronear

purr² *n* : ronroneo *m*

purse¹ [ˈpərs] *vt* **pursed; pursing** : fruncir ⟨to purse one's lips : fruncir la boca⟩

purse² *n* **1** HANDBAG : cartera *f*, bolso *m*, bolsa *f* *Mex* ⟨a change purse : un monedero⟩ **2** FUNDS : fondos *mpl* **3** PRIZE : premio *m*

pursue [pərˈsuː] *vt* **-sued; -suing 1** CHASE : perseguir **2** SEEK : buscar, tratar de encontrar ⟨to pursue pleasure : buscar el placer⟩ **3** FOLLOW : seguir ⟨the road pursues a northerly course : el camino sigue hacia el norte⟩ **4** : dedicarse a ⟨to pursue a hobby : dedicarse a un pasatiempo⟩

pursuer [pərˈsuːər] *n* : perseguidor *m*, -dora *f*

pursuit [pərˈsuːt] *n* **1** CHASE : persecución *f* **2** SEARCH : búsqueda *f*, busca *f* **3** ACTIVITY : actividad *f*, pasatiempo *m*

purveyor [pərˈveɪər] *n* : proveedor *m*, -dora *f*

pus [ˈpʌs] *n* : pus *m*

push¹ [ˈpʊʃ] *vt* **1** SHOVE : empujar **2** PRESS : apretar, pulsar ⟨push that button : aprieta ese botón⟩ **3** PRESSURE, URGE : presionar **4 to push around** BULLY : intimidar, mangonear — *vi* **1** SHOVE : empujar **2** INSIST : insistir, presionar **3 to push off** LEAVE : marcharse, irse, largarse *fam* **4 to push on** PROCEED : seguir

push² *n* **1** SHOVE : empujón *m* **2** DRIVE : empuje *m*, energía *f*, dinamismo *m* **3** EFFORT : esfuerzo *m*

push–button [ˈpʊʃˌbʌtən] *adj* : de botones

pushcart [ˈpʊʃˌkɑrt] *n* : carretilla *f* de mano

pushy [ˈpʊʃi] *adj* **pushier; -est** : mandón, prepotente

pussy [ˈpʊsi] *n, pl* **pussies** : gatito *m*, -ta *f*; minino *m*, -na *f*

pussy willow *n* : sauce *m* blanco

pustule [ˈpʌsˌtʃuːl] *n* : pústula *f*

put [ˈpʊt] *v* **put; putting** *vt* **1** PLACE : poner, colocar ⟨put it on the table : ponlo en la mesa⟩ **2** INSERT : meter **3** (*indicating causation of a state or feeling*) : poner ⟨it put her in a good mood : la puso de buen humor⟩ ⟨to put into effect : poner en práctica⟩ **4** IMPOSE : poner ⟨they put a tax on it : lo gravaron con un impuesto⟩ **5** SUBJECT : someter, poner ⟨to put to the test : poner a prueba⟩ ⟨to put to death : ejecutar⟩ **6** EXPRESS : expresar, decir ⟨he put it

simply : lo dijo sencillamente⟩ **7** APPLY : aplicar ⟨to put one's mind to something : proponerse hacer algo⟩ **8** SET : poner ⟨I put him to work : lo puse a trabajar⟩ **9** ATTACH : dar ⟨to put a high value on : dar gran valor a⟩ **10** PRESENT : presentar, exponer ⟨to put a question to someone : hacer una pregunta a alguien⟩ — *vi* **1 to put to sea** : hacerse a la mar **2 to put up with** : aguantar, soportar

put away *vt* **1** KEEP : guardar **2** *or* **put aside** : dejar a un lado

put by *vt* SAVE : ahorrar

put down *vt* **1** SUPPRESS : aplastar, suprimir **2** ATTRIBUTE : atribuir ⟨she put it down to luck : lo atribuyó a la suerte⟩

put in *vi* : presentarse ⟨I've put in for the position : me presenté para el puesto⟩ — *vt* DEVOTE : dedicar (unas horas, etc.)

put off *vt* DEFER : aplazar, posponer

put on *vt* **1** ASSUME : afectar, adoptar **2** PRODUCE : presentar (una obra de teatro, etc.) **3** WEAR : ponerse

put out *vt* INCONVENIENCE : importunar, incomodar

putrefy [ˈpjuːtrəˌfaɪ] *v* **-fied; -fying** *vt* : pudrir — *vi* : pudrirse

putrid [ˈpjuːtrɪd] *adj* : putrefacto, pútrido

putter [ˈpʌtər] *vi or* **to putter around** : entretenerse

putty¹ [ˈpʌti] *vt* **-tied; -tying** : poner masilla en

putty² *n, pl* **-ties** : masilla *f*

put up *vt* **1** LODGE : alojar **2** CONTRIBUTE : contribuir, pagar

puzzle¹ [ˈpʌzəl] *vt* **-zled; -zling 1** CONFUSE : confundir, dejar perplejo **2 to puzzle out** : dar vueltas a, tratar de resolver

puzzle² *n* **1** : rompecabezas *m* ⟨a crossword puzzle : un crucigrama⟩ **2** MYSTERY : misterio *m*, enigma *m*

puzzlement [ˈpʌzəlmənt] *n* : desconcierto *m*, perplejidad *f*

pygmy¹ [ˈpɪgmi] *adj* : enano, pigmeo

pygmy² *n, pl* **-mies** DWARF : enano *m*, -na *f* **2 Pygmy** : pigmeo *m*, -mea *f*

pylon [ˈpaɪˌlɑn, -lən] *n* **1** : torre *f* de conducta eléctrica **2** : pilón *m* (de un puente)

pyramid [ˈpɪrəˌmɪd] *n* : pirámide *f*

pyre [ˈpaɪr] *n* : pira *f*

pyromania [ˌpaɪroˈmeɪniə] *n* : piromanía *f*

pyromaniac [ˌpaɪroˈmeɪniˌæk] *n* : pirómano *m*, -na *f*

pyrotechnics [ˌpaɪrəˈtɛknɪks] *npl* **1** FIREWORKS : fuegos *mpl* artificiales **2** DISPLAY, SHOW : espectáculo *m*, muestra *f* de virtuosismo ⟨computer pyrotechnics : efectos especiales hechos por computadora⟩

python [ˈpaɪθən, -θən] *n* : pitón *f*, serpiente *f* pitón

Q

q ['kju:] *n, pl* **q's** *or* **qs** ['kju:z] : decimoséptima letra del alfabeto inglés

quack¹ ['kwæk] *vi* : graznar

quack² *n* **1** : graznido *m* (de pato) **2** CHARLATAN : curandero *m*, -ra *f*; matasanos *m fam*

quadrangle ['kwɑ,dræŋgəl] *n* **1** COURTYARD : patio *m* interior **2** → quadrilateral

quadrant ['kwɑdrənt] *n* : cuadrante *m*

quadrilateral [,kwɑdrə'læţərəl] *n* : cuadrilátero *m*

quadruple ['kwɑdrə,pɛd] *n* : cuadrúpedo *m*

quadruple [kwɑ'dru:pəl, -'drʌ-; 'kwɑdrə-] *v* -**pled**; -**pling** *vt* : cuadruplicar — *vi* : cuadruplicarse

quadruplet [kwɑ'dru:plət, -'drʌ-; 'kwɑdrə-] *n* : cuatrillizo *m*, -za *f*

quagmire ['kwæg,mair, 'kwag-] *n* **1** : lodazal *m*, barrizal *m* **2** PREDICAMENT : atolladero *m*

quail¹ ['kweil] *vi* : encogerse, acobardarse

quail² *n, pl* **quail** *or* **quails** : codorniz *f*

quaint ['kweint] *adj* **1** ODD : extraño, curioso **2** PICTURESQUE : pintoresco — **quaintly** *adv*

quaintness ['kweintnəs] *n* : rareza *f*, lo curioso

quake¹ ['kweik] *vi* **quaked**; **quaking** : temblar

quake² *n* : temblor *m*, terremoto *m*

qualification [,kwɑləfə'keifən] *n* **1** LIMITATION, RESERVATION : reserva *f*, limitación *f* ⟨without qualification : sin reservas⟩ **2** REQUIREMENT : requisito *m* **3 qualifications** *npl* ABILITY : aptitud *f*, capacidad *f*

qualified ['kwɑlə,faid] *adj* : competente, capacitado

qualifier ['kwɑlə,faiər] *n* **1** : clasificado *m*, -da *f* (en deportes) **2** : calificativo *m* (en gramática)

qualify ['kwɑlə,fai] *v* -**fied**; -**fying** *vt* **1** : matizar ⟨to qualify a statement : matizar una declaración⟩ **2** MODIFY : calificar (en gramática) **3** : habilitar ⟨the certificate qualified her to teach : el certificado la habilitó para enseñar⟩ — *vi* **1** : obtener el título, recibirse ⟨to qualify as an engineer : recibirse de ingeniero⟩ **2** : clasificarse (en deportes)

quality ['kwɑləţi] *n, pl* -**ties 1** NATURE : carácter *m* **2** ATTRIBUTE : cualidad *f* **3** GRADE : calidad *f* ⟨of good quality : de buena calidad⟩

qualm ['kwɑm, 'kwɑlm, 'kwɔm] *n* **1** MISGIVING : duda *f*, aprensión *f* **2** RESERVATION, SCRUPLE : escrúpulo *m*, reparo *m*

quandary ['kwɑndri] *n, pl* -**ries** : dilema *m*

quantitative ['kwɑntə,teiţiv] *adj* : cuantitativo

quantity ['kwɑntəţi] *n, pl* -**ties** : cantidad *f*

quantum¹ ['kwɑntəm] *n* : cuanto *m* (en física)

quantum² *adj* : cuántico

quantum theory ['kwɑntəm] *n* : teoría *f* cuántica

quarantine¹ ['kwɔrən,ti:n] *vt* -**tined**; -**tining** : poner en cuarentena

quarantine² *n* : cuarentena *f*

quarrel¹ ['kwɔrəl] *vi* -**reled** *or* -**relled**; -**reling** *or* -**relling** : pelearse, reñir, discutir

quarrel² *n* : pelea *f*, riña *f*, disputa *f*

quarrelsome ['kwɔrəlsəm] *adj* : pendenciero, discutidor

quarry¹ ['kwɔri] *vt* **quarried**; **quarrying 1** EXTRACT : extraer, sacar ⟨to quarry marble : extraer mármol⟩ **2** EXCAVATE : excavar ⟨to quarry a hill : excavar un cerro⟩

quarry² *n, pl* **quarries 1** PREY : presa *f* **2** *or* **stone quarry** : cantera *f*

quart ['kwɔrt] *n* : cuarto *m* de galón

quarter¹ ['kwɔrţər] *vt* **1** : dividir en cuatro partes **2** LODGE : alojar, acuartelar (tropas)

quarter² *n* **1** : cuarto *m*, cuarta parte *f* ⟨a foot and a quarter : un pie y cuarto⟩ ⟨a quarter after three : las tres y cuarto⟩ **2** : moneda *f* de 25 centavos, cuarto *m* de dólar **3** DISTRICT : barrio *m* ⟨business quarter : barrio comercial⟩ **4** PLACE : parte *f* ⟨from all quarters : de todas partes⟩ ⟨at close quarters : de muy cerca⟩ **5** MERCY : clemencia *f*, cuartel *m* ⟨to give no quarter : no dar cuartel⟩ **6 quarters** *npl* LODGING : alojamiento *m*, cuartel *m* (militar)

quarterback ['kwɔrţər,bæk] *n* : mariscal *m* de campo

quarterly¹ ['kwɔrţərli] *adv* : cada tres meses, trimestralmente

quarterly² *adj* : trimestral

quarterly³ *n, pl* -**lies** : publicación *f* trimestral

quartermaster ['kwɔrţər,mæstər] *n* : intendente *mf*

quartet [kwɔr'tɛt] *n* : cuarteto *m*

quartz ['kwɔrts] *n* : cuarzo *m*

quash ['kwɑʃ, 'kwɔʃ] *vt* **1** ANNUL : anular **2** QUELL : sofocar, aplastar

quaver¹ ['kweivər] *vi* **1** SHAKE : temblar ⟨her voice was quavering : le temblaba la voz⟩ **2** TRILL : trinar

quaver² *n* : temblor *m* (de la voz)

quay ['ki:, 'kei, 'kwei] *n* : muelle *m*

queasiness ['kwi:zinəs] *n* : mareo *m*, náusea *f*

queasy ['kwi:zi] *adj* -**sier**; -**est** : mareado

queen ['kwi:n] *n* : reina *f*

queenly ['kwi:nli] *adj* -**lier**; -**est** : de reina, regio

queer ['kwir] *adj* : extraño, raro, curioso — **queerly** *adv*

quell ['kwɛl] *vt* : aplastar, sofocar

quench ['kwɛntʃ] vt 1 EXTINGUISH : apagar, sofocar 2 SATISFY : saciar, satisfacer (la sed)

querulous ['kwɛrələs, 'kwɛrjələs, 'kwɪr-] adj : quejumbroso, quejoso — **querulously** adv

query¹ ['kwɪri, 'kwɛr-] vt -ried; -rying 1 ASK : preguntar, interrogar ⟨we queried the professor : preguntamos al profesor⟩ 2 QUESTION : cuestionar, poner en duda ⟨to query a matter : cuestionar un asunto⟩

query² n, pl -ries 1 QUESTION : pregunta f 2 DOUBT : duda f

quest¹ ['kwɛst] v : buscar

quest² n : búsqueda f

question¹ ['kwɛstʃən] vt 1 ASK : preguntar 2 DOUBT : poner en duda, cuestionar 3 INTERROGATE : interrogar — vi INQUIRE : inquirir, preguntar

question² n 1 QUERY : pregunta f 2 ISSUE : asunto m, problema f, cuestión f 3 POSSIBILITY : posibilidad f ⟨it's out of the question : es indiscutible⟩ 4 DOUBT : duda f ⟨to call into question : poner en duda⟩

questionable ['kwɛstʃənəbəl] adj : dudoso, discutible, cuestionable ⟨questionable results : resultados discutibles⟩ ⟨questionable motives : motivos sospechosos⟩

questioner ['kwɛstʃənər] n : interrogador m, -dora f

question mark n : signo m de interrogación

questionnaire [,kwɛstʃə'nær] n : cuestionario m

queue¹ ['kju:] vi queued; queuing or queueing : hacer cola

queue² n 1 PIGTAIL : coleta f, trenza f 2 LINE : cola f, fila f

quibble¹ ['kwɪbəl] vi -bled; -bling : quejarse por nimiedades, andar con sutilezas

quibble² n : objeción f de poca monta, queja f insignificante

quick¹ ['kwɪk] adv : rápidamente

quick² adj 1 RAPID : rápido 2 ALERT, CLEVER : listo, vivo, agudo 3 **a quick temper** : un genio vivo

quick³ n 1 FLESH : carne f viva 2 **to cut someone to the quick** : herir a alguien en lo más vivo

quicken ['kwɪkən] vt 1 REVIVE : resucitar 2 AROUSE : estimular, despertar 3 HASTEN : acelerar ⟨she quickened her pace : aceleró el paso⟩

quickly ['kwɪkli] adv : rápidamente, rápido, de prisa

quickness ['kwɪknəs] n : rapidez f

quicksand ['kwɪk,sænd] n : arena f movediza

quicksilver ['kwɪk,sɪlvər] n : mercurio m, azogue m

quick-tempered ['kwɪk'tɛmpərd] adj : irascible, de genio vivo

quick-witted ['kwɪk'wɪtəd] adj : agudo

quiet¹ ['kwaɪət] vt 1 SILENCE : hacer callar, acallar 2 CALM : calmar, tranquilizar — vi **to quiet down** : calmarse, tranquilizarse

quiet² adv : silenciosamente ⟨a quiet-running engine : un motor silencioso⟩

quiet³ adj 1 CALM : tranquilo, calmoso 2 MILD : sosegado, suave ⟨a quiet disposition : un temperamento sosegado⟩ 3 SILENT : silencioso 4 UNOBTRUSIVE : discreto 5 SECLUDED : aislado ⟨a quiet nook : un rincón aislado⟩ — **quietly** adv

quiet⁴ n 1 CALM : calma f, tranquilidad f 2 SILENCE : silencio m

quietness ['kwaɪətnəs] n : suavidad f, tranquilidad f, quietud f

quietude ['kwaɪə,tu:d, -,tju:d] n : quietud f, reposo m

quill ['kwɪl] n 1 SPINE : púa f (de un puerco espín) 2 : pluma f (para escribir)

quilt¹ ['kwɪlt] vt : acolchar

quilt² n : colcha f, edredón m

quince ['kwɪnts] n : membrillo m

quinine ['kwaɪ,naɪn] n : quinina f

quintessence [kwɪn'tɛsənts] n : quintaesencia f

quintet [kwɪn'tɛt] n : quinteto m

quintuple [kwɪn'tu:pəl, -'tju:-, -'tʌ-; 'kwɪntə-] adj : quíntuplo

quintuplet [kwɪn'tʌplət, -'tu:-, -'tju:-; 'kwɪntə-] n : quintillizo m, -za f

quip¹ ['kwɪp] vi quipped; quipping : bromear

quip² n : ocurrencia f, salida f

quirk ['kwərk] n : peculiaridad f, rareza f ⟨a quirk of fate : un capricho del destino⟩

quirky ['kwərki] adj -kier; -est : peculiar, raro

quit ['kwɪt] v quit; quitting vt : dejar, abandonar ⟨to quit smoking : dejar de fumar⟩ — vi 1 STOP : parar 2 RESIGN : dimitir, renunciar

quite ['kwaɪt] adv 1 COMPLETELY : completamente, totalmente 2 RATHER : bastante ⟨quite near : bastante cerca⟩

quits ['kwɪts] adj **to call it quits** : quedar en paz

quitter ['kwɪtər] n : derrotista mf

quiver¹ ['kwɪvər] vi : temblar, estremecerse, vibrar

quiver² n 1 : carcaj m, aljaba f (para flechas) 2 TREMBLING : temblor m, estremecimiento m

quixotic [kwɪk'sɑtɪk] adj : quijotesco

quiz¹ ['kwɪz] vt quizzed; quizzing : interrogar, hacer una prueba a (en el colegio)

quiz² n, pl quizzes : examen m corto, prueba f

quizzical ['kwɪzɪkəl] adj 1 TEASING : burlón 2 CURIOUS : curioso, interrogativo

quorum ['kworəm] n : quórum m

quota [ˈkwoːtə] n : cuota f, cupo m
quotable [ˈkwoːtəbəl] adj : citable
quotation [kwoˈteɪʃən] n 1 CITATION
: cita f 2 ESTIMATE : presupuesto m,
estimación f 3 PRICE : cotización f
quotation marks npl : comillas fpl

quote¹ [ˈkwoːt] vt **quoted; quoting** 1
CITE : citar 2 VALUE : cotizar (en finanzas)
quote² n 1 → quotation 2 **quotes** npl
→ quotation marks
quotient [ˈkwoːʃənt] n : cociente m

R

r [ˈɑr] n, pl **r's** or **rs** [ˈɑrz] : decimoctava
letra del alfabeto inglés
rabbi [ˈræˌbaɪ] n : rabino m, -na f
rabbit [ˈræbət] n, pl **-bit** or **-bits** : conejo m, -ja f
rabble [ˈræbəl] n 1 MASSES : populacho
m 2 RIFFRAFF : chusma f, gentuza f
rabid [ˈræbɪd] adj 1 : rabioso, afectado
con la rabia 2 FURIOUS : furioso 3
FANATIC : fanático
rabies [ˈreɪbiːz] ns & pl : rabia f
raccoon [ræˈkuːn] n, pl **-coon** or **-coons**
: mapache m
race¹ [ˈreɪs] vi **raced; racing** 1 : correr,
competir (en una carrera) 2 RUSH : ir
a toda prisa, ir corriendo
race² n 1 CURRENT : corriente f (de
agua) 2 : carrera f ⟨dog race : carrera
de perros⟩ ⟨the presidential race : la
carrera presidencial⟩ 3 : raza f ⟨the
black race : la raza negra⟩ ⟨the human
race : el género humano⟩
racecourse [ˈreɪsˌkors] n : pista f (de carreras)
racehorse [ˈreɪsˌhors] n : caballo m de
carreras
racer [ˈreɪsər] n : corredor m, -dora f
racetrack [ˈreɪsˌtræk] n : pista f (de carreras)
racial [ˈreɪʃəl] adj : racial — **racially** adv
racism [ˈreɪˌsɪzəm] n : racismo m
racist [ˈreɪsɪst] n : racista m
rack¹ [ˈræk] vt 1 : atormentar ⟨racked
with pain : atormentado por el dolor⟩
2 to rack one's brains : devanarse los
sesos
rack² n 1 SHELF, STAND : estante m ⟨a
luggage rack : un portaequipajes⟩ ⟨a
coatrack : un perchero, una percha⟩ 2
: potro m (instrumento de la tortura)
racket [ˈrækət] n 1 : raqueta f (en deportes) 2 DIN : estruendo m, bulla f,
jaleo m fam 3 SWINDLE : estafa f, timo
m fam
racketeer [ˌrækəˈtɪr] n : estafador m,
-dora f
raconteur [ˌræˌkɑnˈtər] n : anecdotista
mf
racy [ˈreɪsi] adj **racier; -est** : subido de
tono, picante
radar [ˈreɪˌdɑr] n : radar m
radial [ˈreɪdiəl] adj : radial
radiance [ˈreɪdiəns] n : resplandor m
radiant [ˈreɪdiənt] adj : radiante — **radiantly** adv
radiate [ˈreɪdiˌeɪt] v **-ated; -ating** vt : irradiar, emitir ⟨to radiate heat : irradi-

ar el calor⟩ ⟨to radiate happiness : rebosar de alegría⟩ — vi 1 : irradiar 2
SPREAD : salir, extenderse ⟨to radiate
(out) from the center : salir del centro⟩
radiation [ˌreɪdiˈeɪʃən] n : radiación f
radiator [ˈreɪdiˌeɪtər] n : radiador m
radical¹ [ˈrædɪkəl] adj : radical — **radically** [-kli] adv
radical² n : radical mf
radicalism [ˈrædɪkəˌlɪzəm] n : radicalismo m
radii → **radius**
radio¹ [ˈreɪdiˌoː] v : llamar por radio,
transmitir por radio
radio² n, pl **-dios** : radio m (aparato), radio f (emisora, radiodifusión)
radioactive [ˌreɪdioˈæktɪv] adj : radiactivo, radioactivo
radioactivity [ˌreɪdioˌækˈtɪvəti] n, pl
-ties : radiactividad f, radioactividad f
radiologist [ˌreɪdiˈɑləd͡ʒɪst] n : radiólogo
m, -ga f
radiology [ˌreɪdiˈɑləd͡ʒi] n : radiología f
radish [ˈrædɪʃ] n : rábano m
radium [ˈreɪdiəm] n : radio m
radius [ˈreɪdiəs] n, pl **radii** [-diˌaɪ] : radio
m, -ga f
radon [ˈreɪˌdɑn] n : radón m
raffle¹ [ˈræfəl] vt **-fled; -fling** : rifar,
sortear
raffle² n : rifa f, sorteo m
raft [ˈræft] n 1 : balsa f ⟨rubber rafts
: balsas de goma⟩ 2 LOT, SLEW : montón m ⟨a raft of documents : un montón de documentos⟩
rafter [ˈræftər] n : par m, viga f
rag [ˈræg] n 1 CLOTH : trapo m 2 **rags**
npl TATTERS : harapos mpl, andrajos
mpl
ragamuffin [ˈrægəˌmʌfɪn] n : pilluelo m,
-la f
rage¹ [ˈreɪd͡ʒ] vi **raged; raging** 1 : estar
furioso, rabiar ⟨to fly into a rage : enfurecerse⟩ 2 : bramar, hacer estragos
⟨the wind was raging : el viento bramaba⟩ ⟨flue raged through the school : la
gripe hizo estragos por el colegio⟩
rage² n 1 ANGER : furia f, ira f, cólera f
2 FAD : moda f, furor m
ragged [ˈrægəd] adj 1 UNEVEN : irregular, desigual 2 TORN : hecho jirones
3 TATTERED : andrajoso, harapiento
ragout [ræˈguː] n : ragú m, estofado m
ragtime [ˈrægˌtaɪm] n : ragtime m
ragweed [ˈrægˌwiːd] n : ambrosía f
raid¹ [ˈreɪd] vt 1 : invadir, hacer una incursión en ⟨raided by enemy troops

: invadido por tropas enemigas⟩ **2**
: asaltar, atracar ⟨the gang raided the
warehouse : la pandilla asaltó el al-
macén⟩ **3** : allanar, hacer una redada
en ⟨police raided the house : la policía
allanó la vivienda⟩

raid² *n* **1** : invasión *f* (militar) **2** : asalto
m (por delincuentes) **3** : redada *f*, allanamiento *m* (por la policía)

raider ['reɪdər] *n* **1** ATTACKER : asaltante
mf; invasor *m*, -sora *f* **2 corporate
raider** : tiburón *m*

rail¹ ['reɪl] *vi* **1 to rail against** REVILE
: denostar contra **2 to rail at** SCOLD
: regañar, reprender

rail² *n* **1** BAR : barra *f*, barrera *f* **2**
HANDRAIL : pasamanos *m*, barandilla
f **3** TRACK : riel *m* (para ferrocarriles)
4 RAILROAD : ferrocarril *m*

railing ['reɪlɪŋ] *n* **1** : baranda *f* (de un
balcón, etc.) **2** RAILS : verja *f*

raillery ['reɪləri] *n, pl* **-leries** : bromas *fpl*

railroad ['reɪl,roːd] *n* : ferrocarril *m*

railway ['reɪl,weɪ] → **railroad**

raiment ['reɪmənt] *n* : vestiduras *fpl*

rain¹ ['reɪn] *vi* **1** : llover ⟨it's raining : está
lloviendo⟩ **2 to rain down** SHOWER
: llover ⟨insults rained down on him : le
llovieron los insultos⟩

rain² *n* : lluvia *f*

rainbow ['reɪn,boː] *n* : arco *m* iris

raincoat ['reɪn,koːt] *n* : impermeable *m*

raindrop ['reɪn,drɑp] *n* : gota *f* de lluvia

rainfall ['reɪn,fɔl] *n* : lluvia *f*, precipitación *f*

rainstorm ['reɪn,stɔrm] *n* : temporal *m*
(de lluvia)

rainwater ['reɪn,wɔtər] *n* : agua *f* de lluvia

rainy ['reɪni] *adj* **rainier; -est** : lluvioso

raise¹ ['reɪz] *vt* **raised; raising 1** LIFT
: levantar, subir, alzar ⟨to raise one's
spirits : levantar el ánimo a alguien⟩
2 ERECT : levantar, erigir **3** COLLECT
: recaudar ⟨to raise money : recaudar
dinero⟩ **4** REAR : criar ⟨to raise one's
children : criar uno a sus niños⟩ **5**
GROW : cultivar **6** INCREASE : aumentar, subir **7** PROMOTE : ascender **8**
PROVOKE : provocar ⟨it raised a laugh
: provocó una risa⟩ **9** BRING UP : sacar
(temas, objeciones, etc.)

raise² *n* : aumento *m*

raisin ['reɪzən] *n* : pasa *f*

raja *or* **rajah** ['rɑdʒə, -ˌdʒɑ, -ˌʒɑ] *n* : rajá
m

rake¹ ['reɪk] *v* **raked; raking** *vt* **1** : rastrillar ⟨to rake leaves : rastrillar las ho-
jas⟩ **2** SWEEP : barrer ⟨raked with gunfire : barrido con metralla⟩ — *vi* **to rake
through** : revolver, hurgar en

rake² *n* **1** : rastrillo *m* **2** LIBERTINE : libertino *m*, -na *f* : calavera *m*

rakish ['reɪkɪʃ] *adj* **1** JAUNTY : desenvuelto, desenfadado **2** DISSOLUTE
: libertino, disoluto

rally¹ ['ræli] *v* **-lied; -lying** *vi* **1** MEET,
UNITE : reunirse, congregarse **2** RE-

COVER : recuperarse — *vt* **1** ASSEMBLE
: reunir (tropas, etc.) **2** RECOVER : recobrar (la fuerza, el ánimo, etc.)

rally² *n, pl* **-lies** : reunión *f*, mitin *m*, manifestación *f*

ram¹ ['ræm] *v* **rammed; ramming** *vt* **1**
DRIVE : hincar, clavar ⟨he rammed it
into the ground : lo hincó en la tierra⟩
2 SMASH : estrellar, embestir — *vi* COL-
LIDE : chocar (contra), estrellarse

ram² *n* **1** : carnero *m* (animal) **2 battering ram** : ariete *m*

RAM ['ræm] *n* : RAM *f*

ramble¹ ['ræmbəl] *vi* **-bled; -bling 1**
WANDER : pasear, deambular **2 to ram-
ble on** : divagar, perder el hilo **3**
SPREAD : trepar (dícese de una planta)

ramble² *n* : paseo *m*, excursión *f*

rambler ['ræmblər] *n* **1** WALKER : excursionista *mf* **2** ROSE : rosa *f* trepadora

rambunctious [ræm'bʌŋkʃəs] *adj* UN-
RULY : alborotado

ramification [ˌræməfə'keɪʃən] *n* : ramificación *f*

ramify ['ræmə,faɪ] *vi* **-fied; -fying** : ramificarse

ramp ['ræmp] *n* : rampa *f*

rampage¹ ['ræm,peɪdʒ, ræm'peɪdʒ] *vi*
-paged; -paging : andar arrasando
todo, correr destrozando

rampage² ['ræm,peɪdʒ] *n* : alboroto *m*,
frenesí *m* (de violencia)

rampant ['ræmpənt] *adj* : desenfrenado

rampart ['ræm,pɑrt] *n* : terraplén *m*, muralla *f*

ramrod ['ræm,rɑd] *n* : baqueta *f*

ramshackle ['ræm,ʃækəl] *adj* : destartalado

ran → **run**

ranch ['rænʧ] *n* **1** : hacienda *f*, rancho
m, finca *f* ganadera **2** FARM : granja *f*
⟨fruit ranch : granja de frutas⟩

rancher ['rænʧər] *n* : estanciero *m*, -ra
f; ranchero *m*, -ra *f*

rancid ['ræntsɪd] *adj* : rancio

rancor ['ræŋkər] *n* : rencor *m*

random ['rændəm] *adj* **1** : fortuito,
aleatorio **2 at ~** : al azar — **randomly** *adv*

rang → **ring**

range¹ ['reɪndʒ] *v* **ranged; ranging** *vt*
ARRANGE : alinear, ordenar, arreglar
— *vi* **1** ROAM : deambular ⟨to range
through the town : deambular por el
pueblo⟩ **2** EXTEND : extenderse ⟨the
results range widely : los resultados se
extienden mucho⟩ **3** VARY : variar
⟨discounts range from 20% to 40% : los
descuentos varían entre 20% y 40%⟩

range² *n* **1** ROW : fila *f*, hilera *f* ⟨a mountain range : una cordillera⟩ **2** GRASS-
LAND : pradera *f*, pampa *f* **3** STOVE
: cocina *f* **4** VARIETY : variedad *f*, gama
f **5** SPHERE : ámbito *m*, esfera *f*, campo *m* **6** REACH : registro *m* (de la voz),
alcance *m* (de un arma de fuego) **7
shooting range** : campo *m* de tiro

ranger ['reɪndʒər] *n or* **forest ranger** : guardabosque *mf*

rangy ['reɪndʒi] *adj* **rangier; -est** : alto y delgado

rank¹ ['ræŋk] *vt* **1** RANGE : alinear, ordenar, poner en fila **2** CLASSIFY : clasificar — *vi* **1 to rank above** : ser superior a **2 to rank among** : encontrarse entre, figurar entre

rank² *adj* **1** LUXURIANT : lozano, exuberante (dícese de una planta) **2** SMELLY : fétido, maloliente **3** OUTRIGHT : completo, absoluto ⟨a rank injustice : una injusticia manifiesta⟩

rank³ *n* **1** LINE, ROW : fila *f* ⟨to close ranks : cerrar filas⟩ **2** GRADE, POSITION : grado *m*, rango *m* (militar) ⟨to pull rank : abusar de su autoridad⟩ **3** CLASS : categoría *f*, clase *f* **4 ranks** *npl* : soldados *mpl* rasos

rank and file 1 RANKS : soldados *mpl* rasos **2** : bases *fpl* (de un partido, etc.)

rankle ['ræŋkəl] *v* **-kled; -kling** *vi* : doler — *vt* : irritar, herir

ransack ['ræn,sæk] *vt* : revolver, desvalijar, registrar de arriba abajo

ransom¹ ['rænsəm] *vt* : rescatar, pagar un rescate por

ransom² *n* : rescate *m*

rant ['rænt] *vi or* **to rant and rave** : despotricar, desvariar

rap¹ ['ræp] *v* **rapped; rapping** *vt* **1** KNOCK : golpetear, dar un golpe en **2** CRITICIZE : criticar — *vi* **1** CHAT : charlar, cotorrear *fam* **2** KNOCK : dar un golpe

rap² *n* **1** BLOW, KNOCK : golpe *m*, golpecito *m* **2** CHAT : charla *f* **3** *or* **rap music** : rap *m* **4 to take the rap** : pagar el pato *fam*

rapacious [rə'peɪʃəs] *adj* **1** GREEDY : avaricioso, codicioso **2** PREDATORY : rapaz, de rapiña **3** RAVENOUS : voraz

rape¹ ['reɪp] *vt* **raped; raping** : violar

rape² *n* **1** : colza *f* (planta) **2** : violación *f* (de una persona)

rapid ['ræpɪd] *adj* : rápido — **rapidly** *adv*

rapidity [rə'pɪdəṭi] *n* : rapidez *f*

rapids ['ræpɪdz] *npl* : rápidos *mpl*

rapier ['reɪpiər] *n* : estoque *m*

rapist ['reɪpɪst] *n* : violador *m*, -dora *f*

rapper ['ræpər] *n* : cantante *mf* de rap; rapero *m*, -ra *f*

rapport [ræ'por] *n* : relación *f* armoniosa, entendimiento *m*

rapt ['ræpt] *adj* : absorto, embelesado

rapture ['ræptʃər] *n* : éxtasis *m*

rapturous ['ræptʃərəs] *adj* : extasiado, embelesado

rare ['rær] *adj* **rarer; rarest 1** RAREFIED : enrarecido **2** FINE : excelente, excepcional ⟨a rare talent : un talento excepcional⟩ **3** UNCOMMON : raro, poco común **4** : poco cocido (dícese de la carne)

rarefy ['ræra,faɪ] *vt* **-fied; -fying** : rarificar, enrarecer

rarely ['rærli] *adv* SELDOM : pocas veces, rara vez

raring ['ræren, -ɪŋ] *adj* : lleno de entusiasmo, con muchas ganas

rarity ['ræroṭi] *n, pl* **-ties** : rareza *f*

rascal ['ræskəl] *n* : pillo *m*, -lla *f*; pícaro *m*, -ra *f*

rash¹ ['ræʃ] *adj* : imprudente, precipitado — **rashly** *adv*

rash² *n* : sarpullido *m*, erupción *f*

rashness ['ræʃnəs] *n* : precipitación *f*, impetuosidad *f*

rasp¹ ['ræsp] *vt* **1** SCRAPE : raspar, escofinar **2 to rasp out** : decir en voz áspera

rasp² *n* : escofina *f*

raspberry ['ræz,bɛri] *n, pl* **-ries** : frambuesa *f*

rat ['ræt] *n* : rata *f*

ratchet ['rætʃət] *n* : trinquete *m*

rate¹ ['reɪt] *vt* **rated; rating 1** CONSIDER, REGARD : considerar, estimar **2** DESERVE : merecer

rate² *n* **1** PACE, SPEED : velocidad *f*, ritmo *m* ⟨at this rate : a este paso⟩ **2** : índice *m*, tasa *f* ⟨birth rate : índice de natalidad⟩ ⟨interest rate : tasa de interés⟩ **3** CHARGE, PRICE : precio *m*, tarifa *f*

rather ['ræðər, 'rʌ-, 'rɑ-] *adv* **1** (*indicating preference*) ⟨she would rather stay in the house : preferiría quedarse en casa⟩ ⟨I'd rather not : mejor que no⟩ **2** (*indicating preciseness*) ⟨my father, or rather my stepfather : mi padre, o mejor dicho mi padrastro⟩ **3** INSTEAD : sino que, más que, al contrario ⟨I'm not pleased; rather I'm disappointed : no estoy satisfecho, sino desilusionado⟩ **4** SOMEWHAT : algo, un tanto ⟨rather strange : un poco extraño⟩ **5** QUITE : bastante ⟨rather difficult : bastante difícil⟩

ratification [,ræṭəfə'keɪʃən] *n* : ratificación *f*

ratify ['ræṭə,faɪ] *vt* **-fied; -fying** : ratificar

rating ['reɪṭɪŋ] *n* **1** STANDING : clasificación *f*, posición *f* **2 ratings** *npl* : índice *m* de audiencia

ratio ['reɪʃio] *n, pl* **-tios** : proporción *f*, relación *f*

ration¹ ['ræʃən, 'reɪʃən] *vt* : racionar

ration² *n* **1** : ración *f* **2 rations** *npl* PROVISIONS : víveres *mpl*

rational ['ræʃənəl] *adj* : racional, razonable, lógico — **rationally** *adv*

rationale [,ræʃə'næl] *n* **1** EXPLANATION : explicación *f* **2** BASIS : base *f*, razones *fpl*

rationality [,ræʃə'næləṭi] *n, pl* **-ties** : racionalidad *f*

rationalization [,ræʃənələ'zeɪʃən] *n* : racionalización *f*

rationalize ['ræʃənə,laɪz] *vt* **-ized; -izing** : racionalizar

rattle¹ ['ræṭəl] *v* **-tled; -tling** *vi* **1** CLATTER : traquetear, hacer ruido **2 to rattle on** CHATTER : parlotear *fam* — *vt*

1 : hacer sonar, agitar ⟨the wind rattled the door : el viento sacudió la puerta⟩ **2** DISCONCERT, WORRY : desconcertar, poner nervioso **3 to rattle off** : despachar, recitar, decir de corrido

rattle² *n* **1** CLATTER : traqueteo *m*, ruido *m* **2 or baby's rattle** : sonajero *m* **3** : cascabel *m* (de una culebra)

rattler ['rætələr] → **rattlesnake**

rattlesnake ['rætəl,sneɪk] *n* : serpiente *f* de cascabel

ratty ['ræti] *adj* rattier; -est : raído, andrajoso

raucous ['rɔkəs] *adj* **1** HOARSE : ronco **2** BOISTEROUS : escandaloso, bullicioso — **raucously** *adv*

ravage¹ ['rævɪdʒ] *vt* -aged; -aging : devastar, arrasar, hacer estragos

ravage² *n* : destrozo *m*, destrucción *f* ⟨the ravages of war : los estragos de la guerra⟩

rave ['reɪv] *vi* raved; raving **1** : delirar, desvariar ⟨to rave like a maniac : desvariar como un loco⟩ **2 to rave about** : hablar con entusiasmo sobre, entusiasmarse por

ravel ['rævəl] *v* -eled *or* -elled; -eling *or* -elling *vt* UNRAVEL : desenredar, desenmarañar — *vi* FRAY : deshilacharse

raven ['reɪvən] *n* : cuervo *m*

ravenous ['rævənəs] *adj* : hambriento, voraz — **ravenously** *adv*

ravine [rə'viːn] *n* : barranco *m*, quebrada *f*

ravish ['rævɪʃ] *vt* **1** PLUNDER : saquear **2** ENCHANT : embelesar, cautivar, encantar

raw ['rɔ] *adj* rawer; rawest **1** UNCOOKED : crudo **2** UNTREATED : sin tratar, sin refinar, puro ⟨raw data : datos en bruto⟩ ⟨raw materials : materias primas⟩ **3** INEXPERIENCED : novato, inexperto **4** OPEN : abierto, en carne viva ⟨a raw sore : una llaga abierta⟩ **5** : frío y húmedo ⟨a raw day : un día crudo⟩ **6** UNFAIR : injusto ⟨a raw deal : un trato injusto, una injusticia⟩

rawhide ['rɔ,haɪd] *n* : cuero *m* sin curtir

ray ['reɪ] *n* **1** : rayo *m* (de la luz, etc.) ⟨a ray of hope : un resquicio de esperanza⟩ **2** : raya *f* (pez)

rayon ['reɪ,ɑn] *n* : rayón *m*

raze ['reɪz] *vt* razed; razing : arrasar, demoler

razor ['reɪzər] *n* **1** *or* **straight razor** : navaja *f* (de afeitar) **2** *or* **safety razor** : maquinilla *f* de afeitar, rastrillo *m* Mex **3** SHAVER : afeitadora *f*, rasuradora *f*

reach¹ ['riːtʃ] *vt* **1** EXTEND : extender, alargar ⟨to reach out one's hand : extender la mano⟩ **2** : alcanzar ⟨I couldn't reach the apple : no pude alcanzar la manzana⟩ **3** : llegar a, llegar hasta ⟨the shadow reached the wall : la sombra llegó hasta la pared⟩ **4** CONTACT : contactar, ponerse en contacto con — *vi* **1 or to reach out** : extender la mano **2** STRETCH : extenderse **3 to reach for** : tratar de agarrar

reach² *n* : alcance *m*, extensión *f*

react [ri'ækt] *vi* : reaccionar

reaction [ri'ækʃən] *n* : reacción *f*

reactionary¹ [ri'ækʃə,nɛri] *adj* : reaccionario

reactionary² *n, pl* -ries : reaccionario *m*, -ria *f*

reactor [ri'æktər] *n* : reactor *m* ⟨nuclear reactor : reactor nuclear⟩

read¹ ['riːd] *v* read ['rɛd]; reading *vt* **1** : leer ⟨to read a story : leer un cuento⟩ **2** INTERPRET : interpretar ⟨it can be read two ways : se puede interpretar de dos maneras⟩ **3** : decir, poner ⟨the sign read "No smoking" : el letrero decía "No Fumar"⟩ **4** : marcar ⟨the thermometer reads 70° : el termómetro marca 70°⟩ — *vi* **1** : leer ⟨he can read : sabe leer⟩ **2** SAY : decir ⟨the list reads as follows : la lista dice lo siguiente⟩

read² *n* **to be a good read** : ser una lectura amena

readable ['riːdəbəl] *adj* : legible — **readably** [-bli] *adv*

reader ['riːdər] *n* : lector *m*, -tora *f*

readily ['rɛdəli] *adv* **1** WILLINGLY : de buena gana, con gusto **2** EASILY : fácilmente, con facilidad

readiness ['rɛdinəs] *n* **1** WILLINGNESS : buena disposición *f* **2 to be in readiness** : estar preparado

reading ['riːdɪŋ] *n* : lectura *f*

readjust [,riːə'dʒʌst] *vt* : reajustar — *vi* : volverse a adaptar

readjustment [,riːə'dʒʌstmənt] *n* : reajuste *m*

ready¹ ['rɛdi] *vt* readied; readying : preparar

ready² *adj* readier; -est **1** PREPARED : listo, preparado **2** WILLING : dispuesto **3** : a punto de ⟨ready to cry : a punto de llorar⟩ **4** AVAILABLE : disponible ⟨ready cash : efectivo⟩ **5** QUICK : vivo, agudo ⟨a ready wit : un ingenio agudo⟩

ready–made ['rɛdi'meɪd] *adj* : preparado, confeccionado

reaffirm [,riːə'fərm] *vt* : reafirmar

real¹ ['riːl] *adv* VERY : muy ⟨we had a real good time : lo pasamos muy bien⟩

real² *adj* **1** : inmobiliario ⟨real property : bien inmueble, bien raíz⟩ **2** GENUINE : auténtico, genuino **3** ACTUAL, TRUE : real, verdadero ⟨a real friend : un verdadero amigo⟩ **4 for real** SERIOUSLY : de veras, de verdad

real estate *n* : propiedad *f* inmobiliaria, bienes *mpl* raíces

realign [,riːə'laɪn] *vt* : realinear

realignment [,riːə'laɪnmənt] *n* : realineamiento *m*

realism ['riːə,lɪzəm] *n* : realismo *m*

realist ['riːəlɪst] *n* : realista *mf*

realistic [,riːə'lɪstɪk] *adj* : realista

realistically [,riːə'lɪstɪkli] *adv* : de manera realista

reality [ri'æləti] *n, pl* **-ties** : realidad *f*

realizable [ˌriːə'laɪzəbəl] *adj* : feasible, attainable

realization [ˌriːələ'zeɪʃən] *n* : realización *f*

realize ['riːəˌlaɪz] *vt* **-ized; -izing** **1** AC-COMPLISH : realizar, llevar a cabo **2** GAIN : obtener, realizar, sacar ⟨to realize a profit : realizar beneficios⟩ **3** UNDERSTAND : darse cuenta de, saber

really ['riːli, 'riː-] *adv* **1** ACTUALLY : de verdad, en realidad **2** TRULY : verdaderamente, realmente **3** FRANKLY : francamente, en serio

realm ['rɛlm] *n* **1** KINGDOM : reino *m* **2** SPHERE : esfera *f*, campo *m*

ream¹ ['riːm] *vt* : escariar

ream² *n* **1** : resma *f* (de papel) **2 reams** *npl* LOADS : montones *mpl*

reap ['riːp] *v* : cosechar

reaper ['riːpər] *n* **1** : cosechador *m*, -dora *f* (persona) **2** : cosechadora *f* (máquina)

reappear [ˌriːə'pɪr] *vi* : reaparecer

reappearance [ˌriːə'pɪrənts] *n* : reaparición *f*

rear¹ ['rɪr] *vt* **1** LIFT, RAISE : levantar **2** BREED, BRING UP : criar — *vi or* **to rear up** : encabritarse

rear² *adj* : trasero, posterior, de atrás

rear³ *n* **1** BACK : parte *f* de atrás ⟨to bring up the rear : cerrar la marcha⟩ **2** *or* **rear end** : trasero *m*

rear admiral *n* : contraalmirante *mf*

rearrange [ˌriːə'reɪndʒ] *vt* **-ranged; -ranging** : colocar de otra manera, volver a arreglar, reorganizar

rearview mirror ['rɪrˌvjuː-] *n* : retrovisor *m*

reason¹ ['riːzən] *vt* THINK : pensar — *vi* : razonar ⟨I can't reason with her : no puedo razonar con ella⟩

reason² *n* **1** CAUSE, GROUND : razón *f*, motivo *m* ⟨the reason for his trip : el motivo de su viaje⟩ ⟨for this reason : por esta razón, por lo cual⟩ ⟨the reason why : la razón por la cual, el porqué⟩ **2** SENSE : razón *f* ⟨to lose one's reason : perder los sesos⟩ ⟨to listen to reason : avenirse a razones⟩

reasonable ['riːzənəbəl] *adj* **1** SENSIBLE : razonable **2** INEXPENSIVE : barato, económico

reasonably ['riːzənəbli] *adv* **1** SENSIBLY : razonablemente **2** FAIRLY : bastante

reasoning ['riːzənɪŋ] *n* : razonamiento *m*, raciocinio *m*, argumentos *mpl*

reassess [ˌriːə'sɛs] *vt* : revaluar, reconsiderar

reassurance [ˌriːə'ʃʊrənts] *n* : consuelo *m*, palabras *fpl* alentadoras

reassure [ˌriːə'ʃʊr] *vt* **-sured; -suring** : tranquilizar

reassuring [ˌriːə'ʃʊrɪŋ] *adj* : tranquilizador

reawaken [ˌriːə'weɪkən] *vt* : volver a despertar, reavivar

rebate ['riːˌbeɪt] *n* : reembolso *m*, devolución *f*

rebel¹ [rɪ'bɛl] *vi* **-belled; -belling** : rebelarse, sublevarse

rebel² ['rɛbəl] *adj* : rebelde

rebel³ ['rɛbəl] *n* : rebelde *mf*

rebellion [rɪ'bɛljən] *n* : rebelión *f*

rebellious [rɪ'bɛljəs] *adj* : rebelde

rebelliousness [rɪ'bɛljəsnəs] *n* : rebeldía *f*

rebirth [ˌriː'bərθ] *n* : renacimiento *m*

reboot [riː'buːt] *vt* : reiniciar (una computadora)

reborn [riː'bɔrn] *adj* **to be reborn** : renacer

rebound¹ ['riːˌbaʊnd, ˌriː'baʊnd] *vi* : rebotar

rebound² ['riːˌbaʊnd] *n* : rebote *m*

rebuff¹ [rɪ'bʌf] *vt* : desairar, rechazar

rebuff² *n* : desaire *m*, rechazo *m*

rebuild [ˌriː'bɪld] *vt* **-built** [-'bɪlt]; **-building** : reconstruir

rebuke¹ [rɪ'bjuːk] *vt* **-buked; -buking** : reprender, regañar

rebuke² *n* : reprimenda *f*, reproche *m*

rebut [rɪ'bʌt] *vt* **-butted; -butting** : rebatir, refutar

rebuttal [rɪ'bʌtəl] *n* : refutación *f*

recalcitrant [rɪ'kælsətrənt] *adj* : recalcitrante

recall¹ [rɪ'kɔl] *vt* **1** : llamar, retirar ⟨recalled to active duty : llamado al servicio activo⟩ **2** REMEMBER : recordar, acordarse de **3** REVOKE : revocar

recall² [rɪ'kɔl, 'riːˌkɔl] *n* **1** : retirada *f* (de personas o mercancías) **2** MEMORY : memoria *f* ⟨to have total recall : poder recordar todo⟩

recant [rɪ'kænt] *vt* : retractarse de — *vi* : retractarse, renegar

recapitulate [ˌriːkə'pɪtʃəˌleɪt] *v* **-lated; -lating** : resumir, recapitular

recapture [ˌriː'kæptʃər] *vt* **-tured; -turing** **1** REGAIN : volver a tomar, reconquistar **2** RELIVE : revivir (la juventud, etc.)

recast [riː'kæst] *vt* **-cast; -casting** **1** : refundir (metales) **2** REWRITE : refundir, modificar

recede [rɪ'siːd] *vi* **-ceded; -ceding** **1** WITHDRAW : retirarse, retroceder **2** FADE : desvanecerse, alejarse **3** SLANT : inclinarse **4 to have a receding hairline** : tener entradas

receipt [rɪ'siːt] *n* **1** : recibo *m* **2 receipts** *npl* : ingresos *mpl*, entradas *fpl*

receivable [rɪ'siːvəbəl] *adj* **accounts receivable** : cuentas por cobrar

receive [rɪ'siːv] *vt* **-ceived; -ceiving** **1** GET : recibir ⟨to receive a letter : recibir una carta⟩ ⟨to receive a blow : recibir un golpe⟩ **2** WELCOME : acoger, recibir ⟨to receive guests : tener invitados⟩ **3** : recibir, captar (señales de radio)

receiver [rɪ'siːvər] *n* **1** : receptor *m*, -tora *f* (en futbol americano) **2** : receptor *m* (de radio o televisión) **3 telephone receiver** : auricular *m*

recent ['riːsənt] *adj* : reciente — **recently** *adv*

receptacle [ri'sɛptɪkəl] n : receptáculo m, recipiente m

reception [ri'sɛpʃən] n : recepción f

receptionist [ri'sɛpʃənɪst] n : recepcionista mf

receptive [ri'sɛptɪv] adj : receptivo

receptivity [ˌriːˌsɛp'tɪvəti] n : receptividad f

recess[1] [ri'sɛs, rɪ'sɛs] vt 1 : poner en un hueco ⟨recessed lighting : iluminación empotrada⟩ 2 ADJOURN : suspender, levantar

recess[2] n 1 ALCOVE : hueco m, nicho m 2 BREAK : receso m, descanso m, recreo m (en el colegio)

recession [ri'sɛʃən] n : recesión f, depresión f económica

recessive [ri'sɛsɪv] adj : recesivo

recharge [ˌriː'tʃɑrdʒ] vt -charged; -charging : recargar

rechargeable [ˌriː'tʃɑrdʒəbəl] adj : recargable

recipe ['rɛsəˌpiː] n : receta f

recipient [ri'sɪpiənt] n : recipiente mf

reciprocal [ri'sɪprəkəl] adj : recíproco

reciprocate [ri'sɪprəˌkeɪt] vi -cated; -cating : reciprocar

reciprocity [ˌrɛsə'prɑsəti] n, pl -ties : reciprocidad f

recital [ri'saɪtəl] n 1 PERFORMANCE : recital m 2 ENUMERATION : relato m, enumeración f

recitation [ˌrɛsə'teɪʃən] n : recitación f

recite [ri'saɪt] vt -cited; -citing 1 : recitar (un poema, etc.) 2 RECOUNT : narrar, relatar, enumerar

reckless ['rɛkləs] adj : imprudente, temerario — **recklessly** adv

recklessness ['rɛkləsnəs] n : imprudencia f, temeridad f

reckon ['rɛkən] vt 1 CALCULATE : calcular, contar 2 CONSIDER : considerar

reckoning ['rɛkənɪŋ] n 1 CALCULATION : cálculo m 2 SETTLEMENT : ajuste m de cuentas ⟨day of reckoning : día del juicio final⟩

reclaim [ri'kleɪm] vt 1 : ganar, sanear ⟨to reclaim marshy land : sanear las tierras pantanosas⟩ 2 RECOVER : recobrar, reciclar ⟨to reclaim old tires : reciclar llantas desechadas⟩ 3 REGAIN : reclamar, recuperar ⟨to reclaim one's rights : reclamar unos sus derechos⟩

recline [ri'klaɪn] vi -clined; -clining 1 LEAN : reclinarse 2 REPOSE : recostarse

recluse ['rɛˌkluːs, ri'kluːs] n : solitario m, -ria f

recognition [ˌrɛkɪg'nɪʃən] n : reconocimiento m

recognizable ['rɛkəgˌnaɪzəbəl] adj : reconocible

recognize ['rɛkɪgˌnaɪz] vt -nized; -nizing : reconocer

recoil[1] [ri'kɔɪl] vi : retroceder, dar un culatazo

recoil[2] ['riːˌkɔɪl, ri'-] n : retroceso m, culatazo m

recollect [ˌrɛkə'lɛkt] v : recordar

recollection [ˌrɛkə'lɛkʃən] n : recuerdo m

recommend [ˌrɛkə'mɛnd] vt 1 : recomendar ⟨she recommended the medicine : recomendó la medicina⟩ 2 ADVISE, COUNSEL : aconsejar, recomendar

recommendation [ˌrɛkəmən'deɪʃən] n : recomendación f

recompense[1] ['rɛkəmˌpɛnts] vt -pensed; -pensing : indemnizar, recompensar

recompense[2] n : indemnización f, compensación f

reconcile ['rɛkənˌsaɪl] v -ciled; -ciling vt 1 : reconciliar (personas), conciliar (ideas, etc.) 2 to reconcile oneself to : resignarse a — vi MAKE UP : reconciliarse, hacer las paces

reconciliation [ˌrɛkənˌsɪli'eɪʃən] n : reconciliación f (con personas), conciliación f (con ideas, etc.)

recondite ['rɛkənˌdaɪt, ri'kɑn-] adj : recóndito, abstruso

recondition [ˌriːkən'dɪʃən] vt : reacondicionar

reconnaissance [ri'kɑnəzənts, -sənts] n : reconocimiento m

reconnoiter or **reconnoitre** [ˌriːkə'nɔɪtər, ˌrɛkə-] v -tered or -tred; -tering or -tring vt : reconocer — vi : hacer un reconocimiento

reconsider [ˌriːkən'sɪdər] vt : reconsiderar, repensar

reconsideration [ˌriːkənˌsɪdə'reɪʃən] n : reconsideración f

reconstruct [ˌriːkən'strʌkt] vt : reconstruir

reconstruction [ˌriːkən'strʌkʃən] n : reconstrucción f

record[1] [ri'kɔrd] vt 1 WRITE DOWN : anotar, apuntar 2 REGISTER : registrar, hacer constar 3 INDICATE : marcar (una temperatura, etc.) 4 TAPE : grabar

record[2] ['rɛkərd] n 1 DOCUMENT : registro m, documento m oficial 2 HISTORY : historial m ⟨a good academic record : un buen historial académico⟩ ⟨criminal record : antecedentes penales⟩ 3 : récord m ⟨the world record : el récord mundial⟩ 4 : disco m (de música, etc.) ⟨to make a record : grabar un disco⟩

recorder [ri'kɔrdər] n 1 : flauta f dulce (instrumento de viento) 2 tape recorder : grabadora f

recording [ri'kɔrdɪŋ] n : grabación f

recount[1] [ri'kaʊnt] vt 1 NARRATE : narrar, relatar 2 : volver a contar (votos, etc.)

recount[2] ['riːˌkaʊnt, ˌri'-] n : recuento m

recoup [ri'kuːp] vt : recuperar, recobrar

recourse ['riːˌkors, ri'-] n : recurso m ⟨to have recourse to : recurrir a⟩

recover [ri'kʌvər] vt REGAIN : recobrar — vi RECUPERATE : recuperarse

recovery [ri'kʌvəri] *n, pl* **-eries** : recuperación *f*

re–create [ˌri:kri'eit] *vt* **-ated**; **-ating** : recrear

recreation [ˌrɛkri'eiʃən] *n* : recreo *m*, esparcimiento *m*, diversión *f*

recreational [ˌrɛkri'eiʃənəl] *adj* : recreativo, de recreo

recrimination [ri,krimə'neiʃən] *n* : recriminación *f*

recruit[1] [ri'kru:t] *vt* : reclutar

recruit[2] *n* : recluta *mf*

recruitment [ri'kru:tmənt] *n* : reclutamiento *m*, alistamiento *m*

rectal ['rɛktəl] *adj* : rectal

rectangle ['rɛkˌtæŋgəl] *n* : rectángulo *m*

rectangular [rɛk'tæŋgjələr] *adj* : rectangular

rectify ['rɛktəˌfai] *vt* **-fied**; **-fying** : rectificar

rectitude ['rɛktəˌtu:d, -ˌtju:d] *n* : rectitud *f*

rector ['rɛktər] *n* : rector *m*, -tora *f*

rectory ['rɛktəri] *n, pl* **-ries** : rectoría *f*

rectum ['rɛktəm] *n, pl* **-tums** *or* **-ta** [-tə] : recto *m*

recuperate [ri'ku:pəˌreit, -'kju:-] *v* **-ated**; **-ating** *vt* : recuperar — *vi* : recuperarse, restablecerse

recuperation [ri,ku:pə'reiʃən, -ˌkju:-] *n* : recuperación *f*

recur [ri'kər] *vi* **-curred**; **-curring** : volver a ocurrir, volver a producirse, repetirse

recurrence [ri'kərənts] *n* : repetición *f*, reaparición *f*

recurrent [ri'kərənt] *adj* : recurrente, que se repite

recyclable [ri'saikələbəl] *adj* : reciclable

recycle [ri'saikəl] *vt* **-cled**; **-cling** : reciclar

recycling [ri'saikəliŋ] *n* : reciclaje *m*

red[1] ['rɛd] *adj* **1** : rojo, colorado ⟨to be red in the face : ponerse colorado⟩ ⟨to have red hair : ser pelirrojo⟩ **2** COMMUNIST : rojo, comunista

red[2] *n* **1** : rojo *m*, colorado *m* **2** Red COMMUNIST : comunista *mf*

red blood cell *n* : glóbulo *m* rojo

red–blooded ['rɛd'blʌdəd] *adj* : vigoroso

redcap ['rɛdˌkæp] → **porter**

redden ['rɛdən] *vt* : enrojecer — *vi* BLUSH : enrojecerse, ruborizarse

reddish ['rɛdiʃ] *adj* : rojizo

redecorate [ˌri:'dɛkəˌreit] *vt* **-rated**; **-rating** : renovar, pintar de nuevo

redeem [ri'di:m] *vt* **1** RESCUE, SAVE : rescatar, salvar **2** : desempeñar ⟨she redeemed it from the pawnshop : lo desempeñó de la casa de empeños⟩ **3** : redimir (en religión) **4** : canjear, vender ⟨to redeem coupons : canjear cupones⟩

redeemer [ri'di:mər] *n* : redentor *m*, -tora *f*

redefine [ˌri:di'fain] *vt* : redefinir

redemption [ri'dɛmpʃən] *n* : redención *f*

redesign [ˌri:di'zain] *vt* : rediseñar

red–handed ['rɛd'hændəd] *adj* : con las manos en la masa

redhead ['rɛdˌhɛd] *n* : pelirrojo *m*, -ja *f*

red–hot ['rɛd'hɑt] *adj* **1** : al rojo vivo, candente **2** CURRENT : de candente actualidad **3** POPULAR : de gran popularidad

rediscover [ˌri:di'skʌvər] *vt* : redescubrir

redistribute [ˌri:di'striˌbju:t] *vt* **-uted**; **-uting** : redistribuir

red–letter ['rɛd'lɛtər] *adj* red–letter day : día *m* memorable

redness ['rɛdnəs] *n* : rojez *f*

redo [ˌri:'du:] *vt* **-did** [-did]; **-done** [-'dʌn]; **-doing** **1** : hacer de nuevo **2** → **redecorate**

redolence ['rɛdələnts] *n* : fragancia *f*

redolent ['rɛdələnt] *adj* **1** FRAGRANT : fragante, oloroso **2** SUGGESTIVE : evocador

redouble [ri'dʌbəl] *vt* **-bled**; **-bling** : redoblar, intensificar (esfuerzos, etc.)

redoubtable [r'dautəbəl] *adj* : temible

redress [ri'drɛs] *vt* : reparar, remediar, enmendar

red snapper *n* : pargo *m*, huachinango *m* Mex

red tape *n* : papeleo *m*

reduce [ri'du:s, -'dju:s] *v* **-duced**; **-ducing** *vt* **1** LESSEN : reducir, disminuir, rebajar (precios) **2** DEMOTE : bajar de categoría, degradar **3** to be reduced to : verse rebajado a, verse forzado a **4** to reduce someone to tears : hacer llorar a alguien — *vi* SLIM : adelgazar

reduction [ri'dʌkʃən] *n* : reducción *f*, rebaja *f*

redundancy [ri'dʌndəntsi] *n, pl* **-cies** **1** : superfluidad *f* **2** REPETITION : redundancia *f*

redundant [ri'dʌndənt] *adj* : superfluo, redundante

redwood ['rɛdˌwud] *n* : secoya *f*

reed ['ri:d] *n* **1** : caña *f*, carrizo *m*, junco *m* **2** : lengüeta *f* (para instrumentos de viento)

reef ['ri:f] *n* : arrecife *m*, escollo *m*

reek[1] ['ri:k] *vi* : apestar

reek[2] *n* : hedor *m*

reel[1] ['ri:l] *vt* **1** to reel in : enrollar, sacar (un pez) del agua **2** to reel off : recitar de un tirón — *vi* **1** SPIN, WHIRL : girar, dar vueltas **2** STAGGER : tambalearse

reel[2] *n* **1** : carrete *m* (de pescar etc.), rollo *m* (de fotos) **2** : baile *m* escocés **3** STAGGER : tambaleo *m*

reelect [ˌri:i'lɛkt] *vt* : reelegir

reenact [ˌri:i'nækt] *vt* : representar de nuevo, reconstruir

reenter [ˌri:'ɛntər] *vt* : volver a entrar

reestablish [ˌri:i'stæbliʃ] *vt* : restablecer

reevaluate [ˌri:i'væljuˌeit] *vt* **-ated**; **-ating** : revaluar

reevaluation [ˌri:iˌvælju'eiʃən] *n* : revaluación *f*

reexamine [ˌriːɪɡˈzæmən, -g-] vt **-ined;**
-ining : volver a examinar, reexaminar
refer [rɪˈfər] v **-ferred; -ferring** vt DIRECT,
SEND : remitir, enviar ⟨to refer a pa-
tient to a specialist : enviar a un paciente a un especialista⟩ — vi **to refer**
to MENTION : referirse a, aludir a
referee[1] [ˌrefəˈriː] v **-eed; -eeing** : arbitrar
referee[2] n : árbitro m, -tra f; réferi mf
reference [ˈrefrənts, ˈrefə-] n **1** ALLU-
SION : referencia f, alusión f ⟨to make
reference to : hacer referencia a⟩ **2**
CONSULTATION : consulta f ⟨for future
reference : para futuras consultas⟩ **3**
or **reference book** : libro m de consulta
4 TESTIMONIAL : informe m, referencia f, recomendación f
referendum [ˌrefəˈrendəm] n, pl **-da** [-də]
or **-dums** : referéndum m
refill[1] [ˈriːˈfɪl] vt : rellenar
refill[2] [ˈriːˌfɪl] n : recambio m
refinance [ˌriːˈfaɪˌnænts] vt **-nanced;**
-nancing : refinanciar
refine [rɪˈfaɪn] vt **-fined; -fining 1** : refinar (azúcar, petróleo, etc.) **2** PERFECT
: perfeccionar, pulir
refined [rɪˈfaɪnd] adj **1** : refinado (dícese
del azúcar, etc.) **2** CULTURED : culto,
educado
refinement [rɪˈfaɪnmənt] n : refinamiento m, fineza f, finura f
refinery [rɪˈfaɪnəri] n, pl **-eries** : refinería f
reflect [rɪˈflɛkt] vt **1** : reflejar ⟨to reflect
light : reflejar la luz⟩ ⟨happiness is reflected in her face : la felicidad se refleja en su cara⟩ **2 to reflect that** : pensar que, considerar que — vi **1 to**
reflect on : reflexionar sobre **2 to re-**
flect badly on : desacreditar, perjudicar
reflection [rɪˈflɛkʃən] n **1** : reflexión f,
reflejo m (de la luz, de imágenes, etc.)
2 THOUGHT : reflexión f, meditación f
reflective [rɪˈflɛktɪv] adj **1** THOUGHT-
FUL : reflexivo, pensativo **2** : reflectante (en física)
reflector [rɪˈflɛktər] n : reflector m
reflex [ˈriːˌflɛks] n : reflejo m
reflexive [rɪˈflɛksɪv] adj : reflexivo ⟨a reflexive verb : un verbo reflexivo⟩
reform[1] [rɪˈfɔrm] vt : reformar — vi : reformarse
reform[2] n : reforma f
reformation [ˌrefərˈmeɪʃən] n : reforma
f ⟨the Reformation : la Reforma⟩
reformatory [rɪˈfɔrməˌtori] n, pl **-ries**
: reformatorio m
reformer [rɪˈfɔrmər] n : reformador m,
-dora f
refract [rɪˈfrækt] vt : refractar — vi : refractarse
refraction [rɪˈfrækʃən] n : refracción f
refractory [rɪˈfræktəri] adj OBSTINATE
: refractario, obstinado
refrain[1] [rɪˈfreɪn] vi **to refrain from** : abstenerse de

refrain[2] n : estribillo m (en música)
refresh [rɪˈfrɛʃ] vt : refrescar ⟨to refresh
one's memory : refrescarle la memoria
a uno⟩
refreshing [rɪˈfrɛʃɪŋ] adj : refrescante ⟨a
refreshing sleep : un sueño reparador⟩
refreshment [rɪˈfrɛʃmənt] n **1** : refresco m **2 refreshments** npl : refrigerio
m
refrigerate [rɪˈfrɪdʒəˌreɪt] vt **-ated; -ating**
: refrigerar
refrigeration [rɪˌfrɪdʒəˈreɪʃən] n : refrigeración f
refrigerator [rɪˈfrɪdʒəˌreɪtər] n : refrigerador m, -dora f, nevera f
refuel [riːˈfjuːəl] v **-eled** or **-elled; -eling**
or **-elling** vi : repostar — vt : llenar de
combustible
refuge [ˈrɛˌfjuːdʒ] n : refugio m
refugee [ˌrɛfjuˈdʒiː] n : refugiado m, -da
f
refund[1] [rɪˈfʌnd, ˈriːˌfʌnd] vt : reembolsar, devolver
refund[2] [ˈriːˌfʌnd] n : reembolso m, devolución f
refundable [rɪˈfʌndəbəl] adj : reembolsable
refurbish [rɪˈfərbɪʃ] vt : renovar, restaurar
refusal [rɪˈfjuːzəl] n : negativa f, rechazo m, denegación f (de una petición)
refuse[1] [rɪˈfjuːz] vt **-fused; -fusing** RE-
JECT : rechazar, rehusar **2** DENY : negar, rehusar, denegar ⟨to refuse permission : negar el permiso⟩ **3 to refuse**
to : negarse a
refuse[2] [ˈrɛˌfjuːs, -ˌfjuːz] n : basura f,
desechos mpl, desperdicios mpl
refutation [ˌrɛfjuˈteɪʃən] n : refutación f
refute [rɪˈfjuːt] vt **-futed; -futing 1** DENY
: desmentir, negar **2** DISPROVE : refutar, rebatir
regain [rɪˈɡeɪn] vt **1** RECOVER : recuperar, recobrar **2** REACH : alcanzar ⟨to
regain the shore : llegar a la tierra⟩
regal [ˈriːɡəl] adj : real, regio
regale [rɪˈɡeɪl] vt **-galed; -galing 1** EN-
TERTAIN : agasajar, entretener **2**
AMUSE, DELIGHT : deleitar, divertir
regalia [rɪˈɡeɪliə] npl : ropaje m,
vestiduras fpl, adornos mpl
regard[1] [rɪˈɡɑrd] vt **1** OBSERVE : observar, mirar **2** HEED : tener en cuenta,
hacer caso de **3** CONSIDER : considerar **4** RESPECT : respetar ⟨highly regarded : muy estimado⟩ **5 as regards**
: en cuanto a, en lo que se refiere a
regard[2] n **1** CONSIDERATION : consideración f **2** ESTEEM : respeto m, estima f **3** PARTICULAR : aspecto m, sentido m ⟨in this regard : en este sentido⟩
4 regards npl : saludos mpl, recuerdos
mpl **5 with regard to** : con relación a,
con respecto a
regarding [rɪˈɡɑrdɪŋ] prep : con respecto a, en cuanto a
regardless [rɪˈɡɑrdləs] adv : a pesar de
todo

regardless of *prep* : a pesar de, sin tener en cuenta ⟨regardless of our mistakes : a pesar de nuestros errores⟩ ⟨regardless of age : sin tener en cuenta la edad⟩

regenerate [ri'dʒɛnə,reɪt] *v* **-ated; -ating** *vt* : regenerar — *vi* : regenerarse

regeneration [ri,dʒɛnə'reɪʃən] *n* : regeneración *f*

regent ['ri:dʒənt] *n* **1** RULER : regente *mf* **2** : miembro *m* de la junta directiva (de una universidad, etc.)

regime [reɪ'ʒi:m, rɪ-] *n* : régimen *m*

regimen ['rɛdʒəmən] *n* : régimen *m*

regiment¹ ['rɛdʒə,ment] *vt* : reglamentar

regiment² ['rɛdʒəmənt] *n* : regimiento *m*

region ['ri:dʒən] *n* **1** : región *f* **2 in the region of** : alrededor de

regional ['ri:dʒənəl] *adj* : regional — **regionally** *adv*

register¹ ['rɛdʒəstər] *vt* **1** RECORD : registrar, inscribir **2** INDICATE : marcar (temperatura, medidas, etc.) **3** REVEAL : manifestar, acusar ⟨to register surprise : acusar sorpresa⟩ **4** : certificar (correo) — *vi* ENROLL : inscribirse, matricularse

register² *n* : registro *m*

registrar ['rɛdʒə,strar] *n* : registrador *m*, -dora *f* oficial

registration [,rɛdʒə'streɪʃən] *n* **1** REGISTERING : inscripción *f*, matriculación *f*, registro *m* **2** *or* **registration number** : matrícula *f*, número *m* de matrícula

registry ['rɛdʒəstri] *n*, *pl* **-tries** : registro *m*

regress [ri'grɛs] *vi* : retroceder

regression [ri'grɛʃən] *n* : retroceso *m*, regresión *f*

regressive [ri'grɛsɪv] *adj* : regresivo

regret¹ [ri'grɛt] *vt* **-gretted; -gretting** : arrepentirse de, lamentar ⟨he regrets nothing : no se arrepiente de nada⟩ ⟨I regret to tell you : lamento decirle⟩

regret² *n* **1** REMORSE : arrepentimiento *m*, remordimientos *mpl* **2** SADNESS : pesar *m*, dolor *m* **3 regrets** *npl* : excusas *fpl* ⟨to send one's regrets : excusarse⟩

regretful [ri'grɛtfəl] *adj* : arrepentido, pesaroso

regretfully [ri'grɛtfəli] *adv* : con pesar

regrettable [ri'grɛtəbəl] *adj* : lamentable — **regrettably** [-bli] *adv*

regular¹ ['rɛgjələr] *adj* **1** NORMAL : regular, normal, usual **2** STEADY : uniforme, regular ⟨a regular pace : un paso regular⟩ **3** CUSTOMARY, HABITUAL : habitual, de costumbre

regular² *n* : cliente *mf* habitual

regularity [,rɛgjə'lærəti] *n*, *pl* **-ties** : regularidad *f*

regularly ['rɛgjələrli] *adv* : regularmente, con regularidad

regulate ['rɛgjə,leɪt] *vt* **-lated; -lating** : regular

regulation [,rɛgjə'leɪʃən] *n* **1** REGULATING : regulación *f* **2** RULE : regla *f*,

reglamento *m*, norma *f* ⟨safety regulations : reglas de seguridad⟩

regulator ['rɛgjə,leɪtər] *n* **1** : regulador *m* (mecanismo) **2** : persona *f* que regula

regulatory ['rɛgjələ,tori] *adj* : regulador

regurgitate [ri'gərdʒə,teɪt] *v* **-tated; -tating** : regurgitar, vomitar

rehabilitate [,ri:hə'bɪlə,teɪt, ,ri:ə-] *vt* **-tated; -tating** : rehabilitar

rehabilitation [,ri:hə,bɪlə'teɪʃən, ,ri:ə-] *n* : rehabilitación *f*

rehearsal [ri'hərsəl] *n* : ensayo *m*

rehearse [ri'hərs] *v* **-hearsed; -hearsing** : ensayar

reheat [,ri:'hi:t] *vt* : recalentar

reign¹ [reɪn] *vi* **1** RULE : reinar **2** PREVAIL : reinar, predominar ⟨the reigning champion : el actual campeón⟩

reign² *n* : reinado *m*

reimburse [,ri:əm'bərs] *vt* **-bursed; -bursing** : reembolsar

reimbursement [,ri:əm'bərsmənt] *n* : reembolso *m*

rein¹ [reɪn] *vt* : refrenar (un caballo)

rein² *n* **1** : rienda *f* ⟨to give free rein to : dar rienda suelta a⟩ **2** CHECK : control *m* ⟨to keep a tight rein on : llevar un estricto control de⟩

reincarnation [,ri:ɪn,kar'neɪʃən] *n* : reencarnación *f*

reindeer ['reɪn,dɪr] *n* : reno *m*

reinforce [,ri:ən'fors] *vt* **-forced; -forcing** : reforzar

reinforcement [,ri:ən'forsmənt] *n* : refuerzo *m*

reinstate [,ri:ən'steɪt] *vt* **-stated; -stating** **1** : reintegrar, restituir (una persona) **2** RESTORE : restablecer (un servicio, etc.)

reinstatement [,ri:ən'steɪtmənt] *n* : reintegración *f*, restitución *f*, restablecimiento *m*

reiterate [ri'ɪtə,reɪt] *vt* **-ated; -ating** : reiterar, repetir

reiteration [ri,ɪtə'reɪʃən] *n* : reiteración *f*, repetición *f*

reject¹ [ri'dʒɛkt] *vt* : rechazar

reject² ['ri:,dʒɛkt] *n* : desecho *m* (cosa), persona *f* rechazada

rejection [ri'dʒɛkʃən] *n* : rechazo *m*

rejoice [ri'dʒɔɪs] *vi* **-joiced; -joicing** : alegrarse, regocijarse

rejoin [,ri:'dʒɔɪn] *vt* **1** : reincorporarse a, reintegrarse a ⟨he rejoined the firm : se reincorporó a la firma⟩ **2** [ri'-] REPLY, RETORT : replicar

rejoinder [ri'dʒɔɪndər] *n* : réplica *f*

rejuvenate [ri'dʒu:və,neɪt] *vt* **-nated; -nating** : rejuvenecer

rejuvenation [ri,dʒu:və'neɪʃən] *n* : rejuvenecimiento *m*

rekindle [,ri:'kɪndəl] *v* **-dled; -dling** : reavivar

relapse¹ [ri'læps] *vi* **-lapsed; -lapsing** : recaer, volver a caer

relapse² ['ri:,læps, ri'læps] *n* : recaída *f*

relate [ri'leɪt] v **-lated; -lating** vt **1** TELL : relatar, contar **2** ASSOCIATE : relacionar, asociar ⟨to relate crime to poverty : relacionar la delincuencia a la pobreza⟩ — vi **1** CONNECT : conectar, estar relacionado (con) **2** INTERACT : relacionarse (con), llevarse bien (con) **3** to relate to UNDERSTAND : identificarse con, simpatizar con

related [ri'leɪtəd] adj : emparentado ⟨to be related to : ser pariente de⟩

relation [ri'leɪʃən] n **1** NARRATION : relato m, narración f **2** RELATIVE : pariente mf, familiar mf **3** RELATIONSHIP : relación f ⟨in relation to : en relación con, con relación a⟩ **4** relations npl : relaciones fpl ⟨public relations : relaciones públicas⟩

relationship [ri'leɪʃən,ʃɪp] n **1** CONNECTION : relación f **2** KINSHIP : parentesco m

relative¹ [ˈrɛlətɪv] adj : relativo — **relatively** adv

relative² n : pariente mf, familiar mf

relativism [ˈrɛlətɪ,vɪzəm] n : relativismo m

relativity [ˌrɛlə'tɪvəti] n, pl **-ties** : relatividad f

relax [ri'læks] vt : relajar, aflojar — vi : relajarse

relaxation [ˌriːˌlæk'seɪʃən] n **1** RELAXING : relajación f, aflojamiento m **2** DIVERSION : esparcimiento m, distracción f

relaxing [ri'læksɪŋ] adj : relajante

relay¹ [ˈriːˌleɪ, ri'leɪ] vt **-layed; -laying** : transmitir

relay² [ˈriːˌleɪ] n **1** : relevo m **2** or **relay race** : carrera de relevos

release¹ [ri'liːs] vt **-leased; -leasing 1** FREE : liberar, poner en libertad **2** LOOSEN : soltar, aflojar ⟨to release the brake : soltar el freno⟩ **3** RELINQUISH : renunciar a, ceder **4** ISSUE : publicar (un libro), estrenar (una película), sacar (un disco)

release² n **1** LIBERATION : liberación f, puesta f en libertad **2** RELINQUISHMENT : cesión f (de propiedad, etc.) **3** ISSUE : estreno m (de una película), puesta f en venta (de un disco), publicación f (de un libro) **4** ESCAPE : escape m, fuga f (de un gas)

relegate [ˈrɛlə,geɪt] vt **-gated; -gating** : relegar

relent [ri'lɛnt] vi : ablandarse, ceder

relentless [ri'lɛntləs] adj : implacable, sin tregua

relentlessly [ri'lɛntləsli] adv : implacablemente

relevance [ˈrɛləvənts] : pertinencia f, relación f

relevant [ˈrɛləvənt] adj : pertinente — **relevantly** adv

reliability [ri,laɪə'bɪləti] n, pl **-ties 1** : fiabilidad f, seguridad f (de una cosa) **2** : formalidad f, seriedad f (de una persona)

reliable [ri'laɪəbəl] adj : confiable, fiable, fidedigno, seguro

reliably [ri'laɪəbli] adv : sin fallar ⟨to be reliably informed : saber (algo) de fuentes fidedignas⟩

reliance [ri'laɪənts] n **1** DEPENDENCE : dependencia f **2** CONFIDENCE : confianza f

reliant [ri'laɪənt] adj : dependiente

relic [ˈrɛlɪk] n **1** : reliquia f **2** VESTIGE : vestigio m

relief [ri'liːf] n **1** : alivio m, desahogo m ⟨relief from pain : alivio del dolor⟩ **2** AID, WELFARE : ayuda f (benéfica), asistencia f social **3** : relieve m (en la escultura) ⟨relief map : mapa en relieve⟩ **4** REPLACEMENT : relevo m

relieve [ri'liːv] vt **-lieved; -lieving 1** ALLEVIATE : aliviar, mitigar ⟨to feel relieved : sentirse aliviado⟩ **2** FREE : liberar, eximir ⟨to relieve someone of responsibility for : eximir a alguien de la responsabilidad de⟩ **3** REPLACE : relevar (a un centinela, etc.) **4** BREAK : romper ⟨to relieve the monotony : romper la monotonía⟩

religion [ri'lɪdʒən] n : religión f

religious [ri'lɪdʒəs] adj : religioso — **religiously** adv

relinquish [ri'lɪŋkwɪʃ, -'lɪn-] vt **1** GIVE UP : renunciar a, abandonar **2** RELEASE : soltar

relish¹ [ˈrɛlɪʃ] vt : saborear (comida), disfrutar con (una idea, una perspectiva, etc.)

relish² n **1** ENJOYMENT : gusto m, deleite m **2** : salsa f (condimento)

relive [ˌriː'lɪv] vt **-lived; -living** : revivir

relocate [ˌriː'loːˌkeɪt, ˌriːlo'keɪt] v **-cated; -cating** vt : reubicar, trasladar — vi : trasladarse

relocation [ˌriːlo'keɪʃən] n : reubicación f, traslado m

reluctance [ri'lʌktənts] n : renuencia f, reticencia f, desgana f

reluctant [ri'lʌktənt] adj : renuente, reacio, reticente

reluctantly [ri'lʌktəntli] adv : a regañadientes

rely [ri'laɪ] vi **-lied; -lying 1** DEPEND : depender (de), contar (con) **2** TRUST : confiar (en)

remain [ri'meɪn] vi **1** : quedar ⟨very little remains : queda muy poco⟩ ⟨the remaining 10 minutes : los 10 minutos que quedan⟩ **2** STAY : quedarse, permanecer **3** CONTINUE : continuar, seguir ⟨to remain the same : continuar siendo igual⟩ **4** to remain to : quedar por ⟨to remain to be done : quedar por hacer⟩ ⟨it remains to be seen : está por ver⟩

remainder [ri'meɪndər] n : resto m, remanente m

remains [ri'meɪnz] npl : restos mpl ⟨mortal remains : restos mortales⟩

remake¹ [riː'meɪk] vt **-made; -making 1** TRANSFORM : rehacer **2** : hacer una nueva versión de (una película, etc.)

remake² [ˈriːˌmeɪk] n : nueva versión f

remark¹ [rɪˈmɑrk] vt **1** NOTICE : observar **2** SAY : comentar, observar — vi **to remark on** : hacer observaciones sobre

remark² n : comentario m, observación f

remarkable [rɪˈmɑrkəbəl] adj : extraordinario, notable — **remarkably** [-bli] adv

rematch [ˈriːˌmætʃ] n : revancha f

remedial [rɪˈmiːdiəl] adj : correctivo ⟨remedial classes : clases para alumnos atrasados⟩

remedy¹ [ˈrɛmədi] vt **-died; -dying** : remediar

remedy² n, pl **-dies** : remedio m, medicamento m

remember [rɪˈmɛmbər] vt **1** RECOLLECT : acordarse de, recordar **2** : no olvidar ⟨remember my words : no olvides mis palabras⟩ ⟨to remember to : acordarse de⟩ **3** : dar saludos, dar recuerdos ⟨remember me to her : dale saludos de mi parte⟩ **4** COMMEMORATE : recordar, conmemorar

remembrance [rɪˈmɛmbrəns] n **1** RECOLLECTION : recuerdo m ⟨in remembrance of : en conmemoración de⟩ **2** MEMENTO : recuerdo m

remind [rɪˈmaɪnd] vt : recordar ⟨remind me to do it : recuérdame que lo haga⟩ ⟨she reminds me of Clara : me recuerda de Clara⟩

reminder [rɪˈmaɪndər] n : recuerdo m

reminisce [ˌrɛməˈnɪs] vi **-nisced; -niscing** : rememorar los viejos tiempos

reminiscence [ˌrɛməˈnɪsənts] n : recuerdo m, reminiscencia f

reminiscent [ˌrɛməˈnɪsənt] adj **1** NOSTALGIC : reminiscente, nostálgico **2** SUGGESTIVE : evocador, que recuerda — **reminiscently** adv

remiss [rɪˈmɪs] adj : negligente, descuidado, remiso

remission [rɪˈmɪʃən] n : remisión f

remit [rɪˈmɪt] vt **-mitted; -mitting 1** PARDON : perdonar **2** SEND : remitir, enviar (dinero)

remittance [rɪˈmɪtənts] n : remesa f

remnant [ˈrɛmnənt] n : restos mpl, vestigio m

remodel [riˈmɑdəl] vt **-eled** or **-elled; -eling** or **-elling** : remodelar, reformar

remonstrate [rɪˈmɑnˌstreɪt] vi **-strated; -strating** : protestar ⟨to remonstrate with someone : quejarse a alguien⟩

remorse [rɪˈmɔrs] n : remordimiento m

remorseful [rɪˈmɔrsfəl] adj : arrepentido, lleno de remordimiento

remorseless [rɪˈmɔrsləs] adj **1** PITILESS : despiadado **2** RELENTLESS : implacable

remote [rɪˈmoːt] adj **-moter; -est 1** FAROFF : lejano, remoto ⟨remote countries : países remotos⟩ ⟨in the remote past : en el pasado lejano⟩ **2** SECLUDED : recóndito **3** : a distancia, remoto ⟨remote control : control remoto⟩ **4** SLIGHT : remoto **5** ALOOF : distante

remotely [rɪˈmoːtli] adv **1** SLIGHTLY : remotamente **2** DISTANTLY : en un lugar remoto, muy lejos

remoteness [rɪˈmoːtnəs] n : lejanía f

removable [rɪˈmuːvəbəl] adj : removible

removal [rɪˈmuːvəl] n : separación f, extracción f, supresión f (en algo escrito), eliminación f (de problemas, etc.)

remove [rɪˈmuːv] vt **-moved; -moving 1** : quitar, quitarse ⟨remove the lid : quite la tapa⟩ ⟨to remove one's hat : quitarse el sombrero⟩ **2** EXTRACT : sacar, extraer ⟨to remove the contents of : sacar el contenido de⟩ **3** ELIMINATE : eliminar, disipar

remunerate [rɪˈmjuːnəˌreɪt] vt **-ated; -ating** : remunerar

remuneration [rɪˌmjuːnəˈreɪʃən] n : remuneración f

remunerative [rɪˈmjuːnərətɪv, -ˌreɪ-] adj : remunerativo

renaissance [ˌrɛnəˈsɑnts, -ˈzɑnts; ˈrɛnəˌ-] n : renacimiento m ⟨the Renaissance : el Renacimiento⟩

renal [ˈriːnəl] adj : renal

rename [ˌriːˈneɪm] vt **-named; -naming** : ponerle un nombre nuevo a

rend [ˈrɛnd] vt **rent** [ˈrɛnt]; **rending** : desgarrar

render [ˈrɛndər] vt **1** : derretir ⟨to render lard : derretir la manteca⟩ **2** GIVE : prestar, dar ⟨to render aid : prestar ayuda⟩ **3** MAKE : hacer, volver, dejar ⟨it rendered him helpless : lo dejó incapacitado⟩ **4** TRANSLATE : traducir, verter ⟨to render into English : traducir al inglés⟩

rendezvous [ˈrɑndɪˌvuː, -deɪ-] ns & pl : encuentro m, cita f

rendition [rɛnˈdɪʃən] n : interpretación f

renegade [ˈrɛnɪˌgeɪd] n : renegado m, -da f

renege [rɪˈnɪg, -ˈnɛg] vi **-neged; -neging** : no cumplir con (una promesa, etc.)

renew [rɪˈnuː, -ˈnjuː] vt **1** REVIVE : renovar, reavivar ⟨to renew the sentiments of youth : renovar los sentimientos de la juventud⟩ **2** RESUME : reanudar **3** EXTEND : renovar ⟨to renew a subscription : renovar una suscripción⟩

renewable [rɪˈnuːəbəl, -ˈnjuː-] adj : renovable

renewal [rɪˈnuːəl, -ˈnjuː-] n : renovación f

renounce [rɪˈnaunts] vt **-nounced; -nouncing** : renunciar a

renovate [ˈrɛnəˌveɪt] vt **-vated; -vating** : restaurar, renovar

renovation [ˌrɛnəˈveɪʃən] n : restauración f, renovación f

renown [rɪˈnaun] n : renombre m, fama f, celebridad f

renowned [rɪˈnaund] adj : renombrado, célebre, famoso

rent¹ [ˈrɛnt] vt : rentar, alquilar

rent² *n* **1** : renta *f*, alquiler *m* ‹for rent : se alquila› **2** RIP : rasgadura *f*
rental¹ [ˈrɛntəl] *adj* RENT : de alquiler
rental² *n* : alquiler *m*
renter [ˈrɛntər] *n* : arrendatario *m*, -ria *f*
renunciation [rɪˌnʌntsiˈeɪʃən] *n* : renuncia *f*
reopen [ˌriːˈoːpən] *vt* : volver a abrir
reorganization [ˌriːˌɔrgənəˈzeɪʃən] *n* : reorganización *f*
reorganize [ˌriːˈɔrgənˌaɪz] *vt* **-nized; -nizing** : reorganizar
repair¹ [rɪˈpær] *vt* : reparar, arreglar, refaccionar
repair² *n* **1** : reparación *f*, arreglo *m* **2** CONDITION : estado *m* ‹in bad repair : en mal estado›
reparation [ˌrɛpəˈreɪʃən] *n* **1** AMENDS : reparación *f* **2 reparations** *npl* COMPENSATION : indemnización *f*
repartee [ˌrɛpərˈtiː, -ˌpɑr-, -ˈteɪ] *n* : intercambio *m* de réplicas ingeniosas
repast [rɪˈpæst, ˈriːˌpæst] *n* : comida *f*
repatriate [riˈpeɪtriˌeɪt] *vt* **-ated; -ating** : repatriar
repay [riˈpeɪ] *vt* **-paid; -paying** : pagar, devolver, reembolsar
repeal¹ [rɪˈpiːl] *vt* : abrogar, revocar
repeal² *n* : abrogación *f*, revocación *f*
repeat¹ [rɪˈpiːt] *vt* : repetir
repeat² *n* : repetición *f*
repeatedly [rɪˈpiːtədli] *adv* : repetidamente, repetidas veces
repel [rɪˈpɛl] *vt* **-pelled; -pelling 1** REPULSE : repeler ‹an enemigo, etc.› **2** RESIST : repeler **3** REJECT : rechazar, repeler **4** DISGUST : repugnar, darle asco (a alguien)
repellent *or* **repellant** [rɪˈpɛlənt] *n* : repelente *m*
repent [rɪˈpɛnt] *vi* : arrepentirse
repentance [rɪˈpɛntənts] *n* : arrepentimiento *m*
repentant [rɪˈpɛntənt] *adj* : arrepentido
repercussion [ˌriːpərˈkʌʃən, ˌrɛpər-] *n* : repercusión *f*
repertoire [ˈrɛpərˌtwɑr] *n* : repertorio *m*
repertory [ˈrɛpərˌtori] *n*, *pl* **-ries** : repertorio *m*
repetition [ˌrɛpəˈtɪʃən] *n* : repetición *f*
repetitious [ˌrɛpəˈtɪʃəs] *adj* : repetitivo, reiterativo — **repetitiously** *adv*
repetitive [rɪˈpɛtətɪv] *adj* : repetitivo, reiterativo
replace [rɪˈpleɪs] *vt* **-placed; -placing 1** : volver a poner ‹replace it in the drawer : vuelve a ponerlo en el cajón› **2** SUBSTITUTE : reemplazar, sustituir **3** : reponer ‹to replace the worn carpet : reponer la alfombra raída›
replaceable [rɪˈpleɪsəbəl] *adj* : reemplazable
replacement [rɪˈpleɪsmənt] *n* **1** SUBSTITUTION : reemplazo *m*, sustitución *f* **2** SUBSTITUTE : sustituto *m*, -ta *f*; suplente *mf* (persona) **3** REPLACEMENT PART : repuesto *m*, pieza *f* de recambio
replenish [rɪˈplɛnɪʃ] *vt* : rellenar, llenar de nuevo

replenishment [rɪˈplɛnɪʃmənt] *n* : reabastecimiento *m*
replete [rɪˈpliːt] *adj* : repleto, lleno
replica [ˈrɛplɪkə] *n* : réplica *f*, reproducción *f*
replicate [ˈrɛpləˌkeɪt] *v* **-cated; -cating** *vt* : duplicar, repetir — *vi* : duplicarse
replication [ˌrɛpləˈkeɪʃən] *n* **1** REPRODUCTION : reproducción *f* **2** REPETITION : repetición *f* **3** : replicación *f* (celular)
reply¹ [rɪˈplaɪ] *vi* **-plied; -plying** : contestar, responder
reply² *n*, *pl* **-plies** : respuesta *f*, contestación *f*
report¹ [rɪˈport] *vt* **1** ANNOUNCE : relatar, anunciar **2** : dar parte de, informar de, reportar ‹he reported an accident : dio parte de un accidente› ‹to report a crime : denunciar un delito› **3** : informar acerca de (en un periódico, la televisión, etc.) — *vi* **1** : hacer un informe, informar **2 to report for duty** : presentarse, reportarse
report² *n* **1** RUMOR : rumor *m* **2** REPUTATION : reputación *f* ‹people of evil report : personas de mala fama› **3** ACCOUNT : informe *m*, reportaje *m* (en un periódico, etc.) **4** BANG : estallido *m* (de un arma de fuego)
report card *n* : boletín *m* de calificaciones, boletín *m* de notas
reportedly [rɪˈportədli] *adv* : según se dice, según se informa
reporter [rɪˈportər] *n* : periodista *mf*; reportero *m*, -ra *f*
repose¹ [rɪˈpoːz] *vi* **-posed; -posing** : reposar, descansar
repose² *n* **1** : reposo *m*, descanso *m* **2** CALM : calma *f*, tranquilidad *f*
repository [rɪˈpɑzəˌtori] *n*, *pl* **-ries** : depósito *m*
repossess [ˌriːpəˈzɛs] *vt* : recuperar, recobrar la posesión de
reprehensible [ˌrɛprɪˈhɛntsəbəl] *adj* : reprensible — **reprehensibly** *adv*
represent [ˌrɛprɪˈzɛnt] *vt* **1** SYMBOLIZE : representar ‹the flag represents our country : la bandera representa a nuestro país› **2** : representar, ser un representante de ‹an attorney who represents his client : un abogado que representa su cliente› **3** PORTRAY : presentar ‹he represents himself as a friend : se presenta como amigo›
representation [ˌrɛprɪˌzɛnˈteɪʃən, -zən-] *n* : representación *f*
representative¹ [ˌrɛprɪˈzɛntətɪv] *adj* : representativo
representative² *n* **1** : representante *mf* **2** : diputado *m*, -da *f* (en la política)
repress [rɪˈprɛs] *vt* : reprimir
repression [rɪˈprɛʃən] *n* : represión *f*
repressive [rɪˈprɛsɪv] *adj* : represivo
reprieve¹ [rɪˈpriːv] *vt* **-prieved; -prieving** : indultar
reprieve² *n* : indulto *m*
reprimand [ˈrɛprəˌmænd] *vt* : reprender

reprimand² *n* : reprimenda *f*

reprint¹ [riˈprɪnt] *vt* : reimprimir

reprint² [ˈriːˌprɪnt, riˈprɪnt] *n* : reedición *f*

reprisal [riˈpraɪzəl] *n* : represalia *f*

reproach¹ [riˈproːʧ] *vt* : reprochar

reproach² *n* **1** DISGRACE : deshonra *f* **2** REBUKE : reproche *m*, recriminación *f*

reproachful [riˈproːʧfəl] *adj* : de reproche

reproduce [ˌriːprəˈduːs, -ˈdjuːs] *v* **-duced; -ducing** *vt* : reproducir — *vi* BREED : reproducirse

reproduction [ˌriːprəˈdʌkʃən] *n* : reproducción *f*

reproductive [ˌriːprəˈdʌktɪv] *adj* : reproductor

reproof [riˈpruːf] *n* : reprobación *f*, reprimenda *f*, reproche *m*

reprove [riˈpruːv] *vt* **-proved; -proving** : reprender, censurar

reptile [ˈrɛpˌtaɪl] *n* : reptil *m*

republic [riˈpʌblɪk] *n* : república *f*

republican¹ [riˈpʌblɪkən] *adj* : republicano

republican² *n* : republicano *m*, -na *f*

repudiate [riˈpjuːdiˌeɪt] *vt* **-ated; -ating 1** REJECT : rechazar **2** DISOWN : repudiar, renegar de

repudiation [riˌpjuːdiˈeɪʃən] *n* : rechazo *m*, repudio *m*

repugnance [riˈpʌɡnənts] *n* : repugnancia *f*

repugnant [riˈpʌɡnənt] *adj* : repugnante, asqueroso

repulse¹ [riˈpʌls] *vt* **-pulsed; -pulsing 1** REPEL : repeler **2** REBUFF : desairar, rechazar

repulse² *n* : rechazo *m*

repulsive [riˈpʌlsɪv] *adj* : repulsivo, repugnante, asqueroso — **repulsively** *adv*

reputable [ˈrɛpjətəbəl] *adj* : acreditado, de buena reputación

reputation [ˌrɛpjəˈteɪʃən] *n* : reputación *f*, fama *f*

repute [riˈpjuːt] *n* : reputación *f*, fama *f*

reputed [riˈpjuːtəd] *adj* : reputado, supuesto ⟨she's reputed to be the best : tiene fama de ser la mejor⟩

reputedly [riˈpjuːtədli] *adv* : supuestamente, según se dice

request¹ [rɪˈkwɛst] *vt* : pedir, solicitar, rogar ⟨to request assistance : solicitar asistencia, pedir ayuda⟩ ⟨I requested him to do it : le pedí que lo hiciera⟩

request² *n* : petición *f*, solicitud *f*, pedido *m*

requiem [ˈrɛkwiəm, ˈreɪ-] *n* : réquiem *m*

require [rɪˈkwaɪr] *vt* **-quired; -quiring 1** CALL FOR, DEMAND : requerir, exigir ⟨if required : si se requiere⟩ ⟨to require that something be done : exigir que algo se haga⟩ **2** NEED : necesitar, requerir

requirement [rɪˈkwaɪrmənt] *n* **1** NECESSITY : necesidad *f* **2** DEMAND : requisito *m*, demanda *f*

requisite¹ [ˈrɛkwəzɪt] *adj* : esencial, necesario

requisite² *n* : requisito *m*, necesidad *f*

requisition¹ [ˌrɛkwəˈzɪʃən] *vt* : requisar

requisition² *n* : requisición *f*, requisa *f*

reread [ˌriːˈriːd] *vt* **-read; -reading** : releer

reroute [ˌriːˈruːt, -ˈraʊt] *vt* **-routed; -routing** : desviar

rerun¹ [ˌriːˈrʌn] *vt* **-ran; -run; -running** : reponer (un programa televisivo)

rerun² [ˈriːˌrʌn] *n* **1** : reposición *f* (de un programa televisivo) **2** REPEAT : repetición *f*

resale [ˈriːˌseɪl, ˌriːˈseɪl] *n* : reventa *f* ⟨resale price : precio de venta⟩

rescind [riˈsɪnd] *vt* **1** CANCEL : rescindir, cancelar **2** REPEAL : abrogar, revocar

rescue¹ [ˈrɛsˌkjuː] *vt* **-cued; -cuing** : rescatar, salvar

rescue² *n* : rescate *m*

rescuer [ˈrɛskjuər] *n* : salvador *m*, -dora *f*

research¹ [riˈsərʧ, ˈriːˌsərʧ] *v* : investigar

research² *n* : investigación *f*

researcher [riˈsərʧər, ˈriːˌ-] *n* : investigador *m*, -dora *f*

resemblance [riˈzɛmbləns] *n* : semejanza *f*, parecido *m*

resemble [riˈzɛmbəl] *vt* **-sembled; -sembling** : parecerse a, asemejarse a

resent [riˈzɛnt] *vt* : resentirse de, ofenderse por

resentful [riˈzɛntfəl] *adj* : resentido, rencoroso — **resentfully** *adv*

resentment [riˈzɛntmənt] *n* : resentimiento *m*

reservation [ˌrɛzərˈveɪʃən] *n* **1** : reservación *f*, reserva *f* ⟨to make a reservation : hacer una reservación⟩ **2** DOUBT, MISGIVING : reserva *f*, duda *f* ⟨without reservations : sin reservas⟩ **3** : reserva *f* (de indios americanos)

reserve¹ [riˈzərv] *vt* **-served; -serving** : reservar

reserve² *n* **1** STOCK : reserva *f* ⟨to keep in reserve : guardar en reserva⟩ **2** RESTRAINT : reserva *f*, moderación *f* **3 reserves** *npl* : reservas *fpl* (militares)

reserved [riˈzərvd] *adj* : reservado

reservoir [ˈrɛzərˌvwɑr, -ˌvwɔr, -ˌvɔr] *n* : embalse *m*

reset [ˌriːˈsɛt] *vt* **-set; -setting** : reajustar, poner en hora (un reloj), reiniciar (una computadora)

reside [riˈzaɪd] *vi* **-sided; -siding 1** DWELL : residir **2** LIE : radicar, residir ⟨the power resides in the presidency : el poder radica en la presidencia⟩

residence [ˈrɛzədənts] *n* : residencia *f*

resident¹ [ˈrɛzədənt] *adj* : residente

resident² *n* : residente *mf*

residential [ˌrɛzəˈdɛnʧəl] *adj* : residencial

residual [riˈzɪʤuəl] *adj* : residual

residue [ˈrɛzəˌduː, -ˌdjuː] *n* : residuo *m*, resto *m*

resign [ri'zaɪn] *vt* **1** QUIT : dimitir, renunciar **2 to resign oneself** : aguantarse, resignarse

resignation [ˌrezɪg'neɪʃən] *n* : resignación *f*

resignedly [ri'zaɪnədli] *adv* : con resignación

resilience [ri'zɪljənts] *n* **1** : capacidad *f* de recuperación, adaptabilidad *f* **2** ELASTICITY : elasticidad *f*

resiliency [ri'zɪljəntsi] → **resilience**

resilient [ri'zɪljənt] *adj* **1** STRONG : resistente, fuerte **2** ELASTIC : elástico

resin ['rezən] *n* : resina *f*

resist [ri'zɪst] *vt* **1** WITHSTAND : resistir ⟨to resist heat : resistir el calor⟩ **2** OPPOSE : oponerse a

resistance [ri'zɪstənts] *n* : resistencia *f*

resistant [ri'zɪstənt] *adj* : resistente

resolute ['rezə,lu:t] *adj* : firme, resuelto, decidido

resolutely ['rezə,lu:tli, ˌrezə'-] *adv* : resueltamente, firmemente

resolution [ˌrezə'lu:ʃən] *n* **1** SOLUTION : solución *f* **2** RESOLVE : resolución *f*, determinación *f* **3** DECISION : propósito *m*, decisión *f* ⟨New Year's resolutions : propósitos para el Año Nuevo⟩ **4** MOTION, PROPOSAL : moción *f*, resolución *f* (legislativa)

resolve¹ [ri'zɑlv] *vt* **-solved; -solving** **1** SOLVE : resolver, solucionar **2** DECIDE : resolver ⟨she resolved to get more sleep : resolvió dormir más⟩

resolve² *n* : resolución *f*, determinación *f*

resonance ['rezənənts] *n* : resonancia *f*

resonant ['rezənənt] *adj* : resonante, retumbante

resort¹ [ri'zɔrt] *vi* **to resort to** : recurrir ⟨to resort to force : recurrir a la fuerza⟩

resort² *n* **1** RECOURSE : recurso *m* ⟨as a last resort : como último recurso⟩ **2** HANGOUT : lugar *m* popular, lugar *m* muy frecuentado **3** : lugar *m* de vacaciones ⟨tourist resort : centro turístico⟩

resound [ri'zaʊnd] *vi* : retumbar, resonar

resounding [ri'zaʊndɪŋ] *adj* **1** RESONANT : retumbante, resonante **2** ABSOLUTE, CATEGORICAL : rotundo, tremendo ⟨a resounding success : un éxito rotundo⟩

resource ['ri:,sɔrs, ri'sɔrs] *n* **1** RESOURCEFULNESS : ingenio *m*, recursos *mpl* **2 resources** *npl* : recursos *mpl* ⟨natural resources : recursos naturales⟩ **3 resources** *npl* MEANS : recursos *mpl*, medios *mpl*, fondos *mpl*

resourceful [ri'sɔrsfəl, -'zɔrs-] *adj* : ingenioso

resourcefulness [ri'sɔrsfəlnəs, -'zɔrs-] *n* : ingenio *m*, recursos *mpl*, inventiva *f*

respect¹ [ri'spekt] *vt* : respetar, estimar

respect² *n* **1** REFERENCE : relación *f*, respeto *m* ⟨with respect to : en lo que respecta a⟩ **2** ESTEEM : respeto *m*, es-

tima *f* **3** DETAIL, PARTICULAR : detalle *m*, sentido *m*, respeto *m* ⟨in some respects : en algunos sentidos⟩ **4** respects *npl* : respetos *mpl* ⟨to pay one's respects : presentar sus susreptetos⟩

respectability [ri,spektə'biləti] *n* : respetabilidad *f*

respectable [ri'spektəbəl] *adj* **1** PROPER : respetable, decente **2** CONSIDERABLE : considerable, respetable ⟨a respectable amount : una cantidad respetable⟩ — **respectably** [-bli] *adv*

respectful [ri'spektfəl] *adj* : respetuoso — **respectfully** *adv*

respectfulness [ri'spektfəlnəs] *n* : respetuosidad *f*

respective [ri'spektɪv] *adj* : respectivo ⟨their respective homes : sus casas respectivas⟩ — **respectively** *adv*

respiration [ˌrespə'reɪʃən] *n* : respiración *f*

respirator ['respə,reɪtər] *n* : respirador *m*

respiratory ['respərə,tori, ri'spaɪrə-] *adj* : respiratorio

respite ['respɪt, ri'spaɪt] *n* : respiro *m*, tregua *f*

resplendent [ri'splendənt] *adj* : resplandeciente — **resplendently** *adv*

respond [ri'spɑnd] *vi* **1** ANSWER : contestar, responder **2** REACT : responder, reaccionar ⟨to respond to treatment : responder al tratamiento⟩

response [ri'spɑnts] *n* : respuesta *f*

responsibility [ri,spɑntsə'biləti] *n*, *pl* **-ties** : responsabilidad *f*

responsible [ri'spɑntsəbəl] *adj* : responsable — **responsibly** [-bli] *adv*

responsive [ri'spɑntsɪv] *adj* **1** ANSWERING : que responde **2** SENSITIVE : sensible, receptivo

responsiveness [ri'spɑntsɪvnəs] *n* : receptividad *f*, sensibilidad *f*

rest¹ ['rest] *vi* **1** REPOSE : reposar, descansar **2** RELAX : quedarse tranquilo **3** STOP : pararse, detenerse **4** DEPEND : basarse (en), descansar (sobre), depender (de) ⟨the decision rests with her : la decisión pesa sobre ella⟩ **5 to rest on** : apoyarse en, descansar sobre ⟨to rest on one's arm : apoyarse en el brazo⟩ — *vt* **1** RELAX : descansar **2** SUPPORT : apoyar **3 to rest one's eyes on** : fijar la mirada en

rest² *n* **1** RELAXATION, REPOSE : reposo *m*, descanso *m* **2** SUPPORT : soporte *m*, apoyo *m* **3** : silencio *m* (en música) **4** REMAINDER : resto *m* **5 to come to rest** : pararse

restart [ri'start] *vt* **1** : volver a empezar **2** RESUME : reanudar **3** : volver a arrancar (un motor), reiniciar (una computadora) — *vi* **1** : reanudarse **2** : volver a arrancar

restatement [ˌri'steɪtmənt] *n* : repetición *f*

restaurant ['restə,rɑnt, -rənt] *n* : restaurante *m*

restful ['rɛstfəl] *adj* **1** RELAXING : relajante **2** PEACEFUL : tranquilo, sosegado

restitution [ˌrɛstə'tu:ʃən, -'tju:-] *n* : restitución *f*

restive ['rɛstɪv] *adj* : inquieto, nervioso

restless ['rɛstləs] *adj* **1** FIDGETY : inquieto, agitado **2** IMPATIENT : impaciente **3** SLEEPLESS : desvelado ⟨a restless night : una noche en blanco⟩

restlessly ['rɛstləsli] *adv* : nerviosamente

restlessness ['rɛstləsnəs] *n* : inquietud *f*, agitación *f*

restoration [ˌrɛstə'reɪʃən] *n* : restauración *f*, restablecimiento *m*

restore [rɪ'stor] *vt* **-stored; -storing 1** RETURN : volver **2** REESTABLISH : restablecer **3** REPAIR : restaurar

restrain [rɪ'streɪn] *vt* **1** : refrenar, contener **2 to restrain oneself** : contenerse

restrained [rɪ'streɪnd] *adj* : comedido, templado, contenido

restraint [rɪ'streɪnt] *n* **1** RESTRICTION : restricción *f*, limitación *f*, control *m* **2** CONFINEMENT : encierro *m* **3** RESERVE : reserva *f*, control *m* de sí mismo

restrict [rɪ'strɪkt] *vt* : restringir, limitar, constreñir

restricted [rɪ'strɪktəd] *adj* **1** LIMITED : limitado, restringido **2** CLASSIFIED : secreto, confidencial

restriction [rɪ'strɪkʃən] *n* : restricción *f*

restrictive [rɪ'strɪktɪv] *adj* : restrictivo — **restrictively** *adv*

rest room *n* : servicios *mpl*, baño *m*

restructure [rɪ'strʌktʃər] *vt* **-tured; -turing** : reestructurar

result¹ [rɪ'zʌlt] *vi* : resultar ⟨to result in : resultar en, tener por resultado⟩

result² *n* : resultado *m*, consecuencia *f* ⟨as a result of : como consecuencia de⟩

resultant [rɪ'zʌltənt] *adj* : resultante

resume [rɪ'zu:m] *v* **-sumed; -suming** *vt* : reanudar — *vi* : reanudarse

résumé *or* **resume** *or* **resumé** ['rɛzə‚meɪ, ‚rɛzə'-] *n* **1** SUMMARY : resumen *m* **2** CURRICULUM VITAE : currículum *m*, currículo *m*

resumption [rɪ'zʌmpʃən] *n* : reanudación *f*

resurface [ˌri:'sərfəs] *v* **-faced; -facing** *vt* : pavimentar (una carretera) de nuevo — *vi* : volver a salir en la superficie

resurgence [rɪ'sərdʒənts] *n* : resurgimiento *m*

resurrect [ˌrɛzə'rɛkt] *vt* : resucitar, desempolvar

resurrection [ˌrɛzə'rɛkʃən] *n* : resurrección *f*

resuscitate [rɪ'sʌsə‚teɪt] *vt* **-tated; -tating** : resucitar, revivir

resuscitation [rɪ‚sʌsə'teɪʃən] *n* : reanimación *f*, resucitación *f*

retail¹ ['ri:‚teɪl] *vt* : vender al por menor, vender al detalle

retail² *adv* : al por menor, al detalle

retail³ *adj* : detallista, minorista

retail⁴ *n* : venta *f* al detalle, venta *f* al por menor

retailer ['ri:‚teɪlər] *n* : detallista *mf*, minorista *mf*

retain [rɪ'teɪn] *vt* : retener, conservar, guardar

retainer [rɪ'teɪnər] *n* **1** SERVANT : criado *m*, -da *f* **2** ADVANCE : anticipo *m*

retaliate [rɪ'tæli‚eɪt] *vi* **-ated; -ating** : responder, contraatacar, tomar represalias

retaliation [rɪ‚tæli'eɪʃən] *n* : represalia *f*, retaliación *f*

retard [rɪ'tɑrd] *vt* : retardar, retrasar

retardation [ˌri:‚tɑr'deɪʃən] *n* **1** : retardación *f* **2 or mental retardation** : retraso *m* mental

retarded [rɪ'tɑrdəd] *adj* : retrasado

retch ['rɛtʃ] *vi* : hacer arcadas

retention [rɪ'tɛnʃən] *n* : retención *f*

retentive [rɪ'tɛntɪv] *adj* : retentivo

rethink [ri:'θɪŋk] *vt* **-thought; -thinking** : reconsiderar, repensar

reticence ['rɛtəsənts] *n* : reticencia *f*

reticent ['rɛtəsənt] *adj* : reticente

retina ['rɛtənə] *n, pl* **-nas** *or* **-nae** [-əni, -ən‚aɪ] : retina *f*

retinue ['rɛtən‚u:, -‚ju:] *n* : séquito *m*, comitiva *f*, cortejo *m*

retire [rɪ'taɪr] *vi* **-tired; -tiring 1** RETREAT, WITHDRAW : retirarse, retraerse **2** : retirarse, jubilarse (de su trabajo) **3** : acostarse, irse a dormir

retiree [rɪ‚taɪ'ri:] *n* : jubilado *m*, -da *f*

retirement [rɪ'taɪrmənt] *n* : jubilación *f*

retiring [rɪ'taɪrɪŋ] *adj* SHY : retraído

retort¹ [rɪ'tort] *vt* : replicar

retort² *n* : réplica *f*

retrace [ˌri:'treɪs] *vt* **-traced; -tracing** : volver sobre, desandar ⟨to retrace one's steps : volver uno sobre sus pasos⟩

retract [rɪ'trækt] *vt* **1** TAKE BACK, WITHDRAW : retirar, retractarse de **2** : retraer (las garras) — *vi* : retractarse

retractable [rɪ'træktəbəl] *adj* : retractable

retrain [ˌri:'treɪn] *vt* : reciclar, reconvertir

retreat¹ [rɪ'tri:t] *vi* : retirarse

retreat² *n* **1** WITHDRAWAL : retirada *f*, repliegue *m*, retiro *m* ⟨to beat a retreat : batirse en retirada⟩ **2** REFUGE : retiro *m*, refugio *m*

retrench [rɪ'trɛntʃ] *vt* : reducir (gastos) — *vi* : economizar

retribution [ˌrɛtrə'bju:ʃən] *n* PUNISHMENT : castigo *m*, pena *f* merecida

retrieval [rɪ'tri:vəl] *n* : recuperación *f* ⟨beyond retrieval : irrecuperable⟩ ⟨data retrieval : recuperación de datos⟩

retrieve [rɪ'tri:v] *vt* **-trieved; -trieving 1** : cobrar ⟨to retrieve game : cobrar la caza⟩ **2** RECOVER : recuperar

retriever [rɪ'tri:vər] *n* : perro *m* cobrador

retroactive [ˌretroˈæktɪv] adj : retroactivo — **retroactively** adv

retrograde [ˈretrəˌgreɪd] adj : retrógrado

retrospect [ˈretrəˌspekt] n **in retrospect** : mirando hacia atrás, retrospectivamente

retrospective [ˌretrəˈspektɪv] adj : retrospectivo

return¹ [rɪˈtərn] vi **1** : volver, regresar ⟨to return home : regresar a casa⟩ **2** REAPPEAR : reaparecer, resurgir **3** ANSWER : responder — vt **1** REPLACE, RESTORE : devolver, volver (a poner), restituir ⟨to return something to its place : volver a poner algo en su lugar⟩ **2** YIELD : producir, redituar, rendir **3** REPAY : pagar, devolver ⟨to return a compliment : devolver un cumplido⟩

return² adj : de vuelta

return³ n **1** RETURNING : regreso m, vuelta f, retorno m **2** or **tax return** : declaración f de impuestos **3** YIELD : rédito m, rendimiento m, ganancia f **4** **returns** npl DATA, RESULTS : resultados mpl, datos mpl

reunion [riˈjuːnjən] n : reunión f, reencuentro m

reunite [ˌriːjuˈnaɪt] v **-nited; -niting** vt : (volver a) reunir — vi : (volver a) reunirse

reusable [ˈriːˈjuːzəbəl] adj : reutilizable

reuse [riˈjuːz] vt **-used; -using** : reutilizar, usar de nuevo

revamp [riˈvæmp] vt : renovar

reveal [rɪˈviːl] vt **1** DIVULGE : revelar, divulgar ⟨to reveal a secret : revelar un secreto⟩ **2** SHOW : manifestar, mostrar, dejar ver

revealing [rɪˈviːlɪŋ] adj : revelador

reveille [ˈrevəli] n : toque m de diana

revel¹ [ˈrevəl] vi **-eled** or **-elled; -eling** or **-elling** **1** CAROUSE : ir de juerga **2 to revel in** : deleitarse en

revel² n : juerga f, parranda f fam

revelation [ˌrevəˈleɪʃən] n : revelación f

reveler or **reveller** [ˈrevələr] n : juerguista m f

revelry [ˈrevəlri] n, pl **-ries** : juerga f, parranda f fam, jarana f fam

revenge¹ [rɪˈvendʒ] vt **-venged; -venging** : vengar ⟨to revenge oneself on : vengarse de⟩

revenge² n : venganza f

revenue [ˈrevəˌnuː, -ˌnjuː] n : ingresos mpl, rentas fpl

reverberate [rɪˈvərbəˌreɪt] vi **-ated; -ating** : reverberar

reverberation [rɪˌvərbəˈreɪʃən] n : reverberación f

revere [rɪˈvɪr] vt **-vered; -vering** : reverenciar, venerar

reverence [ˈrevərənts] n : reverencia f, veneración f

reverend [ˈrevərənd] adj : reverendo ⟨the Reverend John Chapin : el reverendo John Chapin⟩

reverent [ˈrevərənt] adj : reverente — **reverently** adv

reverie [ˈrevəri] n, pl **-eries** : ensueño m

reversal [rɪˈvərsəl] n **1** INVERSION : inversión f (del orden normal) **2** CHANGE : cambio m total **3** SETBACK : revés m, contratiempo m

reverse¹ [rɪˈvərs] v **-versed; -versing** vt **1** INVERT : invertir **2** CHANGE : cambiar totalmente **3** ANNUL : anular, revocar — vi : dar marcha atrás

reverse² adj **1** : inverso ⟨in reverse order : en orden inverso⟩ ⟨the reverse side : el reverso⟩ **2** OPPOSITE : contrario, opuesto

reverse³ n **1** OPPOSITE : lo contrario, lo opuesto **2** SETBACK : revés m, contratiempo m **3** BACK : reverso m, dorso m, revés m **4** or **reverse gear** : marcha f atrás, reversa f Col, Mex

reversible [rɪˈvərsəbəl] adj : reversible

reversion [rɪˈvərʒən] n : reversión f, vuelta f

revert [rɪˈvərt] vi : revertir

review¹ [rɪˈvjuː] vt **1** REEXAMINE : volver a examinar, repasar (una lección) **2** CRITICIZE : reseñar, hacer una crítica de **3** EXAMINE : examinar, analizar ⟨to review one's life : examinar su vida⟩ **4 to review the troops** : pasar revista a las tropas

review² n **1** INSPECTION : revista f (de tropas) **2** ANALYSIS, OVERVIEW : resumen m, análisis m ⟨a review of current affairs : un análisis de las actualidades⟩ **3** CRITICISM : reseña f, crítica f (de un libro, etc.) **4** : repaso m (para un examen) **5** REVUE : revista f (musical)

reviewer [rɪˈvjuːər] n : crítico m, -ca f

revile [rɪˈvaɪl] vt **-viled; -viling** : injuriar, denostar

revise [rɪˈvaɪz] vt **-vised; -vising** : revisar, corregir, refundir ⟨to revise a dictionary : corregir un diccionario⟩

revision [rɪˈvɪʒən] n : revisión f

revival [rɪˈvaɪvəl] n **1** : renacimiento m (de ideas, etc.), restablecimiento m (de costumbres, etc.), reactivación f (de la economía) **2** : reanimación f, resucitación f (en medicina) **3** or **revival meeting** : asamblea f evangelista

revive [rɪˈvaɪv] v **-vived; -viving** vt **1** REAWAKEN : reavivar, reanimar, reactivar (la economía), resucitar (a un paciente) **2** REESTABLISH : restablecer — vi **1** : renacer, reanimarse, reactivarse **2** COME TO : recobrar el sentido, volver en sí

revoke [rɪˈvoːk] vt **-voked; -voking** : revocar

revolt¹ [rɪˈvoːlt] vi **1** REBEL : rebelarse, sublevarse **2 to revolt at** : sentir repugnancia por — vt DISGUST : darle asco (a alguien), repugnar

revolt² n REBELLION : rebelión f, revuelta f, sublevación f

revolting [rɪˈvoːltɪŋ] adj : asqueroso, repugnante

revolution [ˌrɛvəˈluːʃən] *n* : revolución *f*

revolutionary[1] [ˌrɛvəˈluːʃənɛˌri] *adj* : revolucionario

revolutionary[2] *n, pl* **-aries** : revolucionario *m*, -ria *f*

revolutionize [ˌrɛvəˈluːʃənˌaɪz] *vt* **-ized**; **-izing** : cambiar radicalmente, revolucionar

revolve [rɪˈvalv] *v* **-volved**; **-volving** *vt* ROTATE : hacer girar — *vi* **1** ROTATE : girar ⟨to revolve around : girar alrededor de⟩ **2 to revolve in one's mind** : darle vueltas en la cabeza a alguien

revolver [rɪˈvalvər] *n* : revólver *m*

revue [rɪˈvjuː] *n* : revista *f* (musical)

revulsion [rɪˈvalʃən] *n* : repugnancia *f*

reward[1] [rɪˈwɔrd] *vt* : recompensar, premiar

reward[2] *n* : recompensa *f*

rewrite [ˌriːˈraɪt] *vt* **-wrote**; **-written**; **-writing** : escribir de nuevo, volver a escribir

rhapsody [ˈræpsədi] *n, pl* **-dies 1** : elogio *m* excesivo ⟨to go into rhapsodies over : extasiarse por⟩ **2** : rapsodia *f* (en música)

rhetoric [ˈrɛtərɪk] *n* : retórica *f*

rhetorical [rɪˈtɔrɪkəl] *adj* : retórico

rheumatic [ruˈmætɪk] *adj* : reumático

rheumatism [ˈruːməˌtɪzəm, ˈrʊ-] *n* : reumatismo *m*

rhinestone [ˈraɪnˌstoːn] *n* : diamante *m* de imitación

rhino [ˈraɪˌnoː] *n, pl* **rhino** *or* **rhinos** → rhinoceros

rhinoceros [raɪˈnɑsərəs] *n, pl* **-eroses** *or* **-eros** *or* **-eri** [-ˌraɪ] : rinoceronte *m*

rhododendron [ˌroːdəˈdɛndrən] *n* : rododendro *m*

rhombus [ˈrɑmbəs] *n, pl* **-buses** *or* **-bi** [-ˌbaɪ, -bi] : rombo *m*

rhubarb [ˈruːˌbarb] *n* : ruibarbo *m*

rhyme[1] [ˈraɪm] *vi* **rhymed**; **rhyming** : rimar

rhyme[2] *n* **1** : rima *f* **2** VERSE : verso *m* (en rima)

rhythm [ˈrɪðəm] *n* : ritmo *m*

rhythmic [ˈrɪðmɪk] *or* **rhythmical** [-mɪkəl] *adj* : rítmico — **rhythmically** [-mɪkli] *adv*

rib[1] [ˈrɪb] *vt* **ribbed**; **ribbing 1** : hacer en canalé ⟨a ribbed sweater : un suéter en canalé⟩ **2** TEASE : tomarle el pelo (a alguien)

rib[2] *n* **1** : costilla *f* (de una persona o un animal) **2** : nervio *m* (de una bóveda o una hoja), varilla *f* (de un paraguas), canalé *m* (de una prenda tejida)

ribald [ˈrɪbəld] *adj* : escabroso, procaz

ribbon [ˈrɪbən] *n* **1** : cinta *f* **2 to tear to ribbons** : hacer jirones

rice [ˈraɪs] *n* : arroz *m*

rich [ˈrɪtʃ] *adj* **1** WEALTHY : rico **2** SUMPTUOUS : suntuoso, lujoso **3** : pesado ⟨rich foods : comida pesada⟩ **4** ABUNDANT : abundante **5** : vivo, intenso ⟨rich colors : colores vivos⟩ **6** FERTILE : fértil, rico

riches [ˈrɪtʃəz] *npl* : riquezas *fpl*

richly [ˈrɪtʃli] *adv* **1** SUMPTUOUSLY : suntuosamente, ricamente **2** ABUNDANTLY : abundantemente **3 richly deserved** : bien merecido

richness [ˈrɪtʃnəs] *n* : riqueza *f*

rickets [ˈrɪkəts] *n* : raquitismo *m*

rickety [ˈrɪkəti] *adj* : desvencijado, destartalado

ricksha *or* **rickshaw** [ˈrɪkˌʃɔ] *n* : cochecillo *m* tirado por un hombre

ricochet[1] [ˈrɪkəˌʃeɪ] *vi* **-cheted** [-ˌʃeɪd] *or* **-chetted** [-ˌʃɛtəd]; **-cheting** [-ˌʃeɪɪŋ] *or* **-chetting** [-ˌʃɛtɪŋ] : rebotar

ricochet[2] *n* : rebote *m*

rid [ˈrɪd] *vt* **rid**; **ridding 1** FREE : librar ⟨to rid the city of thieves : librar la ciudad de ladrones⟩ **2 to rid oneself of** : desembarazarse de

riddance [ˈrɪdənts] *n* : libramiento *m* ⟨good riddance! : ¡adiós y buen viaje!, ¡vete con viento fresco!⟩

riddle[1] [ˈrɪdəl] *vt* **-dled**; **-dling** : acribillar ⟨riddled with bullets : acribillado a balazos⟩ ⟨riddled with errors : lleno de errores⟩

riddle[2] *n* : acertijo *m*, adivinanza *f*

ride[1] [ˈraɪd] *v* **rode** [ˈroːd]; **ridden** [ˈrɪdən]; **riding** *vt* **1** : montar, ir, andar ⟨to ride a horse : montar a caballo⟩ ⟨to ride a bicycle : montar en bicicleta, andar en bicicleta⟩ ⟨to ride the bus : ir en autobús⟩ **2** TRAVERSE : recorrer ⟨he rode 5 miles : recorrió 5 millas⟩ **3** TEASE : burlarse de, ridiculizar **4** CARRY : llevar **5** WEATHER : capear ⟨they rode out the storm : capearon el temporal⟩ **6 to ride the waves** : surcar los mares — *vi* **1** : montar a caballo, cabalgar **2** TRAVEL : ir, viajar (en coche, en bicicleta, etc.) **3** RUN : andar, marchar ⟨the car rides well : el coche anda bien⟩ **4 to ride at anchor** : estar fondeado **5 to let things ride** : dejar pasar las cosas

ride[2] *n* **1** : paseo *m*, vuelta *f* (en coche, en bicicleta, a caballo) ⟨to go for a ride : dar una vuelta⟩ ⟨to give someone a ride : llevar en coche a alguien⟩ **2** : aparato *m* (en un parque de diversiones)

rider [ˈraɪdər] *n* **1** : jinete *mf* ⟨the rider fell off his horse : el jinete se cayó de su caballo⟩ **2** CYCLIST : ciclista *mf* **3** MOTORCYCLIST : motociclista *mf* **4** CLAUSE : cláusula *f* añadida

ridge [ˈrɪdʒ] *n* **1** CHAIN : cadena *f* (de montañas o cerros) **2** : caballete *m* (de un techo), cresta *f* (de una ola o una montaña), cordoncillo *m* (de telas)

ridicule[1] [ˈrɪdəˌkjuːl] *vt* **-culed**; **-culing** : burlarse de, mofarse de, ridiculizar

ridicule[2] *n* : burlas *fpl*

ridiculous [rəˈdɪkjələs] *adj* : ridículo, absurdo

ridiculously [rəˈdɪkjələsli] *adv* : de forma ridícula

rife [ˈraɪf] *adj* : abundante, común ⟨to be rife with : estar plagado de⟩

riffraff ['rɪf₁ræf] n : chusma f, gentuza f

rifle¹ ['raɪfəl] v **-fled; -fling** vt RANSACK : desvalijar, saquear — vi **to rifle through** : revolver

rifle² n : rifle m, fusil m

rift ['rɪft] n **1** FISSURE : grieta f, fisura f **2** BREAK : ruptura f (entre personas), división f (dentro de un grupo)

rig¹ ['rɪg] vt **rigged; rigging 1** : aparejar (un barco) **2** EQUIP : equipar **3** FIX : amañar (una elección, etc.) **4 to rig up** CONSTRUCT : construir, erigir **5 to rig oneself out as** : vestirse de

rig² n **1** : aparejo m (de un barco) **2** or **oil rig** : torre f de perforación, plataforma f petrolífera

rigging ['rɪgɪŋ, -gən] n : jarcia f, aparejo m

right¹ ['raɪt] vt **1** FIX, RESTORE : reparar ⟨to right the economy : reparar la economía⟩ **2** STRAIGHTEN : enderezar

right² adv **1** : bien ⟨to live right : vivir bien⟩ **2** PRECISELY : precisamente, justo ⟨right in the middle : justo en medio⟩ **3** DIRECTLY, STRAIGHT : derecho, directamente ⟨he went right home : fue derecho a casa⟩ **4** IMMEDIATELY : inmediatamente ⟨right after lunch : inmediatamente después del almuerzo⟩ **5** COMPLETELY : completamente ⟨he felt right at home : se sintió completamente cómodo⟩ **6** : a la derecha ⟨to look left and right : mirar la izquierda y a la derecha⟩

right³ adj **1** UPRIGHT : bueno, honrado ⟨right conduct : conducta honrada⟩ **2** CORRECT : correcto ⟨the right answer : la respuesta correcta⟩ **3** APPROPRIATE : apropiado, adecuado, debido ⟨the right man for the job : el hombre perfecto para el trabajo⟩ **4** STRAIGHT : recto ⟨a right line : una línea recta⟩ **5** : derecho ⟨the right hand : la mano derecha⟩ **6** SOUND : bien ⟨he's not in his right mind : no está bien de la cabeza⟩

right⁴ n **1** GOOD : bien m ⟨to do right : hacer el bien⟩ **2** : derecha f ⟨on the right : a la derecha⟩ **3** or **right hand** : mano f derecha **4** ENTITLEMENT : derecho m ⟨the right to vote : el derecho a votar⟩ ⟨women's rights : los derechos de la mujer⟩ **5 the Right** : la derecha (en la política)

right angle n : ángulo m recto

right-angled ['raɪt₁æŋgəld] or **right-angle** [-gəl] adj **1** : en ángulo recto **2 right-angled triangle** : triángulo m rectángulo

righteous ['raɪtʃəs] adj : recto, honrado — **righteously** adv

righteousness ['raɪtʃəsnəs] n : rectitud f, honradez f

rightful ['raɪtfəl] adj **1** JUST : justo **2** LAWFUL : legítimo — **rightfully** adv

right-hand ['raɪt₁hænd] adj **1** : situado a la derecha **2** RIGHT-HANDED : para

la mano derecha, con la mano derecha **3 right-hand man** : brazo m derecho

right-handed ['raɪt₁hændəd] adj **1** : diestro ⟨a right-handed pitcher : un lanzador diestro⟩ **2** : para la mano derecha, con la mano derecha **3** CLOCKWISE : en la dirección de las manecillas del reloj

rightly ['raɪtli] adv **1** JUSTLY : justamente, con razón **2** PROPERLY : debidamente, apropiadamente **3** CORRECTLY : correctamente

right-of-way ['raɪtə₁weɪ, -əv-] n, pl **rights-of-way 1** : preferencia f (del tráfico) **2** ACCESS : derecho m de paso

rightward ['raɪtwərd] adj : a la derecha, hacia la derecha

right-wing ['raɪt₁wɪŋ] adj : derechista

right wing n **the right wing** : la derecha

right-winger ['raɪt₁wɪŋər] n : derechista mf

rigid ['rɪdʒɪd] adj : rígido — **rigidly** adv

rigidity [rɪ'dʒɪdəti] n, pl **-ties** : rigidez f

rigmarole ['rɪgmə₁roːl, 'rɪgə-] n **1** NONSENSE : galimatías m, disparates mpl **2** PROCEDURES : trámites mpl

rigor ['rɪgər] n : rigor m

rigor mortis [₁rɪgər'mortəs] n : rigidez f cadavérica

rigorous ['rɪgərəs] adj : riguroso — **rigorously** adv

rile ['raɪl] vt **riled; riling** : irritar

rill ['rɪl] n : riachuelo m

rim ['rɪm] n **1** EDGE : borde m **2** : llanta f, rin m Col, Mex (de una rueda) **3** FRAME : montura f (de anteojos)

rime ['raɪm] n : escarcha f

rind ['raɪnd] n : corteza f

ring¹ ['rɪŋ] v **rang** ['ræŋ]; **rung** ['rʌŋ]; **ringing** vi **1** : sonar ⟨the doorbell rang : el timbre sonó⟩ **2** or **to ring for** : llamar **2** RESOUND : resonar **3** SEEM : parecer ⟨to ring true : parecer cierto⟩ — vt **1** : tocar, hacer sonar (un timbre, una alarma, etc.) **2** SURROUND : cercar, rodear

ring² n **1** : anillo m, sortija f ⟨wedding ring : anillo de matrimonio⟩ **2** BAND : aro m, anillo m ⟨piston ring : aro de émbolo⟩ **3** CIRCLE : círculo m **4** ARENA : arena f, ruedo m ⟨a boxing ring : un cuadrilátero, un ring⟩ **5** GANG : banda f (de ladrones, etc.) **6** SOUND : timbre m, sonido m **7** CALL : llamada f (por teléfono)

ringer ['rɪŋər] n **to be a dead ringer for** : ser un vivo retrato de

ringleader ['rɪŋ₁liːdər] n : cabecilla f

ringlet ['rɪŋlət] n : sortija f, rizo m

ringworm ['rɪŋ₁wərm] n : tiña f

rink ['rɪŋk] n : pista f ⟨skating rink : pista de patinaje⟩

rinse¹ ['rɪns] vt **rinsed; rinsing** : enjuagar ⟨to rinse out one's mouth : enjuagarse la boca⟩

rinse² n : enjuague m

riot¹ ['raɪət] vi : amotinarse

riot² n : motín m, tumulto m, alboroto m

rioter ['raɪət̬ər] n : alborotador m, -dora f

riotous ['raɪət̬əs] adj **1** UNRULY, WILD : desenfrenado, alborotado **2** ABUNDANT : abundante

rip¹ ['rɪp] v **ripped; ripping** vt : rasgar, arrancar, desgarrar — vi : rasgarse, desgarrarse

rip² n : rasgón m, desgarrón m

ripe ['raɪp] adj **riper; ripest 1** MATURE : maduro ⟨ripe fruit : fruta madura⟩ **2** READY : listo, preparado

ripen ['raɪpən] v : madurar

ripeness ['raɪpnəs] n : madurez f

rip-off ['rɪp,ɒf] n **1** THEFT : robo m **2** SWINDLE : estafa f, timo m fam

rip off vt **1** : rasgar, arrancar, desgarrar **2** SWINDLE fam : estafar, tifar

ripple¹ ['rɪpəl] v **-pled; -pling** vi : rizarse, ondear, ondular — vt : rizar

ripple² n : onda f, ondulación f

rise¹ ['raɪz] vi **rose** ['roːz]; **risen** ['rɪz-ən]; **rising 1** GET UP : levantarse ⟨to rise to one's feet : ponerse de pie⟩ **2** : elevarse, alzarse ⟨the mountains rose to the west : las montañas se elevaron al oeste⟩ **3** : salir (dícese del sol y de la luna) **4** : subir (dícese de las aguas, del humo, etc.) ⟨the river rose : las aguas subieron de nivel⟩ **5** INCREASE : aumentar, subir **6** ORIGINATE : nacer, proceder **7** to rise in rank : ascender **8** to rise up REBEL : sublevarse, rebelarse

rise² n **1** ASCENT : ascensión f, subida f **2** ORIGIN : origen m **3** ELEVATION : elevación f **4** INCREASE : subida f, aumento m, alzamiento m **5** SLOPE : pendiente f, cuesta f

riser ['raɪzər] n **1** : contrahuella f (de una escalera) **2** early riser : madrugador m, -dora f **3** late riser : dormilón m, -lona f

risk¹ ['rɪsk] vt : arriesgar

risk² n : riesgo m, peligro m ⟨at risk : en peligro⟩ ⟨at your own risk : por su cuenta y riesgo⟩

risky ['rɪski] adj **riskier; -est** : arriesgado, peligroso, riesgoso

risqué [rɪ'skeɪ] adj : escabroso, picante, subido de tono

rite ['raɪt] n : rito m

ritual¹ ['rɪtʃuəl] adj : ritual — **ritually** adv

ritual² n : ritual m

rival¹ ['raɪvəl] vt **-valed** or **-valled; -valing** or **-valling** : rivalizar con, competir con

rival² adj : competidor, rival

rival³ n : rival mf; competidor m, -dora f

rivalry ['raɪvəlri] n, pl **-ries** : rivalidad f, competencia f

river ['rɪvər] n : río m

riverbank ['rɪvər,bæŋk] n : ribera f, orilla f

riverbed ['rɪvər,bɛd] n : cauce m, lecho m

riverside ['rɪvər,saɪd] n : ribera f, orilla f

rivet¹ ['rɪvət] vt **1** : remachar **2** FIX : fijar (los ojos, etc.) **3** FASCINATE : fascinar, cautivar

rivet² n : remache m

rivulet ['rɪvjələt] n : arroyo m, riachuelo m ⟨rivulets of sweat : gotas de sudor⟩

roach ['roːtʃ] → **cockroach**

road ['roːd] n **1** : carretera f, calle f, camino m **2** PATH : camino m, sendero m, vía f ⟨on the road to a solution : en vías de una solución⟩

roadblock ['roːd,blɒk] n : control m

roadrunner ['roːd,rʌnər] n : correcaminos m

roadside ['roːd,saɪd] n : borde m de la carretera

roadway ['roːd,weɪ] n : carretera f, calzada f

roam ['roːm] vi : vagar, deambular, errar — vt : vagar por

roan¹ ['roːn] adj : ruano

roan² n : caballo m ruano

roar¹ ['ror] vi : rugir, bramar ⟨to roar with laughter : reírse a carcajadas⟩ — vt : decir a gritos

roar² n **1** : rugido m, bramido m (de un animal) **2** DIN : clamor m (de gente), fragor m (del trueno), estruendo m (del tráfico, etc.)

roast¹ ['roːst] vt : asar (carne, papas), tostar (café, nueces) — vi : asarse

roast² adj : asado ⟨roast chicken : pollo asado⟩ **2** roast beef : rosbif m

roast³ n : asado m

rob ['rɑb] v **robbed; robbing** vt **1** STEAL : robar **2** DEPRIVE : privar, quitar — vi : robar

robber ['rɑbər] n : ladrón m, -drona f

robbery ['rɑbəri] n, pl **-beries** : robo m

robe¹ ['roːb] v **robed; robing** : vestirse

robe² n **1** : toga f (de magistrados, etc.), sotana f (de eclesiásticos) ⟨robe of office : traje de ceremonias⟩ **2** BATHROBE : bata f

robin ['rɑbən] n : petirrojo m

robot ['roː,bɑt, -bət] n : robot m

robotic [roː'bɑt̬ɪk] adj : robótico, robotizado

robotics [roː'bɑt̬ɪks] ns & pl : robótica f

robust [roː'bʌst, 'roː,bʌst] adj : robusto, fuerte — **robustly** adv

rock¹ ['rɑk] vt **1** : acunar (a un niño), mecer (una cuna) **2** SHAKE : sacudir — vi SWAY : mecerse, balancearse

rock² adj : de rock

rock³ n **1** ROCKING : balanceo m **2** or **rock music** : rock m, música f rock **3** : roca f (substancia) **4** STONE : piedra f

rock and roll n : rock and roll m

rocker ['rɑkər] n **1** : balancín m **2** or **rocking chair** : mecedora f, balancín m **3** to be off one's rocker : estar chiflado, estar loco

rocket¹ ['rɑkət] vi : dispararse, subir rápidamente

rocket² n : cohete m

rocking horse *n* : caballito *m* (de balancín)

rock salt *n* : sal *f* gema

rocky ['rɑki] *adj* **rockier; -est 1** : rocoso, pedregoso **2** UNSTEADY : inestable

rod ['rɑd] *n* **1** BAR : barra *f*, varilla *f*, vara *f* (de madera) ⟨a fishing rod : una caña (de pescar)⟩ **2** : medida *f* de longitud equivalente a 5.03 metros (5 yardas)

rode → **ride¹**

rodent ['ro:dənt] *n* : roedor *m*

rodeo ['ro:di,o:, ro'dei,o:] *n*, *pl* **-deos** : rodeo *m*

roe ['ro:] *n* : hueva *f*

rogue ['ro:g] *n* SCOUNDREL : pícaro *m*, -ra *f*; pillo *m*, -lla *f*

roguish ['ro:gɪʃ] *adj* : pícaro, travieso

role ['ro:l] *n* : papel *m*, función *f*, rol *m*

roll¹ ['ro:l] *vt* **1** : hacer rodar ⟨to roll the ball : hacer rodar la pelota⟩ ⟨to roll one's eyes : poner los ojos en blanco⟩ **2** : liar (un cigarrillo) **3** *or* **to roll up** : enrollar ⟨to roll (oneself) up into a ball : hacerse una bola⟩ **4** FLATTEN : estirar (masa), laminar (metales), pasar el rodillo por (el césped) **5 to roll up one's sleeves** : arremangarse — *vi* **1** : rodar ⟨the ball kept on rolling : la pelota siguió rodando⟩ **2** SWAY : balancearse ⟨the ship rolled in the waves : el barco se balanceó en las olas⟩ **3** REVERBERATE, SOUND : tronar (dícese del trueno), redoblar (dícese de un tambor) **4 to roll along** PROCEED : ponerse en marcha **5 to roll around** : revolcarse **6 to roll by** : pasar **7 to roll over** : dar una vuelta

roll² *n* **1** LIST : lista *f* ⟨to call the roll : pasar lista⟩ ⟨to have on the roll : tener inscrito⟩ **2** *or* **bread roll** : panecito *m*, bolillo *m Mex* **3** : rollo *m* (de papel, de tela, etc.) ⟨a roll of film : un carrete⟩ ⟨a roll of bills : un fajo⟩ **4** : redoble *m* (de tambores), retumbo *m* (del trueno, etc.) **5** ROLLING, SWAYING : balanceo *m*

roller ['ro:lər] *n* **1** : rodillo *m* **2** CURLER : rulo *m*

roller coaster ['ro:lər,ko:stər] *n* : montaña *f* rusa

roller-skate ['ro:lər,skeɪt] *vi* **-skated; -skating** : patinar (sobre ruedas)

roller skate *n* : patín *m* (de ruedas)

rollicking ['rɑlɪkɪŋ] *adj* : animado, alegre

rolling pin *n* : rodillo *m*

Roman¹ ['ro:mən] *adj* : romano

Roman² *n* : romano *m*, -na *f*

Roman Catholic *n* : católico *m*, -ca *f* — **Roman Catholic** *adj*

Roman Catholicism *n* : catolicismo *m*

romance¹ [ro'mæns, 'ro:,mænts] *vi* **-manced; -mancing** FANTASIZE : fantasear

romance² *n* **1** : romance *m*, novela *f* de caballerías **2** : novela *f* de amor, novela *f* romántica **3** AFFAIR : romance *m*, amorío *m*

Romanian [ru'meiniən, ro-] *n* **1** : rumano *m*, -na *f* **2** : rumano *m* (idioma) — **Romanian** *adj*

Roman numeral *n* : número *m* romano

romantic [ro'mæntɪk] *adj* : romántico — **romantically** [-tɪkli] *adv*

romp¹ ['rɑmp] *vi* FROLIC : retozar, juguetear

romp² *n* : retozo *m*

roof¹ ['ru:f, 'rʊf] *vt* : techar

roof² *n*, *pl* **roofs** ['ru:fs, 'rʊfs; 'ru:vz, 'rʊvz] **1** : techo *m*, tejado *m*, techado *m* **2 roof of the mouth** : paladar *m*

roofing ['ru:fɪŋ, 'rʊfɪŋ] *n* : techumbre *f*

rooftop ['ru:f,tɑp, 'rʊf-] *n* ROOF : tejado *m*

rook¹ ['rʊk] *vt* CHEAT : defraudar, estafar, timar

rook² *n* **1** : grajo *m* (ave) **2** : torre *f* (en ajedrez)

rookie ['rʊki] *n* : novato *m*, -ta *f*

room¹ ['ru:m, 'rʊm] *vi* LODGE : alojarse, hospedarse

room² *n* **1** SPACE : espacio *m*, sitio *m*, lugar *m* ⟨to make room for : hacer lugar para⟩ **2** : cuarto *m*, habitación *f* (en una casa), sala *f* (para reuniones, etc.) **3** BEDROOM : dormitorio *m*, habitación *f*, pieza *f* **4** (*indicating possibility or opportunity*) ⟨room for improvement : posibilidad de mejorar⟩ ⟨there's no room for error : no hay lugar para errores⟩

roomer ['ru:mər, 'rʊmər] *n* : inquilino *m*, -na *f*

rooming house *n* : pensión *f*

roommate ['ru:m,meɪt, 'rʊm-] *n* : compañero *m*, -ra *f* de cuarto

roomy ['ru:mi, 'rʊmi] *adj* **roomier; -est 1** SPACIOUS : espacioso, amplio **2** LOOSE : suelto, holgado ⟨a roomy blouse : una blusa holgada⟩

roost¹ ['ru:st] *vi* : posarse, dormir (en una percha)

roost² *n* : percha *f*

rooster ['ru:stər, 'rʊs-] *n* : gallo *m*

root¹ ['ru:t, 'rʊt] *vi* **1** : arraigar ⟨the plant rooted easily : la planta arraigó con facilidad⟩ ⟨deeply rooted traditions : tradiciones profundamente arraigadas⟩ **2** : hozar (dícese de los cerdos) ⟨to root around in : hurgar en⟩ **3 to root for** : apoyar a, alentar — *vt* **to root out** *or* **to root up** : desarraigar (plantas), extirpar (problemas, etc.)

root² *n* **1** : raíz *f* (de una planta) **2** ORIGIN : origen *m*, raíz *f* **3** CORE : centro *m*, núcleo *m* ⟨to get to the root of the matter : ir al centro del asunto⟩

rootless ['ru:tləs, 'rʊt-] *adj* : desarraigado

rope¹ ['ro:p] *vt* **roped; roping 1** TIE : amarrar, atar **2** LASSO : lazar **3 to rope off** : acordonar

rope² *n* : soga *f*, cuerda *f*

rosary ['ro:zəri] *n*, *pl* **-ries** : rosario *m*

rose¹ → **rise¹**

rose² ['ro:z] *adj* : rosa, color de rosa

rose[3] n 1 : rosal m (planta), rosa f (flor) 2 : rosa m (color)

rosebush ['ro:z,bʊʃ] n : rosal m

rosemary ['ro:z,mɛri] n, pl **-maries** : romero m

rosette [ro'zɛt] n : escarapela f (hecho de cintas), roseta f (en arquitectura)

Rosh Hashanah [,raʃə'ʃɑnə, ,ro:ʃ-] n : el Año Nuevo judío

rosin ['razən] n : colofonia f

roster ['rastər] n : lista f

rostrum ['rastrəm] n, pl **-trums** or **-tra** [-trə] : tribuna f, estrado m

rosy ['ro:zi] adj **rosier; -est** 1 : sonrosado, de color rosa 2 PROMISING : prometedor, halagüeño

rot[1] ['rat] v **rotted; rotting** vi : pudrirse, descomponerse — vt : pudrir, descomponer

rot[2] n : putrefacción f, descomposición f, podredumbre f

rotary[1] ['ro:təri] adj : rotativo, rotatorio

rotary[2] n, pl **-ries** 1 : máquina f rotativa 2 TRAFFIC CIRCLE : rotonda f, glorieta f

rotate ['ro:,teɪt] v **-tated; -tating** vi REVOLVE : girar, rotar — vt 1 TURN : hacer girar, darle vueltas a 2 ALTERNATE : alternar

rotation [ro'teɪʃən] n : rotación f

rote ['ro:t] n **to learn by rote** : aprender de memoria

rotor ['ro:tər] n : rotor m

rotten ['ratən] adj 1 PUTRID : podrido, putrefacto 2 CORRUPT : corrompido 3 BAD : malo ⟨a rotten day : un día malísimo⟩

rottenness ['ratənnəs] n : podredumbre f

rotund [ro'tʌnd] adj 1 ROUNDED : redondeado 2 PLUMP : regordete fam, llenito fam

rouge ['ru:ʒ, 'ru:dʒ] n : colorete m

rough[1] ['rʌf] v 1 ROUGHEN : poner áspero 2 **to rough out** SKETCH : esbozar, bosquejar 3 **to rough up** BEAT : darle una paliza a (alguien) 4 **to rough it** : vivir sin comodidades

rough[2] adj 1 COARSE : áspero, basto 2 UNEVEN : desigual, escabroso, accidentado (dícese del terreno) 3 : agitado (dícese del mar), tempestuoso (dícese del tiempo), violento (dícese del viento) 4 VIOLENT : violento, brutal ⟨a rough neighborhood : un barrio peligroso⟩ 5 DIFFICULT : duro, difícil 6 CRUDE : rudo, tosco, burdo ⟨a rough cottage : una casita tosca⟩ ⟨a rough draft : un borrador⟩ ⟨a rough sketch : un bosquejo⟩ 7 APPROXIMATE : aproximado ⟨a rough idea : una idea aproximada⟩

rough[3] n 1 **the rough** : el rough (en golf) 2 **in the rough** : en borrador

roughage ['rʌfɪdʒ] n : fibra f

roughen ['rʌfən] vt : poner áspero — vi : ponerse áspero

roughly ['rʌfli] adv 1 : bruscamente ⟨to treat roughly : maltratar⟩ 2 CRUDELY : burdamente 3 APPROXIMATELY : aproximadamente, más o menos

roughneck ['rʌf,nɛk] n : matón m

roughness ['rʌfnəs] n : rudeza f, aspereza f

roulette [ru:'lɛt] n : ruleta f

round[1] ['raʊnd] vt 1 : redondear ⟨she rounded the edges : redondeó los bordes⟩ 2 TURN : doblar ⟨to round the corner : dar la vuelta a la esquina⟩ 3 **to round off** : redondear (un número) 4 **to round off** or **to round out** COMPLETE : rematar, terminar 5 **to round up** GATHER : reunir

round[2] adv → **around**[1]

round[3] adj 1 : redondo ⟨a round table : una mesa redonda⟩ ⟨in round numbers : en números redondos⟩ ⟨round shoulders : espaldas cargadas⟩ 2 **round trip** : viaje m de ida y vuelta

round[4] n 1 CIRCLE : círculo m 2 SERIES : serie f, sucesión f ⟨a round of talks : una ronda de negociaciones⟩ ⟨the daily round : la rutina cotidiana⟩ 3 : asalto m (en boxeo), recorrido m (en golf), vuelta f (en varios juegos) 4 : salva f (de aplausos) 5 **round of drinks** : ronda f 6 **round of ammunition** : disparo m, cartucho m 7 **rounds** npl : recorridos mpl (de un cartero), rondas fpl (de un vigilante), visitas fpl (de un médico) ⟨to make the rounds : hacer visitas⟩

round[5] prep → **around**[2]

roundabout ['raʊndə,baʊt] adj : indirecto ⟨to speak in a roundabout way : hablar con rodeos⟩

roundly ['raʊndli] adv 1 THOROUGHLY : completamente 2 BLUNTLY : francamente, rotundamente 3 VIGOROUSLY : con vigor

roundness ['raʊndnəs] n : redondez f

roundup ['raʊnd,ʌp] n 1 : rodeo m (de animales), redada f (de delincuentes, etc.) 2 SUMMARY : resumen m

round up vt 1 : rodear (ganado), reunir (personas) 2 SUMMARIZE : hacer un resumen de

roundworm ['raʊnd,wərm] n : lombriz f intestinal

rouse ['raʊz] vt **roused; rousing** 1 AWAKE : despertar 2 EXCITE : excitar ⟨it roused him to fury : lo enfureció⟩

rout[1] ['raʊt] vt 1 DEFEAT : derrotar, aplastar 2 **to rout out** : hacer salir

rout[2] n 1 DISPERSAL : desbandada f, dispersión f 2 DEFEAT : derrota f aplastante

route[1] ['ru:t, 'raʊt] vt **routed; routing** : dirigir, enviar, encaminar

route[2] n : camino m, ruta f, recorrido m

routine[1] [ru:'ti:n] adj : rutinario — **routinely** adv

routine[2] n : rutina f

rove ['ro:v] v **roved; roving** vi : vagar, errar — vt : errar por

rover ['ro:vər] n : vagabundo m, -da f

row¹ ['ro:] *vt* **1** : avanzar a remo ⟨to row a boat : remar⟩ **2** : llevar a remo ⟨he rowed me to shore : me llevó hasta la orilla⟩ — *vi* : remar

row² ['rau] *n* **1** : paseo *m* en barca ⟨to go for a row : salir a remar⟩ **2** LINE, RANK : fila *f*, hilera *f* **3** SERIES : serie *f* ⟨three days in a row : tres días seguidos⟩ **4** RACKET : estruendo *m*, bulla *f* **5** QUARREL : pelea *f*, riña *f*

rowboat ['ro:,bo:t] *n* : bote *m* de remos

rowdiness ['raudinəs] *n* : bulla *f*

rowdy¹ ['raudi] *adj* **-dier; -est** : escandaloso, alborotador

rowdy² *n, pl* **-dies** : alborotador *m*, -dora *f*

rower ['ro:ər] *n* : remero *m*, -ra *f*

royal¹ ['rɔiəl] *adj* : real — **royally** *adv*

royal² *n* : persona de linaje real, miembro de la familia real

royalty ['rɔiəlti] *n, pl* **-ties 1** : realeza *f* (posición) **2** : miembros *mpl* de la familia real **3 royalties** *npl* : derechos *mpl* de autor

rub¹ ['rʌb] *v* **rubbed; rubbing** *vt* **1** : frotar, restregar ⟨to rub one's hands together : frotarse las manos⟩ **2** MASSAGE : friccionar, masajear **3** CHAFE : rozar **4** POLISH : frotar, pulir **5** SCRUB : fregar **6 to rub elbows with** : codearse con **7 to rub someone the wrong way** : sacar de quicio a alguien, caerle mal a alguien — *vi* **to rub against** : rozar

rub² *n* **1** RUBBING : frotamiento *m*, fricción *f* **2** DIFFICULTY : problema *m*

rubber ['rʌbər] *n* **1** : goma *f*, caucho *m*, hule *m* *Mex* **2 rubbers** *npl* OVERSHOES : chanclos *mpl*

rubber band *n* : goma *f* (elástica), gomita *f*

rubber–stamp ['rʌbər'stæmp] *vt* **1** APPROVE : aprobar, autorizar **2** STAMP : sellar

rubber stamp *n* : sello *m* (de goma)

rubbery ['rʌbəri] *adj* : gomoso

rubbish ['rʌbɪʃ] *n* : basura *f*, desechos *mpl*, desperdicios *mpl*

rubble ['rʌbəl] *n* : escombros *mpl*, ripio *m*

ruble ['ru:bəl] *n* : rublo *m*

ruby ['ru:bi] *n, pl* **-bies 1** : rubí *m* (gema) **2** : color *m* de rubí

rudder ['rʌdər] *n* : timón *m*

ruddy ['rʌdi] *adj* **-dier; -est** : rubicundo (dícese de la cara, etc.), rojizo (dícese del cielo)

rude ['ru:d] *adj* **ruder; rudest 1** CRUDE : tosco, rústico **2** IMPOLITE : grosero, descortés, maleducado **3** ABRUPT : brusco ⟨a rude awakening : una sorpresa desagradable⟩

rudely ['ru:dli] *adv* : groseramente

rudeness ['ru:dnəs] *n* **1** IMPOLITENESS : grosería *f*, descortesía *f*, falta *f* de educación **2** ROUGHNESS : tosquedad *f* **3** SUDDENNESS : brusquedad *f*

rudiment ['ru:dəmənt] *n* : rudimento *m*, noción *f* básica ⟨the rudiments of Spanish : los rudimentos del español⟩

rudimentary [,ru:də'mɛntəri] *adj* : rudimentario, básico

rue ['ru:] *vt* **rued; ruing** : lamentar, arrepentirse de

rueful ['ru:fəl] *adj* **1** PITIFUL : lastimoso **2** REGRETFUL : arrepentido, pesaroso

ruffian ['rʌfiən] *n* : matón *m*

ruffle¹ ['rʌfəl] *vt* **-fled; -fling 1** AGITATE : agitar, rizar (agua) **2** RUMPLE : arrugar (ropa), despeinar (pelo) **3** ERECT : erizar (plumas) **4** VEX : alterar, irritar, perturbar **5** : fruncir volantes en (tela)

ruffle² *n* FLOUNCE : volante *m*

ruffly ['rʌfəli] *adj* : con volantes

rug ['rʌg] *n* : alfombra *f*, tapete *m*

rugged ['rʌgəd] *adj* **1** ROUGH, UNEVEN : accidentado, escabroso ⟨rugged mountains : montañas accidentadas⟩ **2** HARSH : duro, severo **3** ROBUST, STURDY : robusto, fuerte

ruin¹ ['ru:ən] *vt* **1** DESTROY : destruir, arruinar **2** BANKRUPT : arruinar, hacer quebrar

ruin² *n* **1** : ruina *f* ⟨to fall into ruin : caer en ruinas⟩ **2** : ruina *f*, perdición *f* ⟨to be the ruin of : ser la perdición de⟩ **3 ruins** *npl* : ruinas *fpl*, restos *mpl* ⟨the ruins of the ancient temple : las ruinas del templo antiguo⟩

ruinous ['ru:ənəs] *adj* : ruinoso

rule¹ ['ru:l] *v* **ruled; ruling** *vt* **1** CONTROL, GOVERN : gobernar (un país), controlar (las emociones) **2** DECIDE : decidir, fallar ⟨the judge ruled that ... : el juez falló que ...⟩ **3** DRAW : trazar con una regla — *vi* **1** GOVERN : gobernar, reinar **2** PREVAIL : prevalecer, imperar **3 to rule against** : fallar en contra de

rule² *n* **1** REGULATION : regla *f*, norma *f* **2** CUSTOM, HABIT : regla *f* general ⟨as a rule : por lo general⟩ **3** GOVERNMENT : gobierno *m*, dominio *m* **4** RULER : regla *f* (para medir)

ruler ['ru:lər] *n* **1** LEADER, SOVEREIGN : gobernante *mf*, soberano *m*, -na *f* **2** : regla *f* (para medir)

ruling ['ru:lɪŋ] *n* : resolución *f*, fallo *m*

rum ['rʌm] *n* : ron *m*

Rumanian [ru'meiniən] → **Romanian**

rumble¹ ['rʌmbəl] *vi* **-bled; -bling** : retumbar, hacer ruidos (dícese del estómago)

rumble² *n* : estruendo *m*, ruido *m* sordo, retumbo *m*

ruminant¹ ['ru:mənənt] *adj* : rumiante

ruminant² *n* : rumiante *m*

ruminate ['ru:mə,neit] *vi* **-nated; -nating 1** : rumiar (en zoología) **2** REFLECT : reflexionar, rumiar

rummage ['rʌmɪdʒ] *v* **-maged; -maging** *vi* : hurgar — *vt* RANSACK : revolver ⟨they rummaged the attic : revolvieron el ático⟩

rummy ['rʌmi] *n* : rummy *m* (juego de naipes)

rumor[1] ['ru:mər] *vt* : rumorear ⟨it is rumored that . . . : se rumorea que . . ., se dice que . . .⟩

rumor[2] *n* : rumor *m*

rump ['rʌmp] *n* **1** : ancas *fpl*, grupa *f* (de un animal) **2** : cadera *f* ⟨rump steak : filete de cadera⟩

rumple ['rʌmpəl] *vt* **-pled; -pling** : arrugar (ropa, etc.), despeinar (pelo)

rumpus ['rʌmpəs] *n* : lío *m*, jaleo *m fam*

run[1] ['rʌn] *v* **ran** ['ræn]; **run; running** *vi* **1** : correr ⟨she ran to catch the bus : corrió para alcanzar el autobús⟩ ⟨run and fetch the doctor : corre a buscar al médico⟩ **2** : circular, correr ⟨the train runs between Detroit and Chicago : el tren circula entre Detroit y Chicago⟩ ⟨to run on time : ser puntual⟩ **3** FUNCTION : funcionar, ir ⟨the engine runs on gasoline : el motor funciona con gasolina⟩ ⟨to run smoothly : ir bien⟩ **4** FLOW : correr, ir **5** LAST : durar ⟨the movie runs for two hours : la película dura dos horas⟩ ⟨the contract runs for three years : el contrato es válido por tres años⟩ **6** : desteñir, despintar (dícese de los colores) **7** EXTEND : correr, extenderse **8 to run for office** : postularse, presentarse — *vt* **1** : correr ⟨to run 10 miles : correr 10 millas⟩ ⟨to run errands : hacer los mandados⟩ ⟨to run out of town : hacer salir del pueblo⟩ **2** PASS : pasar **3** DRIVE : llevar en coche **4** OPERATE : hacer funcionar (un motor, etc.) **5** : echar ⟨to run water : echar agua⟩ **6** MANAGE : dirigir, llevar (un negocio, etc.) **7** EXTEND : tender (un cable, etc.) **8 to run a risk** : correr un riesgo

run[2] *n* **1** : carrera *f* ⟨at a run : a la carrera, corriendo⟩ ⟨to go for a run : ir a correr⟩ **2** TRIP : vuelta *f*, paseo *m* (en coche), viaje *m* (en avión) **3** SERIES : serie *f* ⟨a run of disappointments : una serie de desilusiones⟩ ⟨in the long run : a la larga⟩ ⟨in the short run : a corto plazo⟩ **4** DEMAND : gran demanda *f* ⟨a run on the banks : una corrida bancaria⟩ **5** (*used for theatrical productions and films*) ⟨to have a long run : mantenerse mucho tiempo en la cartelera⟩ **6** TYPE : tipo *m* ⟨the average run of students : el tipo más común de estudiante⟩ **7** : carrera *f* (en béisbol) **8** : carrera *f* (en una media) **9 to have the run of** : tener libre acceso de (una casa, etc.) **10 ski run** : pista *f* (de esquí)

runaway[1] ['rʌnə,wei] *adj* **1** FUGITIVE : fugitivo **2** UNCONTROLLABLE : incontrolable, fuera de control ⟨runaway inflation : inflación desenfrenada⟩ ⟨a runaway success : un éxito aplastante⟩

runaway[2] *n* : fugitivo *m*, -va *f*

rundown ['rʌn,daun] *n* SUMMARY : resumen *m*

run–down ['rʌn'daun] *adj* **1** DILAPIDATED : ruinoso, destartalado **2** SICKLY, TIRED : cansado, débil

rung[1] *pp* → **ring**[1]

rung[2] ['rʌŋ] *n* : peldaño *m*, escalón *m*

run–in ['rʌn,ın] *n* : disputa *f*, altercado *m*

runner ['rʌnər] *n* **1** RACER : corredor *m*, -dora *f* **2** MESSENGER : mensajero *m*, -ra *f* **3** TRACK : riel *m* (de un cajón, etc.) **4** : patín *m* (de un trineo), cuchilla *f* (de un patín) **5** : estolón *m* (planta)

runner–up [,rʌnər'ʌp] *n, pl* **runners–up** : subcampeón *m*, -peona *f*

running ['rʌnıŋ] *adj* **1** FLOWING : corriente ⟨running water : agua corriente⟩ **2** CONTINUOUS : continuo ⟨a running battle : una lucha continua⟩ **3** CONSECUTIVE : seguido ⟨six days running : por seis días seguidos⟩

runny ['rʌni] *adj* **-nier; -est 1** WATERY : caldoso **2 to have a runny nose** : moquear

run over *vt* : atropellar — *vi* OVERFLOW : rebosar

runt ['rʌnt] *n* : animal *m* pequeño ⟨the runt of the litter : el más pequeño de la camada⟩

runway ['rʌn,wei] *n* : pista *f* de aterrizaje

rupee [ru:'pi:, 'ru:,-] *n* : rupia *f*

rupture[1] ['rʌpʧər] *v* **-tured; -turing** *vt* **1** BREAK, BURST : romper, reventar **2** : causar una hernia en — *vi* : reventarse

rupture[2] *n* **1** BREAK : ruptura *f* **2** HERNIA : hernia *f*

rural ['rurəl] *adj* : rural, campestre

ruse ['ru:s, 'ru:z] *n* : treta *f*, ardid *m*, estratagema *f*

rush[1] ['rʌʃ] *vi* : correr, ir de prisa ⟨to rush around : correr de un lado a otro⟩ ⟨to rush off : irse corriendo⟩ — *vt* **1** HURRY : apresurar, apurar **2** ATTACK : abalanzarse sobre, asaltar

rush[2] *adj* : urgente

rush[3] *n* **1** HASTE : prisa *f*, apuro *m* **2** SURGE : ráfaga *f* (de aire), torrente *m* (de aguas), avalancha *f* (de gente) **3** DEMAND : demanda *f* ⟨a rush on sugar : una gran demanda para el azúcar⟩ **4** : carga *f* (en futbol americano) **5** : junco *m* (planta)

russet ['rʌsət] *n* : color *m* rojizo

Russian ['rʌʃən] *n* **1** : ruso *m*, -sa *f* **2** : ruso *m* (idioma) — **Russian** *adj*

rust[1] ['rʌst] *vi* : oxidarse — *vt* : oxidar

rust[2] *n* **1** : herrumbre *f*, orín *m*, óxido *m* (en los metales) **2** : roya *f* (en las plantas)

rustic[1] ['rʌstık] *adj* : rústico, campestre — **rustically** [-tıkli] *adv*

rustic[2] *n* : rústico *m*, -ca *f*; campesino *m*, -na *f*

rustle[1] ['rʌsəl] *v* **-tled; -tling** *vt* **1** : hacer susurrar, hacer crujir ⟨to rustle a newspaper : hacer crujir un periódico⟩ **2** STEAL : robar (ganado) — *vi* : susurrar, crujir

rustle[2] *n* : murmullo *m*, susurro *m*, crujido *m*
rustler ['rʌslər] *n* : ladrón *m*, -drona *f* de ganado
rusty ['rʌsti] *adj* **rustier; -est** : oxidado, herrumbroso
rut ['rʌt] *n* **1 GROOVE, TRACK** : rodada *f*, surco *m* **2 to be in a rut** : ser esclavo de la rutina

ruthless ['ruːθləs] *adj* : despiadado, cruel — **ruthlessly** *adv*
ruthlessness ['ruːθləsnəs] *n* : crueldad *f*, falta *f* de piedad
Rwandan [ru'andən] *n* : ruandés *m*, -desa *f* — **Rwandan** *adj*
rye ['raɪ] *n* **1** : centeno *m* **2 or rye whiskey** : whisky *m* de centeno

S

s ['ɛs] *n, pl* **s's** *or* **ss** ['ɛsəz] : decimonovena letra del alfabeto inglés
Sabbath ['sæbəθ] *n* **1** : sábado *m* (en el judaísmo) **2** : domingo *m* (en el cristianismo)
saber ['seɪbər] *n* : sable *m*
sable ['seɪbəl] *n* **1 BLACK** : negro *m* **2** : marta *f* cebellina (animal)
sabotage[1] ['sæbə,tɑːʒ] *vt* **-taged; -taging** : sabotear
sabotage[2] *n* : sabotaje *m*
sac ['sæk] *n* : saco *m* (anatómico)
saccharin ['sækərən] *n* : sacarina *f*
saccharine ['sækərən, -,riːn, -,raɪn] *adj* : meloso, empalagoso
sachet [sæ'ʃeɪ] *n* : bolsita *f* (perfumada)
sack[1] ['sæk] *vt* **1 FIRE** : echar (del trabajo), despedir **2 PLUNDER** : saquear
sack[2] *n* **BAG** : saco *m*
sacrament ['sækrəmənt] *n* : sacramento *m*
sacramental [,sækrə'mɛntəl] *adj* : sacramental
sacred ['seɪkrəd] *adj* **1 RELIGIOUS** : sagrado, sacro ⟨sacred texts : textos sagrados⟩ **2 HOLY** : sagrado **3 sacred to** : consagrado a
sacrifice[1] ['sækrə,faɪs] *vt* **-ficed; -ficing 1** : sacrificar **2 to sacrifice oneself** : sacrificarse
sacrifice[2] *n* : sacrificio *m*
sacrilege ['sækrəlɪʤ] *n* : sacrilegio *m*
sacrilegious [,sækrə'lɪʤəs, -'liː-] *adj* : sacrílego
sacrosanct ['sækro,sæŋkt] *adj* : sacrosanto
sad ['sæd] *adj* **sadder; saddest** : triste — **sadly** *adv*
sadden ['sædən] *vt* : entristecer
saddle[1] ['sædəl] *vt* **-dled; -dling** : ensillar
saddle[2] *n* : silla *f* (de montar)
sadism ['seɪ,dɪzəm, 'sæ-] *n* : sadismo *m*
sadist ['seɪdɪst, 'sæ-] *n* : sádico *m*, -ca *f*
sadistic [sə'dɪstɪk] *adj* : sádico — **sadistically** [-tɪkli] *adv*
sadness ['sædnəs] *n* : tristeza *f*
safari [sə'fɑri, -'fær-] *n* : safari *m*
safe[1] ['seɪf] *adj* **safer; safest 1 UNHARMED** : ileso ⟨safe and sound : sano y salvo⟩ **2 SECURE** : seguro **3 to be on the safe side** : para mayor seguridad **4 to play it safe** : ir a la segura
safe[2] *n* : caja *f* fuerte

safeguard[1] ['seɪf,gɑrd] *vt* : salvaguardar, proteger
safeguard[2] *n* : salvaguarda *f*, protección *f*
safekeeping ['seɪf'kiːpɪŋ] *n* : custodia *f*, protección *f* ⟨to put into safekeeping : poner en buen recaudo⟩
safely ['seɪfli] *adv* **1 UNHARMED** : sin incidentes, sin novedades ⟨they landed safely : aterrizaron sin novedades⟩ **2 SECURELY** : con toda seguridad, sin peligro
safety ['seɪfti] *n, pl* **-ties** : seguridad *f*
safety belt *n* : cinturón *m* de seguridad
safety pin *n* : alfiler *m* de gancho, alfiler *m* de seguridad, imperdible *m* *Spain*
saffron ['sæfrən] *n* : azafrán *m*
sag[1] ['sæg] *vi* **sagged; sagging 1 DROOP, SINK** : combarse, hundirse, inclinarse **2** : colgar, caer ⟨his jowls sagged : le colgaban las mejillas⟩ **3 FLAG** : flaquear, decaer ⟨his spirits sagged : se le flaqueó el ánimo⟩
sag[2] *n* : combadura *f*
saga ['sɑgə, 'sæ-] *n* : saga *f*
sagacious [sə'geɪʃəs] *adj* : sagaz
sage[1] ['seɪʤ] *adj* **sager; -est** : sabio — **sagely** *adv*
sage[2] *n* **1** : sabio *m*, -bia *f* **2** : salvia *f* (planta)
sagebrush ['seɪʤ,brʌʃ] *n* : artemisa *f*
Sagittarius [,sæʤə'tɛriəs] *n* : Sagitario *mf*
said → **say**
sail[1] ['seɪl] *vi* **1** : navegar (en un barco) **2** : ir fácilmente ⟨we sailed right in : entramos sin ningún problema⟩ — *vt* **1** : gobernar (un barco) **2 to sail the seas** : cruzar los mares
sail[2] *n* **1** : vela *f* (de un barco) **2** : viaje *m* en velero ⟨to go for a sail : salir a navegar⟩
sailboat ['seɪl,boːt] *n* : velero *m*, barco *m* de vela
sailfish ['seɪl,fɪʃ] *n* : pez *m* vela
sailor ['seɪlər] *n* : marinero *m*
saint ['seɪnt, *before a name* ,seɪnt *or* sənt] *n* : santo *m*, -ta *f* ⟨Saint Francis : San Francisco⟩ ⟨Saint Rose : Santa Rosa⟩
saintliness ['seɪntlinəs] *n* : santidad *f*
saintly ['seɪntli] *adj* **saintlier; -est** : santo
sake ['seɪk] *n* **1 BENEFIT** : bien *m* ⟨for the children's sake : por el bien de los

niños⟩ **2** (indicating an end or a purpose) ⟨art for art's sake : el arte por el arte⟩ ⟨let's say, for argument's sake, that he's wrong : pongamos que está equivocado⟩ **3 for goodness' sake!** : ¡por el amor de Dios!

salable or **saleable** ['seɪləbəl] adj : vendible

salacious [sə'leɪʃəs] adj : salaz — **salaciously** adv

salad ['sæləd] n : ensalada f

salamander ['sælə,mændər] n : salamandra f

salami [sə'lɑmi] n : salami m

salary ['sæləri] n, pl **-ries** : sueldo m

sale ['seɪl] n **1** SELLING : venta f **2** : liquidación f, rebajas fpl ⟨on sale : de rebaja⟩ **3 sales** npl : ventas fpl ⟨to work in sales : trabajar en ventas⟩

salesman ['seɪlzmən] n, pl **-men** [-mən, -,mɛn] **1** : vendedor m, dependiente m (en una tienda) **2 traveling salesman** : viajante m, representante m

salesperson ['seɪlz,pərsən] n : vendedor m, -dora f; dependiente m, -ta f (en una tienda)

saleswoman ['seɪlz,wʊmən] n, pl **-women** [-,wɪmən] **1** : vendedora f, dependienta f (en una tienda) **2 traveling saleswoman** : viajante f, representante f

salient ['seɪljənt] adj : saliente, sobresaliente

saline ['seɪ,li:n, -,laɪn] adj : salino

saliva [sə'laɪvə] n : saliva f

salivary ['sælə,veri] adj : salival ⟨salivary gland : glándula salival⟩

salivate ['sælə,veɪt] vi **-vated; -vating** : salivar

sallow ['sælo:] adj : amarillento, cetrino

sally¹ ['sæli] vi **-lied; -lying** SET OUT : salir, hacer una salida

sally² n, pl **-lies 1** : salida f (militar), misión f **2** QUIP : salida f, ocurrencia f

salmon ['sæmən] ns & pl **1** : salmón m (pez) **2** : color m salmón

salon [sə'lɑn, 'sæ,lɑn, sæ'lɔ̃] n : salón m ⟨beauty salon : salón de belleza⟩

saloon [sə'lu:n] n **1** HALL : salón m (en un barco) **2** BARROOM : bar m

salsa ['sɔlsə, 'sɑl-] n : salsa f mexicana, salsa f picante

salt¹ ['sɔlt] vt : salar, echarle sal a

salt² adj : salado

salt³ n : sal f

saltwater ['sɔlt,wɔtər, -,wɑ-] adj : de agua salada

salty ['sɔlti] adj **saltier; -est** : salado

salubrious [sə'lu:briəs] adj : salubre

salutary ['sæljə,teri] adj : saludable, salubre

salutation [,sælju'teɪʃən] n : saludo m, salutación f

salute¹ [sə'lu:t] v **-luted; -luting 1** : saludar (con gestos o ceremonias) **2** ACCLAIM : reconocer, aclamar — vi : hacer un saludo

salute² n **1** : saludo m (gesto), salva f (de cañonazos) **2** TRIBUTE : reconocimiento m, homenaje m

Salvadoran [,sælvə'dorən] → **El Salvadoran**

salvage¹ ['sælvɪdʒ] vt **-vaged; -vaging** : salvar, rescatar

salvage² n **1** SALVAGING : salvamento m, rescate m **2** : objetos mpl salvados

salvation [sæl'veɪʃən] n : salvación f

salve¹ ['sæv, 'sɑv] vt **salved; salving** : calmar, apaciguar ⟨to salve one's conscience : aliviarse la conciencia⟩

salve² n : ungüento m

salvo ['sæl,vo:] n, pl **-vos** or **-voes** : salva f

same¹ ['seɪm] adj : mismo, igual ⟨the results are the same : los resultados son iguales⟩ ⟨he said the same thing as you : dijo lo mismo que tú⟩

same² pron : mismo ⟨it's all the same to me : me da lo mismo⟩ ⟨the same to you! : ¡igualmente!⟩

sameness ['seɪmnəs] n **1** SIMILARITY : identidad f, semejanza f **2** MONOTONY : monotonía f

sample¹ ['sæmpəl] vt **-pled; -pling** : probar

sample² n : muestra f, prueba f

sampler ['sæmplər] n **1** : dechado m (de bordado) **2** COLLECTION : colección f **3** ASSORTMENT : surtido m

sanatorium [,sænə'toriəm] n, pl **-riums** or **-ria** [-iə] : sanatorio m

sanctify ['sæŋktə,faɪ] vt **-fied; -fying** : santificar

sanctimonious [,sæŋktə'mo:niəs] adj : beato, santurrón

sanction¹ ['sæŋkʃən] vt : sancionar, aprobar

sanction² n **1** AUTHORIZATION : sanción f, autorización f **2 sanctions** npl : sanciones fpl ⟨to impose sanctions on : imponer sanciones a⟩

sanctity ['sæŋktəti] n, pl **-ties** : santidad f

sanctuary ['sæŋktʃu,eri] n, pl **-aries 1** : presbiterio m (en una iglesia) **2** REFUGE : refugio m, asilo m

sand¹ ['sænd] vt : lijar (madera)

sand² n : arena f

sandal ['sændəl] n : sandalia f

sandbank ['sænd,bæŋk] n : banco m de arena

sandpaper n : papel m de lija

sandpiper ['sænd,paɪpər] n : andarríos m

sandstone ['sænd,sto:n] n : arenisca f

sandstorm ['sænd,stɔrm] n : tormenta f de arena

sandwich¹ ['sænd,wɪtʃ] vt : intercalar, encajonar, meter (entre dos cosas)

sandwich² n : sándwich m, emparedado m, bocadillo m Spain

sandy ['sændi] adj **sandier; -est** : arenoso

sane ['seɪn] adj **saner; sanest 1** : cuerdo **2** SENSIBLE : sensato, razonable

sang → **sing**

sanguine ['sæŋgwən] *adj* **1** RUDDY : sanguíneo, rubicundo **2** HOPEFUL : optimista

sanitarium [,sænə'tɛriəm] *n, pl* **-iums** *or* **-ia** [-iə] → **sanatorium**

sanitary ['sænəteri] *adj* **1** : sanitario ⟨sanitary measures : medidas sanitarias⟩ **2** HYGIENIC : higiénico **3** sanitary napkin : compresa *f*, paño *m* higiénico

sanitation [,sænə'teɪʃən] *n* : sanidad *f*

sanitize ['sænə,taɪz] *vt* **-tized; -tizing 1** : desinfectar **2** EXPURGATE : expurgar

sanity ['sænəti] *n* : cordura *f*, razón *f* ⟨to lose one's sanity : perder el juicio⟩

sank → **sink**

Santa Claus ['sæntə,klɔz] *n* : Papá Noel, San Nicolás

sap[1] ['sæp] *vt* **sapped; sapping 1** UNDERMINE : socavar **2** WEAKEN : minar, debilitar

sap[2] *n* **1** : savia *f* (de una planta) **2** SUCKER : inocentón *m*, -tona *f*

sapling ['sæplɪŋ] *n* : árbol *m* joven

sapphire ['sæ,faɪr] *n* : zafiro *m*

sarcasm ['sɑr,kæzəm] *n* : sarcasmo *m*

sarcastic [sɑr'kæstɪk] *adj* : sarcástico — **sarcastically** [-tɪkli] *adv*

sarcophagus [sɑr'kɑfəgəs] *n, pl* **-gi** [-,gaɪ, -,dʒaɪ] : sarcófago *m*

sardine [sɑr'di:n] *n* : sardina *f*

sardonic [sɑr'dɑnɪk] *adj* : sardónico — **sardonically** [-nɪkli] *adv*

sarsaparilla [,sæspə'rɪlə, ,sɑrs-] *n* : zarzaparrilla *f*

sash ['sæʃ] *n* **1** : faja *f* (de un vestido), fajín *m* (de un uniforme) **2** *pl* **sash** : marco *m* (de una ventana)

sassafras ['sæsə,fræs] *n* : sasafrás *m*

sassy ['sæsi] *adj* **sassier; -est** → **saucy**

sat → **sit**

Satan ['seɪtən] *n* : Satanás *m*, Satán *m*

satanic [sə'tænɪk, seɪ-] *adj* : satánico — **satanically** [-nɪkli] *adv*

satchel ['sætʃəl] *n* : cartera *f*, saco *m*

sate ['seɪt] *vt* **sated; sating** : saciar

satellite ['sætə,laɪt] *n* : satélite *m* ⟨spy satellite : satélite espía⟩

satiate ['seɪʃi,eɪt] *vt* **-ated; -ating** : saciar, hartar

satin ['sætən] *n* : raso *m*, satín *m*, satén *m*

satire ['sæ,taɪr] *n* : sátira *f*

satiric [sə'tɪrɪk] *or* **satirical** [-ɪkəl] *adj* : satírico

satirize ['sætə,raɪz] *vt* **-rized; -rizing** : satirizar

satisfaction [,sætəs'fækʃən] *n* : satisfacción *f*

satisfactory [,sætəs'fæktəri] *adj* : satisfactorio, bueno — **satisfactorily** [-rəli] *adv*

satisfy ['sætəs,faɪ] *v* **-fied; -fying** *vt* **1** PLEASE : satisfacer, contentar **2** CONVINCE : convencer **3** FULFILL : satisfacer, cumplir con, llenar **4** SETTLE : pagar, saldar (una cuenta) — *vi* SUFFICE : bastar

saturate ['sætʃə,reɪt] *vt* **-rated; -rating 1** SOAK : empapar **2** FILL : saturar

saturation [,sætʃə'reɪʃən] *n* : saturación *f*

Saturday ['sætər,deɪ, -di] *n* : sábado *m*

Saturn ['sætərn] *n* : Saturno *m*

satyr ['seɪtər, 'sæ-] *n* : sátiro *m*

sauce ['sɔs] *n* : salsa *f*

saucepan ['sɔs,pæn] *n* : cacerola *f*, cazo *m*, cazuela *f*

saucer ['sɔsər] *n* : platillo *m*

sauciness ['sɔsinəs] *n* : descaro *m*, frescura *f*

saucy ['sɔsi] *adj* **saucier; -est** IMPUDENT : descarado, fresco *fam* — **saucily** *adv*

Saudi ['saudi, 'sɔ-] → **Saudi Arabian**

Saudi Arabian *n* : saudita *mf*, saudí *mf* — **Saudi Arabian** *adj*

sauna ['sɔnə, 'saunə] *n* : sauna *mf*

saunter ['sɔntər, 'sɑn-] *vi* : pasear, parsearse

sausage ['sɔsɪdʒ] *n* : salchicha *f*, embutido *m*

sauté [sɔ'teɪ, so:-] *vt* **-téed** *or* **-téd; -téing** : saltear, sofreír

savage[1] ['sævɪdʒ] *adj* : salvaje, feroz — **savagely** *adv*

savage[2] *n* : salvaje *mf*

savagery ['sævɪdʒri, -dʒəri] *n, pl* **-ries 1** FEROCITY : ferocidad *f* **2** WILDNESS : salvajismo *m*

savanna [sə'vænə] *n* : sabana *f*

save[1] ['seɪv] *vt* **saved; saving 1** RESCUE : salvar, rescatar **2** PRESERVE : preservar, conservar **3** KEEP : guardar, ahorrar (dinero), almacenar (alimentos) **4** : guardar (en informática)

save[2] *prep* EXCEPT : salvo, excepto, menos

savior ['seɪvjər] *n* **1** : salvador *m*, -dora *f* **2** the Savior : el Salvador *m*

savor[1] ['seɪvər] *vt* : saborear

savor[2] *n* : sabor *m*

savory ['seɪvəri] *adj* : sabroso

saw[1] → **see**

saw[2] ['sɔ] *vt* **sawed; sawed** *or* **sawn** ['sɔn], **sawing** : serrar, cortar (con sierra)

saw[3] *n* : sierra *f*

sawdust ['sɔ,dʌst] *n* : aserrín *m*, serrín *m*

sawhorse ['sɔ,hɔrs] *n* : caballete *m*, burro *m* (en carpintería)

sawmill ['sɔ,mɪl] *n* : aserradero *m*

saxophone ['sæksə,fo:n] *n* : saxofón *m*

say[1] ['seɪ] *v* **said** ['sɛd]; **saying; says** ['sɛz] *vt* **1** EXPRESS, UTTER : decir, expresar ⟨to say no : decir que no⟩ ⟨that goes without saying : ni que decir tiene⟩ ⟨no sooner said than done : dicho y hecho⟩ ⟨to say again : repetir⟩ ⟨to say one's prayers : rezar⟩ **2** INDICATE : marcar, poner ⟨my watch says three o'clock : mi reloj marca las tres⟩ ⟨what does the sign say? : ¿qué pone el letrero?⟩ **3** ALLEGE : decir ⟨it's said that she's pretty : se dice que es bonita⟩ — *vi* : decir

say[2] *n*, *pl* **says** ['seɪz] : voz *f*, opinión *f* ⟨to have no say : no tener ni voz ni voto⟩ ⟨to have one's say : dar uno su opinión⟩

saying ['seɪɪŋ] *n* : dicho *m*, refrán *m*

scab ['skæb] *n* **1** : costra *f*, postilla *f* (en una herida) **2** STRIKEBREAKER : rompehuelgas *mf*, esquirol *m*

scabbard ['skæbərd] *n* : vaina *f* (de una espada), funda *f* (de un puñal, etc.)

scabby ['skæbi] *adj* **scabbier; -est** : lleno de costras

scaffold ['skæfəld, -ˌfo:ld] *n* **1** *or* **scaffolding** : andamio *m* (para obreros, etc.) **2** : patíbulo *m*, cadalso *m* (para ejecuciones)

scald ['skɔld] *vt* **1** BURN : escaldar **2** HEAT : calentar (hasta el punto de ebullición)

scale[1] ['skeɪl] *v* **scaled; scaling** *vt* **1** : escamar (un pescado) **2** CLIMB : escalar (un muro, etc.) **3 to scale down** : reducir — *vi* WEIGH : pesar ⟨he scaled in at 200 pounds : pesó 200 libras⟩

scale[2] *n* **1** *or* **scales** : balanza *f*, báscula *f* (para pesar) **2** : escama *f* (de un pez, etc.) **3** EXTENT : escala *f*, proporción *f* ⟨wage scale : escala salarial⟩ **4** : escala *f* (en música, en cartografía, etc.) ⟨to draw to scale : dibujar a escala⟩

scallion ['skæljən] *n* : cebollino *m*, cebolleta *f*

scallop ['skɑləp, 'skæ-] *n* **1** : vieira *f* (molusco) **2** : festón *m* (decoración)

scalp[1] ['skælp] *vt* : arrancar la cabellera a

scalp[2] *n* : cuero *m* cabelludo

scalpel ['skælpəl] *n* : bisturí *m*, escalpelo *m*

scaly ['skeɪli] *adj* **scalier; -est** : escamoso

scam ['skæm] *n* : estafa *f*, timo *m* *fam*, chanchullo *m* *fam*

scamp ['skæmp] *n* : bribón *m*, -bona *f*; granuja *mf*; travieso *m*, -sa *f*

scamper ['skæmpər] *vi* : corretear

scan[1] ['skæn] *vt* **scanned; scanning** **1** : escandir (versos) **2** SCRUTINIZE : escudriñar, escrutar ⟨to scan the horizon : escudriñar el horizonte⟩ **3** PERUSE : echarle un vistazo a (un periódico, etc.) **4** EXPLORE : explorar (con radar), hacer un escáner de (en ecografía) **5** : escanear (una imagen)

scan[2] *n* **1** : ecografía *f*, examen *m* ultrasónico (en medicina) **2** : imagen *f* escaneada (en una computadora)

scandal ['skændəl] *n* **1** DISGRACE, OUTRAGE : escándalo *m* **2** GOSSIP : habladurías *fpl*, chismes *mpl*

scandalize ['skændəˌaɪz] *vt* **-ized; -izing** : escandalizar

scandalous ['skændələs] *adj* : de escándalo

Scandinavian[1] [ˌskændəˈneɪviən] *adj* : escandinavo

Scandinavian[2] *n* : escandinavo *m*, -va *f*

scanner ['skænər] *n* : escáner *m*, scanner *m*

scant ['skænt] *adj* : escaso

scanty ['skænti] *adj* **scantier; -est** : exiguo, escaso ⟨a scanty meal : una comida insuficiente⟩ — **scantily** [-təli] *adv*

scapegoat ['skeɪpˌgo:t] *n* : chivo *m* expiatorio, cabeza *f* de turco

scapula ['skæpjələ] *n*, *pl* **-lae** [-ˌli:, -ˌlaɪ] *or* **-las** → **shoulder blade**

scar[1] ['skɑr] *v* **scarred; scarring** *vt* : dejar una cicatriz en — *vi* : cicatrizar

scar[2] *n* : cicatriz *f*, marca *f*

scarab ['skærəb] *n* : escarabajo *m*

scarce ['skers] *adj* **scarcer; -est** : escaso

scarcely ['skersli] *adv* **1** BARELY : apenas **2** : ni mucho menos, ni nada que se le parezca ⟨he's scarcely an expert : ciertamente no es experto⟩

scarcity ['skersəti] *n*, *pl* **-ties** : escasez *f*

scare[1] ['sker] *vt* **scared; scaring** : asustar, espantar

scare[2] *n* **1** FRIGHT : susto *m*, sobresalto *m* **2** ALARM : pánico *m*

scarecrow ['skerˌkro:] *n* : espantapájaros *m*, espantajo *m*

scarf ['skɑrf] *n*, *pl* **scarves** ['skɑrvz] *or* **scarfs** **1** MUFFLER : bufanda *f* **2** KERCHIEF : pañuelo *m*

scarlet ['skɑrlət] *n* : escarlata *f* — **scarlet** *adj*

scarlet fever *n* : escarlatina *f*

scary ['skeri] *adj* **scarier; -est** : espantoso, pavoroso

scathing ['skeɪðɪŋ] *adj* : mordaz, cáustico

scatter ['skætər] *vt* : esparcir, desparramar — *vi* DISPERSE : dispersarse

scavenge ['skævəndʒ] *v* **-venged; -venging** *vt* : rescatar (de la basura), pepenar *CA*, *Mex* — *vi* : rebuscar, hurgar en la basura ⟨to scavenge for food : andar buscando comida⟩

scavenger ['skævəndʒər] *n* **1** : persona *f* que rebusca en las basuras; pepenador *m*, -dora *f* *CA*, *Mex* **2** : carroñero *m*, -ra *f* (animal)

scenario [səˈnæriˌoː, -ˈnɑr-] *n*, *pl* **-ios** **1** PLOT : argumento *m* (en teatro), guión *m* (en cine) **2** SITUATION : situación *f* hipotética ⟨in the worst-case scenario : en el peor de los casos⟩

scene ['si:n] *n* **1** : escena *f* (en una obra de teatro) **2** SCENERY : decorado *m* (en el teatro) **3** VIEW : escena *f* **4** LOCALE : escenario *m* **5** COMMOTION, FUSS : escándalo *m*, escena *f* ⟨to make a scene : armar un escándalo⟩

scenery ['si:nəri] *n*, *pl* **-eries** **1** : decorado *m* (en el teatro) **2** LANDSCAPE : paisaje *m*

scenic ['si:nɪk] *adj* : pintoresco

scent[1] ['sent] *vt* **1** SMELL : oler, olfatear **2** PERFUME : perfumar **3** SENSE : sentir, percibir

scent[2] *n* **1** ODOR : olor *m*, aroma *m* **2** : olfato *m* ⟨a dog with a keen scent : un perro con un buen olfato⟩ **3** PERFUME : perfume *m*

scented [ˈsɛntəd] *adj* : perfumado

scepter [ˈsɛptər] *n* : cetro *m*

sceptic [ˈskɛptɪk] → **skeptic**

schedule[1] [ˈskɛˌdʒuːl, -dʒəl, *esp Brit* ˈʃɛdˌjuːl] *vt* -**uled**; -**uling** : planear, programar

schedule[2] *n* **1** PLAN : programa *m*, plan *m* ⟨on schedule : según lo previsto⟩ ⟨behind schedule : atrasado, con retraso⟩ **2** TIMETABLE : horario *m*

scheme[1] [ˈskiːm] *vi* **schemed**; **scheming** : intrigar, conspirar

scheme[2] *n* **1** PLAN : plan *m*, proyecto *m* **2** PLOT, TRICK : intriga *f*, ardid *m* **3** FRAMEWORK : esquema *f* ⟨a color scheme : una combinación de colores⟩

schemer [ˈskiːmər] *n* : intrigante *mf*

schism [ˈsɪzəm, ˈskɪ-] *n* : cisma *m*

schizophrenia [ˌskɪtsəˈfriːniə, ˌskɪzə-, -ˈfrɛ-] *n* : esquizofrenia *f*

schizophrenic [ˌskɪtsəˈfrɛnɪk, ˌskɪzə-] *n* : esquizofrénico *m*, -ca *f* — **schizophrenic** *adj*

scholar [ˈskɑlər] *n* **1** STUDENT : escolar *mf*; alumno *m*, -na *f* **2** EXPERT : especialista *mf*

scholarly [ˈskɑlərli] *adj* : erudito

scholarship [ˈskɑlərˌʃɪp] *n* **1** LEARNING : erudición *f* **2** GRANT : beca *f*

scholastic [skəˈlæstɪk] *adj* : académico

school[1] [ˈskuːl] *vt* : instruir, enseñar

school[2] *n* **1** : escuela *f*, colegio *m* (institución) **2** : estudiantes *mfpl* y profesores *mpl* (de una escuela) **3** : escuela *f* (en pintura, etc.) ⟨the Flemish school : la escuela flamenca⟩ **4** school of fish : banco *m*, cardumen *m*

schoolboy [ˈskuːlˌbɔɪ] *n* : escolar *m*, colegial *m*

schoolgirl [ˈskuːlˌgərl] *n* : escolar *f*, colegiala *f*

schoolhouse [ˈskuːlˌhaʊs] *n* : escuela *f*

schoolmate [ˈskuːlˌmeɪt] *n* : compañero *m*, -ra *f* de escuela

schoolroom [ˈskuːlˌruːm, -ˌrʊm] → **classroom**

schoolteacher [ˈskuːlˌtiːtʃər] *n* : maestro *m*, -tra *f*; profesor *m*, -sora *f*

schoolwork [ˈskuːlˌwərk] *n* : trabajo *m* escolar

schooner [ˈskuːnər] *n* : goleta *f*

science [ˈsaɪənts] *n* : ciencia *f*

science fiction *n* : ciencia ficción *f*

scientific [ˌsaɪənˈtɪfɪk] *adj* : científico — **scientifically** [-fɪkli] *adv*

scientist [ˈsaɪəntɪst] *n* : científico *m*, -ca *f*

scintillating [ˈsɪntəˌleɪtɪŋ] *adj* : chispeante, brillante

scissors [ˈsɪzərz] *npl* : tijeras *fpl*

sclerosis [skləˈroːsəs] *n, pl* -**roses** : esclerosis *f*

scoff [ˈskɑf] *vi* to scoff at : burlarse de, mofarse de

scold [ˈskoːld] *vt* : regañar, reprender, reñir

scoop[1] [ˈskuːp] *vt* **1** : sacar (con pala o cucharón) **2** to scoop out HOLLOW : vaciar, ahuecar

scoop[2] *n* : pala *f* (para harina, etc.), cucharón *m* (para helado, etc.)

scoot [ˈskuːt] *vi* : ir rápidamente ⟨she scooted around the corner : volvió la esquina a toda prisa⟩

scooter [ˈskuːtər] *n* : patineta *f*, monopatín *m*, patinete *m*

scope [ˈskoːp] *n* **1** RANGE : alcance *m*, ámbito *m*, extensión *f* **2** OPPORTUNITY : posibilidades *fpl*, libertad *f*

scorch [ˈskɔrtʃ] *vt* : chamuscar, quemar

score[1] [ˈskor] *v* **scored**; **scoring** *vt* **1** RECORD : anotar **2** MARK, SCRATCH : marcar, rayar **3** : marcar, meter (en deportes) **4** GAIN : ganar, apuntarse **5** GRADE : calificar (exámenes, etc.) **6** : instrumentar, orquestar (música) — *vi* **1** : marcar (en deportes) **2** : obtener una puntuación (en un examen)

score[2] *n, pl* **scores** **1** *or pl* **score** TWENTY : veintena *f* **2** LINE, SCRATCH : línea *f*, marca *f* **3** : resultado *m* (en deportes) ⟨what's the score? : ¿cómo va el marcador?⟩ **4** GRADE, POINTS : calificación *f* (en un examen), puntuación *f* (en un concurso) **5** ACCOUNT : cuenta *f* ⟨to settle a score : ajustar una cuenta⟩ ⟨on that score : a ese respecto⟩ **6** : partitura *f* (musical)

scorn[1] [ˈskɔrn] *vt* : despreciar, menospreciar, desdeñar

scorn[2] *n* : desprecio *m*, menosprecio *m*, desdén *m*

scornful [ˈskɔrnfəl] *adj* : desdeñoso, despreciativo — **scornfully** *adv*

Scorpio [ˈskɔrpiˌoː] *n* : Escorpio *mf*, Escorpión *mf*

scorpion [ˈskɔrpiən] *n* : alacrán *m*, escorpión *m*

Scot [ˈskɑt] *n* : escocés *m*, -cesa *f*

Scotch[1] [ˈskɑtʃ] *adj* → **Scottish**[1]

Scotch[2] *npl* the Scotch : los escoceses

scot-free [ˈskɑtˈfriː] *adj* to get off scot-free : salir impune, quedar sin castigo

Scots [ˈskɑts] *n* : escocés *m* (idioma)

Scottish[1] [ˈskɑtɪʃ] *adj* : escocés

Scottish[2] *n* → **Scots**

scoundrel [ˈskaʊndrəl] *n* : sinvergüenza *mf*; bellaco *m*, -ca *f*

scour [ˈskaʊər] *vt* **1** EXAMINE, SEARCH : registrar (un área), revisar (documentos, etc.) **2** SCRUB : fregar, restregar

scourge[1] [ˈskərdʒ] *vt* **scourged**; **scourging** : azotar

scourge[2] *n* : azote *m*

scout[1] [ˈskaʊt] *vi* **1** RECONNOITER : reconocer **2** to scout around for : explorar en busca de

scout[2] *n* **1** : explorador *m*, -dora *f* **2** *or* talent scout : cazatalentos *mf*

scow [ˈskaʊ] *n* : barcaza *f*, gabarra *f*

scowl[1] [ˈskaʊl] *vi* : fruncir el ceño

scowl[2] *n* : ceño *m* fruncido

scram ['skræm] *vi* **scrammed; scramming** : largarse

scramble¹ ['skræmbəl] *v* **-bled; -bling** *vi* **1** : trepar, gatear (con torpeza) ⟨he scrambled over the fence : se trepó a la cerca con dificultad⟩ **2** STRUGGLE : pelearse (por) ⟨they scrambled for seats : se pelearon por los asientos⟩ — *vt* **1** JUMBLE : mezclar **2 to scramble eggs** : hacer huevos revueltos

scramble² *n* : rebatiña *f*, pelea *f*

scrap¹ ['skræp] *v* **scrapped; scrapping** *vt* DISCARD : desechar — *vi* FIGHT : pelearse

scrap² *n* **1** FRAGMENT : pedazo *m*, trozo *m* **2** FIGHT : pelea *f* **3** *or* **scrap metal** : chatarra *f* **4** **scraps** *npl* LEFTOVERS : restos *mpl*, sobras *fpl*

scrapbook ['skræp,bʊk] *n* : álbum *m* de recortes

scrape¹ ['skreɪp] *v* **scraped; scraping** *vt* **1** GRAZE, SCRATCH : rozar, rascar ⟨to scrape one's knee : rasparse la rodilla⟩ **2** CLEAN : raspar ⟨to scrape carrots : raspar zanahorias⟩ **3 to scrape off** : raspar (pintura, etc.) **4 to scrape up** *or* **to scrape together** : juntar, reunir poco a poco — *vi* **1** RUB : rozar **2 to scrape by** : arreglárselas, ir tirando

scrape² *n* **1** SCRAPING : raspadura *f* **2** SCRATCH : rasguño *m* **3** PREDICAMENT : apuro *m*, aprieto *m*

scratch¹ ['skrætʃ] *vt* **1** : arañar, rasguñar ⟨to scratch an itch : rascarse⟩ **2** MARK : rayar, marcar **3 to scratch out** : tachar

scratch² *n* **1** : rasguño *m*, arañazo *m* (en la piel), rayón *m* (en un mueble, etc.) **2** : sonido *m* rasposo ⟨I heard a scratch at the door : oí como que raspaban a la puerta⟩

scratchy ['skrætʃi] *adj* **scratchier; -est** : áspero, que pica ⟨a scratchy sweater : un suéter que pica⟩

scrawl¹ ['skrɔl] *v* : garabatear

scrawl² *n* : garabato *m*

scrawny ['skrɔni] *adj* **scrawnier; -est** : flaco, escuálido

scream¹ ['skri:m] *vi* : chillar, gritar

scream² *n* : chillido *m*, grito *m*

screech¹ ['skri:tʃ] *vi* : chillar (dícese de las personas o de los animales), chirriar (dícese de los frenos, etc.)

screech² *n* **1** : chillido *m*, grito *m* (de una persona o un animal) **2** : chirrido *m* (de frenos, etc.)

screen¹ ['skri:n] *vt* **1** SHIELD : proteger **2** CONCEAL : tapar, ocultar **3** EXAMINE : someter a una revisión, hacerle un chequeo (a un paciente) **4** SIEVE : cribar

screen² *n* **1** PARTITION : biombo *m*, pantalla *f* **2** SIEVE : criba *f* **3** : pantalla *f* (de un televisor, una computadora, etc.) **4** MOVIES : cine *m* **5** *or* **window screen** : ventana *f* de tela metálica

screenplay ['skri:n,pleɪ] *n* SCRIPT : guión *m*

screw¹ ['skru:] *vt* : atornillar — *vi* **1 to screw in** : atornillarse **2 to screw up** *fam* : meter la pata

screw² *n* **1** : tornillo *m* (para fijar algo) **2** TWIST : vuelta *f* **3** PROPELLER : hélice *f*

screwdriver ['skru:,draɪvər] *n* : destornillador *m*, desarmador *m Mex*

scribble¹ ['skrɪbəl] *v* **-bled; -bling** : garabatear

scribble² *n* : garabato *m*

scribe ['skraɪb] *n* : escriba *m*

scrimmage ['skrɪmɪdʒ] *n* : escaramuza *f*

scrimp ['skrɪmp] *vi* **1 to scrimp on** : escatimar **2 to scrimp and save** : hacer economías

script ['skrɪpt] *n* **1** HANDWRITING : letra *f*, escritura *f* **2** : guión *m* (de una película, etc.)

scriptural ['skrɪptʃərəl] *adj* : bíblico

scripture ['skrɪptʃər] *n* **1** : escritos *mpl* sagrados (de una religión) **2 the Scriptures** *npl* : las Sagradas Escrituras

scriptwriter ['skrɪpt,raɪtər] *n* : guionista *mf*, libretista *mf Mex*

scroll ['skro:l] *n* **1** : rollo *m* (de pergamino, etc.) **2** : voluta *f* (adorno en arquitectura)

scrotum ['skro:təm] *n, pl* **scrota** [-tə] *or* **scrotums** : escroto *m*

scrounge ['skraʊndʒ] *v* **scrounged; scrounging** *vt* **1** BUM : gorrear *fam*, sablear *fam* (dinero) **2 to scrounge around for** : buscar, andar a la busca de — *vi* **to scrounge off someone** : vivir a costa de alguien

scrub¹ ['skrʌb] *vt* **scrubbed; scrubbing** : restregar, fregar

scrub² *n* **1** THICKET, UNDERBRUSH : maleza *f*, matorral *m*, matorrales *mpl* **2** SCRUBBING : fregado *m*, restregadura *f*

scrubby ['skrʌbi] *adj* **-bier; -est 1** STUNTED : achaparrado **2** : cubierto de maleza

scruff ['skrʌf] *n* **by the scruff of the neck** : por el cogote, por el pescuezo

scrumptious ['skrʌmpʃəs] *adj* : delicioso, muy rico

scruple ['skru:pəl] *n* : escrúpulo *m*

scrupulous ['skru:pjələs] *adj* : escrupuloso — **scrupulously** *adv*

scrutinize ['skru:tən,aɪz] *vt* **-nized; -nizing** : escrutar, escudriñar

scrutiny ['skru:təni] *n, pl* **-nies** : escrutinio *m*, inspección *f*

scuba ['sku:bə] *n* **1** *or* **scuba gear** : equipo *m* de submarinismo **2 scuba diver** : submarinista *mf* **3 scuba diving** : submarinismo *m*

scuff ['skʌf] *vt* : rayar, raspar ⟨to scuff one's feet : arrastrar los pies⟩

scuffle¹ ['skʌfəl] *vi* **-fled; -fling 1** TUSSLE : pelearse **2** SHUFFLE : caminar arrastrando los pies

scuffle² *n* **1** TUSSLE : refriega *f*, pelea *f* **2** SHUFFLE : arrastre *m* de los pies

scull¹ ['skʌl] *vi* : remar (con espadilla)

scull² *n* OAR : espaldilla *f*
sculpt ['skʌlpt] *v* : esculpir
sculptor ['skʌlptər] *n* : escultor *m*, -tora *f*
sculptural ['skʌlptʃərəl] *adj* : escultórico
sculpture¹ ['skʌlptʃər] *vt* -tured; -turing : esculpir
sculpture² *n* : escultura *f*
scum ['skʌm] *n* 1 FROTH : espuma *f*, nata *f* 2 : verdín *m* (encima de un líquido)
scurrilous ['skərələs] *adj* : difamatorio, calumnioso, injurioso
scurry ['skəri] *vi* -ried; -rying : corretear
scurvy ['skərvi] *n* : escorbuto *m*
scuttle¹ ['skʌtəl] *v* -tled; -tling *vt* : hundir (un barco) — *vi* SCAMPER : corretear
scuttle² *n* : cubo *m* (para carbón)
scythe ['saið] *n* : guadaña *f*
sea¹ ['si:] *adj* : del mar
sea² *n* 1 : mar *mf* ⟨the Black Sea : el Mar Negro⟩ ⟨on the high seas : en alta mar⟩ ⟨heavy seas : mar gruesa, mar agitada⟩ 2 MASS : mar *m*, multitud *f* ⟨a sea of faces : un mar de rostros⟩
seabird ['si:,bərd] *n* : ave *f* marina
seaboard ['si:,bord] *n* : litoral *m*
seacoast ['si:,ko:st] *n* : costa *f*, litoral *m*
seafarer ['si:,færər] *n* : marinero *m*
seafaring¹ ['si:,færiŋ] *adj* : marinero
seafaring² *n* : navegación *f*
seafood ['si:,fu:d] *n* : mariscos *mpl*
seagull ['si:,gʌl] *n* : gaviota *f*
sea horse ['si:,hɔrs] *n* : hipocampo *m*, caballo *m* de mar
seal¹ ['si:l] *vt* 1 CLOSE : sellar, cerrar ⟨to seal a letter : cerrar una carta⟩ ⟨to seal an agreement : sellar un acuerdo⟩ 2 to seal up : tapar, rellenar (una grieta, etc.)
seal² *n* 1 : foca *f* (animal) 2 : sello *m* ⟨seal of approval : sello de aprobación⟩ 3 CLOSURE : cierre *m*, precinto *m*
sea level *n* : nivel *m* del mar
sea lion *n* : león *m* marino
sealskin ['si:l,skɪn] *n* : piel *f* de foca
seam¹ ['si:m] *vt* 1 STITCH : unir con costuras 2 MARK : marcar
seam² *n* 1 STITCHING : costura *f* 2 LODE, VEIN : veta *f*, filón *m*
seaman ['si:mən] *n*, *pl* -men [-mən, -ˌmɛn] 1 SAILOR : marinero *m* 2 : marino *m* (en la armada)
seamless ['si:mləs] *adj* 1 : sin costuras, de una pieza 2 : perfecto ⟨a seamless transition : una transición fluida⟩
seamstress ['si:mpstrəs] *n* : costurera *f*
seamy ['si:mi] *adj* seamier; -est : sórdido
séance ['seɪˌɑnts] *n* : sesión *f* de espiritismo
seaplane ['si:,pleɪn] *n* : hidroavión *m*
seaport ['si:,port] *n* : puerto *m* marítimo
sear ['sɪr] *vt* 1 PARCH, WITHER : secar, resecar 2 SCORCH : chamuscar, quemar

search¹ ['sərtʃ] *vt* : registrar (un edificio, un área), cachear (a una persona), buscar en — *vi* to search for : buscar
search² *n* : búsqueda *f*, registro *m* (de un edificio, etc.), cacheo *m* (de una persona)
searchlight ['sərtʃ,laɪt] *n* : reflector *m*
seashell ['si:,ʃɛl] *n* : concha *f* (marina)
seashore ['si:,ʃor] *n* : orilla *f* del mar
seasick ['si:,sɪk] *adj* : mareado ⟨to get seasick : marearse⟩
seasickness ['si:,sɪknəs] *n* : mareo *m*
seaside → **seacoast**
season¹ ['si:zən] *vt* 1 FLAVOR, SPICE : sazonar, condimentar 2 CURE : curar, secar ⟨seasoned wood : madera seca⟩ ⟨a seasoned veteran : un veterano avezado⟩
season² *n* 1 : estación *f* (del año) 2 : temporada *f* (en deportes, etc.) ⟨baseball season : temporada de beisbol⟩
seasonable ['si:zənəbəl] *adj* 1 : propio de la estación (dícese del tiempo, de las temperaturas, etc.) 2 TIMELY : oportuno
seasonal ['si:zənəl] *adj* : estacional — **seasonally** *adv*
seasoning ['si:zənɪŋ] *n* : condimento *m*, sazón *f*
seat¹ ['si:t] *vt* 1 SIT : sentar ⟨please be seated : siéntense, por favor⟩ 2 HOLD : tener cabida para ⟨the stadium seats 40,000 : el estadio tiene 40,000 asientos⟩
seat² *n* 1 : asiento *m*, plaza *f* (en un vehículo) ⟨take a seat : tome asiento⟩ 2 BOTTOM : fondillos *mpl* (de la ropa), trasero *m* (del cuerpo) 3 : sede *f* (de un gobierno, etc.)
seat belt *n* : cinturón *m* de seguridad
sea urchin *n* : erizo *m* de mar
seawall ['si:,wɑl] *n* : rompeolas *m*, dique *m* marítimo
seawater ['si:,wɔtər, -ˌwɑ-] *n* : agua *f* de mar
seaweed ['si:,wi:d] *n* : alga *f* marina
seaworthy ['si:,wərði] *adj* : en condiciones de navegar
secede [sɪ'si:d] *vi* -ceded; -ceding : separarse (de una nación, etc.)
seclude [sɪ'klu:d] *vt* -cluded; -cluding : aislar
seclusion [sɪ'klu:ʒən] *n* : aislamiento *m*
second¹ ['sɛkənd] *vt* : secundar, apoyar (una moción)
second² *or* **secondly** ['sɛkəndli] *adv* : en segundo lugar
second³ *adj* : segundo
second⁴ *n* 1 : segundo *m*, -da *f* (en una serie) 2 : segundo *m*, ayudante *m* (en deportes) 3 MOMENT : segundo *m*, momento *m*
secondary ['sɛkən,dri] *adj* : secundario
secondhand ['sɛkənd'hænd] *adj* : de segunda mano
second lieutenant *n* : alférez *mf*, subteniente *mf*
second–rate ['sɛkənd'reɪt] *adj* : mediocre, de segunda categoría

secrecy ['si:krəsi] *n, pl* **-cies** : secreto *m*

secret[1] ['si:krət] *adj* : secreto — **secretly** *adv*

secret[2] *n* : secreto *m*

secretarial [ˌsɛkrə'triəl] *adj* : de secretario, de oficina

secretariat [ˌsɛkrə'triət] *n* : secretaría *f*, secretariado *m*

secretary ['sɛkrəˌtri] *n, pl* **-taries** 1 : secretario *m*, -ria *f* (en una oficina, etc.) 2 : ministro *m*, -tra *f*; secretario *m*, -ria *f* ⟨Secretary of State : Secretario de Estado⟩

secrete [sɪ'kri:t] *vt* **-creted; -creting** 1 : secretar, segregar (en fisiología) 2 HIDE : ocultar

secretion [sɪ'kri:ʃən] *n* : secreción *f*

secretive ['si:krətɪv, sɪ'kri:tɪv] *adj* : reservado, callado, secreto

sect [sɛkt] *n* : secta *f*

sectarian [sɛk'triən] *adj* : sectario

section ['sɛkʃən] *n* : sección *f*, parte *f* (de un mueble, etc.), sector *m* (de la población), barrio *m* (de una ciudad)

sectional ['sɛkʃənəl] *adj* 1 : en sección, en corte ⟨a sectional diagram : un gráfico en corte⟩ 2 FACTIONAL : de grupo, entre facciones 3 : modular ⟨sectional furniture : muebles modulares⟩

sector ['sɛktər] *n* : sector *m*

secular ['sɛkjələr] *adj* 1 : secular, laico ⟨secular life : la vida secular⟩ 2 : seglar (dícese de los sacerdotes, etc.)

secure[1] [sɪ'kjʊr] *vt* **-cured; -curing** 1 FASTEN : asegurar (una puerta, etc.), sujetar 2 GET : conseguir

secure[2] *adj* **-curer; -est** : seguro — **securely** *adv*

security [sɪ'kjʊrəti] *n, pl* **-ties** 1 SAFETY : seguridad *f* 2 GUARANTEE : garantía *f* 3 **securities** *npl* : valores *mpl*

sedan [sɪ'dæn] *n* 1 *or* **sedan chair** : silla *f* de manos 2 : sedán *m* (automóvil)

sedate[1] [sɪ'deɪt] *vt* **-dated; -dating** : sedar

sedate[2] *adj* : sosegado — **sedately** *adv*

sedation [sɪ'deɪʃən] *n* : sedación *f*

sedative[1] ['sɛdətɪv] *adj* : sedante

sedative[2] *n* : sedante *m*, calmante *m*

sedentary ['sɛdənˌteri] *adj* : sedentario

sedge [sɛdʒ] *n* : juncia *f*

sediment ['sɛdəmənt] *n* : sedimento *m* (geológico), poso *m* (en un líquido)

sedimentary [ˌsɛdə'mɛntəri] *adj* : sedimentario

sedition [sɪ'dɪʃən] *n* : sedición *f*

seditious [sɪ'dɪʃəs] *adj* : sedicioso

seduce [sɪ'du:s, -'dju:s] *vt* **-duced; -ducing** : seducir

seduction [sɪ'dʌkʃən] *n* : seducción *f*

seductive [sɪ'dʌktɪv] *adj* : seductor, seductivo

see[1] ['si:] *v* **saw** ['sɔ]; **seen** ['si:n]; **seeing** *vt* 1 : ver ⟨I saw a dog : vi un perro⟩ ⟨see you later! : ¡hasta luego!⟩ 2 EXPERIENCE : ver, conocer 3 UNDERSTAND : ver, entender 4 ENSURE : asegurarse ⟨see that it's correct : asegúrese de que sea correcto⟩ 5 ACCOMPANY : acompañar 6 **to see off** : despedir, despedirse de — *vi* 1 : ver ⟨seeing is believing : ver para creer⟩ 2 UNDERSTAND : entender, ver ⟨now I see! : ¡ya entiendo!⟩ 3 CONSIDER : ver ⟨let's see : vamos a ver⟩ 4 **to see to** : ocuparse de

see[2] *n* : sede *f* ⟨the Holy See : la Santa Sede⟩

seed[1] ['si:d] *vt* 1 SOW : sembrar 2 : despepitar, quitarle las semillas a

seed[2] *n, pl* **seed** *or* **seeds** 1 : semilla *f*, pepita *f* (de una fruta) 2 SOURCE : germen *m*, semilla *f*

seedless ['si:dləs] *adj* : sin semillas

seedling ['si:dlɪŋ] *n* : plantón *m*

seedpod ['si:dˌpɑd] → **pod**

seedy ['si:di] *adj* **seedier; -est** 1 : lleno de semillas 2 SHABBY : raído (dícese de la ropa) 3 RUN-DOWN : ruinoso (dícese de los edificios, etc.), sórdido

seek ['si:k] *v* **sought** ['sɔt]; **seeking** *vt* 1 : buscar ⟨to seek an answer : buscar una solución⟩ 2 REQUEST : solicitar, pedir 3 **to seek to** : tratar de, intentar de — *vi* SEARCH : buscar

seem ['si:m] *vi* : parecer

seeming ['si:mɪŋ] *adj* : aparente, ostensible

seemingly ['si:mɪŋli] *adv* : aparentemente, según parece

seemly ['si:mli] *adj* **seemlier; -est** : apropiado, decoroso

seep ['si:p] *vi* : filtrarse

seer ['si:ər] *n* : vidente *mf*, clarividente *mf*

seesaw[1] ['si:ˌsɔ] *vi* 1 : jugar en un subibaja 2 VACILLATE : vacilar, oscilar

seesaw[2] *n* : balancín *m*, subibaja *m*

seethe ['si:ð] *vi* **seethed; seething** 1 : bullir, hervir 2 **to seethe with anger** : rabiar, estar furioso

segment ['sɛgmənt] *n* : segmento *m*

segmented ['sɛgˌmɛntəd, sɛg'mɛn-] *adj* : segmentado

segregate ['sɛgrɪˌgeɪt] *vt* **-gated; -gating** : segregar

segregation [ˌsɛgrɪ'geɪʃən] *n* : segregación *f*

seismic ['saɪzmɪk, 'saɪs-] *adj* : sísmico

seize ['si:z] *v* **seized; seizing** *vt* 1 CAPTURE : capturar, tomar, apoderarse de 2 ARREST : detener 3 CLUTCH, GRAB : agarrar, coger, aprovechar (una oportunidad) 4 **to be seized with** : estar sobrecogido por — *vi or* **to seize up** : agarrotarse

seizure ['si:ʒər] *n* 1 CAPTURE : toma *f*, captura *f* 2 ARREST : detención *f* 3 : ataque *m* ⟨an epileptic seizure : un ataque epiléptico⟩

seldom ['sɛldəm] *adv* : pocas veces, rara vez, casi nunca

select[1] [sə'lɛkt] *vt* : escoger, elegir, seleccionar (a un candidato, etc.)

select[2] *adj* : selecto

selection [sə'lɛkʃən] *n* : selección *f*, elección *f*

selective [sə'lɛktɪv] *adj* : selectivo
selenium [sə'li:niəm] *n* : selenio *m*
self ['sɛlf] *n, pl* **selves** ['sɛlvz] **1** : ser *m*, persona *f* ⟨the self : el yo⟩ ⟨with his whole self : con todo su ser⟩ ⟨her own self : su propia persona⟩ **2** SIDE : lado (de la personalidad) ⟨his better self : su lado bueno⟩
self–addressed [,sɛlfə'drst] *adj* : con la dirección del remitente ⟨include a self-addressed envelope : incluya un sobre con su nombre y dirección⟩
self–appointed [,sɛlfə'pɔɪntəd] *adj* : autoproclamado, autonombrado
self–assurance [,sɛlfə'ʃʊrənts] *n* : seguridad *f* en sí mismo
self–assured [,sɛlfə'ʃʊrd] *adj* : seguro de sí mismo
self–centered [,sɛlf'sɛntərd] *adj* : egocéntrico
self–confidence [,sɛlf'kanfədənts] *n* : confianza *f* en sí mismo
self–confident [,sɛlf'kanfədənt] *adj* : seguro de sí mismo
self–conscious [,sɛlf'kantʃəs] *adj* : cohibido, tímido
self–consciously [,sɛlf'kantʃəsli] *adv* : de manera cohibida
self–consciousness [,sɛlf'kantʃəsnəs] *n* : vergüenza *f*, timidez *f*
self–contained [,sɛlfkən'teɪnd] *adj* **1** INDEPENDENT : independiente **2** RESERVED : reservado
self–control [,sɛlfkən'troːl] *n* : autocontrol *m*, control *m* de sí mismo
self–defense [,sɛlfdɪ'fɛnts] *n* : defensa *f* propia, defensa *f* personal ⟨to act in self-defense : actuar en defensa propia⟩ ⟨self-defense class : clase de defensa personal⟩
self–denial [,sɛlfdɪ'naɪəl] *n* : abnegación *f*
self–destructive [,sɛlfdɪ'strʌktɪv] *adj* : autodestructivo
self–determination [,sɛlfdɪ,tərmə'neɪʃən] *n* : autodeterminación *f*
self–discipline [,sɛlf'dɪsəplən] *n* : autodisciplina *f*
self–employed [,sɛlfɪm'plɔɪd] *adj* : que trabaja por cuenta propia, autónomo
self–esteem [,sɛlfɪ'stiːm] *n* : autoestima *f*, amor *m* propio
self–evident [,sɛlf'ɛvədənt] *adj* : evidente, manifiesto
self–explanatory [,sɛlfɪk'splænə,tori] *adj* : fácil de entender, evidente
self–expression [,sɛlfɪk'sprʃən] *n* : expresión *f* personal
self–government [,sɛlf'gʌvərmənt, -vərn-] *n* : autogobierno *m*
self–help [,sɛlf'hɛlp] *n* : autoayuda *f*
self–important [,sɛlfɪm'pɔrtənt] *adj* **1** VAIN : vanidoso, presumido **2** ARROGANT : arrogante
self–indulgent [,sɛlfɪn'dʌldʒənt] *adj* : que se permite excesos
self–inflicted [,sɛlfɪn'flɪktəd] *adj* : autoinfligido

self–interest [,sɛlf'ɪntrəst, -tə,rst] *n* : interés *m* personal
selfish ['sɛlfɪʃ] *adj* : egoísta
selfishly ['sɛlfɪʃli] *adv* : de manera egoísta
selfishness ['sɛlfɪʃnəs] *n* : egoísmo *m*
selfless ['sɛlfləs] *adj* UNSELFISH : desinteresado
self–made [,sɛlf'meɪd] *adj* : próspero gracias a sus propios esfuerzos
self–pity [,sɛlf'pɪti] *n, pl* **-ties** : autocompasión *f*
self–portrait [,sɛlf'pɔrtrət] *n* : autorretrato *m*
self–propelled [,sɛlfprə'pɛld] *adj* : autopropulsado
self–reliance [,sɛlfri'laɪənts] *n* : independencia *f*, autosuficiencia *f*
self–respect [,sɛlfri'spɛkt] *n* : autoestima *f*, amor *m* propio
self–restraint [,sɛlfri'streɪnt] *n* : autocontrol *m*, moderación *f*
self–righteous [,sɛlf'raɪtʃəs] *adj* : santurrón, moralista
self–sacrifice [,sɛlf'sækrə,faɪs] *n* : abnegación *f*
selfsame ['sɛlf,seɪm] *adj* : mismo
self–service [,sɛlf'sərvɪs] *adj* **1** : de autoservicio **2 self-service restaurant** : autoservicio *m*
self–sufficiency [,sɛlfsə'fɪʃəntsi] *n* : autosuficiencia *f*
self–sufficient [,sɛlfsə'fɪʃənt] *adj* : autosuficiente
self–taught [,sɛlf'tɔt] *adj* : autodidacta
sell ['sɛl] *v* **sold** ['soːld]; **selling** *vt* : vender — *vi* : venderse
seller ['sɛlər] *n* : vendedor *m*, -dora *f*
selves → **self**
semantic [sɪ'mæntɪk] *adj* : semántico
semantics [sɪ'mæntɪks] *ns & pl* : semántica *f*
semaphore ['sɛmə,for] *n* : semáforo *m*
semblance ['sɛmblənts] *n* : apariencia *f*
semen ['siːmən] *n* : semen *m*
semester [sə'mɛstər] *n* : semestre *m*
semicolon ['sɛmi,koːlən, 'sɛ,maɪ-] *n* : punto y coma *m*
semiconductor ['sɛmikən,dʌktər, 'sɛ,maɪ-] *n* : semiconductor *m*
semifinal ['sɛmi,faɪnəl, 'sɛ,maɪ-] *n* : semifinal *f*
seminar ['sɛmə,nar] *n* : seminario *m*
seminary ['sɛmə,nɛri] *n, pl* **-naries** : seminario *m*
Semitic [sə'mɪtɪk] *adj* : semita
senate ['sɛnət] *n* : senado *m*
senator ['sɛnətər] *n* : senador *m*, -dora *f*
send ['sɛnd] *vt* **sent** ['sɛnt]; **sending 1** : mandar, enviar ⟨to send a letter : mandar una carta⟩ ⟨to send word : avisar, mandar decir⟩ **2** PROPEL : mandar, lanzar ⟨he sent it into left field : lo mandó al jardín izquierdo⟩ ⟨to send up dust : alzar polvo⟩ **3 to send into a rage** : poner furioso
sender ['sɛndər] *n* : remitente *mf* (de una carta, etc.)

Senegalese [ˌsɛnəgəˈliːz, -ˈliːs] *n* : senegalés *m*, -lesa *f* — **Senegalese** *adj*
senile [ˈsiːˌnaɪl] *adj* : senil
senility [sɪˈnɪləti] *n* : senilidad *f*
senior[1] [ˈsiːnjər] *adj* **1** ELDER : mayor ⟨John Doe, Senior : John Doe, padre⟩ **2** : superior (en rango), más antiguo (en años de servicio) ⟨a senior official : un alto oficial⟩
senior[2] *n* **1** : superior *m* (en rango) **2 to be someone's senior** : ser mayor que alguien ⟨she's two years my senior : me lleva dos años⟩
senior citizen *n* : persona *f* de la tercera edad
seniority [ˌsiːˈnjɔːrəti] *n* : antigüedad *f* (en años de servicio)
sensation [sɛnˈseɪʃən] *n* : sensación *f*
sensational [sɛnˈseɪʃənəl] *adj* : que causa sensación ⟨sensational stories : historias sensacionalistas⟩
sense[1] [ˈsɛns] *vt* **sensed; sensing** : sentir ⟨he sensed danger : se dio cuenta del peligro⟩
sense[2] *n* **1** MEANING : sentido *m*, significado *m* **2** : sentido *m* ⟨the sense of smell : el sentido del olfato⟩ **3 to make sense** : tener sentido
senseless [ˈsɛnsləs] *adj* **1** MEANINGLESS : sin sentido, sin razón **2** UNCONSCIOUS : inconsciente
senselessly [ˈsɛnsləsli] *adv* : sin sentido
sensibility [ˌsɛntsəˈbɪləti] *n, pl* **-ties** : sensibilidad *f*
sensible [ˈsɛntsəbəl] *adj* **1** PERCEPTIBLE : sensible, perceptible **2** AWARE : consciente **3** REASONABLE : sensato ⟨a sensible man : un hombre sensato⟩ ⟨sensible shoes : zapatos prácticos⟩ — **sensibly** [-bli] *adv*
sensibleness [ˈsɛntsəbəlnəs] *n* : sensatez *f*, solidez *f*
sensitive [ˈsɛntsətɪv] *adj* **1** : sensible, delicado ⟨sensitive skin : piel sensible⟩ **2** IMPRESSIONABLE : sensible, impresionable **3** TOUCHY : susceptible
sensitiveness [ˈsɛntsətɪvnəs] → **sensitivity**
sensitivity [ˌsɛntsəˈtɪvəti] *n, pl* **-ties** : sensibilidad *f*
sensitize [ˈsɛntsəˌtaɪz] *vt* **-tized; -tizing** : sensibilizar
sensor [ˈsɛnˌsɔr, ˈsɛntsər] *n* : sensor *m*
sensory [ˈsɛntsəri] *adj* : sensorial
sensual [ˈsɛntʃuəl] *adj* : sensual — **sensually** *adv*
sensuality [ˌsɛntʃəˈwæləti] *n, pl* **-ties** : sensualidad *f*
sensuous [ˈsɛntʃuəs] *adj* : sensual
sent → **send**
sentence[1] [ˈsɛntənts, -ənz] *vt* **-tenced; -tencing** : sentenciar
sentence[2] *n* **1** JUDGMENT : sentencia *f* **2** : oración *f*, frase *f* (en gramática)
sentiment [ˈsɛntəmənt] *n* **1** BELIEF : opinión *f* **2** FEELING : sentimiento *m* **3** → **sentimentality**

sentimental [ˌsɛntəˈmɛntəl] *adj* : sentimental
sentimentality [ˌsɛntəˌmɛnˈtæləti] *n, pl* **-ties** : sentimentalismo *m*, sensiblería *f*
sentinel [ˈsɛntənəl] *n* : centinela *mf*, guardia *mf*
sentry [ˈsɛntri] *n, pl* **-tries** : centinela *mf*
sepal [ˈsiːpəl, ˈsɛ-] *n* : sépalo *m*
separable [ˈsɛpərəbəl] *adj* : separable
separate[1] [ˈsɛpəˌreɪt] *v* **-rated; -rating** *vt* **1** DETACH, SEVER : separar **2** DISTINGUISH : diferenciar, distinguir — *vi* PART : separarse
separate[2] [ˈsɛprət, ˈsɛpə-] *adj* **1** INDIVIDUAL : separado, aparte ⟨a separate state : un estado separado⟩ ⟨in a separate envelope : en un sobre aparte⟩ **2** DISTINCT : distinto
separately [ˈsɛprətli, ˈsɛpə-] *adv* : por separado, separadamente, aparte
separation [ˌsɛpəˈreɪʃən] *n* : separación *f*
sepia [ˈsiːpiə] *n* : color *m* sepia
September [sɛpˈtɛmbər] *n* : septiembre *m*, setiembre *m*
septic [ˈsɛptɪk] *adj* : séptico ⟨septic tank : fosa séptica⟩
sepulchre [ˈsɛpəlkər] *n* : sepulcro *m*
sequel [ˈsiːkwəl] *n* **1** CONSEQUENCE : secuela *f*, consecuencia *f* **2** : continuación *f* (de una película, etc.)
sequence [ˈsiːkwənts] *n* **1** SERIES : serie *f*, sucesión *f*, secuencia *f* (matemática o musical) **2** ORDER : orden *m*
sequester [sɪˈkwɛstər] *vt* : aislar
sequin [ˈsiːkwən] *n* : lentejuela *f*
sequoia [sɪˈkwoɪə] *n* : secoya *f*, secuoya *f*
sera → **serum**
Serb [ˈsərb] *or* **Serbian** [ˈsərbiən] *n* **1** : serbio *m*, -bia *f* **2** : serbio *m* (idioma) — **Serb** *or* **Serbian** *adj*
Serbo–Croatian [ˌsərbokroˈeɪʃən] *n* : serbocroata *m* (idioma) — **Serbo-Croatian** *adj*
serenade[1] [ˌsɛrəˈneɪd] *vt* **-naded; -nading** : darle una serenata (a alguien)
serenade[2] *n* : serenata *f*
serene [səˈriːn] *adj* : sereno — **serenely** *adv*
serenity [səˈrɛnəti] *n* : serenidad *f*
serf [ˈsərf] *n* : siervo *m*, -va *f*
serge [ˈsərdʒ] *n* : sarga *f*
sergeant [ˈsɑrdʒənt] *n* : sargento *mf*
serial[1] [ˈsɪriəl] *adj* : seriado
serial[2] *n* : serie *f*, serial *m* (de radio o televisión), publicación *f* por entregas
serially [ˈsɪriəli] *adv* : en serie
series [ˈsɪrˌiːz] *n, pl* **series** : serie *f*, sucesión *f*
serious [ˈsɪriəs] *adj* **1** SOBER : serio **2** DEDICATED, EARNEST : serio, dedicado ⟨to be serious about something : tomar algo en serio⟩ **3** GRAVE : serio, grave ⟨serious problems : problemas graves⟩
seriously [ˈsɪriəsli] *adv* **1** EARNESTLY : seriamente, con seriedad, en serio **2** SEVERELY : gravemente

seriousness ['sɪriəsnəs] *n* : seriedad *f*, gravedad *f*

sermon ['sərmən] *n* : sermón *m*

serpent ['sərpənt] *n* : serpiente *f*

serrated [sə'reɪtəd, 'sɛr,eɪtəd] *adj* : dentado, serrado

serum ['sɪrəm] *n, pl* **serums** *or* **sera** ['sɪrə] : suero *m*

servant ['sərvənt] *n* : criado *m*, -da *f*; sirviente *m*, -ta *f*

serve ['sərv] *v* **served; serving** *vi* 1 : servir ⟨to serve in the navy : servir en la armada⟩ ⟨to serve on a jury : ser miembro de un jurado⟩ 2 DO, FUNCTION : servir ⟨to serve as : servir de, servir como⟩ 3 : sacar (en deportes) — *vt* 1 : servir ⟨to serve God : servir a Dios⟩ 2 HELP : servir ⟨it serves no purpose : no sirve para nada⟩ 3 : servir (comida o bebida) ⟨dinner is served : la cena está servida⟩ 4 SUPPLY : abastecer 5 CARRY OUT : cumplir, hacer ⟨to serve time : servir una pena⟩ 6 **to serve a summons** : entregar una citación

server ['sərvər] *n* 1 : camarero *m*, -ra *f*; mesero *m*, -ra *f* (en un restaurante) 2 *or* **serving dish** : fuente *f* (para servir comida) 3 : servidor *m* (en informática)

service¹ ['sərvəs] *vt* **-viced; -vicing** 1 MAINTAIN : darle mantenimiento a (una máquina), revisar 2 REPAIR : arreglar, reparar

service² *n* 1 HELP, USE : servicio *m* ⟨to do someone a service : hacerle un servicio a alguien⟩ ⟨at your service : a sus órdenes⟩ ⟨to be out of service : no funcionar⟩ 2 CEREMONY : oficio *m* (religioso) 3 DEPARTMENT, SYSTEM : servicio *m* ⟨social services : servicios sociales⟩ ⟨train service : servicio de trenes⟩ 4 SET : juego *m*, servicio *m* ⟨tea service : juego de té⟩ 5 MAINTENANCE : mantenimiento *m*, revisión *f*, servicio *m* 6 : saque *m* (en deportes) 7 **armed services** : fuerzas *fpl* armadas

serviceable ['sərvəsəbəl] *adj* 1 USEFUL : útil 2 DURABLE : duradero

serviceman ['sərvəs,mæn, -mən] *n, pl* **-men** [-mən, -,mɛn] : militar *m*

service station → gas station

servicewoman ['sərvəs,wʊmən] *n, pl* **-women** [-,wɪmən] : militar *f*

servile ['sərvəl, -,vaɪl] *adj* : servil

serving ['sərvɪŋ] *n* HELPING : porción *f*, ración *f*

servitude ['sərvə,tuːd, -,tjuːd] *n* : servidumbre *f*

sesame ['sɛsəmi] *n* : ajonjolí *m*, sésamo *m*

session ['sɛʃən] *n* : sesión *f*

set¹ ['sɛt] *v* **set; setting** *vt* 1 SEAT : sentar 2 *or* **set down** PLACE : poner, colocar 3 ARRANGE : fijar, establecer ⟨to set the date : poner la fecha⟩ ⟨he set the agenda : estableció la agenda⟩ 4 ADJUST : poner (un reloj, etc.) 5 (*indicating the causing of a certain condition*) ⟨to set fire to : prenderle fuego a⟩ ⟨she

set it free : lo soltó⟩ 6 MAKE, START : poner, hacer ⟨I set them working : los puse a trabajar⟩ — *vi* 1 SOLIDIFY : fraguar (dícese del cemento, etc.), cuajar (dícese de la gelatina, etc.) 2 : ponerse (dícese del sol o de la luna)

set² *adj* 1 ESTABLISHED, FIXED : fijo, establecido 2 RIGID : inflexible ⟨to be set in one's ways : tener costumbres muy arraigadas⟩ 3 READY : listo, preparado

set³ *n* 1 COLLECTION : juego *m* ⟨a set of dishes : un juego de platos, una vajilla⟩ ⟨a tool set : una caja de herramientas⟩ 2 *or* **stage set** : decorado *m* (en el teatro), plató *m* (en el cine) 3 APPARATUS : aparato *m* ⟨a television set : un televisor⟩ 4 : conjunto *m* (en matemáticas)

setback ['sɛt,bæk] *n* : revés *m*, contratiempo *m*

set in *vi* BEGIN : comenzar, empezar

set off *vt* 1 PROVOKE : provocar 2 EXPLODE : hacer estallar (una bomba, etc.) — *vi or* **set forth** : salir

set out *vi* : salir (de viaje) — *vt* INTEND : proponerse

settee [sɛ'tiː] *n* : sofá *m*

setter ['sɛtər] *n* : setter *mf* ⟨Irish setter : setter irlandés⟩

setting ['sɛtɪŋ] *n* 1 : posición *f*, ajuste *m* (de un control) 2 : engaste *m*, montura *f* (de una gema) 3 SCENE : escenario *m* (de una novela, etc.) 4 SURROUNDINGS : ambiente *m*, entorno *m*, marco *m*

settle ['sɛtəl] *v* **settled; settling** *vi* 1 ALIGHT, LAND : posarse (dícese de las aves), depositarse (dícese del polvo) 2 SINK : asentarse (dícese de los edificios) ⟨he settled into the chair : se arrellanó en la silla⟩ 3 : instalarse (en una casa), establecerse (en una ciudad o región) 4 **to settle down** : calmarse, tranquilizarse ⟨settle down! : ¡tranquilízate!, ¡cálmate!⟩ 5 **to settle down** : sentar cabeza, hacerse sensato ⟨to marry and settle down : casarse y sentar cabeza⟩ — *vt* 1 ARRANGE, DECIDE : fijar, decidir, acordar (planes, etc.) 2 RESOLVE : resolver, solucionar ⟨to settle an argument : resolver una discusión⟩ 3 PAY : pagar ⟨to settle an account : saldar una cuenta⟩ 4 CALM : calmar (los nervios), asentar (el estómago) 5 COLONIZE : colonizar 6 **to settle oneself** : acomodarse, hacerse cómodo

settlement ['sɛtəlmənt] *n* 1 PAYMENT : pago *m*, liquidación *f* 2 COLONY : asentamiento *m* 3 RESOLUTION : acuerdo *m*

settler ['sɛtələr] *n* : poblador *m*, -dora *f*; colono *m*, -na *f*

setup ['sɛt,ʌp] *n* 1 ASSEMBLY : montaje *m*, ensamblaje *m* 2 ARRANGEMENT : disposición *f* 3 PREPARATION : preparación *f* 4 TRAP, TRICK : encerrona *f*

set up *vt* 1 ASSEMBLE : montar, armar 2 ERECT : levantar, erigir 3 ESTABLISH : establecer, fundar, montar (un negocio) 4 CAUSE : armar ⟨they set up a clamor : armaron un alboroto⟩

seven[1] ['sɛvən] *adj* : siete

seven[2] *n* : siete *m*

seven hundred[1] *adj* : setecientos

seven hundred[2] *n* : setecientos *m*

seventeen[1] [,sɛvən'ti:n] *adj* : diecisiete

seventeen[2] *n* : diecisiete *m*

seventeenth[1] [,sɛvən'ti:nθ] *adj* : decimoséptimo

seventeenth[2] *n* 1 : decimoséptimo *m*, -ma *f* (en una serie) 2 : diecisieteavo *m*, diecisieteava parte *f*

seventh[1] ['sɛvənθ] *adj* : séptimo

seventh[2] *n* 1 : séptimo *m*, -ma *f* (en una serie) 2 : séptimo *m*, séptima parte *f*

seventieth[1] ['sɛvəntiəθ] *adj* : septuagésimo

seventieth[2] *n* 1 : septuagésimo *m*, -ma *f* (en una serie) 2 : setentavo *m*, setentava parte *f*, septuagésima parte *f*

seventy[1] ['sɛvənti] *adj* : setenta

seventy[2] *n, pl* **-ties** : setenta *m*

sever ['sɛvər] *vt* **-ered; -ering** : cortar, romper

several[1] ['sɛvrəl, 'sɛvə-] *adj* 1 DISTINCT : distinto 2 SOME : varios ⟨several weeks : varias semanas⟩

several[2] *pron* : varios, varias

severance ['sɛvrəns, 'sɛvə-] *n* 1 : ruptura *f* (de relaciones, etc.) 2 **severance pay** : indemnización *f* (por despido)

severe [sə'vɪr] *adj* **severer; -est** 1 STRICT : severo 2 AUSTERE : sobrio, austero 3 SERIOUS : grave ⟨a severe wound : una herida grave⟩ ⟨severe aches : dolores fuertes⟩ 4 DIFFICULT : duro, difícil — **severely** *adv*

severity [sə'vrəti] *n* 1 HARSHNESS : severidad *f* 2 AUSTERITY : sobriedad *f*, austeridad *f* 3 SERIOUSNESS : gravedad *f* (de una herida, etc.)

sew ['so:] *v* **sewed; sewn** ['so:n] *or* **sewed; sewing** : coser

sewage ['su:ɪʤ] *n* : aguas *fpl* negras, aguas *fpl* residuales

sewer[1] ['so:ər] *n* : uno que cose

sewer[2] ['su:ər] *n* : alcantarilla *f*, cloaca *f*

sewing ['so:ɪŋ] *n* : costura *f*

sex ['sɛks] *n* 1 : sexo *m* ⟨the opposite sex : el sexo opuesto⟩ 2 COPULATION : relaciones *fpl* sexuales

sexism ['sɛk,sɪzəm] *n* : sexismo *m*

sexist[1] ['sɛksɪst] *adj* : sexista

sexist[2] *n* : sexista *mf*

sextant ['sɛkstənt] *n* : sextante *m*

sextet [sɛk'stɛt] *n* : sexteto *m*

sexton ['sɛkstən] *n* : sacristán *m*

sexual ['sɛkʃʊəl] *adj* : sexual — **sexually** *adv*

sexuality [,sɛkʃʊ'æləti] *n* : sexualidad *f*

sexy ['sɛksi] *adj* **sexier; -est** : sexy

shabbily ['ʃæbəli] *adv* 1 : pobremente ⟨shabbily dressed : pobremente vestido⟩ 2 UNFAIRLY : mal, injustamente

shabbiness ['ʃæbinəs] *n* 1 : lo gastado (de ropa, etc.) 2 : lo mal vestido (de personas) 3 UNFAIRNESS : injusticia *f*

shabby ['ʃæbi] *adj* **shabbier; -est** 1 : gastado (dícese de la ropa, etc.) 2 : mal vestido (dícese de las personas) 3 UNFAIR : malo, injusto ⟨shabby treatment : mal trato⟩

shack ['ʃæk] *n* : choza *f*, rancho *m*

shackle[1] ['ʃækəl] *vt* **-led; -ling** : ponerle grilletes (a alguien)

shackle[2] *n* : grillete *m*

shad ['ʃæd] *n* : sábalo *m*

shade[1] ['ʃeɪd] *v* **shaded; shading** *vt* 1 SHELTER : proteger (del sol o de la luz) 2 *or* **to shade in** : matizar los colores de — *vi* : convertirse gradualmente ⟨his irritation shaded into rage : su irritación iba convirtiéndose en furia⟩

shade[2] *n* 1 : sombra *f* ⟨to give shade : dar sombra⟩ 2 : tono *m* (de un color) 3 NUANCE : matiz *m* 4 : pantalla *f* (de una lámpara), persiana *f* (de una ventana)

shadow[1] ['ʃædo:] *vt* 1 DARKEN : ensombrecer 2 TRAIL : seguir de cerca, seguirle la pista (a alguien)

shadow[2] *n* 1 : sombra *f* 2 DARKNESS : oscuridad *f* 3 TRACE : sombra *f*, atisbo *m*, indicio *m* ⟨without a shadow of a doubt : sin sombra de duda, sin lugar a dudas⟩ 4 **to cast a shadow over** : ensombrecer

shadowy ['ʃædowi] *adj* 1 INDISTINCT : vago, indistinto 2 DARK : oscuro

shady ['ʃeɪdi] *adj* **shadier; -est** 1 : sombreado (dícese de un lugar), que da sombra (dícese de un árbol) 2 DISREPUTABLE : sospechoso (dícese de una persona), turbio (dícese de un negocio, etc.)

shaft ['ʃæft] *n* 1 : asta *f* (de una lanza), astil *m* (de una flecha), mango *m* (de una herramienta) 2 *or* **mine shaft** : pozo *m*

shaggy ['ʃægi] *adj* **shaggier; -est** 1 HAIRY : peludo ⟨a shaggy dog : un perro peludo⟩ 2 UNKEMPT : enmarañado, despeinado (dícese del pelo, de las barbas, etc.)

shake[1] ['ʃeɪk] *v* **shook** ['ʃʊk]; **shaken** ['ʃeɪkən]; **shaking** *vt* 1 : sacudir, agitar, hacer temblar ⟨he shook his head : negó con la cabeza⟩ 2 WEAKEN : debilitar, hacer flaquear ⟨it shook her faith : debilitó su confianza⟩ 3 UPSET : afectar, alterar 4 **to shake hands with someone** : darle la mano a alguien, estrecharle la mano a alguien — *vi* : temblar, sacudirse

shake[2] *n* : sacudida *f*, apretón *m* (de manos)

shaker ['ʃeɪkər] *n* 1 **salt shaker** : salero *m* 2 **pepper shaker** : pimentero *m* 3 **cocktail shaker** : coctelera *f*

shake–up ['ʃeɪk,ʌp] *n* : reorganización *f*

shakily ['ʃeɪkəli] *adv* : temblorosamente

shaky ['ʃeɪki] *adj* **shakier; -est 1** SHAK-ING : tembloroso **2** UNSTABLE : poco firme, inestable **3** PRECARIOUS : precario, incierto **4** QUESTIONABLE : dudoso, cuestionable ⟨shaky arguments : argumentos discutibles⟩

shale ['ʃeɪl] *n* : esquisto *m*

shall ['ʃæl] *v aux, past* **should** ['ʃʊd] *present s & pl* **shall 1** *(used to express a command)* ⟨you shall do as I say : harás lo que te digo⟩ **2** *(used to express futurity)* ⟨we shall see : ya veremos⟩ ⟨when shall we expect you? : ¿cuándo te podemos esperar?⟩ **3** *(used to express determination)* ⟨you shall have the money : tendrás el dinero⟩ **4** *(used to express a condition)* ⟨if he should die : si muriera⟩ ⟨if they should call, tell me : si llaman, dímelo⟩ **5** *(used to express obligation)* ⟨he should have said it : debería haberlo dicho⟩ **6** *(used to express probability)* ⟨they should arrive soon : deben (de) llegar pronto⟩ ⟨why should he lie? : ¿porqué ha de mentir?⟩

shallow ['ʃælo] *adj* **1** : poco profundo (dícese del agua, etc.) **2** SUPERFICIAL : superficial

shallows ['ʃæloːz] *npl* : bajío *m*, bajos *mpl*

sham¹ ['ʃæm] *v* **shammed; shamming** : fingir

sham² *adj* : falso, fingido

sham³ *n* **1** FAKE, PRETENSE : farsa *f*, simulación *f*, imitación *f* **2** FAKER : impostor *m*, -tora *f*; farsante *mf*

shamble ['ʃæmbəl] *vi* **-bled; -bling** : caminar arrastrando los pies

shambles ['ʃæmbəlz] *ns & pl* : caos *m*, desorden *m*, confusión *f*

shame¹ ['ʃeɪm] *v* **shamed; shaming 1** : avergonzar ⟨he was shamed by their words : sus palabras le dieron vergüenza⟩ **2** DISGRACE : deshonrar

shame² *n* **1** : vergüenza *f* ⟨to have no shame : no tener vergüenza⟩ **2** DISGRACE : vergüenza *f*, deshonra *f* **3** PITY : lástima *f*, pena *f* ⟨what a shame! : ¡qué pena!⟩

shamefaced ['ʃeɪm‚feɪst] *adj* : avergonzado

shameful ['ʃeɪmfəl] *adj* : vergonzoso — **shamefully** *adv*

shameless ['ʃeɪmləs] *adj* : descarado, desvergonzado — **shamelessly** *adv*

shampoo¹ [ʃæm'puː] *vt* : lavar (el pelo)

shampoo² *n, pl* **-poos** : champú *m*

shamrock ['ʃæm‚rak] *n* : trébol *m*

shank ['ʃæŋk] *n* : parte *f* baja de la pierna

shan't ['ʃænt] *(contraction of* **shall not)** → **shall**

shanty ['ʃænti] *n, pl* **-ties** : choza *f*, rancho *m*

shape¹ ['ʃeɪp] *v* **shaped; shaping** *vt* **1** : dar forma a, modelar (arcilla, etc.), tallar (madera, piedra), formar (carácter) ⟨to be shaped like : tener forma de⟩ **2** DETERMINE : decidir, determi-

nar — *vi or* **to shape up** : tomar forma

shape² *n* **1** : forma *f*, figura *f* ⟨in the shape of a circle : en forma de círculo⟩ **2** CONDITION : estado *m*; condiciones *fpl*, forma *f* (física) ⟨to get in shape : ponerse en forma⟩

shapeless ['ʃeɪpləs] *adj* : informe

shapely ['ʃeɪpli] *adj* **shapelier; -est** : curvilíneo, bien proporcionado

shard ['ʃard] *n* : fragmento *m*, casco *m* (de cerámica, etc.)

share¹ ['ʃɛr] *v* **shared; sharing** *vt* **1** APPORTION : dividir, repartir **2** : compartir ⟨they share a room : comparten una habitación⟩ — *vi* : compartir

share² *n* **1** PORTION : parte *f*, porción *f* ⟨one's fair share : lo que le corresponde a uno⟩ **2** : acción *f* (en una compañía) ⟨to hold shares : tener acciones⟩

sharecropper ['ʃɛr‚krapər] *n* : aparcero *m*, -ra *f*

shareholder ['ʃɛr‚hoːldər] *n* : accionista *mf*

shark ['ʃark] *n* : tiburón *m*

sharp¹ ['ʃarp] *adv* : en punto ⟨at two o'clock sharp : a las dos en punto⟩

sharp² *adj* **1** : afilado, filoso ⟨a sharp knife : un cuchillo afilado⟩ **2** PENETRATING : cortante, fuerte **3** CLEVER : agudo, listo, perspicaz **4** ACUTE : agudo ⟨sharp eyesight : vista aguda⟩ **5** HARSH, SEVERE : duro, severo, agudo ⟨a sharp rebuke : una reprimenda mordaz⟩ **6** STRONG : fuerte ⟨sharp cheese : queso fuerte⟩ **7** ABRUPT : brusco, repentino **8** DISTINCT : nítido, definido ⟨a sharp image : una imagen bien definida⟩ **9** ANGULAR : anguloso (dícese de la cara) **10** : sostenido (en música)

sharp³ *n* : sostenido *m* (en música)

sharpen ['ʃarpən] *vt* : afilar, aguzar ⟨to sharpen a pencil : sacarle punta a un lápiz⟩ ⟨to sharpen one's wits : aguzar el ingenio⟩

sharpener ['ʃarpənər] *n* : afilador *m* (para cuchillos, etc.), sacapuntas *m* (para lápices)

sharply ['ʃarpli] *adv* **1** ABRUPTLY : bruscamente **2** DISTINCTLY : claramente, marcadamente

sharpness ['ʃarpnəs] *n* **1** : lo afilado (de un cuchillo, etc.) **2** ACUTENESS : agudeza *f* (de los sentidos o de la mente) **3** INTENSITY : intensidad *f*, agudeza *f* (de dolores, etc.) **4** HARSHNESS : dureza *f*, severidad *f* **5** ABRUPTNESS : brusquedad *f* **6** CLARITY : nitidez *f*

sharpshooter ['ʃarp‚fuːtər] *n* : tirador *m*, -dora *f* de primera

shatter ['ʃætər] *vt* **1** : hacer añicos ⟨to shatter the silence : romper el silencio⟩ **2 to be shattered by** : quedar destrozado por — *vi* : hacerse añicos, romperse en pedazos

shave[1] [ˈʃeɪv] v **shaved**; **shaved** or **shaven** [ˈʃeɪvən]; **shaving** vt **1** : afeitar, rasurar ⟨she shaved her legs : se rasuró las piernas⟩ ⟨they shaved (off) his beard : le afeitaron la barba⟩ **2** SLICE : cortar (en pedazos finos) — vi : afeitarse, rasurarse

shave[2] n : afeitada f, rasurada f

shaver [ˈʃeɪvər] n : afeitadora f, máquina f de afeitar, rasuradora f

shawl [ˈʃɔl] n : chal m, mantón m, rebozo m

she [ˈʃiː] pron : ella

sheaf [ˈʃiːf] n, pl **sheaves** [ˈʃiːvz] : gavilla f (de cereales), haz m (de flechas), fajo m (de papeles)

shear [ˈʃɪr] vt **sheared**; **sheared** or **shorn** [ˈʃɔrn]; **shearing 1** : esquilar, trasquilar ⟨to shear sheep : trasquilar ovejas⟩ **2** CUT : cortar (el pelo, etc.)

shears [ˈʃɪrz] npl : tijeras fpl (grandes)

sheath [ˈʃiːθ] n, pl **sheaths** [ˈʃiːðz, ˈʃiːθs] : funda f, vaina f

sheathe [ˈʃiːð] vt **sheathed**; **sheathing** : envainar, enfundar

shed[1] [ˈʃd] vt **shed**; **shedding 1** : derramar (sangre o lágrimas) **2** EMIT : emitir (luz) ⟨to shed light on : aclarar⟩ **3** DISCARD : mudar (la piel, etc.) ⟨to shed one's clothes : quitarse uno la ropa⟩

shed[2] n : cobertizo m

she'd [ˈʃiːd] (contraction of **she had** or **she would**) → **have**, **would**

sheen [ˈʃiːn] n : brillo m, lustre m

sheep [ˈʃiːp] ns & pl : oveja f

sheepfold [ˈʃiːpˌfoːld] n : redil m

sheepish [ˈʃiːpɪʃ] adj : avergonzado

sheepskin [ˈʃiːpˌskɪn] n : piel f de oveja, piel f de borrego

sheer[1] [ˈʃɪr] adv **1** COMPLETELY : completamente, totalmente **2** VERTICALLY : verticalmente

sheer[2] adj **1** TRANSPARENT : vaporoso, transparente **2** ABSOLUTE, UTTER : puro ⟨by sheer luck : por pura suerte⟩ **3** STEEP : escarpado, vertical

sheet [ˈʃiːt] n **1** or **bedsheet** [ˈbed-ˌʃiːt] : sábana f **2** : hoja f (de papel) **3** : capa f (de hielo, etc.) **4** : lámina f, placa f (de vidrio, metal, etc.), plancha f (de metal, madera, etc.) ⟨baking sheet : placa f de horno⟩

sheikh or **sheik** [ˈʃiːk, ˈʃeɪk] n : jeque m

shelf [ˈʃelf] n, pl **shelves** [ˈʃelvz] **1** : estante m, anaquel m (en una pared) **2** : banco m, arrecife m (en geología) ⟨continental shelf : plataforma continental⟩

shell[1] [ˈʃel] vt **1** : desvainar (chícharos), pelar (nueces, etc.) **2** BOMBARD : bombardear

shell[2] n **1** SEASHELL : concha f **2** : cáscara f (de huevos, nueces, etc.), vaina f (de chícharos, etc.), caparazón m (de crustáceos, tortugas, etc.) **3** : cartucho m, casquillo m ⟨a .45 caliber shell : un cartucho calibre .45⟩ **4** or **racing shell** : bote m (para hacer regatas de remos)

she'll [ˈʃiːl, ˈʃɪl] (contraction of **she shall** or **she will**) → **shall**, **will**

shellac[1] [ʃəˈlæk] vt **-lacked**; **-lacking 1** : laquear (madera, etc.) **2** DEFEAT : darle una paliza (a alguien), derrotar

shellac[2] n : laca f

shellfish [ˈʃelˌfɪʃ] n : marisco m

shelter[1] [ˈʃeltər] n **1** PROTECT : proteger, abrigar **2** HARBOR : dar refugio a, albergar

shelter[2] n : refugio m, abrigo m ⟨to take shelter : refugiarse⟩

shelve [ˈʃelv] vt **shelved**; **shelving 1** : poner en estantes **2** DEFER : dar carpetazo a

shenanigans [ʃəˈnænɪɡənz] npl **1** TRICKERY : artimañas fpl **2** MISCHIEF : travesuras fpl

shepherd[1] [ˈʃepərd] vt **1** : cuidar (ovejas, etc.) **2** GUIDE : conducir, guiar

shepherd[2] n : pastor m

shepherdess [ˈʃepərdəs] n : pastora f

sherbet [ˈʃɔrbət] or **sherbert** [-bərt] n : sorbete m, nieve f Cuba, Mex, PRi

sheriff [ˈʃerɪf] n : sheriff mf

sherry [ˈʃeri] n, pl **-ries** : jerez m

she's [ˈʃiːz] (contraction of **she is** or **she has**) → **be**, **have**

shield[1] [ˈʃiːld] vt **1** PROTECT : proteger **2** CONCEAL : ocultar ⟨to shield one's eyes : taparse los ojos⟩

shield[2] n **1** : escudo m (armadura) **2** PROTECTION : protección f, blindaje m (de un cable)

shier, shiest → **shy**

shift[1] [ˈʃɪft] vt **1** CHANGE : cambiar ⟨to shift gears : cambiar de velocidad⟩ **2** MOVE : mover **3** TRANSFER : transferir ⟨to shift the blame : echarle la culpa (a otro)⟩ — vi **1** CHANGE : cambiar **2** MOVE : moverse **3 to shift for oneself** : arreglárselas solo

shift[2] n **1** CHANGE, TRANSFER : cambio m ⟨a shift in priorities : un cambio de prioridades⟩ **2** : turno m ⟨night shift : turno de noche⟩ **3** DRESS : vestido m (suelto) **4** → **gearshift**

shiftless [ˈʃɪftləs] adj : perezoso, vago, holgazán

shifty [ˈʃɪfti] adj **shiftier; -est** : taimado, artero ⟨a shifty look : una mirada huidiza⟩

shilling [ˈʃɪlɪŋ] n : chelín m

shimmer [ˈʃɪmər] vi GLIMMER : brillar con luz trémula

shin[1] [ˈʃɪn] vi **shinned**; **shinning** : trepar, subir ⟨she shinned up the pole : subió al poste⟩

shin[2] n : espinilla f, canilla f

shine[1] [ˈʃaɪn] v **shone** [ˈʃoːn] or **shined**; **shining** vi **1** : brillar, relucir ⟨the stars were shining : las estrellas brillaban⟩ **2** EXCEL : brillar, lucirse — vt **1** : alumbrar ⟨he shined the flashlight at it : lo alumbró con la linterna⟩ **2** POLISH : sacarle brillo a, lustrar

shine[2] n : brillo m, lustre m

shingle[1] [ˈʃɪŋɡəl] vt **-gled; -gling** : techar

shingle² *n* : tablilla *f* (para techar)

shingles ['ʃɪŋgəlz] *npl* : herpes *m*

shinny ['ʃɪni] *vi* **-nied; -nying → shin¹**

shiny ['ʃaɪni] *adj* **shinier; -est** : brillante

ship¹ ['ʃɪp] *vt* **shipped; shipping** 1 LOAD : embarcar (en un barco) 2 SEND : transportar (en barco), enviar ⟨to ship by air : enviar por avión⟩

ship² *n* 1 : barco *m*, buque *m* 2 → **spaceship**

shipboard ['ʃɪp,bord] *n* **on ~** : a bordo

shipbuilder ['ʃɪp,bɪldər] *n* : constructor *m*, -tora *f* naval

shipment ['ʃɪpmənt] *n* 1 SHIPPING : transporte *m*, embarque *m* 2 : envío *m*, remesa *f* ⟨a shipment of medicine : un envío de medicina⟩

shipping ['ʃɪpɪŋ] *n* 1 SHIPS : barcos *mpl*, embarcaciones *fpl* 2 TRANSPORTATION : transporte *m* (de mercancías)

shipshape ['ʃɪp,ʃeɪp] *adj* : ordenado

shipwreck¹ ['ʃɪp,rɛk] *vt* **to be shipwrecked** : naufragar

shipwreck² *n* : naufragio *m*

shipyard ['ʃɪp,jard] *n* : astillero *m*

shirk ['ʃərk] *vt* : eludir, rehuir ⟨to shirk one's responsibilities : esquivar uno sus responsabilidades⟩

shirt ['ʃərt] *n* : camisa *f*

shiver¹ ['ʃɪvər] *vi* 1 : tiritar (de frío) 2 TREMBLE : estremecerse, temblar

shiver² *n* : escalofrío *m*, estremecimiento *m*

shoal ['ʃoːl] *n* : banco *m*, bajío *m*

shock¹ ['ʃɑk] *vt* 1 UPSET : conmover, conmocionar 2 STARTLE : asustar, sobresaltar 3 SCANDALIZE : escandalizar 4 : darle una descarga eléctrica a

shock² *n* 1 COLLISION, JOLT : choque *m*, sacudida *f* 2 UPSET : conmoción *f*, golpe *m* emocional 3 : shock *m* (en medicina) 4 *or* **electric shock** : descarga *f* eléctrica 5 SHEAVES : gavillas *fpl* 6 **shock of hair** : mata *f* de pelo

shock absorber *n* : amortiguador *m*

shocking ['ʃɑkɪŋ] *adj* 1 : chocante 2 **shocking pink** : rosa *m* estridente

shoddy ['ʃɑdi] *adj* **shoddier; -est** : de mala calidad ⟨a shoddy piece of work : un trabajo chapucero⟩

shoe¹ ['ʃuː] *vt* **shod** ['ʃɑd]; **shoeing** : herrar (un caballo)

shoe² *n* 1 : zapato *m* ⟨the shoe industry : la industria del calzado⟩ 2 HORSESHOE : herradura *f* 3 **brake shoe** : zapata *f*

shoelace ['ʃuː,leɪs] *n* : cordón *m* (de zapatos)

shoemaker ['ʃuː,meɪkər] *n* : zapatero *m*, -ra *f*

shone → shine

shook → shake

shoot¹ ['ʃuːt] *v* **shot** ['ʃɑt]; **shooting** *vt* 1 : disparar, tirar ⟨to shoot a bullet : tirar una bala⟩ 2 : pegarle un tiro a, darle un balazo a ⟨he shot her : le pegó un tiro⟩ ⟨they shot and killed him : lo mataron a balazos⟩ 3 THROW : lanzar (una pelota, etc.), echar (una mirada) 4 PHOTOGRAPH : fotografiar 5 FILM : filmar — *vi* 1 : disparar (con un arma de fuego) 2 DART : ir rápidamente ⟨it shot past : pasó como una bala⟩

shoot² *n* : brote *m*, retoño *m*, vástago *m*

shooting star *n* : estrella *f* fugaz

shop¹ ['ʃɑp] *vi* **shopped; shopping** : hacer compras ⟨to go shopping : ir de compras⟩

shop² *n* 1 WORKSHOP : taller *m* 2 STORE : tienda *f*

shopkeeper ['ʃɑp,kiːpər] *n* : tendero *m*, -ra *f*

shoplift ['ʃɑp,lɪft] *vi* : hurtar mercancía (de una tienda) — *vt* : hurtar (de una tienda)

shoplifter ['ʃɑp,lɪftər] *n* : ladrón *m*, -drona *f* (que roba en una tienda)

shopper ['ʃɑpər] *n* : comprador *m*, -dora *f*

shore¹ ['ʃor] *vt* **shored; shoring** : apuntalar ⟨they shored up the wall : apuntalaron la pared⟩

shore² *n* 1 : orilla *f* (del mar, etc.) 2 PROP : puntal *m*

shoreline ['ʃor,laɪn] *n* : orilla *f*

shorn → shear

short¹ ['ʃort] *adv* 1 ABRUPTLY : repentinamente, súbitamente ⟨the car stopped short : el carro se paró en seco⟩ 2 **to fall short** : no alcanzar, quedarse corto

short² *adj* 1 : corto (de medida), bajo (de estatura) 2 BRIEF : corto ⟨short and sweet : corto y bueno⟩ ⟨a short time ago : hace poco⟩ 3 CURT : brusco, cortante, seco 4 : corto (de tiempo, de dinero) ⟨I'm one dollar short : me falta un dólar⟩

short³ *n* 1 **shorts** *npl* : shorts *mpl*, pantalones *mpl* cortos 2 → **short circuit**

shortage ['ʃortɪdʒ] *n* : falta *f*, escasez *f*, carencia *f*

shortcake ['ʃort,keɪk] *n* : tarta *f* de fruta

shortchange ['ʃort'tʃeɪndʒ] *vt* **-changed; -changing** : darle mal el cambio (a alguien)

short circuit *n* : cortocircuito *m*, corto *m* (eléctrico)

shortcoming ['ʃort,kʌmɪŋ] *n* : defecto *m*

shortcut ['ʃort,kʌt] *n* 1 : atajo *m* ⟨to take a shortcut : cortar camino⟩ 2 : alternativa *f* fácil, método *m* rápido

shorten ['ʃortən] *vt* : acortar — *vi* : acortarse

shorthand ['ʃort,hænd] *n* : taquigrafía *f*

short-lived ['ʃort'lɪvd, -'laɪvd] *adj* : efímero

shortly ['ʃortli] *adv* 1 BRIEFLY : brevemente ⟨to put it shortly : para decirlo en pocas palabras⟩ 2 SOON : dentro de poco

shortness ['ʃortnəs] *n* 1 : lo corto ⟨shortness of stature : estatura baja⟩ 2 BREVITY : brevedad *f* 3 CURTNESS : brusquedad *f* 4 SHORTAGE : falta *f*, escasez *f*, carencia *f*

shortsighted ['ʃɔrt,saɪtəd] → **near-sighted**

shot ['ʃɑt] n 1 : disparo m, tiro m ⟨to fire a shot : disparar⟩ 2 PELLETS : perdigones mpl 3 : tiro m (en deportes) 4 ATTEMPT : intento m, tentativa f ⟨to have a shot at : hacer un intento por⟩ 5 RANGE : alcance m ⟨a long shot : una posibilidad remota⟩ 6 PHOTOGRAPH : foto f 7 INJECTION : inyección f 8 : trago m (de licor)

shotgun ['ʃɑt,ɡʌn] n : escopeta f

should → **shall**

shoulder[1] ['ʃo:ldər] vt 1 JOSTLE : empujar (con el hombro) 2 : ponerse al hombro (una mochila, etc.) 3 : cargar con (la responsabilidad, etc.)

shoulder[2] n 1 : hombro m ⟨to shrug one's shoulders : encogerse los hombros⟩ 2 : arcén m (de una carretera)

shoulder blade n : omóplato m, omoplato m, escápula f

shouldn't ['ʃudənt] (contraction of should not) → **shall**

shout[1] ['ʃaʊt] v : gritar, vocear

shout[2] n : grito m

shove[1] ['ʃʌv] v **shoved; shoving** : empujar bruscamente

shove[2] n : empujón m, empellón m

shovel[1] ['ʃʌvəl] vt -**veled** or -**velled**; -**veling** or -**velling** 1 : mover con (una) pala ⟨they shoveled the dirt out : sacaron la tierra con palas⟩ 2 DIG : cavar (con una pala)

shovel[2] n : pala f

show[1] ['ʃo:] v **showed; shown** ['ʃo:n] or **showed; showing** vt 1 DISPLAY : mostrar, enseñar 2 REVEAL : demostrar, manifestar, revelar ⟨he showed himself to be a coward : se reveló como cobarde⟩ 3 TEACH : enseñar 4 PROVE : demostrar, probar 5 CONDUCT, DIRECT : llevar, acompañar ⟨to show someone the way : indicarle el camino a alguien⟩ 6 : proyectar (una película), dar (un programa de televisión) — vi 1 : notarse, verse ⟨the stain doesn't show : la mancha no se ve⟩ 2 APPEAR : aparecer, dejarse ver

show[2] n 1 : demostración f ⟨a show of force : una demostración de fuerza⟩ 2 EXHIBITION : exposición f, exhibición f ⟨flower show : exposición de flores⟩ ⟨to be on show : estar expuesto⟩ 3 : espectáculo m (teatral), programa m (de televisión, etc.) ⟨to go to a show : ir al teatro⟩

showcase ['ʃo:,keɪs] n : vitrina f

showdown ['ʃo:,daʊn] n : confrontación f (decisiva)

shower[1] ['ʃaʊər] vt 1 SPRAY : regar, mojar 2 HEAP : colmar ⟨they showered him with gifts : lo colmaron de regalos, le llovieron los regalos⟩ — vi 1 BATHE : ducharse, darse una ducha 2 RAIN : llover

shower[2] n 1 : chaparrón m, chubasco m ⟨a chance of showers : una posibil-idad de chaparrones⟩ 2 : ducha f ⟨to take a shower : ducharse⟩ 3 PARTY : fiesta f ⟨a bridal shower : una despedida de soltera⟩

show off vt : hacer alarde de, ostentar — vi : lucirse

show up vi APPEAR : aparecer — vt EXPOSE : revelar

showy ['ʃo:i] adj **showier; -est** : llamativo, ostentoso — **showily** adv

shrank → **shrink**

shrapnel ['ʃræpnəl] ns & pl : metralla f

shred[1] ['ʃred] vt **shredded; shredding** : hacer trizas, desmenuzar (con las manos), triturar (con una máquina) ⟨to shred vegetables : cortar verduras en tiras⟩

shred[2] n 1 STRIP : tira f, jirón m (de tela) 2 BIT : pizca f ⟨not a shred of evidence : ni la mínima prueba⟩

shrew ['ʃru:] n 1 : musaraña f (animal) 2 : mujer f regañona, arpía f

shrewd ['ʃru:d] adj : astuto, inteligente, sagaz — **shrewdly** adv

shrewdness ['ʃru:dnəs] n : astucia f

shriek[1] ['ʃri:k] vi : chillar, gritar

shriek[2] n : chillido m, alarido m, grito m

shrill ['ʃrɪl] adj : agudo, estridente

shrilly ['ʃrɪli] adv : agudamente

shrimp ['ʃrɪmp] n : camarón m, langostino m

shrine ['ʃraɪn] n 1 TOMB : sepulcro m (de un santo) 2 SANCTUARY : lugar m sagrado, santuario m

shrink ['ʃrɪŋk] vi **shrank** ['ʃræŋk] or **shrunk** ['ʃrʌŋk]; **shrunk** or **shrunken** ['ʃrʌŋkən]; **shrinking** 1 RECOIL : retroceder ⟨he shrank back : se echó para atrás⟩ 2 : encogerse (dícese de la ropa)

shrinkage ['ʃrɪŋkɪʤ] n : encogimiento m (de ropa, etc.), contracción f, reducción f

shrivel ['ʃrɪvəl] vi -**veled** or -**velled**; -**veling** or -**velling** : arrugarse, marchitarse

shroud[1] ['ʃraʊd] vt : envolver

shroud[2] n 1 : sudario m, mortaja f 2 VEIL : velo m ⟨wrapped in a shroud of mystery : envuelto en un aura de misterio⟩

shrub ['ʃrʌb] n : arbusto m, mata f

shrubbery ['ʃrʌbəri] n, pl -**beries** : arbustos mpl, matas fpl

shrug ['ʃrʌɡ] vi **shrugged; shrugging** : encogerse de hombros

shrunk → **shrink**

shuck[1] ['ʃʌk] vt : pelar (mazorcas, etc.), abrir (almejas, etc.)

shuck[2] n 1 HUSK : cascarilla f, cáscara f (de una nuez, etc.), hojas fpl (de una mazorca) 2 SHELL : concha f (de una almeja, etc.)

shudder[1] ['ʃʌdər] vi : estremecerse

shudder[2] n : estremecimiento m, escalofrío m

shuffle[1] ['ʃʌfəl] v -**fled; -fling** vt MIX : mezclar, revolver, barajar (naipes) — vi : caminar arrastrando los pies

shuffle² n 1 : acto m de revolver ⟨each player gets a shuffle : a cada jugador le toca barajar⟩ 2 JUMBLE : revoltijo m 3 : arrastramiento m de los pies

shun [ˈʃʌn] vi **shunned; shunning** : evitar, esquivar, eludir

shunt [ˈʃʌnt] vt : desviar, cambiar de vía (un tren)

shut [ˈʃʌt] v **shut; shutting** vt 1 CLOSE : cerrar ⟨shut the lid : tápalo⟩ 2 **to shut out** EXCLUDE : excluir, dejar fuera a (personas), no dejar que entre (luz, ruido, etc.) 3 **to shut up** CONFINE : encerrar — vi : cerrarse ⟨the factory shut down : la fábrica cerró suspuertas⟩

shut–in [ˈʃʌtˌɪn] n : inválido m, -da f (que no puede salir de casa)

shutter [ˈʃʌtər] n 1 : contraventana f, postigo m (de una ventana o puerta) 2 : obturador m (de una cámara)

shuttle¹ [ˈʃʌtəl] v **-tled; -tling** vt : transportar ⟨she shuttled him back and forth : lo llevaba de acá para allá⟩ — vi : ir y venir

shuttle² n 1 : lanzadera f (para tejer) 2 : vehículo m que hace recorridos cortos 3 → **space shuttle**

shuttlecock [ˈʃʌtəlˌkɑk] n : volante m

shut up vi : callarse ⟨shut up! : ¡cállate (la boca)!⟩

shy¹ [ˈʃaɪ] vi **shied; shying** : retroceder, asustarse

shy² adj **shier** or **shyer** [ˈʃaɪər]; **shiest** or **shyest** [ˈʃaɪəst] 1 TIMID : tímido 2 WARY : cauteloso ⟨he's not shy about asking : no vacila en preguntar⟩ 3 SHORT : corto (de dinero, etc.) ⟨I'm two dollars shy : me faltan dos dólares⟩

shyly [ˈʃaɪli] adv : tímidamente

shyness [ˈʃaɪnəs] n : timidez f

Siamese¹ [ˌsaɪəˈmiːz, -ˈmiːs-] adj : siamés ⟨Siamese twins : hermanos siameses⟩

Siamese² n 1 : siamés m, -mesa f 2 : siamés m (idioma) 3 or **Siamese cat** : gato m siamés

sibling [ˈsɪblɪŋ] n : hermano m, hermana f

Sicilian [səˈsɪljən] n : siciliano m, -na f — **Sicilian** adj

sick [ˈsɪk] adj 1 : enfermo 2 NAUSEOUS : mareado, con náuseas ⟨to get sick : vomitar⟩ 3 : para uso de enfermos ⟨sick day : día de permiso (por enfermedad)⟩

sickbed [ˈsɪkˌbɛd] n : lecho m de enfermo

sicken [ˈsɪkən] vt 1 : poner enfermo 2 REVOLT : darle asco (a alguien) — vi : enfermar(se), caer enfermo

sickening [ˈsɪkənɪŋ] adj : asqueroso, repugnante, nauseabundo

sickle [ˈsɪkəl] n : hoz f

sickly [ˈsɪkli] adj **sicklier; -est** 1 : enfermizo 2 → **sickening**

sickness [ˈsɪknəs] n 1 : enfermedad f 2 NAUSEA : náuseas fpl

side [ˈsaɪd] n 1 : lado m, costado m (de una persona), ijada f (de un animal) 2

: lado m, cara f (de una moneda, etc.) 3 : lado m, parte f ⟨he's on my side : está de mi parte⟩ ⟨to take sides : tomar partido⟩

sideboard [ˈsaɪdˌbord] n : aparador m

sideburns [ˈsaɪdˌbərnz] npl : patillas fpl

sided [ˈsaɪdəd] adj : que tiene lados ⟨one-sided : de un lado⟩

side effect n : efecto m secundario

sideline [ˈsaɪdˌlaɪn] n 1 : línea f de banda (en deportes) 2 : actividad f suplementaria (en negocios) 3 **to be on the sidelines** : estar al margen

sidelong [ˈsaɪdˌlɔŋ] adj : de reojo, de soslayo

sideshow [ˈsaɪdˌʃoː] n : espectáculo m secundario, atracción f secundaria

sidestep [ˈsaɪdˌstɛp] v **-stepped; -stepping** vt : dar un paso hacia un lado — vt AVOID : esquivar, eludir

sidetrack [ˈsaɪdˌtræk] vt : desviar (una conversación, etc.), distraer (a una persona)

sidewalk [ˈsaɪdˌwɔk] n : acera f, vereda f, andén m CA, Col, banqueta f Mex

sideways¹ [ˈsaɪdˌweɪz] adv 1 : hacia un lado ⟨it leaned sideways : se inclinaba hacia un lado⟩ 2 : de lado, de costado ⟨lie sideways : acuéstese de costado⟩

sideways² adj : hacia un lado ⟨a sideways glance : una mirada de reojo⟩

siding [ˈsaɪdɪŋ] n 1 : apartadero m (para trenes) 2 : revestimiento m exterior (de un edificio)

sidle [ˈsaɪdəl] vi **-dled; -dling** : moverse furtivamente

siege [ˈsiːdʒ, ˈsiːʒ] n : sitio m ⟨to be under siege : estar sitiado⟩

siesta [siˈɛstə] n : siesta f

sieve [ˈsɪv] n : tamiz m, cedazo m, criba f (en mineralogía)

sift [ˈsɪft] vt 1 : tamizar, cerner ⟨sift the flour : tamice la harina⟩ 2 or **to sift through** : examinar cuidadosamente, pasar por el tamiz

sifter [ˈsɪftər] n : tamiz m, cedazo m

sigh¹ [ˈsaɪ] vi : suspirar

sigh² n : suspiro m

sight¹ [ˈsaɪt] vt : ver (a una persona), divisar (la tierra, un barco)

sight² n 1 : vista f (facultad) ⟨out of sight : fuera de vista⟩ 2 : algo visto ⟨it's a familiar sight : se ve con frecuencia⟩ ⟨she's a sight for sore eyes : da gusto verla⟩ 3 : lugar m de interés (para turistas, etc.) 4 : mira f (de un rifle, etc.) 5 GLIMPSE : mirada f breve ⟨I caught sight of her : la divisé, alcancé a verla⟩

sighting [ˈsaɪtɪŋ] n : avistamiento m

sightless [ˈsaɪtləs] adj : invidente, ciego

sightseer [ˈsaɪtˌsiːər] n : turista mf

sign¹ [ˈsaɪn] vt 1 : firmar ⟨to sign a check : firmar un cheque⟩ 2 or **to sign on** HIRE : contratar (a un empleado), fichar (a un jugador) — vi 1 : hacer una seña ⟨she signed for him to stop : le hizo una seña para que se parara⟩ 2 : comunicarse por señas

sign² *n* **1** SYMBOL : símbolo *m*, signo *m* ⟨minus sign : signo de menos⟩ **2** GESTURE : seña *f*, señal *f*, gesto *m* **3** : letrero *m*, cartel *m* ⟨neon sign : letrero de neón⟩ **4** TRACE : señal *f*, indicio *m*

signal¹ ['sɪɡnəl] *vt* **-naled** *or* **-nalled; -naling** *or* **-nalling 1** : hacerle señas (a alguien) ⟨she signaled me to leave : me hizo señas para que saliera⟩ **2** INDICATE : señalar, indicar — *vi* : hacer señas, comunicar por señas

signal² *adj* NOTABLE : señalado, notable

signal³ *n* : señal *f*

signature ['sɪɡnə,tʃʊr] *n* : firma *f*

signet ['sɪɡnət] *n* : sello *m*

significance [sɪɡ'nɪfɪkənts] *n* **1** MEANING : significado *m* **2** IMPORTANCE : importancia *f*

significant [sɪɡ'nɪfɪkənt] *adj* **1** IMPORTANT : importante **2** MEANINGFUL : significativo — **significantly** *adv*

signify ['sɪɡnə,faɪ] *vt* **-fied; -fying 1** : indicar ⟨he signified his desire for more : haciendo señas indicó que quería más⟩ **2** MEAN : significar

sign language *n* : lenguaje *m* por señas

signpost ['saɪn,po:st] *n* : poste *m* indicador

silence¹ ['saɪlənts] *vt* **-lenced; -lencing** : silenciar, acallar

silence² *n* : silencio *m*

silent ['saɪlənt] *adj* **1** : callado ⟨to remain silent : quedarse callado, guardar silencio⟩ **2** QUIET, STILL : silencioso **3** MUTE : mudo ⟨a silent letter : una letra muda⟩

silently ['saɪləntli] *adv* : silenciosamente, calladamente

silhouette¹ [,sɪlə'wɛt] *vt* **-etted; -etting** : destacar la silueta de ⟨it was silhouetted against the sky : se perfilaba contra el cielo⟩

silhouette² *n* : silueta *f*

silica ['sɪlɪkə] *n* : sílice *f*

silicon ['sɪlɪkən, -,kɑn] *n* : silicio *m*

silk ['sɪlk] *n* : seda *f*

silken ['sɪlkən] *adj* **1** : de seda ⟨a silken veil : un velo de seda⟩ **2** SILKY : sedoso ⟨silken hair : cabellos sedosos⟩

silkworm ['sɪlk,wərm] *n* : gusano *m* de seda

silky ['sɪlki] *adj* **silkier; -est** : sedoso

sill ['sɪl] *n* : alféizar *m* (de una ventana), umbral *m* (de una puerta)

silliness ['sɪlinəs] *n* : tontería *f*, estupidez *f*

silly ['sɪli] *adj* **sillier; -est** : tonto, estúpido, ridículo

silo ['saɪ,lo:] *n, pl* **silos** : silo *m*

silt ['sɪlt] *n* : cieno *m*

silver¹ ['sɪlvər] *adj* **1** : de plata ⟨a silver spoon : una cuchara de plata⟩ **2** → silvery

silver² *n* **1** : plata *f* **2** COINS : monedas *fpl* **3** → silverware **4** : color *m* plata

silverware ['sɪlvər,wær] *n* **1** : artículos *mpl* de plata, platería *f* **2** FLATWARE : cubertería *f*

silvery ['sɪlvəri] *adj* : plateado

similar ['sɪmələr] *adj* : similar, parecido, semejante

similarity [,sɪmə'lærəṭi] *n, pl* **-ties** : semejanza *f*, parecido *m*

similarly ['sɪmələrli] *adv* : de manera similar

simile ['sɪmə,li:] *n* : símil *m*

simmer ['sɪmər] *v* : hervir a fuego lento

simper¹ ['sɪmpər] *vi* : sonreír como un tonto

simper² *n* : sonrisa *f* tonta

simple ['sɪmpəl] *adj* **simpler; -plest 1** INNOCENT : inocente **2** PLAIN : sencillo, simple **3** EASY : simple, sencillo, fácil **4** STRAIGHTFORWARD : puro, simple ⟨the simple truth : la pura verdad⟩ **5** NAIVE : ingenuo, simple

simpleton ['sɪmpəltən] *n* : bobo *m*, -ba *f*; tonto *m*, -ta *f*

simplicity [sɪm'plɪsəṭi] *n* : simplicidad *f*, sencillez *f*

simplification [,sɪmpləfə'keɪʃən] *n* : simplificación *f*

simplify ['sɪmplə,faɪ] *vt* **-fied; -fying** : simplificar

simply ['sɪmpli] *adv* **1** PLAINLY : sencillamente **2** SOLELY : simplemente, sólo **3** REALLY : absolutamente

simulate ['sɪmjə,leɪt] *vt* **-lated; -lating** : simular

simulation [,sɪmjə'leɪʃən] *n* : simulación *f*

simultaneous [,saɪməl'teɪniəs] *adj* : simultáneo — **simultaneously** *adv*

sin¹ ['sɪn] *vi* **sinned; sinning** : pecar

sin² *n* : pecado *m*

since¹ ['sɪnts] *adv* **1** : desde entonces ⟨they've been friends ever since : desde entonces han sido amigos⟩ ⟨she's since become mayor : más tarde se hizo alcalde⟩ **2** AGO : hace ⟨he's long since dead : murió hace mucho⟩

since² *conj* **1** : desde que ⟨since he was born : desde que nació⟩ **2** INASMUCH AS : ya que, puesto que, dado que

since³ *prep* : desde

sincere [sɪn'sɪr] *adj* **-cerer; -est** : sincero — **sincerely** *adv*

sincerity [sɪn'sɛrəṭi] *n* : sinceridad *f*

sinew ['sɪnju:, 'sɪ,nu:] *n* **1** TENDON : tendón *m*, nervio *m* (en la carne) **2** POWER : fuerza *f*

sinewy ['sɪnjui, 'sɪnʊi] *adj* **1** STRINGY : fibroso **2** STRONG, WIRY : fuerte, nervudo

sinful ['sɪnfəl] *adj* : pecador (dícese de las personas), pecaminoso

sing ['sɪŋ] *v* **sang** ['sæŋ] *or* **sung** ['sʌŋ]; **sung; singing** : cantar

singe ['sɪndʒ] *vt* **singed; singeing** : chamuscar, quemar

singer ['sɪŋər] *n* : cantante *mf*

single¹ ['sɪŋgəl] *vt* **-gled; -gling** *or* **to single out** **1** SELECT : escoger **2** DISTINGUISH : señalar

single² *adj* **1** UNMARRIED : soltero **2** SOLE : solo ⟨a single survivor : un solo sobreviviente) ⟨every single one : cada uno, todos⟩

single³ *n* **1** : soltero *m*, -ra *f* ⟨for married couples and singles : para los matrimonios y los solteros⟩ **2** *or* **single room** : habitación *f* individual **3** DOLLAR : billete *m* de un dólar

single–handed ['sɪŋɡəl'hændəd] *adj* : sin ayuda, solo

singly ['sɪŋɡli] *adv* : individualmente, uno por uno

singular¹ ['sɪŋɡjələr] *adj* **1** : singular (en gramática) **2** OUTSTANDING : singular, sobresaliente **3** STRANGE : singular, extraño

singular² *n* : singular *m*

singularity [,sɪŋɡjə'lærəṭi] *n*, *pl* **-ties** : singularidad *f*

singularly ['sɪŋɡjələrli] *adv* : singularmente

sinister ['sɪnəstər] *adj* : siniestro

sink¹ ['sɪŋk] *v* **sank** ['sæŋk] *or* **sunk** ['sʌŋk]; **sunk; sinking** *vi* **1** : hundirse (dícese de un barco) **2** DROP, FALL : descender, caer ⟨to sink into a chair : dejarse caer en una silla⟩ ⟨his heart sank : se le cayó el alma a los pies⟩ **3** DECREASE : bajar — *vt* **1** : hundir (un barco, etc.) **2** EXCAVATE : excavar (un pozo para minar), perforar (un pozo de agua) **3** PLUNGE, STICK : clavar, hincar **4** INVEST : invertir (fondos)

sink² *n* **1** kitchen sink : fregadero *m*, lavaplatos *m* *Chile, Col, Mex* **2** bathroom sink : lavabo *m*, lavamanos *m*

sinner ['sɪnər] *n* : pecador *m*, -dora *f*

sinuous ['sɪnjʊəs] *adj* : sinuoso — **sinuously** *adv*

sinus ['saɪnəs] *n* : seno *m*

sip¹ ['sɪp] *v* **sipped; sipping** *vt* : sorber — *vi* : beber a sorbos

sip² *n* : sorbo *m*

siphon¹ ['saɪfən] *vt* : sacar con sifón

siphon² *n* : sifón *m*

sir ['sər] *n* **1** (*in titles*) : sir *m* **2** (*as a form of address*) : señor *m* ⟨Dear Sir : Muy señor mío⟩ ⟨yes sir! : ¡sí, señor!⟩

sire¹ ['saɪr] *vt* **sired; siring** : engendrar, ser el padre de

sire² *n* : padre *m*

siren ['saɪrən] *n* : sirena *f*

sirloin ['sər,lɔɪn] *n* : solomillo *m*

sirup → syrup

sisal ['saɪsəl, -zəl] *n* : sisal *m*

sissy ['sɪsi] *n*, *pl* **-sies** : mariquita *f fam*

sister ['sɪstər] *n* **1** : hermana *f* **2 Sister** : hermana *f*, Sor *f* ⟨Sister Mary : Sor María⟩

sisterhood ['sɪstər,hʊd] *n* **1** : condición *f* de ser hermana **2** : sociedad *f* de mujeres

sister–in–law ['sɪstərɪn,lɔ] *n*, *pl* **sisters–in–law** : cuñada *f*

sisterly ['sɪstərli] *adj* : de hermana

sit ['sɪt] *v* **sat** ['sæt]; **sitting** *vi* **1** : sentarse, estar sentado ⟨he sat down : se sentó⟩ **2** ROOST : posarse **3** : sesionar ⟨the legislature is sitting : la legislatu-

ra está en sesión⟩ **4** POSE : posar (un retrato) **5** LIE, REST : estar (ubicado) ⟨the house sits on a hill : la casa está en una colina⟩ — *vt* SEAT : sentar, colocar ⟨I sat him on the sofa : lo senté en el sofá⟩

sitcom ['sɪt,kɑm] **→ situation comedy**

site ['saɪt] *n* **1** PLACE : sitio *m*, lugar *m* **2** LOCATION : emplazamiento *m*, ubicación *f*

sitter ['sɪtər] **→ baby–sitter**

sitting room → living room

situated ['sɪtʃʊ,eɪṭəd] *adj* LOCATED : ubicado, situado

situation [,sɪtʃʊ'eɪʃən] *n* **1** LOCATION : situación *f*, ubicación *f*, emplazamiento *m* **2** CIRCUMSTANCES : situación *f* **3** JOB : empleo *m*

situation comedy *n* : comedia *f* de situación

six¹ ['sɪks] *adj* : seis

six² *n* : seis *m*

six–gun ['sɪks,ɡʌn] *n* : revólver *m* (con seis cámaras)

six hundred¹ *adj* : seiscientos

six hundred² *n* : seiscientos *m*

six–shooter ['sɪks,ʃuːṭər] **→ six–gun**

sixteen¹ [sɪks'tiːn] *adj* : dieciséis

sixteen² *n* : dieciséis *m*

sixteenth¹ [sɪks'tiːnθ] *adj* : decimosexto

sixteenth² *n* **1** : decimosexto *m*, -ta *f* (en una serie) **2** : dieciseisavo *m*, dieciseisava parte *f*

sixth¹ ['sɪksθ, 'sɪkst] *adj* : sexto

sixth² *n* **1** : sexto *m*, -ta *f* (en una serie) **2** : sexto *m*, sexta parte *f*

sixtieth¹ ['sɪkstiəθ] *adj* : sexagésimo

sixtieth² *n* **1** : sexagésimo *m*, -ma *f* (en una serie) **2** : sesentavo *m*, sesentava parte *f*

sixty¹ ['sɪksti] *adj* : sesenta

sixty² *n*, *pl* **-ties** : sesenta *m*

sizable *or* **sizeable** ['saɪzəbəl] *adj* : considerable

size¹ ['saɪz] *vt* **sized; sizing 1** : clasificar según el tamaño **2 to size up** : evaluar, apreciar

size² *n* **1** DIMENSIONS : tamaño *m*, talla *f* (de ropa), número *m* (de zapatos) **2** MAGNITUDE : magnitud *f*

sizzle ['sɪzəl] *vi* **-zled; -zling** : chisporrotear

skate¹ ['skeɪt] *vi* **skated; skating** : patinar

skate² *n* **1** : patín *m* ⟨roller skate : patín de ruedas⟩ **2** : raya *f* (pez)

skateboard ['skeɪt,bɔrd] *n* : monopatín *m*

skater ['skeɪṭər] *n* : patinador *m*, -dora *f*

skein ['skeɪn] *n* : madeja *f*

skeletal ['skljtal] *adj* **1** : óseo (en anatomía) **2** EMACIATED : esquelético

skeleton ['skɛlətən] *n* **1** : esqueleto *m* (anatómico) **2** FRAMEWORK : armazón *mf*

skeptic ['skɛptɪk] *n* : escéptico *m*, -ca *f*

skeptical ['skɛptɪkəl] *adj* : escéptico

skepticism ['skɛptə,sɪzəm] *n* : escepticismo *m*

sketch¹ ['skɛtʃ] *vt* : bosquejar — *vi* : hacer bosquejos

sketch² *n* **1** DRAWING, OUTLINE : esbozo *m*, bosquejo *m* **2** ESSAY : ensayo *m*

sketchy ['skɛtʃi] *adj* **sketchier; -est** : incompleto, poco detallado

skewer¹ ['skju:ər] *vt* : ensartar (carne, etc.)

skewer² *n* : brocheta *f*, broqueta *f*

ski ['ski:] *vi* **skied; skiing** : esquiar

ski² *n, pl* **skis** : esquí *m*

skid¹ ['skɪd] *vi* **skidded; skidding** : derrapar, patinar

skid² *n* : derrape *m*, patinazo *m*

skier ['ski:ər] *n* : esquiador *m*, -dora *f*

skiff ['skɪf] *n* : esquife *m*

skill ['skɪl] *n* **1** DEXTERITY : habilidad *f*, destreza *f* **2** CAPABILITY : capacidad *f*, arte *m*, técnica *f* ⟨organizational skills : la capacidad para organizar⟩

skilled ['skɪld] *adj* : hábil, experto

skillet ['skɪlət] *n* : sartén *mf*

skillful ['skɪlfəl] *adj* : hábil, diestro

skillfully ['skɪlfəli] *adv* : con habilidad, con destreza

skim¹ ['skɪm] *vt* **skimmed; skimming 1** *or* **to skim off** : espumar, descremar (leche) **2** : echarle un vistazo a (un libro, etc.), pasar rozando (una superficie)

skim² *adj* : descremado ⟨skim milk : leche descremada⟩

skimp ['skɪmp] *vi* **to skimp on** : escatimar

skimpy ['skɪmpi] *adj* **skimpier; -est** : exiguo, escaso, raquítico

skin¹ ['skɪn] *vt* **skinned; skinning** : despellejar, desollar

skin² *n* **1** : piel *f*, cutis *m* (de la cara) ⟨dark skin : piel morena⟩ **2** RIND : piel *f*

skin diving *n* : buceo *m*, submarinismo *m*

skinflint ['skɪn,flɪnt] *n* : tacaño *m*, -ña *f*

skinned ['skɪnd] *adj* : de piel ⟨tough-skinned : de piel dura⟩

skinny ['skɪni] *adj* **skinnier; -est** : flaco

skip¹ ['skɪp] *vi* **skipped; skipping** : ir dando brincos — *vt* : saltarse

skip² *n* : brinco *m*, salto *m*

skipper ['skɪpər] *n* : capitán *m*, -tana *f*

skirmish¹ ['skərmɪʃ] *vi* : escaramuzar

skirmish² *n* : escaramuza *f*, refriega *f*

skirt¹ ['skərt] *vt* **1** BORDER : bordear **2** EVADE : evadir, esquivar

skirt² *n* : falda *f*, pollera *f*

skit ['skɪt] *n* : sketch *m* (teatral)

skittish ['skɪtɪʃ] *adj* : asustadizo, nervioso

skulk ['skʌlk] *vi* : merodear

skull ['skʌl] *n* **1** : cráneo *m*, calavera *f* **2 skull and crossbones** : calavera *f* (bandera pirata)

skunk ['skʌŋk] *n* : zorrillo *m*, mofeta *f*

sky ['skaɪ] *n, pl* **skies** : cielo *m*

skylark ['skaɪ,lɑrk] *n* : alondra *f*

skylight ['skaɪ,laɪt] *n* : claraboya *f*, tragaluz *m*

skyline ['skaɪ,laɪn] *n* : horizonte *m*

skyrocket ['skaɪ,rɑkət] *vi* : dispararse

skyscraper ['skaɪ,skreɪpər] *n* : rascacielos *m*

slab ['slæb] *n* : losa *f* (de piedra), tabla *f* (de madera), pedazo *m* grueso (de pan, etc.)

slack¹ ['slæk] *adj* **1** CARELESS : descuidado, negligente **2** LOOSE : flojo **3** SLOW : de poco movimiento

slack² *n* **1** : parte *f* floja ⟨to take up the slack : tensar (una cuerda, etc.)⟩ **2 slacks** *npl* : pantalones *mpl*

slacken ['slækən] *vt* : aflojar — *vi* : aflojarse

slacker ['slækər] *n* : vago *m*, -ga *f*; holgazán *m*, -zana *f*

slag ['slæg] *n* : escoria *f*

slain → **slay**

slake ['sleɪk] *vt* **slaked; slaking** : saciar (la sed), satisfacer (la curiosidad)

slam¹ ['slæm] *v* **slammed; slamming** *vt* **1** : cerrar de golpe ⟨he slammed the door : dio un portazo⟩ **2** : tirar o dejar caer de golpe ⟨he slammed down the book : dejó caer el libro de un golpe⟩ — *vi* **1** : cerrarse de golpe **2 to slam into** : chocar contra

slam² *n* : golpe *m*, portazo *m* (de una puerta)

slander¹ ['slændər] *vt* : calumniar, difamar

slander² *n* : calumnia *f*, difamación *f*

slanderous ['slændərəs] *adj* : difamatorio, calumnioso

slang ['slæŋ] *n* : argot *m*, jerga *f*

slant¹ ['slænt] *vi* : inclinarse, ladearse — *vt* **1** SLOPE : inclinar **2** ANGLE : sesgar, orientar, dirigir ⟨a story slanted towards youth : un artículo dirigido a los jóvenes⟩

slant² *n* **1** INCLINE : inclinación *f* **2** PERSPECTIVE : perspectiva *f*, enfoque *m*

slap¹ ['slæp] *vt* **slapped; slapping** : abofetear, cachetear, dar una palmada (en la espalda, etc.)

slap² *n* : bofetada *f*, cachetada *f*, palmada *f*

slash¹ ['slæʃ] *vt* **1** GASH : cortar, hacer un tajo en **2** REDUCE : reducir, rebajar (precios)

slash² *n* : tajo *m*, corte *m*

slat ['slæt] *n* : tablilla *f*, listón *m*

slate ['sleɪt] *n* **1** : pizarra *f* ⟨a slate roof : un techo de pizarra⟩ **2** : lista *f* de candidatos (políticos)

slaughter¹ ['slɔtər] *vt* **1** BUTCHER : matar (animales) **2** MASSACRE : masacrar (personas)

slaughter² *n* **1** : matanza *f* (de animales) **2** MASSACRE : masacre *f*, carnicería *f*

slaughterhouse ['slɔtər,haʊs] *n* : matadero *m*

Slav ['slɑv, 'slæv] *n* : eslavo *m*, -va *f*

slave¹ ['sleɪv] *vi* **slaved; slaving** : trabajar como un burro

slave² *n* : esclavo *m*, -va *f*

slaver ['slævər, 'sleɪ-] *vi* : babear

slavery ['sleɪvəri] *n* : esclavitud *f*
Slavic ['slɑvɪk, 'slæ-] *adj* : eslavo
slavish ['sleɪvɪʃ] *adj* 1 SERVILE : servil 2 IMITATIVE : poco original
slay ['sleɪ] *vt* slew ['sluː]; slain ['sleɪn]; slaying : asesinar, matar
slayer ['sleɪər] *n* : asesino *m*, -na *f*
sleazy ['sliːzi] *adj* sleazier; -est 1 SHODDY : chapucero, de mala calidad 2 DILAPIDATED : ruinoso 3 DISREPUTABLE : de mala fama
sled¹ ['slɛd] *v* sledded; sledding *vi* : ir en trineo — *vt* : transportar en trineo
sled² *n* : trineo *m*
sledge ['slɛdʒ] *n* 1 : trineo *m* (grande) 2 → sledgehammer
sledgehammer ['slɛdʒ,hæmər] *n* : almádena *f*, combo *m* Chile, Peru
sleek¹ ['sliːk] *vt* SLICK : alisar
sleek² *adj* : liso y brillante
sleep¹ ['sliːp] *vi* slept ['slɛpt]; sleeping : dormir
sleep² *n* 1 : sueño *m* 2 to go to sleep : dormirse
sleeper ['sliːpər] *n* 1 : durmiente *mf* ⟨to be a light sleeper : tener el sueño ligero⟩ 2 *or* sleeping car : coche *m* cama, coche *m* dormitorio
sleepily ['sliːpəli] *adv* : de manera somnolienta
sleepiness ['sliːpinəs] *n* : somnolencia *f*
sleepless ['sliːpləs] *adj* : sin dormir, desvelado ⟨to have a sleepless night : pasar la noche en blanco⟩
sleepwalker ['sliːp,wɔkər] *n* : sonámbulo *m*, -la *f*
sleepy ['sliːpi] *adj* sleepier; -est 1 DROWSY : somnoliento, soñoliento ⟨to be sleepy : tener sueño⟩ 2 LETHARGIC : aletargado, letárgico
sleet¹ ['sliːt] *vi* to be sleeting : caer aguanieve
sleet² *n* : aguanieve *f*
sleeve ['sliːv] *n* : manga *f* (de una camisa, etc.)
sleeveless ['sliːvləs] *adj* : sin mangas
sleigh¹ ['sleɪ] *vi* : ir en trineo
sleigh² *n* : trineo *m* (tirado por caballos)
sleight of hand [,slaɪtəv'hænd] : prestidigitación *f*, juegos *mpl* de manos
slender ['slɛndər] *adj* 1 SLIM : esbelto, delgado 2 SCANTY : exiguo, escaso ⟨a slender hope : una esperanza lejana⟩
sleuth ['sluːθ] *n* : detective *mf*; sabueso *m*, -sa *f*
slew → slay
slice¹ ['slaɪs] *vt* sliced; slicing : cortar
slice² *n* : rebanada *f*, tajada *f*, lonja *f* (de carne, etc.), rodaja *f* (de una verdura, fruta, etc.), trozo *m* (de pastel, etc.)
slick¹ ['slɪk] *vt* : alisar
slick² *adj* 1 SLIPPERY : resbaladizo, resbaloso 2 CRAFTY : astuto, taimado
slicker ['slɪkər] *n* : impermeable *m*
slide¹ ['slaɪd] *v* slid ['slɪd]; sliding ['slaɪdɪŋ] *vi* 1 SLIP : resbalar 2 GLIDE : deslizarse 3 DECLINE : bajar ⟨to let

things slide : dejar pasar las cosas⟩ — *vt* : correr, deslizar
slide² *n* 1 SLIDING : deslizamiento *m* 2 SLIP : resbalón *m* 3 : tobogán *m* (para niños) 4 TRANSPARENCY : diapositiva *f* (fotográfica) 5 DECLINE : descenso *m*
slier, sliest → sly
slight¹ ['slaɪt] *vt* : desairar, despreciar
slight² *adj* 1 SLENDER : esbelto, delgado 2 FLIMSY : endeble 3 TRIFLING : leve, insignificante ⟨a slight pain : un leve dolor⟩ 4 SMALL : pequeño, ligero ⟨not in the slightest : en absoluto⟩
slight³ *n* SNUB : desaire *m*
slightly ['slaɪtli] *adv* : ligeramente, un poco
slim¹ ['slɪm] *v* slimmed; slimming : adelgazar
slim² *adj* slimmer; slimmest 1 SLENDER : esbelto, delgado 2 SCANTY : exiguo, escaso
slime ['slaɪm] *n* 1 : baba *f* (secretada por un animal) 2 MUD, SILT : fango *m*, cieno *m*
slimy ['slaɪmi] *adj* slimier; -est : viscoso
sling¹ ['slɪŋ] *vt* slung ['slʌŋ]; slinging 1 THROW : lanzar, tirar 2 HANG : colgar
sling² *n* 1 : honda *f* (arma) 2 : cabestrillo *m* ⟨my arm is in a sling : llevo el brazo en cabestrillo⟩
slingshot ['slɪŋ,ʃɑt] *n* : tiragomas *m*, resortera *f* Mex
slink ['slɪŋk] *vi* slunk ['slʌŋk]; slinking : caminar furtivamente
slip¹ ['slɪp] *v* slipped; slipping *vi* 1 STEAL : ir sigilosamente ⟨to slip away : escabullirse⟩ ⟨to slip out the door : escaparse por la puerta⟩ 2 SLIDE : resbalarse, deslizarse 3 LAPSE : caer ⟨to slip into error : equivocarse⟩ 4 to let slip : dejar escapar 5 to slip into PUT ON : ponerse — *vt* 1 PUT : meter, poner 2 PASS : pasar ⟨she slipped me a note : me pasó una nota⟩ 3 to slip one's mind : olvidársele a uno
slip² *n* 1 PIER : atracadero *m* 2 MISHAP : percance *m*, contratiempo *m* 3 MISTAKE : error *m*, desliz *m* ⟨a slip of the tongue : un lapsus⟩ 4 PETTICOAT : enagua *f* 5 : injerto *m*, esqueje *m* (de una planta) 6 slip of paper : papelito *m*
slipper ['slɪpər] *n* : zapatilla *f*, pantufla *f*
slipperiness ['slɪpərinəs] *n* 1 : lo resbaloso, lo resbaladizo 2 TRICKINESS : astucia *f*
slippery ['slɪpəri] *adj* slipperier; -est 1 : resbaloso, resbaladizo ⟨a slippery road : un camino resbaloso⟩ 2 TRICKY : artero, astuto, taimado 3 ELUSIVE : huidizo, escurridizo
slipshod ['slɪp,ʃɑd] *adj* : descuidado, chapucero
slip up *vi* : equivocarse
slit¹ ['slɪt] *vt* slit; slitting : cortar, abrir por lo largo

slit² *n* **1** OPENING : abertura *f*, rendija *f* **2** CUT : corte *m*, raja *f*, tajo *m*

slither ['slɪðər] *vi* : deslizarse

sliver ['slɪvər] *n* : astilla *f*

slob ['slɑb] *n* : persona *f* desaliñada ⟨what a slob! : ¡qué cerdo!⟩

slobber¹ ['slɑbər] *vi* : babear

slobber² *n* : baba *f*

slogan ['slo:gən] *n* : lema *m*, eslogan *m*

sloop ['slu:p] *n* : balandra *f*

slop¹ ['slɑp] *v* **slopped; slopping** *vt* : derramar — *vi* : derramarse

slop² *n* : bazofia *f*

slope¹ ['slo:p] *vi* **sloped; sloping** : inclinarse ⟨the road slopes upward : el camino sube (en pendiente)⟩

slope² *n* : inclinación *f*, pendiente *f*, declive *m*

sloppy ['slɑpi] *adj* **sloppier; -est 1** MUDDY, SLUSHY : lodoso, fangoso **2** UNTIDY : descuidado (en el trabajo, etc.), desaliñado (de aspecto)

slot ['slɑt] *n* : ranura *f*

sloth ['slɔθ, 'slo:θ] *n* **1** LAZINESS : pereza *f* **2** : perezoso *m* (animal)

slouch¹ ['slaʊtʃ] *vi* : andar con los hombros caídos, repantigarse (en un sillón)

slouch² *n* **1** SLUMPING : mala postura *f* **2** BUNGLER, IDLER : haragán *m*, -gana *f*; inepto *m*, -ta *f* ⟨to be no slouch : no quedarse atrás⟩

slough¹ ['slʌf] *vt* : mudar de (piel)

slough² ['slu:, 'slaʊ] *n* SWAMP : ciénaga *f*

Slovak ['slo:vɑk, -væk] *or* **Slovakian** [slo:'vɑkiən, -'væ-] *n* : eslovaco *m*, -ca *f* — **Slovak** *or* **Slovakian** *adj*

Slovene ['slo:vi:n] *or* **Slovenian** [slo:'vi:niən] *n* : esloveno *m*, -na *f* — **Slovene** *or* **Slovenian** *adj*

slovenly ['slʌvənli, 'slɑv-] *adj* : descuidado (en el trabajo, etc.), desaliñado (de aspecto)

slow¹ [slo:] *vt* : retrasar, reducir la marcha de — *vi* : ir más despacio

slow² *adv* : despacio, lentamente

slow³ *adj* **1** : lento ⟨a slow process : un proceso lento⟩ **2** : atrasado ⟨my watch is slow : mi reloj está atrasado, mi reloj se atrasa⟩ **3** SLUGGISH : lento, poco activo **4** STUPID : lento, torpe, corto de alcances

slowly [slo:li] *adv* : lentamente, despacio

slowness [slo:nəs] *n* : lentitud *f*, torpeza *f*

sludge ['slʌdʒ] *n* : aguas *fpl* negras, aguas *fpl* residuales

slug¹ ['slʌg] *vt* **slugged; slugging** : pegarle un porrazo (a alguien)

slug² *n* **1** : babosa *f* (molusco) **2** BULLET : bala *f* **3** TOKEN : ficha *f* **4** BLOW : porrazo *m*, puñetazo *m*

sluggish ['slʌgɪʃ] *adj* : aletargado, lento

sluice¹ ['slu:s] *vt* **sluiced; sluicing** : lavar en agua corriente

sluice² *n* : canal *m*

slum ['slʌm] *n* : barriada *f*, barrio *m* bajo

slumber¹ ['slʌmbər] *vi* : dormir

slumber² *n* : sueño *m*

slump¹ ['slʌmp] *vi* **1** DECLINE, DROP : disminuir, bajar **2** SLOUCH : encorvarse, dejarse caer (en una silla, etc.)

slump² *n* : bajón *m*, declive *m* (económico)

slung → **sling**

slunk → **slink**

slur¹ ['slər] *vt* **slurred; slurring** : ligar (notas musicales), tragarse (las palabras)

slur² *n* **1** : ligado *m* (en música), mala pronunciación *f* (de las palabras) **2** ASPERSION : calumnia *f*, difamación *f*

slurp¹ ['slərp] *vi* : beber o comer haciendo ruido — *vt* : sorber ruidosamente

slurp² *n* : sorbo *m* (ruidoso)

slush ['slʌʃ] *n* : nieve *f* medio derretida

slut ['slʌt] *n* PROSTITUTE : ramera *f*, fulana *f*

sly ['slaɪ] *adj* **slier** ['slaɪər]; **sliest** ['slaɪəst] **1** CUNNING : astuto, taimado **2** UNDERHANDED : soplado — **slyly** *adv*

slyness ['slaɪnəs] *n* : astucia *f*

smack¹ ['smæk] *vi* **to smack of** : oler a, saber a — *vt* **1** KISS : besar, plantarle un beso a (alguien) **2** SLAP : pegarle una bofetada a (alguien) **3 to smack one's lips** : relamerse

smack² *adv* : justo, exactamente ⟨smack in the face : en plena cara⟩

smack³ *n* **1** TASTE, TRACE : sabor *m*, indicio *m* **2** : chasquido *m* (de los labios) **3** SLAP : bofetada *f* **4** KISS : beso *m*

small ['smɔl] *adj* **1** : pequeño, chico ⟨a small house : una casa pequeña⟩ ⟨small change : monedas de poco valor⟩ **2** TRIVIAL : pequeño, insignificante

smallness ['smɔlnəs] *n* : pequeñez *f*

smallpox ['smɔl.pɑks] *n* : viruela *f*

smart¹ ['smɑrt] *vi* **1** STING : escocer, picar, arder **2** HURT : dolerse, resentirse ⟨to smart under a rejection : dolerse ante un rechazo⟩

smart² *adj* **1** BRIGHT : listo, vivo, inteligente **2** STYLISH : elegante — **smartly** *adv*

smart³ *n* **1** PAIN : escozor *m*, dolor *m* **2 smarts** *npl* : inteligencia *f*

smartness ['smɑrtnəs] *n* **1** INTELLIGENCE : inteligencia *f* **2** ELEGANCE : elegancia *f*

smash¹ ['smæʃ] *vt* **1** BREAK : romper, quebrar, hacer pedazos **2** WRECK : destrozar, arruinar **3** CRASH : estrellar, chocar — *vi* **1** SHATTER : hacerse pedazos, hacerse añicos **2** COLLIDE, CRASH : estrellarse, chocar

smash² *n* **1** BLOW : golpe *m* **2** COLLISION : choque *m* **3** BANG, CRASH : estrépito *m*

smattering ['smætərɪŋ] *n* **1** : nociones *fpl* ⟨she has a smattering of programming : tiene nociones de programación⟩ **2** : un poco, unos cuantos ⟨a smattering of spectators : unos cuantos espectadores⟩

smear¹ ['smɪr] vt 1 DAUB : embadurnar, untar (mantequilla, etc.) 2 SMUDGE : emborronar 3 SLANDER : calumniar, difamar

smear² n 1 SMUDGE : mancha f 2 SLANDER : calumnia f

smell¹ ['smɛl] v smelled or smelt ['smɛlt]; smelling vt : oler, olfatear ⟨to smell danger : olfatear el peligro⟩ — vi : oler ⟨to smell good : oler bien⟩

smell² n 1 : olfato m, sentido m del olfato 2 ODOR : olor m

smelly ['smɛli] adj smellier; -est : maloliente

smelt¹ ['smɛlt] vt : fundir

smelt² n, pl smelts or smelt : eperlano m (pez)

smile¹ ['smaɪl] vi smiled; smiling : sonreír

smile² n : sonrisa f

smirk¹ ['smərk] vi : sonreír con suficiencia

smirk² n : sonrisa f satisfecha

smite ['smaɪt] vt smote ['smo:t]; smitten ['smɪtən] or smote; smiting 1 STRIKE : golpear 2 AFFLICT : afligir

smith ['smɪθ] n : herrero m, -ra f

smithy ['smɪθi] n, pl smithies : herrería f

smock ['smɑk] n : bata f, blusón m

smog ['smɑg, 'smɔg] n : smog m

smoke¹ ['smo:k] v smoked; smoking vi 1 : echar humo, humear ⟨a chimney that smokes : una chimenea que echa humo⟩ 2 : fumar ⟨I don't smoke : no fumo⟩ — vt : ahumar (carne, etc.)

smoke² n : humo m

smoke detector [dɪ'tɛktər] n : detector m de humo

smoker ['smo:kər] n : fumador m, -dora f

smokestack ['smo:k,stæk] n : chimenea f

smoky ['smo:ki] adj smokier; -est 1 SMOKING : humeante 2 : a humo ⟨a smoky flavor : un sabor a humo⟩ 3 : lleno de humo ⟨a smoky room : un cuarto lleno de humo⟩

smolder ['smo:ldər] vi 1 : arder sin llama 2 : arder (en el corazón) ⟨his anger smoldered : su rabia ardía⟩

smooth¹ ['smu:ð] vt : alisar

smooth² adj 1 : liso (dícese de una superficie) ⟨smooth skin : piel lisa⟩ 2 : suave (dícese de un movimiento) ⟨a smooth landing : un aterrizaje suave⟩ 3 : sin grumos ⟨a smooth sauce : una salsa sin grumos⟩ 4 : fluido ⟨smooth writing : escritura fluida⟩

smoothly ['smu:ðli] adv 1 GENTLY, SOFTLY : suavemente 2 EASILY : con facilidad, sin problemas

smoothness ['smu:ðnəs] n : suavidad f

smother ['smʌðər] vt 1 SUFFOCATE : ahogar, sofocar 2 COVER : cubrir 3 SUPPRESS : contener — vi : asfixiarse

smudge¹ ['smʌdʒ] v smudged; smudging vt : emborronar — vi : correrse

smudge² n : mancha f, borrón m

smug ['smʌg] adj smugger; smuggest : suficiente, pagado de sí mismo

smuggle ['smʌgəl] vt -gled; -gling : contrabandear, pasar de contrabando

smuggler ['smʌgələr] n : contrabandista mf

smugly ['smʌgli] adv : con suficiencia

smut ['smʌt] n 1 SOOT : tizne m, hollín m 2 FUNGUS : tizón m 3 OBSCENITY : obscenidad f, inmundicia f

smutty ['smʌti] adj smuttier; -est 1 SOOTY : tiznado 2 OBSCENE : obsceno, indecente

snack ['snæk] n : refrigerio m, bocado m, tentempié m fam ⟨an afternoon snack : una merienda⟩

snag¹ ['snæg] v snagged; snagging vt : enganchar — vi : engancharse

snag² n : problema m, inconveniente m

snail ['sneɪl] n : caracol m

snake ['sneɪk] n : culebra f, serpiente f

snakebite ['sneɪk,baɪt] n : mordedura f de serpiente

snap¹ ['snæp] v snapped; snapping vi 1 : intentar morder (dícese de un perro, etc.), picar (dícese de un pez) 2 : hablar con severidad ⟨he snapped at me! : ¡me gritó!⟩ 3 BREAK : romperse, quebrarse (haciendo un chasquido) — vt 1 BREAK : partir (en dos), quebrar 2 : hacer (algo) de un golpe ⟨to snap open : abrir de golpe⟩ 3 RETORT : decir bruscamente 4 CLICK : chasquear ⟨to snap one's fingers : chasquear los dedos⟩

snap² n 1 CLICK, CRACK : chasquido m 2 FASTENER : broche m 3 CINCH : cosa f fácil ⟨it's a snap : es facilísimo⟩

snapdragon ['snæp,drægən] n : dragón m (flor)

snapper ['snæpər] → red snapper

snappy ['snæpi] adj snappier; -est 1 FAST : rápido ⟨make it snappy! : ¡date prisa!⟩ 2 LIVELY : vivaz 3 CHILLY : frío 4 STYLISH : elegante

snapshot ['snæp,ʃɑt] n : instantánea f

snare¹ ['snær] vt snared; snaring : atrapar

snare² n : trampa f, red f

snare drum n : tambor m con bordón

snarl¹ ['snɑrl] vi 1 TANGLE : enmarañar, enredar 2 GROWL : gruñir

snarl² n 1 TANGLE : enredo m, maraña f 2 GROWL : gruñido m

snatch¹ ['snætʃ] vt : arrebatar

snatch² n : fragmento m

sneak¹ ['sni:k] vi : ir a hurtadillas — vt : hacer furtivamente ⟨to sneak a look : mirar con disimulo⟩ ⟨he sneaked a smoke : fumó un cigarrillo a escondidas⟩

sneak² n : soplón m, -plona f

sneakers ['sni:kərz] npl : tenis mpl, zapatillas fpl

sneaky ['sni:ki] adj sneakier; -est : solapado

sneer¹ ['snɪr] *vi* : sonreír con desprecio
sneer² *n* : sonrisa *f* de desprecio
sneeze¹ ['sni:z] *vi* **sneezed; sneezing** : estornudar
sneeze² *n* : estornudo *m*
snicker¹ ['snɪkər] *vi* : reírse disimuladamente
snicker² *n* : risita *f*
snide ['snaɪd] *adj* : sarcástico
sniff¹ ['snɪf] *vi* **1** SMELL : oler, husmear (dícese de los animales) **2 to sniff at** : despreciar, desdeñar — *vt* **1** SMELL : oler **2 to sniff out** : olerse, husmear
sniff² *n* **1** SNIFFING : aspiración *f* por la nariz **2** SMELL : olor *m*
sniffle ['snɪfəl] *vi* **-fled; -fling** : respirar con la nariz congestionada
sniffles ['snɪfəlz] *npl* : resfriado *m*
snip¹ ['snɪp] *vt* **snipped; snipping** : cortar (con tijeras)
snip² *n* : tijeretada *f*, recorte *m*
snipe¹ ['snaɪp] *vi* **sniped; sniping** : disparar
snipe² *n, pl* **snipes** *or* **snipe** : agachadiza *f*
sniper ['snaɪpər] *n* : francotirador *m*, -dora *f*
snippet ['snɪpət] *n* : fragmento *m* (de un texto, etc.)
snivel ['snɪvəl] *vi* **-veled** *or* **-velled; -veling** *or* **-velling 1** → **snuffle 2** WHINE : lloriquear
snob ['snɑb] *n* : esnob *mf*, snob *mf*
snobbery ['snɑbəri] *n, pl* **-beries** : esnobismo *m*
snobbish ['snɑbɪʃ] *adj* : esnob, snob
snobbishness ['snɑbɪʃnəs] *n* : esnobismo *m*
snoop¹ ['snu:p] *vi* : husmear, curiosear
snoop² *n* : fisgón *m*, -gona *f*
snooze¹ ['snu:z] *vi* **snoozed; snoozing** : dormitar
snooze² *n* : siestecita *f*, siestita *f*
snore¹ ['snor] *vi* **snored; snoring** : roncar
snore² *n* : ronquido *m*
snort¹ ['snɔrt] *vi* : bufar, resoplar
snort² *n* : bufido *m*, resoplo *m*
snout ['snaʊt] *n* : hocico *m*, morro *m*
snow¹ ['sno:] *vi* **1** : nevar ⟨I'm snowed in : estoy aislado por la nieve⟩ **2 to be snowed under** : estar inundado
snow² *n* : nieve *f*
snowball ['sno:ˌbɔl] *n* : bola *f* de nieve
snowdrift ['sno:ˌdrɪft] *n* : ventisquero *m*
snowfall ['sno:ˌfɔl] *n* : nevada *f*
snowplow ['sno:ˌplaʊ] *n* : quitanieves *m*
snowshoe ['sno:ˌʃu:] *n* : raqueta *f* (para nieve)
snowstorm ['sno:ˌstɔrm] *n* : tormenta *f* de nieve, ventisca *f*
snowy ['sno:i] *adj* **snowier; -est** : nevoso ⟨a snowy road : un camino nevado⟩
snub¹ ['snʌb] *vt* **snubbed; snubbing** : desairar
snub² *n* : desaire *m*
snub–nosed ['snʌbˌno:zd] *adj* : de nariz respingada

snuff¹ ['snʌf] *vt* **1** : apagar (una vela) **2** : sorber (algo) por la nariz
snuff² *n* : rapé *m*
snuffle ['snʌfəl] *vi* **-fled; -fling** : respirar con la nariz congestionada
snug ['snʌg] *adj* **snugger; snuggest 1** COMFORTABLE : cómodo **2** TIGHT : ajustado, ceñido ⟨snug pants : pantalones ajustados⟩
snuggle ['snʌgəl] *vi* **-gled; -gling** : acurrucarse ⟨to snuggle up to someone : arrimársele a alguien⟩
snugly ['snʌgli] *adv* **1** COMFORTABLY : cómodamente **2** : de manera ajustada ⟨the shirt fits snugly : la camisa queda ajustada⟩
so¹ ['so:] *adv* **1** (*referring to something indicated or suggested*) ⟨do you think so? : ¿tú crees?⟩ ⟨so it would seem : eso parece⟩ ⟨I told her so : se lo dije⟩ ⟨he's ready, or so he says : según dice, está listo⟩ ⟨it so happened that . . . : resultó que . . .⟩ ⟨do it like so : hazlo así⟩ ⟨so be it : así sea⟩ **2** ALSO : también ⟨so do I : yo también⟩ **3** THUS : así, de esta manera **4** : tan ⟨he'd never been so happy : nunca había estado tan contento⟩ **5** CONSEQUENTLY : por lo tanto
so² *conj* **1** THEREFORE : así que **2** *or* **so that** : para que, así que, de manera que ⟨**3 so what?** : ¿y qué?
soak¹ ['so:k] *vi* : estar en remojo — *vt* **1** : poner en remojo **2 to soak up** ABSORB : absorber
soak² *n* : remojo *m*
soap¹ ['so:p] *vt* : enjabonar
soap² *n* : jabón *m*
soapsuds ['so:pˌsʌdz] → **suds**
soapy ['so:pi] *adj* **soapier; -est** : jabonoso ⟨a soapy taste : un gusto a jabón⟩ ⟨a soapy texture : una textura de jabón⟩
soar ['sor] *vi* **1** FLY : volar **2** RISE : remontar el vuelo (dícese de las aves) ⟨her hopes soared : su esperanza renació⟩ ⟨prices are soaring : los precios están subiendo vertiginosamente⟩
sob¹ ['sɑb] *vi* **sobbed; sobbing** : sollozar
sob² *n* : sollozo *m*
sober ['so:bər] *adj* **1** : sobrio ⟨he's not sober enough to drive : está demasiado borracho para manejar⟩ **2** SERIOUS : serio
soberly ['so:bərli] *adv* **1** : sobriamente **2** SERIOUSLY : seriamente
sobriety [sə'braɪəṭi, so-] *n* **1** : sobriedad *f* ⟨sobriety test : prueba de alcoholemia⟩ **2** SERIOUSNESS : seriedad *f*
so–called ['so:ˈkɔld] *adj* : supuesto, presunto ⟨the so-called experts : los expertos, así llamados⟩
soccer ['sɑkər] *n* : futbol *m*, fútbol *m*
sociable ['so:ʃəbəl] *adj* : sociable
social¹ ['so:ʃəl] *adj* : social — **socially** *adv*
social² *n* : reunión *f* social

socialism [ˈsoːʃəˌlɪzəm] n : socialismo m
socialist[1] [ˈsoːʃəlɪst] adj : socialista
socialist[2] n : socialista mf
socialize [ˈsoːʃəˌlaɪz] v -ized; -izing vt 1
NATIONALIZE : nacionalizar 2 : so-
cializar (en psicología) — vi : alternar,
circular ⟨to socialize with friends : alternar con amigos⟩
social work n : asistencia f social
society [səˈsaɪəti] n, pl -eties 1 COM-
PANIONSHIP : compañía f 2 : sociedad
f ⟨a democratic society : una sociedad
democrática⟩ ⟨high society : alta so-
ciedad⟩ 3 ASSOCIATION : sociedad f,
asociación f
socioeconomic [ˌsoːsioˌiːkəˈnɑmɪk,
-ˌɛkə-] adj : socioeconómico
sociology [ˌsoːsiˈɑlədʒi] n : sociología f
sociological [ˌsoːsiəˈlɑdʒɪkəl] adj : sociológico
sociologist [ˌsoːsiˈɑlədʒɪst] n : sociólogo
m, -ga f
sock[1] [ˈsɑk] vt : pegar, golpear, darle un
puñetazo a
sock[2] n 1 pl socks or sox [ˈsɑks] : calcetín m, media f ⟨shoes and socks : zapatos y calcetines⟩ 2 pl socks [ˈsɑks]
PUNCH : puñetazo m
socket [ˈsɑkət] n 1 or electric socket
: enchufe m, toma f de corriente 2 : glena f (de una articulación) ⟨shoulder
socket : glena del hombro⟩ 3 eye socket : órbita f, cuenca f
sod[1] [ˈsɑd] vt sodded; sodding : cubrir
de césped
sod[2] n TURF : césped m, tepe m
soda [ˈsoːdə] n 1 or soda water : soda f
2 or soda pop : gaseosa f, refresco m
3 or ice-cream soda : refresco m con
helado
sodden [ˈsɑdən] adj SOGGY : empapado
sodium [ˈsoːdiəm] n : sodio m
sodium bicarbonate n : bicarbonato m
de soda
sodium chloride → salt
sofa [ˈsoːfə] n : sofá m
soft [ˈsɔft] adj 1 : blando ⟨a soft pillow
: una almohada blanda⟩ 2 SMOOTH
: suave (dícese de las texturas, de los
sonidos, etc.) 3 NONALCOHOLIC : no
alcohólico ⟨a soft drink : un refresco⟩
softball [ˈsɔftˌbɔl] n : softbol m
soften [ˈsɔfən] vt : ablandar (algo sólido), suavizar (la piel, un golpe, etc.),
amortiguar (un impacto) — vi : ablandarse, suavizarse
softly [ˈsɔftli] adv : suavemente ⟨she
spoke softly : habló en voz baja⟩
softness [ˈsɔftnəs] n 1 : blandura f, lo
blando (de una almohada, de la mantequilla, etc.) 2 SMOOTHNESS : suavidad f
software [ˈsɔftˌwær] n : software m
soggy [ˈsɑgi] adj soggier; -est : empapado
soil[1] [ˈsɔɪl] vt : ensuciar — vi : ensuciarse

soil[2] n 1 DIRTINESS : suciedad f 2 DIRT,
EARTH : suelo m, tierra f 3 COUNTRY
: patria f ⟨her native soil : su tierra na-
tal⟩
sojourn[1] [ˈsoːˌdʒərn, soˈdʒərn] vi : pasar
una temporada
sojourn[2] n : estadía f, estancia f, permanencia f
solace [ˈsɑləs] n : consuelo m
solar [ˈsoːlər] adj : solar ⟨the solar system : el sistema solar⟩
sold → sell
solder[1] [ˈsɑdər, ˈsɔ-] vt : soldar
solder[2] n : soldadura f
soldier[1] [ˈsoːldʒər] vi : servir como soldado
soldier[2] n : soldado mf
sole[1] [ˈsoːl] adj : único
sole[2] n 1 : suela f (de un zapato) 2
: lenguado m (pez)
solely [ˈsoːli] adv : únicamente, sólo
solemn [ˈsɑləm] adj : solemne, serio —
solemnly adv
solemnity [səˈlɛmnəti] n, pl -ties : solemnidad f
solicit [səˈlɪsət] vt : solicitar
solicitous [səˈlɪsətəs] adj : solícito
solicitude [səˈlɪsəˌtuːd, -ˌtjuːd] n : solicitud f
solid[1] [ˈsɑləd] adj 1 : macizo ⟨a solid
rubber ball : una bola maciza de cau-
cho⟩ 2 CUBIC : tridimensional 3 COM-
PACT : compacto, denso 4 STURDY
: sólido 5 CONTINUOUS : seguido, continuo ⟨two solid hours : dos horas
seguidas⟩ ⟨a solid line : una línea con-
tinua⟩ 6 UNANIMOUS : unánime 7 DE-
PENDABLE : serio, fiable 8 PURE : macizo, puro ⟨solid gold : oro macizo⟩
solid[2] n : sólido m
solidarity [ˌsɑləˈdærəti] n : solidaridad f
solidify [səˈlɪdəˌfaɪ] v -fied; -fying vt : solidificar — vi : solidificarse
solidity [səˈlɪdəti] n, pl -ties : solidez f
solidly [ˈsɑlədli] adv 1 : sólidamente 2
UNANIMOUSLY : unánimemente
soliloquy [səˈlɪləkwi] n, pl -quies : soliloquio m
solitaire [ˈsɑləˌtær] n : solitario m
solitary [ˈsɑləˌteri] adj 1 ALONE : solitario 2 SECLUDED : apartado, retirado
3 SINGLE : solo
solitude [ˈsɑləˌtuːd, -ˌtjuːd] n : soledad f
solo[1] [ˈsoːˌloː] vi : volar en solitario
(dícese de un piloto)
solo[2] adv & adj : en solitario, a solas
solo[3] n, pl solos : solo m
soloist [ˈsoːloɪst] n : solista mf
solstice [ˈsɑlstɪs] n : solsticio m
soluble [ˈsɑljəbəl] adj : soluble
solution [səˈluːʃən] n : solución f
solve [ˈsɑlv] vt solved; solving : resolver, solucionar
solvency [ˈsɑlvənsi] n : solvencia f
solvent [ˈsɑlvənt] n : solvente m
Somali [soˈmɑli, sə-] n : somalí mf —
Somali adj
somber [ˈsɑmbər] adj 1 DARK : sombrío, oscuro ⟨somber colors : colores

oscuros⟩ **2** GRAVE : sombrío, serio **3**
MELANCHOLY : sombrío, lúgubre
sombrero [səm'brɛɾˌo:] *n, pl* **-ros** : sombrero *m* (mexicano)

some[1] ['sʌm] *adj* **1** : un, algún ⟨some
lady stopped me : una mujer me detuvo⟩ ⟨some distant galaxy : alguna
galaxia lejana⟩ **2** : algo de, un poco de
⟨he drank some water : tomó (un poco
de) agua⟩ **3** : unos ⟨do you want some
apples? : ¿quieres unas manzanas?⟩
⟨some years ago : hace varios años⟩

some[2] *pron* **1** : algunos ⟨some went,
others stayed : algunos se fueron, otros
se quedaron⟩ **2** : un poco, algo ⟨there's
some left : queda un poco⟩ ⟨I have
gum; do you want some? : tengo chicle, ¿quieres?⟩

somebody ['sʌmˌbədi, -ˌbadi] *pron* : alguien

someday ['sʌmˌdeɪ] *adv* : algún día

somehow ['sʌmˌhaʊ] *adv* **1** : de alguna
manera, de algún modo ⟨I'll do it somehow : lo haré de alguna manera⟩ **2** : por
alguna razón ⟨somehow I don't trust
her : por alguna razón no me fío de
ella⟩

someone ['sʌmˌwʌn] *pron* : alguien

someplace ['sʌmˌpleɪs] → **somewhere**

somersault[1] ['sʌmərˌsɔlt] *vi* : dar
volteretas, dar un salto mortal

somersault[2] *n* : voltereta *f*, salto *m* mortal

something ['sʌmθɪŋ] *pron* : algo ⟨I want
something else : quiero otra cosa⟩
⟨she's writing a novel or something
: está escribiendo una novela o no sé
qué⟩

sometime ['sʌmˌtaɪm] *adv* : algún día,
en algún momento ⟨sometime next
month : durante el mes que viene⟩

sometimes ['sʌmˌtaɪmz] *adv* : a veces,
algunas veces, de vez en cuando

somewhat ['sʌmˌhwʌt, -ˌhwɑt] *adv*
: algo, un tanto

somewhere ['sʌmˌhwɛr] *adv* **1** (*indicating location*) : en algún lugar ⟨it must
be somewhere else : estará en otra
parte⟩ **2** (*indicating destination*) : a algún lugar

son ['sʌn] *n* : hijo *m*

sonar ['so:ˌnɑr] *n* : sonar *m*

sonata [sə'nɑtə] *n* : sonata *f*

song ['sɔŋ] *n* : canción *f*, canto *m* (de un
pájaro)

songbird ['sɔŋˌbərd] *n* : pájaro *m* cantor

songwriter ['sɔŋˌraɪtər] *n* : compositor
m, -tora *f*

sonic ['sɑnɪk] *adj* **1** : sónico **2** sonic
boom : estampido *m* sónico

son–in–law ['sʌnɪnˌlɔ] *n, pl* **sons–
in–law** : yerno *m*, hijo *m* político

sonnet ['sɑnət] *n* : soneto *m*

sonorous ['sɑnərəs, sə'nɔrəs] *adj*
: sonoro

soon ['su:n] *adv* **1** : pronto, dentro de
poco ⟨he'll arrive soon : llegará pron-

to⟩ **2** QUICKLY : pronto ⟨as soon as
possible : lo más pronto posible⟩ ⟨the
sooner the better : cuanto antes mejor⟩
3 : de buena gana ⟨I'd rather walk
: prefiero caminar⟩

soot ['sʊt, 'su:t, 'sʌt] *n* : hollín *m*, tizne
m

soothe ['su:ð] *vt* soothed; soothing **1**
CALM : calmar, tranquilizar **2** RELIEVE
: aliviar

soothsayer ['su:θˌseɪər] *n* : adivino *m*,
-na *f*

sooty ['sʊti, 'su:-, 'sʌ-] *adj* sootier; -est
: cubierto de hollín, tiznado

sop[1] ['sɑp] *vt* sopped; sopping **1** DIP
: mojar **2** SOAK : empapar **3 to sop up**
: rebañar, absorber

sop[2] *n* **1** CONCESSION : concesión *f* **2**
BRIBE : soborno *m*

sophisticated [sə'fɪstəˌkeɪtəd] *adj* **1**
COMPLEX : complejo **2** WORLDLY-
WISE : sofisticado

sophistication [səˌfɪstə'keɪʃən] *n* **1**
COMPLEXITY : complejidad *f* **2** UR-
BANITY : sofisticación *f*

sophomore ['sɑfˌmor, 'sɑfəˌmor] *n* : estudiante *mf* de segundo año

soporific [ˌsɑpə'rɪfɪk, ˌso:-] *adj* : soporífico

soprano [sə'præˌno:] *n, pl* -nos : soprano *mf*

sorcerer ['sɔrsərər] *n* : hechicero *m*, brujo *m*, mago *m*

sorceress ['sɔrsərəs] *n* : hechicera *f*, bruja *f*, maga *f*

sorcery ['sɔrsəri] *n* : hechicería *f*, brujería *f*

sordid ['sɔrdɪd] *adj* : sórdido

sore[1] ['sor] *adj* sorer; sorest **1** PAINFUL
: dolorido, doloroso ⟨I have a sore
throat : me duele la garganta⟩ **2**
ACUTE, SEVERE : extremo, grande ⟨in
sore straits : en grandes apuros⟩ **3** AN-
GRY : enojado, enfadado

sore[2] *n* : llaga *f*

sorely ['sorli] *adv* : muchísimo ⟨it was
sorely needed : se necesitaba urgentemente⟩ ⟨she was sorely missed : la echaban mucho de menos⟩

soreness ['sornəs] *n* : dolor *m*

sorghum ['sɔrgəm] *n* : sorgo *m*

sorority [sə'rɔrəti] *n, pl* -ties : hermandad *f* (de estudiantes femeninas)

sorrel ['sɔrəl] *n* **1** : alazán *m* (color o animal) **2** : acedera *f* (hierba)

sorrow ['sarˌo:] *n* : pesar *m*, dolor *m*,
pena *f*

sorrowful ['sarəfəl] *adj* : triste, afligido,
apenado

sorrowfully ['sarəfəli] *adv* : con tristeza

sorry ['sari] *adj* sorrier; -est **1** PITIFUL
: lastimero, lastimoso **2 to be sorry**
: sentir, lamentar ⟨I'm sorry : lo siento⟩ **3 to feel sorry for** : compadecer ⟨I
feel sorry for him : me da pena⟩

sort[1] ['sɔrt] *vt* **1** : dividir en grupos **2**
CLASSIFY : clasificar **3 to sort out** OR-
GANIZE : poner en orden **4 to sort out**
RESOLVE : resolver

sort² n 1 KIND : tipo m, clase f ⟨a sort of writer : una especie de escritor⟩ 2 NATURE : índole f 3 out of sorts : de mal humor

sortie [ˈsɔrti, sɔrˈtiː] n : salida f

SOS [ˌɛsˌoːˈɛs] n : SOS m

so-so [ˈsoːˈsoː] adj & adv : así así, de modo regular

soufflé [suːˈfleɪ] n : suflé m

sought → seek

soul [ˈsoːl] n 1 SPIRIT : alma f 2 ESSENCE : esencia f 3 PERSON : persona f, alma f

soulful [ˈsoːlfəl] adj : conmovedor, lleno de emoción

sound¹ [ˈsaʊnd] vt 1 : sondar (en navegación) 2 or to sound out PROBE : sondear 3 : hacer sonar, tocar (una trompeta, etc.) — vi 1 : sonar ⟨the alarm sounded : la alarma sonó⟩ 2 SEEM : parecer

sound² adj 1 HEALTHY : sano ⟨safe and sound : sano y salvo⟩ ⟨of sound mind and body : en pleno uso de sus facultades⟩ 2 FIRM, SOLID : sólido 3 SENSIBLE : lógico, sensato 4 DEEP : profundo ⟨a sound sleep : un sueño profundo⟩

sound³ n 1 : sonido m ⟨the speed of sound : la velocidad del sonido⟩ 2 NOISE : sonido m, ruido m ⟨I heard a sound : oí un sonido⟩ 3 CHANNEL : brazo m de mar, canal m (ancho)

soundless [ˈsaʊndləs] adj : sordo

soundlessly [ˈsaʊndləsli] adv : silenciosamente

soundly [ˈsaʊndli] adv 1 SOLIDLY : sólidamente 2 SENSIBLY : lógicamente, sensatamente 3 DEEPLY : profundamente ⟨sleeping soundly : durmiendo profundamente⟩

soundness [ˈsaʊndnəs] n 1 SOLIDITY : solidez f 2 SENSIBLENESS : sensatez f, solidez f

soundproof [ˈsaʊndˌpruːf] adj : insonorizado

soundtrack [ˈsaʊndˌtræk] n : banda f sonora

sound wave n : onda f sonora

soup [ˈsuːp] n : sopa f

sour¹ [ˈsaʊər] vi : agriarse, cortarse (dícese de la leche) — vt : agriar, cortar (leche)

sour² adj 1 ACID : agrio, ácido (dícese de la fruta, etc.), cortado (dícese de la leche) 2 DISAGREEABLE : desagradable, agrio

source [ˈsors] n : fuente f, origen m, nacimiento m (de un río)

sourness [ˈsaʊərnəs] n : acidez f

south¹ [ˈsaʊθ] adv : al sur, hacia el sur ⟨the window looks south : la ventana mira al sur⟩ ⟨she continued south : continuó hacia el sur⟩

south² adj : sur, del sur ⟨the south entrance : la entrada sur⟩ ⟨South America : Sudamérica, América del Sur⟩

south³ n : sur m

South African n : sudafricano m, -na f — **South African** adj

South American¹ adj : sudamericano, suramericano

South American² n : sudamericano m, -na f; suramericano m, -na f

southbound [ˈsaʊθˌbaʊnd] adj : con rumbo al sur

southeast¹ [saʊˈθiːst] adj : sureste, sudeste, del sureste

southeast² n : sureste m, sudeste m

southeasterly [saʊˈθiːstərli] adv & adj 1 : del sureste (dícese del viento) 2 : hacia el sureste

southeastern [saʊˈθiːstərn] adj → southeast¹

southerly [ˈsʌðərli] adv & adj : del sur

southern [ˈsʌðərn] adj : sur, sureño, meridional, austral ⟨a southern city : una ciudad del sur del país, una ciudad meridional⟩ ⟨the southern side : el lado sur⟩

Southerner [ˈsʌðərnər] n : sureño m, -ña f

South Pole : Polo m Sur

southward [ˈsaʊθwərd] or **southwards** [-wərdz] adv & adj : hacia el sur

southwest¹ [saʊθˈwɛst, as a nautical term often saʊˈwɛst] adj : suroeste, sudoeste, del suroeste

southwest² n : suroeste m, sudoeste m

southwesterly [saʊθˈwɛstərli] adv & adj 1 : del suroeste (dícese del viento) 2 : hacia el suroeste

southwestern [saʊθˈwɛstərn] adj → southwest¹

souvenir [ˌsuːvəˈnɪr, ˈsuːvəˌ-] n : recuerdo m, souvenir m

sovereign¹ [ˈsɑvərən] adj : soberano

sovereign² n 1 : soberano m, -na f (monarca) 2 : soberano m (moneda)

sovereignty [ˈsɑvərənti] n, pl **-ties** : soberanía f

Soviet [ˈsoːviˌɛt, ˈsɑ-, -viət] adj : soviético

sow¹ [ˈsoː] vt **sowed**; **sown** [ˈsoːn] or **sowed**; **sowing** 1 PLANT : sembrar 2 SCATTER : esparcir

sow² [ˈsaʊ] n : cerda f

sox → sock

soy [ˈsɔɪ] n : soya f, soja f

soybean [ˈsɔɪˌbiːn] n : soya f, soja f

spa [ˈspɑ] n : balneario m

space¹ [ˈspeɪs] vt **spaced**; **spacing** : espaciar

space² n 1 PERIOD : espacio m, lapso m, período m 2 ROOM : espacio m, sitio m, lugar m ⟨is there space for me? : ¿hay sitio para mí?⟩ 3 : espacio m ⟨blank space : espacio en blanco⟩ 4 : espacio m (en física) 5 PLACE : plaza f, sitio m ⟨to reserve space : reservar plazas⟩ ⟨parking space : sitio para estacionarse⟩

spacecraft [ˈspeɪsˌkræft] n : nave f espacial

spaceflight [ˈspeɪsˌflaɪt] n : vuelo m espacial

spaceman ['speɪsmən, -ˌmæn] n, pl **-men** [-mən, -ˌmɛn] : astronauta m, cosmonauta m

spaceship ['speɪsˌʃɪp] n : nave f espacial

space shuttle n : transbordador m espacial

space suit n : traje m espacial

spacious ['speɪʃəs] adj : espacioso, amplio

spade¹ ['speɪd] v **spaded**; **spading** vt : palear — vi : usar una pala

spade² n 1 SHOVEL : pala f 2 : pica f (naipe)

spaghetti [spə'ɡɛti] n : espagueti m, espaguetis mpl, spaghetti mpl

spam ['spæm] n : spam m, correo m electrónico no solicitado

span¹ ['spæn] vt **spanned**; **spanning** : abarcar (un período de tiempo), extenderse sobre (un espacio)

span² n 1 : lapso m, espacio m (de tiempo) ⟨life span : duración f de la vida⟩ 2 : luz f (entre dos soportes)

spangle ['spæŋɡəl] n : lentejuela f

Spaniard ['spænjərd] n : español m, -ñola f

spaniel ['spænjəl] n : spaniel m

Spanish¹ ['spænɪʃ] adj : español

Spanish² n 1 : español m (idioma) 2 **the Spanish** : los españoles

spank ['spæŋk] vt : darle nalgadas (a alguien)

spar¹ ['spɑr] vi **sparred**; **sparring** : entrenarse (en boxeo)

spar² n : palo m, verga f (de un barco)

spare¹ ['spær] vt **spared**; **sparing** 1 : perdonar ⟨to spare someone's life : perdonar la vida a alguien⟩ 2 SAVE : ahorrar, evitar ⟨I'll spare you the trouble : le evitaré la molestia⟩ 3 : prescindir de ⟨I can't spare her : no puedo prescindir de ella⟩ ⟨can you spare a dollar? : ¿me das un dólar?⟩ 4 STINT : escatimar ⟨they spared no expense : no repararon en gastos⟩ 5 **to spare** : de sobra

spare² adj 1 : de repuesto, de recambio ⟨spare tire : llanta de repuesto⟩ 2 EXCESS : de más, de sobra ⟨spare time : tiempo libre⟩ 3 LEAN : delgado

spare³ n or **spare part** : repuesto m, recambio m

sparing ['spærɪŋ] adj : parco, económico — **sparingly** adv

spark¹ ['spɑrk] vi : chispear, echar chispas — vt PROVOKE : despertar, provocar ⟨to spark interest : despertar interés⟩

spark² n 1 : chispa f ⟨to throw off sparks : echar chispas⟩ 2 GLIMMER, TRACE : destello m, pizca f

sparkle¹ ['spɑrkəl] vi **-kled**; **-kling** 1 FLASH, SHINE : destellar, centellear, brillar 2 : estar muy animado (dícese de una conversación, etc.)

sparkle² n : destello m, centelleo m

sparkler ['spɑrklər] n : luz f de bengala

spark plug n : bujía f

sparrow ['spæroʊ] n : gorrión m

sparse ['spɑrs] adj **sparser**; **-est** : escaso — **sparsely** adv

spasm ['spæzəm] n 1 : espasmo m (muscular) 2 BURST, FIT : arrebato m

spasmodic [spæz'mɑdɪk] adj 1 : espasmódico 2 SPORADIC : irregular, esporádico — **spasmodically** [-dɪkli] adv

spastic ['spæstɪk] adj : espástico

spat¹ → **spit¹**

spat² ['spæt] n : discusión f, disputa f, pelea f

spatial ['speɪʃəl] adj : espacial

spatter¹ ['spæt̬ər] v : salpicar

spatter² n : salpicadura f

spatula ['spætʃələ] n : espátula f, paleta f (para servir)

spawn¹ ['spɔn] vi : desovar, frezar — vt GENERATE : generar, producir

spawn² n : hueva f, freza f

spay ['speɪ] vt : esterilizar (una perra, etc.)

speak ['spiːk] v **spoke** ['spoːk]; **spoken** ['spoːkən]; **speaking** vi 1 TALK : hablar ⟨to speak to someone : hablar con alguien⟩ ⟨who's speaking? : ¿de parte de quien?⟩ ⟨so to speak : por así decirlo⟩ 2 **to speak out** : hablar claramente 3 **to speak out against** : denunciar 4 **to speak up** : hablar en voz alta 5 **to speak up for** : defender — vt 1 SAY : decir ⟨she spoke her mind : habló con franqueza⟩ 2 : hablar (un idioma)

speaker ['spiːkər] n 1 : hablante mf ⟨a native speaker : un hablante nativo⟩ 2 : orador m, -dora f ⟨the keynote speaker : el orador principal⟩ 3 LOUDSPEAKER : altavoz m, altoparlante m

spear¹ ['spɪr] vt : atravesar con una lanza

spear² n : lanza f

spearhead¹ ['spɪrˌhɛd] vt : encabezar

spearhead² n : punta f de lanza

spearmint ['spɪrˌmɪnt] n : menta f verde

special ['spɛʃəl] adj : especial ⟨nothing special : nada en especial, nada en particular⟩ — **specially** adv

specialist ['spɛʃəlɪst] n : especialista mf

specialization [ˌspɛʃələ'zeɪʃən] n : especialización f

specialize ['spɛʃəˌlaɪz] vi **-ized**; **-izing** : especializarse

specialty ['spɛʃəlti] n, pl **-ties** : especialidad f

species ['spiːˌʃiːz, -ˌsiːz] ns & pl : especie f

specific [spɪ'sɪfɪk] adj : específico, determinado — **specifically** [-fɪkli] adv

specification [ˌspɛsəfə'keɪʃən] n : especificación f

specify ['spɛsəˌfaɪ] vt **-fied**; **-fying** : especificar

specimen ['spɛsəmən] n 1 SAMPLE : espécimen m, muestra f 2 EXAMPLE : espécimen m, ejemplar m

speck ['spɛk] n 1 SPOT : manchita f 2 BIT, TRACE : mota f, pizca f, ápice m

speckled ['spɛkəld] adj : moteado

spectacle ['spɛktɪkəl] n 1 : espectáculo m 2 **spectacles** npl GLASSES : lentes fpl, gafas fpl, anteojos mpl, espejuelos mpl

spectacular [spɛk'tækjələr] adj : espectacular

spectator ['spɛk,teɪtər] n : espectador m, -dora f

specter or **spectre** ['spɛktər] n : espectro m, fantasma m

spectrum ['spɛktrəm] n, pl **spectra** [-trə] or **spectrums** 1 : espectro m (de colores, etc.) 2 RANGE : gama f, abanico m

speculate ['spɛkjə,leɪt] vi -**lated**; -**lating** 1 : especular (en finanzas) 2 WONDER : preguntarse, hacer conjeturas

speculation [,spɛkjə'leɪʃən] n : especulación f

speculative ['spɛkjə,leɪtɪv] adj : especulativo

speculator ['spɛkjə,leɪtər] n : especulador m, -dora f

speech ['spiːtʃ] n 1 : habla f, modo m de hablar, expresión f 2 ADDRESS : discurso m

speechless ['spiːtʃləs] adj : enmudecido, estupefacto

speed¹ ['spiːd] v **sped** ['spɛd] or **speeded**; **speeding** vi 1 : ir a toda velocidad, correr a toda prisa ⟨he sped off : se fue a toda velocidad⟩ 2 : conducir a exceso de velocidad ⟨a ticket for speeding : una multa por exceso de velocidad⟩ — vt **to speed up** : acelerar

speed² n 1 SWIFTNESS : rapidez f 2 VELOCITY : velocidad f

speedboat ['spiːd,boːt] n : lancha f motora

speed bump n : badén m

speed limit n : velocidad f máxima, límite m de velocidad

speedometer [spɪ'dɑmətər] n : velocímetro m

speedup ['spiːd,ʌp] n : aceleración f

speedy ['spiːdi] adj **speedier**; -**est** : rápido — **speedily** [-dəli] adv

spell¹ ['spɛl] vt 1 : escribir, deletrear (verbalmente) ⟨how do you spell it? : ¿cómo se escribe?, ¿cómo se deletrea?⟩ 2 MEAN : significar ⟨that could spell trouble : eso puede significar problemas⟩ 3 RELIEVE : relevar

spell² n 1 TURN : turno m 2 PERIOD, TIME : período m (de tiempo) 3 ENCHANTMENT : encanto m, hechizo m, maleficio m

spellbound ['spɛl,baʊnd] adj : embelesado

speller ['spɛlər] n : persona f que escribe ⟨she's a good speller : tiene buena ortografía⟩

spelling ['spɛlɪŋ] n : ortografía f

spend ['spɛnd] vt **spent** ['spɛnt]; **spending** 1 : gastar (dinero, etc.) 2 PASS : pasar (el tiempo) ⟨to spend time on : dedicar tiempo a⟩

spendthrift ['spɛnd,θrɪft] n : derrochador m, -dora f; despilfarrador m, -dora f

sperm ['spərm] n, pl **sperm** or **sperms** : esperma mf

spew ['spjuː] vi : salir a chorros — vt : vomitar, arrojar (lava, etc.)

sphere ['sfɪr] n : esfera f

spherical ['sfɪrɪkəl, 'sfɛr-] adj : esférico

spice¹ ['spaɪs] vt **spiced**; **spicing** 1 SEASON : condimentar, sazonar 2 or **to spice up** : salpimentar, hacer más interesante

spice² n 1 : especia f 2 FLAVOR, INTEREST : sabor m ⟨the spice of life : la sal de la vida⟩

spick–and–span ['spɪkənd'spæn] adj : limpio y ordenado

spicy ['spaɪsi] adj **spicier**; -**est** 1 SPICED : condimentado, sazonado 2 HOT : picante 3 RACY : picante

spider ['spaɪdər] n : araña f

spigot ['spɪgət, -kət] n : llave f, grifo m, canilla f Arg, Uru

spike¹ ['spaɪk] vt **spiked**; **spiking** 1 FASTEN : clavar (con clavos grandes) 2 PIERCE : atravesar 3 : añadir alcohol a ⟨he spiked her drink with rum : le puso ron a la bebida⟩

spike² n 1 : clavo m grande 2 CLEAT : clavo m 3 : remache m (en voleibol) 4 PEAK : pico m

spill¹ ['spɪl] vt 1 SHED : derramar, verter ⟨to spill blood : derrame sangre⟩ 2 DIVULGE : revelar, divulgar — vi : derramarse

spill² n 1 SPILLING : derrame m, vertido m ⟨oil spill : derrame de petróleo⟩ 2 FALL : caída f

spin¹ ['spɪn] v **spun** ['spʌn]; **spinning** vi 1 : hilar 2 TURN : girar 3 REEL : dar vueltas ⟨my head is spinning : la cabeza me está dando vueltas⟩ — vt 1 : hilar (hilo, etc.) 2 : tejer ⟨to spin a web : una telaraña⟩ 3 TWIRL : hacer girar

spin² n : vuelta f, giro m ⟨to go for a spin : dar una vuelta (en coche)⟩

spinach ['spɪnɪtʃ] n : espinacas fpl, espinaca f

spinal column ['spaɪnəl] n BACKBONE : columna f vertebral

spinal cord n : médula f espinal

spindle ['spɪndəl] n 1 : huso m (para hilar) 2 : eje m (de un mecanismo)

spindly ['spɪndli] adj : larguirucho fam, largo y débil (dícese de una planta)

spine ['spaɪn] n 1 BACKBONE : columna f vertebral, espina f dorsal 2 QUILL : púa f (de un animal) 3 THORN : espina f 4 : lomo m (de un libro)

spineless ['spaɪnləs] adj 1 : sin púas, sin espinas 2 INVERTEBRATE : invertebrado 3 WEAK : débil (de carácter)

spinet ['spɪnət] n : espineta f

spinster ['spɪnstər] n : soltera f

spiny ['spaɪni] adj **spinier**; -**est** : con púas (dícese de los animales), espinoso (dícese de las plantas)

spiral[1] ['spaɪrəl] vi -raled or -ralled; -raling or -ralling : ir en espiral

spiral[2] adj : espiral, en espiral ⟨a spiral staircase : una escalera de caracol⟩

spiral[3] n : espiral f

spire ['spaɪr] n : aguja f

spirit[1] ['spɪrət] vt to spirit away : hacer desaparecer

spirit[2] n 1 : espíritu m ⟨body and spirit : cuerpo y espíritu⟩ 2 GHOST : espíritu m, fantasma m 3 MOOD : espíritu m, humor m ⟨in the spirit of friendship : en el espíritu de amistad⟩ ⟨to be in good spirits : estar de buen humor⟩ 4 ENTHUSIASM, VIVACITY : espíritu m, ánimo m, brío m 5 spirits npl : licores mpl

spirited ['spɪrətəd] adj : animado, enérgico

spiritless ['spɪrətləs] adj : desanimado

spiritual[1] ['spɪrɪtʃuəl, -tʃəl] adj : espiritual — **spiritually** adv

spiritual[2] n : espiritual m (canción)

spiritualism ['spɪrɪtʃuəˌlɪzəm, -tʃə-] n : espiritismo m

spirituality [ˌspɪrɪtʃuˈæləti] n, pl -ties : espiritualidad f

spit[1] ['spɪt] v spit or spat ['spæt]; spitting : escupir

spit[2] n 1 SALIVA : saliva f 2 ROTISSERIE : asador m 3 POINT : lengua f (de tierra)

spite[1] ['spaɪt] vt spited; spiting : fastidiar, molestar

spite[2] n 1 : despecho m, rencor m 2 in spite of : a pesar de (que), pese a (que)

spiteful ['spaɪtfəl] adj : malicioso, rencoroso

spitting image n to be the spitting image of : ser el vivo retrato de

spittle ['spɪtəl] n : saliva f

splash[1] ['splæʃ] vt : salpicar — vi 1 : salpicar 2 to splash around : chapotear

splash[2] n 1 SPLASHING : salpicadura f 2 SQUIRT : chorrito m 3 SPOT : mancha f

splatter ['splætər] → spatter

splay ['spleɪ] vt : extender (hacia afuera) ⟨to splay one's fingers : abrir los dedos⟩ — vi : extenderse (hacia afuera)

spleen ['spli:n] n 1 : bazo m (órgano) 2 ANGER, SPITE : ira f, rencor m

splendid ['splɛndəd] adj : espléndido — **splendidly** adv

splendor ['splɛndər] n : esplendor m

splice[1] ['splaɪs] vt spliced; splicing : empalmar, unir

splice[2] n : empalme m, unión f

splint ['splɪnt] n : tablilla f

splinter[1] ['splɪntər] vt : astillar — vi : astillarse

splinter[2] n : astilla f

split[1] ['splɪt] v split; splitting vt 1 CLEAVE : partir, hender ⟨to split wood : partir madera⟩ 2 BURST : romper, rajar ⟨to split open : abrir⟩ 3 DIVIDE, SHARE : dividir, repartir — vi 1 : par-

tirse (dícese de la madera, etc.) 2 BURST, CRACK : romperse, rajarse 3 or to split up : dividirse

split[2] n 1 CRACK : rajadura f 2 TEAR : rotura f 3 DIVISION : división f, escisión f

splurge[1] ['splərdʒ] v splurged; splurging vt : derrochar — vi : derrochar dinero

splurge[2] n : derroche m

spoil[1] ['spɔɪl] vt 1 PILLAGE : saquear 2 RUIN : estropear, arruinar 3 PAMPER : consentir, mimar — vi : estropearse, echarse a perder

spoil[2] n PLUNDER : botín m

spoke[1] → speak

spoke[2] ['spo:k] n : rayo m (de una rueda)

spoken → speak

spokesman ['spo:ksmən] n, pl -men [-mən, -ˌmɛn] : portavoz mf; vocero m, -ra f

spokeswoman ['spo:ksˌwʊmən] n, pl -women [-ˌwɪmən] : portavoz f, vocera f

sponge[1] ['spʌndʒ] vt sponged; sponging : limpiar con una esponja

sponge[2] n : esponja f

spongy ['spʌndʒi] adj spongier; -est : esponjoso

sponsor[1] ['spʌntsər] vt : patrocinar, auspiciar, apadrinar (a una persona)

sponsor[2] n : patrocinador m, -dora f; padrino m, madrina f

sponsorship ['spʌntsərˌʃɪp] n : patrocinio m, apadrinamiento m

spontaneity [ˌspʌntəˈni:əti, -ˈneɪ-] n : espontaneidad f

spontaneous [spʌnˈteɪniəs] adj : espontáneo — **spontaneously** adv

spoof ['spu:f] n : burla f, parodia f

spook[1] ['spu:k] vt : asustar

spook[2] n : fantasma m, espíritu m, espectro m

spooky ['spu:ki] adj spookier; -est : que da miedo, espeluznante

spool ['spu:l] n : carrete m

spoon[1] ['spu:n] vt : comer, servir, o echar con cuchara

spoon[2] n : cuchara f

spoonful ['spu:nˌfʊl] n : cucharada f ⟨by the spoonful : a cucharadas⟩

spoor ['spʊr, 'spɔr] n : rastro m, pista f

sporadic [spəˈrædɪk] adj : esporádico — **sporadically** [-dɪkli] adv

spore ['spɔr] n : espora f

sport[1] ['spɔrt] vi FROLIC : retozar, juguetear — vt SHOW OFF : lucir, ostentar

sport[2] n 1 : deporte m ⟨outdoor sports : deportes al aire libre⟩ 2 JEST : broma f 3 to be a good sport : tener espíritu deportivo

sporting ['spɔrtɪŋ] adj : deportivo ⟨a sporting chance : buenas posibilidades⟩

sportsman ['spɔrtsmən] n, pl -men [-mən, -ˌmɛn] : deportista m

sportsmanship ['sportsmən,ʃɪp] n : espíritu m deportivo, deportividad f *Spain*

sportswoman ['sports,wʊmən] n, pl **-women** [-,wɪmən] : deportista f

sporty ['sporti] adj **sportier; -est** : deportivo

spot¹ ['spat] v **spotted; spotting** vt 1 STAIN : manchar 2 RECOGNIZE, SEE : ver, reconocer ⟨to spot an error : descubrir un error⟩ — vi : mancharse

spot² adj : hecho al azar ⟨a spot check : un vistazo, un control aleatorio⟩

spot³ n 1 STAIN : mancha f 2 DOT : punto m 3 PIMPLE : grano m ⟨to break out in spots : salirle granos a alguien⟩ 4 PREDICAMENT : apuro m, aprieto m, lío m ⟨in a tight spot : en apuros⟩ 5 PLACE : lugar m, sitio m ⟨to be on the spot : estar en el lugar⟩

spotless ['spatləs] adj : impecable, inmaculado — **spotlessly** adv

spotlight¹ ['spat,laɪt] vt **-lighted** or **-lit** [-,lɪt]; **-lighting** 1 LIGHT : iluminar (con un reflector) 2 HIGHLIGHT : destacar, poner en relieve

spotlight² n 1 : reflector m, foco m 2 **to be in the spotlight** : ser el centro de atención

spotty ['spati] adj **spottier; -est** : irregular, desigual

spouse ['spaʊs] n : cónyuge mf

spout¹ ['spaʊt] vt 1 : lanzar chorros de 2 DECLAIM : declamar — vi : salir a chorros

spout² n 1 : pico m (de una jarra, etc.) 2 STREAM : chorro m

sprain¹ ['spreɪn] vt : sufrir un esguince en

sprain² n : esguince m, torcedura f

sprawl¹ ['sprɔl] vi 1 LIE : tumbarse, echarse, despatarrarse 2 EXTEND : extenderse

sprawl² n 1 : postura f despatarrada 2 SPREAD : extensión f, expansión f

spray¹ ['spreɪ] vt : rociar (una superficie), pulverizar (un líquido)

spray² n 1 BOUQUET : ramillete m 2 MIST : rocío m 3 ATOMIZER : atomizador m, pulverizador m

spray gun n : pistola f

spread¹ ['spred] v **spread; spreading** vt 1 or **to spread out** : desplegar, extender 2 SCATTER, STREW : esparcir 3 SMEAR : untar (mantequilla, etc.) 4 DISSEMINATE : difundir, sembrar, propagar — vi 1 : difundirse, correr, propagarse 2 EXTEND : extenderse

spread² n 1 EXTENSION : extensión f, difusión f (de noticias, etc.), propagación f (de enfermedades, etc.) 2 : colcha f (para una cama), mantel m (para una mesa) 3 PASTE : pasta f ⟨cheese spread : pasta de queso⟩

spreadsheet ['spred,ʃi:t] n : hoja f de cálculo

spree ['spri] n 1 : acción f desenfrenada ⟨to go on a shopping spree : comprar como loco⟩ 2 BINGE : parranda f, juerga ⟨on a spree : de parranda, de juerga⟩

sprig ['sprɪg] n : ramita f, ramito m

sprightly ['spraɪtli] adj **sprightlier; -est** : vivo, animado ⟨with a sprightly step : con paso ligero⟩

spring¹ ['sprɪŋ] v **sprang** ['spræŋ] or **sprung** ['sprʌŋ]; **sprung; springing** vi 1 LEAP : saltar 2 : mover rápidamente ⟨the lid sprang shut : la tapa se cerró de un golpe⟩ ⟨he sprang to his feet : se paró de un salto⟩ 3 **to spring up** : brotar (dícese de las plantas), surgir 4 **to spring from** : surgir de — vt 1 RELEASE : soltar (de repente) ⟨to spring the news on someone : sorprender a alguien con las noticias⟩ ⟨to spring a trap : hacer saltar una trampa⟩ 2 ACTIVATE : accionar (un mecanismo) 3 **to spring a leak** : hacer agua

spring² n 1 SOURCE : fuente f, origen m 2 : manantial m, fuente f ⟨hot spring : fuente termal⟩ 3 : primavera f ⟨spring and summer : la primavera y el verano⟩ 4 : resorte m, muelle m (de metal, etc.) 5 LEAP : salto m, brinco m 6 RESILIENCE : elasticidad f

springboard ['sprɪŋ,bord] n : trampolín m

springtime ['sprɪŋ,taɪm] n : primavera f

springy ['sprɪŋi] adj **springier; -est** 1 RESILIENT : elástico 2 LIVELY : enérgico

sprinkle¹ ['sprɪŋkəl] vt **-kled; -kling** : rociar (con agua), espolvorear (con azúcar, etc.), salpicar

sprinkle² n : llovizna f

sprinkler ['sprɪŋkələr] n : rociador m, aspersor m

sprint¹ ['sprɪnt] vi : echar la carrera, esprintar (en deportes)

sprint² n : esprint m (en deportes)

sprinter ['sprɪntər] n : esprínter mf

sprite ['spraɪt] n : hada f, elfo m

sprocket ['sprakət] n : diente m (de una rueda dentada)

sprout¹ ['spraʊt] vi : brotar

sprout² n : brote m, retoño m, vástago m

spruce¹ ['spru:s] v **spruced; sprucing** vt : arreglar — vi or **to spruce up** : arreglarse, acicalarse

spruce² adj **sprucer; sprucest** : pulcro, arreglado

spruce³ n : picea f (árbol)

spry ['spraɪ] adj **sprier** or **spryer** ['spraɪər]; **spriest** or **spryest** ['spraɪəst] : ágil, activo

spun → **spin**

spunk ['spʌŋk] n : valor m, coraje m, agallas fpl fam

spunky ['spʌŋki] adj **spunkier; -est** : animoso, corajudo

spur¹ ['spər] vt **spurred; spurring** or **to spur on** : espolear (un caballo), motivar (a una persona, etc.)

spur² *n* **1** : espuela *f*, acicate *m* **2** STIM-
ULUS : acicate *m* **3** : espolón *m* (de aves
gallináceas)

spurious ['spjurɪəs] *adj* : espurio

spurn ['spərn] *vt* : desdeñar, rechazar

spurt¹ ['spərt] *vt* SQUIRT : lanzar un chorro de — *vi* SPOUT : salir a chorros

spurt² *n* **1** : actividad *f* repentina ⟨a
spurt of energy : una explosión de ener-
gía⟩ ⟨to do in spurts : hacer por
rachas⟩ **2** JET : chorro *m* (de agua, etc.)

sputter¹ ['spʌtər] *vi* **1** JABBER : farfullar
2 : chisporrotear (dícese de la grasa,
etc.), petardear (dícese de un motor)

sputter² *n* **1** JABBER : farfulla *f* **2** : chisporroteo *m* (de grasa, etc.), petardeo *m*
(de un motor)

spy¹ ['spaɪ] *vt* **spied**; **spying** *vt* SEE : ver,
divisar — *vi* : espiar ⟨to spy on some-
one : espiar a alguien⟩

spy² *n* : espía *mf*

squab ['skwab] *n, pl* **squabs** *or* **squab**
: pichón *m*

squabble¹ ['skwabəl] *vi* **-bled**; **-bling**
: reñir, pelearse, discutir

squabble² *n* : riña *f*, pelea *f*, discusión *f*

squad ['skwad] *n* : pelotón *m* (militar),
brigada *f* (de policías), cuadrilla *f* (de
obreros, etc.)

squadron ['skwadrən] *n* : escuadrón *m*
(de militares), escuadrilla *f* (de
aviones), escuadra *f* (de naves)

squalid ['skwalɪd] *adj* : miserable

squall ['skwɔl] *n* **1** : aguacero *m* tormentoso, chubasco *m* tormentoso **2**
snow squall : tormenta *f* de nieve

squalor ['skwalər] *n* : miseria *f*

squander ['skwandər] *vt* : derrochar
(dinero, etc.), desaprovechar (una
oportunidad, etc.), desperdiciar (talen-
tos, energías, etc.)

square¹ ['skwær] *vt* **squared**; **squaring**
1 : cuadrar **2** : elevar al cuadrado (en
matemáticas) **3** CONFORM : conciliar
(con), ajustar (con) **4** SETTLE : saldar
(una cuenta) ⟨I squared it with him : lo
arreglé con él⟩

square² *adj* **squarer**; **-est 1** : cuadrado
⟨a square house : una casa cuadrada⟩
2 RIGHT-ANGLED : a escuadra, en ángulo recto **3** : cuadrado (en matemáticas) ⟨a square mile : una milla cuadra-
da⟩ **4** HONEST : justo ⟨a square deal
: un buen acuerdo⟩ ⟨fair and square
: en buena lid⟩

square³ *n* **1** : escuadra *f* (instrumento)
2 : cuadrado *m*, cuadro *m* ⟨to fold into
squares : plegar en cuadrados⟩ **3**
: plaza *f* (de una ciudad) **4** : cuadrado
m (en matemáticas)

squarely ['skwærli] *adv* **1** EXACTLY : exactamente, directamente, justo **2** HON-
ESTLY : honradamente, justamente

square root *n* : raíz *f* cuadrada

squash¹ ['skwaʃ, 'skwɔʃ] *vt* **1** CRUSH
: aplastar **2** SUPPRESS : acallar (protestas), sofocar (una rebelión)

squash² *n* **1** *pl* **squashes** *or* **squash**
: calabaza *f* (vegetal) **2** *or* **squash rac-
quets** : squash *m* (deporte)

squat¹ ['skwat] *vi* **squatted; squatting**
1 CROUCH : agacharse, ponerse en cuclillas **2** : ocupar un lugar sin derecho

squat² *adj* **squatter; squattest** : bajo y
ancho, rechoncho *fam* (dícese de una
persona)

squat³ *n* **1** : posición *f* en cuclillas **2**
: ocupación *f* ilegal (de un lugar)

squaw ['skwɔ] *n* : india *f* (norteameri-
cana)

squawk¹ ['skwɔk] *vi* : graznar (dícese de
las aves), chillar

squawk² *n* : graznido *m* (de un ave),
chillido *m*

squeak¹ ['skwiːk] *vi* : chillar (dícese de
un animal), chirriar (dícese de un objeto)

squeak² *n* : chillido *m*, chirrido *m*

squeaky ['skwiːki] *adj* **squeakier; -est**
: chirriante ⟨a squeaky voice : una voz
chillona⟩

squeal¹ ['skwiːl] *vi* **1** : chillar (dícese de
las personas o los animales), chirriar
(dícese de los frenos, etc.) **2** PROTEST
: quejarse

squeal² *n* **1** : chillido *m* (de una persona
o un animal) **2** SCREECH : chirrido *m*
(de frenos, etc.)

squeamish ['skwiːmɪʃ] *adj* : impresionable, sensible ⟨he's squeamish about
cockroaches : las cucarachas le dan
asco⟩

squeeze¹ ['skwiːz] *vt* **squeezed;
squeezing 1** PRESS : apretar, exprimir (naranjas, etc.) **2** EXTRACT : extraer
(jugo, etc.)

squeeze² *n* : apretón *m*

squelch ['skwɛltʃ] *vt* : aplastar (una rebelión, etc.)

squid ['skwɪd] *n, pl* **squid** *or* **squids**
: calamar *m*

squint¹ ['skwɪnt] *vi* : mirar con los ojos
entornados

squint² *adj* *or* **squint–eyed** ['skwɪnt,aɪd]
: bizco

squint³ *n* : ojos *mpl* bizcos, bizquera *f*

squire ['skwaɪr] *n* : hacendado *m*, -da *f*;
terrateniente *mf*

squirm ['skwərm] *vi* : retorcerse

squirrel ['skwərəl] *n* : ardilla *f*

squirt¹ ['skwərt] *vt* : lanzar un chorro de
— *vi* SPURT : salir a chorros

squirt² *n* : chorrito *m*

stab¹ ['stæb] *vt* **stabbed; stabbing 1**
KNIFE : acuchillar, apuñalar **2** STICK
: clavar (con una aguja, etc.), golpear
(con el dedo, etc.)

stab² *n* **1** : puñalada *f*, cuchillada *f* **2**
JAB : pinchazo *m* (con una aguja, etc.),
golpe *m* (con un dedo, etc.) **3 to take
a stab at** : intentar

stability [stə'bɪləti] *n, pl* **-ties** : estabilidad *f*

stabilize ['steɪbə,laɪz] *v* **-lized; -lizing** *vt*
: estabilizar — *vi* : estabilizarse

stable¹ ['steɪbəl] vt -bled; -bling : poner (ganado) en un establo, poner (caballos) en una caballeriza

stable² adj -bler; -blest 1 FIXED, STEADY : fijo, sólido, estable 2 LASTING : estable, perdurable ⟨a stable government : un gobierno estable⟩ 3 : estacionario (en medicina), equilibrado (en psicología)

stable³ n : establo m (para ganado), caballeriza f o cuadra f (para caballos)

staccato [stə'kɑːto] adj : staccato

stack¹ ['stæk] vt 1 PILE : amontonar, apilar 2 COVER : cubrir, llenar ⟨he stacked the table with books : cubrió la mesa de libros⟩

stack² n 1 PILE : montón m, pila f 2 SMOKESTACK : chimenea f

stadium ['steɪdiəm] n, pl -dia [-diə] or -diums : estadio m

staff¹ ['stæf] vt : proveer de personal

staff² n, pl staffs ['stæfs, stævz] or staves ['stævz, 'steɪvz] 1 : bastón m (de mando), báculo m (de obispo) 2 pl staffs PERSONNEL : personal m 3 or stave : pentagrama m (en música)

stag¹ ['stæg] adv : solo, sin pareja ⟨to go stag : ir solo⟩

stag² adj : sólo para hombres

stag³ n, pl stags or stag : ciervo m, venado m

stage¹ ['steɪdʒ] vt staged; staging : poner en escena (una obra de teatro)

stage² n 1 PLATFORM : estrado m, tablado m, escenario m (de un teatro) 2 PHASE, STEP : fase f, etapa f ⟨stage of development : fase de desarrollo⟩ ⟨in stages : por etapas⟩ 3 the stage : el teatro m

stagecoach ['steɪdʒˌkoːtʃ] n : diligencia f

stagger¹ ['stægər] vi TOTTER : tambalearse — vt 1 ALTERNATE : alternar, escalonar (turnos de trabajo) 2 : hacer tambalear ⟨to be staggered by : quedarse estupefacto por⟩

stagger² n : tambaleo m

staggering ['stægərɪŋ] adj : asombroso

stagnant ['stægnənt] adj : estancado

stagnate ['stæg,neɪt] vi -nated; -nating : estancarse

staid ['steɪd] adj : serio, sobrio

stain¹ ['steɪn] vt 1 DISCOLOR : manchar 2 DYE : teñir (madera, etc.) 3 SULLY : manchar, empañar

stain² n 1 SPOT : mancha f 2 DYE : tinte m, tintura f 3 BLEMISH : mancha f, mácula f

stainless ['steɪnləs] adj : sin mancha ⟨stainless steel : acero inoxidable⟩

stair ['stær] n 1 STEP : escalón m, peldaño m 2 stairs npl : escalera f, escaleras fpl

staircase ['stær,keɪs] n : escalera f, escaleras fpl

stairway ['stær,weɪ] n : escalera f, escaleras fpl

stake¹ ['steɪk] vt staked; staking 1 : estacar, marcar con estacas (una

propiedad) 2 BET : jugarse, apostar 3 **to stake a claim to** : reclamar, reivindicar

stake² n 1 POST : estaca f 2 BET : apuesta f ⟨to be at stake : estar en juego⟩ 3 INTEREST, SHARE : interés m, participación f

stalactite [stə'læk,taɪt] n : estalactita f

stalagmite [stə'læg,maɪt] n : estalagmita f

stale ['steɪl] adj staler; stalest : viejo ⟨stale bread : pan duro⟩ ⟨stale news : viejas noticias⟩

stalemate ['steɪl,meɪt] n : punto m muerto, impasse m

stalk¹ ['stɔk] vt : acechar — vi : caminar rígidamente (por orgullo, ira, etc.)

stalk² n : tallo m (de una planta)

stall¹ ['stɔl] vt 1 : parar (un motor) 2 DELAY : entretener (a una persona), demorar — vi 1 : pararse (dícese de un motor) 2 DELAY : demorar, andar con rodeos

stall² n 1 : compartimiento m (de un establo) 2 : puesto m (en un mercado, etc.)

stallion ['stæljən] n : caballo m semental

stalwart ['stɔlwərt] adj 1 STRONG : fuerte ⟨a stalwart supporter : un firme partidario⟩ 2 BRAVE : valiente, valeroso

stamen ['steɪmən] n : estambre m

stamina ['stæmənə] n : resistencia f

stammer¹ ['stæmər] vi : tartamudear, titubear

stammer² n : tartamudeo m, titubeo m

stamp¹ ['stæmp] vt 1 : pisotear (con los pies) ⟨to stamp one's feet : patear, dar una patada⟩ 2 IMPRESS, IMPRINT : sellar (una factura, etc.), acuñar (monedas) 3 : franquear, ponerle estampillas a (correo)

stamp² n 1 : sello m (para documentos, etc.) 2 DIE : cuño m (para monedas) 3 or postage stamp : sello m, estampilla f, timbre m CA, Mex

stampede¹ [stæm'piːd] vi -peded; -peding : salir en estampida

stampede² n : estampida f

stance ['stænts] n : postura f

stanch ['stɔntʃ, 'stɑntʃ] vt : detener, estancar (un líquido)

stand¹ ['stænd] v stood ['stʊd]; standing vi 1 : estar de pie, estar parado ⟨I was standing on the corner : estaba parada en la esquina⟩ 2 or **to stand up** : levantarse, pararse, ponerse de pie 3 (indicating a specified position or location) ⟨they stand third in the country : ocupan el tercer lugar en el país⟩ ⟨the machines are standing idle : las máquinas están paradas⟩ 4 (referring to an opinion) ⟨how does he stand on the matter? : ¿cuál es su postura respecto al asunto?⟩ 5 BE : estar ⟨the house stands on a hill : la casa está en una colina⟩ 6 CONTINUE : seguir ⟨the order still stands : el mandato sigue vigente⟩ — vt 1 PLACE, SET : poner, colocar ⟨he stood them in a row : los colocó en hilera⟩ 2 TOLERATE : aguantar, soportar ⟨he can't stand her : no la puede tragar⟩ 3 to stand firm : mantenerse firme 4 to stand guard : hacer la guardia

stand² n 1 RESISTANCE : resistencia f ⟨to make a stand against : resistir a⟩ 2 BOOTH, STALL : stand m, puesto m, kiosko m (para vender periódicos, etc) 3 BASE : pie m, base f 4 : grupo m (de árboles, etc) 5 POSITION : posición f, postura f 6 stands npl GRANDSTAND : tribuna f

standard¹ ['stændərd] adj 1 ESTABLISHED : estándar, oficial ⟨standard measures : medidas oficiales⟩ ⟨standard English : el inglés estándar⟩ 2 NORMAL : normal, estándar, común 3 CLASSIC : estándar, clásico ⟨a standard work : una obra clásica⟩

standard² n 1 BANNER : estandarte m 2 CRITERION : criterio m 3 RULE : estándar m, norma f, regla f 4 LEVEL : nivel m ⟨standard of living : nivel de vida⟩ 5 SUPPORT : poste m, soporte m

standardization [ˌstændərdəˈzeɪʃən] n : estandarización f

standardize ['stændərˌdaɪz] vt -ized; -izing : estandarizar

standard time n : hora f oficial

stand by vt : atenerse a, cumplir con (una promesa, etc.) — vi 1 : mantenerse aparte ⟨to stand by and do nothing : mirar sin hacer nada⟩ 2 : estar preparado, estar listo (para un anuncio, un ataque, etc.)

stand for vt 1 REPRESENT : significar 2 PERMIT, TOLERATE : permitir, tolerar

standing ['stændɪŋ] n 1 POSITION, RANK : posición f 2 DURATION : duración f

stand out vi 1 : destacar(se) ⟨she stands out from the rest : se destaca entre los otros⟩ 2 to stand out against RESIST : oponerse a

standpoint ['stændˌpɔɪnt] n : punto m de vista

standstill ['stændˌstɪl] n 1 STOP : detención f, paro m ⟨to come to a standstill : pararse⟩ 2 DEADLOCK : punto m muerto, impasse m

stand up vt : dejar plantado ⟨he stood me up again : otra vez me dejó plantado⟩ — vi 1 ENDURE : durar, resistir 2 to stand up for : defender 3 to stand up to : hacerle frente (a alguien)

stank → stink

stanza ['stænzə] n : estrofa f

staple¹ ['steɪpəl] vt -pled; -pling : engrapar, grapar

staple² adj : principal, básico ⟨a staple food : un alimento básico⟩

staple³ n 1 : producto m principal 2 : grapa f (para engrapar papeles)

stapler ['steɪplər] n : engrapadora f, grapadora f

star¹ ['star] v starred; starring vt 1 : marcar con una estrella o un aster-

isco 2 FEATURE : estar protagonizado por — vi : tener el papel principal ⟨to star in : protagonizar⟩

star² n : estrella f

starboard ['starbərd] n : estribor m

starch¹ ['startʃ] vt : almidonar

starch² n : almidón m, fécula f (comida)

starchy ['startʃi] adj starchier; -est : lleno de almidón ⟨a starchy diet : una dieta feculenta⟩

stardom ['stardəm] n : estrellato m

stare¹ ['stær] vi stared; staring : mirar fijamente

stare² n : mirada f fija

starfish ['star,fɪʃ] n : estrella f de mar

stark¹ ['stark] adv : completamente ⟨stark raving mad : loco de remate⟩ ⟨stark naked : completamente desnudo⟩

stark² adj 1 ABSOLUTE : absoluto 2 BARREN, DESOLATE : desolado, desierto 3 BARE : desnudo 4 HARSH : severo, duro

starlight ['star,laɪt] n : luz f de las estrellas

starling ['starlɪŋ] n : estornino m

starry ['stari] adj starrier; -est : estrellado

start¹ ['start] vi 1 JUMP : levantarse de un salto, sobresaltarse, dar un respingo 2 BEGIN : empezar, comenzar 3 SET OUT : salir (de viaje, etc.) 4 : arrancar (dícese de un motor) — vt 1 BEGIN : empezar, comenzar, iniciar 2 CAUSE : provocar, causar 3 ESTABLISH : fundar, montar, establecer ⟨to start a business : montar un negocio⟩ 4 : arrancar, poner en marcha, encender ⟨to start the car : arrancar el motor⟩

start² n 1 JUMP : sobresalto m, respingo m 2 BEGINNING : principio m, comienzo m ⟨to get an early start : salir temprano⟩

starter ['startər] n 1 : participante mf (en una carrera, etc.); jugador m inicial, jugadora f titular (en beisbol, etc.) 2 APPETIZER : entremés m, aperitivo m 3 or starter motor : motor m de arranque

startle ['startəl] vt -tled; -tling : asustar, sobresaltar

start-up ['start,ʌp] adj : de puesta en marcha

starvation [star'veɪʃən] n : inanición f, hambre f

starve ['starv] v starved; starving vi : morirse de hambre — vt : privar de comida

stash ['stæʃ] vt : esconder, guardar (en un lugar secreto)

stat ['stæt] → statistic

state¹ ['steɪt] vt stated; stating 1 REPORT : puntualizar, exponer (los hechos, etc.) ⟨state your name : diga su nombre⟩ 2 ESTABLISH, FIX : establecer, fijar

state² n 1 CONDITION : estado m, condición f ⟨a liquid state : un estado líquido⟩ ⟨state of mind : estado de ánimo⟩

⟨in a bad state : en malas condiciones⟩
2 NATION : estado *m*, nación *f* **3** : estado *m* (dentro de un país) ⟨the States : los Estados Unidos⟩

stateliness ['steɪtlinəs] *n* : majestuosidad *f*

stately ['steɪtli] *adj* **statelier; -est** : majestuoso

statement ['steɪtmənt] *n* **1** DECLARATION : declaración *f*, afirmación *f* **2 or bank statement** : estado *m* de cuenta

stateroom ['steɪt,ru:m, -,rʊm] *n* : camarote *m*

statesman ['steɪtsmən] *n*, *pl* **-men** [-mən, -,mɛn] : estadista *mf*

static[1] ['stætɪk] *adj* : estático

static[2] *n* : estática *f*, interferencia *f*

station[1] ['steɪʃən] *vt* : apostar, estacionar

station[2] *n* **1** : estación *f* (de trenes, etc.) **2** RANK, STANDING : condición *f* (social) **3** : canal *m* (de televisión), estación *f* o emisora *f* (de radio) **4 police station** : comisaría *f* **5 fire station** : estación *f* de bomberos, cuartel *m* de bomberos

stationary ['steɪʃə,nɛri] *adj* **1** IMMOBILE : estacionario, inmovible **2** UNCHANGING : inmutable, inalterable

stationery ['steɪʃə,nɛri] *n* : papel *m* y sobres *mpl* (para correspondencia)

station wagon *n* : camioneta *f* ranchera, camioneta *f* guayín *Mex*

statistic [stə'tɪstɪk] *n* : estadística *f* ⟨according to statistics : según las estadísticas⟩

statistical [stə'tɪstɪkəl] *adj* : estadístico

statistician [,stætə'stɪʃən] *n* : estadístico *m*, -ca *f*

statue ['stæ,tʃu:] *n* : estatua *f*

statuesque [,stætʃʊ'ɛsk] *adj* : escultural

statuette [,stætʃʊ'ɛt] *n* : estatuilla *f*

stature ['stætʃər] *n* **1** HEIGHT : estatura *f*, talla *f* **2** PRESTIGE : talla *f*, prestigio *m*

status ['steɪtəs, 'stæ-] *n* : condición *f*, situación *f*, estatus *m* (social) ⟨marital status : estado civil⟩

statute ['stæ,tʃu:t] *n* : ley *f*, estatuto *m*

staunch ['stɔntʃ] *adj* : acérrimo, incondicional, leal ⟨a staunch supporter : un partidario incondicional⟩ — **staunchly** *adv*

stave[1] ['steɪv] *vt* **staved** *or* **stove** ['sto:v]; **staving 1 to stave in** : romper **2 to stave off** : evitar (un ataque), prevenir (un problema)

stave[2] *n* : duela *f* (de un barril)

staves → **staff**

stay[1] ['steɪ] *vi* **1** REMAIN : quedarse, permanecer ⟨to stay in : quedarse en casa⟩ ⟨he stayed in the city : permaneció en la ciudad⟩ **2** CONTINUE : seguir, quedarse ⟨it stayed cloudy : siguió nublado⟩ ⟨to stay awake : mantenerse despierto⟩ **3** LODGE : hospedarse, alojarse (en un hotel, etc.) — *vt* **1** HALT : detener, suspender (una ejecución, etc.) **2 to stay the course** : aguantar hasta el final

stay[2] *n* **1** SOJOURN : estadía *f*, estancia *f*, permanencia *f* **2** SUSPENSION : suspensión *f* (de una sentencia) **3** SUPPORT : soporte *m*

stead ['stɛd] *n* **1** : lugar *m* ⟨she went in his stead : fue en su lugar⟩ **2 to stand (someone) in good stead** : ser muy útil a, servir de mucho a

steadfast ['stɛd,fæst] *adj* : firme, resuelto ⟨a steadfast friend : un fiel amigo⟩ ⟨a steadfast refusal : una negativa categórica⟩

steadily ['stɛdəli] *adv* **1** CONSTANTLY : continuamente, sin parar **2** FIRMLY : con firmeza **3** FIXEDLY : fijamente

steady[1] ['stɛdi] *v* **steadied; steadying** *vt* : sujetar ⟨she steadied herself : recobró el equilibrio⟩ — *vi* : estabilizarse

steady[2] *adj* **steadier; -est** **1** FIRM, SURE : seguro, firme ⟨to have a steady hand : tener buen pulso⟩ **2** FIXED, REGULAR : fijo ⟨a steady income : ingresos fijos⟩ **3** CALM : tranquilo, ecuánime ⟨she has steady nerves : es imperturbable⟩ **4** DEPENDABLE : responsable, fiable **5** CONSTANT : constante

steak ['steɪk] *n* : bistec *m*, filete *m*, churrasco *m*, bife *m* *Arg, Chile, Uru*

steal ['sti:l] *v* **stole** ['sto:l]; **stolen** ['sto:lən]; **stealing** *vt* : robar, hurtar — *vi* **1** : robar, hurtar **2** : ir sigilosamente ⟨to steal away : escabullirse⟩

stealth ['stɛlθ] *n* : sigilo *m*

stealthily ['stɛlθəli] *adv* : furtivamente

stealthy ['stɛlθi] *adj* **stealthier; -est** : furtivo, sigiloso

steam[1] ['sti:m] *vi* : echar vapor ⟨to steam away : moverse echando vapor⟩ — *vt* **1** : cocer al vapor (en cocina) **2 to steam open** : abrir con vapor

steam[2] *n* **1** : vapor *m* **2 to let off steam** : desahogarse

steamboat ['sti:m,bo:t] → **steamship**

steam engine *n* : motor *m* de vapor

steamroller ['sti:m,ro:lər] *n* : apisonadora *f*

steamship ['sti:m,ʃɪp] *n* : vapor *m*, barco *m* de vapor

steamy ['sti:mi] *adj* **steamier; -est** **1** : lleno de vapor **2** EROTIC : erótico ⟨a steamy romance : un tórrido romance⟩

steed ['sti:d] *n* : corcel *m*

steel[1] ['sti:l] *vt* **to steel oneself** : armarse de valor

steel[2] *adj* : de acero

steel[3] *n* : acero *m*

steely ['sti:li] *adj* **steelier; -est** : como acero ⟨a steely gaze : una mirada fría⟩ ⟨steely determination : determinación férrea⟩

steep[1] ['sti:p] *vt* : remojar, dejar (té, etc.) en infusión

steep[2] *adj* **1** : empinado, escarpado ⟨a steep cliff : un precipicio escarpado⟩ **2** CONSIDERABLE : considerable, marcado **3** EXCESSIVE : excesivo ⟨steep prices : precios muy altos⟩

steeple ['sti:pəl] *n* : aguja *f*, campanario *m*

steeplechase ['stiːpəlˌtʃeɪs] n : carrera f de obstáculos

steeply ['stiːpli] adv : abruptamente

steer¹ ['stɪr] vt 1 : conducir (un coche), gobernar (un barco) 2 GUIDE : dirigir, guiar

steer² n : buey m

steering wheel n : volante m

stein ['staɪn] n : jarra f (para cerveza)

stellar ['stɛlər] adj : estelar

stem¹ ['stɛm] v **stemmed; stemming** vt : detener, contener, parar ⟨to stem the tide : detener el curso⟩ — vi **to stem from** : provenir de, ser el resultado de

stem² n : tallo m (de una planta)

stench ['stɛntʃ] n : hedor m, mal olor m

stencil¹ ['stɛntsəl] vt **-ciled** or **-cilled; -ciling** or **-cilling** : marcar utilizando una plantilla

stencil² n : plantilla f (para marcar)

stenographer [stəˈnɑɡrəfər] n : taquígrafo m, -fa f

stenographic [ˌstɛnəˈɡræfɪk] adj : taquigráfico

stenography [stəˈnɑɡrəfi] n : taquigrafía f

step¹ ['stɛp] vi **stepped; stepping** 1 : dar un paso ⟨step this way, please : pase por aquí, por favor⟩ ⟨he stepped outside : salió⟩ 2 **to step on** : pisar

step² n 1 : paso m ⟨step by step : paso por paso⟩ 2 STAIR : escalón m, peldaño m 3 RUNG : escalón m, travesaño m 4 MEASURE, MOVE : medida f, paso m ⟨to take steps : tomar medidas⟩ 5 STRIDE : paso m ⟨with a quick step : con paso rápido⟩

stepbrother ['stɛpˌbrʌðər] n : hermanastro m

stepdaughter ['stɛpˌdɔtər] n : hijastra f

stepfather ['stɛpˌfɑðər, -ˌfɑ-] n : padrastro m

stepladder ['stɛpˌlædər] n : escalera f de tijera

stepmother ['stɛpˌmʌðər] n : madrastra f

steppe ['stɛp] n : estepa f

stepping–stone ['stɛpɪŋˌstoːn] n : pasadera f (en un río, etc.), trampolín m (al éxito)

stepsister ['stɛpˌsɪstər] n : hermanastra f

stepson ['stɛpˌsʌn] n : hijastro m

step up vt INCREASE : aumentar

stereo¹ ['stɛriˌoː, 'stɪr-] adj : estéreo

stereo² n, pl **stereos** : estéreo m

stereophonic [ˌstɛrioˈfɑnɪk, ˌstɪr-] adj : estereofónico

stereotype¹ ['stɛrioˌtaɪp, 'stɪr-] **-typed; -typing** : estereotipar

stereotype² n : estereotipo m

sterile ['stɛrəl] adj : estéril

sterility [stəˈrɪləti] n : esterilidad f

sterilization [ˌstɛrələˈzeɪʃən] n : esterilización f

sterilize ['stɛrəˌlaɪz] vt **-ized; -izing** : esterilizar

sterling ['stərlɪŋ] adj 1 : de ley ⟨sterling silver : plata de ley⟩ 2 EXCELLENT : excelente

stern¹ ['stərn] adj : severo, adusto — **sternly** adv

stern² n : popa f

sternness ['stərnnəs] n : severidad f

sternum ['stərnəm] n, pl **sternums** or **sterna** [-nə] : esternón m

stethoscope ['stɛθəˌskoːp] n : estetoscopio m

stevedore ['stiːvəˌdor] n : estibador m, -dora f

stew¹ ['stuː, 'stjuː] vt : estofar, guisar — vi 1 : cocer (dícese de la carne, etc.) 2 FRET : preocuparse

stew² n 1 : estofado m, guiso m 2 **to be in a stew** : estar agitado

steward ['stuːərd, 'stjuː-] n 1 MANAGER : administrador m 2 : auxiliar m de vuelo (en un avión), camarero m (en un barco)

stewardess ['stuːərdəs, 'stjuː-] n 1 MANAGER : administradora f 2 : camarera f (en un barco) 3 : auxiliar f de vuelo, azafata f, aeromoza f (en un avión)

stick¹ ['stɪk] v **stuck** ['stʌk]; **sticking** vt 1 STAB : clavar 2 ATTACH : pegar 3 PUT : poner 4 **to stick out** : sacar (la lengua, etc.), extender (la mano) — vi 1 ADHERE : pegarse, adherirse 2 JAM : atascarse 3 **to stick around** : quedarse 4 **to stick out** PROJECT : sobresalir (de una superficie), asomar (por detrás o debajo de algo) 5 **to stick to** : no abandonar ⟨stick to your guns : manténgase firme⟩ 6 **to stick up** : estar parado (dícese del pelo, etc.), sobresalir (de una superficie) 7 **to stick with** : serle fiel a (una persona), seguir con (una cosa) ⟨I'll stick with what I know : prefiero lo conocido⟩

stick² n 1 BRANCH, TWIG : ramita f 2 : palo m, vara f ⟨a walking stick : un bastón⟩

sticker ['stɪkər] n : etiqueta f adhesiva

stickler ['stɪklər] n : persona f exigente ⟨to be a stickler for : insistir mucho en⟩

sticky ['stɪki] adj **stickier; -est** 1 ADHESIVE : pegajoso, adhesivo 2 MUGGY : bochornoso 3 DIFFICULT : difícil

stiff ['stɪf] adj 1 RIGID : rígido, tieso ⟨a stiff dough : una masa firme⟩ 2 : agarrotado, entumecido ⟨stiff muscles : músculos entumecidos⟩ 3 STILTED : acartonado, poco natural 4 STRONG : fuerte (dícese del viento, etc.) 5 DIFFICULT, SEVERE : severo, difícil, duro

stiffen ['stɪfən] vt 1 STRENGTHEN : fortalecer, reforzar (tela, etc.) 2 : hacer más duro (un castigo, etc.) — vi 1 HARDEN : endurecerse 2 : entumecerse (dícese de los músculos)

stiffly ['stɪfli] adv 1 RIGIDLY : rígidamente 2 COLDLY : con frialdad

stiffness ['stɪfnəs] n 1 RIGIDITY : rigidez f 2 COLDNESS : frialdad f 3 SEVERITY : severidad f

stifle ['staɪfəl] *vt* **-fled; -fling** SMOTHER, SUPPRESS : sofocar, reprimir, contener ⟨to stifle a yawn : reprimir un bostezo⟩

stigma ['stɪgmə] *n, pl* **stigmata** [stɪg-'mɑtə, 'stɪgmətə] *or* **stigmas** : estigma *m*

stigmatize ['stɪgmə,taɪz] *vt* **-tized; -tizing** : estigmatizar

stile ['staɪl] *n* : escalones *mpl* para cruzar un cerco

stiletto [stə'lɛ,to:] *n, pl* **-tos** *or* **-toes** : estilete *m*

still¹ ['stɪl] *vt* CALM : pacificar, apaciguar — *vi* : pacificarse, apaciguarse

still² *adv* **1** QUIETLY : quieto ⟨sit still! : ¡quédate quieto!⟩ **2** : de todos modos, aún, todavía ⟨she still lives there : aún vive allí⟩ ⟨it's still the same : sigue siendo lo mismo⟩ **3** IN ANY CASE : de todos modos, aún así ⟨he still has doubts : aún así le quedan dudas⟩ ⟨I still prefer that you stay : de todos modos prefiero que te quedes⟩

still³ *adj* **1** MOTIONLESS : quieto, inmóvil **2** SILENT : callado

still⁴ *n* **1** SILENCE : quietud *f*, calma *f* **2** : alambique *m* (para destilar alcohol)

stillborn ['stɪl,bɔrn] *adj* : nacido muerto

stillness ['stɪlnəs] *n* : calma *f*, silencio *m*

stilt ['stɪlt] *n* : zanco *m*

stilted ['stɪltəd] *adj* : afectado, poco natural

stimulant ['stɪmjələnt] *n* : estimulante *m* — **stimulant** *adj*

stimulate ['stɪmjə,leɪt] *vt* **-lated; -lating** : estimular

stimulation [,stɪmjə'leɪʃən] *n* **1** STIMULATING : estimulación *f* **2** STIMULUS : estímulo *m*

stimulus ['stɪmjələs] *n, pl* **-li** [-,laɪ] **1** : estímulo *m* **2** INCENTIVE : acicate *m*

sting¹ ['stɪŋ] *v* **stung** ['stʌŋ]; **stinging** *vt* **1** : picar ⟨a bee stung him : le picó una abeja⟩ **2** HURT : hacer escocer (físicamente), herir (emocionalmente) — *vi* **1** : picar (dícese de las abejas, etc.) **2** SMART : escocer, arder

sting² *n* : picadura *f* (herida), escozor *m* (sensación)

stinger ['stɪŋər] *n* : aguijón *m* (de una abeja, etc.)

stinginess ['stɪndʒinəs] *n* : tacañería *f*

stingy ['stɪndʒi] *adj* **stingier; -est 1** MISERLY : tacaño, avaro **2** PALTRY : mezquino, mísero

stink¹ ['stɪŋk] *vi* **stank** ['stæŋk] *or* **stunk** ['stʌŋk]; **stunk; stinking** : apestar, oler mal

stink² *n* : hedor *m*, mal olor *m*, peste *f*

stint¹ ['stɪnt] *vt* : escatimar ⟨to stint oneself of : privarse de⟩ — *vi* **to stint on** : escatimar

stint² *n* : período *m*

stipend ['staɪ,pɛnd, -pənd] *n* : estipendio *m*

stipulate ['stɪpjə,leɪt] *vt* **-lated; -lating** : estipular

stipulation [,stɪpjə'leɪʃən] *n* : estipulación *f*

stir¹ ['stər] *v* **stirred; stirring** *vt* **1** AGITATE : mover, agitar **2** MIX : revolver, remover **3** INCITE : incitar, impulsar, motivar **4** *or* **to stir up** AROUSE : despertar (memorias, etc.), provocar (ira, etc.) — *vi* : moverse, agitarse

stir² *n* **1** MOTION : movimiento *m* **2** COMMOTION : revuelo *m*

stirrup ['stərəp, 'stɪr-] *n* : estribo *m*

stitch¹ ['stɪtʃ] *vt* : coser, bordar (para decorar) — *vi* : coser

stitch² *n* **1** : puntada *f* **2** TWINGE : punzada *f*, puntada *f*

stock¹ ['stɑk] *vt* : surtir, abastecer, vender — *vi* **to stock up** : abastecerse

stock² *n* **1** SUPPLY : reserva *f*, existencias *fpl* (en comercio) ⟨to be out of stock : estar agotadas las existencias⟩ **2** SECURITIES : acciones *fpl*, valores *mpl* **3** LIVESTOCK : ganado *m* **4** ANCESTRY : linaje *m*, estirpe *f* **5** BROTH : caldo *m* **6 to take stock** : evaluar

stockade [stɑ'keɪd] *n* : estacada *f*

stockbroker ['stɑk,bro:kər] *n* : corredor *m*, -dora *f* de bolsa

stockholder ['stɑk,ho:ldər] *n* : accionista *mf*

stocking ['stɑkɪŋ] *n* : media *f* ⟨a pair of stockings : unas medias⟩

stock market *n* : bolsa *f*

stockpile¹ ['stɑk,paɪl] *vt* **-piled; -piling** : acumular, almacenar

stockpile² *n* : reservas *fpl*

stocky ['stɑki] *adj* **stockier; -est** : robusto, fornido

stockyard ['stɑk,jard] *n* : corral *m*

stodgy ['stɑdʒi] *adj* **stodgier; -est 1** DULL : aburrido, pesado **2** OLD-FASHIONED : anticuado

stoic¹ ['sto:ɪk] *or* **stoical** [-ɪkəl] *adj* : estoico — **stoically** [-ɪkli] *adv*

stoic² *n* : estoico *m*, -ca *f*

stoicism ['sto:ə,sɪzəm] *n* : estoicismo *m*

stoke ['sto:k] *vt* **stoked; stoking** : atizar (un fuego), echarle carbón a (un horno)

stole¹ → **steal**

stole² ['sto:l] *n* : estola *f*

stolen → **steal**

stolid ['stɑlɪd] *adj* : impasible, imperturbable — **stolidly** *adv*

stomach¹ ['stʌmɪk] *vt* : aguantar, soportar

stomach² *n* **1** : estómago *m* **2** BELLY : vientre *m*, barriga *f*, panza *f* **3** DESIRE : ganas *fpl* ⟨he had no stomach for a fight : no quería pelea⟩

stomachache ['stʌmɪk,eɪk] *n* : dolor *m* de estómago

stomp ['stɑmp, 'stɔmp] *vt* : pisotear — *vi* : pisar fuerte

stone¹ ['sto:n] *vt* **stoned; stoning** : apedrear, lapidar

stone² *n* **1** : piedra *f* **2** PIT : hueso *m*, pepa *f* (de una fruta)

Stone Age *n* : Edad *f* de Piedra

stony ['sto:ni] *adj* **stonier; -est 1** ROCKY : pedregoso **2** UNFEELING : insensible, frío ⟨a stony stare : una mirada glacial⟩

stood → stand

stool ['stu:l] *n* **1** SEAT : taburete *m*, banco *m* **2** FOOTSTOOL : escabel *m* **3** FECES : deposición *f* de heces

stoop¹ ['stu:p] *vi* **1** CROUCH : agacharse **2 to stoop to** : rebajarse a

stoop² *n* **1** : espaldas *fpl* encorvadas ⟨to have a stoop : ser encorvado⟩ **2** : entrada *f* (de una casa)

stop¹ ['stɑp] *v* **stopped; stopping** *vt* **1** PLUG : tapar **2** PREVENT : impedir, evitar ⟨she stopped me from leaving : me impidió que saliera⟩ **3** HALT : parar, detener **4** CEASE : dejar de ⟨he stopped talking : dejó de hablar⟩ — *vi* **1** HALT : detenerse, parar **2** CEASE : cesar, terminar ⟨the rain won't stop : no deja de llover⟩ **3** STAY : quedarse ⟨she stopped with friends : se quedó en casa de unos amigos⟩ **4 to stop by** : visitar

stop² *n* **1** STOPPER : tapón *m* **2** HALT : parada *f*, alto *m* ⟨to come to a stop : pararse, detenerse⟩ ⟨to put a stop to : poner fin a⟩ **3** : parada *f* ⟨bus stop : parada de autobús⟩

stopgap ['stɑp,gæp] *n* : arreglo *m* provisorio

stoplight ['stɑp,laɪt] *n* : semáforo *m*

stoppage ['stɑpɪʤ] *n* : acto *m* de parar ⟨a work stoppage : un paro⟩

stopper ['stɑpər] *n* : tapón *m*

storage ['storɪʤ] *n* : almacenamiento *m*, almacenaje *m*

storage battery *n* : acumulador *m*

store¹ ['stor] *vt* **stored; storing** : guardar, almacenar

store² *n* **1** RESERVE, SUPPLY : reserva *f* **2** SHOP : tienda *f* ⟨grocery store : tienda de comestibles⟩

storehouse ['stor,haus] *n* : almacén *m*, depósito *m*

storekeeper ['stor,ki:pər] *n* : tendero *m*, -ra *f*

storeroom ['stor,ru:m, -,rum] *n* : almacén *m*, depósito *m*

stork ['stork] *n* : cigüeña *f*

storm¹ ['storm] *vi* **1** : llover o nevar tormentosamente **2** RAGE : ponerse furioso, vociferar **3 to storm out** : salir echando pestes — *vt* ATTACK : asaltar

storm² *n* **1** : tormenta *f*, tempestad *f* **2** UPROAR : alboroto *m*, revuelo *m*, escándalo *m* ⟨a storm of abuse : un torrente de abusos⟩

stormy ['stormi] *adj* **stormier; -est** : tormentoso

story ['stori] *n, pl* **stories 1** NARRATIVE : cuento *m*, relato *m* **2** ACCOUNT : historia *f*, relato *m* **3** : piso *m*, planta *f* (de un edificio) ⟨first story : planta baja⟩

stout ['staut] *adj* **1** FIRM, RESOLUTE : firme, resuelto **2** STURDY : fuerte, sólido **3** FAT : corpulento, gordo

stove¹ ['sto:v] *n* : cocina *f* (para cocinar), estufa *f* (para calentar)

stove² → stave¹

stow ['sto:] *vt* **1** STORE : poner, meter, guardar **2** LOAD : cargar **— to stow away** : viajar de polizón

stowaway ['sto:ə,weɪ] *n* : polizón *m*

straddle ['strædəl] *vt* **-dled; -dling** : sentarse a horcajadas sobre

straggle ['strægəl] *vi* **-gled; -gling** : rezagarse, quedarse atrás

straggler ['stræglər] *n* : rezagado *m*, -da *f*

straight¹ ['streɪt] *adv* **1** : derecho, directamente ⟨go straight, then turn right : sigue derecho, luego gira a la derecha⟩ **2** HONESTLY : honestamente ⟨to go straight : enmendarse⟩ **3** CLEARLY : con claridad **4** FRANKLY : francamente, con franqueza

straight² *adj* **1** : recto (dícese de las líneas, etc.), derecho (dícese de algo vertical), lacio (dícese del pelo) **2** HONEST, JUST : honesto, justo **3** NEAT, ORDERLY : arreglado, ordenado

straighten ['streɪtən] *vt* **1** : enderezar, poner derecho **2 to straighten up** : arreglar, ordenar ⟨he straightened up the house : arregló la casa⟩

straightforward [streɪt'fɔrwərd] *adj* **1** FRANK : franco, sincero **2** CLEAR, PRECISE : puro, simple, claro

straightway ['streɪt,weɪ, -,weɪ] *adv* : inmediatamente

strain¹ ['streɪn] *vt* **1** EXERT : forzar (la vista, la voz) ⟨to strain oneself : hacer un gran esfuerzo⟩ **2** FILTER : colar, filtrar **3** INJURE : lastimarse, hacerse daño en ⟨to strain a muscle : sufrir un esguince⟩

strain² *n* **1** LINEAGE : linaje *m*, abolengo *m* **2** STREAK, TRACE : veta *f* **3** VARIETY : tipo *m*, variedad *f* **4** STRESS : tensión *f*, presión *f* **5** SPRAIN : esguince *m*, torcedura *f* (del tobillo, etc.) **6 strains** *npl* TUNE : melodía *f*, acordes *mpl*, compases *fpl*

strainer ['streɪnər] *n* : colador *m*

strait ['streɪt] *n* **1** : estrecho *m* **2 straits** *npl* DISTRESS : aprietos *mpl*, apuros *mpl* ⟨in dire straits : en serios aprietos⟩

straitened ['streɪtənd] *adj* **in straitened circumstances** : en apuros económicos

strand¹ ['strænd] *vt* **1** : varar **2 to be left stranded** : quedar(se) varado, quedar colgado ⟨they left me stranded : me dejaron abandonado⟩

strand² *n* **1** : hebra *f* (de hilo, etc.) ⟨a strand of hair : un pelo⟩ **2** BEACH : playa *f*

strange ['streɪnʤ] *adj* **stranger; -est 1** QUEER, UNUSUAL : extraño, raro **2** UNFAMILIAR : desconocido, nuevo

strangely ['streɪnʤli] *adv* ODDLY : de manera extraña ⟨to behave strangely : portarse de una manera rara⟩ ⟨strangely, he didn't call : curiosamente, no llamó⟩

strangeness ['streɪndʒnəs] *n* **1** ODD-NESS : rareza *f* **2** UNFAMILIARITY : lo desconocido

stranger ['streɪndʒər] *n* : desconocido *m*, -da *f*; extraño *m*, -ña *f*

strangle ['stræŋgəl] *vt* **-gled; -gling** : estrangular

strangler ['stræŋglər] *n* : estrangulador *m*, -dora *f*

strap¹ ['stræp] *vt* **strapped; strapping 1** FASTEN : sujetar con una correa **2** FLOG : azotar (con una correa)

strap² *n* **1** : correa *f* **2 shoulder strap** : tirante *m*

strapless ['stræpləs] *n* : sin tirantes

strapping ['stræpɪŋ] *adj* : robusto, fornido

stratagem ['strætədʒəm, -ˌdʒɛm] *n* : estratagema *f*, artimaña *f*

strategic [strə'tiːdʒɪk] *adj* : estratégico

strategist ['strætədʒɪst] *n* : estratega *m*

strategy ['strætədʒi] *n, pl* **-gies** : estrategia *f*

stratified ['strætəˌfaɪd] *adj* : estratificado

stratosphere ['strætəˌsfɪr] *n* : estratosfera *f*

stratospheric [ˌstrætə'sfɪrɪk, -'sfɛr-] *adj* : estratosférico

stratum ['streɪtəm, 'stræ-] *n, pl* **strata** [-ˌtə] : estrato *m*, capa *f*

straw *n* **1** : paja *f* ⟨the last straw : el colmo⟩ **2** *or* **drinking straw** : pajita *f*, popote *m* Mex

strawberry ['strɔˌbɛri] *n, pl* **-ries** : fresa *f*

stray¹ ['streɪ] *vi* **1** WANDER : alejarse, extraviarse ⟨the cattle strayed away : el ganado se descarrió⟩ **2** DIGRESS : desviarse, divagar

stray² *adj* : perdido, callejero (dícese de un perro o un gato), descarriado (dícese del ganado)

stray³ *n* : animal *m* perdido, animal *m* callejero

streak¹ ['striːk] *vt* : hacer rayas en ⟨blue streaked with grey : azul veteado con gris⟩ — *vi* : ir como una flecha

streak² *n* **1** : raya *f*, veta *f* (en mármol, queso, etc.), mechón *m* (en el pelo) **2** : rayo *m* (de luz) **3** TRACE : veta *f* **4** : racha *f* ⟨a streak of luck : una racha de suerte⟩

stream¹ ['striːm] *vi* : correr, salir a chorros ⟨tears streamed from his eyes : las lágrimas brotaban de sus ojos⟩ — *vt* : derramar, dejar correr ⟨to stream blood : derramar sangre⟩

stream² *n* **1** BROOK : arroyo *m*, riachuelo *m* **2** RIVER : río *m* **3** FLOW : corriente *f*, chorro *m*

streamer ['striːmər] *n* **1** PENNANT : banderín *m* **2** RIBBON : serpentina *f* (de papel), cinta *f* (de tela)

streamlined ['striːmˌlaɪnd] *adj* **1** : aerodinámico (dícese de los automóviles, etc.) **2** EFFICIENT : eficiente, racionalizado

street ['striːt] *n* : calle *f*

streetcar ['striːtˌkɑr] *n* : tranvía *m*

strength ['strɛŋkθ] *n* **1** POWER : fuerza *f* **2** SOLIDITY, TOUGHNESS : solidez *f*, resistencia *f*, dureza *f* **3** INTENSITY : intensidad *f* (de emociones, etc.), lo fuerte (de un sabor, etc.) **4** : punto *m* fuerte ⟨strengths and weaknesses : virtudes y defectos⟩ **5** NUMBER : número *m*, complemento *m* ⟨in full strength : en gran número⟩

strengthen ['strɛŋkθən] *vt* **1** : fortalecer (los músculos, el espíritu, etc.) **2** REINFORCE : reforzar **3** INTENSIFY : intensificar, redoblar (esfuerzos, etc.) — *vi* **1** : fortalecerse, hacerse más fuerte **2** INTENSIFY : intensificarse

strenuous ['strɛnjuəs] *adj* **1** VIGOROUS : vigoroso, enérgico **2** ARDUOUS : duro, riguroso

strenuously ['strɛnjuəsli] *adv* : vigorosamente, duro

stress¹ ['strɛs] *vt* **1** : someter a tensión (física) **2** EMPHASIZE : enfatizar, recalcar **3** to stress out : intensificar

stress² *n* **1** : tensión *f* (en un material) **2** EMPHASIS : énfasis *m*, acento *m* (en lingüística) **3** TENSION : tensión *f* (nerviosa), estrés *m*

stressful ['strɛsfəl] *adj* : estresante

stretch¹ ['strɛtʃ] *vt* **1** EXTEND : estirar, extender, desplegar (alas) **2 to stretch the truth** : forzar la verdad, exagerar — *vi* : estirarse

stretch² *n* **1** STRETCHING : extensión *f*, estiramiento *m* (de músculos) **2** ELASTICITY : elasticidad *f* **3** EXPANSE : tramo *m*, trecho *f* ⟨the home stretch : la recta final⟩ **4** PERIOD : período *m* (de tiempo)

stretcher ['strɛtʃər] *n* : camilla *f*

strew ['struː] *vt* **strewed; strewed** *or* **strewn** ['struːn] **strewing 1** SCATTER : esparcir (semillas, etc.), desparramar (papeles, etc.) **2 to strew with** : cubrir de

stricken ['strɪkən] *adj* **stricken with** : aquejado de (una enfermedad), afligido por (tristeza, etc.)

strict ['strɪkt] *adj* : estricto — **strictly** *adv*

strictness ['strɪktnəs] *n* : severidad *f*, lo estricto

stricture ['strɪktʃər] *n* : crítica *f*, censura *f*

stride¹ ['straɪd] *vi* **strode** ['stroːd]; **stridden** ['strɪdən]; **striding** : ir dando trancos, ir dando zancadas

stride² *n* : tranco *m*, zancada *f*

strident ['straɪdənt] *adj* : estridente

strife ['straɪf] *n* : conflictos *mpl*, disensión *f*

strike¹ ['straɪk] *v* **struck** ['strʌk]; **striking** *vt* **1** HIT : golpear (a una persona) ⟨to strike a blow : pegar un golpe⟩ **2** DELETE : suprimir, tachar **3** COIN, MINT : acuñar (monedas) **4** : dar (la hora) **5** AFFLICT : sobrevenir ⟨he was stricken with a fever : le sobrevino una fiebre⟩ **6** IMPRESS : impresionar, parecer ⟨her voice struck me : su voz me impresionó⟩ ⟨it struck him as funny : le pareció chistoso⟩ **7** : encender (un fósforo) **8** FIND : descubrir (oro, petróleo) **9** ADOPT : adoptar (una pose, etc.) — *vi* **1** HIT : golpear ⟨to strike against : chocar contra⟩ **2** ATTACK : atacar **3** : declararse en huelga

strike² *n* **1** BLOW : golpe *m* **2** : huelga *f*, paro *m* ⟨to be on strike : estar en huelga⟩ **3** ATTACK : ataque *m*

strikebreaker ['straɪk,breɪkər] *n* : rompehuelgas *mf*, esquirol *mf*

strike out *vi* **1** HEAD : salir (para) **2** : ser ponchado (en béisbol) ⟨the batter struck out : poncharon al bateador⟩

striker ['straɪkər] *n* : huelguista *mf*

strike up *vt* START : entablar, empezar

striking ['straɪkɪŋ] *adj* : notable, sorprendente, llamativo ⟨a striking beauty : una belleza imponente⟩ — **strikingly** *adv*

string¹ ['strɪŋ] *vt* strung ['strʌŋ]; stringing **1** THREAD : ensartar ⟨to string beads : ensartar cuentas⟩ **2** HANG : colgar (con un cordel)

string² *n* **1** : cordel *m*, cuerda *f* **2** SERIES : serie *f*, sarta *f* (de insultos, etc.) **3** strings *npl* : cuerdas *fpl* (en música)

string bean *n* : judía *f*, ejote *m* *Mex*

stringent ['strɪndʒənt] *adj* : estricto, severo

stringy ['strɪŋi] *adj* stringier; -est : fibroso

strip¹ ['strɪp] *v* stripped; stripping *vt* : quitar (ropa, pintura, etc.), desnudar, despojar — *vi* UNDRESS : desnudarse

strip² *n* : tira *f* ⟨a strip of land : una faja⟩

stripe¹ ['straɪp] *vt* striped ['straɪpt]; striping : marcar con rayas o listas

stripe² *n* **1** : raya *f*, lista *f* **2** BAND : franja *f*

striped ['straɪpt, 'straɪpəd] *adj* : a rayas, de rayas, rayado, listado

strive ['straɪv] *vi* strove ['stroːv]; striven ['strɪvən] *or* strived; striving **1** to strive for : luchar por lograr **2** to strive to : esforzarse por

strobe ['stroːb] *or* strobe light *n* : luz *f* estroboscópica

strode → stride

stroke¹ ['stroːk] *vt* stroked; stroking : acariciar

stroke² *n* : golpe *m* ⟨a stroke of luck : un golpe de suerte⟩

stroll¹ ['stroːl] *vi* : pasear, pasearse, dar un paseo

stroll² *n* : paseo *m*

stroller ['stroːlər] *n* : cochecito *m* (para niños)

strong ['strɔŋ] *adj* **1** : fuerte **2** HEALTHY : sano **3** ZEALOUS : ferviente

stronghold ['strɔŋ,hoːld] *n* : fortaleza *f*, fuerte *m*, bastión *m* ⟨a cultural stronghold : un baluarte de la cultura⟩

strongly ['strɔŋli] *adv* **1** POWERFULLY : fuerte, con fuerza **2** STURDILY

: fuertemente, sólidamente **3** INTENSELY : intensamente, profundamente **4** WHOLEHEARTEDLY : totalmente

struck → strike¹

structural ['strʌktʃərəl] *adj* : estructural

structure¹ ['strʌktʃər] *vt* -tured; -turing : estructurar

structure² *n* **1** BUILDING : construcción *f* **2** ARRANGEMENT, FRAMEWORK : estructura *f*

struggle¹ ['strʌgəl] *vi* -gled; -gling **1** CONTEND : forcejear (físicamente), luchar, contender **2** : hacer con dificultad ⟨she struggled forward : avanzó con dificultad⟩

struggle² *n* : lucha *f*, pelea *f* (física)

strum ['strʌm] *vt* strummed; strumming : rasguear

strung → string¹

strut¹ ['strʌt] *vi* strutted; strutting : pavonearse

strut² ['strʌt] *n* **1** : pavoneo *m* ⟨he walked with a strut : se pavoneaba⟩ **2** : puntal *m* (en construcción, etc.)

strychnine ['strɪk,naɪn, -nən, -,niːn] *n* : estricnina *f*

stub¹ ['stʌb] *vt* stubbed; stubbing **1** to stub one's toe : darse en el dedo (del pie) **2** to stub out : apagarse

stub² *n* : colilla *f* (de un cigarrillo), cabo *m* (de un lápiz, etc.), talón *m* (de un cheque)

stubble ['stʌbəl] *n* **1** : rastrojo *m* (de plantas) **2** BEARD : barba *f*

stubborn ['stʌbərn] *adj* **1** OBSTINATE : terco, obstinado, empecinado **2** PERSISTENT : pertinaz, persistente — **stubbornly** *adv*

stubbornness ['stʌbərnnəs] *n* **1** OBSTINACY : terquedad *f*, obstinación *f* **2** PERSISTENCE : persistencia *f*

stubby ['stʌbi] *adj* stubbier; -est : corto y grueso ⟨stubby fingers : dedos regordetes⟩

stucco ['stʌkoː] *n*, *pl* stuccos *or* stuccoes : estuco *m*

stuck → stick¹

stuck–up ['stʌk,ʌp] *adj* : engreído, creído *fam*

stud¹ ['stʌd] *vt* studded; studding : tachonar, salpicar

stud² *n* **1** *or* stud horse : semental *m* **2** : montante *m* (en construcción) **3** HOBNAIL : tachuela *f*, tachón *m*

student ['stuːdənt, 'stjuː-] *n* : estudiante *mf*; alumno *m*, -na *f* (de un colegio)

studied ['stʌdid] *adj* : intencionado, premeditado

studio ['stuːdi,oː, 'stjuː-] *n*, *pl* studios : estudio *m*

studious ['stuːdiəs, 'stjuː-] *adj* : estudioso — **studiously** *adv*

study¹ ['stʌdi] *v* studied; studying **1** : estudiar **2** EXAMINE : examinar, estudiar

study² *n*, *pl* studies **1** STUDYING : estudio *m* **2** OFFICE : estudio *m*, gabinete *m* (en una casa) **3** RESEARCH : investigación *f*, estudio *m*

stuff¹ [ˈstʌf] *vt* : rellenar, llenar, atiborrar ⟨a stuffed toy : un juguete de peluche⟩

stuff² *n* **1** POSSESSIONS : cosas *fpl* **2** ESSENCE : esencia *f* **3** SUBSTANCE : cosa *f*, cosas *fpl* ⟨some sticky stuff : una cosa pegajosa⟩ ⟨she knows her stuff : es experta⟩

stuffing [ˈstʌfɪŋ] *n* : relleno *m*

stuffy [ˈstʌfi] *adj* **stuffier; -est 1** CLOSE : viciado, cargado ⟨a stuffy room : una sala mal ventilada⟩ ⟨stuffy weather : tiempo bochornoso⟩ **2** : tapado (dícese de la nariz) **3** STODGY : pesado, aburrido

stumble¹ [ˈstʌmbəl] *vi* **-bled; -bling 1** TRIP : tropezar, dar un traspié **2** FLOUNDER : quedarse sin saber qué hacer o decir **3 to stumble across** *or* **to stumble upon** : dar con, tropezar con

stumble² *n* : tropezón *m*, traspié *m*

stump¹ [ˈstʌmp] *vt* : dejar perplejo ⟨to be stumped : no tener respuesta⟩

stump² *n* **1** : muñón *m* (de un brazo o una pierna) **2** *or* **tree stump** : cepa *f*, tocón *m* **3** STUB : cabo *m*

stun [ˈstʌn] *vt* **stunned; stunning 1** : aturdir (con un golpe) **2** ASTONISH, SHOCK : dejar estupefacto, dejar atónito, aturdir

stung → **sting¹**

stunk → **stink¹**

stunning [ˈstʌnɪŋ] *adj* **1** ASTONISHING : asombroso, pasmoso, increíble **2** STRIKING : imponente, impresionante (dícese de la belleza)

stunt¹ [ˈstʌnt] *vt* : atrofiar

stunt² *n* : proeza *f* (acrobática)

stupefy [ˈstuːpəˌfaɪ, ˈstjuː-] *vt* **-fied; -fying 1** : aturdir, atontar (con drogas, etc.) **2** AMAZE : dejar estupefacto, dejar atónito

stupendous [stuˈpɛndəs, stjuˈ-] *adj* **1** MARVELOUS : estupendo, maravilloso **2** TREMENDOUS : tremendo — **stupendously** *adv*

stupid [ˈstuːpəd, ˈstjuː-] *adj* **1** IDIOTIC, SILLY : tonto, bobo, estúpido **2** DULL, OBTUSE : lento, torpe, lerdo

stupidity [stuˈpɪdəti, stjuˈ-] *n* : tontería *f*, estupidez *f*

stupidly [ˈstuːpədli, ˈstjuː-] *adv* **1** IDIOTICALLY : estúpidamente, tontamente **2** DENSELY : densamente

stupor [ˈstuːpər, ˈstjuː-] *n* : estupor *m*

sturdily [ˈstərdəli] *adv* : sólidamente

sturdiness [ˈstərdinəs] *n* : solidez *f* (de muebles, etc.), robustez *f* (de una persona)

sturdy [ˈstərdi] *adj* **sturdier; -est** : fuerte, robusto, sólido

sturgeon [ˈstərdʒən] *n* : esturión *m*

stutter¹ [ˈstʌtər] *vi* : tartamudear

stutter² *n* STAMMER : tartamudeo *m*

sty [ˈstaɪ] *n* **1** *pl* **sties** PIGPEN : chiquero *m*, pocilga *f* **2** *pl* **sties** *or* **styes** : orzuelo *m* (en el ojo)

style¹ [ˈstaɪl] *vt* **styled; styling 1** NAME : llamar **2** : peinar (pelo), diseñar (vestidos, etc.) ⟨carefully styled prose : prosa escrita con gran esmero⟩

style² *n* **1** : estilo *m* ⟨that's just his style : él es así⟩ ⟨to live in style : vivir a lo grande⟩ **2** FASHION : moda *f*

stylish [ˈstaɪlɪʃ] *adj* : de moda, elegante, chic

stylishly [ˈstaɪlɪʃli] *adv* : con estilo

stylishness [ˈstaɪlɪʃnəs] *n* : estilo *m*

stylist [ˈstaɪlɪst] *n* : estilista *mf*

stylize [ˈstaɪˌlaɪz, ˈstaɪlə-] *vt* : estilizar

stylus [ˈstaɪləs] *n, pl* **styli** [ˈstaɪˌlaɪ] **1** PEN : estilo *m* **2** NEEDLE : aguja *f* (de un tocadiscos)

stymie [ˈstaɪmi] *vt* **-mied; -mieing** : obstaculizar

suave [ˈswɑv] *adj* : fino, urbano

sub¹ [ˈsʌb] *vi* **subbed; subbing** → **substitute¹**

sub² *n* **1** → **substitute²** **2** → **submarine**

subcommittee [ˈsʌbkəˌmɪti] *n* : subcomité *m*

subconscious¹ [ˌsʌbˈkɑntʃəs] *adj* : subconsciente — **subconsciously** *adv*

subconscious² *n* : subconsciente *m*

subcontract [ˌsʌbˈkɑnˌtrækt] *vt* : subcontratar

subculture [ˈsʌbˌkʌltʃər] *n* : subcultura *f*

subdivide [ˌsʌbdəˈvaɪd, ˈsʌbdəˌvaɪd] *vt* **-vided; -viding** : subdividir

subdivision [ˈsʌbdəˌvɪʒən] *n* : subdivisión *f*

subdue [səbˈduː, -ˈdjuː] *vt* **-dued; -duing 1** OVERCOME : sojuzgar (a un enemigo), vencer, superar **2** CONTROL : dominar **3** SOFTEN : suavizar, atenuar (luz, etc.), moderar (lenguaje)

subgroup [ˈsʌbˌgruːp] *n* : subgrupo *m*

subhead [ˈsʌbˌhɛd] *or* **subheading** [-ˌhɛdɪŋ] *n* : subtítulo *m*

subject¹ [səbˈdʒɛkt] *vt* **1** CONTROL, DOMINATE : controlar, dominar **2** : someter ⟨they subjected him to pressure : lo sometieron a presiones⟩

subject² [ˈsʌbdʒɪkt] *adj* **1** : subyugado, sometido ⟨a subject nation : una nación subyugada⟩ **2** PRONE : sujeto, propenso ⟨subject to colds : sujeto a resfriarse⟩ **3 subject to** : sujeto a ⟨subject to congressional approval : sujeto a la aprobación del congreso⟩

subject³ [ˈsʌbdʒɪkt] *n* **1** : súbdito *m*, -ta *f* (de un gobierno) **2** TOPIC : tema *m* **3** : sujeto *m* (en gramática)

subjection [səbˈdʒɛkʃən] *n* : sometimiento *m*

subjective [səbˈdʒɛktɪv] *adj* : subjetivo — **subjectively** *adv*

subjectivity [ˌsʌbˌdʒɛkˈtɪvəti] *n* : subjetividad *f*

subjugate [ˈsʌbdʒɪˌgeɪt] *vt* **-gated; -gating** : subyugar, someter, sojuzgar

subjunctive [səb'dʒʌŋktɪv] *n* : subjunti-
vo *m* — **subjunctive** *adj*
sublet ['sʌb,lɛt] *vt* -let; -letting : subarrendar
sublime [sə'blaɪm] *adj* : sublime
sublimely [sə'blaɪmli] *adv* 1 : de manera sublime 2 UTTERLY : absolutamente, completamente
submarine[1] ['sʌbmə,riːn, ˌsʌbmə'-] *adj*
: submarino
submarine[2] *n* : submarino *m*
submerge [səb'mərdʒ] *v* -merged;
-merging *vt* : sumergir — *vi* : sumergirse
submission [səb'mɪʃən] *n* 1 YIELDING
: sumisión *f* 2 PRESENTATION : presentación *f*
submissive [səb'mɪsɪv] *adj* : sumiso, dócil
submit [səb'mɪt] *v* -mitted; -mitting *v*
YIELD : rendirse ⟨to submit to : someterse a⟩ — *vt* PRESENT : presentar
subnormal [ˌsʌb'nɔrməl] *adj* : por debajo de lo normal
subordinate[1] [sə'bɔrdən,eɪt] *vt* -nated;
-nating : subordinar
subordinate[2] [sə'bɔrdənət] *adj* : subordinado ⟨a subordinate clause : una
oración subordinada⟩
subordinate[3] *n* : subordinado *m*, -da *f*;
subalterno *m*, -na *f*
subordination [sə,bɔrdən'eɪʃən] *n* : subordinación *f*
subpoena[1] [sə'piːnə] *vt* -naed; -naing
: citar
subpoena[2] *n* : citación *f*, citatorio *m*
subscribe [səb'skraɪb] *vi* -scribed;
-scribing 1 : suscribirse (a una revista,
etc.) 2 to subscribe to : suscribir (una
opinión, etc.), estar de acuerdo con
subscriber [səb'skraɪbər] *n* : suscriptor
m, -tora *f* (de una revista, etc.); abonado *m*, -da *f* (de un servicio)
subscription [səb'skrɪpʃən] *n* : suscripción *f*
subsequent ['sʌbsɪkwənt, -sə,kwɛnt]
adj : subsiguiente ⟨subsequent to : posterior a⟩
subsequently ['sʌb,sɪkwɛntli, -kwənt-]
adv : posteriormente
subservient [səb'sərviənt] *adj* : servil
subside [səb'saɪd] *vi* -sided; -siding 1
SINK : hundirse, descender 2 ABATE
: calmarse (dícese de las emociones),
amainar (dícese del viento, etc.)
subsidiary[1] [səb'sɪdi,ɛri] *adj* : secundario
subsidiary[2] *n*, *pl* -ries : filial *f*, subsidiaria *f*
subsidize ['sʌbsə,daɪz] *vt* -dized; -dizing
: subvencionar, subsidiar
subsidy ['sʌbsədi] *n*, *pl* -dies : subvención *f*, subsidio *m*
subsist [səb'sɪst] *vi* : subsistir, mantenerse, vivir
subsistence [səb'sɪstənts] *n* : subsistencia *f*

substance ['sʌbstənts] *n* 1 ESSENCE
: sustancia *f*, esencia *f* 2 : sustancia *f*
⟨a toxic substance : una sustancia tóx-
ica⟩ 3 WEALTH : riqueza *f* ⟨a woman
of substance : una mujer acaudalada⟩
substandard [ˌsʌb'stændərd] *adj* : inferior, deficiente
substantial [səb'stænʧəl] *adj* 1 ABUN-
DANT : sustancioso ⟨a substantial meal
: una comida sustanciosa⟩ 2 CONSID-
ERABLE : considerable, apreciable 3
SOLID, STURDY : sólido
substantially [səb'stænʧəli] *adv* : considerablemente
substantiate [səb'stænʧi,eɪt] *vt* -ated;
-ating : confirmar, probar, justificar
substitute[1] ['sʌbstə,tuːt, -,tjuːt] *v* -tuted;
-tuting *vt* : sustituir — *vi* to substitute
for : sustituir
substitute[2] *n* 1 : sustituto *m*, -ta *f*; suplente *mf* (persona) 2 : sucedáneo *m*
⟨sugar substitute : sucedáneo de azú-
car⟩
substitute teacher *n* : profesor *m*, -sora
f suplente
substitution [ˌsʌbstə'tuːʃən, -'tjuː-] *n*
: sustitución *f*
subterfuge ['sʌbtər,fjuːdʒ] *n* : subterfugio *m*
subterranean [ˌsʌbtə'reɪniən] *adj* : subterráneo
subtitle ['sʌb,taɪtəl] *n* : subtítulo *m*
subtle ['sʌtəl] *adj* -tler; -tlest 1 DELI-
CATE, ELUSIVE : sutil, delicado 2
CLEVER : sutil, ingenioso
subtlety ['sʌtəlti] *n*, *pl* -ties : sutileza *f*
subtly ['sʌtəli] *adv* : sutilmente
subtotal ['sʌb,toːtəl] *n* : subtotal *m*
subtract [səb'trækt] *v* : restar, sustraer
subtraction [səb'trækʃən] *n* : resta *f*, sustracción *f*
suburb ['sʌ,bərb] *n* : municipio *m* periférico, suburbio *m*
suburban [sə'bərbən] *adj* : de las afueras
(de una ciudad), suburbano
subversion [səb'vərʒən] *n* : subversión
f
subversive [səb'vərsɪv] *adj* : subversivo
subway ['sʌb,weɪ] *n* : metro *m*, subterráneo *m* Arg, Uru
succeed [sək'siːd] *vt* FOLLOW : suceder
a — *vi* : tener éxito (dícese de las personas), dar resultado (dícese de los
planes, etc.) ⟨she succeeded in finishing : logró terminar⟩
success [sək'sɛs] *n* : éxito *m*
successful [sək'sɛsfəl] *adj* : exitoso, logrado — **successfully** *adv*
succession [sək'sɛʃən] *n* : sucesión *f* ⟨in
succesion : sucesivamente⟩
successive [sək'sɛsɪv] *adj* : sucesivo,
consecutivo — **successively** *adv*
successor [sək'sɛsər] *n* : sucesor *m*,
-sora *f*
succinct [sək'sɪŋkt, sə'sɪŋkt] *adj* : sucinto — **succinctly** *adv*
succor[1] ['sʌkər] *vt* : socorrer
succor[2] *n* : socorro *m*

succotash [ˈsʌkəˌtæʃ] *n* : guiso *m* de maíz y frijoles

succulent[1] [ˈsʌkjələnt] *adj* : suculento, jugoso

succulent[2] *n* : suculenta *f* (planta)

succumb [səˈkʌm] *vi* : sucumbir

such[1] [ˈsʌtʃ] *adv* **1** SO : tan ⟨such tall buildings : edificios tan grandes⟩ **2** VERY : muy ⟨he's not in such good shape : anda un poco mal⟩ **3 such that** : de tal manera que

such[2] *adj* : tal ⟨there's no such thing : no existe tal cosa⟩ ⟨in such cases : en tales casos⟩ ⟨animals such as cows and sheep : animales como vacas y ovejas⟩

such[3] *pron* **1** : tal ⟨such was the result : tal fue el resultado⟩ ⟨he's a child, and acts as such : es un niño, y se porta como tal⟩ **2** : algo o alguien semejante ⟨books, papers and such : libros, papeles y cosas por el estilo⟩

suck [ˈsʌk] *vt* **1** : chupar (por la boca), aspirar (dícese de las máquinas) **2** SUCKLE : mamar — *vt* : sorber (bebidas), chupar (dulces, etc.)

sucker [ˈsʌkər] *n* **1** : ventosa *f* (de un insecto, etc.) **2** : chupón *m* (de una planta) **3** → lollipop **4** FOOL : tonto *m*, -ta *f*; idiota *mf*

suckle [ˈsʌkəl] *v* **-led; -ling** *vt* : amamantar — *vi* : mamar

suckling [ˈsʌklɪŋ] *n* : lactante *mf*

sucrose [ˈsuːˌkroːs, -ˌkroːz] *n* : sacarosa *f*

suction [ˈsʌkʃən] *n* : succión *f*

Sudanese [ˌsuːdənˈiːz, -ˈiːs] *n* : sudanés *m*, -nesa *f* — **Sudanese** *adj*

sudden [ˈsʌdən] *adj* **1** : repentino, súbito ⟨all of a sudden : de pronto, de repente⟩ **2** UNEXPECTED : inesperado, improviso **3** ABRUPT, HASTY : precipitado, brusco

suddenly [ˈsʌdənli] *adv* **1** : de repente, de pronto **2** ABRUPTLY : bruscamente

suddenness [ˈsʌdənnəs] *n* **1** : lo repentino **2** ABRUPTNESS : brusquedad *f* **3** HASTINESS : lo precipitado

suds [ˈsʌdz] *npl* : espuma *f* (de jabón)

sue [ˈsuː] *v* **sued; suing** *vt* : demandar — *vi* **to sue for** : demandar por (daños, etc.)

suede [ˈsweɪd] *n* : ante *m*, gamuza *f*

suet [ˈsuːət] *n* : sebo *m*

suffer [ˈsʌfər] *vi* : sufrir — *vt* **1** : sufrir, padecer (dolores, etc.) **2** PERMIT : permitir, dejar

sufferer [ˈsʌfərər] *n* : persona que padece (una enfermedad, etc.)

suffering [ˈsʌfərɪŋ] *n* : sufrimiento *m*

suffice [səˈfaɪs] *vi* **-ficed; -ficing** : ser suficiente, bastar

sufficient [səˈfɪʃənt] *adj* : suficiente

sufficiently [səˈfɪʃəntli] *adv* : (lo) suficientemente, bastante

suffix [ˈsʌˌfɪks] *n* : sufijo *m*

suffocate [ˈsʌfəˌkeɪt] *v* **-cated; -cating** *vt* : asfixiar, ahogar — *vi* : asfixiarse, ahogarse

suffocation [ˌsʌfəˈkeɪʃən] *n* : asfixia *f*, ahogo *m*

suffrage [ˈsʌfrɪdʒ] *n* : sufragio *m*, derecho *m* al voto

suffuse [səˈfjuːz] *vt* **-fused; -fusing** : impregnar (de olores, etc.), bañar (de luz), teñir (de colores), llenar (de emociones)

sugar[1] [ˈʃʊgər] *vt* : azucarar

sugar[2] *n* : azúcar *mf*

sugarcane [ˈʃʊgərˌkeɪn] *n* : caña *f* de azúcar

sugary [ˈʃʊgəri] *adj* **1** : azucarado ⟨sugary desserts : postres azucarados⟩ **2** SACCHARINE : empalagoso

suggest [səgˈdʒest, sə-] *vt* **1** PROPOSE : sugerir **2** IMPLY : indicar, dar a entender

suggestible [səgˈdʒestəbəl, sə-] *adj* : influenciable

suggestion [səgˈdʒestʃən, sə-] *n* **1** PROPOSAL : sugerencia *f* **2** INDICATION : indicio *m* **3** INSINUATION : insinuación *f*

suggestive [səgˈdʒestɪv, sə-] *adj* : insinuante — **suggestively** *adv*

suicidal [ˌsuːəˈsaɪdəl] *adj* : suicida

suicide [ˈsuːəˌsaɪd] *n* **1** : suicidio *m* (acto) **2** : suicida *mf* (persona)

suit[1] [ˈsuːt] *vt* **1** ADAPT : adaptar **2** BEFIT : convenir a, ser apropiado a **3** BECOME : favorecer, quedarle bien (a alguien) ⟨the dress suits you : el vestido te queda bien⟩ **4** PLEASE : agradecer, satisfacer, convenirle bien (a alguien) ⟨does Friday suit you? : ¿le conviene el viernes?⟩ ⟨suit yourself! : ¡como quieras!⟩

suit[2] *n* **1** LAWSUIT : pleito *m*, litigio *m* **2** : traje *m* (ropa) **3** : palo *m* (de naipes)

suitability [ˌsuːtəˈbɪlətʃi] *n* : idoneidad *f*, lo apropiado

suitable [ˈsuːtəbəl] *adj* : apropiado, idóneo — **suitably** [-bli] *adv*

suitcase [ˈsuːtˌkeɪs] *n* : maleta *f*, valija *f*, petaca *f Mex*

suite [ˈswiːt, *for 2 also* ˈsuːt] *n* **1** : suite *f* (de habitaciones) **2** SET : juego *m* (de muebles)

suitor [ˈsuːtər] *n* : pretendiente *m*

sulfur [ˈsʌlfər] *n* : azufre *m*

sulfuric acid [ˌsʌlˈfjʊrɪk] *adj* : ácido *m* sulfúrico

sulfurous [ˌsʌlˈfjʊrəs, ˈsʌlfərəs, ˈsʌlfjə-] *adj* : sulfuroso

sulk[1] [ˈsʌlk] *vi* : estar de mal humor, enfurruñarse *fam*

sulk[2] *n* : mal humor *m*

sulky [ˈsʌlki] *adj* **sulkier; -est** : malhumorado, taimado *Chile*

sullen [ˈsʌlən] *adj* **1** MOROSE : hosco, taciturno **2** DREARY : sombrío, deprimente

sullenly [ˈsʌlənli] *adv* **1** MOROSELY : hoscamente **2** GLOOMILY : sombríamente

sully [ˈsʌli] *vt* **sullied; sullying** : manchar, empañar

sultan ['sʌltən] *n* : sultán *m*

sultry ['sʌltri] *adj* **sultrier; -est 1** : bochornoso ⟨sultry weather : tiempo sofocante, tiempo bochornoso⟩ **2** SENSUAL : sensual, seductor

sum[1] ['sʌm] *vt* **summed; summing 1** : sumar (números) **2 → sum up**

sum[2] *n* **·1** AMOUNT : suma *f*, cantidad *f* **2** TOTAL : suma *f*, total *f* **3** : suma *f*, adición *f* (en matemáticas)

sumac ['ʃuː,mæk, 'suː-] *n* : zumaque *m*

summarize ['sʌmə,raɪz] *v* **-rized; -rizing** : resumir, compendiar

summary[1] ['sʌməri] *adj* **1** CONCISE : breve, conciso **2** IMMEDIATE : inmediato ⟨a summary dismissal : un despido inmediato⟩

summary[2] *n, pl* **-ries** : resumen *m*, compendio *m*

summer ['sʌmər] *n* : verano *m*

summery ['sʌməri] *adj* : veraniego

summit ['sʌmət] *n* **1** : cumbre *f*, cima *f* (de una montaña) **2** *or* **summit conference** : cumbre *f*

summon ['sʌmən] *vt* **1** CALL : convocar (una reunión, etc.), llamar (a una persona) **2** : citar (en derecho) **3 to summon up** : armarse de (valor, etc.) ⟨to summon up one's strength : reunir fuerzas⟩

summons ['sʌmənz] *n, pl* **summonses 1** SUBPOENA : citación *f*, citatorio *m Mex* **2** CALL : llamada *f*, llamamiento *m*

sumptuous ['sʌmptʃuəs] *adj* : suntuoso

sum up *vt* **1** SUMMARIZE : resumir **2** EVALUATE : evaluar — *vi* : recapitular

sun[1] ['sʌn] *vt* **sunned; sunning 1** : poner al sol **2 to sun oneself** : asolearse, tomar el sol

sun[2] *n* **1** : sol *m* **2** SUNSHINE : luz *f* del sol

sunbeam ['sʌn,biːm] *n* : rayo *m* de sol

sunblock ['sʌn,blɑk] *n* : filtro *m* solar

sunburn[1] ['sʌn,bərn] *vi* **-burned [-,bərnd]** *or* **-burnt [-,bərnt]; -burning** : quemarse por el sol

sunburn[2] ['sʌn,bərn] *n* : quemadura *f* de sol

sundae ['sʌndi] *n* : sundae *m*

Sunday ['sʌn,deɪ, -di] *n* : domingo *m*

sundial ['sʌn,daɪl] *n* : reloj *m* de sol

sundown ['sʌn,daʊn] → **sunset**

sundries ['sʌndriz] *npl* : artículos *mpl* diversos

sundry ['sʌndri] *adj* : varios, diversos

sunflower ['sʌn,flaʊər] *n* : girasol *m*, mirasol *m*

sung → **sing**

sunglasses ['sʌn,glæsəz] *npl* : gafas *fpl* de sol, lentes *mpl* de sol

sunk → **sink**[1]

sunken ['sʌnkən] *adj* : hundido

sunlight ['sʌn,laɪt] *n* : sol *m*, luz *f* del sol

sunny ['sʌni] *adj* **sunnier; -est** : soleado

sunrise ['sʌn,raɪz] *n* : salida *f* del sol

sunscreen ['sʌn,skriːn] *n* : filtro *m* solar

sunset ['sʌn,sɛt] *n* : puesta *f* del sol

sunshine ['sʌn,ʃaɪn] *n* : sol *m*, luz *f* del sol

sunspot ['sʌn,spɑt] *n* : mancha *f* solar

sunstroke ['sʌn,stroːk] *n* : insolación *f*

suntan ['sʌn,tæn] *n* : bronceado *m*

sup ['sʌp] *vi* **supped; supping** : cenar

super ['suːpər] *adj* : súper ⟨super! : ¡fantástico!⟩

superabundance [,suːpərə'bʌndənts] *n* : superabundancia *f*

superb [sʊ'pərb] *adj* : magnífico, espléndido — **superbly** *adv*

supercilious [,suːpər'sɪliəs] *adj* : altivo, altanero, desdeñoso

supercomputer ['suːpərkəm,pjuːtər] *n* : supercomputadora *f*

superficial [,suːpər'fɪʃəl] *adj* : superficial — **superficially** *adv*

superfluous [sʊ'pərfluəs] *adj* : superfluo

superhighway ['suːpər,haɪ,weɪ, ,suː-pər'-] *n* : autopista *f*

superhuman [,suːpər'hjuːmən] *adj* **1** SUPERNATURAL : sobrenatural **2** HERCULEAN : sobrehumano

superimpose [,suːpərɪm'poːz] *vt* **-posed; -posing** : superponer, sobreponer

superintend [,suːpərɪn'tɛnd] *vt* : supervisar

superintendent [,suːpərɪn'tɛndənt] *n* **1** : portero *m*, -ra *f* (de un edificio); director *m*, -tora *f* (de una escuela, etc.); superintendente *mf* (de policía)

superior[1] [sʊ'piriər] *adj* **1** BETTER : superior **2** HAUGHTY : altivo, altanero

superior[2] *n* : superior *m*

superiority [sʊ,piri'orəti] *n, pl* **-ties** : superioridad *f*

superlative[1] [sʊ'pərlətɪv] *adj* **1** : superlativo (en gramática) **2** SUPREME : supremo **3** EXCELLENT : excelente, excepcional

superlative[2] *n* : superlativo *m*

supermarket ['suːpər,mɑrkət] *n* : supermercado *m*

supernatural [,suːpər'nætʃərəl] *adj* : sobrenatural

supernaturally [,suːpər'nætʃərəli] *adv* : de manera sobrenatural

superpower ['suːpər,paʊər] *n* : superpotencia *f*

supersede [,suːpər'siːd] *vt* **-seded; -seding** : suplantar, reemplazar, sustituir

supersonic [,suːpər'sɑnɪk] *adj* : supersónico

superstar ['suːpər,stɑr] *n* : superestrella *f*

superstition [,suːpər'stɪʃən] *n* : superstición *f*

superstitious [,suːpər'stɪʃəs] *adj* : supersticioso

superstructure ['suːpər,strʌktʃər] *n* : superestructura *f*

supervise ['suːpər,vaɪz] *vt* **-vised; -vising** : supervisar, dirigir

supervision [,suːpər'vɪʒən] *n* : supervisión *f*, dirección *f*

supervisor [ˈsuːpərˌvaɪzər] n : supervisor m, -sora f

supervisory [ˌsuːpərˈvaɪzəri] adj : de supervisor

supine [suˈpaɪn] adj 1 : en decúbito supino, en decúbito dorsal 2 ABJECT, INDIFFERENT : indiferente, apático

supper [ˈsʌpər] n : cena f, comida f

supplant [səˈplænt] vt : suplantar

supple [ˈsʌpəl] adj -pler; -plest : flexible

supplement¹ [ˈsʌpləˌmɛnt] vt : complementar, completar

supplement² [ˈsʌpləmənt] n 1 : complemento m ⟨dietary supplement : complemento alimenticio⟩ 2 : suplemento m (de un libro o periódico)

supplementary [ˌsʌpləˈmɛntəri] adj : suplementario

supplicate [ˈsʌpləˌkeɪt] v -cated; -cating vi : rezar — vt : suplicar

supplier [səˈplaɪər] n : proveedor m, -dora f; abastecedor m, -dora f

supply¹ [səˈplaɪ] vt -plied; -plying : suministrar, proveer de, proporcionar

supply² n, pl -plies 1 PROVISION : provisión f, suministro m ⟨supply and demand : la oferta y la demanda⟩ 2 STOCK : reserva f, existencias fpl (de un negocio) 3 supplies npl PROVISIONS : provisiones fpl, víveres mpl, despensa f

support¹ [səˈport] vt 1 BACK : apoyar, respaldar 2 MAINTAIN : mantener, sostener, sustentar 3 PROP UP : sostener, apoyar, apuntalar, soportar

support² n 1 : apoyo m (moral), ayuda f (económica) 2 PROP : soporte m, apoyo m

supporter [səˈportər] n : partidario m, -ria f

supportive [səˈportɪv] adj : que apoya ⟨his family is very supportive : su familia lo apoya mucho⟩

suppose [səˈpoːz] vt -posed; -posing 1 ASSUME : suponer, imaginarse 2 BELIEVE : suponer, creer 3 to be supposed to : tener que, deber

supposed [səˈpoːzd, -ˈpoːzəd] adj : supuesto — **supposedly** [səˈpoːzədli] adv

supposition [ˌsʌpəˈzɪʃən] n : suposición f

suppository [səˈpɑːzəˌtori] n, pl -ries : supositorio m

suppress [səˈprɛs] vt 1 SUBDUE : sofocar, suprimir, reprimir (una rebelión, etc.) 2 : suprimir, ocultar (información) 3 REPRESS : reprimir, contener ⟨to suppress a yawn : reprimir un bostezo⟩

suppression [səˈprɛʃən] n 1 SUBDUING : represión f 2 : supresión f (de información) 3 REPRESSION : represión f, inhibición f

supremacy [suˈprɛməsi] n, pl -cies : supremacía f

supreme [suˈpriːm] adj : supremo

Supreme Being n : Ser m Supremo

supremely [suˈpriːmli] adv : totalmente, sumamente

surcharge [ˈsərˌtʃɑːrdʒ] n : recargo m

sure¹ [ˈʃʊr] adv 1 ALL RIGHT : por supuesto, claro 2 (used as an intensifier) ⟨it sure is hot! : ¡hace tanto calor!⟩ ⟨she sure is pretty! : ¡qué linda es!⟩

sure² adj surer; -est : seguro ⟨to be sure about something : estar seguro de algo⟩ ⟨a sure sign : una clara señal⟩ ⟨for sure : seguro, con seguridad⟩

surely [ˈʃʊrli] adv 1 CERTAINLY : seguramente 2 (used as an intensifier) ⟨you surely don't mean that! : ¡no me digas que estás hablando en serio!⟩

sureness [ˈʃʊrnəs] n : certeza f, seguridad f

surety [ˈʃʊrəti] n, pl -ties : fianza f, garantía f

surf¹ [ˈsərf] n 1 WAVES : oleaje m 2 FOAM : espuma f

surface¹ [ˈsərfəs] v -faced; -facing vi : salir a la superficie — vt : revestir (una carretera)

surface² n 1 : superficie f 2 on the surface : en apariencia

surfboard [ˈsərfˌbord] n : tabla f de surf, tabla f de surfing

surfeit [ˈsərfət] n : exceso m

surfer [ˈsərfər] n : surfista mf

surfing [ˈsərfɪŋ] n : surf m, surfing m

surge¹ [ˈsərdʒ] vi surged; surging 1 : hincharse (dícese del mar), levantarse (dícese de las olas) 2 SWARM : salir en tropel (dícese de la gente, etc.)

surge² n 1 : oleaje m (del mar), oleada f (de gente) 2 FLUSH : arranque m, arrebato m (de ira, etc.) 3 INCREASE : aumento m (súbito)

surgeon [ˈsərdʒən] n : cirujano m, -na f

surgery [ˈsərdʒəri] n, pl -geries : cirugía f

surgical [ˈsərdʒɪkəl] adj : quirúrgico — **surgically** [-kli] adv

surly [ˈsərli] adj surlier; -est : hosco, arisco

surmise¹ [sərˈmaɪz] vt -mised; -mising : conjeturar, suponer, concluir

surmise² n : conjetura f

surmount [sərˈmaʊnt] vt 1 OVERCOME : superar, vencer, salvar 2 CLIMB : escalar 3 CAP, TOP : coronar

surname [ˈsərˌneɪm] n : apellido m

surpass [sərˈpæs] vt : superar, exceder, rebasar, sobrepasar

surplus [ˈsərˌplʌs] n 1 : excedente m, sobrante m, superávit m (de dinero)

surprise¹ [səˈpraɪz, sər-] vt -prised; -prising : sorprender

surprise² n : sorpresa f ⟨to take by surprise : sorprender⟩

surprising [səˈpraɪzɪŋ, sər-] adj : sorprendente — **surprisingly** adv

surrender¹ [səˈrɛndər] vt 1 : entregar, rendir 2 to surrender oneself : entregarse — vi : rendirse

surrender² n : rendición m (de una ciudad, etc.), entrega f (de posesiones)

surreptitious [ˌsərəpˈtɪʃəs] *adj* : subrepticio — **surreptitiously** *adv*

surrogate [ˈsərəgət, -ˌgeɪt] *n* : sustituto *m*

surround [səˈraʊnd] *vt* : rodear

surroundings [səˈraʊndɪŋz] *npl* : ambiente *m*, entorno *m*

surveillance [sərˈveɪlənts, -ˈveɪjənts, -ˈveɪənts] *n* : vigilancia *f*

survey[1] [sərˈveɪ] *vt* **-veyed; -veying 1** : medir (un terreno) **2** EXAMINE : inspeccionar, examinar, revisar **3** POLL : hacer una encuesta de, sondear

survey[2] [ˈsərˌveɪ] *n, pl* **-veys 1** INSPECTION : inspección *f*, revisión *f* **2** : medición *f* (de un terreno) **3** POLL : encuesta *f*, sondeo *m*

surveyor [sərˈveɪər] *n* : agrimensor *m*, -sora *f*

survival [sərˈvaɪvəl] *n* : supervivencia *f*, sobrevivencia *f*

survive [sərˈvaɪv] *v* **-vived; -viving** *vi* : sobrevivir — *vt* OUTLIVE : sobrevivir a

survivor [sərˈvaɪvər] *n* : superviviente *mf*, sobreviviente *mf*

susceptibility [səˌsɛptəˈbɪləti] *n, pl* **-ties** : vulnerabilidad *f*, propensión *f* (a enfermedades, etc.)

susceptible [səˈsɛptəbəl] *adj* **1** VULNERABLE : vulnerable, sensible ⟨susceptible to flattery : sensible a halagos⟩ **2** PRONE : propenso ⟨susceptible to colds : propenso a resfriarse⟩

suspect[1] [səˈspɛkt] *vt* **1** DISTRUST : dudar de **2** : sospechar (algo), sospechar de (una persona) **3** IMAGINE, THINK : imaginarse, creer

suspect[2] [ˈsʌsˌpɛkt, səˈspɛkt] *adj* : sospechoso, dudoso, cuestionable

suspect[3] [ˈsʌsˌpɛkt] *n* : sospechoso *m*, -sa *f*

suspend [səˈspɛnd] *vt* : suspender

suspenders [səˈspɛndərz] *npl* : tirantes *mpl*

suspense [səˈspɛnts] *n* : incertidumbre *f*, suspenso *m* (en una película, etc.)

suspenseful [səˈspɛntsfəl] *adj* : de suspenso

suspension [səˈspɛntʃən] *n* : suspensión *f*

suspicion [səˈspɪʃən] *n* **1** : sospecha *f* **2** TRACE : pizca *f*, atisbo *m*

suspicious [səˈspɪʃəs] *adj* **1** QUESTIONABLE : sospechoso, dudoso **2** DISTRUSTFUL : suspicaz, desconfiado

suspiciously [səˈspɪʃəsli] *adv* : de modo sospechoso, con recelo

sustain [səˈsteɪn] *vt* **1** NOURISH : sustentar **2** PROLONG : sostener **3** SUFFER : sufrir **4** SUPPORT, UPHOLD : apoyar, respaldar, sostener

sustainable [səˈsteɪnəbəl] *adj* : sostenible

sustenance [ˈsʌstənənts] *n* **1** NOURISHMENT : sustento *m* **2** SUPPORT : sostén *m*

svelte [ˈsfɛlt] *adj* : esbelto

swab[1] [ˈswɑb] *vt* **swabbed; swabbing 1** CLEAN : lavar, limpiar **2** : aplicar a (con hisopo)

swab[2] *n or* **cotton swab** : hisopo *m* (para aplicar medicinas, etc.)

swaddle [ˈswɑdəl] *vt* **-dled; -dling** [ˈswɑdəlɪŋ] : envolver (en pañales)

swagger[1] [ˈswægər] *vi* : pavonearse

swagger[2] *n* : pavoneo *m*

swallow[1] [ˈswɑloː] *vt* **1** : tragar (comida, etc.) **2** ENGULF : tragar, envolver **3** REPRESS : tragarse (insultos, etc.) — *vi* : tragar

swallow[2] *n* **1** : golondrina *f* (pájaro) **2** GULP : trago *m*

swam → swim

swamp[1] [ˈswɑmp] *vt* : inundar

swamp[2] *n* : pantano *m*, ciénaga *f*

swampy [ˈswɑmpi] *adj* **swampier; -est** : pantanoso, cenagoso

swan [ˈswɑn] *n* : cisne *f*

swap[1] [ˈswɑp] *vt* **swapped; swapping** : cambiar, intercambiar ⟨to swap places : cambiarse de sitio⟩

swap[2] *n* : cambio *m*, intercambio *m*

swarm[1] [ˈswɔrm] *vi* : enjambrar

swarm[2] *n* : enjambre *m*

swarthy [ˈswɔrði, -θi] *adj* **swarthier; -est** : moreno

swashbuckling [ˈswɑʃˌbʌklɪŋ] *adj* : de aventurero

swat[1] [ˈswɑt] *vt* **swatted; swatting** : aplastar (un insecto), darle una palmada (a alguien)

swat[2] *n* : palmada *f* (con la mano), golpe *m* (con un objeto)

swatch [ˈswɑtʃ] *n* : muestra *f*

swath [ˈswɑθ, ˈswɔθ] *or* **swathe** [ˈswɑð, ˈswɔð, ˈsweɪð] *n* : franja *f* (de grano segado)

swathe [ˈswɑð, ˈswɔð, ˈsweɪð] *vt* **swathed; swathing** : envolver

swatter [ˈswɑtər] → **flyswatter**

sway[1] [ˈsweɪ] *vi* : balancearse, mecerse — *vt* INFLUENCE : influir en, convencer

sway[2] *n* **1** SWINGING : balanceo *m* **2** INFLUENCE : influjo *m*

swear [ˈswær] *v* **swore** [ˈswor]; **sworn** [ˈsworn]; **swearing** *vi* **1** VOW : jurar **2** CURSE : decir palabrotas — *vt* : jurar

swearword [ˈswærˌwərd] *n* : mala palabra *f*, palabrota *f*

sweat[1] [ˈswɛt] *vi* **sweat** *or* **sweated; sweating 1** PERSPIRE : sudar, transpirar **2** OOZE : rezumar **3 to sweat over** : sudar la gota gorda por

sweat[2] *n* : sudor *m*, transpiración *f*

sweater [ˈswɛtər] *n* : suéter *m*

sweatshirt [ˈswɛtˌʃərt] *n* : sudadera *f*

sweaty [ˈswɛti] *adj* **sweatier; -est** : sudoroso, sudado, transpirado

Swede [ˈswiːd] *n* : sueco *m*, -ca *f*

Swedish[1] [ˈswiːdɪʃ] *adj* : sueco

Swedish[2] *n* **1** : sueco *m* (idioma) **2 the Swedish** *npl* : los suecos

sweep[1] [ˈswiːp] *v* **swept** [ˈswɛpt]; **sweeping** *vt* **1** : barrer (el suelo, etc.), limpiar (suciedad, etc.) ⟨he swept the books aside : apartó los libros de un manotazo⟩ 2 *or* **to sweep through** : extenderse por (dícese del fuego, etc.), azotar (dícese de una tormenta) — *vi* 1 : barrer, limpiar 2 : extenderse (en una curva), describir una curva ⟨the sun swept across the sky : el sol describía una curva en el cielo⟩

sweep² *n* 1 : barrido *m*, barrida *f* (con una escoba) 2 : movimiento *m* circular 3 SCOPE : alcance *m*

sweeper ['swi:pər] *n* : barrendero *m*, -ra *f*

sweeping ['swi:pɪŋ] *adj* 1 WIDE : amplio (dícese de un movimiento) 2 EXTENSIVE : extenso, radical 3 INDISCRIMINATE : indiscriminado, demasiado general 4 OVERWHELMING : arrollador, aplastante

sweepstakes ['swi:pˌsteɪks] *ns & pl* 1 : carrera *f* (en que el ganador se lleva el premio entero) 2 LOTTERY : lotería *f*

sweet¹ ['swi:t] *adj* 1 : dulce ⟨sweet desserts : postres dulces⟩ 2 FRESH : fresco 3 : sin sal (dícese de la mantequilla, etc.) 4 PLEASANT : dulce, agradable 5 DEAR : querido

sweet² *n* : dulce *m*

sweeten ['swi:tən] *vt* : endulzar

sweetener ['swi:tənər] *n* : endulzante *m*

sweetheart ['swi:tˌhɑrt] *n* : novio *m*, -via *f* ⟨thanks, sweetheart : gracias, cariño⟩

sweetly ['swi:tli] *adv* : dulcemente

sweetness ['swi:tnəs] *n* : dulzura *f*

sweet potato *n* : batata *f*, boniato *m*

swell¹ ['swel] *vi* **swelled; swelled** *or* **swollen** ['swo:lən, 'swɑl-]; **swelling** 1 *or* **to swell up** : hincharse ⟨her ankle swelled : se le hinchó el tobillo⟩ 2 *or* **to swell out** : inflarse, hincharse (dícese de las velas, etc.) 3 INCREASE : aumentar, crecer

swell² *n* 1 : oleaje *m* (del mar) 2 → **swelling**

swelling ['swelɪŋ] *n* : hinchazón *f*

swelter ['sweltər] *vi* : sofocarse de calor

swept → **sweep¹**

swerve¹ ['swərv] *vi* **swerved; swerving** : virar bruscamente

swerve² *n* : viraje *m* brusco

swift¹ ['swɪft] *adj* 1 FAST : rápido, veloz 2 SUDDEN : repentino, súbito — **swiftly** *adv*

swift² *n* : vencejo *m* (pájaro)

swiftness ['swɪftnəs] *n* : rapidez *f*, velocidad *f*

swig¹ ['swɪg] *vi* **swigged; swigging** : tomar a tragos, beber a tragos

swig² *n* : trago *m*

swill¹ ['swɪl] *vt* : chupar, beber a tragos grandes

swill² *n* 1 SLOP : bazofia *f* 2 GARBAGE : basura *f*

swim¹ ['swɪm] *vi* **swam** ['swæm]; **swum** ['swʌm]; **swimming** 1 : nadar 2 FLOAT : flotar 3 REEL : dar vueltas ⟨his head was swimming : la cabeza le daba vueltas⟩

swim² *n* : baño *m*, chapuzón *m* ⟨to go for a swim : ir a nadar⟩

swimmer ['swɪmər] *n* : nadador *m*, -dora *f*

swindle¹ ['swɪndəl] *vt* **-dled; -dling** : estafar, timar

swindle² *n* : estafa *f*, timo *m fam*

swindler ['swɪndlər] *n* : estafador *m*, -dora *f*; timador *m*, -dora *f*

swine ['swaɪn] *ns & pl* : cerdo *m*, -da *f*

swing¹ ['swɪŋ] *v* **swung** ['swʌŋ]; **swinging** *vt* 1 : describir una curva con ⟨he swung the ax at the tree : le dio al árbol con el hacha⟩ : balancear (los brazos, etc.), hacer oscilar 2 SUSPEND : colgar — *vi* 1 SWAY : balancearse (dícese de los brazos, etc.), oscilar (dícese de un objeto), columpiarse, mecerse (en un columpio) 2 SWIVEL : girar (en un pivote) ⟨the door swung shut : la puerta se cerró⟩ 3 CHANGE : virar, cambiar (dícese de las opiniones, etc.)

swing² *n* 1 SWINGING : vaivén *m*, balanceo *m* 2 CHANGE, SHIFT : viraje *m*, movimiento *m* 3 : columpio *m* (para niños) 4 **to take a swing at someone** : intentar pegarle a alguien

swipe¹ ['swaɪp] *vt* **swiped; swiping** 1 STRIKE : dar, pegar (con un movimiento amplio) 2 WIPE : limpiar 3 STEAL : birlar *fam*, robar

swipe² *n* BLOW : golpe *m*

swirl¹ ['swərl] *vi* : arremolinarse

swirl² *n* 1 EDDY : remolino *m* 2 SPIRAL : espiral *f*

swish¹ ['swɪʃ] *vt* : mover (produciendo un sonido) ⟨she swished her skirt : movía la falda⟩ — *vi* : moverse (produciendo un sonido) ⟨the cars swished by : se oían pasar los coches⟩

swish² *n* : silbido *m* (de un látigo, etc.), susurro *m* (de agua), crujido *m* (de ropa, etc.)

Swiss ['swɪs] *n* : suizo *m*, -za *f* — **Swiss** *adj*

swiss chard *n* : acelga *f*

switch¹ ['swɪtʃ] *vt* 1 LASH, WHIP : azotar 2 CHANGE : cambiar de 3 EXCHANGE : intercambiar 4 **to switch on** : encender, prender 5 **to switch off** : apagar — *vi* 1 : moverse de un lado al otro 2 CHANGE : cambiar 3 SWAP : intercambiarse

switch² *n* 1 WHIP : vara *f* 2 CHANGE, SHIFT : cambio *m* 3 : interruptor *m*, llave *f* (de la luz, etc.)

switchboard ['swɪtʃˌbord] *n* : conmutador *m*, centralita *f*

swivel¹ ['swɪvəl] *vi* **-veled** *or* **-velled; -veling** *or* **-velling** : girar (sobre un pivote)

swivel² *n* : base *f* giratoria

swollen *pp* → **swell¹**

swoon¹ ['swu:n] *vi* : desvanecerse, desmayarse

swoon² *n* : desvanecimiento *m*, desmayo *m*

swoop¹ ['swu:p] *vi* : abatirse (dícese de las aves), descender en picada (dícese de un avión)

swoop² *n* : descenso *m* en picada

sword ['sɔrd] *n* : espada *f*

swordfish ['sɔrd,fɪʃ] *n* : pez *m* espada

swore, sworn → **swear**

swum *pp* → **swim**¹

swung → **swing**¹

sycamore ['sɪkə,mor] *n* : sicomoro *m*

sycophant ['sɪkəfənt, -,fænt] *n* : adulador *m*, -dora *f*

syllabic [sə'læbɪk] *adj* : silábico

syllable ['sɪləbəl] *n* : sílaba *f*

syllabus ['sɪləbəs] *n, pl* **-bi** [-,baɪ] *or* **-buses** : programa *m* (de estudios)

symbol ['sɪmbəl] *n* : símbolo *m*

symbolic [sɪm'balɪk] *adj* : simbólico — **symbolically** [-kli] *adv*

symbolism ['sɪmbə,lɪzəm] *n* : simbolismo *m*

symbolize ['sɪmbə,laɪz] *vt* **-ized; -izing** : simbolizar

symmetrical [sə'mɛtrɪkəl] *or* **symmetric** [-trɪk] *adj* : simétrico — **symmetrically** [-trɪkli] *adv*

symmetry ['sɪmətri] *n, pl* **-tries** : simetría *f*

sympathetic [,sɪmpə'θɛtɪk] *adj* **1** PLEASING : agradable **2** RECEPTIVE : receptivo, favorable **3** COMPASSIONATE, UNDERSTANDING : compasivo, compasivo

sympathetically [,sɪmpə'θɛtɪkli] *adv* : con compasión, con comprensión

sympathize ['sɪmpə,θaɪz] *vi* **-thized; -thizing** : compadecer ⟨I sympathize with you : te compadezco⟩

sympathy ['sɪmpəθi] *n, pl* **-thies 1** COMPASSION : compasión *f* **2** UNDERSTANDING : comprensión *f* **3** AGREEMENT : solidaridad *f* ⟨in sympathy with : de acuerdo con⟩ **4** CONDOLENCES : pésame *m*, condolencias *fpl*

symphonic [sɪm'fanɪk] *adj* : sinfónico

symphony ['sɪmfəni] *n, pl* **-nies** : sinfonía *f*

symposium [sɪm'po:ziəm] *n, pl* **-sia** [-ziə] *or* **-siums** : simposio *m*

symptom ['sɪmptəm] *n* : síntoma *m*

symptomatic [,sɪmptə'mætɪk] *adj* : sintomático

synagogue ['sɪnə,gag, -,gɔg] *n* : sinagoga *f*

sync ['sɪŋk] *n* : sincronización *f* ⟨in sync : sincronizado⟩

synchronize ['sɪŋkrə,naɪz, 'sɪn-] *v* **-nized; -nizing** *vi* : estar sincronizado — *vt* : sincronizar

syncopate ['sɪŋkə,peɪt, 'sɪn-] *vt* **-pated; -pating** : sincopar

syncopation [,sɪŋkə'peɪʃən, ,sɪn-] *n* : síncopa *f*

syndicate¹ ['sɪndə,keɪt] *vi* **-cated; -cating** : formar una asociación

syndicate² ['sɪndɪkət] *n* : asociación *f*, agrupación *f*

syndrome ['sɪn,dro:m] *n* : síndrome *m*

synonym ['sɪnə,nɪm] *n* : sinónimo *m*

synonymous [sə'nanəməs] *adj* : sinónimo

synopsis [sə'napsɪs] *n, pl* **-opses** [-,si:z] : sinopsis *f*

syntactic [sɪn'tæktɪk] *adj* : sintáctico

syntax ['sɪn,tæks] *n* : sintaxis *f*

synthesis ['sɪnθəsɪs] *n, pl* **-theses** [-,si:z] : síntesis *f*

synthesize ['sɪnθə,saɪz] *vt* **-sized; -sizing** : sintetizar

synthetic¹ [sɪn'θɛtɪk] *adj* : sintético, artificial — **synthetically** [-,tɪkli] *adv*

synthetic² *n* : producto *m* sintético

syphilis ['sɪfələs] *n* : sífilis *f*

Syrian ['sɪriən] *n* : sirio *m*, -ria *f* — **Syrian** *adj*

syringe [sə'rɪndʒ, 'sɪrɪndʒ] *n* : jeringa *f*, jeringuilla *f*

syrup ['sərəp, 'sɪrəp] *n* : jarabe *m*, almíbar *m* (de azúcar y agua)

system ['sɪstəm] *n* **1** METHOD : sistema *m*, método *m* **2** APPARATUS : sistema *m*, instalación *f*, aparato *m* ⟨electrical system : instalación eléctrica⟩ ⟨digestive system : aparato digestivo⟩ **3** BODY : organismo *m*, cuerpo *m* ⟨diseases that affect the whole system : enfermedades que afectan al organismo entero⟩ **4** NETWORK : red *f*

systematic [,sɪstə'mætɪk] *adj* : sistemático — **systematically** [-tɪkli] *adv*

systematize ['sɪstəmə,taɪz] *vt* **-tized; -tizing** : sistematizar

systemic [sɪs'tɛmɪk] *adj* : sistémico

T

t ['ti:] *n, pl* **t's** *or* **ts** ['ti:z] : vigésima letra del alfabeto inglés

tab ['tæb] *n* **1** FLAP, TAG : lengüeta *f* (de un sobre, una caja, etc.), etiqueta *f* (de ropa) **2** → **tabulator 3** BILL, CHECK : cuenta *f* **4 to keep tabs on** : tener bajo vigilancia

tabby ['tæbi] *n, pl* **-bies 1** *or* **tabby cat** : gato *m* atigrado **2** : gata *f*

tabernacle ['tæbər,nækəl] *n* : tabernáculo *m*

table ['teɪbəl] *n* **1** : mesa *f* ⟨a table for two : una mesa para dos⟩ **2** LIST : tabla *f* ⟨multiplication table : tabla de multiplicar⟩ **3 table of contents** : índice *m* de materias

tableau [tæ'blo:, 'tæ,-] *n, pl* **-leaux** [-'blo:z, -,blo:z] : retablo *m*, cuadro *m* vivo (en teatro)

tablecloth ['teɪbəl,klɔθ] *n* : mantel *m*

tablespoon ['teɪbəl,spu:n] *n* **1** : cuchara *f* (de mesa) **2** → **tablespoonful**

tablespoonful [ˈteɪbəlˌspuːnˌfʊl] *n* : cucharada *f*

tablet [ˈtæblət] *n* **1** PLAQUE : placa *f* **2** PAD : bloc *m* (de papel) **3** PILL : tableta *f*, pastilla *f*, píldora *f* ⟨an aspirin tablet : una tableta de aspirina⟩

table tennis *n* : tenis *m* de mesa

tableware [ˈteɪbəlˌwær] *n* : vajillas *fpl*, cubiertos *mpl* (de mesa)

tabloid [ˈtæˌblɔɪd] *n* : tabloide *m*

taboo¹ [təˈbuː, tæ-] *adj* : tabú

taboo² *n* : tabú *m*

tabular [ˈtæbjələr] *adj* : tabular

tabulate [ˈtæbjəˌleɪt] *vt* -lated; -lating : tabular

tabulator [ˈtæbjəˌleɪtər] *n* : tabulador *m*

tacit [ˈtæsət] *adj* : tácito, implícito — **tacitly** *adv*

taciturn [ˈtæsəˌtərn] *adj* : taciturno

tack¹ [ˈtæk] *vt* **1** : sujetar con tachuelas **2 to tack on** ADD : añadir, agregar

tack² *n* **1** : tachuela *f* **2** COURSE : rumbo *m* ⟨to change tack : cambiar de rumbo⟩

tackle¹ [ˈtækəl] *vt* -led; -ling **1** : taclear (en futbol americano) **2** CONFRONT : abordar, enfrentar, emprender (un problema, un trabajo, etc.)

tackle² *n* **1** EQUIPMENT, GEAR : equipo *m*, aparejo *m* **2** : aparejo *m* (de un buque) **3** : tacleada *f* (en futbol americano)

tacky [ˈtæki] *adj* **tackier; -est 1** STICKY : pegajoso **2** CHEAP, GAUDY : de mal gusto, naco *Mex*

tact [ˈtækt] *n* : tacto *m*, delicadeza *f*, discreción *f*

tactful [ˈtæktfəl] *adj* : discreto, diplomático, de mucho tacto

tactfully [ˈtæktfəli] *adv* : discretamente, con mucho tacto

tactic [ˈtæktɪk] *n* : táctica *f*

tactical [ˈtæktɪkəl] *adj* : táctico, estratégico

tactics [ˈtæktɪks] *ns & pl* : táctica *f*, estrategia *f*

tactile [ˈtæktəl, -ˌtaɪl] *adj* : táctil

tactless [ˈtæktləs] *adj* : indiscreto, poco delicado

tactlessly [ˈtæktləsli] *adv* : rudamente, sin tacto

tadpole [ˈtædˌpoːl] *n* : renacuajo *m*

taffeta [ˈtæfətə] *n* : tafetán *m*, tafeta *f* *Arg, Mex, Uru*

taffy [ˈtæfi] *n, pl* **-fies** : caramelo *m* de melaza, chicloso *m Mex*

tag¹ [ˈtæg] *v* **tagged; tagging** *vt* **1** LABEL : etiquetar **2** TAIL : seguir de cerca **3** TOUCH : tocar (en varios juegos) — *vi* **to tag along** : pegarse, acompañar

tag² *n* **1** LABEL : etiqueta *f* **2** SAYING : dicho *m*, refrán *m*

tail¹ [ˈteɪl] *vt* FOLLOW : seguir de cerca, pegarse

tail² *n* **1** : cola *f*, rabo *m* (de un animal) **2** : cola *f*, parte *f* posterior ⟨a comet's tail : la cola de un cometa⟩ **3 tails** *npl* : cruz *f* (de una moneda) ⟨heads or tails : cara o cruz⟩

tailed [ˈteɪld] *adj* : que tiene cola

tailgate¹ [ˈteɪlˌgeɪt] *vi* -gated; -gating : seguir a un vehículo demasiado de cerca

tailgate² *n* : puerta *f* trasera (de un vehículo)

taillight [ˈteɪlˌlaɪt] *n* : luz *f* trasera (de un vehículo), calavera *f Mex*

tailor¹ [ˈteɪlər] *vt* **1** : confeccionar o alterar (ropa) **2** ADAPT : adaptar, ajustar

tailor² *n* : sastre *m*, -tra *f*

tailpipe [ˈteɪlˌpaɪp] *n* : tubo *m* de escape

tailspin [ˈteɪlˌspɪn] *n* : barrena *f*

taint¹ [ˈteɪnt] *vt* : contaminar, corromper

taint² *n* : corrupción *f*, impureza *f*

take¹ [ˈteɪk] *v* **took** [ˈtʊk]; **taken** [ˈteɪkən]; **taking** *vt* **1** CAPTURE : capturar, apresar **2** GRASP : tomar, agarrar ⟨to take the bull by the horns : tomar al toro por los cuernos⟩ **3** CATCH : tomar, agarrar ⟨taken by surprise : tomado por sorpresa⟩ **4** CAPTIVATE : encantar, fascinar **5** INGEST : tomar, ingerir ⟨take two pills : tome dos píldoras⟩ **6** REMOVE : sacar, extraer ⟨take an orange : saca una naranja⟩ **7** : tomar, coger (un tren, un autobús, etc.) **8** NEED, REQUIRE : tomar, requerir ⟨these things take time : estas cosas toman tiempo⟩ **9** BRING, CARRY : llevar, sacar, cargar ⟨take them with you : llévalos contigo⟩ ⟨take the trash out : saca la basura⟩ **10** BEAR, ENDURE : soportar, aguantar (dolores, etc.) **11** ACCEPT : aceptar (un cheque, etc.), seguir (consejos), asumir (la responsabilidad) **12** SUPPOSE : suponer ⟨I take it that . . . : supongo que . . . ⟩ **13** (*indicating an action or an undertaking*) ⟨to take a walk : dar un paseo⟩ ⟨to take a class : tomar una clase⟩ **14 to take place** HAPPEN : tener lugar, suceder, ocurrir — *vi* : agarrar (dícese de un tinte), prender (dícese de una vacuna)

take² *n* **1** PROCEEDS : recaudación *f*, ingresos *mpl*, ganancias *fpl* **2** : toma *f* (de un rodaje o una grabación)

take back *vt* : retirar (palabras, etc.)

take in *vt* **1** : tomarle a, achicar (un vestido, etc.) **2** INCLUDE : incluir, abarcar **3** ATTEND : ir a ⟨to take in a movie : ir al cine⟩ **4** GRASP, UNDERSTAND : captar, entender **5** DECEIVE : engañar

takeoff [ˈteɪkˌɔf] *n* **1** PARODY : parodia *f* **2** : despegue *m* (de un avión o cohete)

take off *vt* REMOVE : quitar ⟨take off your hat : quítate el sombrero⟩ — *vi* **1** : despegar (dícese de un avión o un cohete) **2** LEAVE : irse, partir

take on *vt* **1** TACKLE : abordar, emprender (problemas, etc.) **2** ACCEPT : aceptar, encargarse de, asumir (una responsabilidad) **3** CONTRACT : contratar (trabajadores) **4** ASSUME : adoptar, asumir, adquirir ⟨the neighborhood took on a dingy look : el barrio asumió una apariencia deprimente⟩

takeover ['teɪk₁oːvər] *n* : toma *f* (de poder o de control), adquisición *f* (de una empresa por otra)

take over *vt* : tomar el poder de, tomar las riendas de — *vi* : asumir el mando

taker ['teɪkər] *n* : persona *f* interesada ⟨available to all takers : disponible a cuantos estén interesados⟩

take up *vt* **1** LIFT : levantar **2** SHORTEN : acortar (una falda, etc.) **3** BEGIN : empezar, dedicarse a (un pasatiempo, etc.) **4** OCCUPY : ocupar, llevar (tiempo, espacio) **5** PURSUE : volver a (una cuestión, un asunto) **6** CONTINUE : seguir con

talc ['tælk] *n* : talco *m*

talcum powder ['tælkəm] *n* : talco *m*, polvos *mpl* de talco

tale ['teɪl] *n* **1** ANECDOTE, STORY : cuento *m*, relato *m*, anécdota *f* **2** FALSEHOOD : cuento *m*, mentira *f*

talent ['tælənt] *n* : talento *m*, don *m*

talented ['tæləntəd] *adj* : talentoso

talisman ['tælɪsmən, -lɪz-] *n*, *pl* **-mans** : talismán *m*

talk¹ ['tɔk] *vi* **1** : hablar ⟨he talks for hours : se pasa horas hablando⟩ **2** CHAT : charlar, platicar — *vt* **1** SPEAK : hablar ⟨to talk French : hablar francés⟩ ⟨to talk business : hablar de negocios⟩ **2** PERSUADE : influenciar, convencer ⟨she talked me out of it : me convenció que no lo hiciera⟩ **3** to talk over DISCUSS : hablar de, discutir

talk² *n* **1** CONVERSATION : charla *f*, plática *f*, conversación *f* **2** GOSSIP, RUMOR : chisme *m*, rumores *mpl*

talkative ['tɔkətɪv] *adj* : locuaz, parlanchín, charlatán

talker ['tɔkər] *n* : conversador *m*, -dora *f*; hablador *m*, -dora *f*

talk show *n* : programa *m* de entrevistas

tall ['tɔl] *adj* : alto ⟨how tall is he? : ¿cuánto mide?⟩

tallness ['tɔlnəs] *n* HEIGHT : estatura *f* (de una persona), altura *f* (de un objeto)

tallow ['tælo:] *n* : sebo *m*

tally¹ ['tæli] *v* **-lied; -lying** *vt* RECKON : contar, hacer una cuenta de — *vi* MATCH : concordar, corresponder, cuadrar

tally² *n*, *pl* **-lies** : cuenta *f* ⟨to keep a tally : llevar la cuenta⟩

talon ['tælən] *n* : garra *f* (de un ave de rapiña)

tambourine [₁tæmbə'riːn] *n* : pandero *m*, pandereta *f*

tame¹ ['teɪm] *vt* **tamed; taming** : domar, amansar, domesticar

tame² *adj* **tamer; -est 1** DOMESTICATED : domesticado, manso **2** DOCILE : manso, dócil **3** DULL : aburrido, soso

tamely ['teɪmli] *adv* : mansamente, dócilmente

tamer ['teɪmər] *n* : domador *m*, -dora *f*

tamp ['tæmp] *vt* : apisonar

tamper ['tæmpər] *vi* **to tamper with** : adulterar (una sustancia), forzar (un sello, una cerradura), falsear (documentos), manipular (una máquina)

tampon ['tæm₁pɑn] *n* : tampón *m*

tan¹ ['tæn] *v* **tanned; tanning** *vt* **1** : curtir (pieles) **2** : broncear — *vi* : broncearse

tan² *n* **1** SUNTAN : bronceado *m* ⟨to get a tan : broncearse⟩ **2** : color *m* canela, color *m* café con leche

tandem¹ ['tændəm] *adv* or **in tandem** : en tándem

tandem² *n* : tándem *m* (bicicleta)

tang ['tæŋ] *n* : sabor *m* fuerte

tangent ['tændʒənt] *n* : tangente *f* ⟨to go off on a tangent : irse por la tangente⟩

tangerine ['tændʒə₁riːn, ₁tændʒə'-] *n* : mandarina *f*

tangible ['tændʒəbəl] *adj* : tangible, palpable — **tangibly** [-bli] *adv*

tangle¹ ['tæŋgəl] *v* **-gled; -gling** *vt* : enredar, enmarañar — *vi* : enredarse

tangle² *n* : enredo *m*, maraña *f*

tango¹ ['tæŋ₁goː] *vi* : bailar el tango

tango² *n*, *pl* **-gos** : tango *m*

tangy ['tæŋi] *adj* **tangier; -est** : que tiene un sabor fuerte

tank ['tæŋk] *n* : tanque *m*, depósito *m* ⟨fuel tank : depósito de combustibles⟩

tankard ['tæŋkərd] *n* : jarra *f*

tanker ['tæŋkər] *n* : buque *m* cisterna, camión *m* cisterna, avión *m* cisterna ⟨an oil tanker : un petrolero⟩

tanner ['tænər] *n* : curtidor *m*, -dora *f*

tannery ['tænəri] *n*, *pl* **-neries** : curtiduría *f*, tenería *f*

tannin ['tænən] *n* : tanino *m*

tantalize ['tæntə₁laɪz] *vt* **-lized; -lizing** : tentar, atormentar (con algo inasequible)

tantalizing ['tæntə₁laɪzɪŋ] *adj* : tentador, seductor

tantamount ['tæntə₁maʊnt] *adj* : equivalente

tantrum ['tæntrəm] *n* : rabieta *f*, berrinche *m* ⟨to throw a tantrum : hacer un berrinche⟩

tap¹ ['tæp] *vt* **tapped; tapping 1** : ponerle una espita a, sacar líquido de (un barril, un tanque, etc.) **2** : intervenir (una línea telefónica) **3** PAT, TOUCH : tocar, golpear ligeramente ⟨he tapped me on the shoulder : me tocó en el hombro⟩

tap² *n* **1** FAUCET : llave *f*, grifo *m* ⟨beer on tap : cerveza de barril⟩ **2** : extracción *f* (de líquido) ⟨a spinal tap : una punción lumbar⟩ **3** PAT, TOUCH : golpecito *m*, toque *m*

tape¹ ['teɪp] *vt* **taped; taping 1** : sujetar o arreglar con cinta adhesiva **2** RECORD : grabar

tape² *n* **1** : cinta *f* (adhesiva, magnética, etc.) **2 → tape measure**

tape measure *n* : cinta *f* métrica

taper¹ ['teɪpər] *vi* **1** : estrecharse gradualmente ⟨its tail tapers towards the tip : su cola va estrechándose hacia la punta⟩ **2** *or* **to taper off** : disminuir gradualmente

taper[2] *n* **1** CANDLE : vela *f* larga y delgada **2** TAPERING : estrechamiento *m* gradual

tapestry ['tæpəstri] *n, pl* **-tries** : tapiz *m*

tapeworm ['teɪp,wərm] *n* : solitaria *f*, tenia *f*

tapioca [,tæpi'o:kə] *n* : tapioca *f*

tar[1] ['tɑr] *vt* **tarred; tarring** : alquitranar

tar[2] *n* : alquitrán *m*, brea *f*, chapopote *m* *Mex*

tarantula [tə'ræntʃələ, -'ræntələ] *n* : tarántula *f*

tardiness ['tɑrdinəs] *n* : tardanza *f*, retraso *m*

tardy ['tɑrdi] *adj* **-dier; -est** LATE : tardío, de retraso

target[1] ['tɑrgət] *vt* : fijar como objetivo, dirigir, destinar

target[2] *n* **1** : blanco *m* ⟨target practice : tiro al blanco⟩ **2** GOAL, OBJECTIVE : meta *f*, objetivo *m*

tariff ['tærɪf] *n* DUTY : tarifa *f*, arancel *m*

tarnish[1] ['tɑrnɪʃ] *vt* **1** DULL : deslustrar **2** SULLY : empañar, manchar (una reputación, etc.) — *vi* : deslustrarse

tarnish[2] *n* : deslustre *m*

tarpaulin [tɑr'pɔlən, 'tɑrpə-] *n* : lona *f* (impermeable)

tarragon ['tærə,gɑn, -gən] *n* : estragón *m*

tarry[1] ['tæri] *vi* **-ried; -rying** : demorarse, entretenerse

tarry[2] ['tɑri] *adj* **1** : parecido al alquitrán **2** : cubierto de alquitrán

tart[1] ['tɑrt] *adj* **1** SOUR : ácido, agrio **2** CAUSTIC : mordaz, acrimonioso — **tartly** *adv*

tart[2] *n* : tartaleta *f*

tartan ['tɑrtən] *n* : tartán *m*

tartar ['tɑrtər] *n* **1** : tártaro *m* ⟨tartar sauce : salsa tártara⟩ **2** : sarro *m* (dental)

tartness ['tɑrtnəs] *n* **1** SOURNESS : acidez *f* **2** ACRIMONY, SHARPNESS : mordacidad *f*, acrimonia *f*, acritud *f*

task ['tæsk] *n* : tarea *f*, trabajo *m*

taskmaster ['tæsk,mæstər] *n* **to be a hard taskmaster** : ser exigente, ser muy estricto

tassel ['tæsəl] *n* : borla *f*

taste[1] ['teɪst] *v* **tasted; tasting** *vt* : probar (alimentos), degustar, catar (vinos) ⟨taste this soup : prueba esta sopa⟩ — *vi* : saber ⟨this tastes good : esto sabe bueno⟩

taste[2] *n* **1** SAMPLE : prueba *f*, bocado *m* (de comida), trago *m* (de bebidas) **2** FLAVOR : gusto *m*, sabor *m* **3** : gusto *m* ⟨she has good taste : tiene buen gusto⟩ ⟨in bad taste : de mal gusto⟩

taste bud *n* : papila *f* gustativa

tasteful ['teɪstfəl] *adj* : de buen gusto

tastefully ['teɪstfəli] *adv* : con buen gusto

tasteless ['teɪstləs] *adj* **1** FLAVORLESS : sin sabor, soso, insípido **2** : de mal

gusto ⟨a tasteless joke : un chiste de mal gusto⟩

taster ['teɪstər] *n* : degustador *m*, -dora *f*; catador *m*, -dora *f* (de vinos)

tastiness ['teɪstinəs] *n* : lo sabroso

tasty ['teɪsti] *adj* **tastier; -est** : sabroso, gustoso

tatter ['tætər] *n* **1** SHRED : tira *f*, jirón *m* (de tela) **2 tatters** *npl* : andrajos *mpl*, harapos *mpl* ⟨to be in tatters : estar por los suelos⟩

tattered ['tætərd] *adj* : andrajoso, en jirones

tattle ['tætəl] *vi* **-tled; -tling 1** CHATTER : parlotear *fam*, cotorrear *fam* **2 to tattle on someone** : acusar a alguien

tattletale ['tætəl,teɪl] *n* : soplón *m*, -plona *f fam*

tattoo[1] [tæ'tu:] *vt* : tatuar

tattoo[2] *n* : tatuaje *m* ⟨to get a tattoo : tatuarse⟩

taught → **teach**

taunt[1] ['tɔnt] *vt* MOCK : mofarse de, burlarse de

taunt[2] *n* : mofa *f*, burla *f*

Taurus ['tɔrəs] *n* : Tauro *mf*

taut ['tɔt] *adj* : tirante, tenso — **tautly** *adv*

tautness ['tɔtnəs] *n* : tirantez *f*, tensión *f*

tavern ['tævərn] *n* : taberna *f*

tawdry ['tɔdri] *adj* **-drier; -est** : chabacano, vulgar

tawny ['tɔni] *adj* **-nier; -est** : leonado

tax[1] ['tæks] *vt* **1** : gravar, cobrar un impuesto sobre **2** CHARGE : acusar ⟨they taxed him with neglect : fue acusado de incumplimiento⟩ **3 to tax someone's strength** : ponerle a prueba las fuerzas (a alguien)

tax[2] *n* **1** : impuesto *m*, tributo *m* **2** BURDEN : carga *f*

taxable ['tæksəbəl] *adj* : sujeto a un impuesto

taxation [tæk'seɪʃən] *n* : impuestos *mpl*

tax–exempt ['tæksɪg'zɛmpt, -ɛg-] *adj* : libre de impuestos

taxi[1] ['tæksi] *vi* **taxied; taxiing** *or* **taxying; taxis** *or* **taxies 1** : ir en taxi **2** : rodar sobre la pista de aterrizaje (dícese de un avión)

taxi[2] *n, pl* **taxis** : taxi *m*, libre *m Mex*

taxicab ['tæksi,kæb] *n* → **taxi**[2]

taxidermist ['tæksə,dərmɪst] *n* : taxidermista *mf*

taxidermy ['tæksə,dərmi] *n* : taxidermia *f*

taxpayer ['tæks,peɪər] *n* : contribuyente *mf*, causante *mf Mex*

TB [,ti'bi:] → **tuberculosis**

tea ['ti:] *n* **1** : té *m* (planta y bebida) **2** : merienda *f*, té *m* (comida)

teach ['ti:tʃ] *v* **taught; teaching** *vt* : enseñar, dar clases de ⟨she teaches math : da clases de matemáticas⟩ ⟨she taught me everything I know : me enseñó todo lo que sé⟩ — *vi* : enseñar, dar clases

teacher ['ti:ʧər] n : maestro m, -tra f (de enseñanza primaria); profesor m, -sora f (de enseñanza secundaria)

teaching ['ti:ʧɪŋ] n : enseñanza f

teacup ['ti:ˌkʌp] n : taza f para té

teak ['ti:k] n : teca f

teakettle ['ti:ˌkɛtəl] n : tetera f

teal ['ti:l] n, pl **teal** or **teals** : cerceta f (pato)

team¹ ['ti:m] vi to team up 1 : formar un equipo (en deportes) 2 COLLABO-RATE : asociarse, juntarse, unirse

team² adj : de equipo

team³ n 1 : tiro m (de caballos), yunta f (de bueyes o mulas) 2 : equipo m (en deportes, etc.)

teammate ['ti:mˌmeɪt] n : compañero m, -ra f de equipo

teamster ['ti:mstər] n : camionero m, -ra f

teamwork ['ti:mˌwərk] n : trabajo m en equipo, cooperación f

teapot ['ti:ˌpɑt] n : tetera f

tear¹ ['tær] v **tore** ['tor]; **torn** ['torn]; **tearing** vt 1 RIP : desgarrar, romper, rasgar (tela) ⟨to tear to pieces : hacer pedazos⟩ 2 or to tear apart DIVIDE : dividir 3 REMOVE : arrancar ⟨torn from his family : arrancado de su familia⟩ 4 to tear down : derribar — vi 1 RIP : desgarrarse, romperse 2 RUSH : ir a gran velocidad ⟨she went tearing down the street : se fue como rayo por la calle⟩

tear² n : desgarradura f, rotura f, desgarro m (muscular)

tear³ ['tɪr] n : lágrima f

teardrop ['tɪrˌdrɑp] n → tear³

tearful ['tɪrfəl] adj : lloroso, triste — **tearfully** adv

tease¹ ['ti:z] vt **teased**; **teasing** 1 MOCK : burlarse de, mofarse de 2 ANNOY : irritar, fastidiar

tease² n 1 TEASING : burla f, mofa f 2 : bromista mf; guasón m, -sona f

teaspoon ['ti:ˌspu:n] n 1 : cucharita f 2 → teaspoonful

teaspoonful ['ti:ˌspu:nˌfʊl] n, pl **-spoonfuls** [-ˌfʊlz] or **-spoonsful** [-ˌspu:nzˌfʊl] : cucharadita f

teat ['ti:t] n : tetilla f

technical ['tɛknɪkəl] adj : técnico — **technically** [-kli] adv

technicality [ˌtɛknəˈkæləti] n, pl **-ties** : detalle m técnico

technician [tɛkˈnɪʃən] n : técnico m, -ca f

technique [tɛkˈni:k] n : técnica f

technological [ˌtɛknəˈlɑʤɪkəl] adj : tecnológico

technology [tɛkˈnɑləʤi] n, pl **-gies** : tecnología f

teddy bear ['tɛdi] n : oso m de peluche

tedious ['ti:diəs] adj : aburrido, pesado, monótono — **tediously** adv

tediousness ['ti:diəsnəs] n : lo aburrido, lo pesado

tedium ['ti:diəm] n : tedio m, pesadez f

tee ['ti:] n : tee mf

teem ['ti:m] vi to teem with : estar repleto de, estar lleno de

teenage ['ti:nˌeɪʤ] or **teenaged** [-eɪʤd] adj : adolescente, de adolescencia

teenager ['ti:nˌeɪʤər] n : adolescente mf

teens ['ti:nz] npl : adolescencia f

teepee → tepee

teeter ['ti:tər] vi : balancearse, tambalearse

teeter–totter ['ti:tər-ˌtɑtər] n or **teeter–totter** → seesaw

teeth → tooth

teethe ['ti:ð] vi **teethed**; **teething** : formársele a uno los dientes ⟨the baby's teething : le están saliendo los dientes al niño⟩

telecast¹ ['tɛləˌkæst] vt **-cast**; **-casting** : televisar, transmitir por televisión

telecast² n : transmisión f por televisión

telecommunication [ˌtɛləkəˌmju:nəˈkeɪʃən] n : telecomunicación f

telegram ['tɛləˌgræm] n : telegrama m

telegraph¹ ['tɛləˌgræf] v : telegrafiar

telegraph² n : telégrafo m

telepathic [ˌtɛləˈpæθɪk] adj : telepático — **telepathically** [-θɪkli] adv

telepathy [təˈlɛpəθi] n : telepatía f

telephone¹ ['tɛləˌfo:n] v **-phoned**; **-phoning** vt : llamar por teléfono a, telefonear — vi : telefonear

telephone² n : teléfono m

telescope¹ ['tɛləˌsko:p] vi **-scoped**; **-scoping** : plegarse (como un telescopio)

telescope² n : telescopio m

telescopic [ˌtɛləˈskɑpɪk] adj : telescópico

televise ['tɛləˌvaɪz] vt **-vised**; **-vising** : televisar

television ['tɛləˌvɪʒən] n : televisión f

tell ['tɛl] v **told** ['to:ld]; **telling** vt 1 COUNT : contar, enumerar ⟨all told : en total⟩ 2 INSTRUCT : decir ⟨he told me how to fix it : me dijo cómo arreglarlo⟩ ⟨they told her to wait : le dijeron que esperara⟩ 3 RELATE : contar, relatar, narrar ⟨to tell a story : contar una historia⟩ 4 DIVULGE, REVEAL : revelar, divulgar ⟨he told me everything about her : me contó todo acerca de ella⟩ 5 DISCERN : discernir, notar ⟨I can't tell the difference : no noto la diferencia⟩ — vi 1 SAY : decir ⟨I won't tell : no voy a decírselo a nadie⟩ 2 KNOW : saber ⟨you never can tell : nunca se sabe⟩ 3 SHOW : notarse, hacerse sentir ⟨the strain is beginning to tell : la tensión se empieza a notar⟩

teller ['tɛlər] n 1 NARRATOR : narrador m, -dora f 2 or bank teller : cajero m, -ra f

temerity [təˈmɛrəti] n, pl **-ties** : temeridad f

temp ['tɛmp] n : empleado m, -da f temporal

temper¹ ['tɛmpər] vt 1 MODERATE : moderar, temperar 2 ANNEAL : templar (acero, etc.)

temper[2] *n* **1** DISPOSITION : carácter *m*, genio *m* **2** HARDNESS : temple *m*, dureza *f* (de un metal) **3** COMPOSURE : calma *f*, serenidad *f* ⟨to lose one's temper : perder los estribos⟩ **4** RAGE : furia *f* ⟨to fly into a temper : ponerse furioso⟩

temperament [ˈtɛmpərmənt, -prə-, -pərə-] *n* : temperamento *m*

temperamental [ˌtɛmpərˈmɛntəl, -prə-, -pərə-] *adj* : temperamental

temperance [ˈtɛmprənts] *n* : templanza *f*, temperancia *f*

temperate [ˈtɛmpərət] *adj* : templado (dícese del clima, etc.), moderado

temperature [ˈtɛmpərˌtʃur, -prə-, -pərə-, -tʃər] *n* **1** : temperatura *f* **2** FEVER : calentura *f*, fiebre *f*

tempest [ˈtɛmpəst] *n* : tempestad *f*

tempestuous [tɛmˈpɛstʃuəs] *adj* : tempestuoso

temple [ˈtɛmpəl] *n* **1** : templo *m* (en religión) **2** : sien *f* (en anatomía)

tempo [ˈtɛmˌpoː] *n*, *pl* **-pi** [-ˌpiː] *or* **-pos** : ritmo *m*, tempo *m* (en música)

temporal [ˈtɛmpərəl] *adj* : temporal

temporarily [ˌtɛmpəˈrɛrəli] *adv* : temporalmente, provisionalmente

temporary [ˈtɛmpəˌrɛri] *adj* : temporal, provisional, provisorio

tempt [ˈtɛmpt] *vt* : tentar

temptation [tɛmpˈteɪʃən] *n* : tentación *f*

tempter [ˈtɛmptər] *n* : tentador *m*

temptress [ˈtɛmptrəs] *n* : tentadora *f*

ten[1] [ˈtɛn] *adj* : diez

ten[2] *n* **1** : diez *m* (número) **2** : decena *f* ⟨tens of thousands : decenas de millares⟩

tenable [ˈtɛnəbəl] *adj* : sostenible, defendible

tenacious [təˈneɪʃəs] *adj* : tenaz

tenacity [təˈnæsəti] *n* : tenacidad *f*

tenancy [ˈtɛnəntsi] *n*, *pl* **-cies** : tenencia *f*, inquilinato *m* (de un inmueble)

tenant [ˈtɛnənt] *n* : inquilino *m*, -na *f*; arrendatario *m*, -ria *f*

tend [ˈtɛnd] *vt* : atender, cuidar (de), ocuparse de — *vi* : tender ⟨it tends to benefit the consumer : tiende a beneficiar al consumidor⟩

tendency [ˈtɛndəntsi] *n*, *pl* **-cies** : tendencia *f*, proclividad *f*, inclinación *f*

tender[1] [ˈtɛndər] *vt* : entregar, presentar ⟨I tendered my resignation : presenté mi renuncia⟩

tender[2] *adj* **1** : tierno, blando ⟨tender steak : bistec tierno⟩ **2** AFFECTIONATE, LOVING : tierno, cariñoso, afectuoso **3** DELICATE : tierno, sensible, delicado

tender[3] *n* **1** OFFER : propuesta *f*, oferta *f* (en negocios) **2** legal tender : moneda *f* de curso legal

tenderize [ˈtɛndəˌraɪz] *vt* **-ized; -izing** : ablandar (carnes)

tenderloin [ˈtɛndrˌlɔɪn] *n* : lomo *f* (de res o de puerco)

tenderly [ˈtɛndərli] *adv* : tiernamente, con ternura

tenderness [ˈtɛndərnəs] *n* : ternura *f*

tendon [ˈtɛndən] *n* : tendón *m*

tendril [ˈtɛndrɪl] *n* : zarcillo *m*

tenement [ˈtɛnəmənt] *n* : casa *f* de vecindad

tenet [ˈtɛnət] *n* : principio *m*

tennis [ˈtɛnəs] *n* : tenis *m*

tenor [ˈtɛnər] *n* **1** PURPORT : tenor *m*, significado *m* **2** : tenor *m* (en música)

tenpins [ˈtɛnˌpɪnz] *npl* : bolos *mpl*, boliche *m*

tense[1] [ˈtɛnts] *v* **tensed; tensing** *vt* : tensar — *vi* : tensarse, ponerse tenso

tense[2] *adj* **tenser; tensest** **1** TAUT : tenso, tirante **2** NERVOUS : tenso, nervioso

tense[3] *n* : tiempo *m* (de un verbo)

tensely [ˈtɛntsli] *adv* : tensamente

tenseness [ˈtɛntsnəs] → **tension**

tension [ˈtɛntʃən] *n* **1** TAUTNESS : tensión *f*, tirantez *f* **2** STRESS : tensión *f*, nerviosismo *m*, estrés *m*

tent [ˈtɛnt] *n* : tienda *f* de campaña

tentacle [ˈtɛntɪkəl] *n* : tentáculo *m*

tentative [ˈtɛntətɪv] *adj* **1** HESITANT : indeciso, vacilante **2** PROVISIONAL : sujeto a cambios, provisional

tentatively [ˈtɛntətɪvli] *adv* : provisionalmente

tenth[1] [ˈtɛnθ] *adj* : décimo

tenth[2] *n* **1** : décimo *m*, -ma *f* (en una serie) **2** : décimo *m*, décima parte *f*

tenuous [ˈtɛnjuəs] *adj* : tenue, débil ⟨tenuous reasons : razones poco convincentes⟩

tenuously [ˈtɛnjuəsli] *adv* : tenuemente, ligeramente

tenure [ˈtɛnjər] *n* : tenencia *f* (de un cargo o una propiedad), titularidad *f* (de un puesto académico)

tepee [ˈtiːˌpiː] *n* : tipi *m*

tepid [ˈtɛpɪd] *adj* : tibio

tequila [təˈkiːlə] *n* : tequila *m*

term[1] [ˈtərm] *vt* : calificar de, llamar, nombrar

term[2] *n* **1** PERIOD : término *m*, plazo *m*, período *m* **2** : término *m* (en matemáticas) **3** WORD : término *m*, vocablo *m* ⟨legal terms : términos legales⟩ **4** **terms** *npl* CONDITIONS : términos *mpl*, condiciones *fpl* **5** **terms** *npl* RELATIONS : relaciones *fpl* ⟨to be on good terms with : tener buenas relaciones con⟩ **6 in terms of** : con respecto a, en cuanto a

terminal[1] [ˈtərmənəl] *adj* : terminal

terminal[2] *n* **1** : terminal *m*, polo *m* (en electricidad) **2** : terminal *m* (de una computadora) **3** STATION : terminal *f*, estación *f* (de transporte público)

terminate [ˈtərməˌneɪt] *v* **-nated; -nating** *vi* : terminar(se), concluirse — *vt* : terminar, poner fin a

termination [ˌtərməˈneɪʃən] *n* : cese *m*, terminación *f*

terminology [ˌtərməˈnɑlədʒi] *n*, *pl* **-gies** : terminología *f*

terminus [ˈtərmənəs] *n*, *pl* **-ni** [-ˌnaɪ] *or* **-nuses** **1** END : término *m*, fin *m* **2** : terminal *f* (de transporte público)

termite [ˈtərˌmaɪt] *n* : termita *f*
tern [ˈtərn] *n* : golondrina *f* de mar
terrace[1] [ˈterəs] *vt* **-raced; -racing** : formar en terrazas, disponer en bancales
terrace[2] *n* **1** PATIO : terraza *f*, patio *m* **2** : terraplén *m*, terraza *f*, bancal *m* (en agricultura)
terra–cotta [ˌterəˈkɑtə] *n* : terracota *f*
terrain [təˈreɪn] *n* : terreno *m*
terrapin [ˈterəpɪn] *n* : galápago *m* norteamericano
terrarium [təˈræriəm] *n, pl* **-ia** [-iə] *or* **-iums** : terrario *m*
terrestrial [təˈrestriəl] *adj* : terrestre
terrible [ˈterəbəl] *adj* : atroz, horrible, terrible
terribly [ˈterəbli] *adv* **1** BADLY : muy mal **2** EXTREMELY : terriblemente, extremadamente
terrier [ˈteriər] *n* : terrier *mf*
terrific [təˈrɪfɪk] *adj* **1** FRIGHTFUL : aterrador **2** EXTRAORDINARY : extraordinario, excepcional **3** EXCELLENT : excelente, estupendo
terrify [ˈterəˌfaɪ] *vt* **-fied; -fying** : aterrorizar, aterrar, espantar
terrifying [ˈterəˌfaɪɪŋ] *adj* : espantoso, aterrador
territory [ˈterəˌtori] *n, pl* **-ries** : territorio *m* — **territorial** [ˌterəˈtoriəl] *adj*
terror [ˈterər] *n* : terror *m*
terrorism [ˈterərˌɪzəm] *n* : terrorismo *m*
terrorist[1] [ˈterərɪst] *adj* : terrorista
terrorist[2] *n* : terrorista *mf*
terrorize [ˈterərˌaɪz] *vt* **-ized; -izing** : aterrorizar
terry [ˈteri] *n, pl* **-ries** *or* **terry cloth** : (tela de) toalla *f*
terse [ˈtərs] *adj* **terser; tersest** : lacónico, conciso, seco — **tersely** *adv*
tertiary [ˈtərʃiˌeri] *adj* : terciario
test[1] [ˈtest] *vt* : examinar, evaluar — *vi* : hacer pruebas
test[2] *n* : prueba *f*, examen *m*, test *m* ⟨to put to the test : poner a prueba⟩
testament [ˈtestəmənt] *n* **1** WILL : testamento *m* **2** : Testamento *m* (en la Biblia) ⟨the Old Testament : el Antiguo Testamento⟩
testicle [ˈtestɪkəl] *n* : testículo *m*
testify [ˈtestəˌfaɪ] *v* **-fied; -fying** *vi* : testificar, atestar, testimoniar — *vt* : testificar
testimonial [ˌtestəˈmoːniəl] *n* **1** REFERENCE : recomendación *f* **2** TRIBUTE : homenaje *m*, tributo *m*
testimony [ˈtestəˌmoːni] *n, pl* **-nies** : testimonio *m*, declaración *f*
test tube *n* : probeta *f*, tubo *m* de ensayo
testy [ˈtesti] *adj* **-tier; -est** : irritable
tetanus [ˈtetənəs] *n* : tétano *m*, tétanos *m*
tête–à–tête [ˌtetəˈtet, ˌteɪtəˈteɪt] *n* : conversación *f* en privado
tether[1] [ˈteðər] *vt* : atar (con una cuerda), amarrar
tether[2] *n* : atadura *f*, cadena *f*, correa *f*

text [ˈtekst] *n* **1** : texto *m* **2** TOPIC : tema *m* **3** → **textbook**
textbook [ˈtekstˌbʊk] *n* : libro *m* de texto
textile [ˈtekˌstaɪl, ˈtekstəl] *n* : textil *m*, tela *f* ⟨the textile industry : la industria textil⟩
textual [ˈtekstʃuəl] *adj* : textual
texture [ˈtekstʃər] *n* : textura *f*
Thai [ˈtaɪ] *n* **1** : tailandés *m*, -desa *f* **2** : tailandés *m* (idioma) — **Thai** *adj*
than[1] [ˈðæn] *conj* : que, de ⟨it's worth more than that : vale más que eso⟩ ⟨more than you think : más de lo que piensas⟩
than[2] *prep* : que, de ⟨you're better than he is : eres mejor que él⟩ ⟨more than once : más de una vez⟩
thank [ˈθæŋk] *vt* : agradecer, darle (las) gracias (a alguien) ⟨thank you! : ¡gracias!⟩ ⟨I thanked her for the present : le di las gracias por el regalo⟩ ⟨I thank you for your help : le agradezco su ayuda⟩
thankful [ˈθæŋkfəl] *adj* : agradecido
thankfully [ˈθæŋkfəli] *adv* **1** GRATEFULLY : con agradecimiento **2** FORTUNATELY : afortunadamente, por suerte ⟨thankfully, it's over : se acabó, gracias a Dios⟩
thankfulness [ˈθæŋkfəlnəs] *n* : agradecimiento *m*, gratitud *f*
thankless [ˈθæŋkləs] *adj* : ingrato ⟨a thankless task : un trabajo ingrato⟩
thanks [ˈθæŋks] *npl* **1** : agradecimiento *m* **2** thanks! : ¡gracias!
Thanksgiving [θæŋksˈgɪvɪŋ, ˈθæŋksˌ-] *n* : el día de Acción de Gracias (fiesta estadounidense)
that[1] [ˈðæt] *adv* (*in negative constructions*) : tan ⟨it's not that expensive : no es tan caro⟩ ⟨not that much : no tanto⟩
that[2] *adj, pl* **those** : ese, esa, aquel, aquella ⟨do you see those children? : ¿ves a aquellos niños?⟩
that[3] *conj & pron* : que ⟨he said that he was afraid : dijo que tenía miedo⟩ ⟨the book that he wrote : el libro que escribió⟩
that[4] *pron, pl* **those** [ˈðoːz] **1** : ése, ésa, eso ⟨that's my father : ése es mi padre⟩ ⟨those are the ones he likes : ésos son los que le gustan⟩ ⟨what's that? : ¿qué es eso?⟩ **2** (*referring to more distant objects or time*) : aquél, aquélla, aquello ⟨those are maples and these are elms : aquéllos son arces y éstos son olmos⟩ ⟨that came to an end : aquello se acabó⟩
thatch[1] [ˈθætʃ] *vt* : cubrir o techar con paja
thatch[2] *n* : paja *f* (usada para techos)
thaw[1] [ˈθɔ] *vt* : descongelar — *vi* **1** : derretirse (dícese de la nieve), descongelarse (dícese de los alimentos)
thaw[2] *n* : deshielo *m*

the¹ [ðə, *before vowel sounds usu* ði:] *adv*
1 (*used to indicate comparison*) ⟨the sooner the better : cuanto más pronto, mejor⟩ ⟨she likes this one the best : éste es el que más le gusta⟩ **2** (*used as a conjunction*) : cuanto ⟨the more I learn, the less I understand : cuanto más aprendo, menos entiendo⟩

the² *art* : el, la, los, las ⟨the gloves : los guantes⟩ ⟨the suitcase : la maleta⟩ ⟨forty cookies to the box : cuarenta galletas por caja⟩

theater *or* **theatre** [ˈθiːətər] *n* **1** : teatro *m* (edificio) **2** DRAMA : teatro *m*, drama *m*

theatrical [θiˈætrɪkəl] *adj* : teatral, dramático

thee [ˈðiː] *pron* : te, ti

theft [ˈθɛft] *n* : robo *m*, hurto *m*

their [ˈðɛr] *adj* : su ⟨their friends : sus amigos⟩

theirs [ˈðɛrz] *pron* : (el) suyo, (la) suya, (los) suyos, (las) suyas ⟨they came for theirs : vinieron por el suyo⟩ ⟨theirs is bigger : la suya es más grande, la de ellos es más grande⟩ ⟨a brother of theirs : un hermano suyo, un hermano de ellos⟩

them [ˈðɛm] *pron* **1** (*as a direct object*) : los (*Spain sometimes* les), las ⟨I know them : los conozco⟩ **2** (*as indirect object*) : les, se ⟨I sent them a letter : les mandé una carta⟩ ⟨give it to them : dáselo (a ellos)⟩ **3** (*as object of a preposition*) : ellos, ellas ⟨go with them : ve con ellos⟩ **4** (*for emphasis*) : ellos, ellas ⟨I wasn't expecting them : no los esperaba a ellos⟩

thematic [θiˈmætɪk] *adj* : temático

theme [ˈθiːm] *n* **1** SUBJECT, TOPIC : tema *m* **2** COMPOSITION : composición *f*, trabajo *m* (escrito) **3** : tema *m* (en música)

themselves [ðəmˈsɛlvz, ðɛm-] *pron* **1** (*as a reflexive*) : se, sí ⟨they enjoyed themselves : se divirtieron⟩ ⟨they divided it among themselves : lo repartieron entre sí, se lo repartieron⟩ **2** (*for emphasis*) : ellos mismos, ellas mismas ⟨they built it themselves : ellas mismas lo construyeron⟩

then¹ [ˈðɛn] *adv* **1** : entonces, en ese tiempo ⟨I was sixteen then : tenía entonces dieciséis años⟩ ⟨since then : desde entonces⟩ **2** : después, luego ⟨we'll go to Toronto, then to Winnipeg : iremos a Toronto, y luego a Winnipeg⟩ **3** BESIDES : además, aparte ⟨then there's the tax : y aparte está el impuesto⟩ **4** : entonces, en ese caso ⟨if you like music, then you should attend : si te gusta la música, entonces deberías asistir⟩

then² *adj* : entonces ⟨the then governor of Georgia : el entonces gobernador de Georgia⟩

thence [ˈðɛnts, ˈθɛnts] *adv* : de ahí, de ahí en adelante

theologian [ˌθiːəˈloːdʒən] *n* : teólogo *m*, -ga *f*

theological [ˌθiːəˈlɑdʒɪkəl] *adj* : teológico

theology [θiˈɑlədʒi] *n, pl* **-gies** : teología *f*

theorem [ˈθiːərəm, ˈθɪrəm] *n* : teorema *m*

theoretical [ˌθiːəˈrɛtɪkəl] *adj* : teórico — **theoretically** *adv*

theorist [ˈθiːərɪst] *n* : teórico *m*, -ca *f*

theorize [ˈθiːəˌraɪz] *vi* **-rized; -rizing** : teorizar

theory [ˈθiːəri, ˈθɪri] *n, pl* **-ries** : teoría *f*

therapeutic [ˌθɛrəˈpjuːtɪk] *adj* : terapéutico — **therapeutically** *adv*

therapist [ˈθɛrəpɪst] *n* : terapeuta *mf*

therapy [ˈθɛrəpi] *n, pl* **-pies** : terapia *f*

there¹ [ˈðær] *adv* **1** : ahí, allí, allá ⟨stand over there : párate ahí⟩ ⟨over there : por allí, por allá⟩ ⟨who's there? : ¿quién es?⟩ **2** : ahí, en esto, en eso ⟨there is where we disagree : en eso es donde no estamos de acuerdo⟩

there² *pron* **1** (*introducing a sentence or clause*) ⟨there comes a time to decide : llega un momento en que tiene uno que decidir⟩ **2** there is, there are : hay ⟨there are many children here : aquí hay muchos niños⟩ ⟨there's a good hotel downtown : hay un buen hotel en el centro⟩

thereabouts [ˌðærəˈbauts, ˈðærə-] *or* **thereabout** [-ˈbaut, -ˌbaut] *adv or* **thereabouts** : por ahí, más o menos ⟨at five o'clock or thereabouts : por ahí de las cinco⟩

thereafter [ðærˈæftər] *adv* : después ⟨shortly thereafter : poco después⟩

thereby [ðærˈbaɪ, ˈðærˌbaɪ] *adv* : de tal modo, de ese manera, así

therefore [ˈðærˌfor] *adv* : por lo tanto, por consiguiente

therein [ðærˈɪn] *adv* **1** : allí adentro, ahí adentro ⟨the contents therein : lo que allí se contiene⟩ **2** : allí, en ese aspecto ⟨therein lies the problem : allí está el problema⟩

thereof [ðærˈʌv, -ˈɑv] *adv* : de eso, de esto

thereupon [ˈðærəˌpɑn, -ˌpɔn; ˌðærəˈpɑn, -ˈpɔn] *adv* : acto seguido, inmediatamente (después)

therewith [ðærˈwɪθ, -ˈwɪθ] *adv* : con eso, con ello

thermal [ˈθərməl] *adj* **1** : térmico (en física) **2** HOT : termal

thermodynamics [ˌθərmoʊdaɪˈnæmɪks] *ns & pl* : termodinámica *f*

thermometer [θərˈmɑmətər] *n* : termómetro *m*

thermos [ˈθərməs] *n* : termo *m*

thermostat [ˈθərməˌstæt] *n* : termostato *m*

thesaurus [θɪˈsɔrəs] *n, pl* **-sauri** [-ˈsɔrˌaɪ] *or* **-sauruses** [-ˈsɔrəsəz] : diccionario *m* de sinónimos

these → **this**

thesis ['θi:sɪs] n, pl **theses** ['θi:ˌsi:z] : tesis f

they ['ðeɪ] pron : ellos, ellas ⟨they are here : están aquí⟩ ⟨they don't know : ellos no saben⟩

they'd ['ðeɪd] (contraction of **they had** or **they would**) → **have, would**

they'll ['ðeɪl, 'ðɛl] (contraction of **they shall** or **they will**) → **shall, will**

they're ['ðɛr] (contraction of **they are**) → **be**

they've ['ðeɪv] (contraction of **they have**) → **have**

thiamine ['θaɪəmɪn, -ˌmi:n] n : tiamina f

thick¹ ['θɪk] adj **1** : grueso ⟨a thick plank : una tabla gruesa⟩ **2** : espeso, denso ⟨thick syrup : jarabe espeso⟩ — **thickly** adv

thick² n **1 in the thick of** : en medio de ⟨in the thick of the battle : en lo más reñido de la batalla⟩ **2 through thick and thin** : a las duras y a las maduras

thicken ['θɪkən] vt : espesar (un líquido) — vi : espesarse

thickener ['θɪkənər] n : espesante m

thicket ['θɪkət] n : matorral m, maleza f, espesura f

thickness ['θɪknəs] n : grosor m, grueso m, espesor m

thickset ['θɪk'sɛt] adj STOCKY : robusto, fornido

thick–skinned ['θɪk'skɪnd] adj : poco sensible, que no se ofende fácilmente

thief ['θi:f] n, pl **thieves** ['θi:vz] : ladrón m, -drona f

thieve ['θi:v] v **thieved; thieving** : hurtar, robar

thievery ['θi:vəri] n : hurto m, robo m, latrocinio m

thigh ['θaɪ] n : muslo m

thighbone ['θaɪˌbo:n] n : fémur m

thimble ['θɪmbəl] n : dedal m

thin¹ ['θɪn] v **thinned; thinning** vt : hacer menos denso, diluir, aguar (un líquido), enrarecer (un gas) — vi : diluirse, aguarse (dícese de un líquido), enrarecerse (dícese de un gas)

thin² adj **thinner; -est 1** LEAN, SLIM : delgado, esbelto, flaco **2** SPARSE : ralo, escaso ⟨a thin beard : una barba rala⟩ **3** WATERY : claro, aguado, diluido **4** FINE : delgado, fino ⟨thin slices : rebanadas finas⟩

thing ['θɪŋ] n **1** AFFAIR, MATTER : cosa f, asunto m ⟨don't talk about those things : no hables de esas cosas⟩ ⟨how are things? : ¿cómo van las cosas?⟩ **2** ACT, EVENT : cosa f, suceso m, evento m ⟨the flood was a terrible thing : la inundación fue una cosa terrible⟩ **3** OBJECT : cosa f, objeto m ⟨don't forget your things : no olvides tus cosas⟩

think ['θɪŋk] v **thought** ['θɔt]; **thinking** vt **1** : pensar ⟨I thought to return early : pensaba regresar temprano⟩ **2** BELIEVE : pensar, creer, opinar **3** PONDER : pensar, reflexionar **4** CONCEIVE : ocurrirse, concebir ⟨we've thought up a plan : se nos ha ocurrido un plan⟩ —

vi **1** REASON : pensar, razonar **2** CONSIDER : pensar, considerar ⟨think of your family first : primero piensa en tu familia⟩

thinker ['θɪŋkər] n : pensador m, -dora f

thinly ['θɪnli] adv **1** LIGHTLY : ligeramente **2** SPARSELY : escasamente ⟨thinly populated : poco populado⟩ **3** BARELY : apenas

thinness ['θɪnnəs] n : delgadez f

thin–skinned ['θɪn'skɪnd] adj : susceptible, muy sensible

third¹ ['θərd] or **thirdly** [-li] adv : en tercer lugar ⟨she came in third : llegó en tercer lugar⟩

third² adj : tercero ⟨the third day : el tercer día⟩

third³ n **1** : tercero m, -ra f (en una serie) **2** : tercero m, tercera parte f

third world n the Third World : el Tercer Mundo m

thirst¹ ['θərst] vi **1** : tener sed **2 to thirst for** DESIRE : tener sed de, estar sediento de

thirst² n : sed f

thirsty ['θərsti] adj **thirstier; -est** : sediento, que tiene sed ⟨I'm thirsty : tengo sed⟩

thirteen¹ [ˌθərˈti:n] adj : trece

thirteen² n : trece m

thirteenth¹ [ˌθərˈti:nθ] adj : décimo tercero

thirteenth² n **1** : decimotercero m, -ra f (en una serie) **2** : treceavo m, treceava parte f

thirtieth¹ ['θərt̬iəθ] adj : trigésimo

thirtieth² n **1** : trigésimo m, -ma f (en una serie) **2** : treintavo m, treintava parte f

thirty¹ ['θərt̬i] adj : treinta

thirty² n, pl **thirties** : treinta m

this¹ ['ðɪs] adv : así, a tal punto ⟨this big : así de grande⟩

this² adj, pl **these** ['ði:z] : este ⟨these things : estas cosas⟩ ⟨read this book : lee este libro⟩

this³ pron, pl **these** : esto ⟨what's this? : ¿qué es esto?⟩ ⟨this wasn't here yesterday : esto no estaba aquí ayer⟩

thistle ['θɪsəl] n : cardo m

thong ['θɔŋ] n **1** STRAP : correa f, tira f **2** FLIP-FLOP : chancla f, chancleta f

thorax ['θɔrˌæks] n, pl **-raxes** or **-races** ['θɔrəˌsi:z] : tórax m

thorn ['θɔrn] n : espina f

thorny ['θɔrni] adj **thornier; -est** : espinoso

thorough ['θəro:] adj **1** CONSCIENTIOUS : concienzudo, meticuloso **2** COMPLETE : absoluto, completo — **thoroughly** adv

thoroughbred ['θərəˌbred] adj : de pura sangre (dícese de un caballo)

Thoroughbred n or **Thoroughbred horse** : pura sangre mf

thoroughfare ['θəroˌfær] n : vía f pública, carretera f

thoroughness ['θərənəs] n : esmero m, meticulosidad f

those → that

thou [ˈðaʊ] *pron* : tú

though[1] [ˈðoː] *adv* **1** HOWEVER, NEVERTHELESS : sin embargo, no obstante **2 as ~** : como si ⟨as though nothing had happened : como si nada hubiera pasado⟩

though[2] *conj* : aunque, a pesar de ⟨though it was raining, we went out : salimos a pesar de la lluvia⟩

thought[1] → **think**

thought[2] [ˈθɔt] *n* **1** THINKING : pensamiento, ideas *fpl* ⟨Western thought : el pensamiento occidental⟩ **2** COGITATION : pensamiento *m*, reflexión *f*, raciocinio *m* **3** IDEA : idea *f*, ocurrencia *f* ⟨it was just a thought : fue sólo una idea⟩

thoughtful [ˈθɔtfəl] *adj* **1** PENSIVE : pensativo, meditabundo **2** CONSIDERATE : considerado, atento, cortés — **thoughtfully** *adv*

thoughtfulness [ˈθɔtfəlnəs] *n* : consideración *f*, atención *f*, cortesía *f*

thoughtless [ˈθɔtləs] *adj* **1** CARELESS : descuidado, negligente **2** INCONSIDERATE : desconsiderado — **thoughtlessly** *adv*

thousand[1] [ˈθaʊzənd] *adj* : mil

thousand[2] *n, pl* **-sands** *or* **-sand** : mil *m*

thousandth[1] [ˈθaʊzəntθ] *adj* : milésimo

thousandth[2] *n* **1** : milésimo *m*, -ma *f* (en una serie) **2** : milésimo *m*, milésima parte *f*

thrash [ˈθræʃ] *vt* **1** → **thresh 2** BEAT : golpear, azotar, darle una paliza (a alguien) **3** FLAIL : sacudir, agitar bruscamente

thread[1] [ˈθrɛd] *vt* **1** : enhilar, enhebrar (una aguja) **2** STRING : ensartar (cuentas en un hilo) **3 to thread one's way** : abrirse paso

thread[2] *n* **1** : hilo *m*, hebra *f* ⟨needle and thread : aguja e hilo⟩ ⟨the thread of an argument : el hilo de un debate⟩ **2** : rosca *f*, filete *m* (de un tornillo)

threadbare [ˈθrɛdˌbær] *adj* **1** SHABBY, WORN : raído, gastado **2** TRITE : trillado, tópico, manido

threat [ˈθrɛt] *n* : amenaza *f*

threaten [ˈθrɛtən] *v* : amenazar

threatening [ˈθrɛtənɪŋ] *adj* : amenazador — **threateningly** *adv*

three[1] [ˈθriː] *adj* : tres

three[2] *n* : tres *m*

3–D [ˈθriːˈdiː] *adj* → **three–dimensional**

three–dimensional [ˌθriːdəˈmɛntʃənəl] *adj* : tridimensional

threefold [ˈθriːˌfoːld] *adj* TRIPLE : triple

three hundred[1] *adj* : trescientos

three hundred[2] *n* : trescientos *m*

threescore [ˈθriːˈskor] *adj* SIXTY : sesenta

thresh [ˈθrɛʃ] *vt* : trillar (grano)

thresher [ˈθrɛʃər] *n* : trilladora *f*

threshold [ˈθrɛʃˌhoːld, -ˌoːld] *n* : umbral *m*

threw → throw[1]

thrice [ˈθraɪs] *adv* : tres veces

thrift [ˈθrɪft] *n* : economía *f*, frugalidad *f*

thriftless [ˈθrɪftləs] *adj* : despilfarrador, manirroto

thrifty [ˈθrɪfti] *adj* **thriftier; -est** : económico, frugal — **thriftily** [ˈθrɪftəli] *adv*

thrill[1] [ˈθrɪl] *vt* : emocionar — *vi* **to thrill to** : dejarse conmover por, estremecerse con

thrill[2] *n* : emoción *f*

thriller [ˈθrɪlər] *n* **1** : evento *m* emocionante **2** : obra *f* de suspenso

thrilling [ˈθrɪlɪŋ] *adj* : emocionante, excitante

thrive [ˈθraɪv] *vi* **throve** [ˈθroːv] *or* **thrived; thriven** [ˈθrɪvən] **1** FLOURISH : florecer, crecer abundantemente **2** PROSPER : prosperar

throat [ˈθroːt] *n* : garganta *f*

throaty [ˈθroːti] *adj* **throatier; -est** : ronco (dícese de la voz)

throb[1] [ˈθrɑb] *vi* **throbbed; throbbing** : palpitar, latir (dícese del corazón), vibrar (dícese de un motor, etc.)

throb[2] *n* : palpitación *f*, latido *m*, vibración *f*

throe [ˈθroː] *n* **1** PAIN, SPASM : espasmo *m*, dolor *m* ⟨the throes of childbirth : los dolores de parto⟩ **2 throes** *npl* : lucha *f* larga y ardua ⟨in the throes of : en el medio de⟩

throne [ˈθroːn] *n* : trono *m*

throng[1] [ˈθrɔŋ] *vt* CROWD : atestar, atiborrar, llenar — *vi* : aglomerarse, amontonarse

throng[2] *n* : muchedumbre *f*, gentío *m*, multitud *f*

throttle[1] [ˈθrɑtəl] *vt* **-tled; -tling 1** STRANGLE : estrangular, ahogar **2 to throttle down** : desacelerar (un motor)

throttle[2] *n* **1** : válvula *f* reguladora **2 at full throttle** : a toda máquina

through[1] [ˈθruː] *adv* **1** : a través, de un lado a otro ⟨let them through : déjenlos pasar⟩ **2** : de principio a fin ⟨she read the book through : leyó el libro de principio a fin⟩ **3** COMPLETELY : completamente ⟨soaked through : completamente empapado⟩

through[2] *adj* **1** DIRECT : directo ⟨a through train : un tren directo⟩ **2** FINISHED : terminado, acabado ⟨we're through : hemos terminado⟩

through[3] *prep* **1** : a través de, por ⟨through the door : por la puerta⟩ ⟨a road through the woods : un camino que atraviesa el bosque⟩ **2** BETWEEN : entre ⟨a path through the trees : un sendero entre los árboles⟩ **3** BECAUSE OF : a causa de, como consecuencia de **4** (*in expressions of time*) ⟨through the night : durante la noche⟩ ⟨to go through an experience : pasar por una experiencia⟩ **5** : a, hasta ⟨from Monday through Friday : de lunes a viernes⟩

throughout[1] [θru:'aʊt] *adv* **1** EVERY-
WHERE : por todas partes **2** THROUGH
: desde el principio hasta el fin de (algo)
throughout[2] *prep* **1** : en todas partes de,
a través de ⟨throughout the United
States : en todo Estados Unidos⟩ **2** : de
principio a fin de, durante ⟨through-
out the winter : durante todo el in-
vierno⟩

throve → **thrive**

throw[1] [θro:] *vt* **threw** [θru:]; **thrown**
[θro:n]; **throwing 1** TOSS : tirar, lanzar, echar, arrojar, aventar *Col, Mex*
⟨to throw a ball : tirar una pelota⟩ **2**
UNSEAT : desmontar (a un jinete) **3**
CAST : proyectar ⟨it threw a long shadow : proyectó una sombra larga⟩ **4 to
throw a party** : dar una fiesta **5 to
throw into confusion** : desconcertar **6
to throw out** DISCARD : botar, tirar (en
la basura)

throw[2] *n* TOSS : tiro *m*, tirada *f*, lanzamiento *m*, lance *m* (de dados)

thrower [θro:ər] *n* : lanzador *m*, -dora *f*

throw up *v* VOMIT : vomitar, devolver

thrush [θrʌʃ] *n* : tordo *m*, zorzal *m*

thrust[1] [θrʌst] *vt* **thrust; thrusting 1**
SHOVE : empujar bruscamente **2**
PLUNGE, STAB : apuñalar, clavar ⟨he
thrust a dagger into her heart : la
apuñaló en el corazón⟩ **3 to thrust
one's way** : abrirse paso **4 to thrust
upon** : imponer a

thrust[2] *n* **1** PUSH, SHOVE : empujón *m*,
empellón *m* **2** LUNGE : estocada *f* (en
esgrima) **3** IMPETUS : ímpetu *m*, impulso *m*, propulsión *f* (de un motor)

thud[1] [θʌd] *vi* **thudded; thudding** : producir un ruido sordo

thud[2] *n* : ruido *m* sordo (que produce
un objeto al caer)

thug [θʌɡ] *n* : matón *m*

thumb[1] [θʌm] *vt* : hojear (con el pulgar)

thumb[2] *n* : pulgar *m*, dedo *m* pulgar

thumbnail [θʌm,neɪl] *n* : uña *f* del pulgar

thumbtack [θʌm,tæk] *n* : tachuela *f*,
chinche *f*

thump[1] [θʌmp] *vt* POUND : golpear,
aporrear — *vi* : latir con vehemencia
(dícese del corazón)

thump[2] *n* THUD : ruido *m* sordo

thunder[1] [θʌndər] *vi* **1** : tronar ⟨it
rained and thundered all night : llovió
y tronó durante la noche⟩ **2** BOOM : retumbar, bramar, resonar — *vt* ROAR,
SHOUT : decir a gritos, vociferar

thunder[2] *n* : truenos *mpl*

thunderbolt [θʌndər,bo:lt] *n* : rayo *m*

thunderclap [θʌndər,klæp] *n* : trueno
m

thunderous [θʌndərəs] *adj* : atronador,
ensordecedor, estruendoso

thundershower [θʌndər,ʃaʊər] *n* : lluvia *f* con truenos y relámpagos

thunderstorm [θʌndər,stɔrm] *n* : tormenta *f* con truenos y relámpagos

thunderstruck [θʌndər,strʌk] *adj*
: atónito

Thursday [θərz,deɪ, -di] *n* : jueves *m*

thus [ðʌs] *adv* **1** : así, de esta manera **2**
SO : hasta (cierto punto) ⟨the weath-
er's been nice thus far : hasta ahora ha
hecho buen tiempo⟩ **3** HENCE : por
consiguiente, por lo tanto

thwart [θwɔrt] *vt* : frustrar

thy [ðaɪ] *adj* : tu

thyme [taɪm, θaɪm] *n* : tomillo *m*

thyroid [θaɪ,rɔɪd] *n or* **thyroid gland**
: tiroides *mf*, glándula *f* tiroidea

thyself [ðaɪ'self] *pron* : ti, ti mismo

tiara [ti'ærə, -'ɑr-] *n* : diadema *f*

Tibetan [tə'betən] *n* **1** : tibetano *m*, -na
f **2** : tibetano *m* (idioma) — **Tibetan**
adj

tibia [tɪbiə] *n, pl* **-iae** [-bi,i:] : tibia *f*

tic [tɪk] *n* : tic *m*

tick[1] [tɪk] *vi* **1** : hacer tictac **2** OPER-
ATE, RUN : operar, andar (dícese de un
mecanismo) ⟨what makes him tick?
: ¿qué es lo que lo mueve?⟩ — *vt or* **to
tick off** CHECK : marcar

tick[2] *n* **1** : tictac *m* (de un reloj) **2** CHECK
: marca *f* **3** : garrapata *f* (insecto)

ticket[1] [tɪkət] *vt* LABEL : etiquetar

ticket[2] *n* **1** : boleto *m*, entrada *f* (de un
espectáculo), pasaje *m* (de avión, tren,
etc.) **2** SLATE : lista *f* de candidatos

tickle[1] [tɪkəl] *v* **-led; -ling** *vt* **1** AMUSE
: divertir, hacerle gracia (a alguien) **2**
: hacerle cosquillas (a alguien) ⟨don't
tickle me! : ¡no me hagas cosquillas!⟩
— *vi* : picar

tickle[2] *n* : cosquilleo *m*, cosquillas *fpl*,
picor *m* (en la garganta)

ticklish [tɪkliʃ] *adj* **1** : cosquilloso
(dícese de una persona) **2** DELICATE,
TRICKY : delicado, peliagudo

tidal [taɪdəl] *adj* : de marea, relativo a
la marea

tidal wave *n* : maremoto *m*

tidbit [tɪd,bɪt] *n* **1** BITE, SNACK : bocado *m*, golosina *f* **2** : dato *m* o noticia *f*
interesante ⟨useful tidbits of information : informaciones útiles⟩

tide[1] [taɪd] *vt* **tided; tiding** *or* **to tide over**
: proveer lo necesario para aguantar
una dificultad ⟨this money will tide you
over until you find work : este dinero
te mantendrá hasta que encuentres em-
pleo⟩

tide[2] *n* **1** : marea *f* **2** CURRENT : corriente *f* (de eventos, opiniones, etc.)

tidily [taɪdəli] *adv* : ordenadamente

tidiness [taɪdinəs] *n* : aseo *m*, limpieza
f, orden *m*

tidings [taɪdɪŋz] *npl* : nuevas *fpl*

tidy[1] [taɪdi] *vt* **-died; -dying** : asear,
limpiar, poner en orden

tidy[2] *adj* **-dier; -est 1** CLEAN, NEAT
: limpio, aseado, en orden **2** SUBSTAN-
TIAL : grande, considerable ⟨a tidy sum
: una suma considerable⟩

tie[1] [taɪ] *vt* **tied** *or* **tying** *or* **tieing** *vt* **1** : atar,
amarrar ⟨to tie a knot : atar un nudo⟩
⟨to tie one's shoelaces : atarse los cor-
dones⟩ **2** BIND, UNITE : ligar, atar **3**
: empatar ⟨they tied the score : em-

pataron el marcador⟩ — vi : empatar ⟨the two teams were tied : los dos equipos empataron⟩

tie² n 1 : ligadura f, cuerda f, cordón m (para atar algo) 2 BOND, LINK : atadura f, ligadura f, vínculo m, lazo m ⟨family ties : lazos familiares⟩ 3 or **railroad tie** : traviesa f 4 DRAW : empate m (en deportes) 5 NECKTIE : corbata f

tier ['tɪr] n : hilera f, escalón m

tiff ['tɪf] n : disgusto m, disputa f

tiger ['taɪgər] n : tigre m

tight¹ ['taɪt] adv TIGHTLY : bien, fuerte ⟨shut it tight : ciérralo bien⟩

tight² adj 1 : bien cerrado, hermético ⟨a tight seal : un cierre hermético⟩ 2 STRICT : estricto, severo 3 TAUT : tirante, tenso 4 SNUG : apretado, ajustado, ceñido ⟨a tight dress : un vestido ceñido⟩ 5 DIFFICULT : difícil ⟨to be in a tight spot : estar en un aprieto⟩ 6 STINGY : apretado, avaro, agarrado fam 7 CLOSE : reñido ⟨a tight game : un juego reñido⟩ 8 SCARCE : escaso ⟨money is tight : escasea el dinero⟩

tighten ['taɪtən] vt : tensar (una cuerda, etc.), apretar (un nudo, un tornillo, etc.), apretarse (el cinturón), reforzar (las reglas)

tightly ['taɪtli] adv : bien, fuerte

tightness ['taɪtnəs] n : lo apretado, lo tenso, tensión f

tightrope ['taɪt‚ro:p] n : cuerda f floja

tights ['taɪts] npl : leotardo m, malla f

tightwad ['taɪt‚wɑd] n : avaro m, -ra f; tacaño m, -ña f

tigress ['taɪgrəs] n : tigresa f

tile¹ ['taɪl] vt **tiled; tiling** : embaldosar (un piso), revestir de azulejos (una pared), tejar (un techo)

tile² n 1 or **floor tile** : losa f, baldosa f, mosaico m Mex (de un piso) 2 : azulejo m (de una pared) 3 : teja f (de un techo)

till¹ ['tɪl] vt : cultivar, labrar

till² n : caja f, caja f registradora

till³ prep & conj → until

tiller ['tɪlər] n 1 : cultivador m, -dora f (de la tierra) 2 : caña f del timón (de un barco)

tilt¹ ['tɪlt] vt : ladear, inclinar — vi : ladearse, inclinarse

tilt² n 1 SLANT : inclinación f 2 **at full tilt** : a toda velocidad

timber ['tɪmbər] n 1 : madera f (para construcción) 2 BEAM : viga f

timberland ['tɪmbər‚lænd] n : bosque m maderero

timbre ['tæmbər, 'tɪm-] n : timbre m

time¹ ['taɪm] vt **timed; timing** 1 SCHEDULE : fijar la hora de, calcular el momento oportuno para 2 CLOCK : cronometrar, medir el tiempo de (una competencia, etc.)

time² n 1 : tiempo m ⟨the passing of time : el paso del tiempo⟩ ⟨she doesn't have time : no tiene tiempo⟩ 2 MOMENT : tiempo m, momento m ⟨this is not the time to bring it up : no es el momento

de sacar el tema⟩ 3 : vez f ⟨she called you three times : te llamó tres veces⟩ ⟨three times greater : tres veces mayor⟩ 4 AGE : tiempo m, era f ⟨in your grandparents' time : en el tiempo de tus abuelos⟩ 5 TEMPO : tiempo m, ritmo m (en música) 6 : hora f ⟨what time is it? : ¿qué hora es?⟩ ⟨it's time for dinner : es hora de comer⟩ ⟨at the usual time : a la hora acostumbrada⟩ ⟨to keep time : ir a la hora⟩ ⟨to lose time : atrasar⟩ 7 EXPERIENCE : rato m, experiencia f ⟨we had a nice time together : pasamos juntos un rato agradable⟩ ⟨to have a rough time : pasarlo mal⟩ ⟨have a good time! : ¡que se diviertan!⟩ 8 **at times** SOMETIMES : a veces 9 **for the time being** : por el momento, de momento 10 **from time to time** OCCASIONALLY : de vez en cuando 11 **in time** PUNCTUALLY : a tiempo 12 **in time** EVENTUALLY : con el tiempo 13 **time after time** : una y otra vez

timekeeper ['taɪm‚ki:pər] n : cronometrador m, -dora f

timeless ['taɪmləs] adj : eterno

timely ['taɪmli] adj **-lier; -est** : oportuno

timepiece ['taɪm‚pi:s] n : reloj m

timer ['taɪmər] n : temporizador m, cronómetro m

times ['taɪmz] prep : por ⟨3 times 4 is 12 : 3 por 4 son 12⟩

timetable ['taɪm‚teɪbəl] n : horario m

timid ['tɪmɪd] adj : tímido — **timidly** adv

timidity [tə'mɪdəti] n : timidez f

timorous ['tɪmərəs] adj : timorato, miedoso

timpani ['tɪmpəni] npl : timbales mpl

tin ['tɪn] n 1 : estaño m, hojalata f (metal) 2 CAN : lata f, bote m, envase m

tincture ['tɪŋktʃər] n : tintura f

tinder ['tɪndər] n : yesca f

tine ['taɪn] n : diente m (de un tenedor, etc.)

tinfoil ['tɪn‚fɔɪl] n : papel m (de) aluminio

tinge¹ ['tɪndʒ] vt **tinged; tingeing** or **tinging** ['tɪndʒɪŋ] TINT : matizar, teñir ligeramente

tinge² n 1 TINT : matiz m, tinte m sutil 2 TOUCH : dejo m, sensación f ligera

tingle¹ ['tɪŋgəl] vi **-gled; -gling** : sentir (un) hormigueo, sentir (un) cosquilleo

tingle² n : hormigueo m, cosquilleo m

tinker ['tɪŋkər] vi to tinker with : arreglar con pequeños ajustes, toquetear (con intento de arreglar)

tinkle¹ ['tɪŋkəl] vi **-kled; -kling** : tintinear

tinkle² n : tintineo m

tinsel ['tɪntsəl] n : oropel m

tint¹ ['tɪnt] vt : teñir, colorear

tint² n : tinte m

tiny ['taɪni] adj **-nier; -est** : diminuto, minúsculo

tip¹ ['tɪp] v **tipped; tipping** vt 1 or **to tip over** : volcar, voltear, hacer caer 2 TILT : ladear, inclinar ⟨to tip one's hat : saludar con el sombrero⟩ 3 TAP : tocar, golpear ligeramente **4** : darle una propina (a un mesero, etc.) ⟨I tipped him $5 : le di $5 de propina⟩ **5** : adornar o cubrir la punta de ⟨wings tipped in red : alas que tienen las puntas rojas⟩ **6 to tip off** : dar información a — *vi* TILT : ladearse, inclinarse

tip² *n* **1** END, POINT : punta *f*, extremo *m* ⟨on the tip of one's tongue : en la punta de la lengua⟩ **2** GRATUITY : propina *f* **3** ADVICE, INFORMATION : consejo *m*, información *f* (confidencial)

tip-off ['tɪp,ɔf] *n* **1** SIGN : indicación *f*, señal *f* **2** TIP : información *f* (confidencial)

tipple ['tɪpəl] *vi* -pled; -pling : tomarse unas copas

tipsy ['tɪpsi] *adj* -sier; -est : achispado

tiptoe¹ ['tɪp,to:] *vi* -toed; -toeing : caminar de puntillas

tiptoe² *adv* : de puntillas

tiptoe³ *n* : punta *f* del pie

tip-top¹ ['tɪp'tɑp, -,tɑp] *adj* EXCELLENT : excelente

tip-top² *n* SUMMIT : cumbre *f*, cima *f*

tirade ['taɪ,reɪd] *n* : diatriba *f*

tire¹ ['taɪr] *v* tired; tiring *vt* : cansar, agotar, fatigar — *vi* : cansarse

tire² *n* : llanta *f*, neumático *m*, goma *f*

tired ['taɪrd] *adj* : cansado, agotado, fatigado ⟨to get tired : cansarse⟩

tireless ['taɪrləs] *adj* : incansable, infatigable — **tirelessly** *adv*

tiresome ['taɪrsəm] *adj* : fastidioso, pesado, tedioso — **tiresomely** *adv*

tissue ['tɪ,ʃu:] *n* **1** : pañuelo *m* de papel **2** : tejido *m* ⟨lung tissue : tejido pulmonar⟩

titanic [taɪ'tænɪk, tə-] *adj* GIGANTIC : titánico, gigantesco

titanium [taɪ'teɪniəm, tə-] *n* : titanio *m*

titillate ['tɪtəl,eɪt] *vt* -lated; -lating : excitar, estimular placenteramente

title¹ ['taɪtəl] *vt* -tled; -tling : titular, intitular

title² *n* : título *m*

titter¹ ['tɪtər] *vi* GIGGLE : reírse tontamente

titter² *n* : risita *f*, risa *f* tonta

tizzy ['tɪzi] *n*, *pl* **tizzies** : estado *m* agitado o nervioso ⟨I'm all in a tizzy : estoy todo alterado⟩

TNT [,ti:,ɛn'ti:] *n* : TNT *m*

to¹ ['tu:] *adv* **1** : a un estado consciente ⟨to come to : volver en sí⟩ **2 to and fro** : de aquí para allá, de un lado para otro

to² *prep* **1** (*indicating a place*) : a ⟨to go to the doctor : ir al médico⟩ ⟨I'm going to John's : voy a la casa de John⟩ **2** TOWARD : a, hacia ⟨two miles to the south : dos millas hacia el sur⟩ **3** ON : en, sobre ⟨apply salve to the wound : póngale ungüento a la herida⟩ **4** UP TO : hasta, ⟨to a degree : hasta cierto grado⟩ ⟨from head to toe : de pies a cabeza⟩ **5** (*in expressions of time*) ⟨it's quarter to seven : son las siete menos

cuarto⟩ **6** UNTIL : a, hasta ⟨from May to December : de mayo a diciembre⟩ **7** (*indicating belonging or possession*) : de, a ⟨the key to the lock : la llave del candado⟩ **8** (*indicating response*) : a ⟨dancing to the rhythm : bailando al compás⟩ **9** (*indicating comparison or proportion*) : a ⟨it's similar to mine : es parecido al mío⟩ ⟨they won 4 to 2 : ganaron 4 a 2⟩ **10** (*indicating agreement or conformity*) : a, de acuerdo con ⟨made to order : hecho a la orden⟩ ⟨to my knowledge : a mi saber⟩ **11** (*indicating inclusion*) : en cada, por ⟨twenty to the box : veinte por caja⟩ **12** (*used to form the infinitive*) ⟨to understand : entender⟩ ⟨to go away : irse⟩

toad ['to:d] *n* : sapo *m*

toadstool ['to:d,stu:l] *n* : hongo *m* (no comestible)

toady ['to:di] *n*, *pl* **toadies** : adulador *m*, -dora *f*

toast¹ ['to:st] *vt* **1** : tostar (pan) **2** : brindar por ⟨to toast the victors : brindar por los vencedores⟩ **3** WARM : calentar ⟨to toast oneself : calentarse⟩

toast² *n* **1** : pan *m* tostado, tostadas *fpl* **2** : brindis *m* ⟨to propose a toast : proponer un brindis⟩

toaster ['to:stər] *n* : tostador *m*

tobacco [tə'bæko:] *n*, *pl* **-cos** : tabaco *m*

toboggan¹ [tə'bɑgən] *vi* : deslizarse en tobogán

toboggan² *n* : tobogán *m*

today¹ [tə'deɪ] *adv* **1** : hoy ⟨she arrives today : hoy llega⟩ **2** NOWADAYS : hoy en día

today² *n* : hoy *m* ⟨today is a holiday : hoy es día de fiesta⟩

toddle ['tɑdəl] *vi* -dled; -dling : hacer pininos, hacer pinitos

toddler ['tɑdlər] *n* : niño *m* pequeño, niña *f* pequeña (que comienza a caminar)

to-do [tə'du:] *n*, *pl* **to-dos** [-'du:z] FUSS : lío *m*, alboroto *m*

toe ['to:] *n* : dedo *m* del pie

toenail ['to:,neɪl] *n* : uña *f* del pie

toffee *or* **toffy** ['tɔfi, 'tɑ-] *n*, *pl* **toffees** *or* **toffies** : caramelo *m* elaborado con azúcar y mantequilla

toga ['to:gə] *n* : toga *f*

together [tə'gɛðər] *adv* **1** : juntamente, juntos (el uno con el otro) ⟨Susan and Sarah work together : Susan y Sarah trabajan juntas⟩ **2 ~ with** : con

togetherness [tə'gɛðərnəs] *n* : unión *f*, compañerismo *m*

togs ['tɑgz, 'tɔgz] *npl* : ropa *f*

toil¹ ['tɔɪl] *vi* : trabajar arduamente

toil² *n* : trabajo *m* arduo

toilet ['tɔɪlət] *n* **1** : arreglo *m* personal **2** BATHROOM : (cuarto de) baño *m*, servicios *mpl* (públicos), sanitario *m* Col, Mex, Ven **3** : inodoro *m* ⟨to flush the toilet : jalar la cadena⟩

toilet paper *n* : papel *m* higiénico

toiletries ['tɔɪlətriz] *npl* : artículos *mpl* de tocador

token ['to:kən] *n* 1 PROOF, SIGN : prueba *f*, muestra *f*, señal *m* 2 SYMBOL : símbolo *m* 3 SOUVENIR : recuerdo *m* 4 : ficha *f* (para transporte público, etc.)

told → **tell**

tolerable ['tɑlərəbəl] *adj* : tolerable — **tolerably** [-bli] *adv*

tolerance ['tɑlərən*t*s] *n* : tolerancia *f*

tolerant ['tɑlərənt] *adj* : tolerante — **tolerantly** *adv*

tolerate ['tɑlə,reɪt] *vt* -**ated; -ating** 1 ACCEPT : tolerar, aceptar 2 BEAR, ENDURE : tolerar, aguantar, soportar

toleration [,tɑlə'reɪʃən] *n* : tolerancia *f*

toll[1] ['to:l] *vt* : tañer, sonar (una campana) — *vi* : sonar, doblar (dícese de las campanas)

toll[2] *n* 1 : peaje *m* (de una carretera, un puente, etc.) 2 CASUALTIES : pérdida *f*, número *m* de víctimas 3 TOLLING : tañido *m* (de campanas)

tollbooth ['to:l,bu:θ] *n* : caseta *f* de peaje

tollgate ['to:l,geɪt] *n* : barrera *f* de peaje

tomahawk ['tɑmə,hɔk] *n* : hacha *f* de guerra (de los indígenas norteamericanos)

tomato [tə'meɪto, -'mɑ-] *n, pl* -**toes** : tomate *m*

tomb ['tu:m] *n* : sepulcro *m*, tumba *f*

tomboy ['tɑm,bɔɪ] *n* : marimacho *mf*; niña *f* que se porta como muchacho

tombstone ['tu:m,sto:n] *n* : lápida *f*

tomcat ['tɑm,kæt] *n* : gato *m* (macho)

tome ['to:m] *n* : tomo *m*

tomorrow[1] [tə'mɑro] *adv* : mañana

tomorrow[2] *n* : mañana *m*

tom—tom ['tɑm,tɑm] *n* : tam-tam *m*

ton ['tʌn] *n* : tonelada *f*

tone[1] ['to:n] *vt* **toned; toning** 1 *or* to **tone down** : atenuar, suavizar, moderar 2 *or* to **tone up** STRENGTHEN : tonificar, vigorizar

tone[2] *n* : tono *m* ⟨in a friendly tone : en tono amistoso⟩ ⟨a greyish tone : un tono grisáceo⟩

tongs ['tɑŋz, 'tɔŋz] *npl* : tenazas *fpl*

tongue ['tʌŋ] *n* 1 : lengua *f*, idioma *m* 2 LANGUAGE : lengua *f*, idioma *m*

tongue—tied ['tʌŋ,taɪd] *adj* to get **tongue—tied** : trabársele la lengua a uno

tonic[1] ['tɑnɪk] *adj* : tónico

tonic[2] *n* 1 : tónico *m* 2 *or* **tonic water** : tónica *f*

tonight[1] [tə'naɪt] *adv* : esta noche

tonight[2] *n* : esta noche *f*

tonsil ['tɑn*t*səl] *n* : amígdala *f*, angina *f* *Mex*

tonsillitis [,tɑn*t*sə'laɪtəs] *n* : amigdalitis *f*, anginas *fpl Mex*

too ['tu:] *adv* 1 ALSO : también 2 EXCESSIVELY : demasiado ⟨it's too hot in here : aquí hace demasiado calor⟩

took → **take**[1]

tool[1] ['tu:l] *vt* 1 : fabricar, confeccionar (con herramientas) 2 EQUIP : instalar maquinaria en (una fábrica)

tool[2] *n* : herramienta *f*

toolbox ['tu:l,bɑks] *n* : caja *f* de herramientas

toot[1] ['tu:t] *vt* : sonar (un claxon o un pito)

toot[2] *n* : pitido *m*, bocinazo *m* (de un claxon)

tooth ['tu:θ] *n, pl* **teeth** ['ti:θ] : diente *m*

toothache ['tu:θ,eɪk] *n* : dolor *m* de muelas

toothbrush ['tu:θ,brʌʃ] *n* : cepillo *m* de dientes

toothless ['tu:θləs] *adj* : desdentado

toothpaste ['tu:θ,peɪst] *n* : pasta *f* de dientes, crema *f* dental, dentífrico *m*

toothpick ['tu:θ,pɪk] *n* : palillo *m* (de dientes), mondadientes *m*

top[1] ['tɑp] *vt* **topped; topping** 1 COVER : cubrir, coronar 2 SURPASS : sobrepasar, superar 3 CLEAR : pasar por encima de

top[2] *adj* : superior ⟨the top shelf : la repisa superior⟩ ⟨one of the top lawyers : uno de los mejores abogados⟩

top[3] *n* 1 : parte *f* superior, cumbre *f*, cima *f* (de un monte, etc.) ⟨to climb to the top : subir a la cumbre⟩ 2 COVER : tapa *f*, cubierta *f* 3 : trompo *m* (juguete) 4 **on top of** : encima de

topaz ['to:,pæz] *n* : topacio *m*

topcoat ['tɑp,ko:t] *n* : sobretodo *m*, abrigo *m*

topic ['tɑpɪk] *n* : tema *m*, tópico *m*

topical ['tɑpɪkəl] *adj* : de interés actual

topmost ['tɑp,mo:st] *adj* : más alto

top—notch ['tɑp'nɑtʃ] *adj* : de lo mejor, de primera categoría

topographic [,tɑpə'græfɪk] *or* **topographical** [-fɪkəl] *adj* : topográfico

topography [tə'pɑgrəfi] *n, pl* -**phies** : topografía *f*

topple ['tɑpəl] *v* -**pled; -pling** *vi* : caerse, venirse abajo — *vt* : volcar, derrocar (un gobierno, etc.)

topsoil ['tɑp,sɔɪl] *n* : capa *f* superior del suelo

topsy—turvy [,tɑpsi'tərvi] *adv & adj* : patas arriba, al revés

torch ['tɔrtʃ] *n* : antorcha *f*

tore → **tear**[1]

torment[1] [tɔr'mɛnt, 'tɔr,-] *vt* : atormentar, torturar, martirizar

torment[2] ['tɔr,mɛnt] *n* : tormento *m*, suplicio *m*, martirio *m*

tormentor [tɔr'mɛntər] *n* : atormentador *m*, -dora *f*

torn *pp* → **tear**[1]

tornado [tɔr'neɪdo] *n, pl* -**does** *or* -**dos** : tornado *m*

torpedo[1] [tɔr'pi:do] *vt* : torpedear

torpedo[2] *n, pl* -**does** : torpedo *m*

torpid ['tɔrpɪd] *adj* 1 SLUGGISH : aletargado 2 APATHETIC : apático

torpor ['tɔrpər] *n* : letargo *m*, apatía *f*

torrent ['tɔrənt] *n* : torrente *m*

torrential [tɔ'rɛntʃəl, tə-] *adj* : torrencial

torrid ['tɔrɪd] *adj* : tórrido

torso ['tɔr,so:] *n, pl* -**sos** *or* -**si** [-,si:] : torso *m*

tortilla [tɔr'ti:jə] n : tortilla f (de maíz)
tortoise ['tɔrṭəs] n : tortuga f (terrestre)
tortoiseshell ['tɔrṭəs,ʃɛl] n : carey m, concha f
tortuous ['tɔrtʃuəs] adj : tortuoso
torture¹ ['tɔrtʃər] vt -tured; -turing : torturar, atormentar
torture² n : tortura f, tormento m ⟨it was sheer torture! : ¡fue un verdadero suplicio!⟩
torturer ['tɔrtʃərər] n : torturador m, -dora f
toss¹ ['tɔs, 'tɑs] vt 1 AGITATE, SHAKE : sacudir, agitar, mezclar (una ensalada) 2 THROW : tirar, echar, lanzar — vi : sacudirse, moverse agitadamente ⟨to toss and turn : dar vueltas⟩
toss² n THROW : lanzamiento m, tiro m, tirada f, lance m (de dados, etc.)
toss–up ['tɔs,ʌp] n : posibilidad f igual ⟨it's a toss-up : quizá sí, quizá no⟩
tot ['tɑt] n : pequeño m, -ña f
total¹ [to'təl] vt -taled or -talled; -taling or -talling 1 or to total up ADD : sumar, totalizar 2 AMOUNT TO : ascender a, llegar a
total² adj : total, completo, absoluto — **totally** adv
total³ n : total m
totalitarian [to:,tælə'tɛriən] adj : totalitario
totalitarianism [to:,tælə'tɛriə,nɪzəm] n : totalitarismo m
totality [to:'tæləti] n, pl -ties : totalidad f
tote ['to:t] vt toted; toting : cargar, llevar
totem ['to:təm] n : tótem m
totter ['tɑtər] vi : tambalearse
touch¹ ['tʌtʃ] vt 1 FEEL, HANDLE : tocar, tentar 2 AFFECT, MOVE : conmover, afectar, tocar ⟨his gesture touched our hearts : su gesto nos tocó el corazón⟩ — vi : tocarse
touch² n 1 : tacto m (sentido) 2 DETAIL : toque m, detalle m ⟨a touch of color : un toque de color⟩ 3 BIT : pizca f, gota f, poco m 4 ABILITY : habilidad f ⟨to lose one's touch : perder la habilidad⟩ 5 CONTACT : contacto m, comunicación f ⟨to keep in touch : mantenerse en contacto⟩
touchdown ['tʌtʃ,daʊn] n : touchdown m (en futbol americano)
touching ['tʌtʃɪŋ] adj MOVING : conmovedor
touchstone ['tʌtʃ,sto:n] n : piedra f de toque
touch up vt : retocar
touchy ['tʌtʃi] adj touchier; -est 1 : sensible, susceptible (dícese de una persona) 2 : delicado ⟨a touchy subject : un tema delicado⟩
tough¹ ['tʌf] adj 1 STRONG : fuerte, resistente (dícese de materiales) 2 LEATHERY : correoso ⟨a tough steak : un bistec duro⟩ 3 HARDY : fuerte, robusto (dícese de una persona) 4 STRICT

: severo, exigente 5 DIFFICULT : difícil 6 STUBBORN : terco, obstinado
tough² n : matón m, persona f ruda y brusca
toughen ['tʌfən] vt : fortalecer, endurecer — vi : endurecerse, hacerse más fuerte
toughness ['tʌfnəs] n : dureza f
toupee [tu:'peɪ] n : peluquín m, bisoñé m
tour¹ ['tʊr] vi : tomar una excursión, viajar — vt : recorrer, hacer una gira por
tour² n 1 : gira f, tour m, excursión f 2 **tour of duty** : período m de servicio
tourism ['tʊr,ɪzəm] n : turismo m
tourist ['tʊrɪst, 'tər-] n : turista mf
tournament ['tərnəmənt, 'tʊr-] n : torneo m
tourniquet ['tərnɪkət, 'tʊr-] n : torniquete m
tousle ['taʊzəl] vt -sled; -sling : desarreglar, despeinar (el cabello)
tout ['taʊt] vt : promocionar, elogiar (con exageración)
tow¹ ['to:] vt : remolcar
tow² n : remolque m
toward ['tord, tə'word] or **towards** ['tordz, tə'wordz] prep 1 (indicating direction) : hacia, rumbo a ⟨heading toward town : dirigiéndose rumbo al pueblo⟩ ⟨efforts towards peace : esfuerzos hacia la paz⟩ 2 (indicating time) : alrededor de ⟨toward midnight : alrededor de la medianoche⟩ 3 REGARDING : hacia, con respecto a ⟨his attitude toward life : su actitud hacia la vida⟩ 4 FOR : para, como pago parcial de (una compra o deuda)
towel ['taʊəl] n : toalla f
tower¹ ['taʊər] vi **to tower over** : descollar sobre, elevarse sobre, dominar
tower² n : torre f
towering ['taʊərɪŋ] adj : altísimo, imponente
town ['taʊn] n : pueblo m, ciudad f (pequeña)
township ['taʊn,ʃɪp] n : municipio m
tow truck ['to:,trʌk] n : grúa f
toxic ['tɑksɪk] adj : tóxico
toxicity [tɑk'sɪsəti] n, pl -ties : toxicidad f
toxin ['tɑksɪn] n : toxina f
toy¹ ['tɔɪ] vi : juguetear, jugar
toy² adj : de juguete ⟨a toy rifle : un rifle de juguete⟩
toy³ n : juguete m
trace¹ ['treɪs] vt traced; tracing 1 : calcar (un dibujo, etc.) 2 OUTLINE : delinear, trazar (planes, etc.) 3 TRACK : describir (un curso, una historia) 4 FIND : localizar, ubicar
trace² n 1 SIGN, TRACK : huella f, rastro m, indicio m, vestigio m ⟨he disappeared without a trace : desapareció sin dejar rastro⟩ 2 BIT, HINT : pizca f, ápice m, dejo m
trachea ['treɪkiə] n, pl -cheae [-ki,i:] : tráquea f

tracing paper n : papel m de calcar

track¹ [ˈtræk] vt **1** TRAIL : seguir la pista de, rastrear **2** : dejar huellas de ⟨he tracked mud all over : dejó huellas de lodo por todas partes⟩

track² n **1** : rastro m, huella f (de animales), pista f (de personas) **2** PATH : pista f, sendero m, camino m **3** or **railroad track** : vía f (férrea) **4** → **racetrack 5** : oruga f (de un tanque, etc.) **6** : pista f (deporte) **7 to keep track of** : llevar la cuenta de

track–and–field [ˈtrækəndˈfiːld] adj : de pista y campo

tract [ˈtrækt] n **1** AREA : terreno m, extensión f, área f **2** : tracto m ⟨digestive tract : tracto digestivo⟩ **3** PAMPHLET : panfleto m, folleto m

traction [ˈtrækʃən] n : tracción f

tractor [ˈtræktər] n **1** : tractor m (vehículo agrícola) **2** TRUCK : camión m (con remolque)

trade¹ [ˈtreɪd] v **traded; trading** vi : comerciar, negociar — vt EXCHANGE : intercambiar, canjear

trade² n **1** OCCUPATION : oficio m, profesión f, ocupación f ⟨a carpenter by trade : carpintero de oficio⟩ **2** COMMERCE : comercio m, industria f ⟨free trade : libre comercio⟩ ⟨the book trade : la industria del libro⟩ **3** EXCHANGE : intercambio m, canje m

trade–in [ˈtreɪdˌɪn] n : artículo m que se canjea por otro

trademark [ˈtreɪdˌmɑrk] n **1** : marca f registrada **2** CHARACTERISTIC : sello m característico (de un grupo, una persona, etc.)

trader [ˈtreɪdər] n : negociante mf, tratante mf, comerciante mf

tradesman [ˈtreɪdzmən] n, pl **-men** [-mən, -ˌmen] **1** CRAFTSMAN : artesano m, -na f **2** SHOPKEEPER : tendero m, -ra f; comerciante mf

trade wind n : viento m alisio

tradition [trəˈdɪʃən] n : tradición f

traditional [trəˈdɪʃənəl] adj : tradicional — **traditionally** adv

traffic¹ [ˈtræfɪk] vi **trafficked; trafficking** : traficar (con)

traffic² n **1** COMMERCE : tráfico m, comercio m ⟨the drug traffic : el narcotráfico⟩ **2** : tráfico m, tránsito m, circulación f (de vehículos, etc.)

traffic circle n : rotonda f, glorieta f

trafficker [ˈtræfɪkər] n : traficante mf

traffic light n : semáforo m, luz f (de tránsito)

tragedy [ˈtrædʒədi] n, pl **-dies** : tragedia f

tragic [ˈtrædʒɪk] adj : trágico — **tragically** adv

trail¹ [ˈtreɪl] vi **1** DRAG : arrastrarse **2** LAG : quedarse atrás, retrasarse **3 to trail away** or **to trail off** : disminuir, menguar, desvanecerse — vt **1** DRAG : arrastrar **2** PURSUE : perseguir, seguir la pista de

trail² n **1** TRACK : rastro m, huella f, pista f ⟨a trail of blood : un rastro de sangre⟩ **2** : cola f, estela f (de un meteoro) **3** PATH : sendero m, camino m, vereda f

trailer [ˈtreɪlər] n **1** : remolque m, tráiler m (de un camión) **2** : caravana f (vivienda ambulante)

train¹ [ˈtreɪn] vt **1** : adiestrar, entrenar (atletas), capacitar (trabajadores), amaestrar (animales) **2** POINT : apuntar (un arma, etc.) — vi : entrenar(se) (físicamente), prepararse (profesionalmente) ⟨she's training at the gym : se está entrenando en el gimnasio⟩

train² n **1** : cola f (de un vestido) **2** RETINUE : cortejo m, séquito m **3** SERIES : serie f (de eventos) **4** : tren m ⟨passenger train : tren de pasajeros⟩

trainee [treɪˈniː] n : aprendiz m, -diza f

trainer [ˈtreɪnər] n : entrenador m, -dora f

training [ˈtreɪnɪŋ] n : adiestramiento m, entrenamiento m (físico), capacitación f (de trabajadores)

traipse [ˈtreɪps] vi **traipsed; traipsing** : andar de un lado para otro, vagar

trait [ˈtreɪt] n : rasgo m, característica f

traitor [ˈtreɪtər] n : traidor m, -dora f

traitorous [ˈtreɪtərəs] adj : traidor

trajectory [trəˈdʒektəri] n, pl **-ries** : trayectoria f

tramp¹ [ˈtræmp] vi : caminar (a paso pesado) — vt : deambular por, vagar por ⟨to tramp the streets : vagar por las calles⟩

tramp² n **1** VAGRANT : vagabundo m, -da f **2** HIKE : caminata f

trample [ˈtræmpəl] vt **-pled; -pling** : pisotear, hollar

trampoline [ˌtræmpəˈliːn, ˈtræmpəˌ-] n : trampolín m, cama f elástica

trance [ˈtræn(t)s] n : trance m

tranquil [ˈtræŋkwəl] adj : calmo, tranquilo, sereno — **tranquilly** adv

tranquilize [ˈtræŋkwəˌlaɪz] vt **-ized; -izing** : tranquilizar

tranquilizer [ˈtræŋkwəˌlaɪzər] n : tranquilizante m

tranquillity or **tranquility** [træŋˈkwɪləti] n : sosiego m, tranquilidad f

transact [trænˈzækt] vt : negociar, gestionar, hacer (negocios)

transaction [trænˈzækʃən] n **1** : transacción f, negocio m, operación f **2 transactions** npl RECORDS : actas fpl

transatlantic [ˌtrænsətˈlæntɪk, ˌtrænz-] adj : transatlántico

transcend [trænˈsend] vt : trascender, sobrepasar

transcendent [trænˈsendənt] adj : trascendente — **transcendence** [trænˈsendən(t)s] n

transcendental [ˌtrænˌsenˈdentəl, -sən-] adj : trascendental ⟨transcendental meditation : meditación trascendental⟩

transcribe [træn'skraɪb] *vt* -scribed; -scribing : transcribir

transcript ['træn,skrɪpt] *n* : copia *f* oficial

transcription [træn'skrɪpʃən] *n* : transcripción *f*

transfer¹ [træns'fər, 'træns,fər] *v* -ferred; -ferring *vt* 1 : trasladar (a una persona), transferir (fondos) 3 PRINT : imprimir (un diseño) — *vi* 1 MOVE : trasladarse, cambiarse 2 CHANGE : transbordar, cambiar (de un transporte a otro) ⟨he transfers at E Street : hace un transbordo a la calle E⟩

transfer² ['træns,fər] *n* 1 TRANSFERRING : transferencia *f* (de fondos, de propiedad, etc.), traslado *m* (de una persona) 2 DECAL : calcomanía *f* 3 : boleto *m* (para cambiar de un avión, etc., a otro)

transferable [træns'fərəbəl] *adj* : transferible

transference [træns'fərənts] *n* : transferencia *f*

transfigure [træns'fɪgjər] *vt* -ured; -uring : transfigurar, transformar

transfix [træns'fɪks] *vt* 1 PIERCE : traspasar, atravesar 2 IMMOBILIZE : paralizar

transform [træns'fɔrm] *vt* : transformar

transformation [,trænsfər'meɪʃən] *n* : transformación *f*

transformer [træns'fɔrmər] *n* : transformador *m*

transfusion [træns'fju:ʒən] *n* : transfusión *f*

transgress [træns'grɛs, trænz-] : transgredir, infringir

transgression [træns'grɛʃən, trænz-] *n* : transgresión *f*

transient¹ ['trænʃənt, 'trænziənt] *adj* : pasajero, transitorio — **transiently** *adv*

transient² *n* : transeúnte *mf*

transistor [træn'zɪstər, -'sɪs-] *n* : transistor *m*

transit ['trænsɪt, 'trænzɪt] *n* 1 PASSAGE : pasaje *m*, tránsito *m* ⟨in transit : en tránsito⟩ 2 TRANSPORTATION : transporte *m* (público) 3 : teodolito *m* (instrumento topográfico)

transition [træn'sɪʃən, -'zɪʃ-] *n* : transición *f*

transitional [træn'sɪʃənəl, -'zɪʃ-] *adj* : de transición

transitive ['trænsətɪv, 'trænzə-] *adj* : transitivo

transitory ['trænsə,tori, 'trænzə-] *adj* : transitorio

translate [træns'leɪt, trænz-; 'træns,-, 'trænz,-] *vt* -lated; -lating : traducir

translation [træns'leɪʃən, trænz-] *n* : traducción *f*

translator [træns'leɪtər, trænz-; 'træns,-, 'trænz,-] *n* : traductor *m*, -tora *f*

translucent [træns'lu:sənt, trænz-] *adj* : translúcido

transmission [trænts'mɪʃən, trænz-] *n* : transmisión *f*

transmit [trænts'mɪt, trænz-] *vt* -mitted; -mitting : transmitir

transmitter [trænts'mɪtər, trænz-; 'trænts,-, 'trænz,-] *n* : transmisor *m*, emisor *m*

transom ['træntsəm] *n* : montante *m* (de una puerta), travesaño *m* (de una ventana)

transparency [trænts'pærəntsi] *n*, *pl* -cies : transparencia *f*

transparent [trænts'pærənt] *adj* 1 : transparente, traslúcido ⟨a transparent fabric : una tela transparente⟩ 2 OBVIOUS : transparente, obvio, claro — **transparently** *adv*

transpiration [,træntspə'reɪʃən] *n* : transpiración *f*

transpire [trænts'paɪr] *vi* -spired; -spiring 1 : transpirar (en biología y botánica) 2 TURN OUT : resultar 3 HAPPEN : suceder, ocurrir, tener lugar

transplant¹ [trænts'plænt] *vt* : trasplantar

transplant² ['trænts,plænt] *n* : trasplante *m*

transport¹ [trænts'port, 'trænts,-] *vt* 1 CARRY : transportar, acarrear 2 ENRAPTURE : transportar, extasiar

transport² ['trænts,port] *n* 1 TRANSPORTATION : transporte *m*, transportación *f* 2 RAPTURE : éxtasis *m* 3 *or* **transport ship** : buque *m* de transporte (de personal militar)

transportation [,træntspər'teɪʃən] *n* : transporte *m*, transportación *f*

transpose [trænts'po:z] *vt* -posed; -posing : trasponer, trasladar, transportar (una composición musical)

transverse [trænts'vərs, trænz-] *adj* : transversal, transverso, oblicuo — **transversely** *adv*

trap¹ ['træp] *vt* trapped; trapping : atrapar, apresar (en una trampa)

trap² *n* : trampa *f* ⟨to set a trap : tender una trampa⟩

trapdoor ['træp'dor] *n* : trampilla *f*, escotillón *m*

trapeze [træ'pi:z] *n* : trapecio *m*

trapezoid ['træpə,zɔɪd] *n* : trapezoide *m*, trapecio *m*

trapper ['træpər] *n* : trampero *m*, -ra *f*; cazador *m*, -dora *f* (que usa trampas)

trappings ['træpɪŋz] *npl* 1 : arreos *mpl*, jaeces *mpl* (de un caballo) 2 ADORNMENTS : adornos *mpl*, pompa *f*

trash ['træʃ] *n* : basura *f*

trashy ['træʃi] *adj* : de pacotilla

trauma ['troumə, 'trau-] *n* : trauma *m*

traumatic [trə'mætɪk, trɔ-, trau-] *adj* : traumático

travel¹ ['trævəl] *vi* -eled *or* -elled; -eling *or* -elling 1 JOURNEY : viajar 2 GO, MOVE : desplazarse, moverse, ir ⟨the waves travel at uniform speed : las ondas se desplazan a una velocidad uniforme⟩

travel² n or **travels** npl : viajes mpl

traveler or **traveller** ['trævələr] n : viajero m, -ra f

traverse [trə'vərs, træ'vərs, 'trævərs] vt **-versed; -versing** CROSS : atravesar, extenderse a través de, cruzar

travesty ['trævəsti] n, pl **-ties** : parodia f

trawl¹ ['trɔl] vi : pescar con red de arrastre, rastrear

trawl² n or **trawl net** : red f de arrastre

trawler ['trɔlər] n : barco m de pesca (utilizado para rastrear)

tray ['treɪ] n : bandeja f, charola f Bol, Mex, Peru

treacherous ['tretʃərəs] adj 1 TRAITOR-OUS : traicionero, traidor 2 DANGER-OUS : peligroso

treacherously ['tretʃərəsli] adv : a traición

treachery ['tretʃəri] n, pl **-eries** : traición f

tread¹ ['tred] v **trod** ['trɑd]; **trodden** ['trɑdən] or **trod; treading** vt TRAMPLE : pisotear, hollar — vi 1 WALK : caminar, andar 2 **to tread on** : pisar

tread² n 1 STEP : paso m, andar m 2 : banda f de rodadura (de un neumático, etc.) 3 : escalón m (de una escalera)

treadle ['tredəl] n : pedal m (de una máquina)

treadmill ['tred,mɪl] n 1 : rueda f de andar 2 ROUTINE : rutina f

treason ['triːzən] n : traición f (a la patria, etc.)

treasure¹ ['treʒər, 'treɪ-] vt **-sured; -suring** : apreciar, valorar

treasure² n : tesoro m

treasurer ['treʒərər, 'treɪ-] n : tesorero m, -ra f

treasury ['treʒəri, 'treɪ-] n, pl **-suries** : tesorería f, tesoro m

treat¹ ['triːt] vt 1 DEAL WITH : tratar (un asunto) ⟨the article treats of poverty : el artículo trata de la pobreza⟩ 2 HAN-DLE : tratar (a una persona), manejar (un objeto) ⟨to treat something as a joke : tomar(se) algo a broma⟩ 3 IN-VITE : invitar, convidar ⟨he treated me to a meal : me invitó a comer⟩ 4 : tratar, atender (en medicina) 5 PROCESS : tratar ⟨to treat sewage : tratar las aguas negras⟩

treat² n : gusto m, placer m ⟨it was a treat to see you : fue un placer verte⟩ ⟨it's my treat : yo invito⟩

treatise ['triːtɪs] n : tratado m, estudio m

treatment ['triːtmənt] n : trato m, tratamiento m (médico)

treaty ['triːti] n, pl **-ties** : tratado m, convenio m

treble¹ ['trebəl] vt **-bled; -bling** : triplicar

treble² adj 1 → triple 2 : de tiple, soprano (en música) 3 **treble clef** : clave f de sol

treble³ n : tiple m, parte f de soprano

tree ['triː] n : árbol m

treeless ['triːləs] adj : carente de árboles

trek¹ ['trek] vi **trekked; trekking** : hacer un viaje largo y difícil

trek² n : viaje m largo y difícil

trellis ['trelɪs] n : enrejado m, espaldera f, celosía f

tremble ['trembəl] vi **-bled; -bling** : temblar

tremendous [trɪ'mendəs] adj : tremendo — **tremendously** adv

tremor ['tremər] n : temblor m

tremulous ['tremjələs] adj : trémulo, tembloroso

trench ['trentʃ] n 1 DITCH : zanja f 2 : trinchera f (militar)

trenchant ['trentʃənt] adj : cortante, mordaz

trend¹ ['trend] vi : tender, inclinarse

trend² n 1 TENDENCY : tendencia f 2 FASHION : moda f

trendy ['trendi] adj **trendier; -est** : de moda

trepidation [,trepə'deɪʃən] n : inquietud f, ansiedad f

trespass¹ ['trespəs, -,pæs] vi 1 SIN : pecar, transgredir 2 : entrar ilegalmente (en propiedad ajena)

trespass² n 1 SIN : pecado m, transgresión f ⟨forgive us our trespasses : perdónanos nuestras deudas⟩ 2 : entrada f ilegal (en propiedad ajena)

tress ['tres] n : mechón m

trestle ['tresəl] n 1 : caballete m (armazón) 2 or **trestle bridge** : puente m de caballete

triad ['traɪ,æd] n : tríada f

trial¹ ['traɪəl] adj : de prueba ⟨trial period : período de prueba⟩

trial² n 1 : juicio m, proceso m ⟨to stand trial : ser sometido a juicio⟩ 2 AF-FLICTION : aflicción f, tribulación f 3 TEST : prueba f, ensayo m

triangle ['traɪ,æŋgəl] n : triángulo m

triangular [traɪ'æŋgjələr] adj : triangular

tribal ['traɪbəl] adj : tribal

tribe ['traɪb] n : tribu f

tribesman ['traɪbzmən] n, pl **-men** [-mən, -,men] : miembro m de una tribu

tribulation [,trɪbjə'leɪʃən] n : tribulación f

tribunal [traɪ'bjuːnəl, trɪ-] n : tribunal m, corte f

tributary ['trɪbjə,teri] n, pl **-taries** : afluente m

tribute ['trɪb,juːt] n : tributo m

trick¹ ['trɪk] vt : engañar, embaucar

trick² n 1 RUSE : trampa f, treta f, artimaña f 2 PRANK : broma f ⟨we played a trick on her : le gastamos una broma⟩ 3 : truco m ⟨magic tricks : trucos de magia⟩ ⟨the trick is to wait five minutes : el truco está en esperar cinco minutos⟩ 4 MANNERISM : peculiaridad f, manía f 5 : baza f (en juegos de naipes)

trickery ['trɪkəri] n : engaños mpl, trampas fpl

trickle¹ ['trɪkəl] vi **-led; -ling** : gotear, chorrear

trickle² *n* : goteo *m*, hilo *m*
trickster ['trɪkstər] *n* : estafador *m*, -dora *f*; embaucador *m*, -dora *f*
tricky ['trɪki] *adj* **trickier; -est 1** SLY : astuto, taimado **2** DIFFICULT : delicado, peliagudo, difícil
tricycle ['traɪsɪkəl, -,sɪkəl] *n* : triciclo *m*
trident ['traɪdənt] *n* : tridente *m*
triennial [traɪ'ɛniəl] *adj* : trienal
trifle¹ ['traɪfəl] *vi* **-fled; -fling** : jugar, juguetear
trifle² *n* : nimiedad *f*, insignificancia *f*
trifling ['traɪflɪŋ] *adj* : trivial, insignificante
trigger¹ ['trɪgər] *vt* : causar, provocar
trigger² *n* : gatillo *m*
trigonometry [,trɪgə'nɑmətri] *n* : trigonometría *f*
trill¹ ['trɪl] *vi* QUAVER : trinar, gorjear — *vt* : vibrar ⟨to trill the *r* : vibrar la *r*⟩
trill² *n* **1** QUAVER : trino *m*, gorjeo *m* **2** : vibración *f* (en fonética)
trillion ['trɪljən] *n* : billón *m*
trilogy ['trɪlədʒi] *n, pl* **-gies** : trilogía *f*
trim¹ ['trɪm] *vt* **trimmed; trimming 1** DECORATE : adornar, decorar **2** CUT : recortar **3** REDUCE : recortar, reducir ⟨to trim the excess : recortar el exceso⟩
trim² *adj* **trimmer; trimmest 1** SLIM : esbelto **2** NEAT : limpio y arreglado, bien cuidado
trim³ *n* **1** CONDITION : condición *f*, estado *m* ⟨to keep in trim : mantenerse en buena forma⟩ **2** CUT : recorte *m* **3** TRIMMING : adornos *mpl*
trimming ['trɪmɪŋ] *n* : adornos *mpl*, accesorios *mpl*
Trinity ['trɪnəti] *n* : Trinidad *f*
trinket ['trɪŋkət] *n* : chuchería *f*, baratija *f*
trio ['tri:,o:] *n, pl* **trios** : trío *m*
trip¹ ['trɪp] *v* **tripped; tripping** *vi* **1** : caminar (a paso ligero) **2** STUMBLE : tropezar **3** to trip up ERR : equivocarse, cometer un error — *vt* **1** : hacerle una zancadilla (a alguien) ⟨you tripped me on purpose! : ¡me hiciste la zancadilla a propósito!⟩ **2** ACTIVATE : activar (un mecanismo) **3** to trip up : hacer equivocar (a alguien)
trip² *n* **1** JOURNEY : viaje *m* ⟨to take a trip : hacer un viaje⟩ **2** STUMBLE : tropiezo *m*, traspié *m*
tripartite [traɪ'pɑr,taɪt] *adj* : tripartito
tripe ['traɪp] *n* **1** : mondongo *m*, callos *mpl*, pancita *f Mex* **2** TRASH : porquería *f*
triple¹ ['trɪpəl] *vt* **-pled; -pling** : triplicar
triple² *adj* : triple
triple³ *n* : triple *m*
triplet ['trɪplət] *n* **1** : terceto *m* (en poesía, música, etc.) **2** : trillizo *m*, -za *f* (persona)
triplicate ['trɪplɪkət] *n* : triplicado *m*
tripod ['traɪ,pɑd] *n* : trípode *m*
trite ['traɪt] *adj* **triter; tritest** : trillado, tópico, manido

triumph¹ ['traɪəm,pf] *vi* : triunfar
triumph² *n* : triunfo *m*
triumphal [traɪ'ʌmpfəl] *adj* : triunfal
triumphant [traɪ'ʌmpfənt] *adj* : triunfante, triunfal — **triumphantly** *adv*
trivia ['trɪviə] *ns & pl* : trivialidades *fpl*, nimiedades *fpl*
trivial ['trɪviəl] *adj* : trivial, intrascendente, insignificante
triviality [,trɪvi'æləti] *n, pl* **-ties** : trivialidad *f*
trod, trodden → **tread¹**
troll ['tro:l] *n* : duende *m* o gigante *m* de cuentos folklóricos
trolley ['trɑli] *n, pl* **-leys** : tranvía *m*
trombone [trɑm'bo:n] *n* : trombón *m*
trombonist [trɑm'bo:nɪst] *n* : trombón *m*
troop¹ ['tru:p] *vi* : desfilar, ir en tropel
troop² *n* **1** : escuadrón *m* (de caballería) **2** GROUP : grupo *m*, banda *f* (de personas) **3 troops** *npl* SOLDIERS : tropas *fpl*, soldados *mpl*
trooper ['tru:pər] *n* **1** : soldado *m* (de caballería) **2** : policía *m* montado **3** : policía *m* (estatal)
trophy ['tro:fi] *n, pl* **-phies** : trofeo *m*
tropic¹ ['trɑpɪk] *or* **tropical** [-pɪkəl] *adj* : tropical
tropic² *n* **1** : trópico *m* ⟨tropic of Cancer : trópico de Cáncer⟩ **2 the tropics** : el trópico
trot¹ ['trɑt] *vi* **trotted; trotting** : trotar
trot² *n* : trote *m*
trouble¹ ['trʌbəl] *v* **-bled; -bling** *vt* **1** DISTURB, WORRY : molestar, perturbar, inquietar **2** AFFLICT : afligir, afectar — *vi* : molestarse, hacer un esfuerzo ⟨they didn't trouble to come : no se molestaron en venir⟩
trouble² *n* **1** PROBLEMS : problemas *mpl*, dificultades *fpl* ⟨to be in trouble : estar en un aprieto⟩ ⟨heart trouble : problemas de corazón⟩ **2** EFFORT : molestia *f*, esfuerzo *m* ⟨to take the trouble : tomarse la molestia⟩ ⟨it's not worth the trouble : no vale la pena⟩
troublemaker ['trʌbəl,meɪkər] *n* : agitador *m*, -dora *f*; alborotador *m*, -dora *f*
troublesome ['trʌbəlsəm] *adj* : problemático, dificultoso — **troublesomely** *adv*
trough ['trɒf] *n, pl* **troughs** ['trɒfs, 'trɒvz] **1** : comedero *m*, bebedero *m* (de animales) **2** CHANNEL, HOLLOW : depresión *f* (en el suelo), seno *m* (de olas)
trounce ['traunts] *vt* **trounced; trouncing 1** THRASH : apalear, darle una paliza (a alguien) **2** DEFEAT : derrotar contundentemente
troupe ['tru:p] *n* : troupe *f*
trousers ['trauzərz] *npl* : pantalón *m*, pantalones *mpl*
trout ['traut] *n, pl* **trout** : trucha *f*
trowel ['trauəl] *n* **1** : llana *f*, paleta *f* (de albañil) **2** : desplantador *m* (de jardinero)
truant ['tru:ənt] *n* : alumno *m*, -na *f* que falta a clase sin permiso

truce ['tru:s] *n* : tregua *f*, armisticio *m*
truck¹ ['trʌk] *vt* : transportar en camión
truck² *n* **1** : camión *m* (vehículo automóvil), carro *m* (manual) **2** DEALINGS : tratos *mpl* ⟨to have no truck with : no tener nada que ver con⟩
trucker ['trʌkər] *n* : camionero *m*, -ra *f*
truculent ['trʌkjələnt] *adj* : agresivo, beligerante
trudge ['trʌdʒ] *vi* **trudged; trudging** : caminar a paso pesado
true¹ ['tru:] *vt* **trued; trueing** : aplomar (algo vertical), nivelar (algo horizontal), centrar (una rueda)
true² *adv* **1** TRUTHFULLY : lealmente, sinceramente **2** ACCURATELY : exactamente, certeramente
true³ *adj* **truer; truest 1** LOYAL : fiel, leal **2** : cierto, verdadero, verídico ⟨it's true : es cierto, es la verdad⟩ ⟨a true story : una historia verídica⟩ **3** GENUINE : auténtico, genuino — **truly** *adv*
true–blue ['tru:'blu:] *adj* LOYAL : leal, fiel
truffle ['trʌfəl] *n* : trufa *f*
truism ['tru:ˌɪzəm] *n* : perogrullada *f*, verdad *f* obvia
trump¹ ['trʌmp] *vt* : matar (en juegos de naipes)
trump² *n* : triunfo *m* (en juegos de naipes)
trumped–up ['trʌmpt'ʌp] *adj* : inventado, fabricado ⟨trumped-up charges : falsas acusaciones⟩
trumpet¹ ['trʌmpət] *vi* **1** : sonar una trompeta **2** : berrear, bramar (dícese de un animal) — *vt* : proclamar a los cuatro vientos
trumpet² *n* : trompeta *f*
trumpeter ['trʌmpətər] *n* : trompetista *mf*
truncate ['trʌnˌkeɪt, 'trʌn-] *vt* **-cated; -cating** : truncar
trundle ['trʌndəl] *v* **-dled; -dling** *vi* : rodar lentamente — *vt* : hacer rodar, empujar lentamente
trunk ['trʌŋk] *n* **1** : tronco *m* (de un árbol o del cuerpo) **2** : trompa *f* (de un elefante) **3** CHEST : baúl *m* **4** : maletero *m*, cajuela *f Mex* (de un auto) **5 trunks** *npl* : traje *m* de baño (de caballero)
truss¹ ['trʌs] *vt* : atar (con fuerza)
truss² *n* **1** FRAMEWORK : armazón *m* (de una estructura) **2** : braguero *m* (en medicina)
trust¹ ['trʌst] *vi* : confiar, esperar ⟨to trust in God : confiar en Dios⟩ — *vt* **1** ENTRUST : confiar, encomendar **2** : confiar en, tenerle confianza a ⟨I trust you : te tengo confianza⟩
trust² *n* **1** CONFIDENCE : confianza *f* **2** HOPE : esperanza *f*, fe *f* **3** CREDIT : crédito *m* ⟨to sell on trust : fiar⟩ **4** : fideicomiso *m* ⟨to hold in trust : guardar en fideicomiso⟩ **5** : trust *m* (consorcio empresarial) **6** CUSTODY : responsabilidad *f*, custodia *f*
trustee [ˌtrʌs'ti:] *n* : fideicomisario *m*, -ria *f*; fiduciario *m*, -ria *f*

trustful ['trʌstfəl] *adj* : confiado — **trustfully** *adv*
trustworthiness ['trəst,wərðinəs] *n* : integridad *f*, honradez *f*
trustworthy ['trəst,wərði] *adj* : digno de confianza, confiable
trusty ['trʌsti] *adj* **trustier; -est** : fiel, confiable
truth ['tru:θ] *n*, *pl* **truths** ['tru:ðz, 'tru:θs] : verdad *f*
truthful ['tru:θfəl] *adj* : sincero, veraz — **truthfully** *adv*
truthfulness ['tru:θfəlnəs] *n* : sinceridad *f*, veracidad *f*
try¹ ['traɪ] *v* **tried; trying** *vt* **1** : enjuiciar, juzgar, procesar ⟨he was tried for murder : fue procesado por homicidio⟩ **2** : probar ⟨did you try the salad? : ¿probaste la ensalada?⟩ **3** TEST : tentar, poner a prueba ⟨to try one's patience : tentarle la paciencia a uno⟩ **4** ATTEMPT : tratar (de), intentar **5** *or* **to try on** : probarse (ropa) — *vi* : tratar, intentar
try² *n*, *pl* **tries** : intento *m*, tentativa *f*
tryout ['traɪˌaʊt] *n* : prueba *f*
tsar ['zɑr, 'tsɑr, 'sɑr] → **czar**
T-shirt ['ti:ˌʃərt] *n* : camiseta *f*
tub ['tʌb] *n* **1** CASK : cuba *f*, barril *m*, tonel *m* **2** CONTAINER : envase *m* (de plástico, etc.) ⟨a tub of margarine : un envase de margarina⟩ **3** BATHTUB : tina *f* (de baño), bañera *f*
tuba ['tu:bə, 'tju:-] *n* : tuba *f*
tube ['tu:b, 'tju:b] *n* **1** PIPE : tubo *m* ⟨tubo *m* (de dentífrico, etc.) **3** *or* **inner tube** : cámara *f* **4** : tubo *m* (de un aparato electrónico) **5** : trompa *f* (en anatomía)
tubeless ['tu:bləs, 'tju:b-] *adj* : sin cámara (dícese de una llanta)
tuber ['tu:bər, 'tju:-] *n* : tubérculo *m*
tubercular [tʊ'bərkjələr, tjʊ-] → **tuberculous**
tuberculosis [tʊˌbərkjə'lo:sɪs, tjʊ-] *n*, *pl* **-loses** [-ˌsi:z] : tuberculosis *f*
tuberculous [tʊ'bərkjələs, tjʊ-] *adj* : tuberculoso
tuberous ['tu:bərəs, 'tju:-] *adj* : tuberoso
tubing ['tu:bɪŋ, 'tju:-] *n* : tubería *f*
tubular ['tu:bjələr, 'tju:-] *adj* : tubular
tuck¹ ['tʌk] *vt* **1** PLACE, PUT : meter, colocar ⟨tuck in your shirt : métete la camisa⟩ **2** : guardar, esconder ⟨to tuck away one's money : guardar uno bien su dinero⟩ **3** COVER : arropar (a un niño en la cama)
tuck² *n* : pliegue *m*, alforza *f*
Tuesday ['tu:zˌdeɪ, 'tju:z-, -di] *n* : martes *m*
tuft ['tʌft] *n* : penacho *m* (de plumas), copete *m* (de pelo)
tug¹ ['tʌg] *v* **tugged; tugging** *vi* : tirar, jalar, dar un tirón — *vt* : jalar, arrastrar, remolcar (con un barco)
tug² *n* **1** : tirón *m*, jalón *m* **2** → **tugboat**
tugboat ['tʌgˌbo:t] *n* : remolcador *m*

tug–of–war [ˌtʌɡə'wɔr] n, pl **tugs–of–war** : tira y afloja m

tuition [tu'ɪʃən] n or **tuition fees** : tasas fpl de matrícula, colegiatura f Mex

tulip ['tu:lɪp, 'tju:-] n : tulipán m

tumble[1] ['tʌmbəl] v **-bled; -bling** vi 1 : dar volteretas (en acrobacia) 2 FALL : caerse, venirse abajo — vt 1 TOPPLE : volcar 2 TOSS : hacer girar

tumble[2] n : voltereta f, caída f

tumbler ['tʌmblər] n 1 ACROBAT : acróbata mf, saltimbanqui mf 2 GLASS : vaso m (de mesa) 3 : clavija f (de una cerradura)

tummy ['tʌmi] n, pl **-mies** BELLY : panza f, vientre m

tumor ['tu:mər, 'tju:-] n : tumor m

tumult ['tu:ˌmʌlt, 'tju:-] n : tumulto m, alboroto m

tumultuous [tu'mʌltʃuəs, tju-] adj : tumultuoso

tuna ['tu:nə, 'tju:-] n, pl **-na** or **-nas** : atún m

tundra ['tʌndrə] n : tundra f

tune[1] ['tu:n, 'tju:n] v **tuned; tuning** vt 1 ADJUST : ajustar, hacer más preciso, afinar (un motor) 2 : afinar (un instrumento musical) 3 : sintonizar (un radio o televisor) — vi **to tune in** : sintonizar (con una emisora)

tune[2] n 1 MELODY : tonada f, canción f, melodía f 2 **in tune** : afinado (dícese de un instrumento o de la voz), sintonizado, en sintonía

tuneful ['tu:nfəl, 'tju:n-] adj : armonioso, melódico

tuner ['tu:nər, 'tju:-] n : afinador m, -dora f (de instrumentos); sintonizador m (de un radio o un televisor)

tungsten ['tʌŋkstən] n : tungsteno m

tunic ['tu:nɪk, 'tju:-] n : túnica f

tuning fork n : diapasón m

Tunisian [tu:'ni:ʒən, tju:'nɪziən] n : tunecino m, -na f — **Tunisian** adj

tunnel[1] ['tʌnəl] vi **-neled** or **-nelled; -neling** or **-nelling** : hacer un túnel

tunnel[2] n : túnel m

turban ['tərbən] n : turbante m

turbid ['tərbid] adj : turbio

turbine ['tərbən, -ˌbaɪn] n : turbina f

turboprop ['tərboˌprɑp] n : turbopropulsor m (motor), avión m turbopropulsado

turbulence ['tərbjələnts] n : turbulencia f

turbulent ['tərbjələnt] adj : turbulento — **turbulently** adv

tureen [tə'ri:n, tju-] n : sopera f

turf ['tərf] n : tepe m

turgid ['tərdʒid] adj 1 SWOLLEN : turgente 2 : ampuloso, hinchado ⟨turgid style : estilo ampuloso⟩

Turk ['tərk] n : turco m, -ca f

turkey ['tərki] n, pl **-keys** : pavo m

Turkish[1] ['tərkiʃ] adj : turco

Turkish[2] n : turco m (idioma)

turmoil ['tərˌmɔil] n : agitación f, desorden m, confusión f

turn[1] ['tərn] vt 1 : girar, voltear, volver ⟨to turn one's head : voltear la cabeza⟩ ⟨she turned her chair toward the fire : giró su asiento hacia la hoguera⟩ 2 ROTATE : darle vuelta a, hacer girar ⟨turn the handle : dale vuelta a la manivela⟩ 3 SPRAIN, WRENCH : dislocar, torcer 4 UPSET : revolver (el estómago) 5 TRANSFORM : convertir ⟨to turn water into wine : convertir el agua en vino⟩ 6 SHAPE : tornear (en carpintería) — vi 1 ROTATE : girar, dar vueltas 2 : girar, doblar, dar una vuelta ⟨turn left : doble a la izquierda⟩ ⟨to turn around : dar la media vuelta⟩ 3 BECOME : hacerse, volverse, ponerse 4 SOUR : agriarse, cortarse (dícese de la leche) 5 **to turn to** : recurrir a ⟨they have no one to turn to : no tienen quien les ayude⟩

turn[2] n 1 : vuelta f, giro m ⟨a sudden turn : una vuelta repentina⟩ 2 CHANGE : cambio m 3 CURVE : curva f (en un camino) 4 : turno m ⟨they're awaiting their turn : están esperando su turno⟩ ⟨whose turn is it? : ¿a quién le toca?⟩

turnaround ['tərnəˌraʊnd] n PROCESSING : procesamiento m

turncoat ['tərnˌko:t] n : traidor m, -dora f

turn down vt 1 REFUSE : rehusar, rechazar ⟨they turned down our invitation : rehusaron nuestra invitación⟩ 2 LOWER : bajar (el volumen)

turn in vt : entregar ⟨to turn in one's work : entregar uno su trabajo⟩ ⟨they turned in the suspect : entregaron al sospechoso⟩ — vi : acostarse, irse a la cama

turnip ['tərnəp] n : nabo m

turn off vt : apagar (la luz, la radio, etc.)

turn on vt : prender (la luz, etc.), encender (un motor, etc.)

turnout ['tərnˌaʊt] n : concurrencia f

turn out vt 1 EVICT, EXPEL : expulsar, echar, desalojar 2 PRODUCE : producir 3 → **turn off** — vi 1 : concurrir, presentarse ⟨many turned out to vote : muchos concurrieron a votar⟩ 2 PROVE, RESULT : resultar

turnover ['tərnˌo:vər] n 1 : empanada f (salada o dulce) 2 : volumen m (de ventas) 3 : rotación f (de personal) ⟨a high turnover : un alto nivel de rotación⟩

turn over vt 1 TRANSFER : entregar, transferir (un cargo o una responsabilidad) 2 : voltear, darle la vuelta a ⟨turn the cassette over : voltea el cassette⟩

turnpike ['tərnˌpaɪk] n : carretera f de peaje

turnstile ['tərnˌstaɪl] n : torniquete m (de acceso)

turntable ['tərnˌteɪbəl] n : tornamesa mf

turn up vi 1 APPEAR : aparecer, presentarse 2 HAPPEN : ocurrir, suceder (inesperadamente) — vt : subir (el volumen)

turpentine ['tərpənˌtaɪn] n : aguarrás m, trementina f

turquoise ['tər,kɔɪz, -,kwɔɪz] n : turquesa f

turret ['tərət] n 1 TOWER : torre f pequeña 2 : torreta f (de un tanque, un avión, etc.)

turtle ['tərṭəl] n : tortuga f (marina)

turtledove ['tərṭəl,dʌv] n : tórtola f

turtleneck ['tərṭəl,nɛk] n : cuello m de tortuga, cuello m alto

tusk ['tʌsk] n : colmillo m

tussle[1] ['tʌsəl] vi -**sled; -sling** SCUFFLE : pelearse, reñir

tussle[2] n : riña f, pelea f

tutor[1] ['tu:tər, 'tju:-] vt : darle clases particulares (a alguien)

tutor[2] n : tutor m, -tora f; maestro m, -tra f (particular)

tuxedo [,tʌk'si:,do:] n, pl -**dos** or -**does** : esmoquin m, smoking m

TV [,ti:'vi:, 'ti:,vi:] → television

twain ['twein] n : dos m

twang[1] ['twæŋ] vt : pulsar la cuerda de (una guitarra) — vi : hablar en tono nasal

twang[2] n 1 : tañido m (de una cuerda de guitarra) 2 : tono m nasal (de voz)

tweak[1] ['twi:k] vt : pellizcar

tweak[2] n : pellizco m

tweed ['twi:d] n : tweed m

tweet[1] ['twi:t] vi : piar

tweet[2] n : gorjeo m, pío m

tweezers ['twi:zərz] npl : pinzas fpl

twelfth[1] ['twɛlfθ] adj : duodécimo

twelfth[2] n 1 : duodécimo m, -ma f (en una serie) 2 : doceavo m, doceava parte f

twelve[1] ['twɛlv] adj : doce

twelve[2] n : doce m

twentieth[1] ['twʌntiəθ, 'twɛn-] adj : vigésimo

twentieth[2] n 1 : vigésimo m, -ma f (en una serie) 2 : veinteavo m, veinteava parte f

twenty[1] ['twʌnti, 'twɛn-] adj : veinte

twenty[2] n, pl -**ties** : veinte m

twice ['twais] adv : dos veces ⟨twice a day : dos veces al día⟩ ⟨it costs twice as much : cuesta el doble⟩

twig ['twig] n : ramita f

twilight ['twai,lait] n : crepúsculo m

twill ['twil] n : sarga f, tela f cruzada

twin[1] ['twin] adj : gemelo, mellizo

twin[2] n : gemelo m, -la f; mellizo m, -za f

twine[1] ['twain] v **twined; twining** vt : entrelazar, entrecruzar — vi : enroscarse (alrededor de algo)

twine[2] n : cordel m, cuerda f, mecate m CA, Mex, Ven

twinge[1] ['twindʒ] vi **twinged; twinging** or **twingeing** : sentir punzadas

twinge[2] n : punzada f, dolor m agudo

twinkle[1] ['twiŋkəl] vi -**kled; -kling** 1 : centellear, titilar (dícese de las estrellas o de la luz) 2 : chispear, brillar (dícese de los ojos)

twinkle[2] n : centelleo m (de las estrellas), brillo m (de los ojos)

twirl[1] ['twərl] vt : girar, darle vueltas a — vi : girar, dar vueltas (rápidamente)

twirl[2] n : giro m, vuelta f

twist[1] ['twist] vt : torcer, retorcer ⟨twisted my arm : me torció el brazo⟩ — vi : retorcerse, enroscarse, serpentear (dícese de un río, un camino, etc.)

twist[2] n 1 BEND : vuelta f, recodo m (en el camino, el río, etc.) 2 TURN : giro m ⟨give it a twist : hazlo girar⟩ 3 SPIRAL : espiral f ⟨a twist of lemon : una rodajita de limón⟩ 4 : giro m inesperado (de eventos, etc.)

twisted ['twistəd] adj : retorcido ⟨a twisted mind : una mente retorcida⟩

twister ['twistər] 1 → **tornado** 2 → **waterspout**

twitch[1] ['twitʃ] vi : moverse nerviosamente, contraerse espasmódicamente (dícese de un músculo)

twitch[2] n : espasmo m, sacudida f ⟨a nervous twitch : un tic nervioso⟩

twitter[1] ['twitər] vi CHIRP : gorjear, cantar (dícese de los pájaros)

twitter[2] n : gorjeo m

two[1] ['tu:] adj : dos

two[2] n, pl **twos** : dos m

twofold[1] ['tu:,fo:ld] adv : al doble

twofold[2] ['tu:,fo:ld] adj : doble

two hundred[1] adj : doscientos

two hundred[2] n : doscientos m

twosome ['tu:səm] n COUPLE : pareja f

tycoon [tai'ku:n] n : magnate mf

tying → **tie**[1]

type[1] ['taip] v **typed; typing** vt 1 TYPEWRITE : escribir a máquina, pasar (un texto) a máquina 2 CATEGORIZE : categorizar, identificar — vi : escribir a máquina

type[2] n 1 KIND : tipo m, clase f, categoría f 2 or printing type : tipo m

typeface ['taip,feis] n : tipo m de imprenta

typewrite ['taip,rait] v -**wrote; -written** : escribir a máquina

typewriter ['taip,raitər] n : máquina f de escribir

typhoid[1] ['tai,fɔid, tai'-] adj : relativo al tifus o a la tifoidea

typhoid[2] n or typhoid fever : tifoidea f

typhoon [tai'fu:n] n : tifón m

typhus ['taifəs] n : tifus m, tifo m

typical ['tipikəl] adj : típico, característico — **typically** adv

typify ['tipə,fai] vt -**fied; -fying** : ser típico o representativo de (un grupo, una clase, etc.)

typist ['taipist] n : mecanógrafo m, -fa f

typographic [,taipə'græfik] or **typographical** [-fikəl] adj : tipográfico — **typographically** [-fikli] adv

typography [tai'pagrəfi] n : tipografía f

tyrannical [tə'rænikəl, tai-] adj : tiránico — **tyrannically** [-nikli] adv

tyrannize ['tirə,naiz] vt -**nized; -nizing** : tiranizar

tyranny ['tirəni] n, pl -**nies** : tiranía f

tyrant ['tairənt] n : tirano m, -na f

tzar ['zar, 'tsar, 'sar] → **czar**

U

u [ˈjuː] *n, pl* **u's** *or* **us** [ˈjuːz] : vigésima primera letra del alfabeto inglés

ubiquitous [juːˈbɪkwətəs] *adj* : ubicuo, omnipresente

udder [ˈʌdər] *n* : ubre *f*

UFO [ˈjuːˌefˈoː, ˈjuːˌfoː] *n, pl* **UFO's** *or* **UFOs** (*unidentified flying object*) : ovni *m*, OVNI *m*

Ugandan [juːˈɡændən, -ˈɡɑn-; uːˈɡɑn-] *n* : ugandés *m*, -desa *f* — **Ugandan** *adj*

ugliness [ˈʌɡlinəs] *n* : fealdad *f*

ugly [ˈʌɡli] *adj* **uglier; -est** **1** UNATTRACTIVE : feo **2** DISAGREEABLE : desagradable, feo ⟨ugly weather : tiempo feo⟩ ⟨to have an ugly temper : tener mal genio⟩

Ukrainian [juːˈkreɪniən, -ˈkraɪ-] *n* **1** : ucraniano *m*, -na *f* **2** : ucraniano *m* (idioma) — **Ukrainian** *adj*

ukulele [ˌjuːkəˈleɪli] *n* : ukelele *m*

ulcer [ˈʌlsər] *n* : úlcera *f* (interna), llaga *f* (externa)

ulcerate [ˈʌlsəˌreɪt] *vi* **-ated; -ating** : ulcerarse

ulceration [ˌʌlsəˈreɪʃən] *n* **1** : ulceración *f* **2** ULCER : úlcera *f*, llaga *f*

ulcerous [ˈʌlsərəs] *adj* : ulceroso

ulna [ˈʌlnə] *n* : cúbito *m*

ulterior [ˌʌlˈtɪriər] *adj* : oculto ⟨ulterior motive : motivo oculto, segunda intención⟩

ultimate [ˈʌltəmət] *adj* **1** FINAL : último, final **2** SUPREME : supremo, máximo **3** FUNDAMENTAL : fundamental, esencial

ultimately [ˈʌltəmətli] *adv* **1** FINALLY : por último, finalmente **2** EVENTUALLY : a la larga, con el tiempo

ultimatum [ˌʌltəˈmeɪtəm, -ˈmɑ-] *n, pl* **-tums** *or* **-ta** [-t̬ə] : ultimátum *m*

ultrasound [ˈʌltrəˌsaʊnd] *n* **1** : ultrasonido *m* **2** : ecografía *f* (técnica o imagen)

ultraviolet [ˌʌltrəˈvaɪələt] *adj* : ultravioleta

umbilical cord [ˌʌmˈbɪlɪkəl] *n* : cordón *m* umbilical

umbrage [ˈʌmbrɪʤ] *n* **to take umbrage at** : ofenderse por

umbrella [ˌʌmˈbrelə] *n* **1** : paraguas *m* **2 beach umbrella** : sombrilla *f*

umpire¹ [ˈʌmˌpaɪr] *v* **-pired; -piring** : arbitrar

umpire² *n* : árbitro *m*, -tra *f*

umpteenth [ˌʌmpˈtiːnθ] *adj* : enésimo

unable [ˌʌnˈeɪbəl] *adj* : incapaz ⟨to be unable to : no poder⟩

unabridged [ˌʌnəˈbrɪʤd] *adj* : íntegro

unacceptable [ˌʌnɪkˈsɛptəbəl] *adj* : inaceptable

unaccompanied [ˌʌnəˈkʌmpənid] *adj* : solo, sin acompañamiento (en música)

unaccountable [ˌʌnəˈkaʊntəbəl] *adj* : inexplicable, incomprensible — **unaccountably** [-bli] *adv*

unaccustomed [ˌʌnəˈkʌstəmd] *adj* **1** UNUSUAL : desacostumbrado, ínusual **2** UNUSED : inhabituado ⟨unaccustomed to noise : inhabituado al ruido⟩

unacquainted [ˌʌnəˈkweɪnt̬əd] *adj* **to be unacquainted with** : desconocer, ignorar

unadorned [ˌʌnəˈdɔrnd] *adj* : sin adornos, puro y simple

unadulterated [ˌʌnəˈdʌltəˌreɪt̬əd] *adj* **1** PURE : puro ⟨unadulterated food : comida pura⟩ **2** ABSOLUTE : completo, absoluto

unaffected [ˌʌnəˈfɛktəd] *adj* **1** : no afectado, indiferente **2** NATURAL : sin afectación, natural

unaffectedly [ˌʌnəˈfɛktədli] *adv* : de manera natural

unafraid [ˌʌnəˈfreɪd] *adj* : sin miedo

unaided [ˌʌnˈeɪdəd] *adj* : sin ayuda, solo

unambiguous [ˌʌnæmˈbɪɡjuəs] *adj* : inequívoco

unanimity [ˌjuːnəˈnɪməti] *n* : unanimidad *f*

unanimous [juˈnænəməs] *adj* : unánime — **unanimously** *adv*

unannounced [ˌʌnəˈnaʊnst] *adj* : sin dar aviso

unanswered [ˌʌnˈænsərd] *adj* : sin contestar

unappealing [ˌʌnəˈpiːlɪŋ] *adj* : desagradable

unappetizing [ˌʌnˈæpəˌtaɪzɪŋ] *adj* : poco apetitoso, poco apetecible

unarmed [ˌʌnˈɑrmd] *adj* : sin armas, desarmado

unassisted [ˌʌnəˈsɪstəd] *adj* : sin ayuda

unassuming [ˌʌnəˈsuːmɪŋ] *adj* : modesto, sin pretensiones

unattached [ˌʌnəˈtæʧt] *adj* **1** LOOSE : suelto **2** INDEPENDENT : independiente **3** : solo (ni casado ni prometido)

unattractive [ˌʌnəˈtræktɪv] *adj* : poco atractivo

unauthorized [ˌʌnˈɔθəˌraɪzd] *adj* : sin autorización, no autorizado

unavailable [ˌʌnəˈveɪləbəl] *adj* : no disponible

unavoidable [ˌʌnəˈvɔɪdəbəl] *adj* : inevitable, ineludible

unaware¹ [ˌʌnəˈwær] *adv* → **unawares**

unaware² *adj* : inconsciente

unawares [ˌʌnəˈwærz] *adv* **1** : por sorpresa ⟨to catch someone unawares : agarrar a alguien desprevenido⟩ **2** UNINTENTIONALLY : inconscientemente, inadvertidamente

unbalanced [ˌʌnˈbælən(t)st] *adj* : desequilibrado

unbearable [ˌʌnˈbærəbəl] *adj* : insoportable, inaguantable — **unbearably** [-bli] *adv*

unbecoming [ˌʌnbɪˈkʌmɪŋ] *adj* **1** UNSEEMLY : impropio, indecoroso **2** UNFLATTERING : poco favorecedor

unbelievable [ˌʌnbə'li:vəbəl] *adj* : increíble — **unbelievably** [-bli] *adv*

unbend [ˌʌn'bɛnd] *vi* **-bent** [-'bɛnt]; **-bending** RELAX : relajarse

unbending [ˌʌn'bɛndɪŋ] *adj* : inflexible

unbiased [ˌʌn'baɪəst] *adj* : imparcial, objetivo

unbind [ˌʌn'baɪnd] *vt* **-bound** [-'baʊnd]; **-binding 1** UNFASTEN, UNTIE : desatar, desamarrar **2** RELEASE : liberar

unbolt [ˌʌn'bo:lt] *vt* : abrir el cerrojo de, descorrer el pestillo de

unborn [ˌʌn'bɔrn] *adj* : aún no nacido, que va a nacer

unbosom [ˌʌn'buzəm, -'bu:-] *vt* : revelar, divulgar

unbreakable [ˌʌn'breɪkəbəl] *adj* : irrompible

unbridled [ˌʌn'braɪdəld] *adj* : desenfrenado

unbroken [ˌʌn'bro:kən] *adj* **1** INTACT : intacto, sano **2** CONTINUOUS : continuo, ininterrumpido

unbuckle [ˌʌn'bʌkəl] *vt* **-led; -ling** : desabrochar

unburden [ˌʌn'bərdən] *vt* **1** UNLOAD : descargar **2 to unburden oneself** : desahogarse

unbutton [ˌʌn'bʌtən] *vt* : desabrochar, desabotonar

uncalled–for [ˌʌn'kɔld.fɔr] *adj* : inapropiado, innecesario

uncanny [ən'kæni] *adj* **-nier; -est 1** STRANGE : extraño **2** EXTRAORDINARY : raro, extraordinario — **uncannily** [-'kænəli] *adv*

unceasing [ˌʌn'si:sɪŋ] *adj* : incesante, continuo — **unceasingly** *adv*

unceremonious [ˌʌn.sɛrə'mo:niəs] *adj* **1** INFORMAL : sin ceremonia, sin pompa **2** ABRUPT : abrupto, brusco — **unceremoniously** *adv*

uncertain [ˌʌn'sərtən] *adj* **1** INDEFINITE : indeterminado **2** UNSURE : incierto, dudoso **3** CHANGEABLE : inestable, variable ⟨uncertain weather : tiempo inestable⟩ **4** HESITANT : indeciso **5** VAGUE : poco claro

uncertainly [ˌʌn'sərtənli] *adv* : dudosamente, con desconfianza

uncertainty [ˌʌn'sərtənti] *n, pl* **-ties** : duda *f*, incertidumbre *f*

unchangeable [ˌʌn'tʃeɪndʒəbəl] *adj* : inalterable, inmutable

unchanged [ˌʌn'tʃeɪndʒd] *adj* : sin cambiar

unchanging [ˌʌn'tʃeɪndʒɪŋ] *adj* : inalterable, inmutable, firme

uncharacteristic [ˌʌn.kærɪktə'rɪstɪk] *adj* : inusual, desacostumbrado

uncharged [ˌʌn'tʃɑrdʒd] *adj* : sin carga (eléctrica)

uncivilized [ˌʌn'sɪvə.laɪzd] *adj* **1** BARBAROUS : incivilizado, bárbaro **2** WILD : salvaje

uncle ['ʌŋkəl] *n* : tío *m*

unclean [ˌʌn'kli:n] *adj* **1** IMPURE : impuro **2** DIRTY : sucio

unclear [ˌʌn'klɪr] *adj* : confuso, borroso, poco claro

Uncle Sam ['sæm] *n* : el Tío Sam

unclog [ˌʌn'klɑg] *vt* **-clogged; -clogging** : desatascar, destapar

unclothed [ˌʌn'klo:ðd] *adj* : desnudo

uncomfortable [ˌʌn'kʌmpfərtəbəl] *adj* **1** : incómodo (dícese de una silla, etc.) **2** UNEASY : inquieto, incómodo

uncommitted [ˌʌnkə'mɪtəd] *adj* : sin compromiso

uncommon [ˌʌn'kɑmən] *adj* **1** UNUSUAL : raro, poco común **2** REMARKABLE : excepcional, extraordinario

uncommonly [ˌʌn'kɑmənli] *adv* : extraordinariamente

uncompromising [ˌʌn'kɑmprə.maɪzɪŋ] *adj* : inflexible, intransigente

unconcerned [ˌʌnkən'sərnd] *adj* : indiferente — **unconcernedly** [-'sərnədli] *adv*

unconditional [ˌʌnkən'dɪʃənəl] *adj* : incondicional — **unconditionally** *adv*

unconscious¹ [ˌʌn'kɑntʃəs] *adj* : inconsciente — **unconsciously** *adv*

unconscious² *n* : inconsciente *m*

unconsciousness [ˌʌn'kɑntʃəsnəs] *n* : inconsciencia *f*

unconstitutional [ˌʌn.kɑnstə'tu:ʃənəl, -'tju:-] *adj* : inconstitucional

uncontrollable [ˌʌnkən'tro:ləbəl] *adj* : incontrolable, incontenible — **uncontrollably** [-bli] *adv*

uncontrolled [ˌʌnkən'tro:ld] *adj* : incontrolado

unconventional [ˌʌnkən'vɛntʃənəl] *adj* : poco convencional

unconvincing [ˌʌnkən'vɪnʃsɪŋ] *adj* : poco convincente

uncouth [ˌʌn'ku:θ] *adj* CRUDE, ROUGH : grosero, rudo

uncover [ˌʌn'kʌvər] *vt* **1** : destapar (un objeto), dejar al descubierto **2** EXPOSE, REVEAL : descubrir, revelar, exponer

uncultivated [ˌʌn'kʌltə.veɪtəd] *adj* : inculto

uncurl [ˌʌn'kərl] *vt* UNROLL : desenrollar — *vi* : desenrollarse, desrizarse (dícese del pelo)

uncut [ˌʌn'kʌt] *adj* **1** : sin cortar ⟨uncut grass : hierba sin cortar⟩ **2** : sin tallar, en bruto ⟨an uncut diamond : un diamante en bruto⟩ **3** UNABRIDGED : completo, íntegro

undaunted [ˌʌn'dɔntəd] *adj* : impávido

undecided [ˌʌndi'saɪdəd] *adj* **1** IRRESOLUTE : indeciso, irresoluto **2** UNRESOLVED : pendiente, no resuelto

undefeated [ˌʌndi'fi:təd] *adj* : invicto

undeniable [ˌʌndi'naɪəbəl] *adj* : innegable — **undeniably** [-bli] *adv*

under¹ ['ʌndər] *adv* **1** LESS : menos ⟨$10 or under : $10 o menos⟩ **2** UNDERWATER : debajo del agua **3** : bajo los efectos de la anestesia

under² *adj* **1** LOWER : (más) bajo, inferior **2** SUBORDINATE : inferior **3** : insuficiente ⟨an under dose of medicine : una dosis insuficiente de medicina⟩

under³ *prep* **1** BELOW, BENEATH : debajo de, abajo de ⟨under the table : abajo de la mesa⟩ ⟨we walked under the arch : pasamos por debajo del arco⟩ ⟨under the sun : bajo el sol⟩ **2** : menos de ⟨in under 20 minutes : en menos de 20 minutos⟩ **3** (*indicating rank or authority*) : bajo ⟨under the command of : bajo las órdenes de⟩ **4** SUBJECT TO : bajo ⟨under suspicion : bajo sospecha⟩ ⟨under the circumstances : dadas las circunstancias⟩ **5** ACCORDING TO : según, de acuerdo con, conforme a ⟨under the present laws : según las leyes actuales⟩

underage [ˌʌndərˈeɪdʒ] *adj* : menor de edad

underbrush [ˈʌndərˌbrəʃ] *n* : maleza *f*

underclothes [ˈʌndərˌkloːz, -ˌkloːðz] → **underwear**

underclothing [ˈʌndərˌkloːðɪŋ] → **underwear**

undercover [ˌʌndərˈkʌvər] *adj* : secreto, clandestino

undercurrent [ˈʌndərˌkərənt] *n* **1** : corriente *f* submarina **2** UNDERTONE : corriente *f* oculta, trasfondo *m*

undercut [ˌʌndərˈkʌt] *vt* -cut; -cutting : vender más barato que

underdeveloped [ˌʌndərdɪˈvɛləpt] *adj* : subdesarrollado, atrasado

underdog [ˈʌndərˌdɔg] *n* : persona *f* que tiene menos posibilidades

underdone [ˌʌndərˈdʌn] *adj* RARE : poco cocido

underestimate [ˌʌndərˈɛstəˌmeɪt] *vt* -mated; -mating : subestimar, menospreciar

underexposed [ˌʌndərɪkˈspoːzd] *adj* : subexpuesto (en fotografía)

underfoot [ˌʌndərˈfʊt] *adv* **1** : bajo los pies ⟨to trample underfoot : pisotear⟩ **2 to be underfoot** : estorbar ⟨they're always underfoot : están siempre estorbando⟩

undergarment [ˈʌndərˌgɑrmənt] *n* : prenda *f* íntima

undergo [ˌʌndərˈgoː] *vt* -went [-ˈwɛnt]; -gone [-ˈgɔn]; -going : sufrir, experimentar ⟨to undergo an operation : someterse a una intervención quirúrgica⟩

undergraduate [ˌʌndərˈgrædʒuət] *n* : estudiante *m* universitario, estudiante *f* universitaria

underground¹ [ˌʌndərˈgraʊnd] *adv* **1** : bajo tierra **2** SECRETLY : clandestinamente, en secreto ⟨to go underground : pasar a la clandestinidad⟩

underground² [ˈʌndərˌgraʊnd] *adj* **1** SUBTERRANEAN : subterráneo **2** SECRET : secreto, clandestino

underground³ [ˈʌndərˌgraʊnd] *n* : movimiento *m* o grupo *m* clandestino

undergrowth [ˈʌndərˌgroːθ] *n* : maleza *f*, broza *f*

underhand¹ [ˈʌndərˌhænd] *adv* **1** SECRETLY : de manera clandestina **2 or**

underhanded : sin levantar el brazo por encima del hombro (en deportes)

underhand² *adj* **1** SLY : solapado **2** : por debajo del hombro (en deportes)

underhanded [ˌʌndərˈhændəd] *adj* **1** SLY : solapado **2** SHADY : turbio, poco limpio

underline [ˈʌndərˌlaɪn] *vt* -lined; -lining **1** : subrayar **2** EMPHASIZE : subrayar, acentuar, hacer hincapié en

underlying [ˌʌndərˈlaɪŋ] *adj* **1** : subyacente ⟨the underlying rock : la roca subyacente⟩ **2** FUNDAMENTAL : fundamental, esencial

undermine [ˌʌndərˈmaɪn] *vt* -mined; -mining **1** : socavar (una estructura, etc.) **2** SAP, WEAKEN : minar, debilitar

underneath¹ [ˌʌndərˈniːθ] *adv* : debajo, abajo ⟨the part underneath : la parte de abajo⟩

underneath² *prep* : debajo de, abajo de

undernourished [ˌʌndərˈnərɪʃt] *adj* : desnutrido

underpants [ˈʌndərˌpænts] *npl* : calzoncillos *mpl*, calzones *mpl*

underpass [ˈʌndərˌpæs] *n* : paso *m* a desnivel

underprivileged [ˌʌndərˈprɪvlɪdʒd] *adj* : desfavorecido

underrate [ˌʌndərˈreɪt] *vt* -rated; -rating : subestimar, menospreciar

underscore [ˈʌndərˌskor] *vt* -scored; -scoring → **underline**

undersea¹ [ˌʌndərˈsiː] *or* **underseas** [-ˈsiːz] *adv* : bajo la superficie del mar

undersea² *adj* : submarino

undersecretary [ˌʌndərˈsɛkrəˌtɛri] *n, pl* -ries : subsecretario *m*, -ria *f*

undersell [ˌʌndərˈsɛl] *vt* -sold; -selling : vender más barato que

undershirt [ˈʌndərˌʃərt] *n* : camiseta *f*

undershorts [ˈʌndərˌʃorts] *npl* : calzoncillos *mpl*

underside [ˈʌndərˌsaɪd, ˌʌndərˈsaɪd] *n* : parte *f* de abajo

undersized [ˌʌndərˈsaɪzd] *adj* : más pequeño de lo normal

understand [ˌʌndərˈstænd] *v* -stood [-ˈstʊd]; -standing *vt* **1** COMPREHEND : comprender, entender ⟨I don't understand it : no lo entiendo⟩ ⟨that's understood : eso se comprende⟩ ⟨to make oneself understood : hacerse entender⟩ **2** BELIEVE : entender ⟨to give someone to understand : dar a alguien a entender⟩ **3** INFER : tener entendido ⟨I understand that she's leaving : tengo entendido que se va⟩ — *vi* : comprender, entender

understandable [ˌʌndərˈstændəbəl] *adj* : comprensible

understanding¹ [ˌʌndərˈstændɪŋ] *adj* : comprensivo, compasivo

understanding² *n* **1** GRASP : comprensión *f*, entendimiento *m* **2** SYMPATHY : comprensión *f* (mutua) **3** INTERPRETATION : interpretación *f* ⟨it's my understanding that . . . : tengo la impresión de que . . ., tengo entendido que . . . 〉 **4** AGREEMENT : acuerdo *m*, arreglo *m*

understate [ˌʌndərˈsteɪt] *vt* **-stated; -stating** : minimizar, subestimar

understatement [ˌʌndərˈsteɪtmənt] *n* : atenuación *f* 〈that's an understatement : decir sólo eso es quedarse corto〉

understudy [ˈʌndərˌstʌdi] *n*, *pl* **-dies** : sobresaliente *mf*, suplente *mf* (en el teatro)

undertake [ˌʌndərˈteɪk] *vt* **-took** [-ˈtʊk]; **-taken** [-ˈteɪkən]; **-taking 1** : emprender (una tarea), asumir (una responsabilidad) **2** PROMISE : comprometerse (a hacer algo)

undertaker [ˈʌndərˌteɪkər] *n* : director *m*, -tora *f* de funeraria

undertaking [ˈʌndərˌteɪkɪŋ, ˌʌndərˈ-] *n* **1** ENTERPRISE, TASK : empresa *f*, tarea *f* **2** PLEDGE : promesa *f*, garantía *f*

undertone [ˈʌndərˌtoːn] *n* **1** : voz *f* baja 〈to speak in an undertone : hablar en voz baja〉 **2** HINT, UNDERCURRENT : trasfondo *m*, matiz *m*

undertow [ˈʌndərˌtoː] *n* : resaca *f*

undervalue [ˌʌndərˈvæljuː] *vt* **-ued; -uing** : menospreciar, subestimar

underwater[1] [ˌʌndərˈwɔtər, -ˈwɑ-] *adv* : debajo (del agua)

underwater[2] *adj* : submarino

under way [ˌʌndərˈweɪ] *adv* : en marcha, en camino 〈to get under way : ponerse en marcha〉

underwear [ˈʌndərˌwær] *n* : ropa *f* interior, ropa *f* íntima

underworld [ˈʌndərˌwərld] *n* **1** HELL : infierno *m* **2 the underworld** CRIMINALS : la hampa, los bajos fondos

underwrite [ˈʌndərˌraɪt, ˌʌndərˈ-] *vt* **-wrote** [-ˌroːt, -ˈroːt]; **-written** [-ˌrɪtən, -ˈrɪtən]; **-writing 1** INSURE : asegurar **2** FINANCE : financiar **3** BACK, ENDORSE : suscribir, respaldar

underwriter [ˈʌndərˌraɪtər, ˌʌndərˈ-] *n* INSURER : asegurador *m*, -dora *f*

undeserving [ˌʌndɪˈzərvɪŋ] *adj* : indigno

undesirable[1] [ˌʌndɪˈzaɪrəbəl] *adj* : indeseable

undesirable[2] *n* : indeseable *mf*

undeveloped [ˌʌndɪˈvɛləpt] *adj* : sin desarrollar, sin revelar (dícese de una película)

undies [ˈʌndiːz] → **underwear**

undignified [ˌʌnˈdɪɡnəˌfaɪd] *adj* : indecoroso

undiluted [ˌʌndaɪˈluːtəd, -də-] *adj* : sin diluir, concentrado

undiscovered [ˌʌndɪˈskʌvərd] *adj* : no descubierto

undisputed [ˌʌndɪˈspjuːtəd] *adj* : indiscutible

undisturbed [ˌʌndɪˈstərbd] *adj* : tranquilo (dícese de una persona), sin tocar (dícese de un objeto)

undivided [ˌʌndɪˈvaɪdəd] *adj* : íntegro, completo

undo [ˌʌnˈduː] *vt* **-did** [-ˈdɪd]; **-done** [-ˈdʌn]; **-doing 1** UNFASTEN : desabrochar, desatar, abrir **2** ANNUL : anular **3** REVERSE : deshacer, reparar (daños, etc.) **4** RUIN : arruinar, destruir

undoing [ˌʌnˈduːɪŋ] *n* : ruina *f*, perdición *f*

undoubted [ˌʌnˈdaʊtəd] *adj* : cierto, indudable — **undoubtedly** *adv*

undress [ˌʌnˈdrɛs] *vt* : desvestir, desabrigar, desnudar — *vi* : desvestirse, desnudarse

undrinkable [ˌʌnˈdrɪŋkəbəl] *adj* : no potable

undue [ˌʌnˈduː, -ˈdjuː] *adj* : excesivo, indebido — **unduly** *adv*

undulate [ˈʌndʒəˌleɪt] *vi* **-lated; -lating** : ondular

undulation [ˌʌndʒəˈleɪʃən] *n* : ondulación *f*

undying [ˌʌnˈdaɪɪŋ] *adj* : perpetuo, imperecedero

unearth [ˌʌnˈərθ] *vt* **1** EXHUME : desenterrar, exhumar **2** DISCOVER : descubrir

unearthly [ˌʌnˈərθli] *adj* **-lier; -est** : sobrenatural, de otro mundo

uneasily [ˌʌnˈiːzəli] *adv* : inquietamente, con inquietud

uneasiness [ˌʌnˈiːzinəs] *n* : inquietud *f*

uneasy [ˌʌnˈiːzi] *adj* **-easier; -est 1** AWKWARD : incómodo **2** WORRIED : preocupado, inquieto **3** RESTLESS : inquieto, agitado

uneducated [ˌʌnˈɛdʒəˌkeɪtəd] *adj* : inculto, sin educación

unemployed [ˌʌnɪmˈplɔɪd] *adj* : desempleado

unemployment [ˌʌnɪmˈplɔɪmənt] *n* : desempleo *m*

unending [ˌʌnˈɛndɪŋ] *adj* : sin fin, interminable

unendurable [ˌʌnɪnˈdʊrəbəl, -ɛn-, -ˈdjʊr-] *adj* : insoportable, intolerable

unequal [ˌʌnˈiːkwəl] *adj* **1** : desigual **2** INADEQUATE : incapaz, incompetente 〈to be unequal to a task : no estar a la altura de una tarea〉

unequaled *or* **unequalled** [ˌʌnˈiːkwəld] *adj* : sin igual

unequivocal [ˌʌnɪˈkwɪvəkəl] *adj* : inequívoco, claro — **unequivocally** *adv*

unerring [ˌʌnˈɛrɪŋ, -ˈər-] *adj* : infalible

unethical [ˌʌnˈɛθɪkəl] *adj* : poco ético

uneven [ˌʌnˈiːvən] *adj* **1** ODD : impar (dícese de un número) **2** : desigual, desnivelado (dícese de una superficie) 〈uneven terrain : terreno accidentado〉 **3** IRREGULAR : irregular, poco uniforme **4** UNEQUAL : desigual

unevenly [ˌʌnˈiːvənli] *adv* : desigualmente, irregularmente

uneventful [ˌʌnɪˈvɛntfəl] *adj* : sin incidentes, tranquilo

unexpected [ˌʌnɪkˈspɛktəd] *adj* : imprevisto, inesperado — **unexpectedly** *adv*

unfailing [ˌʌnˈfeɪlɪŋ] *adj* 1 CONSTANT : constante 2 INEXHAUSTIBLE : inagotable 3 SURE : a toda prueba, indefectible

unfair [ˌʌnˈfær] *adj* : injusto — **unfairly** *adv*

unfairness [ˌʌnˈfærnəs] *n* : injusticia *f*

unfaithful [ˌʌnˈfeɪθfəl] *adj* : desleal, infiel — **unfaithfully** *adv*

unfaithfulness [ˌʌnˈfeɪθfəlnəs] *n* : infidelidad *f*, deslealtad *f*

unfamiliar [ˌʌnfəˈmɪljər] *adj* 1 STRANGE : desconocido, extraño ⟨an unfamiliar place : un lugar nuevo⟩ 2 to be unfamiliar with : no estar familiarizado con, desconocer

unfamiliarity [ˌʌnfəˌmɪliˈærəti] *n* : falta *f* de familiaridad

unfashionable [ˌʌnˈfæʃənəbəl] *adj* : fuera de moda

unfasten [ˌʌnˈfæsən] *vt* : desabrochar, desatar (una cuerda, etc.), abrir (una puerta)

unfavorable [ˌʌnˈfeɪvərəbəl] *adj* : desfavorable, mal — **unfavorably** [-bli] *adv*

unfeeling [ˌʌnˈfiːlɪŋ] *adj* : insensible — **unfeelingly** *adv*

unfinished [ˌʌnˈfɪnɪʃd] *adj* : inacabado, incompleto

unfit [ˌʌnˈfɪt] *adj* 1 UNSUITABLE : inadecuado, impropio 2 UNSUITED : no apto, incapaz 3 : incapacitado (físicamente) ⟨to be unfit : no estar en forma⟩

unflappable [ˌʌnˈflæpəbəl] *adj* : imperturbable

unflattering [ˌʌnˈflætərɪŋ] *adj* : poco favorecedor

unfold [ˌʌnˈfoːld] *vt* 1 EXPAND : desplegar, desdoblar, extender ⟨to unfold a map : desplegar un mapa⟩ 2 DISCLOSE, REVEAL : revelar, exponer (un plan, etc.) — *vi* 1 DEVELOP : desarrollarse, desenvolverse ⟨the story unfolded : el cuento se desarrollaba⟩ 2 EXPAND : extenderse, desplegarse

unforeseeable [ˌʌnforˈsiːəbəl] *adj* : imprevisible

unforeseen [ˌʌnforˈsiːn] *adj* : imprevisto

unforgettable [ˌʌnfərˈgɛtəbəl] *adj* : inolvidable, memorable — **unforgettably** [-bli] *adv*

unforgivable [ˌʌnfərˈgɪvəbəl] *adj* : imperdonable

unfortunate¹ [ˌʌnˈfɔrtʃənət] *adj* 1 UNLUCKY : desgraciado, infortunado, desafortunado ⟨how unfortunate! : ¡qué mala suerte!⟩ 2 INAPPROPRIATE : inoportuno ⟨an unfortunate comment : un comentario poco feliz⟩

unfortunate² *n* : desgraciado *m*, -da *f*

unfortunately [ˌʌnˈfɔrtʃənətli] *adv* : desafortunadamente

unfounded [ˌʌnˈfaʊndəd] *adj* : infundado

unfreeze [ˌʌnˈfriːz] *v* **-froze** [-ˈfroːz]; **-frozen** [-ˈfroːzən]; **-freezing** *vt* : descongelar — *vi* : descongelarse

unfriendliness [ˌʌnˈfrɛndlinəs] *n* : hostilidad *f*, antipatía *f*

unfriendly [ˌʌnˈfrɛndli] *adj* **-lier; -est** : poco amistoso, hostil

unfurl [ˌʌnˈfərl] *vt* : desplegar, desdoblar — *vi* : desplegarse

unfurnished [ˌʌnˈfərnɪʃt] *adj* : desamueblado

ungainly [ˌʌnˈgeɪnli] *adj* : desgarbado

ungodly [ˌʌnˈgɑdli, -ˈgɑd-] *adj* 1 IMPIOUS : impío 2 OUTRAGEOUS : atroz, terrible ⟨at an ungodly hour : a una hora intempestiva⟩

ungrateful [ˌʌnˈgreɪtfəl] *adj* : desagradecido, ingrato — **ungratefully** *adv*

ungratefulness [ˌʌnˈgreɪtfəlnəs] *n* : ingratitud *f*

unhappily [ˌʌnˈhæpəli] *adv* 1 SADLY : tristemente 2 UNFORTUNATELY : desafortunadamente, lamentablemente

unhappiness [ˌʌnˈhæpinəs] *n* : infelicidad *f*, tristeza *f*, desdicha *f*

unhappy [ˌʌnˈhæpi] *adj* **-pier; -est** 1 UNFORTUNATE : desafortunado, desventurado 2 MISERABLE, SAD : infeliz, triste, desdichado 3 INOPPORTUNE : inoportuno, poco feliz

unharmed [ˌʌnˈhɑrmd] *adj* : salvo, ileso

unhealthy [ˌʌnˈhɛlθi] *adj* **-thier; -est** 1 UNWHOLESOME : insalubre, malsano, nocivo a la salud ⟨an unhealthy climate : un clima insalubre⟩ 2 SICKLY : de mala salud, enfermizo

unheard-of [ˌʌnˈhɜrdˌʌv] *adj* : sin precedente, inaudito, insólito

unhinge [ˌʌnˈhɪndʒ] *vt* **-hinged; -hinging** 1 : desquiciar (una puerta, etc.) 2 DISRUPT, UNSETTLE : trastornar, perturbar

unholy [ˌʌnˈhoːli] *adj* **-lier; -est** 1 : profano, impío 2 UNGODLY : atroz, terrible

unhook [ˌʌnˈhʊk] *vt* 1 : desenganchar, descolgar (de algo) 2 UNDO : desabrochar

unhurt [ˌʌnˈhɜrt] *adj* : ileso

unicorn [ˈjuːnəˌkɔrn] *n* : unicornio *m*

unidentified [ˌʌnaɪˈdɛntəˌfaɪd] *adj* : no identificado ⟨unidentified flying object : objeto volador no identificado⟩

unification [ˌjuːnəfəˈkeɪʃən] *n* : unificación *f*

uniform¹ [ˈjuːnəˌfɔrm] *adj* : uniforme, homogéneo, constante

uniform² *n* : uniforme *m*

uniformed [ˈjuːnəˌfɔrmd] *adj* : uniformado

uniformity [ˌjuːnəˈfɔrməti] *n, pl* **-ties** : uniformidad *f*

unify [ˈjuːnəˌfaɪ] *vt* **-fied; -fying** : unificar, unir

unilateral [ˌjuːnəˈlætərəl] *adj* : unilateral — **unilaterally** *adv*

unimaginable [ˌʌnɪˈmædʒənəbəl] *adj* : inimaginable, inconcebible

unimportant [ˌʌnɪmˈpɔrtənt] *adj* : intrascendente, insignificante, sin importancia

uninhabited [ˌʌnɪnˈhæbətəd] *adj* : deshabitado, desierto, despoblado

uninhibited [ˌʌnɪnˈhɪbətəd] *adj* : desenfadado, desinhibido, sin reservas

uninjured [ˌʌnˈɪndʒərd] *adj* : ileso

unintelligent [ˌʌnɪnˈtɛlədʒənt] *adj* : poco inteligente

unintelligible [ˌʌnɪnˈtɛlədʒəbəl] *adj* : ininteligible, incomprensible

unintentional [ˌʌnɪnˈtɛntʃənəl] *adj* : no deliberado, involuntario

unintentionally [ˌʌnɪnˈtɛntʃənəli] *adv* : involuntariamente, sin querer

uninterested [ˌʌnˈɪntəˌrɛstəd, -ˌtrɛstəd] *adj* : indiferente

uninteresting [ˌʌnˈɪntəˌrɛstɪŋ, -ˌtrɛstɪŋ] *adj* : poco interesante, sin interés

uninterrupted [ˌʌnˌɪntəˈrʌptəd] *adj* : ininterrumpido, continuo

union [ˈjuːnjən] *n* 1 : unión *f* 2 *or* labor **union** : sindicato *m*, gremio *m*

unionize [ˈjuːnjəˌnaɪz] *v* **-ized; -izing** *vt* : sindicalizar, sindicar — *vi* : sindicalizarse

unique [juˈniːk] *adj* 1 SOLE : único, solo 2 UNUSUAL : extraordinario

uniquely [juˈniːkli] *adv* 1 EXCLUSIVELY : exclusivamente 2 EXCEPTIONALLY : excepcionalmente

unison [ˈjuːnəsən, -zən] *n* 1 : unísono *m* (en música) 2 CONCORD : acuerdo *m*, armonía *f*, concordia *f* 3 in ~ SIMULTANEOUSLY : simultáneamente, al unísono

unit [ˈjuːnɪt] *n* 1 : unidad *f* 2 : módulo *m* (de un mobiliario)

unitary [ˈjuːnəˌteri] *adj* : unitario

unite [juˈnaɪt] *v* **united; uniting** *vt* : unir, juntar, combinar — *vi* : unirse, juntarse

unity [ˈjuːnəti] *n*, *pl* **-ties** 1 UNION : unidad *f*, unión *f* 2 HARMONY : armonía *f*, acuerdo *m*

universal [ˌjuːnəˈvərsəl] *adj* 1 GENERAL : general, universal ⟨a universal rule : una regla universal⟩ 2 WORLDWIDE : universal, mundial — **universally** *adv*

universe [ˈjuːnəˌvərs] *n* : universo *m*

university [ˌjuːnəˈvərsəti] *n*, *pl* **-ties** : universidad *f*

unjust [ˌʌnˈdʒʌst] *adj* : injusto — **unjustly** *adv*

unjustifiable [ˌʌnˌdʒʌstəˈfaɪəbəl] *adj* : injustificable

unjustified [ˌʌnˈdʒʌstəˌfaɪd] *adj* : injustificado

unkempt [ˌʌnˈkɛmpt] *adj* : descuidado, desaliñado, despeinado (dícese del pelo)

unkind [ˌʌnˈkaɪnd] *adj* : poco amable, cruel — **unkindly** *adv*

unkindness [ˌʌnˈkaɪndnəs] *n* : crueldad *f*, falta *f* de amabilidad

unknowing [ˌʌnˈnoːɪŋ] *adj* : inconsciente, ignorante — **unknowingly** *adv*

unknown [ˌʌnˈnoːn] *adj* : desconocido

unlawful [ˌʌnˈlɔːfəl] *adj* : ilícito, ilegal — **unlawfully** *adv*

unleash [ˌʌnˈliːʃ] *vt* : soltar, desatar

unless [ənˈlɛs] *conj* : a menos que, salvo que, a no ser que

unlike¹ [ˌʌnˈlaɪk] *adj* 1 DIFFERENT : diferente, distinto 2 UNEQUAL : desigual

unlike² *prep* 1 : diferente de, distinto de ⟨unlike the others : distinto a los demás⟩ 2 : a diferencia de ⟨unlike her sister, she is shy : a diferencia de su hermana, es tímida⟩

unlikelihood [ˌʌnˈlaɪkliˌhʊd] *n* : improbabilidad *f*

unlikely [ˌʌnˈlaɪkli] *adj* **-lier; -est** 1 IMPROBABLE : improbable, poco probable 2 UNPROMISING : poco prometedor

unlimited [ˌʌnˈlɪmətəd] *adj* : ilimitado

unload [ˌʌnˈloːd] *vt* 1 REMOVE : descargar, desembarcar (mercancías o pasajeros) 2 : descargar (un avión, un camión, etc.) 3 DUMP : deshacerse de — *vi* : descargar (dícese de un avión, un camión, etc.)

unlock [ˌʌnˈlɑk] *vt* 1 : abrir (con llave) 2 DISCLOSE, REVEAL : revelar

unluckily [ˌʌnˈlʌkəli] *adv* : desgraciadamente

unlucky [ˌʌnˈlʌki] *adj* **-luckier; -est** 1 : de mala suerte, desgraciado, desafortunado ⟨an unlucky year : un año de mala suerte⟩ 2 INAUSPICIOUS : desfavorable, poco propicio 3 REGRETTABLE : lamentable

unmanageable [ˌʌnˈmænɪdʒəbəl] *adj* : difícil de controlar, poco manejable, ingobernable

unmarried [ˌʌnˈmærid] *adj* : soltero

unmask [ˌʌnˈmæsk] *vt* EXPOSE : desenmascarar

unmerciful [ˌʌnˈmərsɪfəl] *adj* MERCILESS : despiadado — **unmercifully** *adv*

unmistakable [ˌʌnmɪˈsteɪkəbəl] *adj* : evidente, inconfundible, obvio — **unmistakably** [-bli] *adv*

unmoved [ˌʌnˈmuːvd] *adj* : impasible ⟨to be unmoved by : permanecer impasible ante⟩

unnatural [ˌʌnˈnætʃərəl] *adj* 1 ABNORMAL, UNUSUAL : anormal, poco natural, poco normal 2 AFFECTED : afectado, forzado ⟨an unnatural smile : una sonrisa forzada⟩ 3 PERVERSE : perverso, antinatural

unnecessary [ˌʌnˈnɛsəˌseri] *adj* : innecesario — **unnecessarily** [-ˌnɛsəˈsɛrəli] *adv*

unnerve [ˌʌnˈnərv] *vt* **-nerved; -nerving** : turbar, desconcertar, poner nervioso

unnoticed [ˌʌnˈnoːtəst] *adj* : inadvertido ⟨to go unnoticed : pasar inadvertido⟩

unobstructed [ˌʌnəbˈstrʌktəd] *adj* : libre, despejado

unobtainable [ˌʌnəbˈteɪnəbəl] *adj* : inasequible

unobtrusive [ˌʌnəbˈstruːsɪv] *adj* : discreto

unoccupied [ˌʌnˈɑkjəˌpaɪd] *adj* 1 IDLE : desempleado, desocupado 2 EMPTY : desocupado, libre, deshabitado

unofficial [ˌʌnəˈfɪʃəl] *adj* : extraoficial, oficioso, no oficial

unorganized [ˌʌnˈɔrgəˌnaɪzd] *adj* : desorganizado

unorthodox [ˌʌnˈɔrθəˌdɑks] *adj* : poco ortodoxo, poco convencional

unpack [ˌʌnˈpæk] *vt* : desempacar — *vi* : desempacar, deshacer las maletas

unpaid [ˌʌnˈpeɪd] *adj* : no remunerado, no retribuido ⟨an unpaid bill : una cuenta pendiente⟩

unparalleled [ˌʌnˈpærəˌlɛld] *adj* : sin igual

unpatriotic [ˌʌnˌpeɪtriˈɑtɪk] *adj* : antipatriótico

unpleasant [ˌʌnˈplɛzənt] *adj* : desagradable — **unpleasantly** *adv*

unplug [ˌʌnˈplʌg] *vt* -**plugged**; -**plugging** **1** UNCLOG : destapar, desatascar **2** DISCONNECT : desconectar, desenchufar

unpopular [ˌʌnˈpɑpjələr] *adj* : impopular, poco popular

unpopularity [ˌʌnˌpɑpjəˈlærəti] *n* : impopularidad *f*

unprecedented [ˌʌnˈprɛsəˌdɛntəd] *adj* : sin precedentes, inaudito, nunca visto

unpredictable [ˌʌnprɪˈdɪktəbəl] *adj* : impredecible

unprejudiced [ˌʌnˈprɛdʒədəst] *adj* : imparcial, objetivo

unprepared [ˌʌnprɪˈpærd] *adj* : no preparado ⟨an unprepared speech : un discurso improvisado⟩

unpretentious [ˌʌnprɪˈtɛntʃəs] *adj* : modesto, sin pretensiones

unprincipled [ˌʌnˈprɪntsəpəld] *adj* : sin principios, carente de escrúpulos

unproductive [ˌʌnprəˈdʌktɪv] *adj* : improductivo

unprofitable [ˌʌnˈprɑfətəbəl] *adj* : no rentable, poco provechoso

unpromising [ˌʌnˈprɑməsɪŋ] *adj* : poco prometedor

unprotected [ˌʌnprəˈtɛktəd] *adj* : sin protección, desprotegido

unprovoked [ˌʌnprəˈvoːkt] *adj* : no provocado

unpublished [ˌʌnˈpʌblɪʃt] *adj* : inédito

unpunished [ˌʌnˈpʌnɪʃt] *adj* : impune ⟨to go unpunished : escapar sin castigo⟩

unqualified [ˌʌnˈkwɑləˌfaɪd] *adj* **1** : no calificado, sin título **2** COMPLETE : completo, absoluto ⟨an unqualified denial : una negación incondicional⟩

unquestionable [ˌʌnˈkwɛstʃənəbəl] *adj* : incuestionable, indudable, indiscutible — **unquestionably** [-bli] *adv*

unquestioning [ˌʌnˈkwɛstʃənɪŋ] *adj* : incondicional, absoluto, ciego

unravel [ˌʌnˈrævəl] *v* -**eled** *or* -**elled**; -**eling** *or* -**elling** *vt* **1** DISENTANGLE : desenmarañar, desenredar **2** SOLVE : aclarar, desenmarañar, desentrañar — *vi* : deshacerse

unreal [ˌʌnˈriːl] *adj* : irreal

unrealistic [ˌʌnˌriːəˈlɪstɪk] *adj* : poco realista

unreasonable [ˌʌnˈriːzənəbəl] *adj* **1** IRRATIONAL : poco razonable, irrazonable, irracional **2** EXCESSIVE : excesivo ⟨unreasonable prices : precios excesivos⟩

unreasonably [ˌʌnˈriːzənəbli] *adv* **1** IRRATIONALLY : irracionalmente, de manera irrazonable **2** EXCESSIVELY : excesivamente

unrefined [ˌʌnriˈfaɪnd] *adj* **1** : no refinado, sin refinar (dícese del azúcar, de la harina, etc.) **2** : poco refinado, inculto (dícese de una persona)

unrelated [ˌʌnriˈleɪtəd] *adj* : no relacionado, inconexo

unrelenting [ˌʌnriˈlɛntɪŋ] *adj* **1** STERN : severo, inexorable **2** CONSTANT, RELENTLESS : constante, implacable

unreliable [ˌʌnriˈlaɪəbəl] *adj* : que no es de fiar, de poca confianza, inestable (dícese del tiempo)

unrepentant [ˌʌnriˈpɛntənt] *adj* : impenitente

unresolved [ˌʌnriˈzɑlvd] *adj* : pendiente, no resuelto

unrest [ˌʌnˈrɛst] *n* : inquietud *f*, malestar *m* ⟨political unrest : disturbios políticos⟩

unrestrained [ˌʌnriˈstreɪnd] *adj* : desenfrenado, incontrolado

unrestricted [ˌʌnriˈstrɪktəd] *adj* : sin restricción ⟨unrestricted access : libre acceso⟩

unrewarding [ˌʌnriˈwɔrdɪŋ] *adj* THANKLESS : ingrato

unripe [ˌʌnˈraɪp] *adj* : inmaduro, verde

unrivaled *or* **unrivalled** [ˌʌnˈraɪvəld] *adj* : incomparable

unroll [ˌʌnˈroːl] *vt* : desenrollar — *vi* : desenrollarse

unruffled [ˌʌnˈrʌfəld] *adj* **1** SERENE : sereno, tranquilo **2** SMOOTH : tranquilo, liso ⟨unruffled waters : aguas tranquilas⟩

unruliness [ˌʌnˈruːlinəs] *n* : indisciplina *f*

unruly [ˌʌnˈruːli] *adj* : indisciplinado, díscolo, rebelde

unsafe [ˌʌnˈseɪf] *adj* : inseguro

unsaid [ˌʌnˈsɛd] *adj* : sin decir ⟨to leave unsaid : quedar por decir⟩

unsanitary [ˌʌnˈsænəˌteri] *adj* : antihigiénico

unsatisfactory [ˌʌnˌsætəsˈfæktəri] *adj* : insatisfactorio

unsatisfied [ˌʌnˈsætəsˌfaɪd] *adj* : insatisfecho

unscathed [ˌʌnˈskeɪðd] *adj* UNHARMED : ileso

unscheduled [ˌʌnˈskɛˌdʒuːld] *adj* : no programado, imprevisto

unscientific [ˌʌnˌsaɪənˈtɪfɪk] *adj* : poco científico

unscrupulous [ˌʌnˈskruːpjələs] *adj* : inescrupuloso, sin escrúpulos — **unscrupulously** *adv*

unseal [ˌʌnˈsiːl] *vt* : abrir, quitarle el sello a

unseasonable [ˌʌnˈsiːzənəbəl] *adj* 1
: extemporáneo ⟨unseasonable rain
: lluvia extemporánea⟩ 2 UNTIMELY
: extemporáneo, inoportuno

unseemly [ˌʌnˈsiːmli] *adj* **-lier; -est** 1 IN-
DECOROUS : indecoroso 2 INAPPRO-
PRIATE : impropio, inapropiado

unseen [ˌʌnˈsiːn] *adj* 1 UNNOTICED : inadvertido 2 INVISIBLE : oculto, invisible

unselfish [ˌʌnˈsɛlfɪʃ] *adj* : generoso,
desinteresado — **unselfishly** *adv*

unselfishness [ˌʌnˈsɛlfɪʃnəs] *n* : generosidad *f*, desinterés *m*

unsettle [ˌʌnˈsɛtəl] *vt* **-tled; -tling** DIS-
TURB : trastornar, alterar, perturbar

unsettled [ˌʌnˈsɛtəld] *adj* 1 CHANGE-
ABLE : inestable, variable ⟨unsettled
weather : tiempo inestable⟩ 2 DIS-
TURBED : agitado, inquieto ⟨unsettled
waters : aguas agitadas⟩ 3 UNDECID-
ED : pendiente (dícese de un asunto),
indeciso (dícese de una persona) 4 UN-
PAID : sin saldar, pendiente 5 UNIN-
HABITED : despoblado, no colonizado

unshaped [ˌʌnˈʃeɪpt] *adj* : sin forma, informe

unsightly [ˌʌnˈsaɪtli] *adj* UGLY : feo, de
aspecto malo

unskilled [ˌʌnˈskɪld] *adj* : no calificado

unskillful [ˌʌnˈskɪlfəl] *adj* : inexperto,
poco hábil

unsnap [ˌʌnˈsnæp] *vt* **-snapped; -snap-
ping** : desabrochar

unsociable *adj* : poco sociable

unsolved [ˌʌnˈsɑlvd] *adj* : no resuelto,
sin resolver

unsophisticated [ˌʌnsəˈfɪstəˌkeɪtəd] *adj*
1 NAIVE, UNWORLDLY : ingenuo, de
poco mundo 2 SIMPLE : simple, poco
sofisticado, rudimentario

unsound [ˌʌnˈsaʊnd] *adj* 1 UNHEALTHY
: enfermizo, de mala salud 2 : poco
sólido, defectuoso (dícese de una estructura, etc.) 3 INVALID : inválido, erróneo 4 **of unsound mind** : mentalmente incapacitado

unspeakable [ˌʌnˈspiːkəbəl] *adj* 1 IN-
DESCRIBABLE : indecible, inexpresable, incalificable 2 HEINOUS
: atroz, nefando, abominable — **un-
speakably** [-bli] *adv*

unspecified [ˌʌnˈspɛsəˌfaɪd] *adj* : indeterminado, sin especificar

unspoiled [ˌʌnˈspɔɪld] *adj* 1 : conserva-
do, sin estropear (dícese de un lugar)
2 : que no está mimado (dícese de un
niño)

unstable [ˌʌnˈsteɪbəl] *adj* 1 CHANGE-
ABLE : variable, inestable, cambiable
⟨an unstable pulse : un pulso irregu-
lar⟩ 2 UNSTEADY : inestable, poco sólido (dícese de una estructura)

unsteadily [ˌʌnˈstɛdəli] *adv* : de modo inestable

unsteadiness [ˌʌnˈstɛdinəs] *n* : inestabilidad *f*, inseguridad *f*

unsteady [ˌʌnˈstɛdi] *adj* 1 UNSTABLE
: inestable, variable 2 SHAKY : tembloroso

unstoppable [ˌʌnˈstɑpəbəl] *adj* : irrefrenable, incontenible

unsubstantiated [ˌʌnsəbˈstænʃiˌeɪtəd]
adj : no corroborado, no demostrado

unsuccessful [ˌʌnsəkˈsɛsfəl] *adj* : fracasado, infructuoso

unsuitable [ˌʌnˈsuːtəbəl] *adj* : inadecuado, impropio, inapropiado ⟨an unsuitable time : una hora inconveniente⟩

unsuited [ˌʌnˈsuːtəd] *adj* : inadecuado,
inepto

unsung [ˌʌnˈsʌŋ] *adj* : olvidado

unsure [ˌʌnˈʃʊr] *adj* : incierto, dudoso

unsurpassed [ˌʌnsərˈpæst] *adj* : sin par,
sin igual

unsuspecting [ˌʌnsəˈspɛktɪŋ] *adj* : desprevenido, desapercibido, confiado

unsympathetic [ˌʌnˌsɪmpəˈθɛtɪk] *adj*
: poco comprensivo, indiferente

untangle [ˌʌnˈteɪŋɡəl] *vt* **-gled; -gling**
: desenmarañar, desenredar

unthinkable [ˌʌnˈθɪŋkəbəl] *adj* : inconcebible, impensable

unthinking [ˌʌnˈθɪŋkɪŋ] *adj* : irreflexivo,
inconsciente — **unthinkingly** *adv*

untidy [ˌʌnˈtaɪdi] *adj* 1 SLOVENLY : desaliñado 2 DISORDERLY : desordena-
do, desarreglado

untie [ˌʌnˈtaɪ] *vt* **-tied; -tying** *or* **-tieing**
: desatar, deshacer

until[1] [ʌnˈtɪl] *prep* : hasta ⟨until now
: hasta ahora⟩

until[2] *conj* : hasta que ⟨until they left
: hasta que salieron⟩ ⟨don't answer until you're sure : no contestes hasta que
(no) estés seguro⟩

untimely [ˌʌnˈtaɪmli] *adj* 1 PREMATURE
: prematuro ⟨an untimely death : una
muerte prematura⟩ 2 INOPPORTUNE
: inoportuno, intempestivo

untold [ˌʌnˈtoːld] *adj* 1 : nunca dicho
⟨the untold secret : el secreto sin con-
tar⟩ 2 INCALCULABLE : incalculable,
indecible

untouched [ˌʌnˈtʌt͡ʃt] *adj* 1 INTACT : intacto, sin tocar, sin probar (dícese de
la comida) 2 UNAFFECTED : insensible, indiferente

untoward [ˌʌnˈtɔrd, -ˈtoːərd, -tə-ˈwɔrd]
adj 1 : indecoroso, impropio (dícese
del comportamiento) 2 ADVERSE, UN-
FORTUNATE : desafortunado, adverso
⟨untoward effects : efectos perjudi-
ciales⟩ 3 UNSEEMLY : indecoroso

untrained [ˌʌnˈtreɪnd] *adj* : inexperto, no
capacitado

untreated [ˌʌnˈtriːtəd] *adj* : no tratado
(dícese de una enfermedad, etc.), sin
tratar (dícese de un material)

untroubled [ˌʌnˈtrʌbəld] *adj* : tranquilo
⟨to be untroubled by : no estar afectado por⟩

untrue [ˌʌnˈtruː] *adj* 1 UNFAITHFUL : infiel 2 FALSE : falso

untrustworthy [ˌʌnˈtrʌstˌwərði] *adj* : de
poca confianza (dícese de una per-

sona), no fidedigno (dícese de la información)

untruth [ˌʌn'truːθ, 'ʌn-] n : mentira f, falsedad f

untruthful [ˌʌn'truːθfəl] adj : mentiroso, falso

unusable [ˌʌn'juːzəbəl] adj : inútil, inservible

unused [ˌʌn'juːzd, in sense 1 usually -'juːst] adj **1** UNACCUSTOMED : inhabituado **2** NEW : nuevo **3** IDLE : no utilizado (dícese de la tierra) **4** REMAINING : restante (the unused portion : la porción restante)

unusual [ˌʌn'juːʒʊəl] adj : inusual, poco común, raro

unusually [ˌʌn'juːʒʊəli, -'juːʒəli] adv : excepcionalmente, extraordinariamente, fuera de lo común

unwanted [ˌʌn'wɑntəd] adj : superfluo, de sobre

unwarranted [ˌʌn'wɔrəntəd] adj : injustificado

unwary [ˌʌn'wæri] adj : incauto

unwavering [ˌʌn'weɪvərɪŋ] adj : firme, inquebrantable (an unwavering gaze : una mirada fija)

unwelcome [ˌʌn'wɛlkəm] adj : importuno, molesto

unwell [ˌʌn'wɛl] adj : enfermo, mal

unwholesome [ˌʌn'hoːlsəm] adj **1** UNHEALTHY : malsano, insalubre **2** PERNICIOUS : pernicioso **3** LOATHSOME : repugnante, muy desagradable

unwieldy [ˌʌn'wiːldi] adj CUMBERSOME : difícil de manejar, torpe y pesado

unwilling [ˌʌn'wɪlɪŋ] adj : poco dispuesto (to be unwilling to : no estar dispuesto a)

unwillingly [ˌʌn'wɪlɪŋli] adv : a regañadientes, de mala gana

unwind [ˌʌn'waɪnd] v **-wound** [-'waʊnd]; **-winding** vt UNROLL : desenrollar — vi **1** : desenrollarse **2** RELAX : relajar

unwise [ˌʌn'waɪz] adj : imprudente, desacertado, poco aconsejable

unwisely [ˌʌn'waɪzli] adv : imprudentemente

unwitting [ˌʌn'wɪtɪŋ] adj **1** UNAWARE : inconsciente **2** INADVERTENT : involuntario, inadvertido (an unwitting mistake : un error inadvertido) — **unwittingly** adv

unworthiness [ˌʌn'wərðinəs] n : falta f de valía

unworthy [ˌʌn'wərði] adj **1** UNDESERVING : indigno (to be unworthy of : no ser digno de) **2** UNMERITED : inmerecido

unwrap [ˌʌn'ræp] vt **-wrapped; -wrapping** : desenvolver, deshacer

unwritten [ˌʌn'rɪtən] adj : no escrito

unyielding [ˌʌn'jiːldɪŋ] adj : firme, inflexible, rígido

unzip [ˌʌn'zɪp] vt **-zipped; -zipping** : abrir el cierre de

up¹ ['ʌp] v **upped** ['ʌpt]; **upping; ups** vt INCREASE : aumentar, subir (they upped the prices : aumentaron los pre-

cios) — vi **to up and** : agarrar y fam (she up and left : agarró y se fue)

up² adv **1** ABOVE : arriba, en lo alto (up in the mountains : arriba en las montañas) **2** UPWARDS : hacia arriba (push it up : empújalo hacia arriba) (the sun came up : el sol salió) (prices went up : los precios subieron) **3** (indicating an upright position or waking state) (to sit up : ponerse derecho) (they got up late : se levantaron tarde) (I stayed up all night : pasé toda la noche sin dormir) **4** (indicating volume or intensity) (to speak up : hablar más fuerte) **5** (indicating a northerly direction) (the climate up north : el clima del norte) (I'm going up to Canada : voy para Canadá) **6** (indicating the appearance or existence of something) (the book turned up : el libro apareció) **7** (indicating consideration) (she brought the matter up : mencionó el asunto) **8** COMPLETELY : completamente (eat it up : cómetelo todo) **9** : en pedazos (he tore it up : lo rompió en pedazos) **10** (indicating a stopping) (the car pulled up to the curb : el carro paró al borde de la acera) **11** (indicating an even score) (the game was 10 up : empataron a 10)

up³ adj **1** (risen above the horizon) (the sun is up : ha salido el sol) **2** (being above a normal or former level) (prices are up : los precios han aumentado) (the river is up : las aguas están altas) **3** : despierto, levantado (up all night : despierto toda la noche) **4** BUILT : construido (the house is up : la casa está construida) **5** OPEN : abierto (the windows are up : las ventanas están abiertas) **6** (moving or going upward) (the up staircase : la escalera para subir) **7** ABREAST : enterado, al día, al corriente (to be up on the news : estar al corriente de las noticias) **8** PREPARED : preparado (we were up for the test : estuvimos preparados para el examen) **9** FINISHED : terminado, acabado (time is up : se ha terminado el tiempo permitido) **10** to be up : pasar (what's up? : ¿qué pasa?)

up⁴ prep **1** (to, toward, or at a higher point of) (he went up the stairs : subió la escalera) **2** (to or toward the source of) (to go up the river : ir río arriba) **3** ALONG : a lo largo, por (up the coast : a lo largo de la costa) (just up the way : un poco más adelante) (up and down the city : por toda la ciudad)

upbraid [ˌʌp'breɪd] vt : reprender, regañar

upbringing ['ʌpˌbrɪŋɪŋ] n : crianza f, educación f

upcoming [ˌʌp'kʌmɪŋ] adj : próximo

update¹ [ˌʌp'deɪt] vt **-dated; -dating** : poner al día, poner al corriente, actualizar

update² ['ʌpˌdeɪt] n : actualización f, puesta f al día

upend [ˌʌpˈɛnd] vt 1 : poner vertical 2 OVERTURN : volcar

upgrade¹ [ˈʌpˌgreɪd, ˌʌpˈ-] vt -graded; -grading 1 PROMOTE : ascender 2 IMPROVE : mejorar

upgrade² [ˈʌpˌgreɪd] n 1 SLOPE : cuesta f, pendiente f 2 RISE : aumento m de categoría (de un puesto), ascenso m (de un empleado) 3 IMPROVEMENT : mejoramiento m

upheaval [ˌʌpˈhiːvəl] n 1 : levantamiento m (en geología) 2 DISTURBANCE, UPSET : trastorno m, agitación f, conmoción f

uphill¹ [ˌʌpˈhɪl] adv : cuesta arriba

uphill² [ˈʌpˌhɪl] adj 1 ASCENDING : en subida 2 DIFFICULT : difícil, arduo

uphold [ˌʌpˈhoːld] vt -held; -holding 1 SUPPORT : sostener, apoyar, mantener 2 RAISE : levantar 3 CONFIRM : confirmar (una decisión judicial)

upholster [ˌʌpˈhoːlstər] vt : tapizar

upholsterer [ˌʌpˈhoːlstərər] n : tapicero m, -ra f

upholstery [ˌʌpˈhoːlstəri] n, pl -steries : tapicería f

upkeep [ˈʌpˌkiːp] n : mantenimiento m

upland [ˈʌplənd, -ˌlænd] n : altiplanicie f, altiplano m

uplift¹ [ˌʌpˈlɪft] vt 1 RAISE : elevar, levantar 2 ELEVATE : elevar, animar (el espíritu, la mente, etc.)

uplift² [ˈʌpˌlɪft] n : elevación f

upon [əˈpɔn, əˈpɑn] prep : en, sobre ⟨upon the desk : sobre el escritorio⟩ ⟨upon leaving : al salir⟩ ⟨questions upon questions : pregunta tras pregunta⟩

upper¹ [ˈʌpər] adj 1 HIGHER : superior ⟨the upper classes : las clases altas⟩ 2 : alto (en geografía) ⟨the upper Mississippi : el alto Mississippi⟩

upper² n : parte f superior (del calzado, etc.)

uppercase [ˌʌpərˈkeɪs] adj : mayúsculo

upper hand n : ventaja f, dominio m

uppermost [ˈʌpərˌmoːst] adj : más alto ⟨it was uppermost in his mind : era lo que más le preocupaba⟩

upright¹ [ˈʌpˌraɪt] adj 1 VERTICAL : vertical 2 ERECT : erguido, derecho 3 JUST : recto, honesto, justo

upright² n : montante m, poste m, soporte m

uprising [ˈʌpˌraɪzɪŋ] n : insurrección f, revuelta f, alzamiento m

uproar [ˈʌpˌror] n COMMOTION : alboroto m, jaleo m, escándalo m

uproarious [ˌʌpˈroriəs] adj 1 CLAMOROUS : estrepitoso, clamoroso 2 HILARIOUS : muy divertido, hilarante — **uproariously** adv

uproot [ˌʌpˈruːt, -ˈrʊt] vt : desarraigar

upset¹ [ˌʌpˈsɛt] vt -set; -setting 1 OVERTURN : volcar 2 SPILL : derramar 3 DISTURB : perturbar, disgustar, inquietar, alterar 4 SICKEN : sentar mal a ⟨it upsets my stomach : me sienta mal

al estómago⟩ 5 DISRUPT : trastornar, desbaratar (planes, etc.) 6 DEFEAT : derrotar (en deportes)

upset² adj 1 DISPLEASED, DISTRESSED : disgustado, alterado 2 **to have an upset stomach** : estar mal del estómago, estar descompuesto (de estómago)

upset³ [ˈʌpˌsɛt] n 1 OVERTURNING : vuelco m 2 DISRUPTION : trastorno m (de planes, etc.) 3 DEFEAT : derrota f (en deportes)

upshot [ˈʌpˌʃɑt] n : resultado m final

upside–down [ˌʌpˌsaɪdˈdaʊn] adj : al revés

upside down [ˌʌpˌsaɪdˈdaʊn] adv 1 : al revés 2 : en confusión, en desorden

upstairs¹ [ˌʌpˈstærz] adv : arriba, en el piso superior

upstairs² [ˈʌpˌstærz, ˌʌpˈ-] adj : de arriba

upstairs³ [ˈʌpˌstærz, ˌʌpˈ-] ns & pl : piso m de arriba, planta f de arriba

upstanding [ˌʌpˈstændɪŋ, ˈʌpˌ-] adj HONEST, UPRIGHT : honesto, íntegro, recto

upstart [ˈʌpˌstɑrt] n : advenedizo m, -za f

upswing [ˈʌpˌswɪŋ] n : alza f, mejora f notable ⟨to be on the upswing : estar mejorándose⟩

uptight [ˌʌpˈtaɪt] adj : tenso, nervioso

up to prep 1 : hasta ⟨up to a year : hasta un año⟩ ⟨in mud up to my ankles : en barro hasta los tobillos⟩ 2 **to be up to** : estar a la altura de ⟨I'm not up to going : no estoy en condiciones de ir⟩ 3 **to be up to** : depender de ⟨it's up to the director : depende del director⟩

up-to-date [ˌʌptəˈdeɪt] adj 1 CURRENT : corriente, al día ⟨to keep up-to-date : mantenerse al corriente⟩ 2 MODERN : moderno

uptown [ˈʌpˌtaʊn] adv : hacia la parte alta de la ciudad, hacia el distrito residencial

upturn [ˈʌpˌtərn] n : mejora f, auge m (económico)

upward¹ [ˈʌpwərd] or **upwards** [-wərdz] adv 1 : hacia arriba 2 **~ of** : más de

upward² adj : ascendente, hacia arriba

upwind [ˌʌpˈwɪnd] adv & adj : contra el viento

uranium [jʊˈreɪniəm] n : uranio m

Uranus [jʊˈreɪnəs, ˈjʊrənəs] n : Urano m

urban [ˈərbən] adj : urbano

urbane [ˌərˈbeɪn] adj : urbano, cortés

urchin [ˈərʧən] n 1 SCAMP : granuja mf; pillo m, -lla f 2 **sea urchin** : erizo m de mar

Urdu [ˈʊrduː, ˈər-] n : urdu m

urethra [jʊˈriːθrə] n, pl -thras or -thrae [-ˌθriː] : uretra f

urge¹ [ˈərʤ] vt **urged; urging** 1 PRESS : instar, apremiar, insistir ⟨we urged him to come : insistimos en que viniera⟩ 2 ADVOCATE : recomendar, abogar por 3 **urge on** : animar, alentar

urge² n : impulso m, ganas fpl, compulsión f

urgency [ˈərdʒəntsi] *n, pl* **-cies** : urgencia *f*

urgent [ˈərdʒənt] *adj* **1** PRESSING : urgente, apremiante **2** INSISTENT : insistente **3 to be urgent** : urgir

urgently [ˈərdʒəntli] *adv* : urgentemente

urinal [ˈjurənəl, *esp Brit* juˈraɪnəl] *n* : orinal *m* (recipiente), urinario *m* (lugar)

urinary [ˈjurəˌneri] *adj* : urinario

urinate [ˈjurəˌneɪt] *vi* **-nated; -nating** : orinar

urination [ˌjurəˈneɪʃən] *n* : orinación *f*

urine [ˈjurən] *n* : orina *f*

urn [ˈərn] *n* **1** VASE : urna *f* **2** : recipiente *m* (para servir café, etc.)

Uruguayan [ˌurəˈgwaɪən, ˌjur-, -ˈgwei-] *n* : uruguayo *m*, -ya *f* — **Uruguayan** *adj*

us [ˈʌs] *pron* **1** (*as direct object*) : nos ⟨they were visiting us : nos visitaban⟩ **2** (*as indirect object*) : nos ⟨he gave us a present : nos dio un regalo⟩ **3** (*as object of preposition*) : nosotros, nosotras ⟨stay with us : quédese con nosotros⟩ ⟨both of us : nosotros dos⟩ **4** (*for emphasis*) : nosotros ⟨it's us! : ¡somos nosotros!⟩

usable [ˈjuːzəbəl] *adj* : utilizable

usage [ˈjuːsɪdʒ, -zɪdʒ] *n* **1** HABIT : costumbre *f*, hábito *m* **2** USE : uso *m*

use¹ [ˈjuːz] *v* **used** [ˈjuːzd, *in phrase* "used to" usually ˈjuːstuː]; **using** *vt* **1** EMPLOY : emplear, usar **2** CONSUME : consumir, tomar (drogas, etc.) **3** UTILIZE : usar, utilizar ⟨to use tact : usar tacto⟩ ⟨he used his friends to get ahead : usó a sus amigos para mejorar su posición⟩ **4** TREAT : tratar ⟨they used the horse cruelly : maltrataron al caballo⟩ **5 to use up** : agotar, consumir, gastar — *vi* (*used in the past with* **to** *to indicate a former fact or state*) : soler, acostumbrar ⟨winters used to be colder : los inviernos solían ser más fríos, los inviernos eran más fríos⟩ ⟨she used to dance : acostumbraba bailar⟩

use² [ˈjuːs] *n* **1** APPLICATION, EMPLOYMENT : uso *m*, empleo *m*, utilización *f* ⟨out of use : en desuso⟩ ⟨ready for use : listo para usar⟩ ⟨to be in use : usarse, estar funcionando⟩ ⟨to make use of : servirse de, aprovechar⟩ **2** USEFULNESS : utilidad *f* ⟨to be of no use : no servir (para nada)⟩ ⟨it's no use! : ¡es inútil!⟩ **3 to have the use of** : poder usar, tener acceso a **4 to have no use for**

: no necesitar ⟨she has no use for poetry : a ella no le gusta la poesía⟩

used [ˈjuːzd] *adj* **1** SECONDHAND : usado, de segunda mano ⟨used cars : coches usados⟩ **2** ACCUSTOMED : acostumbrado ⟨used to the heat : acostumbrado al calor⟩

useful [ˈjuːsfəl] *adj* : útil, práctico — **usefully** *adv*

usefulness [ˈjuːsfəlnəs] *n* : utilidad *f*

useless [ˈjuːsləs] *adj* : inútil — **uselessly** *adv*

uselessness [ˈjuːsləsnəs] *n* : inutilidad *f*

user [ˈjuːzər] *n* : usuario *m*, -ria *f*

usher¹ [ˈʌʃər] *vt* **1** ESCORT : acompañar, conducir **2 to usher in** : hacer pasar (a alguien) ⟨to usher in a new era : anunciar una nueva época⟩

usher² *n* : acomodador *m*, -dora *f*

usherette [ˌʌʃəˈret] *n* : acomodadora *f*

usual [ˈjuːʒuəl] *adj* **1** NORMAL : usual, normal **2** CUSTOMARY : acostumbrado, habitual, de costumbre **3** ORDINARY : ordinario, típico

usually [ˈjuːʒuəli, ˈjuːʒəli] *adv* : usualmente, normalmente

usurp [juˈsərp, -ˈzərp] *vt* : usurpar

usurper [juˈsərpər, -ˈzər-] *n* : usurpador *m*, -dora *f*

utensil [juˈtɛntsəl] *n* **1** : utensilio *m* (de cocina) **2** IMPLEMENT : implemento *m*, útil *m* (de labranza, etc.)

uterine [ˈjuːtəˌraɪn, -rən] *adj* : uterino

uterus [ˈjuːtərəs] *n, pl* **uteri** [-ˌraɪ] : útero *m*, matriz *f*

utilitarian [juˌtɪləˈteriən] *adj* : utilitario

utility [juˈtɪləti] *n, pl* **-ties** **1** USEFULNESS : utilidad *f* **2 public utility** : empresa *f* de servicio público

utilization [ˌjuːtələˈzeɪʃən] *n* : utilización *f*

utilize [ˈjuːtəlˌaɪz] *vt* **-lized; -lizing** : utilizar, hacer uso de

utmost¹ [ˈʌtˌmoːst] *adj* **1** FARTHEST : extremo, más lejano **2** GREATEST : sumo, mayor ⟨of the utmost importance : de suma importancia⟩

utmost² *n* : lo más posible ⟨to the utmost : al máximo⟩

utopia [juˈtoːpiə] *n* : utopía *f*

utopian [juˈtoːpiən] *adj* : utópico

utter¹ [ˈʌtər] *vt* : decir, articular, pronunciar (palabras)

utter² *adj* : absoluto — **utterly** *adv*

utterance [ˈʌtərənts] *n* : declaración *f*, articulación *f*

V

v [ˈviː] *n, pl* **v's** *or* **vs** [ˈviːz] : vigésima segunda letra del alfabeto inglés

vacancy [ˈveɪkəntsi] *n, pl* **-cies** **1** EMPTINESS : vacío *m*, vacuidad *f* **2** : vacante *f*, puesto *m* vacante ⟨to fill a vacancy

: ocupar un puesto⟩ **3** : habitación *f* libre (en un hotel) ⟨no vacancies : completo⟩

vacant [ˈveɪkənt] *adj* **1** EMPTY : libre, desocupado (dícese de los edificios,

etc.) **2** : vacante (dícese de los puestos)
3 BLANK : vacío, ausente ⟨a vacant
stare : una mirada ausente⟩

vacate [ˈveɪˌkeɪt] vt **-cated; -cating** : desalojar, desocupar

vacation[1] [veɪˈkeɪʃən, və-] vi : pasar las vacaciones, vacacionar Mex

vacation[2] n : vacaciones fpl ⟨to be on vacation : estar de vacaciones⟩

vacationer [veɪˈkeɪʃənər, və-] n : turista mf, veraneante mf, vacacionista mf CA, Mex

vaccinate [ˈvæksəˌneɪt] vt **-nated; -nating** : vacunar

vaccination [ˌvæksəˈneɪʃən] n : vacunación f

vaccine [vækˈsiːn, ˈvækˌ-] n : vacuna f

vacillate [ˈvæsəˌleɪt] vi **-lated; -lating 1** HESITATE : vacilar **2** SWAY : oscilar

vacillation [ˌvæsəˈleɪʃən] n : indecisión f, vacilación f

vacuous [ˈvækjʊəs] adj **1** EMPTY : vacío **2** INANE : vacuo, necio, estúpido

vacuum[1] [ˈvæˌkjuːm, -kjəm] vt : limpiar con aspiradora, pasar la aspiradora por

vacuum[2] n, pl **vacuums** or **vacua** [ˈvækjʊə] : vacío m

vacuum cleaner n : aspiradora f

vagabond[1] [ˈvægəˌbɑnd] adj : vagabundo

vagabond[2] n : vagabundo m, -da f

vagary [ˈveɪɡəri, vəˈɡeri] n, pl **-ries** : capricho m

vagina [vəˈdʒaɪnə] n, pl **-nae** [-ˌniː, -ˌnaɪ] or **-nas** : vagina f

vagrancy [ˈveɪɡrəntsi] n, pl **-cies** : vagancia f

vagrant[1] [ˈveɪɡrənt] adj : vagabundo

vagrant[2] n : vagabundo m, -da f

vague [ˈveɪɡ] adj **vaguer; -est 1** IMPRECISE : vago, impreciso ⟨a vague feeling : una sensación indefinida⟩ ⟨I haven't the vaguest idea : no tengo la más remota idea⟩ **2** UNCLEAR : borroso, poco claro ⟨a vague outline : un perfil indistinto⟩ **3** ABSENTMINDED : distraído

vaguely [ˈveɪɡli] adv : vagamente, de manera imprecisa

vagueness [ˈveɪɡnəs] n : vaguedad f, imprecisión f

vain [ˈveɪn] adj **1** WORTHLESS : vano **2** FUTILE : vano, inútil ⟨in vain : en vano⟩ **3** CONCEITED : vanidoso, presumido

vainly [ˈveɪnli] adv : en vano, vanamente, inútilmente

valance [ˈvælənts, ˈveɪ-] n **1** FLOUNCE : volante m (de una cama, etc.) **2** : galería f de cortina (sobre una ventana)

vale [ˈveɪl] n : valle m

valedictorian [ˌvælədɪkˈtoriən] n : estudiante mf que pronuncia el discurso de despedida en ceremonia de graduación

valedictory [ˌvæləˈdɪktəri] adj : de despedida

valentine [ˈvælənˌtaɪn] n : tarjeta f que se manda el Día de los Enamorados (el 14 de febrero)

Valentine's Day n : Día m de los Enamorados

valet [ˈvæˌleɪ, væˈleɪ, ˈvælət] n : ayuda m de cámara

valiant [ˈvæljənt] adj : valiente, valeroso

valiantly [ˈvæljəntli] adv : con valor, valientemente

valid [ˈvæləd] adj : válido

validate [ˈvæləˌdeɪt] vt **-dated; -dating** : validar, dar validez a

validity [vəˈlɪdəti, væ-] n : validez f

valise [vəˈliːs] n : maleta f (de mano)

valley [ˈvæli] n, pl **-leys** : valle m

valor [ˈvælər] n : valor m, valentía f

valorous [ˈvælərəs] adj : valeroso, valiente

valuable[1] [ˈvæljʊəbəl, ˈvæljəbəl] adj **1** EXPENSIVE : valioso, de valor **2** WORTHWHILE : valioso, apreciable

valuable[2] n : objeto m de valor

valuation [ˌvæljuˈeɪʃən] n **1** APPRAISAL : valoración f, tasación f **2** VALUE : valuación f

value[1] [ˈvælˌjuː] vt **-ued; -uing 1** APPRAISE : valorar, avaluar, tasar **2** APPRECIATE : valorar, apreciar

value[2] n **1** : valor m ⟨of little value : de poco valor⟩ ⟨to be a good value : estar bien de precio, tener buen precio⟩ ⟨at face value : en su sentido literal⟩ **2** values npl : valores mpl (morales), principios mpl

valueless [ˈvæljuːləs] adj : sin valor

valve [ˈvælv] n : válvula f

vampire [ˈvæmˌpaɪr] n **1** : vampiro m **2** or **vampire bat** : vampiro m

van[1] [ˈvæn] → vanguard

van[2] n : furgoneta f, camioneta f

vanadium [vəˈneɪdiəm] n : vanadio m

vandal [ˈvændəl] n : vándalo m

vandalism [ˈvændəlˌɪzəm] n : vandalismo m

vandalize [ˈvændəlˌaɪz] vt : destrozar, destruir, estropear

vane [ˈveɪn] n or **weather vane** : veleta f

vanguard [ˈvænˌɡɑrd] n : vanguardia f

vanilla [vəˈnɪlə, -ˈne-] n : vainilla f

vanish [ˈvænɪʃ] vi : desaparecer, disiparse, desvanecerse

vanity [ˈvænəti] n, pl **-ties 1** : vanidad f **2** or **vanity table** : tocador m

vanquish [ˈvæŋkwɪʃ, ˈvæn-] vt : vencer, conquistar

vantage point [ˈvæntɪdʒ] n : posición f ventajosa

vapid [ˈvæpəd, ˈveɪ-] adj : insípido, insulso

vapor [ˈveɪpər] n : vapor m

vaporize [ˈveɪpəˌraɪz] v **-rized; -rizing** vt : vaporizar — vi : vaporizarse, evaporarse

vaporizer [ˈveɪpəˌraɪzər] n : vaporizador m

variability [ˌveriəˈbɪləti] n, pl **-ties** : variabilidad f

variable[1] [ˈveriəbəl] adj : variable ⟨variable cloudiness : nubosidad variable⟩

variable² *n* : variable *f*, factor *m*

variance ['verɪənts] *n* **1** DISCREPANCY : varianza *f*, discrepancia *f* **2** DISAGREEMENT : desacuerdo *m* ⟨at variance with : en desacuerdo con⟩

variant¹ ['veriənt] *adj* : variante, divergente

variant² *n* : variante *f*

variation [ˌveri'eɪʃən] *n* : variación *f*, diferencias *fpl*

varicose ['verə,ko:s] *adj* : varicoso

varicose veins *npl* : varices *fpl*, várices *fpl*

varied ['verɪd] *adj* : variado, dispar, diferente

variegated ['veriə,geɪtɪd] *adj* : abigarrado, multicolor

variety [və'raɪəti] *n*, *pl* **-ties 1** DIVERSITY : diversidad *f*, variedad *f* **2** ASSORTMENT : surtido *m* ⟨for a variety of reasons : por diversas razones⟩ **3** SORT : clase *f* **4** BREED : variedad *f* (de plantas)

various ['veriəs] *adj* : varios, diversos

varnish¹ ['vɑrnɪʃ] *vt* : barnizar

varnish² *n* : barniz *m*

varsity ['vɑrsəti] *n*, *pl* **-ties** : equipo *m* universitario

vary ['veri] *v* **varied; varying** *vt* : variar, diversificar — *vi* **1** CHANGE : variar, cambiar **2** DEVIATE : desviarse

vascular ['væskjələr] *adj* : vascular

vase ['veis, 'veiz, 'vɑz] *n* : jarrón *m*, florero *m*

vassal ['væsəl] *n* : vasallo *m*, -lla *f*

vast ['væst] *adj* : inmenso, enorme, vasto

vastly ['væstli] *adv* : enormemente

vastness ['væstnəs] *n* : vastedad *f*, inmensidad *f*

vat ['væt] *n* : cuba *f*, tina *f*

vaudeville ['vɑdvəl, -,vɪl; 'vɑdə,vɪl] *n* : vodevil *m*

vault¹ ['vɔlt] *vi* LEAP : saltar

vault² *n* **1** JUMP : salto *m* ⟨pole vault : salto de pértiga, salto con garrocha⟩ **2** DOME : bóveda *f* **3** : bodega *f* (para vino), bóveda *f* de seguridad (de un banco) **4** CRYPT : cripta *f*

vaulted ['vɔltəd] *adj* : abovedado

vaunted ['vɔntəd] *adj* : cacareado, alardeado ⟨a much vaunted wine : un vino muy alardeado⟩

VCR [ˌvi:ˌsi:'ɑr] *n* : video *m*, videocasetera *f*

veal ['vi:l] *n* : ternera *f*, carne *f* de ternera

veer ['vɪr] *vi* : virar (dícese de un barco), girar (dícese de un coche), torcer (dícese de un camino)

vegetable¹ ['vedʒtəbəl, 'vedʒətə-] *adj* : vegetal

vegetable² *n* **1** : vegetal *m* ⟨the vegetable kingdom : el reino vegetal⟩ **2** : verdura *f*, hortaliza *f* (para comer)

vegetarian [ˌvedʒə'teriən] *n* : vegetariano *mf*

vegetarianism [ˌvedʒə'teriə,nɪzəm] *n* : vegetarianismo *m*

vegetate ['vedʒə,teɪt] *vi* **-tated; -tating** : vegetar

vegetation [ˌvedʒə'teɪʃən] *n* : vegetación *f*

vegetative ['vedʒə,teɪtɪv] *adj* : vegetativo

vehemence ['vi:əmənts] *n* : intensidad *f*, vehemencia *f*

vehement ['vi:əmənt] *adj* : intenso, vehemente

vehemently ['vi:əməntli] *adv* : vehementemente, con vehemencia

vehicle ['vi:əkəl, 'vi:,hɪkəl] *n* **1** *or motor vehicle* : vehículo *m* **2** MEDIUM : vehículo *m*, medio *m*

vehicular [vi'hɪkjələr, və-] *adj* : vehicular ⟨vehicular homicide : muerte *f* por atropello⟩

veil¹ ['veil] *vt* **1** CONCEAL : velar, disimular **2** : cubrir con un velo ⟨to veil one's face : cubrirse con un velo⟩

veil² *n* : velo *m* ⟨bridal veil : velo de novia⟩

vein ['vein] *n* **1** : vena *f* (en anatomía, botánica, etc.) **2** LODE : veta *f*, vena *f*, filón *m* **3** STYLE : vena *f* ⟨in a humorous vein : en vena humorística⟩

veined ['veind] *adj* : veteado (dícese del queso, de los minerales, etc.)

velocity [və'lɑsəti] *n*, *pl* **-ties** : velocidad *f*

velour [və'lʊr] *or* **velours** [-'lʊrz] *n* : velour *m*

velvet¹ ['vɛlvət] *adj* **1** : de terciopelo **2** → **velvety**

velvet² *n* : terciopelo *m*

velvety ['vɛlvəti] *adj* : aterciopelado

venal ['vi:nəl] *adj* : venal, sobornable

vend ['vɛnd] *vt* : vender

vendetta [vɛn'dɛtə] *n* : vendetta *f*

vendor ['vɛndər] *n* : vendedor *m*, -dora *f*; puestero *m*, -ra *f*

veneer¹ [və'nɪr] *vt* : enchapar, chapar

veneer² *n* **1** : enchapado *m*, chapa *f* **2** APPEARANCE : apariencia *f*, barniz *m* ⟨a veneer of culture : un barniz de cultura⟩

venerable ['vɛnərəbəl] *adj* : venerable

venerate ['vɛnə,reɪt] *vt* **-ated; -ating** : venerar

veneration [ˌvɛnə'reɪʃən] *n* : veneración *f*

venereal disease [və'nɪriəl] *n* : enfermedad *f* venérea

venetian blind [və'ni:ʃən] *n* : persiana *f* veneciana

Venezuelan [ˌvɛnə'zweɪlən, -zʊ'ei-] *n* : venezolano *m*, -na *f* — **Venezuelan** *adj*

vengeance ['vɛndʒənts] *n* : venganza *f* ⟨to take vengeance on : vengarse de⟩

vengeful ['vɛndʒfəl] *adj* : vengativo

venial ['vi:niəl] *adj* : venial ⟨a venial sin : un pecado venial⟩

venison ['vɛnəsən, -zən] *n* : venado *m*, carne *f* de venado

venom ['vɛnəm] *n* **1** : veneno *m* **2** MALICE : veneno *m*, malevolencia *f*

venomous [ˈvɛnəməs] *adj* : venenoso

vent¹ [ˈvɛnt] *vt* : desahogar, dar salida a ⟨to vent one's feelings : desahogarse⟩

vent² *n* **1** OPENING : abertura *f* (de escape), orificio *m* **2** *or* **air vent** : respiradero *m*, rejilla *f* de ventilación **3** OUTLET : desahogo *m* ⟨to give vent to one's anger : desahogar la ira⟩

ventilate [ˈvɛntəlˌeɪt] *vt* **-lated; -lating** : ventilar

ventilation [ˌvɛntəlˈeɪʃən] *n* : ventilación *f*

ventilator [ˈvɛntəlˌeɪtər] *n* : ventilador *m*

ventricle [ˈvɛntrɪkəl] *n* : ventrículo *m*

ventriloquism [vɛnˈtrɪləˌkwɪzəm] *n* : ventriloquia *f*

ventriloquist [vɛnˈtrɪləˌkwɪst] *n* : ventrílocuo *m*, -cua *f*

venture¹ [ˈvɛntʃər] *v* **-tured; -turing** *vt* **1** RISK : arriesgar **2** OFFER : aventurar ⟨to venture an opinion : aventurar una opinión⟩ — *vi* : arriesgarse, atreverse, aventurarse

venture² *n* **1** UNDERTAKING : empresa *f* **2** GAMBLE, RISK : aventura *f*, riesgo *m*

venturesome [ˈvɛntʃərsəm] *adj* **1** ADVENTUROUS : audaz, atrevido **2** RISKY : arriesgado

venue [ˈvɛnˌjuː] *n* **1** PLACE : lugar *m* **2** : jurisdicción *f* (en derecho)

Venus [ˈviːnəs] *n* : Venus *m*

veracity [vəˈræsəti] *n*, *pl* **-ties** : veracidad *f*

veranda *or* **verandah** [vəˈrændə] *n* : terraza *f*, veranda *f*

verb [ˈvərb] *n* : verbo *m*

verbal [ˈvərbəl] *adj* : verbal

verbalize [ˈvərbəˌlaɪz] *vt* **-ized; -izing** : expresar con palabras, verbalizar

verbally [ˈvərbəli] *adv* : verbalmente, de palabra

verbatim¹ [vərˈbeɪtəm] *adv* : palabra por palabra, textualmente

verbatim² *adj* : literal, textual

verbose [vərˈboːs] *adj* : verboso, prolijo

verdant [ˈvərdənt] *adj* : verde, verdeante

verdict [ˈvərdɪkt] *n* **1** : veredicto *m* (de un jurado) **2** JUDGMENT, OPINION : juicio *m*, opinión *f*

verge¹ [ˈvərdʒ] *vi* **verged; verging** : estar al borde, rayar ⟨it verges on madness : raya en la locura⟩

verge² *n* **1** EDGE : borde *m* **2 to be on the verge of** : estar a pique de, estar al borde de, estar a punto de

verification [ˌvɛrəfəˈkeɪʃən] *n* : verificación *f*

verify [ˈvɛrəˌfaɪ] *vt* **-fied; -fying** : verificar, comprobar, confirmar

veritable [ˈvɛrətəbəl] *adj* : verdadero, **veritably** *adv*

vermicelli [ˌvərməˈtʃɛli, -ˈsɛli] *n* : fideos *mpl* finos

vermin [ˈvərmən] *ns & pl* : alimañas *fpl*, bichos *mpl*, sabandijas *fpl*

vermouth [vərˈmuːθ] *n* : vermut *m*

vernacular¹ [vərˈnækjələr] *adj* : vernáculo

vernacular² *n* : lengua *f* vernácula

versatile [ˈvərsətəl] *adj* : versátil

versatility [ˌvərsəˈtɪləti] *n* : versatilidad *f*

verse [ˈvərs] *n* **1** LINE, STANZA : verso *m*, estrofa *f* **2** POETRY : poesía *f* **3** : versículo *m* (en la Biblia)

versed [ˈvərst] *adj* : versado ⟨to be well versed in : ser muy versado en⟩

version [ˈvərʒən] *n* : versión *f*

versus [ˈvərsəs] *prep* : versus

vertebra [ˈvərtəbrə] *n*, *pl* **-brae** [-ˌbreɪ, -ˌbriː] *or* **-bras** : vértebra *f*

vertebrate¹ [ˈvərtəbrət, -ˌbreɪt] *adj* : vertebrado

vertebrate² *n* : vertebrado *m*

vertex [ˈvərˌtɛks] *n*, *pl* **vertices** [ˈvərtəˌsiːz] **1** : vértice *m* (en matemáticas y anatomía) **2** SUMMIT, TOP : ápice *m*, cumbre *f*, cima *f*

vertical¹ [ˈvərtɪkəl] *adj* : vertical — **vertically** *adv*

vertical² *n* : vertical *f*

vertigo [ˈvərtɪˌgoː] *n*, *pl* **-goes** *or* **-gos** : vértigo *m*

verve [ˈvərv] *n* : brío *m*

very¹ [ˈvɛri] *adv* **1** EXTREMELY : muy, sumamente ⟨very few : muy pocos⟩ ⟨I am very sorry : lo siento mucho⟩ **2** (*used for emphasis*) ⟨at the very least : por lo menos, como mínimo⟩ ⟨the very same dress : el mismo vestido⟩

very² *adj* **verier; -est 1** EXACT, PRECISE : mismo, exacto ⟨at that very moment : en ese mismo momento⟩ ⟨it's the very thing : es justo lo que hacía falta⟩ **2** BARE, MERE : solo, mero ⟨the very thought of it : sólo pensarlo⟩ **3** EXTREME : extremo, de todo ⟨at the very top : arriba de todo⟩

vesicle [ˈvɛsɪkəl] *n* : vesícula *f*

vespers [ˈvɛspərz] *npl* : vísperas *fpl*

vessel [ˈvɛsəl] *n* **1** CONTAINER : vasija *f*, recipiente *m* **2** BOAT, CRAFT : nave *f*, barco *m*, buque *m* **3** : vaso *m* ⟨blood vessel : vaso sanguíneo⟩

vest¹ [ˈvɛst] *vt* **1** CONFER : conferir ⟨to vest authority in : conferirle la autoridad a⟩ **2** CLOTHE : vestir

vest² *n* **1** : chaleco *m* **2** UNDERSHIRT : camiseta *f*

vestibule [ˈvɛstəˌbjuːl] *n* : vestíbulo *m*

vestige [ˈvɛstɪdʒ] *n* : vestigio *m*, rastro *m*

vestment [ˈvɛstmənt] *n* : vestidura *f*

vestry [ˈvɛstri] *n*, *pl* **-tries** : sacristía *f*

vet [ˈvɛt] *n* **1** → **veterinarian 2** → **veteran**

veteran¹ [ˈvɛtərən, ˈvɛtrən] *adj* : veterano

veteran² *n* : veterano *m*, -na *f*

Veterans Day *n* : día *m* del Armisticio (celebrado el 11 de noviembre en los Estados Unidos)

veterinarian [ˌvɛtərəˈnɛriən, ˌvɛtəˈnɛr-] *n* : veterinario *m*, -ria *f*

veterinary [ˈvɛtərəˌnɛri] *adj* : veterinario

veto¹ [ˈviːtoː] *vt* **1** FORBID : prohibir **2** : vetar ⟨to veto a bill : vetar un proyecto de ley⟩

veto² *n, pl* **-toes 1** : veto *m* ⟨the power of veto : el derecho de veto⟩ **2** BAN : veto *m*, prohibición *f*

vex ['vɛks] *vt* : contrariar, molestar, irritar

vexation [vɛk'seɪʃən] *n* : contrariedad *f*, irritación *f*

via ['vaɪə, 'viːə] *prep* : por, vía

viability [ˌvaɪə'bɪləti] *n* : viabilidad *f*

viable ['vaɪəbəl] *adj* : viable

viaduct ['vaɪəˌdʌkt] *n* : viaducto *m*

vial ['vaɪəl] *n* : frasco *m*

vibrant ['vaɪbrənt] *adj* **1** LIVELY : vibrante, animado, dinámico **2** BRIGHT : fuerte, vivo (dícese de los colores)

vibrate ['vaɪˌbreɪt] *vi* **-brated; -brating 1** OSCILLATE : vibrar, oscilar **2** THRILL : bullir ⟨to vibrate with excitement : bullir de emoción⟩

vibration [vaɪ'breɪʃən] *n* : vibración *f*

vicar ['vɪkər] *n* : vicario *m*, -ria *f*

vicarious [vaɪ'kæriːəs, vɪ-] *adj* : indirecto — **vicariously** *adv*

vice ['vaɪs] *n* : vicio *m*

vice admiral *n* : vicealmirante *mf*

vice president *n* : vicepresidente *m*, -ta *f*

viceroy ['vaɪsˌrɔɪ] *n* : virrey *m*, -rreina *f*

vice versa [ˌvaɪsi'vərsə, ˌvaɪs'vər-] *adv* : viceversa

vicinity [və'sɪnəti] *n, pl* **-ties 1** NEIGHBORHOOD : vecindad *f*, inmediaciones *fpl* **2** NEARNESS : proximidad *f*

vicious ['vɪʃəs] *adj* **1** DEPRAVED : depravado, malo **2** SAVAGE : malo, fiero, salvaje ⟨a vicious dog : un perro feroz⟩ **3** MALICIOUS : malicioso

viciously ['vɪʃəsli] *adv* : con saña, brutalmente

viciousness ['vɪʃəsnəs] *n* : brutalidad *f*, ferocidad *f* (de un animal), malevolencia *f* (de un comentario, etc.)

vicissitudes [və'sɪsəˌtuːdz, vaɪ-, -ˌtjuːdz] *npl* : vicisitudes *fpl*

victim ['vɪktəm] *n* : víctima *f*

victimize ['vɪktəˌmaɪz] *vt* **-mized; -mizing** : tomar como víctima, perseguir, victimizar *Arg, Mex*

victor ['vɪktər] *n* : vencedor *m*, -dora *f*

Victorian [vɪk'toːriən] *adj* : victoriano

victorious [vɪk'toːriəs] *adj* : victorioso — **victoriously** *adv*

victory ['vɪktəri] *n, pl* **-ries** : victoria *f*, triunfo *m*

victuals ['vɪtəlz] *npl* : víveres *mpl*, provisiones *fpl*

video¹ ['vɪdiˌoː] *adj* : de video ⟨video recording : grabación de video⟩

video² *n* **1** : video *m* (medio o grabación) **2** → **videotape²**

video camera *n* : videocámara *f*

videocassette [ˌvɪdiokə'sɛt] *n* : videocasete *m*, videocassette *m*

videocassette recorder → **VCR**

video game *n* : videojuego *m*, juego *m* de video

videotape¹ ['vɪdioˌteɪp] *vt* **-taped; -taping** : grabar en video, videograbar

videotape² *n* : videocinta *f*

vie ['vaɪ] *vi* **vied; vying** ['vaɪɪŋ] : competir, rivalizar

Vietnamese [viˌɛtnə'miːz, -'miːs] *n* **1** : vietnamita *mf* **2** : vietnamita *m* (idioma) — **Vietnamese** *adj*

view¹ ['vjuː] *vt* **1** OBSERVE : mirar, ver, observar **2** CONSIDER : considerar, contemplar

view² *n* **1** SIGHT : vista *f* ⟨to come into view : aparecer⟩ **2** ATTITUDE, OPINION : opinión *f*, parecer *m*, actitud *f* ⟨in my view : en mi opinión⟩ **3** SCENE : vista *f*, panorama *f* **4** INTENTION : idea *f*, vista *f* ⟨with a view to : con vistas a, con la idea de⟩ **5** in view of : dado que, en vista de (que)

viewer ['vjuːər] *n or* **television viewer** : telespectador *m*, -dora *f*; televidente *mf*

viewpoint ['vjuːˌpɔɪnt] *n* : punto *m* de vista

vigil ['vɪdʒəl] *n* **1** : vigilia *f*, vela *f* **2 to keep vigil** : velar

vigilance ['vɪdʒələnts] *n* : vigilancia *f*

vigilant ['vɪdʒələnt] *adj* : vigilante

vigilante [ˌvɪdʒə'læn,ti] *n* : integrante *mf* de un comité de vigilancia (que actúa como policía)

vigilantly ['vɪdʒələntli] *adv* : con vigilancia

vigor ['vɪgər] *n* : vigor *m*, energía *f*, fuerza *f*

vigorous ['vɪgərəs] *adj* : vigoroso, enérgico — **vigorously** *adv*

Viking ['vaɪkɪŋ] *n* : vikingo *m*, -ga *f*

vile ['vaɪl] *adj* **viler; vilest 1** WICKED : vil, infame **2** REVOLTING : asqueroso, repugnante **3** TERRIBLE : horrible, atroz ⟨vile weather : tiempo horrible⟩ ⟨to be in a vile mood : estar de un humor de perros⟩

vilify ['vɪləˌfaɪ] *vt* **-fied; -fying** : vilipendiar, denigrar, difamar

villa ['vɪlə] *n* : casa *f* de campo, quinta *f*

village ['vɪlɪdʒ] *n* : pueblo *m* (grande), aldea *f* (pequeña)

villager ['vɪlɪdʒər] *n* : vecino *m*, -na *f* (de un pueblo); aldeano *m*, -na *f* (de una aldea)

villain ['vɪlən] *n* : villano *m*, -na *f*; malo *m*, -la *f* (en ficción, películas, etc.)

villainess ['vɪlənəs, -ˌnɛs] *n* : villana *f*

villainous ['vɪlənəs] *adj* : infame, malvado

villainy ['vɪləni] *n, pl* **-lainies** : vileza *f*, maldad *f*

vim ['vɪm] *n* : brío *m*, vigor *m*, energía *f*

vindicate ['vɪndəˌkeɪt] *vt* **-cated; -cating 1** EXONERATE : vindicar, disculpar **2** JUSTIFY : justificar

vindication [ˌvɪndə'keɪʃən] *n* : vindicación *f*, justificación *f*

vindictive [vɪn'dɪktɪv] *adj* : vengativo

vine ['vaɪn] *n* **1** GRAPEVINE : vid *f*, parra *f* **2** : planta *f* trepadora, enredadera *f*

vinegar ['vɪnɪgər] *n* : vinagre *m*

vinegary ['vɪnɪgəri] *adj* : avinagrado
vineyard ['vɪnjərd] *n* : viña *f*, viñedo *m*
vintage¹ ['vɪntɪʤ] *adj* **1** : añejo (dícese de un vino) **2** CLASSIC : clásico, de época
vintage² *n* **1** : cosecha *f* ⟨the 1947 vintage : la cosecha de 1947⟩ **2** ERA : época *f*, era *f* ⟨slang of recent vintage : argot de la época reciente⟩
vinyl ['vaɪnəl] *n* : vinilo
viola [vi:'o:lə] *n* : viola *f*
violate ['vaɪə,leɪt] *vt* **-lated; -lating 1** BREAK : infringir, violar, quebrantar ⟨to violate the rules : violar las reglas⟩ **2** RAPE : violar **3** DESECRATE : profanar
violation [,vaɪə'leɪʃən] *n* **1** : violación *f*, infracción *f* (de una ley) **2** DESECRATION : profanación *f*
violence ['vaɪələns, 'vaɪ-] *n* : violencia *f*
violent ['vaɪlənt, 'vaɪə-] *adj* : violento
violently ['vaɪləntli, 'vaɪə-] *adv* : violentamente, con violencia
violet ['vaɪlət, 'vaɪə-] *n* : violeta *f*
violin [,vaɪə'lɪn] *n* : violín *m*
violinist [,vaɪə'lɪnɪst] *n* : violinista *mf*
violoncello [,vaɪələn't'ɛlo:, ,vi:-] → **cello**
VIP [,vi:,aɪ'pi:] *n, pl* **VIPs** [-'pi:z] : VIP *mf*, persona *f* de categoría
viper ['vaɪpər] *n* : víbora *f*
viral ['vaɪrəl] *adj* : viral, vírico ⟨viral pneumonia : pulmonía viral⟩
virgin¹ ['vərʤən] *adj* **1** CHASTE : virginal ⟨the virgin birth : el alumbramiento virginal⟩ **2** : virgen, intacto ⟨a virgin forest : una selva virgen⟩ ⟨virgin wool : lana virgen⟩
virgin² *n* : virgen *mf*
virginity [vər'ʤɪnəti] *n* : virginidad *f*
Virgo ['vər,go:, 'vɪr-] *n* : Virgo *mf*
virile ['vɪrəl, -,aɪl] *adj* : viril, varonil
virility [və'rɪləti] *n* : virilidad *f*
virtual ['vərtʃuəl] *adj* : virtual ⟨a virtual dictator : un virtual dictador⟩ ⟨virtual reality : realidad virtual⟩
virtually ['vərtʃuəli, 'vərtʃəli] *adv* : en realidad, de hecho, casi
virtue ['vər,tʃu:] *n* **1** : virtud *f* **2 by virtue of** : en virtud de, debido a
virtuosity [,vərtʃu'asəti] *n, pl* **-ties** : virtuosismo *m*
virtuoso [,vərtʃu'o:so:, -zo:] *n, pl* **-sos** or **-si** [-,si:, -,zi:] : virtuoso *m*, -sa *f*
virtuous ['vərtʃuəs] *adj* : virtuoso, bueno — **virtuously** *adv*
virulence ['vɪrələns, 'vɪrjə-] *n* : virulencia *f*
virulent ['vɪrələnt, 'vɪrjə-] *adj* : virulento
virus ['vaɪrəs] *n* : virus *m*
visa ['vi:zə, -sə] *n* : visa *f*
vis-à-vis [,vi:zə'vi:, -sə-] *prep* : con relación a, con respecto a
viscera ['vɪsərə] *npl* : vísceras *fpl*
visceral ['vɪsərəl] *adj* : visceral
viscosity [vɪs'kasəti] *n, pl* **-ties** : viscosidad *f*
viscount ['vaɪ,kæunt] *n* : vizconde *m*

viscountess ['vaɪ,kæuntɪs] *n* : vizcondesa *f*
viscous ['vɪskəs] *adj* : viscoso
vise ['vaɪs] *n* : torno *m* de banco, tornillo *m* de banco
visibility [,vɪzə'bɪləti] *n, pl* **-ties** : visibilidad *f*
visible ['vɪzəbəl] *adj* **1** : visible ⟨the visible stars : las estrellas visibles⟩ **2** OBVIOUS : evidente, patente
visibly ['vɪzəbli] *adv* : visiblemente
vision ['vɪʒən] *n* **1** EYESIGHT : vista *f*, visión *f* **2** APPARITION : visión *f*, aparición *f* **3** FORESIGHT : visión *f* (del futuro), previsión *f* **4** IMAGE : imagen *f* ⟨she had visions of a disaster : se imaginaba un desastre⟩
visionary¹ ['vɪʒə,neri] *adj* **1** FARSIGHTED : visionario, con visión de futuro **2** UTOPIAN : utópico, poco realista
visionary² *n, pl* **-ries** : visionario *m*, -ria *f*
visit¹ ['vɪzət] *vt* **1** : visitar, ir a ver **2** AFFLICT : azotar, afligir ⟨visited by troubles : afligido con problemas⟩ — *vi* : hacer (una) visita
visit² *n* : visita *f*
visitor ['vɪzətər] *n* : visitante *mf* (a una ciudad, etc.), visita *f* (a una casa)
visor ['vaɪzər] *n* : visera *f*
vista ['vɪstə] *n* : vista *f*
visual ['vɪʒuəl] *adj* : visual ⟨the visual arts : las artes visuales⟩ — **visually** *adv*
visualize ['vɪʒuə,laɪz] *vt* **-ized; -izing** : visualizar, imaginarse, hacerse una idea de — **visualization** [,vɪʒəwələ-'zeɪʃən] *n*
vital ['vaɪtəl] *adj* **1** : vital ⟨vital organs : órganos vitales⟩ **2** CRUCIAL : esencial, crucial, decisivo ⟨of vital importance : de suma importancia⟩ **3** LIVELY : enérgico, lleno de vida, vital
vitality [vaɪ'tæləti] *n, pl* **-ties** : vitalidad *f*, energía *f*
vitally ['vaɪtəli] *adv* : sumamente
vital statistics *npl* : estadísticas *fpl* demográficas
vitamin ['vaɪtəmən] *n* : vitamina *f* ⟨vitamin deficiency : carencia vitamínica⟩
vitreous ['vɪtriəs] *adj* : vítreo
vitriolic [,vɪtri'alɪk] *adj* : mordaz, virulento
vituperation [vaɪ,tu:pə'reɪʃən, -,tju:-] *n* : vituperio *m*
vivacious [və'veɪʃəs, vaɪ-] *adj* : vivaz, animado, lleno de vida
vivaciously [və'veɪʃəsli, vaɪ-] *adv* : con vivacidad, animadamente
vivacity [və'væsəti, vaɪ-] *n* : vivacidad *f*
vivid ['vɪvəd] *adj* **1** LIVELY : lleno de vitalidad **2** BRILLIANT : vivo, intenso ⟨vivid colors : colores vivos⟩ **3** INTENSE, SHARP : vívido, gráfico ⟨a vivid dream : un sueño vívido⟩
vividly ['vɪvədli] *adv* **1** BRIGHTLY : con colores vivos **2** SHARPLY : vívidamente
vividness ['vɪvədnəs] *n* **1** BRIGHTNESS : intensidad *f*, viveza *f* **2** SHARPNESS : lo gráfico, nitidez *f*

vivisection [ˌvɪvəˈsɛkʃən, ˈvɪvəˌ-] *n* : vivisección *f*

vixen [ˈvɪksən] *n* : zorra *f*, raposa *f*

vocabulary [voˈkæbjəˌlɛri] *n, pl* **-laries 1** : vocabulario *m* **2** LEXICON : léxico *m*

vocal [ˈvoːkəl] *adj* **1** : vocal **2** LOUD, OUTSPOKEN : ruidoso, muy franco

vocal cords *npl* : cuerdas *fpl* vocales

vocalist [ˈvoːkəlɪst] *n* : cantante *mf*, vocalista *mf*

vocalize [ˈvoːkəlˌaɪz] *vt* **-ized; -izing** : vocalizar

vocation [voˈkeɪʃən] *n* : vocación *f* ⟨to have a vocation for : tener vocación de⟩

vocational [voˈkeɪʃənəl] *adj* : profesional ⟨vocational guidance : orientación profesional⟩

vociferous [voˈsɪfərəs] *adj* : ruidoso, vociferante

vodka [ˈvɑdkə] *n* : vodka *m*

vogue [ˈvoːɡ] *n* : moda *f*, boga *f* ⟨to be in vogue : estar de moda, estar en boga⟩

voice¹ [ˈvɔɪs] *vt* **voiced; voicing** : expresar

voice² *n* **1** : voz *f* ⟨in a low voice : en voz baja⟩ ⟨to lose one's voice : quedarse sin voz⟩ ⟨the voice of the people : la voz del pueblo⟩ **2** to make one's voice heard : hacerse oír

voice box → larynx

voiced [ˈvɔɪst] *adj* : sonoro

voice mail *n* : correo *m* de voz

void¹ [ˈvɔɪd] *vt* : anular, invalidar ⟨to void a contract : anular un contrato⟩

void² *adj* **1** EMPTY : vacío, desprovisto ⟨void of content : desprovisto de contenido⟩ **2** INVALID : inválido, nulo

void³ *n* : vacío *m*

volatile [ˈvɑlətəl] *adj* : volátil, inestable

volatility [ˌvɑləˈtɪləti] *n* : volatilidad *f*, inestabilidad *f*

volcanic [vɑlˈkænɪk] *adj* : volcánico

volcano [vɑlˈkeɪˌnoː] *n, pl* **-noes** *or* **-nos** : volcán *m*

vole [ˈvoːl] *n* : campañol *m*

volition [voˈlɪʃən] *n* : volición *f*, voluntad *f* ⟨of one's own volition : por voluntad propia⟩

volley [ˈvɑli] *n, pl* **-leys 1** : descarga *f* (de tiros) **2** : torrente *m*, lluvia *f* (de insultos, etc.) **3** : salva *f* (de aplausos) **4** : volea *f* (en deportes)

volleyball [ˈvɑliˌbɔl] *n* : voleibol *m*

volt [ˈvoːlt] *n* : voltio *m*

voltage [ˈvoːltɪdʒ] *n* : voltaje *m*

volubility [ˌvɑljəˈbɪləti] *n* : locuacidad *f*

voluble [ˈvɑljəbəl] *adj* : locuaz

volume [ˈvɑljəm, -ˌjuːm] *n* **1** BOOK : volumen *m*, tomo *m* **2** SPACE : capacidad *f*, volumen *m* (en física) **3** AMOUNT : cantidad *f*, volumen *m* **4** LOUDNESS : volumen *m*

voluminous [vəˈluːmənəs] *adj* : voluminoso

voluntary [ˈvɑlənˌtɛri] *adj* : voluntario — **voluntarily** [ˌvɑlənˈtɛrəli] *adv*

volunteer¹ [ˌvɑlənˈtɪr] *vt* : ofrecer, dar ⟨to volunteer one's assistance : ofrecer la ayuda⟩ — *vi* : ofrecerse, alistarse como voluntario

volunteer² *n* : voluntario *m*, -ria *f*

voluptuous [vəˈlʌptʃuəs] *adj* : voluptuoso

vomit¹ [ˈvɑmət] *v* : vomitar

vomit² *n* : vómito *m*

voodoo [ˈvuːˌduː] *n, pl* **voodoos** : vudú *m*

voracious [voˈreɪʃəs, və-] *adj* : voraz

voraciously [voˈreɪʃəsli, və-] *adv* : vorazmente, con voracidad

vortex [ˈvɔrˌtɛks] *n, pl* **vortices** [ˈvɔrtəˌsiːz] : vórtice *m*

vote¹ [ˈvoːt] *vi* **voted; voting** : votar ⟨to vote Democratic : votar por los demócratas⟩

vote² *n* **1** : voto *m* **2** SUFFRAGE : sufragio *m*, derecho *m* al voto

voter [ˈvoːtər] *n* : votante *mf*

voting [ˈvoːtɪŋ] *n* : votación *f*

vouch [ˈvaʊtʃ] *vi* to vouch for : garantizar (algo), responder de (algo), responder por (alguien)

voucher [ˈvaʊtʃər] *n* **1** RECEIPT : comprobante *m* **2** : vale *m* ⟨travel voucher : vale de viajar⟩

vow¹ [ˈvaʊ] *vt* : jurar, prometer, hacer voto de

vow² *n* : promesa *f*, voto *m* (en la religión) ⟨a vow of poverty : un voto de pobreza⟩

vowel [ˈvaʊəl] *n* : vocal *f*

voyage¹ [ˈvɔɪɪdʒ] *vi* **-aged; -aging** : viajar

voyage² *n* : viaje *m*

voyager [ˈvɔɪɪdʒər] *n* : viajero *m*, -ra *f*

vulcanize [ˈvʌlkəˌnaɪz] *vt* **-nized; -nizing** : vulcanizar

vulgar [ˈvʌlɡər] *adj* **1** COMMON, PLEBIAN : ordinario, populachero, del vulgo **2** COARSE, CRUDE : grosero, de mal gusto, majadero *Mex* **3** INDECENT : indecente, colorado (dícese de un chiste, etc.)

vulgarity [ˌvʌlˈɡærəti] *n, pl* **-ties** : grosería *f*, vulgaridad *f*

vulgarly [ˈvʌlɡərli] *adv* : vulgarmente, groseramente

vulnerability [ˌvʌlnərəˈbɪləti] *n, pl* **-ties** : vulnerabilidad *f*

vulnerable [ˈvʌlnərəbəl] *adj* : vulnerable

vulture [ˈvʌltʃər] *n* : buitre *m*, zopilote *m* CA, Mex

vying → vie

W

w ['dʌbəl,ju:] *n*, *pl* **w's** *or* **ws** [-ju:z] : vigésima tercera letra del alfabeto inglés

wad¹ ['wɑd] *vt* **wadded; wadding 1** : hacer un taco con, formar en una masa **2** STUFF : rellenar

wad² *n* : taco *m* (de papel), bola *f* (de algodón, etc.), fajo *m* (de billetes)

waddle¹ ['wɑdəl] *vi* **-dled; -dling** : andar como un pato

waddle² *n* : andar *m* de pato

wade ['weɪd] *v* **waded; wading** *vi* **1** : caminar por el agua **2 to wade through** : leer (algo) con dificultad — *vt or* **to wade across** : vadear

wading bird *n* : zancuda *f*, ave *f* zancuda

wafer ['weɪfər] *n* : barquillo *m*, galleta *f* de barquillo

waffle ['wɑfəl] *n* **1** : wafle *m* **2 waffle iron** : waflera *f*

waft ['wɑft, 'wæft] *vt* : llevar por el aire — *vi* : flotar

wag¹ ['wæg] *v* **wagged; wagging** *vt* : menear — *vi* : menearse, moverse

wag² *n* **1** : meneo *m* (de la cola) **2** JOKER, WIT : bromista *mf*

wage¹ ['weɪʤ] *vt* **waged; waging** : hacer, librar ⟨to wage war : hacer la guerra⟩

wage² *n or* **wages** *npl* : sueldo *m*, salario *m* ⟨minimum wage : salario mínimo⟩

wager¹ ['weɪʤər] *v* : apostar

wager² *n* : apuesta *f*

waggish ['wægɪʃ] *adj* : burlón, bromista (dícese de una persona), chistoso (dícese de un comentario)

waggle ['wægəl] *vt* **-gled; -gling** : menear, mover (de un lado a otro)

wagon ['wægən] *n* **1** : carro *m* (tirado por caballos) **2** CART : carrito *m* **3** → **station wagon**

waif ['weɪf] *n* : niño *m* abandonado, animal *m* sin hogar

wail¹ ['weɪl] *vi* : gemir, lamentarse

wail² *n* : gemido *m*, lamento *m*

wainscot ['weɪnskət, -,skɑt, -,sko:t] *or* **wainscoting** [-skətɪŋ, -,skɑ-, -,sko:-] *n* : boiserie *f*, revestimiento *m* de paneles de madera

waist ['weɪst] *n* : cintura *f* (del cuerpo humano), talle *m* (de ropa)

waistline ['weɪst,laɪn] → **waist**

wait¹ ['weɪt] *vi* : esperar ⟨to wait for something : esperar algo⟩ ⟨wait and see! : ¡espera y verás!⟩ ⟨I can't wait : me muero de ganas⟩ — *vt* **1** AWAIT : esperar **2** DELAY : retrasar ⟨don't wait lunch : no retrase el almuerzo⟩ **3** SERVE : servir, atender ⟨to wait tables : servir (a la mesa)⟩

wait² *n* **1** : espera *f* **2 to lie in wait** : estar al acecho

waiter ['weɪt̬ər] *n* : mesero *m*, camarero *m*, mozo *m Arg, Chile, Col, Peru*

waiting room *n* : sala *f* de espera

waitress ['weɪtrəs] *n* : mesera *f*, camarera *f*, moza *f Arg, Chile, Col, Peru*

waive ['weɪv] *vt* **waived; waiving** : renunciar a ⟨to waive one's rights : renunciar a sus derechos⟩ ⟨to waive the rules : no aplicar las reglas⟩

waiver ['weɪvər] *n* : renuncia *f*

wake¹ ['weɪk] *v* **woke** ['wo:k]; **woken** ['wo:kən] *or* **waked; waking** *vi or* **to wake up** : despertar(se) ⟨he woke at noon : se despertó al mediodía⟩ ⟨wake up! : ¡despiértate!⟩ — *vt* : despertar

wake² *n* **1** VIGIL : velatorio *m*, velorio *m* (de un difunto) **2** TRAIL : estela *f* (de un barco, un huracán, etc.) **3** AFTERMATH : consecuencias *fpl* ⟨in the wake of : tras, como consecuencia de⟩

wakeful ['weɪkfəl] *adj* **1** SLEEPLESS : desvelado **2** VIGILANT : alerta, vigilante

waken ['weɪkən] → **awake**

walk¹ ['wɔk] *vi* **1** : caminar, andar, pasear ⟨you're walking too fast : estás caminando demasiado rápido⟩ ⟨to walk around the city : pasearse por la ciudad⟩ **2** : ir andando, ir a pie ⟨we had to walk home : tuvimos que ir a casa a pie⟩ **3** : darle base por bolas (a un bateador) — *vt* **1** : recorrer, caminar ⟨she walked two miles : caminó dos millas⟩ **2** ACCOMPANY : acompañar **3** : sacar a pasear (a un perro)

walk² *n* **1** : paseo *m*, caminata *f* ⟨to go for a walk : ir a caminar, dar un paseo⟩ **2** PATH : camino *m* **3** GAIT : andar *m* **4** : marcha *f* (en beisbol) **5 walk of life** : esfera *f*, condición *f*

walker ['wɔkər] *n* **1** : paseante *mf* **2** HIKER : excursionista *mf* **3** : andador *m* (aparato)

walking stick *n* : bastón *m*

walkout ['wɔk,aʊt] *n* STRIKE : huelga *f*

walk out *vi* **1** STRIKE : declararse en huelga **2** LEAVE : salir, irse **3 to walk out on** : abandonar, dejar

walkway ['wɔk,weɪ] *n* **1** SIDEWALK : ácera *f* **2** PATH : sendero *m* **3** PASSAGEWAY : pasadizo *m*

wall¹ ['wɔl] *vt* **1 to wall in** : cercar con una pared o un muro, tapiar, amurallar **2 to wall off** : separar con una pared o un muro **3 to wall up** : tapiar, condenar (una ventana, etc.)

wall² *n* **1** : muro *m* (exterior) ⟨the walls of the city : las murallas de la ciudad⟩ **2** : pared *f* (interior) **3** BARRIER : barrera *f* ⟨a wall of mountains : una barrera de montañas⟩ **4** : pared *f* (en anatomía)

wallaby ['wɑləbi] *n*, *pl* **-bies** : ualabí *m*

walled ['wɔld] *adj* : amurallado

wallet ['wɑlət] *n* : billetera *f*, cartera *f*

wallflower ['wɔl,flaʊər] *n* **1** : alhelí *m* (flor) **2 to be a wallflower** : comer pavo

wallop ['wɑləp] *vt* **1** TROUNCE : darle una paliza (a alguien) **2** SOCK : pegar fuerte

wallop² *n* : golpe *m* fuerte, golpazo *m*

wallow¹ ['wɑ,lo:] *vi* **1** ⟨to wallow in the mud : revolcarse en el lodo⟩ **2** DELIGHT : deleitarse ⟨to wallow in luxury : nadar en lujos⟩

wallow² *n* : revolcadero *m* (para animales)

wallpaper¹ ['wɔl,peɪpər] *vt* : empapelar

wallpaper² *n* : papel *m* pintado

walnut ['wɔl,nʌt] *n* **1** : nuez *f* (fruta) **2** : nogal *m* (árbol y madera)

walrus ['wɔlrəs, 'wɑl-] *n, pl* **-rus** *or* **-ruses** : morsa *f*

waltz¹ ['wɔlts] *vi* **1** : valsar, bailar el vals **2** BREEZE : pasar con ligereza ⟨to waltz in : entrar tan campante⟩

waltz² *n* : vals *m*

wan ['wɑn] *adj* **wanner; -est 1** PALLID : pálido **2** DIM : tenue ⟨wan light : luz tenue⟩ **3** LANGUID : lánguido ⟨a wan smile : una sonrisa lánguida⟩ — **wanly** *adv*

wand ['wɑnd] *n* : varita *f* (mágica)

wander ['wɑndər] *vi* **1** RAMBLE : deambular, vagar, vagabundear **2** STRAY : alejarse, desviarse, divagar ⟨she let her mind wander : dejó vagar la imaginación⟩ — *vt* : recorrer ⟨to wander the streets : vagar por las calles⟩

wanderer ['wɑndərər] *n* : vagabundo *m*, -da *f*; viajero *m*, -ra *f*

wanderlust ['wɑndər,lʌst] *n* : pasión *f* por viajar

wane¹ ['weɪn] *vi* **waned; waning 1** : menguar (dícese de la luna) **2** DECLINE : disminuir, decaer, menguar

wane² *n* **on the wane** : decayendo, en decadencia

wangle ['wæŋɡəl] *vt* **-gled; -gling** FINAGLE : arreglárselas para conseguir

wannabe ['wɑnə,bi:] *n* : aspirante *mf* (a algo); imitador *m*, -dora *f* (de alguien)

want¹ ['wɑnt, 'wɔnt] *vt* **1** LACK : faltar **2** REQUIRE : requerir, necesitar **3** DESIRE : querer, desear

want² *n* **1** LACK : falta *f* **2** DESTITUTION : indigencia *f*, miseria *f* **3** DESIRE, NEED : deseo *m*, necesidad *f*

wanting ['wɑntɪŋ, 'wɔn-] *adj* **1** ABSENT : ausente **2** DEFICIENT : deficiente ⟨he's wanting in common sense : le falta sentido común⟩

wanton ['wɑntən, 'wɔn-] *adj* **1** LEWD, LUSTFUL : lascivo, lujurioso, licencioso **2** INHUMANE, MERCILESS : despiadado ⟨wanton cruelty : crueldad despiadada⟩

wapiti ['wɑpəti] *n, pl* **-ti** *or* **-tis** : uapití *m*

war¹ ['wɔr] *vi* **warred; warring** : combatir, batallar, hacer la guerra

war² *n* : guerra *f* ⟨to go to war : entrar en guerra⟩

warble¹ ['wɔrbəl] *vi* **-bled; -bling** : gorjear, trinar

warble² *n* : trino *m*, gorjeo *m*

warbler ['wɔrblər] *n* : pájaro *m* gorjeador, curruca *f*

ward¹ ['wɔrd] *vt* **to ward off** : desviar, protegerse contra

ward² *n* **1** : sala *f* (de un hospital, etc.) ⟨maternity ward : sala de maternidad⟩ **2** : distrito *m* electoral o administrativo (de una ciudad) **3** : pupilo *m*, -la *f* (de un tutor, etc.)

warden ['wɔrdən] *n* **1** KEEPER : guarda *mf*; guardián *m*, -diana *f* ⟨game warden : guardabosque⟩ **2** *or* **prison warden** : alcaide *m*

wardrobe ['wɔrd,ro:b] *n* **1** CLOSET : armario *m* **2** CLOTHES : vestuario *m*, guardarropa *f*

ware ['wær] *n* **1** POTTERY : cerámica *f* **2 wares** *npl* GOODS : mercancía *f*, mercadería *f*

warehouse ['wær,haus] *n* : depósito *m*, almacén *m*, bodega *f* Chile, Col, Mex

warfare ['wɔr,fær] *n* **1** WAR : guerra *f* **2** STRUGGLE : lucha *f* ⟨the warfare against drugs : la lucha contra las drogas⟩

warhead ['wɔr,hɛd] *n* : ojiva *f*, cabeza *f* (de un misil)

warily ['wærəli] *adv* : cautelosamente, con cautela

wariness ['wærinəs] *n* : cautela *f*

warlike ['wær,laɪk] *adj* : belicoso, guerrero

warm¹ ['wɔrm] *vt* **1** HEAT : calentar, recalentar **2 to warm one's heart** : reconfortar a uno, alegrar el corazón **3 to warm up** : calentar (los músculos, un automóvil, etc.) — *vi* **1** : calentarse **2 to warm to** : tomarle simpatía (a alguien), entusiasmarse con (algo)

warm² *adj* **1** LUKEWARM : tibio, templado **2** : caliente, cálido, caluroso ⟨a warm wind : un viento cálido⟩ ⟨a warm day : un día caluroso, un día de calor⟩ ⟨warm hands : manos calientes⟩ **3** : caliente, que abriga ⟨warm clothes : ropa de abrigo⟩ ⟨I feel warm : tengo calor⟩ **4** CARING, CORDIAL : cariñoso, cordial **5** : cálido (dícese de colores) **6** FRESH : fresco, reciente ⟨a warm trail : un rastro reciente⟩ **7** (*used for riddles*) : caliente

warm–blooded ['wɔrm'blʌdəd] *adj* : de sangre caliente

warmhearted ['wɔrm'hɑrtəd] *adj* : cariñoso

warmly ['wɔrmli] *adv* **1** AFFECTIONATELY : calurosamente, afectuosamente **2 to dress warmly** : abrigarse

warmonger ['wɔr,mɑŋɡər, -,mʌŋ-] *n* : belicista *mf*

warmth ['wɔrmθ] *n* **1** : calor *m* **2** AFFECTION : cariño *m*, afecto *m* **3** ENTHUSIASM : ardor *m*, entusiasmo *m*

warm–up ['wɔrm,ʌp] *n* : calentamiento *m*

warn ['wɔrn] *vt* **1** CAUTION : advertir, alertar **2** INFORM : avisar, informar

warning ['wɔrnɪŋ] *n* **1** ADVICE : advertencia *f*, aviso *m* **2** ALERT : alerta *f*, alarma *f*

warp¹ ['wɔrp] *vt* **1** : alabear, combar **2** PERVERT : pervertir, deformar — *vi* : pandearse, alabearse, combarse

warp² *n* **1** : urdimbre *f* ⟨the warp and the weft : la urdimbre y la trama⟩ **2** : alabeo *m* (en la madera, etc.)

warrant¹ ['wɔrənt] *vt* **1** ASSURE : asegurar, garantizar **2** GUARANTEE : garantizar **3** JUSTIFY, MERIT : justificar, merecer

warrant² *n* **1** AUTHORIZATION : autorización *f*, permiso *m* ⟨an arrest warrant : una orden de detención⟩ **2** JUSTIFICATION : justificación *f*

warranty ['wɔrənti, ˌwɔrən'ti:] *n, pl* **-ties** : garantía *f*

warren ['wɔrən] *n* : madriguera *f* (de conejos)

warrior ['wɔriər] *n* : guerrero *m*, -ra *f*

warship ['wɔrˌʃip] *n* : buque *m* de guerra

wart ['wɔrt] *n* : verruga *f*

wartime ['wɔrˌtaɪm] *n* : tiempo *m* de guerra

wary ['wæri] *adj* **warier; -est** : cauteloso, receloso ⟨to be wary of : desconfiar de⟩

was → be

wash¹ ['wɔʃ, 'wɑʃ] *vt* **1** CLEAN : lavar(se), limpiar, fregar ⟨to wash the dishes : lavar los platos⟩ ⟨to wash one's hands : lavarse las manos⟩ **2** DRENCH : mojar **3** LAP : bañar ⟨waves were washing the shore : las olas bañaban la orilla⟩ **4** CARRY, DRAG : arrastrar **5 to wash away** : llevarse (un puente, etc.) — *vi* **1** : lavarse (dícese de una persona o la ropa) ⟨the dress washes well : el vestido se lava bien⟩ **2 to wash against** *or* **to wash over** : bañar

wash² *n* **1** : lavado *m* ⟨to give something a wash : lavar algo⟩ **2** LAUNDRY : artículos *mpl* para lavar, ropa *f* sucia **3** : estela *f* (de un barco)

washable ['wɔʃəbəl, 'wɑ-] *adj* : lavable

washboard ['wɔʃˌbord, 'wɑʃ-] *n* : tabla *f* de lavar

washbowl ['wɔʃˌboːl, 'wɑʃ-] *n* : lavabo *m*, lavamanos *m*

washcloth ['wɔʃˌklɔθ, 'wɑʃ-] *n* : toallita *f* (para lavarse)

washed–out ['wɔʃt'aʊt, 'wɑʃt-] *adj* **1** : desvaído (dícese de colores) **2** EXHAUSTED : agotado, desanimado

washed–up ['wɔʃt'ʌp, 'wɑʃt-] *adj* : acabado (dícese de una persona), fracasado (dícese de un negocio, etc.)

washer ['wɔʃər, 'wɑ-] *n* **1 → washing machine 2** : arandela *f* (de una llave, etc.)

washing ['wɔʃɪŋ, 'wɑ-] *n* WASH : ropa *f* para lavar

washing machine *n* : máquina *f* de lavar, lavadora *f*

washout ['wɔʃˌaʊt, 'wɑʃ-] *n* **1** : erosión *f* (de la tierra) **2** FAILURE : fracaso *m* ⟨she's a washout : es un desastre⟩

washroom ['wɔʃˌruːm, 'wɑʃ-, -ˌrʊm] *n* : servicios *mpl* (públicos), baño *m*, sanitario *m* Col, Mex, Ven

wasn't ['wʌzənt] (*contraction of* was not) → be

wasp ['wɑsp] *n* : avispa *f*

waspish ['wɑspɪʃ] *adj* **1** IRRITABLE : irritable, irascible **2** CAUSTIC : cáustico, mordaz

waste¹ ['weɪst] *v* **wasted; wasting** *vt* **1** DEVASTATE : arrasar, arruinar, devastar **2** SQUANDER : desperdiciar, despilfarrar, malgastar ⟨to waste time : perder tiempo⟩ — *vi or* **to waste away** : consumirse, chuparse

waste² *adj* **1** BARREN : yermo, baldío **2** DISCARDED : de desecho **3** EXCESS : sobrante

waste³ *n* **1 → wasteland 2** MISUSE : derroche *m*, desperdicio *m*, despilfarro *m* ⟨a waste of time : una pérdida de tiempo⟩ **3** RUBBISH : basura *f*, desechos *mpl*, desperdicios *mpl* **4** EXCREMENT : excremento *m*

wastebasket ['weɪstˌbæskət] *n* : cesto *m* (de basura), papelera *f*, zafacón *m* Car

wasteful ['weɪstfəl] *adj* : despilfarrador, derrochador, pródigo

wastefulness ['weɪstfəlnəs] *n* : derroche *m*, despilfarro *m*

wasteland ['weɪstˌlænd, -lənd] *n* : baldío *m*, yermo *m*, desierto *m*

watch¹ ['wɑtʃ] *vi* **1 or to keep watch** : velar **2** OBSERVE : mirar, ver, observar **3 to watch for** : AWAIT : esperar, quedar a la espera de **4 to watch out** : tener cuidado ⟨watch out! : ¡ten cuidado!, ¡ojo!⟩ — *vt* **1** OBSERVE : mirar, observar **2 or to watch over** : vigilar, cuidar **3** : tener cuidado de ⟨watch what you do : ten cuidado con lo que haces⟩

watch² *n* **1** : guardia *f* ⟨to be on watch : estar de guardia⟩ **2** SURVEILLANCE : vigilancia *f* **3** LOOKOUT : guardia *mf*, centinela *m*, vigía *mf* **4** TIMEPIECE : reloj *m*

watchdog ['wɑtʃˌdɔg] *n* : perro *m* guardián

watcher ['wɑtʃər] *n* : observador *m*, -dora *f*

watchful ['wɑtʃfəl] *adj* : alerta, vigilante, atento

watchfulness ['wɑtʃfəlnəs] *n* : vigilancia *f*

watchman ['wɑtʃmən] *n, pl* **-men** [-mən, -ˌmɛn] : vigilante *m*, guarda *m*

watchword ['wɑtʃˌwərd] *n* **1** PASSWORD : contraseña *f* **2** SLOGAN : lema *m*, eslogan *m*

water¹ ['wɔtər, 'wɑ-] *vt* **1** : regar (el jardín, etc.) **2 to water down** DILUTE : diluir, aguar — *vi* : lagrimear (dícese de los ojos), hacérsele agua la boca a uno ⟨my mouth is watering : se me hace agua la boca⟩

water² *n* : agua *f*

water buffalo *n* : búfalo *m* de agua

watercolor ['wɔtərˌkʌlər, 'wɑ-] *n* : acuarela *f*

watercourse ['wɔtərˌkors, 'wɑ-] *n* : curso *m* de agua

watercress ['wɔtərˌkrɛs, 'wɑ-] *n* : berro *m*

waterfall ['wɔtər,fɔl, 'wɑ-] n : cascada f, salto m de agua, catarata f

waterfowl ['wɔtər,faʊl, 'wɑ-] n : ave f acuática

waterfront ['wɔtər,frʌnt, 'wɑ-] n 1 : tierra f que bordea un río, un lago, o un mar 2 WHARF : muelle m

water lily n : nenúfar m

waterlogged ['wɔtər,lɔgd, 'wɑtər-,lɑgd] adj : lleno de agua, empapado, inundado (dícese del suelo)

watermark ['wɔtər,mɑrk, 'wɑ-] n 1 : marca f del nivel de agua 2 : filigrana f (en el papel)

watermelon ['wɔtər,mɛlən, 'wɑ-] n : sandía f

water moccasin → **moccasin**

waterpower ['wɔtər,paʊər, 'wɑ-] n : energía f hidráulica

waterproof¹ ['wɔtər,pru:f, 'wɑ-] vt : hacer impermeable, impermeabilizar

waterproof² adj : impermeable, a prueba de agua

watershed ['wɔtər,ʃed, 'wɑ-] n 1 : línea f divisoria de aguas 2 BASIN : cuenca f (de un río)

waterskiing ['wɔtər,ski:ɪŋ, 'wɑ-] n : esquí m acuático

waterspout ['wɔtər,spaʊt, 'wɑ-] n WHIRLWIND : tromba f marina

watertight ['wɔtər,taɪt, 'wɑ-] adj 1 : hermético 2 IRREFUTABLE : irrebatible, irrefutable ⟨a watertight contract : un contrato sin lagunas⟩

waterway ['wɔtər,weɪ, 'wɑ-] n : vía f navegable

waterworks ['wɔtər,wərks, 'wɑ-] npl : central f de abastecimiento de agua

watery ['wɔtəri, 'wɑ-] adj 1 : acuoso, como agua 2 : aguado, diluido ⟨watery soup : sopa aguada⟩ 3 : lloroso ⟨watery eyes : ojos llorosos⟩ 4 WASHEDOUT : desvaído (dícese de colores)

watt ['wɑt] n : vatio m

wattage ['wɑtɪdʒ] n : vataje m

wattle ['wɑtəl] n : carúncula f (de un ave, etc.)

wave¹ ['weɪv] v **waved; waving** vi 1 : saludar con la mano, hacer señas con la mano ⟨she waved at him : lo saludó con la mano⟩ 2 FLUTTER, SHAKE : ondear, agitarse 3 UNDULATE : ondular — vt 1 SHAKE : agitar 2 BRANDISH : blandir 3 CURL : ondular, marcar (el pelo) 4 SIGNAL : hacerle señas a ⟨he waved farewell : se despidió con la mano⟩

wave² n 1 : ola f (de agua) 2 CURL : onda f (en el pelo) 3 : onda f (en física) 4 SURGE : oleada f ⟨a wave of enthusiasm : una oleada de entusiasmo⟩ 5 GESTURE : señal f con la mano, saludo m con la mano

wavelength ['weɪv,lɛŋkθ] n : longitud f de onda

waver ['weɪvər] vi 1 VACILLATE : vacilar, fluctuar 2 FLICKER : parpadear, titilar, oscilar 3 FALTER : flaquear, tambalearse

wavy ['weɪvi] adj **wavier; -est** : ondulado

wax¹ ['wæks] vi 1 : crecer (dícese de la luna) 2 BECOME : volverse, ponerse ⟨to wax indignant : indignarse⟩ — vt : encerar

wax² n 1 BEESWAX : cera f de abejas 2 : cera f ⟨floor wax : cera para el piso⟩ 3 or **earwax** ['ɪr,wæks] : cerilla f, cerumen m

waxen ['wæksən] adj : de cera

waxy ['wæksi] adj **waxier; -est** : ceroso

way ['weɪ] n 1 PATH, ROAD : camino m, vía f 2 ROUTE : camino m, ruta f ⟨to go the wrong way : equivocarse de camino⟩ ⟨I'm on my way : estoy de camino⟩ 3 : línea f de conducta, camino m ⟨he chose the easy way : optó por el camino fácil⟩ 4 MANNER, MEANS : manera f, modo m, forma f ⟨in the same way : del mismo modo, igualmente⟩ ⟨there are two ways about it : no cabe la menor duda⟩ ⟨no way! : ¡de ninguna manera!⟩ 5 (indicating a wish) ⟨have it your way : como tú quieras⟩ ⟨to get one's own way : salirse uno con la suya⟩ 6 STATE : estado m ⟨things are in a bad way : las cosas marchan mal⟩ 7 RESPECT : aspecto m, sentido m 8 CUSTOM : costumbre f ⟨to mend one's ways : dejar las malas costumbres⟩ 9 PASSAGE : camino m ⟨to get in the way : meterse en el camino⟩ 10 DISTANCE : distancia f ⟨to come a long way : hacer grandes progresos⟩ 11 DIRECTION : dirección f ⟨come this way : venga por aquí⟩ ⟨which way did he go? : ¿por dónde fue?⟩ 12 **by the way** : a propósito, por cierto 13 **by way of** VIA : vía, pasando por 14 **out of the way** REMOTE : remoto, recóndito 15 → **under way**

wayfarer ['weɪ,færər] n : caminante mf

waylay ['weɪ,leɪ] vt **-laid** [-,leɪd]; **-laying** ACCOST : abordar

wayside ['weɪ,saɪd] n : borde m del camino

wayward ['weɪwərd] adj 1 UNRULY : díscolo, rebelde 2 UNTOWARD : adverso

we ['wi:] pron : nosotros, nosotras

weak ['wi:k] adj 1 FEEBLE : débil, endeble 2 : flojo, pobre ⟨a weak excuse : una excusa poco convincente⟩ 3 DILUTED : aguado, diluido ⟨weak tea : té poco cargado⟩ 4 FAINT : tenue (dícese de los colores, las luces, los sonidos, etc.)

weaken ['wi:kən] vt : debilitar — vi : debilitarse, flaquear

weakling ['wi:klɪŋ] n : alfeñique m fam; debilucho m, -cha f

weakly¹ ['wi:kli] adv : débilmente

weakly² adj **weaklier; -est** : débil, enclenque

weakness ['wi:knəs] n 1 FEEBLENESS : debilidad f 2 FAULT, FLAW : flaqueza f, punto m débil

wealth [ˈwɛlθ] n 1 RICHES : riqueza f 2 PROFUSION : abundancia f, profusión f

wealthy [ˈwɛlθi] adj **wealthier; -est** : rico, acaudalado, adinerado

wean [ˈwiːn] vt 1 : destetar (a los niños o las crías) 2 **to wean someone away from** : quitarle a alguien la costumbre de

weapon [ˈwɛpən] n : arma f

weaponless [ˈwɛpənləs] adj : desarmado

weaponry [ˈwɛpənri] n : armamento m

wear[1] [ˈwær] v **wore** [ˈwor]; **worn** [ˈworn]; **wearing** vt 1 : llevar (ropa, un reloj, etc.), calzar (zapatos) ⟨to wear a happy smile : sonreír alegremente⟩ 2 or **to wear away** : desgastar, erosionar (rocas, etc.) 3 **to wear out** : gastar ⟨he wore out his shoes : gastó sus zapatos⟩ 4 **to wear out** EXHAUST : agotar, fatigar ⟨to wear oneself out : agotarse⟩ — vi 1 LAST : durar 2 **to wear off** DIMINISH : disminuir 3 **to wear out** : gastarse

wear[2] n 1 USE : uso m ⟨for everyday wear : para todos los días⟩ 2 CLOTHING : ropa f ⟨children's wear : ropa de niños⟩ 3 DETERIORATION : desgaste m ⟨to be the worse for wear : estar deteriorado⟩

wearable [ˈwærəbəl] adj : que puede ponerse (dícese de una prenda)

wear and tear n : desgaste m

weariness [ˈwɪrinəs] n : fatiga f, cansancio m

wearisome [ˈwɪrisəm] adj : aburrido, pesado, cansado

weary[1] [ˈwɪri] v **-ried; -rying** vt 1 TIRE : cansar, fatigar 2 BORE : hastiar, aburrir — vi : cansarse

weary[2] adj **-rier; -est** 1 TIRED : cansado 2 FED UP : harto 3 BORED : aburrido

weasel [ˈwiːzəl] n : comadreja f

weather[1] [ˈwɛðər] vt 1 WEAR : erosionar, desgastar 2 ENDURE : aguantar, sobrellevar, capear ⟨to weather the storm : capear el temporal⟩

weather[2] n : tiempo m

weather-beaten [ˈwɛðərˌbiːtən] adj : curtido

weatherman [ˈwɛðərˌmæn] n, pl **-men** [-mən, -ˌmɛn] METEOROLOGIST : meteorólogo m, -ga f

weatherproof [ˈwɛðərˌpruːf] adj : que resiste a la intemperie, impermeable

weather vane → **vane**

weave[1] [ˈwiːv] v **wove** [ˈwoːv] or **weaved**; **woven** [ˈwoːvən] or **weaved**; **weaving** vt 1 : tejer (tela) 2 INTERLACE : entretejer, entrelazar 3 **to weave one's way through** : abrirse camino por — vi 1 : tejer 2 WIND : serpentear, zigzaguear

weave[2] n : tejido m, trama f

weaver [ˈwiːvər] n : tejedor m, -dora f

web[1] [ˈwɛb] vt **webbed; webbing** : cubrir o proveer con una red

web[2] n 1 COBWEB, SPIDERWEB : telaraña f, tela f de araña 2 ENTANGLEMENT, SNARE : red f, enredo m ⟨a web of intrigue : una red de intriga⟩ 3 : membrana f interdigital (de aves) 4 NETWORK : red f ⟨a web of highways : una red de carreteras⟩ 5 **the Web** : la web

webbed [ˈwɛbd] adj : palmeado ⟨webbed feet : patas palmeadas⟩

Web site n : sitio m web

wed [ˈwɛd] vt **wedded; wedding** 1 MARRY : casarse con 2 UNITE : ligar, unir

we'd [ˈwiːd] (contraction of we had, we should, or we would) → **have, should, would**

wedding [ˈwɛdɪŋ] n : boda f, casamiento m

wedge[1] [ˈwɛdʒ] vt **wedged; wedging** 1 : apretar (con una cuña) ⟨to wedge open : mantener abierto con una cuña⟩ 2 CRAM : meter, embutir

wedge[2] n 1 : cuña f 2 PIECE : porción f, trozo m

wedlock [ˈwɛdˌlɑk] → **marriage**

Wednesday [ˈwɛnzˌdeɪ, -di] n : miércoles m

wee [ˈwiː] adj : pequeño, minúsculo ⟨in the wee hours : a las altas horas⟩

weed[1] [ˈwiːd] vt 1 : desherbar, desyerbar 2 **to weed out** : eliminar, quitar

weed[2] n : mala hierba f

weedy [ˈwiːdi] adj **weedier; -est** 1 : cubierto de malas hierbas 2 LANKY, SKINNY : flaco, larguirucho fam

week [ˈwiːk] n : semana f

weekday [ˈwiːkˌdeɪ] n : día m laborable

weekend [ˈwiːkˌɛnd] n : fin m de semana

weekly[1] [ˈwiːkli] adv : semanalmente

weekly[2] adj : semanal

weekly[3] n, pl **-lies** : semanario m

weep [ˈwiːp] v **wept** [ˈwɛpt]; **weeping** : llorar

weeping willow n : sauce m llorón

weepy [ˈwiːpi] adj **weepier; -est** : lloroso, triste

weevil [ˈwiːvəl] n : gorgojo m

weft [ˈwɛft] n : trama f

weigh [ˈweɪ] vt 1 : pesar 2 CONSIDER : considerar, sopesar 3 **to weigh anchor** : levar anclas 4 **to weigh down** : sobrecargar (con una carga), abrumar (con preocupaciones, etc.) — vi 1 : pesar ⟨it weighs 10 pounds : pesa 10 libras⟩ 2 COUNT : tener importancia, contar 3 **to weigh on one's mind** : preocuparle a uno

weight[1] [ˈweɪt] vt 1 : poner peso en, sujetar con un peso 2 BURDEN : cargar, oprimir

weight[2] n 1 HEAVINESS : peso m ⟨to lose weight : bajar de peso, adelgazar⟩ 2 : peso m ⟨weights and measures : pesos y medidas⟩ 3 : pesa f ⟨to lift weights : levantar pesas⟩ 4 BURDEN : peso m, carga f ⟨to take a weight off one's mind : quitarle un peso de encima a uno⟩ 5

IMPORTANCE : peso *m* **6** INFLUENCE : influencia *f*, autoridad *f* ⟨to throw one's weight around : hacer sentir su influencia⟩

weighty [ˈweɪti] *adj* **weightier; -est 1** HEAVY : pesado **2** IMPORTANT : importante, de peso

weird [ˈwɪrd] *adj* **1** MYSTERIOUS : misterioso **2** STRANGE : extraño, raro — **weirdly** *adv*

welcome¹ [ˈwɛlkəm] *vt* **-comed; -coming** : darle la bienvenida a, recibir

welcome² *adj* : bienvenido ⟨to make someone welcome : acoger bien a alguien⟩ ⟨you're welcome! : ¡de nada!, ¡no hay de qué!⟩

welcome³ *n* : bienvenida *f*, recibimiento *m*, acogida *f*

weld¹ [ˈwɛld] *v* : soldar

weld² *n* : soldadura *f*

welder [ˈwɛldər] *n* : soldador *m*, -dora *f*

welfare [ˈwɛlˌfær] *n* **1** WELL-BEING : bienestar *m* **2** : asistencia *f* social

well¹ [ˈwɛl] *vi* **or to well up** : brotar, manar

well² *adv* **better** [ˈbɛtər]; **best** [ˈbɛst] **1** RIGHTLY : bien, correctamente **2** SATISFACTORILY : bien ⟨to turn out well : resultar bien, salir bien⟩ **3** COMPLETELY : completamente ⟨well-hidden : completamente escondido⟩ **4** INTIMATELY : bien ⟨I knew him well : lo conocía bien⟩ **5** CONSIDERABLY, FAR : muy, bastante ⟨well ahead : muy adelante⟩ ⟨well before the deadline : bastante antes de la fecha⟩ **6 as well** ALSO : también **7 → as well as**

well³ *adj* **1** SATISFACTORY : bien ⟨all is well : todo está bien⟩ **2** DESIRABLE : conveniente ⟨it would be well if you left : sería conveniente que te fueras⟩ **3** HEALTHY : bien, sano

well⁴ *n* **1** : pozo *m* (de agua, petróleo, gas, etc.), aljibe *m* (de agua) **2** SOURCE : fuente *f* ⟨a well of information : una fuente de información⟩ **3** *or* **stairwell** : caja *f*, hueco *m* (de la escalera)

well⁵ *interj* **1** (*used to introduce a remark*) : bueno **2** (*used to express surprise*) : ¡vaya!

we'll [ˈwiːl, wɪl] (*contraction of* **we shall** *or* **we will**) **→ shall, will**

well-balanced [ˈwɛlˈbælənst] *adj* : equilibrado

well-being [ˈwɛlˈbiːɪŋ] *n* : bienestar *m*

well-bred [ˈwɛlˈbrɛd] *adj* : fino, bien educado

well-defined [ˌwɛldɪˈfaɪnd] *adj* : bien definido

well-done [ˈwɛlˈdʌn] *adj* **1** : bien hecho ⟨well-done! : ¡bravo!⟩ **2** : bien cocido

well-known [ˈwɛlˈnoːn] *adj* : famoso, bien conocido

well-meaning [ˈwɛlˈmiːnɪŋ] *adj* : bienintencionado, que tiene buenas intenciones

well-nigh [ˈwɛlˈnaɪ] *adv* : casi ⟨well-nigh impossible : casi imposible⟩

well-off [ˈwɛlˈɔf] **→ well-to-do**

well-rounded [ˈwɛlˈraʊndəd] *adj* : completo, equilibrado

well-to-do [ˌwɛltəˈduː] *adj* : próspero, adinerado, rico

Welsh [ˈwɛlʃ] *n* **1** : galés *m*, galesa *f* **2** : galés *m* (idioma) — **Welsh** *adj*

welt [ˈwɛlt] *n* **1** : vira *f* (de un zapato) **2** WHEAL : verdugón *m*

welter [ˈwɛltər] *n* : fárrago *m*, revoltijo *m* ⟨a welter of data : un fárrago de datos⟩

wend [ˈwɛnd] *vi* **to wend one's way** : ponerse en camino, encaminar sus pasos

went → go¹

wept → weep

were → be

we're [ˈwɪr, ˈwər, ˈwiːər] (*contraction of* **we are**) **→ be**

werewolf [ˈwɪrˌwʊlf, ˈwɛr-, ˈwər-, -ˌwʌlf] *n, pl* **-wolves** [-ˌwʊlvz, -ˌwʌlvz] : hombre *m* lobo

west¹ [ˈwɛst] *adv* : al oeste

west² *adj* : oeste, del oeste, occidental ⟨west winds : vientos del oeste⟩

west³ *n* **1** : oeste *m* **2 the West** : el Oeste, el Occidente

westerly [ˈwɛstərli] *adv & adj* : del oeste

western [ˈwɛstərn] *adj* **1** : Occidental, del Oeste **2** : occidental, del oeste

Westerner [ˈwɛstərnər] *n* : habitante *mf* del oeste

West Indian *n* : antillano *m*, -na *f* — **West Indian** *adj*

westward [ˈwɛstwərd] *adv & adj* : hacia el oeste

wet¹ [ˈwɛt] *vt* **wet** *or* **wetted; wetting** : mojar, humedecer

wet² *adj* **wetter; wettest 1** : mojado, húmedo ⟨wet clothes : ropa mojada⟩ **2** RAINY : lluvioso **3 wet paint** : pintura *f* fresca

wet³ *n* **1** MOISTURE : humedad *f* **2** RAIN : lluvia *f*

we've [ˈwiːv] (*contraction of* **we have**) **→ have**

whack¹ [ˈhwæk] *vt* : golpear (fuertemente), aporrear

whack² *n* **1** : golpe *m* fuerte, porrazo *m* **2** ATTEMPT : intento *m*, tentativa *f*

whale¹ [ˈhweɪl] *vi* **whaled; whaling** : cazar ballenas

whale² *n, pl* **whales** *or* **whale** : ballena *f*

whaleboat [ˈhweɪlˌboːt] *n* : ballenero *m*

whalebone [ˈhweɪlˌboːn] *n* : barba *f* de ballena

whaler [ˈhweɪlər] *n* **1** : ballenero *m*, -ra *f* **2 → whaleboat**

wharf [ˈhwɔrf] *n, pl* **wharves** [ˈhwɔrvz] : muelle *m*, embarcadero *m*

what¹ [ˈhwɑt, ˈhwʌt] *adv* HOW : cómo, cuánto ⟨what he suffered! : ¡cómo sufría!⟩ **2 what with** : entre ⟨what with one thing and another : entre una cosa y otra⟩

what² *adj* **1** (*used in questions*) : qué ⟨what more do you want? : ¿qué más quieres?⟩ ⟨what color is it? : ¿de qué color es?⟩ **2** (*used in exclamations*) : qué ⟨what an idea! : ¡qué idea!⟩ **3** ANY, WHATEVER : cualquier ⟨give what help you can : da cualquier contribución que puedas⟩

what³ *pron* **1** (*used in direct questions*) : qué ⟨what happened? : ¿qué pasó?⟩ ⟨what does it cost? : ¿cuánto cuesta?⟩ **2** (*used in indirect statements*) : lo que, que ⟨I don't know what to do : no sé que hacer⟩ ⟨do what I tell you : haz lo que te digo⟩ **3** what for → WHY : porqué **4 what if** : y si ⟨what if he knows? : ¿y si lo sabe?⟩

whatever¹ [ˌhwʌtˈɛvər, ˌhwʌt-] *adj* **1** ANY : cualquier, cualquier . . . que ⟨whatever way you prefer : de cualquier manera que prefiera, como prefiera⟩ **2** (*in negative constructions*) ⟨there's no chance whatever : no hay ninguna posibilidad⟩ ⟨nothing whatever : nada en absoluto⟩

whatever² *pron* **1** ANYTHING : (todo) lo que ⟨I'll do whatever I want : haré lo que quiera⟩ **2** (*no matter what*) ⟨whatever it may be : sea lo que sea⟩ **3** WHAT : qué ⟨whatever do you mean? : ¿qué quieres decir?⟩

whatsoever¹ [ˌhwʌtsoˈɛvər, ˌhwʌt-] *adj* → **whatever¹**

whatsoever² *pron* → **whatever²**

wheal [ˈhwiːl] *n* : verdugón *m*

wheat [ˈhwiːt] *n* : trigo *m*

wheaten [ˈhwiːtən] *adj* : de trigo

wheedle [ˈhwiːdəl] *vt* **-dled; -dling** CAJOLE : engatusar ⟨to wheedle something out of someone : sonsacarle algo a alguien⟩

wheel¹ [ˈhwiːl] *vt* : empujar (una bicicleta, etc.), mover (algo sobre ruedas) —*vi* **1** ROTATE : girar, rotar **2 to wheel around** TURN : darse la vuelta

wheel² *n* **1** : rueda *f* **2 or steering wheel** : volante *m* (de automóviles, etc.), timón *m* (de barcos o aviones) **3 wheels** *npl* : maquinaria *f*, fuerza *f* impulsora ⟨the wheels of government : la maquinaria del gobierno⟩

wheelbarrow [ˈhwiːlˌbær.oː] *n* : carretilla *f*

wheelchair [ˈhwiːlˌtʃær] *n* : silla *f* de ruedas

wheeze¹ [ˈhwiːz] *vi* **wheezed; wheezing** : resollar, respirar con dificultad

wheeze² *n* : resuello *m*

whelk [ˈhwɛlk] *n* : buccino *m*

whelp¹ [ˈhwɛlp] *vi* : parir

whelp² *n* : cachorro *m*, -rra *f*

when¹ [ˈhwɛn] *adv* : cuándo ⟨when will you return? : ¿cuándo volverás?⟩ ⟨he asked me when I would be home : me preguntó cuándo estaría en casa⟩

when² *conj* **1** (*referring to a particular time*) : cuando, en que ⟨when you are ready : cuando estés listo⟩ ⟨the days when I clean the house : los días en que limpio la casa⟩ **2** IF : cuando, si ⟨how can I go when I have no money? :

¿cómo voy a ir si no tengo dinero?⟩ **3** ALTHOUGH : cuando ⟨you said it was big when actually it's small : dijiste que era grande cuando en realidad es pequeño⟩

when³ *pron* : cuándo ⟨since when are you the boss? : ¿desde cuándo eres el jefe?⟩

whence [ˈhwɛnʦ] *adv* : de donde

whenever¹ [hwɛnˈvər] *adv* **1** : cuando sea ⟨tomorrow or whenever : mañana o cuando sea⟩ **2** (*in questions*) : cuándo

whenever² *conj* **1** : siempre que, cada vez que ⟨whenever I go, I'm disappointed : siempre voy, quedo desilusionado⟩ **2** WHEN : cuando ⟨whenever you like : cuando quieras⟩

where¹ [ˈhwɛr] *adv* : dónde, adónde ⟨where is he? : ¿dónde está?⟩ ⟨where did they go? : ¿adónde fueron?⟩

where² *conj* : donde, adonde ⟨she knows where the house is : sabe donde está la casa⟩ ⟨she goes where she likes : va adonde quiera⟩

where³ *pron* : donde ⟨Chicago is where I live : Chicago es donde vivo⟩

whereabouts¹ [ˈhwɛrəˌbaʊts] *adv* : dónde, por dónde ⟨whereabouts is the house? : ¿dónde está la casa?⟩

whereabouts² *ns & pl* : paradero *m*

whereas [hwɛrˈæz] *conj* **1** : considerando que (usado en documentos legales) **2** : mientras que ⟨I like the white one whereas she prefers the black : me gusta el blanco mientras que ella prefiere el negro⟩

whereby [hwɛrˈbaɪ] *adv* : por lo cual

wherefore [ˈhwɛrˌfor] *adv* : por qué

wherein [hwɛrˈɪn] *adv* : en el cual, en el que

whereof [hwɛrˈʌv, -ˈɑv] *conj* : de lo cual

whereupon [ˈhwɛrəˌpɑn, -ˌpɔn] *conj* : con lo cual, después de lo cual

wherever¹ [hwɛrˈɛvər] *adv* **1** WHERE : dónde, adónde **2** : en cualquier parte ⟨or wherever : o donde sea⟩

wherever² *conj* : dondequiera que, donde sea ⟨wherever you go : dondequiera que vayas⟩

wherewithal [ˈhwɛrwɪˌðɔl, -ˌθɔl] *n* : medios *mpl*, recursos *mpl*

whet [ˈhwɛt] *vt* **whetted; whetting 1** SHARPEN : afilar **2** STIMULATE : estimular ⟨to whet the appetite : estimular el apetito⟩

whether [ˈhwɛðər] *conj* **1** : si ⟨I don't know whether it is finished : no sé si está acabado⟩ ⟨we doubt whether he'll show up : dudamos que aparezca⟩ **2** (*used in comparisons*) ⟨whether I like it or not : tanto si quiero como si no⟩ ⟨whether he comes or he doesn't : venga o no⟩

whetstone [ˈhwɛtˌstoːn] *n* : piedra *f* de afilar

whey [ˈhweɪ] *n* : suero *m* (de la leche)

which¹ [ˈhwɪtʃ] *adj* : qué, cuál ⟨which tie do you prefer : ¿cuál corbata prefieres?⟩ ⟨which ones? : ¿cuáles?⟩ ⟨tell me which house is yours : dime qué casa es la tuya⟩

which² *pron* **1** : cuál ⟨which is the right answer? : ¿cuál es la respuesta correcta?⟩ **2** : que, el (la) cual ⟨the cup which broke : la taza que se quebró⟩ ⟨the house, which is made of brick : la casa, la cual es de ladrillo⟩

whichever¹ [ʰwɪtʃʰɛvər] *adj* : el (la) que, cualquiera que ⟨whichever book you like : cualquier libro que te guste⟩

whichever² *pron* : el (la) que, cualquiera que ⟨take whichever you want : toma el que quieras⟩ ⟨whichever I choose : cualquiera que elija⟩

whiff¹ [ʰwɪf] *v* PUFF : soplar

whiff² *n* **1** PUFF : soplo *m*, ráfaga *f* **2** SNIFF : olor *m* HINT : dejo *m*, pizca *f*

while¹ [ʰwaɪl] *vt* whiled; whiling : pasar ⟨to while away the time : matar el tiempo⟩

while² *n* **1** TIME : rato *m*, tiempo *m* ⟨after a while : después de un rato⟩ ⟨in a while : dentro de poco⟩ **2 to be worth one's while** : valer la pena

while³ *conj* **1** : mientras ⟨whistle while you work : silba mientras trabajas⟩ **2** WHEREAS : mientras que **3** ALTHOUGH : aunque ⟨while it's very good, it's not perfect : aunque es muy bueno, no es perfecto⟩

whim [ʰwɪm] *n* : capricho *m*, antojo *m*

whimper¹ [ʰwɪmpər] *vi* : lloriquear, gimotear

whimper² *n* : quejido *m*

whimsical [ʰwɪmzɪkəl] *adj* **1** CAPRICIOUS : caprichoso, fantasioso **2** ERRATIC : errático — **whimsically** *adv*

whine¹ [ʰwaɪn] *vi* whined; whining **1** : lloriquear, gimotear, gemir **2** COMPLAIN : quejarse

whine² *n* : quejido *m*, gemido *m*

whinny¹ [ʰwɪni] *vi* -nied; -nying : relinchar

whinny² *n, pl* -nies : relincho *m*

whip¹ [ʰwɪp] *v* whipped; whipping *vt* **1** SNATCH : sacar (rápidamente), arrebatar ⟨she whipped the cloth off the table : arrebató el mantel de la mesa⟩ **2** LASH : azotar **3** DEFEAT : vencer, derrotar **4** INCITE : incitar, despertar ⟨to whip up enthusiasm : despertar el entusiasmo⟩ **5** BEAT : batir (huevos, crema, etc.) — *vi* FLAP : agitarse

whip² *n* **1** : látigo *m*, azote *m*, fusta *f* (de jinete) **2** : miembro *m* de un cuerpo legislativo encargado de disciplina

whiplash [ʰwɪp,læʃ] *n or* **whiplash injury** : traumatismo *m* cervical

whippet [ʰwɪpət] *n* : galgo *m* pequeño, galgo *m* inglés

whir¹ [ʰwər] *vi* whirred; whirring : zumbar

whir² *n* : zumbido *m*

whirl¹ [ʰwərl] *vi* **1** SPIN : dar vueltas, girar ⟨my head is whirling : la cabeza me

está dando vueltas⟩ **2 to whirl about** : arremolinarse, moverse rápidamente

whirl² *n* **1** SPIN : giro *m*, vuelta *f*, remolino *m* (dícese del polvo, etc.) **2** BUSTLE : bullicio *m*, torbellino *m* (de actividad, etc.) **3 to give it a whirl** : intentar hacer, probar

whirlpool [ʰwərl,pu:l] *n* : vorágine *f*, remolino *m*

whirlwind [ʰwərl,wɪnd] *n* : remolino *m*, torbellino *m*, tromba *f*

whisk¹ [ʰwɪsk] *vt* **1** : llevar ⟨she whisked the children off to bed : llevó a los niños a la cama⟩ **2** : batir ⟨to whisk eggs : batir huevos⟩ **3 to whisk away** *or* **to whisk off** : sacudir

whisk² *n* **1** WHISKING : sacudida *f* (movimiento) **2** : batidor *m* (para batir huevos, etc.)

whisk broom *n* : escobilla *f*

whisker [ʰwɪskər] *n* **1** : pelo *m* (de la barba o el bigote) **2 whiskers** *npl* : bigotes *mpl* (de animales)

whiskey *or* **whisky** [ʰwɪski] *n, pl* -keys *or* -kies : whisky *m*

whisper¹ [ʰwɪspər] *vi* : cuchichear, susurrar — *vt* : decir en voz baja, susurrar

whisper² *n* **1** WHISPERING : susurro *m*, cuchicheo *m* **2** RUMOR : rumor *m* **3** TRACE : dejo *m*, pizca *f*

whistle¹ [ʰwɪsəl] *v* -tled; -tling *vi* : silbar, chiflar, pitar (dícese de un tren, etc.) — *vt* : silbar ⟨to whistle a tune : silbar una melodía⟩

whistle² *n* **1** WHISTLING : chiflido *m*, silbido *m* **2** : silbato *m*, pito *m* (instrumento)

whit [ʰwɪt] *n* BIT : ápice *m*, pizca *f*

white¹ [ʰwaɪt] *adj* whiter; -est : blanco

white² *n* **1** : blanco *m* (color) **2** : clara *f* (de huevos) **3 or white person** : blanco *m*, -ca *f*

white blood cell *n* : glóbulo *m* blanco

whitecaps [ʰwaɪt,kæps] *npl* : cabrillas *fpl*

white-collar [ʰwaɪtˈkɑlər] *adj* **1** : de oficina **2 white-collar worker** : oficinista *mf*

whitefish [ʰwaɪt,fɪʃ] *n* : pescado *m* blanco

whiten [ʰwaɪtən] *vt* : blanquear — *vi* : ponerse blanco

whiteness [ʰwaɪtnəs] *n* : blancura *f*

white-tailed deer [ʰwaɪtˈteɪld] *n* : ciervo *f* de Virginia

whitewash¹ [ʰwaɪt,wɔʃ] *vt* **1** : enjalbegar, blanquear ⟨to whitewash a fence : enjalbegar una valla⟩ **2** CONCEAL : encubrir (un escándalo, etc.)

whitewash² *n* **1** : jalbegue *m*, lechada *f* **2** COVER-UP : encubrimiento *m*

whither [ʰwɪðər] *adv* : adónde

whiting [ʰwaɪtɪŋ] *n* : merluza *f*, pescadilla *f* (pez)

whitish [ʰwaɪtɪʃ] *adj* : blancuzco

whittle [ʰwɪtəl] *vt* -tled; -tling **1** : tallar (madera) **2 to whittle down** : reducir, recortar ⟨to whittle down expenses : reducir los gastos⟩

whiz[1] *or* **whizz** [ˈʰwɪz] *vi* **whizzed; whizzing 1** BUZZ : zumbar **2 to whiz by** : pasar muy rápido, pasar volando

whiz[2] *or* **whizz** *n, pl* **whizzes 1** BUZZ : zumbido *m* **2 to be a whiz** : ser un prodigio, ser muy hábil

who [ˈhuː] *pron* **1** (*used in direct and indirect questions*) : quién ⟨who is that? : ¿quién es ese?⟩ ⟨who did it? : ¿quién lo hizo?⟩ ⟨we know who they are : sabemos quiénes son⟩ **2** (*used in relative clauses*) : que, quien ⟨the lady who lives there : la señora que vive allí⟩ ⟨for those who wait : para los que esperan, para quienes esperan⟩

whodunit [huːˈdʌnɪt] *n* : novela *f* policíaca

whoever [huːˈɛvər] *pron* **1** : quienquiera que, quien ⟨whoever did it : quienquiera que lo hizo⟩ ⟨give it to whoever you want : dalo a quien quieras⟩ **2** (*used in questions*) : quién ⟨whoever could that be? : ¿quién podría ser?⟩

whole[1] [ˈhoːl] *adj* **1** UNHURT : ileso **2** INTACT : intacto, sano **3** ENTIRE : entero, íntegro ⟨the whole island : toda la isla⟩ ⟨whole milk : leche entera⟩ **4 a whole lot** : muchísimo

whole[2] *n* **1** : todo *m* **2 as a whole** : en conjunto **3 on the whole** : en general

wholehearted [ˈhoːlˈhɑrtəd] *adj* : sin reservas, incondicional

whole number *n* : entero *m*

wholesale[1] [ˈhoːlˌseɪl] *v* **-saled; -saling** *vt* : vender al por mayor — *vi* : venderse al por mayor

wholesale[2] *adv* : al por mayor

wholesale[3] *adj* **1** : al por mayor ⟨wholesale grocer : tendero al por mayor⟩ **2** TOTAL : total, absoluto ⟨wholesale slaughter : matanza sistemática⟩

wholesale[4] *n* : mayoreo *m*

wholesaler [ˈhoːlˌseɪlər] *n* : mayorista *mf*

wholesome [ˈhoːlsəm] *adj* **1** : sano ⟨wholesome advice : consejo sano⟩ **2** HEALTHY : sano, saludable

whole wheat *adj* : de trigo integral

wholly [ˈhoːli] *adv* **1** COMPLETELY : completamente **2** SOLELY : exclusivamente, únicamente

whom [ˈhuːm] *pron* **1** (*used in direct questions*) : a quién ⟨whom did you choose? : ¿a quién elegiste?⟩ **2** (*used in indirect questions*) : de quién, con quién, en quién ⟨I don't know whom to consult : no sé con quién consultar⟩ **3** (*used in relative clauses*) : que, a quien ⟨the lawyer whom I recommended to you : el abogado que te recomendé⟩

whomever [huːmˈɛvər] *pron* WHOEVER : quienquiera, quien ⟨marry whomever you please : cásate con quien quieras⟩

whoop[1] [ˈʰwuːp, ˈʰwʊp] *vi* : gritar, chillar

whoop[2] *n* : grito *m*

whooping cough *n* : tos *f* ferina

whopper [ˈʰwɑpər] *n* **1** : cosa *f* enorme **2** LIE : mentira *f* colosal

whopping [ˈʰwɑpɪŋ] *adj* : enorme

whore [ˈhor] *n* : puta *f*, ramera *f*

whorl [ˈʰworl, ˈʰwərl] *n* : espiral *f*, espira *f* (de una concha), línea *f* (de una huella digital)

whose[1] [ˈhuːz] *adj* **1** (*used in questions*) : de quién ⟨whose truck is that? : ¿de quién es ese camión?⟩ **2** (*used in relative clauses*) : cuyo ⟨the person whose work is finished : la persona cuyo trabajo está terminado⟩

whose[2] *pron* : de quién ⟨tell me whose it was : dime de quién era⟩

why[1] [ˈʰwaɪ] *adv* : por qué ⟨why did you do it? : ¿por qué lo hizo?⟩

why[2] *n, pl* **whys** REASON : porqué *m*, razón *f*

why[3] *conj* : por qué ⟨I know why he left : yo sé por qué salió⟩ ⟨there's no reason why it should exist : no hay razón para que exista⟩

why[4] *interj* (*used to express surprise*) : ¡vaya!, ¡mira!

wick [ˈwɪk] *n* : mecha *f*

wicked [ˈwɪkəd] *adj* **1** EVIL : malo, malvado **2** MISCHIEVOUS : travieso, pícaro ⟨a wicked grin : una sonrisa traviesa⟩ **3** TERRIBLE : terrible, horrible ⟨a wicked storm : una tormenta horrible⟩

wickedly [ˈwɪkədli] *adv* : con maldad

wickedness [ˈwɪkədnəs] *n* : maldad *f*

wicker[1] [ˈwɪkər] *adj* : de mimbre

wicker[2] *n* **1** : mimbre *m* **2** → **wickerwork**

wickerwork [ˈwɪkər,wərk] *n* : artículos *mpl* de mimbre

wicket [ˈwɪkət] *n* **1** WINDOW : ventanilla *f* **2** *or* **wicket gate** : postigo *m* **3** : aro *m* (en croquet), palos *mpl* (en críquet)

wide[1] [ˈwaɪd] *adv* **wider; widest 1** WIDELY : por todas partes ⟨to travel far and wide : viajar por todas partes⟩ **2** COMPLETELY : completamente, totalmente ⟨wide open : abierto de par en par⟩ **3 wide apart** : muy separados

wide[2] *adj* **wider; widest 1** VAST : vasto, extensivo ⟨a wide area : una área extensiva⟩ **2** : ancho ⟨three meters wide : tres metros de ancho⟩ **3** BROAD : ancho, amplio **4** *or* **wide-open** : muy abierto **5 wide of the mark** : desviado, lejos del blanco

wide-awake [ˈwaɪdˈweɪk] *adj* : (completamente) despierto

wide-eyed [ˈwaɪdˈaɪd] *adj* **1** : con los ojos muy abiertos **2** NAIVE : inocente, ingenuo

widely [ˈwaɪdli] *adv* : extensivamente, por todas partes

widen [ˈwaɪdən] *vt* : ampliar, ensanchar — *vi* : ampliarse, ensancharse

widespread [ˈwaɪdˈsprɛd] *adj* : extendido, extenso, difuso

widow[1] [ˈwɪˌdoː] *vt* : dejar viuda ⟨to be widowed : enviudar⟩

widow[2] *n* : viuda *f*

widower ['wɪdəwər] *n* : viudo *m*

width ['wɪdθ] *n* : ancho *m*, anchura *f*

wield ['wi:ld] *vt* **1** USE : usar, manejar ⟨to wield a broom : usar una escoba⟩ **2** EXERCISE : ejercer ⟨to wield influence : influir⟩

wiener ['wi:nər] → **frankfurter**

wife ['waɪf] *n, pl* **wives** ['waɪvz] : esposa *f*, mujer *f*

wifely ['waɪfli] *adj* : de esposa, conyugal

wig ['wɪg] *n* : peluca *f*

wiggle[1] ['wɪgəl] *v* **-gled; -gling** *vt* : menear, contonear ⟨to wiggle one's hips : contonearse⟩ — *vi* : menearse

wiggle[2] *n* : meneo *m*, contoneo *m*

wiggly ['wɪgəli] *adj* **-glier; -est 1** : que se menea **2** WAVY : ondulado

wigwag ['wɪg,wæg] *vi* **-wagged; -wagging** : comunicar por señales

wigwam ['wɪg,wɑm] *n* : wigwam *m*

wild[1] ['waɪld] *adv* **1** → **wildly 2 to run wild** : descontrolarse

wild[2] *adj* **1** : salvaje, silvestre, cimarrón ⟨wild horses : caballos salvajes⟩ ⟨wild rice : arroz silvestre⟩ **2** DESOLATE : yermo, agreste **3** UNRULY : desenfrenado **4** CRAZY : loco, fantástico ⟨wild ideas : ideas locas⟩ **5** BARBAROUS : salvaje, bárbaro **6** ERRATIC : errático ⟨a wild throw : un tiro errático⟩

wild[3] *n* → **wilderness**

wild card *n* **1** : factor *m* desconocido **2** : comodín (carta o símbolo)

wildcat ['waɪld,kæt] *n* **1** : gato *m* montés **2** BOBCAT : lince *m* rojo

wilderness ['wɪldərnəs] *n* : yermo *m*, desierto *m*

wildfire ['waɪld,faɪr] *n* **1** : fuego *m* descontrolado **2 to spread like wildfire** : propagarse como un reguero de pólvora

wildflower ['waɪld,flaʊər] *n* : flor *f* silvestre

wildfowl ['waɪld,faʊl] *n* : ave *f* de caza

wildlife ['waɪld,laɪf] *n* : fauna *f*

wildly ['waɪldli] *adv* **1** FRANTICALLY : frenéticamente, como un loco **2** EXTREMELY : extremadamente ⟨wildly happy : loco de felicidad⟩

wile[1] ['waɪl] *vt* **wiled; wiling** LURE : atraer

wile[2] *n* : ardid *m*, artimaña *f*

will[1] ['wɪl] *v, past* **would** ['wʊd]; *pres sing & pl* **will** *vt* WISH : querer ⟨do what you will : haz lo que quieras⟩ — *v aux* **1** (*expressing willingness*) ⟨no one would take the job : nadie aceptaría el trabajo⟩ ⟨I won't do it : no lo haré⟩ **2** (*expressing habitual action*) ⟨he will get angry over nothing : se pone furioso por cualquier cosa⟩ **3** (*forming the future tense*) ⟨tomorrow we will go shopping : mañana iremos de compras⟩ **4** (*expressing capacity*) ⟨the couch will hold three people : en el sofá cabrán tres personas⟩ **5** (*expressing determination*) ⟨I will go despite them : iré a pesar de ellos⟩ **6** (*expressing probability*) ⟨that will be the mailman : eso ha de ser el cartero⟩ **7** (*expressing inevitability*) ⟨accidents will happen : los accidentes ocurrirán⟩ **8** (*expressing a command*) ⟨you will do as I say : harás lo que digo⟩

will[2] *vt* **1** ORDAIN : disponer, decretar ⟨if God wills it : si Dios lo dispone, si Dios quiere⟩ **2** : lograr a fuerza de voluntad ⟨they were willing him to succeed : estaban deseando que tuviera éxito⟩ **3** BEQUEATH : legar

will[3] *n* **1** DESIRE : deseo *m*, voluntad *f* **2** VOLITION : voluntad *f* ⟨free will : libre albedrío⟩ **3** WILLPOWER : voluntad *f*, fuerza *f* de voluntad ⟨a will of iron : una voluntad férrea⟩ **4** : testamento *m* ⟨to make a will : hacer testamento⟩

willful *or* **wilful** ['wɪlfəl] *adj* **1** OBSTINATE : obstinado, terco **2** INTENTIONAL : intencionado, deliberado — **willfully** *adv*

willing ['wɪlɪŋ] *adj* **1** INCLINED, READY : listo, dispuesto **2** OBLIGING : servicial, complaciente

willingly ['wɪlɪŋli] *adv* : con gusto

willingness ['wɪlɪŋnəs] *n* : buena voluntad *f*

willow ['wɪ,lo:] *n* : sauce *m*

willowy ['wɪloi] *adj* : esbelto

willpower ['wɪl,paʊər] *n* : voluntad *f*, fuerza *f* de voluntad

wilt ['wɪlt] *vi* **1** : marchitarse (dícese de las flores) **2** LANGUISH : debilitarse, languidecer

wily ['waɪli] *adj* **wilier; -est** : artero, astuto

wimp ['wɪmp] *n* **1** COWARD : gallina *f*, cobarde *mf* **2** WEAKLING : debilucho *m*, -cha *f*, alfeñique *m*

win[1] ['wɪn] *v* **won** ['wʌn]; **winning** *vi* : ganar — *vt* **1** : ganar, conseguir **2 to win over** : ganarse a **3 to win someone's heart** : conquistar a alguien

win[2] *n* : triunfo *m*, victoria *f*

wince[1] ['wɪnts] *vi* **winced; wincing** : estremecerse, hacer una mueca de dolor

wince[2] *n* : mueca *f* de dolor

winch ['wɪntʃ] *n* : torno *m*

wind[1] ['wɪnd] *vt* : dejar sin aliento ⟨to be winded : quedarse sin aliento⟩

wind[2] ['waɪnd] *v* **wound** ['waʊnd]; **winding** *vi* MEANDER : serpentear — *vt* **1** COIL, ROLL : envolver, enrollar **2** TURN : hacer girar ⟨to wind a clock : darle cuerda a un reloj⟩

wind[3] ['wɪnd] *n* **1** : viento *m* ⟨against the wind : contra el viento⟩ **2** BREATH : aliento *m* **3** FLATULENCE : flatulencia *f*, ventosidad *f* **4 to get wind of** : enterarse de

wind[4] ['waɪnd] *n* **1** TURN : vuelta *f* **2** BEND : recodo *m*, curva *f*

windbreak ['wɪnd,breɪk] *n* : barrera *f* contra el viento, abrigadero *m*

windfall ['wɪnd,fɔl] *n* **1** : fruta *f* caída **2** : beneficio *m* imprevisto

wind instrument *n* : instrumento *m* de viento

windlass [ˈwɪndləs] *n* : cabrestante *m*

windmill [ˈwɪndˌmɪl] *n* : molino *m* de viento

window [ˈwɪnˌdoː] *n* 1 : ventana *f* (de un edificio o una computadora), ventanilla *f* (de un vehículo o avión), vitrina *f* (de una tienda) 2 → **windowpane**

windowpane [ˈwɪnˌdoːˌpeɪn] *n* : vidrio *m*

window–shop [ˈwɪndoˌʃɑp] *vi* -**shopped**; -**shopping** : mirar las vitrinas

windpipe [ˈwɪndˌpaɪp] *n* : tráquea *f*

windshield [ˈwɪndˌʃiːld] *n* 1 : parabrisas *m* 2 **windshield wiper** : limpiaparabrisas *m*

windup [ˈwaɪndˌʌp] *n* : conclusión *f*

wind up *vt* END : terminar, concluir — *vi* : terminar, acabar

windward[1] [ˈwɪndwərd] *adj* : de barlovento

windward[2] *n* : barlovento *m*

windy [ˈwɪndi] *adj* **windier**; -**est** 1 : ventoso ⟨it's windy : hace viento⟩ 2 VERBOSE : verboso, prolijo

wine[1] [ˈwaɪn] *v* **wined**; **wining** *vi* : beber vino — *vt* to **wine and dine** : agasajar

wine[2] *n* : vino *m*

wing[1] [ˈwɪŋ] *vi* FLY : volar

wing[2] *n* 1 : ala *f* (de un ave, un avión, o un edificio) 2 FACTION : ala *f* ⟨the right wing of the party : el ala derecha del partido⟩ 3 **wings** *npl* : bastidores *mpl* (de un teatro) 4 **on the wing** : al vuelo, volando 5 **under one's wing** : bajo el cargo de uno

winged [ˈwɪŋd, ˈwɪŋəd] *adj* : alado

wink[1] [ˈwɪŋk] *vi* 1 : guiñar el ojo 2 BLINK : pestañear, parpadear 3 FLICKER : parpadear, titilar

wink[2] *n* 1 : guiño *m* (del ojo) 2 NAP : siesta *f* ⟨not to sleep a wink : no pegar el ojo⟩

winner [ˈwɪnər] *n* : ganador *m*, -dora *f*

winning [ˈwɪnɪŋ] *adj* 1 VICTORIOUS : ganador 2 CHARMING : encantador

winnings [ˈwɪnɪŋz] *npl* : ganancias *fpl*

winnow [ˈwɪˌnoː] *vt* : aventar (el grano, etc.)

winsome [ˈwɪnsəm] *adj* CHARMING : encantador

winter[1] [ˈwɪntər] *adj* : invernal, de invierno

winter[2] *n* : invierno *m*

wintergreen [ˈwɪntərˌgriːn] *n* : gaulteria *f*

wintertime [ˈwɪntərˌtaɪm] *n* : invierno *m*

wintry [ˈwɪntri] *adj* **wintrier**; -**est** 1 WINTER : invernal, de invierno 2 COLD : frío ⟨she gave us a wintry greeting : nos saludó fríamente⟩

wipe[1] [ˈwaɪp] *vt* **wiped**; **wiping** 1 : limpiar, pasarle un trapo a ⟨to wipe one's feet : limpiarse los pies⟩ 2 **to wipe away** : enjugar (lágrimas), borrar (una memoria) 3 **to wipe out** ANNIHILATE : aniquilar, destruir

wipe[2] *n* : pasada *f* (con un trapo, etc.)

wire[1] [ˈwaɪr] *vt* **wired**; **wiring** 1 : instalar el cableado en (una casa, etc.) 2 BIND : atar con alambre 3 TELEGRAPH : telegrafiar, mandarle un telegrama (a alguien)

wire[2] *n* 1 : alambre *m* ⟨barbed wire : alambre de púas⟩ 2 : cable *m* (eléctrico o telefónico) 3 CABLEGRAM, TELEGRAM : telegrama *m*, cable *m*

wireless [ˈwaɪrləs] *adj* : inalámbrico

wiretapping [ˈwaɪrˌtæpɪŋ] *n* : intervención *f* electrónica

wiring [ˈwaɪrɪŋ] *n* : cableado *m*

wiry [ˈwaɪri] *adj* **wirier**; -**est** 1 : hirsuto, tieso (dícese del pelo) 2 : esbelto y musculoso (dícese del cuerpo)

wisdom [ˈwɪzdəm] *n* 1 KNOWLEDGE : sabiduría *f* 2 JUDGMENT, SENSE : sensatez *f*

wisdom tooth *n* : muela *f* de juicio

wise[1] [ˈwaɪz] *adj* **wiser**; **wisest** 1 LEARNED : sabio 2 SENSIBLE : sabio, sensato, prudente 3 KNOWLEDGEABLE : entendido, enterado ⟨they're wise to his tricks : conocen muy bien sus mañas⟩

wise[2] *n* : manera *f*, modo *m* ⟨in no wise : de ninguna manera⟩

wisecrack [ˈwaɪzˌkræk] *n* : broma *f*, chiste *m*

wisely [ˈwaɪzli] *adv* : sabiamente, sensatamente

wish[1] [ˈwɪʃ] *vt* 1 WANT : desear, querer 2 **to wish (something) for** : desear ⟨they wished me well : me desearon lo mejor⟩ — *vi* 1 : pedir (como deseo) 2 : querer ⟨as you wish : como quieras⟩

wish[2] *n* 1 : deseo *m* ⟨to grant a wish : conceder un deseo⟩ 2 **wishes** *npl* : saludos *mpl*, recuerdos *mpl* ⟨to send best wishes : mandar muchos recuerdos⟩

wishbone [ˈwɪʃˌboːn] *n* : espoleta *f*

wishful [ˈwɪʃfəl] *adj* 1 HOPEFUL : deseoso, lleno de esperanza 2 **wishful thinking** : ilusiones *fpl*

wishy–washy [ˈwɪʃiˌwɑʃi, -ˌwɑʃi] *adj* : insípido, soso

wisp [ˈwɪsp] *n* 1 BUNCH : manojo *m* (de paja) 2 STRAND : mechón *m* (de pelo) 3 : voluta *f* (de humo)

wispy [ˈwɪspi] *adj* **wispier**; -**est** : tenue, ralo (dícese del pelo)

wisteria [wɪsˈtɪriə] *n* : glicinia *f*

wistful [ˈwɪstfəl] *adj* : añorante, anhelante, melancólico — **wistfully** *adv*

wistfulness [ˈwɪstfəlnəs] *n* : añoranza *f*, melancolía *f*

wit [ˈwɪt] *n* 1 INTELLIGENCE : inteligencia *f* 2 CLEVERNESS : ingenio *m*, gracia *f*, agudeza *f* 3 HUMOR : humorismo *m* 4 JOKER : chistoso *m*, -sa *f* 5 **wits** *npl* : razón *f*, buen juicio *m* ⟨scared out of one's wits : muerto de miedo⟩ ⟨to be at one's wits' end : estar desesperado⟩

witch [ˈwɪtʃ] *n* : bruja *f*

witchcraft [ˈwɪtʃˌkræft] *n* : brujería *f*, hechicería *f*

witch doctor n : hechicero m, -ra f
witchery ['wɪtʃəri] n, pl **-eries 1** → **witch-craft 2** CHARM : encanto m
witch–hunt ['wɪtʃ,hʌnt] n : caza f de brujas
with ['wɪð, 'wɪθ] prep **1** : con 〈I'm going with you : voy contigo〉 〈coffee with milk : café con leche〉 **2** AGAINST : con 〈to argue with someone : discutir con alguien〉 **3** (used in descriptions) : con, de 〈the girl with red hair : la muchacha de pelo rojo〉 **4** (indicating manner, means, or cause) : con 〈to cut with a knife : cortar con un cuchillo〉 〈fix it with tape : arréglalo con cinta〉 〈with luck : consuerte〉 **5** DESPITE : a pesar de, aún con 〈with all his work, the business failed : a pesar de su trabajo, el negocio fracasó〉 **6** REGARDING : respecto a, con 〈the trouble with your plan : el problema con su plan〉 **7** AC-CORDING TO : según 〈it varies with the season : varía según la estación〉 **8** (indicating support or understanding) : con 〈I'm with you all the way : estoy contigo hasta el fin〉
withdraw [wɪð'drɔ, wɪθ-] v **-drew** [-'dru:]; **-drawn** [-'drɔn]; **-drawing** vt **1** REMOVE : retirar, apartar, sacar (dinero) **2** RE-TRACT : retractarse de — vi : retirarse, recluirse (de la sociedad)
withdrawal [wɪð'drɔəl, wɪθ-] n **1** : retirada f, retiro m (de fondos, etc.), re-traimiento m (social) **2** RETRACTION : retractación f **3** **withdrawal symp-toms** : síndrome m de abstinencia
withdrawn [wɪð'drɔn, wɪθ-] adj : retraí-do, reservado, introvertido
wither ['wɪðər] vt : marchitar, agostar — vi **1** WILT : marchitarse **2** WEAKEN : de-caer, debilitarse
withhold [wɪθ'ho:ld, wɪð-] vt **-held** [-'hld]; **-holding** : retener (fondos), aplazar (una decisión), negar (permiso, etc.)
within¹ [wɪð'ɪn, wɪθ-] adv : dentro
within² prep **1** : dentro de 〈within the limits : dentro de los límites〉 **2** (in ex-pressions of distance) : a menos de 〈within 10 miles of the ocean : a menos de 10 millas del mar〉 **3** (in expressions of time) : dentro de 〈within an hour : dentro de una hora〉 〈within a month of her birthday : a poco menos de un mes de su cumpleaños〉
without¹ [wɪð'aʊt, wɪθ-] adv **1** OUTSIDE : fuera **2** **to do without** : pasar sin algo
without² prep **1** OUTSIDE : fuera de **2** : sin 〈without fear : sin temor〉 〈he left without his briefcase : se fue sin su portafolios〉
withstand [wɪθ'stænd, wɪð-] vt **-stood** [-'stʊd]; **-standing 1** BEAR : aguantar, soportar **2** RESIST : resistir, resistirse a
witless ['wɪtləs] adj : estúpido, tonto
witness¹ ['wɪtnəs] vt **1** SEE : presenciar, ver, ser testigo de **2** : atestiguar (una firma, etc.) — vi TESTIFY : atestiguar, testimoniar

witness² n **1** TESTIMONY : testimonio m 〈to bear witness : atestiguar, testimo-niar〉 **2** : testigo mf 〈witness for the prosecution : testigo de cargo〉
witticism ['wɪtə,sɪzəm] n : agudeza f, ocurrencia f
witty ['wɪti] adj **-tier; -est** : ingenioso, ocurrente, gracioso
wives → **wife**
wizard ['wɪzərd] n **1** SORCERER : mago m, brujo m, hechicero m **2** : genio m 〈a math wizard : un genio en matemáticas〉
wizened ['wɪzənd, 'wi:-] adj : arrugado, marchito
wobble¹ ['wabəl] vi **-bled; -bling** : bam-bolearse, tambalearse, temblar (dícese de la voz)
wobble² n : tambaleo m, bamboleo m
wobbly ['wabəli] adj : bamboleante, tambaleante, inestable
woe ['wo:] n **1** GRIEF, MISFORTUNE : desgracia f, infortunio m, aflicción f **2** **woes** npl TROUBLES : penas fpl, males mpl
woeful ['wo:fəl] adj **1** SORROWFUL : afligido, apenado, triste **2** UNFORTU-NATE : desgraciado, infortunado **3** DE-PLORABLE : lamentable
woke, woken → **wake¹**
wolf¹ ['wʊlf] vt or **to wolf down** : engu-llir
wolf² n, pl **wolves** ['wʊlvz] : lobo m, -ba f
wolfram ['wʊlfrəm] → **tungsten**
wolverine [,wʊlvə'ri:n] n : glotón m (ani-mal)
woman ['wʊmən] n, pl **women** ['wɪmən] : mujer f
womanhood ['wʊmən,hʊd] n **1** : condi-ción f de mujer **2** WOMEN : mujeres fpl
womanly ['wʊmənli] adj : femenino
womb ['wu:m] n : útero m, matriz f
won → **win**
wonder¹ ['wʌndər] vi **1** SPECULATE : preguntarse, pensar 〈to wonder about : preguntarse por〉 **2** MARVEL : asom-brarse, maravillarse — vt : preguntarse 〈I wonder if they're coming : me pregun-to si vendrán〉
wonder² n **1** MARVEL : maravilla f, mi-lagro m 〈to work wonders : hacer mar-avillas〉 **2** AMAZEMENT : asombro m
wonderful ['wʌndərfəl] adj : maravi-lloso, estupendo
wonderfully ['wʌndərfəli] adv : maravi-llosamente, de maravilla
wonderland ['wʌndər,lænd, -lənd] n : país m de las maravillas
wonderment ['wʌndərmənt] n : asom-bro m
wondrous ['wʌndrəs] → **wonderful**
wont¹ ['wɔnt, 'wo:nt, 'wʌnt] adj : acos-tumbrado, habituado
wont² n : hábito m, costumbre f
won't ['wo:nt] (contraction of will not) → **will¹**
woo ['wu:] vt **1** COURT : cortejar **2** : bus-car el apoyo de (clientes, votantes, etc.)

wood¹ ['wʊd] *adj* : de madera

wood² *n* **1** *or* **woods** *npl* FOREST : bosque *m* **2** : madera *f* (materia) **3** FIREWOOD : leña *f*

woodchuck ['wʊd,tʃʌk] *n* : marmota *f* de América

woodcut ['wʊd,kʌt] *n* **1** : plancha *f* de madera (para imprimir imágenes) **2** : grabado *m* en madera

woodcutter ['wʊd,kʌtər] *n* : leñador *m*, -dora *f*

wooded ['wʊdəd] *adj* : arbolado, boscoso

wooden ['wʊdən] *adj* **1** : de madera ⟨a wooden cross : una cruz de madera⟩ **2** STIFF : rígido, inexpresivo (dícese del estilo, de la cara, etc.)

woodland ['wʊdlənd, -,lænd] *n* : bosque *m*

woodpecker ['wʊd,pɛkər] *n* : pájaro *m* carpintero

woodshed ['wʊd,ʃɛd] *n* : leñera *f*

woodsman ['wʊdzmən] → **woodcutter**

woodwind ['wʊd,wɪnd] *n* : instrumento *m* de viento de madera

woodworking ['wʊd,wərkɪŋ] *n* : carpintería *f*

woody ['wʊdi] *adj* **woodier; -est 1** → **wooded 2** : leñoso ⟨woody plants : plantas leñosas⟩ **3** : leñoso (dícese de la textura), a madera (dícese del aroma, etc.)

woof ['wʊf] → **weft**

wool ['wʊl] *n* : lana *f*

woolen¹ *or* **woollen** ['wʊlən] *adj* : de lana

woolen² *or* **woollen** *n* **1** : lana *f* (tela) **2** **woolens** *npl* : prendas *fpl* de lana

woolly ['wʊli] *adj* **-lier; -est 1** : lanudo **2** CONFUSED : confuso, vago

woozy ['wu:zi] *adj* **-zier; -est** : mareado

word¹ ['wərd] *vt* : expresar, formular, redactar

word² *n* **1** : palabra *f*, vocablo *m*, voz *f* ⟨word for word : palabra por palabra⟩ ⟨in one's own words : en sus propias palabras⟩ ⟨words fail me : me quedo sin habla⟩ **2** REMARK : palabra *f* ⟨by word of mouth : de palabra⟩ ⟨to have a word with : hablar (dos palabras) con⟩ **3** COMMAND : orden *f* ⟨to give the word : dar la orden⟩ ⟨just say the word : no tienes que decirlo⟩ **4** MESSAGE, NEWS : noticias *fpl* ⟨is there any word from her? : ¿hay noticias de ella?⟩ ⟨to send word : mandar un recado⟩ **5** PROMISE : palabra *f* ⟨to keep one's word : cumplir uno su palabra⟩ **6 words** *npl* QUARREL : palabra *f*, riña *f* ⟨to have words with : tener unas palabras con, reñir con⟩ **7 words** *npl* TEXT : letra *f* (de una canción, etc.)

wordiness ['wərdinəs] *n* : verbosidad *f*

wording ['wərdɪŋ] *n* : redacción *f*, lenguaje *m* (de un documento)

word processing *n* : procesamiento *m* de textos

word processor *n* : procesador *m* de textos

wordy ['wərdi] *adj* **wordier; -est** : verboso, prolijo

wore → **wear¹**

work¹ ['wərk] *v* **worked** ['wərkt] *or* **wrought** ['rɔt]; **working** *vt* **1** OPERATE : trabajar, operar ⟨to work a machine : operar una máquina⟩ **2** : lograr, conseguir (algo) con esfuerzo ⟨to work one's way up : lograr subir por sus propios esfuerzos⟩ **3** EFFECT : efectuar, llevar a cabo, obrar (milagros) **4** MAKE, SHAPE : elaborar, fabricar, formar ⟨a beautifully wrought vase : un florero bellamente elaborado⟩ **5** to **work up** : estimular, excitar ⟨don't get worked up : no te agites⟩ — *vi* **1** LABOR : trabajar ⟨to work full-time : trabajar a tiempo completo⟩ **2** FUNCTION : funcionar, servir

work² *adj* : laboral

work³ *n* **1** LABOR : trabajo *m*, labor *f* **2** EMPLOYMENT : trabajo *m*, empleo *m* **3** TASK : tarea *f*, faena *f* **4** DEED : obra *f*, labor *f* ⟨works of charity : obras de caridad⟩ **5** : obra *f* (de arte o literatura) **6** → **workmanship 7 works** *npl* FACTORY : fábrica *f* **8 works** *npl* MECHANISM : mecanismo *m*

workable ['wərkəbəl] *adj* **1** : explotable (dícese de una mina, etc.) **2** FEASIBLE : factible, realizable

workaday ['wərkə,dei] *adj* : ordinario, banal

workbench ['wərk,bɛntʃ] *n* : mesa *f* de trabajo

workday ['wərk,dei] *n* **1** : jornada *f* laboral **2** WEEKDAY : día *m* hábil, día *m* laborable

worker ['wərkər] *n* : trabajador *m*, -dora *f*; obrero *m*, -ra *f*

working ['wərkɪŋ] *adj* **1** : que trabaja ⟨working mothers : madres que trabajan⟩ ⟨the working class : la clase obrera⟩ **2** : de trabajo ⟨working hours : horas de trabajo⟩ **3** FUNCTIONING : que funciona, operativo **4** SUFFICIENT : suficiente ⟨a working majority : una mayoría suficiente⟩ ⟨working knowledge : conocimientos básicos⟩

workingman ['wərkɪŋ,mæn] *n, pl* **-men** [-mən, -,mɛn] : obrero *m*

workman ['wərkmən] *n, pl* **-men** [-mən, -,mɛn] **1** → **workingman 2** ARTISAN : artesano *m*

workmanlike ['wərkmən,laɪk] *adj* : bien hecho, competente

workmanship ['wərkmən,ʃɪp] *n* **1** WORK : ejecución *f*, trabajo *m* **2** CRAFTSMANSHIP : artesanía *f*, destreza *f*

workout ['wərk,aʊt] *n* : ejercicios *mpl* físicos, entrenamiento *m*

work out *vt* **1** DEVELOP, PLAN : idear, planear, desarrollar **2** RESOLVE : solucionar, resolver ⟨to work out the answer : calcular la solución⟩ — *vi* **1** TURN OUT : resultar **2** SUCCEED : lograr, dar resultado, salir bien **3** EXERCISE : hacer ejercicio

workroom ['wərk₁ru:m, -₁rʊm] *n* : taller *m*

workshop ['wərk₁ʃɑp] *n* : taller *m* ⟨ceramics workshop : taller de cerámica⟩

workstation ['wərk₁steɪʃən] *n* : estación *f* de trabajo (en informática)

world¹ ['wərld] *adj* : mundial, del mundo ⟨world championship : campeonato mundial⟩

world² *n* : mundo *m* ⟨around the world : alrededor del mundo⟩ ⟨a world of possibilities : un mundo de posibilidades⟩ ⟨to think the world of someone : tener a alguien en gran estima⟩ ⟨to be worlds apart : no tener nada que ver (uno con otro)⟩

worldly ['wərldli] *adj* **1** : mundano ⟨wordly goods : bienes materiales⟩ **2** SOPHISTICATED : sofisticado, de mundo

worldwide¹ ['wərld'waɪd] *adv* : mundialmente, en todo el mundo

worldwide² *adj* : global, mundial

World Wide Web *n* : World Wide Web *f*

worm¹ ['wərm] *vi* CRAWL : arrastrarse, deslizarse (como gusano) — *vt* **1** : desparasitar (un animal) **2 to worm one's way into** : introducirse en ⟨he wormed his way into her confidence : se ganó su confianza⟩ **3 to worm something out of someone** : sonsacarle algo a alguien

worm² *n* **1** : gusano *m*, lombriz *f* **2 worms** *npl* : lombrices *fpl* (parásitos)

wormy ['wərmi] *adj* **wormier; -est** : infestado de gusanos

worn *pp* → **wear**¹

worn-out ['worn'aʊt] *adj* **1** USED : gastado, desgastado **2** TIRED : agotado

worried ['wərid] *adj* : inquieto, preocupado

worrier ['wəriər] *n* : persona *f* que se preocupa mucho

worrisome ['wərisəm] *adj* **1** DISTURBING : preocupante, inquietante **2** : que se preocupa mucho (dícese de una persona)

worry¹ ['wəri] *v* **-ried; -rying** *vt* : preocupar, inquietar — *vi* : preocuparse, inquietarse, angustiarse

worry² *n, pl* **-ries** : preocupación *f*, inquietud *f*, angustia *f*

worse¹ ['wərs] *adv* (*comparative of* **bad** *or of* **ill**) : peor

worse² *adj* (*comparative of* **bad** *or of* **ill**) : peor ⟨from bad to worse : de mal en peor⟩ ⟨to get worse : empeorar⟩ ⟨to feel worse : sentirse peor⟩

worse³ *n* : estado *m* peor ⟨to take a turn for the worse : ponerse peor⟩ ⟨so much the worse : tanto peor⟩

worsen ['wərsən] *vt* : empeorar — *vi* : empeorar(se)

worship¹ ['wərʃəp] *v* **-shiped** *or* **-shipped; -shiping** *or* **-shipping** *vt* : adorar, venerar ⟨to worship God : adorar a Dios⟩ — *vi* : practicar una religión

worship² *n* : adoración *f*, culto *m*

worshiper *or* **worshipper** ['wərʃəpər] *n* : devoto *m*, -ta *f*; adorador *m*, -dora *f*

worst¹ ['wərst] *vt* DEFEAT : derrotar

worst² *adv* (*superlative of* **ill** *or of* **bad** *or* **badly**) : peor ⟨the worst dressed of all : el peor vestido de todos⟩

worst³ *adj* (*superlative of* **bad** *or of* **ill**) : peor ⟨the worst movie : la peor película⟩

worst⁴ *n* **the worst** : lo peor, el (la) peor ⟨the worst is over : ya ha pasado lo peor⟩

worsted ['wʊstəd, 'wərstəd] *n* : estambre *m*

worth¹ ['wərθ] *n* **1** : valor *m* (monetario) ⟨ten dollars' worth of gas : diez dólares de gasolina⟩ **2** MERIT : valor *m*, mérito *m*, valía *f* ⟨an employee of great worth : un empleado de gran valía⟩

worth² *prep* **to be worth** : valer ⟨her holdings are worth a fortune : sus propiedades valen una fortuna⟩ ⟨it's not worth it : no vale la pena⟩

worthiness ['wərðinəs] *n* : mérito *m*

worthless ['wərθləs] *adj* **1** : sin valor ⟨worthless trinkets : chucherías sin valor⟩ **2** USELESS : inútil

worthwhile [wərθ'hwaɪl] *adj* : que vale la pena

worthy ['wərði] *adj* **-thier; -est 1** : digno ⟨worthy of promotion : digno de un ascenso⟩ **2** COMMENDABLE : meritorio, encomiable

would ['wʊd] *past of* **will 1** (*expressing preference*) ⟨I would rather go alone than with her : preferiría ir sola que con ella⟩ **2** (*expressing intent*) ⟨those who would ban certain books : aquellos que prohibirían ciertos libros⟩ **3** (*expressing habitual action*) ⟨he would often take his kids to the park : solía llevar a sus hijos al parque⟩ **4** (*expressing contingency*) ⟨I would go if I had the money : iría yo si tuviera el dinero⟩ **5** (*expressing probability*) ⟨she would have won if she hadn't tripped : habría ganado si no hubiera tropezado⟩ **6** (*expressing a request*) ⟨would you kindly help me with this? : ¿tendría la bondad de ayudarme con esto?⟩

would-be ['wʊd'bi:] *adj* : potencial ⟨a would-be celebrity : un aspirante a celebridad⟩

wouldn't ['wʊdənt] (*contraction of* **would not**) → **would**

wound¹ ['wu:nd] *vt* : herir

wound² *n* : herida *f*

wound³ ['waʊnd] → **wind**²

wove, woven → **weave**¹

wow ['waʊ] *interj* : ¡guau!, ¡híjole! *Mex*, ¡hala! *Spain*

wrangle¹ ['ræŋgəl] *vi* **-gled; -gling** : discutir, reñir ⟨to wrangle over : discutir por⟩

wrangle² *n* : riña *f*, disputa *f*

wrap¹ ['ræp] *v* **wrapped; wrapping** *vt* **1** COVER : envolver, cubrir ⟨to wrap a package : envolver un paquete⟩

⟨wrapped in mystery : envuelto en misterio⟩ **2** ENCIRCLE : rodear, ceñir ⟨to wrap one's arms around someone : estrechar a alguien⟩ **3 to wrap up** FINISH : darle fin a (algo) — *vi* **1** COIL : envolverse, enroscarse **2 to wrap up** DRESS : abrigarse ⟨wrap up warmly : abrígate bien⟩

wrap² *n* **1** WRAPPER : envoltura *f* **2** : prenda *f* que envuelve (como un chal, una bata, etc.)

wrapper ['ræpər] *n* : envoltura *f*, envoltorio *m*

wrapping ['ræpɪŋ] *n* : envoltura *f*, envoltorio *m*

wrath ['ræθ] *n* : ira *f*, cólera *f*

wrathful ['ræθfəl] *adj* : iracundo

wreak ['ri:k] *vt* : infligir, causar ⟨to wreak havoc : crear caos, causar estragos⟩

wreath ['ri:θ] *n, pl* **wreaths** ['ri:ðz, 'ri:θs] : corona *f* (de flores, etc.)

wreathe ['ri:ð] *vt* **wreathed; wreathing 1** ADORN : coronar (de flores, etc.) **2** ENVELOP : envolver ⟨wreathed in mist : envuelto en niebla⟩

wreck¹ ['rɛk] *vt* : destruir, arruinar, estrellar (un automóvil), naufragar (un barco)

wreck² *n* **1** WRECKAGE : restos *mpl* de un buque naufragado, un avión siniestrado, etc.) **2** RUIN : ruina *f*, desastre *m* ⟨this place is a wreck! : ¡este lugar está hecho un desastre!⟩ ⟨to be a nervous wreck : tener los nervios destrozados⟩

wreckage ['rɛkɪʤ] *n* : restos *mpl* (de un buque naufragado, un avión siniestrado, etc.), ruinas *fpl* (de un edificio)

wrecker ['rɛkər] *n* **1** TOW TRUCK : grúa *f* **2** : desguazador *m* (de autos, barcos, etc.), demoledor *m* (de edificios)

wren ['rɛn] *n* : chochín *m*

wrench¹ ['rɛntʃ] *vt* **1** PULL : arrancar (de un tirón) **2** SPRAIN, TWIST : torcerse (un tobillo, un músculo, etc.)

wrench² *n* **1** TUG : tirón *m*, jalón *m* **2** SPRAIN : torcedura *f* **3** *or* **monkey wrench** : llave *f* inglesa

wrest ['rɛst] *vt* : arrancar

wrestle¹ ['rɛsəl] *v* **-tled; -tling** *vi* **1** : luchar, practicar la lucha (en deportes) **2** STRUGGLE : luchar ⟨to wrestle with a dilemma : lidiar con un dilema⟩ — *vt* : luchar contra

wrestle² *n* STRUGGLE : lucha *f*

wrestler ['rɛsələr] *n* : luchador *m*, -dora *f*

wrestling ['rɛsəlɪŋ] *n* : lucha *f*

wretch ['rɛtʃ] *n* : infeliz *mf*; desgraciado *m*, -da *f*

wretched ['rɛtʃəd] *adj* **1** MISERABLE, UNHAPPY : desdichado, afligido ⟨I feel wretched : me siento muy mal⟩ **2** UNFORTUNATE : miserable, desgraciado, lastimoso ⟨wretched weather : tiempo espantoso⟩ **3** INFERIOR : inferior, malo

wretchedly ['rɛtʃədli] *adv* : miserablemente, lamentablemente

wriggle ['rɪgəl] *vi* **-gled; -gling** : retorcerse, menearse

wring ['rɪŋ] *vt* **wrung** ['rʌŋ]; **wringing 1** *or* **to wring out** : escurrir, exprimir (el lavado) **2** EXTRACT : arrancar, sacar (por la fuerza) **3** TWIST : torcer, retorcer **4 to wring someone's heart** : partirle el corazón a alguien

wringer ['rɪŋər] *n* : escurridor *m*

wrinkle¹ ['rɪŋkəl] *v* **-kled; -kling** *vt* : arrugar — *vi* : arrugarse

wrinkle² *n* : arruga *f*

wrinkly ['rɪŋkəli] *adj* **wrinklier; -est** : arrugado

wrist ['rɪst] *n* **1** : muñeca *f* (en anatomía) **2** *or* **wristband** ['rɪst-ˌbænd] CUFF : puño *m*

writ ['rɪt] *n* : orden *f* (judicial)

write ['raɪt] *v* **wrote** ['ro:t]; **written** ['rɪtən]; **writing** : escribir

write down *vt* : apuntar, anotar

write off *vt* CANCEL : cancelar

writer ['raɪtər] *n* : escritor *m*, -tora *f*

writhe ['raɪð] *vi* **writhed; writhing** : retorcerse

writing ['raɪtɪŋ] *n* **1** : escritura *f* **2** HANDWRITING : letra *f* **3 writings** *npl* WORKS : escritos *mpl*, obra *f*

wrong¹ ['rɔŋ] *vt* **wronged; wronging** : ofender, ser injusto con

wrong² *adv* : mal, incorrectamente

wrong³ *adj* **wronger** ['rɔŋər]; **wrongest** ['rɔŋəst] **1** EVIL, SINFUL : malo, injusto, inmoral **2** IMPROPER, UNSUITABLE : inadecuado, inapropiado, malo **3** INCORRECT : incorrecto, erróneo, malo ⟨a wrong answer : una mala respuesta⟩ **4 to be wrong** : equivocarse, estar equivocado

wrong⁴ *n* **1** INJUSTICE : injusticia *f*, mal *m* **2** OFFENSE : ofensa *f*, agravio *m* (en derecho) **3 to be in the wrong** : haber hecho mal, estar equivocado

wrongdoer ['rɔŋˌduːər] *n* : malhechor *m*, -chora *f*

wrongdoing ['rɔŋˌduːɪŋ] *n* : fechoría *f*, maldad *f*

wrongful ['rɔŋfəl] *adj* **1** UNJUST : injusto **2** UNLAWFUL : ilegal

wrongly ['rɔŋli] *adv* **1** : injustamente **2** INCORRECTLY : erróneamente, incorrectamente

wrote → **write**

wrought ['rɔt] *adj* **1** SHAPED : formado, forjado ⟨wrought iron : hierro forjado⟩ **2** *or* **wrought up** : agitado, excitado

wrung → **wring**

wry ['raɪ] *adj* **wrier** ['raɪər]; **wriest** ['raɪəst] **1** TWISTED : torcido ⟨a wry neck : un cuello torcido⟩ **2** : irónico, sardónico (dícese del humor)

X

x¹ *n, pl* x's *or* xs ['ɛksəz] 1 : vigésima cuarta letra del alfabeto inglés 2 : incógnita *f* (en matemáticas)

x² ['ks] *vt* x-ed ['ɛkst]; x-ing *or* x'ing ['ɛksɪŋ] DELETE : tachar

xenon ['zi:ˌnɑn, 'zɛ-] *n* : xenón *m*

xenophobia [ˌzɛnə'fo:biə, ˌzi:-] *n* : xenofobia *f*

Xmas ['krɪsməs] *n* : Navidad *f*

x-ray ['ɛksˌreɪ] *vt* : radiografiar

X ray ['ɛksˌreɪ] *n* 1 : rayo *m* X 2 *or* X–ray photograph : radiografía *f*

xylophone ['zaɪləˌfo:n] *n* : xilófono *m*

Y

y ['waɪ] *n, pl* y's *or* ys ['waɪz] : vigésima quinta letra del alfabeto inglés

yacht¹ ['jɑt] *vi* : navegar (a vela), ir en yate ⟨to go yachting : irse a navegar⟩

yacht² *n* : yate *m*

yak ['jæk] *n* : yac *m*

yam ['jæm] *n* 1 : ñame *m* 2 SWEET POTATO : batata *f*, boniato *m*

yank¹ ['jæŋk] *vt* : tirar de, jalar, darle un tirón a

yank² *n* : tirón *m*

Yankee ['jæŋki] *n* : yanqui *mf*

yap¹ ['jæp] *vi* yapped; yapping 1 BARK, YELP : ladrar, gañir 2 CHATTER : cotorrear *fam*, parlotear *fam*

yap² *n* : ladrido *m*, gañido *m*

yard ['jɑrd] *n* 1 : yarda *f* (medida) 2 SPAR : verga *f* (de un barco) 3 COURTYARD : patio *m* 4 : jardín *m* (de una casa) 5 : depósito *m* (de mercancías, etc.)

yardage ['jɑrdɪdʒ] *n* : medida *f* en yardas

yardarm ['jɑrdˌɑrm] *n* : penol *m*

yardstick ['jɑrdˌstɪk] *n* 1 : vara *f* 2 CRITERION : criterio *m*, norma *f*

yarn ['jɑrn] *n* 1 : hilado *m* 2 TALE : historia *f*, cuento *m* ⟨to spin a yarn : inventar una historia⟩

yawl ['jɔl] *n* : yola *f*

yawn¹ ['jɔn] *vi* 1 : bostezar 2 OPEN : abrirse

yawn² *n* : bostezo *m*

ye ['ji:] *pron* : vosotros, vosotras

yea¹ ['jeɪ] *adv* YES : sí

yea² *n* : voto *m* a favor

year ['jɪr] *n* 1 : año *m* ⟨last year : el año pasado⟩ ⟨he's ten years old : tiene diez años⟩ 2 : curso *m*, año *m* (escolar) 3 years *npl* AGES : siglos *mpl*, años *mpl* ⟨I haven't seen them in years : hace siglos que no los veo⟩

yearbook ['jɪrˌbʊk] *n* : anuario *m*

yearling ['jɪrlɪŋ, 'jərlən] *n* : animal *m* menor de dos años

yearly¹ ['jɪrli] *adv* : cada año, anualmente

yearly² *adj* : anual

yearn ['jərn] *vi* : anhelar, ansiar

yearning ['jərnɪŋ] *n* : anhelo *m*

yeast ['ji:st] *n* : levadura *f*

yell¹ ['jɛl] *vi* : gritar, chillar — *vt* : gritar

yell² *n* : grito *m*, alarido *m* ⟨to let out a yell : dar un grito⟩

yellow¹ ['jɛlo] *vi* : ponerse amarillo, volverse amarillo

yellow² *adj* 1 : amarillo 2 COWARDLY : cobarde

yellow³ *n* : amarillo *m*

yellow fever *n* : fiebre *f* amarilla

yellowish ['jɛloɪʃ] *adj* : amarillento

yellow jacket *n* : avispa *f* (con rayas amarillas)

yelp¹ ['jɛlp] *vi* : dar un gañido (dícese de un animal), dar un grito (dícese de una persona)

yelp² *n* : gañido *m* (de un animal), grito *m* (de una persona)

yen ['jɛn] *n* 1 DESIRE : deseo *m*, ganas *fpl* 2 : yen *m* (moneda japonesa)

yeoman ['jo:mən] *n, pl* -men [-mən, -mɛn] : suboficial *mf* de marina

yes¹ ['jɛs] *adv* : sí ⟨to say yes : decir que sí⟩

yes² *n* : sí *m*

yesterday¹ ['jɛstərˌdeɪ, -di] *adv* : ayer

yesterday² *n* 1 : ayer *m* 2 the day before yesterday : anteayer

yet¹ ['jɛt] *adv* 1 BESIDES, EVEN : aún ⟨yet more problems : más problemas aún⟩ ⟨yet again : otra vez⟩ 2 SO FAR : aún, todavía ⟨not yet : todavía no⟩ ⟨as yet : hasta ahora, todavía⟩ 3 : ya ⟨has he come yet? : ¿ya ha venido?⟩ 4 EVENTUALLY : todavía, algún día 5 NEVERTHELESS : sin embargo

yet² *conj* : pero

yew ['ju:] *n* : tejo *m*

yield¹ ['ji:ld] *vt* 1 SURRENDER : ceder ⟨to yield the right of way : ceder el paso⟩ 2 PRODUCE : producir, dar, rendir (en finanzas) — *vi* 1 GIVE : ceder ⟨to yield under pressure : ceder por la presión⟩ 2 GIVE IN, SURRENDER : ceder, rendirse, entregarse

yield² *n* : rendimiento *m*, rédito *m* (en finanzas)

yin and yang ['jɪnænd'jæŋ, -'jɑŋ] *n* : yin *m* y yang *m*

yodel¹ ['jo:dəl] *vi* -deled *or* -delled; -deling *or* -delling : cantar al estilo tirolés

yodel² *n* : canción *f* al estilo tirolés

yoga ['jo:gə] *n* : yoga *m*

yogurt ['jo:gərt] *n* : yogur *m*, yogurt *m*

yoke¹ ['jo:k] *vt* yoked; yoking : uncir (animales)

yoke² *n* 1 : yugo *m* (para uncir animales)

⟨the yoke of oppression : el yugo de la opresión⟩ **2** TEAM : yunta *f* (de bueyes) **3** : canesú *m* (de ropa)

yokel [ˈjoːkəl] *n* : palurdo *m*, -da *f*

yolk [ˈjoːk] *n* : yema *f* (de un huevo)

Yom Kippur [ˌjoːmkɪˈpʊr, ˌjɑm-, -ˈkɪpər] *n* : el Día *m* del Perdón, Yom Kippur

yon [ˈjɑn] → **yonder**

yonder[1] [ˈjɑndər] *adv* : allá ⟨over yonder : allá lejos⟩

yonder[2] *adj* : aquel ⟨yonder hill : aquella colina⟩

yore [ˈjoːr] *n* in days of yore : antaño

you [ˈjuː] *pron* **1** (*used as subject — familiar*) : tú; vos (*in some Latin American countries*); ustedes *pl*; vosotros, vosotras *pl Spain* **2** (*used as subject — formal*) : usted, ustedes *pl* **3** (*used as indirect object — familiar*) : te, les *pl* (se before lo, la, los, las), os *pl Spain* ⟨he told it to you : te lo contó⟩ ⟨I gave them to (all of, both of) you : se los di⟩ **4** (*used as indirect object — formal*) : lo (*Spain sometimes* le), la; los (*Spain sometimes* les), las *pl* **5** (*used after a preposition — familiar*) : ti; vos (*in some Latin American countries*); ustedes *pl*; vosotros, vosotras *pl Spain* **6** (*used after a preposition — formal*) : usted, ustedes *pl* **7** (*used as an impersonal subject*) (*you never know* : nunca se sabe⟩ ⟨you have to be aware : hay que ser consciente⟩ ⟨you mustn't do that : eso no se hace⟩ **8 with you** (*familiar*) : contigo; con ustedes *pl*; con vosotros, con vosotras *pl Spain* **9 with you** (*formal*) : con usted, con ustedes *pl*

you'd [ˈjuːd, ˈjud] (*contraction of* you had *or* you would) → **have**, **would**

you'll [ˈjuːl, ˈjul] (*contraction of* you shall *or* you will) → **shall**, **will**

young[1] [ˈjʌŋ] *adj* **younger** [ˈjʌŋgər]; **youngest** [-gəst] **1** : joven, pequeño, menor ⟨young people : los jóvenes⟩ ⟨my younger brother : mi hermano menor⟩ ⟨she is the youngest : es la más pequeña⟩ **2** FRESH, NEW : tierno (dícese de las verduras), joven (dícese del vino) **3** YOUTHFUL : joven, juvenil

young[2] *npl* : jóvenes *mfpl* (de los humanos), crías *fpl* (de los animales)

youngster [ˈjʌŋkstər] *n* **1** YOUTH : joven *mf* **2** CHILD : chico *m*, -ca *f*; niño *m*, -ña *f*

your [ˈjʊr, ˈjoːr, jər] *adj* **1** (*familiar singular*) : tu ⟨your cat : tu gato⟩ ⟨your books : tus libros⟩ ⟨wash your hands : lávate las manos⟩ **2** (*familiar plural*) : su, vuestro *Spain* ⟨your car : su coche, el coche de ustedes⟩ **3** (*formal*) : su ⟨your houses : sus casas⟩ **4** (*impersonal*) : el, la, los, las ⟨on your left : a la izquierda⟩

you're [ˈjʊr, ˈjoːr, ˈjər, ˈjuːər] (*contraction of* you are) → **be**

yours [ˈjʊrz, ˈjoːrz] *pron* **1** (*belonging to one person — familiar*) : (el) tuyo, (la) tuya, (los) tuyos, (las) tuyas ⟨those are mine; yours are there : ésas son mías; las tuyas están allí⟩ ⟨is this one yours? : ¿éste es tuyo?⟩ **2** (*belonging to more than one person — familiar*) : (el) suyo, (la) suya, (los) suyos, (las) suyas; (el) vuestro, (la) vuestra, (los) vuestros, (las) vuestras *Spain* ⟨our house and yours : nuestra casa y la suya⟩ **3** (*formal*) : (el) suyo, (la) suya, (los) suyos, (las) suyas

yourself [jərˈsɛlf] *pron*, *pl* **yourselves** [-ˈslvz] **1** (*used reflexively — familiar*) : te, se *pl*, os *pl Spain* ⟨wash yourself : lávate⟩ ⟨you dressed yourselves : se vistieron, os vestisteis⟩ **2** (*used reflexively — formal*) : se ⟨did you hurt yourself? : ¿se hizo daño?⟩ ⟨you've gotten yourselves dirty : se ensuciaron⟩ **3** (*used for emphasis*) : tú mismo, tú misma; usted mismo, usted misma; ustedes mismos, ustedes mismas *pl*; vosotros mismos, vosotras mismas *pl Spain* ⟨you did it yourselves? : ¿lo hicieron ustedes mismos?, ¿lo hicieron por sí solos?⟩

youth [ˈjuːθ] *n*, *pl* **youths** [ˈjuːðz, ˈjuːθs] **1** : juventud *f* ⟨in her youth : en su juventud⟩ **2** BOY : joven *m* **3** : jóvenes *mfpl*, juventud *f* ⟨the youth of our city : los jóvenes de nuestra ciudad⟩

youthful [ˈjuːθfəl] *adj* **1** : de juventud **2** YOUNG : joven **3** JUVENILE : juvenil

youthfulness [ˈjuːθfəlnəs] *n* : juventud *f*

you've [ˈjuːv] (*contraction of* you have) → **have**

yowl[1] [ˈjæʊl] *vi* : aullar

yowl[2] *n* : aullido *m*

yo-yo [ˈjoːˌjoː] *n*, *pl* **-yos** : yoyo *m*, yoyó *m*

yucca [ˈjʌkə] *n* : yuca *f*

Yugoslavian [ˌjuːgoˈslaviən] *n* : yugoslavo *m*, -va *f* — **Yugoslavian** *adj*

yule [ˈjuːl] *n* CHRISTMAS : Navidad *f*

yuletide [ˈjuːlˌtaɪd] *n* : Navidades *fpl*

yuppie [ˈjʌpi] *n* : yuppy *mf*

Z

z ['zi:] n, pl z's or zs : vigésima sexta letra del alfabeto inglés

Zambian ['zæmbiən] n : zambiano m, -na f — **Zambian** adj

zany[1] ['zeɪni] adj -nier; -est : alocado, disparatado

zany[2] n, pl -nies : bufón m, -fona f

zap[1] ['zæp] vt zapped; zapping 1 ELIMINATE : eliminar 2 : enviar o transportar rápidamente — vi : ir rápidamente

zap[2] n 1 ZEST : sabor m, sazón f 2 BLAST : golpe m fuerte

zap[3] interj : ¡zas!

zeal ['zi:l] n : fervor m, celo m, entusiasmo m

zealot ['zɛlət] n : fanático m, -ca f

zealous ['zɛləs] adj : celoso — **zealously** adv

zebra ['zi:brə] n : cebra f

zenith ['zi:nəθ] n 1 : cenit m (en astronomía) 2 PEAK : apogeo m, cenit m ⟨at the zenith of his career : en el apogeo de su carrera⟩

zephyr ['zɛfər] n : céfiro m

zeppelin ['zɛplən, -pəlɪn] n : zepelín m

zero[1] ['zi:ro, 'zɪro] vi to zero in on : apuntar hacia, centrarse en (un problema, etc.)

zero[2] adj : cero, nulo ⟨zero degrees : cero grados⟩ ⟨zero opportunities : oportunidades nulas⟩

zero[3] n, pl -ros : cero m ⟨below zero : bajo cero⟩

zest ['zɛst] n 1 GUSTO : entusiasmo m, brío m 2 FLAVOR : sabor m, sazón f

zestful ['zɛstfəl] adj : brioso

zigzag[1] ['zɪg,zæg] vi -zagged; -zagging : zigzaguear

zigzag[2] adv & adj : en zigzag

zigzag[3] n : zigzag m

Zimbabwean [zɪm'babwiən, -bweɪ-] n : zimbabuense mf — **Zimbabwean** adj

zinc ['zɪŋk] n : cinc m, zinc m

zing ['zɪŋ] n 1 HISS, HUM : zumbido m, silbido m 2 ENERGY : brío m

zinnia ['zɪniə, 'zi:-, -njə] n : zinnia f

Zionism ['zaɪə,nɪzəm] n : sionismo m

Zionist ['zaɪənɪst] n : sionista mf

zip[1] ['zɪp] v zipped; zipping vt or to zip up : cerrar el cierre de — vi 1 SPEED : pasarse volando ⟨the day zipped by : el día se pasó volando⟩ 2 HISS, HUM : silbar, zumbar

zip[2] n 1 ZING : zumbido m, silbido m 2 ENERGY : brío m

zip code n : código m postal

zipper ['zɪpər] n : cierre m, cremallera f, zíper m CA, Mex

zippy ['zɪpi] adj -pier; -est : brioso

zircon ['zər,kan] n : circón m, zircón m

zirconium [ˌzər'ko:niəm] n : circonio m

zither ['zɪðər, -θər] n : cítara f

zodiac ['zo:di,æk] n : zodíaco m

zombie ['zambi] n : zombi m/f, zombie mf

zone[1] ['zo:n] vt zoned; zoning 1 : dividir en zonas 2 DESIGNATE : declarar ⟨to zone for business : declarar como zona comercial⟩

zone[2] n : zona f

zoo ['zu:] n, pl zoos : zoológico m, zoo m

zoological [ˌzo:ə'ladʒɪkəl, ˌzu:ə-] adj : zoológico

zoologist [zo'alədʒɪst, zu:-] n : zoólogo m, -ga f

zoology [zo'alədʒi, zu:-] n : zoología f

zoom[1] ['zu:m] vi 1 : zumbar, ir volando ⟨to zoom past : pasar volando⟩ 2 CLIMB : elevarse ⟨the plane zoomed up : el avión se elevó⟩

zoom[2] n 1 : zumbido m ⟨the zoom of an engine : el zumbido de un motor⟩ 2 : subida f vertical (de un avión, etc.) 3 or **zoom lens** : zoom m

zucchini [zu'ki:ni] n, pl -ni or -nis : calabacín m, calabacita f Mex

Zulu ['zu:lu:] n 1 : zulú mf 2 : zulú m (idioma) — **Zulu** adj

zygote ['zaɪ,go:t] n : zigoto m, cigoto m

Common Spanish Abbreviations

abr.	abril	Apr.	April
A.C., a.C.	antes de Cristo	BC	before Christ
a. de J.C.	antes de Jesucristo	BC	before Christ
admon., admón.	administración	—	administration
a/f	a favor	—	in favor
ago.	agosto	Aug.	August
Apdo.	apartado (de correos)	—	P.O. box
aprox.	aproximadamente	approx.	approximately
Aptdo.	apartado (de correos)	—	P.O. box
Arq.	arquitecto	arch.	architect
A.T.	Antiguo Testamento	O.T.	Old Testament
atte.	atentamente	—	sincerely
atto., atta.	atento, atenta	—	kind, courteous
av., avda.	avenida	ave.	avenue
a/v.	a vista	—	on receipt
BID	Banco Interamericano de Desarrollo	IDB	Interamerican Development Bank
Bo	banco	—	bank
BM	Banco Mundial	—	World Bank
c/, C/	calle	st.	street
C	centígrado, Celsius	C	centigrade, Celsius
C.	compañía	Co.	company
CA	corriente alterna	AC	alternating current
cap.	capítulo	ch., chap.	chapter
c/c	cuenta corriente	—	current account, checking account
c.c.	centímetros cúbicos	cu. cm	cubic centimeters
CC	corriente continua	DC	direct current
c/d	con descuento	—	with discount
Cd.	ciudad	—	city
CE	Comunidad Europea	EC	European Community
CEE	Comunidad Económica Europea	EEC	European Economic Community
cf.	confróntese	cf.	compare
cg.	centígramo	cg	centigram
CGT	Confederación General de Trabajadores or del Trabajo	—	confederation of workers, workers' union
CI	coeficiente intelectual or de inteligencia	IQ	intelligence quotient
Cía.	compañía	Co.	company
cm.	centímetro	cm	centimeter
Cnel.	coronel	Col.	colonel
col.	columna	col.	column
Col. Mex	colonia	—	residential area
Com.	comandante	Cmdr.	commander
comp.	compárese	comp.	compare
Cor.	coronel	Col.	colonel

SPANISH ABBREVIATION AND EXPANSION		ENGLISH EQUIVALENT	
C.P.	código postal	—	zip code
CSF, c.s.f.	coste, seguro y flete	c.i.f.	cost, insurance, and freight
cta.	cuenta	ac., acct.	account
cte.	corriente	cur.	current
c/u	cada uno, cada una	ea.	each
CV	caballo de vapor	hp	horsepower
D.	Don	—	—
Da., D.ª	Doña	—	—
d.C.	después de Cristo	AD	anno Domini (in the year of our Lord)
dcha.	derecha	—	right
d. de J.C.	después de Jesucristo	AD	anno Domini (in the year of our lord)
dep.	departamento	dept.	department
DF, D.F.	Distrito Federal	—	Federal District
dic.	diciembre	Dec.	December
dir.	director, directora	dir.	director
dir.	dirección		address
Dña.	Doña	—	—
do.	domingo	Sun.	Sunday
dpto.	departamento	dept.	department
Dr.	doctor	Dr.	doctor
Dra.	doctora	Dr.	doctor
dto.	descuento	—	discount
E, E.	Este, este	E	East, east
Ed.	editorial	—	publishing house
Ed., ed.	edición	ed.	edition
edif.	edificio	bldg.	building
edo.	estado	st.	state
EEUU, EE.UU.	Estados Unidos	US, U.S.	United States
ej.	por ejemplo	e.g.	for example
E.M.	esclerosis multiple	MS	multiple sclerosis
ene.	enero	Jan.	January
etc.	etcétera	etc.	et cetera
ext.	extensión	ext.	extension
F	Fahrenheit	F	Fahrenheit
f.a.b.	franco a bordo	f.o.b.	free on board
FC	ferrocarril	RR	railroad
feb.	febrero	Feb.	February
FF AA, FF.AA.	Fuerzas Armadas	—	armed forces
FMI	Fondo Monetario Internacional	IMF	International Monetary Fund
g.	gramo	g., gm, gr	gram
G.P.	giro postal	M.O.	money order
gr.	gramo	g., gm, gr	gram
Gral.	general	Gen.	general
h.	hora	hr.	hour
Hnos.	hermanos	Bros.	brothers
I + D, I & D, I y D	investigación y desarrollo	R & D	research and development
i.e.	esto es, es decir	i.e.	that is
incl.	inclusive	incl.	inclusive, inclusively
Ing.	ingeniero, ingeniera	eng.	engineer

SPANISH ABBREVIATION AND EXPANSION		ENGLISH EQUIVALENT	
IPC	índice de precios al consumo	**CPI**	consumer price index
IVA	impuesto al valor agregado	**VAT**	value-added tax
izq.	izquierda	l.	left
juev.	jueves	**Thurs.**	Thursday
jul.	julio	**Jul.**	July
jun.	junio	**Jun.**	June
kg.	kilogramo	**kg**	kilogram
km.	kilómetro	**km**	kilometer
km/h	kilómetros por hora	**kph**	kilometers per hour
kv, kV	kilovatio	**kw, kW**	kilowatt
l.	litro	**l, lit.**	liter
Lic.	licenciado, licenciada	**—**	**—**
Ltda.	limitada	**Ltd.**	limited
lun.	lunes	**Mon.**	Monday
m	masculino	**m**	masculine
m	metro	**m**	meter
m	minuto	**m**	minute
mar.	marzo	**Mar.**	March
mart.	martes	**Tues.**	Tuesday
mg.	miligramo	**mg**	milligram
miérc.	miércoles	**Wednes.**	Wednesday
min	minuto	**min.**	minute
mm.	milímetro	**mm**	millimeter
M-N, m/n	moneda nacional	**—**	national currency
Mons.	monseñor	**Msgr.**	monsignor
Mtra.	maestra	**—**	teacher
Mtro.	maestro	**—**	teacher
N, N.	Norte, norte	**N, no.**	North, north
n/o	nuestro	**—**	our
n.º	número	**no.**	number
N. de (la) R.	nota de (la) redacción	**—**	editor's note
NE	nordeste	**NE**	northeast
NN.UU.	Naciones Unidas	**UN**	United Nations
NO	noroeste	**NW**	northwest
nov.	noviembre	**Nov.**	November
N.T.	Nuevo Testamento	**N.T.**	New Testament
ntra., ntro.	nuestra, nuestro	**—**	our
NU	Naciones Unidas	**UN**	United Nations
núm.	número	**num.**	number
O, O.	Oeste, oeste	**W**	West, west
oct.	octubre	**Oct.**	October
OEA, O.E.A.	Organización de Estados Americanos	**OAS**	Organization of American States
OMS	Organización Mundial de la Salud	**WHO**	World Health Organization
ONG	organización no gubernamental	**NGO**	non-governmental organization
ONU	Organización de las Naciones Unidas	**UN**	United Nations
OTAN	Organización del Tratado del Atlántico Norte	**NATO**	North Atlantic Treaty Organization
p.	página	**p.**	page
P, P.	padre	**Fr.**	father

SPANISH ABBREVIATION AND EXPANSION		ENGLISH EQUIVALENT	
pág.	página	**pg.**	page
pat.	patente	**pat.**	patent
PCL	pantalla de cristal líquido	**LCD**	liquid crystal display
P.D.	post data	**P.S.**	postscript
p. ej.	por ejemplo	**e.g.**	for example
PNB	Producto Nacional Bruto	**GNP**	gross national product
p^o	paseo	**Ave.**	avenue
p.p.	porte pagado	**ppd.**	postpaid
PP, p.p.	por poder, por poderes	**p.p.**	by proxy
prom.	promedio	**av., avg.**	average
ptas., pts.	pesetas		
q.e.p.d.	que en paz descanse	**R.I.P.**	may he/she rest in peace
R, R/	remite	—	sender
RAE	Real Academia Española	—	—
ref., ref.^a	referencia	**ref.**	reference
rep.	república	**rep.**	republic
r.p.m.	revoluciones por minuto	**rpm.**	revolutions per minute
rte.	remite, remitente	—	sender
's.	siglo	**c., cent.**	century
s/	su, sus	—	his, her, your, their
S, S.	Sur, sur	**S, so.**	South, south
S.	san, santo	**St.**	saint
S.A.	sociedad anónima	**Inc.**	incorporated (company)
sáb.	sábado	**Sat.**	Saturday
s/c	su cuenta	—	your account
SE	sudeste, sureste	**SE**	southeast
seg.	segundo, segundos	**sec.**	second, seconds
sep., sept.	septiembre	**Sept.**	September
s.e.u.o.	salvo error u omisión	—	errors and omissions excepted
Sgto.	sargento	**Sgt.**	sergeant
S.L.	sociedad limitada	**Ltd.**	limited (corporation)
S.M.	Su Majestad	**HM**	His Majesty, Her Majesty
s/n	sin número	—	no (street) number
s.n.m.	sobre el nivel de mar	**a.s.l.**	above sea level
SO	sudoeste/suroeste	**SW**	southwest
S.R.C.	se ruega contestación	**R.S.V.P.**	please reply
ss.	siguientes	—	the following ones
SS, S.S.	Su Santidad	**H.H.**	His Holiness
Sta.	santa	**St.**	Saint
Sto.	santo	**St.**	saint
t, t.	tonelada	**t., tn.**	ton
TAE	tasa anual efectiva	**APR**	annual percentage rate
tb.	también	—	also
tel., Tel.	teléfono	**tel.**	telephone
Tm.	tonelada métrica	**MT**	metric ton
Tn.	tonelada	**t., tn.**	ton
trad.	traducido	**tr., trans., transl.**	translated

SPANISH ABBREVIATION AND EXPANSION		ENGLISH EQUIVALENT	
UE	Unión Europea	EU	European Union
Univ.	universidad	Univ., U.	university
UPC	unidad procesadora central	CPU	central processing unit
Urb.	urbanización	—	residential area
v	versus	v., vs.	versus
v	verso	v., ver., vs.	verse
v.	véase	vid.	see
Vda.	viuda	—	widow
v.g., v.gr.	verbigracia	e.g.	for example
vier., viern.	viernes	Fri.	Friday
V.M.	Vuestra Majestad	—	Your Majesty
VºBº, V.ºB.º	visto bueno	—	OK, approved
vol, vol.	volumen	vol.	volume
vra., vro.	vuestra, vuestro	—	your

Common English Abbreviations

ENGLISH ABBREVIATION AND EXPANSION		SPANISH EQUIVALENT	
AAA	American Automobile Association	—	—
AD	anno Domini (in the year of our Lord)	d.C., d. de J.C.	después de Cristo, después de Jesucristo
AK	Alaska	—	Alaska
AL, Ala.	Alabama	—	Alabama
Alas.	Alaska	—	Alaska
a.m., AM	ante meridiem	a.m.	ante meridiem (de la mañana)
Am., Amer.	America, American	—	América, americano
amt.	amount	—	cantidad
anon.	anonymous	—	anónimo
ans.	answer	—	respuesta
Apr.	April	abr.	abril
AR	Arkansas	—	Arkansas
Ariz.	Arizona	—	Arizona
Ark.	Arkansas	—	Arkansas
asst.	assistant	ayte.	ayudante
atty.	attorney	—	abogado, -da
Aug.	August	ago.	agosto
ave.	avenue	av., avda.	avenida
AZ	Arizona	—	Arizona
BA	Bachelor of Arts	Lic.	Licenciado, -da en Filosofía y Letras
BA	Bachelor of Arts (degree)	—	Licenciatura en Filosofía y Letras
BC	before Christ	a.C., A.C., a. de J.C.	antes de Cristo, antes de Jesucristo
BCE	before the Christian Era, before the Common Era	—	antes de la era cristiana, antes de la era común
bet.	between	—	entre
bldg.	building	edif.	edificio
blvd.	boulevard	blvar., br.	bulevar
Br., Brit.	Britain, British	—	Gran Bretaña, británico
Bro(s).	brother(s)	Hno(s).	hermano(s)
BS	Bachelor of Science	Lic.	Licenciado, -da en Ciencias
BS	Bachelor of Science (degree)	—	Licenciatura en Ciencias
c	carat	—	quilate
c	cent	—	centavo
c	centimeter	cm.	centímetro
c	century	s.	siglo
c	cup	—	taza
C	Celsius, centigrade	C	Celsius, centígrado
CA, Cal., Calif.	California	—	California
Can., Canad.	Canada, Canadian	—	Canadá, canadiense
cap.	capital	—	capital
cap.	capital	—	mayúscula
Capt.	captain	—	capitán

ENGLISH ABBREVIATION AND EXPANSION		SPANISH EQUIVALENT	
cent.	century	s.	siglo
CEO	chief executive officer	—	presidente, -ta (de una corporación)
ch., chap.	chapter	cap.	capítulo
CIA	Central Intelligence Agency	—	—
cm	centimeter	cm.	centímetro
Co.	company	C., Cía.	compañía
co.	county	—	condado
CO	Colorado	—	Colorado
c/o	care of	a/c	a cargo de
COD	cash on delivery, collect on delivery	—	(pago) contra reembolso
col.	column	col.	columna
Col., Colo.	Colorado	—	Colorado
Conn.	Connecticut	—	Connecticut
corp.	corporation	—	corporación
CPR	cardiopulmonary resuscitation	RCP	reanimación cardiopulmonar, resucitación cardiopulmonar
ct.	cent	—	centavo
CT	Connecticut	—	Connecticut
D.A.	district attorney	—	fiscal (del distrito)
DC	District of Columbia	—	—
DDS	Doctor of Dental Surgery	—	doctor de cirugía dental
DE	Delaware	—	Delaware
Dec.	December	dic.	diciembre
Del.	Delaware	—	Delaware
DJ	disc jockey	—	disc-jockey
dept.	department	dep., dpto.	departamento
DMD	Doctor of Dental Medicine	—	doctor de medicina dental
doz.	dozen	—	docena
Dr.	doctor	Dr., Dra.	doctor, doctora
DST	daylight saving time	—	—
DVM	Doctor of Veterinary Medicine	—	doctor de medicina veterinaria
E	East, east	E, E.	Este, este
ea.	each	c/u	cada uno, cada una
e.g.	for example (exempli gratia)	v.g., v.gr.	verbigracia
EMT	emergency medical technician	—	técnico, -ca en urgencias médicas
Eng.	England, English	—	Inglaterra, inglés
esp.	especially	—	especialmente
EST	eastern standard time	—	—
etc.	et cetera	etc.	etcétera
f	false	—	falso
f	female	f	femenino
F	Fahrenheit	F	Fahrenheit
FBI	Federal Bureau of Investigation	—	—
Feb.	February	feb.	febrero
fem.	feminine	—	femenino
FL, Fla.	Florida	—	Florida

ENGLISH ABBREVIATION AND EXPANSION		SPANISH EQUIVALENT	
Fri.	Friday	vier., viern.	viernes
ft.	feet, foot	—	pie(s)
g	gram	g., gr.	gramo
Ga., GA	Georgia	—	Georgia
gal.	gallon	—	galón
Gen.	general	Gral.	general
gm	gram	g., gr.	gramo
gov.	governor	—	gobernador, -dora
govt.	government	—	gobierno
gr.	gram	g., gr.	gramo
HI	Hawaii	—	Hawai, Hawaii
hr.	hour	h.	hora
HS	high school	—	colegio secundario
ht.	height	—	altura
Ia., IA	Iowa	—	Iowa
ID	Idaho	—	Idaho
i.e.	that is (id est)	i.e.	id est (esto es, es decir)
IL, Ill.	Illinois	—	Illinois
in.	inch	—	pulgada
IN	Indiana	—	Indiana
Inc.	incorporated	S.A.	sociedad anónima
Ind.	Indian, Indiana	—	Indiana
Jan.	January	ene.	enero
Jul.	July	jul.	julio
Jun.	June	jun.	junio
Jr., Jun.	Junior	Jr.	Júnior
Kan., Kans.	Kansas	—	Kansas
kg	kilogram	kg.	kilogramo
km	kilometer	km.	kilómetro
KS	Kansas	—	Kansas
Ky., KY	Kentucky	—	Kentucky
l	liter	l.	litro
l.	left	izq.	izquierda
L	large	G	(talla) grande
La., LA	Louisiana	—	Luisiana, Louisiana
lb.	pound	—	libra
Ltd.	limited	S.L.	sociedad limitada
m	male	m	masculino
m	meter	m	metro
m	mile	—	milla
M	medium	M	(talla) mediana
MA	Massachusetts	—	Massachusetts
Maj.	major	—	mayor
Mar.	March	mar.	marzo
masc.	masculine	—	masculino
Mass.	Massachusetts	—	Massachusetts
Md., MD	Maryland	—	Maryland
M.D.	Doctor of Medicine	—	doctor de medicina
Me., ME	Maine	—	Maine
Mex.	Mexican, Mexico	Méx.	mexicano, México
mg	milligram	mg.	miligramo
mi.	mile	—	milla
MI, Mich.	Michigan	—	Michigan
min.	minute	min	minuto
Minn.	Minnesota	—	Minnesota
Miss.	Mississippi	—	Mississippi, Misisipí
ml	mililiter	ml.	mililitro

ENGLISH ABBREVIATION AND EXPANSION		SPANISH EQUIVALENT	
mm	millimeter	mm.	milímetro
MN	Minnesota	—	Minnesota
mo.	month	—	mes
Mo., MO	Missouri	—	Missouri
Mon.	Monday	lun.	lunes
Mont.	Montana	—	Montana
mpg	miles per gallon	—	millas por galón
mph	miles per hour	—	millas por hora
MS	Mississippi	—	Mississippi, Misisipí
mt.	mount, mountain	—	monte, montaña
MT	Montana	—	Montana
mtn.	mountain	—	montaña
N	North, north	N	Norte, norte
NASA	National Aeronautics and Space Administration	—	—
NC	North Carolina	—	Carolina del Norte, North Carolina
ND, N. Dak.	North Dakota	—	Dakota del Norte, North Dakota
NE	northeast	NE	nordeste
NE, Neb., Nebr.	Nebraska	—	Nebraska
Nev.	Nevada	—	Nevada
NH	New Hampshire	—	New Hampshire
NJ	New Jersey	—	Nueva Jersey, New Jersey
NM, N. Mex.	New Mexico	—	Nuevo México, New Mexico
no.	north	N	norte
no.	number	n.⁰	número
Nov.	November	nov.	noviembre
N.T.	New Testament	N.T.	Nuevo Testamento
NV	Nevada	—	Nevada
NW	northwest	NO	noroeste
NY	New York	NY	Nueva York, New York
O	Ohio	—	Ohio
Oct.	October	oct.	octubre
OH	Ohio	—	Ohio
OK, Okla.	Oklahoma	—	Oklahoma
OR, Ore., Oreg.	Oregon	—	Oregon
O.T.	Old Testament	A.T.	Antiguo Testamento
oz.	ounce, ounces	—	onza, onzas
p.	page	p.	página
Pa., PA	Pennsylvania	—	Pennsylvania, Pensilvania
pat.	patent	pat.	patente
PD	police department	—	departamento de policía
PE	physical education	—	educación física
Penn., Penna.	Pennsylvania	—	Pennsylvania, Pensilvania
pg.	page	pág.	página
PhD	Doctor of Philosophy	—	doctor, -tòra (en filosofía)

ENGLISH ABBREVIATION AND EXPANSION			SPANISH EQUIVALENT
pkg.	package	—	paquete
p.m., PM	post meridiem	p.m.	post meridiem (de la tarde)
P.O.	post office	—	oficina de correos, correo
pp.	pages	págs.	páginas
PR	Puerto Rico	PR	Puerto Rico
pres.	present	—	presente
pres.	president	—	presidente, -ta
prof.	professor	—	profesor, -sora
P.S.	postscript	P.D.	postdata
P.S.	public school	—	escuela pública
pt.	pint	—	pinta
pt.	point	pto.	punto
PTA	Parent-Teacher Association	—	—
PTO	Parent-Teacher Organization	—	—
q, qt.	quart	—	cuarto de galón
r.	right	dcha.	derecha
rd.	road	c/, C/	calle
RDA	recommended daily allowance	—	consumo diario recomendado
recd.	received	—	recibido
Rev.	reverend	Rdo.	reverendo
RI	Rhode Island	—	Rhode Island
rpm	revolutions per minute	r.p.m.	revoluciones por minuto
RR	railroad	FC	ferrocarril
R.S.V.P.	please reply (répondez s'il vous plaît)	S.R.C.	se ruega contestación
rt.	right	dcha.	derecha
rte.	route	—	ruta
S	small	P	(talla) pequeña
S	South, south	S	Sur, sur
S.A.	South America	—	Sudamérica, América del Sur
Sat.	Saturday	sáb.	sábado
SC	South Carolina	—	Carolina del Sur, South Carolina
SD, S. Dak.	South Dakota	—	Dakota del Sur, South Dakota
SE	southeast	SE	sudeste, sureste
Sept.	September	sep., sept.	septiembre
so.	south	S	sur
sq.	square	—	cuadrado
Sr.	Senior	Sr.	Sénior
Sr.	sister	—	sor
st.	state	—	estado
st.	street	c/, C/	calle
St.	saint	S., Sto., Sta.	santo, santa
Sun.	Sunday	dom.	domingo
SW	southwest	SO	sudoeste, suroeste
t.	teaspoon	—	cucharadita
T, tb., tbsp.	tablespoon	—	cucharada (grande)
Tenn.	Tennessee	—	Tennessee

ENGLISH ABBREVIATION AND EXPANSION		SPANISH EQUIVALENT	
Tex.	Texas	—	Texas
Thu., Thur., Thurs.	Thursday	**juev.**	jueves
TM	trademark	—	marca (de un producto)
TN	Tennessee	—	Tennessee
tsp.	teaspoon	—	cucharadita
Tue., Tues.	Tuesday	**mart.**	martes
TX	Texas	—	Texas
UN	United Nations	**NU, NN.UU.**	Naciones Unidas
US	United States	**EEUU, EE.UU.**	Estados Unidos
USA	United States of America	**EEUU, EE.UU.**	Estados Unidos de América
usu.	usually	—	usualmente
UT	Utah	—	Utah
v.	versus	**v**	versus
Va., VA	Virginia	—	Virginia
vol.	volume	**vol.**	volumen
VP	vice president	—	vicepresidente, -ta
vs.	versus	**v**	versus
Vt., VT	Vermont	—	Vermont
W	West, west	**O**	Oeste, oeste
WA, Wash.	Washington (estado)	—	Washington
Wed.	Wednesday	**miérc.**	miércoles
WI, Wis., Wisc.	Wisconsin	—	Wisconsin
wt.	weight	—	peso
WV, W. Va.	West Virginia	—	Virginia del Oeste, West Virginia
WY, Wyo.	Wyoming	—	Wyoming
yd.	yard	—	yarda
yr.	year	—	año

Spanish Numbers

	Cardinal Numbers		
1	uno	28	veintiocho
2	dos	29	veintinueve
3	tres	30	treinta
4	cuatro	31	treinta y uno
5	cinco	40	cuarenta
6	seis	50	cincuenta
7	siete	60	sesenta
8	ocho	70	setenta
9	nueve	80	ochenta
10	diez	90	noventa
11	once	100	cien
12	doce	101	ciento uno
13	trece	200	doscientos
14	catorce	300	trescientos
15	quince	400	cuatrocientos
16	dieciséis	500	quinientos
17	diecisiete	600	seiscientos
18	dieciocho	700	setecientos
19	diecinueve	800	ochocientos
20	veinte	900	novecientos
21	veintiuno	1,000	mil
22	veintidós	1,001	mil uno
23	veintitrés	2,000	dos mil
24	veinticuatro	100,000	cien mil
25	veinticinco	1,000,000	un millón
26	veintiséis	1,000,000,000	mil millones
27	veintisiete	1,000,000,000,000	un billón

Ordinal Numbers

1st	primero, -ra	18th	decimoctavo, -va
2nd	segundo, -da	19th	decimonoveno, -na;
3rd	tercero, -ra		*or* decimonono, -na
4th	cuarto, -ta	20th	vigésimo, -ma
5th	quinto, -ta	21st	vigésimoprimero,
6th	sexto, -ta		vigésimaprimera
7th	séptimo, -ta	22nd	vigésimosegundo,
8th	octavo, -ta		vigésimasegunda
9th	noveno, -na	30th	trigésimo, -ma
10th	décimo, -ma	40th	cuadragésimo, -ma
11th	undécimo, -ca	50th	quincuagésimo, -ma
12th	duodécimo, -ma	60th	sexagésimo, -ma
13th	decimotercero, -ra	70th	septuagésimo, -ma
14th	decimocuarto, -ta	80th	octogésimo, -ma
15th	decimoquinto, -ta	90th	nonagésimo, -ma
16th	decimosexto, -ta	100th	centésimo, -ma
17th	decimoséptimo, -ma	1,000th	milésimo, -ma

English Numbers

Cardinal Numbers

1	one	50	fifty
2	two	60	sixty
3	three	70	seventy
4	four	80	eighty
5	five	90	ninety
6	six	100	one hundred
7	seven	101	one hundred and one
8	eight	200	two hundred
9	nine	300	three hundred
10	ten	400	four hundred
11	eleven	500	five hundred
12	twelve	600	six hundred
13	thirteen	700	seven hundred
14	fourteen	800	eight hundred
15	fifteen	900	nine hundred
16	sixteen	1,000	one thousand
17	seventeen	1,001	one thousand and one
18	eighteen	2,000	two thousand
19	nineteen	10,000	ten thousand
20	twenty	100,000	one hundred thousand
21	twenty-one	1,000,000	one million
30	thirty	1,000,000,000	one billion
40	forty	1,000,000,000,000	one trillion

Ordinal Numbers

1st	first	17th	seventeenth
2nd	second	18th	eighteenth
3rd	third	19th	nineteenth
4th	fourth	20th	twentieth
5th	fifth	21st	twenty-first
6th	sixth	30th	thirtieth
7th	seventh	40th	fortieth
8th	eighth	50th	fiftieth
9th	ninth	60th	sixtieth
10th	tenth	70th	seventieth
11th	eleventh	80th	eightieth
12th	twelfth	90th	ninetieth
13th	thirteenth	100th	hundredth
14th	fourteenth	1,000th	thousandth
15th	fifteenth	1,000,000th	millionth
16th	sixteenth	1,000,000,000th	billionth

Nations of the World

Africa/África

English	Spanish
Algeria	Argelia
Angola	Angola
Benin	Benin
Botswana	Botswana, Botsuana
Burkina Faso	Burkina Faso
Burundi	Burundi
Cameroon	Camerún
Cape Verde	Cabo Verde
Central African Republic	República Centroafricana
Chad	Chad
Comoro Islands	Islas Comores, Comoras
Congo	Congo
Democratic Republic of Congo	Congo, República Democrática del
Djibouti	Djibouti, Djibuti
Egypt	Egipto
Equatorial Guinea	Guinea Ecuatorial
Eritrea	Eritrea
Ethiopia	Etiopía
Gabon	Gabón
Gambia	Gambia
Ghana	Ghana
Guinea	Guinea
Guinea-Bissau	Guinea-Bissau
Ivory Coast	Costa de Marfil
Kenya	Kenya, Kenia
Lesotho	Lesotho, Lesoto
Liberia	Liberia
Libya	Libia
Madagascar	Madagascar
Malawi	Malawi, Malaui
Mali	Malí
Mauritania	Mauritania
Mauritius	Mauricio
Morocco	Marruecos
Mozambique	Mozambique
Namibia	Namibia
Niger	Níger
Nigeria	Nigeria
Rwanda	Ruanda, Rwanda
São Tomé and Principe	Santo Tomé y Príncipe
Senegal	Senegal
Seychelles	Seychelles
Sierra Leone	Sierra Leona
Somalia	Somalia
South Africa, Republic of	Sudáfrica, República de
Sudan	Sudán
Swaziland	Suazilandia, Swazilandia
Tanzania	Tanzanía, Tanzania
Togo	Togo